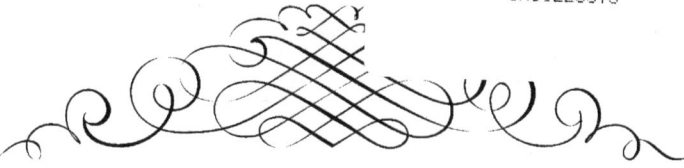

ISBN 978-1-5283-9245-7
PIBN 10978831

FB &c Ltd, Dalton House, 60 Windsor Avenue, London, SW19 2RR.
Company number 08720141. Registered in England and Wales.

For support please visit www.forgottenbooks.com

A New World of Cleanliness

The Easiest, Quickest, Cheapest, Most Thorough Way to Clean — and KEEP CLEAN — Your Home, Office or Other Building Is with AIR :: ::

No Expensive Plant Required : No Piping, Wiring, or Installation of Any Kind

Can be used in any building that has electricity—either alternating or direct current.

A child's strength will operate it, and green servants secure perfect results.

THE "INVINCIBLE" ELECTRIC RENOVATOR

GETS *ALL* THE DIRT *ALL* THE TIME

A handy, portable machine, ready for instant use. Runs by electric motor. Creates a strong suction, or "draw." A hose is attached, and to that a nozzle, or tool, which is passed over the object, or surface, to be cleaned.

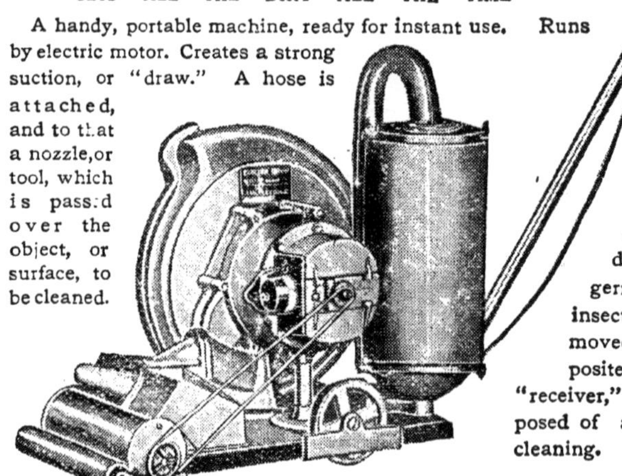

Every particle of dust, dirt, disease germs, moths, insects are removed and deposited in a "receiver," to be disposed of after the cleaning.

The method is almost noiseless, and absolutely dustless. No flying particles. Cleaning and dusting all in the one operation without removal of a single article.

Infinitely better and more thorough than the broom. Saves wear and tear on fabrics and furniture; preserves the newness and lengthens the life. Saves time, help, actual money cost, supervision and worry.

READ THE WHOLE STORY ABOUT THIS NEW SANITARY METHOD OF CLEANING

Our "TWO BOOKLETS" contain a world of information and living facts about the "INVINCIBLE;" also give large list of enthusiastic users. While you have it in mind, write. Dept. 6

The ELECTRIC RENOVATOR MANUFACTURING COMPANY

900 FARMERS' BANK BUILDING : : PITTSBURGH, PA.

A Barrel of Whiskey

FOR $4.00

We Ship Direct to Consumer. Price **4** Dollars

We Pay All Express Charges. Price **4** Dollars

Each barrel has a wooden stand, a drinking glass and spigot. The Best Whiskey In America for the price

On receipt of $4 we will deliver direct to you one of our celebrated Baby Barrels free of any other cost. Friedenwald's Baby Barrel is a little oak barrel containing one gallon of either FRIEDENWALD'S Maryland Whiskey or Kentucky Bourbon.

We guarantee its perfect purity, which makes Friedenwald's Baby Barrel especially valuable for medicinal use. We ship this whiskey just as we receive it from our distillery in these small oak barrels—which are made from the original oak staves of large whiskey barrels. Each baby barrel has a small spigot, drinking glass and wooden stand, making it the most unique package ever offered to the public. Its advantages are that whiskey is better in wood than in bottles and the greatest advantage that there is absolutely no danger from breakage as you know that often you receive bottles and some are broken—you are the loser. Our way—goods shipped in baby barrels—you always get what you pay for—absolutely no breakage. Order one at once. We pay express charges.

J. H. FRIEDENWALD & CO.

90-92-94-96-98-100 N. Eutaw St. - - BALTIMORE, MD.

REFERENCES: Western National Bank, or any Commercial Agency.

All orders west of Mississippi must call for not less than Six Baby Barrels.

IMPROVED RIDING GALLERY
HERSCHELL, SPILLMAN & CO.
NORTH TONAWANDA, N.Y. U.S.A.

ICE HOUSE
WASH HOUSE
TRAIN HOUSE
Tam o' Shanter
ALE
BARTHOLOMAY BREWER
ROCHESTER, N.Y.
rtholomay
Rienzi
BEER
ROCHESTER N.Y.
OVER fifty years' experience in furthering the quality of the
BARTHOLOMAY
brews has accomplished perfection.
EITHER at home, in the club or on your travels drink
RIENZI BEER
the beer with a reputation, or
Tam o'Shanter Ale
which is pronounced "as fine as rare old wine."
Our Leading Brands in Bottles Only.
BARTHOLOMAY BREWERY CO.
ROCHESTER, N. Y.

Antikamnia Tablets

OPPOSED TO PAIN.

Fac-simile

Adult Dose: Two every two or three hours.

Fac-simile

FOR PAIN and FEVER

HEADACHES, NEURALGIAS, WOMEN'S ACHES and ILLS

AND THE PAINFUL AFTER-EFFECTS

PRESCRIPTIONS

Showing Uses for Antikamnia Tablets

ANY PAIN (No matter where)
Dose:—Two tablets every three hours.

COLD-IN-THE-HEAD
Dose:—Two every three hours.

DISSIPATION—(To relieve after-effects)
Dose:—One every two hours.

FACIAL NEURALGIA
Dose:—One every half hour until four are taken.

FEVER—(Feverish Conditions)
Dose:—One every two hours.

HEADACHE—(Dyspepsia, Indigestion)
Dose:—Two, and repeat in three hours.

HEADACHE—(Menstrual or Monthly)
Dose:—Two, and repeat in three hours.

HEADACHE—(Nervous or Daily)
Dose:—Two. Repeat in two hours.

HEAT EFFECTS—(Dizziness or Sun Pains)
Dose:—One or two every three hours. Ice water applications.

HICCOUGH AND SOUR STOMACH
Dose:—One dissolved upon the tongue. Repeat every hour if needed.

LIGHT ON PAIN

PRESCRIPTIONS

Showing Uses for Antikamnia Tablets

NERVOUSNESS—(Overwork or Excesses)
Dose:—One tablet every two or three hours and at bedtime.

NEURALGIA—(All kinds)
Dose:—One every two or three hours.

RHEUMATIC PAIN—(General)
Dose:—One or two every three hours.

SEA AND CAR SICKNESS
Dose:—One or two tablets every three hours. Fresh air.

SHOPPERS' OR SIGHTSEERS' HEADACHE
Dose:—Two every three hours.

SUMMER COLDS—(Coryza)
Dose:—Two tablets every three hours.

TOOTHACHE—(Pain about the Teeth)
Dose:—Two every three hours.

VOMITING—(Pregnancy or Indigestion)
Dose:—One or two every three hours.

WOMEN'S PAINS
Dose:—Two tablets every three hours.

WORRY—(Nervousness; "The Blues")
Dose:—One or two every three hours.

For Information, Samples and Literature address

THE ANTIKAMNIA CHEMICAL COMPANY, St. Louis, U.S.A.

ANTIKAMNIA & CODEINE TABLETS
FOR ALL COUGHS, TICKLING OR DEEP-SEATED

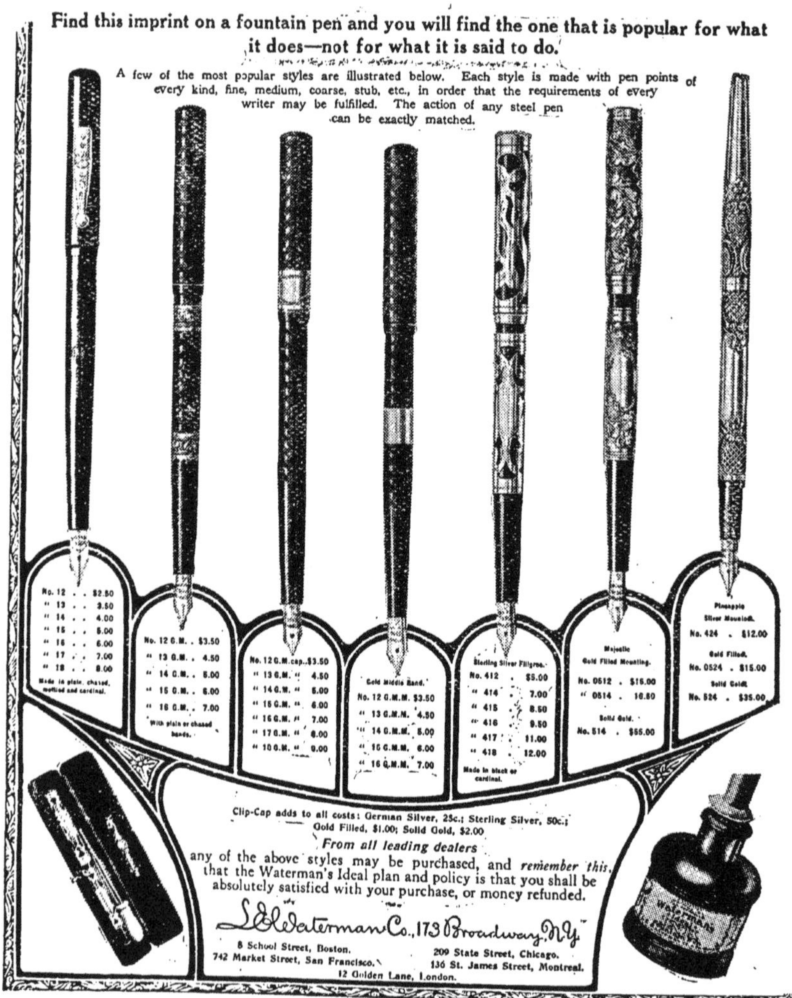
Find this imprint on a fountain pen and you will find the one that is popular for what it does—not for what it is said to do.
A few of the most popular styles are illustrated below. Each style is made with pen points of every kind, fine, medium, coarse, stub, etc., in order that the requirements of every writer may be fulfilled. The action of any steel pen can be exactly matched.
No. 12 . . $2.50
" 13 . . 3.50
" 14 . . 4.00
" 15 . . 5.00
" 16 . . 6.00
" 17 . . 7.00
" 18 . . 8.00
Made in plain, chased, mottled and cardinal.
No. 12 G.M. . $3.50
" 13 G.M. . 4.50
" 14 G.M. . 5.00
" 15 G.M. . 6.00
" 16 G.M. . 7.00
With plain or chased bands.
No. 12 G.M. cap. .$3.50
" 13 G.M. " 4.50
" 14 G.M. " 5.00
" 15 G.M. " 6.00
" 16 G.M. " 7.00
" 17 G.M. " 8.00
" 18 G.M. " 9.00
Gold Middle Band.
No. 12 G.M.M. $3.50
" 13 G.M.M. 4.50
" 14 G.M.M. 5.00
" 15 G.M.M. 6.00
" 16 G.M.M. 7.00
Sterling Silver Filigree.
No. 412 . $5.00
" 414 . 7.00
" 415 . 8.50
" 416 . 9.50
" 417 . 11.00
" 418 . 12.00
Made in black or cardinal.
Majestic
Gold Filled Mounting.
No. 0512 . $15.00
" 0514 . 16.50
Solid Gold.
No. 514 . $55.00
Pineapple
Silver Mounted.
No. 424 . $12.00
Gold Filled.
No. 0524 . $15.00
Solid Gold.
No. 524 . $35.00
Clip-Cap adds to all costs: German Silver, 25c.; Sterling Silver, 50c.; Gold Filled, $1.00; Solid Gold, $2.00
From all leading dealers
any of the above styles may be purchased, and remember this, that the Waterman's Ideal plan and policy is that you shall be absolutely satisfied with your purchase, or money refunded.
L. E. Waterman Co., 173 Broadway, N.Y.
8 School Street, Boston.
742 Market Street, San Francisco.
209 State Street, Chicago.
136 St. James Street, Montreal.
12 Golden Lane, London.
WATERMAN'S

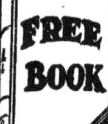

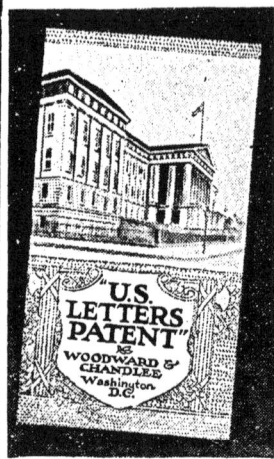

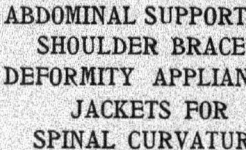

Genius of Invention

The Automatic Time Stamp

AARON'S CHILLED PLATINUM
TRADE MARK.

CLASSIFIED SANITARIUM DIRECTORY
of
EASTERN UNITED STATES

(By special arrangement with Mr. G. L. HARRINGTON, publisher Long Island Medical Journal.)

Alphabetical List by States

CONNECTICUT.

	Elevation	Established
Barnes' Sanitarium, Dr., F. H. Barnes, Stamford	500	1895
Bowman's Sanitarium, Dr., J. E. Bowman, Greenwich	28	1895
Brooks' Sanatorium, Dr., M. J. Brooks, New Canaan	340	1896
Cedar Wild Sanitarium, A. L. Fitch, Darien	66	1900
Cheney's Sanatorium, Dr. B. Austin; B. A. Cheney, New Haven	10	1893
Crest View Sanatorium, H. M. Hitchcock, Greenwich	300	1894
Cromwell Hall, F. K. Hallock, Cromwell	250	1877
Elmcroft Sanatorium, E. S. Vail, Enfield	78	1890
Givens' Sanitarium, Dr., A. J. Givens, Stamford	150	1890
Grand View Sanatorium, W. P. S. Keating, South Windham	800	1894
Keeley Institute, The, W. H. Boals, 307 Beach Street, West Haven	64	1892
McFarland's Sanitarium, Dr., D. W. McFarland, Greens Farms	100	1898
Moss Hill Villa, A. D. Wadsworth, South Norwalk	300	1903
Newhope Private Sanitarium, C. E. Skinner, 61-63 Grove Street, New Haven	10	1900
"On-the-Hill" Sanatorium, C. W. Jackson, Watertown	600	1903
Spring Hill Home, J. L. Buel, Litchfield	1,150	1858
Styles' Sanitarium, Dr., E. L. Styles, New Britain	199	1896
Westport Sanitarium, F. D. Ruland, Westport	26	1891
Wilson Sanitarium, ——— 151 Retreat Avenue, Hartford	38	1898
Woodland Sanatorium, M. M. Johnson, 122 Woodland Street, Hartford	38	1890

DISTRICT OF COLUMBIA.

	Elevation	Established
Francis Private Sanitarium, John R., John R. Francis, 2112 Pennsylvania Avenue, N. W., Washington	25	....
Keeley Institute, E. C. Barstow, 211 North Capital Street, Washington	25	1897

INDIANA.

	Elevation	Established
Bourbon Sanitarium, A. C. Matchette, Bourbon	800	1901
Bye Sanitarium, Dr. Benj. Bye, Indianapolis	700	1896
Columbus Sanitarium, John Little Morris, Columbus	600	1890
Crescent Sanitarium, Drs. A. M. Hayden and J. W. Phares, Evansville	431	1899
Evansville Sanitarium, Edw. Walker and J. Welbron, 712 Twentieth Street, Evansville	370	1893
Fayette Sanitarium, W. H. Worster, Connersville	800	1902
Fletcher's Sanitarium, Dr. W. B., W. B. Fletcher, Indianapolis	700	1888
Gilbert Memorial Sanitarium, Dr. Wm. Gilbert, Evansville	300	1897
Glen View, M. C. Benham, Richmond	915	1881
Home Lawn Mineral Springs, W. E. Hendricks, Martinsville	500	1890
Hotel Lithia, C. J. Finney, Attica	500	....
Highland Sanitarium, A. S. Tilford, Martinsville	500	1894
Interlaken Sanitarium, W. Wardner, La Porte	300	1870
Invalids' Home Sanitarium, R. B. Jackson, Kokomo	575	1873
Knapp Sanitarium, Dr. Geo. H. C. Knapp, cor. Fourth Street and Broadway, Vincennes	400	1898
Martinsville Sanitarium, E. V. Green, Martinsville	600	1889
"Norways," A. E. Sterne, 1820 East Tenth Street, Indianapolis	450	1898
Shelbyville, ————, Shelbyville	1,844	1900
Vigo Sanitarium, Drs. Stock and Howe, 324 South Third Street, Terre Haute	400	1900
Winona Lake Health Resort, J. G. Nebras, Winona Lake	800	1903

MAINE.

	Elevation	Established
Maine State Sanatorium, E. Nichols, Hebron	1,200	1905

MARYLAND.

	Elevation	Established
Barnard Sanatorium, J. S. Barnard, 2724 Charles Street, North Baltimore	130	1900
Brewster Park Hotel Sanitarium, F. A. Brewster, Laurel	1,000	1905
Carroll Springs Sanitarium, G. H. Wright, Forest Glen	300	1889
Fort Hill Private Home for Backward and Nervous Children, S. J. Fort, near Ellicott City, Howard County	500	1886
Gundry Sanitarium, A. T. Gundry, Catonsville	500	1900
Miller Sanitarium, I. Miller, 1734 St. Paul Street, Baltimore	200	1896
Mt. Hope Retreat, F. J. Flannery and C. G. Hill, Mt. Hope	460	1840
Riggs' Cottage, G. H. Riggs, Ijamsville	750	1896
Sanitarium, H. A. Kelly, 1418 Eutaw Place, Baltimore	1,000	1892
Sheppard and Enoch Pratt Hospital, E. N. Brush, Towson (Station A, Baltimore)	456	1853
Springer Sanitarium, N A. Springer and J. R. Green, Towson (Station A, Baltimore)	130	1890
Wills Mountain Sanatorium, H. D. Fry and J. T. Johnson, (near) Cumberland	1,800	1903

MASSACHUSETTS.

	Elevation	Established
Adams Nervine Asylum, D. H. Fuller, Jamaica Plain, Boston	80	1877
Attleboro and Martha's Vineyard Sanitarium, The, L. V. Gustin-Mackie. June to October, Cottage City; October to June, Attleboro	100	1880
Baker Sanitarium, Walter, F. L. Taylor, Roxbury, Boston	80	1892

(Continued on page XXX)

MASSACHUSETTS—Continued.

	Elevation	Established
Berkshire Hills Sanatorium, The, W. E. Brown, North Adams	927	1877
Buscall's Home, I. Buscall, Springfield	100	1890
Children's Island Sanitarium, H. J. Hall, Salem Harbor, Marblehead	50	1866
Douglas' Sanatorium, Dr., C. J. Douglas, 321 Center Street, Dorchester, Boston	80	....
Framingham Nervine, E. L. Keith, Winter Street, Framingham	300	1896
Greystone Towers Sanatorium, E. S. Le Lacheur, West Bridgewater	....	1904
Highlands, The, F. W. Russell, A. B., Winchendon	1,100	1875
Keeley Institute, J. H. Kane, Lexington	200	1892
Maquan Sanitarium, F. S. Thomas, South Hanson	60	1894
Millet Sanatorium, The, C. S. Millet, East Bridgewater	200	1900
Nauheim Sanitarium, Mary Sanderson, Springfield	200	1905
New England Sanitarium, W. E. Bliss, Melrose	300	1899
Newton Nervine, N. E. Paine, West Newton	40	1892
Newton Sanatorium, N. E. Paine, West Newton	40	1900
Ocean View, W. S. Birge, Provincetown	300	1902
Ring's Sanatorium, Dr., A. M. Ring, Arlington Heights, Boston	400	1879
Riverview Sanitarium, W. F. Robie, Baldwinville	1,000	1885
Sharon Sanatorium, V. Y. Bowditch, Sharon	300	1891
Somerville Sanitarium, H. Hull, 16 Austin Street, Somerville	500	1895
Tothill Lodge, A. H. Tuttle, Charles River Road, Cambridge	70	1901
Wheeler Sanitarium, Mrs. M. H. Paul, Superintendent, 32 Copeland Street, Roxbury District, Boston	80	1888
Wellesley Nervine, E. H. Wiswall, Wellesley	200	1897
Woodside Cottages, F. W. Patch, Framingham	350	1900
Worcester Sanitarium, "The Pines," H. A. Gibbs, Worcester	500	1897

NEW JERSEY.

	Elevation	Established
"Fair Oaks," Eliot Gorton, Summit	580	1902
Galen Hall, ———, Atlantic City	10	1894
Idylease Inn, E. A. Day, Newfoundland	1,000	1902
Oak Hill Sanitarium, D. M. Gardiner, Caldwell	500	1899
Plainfield Sanitarium, J. H. Cooley, Somerset Street, Plainfield	100	1879
Riverlawn, D. T. Millspaugh, 45 Totowa Avenue, Paterson	120	1891
Summit Grove Place Sanitarium, S. S. Nivison, Hammonton	100	....
Vaughan's Private Sanitarium, H. D. Van Gasbeek, Sussex	800	1895

NEW HAMPSHIRE.

	Elevation	Established
Highland Springs Sanatorium, A. E. Browning, Nashua	1,000	1900
Pembroke Sanatorium, H. T. Fontaine, Pembroke, P. O. Address, R. F. D. No. 14, Concord	700	1901

NEW YORK STATE.

	Elevation	Established
Adirondack Cottage Sanitarium, E. L. Trudeau, Saranac Lake	1,650	1884
Avon Springs Sanitarium, W. K. Quackenbush, Avon	700	1872
Bay Ridge Home, Mrs. A. A. R. Henrichsen, Supt., 224 Seventy-eighth Street, Brooklyn	90	....
Bethesda Sanitarium, The, W. H. Person, 192-194 St. Marks Avenue, Brooklyn	90	....
Bethesda Sanitarium, C. D. Clawson, Montour Falls	400	1879
Bond's House, Dr., G. F. M. Bond, 960 N. Broadway, Yonkers	350	1901
Breezehurst Terrace, D. A. Harrison, Whitestone, L. I.	140	1890
Brigham Hall Hospital, D. R. Burrell, Canandaigua	700	1855
Buffalo Electric Sanitarium, J. T. Pitkin, 206 Connecticut Street, Buffalo	500	1888
Clifton Springs Sanitarium, F. W. Spaulding, Clifton Springs	300	1850
Combes' Sanitarium, Dr., R. C. F. Combes, Flushing, N. Y. City	65	1889
Corwin Sanitarium, Elizabeth Corwin, Binghamton	800	1893
Dryden Spa Place Sanitarium, S. S. Nivison, Dryden	2,500	1862
Everett's House, Dr., E. A. Everett, 861 College Avenue, Elmira	1,000	1905
"Falkirk," ———, Central Valley	....	1890
Gabriels' Sanatorium, W. H. Clancy, Gabriels, Franklin County	1,800	1896
Gleason Health Resort, J. C. Fisher, Elmira	1,000	1852
Glens Springs Sanitarium, W. E. Leffingwell, Watkins	1,000	1890
Glenwood Sanitarium, J. W. Wherry, Dansville	980	1905
Graham Highland Park Sanatorium and Maternity Hospital, C. T. Graham, Rochester	500	1900
Greenmont Sanitarium, R. L. Parsons, Ossining	300	1880
"Interpines," F. W. Seward, Goshen	800	1890
Jackson Health Resort, J. H. Jackson, Dansville	900	1858
Keeley Institute, J. A. Boon, White Plains	300	1892
Keeley Institute, M. J. O'Connell, 799 Niagara Street, Buffalo	....	1894
Kellogg's House, Dr. T. H. Kellogg, Riverdale, New York City	50	1898
Knickerbocker Hall, J. R. Harding, College Point, L. I.	40	1902
Lexington Heights Hospital, D. G. Wilcox, 173 Lexington Avenue, Buffalo	500	1890
Long Island Home, O. J. Wilsey, Amityville, L. I.	12	1882
Loomis Sanatorium, H. M. King, Liberty, Sullivan County	2,300	1896
Louden Hall, J. Louden, Supt., Amityville, L. I.	29	1886
MacDonald's House, Dr., C. F. MacDonald, Pleasantville Station, Westchester County	350	1896
Marshall Sanatorium, H. Elliott, Troy	200	1851
McMichael's Sanatorium, Dr. G. H. McMichael, 75 West Tupper Street, Buffalo	500	1891
Middletown Sanitarium, Middletown, N. Y.	600	1902

(Concluded on page XXXII)

NEW YORK STATE.—Continued.

	Elevation	Established
Montefiore Home Country Sanatorium, L. Rosenberg, Bedford Station	450	1897
Morton's Private House, Dr., D. J. Morton, Eighty-eighth Street and Fort Hamilton Parkway, Brooklyn	90	1902
Muncie Sanitarium, E. H. Muncie, 117 Macon Street, Brooklyn	90	1896
Muncie Sanatorium Hotel, E. H. & L. H. Muncie, Muncie Island, Babylon, L. I.	150	1898
Murray Hill Sanitarium, E. V. Magnet, Supt., 148 East Thirty-fifth Street, New York City	56	....
New York Christian Home for Intemperate Men, Rev. G. L. Avery, Manager	50	1877
Olean Sanitarium, W. I. Hewitt, Olean	1,600	1894
Oppenheimer Institute, 317 West Fifty-seventh Street, New York City	50	1902
Parkside Sanitarium, S. A. Dunnam, Buffalo	500	1902
Private Sanitarium, A. J. Sherman, 126 East Sixtieth Street, New York City	50	1894
Providence Retreat, J. J. Twohey, 2157 Main Street, Buffalo	500	1860
River Crest, W. E. Dold, Astoria, L. I., New York City	50	....
Riverview, J. R. Bolton, Fishkill-on-the-Hudson	175	1870
Ross Health Resort, W. H. Ross, Brentwood, L. I.	80	1900
Sahler Sanitarium, The Dr. C. O., C. O Sahler, Kingston	180	1893
St. Vincent's Retreat, S. J. Brooks, Harrison, Westchester County (Women only)	300	1879
Sanford Hall, W. S. Brown, Flushing, New York City	30	1841
Shepard's Sanitarium, Dr., C. H. Shepard, 81 Columbia Heights, Brooklyn	90	1861
Spa Sanitarium, The, A. I. Thayer, 65 High Street, Ballston, Spa	400	1901
Steuben Sanitarium, J. E. Walker, Hornellsville	1,400	1892
Stony Wold Sanitarium, H. S. Goodall, Lake Kushaqua	1,725	1901
Stroug's, Dr., S. E. Strong, Saratoga Springs	300	1855
Telfair Sanitarium, W. G. Telfair, 568 West Avenue, Rochester	500	1892
Vitalist School of Physical Training, The, A. H. Terry, Blue Point, L. I.	70	1906
Waldmere-on-the-Sound, E. N. Carpenter, Mamaroneck	10	1889
Whitesboro Sanitarium, F. P. Bayliss, Whitesboro	500	1893
Williamson Sanitarium, A. N. Williamson, Dobb's Ferry	10	1880
Willis Sanitarium, H. Willis, 1453 Pacific Street, Brooklyn	90	1901

OHIO.

	Elevation	Established
Barnhill Sanitarium, T. G. Barnhill, Findlay	700	1895
"Brown Cure, The J. S.," C. J. Turner, Main Street, Greenspring	800	1865
Brunton Sanitarium, H. O. Brunton, Conneaut	200	1902
Cincinnati Sanitarium, F. W. Langdon, College Hill, Station K, Cincinnati	900	1873
Fair Oaks Villa, W. A. Searl, Cuyahoga Falls	1,100	1894
Geiger's Sanitarium, G. H. Geiger, 118 East Second Street, Dayton	700	1890
Good Samaritan Hospital, H. T. Sutton, Zanesville	690	1895
Grandview Sanitarium, Price Hill, B. T. Beebe, Cincinnati	800	1901
Hartman Sanitarium, D. R. Summy, 247 South Fourth Street, Columbus	450	1890
Langcoy's Bathatorium and Electric Health Home, J. Miller Langcoy's, Lime, Allen County	835	1900
Mansfield Sanitarium, B. F. Harding, Mansfield	1,300	1902
McMillen Sanitarium, Bishop McMillen, Shepard	600	1894
Mowry's Sanitarium and Treatment Rooms, Dr. D. Mowry, 203 Fountain Pl., Bellefontaine	1,100	1895
Park View Sanitarium, H. A. Rodebaugh, 664 N. Park Street, Columbus	790	1901
Oxford Retreat, G. F. Cook, Oxford	900	1885
Sawyer Sanitarium, C. E. Sawyer, Marion	240	1895
Sigler's Electrical Sanitarium, J. B. Claypool, Niles	870	1874
Shepard Sanitarium, W. E. Postle, Shepard	....	1853
University Sanitarium, C. A. Palmer, 773 Republic, Cleveland	600	1900

PENNSYLVANIA.

	Elevation	Established
Erastou Sanitarium, C. S. Kinney, Easton	300	....
Grand View Sanitarium, R. D. Wenrich, Wernersville	800	1847
Inwood Sanitarium, S. E. Winter, West Conshohocken	1,100	1898
Lebanon Sanitarium, A. B. Gloninger, Lebanon	600	1904
Lititz Springs Sanitarium, J. B. Brobst, Lititz	700	1902
Markleton Sanatorium, J. L. Martin, Markleton	2,000	1891
Mercer Sanitarium, The, M. L. McKinstry, Mercer	2,500	1900
Mountain Side Sanatorium, A. M. Rothrock, Mont Alto	2,000	1905
Pennsylvania Sanitarium, H. B. Knapp, 1929 Girard Avenue, Philadelphia	300	1902
South Mountain Camp Sanatorium, A. M. Rothrock, Mont Alto	1,650	1903
Sunnyrest Sanatorium, E. Stockdale, White Haven	1,200	1901
Walter Sanatorium, The, R. Walter, Walters Park	800	1874
White Haven Sanatorium, L. F. Flick, White Haven	1,500	1901

RHODE ISLAND.

	Elevation	Established
Bates' Electropathic Sanitarium, Dr., W. L. Bates, 141 Benefit Street, Providence	70	1893
Hopeworth Sanitarium, W. C. Canfield, Bristol	75	1883
Keeley Institute, The, T. J. Stringfield, Providence	70	1892

VERMONT.

	Elevation	Established
Lakeview Sanitarium, W. D. Berry, Burlington	300	1882
Prime's Vermont Sanitarium, Dr. W. R. Prime, 244 Pearl Street, Burlington	260	1895
Randolph Sanatorium, The, J. P. Gifford, Randolph	1,800	1905
Sparhawk Sanitarium, S. Sparhawk, Burlington	300	1887

Manufacturer and Builder of

SUMMER HOUSES : BRIDGES : ARBORS
HANGING BASKETS : WINDOW BOXES
SETTEES : TABLES : CHAIRS, Etc.

OFFICE AND SALESROOM
84 CORTLANDT ST. - NEW YORK
PHONE, 5259 CORTLANDT

Designs, Estimates and Illustrative Catalogue on Application : Park Furniture a Specialty.

HERMAN LIPS

LANDSCAPE GARDENER

84 Cortlandt St. - - - NEW YORK

Nurseries in Massachusetts Telephone, 5259 Cortlandt **Nurseries in New Jersey**

Detailed planting plans supplied and work carried out complete by contract or commission :: Estimates Cheerfully Given

IDEAL SUBURBAN TOWNS

The well-known fact that during the last few years there has been a great increase in the permanent population of the towns and villages constituting the suburbs of the large business centres, is particularly true of the delightful suburban places along the Long Island Railroad.

Those residing in cities have of late years been greatly interested in the advantages of living in the country the year round, and business men who must needs be at their desks or stores daily, are locating their families where they may have all the benefits of the country and where they themselves may spend each night without making the journey to and from the city a tiresome feature of their daily life.

Probably the most essential thing in living in a suburban town is quick and satisfactory transportation facilities to the city, and in referring to Long Island it is sufficient to say that the frequent and well regulated service of the Long Island Railroad is all that can be asked for.

Long Island's topographical variations range themselves into three main classes, each served by a separate branch of the Long Island R.R. On the southern shore is a charming stretch of land overlooking the Atlantic Ocean and the Great South Bay, with fine beaches (the only extensive east and west beach on the Atlantic Coast), unexcelled for surf and still-water bathing; the central section is level though in places rolling country, made up of farms and woodland; the northern reaches of the island are generally hilly, covered with a thick growth of trees.

The great diversity of scenery and natural characteristics make Long Island a most popular Summer and residential territory. Its nearness to New York City, the superiority of the railroad service, the excellence of its school system, the high quality of its society—pure water, refreshing breezes, cooled by the ocean in the Summer—churches of all denominations, clubs, libraries and well-stocked stores—all unite in producing conditions that are ideal for a home, which is proven by the fact that many handsome residences have long since been established there and are occupied the entire year by their owners.

No other suburban territory can make so strong an appeal to the seekers of a quiet, restful, healthful, home section as Long Island.

For Illustrated and Descriptive Books Write to the General Passenger Agent of the

LONG ISLAND RAILROAD

263 Fifth Avenue, New York

A. L. LANGDON, Traffic Manager. **HOWARD M. SMITH,** General Passenger Agent.

Street Directory.

CROSS STREET CORNER NUMBERS ON BROADWAY AND THE AVENUES, N. Y. CITY.

BROADWAY.

1 Battery Pl.	210 Fulton.	362 Franklin.	694 Fourth.	901 E. 20th.	1291 W 33d.	1549 W. 46th.
8 Beaver.	222 Ann.	378 White.	713 Wash'ton Pl.	919 E. 21st.	Sixth Avenue.	1569 W. 47th.
27 Morris.	Vesey.	398 Walker.	727 Waverley Pl.	939 E. 22d.	1311 W. 34th.	1589 W. 48th.
55 Exchange Al.	227 Barclay.	413 Lispenard.	744 Astor Place.	957 E. 23d.	1329 W. 35th.	1609 W. 49th.
56 Exchange Pl.	237 Park Place.	416 Canal.	755 Eighth.	957 Fifth Ave.	1349 W. 36th.	1629 W. 50th.
73 Rector.	247 Murray.	432 Howard.	770 E. 9th.	Madison Square.	1369 W. 37th.	1649 W. 51st.
86 Wall.	259 Warren.	458 Grand.	784 E. 10th.	1099 W. 24th.	1391 W. 38th.	1665 W. 52d.
100 Pine.	271 Chambers.	486 Broome.	801 E. 11th.	1119 W. 25th.	1409 W. 39th.	1687 W. 53d.
114 Thames.	287 Reade.	526 Spring.	824 E. 12th.	1139 W. 26th.	1429 W. 40th.	1709 W. 54th.
119 Cedar.	303 Duane.	566 Prince.	840 E. 13th.	1159 W. 27th.	1447 W. 41st.	1729 W. 55th.
145 Liberty.	317 Thomas.	608 Houston.	858 E. 14th.	1183 W. 28th.	1467 W. 42d.	1749 W. 56th.
171 Cortlandt.	318 Pearl.	640 Bleecker.	Union Square.	1203 W. 29th.	1489 W. 43d.	1769 W. 57th.
172 Maiden Lane.	334 Worth.	658 Bond.	857 E. 17th.	1227 W. 30th.	1505 W. 44th.	1787 W. 58th.
184 John.	344 Catharine La.	681 W. 3d.	871 E. 18th.	1251 W. 31st.	1525 W. 45th.	1805 W. 59th.
191 Dey.	348 Leonard	682 Great Jones.	887 E. 19th.	1273 W. 32d.	Seventh Avenue.	Central Park.

FIFTH AVENUE.

1 Wash'ton Sq.	185 23d.	439 39th.	703 55th.	889 70th.	1039 85th.	1189 100th.
7 Clinton Pl.	Broadway.	457 40th.	719 56th.	899 71st.	1049 86th.	1199 101st.
21 9th.	25th.	477 41st.	737 57th.	909 72d.	1059 87th.	1209 102d.
33 10th.	216 26th.	499 42d.	751 58th.	919 73d.	1069 88th.	1219 103d.
41 11th.	231 27th.	511 43d.	769 59th.	929 74th.	1079 89th.	1229 104th.
51 12th.	249 28th.	529 44th.	787 60th.	939 75th.	1089 90th.	1239 105th.
61 13th.	263 29th.	545 45th.	799 61st.	949 76th.	1099 91st.	1249 106th.
67 14th.	281 30th.	561 46th.	809 62d.	959 77th.	1109 92d.	1259 107th.
96 15th.	299 31st.	575 47th.	817 63d.	969 78th.	1119 93d	1269 108th.
81 16th.	315 32d.	593 48th.	829 64th.	979 79th.	1129 94th.	1279 109th.
95 17th.	331 33d.	609 49th.	839 65th.	989 80th.	1139 95th.	2002 124th.
107 18th.	353 34th.	623 50th.	849 66th.	999 81st.	1149 96th.	2020 125th.
115 19th.	371 35th.	637 51st.	856 67th	1009 82d.	1159 97th.	2040 126th.
133 20th.	387 36th.	653 52d.	869 68th.	1019 83d.	1169 98th.	2056 127th.
147 21st.	405 37th.	671 53d.	879 69th.	1029 84th.	1179 99th.	2076 128th.
165 22d.	421 38th	685 54th.				

THIRD AVENUE.

1 Seventh.	819 E. 24th.	657 E. 42d.	1009 E 60th.	1371 E. 78th.	1722 E. 96th.	2082 E. 114th.
Astor Place.	337 E. 25th.	679 E. 43d.	1029 E. 61st.	1389 E. 79th.	E. 97th.	2100 E. 115th.
19 St. Mark's Pl.	355 E. 26th.	701 E. 44th.	1047 E. 62d.	1409 E. 80th.	E. 98th.	2123 E. 116th.
28 E. 9th.	373 E. 27th.	721 E. 45th.	1069 E. 63d.	1433 E. 81st.	1781 E. 99th.	2141 E. 117th.
45 E. 10th.	391 E. 28th.	739 E. 46th.	1089 E. 64th.	1451 E. 82d.	1800 E. 100th.	2161 E. 118th.
63 E. 11th.	411 E. 29th.	755 E. 47th.	1109 E. 65th.	1469 E. 83d.	1816 E. 101st.	2181 E. 119th.
83 E. 12th.	429 E. 30th.	773 E. 48th.	1129 E. 66th.	1487 E. 84th.	1843 E. 102d.	2199 E. 120th.
103 E. 13th.	449 E. 31st.	793 E. 49th.	1148 E. 67th.	1505 E. 85th.	1861 E. 103d.	2217 E. 121st.
123 E. 14th.	467 E. 32d.	813 E. 50th.	1160 E. 68th.	1525 E. 86th.	1881 E. 104th.	2241 E. 122d.
145 E. 15th.	487 E. 33d.	835 E. 51st.	1185 E. 69th.	1545 E. 87th.	1897 E. 105th.	2261 E. 123d.
165 E. 16th.	505 E. 34th.	857 E. 52d.	1205 E. 70th.	1565 E. 88th.	1923 E. 106th.	2281 E. 124th.
185 E. 17th.	523 E. 35th.	875 E. 53d.	1229 E. 71st.	1583 E. 89th.	1943 E. 107th.	2297 E. 125th.
203 E 18th.	541 E. 36th.	895 E. 54th.	1245 E. 72d.	1605 E. 90th.	1965 E. 108th.	2319 E. 126th.
223 E. 19th.	557 E. 37th.	913 E. 55th.	1265 E. 73d.	1627 E. 91st.	1981 E. 109th.	2339 E. 127th.
243 E. 20th.	577 E. 38th.	933 E. 56th.	1289 E. 74th.	1643 E. 92d.	2007 E. 110th.	2359 E. 128th.
261 E. 21st.	597 E 39th.	951 E. 57th.	1309 E. 75th.	1657 E. 93d.	2023 E. 111th.	2375 E. 129th.
281 E. 22d.	617 E. 40th.	969 E. 58th.	1329 E. 76th	1677 E. 94th.	2041 E. 112th.	2398 E. 130th.
299 E. 23d.	635 E. 41st.	989 E. 59th.	1349 E. 77th.	1693 E. 95th.	2063 E. 113th.	Harlem River.

LEXINGTON AVENUE.

1 E. 21st.	293 E. 37th.	593 E. 52d.	901 E. 67th.	1209 E. 82d.	1629 E. 103d.	1895 E. 118th.
9 E. 22d.	311 E. 38th.	615 E. 53d.	921 E. 68th.	1221 E. 83d.	1645 E. 104th.	1915 E. 119th.
17 E. 23d.	331 E. 39th.	635 E. 54th.	941 E. 69th.	1241 E. 84th.	1673 E. 105th.	1944 E. 120th.
39 E. 24th.	353 E. 40th.	655 E. 55th.	961 E. 70th.	1249 E. 85th.	1689 E. 106th.	1980 E. 121st.
59 E. 25th.	373 E. 41st.	675 E. 56th.	979 E. 71st.	1271 E. 86th.	1705 E. 107th.	2001 E. 122d.
77 E. 26th.	389 E. 42d.	695 E. 57th.	995 E 72d.	1289 E. 87th.	1733 E. 108th.	2025 E. 123d.
91 E. 27th.	413 E. 43d.	721 E. 58th.	1023 E. 73d.	1309 E. 88th.	1755 E. 109th.	E. 124th.
115 E. 28th.	435 E. 44th.	741 E. 59th.	1031 E. 74th.	1328 E. 89th.	1773 E. 110th.	2056 E. 125th.
135 E. 29th.	449 E. 45th	751 E. 60th.	1055 E. 75th.	1348 E. 90th.	1787 E. 111th.	2085 E. 126th.
159 E. 30th.	473 E. 46th.	781 E. 61st.	1077 E. 76th.	1362 E. 91st.	1801 E. 112th.	2102 E. 127th.
177 E. 31st.	491 E. 47th.	801 E. 62d.	1099 E. 77th.	1380 E. 92d.	1813 E. 113th.	2125 E. 128th.
197 E. 32d.	513 E. 48th.	821 E. 63d.	1113 E. 78th.	1423 E. 93d.	1841 E. 114th.	2143 E. 129th.
217 E. 33d.	537 E. 49th.	841 E 64th.	1135 E. 79th.	1447 E. 94th.	1856 E. 115th.	2168 E. 130th.
237 E. 34th.	555 E. 50th.	861 E. 65th.	1159 E. 80th.	1469 E. 95th.	1869 E. 116th.	E. 131st.
253 E. 35th.	571 E. 51st.	881 E. 66th.	1187 E. 81st.	1613 E. 102d.	1877 E. 117th.	Harlem River.
271 E. 36th.						

FOURTH AVENUE.

2 Bowery.	Eighth.	111 E. 12th.	250 E. 20th.	322 E. 24th.	384 E. 27th.	440 E. 30th.
Sixth.	55 E. 9th.	135 E. 13th.	265 E. 21st.	342 E. 25th.	402 E. 28th.	460 E. 31st.
Seventh.	73 E. 10th.	157 E. 14th.	283 E. 22d.	362 E. 26th.	422 E. 29th.	478 E. 32d.
37 Astor Place.	91 E. 11th.	Union Square.	289 E. 23d.			

PARK AVENUE.

1 E. 34th.	375 E. 53d.	650 E. 67th.	935 E. 81st.	1217 E. 95th.	1489 E. 109th.	E. 123d.
18 E. 35th.	395 E. 54th.	E. 68th.	957 E. 82d.	1236 E. 96th.	1507 E. 110th.	1796 E. 124th.
37 E. 36th.	413 E. 55th.	692 E. 69th.	979 E. 83d.	1253 E. 97th.	1526 E. 111th.	1817 E. 125th.
47 E. 37th.	435 E. 56th.	717 E. 70th.	997 E. 84th.	1269 E. 98th.	1555 E. 112th.	1837 E. 126th.
65 E. 38th.	455 E. 57th.	731 E. 71st.	1015 E. 85th.	E. 99th.	1571 E. 113th.	1851 E. 127th.
79 E. 39th.	479 E. 58th.	757 E. 72d.	1037 E. 86th.	1316 E. 100th.	1590 E. 114th.	1875 E. 128th.
99 E. 40th.	497 E. 59th.	779 E. 73d.	1055 E. 87th.	1336 E. 101st.	1617 E. 115th.	1895 E. 129th.
115 E. 41st	513 E. 60th.	795 E. 74th.	1075 E. 88th.	1353 E. 102d.	1635 E. 116th.	1915 E. 130th.
135 E. 42d.	525 E. 61st.	819 E. 75th.	1097 E. 89th.	E. 103d.	1649 E. 117th.	1937 E. 131st.
R. R. Yard.	549 E. 62d.	833 E. 76th.	1115 E. 90th.	E. 104th	1673 E. 118th.	1957 E. 132d.
E. 48th.	573 E. 63d.	E. 77th.	1135 E. 91st.	1408 E. 105th.	1695 E. 119th.	1978 E. 133d.
E. 49th.	593 E. 64th.	879 E. 78th.	1155 E. 92d.	1424 E. 106th.	1711 E. 120th.	E. 134th.
E. 50th.	607 E. 65th.	895 E. 79th.	1177 E. 93d.	1455 E. 107th.	1737 E. 121st.	E. 135th.
E. 51st.	637 E. 66th.	911 E. 80th.	1197 E. 94th.	1475 E. 108th.	1755 E. 122d.	Harlem River.
E. 52d.						

MADISON AVENUE.

1 E. 23d.	228 E. 37th.	E. 51st.	750 E. 65th.	1029 E. 79th.	1689 E. 112th.	1969 E. 126th.
11 E. 24th.	244 E. 38th.	E. 52d.	770 E. 66th.	1047 E. 80th.	1709 E. 113th.	1991 E. 127th.
21 E. 25th.	262 E. 39th.	510 E. 53d.	790 E. 67th.	1071 E. 81st.	1729 E. 114th.	2013 E. 128th.
37 E. 26th.	280 E. 40th.	530 E. 54th.	811 E. 68th.	E. 82d.	1749 E. 115th.	2029 E. 129th.
60 E. 27th.	298 E. 41st.	540 E. 55th.	826 E. 69th.	1103 E. 83d.	1769 E. 116th.	2049 E. 130th.
78 E. 28th.	314 E. 42d.	570 E. 56th.	846 E. 70th.	1121 E. 84th.	1789 E. 117th.	2071 E. 131st.
96 E. 29th.	330 E. 43d.	578 E. 57th.	E. 71st.	* * *	1809 E. 118th.	2099 E. 132d.
116 E. 30th.	344 E. 44th.	606 E. 58th.	E. 72d.	1549 E. 105th.	1829 E. 119th.	2119 E. 133d.
132 E. 31st.	350 E. 45th.	634 E. 59th.	875 E. 73d.	1569 E. 106th.	1849 E. 120th.	2139 E. 134th.
150 E. 32d.	E. 46th.	650 E. 60th.	931 E. 74th.	1589 E. 107th.	1869 E. 121st.	2149 E. 135th.
168 E. 33d.	E. 47th.	670 E. 61st.	951 E. 75th.	1609 E. 108th.	1889 E. 122d.	E. 136th.
184 E. 34th.	412 E. 48th.	686 E. 62d.	971 E. 76th.	1629 E. 109th.	1909 E. 123d.	E. 137th.
198 E. 35th.	430 E. 49th.	708 E. 63d.	987 E. 77th.	1649 E. 110th.	1929 E. 124th.	E. 138th.
214 E. 36th.	450 E. 50th.	726 E. 64th.	1009 E. 78th.	1669 E. 111th.	1949 E. 125th.	Harlem River.

SIXTH AVENUE.

1 Carmine.	112 W. 9th.	267 W. 17th.	427 W. 26th.	B'way W. 35th.	771 W. 44th.	933 W. 53d.
2 Minetta Lane.	132 W. 10th.	287 W. 18th.	447 W. 27th.	609 W. 36th.	791 W. 45th.	951 W. 54th.
16 W. 3d.	139 Milligan Pl.	303 W. 19th.	465 W. 28th.	631 W. 37th.	813 W. 46th.	971 W. 55th.
39 W. 4th.	149 W. 11th.	319 W. 20th.	483 W. 29th.	651 W. 38th.	829 W. 47th.	991 W. 56th.
57 Wash'ton Pl.	169 W. 12th.	337 W. 21st.	499 W. 30th.	677 W. 39th.	847 W. 48th.	1011 W. 57th.
75 Waverley Pl.	187 W. 13th.	355 W. 22d.	519 W. 31st.	697 W. 40th.	867 W. 49th.	1031 W. 58th.
94 Clinton Pl.	207 W. 14th.	373 W. 23d.	533 W. 32d.	717 W. 41st.	885 W. 50th.	1051 W. 59th.
105 Greenwich	227 W. 15th.	389 W. 24th.	B'way W. 33d.	735 W. 42d.	899 W. 51st.	Central Park.
Ave.	251 W. 16th.	409 W. 25th.	B'way W. 34th.	755 W. 43d.	917 W. 52d.	

FIRE! FIRE!! FIRE!!!

THE CRY MAY CAUSE ALARM

BUT WITH THE PROTECTION OF AN

"ACME" FIRE EXTINGUISHER

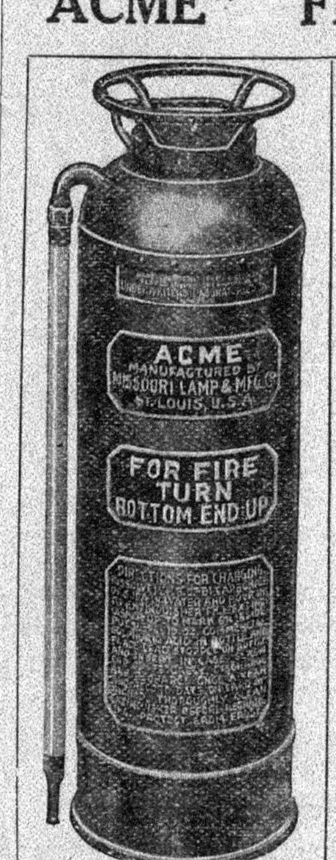

THE DAMAGE IS AVOIDED WHERE USUALLY 100 GALLONS OF WATER ARE APPLIED.

Our Celebrated "ACME" Does the Work

No Business Place, Factory or Home Should Be Without FIRE PROTECTION.

CONSIDER ITS VALUE BEFORE ITS NECESSITY

Be on the safe side by writing us to-day for Free Illustrated Circular, with prices.

We are the patentees and manufacturers of the famous REX —ROYAL—PHOENIX—MISSOURI — U. S. — AJAX — ADVANCE.

APPROVED NOV. 15, 1901
BY THE
National Fire Protection Ass'n.

LARGEST MANUFACTURERS OF
CHEMICAL FIRE EXTINGUISHERS
IN THE WORLD

MISSOURI LAMP AND M'F'G CO., ST. LOUIS, MO., U. S. A 111a ELM STREET

Electricity Now Does All the Washing and Wringing

We now attach an electric motor to the famous 1900 Washer. It operates the wringer, too. Connect it with a light fixture as you connect a table lamp. Turn on the current as you turn on the light. The washer then operates just like our hand washer, only you don't need to touch it.

When the washing is done, move a small lever and the motor connects with the wringer. The one motor, operating both the washer and wringer, does every whit of the work. Please think what that means. The hardest drudgery there is about housework done by two cents' worth of electricity.

Servants happy; laundry bills saved; clothes lasting twice as long. For the "1900" does washing better than any other method known.

Now electricity makes the washer go. Doesn't that sound like a new era for women?

The Electric Washer and Wringer

You can now have your washings done by electricity. The 1900 Electric Washer Outfit (Washer, Wringer and Motor complete) does all the heavy work of washing and wrings out the clothes.

Any electric light current furnishes the power needed. You connect up the washer the same way you put an electric light globe into its socket. Then all there is to do to start the washer is—turn on the electricity. The motion of the tub (driven by the electricity) and the water and soap in the tub wash the clothes clean. Washing is done quicker and easier, and more thoroughly and economically this way than ever before.

Servants will stay contented—laundry bills will be saved—clothes will last twice as long—where there is a 1900 Electric Washer to do the washing.

These washers save so much work and worry and trouble, that they *sell themselves*. This is the way of it—

30 DAYS' FREE TRIAL—FREIGHT PREPAID

We ship you an Electric Washer and *prepay the freight*.

Use the washer a month. Wash your linens and laces—wash your blankets and quilts—wash your rugs.

Then—when the month is up if you are not convinced the washer is all we say—don't keep it. Tell us you don't want the washer and that will settle the matter. We won't charge anything for the use you have had of it.

This is the *only* washer outfit that does *all* the drudgery of the washing—*washes* and *wrings* clothes—saves them from wear and tear—and keeps your servants contented. Our washer book tells how our washers are made and how they work. Send for this book to-day.

Don't mortgage your pleasure in life to dread of wash-day and wash-day troubles with servants.

Let the 1900 Electric Washer and Wringer shoulder your wash-day burden—save your clothes and money, and keep your servants contented.

Write for our Washer Book at once. Address—

The 1900 *Washer Co.*, 973 *Henry Street, Binghamton, N. Y.* (*If you live in Canada, write to the Canadian* 1900 *Washer Co.*, 355 *Yonge Street, Toronto Ont.*)

We also offer the "1900" gravity washer for those not using electricity.

Simply ask us to show you the "1900" Gravity Washer. We will send it to you, freight prepaid. You pay no deposit, give no security; you are under no obligation.

Use it for 30 days; do four washings with it. Learn how it saves your labor, and how it saves your clothes.

Then if you want it, pay a little each week, or a little each month. No hurry; just suit yourself. If you don't want it simply send it back.

The "1900" saves so much, and costs so little, that it is far cheaper to have it than to go without it. So send us this coupon now for our new Washer Book, showing the different styles. Then tell us which you want to see, and we'll send it. Do this in justice to yourself.

Mail Us This Coupon

The 1900 Washer Co.,
973 Henry St., Binghamton, N. Y.

Send me your Free Washer Book

Name..

Address..

We have a Canadian Factory at Toronto.

The "1900" Gravity Washer

BETTER
FIRE PROTECTION
THE
PITTSBURGH
TO USE
TURN BOTTOM UP
TO STOP TURN BACK
SAFETY
FIRE BUCK
TANK
NEW YORK
THE PITTSBURGH
APPROVED
FIRE EXTINGUISHER
three-gallon capacity, polished copper, tested to 350 pounds pressure, made according to the requirements of the National Board of Fire Underwriters, bearing label of the Underwriters' Laboratories.

THE SAFETY

FIRE BUCKET TANK contains six fire buckets with self-raising handles, submerged in a Steel Tank filled with twenty-five to forty gallons of chemical solution.

Six men can each take a bucket.

There is no evaporation, no fouling, nothing to get out of order.

The chemical solution will not freeze at twenty-five degrees below zero.

Requires no attention. Always ready for immediate use.

Send for booklet "Better Fire Protection."

THE SAFETY FIRE EXTINGUISHER COMPANY

29-33 WEST 42D STREET : NEW YORK

Telephone : Bryant 2491

Anglo-American Telegraph Co., Ltd.

ESTABLISHED 1866

THE PIONEER ATLANTIC CABLE COMPANY.

Direct Communication Between America and Europe by Four Cables.

AUTOMATIC DUPLEX SYSTEM.

NEW CABLES TO FRANCE, HOLLAND, AND BELGIUM

GOOD COMMUNICATION WITH GERMANY.

Telegrams can be forwarded "VIA ANGLO CABLES," to Europe, Egypt, East and West Coasts of Africa, Turkey, India, China, Cochin China, Corea, Manila, Japan, Australia, New Zealand, South America, Zanzibar, Mozambique, Arabia, Cape of Good Hope, Cape Verde, Madeira, and the Canary Islands, etc., etc.,

FROM THE FOLLOWING AMERICAN STATIONS:

NEW YORK OFFICES:
- Head Office, 8 Broad Street (Stock Exchange Bldg.), Tel. No. 3635 Rector.
- 68 Broad Street (Morris Bldg.), Tel. No. 3635 Rector.
- Produce Exchange Building, Tel. No. 870 Broad.
- 445 Broome Street (Silk Exchange Bldg.), Tel. No. 691 Spring.

MONTREAL OFFICE: 51 St. Francois Xavier Street, Tel. No. Bell 1027.

OFFICES IN EUROPE:

LONDON: 63 Old Broad Street, E. C.
" 109 Fenchurch Street, E. C.
" 46 Mark Lane, E. C.
" Baltic Exchange Chambers, St. Mary Axe, E. C.
" 2 Northumberland Avenue, Charing Cross, W. C.
" 48 Tooley Street, S. E.
LIVERPOOL: A1 The Exchange.
BRADFORD: 10 Forster Square.
BRISTOL: Back Hall Chambers, Baldwin Street.
DUNDEE: 1 Panmure Street.
EDINBURGH: 50 Frederick Street.

GLASGOW: 113 Hope Street.
LEITH: Exchange Buildings.
MANCHESTER: 31 Brown Street.
NEWCASTLE-ON-TYNE: 1 Side.
PARIS AGENCY: 37 Rue Caumartin.
CARDIFF " Atlantic Buildings.
ANTWERP " 26 Rue du Menuisiers.
ROME " 49 Via venti Settembre.
AMSTERDAM AGENCY: Weesperzyde 4.
BARCELONA " 96 Paseo de Gracia.
COPENHAGEN " 2 I Chr. Wintersvej.
HAVRE: 118 Boulevard Strasbourg.

CHRISTIANIA: P. O. box 3.

THE SHORTEST AND QUICKEST ROUTES ACROSS THE ATLANTIC.

Used by all the principal stockbrokers of New York, London, Liverpool, etc., to whom the QUICKEST OBTAINABLE SERVICE is essential.

THIS COMPANY, whose CARRYING CAPACITY IS FAR IN EXCESS OF ANY OTHER ATLANTIC CABLE COMPANY, is naturally favorable to the MAINTENANCE OF A LOW RATE WITH AN INCREASING VOLUME OF TRAFFIC.

"WELL! WELL! I HEAR YOU PERFECTLY NOW!"
"I hear you anywhere in the Room; why I could not hear ordinary conversation one foot away.
"I have had the Acousticon now for nearly a year and it is all in all to me. Gold could not buy it if I could not get another."
GARRET BROWN, St. Louis, Mo.
The experience of Mr. Brown is the same as that of thousands who are now using the Acousticon—To them we have said as we now say to you:
Test the Acousticon and let us prove that it will make you hear easily, distinctly and clearly
Entirely At Our Expense
If you are not convenient to one of our many offices, you can test it at your own home and if you do not hear satisfactorily the trial will not cost you one cent. No trial fee, no penalty, no expense whatever if you do not hear.
The Acousticon is the original electrical hearing device, fully protected by U. S. patents and you cannot secure anything as efficient under another name.
Write for particulars of the Free Test, Booklet, etc. to
THE GENERAL ACOUSTIC CO.
832 BROWNING BUILDING,
Broadway and 32d St., New York City.

Be a Producer!

—The man who is a producer of business is never in danger of being without a good position.

The house cannot exist without him. It must have him. He is a money-maker. He keeps the wheels of business turning. Take him off the job and business stops entirely. Hard times or no hard times, he is sure of a place because he pays his own way—and a good deal more.

Why not be a star salesman?

Why not become the kind of a producing man they cannot get along without?

Salesmanship pays better than any other profession—better than law, or medicine, or engineering—better than nearly any kind of technical work you could take up. And it pays quicker! Capable salesmen earn good money **from the start.**

Salesmanship is a broad field—it is not confined to any line of business or profession.

The Sheldon School helps make salesmen.

Studying the Sheldon Science of Salesmanship will fit any man to enter the production side of business, and to be successful there.

Study Scientific Salesmanship as taught by Sheldon by correspondence, and make yourself the kind of man there is a demand for, the kind they can't get along without, the producing kind of man.

If you are a salesman already, Sheldon can help you become a better salesman. He has helped 33,000 others, representing every line of business.

We maintain an employment division to help locate our graduates when they need it. We do not guarantee to get them positions, but the fact that in this department we have requests for three times as many men as we have men asking for postions shows that Sheldon graduates are in demand and that they have little trouble getting a good position through us if they need it.

Send coupon **today** for free booklet outlining the Course in Salesmanship. **Don't wait. Investigate** this success-building plan at any rate.

If you live in Chicago, New York, Cleveland, San Francisco, Los Angeles, Denver, or wherever we have a branch office, we will give you a free personal lesson in Salesmanship to show you the value of this great course.

Every day you delay adopting some definite plan for increasing your efficiency you become less essential to the business world. You have "intended" making this start long enough. Now make it. Check off the coupon below, sign it and send it in, or write us.

The Sheldon School,
1217 Republic Bldg., Chicago, Ill.

THE SHELDON SCHOOL,
1217 Republic Building, Chicago.

Please send me your free book on Salesmanship. I am interested specially in the subjects I have checked below:

....Salesmanship
....Advertising
....Business Logic
....Business Psychology
....Promotion
....Self Development
....System and Costs
....Self Education
....Science of Retail Merchandising.

Name..

Address..

Town...................... *State*................

Position.................. *Business*.............

All instruction by correspondence.

Do you use Press Clippings?

If you do not, drop a postal card to

Romeike's Press Clipping Bureau

and we will show you how Press Clippings can be used to your advantage.

Press Clippings are always interesting and profitable, they are indispensable to professional and business men alike.

Authors, artists, actors, singers and society leaders are supplied with reviews and criticisms.

We collect obituary notices and bind them in scrapbooks.

Lawyers, bankers, brokers, financial institutes depend largely on quick information from the columns of the press; we supply them.

To the manufacturer we show through the Clippings new markets for his products.

The inventor, the politician, the social reformer, in fact all who attract the attention of the press, are informed and kept up to date by Press Clippings.

A postal card will bring all the information.

HENRY ROMEIKE, Inc.

110-112 West 26th St. - New York City

Telephone, 3923 Madison Square

DICTIONARY INDEX

An Aid to the Student and the Teacher

not only in saving time, but in preserving continuity of thought. The late President CHARLES KENDALL ADAMS said of this index: "It is of especial value to those learning a foreign language." APPLICABLE TO ALL DICTIONARIES, BOOKS OF REFERENCE, SCIENTIFIC AND TECHNICAL. Ask your bookdealer for it or apply directly to

DENISON & SILVERA, 152 E. 23d St., N. Y.

TELEPHONE 150 GRAMERCY

PATENT Your Inventions

Our free Hand-Book for Inventors tells what you want to know about PROTECTIVE patents, how to obtain them, the cost, and our PERSONAL SERVICE. Advice free. We are the only attorneys who agree to return our entire attorney fee if FOR ANY REASON WHATEVER we fail to secure patent. Our Mr. Beeler was for ten years an Examiner in the U. S. Patent Office before becoming a member of our firm. References furnished. BEELER & ROBB, U. S. and Foreign Patents, 105-109 McGill Building, Washington, D. C.

TRADE-MARKS REGISTERED IN THE U. S. PATENT OFFICE.

REDDING & CO.

MASONIC BOOKS AND GOODS

Regalia, Jewels, Badges, Pins, Charms and Lodge Supplies

Send for Catalogue **212 BROADWAY, NEW YORK** (Entrance on Fulton Street)

WHEN YOU PATRONIZE THE ADVERTISERS, KINDLY MENTION THE WORLD ALMANAC.

Strickland Cleaner Plants

High Grade Vacuum Devices for Sanitary Clean:ng

Made in 3 sizes for

Residences

Hotels

Hospitals

Institutions

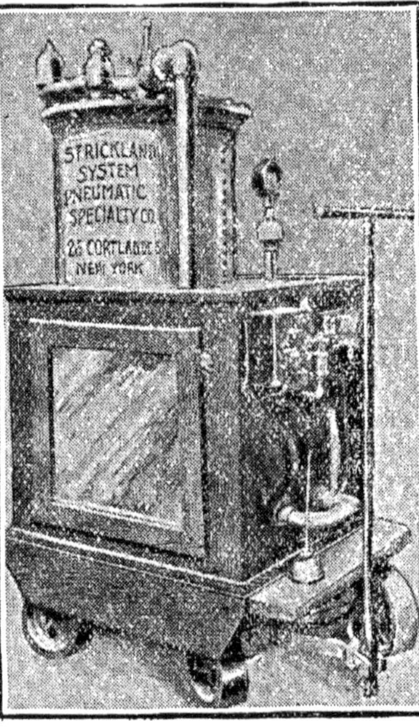

Office Buildings

Railway Cars and Terminals

Steamships etc.

Provides a complete service, which is distributed throughout the building.

The dirt, dust and grit is collected in a receptacle near the apparatus.

Eradicates dust, dirt and germs from the upholstered portions of furniture without injury to the fabric.

Portable Size No. 2

Enables the maid or porter to house-clean at any time instead of making it an annual or semi-annual event.

Removes dust and deposits from curtains, draperies, walls, ceilings and decorations, preventing their discoloration from that cause.

Dispels the necessity of taking up and sending out carpets, rugs and mattings for cleaning purposes.

Renovates and aerates bedding, mattresses, clothing, quilts, etc.

Will keep the general interior in a cleanly and more healthful condition than is possible with other methods.

Does all work in a DUSTLESS and SANITARY manner with little effort on the part of the operator and in much less time than is necessary by old-fashioned ways.

Send for Illustrated Folder, or, better still, let us send our representative to arrange for demonstration.

Pneumatic Specialty Company

26 CORTLANDT STREET

Havemeyer Building NEW YORK CITY

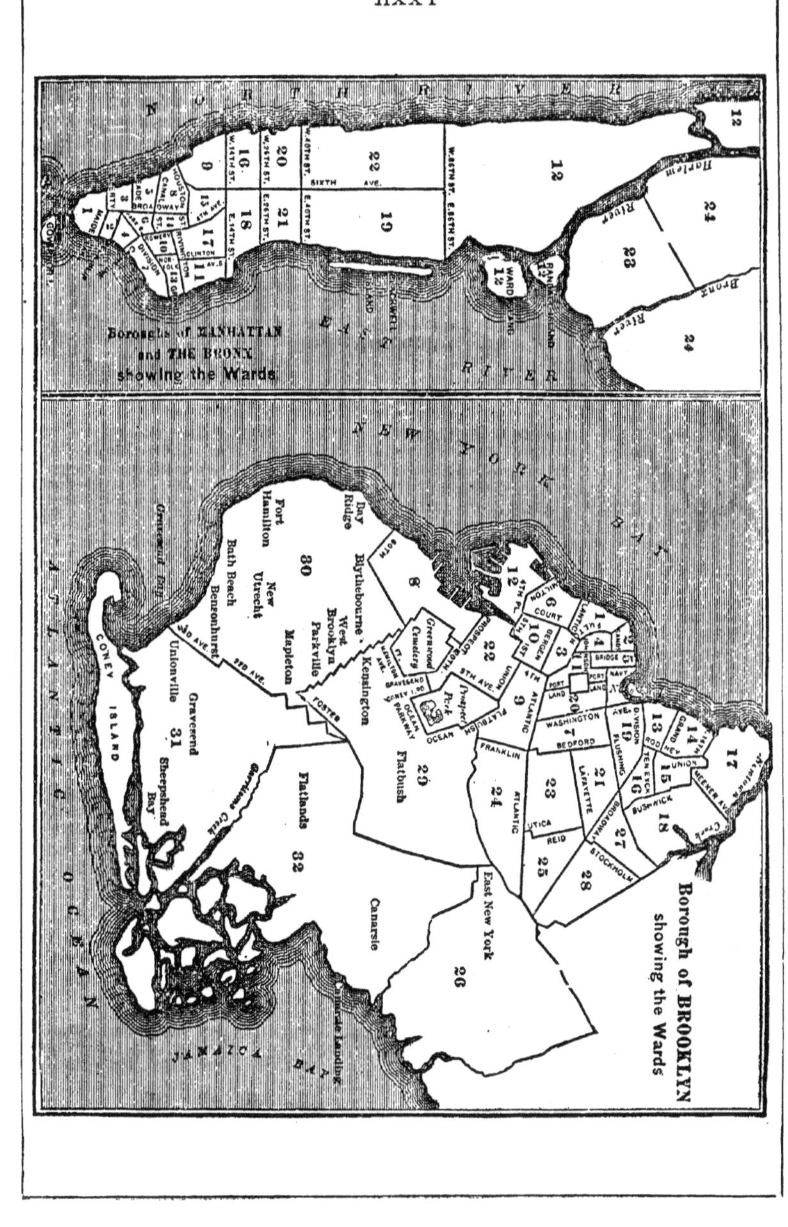
Borough of BROOKLYN
showing the Wards
Boroughs of MANHATTAN
and THE BRONX
showing the Wards
East New York
Canarsie
Flatlands
Flatbush
Kensington
Blythebourne
West Brooklyn
Parkville
Mapleton
New Utrecht
Bath Beach
Bensonhurst
Gravesend
Unionville
Sheepshead Bay
Fort Hamilton
Bay Ridge
Coney Island
Gravesend Bay
Gerritsens Creek
Canarsie Landing
Jamaica Bay
Prospect Park
Greenwood Cemetery
Newtown Creek
New York Bay
Atlantic Ocean
East River
North River
Harlem River
Bronx River
Blackwells Island
Wards Island
Randalls Island

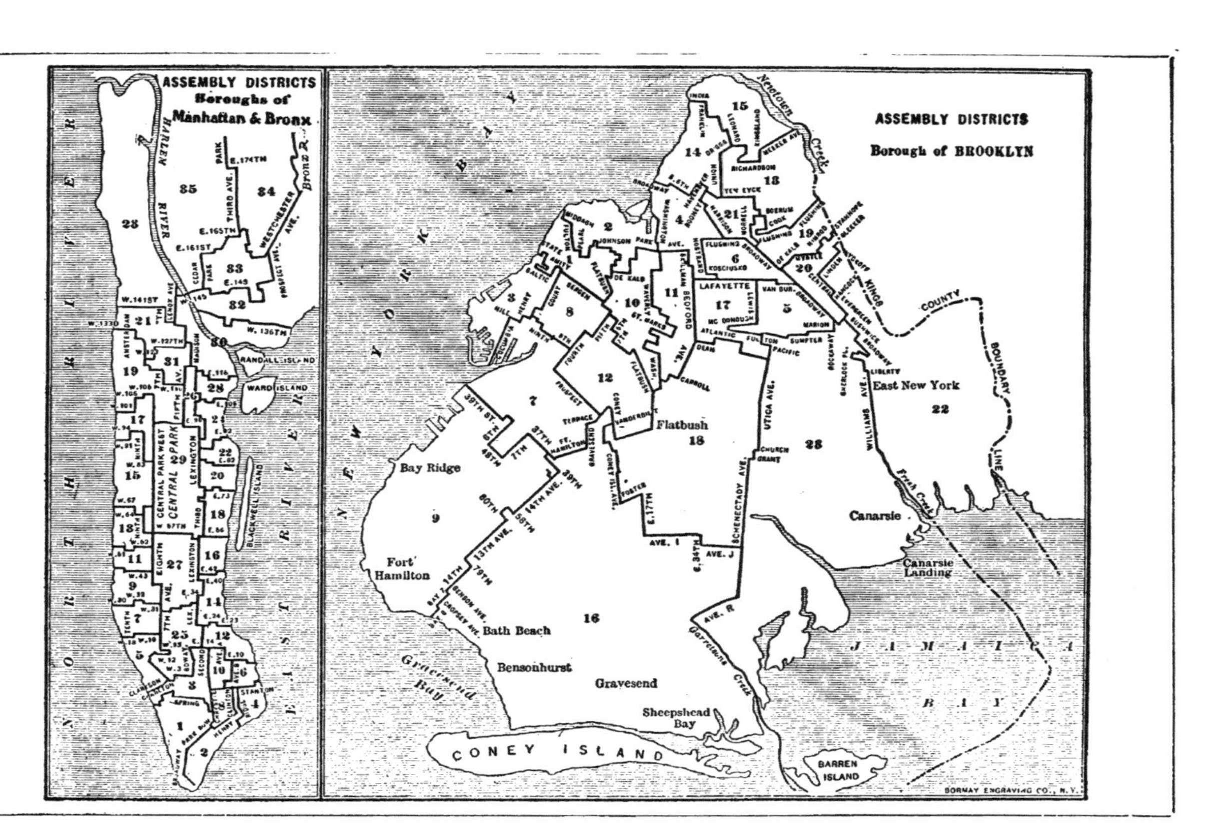
ASSEMBLY DISTRICTS
Boroughs of Manhattan & Bronx
HARLEM RIVER
WARD ISLAND
RANDALL ISLAND
BLACKWELL ISLAND
CENTRAL PARK
ASSEMBLY DISTRICTS
Borough of BROOKLYN
East New York
Canarsie
Canarsie Landing
Flatbush
Gravesend
Sheepshead Bay
CONEY ISLAND
Bensonhurst
Bath Beach
Fort Hamilton
Bay Ridge
Gravesend Bay
BARREN ISLAND

The American Standard Car

Is a Title Deserved in So Great a Degree by No Other Car Than

The "Maxwell"

The Maxwell serves the needs of a greater variety of users. It gives unqualified satisfaction to the man to whom economy of upkeep is a consideration as well as to him who in using a Maxwell finds excessive first outlay unnecessary.

Whether the motorist travels about in a Maxwell Junior $500 Standard American Runabout; whether he uses a 2-cylinder 14 H. P. Runabout, which is sold, fully equipped, at $825; the 2-cylinder 20 H. P. "Doctor" Maxwell—the ideal physician's car, at $1,350, fully equipped; the 2-cylinder 20 H. P. five-passenger Touring Car, at $1,450, fully equipped; or one of our 4-cylinder 30 H. P. cars of the five-bearing crankshaft type, selling at $1,750—every one of these models represents the highest value ever produced by the American automobile industry.

Maxwell Model D A, 4-cylinder, 30 H. P. Touring Car, $1,750

Some cars use THREE-POINT SUSPENSION; others THERMO SYPHON COOLING, UNIT CONSTRUCTION, MULTIPLE-DISC CLUTCHES—but no other American car combines all these important features in a single design, except THE MAXWELL.

Our 4-cylinder 30 H. P. types use five-bearing crankshafts—a construction more expensive to make, but certain to produce the satisfaction that is genuine Maxwell satisfaction, the pleasant certainty that the problem of owning a Maxwell is PERFECTLY SIMPLE, because the car itself—no matter which of the Maxwell models you choose— is SIMPLY PERFECT.

You should be interested to learn more about Maxwells. Drop us a line.

Benj Briscoe
President

Maxwell-Briscoe Motor Company

P. O. Box 116, Tarrytown, N. Y.

Factories: New Castle Tarrytown Pawtucket

PIERCE CYCLES
Chain Model with Cushion Frame and Spring Forks
WHAT a good bicycle can do for you! It will preserve or renew your health; give you a clear brain; prove a means of infinite pleasure and recreation; and besides all this save for you both time and money.
The Pierce line, which, as every one knows, is by far the best in the world, includes the Famous Cushion Frames, the Racer, the Road Model and the Heavy Service Model.
We guarantee our products and you will never repent of any confidence placed in Pierce constructions.
Write us for Catalog W, giving full details.
Makers of the Pierce Vibrationless Motorcycle.
The PIERCE CYCLE CO.
MANUFACTURERS
10 Hanover Street,
Buffalo, N. Y.

"YOU LIVE AS LONG AS YOU BREATHE."

—Prof. Charles Munter.

Prof. Charles Munter's

For Man, Woman and Child

COMPELS DEEP BREATHING

BY

Straightening Round Shoulders Instantly

PROFESSOR CHARLES MUNTER, the inventor of Nulife, has demonstrated the wonders of Nulife for many years and shown why it is one of the most remarkable discoveries and yet the simplest method of improving health that has ever been offered to humanity. The chief beauty of it is that IT PERMITS NATURE TO DO HER OWN CURING, and no drugs, with their after-effects, to mar the good it does.

Prof. Charles Munter's Nulife

Makes you use all of your lungs all of the time, and insures perfect health without resorting to the tiring exercises of physical culture, medicines or other artificial means.

Fresh air is the most vital substance necessary to life. Very few people inhale sufficient air into their lungs regularly to keep them in good health, and when the supply of fresh air is reduced in the lungs the internal organs become overheated, which is the forerunner of sickness. Fresh air is the deadliest foe to all germs that settle in the human body, and the more air that is breathed into the lungs the more assured the body is against sickness. Stooping shoulders, sunken chest, a curved spine, sagging from tired and exhausted effort, are the reasons why the body is prevented from breathing all the air necessary to its perfect existence.

NULIFE holds your head erect, your shoulders back, expands your chest; your abdomen is drawn in while supporting the spine, thereby compelling you to breathe all the air in your lungs necessary. The body is put in this perfect physical condition, which we guarantee, and all ailments are prevented. NULIFE gives to man that military, commanding appearance so much desired; improves a woman's figure instantly by filling out the hollows in the neck, giving graceful lines of beauty and that perfect form demanded by health and fashion. Children wearing NULIFE grow erect, robust and strong.

BEWARE of Imitations. Genuine NULIFE Stamped on Every Garment

NULIFE formerly sold by agents everywhere at $5.00 each, but with my improved facilities and the increased demand for NULIFE from all classes of people throughout the world, I have decided to place NULIFE within the reach of every man, woman and child, as it is essential to perpetual health and physical beauty, and I will send it direct to your home prepaid for $3.00 and guarantee it satisfactory.

When ordering send me $3.00 with your name and address plainly written and your height, weight and chest (not bust) measure, state if male or female, or, if you prefer, fill out the attached coupon.

Read My Book, " What NULIFE Will Do for You," Which I Will Send you Free on Application, by Addressing

PROF. CHAS. MUNTER

Dept. W. A., 13-15 W. 34th St., near Fifth Ave., N.Y. City

Clip Out and Fill in This Coupon.

PROFESSOR CHARLES MUNTER,
13-15 West 34th Street, New York.

Enclosed find $3.00, for which please send me a NULIFE.

My name is............................
My weight is............................
My height is............................
My chest measure is..................
My address is..........................
(Town or City)
Dept..
W. A. (State)

Commercial School

FIFTY-FIRST YEAR

101, 103 and 105 East 23d Street, New York. 'Phone, Gramercy 101.

Commercial and Stenographic Courses

Day and Evening.

Enter at Any Time.

CALL OR WRITE FOR CATALOGUE.

NATURE'S BEST

SCALP FOOD and HAIR TONIC

MADE FROM BEST CRUDE PETROLEUM.

Free from Every Drug and Injurious Ingredient.

Odorless, Anti septic, Nourishing, Cooling, Refreshing.

CRUDOL

CRUDOL Removes Dandruff, Stops That "Itching," Gives New Life to the Scalp, Tone and Lustre to the Hair, and Promotes Its Growth. Put Up in Pure Tin Tubes Only. **In 25 and 50 Cent Sizes** Mailed to You Postage Prepaid.

The Crudol Company
1777 Broadway, New York City

MORE LIGHT FOR LESS MONEY

If we can save you one-third of what your present system costs and give you better light are you interested? Understand us rightly. We mean we will **prove** saving, **prove** improved illuminating, **prove** increased convenience. That's the proposition we make you.

We will send you any lamp listed in our catalog "28" on trial to prove that The Angle Lamp is the one perfect substitute for gas or electricity. Like gas, it is always ready to light at the turning of a button and the striking of a match. Like gas, it can be burned at full height or left **burning dimly** without a trace of smoke or odor. **Unlike** gas, it costs even less than the troublesome old style lamp—fully one-third less.

THE ANGLE LAMP

"The Angle Lamp is worth all the gas or gasoline lights ever made," writes one user. "Saved 20 times its cost," says another, "in oil, burners, chimneys and cuss words." "It has made me wonder why there are any ordinary lamps left to tell their tale of discomfort," adds a third.

Five thousand people voluntarily wrote us letters of indorsement and praise last year. The explanation is—new method.

Let us show you what wonders they have worked in oil lighting. WRITE FOR OUR DESCRIPTIVE CATALOG "28." A mere postal card request will bring you this booklet describing a light which, burning common kerosene in a new way, is so completely satisfactory that such particular people as Mrs. Grover Cleveland, the Rockefellers, Carnegies, etc., use it for lighting their homes and estates in preference to any other system. And it will also bring our offer of

THIRTY DAYS' TRIAL.

The Angle Lamp is made in thirty-two varieties from $2.00 up—a lamp for EVERY purpose. SEND FOR OUR CATALOG "28" showing just the style to suit you and explaining our trial offer.

ANGLE MFG. CO.

159-161 W. 24th St., N. Y. City

THE DUPLEX

Flat Bed Web-Perfecting Newspaper Press

IN USE THROUGHOUT THE WORLD

Prints 5,000 to 6,000 per hour of either 4, 6, 8, 10 or 12 pages WITHOUT STEREOTYPING

Duplex Printing Press Co.

BATTLE CREEK, MICH.

THE THERMOS BOTTLE

Keeps Hot Drinks Steaming Hot Without Fire 24 Hours

Keeps Cold Drinks Freezing Cold Without Ice 3 Days

Fill your Thermos Bottle with steaming hot coffee, and it will be steaming hot next day. Or, if there's a baby in the house, keep its sterilized milk at feeding temperature all day and all night in a Thermos Bottle.

There are so many uses for Thermos Bottles in the home and out-of-doors that you really ought to have one or two. Get at least one at once.

Fill Thermos Bottles with ice-cold drinks for your Outing, Hunting, Motoring, Yachting or Fishing Trips, or for any journey—and any time, night or day, for three days afterward you can count on your Thermos Bottle for a pure, fresh, ice-cold drink.

The Thermos Bottle is one bottle inside another, with a vacuum between. The same Thermos Bottle keeps liquids either hot or cold. No chemicals. Filled, cleaned, emptied same as any ordinary bottle.

DO NOT BE DECEIVED BY IMITATIONS AND INFRINGEMENTS

The Thermos is the original and only perfect temperature retaining bottle. Temperature tests prove the falsity of extravagant claims made for infringing bottles.

The Thermos Bottle is guaranteed by over 30,000 dealers throughout the world. If your dealer cannot supply you we will ship direct, prepaid, on receipt of price. Pints, $3.75. Quarts, $5.75.

Write To-Day for Our Free Booklet "A"

AMERICAN THERMOS BOTTLE COMPANY OF NEW YORK

527 FIFTH AVENUE, NEW YORK CITY

ADVERTISERS IN THE WORLD ALMANAC

A PAGE

Aaron, The D. C., Pen Co......xxiv
Actina Appliance Co........721-725
Advance Thresher Co......lxxxii
Alexander, MacDonald and Greene.........................lxi
Alpine Wax Oil Polish Co....xxiv
America-Europe Co.........lxxxiv
American College of Mechano-Therapy...........................722
American Felt Co..................734
American Poultry Advocate....iv
American Steel & Wire Co....693
American Thermos Bottle Co...xci
American Type Founders' Co..720
American Underwriters' Corporation...........................713
American Wine Growers' Association...............16a-16b
American Wine Press..........16b
Andrews, J. H......................724
Anglo-Am. Telegraph Co......lxii
Angle Mfg. Co.....................lxxxv
Antikamnia Chemical Co......xv
Art Students' League...........709
Art Metal Construction Co...ii
Autographic Register Co.......732
Automatic Time Stamp Co...xxiv

B

Bank's Sons, John..............xliv
Barnes' Sanitarium, Dr.......xxxi
Barnes, Walter F.....................xii
Barrow, Wade, Guthrie & Co..727
Bartholomay Brewery Co.......xiv
Beaumel & Co., D. W.............xvii
Beeler & Robb......................lxvii
Behringer, E..........................735
Bendiner & Schlesinger.......xxxix
Best, Edward H., & Co...............xl
Best Light Co..........................726
Black, A. Parks....718, 722, 727, 734
Blickensderfer Mfg. Co.........viii
Bobo, W. Thompson..............xxvi
Breathe-Rite Co..................lxxxvii
Brentano's............................xxiv
Bromley Co., Dr....................xliii
Brooks, C. E...........................725
Brown, S. A., Pharmacy..........699
Bureau of Navigation.............687
Buchanan, James & Co...........736
Burham Safety Razor Co.......720
Burt Mfg. Co............................iii

C

Caldwell Mfg. Co.......................xx
Caldwell, Dr. W. B..............xlviii
Callanan, L. J...........733, 734, 735
Chase, O. L...............................xix
Chu Fong..................................733
Cluthe, Chas. W........................16q
Cobb, George W., Jr...............16-O
Coleman, Watson E..............lxvi
Collins Ink Eradicator Co.......717
Columbian Rope Co...............xliv
Columbia Warehouses...........735
Commercial Correspondence Schools....................717-724
Conti, Cesare...............lxxxi-732
Conway Hall............................735
Cook's Sons, Adam.................691
Cooper Medicine Co....................l
Country Hydrant Co..............16m
Couse & Bolton......................xliv
Crest View Sanitarium.........xxix
Crex Carpet Co..........................xli
Cross Co.................................xviii
Crudol Co..............................lxxxv

D

Deming Co...........................lxxxiii
Denison & Silvera...................lxvii
Ditman, A. J............................729
Divine, Fred. D., Co..............xxvii

D PAGE

Drake Schools.........................708
Dun, R. G., & Co...............733-734
Duck, J. J.....................................ix
Duplex Printing Press Co.......xc

E

Eagle Typewriter Co...............735
Eclipse Machine Co..............lxxxvi
Electric Renovator Mfg. Co......vi
Electro-Chemical Ring Co.........li
Electro Importing Co...............16f
Empire Electric Sign Co..........733
Empire Storage Warehouse....735
Erkenbrach, Geo. A., & Co......733
Evans, Victor J., & Co...........xiii

F

Faber, Eberhard.....................xlvi
Fitzgerald & Co......................690
Fletcher-Stanley Co.......Cover 1
Florida Military Academy......735
Freeman & Sons Mfg. Co., S....716
Fried, Chas.............................699
Friedenwald, J. H., & Co.........vii
Fuller, Geo. R., Co....................xx
Fuller's N. Y. Detective Bureau 733

G

General Acoustic Co...........lxiii
Gillmann, C. F., Co.................716
Gloeckner & Newby...............733
Godfrey, Charles J., Co..........16f
Good Health Co..................lxxviii
Gregg Publishing Co.............lxix

H

Haffen, J. & M. Brewing Co. lxxxvi
Hastings & McIntosh Truss Co.724
Hay's Hair Health..............lxxxiv
Herschell-Spillman Co...........xii
Hicks Almanac......................lxiii
Hocking, W. C., & Co.............697
Hoe, R., & Co..............................lx
Hoffman, Geo. Wm...................xxi
Holeproof Hosiery Co..........xxxv
Holy Cross College.................735
Home Correspondence School.lxvi
Hough, Franklin H..............xxxiii

I

Ideal Co.....................................xlv
Interborough Rapid Transit Co...........705, 706, 707, 708
International Correspondence Schools..............................16j
International Sprinkler Co., lxxxix
International Stock Food Co...lxx
International Time Recording Co..719

J

Jackson Health Resort........xxix
Jagels & Bellis........................16e
Johnson's Foot Soap..............16f
Jones, C. L., Co.....................xxxiii

K

Kasner, A. H............................732
Kemp, C. M., Mfg. Co..............719
Kenny Publishing Co.........lxxxvi
Kimball, S F..............................735
Kinsman, Dr. F. G.....................xxv
Klumpp's Sons, John G...........732
Koberlein's Transfer................734
Koven, L. O., & Bro..................718

L

Lacey, R. S. & A. B.................xvii
Lincoln-Pope Mercantile Co..699
Lincoln Safe Deposit Co...........lv
Lips, Herman.........................xxxiv
Long Island Railroad........xxxviii
Longman's Sons, R...................734
Loring & Co., Ltd....................xxvii

L PAGE

Lorrimer Institute...................689
Lotz, Henry W...........................734
Lung Germine Co......................728

M

Mager & Gougelmann..............732
Magic Foot Draft Co................688
Malcom, Mme...........................734
Manhattan Office Partition Co.16-O
Mark Sons, Jacob....................735
Marsh, M. & Son, Inc..................xi
Mason, Fenwick & Lawrence..xxii
Maxwell-Briscoe Motor Co..lxxv
McLain Orthopedic Sanitarium 731
McLaughlin Typewriter Exchange..730
McLeod, Ward & Co........710-726
Meilink Mfg. Co............................v
Merchant & Evans Co..........xxxvii
Merriam, G. & C., Co................712
Michigan Business Institute...710
Missouri Lamp & Mfg. Co.....xlix
Modern Electrics......................16f
Monarch Typewriter Co..........lxiv
Mount & Robertson..................16n
Muller, Wm. H.........................16p
Munn & Co.................................730
Munter, Prof. Chas.................lxxix

N

Nassau Bank........................xiii-lix
Nathan Novelty Mfg. Co..........726
Negreen, Joseph.......................735
New Jersey Military Academy..735
New York Camera Exchange, 724, 732
New York Commercial Sales Co.688
New York Electrical Trade School......................................710
New York Homœopathic Medical College and Flower Hospital...709
New York Physical Culture School......................................732
New York Post-Graduate Medical School and Hospital......704
New York Preparatory School...14
New York Rustic Works.....xxxiv
New York School of Automobile Engineers................................xxii
New York Standard Ash Can Mfg. Co.....................................732
New York Sunday World........lvi
Nichols, C. A., Co......................712
Nineteen Hundred Washer Co..liii
Noll, Henry......................691, 698

O

Ogilvie, J. S. Pub'g Co..............714
Ohio Carriage Mfg. Co..............xxv
Oliver Typewriter Co..694, 700, 723
O'Meara & Brock......................695
Omnigraph Mfg. Co...................735

P

Pabst Extract Co.....................xlvii
Packard Commercial School.lxxxv
Pain Manufacturing Co............734
Pall Mall Electric Co.................701
Paris Medicine Co.....................697
Parker, C. L..................................xii
Peebles Institute, Dr...............xxvi
Pettes & Randall Co..................733
Philo-Burt Mfg. Co....................721
Pierce Cycle Co.....................lxxvii
Plainfield Sanitarium..............xxxi
Pleasant Valley Wine Co.........16c
Pneumatic Specialty Co.......lxviii
Pompeian Mfg. Co.........................2
Powers Photo-Engraving Co.ix-16g
Press Co......................................727

Q

Quencer, W. J.............................16p

ADVERTISERS IN THE WORLD ALMANAC

R PAGE

Rapid Addressing Machine Co. 732
Rathbone, R. C., & Son xiv
Ray, William H., Printing Ink Mfg. Co. Cover 3
Reading Standard Co. lxxxiv
Redding & Co. lxvii
Reuter, Carl H. lxxxvi
Ricketts & Banks 732
Rieger, J. & Co. liv
Rife Automatic Ram Co. 718
Ripin & Co. 16d
Robinson, Geo. 730
Romeike, Henry lxvii
Royal Manufacturing Co. 690
Rust, Wm., & Sons 724
Ryan, P. 734

S

Safety Car Heating and Lighting Co., The 733
Safety Fire Extinguisher Co. lviii
Sanden, Alfred 696
Sandholm Drug Co. lvii
Sargent Co 734
Schiavone, L., & Co. 732
Schaefer, Dr. W. A. 701
Schnoter, J. C., Co. 715, 730, 732
Schulte, A. 733
Schwarzschild & Sulzberger Co. 690
Scranton, S. S., Co. 711

S PAGE

Sheldon School lxv
Sinn, A W. 734
Spiro Mfg. Co. lxxxvi
Sprague Correspondence School of Law 715
Springfield Elastic Tread Co. 715
Springfield Metallic Casket Co. 703
Standard Folding Typewriter Sales Co 16-L
Steinway & Sons 16h
Stolz Electrophone Co. xxv
St. James Society 722
St. John's College 735
Stuart Plaster-Pad Co. 728
Sun Kim Lung Co. 733

T

Talbot's Vans, Wm. J. 734
Thorburn, J. M. & Co. i
Three-in-One Oil Co. lxxi
Trautman, Ira F. 732
Travelers' Insurance Co. xcvi
Trommer's Evergreen Brewery x
Tucker, Thos. H. 699
Twinlock Co. lxxxviii
Tyrrell's Hygienic Institute xxvi

U

Ullrich, J. & Co. lxxiv
Underwood Typewriter Co. 695
Universal Business Institute 16k
Universal Novelty Co. 691

V PAGE

Valley Female Seminary 735
Vallely, P. W. 726
Van Gordon D. P. xxxiv
Van Vleck, Dr., Co. 695
Victor Safe & Lock Co. xxiii
Vir Publishing Co. 711
Vogt-Applegate Co. xxxvi

W

Wadsworth's Sanitarium xxxiii
Walter & Co. 732
Waterman, L. E., Co. xvi-Cover 4
Waterous Engine Works Co. 698
Welch, Wilbur A. 16f
Wells, Dr. Rupert 697
Westlotorn's Detective Agency 733
Wilbur Stock Food Co. 729
Williamson Sign System 699
Wilson Bros. 730
Winchester & Co. 16g
Woodlawn Cemetery 733
Woodward & Chandlee xviii
Wurlitzer, Rudolph Co. 717
Wycil & Co. lxvi

Y

Yonkerman Consumption Remedy Co. iii
Young, W. F. lxxx

ADVERTISING INDEX.

PAGE

Ales and Beer.
Bartholomay Brewery Co. xiv

Amusement Outfitters.
Hirschell-Spillman Co. xii

Appliances for Deafness.
Actina Appliance Co. 721
General Acoustic Co. lxii
Stolz Electrophone Co. xxv

Artificial Eyes.
Chas Fried 699

Artificial Limbs, etc.
A. J. Ditman 729
Geo. R. Fuller Co. xx

Automatic Sprinklers.
International Sprinkler Co. lxxxix

Automobiles.
Maxwell-Briscoe Motor Co. lxxv

Bandages—Suspensories.
A. Parks Black 718, 722, 727

Banks.
Nassau Bank xiii

Bicycles.
Pierce Cycle Co. lxxvi

Bookkeeping
Michigan Business Institute 710

Booksellers.
Brentano's xxiv

Breweries.
Bartholomay Brewery Co. xiv
J. & M. Haffen Brewing Co. lxxxvi
Trommer's Evergreen Brew'ry x

Cable Lines.
Anglo-American Telegraph Co. lxii

Cameras.
N. Y. Camera Exchange 724

Carousselles.
Herschell-Spillman Co. xii

PAGE

Carpets.
Crex Carpet Co. xli

Carriages.
Ohio Carriage Mfg. Co. xxv

Caskets.
Springfield Metallic Casket Co. 703

Cigars.
M. Marsh & Son xi

Cigar Lighters.
Universal Novelty Co. 691

Coal.
Jagels & Bellis 16e

Coaster Brakes.
Eclipse Machine Co. lxxvi

Corpulence Belts.
A. Parks Black 718, 722, 727

Corsets.
Pall Mall Electric Co. 701

Dictionaries.
G. & C. Merriam Co. 712

Dictionary Index.
Denison & Silvera lxvii

Educational.
Packard Commercial School lxxxv
American College of Mechano-Therapy 722
Art Students' League 709
Commercial Correspondence Schools 717, 724
Cross Co. xviii
Drake School 708
Gregg Publishing Co. lxix
Home Correspondence School lxvi
International Correspondence Schools 16j
N. Y. Electrical Trade School 710
New York Homoeopathic Medical College 709
New York Post-Graduate Medical School 704

PAGE

Educational.
N. Y. School of Auto. Engin's. xxii
N. Y. Preparatory School 14
Sheldon School lxv
Sprague Correspondence School of Law 715
Universal Business Institute 16k
Williamson Sign System 699
Wycil & Co. lxvi

Elastic Hosiery.
A. J. Ditman 729
A. Parks Black 718, 722, 727
Geo. R. Fuller Co. xx

Electric Belts.
Alfred Sanden 696

Electrical Novelties.
J. J. Duck ix

Electrical Supplies and Specialties.
Electro Importing Co. 16f
Fletcher-Stanley Co. Cover 2
J. J. Duck ix

Farm and Household Supplies.
Lincoln-Pope Mercantile Co. 699

Farm Machinery.
Advance Thresher Co. lxxxii
S. Freeman & Sons Mfg. Co. 716
Wilson Bros. 730

Fence.
American Steel & Wire Co. 693

Fire Engines.
Waterous Engine Works Co. 698

Fire Extinguishers.
International Sprinkler Co. lxxxix
Missouri Lamp & Mfg. Co. xlix
Safety Fire Extinguisher Co. lviii

Fishing Rods.
Fred D. Divine Co. xxvii

Floor and Furniture Polish.
Alpine Wax Oil Polish Co. xxiv

ADVERTISING INDEX.

Fountain Pens. PAGE
D. W. Beaumel & Co..........xvii
L. E. Waterman Co.... xvi-Cover 4

Gas Plants.
C. M. Kemp Mfg. Co............719

Gasoline Tanks.
L. O. Koven & Bro............718

Hair Restoratives.
Bendiner & Schlesinger.....xxxix
Crudol Co...................lxxxv
Hay's Hair Health... lxxxiv
Lorrimer Institute..............695

Hair Brushes.
Pall Mall Electric Co..............701

Health Appliances.
Actina Appliance Co........721-725
Breathe-Rite Co...........lxxxvii
C. E. Brooks.........................725
Dr. W. A. Schaeler 701
Electro-Chemical Ring Co.........li
Ideal Co...............................xlv
L. C. McLain Sanitarium.......731
Magic Foot Draft Co..............688
Philo-Burt Mfg. Co..............721
Prof. Chas Munter............lxxix
Stolz Electrophone Co. xxv
Stuart Plaster Pad Co...........728
Tyrrell Hygienic Institute...xxvi

Hernia—Trusses.
A. Parks Black.........718, 722, 727

Hotel Directories.
Kenny's Hotel Directory,.lxxxvi

Household Articles.
Royal Mfg. Co....................690

Hosiery.
Holeproof Hosiery Co.........xxxv

House-Cleaning Apparatus.
Electric Renovator Mfg. Co.....vi
Pneumatic Specialty Co.....lxviii

Ink Pencils.
J. Ullrich & Co..... lxxiv
Universal Novelty Co...........691

Insurance.
Travelers Insurance Co..... xcvi
R. C. Rathbone & Son, Inc....xlv

Jockey Straps.
A. Parks Black...........718, 722, 727

Landscape Gardener.
Herman Lips..... xxxiv

Lawyers.
Geo. Robinson....................730

Lead Pencils.
Eberhard Faber................xlvi

Leather Belting.
Couse & Bolton..................xliv

Liquors and Cordials.
America-Europe Co.........lxxxiv

Lighting Systems.
Angle Mfg Co................lxxxv
Best Light Co.....................726

Lubricants.
Adam Cook's Sons..............691

Machinery.
Advance Thresher Co.......lxxxii
C. M. Kemp Mfg. Co...........719
Deming Co...................lxxxiii
Rife Automatic Ram Co.......718
S. Freeman & Sons Mfg. Co....716

Machinery. PAGE
Waterous Engine Works Co....698
Wilson Bros......................730

Masonic Supplies.
Redding & Co....................lxvii

Medical.
Antikamnia Chemical Co......xv
Bendiner & Schlesinger.....xxxix
Crudol Co.......................lxxxv
Cooper Medicine Co..................l
C. L. Jones Co.....................xxxiii
Dr. F. G. Kinsman..............xxv
Dr. W. B. Caldwell............xlviii
Dr. Bromley Co.....................xliii
Dr. Peebles Institute..........xxvi
Dr. Rupert Wells.................697
Dr. Van Vleck Co.................695
Good Health Co.............lxxviii
Hay's Hair Health........lxxxiv
Loring Co.............................xxvii
Lorrimer Institute..............689
Lung Germine Co.................728
Pabst Extract Co..................xlvii
Paris Medicine Co................697
S. A. Brown Pharmacy.........699
Sandholm Drug Co..............lvii
St. James Society...................722
W. F. Young.....................lxxx
W. J. Quencer.....................16p
Wm. H. Muller........... .....16p
Winchester & Co.................16g
W. Thompson Bobo...........xxvi
YonkermanCom'ptionRe'dyCo.lii

Merry-Go-Rounds, Etc.
Herschell-Spillman Co.........xii

Metals.
Merchant & Evans Co.......xxxvii

Metal Polish.
Geo. W. Hoffman...............xxi

Motorcycles.
Reading Standard Co......lxxxiv

Moving Vans.
John Banks' Sons.............xliv

Musical Instruments.
Rudolph Wurlitzer Co..........717

Navy Training Stations.
Bureau of Navigation..........687

Newspapers.
New York Sunday World......lvi

Obesity Belts.
A. Parks Black..........718-722-727
Henry Noll..........................691

Office Fixtures & Furniture
Art Metal Construction Co.......ii
Geo W. Cobb, Jr..............16-O
P. W. Vallely.........................726
Walter F. Barnes..................xii

Office Specialties and Supplies.
Automatic Time Stamp Co...xxiv
C. F. Gillmann & Co...............716
Carl H. Reuter...............lxxxvi
Collins Ink Eradicator Co. 717
D. C. Aaron Pen Co...... xxiv
Eberhard Faber...............xlvi
International Time Recording Co....................................719
J. Ullrich & Co................lxxiv
McLeod, Ward & Co...........710-726
New York Commercial Sales Co.688
Spiro Mfg. Co...............lxxxvi
S. S. Scranton Co....... 711
Twinlock Co................lxxxviii
Universal Novelty Co...........691

Office Partitions.
Manhattan Office Partition Co.16 O
Mount & Robertson......... ..16n

Office Railings. PAGE
Manhattan Office Partition Co.16-O
Mount & Robertson............16n

Oil and Greases.
Adam Cook's Sons..............691
Three-in-One Oil Co.............lxxi

Oil and Water Tanks.
L. O. Koven & Bro...............718

Packing Houses.
Schwarzschild & Sulzberger....690

Paint.
O. L. Chase.......................xix

Patents.
Beeler & Robb.................lxvii
C. L. Parker......................xii
Franklin H. Hough..........xxxiii
Mason, Fenwick & Lawrence.xxii
Munn & Co.........................730
O'Meara & Brock.................695
R. S. & A. B. Lacey.............xvii
Victor J. Evans & Co............xiii
Watson E. Coleman............lxvi
Fitzgerald & Co....................690
Woodward & Chandlee.......xviii

Pens.
D.C. Aaron Pen Co...........xxiv

Photo-Engravers.
Powers Photo-En'ing Co...ix-16G

Pianos.
Steinway & Sons................16h

Piano Movers.
John Banks's Sons.............xliv

Poultry Publications.
American Poultry Advocate....iv

Poultry Supplies.
Wm. Rust & Sons................724

Press Blankets.
Edward H. Best & Co. xl

Press Clipping Bureaus.
Henry Romeike....... lxvii

Printing Ink Manufacturers
Wm. H. Ray Printing Ink Mfg. Co...................Cover 3

Printing Presses.
Duplex Printing Press Co xc
The Press Co.......................727

Public Accountants.
Barrow, Wade, Guthrie & Co..727

Publishers.
Brentano's.......................xxiv
American Underwriters Corp'n.............................713
C. A. Nichols Co. 712
G. & C. Merriam Co..............712
Gregg Publishing Co............lxix
J. S. Ogilvie Pub. Co.............711
S. S. Scranton Co..................711
Vir Publishing Co...................711

Publications.
American Poultry Advocate...iv
American Wine Press..........16b
Hicks' Almanac................lxiii
Modern Electrics................16f
New York Sunday World.......lvi

Pumps.
The Deming Co........... lxxxiii

Railroads.
Long Island Railroad xxxviii
Interborough Rapid Transit Co 705, 706, 707, 708

ADVERTISING INDEX.

Rheumatic Rings. PAGE
Electro-Chemical Ring Co. li
Roofing Material.
Merchant & Evans Co. xxxvii
Rope.
Columbia Rope Co...............xliv
Rubber Heels.
Nathan Novelty Mfg. Co.......726
Springfield Elastic Tread Co....715
Rupture Cure.
C. E. Brooks.....................725
Stuart Plaster Pad Co..........728
Rustic Works.
New York Rustic Works... xxxiv
Safes.
Victor Safe & Lock Co........xviii
Meilink Mfg. Co. v
Safe Deposit Vaults.
Lincoln Safe Deposit Co..........lv
Nassau Bank......................lix
Safety Razors.
Burham Safety Razor Co.......720
Sanitariums.
Crest View Sanitarium.......xxix
Dr. Barnes' Sanitarium......xxx
Dr. Wadsworth's Sanitarium xxxiii
Jackson Health Resort.......xxix
L. C. McLain Sanitarium.....731
Plainfield Sanitarium........xxxi
Schools and Colleges.
American College of Mechano-Therapy......................722
Art Students' League..........709
Commercial Correspondence Schools........... ....717, 724
Cross Co........................xvii
Drake Schools...........708
International Correspondence Schools.........................16j
New York Homoeopathic Medical College...............709
New York Electrical Trade School...........................710
N. Y. School of Automobile Engineers......................xxi
N. Y. Preparatory School.......14
Sprague Correspondence School of Law.................715
Universal Business Institute...16k
Sheldon School.................lxv
Home Correspondence School.lxv
Gregg Publishing Co............lxix

Schools and Colleges. PAGE
Packard's Commercial School lxxxv
New York Post-Graduate Medical School................704
Scissors.
W. C. Hocking & Co.............697
Seeds and Bulbs.
J. M. Thorburn & Co..............I
Shaving Glasses.
Caldwell Mfg. Co.................xx
Shoulder Braces.
Geo. R. Fuller Co..................xx
J. C. Schnoter Co...........715, 730
Soap.
Johnson's Foot Soap...........16f
Sporting Goods.
Chas. J. Godfrey Co............16f
Fred D. Divine Co.............xxvii
Sprinklers, Automatic.
International Sprinkler Co.lxxxix
Stenography.
Michigan Business Institute...710
Stereotype and Press-Room Supplies.
Edward H. Best & Co............xl
R. Hoe & Co.........................lx
Stogies.
M. Marsh & Son.................xi
Stock Food.
International Stock Food Co..lxx
Wilbur Stock Food Co..........729
Storage Warehouses.
John Banks's Sons...........xliv
Suspensories.
J. C. Schnoter Co............715, 730
Surgical Bandages.
A. Parks Black..........718-722, 727
Telegraphy.
Michigan Business Institute...710
Telegraph Lines.
Anglo-Am'n Telegraph Co....lxii
Thermos Bottle.
American Thermos Bottle Co..xci
Time Stamps.
Automatic Time Stamp Co..xxiv
C. F. Gillmann & Co............716
International Time Recording Co...............................719

Toilet Preparations. PAGE
Pompeian Mfg. Co................2
Trusses.
Chas. W. Cluthe................16q
Geo. R. Fuller Co..................xx
Hastings & McIntosh Truss Co..............................724
Henry Noll........................698
J. C. Schnoter Co..........715, 730
Type Founders.
American Type Founders Co..720
Typewriters.
Alexander, MacDonald & Greene.............................lxi
Blickensderfer Mfg. Co.. viii
McLaughlin Typewriter Exchange........................730
Monarch Typewriter Co.......lxiv
Oliver Typewriter Co.. 694, 700, 723
Standard Folding Typewriter Sales Co.....................16-T
Underwood Typewriter Co.....695
Vaults.
Meilink Mfg. Co...................v
Victor Safe & Lock Co........xxiii
Ventilators.
Merchant & Evans Co......xxxvii
Burt Mfg. Co. iii
Washing Machines.
1900 Washer Co liii
Whiskey.
Cesare Conti....................lxxxi
J. H. Friedenwald & Co....... vii
J. Rieger & Co....................liv
James Buchanan & Co...........736
Vogt-Applegate Co.........xxxvi
Water Systems.
Country Hydrant Co..........16m
Rife Automatic Ram Co... 718
Wine Growers.
American Wine Growers' Association..............16a-16b
Pleasant Valley Wine Co..... 16c
Wine Merchants.
Cesare Conti....................lxxxi
Ripin & Co........................16d

ADVERTISED IN THE CLASSIFIED DEPARTMENT
THE ADDENDA

PAGE 732.

Abdominal Supporters.
Addressing.
Artificial Eyes.
Ash Cans.
Assayers and Chemists.
Athletic Goods.
Automobile Tires.
Auto Tires Bought.
Autographic Registers.
Bankers and Brokers.
Bowling Alley Supplies.
Business Opportunities.
Cameras and Lenses.

PAGE 733.

Cameras and Lenses.
Car Lighting.
Cemeteries.
Chemicals.
Chinese Goods.
Cigars.
Electric Signs.
Clocks.
Coffee.
Collections.
Detective Agencies.

PAGE 734.

Felt.
Fireworks.
Gray Hair Restored.
Hernia, Trusses, &c.
Invalid Chairs.
Lame People.
Mercantile Agencies.
Moving Vans.
Old Gold and Silver.
Olive Oil.
Packing Boxes.
Piano Movers.

PAGE 735.

Postage Stamps.
Rheumatism.
Schools and Colleges.
Special Sheet and Metal Workers.
Storage Warehouses.
Telegraphy.
Typewriters.
Vault Lights.
Whiskey.

The  World

The World Almanac

AND

Encyclopedia

1909

ISSUED BY
THE PRESS PUBLISHING CO., NEW YORK WORLD,
PULITZER BUILDING,
NEW YORK.

GENERAL INDEX.

A

PAGE
A. A. U. NATIONAL..........201
Academicians, National........363
" Royal.........................364
Academy of Design, National363
" Science, National..........299
Accidents, Railroad..............274
Accounts, When Outlawed....616
Acknowledgment of Deeds....252
Actors, Birthplaces, etc....287-289
Actors' Church Alliance.......332
" Fund of America.........332
Acts of 60th Congress........... 88
Act Prohibiting Money Contributions..........104
Actuarial Society of America..296
Administration of Deceased Persons' Estate................607
Aeronautics in 1908.........240-243
" Records.......................222
Afghanistan.........................546
Africa, Area and Population.67,396
" Division of.......................410
Age of the Earth......................65
Agricultural Implements.492,497
" Statistics......................523
" Science, Society for Promotion of......................299
Agriculture Dep't Officials.......557
" Secretaries of..................448
Alabama Election Returns....619
Alaska-Yukon-Pacific Exposition...................541
Alcohol Statistics..................530
Aldermen, N. Y. City.........668
Alfred B. Nobel Prizes.........550
Alliance Française..............332
" of Reformed Churches..342
Altar Colors........................... 36
Altitudes, Greatest in States... 59
Aluminum, Production of......521
Amateur A.U. Records for 1908.201
Ambassadors.......402,450-453,584
Amendments to U. S. Constitution.......................84-85
America, Area and Population. 67
" British, Area, etc.........396
American Acad. of Medicine..296
" Academy Political and Social Science...............296
" Anatomists' Association..298
" and Foreign Shipping.....490
" Anti-Tuberculosis League......................296
" Antiquarian Society.......296
" Asiatic Association........296
" Association for Advancement of Science..........296
" Asso. of Obstetricians and Gynæcologists..............296
" Bar Association...............296
" Battle Dates.....................515
" Benefit Society.................293
" Bible Society....................346
" Board of Foreign Missions..........................345
" Bonapartes........................539
" Chemical Society...............296
" Civic Alliance....................332
" Civic Association...............429
" Climatological Ass'n.........296
" College Fraternities...322-323
PAGE
American Continentals.........381
" Cross of Honor...............381
" Dermatological Ass'n.....296
" Dialect Society................296
" Economic Association....296
" Electro-Therapeutic Association.....................296
" Entomological Society....296
" Federation of Catholic Societies..........................469
" Federation of Labor.......139
" Fisheries Society............296
" Flag Association..............377
" Folklore Society..............296
" Forestry Association..177,297
" Geographical Society......297
" Guild...............................293
" Gynæcological Society....297
" Historical Association....297
" Hog...................................529
" Humane Society............332
" Indian..............................101
" Institute of Architects....297
" Institute of Civics...........538
" Inst. Electrical Eng'rs....297
" Inst. of Homœopathy......297
" Inst. Mining Engineers...297
" Inst Social Service.........332
" and Japanese Agreement.431
" Laryngological, Rhinological and Otological Soc..297
" Laryngological Ass'n.....297
" Learned Societies.....296-299
" Mathematical Society....297
" Mechanics, United.........295
" Medical Association.......297
" Medico - Psychological Ass'n.............................297
" Microscopical Society.....297
" Multi-Millionaires......471-479
" Municipalities League....429
" National Red Cross........383
" Neurological Association..297
" Numismatic Society.......297
" Ophthalmological Society.297
" Oriental Society.............297
" Ornithologists' Union.....297
" Orthopedic Association...297
" Osteopathic Society.......297
" Otological Society..........298
" Pediatric Society............298
" Philological Association.298
" Philosophical Society.....298
" Physical Society.............298
" Physicians, Ass'n of.......298
" Proctologic Society.........298
" Psychological Association.298
" Public Health Ass'n......298
" Revolution, Daughters of..378
" Revolution, Sons of........375
" Rivers, Principal.......... 70
" Roentgen Ray Society....298
" S. P. C. A. Society...........332
" Social Science Association.298
" Society of Civil Engineers298
" Soc'ty of Curio Collectors.298
" Society of International Law..................................292
" Society of Mechanical Engineers.........................298
" Society of Naturalists....298
" Sociological Society.........469
PAGE
American Statistical Associa'n.298
" Sunday School Union.....347
" Surgical Association.......298
" Therapeutic Society........298
" Tract Society..................346
" Turf.........................210-212
" Unitarian Association.....338
" Urological Association....298
" Whist.......................230-235
Amusements, N. Y. City...672-673
Anarchistic Literature Excluded from Mails.............100
Ancient and Modern Year.....60
Andrew and Philip, Brotherhood of............................349
Animals, Domestic, in U. S...524
Annapolis Naval Academy....615
Anniversaries, List of..............33
Antarctic Exploration.........369
Antimony Production......520-521
Antiquarian, American Society.296
Anti-Rebate Law Prosecutions 461
Anti-Saloon League, The......537
Apoplexy, Deaths from..........536
Apothecaries' Weights......... 74
Appellate Division, Supreme Court, N. Y. City..............670
Appendicitis, Deaths from.....536
Apple Crop..............................524
Apportionment of Congress...590
Appraisers, U. S. General....686n
Appropriations by Congress...501
Arabic Numerals............... 77
Arbitration and Mediation Board, N. Y. State.......600
" Treaties..........................522
Arbor Day..............................177
Archery Records.....................185
Archæological Institute.........298
Archæology...........................365
Arctic Club............................298
" Exploration....................369
Area, Cities in U. S...............551
" Continents....................67
" Extreme of Counties.....417
" Foreign Countries..........546
" of Africa........................396
" of British Empire..........396
" of Canada......................407
" of Great Lakes..............538
" of London......................404
" of Mexico......................409
" of States........................554
" of United States........110,546
Argentine Republic, Area, etc.546
" Army and Navy............614
" Battleships...................388
Arizona Election Returns......620
Arkansas Election Returns....620
Armed Strength of World......614
Armies and Navies, Cost of Maintaining.....................502
Armories, N. Y. City..........686q
Army and Navy of Confederate States, Society......382
" and Navy Union.......351,373
" British..............401,502,614
" General Officers Retired 562-563
" Generals, U. S.................561
" of Cumberland Society....352
" of Philippines Society....380
" of Potomac Society........352
" of Santiago Society........380

SEE ADVERTISING INDEX ON PAGES XCII TO XCV.

PAGE

Army of Tennessee Society....352
" of U. S., General Staff.....561
" of U.S. in New York City.686x
" Rank of Officers.......564-568
" U. S., Organization.......563
Art Galleries, N. Y.............686q
Artillery Corps, Field Officers.568
Ash Wednesday, 1909.......... 26
Asia, Statistics of............67, 396
Assembly Dists., N. Y. City..lxxiii
" New York State.......601-602
Assessed Valuation of Property in U. S.........501, 551
Assessors, Board of, N. Y. City669
Assistant Treasurers, U. S.....558
Associated Press...............331
Asteroids..............................49
Astor Battery Ass'n...........380
" Library, N. Y. City.........300
Astronomical and Astrophysical Society of America........298
Astronomical Phenomena for 1909.......................52-53
" Signs and Symbols........ 52
Astronomy in 1908.............365
Asylums, N. Y. City........680-681
Athletic Championships....201-204
Athletic Records............198-200
Atmosphere of the Earth..... 49
Attorney-Generals, U. S....... .448
Australasia..................67, 396
Austria, Diplomatic Intercourse, 451
" Hungary, Army and Navy, 387, 406, 614
" " Ministry..........391
" " Royal Family..392
Austrian-Hungarian Gov't....406
Austro-Hungarian Empire......546
Austro-Hungary Battleships... 386-387
Automobile Industry.......236-238
" Records..............238-239, 248
Autumn, Beginning of, 1909.... 26
Aztec Club of 1847..............375

B

BACON, PRODUCTION OF.......529
Baggage Examination Rules...116
Ballooning.........................243
Ballots for Candidates for President........................617
Baltimore Exposition.......... 540
Banking Statistics..........110, 508
Bankruptcy Law, U. S.........511
Banks in N. Y. City.........677-678
Baptist Churches, N. Y. City 682, 686a
" Young People's Union.....345
Baptists, Number of.........333-324
Bar Association, American....296
" " N. Y. City......686n
Barley, Production of...........523
Barometer Indications........... 56
Baseball Records...........215-221
Basket Ball........................195
Battle Dates, American........515
Battles of Civil War............376
Battleship Fleet, U. S..........583
Battleships of Naval Powers 384-388
Battleships, U. S............575, 581
Bavarian Royal Family........392
Beer Consumption...............530
Belgian Royal Family 392
Belgium, Area, etc..............546
" Army and Navy..........614
" Ministry....................391
Ben-Hur, Tribe of..............293
Benefactions of 1908.......356-358
Benzine Production............519
Beverages, When to Serve....531
Bible Society, American.......316
Bicycling Records...... 15, 223-225
Billiard Records 194, 248
Births................................534
Bishops, English..................401
" of Religious Denominations.............15, 336-338
Blacklisting Laws..............137
Blind Persons in U. S..........534
B'nai B'rith, Order of..........293
Board of Education, N. Y..669, 686k
" of Estimate and Apportionment, N. Y. City......669
Boat-Racing Records............190
Boiling Points..................... 78
Bolivia, Army of.................614
Bolivia, Statistics of............546
Bonaparte Family...............395
Bonapartes, American..........539
Bonded Debts of States.........501
Books Postage....................169
Books, Production of 359
" of 1908.....................360-362
Borough Presidents, N. Y.....668
Botanical Society.................298
Bourbon-Orleanist Family.....395
Bowling..............................188
Boxing........................243-244
Boycotting Laws.................137
Brandy, Production of.........530
Brazil, Area and Population....546
" Army and Navy of.......614
Brazilian Battleships............388
Bridges, N. Y. City............686w
Brighton Handicap..............211
Brigadier-Generals, U. S. A....561
Brith Abraham Order......... 293
British Army...........401, 502, 614
" Battleships 384
" Colonies...............396, 402
" Courts of Law 400
" Diplomatic Intercourse, 402, 451
" Dukes 403
" Empire, Statistics..396, 403, 546
" Government.................400
" King's Title and Oath.....399
" Measures and Weights.... 74
" Navy.............384, 401, 502, 614
" Parliament..................403
" Population.........396, 404, 546
" Premiers......................399
" Royal Family..........389, 397
" Throne, Order of Succession 398
Bronchitis, Deaths from.......536
Brooklyn Churches............ 686a
" Handicap......................211
" Navy Yard.................686g
Brotherhood of Am. Yeomen..293
" of Andrew and Philip.... 349
" of Red Diamond...........350
" of St. Andrew...............345
Brussels Universal and International Exposition........539
Buckwheat, Production of.....523
Buddhism 333
Building and Loan Associations518
Building Commissioners, Soc..429
Buildings, Height of, in N. Y.686g
Bulgarian Army..................614
Bullion, Value of Silver.........504
Bureau of Buildings, N. Y.....668
Bureaus of Labor................138
Bushel Weights................... 73
Business Failures in U. S......511
" Pursuits in U. S.......421-422
Butter Production................524

C

CABINET OFFICERS SINCE 1789.....................447-449
" of President Roosevelt....556
Cable Telegraph Rates.........283
Cables, Submarine...............285
Calendar for 200 Years.......... 35
" Greek & Russian, for 1909. 36
" Gregorian..................... 32
" Jewish, for 1909 36
" Mohammedan, for 1909... 36
" Ready-Reference.........34-35
" Ritualistic 36
Calendars for 1909 and 1910...... 33
" Monthly for 1909.........37-48
California Election Returns 621
Canada, Dominion of.........407-408
Canal Board, N. Y. State.......600
" Panama...................455-457
Canals................................286
Cancer, Deaths from............536
Canoe Racing......................195
Capital Punishment... 537
Capitals, Foreign.................546
" of States......................554
Capitol, U. S......................111
Captains, U. S. Army...........561
" " Navy...............573
Cardinals, College of............336
Carnegie Hero Fund............353
" Institution....................299
" Libraries......................353
Carter Handicap..................210
Casualty Insurance in U. S.....538
Catholic Benevolent Legion...293
" Bishops.....................15, 336
" Churches in N. Y. City...682
" Knights of America.......293
" Mutual Benefit Ass'n....293
" Roman, Hierarchy....15, 336
" Societies, Federation of .469
" Summer School...........355
Catholics, Number of.......333-334
Cattle, Value of, in U. S.........524
Cement Production..............520
Cemeteries, National............606
Cemeteries, New York City. ..692
Census, U. S................ 150-152
Central and South American Trade..........................410
Centre of Population in U. S...422
Cereal Crops.......................524
Chamber of Commerce....... 686v
Champagne Statistics............530
Charities and Correction, N. Y..669
Chautauqua Institution........302
Checkers........................... 248
Checks and Notes................252
Cheese Production...............524
Chemical Industry Society......299
" Society, American........296
Chemicals, Manufacture of.....427
Chemistry in 1908...............366
Chess................................229
Children's Court. N. Y. City.....670
Chile, Army and Navy.........614
" Statistics of...................546
Chilian Battleships.............388
China, Area and Population...546
" Army and Navy...........614
Chinese in U. S. 411
" Indemnity, The.............100
Christian & Mission Alliance..348
" Endeavor Society..........345
" " Union..........348
" Science 343
Christians, Number of..........333
Chronological Cycles and Eras. 26
Church Days in 1909............. 26
" Established, of England. 401
" Temperance Society.......348
Churches, N. Y. City 682-686f
" in the U. S 334
" in the World..................333
Cigars and Cigarettes............487
Cincinnati, Society of......374-375
Circuit Courts of U. S.......559, 671
Cities, Finances of.............499, 551
" Largest of the Earth......411
" of U. S., Population of.423, 551

PAGE

Cities of U. S., Statistics of.....551
Civic Ass'n, American.........429
" Organizations in U. S......429
Civil Engineers' Society.......298
" Lists of Sovereigns.......546
" Service Comm'rs, U. S....557
" " " N. Y. State..600
" " N. Y. City.... 147
" " Rules of, U. S...15,146
Claims, U. S. Court of..........559
Clearing-House Statistics..509,677
Closing of Navigation............ 69
Clubs, New York City.........686z
Coal Statistics...... 518,520
Cocoa...........................528
Coffee Production..............528
Coinage at U. S. Mints.........506
" of Nations.................503
Coins, Foreign, Value of........481
Coke Production................520
Collectors of Customs..........558
College Colors..................321
" Commencements.........310
" Enrolment.................326
" Fraternities...........322-325
" Presidents........,......305-310
" Reference Marks.. 320
" Tuition Fees, etc......315-319
College of Cardinals.............336
Colleges in N. Y. City.........686k
" of U. S., Statistics of...305-328
Colombia, Statistics of..........546
Colonels of U. S. Army 561
Colonial Dames of America.. ..377
" Governors, British........402
" Society of America........381
" Wars, Society of...........383
Colorado Election Returns.....622
Colored Population in U S. 414,419
Comets, Periodic.................12
Commanders, U. S. Navy.......574
Commerce and Labor, Department of....................449,557
Commerce of New York.......681
Commission on Country Life...117
Committees, N. Y. State Dem.436
" National....................438
" N. Y. State Republican..437
Common Schools, U. S..........326
Commons, House of. 403
Compound Interest Table...... 77
Comptroller's Office, N. Y......668
Confederacy, U'ted Daughters.382
Confederate States, Army and Navy Society............382
" Veterans....................382
Confucianism....................333
Congo State......................546
Congregational Churches, N. Y. City..................682, 686b
" National Council..........338
Congregationalists..........333-334
Congress, Acts of Sixtieth...... 88
" Appropriations by.........501
" Library of...................301
" Party Divisions in.........591
" Sixtieth 592
Congressional Apportionment.590
Connecticut Election Returns..623
Conservation of Natural Resources....................105-107
Constitution of the U. S......81-85
Consuls, Foreign, in U. S.......588
" " N. Y. City.....692
" U. S., Abroad.............584
Consumption, Deaths from.....536
Continents, Statistics of......... 67
Contracts, Law of...........254,255
Conventions, Political..........486
Copper Production... ......519, 521
Copyright Law...................330
Corn Crop, Statistics of... .523,524
Coroners, N. Y. City............668
Corporate Schools, N. Y. City, 686k
Corporation Counsel, N. Y.....668

PAGE

Cotton Exports and Imports...526
" Manufacturers............497
" Supply and Crop......524,525
Counties, Debts of..............499
Counties, Largest and Smallest.417
Countries, Production of.......495
Countries of the World.........546
County Officers, N. Y. City 669
Court of Arbitration, N. Y.....671
" of Claims, N. Y.......... 600
" of Honor....................293
Court Tennis.....................181
Courts, British 400
Courts of New York City........670
" State (see each State Election Returns).
" of New York State 603
Courts of United States.......559,670
Cows, Value of, U. S...........524
Creeds, Population of Earth by.333
Cricket...........................186
Criminal Courts in N. Y. City..670
Crops, Statistics of...........15,523
Cross Country and Marathon Races ....,...15,247
Cruisers, United States.........576
Cuba, Commerce................494
" Statistics of...............546
Cuban Occupation in 1908.......462
Cubic Measure..............72, 74
Cumberland Society, Army.....352
Curling..........................183
Currency Act, The............89-92
Currency Circulation, U. S......110
Customs Act of 1908.............115
Custom-House, N. Y. City.....686u
Customs, Collectors, N. Y. City 686u
" Officials 558
" Tariff, U. S.............114-115
Cycles, Chronological 26
Cycling Events of 1908............225

D

DAIRY PRODUCTS..............529
Dames of the Revolution.......378
Danish Battleships..............387
Dates, Memorable.............. 30
Daughters of Revolution.........378
" of the Amer. Revolution..378
" of Confederacy, United.. 382
" of the King.................349
" of 1812, United.............378
Day of Week, How to Find...34-35
Days Between Two Dates...... 27
Deaf Mutes in U. S.............534
Death Roll of 1908.......15,466-.469
" Statistics...................535
Debt of United States, Public.. 110, 496
Debts of Nations........ 500
" of States in U. S............501
" of United States Cities.....551
" When Outlawed......... .616
Deceased Persons' Estates 607,613
Declaration of Independence.. 86
Deeds, Acknowledgment of, ..252
Deer, Season for Shooting......178
Defective Classes 534
Delaware Election Returns......623
Democratic National and State Committees..............436
" Conventions................486
" League National 502
" Party Platforms.......153-157
Denmark and Colonies.........546
" Army and Navy...........614
" Royal Family............ 392
Denominations, Religious......333
Density of Population in U. S..415
Dental Examinations, N. Y....148
" Schools in U. S.............326
Deposits in Banks.......110,510,677
Derby, English 211
Dialect Society, American.....296

PAGE

Dickens Fellowship, The......303
Diplomatic Consular List.......588
" Intercourse..........402,450-453
Displacement of Steamers.....280
Distance to Moon............... 49
" from Sun................... 49
Distances Between Cities.......173
Distilled Spirits..................530
Distribution of Population in U. S..................... 418
District-Att'y's Office, N. Y,....670
" " U. S. 560
" Courts of U. S...............559
" Leaders, N. Y. City......686y
" of Columbia Gov't.........552
Division of Africa...............410
Divisions of Time............... 32
Divorce Laws 249-251
" Statistics....... 251
Dock Dept., N. Y. City........669
Domestic Animals in U. S. 524
" Money Orders in 1908......516
" Rates of Postage......168-171
" Weights & Measures...... 74
Dramatic People................287
Druids, Order of..................293
Dry Measure.................72, 74
Dukes, Table of British 403
Dumbells, Records of.............199
Duration of Life.................. 67
Duties, Customs, U. S......114,115
Dwellings in U. S................415

E

EAGLES, ORDER OF........... 293
Earnings of Wage-Earners, 135-136
Earth, Age of..................... 65
Earth, Facts About..........49, 67
Earth's Atmosphere............. 49
" Population................. 67
Earthquake Areas of the World 63
Easter in 1909..................... 26
" Table of Dates 27
Eclipses in 1909.................. 52
Economic Ass'n, American....296
Education, Dept. of, N. Y. 669, 686k
" Ass'n, Religious..........350
" General Board.......... ..302
" John F. Slater Fund.......302
" Peabody Fund.............302
" Southern Board 302
" Statistics of............327-328
Eggs, Production of............529
Egypt, Area, etc.................546
Eight-Hour Labor Laws....137-138
Election Returns Begin..........619
Elections Bureau, N. Y. City..669
" Presidential.................618
" State, When Next Occur. 555
Election, Presidential of 1912..439
Electoral Vote for President, 439, 441-442, 617
" " of the States...439
Electric Lighting................371
" Railway Progress.........371
Electrical Engineers, American Institute........................297
Electrical Progress in 1908..370-372
Electrical Units.................. 75
Electro-chemistry................371
Elevated R. Rs. in N. Y.....705-707
Elks, Order of.....................293
Ember Days........................ 29
Emigrants, see "Immigration."
Emmanuel Movement. 341
Employers' Liability Law...... 99
Encyclical on Modernism..339-340
Endurance Records 204
Engineering 367
Engineering Education, Society for Promotion of..........299

SEE ADVERTISING INDEX ON PAGES XCII TO XCV

PAGE

England, see "British."
" Area and Population......396
English Derby......211
" Established Church......401
" Mile...... 76
" Speaking Religious Communities......333
Entomological Society, Amer. 296
Epiphany in 1909...... 26
Episcopal Bishops......337
Episcopalians......333, 335
Epochs, Beginning of...... 26
Epworth League......349
Eras, Chronological...... 26
Esperanto, An International Language......358
Europe, Area and Population......67, 396, 546
European Banking Statistics..509
" Languages Spoken...... 67
" Military Resources...... 614
" Ministries......391
" Sovereigns......389
" " Civil List......546
Events, Historical...... 33
" Record of, 1908......15, 464-465
Excelsior Handicap......210
Excise Dept., N. Y. City......669
Expenditures, U. S. Govt..110, 489
Exports......110, 492, 493, 495
Expositions......539, 540, 541
Express Business in U. S......491
" on Railroads......258

F

FACTS ABOUT THE EARTH.... 67
Failures in U. S......511
Families in U. S......415
Famous Old People of 1909......470
" Universities......325
Farm Productions in U.S.15, 110, 524
Fastest Ocean Passages...... 281
Federal Council of Churches of Christ......350
Federal Government......556 557
" Officers in N. Y. City......686n
Federation of Labor, Amer......139
Feeble-Minded......534
Fencing......182
Fermented Liquors......530
Ferries from New York City..686t
Fiction in 1908......360-362
Field Officers U. S. Army..568-569
" Days, Sunday World......209
Finance Dep't, N. Y. City......668
Finances of Larger Cities......551
" of Nations......500
Financial Statistics, Begin......498
Fire Dept., N. Y. City..12, 669, 686aa
" Insurance Statistics......549
Fires, Loss by, in United States.549
Fisheries of U. S......502
Fishing, Open Seasons for...... 178
Flag, National...... 85
" Ass'n, American......377
Flags, Storm & Weather Sig...15, 60
" Transatlantic Lines......281
Flaxseed Crop......524
Florida Election Returns......624
Flowers, State......616
Folklore Society, American...296
Food, Law, Pure......15, 96-97
Football Records......245-246, 248
Foreign Bank Statistics......509
" Coins, Value of......481
" Consuls in N. Y. City......692
" Consuls in U. S......588
" Countries, Exports and Imports......492
" Legations in U. S......587
" Mails......171-173

PAGE

Foreign Ministries......391
" Missions, American Board 345
" Moneys...... 75
" Population in U. S......426
" Shipping......490
" Trade of the U. S......492
" Wars, Military Order of..373
Foresters, Order of......293
Forestry Statistics......175-177
Forts. N. Y. City......686x
Forty Immortals......353
Founders and Patriots of America......383
Fourth of July Casualties......31
France and Colonies...... 546
" Army and Navy.386, 405, 502, 614
France, Diplomatic Intercourse......452
" Government of......405
" Rulers of......389
Fraternal Brotherhood......293-294
" Organizations......293-295, 544
" Union of America......293
Fraternities, College......322-323
Free Baptist Young People....345
" Sons of Israel......294
Freemasonry......542
Free Thinkers, Number of....333
Freezing and Fusing Points....78
French Academy......353
" Battleships......386
" Ministry......391
" Pretenders......395
" Revolutionary Era...... 30
Funnel Marks of Steamers... 281
Futurity, The......211

G

GAME LAWS......178-179
Gasoline Production......519
General Education Board......302
Generals, U. S. Army......561
Geographic Board, U. S......331
" Society, National......299
Geographical Research.....367-369
" Society, American......297
Geological Society of America, 298
Geometrical Progression...... 76
Georgia Election Returns......624
Geological Strata...... 66
Geology......366
German Army and Navy..385, 405, 502, 614
" Battleships......385
" Diplomatic Intercourse...452
" Empire......546
" Government of......405
" Ministry......391
" Royal Family......393
Gin, Production of......530
Gleaners, Order of......295
Goats in U. S., Value of......524
Gold Certificates, U. S......110, 508
" Coins in Circulation......361
" in Circulation......110, 508
" Mines, Product......505
" Production of......110, 521, 505
" Source of, in U. S......504
Golden Cross, Order of......294
Golf......187, 188
Good Friday in 1909...... 26
" Roads Ass'n, Nat'l......429
" Templars, Order of......544
Government City of N. Y......668
Governments of the Earth......405
Governors of New York......454
" of States in U. S......555
Grain Production of U. S......523
Grand Army of the Republic....379
Gravity, Specific...... 78
Great Britain, see "British."
Greece, Army and Navy of......614

PAGE

Greece, Statistics of......546
Grecian Battleships......388
Greek Calendar for 1909...... 36
" Church Adherents......333
" Royal Family......393
Gregorian Calendar...... 32
Guam......412, 483, 554, 546
Gymnastics......185

H

HALL OF FAME......303
Hams, Production of......529
Hammer Throwing Records..199
Harness Racing......213-214
Harvard Boat Races......190
Hawaii......483, 554, 546
" Commerce......494
" Population......412, 546
Hay, Production of......524
Heads of Governments......390
Health Dept., N. Y. City......668
" Public...... 98
Heart Disease, Deaths from...536
Height of Buildings in N. Y...686g
" of Mountains......59, 67
" and Weight of Men and Women...... 78
Hemp Crop......524
Heptasophs, Order of......294
Hibernians, Order of......294
Hierarchy, Roman Catholic.15, 336
High-Tide Tables...... 62
Highways, Bureau of, N. Y. C...668
Hindooism......343
Historical Ass'n, American...297
" Events, Dates of...... 33
Hockey Records......185
Hog Statistics......529
Holidays...... 29
Homes and Asylums in New York City......680-681
Homes for Soldiers......606
" in United States......415
Homicide in United States.... 537
Homing Pigeons......225
Homœopathy, American Institute......297
Hops, Production of......524
Hopping Records......199
Horse-Racing Records......210
Horses, Value of, in U. S......524
Hospitals, N. Y. City......686h
Hotel Liquor Licenses, N. Y...531
House Flags on Steamers......281
" of Commons......403
" of Lords......400, 403
" of Representatives......593
Hudson-Fulton Celebration...255
Huguenot Society......383
Human Family...... 67
Humane Society, American...332
Hunting and Game Laws..178-179
Hurdle-Racing Records......198
Hurricane Warnings......15, 61

I

ICE YACHT CLUB RACES......192
I. C. A. A. A. A. Records......200
Idaho Election Returns......626
Illinois Election Returns......627
Illiterate Population in U. S...416
Immigration into U. S......282
" Commissioner, N. Y......686n
Imports......110, 492-493, 495
Indebtedness of Nations......500
Independence Declaration.. 86-87
Independence Party Convention......486
Independence Party Platform......162-165

PAGE

India, Government of....402
Indian, American....101
" Commissioners, Board....557
" Corn Production....523
" Population in U. S....414
" Wars, Order of....373
Indiana Election Returns....628
Indians, Expenditure, U.S....489
Indoor Athletic Records....203
Industrial Progress, U. S....110
"In God We Trust," When First Used on Coins....95
Inhabitants of Earth....67
Inhabitants of U. S. see "Population."
Inheritance Tax Laws....607
Initiative and Referendum....149
Insanity Statistics....534
Inspection of Steam Vessels.686u
Insular Possessions of U. S.482-484
Insurance Statistics....547
Interborough Rapid Transit, 705-708
Intercollegiate Varsity Races.190
Interest Rates in N. Y. Savings Banks....677-678
" Tables and Laws....76-77,616
Interior Department Officials..557
" Secretaries of the....448
Internal Revenue Officers, N. Y....686u
" Revenue Receipts....487
Internal Revenue Taxes....488
International Boat Races....193
" Bureau of American Republics....99
" League of Press Clubs....381
" Reform Bureau....429
International Red Cross Treaty....102
Interscholastic, Records....201
Interstate Commerce Com....557
" Commerce Law....112
" National Guard Ass'n....381
Intestate's Personal Estate 253-254
Intimidation Laws....137
Iowa Election Returns....630
Ireland, Area and Population, 396,404
" Government of....400
Irish Catholic Benev. Union...294
Iron and Steel Tonnage in U. S. 490
" World's Production of....520
Israel, Free Sons of....294
Italian Government....406
" Ministry....391
" Royal Family....393
Italy and Colonies....546
" Army and Navy of.386,406, 502,614
" Diplomatic Intercourse ...453

J

JAPAN, AREA AND POPULATION....546
" Army and Navy....502,614
Japanese in the U. S....414
" Battleships....385
" National Exposition....540
Jewish Calendar for 1909....36
" Churches in N.Y.City 682-686b
" Era....26
" Historical Society....298
Jews, Number of....333-334
Judgments, When Outlawed..616
Judiciary of New York City....670
" of New York State....603
" of States. (See Each State Election Returns.)
Judiciary of United States....559
Julian Period and Year....26

PAGE

Jumping Records....199
Jupiter, Planet....26, 49
Jury Duty, New York City....686v
Justice, U. S. Department of...557
Justices of the U. S. Supreme Court Since 1789....531

K

KANSAS ELECTION RETURNS, 631
Kentucky Derby....210
Kentucky Election Returns. 632
King's Daughters and Sons....349
Knights and Ladies of Honor..294
" of Columbus....294
" of Golden Eagle....294
" of Honor....294
" of Labor....141
" of Maccabees....294
" of Malta....294
" of Pythias....545
" of St. John and Malta....294
" Templars....543
Knots and Miles....75
Korea, Statistics of....546

L

LABOR COMMISSION, N. Y. STATE....600
Labor Information....137,141
Lacrosse Records....200
Ladies' Catholic Benev. Ass'n 294
Ladies of the Maccabees of the World....294
Lakes, Great, Area of....538
Lake Mohonk Conference....507
Lambeth Encyclical....354-355
Land Forces of Europe....614
Land, Lowest Point....59
Lands, Public, in U. S....439
Languages Spoken, European. 67
Lard, Production of....529
Latitude and Longitude....68
Latter-Day Saints....334, 347
Law Courts, N. Y. City....670
" Examinations in N.Y....254
" Schools in U. S....326
Law of Contracts....254
Lawn-Tennis Records...15, 180-181
Lawyers' Club, N. Y. City...686u
Lead, Production of....520-521
Leaders, District, N. Y. City.686y
League of American Municipalities....429
Leap Years....34
Learned Societies, American 296-299
Legal Holidays....29
Legations, Foreign, in U. S....587
Legislation State, Regulating R. R. Rates....15,458
" State....118-131
Legislature, N. Y. State....601
Legislatures, Pay and Terms of Members....555
Legislatures. (See Each State Election Returns.)
Legislatures, State, When Next Sessions Begin....555
Lenox Library....300
Lent in 1909....26
Letter Carriers, N. Y. City....686r
" Postage....15,168,171-172
Liberia, Statistics of....546
Libraries, N. Y. City....300,702
Library of Congress....301
Licences, Bureau of, N. Y. City.668

PAGE

Licences, Number of Hotel....531
Life, Human, Duration of....67
" Insurance Statistics...547-548
Life-Saving Service....553,686u
Lifting Records....200
Light-House Establishment...517
Lightning, Loss by....61
Limitations, Statutes of....616
Lincoln Centennial....428
Lincoln's Gettysburg Speech..428
Linear Measure....72
Liquid Measure....72.74
Liquor Prohibition Movement.532
" Statistics....530-531
Literature in 1908....360,362
Lockouts, Strikes, etc....132-133
Locomotives....257,278
London Officials & Population.. 404
Long Measure....74
Longitude Table....68
Lords, House of....400,403
Louisiana Election Returns....634
Loyal Americans of the Republic....294
Loyal Legion, Military Order...352
Lumber in U. S....174,176
Luther League of America....349
Lutheran Churches in N. Y. City....683,686b
Lutherans, Number of....333-334

M

MACCABEES, KNIGHTS OF....294
Magnetic Declinations....57
Magistrates, N. Y. City....670
Mails, Domestic and Foreign....15,168-173
Mail Time to Cities....173
Maine Election Returns....635
Major-Generals, U. S. Army..561
Malt Liquors, Statistics....530
Manhattan El. R. R....705
Manufactures....496-497
Map Elevated Ry., N. Y....707
" N. Y. City Assembly Districts and Wards....lxxll
" of Subway, N. Y....706
Marathon Races....15,247
Marine Corps, United States.573,614
" Engineers, Society....299
" Insurance....538
Mariner's Measure....74
Marriage & Divorce Laws..249-251
Married Persons in U. S....416
Mars, Planet....26, 49
Marshals, United States....560
Maryland Election Returns....635
Masonic Grand Lodges, U. S.. 542-543
Masonry, Sovereign Sanctuary 543
Masons, Colored....543
" Knights Templars....543
" Royal Arch....543
" Scottish Rite....542
Massachusetts Election Ret'ns. 636
Materials, Tensile Strength of. 79
Mathematical Society, Amer..297
Mayflower Descendants Soc...383
Mayors of New York City....454
" of Cities in United States.551
Measures, Ancient Greek and Roman....75
" Domestic....74
" Metric System of....71-73
" Used in Great Britain....74
Meat Inspection Law....97

SEE ADVERTISING INDEX ON PAGES XCII TO XCV.

PAGE

Mechanical Engineers, American Society....298
Mechanics, United American..295
Medal of Honor Legion....351
Medical Association, Amer....297
" Assn. of the Southwest...299
" Examinations, N. Y......148
" Schools in U S.....326
" Signs and Abbreviations 74
Medicine, American Academy.296
Medico-Legal Society....299
Medico-Psychological Ass'n..297
Memorable Dates....30
Merchant Marine....490
Merchant Navies of the World.490
Mercury, Planet....49,26
Metals, Production of....521
Methodist Bishops....337
" Churches in N.Y.City.683,686c
Methodists, Number of....333,334
Metric System....71-73
Metropolitan Handicap....210
Mexico,Army and Navy of.409,614
Mexico,Statistics of....409,548
Mica, Production of....520
Michigan Election Returns....637
Mile, English....76
Military Academy of U. S....615
" Departments, U. S....569
" Order Foreign Wars....373
" Order Loyal Legion....352
" Resources of Europe....614
Militia Act, The....93-95
Militia in N. Y. City....686q
" Naval....570,686q
" of the States....571
Milk Production....524
Millionaires, American....471
Mineral Products of U. S....520-521
Minimum, Weight of Produce. 73
Ministers, Foreign, in U. S.391-450
of European Countries....391
U. S., Abroad....450
Minnesota Election Returns....639
Mint, Directors of....450
Mints, Coinage of....506
" Superintendents of....558
Missions, Am. Board Foreign. 345
Mississippi Election Ret'ns....640
Missouri Election Returns....641
Modernism, Encyclical on.339-340
Mohammedan Calendar....36
Mohammedanism....333
Molasses Production....524
Monarchies and Republics.... 67
Monetary Statistics....503
Money Contributions, Act Prohibiting.... 104
" Orders in 1908.... 517
" Orders, Postal....170, 173
Moneys, Foreign.... 75
Monroe Doctrine....522
Montana Election Returns....642
Monthly Calendars for 1909...36-48
" Wage Table.... 77
Moon, Information About....36,49-50
" Eclipses of.... 52
Moonlight Chart for 1909.... 51
Moon's Phases in 1909.... 50
Moravians in U. S....335
Morocco, Statistics of....546
Mortality Statistics....535
Motor Boats....194,228
Motor Cycle....235,248
Mountains, Highest....59,67
Mount Vernon Ladies' Association....383
Mules, Value of, in U. S....524
Multi-Millionaries, American.471-479
Municipal Civil Service, N. Y.669
" and Civic Organizations..429
" Courts, N. Y. City....671
" Research Bureau,N. Y....668

PAGE

Municipal Statistics, Bureau, N. Y....668
Municipalities, Amer. League.429
Murders in U. S....537
Museums & Music Halls, N.Y..672
Musical People, Ages, etc..287-289
Mystic Circle, Order of....294
" Shrine, Nobles of the....543
" Workers of the World....294

N

NAPHTHA PRODUCTION....519
National Academy of Design..363
" A. A. U. Championships...201
" Academy of Sciences....299
" Association for Study of Epilepsy....299
" Ass'n for Study and Prevention of Tuberculosis.299
" Ass'n of Postmasters....516
" Association of R. R. Commissioners....274
" Bank Examiner, N. Y. City....686u
" Bank Notes....110,508
" Bank Statistics....110,508,677
" Cemeteries....606
" Civic Federation....134-135
" Conventions of Political Parties in 1908....486
" Council of Congregational Churches....338
" Democratic League....502
" Encampments....379
" Flag.... 85
" Geographic Society....299
" Good Roads Ass'n.... 429
" Guard....571,686q
" Home Disabled Volunt's.606
" Meat Inspection Law.... 97
" Municipal and Civic Organizations.... 429
" Municipal League....429
" Parks....177
" Party Platforms....153-167
" Provident Union....294
" Pure Food Law.... 15,96-97
" Purity Federation....350
" Republican League....491
" Sculpture Society....364
" Spiritualists' Association.344
" Union....295
" Unions....141
Nations, Indebtedness of....500
" Wealth of....500
Naturalists' Society, American.298
Naturalization Laws of United States....432
Naval Academy of U. S....615
" and Military Order, Spanish-American War....380
" Architects, Society of....299
" Enlistment....580
" Militia....570, 686q
" Officers, Customs....558
" Order of the United States.351
" Veterans, Nat'l Ass'n....351
Navies of the World....502,614
Navigation, Opening & Closing. 69
Navy, British....384,502
" Captains and Commanders....572-574
" Dep't Expenditures....489
" Department Officials....556
" Flag Officers....572
" League of the U.S....351
" Pay Table....583
" Rank of Officers....580
" Retired List....572
" Secretaries of the....448
" U. S. Official List.... 572
" United States....502,572-583
" U. S., Vessels..490,575-579,581
" Yards, United States....582

PAGE

Nebraska Election Returns....643
Necrology of 1908....15,466-469
Negroes in U. S....419,414
Neptune, Planet.... 49
Netherlands and Colonies....546
" Army and Navy....614
" Battleships....387
" Ministry....391
" Royal Family of....393
Nevada Election Returns....644
New Eng. Order Protection... 295
New Hampshire Election Returns....645
New Jersey Election Returns..644
New Mexico Election Returns....645
Newspaper Postage....169
" Measure, Standard.... 76
" Statistics....331
New Thought....550
N. Y. City Civil Service....147
" " Clearing-House.509,677
" " Government....668-669
" " Information Begins.672
" " Judiciary....670
" " National Guard... 686q
N.Y. City Populat'n..411,552,686y
" " Public Library....300
" " Tax Rate.... 552
" " Vote....646-649
New York Counties, Political and Judicial Divisions...605
" " State Commissioners of Excise....600
" " Counties, Order of Creation....605
" " State Civil Service Commissioners....600
" " Election Returns....646
" " Government....600
" " Judiciary....603
" " Legislature....601
" " Public Service Commissioners...290-292,600
" " Pub. Service Act. 290-292
" " Zoological Society....299
Nickel Production....521
Night Signals on Steamers....281
Nobel Prizes....550
Nobles of the Mystic Shrine...543
No. Carolina Election Returns. 650
North America, Population of..67
North Dakota Election Returns.651
Norway, Area and Population.546
" Army and Navy....614
" Ministries....391
Norwegian Battleships....387
Norwegian Royal Family....393
Notes, Promissory....252
" When Outlawed.... 616
Novels of 1908....360
Numerals, Roman and Arabic..77
Numismatic and Archæological Society....297
Nurse Training Schools....326
Nurses, Registration of....148

O

OAT CROP STATISTICS....523,524
Obituary Roll of 1908....15,466-469
Objects Visible at Sea-Level... 56
Occupations in U. S....421-422
Occurrences During Printing....15
Ocean Steamers....279-281,686s
Oceans, Depth of.... 67
Odd Fellowship, Information. 544
Ohio Election Returns.... 652
Oklahoma Election Returns...653
Old People of 1909, Famous....470
Olympic Championships....197
Opening and Closing of Navigation.... 69

PAGE
Oregon Election Returns.......655
Organization of the Army.....563
Oriental Society, American....297
Ornithologists' Union, Amer. 297
Owls, Order of.................295
Oxford-Cambridge Boat Races.192

P

PACING RECORDS..... 214
Painting and Sculpture.... 363
Palm Sunday in 1909........... 26
Panama Canal..............455-458
" " Zone...........484
" Statistics of..........546, 554
Paper Measure.................. 74
Paralysis, Deaths from........536
Parcels Post...................171
Parks, National...............177
" New York City 686p, 686v
Parliament, British............403
Party Divisions in Congress....591
" Platforms..............153-167
Passenger Stations, N.Y.......702
Passport F gulations..........113
Pastors of Churches in N. Y. City...... 682
Patents, Commissioners of.....450
Patent Office...............144-145
Patriots of America, Order of...383
Pawnbrokers' Regulations, New York........... ....686h
Peabody Education Fund......302
Peach and Pear Crop.......... 524
Peanut Crop....................524
Penalties for Usury 616
Pennsylvania Elect'n Returns.655
Pension Agencies.........557, 686n
" Commissioners.............450
" Statistics.. ....142-143, 557
People's Party Convention....486
People's Party Platform..161-162
People's Party National Committee 428
Per Capita Statistics........110, 503
Periodic Comets.................. 12
Periods, Chronological.......... 26
Persia, Statistics of.............546
Personal Estate, Distribution..253
Personalty in U.S...........501, 551
Peru, Army and Navy of......416
" Statistics of.................546
Petroleum, Production of.... .519
Pharmacy Examinations......148
Phi Beta Kappa................323
Philippine Commerce..........494
" Islands. 482
Philippine Area and Population......................412, 546, 554
Philological Association, American. 298
Philosophical Society, Am.....298
Physical Society, American. ..298
Physicians, American Association.............................298
Piers, New York City........686x
Pig Iron Production........519, 521
Pilgrim Fathers, Order of......295
Pilot Commissioners 669
Pistol Records...............208
Planetary Configurations, 1909...... 53
Platforms, National.......153-167
Platinum Production...........521
Plays of 1908....................674
Pneumonia, Deaths from......536
Polar Research..........369, 485-486
" Regions, Area and Population.................... 67
Pole Star, Mean Time of Transit..........................54-55
Police Dept., N.Y. City. 668, 686b
Political and Social Science Academy.....................296
Political Committees............438
" Conventions..................486
" Divisions in Congress.....591
" Platforms....................153
Polo.................................182
Polar Commission, International 539
Polytheism.......................333
Pool Records.............. 195, 248
Pope Pius X Encyclical on Modernism..............339
Popular Vote, President, 441-442, 617
Population, According to Age, Conjuga' Condition, Illiteracy.. 416
" According to School Age and Voting. 417
" According to Sex, Nativity, and Color.........414
" According to Vote Cast..418
" All Countries..............546
" by Dwellings, Families, Density, etc..............415
" by Governors of States... 420
" by State Censuses in 1905..413
" by Topographic Divs......418
" Centre of 422
" Each Census, 1790 to 1900..412
" Foreign in United States, 418, 426
" Indian...... ....101, 414
" of Africa...........67, 396, 546
" of America (British)......396
" of Asia..................67, 396
" of Australia..................396
" of British Empire 396
" of Canada...................407
" of Cities of U.S........... 423-425, 551
" of Cuba.......................546
" of Earth According to Race.................. 67
" of Earth, by Continents.. 67
" of Foreign Countries.......546
" of Gt. Britain and Ireland, 396
" of Incorporated Places in U.S.....................423-425
" of Largest Cities of Earth.411
" of London..............404, 411
" of Mexico....................409
" of New England Towns...425
" of New York City 411, 552, 686y
" of U. S..110, 412, 420, 426, 508, 546
" Rank of States.............422
" Urban, in U. S.............422
" Which Cannot Speak English.......................416
Pork, Production of............529
Porto Rico..............482, 546, 554
" " Commerce..............494
" " Population.......412, 546
Portugal and Colonies..........546
" Army and Navy..........614
Portuguese Battleships.........388
" Royal Family..............394
Port Wardens, N. Y. City......669
Postal Information 15, 168-173
Postmasters of Cities in United States.............................558
Postmasters-General, List of...448
Postmasters, National Assn....516
Post-Office Dep't Officials. . 557
" " N.Y. City......16, 686r
" " Statistics.......516-517
Potato Crop in U. S.............524
Potentiality of U. S.............507
Potomac, Society of Army 352
Poultry and Eggs, Production of.................................529
Power Transmission 372
Precious Metals, Statistics..... . 505
" Stones, Production........521
Presbyterian Assemblies.......342
" Churches in N. Y. City.684-686d
Presbyterians, Number of..333, 335
Presidents of the U. S..........443
" of the U. S. Senate........446
" Salary... 440
Presidential Cabinet Officers, 447-449
" Elections...............440, 617
" Election of 1912.:.......... .439
" Elections, 1789 to 1908..441-442
" Succession 445
" Vote.....................439, 617
Press Clubs, League 331
" Statistics of............ ...331
Prices of Commodities.........485
Printed Matter, Postage.......169
Prisoners Commutation Table.537
Produce, Minimum Weights of. 73
Production, Countries Excelling in.......................495
Professional Schools in U.S....326
Progress of United States..110-111
Prohibition Movement.........532
Prohibition Nat'l Committee..438
" Party Convention...........486
" Platform.....................167
Promissory Notes and Checks.252
Property, Assessed Valuation in U.S..................501, 551
Protected Home Circle.... 295
Protestant Episcopal Bishops..337
" Episcopal Churches, in N. Y. City..........684, 686d
Protestants, Number of....333, 335
Provident Loan Society.......686h
Public Administrator, N.Y....669
" Buildings, N. Y. City......702
" Debt of U. S...........110, 499
" " Cities in U. S.....551
" Health Ass'n, American.298
" Health........................ 98
" Lands of U. S............ 430
" Porters.....................686r
" Schools Athletic League 206-207
" Schools in N. Y. City 686j-686m
" Service Act, N. Y.....290-292
" Service Comm'rs.290, 600, 669
" Works Dept., N. Y. City. 668
Pugilism.................243-244, 248
Pupils, School, in U. S........326
Pure Food Law...........15, 96-97
Purity Federation, National...350
Pythias, Knights of............545

Q

QUALIFICATIONS FOR VOTING. 433-434
Quarantine Commissioners.....669
Quicksilver, Production of..... 521
Quoits Records..................183

R

RACE, POPULATION ACCORDING TO.............................. 67
Racquets and Court Tennis....181
Railroad Accidents..............274
" Cars, Cost and Weight....278
" Commissioners..............277
" Earnings and Expenses. ..257
" Employés, British, Wages.276
" Employés in U.S...........274
" Expresses.....................258
" "Grouped" by Capitalists..... 278

SEE ADVERTISING INDEX ON PAGES XCII TO XCV.

PAGE
Railroad Equipment............278
" Mileage..................257-276
" Officials...........258-273,277
" Passenger Stations.........702
" Rates, Regulation.......15,460
" Speed Records...............275
" Statistics of U. S.......257-278
" Stockholders...................273
" Stocks, List......................512
" Traffic.......................257,276
Rainfall, Normal, in the U. S.. 58
" of Foreign Cities.......... 59
Rank of Officers, Army and Navy.............................564,580
Rates of Postage..............15,168
Ratio of Silver to Gold...........504
Ready-Reference Calendars.34-35
Realty and Personalty.......501,551
Rear-Admirals, U. S. Navy....572
Receipts & Expenditures, U. S.489
Rechabites, Order of............295
Reciprocity Treaties 592
Record of Events in 1908....15,464
Red Cross, American Nat'l....382
" " Treaty International.102
Red Men, Order of...............295
Reformed Churches, Alliance .342
" Church in America.........338
" Episcopal Bishops..........338
" Number of..............333,337
Regattas in 1908......................191
Regents' Examinations, N. Y..148
Regents of University, N. Y....600
Regiments, U. S., Field Officers.....................................568
Registration of Mail Matter170-171
" of Trade-Marks............152
" of Voters...........................435
Regulation of R. R. Rates...15,460
Relay Racing.........................199
Reigning Families of Europe....392
Religious Statistics...................333
Representatives in Congr's.593-598
" Salary of...........................595
Republic, Grand Army of.........379
Republican National and State Committees........................435
" Conventions.....................486
" League, National..........491
" Party Platforms...............157
Republics and Monarchies. ... 67
Revenue Cutter Service..........553
Revenues, U.S. Government....489
Revolution, Daughters of.......378
" American, Daughters of..378
" American, Sons of..........375
" Sons of the......................375
Rhode Island Election Returns.......................................657
Rhodes Scholarship................480
Rice Crop..................................524
Rifle & Revolver Shooting.207,248
Ritualistic Calendar................ 36
Rivers, Principal American.... 70
Rod and Reel-Casting Records.189
Roentgen Ray Society..........298
Rogation Days......................... 29
Roller Skating...............204,248
Roman Catholic Churches in N. Y. City............... 686,686e
" Catholic Hierarchy.....15,336
" Catholics, Number of...333-334
" Era...................................... 26
" Numerals............................ 77
Roosevelt African Expedition. 31
Rope Climbing Records.........200
Roque......................................183
Roumania, Statistics of..........546
Roumanian Army...................614
Rowing Records.............190-192
Royal Academy.....................364
" Arcanum.........................545
" Arch Masons....................543
" Families of Europe.........392
" League.............................295

PAGE
Rulers of Nations...............390
Rum, Production of.............530
Running Records..................198
Russia, Army and Navy.406,502,614
" Diplomatic Intercourse...450
Russian Calendar for 1909...... 36
" Battleships......................387
" Empire, Population, etc..546
" Government.....................406
" Imperial Family.............394
" Ministry...........................391
Rye, Production of...............523

S

SACK RACING......................199
Safe Deposit Cos. in N. Y..678,702
Salaries of Governors of States in U. S..........................555
" of Members of State Legislatures in U. S................555
" of Representatives in U. S. Congress......................595
" of U. S. Cabinet Officers ..556
" of U. S. Senators.............596
Salary of the President..........440
Saloons in N. Y. City..............531
Salt, Production of.................520
Salvation Army...............335,344
Samoa, American Population of.....................................412,546
Saratoga Handicap.................211
Saturn, Planet.....................26,49
Savings Banks, N. Y. City..677-678
" Banks Statistics...110,508,510
Saxon Royal Family...............394
Schools in U. S.......................326
" & College Enrolment.......326
" New York City.....686j-686m
" of Pharmacy....................326
Sciences, Nat'l Academy.......299
Scientific Progress in 1908...365-367
Scotland, Government of.......400
" Area and Population..396,401
Scottish Clans, Order of.........295
" Rite Masons.....................542
Sculpture..............................363
" National Society.............364
Seaports, Greatest..................495
Seasons, The.......................... 26
Secretaries, Cabinet, List...447-448
Seed Planting in U. S............ 80
Senate, N. Y. State..................601
" U. S. Presidents pro tempore.................................446
Senators, U. S...................592,595
" U. S., Salary of...............596
Servia, Statistics of................546
Servian Army........................614
" Royal Family..................395
Sewers, Bureau of, N. Y. City..668
Sex Proportion in U. S..........413
Shakespearean Table..............673
Sheep in U. S................110,524
Sheriff, N. Y. City....................669
Shield of Honor.......................295
Shintoism.................................333
Shipbuilding in U. S...............490
Shipping, American & Foreign.490
Shot-Putting Records..............199
Shooting Records....................207
Siam, Statistics of...................546
Sidewalks, New York City....686l
Signals, Weather.................15,60
Signers of the Declaration of Independence..................... 87
Silver Bay Association...........502
Silver Certificates, U. S.....110,506
" In Circulation..............110,508

PAGE
Silver Mines Product............505
" Production of......110,503,521
" Purchases by U. S.........504
" Ratio to Gold..................504
" Source of, in U. S...........504
Simple Interest Table........... 76
Single Tax............................686ff
Sixtieth Congress..................593
Sixty-first Congress...............596
Skating Records........ 184,204,248
Ski Records...........................194
Slate, Production of..............520
Slater, John. F., Fund............302
Slaves in U. S. in 1790...........419
Smithsonian Institution..........304
Snuff.......................................487
Social Science Ass'n, American.298
Socialist Labor National Committee.....................................438
" Labor Party Convention..486
" Labor Party Platform 167
" Party Convention...........486
" Party Nat'l Committee...438
" Party Platform...............165
Sociological Society, Amer....469
Societies in N. Y. City.........686n
" of War of 1812.................377
Society of The Cincinnati..374-375
Solar System.......................... 49
Soldiers' Homes.....................605
Sons of Temperance...............545
Sons of the American Revolution..375
Sons of the Revolution...........375
" of Veterans, U. S. A........380
South America, Population of. 67
South & Central Amer. Trade..410
" American Armies and Navies.................................614
S. Carolina Election Returns.657
S. Dakota Election Returns....658
Southern Education Board....302
" Medical Ass'n...................299
Sovereigns of Europe.......389,546
Spain, Area and Population....546
" Army and Navy..............614
" Diplomatic Intercourse...453
Spanish-American Claims.....557
" Battleships......................388
" Ministry..........................391
" Royal Family..................394
" War Veterans..................380
Speakers of U.S. House of Representatives..........................446
Special Sessions, Court..........640
Specific Gravity......................78
Speed of Railroad Trains.......275
" of Steamships...................281
Spindles in Operation............525
Spirits, Statistics of..............530
Spiritualists, National Association..341
Spiritualists, number of........335
Sporting Records.........15,178-259
Spring, Beginning of, 1909...... 28
Square Measure...................72, 74
Squash Records.....................189
Stage, The........................287,684
Standard Oil Co. Prosecution...463
" Time..............................83
Star Table.............................. 55
" of Bethlehem Order.........295
Stars, Morning and Evening... 26
State and Territorial Governments.....................................555
" and Territorial Statistics..554
" Banks, Loan & Trust Cos...508
" " in N. Y. City.........676
" Capitals...........................554
" Committees Political 436-437
" Department Officials 556
" Elections................begin 619
" Flowers...........................616

PAGE

State Labor Bureaus.............138
" Legislation............118-121
" Legislatures...........555, 619
" Legislation Regulating R.R. Rates...........15, 458
" Militia...................571
" Officers in N. Y. City.... 669
" Officers, (See Each State Election Returns.)
" Rank According to Population...................422
States and the Union 554
" Area of....................554
" Debts of...................501
Statistical Ass'n, American....298
Statutes of Limitations.........616
Steamboat Inspection, U.S......480
Steamships from N.Y.279-280, 686u
Steam, Temperature of......... 79
Steam Vessel, Inspectors.....686u
Steel, Production of............519
" Tonnage in U. S............490
Stockholders, Railroad.........278
Stocks, Prices of Leading....512-515
Stone Gathering Records.......199
Storm Warnings..............15, 61
Street-Cleaning Dept., N. Y....668
Street Openings, Bureau of N. Y. City.................668
Strikes and Lockouts.......132-123
St. Andrew, Brotherhood of....345
St. Vincent de Paul Society....348
Students in U. S...............328
Submarine Cables 285
Sub-Treasury, N. Y. City.......686
Suburban Handicap............211
Subways in New York......706, 708
Suffrage Qualifications......433-434
" Right of....................432
" Woman......................435
Sugar Production...........524, 528
Suicide, Statistics of.........534, 536
Sulphur Production............520
Summer, Beginning of, 1909.... 26
Sun, Eclipse of................. 52
" Mean Distance of.......... 49
" on Meridian.............36-48
" Rises and Sets............36-48
Sun's Declination............... 54
Sunday-School Statistics.......335
" World Field Days..........209
Supreme Court of U. S......531, 559
" " N. Y.......603, 670
Surgical Ass'n, American......298
Surrogate's Court, N. Y.......671
Surveyors of Customs..........558
Sweden, Area, etc..............546
" Army and Navy...........614
" Ministry of................391
Swedish Battleships...........387
" Royal Family..............395
Swimming Records 226, 248
Swine in U.S...................524
Switzerland, Army of..........614
" Statistics of................546

T

TAMMANY, SOCIETY OF.........373
Tampa Isthmian Canal Exposition.........................540
Taoism.........................333
Tariff Rates, U. S...........114-115
Tax Department, N. Y. City...669
" Rate, U. S. Cities..........551
" Rates of States.............501
Taxable Property U.S. Cities.501, 551
Taxes, Internal Revenue.......488
" Receiver of, N. Y. City.....668

Tea and Coffee..................528
Teachers in U. S. Schools......326
Telegraph Information.283-284, 370
Telephone Statistics....284, 286, 370
Temperance, Sons of...........545
Temperature of Foreign Cities. 59
" Normal, in U. S............ 58
Temperature of Steam.......... 79
Tennessee Election Returns......658
Tennis Records...............15, 180
Tensile Strength of Materials.. 79
Territorial Expansion of U. S..484
Territories of United States.... 554
Texas Election Returns.........660
" Land Measure............. 74
Theatres, New York City......672
Theatrical Runs.................674
Theodore Roosevelt's African Expedition.................... 81
Theological Schools in U. S....326
Theosophical Society, The..335, 343
Thermometers.................. 56
Thirteenth Army Corps Ass'n 352
Tide Tables...................62-63
Timber in U. S.................174
Time Difference................ 28
" Divisions of............... 32
" Measure................... 74
" Standard................... 32
Tin, Production of..........519, 520
Tobacco, Production of.....521, 524
Tonnage, Maritime 490
Torpedo Boats, U. S....578-579, 582
Tract Society, American......346
Trade, Foreign, of U. S.........492
Trade Marks, Registration....152
Transportation by Water...108-109
Transatlantic Steamers....279, 686u
Trap Shooting.................. 205
Treasury Department Officials.556
" Secretaries of the......... 447
Treaties, Arbitration...........522
" Reciprocity..................522
Tribe of Ben Hur...............293
Trinity Sunday in 1909.......... 26
Tropical Year................... 32
Trotting Records...............213
Trust Companies in N. Y.......679
Trusts in Party Platforms..154, 158, 161, 164
" Prosecution of, by U. S. 463
Turf, The American....210-212, 248
Turkey, Army & Navy of......614
Turkish Battleships............388
" Empire....................546
Tutuila, Area and Population 483, 546, 554
Twilight Tables..............36-48
Typhoid Fever, Deaths from...536

U

UNION ARMY SOCIETIES.......352
" Fraternal League..........295
" Veteran Legion...........381
Unions, Labor..............139-141
Unitarian Ass'n, American....338
Unitarians, Number of.....333, 335
United American Mechanics.. 295
" Confederate Veterans.....382
" Daughters of Confederacy.382
" Sons Confederate Vets....382
" Spanish War Veterans....380
" Volunteer Ass'n...........380
" Workmen, Order of 295
United States Area. 110, 546
" Army.............502, 561-570
" Army and Navy Union....373
" Army in New York City.686u
" Assay Office in N. Y......686u

United States Assistant Treasurers.......................558
" Bankruptcy Law...........511
" Battleship Fleet............583
" Census.......................150
" Civil Service Commission..557
" Civil Service Rules.....15, 146
" Constitution..............81-85
" Consuls Abroad............584
" Courts.......................559
" Courts in N. Y. City.......671
" Customs Duties........114-115
" Daughters 1812, Society....378
" District-Attorneys.........560
" Foreign Trade............. 492
" Forestry Statistics.....175-177
" General Appraisers.......686u
" Geographic Board.........331
" Government.............556-557
" Government Print'g Office 517
" Industries....................110
" Insular Possessions....482-484
" Internal Revenue Receipts.487
" Internal Revenue Taxes..488
" Judiciary....................559
" Land Offices..................430
" Life-Saving Service...553, 686u
" Lighthouse Establishm't. 517
" Manufactures..........496-497
" Marine Corps...............573
" Military Academy.........615
" Ministers Abroad.450-453, 584
" Naval Academy.............615
" Naval Enlistment and Pay.....................580, 583
" Navy.....................572, 614
" Navy Vessels 575-576
" Navy Yards..................582
" Pension Statistics..110-142, 557
" Population.....110, 412, 420, 426, 508, 546
" Postmasters..................558
" Post-Office Statistics.........516
" Progress..................110-111
" Public Debt..............110, 498
" Public Lands.................430
" Receipts & Expenditures, 110, 489
" Revenue Cutter Service...553
" Secret Service..............517
" Senate, Presidents pro tempore......................446
" Senators..................592, 596
" Shipping Com'r, N. Y.....686u
" Steamboat Inspection Service..........................480
" Supreme Court.............559
" Vessels in 1908.............490
" Wars......................376, 515
" Warships...............575, 581
" Wealth of...............110, 507
Universal Brotherhood.........343
Universalist Gen'l Convention.338
Universalists in U. S..........335
Universities of U. S....305, 320, 327
Uranus, Planet.................. 49
Urban Population in U. S......422
Usury, Penalty for.............616
Utah Election Returns..........662

V

VALUATION, ASSESSED, OF PROPERTY IN U. S......501, 551
Vaulting Records...............199
Vedanta Society.................347
Velocity of Winds in U. S...... 61
Venezuela, Area & Population.546

PAGE

Venezuela, Army of..........416
Venus, Planet..........26, 49
Vermont Election Returns..........662
Vessels of U. S. Navy..575,579,582
Veterans of Indian Wars, Soc. of..........373
Veterans, Sons of U. S. Army..380
Veterinary Examinations..........148
" Schools..........326
Vice-Presidents of U.S., List...446
" " Vote..........441
Virginia Election Returns..........663
Volcanic Deposits in U. S....64-65
Volunteers of America.......... 344
Vote of New York City.....646,649
" Popular and Electoral 441-442
Voters, Registration of..........435
" Qualifications for......433-434
Voting Population of U. S......420

W

WAGE-EARNERS IN U. S...135, 496-497
Wage Table, Monthly.......... 77
Wake Island..........483
Wales, Population of 396,404
Walking Records..........198
War Dep't Expenditures......489
Wards in N. Y. City..........lxxii
Wars, U. S. 376,515

PAGE

Washington State Election Returns..........665
Water Polo..........227
" Supply Board N. Y. City,..663
" Measures..........73
Water, Transportation By.108-109
Wealth of U. S..........110,507
Wealth of Nations..........500
Weather Bureau, N. Y. City..68-69
" Flags.......... 60
" Rules for Foretelling..... 56
" Wisdom 56
Weight-Throwing Records....199
Weights..........71-75
Weights, Ancient Greek and Roman.......... 75
Weight and Height of Women. 78
West Point Military Academy..615
W. Virginia Election Returns..665
Western Surgical Gynecological Ass'n..........299
Wheat Statistics..........523,524
Whiskey, Production of..........530
Whistle Weather Signals...... 60
Whist, American..........230-235
Whist Records..........248
Wills..........252
Winds, Velocity of, in U. S..... 61
Wine Production of the World, 529
" Statistics of..........530,531
Winter, Beginning of, 1909..... 26
Wireless Telegraphy..........370
Wisconsin Election Returns... 666

PAGE

Withdrawals for Consumption..........487
Woman Suffrage..........435
Woman's Christian Temperance Union..........248
" Relief Corps. 380
Women at Work in U. S..........329
Wool Manufacturers..........527
Women's Patriotic Societies...377
Woodland Area in U. S..........175
Woodmen, Fraternal Order....295
Wool, Statistics of..........524-527
World, Statistics of Countries of.546
World's Wonderful Progress.. 28
" Young Women's Christian Association..........346
Wrestling..........184
Würtemberg, Royal Family...395
Wyoming Election Returns...667

Y

YACHTING RECORDS 193
Yale Boat Races..........190
Yeomen of America..........295
Young Men's Christ. Ass'ns....346
" People's Christ'n Union..348

Z

ZINC, PRODUCTION OF......519,520
Zoological Society, New York. 299

Periodic Comets.

NAME.	Perihelion Passage.	Period (Years).	Perihel. Dist. Earth's Orbit=1.	Eccentricity.	NAME.	Perihelion Passage.	Period (Years).	Perihel. Dist. Earth's Orbit=1.	Eccentricity.
Encke........	1885, Mar. 7	3.3	0.34	0.846	Biela.........	1882, Sept. 23	6.6	0.86	0.755
Tempel.......	1884, Nov. 20	5.2	1.34	0.553	D'Arrest.....	1884, Jan. 13	6.7	1.33	0.626
Barnard......	1890, Feb.	5.4	1.28	0.582	Faye.........	1881, Jan. 22	7.6	1.74	0.549
Tempel-Swift	1886, May 9	5.5	1.07	0.656	Tuttle.........	1885, Sept. 11	13.8	1.02	0.821
Brorsen.......	1879, Mar. 30	5.5	0.59	0.810	Pons-Brooks.	1884, Jan. 25	71.5	0.77	0.955
Winnecke...	1886, Sept. 4	5.8	0.88	0.727	Olbers........	1887, Oct. 8	72.6	1.20	0.931
Tempel.......	1885, Sept. 25	6.5	2.07	0.405	Halley........	1835, Nov. 15	76.4	0.59	0.967

Fire Engine Companies in Brooklyn and Queens.

(Headquarters, 365 Jay Street, Brooklyn.)

101—1233 4th Ave.
102—Van Brunt St., nr. Seabring.
103—Hicks St., near Degraw St.
104—Degraw St., near Court St.
105—Pierrepont St., near Fulton.
106—Pearl St., near Nassau St.
107—Pearl St., near Concord St.
108—Front St., near Bridge St.
109—Graham Ave., n. Myrtle Av.
110—Carlton Ave., n. Myrtle Ave.
111—Clymer St., nr. Bedford Ave.
112—Wythe Ave., near N. 8th St.
113—Powers St., n. Manhattan Av.
114—Herkimer St., nr. N. Y. Ave.
115—India St., near Franklin St.
116—Scholes St., near Union Ave.
117—De Kalb Ave., n. Lewis Ave.
118—Hart St., near Central Ave.
119—Dean St., n. Vanderbilt Ave.
120—11th St., near 7th Ave.
121—S. 2d St., near Bedford Ave.
122—Quincy St., n. Patchen Ave.
123—Fireboat Seth Low, Pier ft. 42d St.
124—274 Hicks St.
125—Liberty Ave., n. Ashford St.
126—State St., near Nevins St.
127—Herkimer St., n. Ralph Ave.
128—39th St., cor. 5th Ave.
129—Kingsland Ave., cor. Frost.
130—Ellery St., near Marcy Ave.
131—Watkins St. and Glenmore Ave.
132—Fireboat David A. Boody, Pier ft. N. 8th St.
133—Hull St., near Broadway.
134—Bergen St., near Troy Ave.
135—Monroe St., n. Nostrand Av.
136—Liberty Ave., nr. Market St.
137—Morgan Ave., cor. Grattan.
138—Norman Ave., nr. Diamond.
139—4th Ave., near 6th St.
140—Prospect Av., n. Greenwood.
141—Bay Ridge Ave., nr. 2d Ave.
142—5th Ave., near 92d St.
143—18th Ave. and 86th St.
144—W. 15th St., near Surf Ave.
145—W. 8th St., near Surf Ave.
146—E. 23d St., nr. Voorhees Av.
147—60th St., n. New Utrecht Ave.
148—Church Ave., n. Bedford Av.
149—Rogers Ave., nr. Midwood.
150—Lawrence Ave., near 2d Av.
151—Wallabout Market.
152—Central Ave., n. Decatur St.
153—86th St., near 24th Ave.
154—Town Hall, Gravesend.
155—Rogers Ave., near Ave. F.
156—124 De Kalb Ave.
157—Rockaway Ave and Canarsie R. R., Flatlands.
158—136 8th St., L. I. City.
159—71 Gale St., L. I. City.
160—687 Vernon Ave., L. I. City.
161—231 Radde St., L. I. City.
162—80 Main St., L. I. City.
163—354 Flushing Ave., L. I. City.
164—Central Ave., near Cleveland St., Far Rockaway.
165—Boulevard, near Ammerman Ave., Arverne.
166—Grove St., near Boulevard, Rockaway.
167—Boulevard, near Henry St., Rockaway.
168—Washington and Beach Avs., Rockway Park.
169—Union St. and 7th Ave.
170—Willow St., bet. Fulton and Hillside Ave., Richmond Hill.
Chemical Engine Co. No. 1, 712 Driggs Ave.
Water Tower No. 1, 365 Jay St.
Search Light No. 3, St. Edwards and Bolivar Sts.

SEE CLASSIFIED ADVERTISING ON PAGES 732 TO 735.

Index

OF NOTEWORTHY ARTICLES OR PARAGRAPHS IN PRECEDING VOLUMES OF "THE WORLD ALMANAC."

Articles.	Volume.	Page.
Alaska Boundary Award	1904	148
Alcoholic Drinks, Consumption of	1890	108
Alien Landholders in the United States	1888	90
America, Four Centuries of	1901	106
Arbitration, International Court of	1902	84
Arbitration Treaty with Great Britain	1898	87
Army, U. S., General Officers Who Have Risen from the Ranks	1900	409
Army, U. S., Regimental Records	1904	351
Australian Ballot System	1892	90
Australian Federation	1901	382
Barge Canal, New York	1904	150
Bartholdi Statue Described	1887	24
Battle Calendar of the Republic	1899	85
Bell Time on Shipboard	1902	27
Bible Statistics	1894	219
Boodle Aldermen of New York, List of	1888	118
Bryant's Index Expurgatorius	1907	318
Canada, Boundary Line Controversy	1902	184
Census, Eleventh U. S., How Taken	1890	57
Census, Twelfth U. S., How Taken	1900	102
Centuries Ago	1894	42
" "	1896	44
Chicago, Information About	1893	423
Chicago, Maps of	1893	423
Chicago, World's Fair	1894	81
China Boxer Rising	1902	153
Chinese Exclusion Act of 1892	1894	106
Chinese Treaty with the U. S	1895	100
Clearing-Houses of World, Statistics of	1890	96
Colleges, American, Locations of	1902	318
Columbian Postage Stamps Described	1893	150
Columbus to Veragua, Pedigree	1894	82
Conemaugh Flood	1891	67
Confederate States of America	1908	337
Conflagrations, Great Historic	1908	415
Constitution of the State of New York	1908	164
Constitutions, State	1902	156
Constitutional Amendments, Proposed	1890	78
Counterfeits, Dangerous	1890	136
Cuban Reciprocity Treaty	1904	146
Cuba, Intervention in 1906	1907	136
Cyclones, Statistics for 87 Years	1889	24
Czar's Universal Peace Proposal	1899	106
Dispensary Liquor Law of S. Carolina	1894	108
Earthquakes, Their Cause and Result	1907	65
Electricity, Death Penalty by	1889	114
Events, A Quarter Century Record of	1908	52
Faribault System of Education	1893	185
Fecundity, Statistics of	1895	231
Financial Stringency of 1907	1908	388
Floriculture in the United States	1892	140
Generals of the U. S. Army Since 1776	1902	410
Gold Standard Act of 1900	1901	91
Governors of States Since the Adoption of Their Constitutions	1906	120
Hague Peace Conference, 1899	1900	98
" 1907	1908	292
Harvest Moon	1902	49
Hawaii, Joint Resolution Annexing	1899	96
Hundred Best Books, Lubbock	1895	247
Immigration Law of 1907	1908	184
Income Tax of 1894	1895	92
Influence of the Moon on the Weather	1898	52
Inheritance, Law of	1903	229
Inter-Continental Railway	1907	245
Inter-Parliamentary Union of 1906	1907	382
International Marine Conference	1890	56
Isthmian Canal Act	1903	156
Italian Art Exposition	1902	293
Jamestown Exposition	1907	300
Labor Movement in U. S., Chronology of	1892	93
Labor Strikes, Tabular History of	1895	96
Land Areas in the U. S. and Europe	1890	96
Landowners, Alien, Number of, in the United States	1888	90
Legislative Assemblies of the World	1906	372
Lewis and Clark Centennial Exposition	1905	12
Literary Pseudonyms	1904	292
Luminiferous Ether, The	1904	52
Mars, The Planet	1902	30
Masonry, Degrees in	1902	324
Mayflower Passengers	1908	336
Medal of Honor, U. S. Military, List of Persons Awarded	1899	84
Medical and Surgical Progress in the Nineteenth Century	1901	298
Meteorites	1903	59
Milky Way, The	1903	59
Millionaries, The American	1902	135
Mormons, The	1897	329
Mottoes and Popular Names of States	1908	372
Naval Guns, Range of	1892	252
Navy, U. S., Historic Vessels of	1904	355
New Testament Chronology	1901	28
New York City, Reconstruction of	1903	389
New York State Constitution	1908	164
Nicaragua Canal Treaty	1902	157
Novels, Hundred Greatest	1895	246
Panama Canal, Acquisition of	1905	126
Panama, Treaty with	1904	142
Pan-American Conference of 1889	1890	60
Pan-American Conference of 1906	1907	135
Pilgrims of 1620	1908	336
Poisons and Their Antidotes	1904	235
Porto Rico, Act for Civil Government	1901	93
Postage Stamps, Old, Prices of	1893	150
Prohibition Party, Growth of	1889	97
Pseudonyms, Literary	1904	292
Railroad Facts	1892	154
Railroad Strike of July, 1894	1895	98
Railway Between North and South America	1907	245
Rifles Used by Principal Armies	1902	360
Roosevelt, Theodore, Pedigree	1908	334
Russian Duma Called	1906	141
Russian-Japanese War. First Year	1905	133
Russian-Japanese War. Second Year	1906	136
Samoan Treaty	1901	92
Santo Domingo Treaty	1908	295
Seismic Disturbances of 1902	1903	278
" " in 1903	1904	28
" " of 1906	1907	65
Senators, U. S., from 1789	1904	116
Ship Subsidy Bill	1908	227
Silver Purchase Repeal Legislation	1894	102
Silver Question	1886	50
" "	1888	68
Simplified Spelling Movement	1907	316
Socialist Demands	1907	119
Solar Energy, Source and Maintenance of	1908	134
South African War and Map	1900	94
South Carolina Exposition	1902	295
South Carolina Liquor Law	1894	108
Spain, Treaty of Peace with	1900	88
Spanish-American War, History of	1899	64
Stars, The Fixed	1900	34
Sub-Treasury Scheme of the Farmers' Alliance	1892	91
Sunshine, Duration of, on U. S. Territory	1901	53
Sun Spots, Their Influence on the Earth	1901	49
Telescopes in the U. S., Large	1889	124
Tornadoes, Statistics of, for 87 Years	1900	35
Torpedo Service of the World	1886	65
Truck Farming in the United States	1892	140
Trusts, Principal	1908	306
Utah Commission, Report of	1890	161
Venezuelan Boundary Treaty	1896	67
Veto Power of the Executive in All the States	1888	58
Vine Cultivation in the United States	1892	140
Volapük	1892	195
Warships of U. S. Since 1775	1900	356
Women, American, Who Have Married Foreign Titles	1908	319
World's Columbian Exposition	1893	75
" " "	1894	81
World's International Expositions, List of	1892	74
World, The, A Quarter Century History of	1908	19

New York Preparatory School

15 West 43d Street
Near Fifth Avenue
NEW YORK
Telephone 2956 Bryant

200 Joralemon Street
Cor. Court Street
BROOKLYN
Telephone 1908 Main

Law, Medical, Dental, Veterinary Students, Nurses, Pharmacy, Certified Public Accountants, thoroughly and rapidly prepared for

Regents' Examinations

Day and Evening Sessions for Young Men and Women

College Preparatory Course

CIVIL SERVICE, FEDERAL, STATE, MUNICIPAL

Annual Catalogue and Pamphlet, "SUCCESS IN REGENTS' EXAMINATIONS," sent on application to the registrar.

SAMUEL F. BATES, Registrar.

EMIL E. CAMERER, M. A., LL. B., Principal.

SOME weeks are occupied in printing a volume so bulky as THE WORLD ALMANAC, and it is necessarily put to press in parts or "forms." Changes are in the meantime occurring. Advantage is taken of the going to press of the last form of the First Edition to insert information of the latest possible date, which is done below. The readers of the ALMANAC are requested to observe these additions, corrections and changes, and it would be well to make note of them on the pages indicated.

336. Roman Catholic Hierarchy. Rt. Rev. John L. Spalding, Bishop of Peoria, has resigned the bishopric.

146. United States Executive Civil Service—On December 1 the President issued an order applying the Civil Service rules to fourth-class postmasters in all States east of the Mississippi River and north of the Ohio. The order is experimental. If it proves satisfactory in the States to which it has been applied it will be made general. The Civil Service Commission will order examinations in all the counties in the States indicated.

458. Railroad Rates, Legislation Regulating—The Supreme Court of the United States, November 30, reversed the decision of the United States Circuit Court for the Eastern District of Virginia, which held unconstitutional the order of the State Railroad Commission fixing a two-cent passenger rate on State business. The effect of the decision was the upholding of the order.

168. Postal Information—The United States and Germany have agreed to an arrangement, effective January 1, 1909, providing for a 2-cent letter rate between the two countries in the place of the 5-cent rate when the letters are exchanged by sea direct—that is by the North German Lloyd and Hamburg-American lines. Letters despatched by way of Great Britain or France must be paid at the Postal Union rate of 5 cents for the first ounce and 3 cents for each additional ounce.

96. The National Pure Food Law—After January 1, according to a decision of the Board, the phrase "Guaranteed under the Food and Drug act, June 30, 1906," must be changed, so as to show plainly that the guarantee is that of the manufacturer and not of the Government. But because of the large sums of money invested in good faith in labels and plates, the old form of labels now in use, representing guarantees already filed with the Department, will be recognized for two years.

60. Storm and Hurricane Warnings—The Chief of the Weather Bureau, Washington, has announced that on and after January 1, 1909, in the display of night storm warnings a red light alone will indicate easterly winds and a white light below a red light will indicate westerly winds. The foregoing action reverses the positions formerly occupied by the red and white lights in indicating westerly winds.

464. Record of Events—December 8—Milton Tercentenary celebrated. December 12—The Netherlands naval cruiser Gelderland seized the Venezuelan coast-guard ship Alix on the Venezuelan Coast. December 12—Dynamite explosion on the Panama Canal killed 24 workmen and others.

466. Death Roll of 1908—Additional. Francis Marinus Caldwell (70), Treasurer-General of the Society of The Cincinnati, Philadelphia, Pa., December 1; Oliver Wolcott Gibbs (86), Professor of Applied Science, and Senior Member of the Faculty of Harvard University, Newport, R. I., December 9; Henry Jackson (71), Brigadier-General, U. S. A., retired, Leavenworth, Kan., December 10; Mrs. Nicholas Fish (60), widow of the New York banker and diplomatist, Washington, D. C., December 11.

88. Acts of Congress—Recommendations in the President's Message, December 8, 1908. Legislation to remedy defects in the currency system. Amendment of the Sherman Anti-Trust law, exempting railroads from its provisions. Placing the railroads under the control of the Interstate Commerce Commission and allowing them to make combinations and traffic agreements subject to the Commission's approval. Placing telegraph and telephone companies doing an interstate business under the control of the Commission. Passage of an employers' liability bill. Less delay in the administration of justice; larger salaries for Federal judges and further safeguards against abuse of the power of injunction. Progressive income tax on large inheritances. Obliteration of bureau organization of the navy, creation of a general staff and building of four all-big-gun battleships. Promotion in the army and navy for merit rather than seniority. Admission of New Mexico and Arizona as States. Establishment of postal savings bank and parcels post in rural districts. Conferring of citizenship on Porto Ricans.

110. Farm Productions of the United States—The twelfth annual report of the Department of Agriculture, made public Dec. 13, gave value of all farm products of the United States in 1908 as $7,778,000,000, of which the value of the Indian corn crop of 2,643,000,000 bushels is $1,615,000,000; of the hay crop of 63,000 tons, $621,000,000; of 660,000,000 bushels of wheat, $620,000,000; of 789,000,000 bushels of oats $321,000,000; of 167,000,000 of barley, $86,000,000. In the past ten years the wealth production of the farms of the United States has exceeded $60,000,000,000.

464. Governor Hughes, of New York, on December 14 appointed a committee of nine bankers, economists and business men to inquire into the facts surrounding the business of Exchanges in New York, and to suggest "what changes, if any, are advisable in the laws of the State bearing upon speculation in securities and commodities, or relating to the protection of investors, or with regard to the instrumentalities and organizations used in dealing in securities and commodities which are the subject of speculation." The committee named is composed of Horace White, author and editor; Charles A. Schieren, merchant, formerly Mayor of Brooklyn; David Leventritt, former Justice of the Supreme Court; Clark Williams, State Superintendent of Banking; John B. Clark, Professor of Political Economy in Columbia University; Willard V. King, banker, President Columbia Trust Company; Samuel H. Ordway, lawyer, New York; Edward D. Page, of New York, member of the firm of Faulkner, Page & Co., and Charles Sprague Smith, Director of the People's Institute, all of New York City.

223. Sporting Records. Six-Day Bicycle Race, New York, 1908—Order of finish: MacFarland-Moran, Rutt-Stol, Hill-DeMara, 2,737 1-10 miles (new record); Walthour-Root, 2,737; Collins-Mitten, 2,736 9-10; Galvin-Wiley, 2,736 8-10; Anderson-Vanoni and Palmer-Drobach, 2,723 4-10 miles. Former record, 2,733 4-10, by Miller-Waller, 1899. MacFarland, Rutt and DeMara rode last mile, finishing in order named.

Longboat-Dorando Marathon—Tom Longboat, the Onondaga Indian, defeated Dorando Pietri, of Italy, in a Marathon race of 26 miles, 385 yards, in Madison Square Garden, December 15, 1908. Dorando collapsed in last mile. Longboat's time, 2:45:05 2-5.

World's Lawn Tennis Championship for Davis Cup, Melbourne, Australia, November 28-30, 1908.—Norman Brookes and A. F. Wilding, Australia, easily defeated Beals C. Wright and F. B. Alexander, America, challengers, in doubles, and Wilding defeated Alexander in singles.

EDWARD M. MORGAN, Postmaster; THOMAS F. MURPHY, Assistant Postmaster.

OFFICES AND OFFICE HOURS—SECOND FLOOR.

Postmaster.—Room 1, south end. Office hours, 9 A. M. to 3 P. M.

Assistant Postmaster.—Room 2, Broadway side. Office hours, 9 A. M. to 4 P. M. Secretary to the Postmaster, Room 1, south end. Office hours 9 A. M. to 3 P. M.

Superintendent of Delivery.—Room 5, Park Row side. Office hours, 9 A. M. to 4 P. M.

Auditor.—Rooms 9 and 17, Park Row side. Office hours, 9 A. M. to 4 P. M.

Cashier.—Rooms 21 and 15, Park Row side. Office hours, 10 A. M. to 3 P. M.

Money-Orders.—Superintendent of Department, Room 42, City Hall side. Office hours, 9 A. M. to 4 P. M. Domestic Money-Orders, Rooms 40 and 41, City Hall side. Office hours, 9 A. M. to 5 P. M. International, Room 41, City Hall side. Domestic and Foreign Money-Orders issued also from 5 P. M. to 12 P. M. Window No. 3, Broadway side, Ground Floor.

Inquiry Office for Missing Letters, etc.—Room 14, B'way side. Office hours, 9 A. M. to 4 P. M.

MEZZANINE FLOOR.—First landing at the head of main stairway, south end of building.

Superintendent Carriers' Department (General P. O. District).—Park Row side.

Assistant Custodian.—An officer of the Treasury Department in charge of the building and watch. Room 9, Park Row side. Office hours, 9 A. M. to 4 P. M.

Registered Letters and Parcels Department.—Windows for reception, Rooms 4 and 6, Broadway side. Office hours, 8 A. M. to 8 P. M. Windows for Delivery, Rooms 4 and 6, Broadway side. Office hours, 8 A. M. to 8 P. M.

[All offices on the Second and Mezzanine and Fifth Floors are closed on Sundays, and at 10 A. M. on holidays. No Money-Order business transacted on these days.] No Registry business transacted on Sundays.

FIFTH FLOOR.

Order Department of Instruction.—Room 161A, B'way side. Office hours, 9 A. M. to 4 P. M.

ENTRANCE FLOOR.

Superintendent of Mails.—Sec. 26, Park Row side. Office hours, 9 A. M. to 4 P. M.

Bureau of Information.—South end (Retail Stamp Window).

Bank Window.—Sec. 15, Park Row side.

General Delivery (Park Row side).—Men's Window, sec. 5; Advertised Letter Window, sec. 6; Foreign Advertised Letter Window, sec. 7; Ladies' Window, sec. 9.

Foreign Supplementary Mail Window.—Sec. 24, Park Row side.

Parcels Post Mails.—Sec. 24, Park Row side. Office hours, 9 A. M. to 5 P. M.

Postage Stamps, etc.—Stamped envelopes and newspaper wrappers and postal cards. Sales in sums over $1: Windows 1 and 2, sec. 19, Broadway side, and 6 and 9, south end. Sales in sums of less than $1: Windows 4 and 5, secs. 17 and 18, Broadway side; windows 7 and 8, sec. 3, south end, and booths 10 and 11, Park Row side.

OPEN ALWAYS.—Outgoing Domestic Letter Mails Department—Sec. 17, Broadway side. **General Post-Office Delivery Department**—Sec. 11, Park Row side.

On general holidays, viz.: January 1, February 12, 22, May 30, July 4, Labor Day, Election Day, Thanksgiving Day, December 25, and such days as the President of the United States, or the laws, or Governor of the State may designate as holidays, fast, and thanksgiving days, all mails are closed as on other days of the week, but only such carrier deliveries are made as may have been previously announced.

Mail in Quantities.—For New York City delivery, received at sec. 10, Broadway side. Letters for outgoing domestic mails received principally at the Hudson Terminal station, 30 Church Street, and at General Post-Office, sec. 16, Broadway side. Letters for foreign countries received at sec. 16, Broadway side. Circulars received at sec. 12, Broadway side. Mail in quantities must be assorted by States by the sender before mailing.

Delivery for Newspaper Exchanges.—Sec. 23, Park Row side.

Drops.—For outgoing domestic mails, sec. 23, Park Row side and secs. 12, 13, 14, 15, Broadway side. For New York City delivery, sec. 3, South End, sec. 13, Park Row side, and sec. 11, Broadway side. For foreign countries, sec. 25, Park Row side, and sec. 16, Broadway side.

Special Delivery Letters for New York City or Elsewhere.—Sec. 13, Park Row side, and sec. 13, Broadway side.

Lock-Boxes.—South end and B'way side. Lock-boxes for newspaper exchanges, Park Row side.

CARRIER STATIONS IN MANHATTAN AND BRONX.

A—136-138 Greene St., bet. Prince and Houston Sts.
B—Grand St., southeast cor. Attorney St.
C—West 13th St. and Ninth Ave.
D—103-105 East 12th St.
E—110-114 West 32d St., near Sixth Ave.
F—34th St., near Lexington Ave.
G—1648 Broadway, cor. 51st St.
H—43d St. and Madison Ave.
I—Columbus Ave., cor. 105th St.
J—2309-2311 Eighth Ave., cor. 124th St.
K—202-204 East 88th St., near Third Ave.
L—141 East 125th St., cor. Lexington Ave.
M—1965 Amsterdam Ave., bet. 157th and 158th Sts.
N—Broadway, cor. 69th St.
O—122-124 Fifth Ave.
P—Custom House Building.
R—Third Ave., cor. 150th St. (Morrisania).
S—Broadway, cor. Howard St.
T—507-509 East 165th St.
U—Third Ave., cor. 103d St.
V—Southeast cor. West Broadway and Canal St.
W—498 Columbus Ave., cor. 84th St.
X—631-633 East 138th St., near Willis Ave.
Y—1160-1162 Third Ave., near 68th St.

City Island—Main St. and Bay Ave.
Foreign—West St., cor. Morton St.
Fox St.—Fox St., bet. 167th and 169th Sts.
High Bridge—Depot Place, near Sedgwick Ave.
Hudson Terminal Station.—30 Church St.
Jay St.—Jay and Greenwich Sts. (not a carrier station).
Kingsbridge—Kingsbridge, near R. R. Station.
Madison Square—310 4th Ave., near 23d St.
Times Square—239 West 39th St.
Tompkins Square—12th St. and Ave. B.
Tremont—1931 Washington Ave., between 177th and 178th Sts.
University Heights—New York University.
Wall St.—60 Wall St.
Washington Bridge—Amsterdam Ave., near 180th St.
Westchester—Main St., near West Farms Road.
Williamsbridge—White Plains Ave., near Briggs Ave.
Fordham—2519 Webster Ave., near Fordham Road.
College—305-307 West 140th St.

[All carrier stations are opened on week days from 7 A. M. to 8 P. M., for Money-Order business from 8 A. M. to 8 P. M., for the registry of letters from 8 A. M. to 8 P. M. On Sundays stations are opened from 9 to 11 A. M., and on holidays from 7 to 10 A. M. No Money-Order or registry business transacted on Sundays or holidays.]

The Juice of the Grape as a Temperance Beverage—The Increased Use of Light Table Wines in This Country.

THE grape is the choicest of our fruits. The juice of the grape makes one of the most pleasant and healthful drinks. The effect of good wine in aiding digestion and in restoring strength is wonderful, for wine is both food and drink, and the medical profession agrees in recommending pure wine either as a beverage or as a tonic.

Within the past few years a great change has taken place in the attitude of the press and people with reference to the drinking of our pure native wines. Thus, one New York paper recently said it was a matter of congratulation that the consumption of strong drinks was decreasing, while the consumption of mild beverages, such as wine, was on the increase. This is largely due to the fact that many thousands of Americans have learned to drink light wines at the table with their meals. Then, again, our large foreign population coming from the wine-growing countries of Europe take kindly to wine in preference to beer and whiskey, and they are the most temperate people in the world.

In France and Italy, for example, where every one, women as well as men, drink wine like water, no one uses strong liquors, and therefore alcoholism or drunkenness is practically unknown. In the countries of continental Europe the legislators recognize so well the fact that the drinking of wine is a good thing that they favor the sale of wine in every way. We should have the same kind of laws in the United States, and then wines could be sold separate from beer and whiskey. There is no good reason why wine—which is both a food and drink—should not be sold in the same way and in the same places as other foods—for example, in the grocery and other stores, where families get their provisions or supplies.

The big increase in the consumption of light wines in this country should be regarded with favor as conducing to temperance. The people who drink wine do not go to the saloons, as little or no wine is sold in saloons. Almost all of the wine is used at home and in the family. The time to drink wine is at mealtime; the place to drink wine is at the table.

THE USE OF WINE MAKES FOR TEMPERANCE.

There is a growing sentiment that temperance is best promoted by providing people with a beverage which is cheap, pleasant to the taste, and a harmless tonic unless used in excessive quantities. Such a beverage and tonic is good wine. It is the pure juice of the grape, and the low percentage of alcohol acts as a tonic and stimulant. Our leading medical authorities say that alcohol in such small amounts as are found in light wines have and never will make a drunkard; but, on the contrary, the daily and moderate use of wine at the table makes for temperance. Thus, the moderate drinking of light wines generally takes away the thirst or desire for strong or spirituous liquors.

This important fact is abundantly proved by the statistics of the wine-drinking countries of Europe, where the per capita consumption of alcoholic liquors is about a gallon, but the consumption of wine in France and Italy is 35 gallons for every person in a year. And yet, owing to the large use of strong liquors, there is more intemperance in the United States than there is in France and Italy put together. When the people of this country learn to drink light wines daily at the table with their meals they will become most temperate, and the so-called "temperance question" will be in a large measure solved.

AMERICAN WINES THE PUREST AND BEST IN THE WORLD.

It is interesting to note that the superior qualities of American wines are becoming more and more appreciated, while, on account of their known purity, our native wines are preferred to the foreign. American wines are as good as any in the world. They are made from the choicest grapes, with the greatest care, and with the highest skill. Americans should be proud of their success in producing fine American wines and champagnes. The steady growth of our wine industry has resulted in a falling off in the use of foreign wines and champagnes. The official figures show that just about eight times as much of American wines are produced and consumed in this country as there are of foreign wines. Our annual production is now about 45,000,000 to 50,000,000 gallons of wine. There are about 350,000 acres of vineyards in the United States. The State of California leads with about 225,000 acres of vines; New York State is second with 60,000 acres of vineyards. The capital invested in our vineyard lands in wine cellars or plants, machinery, warehouses, stock of wines, etc., is put at about $125,000,000.

The largest and leading wine growers from the Atlantic to the Pacific are united into an organization called the American Wine Growers' Association. This association has done much to improve the conditions of the wine trade, to raise the standard of our wines, and the members guarantee the purity and quality of their wines. Those who are interested in getting wines for their own use should write to the American Wine Growers' Association, 245 Broadway, New York.

AMERICAN WINES THE BEST

Good Wines for Good Health

WHEN You find Whiskey too Strong
WHEN You get Tired of Beer
WHEN Tea and Coffee Doesn't Agree with You
WHEN You turn against Colored and Flavored Soft Drinks

THEN FOLLOW PAUL'S ADVICE

"Use a Little Wine for Your Stomach's Sake."

GOOD WINE IS BOTH A FOOD AND A TONIC

AS A FOOD—Wine should be taken with Food—that is, at Mealtime.
AS A TONIC—Wine should be taken before Meals—that is, to Improve the Appetite and Aid Digestion.

HOW TO USE DIFFERENT WINES

Dry Wines—Claret, Riessling, Dry Catawba, Etc., with or without a little water, add Zest and Pleasure to every Meal.

Sweet Wines—Port, Sherry, Sweet Catawba, Muscatel, Etc., are to be served with Cake or with the Dessert.

American Champagnes—Equal to the imported kinds in every way, and at half the price.

Why take Patent Medicine when you can get Good American Wine?

Consult Your Doctor If You Are Sick and Need Medicine.

An Interesting Booklet on "The Food Value of Wine," by Prof. E. H. Twight, will be Sent Free on application to AMERICAN WINE PRESS, 240 Broadway, New York.

It is pure of the purest, with a sparkle its own,
Of the delicate flavor that long lingers on;
Thorough-bred, thorough-ripened, for long years it has lain,
Till it's rich, rare and royal—The Great Western Champagne.

Great Western

Extra Dry

Champagne

Produced by the Oldest and Largest
Champagne House in America

The only Champagne awarded a GOLD MEDAL at the Paris Exposition in 1900, many others competing : : : :

Pleasant Valley Wine Company, Sole Makers

RHEIMS, NEW YORK

Sold by Dealers in fine Wines, and served in Hotels, Restaurants and Cafes.

The New Steinway

Five-Foot-Ten-Inch

Miniature Grand Piano

(Trade Marked)

Is proving a constant and increasing source of wonderment and delight to all musicians and music-lovers. Scientific experiments and acoustical researches have determined the exact size, namely FIVE FEET TEN INCHES, necessary to reproduce the REMARKABLE attributes and qualities of our larger Grand Pianos. Any Grand under this size crosses the danger line, as it cannot yield a tonal result superior to that of the discarded Square or the present Upright Piano. The full, rich and sweet tone of the Steinway Miniature Grand and its dainty appearance are already giving the utmost satisfaction to thousands of purchasers, and we recommend a thorough examination and trial of this unique instrument to anybody desirous of possessing a Grand Piano, but who does not wish to exceed the investment of $800 in a Piano Purchase.

STEINWAY & SONS

Steinway Hall, 107 and 109 East 14th St., New York

(Subway Express Station at the Door)

"Yes, I'm sorry, too, that you can not fill the position, but what I need is a TRAINED man—a man who thoroughly understands the work."

"No, there's no other position open—we've hundreds of applicants now on the list waiting for the little jobs. This position calls for a TRAINED man. Good day."

That's it. There's a big call for the **trained** man—the man who can handle the big things—the man who is an expert.

You can easily receive the training that will put you in the class of well-paid men. You can't begin to understand how quickly the little coupon below will bring you success. Already it has helped thousands of men to better-paying positions and more congenial work. It will cost you only a two-cent stamp to learn how it is all done. Just mark the coupon as directed and mail it today. The International Correspondence Schools have a way to help you.

During the last year over 4,000 students voluntarily reported better positions and higher salaries secured through I. C. S. training. To only this small percentage of our student body there was brought increased salaries amounting in one year to over Two Million Dollars!

Don't fill a little job all your life when you can so easily move up in the world.

NOW is the time to mark the coupon.

International Correspondence Schools
Box 1900, Scranton, Pa.

Please explain, without further obligation on my part, how I can qualify for a larger salary in the position before which I have marked X.

Bookkeeper	Mechan'l Draftsman
Stenographer	Foreman Plumber
Advertisement Writer	Elec.-Lighting Supt.
Show-Card Writer	Mechan. Engineer
Window Trimmer	Surveyor
Commercial Law	Stationary Engineer
Banking Expert	Civil Engineer
Illustrator	Building Contractor
Civil Service	Architec'l Draftsman
Chemist	Architect
Textile-Mill Supt.	Structural Engineer
Electrician	Bridge Engineer
Elec. Engineer	Mining Engineer

Name ______________________

St. & No. ______________________

City ______________ *State* __________

LEARN BY MAIL. BE A
CERTIFIED PUBLIC ACCOUNTANT.
COST ACCOUNTANT.
$2500 - $25,000 according to ability.
THE ONLY PROFESSIONS IN WHICH THE DEMAND FOR CAPABLE MEN EXCEEDS THE SUPPLY
AS A CERTIFIED PUBLIC ACCOUNTANT — Your earnings can easily reach the top mark, lifting you from the irksome, ill-paid grind and long hours to positions of honor, importance and profit.
The profession is now universally recognized, same as medicine and law.
Our Certified Public Accountancy Course is the most perfect and most efficient ever arranged. Written by the best men in the field and taught by Certified Public Accountants and Counsellors at Law of highest standing in actual practice, it is receiving the recognition which it merits.
Our Courses include
Theory of Accounts,
Practical Accounting,
Cost Accounting,
Auditing,
Commercial Law,
Book-keeping and
Business Practice.
Successful students throughout the world to whom we can refer.
AS A COST ACCOUNTANT—If you are skilled in the higher branches of Accountancy you need the Cost Accounting Course to complete your equipment and make you a master in your field.
Manufacturing costs are no longer simply material and labor. Fractional differences determine the manufacturer's success or failure to-day. Hence his absolute dependence upon the Cost Accountant who thus becomes the most important and best paid man in the business.
Our Course was written and arranged by one of the ablest expert Cost Accountants in the world. It embraces two superb volumes of 12 lessons, including color charts and worked-out examples, taken from actual business experience covering a busy life of over 40 years.
It is clear, concise, stripped of complexity, yet its scope is all-embracing.
This institute is in a class by itself and is so recognized throughout the world. Our Instruction is thorough, capable and intensely practical.
We guarantee the practicability of Our Courses and undertake to make you proficient. Your instruction is individual and is conveyed to you by mail as effectively as if an instructor were at your side. Hence you cannot fail. Satisfaction guaranteed.
BOARD OF INSTRUCTORS:
EDWARD H. HYANS, C. P. A.
JOHN MOULL, C. P. A.
ARTHUR WOLFF, C. P. A.
MEYER B. CUSHNER, LL. B.
C. E. WOODS, E. E., M. E., Industrial Engineer.
Members N. Y. State Society, C. P. A., Fellows of American Association of Public Accountants, Members of New York Bar.
Write for Booklet J, mentioning courses that interest you.
UNIVERSAL BUSINESS INSTITUTE, Inc., Dept. J.
27-29 East 22nd Street, New York.

THE FOLDING TYPEWRITER
VISIBLE WRITING
MECHANICAL MARVEL
STEEL TYPE AND BARS
SIMPLICITY
DURABILITY
MADE OF ALUMINUM
PRICE $50.00
WEIGHS ONLY 5½ POUNDS
BICHROME RIBBON

Open, Ready for Use

Folded, for Carrying, Occupies Space 5x7⅛x10 inches

Guaranteed to turn out good clean work. Only PORTABLE MACHINE to successfully compete with the high priced ones. It is positively the neatest, most compact and complete machine made. **The only FOLDING Typewriter in the world.** Easy touch. Unlimited speed. Permanent alignment. Steel type. Uniform depression. Excellent manifolder.

Every live dealer should sell the Standard Folding Typewriter
We have some territory open for exclusive agents. Write us

Standard Folding Typewriter Sales Co.

309 Broadway : New York

FRESH RUNNING, DRINKABLE, AERATED WATER CONVENIENCES in your country home, mean modern comfort to yourself and family.

THE BETHALTO WATER SYSTEM

(Patented)

(Study above illustration and see the simplicity and superiority over all others.)

Your suburban or country home, farm, etc., can thus be supplied with FRESH COOL, AERATED WATER, conveyed from YOUR OWN well, cistern or spring, direct to the faucets wherever water is desired. **You can thus enjoy kitchen, bathroom, laundry and sprinkling conveniences, the same as in a large city.** This system is as practical in Winter as in Summer, and is superior to any other water system in that it furnishes fresh, cool and drinkable water to all parts of your house and premises WITHOUT USING ELEVATED TANK, in which the water freezes in Winter and becomes warm and stale in Summer. This system also affords you a

PROTECTION AGAINST FIRES

You have full control over the pressure, and in case of fire a simple turn of the regulator will **momentarily** increase the pressure, and thus a reliable **Fire Protection** is at your immediate command.

EASILY OPERATED

The only labor required is to pump air into the air receiver. With this system **you pump air only** (not air and water), and the air forces the water to any place you desire it. **Hand** or **Power** Systems furnished. Unlimited testimonials can be furnished from satisfied and enthusiastic users. Prices are very reasonable, and full guarantee goes with each system.

The Bethalto Water System received the highest award at the Louisiana Purchase Exposition, St. Louis, U. S. A., 1904.

WRITE FOR CATALOGUE AND FULL PARTICULARS

THE COUNTRY HYDRANT CO.

(Patentees and Sole Manufacturers)

904 South Fourth St. - - - ST. LOUIS, MO.

The World.

JOSEPH PULITZER.

In epitomizing a year's work of THE WORLD, merely a few of its more notable accomplishments can be mentioned. Day by day it serves the people, giving them the news from all parts of the globe and waging editorially their battles, without fear or favor. It is always the same old WORLD in principles, yet it is ever new in presenting an infinite variety of stories of happenings up to within a few minutes of going to press.

In the history of THE WORLD the year 1908 will ever be memorable for having included in its days the twenty-fifth anniversary of the dedication of THE WORLD to progress and public service, May 10, 1883, and the opening of the new Pulitzer Building.

AN HISTORIC CELEBRATION.

On the night of May 9 the completion of the twenty-fifth year of the control of THE WORLD by Mr. Joseph Pulitzer was celebrated in an unparalleled manner, the event attracting international attention. The splendid new Pulitzer Building, just completed, was thrown open to invited guests, while 50,000 people, massed in City Hall Park and on the roofs of adjacent skyscrapers, witnessed a magnificent display of Pain's fireworks, visible many miles away in Greater New York and New Jersey.

Inside the building were gathered eminent men, leaders in all branches of commerce and trade, lawmakers of the nation, State and municipality, scientists, authors, judges, clergymen, and a vast host of others, representing practically every phase of the nation's life.

A special train from Washington over the Pennsylvania road brought a notable company of statesmen, members of the United States Senate and House of Representatives, and leaders of the various executive departments of the nation to the celebration.

On the twelfth floor of the building, the space devoted to the library, the biographical department and the editorial department of the morning edition of THE WORLD, was converted into an auditorium. Chairs for nearly a thousand guests had been provided, but several hundred more persons had to stand. This temporary auditorium was decorated only with the national colors. Over the platform was John S. Sargent's portrait of Joseph Pulitzer. Beneath the picture was a small platform, where, soon after 9 o'clock, the gentlemen who were to speak and others took their seats. Among them were Senator William Alden Smith, of Michigan; Senator T. P. Gore, of Oklahoma; Lieut.-Gov. L. S. Chanler, Acting-Mayor P. F. McGowan, Congressman Henry T. Rainey, of Illinois; Congressman William Sulzer, of New York; Governor Mead, of Washington; Congressman J. L. Slayden, of Texas.

Close around the platform were many of New York's prominent citizens, intermingled with representatives from other cities. Comptroller Metz and Police Commissioner Bingham were near to Congressman John Wesley Gaines, of Tennessee, and Secretary of State John S. Whalen, from Albany, and Senator McCarren, of Brooklyn. Former Mayor Fitzgerald of Boston, had a front seat. Bankers, business men, merchant princes, lawyers, professors, editors and politicians were at every hand.

Mr. Ralph Pulitzer called the assemblage to order to express thanks for the presence of so many guests and their kindly expressions of good will. Mr. Pulitzer said, in opening his address:

"On my father's behalf I bid you welcome here to-night to help us celebrate the twenty-fifth anniversary of his ownership of THE WORLD. I am sure you will all regret as deeply as I do that he cannot be with us to-night. But the darkened sight and the broken health, which he sacrificed to make this paper possible, make his presence at its twenty-fifth birthday impossible. And so we must rest satisfied with the feeling that, though he be physically absent to-night, at least he is present among us in that constructive imagination, that power of intellectual projection, that power of transmitting the enthusiasm of convictions which has reached across oceans and continents for all these years to keep THE WORLD on the course which he laid out for it a quarter of a century ago. Fortunately, gentlemen, it is not necessary for me to boast that in that quarter of a century THE WORLD has succeeded. Its material accomplishment has a solid sponsor in this building which we are opening to-night, which has just been doubled in size to accommodate our growth."

Mr. Pulitzer was followed by Acting-Mayor McGowan, Lieutenant-Governor Chanler, William Alden Smith, Governor Mead, United States Senator Gore, Mark Smith, of Arizona; Congressman Slater and Congressman Keifer. All these speakers paid high tribute to Mr. Joseph Pulitzer's genius and energy as exemplified by the gigantic success of THE WORLD. Letters and telegrams of regret at inability to be present, but extending warm congratulations to Mr. Pulitzer and THE WORLD, were received from Justice David J. Brewer, of the United States Supreme Court; Speaker Joseph G. Cannon, President Woodrow Wilson, of Princeton University; Justice Gray, of the United States Circuit Court; Gov. J. Franklin Fort, of New Jersey; Stuyvesant Fish, Minister Sternberg, James J. Freel, United States Senator Briggs, Jacob H. Schiff, Justice Edgar M. Cullen, Gov. James H. Higgins, of Rhode Island; Editor H. M. Alden, of Harper's Magazine; Charles S. Diehl, of the Associated Press, and other friends of THE WORLD.

MR. PULITZER'S CABLED GREETING.

The following cablegram from Mr. Joseph Pulitzer was read by Mr. Ralph Pulitzer:

"Not self-admiration but self-criticism and self-improvement are the passions of THE WORLD.

"Twenty-five years ago it was dedicated to truly democratic ideas, to the cause of the people.

"Nineteen years ago the cornerstone of this building was laid with the invocation:

" 'Let it ever be remembered that this edifice owes its existence to the public, that its architect is popular favor, that its moral cornerstone is love of liberty and justice, that its every stone comes from the people and represents public approval for public service rendered.'

"What was said then may be said with double force to-day. THE WORLD may have committed a thousand faults of overzeal, but they were faults of the hand, not those of head or heart. Without public approval a newspaper cannot live; the people can destroy it any day by merely refusing it. In its last analysis, nay in its first and every analysis, step by step, day after day, the existence of a newspaper is dependent upon the approval of the public.

"Editors submit their work morning after morning to the only real referendum and recall, that of a constituency having virtual power of life and death over their journals. Yet a newspaper can never be influential if it seeks no more than to please the unthinking, or echo the cries of ignorance and passion. Indeed, to become truly commanding, a newspaper must have convictions, must sometimes fearlessly oppose the will of the very public upon which its existence depends.

"Editors who are worthy of their calling do not mistake the clamor of a demagogue for the voice of the people, nor the schemes of the cunning for counsels of wisdom. They do not confuse true democracy with partisanship. They maintain a fearless independence. Their work is performed with integrity, public spirit, and self-sacrifice. Their thoughts, their energies, and virtually their lives are devoted to a ceaseless study of public affairs, and to work for the public good.

"Thus the newspaper becomes a public institution.

"Twenty-five years ago THE WORLD said, 'There is room in this great and growing republic for a journal that is truly democratic.'

"Do not these words apply to-day?

"What is truly democratic?

"Not party but country. Not party but humanity. Not party but liberty. Not party but equality. Not party but equal opportunity. Not party but equal Justice. Not party for Privilege, Plutocracy, Prohibitive Protection and Monopoly, but for the Harmony, Happiness and Prosperity of all the people.

"Not party ruled by a demagogue.

"Not party ruled by an autocrat.

"Not party submitting to an autocrat's contempt of Congress, Courts and Constitution, and usurpation of powers.

"Democracy is far stronger than the Democratic party, and the Democratic party is far weaker than democracy.

"Is corruption truly democratic?

"Is socialism truly democratic?

"Truly democratic ideas mean popular government by the best, by the wisest, by the most virtuous. They are the permanent protest against Privilege; they are the eternal vigilance over Public Liberty; they are the inherent impulse for Progress and Reform, against stagnation and injustice; they are rooted in the human heart; they are inalienable; they are stronger than the nation itself.

"THE WORLD will remain forever independent, detached from party. THE WORLD will persevere with burning zeal in fighting corruption and privilege, regardless of party. But it will also fight humbugs and demagogues, faithless office-holders and shameless office-seekers, who, under the pretense of hating corruption, posing as friends of the people, pursue their own personal, political and pecuniary ambition.

"THE WORLD will continue to expose all fraud and sham, fight all public evils and abuses,' and in the precise language dedicating the cornerstone of the building which to-day stands completed, doubled in size, this invocation is repeated:

"'God grant that THE WORLD may forever strive toward the highest ideals, be both a daily schoolhouse and a daily forum, both a daily teacher and a daily tribune, an instrument of justice, a terror to crime, an aid to education, an exponent of true Americanism. JOSEPH PULITZER."

THE WORLD'S FAMOUS ANNIVERSARY NUMBER.

On Sunday, May 10, THE WORLD circulated the biggest and best newspaper ever printed. This marvel of modern journalism contained 200 pages, and many men and women of world-wide reputation contributed to its columns. Half a million copies of this prodigious issue found their way to the four corners of the globe, and in thousands of homes the paper is still preserved as a souvenir and in libraries and museums as an example of newspaper enterprise.

This enormous paper was divided into sections, these divisions being known respectively as the National, Industrial, Musical, Real Estate, Magazine, News, Comic, Automobile and Metropolitan; and each was filled with the work of expert writers and artists. No paper ever printed has approached this issue in variety of contents and beauty of illustrations.

Among the well-known newspaper men whose congratulatory letters appeared in the anniversary edition of THE WORLD were St. Clair McKelway, Brooklyn Eagle; Page M. Baker, New Orleans Times-Democrat; George Harvey, North American Review; J. C. Hemphill, Charleston News and Courier; Charles H. Taylor, Boston Globe; Medill McCormick, Chicago Tribune; Ambassador Whitelaw Reid, New York Tribune; Thomas G. Rapier, New Orleans Picayune; Herman Ridder, New York Staats-Zeitung; M. H. de Young, San Francisco Chronicle; E. B. Stahlman, Nashville Banner; Melville E. Stone, Associated Press; William R. Nelson, Kansas City Star and Times; Adolph S. Ochs, New York Times; Frank B. Noyes, Chicago Record-Herald; Harvey W. Scott, Portland Oregonian; Victor F. Lawson, Chicago Daily News; Samuel Bowles, Springfield Republican; E. A. Grozier, Boston Post; Henry L. Stoddard, New York Mail; Edward H. Butler, Buffalo News; Delavan Smith, Indianapolis News, and Frank A. Munsey, Munsey's Magazine.

The past, present and future accomplishments of great newspapers formed a theme of discussion by President Taylor, of Vassar College; President Schurman, of Cornell University, and forty other heads of educational institutions; Samuel Gompers, Hamlin Garland, Artists J. G. Brown, J. Carroll Beckwith and Frank Fowler; Mrs. Frank Leslie (Baroness de Bazus), President J. L. Waite, of the National Association of Postmasters; Prof. Walter Damrosch, Mrs. Donald McLean, Booth Tarkington, Hon. J. Sloat Fassett, Hon. James W. Wadsworth, Homer Folks, Secretary of State John Sibley Whalen, of Albany; Rev. Dr. Francis E. Clark, Mrs. Frederic Schoff, of Philadelphia, and many others.

To the National Section Hon. William H. Taft contributed a paper on "Journalism;" William Watson, a poem, "To the Invincible Republic;" Right Hon. Augustine Birrell, Chief Secretary for Ireland, an article on "Democracy;" United States Senator W. B. Allison, a review, "Our Country's Growth." In this section also appeared signed articles by Secretary Oscar S. Straus, of the Department of Commerce and Labor; Speaker Cannon, of the House of Representatives; S. D. N. North, Director of the Census; Representatives Hobson, Kuestermann, Loudenslager, Tawney, Clark and Williams; United States Senators Perkins, Nelson, Bede, Hopkins, Warren, Clay, Burrows, Ankeny, Gallinger and Elkins; Chaplain Edward Everett Hale, of the United States Senate; Rev. Dr. Charles F. Aked, Arthur von Briesen, Rev. Phoebe A. Hanaford, Margaret E. Sangster, the Governors of thirty-two States of the Union, Baron Kogoro Takahira, Japanese Ambassador; Theodore Barth, of Berlin; Signor Luigi Luzzatti, the eminent Italian financial authority; Maarten Maartens, the Dutch poet; Editor A. G. Gardiner, of the London Daily News; Count Henri de Frankenstein, of Italy; Benito Perez Galdoz, Spanish statesman; S. S. McClure, of McClure's Magazine; T. P. O'Conner, M. P.; Joaquin Nabuco, Brazilian Ambassador; Prof. Carl von Noorden, of Vienna; Deputy E. Van der Velde, of Belgium; Prof. D. H. Vambery, the Hungarian publicist; Marquess del Valdeiglesia, Spanish Senator and editor; Prof. Luigi, Pietrobono, President of the Nazarene College, Rome; Robert Donald, editor of the London Daily Chronicle; H. W. Massingham, editor of the Nation, London; Ernestio Teodoro Moneta, the veteran Italian journalist; V. Karnebeek, member of the Dutch Chamber, and many others eminent in their respective walks of life at home and abroad.

THE NEW PULITZER BUILDING.

THE WORLD'S new home is the largest and most completely equipped newspaper plant in the country. The entire main floor to the right of the marble corridor which runs through from Park Row entrance to William Street is devoted to the business offices of the paper.

The new editorial floor of THE WORLD easily surpasses in size, light and conveniences any other editorial department in existence. In the front of the building the MORNING and SUNDAY WORLD have their quarters, and in the rear of these are the commodious rooms devoted to the editorial staff of THE EVENING WORLD, to the artists and to photograph files. On this floor also the library, with 20,000 volumes, and the biographical departments are located.

THE WORLD'S composing room, occupying the entire thirteenth floor, can only be compared with that of the Government Printing Office at Washington, and will not suffer by the comparison. In newspaper offices there is nothing to equal it. In the front, sixty-four linotype machines, fifty of which are run by independent motors, and all of which will be so run in the near future, are used to set the news columns of the various editions of THE WORLD. There are 380 men in the composing room force. In the new part of the building THE WORLD'S job department, conducted exclusively for THE WORLD'S use, is located. The light and ventilation of this huge room, which are perfect, can never be interfered with.

On the fourteenth floor of the building is the photo-engraving plant of THE WORLD, together with every appointment of an up-to-date photograph gallery. In the old dome, beneath the observatory which has been the mecca of hundreds of thousands of visitors since its erection, are still located the private rooms of editorial writers and editors of the MORNING or SUNDAY WORLD, several studios for artists, the TRI-WEEKLY WORLD'S editorial room, THE WORLD ALMANAC department and the main telephone switchboard, which connects the many desk telephones of THE WORLD. In THE WORLD ALMANAC quarters throughout the year goes on the work of gathering from original sources the facts and figures which have made the publication a necessity to a million readers yearly.

MARVELS OF THE WORLD PRESSROOM.

While the general public quite naturally associates THE WORLD and its work with the Pulitzer Building as the structure appears above ground, the wonders of the mechanical department are located far beneath the surface, the lowest floor being located but twelve inches above ocean level, or thirty-six feet below Park Row. Here the giant presses roar, the stereotype plates are made, the paper is stored, the power and water plants are located, and marvels of basic structural work are shown.

THE WORLD'S two latest improved double octuple, duodecuple and quadriquadruple combination presses, with central folders, are not only the two largest presses THE WORLD pressroom ever received, but they are also the largest in any pressroom in the world. Each of these presses is practically four quadruple presses in combination, yet they can be operated as four units, or separate quadruple machines independent of each other, or as a double octuple or two separate octuples, or two sextuples with color.

These presses are 37 feet long, 12 feet wide, 19 feet 6 inches high and weigh 160 tons. They are from entirely new designs, and each press contains more than 75,000 pieces. The two presses have 32 pairs of plate and impression cylinders, which require a complement of 256 plates, weighing 12,000 pounds. They carry 32 rolls of paper 73 inches wide. As each roll weighs about 1,500 pounds, twenty-four tons of white paper are required to start both presses. The composition rollers, 560 in number, weigh fourteen tons. The two presses have 32 ink fountains, each containing 100 pounds of ink, a total of 3,200 pounds, or one and three-fifths tons. Twenty-four paste fountains paste the papers.

At a running speed these monster presses will produce 400,000 four, six or eight page papers an hour; 200,000 ten to sixteen page papers, all inset and delivered folded, pasted and counted in lots of fifty; 100,000 eighteen to thirty-two page papers, all inset or composed of two uneven sections, at will, as one paper, or 50,000 thirty-six to sixty-four page papers, composed of four even or four uneven sections, all delivered as one paper. In addition to this the presses will print in color.

To THE WORLD'S pressroom a new color press has been added, a duplicate of the eleven-cylinder, multi-color, half-tone, electrotype web press already used to print the color magazines and comic sections of the SUNDAY WORLD. These two presses, representing an outlay of $120,000, have a running speed per hour of 100,000 twelve-page magazines, with covers, printed in three colors and black, or 50,000 twenty-page magazines with a four-page comic. Many other combinations are possible. These color presses are 40 feet long, 12 feet wide and 15 feet high, and run from electrotype plates only.

The immensity of the combined capacity of the presses in THE WORLD'S pressrooms may be judged by the fact that they will print 1,300,000 four, six or eight page papers an hour; 725,000 ten or twelve page papers; 575,000 fourteen or sixteen page papers, or 361,000 eighteen, twenty, twenty-two or twenty-four page papers, and the larger number of pages in proportion. To this must be added the product of the two large color presses.

THE WORLD is the greatest buyer of presses in the world. There are now in the pressroom of THE WORLD fifteen presses, viz.: Five quadruples, one double, one color web, two sextuples, three octuples, two double octuples and one double multi-color. Besides these, since 1883, THE WORLD, which then had but two single presses, has bought three single, four double, three double supplement and one quadruple presses, a total of eleven machines, making with the ones now in use a total of twenty-six since Mr. Pulitzer took charge of the paper; or, with the original two, a grand total of twenty-eight presses purchased for the exclusive use of THE WORLD.

THE MAP OF BRYANISM.

Immediately after Mr. Bryan's speech at Madison Square Garden, August 31, 1906, in which he declared himself in favor of Government ownership of railroads, THE WORLD began its opposition to his nomination for President. During the time that elasped between the Madison Square Garden speech and the Denver Convention, THE WORLD warned Mr. Bryan no fewer than seventy-five times that his nomination meant certain Democratic defeat.

These warnings were definite and unequivocal, as the following extracts prove:

Sept. 23, 1907, THE WORLD said:

Roosevelt would obliterate him. Taft, Knox, Hughes or La Follette would beat him hands down.

Nov. 11, 1907, it said:

It is manifest that Mr. Bryan's nomination would mean a walkover for Roosevelt, for Taft, for anybody a Republican convention would be likely to nominate.

Jan. 13, 1908, it said:

Bryan against Taft could mean only a Taft walkover.

Jan. 16 it said:

Mr. Bryan would not have a ghost of a chance in New York and New Jersey.

Feb. 27 it said:

He could not carry New York against Mr. Taft even if 100,000 of the Republicans who voted for Roosevelt should stay at home.

March 10 it said:

To nominate Mr. Bryan is to throw away the election in advance.

April 13 it said:

If Mr. Bryan is nominated there will not be the remotest possibility of carrying New York.

The morning after Mr. Taft's nomination in Chicago, THE WORLD declared without reservation that "Bryan's nomination means Taft's election."

In the furtherance of this campaign THE WORLD issued on February 1, 1908, its pamphlet, "The Map of Bryanism," reviewing the results of Mr. Bryan's twelve years of leadership and proving the certainty of another disastrous defeat in the event of his third nomination. The pamphlet took the name from the political map that first appeared in THE WORLD Nov. 11, 1907, showing how Bryanism had all but obliterated the Democratic party in the North, as a National organization, and that the disintegration of even the solid South had begun, as indicated by Republican victories in Missouri and Kentucky, with Maryland wavering in the balance.

THAT PROPHETIC MAP.

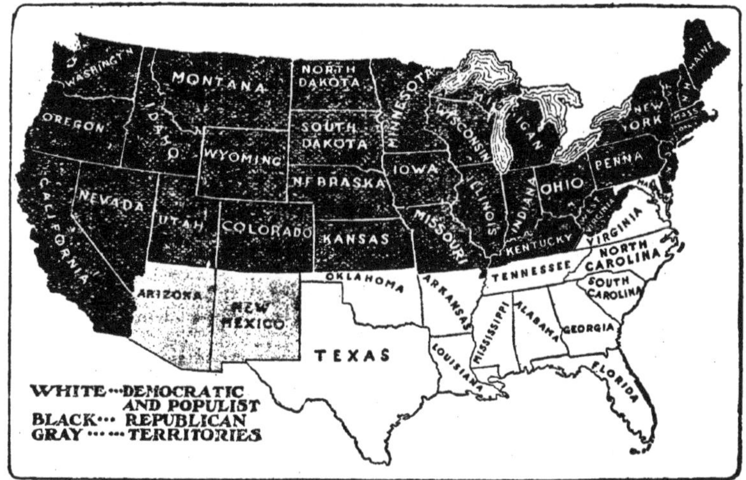

(FIRST PRINTED IN THE WORLD NOVEMBER 11, 1907).

THE WORLD'S appeal to the independent Democratic thought of the country was based specifically on Mr. Bryan's statement of November 14, 1907, announcing his readiness to accept the nomination.

The pamphlet began with a recitation of the condition of the Democratic party at the end of the twelve years in which Mr. Bryan had been its leader and particularly its dictator. Excepting Thomas Jefferson and Andrew Jackson, no other Democrat had dominated his party so long or so completely. Of the twenty-eight years of Jefferson's active leadership, the party was in power twenty-four; of the sixteen years of Jackson's active leadership the party was in power twelve; under Mr. Bryan's leadership the party has not been in power a single day, a single hour, a single minute.

The pamphlet enumerated the results of Mr. Bryan's leadership in the following words:

"The Democratic party went out of power in the nation March 4, 1897. Four years earlier it controlled 23 of the 44 States, the Republicans 17 and the Populists 4.

"In Congress the party division was as follows: Senate—Democrats, 44; Republicans, 38; Independent, 1; Alliance, 2; vacancies, 3. House—Democrats, 220; Republicans, 128; Populists, 8.

"The popular vote in 1892 was: Democratic, 5,556,918; Republican, 5,176,108; Populist, 1,041,028 (Weaver, for whom you voted).

"The electoral vote in the same year was: Democratic, 277; Republican, 145; Populist, 22.

"What was the situation November 14, 1907, Mr. Bryan, after eleven years of your leadership, when you announced your receptive candidacy?

"Of the 46 States the Democrats controlled 13 and the Republicans 33.

"The popular vote in the Presidential election of 1904 was: Republicans, 7,623,486; Democratic, 5,077,971; Socialist, 402,283. The electoral vote was: Republican, 336; Democratic, 140.

"In Congress the party division now is: Senate—Republicans, 61; Democrats, 31. House—Republicans, 223; Democrats, 168.

"In 1893 there were Democratic United States Senators from California, Illinois, Indiana, Montana, New Jersey, New York, Ohio and Wisconsin. In 1907, when you reviewed your work and found Democratic conditions and prospects so pleasing, there was not a single anti-Republican Senator from a Northern State except two silver men from Colorado and Nevada respectively. The Republicans had gained a Senator, not only in Colorado, but in Missouri.

"Whole States at the North are without Democratic representation in Congress, and from the Atlantic to the Pacific, north of the Ohio River, there are but six Democratic Governors, viz.: James M. Higgins, Rhode Island; John A. Johnson, Minnesota; Joseph K. Toole, Montana; John Sparks, Nevada; John Burke, North Dakota, and George E. Chamberlain, Oregon. Singularly enough, these are all found in States which are normally Republican or Populistic. Kentucky has just gone Republican, electing an entire State ticket by the second largest majority the State has given to any candidate in fifteen years.

"Throughout the North, in the cities and in the counties, Democrats have been driven from places which the party has controlled for generations, and in hundreds of localities no representative of the party holds a public position, except as he may have been appointed thereto by some considerate or patronizing Republican or is protected by the provisions of a civil service law.

"Such to-day is the condition of the historic Democratic party, Mr. Bryan, after twelve years of your leadership."

The pamphlet then recited the history of Mr. Bryan's leadership, beginning with the crown of thorns speech in the 1896 convention, which won him his first nomination for President. Separate chapters were devoted to the sacrifice of Democratic principle for Populist support; to the silver interests, which financed Mr. Bryan's 1896 campaign; to the assault upon the courts; to the rise and fall of anti-imperialism and the campaign of 1900; to Mr. Bryan's attacks upon Democrats who differed with him; to Government ownership of railroads; to the initiative and referendum, and to the Populistic origin of all Mr. Bryan's important economic issues.

An examination was made of the Democratic, Populistic and Silver Republican platforms in Nebraska, framed and supported by Mr. Bryan since 1892, when he voted for the Populistic candidate for President. These platforms proved that Mr. Bryan had indorsed at one time or another the following Populistic principles:

Free silver, 16 to 1, without the concurrence of other nations.
Government loans to farmers.
Government ownership and operation of railroads.
Greenback inflation (irredeemable).
Government ownership and operation of telegraph and telephone lines.
Election of United States Senators by popular vote.
Initiative and referendum.
Election of United States Judges by direct vote and for short terms.
A promise to pack the Supreme Court of the United States.
No government "by injunction."
Opposition to private contracts providing for the payment of gold.
Government ownership of interstate railroads and State ownership of State railroads.
Municipal ownership of all public utilities in cities.
Crippling the United States courts and contracting their jurisdiction over questions arising under the Constitution.

The consequences of this Populistic domination of the Democratic party were summarized as follows:

(1) The return of the Republican party to power; (2) Hannaism and the open partnership between the Government and the corporations; (3) the obstruction and delay of the natural progress of reform and the natural expression of public opinion against trusts through the general alarm awakened by your policies; (4) Wall Street's opportunity to loot the public under pretext of maintaining the public credit and vindicating the "National honor;" (5) the growth of Socialism through the disintegrating of the Democratic party.

The pamphlet proceeded to show that even if Mr. Bryan had not rendered his defeat certain by such economic and political vagaries as free silver, Government ownership, the initiative and referendum and the like, he had disqualified himself to lead an Opposition party in a campaign, in which Mr. Roosevelt, Mr. Roosevelt's policies and Mr. Roosevelt's administration must be the paramount issues.

Mr. Bryan had undertaken to make the Democratic party a mere annex to the Roosevelt administration. He had endorsed Mr. Roosevelt politically, morally, administratively and personally. He had ventured to declare himself heir to the Roosevelt vote in these words printed in the Commoner of December 20, 1907:

"While the Democrats will be glad to know of the President's fixed purpose not to be a candidate, their opposition to his candidacy was not on account of his popularity, for it is not at all certain that he could have polled more votes than any other Republican, but President Roosevelt's candidacy would make it impossible for the Democrats to secure the support of Roosevelt Republicans."

He had absolved Mr. Roosevelt from all blame for financial disturbances of 1907, insisting that the President's reckless, passionate speeches and his government by denunciation had nothing to do with bringing on the panic, but that the full responsibility rested upon those unknown persons whom Mr. Roosevelt was accustomed to denounce as malefactors of great wealth. He had, moreover, urged the Democrats in Congress to take up Mr. Roosevelt's more radical policies and try to force an issue on the theory that "the natural fight is between the Democratic party and the reactionary Republican party."

Of this attempt on Mr. Bryan's part to declare himself heir to Mr. Roosevelt's policies the pamphlet said:

"Do not deceive yourself, Mr. Bryan. In your Freeport speech of December 7, 1907, you conceded that Mr. Roosevelt could be re-elected. If you were the Democratic candidate not only would Mr. Roosevelt be elected, but so would Taft or Hughes or Cannon or any man that a Republican convention would be likely to nominate.

In conclusion, the unsurmountable objections to Mr. Bryan's nomination were expressed in the following paragraphs:

"In a period of great financial disturbance the party must have a leader who can appeal to public confidence, not one who can appeal only to public distrust. You are still utterly unsafe on the money question. With great issues like currency and banking reform to be dealt with, and the question of a central bank to be considered, you are one of the last public men in the country who could be regarded as a safe and trustworthy counsellor. You have learned nothing about finance in eleven years, but the American people have learned much. For one thing, they know how little you knew then. In the midst of financial depression the American people need statesmanship, not Populistic agitation, and they will not accept you as a trustworthy guide and leader. Least of all will they accept you when you continue to assert, as you did at Freeport, that your 16-to-1 campaign has been vindicated by events. If the election of 1896 was disastrous to the Democratic party, with you as its candidate, the election of 1908 would be doubly disastrous. There is enough menace to legitimate business now without deliberately electing a new and unnecessary menace to the Presidency of the United States. * * *

"The vital fact confronting you and the Democratic party is this:

"You cannot possibly be elected.

"Why, then, should you receive the nomination?"

Editorially THE WORLD'S opposition to Mr. Bryan's nomination was continued until the very day the Democratic National Convention named him as candidate. THE WORLD made the fight practically alone and unaided in the face of almost certain defeat. It had little expectation of preventing Mr. Bryan's nomination, but it was determined that the Democratic leaders should be forced to appreciate the seriousness of the situation that confronted their party.

THE WORLD dropped its opposition to Mr. Bryan after his nomination as useless; his defeat was absolutely certain, and it became a mere choice between Mr. Roosevelt's candidate, Mr. Roosevelt's principles and Mr. Roosevelt's policies, and saving the Democratic party from absolute destruction. Believing in the vital necessity for maintaining the Democracy as an opposition to the Republican majority, THE WORLD rendered such support as it conscientiously could to the Democratic ticket in the campaign.

The results of the election that followed vindicated every statement that it made in regard to the folly of nominating Mr. Bryan and as to the absolute certainty of his defeat. The popular plurality against Mr. Bryan in the election of 1908 was greater than the popular plurality against him in 1900, which in turn was greater than the popular plurality against him than in 1896. In all but four States of the Union Mr. Bryan proved himself weaker than his party. Although Mr. Taft carried Ohio, Indiana, Minnesota, Montana and North Dakota, the Democratic candidates for Governor were elected in all these States. In New York, Mr. Bryan ran 135,000 behind the Democratic candidate for Governor. He lost the Greater City of New York, thereby duplicating his defeat of 1896. In Illinois Mr. Bryan ran about 150,000 behind his ticket, and in Michigan approximately 150,000. Although he carried his own State, Nebraska, he ran behind the Democratic candidate for Governor. He lost Missouri, a State which was considered impregnably Democratic until after the Democratic party surrendered itself to the leadership of Mr. Bryan, and which even Mr. Bryan himself carried in 1896 and 1900.

Although he obtained 6 electoral votes in Maryland against Taft's 2, this victory was obtained only by reason of the complicated ballot employed in that State by which many thousands of illiterate Republicans were unable to mark their ticket correctly.

Although Mr. Bryan polled 1,315,211 more votes than Judge Parker, in 1904, Mr. Taft's popular plurality was 1,208,998. In 1900 Mr. McKinley's popular plurality over Mr. Bryan was 849,790, and in 1896 it was only 601,854. Including Oklahoma, which was admitted since 1900, Mr. Bryan polled fewer votes this year than eight years ago.

At the same time, the wisdom of THE WORLD'S course during the campaign is demonstrated by the fact that the Democratic party is in better condition to-day than at any other time since 1892. New leaders are coming to the front. Strong men have been elected Governors in Ohio, Indiana, Minnesota, Nebraska, Colorado, North Dakota and Montana. A United States Senator is gained in Indiana and probably another in Oregon. The Republican majority in the House of Representatives is thirty-one fewer than in 1904. THE WORLD'S question, "Shall the Democratic party die?" can be answered by an emphatic "No!"

THE WORLD AND GOVERNOR HUGHES.

THE WORLD consistently and sturdily urged the renomination of Governor Charles E. Hughes in the best interests of the State of New York and condemned the movement to name him as the Republican candidate for the Presidency. As early as January 2 THE WORLD concluded a long editorial on this subject with the words: "What folly it would be to remove Charles E. Hughes from Albany to Washington before the State and Nation have reaped the priceless fruits of his administration as Governor of New York!"

THE WORLD announced itself as being in hearty accord with the most important recommendations of Governor Hughes's message on the first day of the new year. They were:

The destruction of race-track gambling.

The reform of bank and trust-company laws and management.

The extension of the authority of the Public Service Commissions over telegraph and telephone companies.

The revision of the charter of the City of New York.

The reform of the election laws, with a simplified ballot.

The reform of the primary election laws, with a provision for direct nominations.

The extension of the city's subway system, and as a means to that end a constitutional amendment excluding from the debt limit bonds issued for purposes which produce revenue in excess of their maintenance charges.

The petty Republican bosses of the State of New York did their best to defeat the renomination of Hughes, but he easily routed them in the State Convention. The Democrats opposed him with Lewis Stuyvesant Chanler, who made a weak campaign, with no assuring pledges to the people. Naturally, Chanler was beaten. On the morning after election THE WORLD gave the reasons in these words: "Governor Hughes's re-election is a great moral victory. He won it himself by appealing to the moral sense of the better citizenship. And it was accomplished by Democratic votes over an enormous Republican defection. Against him were the votes and money of Wall Street, the Stock Exchange, the traction merger, the life-insurance companies and the petty Republican bosses whom he had offended. Governor Hughes won because the people trust him to carry on the great reforms he has begun. They want the government of this State to go forward and not backward."

FIGHTING FOR SUBWAY EXTENSION.

THE WORLD, the pioneer champion of an adequate subway system for Greater New York, continued in 1908 its battle for extension. When Comptroller Metz declared that the city had no money with which to build subways and that the municipal debt limit had been reached, THE WORLD on March 7 published the offer of a responsible contractor to build the East Side Subway at an estimated cost of $60,000,000 and take his pay as the city might be able to liquidate the debt, according to the standing of the debt limit. THE WORLD later showed how the Public Service Commission can legally let contracts to the amount of $23,000,000 annually and thus within four or five years complete the tri-borough subway which would carry a passenger from the Bronx to Coney Island for one fare. Judge Dillon declared that THE WORLD'S pay-as-you-go plan is legal, and said that the city could begin the construction of subways at once. This opinion of the greatest American authority on municipal law was coincided in by Corporation Counsel Pendleton. And as THE WORLD'S confident prediction of "from City Hall to Harlem in fifteen minutes" became a triumphant fact, so will "from the Bronx to Coney Island for five cents" be yet brought about.

AMATEUR ATHLETICS ENCOURAGED.

THE SUNDAY WORLD Field Days, instituted by THE WORLD in 1906 among the grammar school boys of the city were observed in 1908 with even greater success than ever before. The number of schools represented in 1908 was increased to 114, and 25,000 boys competed in the games, with an added 1,400 at the final meet held in October at the Curtis Athletic Field, on Staten Island. It is estimated that 150,000 school children witnessed the year's competitions for THE WORLD'S medals and class banners. Nearly 700 school principals and teachers officiated at the meets.

In 1908 THE SUNDAY WORLD also gave a number of handsome silver trophies as prizes in a series of tennis games, and 300 medals and other prizes for baseball games during the school vacation under the direction of the New York Park and Playgrounds Association. In this great series 150 baseball teams played for THE WORLD medals. The competitors were boys under 17 years of age.

Commenting on the field days, Dr. Luther Henry Gulick, director of physical training in the New York public schools and secretary of the Public Schools Athletic League, wrote: "The work that has been done by THE SUNDAY WORLD in this connection in the past two years has been of the utmost service to the boys of Greater New York. You have furnished to these schools the opportunity without which a very large number of boys would not have had athletics at all."

THE WORLD'S AID TO CHEAP POSTAGE.

THE WORLD has reason to feel particular pride in the establishment on October 1, 1908, of two-cent postage between the United States and Great Britain. On the day it went into effect, John Henniker Heaton, M. P., who has been a lifelong agitator for a universal two-cent postage law, and who had a foremost part in establishing the cheap postal rate, sent the following message to THE WORLD:

"Penny postage would have been delayed ten years but for the American Postmaster-General. His tact and skill broke down all opposition to this important piece of progress. The British authorities, with the Franco-British exhibition in mind, wanted to establish a penny postage with France first, but we urged that the privilege be given first to an English-speaking race, and Postmaster-General Meyer put the case so forcibly that we won out.

"I think the most striking result of the new system, besides the extended opportunities for intercourse between America and England, will be the boon to poor Irish peasants who maintain a constant correspondence with relatives in America. The five cents for postage on the weekly letter to America was severely felt by a people whose pecuniary means are incredibly low. John Redmond took a very active part in helping my campaign.

"The first letters posted with the two-cent stamps will be some I am sending this midnight. I have written to President Roosevelt, Postmaster-General Meyer, John Wanamaker, Nicholas Longworth and to the editor of THE WORLD.

"When I first went to New York on this project eighteen years ago, THE WORLD took up my case and has helped me ever since."

A TWENTY YEARS' FIGHT WON.

November 23, 1908, saw the culmination of THE WORLD'S fight for twenty years to obtain publicity of campaign contributions. On that date the treasurers of the Republican and Democratic National, State and local campaign committees filed at Albany statements of the amounts received by their respective parties for campaign expenses. The Republican list totalled $1,655,518.27, and the Democratic $620,644.77. The Republican treasurer, Mr. Sheldon, informed the Secretary of State that a supplemental statement showing expenditures in the West would be filed later. Twenty years ago THE WORLD started its fight to obtain publicity of campaign contributions, and this action by the various campaign treasurers marked the first great victory in the insistent and persistent effort which has at last been crystallized into law to reveal the sources of income enjoyed by the various parties.

EVER FIGHTING MUNICIPAL CORRUPTION.

During 1908 THE WORLD continued to arraign the local government for its many extravagances. Chief among the unwarranted expenditures of the people's money, needed for subways and other improvements, is the building of the new Catskill reservoir. THE WORLD showed that the Croton water waste is 80,000,000,000 gallons a year, worth $101,000,000, over the spillway of Croton dam. This is more water than flows through Esopus Creek, the new source of water supply. THE WORLD also denounced the existence of a land-option ring organized to speculate in the Catskill aqueduct territory and charge $150 an acre for swamp land which cost the ring $8 an acre. This profit was made possible by the Water Supply Board moving the line of the aqueduct six miles. The entire reckless, wasteful Catskill scheme, on a par with the Ramapo scheme killed a few years ago by THE WORLD, has been thoroughly uncovered by this, the people's paper.

The loss of life and property through the use of rotten fire hose bought by city authorities at exorbitant prices was another theme of warm discussion by THE WORLD in 1908.

A FEW OF MANY PUBLIC SERVICES IN 1908.

In January THE WORLD exposed the intolerable state of affairs in the Brooklyn courts, showing that because of congested dockets it would take six years to catch up with the cases even if three more judges were provided, which could not be done until 1911. THE WORLD therefore secured the introduction of a bill at Albany to secure a constitutional amendment insuring the necessary relief.

When detectives failed to identify the body of Mrs. Theodore S. Whitemore, of Brooklyn, the victim of a Jersey swamp murder, THE WORLD identified the corpse through a bit of embroidery on a red coat which she wore.

THE WORLD was the first newspaper to expose the true character of Mrs. Ada Jean McKey, originator of swindling schemes and passer of spurious checks, who fooled fashionable society of New York through her relations with them in her sumptuous offices in Fifth Avenue.

It was THE WORLD that proved, through its expert criminologist, William M. Clemens, that Hazel Drew, the pretty Troy girl who was brutally murdered, was killed by strangulation, and not by a blow. Although the murderer has not yet been captured, THE WORLD did valuable service in exposing the falsity of many "clues" which detectives and officials were following after the discovery of Miss Drew's body.

Ever consistently against jingoism, THE WORLD sternly rebuked the agitators of war between the United States and Japan last Spring and gave abundant evidence of the good-will existing between the two nations.

On January 18 and on subsequent dates THE WORLD exposed the looseness of methods in the city's Night Court and proved that women convicted of disorderly conduct could be paroled or otherwise liberated from prison upon cash payments. This story of irregularities caused a sensation, and THE WORLD demanded the resignation of Magistrate Droege. The latter, in a public statement, admitted: "I convict myself of folly."

On July 19 THE WORLD published a remarkable story clearing up the history of Charlotte Wood, who deserted the baronet she had unwillingly wed, lived with John C. Mather, was condemned to death as a poisoner, had her sentence commuted to life imprisonment, died in Matteawan and was buried in the potter's field of the asylum.

After the country was appalled, in March, by the holocaust in the Collingwood (Ohio) schoolhouse, when 180 children lost their lives, THE WORLD fought vigorously for safer school buildings and promptly showed which school structures in Greater New York demanded the immediate attention of the building authorities. Echoes of THE WORLD'S crusade came from many outside towns and cities, where unsafe school buildings were at once supplied with fire-escapes and were in other ways also made less dangerous.

THE EVENING AND SUNDAY WORLDS.

No less energetic than THE MORNING WORLD as a newspaper and champion of public rights, THE EVENING WORLD continued to be the favorite afternoon daily of the metropolis during 1908. Argus-eyed for news and generally first on the street with details of important happenings, furnishing a bright magazine for all the family for a cent a day, recognized as the best sporting medium; snappy, fearless and full of life, THE EVENING WORLD easily maintained its long lead over even the most sprightly of its city contemporaries.

THE SUNDAY WORLD, the giant of Sunday journalism, carried news, good cheer and education into hundreds of thousands of homes fifty-two weeks during the year 1908. Like the daily WORLD, it was chosen as a forum by eminent men and women for expression of their views. At home and abroad its mighty and ever-growing prowess was recognized in the realm of discussion of problems of human interest. The Magazine section of THE SUNDAY WORLD in 1908 set a standard of attainment so high that the best efforts of other journals failed to reach it.

The THRICE-A-WEEK WORLD, issued every forty-eight hours and containing the cream of the news and other features of the daily WORLD, brightens the homes of farmers and other country subscribers all over the United States. Its combinations with agricultural and household journals have proved to be favorites.

Thus THE WORLD rounds out its silver jubilee year with all promises fulfilled and with reiteration of its pledges to serve the public's best interests without fear or favor. In twenty-five years it has accomplished much, and it expects to accomplish much more. The dawn of 1909 finds its power not one whit abated and its devotion to principle stronger than ever. PUBLICITY is still its watchword.

THE astronomical calculations in this work were expressly made for it by Dr. J. Morrison, and are given in local *Mean Time.*

Chronological Eras.

The year 1909 corresponds to the year 7417-18 of the Byzantine era; to 5669-70 of the Jewish era, the year 5670 commencing at sunset on September 15; to 2662 since the foundation of Rome according to Varro; to 2685 of the Olympiads (the first year of the 672d Olympiad commencing July 1, 1909); to 2569 of the Japanese era, and to the 42d of the Meiji; to 1326-27 of the Mohammedan era, the year 1327 commencing on January 23, 1909. The 134th year of the Independence of the United States of America begins on July 4, 1909.

Date of Beginning of Epochs, Eras, and Periods.

Name.		*Began.*	*Name.*		*Began.*
Grecian Mundane Era	B. C.	5598, Sept. 1	Grecian or Syro-Macedonian Era	B. C.	312, Sept. 1
Civil Era of Constantinople	"	5508, Sept. 1	Era of Maccabees	"	166, Nov. 24
Alexandrian Era	"	5502, Aug. 29	Tyrian Era	"	125, Oct. 19
Julian Period	"	4713, Jan. 1	Sidonian Era	"	110, Oct. 1
Mundane Era	"	4008, Oct. 1	Julian Year	"	45, Jan. 1
Jewish Mundane Era	"	3761, Oct. 1	Spanish Era	"	38, Jan. 1
Era of Abraham	"	2015, Oct. 1	Augustan Era	"	27, Feb. 14
Era of the Olympiads	"	776, July 1	Vulgar Christian Era	A. D.	1, Jan. 1
Roman Era (A. U. C.)	"	753, Apr. 24	Destruction of Jerusalem	"	69, Sept. 1
Metonic Cycle	"	432, July 15	Mohammedan Era	"	622, July 16

Chronological Cycles.

Dominical Letters	C	Lunar Cycle (Golden Number)	10	Roman Indiction	7
Epact	8	Solar Cycle	14	Julian Period	6622

The Seasons.

			D.	H.		
Vernal Equinox,	Spring begins	March	21	1	A. M.	*Washington Mean Time.*
Summer Solstice,	Summer begins	June	21	9	P. M.	
Autumnal Equinox,	Autumn begins	September	23	12	P. M.	
Winter Solstice,	Winter begins	December	22	6	A. M.	

Morning Stars.

MERCURY.—February 11 to April 21; June 14 to August 4; October 12 to December 3.

VENUS.—January 1 to April 28.

MARS.—January 1 to September 24.

JUPITER.—January 1 to February 28; September 18 to end of year.

SATURN.—April 3 to October 13.

Evening Stars.

MERCURY.—January 1 to February 11; April 21 to June 14; August 4 to October 12; December 3 to end of year.

VENUS.—April 28 to end of year.

MARS.—September 24 to end of year.

JUPITER.—February 28 to September 18.

SATURN.—January 1 to April 3; October 13 to end of year.

Church Memoranda for 1909.

January.

1 Friday.
6 Epiphany.
10 i. Sun. aft. Epiphany
17 ii. " " "
24 iii. " " "
31 iv. " " "

February.

1 Monday.
7 Septuagesima Sunday
14 Sexagesima Sunday.
21 Quinquagesima Sun.
24 Ash Wednesday.
28 i. Sunday in Lent.

March.

1 Monday.
7 ii. Sunday in Lent.
14 iii. " " "
18 Thurs. (Mi-Careme).
21 iv. Sunday in Lent.
28 v. " " "

April.

1 Thursday.
4 Palm Sunday.
9 Good Friday.
11 Easter Sunday.
18 i. Sunday aft. Easter.
25 ii. " " "

May.

1 Saturday.
2 iii. Sunday aft. Easter.
9 iv. " " "
16 v. " " "
20 Ascension.
23 Sunday aft. Ascension
30 Whit Sunday.

June.

1 Tuesday.
6 Trinity Sunday.
13 i. Sunday aft. Trinity.
20 ii " " "
24 St. John Baptist.
27 iii. Sunday aft. Trinity

July.

1 Thursday.
4 iv. Sunday aft. Trinity
11 v. " " "
18 vi. " " "
25 vii. " " "

August.

1 viii. Sun. aft. Trinity.
8 ix. " " "
15 x. " " "
22 xi. " " "
24 St. Bartholomew.
29 xii. Sun. aft. Trinity.

September.

1 Wednesday.
5 xiii. Sun. aft. Trinity.
12 xiv. " " "
19 xv. " " "
26 xvi. " " "

October.

1 Friday.
3 xvii. Sun. aft. Trinity.
10 xviii. " " "
17 xix. " " "
18 St. Luke.
24 xx. Sun. aft. Trinity.
31 xxi. " " "

November.

1 Monday.
7 xxii. Sun. aft. Trinity.
14 xxiii. " " "
21 xxiv. " " "
28 Advent Sunday.
30 St. Andrew.

December.

1 Wednesday.
5 i. Sunday in Advent.
12 ii. " " "
19 iii. " " "
21 St. Thomas.
25 Christmas.
26 Sun. aft. Christmas.
27 St. John Evangelist.
31 Friday.

Table of Days Between Two Dates.

A TABLE OF THE NUMBER OF DAYS BETWEEN ANY TWO DAYS WITHIN TWO YEARS.

Day Mo.	Jan.	Feb.	Mar.	April.	May.	June.	July.	Aug.	Sept.	Oct.	Nov.	Dec.	Day Mo.	Jan.	Feb.	Mar.	April.	May.	June.	July.	Aug.	Sept.	Oct.	Nov.	Dec.
1	1	32	60	91	121	152	182	213	244	274	305	335	1	366	397	425	456	486	517	547	578	609	639	670	700
2	2	33	61	92	122	153	183	214	245	275	306	336	2	367	398	426	457	487	518	548	579	610	640	671	701
3	3	34	62	93	123	154	184	215	246	276	307	337	3	368	399	427	458	488	519	549	580	611	641	672	702
4	4	35	63	94	124	155	185	216	247	277	308	338	4	369	400	428	459	489	520	550	581	612	642	673	703
5	5	36	64	95	125	156	186	217	248	278	309	339	5	370	401	429	460	490	521	551	582	613	643	674	704
6	6	37	65	96	126	157	187	218	249	279	310	340	6	371	402	430	461	491	522	552	583	614	644	675	705
7	7	38	66	97	127	158	188	219	250	280	311	341	7	372	403	431	462	492	523	553	584	615	645	676	706
8	8	39	67	98	128	159	189	220	251	281	312	342	8	373	404	432	463	493	524	554	585	616	646	677	707
9	9	40	68	99	129	160	190	221	252	282	313	343	9	374	405	433	464	494	525	555	586	617	647	678	708
10	10	41	69	100	130	161	191	222	253	283	314	344	10	375	406	434	465	495	526	556	587	618	648	679	709
11	11	42	70	101	131	162	192	223	254	284	315	345	11	376	407	435	466	496	527	557	588	619	649	680	710
12	12	43	71	102	132	163	193	224	255	285	316	346	12	377	408	436	467	497	528	558	589	620	650	681	711
13	13	44	72	103	133	164	194	225	256	286	317	347	13	378	409	437	468	498	529	559	590	621	651	682	712
14	14	45	73	104	134	165	195	226	257	287	318	348	14	379	410	438	469	499	530	560	591	622	652	683	713
15	15	46	74	105	135	166	196	227	258	288	319	349	15	380	411	439	470	500	531	561	592	623	653	684	714
16	16	47	75	106	136	167	197	228	259	289	320	350	16	381	412	440	471	501	532	562	593	624	654	685	715
17	17	48	76	107	137	168	198	229	260	290	321	351	17	382	413	441	472	502	533	563	594	325	655	686	716
18	18	49	77	108	138	169	199	230	261	291	322	352	18	383	414	442	473	503	534	564	595	626	656	687	717
19	19	50	78	109	139	170	200	231	262	292	323	353	19	384	415	443	474	504	535	565	596	627	657	688	718
20	20	51	79	110	140	171	201	232	263	293	324	354	20	385	416	444	475	505	536	566	597	628	658	589	719
21	21	52	80	111	141	172	202	233	264	294	325	355	21	386	417	445	476	506	537	567	598	629	659	690	720
22	22	53	81	112	142	173	203	234	265	295	326	356	22	387	418	446	477	507	538	568	599	630	660	691	721
23	23	54	82	113	143	174	204	235	266	296	327	357	23	388	419	447	478	508	539	569	600	631	661	692	722
24	24	55	83	114	144	175	205	236	267	297	328	358	24	389	420	448	479	509	540	570	601	632	662	693	723
25	25	56	84	115	145	176	206	237	268	298	329	359	25	390	421	449	480	510	541	571	602	633	663	591	724
26	26	57	85	116	146	177	207	238	269	299	330	350	26	391	422	450	481	511	542	572	603	634	664	695	725
27	27	58	86	117	147	178	208	239	270	300	331	361	27	392	425	451	482	512	543	573	604	635	665	696	726
28	28	59	87	118	148	179	209	240	271	301	332	362	28	393	424	452	483	513	544	574	605	636	666	697	727
29	29	..	88	119	149	180	210	241	272	302	333	363	29	394	....	453	484	514	545	575	606	637	667	698	728
30	30	..	89	120	150	181	211	242	273	303	334	364	30	395	....	454	485	515	546	576	607	638	668	699	729
31	31	.	90	...	151	...	212	243	....	304	....	265	31	396	...	455	....	516	....	577	608	...	669	. .	730

The above table applies to ordinary years only. For leap year, one day must be added to each number of days after February 28.

EXAMPLE.—To find the number of days between June 3, 1900, and February 16, 1901: The figures opposite the third day in the first June column are 154; those opposite the sixteenth day in the second February column are 412. Subtract the first from the second product—*i. e.*, 154 from 412, and the result is 258, the number of days between the two dates.

Easter Sunday.

A TABLE SHOWING THE DATE OF EASTER SUNDAY IN EACH YEAR OF THE NINETEENTH AND TWENTIETH CENTURIES.

1801—April 5.	1835—April 19.	1869—Mar. 28.	1902—Mar. 30.	1935—April 21.	1968—April 14.
1802—April 18.	1836—April 3.	1870—April 17.	1903—April 12.	1936—April 12.	1969—April 6.
1803—April 10.	1837—Mar. 26.	1871—April 9.	1904—April 3.	1937—Mar. 28.	1970—Mar. 29.
1804—April 1.	1838—April 15.	1872—Mar. 31.	1905—April 23.	1938—April 17.	1971—April 11.
1805—April 14	1839—Mar. 31.	1873—April 13.	1906—April 15.	1939—April 9.	1972—April 2.
1806—April 6.	1840—April 19.	1874—April 5.	1907—Mar. 31.	1940—Mar. 24.	1973—April 22.
1807—Mar. 29.	1841—April 11.	1875—Mar. 28.	1908—April 19.	1941—April 13.	1974—April 14.
1808—April 17.	1842—Mar. 27.	1876—April 16.	1909—April 11.	1942—April 5.	1975—Mar. 30.
1809—April 2.	1843—April 16.	1877—April 1.	1910—Mar. 27.	1943—April 25.	1976—April 18.
1810—April 22.	1844—April 7.	1878—April 21.	1911—April 16.	1944—April 9.	1977—April 10.
1811—April 14.	1845—Mar. 23.	1879—April 13.	1912—April 7.	1945—April 1.	1978—Mar. 26.
1812—Mar. 29.	1846—April 12.	1880—Mar. 28.	1913—Mar. 23.	1946—April 21.	1979—April 15.
1813—April 18.	1847—April 4.	1881—April 17.	1914—April 12.	1947—April 6.	1980—April 6.
1814—April 10.	1848—April 23.	1882—April 9.	1915—April 4.	1948—Mar. 28.	1981—April 19.
1815—Mar. 26.	1849—April 8.	1883—Mar. 25.	1916—April 23.	1949—April 17.	1982—April 11.
1816—April 14.	1850—Mar. 31.	1884—April 13.	1917—April 8.	1950—April 9.	1983—April 3.
1817—April 6.	1851—April 20.	1885—April 5.	1918—Mar. 31.	1951—Mar. 25.	1984—April 22.
1818—Mar. 22.	1852—April 11.	1886—April 25.	1919—April 20.	1952—April 13.	1985—April 7.
1819—April 11.	1853—Mar. 27.	1887—April 10.	1920—April 4.	1953—April 5.	1986—Mar. 30.
1820—April 2.	1854—April 16.	1888—April 1.	1921—Mar. 27.	1954—April 18.	1987—April 19.
1821—April 22.	1855—April 8.	1889—April 21.	1922—April 16.	1955—April 10.	1988—April 3
1822—April 7.	1856—Mar. 23.	1890—April 6.	1923—April 1.	1956—April 1.	1989—Mar. 26.
1823—Mar. 30.	1857—April 12.	1891—Mar. 29.	1924—April 20.	1957—April 21.	1990—April 15.
1824—April 18	1858—April 4.	1892—April 17.	1925—April 12.	1958—April 6	1991—Mar. 31.
1825—April 3.	1859—April 24.	1893—April 2.	1926—April 4.	1959—Mar. 29.	1992—April 19.
1826—Mar 26	1860—April 8.	1894—Mar. 25.	1927—April 17.	1960—April 17.	1993—April 11.
1827—April 15.	1861—Mar. 31.	1895—April 14.	1928—April 8.	1961—April 2.	1994—April 3.
1828—April 6.	1862—April 20.	1896—April 5.	1929—Mar. 31.	1962—April 22.	1995—April 16.
1829—April 19.	1863—April 5.	1897—April 18.	1930—April 20.	1963—April 14.	1996—April 7.
1830—April 11.	1864—Mar. 27.	1898—April 10.	1931—April 5.	1964—Mar. 29.	1997—Mar. 30.
1831—April 3.	1865—April 16.	1899—April 2.	1932—Mar. 27.	1965—April 18.	1998—April 12.
1832—April 22.	1866—April 1.	1900—April 15	1933—April 16.	1966—April 10.	1999—April 4.
1833—April 7.	1867—April 21.	1901—April 7.	1934—April 1.	1967—Mar. 26.	2000—April 23.
1834—Mar. 30.	1868—April 12.				

Time Difference.

Places.	When it is 12 o'Clock Noon According to — Standard Time in the United States: Eastern (a)	Central (b)	Mountain (c)	Pacific (d)	At London.	At Paris.
IT IS AT						
Aden ... Arabia	8.00 P. M.	9.00 P. M.	10.00 P. M.	11 00 P. M.	3.00 P. M.	2.51 P. M.
Amsterdam ... Holland	5.20 P. M.	6.20 P. M.	7.20 P. M.	8.20 P. M.	12.20 P. M.	12.10 P. M.
Athens ... Greece	6.35 P. M.	7.35 P. M.	8.35 P. M.	9.35 P. M.	1.35 P. M.	1.26 P. M.
Berlin ... Germany	5.54 P. M.	6.54 P. M.	7.54 P. M.	8.54 P. M.	12.54 P. M.	12.45 P. M.
Bombay ... India	9.51 P. M.	10.51 P. M.	11.51 P. M.	12.51 A. M.	4.51 P. M.	4.42 P. M.
Bremen ... Germany	5.33 P. M.	6.33 P. M.	7.33 P. M.	8.33 P. M.	12.33 P. M.	12.23 P. M.
Central Time (b) ... United States	11.00 A. M.	....	1.00 P. M.	2.00 P. M.	6.00 A. M.	5.51 A. M.
Constantinople ... Turkey	6.56 P. M.	7.56 P. M.	8.56 P. M.	9.56 P. M.	1.56 P. M.	1.47 P. M.
Copenhagen ... Denmark	5.50 P. M.	6.50 P. M.	7.50 P. M.	8.50 P. M.	12.50 P. M	12.41 P. M.
Dublin ... Ireland	4.34 P. M.	5.35 P. M.	6.35 P. M.	7.35 P. M.	11.35 A. M.	11.26 A. M.
Eastern Time (a) ... United States	....	1.00 P. M.	2.00 P. M.	3.00 P. M.	7.00 A. M.	6.51 A. M.
Hamburg ... Germany	5.10 P. M.	6.40 P. M.	7.40 P. M.	8.40 P. M.	12.40 P. M.	12.31 P. M.
Havre ... France	5.00 P. M.	6.00 P. M.	7.00 P. M.	8.00 P. M.	12 NOON	11.51 A. M.
Hong Kong ... China	12.37 A. M.*	1.37 A. M.*	2.37 A. M.*	3.37 A. M.*	7.37 P. M.	7 27 P. M.
Honolulu ... Hawaii	6.29 A. M.	7.29 A. M.	8.29 A. M.	9.29 A. M.	1.29 A. M.	1.19 A. M.
Liverpool ... England	4.48 P. M.	5.48 P. M.	6.48 P. M.	7.48 P. M.	11.48 A. M.	11.39 A. M.
London ... England	5.00 P. M.	6.00 P. M.	7.00 P. M.	8.00 P. M.	....	11.51 A. M.
Madrid ... Spain	4.45 P. M.	5.45 P. M.	6.45 P. M.	7.45 P. M.	11.45 A. M.	11.36 A. M.
Manila ... Philippine Islands	1.04 A. M.*	2.04 A. M.*	3.04 A. M.*	4.04 A. M.*	8.04 P. M.	7.54 P. M.
Melbourne ... Australia	2.40 A. M.*	3.40 A. M.*	4.40 A. M.*	5.40 A. M.*	9.40 P. M.	9.31 P. M.
Mountain Time (c) ... United States	10.00 A. M.	11.00 A. M.	....	1.00 P. M.	5.00 A. M.	4.51 A. M.
Pacific Time (d) ... United States	9.00 A. M.	10.00 A. M.	11.00 A. M.	....	4.00 A. M.	3.51 A. M.
Paris ... France	5.09 P. M.	6.09 P. M.	7.09 P. M.	8.09 P. M.	12.09 P. M.	....
Rome ... Italy	5.50 P. M.	6.50 P. M.	7.50 P. M.	8.50 P. M.	12.50 P. M.	12.41 P. M.
Stockholm ... Sweden	6.12 P. M.	7.12 P. M.	8.12 P. M.	9.12 P. M.	1.12 P. M.	1.03 P. M.
St. Petersburg ... Russia	7.01 P. M.	8.01 P M.	9.01 P. M.	10.01 P. M.	2.01 P. M.	1.52 P. M.
Vienna ... Austria	6.06 P. M.	7.06 P. M.	8.06 P. M.	9.06 P. M.	1.06 P. M.	12.57 P. M.
Yokohama ... Japan	2.19 A. M.*	3.19 A. M.*	4.19 A. M.*	5.19 A. M.*	9.19 P. M.	9.09 P. M.

* At places marked * the time noted is in the morning of the FOLLOWING day.

(a) "EASTERN" includes: New York, Boston, Philadelphia, Baltimore, Washington, Richmond, Norfolk, Charleston, Buffalo, Pittsburgh, Montreal, Quebec, Ottawa, Toronto, etc.

(b) "CENTRAL" includes: Chicago, St. Louis, Minneapolis, St. Paul, Milwaukee, Kansas City, Omaha, Indianapolis, Cincinnati, Cleveland, Detroit, New Orleans, Memphis, Savannah, Pensacola, Winnipeg. etc.

(c) "MOUNTAIN" includes: Denver, Leadville, Colorado Springs, Helena, Regina (N. W. T.), etc.

(d) "PACIFIC" includes: San Francisco, Portland (Oregon), Victoria, Vancouver, Tacoma, Seattle, etc.

The World's Wonderful Progress.

The following twenty-five impressive WORLD facts connected with its unrivalled history of a quarter of a century give some impression of the vastness of the operations of the country's greatest paper:

I.	Total number of WORLDS printed in 25 years, to May 1, 1908	4,407,776,917
II.	This is equivalent, in 8-page papers, to	8,868,928,117
III.	Total consumption of white paper in pounds, in 25 years	1,016,865,553
IV.	Total consumption in week ending May 1, 1908 .... 805 tons, or	1,610,000 lbs.
V.	Total consumption in corresponding week of 1883	12,300 lbs.
VI.	Cost of white paper consumed by THE WORLD in 25 years past	$21,874,679.28
VII.	Cost of white paper consumed by THE WORLD in the year 1907	$1,632,593.00
VIII.	Total number of columns of advertising printed in THE WORLD, May 10, 1883, to April 30, 1908	738,585
IX.	Number of separate advertisements printed in THE WORLD in the month of April, 1908	108,009
X.	Gain over the corresponding month of April, 1883, when 7,666 separate advertisements were printed	100,343
XI.	Number of answers received at THE WORLD office to advertisements bearing box number addresses during the year 1907	1,067,949
XII.	Total composition, ems	15,724,845,844
XIII.	Cost of WORLD composition in 25 years	$8,169,580.37
XIV.	Total ink used, pounds, in 25 years	14,124,375
XV.	Paid for expressage and postage to U. S. Government since 1883	$2,585,197.44
XVI.	Total payrolls since May 10, 1883	$33,391,429.76
XVII.	Number of employees (home office only)	1,572
XVIII.	Total cash receipts, May 10, 1883, to April 30, 1908	$95,445,062.60
XIX.	Total floor space of THE WORLD plant	100,000 sq. ft.
XX.	Combined hourly press capacity in 8-page papers	1,300,000
XXI.	Three minor newspaper expenses—wrapping paper, paste and twine—totalled for the year 1907	$23,210
XXII.	Annual wire news charges (cable, telegraph, telephone, wireless) for 1907	$152,723
XXIII.	Horse power (electrical units) of THE WORLD plant	1,750
XXIV.	Stereotype page-plates cast in one year in THE WORLD'S foundry ...	520,962
XXV.	The average week-day output of THE WORLD in April, 1883, was 56 columns. The average for April, 1908, morning and evening, was 253 columns, nearly	5 times greater

Legal Holidays in the Various States.

JANUARY 1. NEW YEAR'S DAY: In all the States (including the District of Columbia, Arizona, and New Mexico), except Massachusetts, Mississippi, and New Hampshire.

JANUARY 8. ANNIVERSARY OF THE BATTLE OF NEW ORLEANS: In Louisiana.

JANUARY 19. LEE'S BIRTHDAY: In Florida, Georgia, North Carolina, South Carolina, Virginia, Alabama, and Arkansas.

FEBRUARY. MARDI-GRAS: In Alabama and the parish of Orleans, Louisiana.

FEBRUARY 12. LINCOLN'S BIRTHDAY: In Colorado, Connecticut, Delaware, Illinois, Kansas, Massachusetts, Minnesota, Nevada. New Jersey, New York, North Dakota, Pennsylvania, Washington, and Wyoming.

FEBRUARY 22. WASHINGTON'S BIRTHDAY: In all the States, District of Columbia, and Arizona, except Mississippi, where it is observed by exercises in the public schools.

FEBRUARY (Third Tuesday) SPRING ELECTION DAY: In Pennsylvania.

MARCH 2. ANNIVERSARY OF TEXAN INDEPENDENCE: In Texas.

APRIL 9, 1909. GOOD FRIDAY: In Alabama, Connecticut, Delaware, Florida, Louisiana, Maryland, Minnesota, New Jersey, Pennsylvania, Tennessee.

APRIL 19. PATRIOTS' DAY: In Maine and Massachusetts.

APRIL 21. ANNIVERSARY OF THE BATTLE OF SAN JACINTO: In Texas.

APRIL 26. CONFEDERATE MEMORIAL DAY: In Alabama, Florida, Georgia, and Mississippi.

MAY 10. CONFEDERATE MEMORIAL DAY: In North Carolina and South Carolina.

MAY (Second Friday) CONFEDERATE DAY: In Tennessee.

MAY 20. ANNIVERSARY OF THE SIGNING OF THE MECKLENBURG DECLARATION OF INDEPENDENCE: In North Carolina.

MAY (last Friday) PIONEER DAY: In Montana, observed in public schools.

MAY 30. DECORATION DAY: In all the States and Territories (and District of Columbia), except Florida, Georgia, Idaho, Louisiana, Mississippi, North Carolina, South Carolina, Tennessee, Texas. In Virginia, known as "Confederate Memorial Day."

JUNE 3. JEFFERSON DAVIS'S BIRTHDAY: In Florida, Georgia, Alabama, Mississippi, Tennessee, Texas, and South Carolina. In Louisiana known as "Confederate Memorial Day." In Virginia, in public schools.

JULY 4. INDEPENDENCE DAY: In all the States, District of Columbia, and Territories.

JULY 24. PIONEERS' DAY: In Utah.

JULY (Fourth Saturday) PRIMARY ELECTION DAY: In Texas.

AUGUST. PRIMARY ELECTION DAYS: In Missouri.

AUGUST 16. BENNINGTON BATTLE DAY: In Vermont.

SEPTEMBER 6, 1909. LABOR DAY: In all the States and Territories (and District of Columbia), except North Dakota. In Louisiana, observed in Orleans Parish. In Wyoming by proclamation of the Governor.

SEPTEMBER (First Tuesday) PRIMARY ELECTION DAY: In Wisconsin. In Michigan in even years.

SEPTEMBER 9. ADMISSION DAY: In California.

SEPTEMBER 12. "OLD DEFENDERS' DAY": In Baltimore, Md.

OCTOBER 31. ADMISSION DAY: In Nevada.

NOVEMBER 1. ALL SAINTS' DAY: In Louisiana.

NOVEMBER — GENERAL ELECTION DAY: In Arizona, California, Colorado, Delaware, Florida, Idaho (Illinois in Chicago, Springfield and East St. Louis only), Indiana, Iowa, Kansas, Kentucky. Louisiana, Maryland, Michigan, Minnesota, Missouri, Montana, Nevada, New Hampshire, New Jersey, New Mexico, New York, North Carolina, North Dakota, Ohio (from 5.30 A.M. 9 to A.M. only), Oklahoma, Oregon, Pennsylvania, Rhode Island, South Carolina, South Dakota, Tennessee, Texas, West Virginia, Washington, Wisconsin, and Wyoming, in the years when elections are held therein. In 1909 in States holding such elections the date is November 2.

NOVEMBER — 1909. THANKSGIVING DAY (usually the fourth Thursday in November): Is observed in all the States, and in the District of Columbia, Arizona, and New Mexico, though in some States it is not a statutory holiday.

DECEMBER 25. CHRISTMAS DAY: In all the States, District of Columbia, and Territories.

Sundays and Fast Days are legal holidays in all the States which designate them as such.

There are no statutory holidays in Mississippi, but by common consent the Fourth of July, Thanksgiving and Christmas are observed. In New Mexico, Washington's Birthday, Decoration Day, Labor Day, Flag Day (June 14), and Arbor Day are holidays when so designated by the Governor. In South Carolina, Thursday of Fair Week is a legal holiday.

ARBOR DAY is a legal holiday in Arizona, Maine, Maryland, New Mexico, Wisconsin, and Wyoming, the day being set by the Governor; in Texas, February 22; Nebraska, April 22; Utah, April 15; Rhode Island, second Friday in May; Montana, second Tuesday in May; Georgia, first Friday in December; Colorado (school holiday only), third Friday in April; in Oklahoma, the Friday following the second Monday in March; in Arkansas, first Saturday in March.

Every Saturday after 12 o'clock noon is a legal holiday in California in public offices, Illinois (in cities of 200,000 or more inhabitants), Maryland, Michigan, New York, New Jersey, Ohio, Pennsylvania, Rhode Island, Virginia, the District of Columbia (for banking purposes), and in New Orleans, La., and Charleston, S. C.; in Louisiana and Missouri in cities of 100,000 or more inhabitants; in Tennessee, for State and county officers, and in Colorado during June, July, and August; in Indiana, first Saturday in June to last Saturday in October, inclusive, for all public offices in counties having a county-seat of 100,000 population or more.

There is no national holiday, not even the Fourth of July. Congress has at various times appointed special holidays. In the second session of the Fifty-third Congress it passed an act making Labor Day a public holiday in the District of Columbia, and it has recognized the existence of certain days as holidays for commercial purposes, but, with the exception named, there is no general statute on the subject. The proclamation of the President designating a day of Thanksgiving only makes it a legal holiday in the District of Columbia and the Territories.

Ember and Rogation Days.

EMBER and Rogation Days are certain periods of the year devoted to prayer and fasting. Ember Days (twelve annually) are the Wednesday, Friday, and Saturday after the first Sunday in Lent, after the feast of Pentecost (Whit Sunday), after the festival of the Holy Cross, and after the festival of St. Lucia. Ember Weeks are the weeks in which the Ember Days appear.

Rogation Days are the three days immediately preceding Holy Thursday or Ascension Day.

Table of Memorable Dates.

B. C.

1183 Fall of Troy.
1082 Era of the Great Pyramid.
878 Carthage founded.
776 Olympic Era began.
753 Foundation of Rome.
588 Jerusalem taken by Nebuchadnezzar.
536 Restoration of the Jews under Cyrus.
509 Expulsion of Tarquins from Rome.
480 Xerxes defeated Greeks at Thermopylæ.
55 Cæsar conquered Britain.
4 Birth of Jesus Christ.

A. D.

29 The Crucifixion.
70 Jerusalem was destroyed by Titus.
313 Constantine converted toChristianity
410 The Romans abandoned Britain.
827 Egbert, first king of all England, Oct. 14.
1066 Battle of Hastings, Norman Conquest
1096 The Crusades began.
1172 Ireland was conquered by Henry II.
1215 King John granted Magna Charta, June 15.
1265 First Representative Parliament in England.
1415 Battle of Agincourt, Oct. 25.
1431 Joan of Arc was burnt, May 30.
1453 Constantinople taken by the Turks.
1455 The Wars of the Roses began.
1462 The Bible was first printed at Mentz.
1471 Caxton set up his printing press.
1486 The feuds of York and Lancaster ended.
1492 Columbus discovered America, Oct.12
1517 The Reformation began in Germany.
1519 Cortez began the conquest of Mexico.
1535 The first English Bible printed.
1539 Monasteries were closed in England.
1558 Accession of Queen Elizabeth, Nov.17
1565 Revolt of the Netherlands began.
1565 St. Augustine, Florida, settled.
1572 The St. Bartholomew Massacre, Aug.24
1588 The Spanish Armada defeated, July.
1600 East India Company first chartered.
1603 Union of England and Scotland.
1605 The Gunpowder Plot in England.
1607 Jamestown, Va., was settled.
1609 Hudson River first explored.
1616 Shakespeare died, April 23.
1618 Thirty Years' War in Germany began.
1620 Pilgrims by the Mayflower landed.
1623 Manhattan Island settled.
1634 Maryland settled by Roman Catholics
1636 Rhode Island settled by Roger Williams.
1640 Cromwell's Long Parliament assembled.
1649 Charles I. was beheaded, Jan. 30.
1653 Oliver Cromwell became Lord Protector.
1660 Restoration of the Stuarts.
1664 New York conquered from the Dutch.
1664 The great plague of London.
1666 The great fire of London began Sept.2.
1679 Habeas Corpus Act passed in England.

A. D.

1682 Pennsylvania settled by William Penn.
1685 Revocation of the Edict of Nantes, Oct. 22.
1688 James II. abdicated, Dec. 11.
1690 Battle of the Boyne, July 1.
1690 First newspaper in America; at Boston.
1704 Gibraltar was taken by the English.
1713 Peace of Utrecht, April 11.
1714 Accession of House of Hanover, Aug.1
1715 First Jacobite Rebellion in Great Britain.
1720 South Sea Bubble.
1745 Battle of Fontenoy, April 30.
1745 Second Jacobite Rebellion in Great Britain.
1756 Black Hole Suffocation in Calcutta.
1757 Clive won Battle of Plassey in India.
1759 Canada was taken from the French.
1765 Stamp Act enacted.
1773 Steam engine perfected by Watt.
1773 Tea destroyed in Boston Harbor, Dec. 16.
1775 Battle of Lexington, April 19.
1775 Battle of Bunker Hill, June 17.
1776 Declaration of Independence, July 4.
1777 Burgoyne's surrender, Oct. 17.
1779 Capt. Cook was killed, Feb. 14.
1781 Cornwallis' surrender at Yorktown, Oct. 19.
1788 First settlement in Australia, Jan. 26.
1789 The French Revolution began July 14
1789 Washington first inaug'ted President
1793 Cotton-gin invented by Whitney.
1793 Louis XVI. of France executed, Jan.21
1796 Vaccination discovered by Jenner.
1798 The Irish Rebellion.
1799 Battle of Seringapatam; death of Tippoo.
1799 Bonaparte declared First Consul, Nov. 10.
1801 Union of Great Britain and Ireland, Jan. 1.
1803 Louisiana purchased from the French
1804 Bonaparte became Emperor of France
1805 Battle of Trafalgar; death of Nelson.
1807 Fulton's first steamboat voyage.
1812 Second war with Great Britain.
1812 The French expedition to Moscow.
1813 Perry's victory on Lake Erie, Sept.10.
1814 The printing machine invented.
1814 Scott's "Waverley" published.
1815 Battle of New Orleans, Jan. 8.
1815 Battle of Waterloo, June 18.
1819 First steamship crossed the Atlantic.
1820 Missouri Compromise adopted.
1823 Monroe Doctrine declared, Dec. 2.
1828 First passenger railroad in U. S.
1830 Revolution in France, Orleanist succession.
1832 South Carolina Nullification Ordinance.
1835 Morse invented the telegraph.
1835 Seminole War in Florida began.
1837 Accession of Queen Victoria, June 20
1845 Texas annexed.

A. D.

1846 Sewing machine completed by Howe.
1846 The Irish Potato Famine.
1846 British Corn laws repealed, June 26.
1846 War with Mexico began.
1848 French Revolution. Republic succeeded.
1848 Gold discovered in California, Sept.
1851 Gold discovered in Australia, Feb. 12
1851 First International Exhibit'n, London
1852 Louis Napoleon became Emperor.
1853 Crimean War began.
1854 Japan opened by Commodore Perry.
1857 The Great Mutiny in India.
1857 The Dred Scott decision.
1857 First Atlantic cable message, Aug. 4.
1859 John Brown's raid into Virginia.
1860 South Carolina seceded, Dec. 20.
1861 Emancipation of the Russian serfs.
1863 Lincoln's Emancipation Proclamation, Jan. 1.
1863 Battle of Gettysburg, July 1-3
1865 Lee surrendered at Appomattox, April 9.
1865 President Lincoln assassinated, April 14.
1866 Battle of Sadowa. Prussia beat Austria.
1867 Emperor Maximilian of Mexico executed.
1867 The Dominion of Canada established
1870 Franco-German War began, July 19.
1870 Capitulation of French at Sedan, Sept. 1.
1870 Rome became the capital of Italy.
1871 The German Empire re-established.
1871 The Irish Church was disestablished.
1871 The great fire in Chicago, Oct. 8-11.
1872 The great fire in Boston, Nov. 9.
1876 Prof. Bell perfected the telephone.
1876 Centennial Exposit'n at Philadelphia
1881 President Garfield shot, July 2.
1889 Brazil became a Republic.
1889 Johnstown, Pa., flood, May 31.
1893 World's Columbian Exposition at Chicago.
1894 Chinese-Japanese War began.
1895 Cuban Revolution began, Feb. 20.
1897 The Turkish-Greek War.
1898 The Spanish-American War.
1899 Universal Peace Conference.
1899 The South African War began.
1900 Boxer Insurrection in China.
1900 The Galveston tornado, Sept. 8.
1901 Death of Queen Victoria.
1901 Assassination of President McKinley
1902 Martinique destroyed by volcanic eruption.
1903 Republic of Panama established.
1904 The Russo-Japanese War began.
1906 San Francisco earthquake and conflagration.
1908 Emperor and Dowager Empress of China died. Pi Yu ascended the throne.
1908 American Battleship fleet nearly circumnavigated the Globe.

The French Revolutionary Era.

In September, 1793, the convention decreed that the common era should be abolished in all civil affairs, and that the new French era should begin on September 22, 1792, the day of the true autumnal equinox, and that each succeeding year should begin at the midnight of the day on which the true autumnal equinox falls. The year was divided into twelve months of thirty days each. In ordinary years there were five extra days, from the 17th to the 21st of our September, and at the end of every fourth year was a sixth complimentary day. This reckoning was first used on November 22, 1793, and was continued until December 31, 1805, when it was discontinued, and the Gregorian calendar, used throughout the rest of Europe, was resumed. The following were the dates for the year 1804, the last complete year of this style of reckoning:

Vendemiaire	(Vintage),	September 23 to October 22.	Germinal	(Budding),	March 22 to April 21.
Brumaire	(Foggy),	October 23 to November 22.	Floreal	(Flowery),	April 21 to May 20.
Frimaire	(Sleety),	November 22 to December 21.	Prairial	(Pasture),	May 21 to June 20.
Nivose	(Snowy),	December 22 to January 21.	Messidor	(Harvest),	June 20 to July 19.
Pluviose	(Rainy),	January 21 to February 20.	Thermidor	(Hot),	July 20 to August 19.
Ventose	(Windy),	February 20 to March 19.	Fructidor	(Fruit),	August 19 to September 18.

The months were divided into three decades of ten days each, but to make up the 365 five were added at the end of September: Primidi, dedicated to Virtue; Duodi, to Genius; Tridi, to Labor; Quartidi, to Opinion, and Quintidi, to Rewards. To Leap Year, called Olympic, a sixth day, September 22 or 23, Sextidi, "the day of the Revolution," was added.

To each tenth day, thirty-six in all, were assigned thirty-six "Fetes Decadaires," decreed by the National Convention on the eighteenth Prairial, in honor of the Supreme Being and Nature, the Human Race, the French People, Benefactors of Humanity, Martyrs for Liberty, Liberty and Equality, the Republic, Liberty of the World, Love of Country, Hatred of Tyrants and Traitors, Truth, Justice, Modesty, Glory and Immortality, Friendship, Frugality, Courage, Good Faith, Heroism, Disinterestedness, Stoicism, Love, Conjugal Fidelity, Paternal Love, Maternal Tenderness, Filial Piety, Infancy, Childhood, Manhood, Old Age, Sickness, Agriculture, Industry, Our Ancestors, Our Posterity, Goodness.

Theodore Roosevelt's African Expedition.

OFFICIAL STATEMENT.

On December 5 Secretary Charles D. Walcott, of the Smithsonian Institution, gave out the following official statement concerning the projected African expedition of Theodore Roosevelt, by authority of the President:

"In March, 1909, Mr. Theodore Roosevelt will head a scientific expedition to Africa outfitted by the Smithsonian Institution, and starting from New York City. This expedition will gather natural history materials for the Government collections, to be deposited by the Smithsonian Institution in the new United States National Museum at Washington, D. C.

"Besides the President and his son, Kermit Roosevelt, the personnel of the party, on leaving New York, will consist of three representatives of the Smithsonian Institution: Major Edgar A. Mearns, Medical Corps, United States Army (retired); Mr. Edmund Heller, and Mr. J. Alden Loring. On arriving in Africa, the party will be enlarged by the addition of Mr. R. J. Cuninghame, who is now in Africa preparing the President's outfit. He will have charge of a number of native porters, who, with necessary animals, will be formed into a small caravan.

"Mr. Roosevelt and his son will kill the big game, the skins and skeletons of which will be prepared and shipped to the United States by other members of the party. Kermit Roosevelt is to be the official photographer of the expedition.

"The national collections are very deficient in natural history materials from the Dark Continent, and an effort will be made by the expedition to gather general collections in zoology and botany to supply some of its deficiencies; but the main effort will be to collect the large and vanishing African animals.

"Mr. R. J. Cuninghame, who is now engaged in assembling the materials for Mr. Roosevelt's use, has been employed to act as guide and manager of the caravan. Mr. Cuninghame is also an experienced collector of natural history specimens, having made collections for the British Museum in Norway and Africa. He is an English fieldman, who has guided numerous hunting parties in Africa and who was chief hunter for the Field Columbian Exposition.

"Mr. Edmund Heller, a graduate of Stanford University, class of 1901, is a thoroughly trained naturalist, whose special work will be the preparation and preservation of specimens of large animals. Mr. Heller is about thirty years of age. His former experience, when associated with Mr. D. G. Eliot and Mr. Ackley, of the Field Columbian Museum, in collecting big game animals in the same portions of Africa which Mr. Roosevelt will visit, will be a valuable asset to the expedition. Mr. Heller has had large experiences in animal collecting in Alaska, British Columbia, United States, Mexico, Central America, and South America. In the year 1898 he made a collecting trip of eleven months to Gallopagos Islands, starting from San Francisco. He is a born enthusiastic collector as well as a well-equipped naturalist. He is also author of scientific papers on mammals, birds, reptiles and fishes. At present he is Assistant Curator of the Museum of Vertebrate Zoology of the University of California.

"J. Alden Loring is a field naturalist, whose training comprises service in the biological survey of the Department of Agriculture and in the Bronx Zoological Park, New York City, as well as on numerous collecting trips through British America, Mexico, and the United States.

"He is about thirty-eight years old, of ardent temperament, and intensely energetic. In August, September, and October, 1898, he made the highest record for a travelling collector, having sent in to the United States National Museum 900 well prepared specimens of small mammals in the three months' journey from London through Sweden, Germany, Switzerland, and Belgium.

"Major Edgar A. Mearns, a retired officer of the Medical Corps of the army, about fifty-three years of age, will be the physician of the trip and have charge of the Smithsonian portion of the party. He had twenty-five years' experience as an army doctor, and is also well known as a naturalist and collector of natural history specimens.

"No fears need be entertained for the President's safety from the attacks of man or beast as every member of the party is an excellent rifle shot.

"The party will reach Mombasa in April, 1909. No detailed itinerary has been decided upon; but the general route will be up the Uganda Railway to Nairobi and Lake Victoria Nyanza, a distance of about 650 miles by rail, thence crossing into Uganda, and, finally, passing down the Nile to Cairo. Much of the hunting will be done in British East Africa, where the Uganda Railroad can be used as a base of supplies and means of ready transportation. At least one great mountain, possibly Mount Kenia, will be visited.

"Khartoum will be reached, if all goes well, about April, 1910. The expedition may be expected to spend about one year on African soil."

Fourth of July Casualties.

The number of Fourth of July casualties in the United States in 1908, according to a record kept by the Journal of the American Medical Association, was 5,623. The number of deaths resulting therefrom was 162.

Church Fasts.

The Roman Catholic Days of fasting are the forty days of Lent, the Ember Days, the Wednesdays and Thursdays of the four weeks in Advent, and certain Vigils or evenings prior to the greater feasts. In the American Episcopal Church the days of fasting or abstinence to be observed, according to the Book of Common Prayer, are the forty days of Lent, the Ember Days, the three Rogation Days, and all the Fridays of the year except Christmas Day. In the Greek Church the four principal fasts are those in Lent, the week succeeding Whitsuntide, the fortnight before the Assumption, and forty Days before Christmas.

Divisions of Time.

The interval between two consecutive transits of a fixed star over any meridian or the interval during which the earth makes one absolute revolution on its axis is called a *Sidereal* Day, and is invariable, while the interval between two consecutive transits of the Sun over any meridian is called an *Apparent* Solar Day, and its length varies from day to day by reason of the variable motion of the earth in its orbit, and the inclination of this orbit to the equator on which time is measured.

A *Mean* Solar Day is the average or mean of all the apparent solar days in a year. *Mean Solar Time* is that shown by a well-regulated clock or watch, while *Apparent Solar Time* is that shown by a well-constructed sun-dial; the difference between the two at any time is the *Equation of Time*, and may amount to 16 minutes and 21 seconds. The Astronomical Day begins at noon and the Civil Day at the preceding midnight. The Sidereal and Mean Solar Days are both invariable, but one day of the latter is equal to 1 day, 3 minutes, and 56.555 seconds of the former.

The interval during which the earth makes one absolute revolution round the Sun is called a *Sidereal Year*, and consists of 365 days, 6 hours, 9 minutes, and 9.6 seconds, which is invariable.

The Tropical Year is the interval between two consecutive returns of the Sun to the Vernal Equinox. If this were a fixed point, the Sidereal and Tropical Years would be identical; but in consequence of the disturbing influence of the Moon and planets on the spheroidal figure of the earth, the Equinox has a slow, retrograde mean motion of 50″.26 annually, so that the Sun returns to the Equinox sooner every year than he otherwise would by 20 minutes 23.6 seconds; the Tropical Year, therefore, consists of 365 days, 5 hours, 48 minutes, and 46 seconds. The Tropical Year is not of uniform length; it is now slowly decreasing at the rate of .595 second per century, but this variation will not always continue.

Julius Cæsar, in B. C. 45, was the first to reform the calendar by ordering that every year whose date number is exactly divisible by 4 contain 366 days, and all other years 365 days. The intercalary day was introduced by counting the *sixth* day before the Kalends of March *twice;* hence the name bissextile, from bis, twice, and sex, six. He also changed the beginning of the year from 1st of March to the 1st of January, and also changed the name of the fifth month (Quintilis) to July, after himself. The average length of the Julian year is therefore 365¼ days, which, however, is too long by 11 minutes and 14 seconds, and this would accumulate in 400 years to about three days. The Julian Calendar continued in use until A. D. 1582, when the date of the beginning of the seasons occurred 10 days later than in B. C. 45, when this mode of reckoning time was introduced.

The Gregorian Calendar was introduced by Pope Gregory XIII. with the view of keeping the Equinox to the same day of the month. It consists of 365 days, but every year exactly divisible by 4 and the centurial years which are exactly divisible by 400 contain 366 days; and if in addition to this arbitrary arrangement the centurial years exactly divisible by 4,000 contain 366 days, the error in the Gregorian system will amount to only one day in about 20 centuries. If, however, 31 leap years were intercalated in 128 years, instead of 32 as at present, the calendar would be practically exact and the error would not amount to more than a day in 100,000 years. The length of the mean Gregorian Year may therefore be set down at 365 days, 5 hours, 49 minutes, 12 seconds. The Gregorian Calendar was introduced into England and her colonies in 1752, at which time the Equinox had retrograded 11 days since the Council of Nice in A. D. 325, when the festival of Easter was established and the Equinox occurred on March 21; hence September 3, 1752, was called September 14, and at the same time the commencement of the legal year was changed from March 25 to January 1, so that the year 1751 lost the months of January and February and the first 24 days of March. The difference between the Julian and Gregorian Calendars is now 13 days. Russia and the Greek Church still employ the Julian Calendar for civil and ecclesiastical purposes.

Standard Time.

Primarily, for the convenience of the railroads, a standard of time was established by mutual agreement in 1883, by which trains are run and local time regulated. According to this system, the United States, extending from 65° to 125° west longitude, is divided into four time sections, each of 15° of longitude, exactly equivalent to one hour, commencing with the 75th meridian. The first (eastern) section includes all territory between the Atlantic Coast and an irregular line drawn from Detroit to Charleston, S. C., the latter being its most southern point. The second (central) section includes all the territory between the last-named line and an irregular line from Bismarck, N. D., to the mouth of the Rio Grande. The third (mountain) section includes all territory between the last-named line and nearly the western borders of Idaho, Utah, and Arizona. The fourth (Pacific) section covers the rest of the country to the Pacific Coast. Standard time is uniform inside each of these sections, and the time of each section differs from that next to it by exactly one hour. Thus at 12 noon in New York City (eastern time), the time at Chicago (central time) is 11 o'clock A. M.; at Denver (mountain time), 10 o'clock A. M., and at San Francisco (Pacific time), 9 o'clock A. M. Standard time is 16 minutes slower at Boston than true local time, 4 minutes slower at New York, 8 minutes faster at Washington, 19 minutes faster at Charleston, 28 minutes slower at Detroit, 18 minutes faster at Kansas City, 10 minutes slower at Chicago, 1 minute faster at St. Louis, 28 minutes faster at Salt Lake City, and 10 minutes faster at San Francisco.

1909

	Sun.	Mon.	Tues.	Wed.	Thur.	Fri.	Sat.		Sun.	Mon.	Tues.	Wed.	Thur.	Fri.	Sat.
Jan.						1	2	July.					1	2	3
	3	4	5	6	7	8	9		4	5	6	7	8	9	10
	10	11	12	13	14	15	16		11	12	13	14	15	16	17
	17	18	19	20	21	22	23		18	19	20	21	22	23	24
	24	25	26	27	28	29	30		25	26	27	28	29	30	31
	31														
Feb.		1	2	3	4	5	6	Aug.	1	2	3	4	5	6	7
	7	8	9	10	11	12	13		8	9	10	11	12	13	14
	14	15	16	17	18	19	20		15	16	17	18	19	20	21
	21	22	23	24	25	26	27		22	23	24	25	26	27	28
	28								29	30	31				
Mar.		1	2	3	4	5	6	Sept.				1	2	3	4
	7	8	9	10	11	12	13		5	6	7	8	9	10	11
	14	15	16	17	18	19	20		12	13	14	15	16	17	18
	21	22	23	24	25	26	27		19	20	21	22	23	24	25
	28	29	30	31					26	27	28	29	30		
April.					1	2	3	Oct.						1	2
	4	5	6	7	8	9	10		3	4	5	6	7	8	9
	11	12	13	14	15	16	17		10	11	12	13	14	15	16
	18	19	20	21	22	23	24		17	18	19	20	21	22	23
	25	26	27	28	29	30			24	25	26	27	28	29	30
									31						
May.							1	Nov.		1	2	3	4	5	6
	2	3	4	5	6	7	8		7	8	9	10	11	12	13
	9	10	11	12	13	14	15		14	15	16	17	18	19	20
	16	17	18	19	20	21	22		21	22	23	24	25	26	27
	23	24	25	26	27	28	29		28	29	30				
	30	31													
June.			1	2	3	4	5	Dec.				1	2	3	4
	6	7	8	9	10	11	12		5	6	7	8	9	10	11
	13	14	15	16	17	18	19		12	13	14	15	16	17	18
	20	21	22	23	24	25	26		19	20	21	22	23	24	25
	27	28	29	30					26	27	28	29	30	31	

1910

	Sun.	Mon.	Tues.	Wed.	Thur.	Fri.	Sat.		Sun.	Mon.	Tues.	Wed.	Thur.	Fri.	Sat.
Jan.							1	July.						1	2
	2	3	4	5	6	7	8		3	4	5	6	7	8	9
	9	10	11	12	13	14	15		10	11	12	13	14	15	16
	16	17	18	19	20	21	22		17	18	19	20	21	22	23
	23	24	25	26	27	28	29		24	25	26	27	28	29	30
	30	31							31						
Feb.			1	2	3	4	5	Aug.		1	2	3	4	5	6
	6	7	8	9	10	11	12		7	8	9	10	11	12	13
	13	14	15	16	17	18	19		14	15	16	17	18	19	20
	20	21	22	23	24	25	26		21	22	23	24	25	26	27
	27	28							28	29	30	31			
Mar.			1	2	3	4	5	Sept.					1	2	3
	6	7	8	9	10	11	12		4	5	6	7	8	9	10
	13	14	15	16	17	18	19		11	12	13	14	15	16	17
	20	21	22	23	24	25	26		18	19	20	21	22	23	24
	27	28	29	30	31				25	26	27	28	29	30	
April.						1	2	Oct.							1
	3	4	5	6	7	8	9		2	3	4	5	6	7	8
	10	11	12	13	14	15	16		9	10	11	12	13	14	15
	17	18	19	20	21	22	23		16	17	18	19	20	21	22
	24	25	26	27	28	29	30		23	24	25	26	27	28	29
									30	31					
May.	1	2	3	4	5	6	7	Nov.			1	2	3	4	5
	8	9	10	11	12	13	14		6	7	8	9	10	11	12
	15	16	17	18	19	20	21		13	14	15	16	17	18	19
	22	23	24	25	26	27	28		20	21	22	23	24	25	26
	29	30	31						27	28	29	30			
June.				1	2	3	4	Dec.					1	2	3
	5	6	7	8	9	10	11		4	5	6	7	8	9	10
	12	13	14	15	16	17	18		11	12	13	14	15	16	17
	19	20	21	22	23	24	25		18	19	20	21	22	23	24
	26	27	28	29	30				25	26	27	28	29	30	31

Anniversaries.

DATES OF HISTORICAL EVENTS CUSTOMARILY OR OCCASIONALLY OBSERVED.

Jan. 1. Emancipation Proclamation by Lincoln. 1863.
Jan. 8. Battle of New Orleans, 1815.
Jan. 17. Franklin born, 1706.
Jan. 19. Robert E. Lee born, 1807.
Jan. 27. German Emperor born, 1859.
Feb. 12. Abraham Lincoln born, 1809.
Feb. 15. Battle-ship Maine blown up, 1898.
Feb. 22. George Washington born, 1732.
March 5. Boston Massacre, 1770.
March 15. Andrew Jackson born, 1767.
March 18. Grover Cleveland born, 1837.
March 19. William J. Bryan born, 1860.
April 9. Lee surrendered at Appomattox, 1865.
April 12. Fort Sumter fired on, 1861.
April 12. Henry Clay born, 1777.
April 13. Thomas Jefferson born, 1743.
April 14 Lincoln assassinated, 1865.
Ap. 18-19. Earthquake and great conflagration at San Francisco, 1906.
April 19. Primrose Day in England, Lord Beaconsfield died, 1881.
Apr'l 19. Battles of Lexington and Concord, 1775.
April 23. Shakespeare born, 1564.
April 27. Gen. U. S. Grant born, 1822.
April 30. Washington was inaugurated first President, 1789.
May 1. Dewey destroyed the Spanish fleet at Manila, 1898.
May 13. First English settlement in America, at Jamestown, 1607.
May 13. Society of The Cincinnati organized by officers of Revolutionary Army, 1783.
May 18. The Czar of Russia born, 1868.
May 20. Mecklenburg, N. C., Declaration of Independence, 1775.
May 24. Queen Victoria born, 1819.
June 14. Flag Day in the United States.
June 15. King John granted Magna Charter at Runnymede, 1215.
June 17. Battle of Bunker Hill, 1775.
June 18 Battle of Waterloo, 1815.
June 28. Battle of Fort Moultrie, Charleston, S. C., 1776.
July 1. Dominion Day in Canada.
July 1-3. Battle of Gettysburg, 1863.
July 3. Cervera's fleet was destroyed off Santiago, 1898.
July 4. Declaration of Independence, 1776.
July 12. Orangemen's Day.
July 14. The Bastile was destroyed, 1789.
July 16. Santiago surrendered. 1898.
July 21. Battle of Bull Run, 1861.
Aug. 7. Gen. Nathanael Greene born, 1742.
Aug. 13. Manila surrendered to the Americans, 1898.
Aug. 16. Battle of Bennington, Vt., 1777.
Sep. 1. Capitulation of Sedan, 1870.
Sep. 6. President McKinley shot at Buffalo, 1901.
Sep. 10. Battle of Lake Erie, Perry's victory, 1813.
Sep. 11. Battle of Lake Champlain, McDonough's victory, 1814.
Sep. 13. Battle of Chapultepec, 1847.
Sep. 14. City of Mexico taken by the U. S. troops, 1847.
Sep. 15. William H. Taft born, 1857.
Sep. 17. Battle of Antietam, 1862.
Sep. 19-20. Battle of Chickamauga, 1863.
Sep. 20. Italians occupied Rome, 1870.
Oct. 8-11. Great fire of Chicago, 1871.
Oct. 12. Columbus discovered America, 1492.
Oct. 17. Burgoyne surrendered at Saratoga, 1777.
Oct. 19. Cornwallis surrendered at Yorktown, 1781.
Oct. 27. Theodore Roosevelt born, 1858.
Nov. 5. Guy Fawkes Day in England. The Gunpowder Plot discovered, 1604.
Nov. 9. King Edward VII. born, 1841.
Nov. 9. Great fire of Boston, 1872.
Nov. 10. Martin Luther born, 1483.
Nov. 25. British evacuated New York, 1783.
Dec. 2. Battle of Austerlitz, 1805.
Dec. 14. Washington died, 1799.
Dec. 16. Boston "Tea Party," 1773.
Dec. 16. The great fire in New York. 1835
Dec. 22. Mayflower pilgrims landed at Plymouth Rock, 1620.
Dec. 25-26. Battle of Trenton, N. J., 1776.

Ready-Reference Calendar.—1.

For ascertaining the Day of the Week for any given Time from the Beginning of the Christian Era to the Year 2200.

RULE.—To the day of the Month, add Factors for Month, Century, and Year, and divide the total by **7.**

If there is no remainder, the day is	Sunday.	Should the total be less than 7, it is to be taken as a remainder.
" 1 is the remainder "	Monday.	
" 2 " "	Tuesday.	
" 3 " "	Wednesday.	
" 4 " "	Thursday.	
" 5 " "	Friday.	
" 6 "	Saturday.	

EXAMPLE:

Week-day of Washington's Birthday, February 22, 1909.

Day.		Factors for Month.		Century.		Year.		
22	+	5	+	5	+	4	=	36

36 divided by 7 leaves 1 remainder, therefore the day will be *Monday.*

MONTHS.
For Leap years figures in heavier type to be taken.

	Jan.	Feb.	Mar.	Apr.	May	June	July	Aug.	Sept.	Oct.	Nov.	Dec.
Factors.	2	5	5	1	3	6	1	4	0	2	5	0
	1	**4**										

CENTURIES (Cardinal Numbers).
The year 00 of Centuries in heavier type was, or will be, a Leap year.

OLD STYLE, ended Sept. 2, 1752—a Wednesday.	**2**	**1**	**0**	**6**	**5**	**4**	**3**
	9	**8**	**7**	**13**	**12**	**11**	**10**
	16	**15**	**14**				**17**
NEW STYLE, began Sept. 14, 1752—a Thursday.	18		17		**20**	19	
	22		21		**24**	23	
	26		25		**28**	27	
	and every succeeding fourth Century.						
Factors.	0	1	2	3	4	5	6

YEARS.
Leap years in heavier type.

00	1	2	3		**4**	5
6	7		**8**	9	10	11
	12	13	14	15		**16**
17	18	19		**20**	21	22
23		**24**	25	26	27	
28	29	30	31		**32**	33
34	35		**36**	37	38	39
	40	41	42	43		**44**
45	46	47		**48**	49	50
51		**52**	53	54	55	
56	57	58	59		**60**	61
62	63		**64**	65	66	67
	68	69	70	71		**72**
73	74	75		**76**	77	78
79		**80**	81	82	83	
84	85	86	87		**88**	89
90	91		**92**	93	94	95
	96	97	98	99		
0	1	2	3	4	5	6

The system of this Calendar is taken from one printed in Whitaker's (London) Almanac.

Ready-Reference Calendar.—2.

For ascertaining any Day of the Week for any given Time within Two Hundred Years from the introduction of the New Style, 1753, to 1952 inclusive.

YEARS 1753 TO 1952.									Jan.	Feb.	Mar.	Apr.	May.	June	July.	Aug.	Sept.	Oct.	Nov.	Dec.
1753g 1754d	1781g 1782d	1800e 1801a	1828q 1829a	1856q 1857a	1884q 1885a	1900g 1901d	1928h 1929d	a	4	7	7	3	5	1	3	6	2	4	7	2
1755e 1756p	1783e 1784p	1802b 1803c	1830b 1831c	1858b 1859c	1886b 1887c	1902e 1903a	1930e 1931a	b	5	1	1	4	6	2	4	7	3	5	1	3
17 7c 1758f	1785c 1786f	1804h 1805d	1832h 1833d	1860h 1861d	1888h 1889d	1904k 1905t	1932k 1933f	c	6	2	2	5	7	3	5	1	4	6	2	4
1759g 1760q	1787g 1788q	1806e 1807a	1834e 1835a	1862e 1863a	1890e 1891a	1906g 1907d	1934g 1935d	d	2	5	5	1	3	6	1	4	7	2	5	7
17 1a 1762b	1789a 1790b	1808k 1809f	1836k 1837f	1864k 1865f	1892k 1893f	1908l 1909b	1936l 1937b	e	3	6	6	2	4	7	2	5	1	3	6	1
1763c 1764h	1791c 1792h	1810g 1811d	1838g 1839d	1866g 1867d	1894g 1895d	1910c 1911f	1938c 1939f	f	7	3	3	6	1	4	6	2	5	7	3	5
1765d 1766e	1793d 1794e	1812l 1813b	1840l 1841b	1868l 1869b	1896l 1897b	1912m 1913e	1940m 1941e	g	1	4	4	7	2	5	7	3	6	1	4	6
17 7a 1768k	1795a 1796k	1814c 1815f	1842c 1843f	1870c 1871f	1898c 1899f	1914a 1915b	1942a 1943b	h	7	3	4	7	2	5	7	3	6	1	4	6
1769f 1770g	1797f 1798g	1816m 1817e	1844m 1845e	1872m 1873e		1916n 1917g	1944n 1945g	k	5	1	2	5	7	3	5	1	4	6	2	4
1771d 1772l	1799d	1818a 1819b	1846a 1847b	1874a 1875b		1918d 1919e	1946d 1947e	l	3	6	7	3	5	1	3	6	2	4	7	2
1773b 1774c		1820n 1821g	1848n 1849g	1876n 1877g		1920p 1921c	1948p 1949c	m	1	4	5	1	3	6	1	4	7	2	5	7
1775f 1776m		1822d 1823e	1850d 1851e	1878d 1879e		1922f 1923g	1950f 1951g	n	6	2	3	6	1	4	6	2	5	7	3	5
1777e 1778a		1824p 1825c	1852p 1853c	1880p 1881c		1924q 1925a	1952q	p	4	7	1	4	6	2	4	7	3	5	1	3
1779b 1780n		1826f 1827g	1854f 1855g	1882f 1883g		1926b 1927c		q	2	5	6	2	4	7	2	5	1	3	6	1

NOTE.—The letters in the list of "*Years* from 1753 to 1952," refer to the table headed with the *Months*, the figures in which refer to the same figures at the head of the table of *Days*. For example: To know on what day July 4, 1909, will fall look for 1909 in the table of *Years*. The letter "b" is attached. Look for the same letter in the table of *Months* and in a parallel line under July is the figure 4, which directs to column 4 in the table of *Days* below, in which it will be seen that July 4 falls on Sunday.

TABLE OF DAYS.

1		2		3		4		5		6		7	
Monday	1	Tuesday	1	Wednesday	1	Thursday	1	Friday	1	Saturday	1	SUNDAY	1
Tuesday	2	Wednesday	2	Thursday	2	Friday	2	Saturday	2	SUNDAY	2	Monday	2
Wednesday	3	Thursday	3	Friday	3	Saturday	3	SUNDAY	3	Monday	3	Tuesday	3
Thursday	4	Friday	4	Saturday	4	SUNDAY	4	Monday	4	Tuesday	4	Wednesday	4
Friday	5	Saturday	5	SUNDAY	5	Monday	5	Tuesday	5	Wednesday	5	Thursday	5
Saturday	6	SUNDAY	6	Monday	6	Tuesday	6	Wednesday	6	Thursday	6	Friday	6
SUNDAY	7	Monday	7	Tuesday	7	Wednesday	7	Thursday	7	Friday	7	Saturday	7
Monday	8	Tuesday	8	Wednesday	8	Thursday	8	Friday	8	Saturday	8	SUNDAY	8
Tuesday	9	Wednesday	9	Thursday	9	Friday	9	Saturday	9	SUNDAY	9	Monday	9
Wednesd.	10	Thursday	10	Friday	10	Saturday	10	SUNDAY	10	Monday	10	Tuesday	10
Thursday	11	Friday	11	Saturday	11	SUNDAY	11	Monday	11	Tuesday	11	Wednesd.	11
Friday	12	Saturday	12	SUNDAY	12	Monday	12	Tuesday	12	Wednesd.	12	Thursday	12
Saturday	13	SUNDAY	13	Monday	13	Tuesday	13	Wednesd.	13	Thursday	13	Friday	13
SUNDAY	14	Monday	14	Tuesday	14	Wednesd.	14	Thursday	14	Friday	14	Saturday	14
Monday	15	Tuesday	15	Wednesd.	15	Thursday	15	Friday	15	Saturday	15	SUNDAY	15
Tuesday	16	Wednesd.	16	Thursday	16	Friday	16	Saturday	16	SUNDAY	16	Monday	16
Wednesd.	17	Thursday	17	Friday	17	Saturday	17	SUNDAY	17	Monday	17	Tuesday	17
Thursday	18	Friday	18	Saturday	18	SUNDAY	18	Monday	18	Tuesday	18	Wednesd.	18
Friday	19	Saturday	19	SUNDAY	19	Monday	19	Tuesday	19	Wednesd.	19	Thursday	19
Saturday	20	SUNDAY	20	Monday	20	Tuesday	20	Wednesd.	20	Thursday	20	Friday	20
SUNDAY	21	Monday	21	Tuesday	21	Wednesd.	21	Thursday	21	Friday	21	Saturday	21
Monday	22	Tuesday	22	Wednesd.	22	Thursday	22	Friday	22	Saturday	22	SUNDAY	22
Tuesday	23	Wednesd.	23	Thursday	23	Friday	23	Saturday	23	SUNDAY	23	Monday	23
Wednesd.	24	Thursday	24	Friday	24	Saturday	24	SUNDAY	24	Monday	24	Tuesday	24
Thursday	25	Friday	25	Saturday	25	SUNDAY	25	Monday	25	Tuesday	25	Wednesd.	25
Friday	26	Saturday	26	SUNDAY	26	Monday	26	Tuesday	26	Wednesd.	26	Thursday	26
Saturday	27	SUNDAY	27	Monday	27	Tuesday	27	Wednesd.	27	Thursday	27	Friday	27
SUNDAY	28	Monday	28	Tuesday	28	Wednesd.	28	Thursday	28	Friday	28	Saturday	28
Monday	29	Tuesday	29	Wednesd.	29	Thursday	29	Friday	29	Saturday	29	SUNDAY	29
Tuesday	30	Wednesd.	30	Thursday	30	Friday	30	Saturday	30	SUNDAY	30	Monday	30
Wednesd.	31	Thursday	31	Friday	31	Saturday	31	SUNDAY	31	Monday	31	Tuesday	31

Ritualistic Calendar.

COLORS FOR THE ALTAR IN USE IN RITUALISTIC EPISCOPAL CHURCHES IN THE UNITED STATES.

White.—From the First Service (First Vespers) of Christmas Day to the Octave of Epiphany, inclusive (except on the Feasts of Martyrs); on Maundy Thursday (for the celebration); from the First Service of Easter Day to the Vigil of Pentecost (except on Feasts of Martyrs and Rogation Days); on Trinity Sunday. Conversion of St. Paul, Purification, Annunciation, St. John Baptist, St. Michael, St. Luke, All Saints, Saints who are not Martyrs, and Patron Saints (Transfiguration and Dedication of Church).

Red.—From First Vespers of Pentecost to the First Vespers of Trinity Sunday (which includes Ember Days), Holy Innocents (if on a Sunday), and Feasts of all Martyrs.

Violet.—From Septuagesima to Maundy Thursday (Easter-Eve); Advent Sunday to Christmas Eve, Vigils, Ember Days (except in Whitsun Week), and Rogation Days; Holy Innocents (unless on Sunday). *Black.*—Good Friday and at funerals. *Green.*—All other days.

These regulations as to colors are general. A more minute code changing with each year is published in the church almanacs.

Jewish Calendar, 1909.

New Moon, Fasts, Feasts, etc.					New Moon, Fasts, Feasts, etc.				
5669.			1909.		5670.			1909.	
Sebat	1	New Moon	Jan.	23	Tisri	1	New Moon (New Year)	Sept.	16
Adar	1	"	Feb.	22	"	3	Fast of Guadaliah	"	18
Nisan	1	"	Mar.	23	"	10	" Expiation (Yom Kippur)	"	25
"	15	Passover	April	[illegible]	"	15	Feast of Tabernacles	"	30
Yiar	1	New Moon	"	22	"	22	" Eighth Day	Oct.	7
"	14	Second Passover	May	5	"	23	" Rejoicing with the Law	"	8
Sivan	1	New Moon	"	21	Hesvan	1	New Moon	"	16
"	6	Pentecost	"	[illegible]6	Kislev	1	"	Nov.	14
Tamuz	1	New Moon	June	20	"	25	Dedication of the Temple	Dec.	8
"	17	Fast of Tamuz	July	6	Tebet	1	New Moon	"	13
Ab	1	New Moon	"	19	"	10	Fast of Tebet	"	22
"	9	Fast of Ab (Destruction of Jerusalem)	"	27				1910.	
					Sebat	1	New Moon	Jan.	11
Elul	1	New Moon	Aug.	18	Adar	1	"	Feb.	10

The year 5669 is an ordinary perfect year of 355 days, and the year 5670 an embolismic imperfect year of 383 days.

Greek Church and Russian Calendar, 1909.

A. D. 1909. A. M. 8018.

New Style.		Holy Days.	Old Style.		New Style.		Holy Days.	Old Style.	
Jan.	14	Circumcision	Jan.	1	Aug.	14	First Day of Fast of Theotokos	Aug.	1
"	19	Theophany (Epiphany)	"	6	"	19	Transfiguration	"	6
Feb.	15	Hypapante (Purification)	Feb.	2	"	28	Repose of Theotokos	"	15
"	21	Carnival Sunday	"	8	Sept.	12	St. Alexander Nevsky*	"	30
"	24	Ash Wednesday	"	11	"	21	Nativity of Theotokos	Sept.	8
April	4	Palm Sunday	Mar.	22	"	27	Exaltation of the Cross	"	14
"	7	Annunciation	"	25	Oct.	14	Patronage of Theotokos	Oct.	1
"	9	Great Friday	"	27	Nov.	28	First Day of Fast of Nativity	Nov.	15
"	11	Holy Pasch (Easter)	"	29	Dec.	4	Entrance of Theotokos	"	21
May	20	Ascension	May	7	"	22	Conception of Theotokos	Dec.	9
"	27	Coronation of Emperor*	"	14	1910.				
"	30	Pentecost	"	17	Jan.	7	Nativity (Christmas)	"	25
"	31	Holy Ghost	"	18				1910.	
July	12	Peter and Paul (Chief Apostles)	June	29	"	14	Circumcision	Jan.	1

*Peculiar to Russia.

Mohammedan Calendar, 1909.

Year.	Names of Months.	Month Begins.	Year.	Names of Months.	Month Begins.
1327	Muharram (New Year)	Jan. 23, 1909	1327	Ramadan (Month of Abstinence)	Sept. 16, 1909
"	Saphar	Feb. 22, "	"	Shawall	Oct. 16, "
"	Rabia I	Mar 23, "	"	Dulkaada	Nov. 14, "
"	Rabia II	April 22, "	"	Dulheggia	Dec. 14, "
"	Jomadi I	May 21, "	1328	Muharram (New Year)	Jan. 13, 1910
"	Jomadi II	June 20, "	"	Saphar	Feb. 12, "
"	Rajab	July 19, "			
"	Shabaan	Aug. 18, "			

Day of the Month.	Day of the Week.	Calendar for Boston, New England, N. Y. State, Michigan, Wisconsin, N. and S. Dakota, Washington, and Oregon.			Calendar for New York City, Connecticut, Pennsylvania, Ohio, Indiana, Illinois, Iowa, Nebraska, Wyoming, and Northern California.			Calendar for Washington, Virginia, Kentucky, Missouri, Kansas, Colorado, Utah, Nevada, and Central California.			Calendar for Charleston, Georgia, Alabama, Louisiana, Arkansas, Texas, New Mexico, Arizona, and Southern California.		
		Sun Rises.	Sun Sets.	Moon R. & S.	Sun Rises.	Sun Sets.	Moon R. & S.	Sun Rises.	Sun Sets.	Moon R. & S.	Sun Rises.	Sun Sets.	Moon R. & S.
		H. M.	H. M.	H. M.	H. M.	H. M.	H. M.	H. M.	H. M.	H. M.	H. M.	H. M.	H. M.
1	Fr	7 30	4.37	2 17	7 24	4 43	2 15	7 19	4 48	2 13	7 4	5 6	2 6
2	Sa	7 30	4 38	3 26	7 24	4 44	3 23	7 19	4 49	3 20	7 4	5 6	3 9
3	**S**	7 30	4 39	4 35	7 24	4 45	4 31	7 19	4 50	4 26	7 4	5 6	4 13
4	M	7 30	4 40	5 42	7 24	4 46	5 37	7 19	4 51	5 31	7 4	5 6	5 15
5	Tu	7 30	4 41	6 43	7 24	4 47	6 38	7 19	4 52	6 32	7 4	5 7	6 14
6	W	7 30	4 42	rises.	7 24	4 48	rises.	7 19	4 53	rises.	7 4	5 7	rises.
7	Th	7 30	4 43	5 48	7 24	4 49	5 54	7 19	4 54	5 59	7 4	5 8	6 15
8	Fr	7 30	4 44	6 48	7 24	4 50	6 54	7 19	4 55	6 58	7 4	5 9	7 12
9	Sa	7 29	4 45	7 50	7 24	4 51	7 53	7 19	4 56	7 57	7 4	5 10	8 9
10	**S**	7 29	4 46	8 51	7 24	4 52	8 53	7 19	4 57	8 56	7 4	5 11	9 4
11	M	7 29	4 47	9 50	7 23	4 53	9 52	7 19	4 58	9 54	7 4	5 12	9 59
12	Tu	7 29	4 48	10 50	7 23	4 54	10 50	7 19	4 59	10 51	7 4	5 12	10 53
13	W	7 29	4 49	11 50	7 23	4 55	11 49	7 18	5 0	11 49	7 4	5 13	11 47
14	Th	7 28	4 50	A. M.	7 23	4 56	A. M.	7 18	5 1	A. M.	7 3	5 14	A. M.
15	Fr	7 28	4 51	12 51	7 22	4 57	12 49	7 18	5 2	12 48	7 3	5 15	12 42
16	Sa	7 27	4 53	1 54	7 22	4 58	1 51	7 17	5 3	1 49	7 3	5 16	1 40
17	**S**	7 27	4 54	3 0	7 21	4 59	2 56	7 17	5 4	2 52	7 3	5 17	2 40
18	M	7 26	4 55	4 9	7 21	5 0	4 4	7 16	5 5	3 59	7 2	5 18	3 43
19	Tu	7 26	4 56	5 17	7 20	5 1	5 11	7 16	5 6	5 6	7 2	5 19	4 48
20	W	7 25	4 58	6 23	7 19	5 2	6 17	7 15	5 7	6 11	7 2	5 20	5 52
21	Th	7 24	4 59	sets.	7 18	5 3	sets.	7 14	5 8	sets.	7 1	5 21	sets.
22	Fr	7 23	5 0	5 50	7 18	5 4	5 55	7 14	5 9	6 0	7 1	5 22	6 15
23	Sa	7 22	5 1	7 9	7 17	5 6	7 12	7 13	5 10	7 16	7 0	5 23	7 27
24	**S**	7 21	5 2	8 27	7 16	5 7	8 29	7 12	5 11	8 32	7 0	5 24	8 38
25	M	7 21	5 3	9 43	7 15	5 9	9 44	7 12	5 13	9 45	7 0	5 25	9 47
26	Tu	7 20	5 5	10 56	7 14	5 10	10 56	7 11	5 14	10 56	6 59	5 26	10 54
27	W	7 20	5 6	A. M.	7 14	5 11	A. M.	7 10	5 15	A. M.	6 59	5 27	11 59
28	Th	7 19	5 7	12 7	7 13	5 12	12 7	7 10	5 16	12 5	6 58	5 28	A. M.
29	Fr	7 18	5 9	1 19	7 13	5 13	1 15	7 9	5 17	1 12	6 58	5 29	1 3
30	Sa	7 17	5 10	2 28	7 12	5 15	2 24	7 8	5 19	2 19	6 58	5 30	2 7
31	**S**	7 16	5 11	3 34	7 12	5 16	3 29	7 8	5 20	3 24	6 57	5 31	3 8

SUN ON MERIDIAN.

Day of Month.	H. M. S.	Day of Month.	H. M. S.	Day of Month.	H. M. S.	Day of Month.	H. M. S.	Day of Month.	H. M. S.
1	12 3 40	8	12 6 49	14	12 9 11	20	12 11 10	26	12 12 43
2	12 4 8	9	12 7 14	15	12 9 32	21	12 11 28	27	12 12 55
3	12 4 36	10	12 7 38	16	12 9 53	22	12 11 44	28	12 13 7
4	12 5 3	11	12 8 2	17	12 10 14	23	12 12 0	29	12 13 18
5	12 5 30	12	12 8 26	18	12 10 33	24	12 12 15	30	12 13 28
6	12 5 57	13	12 8 49	19	12 10 52	25	12 12 29	31	12 13 37
7	12 6 23								

TWILIGHT.

Places.	Jan.	Begins, A. M.	Ends, P. M.	Jan.	Begins, A. M.	Ends, P. M.	Jan.	Begins, A. M.	Ends, P. M.
		H. M.	H. M.		H. M.	H. M.		H. M.	H. M.
Boston	1	5 48	6 19	11	5 48	6 28	21	5 46	6 38
New York..	1	5 46	6 21	11	5 46	6 30	21	5 44	6 39
Wash'ton.	1	5 43	6 24	11	5 44	6 32	21	5 42	6 41
Charleston..	1	5 35	6 23	11	5 36	6 40	21	5 30	6 57

2d Month. FEBRUARY, 1909. 28 Days.

Day of the Month.	Day of the Week.	Calendar for Boston, New England, N. Y. State, Michigan, Wisconsin, N. and S. Dakota, Washington, and Oregon.			Calendar for New York City, Connecticut, Pennsylvania, Ohio, Indiana, Illinois, Iowa, Nebraska, Wyoming, and Northern California.			Calendar for Washington, Virginia, Kentucky, Missouri, Kansas, Colorado, Utah, Nevada, and Central California.			Calendar for Charleston, Georgia, Alabama, Louisiana, Arkansas, Texas, New Mexico, Arizona, and Southern California.		
		Sun Rises.	Sun Sets.	Moon R. & S.	Sun Rises.	Sun Sets.	Moon R. & S.	Sun Rises.	Sun Sets.	Moon R. & S.	Sun Rises.	Sun Sets.	Moon R. & S.
		H. M.	H. M.	H. M.	H. M.	H. M.	H. M.	H. M.	H. M.	H. M.	H. M.	H. M.	H. M.
1	M	7 15	5 13	4 37	7 11	5 17	4 31	7 7	5 21	4 25	6 57	5 32	4 8
2	Tu	7 14	5 14	5 33	7 10	5 18	5 27	7 6	5 22	5 21	6 56	5 32	5 3
3	W	7 13	5 15	6 20	7 9	5 19	6 14	7 5	5 23	6 9	6 55	5 33	5 51
4	Th	7 11	5 16	7 4	7 7	5 20	6 59	7 4	5 24	6 54	6 54	5 34	6 38
5	Fr	7 10	5 18	rises.	7 6	5 22	rises.	7 3	5 25	rises.	6 53	5 35	rises.
6	Sa	7 9	5 19	6 40	7 5	5 23	6 43	7 2	5 26	6 46	6 52	5 36	6 56
7	**S**	7 8	5 20	7 40	7 4	5 24	7 43	7 1	5 27	7 46	6 51	5 37	7 51
8	M	7 7	5 22	8 41	7 3	5 25	8 42	7 0	5 28	8 43	6 50	5 38	8 46
9	Tu	7 6	5 23	9 40	7 2	5 26	9 40	6 59	5 29	9 40	6 49	5 39	9 39
10	W	7 5	5 25	10 40	7 1	5 28	10 39	6 58	5 31	10 38	6 48	5 40	10 34
11	Th	7 4	5 26	11 42	7 0	5 29	11 39	6 57	5 32	11 36	6 47	5 41	11 29
12	Fr	7 2	5 27	A. M.	6 59	5 30	A. M.	6 56	5 33	A. M.	6 46	5 42	A. M.
13	Sa	7 1	5 29	12 45	6 58	5 31	12 41	6 55	5 34	12 38	6 45	5 43	12 27
14	**S**	7 0	5 30	1 50	6 57	5 33	1 46	6 54	5 35	1 41	6 44	5 44	1 27
15	M	6 59	5 31	2 57	6 55	5 34	2 52	6 53	5 36	2 46	6 44	5 45	2 29
16	Tu	6 57	5 32	4 3	6 53	5 36	3 59	6 52	5 38	3 50	6 43	5 46	3 32
17	W	6 55	5 33	5 5	6 52	5 37	4 58	6 50	5 39	4 52	6 42	5 47	4 33
18	Th	6 54	5 35	5 59	6 50	5 38	5 53	6 49	5 40	5 47	6 41	5 48	5 30
19	Fr	6 52	5 37	6 45	6 49	5 40	6 41	6 47	5 41	6 36	6 40	5 49	6 21
20	Sa	6 50	5 39	sets.	6 48	5 41	sets.	6 46	5 42	sets.	6 39	5 50	sets.
21	**S**	6 48	5 40	7 19	6 46	5 42	7 19	6 44	5 43	7 21	6 38	5 51	7 26
22	M	6 47	5 42	8 36	6 45	5 43	8 37	6 43	5 45	8 37	6 37	5 51	8 37
23	Tu	6 45	5 43	9 52	6 43	5 45	9 51	6 41	5 46	9 50	6 36	5 52	9 46
24	W	6 44	5 45	11 08	6 42	5 47	11 5	6 40	5 47	11 2	6 35	5 53	10 54
25	Th	6 43	5 46	A. M.	6 40	5 48	A. M.	6 38	5 48	A. M.	6 34	5 54	11 58
26	Fr	6 41	5 47	12 18	6 38	5 49	12 14	6 37	5 49	12 10	6 33	5 55	A. M.
27	Sa	6 40	5 48	1 27	6 37	5 50	1 22	6 36	5 50	1 17	6 31	5 56	1 2
28	**S**	6 38	5 49	2 32	6 36	5 51	2 26	6 35	5 51	2 20	6 30	5 57	2 3

SUN ON MERIDIAN.

Day of Month.	H. M. S.	Day of Month.	H. M. S.	Day of Month.	H. M. S.	Day of Month.	H. M. S.	Day of Month.	H. M. S.
1	12 13 46	7	12 14 19	13	12 14 24	19	12 14 2	25	12 13 16
2	12 13 53	8	12 14 22	14	12 14 22	20	12 13 56	26	12 13 7
3	12 14 0	9	12 14 24	15	12 14 19	21	12 13 50	27	12 12 56
4	12 14 6	10	12 14 25	16	12 14 16	22	12 13 42	28	12 12 45
5	12 14 11	11	12 14 25	17	12 14 12	23	12 13 34		
6	12 14 16	12	12 14 25	18	12 14 6	24	12 13 26		

TWILIGHT.

Places.	Feb.	Begins, A. M.	Ends, P. M.	Feb.	Begins, A. M.	Ends, P. M.	Feb.	Begins, A. M.	Ends, P. M.
		H. M.	H. M.		H. M.	H. M.		H. M.	H. M.
Boston......	1	5 37	6 50	11	5 27	7 1	21	5 14	7 13
New York.	1	5 36	6 51	11	5 27	7 1	21	5 15	7 13
Wash'ton.	1	5 35	6 52	11	5 26	7 2	21	5 15	7 13
Charleston	1	5 30	6 57	11	5 24	7 5	21	5 15	7 13

MARCH, 1909.

Day of the Month.	Day of the Week.	Calendar for BOSTON, New England, N. Y. State, Michigan, Wisconsin, N. and S. Dakota, Washington, and Oregon.			Calendar for NEW YORK CITY, Connecticut, Pennsylvania, Ohio, Indiana, Illinois, Iowa, Nebraska, Wyoming, and Northern California.			Calendar for WASHINGTON, Virginia, Kentucky, Missouri, Kansas, Colorado, Utah, Nevada, and Central California.			Calendar for CHARLESTON, Georgia, Alabama, Louisiana, Arkansas, Texas, New Mexico, Arizona, and Southern California.		
		Sun Rises.	Sun Sets.	Moon R. & S.	Sun Rises.	Sun Sets.	Moon R. & S.	Sun Rises.	Sun Sets.	Moon R. & S.	Sun Rises.	Sun Sets.	Moon R. & S.
		H. M.	H. M.	H. M.	H. M.	H. M.	H. M.	H. M.	H. M.	H. M.	H. M.	H. M.	H. M.
1	M	6 37	5 50	3 30	6 35	5 52	3 24	6 34	5 52	3 18	6 29	5 57	3 0
2	Tu	6 36	5 50	4 21	6 34	5 52	4 16	6 33	5 53	4 9	6 28	5 58	3 51
3	W	6 34	5 51	5 5	6 32	5 53	4 59	6 31	5 54	4 54	6 27	5 58	4 37
4	Th	6 33	5 52	5 41	6 31	5 54	5 37	6 30	5 55	5 32	6 26	5 59	5 17
5	Fr	6 31	5 53	6 13	6 29	5 55	6 9	6 28	5 56	6 5	6 25	6 0	5 53
6	Sa	6 29	5 55	rises.	6 28	5 56	rises.	6 27	5 57	rises.	6 24	6 1	rises.
7	**S**	6 28	5 56	6 34	6 27	5 57	6 35	6 26	5 58	6 36	6 23	6 1	6 40
8	M	6 26	5 57	7 33	6 25	5 59	7 33	6 24	5 59	7 34	6 22	6 2	7 34
9	Tu	6 25	5 59	8 33	6 24	6 0	8 32	6 23	6 0	8 31	6 21	6 3	8 28
10	W	6 23	6 0	9 34	6 22	6 1	9 32	6 21	6 1	9 30	6 20	6 3	9 23
11	Th	6 21	6 1	10 36	6 20	6 2	10 33	6 19	6 2	10 30	6 19	6 4	10 21
12	Fr	6 19	6 2	11 40	6 18	6 3	11 35	6 18	6 3	11 31	6 17	6 5	11 18
13	Sa	6 17	6 3	A. M.	6 16	6 4	A. M.	6 16	6 4	A. M.	6 16	6 6	A. M.
14	**S**	6 16	6 4	12 45	6 15	6 5	12 40	6 15	6 5	12 35	6 14	6 6	12 18
15	M	6 14	6 5	1 50	6 13	6 6	1 44	6 13	6 6	1 38	6 13	6 7	1 20
16	Tu	6 12	6 7	2 51	6 12	6 7	2 45	6 12	6 7	2 38	6 11	6 8	2 19
17	W	6 10	6 8	3 47	6 10	6 8	3 41	6 10	6 8	3 34	6 10	6 9	3 16
18	Th	6 9	6 9	4 35	6 9	6 9	4 29	6 9	6 9	4 24	6 9	6 10	4 8
19	Fr	6 7	6 10	5 16	6 7	6 10	5 12	6 7	6 10	5 8	6 8	6 11	4 55
20	Sa	6 5	6 11	5 51	6 5	6 11	5 49	6 5	6 11	5 46	6 6	6 11	5 37
21	**S**	6 3	6 12	sets.	6 3	6 12	sets.	6 3	6 12	sets.	6 5	6 12	sets.
22	M	6 2	6 14	7 25	6 2	6 13	7 24	6 2	6 13	7 24	6 3	6 13	7 22
23	Tu	6 0	6 15	8 42	6 1	6 14	8 40	6 1	6 14	8 38	6 2	6 14	8 32
24	W	5 59	6 16	9 59	6 0	6 15	9 55	6 0	6 15	9 52	6 1	6 15	9 41
25	Th	5 57	6 17	11 12	5 58	6 16	11 7	5 58	6 16	11 3	5 59	6 15	10 49
26	Fr	5 55	6 18	A. M.	5 56	6 17	A. M.	5 56	6 17	A. M.	5 58	6 16	11 53
27	Sa	5 53	6 20	12 21	5 54	6 18	12 16	5 54	6 18	12 10	5 56	6 17	A. M.
28	**S**	5 52	6 21	1 24	5 53	6 19	1 18	5 53	6 19	1 12	5 55	6 17	12 53
29	M	5 50	6 22	2 19	5 52	6 20	2 13	5 52	6 20	2 6	5 54	6 18	1 48
30	Tu	5 48	6 23	3 5	5 50	6 21	3 0	5 51	6 20	2 54	5 53	6 19	2 36
31	W	5 46	6 24	3 44	5 48	6 22	3 39	5 49	6 21	3 34	5 52	6 19	3 18

SUN ON MERIDIAN.

Day of Month.	H. M. S.	Day of Month.	H. M. S.	Day of Month.	H. M. S.	Day of Month.	H. M. S.	Day of Month.	H. M. S.
1	12 12 34	8	12 11 0	14	12 9 24	20	12 7 40	26	12 5 51
2	12 12 22	9	12 10 45	15	12 9 7	21	12 7 22	27	12 5 33
3	12 12 9	10	12 10 29	16	12 8 50	22	12 7 4	28	12 5 14
4	12 11 56	11	12 10 13	17	12 8 33	23	12 6 46	29	12 4 56
5	12 11 43	12	12 9 57	18	12 8 15	24	12 6 28	30	12 4 38
6	12 11 29	13	12 9 41	19	12 7 58	25	12 6 9	31	12 4 19
7	12 11 14								

TWILIGHT.

Places.	Mar.	Begins, A. M.	Ends, P. M.	Mar.	Begins, A. M.	Ends, P. M.	Mar.	Begins, A. M.	Ends, P. M.
		H. M.	H. M.		H. M.	H. M.		H. M.	H. M.
Boston......	1	5 2	7 23	11	4 45	7 35	21	4 27	7 47
New York	1	5 3	7 22	11	4 47	7 33	21	4 30	7 45
Wash'ton.	1	5 4	7 21	11	4 49	7 31	21	4 33	7 42
Charleston	1	5 6	7 19	11	4 53	7 27	21	4 40	7 35

Day of the Month.	Day of the Week.	Calendar for BOSTON, New England, N. Y. State, Michigan, Wisconsin, N. and S. Dakota, Washington, and Oregon.			Calendar for NEW YORK CITY, Connecticut, Pennsylvania, Ohio, Indiana, Illinois, Iowa, Nebraska, Wyoming, and Northern California.			Calendar for WASHINGTON, Virginia, Kentucky, Missouri, Kansas, Colorado, Utah, Nevada, and Central California.			Calendar for CHARLESTON, Georgia, Alabama, Louisiana, Arkansas, Texas, New Mexico, Arizona, and Southern California.		
		SUN RISES.	SUN SETS.	MOON R. & S.	SUN RISES.	SUN SETS.	MOON R. & S.	SUN RISES.	SUN SETS.	MOON R. & S.	SUN RISES.	SUN SETS.	MOON R. & S.
		H. M.	H. M.	H. M.	H. M.	H. M.	H. M.	H. M.	H. M.	H. M.	H. M.	H. M.	H. M.
1	Th	5 44	6 25	4 14	5 46	6 23	4 12	5 47	6 22	4 8	5 50	6 19	3 55
2	Fr	5 43	6 26	4 44	5 45	6 24	4 41	5 46	6 23	4 38	5 49	6 20	4 28
3	Sa	5 42	6 28	5 9	5 44	6 26	5 7	5 45	6 24	5 4	5 48	6 21	4 58
4	**S**	5 40	6 29	5 31	5 42	6 27	5 30	5 43	6 25	5 29	5 46	6 22	5 26
5	M	5 38	6 30	rises.	5 40	6 28	rises.	5 41	6 26	rises.	5 45	6 23	rises.
6	Tu	5 36	6 31	7 26	5 38	6 29	7 25	5 40	6 27	7 23	5 44	6 23	7 18
7	W	5 34	6 32	8 29	5 36	6 30	8 26	5 38	6 28	8 23	5 42	6 24	8 14
8	Th	5 32	6 33	9 33	5 34	6 31	9 29	5 36	6 29	9 25	5 41	6 25	9 13
9	Fr	5 31	6 34	10 38	5 33	6 32	10 33	5 35	6 30	10 28	5 39	6 25	10 13
10	Sa	5 29	6 35	11 43	5 31	6 33	11 38	5 33	6 31	11 31	5 38	6 26	11 13
11	**S**	5 27	6 36	A. M.	5 29	6 34	A. M.	5 31	6 32	A. M.	5 37	6 27	A. M.
12	M	5 26	6 37	12 45	5 28	6 35	12 38	5 30	6 33	12 32	5 35	6 27	12 12
13	Tu	5 24	6 38	1 41	5 26	6 36	1 35	5 28	6 34	1 28	5 34	6 28	1 9
14	W	5 23	6 40	2 30	5 25	6 37	2 25	5 27	6 35	2 19	5 33	6 29	2 1
15	Th	5 21	6 41	3 13	5 24	6 38	3 8	5 26	6 36	3 3	5 32	6 29	2 48
16	Fr	5 19	6 42	3 48	5 22	6 39	3 45	5 24	6 37	3 41	5 31	6 30	3 30
17	Sa	5 18	6 43	4 20	5 21	6 40	4 17	5 23	6 38	4 15	5 30	6 30	4 8
18	**S**	5 16	6 44	4 49	5 19	6 41	4 48	5 22	6 39	4 47	5 29	6 31	4 44
19	M	5 14	6 45	sets.	5 17	6 42	sets.	5 20	6 40	sets.	5 28	6 32	sets.
20	Tu	5 13	6 47	7 31	5 16	6 43	7 28	5 19	6 41	7 25	5 27	6 32	7 17
21	W	5 11	6 48	8 47	5 14	6 45	8 43	5 17	6 42	8 40	5 25	6 33	8 27
22	Th	5 10	6 49	10 2	5 13	6 46	9 57	5 16	6 43	9 51	5 24	6 34	9 36
23	Fr	5 8	6 50	11 10	5 11	6 47	11 4	5 14	6 44	10 58	5 23	6 35	10 40
24	Sa	5 6	6 51	A. M.	5 10	6 48	A. M.	5 13	6 45	11 58	5 21	6 36	11 39
25	**S**	5 5	6 52	12 10	5 9	6 49	12 4	5 12	6 46	A. M.	5 20	6 37	A. M.
26	M	5 3	6 53	1 2	5 7	6 50	12 56	5 10	6 47	12 50	5 19	6 37	12 31
27	Tu	5 2	6 54	1 44	5 6	6 51	1 39	5 9	6 48	1 33	5 18	6 38	1 17
28	W	5 1	6 55	2 20	5 5	6 52	2 14	5 8	6 49	2 10	5 17	6 38	1 56
29	Th	4 59	6 56	2 48	5 3	6 53	2 45	5 6	6 50	2 41	5 16	6 39	2 30
30	Fr	4 58	6 58	3 13	5 2	6 54	3 11	5 5	6 50	3 8	5 15	6 39	3 1

SUN ON MERIDIAN.

DAY OF MONTH.	H. M. S.	DAY OF MONTH.	H. M. S.	DAY OF MONTH.	H. M. S.	DAY OF MONTH.	H. M. S.	DAY OF MONTH.	H. M. S.
1	12 4 1	7	12 2 15	13	12 0 36	19	11 59 9	25	11 57 58
2	12 3 43	8	12 1 57	14	12 0 21	20	11 58 56	26	11 57 47
3	12 3 25	9	12 1 41	15	12 0 6	21	11 58 44	27	11 57 37
4	12 3 7	10	12 1 24	16	11 59 51	22	11 58 32	28	11 57 28
5	12 2 49	11	12 1 8	17	11 59 37	23	11 58 20	29	11 57 19
6	12 2 32	12	12 0 52	18	11 59 23	24	11 58 9	30	11 57 10

TWILIGHT.

PLACES.	Apr.	Begins, A. M.	Ends, P. M.	Apr.	Begins, A. M.	Ends, P. M.	Apr.	Begins, A. M.	Ends, P. M.
		H. M.	H. M.		H. M.	H. M.		H. M.	H. M.
Boston......	1	4 6	8 2	11	3 36	8 16	21	3 25	8 32
New York.	1	4 10	7 58	11	3 50	8 12	21	3 31	8 26
Wash'ton.	1	4 14	7 54	11	3 56	8 7	21	3 37	8 20
Charleston	1	4 24	7 43	11	4 10	7 52	21	3 55	8 2

5TH MONTH. **MAY, 1909.** 31 DAYS.

Day of the Month.	Day of the Week.	Calendar for BOSTON, New England, N. Y. State, Michigan, Wisconsin, N. and S. Dakota, Washington, and Oregon. Sun Rises. H. M.	Sun Sets. H. M.	Moon R. & S. H. M.	Calendar for NEW YORK CITY, Connecticut, Pennsylvania, Ohio, Indiana, Illinois, Iowa, Nebraska, Wyoming, and Northern California. Sun Rises. H. M.	Sun Sets. H. M.	Moon R. & S. H. M.	Calendar for WASHINGTON, Virginia, Kentucky, Missouri, Kansas, Colorado, Utah, Nevada, and Central California. Sun Rises. H. M.	Sun Sets. H. M.	Moon R. & S. H. M.	Calendar for CHARLESTON, Georgia, Alabama, Louisiana, Arkansas, Texas, New Mexico, Arizona, and Southern California. Sun Rises. H. M.	Sun Sets. H. M.	Moon R. & S. H. M.
1	Sa	4 56	6 59	3 36	5 0	6 5	3 35	5 3	6 51	3 34	5 14	6 40	3 29
2	**S**	4 55	7 0	3 57	4 59	6 5	3 47	5 2	6 52	3 57	5 13	6 41	3 57
3	M	4 53	7 1	4 19	4 58	6 5	4 0	5 1	6 53	4 21	5 12	6 42	4 23
4	Tu	4 52	7 2	4 41	4 57	6 5	4 3	5 0	6 54	4 44	5 11	6 43	4 50
5	W	4 50	7 3	rises.	4 56	6 5	rises.	4 59	6 55	rises.	5 10	6 44	rises.
6	Th	4 49	7 4	8 29	4 55	7	8 34	4 57	6 56	8 20	5 10	6 45	8 5
7	Fr	4 48	7 5	9 36	4 54	7	9 0	4 56	6 57	9 25	5 9	6 45	9 7
8	Sa	4 47	7 6	10 40	4 53	7	10 4	4 54	6 58	10 27	5 8	6 46	10 8
9	**S**	4 46	7 7	11 38	4 52	7	11 2	4 53	6 59	11 25	5 7	6 47	11 6
10	M	4 45	7 8	A. M.	4 51	7	A. M.	4 52	7 0	A. M.	5 6	6 47	A. M.
11	Tu	4 44	7 9	12 31	4 50	7	12 24	4 51	7 1	12 18	5 5	6 48	12 0
12	W	4 43	7 10	1 13	4 49	7	1 8	4 50	7 2	1 3	5 5	6 49	12 47
13	Th	4 42	7 11	1 50	4 48	7	1 46	4 49	7 3	1 42	5 4	6 49	1 30
14	Fr	4 41	7 12	2 21	4 47	7	2 49	4 48	7 4	2 16	5 3	6 50	2 7
15	Sa	4 40	7 13	2 50	4 46	7 1	2 8	4 47	7 5	2 47	5 2	6 51	2 32
16	**S**	4 39	7 14	3 17	4 45	7 2	3 7	4 46	7 6	3 17	5 2	6 51	3 16
17	M	4 38	7 15	3 44	4 44	7	3 5	4 46	7 7	3 46	5 1	6 52	3 51
18	Tu	4 37	7 16	4 13	4 43	7	4 6	4 45	7 7	4 18	5 1	6 53	4 27
19	W	4 36	7 17	sets.	4 42	7	sets.	4 44	7 8	sets.	5 0	6 53	sets.
20	Th	4 35	7 18	8 49	4 42	7	8 53	4 44	7 9	8 38	5 0	6 54	8 21
21	Fr	4 34	7 19	9 56	4 41	7	9 0	4 43	7 10	9 4	4 59	6 55	9 25
22	Sa	4 33	7 20	10 52	4 40	7	10 6	4 43	7 10	10 4	4 58	6 55	10 21
23	**S**	4 32	7 21	11 40	4 39	7	11 4	4 42	7 1	11 2	4 58	6 56	11 10
24	M	4 32	7 22	A. M.	4 39	7	A. M.	4 42	7 2	A. M.	4 57	6 57	11 53
25	Tu	4 31	7 23	12 18	4 35	7	12 1	4 41	7 3	2 8	4 57	6 57	A. M.
26	W	4 30	7 24	12 54	4 3	7	12 4	4 40	7 14	12 45	4 56	6 58	12 32
27	Th	4 30	7 25	1 17	4 3	7	1 1	4 40	7 15	1 11	4 56	6 59	1 2
28	Fr	4 29	7 26	1 41	4 3	7	1 3	4 39	7 16	1 38	4 55	6 59	1 31
29	Sa	4 29	7 27	2 2	4 35	7	2	4 38	7 16	2 1	4 55	7 0	1 58
30	**S**	4 28	7 28	2 23	4 3	7	2 2	4 38	7 17	2 24	4 54	7 0	2 25
31	M	4 27	7 28	2 45	4 33	7	2 4	4 37	7 18	2 48	4 54	7 1	2 52

SUN ON MERIDIAN.

Day of Month.	H. M. S.	Day of Month.	H. M. S.	Day of Month.	H. M. S.	Day of Month.	H. M. S.	Day of Month.	H. M. S.
1	11 57 2	8	11 56 22	14	11 56 10	20	11 56 19	26	11 56 48
2	11 56 55	9	11 56 19	15	11 56 10	21	11 56 23	27	11 56 54
3	11 56 48	10	11 56 16	16	11 56 11	22	11 56 27	28	11 57 1
4	11 56 42	11	11 56 14	17	11 56 12	23	11 56 31	29	11 57 8
5	11 56 36	12	11 56 12	18	11 56 14	24	11 56 36	30	11 57 16
6	11 56 31	13	11 56 11	19	11 56 16	25	11 56 42	31	11 57 24
7	11 56 26								

TWILIGHT.

Places.	May.	Begins, A. M.	Ends, P. M.	May.	Begins, A. M.	Ends, P. M.	May.	Begins, A. M.	Ends, P. M.
		M.	H. M.		H. M.	H. M.		H. M.	H. M.
Boston. ...	1	6	8 48	11	2 47	9 6	21	2 31	9 22
New York.	1	13	8 40	11	2 36	8 56	21	2 42	9 11
Wash'ton.	1	21	8 33	11	3 5	8 47	21	2 52	9 0
Charleston	1	3 42	8 21	11	3 30	8 22	21	3 21	8 32

Day of the Month.	Day of the Week.	Calendar for BOSTON, New England, N. Y. State, Michigan, Wisconsin, N. and S. Dakota, Washington, and Oregon.			Calendar for NEW YORK CITY, Connecticut, Pennsylvania, Ohio, Indiana, Illinois, Iowa, Nebraska, Wyoming, and Northern California.			Calendar for WASHINGTON, Virginia, Kentucky, Missouri, Kansas, Colorado, Utah, Nevada, and Central California.			Calendar for CHARLESTON, Georgia, Alabama, Louisiana, Arkansas, Texas, New Mexico, Arizona, and Southern California.		
		SUN RISES.	SUN SETS.	MOON R. & S.	SUN RISES.	SUN SETS.	MOON R. & S.	SUN RISES.	SUN SETS.	MOON R. & S.	SUN RISES.	SUN SETS.	MOON R. & S.
		H. M.	H. M.	H. M.	H. M.	H. M.	H. M.	H. M.	H. M.	H. M.	H. M.	H. M.	H. M.
1	Tu	4 26	7 29	3 8	4 32	7 24	3 11	4 37	7 18	3 13	4 54	7 1	3 21
2	W	4 26	7 30	3 35	4 32	7 24	3 39	4 37	7 19	3 43	4 54	7 2	3 54
3	Th	4 25	7 31	4 5	4 31	7 25	4 10	4 37	7 19	4 15	4 53	7 2	4 31
4	Fr	4 25	7 32	rises.	4 31	7 26	rises.	4 36	7 20	rises.	4 53	7 3	rises.
5	Sa	4 24	7 32	9 32	4 30	7 26	9 26	4 36	7 20	9 19	4 53	7 3	9 0
6	**S**	4 24	7 33	10 27	4 30	7 27	10 21	4 36	7 21	10 15	4 53	7 4	9 56
7	M	4 23	7 33	11 13	4 29	7 27	11 8	4 35	7 21	11 2	4 52	7 4	10 46
8	Tu	4 23	7 34	11 53	4 29	7 28	11 48	4 35	7 22	11 44	4 52	7 5	11 30
9	W	4 23	7 35	A. M.	4 29	7 28	A. M.	4 35	7 23	A. M.	4 52	7 5	A. M.
10	Th	4 22	7 36	12 25	4 28	7 29	12 22	4 34	7 23	12 19	4 52	7 6	12 9
11	Fr	4 22	7 36	12 54	4 28	7 30	12 52	4 34	7 24	12 50	4 52	7 6	12 44
12	Sa	4 22	7 37	1 20	4 28	7 30	1 20	4 34	7 24	1 19	4 52	7 7	1 18
13	**S**	4 22	7 37	1 46	4 28	7 31	1 47	4 34	7 25	1 48	4 52	7 7	1 51
14	M	4 22	7 38	2 13	4 28	7 31	2 15	4 34	7 25	2 17	4 52	7 8	2 24
15	Tu	4 22	7 38	2 34	4 28	7 32	2 47	4 34	7 26	2 51	4 52	7 8	3 1
16	W	4 22	7 38	3 18	4 28	7 32	3 23	4 34	7 26	3 28	4 52	7 8	3 42
17	Th	4 22	7 39	sets.	4 28	7 32	sets.	4 34	7 26	sets.	4 52	7 9	sets.
18	Fr	4 22	7 39	8 40	4 28	7 33	8 33	4 34	7 27	8 27	4 52	7 9	8 8
19	Sa	4 22	7 39	9 32	4 28	7 33	9 26	4 34	7 27	9 19	4 52	7 9	9 1
20	**S**	4 22	7 39	10 14	4 28	7 33	10 9	4 34	7 27	10 3	4 52	7 9	9 47
21	M	4 22	7 39	10 49	4 28	7 33	10 44	4 34	7 27	10 40	4 52	7 10	10 26
22	Tu	4 23	7 39	11 18	4 29	7 33	11 15	4 35	7 27	11 11	4 52	7 10	11 1
23	W	4 23	7 40	11 43	4 29	7 34	11 41	4 35	7 28	11 38	4 53	7 10	11 31
24	Th	4 23	7 40	A. M.	4 29	7 34	A. M.	4 35	7 28	A. M.	4 53	7 10	A. M.
25	Fr	4 23	7 40	12 7	4 29	7 34	12 5	4 35	7 28	12 4	4 53	7 11	12 0
26	Sa	4 23	7 40	12 27	4 29	7 34	12 27	4 35	7 28	12 27	4 53	7 11	12 26
27	**S**	4 23	7 40	12 48	4 30	7 34	12 49	4 35	7 29	12 50	4 53	7 11	12 53
28	M	4 24	7 40	1 10	4 30	7 34	1 12	4 36	7 29	1 14	4 54	7 11	1 21
29	Tu	4 24	7 40	1 35	4 30	7 35	1 38	4 36	7 29	1 41	4 54	7 11	1 51
30	W	4 24	7 40	2 3	4 30	7 35	2 8	4 36	7 29	2 12	4 54	7 11	2 25

SUN ON MERIDIAN.

DAY OF MONTH.	H. M. S.	DAY OF MONTH.	H. M. S.	DAY OF MONTH.	H. M. S.	DAY OF MONTH.	H. M. S.	DAY OF MONTH.	H. M. S.
1	11 57 33	7	11 58 33	13	11 59 43	19	12 1 0	25	12 2 18
2	11 57 42	8	11 58 44	14	11 59 56	20	12 1 13	26	12 2 31
3	11 57 51	9	11 58 55	15	12 0 8	21	12 1 26	27	12 2 43
4	11 58 1	10	11 59 7	16	12 0 21	22	12 1 39	28	12 2 56
5	11 58 11	11	11 59 19	17	12 0 34	23	12 1 52	29	12 3 8
6	11 58 22	12	11 59 31	18	12 0 47	24	12 2 5	30	12 3 20

TWILIGHT.

PLACES.	June.	Begins, A. M.	Ends, P. M.	June.	Begins, A. M.	Ends, P. M.	June.	Begins, A. M.	Ends, P. M.
		H. M.	H. M.		H. M.	H. M.		H. M.	H. M.
Boston......	1	2 17	9 38	11	2 9	9 51	21	2 8	9 55
New York..	1	2 29	9 26	11	2 23	9 37	21	2 22	9 41
Wash'ton..	1	2 41	9 14	11	2 36	9 24	21	2 35	9 28
Charleston.	1	3 13	8 43	11	3 9	8 51	21	3 9	8 54

Day of the Month.	Day of the Week.	Calendar for BOSTON, New England, N. Y. State, Michigan, Wisconsin, N. and S. Dakota, Washington, and Oregon.			Calendar for NEW YORK CITY, Connecticut, Pennsylvania, Ohio, Indiana, Illinois, Iowa, Nebraska, Wyoming, and Northern California.			Calendar for WASHINGTON, Virginia, Kentucky, Missouri, Kansas, Colorado, Utah, Nevada, and Central California.			Calendar for CHARLESTON, Georgia, Alabama, Louisiana, Arkansas, Texas, New Mexico, Arizona, and Southern California.		
		SUN RISES.	SUN SETS.	MOON R. & S.	SUN RISES.	SUN SETS.	MOON R. & S.	SUN RISES.	SUN SETS.	MOON R. & S.	SUN RISES.	SUN SETS.	MOON R. & S.
		H. M.	H. M.	H. M.	H. M.	H. M.	H. M.	H. M.	H. M.	H. M.	H. M.	H. M.	H. M.
1	Th	4 25	7 40	2 38	4 3[illegible]	7 3[illegible]	2 43	4 3[illegible]	7 29	2 49	4 55	7 11	3 5
2	Fr	4 25	7 40	3 21	[illegible]	7 [illegible]	3 [illegible]7	[illegible]	7 29	3 33	4 55	7 11	3 52
3	Sa	4 26	7 40	rises.		7	ris[illegible]		7 29	rises.	4 55	7 11	rises.
4	S	4 27	7 40	9 10		7	9 4		7 29	8 58	4 56	7 11	8 41
5	M	4 27	7 39	9 52		7	9 47		7 28	9 42	4 56	7 11	9 27
6	Tu	4 28	7 39	10 27		7	10 24		7 28	10 20	4 57	7 11	10 9
7	W	4 29	7 39	10 57		7	10 55		7 28	10 53	4 57	7 11	10 46
8	Th	4 29	7 39	11 25		7	1 24		7 28	11 23	4 58	7 11	11 20
9	Fr	4 30	7 38	11 51		7	1 51		7 27	11 52	4 58	7 11	11 53
10	Sa	4 31	7 38	A. M.		7	A. M.		7 27	A. M.	4 59	7 10	A. M.
11	S	4 32	7 38	12 17		7	12 19		7 27	12 21	5 0	7 10	12 26
12	M	4 33	7 37	12 46		7	12 48		7 26	12 52	5 0	7 10	1 3
13	Tu	4 33	7 37	1 18		7	1 22		7 26	1 26	5 1	7 10	1 39
14	W	4 34	7 36	1 55		7	2 1		7 25	2 6	5 1	7 9	2 22
15	Th	4 35	7 36	2 40		7	2 46		7 25	2 52	5 2	7 9	3 10
16	Fr	4 36	7 35	3 32		7	3 38		7 24	3 45	5 3	7 9	4 4
17	Sa	4 37	7 34	sets.		7	sets.		7 24	sets.	5 3	7 8	sets.
18	S	4 37	7 34	8 48		7	8 43		7 23	8 38	5 4	7 8	8 23
19	M	4 38	7 33	9 19		7	9 15		7 23	9 11	5 4	7 7	8 59
20	Tu	4 39	7 32	9 45		7	9 42		7 22	9 40	5 5	7 7	9 31
21	W	4 40	7 32	10 9		7	10 7		7 21	10 5	5 5	7 6	10 0
22	Th	4 41	7 31	10 30		7	10 29		7 21	10 29	5 6	7 6	10 27
23	Fr	4 42	7 30	10 51		7	10 52		7 20	10 52	5 7	7 5	10 54
24	Sa	4 43	7 29	11 12		7	11 14		7 19	11 16	5 7	7 5	11 21
25	S	4 44	7 28	11 36		7	11 38		7 18	11 41	5 8	7 4	11 50
26	M	4 45	7 27	A. M.		7	A. M.		7 17	A. M.	5 9	7 3	A. M.
27	Tu	4 46	7 26	12 2		7	12 6		7 17	12 10	5 9	7 3	12 22
28	W	4 47	7 25	12 34		7	2 38		7 16	12 43	5 10	7 2	12 58
29	Th	4 48	7 24	1 12		7	1 [illegible]7		7 15	1 23	5 11	7 1	1 41
30	Fr	4 49	7 23	1 59		7	2 6		7 14	2 12	5 11	7 1	2 32
31	Sa	4 50	7 22	2 58		7	3 5		7 14	3 11	5 12	7 0	3 31

SUN ON MERIDIAN.

DAY OF MONTH.	H. M. S.	DAY OF MONTH.	H. M. S.	DAY OF MONTH.	H. M. S.	DAY OF MONTH.	H. M. S.	DAY OF MONTH.	H. M. S.
1	12 3 3	8	12 4 45	14	12 5 34	20	12 6	26	12 18
2	12 3 4	9	12 4 54	15	12 5 41	21	12 10	27	12 18
3	12 3 5	10	12 5 3	16	12 5 47	22	12 13	28	12 17
4	12 4	11	12 5 12	17	12 5 53	23	12 15	29	12 16
5	12 4 1	12	12 5 20	18	12 5 58	24	12 17	30	12 14
6	12 4 2	13	12 5 27	19	12 6 2	25	12 6 18	31	12 6 11
7	12 4 3[illegible]								

TWILIGHT.

PLACES.	July.	Begins, A. M.	Ends, P. M.	July.	Begins, A. M.	Ends, P. M.	July.	Begins, A. M.	Ends, P. M.
		H. M.	H. M.		H. M.	H. M.		H. M.	H. M.
Boston......	1	2 14	9 54	11	2 24	9 45	21	2 39	9 34
New York.	1	2 27	9 40	11	2 37	9 34	21	2 49	9 23
Wash'ton..	1	2 40	9 27	11	2 49	9 22	21	3 0	9 12
Charleston.	1	3 13	8 54	11	3 20	8 50	21	3 29	8 43

Day of the Month.	Day of the Week.	Calendar for BOSTON, New England, N. Y. State, Michigan, Wisconsin, N. and S. Dakota, Washington, and Oregon.			Calendar for NEW YORK CITY, Connecticut, Pennsylvania, Ohio, Indiana, Illinois, Iowa, Nebraska, Wyoming, and Northern California.			Calendar for WASHINGTON, Virginia, Kentucky, Missouri, Kansas, Colorado, Utah, Nevada, and Central California.			Calendar for CHARLESTON, Georgia, Alabama, Louisiana, Arkansas, Texas, New Mexico, Arizona, and Southern California.		
		SUN RISES.	SUN SETS.	MOON R. & S.	SUN RISES.	SUN SETS.	MOON R. & S.	SUN RISES.	SUN SETS.	MOON R. & S.	SUN RISES.	SUN SETS.	MOON R. & S.
		H. M.	H. M.	H. M.	H. M.	H. M.	H. M.	H. M.	H. M.	H. M.	H. M.	H. M.	H. M.
1	**S**	4 51	7 21	rises.	4 55	7 17	rises.	[illegible] 59	7 13	rises.	5 13	6 59	rises.
2	M	4 52	7 20	8 25	4 56	7 16	8 2[illegible]	0	7 12	8 17	5 14	6 58	8 4
3	Tu	4 53	7 19	8 58	4 57	7 5	8 5	1	7 11	8 52	5 14	6 57	8 44
4	W	4 54	7 18	9 27	4 58	7 4	9 2	[illegible]	7 10	9 24	5 15	6 56	9 20
5	Th	4 55	7 17	9 54	[illegible] 59	7 2	9 5		7 9	9 54	5 16	6 55	9 54
6	Fr	4 56	7 15	10 21	0	7 1	10 2		7 8	10 23	5 16	6 55	10 28
7	Sa	4 57	7 14	10 49	1	7 0	10 5	4	7 7	10 54	5 17	6 54	11 12
8	**S**	4 58	7 13	11 20	2	7 9	1 2	5	7 6	11 27	5 18	6 53	11 40
9	M	4 59	7 11	11 55	3	7 7	A. M.	6	7 4	A. M.	5 19	6 52	A. M.
10	Tu	5 0	7 10	A. M.	4	7 6	12 [illegible]	[illegible]	7 3	12 5	5 19	6 51	12 21
11	W	5 1	7 9	12 37	5	7 5	12 4		7 2	12 49	5 20	6 50	1 7
12	Th	5 2	7 8	1 26	6	7 4	1 [illegible]		7 0	1 39	5 21	6 48	1 58
13	Fr	5 3	7 7	2 22	7	7 3	2	1	6 59	2 34	5 21	6 47	2 53
14	Sa	5 4	7 5	3 22	8	7 1	3	2	6 58	3 34	5 22	6 46	3 51
15	**S**	5 5	7 4	sets.	9	7 0	se .		6 57	sets.	5 23	6 45	sets.
16	M	5 6	7 2	7 47	10	6 58	7 4		6 56	7 40	5 23	6 44	7 31
17	Tu	5 7	7 0	8 12	[illegible]1	6 [illegible]7	8 0		6 54	8 8	5 24	6 43	8 2
18	W	5 8	6 59	8 34	2	6 5	8 3		6 53	8 32	5 25	6 42	8 29
19	Th	5 9	6 57	8 55	3	6 4	8 5		6 52	8 55	5 25	6 41	8 55
20	Fr	5 10	6 55	9 15	4	6 2	9 7		6 50	9 18	5 26	6 40	9 22
21	Sa	5 11	6 54	9 37	5	6 0	9 0		6 49	9 42	5 27	6 39	9 49
22	**S**	5 12	6 52	10 2	6	6 9	10 5		6 48	10 9	5 27	6 38	10 19
23	M	5 13	6 51	10 32	7	6 8	10 37		6 46	10 41	5 28	6 37	10 55
24	Tu	5 14	6 50	11 5	8	6 7	1 10		6 45	11 15	5 29	6 36	11 33
25	W	5 15	6 48	11 47	9	6 6	1 53		6 43	A. M.	5 29	6 34	A. M.
26	Th	5 16	6 47	A. M.	0	6 44	A. M.		6 42	12 0	5 30	6 33	12 18
27	Fr	5 17	6 45	12 40	1	6 42	12 46		6 40	12 53	5 31	6 32	1 13
28	Sa	5 18	6 44	1 43	5 22	6 41	1 49	5 24	6 38	1 55	5 31	6 31	2 15
29	**S**	5 19	6 42	2 56	5 23	6 40	3 1	5 25	6 37	3 7	5 32	6 29	3 23
30	M	5 20	6 40	4 13	5 24	6 38	4 17	5 26	6 36	4 22	5 33	6 28	4 35
31	Tu	5 21	6 39	rises.	5 25	6 37	rises.	5 27	6 34	rises.	5 33	6 27	rises.

SUN ON MERIDIAN.

Day of Month.	H. M. S.	Day of Month.	H. M. S.	Day of Month.	H. M. S.	Day of Month.	H. M. S.	Day of Month.	H. M. S.
1	12 6 8	8	12 5 29	14	12 4 34	20	12 3 19	26	12 1 46
2	12 6 4	9	12 5 21	15	12 4 22	21	12 3 5	27	12 1 29
3	12 6 0	10	12 5 13	16	12 4 11	22	12 2 50	28	12 1 12
4	12 5 55	11	12 5 4	17	12 3 58	23	12 2 35	29	12 0 54
5	12 5 49	12	12 4 54	18	12 3 46	24	12 2 19	30	12 0 36
6	12 5 43	13	12 4 44	19	12 3 32	25	12 2 3	31	12 0 18
7	12 5 36								

TWILIGHT.

PLACES.	Aug.	Begins, A. M.	Ends, P. M.	Aug.	Begins, A. M.	Ends, P. M.	Aug.	Begins, A. M.	Ends, P. M.
		H. M.	H. M.		H. M.	H. M.		H. M.	H. M.
Boston......	1	2 57	9 16	11	3 13	8 57	21	3 29	8 37
New York.	1	3 6	9 6	11	3 22	8 48	21	3 35	8 31
Wash'ton.	1	3 15	8 57	11	3 29	8 41	21	3 41	8 24
Charleston.	1	3 40	8 32	11	3 50	8 20	21	3 59	8 7

Day of the Month.	Day of the Week.	Calendar for BOSTON, New England, N. Y. State, Michigan, Wisconsin, N. and S. Dakota, Washington, and Oregon.			Calendar for NEW YORK CITY, Connecticut, Pennsylvania, Ohio, Indiana, Illinois, Iowa, Nebraska, Wyoming, and Northern California.			Calendar for WASHINGTON, Virginia Kentucky, Missouri, Kansas, Colorado, Utah, Nevada, and Central California.			Calendar for CHARLESTON, Georgia, Alabama, Louisiana, Arkansas, Texas, New Mexico, Arizona, and Southern California.		
		SUN RISES.	SUN SETS.	MOON R. & S.	SUN RISES.	SUN SETS.	MOON R. & S.	SUN RISES.	SUN SETS.	MOON R. & S.	SUN RISES.	SUN SETS.	MOON R. & S.
		H. M.	H. M.	H. M.	H. M.	H. M.	H. M.	H. M.	H. M.	H. M.	H. M.	H. M.	H. M.
1	W	5 23	6 37	7 54	5 26	6 35	7 54	5 28	6 33	7 53	5 34	6 26	7 51
2	Th	5 24	6 35	8 21	5 27	6 34	8 21	5 29	6 31	8 22	5 35	6 25	8 25
3	Fr	5 26	6 33	8 49	5 28	6 33	8 51	5 30	6 30	8 54	5 35	6 24	9 1
4	Sa	5 27	6 32	9 20	5 29	6 30	9 23	5 31	6 29	9 27	5 36	6 22	9 38
5	**S**	5 28	6 30	9 54	5 30	6 28	9 59	5 32	6 27	10 4	5 37	6 21	10 19
6	M	5 29	6 28	10 35	5 31	6 26	10 40	5 33	6 25	10 47	5 37	6 19	11 4
7	Tu	5 30	6 26	11 22	5 32	6 24	11 28	5 34	6 23	11 35	5 38	6 18	11 54
8	W	5 31	6 25	A. M.	5 33	6 23	A. M.	5 35	6 21	A. M.	5 39	6 16	A. M.
9	Th	5 32	6 23	12 16	5 34	6 21	12 22	5 36	6 20	12 29	5 40	6 15	12 48
10	Fr	5 33	6 21	1 15	5 35	6 19	1 21	5 37	6 18	1 27	5 40	6 14	1 45
11	Sa	5 34	6 19	2 18	5 36	6 17	2 23	5 38	6 16	2 28	5 41	6 12	2 44
12	**S**	5 35	6 17	3 20	5 37	6 16	3 25	5 39	6 14	3 30	5 42	6 11	3 42
13	M	5 36	6 15	4 24	5 38	6 14	4 27	5 40	6 12	4 30	5 42	6 9	4 39
14	Tu	5 37	6 14	sets.	5 39	6 13	sets.	5 41	6 10	sets.	5 43	6 8	sets.
15	W	5 38	6 12	7 0	5 40	6 11	7 0	5 41	6 9	6 59	5 44	6 7	6 59
16	Th	5 39	6 10	7 20	5 41	6 9	7 21	5 42	6 7	7 22	5 44	6 6	7 25
17	Fr	5 41	6 8	7 41	5 42	6 7	7 43	5 43	6 5	7 45	5 45	6 5	7 51
18	Sa	5 42	6 6	8 4	5 43	6 5	8 7	5 44	6 4	8 11	5 45	6 4	8 20
19	**S**	5 43	6 5	8 32	5 44	6 4	8 36	5 45	6 2	8 41	5 46	6 3	8 54
20	M	5 44	6 3	9 2	5 45	6 2	9 7	5 46	6 1	9 12	5 47	6 1	9 36
21	Tu	5 45	6 1	9 40	5 45	6 0	9 46	5 47	6 0	9 52	5 47	6 0	10 11
22	W	5 46	6 0	10 27	5 46	5 59	10 33	5 48	5 59	10 40	5 48	5 59	11 0
23	Th	5 47	5 58	11 24	5 47	5 57	11 30	5 49	5 57	11 37	5 48	5 57	11 57
24	Fr	5 48	5 56	A. M.	5 48	5 56	A. M.	5 50	5 56	A. M.	5 49	5 55	A. M.
25	Sa	5 50	5 55	12 30	5 49	5 54	12 36	5 51	5 54	12 42	5 50	5 54	1 0
26	**S**	5 51	5 53	1 44	5 50	5 53	1 49	5 52	5 53	1 54	5 50	5 53	2 9
27	M	5 52	5 51	3 2	5 51	5 51	3 6	5 53	5 51	3 10	5 51	5 51	3 21
28	Tu	5 53	5 49	4 22	5 52	5 49	4 24	5 53	5 49	4 26	5 52	5 50	4 32
29	W	5 54	5 47	rises.	5 53	5 48	rises.	5 54	5 48	rises.	5 52	5 49	rises.
30	Th	5 55	5 46	6 47	5 54	5 47	6 49	5 55	5 46	6 50	5 53	5 48	6 55

SUN ON MERIDIAN.

DAY OF MONTH.	H. M. S.	DAY OF MONTH.	H. M. S.	DAY OF MONTH.	H. M. S.	DAY OF MONTH.	H. M. S.	DAY OF MONTH.	H. M. S.
1	11 59 59	7	11 58 2	13	11 55 58	19	11 53 51	25	11 51 45
2	11 59 40	8	11 57 42	14	11 55 37	20	11 53 30	26	11 51 25
3	11 59 21	9	11 57 21	15	11 55 16	21	11 53 9	27	11 51 5
4	11 59 2	10	11 57 0	16	11 54 55	22	11 52 48	28	11 50 44
5	11 58 42	11	11 56 40	17	11 54 33	23	11 52 27	29	11 50 24
6	11 58 22	12	11 56 19	18	11 54 12	24	11 52 6	30	11 50 5

TWILIGHT.

PLACES.	Sept.	Begins, A. M.	Ends, P. M.	Sept.	Begins, A. M.	Ends, P. M.	Sept.	Begins, A. M.	Ends, P. M.
		H. M.	H. M.		H. M.	H. M.		H. M.	H. M.
Boston......	1	3 45	8 14	11	3 59	7 54	21	4 12	7 34
New York.	1	3 50	8 9	11	4 3	7 50	21	4 15	7 31
Wash'ton.	1	3 55	8 4	11	4 7	7 46	21	4 18	7 28
Charleston	**1**	**4 9**	**7 51**	**11**	**4 17**	**7 36**	**21**	**4 20**	**7 20**

Day of the Month.	Day of the Week.	Calendar for BOSTON, New England, N. Y. State, Michigan, Wisconsin, N. and S. Dakota, Washington, and Oregon.			Calendar for NEW YORK CITY, Connecticut, Pennsylvania, Ohio, Indiana, Illinois, Iowa, Nebraska, Wyoming, and Northern California.			Calendar for WASHINGTON, Virginia, Kentucky, Missouri, Kansas, Colorado, Utah, Nevada, and Central California.			Calendar for CHARLESTON, Georgia, Alabama, Louisiana, Arkansas, Texas, New Mexico, Arizona, and Southern California.		
		SUN RISES.	SUN SETS.	MOON R. & S.	SUN RISES.	SUN SETS.	MOON R. & S.	SUN RISES.	SUN SETS.	MOON R. & S.	SUN RISES.	SUN SETS.	MOON R. & S.
		H. M.	H. M.	H. M.	H. M.	H. M.	H. M.	H. M.	H. M.	H. M.	H. M.	H. M.	H. M.
1	Fr	5 56	5 44	7 16	5 55	5 45	7 19	5 55	5 45	7 22	5 53	5 47	7 32
2	Sa	5 57	5 42	7 51	5 56	5 43	7 55	5 56	5 43	7 59	5 54	5 45	8 12
3	**S**	5 58	5 40	8 30	5 57	5 41	8 35	5 57	5 41	8 41	5 55	5 43	8 57
4	M	5 59	5 39	9 15	5 58	5 40	9 21	5 58	5 40	9 28	5 56	5 42	9 47
5	Tu	6 1	5 38	10 8	6 0	5 39	10 15	5 59	5 38	10 22	5 57	5 41	10 41
6	W	6 2	5 36	11 8	6 1	5 37	11 14	6 0	5 36	11 20	5 58	5 40	11 39
7	Th	6 3	5 34	A. M.	6 2	5 35	A. M.	6 1	5 34	A. M.	5 59	5 39	A. M.
8	Fr	6 4	5 32	12 10	6 3	5 33	12 15	6 2	5 32	12 21	5 59	5 37	12 38
9	Sa	6 5	5 31	1 13	6 4	5 32	1 16	6 3	5 30	1 22	6 0	5 36	1 36
10	**S**	6 6	5 29	2 16	6 5	5 30	2 19	6 4	5 29	2 23	6 1	5 35	2 34
11	M	6 8	5 28	3 18	6 6	5 28	3 20	6 5	5 27	3 23	6 1	5 34	3 30
12	Tu	6 9	5 26	4 18	6 7	5 27	4 20	6 6	5 25	4 21	6 2	5 33	4 24
13	W	6 10	5 24	5 18	6 8	5 25	5 18	6 7	5 23	5 18	6 3	5 31	5 18
14	Th	6 11	5 22	sets.	6 9	5 24	sets.	6 8	5 22	sets.	6 3	5 30	sets.
15	Fr	6 12	5 21	6 9	6 10	5 22	6 12	6 9	5 21	6 15	6 4	5 29	6 23
16	Sa	6 13	5 19	6 33	6 11	5 21	6 37	6 10	5 19	6 41	6 5	5 28	6 53
17	**S**	6 14	5 17	7 5	6 12	5 19	7 9	6 11	5 18	7 15	6 6	5 26	7 30
18	M	6 15	5 15	7 38	6 13	5 17	7 44	6 12	5 16	7 50	6 7	5 25	8 8
19	Tu	6 17	5 14	8 21	6 14	5 16	8 27	6 13	5 15	8 34	6 7	5 24	8 54
20	W	6 18	5 12	9 13	6 15	5 14	9 20	6 14	5 14	9 27	6 8	5 23	9 47
21	Th	6 19	5 11	10 15	6 16	5 13	10 21	6 15	5 13	10 27	6 9	5 22	10 46
22	Fr	6 20	5 9	11 24	6 17	5 12	11 29	6 16	5 11	11 35	6 10	5 21	11 51
23	Sa	6 21	5 8	A. M.	6 18	5 11	A. M.	6 17	5 10	A. M.	6 11	5 19	A. M.
24	**S**	6 22	5 6	12 38	6 19	5 9	12 42	6 18	5 9	12 45	6 12	5 18	12 59
25	M	6 23	5 4	1 54	6 20	5 8	1 57	6 19	5 8	2 0	6 13	5 17	2 9
26	Tu	6 25	5 2	3 11	6 21	5 6	3 13	6 20	5 7	3 14	6 14	5 16	3 19
27	W	6 26	5 0	4 30	6 22	5 5	4 30	6 21	5 6	4 30	6 15	5 15	4 29
28	Th	6 27	4 59	rises.	6 23	5 3	rises.	6 22	5 5	rises.	6 15	5 14	rises.
29	Fr	6 28	4 58	5 44	6 24	5 2	5 48	6 23	5 4	5 51	6 16	5 14	6 3
30	Sa	6 29	4 57	6 21	6 25	5 0	6 25	6 24	5 3	6 31	6 17	5 13	6 46
31	**S**	6 30	4 55	7 4	6 27	4 59	7 10	6 25	5 2	7 16	6 17	5 12	7 35

SUN ON MERIDIAN.

DAY OF MONTH.	H. M. S.	DAY OF MONTH.	H. M. S.	DAY OF MONTH.	H. M. S.	DAY OF MONTH.	H. M. S.	DAY OF MONTH.	H. M. S.
1	11 49 45	8	11 47 38	14	11 46 7	20	11 44 54	26	11 44 4
2	11 49 26	9	11 47 21	15	11 45 53	21	11 44 44	27	11 43 59
3	11 49 7	10	11 47 6	16	11 45 40	22	11 44 35	28	11 43 53
4	11 48 49	11	11 46 50	17	11 45 28	23	11 44 26	29	11 43 49
5	11 48 31	12	11 46 35	18	11 45 16	24	11 44 18	30	11 43 45
6	11 48 13	13	11 46 21	19	11 45 5	25	11 44 11	31	11 43 42
7	11 47 55								

TWILIGHT.

PLACE.	Oct.	Begins, A. M.	Ends, P. M.	Oct.	Begins, A. M.	Ends, P. M.	Oct.	Begins, A. M.	Ends, P. M.
		H. M.	H. M.		H. M.	H. M.		M.	H. M.
Boston	1	4 24	7 15	11	4 35	6 8	21	20	6 12
New York.	1	4 26	7 14	11	4 36	6 7	21	18	6 14
Wash'ton.	1	4 27	7 12	11	4 37	6 6	21	16	6 16
Charleston	1	4 32	7 7	11	4 39	6 54	21	5 10	6 22

Day of the Month.	Day of the Week.	Calendar for Boston, New England, N. Y. State, Michigan, Wisconsin, N. and S. Dakota, Washington, and Oregon.			Calendar for New York City, Connecticut, Pennsylvania, Ohio, Indiana, Illinois, Iowa, Nebraska, Wyoming, and Northern California.			Calendar for Washington, Virginia, Kentucky, Missouri, Kansas, Colorado, Utah, Nevada, and Central California.			Calendar for Charleston, Georgia, Alabama, Louisiana, Arkansas, Texas, New Mexico, Arizona, and Southern California.		
		Sun Rises.	Sun Sets.	Moon R. & S.	Sun Rises.	Sun Sets.	Moon R. & S.	Sun Rises.	Sun Sets.	Moon R. & S.	Sun Rises.	Sun Sets.	Moon R. & S.
		H. M.	H. M.	H. M.	H. M.	H. M.	H. M.	H. M.	H. M.	H. M.	H. M.	H. M.	H. M.
1	M	6 32	4 54	7 56	6 28	4 58	8 3	6 26	5 1	8 9	6 18	5 11	8 29
2	Tu	6 33	4 53	8 55	6 30	4 57	9 2	6 27	5 0	9 8	6 18	5 10	9 28
3	W	6 34	4 52	9 58	6 31	4 56	10 4	6 28	4 59	10 10	6 19	5 9	10 28
4	Th	6 35	4 51	11 3	6 32	4 55	11 8	6 29	4 58	11 13	6 20	5 8	11 28
5	Fr	6 36	4 50	A. M.	6 33	4 54	A. M.	6 30	4 57	A. M.	6 21	5 7	A. M.
6	Sa	6 38	4 49	12 7	6 34	4 53	12 11	6 31	4 56	12 15	6 22	5 7	12 26
7	**S**	6 39	4 47	1 8	6 35	4 52	1 10	6 32	4 55	1 13	6 23	5 6	1 21
8	M	6 40	4 46	2 10	6 36	4 51	2 12	6 33	4 54	2 14	6 24	5 5	2 18
9	Tu	6 42	4 45	3 10	6 38	4 50	3 11	6 35	4 53	3 11	6 25	5 4	3 12
10	W	6 43	4 44	4 10	6 40	4 49	4 9	6 36	4 52	4 8	6 26	5 3	4 6
11	Th	6 45	4 43	5 10	6 41	4 48	5 8	6 37	4 51	5 7	6 27	5 2	5 1
12	Fr	6 46	4 41	sets.	6 42	4 47	sets.	6 39	4 50	sets.	6 28	5 1	sets.
13	Sa	6 48	4 40	5 5	6 43	4 46	5 10	6 40	4 49	5 15	6 29	5 1	5 29
14	**S**	6 50	4 39	5 38	6 44	4 45	5 44	6 41	4 48	5 50	6 30	5 0	6 7
15	M	6 51	4 37	6 19	6 46	4 44	6 26	6 42	4 47	6 32	6 31	4 59	6 52
16	Tu	6 53	4 36	7 9	6 47	4 43	7 15	6 43	4 46	7 22	6 32	4 58	7 42
17	W	6 54	4 35	8 7	6 48	4 42	8 13	6 44	4 45	8 20	6 32	4 58	8 40
18	Th	6 55	4 34	9 15	6 49	4 41	9 20	6 45	4 44	9 26	6 33	4 57	9 43
19	Fr	6 57	4 33	10 23	6 50	4 40	10 28	6 46	4 44	10 33	6 34	4 56	10 47
20	Sa	6 58	4 33	11 36	6 51	4 39	11 40	6 47	4 43	11 43	6 35	4 56	11 54
21	**S**	6 59	4 32	A. M.	6 52	4 38	A. M.	6 48	4 42	A. M.	6 36	4 55	A. M.
22	M	7 0	4 31	12 51	6 53	4 38	12 53	6 49	4 42	12 55	6 36	4 55	1 1
23	Tu	7 2	4 31	2 5	6 54	4 37	2 6	6 50	4 41	2 7	6 37	4 55	2 9
24	W	7 3	4 30	3 21	6 55	4 36	3 21	6 51	4 41	3 20	6 38	4 54	3 17
25	Th	7 4	4 30	4 39	6 56	4 36	4 37	6 52	4 41	4 35	6 39	4 54	4 27
26	Fr	7 5	4 29	5 58	6 58	4 35	5 55	6 53	4 40	5 51	6 40	4 54	5 39
27	Sa	7 6	4 29	rises.	6 59	4 35	rises.	6 54	4 40	rises.	6 40	4 54	rises.
28	**S**	7 7	4 29	5 40	7 0	4 35	5 46	6 55	4 40	5 53	6 41	4 54	6 12
29	M	7 7	4 28	6 37	7 1	4 34	6 43	6 56	4 40	6 50	6 42	4 54	7 10
30	Tu	7 8	4 28	7 40	7 2	4 34	7 47	6 57	4 40	7 53	6 43	4 54	8 11

SUN ON MERIDIAN.

Day of Month.	H. M. S.	Day of Month.	H. M. S.	Day of Month.	H. M. S.	Day of Month.	H. M. S.	Day of Month.	H. M. S.
1	11 43 40	7	11 43 45	13	11 44 21	19	11 45 27	25	11 47 2
2	11 43 39	8	11 43 49	14	11 44 30	20	11 45 41	26	11 47 20
3	11 43 39	9	11 43 53	15	11 44 40	21	11 45 56	27	11 47 40
4	11 43 39	10	11 43 59	16	11 44 50	22	11 46 19	28	11 48 0
5	11 43 40	11	11 44 6	17	11 45 2	23	11 46 27	29	11 48 20
6	11 43 43	12	11 44 13	18	11 45 14	24	11 46 44	30	11 48 42

TWILIGHT.

Places.	Nov.	Begins, A. M.	Ends, P. M.	Nov.	Begins, A. M.	Ends, P. M.	Nov.	Begins, A. M.	Ends, P. M.
		H. M.	H. M.		H. M.	H. M.		H. M.	H. M.
Boston......	1	4 58	6 29	11	5 9	6 19	21	5 20	6 12
New York.	1	4 58	6 29	11	5 8	6 20	21	5 18	6 14
Wash'ton.	1	4 57	6 30	11	5 7	6 21	21	5 16	6 16
Charleston	1	4 54	6 33	11	5 2	6 26	21	5 10	6 22

Day of the Month.	Day of the Week.	Calendar for BOSTON. New England, N. Y. State, Michigan, Wisconsin, N. and S. Dakota, Washington, and Oregon.			Calendar for NEW YORK CITY. Connecticut, Pennsylvania, Ohio, Indiana, Illinois, Iowa, Nebraska, Wyoming, and Northern California			Calendar for WASHINGTON, Virginia Kentucky, Missouri, Kansas, Colorado, Utah, Nevada, and Central California.			Calendar for CHARLESTON, Georgia, Alabama, Louisiana, Arkansas, Texas, New Mexico, Arizona, and Southern California.		
		SUN RISES	SUN SETS.	MOON R. & S.	SUN RISES.	SUN SETS.	MOON R. & S.	SUN RISES.	SUN SETS.	MOON R. & S.	SUN RISES.	SUN SETS.	MOON R. & S.
		H. M.	H. M.	H. M.	H. M.	H. M.	H. M.	H. M.	H. M.	H. M.	H. M.	H. M.	H. M.
1	W	7 9	4 28	8 50	7 [illegible]	4 3[illegible]	8 5[illegible]	6 5[illegible]	4 40	9 0	6 44	4 54	9 16
2	Th	7 10	4 28	9 55		[illegible]3	9 5	7	4 39	10 4	6 44	4 54	10 17
3	Fr	7 11	4 28	10 54			11	7	4 39	11 4	6 45	4 54	11 14
4	Sa	7 12	4 28	A. M.			A. M.	7	4 39	A. M.	6 46	4 54	A. M.
5	S	7 13	4 28	12 0			12 [illegible]	7	4 39	12 4	6 47	4 54	12 10
6	M	7 14	4 28	1 0			1	7	4 38	1 2	6 47	4 54	1 4
7	Tu	7 15	4 28	2 0	1		2	7	4 38	1 59	6 48	4 54	1 58
8	W	7 16	4 28	3 0	1		2 5	7	4 38	2 57	6 49	4 54	2 52
9	Th	7 17	4 28	4 1	1		3 5	7	4 38	3 56	6 50	4 54	3 48
10	Fr	7 18	4 28	5 4	7 1	33	5	7	4 38	4 56	6 50	4 54	4 45
11	Sa	7 19	4 28	6 9	7 1	33	6	7	4 38	5 59	6 51	4 54	5 44
12	S	7 20	4 28	sets.	7 1	33	sets.	7 1	4 38	sets.	6 52	4 55	sets.
13	M	7 21	4 28	5 3	7 1	[illegible]	5 10	7 1	4 38	5 17	6 53	4 55	5 37
14	Tu	7 22	4 28	6 0	7 1		6 6	7	4 39	6 13	6 54	4 55	6 33
15	W	7 23	4 28	7 4	7 1		7 10	7	4 39	7 17	6 55	4 56	7 35
16	Th	7 24	4 29	8 12	7 1		8 19	7	4 39	8 25	6 56	4 56	8 40
17	Fr	7 24	4 29	9 27	7 1		9 31	7	4 40	9 35	6 57	4 57	9 46
18	Sa	7 25	4 29	10 40	7 1	4	10 42	7	4 40	10 45	6 58	4 57	10 53
19	S	7 25	4 30	11 52	7 2	5	1 54	7	4 41	11 55	6 58	4 58	11 58
20	M	7 26	4 30	A. M.	7 2	5	A. M.	7	4 41	A. M.	6 59	4 58	A. M.
21	Tu	7 26	4 30	1 6	7 2	5	1 [illegible]	7	4 42	1 5	6 59	4 59	1 4
22	W	7 27	4 30	2 20	7 2	5	2 1	7	4 42	2 16	7 0	4 59	2 11
23	Th	7 27	4 31	3 35	7 2	6	3 [illegible]	7	4 43	3 29	7 0	5 0	3 20
24	Fr	7 28	4 32	4 52	7 2	6	4	7	4 44	4 43	7 0	5 0	4 29
25	Sa	7 28	4 33	6 8	7 2	6	6	7	4 45	5 57	7 0	5 1	5 40
26	S	7 28	4 33	rises.	7 2	7	rises.	7	4 45	rises.	7 1	5 2	rises.
27	M	7 29	4 34	5 20	7 2	7	5 [illegible]	7	4 46	5 32	7 1	5 2	5 52
28	Tu	7 29	4 34	6 26	7 2	8	6	7	4 46	6 38	7 1	5 3	6 56
29	W	7 29	4 35	7 34	7 2	9	7	7	4 47	7 44	7 2	5 3	7 59
30	Th	7 29	4 35	8 41	7 2	0	8	7	4 47	8 48	7 2	5 4	8 59
31	Fr	7 30	4 36	9 46	7 2	1	9	7	4 48	9 51	7 3	5 4	9 58

SUN ON MERIDIAN.

DAY OF MONTH.	H. M. S.	DAY OF MONTH.	H. M. S.	DAY OF MONTH.	H. M. S.	DAY OF MONTH.	H. M. S.	DAY OF MONTH.	H. M. S.
1	11 49 4	8	11 51 55	14	11 54 42	20	11 57 38	26	12 0 37
2	11 49 26	9	11 52 22	15	11 55 10	21	11 58 8	27	12 1 7
3	11 49 50	10	11 52 49	16	11 55 40	22	11 58 38	28	12 1 37
4	11 50 14	11	11 53 17	17	11 56 9	23	11 59 8	29	12 2 5
5	11 50 38	12	11 53 45	18	11 56 39	24	11 59 38	30	12 2 34
6	11 51 3	13	11 54 13	19	11 57 8	25	12 0 7	31	12 3 3
7	11 51 29								

TWILIGHT.

PLACES.	Dec.	Begins, A. M.	Ends, P. M.	Dec.	Begins, A. M.	Ends, P. M.	Dec.	Begins, A. M.	Ends, P. M.
		H. M.	H. M.		H. M.	H. M.		H. M.	H. M.
Boston......	1	5 29	6 9	11	5 8	6 9	21	5 45	6 12
New York.	1	5 27	6 11	11	5 6	6 11	21	5 42	6 14
Wash'ton..	1	5 25	6 13	11	5 3	6 14	21	5 40	6 17
Charleston.	1	5 17	6 20	11	5 35	6 22	21	5 31	6 26

Moonlight Chart, 1909.

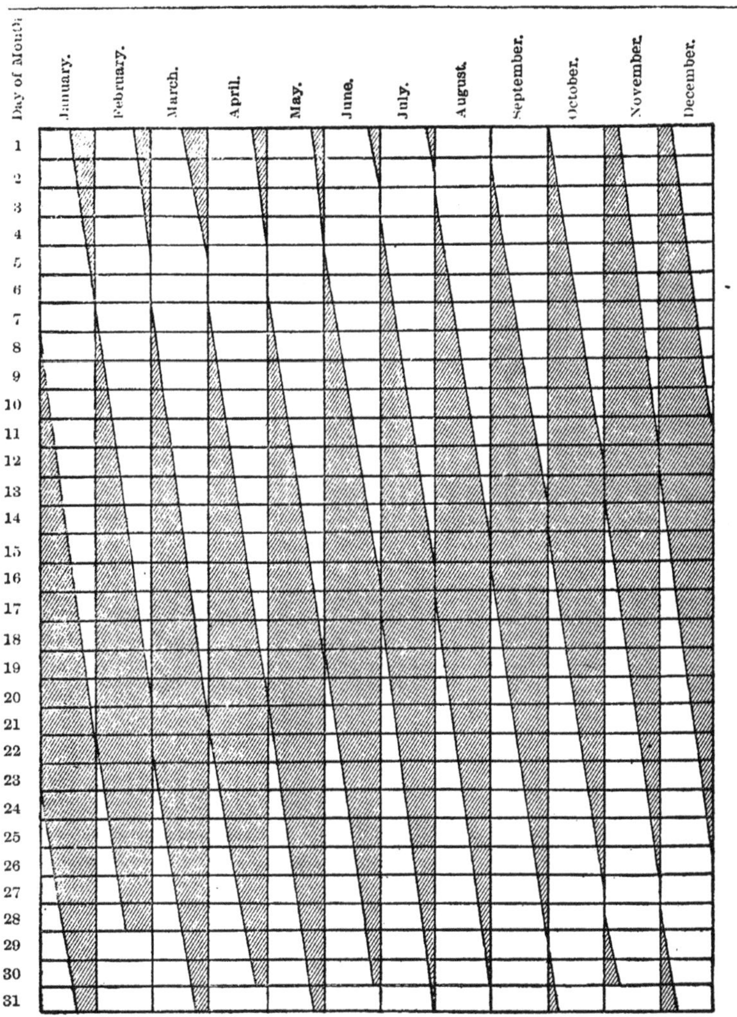

EXPLANATION.—The white spaces show the amount of moonlight each night. January 6, February 5, etc., the time of full moon, when moonlight lasts the whole night: January 13, February 12, etc., the moon rises at or near midnight, and the latter half of the night has moonlight; January 21, February 20, new moon, when there is no moonlight the whole night; January 29, February 28, etc., moon sets at or near midnight, when the half of the night has moonlight.

Astronomical Phenomena for the Year 1909.

ASTRONOMICAL SIGNS AND SYMBOLS.

☉	The Sun.	♂	Mars.	☌	Conjunction.
☾	The Moon.	♃	Jupiter.	□	Quadrature.
☿	Mercury.	♄	Saturn.	☍	Opposition.
♀	Venus.	♅	Uranus.	☊	Ascending Node.
⊕	The Earth.	♆	Neptune.	☋	Descending Node.

Two heavenly bodies are in "conjunction" (☌) when they have the same *Right Ascension*, or are on the *same meridian, i. e.*, when one is due *north* or *south* of the other; if the bodies are near each other as seen from the earth. they will rise and set at the same time; they are in "opposition" (☍) when in opposite quarters of the heavens, or when one rises just as the other is setting. "Quadrature" (□) is half way between conjunction and opposition. By "greatest elongation" is meant the greatest apparent *angular* distance from the sun; the planet is then generally most favorably situated for observation. Mercury can only be seen with the naked eye at this time. When a planet is in its "ascending" (☊) or "descending" (☋) node it is crossing the plane of the earth's orbit. The term "Perihelion" means nearest, and "Aphelion" farthest, from the sun. An "occultation" of a planet or star is an eclipse of it by some other body, usually the moon.

I.—ECLIPSES.

In the year 1909 there will be four eclipses, two of the sun and two of the moon.

1. A total eclipse of the moon June 3, visible generally in North America, except the Northwestern portion; visible also in South America and Europe.

PLACES.	Moon Enters Shadow.	Total Eclipse Begins.	Total Eclipse Ends.	Moon Leaves Shadow.
		H. M.	H. M.	H. M.
Boston	Before Moon Rises	8 13.8 P. M.	9 15.5 P. M.	10 30.1 P. M.
New York	"	8 2.0 P. M.	9 7.3 P. M.	10 18.3 P. M.
Washington	"	7 49.7 P. M.	8 51.4 P. M.	10 6.0 P. M.
Charleston	"	7 29.5 P. M.	8 40.2 P. M.	9 54.8 P. M.
Cincinnati	"	7 20.3 P. M.	8 22.0 P. M.	9 36.6 P. M.
Chicago	"	7 7.6 P. M.	8 9.3 P. M.	9 23.9 P. M.
St. Louis	"	Before Moon Rises	7 58.9 P. M.	9 13.5 P. M.
Denver	"	"	Before Moon Rises	8 14.5 P. M.
Ogden	"	"	"	7 46.3 P. M.

Magnitude of the eclipse 1.16, the moon's diameter = 1.

(*Local Mean Time.*)

2. A central eclipse of the sun June 17, visible as a partial one in the United States and Canada. There will be no eclipse visible south of a line drawn from San Francisco through Tucson, Arizona, to Corpus Christi Bay, Texas. The central eclipse will be annular for a short time, at the beginning and end, and total during the remainder of its course. The path of the central eclipse commences in Siberia in latitude 50° N. and longitude 81°31′.6 E. and moving in a Northeasterly direction and then nearly due North passes nearly over the North Pole, thence along the west coast of Greenland, terminating in the North Atlantic Ocean in latitude 60°23′ N. and longitude 42° W., near Cape Farewell. The following table gives the dates of the eclipse for several important places.

PLACES.	Eclipse Begins.	Eclipse Ends.	Position Angle.
	D. H. M.	H. M.	° ′
Boston	June 17, 7 9.8 P. M.	Sun sets eclipsed	294 34
New York	" 7 2.8 P. M.	" "	299 12
Washington	" 6 56 2 P. M.	" "	302 51
Charleston	" 6 58.3 P. M.	" "	313 49
Cincinnati	" 6 30.7 P. M.	" "	307 13
Chicago	" 6 14.3 P. M.	" "	305 42
Northfield, Minn.	" 5 48.2 P. M.	7 22.7 P. M.	304 56
Denver	" 5 18.4 P. M.	6 34.6 P. M.	322 16
Ogden	" 4 48.0 P. M.	6 2.6 P. M.	325 9
Seattle	" 3 43.7 P. M.	5 14.9 P. M.	318 10

(*Local Mean Time.*)

The position angle is for the beginning and is estimated from the north point of the sun's limb toward the East.

3. A total eclipse of the moon November 26-27, visible in the United States, Canada, Mexico, Central and South America.

PLACES.	Moon Enters Shadow.	Total Eclipse Begins.	Total Eclipse Ends.	Moon Leaves Shadow.
	D. H. M.	D. H. M.	D. H. M.	D. H. M.
Boston	Nov. 27, 2 26.2 A.M.	Nov. 27, 3 29.4 A.M.	Nov. 27, 4 51.2 A.M.	Nov. 27, 5 54.0 A.M.
New York	" 2 15.1 A.M.	" 3 17.7 A.M.	" 4 39.7 A.M.	" 5 42.3 A.M.
Washington	" 2 2.8 A.M.	" 3 5.4 A.M.	" 4 27.4 A.M.	" 5 30.0 A.M.
Charleston	" 1 51.5 A.M.	" 2 54.1 A.M.	" 4 16.1 A.M.	" 5 18.7 A.M.
Cincinnati	" 1 43.3 A.M.	" 2 45.9 A.M.	" 4 7.9 A.M.	" 5 10.5 A.M.
Chicago	" 1 20.6 A.M.	" 2 23.2 A.M.	" 3 45.2 A.M.	" 4 47.8 A.M.
New Orleans	" 1 10.8 A.M.	" 2 13.4 A.M.	" 3 35.4 A.M.	" 4 38.0 A.M.
San Antonio	" 12 37.1 A.M.	" 1 39.7 A.M.	" 3 1.7 A.M.	" 4 4.3 A.M.
Denver	" 12 11.2 A.M.	" 1 13.8 A.M.	" 2 35.8 A.M.	" 3 38.4 A.M.
Ogden	Nov. 26, 11 43.0 P.M.	" 12 45.6 A.M.	" 2 7.6 A.M.	" 3 10.2 A.M.
San Francisco	" 11 1.3 P.M.	" 12 3.9 A.M.	" 1 25.9 A.M.	" 2 28.5 A.M.

(*Local Mean Time.*)

Magnitude of the eclipse 1.37, the moon's diameter = 1.

ASTRONOMICAL PHENOMENA FOR THE YEAR 1909.—*Continued.*

4. A partial eclipse of the sun December 12, invisible in America. This eclipse is visible in the regions around the South Pole, Tasmania, the southern portion of Australia and New Zealand.

II.—OCCULTATION.

There will be an occultation of the planet Mars on September 1, visible in the United States.

PLACES.	Immersion.				Emersion.			
		H.	M.			H.	M.	
Boston	Sept. 1,	9	13.7	P. M.	Sept. 1,	10	13.0	P. M.
New York	"	8	52.7	P. M.	"	9	52.3	P. M.
Washington	"	8	42.4	P. M.	"	9	39.7	P. E.
Charleston	"	8	8.8	P. M.	"	9	6.0	P. M.

(*Local Mean Time.*)

III.—PLANETARY CONFIGURATIONS, 1909.

(*Washington Mean Time.*)

	D.	H.	M.			
Jan.	3	1	0	A. M.	⊕	in perihelion.
	11	2	1	A. M.	☌ ♃ ☾	
	17	6	54	P. M.	☌ ♂ ☾	
	19	11	55	P. M.	☌ ♀ ☾	
	22	11	38	P. M.	☌ ☿ ☾	
	26	12	39	A. M.	☌ ♄ ☾	
	26	1		P. M.	☿ in ☊	
	26	10		P. M.	☿	gr. elong. E. 18° 27′.
	29	2		A. M.	♀ in ☋	
	31	3		A. M.	☿	in perihelion.
Feb.	1	9		P. M.	☿	stationary.
	7	5	4	A. M.	☌ ☾	
	11	9		A. M.	☌ ♃ ☉	inferior.
	13	4		A. M.	♂ in ☋	
	15	3	35	P. M.	☌ ♂ ☾,	♂ N. 1′.
	18	11		P. M.	☌ ♀ ☾	
	19	12	28	A. M.	☌ ☿ ☾	
	19	12		P. M.	☌ ☿ ♀,	♀ N. 4° 1′.
	22	2	20	P. M.	☌ ♄ ☾	
	23	11		A. M.	☿	stationary.
	28	2		P. M.	☍ ☉	
Mar.	4	2		P. M.	♀	in aphelion.
	6	4	41	A. M.	☌ ♃ ☾	
	9	2		P. M.	☿	gr. elong. W. 27° 26′.
	16	3		A. M.	☿	in aphelion.
	16	9	55	A. M.	☌ ☾	
	19	6	27	P. M.	☌ ☾	
	20	7	52	P. M.	☌ ☾	
	22	6	38	A. M.	☌ ☾	
Apr.	2	4	40	A. M.	☌ ☾	
	3	6		A. M.	☌ ☉	
	9	11		A. M.	☌ [illegible] ♄,	N. 0° 58′.
	13	4		P. M.	☌ [illegible] ♄,	☿ N. 0° 39′.
	14	1	43	A. M.	☌ ♂ ☾	
	18	11	3	P. M.	☌ ♄ ☾	
	19	5	36	P. M.	☌ ☿ ☾	
	19	5	51	P. M.	☌ ♀ ☾	
	19	10		P. M.	☌ ☿ ♀	
	21	6		P. M.	☌ ☿ ☉	superior.
	28	12		P. M.	☌ ♀ ☉	superior.
	29	2		A. M.	☿	in perihelion.
	29	8	37	A. M.	☌ ♃ ☾	
May	1	7		P. M.	♃	stationary.
	12	3	19	P. M.	☌ ♂ ☾	
	13	10		A. M.	□ ♂ ☉	
	16	1	32	P. M.	☌ ♄ ☾	
	19	6	26	P. M.	☌ ♀ ☾	
	20	11		A. M.	☿	gr. elong. E. 22° 23′.
	21	1	27	A. M.	☌ ☿ ☾	
	22	5		A. M.	♀ in ☊	
	26	5	57	P. M.	☌ ♃ ☾	
	27	6		A. M.	□ ♃ ☉	
June	2	12		P. M.	☿	stationary.
	7	10		A. M.	☌ ♀,	♀ N. 2° 11′.
	10	2	45	A. M.	☌ ☾	
	13	1		A. M.	☌ ☿ ☾	
	14	6		P. M.	☌ [illegible] ☉	inferior.

	D	H.	M.			
June	17	11	5	A. M.	☌ ☿ ☾	
	18	8	50	P. M.	☌ ♀ ☾	
	23	7	49	A. M.	☌ ♃ ☾	
	24	11		P. M.	♀	in perihelion.
	26	12		P. M.	☿	stationary.
July	3	10		P. M.	⊕	in aphelion.
	8	12		A. M.	☿	gr. elong. W. 21° 12′.
	8	10	37	A. M.	☌ ♂ ☾	
	10	9	38	A. M.	☌ ♄ ☾	
	15	3	28	P. M.	☌ ☿ ☾	
	15	9		P. M.	□ ♄ ☉	
	19	12	42	A. M.	☌ ♀ ☾	
	21	12	31	A. M.	☌ ♃ ☾	
Aug.	4	7		A. M.	☌ ☿ ☉	superior.
	5	11	6	A. M.	☌ ♂ ☾	
	6	5		A. M.	♄	stationary.
	6	4	37	P. M.	☌ ♄ ☾	
	12	2		A. M.	☌ ♀ ♃,	♀ N. 0° 12′.
	13	2		P. M.	♂	in perihelion.
	16	5	48	P. M.	☌ ☾	
	17	6	28	P. M.	☌ ☾	
	18	7	4	A. M.	☌ [illegible] ☾	
	23	10		A. M.	♂	stationary.
	25	7		A. M.	☌ ♃,	♃ N. 0° 40′.
Sept.	1	10	31	P. M.	☌	
	2	11	25	P. M.	☌	
	14	12	43	P. M.	☌ ☾	
	16	2	15	P. M.	☌ [illegible]	
	17	5		A. M.	☿	gr. elong. E. 26° 34′.
	17	4		P. M.	☌ ♀ ☾	
	18	9		A. M.	☌ ♃ ☉	
	24	5		A. M.	☍ ♂ ☉	
	28	9	54	P. M.	☌ ♂ ☾	
	30	6	53	A. M.	☌ ♄ ☾	
Oct.	11	6	50	A. M.	☌ ♃ ☾	
	12	10		A. M.	☌ ☿ ☉	inferior.
	13	1		P. M.	☍ ♄ ☉	
	13	4	11	P. M.	☌ ☿ ☾	
	17	11	32	P. M.	☌ ♀ ☾	
	26	12	58	A.	☌ ♂ ☾	
	26	12		P.	♂ ☾	stationary.
	27	2	40	P.	☌ ♄	
	28	2		A. M.	☿	gr. elong. W. 18° 33′.
Nov.	9	12	35	A. M.	☌ ♃	
	11	5	19	P. M.	☌ ☿	
	16	11	19	P. M.	☌ ♀	
	22	5	2	P. M.	☌ ♂ ☾	
	23	9	45	P. M.	☌ ♄	
Dec.	2	12		P. M.	♀	gr. elong. E. 47° 18′.
	3	1		A.	☌ ☉	
	6	5	27	P. M.	☌	
	13	2	19	A. M.	☌ ☾	
	16	10		A. M.	☌ ☿ [illegible]	
	20	5		P. M.	♄	stationary.
	20	6	46	P. M.	☌ ♂ ☾	
	21	3	53	A. M.	☌ ♄ ☾	
	31	2		P. M.	☌ ♂ ♄,	♂ N. 3° 12′.

The Sun's Declination.

WASHINGTON APPARENT NOON

1909.	January.	February.	March.	April	May.	June
	° ′ ″	° ′ ″	° ′ ″	° ′ ″	° ′ ″	° ′ ″
1	23 1 16 S.	17 8 2 S.	7 37 54 S.	4 29 14 N.	15 1 50 N.	22 2 16 N.
2	22 56 7	16 50 50	7 15 4	4 52 20	15 19 54	22 10 17
3	22 50 32	16 33 21	6 52 9	5 15 21	15 37 42	22 17 56
4	22 24 29	16 15 34	6 29 7	5 38 17	15 55 15	22 25 11
5	22 37 59	15 57 31	6 6 0	6 1 6	16 12 32	22 32 3
6	22 31 2	15 39 12	5 42 49	6 23 49	16 29 33	22 38 31
7	22 23 40	15 20 36	5 19 32	6 46 26	16 46 17	22 44 35
8	22 15 49	15 1 45	4 56 12	7 8 55	17 2 45	22 50 16
9	22 7 33	14 42 39	4 32 48	7 31 18	17 18 56	22 55 32
10	21 58 51	14 23 17	4 9 20	7 53 33	17 34 49	23 0 25
11	21 49 43	14 3 42	3 45 49	8 15 40	17 50 25	23 4 53
12	21 40 10	13 43 53	3 22 15	8 37 39	18 5 43	23 8 57
13	21 30 12	13 23 49	2 58 39	8 59 29	18 20 44	23 12 37
14	21 19 48	13 3 33	2 35 0	9 21 11	18 35 25	23 15 52
15	21 9 1	12 43 4	2 11 21	9 42 44	18 49 48	23 18 42
16	20 57 48	12 22 23	1 47 39	10 4 6	19 3 52	23 21 8
17	20 46 12	12 1 29	1 23 57	10 25 20	19 17 37	23 23 9
18	20 34 11	11 40 24	1 0 14	10 46 23	19 31 3	23 24 45
19	20 21 48	11 19 8	0 36 1	11 7 15	19 44 8	23 25 56
20	20 9 2	10 57 42	0 12 48 S.	11 27 56	19 56 54	23 26 43
21	19 55 52	10 36 5	0 10 54 N.	11 48 27	20 9 19	23 27 5
22	19 42 21	10 14 18	0 34 35	12 8 45	20 21 23	23 27 2
23	19 28 27	9 52 22	0 58 16	12 28 52	20 33 6	23 26 34
24	19 14 12	9 30 18	1 21 54	12 48 46	20 44 28	23 25 41
25	18 59 36	9 8 4	1 45 30	13 8 27	20 55 29	23 24 23
26	18 44 39	8 45 43	2 9 4	13 27 56	21 6 8	23 22 41
27	18 29 21	8 23 14	2 32 35	13 47 11	21 16 25	23 20 34
28	18 13 44	8 0 37 S.	2 56 2	14 6 12	21 26 20	23 18 3
29	17 57 46		3 19 27	14 24 59	21 35 53	23 15 6
30	17 41 30		3 42 47	14 43 32 N.	21 45 3	23 11 46 N.
31	17 24 55 S.		4 6 2 N.		21 53 51 N.	

1909.	July.	August.	September.	October.	November.	December.
	° ′ ″	° ′ ″	° ′ ″	° ′ ″	° ′ ″	° ′ ″
1	23 8 1 N.	18 4 35 N.	8 21 12 N.	3 7 14 S.	14 23 4 S.	21 47 35 S.
2	23 3 52	17 49 24	7 59 23	3 30 30	14 42 23	21 56 46
3	22 59 19	17 33 55	7 37 27	3 53 45	15 1 19	22 5 32
4	22 54 21	17 18 9	7 15 23	4 17 57	15 19 59	22 15 52
5	22 49 0	17 2 6	6 53 12	4 40 6	15 38 25	22 21 47
6	22 43 15	16 45 46	6 39 54	5 3 11	15 56 35	22 29 15
7	22 37 6	16 29 10	6 8 30	5 26 13	16 14 30	22 36 17
8	22 30 34	16 12 19	5 45 59	5 49 11	16 32 8	22 42 53
9	22 23 39	15 55 11	5 23 23	6 12 5	16 49 30	22 49 2
10	22 16 20	15 37 48	5 0 40	6 34 54	17 6 34	22 54 44
11	22 8 38	15 20 10	4 37 53	6 57 38	17 23 21	22 59 59
12	22 0 34	15 2 17	4 15 1	7 20 16	17 39 50	23 4 46
13	21 52 6	14 44 9	3 52 4	7 43 48	17 56 1	23 9 6
14	21 43 16	14 25 48	3 29 3	8 5 14	18 11 53	23 12 58
15	21 34 4	14 7 12	3 5 58	8 27 33	18 27 26	23 16 23
16	21 24 30	13 48 23	2 42 50	8 49 45	18 42 39	23 19 19
17	21 14 34	13 29 21	2 19 38	9 11 49	18 57 32	23 21 48
18	21 4 16	13 10 6	1 56 24	9 33 46	19 12 5	23 23 48
19	20 53 37	12 50 39	1 33 8	9 55 33	19 26 17	23 25 20
20	20 42 37	12 30 59	1 9 49	10 17 13	19 40 8	23 26 24
21	20 31 16	12 11 8	0 46 29	10 38 43	19 53 38	23 26 59
22	20 19 34	11 51 5	0 23 7 N.	11 0 3	20 6 45	23 27 7
23	20 7 31	11 30 50	0 0 16 S.	11 21 14	20 19 31	23 26 46
24	19 55 9	11 10 25	0 23 39	11 42 14	20 31 53	23 25 56
25	19 42 26	10 49 49	0 47 3	12 3 3	20 43 53	23 24 39
26	19 29 24	10 29 4	1 10 27	12 23 41	20 55 30	23 22 53
27	19 16 3	10 8 8	1 33 50	12 45 7	21 6 43	23 20 39
28	19 2 22	9 47 3	1 57 13	13 4 22	21 17 32	23 17 57
29	18 48 23	9 25 48	2 20 34	13 24 24	21 27 58	23 14 46
30	18 34 5	9 4 24	2 43 55 S.	13 44 14	21 37 58 S.	23 11 8
31	18 19 29 N.	8 42 52 N.		14 3 51 S.		23 7 2 S.

Pole Star.

MEAN TIME OF TRANSIT (AT WASHINGTON) AND POLAR DISTANCE OF POLARIS.

1909	January.		February.		March.		April.		May.		June.	
Day of Month.	Upper Transit.	Polar Distance.	Lower Transit.	Polar Distance	Lower Transit.	Polar Distance.	Lower Transit.	Polar Distance.	Lower Transit.	Polar Distance.	Lower Transit.	Polar Distance.
	P. M. H. M. S.	° ′ ″	A. M. H. M. S	° ′ ″	A. M. H. M. S.	° ′ ″	A. M. H. M. S.	° ′ ″	P. M. H. M. S.	° ′ ″	P. M. H. M. S.	° ′ ″
1	6 42 37	1 10 31	4 42 9	1 10 30	2 51 37	1 10 35	12 49 30	1 10 43	10 47 41	1 10 52	8 46 8	1 10 59
11	6 3 6	1 10 30	4 2 39	1 10 31	2 16 9	1 10 37	12 10 11	1 10 46	10 8 27	1 10 55	8 6 59	1 11 0
21	5 23 37	1 10 30	3 23 11	1 10 33	1 32 48	1 10 40	11 26 57 P.M.	1 10 49	9 29 15	1 10 57	7 27 45	1 11 1

POLE STAR—*Continued.*

1909 Day of Month.	JULY. Lower Transit.	JULY. Polar Distance.	AUGUST. Upper Transit.	AUGUST. Polar Distance.	SEPTEMBER. Upper Transit.	SEPTEMBER. Polar Distance.	OCTOBER. Upper Transit.	OCTOBER. Polar Distance.	NOVEMBER. Upper Transit.	NOVEMBER. Polar Distance.	DECEMBER. Upper Transit.	DECEMBER. Polar Distance.
	P. M. H. M. S.	° ′ ″	A. M. H. M. S	° ′ ″	A. M. H. M. S.	° ′ ″	A. M. H. M. S.	° ′ ″	P. M. H. M. S	° ′ ″	P. M. H. M. S.	° ′ ″
1	6 48 41	1 11 1	4 49 16	1 10 58	2 47 49	1 10 50	12 50 9	1 10 40	10 44 23	1 10 28	8 46 13	1 10 18
11	6 9 31	1 11 1	4 10 6	1 10 56	2 8 38	1 10 47	12 10 53	1 10 36	10 5 1	1 10 24	8 6 47	1 10 15
21	5 30 22	1 10 59	3 30 56	1 10 54	1 29 24	1 10 44	11 27 39 P.M.	1 10 32	9 25 38	1 10 21	7 27 18	1 10 13

From June 16 to August 1 both the upper and lower transits take place during daylight. The azimuth at the time of greatest eastern or western elongation can be easily computed from the formula:

$$\sin A = \frac{\sin p}{\cos l}$$

where A denotes the azimuth, p the polar distance, and l the latitude of the place.

DATE OF GREATEST ELONGATION.

To find the time of greatest eastern or western elongation, let H denote the hour angle, and l and p as before, then we shall have

$$\cos H = \tan p \tan l.$$

And the hour angle in *mean time* is

$$H_m = H^\circ \times 0.0664846.$$

This quantity, H_m, added to or subtracted from the time of transit given above, according to the elongation required, will give the *mean time* of the *greatest* elongation at any place whose north latitude is l.

Star Table.

FOR IDENTIFYING THE PRINCIPAL FIXED STARS.

NAME OF STAR.	Declination ° ′	On Meridian. Upper. H. M.	On Meridian. Lower. H. M.	NAME OF STAR.	Declination ° ′	On Meridian. Upper. H. M.	On Meridian. Lower. H. M.
αAndromedæ	N 28 31	— 1 18.0	+10 40.0	αLeonis (Regulus)	N 12 28	+ 8 40.1	+20 38.1
γPegasi (Algenib)	N 14 37	— 1 13.2	+10 44.8	αVirginis (Spica)	S 10 37	+11 56.5	+23 54.5
αCassiopeiæ	N 55 58	— 0 42.2	+11 15.8	αBootis (Arcturus)	N 19 43	+12 47.5	+ 0 45.5
αArietis	N 22 59	+ 0 40.0	+12 38.0	βUrsæ Minoris	N 74 35	+13 27.5	+ 1 25.5
βPersei (Algol)	N 40 34	+ 1 39.9	+13 37.9	αCoronæ Borealis	N 27 4	+13 49.7	+ 1 47.7
αTauri (Aldebaran)	N 16 18	+ 3 8.2	+15 6.2	αScorpii (Antares)	S 26 12	+14 59.3	+ 2 57.3
αAurigæ (Capella)	N 45 54	+ 3 47.1	+15 45.1	αLyræ (Vega)	N 8 41	+17 9.3	+ 5 7 3
βOrionis (Rigel)	S 8 19	+ 3 47.6	+15 45.6	αAquilæ (Altair)	N 8 36	+18 21.4	+ 6 19 4
αOrionis (Betelguese)	N 7 23	+ 4 27.6	+16 25.6	αCygni (Deneb)	N 44 55	+19 13.5	+ 7 11.5
αCanis Majoris (Sirius)	S 16 35	+ 5 18.4	+17 16.4	αCephei	N 62 9	+19 51.5	+ 7 49.5
αGeminorum (Castor)	N 32 7	+ 6 5.7	+18 3.7	αAquarii	S 0 49	+20 35.8	+ 8 33.8
βGeminorum (Pollux)	N 28 16	+ 6 16.6	+18 14.6	αPiscis Aus.	S 30 10	+21 27.1	+ 9 25.1
αCanis Minor	N 5 29	+ 6 11.6	+18 9.6	αPegasi (Markab)	N 14 39	+21 34.7	+ 9 32.7

To find the time of the star's transit add or subtract, according to the sign, the numbers in the second column of figures to the date of the transit of the pole star given above. Thus, for α Andromedæ February 1. Lower Transit of Polar Star is 4 h. 42 m. 9 s. A. M., to which add 10 h. 40 m. and we have 3 h. 22 m. 9 s. P. M.; for December 21, we find 6 h. 9 m. 18 s. P. M., etc.

APPROXIMATE PARALLAX AND DISTANCE IN LIGHT-YEARS OF SOME OF THE PRINCIPAL FIXED STARS.

By light-years is to be understood the number of years light requires to travel from the star to us.

	Parallax. ″	Light-Years.		Parallax. ″	Light-Years.
Polaris (Pole Star)	073	45	α Lyræ (Vega)	0.140	23
α Aurigæ (Capella)	0.046	71	61 Cygni	0.348–0.564	6–8
α Canis Majoris (Sirius)	0.233	15	β Cassiopeiæ	0.187	17
α Canis Minoris (Procyon)	0.123	27	γ Draconis	0.127	26
α Boötis (Arcturus)	0.127	28	85 Pegasi	0.054	60
α Centauri	0.916	3.6			

The determination of stellar parallax is one of the most difficult and refined problems in practical or observational astronomy. It is to find the angle which the semi-diameter of the earth's orbit subtends at the star—an angle always very small as seen from the above table and which cannot be measured directly but by various processes too complicated to be explained here.

Thermometers.

COMPARATIVE SCALES.

Reaumur, 80°.	Centigrade, 100°.	Fahrenheit, 212°.	
76	95	203	WATER BOILS AT SEA-LEVEL.
72	90	194	
68	85	185	
63.1	78.9	174	
60	75	167	Alcohol Boils.
56	70	158	
52	65	149	
48	60	140	
44	55	131	
42.2	52.8	127	Tallow Melts.
40	50	122	
36	45	113	
33.8	42.2	108	
32	40	104	
29.3	36.7	98	Blood Heat.
28	35	95	
25.8	32.2	90	
24	30	86	
21.3	26.7	80	
20	25	77	
16	20	68	
12.4	15.3	60	Temperate.
10.2	12.8	55	
8	10	50	
5.8	7.2	45	
4	5	41	
1.3	1.7	35	
0	0	32	WATER FREEZES.
– 0.9	– 1.1	30	
– 4	– 5	23	
– 5.3	– 6.7	20	
– 8	–10	14	
– 9.8	–12.2	10	
–12	–15	5	
–14.2	–17.8	0	ZERO Fahr.
–16	–20	– 4	
–20	–25	–13	
–24	–30	–22	
–28	–35	–31	
–32	–40	–40	

Rules for Foretelling the Weather.

ADAPTED FOR USE WITH ANEROID BAROMETERS.

A RISING BAROMETER.

A RAPID rise indicates unsettled weather.

A gradual rise indicates settled weather

A rise with dry air and cold increasing in Summer indicates wind from the northward, and if rain has fallen, better weather may be expected.

A rise with moist air and a low temperature indicates wind and rain from the northward.

A rise with southerly winds indicates fine weather.

A STEADY BAROMETER.

With dry air and seasonable temperature indicates a continuance of very fine weather.

A FALLING BAROMETER.

A rapid fall indicates stormy weather.

A rapid fall with westerly wind indicates stormy weather from the northward.

A fall with a northerly wind indicates storm, with rain and hail in Summer, and snow in Winter.

A fall with increased moisture in the air, and heat increasing, indicates wind and rain from the southward.

A fall with dry air and cold increasing in Winter indicates snow.

A fall after very calm and warm weather indicates rain with squally weather.

The barometer rises for northerly winds, including from northwest by north to the eastward for dry, or less wet weather, for less wind, or for more than one of these changes, except on a few occasions, when rain, hail, or snow comes from the northward with strong wind.

The barometer falls for southerly wind, including from southeast by south to the westward, for wet weather, for stronger wind or for more than one of these changes, except on a few occasions, when moderate wind, with rain or snow, comes from the northward.

The above printed rules are in use by the Seawanhaka-Corinthian Yacht Club of New York.

DURATION OF DIFFERENT KINDS OF WEATHER IN THE SEVERAL STORMS—VICINITY OF NEW YORK.

CRITICAL WINDS.	Clear Hours.	Cloudy Hours.	Rain Hours.	Clearing Hours.
South to Southwest	9	8	8.3	14
South to Southeast	14	13.4	15.6	15.4
East to Northeast	20	17.6	31	20.6

WEATHER WISDOM.

SUNSET COLORS.—A gray, lowering sunset, or one where the sky is green or yellowish-green, indicates rain. A red sunrise, with clouds lowering later in the morning, also indicates rain.

HALO (SUN DOGS).—By halo we mean the large circles, or parts of circles, about the sun or moon. A halo occurring after fine weather indicates a storm.

CORONA.—By this term we mean the small colored circles frequently seen around the sun or moon. A corona growing smaller indicates rain; growing larger, fair weather.

RAINBOWS.—A morning rainbow is regarded as a sign of rain; an evening rainbow of fair weather.

SKY COLOR.—A deep-blue color of the sky, even when seen through clouds, indicates fair weather; a growing whiteness, an approaching storm.

FOGS.—Fogs indicate settled weather. A morning fog usually breaks away before noon.

VISIBILITY.—Unusual clearness of the atmosphere, unusual brightness or twinkling of the stars, indicate rain.

FROST.—The first frost and last frost are usually preceded by a temperature very much above the mean.

OBJECTS VISIBLE AT SEA-LEVEL IN CLEAR WEATHER.

The following table shows the distance at sea-level at which objects are visible at certain elevations:

ELEVATION—FEET.	Miles.	ELEVATION—FEET.	Miles.	ELEVATION—FEET.	Miles.
1	1.31	30	7.25	90	12.25
5	2.96	35	7.83	100	13.23
6	3.24	40	8.37	150	16.22
7	3.49	45	8.87	200	18.72
8	3.73	50	9.35	300	22.91
9	3.96	60	10.25	500	29.58
10	4.18	70	11.07	1,000	33.41
20	5.92	80	11.88	1 mile	96.10
25	6.61				

Table of Magnetic Declinations,

OR VARIATION OF COMPASS FOR JANUARY, 1909—WITH THE ANNUAL CHANGE IN 1905 FOR THE PRINCIPAL PLACES IN THE UNITED STATES.

A plus (+) sign to the annual change denotes that the declination is increasing, and a minus (—) sign the reverse.

(Specially prepared for THE WORLD ALMANAC in the Office of the United States Coast and Geodetic Survey.)

State or Territory.	Station.	Approximate Latitude. °	′	Approximate Longitude. °	′	Variation January, 1909 °	′	Annual Change. ′
Ala.	Montgomery	32	22	86	18	2	51 E	+ 1
	Mobile	30	42	88	3	4	33 E	+ 1
	Huntsville	34	44	86	35	3	59 E	+ 1
Alaska	Sitka	57	3	135	20	30	11 E	+ 3
	Kodiak	57	48	152	24	24	8 E	— 2
	St. Michael	63	29	162	1	21	23 E	— 7
	Dutch Harbor	53	53	166	32	17	42 E	— 3
	Kiska	51	58	182	28	8	0 E	
Ariz.	Prescott	34	34	112	30	14	13 E	+ 3
	Yuma	32	44	114	37	14	18 E	+ 3
	Nogales	31	20	110	56	12	3 E	+ 3
Ark.	Little Rock	34	44	92	16	6	52 E	+ 2
Cal.	Sacramento	38	34	121	30	16	59 E	+ 4
	San Francisco	37	48	122	25	17	54 E	+ 4
	Los Angeles	34	4	118	15	15	24 E	+ 4
	San Diego	32	43	117	10	14	13 E	+ 3
Col	Denver	39	45	105	0	14	22 E	+ 2
Conn.	Hartford	41	46	72	40	10	53 W	+ 3
	New Haven	41	18	72	55	10	18 W	+ 3
Del	Dover	39	9	75	31	6	55 W	+ 3
Dist. of Col	Washington	38	53	77	0	5	13 W	+ 3
Florida	Tallahassee	30	26	84	17	2	15 E	0
	Jacksonville	30	20	81	39	1	9 E	— 1
	Key West	24	33	81	48	2	25 E	— 2
Georgia	Atlanta	33	44	84	22	1	36 E	— 1
	Savannah	32	5	81	5	0	34 E	— 1
Idaho	Boisé	43	37	116	12	19	21 E	+ 3
Illinois	Springfield	39	50	89	39	4	14 E	— 1
	Chicago	41	54	87	37	3	49 E	— 1
Indiana	Indianapolis	39	47	86	8	1	17 E	— 1
	Fort Wayne	41	3	85	3	0	4 E	— 1
Iowa	Des Moines	41	36	93	36	8	1 E	+ 1
	Keokuk	40	23	91	23	6	1 E	+ 1
Kansas	Topeka	39	2	95	43	9	19 E	+ 2
	Ness City	38	28	99	54	11	24 E	+ 2
Ky	Lexington	38	4	84	30	0	28 E	— 1
	Paducah	37	5	88	37	4	20 E	0
	Louisville	38	15	85	46	1	14 E	— 1
La	Baton Rouge	30	27	91	11	6	2 E	+ 2
	New Orleans	30	0	90	5	5	37 E	+ 2
	Shreveport	32	30	93	45	7	7 E	+ 2
Maine	Bangor	44	48	68	48	17	35 W	+ 2
	Portland	43	39	70	17	15	3 W	+ 3
	Eastport	44	54	66	59	19	24 W	+ 2
Md.	Annapolis	38	59	76	29	6	3 W	+ 3
	Baltimore	39	16	76	35	6	3 W	+ 3
Mass	Boston	42	22	71	4	13	8 W	+ 3
	Pittsfield	42	27	73	17	11	28 W	+ 3
Mich	Lansing	42	44	84	32	0	22 W	+ 2
	Detroit	42	21	83	3	1	32 W	+ 2
	Marquette	46	33	87	22	2	4 E	— 1
Minn	St. Paul	44	58	93	5	8	46 E	+ 1
	Duluth	46	46	92	4	12	26 E	+ 1
Miss	Jackson	32	19	90	12	6	6 E	+ 1
	Oxford	34	22	89	33	5	41 E	+ 1
Mo	Jefferson City	38	35	92	9	7	42 E	+ 2
	St. Louis	38	38	90	16	5	17 E	+ 2
	Kansas City	39	7	94	38	9	12 E	+ 2
Mon	Helena	46	37	112	2	19	58 E	+ 3
Neb	Lincoln	40	49	96	42	10	21 E	+ 2
	Omaha	41	16	95	58	9	47 E	+ 2
Nevada	Carson City	39	10	119	46	17	13 E	+ 3
	Eureka	39	31	115	58	17	0 E	+ 3
N. H.	Concord	43	12	71	29	12	48 W	+ 3
N. J.	Trenton	40	13	74	44	6	18 W	+ 3
N. Mex.	Santa Fé	35	41	105	57	12	58 E	+ 3
N. Y.	Albany	42	40	73	45	11	18 W	+ 3
	New York	40	43	74	0	9	18 W	+ 3
	Ithaca	42	27	76	29	7	37 W	+ 3
	Buffalo	42	55	78	54	6	24 W	+ 2
N. C.	Raleigh	35	47	78	38	2	42 W	+ 3
	Wilmington	34	13	77	56	3	23 W	+ 3
N. Dak.	Bismarck	46	48	100	47	15	23 E	+ 2
	Pembina	48	58	97	14	11	32 E	+ 2
Ohio	Columbus	40	0	83	0	1	3 W	+ 2
	Cleveland	41	30	81	42	2	36 W	+ 2
	Cincinnati	39	8	84	25	1	1 W	+ 2
Okla	Atoka	34	24	96	9	8	32 E	+ 2
	Guthrie	35	53	97	25	9	42 E	+ 2
Oregon	Portland	45	31	122	41	22	57 E	+ 4
Pa	Harrisburg	40	16	76	53	6	45 W	+ 3
	Philadelphia	39	58	75	10	7	55 W	+ 3
	Allegheny	40	29	80	1	4	12 W	+ 2
R. I.	Providence	41	50	71	24	18	18 W	+ 3
S. C.	Columbia	34	0	81	2	0	3 W	+ 1
	Charleston	32	47	79	5	0	46 W	+ 2
S. Dak.	Pierre	44	22	100	26	13	7 E	+ 2
	Yankton	42	53	97	25	11	24 E	+ 2
Tenn	Nashville	36	9	86	48	3	47 E	0
	Knoxville	35	58	83	55	0	15 W	+ 1
	Memphis	35	8	90	3	5	25 E	0
Tex.	Austin	30	17	97	44	8	27 E	+ 2
	San Antonio	29	27	98	28	9	4 E	+ 2
	Houston	29	47	95	20	8	2 E	+ 2
	Galveston	29	18	94	47	7	34 E	+ 2
	El Paso	31	46	106	29	12	14 E	+ 3
Utah	Salt Lake	40	46	111	54	16	53 E	+ 3
	Ogden	41	13	112	0	17	50 E	+ 3
Vt	Montpelier	44	15	72	32	14	23 W	+ 3
	Burlington	44	28	73	12	12	58 W	+ 3
Va	Richmond	37	32	77	26	4	8 W	+ 3
	Norfolk	36	52	76	17	4	48 W	+ 3
	Lynchburg	37	25	79	9	2	48 W	+ 3
Wash.	Olympia	47	2	122	54	23	29 E	+ 3
	Walla Walla	46	4	118	21	21	48 E	+ 3
W. Va.	Charleston	38	21	81	38	2	31 W	+ 3
	Wheeling	40	3	80	44	1	30 W	+ 2
Wis.	Madison	43	4	89	25	4	55	0
	Milwaukee	43	4	87	53	3	30	0
	La Crosse	43	50	91	14	6	30	0
Wyo	Cheyenne	41	8	104	49	15	5 E	+ 2

EXTREME VALUES.

State or Territory.	Station.	Latitude	Longitude	Variation	Annual Change
Maine	N. E. Corner	..	..	21 0 W	..
Alaska	N. E. Corner	..	..	40 0 E	..

DEPENDENCIES.

State or Territory.	Station.	Lat. °	′	Long. °	′	Var. °	′	Annual Change
Cuba	Havana	23	8	82	22	2	47 E	— 3
	Santiago	20	0	75	50	1	12 E	— 3
Porto Rico.	San Juan	18	29	66	7	1	46 W	+ 6
	Ponce	17	59	66	40	1	36 W	+ 6
Haw'n Islands	Honolulu	21	18	157	52	10	38 E	+ 1
	Hilo	19	44	155	05	8	51 E	+ 1
Philippines	Manila	14	35	120	58	9	56 E	+ 1

Normal Temperature and Rainfall

TABLE SHOWING THE NORMAL TEMPERATURE FOR JANUARY AND JULY, AND THE NORMAL ANNUAL PRECIPITATION AT WEATHER BUREAU STATIONS IN EACH OF THE STATES AND TERRITORIES, ALSO THE HIGHEST AND LOWEST TEMPERATURES EVER REPORTED FROM EACH OF SAID STATIONS, TO JANUARY 1, 1908.
(Prepared in the office of the Chief of the Weather Bureau, U. S. Department of Agriculture, for THE WORLD ALMANAC for 1909.)

States and Territories.	Stations.	Temperature: Mean, January.	Temperature: Mean, July.	Temperature: Extremes, Highest.	Temperature: Extremes, Lowest.	Mean Annual Precipitation, Rain and Melted Snow (inches).
Ala.	Birmingham	45	82	98	2	49.5
	Mobile	50	80	102	–1	62.0
	Montgomery	48	81	107	–5	51.2
Ariz.	Flagstaff	27	65	93	–20	23.0
	Phœnix	50	90	119	12	7.9
	Yuma	55	91	118	22	3.1
Ark.	Fort Smith	38	81	107	–15	41.3
	Little Rock	41	81	106	–12	49.9
Cal.	Fresno	45	82	115	20	9.7
	Los Angeles	53	67	109	28	15.6
	Red Bluff	45	82	115	18	25.0
	Sacramento	46	72	110	19	20.1
	San Diego	54	67	101	32	10.0
	San Francisco	50	57	101	29	22.3
Col.	Denver	29	72	105	–29	14.0
	Grand Junction	25	79	104	–16	8.5
	Pueblo	29	73	104	–27	12.0
Conn.	New Haven	27	72	100	–14	47.2
D. C.	Washington	33	77	104	–15	43.5
Florida	Jacksonville	54	81	104	10	53.2
	Jupiter	64	81	96	24	60.2
	Key West	69	84	100	41	38.7
	Pensacola	52	81	103	7	56.2
	Tampa	57	80	96	19	53.1
Georgia	Atlanta	42	78	100	–8	49.4
	Augusta	46	80	105	3	47.9
	Savannah	50	80	105	8	50.3
Idaho	Boisé	29	73	111	–28	12.7
	Pocatello	25	71	102	–20	12.9
Illinois	Cairo	35	79	106	–16	41.7
	Chicago	24	72	103	–23	33.3
	Springfield	26	76	107	–24	37.0
Indiana	Indianapolis	28	76	106	–25	41.5
Iowa	Des Moines	20	76	109	–30	32.4
	Dubuque	18	75	106	–32	34.0
	Keokuk	24	77	108	–27	35.1
Kansas	Concordia	24	78	106	–25	27.5
	Dodge	27	78	108	–26	20.8
	Wichita	30	79	106	–22	30.6
Ky.	Louisville	34	79	107	–20	44.3
La.	New Orleans	53	81	102	7	57.4
	Shreveport	46	82	107	–5	45.7
Maine	Eastport	20	60	93	–21	43.3
	Portland	22	68	97	–17	42.5
Md.	Baltimore	33	77	104	–7	43.0
Mass.	Boston	27	71	102	–13	43.4
Mich.	Alpena	19	66	98	–27	33.2
	Detroit	24	72	101	–24	32.2
	Marquette	16	65	108	–27	32.6
	Port Huron	22	69	99	–25	30.6
Minn.	Duluth	10	66	99	–41	29.9
	Moorhead	3	69	102	–48	24.9
	St. Paul	12	72	104	–41	28.7
Miss.	Vicksburg	47	80	101	–1	53.7
Mo.	Kansas City	26	78	106	–22	37.3
	St. Louis	31	79	107	–22	37.2
	Springfield	31	76	106	–29	44.6
Mont.	Havre	14	6[illegible]	108	–55	13.7
	Helena	20	67	103	–42	12.8
Mont.	Kalispell	20	64	96	–28	16.9
	Miles City	14	73	111	–49	13.2
Neb.	North Platte	21	74	107	–35	18.9
	Omaha	20	76	106	–32	30.7
	Valentine	18	73	106	–38	22.5
Nevada	Winnemucca	29	72	104	–28	8.4
N. C.	Charlotte	40	79	102	–5	49.2
	Hatteras	46	79	93	8	60.8
	Wilmington	46	79	103	5	51.0
N. Dak.	Bismarck	7	70	106	–44	17.6
	Williston	6	69	107	–49	15.1
N. H.	Concord	21	69	95	–23	40.1
N. J.	Atlantic City	32	72	99	–7	40.8
	Cape May	34	73	96	–7	40.8
N. Mex.	Roswell	39	79	104	–29	15.8
	Santa Fé	28	69	97	–13	14.2
N. Y.	Albany	22	72	100	–24	36.4
	Binghamton	23	70	96	–26	32.9
	Buffalo	25	70	95	–14	37.3
	New York City	30	74	100	–6	44.6
	Oswego	24	70	100	–23	36.2
Ohio	Cincinnati	32	78	105	–17	37.3
	Columbus	29	75	104	–20	36.9
	Toledo	26	74	102	–16	30.6
Okla.	Oklahoma	35	80	104	–17	31.7
Oregon	Portland	39	66	102	–2	45.1
	Roseburg	41	66	106	–6	34.4
Pa.	Erie	26	72	94	–16	38.6
	Philadelphia	32	76	103	–6	41.2
	Pittsburgh	31	75	103	–20	36.4
R. I.	Block Island	31	68	89	–4	44.4
S. C.	Charleston	49	81	104	7	52.1
S. Dak.	Huron	10	72	108	–43	21.1
	Pierre	14	75	110	–40	16.6
	Yankton	16	75	107	–34	25.4
Tenn.	Chattanooga	41	78	101	–10	50.7
	Memphis	40	81	104	–9	50.3
	Nashville	38	79	104	–13	48.5
Texas	Abilene	43	82	110	–6	24.7
	Amarillo	34	76	105	–16	22.6
	El Paso	44	80	113	–5	9.8
	Galveston	53	83	98	8	47.1
	Palestine	46	82	104	–6	43.0
	San Antonio	51	82	108	4	26.8
Utah	Salt Lake City	29	76	102	–20	16.0
Vt.	Burlington	19	71	97	–25	31.6
	Northfield	15	67	95	–32	33.8
Va.	Lynchburg	36	77	102	–6	43.4
	Norfolk	40	78	102	2	49.5
Wash.	Seattle	39	64	96	11	36.6
	Spokane	27	69	104	–30	18.8
	Walla Walla	33	74	113	–17	17.7
W. Va.	Elkins	29	70	94	–2[illegible]	42.8
	Parkersburg	31	76	102	–27	40.2
Wis.	La Crosse	15	73	104	–43	31.2
	Milwaukee	20	70	100	–25	31.4
Wyo.	Cheyenne	26	67	100	–38	13.6
	Lander & Washakie	17	68	100	–54	13.9

The minus (–) sign indicates temperature below zero.

Temperature and Rainfall of Foreign Cities.

Cities.	Mean Annual Temperature.	Annual Average Rainfall Inches.	Cities.	Mean Annual Temperature.	Annual Average Rainfall Inches.	Cities.	Mean Annual Temperature.	Annual Average Rainfall Inches.
Alexandria	69.0	10	Florence	59.2	41	Naples	60.3	30
Algiers	64.3	27	Frankfort	50.0	....	Nice	58.0	29
Amsterdam	49.9	....	Geneva	52.7	32	Odessa	48.0	....
Archangle	33.0	....	Genoa	61.1	47	Para	81.0	71
Astrakhan	50.1	6	Glasgow	49.8	44	Paris	51.3	22
Athens	63.0	....	Hamburg	47.0	....	Peking	53.0	27
Bagdad	74.0	....	Havana	79.1	91	Port Said	....	2
Barcelona	63.0	....	Hong Kong	73.0	101	Prague	50.2	14
Berlin	48.2	24	Honolulu	75.0	....	Quebec	40.3	....
Bermuda	72.0	55	Iceland	39.0	30	Quito	60.9	....
Berne	46.0	46	Jerusalem	62.6	16	Rio de Janeiro	77.2	29
Birmingham	48.2	....	Lima	73.3	....	Rome	60.5	31
Bombay	81.3	75	Lisbon	61.4	27	Rotterdam	51.0	23
Bordeaux	57.0	30	London	50.8	25	San Domingo	81.3	108
Brussels	50.0	29	Lyons	53.0	28	Shanghai	59.0	....
Budapest	51.9	17	Madeira	66.0	25	Smyrna	60.0	24
Buenos Ayres	62.8	....	Madrid	58.2	9	St. Petersburg	39.6	17
Cairo	72.2	....	Malta	66.0	20	Stockholm	42.3	20
Calcutta	82.4	76	Manchester	48.8	36	Sydney	65.8	49
Canton	71.0	39	Manila	78.4	....	The Hague	52.0	....
Cape Town	62.0	23	Maranham	....	277	Tobolsk	32.0	....
Cayenne	....	116	Marseilles	58.3	23	Trieste	55.0	43
Cherrapongee*	....	610	Melbourne	57.0	29	Valdivia	52.0	106
Christiania	41.5	....	Mexico	60.9	....	Valparaiso	64.0	....
Constantinople	56.5	....	Milan	55.1	38	Venice	55.4	....
Copenhagen	46.6	19	Montevideo	62.0	44	Vera Cruz	77.0	180
Delhi	77.0	24	Montreal	44.6	....	Vienna	51.0	19
Dublin	50.1	29	Moscow	40.0	....	Warsaw	56.2	....
Edinburgh	47.1	38	Munich	48.4	....			

* In Southwestern Assam. It is the wettest place in the world. In 1861 the rainfall there reached 905 inches.

NOTE—The mean annual temperature of the globe is 50° Fahr. The average rainfall is 36 inches.

Greatest Altitude in Each State.

FROM THE RECORDS OF THE UNITED STATES GEOLOGICAL SURVEY.

State or Territory.	Name of Place.	Heig't Feet.	State or Territory.	Name of Place.	Heig't Feet.
Alabama	Cheawha Mt. (Talladega Co)	2,407	Montana	Granite Peak	12,600
Alaska	Mt. McKinley	20,464	Nebraska	Lawton (U. P. R. R.)	5,945
Arizona	San Francisco Mt	12,794	Nevada	Wheeler Peak	13,058
Arkansas	Magazine Mt	2,800	N. Hampshire.	Mt. Washington	6,279
California	Mt. Whitney	14,501	New Jersey	High Point	1,800
Colorado	Mt. Elbert	14,421	New Mexico	Truchas Peak	13,275
Connecticut	Bear Mt	2,355	New York	Mt. Marcy (Adirondacks)	5,344
Delaware	Southwood	327	North Carolina	Mt. Mitchell	6,711
D. of Columbia	Tenley	400	North Dakota	Summit (Billings Co.)	2,830
Florida	Mossyhead	274	Ohio	Bellefontaine	1,540
Georgia	Sitting Bull Mt	5,046	Oklahoma	W. end Beaver County	5,000
Idaho	Hyndman Peak	12,078	Oregon	Mt. Hood	11,225
Illinois	Wadham	1,023	Pennsylvania	Blue Knob	3,136
Indiana	Carlos City	1,208	Rhode Island	Durfee Hill	805
Iowa	Primghar Weather Bureau	1,800	South Carolina	Rich Mountain	3,569
Kansas	Kanarado	3,906	South Dakota	Harney Peak	7,216
Kentucky	Big Black Mt. (Harlan Co.)	4,100	Tennessee	Guyot	6,636
Louisiana	Arcadia	368	Texas	El Capitan	8,690
Maine	Katahdin Mt	5,200	Utah	Emmons Peak	13,428
Maryland	Great Backbone Mt	3,400	Vermont	Mt. Mansfield	4,364
Massachusetts	Mt. Greylock	3,535	Virginia	Mt. Rogers (Grayson Co.)	5,719
Michigan	Porcupine Mt	2,023	Washington	Mt. Rainier	14,363
Minnesota	Mesabi Range & Misquah		West Virginia	Spruce Mt. (Pendleton Co.)	4,860
	Hills	2,400	Wisconsin	Rib Hill (Marathon Co.)	1,940
Mississippi	Holly Springs	602	Wyoming	Grand Teton Mt	13,747
Missouri	Cedar Gap	1,683			

The lowest point of dry land in the United States is in Death Valley, Cal., 278 feet below sea level.

NOTE.—The above table was prepared for THE WORLD ALMANAC by the Geographic Branch of the United States Geological Survey. It should be stated in connection with this table that it presents only points whose heights are matters of record, and that in several cases in the high mountain region of the far West and the Pacific Slope it is well known that there are higher points within the State or Territory whose heights are not yet known with accuracy, and consequently cannot be given.

This table was revised by the United States Geological Survey to September 1, 1908.

Weather Flags

OF THE WEATHER BUREAU, U. S. DEPARTMENT OF AGRICULTURE.

THE Weather Bureau furnishes, when practicable, for the benefit of all interests dependent upon weather conditions, the "Forecasts" which are prepared daily at the Central Office in Washington, D. C., and certain designated stations. These forecasts are telegraphed to stations of the Weather Bureau, railway officials, postmasters, and many others, to be communicated to the public by means of flags or steam whistles. The flags adopted for this purpose are five in number, and of the forms and colors indicated below:

EXPLANATION OF WEATHER FLAGS.

No. 1. White Flag.	No. 2. Blue Flag.	No. 3. White and Blue Flag.	No. 4. Black Triangular Flag.	No. 5. White Flag with black square in centre.
Clear or fair weather.	Rain or snow.	Local rain or snow.	Temperature.	Cold wave.

When number 4 is placed above number 1, 2, or 3, it indicates warmer; when below, colder; when not displayed, the temperature is expected to remain about stationary. During the late Spring and early Fall the cold-wave flag is also used to indicate anticipated frosts.

WHISTLE SIGNALS.

A warning blast of from fifteen to twenty seconds duration is sounded to attract attention. After this warning the longer blasts (of from four to six seconds duration) refer to weather, and shorter blasts (of from one to three seconds duration) refer to temperature; those for weather are sounded first.

Blasts.	Indicate.	Blasts.	Indicate.
One long	Fair weather.	One short	Lower temperature.
Two long	Rain or snow.	Two short	Higher temperature.
Three long	Local rain or snow.	Three short	Cold wave.

By repeating each combination a few times, with intervals of ten seconds, liability to error in reading the signals may be avoided.

As far as practicable the forecast messages will be telegraphed at the expense of the Weather Bureau; but if this is impracticable, they will be furnished at the regular commercial rates and sent "collect." In no case will the forecasts be sent to a second address in any place, except at the expense of the applicant.

Persons desiring to display the flags or sound the whistle signals for the benefit of the public should communicate with the Weather Bureau officials in charge of the climatological service of their respective States, the central stations of which are as follows:

Alabama, Montgomery.
Arizona, Phœnix.
Arkansas, Little Rock.
California, San Francisco.
Colorado, Denver.
Florida, Jacksonville.
Georgia, Atlanta.
Idaho, Boisé.
Illinois, Springfield.
Indiana, Indianapolis.
Iowa, Des Moines.
Kansas, Topeka.
Kentucky, Louisville.
Louisiana, New Orleans.
Maryland, Baltimore (for Delaware and Maryland).
Massachusetts, Boston (for New England).
Michigan, Grand Rapids.
Minnesota, Minneapolis.
Mississippi, Vicksburg.
Missouri, Columbia.
Montana, Helena.
Nebraska, Lincoln.
Nevada, Reno.
New Jersey, Atlantic City.
New Mexico, Santa Fé.
New York, Ithaca.
North Carolina, Raleigh.
North Dakota, Bismarck.
Ohio, Columbus.
Oklahoma, Oklahoma.
Oregon, Portland.
Pennsylvania, Philadelphia.
South Carolina, Columbia.
South Dakota, Huron.
Tennessee, Nashville.
Texas, Galveston.
Utah, Salt Lake City.
Virginia, Richmond.
Washington, Seattle.
West Virginia, Parkersburg.
Wisconsin, Milwaukee.
Wyoming, Cheyenne.

The Ancient and Modern Year.

THE Athenians began the year in June, the Macedonians in September, the Romans first in March and afterward in January, the Persians on August 11, the ancient Mexicans on February 23, the Mohammedans in July. The Chinese year, which begins early in February, is similar to the Mohammedan in having 12 months of 29 and 30 days alternately; but in every nineteen years there are seven years which have 13 months. This is not quite correct, and the Chinese have therefore formed a cycle of 60 years, in which period 22 intercalary months occur.

Storm and Hurricane Warnings

OF THE WEATHER BUREAU, U. S. DEPARTMENT OF AGRICULTURE.

STORM WARNINGS.

Northeasterly winds.

Southeasterly winds.

Northwesterly winds.

Southwesterly winds.

Red, black centre.

Storm Warnings.—A red flag with a black centre indicates that a storm of marked violence is expected.

The pennants displayed with the flags indicate the direction of the wind; red, easterly (from northeast to south); white, westerly (from southwest to north). The pennant above the flag indicates that the wind is expected to blow from the northerly quadrants; below, from the southerly quadrants.

By night a red light indicates easterly winds, and a white light below a red light westerly winds.

Hurricane Warnings.—Two red flags with black centres, displayed one above the other, indicate the expected approach of a tropical hurricane, and also one of those extremely severe and dangerous storms which occasionally move across the Lakes and Northern Atlantic Coast.

Velocity of Winds in the United States.

AVERAGE hourly velocity of the wind at selected stations of the United States Weather Bureau, also the highest velocity ever reported for a period of five minutes. (Prepared by W. L. Moore, Chief of the U. S. Weather Bureau, and revised to January 1, 1908, for THE WORLD ALMANAC.)

STATIONS.	Average Hourly Velocity.	Highest Ever Reported.	STATIONS.	Average Hourly Velocity.	Highest Ever Reported.	STATIONS.	Average Hourly Velocity.	Highest Ever Reported.
	Mi.	Mi.		Mi.	Mi.		Mi.	Mi.
Abilene, Texas	11	66	El Paso, Texas	5	78	Philadelphia, Pa	10	75
Albany N. Y	6	70	Fort Smith, Ark	5	66	Pittsburgh, Pa	6	66
Alpena, Mich	9	72	Galveston, Texas	10	*84	Portland, Me	5	60
Atlanta, Ga	9	60	Havre, Mont	11	76	Red Bluff, Cal	7	60
Bismarck, N. D	8	74	Helena, Mont	6	60	Rochester, N. Y	11	78
Boisé, Idaho	4	55	Huron, S. D	10	69	St. Louis, Mo	11	80
Boston, Mass	11	72	Jacksonville, Fla	6	70	St. Paul, Minn	7	102
Buffalo, N. Y	11	90	Keokuk, Iowa	8	60	St. Vincent, Minn.†	9	72
Charlotte, N. C	5	55	Knoxville, Tenn	5	84	Salt Lake City, Utah	5	66
Chattanooga, Tenn	6	60	Leavenworth, Kan.†	7	66	San Diego, Cal	6	40
Chicago, Ill	9	84	Louisville, Ky	7	60	San Francisco, Cal	9	60
Cincinnati, Ohio	7	59	Lynchburg, Va	4	50	Santa Fé, N. M	6	53
Cleveland, Ohio	9	73	Memphis, Tenn	6	75	Savannah, Ga	7	80
Custer, Mont.†	7	72	Montgomery, Ala	5	54	Spokane, Wash	4	52
Denver, Col	7	75	Nashville, Tenn	6	75	Toledo, Ohio	9	72
Detroit, Mich	9	76	New Orleans, La	7	60	Vicksburg, Miss	6	60
Dodge City, Kan	11	75	New York City, N. Y.	9	80	Washington, D. C	5	66
Dubuque, Iowa	5	60	North Platte, Neb	9	96	Wilmington, N. C	7	68
Duluth, Minn	7	78	Omaha, Neb	8	64			
Eastport, Me	9	78	Palestine, Texas	8	60			

*Anemometer blew away, at a velocity of 84 miles per hour, September, 1900. †Stations discontinued.

STANDARD TABLE SHOWING VELOCITY AND FORCE OF WINDS.

DESCRIPTION.	Miles per Hour.	Feet per Minute.	Feet per Second.	Force in lbs. per Square Foot.	DESCRIPTION.	Miles per Hour.	Feet per Minute.	Feet per Second.	Force in lbs. per Square Foot.
Perceptible	1	88	1.47	.005	High wind	30	2,640	44.0	4.428
Just perceptible	2	176	2.93	.020		35	3,080	51.3	6.027
	3	264	4.4	.044	Very high wind	40	3,520	58.6	7.872
Gentle breeze	4	352	5.87	.079		45	3,960	66.0	9.963
	5	440	7.33	.123	Storm	50	4,400	73.3	12.300
Pleasant breeze	10	880	14.67	.492	Great storm	60	5,280	88.0	17.712
	15	1,320	22.0	1.107		70	6,160	102.7	24.108
Brisk wind	20	1,760	29.3	1.968	Hurricane	80	7,040	117·3	31.488
	25	2,200	36.6	3.075		100	8,800	146.6	49.200

Loss by Lightning in the United States.

THE Weather Bureau of the United States Department of Agriculture in October, 1900, issued a bulletin giving these facts: In 1899 the total number of strokes of lightning which caused damage was 5,527; number of buildings injured, 6,256; value of property lost, $3,016,520; number of deaths by lightning during the year, 563; number of persons injured, 820; number of live stock killed in the fields, 4,251; value, $129,955. These are the latest available statistics.

The Chronicle Fire Tables record 3,012 fires caused by lightning in the United States in 1902, the property loss occasioned thereby being $3,396,810. These are the latest reported statistics on the subject.

High-Tide Tables.

FOR GOVERNOR'S ISLAND (NEW YORK HARBOR).

(Specially prepared from the Tide-Tables of the United States Coast and Geodetic Survey for THE WORLD ALMANAC.)

Eastern Time. Standard Time.

1909.	January.		February.		March.		April.		May.		June.	
Day of Month.	A. M.	P. M.	A. M.	P. M.	A. M.	P. M.	A. M.	P. M.	A. M.	P. M.	A. M.	P. M.
	H. M.	H. M.	H. M.	H. M.	H. M.	H. M.	H. M.	H. M.	H. M.	H. M.	H. M.	H. M.
1	3 40	4 5	5 12	6 0	3 54	4 54	5 28	6 12	5 37	6 3	6 2	6 22
2	4 35	5 8	6 4	6 50	4 56	5 51	6 13	6 47	6 16	6 34	6 31	6 56
3	5 27	6 5	6 50	7 34	5 48	6 39	6 52	7 15	6 49	7 2	7 12	7 33
4	6 15	6 56	7 32	8 12	6 36	7 18	7 23	7 40	7 12	7 30	7 51	8 12
5	7 1	7 43	8 10	8 45	7 15	7 48	7 53	8 4	7 45	8 0	8 35	8 55
6	7 45	8 27	8 44	9 14	7 50	8 16	8 17	8 30	8 15	8 35	9 17	9 40
7	8 27	9 7	9 17	9 42	8 21	8 40	8 40	9 0	8 47	9 12	10 6	10 26
8	9 7	9 46	9 46	10 9	8 48	9 3	9 10	9 33	9 28	9 52	11 0	11 17
9	9 43	10 20	10 15	10 42	9 11	9 30	9 46	10 14	10 12	10 38	11 58	....
10	10 20	10 58	10 47	11 20	9 40	10 4	10 27	10 58	11 3	11 30	12 13	1 1
11	10 55	11 35	11 25	......	10 12	10 42	11 15	11 48	....	12 0	1 16	2 10
12	11 32	....	12 6	12 10	10 50	11 27	....	12 10	12 27	1 10	2 25	3 17
13	12 17	12 12	12 59	1 2	11 34	....	12 48	1 17	1 35	2 28	3 35	4 18
14	1 2	1 0	2 0	2 5	12 19	12 29	1 55	2 40	2 50	3 42	4 42	5 15
15	1 56	1 53	3 7	3 20	1 19	1 34	3 16	4 4	4 4	4 45	5 44	6 7
16	2 52	2 51	4 13	4 39	2 28	2 54	4 28	5 10	5 8	5 39	6 42	6 58
17	3 48	3 55	5 14	5 43	3 42	4 22	5 31	6 3	6 4	6 30	7 35	7 45
18	4 42	4 59	6 8	6 40	4 51	5 30	6 25	6 53	6 57	7 18	8 27	8 33
19	5 32	5 54	7 1	7 30	5 51	6 24	7 16	7 40	7 49	8 4	9 15	9 19
20	6 25	6 48	7 49	8 19	6 45	7 14	8 5	8 25	8 38	8 50	10 4	10 5
21	7 12	7 40	8 38	9 5	7 34	8 0	8 52	9 10	9 27	9 37	10 51	10 48
22	8 0	8 30	9 25	9 54	8 22	8 45	9 40	9 57	10 18	10 23	11 37	11 32
23	8 49	9 20	10 12	10 43	9 8	9 32	10 28	10 45	11 10	11 12	...	12 22
24	9 38	10 12	11 4	11 35	9 55	10 20	11 22	11 37	......	12 5	12 14	1 10
25	10 38	11 7	11 58	....	10 45	11 10	....	12 25	12 2	1 4	12 58	1 52
26	11 22	....	12 33	1 2	11 38	....	12 35	1 36	12 59	2 5	1 42	2 37
27	12 3	12 20	1 40	2 18	12 4	12 42	1 39	2 50	2 0	3 0	2 29	3 23
28	1 5	1 22	2 46	3 40	1 5	2 0	2 47	3 58	3 0	3 50	3 20	4 10
29	2 10	2 38	....	....	2 15	3 23	3 54	4 50	3 55	4 32	4 15	4 56
30	3 15	3 52	....	....	3 27	4 35	4 50	5 29	4 45	5 10	5 5	5 40
31	4 16	5 1	....	....	4 32	5 30	....	....	5 25	5 45	......	....

1909.	July.		August.		September.		October.		November.		December.	
Day of Month.	A. M.	P. M.	A. M.	P. M.	A. M.	P. M.	A. M.	P. M.	A. M.	P. M.	A. M.	P. M.
	H. M.	H. M.	H. M.	H. M.	H. M.	H. M.	H. M.	H. M.	H. M.	H. M.	H. M.	H. M.
1	5 54	6 25	7 20	7 40	8 41	9 1	9 6	9 30	10 22	11 4	10 52	11 50
2	6 47	7 11	8 11	8 30	9 30	9 50	9 55	10 22	11 18	....	11 52	....
3	7 33	7 57	9 0	9 18	10 20	10 40	10 46	11 19	12 11	12 17	12 52	12 50
4	8 22	8 43	9 50	10 8	11 10	11 32	11 42	....	1 20	1 24	1 55	1 50
5	9 12	9 30	10 40	10 58	....	12 5	12 21	12 41	2 30	2 32	2 50	2 53
6	10 2	10 20	11 34	11 48	12 31	1 5	1 33	1 48	3 32	3 33	3 41	3 47
7	10 55	11 9	....	12 27	1 39	2 8	2 48	2 56	4 26	4 28	4 24	4 35
8	11 55	....	12 44	1 26	2 55	3 15	4 0	4 2	5 8	5 17	5 0	5 15
9	12 2	12 48	1 46	2 28	4 9	4 20	4 57	4 57	5 43	5 56	5 35	5 52
10	12 59	1 49	2 59	3 32	5 5	5 18	5 43	5 46	6 15	6 31	6 5	6 20
11	2 4	2 52	4 15	4 35	6 8	6 10	6 21	6 30	6 43	7 0	6 40	6 50
12	3 12	3 53	5 23	5 33	6 53	6 55	6 55	7 5	7 12	7 25	7 12	7 25
13	4 22	4 53	6 23	6 26	7 30	7 35	7 24	7 38	7 40	7 52	7 49	8 5
14	5 30	5 48	7 13	7 15	8 2	8 11	7 50	8 5	8 13	8 25	8 28	8 48
15	6 32	6 41	7 58	7 58	8 32	8 43	8 17	8 28	8 49	9 5	9 12	9 37
16	7 25	7 30	8 38	8 38	9 0	9 11	8 47	8 56	9 30	9 50	9 58	10 29
17	8 15	8 16	9 11	9 16	9 27	9 35	9 20	9 30	10 15	10 40	10 49	11 28
18	9 0	9 0	9 44	9 50	9 57	10 5	9 57	10 11	11 6	11 40	11 44	....
19	9 42	9 42	10 12	10 18	10 33	10 41	10 40	10 58	....	12 2	12 33	12 45
20	10 23	10 22	10 43	10 48	11 14	11 21	11 30	11 51	12 47	1 7	1 40	1 52
21	11 0	10 59	11 16	11 18	....	12 1	....	12 26	2 0	2 16	2 46	3 0
22	11 35	11 31	11 55	11 55	12 12	12 55	12 57	1 30	3 9	3 27	3 48	4 16
23	....	12 8	....	12 40	1 10	1 57	2 10	2 40	4 10	4 30	4 45	5 10
24	12 3	12 47	12 40	1 31	2 20	3 5	3 27	3 50	5 5	5 26	5 37	6 8
25	12 38	1 30	1 35	2 31	3 36	4 12	4 31	4 52	5 55	6 20	6 28	7 0
26	1 22	2 20	2 38	3 35	4 47	5 13	5 26	5 48	6 45	7 13	7 11	7 54
27	2 13	3 15	3 52	4 37	5 48	6 10	6 17	6 40	7 33	8 4	8 5	8 45
28	3 13	4 11	5 3	5 36	6 40	7 2	7 5	7 30	8 20	8 56	8 53	9 37
29	4 19	5 7	6 6	6 32	7 30	7 53	7 54	8 20	9 10	9 50	9 40	10 26
30	5 24	6 0	7 1	7 24	8 17	8 41	8 42	9 11	10 0	10 48	10 30	11 18
31	6 24	6 52	7 53	8 14	....	....	9 32	10 5	....	....	11 17	....

HIGH-TIDE TABLES—*Continued.*

TIME OF HIGH WATER AT POINTS ON THE ATLANTIC COAST.

The local time of high water at the following places may be found approximately for each day by adding to or subtracting from the time of high water at Governor's Island, N. Y., the hours and minutes annexed.

	H.	M.		H.	M.
Albany, N. Y. ....add	9	31	New Haven, Ct. ....add	3	1
Annapolis, Md. ....add	8	57	New London, Ct. ....add	1	22
Atlantic City, N. J. ....sub.		20	Newport, R. I. ....sub.		22
Baltimore, Md. ....add	10	52	Norfolk, Va. ....add		58
Bar Harbor, Me. ....add	2	46	Norwich, Ct. ....add	2	0
Beaufort, S. C. ....sub.		8	Old Point Comfort, Va. ....add		39
Block Island, R. I. ....sub.		34	Philadelphia, Pa. ....add	5	41
Boston, Mass. ....add	3	22	Plymouth, Mass. ....add	3	12
Bridgeport, Ct. ....add	3	2	Point Lookout, Md. ....add	4	49
Bristol, R. I. ....sub.		14	Portland, Me. ....add	3	10
Cape May, N. J. ....add		10	Portsmouth, N. H. ....add	3	16
Charleston, S. C. ....sub.		42	Poughkeepsie, N. Y. ....add	3	51
Eastport, Me. ....add	3	0	Providence, R. I. ....add		7
Fernandina, Fla. ....sub.		18	Richmond, Va. ....add	8	48
Gloucester, Mass. ....add	2	55	Rockaway Inlet, N. Y. ....sub.		25
Hell Gate Ferry, East River, N. Y. ..add	1	53	Rockland, Me. ....add	3	1
Isles of Shoals, N. H. ....add	3	11	Rockport, Mass. ....add	2	50
Jacksonville, Fla. ....add		37	Salem, Mass. ....add	3	9
Key West, Fla. ....add	1	24	Sandy Hook, N. J. ....sub.		32
League Island, Pa. ....add	5	23	Savannah, Ga. ....add		7
Marblehead, Mass. ....add	3	2	Southport (Smithville), N. C. ....sub.		43
Nahant, Mass. ....add	3	2	Vineyard Haven, Mass. ....add	3	36
Nantucket, Mass. ....add	4	21	Washington, D. C. ....add	12	1
Newark, N. J. ....add		54	Watch Hill, R. I. ....add		42
New Bedford, Mass. ....sub.		10	West Point, N. Y. ....add	2	47
Newburyport, Mass. ....add	3	16	Wilmington, N. C. ....add	1	0

EXAMPLE.—To find the approximate time of high tide at Atlantic City, N. J., on any day, find first the time of high water at New York under the desired date, and then subtract 20 minutes, as in the above table; the result is the time of high water required.

AVERAGE RISE AND FALL OF TIDE.

PLACES.	Feet.	Inches.	Places.	Feet.	Inches.	Places.	Feet.	Inches.
Baltimore, Md.	1	3	New London, Ct.	3	9	San Diego, Cal.	3	7
Boston, Mass.	9	8	New Orleans, La.	None	None	Sandy Hook, N. J.	4	7
Charleston, S. C.	5	1	Newport, R. I.	9	8	San Francisco, Cal.	4	9
Eastport, Me.	18	2	New York, N. Y.	4	4	Savannah, Ga.	6	5
Galveston, Tex.	1	1	Old Point Comf't, Va.	2	5	Seattle, Wash.	12	2
Key West, Fla.	1	2	Philadelphia, Pa.	6	0	Tampa, Fla.	2	2
Mobile, Ala.	1	2	Portland, Me.	9	1	Washington, D. C.	2	9

Highest tide at Eastport, Me., 218 inches. Lowest tide at Galveston, Tex., 13 inches.

Earthquake Areas of the Earth.

MAJOR DE MONTESSUS DE BALOKE, after years of labor, has drawn up a catalogue of 130,000 shocks, of which trustworthy details have been procured, and this indicates with some scientific accuracy how the symptoms of seismic activity are manifested over the earth's surface. The period of observation includes generally the last fifty years; but there is no reason to suppose that a longer time would materially affect the proportionate numbers. The appended figures, drawn from M. de Montessus's statistics, will give an idea of the general result:

AREA.	Earth-quakes.	AREA.	Earth-quakes.	AREA.	Earth-quakes.
Scandinavia....	646	Greece....	10,306	Atlantic Coast....	937
British Isles....	1,139	Russia....	258	Mexico....	5,586
France....	2,793	Asia Minor....	4,451	Central America....	2,739
Spain and Portugal....	2,656	India....	813	West Indies....	2,561
Switzerland....	3,895	Japan....	27,562	South America....	8,081
Italy....	27,672	Africa....	179	Java....	2,155
Holland and North Germany....	2,326	Atlantic Islands....	1,704	Australia and Tasmania.	83
Sicily....	4,331	United States, Pacific Coast....	4,467	New Zealand....	1,925

The most shaken countries of the world are Italy, Japan, Greece, South America (the Pacific Coast), Java, Sicily, and Asia Minor. The lands most free from these convulsions are Africa, Australia, Russia, Siberia, Scandinavia, and Canada. As a rule, where earthquakes are most frequent they are most severe. But to this general statement there are exceptions—Indian shocks, though less numerous, being often very disastrous. Loss of life in many cases depends, however, on density of population rather than on the intensity of the earth movement. Numerically, also, France has registered more seismic tremors than Spain and Portugal, but France in historic times has experienced no earthquake disaster approaching the havoc wrought by the one calamity at Lisbon.

Volcanic Deposits in the United States.

(Prepared for THE WORLD ALMANAC by Dr. J. Morrison, M. D., Ph. D.)

IN the long series of geologic ages during which North America was being fitted for the occupation of man, four great seismic convulsions are especially to be noted because their permanent results contribute very largely to characterize the physical features of our continent.

The first occurred before the dawn of either animal or vegetable life, during the Azoic age when the Laurentian Mountains of Northern Canada were pushed up in molten or plastic condition from the interior of the earth through the comparatively thin overlying crust of limestone. This igneous rock is known by the name of gray or red granite, occurs in vast unstratified masses and is of course destitute of organic remains. There are many other large deposits of granite scattered over the continent but it is very probable that they were upheaved in subsequent ages.

The Laurentian Mountains are the oldest portion of our continent and their birth antedates that of all other Mountains in the western hemisphere by many millions of years.

THE APPALACHIAN CONVULSION.

The second great convulsion occurred when the Appalachian chain of mountains was heaved up from beneath the briny waves. Some igneous rock was brought to the surface as appears from beds of granite in New Hampshire, in the Adirondacks, and other parts of the chain. There is no evidence of volcanic eruptions of lava throughout its entire course, and if any volcanoes existed they probably emitted hot water, steam and other gases. In the upheaval of this mighty chain of mountains, very extensive cracks or "faults" must have been made both on the east and west sides of the chain. It is along these that recent seismic disturbances have occurred. These cracks are now hermetically and perhaps eternally closed or sealed up by the pressure of the adjacent walls of the crust, but it is very probable that in some places there may be small fissures or vents still open which emit gas or aqueous vapor. This may account for the blue haze or mist which always hangs over the eastern portion of the Appalachian chain and which has given to it the name of the "Blue Ridge" Mountains, while no such haze to any appreciable extent covers the western portions of the range known as the Alleghany and Cumberland mountains.

UPHEAVAL OF THE ROCKY MOUNTAINS.

The third great disturbance was the upheaval of the Rocky Mountain system which is comparatively young as regards the Laurentian and Appalachian systems. This mighty chain with all its outlying spurs and ranges covers a very large area in the western part of the continent, and was for many ages the theatre of violent volcanic eruptions, with the exception of the active volcanoes in Alaska, Mexico and Central America, all the others which, in the remote past, constituted a very prominent feature in this region, are extinct for unnumbered ages. All the conical peaks which are found in great numbers from a few hundred to many thousand feet in height, from the Arctic Ocean to Mexico, were at one time active volcanoes. Mounts McKinley, Logan, Ranier, St. Helena, Whitney, Pike's Peak and others, many of which are now covered with perpetual snow, were once terrific outlets of subterranean fires. In Washington, Idaho, Oregon and California there are thousands of square miles surrounding these now extinct volcanic cones, covered with basalt and other volcanic products. This region was once a veritable "land of fire." Nowhere else, perhaps, was there anything to equal these terrific volcanic outbursts. The western side of this mighty range is still seamed with cracks or "faults" along which seismic disturbances of more or less destructive character have even recently occurred.

A CENTRAL OCEAN.

Between the Appalachian and Rocky Mountains an ocean once extended from the Gulf of Mexico to the Arctic Sea, covering the entire valley of the Mississippi and its numerous tributaries and having probably three outlets, one between the Laurentian and Appalachian Mountains, through what is now the valley of the St. Lawrence; one through the valley of Lake Winnipeg and the Nelson River, into Hudson Bay; but by far the greatest portion extended on through the valley of the Mackenzie River (the Mississippi of the North) to the Arctic Ocean. From the depth of alluvial deposits found in this extensive valley, it is quite evident that this ocean must have existed for many millions of years. The Gulf Stream, which now flows along the eastern side of the United States, then flowed through this ocean to the Arctic Sea and thus softened the climate in the high northern latitudes of this valley, a fact which is attested by the finding of organic remains of animals and plants which belonged to a sub-tropical climate.

After the lapse of ages the floor of this ocean was gradually elevated to its present position, the water flowed off to the north and south and then the great rivers of this region began to cut their channels to the ocean. A long narrow trough or channel, several hundred miles long and from twenty to forty or fifty miles wide, and extending from about the interior of Kansas through Oklahoma and Texas to the Gulf of Mexico, still remained covered with water for an immensely long period. In north western Texas, the terraces and beaches of this ancient arm of the sea can still be easily traced by means of the marine remains deposited at their foot. At some subsequent period this channel was pushed up until the sea water flowed off, carrying away with it whatever loose sedimentary deposits then existed, and leaving a floor of clean limestone rock which in many places consists chiefly of masses of exceedingly small shells,—the solid sarcophagi of countless millions of once living creatures which tenanted these ocean depths.

THE BLACK BELT OF TEXAS.

Another long interval rolls by and during one of the numerous seismic convulsions a mud volcano burst forth somewhere in what is now Kansas or northern Oklahoma. Sea water had percolated through the "faults" and fissures down to the heated interior of the earth, where it was converted into superheated, steam, which, no doubt assisted in disintegrating the rocky masses containing potassium, iron, sulphur, calcium and other minerals, and when the pressure became so great that the overlying crust was inadequate to resist it, a volcano burst out and vomited forth steam and hot black mud which not only filled up the trough or channel but also flowed in a mighty stream to the Gulf of Mexico. This long narrow tract of country is now known as the "Black Belt of Texas." It is of volcanic origin; it was ejected from the interior of the earth long anterior to the Glacial period; its temperature no doubt exceeded that of boiling water, and so deep was it in many places that it required several years to cool. In central and northern Texas and further north, it occurs frequently

VOLCANIC DEPOSITS IN THE UNITED STATES.—*Continued.*

in parallel waves or undulations, the result no doubt of subsequent eruptions when the mud soon became too viscid by cooling to reach the Gulf. These waves or undulations have been worn down by rain storms for hundreds of thousands of years and their present dimensions can give only a very faint idea of what they once were, but they still constitute the only physical feature that diversifies the landscape in certain portions of the "Black Belt." The volcano, from which it was poured out, sank beneath the surface ages ago. The enormous cavity which must have been formed permitted the volcanic cone to collapse, subsequent eruptions may have filled up any cavity that remained, and the hand of time completely obliterated all traces of its site. The falling in of volcanic cones is of frequent occurrence especially in Mexico, and the cone of Vesuvius in Italy has often fallen in several hundred feet. Abundant evidence of the volcanic origin of this black mud or clay is found in the following facts:

First.—It contains no fossils; no remains of either animals or plants can be found in it, except perhaps near the surface, where they are of very recent origin. Now, if it had been deposited at the bottom of an ocean, it would certainly contain shells and other marine remains.

Second.—The limestone rock, on which it for the most part rests, was heated to such an extent that it is almost completely burned limestone. The action of heat can be seen about four or five feet deep, below which the limestone is of the usual blue color. The intensity of the heat could not, of course, be very high, but the quantity of the heat in it must have been prodigious.

Here, perhaps, it will be necessary to digress a little to explain to the untechnical reader what is meant by the intensity and quantity of heat. The heat in a piece of iron wire heated almost to the melting point is of high intensity, but small in quantity, while on the other hand the heat contained in several thousand gallons of boiling water is of low intensity, but great in quantity. The former would have no appreciable effect in heating a large room, but the latter would soon make it uncomfortably warm. So it was with this boiling black mud, the quantity of heat in it was sufficient to burn or decompose the limestone rock, on which it rested, to the depth of four or five feet.

A chemical examination of this black mud shows it to be composed of ordinary blue clay (silicate of aluminum) colored black, with variable quantities of the sulphides of sodium, potassium and iron. It still possesses a slight alkaline reaction. The water of the streams that flow through it is also alkaline, and so also is the water of many of the artesian wells that have been bored through it. It is on the whole very fertile, owing partly to the large amount of vegetable mould which has for ages accumulated on the surface.

OTHER BLACK MUD ERUPTIONS.

As a still further confirmation of its volcanic origin, two recent eruptions of similar black mud may be cited. In May, 1902, the city of St. Pierre, in Martinique, was destroyed by a blast of superheated steam and other gases from Mount Pelee, which subsequently vomited out a large quantity of black waxy mud, which filled up a large ravine and the bed of a river for several miles. About two decades ago one of New Zealand's terrific volcanoes poured out such a quantity of black mud that it completely obliterated the beds of several lakes and rivers, and thoroughly changed the face of the entire landscape.

These tremendous seismic convulsions in remote geologic ages produced great and useful changes in the physical aspect of our globe, but they were all necessary for the accommodation and reception of the coming man who was, however, still hid deep in the womb of the future.

Age of the Earth.

THE following is the estimate of Prof. Lester F. Ward, of Brown University:

Geologic Periods.	Years.	Geologic Periods.	Years.
Archean	18,000,000	Cretaceous	3,000,000
Algonkian	18,000,000	Tertiary	2,675,000
Cambrian	6,000,000	Quarternary	300,000
Silurian	6,000,000	Historic Period	25,000
Devonian	6,000,000		
Carboniferous	6,000,000	Total age of the earth	72,000,000
Triassic	3,000,000	Age of written language	6,000
Jurassic	3,000,000		

The following is the estimate of the existence of the human race on the planet:

Whatever theory we may adopt as to the particular way in which life began, it is at least certain that in some way it did begin about as soon as the conditions of the earth's surface became such as to permit its existence. And we may well accept Professor Lowell's view, shared by many others, that for the origination of life much higher temperatures were required than those which commonly prevail at the present time, although, after having once originated, owing to the slow rate at which the planet cooled, it easily adapted itself to much lower temperatures.

The human race is supposed to have existed between 200,000 and 300,000 years, let us say one-quarter of 1,000,000 years. It has been conscious of its existence only about 10,000 years, and really alive as a psychic being less than 5,000 years. The most that it has accomplished of any value to itself has been done within 2,000 years, and its great work within 200 years. In a word, relatively speaking, man has only just begun to exist. His golden age, as Saint-Simon said, is before him and not behind him. His history is but the threshold of the psychozoic age. The whole of that immense period lies before him. The conditions of existence on this earth are now at their optimum. Abundance of air and water, heat and light, great variety of surface, soil, climate, mineral resources and all the materials and forces of Nature ready to yield to the magic wand of science. There are no indications that these conditions will change in an entire geologic epoch. These favorable conditions are certainly liable to last as long as the tertiary period just closed has lasted, namely, about 3,000,000 years.

The Geological Strata.

THE strata composing the earth's crust is divided by most geologists into two great classes: 1. Those generally attributed to the agency of water. 2. To the action of fire; which may be subdivided as follows: (*a*) Aqueous formations, stratified, rarely crystalline (sedimentary or fossiliferous rocks; metamorphic or unfossiliferous). (*b*) Igneous formations, unstratified, crystalline (volcanic, as basalt; platonic, as granite).

The geological record is classified into five main divisions or periods: 1. The Archæan, lifeless and dawn of life. 2. The Palæozoic (ancient life). 3. The Mesozoic (middle life). 4 The Cenozoic (recent life). 5. Quaternary, the age in which man's first appearance is indicated.

Periods.		Eras.	Series.	Subdivisions.
Quaternary Period.	Age of Primeval Man.	Quaternary or Post Tertiary.	3. Recent. 2. Champlain. 1. Glacial.	Pleistocene.
Cenozoic Period.	Age of Mammals.	Tertiary Era.	4. Pliocene.	English Crag.
			3. Miocene.	Upper Molasse.
			2. Oligocene.	Rupelian and Tongrian of Belgium.
			1. Eocene.	
Mesozoic Period.	Age of Reptiles.	Cretaceous Era.	4. Laramie.	Upper Chalk.
			3. Colorado.	Lower Chalk. Chalk Marl.
			2. Dakota.	Gault.
			1. Lower.	Neocomian. Lower Greensand.
		Jura-Trias. Jurassic	3. Purbeck.	Wealden. Purbeck, Portland, Kimmeridge.
			2. Oōlite.	Oxford Oōlites. Lower or Bath Oōlite.
			1. Lias.	1. Lower Lias. 2. Marlstone. 3. Upper Lias.
		7. Triassic.	4. Rhætic. 3. Upper. 2. Middle. 1. Lower.	Kössen beds, Dachstein beds; Alpine Keuper. [Trias, in part. Muschelkalk Bunter-Sandstein.
Palæozoic Period.	Age of Coal Plants.	Carboniferous Era.	3. Permian.	2. Magnesian Limestone. 1. Lower Red Sandstone, or Rothliegendes.
			2. Carboniferous.	3. Upper Coal-Measures. 2. Lower Coal-Measures.
			1. Subcarboniferous.	1. Millstone Grit. Lower Carboniferous. Mountain Limestone.
	Age of Fishes.	Devonian Era.	5. Catskill and Chemung. 4. Portage. 3. Hamilton. 2. Coniferous. 1. Oriskany.	Catskill Red Sandstone. Chemung. Portage. Genesee Slate. Hamilton beds. Marcellus Shale. Upper Helderberg, Schoharie, Grit. Oriskany Sandstone. } Old Red Sandstone.
	Age of Invertebrates.	Upper Silurian.	3. Lower Helderberg.	Lower Helderberg.
			2. Onondaga.	Onondaga Salt Group. Salina beds. Water Lime.
			1. Niagara.	3. Niagara Group. Wenlock Group. 2. Clinton Group. } Upper 1. Medina Sandstone. } Llandovery.
		Lower Silurian.	3. Trenton.	3. Hudson River beds. Cincinnati Group. Lower Llandovery. 2. Utica Shales. 1. Trenton Limestone. Caradoc and Bala Limestone. Black River Limestone.
			2. Chazy.	Chazy Limestone.
			1. Calciferous.	Calciferous Sandrock. Magnesian stone.
		Cambrian.		Lower, Middle, and Upper Cambrian.
Archæan Period.			Eozoic (dawn of life). Azoic (lifeless).	1. Laurentian. Huronian.

Facts About the Earth.

ACCORDING to Clark, the equatorial semi-diameter is 20,926,202 feet=3963.296 miles, and the polar semi-diameter is 20,854,895 feet=3950.738 miles. One degree of latitude at the pole=69.407 miles. One degree of latitude at the equator=68.704 miles.

POPULATION OF THE EARTH BY CONTINENTS.

CONTINENTAL DIVISIONS.	Area in Square Miles.	INHABITANTS. Number	INHABITANTS. Per Sq. Mile.	CONTINENTAL DIVISIONS.	Area in Square Miles.	INHABITANTS. Number.	INHABITANTS. Per Sq. Mile.
Africa	11,514,000	127,000,000	11.00	Australasia	3,288,000	5,200,000	1.58
America, N..	6,446,000	115,000,000	17.80	Europe..	3,555,000	380,200,000	106.90
America, S..	6,837,000	45,000,000	6.50	Polar Reg...	4,888,800	300,000	0.07
Asia	14,710,000	850,000,000	57.70	Total.........	51,238,800	1,522,700,000	29.60

The above estimate is based upon one made by Ernest George Ravenstein, F.R.G.S., the geographer and statistician in 1890, with the additions in population since that date in the Americas and Australasia bringing it down to 1909.

Ravenstein's estimate of the earth's fertile region, in square miles, is 28,269,200; steppe, 13,901,000; desert, 4,180,000; polar regions, 4,888,800.

The population of the earth at the death of the Emperor Augustus, estimated by Bodio, was 54,000,000. The population of Europe hardly exceeded 50,000,000 before the fifteenth century.—*Mulhall.*

The area and cubic contents of the earth, according to the data of Clark, given above, are: Surface, 196,971,984 square miles; cubic contents, 259,944,035,515 cubic miles.

Murray (Challenger expedition) states the greatest depth of the Atlantic Ocean at 27,366 feet; Pacific Ocean, 30,000 feet; Indian Ocean, 18,582 feet; Southern Ocean, 25,200 feet; Arctic Ocean, 9,000 feet. The Atlantic Ocean has an area, in square miles, of 24,536,000; Pacific Ocean, 50,309,000; Indian Ocean, 17,084,000; Arctic Ocean, 4,781,000; Southern Ocean, 30,592,000. The highest mountain is believed to be Deodhunga or Everest, one of the Himalayas, 29,002 feet.

For population of the earth according to creed, see RELIGIOUS STATISTICS.

POPULATION OF THE EARTH ACCORDING TO RACE.

(Based on estimate by John Bartholomew, F.R.G.S., Edinburgh, revised to 1909.)

RACE.	Location.	Number.	RACE.	Location.	Number.
Indo-Germanic or Aryan (white)...	Europe, Persia, etc.	625,000,000	Hottentot and Bushman (black)............	South Africa	150,000
Mongolian or Turainian (yellow and brown)......................	Greater part of Asia................	630,000,000	Malay and Polynesian (brown)........	Australasia & Polynesia	35,000,000
Semitic or Hamitic (white).....................	North Africa, Arabia	65,000,000	American Indian (red)......	North & So. America......	15,000,000
Negro and Bantu (black).....................	Central Africa....	150,000,000	Total........................	....	1,520,150,000

The human family is subject to fifty principal governments. As to their form they may be classified as follows: *Absolute monarchies*, Abyssinia, Afghanistan, China, Korea, Morocco, Siam; *Limited monarchies*, Austria-Hungary, Belgium, British Empire, Bulgaria, Denmark, Germany, Greece, Italy, Japan, Montenegro, Netherlands, Norway, Persia, Portugal, Roumania, Russia, Servia, Sweden, Spain, Turkey; *Republics*, Argentine Republic, Bolivia, Brazil, Chile, Colombia, Costa Rica, Cuba, Dominican Republic, Ecuador, France, Guatemala, Hayti, Honduras, Liberia, Mexico, Nicaragua, Panama, Paraguay, Peru, Salvador, Switzerland, United States of America, Uruguay, Venezuela. Besides these are the undefined despotisms of Central Africa, and a few insignificant independent States.

The average duration of human life is about 33 years. One-quarter of the people on the earth die before age 6, one-half before age 16, and only about 1 person of each 100 born lives to age 65.

EUROPEAN LANGUAGES SPOKEN.

LANGUAGES.	NUMBER OF PERSONS SPOKEN BY. 1801.	NUMBER OF PERSONS SPOKEN BY. 1901.	PROPORTION OF THE WHOLE. 1801.	PROPORTION OF THE WHOLE. 1901.	LANGUAGES.	NUMBER OF PERSONS SPOKEN BY. 1801.	NUMBER OF PERSONS SPOKEN BY. 1901.	PROPORTION OF THE WHOLE. 1801.	PROPORTION OF THE WHOLE. 1901.
English	20,520,000	130,300,000	12.7	29.2	Portuguese	7,480,000	15,000,000	4.7	3.3
French	31,450,000	52,100,000	19.4	11.7	Russian......	30,770,000	85,000,000	19.0	19.0
German......	30,320,000	84,200,000	18.7	18.8					
Italian	15,070,000	34,000,000	9.3	7.6	Total	161,800,000	447,100,000	100.0	100.0
Spanish	26,190,000	46,500,000	16.2	10.4					

These estimates (that for 1801 being by Mulhall) exhibit the superior growth of the English language in the last century.

Latitude and Longitude Table.

(LONGITUDE RECKONED FROM GREENWICH.)

Specially prepared for THE WORLD ALMANAC.

Place	°	′	″		H.	M.	S.	
Acapulco, Mex.	16	50	56	N.	6	39	41.8	W.
Adelaide, S. Australia*	34	55	38	S.	9	14	20.3	E.
Aden, Arabia	12	46	40	N.	2	59	55.8	E.
Albany, N. Y.*	42	39	13	N.	4	55	6.8	W.
Algiers*	36	47	50	N.	0	12	11.4	E.
Allegheny, Pa.*	40	27	42	N.	5	20	2.9	W.
Alexandria, Egypt	31	11	43	N.	1	59	26.7	E.
Amherst, Mass.*	42	22	17	N.	4	50	4.7	W.
Ann Arbor, Mich.*	42	16	48	N.	5	34	55.2	W.
Annapolis, Md.*	38	58	54	N.	5	5	56.5	W.
Antipodes Island	49	42	0	S.	11	54	52.3	E.
Apia, Samoa	13	48	56	S.	11	26	59.7	E.
Archangel, Russia	64	32	6	N.	2	42	14.0	E.
Armagh, Ireland*	54	21	13	N.	0	26	35.4	W.
Aspinwall, S. A., Lt.	9	22	9	N.	5	19	39.0	W.
Astoria, Ore.	46	11	19	N.	8	15	18.8	W.
Athens, Greece*	37	58	21	N.	1	34	54.9	E.
Attu Island, Alaska	52	56	1	N.	11	32	49.6	E.
Bahia, Brazil	13	0	37	S.	2	34	8.4	W.
Baltimore, Md.	39	17	48	N.	5	6	26.0	W.
Batavia, Java.	6	7	40	S.	7	7	13.7	E.
Belize, Honduras	17	29	20	N.	5	52	46.7	W.
Belle Isle, Lt.	51	53	0	N.	3	41	29.5	W.
Berlin, Prussia*	52	30	17	N.	0	53	34.9	E.
Bermuda, Dock Yard	32	19	24	N.	4	19	18.3	W.
Bombay*	18	53	45	N.	4	51	15.7	E.
Bonn, Germany*	50	43	45	N.	0	28	23.3	E.
Bordeaux, France*	44	50	17	N.	0	2	5.4	W.
Boston State House	42	21	28	N.	4	44	15.3	W.
Bridgetown, Barbados	13	5	42	N.	3	58	29.3	W.
Brussels, Belgium*	50	51	10	N.	0	17	28.6	E.
Buenos Ayres	34	36	30	S.	3	53	28.9	W.
Calcutta	22	33	25	N.	5	53	20.7	E.
Callao, Peru, Lt.	12	4	3	S.	5	9	3.0	W.
Cambridge, Eng.*	52	12	52	N.	0	0	22.7	E.
Cambridge, Mass.*	42	22	48	N.	4	44	31.0	W.
Canton, China	23	6	35	N.	7	33	46.3	E.
Cape Cod, Mass., Lt.	42	2	21	N.	4	40	14.6	W.
C. Hatteras, N. C., Lt.	35	15	14	N.	5	2	5.0	W.
Cape Henry, Va., Lt.	36	55	29	N.	5	4	2.0	W.
Cape Horn	55	58	41	S.	4	29	5.0	W.
Cape May, N. J., Lt.	38	55	56	N.	4	59	50.7	W.
Cape Good Hope, Lt.	34	21	12	S.	1	13	58.0	E.
Cape Prince of Wales	65	33	30	N.	11	11	56.8	W.
Charleston, S. C., Lt.	32	41	44	N.	5	19	32.0	W.
Charlottetown, P. E. I.	46	13	55	N.	4	12	27.5	W.
Cherbourg, France	49	38	54	N.	0	6	32.5	W.
Chicago, Ill.*	41	50	1	N.	5	50	26.7	W.
Christiania, Nor.*	59	54	44	N.	0	42	53.8	E.
Cincinnati, O.*	39	8	19	N.	5	37	41.3	W.
Clinton, N. Y.*	43	3	17	N.	5	1	37.4	W.
Colombo, Ceylon	6	55	40	N.	5	19	21.9	E.
Constantinople	41	0	39	N.	1	56	3.7	E.
Copenhagen*	55	41	13	N.	0	50	18.8	E.
Demerara (Geo'town Lt)	6	49	20	N.	3	52	46.0	W.
Denver, Col.*	39	40	36	N.	6	59	47.6	W.
Dublin, Ireland*	53	23	13	N.	0	25	21.1	W.
Edinburgh*	55	57	23	N.	0	12	43.1	W.
Esquimault, B. C., Lt.	48	25	40	N.	8	13	47.1	W.
Father Point, Que., Lt.	48	31	25	N.	4	33	49.2	W.
Fayal, Azores	38	32	9	N.	1	54	16.0	W.
Fernandina, Fla.	30	40	18	N.	5	25	51.1	W.
Florence, Italy*	43	46	4	N.	0	45	1.5	E.
Funchal, Madeira	32	38	4	N.	1	7	35.6	W.
Galveston, Tex.	29	18	17	N.	6	19	9.7	W.
Geneva, Switzerland*	46	11	59	N.	0	24	36.8	E.
Glasgow, Scotland*	55	52	43	N.	0	17	10.6	W.
Gibraltar	36	6	30	N.	0	21	23.3	W.
Greenwich, Eng.*	51	28	38	N.	0	0	0.0	—
Halifax, N. S.	44	39	38	N.	4	14	21.1	W.
Hamburg, Ger.*	53	33	7	N.	0	39	53.8	E.
Hanover, N. H.*	43	42	15	N.	4	49	7.9	W.
Havana, Cuba	23	9	21	N.	5	29	26.0	W.
Hobart Town, Tas.	42	53	25	S.	9	49	20.5	E.
Hong Kong, China*	22	18	12	N.	7	36	41.9	E.
Honolulu (Reef Lt.)	21	17	55	N.	10	31	28.0	W.
Key West, Fla., Lt.	24	32	58	N.	5	27	12.3	W.
Kingston, Jamaica	17	57	41	N.	5	7	10.7	W.
Lisbon, Portugal*	38	42	31	N.	0	36	44.7	W.
Liverpool*	53	24	5	N.	0	12	17.3	W.

Place	°	′	″		H.	M.	S.	
Madison, Wis.*	43	4	37	N.	5	57	37.8	W.
Madras, India*	13	4	8	N.	5	20	59.4	E.
Madrid, Spain*	40	24	30	N.	0	14	45.4	W.
Manila, Lt.	14	35	25	N.	8	3	50.0	E.
Marseilles*	43	18	18	N.	0	21	34.6	E.
Melbourne, Vic.*	37	49	53	S.	9	39	54.1	E.
Mexico (city)*	19	26	2	N.	6	36	26.7	W.
Monrovia, Liberia	6	19	5	N.	0	43	15.7	W.
Montreal, Que.*	45	30	17	N.	4	54	18.7	W.
Moscow*	55	45	20	N.	2	30	17.2	E.
Mount Hamilton, Cal.*	37	20	24	N.	8	6	34.1	W.
Munich*	48	8	45	N.	0	46	26.1	E.
Nain, Labrador	56	32	51	N.	4	6	42.7	W.
Naples*	40	51	46	N.	0	57	1.8	E.
Nashville, Tenn.*	36	8	54	N.	5	47	12.0	W.
Nassau, Bahamas	25	5	37	N.	5	9	27.8	W.
Natal, S. Africa*	29	50	47	S.	2	4	1.2	E.
New Haven, Ct.*	41	18	36	N.	4	51	42.1	W.
New Orleans (Mint)	29	57	46	N.	6	0	13.9	W.
New York (Colu. Col.)*	40	45	23	N.	4	55	53.6	W.
Nice, France*	43	43	17	N.	0	29	12.2	E.
Norfolk, Va. (Navy Yd)	36	49	33	N.	5	5	11.0	W.
North Cape	71	11	0	N.	1	42	40.5	E.
Northfield, Minn.*	44	27	42	N.	6	12	35.8	W.
Odessa, Russia*	46	28	37	N.	2	3	2.2	E.
Ogden, Utah*	41	13	8	N.	7	27	59.6	W.
Oxford, Eng. (Univ.)*	51	45	34	N.	0	5	0.4	W.
Panama, Colombia	8	57	6	N.	5	18	8.8	W.
Para, Brazil	1	26	59	S.	3	14	0.0	W.
Paris, France*	48	50	12	N.	0	9	20.9	E.
Pensacola, Fla., Lt.	30	20	47	N.	5	49	14.1	W.
Pernambuco, Brazil, Lt.	8	3	22	S.	2	19	27.8	W.
Port au Prince, Hayti	18	33	54	N.	4	49	28.0	W.
Philadelphia, Pa.*	39	57	7	N.	5	0	38.5	W.
Point Barrow†	71	27	0	N.	10	25	0.0	W.
Portland, Me.	43	39	28	N.	4	41	1.2	W.
Port Louis, Mauritius	20	8	46	S.	3	49	57.7	E.
Port Said, Egypt, Lt.	31	15	45	N.	2	9	15.5	E.
Port Spain, Trinidad	10	38	39	N.	4	6	2.5	W.
P. Stanley, Falkland Is.	51	41	10	S.	3	51	26.0	W.
Prague, Bohemia*	50	5	19	N.	0	57	40.3	E.
Princeton, N. J.*	40	20	58	N.	4	58	37.5	W.
Providence, R. I.*	41	49	46	N.	4	45	37.5	W.
Quebec, Que.*	46	47	59	N.	4	44	52.6	W.
Richmond, Va.	37	32	16	N.	5	9	44.0	W.
Rio de Janeiro*	22	54	24	S.	2	52	41.4	W.
Rochester, N. Y.*	43	9	17	N.	5	10	21.8	W.
Rome, Italy*	41	53	54	N.	0	49	55.6	E.
Saigon, Cochin-China*	10	46	47	N.	7	6	48.7	E.
San Diego, Cal.	32	43	6	N.	7	48	38.7	W.
Sandy Hook, N. J., Lt.	40	27	40	N.	4	56	0.6	W.
San Francisco, Cal.*	37	47	28	N.	8	9	42.8	W.
San Juan de Porto Rico	18	28	56	N.	4	24	29.8	W.
Santiago de Cuba	20	0	16	N.	5	3	22.0	W.
Savannah, Ga.	32	4	52	N.	5	24	21.7	W.
Seattle, Wash.	47	35	54	N.	8	9	19.9	W.
Shanghai, China	31	14	42	N.	8	5	55.7	E.
Singapore, India	1	17	11	N.	6	55	25.0	E.
St. Helena Island	15	55	0	S.	0	22	52.0	W.
St. John's, Newfo'land	47	34	2	N.	3	30	43.6	W.
St. Louis, Mo.*	38	38	4	N.	6	0	49.1	W.
St. Petersburg, Russia*	59	56	30	N.	2	1	13.5	E.
Stockholin*	59	20	33	N.	1	12	14.0	E.
Suakim, E. Africa, Lt.	19	7	0	N.	2	29	16.6	E.
Sydney, N. S. W.*	33	51	41	S.	10	4	49.5	E.
Tokio, Japan*	35	39	17	N.	9	18	58.0	E.
Tunis (Goletta Lt.)	36	48	36	N.	0	41	14.5	E.
Utrecht, Netherlands*	52	5	10	N.	0	20	31.7	E.
Valparaiso, Chile	33	1	53	S.	4	46	34.8	W.
Venice, Italy*	45	26	10	N.	0	49	22.1	E.
Vera Cruz, Mex., Lt.	19	12	29	N.	6	24	31.8	W.
Victoria, B. C., Lt.	48	25	26	N.	8	13	33.8	W.
Vienna, Austria*	48	13	55	N.	1	5	21.5	E.
Warsaw, Russia*	52	13	6	N.	1	24	7.4	E.
Washington, D. C.*	38	55	15	N.	5	8	15.7	W.
Wellington, N. Z.*	41	18	1	S.	11	39	6.5	E.
West Point, N. Y.*	41	23	22	N.	4	55	50.6	W.
Williamstown, Mass.*	42	42	30	N.	4	52	50.4	W.
Yokohama, Japan	35	26	24	N.	9	18	36.9	E.
Zanzibar (E. Consulate)	6	9	43	S.	2	36	44.7	E.

* Observatories. Lt. denotes a light-house. † Highest latitude in U. S. territory.

Opening and Closing of Navigation

ON THE HUDSON RIVER AND THE ERIE CANAL, AND OPENING OF LAKE ERIE NAVIGATION.

Navigation of the Hudson River.			Navigation of the Erie Canal.			Opening of Lake Erie.*
River Open.	River Closed.	Days Open.	Canal Open.	Canal Closed.	Navigable Days.	
Mar. 3, 1824	Jan. 5, 1825	308	April 30, 1824	Dec. 4	219	....
Mar. 6, 1825	Dec. 13, 1825	283	April 12, 1825	Dec. 5	238	....
Feb. 25, 1826	Dec. 13, 1826	292	April 25, 1826	Dec. 18	243	....
Mar. 20, 1827	Nov. 25, 1827	251	April 22, 1827	Dec. 18	241	April 21, 1827
Feb. 8, 1828	Dec. 23, 1828	320	Mar. 27, 1828	Dec. 20	269	April 1, 1828
April 1, 1829	Jan. 14, 1830	286	May 2, 1829	Dec. 17	230	May 10, 1829
Mar. 15, 1830	Dec. 25, 1830	283	April 30, 1830	Dec. 17	242	May 5, 1830
Mar. 15, 1831	Dec. 6, 1831	262	April 16, 1831	Dec. 1	230	May 8, 1831
Mar. 25, 1832	Dec. 21, 1832	289	April 25, 1832	Dec. 21	241	April 27, 1832
Mar. 21, 1833	Dec. 13, 1833	277	April 19, 1833	Dec. 12	238	April 23, 1833
Feb. 29, 1834	Dec. 15, 1834	291	April 17, 1834	Dec. 12	240	April 6, 1834
Mar. 25, 1835	Nov. 30, 1835	268	April 15, 1835	Nov. 30	230	May 3, 1835
April 4, 1836	Dec. 7, 1836	244	April 25, 1836	Nov. 26	216	April 27, 1836
Mar. 27, 1837	Dec. 14, 1837	261	April 20, 1837	Dec. 9	234	May 13, 1837
Mar. 19, 1838	Nov. 25, 1838	257	April 11, 1838	Nov. 25	228	March 31, 1838
Mar. 25, 1839	Nov. 18, 1839	286	April 20, 1839	Dec. 16	241	April 11, 1839
Feb. 25, 1840	Nov. 5, 1840	285	April 20, 1840	Dec. 9	228	April 27, 1840
Mar. 24, 1841	Nov. 19, 1841	266	April 24, 1841	Nov. 30	221	April 14, 1841
Feb. 4, 1842	Nov. 28, 1842	303	April 20, 1842	Nov. 28	222	March 7, 1842
April 13, 1843	Dec. 10, 1843	242	May 1, 1843	Nov. 30	214	May 6, 1843
Mar. 18, 1844	Dec. 17, 1844	273	April 18, 1844	Nov. 26	222	March 14, 1844
Feb. 24, 1845	Dec. 3, 1845	283	April 15, 1845	Nov. 29	228	April 3, 1845
Mar. 18, 1846	Dec. 14, 1846	275	April 16, 1846	Nov. 25	234	April 11, 1846
April 7, 1847	Dec. 25, 1847	263	May 1, 1847	Nov. 30	214	April 23, 1847
Mar. 22, 1848	Dec. 27, 1848	292	May 1, 1848	Dec. 9	223	April 9, 1848
Mar. 19, 1849	Dec. 26, 1849	286	May 1, 1849	Dec. 5	219	March 25, 1849
Mar. 10, 1850	Dec. 17, 1850	282	April 22, 1850	Dec. 11	224	March 25, 1850
Feb. 25, 1851	Dec. 14, 1851	293	April 15, 1851	Dec. 5	235	April 2, 1851
Mar. 28, 1852	Dec. 23, 1852	270	April 20, 1852	Dec. 16	239	April 20, 1852
Mar. 23, 1853	Dec. 21, 1853	274	April 20, 1853	Dec. 20	245	April 14, 1853
Mar. 17, 1854	Dec. 8, 1854	266	May 1, 1854	Dec. 3	217	April 29, 1854
Mar. 27, 1855	Dec. 20, 1855	268	May 1, 1855	Dec. 10	224	April 21, 1855
April 11, 1856	Dec. 14, 1856	248	May 5, 1856	Dec. 4	214	May 2, 1856
Feb. 27, 1857	Dec. 27, 1857	303	May 6, 1857	Dec. 15	223	April 27, 1857
Mar. 20, 1858	Dec. 17, 1858	273	April 28, 1858	Dec. 8	225	April 15, 1858
Mar. 13, 1859	Dec. 10, 1859	273	April 15, 1859	Dec. 12	242	April 7, 1859
Mar. 6, 1860	Dec. 14, 1860	283	April 25, 1860	Dec. 12	232	April 17, 1860
Mar. 5, 1861	Dec. 23, 1861	294	May 1, 1861	Dec. 10	224	April 13, 1861
April 4, 1862	Dec. 19, 1862	259	May 1, 1862	Dec. 10	224	April 15, 1862
April 3, 1863	Dec. 11, 1863	252	May 1, 1863	Dec. 9	223	April 3, 1863
Mar. 11, 1864	Dec. 12, 1864	277	April 30, 1864	Dec. 8	223	April 13, 1864
Mar. 22, 1865	Dec. 16, 1865	270	May 1, 1865	Dec. 12	226	April 26, 1865
Mar. 20, 1866	Dec. 15, 1866	270	May 1, 1866	Dec. 12	226	April 28, 1866
Mar. 26, 1867	Dec. 8, 1867	257	May 6, 1867	Dec. 20	229	April 21, 1867
Mar. 24, 1868	Dec. 5, 1868	252	May 4, 1868	Dec. 7	217	April 19, 1868
April 5, 1869	Dec. 9, 1869	248	May 6, 1869	Dec. 10	218	May 1, 1869
Mar. 31, 1870	Dec. 17, 1870	261	May 10, 1870	Dec. 8	213	April 16, 1870
Mar. 12, 1871	Nov. 29, 1871	263	April 24, 1871	Dec. 1	220	April 1, 1871
April 7, 1872	Dec. 9, 1872	247	May 13, 1872	Dec. 1	202	May 6, 1872
April 16, 1873	Nov. 22, 1873	221	May 15, 1873	Dec. 5	205	April 29, 1873
Mar. 19, 1874	Dec. 12, 1874	269	May 5, 1874	Dec. 5	215	April 18, 1874
April 13, 1875	Nov. 29, 1875	229	May 18, 1875	Nov. 30 (by ice)	197	May 12, 1875
April 1, 1876	Dec. 2, 1876	245	May 4, 1876	Dec. 1	211	May 4, 1876
Mar. 30, 1877	Dec. 31, 1877	277	May 8, 1877	Dec. 7	214	April 17, 1877
Mar. 14, 1878	Dec. 20, 1878	282	April 15, 1878	Dec. 7	237	March 24, 1878
April 4, 1879	Dec. 20, 1879	261	May 8, 1879	Dec. 6	212	April 24, 1879
Mar. 5, 1880	Nov. 25, 1880	265	April 16, 1880	Nov. 21 (by ice)	220	March 12, 1880
Mar. 21, 1881	Jan. 2, 1882	287	May 12, 1881	Dec. 8	211	May 1, 1881
Mar. 8, 1882	Dec. 4, 1882	272	April 11, 1882	Dec. 7	241	March 26, 1882
Mar. 29, 1883	Dec. 15, 1883	261	May 7, 1883	Dec. 1	208	May 4, 1883
Mar. 25, 1884	Dec. 19, 1884	269	May 6, 1884	Dec. 1	209	April 25, 1884
April 7, 1885	Dec. 13, 1885	250	May 11, 1885	Dec. 1	205	May 2, 1885
Mar. 30, 1886	Dec. 3, 1886	248	May 1, 1886	Dec. 1	214	April 26, 1886
April 9, 1887	Dec. 20, 1887	256	May 7, 1887	Dec. 1	208	April 17, 1887
April 8, 1888	Dec. 14, 1888	251	May 10, 1888	Dec. 3	207	April 10, 1888
Mar. 19, 1889	Open all Winter	286	May 1, 1889	Nov. 30	214	April 10, 1889
Open all Winter	Dec. 3, 1890	337	April 28, 1890	Nov. 30	216	March 31, 1890
Mar. 22, 1891	Dec. 24, 1891	277	May 5, 1891	Dec. 5	215	April 13, 1891
April 1, 1892	Dec. 22, 1892	266	May 1, 1892	Dec. 5	219	April 14, 1892
April 1, 1893	Dec. 6, 1893	250	May 3, 1893	Nov. 30	212	April 15, 1893
Mar. 18, 1894	Dec. 24, 1894	282	May 1, 1894	Nov. 30	214	April 28, 1894
April 2, 1895	Dec. 9, 1895	252	May 3, 1895	Dec. 5	216	April 4, 1895
April 17, 1896	Dec. 10, 1896	246	May 1, 1896	Dec. 1	214	April 19, 1896
April 29, 1897	Dec. 7, 1897	223	May 8, 1897	Dec. 1	208	April 6, 1897
Mar. 14, 1898	Dec. 12, 1898	274	May 7, 1898	Dec. 10	218	March 25, 1898
Mar. 29, 1899	Dec. 28, 1899	275	April 26, 1899	Dec. 1	219	April 27, 1899
April 9, 1900	Dec. 11, 1900	246	April 25, 1900	Dec. 1	220	April 22, 1900
Mar. 28, 1901	Dec. 1, 1901	248	May 7, 1901	Nov. 30	207	April 20, 1901
Mar. 17, 1902	Dec. 8, 1902	266	April 24, 1902	Dec. 4	224	April 9, 1902
Mar. 14, 1903	Dec. 2, 1903	263	May 2, 1903	Nov. 28	210	April 6, 1903
April 4, 1904	Dec. 4, 1904	244	May 5, 1904	Nov. 26	205	May 10, 1904
April 3, 1905	Dec. 15, 1905	257	May 4, 1905	Nov. 28	209	April 22, 1905
Mar. 22, 1906	Dec. 5, 1906	260	May 2, 1906	Nov. 28	211	April 15, 1906
Mar. 29, 1907	Dec. 6, 1907	253	May 1, 1907	Dec. 10	224	April 6, 1907
Mar. 23, 1908	1908	...	May 5, 1908	....	...	April 25, 1908

* At Buffalo. The record in the above table is kept by the State Superintendent of Public Works.

Names.	Sources.	Mouths.	Length Miles.
Alabama	Junction of Coosa and Talapoosa, Ala	Mobile River	175
Alleghany	Allegany Co., N. Y	Ohio River	460
Androscoggin	Umbagog Lake, Maine	Atlantic Ocean	140
Appalachicola	Junction of Chattahoochee and Flint R. Ga	Gulf of Mexico	110
Arkansas	Rocky Mountains, Col	Mississippi River	2170
Black	Adirondack Lakes, N. Y	Lake Ontario	126
Black Warrior	Formed by Locus and Mulberry, Forks, Ala	Tombigbee River	300
Brazos	Highlands, Texas	Gulf of Mexico	750
Cape Fear	Junction of Haw and Deep Rivers, N. C	Atlantic Ocean	250
Chattahoochee	Alleghany Mountains, Ga	Appalachicola River	430
Chowan	Mott and Meherin, N. C	Albemarle Sound	250
Colorado	Llano Estacado, Tex	Gulf of Mexico	690
Colorado	Junction of Green and Grand Rivers, Utah	Gulf of Colorado	1360
Columbia	Lewis's and Clark's Fork	Pacific Ocean	750
Connecticut	Connecticut Lake, Vt	Long Island Sound	410
Coosa	Junction of Oosteuaula and Etowah Rivers, Ga	Alabama River	275
Cumberland	Junction of Poor and Straight Forks, Ky	Ohio River	560
Delaware	Catskill Mountains, N. Y	Delaware Bay	300
Des Moines	Lake Shetek, Minn	Mississippi River	400
Flint	Alleghany Mountains, Ga	Appalachicola River	275
Genesee	Allegany County, N. Y	Lake Ontario	145
Gila	Sierra Madre Mountains, N. M	Colorado River	650
Grand	Southern Iowa	Missouri River	200
Grand	Highlands, Mich	Lake Michigan	280
Grande del Norte	Rocky Mountains, Col	Gulf of Mexico	1800
Great Pedee	Yadkin River, N. C	Atlantic Ocean	375
Green	Cumberland Mountains, Ky	Ohio River	520
Hudson	Lake Sanford, Adirondack Mountains, N. Y	New York Bay	280
Housatonic	Taghanic Mountains, Mass	Long Island Sound	150
Illinois	Des Plaines River, Wis	Mississippi River	435
James	Jackson and Pastur Rivers, Va	Chesapeake Bay	450
Kalamazoo	Highlands, Mich	Lake Michigan	200
Kanawha	Junction of Greenbrier and New Rivers, Va	Ohio River	400
Kansas	Smoky Hill River, Kan	Missouri River	600
Kaskaskia	Grand Prairie, Ill	Mississippi River	320
Kennebec	Moosehead Lake, Me	Atlantic Ocean	160
Kentucky	"Forks" Cumberland Mountains, Ky	Ohio River	300
Lewis's Fork	Rocky Mountains, Ore	Columbia River	750
Menominee	Junction Brule and Mequacumecum Rivers, Wis	Green Bay	160
Merrimac	White Mountains, N. H.	Atlantic Ocean	150
Minnesota	Eastern Dakota	Mississippi River	334
Mississippi	Itasca Lake, Minn	Gulf of Mexico	3160
Missouri	Rocky Mountains, junction of Jefferson, Madison, Gallatin Rivers, Mont.	Mississippi River	3100
Mobile	Junction of Tombigbee and Ala. R., Ala	Gulf of Mexico	50
Mohawk	Oneida County, N. Y	Hudson River	135
Monongahela	Rich Mountains, W. Va	Ohio River	300
Nebraska	Junction of Sweet Water and North Fork, Wyo	Missouri River	1260
Neenah	Highlands, Wis	Green Bay	180
Neuse	Table-lands, N. C	Pamlico Sound	250
Ocmulgee	Alleghany Mountains, Ga	Altamaha River	250
Ohio	Junction of Alleghany and Monon R., Pa	Mississippi River	950
Ontonagon	Lakes, Wis	Lake Superior	145
Osage	Osage County, Kan	Missouri River	450
Oswegatchie	Cranberry Lake, N. Y	St. Lawrence River	120
Oswego	Onondaga Lake, N. Y	Lake Ontario	24
Pearl	Table-land, Miss	Lake Borgne	250
Penobscot	East, Seboeis Lake, Me	Atlantic Ocean	270
Potomac	Alleghany Mountains, Md	Chesapeake Bay	380
Red	Llano Estacado, Tex	Mississippi River	1600
Red (of the North)	Pine Lake, Minn	Winnipeg Lake	700
Roanoke	Dan and Staunton, Va	Albemarle Sound	255
Rock	Koshkonong Lake, Wis	Mississippi River	330
Sabine	Highlands, Tex	Gulf of Mexico	460
Sacramento	Junction of North and South Fork, Sierra Madre Mountains, Cal	Bay of San Francisco	450
Saginaw	Highlands, Mich	Lake Huron	110
St. Croix	Ontonagon Ridge, Wis	Mississippi River	200
St. Francis	Highlands, Mo	Mississippi River	460
St. John	Everglades, Fla	Atlantic Ocean	230
St. Joseph	Highlands, Ind	Lake Michigan	260
St. Mary	Okefinokee Swamp, Ga	Atlantic Ocean	100
San Joaquin	Sierra Nevada Mountains, Cal	Bay of San Francisco	350
Santee	Junction of Wateree and Congaree, N. C	Atlantic Ocean	350
Savannah	Alleghany Mountains, S. C	Atlantic Ocean	335
Scioto	Table-lands, O	Ohio River	200
Susquehanna	E. Branch, Otsego Lake, N. Y W. Branch, Alleghany Mountains, N. Y Main, Junction of East and West Branches, Pa	256 Susquehanna River... 208 Chesapeake Bay... 153	617
Tallapoosa	Alleghany Mountains, Ga	Alabama River	175
Tennessee	" " N. C	Ohio River	1200
Tombigbee	" " Miss	Mobile River	475
Trinity	Highlands, Tex	Gulf of Mexico	530
Wabash	Table-lands, O	Ohio River	520
Washita	Potean Hills, Ark	Red River	450
White	Boston Mountains, Ark	Arkansas River	650
Willamette	Cascade, Ore	Columbia River	250
Wisconsin	Ontonagon Ridge, Wis	Mississippi River	400
Yazoo	Junction of Coldwater and Tallahatchee Rivers, Miss	Mississippi River	540
Yellowstone	National Park, Yellowstone Lake	Missouri River	1000

Metric System of Weights and Measures.

THE METRIC SYSTEM has been adopted by Mexico, Brazil, Chile, Peru, etc., and except Russia and Great Britain, where it is permissive, by all European nations. Various names of the preceding systems are, however, frequently used: In Germany, ½ kilogram = 1 pound; in Switzerland, 3-10 of a metre = 1 foot, etc. If the first letters of the prefixes *deka*, *hecto*, *kilo*, *myria*, from the Greek, and *deci*, *centi*, *mili*, from the Latin, are used in preference to our plain English, 10, 100, etc., it is best to employ capital letters for the multiples and small letters for the subdivisions, to avoid ambiguities in abbreviations: 1 dekametre or 10 metres = 1 dm.; 1 decimetre or 1-10 of a metre = 1 dm.

The METRE, unit of length, is nearly the ten-millionth part of a quadrant of a meridian, of the distance between Equator and Pole. The International Standard Metre is, practically, nothing else but a length defined by the distance between two lines on a platinum-iridium bar at 0° Centigrade, deposited at the International Bureau of Weights and Measures, Paris, France.

The LITRE, unit of capacity, is derived from the weight of one kilogram pure water at greatest density, a cube whose edge is one-tenth of a metre and, therefore, the one-thousandth part of a metric ton.

The GRAM, unit of weight, is a cube of pure water at greatest density, whose edge is one-hundredth of a metre, and, therefore, the one-thousandth part of a kilogram, and the one-millionth part of a metric ton.

The Metric System was legalized in the United States on July 28, 1866, when Congress enacted as follows:

"The tables in the schedule hereto annexed shall be recognized in the construction of contracts, and in all legal proceedings, as establishing, in terms of the weights and measures now in use in the United States, the equivalents of the weights and measures expressed therein in terms of the metric system, and the tables may lawfully be used for computing, determining, and expressing in customary weights and measures the weights and measures of the metric system."

The following are the tables annexed to the above:

MEASURES OF LENGTH.

Metric Denominations and Values.		Equivalents in Denominations in Use.	
Myriametre	10,000 metres.	6.2137	miles.
Kilometre	1,000 metres.	0.62137	mile, or 3,280 feet 10 inches.
Hectometre	100 metres.	328	feet 1 inch.
Dekametre	10 metres.	393.7	inches.
Metre	1 metre.	39.37	inches.
Decimetre	1-10 of a metre.	3.937	inches.
Centimetre	1-100 of a metre.	0.3937	inch.
Millimetre	1-1000 of a metre.	0.0394	inch.

MEASURES OF SURFACE.

Metric Denominations and Values.		Equivalents in Denominations in Use.	
Hectare	10,000 square metres.	2.471	acres.
Are	100 square metres.	119.6	square yards.
Centare	1 square metre.	1,550	square inches.

MEASURES OF CAPACITY.

METRIC DENOMINATIONS AND VALUES.			EQUIVALENTS IN DENOMINATIONS IN USE.		
Names.	Number of Litres.	Cubic Measure.	Dry Measure.	Liquid or Wine Measure.	
Kilolitre or stere.	1,000	1 cubic metre	1.308 cubic yards	264.17	gallons.
Hectolitre	100	1-10 of a cubic metre.	2 bush. and 3.35 pecks	26.417	gallons.
Dekalitre	10	10 cubic decimetres	9.08 quarts	2.6417	gallons.
Litre	1	1 cubic decimetre	0.908 quart	1.0567	quarts.
Decilitre	1-10	1-10 of a cubic decimetre.	6.1022 cubic inches	0.845	gill.
Centilitre	1-100	10 cubic centimetres	0.6102 cubic inch	0.338	fluid ounce.
Millilitre	1-1000	1 cubic centimetre	0.061 cubic inch	0.27	fluid dram.

METRIC SYSTEM—*Continued.*

WEIGHTS.

Metric Denominations and Values.			Equivalents in Denominations in Use.	
Names.	Number of Grams.	Weight of What Quantity of Water at Maximum Density.	Avoirdupois Weight.	
Miller or tonneau	1,000,000	1 cubic metre	2204.6	pounds.
Quintal	100,000	1 hectolitre	220.46	pounds.
Myriagram	10,000	10 litres	22.046	pounds.
Kilogram or kilo	1,000	1 litre	2.2046	pounds.
Hectogram	100	1 decilitre	3.5274	ounces.
Dekagram	10	10 cubic centimetres	0.3527	ounce.
Gram	1	1 cubic centimetre	15.432	grains.
Decigram	1-10	1-10 of a cubic centimetre	1.5432	grains.
Centigram	1-100	10 cubic millimetres	0.1543	grain.
Milligram	1-1000	1 cubic millimetre	0.0154	grain

TABLES FOR THE CONVERSION OF METRIC WEIGHTS AND MEASURES INTO CUSTOMARY UNITED STATES EQUIVALENTS AND THE REVERSE.

From the legal equivalents are deduced the following tables for converting United States weights and measures:

METRIC TO CUSTOMARY. | CUSTOMARY TO METRIC.

LINEAR MEASURE.

Metres=Ins.	*Metres=Feet.*	*Metres=Yards.*	*Kilometres=Miles.*	*Ins.=Centimetres*	*Feet=Metres.*	*Yards=Metres.*	*Miles=Kilometres.*
1=39.37	1=3.28083	1=1.093611	1=0.62137	1=2.54	1=0.304801	1=0.914402	1=1.60935
2=78.74	2=6.56167	2=2.187222	2=1.24274	2=5.08	2=0.609601	2=1.828804	2=3.21869
3=118.11	3=9.84250	3=3.280833	3=1.86411	3=7.62	3=0.914402	3=2.743205	3=4.82804
4=157.48	4=13.12333	4=4.374444	4=2.48548	4=10.16	4=1.219202	4=3.657607	4=6.43739
5=196.85	5=16.40417	5=5.468056	5=3.10685	5=12.70	5=1.524003	5=4.572009	5=8.04674
6=236.22	6=19.68500	6=6.561667	6=3.72822	6=15.24	6=1.828804	6=5.486411	6=9.65608
7=275.59	7=22.96583	7=7.655278	7=4.34959	7=17.78	7=2.133604	7=6.400813	7=11.26543
8=314.96	8=26.24667	8=8.748989	8=4.97096	8=20.32	8=2.438405	8=7.315215	8=12.87478
9=354.33	9=29.52750	9=9.842500	9=5.59233	9=22.86	9=2.743205	9=8.229616	9=14.48412

SQUARE MEASURE. | CUBIC MEASURE. | SQUARE MEASURE.

Square Centimet's = Square Inches.	*Square Metres = Square Feet.*	*Square Metres = Square Yards.*	*Cubic Metres = Cubic Feet.*	*Cubic Feet = Cubic Metres.*	*Square Inches = Square Centimet's*	*Square Feet = Square Metres.*	*Square Yards = Square Metres.*
1=0.155	1=10.764	1 1.196	1=35.314	1=0.02832	1=6.452	1=0.09290	1=0.836
2=0.310	2=21.528	2=2.392	2=70.629	2=0.05663	2=12.903	2=0.18581	2=1.672
3=0.465	3=32.292	3=3.588	3=105.943	3=0.08495	3=19.354	8=0.27871	3=2.508
4=0.620	4=43.055	4=4.784	4=141.258	4=0.11327	4=25.806	4=0.37161	4=3.344
5=0.775	5=53.819	5=5.980	5=176.572	5=0.14159	5=32.257	5=0.46452	5=4.181
6=0.930	6=64.583	6=7.176	6=211.887	6=0.16990	6=38.709	6=0.55742	6=5.017
7=1.085	7=75.347	7=8.372	7=247.201	7=0.19822	7=45.160	7=0.65032	7=5.853
8=1.240	8=86.111	8=9.568	8=282.516	8=0.22654	8=51.612	8=0.74323	8=6.689
9=1.395	9=96.874	9=10.764	9=317.830	9=0.25485	9=58.063	9=0.83613	9=7.525

LIQUID MEASURE. | DRY MEASURE. | LIQUID MEASURE.

Centilitres = Fluid Ounces.	*Litres = Quarts.*	*Litres = Gallons.*	*Hectolitres = Bushels.*	*Bushels = Hectolitres*	*Fluid Ounces = Centilitres*	*Quarts = Litres.*	*Gallons = Litres.*
1=0.338	1=1.0567	1=0.26417	1=2.8377	1=0.35239	1=2.957	1=0.94636	1=3.78543
2=0.676	2=2.1134	2=0.52834	2=5.6754	2=0.70479	2=5.914	2=1.89272	2=7.57087
3=1.014	3=3.1700	3=0.79251	3=8.5132	3=1.05718	3=8.872	3=2.83908	3=11.35630
4=1.352	4=4.2267	4=1.05668	4=11.3509	4=1.40957	4=11.829	4=3.78544	4=15.14174
5=1.691	5=5.2834	5=1.32085	5=14.1887	5=1.76196	5=14.786	5=4.73180	5=18.92717
6=2.028	6=6.3401	6=1.58502	6=17.0264	6=2.11436	6=17.744	6=5.67816	6=22.71261
7=2.367	7=7.3968	7=1.84919	7=19.8642	7=2.46675	7=20.701	7=6.62452	7=26.49804
8=2.705	8=8.4534	8=2.11336	8=22.7019	8=2.81914	8=23.659	8=7.57088	8=30.28348
9=3.043	9=9.5101	9=2.37753	9=25.5396	9=3.17154	9=26.616	9=8.51724	9=34.06891

METRIC SYSTEM—*Continued.*

WEIGHT (AVOIRDUPOIS).

Centi-grams = Grains.	Kilo-grams = Ounces Av'd'ps.	Kilo-grams = Pounds Av'd'ps.	Metric Tons = Long Tons.	Grains = Centi-grams.	Ounces Av'd'ps = Grams.	Pounds Av'd'ps = Kilo-grams.	Long Tons = Metric Tons.
1=0.1543	1= 35.274	1= 2.20462	1=0.9842	1= 6.4799	1= 28.3495	1=0.45359	1=1.0161
2=0.3086	2= 70.548	2= 4.40924	2=1.9684	2=12.9598	2= 56.6991	2=0.90719	2=2.0321
3=0.4630	3=105.822	3= 6.61386	3=2.9526	3=19.4397	3= 85.0486	3=1.36078	3=3.0482
4=0.6173	4=141.096	4= 8.81849	4=3.9368	4=25.9196	4=113.3981	4=1.81437	4=4.0642
5=0.7716	5=176.370	5=11.02311	5=4.9210	5=32.3995	5=141.7476	5=2.26796	5=5.0803
6=0.9259	6=211.644	6=13.22773	6=5.9052	6=38.8793	6=170.0972	6=2.72156	6=6.0963
7=1.0803	7=246.918	7=15.43235	7=6.8894	7=45.3592	7=198.4467	7=3.17515	7=7.1124
8=1.2346	8=282.192	8=17.63697	8=7.8736	8=51.8391	8=226.7962	8=3.62874	8=8.1284
9=1.3889	9=317.466	9=19.84159	9=8.8578	9=58.3190	9=255.1457	9=4.08233	9=9.1445

THE METRIC SYSTEM SIMPLIFIED.

The following tables of the metric system of weights and measures have been simplified as much as possible for THE WORLD ALMANAC by omitting such denominations as are not in practical, everyday use in the countries where the system is used exclusively.

TABLES OF THE SYSTEM.

Length.—The denominations in practical use are millimetres (mm.), centimetres (cm.), metres (m.), and kilometres (km.).
10 mm. = 1 cm.; 100 cm. = 1 m.; 1,000 m. = 1 km. NOTE.—A decimetre is 10 cm.
Weight.—The denominations in use are grams (g.), kilos* (kg.), and tons (metric tons).
1,000 g. = 1 kg.; 1,000 kg. = 1 metric ton.
Capacity.—The denominations in use are cubic centimetres (c. c.) and litres (l.).
1,000 c.c. = 1 l. NOTE.—A hectolitre is 100 l. (seldom used).
Relation of capacity and weight to length: A cubic decimetre is a litre, and a litre of water weighs a kilo.

APPROXIMATE EQUIVALENTS.

A metre is about a yard; a kilo is about 2 pounds; a litre is about a quart; a centimetre is about ⅖ inch; a metric ton is about same as a ton; a kilometre is about ⅔ mile; a cubic centimetre is about a thimbleful; a nickel weighs about 5 grams.

PRECISE EQUIVALENTS.

1 acre =	.40	hectar	.4047	1 mile =	1.6	kilometres	1.609
1 bushel =	35	litres	35.24	1 millimetre =	.039	inch	.0394
1 centimetre =	.39	inch	.3937	1 ounce (av'd) =	28	grams	28.35
1 cubic centimetre =	.061	cubic inch	.0610	1 ounce (Troy) =	31	grams	31.10
1 cubic foot =	.028	cubic metre	.0283	1 peck =	8.8	litres	8.809
1 cubic inch =	16	cubic cent.†	16.39	1 pint =	.47	litre	.4732
1 cubic metre =	35	cubic feet	35.31	1 pound =	.45	kilo	.4536
1 cubic metre =	1.3	cubic yards	1.308	1 quart (dry) =	1.1	litres	1.101
1 cubic yard =	.76	cubic metre	.7645	1 quart (liquid) =	.95	litre	.9464
1 foot =	30	centimetres	30.48	1 sq. centimetre =	.15	sq. inch	.1550
1 gallon =	3.8	litres	3.785	1 sq. foot =	.093	sq. metre	.0929
1 grain =	.065	gram	.0648	1 sq. inch =	6.5	sq. c'timetr's.	6.452
1 gram =	15	grains	15.43	1 sq. metre =	1.2	sq. yards	1.196
1 hectar =	2.5	acres	2.471	1 sq. metre =	11	sq. feet	10.76
1 inch =	25	millimetres	25.40	1 sq. yard =	.84	sq. metre	.8361
1 kilo =	2.2	pounds	2.205	1 ton (2,000 lbs.) =	.91	metric ton	.9072
1 kilometre =	.62	mile	.6214	1 ton (2,240 lbs.) =	1	metric ton	1.017
1 litre =	.91	quart (dry)	.9081	1 ton (metric) =	1.1	ton (2,000 lbs.)	1.102
1 litre =	1.1	quarts (liq'd)	1.057	1 ton (metric) =	.98	ton (2,240 lbs.)	.9842
1 metre =	3.3	feet	3.281	1 yard =	.91	metre	.9144

* Contraction for kilogram. † Centimetres.

Minimum Weights of Produce.

THE following are minimum weights of certain articles of produce according to the laws of the United States:

	Per Bushel.		Per Bushel.		Per Bushel.
Wheat	60 lbs.	White Potatoes	60 lbs.	Hungarian Grass Seed	50 lbs.
Corn, in the ear	70 "	Sweet Potatoes	55 "	Timothy Seed	45 "
Corn, shelled	56 "	Onions	57 "	Blue Grass Seed	44 "
Rye	56 "	Turnips	55 "	Hemp Seed	44 "
Buckwheat	48 "	Dried Peaches	33 "	Salt (see note below).	
Barley	48 "	Dried Apples	26 "	Corn Meal	48 "
Oats	32 "	Clover Seed	60 "	Ground Peas	24 "
Peas	60 "	Flax Seed	56 "	Malt	34 "
White Beans	60 "	Millet Seed	50 "	Bran	20 "
Castor Beans	46 "				

SALT.—Weight per bushel as adopted by different States ranges from 50 to 80 pounds. Coarse salt in Pennsylvania is reckoned at 80 pounds, and in Illinois at 50 pounds per bushel. Fine salt in Pennsylvania is reckoned at 62 pounds, in Kentucky and Illinois at 55 pounds per bushel.

Measures and Weights of Great Britain.

THE measures of length and the weights are nearly, practically, the same as those in use in the United States. The English ton is 2,240 lbs. avoirdupois, the same as the long ton, or shipping ton of the United States. The English hundredweight is 112 lbs. avoirdupois, the same as the long hundredweight of the United States. The metre has been legalized at 39.37079 inches, but the length of 39.370432 inches, as adopted by France, Germany, Belgium, and Russia, is frequently used.

The Imperial gallon, the basis of the system of capacity, involves an error of about 1 part in 1,836: 10 lbs. of water = 277.123 cubic inches.

The English statute mile is 1,760 yards or 5.280 feet. The following are measures of capacity:

NAMES.	Pounds of Water.		Cubic Inches.	Litres.	United States Equivalents.
4 gills = 1 pint	1.25		34.66	0.56793	1.20032 liquid pints.
2 pints = 1 quart	2.5		69.32	1.13586	1.20032 " quarts.
2 quarts = 1 pottle	5		138.64	2.27173	2.40064 " "
2 pottles = 1 gallon	10		277.27	4.54346	1.20032 " gallons.
2 gallons = 1 peck	20	Dry m'sure	554.55	9.08692	1.03152 dry pecks.
4 pecks = 1 bushel	80	Dry m'sure	2218.19	36.34766	1.03152 " bushels.
4 bushels = 1 coomb	320	Dry m'sure	8872.77	145.39062	4.12606 " "
2 coombs = 1 quarter	640	Dry m'sure	17745.54	290.7813	8 2521 " "

A cubic foot of pure gold weighs 1,210 pounds; pure silver, 655 pounds; cast iron, 450 pounds; copper, 550 pounds; lead, 710 pounds; pure platinum, 1,220 pounds; tin, 456 pounds, aluminum. 163 pounds.

Stone—A measure of weight (avoirdupois) usually equal to half of the quarter of 28 pounds, or one-eighth hundredth weight of 112 pounds (termed the horseman's weight); tor butcher's meat, one-fourteenth of a hundred pounds.

Domestic Weights and Measures.

Apothecaries' Weight: 20 grains = 1 scruple; 3 scruples = 1 dram; 8 drams = 1 ounce; 12 ounces = 1 pound.

Avoirdupois Weight (short ton): 27 11-32 grains = 1 dram; 16 drams = 1 ounce; 16 ounces = 1 pound; 25 pounds = 1 quarter; 4 quarters = 1 cwt.; 20 cwt. = 1 ton.

Avoirdupois Weight (long ton): 27 11-32 grains = 1 dram; 16 drams = 1 ounce; 16 ounces = 1 pound; 112 pounds = 1 cwt.; 20 cwt. = 1 ton.

Troy Weight: 24 grains = 1 pennyweight; 20 pennyweights = 1 ounce; 12 ounces = 1 pound.

Circular Measure: 60 seconds = 1 minute; 60 minutes = 1 degree; 30 degrees = 1 sign; 12 signs = 1 circle or circumference.

Cubic Measure: 1,728 cubic inches = 1 cubic foot; 27 cubic feet = 1 cubic yard.

Dry Measure: 2 pints = 1 quart; 8 quarts = 1 peck; 4 pecks = 1 bushel.

Liquid Measure: 4 gills = 1 pint; 2 pints = 1 quart; 4 quarts = 1 gallon; 31½ gallons = 1 barrel; 2 barrels = 1 hogshead.

Long Measure: 12 inches = 1 foot; 3 feet = 1 yard; 5½ yards = 1 rod or pole; 40 rods = 1 furlong; 8 furlongs = 1 statute mile (1,760 yards or 5,280 feet); 3 miles = 1 league.

Mariner's Measure: 6 feet = 1 fathom; 120 fathoms = 1 cable length; 7⅛ cable lengths = 1 mile; 5,280 feet = 1 statute mile; 6,085 feet = 1 nautical mile.

Paper Measure: 24 sheets = 1 quire; 20 quires = 1 ream (480 sheets); 2 reams = 1 bundle; 5 bundles = 1 bale.

Square Measure: 144 square inehes = 1 square foot; 9 square feet = 1 square yard; 30¼ square yards = 1 square rod or perch; 40 square rods = 1 rood; 4 roods = 1 acre; 640 acres = 1 square mile; 36 square miles (6 miles square) = 1 township.

Time Measure: 60 seconds = 1 minute; 60 minutes = 1 hour; 24 hours = 1 day; 7 days = 1 week; 365 days = 1 year; 366 days = 1 leap year.

MEDICAL SIGNS AND ABBREVIATIONS.

℞ (Lat. Recipe), take; āā, of each; ℔, pound; ℥, ounce; ʒ, drachm; ℈, scruple; ♏, minim, or drop; O or o, pint; f℥, fluid ounce: fʒ, fluid drachm; as, ℥ss, half an ounce; ℥i, one ounce; ℥iss, one ounce and a half; ℥ij, two ounces; gr., grain; Q. S., as much as sufficient; Ft. Mist., let a mixture be made; Ft. Haust., let a draught be made; Ad., add to; Ad lib., at pleasure; Aq., water; M., mix; Mac., macerate; Pulv., powder; Pil., pill; Solv., dissolve; St., let it stand; Sum., to be taken; D., dose; Dil., dilute; Filt., filter; Lot., a wash; Garg., a gargle; Hor. Decub., at bed time; Inject., injection; Gtt., drops; ss, one-half; Ess., essence.

TEXAS LAND MEASURE.

(Also used in Mexico, New Mexico, Arizona, and California.)

26,000,000	square varas (square of 5,099	varas) = 1 league and 1 labor	=	4,605.5	acres.
1,000,000	square varas (square of 1.000	varas) = 1 labor	=	177.136	acres.
25,000,000	square varas (square of 5,000	varas) = 1 league	=	4,428.4	acres.
12,500 000	square varas (square of 3,535.5	varas) = ½ league	=	2,214.2	acres.
8,333,333	square varas (square of 2,886.7	varas) = ⅓ league	=	1.476.13	acres.
6.250,000	square varas (square of 2.500	varas) = ¼ league	=	1,107.1	acres.
7,225.600	square varas (square of 2,688	varas)	=	1,280	acres.
3.612,800	square varas (square of 1,900.8	varas) = 1 section	=	640	acres.
1,806.400	square varas (square of 1,344	varas) = ½ section	=	320	acres.
903,200	square varas (square of 950.44	varas) = ¼ section	=	160	acres.
451.600	square varas (square of 672	varas) = ⅛ section	=	80	acres.
225.800	square varas (square of 475	varas) = 1-16 section	=	40	acres.
5,645.376	square varas (square of 75.137	varas) = 4,840 square yards	=	1	acre.

To find the number of acres in any number of square varas, multiply the latter by 177 (or to be more exact, by 177⅛), and cut off six decimals.

1 vara = 33⅓ inches. 1,900.8 varas = 1 mile.

WEIGHTS AND MEASURES OF THE PHILIPPINES.

1 pulgada (12 linea)	=	.927	inch.	1 libra (16 onzo)	=	1.0144	lb. av.
1 pie	=	11.125	inches.	1 arroba	=	25.360	lb. av.
1 vara	=	33.375	inches.	1 catty (16 tael)	=	1.394	lb. av.
1 gantah	=	.8796	gallon.	1 pecul (100 catty)	=	139.482	lb. av.
1 caban	=	21.991	gallons.				

Knots and Miles.

THE **Statute Mile** is 5,280 feet.
The **British Admiralty Knot** or **Nautical Mile** is 6,080 feet.
The **Statute Knot** is 6,082.66 feet, and is generally considered the standard. The number of feet in a statute knot is arrived at thus: The circumference of the earth is divided into 360 degrees, each degree containing 60 knots or (360x60) 21,600 knots to the circumference. 21,600 divided into 131,385,456—the number of feet in the earth's circumference—gives 6,082.66 feet—the length of a standard mile.

1 knot	= 1.151 miles	4 knots	= 4.606 miles	20 knots	= 23.030 miles	600 feet	= 1 cable
2 knots	= 2.303 miles	5 knots	= 5.757 miles	25 knots	= 28.787 miles	10 cables	= 1 knot
3 knots	= 3.454 miles	10 knots	= 11.515 miles	6 feet	= 1 fathom		

Ancient Greek and Roman Weights and Measures,

WITH AMERICAN EQUIVALENTS.

WEIGHTS.

The Roman libra or pound = 10 oz. 18 pwt. 13 5-7 gr., Troy.
The Attica mina or pound = 11 oz. 7 pwt. 16 2-7 gr., Troy.
The Attica talent (60 minæ) = 56 lbs. 11 oz. 0 pwt 17 1-7 gr., Troy.

DRY MEASURE.

The Roman modus = 1 pk. 2-9 pint.
The Attic chœnix = nearly 1½ pints.
The Attic medimnus = 4 pk. 6 1-10 pints.

LIQUID MEASURE.

The cotyle = a little over ½ pint.
The cyathus = a little over 1⅛ pints.
The chus = a little over 6⅔ pints.

LONG MEASURE.

The Roman foot = 11 3-5 inches.
The Roman cubit = 1 ft. 5⅔ inches.
The Roman pace = 4 ft. 10 niches.
The Roman furlong = 604 ft. 10 inches.
The Roman mile = 4,835 feet.
The Grecian cubit = 1 ft. 6⅛ inches.
The Grecian furlong = 504 ft. 4 1-5 inches.
The Grecian mile = 4030 ft.

MONEY.

The quadrans = 1 1-10 mills.
The as = 1 3-10 mills.
The sestertius = 3 58 + cents.
The sestertium (1,000 sestertii) = $35.80+.
The denarius = 14.35 + cents.
The Attic obolus = 2.39 + cents.
The drachma = 14.35 + cents.*
The mina (100 drachmæ) = $14.35+.
The talent (60 minæ) = $861.00+.
The Greek stater = aureus (same as the Roman †) = $3.58,79.
The stater = daricus = $7.16,66.

*The modern drachma equals 19.3 cents. † Did not remain, at all periods, at this value, but this is the value indicated by Tacitus.

BIBLICAL WEIGHTS REDUCED TO TROY WEIGHT.

	Lbs.	Oz.	Pwt.	Gr.
The Gerah, one-twentieth of a Shekel	0	0	0	12
The Bekah, half a Shekel	0	0	5	0
The Shekel	0	0	10	0
The Maneh, 60 Shekels	2	6	0	0
The Talent, 50 manehs, or 3,000 Shekels	125	0	0	0

Electrical Units.

NAME.	Symbol.	Unit of	How Obtained.	CGS*	Equivalent.
Ohm	R	Resistance	The electrical resistance of a column of mercury 106 centimetres long and of 1 square millimetre section.	10^9	1 true ohm = 1.0112 British Association ohms.
Ampère	C	Current	Is that current of electricity that decomposes .0 009324 gramme of water per second.	10^1	Deposits 1.118 milligrams of silver per second.
Volt	E	Electromotive force	One ampère of current passing through a substance having 1 ohm of resistance = 1 volt.	10^8	.926 of a standard Daniel Cell.
Coulomb	Q	Quantity	A current of 1 ampère during 1 second of time.	10^1	Deposits 1.118 milligrams of silver.
Farad	K	Capacity	The capacity that a current of 1 ampère for 1 second (=1 coulomb) charges it to potential of 1 volt.	10^9	2.5 knots of D. U. S. cable.
Microfarad	"		1-millionth of farad.	10^{15}	
Watt	Pw.	Power	Power of 1 ampère current passing through resistance of 1 ohm.	10^7	.0013405 (or $\frac{1}{746}$) of a horse power.
Jou	W.j.	Work	Is the work done by 1 watt of electrical power in 1 second.	10^7	.238 unit of heat (Therm).

*C. G. S. = Electro-magnetic units. Consult technical works in electricity.

Foreign Moneys.

English Money: 4 farthings = 1 penny (*d*); 12 pence = 1 shilling (*s*); 20 shillings = 1 pound (£). 21 shillings = one guinea; 5 shillings = one crown.
French Money: 10 centimes = 1 decime; 10 decimes = 1 franc.
German Money: 100 pfennig = 1 mark.
Russian Money: 100 copecks = 1 ruble.
Austro-Hungarian Money: 100 kreutzer = 1 florin.
For United States equivalents, see table of "Value of Foreign Coins in U. S. Money."

Table of Geometrical Progression.

(WHEREBY any questions of Geometrical Progression and of Double Ratio may be solved by Inspection, the Number of Terms not exceeding 56.)

1	1	15	16384	29	268435456	43	4398046511104
2	2	16	32768	30	536870912	44	8796093022208
3	4	17	65536	31	1073741824	45	17592186044416
4	8	18	131072	32	2147483648	46	35184372088832
5	16	19	262144	33	4294967296	47	70368744177664
6	32	20	524288	34	8589934592	48	140737488355328
7	64	21	1048576	35	17179869184	49	281474976710656
8	128	22	2097152	36	34359738368	50	562949953421312
9	256	23	4194304	37	68719476736	51	1125899906842624
10	512	24	8388608	38	137438953472	52	2251799813685248
11	1024	25	16777216	39	274877906944	53	4503599627370496
12	2048	26	33554432	40	549755813888	54	9007199254740992
13	4096	27	67108864	41	1099511627776	55	18014398509481984
14	8192	28	134217728	42	2199023255552	56	36008797018963968

ILLUSTRATIONS—The 13th power of 2=8192, and the the 8th root of 256=2.

The English Mile

COMPARED WITH OTHER EUROPEAN MEASURES.

	English Mile.	English Geog. M.	French Kilom.	German Geog. M.	Russian Verst.	Austrian Mile.	Dutch Ure.	Norweg. Mile.	Swedish Mile.	Danish Mile.	Swiss Stunde.
English Statute Mile....	1.000	0.867	1.609	0.217	1.508	0.212	0 289	0.142	0.151	0.213	0.335
English Geog. Mile.....	1.150	1.000	1.855	0.250	1.738	0.245	0.333	0.164	0.169	0.246	0 386
French Kilometer.......	0.621	0.540	1.000	0.135	0.937	0.132	0.180	0 088	0.094	0 133	0.208
German Geog. Mile......	4.610	4.000	7.420	1.000	6.953	0.978	1 333	0.657	0 694	0.985	1.543
Russian Verst............	0 663	0 575	1.067	0.144	1.000	0.141	0.192	0.094	0.100	0.142	0.222
Austrian Mile	4.714	4.089	7.586	1.022	7.112	1.000	1.363	0.672	0.710	1.006	1 578
Dutch Ure................	3.458	3.000	5 565	0.750	5.215	0.734	1.000	0.493	0 520	0.738	1.157
Norwegian Mile.........	7.021	6.091	11 299	1.523	10.589	1.489	2.035	1.000	1.057	1.499	2.350
Swedish Mile............	6.644	5.764	10.692	1.441	10.019	1.409	1.921	0 948	1.000	1.419	2.224
Danish Mile..............	4.682	4.062	7.536	1.016	7.078	0 994	1.354	0.667	0.708	1.000	1.567
Swiss Stunde.............	2.987	2.592	4.808	0.648	4.505	0.634	0 864	0 425	0.449	0 638	1,000

Standard Newspaper Measure.

THE Standard Newspaper Measure, as recognized and now in general use is 13 ems pica. The standard of measurement of all sizes of type is the "em quad," not the letter "m."

The basis of measurements adopted by the International Typographical Union is the lower-case alphabet, from "a" to "z" inclusive, and the ems used are the same body as the type measured.

4½ Point..................18 ems	7 Point....................14 ems	10 Point......................13 ems
5 Point....................17 ems	8 Point....................14 ems	11 Point......................13 ems
5½ Point..................16 ems	9 Point....................13 ems	12 Point......................13 ems
6 Point....................15 ems		

Simple Interest Table.

(Showing at Different Rates the Interest on $1 from 1 Month to 1 Year, and on $100 from 1 Day to 1 Year)

TIME.	4 PER CENT.			5 PER CENT.			6 PER CENT.			7 PER CENT.			8 PER CENT.		
	Dollars.	Cents.	Mills.	Dollars.	Cents.	Mills.	Dollars.	Cents.	Mills.	Dollars.	Cents.	Mills.	Dollars.	Cents.	Mills.
One Dollar 1 month..........	..	..	3	..	..	4	..	..	5	..	..	5	..	..	6
" 2 "	..	..	7	..	..	8	..	1	..	..	1	1	..	1	3
" 3 "	..	1	1	..	1	3	..	1	5	..	1	7	..	2	..
" 6 "	..	2	..	..	2	5	..	3	..	..	3	5	..	4	..
" 12 "	..	4	..	..	5	..	..	6	..	..	7	..	..	8	..
One Hundred Dollars 1 day...	..	1	1	..	1	3	..	1	6	..	1	9	..	2	2
" " 2 " ..	..	2	2	..	2	7	..	3	2	..	3	8	..	4	4
" " 3 " ..	..	3	4	..	4	1	..	5	..	..	5	8	..	6	7
" " 4 " ..	..	4	5	..	5	3	..	6	6	..	7	7	..	8	9
" " 5 " ..	..	5	6	..	6	9	..	8	2	..	9	7	..	11	1
" " 6 " ..	..	6	7	..	8	3	..	10	..	..	11	6	..	13	3
" " 1 month	..	33	4	..	41	6	..	50	..	..	58	3	..	66	7
" " 2 "	..	66	7	..	83	2	1	..	..	1	16	6	1	33	3
" " 3 "	1	..	..	1	25	..	1	50	..	1	75	..	2	..	..
" " 6 "	2	..	..	2	50	..	3	..	..	3	50	..	4	..	..
" " 12 "	4	..	..	5	..	..	6	..	..	7	..	..	8	..	..

Compound Interest Table.

COMPOUND INTEREST ON ONE DOLLAR FOR 100 YEARS.

Amount	Years.	Per cent.	Accumulation.	Amount	Years.	Per cent.	Accumulation.	Amount	Years.	Per cent.	Accumulation.
$1	100	1	$2.70,5	$1	100	4½	$81.58,9	$1	100	10	$13,780.66
1	100	2	7.24,5	1	100	5	131.50,1	1	100	11	34,064.34.6
1	100	2½	11.81.4	1	100	6	339.30.5	1	100	12	83,521.82,7
1	100	3	19.21.8	1	100	7	867.72.1	1	100	15	1,174,302.40
1	100	3½	31.19,1	1	100	8	2,199.78,4	1	100	18	15,424,106.40
1	100	4	50.50,4	1	100	9	5,529.04,4	1	100	24	2,198,720,200

YEARS IN WHICH A GIVEN AMOUNT WILL DOUBLE AT SEVERAL RATES OF INTEREST.

Rate.	At Simple Interest.	At Compound Interest. Compounded Yearly.	At Compound Interest. Compounded Semi-Annually.	At Compound Interest. Compounded Quarterly.	Rate.	At Simple Interest.	At Compound Interest. Compounded Yearly.	At Compound Interest. Compounded Semi-Annually.	At Compound Interest. Compounded Quarterly.
1	100 years.	69.660	69.487	69.237	6	16.67	11.896	11.725	11.639
1½	66.66	46.556	46.382	46.297	6½	15.38	11.007	10.836	10.750
2	50.00	35.003	34.830	34.743	7	14.29	10.245	10.074	9.966
2½	40.00	28.071	27.899	27.748	7½	13.33	9.584	9.414	9.328
3	33.33	23.450	23.278	23.191	8	12.50	9.006	8.837	8.751
3½	28.57	20.149	19.977	19.890	8½	11.76	8.497	8.327	8.241
4	25.00	17.673	17.501	17.415	9	11.11	8.043	7.874	7.788
4½	22.22	15.747	15.576	15.490	9½	10.52	7.638	7.468	7.383
5	20.00	14.207	14.035	13.949	10	10.00	7.273	7.103	7.018
5½	18.18	12.942	12.775	12.689	12	8.34	6.116	5.948	5.862

Monthly Wage Table.*

Days.	$10	$11	$12	$13	$14	$15	$16	$17	$18	$19	$20
1	.38	.42	.46	.50	.54	.58	.62	.65	.69	.73	.77
2	.77	.85	.92	1.00	1.08	1.15	1.23	1.31	1.38	1.46	1.54
3	1.15	1.27	1.38	1.50	1.62	1.73	1.85	1.96	2.08	2.19	2.31
4	1.54	1.69	1.85	2.00	2.15	2.31	2.46	2.62	2.77	2.92	3.08
5	1.92	2.12	2.31	2.50	2.69	2.88	3.08	3.27	3.46	3.65	3.85
6	2.31	2.54	2.77	3.00	3.23	3.46	3.69	3.92	4.15	4.38	4.62
7	2.69	2.96	3.23	3.50	3.77	4.04	4.31	4.58	4.85	5.12	5.38
8	3.08	3.38	3.69	4.00	4.31	4.62	4.92	5.23	5.54	5.85	6.15
9	3.46	3.81	4.15	4.50	4.85	5.19	5.54	5.88	6.23	6.58	6.92
10	3.85	4.23	4.62	5.00	5.38	5.77	6.15	6.54	6.92	7.31	7.69
11	4.23	4.65	5.08	5.50	5.92	6.35	6.77	7.19	7.62	8.04	8.46
12	4.62	5.08	5.44	6.00	6.46	6.92	7.38	7.85	8.31	8.77	9.23
13	5.00	5.50	6.00	6.50	7.00	7.50	8.00	8.50	9.00	9.50	10.00
14	5.38	5.92	6.46	7.00	7.54	8.08	8.62	9.15	9.69	10.23	10.77
15	5.77	6.35	6.92	7.50	8.08	8.65	9.23	9.81	10.38	10.96	11.54
20	7.69	8.46	9.23	10.00	10.77	11.54	12.31	13.08	13.85	14.62	15.38
1 month	10.00	11.00	12.00	13.00	14.00	15.00	16.00	17.00	18.00	19.00	20.00
2	20.00	22.00	24.00	26.00	28.00	30.00	32.00	34.00	36.00	38.00	40.00
3	30.00	33.00	36.00	39.00	42.00	45.00	48.00	51.00	54.00	57.00	60.00
4	40.00	44.00	48.00	52.00	56.00	60.00	64.00	68.00	72.00	76.00	80.00
5	50.00	55.00	60.00	65.00	70.00	75.00	80.00	85.00	90.00	95.00	100.00
6	60.00	66.00	72.00	78.00	84.00	90.00	96.00	102.00	108.00	114.00	120.00
7	70.00	77.00	84.00	91.00	98.00	105.00	112.00	119.00	126.00	133.00	140.00
8	80.00	88.00	96.00	104.00	112.00	120.00	128.00	136.00	144.00	152.00	160.00
9	90.00	99.00	108.00	117.00	126.00	135.00	144.00	153.00	162.00	171.00	180.00
10	100.00	110.00	120.00	130.00	140.00	150.00	160.00	170.00	180.00	190.00	200.00
11	110.00	121.00	132.00	143.00	154.00	165.00	176.00	187.00	198.00	209.00	220.00
1 year	120.00	132.00	144.00	156.00	168.00	180.00	192.00	204.00	216.00	228.00	240.00

*Six working days in the week.

Roman and Arabic Numerals.

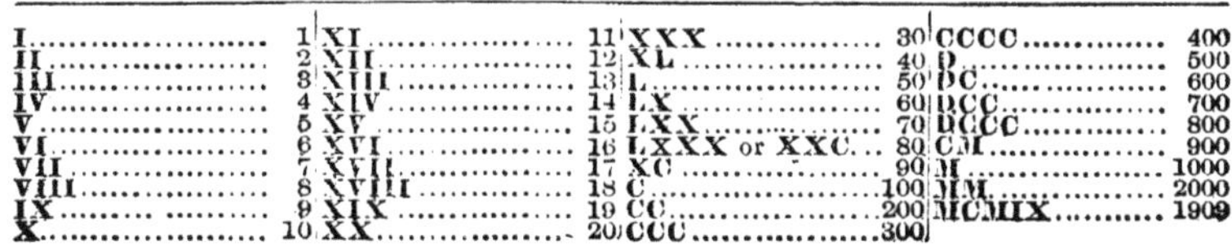

I	1	XI	11	XXX	30	CCCC	400
II	2	XII	12	XL	40	D	500
III	3	XIII	13	L	50	DC	600
IV	4	XIV	14	LX	60	DCC	700
V	5	XV	15	LXX	70	DCCC	800
VI	6	XVI	16	LXXX or XXC	80	CM	900
VII	7	XVII	17	XC	90	M	1000
VIII	8	XVIII	18	C	100	MM	2000
IX	9	XIX	19	CC	200	MCMIX	1909
X	10	XX	20	CCC	300		

Specific Gravity.*

Liquids.		*Timber.*		*Sundries.*		*Metals and Stones.*	
Water	100	Cork	24	Indigo	77	Granite	278
Sea-water	103	Poplar	38	Ice	92	Diamond	353
Dead Sea	124	Fir	55	Gunpowder	93	Cast iron	721
Alcohol	84	Cedar	61	Butter	94	Tin	729
Turpentine	99	Pear	66	Clay	120	Bar iron	779
Wine	100	Walnut	67	Coal	130	Steel	783
Urine	101	Cherry	72	Opium	134	Brass	840
Cider	102	Maple	75	Honey	145	Copper	895
Beer	102	Ash	84	Ivory	183	Silver	1,047
Woman's milk	102	Beech	85	Sulphur	203	Lead	1,135
Cow's "	103	Mahogany	106	Marble	270	Mercury	1,357
Goat's "	104	Oak	117	Chalk	279	Gold	1,926
Porter	104	Ebony	133	Glass	289	Platina	2,150

The weight of a cubic foot of distilled water at a temperature of 60° F. is 1,000 ounces Avoirdupois, *very nearly*, therefore the weight (in ounces, Avoirdupois) of a cubic foot of any of the substances in the above table is found by multiplying the specific gravities by 10, thus:—one cubic foot of oak weighs 1,170 ounces; one cubic foot of marble 2,700 ounces, and so on.

* Compared with water.

Freezing, Fusing, and Boiling Points.

Substances.	Reaumur.	Centigrade.	Fahrenheit.	Substances.	Reaumur.	Centigrade.	Fahrenheit.
Bromine freezes at	— 17.6°	— 22°	— 7.6°	Silver fuses at	800°	1,000°	1,832°
Olive oil freezes at	8	10	50	Sodium fuses at	76.5	95 6	204
Quicksilver freezes at	— 31.5	— 39.4	— 39	Sulphur fuses at	92	115	239
Water freezes at	0	0	32	Tin fuses at	182	228	442
Bismuth metal fuses at	211	264	507	Zinc fuses at	329.6	412	773
Copper fuses at	963	1,204	2,200	Alcohol boils at	63	74.4	167
Gold fuses at	1,105	1,380	2,518	Bromine boils at	50	63	145
Iron fuses at	1,230	1,538	2,800	Ether boils at	28.4	35.5	96
Lead fuses at	260	325	617	Iodine boils at	140	175	347
Potassium fuses at	50	62.5	144.5	Water boils at	80	100	212

Authorities vary on some of these points. The best are given.

Height and Weight of Men.

TABLE OF AVERAGE HEIGHT AND WEIGHT OF MALES, BASED ON ANALYSIS OF 74,162 ACCEPTED APPLICANTS FOR LIFE INSURANCE AS REPORTED TO THE ASSOCIATION OF LIFE INSURANCE MEDICAL DIRECTORS.

Height.	Age. 15–24	Age. 25–29	Age. 30–34	Age. 35–39	Age. 40–44	Age. 45–49	Age. 50–54	Age. 55–59	Age. 60–64	Age. 65–69
	Pounds.	Pounds.	Pounds.	Pounds.	Pounds.	Pounds.	Pounds.	Pounds.	Pounds.	Pounds.
5 feet	120	125	128	131	133	134	134	134	131	....
5 feet 1 inch	122	126	129	131	134	136	136	136	134	....
5 feet 2 inches	124	128	131	133	136	138	138	138	137	....
5 feet 3 inches	127	131	134	136	139	141	141	141	140	140
5 feet 4 inches	131	135	138	140	143	144	145	145	144	143
5 feet 5 inches	134	138	141	143	146	147	149	149	148	147
5 feet 6 inches	138	142	145	147	150	151	153	153	153	151
5 feet 7 inches	142	147	150	152	155	156	158	158	158	156
5 feet 8 inches	146	151	154	157	160	161	163	163	163	162
5 feet 9 inches	150	155	159	162	165	166	167	168	168	168
5 feet 10 inches	154	159	164	167	170	171	172	173	174	174
5 feet 11 inches	159	164	169	173	175	177	177	178	180	180
6 feet	165	170	175	179	180	183	182	183	185	185
6 feet 1 inch	170	177	181	185	186	189	188	189	189	189
6 feet 2 inches	176	184	188	192	194	196	194	194	192	192
6 feet 3 inches	181	190	195	200	203	204	201	198	....	....

A Height and Weight Table compiled by a Committee of the Medical Section of the National Fraternal Congress, 1900, which is the analysis of 133,940 applications of selected risks, in a few instances differed very slightly from the above.

HEIGHT AND WEIGHT OF WOMEN.

The following table gives the relative height and weight of women, all ages. The weight of ordinary clothing, however, is included:

Height.	Average.	Minimum.	Maximum.	Height.	Average.	Minimum.	Maximum.
5 feet	115	98	132	5 feet 7 inches	145	123	167
5 feet 1 inch	120	102	138	5 feet 8 inches	148	126	170
5 feet 2 inches	125	106	144	5 feet 9 inches	155	131	179
5 feet 3 inches	130	111	150	5 feet 10 inches	160	136	184
5 feet 4 inches	1 5	115	155	5 feet 11 inches	165	138	190
5 feet 5 inches	140	119	161	6 feet	170	141	196
5 feet 6 inches	143	121	165				

Water Measures.

WEIGHT OF WATER.

1	cubic inch.........	.03617	pound.	1	cylindrical foot....	6.0	U.S. gals.
12	cubic inches.......	.434	pound.	2.282	cylindrical feet....	112.0	pounds.
1	cubic foot (salt)...	64.3	pounds.	45.64	cylindrical feet....	2240.0	pounds.
1	cubic foot (fresh)..	62.5	pounds.	1	imperial gallon....	10.0	pounds.
1	cubic foot.........	7.48052	U. S. gals.	11.2	imperial gallons...	112.0	pounds.
1.8	cubic feet.........	112.0	pounds.	224	imperial gallons...	2240.0	pounds.
35.84	cubic feet.........	2240.0	pounds.	1	U. S. gallon	8.355	pounds.
1	cylindrical inch...	.02842	pound.	13.44	U. S. gallons......	112.0	pounds.
12	cylindrical inches	.341	pound.	268.8	U. S. gallons......	2240.0	pounds.
1	cylindrical foot....	49.10	pounds.				

NOTE.—The centre of pressure of a body of water is at two-thirds the depth from the surface

THEORETICAL VELOCITY OF WATER IN FEET PER SECOND.

HEAD, FEET.	Velocity, Feet per Second.	HEAD, FEET.	Velocity, Feet per Second.	HEAD, FEET.	Velocity, Feet per Second.	HEAD, FEET.	Velocity, Feet per Second.
10	25.4	25	40.1	55	59.5	85	74.0
12	27.8	30	43.9	60	62.1	90	76.1
15	31.1	35	47.4	65	64.7	95	78.2
18	34.0	40	50.7	70	67.1	100	80.3
20	35.9	45	53.8	75	69.5	125	89.7
22	37.6	50	56.7	80	71.8	150	98.3

PRESSURE OF WATER PER SQUARE INCH AT DIFFERENT ELEVATIONS.

HEIGHT IN INCHES.	Pressure.	HEIGHT IN INCHES.	Pressure.	HEIGHT IN INCHES.	Pressure.	HEIGHT IN INCHES.	Pressure.
6	2.60	35	15.16	90	38.98	160	69.31
8	3.40	40	17.32	100	43.31	170	73.64
10	4.33	45	19.49	110	47.64	180	77.97
15	6.49	50	21.65	120	51.98	190	82.30
20	8.66	60	25.99	130	56.31	200	86.63
25	10.82	70	30.32	140	60.64	215	93.14
30	12.99	80	34.65	150	64.97	230	99.63

Temperature of Steam

ATMOSPHERIC PRESSURE 14.7 DEGREES IN FAHRENHEIT SCALE.

PRESSURE PER SQ. INCH.	Degrees of Temperature.	PRESSURE PER SQ. INCH.	Degrees of Temperature.	PRESSURE PER SQ. INCH.	Degrees of Temperature.	PRESSURE PER SQ. INCH.	Degrees of Temperature.
1	216.3	12	244.3	32	277.0	80	323.9
2	219.4	14	248.3	34	279.6	85	327.6
3	222.4	16	252.1	40	286.9	90	331.1
4	225.2	18	255.7	45	292.5	95	334.5
5	227.9	20	259.2	50	297.8	100	337.8
6	230.5	22	262.5	55	302.7	105	341.0
7	233.0	24	265.6	60	307.4	110	344.0
8	235.4	26	268.6	65	311.8	115	347.0
9	237.7	28	271.5	70	316.0	120	350.0
10	240.0	30	274.3	75	320.0	125	352.8

Steam flows into atmosphere at the rate of 650 feet per second.

Tensile Strength of Materials.

WEIGHT OF POWER REQUIRED TO TEAR ASUNDER ONE SQUARE INCH.

MATERIALS.	Lbs. Avoir.	MATERIALS.	Lbs. Avoir.	MATERIALS.	Lbs. Avoir.	MATERIALS.	Lbs. Avoir.
Brass..................	42,000	Iron, rivets, Am......	53,300	Tin 10, Antimony 1...	11,000	Slate.	12,000
" yellow..........	18,000	" " Eng......	65,000	Zinc.......	3,500	Ash..................	14,000
Bronze, greatest......	56,788	" Wire, Am.......	73,600	" sheet............	16,000	Beech................	11,500
" least.........	17,698	" Wrought wire...	103,000	Brick, fire............	65	Cedar......	11,400
Copper, bolt	36,800	Lead, cast............	1,800	" inferior........	100	Chestnut, sweet......	10,500
" cast Am......	24,250	" milled..........	3,320	" well burned...	750	Cypress..............	6,000
" rolled.........	36,000	" wire............	2,580	Cement, bluestone....	77	Deal, Christiana......	12,400
" wire...........	61,200	Platinum, Wire.......	53,000	" hydraulic....	234	Elm..................	13,400
" wrought......	34,000	Silver, cast..........	40,000	" Portland, 6 mo	414	Fir, strongest........	12,000
Gold, cast....	20,000	Steel, Am. Tool Co....	179,980	Chalk................	118	Locust....	20,500
Iron, cast, Low Moor,		" blistered, soft	104,000	Glass, crown..........	2,346	Mahogany............	21,000
No. 2.............	14,076		133,000	Gutta-percha....	3,500	Maple................	10,500
Iron, Cast Am......	18,000	Steel, cast, maxi'm....	142,000	Ivory.....	16,000	Oak, Am. white......	11,500
	30,000	" " mean......	88,657	Leather belts.........	330	Pear.	9,800
Iron, wrought, best		" plates, crosswise	93,700	Limestone..........	670	Pine, Am. white......	11,500
Swedish bar......	72,000	" " length-			2,800	" pitch...........	12,000
Iron, bolts............	52,250	wise..	96,300	Marble, Italian.......	5,200	Poplar...............	7,000
" hammered.......	53,913	Steel, puddled, ex-		" White.	9,000	Spruce, white.........	10,290
" mean of Am....	31,829	treme.............	173,817	Plaster of Paris.......	72	Sycamore......... ...	13,000
" " Eng....	53,900	Steel, razor...........	150,000	Rope, hemp, tarred...	15,000	Teak.................	14,000
" plates, boiler	48,000	Tin, Banca.......	2,122	" manila.........	9,000	Walnut...............	7,800
American......	62,000	" cast, block.......	5,000	" wire............	37,000	Willow...............	13,000

Tensile Strength is the resistance of the fibres or particles of a body to separation. It is therefore proportional to their number, or to the area of its transverse section. The fibres of wood are strongest near the centre of the trunk or limb of a tree.

Seed Planting in the United States.

(Compiled from reports of the Department of Agriculture.)

Kind of Crop.	Date of Planting.	Best Soil.	Amount of Manure per Acre.	Amount of Seed per Acre (1).	Weeks to Maturity.
NEW ENGLAND.					
Corn	May 10 to 30	Sandy or clay loam	8 to 12 tons	8 to 12 qts.	14-17
Wheat	Fall or Spring	Clay loam	18 tons	2 bush	20
Oats	Apr. to May	Strong loam	6 to 8 tons	2 to 3 bush	11-15
Barley	Apr. to June 20	Strong loam	7 to 8 tons	2 to 3 bush	10-15
Rye	Apr. to May, Sept.	Medium loam	7 to 8 tons	5 to 6 pecks	40
Buckwheat	June 1 to 20	Light loam	4 to 6 tons	1 to 1¼ bush	10-15
White beans	May to June	Sandy loam	7 to 8 tons	8 to 16 qts.	8-14
Potatoes	Apr. 15 to May 1.	Rich loam	15 to 20 tons	8 to 20 bush	12-20
Turnips	July 1 to Aug. 3	Sandy loam	10 tons	1 lb.	10
Mangels	Apr. 15 to May 5	Strong heavy loam	8 to 15 tons	4 to 6 lbs.	17-22
Tobacco	Seed bed Apr.	Sandy loam	8 to 12 tons		9-12
Hay					
MIDDLE STATES.					
Corn	Apr. 20 to May 30	Medium loam	8 to 12 tons manure.	6 to 8 qts.	16-18
Wheat	Sept. 20 to Oct. 20	Loam	8 tons; 300 lbs. fer.	2 bush	41-43
Oats	Mar. to May	Moist clay loam	8 tons; 300 lbs. fer.	2 to 2½ bush	16-17
Barley	Mar. to May	Clay loam	8 tons; 300 lbs. fer.	2 to 2½ bush	13-16
Rye	Sept. 1 to Oct. 1	Sand or gravel loam	8 tons; 300 lbs. fer.	1½ bush	40-43
Buckwheat	June to July	Loam	5 tons	½ to 1½ bush	8-10
White beans	May to June	Sandy loam	8 tons	1½ bush	13-14
Potatoes	Mar. to May	Loam	10 to 18 tons	8 to 15 bush	14-22
Sweet potatoes.	May to June	Sandy loam		10 to 12 bush	10-15
Cabbage	Mar. to July	Clay or sandy loam	300 to 600 lbs. fer.	4 to 8 oz.	8-15
Turnips	July	Loam		2 to 5 lbs.	10-12
Mangels	May	Loam	10 to 20 tons	10 to 15 bush	15-18
Flax	May	Limestone loam		20 qts.	8-10
Tobacco	Seed bed Mar.	Sandy loam	Commercial fer.		15-20
Hay, timothy	Aug. to Oct	Clay loam		6 to 8 qts	
Hay, clover	Feb. to Apr.	Clay loam		6 qts.	
CENTRAL AND WESTERN STATES.					
Corn	Apr. 1 to June 1	Black or sandy loam.	5 to 10 tons	6 qts.	16-20
Wheat	Fall or Spring	Strong loam	8 tons	2 bush	40-42
Oats	Apr. 1 to May 1	Clay loam	8 tons	2 to 3 bush	12-14
Barley	Fall or Spring (1).	Clay loam	8 tons	2 bush	11-13
Rye	Sept. 1 to 30	Light loam	8 tons	1 to 2 bush	35-40
Buckwheat	June	Clay loam	5 tons	1 to 2 bush	10-12
White beans	May 10 to June 10.	Clay loam	8 tons	1½ bush	12
Potatoes	Mar. 15 to June 1	Sandy loam	5 to 10 tons	5 to 10 bush	10-20
Turnips	July 15 to Aug. 30.	Loam or muck	8 to 10 tons	1 to 6 lbs.	10-16
Mangels	Apr. 1 to May 15	Sandy loam	8 to 12 tons	6 to 8 lbs.	22-24
Flax	Mar. 15 to May 15.	Loam	10 to 15 tons	2 to 3 pecks	15-20
Tobacco	Seed bed, Mar.	Sandy loam	8 to 10 tons	Oz. to 6 sq. rd.	15-18
Hay	Apr. to May	Clay loam	10 tons	8 to 15 lbs.	
SOUTHERN STATES.					
Cotton	Feb. to May 15	Sandy loam (2)		1 to 3 bush	20-30
Corn	Feb. to June	Rich loam	10 bush. cot. seed.	8 qts.	18-20
Wheat	Sept. to Nov.	Clay loam (2)	8 tons	2 bush	43
Oats	Feb., May, Sept.	Clay loam (2)	8 to 10 tons	2½ bush	17
Barley	Apr. to May	Clay loam (2)	8 to 10 tons	2½ bush	17
Rye	Sept. to Oct.	Clay loam (2)	10 tons	1½ bush	43
White beans	Mar. to May	Light loam	8 tons	1 to 2 bush	7-8
Cabbage	Oct., Mar. to May.	Light loam	6 to 10 tons	¼ to ½ lbs.	14
Watermelons	Mar. 1 to May 10.	Rich, light loam	5 tons; 300 lbs. fer.	2 to 7 lbs.	16-20
Onions	Feb. 1 to Apr. 10.	Loam or muck			16-24
Potatoes	Jan., Feb. to Apr.	Light loose loam	8 to 12 tons	8 to 10 bush	11-15
Sweet potatoes.	May to June	Sandy loam		10 to 12 bush	12-15
Pumpkins	Apr. 1 to May 1	Rich, light loam		4 to 7 lbs.	17-20
Tomatoes	Jan. 1 to Feb. 19	Rich, sandy loam		4 to 9 oz.	14-20
Turnips	Feb., Aug., Apr.	Rich, light loam		2 to 6 lbs.	8-12
Tobacco	Seed bed, Mar.	Sandy loam	8 to 15 tons	oz. to 6 sq. rd.	18-20
Cow peas	May 1 to July 15.	Sandy loam	200 to 300 lbs. phos.	2 to 5 pecks	6-8

(1) The standard varieties of seed planted in the several sections of the United States are as follows: Corn—New England, leaming, sanford, flint; Middle States, leaming, white dent, yellow dent; Central and Western States, leaming, sanford, flint, white dent; Southern States, hickory king, gourdseed, Cox prolific. Wheat—Middle States, fultz; Central and Western States, fultz, poole, fife; Southern States, fulcaster. Oats—New England, white; Middle States, white, black; Central and Western States, gray Norway, silver mine, Russian; Southern States, Texas rustproof. Barley—Middle States, mansbury; Southern States, Tennessee Winter. Rye—New England, white; Middle States, white, Winter; Central and Western States, Winter; Southern States, excelsior Winter. Buckwheat—Middle States, silver hull; Central and Western States, silver hull. Potatoes—New England, green mountain, carmen 3, rose; Middle States, rose, carmen 3, rural 2; Central and Western States, hebron, rural, early rose, early Ohio. Tobacco—Central and Western States, yellow prior, Spanish, white burley. Hay, clover—Middle States, medium red. Sweet Potatoes—Middle States, yellow Jersey; Southern States, yellow Jersey. Cotton—Southern States, Texas stormproof. Spring wheat is to some extent grown in Ohio, Indiana, Illinois and many other States. It matures in eighteen to twenty weeks.

(2) In Texas the black loam is a good soil for cotton, corn, wheat and most other field crops.

Constitution of the United States.

Preamble.

We, the people of the United States, in order to form a more perfect Union, establish justice, insure domestic tranquillity, provide for the common defence, promote the general welfare, and secure the blessings of liberty to ourselves and our posterity, do ordain and establish this Constitution for the United States of America.

ARTICLE I.

Legislative powers.

Section I. All legislative powers herein granted shall be vested in a Congress of the United States, which shall consist of a Senate and House of Representatives.

House of Representatives.

Section II. 1. The House of Representatives shall be composed of members chosen every second year by the people of the several States, and the electors in each State shall have the qualifications requisite for electors of the most numerous branch of the State Legislature.

Qualifications of Representatives.

2. No person shall be a Representative who shall not have attained to the age of twenty-five years, and been seven years a citizen of the United States, and who shall not, when elected, be an inhabitant of that State in which he shall be chosen.

Apportionment of Representatives.

3. Representatives and direct taxes shall be apportioned among the several States which may be included within this Union according to their respective numbers, which shall be determined by adding to the whole number of free persons, including those bound to service for a term of years, and excluding Indians not taxed, three-fifths of all other persons. The actual enumeration shall be made within three years after the first meeting of the Congress of the United States, and within every subsequent term of ten years, in such manner as they shall by law direct. The number of Representatives shall not exceed one for every thirty thousand, but each State shall have at least one Representative: and until such enumeration shall be made, the State of New Hampshire shall be entitled to choose 3; Massachusetts, 8; Rhode Island and Providence Plantations, 1; Connecticut, 5; New York, 6; New Jersey, 4; Pennsylvania, 8; Delaware, 1; Maryland, 6; Virginia, 10; North Carolina, 5; South Carolina, 5, and Georgia, 3.*

Vacancies, how filled.

4. When vacancies happen in the representation from any State, the Executive Authority thereof shall issue writs of election to fill such vacancies.

Officers, how appointed.

5. The House of Representatives shall choose their Speaker and other officers, and shall have the sole power of impeachment.

Senate.

Section III. 1. The Senate of the United States shall be composed of two Senators from each State, chosen by the Legislature thereof, for six years; and each Senator shall have one vote.

Classification of Senators.

2. Immediately after they shall be assembled in consequence of the first election, they shall be divided as equally as may be into three classes. The seats of the Senators of the first class shall be vacated at the expiration of the second year, of the second class at the expiration of the fourth year, and of the third class at the expiration of the sixth year, so that one-third may be chosen every second year; and if vacancies happen by resignation, or otherwise, during the recess of the Legislature of any State, the Executive thereof may make temporary appointment until the next meeting of the Legislature, which shall then fill such vacancies.

Qualifications of Senators.

3. No person shall be a Senator who shall not have attained to the age of thirty years, and been nine years a citizen of the United States, and who shall not, when elected, be an inhabitant of that State for which he shall be chosen.

President of the Senate.

4. The Vice-President of the United States shall be President of the Senate, but shall have no vote unless they be equally divided.

5. The Senate shall choose their other officers, and also a President pro tempore, in the absence of the Vice-President, or when he shall exercise the office of President of the United States.

Senate a court for trial of impeachments.

6. The Senate shall have the sole power to try all impeachments. When sitting for that purpose, they shall be on oath or affirmation. When the President of the United States is tried, the Chief Justice shall preside; and no person shall be convicted without the concurrence of two-thirds of the members present.

Judgment in case of conviction.

7. Judgment in cases of impeachment shall not extend further than to removal from office, and disqualification to hold and enjoy any office of honor, trust, or profit under the United States; but the party convicted shall nevertheless be liable and subject to indictment, trial, judgment, and punishment, according to law.

Elections of Senators and Representatives.

Section IV. 1. The times, places, and manner of holding elections for Senators and Representatives shall be prescribed in each State by the Legislature thereof; but the Congress may at any time by law make or alter such regulations, except as to places of choosing Senators.

Meeting of Congress.

2. The Congress shall assemble at least once in every year, and such meeting shall be on the first Monday in December, unless they shall by law appoint a different day.

Organization of Congress.

Section V. 1. Each House shall be the judge of the elections, returns, and qualifications of its own members, and a majority of each shall constitute a quorum to do business; but a smaller number may adjourn from day to day, and may be authorized to compel the attendance of absent members in such manner and under such penalties as each House may provide.

Rule of proceedings.

2. Each House may determine the rules of its proceedings, punish its members for disorderly behavior, and with the concurrence of two-thirds expel a member.

Journals of each House.

3. Each House shall keep a journal of its proceedings, and from time to time publish the same, excepting such parts as may in their judgment require secrecy; and the yeas and nays of the members of either House on any question shall, at the desire of one-fifth of those present, be entered on the journal.

Adjournment of Congress.

4. Neither House, during the session of Congress, shall, without the consent of the other, adjourn for more than three days, nor to any other place than that in which the two Houses shall be sitting.

Pay and privileges of members.

Section VI. 1. The Senators and Representatives shall receive a compensation for their services, to be ascertained by law, and paid out of the Treasury of the United States. They shall in all cases, except treason, felony, and breach of the peace, be privileged from arrest during their attendance at the session of their respective Houses, and in going to and returning from the same; and for any speech or debate in either House they shall not be questioned in any other place.

Other offices prohibited.

2. No Senator or Representative shall, during the time for which he was elected, be appointed to any civil office under the authority of the United States which shall have been created, or the emoluments whereof shall have been increased during such time; and no person holding any office under the United States shall be a member of either House during his continuance in office.

Revenue bills.

Section VII. 1. All bills for raising revenue shall originate in the House of Representatives, but the Senate may propose or concur with amendments, as on other bills.

How bills become laws.

2. Every bill which shall have passed the House of Representatives and the Senate shall, before it become a law, be presented to the President of the United States; if he approve, he shall sign it, but if not, he shall return it, with his objections, to that House in which it shall have originated, who shall enter the objections at large on their journal, and proceed to reconsider it. If after such reconsideration two-thirds of that House shall agree to pass the bill, it shall be sent, together with the objections, to the other House, by which it shall likewise be reconsidered; and if approved by two-thirds of that House it shall become a law. But in all such cases the votes of both Houses shall be determined by yeas and nays, and the names of the persons voting for and against the bill shall be entered on the journal of each House respectively. If any bill shall not be returned by the President within ten days (Sundays excepted) after it shall have been presented to him, the same shall be a law in like manner as if he had signed it, unless the Congress by their adjournment prevent its return; in which case it shall not be a law.

---

* See Article XIV., Amendments.

Approval and veto powers of the President. 3. Every order, resolution, or vote to which the concurrence of the Senate and House of Representatives may be necessary (except on a question of adjournment) shall be presented to the President of the United States; and before the same shall take effect shall be approved by him, or being disapproved by him, shall be repassed by two-thirds of the Senate and the House of Representatives, according to the rules and limitations prescribed in the case of a bill.

Powers vested in Congress. SECTION VIII. 1. The Congress shall have power:

To lay and collect taxes, duties, imposts, and excises, to pay the debts and provide for the common defence and general welfare of the United States; but all duties, imposts, and excises shall be uniform throughout the United States.

2. To borrow money on the credit of the United States.

3. To regulate commerce with foreign nations, and among the several States, and with the Indian tribes.

4. To establish an uniform rule of naturalization and uniform laws on the subject of bankruptcies throughout the United States.

5. To coin money, regulate the value thereof, and of foreign coin, and fix the standard of weights and measures.

6. To provide for the punishment of counterfeiting the securities and current coin of the United States.

7. To establish post-offices and post-roads.

8. To promote the progress of science and useful arts by securing for limited times to authors and inventors the exclusive rights to their respective writings and discoveries.

9. To constitute tribunals inferior to the Supreme Court.

10. To define and punish piracies and felonies committed on the high seas, and offences against the law of nations.

11. To declare war, grant letters of marque and reprisal, and make rules concerning captures on land and water.

12. To raise and support armies, but no appropriation of money to that use shall be for a longer term than two years.

13. To provide and maintain a navy.

14. To make rules for the government and regulation of the land and naval forces.

15. To provide for calling forth the militia to execute the laws of the Union, suppress insurrections, and repel invasions.

16. To provide for organizing, arming, and disciplining the militia, and for governing such part of them as may be employed in the service of the United States, reserving to the States respectively the appointment of the officers, and the authority of training the militia according to the discipline prescribed by Congress.

17. To exercise exclusive legislation in all cases whatsoever over such district (not exceeding ten miles square) as may, by cession of particular States and the acceptance of Congress, become the seat of Government of the United States, and to exercise like authority over all places purchased by the consent of the Legislature of the State in which the same shall be, for the erection of forts, magazines, arsenals, dry-docks, and other needful buildings.

18. To make all laws which shall be necessary and proper for carrying into execution the foregoing powers, and all other powers vested by this Constitution in the Government of the United States, or in any department or officer thereof.

Immigrants, how admitted. SECTION IX. 1. The migration or importation of such persons as any of the States now existing shall think proper to admit shall not be prohibited by the Congress prior to the year one thousand eight hundred and eight, but a tax or duty may be imposed on such importation, not exceeding ten dollars for each person.

Habeas corpus. 2. The privilege of the writ of habeas corpus shall not be suspended, unless when in cases of rebellion or invasion the public safety may require it.

Attainder. 3. No bill of attainder or ex post facto law shall be passed.

Direct taxes. 4. No capitation or other direct tax shall be laid, unless in proportion to the census or enumeration hereinbefore directed to be taken.

Regulations regarding customs duties. 5. No tax or duty shall be laid on articles exported from any State.

6. No preference shall be given by any regulation of commerce or revenue to the ports of one State over those of another, nor shall vessels bound to or from one State be obliged to enter, clear, or pay duties in another.

Moneys, how drawn. 7. No money shall be drawn from the Treasury but in consequence of appropriations made by law; and a regular statement and account of the receipts and expenditures of all public money shall be published from time to time.

Titles of nobility prohibited. 8. No title of nobility shall be granted by the United States. And no person holding any office of profit or trust under them shall, without the consent of the Congress, accept of any present, emolument, office, or title of any kind whatever from any king, prince, or foreign state.

Powers of States defined. SECTION X. 1. No State shall enter into any treaty, alliance, or confederation, grant letters of marque and reprisal, coin money, emit bills of credit, make anything but gold and silver coin a tender in payment of debts, pass any bill of attainder, ex post facto law, or law impairing the obligation of contracts, or grant any title of nobility.

2. No State shall, without the consent of the Congress, lay any impost or duties on imports or exports, except what may be absolutely necessary for executing its inspection laws, and the net produce of all duties and imposts, laid by any State on imports or exports, shall be for the use of the Treasury of the United States; and all such laws shall be subject to the revision and control of the Congress.

3. No State shall, without the consent of Congress, lay any duty of tonnage, keep troops or ships of war in time of peace, enter into any agreement or compact with another State, or with a foreign power, or engage in war, unless actually invaded, or in such imminent danger as will not admit of delay.

ARTICLE II.

Executive power, in whom vested. SECTION I. 1. The Executive power shall be vested in a President of the United States of America. He shall hold his office during the term of four years, and, together with the Vice-President, chosen for the same term, be elected as follows:

Electors. 2. Each State shall appoint, in such manner as the Legislature thereof may direct, a number of electors, equal to the whole number of Senators and Representatives to which the State may be entitled in the Congress: but no Senator or Representative or person holding an office of trust or profit under the United States shall be appointed an elector.

Proceedings of electors. 3. [The electors shall meet in their respective States and vote by ballot for two persons, of whom one at least shall not be an inhabitant of the same State with themselves. And they shall make a list of all the persons voted for, and of the number of votes for each, which list they shall sign and certify and transmit, sealed, to the seat of the Government of the United States, directed to the President of the Senate. The President of the Senate shall, in the presence of the Senate and House of Representatives, open all the certificates, and the votes shall then be counted. The person having the greatest number of votes shall be the President, if such number be a majority of the whole number of electors appointed, and if there be more than one who have such majority, and have an equal number of votes, then the House of Representatives shall immediately choose by ballot one of them for President; and if no person have a majority, then from the five highest on the list the said House shall in like manner choose the President. But in choosing the President, the vote shall be taken by States, the representation from each State having one vote. A quorum, for this purpose, shall consist of a member or members from two-thirds of the States, and a majority of all the States shall be necessary to a choice. In every case, after the choice of the President, the person having the greatest number of votes of the electors shall be the Vice-President. But if there should remain two or more who have equal votes, the Senate shall choose from them by ballot the Vice-President.]*

Proceedings of the House of Representatives.

Time of choosing electors. 4. The Congress may determine the time of choosing the electors and the day on which they shall give their votes, which day shall be the same throughout the United States.

* This clause is superseded by Article XII., Amendments.

Qualifications of the President. 5. No person except a natural born citizen, or a citizen of the United States at the time of the adoption of this Constitution, shall be eligible to the office of President; neither shall any person be eligible to that office who shall not have attained to the age of thirty-five years and been fourteen years a resident within the United States.

Provision in case of his disability. 6. In case of the removal of the President from office, or of his death, resignation, or inability to discharge the powers and duties of the said office, the same shall devolve on the Vice-President, and the Congress may by law provide for the case of removal, death, resignation, or inability, both of the President and Vice-President, declaring what officer shall then act as President, and such officer shall act accordingly until the disability be removed or a President shall be elected.

Salary of the President. 7. The President shall, at stated times, receive for his services a compensation which shall neither be increased nor diminished during the period for which he shall have been elected, and he shall not receive within that period any other emolument from the United States, or any of them.

Oath of the President. 8. Before he enter on the execution of his office he shall take the following oath or affirmation:

"I do solemnly swear (or affirm) that I will faithfully execute the office of President of the United States, and will, to the best of my ability, preserve, protect, and defend the Constitution of the United States."

Duties of the President. SECTION II. 1. The President shall be Commander-in-Chief of the Army and Navy of the United States, and of the militia of the several States when called into the actual service of the United States; he may require the opinion, in writing, of the principal officer in each of the executive departments upon any subject relating to the duties of their respective offices, and he shall have power to grant reprieves and pardons for offences against the United States except in cases of impeachment.

May make treaties, appoint ambassadors, judges, etc. 2. He shall have power, by and with the advice and consent of the Senate, to make treaties, provided two-thirds of the Senators present concur; and he shall nominate, and by and with the advice and consent of the Senate shall appoint ambassadors, other public ministers and consuls, judges of the Supreme Court, and all other officers of the United States whose appointments are not herein otherwise provided for, and which shall be established by Law; but the Congress may by law vest the appointment of such inferior officers as they think proper in the President alone, in the courts of law, or in the heads of departments.

May fill vacancies. 3. The President shall have power to fill up all vacancies that may happen during the recess of the Senate by granting commissions, which shall expire at the end of their next session.

May make recommendations to and convene Congress. SECTION III. He shall from time to time give to the Congress information of the state of the Union, and recommend to their consideration such measures as he shall judge necessary and expedient. he may, on extraordinary occasions, convene both Houses, or either of them, and in case of disagreement between them with respect to the time of adjournment, he may adjourn them to such time as he shall think proper. he shall receive ambassadors and other public ministers, he shall take care that the laws be faithfully executed, and shall commission all the officers of the United States.

How officers may be removed. SECTION IV. The President, Vice-President, and all civil officers of the United States shall be removed from office on impeachment for and conviction of treason, bribery, or other high crimes and misdemeanors.

ARTICLE III.

Judicial power, how invested. SECTION I. The judicial power of the United States shall be vested in one Supreme Court, and in such inferior courts as the Congress may from time to time ordain and establish. The judges, both of the Supreme and inferior courts, shall hold their offices during good behavior, and shall at stated times receive for their services a compensation which shall not be diminished during their continuance in office.

To what cases it extends. SECTION II. 1. The judicial power shall extend to all cases in law and equity arising under this Constitution, the laws of the United States, and treaties made, or which shall be made, under their authority; to all cases affecting ambassadors, other public ministers, and consuls; to all cases of admiralty and maritime jurisdiction; to controversies to which the United States shall be a party; to controversies between two or more States, between a State and citizens of another State, between citizens of different States, between citizens of the same State claiming lands under grants of different States, and between a State, or the citizens thereof, and foreign States, citizens, or subjects.

Jurisdiction of the Supreme Court. 2. In all cases affecting ambassadors, other public ministers, and consuls, and those in which a State shall be party, the Supreme Court shall have original jurisdiction. In all the other cases before-mentioned the Supreme Court shall have appellate jurisdiction both as to law and fact, with such exceptions and under such regulations as the Congress shall make.

Rules respecting trials. 3. The trial of all crimes, except in cases of impeachment, shall be by jury, and such trial shall be held in the State where the said crimes shall have been committed, but when not committed within any State the trial shall be at such place or places as the Congress may by law have directed.

Treason defined. SECTION III. 1. Treason against the United States shall consist only in levying war against them, or in adhering to their enemies, giving them aid and comfort. No person shall be convicted of treason unless on the testimony of two witnesses to the same overt act, or on confession in open court.

How punished. 2. The Congress shall have power to declare the punishment of treason, but no attainder of treason shall work corruption of blood or forfeiture except during the life of the person attained.

ARTICLE IV.

Rights of States and records. SECTION I. Full faith and credit shall be given in each State to the public acts, records, and judicial proceedings of every other State. And the Congress may by general laws prescribe the manner in which such acts, records, and proceedings shall be proved, and the effect thereof.

Privileges of citizens. SECTION II. 1. The citizens of each State shall be entitled to all privileges and immunities of citizens in the several States.

Executive requisitions. 2. A person charged in any State with treason, felony, or other crime, who shall flee from justice, and be found in another State, shall, on demand of the Executive authority of the State from which he fled, be delivered up, to be removed to the State having jurisdiction of the crime.

Laws regulating service or labor. 3. No person held to service or labor in one State, under the laws thereof, escaping into another shall, in consequence of any law or regulation therein, be discharged from such service or labor, but shall be delivered up on claim of the party to whom such service or labor may be due.

New States, how formed and admitted. SECTION III. 1. New States may be admitted by the Congress into this Union; but no new State shall be formed or erected within the jurisdiction of any other State, nor any State be formed by the junction of two or more States, or parts of States, without the consent of the Legislatures of the States concerned, as well as of the Congress.

Power of Congress over public lands. 2. The Congress shall have power to dispose of and make all needful rules and regulations respecting the territory or other property belonging to the United States, and nothing in this Constitution shall be so construed as to prejudice any claims of the United States, or of any particular State.

Republican government guaranteed. SECTION IV. The United States shall guarantee to every State in this Union a republican form of government, and shall protect each of them against invasion, and, on application of the Legislature, or of the Executive (when the Legislature cannot be convened), against domestic violence.

ARTICLE V.

Constitution, how amended. The Congress, whenever two-thirds of both Houses shall deem it necessary, shall propose amendments to this Constitution, or, on the application of the Legislatures of two-thirds of the several States, shall call a convention for proposing amendments, which, in either case, shall be valid to all intents and purposes, as part of this Constitution, when ratified by the Legislatures of three-fourths of the several States, or by conventions in three-fourths thereof, as the one or the other mode of ratification may be proposed by the Congress: provided that no amendment which may be made prior to the year one thousand eight hundred and eight shall in any manner affect the first and fourth clauses in the Ninth Section of the First Article; and that no State, without its consent, shall be deprived of its equal suffrage in the Senate.

ARTICLE VI.

Validity of debts recognized. 1. All debts contracted and engagements entered into before the adoption of this Constitution shall be as valid against the United States under this Constitution as under the Confederation.

Supreme law of the land defined. 2. This Constitution and the laws of the United States which shall be made in pursuance thereof and all treaties made, or which shall be made, under the authority of the United States, shall be the supreme law of the land, and the judges in every State shall be bound thereby, anything in the Constitution or laws of any State to the contrary notwithstanding.

Oath; of whom required and for what. 3. The Senators and Representatives before mentioned, and the members of the several State Legislatures, and all executive and judicial officers, both of the United States and of the several States, shall be bound by oath or affirmation to support this Constitution; but no religious test shall ever be required as a qualification to any office or public trust under the United States.

ARTICLE VII.

Ratification of the Constitution. The ratification of the Conventions of nine States shall be sufficient for the establishment of this Constitution between the States so ratifying the same.

AMENDMENTS TO THE CONSTITUTION.

ARTICLE I.

Religion and free speech. Congress shall make no law respecting an establishment of religion, or prohibiting the free exercise thereof; or abridging the freedom of speech or of the press; or the right of the people peaceably to assemble, and to petition the Government for a redress of grievances.

ARTICLE II.

Right to bear arms. A well-regulated militia being necessary to the security of a free State, the right of the people to keep and bear arms shall not be infringed.

ARTICLE III.

Soldiers in time of peace. No soldier shall, in time of peace, be quartered in any house without the consent of the owner, nor in time of war but in a manner to be prescribed by law.

ARTICLE IV.

Right of search. The right of the people to be secure in their persons, houses, papers, and effects, against unreasonable searches and seizures, shall not be violated, and no warrants shall issue but upon probable cause, supported by oath or affirmation, and particularly describing the place to be searched, and the persons or things to be seized.

ARTICLE V.

Capital crimes and arrest therefor. No person shall be held to answer for a capital or other infamous crime unless on a presentment or indictment of a grand jury, except in cases arising in the land or naval forces, or in the militia, when in actual service, in time of war or public danger; nor shall any person be subject for the same offence to be twice put in jeopardy of life or limb; nor shall be compelled in any criminal case to be a witness against himself, nor be deprived of life, liberty, or property, without due process of law; nor shall private property be taken for public use without just compensation.

ARTICLE VI.

Right to speedy trial. In all criminal prosecutions, the accused shall enjoy the right to a speedy and public trial, by an impartial jury of the State and district wherein the crime shall have been committed, which district shall have been previously ascertained by law, and to be informed of the nature and cause of the accusation; to be confronted with the witnesses against him; to have compulsory process for obtaining witnesses in his favor, and to have the assistance of counsel for his defence.

ARTICLE VII.

Trial by jury. In suits at common law, where the value in controversy shall exceed twenty dollars, the right of trial by jury shall be preserved, and no fact tried by a jury shall be otherwise re-examined in any court of the United States than according to the rules of the common law.

ARTICLE VIII.

Excessive bail. Excessive bail shall not be required, nor excessive fines imposed, nor cruel and unusual punishments inflicted.

ARTICLE IX.

Enumeration of rights. The enumeration in the Constitution of certain rights shall not be construed to deny or disparage others retained by the people.

ARTICLE X.

Reserved rights of States. The powers not delegated to the United States by the Constitution, nor prohibited by it to the States, are reserved to the States respectively, or to the people.

ARTICLE XI.

Judicial power. The judicial power of the United States shall not be construed to extend to any suit in law or equity, commenced or prosecuted against one of the United States, by citizens of another State, or by citizens or subjects of any foreign State.

ARTICLE XII.

Electors in Presidential elections. The electors shall meet in their respective States, and vote by ballot for President and Vice-President, one of whom at least shall not be an inhabitant of the same State with themselves; they shall name in their ballots the person voted for as President, and in distinct ballots the person voted for as Vice-President; and they shall make distinct lists of all persons voted for as President, and of all persons voted for as Vice-President, and of the number of votes for each, which list they shall sign and certify, and transmit, sealed, to the seat of the Government of the United States, directed to the President of the Senate; the President of the Senate shall, in the presence of the Senate and House of Representatives, open all the certificates, and the votes shall then be counted; the person having the greatest number of votes for President shall be the President, if such number be a majority of the whole number of electors appointed; and if no person have such majority, then from the persons having the highest numbers, not exceeding three, on the list of those voted for as President, the House of Representatives shall choose immediately, by ballot, the President. But in choosing the President, the votes shall be taken by States, the representation from each State having one vote; a quorum for this purpose shall consist of a member or members from two-thirds of the States, and a majority of all the States shall be necessary to a choice. And if the House of Representatives shall not choose a President, whenever the right of choice shall devolve upon them, before the fourth day of March next following, then the Vice-President shall act as President, as in the case of the death or other constitutional disability of the President.

Vice-President. The person having the greatest number of votes as Vice-President shall be the Vice-President, if such number be a majority of the whole number of electors appointed, and if no person have a majority, then from the two highest numbers on the list the Senate shall choose the Vice-President; a quorum for the purpose shall consist of two-thirds of the whole number of Senators, and a majority of the whole number shall be necessary to a choice. But no person constitutionally ineligible to the office of President shall be eligible to that of Vice-President of the United States.

ARTICLE XIII.

Slavery prohibited. 1. Neither slavery nor involuntary servitude, except as a punishment for crime whereof the party shall have been duly convicted, shall exist within the United States, or any place subject to their jurisdiction.

2. Congress shall have power to enforce this article by appropriate legislation.

ARTICLE XIV.

Protection for all citizens.

1. All persons born or naturalized in the United States, and subject to the jurisdiction thereof, are citizens of the United States and of the State wherein they reside. No State shall make or enforce any law which shall abridge the privileges or immunities of citizens of the United States; nor shall any State deprive any person of life, liberty, or property without due process of law, nor deny to any person within its jurisdiction the equal protection of the laws.

Apportionment of Representatives.

2. Representatives shall be apportioned among the several States according to their respective numbers, counting the whole number of persons in each State, excluding Indians not taxed. But when the right to vote at any election for the choice of electors for President and Vice-President of the United States, Representatives in Congress, the executive and judicial officers of a State, or the members of the Legislature thereof, is denied to any of the male members of such State, being of twenty-one years of age, and citizens of the United States, or in any way abridged, except for participation in rebellion or other crime, the basis of representation therein shall be reduced in the proportion which the number of such male citizens shall bear to the whole number of male citizens twenty-one years of age in such State.

Rebellion against the United States.

3. No person shall be a Senator or Representative in Congress, or elector of President and Vice-President, or holding any office, civil or military, under the United States, or under any State, who, having previously taken an oath, as a member of Congress, or as an officer of the United States, or as a member of any State Legislature, or as an executive or judicial officer of any State, to support the Constitution of the United States, shall have engaged in insurrection or rebellion against the same, or given aid and comfort to the enemies thereof. But Congress may, by a vote of two-thirds of each House, remove such disability.

The public debt.

4. The validity of the public debt of the United States, authorized by law, including debts incurred for payment of pensions and bounties for services in suppressing insurrection and rebellion, shall not be questioned. But neither the United States nor any State shall assume or pay any debt or obligation incurred in aid of insurrection or rebellion against the United States, or any claim for the loss or emancipation of any slave; but all such debts, obligations, and claims shall be held illegal and void.

5. The Congress shall have power to enforce by appropriate legislation the provisions of this article.

ARTICLE XV.

Right of suffrage.

1. The right of the citizens of the United States to vote shall not be denied or abridged by the United States or by any State on account of race, color, or previous condition of servitude.

2. The Congress shall have power to enforce the provisions of this article by appropriate legislation.

RATIFICATION OF THE CONSTITUTION.

The Constitution was ratified by the thirteen original States in the following order:

Delaware, December 7, 1787, unanimously.
Pennsylvania, December 12, 1787, vote 46 to 23.
New Jersey, December 18, 1787, unanimously.
Georgia, January 2, 1788, unanimously.
Connecticut, January 9, 1788, vote 128 to 40.
Massachusetts, February 6, 1788, vote 187 to 168.
Maryland, April 28, 1788, vote 63 to 12.
South Carolina, May 23, 1788, vote 149 to 73.
New Hampshire, June 21, 1788, vote 57 to 46.
Virginia, June 25, 1788, vote 89 to 79.
New York, July 26, 1788, vote 30 to 28.
North Carolina, November 21, 1789, vote 193 to 75.
Rhode Island, May 29, 1790, vote 34 to 32.

RATIFICATION OF THE AMENDMENTS.

I. to X. inclusive were declared in force December 15, 1791.

XI. was declared in force January 8, 1798.

XII., regulating elections, was ratified by all the States except Connecticut, Delaware, Massachusetts, and New Hampshire, which rejected it. It was declared in force September 28, 1804.

XIII. The emancipation amendment was ratified by 31 of the 36 States; rejected by Delaware and Kentucky, not acted on by Texas; conditionally ratified by Alabama and Mississippi. Proclaimed December 18, 1865.

XIV. Reconstruction amendment was ratified by 23 Northern States; rejected by Delaware, Kentucky, Maryland, and 10 Southern States, and not acted on by California. The 10 Southern States subsequently ratified under pressure. Proclaimed July 28, 1868.

XV. Negro citizenship amendment was not acted on by Tennessee, rejected by California, Delaware, Kentucky, Maryland, New Jersey, and Oregon; ratified by the remaining 30 States. New York rescinded its ratification January 5, 1870. Proclaimed, March 30, 1870.

The National Flag.

THE official flag of the United States bears forty-six white stars in a blue field, arranged in six rows—the first, third, fourth and sixth rows having eight stars each, and the other two rows seven stars each. The garrison flag of the Army is made of bunting, thirty-six feet fly and twenty feet hoist; thirteen stripes, and in the upper quarter, next the staff, is the field or "union" of stars, equal to the number of States, on blue field, over one-third length of the flag, extending to the lower edge of the fourth red stripe from the top. The storm flag is twenty feet by ten feet, and the recruiting flag nine feet nine inches by four feet four inches. The "American Jack" is the "union" or blue field of the flag. The Revenue Marine Service flag, authorized by act of Congress, March 2, 1799, was originally prescribed to "consist of sixteen perpendicular stripes, alternate red and white, the union of the ensign bearing the arms of the United States in dark blue on a white field." The sixteen stripes represented the number of States which had been admitted to the Union at that time, and no change has been made since. Prior to 1871 it bore an eagle in the union of the pennant, which was then substituted by thirteen blue stars in a white field, but the eagle and stars are still retained in the flag. June 14, the anniversary of the adoption of the flag, is celebrated as Flag Day in a large part of the Union.

IN ORDER TO SHOW PROPER RESPECT FOR THE FLAG THE FOLLOWING CEREMONY SHOULD BE OBSERVED:

It should not be hoisted before sunrise nor allowed to remain up after sunset.

At "retreat," sunset, civilian spectators should stand at "attention" and uncover during the playing of the "Star Spangled Banner." Military spectators are required by regulation to stand at "attention" and give the military salute.

When the National colors are passing on parade, or in review, the spectator should, if walking, halt, and if sitting, arise and stand at attention and uncover.

When the flag is flown at half staff as a sign of mourning it should be hoisted to full staff at the conclusion of the funeral.

In placing the flag at half staff, it should first be hoisted to the top of the staff and then lowered to position, and preliminary to lowering from half staff, it should be first raised to the top.

On Memorial Day, May 30, the flag should fly at half staff from sunrise to noon and full staff from noon to sunset.—*Sons of the Revolution in the State of New York.*

Declaration of Independence.

IN CONGRESS JULY 4, 1776.

THE unanimous declaration of the thirteen United States of America. When in the Course of human events, it becomes necessary for one people to dissolve the political bands which have connected them with another, and to assume among the powers of the earth, the separate and equal station to which the Laws of Nature and of Nature's God entitles them, a decent respect to the opinions of mankind requires that they should declare the causes which impel them to the separation.

We hold these truths to be self-evident, that all men are created equal, that they are endowed by their Creator with certain unalienable Rights, that among these are Life, Liberty and the pursuit of Happiness. That to secure these rights, Governments are instituted among Men, deriving their just powers from the consent of the governed, That whenever any Form of Government becomes destructive of these ends, it is the Right of the People to alter or to abolish it, and to institute new Government, laying its foundation on such principles and organizing its powers in such form, as to them shall seem most likely to effect their Safety and Happiness. Prudence, indeed, will dictate that Governments long established should not be changed for light and transient causes; and accordingly all experience hath shewn, that mankind are more disposed to suffer, while evils are sufferable, than to right themselves by abolishing the forms to which they are accustomed. But when a long train of abuses and usurpations, pursuing invariably the same Object evinces a design to reduce them under absolute Despotism, it is their right, it is their duty, to throw off such Government, and to provide new Guards for their future security. Such has been the patient sufferance of these Colonies; and such is now the necessity which constrains them to alter their former Systems of Government. The history of the present King of Great Britain is a history of repeated injuries and usurpations, all having in direct object the establishment of an absolute Tyranny over these States. To prove this, let Facts be submitted to a candid world.

He has refused his Assent to Laws, the most wholesome and necessary for the public good.

He has forbidden his Governors to pass Laws of immediate and pressing importance, unless suspended in their operation till his Assent should be obtained; and when so suspended, he has utterly neglected to attend to them.

He has refused to pass other Laws for the accommodation of large districts of people, unless those people would relinquish the right of Representation in the Legislature, a right inestimable to them and formidable to tyrants only.

He has called together legislative bodies at places unusual, uncomfortable, and distant from the depository of their public Records, for the sole purpose of fatiguing them into compliance with his measures.

He has dissolved Representative Houses repeatedly, for opposing with manly firmness his invasions on the rights of the people.

He has refused for a long time, after such dissolutions, to cause others to be elected; whereby the Legislative powers, incapable of Annihilation, have returned to the People at large for their exercise; the State remaining in the meantime exposed to all the dangers of invasion from without, and convulsions within.

He has endeavored to prevent the population of these States; for that purpose obstructing the Laws for Naturalization of Foreigners; refusing to pass others to encourage their migrations hither, and raising the conditions of new Appropriations of Lands.

He has obstructed the Administration of Justice, by refusing his Assent to Laws for establishing Judiciary Powers.

He has made Judges dependent on his Will alone, for the tenure of their offices, and the amount and payment of their salaries.

He has erected a multitude of New Offices, and sent hither swarms of Officers to harass our people, and eat out their substance.

He has kept among us, in times of peace, Standing Armies without the Consent of our legislature.

He has affected to render the Military independent of and superior to the Civil power.

He has combined with others to subject us to a jurisdiction foreign to our constitution, and unacknowledged by our laws; giving his Assent to their Acts of pretended Legislation:

For quartering large bodies of armed troops among us:

For protecting them, by a mock Trial, from punishment for any Murders which they should commit on the Inhabitants of these States:

For cutting off our Trade with all parts of the world:

For imposing Taxes on us without our Consent:

For depriving us in many cases, of the benefits of Trial by jury:

For transporting us beyond Seas to be tried for pretended offences:

For abolishing the free System of English Laws in a neighboring Province, establishing therein an Arbitrary government, and enlarging its Boundaries so as to render it at once an example and fit instrument for introducing the same absolute rule into these Colonies:

For taking away our Charters, abolishing our most valuable Laws, and altering fundamentally the Forms of our Governments:

For suspending our own Legislatures, and declaring themselves invested with power to legislate for us in all cases whatsoever.

He has abdicated Government here, by declaring us out of his Protection and waging War against us.

He has plundered our seas, ravaged our Coasts, burnt our towns, and destroyed the lives of our people.

He is at this time transporting large Armies of foreign Mercenaries to compleat the works of death, desolation and tyranny, already begun with circumstances of Cruelty & perfidy scarcely paralleled in the most barbarous ages, and totally unworthy the Head of a civilized nation.

He has constrained our fellow-Citizens taken captive on the high Seas to bear Arms against their Country, to become the executioners of their friends and Brethren, or to fall themselves by their Hands

He has excited domestic insurrections amongst us, and has endeavored to bring on the inhabitants of our frontiers, the merciless Indian Savages, whose known rule of warfare, is an undistinguished destruction of all ages, sexes and conditions.

In every stage of these Oppressions We have Petitioned for Redress in the most humble terms:

DECLARATION OF INDEPENDENCE—*Continued.*

Our repeated Petitions have been answered only by repeated injury. A Prince, whose character is thus marked by every act which may define a Tyrant, is unfit to be the ruler of a free people.

Nor have We been wanting in attentions to our British brethren. We have warned them from time to time of attempts by their legislature to extend an unwarrantable jurisdiction over us. We have reminded them of the circumstances of our emigration and settlement here. We have appealed to their native justice and magnanimity, and we have conjured them by the ties of our common kindred to disavow these usurpations, which, would inevitably interrupt our connections and correspondence. They too have been deaf to the voice of justice and of consanguinity. We must, therefore, acquiesce in the necessity, which denounces our Separation, and hold them, as we hold the rest of mankind, Enemies in War, In Peace Friends.

WE, THEREFORE, the REPRESENTATIVES of the UNITED STATES OF AMERICA, IN GENERAL CONGRESS, Assembled, appealing to the Supreme Judge of the world for the rectitude of our intentions, do, in the Name, and by authority of the good People of these Colonies, solemnly PUBLISH and DECLARE, That these United Colonies are, and of Right ought to be FREE AND INDEPENDENT States; that they are Absolved from all Allegiance to the British Crown, and that all political connection between them and the State of Great Britain, is and ought to be totally dissolved; and that as FREE AND INDEPENDENT STATES, they have full Power to levy War, conclude Peace, contract Alliances, establish Commerce, and to do all other Acts and Things which INDEPENDENT STATES may of right do. And for the support of this Declaration, with a firm reliance on the protection of Divine Providence, We mutually pledge to each other our Lives, our Fortunes, and our sacred Honor.

SIGNERS OF THE DECLARATION OF INDEPENDENCE.

NAME.	Colony.	Occupation.	Born.	Birthplace.	Died.	Age.
Adams, John	Mass. Bay	Lawyer	Oct. 19, 1735	Braintree, Mass	July 4, 1826	92
Adams, Samuel	Mass. Bay	Merchant	Sep. 22, 1722	Boston, Mass	Oct. 3, 1803	81
Bartlett, Josiah	N. Hamp.	Physician	Nov. 1729	Amesbury, Mass	May 19, 1795	67
Braxton, Carter	Virginia	Planter	Sep. 10, 1736	Newington, Va	Oct. 10, 1797	62
Carroll, Charles	Maryland	Lawyer	Sep. 20, 1737	Annapolis, Md	Nov. 14, 1832	96
Chase, Samuel	Maryland	Lawyer	Apr. 17, 1741	Somerset Co., Md	June 19, 1811	71
Clark, Abraham	N. Jersey	Lawyer	Feb. 15, 1726	Elizabethtown, N. J.	Sept. 1794	69
Clymer, George	Penn	Merchant	Jan. 24, 1739	Philadelphia, Pa	Jan. 23, 1813	75
Ellery, William	Rhode Isl.	Lawyer	Dec. 22, 1727	Newport, R. I	Feb. 15, 1820	93
Floyd, William	New York	Farmer	Dec. 17, 1734	Setauket, N. Y	Aug. 1, 1821	87
Franklin, Benjamin	Penn	Printer	Jan. 17, 1706	Boston, Mass	Apr. 17, 1790	85
Gerry, Elbridge	Mass. Bay	Merchant	July 17, 1744	Marblehead, Mass	Nov. 23, 1814	71
Gwinnett, Button	Georgia	Merchant	1732	England	May 27, 1777	45
Hancock, John	Mass. Bay	Merchant	Jan. 12, 1737	Braintree, Mass	Oct. 8, 1793	57
Hall, Lyman	Georgia	Physician	1731	Ct	1784	53
Harrison, Benj	Virginia	Farmer	1740	Berkeley, Va	Apr. 1791	51
Hart, John	N. Jersey	Farmer	1715	Hopewell, N. J	1780	65
Hewes, Joseph	N. Carolina	Lawyer	1730	Kingston, N. J	Nov 10, 1779	49
Heyward, Jr., Thos.	S. Carolina	Lawyer	1746	St. Luke's, S. C	Mar. 1809	63
Hooper, Wm	N. Carolina	Lawyer	June 17, 1742	Boston, Mass	Oct. 1790	49
Hopkins, Steph	Rhode Isl.	Farmer	Mar. 7, 1707	Scituate, Mass	July 13, 1785	79
Hopkinson, Francis	N. Jersey	Lawyer	1737	Philadelphia, Pa	May 9, 1791	54
Huntington, Sam'l	Ct	Lawyer	July 3, 1732	Windham, Ct	Jan. 5, 1796	64
Jefferson, Thos	Virginia	Lawyer	Apr. 13, 1743	Shadwell, Va	July 4, 1826	83
Lee, Richard Henry	Virginia	Soldier	Jan. 20, 1732	Stratford, Va	June 19, 1794	63
Lee, Francis Lightfoot	Virginia	Farmer	Oct. 14, 1734	Stratford, Va	Apr. 1797	63
Lewis, Francis	New York	Merchant	March, 1713	Llandaff, Wales	Dec. 30, 1803	91
Livingston, Philip	New York	Merchant	Jan. 15, 1716	Albany, N. Y	June 12, 1778	63
Lynch, Jr., Thos	S. Carolina	Lawyer	Aug. 5, 1749	Pr. George's Co. S. C	1779	30
M'Kean, Thos.	Delaware	Lawyer	Mar. 19, 1734	New London, Pa	June 24, 1817	84
Middleton, Arthur	S. Carolina	Lawyer	1743	Middleton Pl., S. C	Jan. 1, 1788	44
Morris, Lewis	New York	Farmer	1726	Morrisania, N. Y.	Jan. 22, 179	72
Morris, Robert	Penn	Merchant	Jan. 20, 1734	Lancashire, Eng	May 8, 1806	73
Morton, John	Penn	Surveyor	1724	Ridley, Pa	Apr. 1777	53
Nelson, Jr., Thos.	Virginia	Statesman	Dec. 26, 1738	York, Va	Jan. 4, 1789	51
Paca, William	Maryland	Lawyer	Oct. 31, 1740	Wye Hall, Md	1799	59
Paine, Robert Treat	Mass. Bay	Lawyer	1731	Boston, Mass	May 11, 1814	84
Penn, John	N. Carolina	Lawyer	May 17, 1741	Caroline Co., Va	Sept. 1788	48
Read, George	Delaware	Lawyer	1734	Cecil Co., Md	1798	64
Rodney, Cæsar	Delaware	General	1730	Dover, Del	1783	53
Ross, George	Penn	Lawyer	1730	Newcastle, Del	July 1779	49
Rush, Benjamin	Penn	Physician	Dec. 24, 1745	Berberry, Pa	Apr. 19, 1813	68
Rutledge, Edward	S. Carolina	Lawyer	Nov. 1749	Charleston, S. C	Jan. 23, 1800	51
Sherman, Roger	Ct	Shoemaker	Apr. 19, 1721	Newton, Mass	July 23, 1793	73
Smith James	Penn	Lawyer	1710	Ireland	July 11, 1806	96
Stockton, Richard	N. Jersey	Lawyer	Oct. 1, 1730	Princeton, N. J	Feb. 28, 1781	51
Stone, Thos	Maryland	Lawyer	1742	Pointoin Manor, Md	Oct. 5, 1787	45
Taylor, Geo	Penn	Physician	1716	Ireland	Feb. 23, 1781	65
Thornton, Matthew	N. Hamp.	Physician	1714	Ireland	June 24, 1803	89
Walton, George	Georgia	Lawyer	1740	Frederick Co., Va	Feb. 2, 1804	64
Whipple, William	Ct	Sailor	1730	Kittery, Me	Nov. 28, 1785	55
Williams, William	Ct	Statesman	Apr. 8, 1731	Lebanon, Ct	Aug. 2, 1811	81
Wilson, James	Penn	Lawyer	1742	St. Andrews, Scot	Aug. 28, 1798	56
Witherspoon, John	N. Jersey	Minister	Feb. 5, 1722	Yester, Scot	Nov. 15, 1794	73
Wolcott, Oliver	Ct	Physician	Nov. 26, 1726	Windsor, Ct	Dec. 1, 1797	72
Wythe, George	Virginia	Lawyer	1726	Elizabeth Co., Va	June 8, 1806	80

Acts of the Sixtieth Congress.

FIRST SESSION.

THE principal bills of a public nature which became laws during the first session of the Sixtieth Congress, beginning December 2, 1907, and ending March 4, 1908 were:

Chapter 76. An act restricting in certain cases the right of appeal to the Supreme Court in habeas corpus proceedings. [March 10, 1908.]

Chapter 149. An act relating to the liability of common carriers by railroad to their employés in certain cases. [April 22, 1908.]

Chapter 151. An act to provide for safety of life on navigable waters during regattas or marine parades. [April 28, 1908.]

Chapter 152. An act to repeal an act approved April 30, 1906 and for other purposes. The act repealed the application of the coastwise laws to the Philippine Islands. [April 29, 1908.]

Chapter 161. An act to amend an act entitled "An act to provide for the reorganization of the consular service of the United States." approved April 5, 1906. The act further abolishes unnecessary consulships and constituted consulships. [May 11, 1908.]

Chapter 164. An act to increase the membership of the Philippine Commission by one member, and for other purposes. [May 11, 1908.]

Chapter 170. An act to amend an act entitled "An act to prevent the importation of impure and unwholesome tea" approved March 2, 1897. [May 16, 1908.]

Chapter 172. An act for the widening of Benning road and for other purposes. The act prohibited gambling at races, baseball, etc., in the District of Columbia. [May 16, 1908.]

Chapter 173. An act providing for the restoration of the motto "In God We Trust" on certain denominations of the gold and silver coins of the United States. [May 18, 1908.]

Chapter 185. An act to provide for participation by the United States in an international exposition to be held at Tokio, Japan, in 1912. [May 22, 1908.]

Chapter 189. An act to amend Section 4885 of the revised statutes. The act amended the patent laws in relation to time of issues and heirs of deceased patentees. [May 23, 1908.]

Chapter 204. An act to further amend the act entitled "An act to promote the efficiency of the militia and for other purposes" approved January 21, 1903. [May 27, 1908.]

Chapter 205. An act to amend an act entitled "An act to simplify the laws in relation to the collection of revenues, etc." approved July 24, 1897. The act changed the customs law in reference to procedure in cases of appeal before the Board of Appraisers. [May 27, 1908.]

Chapter 209. An act to regulate the employment of child labor in the District of Columbia. Intended for a model law on the subject. [May 28, 1908.]

Chapter 225. An act to promote the safety of employés on railroads. [May 30, 1908.]

Chapter 229. An act to amend the national banking laws. [May 30, 1908.]

Chapter 236. An act granting to certain employés of the United States the right to receive from it compensation for injuries sustained in the course of their employment. [May 30, 1908.]

Joint Resolution No. 9. To continue "in full force and effect" An act to provide for the appropriate marking of the graves of the soldiers and sailors of the Confederate Army and Navy who died in Northern prisons, and were buried near the prisons where they died, and for other purposes. [February 26, 1908.]

Joint Resolution No. 11. Authorizing the invitation to governments of other countries to send representatives to the International Congress on Tuberculosis. [March 6, 1908.]

Joint Resolution No. 28. To provide for the remission of a portion of the Chinese Indemnity. [May 25, 1908.]

Other acts increased widows' pensions from $8 to $12 a month; increased the efficiency of the army medical corps; increased the pay of the army and navy; established thirty additional fish hatcheries; established a female nurse corps for navy hospitals and hospital ships; excluded anarchistic publications from the mails; created the Chippewa national forest reserve in Minnesota, and appropriated $29,227,000 for the continued construction of the Panama Canal.

Eleven Hague conventions and twelve arbitration conventions were ratified, also four extradition, two trade marks and three naturalization treaties with other countries.

Three Hague Conventions—Creation of international prize court, affecting status of merchant ships at outbreak of war, and conversion of merchant ships into warships, were disapproved by committee. The wireless convention, international treaty defining duties of wireless telegraph companies, etc., was not ratified.

The number of public acts passed were 152. There were 2,300 invalid pension acts and 700 private pension acts. The number of bills introduced in the Senate during the session was over 7,000; in the House of Representatives over 22,000.

Among the measures left over for the second session were the Census bill, Postal Savings Bank, Parcels Post Reduction, Anti-injunction Legislation, amendments to the Sherman Anti-Trust law, campaign publicity legislation, and Brownsville resolutions, providing for the restorations to the army of certain discharged negro soldiers.

The President sent to Congress twenty messages, including nine transmitting reports of Federal officers, in response to resolutions, etc. Eleven special messages recommended general or special legislation. The most important executive communications were the annual message of December 3, 1907, and special messages, as follows: December 21, asking continuance of biological survey. January 6, urging that additional census employés be subject to Civil Service regulations. January 28, urging pensions, etc., for life saving service. March 25, urging general legislation. April 14, urging authorization of four battleships. April 27, urging general legislation. The President also sent to Congress one veto message, in which he disapproved a bill granting an extension of time to a company previously authorized to dam the Rainy River, in Minnesota, but, with his consent, it was later passed over his veto.

The Currency Act of 1908.

AMENDMENTS TO THE NATIONAL BANKING LAWS.

THE following is Chap. 229 of the acts of the first session of the Sixtieth Congress, entitled "An Act to Amend the National Banking Laws," approved May 30, 1908.

Be it enacted by the Senate and House of Representatives of the United States of America in Congress assembled, That national banking associations, each having an unimpaired capital and a surplus of not less than twenty per centum, not less than ten in number, having an aggregate capital and surplus of at least $5,000,000, may form voluntary associations to be designated as national currency associations. The banks uniting to form such association shall, by their presidents or vice-presidents, acting under authority from the board of directors, make and file with the Secretary of the Treasury a certificate setting forth the names of the banks composing the association, the principal place of business of the association, and the name of the association, which name shall be subject to the approval of the Secretary of the Treasury. Upon the filing of such certificate the associated banks therein named shall become a body corporate, and by the name so designated and approved may sue and be sued and exercise the powers of a body corporate for the purposes hereinafter mentioned: Provided, That not more than one such national currency association shall be formed in any city: Provided further, That the several members of such national currency association shall be taken, as nearly as conveniently may be, from a territory composed of a State or part of a State, or contiguous parts of one or more States: And provided further, That any national bank in such city or territory, having the qualifications herein prescribed for membership in such national currency association, shall, upon its application to and upon the approval of the Secretary of the Treasury, be admitted to membership in a national currency association for that city or territory, and upon such admission shall be deemed and held a part of the body corporate, and as such entitled to all the rights and privileges and subject to all the liabilities of an original member: And provided further, That each national currency association shall be composed exclusively of banks not members of any other national currency association.

The dissolution, voluntary or otherwise, of any bank in such association shall not affect the corporate existence of the association unless there shall then remain less than the minimum number of ten banks: Provided, however, That the reduction of the number of said banks below the minimum of ten shall not affect the existence of the corporation with respect to the assertion of all rights in favor of or against such association. The affairs of the association shall be managed by a board consisting of one representative from each bank. By-laws for the government of the association shall be made by the board, subject to the approval of the Secretary of the Treasury. A president, vice-president, secretary, treasurer, and an executive committee of not less than five members, shall be elected by the board. The powers of such board, except in the election of officers and making of by-laws, may be exercised through its executive committee.

POWERS OF THE NATIONAL CURRENCY ASSOCIATION.

The national currency association herein provided for shall have and exercise any and all powers necessary to carry out the purposes of this section, namely, to render available, under the direction and control of the Secretary of the Treasury, as a basis for additional circulation any securities, including commercial paper, held by a national banking association. For the purpose of obtaining such additional circulation, any bank belonging to any national currency association, having circulating notes outstanding secured by the deposit of bonds of the United States to an amount not less than 40 per centum of its capital stock, and which has its capital unimpaired and a surplus of not less than 20 per centum, may deposit with and transfer to the association, in trust for the United States, for the purpose hereinafter provided, such of the securities above mentioned as may be satisfactory to the board of the association. The officers of the association may thereupon, in behalf of such bank, make application to the Comptroller of the Currency for an issue of additional circulating notes to an amount not exceeding 75 per centum of the cash value of the securities or commercial paper so deposited. The Comptroller of the Currency shall immediately transmit such application to the Secretary of the Treasury with such recommendation as he thinks proper, and, if in the judgment of the Secretary of the Treasury, business conditions in the locality demand additional circulation, and if he be satisfied with the character and value of the securities proposed and that a lien in favor of the United States on the securities so deposited and on the assets of the banks composing the association will be amply sufficient for the protection of the United States, he may direct an issue of additional circulating notes to the association, on behalf of such bank, to an amount in his discretion, not, however, exceeding 75 per centum of the cash value of the securities so deposited: Provided, That upon the deposit of any of the State, city, town, county, or other municipal bonds, of a character described in Sec. 3 of this act, circulating notes may be issued to the extent of not exceeding 90 per centum of the market value of such bonds so deposited: And provided further, That no national banking association shall be authorized in any event to issue circulating notes based on commercial paper in excess of 30 per centum of its unimpaired capital and surplus. The term "commercial paper" shall be held to include only notes representing actual commercial transactions, which when accepted by the association shall bear the names of at least two responsible parties and have not exceeding four months to run.

The banks and the assets of all banks belonging to the association shall be jointly and severally liable to the United States for the redemption of such additional circulation; and to secure such liability the lien created by Sec. 5230 of the Revised Statutes shall extend to and cover the assets of all banks belonging to the association, and to the securities deposited by the banks with the association pursuant to the provisions of this act; but as between the several banks composing such association each bank shall be liable only in the proportion that its capital and surplus bears to the aggregate capital and surplus of all such banks. The association may, at any time, require of any of its constituent banks a deposit of additional securities or commercial paper, or an exchange of the securities already on deposit to secure such additional circulation; and in case of the failure of such bank to make such deposit or exchange the association may, after ten days' notice to the bank, sell the securities and paper already in its hands at public sale, and deposit the proceeds with the Treasurer of the United States as a fund for the redemption of such additional circulation. If such fund be insufficient for that purpose the association may recover from the bank the amount of the deficiency by suit in the Circuit Court of the United States, and shall have the benefit of the lien hereinbefore provided for in favor of the United States upon the assets of such bank. The association or the Secretary of the Treasury may permit or require the withdrawal of any such securities or commercial paper and the substitution of other securities or commercial paper of equal value therefor.

Sec. 2. That whenever any bank belonging to a national currency association shall fail to preserve or make good its redemption fund in the Treasury of the United States, required by Sec. 3 of the Act of June 20, 1874, Chap. 343, and the provisions of this act, the Treasurer of the United States shall notify such national currency association to make good such redemption fund, and upon the failure of such national currency association to make good such fund, the Treasurer of the United States may, in his discretion, apply so much of the redemption fund belonging to the other banks composing such national currency association as may be necessary for that purpose; and such national currency association may, after five days' notice to such bank, proceed to sell at public sale the securities deposited by such bank with the association pursuant to the provisions of Sec. 1 of this act, and deposit the proceeds with the Treasurer of the United States as a fund for the redemption of the additional circulation taken out by such bank under this act.

PROVISION FOR ADDITIONAL CIRCULATION.

Sec. 3. That any national banking association which has circulating notes outstanding, secured by the deposit of United States bonds to an amount of not less than 40 per centum of its capital stock, and which has a surplus of not less than 20 per centum, may make application to the Comptroller of the Currency for authority to issue additional circulating notes to be secured by the deposit of bonds other than bonds of the United States. The Comptroller of the Currency shall transmit immediately the application, with his recommendation, to the Secretary of the Treasury, who shall, if in his judgment business conditions in the locality demand additional circulation, approve the same, and shall determine the time of issue and fix the amount, within the limitations herein imposed, of the additional circulating notes to be issued. Whenever after receiving notice of such approval any such association shall deposit with the Treasurer or any assistant treasurer of the United States such of the bonds described in this section as shall be approved in character and amount by the Treasurer of the United States and the Secretary of the Treasury, it shall be entitled to receive, upon the order of the Comptroller of the Currency, circulating notes in blank, registered and countersigned as provided by law, not exceeding in amount 90 per centum of the market value but not in excess of the par value of any bonds so deposited, such market value to be ascertained and determined under the direction of the Secretary of the Treasury.

BONDS OF STATES, CITIES, ETC.

The Treasurer of the United States, with the approval of the Secretary of the Treasury, shall accept as security for the additional circulating notes provided for in this section, bonds or other interest-bearing obligations of any State of the United States, or any legally authorized bonds issued by any city, town, county, or other legally constituted municipality or district in the United States which has been in existence for a period of ten years, and which for a period of ten years previous to such deposit has not defaulted in the payment of any part of either principal or interest of any funded debt authorized to be contracted by it, and whose net funded indebtedness does not exceed 10 per centum of the valuation of its taxable property, to be ascertained by the last preceding valuation of property for the assessment of taxes. The Treasurer of the United States, with the approval of the Secretary of the Treasury shall accept, for the purposes of this section, securities herein enumerated in such proportions, as he may from time to time determine, and he may with such approval at any time require the deposit of additional securities, or require any association to change the character of the securities already on deposit.

Sec. 4. That the legal title of all bonds, whether coupon or registered, deposited to secure circulating notes issued in accordance with the terms of Sec. 3 of this act shall be transferred to the Treasurer of the United States in trust for the association depositing them, under regulations to be prescribed by the Secretary of the Treasury. A receipt shall be given to the association by the Treasurer or any assistant treasurer of the United States, stating that such bond is held in trust for the association on whose behalf the transfer is made, and as security for the redemption and payment of any circulating notes that have been or may be delivered to such association. No assignment or transfer of any such bond by the Treasurer shall be deemed valid unless countersigned by the Comptroller of the Currency. The provisions of Secs. 5163, 5164, 5165, 5166 and 5167, and Secs. 5224, to 5234, inclusive, of the Revised Statutes respecting United States bonds deposited to secure circulating notes shall, except as herein modified, be applicable to all bonds deposited under the terms of Sec. 3 of this act.

STATUS OF ADDITIONAL CIRCULATING NOTES.

Sec. 5. That the additional circulating notes issued under this act shall be used, held, and treated in the same way as circulating notes of national banking associations heretofore issued and secured by a deposit of United States bonds, and shall be subject to all the provisions of law affecting such notes except as herein expressly modified: Provided,

That the total amount of circulating notes outstanding of any national banking association including notes secured by United States bonds as now provided by law, and notes secured otherwise than by deposit of such bonds, shall not at any time exceed the amount of its unimpaired capital and surplus: And provided further, That there shall not be outstanding at any time circulating notes issued under the provision of this act to an amount of more than $500,000,000.

Sec. 6. That whenever and so long as any national banking association has outstanding any of the additional circulating notes authorized to be issued by the provisions of this act it shall keep on deposit in the Treasury of the United States, in addition to the redemption fund required by Sec. 3 of the Act of June 20, 1874, an additional sum equal to 5 per centum of such additional circulation at any time outstanding, such additional 5 per centum to be treated, held, and used in all respects in the same manner as the original redemption fund provided for by said Sec. 3 of the Act of June 20, 1874.

Sec. 7. In order that the distribution of notes to be issued under the provisions of this act shall be made as equitable as practicable between the various sections of the country, the Secretary of the Treasury shall not approve applications from associations in any State in excess of the amount to which such State would be entitled of the additional notes herein authorized on the basis of the proportion which the unimpaired capital and surplus of the national banking associations in such State bears to the total amount of unimpaired capital and surplus of its national banking associations of the United States: Provided, however, That in case the application from associations in any State shall not be equal to the amount which the association of such State would be entitled to under this method of distribution, the Secretary of the Treasury may, in his discretion, to meet an emergency, assign the amount not thus applied for to any applying association or associations in States in the same section of the country.

Sec. 8. That it shall be the duty of the Secretary of the Treasury to obtain information with reference to the value and character of the securities authorized to be accepted under the provisions of this act, and he shall from time to time furnish information to national banking associations as to such securities as would be acceptable under the provisions of this act.

TAX ON CIRCULATION.

Sec. 9. That Sec. 5214 of the Revised Statutes, as amended, be further amended to read as follows:

"Sec. 5214. National banking associations having on deposit bonds of the United States, bearing interest at the rate of 2 per centum per annum including bonds issued for the construction of the Panama Canal, under the provisions of Sec. 8 of 'An act to provide for the construction of a canal connecting the waters of the Atlantic and Pacific oceans,' approved June 28, 1902, to secure its circulating notes, shall pay to the Treasurer of the United States, in the months of January and July, a tax of one-fourth of 1 per centum each half year upon the average amount of such of its notes in circulation as are based upon the deposit of such bonds; and such associations having on deposit bonds of the United States bearing interest at a rate higher than 2 per centum per annum shall pay a tax of one-half of 1 per centum each half year upon the average amount of such of its notes in circulation as are based upon the deposit of such bonds. National banking associations having circulating notes secured otherwise than by bonds of the United States shall pay for the first month a tax at the rate of 5 per centum per annum upon the average amount of such of their notes in circulation as are based upon the deposit of such securities, and afterward an additional tax of 1 per centum per annum for each month until a tax of 10 per centum per annum is reached, and thereafter such tax of 10 per centum per annum, upon the average amount of such notes. Every national banking association having outstanding circulating notes secured by a deposit of other securities than United States bonds shall make monthly returns, under oath of its president or cashier, to the Treasurer of the United States, in such form as the Treasurer may prescribe, of the average monthly amount of its notes so secured in circulation; and it shall be the duty of the Comptroller of the Currency to cause such reports of notes in circulation to be verified by examination of the banks' records. The taxes received on circulating notes secured otherwise than by bonds of the United States shall be paid into the Division of Redemption of the Treasury and credited and added to the reserve fund held for the redemption of United States and other notes."

RETIRING CIRCULATION.

Sec. 10. That Sec. 9 of the act approved July 12, 1882, as amended by the act approved March 4, 1907, be further amended to read as follows.

"Sec. 9. That any national banking association desiring to withdraw its circulating notes, secured by deposit of United States bonds in the manner provided in Sec. 4 of the act approved June 20, 1874, is hereby authorized for that purpose to deposit lawful money with the Treasurer of the United States and, with the consent of the Comptroller of the Currency and the approval of the Secretary of the Treasury, to withdraw a proportionate amount of bonds held as security for its circulating notes in the order of such deposits: Provided, That not more than $9,000.000 of dollars of lawful money shall be so deposited during any calendar month for this purpose.

"Any national banking association desiring to withdraw any of its circulating notes, secured by the deposit of securities other than bonds of the United States, may make such withdrawal at any time in like manner and effect by the deposit of lawful money or national bank notes with the Treasurer of the United States, and upon such deposit a proportionate share of the securities so deposited may be withdrawn: Provided, That the deposits under this section to retire notes secured by the deposit of securities other than bonds of the United States shall not be covered into the Treasury, as required by Sec. 6 of an act entitled 'An act directing the purchase of silver bullion and the issue of Treasury notes thereon, and for other purposes,' approved July 14, 1890, but shall be retained in the Treasury for the purpose of redeeming the notes of the bank making such deposit."

ISSUE OF NOTES.

Sec. 11. That Sec. 5172 of the Revised Statutes be, and the same is hereby, amended to read as follows:

"Sec. 5172. In order to furnish suitable notes for circulation, the Comptroller of the Currency shall, under the direction of the Secretary of the Treasury, cause plates and dies to be engraved, in the best manner to guard against counterfeiting and fraudulent alterations, and shall have printed therefrom, and numbered, such quantity of circulating notes, in blank, of the denominations of $5, $10, $20, $50, $100, $500, $1,000, and $10,000, as may be required to supply the associations entitled to receive the same. Such notes shall state upon their face that they are secured by United States bonds or other securities, certified by the written or engraved signatures of the Treasurer and Register and by the imprint of the seal of the Treasury. They shall also express upon their face the promise of the association receiving the same to pay on demand, attested by the signature of the president or vice-president and cashier. The Comptroller of the Currency, acting under the direction of the Secretary of the Treasury, shall as soon as practicable cause to be prepared circulating notes in blank, registered and countersigned, as provided by law, to an amount equal to 50 per centum of the capital stock of each national banking association; such notes to be deposited in the Treasury or in the Sub-treasury of the United States nearest the place of business of each association, and to be held for such association, subject to the order of the Comptroller of the Currency, for their delivery as provided by law: Provided, That the Comptroller of the Currency may issue national bank notes of the present form until plates can be prepared and circulating notes issued as above provided: Provided, however, That in no event shall bank notes of the present form be issued to any bank as additional circulation provided for by this act."

Sec. 12. That circulating notes of national banking associations, when presented to the Treasury for redemption, as provided in Sec. 3 of the act approved June 20, 1874, shall be redeemed in lawful money of the United States.

Sec. 13. That all acts and orders of the Comptroller of the Currency and the Treasurer of the United States authorized by this act shall have the approval of the Secretary of the Treasury who shall have power, also, to make any such rules and regulations and exercise such control over the organization and management of national currency associations as may be necessary to carry out the purposes of this act.

Sec. 14. That the provisions of Sec. 5191 of the Revised Statutes, with reference to the reserves of national banking associations, shall not apply to deposits of public moneys by the United States in designated depositaries.

Sec. 15. That all national banking associations designated as regular depositaries of public money shall pay upon all special and additional deposits made by the Secretary of the Treasury in such depositaries, and all such associations designated as temporary depositaries of public money shall pay upon all sums of public money deposited in such associations interest at such rate as the Secretary of the Treasury may prescribe, not less, however, than 1 per centum per annum upon the average monthly amount of such deposits: Provided, however, That nothing contained in this act shall be construed to change or modify the obligation of any association or any of its officers for the safe-keeping of public money: Provided further, That the rate of interest charged upon such deposits shall be equal and uniform throughout the United States.

Sec. 16. That a sum sufficient to carry out the purposes of the preceding sections of this act is hereby appropriated out of any money in the Treasury not otherwise appropriated.

CREATION OF THE NATIONAL MONETARY COMMISSION.

Sec. 17. That a Commission is hereby created, to be called the "National Monetary Commission," to be composed of nine members of the Senate, to be appointed by the presiding officer thereof, and nine members of the House of Representatives, to be appointed by the Speaker thereof; and any vacancy on the Commission shall be filled in the same manner as the original appointment.

Sec. 18. That it shall be the duty of this Commission to inquire into and report to Congress at the earliest date practicable, what changes are necessary or desirable in the monetary system of the United States or in the laws relating to banking and currency, and for this purpose they are authorized to sit during the sessions or recess of Congress, at such times and places as they may deem desirable, to send for persons and papers, to administer oaths, to summons and compel the attendance of witnesses, and to employ a disbursing officer and such secretaries, experts, stenographers, messengers, and other assistants as shall be necessary to carry out the purposes for which said Commission was created. The Commission shall have the power, through sub-committee or otherwise, to examine witnesses and to make such investigations and examinations, in this or other countries, of the subjects committed to their charge as they shall deem necessary.

Sec. 19. That a sum sufficient to carry out the purposes of Secs. 17 and 18 of this act, and to pay the necessary expenses of the Commission and its members, is hereby appropriated, out of any money in the Treasury not otherwise appropriated. Said appropriation shall be immediately available and shall be paid out on the audit and order of the chairman or acting chairman of said Commission, which audit and order shall be conclusive and binding upon all Departments as to the correctness of the accounts of such Commission.

Sec. 20. That this act shall expire by limitation on the 30th day of June, 1914.

Approved, May 30, 1908.

The Militia Act of 1908.

CHAPTER 204 of the acts of the Sixtieth Congress, first session, approved May 27, 1908, entitled "An act to further amend the act entitled 'An act to Promote the Efficiency of the Militia' and for other purposes," approved January 21, 1903, reads as follows:

Be it enacted by the Senate and House of Representatives of the United States of America in Congress assembled, That Sec. 1 of said act be, and is hereby, amended and re-enacted so as to read as follows:

"Section 1. That the militia shall consist of every able-bodied male citizen of the respective States and Territories and the District of Columbia, and every able-bodied male of foreign birth who has declared his intention to become a citizen, who is more than eighteen and less than forty-five years of age, and shall be divided into two classes: The organized militia, to be known as the National Guard of the State, Territory, or District of Columbia, or by such other designations as may be given them by the laws of the respective States or Territories, the remainder to be known as the Reserve Militia: Provided, That the provisions of this act and of Sec. 1661, Revised Statutes, as amended, shall apply only to the militia organized as a land force."

Sec. 2. That Sec. 3 of said act as amended be, and the same is hereby, amended and re-enacted so as to read as follows:

"Sec. 3. That the regularly enlisted, organized, and uniformed active militia in the several States and Territories and the District of Columbia who have heretofore participated or shall hereafter participate in the apportionment of the annual appropriation provided by Sec. 1661 of the Revised Statutes of the United States, as amended, whether known and designated as National Guard, militia or otherwise, shall constitute the organized militia. On and after January 21, 1910, the organization, armament, and discipline of the organized militia in the several States and Territories and the District of Columbia shall be the same as that which is now or may hereafter be prescribed for the Regular Army of the United States, subject in time of peace to such general exceptions as may be authorized by the Secretary of War:

INSPECTORS OF SMALL ARMS.

"Provided, That in peace and war each organized division of militia may have one inspector of small-arms practice with the rank of lieutenant-colonel; each organized brigade of militia one inspector of small-arms practice with the rank of major; each regiment of infantry or cavalry of organized militia one assistant inspector of small-arms practice with the rank of captain, and each separate or unassigned battalion of infantry or engineers or squadron of cavalry of organized militia one assistant inspector of small-arms practice with the rank of first-lieutenant: Provided also, That the President of the United States in time of peace may, by order, fix the minimum number of enlisted men in each company, troop, battery, signal corps, engineer corps, and hospital corps: And provided further, That any corps of artillery, cavalry, and infantry existing in any of the States at the passage of the act of May 8, 1792, which, by the laws, customs, or usages of the said States, have been in continuous existence since the passage of said act, under its provisions and under the provisions of Sec. 232 and Secs. 1625 to 1660, both inclusive, of Title 16 of the Revised Statutes of the United States, relating to the militia, shall be allowed to retain their accustomed privileges, subject, nevertheless, to all other duties required by law, in like manner as the other militia."

TO BE CALLED OUT IN INVASION.

Sec. 3. That Sec. 4 of said Act as amended be, and the same is hereby, amended and re-enacted so as to read as follows:

"Sec. 4. That whenever the United States is invaded or in danger of invasion from any foreign nation, or of rebellion against the authority of the Government of the United States, or the President is unable with the regular forces at his command to execute the laws of the Union, it shall be lawful for the President to call forth such number of the militia of the State or of the States or Territories or of the District of Columbia as he may deem necessary to repel such invasion, suppress such rebellion, or to enable him to execute such laws and to issue his orders for that purpose, through the Governor of the respective State or Territory, or through the commanding-general of the militia of the District of Columbia, from which State, Territory, or district such troops may be called, to such officers of the militia as he may think proper."

TERM OF SERVICE.

Sec. 4. That Sec. 5 of said act as amended be, and the same is hereby, amended and re-enacted so as to read as follows:

"Sec. 5. That whenever the President calls forth the organized militia of any State, Territory, or of the District of Columbia, to be employed in the service of the United States, he may specify in his call the period for which such service is required, and the militia so called shall continue to serve during the term so specified, either within or without the territory of the United States, unless sooner relieved by order of the President: Provided, That no commissioned officer or enlisted man of the organized militia shall be held to service beyond the term of his existing commission or enlistment: Provided further, That when the military needs of the Federal Government arising from the necessity to execute the laws of the Union, suppress insurrection, or repel invasion, cannot be met by the regular forces, the organized militia shall be called into the service of the United States in advance of any volunteer force which it may be determined to raise."

MUSTERING IN.

Sec. 5. That Sec. 7 of said act as amended be, and the same is hereby, amended and re-enacted so as to read as follows:

"Sec. 7. That every officer and enlisted man of the militia who shall be called forth in the manner hereinbefore prescribed, shall be mustered for service without further enlistment, and without further medical examination previous to such muster, except for those States and Territories which have not adopted the standard of medical examination prescribed for the Regular Army: Provided, however, That any officer or enlisted man of the militia who shall refuse or neglect to present himself for such muster, upon being called forth as herein prescribed, shall be subject to trial by court-martial and shall be punished as such court-martial may direct."

COURTS-MARTIAL.

Sec. 6. That Sec. 8 of said act as amended be, and the same is hereby, amended and re-enacted so as to read as follows:

"Sec. 8. That the majority membership of courts-martial for the trial of officers or men of the militia when in the service of the United States shall be composed of militia officers."

COMMENCEMENT OF PAY.

Sec. 7. That Sec. 11 of said act as amended be, and the same is hereby, amended and re-enacted so as to read as follows:

"Sec. 11. That when the militia is called into the actual service of the United States, or any portion of the militia is called forth under the provisions of this act, their pay shall commence from the day of their appearing at the place of company rendezvous, but this provision shall not be construed to authorize any species of expenditure previous to arriving at such place of rendezvous which is not provided by existing laws to be paid after their arrival at such places of rendezvous."

ISSUE OF ARMS.

Sec. 8. That Sec. 13 of said act as amended be, and the same is hereby, amended and re-enacted so as to read as follows:

"Sec. 13. That the Secretary of War is hereby authorized to procure, by purchase or manufacture, and issue from time to time to the organized militia, under such regulations as he may prescribe, such number of the United States service arms, together with all accessories and such other accoutrements, equipments, uniforms, clothing, equipage, and military stores of all kinds required for the Army of the United States, as are necessary to arm, uniform, and equip all of the organized militia in the several States, Territories, and the District of Columbia, in accordance with the requirements of this act, without charging the cost or value thereof, or any expense connected therewith, against the allotment of said State, Territory, or the District of Columbia, out of the annual appropriation provided by Sec 1661 of the Revised Statutes as amended, or requiring payment therefor, and to exchange without receiving any money credit therefor, ammunition or parts thereof suitable to the new arms, round for round, for corresponding ammunition suitable to the old arms heretofore issued to said State, Territory, or the District of Columbia by the United States: Provided, That said property shall remain the property of the United States, except as hereinafter provided, and be annually accounted for by the Governors of the States and Territories as required by law, and that each State, Territory, and the District of Columbia shall, on receipt of new arms or equipments, turn in to the War Department, or otherwise dispose of in accordance with the directions of the Secretary of War, without receiving any money credit therefor and without expense for transportation, all United States property so replaced or condemned. When the organized militia is uniformed as above required, the Secretary of War is authorized to fix an annual clothing allowance to each State, Territory, and the District of Columbia for each enlisted man of the organized militia thereof, and thereafter issues of clothing to such States, Territories, and the District of Columbia shall be in accordance with such allowance, and the Governors of the States and Territories and the commanding general of the militia of the District of Columbia shall be authorized to drop from their returns each year as expended clothing corresponding in value to such allowance. The Secretary of War is hereby further authorized to issue from time to time to the organized militia, under such regulations as he may prescribe, small arms and artillery ammunition upon the requisition of the Governor, in the proportion of fifty per centum of the corresponding Regular Army allowance, without charge to the State's allotment from the appropriation under Sec. 1661, Revised Statutes, as amended. To provide means to carry into effect the provisions of this section, the necessary money to cover the cost of procuring, exchanging, or issuing of arms, accoutrements, equipments, uniforms, clothing, equipage, ammunition, and military stores to be exchanged or issued hereunder is hereby appropriated out of any money in the Treasury not otherwise appropriated: Provided, That the sum expended in the execution of the purchases and issues provided for in this section shall not exceed the sum of $2,000,000 in any fiscal year: Provided also, That the Secretary of War shall annually submit to Congress a report of expenditures made by him in the execution of the requirements of this section."

PARTICIPATION IN REGULAR ARMY ENCAMPMENTS, ETC.

Sec. 9. That Sec. 15 of said act as amended be, and the same is hereby, amended and re-enacted so as to read as follows:

"Sec. 15. That the Secretary of War is authorized to provide for participation by any part of the organized militia of any State or Territory on the request of the Governor therof in the encampment, manoeuvres, and field instruction of any part of the Regular Army at or near any military post or camp or lake or seacoast defences of the United States. In such case the organized militia so participating shall receive the same pay, subsistence, and transportation as is provided by law for the officers and men of the Regular Army, and no part of the sums appropriated for the support of the Regular Army shall be used to pay any part of the expenses of the organized militia of any State, Territory, or District of Columbia while engaged in joint encampments, manoeuvres, and field instruction of the Regular Army and militia, but all payments to the militia under the provisions of this section and all allowances for mileage shall be made solely from the sums appropriated for such purposes: Provided, That the command of such military post or camp and the officers and troops of the United States there stationed shall remain with the regular commander of the post without regard to the rank of the commanding or other officers of the militia temporarily so encamped within its limits or in its vicinity: Provided further, That except as herein specified the right to command during such joint encampments, manoeuvres, and field instruction shall be governed by the rules set out in Articles 122 and 124 of the Rules and Articles for the Government of the Armies of the United States. The sums appropriated for the organized militia for such joint encampment, manoeuvres, and field instruction shall be disbursed as, and for that purpose shall constitute, one fund; and the Secretary of War shall forward to Congress, at each session next after said encampment, a detailed statement of the expenses of such encampments and manoeuvres."

ALLOWANCE.

Sec. 10. That Sec. 16 of said act as amended be, and the same is hereby, amended and re-enacted so as to read as follows:

"Sec. 16. That whenever any officer or enlisted man of the organized militia shall upon the recommendation of the Governor of any State, Territory, or the Commanding-General of the District of Columbia milita, and when authorized by the President, attend and pursue a regular course of study at any military school or college of the United States, such officer or enlisted man shall receive from the annual appropriation for the support of the army the same travel allowances and quarters or commutation of quarters to which an officer or enlisted man of the Regular Army would be entitled for attending such school or college under orders from proper military authority; such officer shall also receive commutation and subsistence at the rate of $1 per day and each enlisted man such subsistence as is furnished to an enlisted man of the Regular Army while in actual attendance upon a course of instruction."

ASSIGNMENT OF ARMY OFFICERS OR MEN WITH THE MILITIA.

Sec. 11. That Sec. 20 of said act as amended be, and the same is hereby, amended and re-enacted so as to read as follows:

"Sec. 20. That upon the application of the Governor of any State or Territory furnished with material of war under the provisions of this act, or former laws of Congress, the Secretary of War may, in his discretion, detail one or more officers or enlisted men of the army to report to the Governor of such State or Territory for duty in connection with the organized militia. All such assignments may be revoked at the request of the Governor of such State or Territory or at the pleasure of the Secretary of War. The Secretary of War is hereby authorized to appoint a board of five officers on the active list of the organized militia so selected as to secure, as far as practicable, equitable representation to all sections of the United States, and which shall, from time to time, as the Secretary of War may direct, proceed to Washington, District of Columbia, for consultation with the Secretary of War respecting the condition, status, and needs of the whole body of the organized militia. Such officers shall be appointed for the term of four years unless sooner relieved by the Secretary of War.

"The actual and necessary travelling expenses of the members of the board, together with a per diem to be established by the Secretary of War, shall be paid to the members of the board. The expenses herein authorized, together with the necessary clerical and office expenses of the division of militia affairs in the office of the Secretary of War, shall constitute a charge against the whole sum annually appropriated under Sec. 1661, Revised Statutes, as amended, and shall be paid therefrom, and not from the allotment duly apportioned to any particular State, Territory, or the District of Columbia; and a list of such expenses shall be submitted to Congress annually by the Secretary of War in connection with his annual report."

Joint Resolution No. 4, approved January 16, 1908, provides that "the time allowed the organized militia of the several States and Territories and the District of Columbia in which to conform their organization, armament and discipline to that which is now or may hereafter be prescribed for the Regular and Volunteer Armies of the United States by Sec. 3 of act approved January 21, 1903, be, and is hereby, extended to January 21, 1910."

"In God We Trust" Restored.

CONGRESS on May 18, 1908, passed the following act restoring the motto "In God We Trust" to the coins:

Be it enacted by the Senate and House of Representatives of the United States of America in Congress assembled, That the motto, "In God We Trust," heretofore inscribed on certain denominations of the gold and silver coins of the United States of America, shall hereafter be inscribed upon all such gold and silver coins of said denominations as heretofore.

The National Pure Food Law.

THE Pure Food Act, approved June 30, 1906, is entitled "An Act for preventing the manufacture, sale, or transportation of adulterated or misbranded or poisonous or deleterious foods, drugs, medicines and liquors, and for regulating traffic therein, and for other purposes." It took effect by its terms on January 1, 1907.

"Under Section 3 of the Act the secretaries of the Departments of the Treasury, Agriculture, and Commerce and Labor are required to make uniform rules for carrying out the provision of the Act. The administration of the law has therefore been placed under the charge of a Commission appointed by these three departments. The Treasury Department is represented by James L. Gerry, the Department of Agriculture by Dr. Harvey W. Wiley, and the Department of Commerce and Labor by S. N. D. North, Director of the Census. Dr. Wiley is chairman. The Commission met and organized in the City of New York September 17, 1906, and proceeded to prepare rules and regulations for carrying out the provisions of the Act.

The first section of the Act makes it unlawful for any person to manufacture within the District of Columbia or any Territory, any article of food or drug which is adulterated or misbranded, under a penalty not to exceed $500, or one year's imprisonment, or both, at the discretion of the court for the first offence, and not to exceed $1,000 and one year's imprisonment, or both, for each subsequent offence.

Section 2 of the Act makes it applicable to food or drugs introduced into any State from any other State, and from or to any foreign country.

The sections descriptive of the articles which come within the scope of the Act are as follows:

"Sec. 6. The term 'drug,' as used in this Act, shall include all medicines and preparations, recognized in the United States Pharmacopoeia or National Formulary for internal or external use, and any substance or mixture of substances intended to be used for the cure, mitigation or prevention of disease of either man or other animals. The term 'food,' as used herein, shall include all articles used for food, drink, confectionery or condiment by man or other animals, whether simple, mixed or compound.

"Sec. 7. For the purposes of this Act an article shall be deemed to be adulterated:"

In case of drugs:

"First. If, when a drug is sold under or by a name recognized in the United States Pharmacopoeia or National Formulary, it differs from the standard of strength, quality or purity, as determined by the test laid down in the United States Pharmacopoeia or National Formulary official at the time of investigation: Provided, That no drug defined in the United States Pharmacopoeia or National Formulary shall be deemed to be adulterated under this provision of the standard of strength, quality or purity be plainly stated upon the bottle, box or other container thereof, although the standard may differ from that determined by the test laid down in the United States Pharmacopoeia or National Formulary.

"Second. If this strength or purity fall below the professed standard or quality under which it is sold."

In the case of confectionery:

"If it contain terra alba, barytes, talc, chrome yellow, or other mineral substance or poisonous color or flavor, or other ingredient deleterious or detrimental to health, or any vinous, malt or spirituous liquor or compound or narcotic drug."

In the case of food:

"First. If any substance has been mixed and packed with it so as to reduce, or lower, or injuriously affect its quality or strength.

"Second. If any substance has been substituted wholly or in part for the article.

"Third. If any valuable constituent of the article has been wholly or in part extracted.

"Fourth. If it be mixed, colored, powdered, coated, or stained in a manner whereby damage or inferiority is concealed.

"Fifth. If it contain any added poisonous or other added deleterious ingredient which may render such article injurious to health: Provided, That when in the preparation of food products for shipment they are preserved by any external application applied in such manner that the preservative is necessarily removed mechanically, or by maceration in water, or otherwise, and directions for the removal of said preservatives shall be printed on the covering of the package, the provisions of this Act shall be construed as applying only when said products are ready for consumption.

"Sixth. If it consists in whole or in part of a filthy, decomposed, or putrid animal or vegetable substance, or any portion of an animal unfit for food, whether manufactured or not, or if it is the product of a diseased animal, or one that has died otherwise than by slaughter.

"Sec. 8. The term 'misbranded,' used herein, shall apply to all drugs, or articles, or food, or articles which enter into the composition of food, the package or label of which shall bear any statement, design, or device regarding such article, or the ingredients or substances contained therein which shall be false or misleading in any particular, and to any food or drug product which is falsely branded as to the State, Territory, or country in which it is manufactured or produced.

"That for the purposes of this Act, an article shall also be deemed to be misbranded."

In case of drugs:

"First. If it be an imitation of or offered for sale under the name of another article.

"Second. If the contents of the package as originally put up shall have been removed, in whole or in part, and other contents shall have been placed in such package, or if the package fail to bear a statement on the label of the quantity or proportion of any alcohol, morphine, opium, cocaine, heroin, alpha or beta eucaine, chloroform, cannabis indica, chloral hydrate or acetanilide, or any derivative or preparation of any such substances contained therein."

In case of food:

"First. If it be an imitation of or offered for sale under the distinctive name of another article.

"Second. If it be labelled or branded so as to deceive or mislead the purchaser, or purport to be a foreign product when not so, or if the contents of the package as originally put up shall have been removed in whole or in part and other contents shall have been placed in such package, or if it fail to bear a statement on the label of the quantity or proportion of any morphine, opium, cocaine, heroin, alpha or beta eucaine, chloroform, cannabis indica, chloral hydrate, or acetanilide, or any derivative or preparation of any such substance contained therein.

"Third. If in package form, and the contents are stated in terms of weight or measure, they are not plainly or correctly stated on the outside of the package.

"Fourth. If the package containing it or its label shall bear any statement, design or device regarding the ingredients or the substances contained therein, which statement, design or device shall be false or misleading, in any particular: Provided, That an article of food which does not contain any added poisonous or deleterious ingredients shall not be deemed to be adulterated or misbranded in the following cases:

"First. In the case of mixtures or compounds which may be now or from time to time hereafter known as articles of food, under their own distinctive names, and not an imitation of or offered for sale under their own distinctive names, and not an imitation of or offered for sale under the distinctive name of another article, if the name be accompanied on the same label or brand with a statement of the place where said article has been manufactured or produced.

"Second. In the case of articles labelled, branded or tagged so as to plainly indicate that they are compounds, imitations or blends, and the word 'compound,' 'imitation' or 'blend,' as the case may be, is plainly stated on the package in which it is offered for sale: Provided, That the term blend as used herein shall be construed to mean a mixture of like substances, not excluding harmless coloring or flavoring ingredients used for the purpose of coloring and flavoring only: And provided further, That nothing in this Act shall be construed as requiring or compelling proprietors or manufacturers of proprietary foods which contain unwholesome added ingredients to disclose their trade formulas, except in so far as the provisions of this Act may require to secure freedom from adulteration or misbranding.

"Sec. 9. No dealer shall be prosecuted under the provisions of this Act, when he can establish a guaranty signed by the wholesaler, jobber, manufacturer or other party residing in the United States, from whom he purchases such articles, to the effect that the same is not adulterated or misbranded within the meaning of this Act, designating it."

The remaining provisions of the Act provide the methods of prosecuting offenders and destroying goods imported or offered for import which are adulterated or falsely labelled.

The National Meat Inspection Law.

IN the Act making appropriations for the Department of Agriculture for the fiscal year ending June 30, 1907, approved June 30, 1906 (confirmed by Act of March 4, 1907), appear the following provisions regulating the inspection of meat foods either in the hoof or carcass or in canning and packing establishments:

"For the purpose of preventing the use in interstate or foreign commerce, as hereinafter provided, of meat and meat food products which are unsound, unhealthful, unwholesome or otherwise unfit for human food, the Secretary of Agriculture, at his discretion, may cause to be made, by inspectors appointed for that purpose, an examination and inspection of all cattle, sheep, swine, and goats, before they shall be allowed to enter into any slaughtering, packing, meat-canning, rendering, or similar establishments in which they are to be slaughtered, and the meat and meat food products thereof are to be used in interstate or foreign commerce; and all cattle, swine, sheep, and goats found on such inspection to show symptoms of disease shall be set apart and slaughtered separately from all other cattle, sheep, swine, or goats, and when so slaughtered the carcasses of said cattle, sheep, swine, or goats, shall be subject to a careful examination and inspection, all as provided by the rules and regulations to be prescribed by the Secretary of Agriculture as herein provided for.

"For the purpose hereinbefore set forth the Secretary of Agriculture shall cause to be made by inspectors appointed for that purpose, as hereinafter provided, a post-mortem examination and inspection of the carcasses and parts thereof of all cattle, sheep, swine, and goats to be prepared for human consumption at any slaughtering, meat-canning, salting, packing, rendering, or similar establishment in any State, Territory, or the District of Columbia for transportation or sale as articles of interstate or foreign commerce: and the carcasses and parts thereof of all such animals found to be sound, healthful, wholesome, and fit for human food, shall be marked, stamped, tagged, or labelled as 'inspected and passed;' and said inspectors shall label, mark, stamp, or tag as 'inspected and condemned' all carcasses and parts thereof of animals found to be unsound, unhealthful, unwholesome, or otherwise unfit for human food; and all carcasses or parts thereof thus inspected and condemned shall be destroyed for food purposes by the said establishment in the presence of an inspector, and the Secretary of Agriculture may remove inspectors from any such establishment which fails to so destroy any such condemned carcass or part thereof, and said inspectors, after said first inspection shall, when they deem it necessary, reinspect said carcasses or parts thereof to determine whether since the first inspection the same have become unsound, unhealthful, unwholesome, or in any way unfit for human food, and if any carcass or any part thereof shall, upon examination and inspection subsequent to the first examination and inspection, be found to be unsound, unhealthful, unwholesome, or otherwise unfit for human food, it shall be destroyed for food purposes by the said establishment in the presence of an inspector, and the Secretary of Agriculture may remove inspectors from any establishment which fails to so destroy any such condemned carcass or part thereof.

"The foregoing provisions shall apply to all carcasses or parts of carcasses of cattle, sheep, swine, and goats, or the meat or meat products thereof which may be brought into any slaughtering, meat-canning, salting, packing, rendering, or similar establishment, and such examination and inspection shall be had before the said carcasses or parts thereof shall be allowed to enter into any department wherein the same are to be treated and prepared for meat food products; and the foregoing provisions shall also apply to all such products which, after having been issued from any slaughtering, meat-canning, salting, packing, rendering, or similar establishment, shall be returned to the same or to any similar establishment where such inspection is maintained.

"For the purposes hereinbefore set forth the Secretary of Agriculture shall cause to be made by inspectors appointed for that purpose an examination and inspection of all meat food products prepared for interstate or foreign commerce in any slaughtering, meat-canning, salting, packing, rendering, or similar establishment, and for the purposes of any examination and inspection said inspectors shall have access at all times, by day or night, whether the establishment be operated or not, to every part of said establishment, and said inspectors shall mark, stamp, tag, or label as 'inspected and passed' all such products found to be sound, healthful, and wholesome, and which contain no dyes, chemicals, preservatives, or ingredients which render such meat or meat food products unsound, unhealthful, unwholesome, or unfit for human food; and said inspectors shall label, mark, stamp, or tag as 'inspected and condemned' all such products found unsound, unhealthful, and unwholesome, or which contain dyes, chemicals, preservatives, or ingredients which render such meat or meat food products unsound, unhealthful, unwholesome, or unfit for human food, and all such condemned meat food products shall be destroyed for food purposes, as hereinbefore provided, and the Secretary of Agriculture may remove inspectors from any establishment which fails to so destroy such condemned meat food product."

Other sections of the law provide for the sanitary examination of slaughtering, packing, and canning establishments, and the labelling of all such inspected articles of food.

The provisions of this Act requiring inspection to be made by the Secretary of Agriculture shall not apply to animals slaughtered by any farmer on the farm and sold and transported as interstate or foreign commerce, nor to retail butchers and retail dealers in meat and meat food products, supplying their customers: Provided, That if any person shall sell or offer for sale or transportation for interstate or foreign commerce any meat or meat food products which are diseased, unsound, unhealthful, unwholesome, or otherwise unfit for human food, knowing that such meat food products are intended for human consumption, he shall be guilty of a misdemeanor, and on conviction thereof shall be punished by a fine not exceeding $1,000 or by imprisonment for a period of not exceeding one year, or by both such fine and imprisonment.

The Public Health.

PROVISION for the Public Health is made by the United States under the following regulations:

The Surgeon-General of the Public Health and Marine-Hospital Service is charged with the supervision of the marine hospitals and other relief stations of the service, and the care of sick and disabled seamen taken from merchant vessels of the United States (ocean, lake and river) and vessels of the Light-House Service and officers and men of the Revenue-Cutter Service, Coast and Geodetic Survey, and surfmen of the Life-Saving Service. This supervision includes the purveying of medical and other supplies, the assignment of orders to medical officers, the examination of requisitions, vouchers, and property returns, and all matters pertaining to the service.

Under his direction all applicants for pilots' licenses are examined for the detection of color-blindness. Ordinary seamen on request of the master or agent are examined physically to determine their fitness before shipment, and a like examination is made of the candidates for admission to the Revenue-Cutter Service and candidates for appointment as surfmen in the United States Life-Saving Service. He examines also and passes upon the medical certificates of claimants for pensions under the laws governing the Life-Saving Service.

Under the act of February 15, 1893, he is charged with the framing of regulations for the prevention of the introduction and spread of contagious disease and is also charged with the conduct of the quarantine service of the United States.

Under the act of July 1, 1902, the name of the Marine-Hospital Service was changed to that of the Public Health and Marine-Hospital Service, and the Surgeon-General, in the interest of the public health, is authorized to call conferences at least once a year of the State and Territorial boards of health, quarantine authorities, and State health officers (the District of Columbia included) for the purpose of considering matters relating to the public health.

Under the law he is charged with the direction of the hygienic laboratory for the investigation of contagious and infectious disease and other matters relating to the public health; with the publication of the weekly Public Health Reports of the United States, including the collection and publication of vital statistics, and is responsible for the proper enforcement of the "Act to regulate the sale of viruses, serums, toxins, and analogous products in the District of Columbia, to regulate interstate traffic in said articles, and for other purposes;" approved July 1, 1902.

Under the law of March 28, 1890, known as the Interstate-Quarantine Law, he is charged with preparing the rules and regulations, under direction of the Secretary of the Treasury, necessary to prevent the introduction of certain contagious diseases from one State to another.

He is charged with the control of an experiment station for the study of the prevention and cure of leprosy, now in course of establishment under the direction of the Secretary of the Treasury.

The Surgeon-General of the Army has the administrative control of the Medical Department of the Army, the disbursement of its appropriations, the designation of the stations of medical officers, the recruitment, instruction and control of the Hospital Corps and of the Army Nurse Corps. He directs the selection, purchase and distribution of the medical supplies of the army. The Army Medical Museum and the general hospitals are under his direct control.

Employers' Liability Law.

ENACTED BY THE SIXTIETH CONGRESS.

THE following is the text of Chap. 149: "An act Relating to the Liability of Common Carriers by Railroad to their Employees in Certain Cases," approved April 22, 1908.

Be it enacted by the Senate and House of Representatives of the United States of America in Congress assembled, That every common carrier by railroad while engaging in commerce between any of the several States or Territories, or between any of the States and Territories, or between the District of Columbia and any of the States or Territories, or between the District of Columbia or any of the States or Territories and any foreign nation or nations, shall be liable in damages to any person suffering injury while he is employed by such carrier in such commerce, or in case of the death of such employee, to his or her personal representative, for the benefit of the surviving widow or husband and children of such employee; and, if none, then of such employee's parents; and, if none, then of the next of kin dependent upon such employee, for such injury or death resulting in whole or in part from the negligence of any of the officers, agents, or employees of such carrier, or by reason of any defect or insufficiency, due to its negligence, in its cars, engines, appliances, machinery, track, roadbed, works, boats, wharves, or other equipment.

Sec. 2. That every common carrier by railroad in the Territories, the District of Columbia, the Panama Canal zone, or other possessions of the United States shall be liable in damages to any person suffering injury while he is employed by such carrier in any of said jurisdictions, or, in case of the death of such employee, to his or her personal representative, for the benefit of the surviving widow or husband and children of such employee; and, if none, then of such employee's parents; and if none, then of the next of kin dependent upon such employee, for such injury or death resulting in whole or in part from the negligence of any of the officers, agents, or employees of such carrier, or by reason of any defect or insufficiency, due to its negligence, in its cars, engines, appliances, machinery, track, roadbed, works, boats, wharves, or other equipment.

Sec. 3. That in all actions hereafter brought against any such common carrier by railroad under or by virtue of any of the provisions of this act to recover damages for personal injuries to an employee, or where such injuries have resulted in his death, the fact that the employee may have been guilty of contributory negligence shall not bar a recovery, but the damages shall be diminished by the jury in proportion to the amount of negligence attributable to such employee: Provided, That no such employee who may be injured or killed shall be held to have been guilty of contributory negligence in any case where the violation by such common carrier of any statute enacted for the safety of employees contributed to the injury or death of such employee.

Sec. 4. That in any action brought against any common carrier under or by virtue of any of the provisions of this act to recover damages for injuries to, or the death of, any of its employees, such employee shall not be held to have assumed the risks of his employment in any case where the violation by such common carrier of any statute enacted for the safety of employees contributed to the injury or death of such employee.

Sec. 5. That any contract, rule, regulation, or device whatsover, the purpose or intent of which shall be to enable any common carrier to exempt itself from any liability created by this act, shall to that extent be void: Provided, That in any action brought against any such common carrier under or by virtue of any of the provisions of this act, such common carrier may set off therein any sum it has contributed or paid to any insurance, relief benefit, or indemnity that may have been paid to the injured employee or the person entitled thereto on account of the injury or death for which said action was brought.

Sec. 6. That no action shall be maintained under this act unless commenced within two years from the day the cause of action accrued.

Sec. 7. That the term "common carrier" as used in this act shall include the receiver or receivers or other persons or corporations charged with the duty of the management and operation of the business of a common carrier.

Sec. 8. That nothing in this act shall be held to limit the duty or liability of common carriers or to impair the rights of their employees under any other act or acts of Congress, or to affect the prosecution of any pending proceeding or right of action under the act of Congress entitled "An act Relating to Liability of Common Carriers in the District of Columbia and Territories, and to common carriers engaged in commerce between the States and between the States and foreign nations to their employees," approved June 11, 1906.

International Bureau of the American Republics.

THE International Bureau of the American Republics was established under the recommendation of the First International American Conference, held in the city of Washington in 1890 for the purpose of maintaining closer relations between the several Republics of the Western Hemisphere. It was reorganized by the Second International American Conference, held in the city of Mexico in 1901, and its scope widened by imposing many new and important duties. A prominent feature of the new arrangement was the foundation of the Columbus Memorial Library. The International Bureau corresponds, through the diplomatic representatives of the several governments in Washington, with the executive departments of these governments, and is required to furnish such information as it possesses or can obtain to any of the Republics making requests. It is the custodian of the archives of the International American Conferences, and is especially charged with the performance of duties imposed upon it by these conferences. The International Bureau is sustained by contributions from the American Republics in proportion to their population, and is governed by a board composed of the diplomatic representatives at Washington from the several countries composing the Union, and the Secretary of State, who is ex-officio its chairman. It publishes a monthly bulletin containing the latest official information respecting the resources, commerce, and general features of the American Republics, as well as maps and geographical sketches of these countries, which publications are considered public documents, and as such are carried free in the mails of all the Republics of the Union.

The Chinese Indemnity.

RESOLUTION OF THE SIXTIETH CONGRESS REMITTING A PORTION.

JOINT resolution No. 29 "to provide for the remission of a portion of the Chinese Indemnity," approved May 25, 1908:

Resolved by the Senate and House of Representatives of the United States of America in Congress assembled, That the President is hereby authorized to consent to a modification of the bond for $24,440,778.81, dated December 15, 1906, received from China pursuant to the protocol of September 7, 1901, for indemnity against losses and expenses incurred by reason of the so-called Boxer disturbances in China during the year 1900, so that the total payment to be made by China under the said bond shall be limited to the sum of $13,655,492.69 and interest at the stipulated rate of four per centum per annum, and that the remainder of the indemnity to which the United States is entitled under the said protocol and bond may be remitted as an act of friendship, such payment and remission to be at such times and in such manner as the President shall deem just.

Provided, That within one year from the passage of this resolution any person whose claim upon the Chinese indemnity, 1900, was presented to the United States Commissioners or to the Department of State and disallowed in whole or in part may present the same by petition to the Court of Claims, which court is hereby invested with jurisdiction to hear and adjudicate such claim, without appeal, and to render such judgments de novo, or in addition to any allowance or allowances heretofore made, as, in each case shall be fully and substantially compensatory for actual losses and expenses of the claimant caused by the anti-foreign disturbances in China during the year 1900, excluding merely speculative claims or elements of damage.

And provided also, That the sum of $2,000,000 be reserved from the Chinese indemnity, 1900, for the payment of such judgments, the same to be paid by the Treasurer of the United States as and when they shall be certified to the Secretary of the Treasury by the said court, and any balance remaining after all such claims have been adjudicated and paid shall be returned to the Chinese Government in such manner as the Secretary of State shall decide, and the Secretary of the Treasury is hereby authorized and directed to so return the same.

And provided further, That all evidence furnished by the claimants, and statements made by them to the said commissioners or to the Department of State, shall be transmitted by the said Department to the said Court of Claims and considered together with such other additional testimony as may be presented by either side, and the Government of the United States shall defend the said claims in the said court by such attorney or attorneys as may be designated for such service by the Attorney-General of the United States.

Provided further, That in no case shall the Court of Claims award a principal sum to any claimant which, together with the principal sums said claimant may have already received by decision of the United States Commissioners and the Department of State, shall exceed the amount originally claimed by said claimant.

Anarchistic Literature Excluded from the Mails.

THE President of the United States on March 22 sent the following communication to the Department of Justice in reference to an anarchistic publication at Paterson, N. J., entitled "La Questione Sociale:"

To the Department of Justice:

By my direction the Postmaster-General is to exclude "La Questione Sociale," of Paterson, N. J., from the mails, and it will not be admitted to the mails unless by order of the court, or unless you advise me that it must be admitted. Please see if it is not possible to prosecute criminally under any section of the law that is available the men that are interested in the sending out of this anarchistic and murderous publication. They are, of course, the enemies of mankind, and every effort should be made to hold them accountable for an offence far more infamous than that of an ordinary murder.

This matter has been brought to my attention by the Mayor of the City of Paterson. I wish every effort made to get at the criminals under the Federal law. It may be found impossible to do this. I shall also, through the Secretary of State, call the attention of the Governor of New Jersey to the circumstances, so that he may proceed under the State law, his attention being further drawn to the fact that the newspaper is circulated in other States. After you have concluded your investigation I wish a report from you to serve as a basis for recommendations by me for action by Congress.

The newspaper article in question advocates murder by dynamite. It specifically advocates the murder of enlisted men of the United States Army and officers of the police force, and the burning of the houses of private citizens. The preaching of murder and arson is certainly as immoral as the circulation of obscene and lascivious literature, and if the practice is not already forbidden by the law it should be forbidden. The Immigration law now prohibits the entry to the United States of any person who entertains or advocates the views expressed in this newspaper article. It is, of course, inexcusable to permit those already here to promulgate such views.

Those who write, publish, and circulate such articles stand on the level with those who use the mails for distributing poisons for the purpose of murder, and convictions have been obtained when the mails have been used for the distribution of poisons. No law should require the Postmaster-General to become an accessory to murder by circulating literature of this kind. THEODORE ROOSEVELT.

In response to the above the Attorney-General wrote an opinion which the President transmitted to Congress with the following message:

To the Senate and House of Representatives:

I herewith submit a letter from the Department of Justice which explains itself. Under this opinion I hold that existing statutes give the President the power to prohibit the Post-

ANARCHISTIC LITERATURE EXCLUDED FROM THE MAILS—*Continued.*

master-General from being used as an instrument in the commission of crime—that is, to prohibit the use of the mails for the advocacy of murder, arson and treason—and I shall act upon such construction. Unquestionably, however, there should be further legislation by Congress in this matter.

When compared with the suppression of anarchy, every other question sinks into insignificance. The Anarchist is the enemy of humanity, the enemy of all mankind and his is a deeper degree of criminality than any other. No immigrant is allowed to come to our shores if he is an Anarchist, and no paper published here or abroad should be permitted circulation in this country if it propagates anarchistic opinions.

The White House, April 9, 1908. THEODORE ROOSEVELT.

THE ATTORNEY-GENERAL'S OPINION.

The opinion of the Attorney-General, which the President transmitted to Congress, embraced a discussion of the whole subject from many legal points of view. His first conclusion was that the article in the Anarchist paper, which advocates the use of arms and dynamite in annihilating police and soldiers that anarchy may prevail, constitutes a "seditious libel." and "is undoubtedly a crime at common law."

He declared that there is no Federal statute which makes such publications an offence against the United States, and that the Federal courts consequently have no jurisdiction. That Congress has full power to make such publications criminal the Attorney-General asserted, and quoted Chief Justice Fuller and Justice Field as authority.

The greater portion of his opinion was devoted to the question of whether, in the absence of any legislation by Congress, the Postmaster-General had the right to exclude such publication from the mails. On this point his conclusion was:

"The Postmaster-General will be justified in excluding from the mails any issue of any periodical, otherwise entitled to the privileges of second-class mail matter, which shall contain any article constituting a seditious libel, and counselling crimes as murder, arson, riot and treason."

In arriving at the latter conclusion the Attorney-General made a clear distinction with reference to the authority of postal officials over sealed and unsealed mail matter. In conveying letters and newspapers to persons to whom they are directed, he said that the United States "undertakes the business of a messenger." He added:

In so far as it conveys sealed documents, its agents not only are not bound to know, but are expressly forbidden to ascertain, what the purport of such messages may be; therefore neither the Government nor its officers can be held either legally or morally responsible for the nature of the letters to which they thus, in intentional ignorance, afford transportation. But in the case of printed matter intended for general circulation and which by virtue of the statutes above mentioned, and in consideration of the reduced rate at which it is transported, the officers of the Post-Office Department have the legal right to thoroughly inspect, it seems obvious that neither these officers nor the Government which employs them can escape responsibility for the consequences if they knowingly transport matter which becomes, and which they must know might be reasonably expected to become, a cause of crime.

ACTION OF CONGRESS.

Revised Statutes of the United States, Sec. 3893, in reference to matter excluded from the mails was amended by Chap. 206 of the Acts of the Sixtieth Congress, approved May 27, 1908, by adding thereto: "And the term indecent within the intendment of this section shall include matter of a character tending to incite arson, murder, or assassination."

The American Indian.

THE annual reports of the agents of the United States Bureau of Indian Affairs in 1907 showed that the Indian population was 298,482, distributed in the several States as follows:

Arizona	38,852	Kansas	1,274	New York	5,419	Washington	8,538
California	18,988	Michigan	6,708	North Carolina	1,550	Wisconsin	10,445
Colorado	807	Minnesota	9,895	North Dakota	7,919	Wyoming	1,701
Florida	358	Montana	10,459	Oklahoma	14,136	Texas	470
Idaho	4,056	Nebraska	3,685	Oregon	3,691	Miscellaneous	713
Indian Ter	102,993	Nevada	5,367	South Dakota	19,685		
Iowa	345	New Mexico	18,564	Utah	1,854	Total	298,472

Of the 274,706 Indian population in 1904, 116,333 wore citizen's dress and 43,602 wore a mixture of Indian and civilized clothing. Those who could read numbered 63,147 and 69,209 could carry on an ordinary conversation in English.

The expenditures of the United States on account of the Indians in the fiscal year ended June 30, 1907, were $15,140,292; The expenditures from 1789 to 1907, inclusive, have been $454,787,382.

The appropriation made by Congress for Indian schools for the fiscal year ending June 30, 1907, was $9,428,983.35. The Government supports 116 boarding schools, and 163 day schools. Indians incidentally under the Indian office, and self-supporting:

The five civilized tribes, Indians and colored—Cherokees, 41,512; Chickasaws, 10,989; Choctaws, 26,615; Creeks, 18,762; Seminoles, 3,124. Total Indians, 100,943; total colored, 23,382; grand total, 124,325 100,943

Pueblos of New Mexico 9,146

Six Nations, Saint Regis, and other Indians of New York 5,419

Eastern Cherokees of North Carolina 1,550

Indians under control of the War Department, prisoners of war (Apaches at Ft. Sill, Okla. 298

International Red Cross Treaty.

CONVENTION FOR THE AMELIORATION OF THE CONDITION OF THE WOUNDED IN THE FIELD.

THE President of the United States proclaimed the following convention August 3, 1907.

Whereas a convention between the United States of America and Germany, the Argentine Republic, Austria-Hungary, Belgium, Bulgaria, Chile, China, the Congo Free State, Denmark, Spain, Brazil, Mexico, France, Great Britain, Greece, Guatemala, Honduras, Italy, Japan, Luxemburg, Montenegro, Norway, the Netherlands, Peru, Persia, Portugal, Roumania, Russia, Servia, Siam, Sweden, Switzerland, and Uruguay, for the amelioration of the condition of the wounded of armies in the field, was signed at Geneva, July 6, 1906, the original of which convention, being in the French language, is word for word as follows:

Here follow the names and titles of the contracting parties, and the names and titles of their plenipotentiaries, and then the text.

CHAPTER I.—The Sick and Wounded.

Article 1. Officers, soldiers, and other persons officially attached to armies, who are sick or wounded, shall be respected and cared for, without distinction of nationality, by the belligerent in whose power they are.

A belligerent, however, when compelled to leave his wounded in the hands of his adversary, shall leave with them, so far as military conditions permit, a portion of the personnel and material of his sanitary service to assist in caring for them.

Art. 2. Subject to the care that must be taken of them under the preceding article, the sick and wounded of an army who fall into the power of the other belligerent become prisoners of war, and the general rules of international law in respect to prisoners become applicable to them.

The belligerents remain free, however, to mutually agree upon such clauses, by way of exception or favor, in relation to the wounded or sick as they may deem proper. They shall especially have authority to agree:

1. To mutually return the sick and wounded left on the field of battle after an engagement.
2. To send back to their own country the sick and wounded who have recovered, or who are in a condition to be transported and whom they do not desire to retain as prisoners.
3. To send the sick and wounded of the enemy to a neutral State, with the consent of the latter and on condition that it shall charge itself with their interment until the close of hostilities.

Art. 3. After every engagement the belligerent who remains in possession of the field of battle shall take measures to search for the wounded and to protect the wounded and dead from robbery and ill treatment.

He will see that a careful examination is made of the bodies of the dead prior to their interment or incineration.

Art. 4. As soon as possible each belligerent shall forward to the authorities of their country or army the marks or military papers of identification found upon the bodies of the dead, together with a list of names of the sick and wounded taken in charge by him.

Belligerents will keep each other mutually advised of interments and transfers, together with admissions to hospitals and deaths which occur among the sick and wounded in their hands. They will collect all objects of personal use, valuables, letters, etc., which are found upon the field of battle, or have been left by the sick or wounded who have died in sanitary formations or other establishments, for transmission to persons in interest through the authorities of their own country.

Art. 5. Military authority may make an appeal to the charitable zeal of the inhabitants to receive and, under its supervision, to care for the sick and wounded of the armies, granting to persons responding to such appeals special protection and certain immunities.

CHAPTER II.—Sanitary Formations and Establishments.

Art. 6. Mobile sanitary formations (i. e., those which are intended to accompany armies in the field) and the fixed establishments belonging to the sanitary service shall be protected and respected by belligerents.

Art. 7. The protection due to sanitary formations and establishments ceases if they are used to commit acts injurious to the enemy.

Art. 8. A sanitary formation or establishment shall not be deprived of the protection accorded by Article 6 by the fact:

1. That the personnel of a formation or establishment is armed and uses its arms in self-defence or in defence of its sick and wounded.
2. That in the absence of armed hospital attendants, the formation is guarded by an armed detachment or by sentinels acting under competent orders.
3. That arms or cartridges, taken from the wounded and not yet turned over to the proper authorities, are found in the formation or establishment.

CHAPTER III.—Personnel.

Art. 9. The personnel charged exclusively with the removal, transportation, and treatment of the sick and wounded, as well as with the administration of sanitary formations and establishments, and the chaplains attached to armies, shall be respected and protected under all circumstances. If they fall into the hands of the enemy they shall not be considered as prisoners of war.

These provisions apply to the guards of sanitary formations and establishments in the case provided for in Section 2 of Article 8.

Art. 10. The personnel of volunteer aid societies, duly recognized and authorized by their own governments, who are employed in the sanitary formations and establishments of armies, are assimilated to the personnel contemplated in the preceding article, upon condition that the said personnel shall be subject to military laws and regulations.

Each State shall make known to the other, either in time of peace or at the opening, or during the progress of hostilities, and in any case before actual employment, the names of the societies which it has authorized to render assistance, under its responsibility, in the official sanitary service of its armies.

Art. 11. A recognized society of a neutral State can only lend the services of its sanitary personnel and formations to a belligerent with the prior consent of its own government and the authority of such belligerent. The belligerent who has accepted such assistance is required to notify the enemy before making any use thereof.

Art. 12. Persons described in Articles 9, 10, and 11 will continue in the exercise of their functions, under the direction of the enemy, after they have fallen into his power.

When their assistance is no longer indispensable they will be sent back to their army or country, within such period and by such route as may accord with military necessity. They will carry with them such effects, instruments, arms, and horses as are their private property.

Art. 13. While they remain in his power, the enemy will secure to the personnel mentioned in Article 9 the same pay and allowances to which persons of the same grade in his own army are entitled.

CHAPTER IV.—Materiel.

Art. 14. If mobile sanitary formations fall into the power of the enemy, they shall retain their materiel, including the teams, whatever may be the means of transportation and the conducting personnel. Competent military authority, however, shall have the right to employ it in caring for the sick and wounded. The restitution of the materiel shall take place in accordance with the conditions prescribed for the sanitary personnel, and, as far as possible, at the same time.

Art. 15. Buildings and materiel pertaining to fixed establishments shall remain subject to the laws of war, but cannot be diverted from their use so long as they are necessary for the sick and wounded. Commanders of troops engaged in operations, however, may use them, in case of important military necessity, if, before such use, the sick and wounded who are in them have been provided for.

Art. 16. The materiel of aid societies admitted to the benefits of this convention, in conformity to the conditions therein established, is regarded as private property, and, as such, will be respected under all circumstances, save that it is subject to the recognized right of requisition by belligerents in conformity to the laws and usages of war.

CHAPTER V.—Convoys of Evacuation.

Art. 17. Convoys of evacuation shall be treated as mobile sanitary formations subject to the following special provisions:

1. A belligerent intercepting a convoy may, if required by military necessity, break up such convoy, charging himself with the care of the sick and wounded whom it contains.

2. In this case the obligation to return the sanitary personnel, as provided for in Article 12, shall be extended to include the entire military personnel employed, under competent orders, in the transportation and protection of the convoy.

The obligation to return the sanitary materiel, as provided for in Article 14, shall apply to railway trains and vessels intended for interior navigation which have been especially equipped for evacuation purposes, as well as to the ordinary vehicles, trains, and vessels which belong to the sanitary service.

Military vehicles, with their teams, other than those belonging to the sanitary service, may be captured.

The civil personnel and the various means of transportation obtained by requisition, including railway materiel and vessels utilized for convoys, are subject to the general rules of international law.

CHAPTER VI.—Distinctive Emblem.

Art. 18. Out of respect to Switzerland the heraldic emblem of the red cross on a white ground, formed by the reversal of the Federal colors, is continued as the emblem and distinctive sign of the sanitary service of armies.

Art. 19. This emblem appears on flags and brassards as well as upon all materiel appertaining to the sanitary service, with the permission of the competent military authority.

Art. 20. The personnel protected in virtue of the first paragraph of Article 9, and Articles 10 and 11, will wear attached to the left arm a brassard bearing a red cross on a white ground, which will be issued and stamped by competent military authority, and accompanied by a certificate of identity in the case of persons attached to the sanitary service of armies who do not have military uniform.

Art. 21. The distinctive flag of the convention can only be displayed over the sanitary formations and establishments which the convention provides shall be respected, and with the consent of the military authorities. It shall be accompanied by the national flag of the belligerent, to whose service the formation or establishment is attached.

Sanitary formations which have fallen into the power of the enemy, however, shall fly no other flag than that of the Red Cross so long as they continue in that situation.

Art. 22. The sanitary formations of neutral countries which, under the conditions set forth in Article 11, have been authorized to render their services, shall fly, with the flag of the convention, the national flag of the belligerent to which they are attached. The provisions of the second paragraph of the preceding article are applicable to them.

Art. 23. The emblem of the red cross on a white ground and the words Red Cross or Geneva Cross may only be used, whether in time of peace or war, to protect or designate sanitary formations and establishments, the personnel and material protected by the convention.

CHAPTER VII.—Application and Execution of the Convention.

Art. 24. The provisions of the present convention are obligatory only on the contracting

powers, in case of war between two or more of them. The said provisions shall cease to be obligatory if one of the belligerent powers should not be signatory to the convention.

Art. 25. It shall be the duty of the commanders-in-chief of the belligerent armies to provide for the details of execution of the foregoing articles, as well as for unforeseen cases, in accordance with the instructions of their respective governments, and conformably to the general principles of this convention.

Art. 26. The signatory governments shall take the necessary steps to acquaint their troops, and particularly the protected personnel, with the provisions of this convention, and to make them known to the people at large.

CHAPTER VIII.—Repression of Abuses and Infractions.

Art. 27. The signatory powers whose legislation may not now be adequate engage to take or recommend to their legislatures such measures as may be necessary to prevent the use, by private persons or by societies other than those upon which this convention confers the right thereto, of the emblem or name of the Red Cross or Geneva Cross, particularly for commercial purposes by means of trade-marks or commercial labels.

The prohibition of the use of the emblem or name in question shall take effect from the time set in each act of legislation, and at the latest five years after this convention goes into effect. After such going into effect, it shall be unlawful to use a trade-mark or commercial label contrary to such prohibition.

Art. 28. In the event of their military penal laws being insufficient, the signatory governments also engage to take, or to recommend to their legislatures, the necessary measures to repress, in time of war, individual acts of robbery and ill treatment of the sick and wounded of the armies, as well as to punish, as usurpations of military insignia, the wrongful use of the flag and brassard of the Red Cross by military persons or private individuals not protected by the present convention.

They will communicate to each other through the Swiss Federal Council the measures taken with a view to such repression, not later than five years from the ratification of the present convention.

GENERAL PROVISIONS.

Art. 29. The present convention shall be ratified as soon as possible. The ratifications will be deposited at Berne.

A record of the deposit of each act of ratification shall be prepared, of which a duly certified copy shall be sent, through diplomatic channels, to each of the contracting powers.

Art. 30. The present convention shall become operative, as to each power, six months after the date of deposit of its ratification.

Art. 31. The present convention, when duly ratified, shall supersede the convention of August 22, 1864, in the relations between the contracting states.

The convention of 1864 remains in force in the relations between the parties who signed it, but who may not also ratify the present convention.

Art. 32. The present convention may, until December 31, proximo, be signed by the powers represented at the conference which opened at Geneva on June 11, 1906, as well as by the powers not represented at the conference who have signed the convention of 1864.

Such of those powers as shall not have signed the present convention on or before December 31, 1906, will remain at liberty to accede to it after that date. They shall signify their adherence in a written notification addressed to the Swiss Federal Council, and communicated to all the contracting powers by the said council.

Other powers may request to adhere in the same manner, but their request shall only be effective if, within the period of one year from its notification to the Federal Council, such council has not been advised of any opposition on the part of any of the contracting powers.

Art. 33. Each of the contracting parties shall have the right to denounce the present convention. This denunciation shall only become operative one year after a notification in writing shall have been made to the Swiss Federal Council, which shall forthwith communicate such notification to all the other contracting parties.

This denunciation shall only become operative in respect to the power which has given it.

In faith whereof the plenipotentiaries have signed the present convention and affixed their seals thereto.

Done at Geneva, the sixth day of July, one thousand nine hundred and six, in a single copy, which shall remain in the archives of the Swiss Confederation and certified copies of which shall be delivered to the contracting parties through diplomatic channels.

(Here follow the signatures.)

Act Prohibiting Money Contributions

FROM CORPORATIONS FOR POLITICAL PURPOSES.

Be it enacted by the Senate and House of Representatives of the United States of America in Congress assembled, That it shall be unlawful for any national bank, or any corporation organized by authority of any laws of Congress, to make a money contribution in connection with any election to any political office. It shall also be unlawful for any corporation whatever to make a money contribution in connection with any election at which Presidential and Vice-Presidential electors, or a Representative in Congress, is to be voted for, or any election by any State Legislature of a United States Senator. Every corporation which shall make any contribution in violation of the foregoing provisions shall be subject to a fine not exceeding $5,000, and every officer or director of any corporation who shall consent to any contribution by the corporation in violation of the foregoing provisions shall, upon conviction, be punished by a fine of not exceeding $1,000 and not less than $250, or by imprisonment for a term of not more than one year, or both, such fine and imprisonment in the discretion of the court.—*Passed by Congress January, 26, 1907.*

Conservation of Natural Resources.

CONFERENCE OF STATE GOVERNORS AND PUBLIC MEN AT THE INVITATION OF THE PRESIDENT.

THE INVITATION BY THE PRESIDENT.

THE President of the United States on November 17, 1907, issued an invitation to the Governors of the States and Territories to meet him at the White House, Washington, on May 13, 14, and 15, 1908, to discuss the question of means to conserve the natural resources of the country. Invitations were also extended to ex-President Cleveland, William J. Bryan, Andrew Carnegie, James J. Hill, John Mitchell, Judge George Gray and other prominent public men.

The following was the text of the invitation to each of the Governors:

"The natural resources of the territory of the United States were, at the time of the settlement, richer, more varied, and more available than those of any other equal area on the surface of the earth. The development of these resources has given up, for more than a century, a rate of increase in population and wealth undreamed of by the men who founded our Government and without parallel in history. It is obvious that the prosperity which we now enjoy rests directly upon these resources. It is equally obvious that the vigor and success which we desire and foresee for this Nation in the future must have this as the ultimate material basis.

"In view of these evident facts, it seems to me time for the country to take account of its natural resources and to inquire how long they are likely to last. We are prosperous now; we should not forget that it will be just as important to our descendants to be prosperous in their time as it is to us to be prosperous in our time.

"Recently I expressed the opinion that there is no other question now before the Nation of equal gravity with the question of the conservation of our natural resources, and I added that it is the plain duty of those of us who, for the moment, are responsible to make inventory of the natural resources which have been handed down to us, to forecast as well as we may the needs of the future, and so to handle the great sources of our prosperity as not to destroy in advance all hope of the prosperity of our descendants.

"It is evident that the abundant natural resources on which the welfare of this Nation rests are becoming depleted, and in not a few cases are already exhausted. This is true of all portions of the United States; it is especially true of the longer settled communities of the East. The gravity of the situation must, I believe, appeal with special force to the Governors of the States, because of their close relations to the people and their responsibility for the welfare of their communities.

"I have therefore decided, in accordance with the suggestion of the Inland Waterways Commission, to ask the Governors of the States and Territories to meet at the White House on May 13, 14, and 15, to confer with the President and with each other upon the conservation of natural resources. It gives me great pleasure to invite you to take part in this conference. I should be glad to have you select three citizens to accompany you and to attend the conference as your assistants or advisers. I shall also invite the Senators and Representatives of the Sixtieth Congress to be present at the sessions, so far as their duties will permit.

"The matters to be considered at this conference are not confined to any region or group of States, but are of Vital concern to the Nation as a whole, and to all the people. Those subjects include the use and conservation of the mineral resources, the resources of the land, and the resources of the waters in every part of our territory.

"In order to open discussion I shall invite a few recognized authorities to present brief descriptions of actual facts and conditions without argument, leaving the conference to deal with each topic as it may elect. The members of the Inland Waterways Commission will be present, in order to share with me the benefit of information and suggestion, and, if desired, to set forth their provisional plans and conclusions.

"Facts which I cannot gainsay force me to believe that the conservation of our natural resources is the most weighty question now before the people of the United States. If this is so, the proposed conference, which is the first of its kind, will be among the most important gatherings in our history in its effect upon the welfare of all our people.

"I earnestly hope, my dear Governor, that you will find it possible to be present. Sincerely yours, "THEODORE ROOSEVELT."

THE CONFERENCE.

The Governors of thirty-seven States and Territories, and many prominent public men, met at the White House May 13, 1908. President Roosevelt presided and made an address reviewing the treatment of natural resources throughout the world, and especially the use and waste of them in our own country during the past century. A wise use of them, he said, was the great material question of the present time. He had called this conference "because the enormous consumption of these resources, and the threat of imminent exhaustion of some of them called for common effort and action."

During the three days of the conference addresses were made by Andrew Carnegie, John Mitchell, Governor John Johnson, of Minnesota; John Hays Hammond, Secretary Elihu Root, James J. Hill, Professor Thomas C. Chamberlain, President Hadley, of Yale University; Governor Glenn, of North Carolina; Governor Folk, of Missouri; William J. Bryan and others.

A committee on resolutions was appointed by the President, composed of Governor

Blanchard, of Louisiana, chairman, and Governors Cutler, of Utah; Davidson, of Wisconsin, and Ansel, of South Carolina.

THE DECLARATION.

The Committee on Resolutions reported the following declaration on the second day, and it was unanimously adopted on the third day of the conference:

"We, the Governors of the States and Territories of the United States of America, in conference assembled, do hereby declare the conviction that the great prosperity of our country rests upon the abundant resources of the land chosen by our forefathers for their homes, and where they laid the foundation of this great nation. We look upon these resources as a heritage to be made use of in establishing and promoting the comfort, prosperity and happiness of the American people, but not to be wasted, deteriorated or needlessly destroyed.

"We agree that our country's future is involved in this; that the great natural resources supply the material basis upon which our civilization must continue to depend, and upon which the perpetuity of the nation itself rests.

"We agree, in the light of facts brought to our knowledge, and from information received from sources which we cannot doubt, that this material basis is threatened with exhaustion. Even as each succeeding generation from the birth of the nation has performed its part in promoting the progress and development of the Republic, so do we in this generation recognize it as a high duty to perform our part, and this duty in large degree in the adoption of measures for the conservation of the natural wealth of the country.

"We declare our firm conviction that this conservation of our natural resources is a subject of transcendent importance, which should engage unremittingly the attention of the nation, the States and the people in earnest co-operation. These natural resources include the land on which we live, and which yields our food; the living waters which fertilize the soil, supply power and form great avenues of commerce; the forests which yield the materials for our homes, prevent erosion of the soil and conserve the navigation and other uses of our streams, and the minerals which form the basis of our industrial life, and supply us with heat, light and power.

"We agree that the land should be so used that erosion and soil wash should cease, that there should be reclamation of arid and semi-arid regions by means of irrigation, and of swamp and overflowed regions by means of drainage; that the waters should be so conserved and used as to promote navigation, to enable the arid regions to be reclaimed by irrigation, and to develop power in the interests of the people; that the forests, which regulate our rivers, support our industries and promote the fertility and productiveness of the soil, should be preserved and perpetuated; that the minerals found so abundantly beneath the surface should be so used as to prolong their utility; that the beauty, healthfulness and habitability of our country should be preserved and increased; that the sources of national wealth exist for the benefit of all the people, and that the monopoly thereof should not be tolerated.

"We commend the wise forethought of the President in sounding the note of warning as to the waste and exhaustion of the natural resources of the country, and signify our high appreciation of his action in calling this conference to consider the same and to seek remedies therefor through co-operation of the Nation and the States.

"We agree that this co-operation should find expression in suitable action by the Congress within the limits of and co-extensive with the national jurisdiction of the subject, and complementary thereto by the Legislatures of the several States within the limits of and co-extensive with their jurisdiction.

"We declare the conviction that in the use of the natural resources States are interdependent and bound together by ties of mutual benefits, responsibilities and duties.

"We agree in the wisdom of future conferences between the President, members of Congress and the Governors of the States regarding the conservation of our natural resources, with the view of continued co-operation and action on the lines suggested. And to this end we advise that from time to time, as in his judgment may seem wise, the President call the Governors of the States, members of Congress and others into conference.

"We agree that further action is advisable to ascertain the present condition of our natural resources and to promote the conservation of the same. And to that end we recommend the appointment by each State of a commission on the conservation of natural resources, to co-operate with each other and with any similar commission on behalf of the Federal Government.

"We urge the continuation and extension of forest policies adapted to secure the husbanding and renewal of our diminishing timber supply, the prevention of soil erosion, the protection of head-waters, and the maintenance of the purity and navigability of the streams. We recognize that the private ownership of forest lands entails responsibilities in the interests of all the people, and we favor the enactment of laws looking to the protection and replacement of privately owned forests.

"We recognize in our waters a most valuable asset of the people of the United States, and we recommend the enactment of laws looking to the conservation of water resources for irrigation, water supply, power and navigation, to the end that navigable and course streams may be brought under complete control and fully utilized for every purpose. We specially urge on the Federal Congress the immediate adoption of a wise, active and thorough waterway policy, providing for the prompt improvement of our streams and conservation of their watersheds required for the uses of commerce and the protection of the interests of our people.

"We recommend the enactment of laws looking to the prevention of waste in the mining and extraction of coal, oil, gas and other minerals, with a view to their wise conservation for the use of the people, and to the protection of human life in the mines.

"Let us conserve the foundations of our prosperity."

After the adjournment of the conference a number of the Governors met and appointed a committee to make arrangements for future conferences.

THE NATIONAL CONSERVATION COMMISSION.

On June 3 the President, in compliance with the suggestion made by the Governors at the conference, appointed a "National Conservation Commission" to consider and advise him on questions relating to the conservation of the natural resources of the country and to co-operate with similar bodies which may be designated by the several States.

The composition of the Commission is as follows, the first name in each branch being that of the chairman:

Executive Committee—Gifford Pinchot, Theodore E. Burton, Reed Smoot, Knute Nelson, John Dalzell, W. J. McGee, Overton W. Price, G. W. Woodruff and Joseph A. Holmes.

Committee on Waters—Representative Theodore E. Burton, Ohio; Senators William B. Allison, Iowa; Francis G. Newlands, Nevada; William Warner, Missouri, and John H. Bankhead, Alabama; W. J. McGee, Bureau of Soils, secretary; F. H. Newell, Reclamation Service; Gifford Pinchot, Forest Service; Herbert Knox Smith, Bureau of Corporations; Representative Joseph E. Ransdell, Louisiana; Prof. George F. Swain, Massachusetts Institute of Technology, the Chief of Engineers, U. S. A.

Committee on Forests—Senators Reed Smoot, Utah; Albert J. Beveridge, Indiana, and Charles A. Culberson, Texas; Representatives Charles F. Scott, Kansas, Champ Clark, Missouri, and J. B. White, Missouri; Prof. Henry S. Graves, Yale Forest School; William Irvine, Wisconsin; ex-Gov. Newton C. Blanchard, Louisiana; Charles L. Pack, New Jersey; Gustav Schwab, National Council of Commerce, New York; Overton W. Price, Forest Service, secretary.

Committee on Lands—Senators Knute Nelson, Minnesota, and Francis E. Warren, Wyoming; Representatives John Sharp Williams, Mississippi; Swagar Sherley, Kentucky; and Herbert Parsons, New York; ex-Gov. George C. Pardee, California; ex-Gov. N. B. Broward, Florida; James J. Hill, Minnesota; Charles McDonald, American Society of Civil Engineers, New York; Murdo MacKenzie, Colorado; Frank C. Goudy, Colorado; George W. Woodruff, Interior Department, secretary.

Committee on Minerals—Representative John Dalzell, Pennsylvania; Senators Joseph M. Dixon, Montana; Frank P. Flint, California, and Lee S. Overman, North Carolina; Representatives Philo Hall, South Dakota, and James L. Slayden, Texas; Andrew Carnegie, New York; Prof. Charles F. Van Hise, Wisconsin; John Mitchell, Illinois; John Hays Hammond, Massachusetts; Dr. Irving Fisher, Yale University; Joseph A. Holmes, Geological Survey, secretary.

Of the work of the Commission Henry Gannett, Geographer of the United States Census Office, writes:

"This National Commission has commenced the task of taking an account of stock of the country's resources in water, land, forests, and minerals, in order, not only to know what we have, but how long, under the probable future rates of consumption, the supplies will last. With this are proceeding also studies of the best means whereby the drain may be lessened without injury to our industries, where waste may be stopped or reduced, and where products may be utilized more fully.

"Some of the matters now under study are: Under the head of water, the amount of rainfall, the amount and character of stream flow, the possibility of improvement of our streams for navigation, under comprehensive plans, the prevention of floods, the present and possible future development of water power, irrigation, etc.; under the head of lands, the status of the Federal land laws, the condition of our soils and their possible improvement to meet the increasing demands of the future, the additional amounts which can be put under cultivation, the condition of our public grazing lands and the steps which may best be taken for their improvement, the extent of our swamp lands and the result of draining them, etc.; under the head of forests, the amount of standing timber remaining to us and the rate at which it is being depleted, the best methods of restricting the cut, preventing destruction by fire and other enemies and of restocking the cut and burned areas, the relations of forests and streams, and many other allied matters; under the head of minerals, the supply in the ground of each ore and mineral and the rate at which these supplies are being exhausted, with studies of the best means of prolonging the supply.

"The supply of game and fish and the rate of their destruction, with the methods in use for their protection and restocking, and many other matters are under study which cannot be recapitulated here.

"These studies are being made by scientists in the various bureaus of the Federal Government, aided by officers of the State Governments and State Conservation Committees. Prominent among the bureaus enlisted in the work are the Census, the Forest Service, the Bureau of Corporations, those of Statistics of the Departments of Agriculture and of Commerce and Labor, those of Plant Industry and of Soils, the office of Experiment Stations, General Land Office, Reclamation Service, and Weather Bureau.

"The work of the National Conservation Commission will consist mainly:

"First—In the collection and digestion of information concerning our resources. So far its work is commercial, or, better, economic geography.

"Second—In the dissemination widely of this information, together with advice and suggestions as to the methods of conservation, and thus to cultivate public sentiment in the practice of economy in our resources.

"Third—In so shaping legislation, both National and State, as most fully to carry out these ends of conservation.

"In order to aid in this work an association of great organizations is being founded, known as the Conservation League of America."

Statistics of Transportation by Water
IN THE UNITED STATES.

United States Census Bulletin 91, issued March 25, 1908, contained a summary of the main features of a census of transportation by water, which covered the year ending December, 31, 1906, prepared by William M. Stenart, Chief Statistician for Manufacturers.

The bulletin includes the statistics for all American vessels or craft of five tons net register or over operated on the coasts and inland waters of the United States, Porto Rico and the Hawaiian Islands, or between the ports of these and other countries. All craft are included except those owned by the Federal Government, those engaged in fishing, and stationary wharfboats and houseboats used largely for residential purpose.

The statistics cover 37,321 active craft with an aggregate gross tonnage of 12,893,429 and 1,762 idle craft with an aggregate gross tonnage of 179,326. In 1889 there were reported 30,485 active craft with an aggregate gross tonnage of 8,359,135 and 1,490 idle craft with an aggregate gross tonnage of 238,639. Of the active craft, the value increased from over $200,000,000 in 1889 to over $500,000,000 in 1906. In the same period the gross income increased from about $162,000,000 to about $295,000,000, or 82 per cent.; the number of employees, from about 114,000 to about 141,000, or 23.8 per cent.; and the wages paid, from about $41,000,000 to about $72,000,000, or 72.7 per cent.

MOST IMPORTANT DIVISION.

By far the largest part of the American shipping, 20,032 vessels with an aggregate tonnage of more than 4,800,000 tons, operates on the Atlantic Coast and Gulf of Mexico. The next greatest number, 9,622 vessels with a tonnage of over 4,400,000, is shown for the Mississippi River and its tributaries. But so many of these vessels reported from the Mississippi River are coal barges and scows, that in spite of the large number and great tonnage the value is only about $23,000,000, and the income only about $17,000,000. The smaller number of vessels on the Great Lakes, 2,990, represented a value of over $130,000,000 and derived an income of over $65,000,000. Shipping on the Pacific Coast showed a great proportionate increase and did business valued at about $49,000,000.

DECREASING USE OF SAILING VESSELS.

The substantial increase in American shipping is due entirely to the increase in steam vessels and in unrigged craft, as the number of sailing vessels decreased over 10 per cent., while their tonnage increased but 1.7 per cent.

Between 1889 and 1906 the number of steam vessels increased from 5,603 to 9,927, or 77.2 per cent.; their tonnage, from 1,710,073 to 4,059,521, or 137.4 per cent.; and their value, from $131,567,427 to $386,772,727, or 194 per cent. This increase, moreover, was general on all waters except the Mississippi River and its tributaries, where the tonnage actually decreased. The greatest absolute increase, except in gross tonnage, is shown for the steam vessels operating on the Atlantic Coast and Gulf of Mexico. In gross tonnage the largest increase—one of 1,319,973 tons—was reported from the Great Lakes, and resulted from the recent construction of large vessels to carry ore and grain.

If the tugs and other towing vessels are regarded as part of the freight equipment, 67.4 per cent. of the steam vessels were engaged as freight and passenger boats. Yachts, although forming a considerable proportion of the number of steam vessels, are of comparatively little commercial importance. Ferryboats, which numbered 536, formed 5.4 per cent. of all steam vessels.

NEARLY ONE MILLION FERRY PASSENGERS DAILY.

During the year 1906, according to the census, ferryboats carried 330,737,639 passengers; over 63 per cent. of whom were carried by the ferries in and around New York harbor. Of the total number, 309,792,584 passengers rode on regular ferryboats and 20,945,055 on municipal ferryboats. While the income of ferryboats is derived largely from carrying these passengers, in some cases, particularly on the Mississippi River and its tributaries, the ferrying of wagons, teams and cattle and the carriage of freight are in excess of the passenger business.

On railroad ferries carrying passenger coaches, it is estimated, 37,455,512 additional persons were carried. These car ferries form connecting links in railway systems and transport for short distances whole trains of cars without disturbing the passengers or the freight.

FREIGHT MORE THAN DOUBLED.

In 1889 nearly 130,000,000 net tons of freight were carried by vessels of the United States; in 1906 over 265,000,000 net tons were so carried, an increase of over 100 per cent. The proportionate increases for freight carried on the Atlantic Coast and Gulf of Mexico and on the Great Lakes were even considerably larger.

On the basis of tonnage moved, coal is the most important item of freight in the water commerce of the United States. The movement, amounting to over 49,000,000 tons, is composed chiefly of shipments of hard coal from railway terminals on the New Jersey coast for consumption in Greater New York, and of soft coal from Atlantic ports further south. Next to coal the greatest tonnage is for iron ore, the transportation of which is concentrated on the Great Lakes. In 1889 shipments of iron ore amounted to about 8,000,000 tons; in 1906, to over 41,000,000 tons, an increase of over 400 per cent. In the Great Lakes region large quantities of grain—8,680,329 tons—were transported by water.

Considerable decreases are shown in the shipments of lumber and of ice. The decrease in the former is due to the exhaustion of the forests near water courses; that in the latter, to the great increase in the use of manufactured ice.

IRON AND STEEL CONSTRUCTION.

One of the striking facts brought out by the report is the rapid increase in use of iron and steel as materials for the construction of vessels. The first census at which the construction of iron and steel and of wooden vessels was given separately was that of 1880. In that year 20.5 per cent. only of the total value of new construction was of iron and steel; in 1890 the proportion was 47.2 per cent.; in 1900, 71.2 per cent.; and in 1906, 81.7 per cent. Or, to state this increase in terms of tonnage instead of value, in 1906 the gross tonnage

STATISTICS OF TRANSPORTATION BY WATER.—*Continued.*

reported for vessels constructed of iron and steel exceeded the gross tonnage reported in 1889 by 2,751,505 tons, an increase of more than 520 per cent. More than half of this increase occurred on the Great Lakes, where the tonnage of wooden vessels actually decreased.

A further separation of the statistics for iron and steel vessels shows the great importance of tonnage for steel as compared with that for iron, wood, or composite materials. In 1906 no less than 62.4 per cent. of the tonnage of the steam vessels was reported for steel vessels.

Because of their comparatively small size, wooden vessels still predominate among the sailing vessels and the unrigged craft.

HORSEPOWER AND CHARACTER OF PROPULSION.

Comparative figures to show the increase in horsepower are wanting, but by assuming that the average horsepower per ton was the same in 1880 as in 1906, namely, 85 one-hundredths of a horsepower, the actual increase is found to be nearly 2,000,000 horsepower. Of the total horsepower reported in 1906, 97.9 per cent. was steam and 2.1 per cent. gasoline; the 88 horsepower reported as electric is in the shape of storage batteries on seven small yachts.

With the increased size of vessels has come the more general use of the screw propeller. Introduced into the United States in 1841, the screw propeller in 1906 was the means of propulsion of 80.1 per cent. of all vessels and of 85.5 per cent. of the entire gross tonnage. Stern wheels were in use on the next largest number of vessels, 70.4 per cent. of which were in the Mississippi River district; the side wheel type still predominates among ferryboats.

INCREASED USE OF CANALS.

In 1880 the amount of freight passing through the canals and canalized rivers of the United States was, in round numbers, 21,000,000 tons; in 1889, 49,000,000 tons; and in 1906, 122,000,000 tons, an increase of over 480 per cent. between 1880 and 1906. This increase has resulted wholly from the increased use of Government canals, which are ship canals and canalized rivers; the use of canals under State and corporation control, largely of the smaller type, has steadily decreased. In 1880 only 24.1 per cent. of the canal traffic was on ship canals; in 1889 the percentage was 79.9; and in 1906, 96.5.

In striking contrast to this great increase in the canal freight movement is the comparatively mall increase in the length of the canals and canalized rivers. The total mileage of canals constructed and of rivers improved by canalization between 1880 and 1906 was 1,296.53 miles. In the same period, however, 887.71 miles were abandoned, so that the increase in the mileage in use was only 408.82 miles. The whole increase comes practically in the canalized rivers; in canals operated under State or corporation ownership the old canals abandoned exceed the new constructed by somewhat over 700 miles.

BUSIEST CANAL IN THE WORLD.

The busiest canal in the world is the St. Mary's Falls canal connecting Lake Superior with Lake Huron. In 1906 the net tonnage of vessels passing through this canal was three times as great as that through the Suez canal and more than seven times as great as that through the Kaiser Wilhelm, or Kiel, canal. This is the more noteworthy since the St. Mary's Falls canal, on account of the severity of the cold, is open to traffic for only about eight months in the year, while the others are open twelve. The increased use of the St. Mary's Falls canal has been tremendous. In 1880 only 1,244,279 tons went through; in 1889, 7,516,022 tons; and in 1906, 41,276,862 tons, an amount 3,217.3 per cent. greater than in 1880 and 449.2 per cent. greater than in 1889.

YACHTS.

The total number of yachts reported in 1906 was 3,770, of which 2,176 were steam yachts with a gross tonnage of 82,275 and valued at $24,281,861, and 1,594 were sail yachts with a gross tonnage of 24,155 and valued at $4,169,253.

While yachts are, as a rule, of small tonnage, the average for the 3,770 included in the census for 1906 was slightly more than 28 gross tons per vessel; for the steam craft it was 38 tons; and for the sail, 15 tons. The average value per vessel was $7,547; for steam, $11,159, and for sail, $2,616. The steam yachts include the gasoline and electric launches and represent 57.7 per cent. of the total number of vessels included in this class. Yachts propelled by machinery are the only kind reported for the Mississippi River and its tributaries, and they also predominate on all the other waters except the Pacific Coast, where there was a larger number of sail craft.

Of the total number of yachts, 3,439, or 91.2 per cent., were owned by individuals; 243, or 6.5 per cent., by firms; 64, or 1.7 per cent., by corporations; and 21, or six-tenths of 1 per cent. by miscellaneous forms of organizations.

FISHING CRAFT.

Vessels employed in the fishing industry are not included in the census of water transportation. They should nevertheless receive consideration as forming an important element of American shipping. The total number of fishing vessels in the United States, according to statistics collected by the Bureau of Fisheries of the Department of Commerce and Labor, was 4,915, with a net tonnage of 97,367 and valued at $8,975,626. The number of "transportation vessels" was 1,995, with net tonnage of 98,765 and valued at $5,077,926. The number of persons employed was 42,319, and were those employed on fishing vessels and in transporting the catch to market and the supplies to the fishing grounds. In addition, 110,484 persons were employed in shore and boat fisheries and 66,756 on shore in canneries and in various other capacities.

The 6,910 vessels reported as fishing and transporting do not include the small boats and launches employed in the industry; these numbered 82,443 and were valued at $5,656,721.

The "outfit" for which the cost or value is shown for both classes of vessels consists of all supplies necessary in the industry except fishing apparatus, including fuel, provisions, preservatives, dories, etc. The value of the fishing apparatus, which includes seines, nets, lobster pots, dredges, etc., amounted to $8,551,808 for all fisheries in the United States.

Progress of the United States

IN AREA, POPULATION AND MATERIAL INDUSTRIES.

(Compiled from a statement prepared by O. P. Austin, Chief of the Bureau of Statistics, Department of Commerce and Labor.)

	1800.	1850.	1880.	1900.	1908.
Area *a*..........square miles.	827,844	2,980,959	3,026,789	3,026,789	3,026,789
Population *b*..........no.	5,308,483	23,191,876	50,155,783	76,303,387	87,189,392
Population per square mile *b*.... no.	6.41	7.78	16.57	25.14	28.71
Wealth *b c*..........dols.	....	7,135,780,000	42,642,000,000	88,517,306,775	*d* 107,104,211,917
Wealth, per capita *b c*..........dols.	....	307.69	850.20	1,164.79	*d* 1,310.11
Public debt, less cash in Treasury *e*..........dols.	82,976,294	63,452,774	1,919,326,748	1,107,711,258	938,132,409
Public debt, per capita..........dols.	15.63	2.74	38.27	14.52	10.76
Interest bearing debt *f*..........dols.	82,976,294	63,452,774	1,723,993,100	1,023,478,860	897,503,990
Annual interest charge..........dols.	3,402,601	3,782,393	79,633,981	33,545,130	21,101,197
Interest per capita..........dols.	0.64	0.16	1.59	0.44	0.24
Gold coined..........dols.	317,760	31,981,739	62,308,279	99,272,943	*y* 131,907,490
Silver coined..........dols.	224,296	1,866,100	27,411,694	36,345,321	*y* 13,178,436
Gold in circulation *g h*..........dols.	} 16,000,000	147,395,456	{ 225,695,779	610,806,472	*y* 614,553,628
Silver in circulation *g h*..........dols.			68,622,345	142,050,334	199,267,923
Gold certificates in circulation, dols.	....	....	7,963,900	200,733,019	788,464,309
Silver certificates in circulat'n, dols.	....	....	5,789,569	408,465,574	465,581,977
United States notes outstanding..........dols.	....	....	327,895,457	313,971,545	340,189,838
National bank notes outstanding..........dols.	...	...	337,415,178	300,115,112	632,431,530
Miscellaneous currency in circulation *i*..........dols.	10,500,000	131,366,526	....	79,008,942	4,968,084
Total circulation of money..........dols.	26,500,000	278,761,982	973,382,228	2,055,150,998	3,045,457,289
Per capita..........dols.	5.00	12.02	19.41	26.94	*k* 34.81
National banks..........no.	....	....	2,076	3,732	6,824
Capital..........dols.	....	....	455,909,565	621,536,461	919,100,850
Bank clearings, New York..........dols.	....	....	37,182,128,621	51,964,588,564	*y* 95,315,421,238
Total United States..........dols.	....	....	....	84,582,450,081	*y* 154,662,515,258
Deposits in National banks..........dols.	....	....	833,701,034	2,458,092,758	4,374,551,208
Deposits in savings banks..........dols.	....	43,431,130	819,106,973	2,389,719,954	*y* 3,495,410,087
Depositors in savings banks..........no.	....	251,354	2,335,582	6,107,083	*y* 8,588,811
Farms and farm property *b*..........dols.	....	3,967,343,580	12,180,501,538	20,514,001,838	....
Farm products, value *b*..........dols.	....	....	2,212,540,927	3,764,177,706	....
Manufacturing establishments *b*..........no.	....	123,025	253,852	512,339	*j k* 216,262
Value of products *b*..........dols.	....	1,019,106,616	5,369,579,191	13,014,287,498	*j k* 11,802,147,087
United States Government receipts—net ordinary *l*..........dols.	10,848,749	43,592,889	333,526,501	567,240,852	599,895,763
Customs..........dols.	9,080,933	39,668,686	186,522,065	233,164,871	285,680,653
Internal revenue..........dols.	809,397	....	124,009,374	295,327,927	250,711,008
United States Government expenditures, net ordinary *m*..........dols.	7,411,370	37,165,990	169,090,062	447,553,458	659,552,125
War..........dols.	2,560,879	9,687,025	38,116,916	134,774,768	110,284,864
Navy..........dols.	3,448,716	7,904,725	13,536,985	55,953,078	118,726,347
Pensions..........dols.	64,131	1,866,886	56,777,174	140,877,316	153,887,995
Interest on public debt..........dols.	3,402,601	3,782,393	95,757,575	40,160,333	21,424,990
Imports of merchandise..........dols.	91,252,768	173,509,526	667,954,746	849,941,184	1,194,341,792
Per capita..........dols.	17.19	7.48	12.51	10.88	13.70
Exports of merchandise..........dols.	70,971,780	144,375,726	835,638,658	1,394,483,082	1,860,773,346
Per capita..........dols.	13.37	6.23	16.43	17.96	21.04
Imports, silk, raw..........lbs.	....	....	2,562,236	13,073,718	16,662,132
Rubber, crude..........lbs.	....	....	16,826,099	49,377,138	62,233,160
Tin plates..........lbs.	....	....	379,902,880	147,963,804	140,739,972
Iron, steel and manufacturers of..........dols.	....	20,145,067	71,266,699	20,478,728	27,607,909
Domestic exports, iron, steel, and manufacturers of..........dols.	52,144	1,953,702	14,716,524	121,913,548	183,982,182
Manufactures..........dols.	....	23,223,106	121,818,298	484,846,235	750,679,881
Farm animals, value..........dols.	....	544,180,516	1,576,917,556	2,228,123,134	4,331,230,000
Cattle..........no.	....	17,778,907	33,258,000	43,902,414	71,267,000
Horses..........no.	....	4,336,719	11,201,800	13,537,524	19,992,000
Sheep..........no.	....	21,773,220	40,765,900	41,883,065	54,631,000
Mules..........no.	....	559,331	1,729,500	2,086,027	3,869,000
Swine..........no.	....	30,354,213	34,034,100	37,079,356	56,084,000
Production of gold..........dols.	....	50,000,000	36,000,000	79,171,000	*y z* 89,620,399
Silver, commercial value..........dols.	....	50,900	34,717,000	35,741,100	*y z* 37,571,580
Coal..........tons	....	6,266,233	63,822,830	240,789,310	428,973,251
Petroleum..........galls.	....	....	1,104,017,166	2,672,062,218	*y z* 6,976,004,070
Pig iron..........tons	....	563,755	3,835,191	13,789,242	25,781,361
Steel..........tons	....	....	1,247,335	10,188,329	*y z* 23,360,000
Tin plates..........lbs.	....	......	....	677,969,600	*p* 1,293,738,880
Copper..........tons	....	650	27,000	270,588	387,945
Wool..........lbs.	....	52,516,959	232,500,000	288,636,621	298,294,750
Wheat..........bush.	......	100,485,944	498,549,868	522,229,505	634,087,000
Corn..........bush.	....	592,071,104	1,717,434,543	2,105,102,516	2,592,320,000

PROGRESS OF THE UNITED STATES—*Continued.*

	1800.	1850.	1880.	1900.	1908.
Cotton .... bales	155,556	2,333,718	5,761,252	9,436,416	*y* 13,510,982
Cane sugar... .... tons	....	110,526	92,802	149,191	*y* 221,[illegible]19
Sugar consumed .... tons	....	239,409	956,784	2,219,847	*y* 2,993,[illegible]
Cotton taken by mills .... bales	....	595,000	1,795,000	3,644,000	*y* 5,005,600
Domestic cotton exported .... lbs.	....	635,381,604	1,822,061,114	3,100,583,188	3,816,998,[illegible]
Railways operated .... miles	....	9,021	93,267	194,262	*p* 22[illegible],635
Passengers carried .... no.	....	....	....	584,695,935	*p* 815,774,118
Freight carried 1 mile .... tons.	....	....	....	141,162,109,413	*p* 216 653,795,696
Rates, ton per mile .... cents	....	....	....	0.75	*p* 0.77
Passenger cars .... no.	....	....	12 788	26,786	*p* 33,896
Freight and other cars .... no.	....	....	554,185	1,358,467	*p* 1,991,962
American vessels built .... tons.	106,261	279,255	157,409	293,790	*y* 471,332
Trading domestic, etc .... tons.	301,919	1,949,743	2,715,224	4,338,145	*y* 6,067,648
Trading foreign .... tons.	669,921	1,585,711	1,352,810	826,694	*y* 871,146
On Great Lakes .... tons.	....	198,266	605,102	1,565,587	*y* 2,439,741
Vessels passing through Sault Ste. Marie Canal .... tons	....	....	1,734,890	22,315,834	*y* 44,087 974
Commercial failures .... no.	....	....	4,735	10,774	*y* 11,725
Amount of liabilities .... dols.	....	....	65,752,000	138 495,673	*y* 197,385,225
Post-Offices .... no.	903	18,417	42,989	76,688	*y* 62,663
Receipts of P. O. Department.. dols.	280,804	5,499,985	33,315,479	102,354,579	*y* 183,585,006
Telegrams sent *w* .... no.	....	....	29,215,509	79,696,227	*x y* 98,480,097
Newspapers, etc.* .... no.	....	2,526	9,723	20,806	*y* 21,735
Public schools, salaries .... dols.	....	....	55,942 972	137,687,746	*p* 186,483,464
Patents issued .... no.	....	993	13,947	26,499	*y* 36,620
Immigrants arrived † .... no.	....	369,980	457,257	448,572	782 870

a Exclusive of Alaska and islands belonging to the United States. *b* Census figures; those for intermediate years estimated. *c* True valuation of real and personal property. *d* 1904. *e* Total debt prior to 1855. *f* Figures for the years 1800 and 1850 include the total public debt. *g* Gold and silver cannot be stated separately prior to 1880. From 1862 to 1875, inclusive, gold and silver were not in circulation except on the Pacific Coast, where it is estimated that the average specie circulation was about $25.000.000, and this estimate is continued for the three following years under the head of gold. After that period gold was available for circulation. *h* Total specie in circulation; gold and silver not separately stated prior to 1880. *i* Includes notes of Bank of United States, State bank notes, demand notes of 1862 and 1863, fractional currency, 1863 to 1878, treasury notes of 1890, 1891 to date; and currency certificates, act of June, 8, 1872, 1892 to 1900. *j* 1905. *k* Exclusive of neighborhood industries and hand trades, included in previous years. *l* "Net ordinary receipts" include receipts from customs, internal revenue, direct tax, public lands, and "miscellaneous." *m* "Net ordinary expenses" include expenditures for war, navy, Indians, pensions, and "miscellaneous." *n* Imports for consumption after 1850. *o* Domestic exports only after 1850. *p* 1906. *pr* Estimate of the Director of the Mint. *w* Western Union to 1880; includes Postal Telegraph after 1880. *x* Not including messages sent by Western Union over leased wires or under railroad contracts. *y* 1907. *z* Preliminary figures. * After 1850, from Rowell's Newspaper Directory † 1850, includes aliens not immigrants; fifteen months ending December 31; after 1850, fiscal years.

The Capitol at Washington.

THE Capitol is situated in latitude 38° 53′ 20″.4 north and longitude 77° 00′ 35″.7 west from Greenwich. It fronts east, and stands on a plateau eighty-eight feet above the level of the Potomac.

The entire length of the building from north to south is seven hundred and fifty-one feet four inches, and its greatest dimension from east to west three hundred and fifty feet. The area covered by the building is 153,112 square feet.

The dome of the original central building was constructed of wood, covered with copper. This was replaced in 1856 by the present structure of cast iron It was completed in 1865. The entire weight of iron used is 8,909,200 pounds.

The dome is crowned by a bronze statue of Freedom, which is nineteen feet, six inches high and weighs 14,985 pounds. It was modelled by Crawford. The height of the dome above the base line of the east front is two hundred and eighty-seven feet five inches. The height from the top of the balustrade of the building is two hundred and seventeen feet eleven inches. The greatest diameter at the base is one hundred and thirty-five feet five inches.

The rotunda is ninety-seven feet six inches in diameter, and its height from the floor to the top of the canopy is one hundred and eighty feet three inches.

The Senate Chamber is one hundred and thirteen feet three inches in length, by eighty feet three inches in width, and thirty-six feet in height. The galleries will accommodate one thousand persons.

The Representatives' Hall is one hundred and thirty-nine feet in length, by ninety-three feet in width, and thirty-six feet in height.

The southeast corner-stone of the original building was laid September 18, 1793, by President Washington with Masonic ceremonies. The corner-stone of the extensions was laid July 4, 1851, by President Fillmore.

The room now occupied by the Supreme Court was, until 1859, occupied as the Senate Chamber. Previous to that time the court occupied the room immediately beneath, now used as a law library.

Interstate Commerce Law.

THE following is a synopsis of the provisions of the Interstate Commerce law and acts amendatory thereof, prepared for the Official Congressional Directory:

Under "An Act to Regulate Commerce," approved February 4, 1887; as amended March 2, 1889; February 10, 1891; February 8, 1895; the "Elkins act" of February 19, 1903, and the amending act approved June 29, 1906, the Interstate Commerce Commission is composed of seven members, each receiving a salary of $10,000 per annum. The regulating statutes apply to all common carriers engaged in the transportation of oil or other commodity, except water and except natural or artificial gas, by means of pipe lines, or partly by pipe line and partly by rail, or partly by pipe line and partly by water, and to common carriers engaged in the transportation of passengers or property wholly by railroad (or partly by railroad and partly by water when both are used under a common control, management, or arrangement for a continuous carriage or shipment). The statutes apply generally to interstate traffic, including import and domestic traffic, and also that which is carried wholly within any territory of the United States. Only traffic transported wholly within a single State is excepted.

The Commission has jurisdiction on complaint, and, after full hearing, to determine and prescribe reasonable rates, regulations, and practices, and order reparation to injured shippers; to require any carriers to cease and desist from unjust discrimination, or undue or unreasonable preference, and to institute and carry on proceedings for enforcement of the law. The Commission may also inquire into the management of the business of all common carriers subject to the provisions of the regulating statutes, and it may prescribe the accounts, records, and memoranda which shall be kept by the carriers, and from time to time inspect the same. The carriers must file annual reports with the Commission, and such other reports as may from time to time be required. Various other powers are conferred upon the Commission. Carriers failing to file and publish all rates and charges, as required by law, are prohibited from engaging in interstate transportation, and penalties are provided in the statute for failure on the part of carriers or of shippers to observe the rates specified in the published tariffs.

The Commission also appoints a Secretary and clerks, whose duties are not specifically defined by the act.

The act of February 11, 1903, provides that suits in equity brought under the act to regulate commerce, wherein the United States is complainant, may be expedited and given precedence over other suits, and that appeals from the Circuit Court lie only to the Supreme Court. The act of February 19, 1903, commonly called the Elkins law, penalizes the offering, soliciting, or receiving of rebates, allows proceedings in the courts by injunction to restrain departures from published rates, and makes the Expediting act of February 11, 1903, include cases prosecuted under the direction of the Attorney-General in the name of the Commission.

Under the act of August 7, 1888, all railroad and telegraph companies to which the United States have granted any subsidy in lands or bonds or loan of credit for the construction of either railroad or telegraph lines are required to file annual reports with the Commission and such other reports as the Commission may call for. The act also directs every such company to file with the Commission copies of all contracts and agreements of every description existing between it and every other person or corporation whatsoever in reference to the ownership, possession, or operation of any telegraph lines over or upon the right of way, and to decide questions relating to the interchange of business between such government-aided telegraph company and any connecting telegraph company. The act provides penalties for failure to perform and carry out within a reasonable time the order or orders of the Commission.

The act of March 2, 1893, known as the "Safety Appliance act," provides that within specified periods railroad cars used in interstate commerce must be equipped with automatic couplers and standard height of drawbars for freight cars, and have grab irons or hand holds in the ends and sides of each car. A further provision is that locomotive engines used in moving interstate traffic shall be fitted with a power driving-wheel brake and appliances for operating the train-brake system, and a sufficient number of cars in the train shall be equipped with power or train brakes The act directs the Commission to lodge with the proper District-Attorneys information of such violations as may come to its knowledge. The Commission is authorized to, from time to time, upon full hearing and for good cause, extend the period within which any common carrier shall comply with the provisions of the statute. The act of March 2, 1903, amended this act so as to make its provisions apply to Territories and the District of Columbia to all cases when couplers of whatever design are brought together, and to all locomotives, cars, and other equipment of any railroad engaged in interstate traffic, except logging cars and cars used upon street railways, and also to power or train brakes used in railway operation.

The act of June 1, 1898, concerning carriers engaged in interstate commerce and their employés, known as the "Arbitration Act," directs the Chairman of the Interstate Commerce Commission and the Commissioner of Labor to use their best efforts, by mediation and conciliation, to settle controversies between railway companies and their employés. Every agreement of arbitration made under the act must be forwarded to the Chairman of the Interstate Commerce Commission, who shall file the same in the office of that Commission. When the agreement of arbitration is signed by employés individually instead of a labor organization, the act provides, if various specified conditions have been complied with, that the Chairman of the Commission shall, by notice in writing, fix a time and place for the meeting of the Board of Arbitrators. If the two arbitrators chosen by the parties fail to select a third within five days after the first meeting, the third arbitrator shall be named by the Chairman of the Interstate Commerce Commission and the Commissioner of Labor.

The act of March 3, 1901, "requiring common carriers engaged in interstate commerce to make reports of all accidents to the Interstate Commerce Commission," makes it the duty of such carrier to monthly report, under oath, all collisions and derailments of its trains and accidents to its passengers, and to its employés while on duty in its service, and to state the nature and causes thereof. The act prescribes that a fine shall be imposed against any such carrier failing to make the report so required,

Passport Regulations.

RULES governing the granting and issuing of passports in the United States:

1. BY WHOM ISSUED AND REFUSAL TO ISSUE.—No one but the Secretary of State may grant and issue passports in the United States (Revised Statutes, sections 4075, 4078), and he is empowered to refuse them in his discretion.

Passports are not issued by American diplomatic and consular officers abroad, except in cases of emergency; and a citizen who is abroad and desires to procure a passport must apply therefor through the nearest diplomatic or consular officer to the Secretary of State.

Applications for passports by persons in Porto Rico or the Philippines should be made to the Chief Executives of those islands. The evidence required of such applicants is the same as that required of applicants in the United States.

2. FEE.—By act of Congress approved March 23, 1888, a fee of one dollar is required to be collected for every citizen's passport. That amount in currency or postal money order should accompany each application made by a citizen of the United States. Orders should be made payable to the Disbursing Clerk of the Department of State. Drafts or checks will not be accepted.

3. APPLICATIONS.—A person who is entitled to receive a passport, if within the United States, must make a written application, in the form of an affidavit, to the Secretary of State. The application must be made by the person to whom the passport is to be issued and signed by him, as it is not competent for one person to apply for another.

The affidavit must be attested by an officer authorized to administer oaths, and if he has an official seal it must be affixed. If he has no seal, his official character must be authenticated by certificate of the proper legal officer.

If the applicant signs by mark, two attesting witnesses to his signature are required. The applicant is required to state the date and place of his birth, his occupation, the place of his permanent residence, to what country or countries he intends to travel, and within what length of time he will return to the United States with the purpose of residing and performing the duties of citizenship.

The applicant must take the oath of allegiance to the Government of the United States.

The application must be accompanied by a description of the person applying, and should state the following particulars, viz.: Age, —— years; stature, —— feet —— inches (English measure); forehead, ——; eyes, ——; nose, ——; mouth, ——; chin, ——; hair, ——; complexion, ——; face, ——.

The application must be accompanied by a certificate from at least one credible witness that the applicant is the person he represents himself to be, and that the facts stated in the affidavit are true to the best of the witness's knowledge and belief.

4. NATIVE CITIZENS.—An application containing the information indicated by rule 3 will be sufficient evidence in the case of native citizens. A person of the Chinese race, alleging birth in the United States, must accompany his application with supporting affidavits from at least two credible witnesses, preferably not of the Chinese race, having personal knowledge of the applicant's birth in the United States. The application and supporting affidavits should be in duplicate, and should be accompanied by three photographs of the applicant, and should state at what port he intends to re-enter the United States.

5. A PERSON BORN ABROAD WHOSE FATHER WAS A NATIVE CITIZEN OF THE UNITED STATES.—In addition to the statements required by rule 3, his application must show that his father was born in the United States, has resided therein, and was a citizen at the time of the applicant's birth. The Department may require that this affidavit be supported by that of one other citizen acquainted with the facts.

6. NATURALIZED CITIZENS.—In addition to the statements required by rule 3, a naturalized citizen must transmit his certificate of naturalization, or a duly certified copy of the court record thereof, with his application. It will be returned to him after inspection. He must state in his affidavit when and from what port he emigrated to this country, what ship he sailed in, where he has lived since his arrival in the United States, when and before what court he was naturalized, and that he is the identical person described in the certificate of naturalization. The signature to the application should conform in orthography to the applicant's name as written in his certificate of naturalization, or an explanation of the difference should be submitted.

7. WOMAN'S APPLICATION.—If she is unmarried, in addition to the statements required by rule 3, she should state that she has never been married. If she is the wife or widow of a native citizen of the United States the fact should be made to appear in her application. If she is the wife or widow of a naturalized citizen, in addition to the statements required by rule 3, she must transmit for inspection her husband's certificate of naturalization, must state that she is the wife (or widow) of the person described therein, and must set forth the facts of his emigration, naturalization, and residence, as required in the rule governing the application of a naturalized citizen. A married woman citizenship follows that of her husband so far as her international status is concerned. It is essential, therefore, that a woman's marital relations be indicated in her application for a passport, and that in the case of a married woman her husband's citizenship be established.

8. THE CHILD OF A NATURALIZED CITIZEN CLAIMING CITIZENSHIP THROUGH THE NATURALIZATION OF THE PARENT.—In addition to the statements required by rule 3, the applicant must state that he or she is the son or daughter, as the case may be, of the person described in the certificate of naturalization, which must be submitted for inspection, and must set forth the facts of emigration naturalization, and residence, as required in the rule governing the application of a naturalized citizen.

9. A RESIDENT OF AN INSULAR POSSESSION OF THE UNITED STATES WHO OWES ALLEGIANCE TO THE UNITED STATES.—In addition to the statements required by rule 3, he must state that he owes allegiance to the United States and that he does not acknowledge allegiance to any other government; and must submit affidavits from at least two credible witnesses having good means of knowledge in substantiation of his statements of birth, residence, and loyalty.

10. EXPIRATION OF PASSPORT.—A passport expires two years from the date of its issuance. A new one will be issued upon a new application, and if the applicant be a naturalized citizen, the old passport will be accepted in lieu of a certificate of naturalization, if the application upon which it was issued is found to contain sufficient information as to the naturalization of the applicant.

11. WIFE, MINOR CHILDREN, AND SERVANTS.—When the applicant is accompanied by his wife, minor children, or servant who would be entitled to receive a passport, it will be sufficient to state the fact, giving the respective ages of the children and the allegiance of the servant, when one passport will suffice for all. For any other person in the party a separate passport will be required. A woman's passport may include her minor children and servant under the above-named conditions. The term servant does not include a governess, tutor, pupil, companion, or person holding like relations to the applicant for a passport.

12. TITLES.—Professional and other titles will not be inserted in passports.

13. BLANK FORMS OF APPLICATION.—They will be furnished by the Department to persons who desire to apply for passports, but are not furnished, except as samples, to those who make a business of procuring passports.

14. ADDRESS.—Communications should be addressed to the Department of State, Bureau of Citizenship, and each communication should give the post-office address of the person to whom the answer is to be directed.

Section 4075 of the Revised Statutes of the United States, as amended by the act of Congress, approved June 14, 1902, providing that "the Secretary of State may grant and issue passports, and cause passports to be granted, issued, and verified in foreign countries by such diplomatic or consular officers of the United States, and by such chief or other executive officer of the insular possessions of the United States, and under such rules as the President shall designate and prescribe for and on behalf of the United States," the foregoing rules are hereby prescribed for the granting and issuing of passports in the United States.

The Secretary of State is authorized to make regulations on the subject of issuing and granting passports additional to these rules and not inconsistent with them.

THEODORE ROOSEVELT.

THE WHITE HOUSE, June 13, 1907.

United States Customs Duties.

A TABLE OF LEADING ARTICLES IMPORTED, GIVING RATE AT ENTRY BY THE TARIFF ACT OF 1897.

N. e. s. indicates "when not elsewhere specified." Tables showing comparison with the Rates by the Tariff of 1883 and the McKinley Tariff of 1890 were printed in THE WORLD ALMANAC for 1895, and the Wilson Tariff of 1894 and the Dingley Tariff of 1897 in the edition of 1898.

Articles.	Tariff Rate.
Alcohol, amylic, or fusel oil	¼c. ⅌ ℔.
Animals for breeding purposes	Free.
Barley, bushel of 48 ℔s.	30c. per bushel.
Beads	35 p. c. ad val.
Beef, mutton, and pork	2c. ⅌ ℔.
Beer, ale, not in bottles	20c. ⅌ gal.
Beer, porter, and ale, in bottles	40c. "
Bindings, cotton	45 p. c. ad val.
Bindings, flax	45 "
Bindings, wool	50c. ⅌ ℔. and 60 p.c. ad val.
Blankets	22c. ⅌ ℔. and 30 p.c. ad val.
Blankets, value 40c. to 50c.	33c. ⅌ ℔. and 35 p.c. ad val. (*a*)
Bonnets, silk	60 p. c. ad val.
Books, charts, maps	25 "
Books, over 20 years old, for public libraries	Free.
Bronze, manufactures of	45 p. c. ad val.
Brushes	40 "
Butter, and substitutes for	6c. ⅌ ℔.
Buttons, sleeve and collar, gilt	50 p. c. ad val.
Canvas for sails	45 "
Caps, fur and leather	35 "
Carpets, treble ingrain	22c. ⅌ sq. yd. & 40 p.c. ad val.
Carpets, two-ply	18c. ⅌ sq. yd. & 40 p.c. ad val.
Carpets, tapestry Brussels	28c. ⅌ sq. yd. & 40 p.c. ad val.
Carpets, Wilton, Axminster, velvet	60c. ⅌ sq. yd. & 40 p.c. ad val.
Cattle (over one year old)	27½ p.c. ad val.
Cheese, all kinds	6c. ⅌ ℔.
Cigars and cigarettes	$4.50 ⅌ ℔. and 25 p.c. ad val.
Clocks, n. e. s.	40 p. c. ad val.
Clothing, ready-made, cotton, n.e.s.	50 "
Clothing, ready-made, linen, silk, and woollen	60 " (*k*)
Coal, anthracite	Free.
Coal, bituminous	67c. ⅌ ton.
Coffee	Free.
Confectionery, all sugar	50 p. c. ad val. (if more than 15c. ⅌ ℔.).
Copper, manufactures of	45 p. c. ad val.
Cotton gloves	50 "
Cotton handkerchiefs, hemmed	45 "
Cotton handkerchiefs, hemstitched	55 "
Cotton hosiery	50c. to $2 ⅌ doz. pairs and 15 p. c. ad val.
Cotton shirts and drawers	60c. to $2.25 ⅌ doz. & 15 p. c. to 50 p. c. ad val.
Cotton plushes, unbleached	9c. ⅌ sq. yd & 25 p.c. ad val.
Cotton webbing	45 p. c. ad val.
Cotton curtains	50 "
Cutlery, more than $3 per doz.	20c. ⅌ piece & 40 p.c. ad val.
Cutlery, razors, over $3 per doz.	$1.75 ⅌ doz. & 20 p.c. ad val.
Cutlery, table knives	16c. each and 15 p.c. ad val.
Cutlery, table knives, over $4 ⅌ doz.	45 p. c. ad val.
Diamonds (uncut, free), cut and set	60 "
Diamonds, cut, but not set	10 "
Drugs (crude, free), not crude	¼c. ⅌ ℔. and 10 p.c. ad val.
Dyewoods, crude	Free.
Dyewoods, extracts of	⅞c. ⅌ ℔.
Earthenware, common	25 p. c. ad val.
Earthenware, porcelain, plain	55 "
Earthenware, porcelain, etc., decorated	60 p. c. ad val.
Eggs	5c. ⅌ doz.
Engravings	25 p. c. ad val.
Extracts, meat	35c. ⅌ ℔.
Fertilizers, guanos, manures	Free.
Firearms	(*b*)
Fish, American fisheries	Free.
Fish, smoked, dried	¾c. ⅌ ℔.
Flannels	22c. ⅌ ℔. and 30 p.c. ad val.
Flannels, value 40c. to 50c.	33c. ⅌ ℔. and 35 p.c. ad val.
Flax, manufactures of, n. e. s.	45 p. c. ad val.
Flowers, artificial	50 "
Fruits, preserved in their own juice.	1c. ⅌ ℔. and 35 p. c. ad val.
Fruits, apples	25c. ⅌ bu.
Fruits, oranges, lemons, n. e. s.	1c. ⅌ ℔.
Fur, manufactures of	35 p. c. ad val.
Furniture, wood	35 "
Glassware, plain and cut	60 "
Glass, polished plate, not over 16x24.	8c. ⅌ sq. foot.
Glass, silvered, not over 16x24	11c. "
Glass bottles, over 1 pint	1c. ⅌ ℔.
Gloves, men's, ladies', children's	*
Glucose	1½c. ⅌ ℔.
Glue, value not over 7c. per lb.	2½c. ⅌ ℔ (*g*).
Gold, manufactures of, not jewelry.	45 p. c. ad val.
Hair of hogs, curled for mattresses.	10 "
Hair manufactures, n. e. s.	35 "
Hair, human, unmanufactured	20 p. c; not drawn, free.
Hams and bacon	5c. ⅌ ℔.
Hay	$4 ⅌ ton.
Hemp cordage	2c. ⅌ ℔.
Hides, raw, dried, salted, pickled	15 p. c. ad val.
Honey	20c. ⅌ gal.
Hoops, iron or steel, baling	5-10c. ⅌ ℔.
Hops	12c. ⅌ ℔.
Horn, manufactures of	30 p. c. ad val.
Horses, mules	$30 ⅌ head (*h*).
India-rubber, manufactures of	30 p. c. ad val.
India-rubber, vulcanized	35 "
Instruments, metal	45 "
Iron, manufactures of, n. e. s.	45 "
Iron screws, ⅛ inch or less in length	12c. ⅌ ℔.
Iron, tinned plates	1½c. ⅌ ℔.
Ivory, manufactures of, n. e. s.	35 p. c. ad val.
Jewelry	60 "
Knit goods, wool, value not over 30c. ⅌ ℔.	44c. ⅌ ℔. and 50 p.c. ad val.
Knit goods, woollen apparel, 30 to 40c. ⅌ ℔.	44c. ⅌ ℔. and 50 p.c. ad val.
Knit goods, woollen apparel, over 40c. ⅌ ℔.	44c. " (*c*)
Knit goods, silk	60 p. c. ad val.
Lard	2c. ⅌ ℔.
Lead, pigs, bars	2⅛c. "
Lead, type metal	1½c. "
Leather manufactures, n. e. s.	35 p. c. ad val.
Linen manufactures, n. e. s.	45 "
Linen, wearing apparel	60 "
Macaroni	1½c. ⅌ ℔.
Malt, barley	45c. ⅌ bu.
Matches, friction, boxed	8c. ⅌ gross.
Matting, cocoa and rattan	6c. ⅌ sq. yard.
Meerschaum pipes	60 p. c. ad val.
Molasses, n. e. s.	40° to 56°, 3c. ⅌ gal. (*i*).
Muffs, fur	35 p. c. ad val.
Musical instruments	45 "
Nails, cut	6-10c. ⅌ ℔.
Nails, horseshoe	2¼c. "
Newspapers, periodicals	Free.

UNITED STATES CUSTOMS DUTIES—*Continued.*

ARTICLES.	Tariff Rate.	ARTICLES.	Tariff Rate.
Oilcloth, value over 25c.	8 to 20c. ⅌ sq. yd. (*j*).	Soap, castile	1¼c. ⅌ ℔.
Oil, olive	50c. ⅌ gal., in bottles, etc.	Soap, toilet, perfumed	15c. ⅌ ℔.
Oil, olive, n. e. s.	40c. ⅌ gal.	Spirits, except bay rum	$2.25 prf. gal.
Oil, whale and seal, foreign, n. e. s.	8c. ⅌ gal.	Straw manufactures, n. e. s.	30 p. c. ad val.
Onions	40c. ⅌ bu.	Sugars, not above 16 Dutch standard	95-100c. ⅌ ℔ (*m*)
Opium, liquid preparations	40 p. c. ad val.	Sugars, above 16 Dutch standard	1 95-100c. "
Opium, crude and unadulterated	$1 ⅌ ℔.	Tea	Free.
Paintings and marble statuary	20 p. c. ad val.	Tin, ore or metal	"
Paper manufactures, n. e. s.	35 "	Tin plates	1½c. ⅌ ℔.
Paper stock, crude	Free.	Tobacco, cigar wrappers, not stemmed	$1.85 "
Pepper, cayenne, unground	2½c. ⅌ ℔.	Tobacco, if stemmed	$2.50 "
Perfumery, alcoholic	60c. ⅌ ℔. and 45 p. c. ad val.	Tobacco, all other leaf, stemmed	50c. "
Photograph albums	35 p. c. ad val.	Tobacco, unmanufactured, not stemmed	35c. "
Photograph slides	25 "	Umbrellas, silk or alpaca	50 p. c. ad val.
Pickles	40 "	Vegetables, natural, n. e. s	25 "
Pins, metallic	35 "	Vegetables, prepared or preserved	40 "
Pipes of clay, common, 40c. ⅌ gross.	15c. ⅌ gross.	Velvets, silk, 75 p. c. or more silk	$1.50 ⅌ ℔. and 15 p.c. ad val.
Poultry, dressed	5c. ⅌ ℔.	Watches and parts of	40 p. c. ad val.
Potatoes	25c. ⅌ bu.	Wheat, bushel of 60 ℔	25c. ⅌ bu.
Pulp wood, for paper-makers	1-12c. ⅌ ℔., mechanically ground (*l*).	Willow for basket-makers	20 p. c. ad val.
Quicksilver	7c. ⅌ ℔.	Willow manufactures, n. e. s.	40 "
Quinine, sulphate, and salts	Free.	Wines, champagne, in ½-pt. bottles or less	$2 ⅌ doz.
Railroad ties, cedar	20 p. c. ad val.	Wines, champagne, in bottles, ½ pt. to 1 pt	$4 "
Rugs, Oriental	10c. ⅌ sq. f. & 40 p.c. ad val.	Wines, champagne, in bottles, 1 pt. to 1 qt	$8 "
Salmon, dried or smoked	¾c. ⅌ ℔.	Wines, still, in casks containing more than 14 p. c. absolute alcohol	50c. ⅌ gal.
Salt	12c. ⅌ 100 ℔., packages; 8c. ⅌ 100 ℔., bulk.	Woods, cabinet, sawed	$1 to $2 ⅌ M ft.
Sauces, n. e. s.	40 p. c. ad val.	Wool, first class	11c. ⅌ ℔.
Sausages, bologna	Free.	Wool, second class	12c. "
Sausages, all other	25 p. c. ad val.	Wool, third class, n. e. s., above 13c. ⅌ ℔	7c. ⅌ ℔. (*e*).
Sealskin sacques	35 "	Wool or worsted yarns, value not over 30c. ⅌ ℔.	27½c. ⅌ ℔. & 40 p.c. ad val.
Silk, raw	Free.	Wool or worsted yarns, value 30c. to 40c. ⅌ ℔.	38½c. ⅌ ℔. & 40 p.c. ad val. (*f*).
Silk, spun in skeins	35 p.c. ad val. (*d*	Wool or worsted yarns, value over 40c. ⅌ ℔.	38½c. ⅌ ℔. & 40 p.c. ad val.
Silk laces, wearing apparel	60 "	Woollen or worsted clothing	44c. ⅌ ℔. & 60 p. c. ad val.
Skins, uncured, raw	Free.		
Skins, tanned and dressed	20 p. c. ad val.		
Slates, manufactures of, n. e. s.	20 "		
Smokers' articles, ex. clay pipes	60 "		

* The Dingley Tariff increases rates on women's and children's gloves uniformly 75c. per dozen pairs; on men's gloves the rates are the same as the Wilson rates. (*a*) Valued at more than 50c. per lb., 33c. per lb. and 40 per cent. ad val. (*b*) Specific duties ranging from $1.50 to $6 on each article and 35 per cent. ad val. (*c*) On goods above 40c. and not above 70c. per lb.; duty on goods above 70c. per lb., 44c. per lb. and 55 per cent. ad val. (*d*) Value $1 per lb., 20c. per lb. and 15 per cent. ad val., with increasing duty of 10c. per lh. for each 50c. additional value up to $2.50; all over $2.50 per lb, 60c. per lb. and 15 per cent. ad val. (*e*) Wool valued at 12c. per lb. or less, 4c. per lb.; above 12c. duty is 7c. per lb. (*f*) Two prices only in Dingley bill, 30c. and less, and above 30c. (*g*) If not over 10c. per lb. (*h*) If valued at $150; if more, 25 per cent. ad val. (*i*) Above 56°, 6c. per gal. (*j*) And 15 to 20 per cent. ad val. (*k*) On woollen an additional duty of 44c. per lb. (*l*) Chemical wood pulp, 1-6c. per lb. (*m*) When not above 75°, but for every additional degree by polariscopic test, 35-1,000c. per pound additional, and fractions of a degree in proportion.

Articles of merchandise entering the United States from Hawaii and Porto Rico and entering those possessions from the United States are exempt from duty.

The act of Congress approved March 2, 1902, provides that the customs duties on articles entering the Philippines from the United States shall be the same as on those entering from foreign countries. On articles entering the United States from the Philippines the full tariff rates shall be collected, except that a 25 per cent. reduction shall be granted on articles prodneed and grown in the Philippines.

CUSTOMS ACT OF 1908.

Chapter 205, of the acts of the Sixtieth Congress, First Session, approved May 27, 1908, amended the revenue act of 1897 by providing that the owner, importer, consignee or agent of imported merchandise may appeal from the decision of the Collector of the Port, as to the rate and amount of duties chargeable, and as to fees and exactions of whatever character (except duties on tonnage) to a Board of three general appraisers, who may be designated by the Secretary of the Treasury, by giving notice in writing to the Collector within fifteen days after the payment of such rates and fees. The decision of the Board or a majority of the members thereof shall be final, except where an application shall be filed in the Circuit Court of the United States for a review of the facts in the case. But the Board may at its discretion grant a rehearing. The general Board of nine general appraisers shall have the power to establish, from time to time, such reasonable rules of practice not inconsistent with the law, as may be deemed necessary for the conduct of the proceedings of the said Board of three general appraisers, and to assign or reassign any case to any of such Boards of three at any time before promulgation of decision, in order to secure uniformity of decision. In case of dissatisfaction with the decision of the general Board as to the construction of the law and the facts, appeal may be made to the Circuit Court of the United States for review, **and to the Circuit Court of Appeals, and Supreme Court of the United States, successively.**

Custom House Examination of Baggage.

THE following "Notice to Passengers" was issued by the Treasury Department July 31, 1907, and is still in force.

The customs laws and the regulations made in pursuance thereof require examination of the baggage and effects of passengers upon arrival in the United States from foreign countries.

Entries prepared and signed by passengers are required. The forms provided for that purpose entitled "Baggage Declaration and Entry," for residents and non-residents, will be distributed to passengers during the early part of the voyage by an officer of the ship designated for that purpose. When a passenger has prepared and signed his declaration and entry, he should detach and retain the coupon at the bottom of the form and return the latter to the officer of the ship. Declarations spoiled in the preparation should not be destroyed by the passenger, but should be turned over to the purser, who will write, or stamp, thereon the word "cancelled," and furnish a new blank declaration to the passenger. After the ship has docked and the baggage and effects of the passenger are landed, he should present the coupon which he has retained to the chief customs officer on the dock, who will detail an inspector to make the examination.

CLASSIFICATION OF PASSENGERS.

For the purposes of customs administration, passengers are divided into two classes, viz:
1. Non-residents of the United States.
2. Residents of the United States.

The division of passengers into non-residents and residents in nowise affects citizenship.
Non-residents are:

(a) Actual residents of other countriés.

(b) Persons who have been abroad with a fixed foreign abode for one year or more, who elect to declare as non-residents.

(c) Persons who have been abroad for two years with or without a fixed place of foreign abode, who elect to declare as non-residents.

Persons of class (c) may erase the second and third lines within the brackets on the "Baggage Declaration and Entry" for non-residents.

Residents are such persons as are not included in the definition of non-residents.

WEARING APPAREL.

There is no limitation as to the value of articles free of duty brought in by persons declaring as non-residents, provided such articles are in the nature of wearing apparel, articles of personal adornment, toilet articles, and similar personal effects actually accompanying the passenger and necessary and appropriate for his or her wear and use for the purposes of the journey and present comfort and convenience, and are not intended for other persons nor for sale.

Persons declaring as residents are entitled to bring with them free of duty all wearing apparel and other personal effects taken by them out of the United States which have not been remodelled or improved abroad so as to increase their value, and articles obtained abroad by purchase or otherwise of a value not exceeding $100, provided they are not for sale; but in the case of a minor, the exemption of $100 worth of articles obtained abroad is restricted to such articles as are intended for the bona fide personal use of such minor.

CIGARS.

Each passenger is entitled to bring in free of duty and internal revenue tax 50 cigars or 300 cigarettes for his or her bona fide personal consumption. Cigars and cigarettes in excess of these quantities are chargeable with internal revenue tax and duties or fines, as the case may be.

Persons declaring as residents should use the form of baggage declaration and entry for residents of the United States. Non-residents should use the form of baggage declaration and entry for non-residents of the United States.

DESCRIPTION OF ARTICLES.

Residents should carefully state in their entries under the captions "Description of Articles" and "Foreign Cost or Value" the articles obtained abroad, with the cost price of each article if purchased, or the foreign market value of each article if obtained otherwise than by purchase.

Non-residents should carefully state in their entries under the captions "Description of Articles" and "Foreign Cost or Value" articles not necessary and appropriate for the wear and use of such non-residents for purposes of the journey and their present comfort and convenience, and articles intended for sale or for the use of any other person or persons, with the cost price of each article if purchased, or the foreign market value of each article if obtained otherwise than by purchase.

The senior member of a family, if a passenger, may make entry for the entire family.

Ladies travelling alone should state the fact in their declarations and entries.

The exact number of pieces of baggage accompanying the passenger should be stated in the entry.

Whenever practicable passengers should present the original receipted bills of foreign purchases.

DISSATISFACTION AND RE-EXAMINATION.

Passengers dissatisfied with values placed upon dutiable articles by the customs officers on the docks may demand a re-examination, but application therefor should be immediately made to the officers there in charge. If for any reason this course is impracticable, the packages containing the articles should be left in customs custody and application for re-appraisement made to the collector of customs, in writing, within two days after the original appraisement. No request for re-appraisement can be entertained after the articles have been removed from customs custody.

Duties will be assessed on used articles of foreign origin at the foreign market values on the date of the owner's departure for the United States, with due allowance for wear or depreciation.

Upon application to the customs officer in charge on the dock, baggage intended for delivery at ports in the United States other than the port of arrival, or in transit through the United States to a foreign country, may be forwarded thereto without the assessment of duty at the port of arrival, by the various railroads and express companies, whose representatives will be found on the pier. Passengers desiring to have their baggage forwarded in bond should so indicate in their declarations and entries.

PAYMENT OF DUTIES ON BAGGAGE.

Government officers are forbidden by law to accept anything but currency in payment of duties, but, if requested, will retain baggage on the piers for twenty-four hours to enable the owner to secure the currency.

GRATUITIES TO OFFICERS FORBIDDEN.

Passengers are advised that to offer gratuities or bribes to customs officers is a violation of law which will be prosecuted, and that customs officers who accept gratuities or bribes will be dismissed from the service.

HOUSEHOLD EFFECTS.

Household effects of persons or families from foreign countries will be admitted free of duty if actually used abroad by them not less than one year, and not intended for any other person nor for sale.

In order to secure prompt identification and thereby facilitate the passage through the customs upon return of valuable personal and household effects, including sealskin garments, taken abroad by persons leaving the United States, the articles may be registered with the collector at the port of departure or the port at which the journey commences.

Commission on Country Life.

In August, 1908, President Roosevelt desirous of improving social, sanitary, and economic conditions on American farms, invited Prof. L. H. Bailey, of the New York College of Agriculture, at Ithaca; Henry Wallace, of "Wallace's Farmer," Des Moines, Ia.; Kenyon L. Butterfield, president of the Massachusetts Agricultural College, at Amherst; Gifford Pinchot, of the United States Forest Service, and Walter H. Page, editor of "The World's Work," New York, to assist him by acting as a committee of investigation, or "commission on country life." "I should be glad," he said, "to have you report before the end of next December," as he proposed to use it in making recommendations to Congress. In a letter to Professor Bailey he set forth his purpose:

"No nation," he said, "has ever achieved permanent greatness unless this greatness was based on the wellbeing of the great farmer class, the men who live on the soil; for it is upon their welfare, material and moral, that the welfare of the rest of the nation ultimately rests." He believed that our farmers are better off than they ever were before, but he asserted that "the social and economic institutions of the open country are not keeping pace with the development of the nation as a whole." In portions of the South there is much unnecessary suffering and loss of efficiency on the farms, their unsanitary condition causing great mortality among children. Continuing the President said:

"I doubt if any other nation can bear comparison with our own in the amount of attention given by the Government, both Federal and State, to agricultural matters. But practically the whole of this effort has hitherto been directed toward increasing the production of crops. Our attention has been concentrated almost exclusively on getting better farming. In the beginning this was unquestionably the right thing to do. The farmer must first of all grow good crops in order to support himself and his family. But when this has been secured the effort for better farming should cease to stand alone, and should be accompanied by the effort for better business and better living on the farm. It is at least as important that the farmer should get the largest possible return in money, comfort and social advantages from the crops he grows as that he should get the largest possible return in crops from the land he farms. Agriculture is not the whole of country life. The great rural interests are human interests, and good crops are of little value to the farmer unless they open the door to a good kind of life on the farm."

"It is especially important that whatever will serve to prepare country children for life on the farm, and whatever will brighten home life in the country and make it richer and more attractive for the mothers, wives and daughters of farmers, should be done promptly, thoroughly and gladly. There is no more important person, measured in influence upon the life of the nation, than the farmer's wife, no more important home than the country home, and it is of national importance to do the best we can for both.

"The farmers have hitherto had less than their full share of public attention along the lines of business and social life. There is too much belief among all our people that the prizes of life lie away from the farm. I am therefore anxious to bring before the people of the United States the question of securing better business and better living on the farm, whether by co-operation between farmers for buying, selling and borrowing, by promoting social advantages and opportunities in the country, or by any other legitimate means that will help to make country life more gainful, more attractive, and fuller of opportunities, pleasures and rewards for the men, women and children of the farms."

He asked the commission to report upon the present condition of country life, upon what means are now available for supplying the deficiencies that exist; and upon the best method of organized permanent effort in investigation and actual work along the lines he indicated.

State Legislation in 1908.

THE following statement of the more important legislation effected by State Legislatures in 1908 is a summary compiled, by permission, from the appendix to the address of the Hon. Jacob M. Dickinson, of Illinois, president of the American Bar Association, at the annual meeting held at Seattle, Wash., in August, 1908.

The Legislatures in session in 1908 were those of the States of Alabama, Illinois, Kansas, Kentucky, Louisiana, Maryland, Massachusetts, Mississippi, Nevada, New Jersey, New York, North Carolina, Ohio, Oklahoma, South Carolina, Virginia, and West Virginia. In Oregon certain acts were submitted to vote under a referendum. When this address was prepared the Legislature of Georgia was still in session, and the acts had not yet been published. The following is the summary:

Agriculture.—Louisiana provided for the establishment by the State Board of Agriculture and Immigration of a branch experimental station at some suitable point in the rice belt of Southwestern Louisiana, for the purpose of carrying on scientific and experimental investigation with reference to the production of rice. That State also passed an act fixing a standard of cotton classification.

Mississippi established county departments of agriculture to disseminate useful information among the farmers and to develop the agricultural resources of the counties. Mississippi also provided rules and regulations to prevent the introduction and spread of insect pests and plant diseases, and to prevent the importation of nursery stock infested with injurious insects or diseases. Inspection by the State entomologists is provided for, and shipments of nursery stock are required to be made under proper certificate. It is made the duty of transportation companies and their agents to notify the State entomologists of any shipments made without such certificate.

Mississippi also provided for the establishment of county agricultural high schools, for the purpose of instructing the white youth of the counties in theoretical and practical agriculture.

Child Labor.—Louisiana, Kentucky, Mississippi, Ohio and Virginia enacted child labor laws.

Kentucky provided that children under fourteen years of age can not be employed in labor during school terms, and in no event except on farms or in domestic work. Those between fourteen and sixteen years of age may work in employments not dangerous to health, morals, life or limb. The act requires safeguarding machinery, prohibits certain work, imposes requirements as to sanitary conditions and provides penalties for the violation of the act.

Mississippi enacted that children under twelve years of age shall not work in mills or factories, that those under sixteen shall not work in factories above ten hours per day, and that no child under sixteen shall be employed to work in any mill, factory or manufacturing establishment without the consent of parent or guardian. It is made the duty of sheriffs and county health officers to visit factories employing children, and of officers and managers to give correct information demanded of them. Violation of the law is punishable by fine or imprisonment, or both. The act only applies to factories working cotton, wool or other fabrics or where children are employed indoors at work injurious to health or in operating dangerous machinery.

Ohio provided that no child under fourteen years of age shall be employed in any factory, workshop, business office, telephone or telegraph office, restaurant, bakery, hotel, apartment house, mercantile or other establishment, or in the distribution or transmission of merchandise or messages. Children between fourteen and sixteen years of age are permitted to be so employed if they have a schooling certificate. Boys under sixteen years of age and girls under eighteen years of age when allowed by law to pursue such employment are not allowed to work more than forty-eight hours in any one week, nor more than eight hours in any one day, nor before seven o'clock in the morning nor after six o'clock in the evening, and shall be entitled to not less than thirty minutes for meal time and the meal time shall not be included as part of the work hours of the week or day.

Any child under the age of sixteen is not permitted to be employed in any of the following occupations: Sewing machine belts in any workshop or factory; adjusting belts, oiling, wiping or cleaning machinery, operating circular or band saws, wood-shapers, wood-jointers, planers, sand-paper or wood-polishing machinery; job or cylinder printing presses operated by power other than foot; emery or polishing wheels for polishing metals; wood-turning or boring machinery; stamping machines; corrugating rolls; steam boilers or other steam generating apparatus; dough brakes or cracker machinery; wire or iron straightening machinery; rolling mill machinery, punches or shears; washing, grinding or mixing mills; calendar rolls in rubber manufacturing; laundering machinery; passenger or freight elevators; preparing compositions in which dangerous or poisonous acids are used; manufacture of paints, colors or white lead; dipping, dyeing or packing matches; manufacturing, packing or storing powder; dynamite, nitro-glycerine, compounds, fuses or other explosives; manufacturing goods for immoral purposes; as pin boys in bowling alleys or in or about any distillery, brewery or any other place where malt or alcoholic liquors are manufactured, packed, wrapped or bottled; nor in any theatre, hotel, concert hall, drug store, saloon or place of amusement wherein intoxicating liquors are sold; in any other employment which may be considered dangerous to their lives, limbs, health or morals.

No female under the age of sixteen years is allowed to be employed in any capacity where such employment compels her to remain standing constantly, nor in assorting, manufacturing or packing tobacco. The act provides for the appointment of eight women visitors. It is made the duty of such visitors to visit all shops and factories in which women and children are employed and carefully inspect the sanitary conditions and means of exit, and machinery that may become dangerous, and to see that the same is guarded and surrounded with sufficient guards to prevent accidents or injury.

Virginia enacted that after March 1, 1909, no child under thirteen years of age, and after March 1, 1910, no child under fourteen years of age, shall be employed in factories, workshops, mines, or mercantile establishments, except in cases of orphans and children with dependent relatives.

Children—Delinquent, Dependent and Abandoned.—Louisiana passed an act regulating the care, treatment and control of neglected and delinquent children, seventeen years of age and under, and providing for the trial of adults charged with the violating of laws for the protection of the physical, moral and mental well-being of children, or with desertion or failure to support wife or children. By the same act a Juvenile Court is created in the Parish of Orleans.

The State of Michigan provided for the care of destitute, homeless, abandoned, or delinquent children, and vested the Probate Court with jurisdiction over them.

Ohio, repealing former acts, passed a new and comprehensive statute relating to the control and care of dependent, neglected and delinquent children.

Corporations.—Louisiana passed an act providing for enforcing the execution of judgments forfeiting or annulling the charters of corporations domiciled in the State.

Maryland provided for incorporation under the general law "for any lawful purpose." The estoppel doctrine was made applicable in cases of attack upon corporate existence. Voting trusts for a period not exceeding five years are made lawful. Provision is made for the protection of minority shareholders in cases of consolidation and merger. The statutory liability of stockholders has been limited, and such liability, where it exists, has been made an asset for equal distribution among all creditors. Shares may be paid for in services and property, but in cases where other than money is accepted in payment for shares, a certificate showing the facts must be recorded. Subject to this restriction, the action of the stockholders in accepting other than money is binding upon creditors in the absence of actual fraud. Owners in the aggregate of five per cent. of the outstanding capital stock may, upon written request, have a statement of the affairs of the corporation under oath, showing in detail the assets and liabilities, within twenty days after such request. Every president or treasurer refusing to file such statement is liable to the person making the request in the sum of $50 for each day's delay. All the books of every corporation are, during business hours, open for inspection to any person or persons holding in the aggregate five per cent. of the outstanding capital stock. Stringent regulations are made to prevent the payment of dividends improperly, and no money can be loaned to any stockholder or director without the assenting officers and directors being personally liable therefor. This, however, does not apply to those corporations whose principal business under their charters is to lend money or to receive money on deposit, or to any life insurance company lending money to its policyholders on their policies. All the usual requirements and obligations in modern legislation applicable to foreign corporations doing business in the State are enacted. All corporations formed under the act and all those created theretofore are given the right of perpetual succession until forfeiture.

Michigan provided that every corporation which has paid a franchise fee and been admitted to do business in the State, which shall thereafter increase its capital stock represented by property used and business done in Michigan, shall pay an additional franchise fee of one-half of one mill on each dollar of increase, represented by property owned and business done in Michigan. Whenever requested by the Secretary of State, a statement under oath shall be filed showing the proportion of the property used and business transacted in Michigan. This provision is incapable of fulfilment by railroad companies with any degree of even approximate accuracy. It is impossible to tell what proportion of a railroad company's property is used in carrying on business within a State, when the same property is being used at the same time for carrying on interstate business. No sound basis has ever yet been reached for making such an estimate. The problem has vexed the most critical accountants, and will probably remain insoluble.

Mississippi enacted that any public service corporation which when sued in any State court shall remove such cause to a Federal court, or which shall institute any suit in the Federal court of that State, which it could not maintain if it were a domestic company incorporated under the laws of the State, shall forfeit its right to carry on interstate commerce within the State and also the right of eminent domain in the State.

Mississippi made it unlawful for any district-attorney or any attorney-at-law associated in practice with any district-attorney, and attorneys for levee boards, to represent in a legal capacity any public service corporation; and any attorney violating the act is guilty of a misdemeanor, and in addition to being subject to a fine, shall forfeit his license to practice law in the State.

Courts, Practice and Remedies.—Alabama enacted that graduates of the Law Department of the University of Alabama, upon presentation of their diplomas, and the payment of license fees and the proof of good moral character, shall be entitled to practice in all the courts of the State.

Louisiana passed an act to prevent the courts of that State from granting writs of injunction maintaining a person removed from office in the possession of the same or restraining his successor from taking possession of the office, books, documents, archives, or emoluments thereof.

Louisiana also enacted that any person who shall practice as an attorney and counseilor-at-law in any court of record in the State without having first been examined and obtained a license as required by law, shall be guilty of a midemeanor, and subject to a fine of not less than $50 nor more than $200, or to imprisonment in the parish jail not exceeding thirty days.

Maryland passed an act prohibiting the practice of law or giving of legal advice without admission to the bar, and providing a penalty of fine or imprisonment for false representation as to membership.

Maryland passed a very stringent and comprehensive law against barratry, which, if enforced, will bear hard on "ambulance chasers" and side-partners in promoting litigation. It provides that:

"Whoever, for his own gain, and having no existing relationship or interest in the issue, directly or indirectly, solicits another to sue at law or in equity, or to make a litigious claim, or to retain his own or another's services in so suing or making a litigious claim; or whoever knowingly prosecutes a case in which his services have been retained as a result of such solicitation; or causes any case to be instituted without authority; or whoever, being an attorney-at-law, directly or indirectly, agrees to procure another to be employed as an expert witness, or otherwise, or procures another to be so employed in consideration of his so soliciting litigious business or undertaking to solicit it, or in any other way compensates or agrees to compensate another for so doing, shall upon conviction thereof, be punished by a fine of not more than $500 or by imprisonment in jail for not more than three months, or by both. Any solicitation as aforesaid shall be prima facie evidence that the person so soliciting is doing so for gain."

Massachusetts passed an act providing that women may be appointed assistant clerks in police, district or municipal courts.

Mississippi provided a direct appeal to the Supreme Court from an order of the Railroad Commission, the validity of which shall be disputed upon the ground that the Commission was without power to make it, or whenever the Commission shall refuse to make an order asked for upon the ground that it is without power to make it. A bill of exceptions is provided for, limited to such facts as may be necessary to present only the question as to the power of the Commission in the premises.

Mississippi abolished the limitation of one year provided for the bringing of suits for injuries producing death.

New Jersey provided for pensioning its judges. They must have reached the age of seventy-three and have served the State for twenty-one years, and on retirement are to receive an amount equal to one-third of the former salary.

Virginia provided that where an injunction is granted without notice, the order shall prescribe the time within which it shall be effective, and after such time, unless previously enlarged, it shall stand dissolved. Within the time designated the party to whom the injunction is awarded may upon notice apply for an enlargement or a further injunction, and the adverse party may move to dissolve the injunction.

The "unwritten law" as interpreted by the courts of Virginia, has been, in its application, modified by a statute of the State which provides that testimony may be admitted as to the truth of the statements which led to the homicide.

Crimes and Corrections.—Louisiana passed an act making it a misdemeanor for any school officer or teacher while employed in the public schools to act as agent for, or receive gifts, rebates; commissions, or fees, directly or indirectly, from individuals or companies that manufacture, handle, or sell in the State of Louisiana any kind of school books, school supplies, school furniture or school building materials.

Louisiana enacted that it shall be a misdemeanor for any person to appear at a picnic, barbecue, children's day celebration, church service, Sunday school celebration, literary society or any other public gathering, or on any railway train in the State, in a drunken or intoxicated condition.

Louisiana enacted a statute to prohibit gambling on horse races "by the operation of betting books, French Mutual pooling devices, auction pools, or any other device," and has made the violation of the act a misdemeanor punishable by fine and imprisonment.

That State also passed an act providing that if any person shall wilfully and maliciously set fire to or burn or blow up or destroy with dynamite, gunpowder or other explosive substance, or set fire to or explode any explosive substance with intent to blow up or destroy any house, building, shed, outhouse, levee, dam, ship, vessel, steamboat, street or railroad car, or other vehicle, or other construction in or on which human beings are customarily to be found, such person shall be guilty of a crime, and on conviction thereof shall suffer the death penalty.

It made it a misdemeanor for any person, firm, association or corporation, intentionally, for the purpose of injuring or destroying the business of a competitor in any locality, to discriminate between different sections, communities, cities or localities in the State, by selling such commodities at a lower rate in one section, community, city or locality, than in another, making due allowance for the grade of commodity and cost of transportation.

Louisiana also passed an act to protect prisoners while in the custody of officers of the law, making it a misdemeanor for any such officer to frighten by threat, or to torture, or to resort to any means of an inhuman nature whatever, to secure a confession from the accused. It also passed an act against blackmail, and an act defining kidnapping and making the offence punishable by imprisonment at hard labor or otherwise for a period not exceeding twenty years, in the discretion of the court. By another act, concubinage between a person of the Caucasian race and a person of the Negro race is made a felony.

Louisiana also passed an act making it a misdemeanor to make, circulate or transmit false statements, rumors, reports or suggestions written, printed or spoken concerning the financial conditions of any bank organized under the laws of the State, and derogatory to the same.

Massachusetts enacted that photographic plates, if the pictures are not intended for sale, may be exposed on the Lord's Day, and that ice cream may be delivered on that day.

New Jersey provided for a Dependency and Criminality Commission to investigate the causes of dependency and crime, and point out methods for their amelioration and elimination.

That State also passed an act making the encouraging of arson and anarchy by any means a high misdemeanor. A laudable effort to destroy petty graft has been made by an enactment of New Jersey providing that it shall be a misdemeanor to give, offer or promise any gift or gratuity to an agent, employee or servant without the knowledge of the principal, employer or master, with intent to influence his action in his employment. The acceptance of such gratuity is likewise a misdemeanor. This is likely to interfere with the close relations existing between butlers and cooks on the one hand and dealers in household articles on the other.

New York prohibited any contract of sale upon credit or margin of any securities or commodities, wherein both parties intend that it shall be settled upon the basis of the public market quotations of prices made on any board of trade upon which such commodities or securities are dealt in, and without intending a bona fide purchase and sale of the same. Any one in any way making any quotations of prices with intent to make any such contracts shall be guilty of a felony. The act defines "bucket shop" as any building, room, apartment, booth, office or store, or any other place, where any contract prohibited by the act is made or offered to be made.

Rhode Island and Virginia also passed acts prohibiting "bucketing, bucket-shopping, and to abolish bucket shops."

Mississippi also made what is commonly known as dealing in futures unlawful, and the parties participating therein guilty of a misdemeanor. The establishment or maintaining any office for such purpose is prohibited, and money lost in such transactions may be recovered. The renting or leasing of an office for such purpose is made a misdemeanor.

New York established a State farm for women, with outdoor treatment of female delinquents. The object is to give them such industrial occupation as will tend to improve the general physical, mental and moral welfare. Such occupation is to be carried on in the open air as far as practicable.

Ohio made it a misdemeanor punishable by fine or imprisonment or both for a stenographer to disclose any matters dictated to such stenographer by his or her employers.

By an act of Ohio of May 9, 1908, courts are permitted to suspend the execution of sentence where it appears to the court that the defendant has never been imprisoned for crime and that the character of the defendant and the circumstances of the case are such that he is not likely again to engage in any offensive course of conduct and that the public good does not demand or require that the defendant shall suffer the penalty imposed by law. Certain heinous crimes are excepted from the provisions of the act. Ohio passed a statute against the use, knowingly, of false weights and measures. Another statute of Ohio makes the malicious cutting down or destroying tobacco belonging to another a criminal offence.

Ohio made it a criminal offence for any person knowingly to make or publish any prospectus concerning the affairs or financial condition or property of any corporation, joint stock association, co-partnership or individual, which contains any statement which is false or wilfully exaggerated and intended to deceive any person or persons as to the real value of securities offered for sale.

Virginia established a death chamber at the penitentiary and provided that all executions shall be by electrocution.

Education.—Kentucky passed an act which makes attendance upon schools by children between seven and fourteen years of age in cities of certain classes compulsory, unless they are taught privately or have acquired the common school advantages of instruction.

Louisiana enacted that all diplomas or degrees, whether literary or scientific, academic or professional, granted by the Board of Supervisors of the Louisiana State University and Agricultural and Mechanical College, shall be recognized by the courts and other officials of Louisiana as entitling the graduates holding the same to the same rights, immunities and privileges in the State of Louisiana as the diplomas or degrees of any other institution of learning whatever.

Maryland provided for retiring its aged and indigent teachers of public schools upon a pension of two hundred dollars per annum.

In order to provide competent colored teachers for colored schools, Maryland has taken over the management of the Baltimore Normal School, to be under the control of the State Board of Education.

Massachusetts incorporated an American College for Girls at Constantinople, in Turkey, authorizing it to grant such degrees as are granted by institutions of learning in Massachusetts. That State also enacted that street or elevated railway companies shall charge school children travelling to and from their schools and their homes only one-half the regular fare charged other passengers between the same points.

North Carolina provided that blind children shall be compelled to attend school, and that parents, guardians or custodians of any blind children between prescribed ages failing to send them to school shall be guilty of a misdemeanor.

Ohio established a Commission for the Blind, defining its powers and duties, and conferring upon it the power to establish schools for industrial training and workshops for the employment of suitable blind persons, and to equip and maintain such schools.

It is noteworthy that in a very comprehensive law passed by West Virginia relating to education it is provided that every person having under control a child between the age of eight and fifteen years of age, shall cause such child to attend some free school for a period of twenty-four weeks yearly, and that for every neglect of such duty the offender shall be subject to a fine of two dollars for the first offence and five dollars for each subsequent offence, the offence consisting in the failure for two days in any week to cause such child to attend school, except in cases of sickness or death in the pupil's family, or other reasonable cause, or unless the pupil be thoroughly and systematically instructed for a like period elsewhere, provided that there be a school in session within two miles of the pupil's home by the nearest travelled road. A truant officer is provided to ascertain any violations of the law, and see to its enforcement. Any employer who induces the absence of such child from school or employs such child unlawfully absent is subject to a fine and imprisonment. Teachers are likewise charged with co-operation in the enforcement of the law.

Virginia provided for the retirement and pensioning of public teachers who have taught in the public schools of the State an aggregate of twenty years, if such persons have maintained a good record and by reason of physical or mental infirmity or old age are incapable of rendering efficient service as teachers. Voluntary application may be made under the same conditions by one who has taught for twenty-five years.

Finance.—Louisiana amended Article 2024 of its Civil Code, relating to interest. Legal interest is fixed at 5 per cent. per annum on all sums which are the subject of a judicial demand, and on sums at banks at the rates fixed by their charters. The amount of conventional interest shall not exceed 8 per cent. per. annum, and the same must be fixed in writing.

Fish and Game.—Various acts were passed by the States in which sessions of the Legislatures were held during the past year, in relation to fish and game, but as such statutes are chiefly of local interest, it is hardly necessary to notice them here. All seasons have generally been accepted as open for the destruction of foxes, but the sporting disposition of the South Carolinians asserted itself in an act which makes it unlawful to take in any manner a fox in certain counties between the fifteenth day of February and the first of September.

It may be noted that Louisiana passed an act declaring diamond-back terrapins the property of the State, and regulating the catching, killing and sale of the same.

Forestry.—Alabama provided for a State Commission of Forestry, defining its duties, and requiring it to publish annually "a report upon the forest conditions in Alabama, with reference to the preservation of forests, the effects of the destruction of forests upon the welfare of the State, and all other matters pertaining to the subject of forestry." It is also made the duty of the commission to report to each session of the Legislature the results of their investigations and to recommend desirable legislation with reference to forestry.

A resolution was passed by the Legislature of Illinois providing for a Forest Preserve District Commission, to investigate and report in regard to the creation of forest preserve districts and to recommend legislation in regard thereto.

Louisiana provided for a commission for the conservation of the natural resources of the State, to be known as the Commission on Natural Resources, and has provided for its administration and duties. By another act, Louisiana established a Chair of Forestry in the State University.

The State of Maryland passed an act consenting to the acquisition by the United States of lands in the mountain region of Maryland for the establishment of a National Forest Reserve, and consented that Congress may pass laws for the management, control and protection of the same.

Massachusetts passed an act to provide for the purchase of forest land and for reforestation. By another act it is provided that land upon which certain specified kinds of trees are planted to the number of not less than 600 per acre shall be exempt from taxation for a period of ten years after said trees have grown in height two feet on the average.

Rhode Island provided that lands worth not more than $25 per acre are exempt from taxation when planted with trees of named kinds, not less than 500 trees to the acre.

Insurance.—Louisiana enacted a number of statutes relating to insurance. By one act the organization of Industrial Life Insurance Companies is authorized, and such companies are required to make a deposit with the State Treasurer. The act provides that stock companies shall have a fully paid up capital and that mutual companies shall have an initial fund, and has provided for the issuance of licenses to them by the Secretary of State before they begin business. Another act was passed to prevent discrimination between policyholders of life insurance companies doing business in the State by the sale of special contracts or other inducements under pretense of making such holders agents of the company, and providing penalties for the enforcement of the act.

Louisiana passed an act providing for the organization of insurance companies on the stock plan in that State; the kinds of insurance which can be transacted, the amount of capital required for such companies other than companies formed for the purpose of transacting life, health, accident, burial or sick benefit insurance on the industrial plan. By another act, fire insurance companies are required to furnish blanks for proof of loss, failure to do so being deemed a waiver of the requirement of any statement or proof of loss at the hands of the insured person, firm or corporation. Prompt settlement by insurance companies for losses is required, and upon failure to settle within the designated time the insurance company becomes liable to a penalty of 12 per cent. on the amount of the loss as damages.

Another act provides for the organization of mutual life insurance companies, and requires a deposit from the same.

Louisiana passed an act providing that no policy thereafter issued by any fire insurance company authorized to do business in the State shall contain any clause or provision requiring the assured to take out or maintain a larger amount of insurance than that covered by such policy, nor in any way providing that the insured shall be liable as co-insurer with the company issuing the policy for any part of the loss or damage which may be occasioned by fire, lightning or windstorm to the property located in the State of Louisiana covered by such loss or damage, or any part thereof, by reason of the failure of the assured to take out and maintain other insurance upon said property.

The State of Louisiana also enacted that life, health and accident companies which issue policies or contracts of insurance to the assured without a medical examination by a physician, shall waive their right to claim forfeiture for misrepresentations under certain conditions.

Ohio passed a very comprehensive up-to-date life insurance law, providing that any one soliciting insurance shall be regarded as the agent of the company, that no such company shall make any discrimination in favor of individuals of the same class and equal expectation of life as to premiums, etc., that the policy must clearly set forth the contract, that there shall be no special favors, that no stock, bonds or other securities shall be disposed of in connection with the policy, that no domestic life insurance company shall disburse $100 or more unless evidenced by voucher, that every company shall file statements as to profit and loss with reference to each kind of insurance, that no misrepresentation shall be made as to funds or assets, and there shall be annual net valuations of all outstanding policies.

South Carolina established a separate and distinct department of the State government, to be known as the Insurance Department, charged with the enforcement and execution of the laws relating to insurance, devolving upon it duties hitherto performed in that respect by the State Treasurer and Comptroller-General. It is given authority to issue and revoke licenses to insurance companies, examination and license of every insurance company being a condition precedent to its right to do business.

By amendment to its existing law, West Virginia brought all companies thereafter engaged in the State in the class of insurance mentioned in the act, and all guarantee, surety and indemnity companies, and all companies of similar character, under the same law which provides for the examination and supervision by the auditor of insurance companies incorporated by the State.

Labor and Factories.—Louisiana passed an act creating a Bureau of Labor and Industrial Statistics, and providing for the appointment of a commissioner, to be known as the Commissioner of Labor and Industrial Statistics of Louisiana, and prescribing his powers and duties.

Another act of Louisiana requires that mechanics employed on all State or public buildings or public works in cities exceeding 10,000 population throughout the State shall be citizens of the State, except under certain conditions, and shall have paid one poll tax; and penalties are provided for a violation of the provisions of the act.

Massachusetts passed an act providing for an employer submitting to the State Board of Conciliation and Arbitration a plan for compensation to injured employees, and approval by said board. Upon approval, it shall be lawful to enter into a contract by which employee shall release employer from all liability and accept in lieu thereof the compensation provided in such plan. Parents and guardians may make an agreement binding a minor. It is provided, however, that the making of such contract by the employee shall not be a condition of employment.

Mississippi abolished the hiring of county prisoners to any individual or corporation for any purpose, and has provided that county farms are to be established by Boards of Supervisors for working county convicts, or they may be kept in jail or may be worked on public roads or any other work of an exclusive character.

Mississippi enacted that any public service corporation blacklisting or refusing employment to telegraph operators only because of their affiliation with a labor organization shall be liable to actual and exemplary damages.

Liquors.—Alabama passed an act prohibiting the manufacture, sale, barter, exchange, or giving away to induce trade of alcohols, spirituous, vinous and malt liquors, except the sale of alcohol in certain cases and upon certain conditions, and except the sale of wines for sacramental purposes. The act does not prohibit the social serving of liquors and beverages in private residences in ordinary social intercourse.

Alabama also enacted that any person who keeps for sale intoxicating drinks within a territory where such sale is prohibited, shall on conviction be fined up to $500 and sentenced to hard labor for not less than six nor more than twelve months. This act provides that wherever any of such liquors are delivered to a carrier for a destination in a prohibition territory c. o. d., the carrier shall be held as the agent of the consignor until delivered, and the servant or agent of the carrier delivering and receiving pay therefor within such prohibition district must on conviction be fined and imprisoned. This act was doubtless intended to apply to liquors carried in interstate commerce. It was approved November 23, 1907, and apparently in ignorance of the decision of the Supreme Court of the United States in Adams Express Company vs. Kentucky, 206 U. S. 129, decided May 13, 1907, which held that a statute similar in terms enacted by the State of Kentucky, was, as applied to shipments from one State to another, an attempt to regulate interstate commerce and beyond the powers of the State.

Another statute of Alabama provides that any person who shall publicly drink intoxicating liquors in the presence of passengers on any car, shall be guilty of a misdemeanor, punishable by fine or imprisonment, but the act is not applicable to smoking compartments, closets, dining or buffet cars. Conductors are invested with police powers to enforce the act.

Louisiana passed an act making it unlawful for any person to drink intoxicating liquors of any kind in or upon any railway passenger train, or coach, or closet, vestibule thereof or platform connected therewith, while said train or coach is in the service of passenger transportation within the State. A penalty by fine or imprisonment is provided for. The act does not apply to the drinking of liquor with meals on regular dining cars.

Mississippi prohibited the manufacture, sale, barter, or giving away to induce trade of any vinous, alcoholic, malt, intoxicating or spirituous liquors, provided that homemade wines may be produced for domestic or household uses only. Druggists may sell under certain limitations pure alcohol for medicinal purposes only, and grain alcohol to chemists and bacteriologists, and wine for sacramental purposes. All licenses to sell liquor shall cease.

Mississippi passed an act amending the law in reference to intoxicating liquors shipped into the State c. o. d. or with the bill of lading attached, providing that the receivers of such liquors shall not remove them more than one hundred feet from the point of delivery by the carrier, that they shall not be disposed of at a greater distance than one hundred feet from the point of receipt, and that it shall be unlawful to sell or give away any part thereof. It is made unlawful for any person in the State to have in possession any intoxicating liquors for the purpose of selling the same or giving same away, and possession by any person of one-half gallon or more of such liquors shipped after the enactment of the law into the State upon condition of payment on delivery is prima facie evidence of guilt.

By another act, Mississippi made more stringent its anti-liquor laws, punishing, with fine or imprisonment or both, persons who sell or give away liquors, making the possession of a United States license or application for retailing liquor presumptive evidence of guilt, and that such liquors shall be seized and destroyed. Any one soliciting orders for the sale of such liquors, whether the delivery shall be within or without the State, it being contemplated that they shall be brought into the State, is guilty of a misdemeanor. If any person carry to any place of amusement or place of entertainment or public assemblage any intoxicating liquors, he is subject to a fine of $50 or imprisonment or both, provided, however, that the act does not prevent the use of liquors in the dispensation of hospitality at one's own house. Debts incurred for liquors are not collectible.

The State of Mississippi passed a resolution on March 21, 1908, that the United States Senators and Representatives in Congress from the State of Mississippi are requested to urge the passage of such measures as will prevent the issuance by the United States Government of revenue licenses for the sale of intoxicating liquors in any State which prohibits such sale.

North Carolina prohibited the manufacture and sale of intoxicating liquors in North Carolina except under certain conditions. The act gives a luminous definition of intoxicating liquors—defining them as "liquors that will produce intoxication." The act empowers counties or municipalities to prohibit the sale of such liquors by pharmacists. The statute, however, was not to go into effect until a majority of the electors shall have voted "against the manufacture and sale of intoxicating liquors."

Another act of North Carolina provided that upon a criminal prosecution of a physician for giving a prescription of liquors to persons not in good faith patients and in need of such liquors, it shall be prima facie evidence of guilt that the person to whom the prescription was given was able to go about from place to place, and that such physician has not previously written for such person any prescription except for such liquors.

An act of Ohio of March 5, 1908, provided for a county unit local option.

South Carolina passed an act to provide for the teaching of physiology and hygiene in the public schools, and that the nature of alcoholic drinks and narcotics, as to their effect upon the human system, shall be included in the branches of study in the public schools. A failure upon the part of the officer or teacher in control to comply with the requirements of the act shall be visited by removal from office.

The same State also passed an act prohibiting the drinking of intoxicating liquors in the presence of any passengers or on any passenger car in the State, and making the offender guilty of a misdemeanor, subject to fine and imprisonment. It provided, however, that the act shall not apply to any dining or buffet car.

West Virginia made all places, including drug stores, clubs, orders or associations, where intoxicating liquors are stored, sold, vended, given away or furnished contrary to law, nuisances, and has invested courts of equity with power to abate them. The court is also vested with power to revoke any license theretofore issued for the sale of intoxicating liquors on the premises. All licensed rooms, except drug stores, where liquors are sold, or kept for sale, either at wholesale or retail, are required to be kept securely locked on Sunday from 12 midnight, Saturday, to 5 o'clock Monday morning, and no person shall be permitted in such room for any purpose during the days and hours specified. Side-door connections are forbidden and the bar and all parts of the room shall be in plain view from the street day and night, unobserved by any device, and a light shall be kept burning in the room during day and night.

Livestock.—Kansas passed an act providing for the inspection of concentrated feeding stuff, and for the marking of the same.

Louisiana established a State Livestock Sanitary Board, with power and authority to regulate livestock sanitary matters, and the right to establish and maintain quarantine lines, prevent the introduction and spread of Texas and tick fever, or any of the infectious or contagious diseases of livestock, and also providing for the appointment of inspectors and fixing their duties. Louisiana also passed an act to regulate the practice of veterinary medicine and veterinary surgery, and to define and punish offences committed in violation of the act.

Mississippi created a livestock sanitary board, for the purpose of dealing with infectious diseases of animals. Such board is to consist of the Commissioner of Agriculture, Professor of Animal Husbandry at the Agricultural and Mechanical College, and Professor of Veterinary Science at the Agricultural and Mechanical College, and two other members appointed by the Governor as representatives of livestock breeders of the State. The importation of infected animals into the State, contrary to the rules and regulations of the board, is forbidden, and violation of this provision of the act is made a misdemeanor punishable by fine or imprisonment. The board is authorized to maintain quarantine lines, to appoint inspectors and to inspect and disinfect livestock and premises.

An act was passed by Mississippi to regulate the sale and inspection and analysis of feeding stuff offered for sale in the State, and manufacturers, dealers or persons soliciting orders for such commercial feeding stuffs are required to submit samples to the State Chemist for inspection and analysis and furnish a statement of constituent elements.

In order to maintain or improve the breed of stock, Maryland provided that owners of stallions or jacks offered for public service shall file with a clerk of court a statement showing the name, age, pedigree and record if known, and if not known, then such fact.

New Jersey provided for the establishment of a Livestock Commission, the purchase and maintenance of stallions of draught and coach type for distribution and use in counties where breeders' associations are organized, and to provide dams for breeding which shall conform to standards established by the commission, and to aid in the selection and distribution of sires and dams. There are provisions for the examination, registration and leasing of all stallions and jacks offered for public service.

Virginia passed an act providing for the inspection of concentrated feeding stuff, and for the marking of same.

Master and Servant.—South Carolina enacted that any person who shall make a contract for personal service and shall fraudulently, with malicious intent to injure his employer, refuse to render such service shall be guilty of a misdemeanor, and provided a reciprocal liability as to the employer, making the failure to perform the contract without sufficient cause and to the injury of the other prima facie evidence of a guilty intent. Similar provisions are made in respect to the procurement of advances of money or other things of value by the employee. A reciprocal relation as to the promise to advance is established in respect to the employer. Such contracts may be either verbal or written.

The punishment is a fine of from $25 to $100 or imprisonment. The act provides that it shall not apply where the inducement or consideration of such contract is money or other thing of value advanced to or for the employee prior to the commencement of service thereunder. The purpose of this provision doubtless is to guard the act from being applied to advances made to immigrant laborers. In all other respects the act is similar to those which are styled peonage acts, the constitutionality of which is now under consideration and the operations of which are being investigated by Congress.

Massachusetts abolished the doctrine of assumed risks and also that of fellow-servants where the employer is a railroad corporation.

Public Health and Safety.—Alabama passed an act "to regulate the practice of pharmacy and the sale of poisons in cities and towns of more than 900 inhabitants."

Alabama provided for the establishment of an epileptic colony, "to secure the humane, curative, scientific and economical care of epileptics, exclusive of violently insane persons who may require treatment at an insane hospital."

Kansas prohibited the use of sulphites and any preparation containing sulphur dioxide, or any secret preparation in the manufacture of meat products, and meat products so treated are declared to be adulterated, and the offender is subject to the penalties relating to adulterated foods.

Kentucky passed a pure food law and an act to encourage the establishment of a tuberculosis sanitarium.

Louisiana created a Board of Osteopathy and provided for regulating the practice of osteopathy.

Louisiana made it unlawful to sell, give, barter or exchange at retail any cocaine or "crown," or concoction of which cocaine is the principal ingredient, except upon the written prescription each time of an authorized physician.

Louisiana also passed an act prohibiting spitting on floors or walls of public buildings.

By another act Louisiana provided regulations for the swinging of scaffolding in construction work in cities of 30,000 or over. That State also passed an act providing that all the doors for ingress and egress to public schoolhouses, churches, courthouses, assembly rooms, halls, theatres, factories with more than twenty employees, and of all other buildings of public resort, where people are wont to assemble, shall be swung so as to open outwardly from the audience rooms, classrooms, halls or workshops. But such doors may be swung on double-jointed hinges. Rhode Island passed a similar act.

Maryland brought professional Christian Science healers within the operation of the statutory regulations concerning practitioners of medicine, by making them applicable to persons who for hire, gratuity or compensation, undertake by mental or other process to cure or heal bodily or mental ailments.

Massachusetts provided for instruction in the public schools as to tuberculosis and its prevention. It prohibits the manufacture and sale of cocaine and articles containing cocaine, and forbids in any place of public amusement or of public resort any lung-testing machine or similar contrivance, the use of which requires the application of any part thereof to the lips.

Massachusetts authorized towns to appropriate money for and to establish and maintain public gymnasiums and swimming baths, and required that every city and town having a population of more than 10,000 shall provide a public playground for the minors of such city or town, and at least one additional one for every additional 20,000 of its population, provided that such cities and towns shall accept the provisions of the act by a vote.

New York passed a law declaring tuberculosis to be an infectious and communicable disease, and requiring reports from physicians and others of all those known to have tuberculosis. It also provides for examination and keeping of a register and for disinfection of premises, and prohibits the occupancy of premises that have been infected, except upon certain conditions. It declares that any person having tuberculosis who shall not exercise proper care, shall be guilty of a nuisance, and upon failure to comply with regulations provided therefor, such person shall be guilty of a misdemeanor.

Ohio passed an act "to authorize the State Board of Health to require the purification of sewage and public water supplies, and to protect streams against pollution."

By another act, somewhat similar to the Federal Pure Food and Drug act, Ohio regulates the branding of drugs and foods.

Ohio made it a criminal offence for any person to sell, exchange or deliver or have in his custody or possession with intent to sell, exchange or deliver, adulterated milk or milk to which water or any foreign substance has been added, or milk from cows fed on wet distillery waste or starch waste, or cows kept in a dairy or place which has been declared to be unclean by a health officer, or from diseased or sick cows.

Ohio passed an act making it a criminal offence to sell, barter or give away alkaloid cocaine except upon the prescription of a physician.

By another act, Ohio provided for compulsory fire drills in every public and private school having an average daily attendance of 50 or more pupils.

Ohio provided for the establishment of county hospitals for the care and treatment of inmates of county infirmaries and other residents of the counties suffering from tuberculosis.

Ohio passed an act to regulate the manufacture and sale of renovated or process butter, and requiring packages containing such butter to be marked with the words "renovated butter" or "process butter."

Ohio established a State Dental Board, prescribing its powers and duties, and provided for the examination and licensing of persons applying for the privilege of practicing dentistry within the State.

For the first time, South Carolina seems to have provided for a State Health Officer, although it previously had a State Board of Health. It also enables cities of more than 20,000 population to establish and maintain public baths, and fix rates for their use.

South Carolina authorized its Board of Medical Examiners to revoke, subject to judicial review, the license of any physician or surgeon who is guilty of a felony or gross immorality, or so addicted to the liquor or drug habit as to render him unfit to practice medicine, or if he has been convicted of illegal practices.

Virginia passed a statute providing for the examination of persons in care of institutions supported from the public funds, and if tuberculosis shall be discovered, for the separation of such persons from the other inmates not so affected. Provisions are made for disinfection. It is made an offence punishable by fine for any person knowingly to permit any one to occupy apartments previously occupied by a consumptive before they shall have been disinfected.

Virginia provided for a Dairy and Food Commissioner, with power to inquire into dairy and food and drink products and articles which are food or drinks or their constituents. He shall cause proceedings to be commenced against any person for the enforcement of the laws relative to adulteration, impure or unwholesome food. He shall examine into the sanitary conditions in the operation of any bakery, confectionery or ice cream plant or place where any food or drink products are manufactured, stored or deposited or sold. He shall seize any food or dairy products, substitutes therefor or imitations thereof, which are contrary to the provisions of the act or other laws. Such property, properly seized, may be forfeited to the State and by it destroyed. He shall encourage the dairy industry of the State, and for that purpose shall investigate the general condition of all plants appertaining thereto, and may cause instructions to be given in order to secure the proper feeding and care of cows and the practical operation of any such plant. Persons violating the law shall be guilty of a misdemeanor punishable by a fine or imprisonment in jail.

A statute was passed by Virginia prohibiting the sale or giving away or otherwise dispensing cocaine, alpha or beta eucaine or any mixture of either, except on the prescription of a licensed physician. The same State has also passed an act to regulate the practice of pharmacy and the composition, branding, possession, dispensing and sale of drugs, poisons and narcotics.

Public Service Corporations—Other Than Railroads.—Louisiana passed an act "requiring all persons and corporations operating telegraph or telephone lines to pay either at the point where the message is to be delivered or at the point where the message is offered for transmission, at the option of the person making the claim, for all damages that may arise from the failure, refusal or neglect to transmit or to deliver, or from any delay made in the transmission or the delivery of any message handled by them, or offered them for transmission, and conferring upon courts at the place where the message is to be delivered, or the courts where the message is offered for transmission, or the courts of the domicile of such person or corporation, jurisdiction, at the option of the party bringing the suit."

Mississippi provided that, in addition to damages, a penalty of $25 may be recovered against telephone and telegraph companies for failure to transmit properly or deliver promptly messages intrusted to them for transmission. It has enacted that an express company shall be subject to a penalty of $25, in addition to damages, for demanding or receiving any charge which has been paid or a greater sum than that for which the company agreed to perform the service, or more than reasonable compensation for any service rendered. It has also provided for a penalty of $25 recoverable for overcharging for telephone or telegraph messages, and the test of liability is whether or not the charge is a reasonable compensation for the service rendered. In the enforcement of this act, it would probably be left to a jury in each particular case to determine whether or not the charge was reasonable, and in one instance the company might be forced to pay a penalty, where in another instance for the same service a jury would decide that the charge was reasonable.

Railroads and Common Carriers.—Alabama probably passed more legislation affecting railroads than any other State within the same period. The Legislature held three sessions during the year 1907. The second session concluded its labors on the seventh of August. The third session began on the seventh of November. Litigation having arisen in respect of the acts previously passed, in order to avoid the effect of the decisions of the Supreme Court of the United States that a State officer charged specially with the enforcement of a statute which would deprive a person of property without the due process of law, could be enjoined, an act was passed excluding from the Railroad Commission and the members thereof and the Attorney-General, all power, authority or duty to enforce any rates, fares or charges for the transportation of any passengers which had been or which may thereafter be prescribed by statute, or which had been or may be established by the Railroad Commission's orders.

A series of laws was enacted prohibiting any representative of any person or corporation operating a railroad as a common carrier in the State from receiving for intrastate transportation a higher rate than that established by statute; prohibiting common carriers from preventing access to passenger trains by the use of any means whatsoever by any person desiring to take passage for intrastate travel, when such person has offered to purchase a ticket at the rate prescribed by law, and the sale has been refused; from publishing or receiving a greater rate of transportation than that prescribed by statute or established by the Railroad Commission; from refusing to receive property or passengers for transportation at such rate, and fixing maximum rates to be charged by common carriers for intrastate traffic.

Severe cumulative penalties are provided for the violation of the various acts. The act, omission or failure of any officer or agent is made the act, omission or failure of the corporation. Besides the civil remedies, every officer or agent violating or aiding in the violation of any law or the order of the Railroad Commission is made guilty of a misdemeanor, punishable by a fine not exceeding $1,000. The violation of the act prohibiting a charge exceeding the maximum rate established is punishable in each instance by a fine up to $2,000, and every officer, agent or employee aiding in charging such excessive rate is guilty of a misdemeanor, punishable by a fine up to $500. To prevent relief, the extraordinary provision is made that no suit for the recovery of such forfeiture shall be instituted by the Railroad Commission or any member thereof or by the Attorney-General, but that any individual may institute and prosecute to judgment such suit in the name of the State of Alabama, without his name appearing in the complaint, and that such individual shall be entitled to one-half of the amount recovered. It is provided that such suit shall be a suit by the State of Alabama.

Ten years is the limitation set upon an action brought for a refusal to carry a person at the rate fixed by law. It is provided that it shall be no defence that the rate under consideration has been enjoined, unless the party plaintiff to the instant action was a party to the injunction proceedings. The several railroad companies doing business in the State are divided by name, arbitrarily, into classes, and the maximum rates which they may charge are established.

The railroad legislation of Alabama passed during the year 1907 fills a volume of 240 pages. The enactments embody almost every restrictive measure covered by the legislation of Congress and of the several States. They are the outgrowth of a very bitter controversy between the common carriers and the State, intensified by the intervention of the Federal courts. * * *

Louisiana enacted that every claim for loss of, or damage to, property or freight while in the possession of any common carrier doing business in the State shall be adjusted and paid within thirty days, in case of shipments wholly within the State, and within sixty days in case of shipments from without the State, after the filing of such claim with the agent of such common carrier at the point of destination of such shipment, provided that no claim shall be filed until after arrival of the shipment or some part thereof at the point of destination or until after the lapse of a reasonable time for the arrival thereof. A penalty of $50 is provided for failure to make such settlement.

Louisiana enacted that it shall be unlawful for any common carrier engaged in intrastate transportation of property, or any officer, agent or employee of such common carrier or for any other person or corporation lawfully authorized by such common carrier to receive information therefrom, knowingly to disclose or to permit to be acquired by any person or corporation other than the shipper or consignee, without the consent of such shipper or consignee, any information concerning the nature, kind, quantity, destination or consignee, or which may improperly disclose his business transactions to a competitor; and has also enacted that it shall be unlawful for any person or corporation to collect or knowingly receive such information which may be so used; provided that nothing in the act shall be construed to prevent the giving of such information in response to legal process or to State or Federal officers in the exercise of their powers, or to any officer or other duly authorized person seeking such information for the prosecution of persons charged with or suspected of crime.

Louisiana enlarged the powers of its Railroad Commission, providing that said Commission shall have power to require railway companies to establish stations for passengers and freight wherever reasonably necessary, to build and maintain suitable cattle guards, to require switch connections between different lines in certain cases, and to require railroad companies to furnish cars for the movement of traffic to the best of their ability and without discrimination when such connections shall have been made.

Another act of Louisiana requires common carriers to pay at the point of delivery for all freight they may fail, refuse or neglect to deliver, or for all damages arising from such failure to deliver, as well as for damages to freight while in transit.

Louisiana passed an act requiring railroad corporations operating within that State and having their repair shops in the State, as a condition precedent to using the power of eminent domain granted under the laws of the State of Louisiana, to repair, renovate and rebuild all defective or broken cars, coaches, locomotives or other equipment in the State of Louisiana, and prohibiting any railroad corporation from sending or removing any defective cars out of the State to be repaired, renovated or rebuilt. The act contains a proviso, however, in the following language: "Provided such railway shall have, or be under obligation to have, proper facilities in the State to do such work, and provided this act shall not be so construed as to require any railroad company to violate the safety appliance law of Congress, and provided, further, that no railway company shall be required to haul disabled equipment a greater distance for repairs at a point in Louisiana than would be necessary to reach repair shops in another State."

Louisiana provided a period of three months after any orders of the Railroad Commission are made and become effective, within which suits may be brought to set aside, alter, change or modify the orders of the Railroad Commission respecting rates, charges, rules, regulations and classifications, affecting railroad, express, telephone, telegraph, steamboat, or other watercraft or sleeping car companies, or other individuals, companies or corporations under the jurisdiction of the Commission requiring the performance of any act by any such company, corporation or individual.

Maryland provided for separate toilet rooms and sleeping cabins for white and colored passengers on steamboats on Chesapeake Bay and its tributaries, and that separate seats must be provided for such passengers in railway cars and electric trolley cars running twenty miles beyond municipal limits.

Maryland authorized railroad companies within and without the State reciprocally to lease connecting railroads under certain prescribed conditions.

Following the example of other States, Maryland has undertaken to prescribe by law what shall constitute a train crew.

Mississippi provided that claims for lost or damaged freight against common carriers doing business in that State must be settled within sixty days from the filing of notice of the loss or damage with the agent of the carrier at the point of destination. Where freight is handled by two or more roads or systems of roads and is lost or damaged, claims therefor shall be settled within ninety days from the filing of written notice by the consignee with the agent at point of destination, and failure to settle within the designated time subjects the carrier to a penalty of $25 in addition to actual damages. The act applies only to claims of $200 or less.

Mississippi abolished the fellow-servants rule as to actions by employees of all corporations and individuals using motive power or cars running on tracks, and gives them the same rights and remedies on account of the acts or omissions of any of their fellow-employees as are allowed to non-employees. Knowledge by the injured party of a defect or unsafe condition of machinery shall not be a defence except as to those in charge of the cars and engines and who voluntarily operate them.

Mississippi passed an act by which railroad companies are prohibited from charging for storage of baggage until after four days have elapsed.

Another act of Mississippi provided that if any common carrier shall violate any law enjoining or prohibiting the performance of an act, or shall fail to comply with any lawful order or reasonable rule or regulation of the Railroad Commission, or shall demand or receive a greater sum for a service than is authorized by law or the Commission, it shall be liable to a penalty of $500 for every such failure or overcharge not otherwise punished. It has also provided that all members of families consisting of father, mother, sons or daughters, shall be entitled to all benefits or privileges to mileage books over railroads in the State as if such member were the original purchaser. It has also delegated to the Railroad Commission the power to require railroad companies to build and maintain side-tracks, spur tracks, loop or switch tracks, and not abandon them without the consent of the Commission.

Mississippi made the term "railroad" include all owners or operators of the railroad as a common carrier, and the term "company" likewise applicable to all such, and has brought car service associations under the authority of the Railroad Commission, making all the powers vested in the Commission in respect of railroads and all penalties fixed by law for disobeying the mandates or orders of the Railroad Commission applicable to them.

North Carolina enacted that a railroad company charging more for the carriage of passengers in the State of North Carolina than two and one-half cents per mile, or half of that rate for children between five and twelve years of age, shall be guilty of a misdemeanor, punishable by fine of not less than $500 and not more than $5,000, and that any agent or employee of a railroad company violating the act shall be subject to fine or imprisonment or both. It also provides that any one accepting free transportation other than provided by law shall be guilty of a misdemeanor.

Ohio made a railroad company liable to its employees for injury or death caused by a defective appliance if such defect might have been discovered by reasonable and proper care, tests or inspection. Proof of a defect is made presumptive evidence of knowledge on the part of the company. An employee having knowledge of such defect is not deemed to have assumed the risk of such defect although continuing in the employ of the railroad company after such knowledge. Such continuance shall not be deemed contributory negligence. The fellow-servant rule is also abolished. By Sec. 2 of the act, the doctrine of comparative negligence is introduced as to all actions brought after the passage of the act. Contributory negligence merely goes to a reduction of damages. All questions of negligence and contributory negligence are made questions for the jury.

It is interesting to note that under a referendum, the State of Oregon at an election held June 1, 1908, rejected an act requiring common carriers to grant free transportation to certain public officers as a condition precedent to the exercise of the right of eminent domain. The vote stood : "Yes, 28,856; No, 59,406."

South Carolina amended its law, adding claims for lost baggage to those which must be adjusted by common carriers within a certain period, under penalty of $50 for every failure.

Virginia passed an act regulating the time and manner in which common carriers doing business in the State shall pay claims for loss or damage to freight and for storage, demurrage and car service, and also an act making railroad companies liable for damage by fire occasioned from sparks or coals thrown from their engines of trains, regardless of the use or condition of spark-arresting appliances. It has by another act magnanimously given railroad companies an insurable interest in the property along its route and authorized them to procure insurance against injury thereto by fire for which such companies might be liable. If a railroad company is engaged in interstate commerce and, as a carrier, must perform service for the public, and must perform such service operated with whatever damages may be incident thereto, even though it shall not be guilty of negligence, a question would arise whether the imposition of such burden by a State is not an interference with the carrying on of interstate commerce.

State Government and Elections.—Illinois passed an act to provide for the holding of primary elections by political parties. The first section of this act provides, among other things, that "the nomination of all candidates for all elective State, Congressional, Senatorial, county, city and Village (including officers of the Municipal Court of Chicago), town and judicial offices, members of the State Board of Equalization, Clerks of the Appellate Courts, Trustees of Sanitary Districts, and for the election of precinct, Senatorial and State Central Committeemen, by all political parties," shall be made in the manner provided in the act, provided that the act shall not apply to township and school elections. By the same section it is provided that the name of no person shall be put on the official ballot, where the act applies, unless such candidate is chosen in accordance with its provisions.

A political party, which at the general election for State and county officers next preceding a primary polled more than 2 per cent. of the entire vote of the State, is declared to be a political party within the State, and must nominate all candidates provided for in the act under the provisions thereof. Similar provisions are made as to Congressional and Senatorial districts, and also as to cities and villages.

Section 6 provides that the primaries shall be held on the second Tuesday in April every year except that then current, the first primary election under the act being held on August 8, 1908. This regular primary, as well as the one held in August, 1908, was for the purpose of nominating candidates for election occurring the following November. A primary in February is provided for the nomination of judicial officers, to be voted on in June, and a primary for the last Tuesday in February is provided for the nomination of officers, to be voted for at the April election on the first Tuesday of that month. A primary is to be held on the second Tuesday in March for the nomination of officers to be voted for on the third Tuesday in April of each year. For the nomination of all other officers falling within the act, primaries shall be held three weeks preceding the election. Various political committees are provided for, provision being made for their election under the primary act, and it is provided that each committee and its officers shall have the powers usually exercised by such committees and officers not inconsistent with the provisions of the act; and the various political parties in existence at the time of the passage of the act are recognized and continued. The time for holding conventions is fixed in the act, and various provisions are made as to calling the same, and indicating the number of delegates thereto. * * *

Kansas enacted a law relating to primary elections, providing that all candidates for elective offices shall be nominated by a primary held in accordance with the act, and that party candidates for the office of United States Senator shall be nominated in the manner therein provided. Certain minor offices are excepted from the operation of the act.

Louisiana passed an act providing for a new registration of voters throughout the State, and also amended its primary election law.

Maryland provided that political parties shall nominate candidates for public office, including candidates for the office of United States Senator, and elect delegates to conventions or managing bodies, county executives or executive committees not appointed by a party convention, through a primary election, to be held on the days designated by party committees or governing bodies; provided that such election shall not be later than the second Monday in September. Elaborate provisions are made for such election and the steps to be taken by candidates to make them eligible.

Maryland amended its act relating to expenses in elections for public office and for nominations thereto, and has provided for judicial inquiries concerning election expenses. Every political committee shall receive and disburse all things of value through a treasurer. No person other than a treasurer or political agent shall pay any election expenses, except that a candidate may pay his own expenses for postage, telegrams, telephoning, stationery, printing, expressage, travelling and board. The permissible expenses of any candidate are graded by the number of votes. The legitimate expenses are specified. Every treasurer and political agent must render a full and detailed sworn account of all expenditures. All candidates, including those for the office of United States Senator, must file itemized statements of expenditures for expenses.

Maryland made it unlawful for any corporation to contribute for any political purpose.

Massachusetts forbade, under punishment by fine, political committees and their representatives from soliciting from candidates for nomination money or promises to pay money as a prerequisite to obtaining nomination papers. It also forbade any business corporation, its officers and agents to pay or contribute for election purposes. An offending corporation is punishable by a fine of not more than $10,000, and an offending officer or agent is punishable by a fine of not more than $5,000 or by imprisonment for not more than six months. It also forbade the employment of more than six persons by political committees in cities in each voting precinct, except as caucus officers. In cities not divided into precincts the number shall not exceed six for each ward.

Michigan enacted a primary law for the nomination of party candidates, to become operative when a majority of the enrolled voters of any political party within designated political divisions shall vote in favor of direct nomination of party candidates, such method being subject, however, to discontinuance whenever a majority of the enrolled voters of such political party in any city, county or district voting thereon shall vote against such method, when re-submitted under the terms of the act. The act is very elaborate, providing with great detail for the full and fair expression of the will of the voters. It is noticeable that party lines will be distinctly drawn by the requirement that voters at primary elections shall be enrolled as members of a particular political party. A change of party affiliation requires a special application and a transfer to another enrolment.

Michigan provided for the casting, registering and counting of votes by means of voting machines.

Mississippi, one of the pioneer States in establishing primary election laws, provided for contesting such an election on the charge of fraud.

Mississippi also passed an act forbidding corporations doing business in that State, or any servant, agent, employee or officer thereof, to contribute money or property of said corporation for the purpose of aiding any political party or candidate to any public office under penalty of not less than $100 nor more than $1,000.

Nevada provided for a State police called "Nevada State Police." The law is quite elaborate and has some notable provisions. Each member is authorized to make arrests, with or without warrant, of any person charged with a crime or suspected of the commission of any offence, and to suppress all riots. When the Governor shall declare martial law or a county shall be in a state of insurrection, the police shall have power to take any steps proper for the preservation of life and property. When martial law shall have been declared the Adjutant-General shall provide the police with rations, subsistence for men and horses, camp equipage, transportation and such forces as shall be necessary to perform their duties. In cases of martial law or insurrection, the rules of discipline and regulations of the Army of the United States shall be applied, so far as applicable, to the government of the police. Members are required to serve for a period of not less than one year, unless dismissed or discharged. Any person intercepting, molesting or insulting by words or behavior any member of the police while on duty is subject to arrest and punishment for breach of the peace. A member of the police is subject to trial according to martial law and military usage.

This legislation was the outcome of the domestic violence which caused the State of Nevada, shortly before the passage of the act, to pass a resolution that application be made to the President of the United States to retain in the Goldfield mining district of Nevada a sufficient force of the United States Army to insure domestic tranquillity.

New York made very extensive amendments to its primary election law, bringing it in its main features in general harmony with the recent primary election laws of other States.

Ohio passed an act making elaborate provisions governing primary elections, to be held upon the same day by all political parties, and to be conducted in the manner of a regular election with the Australian ballot.

Ohio passed an act forbidding corporations, directly or indirectly, to contribute anything to any political party, committee or organization, or for any political purposes. Both the corporation which gives and the person who knowingly receives from the corporation are made subject to criminal penalties. A person so participating is given immunity for his testimony.

The suffragette movement has not become potent in Oregon, for at an election on a referendum held in June, 1908, a constitutional amendment permitting women to vote on equal terms with men was rejected, the vote standing: "Yes, 36,858; No, 58,670."

Oregon, by a vote on referendum, adopted an amendment to the State Constitution giving voters power to call a special election at any time to discharge a public officer and elect his successor. The same State also adopted in the same manner a bill instructing members of the Legislature to elect the candidate for United States Senator who received the highest number of votes at the general election. It also in the same manner passed a bill limiting the amount of money candidates and other persons may spend in election campaigns, and prohibiting attempts on election day to persuade any voter to vote for or against any candidate or candidates, or any measure submitted to the people. It is interesting to note that out of nineteen questions submitted twelve were adopted and seven were rejected.

West Virginia enacted an elaborate law for the registration of voters, and also one providing for official ballots. Under this latter act the State Executive Committee of each political party must adopt a party emblem.

West Virginia also passed an act to prevent corrupt practices in elections, and to limit the expenses of candidates and political committees. Expenses are limited to those for travel of the candidate, rent of hall or room for the delivery of speeches, the payment of reasonable compensation for public speakers and musicians and their travelling expenses, printing and distribution of campaign literature, copying and classifying poll lists, making canvasses of voters, charges for services rendered by carriers, telegraph companies and for postage and messenger services, and reasonable clerk hire.

Every person who shall, after election, solicit any money or valuable consideration on account of having induced any other person to vote at any election shall be guilty of a misdemeanor. Whether this will apply to campaign orators, who in asking for office, in return for party service, boast of their achievements, presents an interesting problem. No candidate for Congress or any public office shall pay or promise to pay, in order to secure his nomination or election, anything in excess of a sum to be determined upon the basis of $250 for 5,000 votes or less, and graduated amounts for any excess over that number. Every candidate for nomination must file with designated officers a sworn written statement setting forth in detail all money contributed, disbursed, expended or promised, in endeavoring to secure his nomination or election, or in connection with the election of any other person at said election.

Failure to comply with this provision is made a misdemeanor, and no emolument of the office shall be received prior to its filing. Every political committee shall collect and disburse its campaign expenses through a treasurer, who shall keep a true account of all sums received or disbursed, showing the person from whom received or to whom paid, and the purpose of the transaction. He shall within thirty days after each election file in the designated office a sworn account, showing all such receipts and disbursements and their objects, and shall also show all unpaid debts and obligations and their nature and to whom owing. These accounts are open to public inspection. Upon failure to comply with the law, the treasurer is guilty of a misdemeanor. No corporation, joint stock company or association shall directly or indirectly contribute for the nomination or election of any one to office, subject to a penalty of not exceedng $1,000.

Taxation.—Louisiana passed an act to prevent double taxation, by making mortgage paper and other evidence of indebtedness taxable only at the situs of the owner and holder thereof.

Massachusetts passed a law exempting bonds, notes and certificates of indebtedness of any county, city or town in the commonwealth issued after the first day of May, 1908, from taxation for State, county, city or town purposes.

Massachusetts authorized the appointment of women as deputy collectors of taxes.

Trusts.—Massachusetts passed an act authorizing proceedings by the Attorney-General to restrain by injunction the carrying out of any agreement for the creation of a monopoly for the sale of articles or commodities in common use.

Mississippi amended its laws on trusts, combines and criminal conspiracy so as to make any corporation, partnership or persons a trust and combine, which shall destroy or attempt to destroy competition in the manufacture or sale of a commodity by offering the same for sale at lower price at one place in the State than at another, or rendering service for a lower price in one locality than in another. It is made a prima facie case of violation to show a sale or offer of sale at a lower price at one place in the State than another, or to show a lower charge for a service in one locality than another.

Mississippi provided for the better enforcement of its anti-trust laws by a proceeding in the nature of quo warranto injunction or any other appropriate remedy. Jurisdiction is conferred upon the chancery courts to determine all suits arising out of the violations of the anti-trust law and authority is given to them to grant injunctions, appoint receivers, impose the penalty provided by law and make such decree as may be necessary to prevent the continued operation of unlawful trusts and combines within the State.

Uniform State Laws.—Massachusetts, Ohio and Rhode Island passed the Uniform Sales act, and Louisiana, Ohio and Rhode Island passed the Uniform Warehouse Receipts act.

Miscellaneous.—The Legislature of Illinois passed a joint resolution providing for the celebration of the hundredth anniversary of the birth of Abraham Lincoln, to be held at Springfield, February 12, 1909.

Kentucky passed an act authorizing tobacco pooling.

Louisiana amended and re-enacted Article 1591 of the Revised Civil Code, providing what persons are absolutely incapable of being witnesses to testaments. They are: 1. Children who have not attained the age of sixteen years complete. 2. Persons insane, deaf, dumb or blind. 3. Persons whom the criminal laws declare incapable of exercising civil functions. 4. Married women to the wills of their husbands.

Louisiana imposed a limitation of one year within which to bring actions for the recovery of damages done to person or property by reason of the grading of streets or alleys by municipalities.

Louisiana enacted that in cases where the employer requires a cash deposit by the employee as a guarantee of the faithful performance of duties imposed on such employee, such employer shall pay interest thereon at the rate of not less than 4 per cent. per annum.

Another act of Louisiana, relating to building contracts in certain cases, provided for the giving of security for the payment of sub-contractors, mechanics, laborers, etc., and confers upon such persons a right of action against the surety on the bond in case of default by the contractor.

Louisiana passed an act to prohibit the owner, lessee, proprietor or manager of any theatre to permit persons to take seats and disturb the audience after the curtain has risen. Persons arriving late are required to wait until an intermission before taking their seats.

Louisiana passed an act establishing a State Board of Accountants, fixing its duties and providing for the issuance of certificates, or licenses to practice the business of expert public accountants.

Mississippi provided for the commission form of government for cities and towns, and that they may adopt such form by an election. The purpose of this is to get away from ward lines and ward politics. A return is provided for to the former system by an election held for that purpose.

New Jersey established a department of Inland Waterways, to increase the efficiency of existing waterways, and construct new ones, and for the improvement and development of the New Jersey coast.

New York provided for the application of the Torrens System of Land Title Registration when desired.

Ohio provided for a Board of Certified Public Accountants and forbade any person using the name of Certified Public Accountant or the abbreviation "C. P. A." who has not received a certificate from such board. A certificate can only be granted to a person over twenty-one years of age, of good moral character, and who is either the graduate of a high school or has received an equivalent education and who has at least three years' experience in the practice of accounting and has successfully passed the examination in the Theory of Accounts, Practical Accounting, Auditing and Commercial Law as affecting accountancy.

Ohio passed an elaborate statute providing for the registration of motor cars with the Secretary of State, and regulating their speed and use.

Rhode Island, also passed a very comprehensive act concerning the registration, numbering, use and speed of motor vehicles and the licensing of operators of such vehicles. This act, it is understood, was passed after a full consideration of all the legislation of other States upon the same subject. It may therefore be considered as fairly representing the advanced stages of automobile regulation.

On May 4, 1776, Rhode Island passed a law severing her connection with England, and in commemoration of this event, that State passed an act establishing May 4 as Rhode Island Independence Day.

Oklahoma.—On the fourth of last July, the forty-sixth star appeared in the field of our national flag for the State of Oklahoma, which, through the amalgamation of the Territories of Oklahoma and Indian Territory, entered into statehood by the adoption of its constitution in September, 1907, and the issuance of the proclamation of the President on the sixteenth of November following. There has been no time for any "noteworthy changes" in the statute law of Oklahoma. It has, however, made some new and notable contributions to the statute law. The first Legislature assembled on the first Monday in December, 1907, and adjourned May 26, 1908. A distinctly new departure was an act providing for the guarantee of depositors in banks against loss. A fund is provided by an assessment of one per cent., upon the average of each State bank. The depositors of any savings bank are immediately subrogated to a right of payment out of this fund, the integrity of which is restored by an additional assessment. The benefits of the act are open to national banks, but the Attorney-General of the United States has given an opinion that national banks so participating are liable to a forfeiture of their charters.

In pursuance of a requirement in the enabling act of Congress, Oklahoma inserted in its constitution a provision that no intoxicants should be sold for a period of twenty-one years in what was formerly Indian Territory, except through State dispensary agents, and then only for medical purposes. There was a submission to a vote of the people of the question whether or not the law should be State wide, but the response was in the affirmative. Pursuant to this action, the Legislature passed a State dispensary law, under which intoxicants are sold solely upon the prescription of physicians.

A graduated tax on all incomes in excess of $3,500, and a tax on inheritance, on land holdings in excess of 640 acres of average value, a tax upon gross incomes of public service corporations, and a tax upon miners of oil and coal were imposed.

An anti-trust bill was passed, but unlike the Sherman act as construed by a majority of the United States Supreme Court, it only operates upon such contracts and combinations in restraint of trade as are "against public policy." Doubtless this aspect of the law is in response to such views as have been recently enunciated by President Roosevelt and others, who have seen the injurious effects of such inelastic statutes as the Sherman law and its congeners. A violation of the act is punishable both by fine and imprisonment, and forfeiture of personal property, at the discretion of the Supreme Court.

In pursuance of the constitutional provision for the initiative and referendum an act was passed putting it into effect. Legislation may be initiated upon petitions signed by 8 per cent. of the regular voters, and a constitutional amendment upon petition signed by 15 per cent. The referendum may be made operative either by legislative act or by petition signed by 5 per cent. of the legal voters.

An act was also passed authorizing cities of a certain class to adopt for themselves a charter form of government. There was also an act authorizing the creation of drainage districts for the reclamation of overflowed land.

Statistics of Strikes and Lockouts.

THE twenty-first annual report of the Commissioner of Labor dealing with the subject of strikes and lockouts in the United States during the years 1881 to 1905, inclusive, a period of twenty-five years, was issued June 5, 1907.

The following tables extracted from the report show the number, duration, causes and result of strikes during the period under observation.

NUMBER OF STRIKES AND LOCKOUTS.

Year.	Strikes.					Lockouts.				
	Number.	Establishments.		Strikers.	Employees thrown out of work.	Number.	Establishments.		Employees locked out.	Employees thrown out of work.
		Number.	Average per Strike.	Number.	Number.		Number.	Average per lockout.	Number.	Number.
1881	471	2,928	6.2	101,070	129,521	6	9	1.5	655	655
1882	454	2,105	4.6	120,860	154,671	22	42	1.9	4,131	4,131
1883	478	2,759	5.8	122.198	149.763	28	117	4.2	20,512	20,512
1884	443	2,367	5.3	117,313	147,054	42	354	8.4	18,121	18,121
1885	645	2,284	3.5	158 584	242,705	50	183	3.7	15 424	15,424
1886	1,432	10,053	7.0	407,152	508,044	140	1,509	10.8	101,980	101,980
1887	1,436	6,589	4.6	272,776	379.676	67	1,281	19.1	57,534	59,630
1888	906	3,506	3.9	103,218	147,704	40	180	4.5	13,787	15.176
1889	1,075	3,786	3.5	205,068	249,559	36	132	3.7	10,471	10,731
1890	1,833	9,424	5.1	285,900	351,944	64	324	5.1	19,233	21,555
1891	1,717	8.116	4.7	245,042	298,939	69	546	7.9	14,116	31,014
1892	1,298	5,540	4.3	163,499	206,671	61	716	11.7	30.050	32,014
1893	1,305	4,555	3.5	195,008	265,914	70	305	4.4	13,016	21,842
1894	1,349	8,196	6.1	505.049	660,425	55	875	15.9	28,548	29.619
1895	1,215	6,973	5.7	285,742	392,403	40	370	9.3	12,754	14,785
1896	1,026	5,462	5.3	183,813	241,170	40	51	1.3	3,675	7,668
1897	1,078	8,492	7.9	332,570	408,391	32	171	5.3	7,651	7,763
1898	1,056	3,809	3.6	182,067	249,002	42	164	3.9	11,038	14,217
1899	1,797	11,317	6.3	308,267	417,072	41	323	7.9	14,698	14,817
1900	1,779	9.248	5.2	399,656	505,066	60	2,281	38.0	46,562	62,653
1901	2,924	10,908	3.7	396,280	543,386	88	451	5.1	16,257	20,457
1902	3,162	14,248	4.5	553,143	659,792	78	1,304	16.7	30,304	31,715
1903	3,494	20,248	5.8	531,682	656,055	154	3,288	21.4	112,332	131,779
1904	2,307	10,202	4.4	375,754	517,211	112	2,316	20.7	44,908	56,604
1905	2,077	8,292	4.0	176,337	221,686	109	1,255	11.5	68,474	80,748
Total	36,757	181,407	4.9	6,728,048	8,703,824	1,546	18,547	12.0	716,231	825,610

A greater number of strikes occurred in the building trades than in any other industry. In that industry during the years from 1881 to 1905 there were 9,564 strikes, 69,899 establishments involved, 917,905 strikers, and 1,083,699 employees thrown out of work in the establishments involved in strikes.

The coal and coke industry was second in importance so far as number of strikes and establishments involved were concerned, but first in number of strikers and employees thrown out of work. In the coal and coke industry there were 3,336 strikes, 17,025 establishments involved, 2,006,353 strikers, and 2,460,743 employees thrown out of work.

RESULTS OF STRIKES AND LOCKOUTS.

Year.	Strikes.						Lockouts.			
	Ordered by labor organization.			Not ordered by labor organization.			Total establishments involved.	Per Cent. of establishments in which lockout—		
	Per Cent. of establishments in which strike—			Per Cent. of establishments in which strike—						
	Succeeded.	Succeeded partly.	Failed.	Succeeded.	Succeeded partly.	Failed.		Succeeded.	Succeeded partly.	Failed.
1881	64.99	6.71	28.30	49.33	7.98	42.69	9	88.89	11.11	......
1882	56.36	9.54	34.10	44.71	3.79	51.50	42	64.29	......	35.71
1883	64.07	18.31	17.62	25.42	3.80	70.78	117	56.41	......	43.59
1884	55.62	3.25	41.13	31.25	7.00	61.75	354	27.97	.28	71.75
1885	62.42	10.58	27.00	27.05	6.60	66.35	183	38.25	3.28	58.47
1886	33.46	20.48	46.06	42.07	7.07	50.86	1,509	21.18	13.11	65.71
1887	48.36	7.19	44.45	27.08	7.24	65.68	1,281	34.19	1.25	64.56
1888	56.17	4.99	38.84	25.00	8.86	66.14	180	74.44	3.89	21.67
1889	45.61	21.37	33.02	49.93	9.26	40.81	132	40.91	25.76	33.33
1890	53.99	10.17	35.84	39.86	8.45	51.69	324	65.74	5.56	28.70
1891	38.46	8.10	53.44	36.76	11.68	51.56	546	63.92	14.29	21.79
1892	39.33	8.75	51.92	39.19	8.16	52.65	716	69.13	25.28	5.59
1893	53.94	10.89	35.17	28.42	6.19	65.39	305	41.90	18.31	39.79
1894	37.35	13.67	48.98	43.94	12.12	43.94	875	11.31	2.40	86.29
1895	59.25	10.05	30.70	27.21	9.18	63.61	370	13.24	27	86.49
1896	62.47	6.55	30.98	29.93	15.69	54.38	51	80.39	1.96	17.65
1897	59.67	29.51	10.82	30.83	12.54	56.63	171	60.82	3.51	35.67
1898	69.74	6.15	24.11	33.96	7.64	58.40	164	63.41	.61	35.98
1899	76.33	14.19	9.48	36.56	14.92	48.52	323	18.01	.62	81.87
1900	48.06	21.95	29.99	29.94	7.03	63.03	2,281	94.30	.31	5.39
1901	50.36	17.19	32.45	30.59	16.44	52.97	451	37.03	42.13	20.84
1902	48.31	23.72	27.97	31.38	8.74	59.88	1,304	78.22	4.06	17.72
1903	41.72	23.77	34.51	22.86	15.43	61.71	3,288	81.39	5.17	13.44
1904	35.75	15.59	48.66	25.48	8.78	65.74	2,316	55.91	23.06	21.03
1905	41.58	11.30	47.12	24.01	13.22	62.74	1,255	31.60	32.64	35.76
Total	49.48	15.87	34.65	33.86	9.83	56.31	18,547	57.20	10.71	32.09

STRIKES AND LOCKOUTS—*Continued.*

PRINCIPAL CAUSES OF STRIKES.

CAUSE OR OBJECT.	Per Cent. of Establishments in which strike—			Strikers.		Employees thrown out of work.	
	Succeeded.	Succeeded partly.	Failed.	Number.	Per Cent. of total (6,728,048).	Number.	Per Cent. of total (8,703,824).
For increase of wages	49.95	18.69	31.36	2,212,195	32.88	2,940,804	33.79
For increase of wages, with various causes	46.87	25.18	27.95	1,331,158	19.79	1,598,199	18.36
Against reduction of wages	34.95	12.74	52.31	856,947	12.74	1,158,435	13.31
Against reduction of wages, with various causes	67.40	6.21	26.39	99,698	1.48	134,744	1.55
For reduction of hours	50.69	10.08	39.23	389,876	5.79	514,496	5.91
For reduction of hours, with various causes	52.35	21.93	25.72	850,694	12.64	1,004,135	11.54
Against increase of hours	50.06	12.85	37.09	65,883	.98	82,808	.95
Against increase of hours, with various causes	61.53	6.15	32.32	22,164	.33	28,686	.33
Recognition of union and union rules	55.48	1.61	42.88	610,088	9.07	743,523	8.54
Recognition of union and union rules, with various causes	38.66	24.58	36.76	795,727	11.83	896,814	10.30
Employment of certain persons	24.81	1.64	73.55	287,883	4.28	402,339	4.62
Employment of certain persons, with various causes	29.03	18.42	52.55	139,767	2.08	163,268	1.88
Method and time of payment, with various causes	55.39	27.60	17.01	225,668	3.50	251,995	2.90
Docking, fines and charges, with various causes	22.07	59.45	18.48	171,404	2.55	177,740	2.04
Working conditions and rules	41.63	3.98	54.39	112,705	1.68	150,769	1.73
Sympathy with strikers and employees locked out elsewhere	20.68	2.79	76.53	259,516	3.85	373,968	4.30

DURATION OF STRIKES AND LOCKOUTS.

The presentation of strikes by years shows that the average duration per establishment for the twenty-five years from 1881 to 1905 was 25.4 days. During these years the average duration of strikes varied from 12.7 days in 1881 to 35.5 days in 1904. Of all establishments involved in strikes during these years 61.38 per cent. were closed, and the average number of days closed per establishment was 20.1. The per cent. of establishments in which strikes occurred which were closed by strikes varied from 45.54 per cent. in 1905 to 85.82 per cent. in 1895. The average days closed per establishment varied from 12.1 in 1881 to 36 9 in 1894.

The average duration of strikes per establishment varied from 4.6 days in agriculture to 83.2 days in ore mining. Industries showing high averages are pottery, 66.5 days; gloves and mittens, 54.6 days; coal and coke, 50.9 days.

An interesting statement in the report is the one showing the per cent. of establishments involved which were closed by strikes. The percentages varied from 9.72 per cent. in slaughtering and meat packing to 96.71 per cent. in coal and coke. Industries showing a low percentage of establishments closed were lithographing 10 per cent. and car building 13.68 per cent. Industries showing a high percentage of establishments closed were water transportation 92.46 per cent., women's clothing 85.20 per cent., ore mining 84.55 per cent., laundry work 83.82 per cent., and men's clothing 82.86 per cent. The average days closed varied from 3.1 in blacksmithing and horseshoeing to 103.4 in the manufacture of pottery.

The average duration of all lockouts per establishment during the twenty-five-year period, 1881 to 1905, was 84.6 days, the percentage of establishments involved which were closed was 68.25 per cent., and the average days closed per establishment were 40.4.

The average duration per establishment varied from twenty-seven days in 1901 to 265.1 days in 1900, the percentage of establishments closed from 30.65 per cent. in 1899 to 91.89 per cent. in 1900, and the average days closed from 10.4 days in 1901 to 95.8 days in 1900.

In the building trades—the industry in which lockouts were of most frequent occurrence—the average days of duration per establishment was 105.3, the percentage of establishments closed was 72.49 per cent., and the average days closed per establishment 49.3. In men's clothing the average duration was 33.8 days, the per cent. closed 86.30, and the average days closed 32.5.

STRIKES AND LOCKOUTS SETTLED BY JOINT AGREEMENT AND ARBITRATION, 1901 TO 1905.

YEAR.	STRIKES.			LOCKOUTS.		
	Number.	Number settled by joint agreement.	Number settled by arbitration.	Number.	Number settled by joint agreement.	Number settled by arbitration.
1901	2,924	149	49	88	10	2
1902	3,162	204	58	78	11	1
1903	3,494	246	66	154	18	3
1904	2,307	130	23	112	17	2
1905	2,077	74	27	109	10	3
Total	13,964	803	223	541	66	11

National Civic Federation.

AN organization of prominent representatives of capital, labor, and the general public formed as the direct outgrowth of conventions held in Chicago and New York in 1900–1901. Its purpose is to organize the best brains of the Nation in an educational movement toward the solution of some of the great problems related to social and industrial progress; to provide for study and discussion of questions of national import; to aid thus in the crystallization of the most enlightened public opinion; and when desirable, to promote legislation in accordance therewith. At the present time the work of the Federation is carried on through the following agencies:

(1) The Trade Agreement Department which consists of employers and representatives of workingmen, who make agreements as to hours, wages and conditions of employment.

(2) The Industrial Conciliation Department dealing entirely with strikes and lockouts, and including in its membership representatives of the general public and the leading organizations of employers and wage-earners. The services of this department have been enlisted in more than five hundred cases involving every phase of industrial controversy.

(3) The Industrial Economics Department organized to promote discussion and to aid in the solution of practical economic and social problems such as "Wages, and the Cost of Living," "The Injunction," "Opened and Closed Shop," "Restriction of Output," "Compulsory Arbitration," "Initiative and Referendum," "The Income Tax," "The Trusts," "Socialism," etc.

(4) Industrial Welfare Department composed of employers of labor in stores, factories, mines and on railroads. It is devoted to interesting employers in improving the conditions under which employés in all industries work and live.

(5) Public Employés' Welfare Department, whose object is to create an interest in improving the working conditions of Federal, State and Municipal employés. The Department is composed of officials who have to do with the working conditions of public employés, chairmen of boards of health, heads of departments of public safety, leading physicians connected with public hospitals, heads of charity boards and others.

(6) The Woman's Department composed largely of women who are themselves stockholders or who are financially interested in industrial organizations through family relationships. The object of this department is to use its influence in securing needed improvements in the working and living conditions of women and men wage-earners in the various industries and governmental institutions, and to co-operate, when practicable, in the general work of the Federation.

(7) Public Ownership Commission composed of one hundred prominent men representing every shade of public opinion on this subject. The investigation by this commission into the facts of public ownership and operation here and abroad is the most thorough yet undertaken.

(8) The Immigration Department composed of men selected to represent all localities in the Union affected by the admission of aliens.

(9) Political Reform Department organized to arouse and promote public interest in representative government in national, State and city politics. The officers of the Federation are:

President, Seth Low; Vice-Presidents, Samuel Gompers, Nahum J. Bachelder, Ellison A. Smyth, Benjamin I. Wheeler; Treasurer, Isaac N. Seligman; Chairman Trade Agreement Department, John Mitchell; Chairman Public Employés' Welfare Department, William H. Tait; Chairman Industrial Welfare Department, Charles A. Moore; Chairman Industrial Economics Department, Nicholas Murray Butler; Ex-officio, Chairman Industrial Conciliation Department, Seth Low; Chairman Public Ownership Commission, Melville E. Ingalls; Chairman Immigration Department, Franklin MacVeagh; Chairman Executive Council, Ralph M. Easley; Secretary, D. L. Cease. Office, 281 Fourth Avenue, New York City. The following compose the executive committee of the Federation:

ON THE PART OF THE PUBLIC:

Andrew Carnegie (Capitalist), New York; Cornelius N. Bliss (Ex-Secretary of the Interior), New York City; Nahum J. Bachelder (Master of the National Grange), Concord, N. H.; John Hays Hammond (Mining Engineer), Gloucester, Mass.; Benjamin I. Wheeler (President University of California), Berkeley, Cal.; William H. Taft (Former Secretary of War), Cincinnati, Ohio; Charles W. Eliot (President Harvard University), Cambridge, Mass.; Nicholas Murray Butler (President Columbia University), New York City; Seth Low (Publicist), New York City; Archbishop John Ireland (of the Roman Catholic Church), St. Paul, Minn.; Charles J. Bonaparte (Attorney-General of United States), Washington, D. C.; David R. Francis (Ex-Secretary of the Interior), St. Louis, Mo.; Isaac N. Seligman (of J. & W. Seligman & Co.), New York City; James Speyer (of Speyer & Co.), New York; V. Everit Macy (Capitalist), New York City; John M. Stahl (President Farmers' National Congress); Ralph M. Easley (Chairman Executive Council National Civic Federation), New Canaan, Ct.

ON THE PART OF EMPLOYERS:

Henry Phipps (Director United States Steel Corporation), New York City; August Belmont (President August Belmont & Co.), New York City; W. A. Clark (President United Verde Copper Co.), Butte, Mont.; Clarence H. Mackay (President Postal Telegraph-Cable Co.), New York City; Marvin Hughitt (President Chicago & Northwestern Railway Co.), Chicago, Ill.; Frederick D. Underwood (President Erie Railroad Co.), New York City; M. H. Taylor (President Pittsburgh Coal Co.), Pittsburgh, Pa.; Melville E. Ingalls, (C. C. C. & St. L. Railway Co.), Cincinnati, Ohio; Samuel Mather (of Pickands, Mather & Co.), Cleveland, Ohio; Charles A. Moore (Manning, Maxwell & Moore), New York City; Franklin MacVeagh (of Franklin MacVeagh & Co.), Chicago, Ill.; Alexander H. Revell (of A. H. Revell & Co.), Chicago, Ill.; Frank A. Munsey (Publisher), New York City; Ellison A. Smyth (President South Carolina Cotton Manufacturers' Association), Pelzer, S. C.; Charles H. Taylor, Jr. (Ex-President American Newspaper Publishers' Association), Boston, Mass.; Dan R. Hanna (of M. A. Hanna & Co.), Cleveland, Ohio; Marcus M. Marks (President National Association of Clothiers), New York City; Otto M. Eidlitz (Former Chairman Board of Governors, Building Trades Employers' Association), New York City.

ON THE PART OF WAGE-EARNERS:

Samuel Gompers (President American Federation of Labor), Washington, D. C.; John Mitchell (Former President United Mine Workers of America), New York City; A. B. Garretson (Grand Chief Conductor, Order of Railway Conductors), Cedar Rapids, Iowa; James Duncan (General Secretary Granite Cutters' International Association of America), Quincy, Mass.; Daniel J. Keefe (President International 'Longshoremen, Marine and Transportworkers' Association), Detroit, Mich.; Warren S. Stone (Grand Chief International Brotherhood of Locomotive Engineers), Cleveland, Ohio; P. H. Morrissey (Grand Master, Brotherhood Railroad Trainmen), Cleveland, Ohio; William D. Mahon (President Amalgamated Association of Street Railway Employés of America), Detroit,

Mich.; Timothy Healy (President International Brotherhood of Stationary Firemen), New York City; William J. Bowen (President Bricklayers' and Masons' International Union), Indianapolis, Ind.; J. J. Hannahan (Grand Master Brotherhood of Locomotive Firemen), Peoria, Ill.; James O'Connell (President International Association of Machinists), Washington, D. C.; John F. Tobin (General President Boot and Shoe Workers' Union), Boston, Mass.; Joseph F. Valentine (President Iron Moulders' Union of North America), Cincinnati, Ohio; James M. Lynch (President International Typographical Union), Indianapolis, Ind.; Denis A. Hayes (President Glass Bottle Blowers' Association of United States and Canada), Philadelphia, Pa.; William D. Huber (President United Brotherhood of Carpenters and Joiners of America), Indianapolis, Ind.

The Woman's Department of the National Civic Federation was organized at Washington, May 12, 1908, with the following officers and executive committee:

Chairman, Mrs. Medill McCormick, Chicago; Vice-Chairmen, Miss Anne Morgan, New York; Mrs. J. Borden Harriman, New York; Mrs. Cornelius Stevenson, Philadelphia; Mrs. John K. Ottley, Georgia; Mrs. Henry Lee Higginson, Massachussets, and Mrs. Benjamin Ide Wheeler, California; Treasurer, Mrs. S. Thurston Ballard, Lousiville; Secretary, Miss Gertrude Beeks, New York.

Executive Committee: Mrs. Horace Brook, Philadelphia; Mrs. Eva McDonald, Valesh, Washington; Mrs. Cyrus H. Orr, Birmingham, Ala.; Mrs. Sarah S. Platt-Decker, Denver; Mrs. B. Frank Mebane, Spray, N. C.; Mrs. Clarence H. Mackay, Roslyn, L. I.; Mrs. Philip McMillan, Detroit; Mrs. Ogden Armour, Chicago; Mrs. Frederick Dent Grant, U. S. A.; Mrs. Bowman S. McCalla, U. S. N.; Mrs. A. F. McKissick, Greenwood, S. C.; Mrs. John R. McLean, Washington; Mrs. Arthur Lee, Elkins, W. Va.; Mrs. George Westinghouse, Pittsburgh; Mrs. Andrew Carnegie, New York; Mrs. Roger Wolcott, Boston, Mrs. Proctor, Cincinnati; Mrs. Wanamaker, Philadelphia; Mrs. Meyerhausen; Mrs. Overton Lea, Nashville, Tenn.; Mrs. Nicholas Longworth, Cincinnati; Mrs. Edwin Farnham Green, Boston; Mrs. John Newbold Hazard, Peacedale, R. I.; Mrs. John D. Rockefeller, Jr., New York; Mrs. Edmund Leighton Tyler, Anniston, Ala.; Mrs. Francis Higginson Cabot, New York; Mrs. Ellen Mason, Boston, and Mrs. Murray Crane, Boston.

Earnings of Wage-Earners

IN THE UNITED STATES.

(From Census Bulletin 93.)

When the material for the Federal census of manufactures was collected in 1905, each manufacturing establishment was requested to report, for the week in 1904 during which the largest number of persons was employed, the number of wage-earners, classified by the amount they earned.

The returns are those of earnings or wages and not of rates of pay. Rates are higher than earnings because they are for a full week, whereas earnings shown in the bulletin were reported for the time actually worked, and this in some instances was less than the full week.

The results of this inquiry were published in Bulletin 93 of the Bureau of the Census in May, 1908, which was prepared under the supervision of William M. Steuart, chief statistician for manufactures.

According to this bulletin satisfactory returns were received from 123,703 establishments, 62.9 per cent. of all manufacturing establishments which employ wage-earners. These establishments from which the returns were received, moreover, employed almost one-half of all the wage-earners engaged in factory industries in the United States, and therefore the statistics are sufficiently representative to give fairly accurate results.

The bulletin now published contains the first regular Census report ever made of classified weekly earnings covering a large number of establishments. Of the 3,297,819 wage-earners covered by the present investigation, 2,619,053, or 70.4 per cent., were men; 588,599, or 17.9 per cent., were women; and 90,167, or 2.7 per cent., were children. The pay rolls of the 123,703 establishments for the week covered amounted to $33,185,791, and of this the men received $29,240,287, or 88.1 per cent.; the women, $3,633,481, or 11 per cent.; and the children, $312,023, or nine-tenths of 1 per cent.

CLASSIFIED EARNINGS, ALL INDUSTRIES.

The important feature of the bulletin is the classification of these wage-earners—men, women, and children—at each amount of earnings. For all wage-earners reported, every industry being represented in the establishments reporting, this classification is as follows:

	Number of wage-earners included in the inquiry.	Percentage in the group.	Cumulative percentage.		Number of wage-earners included in the inquiry.	Percentage in the group.	Cumulative percentage.
Less than $3	132,064	4.0	100.0	$10 to $12	439,208	13.3	44.0
$3 to $4	150,403	4.6	96.0	$12 to $15	464,875	14.1	30.7
$4 to $5	194,301	5.9	91.4	$15 to $20	390,367	11.8	16.6
$5 to $6	206,163	6.2	85.5	$20 to $25	106,700	3.2	4.8
$6 to $7	262,531	8.0	79.3	$25 and over	51,728	1.6	1.6
$7 to $8	266,012	8.1	71.3				
$8 to $9	255,458	7.7	63.2	Total	3,297,819	100.0	....
$9 to $10	378,009	11.5	55.5				

More than half of all the wage-earners included in the bulletin earned $9 and over during the week.

The earnings are classified for totals of States and of industries, while twenty-five industries are shown in detail by States and Territories, and twenty-five States by leading industries. Average earnings are also computed for all the States and industries shown.

AVERAGE WAGE-EARNER GOT $10 A WEEK.

The figures show that in 1904 the average wage-earner employed in manufacturing received $10.06 per week. The average man received $11.16; the average woman, $6.17; and the average child under 16 years of age, $3.46.

DIAMOND CUTTERS EARNED LARGE AMOUNTS.

The highest average weekly earnings reported for the men in any manufacturing industry were $21.68, paid in conducting lapidary work. The principal occupations in this industry—those which cause the high earnings—are connected with the cutting, polishing, and setting of diamonds and other precious stones. Even when power-driven machinery is used, these occupations call for exceptional skill and judgment, and as a result, a successful worker commands high rates.

Other industries which were conspicuous for the high weekly earnings paid to men wage-earners embraced the manufacture of corsets ($16.99), photolithographing and photo-engraving ($16.68,) the manufacture of statuary and art goods ($16.45), and the manufacture of watches ($16.16). The manufacture of watches was also conspicuous for the high average earnings of women ($8.93). No other industry employing any considerable number of women reported so large an amount.

MEN MAKING TURPENTINE AND ROSIN RECEIVED LOW EARNINGS.

The lowest average earnings for men in any industry were $5.23, paid to those engaged in the manufacture of turpentine and rosin. Most of the men employed in this industry were engaged in gathering the crude gum, a task which is in some respects the lowest order of employment reported in connection with the census of manufactures. In the cottonseed oil and cake industry, another in which the average weekly earnings of men ($6.64) were noticeably low, large numbers were engaged in handling the raw material and the finished product, while comparatively few were employed in the operation of machinery and in the actual work of production.

The lowest average earnings for children were $1.84 per week, received by the 105 children engaged in the manufacture of pickles, preserves, and sauces. Of the industries employing a considerable number of women, the grading, roasting, cleaning, and shelling of peanuts is the one in which the earnings of women were lowest. The average weekly earnings of the 392 women in this industry were but $2.26.

MEN IN STEEL WORKS AND ROLLING MILLS EARNED $12.56.

The industries thus far mentioned are of interest, because they were extremes and not because they employed large numbers of wage-earners. The average earnings of the men in some of the more important industries were as follows: Iron and steel, steel works and rolling mills, $12.56; iron and steel, blast furnaces, $11.71; foundry and machine shop products, $11.88; lumber and timber products, $9.25; furniture, $10.16; cotton goods, $7.71; boots and shoes, $11.88; men's clothing, $12.23; women's clothing, $13.52; tobacco, cigars and cigarettes, $11.14; newspaper and periodical printing and publishing, $13.13; and glass, $14.10.

WOMEN IN COTTON MILLS EARNED $6 A WEEK.

The average weekly earnings of women in some of the industries which employ considerable numbers were as follows: Cotton goods, $6.03; hosiery and knit goods, $6.01 silk and silk goods, $6.11; boots and shoes, $7.60; men's clothing, $6.07; women's clothing, $6.85; shirts, $5.69; and glass, $5.08.

The only industries employing considerable numbers of children under 16 years of age were glass, shirts, tobacco, cigars and cigarettes, and the five textile industries. In the cotton industry, which is the most important of the textiles, the average weekly earnings of the children were $3.21. For glass the average weekly earnings were $4.22; for shirts, $2.31; and for tobacco, cigars and cigarettes, $3.

LOW EARNINGS IN SOUTHERN COTTON MILLS.

In connection with the cotton industry, the bulletin makes an interesting comparison of the earnings in the North with those in the South. By confining the comparison to establishments engaged in the manufacture of plain cloths for printing and converting, it eliminates to a considerable extent the differences between the character of the industry in the two sections, and thus presents a fair basis to measure differences in earnings. This comparison shows that the average earnings of men were in New England $8.52; in the South, $5.14—a difference of $3.38. For women the average was, in New England $7.23; in the South, $3.77—a difference of $3.46; while for children the average was, in New England $4.45; in the South, $2.73—a difference of $1.72. For all classes the average weekly earnings in the North were $7.62 as contrasted with but $4.16 in the South.

In explaining the low average earnings prevailing in the Southern States, the Census Bureau calls attention to the recentness of the development of the factory system in that part of the country, to the comparatively large proportion which women and children form of the total number of wage-earners, to the relatively large number of negroes employed, and to the fact that the industries thus far established in the South are those which do not in any part of the country require the most highly paid wage-earners. It is very probable that the further industrial development of the South will result ultimately in a material increase in average earnings.

WESTERN STATES HAD HIGHEST EARNINGS.

The Southern States are moreover generally conspicuous for low average weekly earnings. The rank of the several geographic divisions in respect to the average earnings of all wage-earners included in this inquiry is as follows: Western, $13.65; North Central, $10.62; North Atlantic, $10.11; South Central, $8.33; and South Atlantic, $7.31.

NEW YORK RANKED TWENTY-FIFTH.

The leading States with respect to average weekly earnings were: Montana, $18.19; Nevada, $17.76; Arizona, $16.15; and Wyoming, $15.75. New York was twenty-fifth, with $10.40; Pennsylvania, twenty-third, with $10.51; Illinois, fifteenth, with $11.55; Ohio, twentieth, with $10.63; and Massachusetts, thirty-second, with $9.68. North Carolina, with $4.96, and South Carolina, with $4.68, reported the lowest averages.

Labor Legislation.

BOYCOTTING, BLACKLISTING AND INTIMIDATION LAWS.

THE States having laws prohibiting *boycotting* in terms are Alabama, Colorado, Illinois, Indiana, and Texas.

The States having laws prohibiting *blacklisting* in terms are Alabama, Arkansas, Colorado, Connecticut, Florida, Illinois, Indiana, Iowa, Kansas, Minnesota, Missouri, Montana, Nevada, North Dakota, Oklahoma, Oregon, Texas, Utah, Virginia, Washington, and Wisconsin.

A number of States have enacted laws concerning *intimidation*, conspiracy against workingmen, and interference with employment, viz.: Alabama, Arkansas, Connecticut, Delaware, Florida, Georgia, Illinois, Kansas, Kentucky, Louisiana, Maine, Massachusetts, Michigan, Minnesota, Mississippi, Missouri, New Hampshire, New Jersey, New York, North Dakota, Oklahoma, Oregon, Pennsylvania, Porto Rico, Rhode Island, South Dakota, Texas, Utah, Vermont, Washington, West Virginia, and Wisconsin.

In the following States it is unlawful for an employer to exact any agreement, either written or verbal, from an employé not to join or become a member of a labor organization, as a condition of employment: California, Colorado, Connecticut, Idaho, Indiana, Kansas, Massachusetts, Minnesota, Nevada, New Jersey, Ohio, Oregon, Pennsylvania, Porto Rico and Wisconsin.

EIGHT-HOUR LAWS.

Arizona.—Eight hours constitute a day's labor in all underground mines and workings.

Arkansas.—Eight hours constitute a day's work on public highways and bridges and for railway telegraph operators.

California.—Unless otherwise expressly stipulated, eight hours constitute a day's work. The time of service of all laborers, workmen, and mechanics employed upon any public works of, or work done for, the State, or for any political sub-division thereof, whether the work is to be done by contract or otherwise, is limited and restricted to eight hours in any one calendar day.

Colorado.—A day's work for all workingmen employed by the State, or any county, township, school district, municipality, or incorporated town, and for all employés in underground mines or workings, and in smelting and refining works, is restricted to eight hours.

Connecticut.—Eight hours of labor constitute a lawful day's work unless otherwise agreed. Railroad telegraph operators controlling the movement of trains may work but eight hours, except at stations kept open only in the daytime.

Delaware.—Eight hours constitute a lawful day's work for all municipal employés of the city of Wilmington.

District of Alaska.—Eight hours are a day's labor on the public roads.

District of Columbia.—A day's work for all laborers and mechanics employed by the District of Columbia, or by any contractor or sub-contractor upon any public works of the District, is limited to eight hours.

Hawaii.—For all mechanics, clerks, laborers, and other employés on public works and in public offices eight hours of actual service constitute a day's work.

Idaho.—Eight hours' actual work constitute a lawful day's labor for manual laborers employed by the day on all State, county, and municipal works. Labor in mines and smelters is limited to eight hours per day.

Illinois.—Eight hours are a legal day's work in all mechanical employments, except on farms, and when otherwise agreed; the law does not apply to service by the year, month, or week. Eight hours constitute a day's labor on the public highways.

Indiana.—Eight hours of labor constitute a legal day's work on the public roads, and for all classes of mechanics, workingmen, and laborers, excepting those engaged in agricultural and domestic labor. Overwork by agreement and for extra compensation is permitted.

Iowa.—Eight hours constitute a day's labor on the public roads.

Kansas.—Eight hours are a day's work for all laborers, mechanics, or other persons employed by or on behalf of the State or any county, city, township, or other municipality.

Kentucky.—Eight hours constitute a day's work on the public roads.

Maryland.—No mechanic or laborer employed by the Mayor or City Council of Baltimore, or by any agent or contractor under them, shall be required to work more than eight hours as a day's labor.

Massachusetts.—Eight hours shall constitute a day's work for all laborers, workmen, and mechanics employed by or on behalf of the Commonwealth or any county therein, or of any city or town in the Commonwealth upon acceptance of the statute by a majority of voters present and voting upon the same at any general election.

Minnesota.—Eight hours constitute a day's labor for all laborers, workmen, or mechanics employed by or on behalf of the State, whether the work is done by contract or otherwise.

Mississippi.—Eight hours are a day's labor on highways.

Missouri.—Eight hours constitute a legal day's work. The law does not prevent an agreement to work for a longer or a shorter time and does not apply to agricultural laborers. It is unlawful for employers to work their employés longer than eight hours per day in mines and smelters, or as train despatchers, etc., on railroads, unless the office is open only during the daytime. Eight hours are a day's labor on highways.

Montana.—Eight hours constitute a legal day's work for persons engaged to operate or handle hoisting engines at mines. The law applies only to such plants as are in operation sixteen or more hours per day, or at or in mines where the engine develops fifteen or more horse-power, or where fifteen or more men are employed underground in the twenty-four hours. A day's labor on public works and in smelters and underground mines is limited to eight hours per day.

Nebraska.—Eight hours constitute a day's work on public roads and on all public works in cities of the first class.

Nevada.—For labor on public highways, in underground mines and in smelters, as train despatchers, etc., on railroads, and on all works and undertakings carried on or aided by the State, county, or municipal governments, the hours of labor are fixed at eight per day.

New Mexico.—Eight hours constitute a day's labor on public roads and highways.

LABOR LEGISLATION—*Continued.*

New York.—Eight hours constitute a day's work on highways, and on work done by or for the State, or a municipal corporation, whether directly by contractors or sub-contractors; also for all classes of employés, except in farm or domestic labor, though overwork for extra pay is permitted in private employments.

North Carolina.—Train despatchers, etc., on railroads may work only eight hours, unless otherwise permitted by the corporation commission.

North Dakota.—Eight hours are a day's labor on public roads.

Ohio.—Eight hours shall constitute a day's work in all engagements to labor in any mechanical, manufacturing, or mining business, unless otherwise expressly stipulated in the contract.

Oklahoma.—Eight hours constitute a day's labor on all public works.

Oregon.—Eight hours constitute a day's labor on all public works, and in underground mines yielding metal.

Pennsylvania.—Eight hours of labor shall be deemed and held to be a legal day's work in all cases of labor and service by the day where there is no agreement or contract to the contrary. This does not apply to farm or agricultural labor or to service by the year, month, or week. Eight hours constitute a day's labor for all mechanics, workmen, and laborers in the employ of the State, or of any municipal corporation therein, or otherwise engaged on public works. This act shall be deemed to apply to employés of contractors.

Philippine Islands.—Eight hours constitute a day's work on highways.

Porto Rico.—No laborer may be compelled to work more than eight hours per day on public works.

South Dakota.—For labor on public highways a day's work is fixed at eight hours.

Tennessee.—Eight hours shall be a day's work on the highways.

Texas.—Eight hours constitute a day's work on the highways, and by train despatchers, etc., except at stations where but one operator is employed.

Utah.—Eight hours constitute a day's labor on all works carried on or aided by the State, county, or municipal governments, and in all underground mines or workings, and in smelters and all other establishments for the reduction of ores.

Washington.—Eight hours in any calendar day shall constitute a day's work on any work done for the State, or for any county or municipality.

West Virginia.—Eight hours shall constitute a day's work for all laborers, workmen, and mechanics who may be employed by or on behalf of the State, and for telegraph operators directing the movement of trains where three or more passenger or ten or more freight trains pass in twenty-four hours.

Wisconsin.—In all engagements to labor in any manufacturing or mechanical business, where there is no express contract to the contrary, a day's work shall consist of eight hours, but the law does not apply to contracts for labor by the week, month, or year. Eight hours constitute a day's labor on the public highways, and for train despatchers.

Wyoming.—Eight hours' actual work constitute a legal day's labor in all mines and on all State and municipal works.

United States.—A day's work for all laborers, workmen and mechanics who may be employed by the United States, or by any contractor or sub-contractor upon any of the public works of the United States, is limited to eight hours.

THE WORLD ALMANAC is indebted to Commissioner Charles P. Neill of the U. S. Bureau of Labor for this Summary of Labor Legislation revised to date.

State Labor Bureaus.

LIST OF BUREAUS OF LABOR AND LABOR STATISTICS IN UNITED STATES.

LOCATION.	Title.	Organized.	Chief Officer.	Address.
District of Col.	United States Bureau of Labor	1885	Charles P. Neill	Washington.
California	Bureau of Labor Statistics	1883	J. D. Mackenzie	San Francisco.
Colorado	Bureau of Labor Statistics	1887	Axel Swanson	Denver.
Connecticut	Bureau of Labor Statistics	1893	William H. Scoville	Hartford.
Idaho	Bureau of Labor and Mining Statistics	1895	All n Miller	Boisé.
Illinois	Bureau of Labor Statistics	1879	David Ross	Springfield.
Indiana	Bureau of Statistics	1879	Mary A. Stubbs Moore	Indianapolis.
Iowa	Bureau of Labor Statistics	1884	E. D. Brigham	Des Moines.
Kansas	Bureau of Labor Statistics	1885	W. L. A. Johnson	Topeka.
Kentucky	Bureau of Agriculture, Lab & Statistics	1876	M. C. Rankin	Frankfort.
Louisiana	Bureau of Statistics of Labor	1900	Robert E. Lee	New Orleans, La.
Maine	Bureau of Labor Statistics	1887	Thos. J. Lyons	Augusta.
Maryland	Bureau of Industrial Statistics	1884	Charles J. Fox	Baltimore.
Massachus'tts	Bureau of Statistics of Labor	1869	Chas. F. Gettemy	Boston.
Michigan	Bureau of Labor & Industrial Statistics	1883	R. H. Fletcher	Lansing.
Minnesota	Bureau of Labor	1887	W. H. Williams	St. Paul.
Missouri	Bureau of Labor Statistics & Inspection	1879	J. C. A. Hiller	Jefferson City.
Montana	Bureau of Agriculture, Lab. & Industries	1893	J. A. Ferguson	Helena.
Nebraska	Bureau of Labor & Industrial Statistics	1887	John J. Ryder	Lincoln.
N. Hampshire	Bureau of Labor	1893	Lysander H. Carroll	Concord
New Jersey	Bureau of Statistics of Labor & Printing	1878	W. C. Garrison	Trenton
New York	Department of Labor	1883	John Williams	Albany.
N. Carolina	Bureau of Labor Statistics	1887	Henry B. Varner	Raleigh.
North Dakota	Department of Agriculture and Labor	1890	W. C. Gilbreath	Bismarck.
Ohio	Bureau of Labor Statistics	1877	W. T. Lewis	Columbus.
Oklahoma	Department of Labor	1907	Chas. L. Daugherty	....
Oregon	Bur. Labor Stat. & Insp. Fac. Works'ps	1903	O. P. Hoff	Salem.
Pennsylvania	Bureau of Industrial Statistics	1872	J. L. Rockey	Harrisburg.
Rhode Island	Bureau of Labor Statistics	1887	George H. Webb	Providence.
Tennessee	Bureau of Mines	1891	R. E. Shiflett	Nashville.
Virginia	Bureau of Labor & Industrial Statistics	1898	James B. Doherty	Richmond.
Washington	Bureau of Labor	1897	C. F. Hubbard	Olympia.
West Virginia	Bureau of Labor	1889	I. V. Barton	Wheeling.
Wisconsin	Bureau of Labor Statistics	1883	J. D. Beck	Madison.

General Labor Organizations.

AMERICAN FEDERATION OF LABOR.

PRESIDENT, Samuel Gompers, 423 G Street, N.W., Washington, D.C.; Secretary, Frank Morrison, same address; Treasurer, John B. Lennon, Bloomington, Ill.; First Vice-President, James Duncan, Hancock Building, Quincy, Mass.; Second Vice-President, John Mitchell, 281 Fourth Avenue, New York City; Third Vice-President, James O'Connell, 402 McGill Building, Washington, D. C.; Fourth Vice-President, Max Morris, 315 Appel Building, Denver, Col.; Fifth Vice-President, D. A. Hayes, 930 Witherspoon Building, Philadelphia, Pa.; Sixth Vice-President, Daniel J. Keefe, 407 Elks Temple Building, Detroit, Mich.; Seventh Vice-President, William D. Huber, State Life Building, Indianapolis, Ind.; Eighth Vice-President, Joseph F. Valentine, Commercial Tribune Building, Cincinnati, Ohio.

The Federation is composed of 116 national and international unions, representing approximately 27,000 local unions, 38 State branches, 587 city central unions, and 664 local unions. The approximate paid membership is 1,540,000. The affiliated unions publish about 245 weekly or monthly papers, devoted to the cause of labor. The official organ is the *American Federationist*, edited by Samuel Gompers. There are 926 organizers of local unions acting under the orders of the American Federation of Labor. The objects and aims of the American Federation of Labor are officially stated to render employment and means of subsistence less precarious by securing to the workers an equitable share of the fruits of their labor.

INTERNATIONAL UNIONS COMPRISING THE AMERICAN FEDERATION OF LABOR.

Actors' National Protective Union of America. Lew Morton, 8 Union Square, New York, N. Y.
Asbestos Workers of America, National Association of Heat, Frost, and General Insulators. P. G. Jessen, South Garrison Avenue, St. Louis, Mo.
Bakery and Confectionery Workers' International Union of America. Otto E. Fischer, Metropolitan Block, Room 45, 161-163 Randolph Street, Chicago, Ill.
Barbers' International Union, Journeymen. Jacob Fischer, Security Trust Building, Indianapolis, Ind.
Bill Posters and Billers of America, National Alliance. W. J. Murray, Room 11, Broadway Theatre Building, New York.
Blacksmiths, International Brotherhood of. Charles N. Glover, Suite 570-585 Monon Building, Chicago, Ill.
Boiler-Makers and Iron Shipbuilders of America, Brotherhood of. W. J. Gilthorpe, Room 314, Portsmouth Building, Kansas City, Kan.
Bookbinders, International Brotherhood of. James W. Dougherty, Room 210, 132 Nassau Street, New York, N. Y.
Boot and Shoe Workers' Union. C. L. Baine, 246 Summer Street, Boston, Mass.
Brewery Workmen, International Union of United. Louis Kemper, Rooms 109-110 Odd Fellows' Temple, corner Seventh and Elm Streets, Cincinnati, Ohio.
Brick, Tile, and Terra Cotta Workers' Alliance, International. George Hodge, Room 503, 275 La Salle Street, Chicago, Ill.
Bridge and Structural Iron Workers, International Association of. J. J. McNamara, 422-424 American Central Life Building, Indianapolis, Ind.
Broom and Whisk Makers' Union, International. C. T. Dolan, Yondorff Building, 212 South Halsted Street, Chicago, Ill.
Brushmakers' International Union. John M. McElroy, 1822 Stiles Street, Philadelphia, Pa.
Carpenters and Joiners of America, United Brotherhood of. Frank Duffy, P. O. Box 187, Indianapolis, Ind.
Carpenters and Joiners, Amalgamated Society of. Thomas Atkinson, 332 East 93d Street, N. Y.
Carriage and Wagon Workers, International. John H. Brinkman, 520 Sixth Street, N. W., Washington, D. C.
Carvers' Association of North America, International Wood. John S. Henry, 1220 Third Avenue, New York, N. Y.
Car Workers, International Association of. G. W. Gibson, Rooms 1205-1206 Star Building, 356 Dearborn Street, Chicago, Ill.
Cement Workers, American Brotherhood of. Henry Ullner, 1122 Market Street, San Francisco, Cal.
Chainmakers' National Union of the United States of America. Curtin C. Miller, 289 Wayne Street, Mansfield, Ohio.
Cigar-Makers' International Union of America. George W. Perkins, Room 820, Monon Block, 320 Dearborn Street, Chicago, Ill.
Clerks' International Protective Association, Retail. Max Morris, Box 1581, Denver, Col.
Cloth Hat and Cap Makers of North America, United. Max Zuckerman, 62 East Fourth St., N. Y.
Commercial Telegraphers' Union of America, The. Wesley Russell, 922-930 Monon Building, Chicago, Ill.
Compressed Air Workers, International Union. James Rowan, 138 East 66th Street, New York.
Coopers' International Union of North America. J. A. Cable, Meriwether Building, Kansas City, Kan.
Curtain Operatives of America, Amalgamated Lace. William Borland, 2829 North Reese Street, Philadelphia, Pa.
Cutting Die and Cutter Makers, International Union of. Joseph J. Brady, 576 Central Avenue, Brooklyn, N. Y.
Electrical Workers of America, International Brotherhood of. Peter W. Collins, Pierick Building, Springfield, Ill.
Elevator Constructors, International Union of. William Young, 1952 North 19th Street, Philadelphia, Pa.
Engineers, International Union of Steam. R. A. McKee, 606 Main Street, Peoria, Ill.
Engravers, International Association of Watch Case. George Weidman, Box 263, Canton, Ohio.
Firemen, International Brotherhood of Stationary. C. L. Shamp, Rooms 2-4, 2502 North 18th Street, Omaha, Neb.
Fitters and Helpers of America, International Association of Steam and Hot Water. W. F. Costello, Rooms 82-84 Poli Building, 23 Church Street, New Haven, Ct.
Flour and Cereal Mill Employés, International Union of. A. E. Kellington, 316 Corn Exchange, Minneapolis, Minn.
Foundry Employés, International Brotherhood of. Geo. Bechtold, 1025 Franklin Avenue, St. Louis, Mo.

GENERAL LABOR ORGANIZATIONS—*Continued.*

Freight Handlers and Warehousemen's International Union of America, Interior. J. J. Flynn, Yondorf Building, 210 South Halstead Street, Chicago. Ill.
Fur Workers of the United States and Canada, International Association of. A. V. McCormack, P. O. Box, 124 Toronto, Ontario, Can.
Garment Workers of America. United. B. A. Larger, Rooms 116-117 Bible House, New York, N. Y.
Garment Workers' Union, International Ladies'. John Alex. Dyche, 25-27 Third Avenue, N. Y.
Glass Bottle Blowers' Association of the United States and Canada. William Launer, Rooms 930-931 Witherspoon Building, Juniper and Walnut Streets, Philadelphia, Pa.
Glass Workers' International Association, Amalgamated, William Figolah, 55 North Clark Street, Chicago, Ill.
Glove Workers' Union of America, International. Agnes Nestor, Room 506, Bush Temple of Music, Chicago, Ill.
Gold Beaters' National Protective Union of America, United. Thomas Delaney, 88 Barrow Street, New York, N. Y.
Granite Cutters' International Association of America, The. James Duncan, Hancock Building, Quincy, Mass.
Grinders' and Finishers' National Union, Pocket Knife Blade. F. A. Didsbury, 508 Brook Street, Bridgeport, Ct.
Grinders' National Union, Table Knife. John F. Gleason, 76 Chestnut Street, Bristol, Ct.
Hatters of North America, United. Martin Lawlor, Room 15, 11 Waverley Place, New York, N. Y.
Hod Carriers and Building Laborers' Union of America, International. H. A. Stemburgh, Realty Building, 410-412 East Market Street, Elmira, N. Y.
Horse-Shoers of United States and Canada, International Union of Journeymen. Roady Kenehan, 1548 Wazee Street, Denver, Col.
Hotel and Restaurant Employés' International Alliance and Bartenders' International League of America. Jere. L. Sullivan, Commercial Tribune Building, Cincinnati, Ohio.
Iron, Steel, and Tin Workers, Amalgamated Association of. John Williams, House Building, Smithfield and Water Streets, Pittsburgh, Pa.
Jewelry Workers' Union of America, International. William F. Schade, Box 141, Philadelphia, Pa.
Lathers, International Union of Wood, Wire, and Metal. Ralph V. Brandt, 401 Superior Building, 345 Superior Street, Cleveland, Ohio.
Laundry Workers' International Union, Shirt, Waist and. John J. Manning, 602 Second Avenue, Troy, N. Y.
Leather Workers on Horse Goods, United Brotherhood of. J. J. Pfeiffer, 209-210 Postal Building, Kansas City, Mo.
Leather Workers' Union of America, Amalgamated. F. Victor Turnquist, 125 Fifth Avenue, Lowell, Mass.
Lithographers, International Protective and Beneficial Association of the United States and Canada. James J. McCafferty, 430 Walnut Street, Philadelphia, Pa.
Lobster Fishermen's International Protective Association. J. B. Webster, Vinal Haven, Me.
Longshoremen's Association, International. John J. Joyce, 601-4 Elks Temple, Detroit, Mich.
Machine Printers and Color Mixers of the United States, National Association of. James J. Mulhearn, 233 45th Street, Brooklyn, N. Y.
Machinists, International Association of. George Preston, 908-914 G Street, N. W., McGill Building, Washington, D. C.
Maintenance of Way Employés, International Brotherhood of. S. J. Pegg, 609-25 Benoist Building, St. Louis, Mo.
Marble Workers, International Association of. Stephen C. Hogan, 632 Eagle Avenue, New York, N. Y.
Meat Cutters and Butchers' Workmen of North America, Amalgamated. Homer D. Call. 801 Cortland Avenue, Syracuse, N. Y.
Metal Polishers, Buffers, Platers, and Brass Workers' International Union of North America. Charles R. Atherton, Neave Building, Cincinnati, Ohio.
Metal Workers' International Alliance, Amalgamated Sheet. John E. Bray, 325 Nelson Building, Kansas City, Mo.
Mine Workers of America, United. W. D. Ryan, State Life Building, Indianapolis, Ind.
Moulders' Union of North America, Iron. E. J. Denney, 530 Walnut Street, Cincinnati, Ohio.
Musicians, American Federation of. Owen Miller, 3535 Pine Street, St. Louis, Mo.
Paper-Makers of America, United Brotherhood of. J. J. O'Connor, 22 Smith Building, Watertown, N. Y.
Pattern-Makers' League of North America. James Wilson. Neave Building, Cincinnati, O.
Pavers, Rammermen, Flag Layers, Bridge and Stone Curb Setters, International Union of. John E. Pritchard, 25 Third Avenue, N. Y.
Paving Cutters' Union of the United States of America and Canada. John Sheret, Lock Box 116, Albion, N. Y.
Photo-Engravers' Union of North America, International. H. E. Gudbrandsen, 2830 Fourteenth Avenue south, Minneapolis, Minn.
Piano and Organ Workers' Union of America, International. Charles Dold, 40 Seminary Avenue, Chicago, Ill.
Plate Printers' Union of North America, International Steel and Copper. T. L. Mahan, 319 S Street, N. E., Washington, D. C.
Plumbers, Gas Fitters, Steam Fitters, and Steam Fitters' Helpers, of United States and Canada, United Association of. John R. Alpine. 401-406 Bush Temple of Music, Chicago, Ill.
Post-Office Clerks, National Federation of. George F. Pfeiffer, 377 Albion Street, Milwaukee, Wis.
Potters, National Brotherhood of Operative. Edward Menge, Box 181, East Liverpool, Ohio.
Powder and High Explosive Workers of America, United. James G. McOrindle, Gracedale, Pa.
Print Cutters' Association of America, National. Thos. I. G. Eastwood, 434-436 West 164th Street, New York, N. Y.
Printing Pressmen's Union, International. Patrick McMullen, Rooms 702-705 Lyric Theatre Building, Cincinnati, Ohio.

GENERAL LABOR ORGANIZATIONS—*Continued.*

Quarryworkers' International Union of North America. P. F. McCarthy, Scampini Building, Barre, Vt.
Railroad Telegraphers, Order of. L. W. Quick, Star Building, St. Louis, Mo.
Railway Employés of America, Amalgamated Association of Street and Electric. W. D. Mahon, 45 Hodges Block, Detroit, Mich.
Roofers, Composition, Damp and Waterproof Workers of the United States and Canada. International Brotherhood of. Henry Sands, 236 Washington Street, Newark, N. J.
Sawsmiths' National Union. F. E. Kingsley, 1145 North Beville Avenue, Indianapolis, Ind.
Seamen's Union, International, of America. William H. Frazier, 1½A Lewis Street, Boston, Mass.
Shingle Weavers' Union of America, International. Donald McRae, 317 Labor Temple, Seattle, Wash.
Shipwrights, Joiners. and Caulkers of America, International Union of. Thomas Durett, 108 Marshall Street, Elizabeth, N. J.
Slate and Tile Roofers' Union of America, International. Wm. W. Clark, 1460 St. Louis Avenue, East St. Louis, Ill.
Slate Workers, International Union of. Thomas H. Palmer, Pen Argyle, Pa.
Spinners' International Union. Samuel Ross, Box 367, New Bedford, Mass.
Stage Employés' International Alliance, Theatrical. Lee M. Hart, State Hotel, State and Harrison Streets, Chicago, Ill.
Steel Plate Transferrers' Association of America. The. Frank D. Tichenor, 530 Kosciusko Street, Brooklyn, N. Y.
Stereotypers and Electrotypers' Union of North America, International. George W. Williams, 665 Massachusetts Avenue, Boston, Mass.
Stonecutters' Association of North America, Journeymen. James F. McHugh, 520 Sixth Street, Northwest, Washington, D. C.
Stove Mounters' International Union. J. H. Kaefer, 166 Concord Avenue, Detroit, Mich.
Switchmen's Union of North America. M. R. Welch, 326 Brisbane Building, Buffalo, N. Y.
Tailors' Union of America, Journeymen. John B. Lennon, Box 597, Bloomington, Ill.
Teamsters, International Brotherhood of. Thomas L. Hughes, Room 51, 147 Market Street, Indianapolis, Ind.
Textile Workers of America, United. Albert Hibbert, Box 742, Fall River, Mass.
Tile Layers and Helpers' Union, International Ceramic, Mosaic, and Encaustic. James P. Reynolds, 108 Corry Street, Allegheny, Pa.
Tin Plate Workers' Protective Association of America, International. Charles E. Lawyer, Rooms 20-21, Reilly Block, Wheeling, W. Va.
Tip Printers, International Brotherhood of. T. J. Carolan, care 6 Miller Street, Newark, N. J.
Tobacco Workers' International Union. E. Lewis Evans, Room 56, American National Bank Building, Third and Main Streets, Louisville, Ky.
Travellers' Goods and Leather Novelty Workers' International Union of America. Murt Malone, 240 Jefferson Avenue, Oshkosh, Wis.
Typographical Union, International. J. W. Bramwood, Rooms 640-650, Newton Claypool Building, Indianapolis, Ind.
Upholsterers' International Union of North America. James H. Hatch, 145 East 53d Street, New York, N. Y.
Weavers' Amalgamated Association, Elastic Goring. Alfred Haughton, 50 Cherry Street, Brockton, Mass.
Weavers' Protective Association, American Wire. E. E. Desmond, 184 St. Nicholas Avenue, Brooklyn, N. Y.
Woodmen and Saw Mill Workers, International Brotherhood of. Ernest G. Pape, 1609 Fifth Street, Eureka, Cal.
Wood Workers' International Union of America, Amalgamated. John G. Meiler, 407-410 Bush Temple of Music, Chicago, Ill.

NATIONAL UNIONS

NOT AFFILIATED WITH THE AMERICAN FEDERATION OF LABOR.

American Flint Glass Workers Union. W. P. Clark, Toledo, Ohio.
Bricklayers and Masons' Union. William Dobson, Odd Fellows' Building, Indianapolis, Ind.
Brotherhood of Operative Plasterers. Jos. McIlveen, 2909 Wylie Avenue, Pittsburgh, Pa.
Brotherhood of Locomotive Engineers. Warren S. Stone, Cleveland, Ohio.
Brotherhood of Locomotive Firemen. W. S. Carter, Peoria, Ill.
Brotherhood of Railroad Switchmen. M. R. Welch, 326 Mooney Building, Buffalo, N. Y.
Brotherhood of Railroad Trainmen. A. E. King, Cleveland, Ohio.
Brotherhood of Railway Clerks. R. E. Fisher, Kansas City Life Building, Kansas City, Mo.
National Association of Letter Carriers. E. J. Cantwell, Hutchins Building, Washington, D. C.
National Association of Steam Fitters. W. F. Costello, 33 Olive Street, New Haven, Ct.
Railroad Conductors' Order. W. J. Maxwell, Cedar Rapids, Ia.
Stone Masons' International Union. John Reichwein, 536 Concord Street, Indianapolis, Ind.
Western Federation of Miners. Ernest Mills, 3 Pioneer Building, Denver, Col.

KNIGHTS OF LABOR.

General Master Workman, Simon Burns, 518 Fourth Avenue, Pittsburgh, Pa.; General Worthy Foreman, P. H. Farrell, 444 West 163d Street, New York City. General Secretary-Treasurer, J. Frank O'Meara, Bliss Building, Washington, D. C.; General Executive Board, Simon Burns, Pittsburgh, Pa.; Henry A. Hicks, Hasbrouck Heights, N. J.; John Fernau, Pittsburgh, Pa.; J. Frank O'Meara, Washington, D. C.; Joseph R. Morrison, Watervliet, N. Y.

United States Pension Statistics.

NUMBER OF ARMY AND NAVY PENSIONERS ON THE ROLL JUNE 30, 1908.

Location of Agency.	Regular Establishment.		Civil War. (General Law.)		Civil War. (Act June 27, 1890.)		Civil War. (Act April 19, 1908.)	Service. (Act of Feb. 6, 1907.)	War with Spain.	Number of pensioners on the roll June 30, 1908.	Number of pensioners on the roll June 30, 1907.
	Invalids.	Widows, etc.	Invalids.	Widows, etc.	Invalids.	Minors, etc.	Widows.		Invalids, etc.		
Topeka...	923	145	15,401	6,702	19,761	669	20,928	41,288	2,081	109,579	111,508
Columbus.	564	120	19,350	10,225	14,274	321	17,125	29,153	2,409	93,969	95,829
Chicago...	891	219	11,319	6,657	10,464	35.	13,908	26,898	1,662	73,787	75,099
Knoxville	887	264	5,177	3,139	12,072	605	12,031	20,387	2,727	63,030	63,890
Ind'nap'lis	527	70	18,432	7,940	6,840	263	8,923	14,090	1,923	59,504	60,906
Boston....	592	325	4,416	5,502	5,309	165	15,280	25,701	1,151	58,499	59,236
Philad'ia..	611	326	4,882	4,257	7,296	206	16,123	22,368	993	57,302	58,295
New York	1,024	533	6,788	3,985	5,423	146	15,445	21,355	1,393	53,398	53,888
W'hington	2,716	993	5,433	3,561	9,229	293	10,601	17,383	2,223	53,197	53,640
DesMoines	325	47	9,086	4,175	7,970	168	8,361	20,597	1,080	52,207	53,000
Milwaukee	340	81	7,731	4,205	6,559	196	8,196	19,447	1,277	48,241	48,843
Buffalo...	283	97	7,425	5,125	6,404	100	8,154	14,950	872	48,536	45,069
Pittsburgh	160	51	5,477	3,233	7,110	125	10,544	15,974	797	48,602	44,496
San Fran.	1,103	217	3,838	1,725	7,054	167	6,391	25,903	1,819	43,378	42,713
Detroit...	306	71	8,943	4,289	5,953	126	6,444	12,283	1,417	39,964	40,685
Louisville	375	105	8,810	2,550	4,322	257	5,375	7,670	1,133	26,143	26,854
Augusta..	83	38	3,868	2,189	1,933	48	2,415	5,821	266	16,718	17,303
Concord..	76	20	3,769	2,322	1,627	43	2,601	4,786	342	15,633	16,117
Total....	11,786	3,722	142,044	81,680	140,600	4,249	188,445	338,341	25,665	951,687	967,371

Pensioners of the war of the Revolution—daughters, 2. Pensioners of the war of 1812—widows, 471. Pensioners of the war with Mexico—Survivors, 2,932; widows, 6,914. Indian wars—Survivors, 1,820; widows, 3,018.

NUMBER OF PENSION CLAIMS, PENSIONERS, AND DISBURSEMENTS, 1864-1908.

Fiscal-Year Ending June 30.	Total Number of Applications Filed.	Total Number of Claims Allowed.	Number of Pensioners on the Roll.			Disbursements.
			Invalids.	Widows, etc.	Total.	
1864	53,599	39,487	23,479	27,656	51,135	$4,504,616.92
1865	72,684	40,171	35,880	50,106	85,986	8,525,153.11
1866	65,256	50,177	55,652	71,070	126,722	13,459,969.43
1867	36,753	36,482	69,565	83,618	153,183	18,619,956.46
1868	20,768	28,921	75,957	93,686	169,643	24,010,981.99
1869	26,066	23,196	82,859	105,104	187,963	28,422,884.08
1870	24,851	18,221	87,521	111,165	198,686	27,780,811.81
1871	43,969	16,562	93,394	114,101	207,495	33,077,383.63
1872	26,391	34,333	113,954	118,275	232,299	30,169,341.00
1873	18,303	16,052	119,500	118,911	238,411	29,185,289.62
1874	16,734	10,462	121,628	114,613	236,241	30,593,749.56
1875	18,704	11,152	122,989	111,832	234,821	29,683,116.63
1876	23,523	9,977	124,239	107,898	232,137	28,351,599.69
1877	22,715	11,326	128,723	103,381	232,104	28,580,157.04
1878	44,587	11,962	131,649	92,349	223,998	26,844,415.18
1879	57,118	31,346	138,615	104,140	242,755	33,780,526.19
1880	141,466	19,545	145,410	105,392	250,802	57,240,540.14
1881	31,116	27,394	164,110	104,720	268,830	50,626,538.51
1882	40,939	27,664	182,633	103,064	285,697	54,296,280.54
1883	48,776	38,162	206,042	97,616	303,658	60,431,972.85
1884	41,785	34,192	225,470	97,286	323,756	57,273,536.74
1885	40,918	35,767	247,146	97,979	345,125	65,693,706.72
1886	49,895	40,857	270,346	95,437	365,783	64,584,270.45
1887	72,465	55,194	306,298	99,709	406,007	74,815,486.85
1888	75,726	60,252	343,701	108,856	452,557	79,646,146.37
1889	81,220	51,921	373,699	116,026	489,725	89,131,968.44
1890	105,044	66,637	415,654	122,290	537,944	106,493,890.19
1891	696,941	156,486	536,821	139,339	676,160	118,548,959.71
1892	246,638	224,047	703,242	172,826	876,068	141,086,948.84
1893	119,361	121,630	759,706	206,306	966,012	158,155,342.51
1894	57,141	39,085	754,382	215,162	969,544	140,772,163.78
1895	45,361	39,185	750,951	219,567	970,524	140,959,361.00
1896	42,244	40,374	747,967	222,557	970,678	139,280,075.00
1897	50,585	50,101	746,829	229,185	976,014	140,845,772.00
1898	48,732	52,648	760,853	232,861	993,714	145,748,865.56
1899	53,881	37,077	753,451	238,068	991,519	139,482,696.00
1900	51,964	40,645	751,864	241,674	993,529	139,381,522.73
1901	58,373	44,868	747,999	249,736	997,735	139,582,231.98
1902	47,965	40,173	738,809	260,637	999,446	138,491,822.48
1903	52,325	40,136	728,732	267,813	996,545	138,890,088.64
1904	55,794	44,296	720,315	274,447	994,762	142,092,818.75
1905	52,841	50,027	717,158	281,283	998,441	142,099,286.05
1906	37,193	34,974	712,419	273,552	985,971	138,864,409.45
1907	43,319	29,945	680,934	286,437	967,371	138,030,894.22
1908	......	......	658,071	293,616	951,687	153,093,086.27
Total	*3,113,867	*1,941,015	......	......	......	$3,691,230,634.21

*Exclusive of 1908.

UNITED STATES PENSION STATISTICS—*Continued.*

PENSION AGENCIES AND GEOGRAPHICAL LIMITS, JUNE 30, 1908.

Agencies.	Geographical Limits.	Pay Places Naval Pensioners.	Disbursements.
Augusta	Maine	Boston	$2,945,856.05
Boston	Connecticut, Massachusetts, Rhode Island	Boston	9,046,412.21
Buffalo	Western New York	New York City	6,812,641.35
Chicago	Illinois	Chicago	11,854,787.69
Columbus	Ohio	Chicago	15,940,259.79
Concord	New Hampshire, Vermont	Boston	2,748,387.69
Des Moines	Iowa, Nebraska	Chicago	8,548,546.18
Detroit	Michigan	Chicago	6,917,428.79
Indianapolis	Indiana	Chicago	10,626,002.48
Knoxville	Southern States*	Washington	9,428,559.60
Louisville	Kentucky	Chicago	4,145,360.12
Milwaukee	Minnesota, Dakotas, Wisconsin	Chicago	7,910,832.71
New York	East New York, East New Jersey	New York City	8,068,753.78
Philadelphia	East Pennsylvania, West New Jersey	Philadelphia	8,602,333.47
Pittsburgh	West Pennsylvania	Philadelphia	6,876,520.86
San Francisco	Pacific Coast	San Francisco	6,767,265.76
Topeka	Colorado, Kansas, Missouri, New Mexico	Chicago	17,621,652.81
Washington	Delaware, Maryland, Virginia, W. Va., D. C., Foreign	Washington	8,790,728.39
Total, incl	uding agency expenses		$153,652,329.73

* Excepting the States in the Louisville and Washington districts.

The expenses of the Pension Bureau and of pension agencies in disbursing the pension fund during the fiscal year were $2,800,963.36. From 1866 to 1908 inclusive, this expense has been $112,852,-477.09. The names of the pension agents will be found in the list of officials of the Federal Government.

TOTAL DISBURSEMENTS FOR PENSIONS FOR ALL WARS AND FOR REGULAR ESTABLISHMENT.

War of the Revolution (estimate) $70,000,000; war of 1812 (on account of service without regard to disability) $45,694,665.24; Indian wars (on account of service without regard to disability) $9,355,711.03; war with Mexico (on account of service without regard to disability) $40,876,879.10; civil war, $3,533,593,025.95; war with Spain and insurrection in the Philippine Islands, $22,563,635.41; regular establishment, $12,630,947.88; unclassified, $16,393,945.35. Total disbursements for pensions, $3,751,108,809.96.

PENSIONERS IN EACH STATE AND TERRITORY.

State	No.	State	No.	State	No.	State	No.	State	No.
Alabama	3,788	Idaho	2,223	Minn	15,789	N. Dak	2,108	Vermont	7,815
Alaska T	86	Illinois	66,680	Miss	4,738	Ohio	93,941	Virginia	8,807
Arizona T.	871	Indiana	58,016	Missouri	48,615	Okla.	13,545	Washing'n	10,761
Arkansas	10,724	Iowa	33,362	Montana	2,114	Oregon	7,862	West Va	12,136
California	27,207	Kansas	37,547	Nebras'a	15,405	Penn'a	93,388	Wisconsin	24,595
Colorado	9,098	Kentuc'y	25,657	Nevada	505	R. Island	5,369	Wyoming	946
Conn	11,826	Louis'a	6,447	N. Hamp	7,868	S. Car'a	2,021	Insul. Pos.	131
Delaware	2,705	Maine	17,620	N. Jersey	24,420	S. Dak	4,548	Foreign	5,047
D. of Col	8,683	Maryla'd	12,668	N. Mex	2,250	Tenn	18,755		
Florida	3,870	Mass	40,044	N. York	81,167	Texas	8,895	Total	951,687
Georgia	3,524	Michigan	40,335	N. Car'a	4,091	Utah	1,074		

DAUGHTERS OF REVOLUTIONARY SOLDIERS ON PENSION ROLLS JUNE 30, 1908.

Name.	Age.	Name of Soldier.	Service of Soldier.	Residence.
Hurlbutt, Sarah C.	90	Weeks, Elijah	Massachusetts	Little Marsh, Pa.
Wooley, Phoebe M., now Palmeter	87	Wooley, Jonathan	N. Hampshire.	Brookfield, N. Y.

Daniel F. Bakeman, the last survivor of the War of the Revolution, died in Freedom, Cattaraugus County, N. Y., April 5, 1869, aged 109 years. Esther S. Damon, the last surviving widow of a Revolutionary soldier, who died at Plymouth Union, Vt., November 11, 1906, aged 92 years, was the wife of Noah Damon, who served at various periods as a private in Massachusetts troops from April 19, 1775, to May 11, 1780.

The last survivor of the war of 1812 who was on the pension rolls was Hiram Crook of Ava, N. Y., who died May 13, 1905, aged 105 years. He served in the defence of Sacket Harbor in 1814.

The number of enrolled pension attorneys in 1908 was 25,039.

The following are the ratings per month for disabilities incurred in the service:

Army.—Lieutenant-colonel and all officers of higher rank, $30; major, surgeon, and paymaster, $25; captain and chaplain, $20; first lieutenant and assistant surgeon, $17; second lieutenant and enrolling officer, $15; enlisted men, $8.

Navy.—Captain and all officers of higher rank, commander, surgeon, paymaster, and chief engineer, $30; lieutenant, passed assistant surgeon, surgeon, paymaster, and chief engineer, $25; master, professor of mathematics, and assistant surgeon, $20; first assistant engineer, ensign, and pilot, $15; cadet midshipman, passed midshipman, midshipman, warrant officers, $10; enlisted men, $8.

Patent Office Procedure.

THE following statement has been revised by the Patent Office for THE WORLD ALMANAC for 1909.

Patents are issued in the name of the United States, and under the seal of the Patent Office, to any person who has invented or discovered any new and useful art, machine, manufacture, or composition of matter or any new and useful improvement thereof, or any new original and ornamental design for an article of manufacture, not known or used by others in this country before his invention or discovery thereof, and not patented or described in any printed publication in this or any foreign country, before his invention or discovery thereof or more than two years prior to his application, and not in public use or on sale in the United States for more than two years prior to his application, unless the same is proved to have been abandoned; upon payment of the fees required by law and other due proceedings had.

Every patent contains a grant to the patentee, his heirs or assigns, for the term of seventeen years, except in the case of design patents, of the exclusive right to make, use, and vend the invention or discovery throughout the United States and the Territories, referring to the specification for the particulars thereof.

If it appear that the inventor, at the time of making his application, believed himself to be the first inventor or discoverer, a patent will not be refused on account of the invention or discovery, or any part thereof, having been known or used in any foreign country before his invention or discovery thereof, if it had not been before patented or described in any printed publication.

Joint inventors are entitled to a joint patent; neither can claim one separately. Independent inventors of distinct and independent improvements in the same machine cannot obtain a joint patent for their separate inventions; nor does the fact that one furnishes the capital and another makes the invention entitle them to make application as joint inventors; but in such case they may become joint patentees.

No person otherwise entitled thereto will be debarred from receiving a patent for his invention or discovery, by reason of its having been first patented or caused to be patented by the inventor or his legal representatives or assigns in a foreign country, unless the application for said foreign patent was filed more than twelve months prior to the filing of the application in this country, and four months in cases of designs, in which case no patent shall be granted in this country.

APPLICATIONS.

Applications for a patent must be made in writing to the Commissioner of Patents. The applicant must also file in the Patent Office a written description of the invention or discovery, and of the manner and process of making, constructing, compounding, and using it, in such full, clear, concise, and exact terms as to enable any person skilled in the art or science to which it appertains, or with which it is most nearly connected, to make, construct, compound, and use the same; and in case of a machine, he must explain the principle thereof, and the best mode in which he has contemplated applying that principle, so as to distinguish it from other inventions, and particularly point out and distinctly claim the part, improvement, or combination which he claims as his invention or discovery. The specification and claim must be signed by the inventor and attested by two witnesses.

When the nature of the case admits of drawings, the applicant must furnish a drawing of the required size, signed by the inventor or his attorney in fact, and attested by two witnesses. In all cases which admit of representation by model, the applicant, if required by the Patent Office, shall furnish a model of convenient size to exhibit advantageously the several parts of his invention or discovery.

The applicant shall make oath that he verily believes himself to be the original and first inventor or discoverer of the art, machine, manufacture, composition, or improvement for which he solicits a patent; that he does not know and does not believe that the same was ever before known or used, and shall state of what country he is a citizen and where he resides, and whether he is the sole or joint inventor of the invention claimed in his application. In every original application the applicant must distinctly state under oath that the invention has not been patented to himself or to others with his knowledge or consent in this or any foreign country for more than two years prior to his application, or on an application for a patent filed in any foreign country by himself or his legal representatives or assigns more than twelve months prior to his application in this country, or four months in cases of designs. If any application for patent has been filed in any foreign country by the applicant in this country or by his legal representatives or assigns, prior to his application in this country, he shall state the country or countries in which such application has been filed, giving the date of such application, and shall also state that no application has been filed in any other country or countries than those mentioned; that to the best of his knowledge and belief the invention has not been in public use or on sale in the United States nor described in any printed publication or patent in this or any foreign country for more than two years prior to his application in this country. Such oath may be made before any person within the United States authorized by law to administer oaths, or, when the applicant resides in a foreign country, before any minister, chargé d'affaires, consul, or commercial agent holding commission under the Government of the United States, or before any notary public, judge or magistrate having an official seal and authorized to administer oaths in that country whose authority shall be proved by a certificate of a diplomatic or consular officer of the United States, except that no acknowledgment may be taken by any attorney appearing in the case.

On the filing of such application and the payment of the fees required by law, if, on examination, it appears that the applicant is justly entitled to a patent under the law, and that the same is sufficiently useful and important, the Commissioner will issue a patent therefor.

Every patent or any interest therein shall be assignable in law by an instrument in writing; and the patentee or his assigns or legal representatives may, in like manner, grant and convey an exclusive right under his patent to the whole or any specified part of the United States.

REISSUES.

A reissue is granted to the original patentee, his legal representatives, or the assignees of the entire interest when, by reason of a defective or insufficient specification, or by reason of the patentee claiming as his invention or discovery more than he had a right to claim as new, the original patent is inoperative or invalid, provided the error has arisen from inadvertence, accident, or mistake, and without any fraudulent or deceptive intention. Reissue applications must be made and the specifications sworn to by the inventors, if they be living.

CAVEATS.

A caveat, under the patent law, is a notice given to the office of the caveator's claim as inventor, in order to prevent the grant of a patent to another for the same alleged invention upon an application filed during the life of a caveat without notice to the caveator.

Any person who has made a new invention or discovery, and desires further time to mature the same, may, on payment of a fee of ten dollars, file in the Patent Office a caveat setting forth the

PATENT OFFICE PROCEDURE—*Continued.*

object and the distinguishing characteristics of the invention, and praying protection of his right until he shall have matured his invention. Such caveat shall be filed in the confidential archives of the office and preserved in secrecy, and shall be operative for the term of one year from the filing thereof. The caveat may be renewed, on request in writing, by the payment of a second fee of ten dollars, and it will continue in force for one year from the payment of such second fee.

The caveat must comprise a specification, oath, and, when the nature of the case admits of it, a drawing, and, like the application, must be limited to a single invention or improvement.

FEES.

Fees must be paid in advance, and are as follows: On filing each original application for a patent, $15. On issuing each original patent, $20. In design cases: For three years and six months, $10; for seven years, $15; for fourteen years, $30. On filing each caveat, $10. On every application for the reissue of a patent, $30. On filing each disclaimer, $10. For certified copies of patents and other papers in manuscript, ten cents per hundred words and twenty-five cents for the certificate; for certified copies of printed patents, eighty cents. For uncertified printed copies of specifications and drawings of patents, five cents each. For recording every assignment, agreement, power of attorney, or other paper, of three hundred words or under, $1; of over three hundred and under one thousand words, $2; for each additional thousand words, or fraction thereof, $1. For copies of drawings, the reasonable cost of making them. The Patent Office is prepared to furnish positive photographic copies of any drawing, foreign or domestic, in the possession of the office, in sizes and at rates as follows: Large size, 10x15 inches, twenty-five cents; medium size, 8x12½ inches, fifteen cents. Fee for examining and registering trade-mark, $10, which includes certificate. Stamps cannot be accepted by the Patent Office in payment of fees. Stamps and stamped envelopes should not be sent to the office for replies to letters, as stamps are not required on mail matter emanating from the Patent Office.

PATENT OFFICE STATISTICS.

The receipts of the Patent Office during the year ending December 31, 1907, were $1,910,618.14. and expenditures, $1,631,458.36. Receipts over expenditures, $279,159.78.

The following is a statement of the business of the office for the year ending December 31, 1907:

Number of applications for patents	57,679
Number of applications for design patents	896
Number of applications for reissue patents	187
Total	58,762
Number of caveats filed	1,967
Number of applications for registration of trade-marks	7,722
Number of applications for registration of labels	1,027
Number of applications for prints	403
Number of disclaimers filed	5
Number of appeals on the merits	1,443
Total	12,567
Number of applications, etc., requiring investigation and action	18,540

Number of patents granted, including designs	36,469
Patents reissued	151
Total	36,620
Number of trade-marks registered	7,878
Number of labels registered	667
Number of prints registered	315
Total	8,860
Number of patents expired	25,322
Number of patents withheld for non-payment of final fees	5,541
Number of applications allowed awaiting final fees	11,102
Number of trade-mark applications passed for publication	7,561

The total number of applications filed at the Patent Office in seventy-one years, 1837-1907, was 1,524,748; number of caveats filed, 125,143; number of original patents, including designs and reissues issued, 927,270; net surplus in the U. S. Treasury on account of the patent fund, $6,706,181.64.

The following is a statement of patents and designs issued in 1907 according to residence of patentees:

Alabama, 156; Alaska, 7; Arizona, 38; Arkansas, 150; California, 1,209; Colorado, 460; Connecticut, 920; Delaware, 44; District of Columbia, 296; Florida, 111; Georgia, 264; Hawaii, 16; Idaho, 76; Illinois, 3,470; Indiana, 921; Indian Territory, 61; Iowa, 679; Kansas, 472; Kentucky, 304; Louisiana, 160; Maine, 178; Maryland, 383; Massachusetts, 2,113; Michigan, 1,110; Minnesota, 598; Mississippi, 108; Missouri, 1,130; Montana, 118; Nebraska, 327; Nevada, 39; New Hampshire, 121; New Jersey, 1,504; New Mexico, 27; New York, 5,231; North Carolina, 153; North Dakota, 134; Ohio, 2,493; Oklahoma, 148; Oregon, 219; Panama, 4; Pennsylvania, 3,471; Phillipine Islands, 7; Porto Rico, 10; Rhode Island, 271; South Carolina, 72; South Dakota, 127; Tennessee, 232; Texas, 514; Utah, 101; Vermont, 94; Virginia, 274; Washington, 410; West Virginia, 237; Wisconsin, 758; Wyoming, 22; U. S. Army, 6; U. S. Navy, 15. Total, 32,603.

Foreign countries: Austria-Hungary, 127; Belgium, 58; Canada, 536; Cuba, 21; Denmark, 40; England, 868; France, 334; Germany, 1,182; Italy, 48; Japan, 9; Mexico, 26; Russia, 23; Scotland, 62; Sweden, 77; Switzerland, 121; other countries, 334. Total foreign, 3,866.

GENERAL PATENT STATISTICS.

The following table is compiled from the report of the Commissioner of Patents for 1908. It exhibits the number of patents issued by foreign countries and the United States from the earliest records to December 31, 1907:

Countries.	To 1870 Inclusive.	1871 to 1907.	Total.	Countries.	To 1870 Inclusive.	1871 to 1907.	Total.
Austria	....	50,350	50,350	Russia	1,464	17,796	19,260
Austria-Hungary	15,350	67,583	82,933	Spain	....	38,348	38,348
Belgium	35,044	176,217	211,261	Sweden	1,629	25,186	26,815
Canada	4,081	108,576	112,657	Switzerland	....	39,473	39,473
France	103,934	291,338	395,272	All other foreign countries	228,074	1,483,617	1,711,691
Germany	9,996	202,084	212,080				
Great Britain	53,408	329,709	383,117				
Hungary	....	36,409	36,409	Total foreign	238,437	1,625,899	1,863,836
India	445	9,118	9,563	United States	120,573	765,062	885,635
Italy and Sardinia	4,723	80,195	84,918				
Japan	....	13,235	13,235	Grand total	359,010	2,390,461	2,749,471

United States Executive Civil Service.

(Revised for this issue of THE WORLD ALMANAC by the Secretary of the Civil Service Commission.)

THE purpose of the Civil Service act, as declared in its title, is "to regulate and improve the Civil Service of the United States." It provides for the appointment of three Commissioners, a chief Examiner, a Secretary, and other employés, and makes it the duty of the Commissioners to aid the President as he may request in preparing suitable rules for carrying the act into effect; to make regulations to govern all examinations held under the provisions of the act, and to make investigations and report upon all matters touching the enforcement and effect of the rules and regulations. The address of the Commission is Washington, D. C.

PROVISIONS OF THE RULES.

The act requires the rules to provide, as nearly as the conditions of good administration will warrant, for open competitive practical examinations for testing the fitness of applicants for the classified service; for the filling of all vacancies by selections from among those graded highest; for the apportionment of appointments at Washington among the States upon the basis of population; for a period of probation before absolute appointment; that no person in the public service shall be obliged to contribute service or money for political purposes; that persons in the competitive service, while retaining the right to vote as they please or to express privately their political opinions, shall take no active part in political campaigns; and that no person in said service has any right to use his official authority or influence to coerce the political action of any person or body.

EXTENT OF THE SERVICE.

There are about 352,000 positions in the Executive Civil Service, over half of which, or 206,637, are subject to competitive examination. The expenditure for salaries in the Executive Civil Service is over $200,000,000 a year. The Civil Service act does not require the classification of persons appointed by the President and confirmed by the Senate or of persons employed merely as laborers or workmen. Many positions are excepted in part from the provisions of the rules for various reasons, the largest single class being those of fourth-class postmasters, of which there were 54,312 on July 1, 1908.

APPLICATIONS.

Persons seeking to be examined must file an application blank. The blank for the Departmental Service at Washington, Railway Mail Service, the Indian School Service, and the Government Printing Service should be requested directly of the Civil Service Commission at Washington. The blank for the Customs, Postal, or Internal Revenue Service should be requested of the Civil Service Board of Examiners at the office where service is sought.

Applicants for examination must be citizens of the United States, and of the proper age. No person using intoxicating liquors to excess may be appointed. No discrimination is made on account of sex, color, or political or religious opinions. The limitations of age vary with the different services, but do not apply to any person honorably discharged from the military or naval service of the United States by reason of disability resulting from wounds or sickness incurred in the line of duty.

EXAMINATIONS.

The examinations are open to all persons qualified in respect to age, citizenship, legal residence, character, and health. During the fiscal year ended June 30, 1908, 39,003 persons were appointed. Of those appointed, 4,088 were rural letter-carriers, 14,631 were mechanics and workmen at navy yards appointed on registration tests of fitness given by a board of labor employment at each yard. Several hundr d different kinds of examinations were held, each one of which involved different tests. Two hundred and fifty-six of these examinations contained educational tests, the others being for mechanical trades or skilled occupations and consisting of certificates of employers or fellow-workmen. Examinations are held twice a year in each State and Territory, the places and dates being publicly announced.

APPOINTMENTS.

In case of a vacancy not filled by promotion, reduction, transfer, or reinstatement, the highest three of the sex called for on the appropriate register are certified for appointment, the apportionment being considered in appointments at Washington. In the absence of eligibles, or when the work is of short duration, temporary appointments, without examination, are permitted. The number of women applying for ordinary clerical places is greatly in excess of the calls of appointing officers. The chances of appointment are good for teachers, matrons, seamstresses, and physicians in the Indian Service, for male stenographers and typewriters, draughtsmen, patent examiners, civil, mechanical, and electrical engineers, and for technical and scientific experts.

PREFERENCE CLAIMANTS.

Persons who served in the military or naval service of the United States, and were discharged by reason of disabilities resulting from wounds or sickness incurred in the line of duty, are, under the Civil Service rules, given certain preferences. They are released from all maximum age limitations, are eligible for appointment at a grade of 65, while all others are obliged to obtain a grade of 70, and are certified to appointing officers before all others. Subject to the other conditions of the rules, a veteran of the rebellion or of the war with Spain, or the widow of any such person, or any army nurse of either war, may be reinstated without regard to the length of time he or she has been separated from the service.

INSULAR POSSESSIONS.

Examinations are also held for positions in the Philippines, Porto Rico, and Hawaii, and also for the Isthmian Canal service.

THE UNCLASSIFIED SERVICE.

Under an executive order unclassified laborers are appointed after open, competitive examination upon their physical condition. This action is outside the Civil Service act.

PUBLICATIONS OF THE COMMISSION.

Among the publications of the Commission for free distribution are the following:

Manual of Examinations, giving places and dates of examinations, rules by which papers are rated descriptions of examinations, specimen questions, and general information.

The Civil Service act and rules.

The Annual Reports of the Commission, showing its work. These annual reports, of which twenty-four have been issued, may be consulted at public libraries.

Civil Service Rules in the City of New York.

SYNOPSIS of regulations governing the admission of persons into the civil service of the City of New York. Information may also be had by applying to the Secretary of the Municipal Civil Service Commission, 299 Broadway, New York City.

Under the White Civil Service law, Chapter 370, Laws of 1899, April 19, the rules apply to all positions in the service of the City of New York except officers elected by the people, all legislative officers and employés, heads of any department, or superintendents, principals, or teachers in a public school, academy, or college. This requires "examinations, wherever practicable, to ascertain the fitness of applicants for appointment to the civil service of said city." The Constitution requires that these examinations shall be competitive, "so far as practicable."

APPLICATIONS.

Applications of competitors for positions must be addressed to the "Secretary of the Municipal Civil Service Commission, New York City," and must set forth:

Applications are only received when an examination is ordered for a position.

First—The affidavit of the applicant showing his age, whether a citizen of the United States, giving his place of residence, with the street and number thereof, if any; the place, nature, and extent of his education, and of his business training and experience, and stating whether he has ever been in the civil service of the City of New York, or in the military or naval service of the United States, and if so, when and where.

Second—A statement whether such application is limited to any particular office in the service.

Third—The certificate of four reputable persons of the City of New York, that they have been personally acquainted with the applicant for at least one year, and believe him to be of good moral character, of temperate and industrious habits, and in all respects fit for the service he wishes to enter, and that each of them is willing that such certificate should be published for public information, and will upon request give such further information concerning the applicant as he may possess.

Applicants for the following positions must, before being admitted to examination, present satisfactory evidence as to the following facts:

First—If the position to be filled be that of physician, surgeon, medical officer, inspector of vaccination, or sanitary inspector, that the applicant is duly authorized by the laws of the State of New York to practise medicine and surgery. Second—If the position to be filled be that of chemist or analyzer, that the applicant has received the degree of Bachelor of Sciences, or its equivalent, from some institution duly authorized by law to confer such degree.

In positions where the duties are professional, technical, or expert, the candidates will be required to show what preliminary training or technical education they have undergone to qualify them for such situations before they can be admitted to examination.

In all examinations for professional positions, or positions requiring technical knowledge, no person shall be placed on the eligible list who obtains a rating in technical knowledge of less than 75.

CONDUCT OF EXAMINATIONS.

Applicants shall be admitted to examination upon the production of the official notification to appear for that purpose.

All paper upon which examinations are to be written shall be furnished to the applicants by the examining board and shall bear some suitable official indorsement, stamp, or mark, for the purpose of identifying the same.

All examinations shall be in writing, except such as refer to expertness or physical qualities, and except as herein otherwise provided.

The sheets of questions shall be numbered and shall be given out in the order of their numbers, each, after the first, being given only when the competitor has returned to the examiners the last sheet given to him. In general, no examination shall extend beyond five hours without intermission; and no questions given out at any session, to any candidate, shall be allowed to be answered at another session.

Each examiner shall exercise all due diligence to secure fairness and prevent all collusion and fraud in the examinations.

The time allowed for completing the examination shall be announced before the first paper is given out.

The following municipal departments and offices come under jurisdiction of Civil Service rules:

Accounts, Com. of.
Armory, Board of.
Assessors, Board of.
Aqueduct Commission.
Bellevue and Allied Hospitals.
Board of Water Supply.
Bridges, Dept. of.
Brooklyn Disciplinary Training School for Boys.
Buildings, Dept. of.
Charities, Dept. of Public.
City Record, Supervisor of the.
Civil Service Commission.
College of the City of New York
Correction, Dept. of.
Coroners.
Court, City.
Court, City Magistrate.
Court, Municipal.
Court of Special Sessions.
Docks and Ferries, Dept. of.
Education, Dept. of.
Elections, Board of.
Estimate and Apportionment, Board of.
Examiners, Board of.
Finance Dept.
Fire Dept.
Health Dept.
Law Dept.
Mayor's Office.
Normal College.
Parks, Dept. of.
Police Dept.
Presidents of Boroughs.
Public Works Bureau.
Sinking Fund Commission.
Street Cleaning, Dept. of.
Taxes and Assessm'ts, Dept. of.
Tenement House Dept.
Water Supply, Gas, and Electricity, Dept. of.

The inspectors of elections and poll clerks are exempt from examination. Special patrolmen, appointed pursuant to section 269 of the New York City Consolidation act, are also exempt.

Regents' Examinations in New York State in 1909.

Regents' Examinations under the control of the Education Department of the State of New York (office, Albany, N. Y.) will be held in 1909 at the following times and places: Jan. 25-29 inclusive, at New York, and about 800 academies and high schools; 86 subjects. June 14-18 inclusive, at New York, and about 800 academies and high schools; 87 subjects. Examinations for teachers' certificates are held on the same dates as the Regents, and August 11-13 and 24-28. Sept. 13-15, inclusive, at New York, Albany, Syracuse, Buffalo; 33 subjects. September examinations are for professional and technical students only. Morning session begins 9.15 o'clock. Afternoon session begins 1.15 o'clock.

University Credentials—Preliminary (preacademic) certificate—Reading, writing, spelling, elementary English, arithmetic, geography, and elementary United States history and civics. Medical Student Certificate—All matriculates after Jan. 1, 1897 must secure 60 academic counts or their full equivalent.

Law Student Certificate—For those who filed a clerkship certificate on June 1, 1908, or thereafter, or who began their work in a registered law school on or after that date, the following set subjects passed in Regents' examinations will be accepted: English, 3 years, 10; mathematics, 2 years (algebra and geometry), 10; Latin, 2 years (grammar, composition and Caesar), 10; science, physics, 5; history, 1 year (American history, civics), 5; (1 year, history of Great Britain and Ireland, economics), 5; total, 45. Or any 60 counts passed in Regents' examinations. Four years of High School work in a registered High School, can also be accepted. For those whose clerkship certificates were filed, prior to June 1, 1908, the following is the requirement—Any 60 academic counts or Regents' examinations in the following set subjects: second year English, Latin first year, elementary algebra, plane geometry, American history, history of Great Britain and Ireland (three hour course), civics, economics and arithmetic.

Dental Student Certificate—Any 60 academic counts or their equivalents (for matriculates before Jan. 1, 1905, any 45 academic counts).

Veterinary Student Certificate—Any 60 academic counts or their equivalents (for matriculates before Jan. 1, 1905, any 30 academic counts).

Pharmacy Student Certificate—Any 15 academic counts.

Nurses Preliminary Certificate—After January 1, 1906, 15 counts.

Academic Diploma—For 72 counts. This diploma is based on a four-year curriculum, requiring a student to pursue four subjects of study of at least 18 lesson periods a week. This increase from 15 to 18 lessons a week necessitates a corresponding change in the system of "counts," and 12 counts under the former scheme of values is equal to 15 under the present. For diplomas earned in June, 1909, and thereafter, the requirements are: English 13 counts, mathematics 10, history 8, science 10, elective 31. For the classical academic diploma: English 13, mathematics 10, history 5, science 5, Latin 20, a second foreign language 15, elective 4. There is no time limit, but credentials issued by the Department are good till cancelled for cause. To protect the rights of the weak or of the slowly developing student and at the same time to test the knowledge of the most capable, the following system of differentiated credentials has been adopted: 1. A diploma based on a general average of 65; 2. A diploma, with credit, based on a general average of 75; 3. A diploma, with great credit, based on a general average of 85; 4. A diploma, with highest credit, based on a general average of 90. Answer papers are reviewed in the Department and all papers below standard returned to the candidates. Candidates attending schools in which these examinations are not held should send notice at least ten days in advance at what time and in what studies they wish to be examined, that required desk room may be provided. Candidates who fail to send this advance notice can be admitted only so far as there are unoccupied seats. [See Handbook 3].

Professional Certificates Without Examination—Candidates having credentials which can be accepted in place of examinations should send them to the Education Department—Registration. [See Handbook 23].

Medical Examinations—The regents shall admit to any examination any candidate who pays a fee of $25 and submits satisfactory evidence, verified by oath, if required, that he—1. Is more than twenty-one years of age; 2. Is of good moral character; 3. Has the general education required preliminary to receiving the degree of bachelor or doctor of medicine in this State; 4. Has studied medicine not less than four school years, including four satisfactory courses of at least seven months each in four different calendar years in a medical school registered as maintaining at the time a satisfactory standard. This requirement took effect Jan. 1, 1898, and does not apply to students matriculated before that date who receive their degree before Jan. 1, 1902; 5. Evidence that applicant has received the degree of bachelor or doctor of medicine from some registered medical school, or a diploma or license conferring full rights to practise medicine in some foreign country (original credentials). Examinations for license to practise medicine in this State will be held as follows: Feb. 2-5, May 18-21, June 22-25, Sept. 21-24, at New York, Albany, Syracuse, and Buffalo. (Each candidate is notified as to exact place.)

Dental Examinations—The regents shall admit to examination any candidate who pays a fee of $25 and submits satisfactory evidence, verified by oath, if required, that he—1. Is more than twenty-one years of age; 2. Is of good moral character; 3. Has the general education required preliminary to receiving the degree of doctor of dental surgery in this State. Matriculates in a registered dental school before Jan. 1, 1896, are exempt from the preliminary education requirement for degrees and for admission to the licensing examinations; 4. Subsequently to receiving such preliminary education either has been graduated in course with a dental degree from a registered dental school, or else, having been graduated in course from a registered medical school with a degree of doctor of medicine, has pursued thereafter a course of special study of dentistry for at least two years in a registered dental school, and received therefrom its degree of doctor of dental surgery, or else holds a diploma or license conferring full right to practise dentistry in some foreign country and granted by some registered authority. Dates of dental examinations: Feb. 2-5, May 18-21, June 22-25, and Sept. 21-24, at New York, Albany, Syracuse, and Buffalo. (Each candidate is notified as to exact place.)

Pharmacy Examinations—Applications for examination, accompanied by the proper fee, must be forwarded to the secretary of the branch of the State Board of Pharmacy in which the applicant resides at least ten days previous to the date of examination. A candidate for the grade of licensed pharmacist must pay a fee of $10 and submit evidence of: 1. A minimum age of 21 years: 2. At least four years' practical experience in a pharmacy; 3. A diploma from a registered pharmacy school. For the grade of licensed druggist a candidate must pay a fee of $5, submit proof of three years' practical experience in a pharmacy, and pass examination.

Veterinary Examinations—The regents shall admit to examination any candidate who pays a fee of $10 and submits satisfactory evidence, verified by oath, if required, that he—1. Is more than twenty-one years of age; 2. Is of good moral character; 3. Has the general education required in all cases after July 1, 1897, preliminary to receiving a degree in veterinary medicine. Matriculates in a registered veterinary medical school prior to Jan. 1, 1896, are exempt from the preliminary education requirement; 4. Has studied veterinary medicine not less than three full years, including three satisfactory courses, in three different academic years, in a veterinary medical school registered as maintaining at the time a satisfactory standard; 5. Has received a degree as veterinarian from some registered veterinary medical school. Dates of examinations: Feb. 2-5, May 18-21, June 22-25, Sept. 21-24, at New York, Albany, Syracuse, and Buffalo.

Certified Public Accountants—1. The full C. P. A. certificate is to be granted only to those at least twenty-five years of age who have had three years' satisfactory experience in the study or practice of accounting, one of which shall have been in the office of an expert public accountant; 2. Candidates having the required preliminary education and passing the required examinations, but lacking the age or the three years' experience required for the full C. P. A. certificate, may be certified as junior accountants under the same conditions as to residence and character; 3. Two examinations, in January and in June, are held annually. There are to be four sessions as follows: 1. Theory of accounts; 2. Practical accounting; 3. Auditing; 4. Commercial law; candidates must complete all subjects at a single examination as required in medicine; candidates for either the C. P. A. or the junior accountant certificate must be more than twenty-one years of age, and of good moral character. They must pay a fee of $25, and must have the regents' academic diploma or its equivalent as prescribed for other professional examinations. Dates of examinations: Feb. 2-3 and June 22-23, at New York, Albany, Syracuse, and Buffalo.

Registration of Nurses—Who May Practise as Registered Nurses—Any resident of the State of New York, being over the age of twenty-one years and of good moral character, holding a diploma from a training school for nurses connected with a hospital or sanitarium giving a course of at least two years, and registered by the regents of the University of the State of New York as maintaining in this and other respects proper standards, all of which shall be determined by the said regents, and who shall have received from the said regents a certificate of his or her qualifications to practise as a registered nurse, shall be styled and known as a registered nurse, and no other person shall assume such title, or use the abbreviation R. N. or any other words, letters, or figures to indicate that the person using the name is such a registered nurse. Two examinations will be held annually in January and June respectively. Applications should be made at least ten days in advance to Education Department, Examination Division, Albany, N. Y. Dates: Feb. 2-3, June 22-23, at New York, Albany, Syracuse, and Buffalo. (Each candidate is notified as to exact place.)

THE political institutions known as Initiative and Referendum are those by which the body of the electorate may initiate measures to be enacted by their own vote into laws, and by which laws enacted by the Legislatures are referred to and approved or rejected by the people. The first appearance of these propositions was in Switzerland about the sixteenth century, but made great strides there in recent years, being in effect in every canton except Freiburg. The Referendum may be divided into Referendums of (a) entire constitutions, (b) amendments to constitutions, (c) of laws affecting the whole State, and (d) of laws affecting parts of States or localities only.

REFERENDUMS OF WHOLE CONSTITUTIONS.

Massachusetts in 1778 was the first State to refer its whole constitution to popular approval, followed closely by New Hampshire (1783), Connecticut (1818), and Maine (1819), Rhode Island (1824, rejected), New York (the first State out of New England, in 1821), Virginia (1829), Georgia (1833), Tennessee (1834), North Carolina and Michigan, in 1835. Since 1835 all new Constitutions except those of Delaware (1895), Mississippi (1890), and South Carolina (1895) have been submitted to popular vote after leaving the hands of the Convention or Legislature.

AMENDMENTS TO CONSTITUTIONS.

Amendments to Constitutions are made by Conventions called on a Referendum in thirty States—Alabama, California, Colorado, Delaware, Florida, Idaho, Illinois, Iowa, Kansas, Kentucky, Maryland, Michigan, Minnesota, Missouri, Montana, Nebraska, Nevada, New Hampshire, New York, North Carolina, Ohio, South Carolina, South Dakota, Tennessee, Utah, Virginia, Washington, West Virginia, Wisconsin, and Wyoming—and in fifteen—Arkansas, Connecticut, Georgia, Indiana, Louisiana, Maine, Massachusetts, Mississippi, New Jersey, North Dakota, Oregon, Pennsylvania, Rhode Island, Texas, and Vermont—by the Legislature, and are referable to the people in forty-three States, the exceptions being Delaware and South Carolina.

LAWS AFFECTING THE WHOLE STATE.

1. When the vote of the people is authorized by the Constitution. This is the Referendum in its narrower sense, and in this aspect is now a matter of political interest. The Constitution of South Dakota (1898) provides: "The legislative power of the State shall be vested in a Legislature, which shall consist of a Senate and House of Representatives, except that the people expressly reserve to themselves the right to propose measures (initiative), which measures the Legislature shall enact and submit to a vote of the electors of the State, and also the right to require that any laws which the Legislature may have enacted shall be submitted to a vote of the electors of the State before going into effect." The Constitution of Oregon (1902) contains a similar provision. So far, however, no other State has incorporated this initiative and referendum clause in general terms in its Constitution. Special provisions, nevertheless, are the subject of referendum, as the location of the capital of the State and of State institutions, the limitation of expenditure, or of the debt, and in Colorado, Montana, Idaho, and Utah the maximum tax rate, the franchise and many like questions.

2. When no authorization for such vote is contained in the Constitution. The reference of general laws to the people in the absence of express constitutional authority was early attempted, but has generally been held unconstitutional. Barto vs. Himrod, 4 Seld (N. Y.) 483, is the leading case. But the reference of a time when a law shall take effect has been held constitutional—upon this many of the State prohibitory Liquor Laws are based, as in Michigan (1852), Vermont (1852), Maine (1858), North Carolina (1881). Other matters of a general nature have been so referred—e. g., the seat of Government (California, 1850), free schools (New York, 1849), minority representation on corporations (New Hampshire, 1880), contract labor in prisons (New York, 1883), Chinese immigration (Nevada, 1880), woman suffrage (Massachusetts, 1895).

LAWS AFFECTING PARTS OF STATES OR LOCALITIES ONLY.

The reference of such laws to the vote of the people of the locality affected is held to be not unconstitutional in legislation determining the area, boundaries, etc., of local political districts; the selection of county seats and sites, the selection of a corporate name, and the choice of a city charter or local government, in which the referendum is made obligatory in some States. So, also, propositions to remove the fire and police departments of Jersey City were referred to the inhabitants in 1885; to reform the Civil Service in any city of Illinois (1895); to increase the number of supervisors in Iowa (1897), Nebraska (1897), North Dakota (1895), and Ohio (1896). Every phase of legislation in which there is danger to the legislator is apt at some time to be so referred, including loan bills and financial proposals of all kinds.

THE INITIATIVE.

The initiative is either a right reserved by the people of a State in their Constitution to originate propositions to be enacted into law by the Legislature and ratified by the vote of the people, or that giving a number of voters in a community the right to cause an election to be held upon a permitted question (as whether liquor shall be sold in the town), and if the vote be in favor of a change then the new condition to obtain under a previously passed statute of the State Legislature. The initiative in its larger aspect has authority only in South Dakota and Oregon, and there its operation excludes only matters of emergency, as the preservation of the public peace, health, or safety. In its local aspect it has been called in to inaugurate a vast variety of matters of local interest,—prohibition, county seats, live stock and fencing laws, high-school laws—finding its greatest development in Oregon, South Dakota, Nebraska, California, and Iowa.

The Initiative and Referendum constitute a political force or medium opposed in action to the Legislature as the delegated authority of the people, and the various labor and people's parties have turned to them as a means of holding in their own hands a larger measure of the sovereign power which, under the older theories of government, was entirely delegated to their representatives.

The past year has seen a somewhat enlarged use of the referendum in several of the Western States and in the new State of Oklahoma, where the doctrine is given free rein.

The United States Census.

The Constitution requires that a census of the United States shall be taken decennially. The First Census was taken in 1790 under the supervision of the President; subsequent censuses, to and including that of 1840, were taken under the supervision of the Secretary of State. In 1849 the supervision of the census was transferred to the newly organized Department of the Interior, and continued under the control of that department until the passage of the act of 1903 creating the Department of Commerce and Labor; by this act the Census Office was transferred to the supervision of the new department. Congress, by act approved March 6, 1902, made the Census Office a permanent bureau of the Government.

The last census of the United States was taken in 1900, in accordance with the act of Congress approved March 3, 1899. This act divided the statistical inquiry into two classes: Reports of the Twelfth Census, comprising population, manufactures, agriculture, and vital statistics; and special reports, the insane and feeble-minded, deaf, dumb, and blind; crime, pauperism, and benevolence; deaths and births in registration areas, social statistics of cities, wealth, debt, and taxation; religious bodies, electric light and power, telephones and telegraphs, transportation by water, street railways, express companies, and mines and mining. To these were subsequently added annual statistics of cotton production. The series comprising the main reports of the Twelfth Census were by law ordered compiled and published by July 1, 1902, after which the special reports were to receive consideration. In accordance with this law, ten volumes of the main reports, comprising about 10,000 pages, were published within the period specified, and summaries of these reports will be found on other pages of THE WORLD ALMANAC.

Since July 1, 1902, the Bureau of the Census has been engaged in securing and tabulating statistics relating to the secondary reports, several of which have been completed or are now approaching completion. By act of Congress the President was empowered to instruct the Census Office to compile the census of the Philippine Islands. In compliance with the President's order the tabulation was made and the reports were published in four volumes. An edition in Spanish was also issued. Numerous minor assignments of statistical work have been made to the Bureau. It is likely, indeed, to become the main producer of, or clearing-house for, Federal statistics, as predicted during the discussion that preceded the establishment of the permanent office. Since the publication of the main reports of the Twelfth Census the Bureau has published the Abstract of the Twelfth Census, the Statistical Atlas of the United States, special reports on Employees and Wages, Occupations, Mines and Quarries, Street Railways, Benevolent Institutions, Electric Light and Power Stations, the Blind and the Deaf; Mortality, 1900 to 1904; Supplementary Analysis of the Twelfth Census; the Insane and Feeble-minded in Hospitals and Institutions; Paupers in Almshouses, Manufactures, 1905; Wealth, Debt, and Taxation; Prisoners; Women at Work; Mortality, 1905; and bulletins on Statistics of Cities, Valuation of Railway Operating Property, and Child Labor. It has also completed the census of Manufactures of 1905, and issued the reports on Wages and Transportation by Water. During 1909 the Bureau will be occupied principally in completing the reports on Marriage and Divorce; Religious Bodies; Criminal Judicial Statistics; Express Companies; the annual reports on Mortality and Cotton Production and Consumption, and preliminary work for the 13th Census.

The Director of the Census is appointed by the President of the United States, and receives a salary of $6,000. The present Director is S. N. D. North, of Massachusetts. The office organization consists of chief clerk, William S. Rossiter; a disbursing and appointment clerk, Thomas S. Merrill; four chief statisticians; for population, William C. Hunt; for manufactures, William M. Steuart; for agriculture, Le Grand Powers, and for vital statistics, Cressy L. Wilbur; a geographer, Charles S. Sloane; and such administrative division chiefs as are required by the demands of the office. The entire number of employees in the Bureau on July 1, 1908, was 641. This number does not include special agents employed intermittently in the Southern States for the collection of cotton statistics.

Should the bill now pending before Congress be passed, the Thirteenth Census will be taken as of April 15, 1910, instead of June 1. The office force will be greatly enlarged, and it is estimated that the total number of employees, including enumerators and supervisors, will be approximately 60,000, and the expenditure $14,000,000.

THE CENSUS OF 1910.

The bill providing for taking the Thirteenth Census of the United States, which is pending in Congress and will come up for passage during the second session of the Sixtieth Congress is composed of thirty-three sections and follows in all essentials the original changes introduced by the law of 1899. Like that law, it limits the enumeration strictly to four subjects—population, agriculture, manufactures and mines and quarries—relegating other decennial inquiries to the interval between the censuses. One of the inquiries of 1899, that into deaths in the general population, has been dropped. The reasons are twofold. Fifty years of experiment from 1850 to 1900 has established with certainty the fact that not more than seven-tenths of all the deaths which occur in a given community during a year can be obtained by enumerators asking at the close of that year of each family a report of any deaths which had occurred therein during the preceding twelve months. Tables so imperfect have very little statistical or medical value, and are constantly misunderstood by the public. So wide a margin of error in one branch of the census tends also to discredit more accurate results reached in other divisions. Furthermore, the Federal Census, acting in co-operation with the States and cities having trustworthy local registers of deaths, is now annually publishing returns for about one-half the population of the country, which probably cover 95 per cent. of all deaths occurring within that region, and furnish a far better index to the death rate in the whole country than enumerators' returns for the United States could do.

While this inquiry into deaths outside the registration area is likely to be discontinued, it is proposed to add one other inquiry—that into mines and mining. This is done because the past experience of the Census Office shows that the line between manufacturing, on the one hand, and mining or quarrying, on the other, is one almost impossible for the Census Office to draw, and that the difficulties in doing so are steadily increasing.

Like the law of 1890, the present draft requires the results of the census to be published by the Summer of 1912, and thus prohibits the office from extending its publications into the seventh or eighth year after the census day, as had been done at certain previous censuses.

In a summary of the provisions of the bill Walter F. Willcox in a paper prepared for the Quarterly of the American Statistical Association specifies:

"Probably the most important new feature in the draft of the Census bill is the provision for an almost automatic transfer of the Census Office from a status closely approaching that of the ordinary bureau, which it maintains during the seven years inter-

THE UNITED STATES CENSUS.—*Continued.*

vening between the decennial censuses, to the unusual condition requisite during the three years when the decennial census is being taken. The period from July 1, 1909, to July 1, 1912, is named the decennial census period. During that period the law provides for an Assistant Director, a fifth Chief Statistician, and such other clerks of various classes as may be found necessary. During that period also the Director of the Census may promote or transfer persons from the temporary roll of employees holding office only during the decennial period to the permanent force and vice versa. The whole office works thus as one organization, its energies and personnel being devoted in part to the decennial census, in part to the routine work of the permanent office, as the needs of the work require.

"The funds, like the personnel, are entirely under the control of the Director. During those three years there are no annual appropriations for any work of the office, but all its expenses are to be met out of a single lump appropriation. For the three years a sum of $14,000,000 is provided. During this period the responsibility and the initiative are concentrated in the hands of the Director, and he is solely responsible for the rapid and effective progress of the work. The work of the decennial census must be completed by the end of this decennial census period, and the office then returns to its normal condition. The temporary employees having no standing on the Civil Service roll lose their positions in 1912, and the office reverts to what may be called a peace footing.

"It is proposed to change the census day from June 1 to April 15. June 1 is so late in the Summer that many persons have left their usual places of residence, their houses are closed, and it is extremely difficult to obtain information about them either from the neighbors or by correspondence. This source of danger and of error to a census is increasing with each decade."

PROVISIONS OF THE CENSUS BILL.

The following are the provisions of the pending Census bill which cover some of its most important requirements:

"Section 8. The Thirteenth Census shall be restricted to inquiries relating to population, to agriculture, to manufactures, and to mines and quarries."

POPULATION.

"The schedules relating to population shall include for each inhabitant the name, relationship to head of family, color, sex, age, conjugal condition, place of birth, place of birth of parents, number of years in the United States, citizenship, occupation, school attendance, literacy, and tenure of home."

AGRICULTURE.

"The schedules relating to agriculture shall include name of occupant of each farm, color of occupant, tenure, acreage of farm, value of farm and improvements, value of farm implements, number and value of live stock on farms and ranges, number and value of domestic animals not on farms and ranges, and the acreage of crops as of the date of enumeration, and the acreage of crops and the quantity and value of crops and other farm products for the year ending December 31 next preceding the enumeration."

MANUFACTURES AND MINES.

"The schedules of inquiries relating to manufactures and to mines and quarries shall include the name and location of each establishment; character of organization, whether individual, co-operative, or other form; character of business or kind of goods manufactured; amount of capital invested; number of proprietors, firm members, co-partners, stockholders, and officers and the amount of their salaries: number of employees and the amount of their wages; quantity and cost of materials used in manufactures; amount of miscellaneous expenses; quantity and value of products; time in operation during the census year; character and quantity of power used, and character and number of machines employed.

"The census of manufactures and of mines and quarries shall relate to the year ending December thirty-first next preceding the enumeration of population and shall be confined to mines and quarries and to manufacturing establishments which were in active operation during all or a portion of that year and had a product valued at $500 or more. The census of manufactures shall furthermore be confined to manufacturing establishments conducted under what is known as the factory system, exclusive of the so-called neighborhood or household industries.

"Whenever he shall deem it expedient, the Director of the Census may charge the collection of these statistics upon the special agents or upon detailed employees, to be employed without respect to locality.

"The form and subdivision of inquiries necessary to secure the information under the foregoing topics shall be determined by the Director of the Census."

DUTY OF CITIZENS TO ANSWER QUESTIONS.

"Section 23. That it shall be the duty of all persons over twenty-one years of age when requested by the Director of the Census, or by any supervisor, enumerator, or special agent, or other employee of the Census Office, acting under the instructions of the said Director, to answer correctly, to the best of their knowledge, all questions on the census schedules applying to themselves and to the family to which they belong or are related, and to the farm or farms of which they or their families are the occupants; and any person over twenty-one years of age who, under the conditions hereinbefore stated, shall refuse or wilfully neglect to answer any of these questions, or shall wilfully give answers that are false, shall be guilty of a misdemeanor, and upon conviction thereof shall be fined not exceeding $100.

"And it shall be the duty of every owner, proprietor, manager, superintendent, or agent of a hotel, apartment house, boarding or lodging house, tenement, or other building, when requested by the Director of the Census, or by any supervisor, enumerator, special agent, or other employee of the Census Office, acting under the instructions of the said Director, to furnish the names of the occupants of said hotel, apartment house, boarding or lodging house, tenement, or other building, and to give thereto free ingress and egress to any duly accredited representative of the Census Office, so as to permit of the proper and correct enumeration of all persons having their usual place of abode in said hotel, apartment house, boarding or lodging house, tenement, or other building; and any owner, proprietor, manager, superintendent, or agent of a hotel, apartment house, boarding or lodging house, tenement, or other building who shall refuse or wilfully neglect to give

THE UNITED STATES CENSUS.—*Continued.*

such information or assistance under the conditions hereinbefore stated shall be guilty of a misdemeanor, and upon conviction thereof shall be fined not exceeding $500.

"Section 24. And it shall be the duty of every owner, president, treasurer, secretary, director, or other officer or agent of any manufacturing establishment, mine, quarry, or other establishment of productive industry, whether conducted as a corporation, firm, limited liability company, or by private individuals, when requested by the Director of the Census or by any supervisor, enumerator, special agent, or other employee of the Census Office, acting under the instructions of the said Director, to answer completely and correctly to the best of his knowledge all questions on any census schedule applying to such establishment; and any owner, president, secretary, director, or other officer or agent of any manufacturing establishment, mine, quarry, or other establishment of productive industry, who under the conditions hereinbefore stated shall refuse or wilfully neglect to answer any of these questions, or shall wilfully give answers that are false, shall be guilty of a misdemeanor, and upon conviction thereof shall be fined not exceeding $10,000, or imprisoned for a period not exceeding one year, or both so fined and imprisoned, at the discretion of the court. The provisions of this section shall also apply to the collection of the information required and authorized by the act entitled 'An act to provide for a permanent Census Office,' and by acts amendatory thereof or supplemental thereto."

INFORMATION RECEIVED AS CONFIDENTIAL.

"Section 25. That the information furnished under the provisions of the next preceding section shall be used only for the statistical purposes for which it is supplied. No publication shall be made by the Census Office whereby the data furnished by any particular establishment can be identified, nor shall the Director of the Census permit any one other than the sworn employees of the Census Office to examine the individual reports."

Registration of Trade-Marks

IN THE UNITED STATES.

THE following are extracts from the new "Act to authorize the registration of trade-marks used in commerce with foreign nations, or among the several States or Indian tribes, and to protect the same," passed by the Fifty-eighth Congress, and approved by the President, February 20, 1905, and amended by act passed by the Fifty-ninth Congress, approved March 2, 1907.

"The owner of a trade-mark used in commerce with foreign nations, or among the several States, or with Indian tribes, provided such owner shall be domiciled within the territory of the United States, or resides in or is located in any foreign country which, by treaty, convention, or law, affords similar privileges to the citizens of the United States, may obtain registration for such trade-mark by complying with the following requirements: First, by filing in the Patent Office an application therefor, in writing, addressed to the Commissioner of Patents, signed by the applicant, specifying his name, domicile, location, and citizenship; the class of merchandise and the particular description of goods comprised in such class to which the trade-mark is appropriated; a description of the trade-mark itself, and a statement of the mode in which the same is applied and affixed to goods, and the length of time during which the trade-mark has been used. With this statement shall be filed a drawing of the trade-mark, signed by the applicant, or his attorney, and such number of specimens of the trade-mark, as actually used, as may be required by the Commissioner of Patents. Second, by paying into the Treasury of the United States the sum of ten dollars, and otherwise complying with the requirements of this act and such regulations as may be prescribed by the Commissioner of Patents.

"A certificate of registration shall remain in force for twenty years, except that in the case of trade-marks previously registered in a foreign country such certificates shall cease to be in force on the day on which the trade-mark ceases to be protected in such foreign country, and shall in no case remain in force more than twenty years, unless renewed. Certificates of registration may be, from time to time, renewed for like periods on payment of the renewal fees required by this act, upon request by the registrant, his legal representatives, or transferees of record in the Patent Office, and such request may be made at any time not more than six months prior to the expiration of the period for which the certificates of registration were issued or renewed. Certificates of registration in force at the date at which this act takes effect shall remain in force for the period for which they were issued, but shall be renewable on the same conditions and for the same periods as certificates issued under the provisions of this act, and when so renewed shall have the same force and effect as certificates issued under this act.

"The registration of a trade-mark under the provisions of this act shall be prima facie evidence of ownership who shall, without the consent of the owner thereof, reproduce, counterfeit, copy, or colorably imitate any such trade-mark and affix the same to merchandise of substantially the same descriptive properties as those set forth in the registration, or to labels, signs, prints, packages, wrappers, or receptacles intended to be used upon or in connection with the sale of merchandise of substantially the same descriptive properties as those set forth in such registration, and shall use, or shall have used, such reproduction, counterfeit, copy, or colorable imitation in commerce among the several States, or with a foreign nation, or with the Indian tribes, shall be liable to an action for damages therefor at the suit of the owner thereof; and whenever in any such action a verdict is rendered for the plaintiff, the court may enter judgment therein for any sum above the amount found by the verdict as the actual damages, according to the circumstances of the case, not exceeding three times the amount of such verdict, together with the costs."

No trade-mark shall be granted which "consists of or comprises the flag or coat of arms or other insignia of the United States or any simulation thereof, or of any State or municipality, or of any foreign nation, nor which is identical with or nearly resembling a trade-mark already registered." "No portrait of a living individual may be registered as a trade-mark except by the consent of such individual, evidenced by an instrument in writing."

TRADE-MARK TREATIES WITH FOREIGN NATIONS.

The following is a list of the Governments with which conventions for the reciprocal registration and protection of trade-marks have been entered into by the United States: Austria-Hungary, Belgium, Denmark, France, Germany, Great Britain (including colonies), Italy, Japan, Luxemburg, Russia, Servia, Spain. The laws of Switzerland and the Netherlands being so framed as to afford reciprocal privileges to the citizens or subjects of any Government which affords similar privileges to the people of those countries, the mere exchange of diplomatic notes, giving notice of the fact, accomplishes all the purposes of a formal convention.

National Platforms of Political Parties.

PLATFORM OF THE DEMOCRATIC PARTY, ADOPTED AT DENVER, COL., JULY 10, 1908.

We, the representatives of the Democrats of the United States, in national convention assembled, reaffirm our belief in and pledge our loyalty to the principles of the party.

We rejoice at the increasing signs of an awakening throughout the country. The various investigations have traced graft and political corruption to the representatives of predatory wealth, and laid bare the unscrupulous methods by which they have debauched elections and preyed upon a defenceless public through the subservient officials whom they have raised to place and power.

The conscience of the nation is now aroused to free the government from the grip of those who have made it a business asset of the favor-seeking corporations; it must become again a people's government, and be administered in all its departments according to the Jeffersonian maxim of "equal rights to all and special privileges to none."

"Shall the people rule?" is the overshadowing issue which manifests itself in all the questions now under discussion.

The Misuse of Patronage.—We condemn as a violation of the spirit of our institutions the action of the present Chief Executive in using the patronage of his high office to secure the nomination of one of his Cabinet officers. A forced succession in the Presidency is scarcely less repugnant to public sentiment than is life tenure in that office. No good intention on the part of the executive and no virtue in the one selected can justify the establishment of a dynasty. The right of the people to freely select their officials is inalienable and cannot be delegated.

Publicity of Campaign Contributions.—We demand Federal legislation forever terminating the partnership which has existed between corporations of the country and the Republican party under the expressed or implied agreement that in return for the contributions of great sums of money wherewith to purchase elections they should be allowed to continue substantially unmolested in their efforts to encroach upon the rights of the people.

Any reasonable doubt as to the existence of this relation has been forever dispelled by the sworn testimony of witnesses examined in the insurance investigation in New York and the open admission, unchallenged by the Republican National Committee, of a single individual that he himself, at the personal request of the Republican candidate for the Presidency, raised more than a quarter of a million of dollars to be used in a single State during the closing hours of the last campaign. In order that this practice shall be stopped for all time we demand the passage of a statute punishing with imprisonment any officer of a corporation who shall either contribute on behalf of or consent to the contribution by corporations of any money or thing of value to be used in furthering the election of a President or Vice-President of the United States or of any member of Congress thereof.

We denounce the action of the Republican party, having complete control of the Federal Government, for its failure to pass the bill introduced in the last Congress to compel the publication of the names of contributors and the amounts contributed toward Congress funds, and point to the evidence of their insincerity when they sought by an absolutely irrelevant and impossible amendment to defeat the passage of the bill. As a further evidence of their intention to conduct their campaign in the coming contest with vast sums of money wrested from favor-seeking corporations, we call attention to the fact that the recent Republican National Convention at Chicago refused, when the plank was presented to it, to declare against such practices.

We pledge the Democratic party to the enactment of a law preventing any corporation contributing to a campaign fund, and any individual from contributing an amount above a reasonable minimum, and providing for the publication before election of all such contributions above a reasonable minimum.

The Rights of the States.—Believing, with Jefferson, in "the support of the State Governments in all their rights as the most competent administration for our domestic concerns and the surest bulwark against anti-Republican tendencies," and in "the preservation of the general government in its whole constitutional vigor as the sheet anchor of our peace at home and safety abroad," we are opposed to the centralization implied in the suggestions, now frequently made, that the powers of the general government should be extended by judicial construction. There is no twilight zone between the Nation and the State in which exploiting interests can take refuge from both; and it is as necessary that the Federal Government shall exercise the powers delegated to it as it is that the State Governments shall use the authority reserved to them, but we insist that Federal remedies for the regulation of interstate commerce and for the prevention of private monopoly shall be added to, not substituted for, State remedies.

Tariff.—We welcome the belated promise of tariff reform now affected by the Republican party in tardy recognition of the righteousness of the Democratic position on this question, but the people cannot safely trust the execution of this important work to a party which is so deeply obligated to the highly protected interests as is the Republican party. We call attention to the significant fact that the promised relief was postponed until after the coming election—an election to succeed in which the Republican party must have that same support from the beneficiaries of the high protective tariff as it has always heretofore received from them; and to the further fact that during years of uninterrupted power no action whatever has been taken by the Republican Congress to correct the admittedly existing tariff iniquities.

We favor immediate revision of the tariff by the reduction of import duties. Articles entering into competition with trust controlled products should be placed upon the free list, and material reductions shall be made in the tariff upon the necessaries of life, especially upon articles competing with such American manufactures as are sold abroad more cheaply than at home, and graduated reductions should be made in such other schedules as may be necessary to restore the tariff to a revenue basis.

Existing duties have given to the manufacturers of paper a shelter behind which they have organized combinations to raise the price of pulp and of paper, thus imposing a tax upon the spread of knowledge. We demand the immediate repeal of the tariff on pulp, print paper, lumber, timber and logs and that these articles be placed upon the free list.

Trusts.—A private monopoly is indefensible and intolerable. We therefore favor the vigorous enforcement of the criminal law against guilty trust magnates and officials, and demand the enactment of such additional legislation as may be necessary to make it impossible for a private monopoly to exist in the United States.

Among the additional remedies we specify three: First, a law preventing a duplication of directors among competing corporations; second, a license system which will, without abridging the right of each State to create corporations or its right to regulate as it will foreign corporations doing business within its limits, make it necessary for a manufacturing or trading corporation engaged in interstate commerce to take out a Federal license before it shall be permitted to control as much as 25 per cent. of the product in which it deals, a license to protect the public from watered stock and to prohibit the control by such corporation of more than 50 per cent. of the total amount of any product consumed in the United States; and, third, a law compelling such licensed corporations to sell to all purchasers in all parts of the country on the same terms after making due allowance for cost of transportation.

Railroad Regulation.—We assert the right of Congress to exercise complete control over interstate commerce and the right of each State to exercise like control over commerce within its borders.

We demand such enlargement of the powers of the Interstate Commerce Commission as may be necessary to compel railroads to perform their duties as common carriers and prevent discrimination and extortion.

We favor the efficient supervision and rate regulation of railroads engaged in interstate commerce; to this end we recommend the valuation of railroads by the Interstate Commerce Commission, such valuation to take into consideration the physical value of the property, the original cost and cost of reproduction and all elements of value that will render the valuation made fair and just.

We favor such legislation as will prohibit the railroads from engaging in business which brings them into competition with their shippers; also legislation which will assure such reduction in transportation rates as conditions will permit, care being taken to avoid reductions that would compel a reduction of wages, prevent adequate service or do injustice to legitimate investments. We heartily approve the laws prohibiting the pass and the rebate, and we favor any further necessary legislation to restrain, control and prevent such abuses.

We favor such legislation as will increase the power of the Interstate Commerce Commission, giving to it the initiative with reference to rates and transportation charges put into effect by the railroad companies, and permitting the Interstate Commerce Commission, on its own initiative, to declare a rate illegal and as being more than should be charged for such service. The present law relating thereto is inadequate by reason of the fact that the Interstate Commerce Commission is without power to fix or investigate a rate until complaint has been made to it by the shipper.

We further declare that all agreements of traffic or other associations of railway agents affecting interstate rates, service or classification, shall be unlawful unless filed with and approved by the Interstate Commerce Commission.

We favor the enactment of a law giving to the Interstate Commerce Commission the power to inspect proposed railroad tariff rates or schedules before they shall take effect, and, if they be found to be unreasonable, to initiate an adjustment thereof.

Banking.—The panic of 1907, coming without any legitimate excuse, when the Republican party had for a decade been in complete control of the Federal Government, furnishes additional proof that it is either unwilling or incompetent to protect the interests of the general public. It has so linked the country to Wall Street that the sins of the speculators are visited upon the whole people. While refusing to rescue wealth producers from spoliation at the hands of the stock gamblers and speculators in farm products, it has deposited Treasury funds, without interest and without competition, in favorite banks. It has used an emergency for which it is largely responsible to force through Congress a bill changing the basis of bank currency and inviting market manipulation, and has failed to give to the fifteen million depositors of the country protection in their savings.

We believe that, in so far as the needs of commerce require an emergency currency, such currency should be issued, controlled by the Federal Government and loaned on adequate security to national and State banks. We pledge ourselves to legislation under which the national banks shall be required to establish a guarantee fund for the prompt payment of the depositors of any insolvent national bank under an equitable system which shall be available to all State banking institutions wishing to use it.

We favor a postal savings bank, if the guaranteed bank cannot be secured, and that it be constituted so as to keep the deposited money in the communities where it is established; but we condemn the policy of the Republican party in providing postal savings banks under a plan of conduct by which they will aggregate the deposits of rural communities and redeposit the same while under Government charge in the banks of Wall Street, thus depleting the circulating medium of the producing regions and unjustly favoring the speculative markets.

Income Tax.—We favor an income tax as part of our revenue system, and we urge the submission of a constitutional amendment specifically authorizing Congress to levy and collect a tax upon individual and corporate incomes to the end that wealth may bear its proportionate share of the burdens of the Federal Government.

Labor and Injunctions.—The courts of justice are the bulwark of our liberty, and we yield to none in our purpose to maintain their dignity. Our party has given to the bench a long line of distinguished judges, who have added to the respect and confidence in which this department must be jealously maintained. We resent the attempt of the Republican party to raise false issues respecting the judiciary. It is an unjust reflection upon a great body of our citizens to assume that they lack respect for the courts.

It is the function of the courts to interpret the laws which the people create, and if the laws appear to work economic, social or political injustice, it is our duty to change them. The only basis upon which the integrity of our courts can stand is that of unswerving justice and protection of life, personal liberty and property. If judicial processes may be abused, we should guard them against abuse.

Experience has proven the necessity of a modification of the present law relating to injunctions, and we reiterate the pledge of our national platforms of 1896 and 1904 in favor of the measure which passed the United States Senate in 1896, but which a Republican Congress has ever since refused to enact, relating to contempts in Federal courts and providing for trial by jury in cases of indirect contempt.

Questions of judicial practice have arisen, especially in connection with industrial disputes. We deem that the parties to all judicial proceedings should be treated with rigid impartiality, and that injunctions should not be issued in any cases in which injunctions would not issue if no industrial dispute were involved.

The expanding organization of industry makes it essential that there should be no abridgment of the right of wage earners and producers to organize for the protection of wages and the improvement of labor conditions, to the end that such labor organizations and their members should not be regarded as illegal combinations in restraint of trade.

We favor the eight-hour day on all Government work.

We pledge the Democratic party to the enactment of a law by Congress, as far as the Federal jurisdiction extends, for a general employers' liability act, covering injury to body or loss of life of employees.

We pledge the Democratic party to the enactment of a law creating a department of labor, represented separately in the President's Cabinet, which department shall include the subject of mines and mining.

Merchant Marine.—We believe in the upbuilding of the American merchant marine without new or additional burdens upon the people and without bounties from the public treasury.

The Navy.—The constitutional provision that a navy shall be provided and maintained means an adequate navy, and we believe that the interests of this country would be best served by having a navy sufficient to defend the coasts of this country, and protect American citizens wherever their rights may be in jeopardy.

Protection of American Citizens.—We pledge ourselves to insist upon the just and lawful protection of our citizens at home and abroad and to use all proper methods to secure for them, whether native born or naturalized, and without distinction of race or creed, the equal protection of law and the enjoyment of all rights and privileges open to them under our treaties; and if, under existing conditions, the right of travel and sojourn is denied to American citizens, or recognition is withheld from American passports by any countries on the ground of race or creed, we favor prompt negotiations with the governments of such countries to secure the removal of these unjust discriminations.

We demand that all over the world a duly authorized passport issued by the Government of the United States to an American citizen shall be proof of the fact that he is an American citizen and shall entitle him to the treatment due him as such.

Civil Service.—The laws pertaining to the Civil Service should be honestly and rigidly enforced, to the end that merit and ability shall be the standard of appointment and promotion rather than services rendered to a political party.

Pensions.—We favor a generous pension policy, both as a matter of justice to the surviving veterans and their dependants and because it tends to relieve the country of the necessity of maintaining a large standing army.

Health Bureau.—We advocate the organization of all existing national public health agencies into a national bureau of public health, with such power over sanitary conditions connected with factories, mines, tenements, child labor and such other subjects as are properly within the jurisdiction of the Federal Government and do not interfere with the power of the States controlling public health agencies.

Agricultural and Mechanical Education.—The Democratic party favors the extension of agricultural, mechanical and industrial education. We therefore favor the establishment of district agricultural experiment stations and secondary agricultural and mechanical colleges in the several States.

Popular Election of Senators.—We favor the election of United States Senators by direct vote of the people, and regard this reform as the gateway to other national reforms.

Oklahoma.—We welcome Oklahoma to the sisterhood of States, and heartily congratulate her on the auspicious beginning of a great career.

Arizona and New Mexico.—The national Democratic party has for the last sixteen years labored for the admission of Arizona and New Mexico as separate States of the Federal Union, and recognizing that each possesses every qualification to successfully maintain separate State governments, we favor the immediate admission of these Territories as separate States.

Grazing Lands.—The establishment of rules and regulations, if any such are necessary, in relation to free grazing upon the public lands outside of forest or other reservations until the same shall eventually be disposed of should be left to the people of the States respectively in which such lands may be situated.

Waterways.—Water furnishes the cheapest means of transportation, and the National Government, having the control of navigable waters, should improve them to their fullest capacity. We earnestly favor the immediate adoption of a liberal and comprehensive plan for improving every watercourse in the Union which is justified by the needs of commerce, and to secure that end we favor, when practicable, the connection of the Great Lakes with the navigable rivers and with the Gulf through the Mississippi River, and the navigable rivers with each other, and the rivers, bays and sounds of our coasts with each other by artificial canals, with a view to perfecting a system of inland waterways, to be navigated by vessels of standard draught.

We favor the co-ordination of the various services of the Government connected with waterways in one service, for the purpose of aiding in the completion of such a system of inland waterways; and we favor the creation of a fund ample for continuous work, which shall be conducted under the direction of a commission of experts to be authorized by law.

Post Roads.—We favor Federal aid to State and local authorities in the construction and maintenance of post roads.

Arbitrary Power of Speaker.—The House of Representatives was designed by the fathers of the Constitution to be the popular branch of our Government, responsive to the public will.

The House of Representatives, as controlled in recent years by the Republican party, has ceased to be a deliberative and legislative body, responsive to the will of a majority of its members, but has come under the absolute domination of the Speaker, who has entire control of its deliberations and powers of legislation.

We have observed with amazement the popular branch of our Federal Government helpless to obtain either the consideration or enactment of measures desired by a majority of its members.

Legislative government becomes a failure when one member in the person of the Speaker is more powerful than the entire body.

We demand that the House of Representatives shall again become a deliberative body, controlled by a majority of the people's representatives, and not by the Speaker, and we pledge ourselves to adopt such rules and regulations to govern the House of Representatives as will enable a majority of its members to direct its deliberations and control legislation.

Economy in Administration.—The Republican Congress in the session just ended has made appropriations amounting to $1,008,000,000, exceeding the total expenditures of the last fiscal year by $90,000,000 and leaving a deficit of more than $60,000,000 for the fiscal year. We denounce the needless waste of the people's money which has resulted in this appalling increase as a shameful violation of all prudent conditions of government, as no less than a crime against the millions of working men and women, from whose earnings the great proportion of these colossal sums must be extorted through excessive tariff exactions and other indirect methods. It is not surprising that in the face of this shocking record the Republican platform contains no reference to economical administration or promise thereof in the future. We demand that a stop be put to this frightful extravagance and insist upon the strictest economy in every department compatible with frugal and efficient administration.

Officeholders.—Coincident with the enormous increase in expenditures is a like addition to the number of officeholders. During the last year 23,784 were added, costing $16,156,000, and in the last six years of the Republican administration the total number of new offices created, aside from many commissions, has been 99,319, entailing an additional expenditure of nearly seventy million dollars, as against only 10,279 new offices created under the Cleveland and McKinley administrations, which involved an expenditure of only $6,000,000. We denounce this great and growing increase in the number of officeholders as not only unnecessary and wasteful but also as clearly indicating a deliberate purpose on the part of the administration to keep the Republican party in power at public expense by thus increasing the number of its retainers and dependents. Such procedure we declare to be no less dangerous and corrupt than the open purchase of votes at the polls.

Natural Resources.—We repeat the demand for internal development and for the conservation of our natural resources contained in previous platforms, the enforcement of which Mr. Roosevelt has vainly sought from a reluctant party, and to that end we insist upon the preservation, protection, and replacement of needed forests, the preservation of the public domain for homeseekers, the protection of the national resources in timber, coal, iron and oil against monopolistic control; the development of our waterways for navigation and every other useful purpose, including the irrigation of arid lands, the reclamation of swamp lands, the clarification of streams, the development of water power and the preservation of electric power generated by this natural force from the control of monopoly; and to such end we urge the exercise of all powers, national, State, and municipal, both separately and in co-operation.

We insist upon a policy of administration of our forest reserve which shall relieve it of the abuses which have arisen thereunder, and which shall, as far as practicable, conform to the police regulations of the several States where they are located, which shall enable homesteaders as of right to occupy and acquire title to all portions thereof which are especially adapted to agriculture, and which shall furnish a system of timber sales available as well to the private citizen as to the larger manufacturer and consumer.

Philippines.—We condemn the experiment in imperialism as an inexcusable blunder, which has involved us in an enormous expense, brought us weakness instead of strength, and laid our nation open to the charge of abandoning a fundamental doctrine of self-government. We favor an immediate declaration of the nation's purpose to recognize the independence of the Philippine Islands as soon as a stable government can be established, such independence to be guaranteed by us as we guarantee the independence of Cuba, until the neutralization of the islands can be secured by treaty with other powers. In recognizing the independence of the Philippines our Government should retain such land as may be necessary for coaling stations and naval bases.

Pan-American Relations.—The Democratic party recognizes the importance and advantage of developing closer ties of Pan-American friendship and commerce between the United States and her sister nations of Latin America, and favors the taking of such steps, consistent with Democratic policies, for better acquaintance, greater mutual confidence and larger exchange of trade as will bring lasting benefit not only to the United States but to this group of American republics having constitutions, forms of government, ambitions and interests akin to our own.

Telegraph and Telephone.—We pledge the Democratic party to the enactment of a law to regulate the rates and services of telegraph and telephone companies engaged in the transmission of messages between the States, under the jurisdiction of the Interstate Commerce Commission.

Asiatic Immigration.—We favor full protection, by both national and State governments within their respective spheres, of all foreigners residing in the United States under treaty, but we are opposed to the admission of Asiatic immigrants who cannot be amalgamated with our population, or whose presence among us would raise a race issue and involve us in diplomatic controversies with Oriental powers.

Alaska and Porto Rico.—We demand for the people of Alaska and Porto Rico the full enjoyment of the rights and privileges of a territorial form of government, and the officials appointed to administer the government of all our Territories and the District of Columbia should be thoroughly qualified by previous bona fide residence.

Hawaii.—We favor the application of the principles of the land laws of the United States to our newly acquired Territory, Hawaii, to the end that the public lands of that Territory may be held and utilized for the benefit of bona fide homesteaders.

Panama Canal.—We believe the Panama Canal will prove of great value to our country, and favor its speedy completion.

Foreign Patents.—We believe that where an American citizen holding a patent in a foreign country is compelled to manufacture under his patent within a certain time similar restrictions should be applied in this country to the citizens or subjects of such a country.

Conclusion.—The Democratic party stands for democracy; the Republican has drawn to itself all that is aristocratic and plutocratic.

The Democratic party is the champion of civil rights and opportunities to all; the Republican party is the party of privileges and private monopoly. The Democratic party listens to the voice of the whole people and gauges progress by the prosperity and advancement of the average man; the Republican party is subservient to the comparatively few who are the beneficiaries of governmental favoritism. We invite the co-operation of all, regardless of previous political affiliation or past differences, who desire to preserve a government of the people by the people and for the people, and who favor such an administration of the government as will insure, as far as human wisdom can, that each citizen shall draw from society a reward commensurate with his contribution to the welfare of society.

PLATFORM OF THE REPUBLICAN PARTY, ADOPTED AT CHICAGO, ILL., JUNE 18, 1908.

Once more the Republican party, in national convention assembled, submits its cause to the people. This great historic organization, that destroyed slavery, preserved the Union, restored credit, expanded the national domain, established a sound financial system, developed the industries and resources of the country and gave to the nation her seat of honor in the councils of the world, now meets the new problems of government with the same courage and capacity with which it solved the old.

Republicanism Under Roosevelt.—In this the great era of American advancement the Republican party has reached its highest service under the leadership of Theodore Roosevelt. His administration is an epoch in American history. In no other period since national sovereignty was won under Washington, or preserved under Lincoln, has there been such mighty progress in those ideals of government which make for justice, equality and fair dealing among men.

The highest aspirations of the American people have found a voice. Their most exalted servant represents the best aims and worthiest purposes of all his countrymen. American manhood has been lifted to a nobler sence of duty and obligation. Conscience and courage in public station and higher standards of right and wrong in private life have become cardinal principles of political faith; capital and labor have been brought into closer relations of confidence and interdependence, and the abuse of wealth, the tyranny of power and all the evils of privilege and favoritism have been put to scorn by the simple, manly virtues of justice and fair play.

The great accomplishments of President Roosevelt have been, first and foremost, a brave and impartial enforcement of the law, the prosecution of illegal trusts and monopolies, the exposure and punishment of evildoers in the public service, the more effective regulation of the rates and service of the great transportation lines, the complete overthrow of preferences, rebates and discriminations, the arbitration of labor disputes, the amelioration of the condition of wageworkers everywhere, the conservation of the natural resources of the country, the forward step in the improvement of the inland waterways, and always the earnest support and defence of every wholesome safeguard which has made more secure the guarantees of life, liberty and property.

These are the achievements that will make for Theodore Roosevelt his place in history, but more than all else the great things he has done will be an inspiration to those who have yet greater things to do. We declare our unfaltering adherence to the policies thus inaugurated and pledge their continuance under a Republican administration of the government.

Equality of Opportunity.—Under the guidance of republican principles the American people have become the richest nation in the world. Our wealth to-day exceeds that of England and all her colonies, and that of France and Germany combined. When the Republican party was born the total wealth of the country was $16,000,000,000. It has leaped to $110,000,000,000 in a generation, while Great Britain has gathered but $60,000,000,000 in 500 years. The United States now owns one-fourth of the world's wealth and makes one-third of all modern manufactured products. In the great necessities of civilization, such as coal, the motive power of all activity; iron, the chief basis of all industry; cotton, the staple foundation of all fabrics; wheat, corn and all the agricultural products that feed mankind, America's supremacy is undisputed. And yet her great natural wealth has been scarcely touched. We have a vast domain of 3,000,000 square miles, literally bursting with latent treasure, still waiting the magic of capital and industry to be converted to the practical uses of mankind; a country rich in soil and climate, in the unharnessed energy of its rivers and in all the varied products of the field, the forest and the factory. With gratitude for God's bounty, with pride in the splendid productiveness of the past and with confidence in the plenty and prosperity of the future the Republican party declares for the principle that in the development and enjoyment of wealth so great and blessings so benign there shall be equal opportunity for all.

The Revival of Business.—Nothing so clearly demonstrates the sound basis upon which our commercial, industrial and agricultural interests are founded, and the necessity of promoting their continued welfare through the operation of Republican policies as the recent safe passage of the American people through a financial disturbance which, if appearing in the midst of Democratic rule or the menace of it, might have equalled the familiar Democratic panics of the past. We congratulate the people upon the renewed evidence of American supremacy, and hail with confidence the signs now manifest of a complete restoration of business prosperity in all lines of trade, commerce and manufacturing.

Recent Republican Legislation.—Since the election of William McKinley, in 1896 the people of this country have felt anew the wisdom of intrusting to the Republican party through decisive majorities the control and direction of national legislation.

The many wise and progressive measures adopted at recent sessions of Congress have demonstrated the patriotic resolve of Republican leadership in the legislative department to keep step in the forward march toward better government.

Notwithstanding the indefensible filibustering of a Democratic minority in the House of Representatives during the last session, many wholesome and progressive laws were enacted, and we especially commend the passage of the Emergency Currency bill; the appointment of the national monetary commission; the employers' and government liability laws; the measures for the greater efficiency of the army and navy; the Widows' Pension bill; the child labor law for the District of Columbia; the new statutes for the safety of railroad engineers and firemen and many other acts conserving the public welfare.

Pledges for Future Tariff.—The Republican party declares unequivocally for a revision of the tariff by a special session of Congress immediately following the inauguration of the next President, and commends the steps already taken to this end in the work assigned to the appropriate committees of Congress, which are now investigating the operation and effect of existing schedules. In all tariff legislation the true principle of protection is best maintained by the imposition of such duties as will equal the difference between the cost of production at home and abroad, together with a reasonable profit to American industries. We favor the establishment of maximum and minimum rates to be administered by the President under limitations fixed in the law, the maximum to be available to meet discriminations by foreign countries against American goods entering their markets, and the minimum to represent the normal measure of protection at home; the aim and purpose of the Republican policy being not only to preserve, without excessive duties, that security against foreign competition to which American manufacturers, farmers and producers are entitled, but also to maintain the high standard of living of the wage earners of this country, who are the most direct beneficiaries of the protective system. Between the United States and the Philippines we believe in a free interchange of products with such limitations as to sugar and tobacco as will afford adequate protection to domestic interests.

Currency.—We approve the emergency measures adopted by the Government during the recent financial disturbance, and especially commend the passage by Congress at the last session of the law designed to protect the country from a repetition of such stringency. The Republican party is committed to the development of a permanent currency system, responding to our greater needs, and the appointment of the national monetary commission by the present Congress, which will impartially investigate all proposed methods, insures the early realization of this purpose. The present currency laws have fully justified their adoption, but an expanding commerce, a marvellous growth in wealth and population, multiplying the centres of distribution, increasing the demand for the movement of crops in the West and South and entailing periodic changes in monetary conditions, disclose the need of a more elastic and adaptable system. Such a system must meet the requirements of agriculturists, manufacturers, merchants and business men generally, must be automatic in operation, minimizing the fluctuations in interest rates, and, above all, must be in harmony with that Republican doctrine which insists that every dollar shall be based upon and as good as gold.

Postal Savings.—We favor the establishment of a postal savings bank system for the convenience of the people and the encouragement of thrift.

Trusts.—The Republican party passed the Sherman anti-trust law over Democratic opposition, and enforced it after Democratic dereliction. It has been a wholesome instrument for good in the hands of a wise and fearless administration. But experience has shown that its effectiveness can be strengthened and its real objects better attained by such amendments as will give to the Federal Government greater supervision and control over, and secure greater publicity in, the management of that class of corporations engaged in interstate commerce having power and opportunity to effect monopolies.

Railroads.—We approve the enactment of the Railroad Rate law and the vigorous enforcement by the present administration of the statutes against rebates and discriminations, as a result of which the advantages formerly possessed by the large shipper over the small shipper have substantially disappeared; and in this connection we commend the appropriation by the present Congress to enable the Interstate Commerce Commission to thoroughly investigate, and give publicity to, the accounts of interstate railroads. We believe, however, that the interstate commerce law should be further amended so as to give railroads the right to make and publish traffic agreements subject to the approval of the commission, but maintaining always the principle of competition between naturally competing lines and avoiding the common control of such lines by any means whatsoever. We favor such national legislation and supervision as will prevent the future overissue of stocks and bonds by interstate carriers.

Railroad and Government Employees.—The enactment in constitutional form at the present session of Congress of the employers' liability law, the passage and enforcement of the safety appliance statutes, as well as the additional protection secured for engineers and firemen; the reduction in the hours of labor of trainmen and railroad telegraphers, the successful exercise of the powers of meditation and arbitration between interstate railroads and their employees, and the law making a beginning in the policy of compensation for injured employees of the Government, are among the most commendable accomplishments of the present administration. But there is further work in this direction yet to be done, and the Republican party pledges its continued devotion to every cause that makes for safety and the betterment of conditions among those whose labor contributes so much to the progress and welfare of the country.

Wage Earners Generally.—The same wise policy which has induced the Republican party to maintain protection to American labor, to establish an eight-hour day in the construction of all public works, to increase the list of employees who shall have preferred claims for wages under the bankruptcy laws, to adopt a child labor statute for the District of Columbia, to direct an investigation into the condition of working women and children, and, later, of employees of telephone and telegraph companies engaged in interstate business; to appropriate $150,000 at the recent session of Congress in order to secure a thorough inquiry into the causes of catastrophes, and loss of life in the mines, and to amend and strengthen the law prohibiting the importation of contract labor, will be pursued in every legitimate direction within Federal authority to lighten the burdens and increase the opportunity for happiness and advancement of all who toil. The Republican party recognizes the special needs of wage workers generally, for their wellbeing means the wellbeing of all. But more important than all other considerations is that of good citizenship, and we especially stand for the needs of every American, whatever his occupation, in his capacity as a self-respecting citizen.

Court Procedure.—The Republican party will uphold at all times the authority and integrity of the courts, State and Federal, and will ever insist that their powers to enforce their process and to protect life, liberty and property shall be preserved inviolate. We believe, however, that the rules of procedure in the Federal courts with respect to the issuance of the writ of injunction should be more accurately defined by statute, and that no injunction or temporary restraining order should be issued without notice, except where irreparable injury would result from delay, in which case a speedy hearing thereafter should be granted.

The American Farmer.—Among those whose welfare is as vital to the welfare of the whole country as is that of the wage earner is the American farmer. The prosperity of the country rests peculiarly upon the prosperity of agriculture. The Republican party during the last twelve years has accomplished extraordinary work in bringing the resources of the National Government to the aid of the farmer, not only in advancing agriculture itself, but in increasing the conveniences of rural life. Free rural mail delivery has been established; it now reaches millions of our citizens, and we favor its extension until every community in the land receives the full benefits of the postal service. We recognize the social and economic advantages of good country roads, maintained more and more largely at public expense and less and less at the expense of the abutting owner. In this work we commend the growing practice of State aid, and we approve the efforts of the national Agricultural Department by experiments and otherwise to make clear to the public the best methods of road construction.

The Negro.—The Republican party has been for more than fifty years the consistent friend of the American negro. It gave him freedom and citizenship. It wrote into the organic law the declarations that proclaim his civil and political rights, and it believes to-day that his noteworthy progress in intelligence, industry and good citizenship has earned the respect and encouragement of the nation. We demand equal justice for all men, without regard to race or color; we declare once more, and without reservation, for the enforcement in letter and spirit of the Thirteenth, Fourteenth and Fifteenth amendments to the Constitution, which were designed for the protection and advancement of the negro, and we condemn all devices that have for their real aim his disfranchisement for reasons of color alone, as unfair, un-American and repugnant to the supreme law of the land.

Natural Resources and Waterways.—We indorse the movement inaugurated by the administration for the conservation of natural resources; we approve all measures to prevent the waste of timber; we commend the work now going on for the reclamation of arid lands, and reaffirm the Republican policy of the free distribution of the available areas of the public domain to the landless settler. No obligation of the future is more insistent and none will result in greater blessings to posterity. In line with this splendid undertaking is the further duty, equally imperative, to enter upon a systematic improvement upon a large and comprehensive plan, just to all portions of the country, of the waterways, harbors and Great Lakes, whose natural adaptability to the increasing traffic of the land is one of the greatest gifts of a benign Providence.

The Army and Navy.—The present Congress passed many commendable acts increasing the efficiency of the army and navy; making the militia of the States an integral part of the national establishment; authorizing joint manoeuvres of army and militia; fortifying new naval bases and completing the construction of coaling stations; instituting a female nurse corps for naval hospitals and ships, and adding two new battleships, ten torpedo boat destroyers, three steam colliers and eight submarines to the strength of the navy. Although at peace with all the world and secure in the consciousness that the American people do not desire and will not provoke a war with any other country, we nevertheless declare our unalterable devotion to a policy that will keep this Republic ready at all times to defend her traditional doctrines, and assure her appropriate part in promoting permanent tranquillity among the nations.

Protection of American Citizenship Abroad.—We commend the vigorous efforts made by the administration to protect American citizens in foreign lands and pledge ourselves to insist on the just and equal protection of all our citizens abroad. It is the unquestioned duty of the Government to procure for all our citizens, without distinction, the rights of travel and sojourn in friendly countries, and we declare ourselves in favor of all proper efforts tending to that end.

Extension of Foreign Commerce.—Under the administration of the Republican party the foreign commerce of the United States has experienced a remarkable growth, until it has a present annual valuation of approximately $3,000,000,000 and gives employment to a vast amount of labor and capital which would otherwise be idle. It has inaugurated through the recent visit of the Secretary of State to South America and Mexico a new era of Pan-American commerce and comity which is bringing us into closer touch with our twenty sister American republics, having a common historical heritage, a republican form of government and offering us a limitless field of legitimate commercial expansion.

Arbitration and Hague Treaties.—The conspicuous contributions of American statesmanship to the great cause of international peace so signally advanced in The Hague conferences, are an occasion for just pride and gratification. At the last session of the Senate of the United States eleven Hague conventions were ratified, establishing the rights of neutrals, laws of war on land, restriction of submarine mines, limiting the use of force for the collection of contractual debts, governing the opening of hostilities, extending the application of Geneva principles and in many ways lessening the evils of war and promoting the peaceful settlement of international controversies. At the same session twelve arbitration conventions with great nations were confirmed, and extradition, boundary and neutralization treaties of supreme importance were ratified. We indorse such achievements as the highest duty a people can perform and proclaim the obligation of further strengthening the bonds of friendship and good will with all the nations of the world.

Merchant Marine.—We adhere to the Republican doctrine of encouragement to American shipping and urge such legislation as will revive the merchant marine prestige of the country, so essential to national defence, the enlargement of foreign trade and the industrial prosperity of our own people.

Veterans of the Wars.—Another Republican policy which must ever be maintained is that of generous provision for those who have fought the country's battles and for the widows and orphans of those who have fallen. We commend the increase in the widows' pensions made by the present Congress and declare for a liberal administration of all pension laws, to the end that the people's gratitude may grow deeper as the memories of heroic sacrifice grow more sacred with the passing years.

Civil Service.—We reaffirm our declarations that the Civil Service laws, enacted, extended and enforced by the Republican party, shall continue to be maintained and obeyed.

Public Health.—We commend the efforts designed to secure greater efficiency in national public health agencies and favor such legislation as will effect this purpose.

Bureau of Mines and Mining.—In the interest of the great mineral industries of our country we earnestly favor the establishment of a bureau of mines and mining.

Cuba.—The American Government, in Republican hands, has freed Cuba, given peace and protection to Porto Rico and the Philippines under our flag, and begun the construction of the Panama Canal. The present conditions in Cuba vindicate the wisdom of maintaining between that republic and this imperishable bonds of mutual interest, and the hope is now expressed that the Cuban people will soon again be ready to assume complete sovereignty over their land.

Porto Rico.—In Porto Rico the Government of the United States is meeting loyal and patriotic support; order and prosperity prevail, and the wellbeing of the people is in every respect promoted and conserved.

We believe that the native inhabitants of Porto Rico should be at once collectively made citizens of the United States, and that all others properly qualified under existing laws residing in said island should have the privilege of becoming naturalized.

The Philippines.—In the Philippines insurrection has been suppressed, law is established and life and property are made secure. Education and practical experience there advancing the capacity of the people for government, and the policies of McKinley and Roosevelt are leading the inhabitants step by step to an ever increasing measure of home rule.

The Panama Canal.—Time has justified the selection of the Panama route for the great isthmian canal, and events have shown the wisdom of securing authority over the zone through which it is to be built. The work is now progressing with a rapidity far beyond expectation, and already the realization of the hopes of centuries has come within the vision of the near future.

New Mexico and Arizona.—We favor the immediate admission of the Territories of New Mexico and Arizona as separate States in the Union.

The Lincoln Centenary.—February 12, 1909, will be the one hundredth anniversary of the birth of Abraham Lincoln, an immortal spirit whose fame has brightened with the receding years and whose name stands among the first of those given to the world by the great Republic. We recommend that this centennial anniversary be celebrated throughout the confines of the nation by all the people thereof; and especially by the public schools as an exercise to stir the patriotism of the youth of the land.

Democratic Incapacity.—We call the attention of the American people to the fact that none of the great measures here advocated by the Republican party could be enacted and none of the steps forward here proposed could be taken under a Democratic administration or under one in which party responsibility is divided. The continuance of present policies, therefore, absolutely requires the continuance in power of that party which believes in them and which possesses the capacity to put them into operation.

Beyond all platform declarations there are fundamental differences between the Republican party and its chief opponent which make the one worthy and the other unworthy of public trust.

In history the difference between Democracy and Republicanism is that the one stood for debased currency, the other for honest currency; the one for free silver, the other for sound money; the one for free trade, the other for protection; the one for the contraction of American influence, the other for its expansion; the one has been forced to abandon e ery position taken on the great issues before the people, the other has held and vindicated all.

In experience the difference between Democracy and Republicanism is that one means adversity, while the other means prosperity; one means low wages, the other means high; one means doubt and debt, the other means confidence and thrift.

In principle the difference between Democracy and Republicanism is that one stands for vacillation and timidity in government; the other for strength and purpose; one stands for obstruction, the other for construction; one promises, the other performs; one finds fault, the other finds work.

The present tendencies of the two parties are even more marked by inherent differences. The trend of Democracy is toward socialism, while the Republican party stands for wise and regulated individualism. Socialism would destroy wealth, Republicanism would prevent its abuse. Socialism would give to each an equal right to take; Republicanism would give to each an equal right to earn. Socialism would offer an equality of possession which would soon leave no one anything to possess; Republicanism would give equality of opportunity which would assure to each his share of a constantly increasing sum of possessions. In line with this tendency the Democratic party of to-day believes in Government ownership, while the Republican party believes in Government regulation. Ultimately Democracy would have the nation own the people, while Republicanism would have the people own the nation.

Conclusion.—Upon this platform of principles and purposes, reaffirming our adherence to every Republican doctrine proclaimed since the birth of the party, we go before the country, asking the support not only of those who have acted with us heretofore, but of all our fellow citizens who, regardless of past political differences, unite in the desire to maintain the policies, perpetuate the blessings and make secure the achievements of a greater America.

PLATFORM OF THE PEOPLE'S PARTY, ADOPTED AT ST. LOUIS, MO., APRIL 3, 1903.

Preamble.—The People's Party of the United States, in convention assembled, at St. Louis, Mo., this 2d day of April, 1908, which increased confidence in its contentions, reaffirms the declarations made by its first national convention at Omaha, in 1892.

The admonitions of Washington's farewell address; the state papers of Jefferson, and the words of Lincoln, are the teachings of our greatest apostles of human rights and political liberty. There has been a departure from the teaching of these great patriots during recent administrations. The Government has been controlled so as to place the rights of property above the rights of humanity, and has brought the country to a condition that is full of danger to our national wellbeing. Financial combinations have had too much power over Congress, and too much influence with the administrative departments of the Government.

Prerogatives of government have been unwisely and often corruptly surrendered to corporate monopoly and aggregations of predatory wealth. The supreme duty of the hour is for the people to insist that these functions of government be exercised in their own interest. Not the giver of the "thirty pieces of silver" has been condemned, but the "Judas" who received them, has been execrated through the ages. The sycophants of monopoly deserve no better fate.

Money.—The issuance of money is a function of government and should not be delegated to corporation or individual. The Constitution gives Congress alone the power to issue money and regulate the value thereof; we, therefore, demand that all money shall be issued by the Government direct to the people without the intervention of banks, and shall be a full legal tender for all debts, public and private, and in quantity sufficient to supply the needs of the country.

The issuance and distribution of full legal tender money from the Treasury, shall not be through private banks, preferred or otherwise, but direct to the people without interest, for the construction and purchase of Federal and internal improvements and utilities, and for the employment of labor.

We demand that postal savings banks be established by the Government for the safe deposit of the savings of the people.

Land.—The public domain is a sacred heritage of all the people and should be held for homesteads for actual settlers only. Alien ownership should be forbidden, and lands now held by aliens or by corporations, who have violated the conditions of their grants, should be restored to the public domain.

Trusts and Monopoly.—To prevent unjust discrimination and monopoly, the Government should own and control the railroads and those public utilities, which in their nature are monopolies. To perfect the postal service, the Government should own and operate the general telegraph and telephone systems and provide a parcels post.

As to those trusts and monopolies which are not public utilities or national monopolies, we demand that those special privileges which they now enjoy, and which alone enable them to exist, shall be immediately withdrawn.

Corporations being the creatures of government, should be subjected to such governmental regulation and control as will adequately protect the public.

We demand the taxation of monopoly privileges while they remain in private hands, to the extent of the value of the privilege granted.

We demand that Congress shall enact a general law uniformly regulating the powers and duties of all incorporated companies doing interstate business.

Initiative and Referendum.—As a means of placing all public questions directly under the control of the people, we demand that legal provision be made under which the people may exercise the initiative and referendum, proportional representation, and direct vote for all public officers, with the right of recall.

We recommend a Federal statute that will recognize the principle of the initiative and referendum, and thereby restore to the voters the right to instruct their national representatives.

Labor.—We believe in the right of those who labor, to organize for their mutual protection and benefit, and pledge the efforts of the People's Party to preserve this right inviolate.

We condemn the recent attempt to destroy the power of trades unions through the unjust use of the Federal injunction, substituting government by injunction for free government.

We favor the enactment of legislation looking to the improvement of conditions for wage earners.

We demand the abolition of child labor in factories and mines, and the suppression of sweat-shops.

We oppose the use of convict labor in competition with free labor.

We demand the exclusion from American shores of foreign pauper labor, imported to beat down the wages of intelligent American workingmen.

We favor the eight-hour work day, and legislation protecting the lives and limbs of workmen through the use of safety appliances.

We demand the enactment of an employers' liability act within constitutional bounds.

We declare against the continuation of the criminal carelessness in the operation of mines, through which thousands of miners have lost their lives to increase the dividends of stockholders, and demand the immediate adoption of precautionary measures to prevent a repetition of such horrible catastrophes.

We declare that in times of depression, when workingmen are thrown into enforced idleness, that works of public improvement should be at once inaugurated and work provided for those who cannot otherwise secure employment.

We especially emphasize the declaration of the Omaha platform, that "Wealth belongs to him who creates it and every dollar taken from industry without a just equivalent is robbery."

We congratulate the farmers of the country upon the enormous growth of their splendid organizations, and the good already accomplished through them, securing higher prices for farm products and better conditions generally, for those engaged in agricultural pursuits. We urge the importance of maintaining these organizations and extending their power and influence.

Courts.—We condemn all unwarranted assumption of authority by inferior Federal courts, in annulling, by injunction, the laws of the States, and demand legislative action by Congress, which will prohibit such usurpation, and will restrict to the Supreme Court of the United States, the exercise of power in cases involving State legislation.

Gambling in Futures.—We are opposed to gambling in futures.

Conclusion.—We present to all people the foregoing declaration of principles and policies as our deep, earnest and abiding convictions; and now, before the country and in the name of the great moral, but eternal power in the universe, that makes for right thinking and right living and determines the destiny of nations, this convention pledges that the People's Party will stand by these principles and policies in success and in defeat; that never again will the party by the siren songs and false promises of designing politicians, be tempted to change its course, or be drawn again upon the treacherous rocks of fusion.

PLATFORM OF THE INDEPENDENCE PARTY, ADOPTED AT CHICAGO, ILL., JULY 28, 1908.

We, independent American citizens, representing the Independence party in forty-four States and two Territories, have met in national convention to nominate, absolutely independent of all other political parties, candidates for President and Vice-President of the United States.

Our action is based upon a determination to wrest the conduct of public affairs from the hands of selfish interests, political tricksters and corrupt bosses, and make the Government, as the founders intended, an agency for the common good.

At a period of unexampled national prosperity and promise, a staggering blow was dealt to legitimate business by the unmolested practice of stock watering and dishonest financiering. Multitudes of defenseless investors, thousands of honest business men and an army of idle workingmen are paying the penalty. Year by year, fostered by wasteful and reckless governmental extravagance, by the manipulation of trusts and by a privilege creating tariff, the cost of living mounts higher and higher. Day by day the control of the Government drifts further away from the people and more firmly into the grip of machine politicians and party bosses.

The Republican and Democratic parties are not only responsible for these conditions, but are committed to their indefinite continuance. Prodigal of promises, they are so barren of performance that to a new party of independent voters the country must look for the establishment of a new policy and a return to genuine popular government.

Our object is not to introduce violent innovations or startling new theories. We of the Independence party look back, as Lincoln did, to the Declaration of Independence as the fountain-head of all political inspiration. It is not our purpose to attempt to revolutionize the American system of government, but to restore the action of the Government to the principles of Washington and Jefferson and Lincoln. It is not our purpose, either, to effect a radical change in the American system of government, but to conserve for the citizens of the United States their privileges and liberties won for them by the founders of this Government and to perpetuate the principles and policies upon which the nation's greatness has been built.

The Independence party is, therefore, a conservative force in American politics, devoted to the preservation of American liberty and independence, to honesty in elections, to opportunity in business and to equality before the law. Those who believe in the Independence party and work with it are convinced that a genuine democracy should exist; that a true republican form of government should continue; that the power of government should rest with the majority of the people, and that the Government should be conducted for the benefit of the whole citizenship, rather than for the special advantage of a particular class.

Direct Nominations.—As of first importance in order to restore the power of government to the people, to make their will supreme in the primaries, in the elections and in the control of public officials after they have been elected, we declare for direct nominations, the initiative and referendum and the right of recall.

It is idle to cry out against the evil of bossism while we perpetuate a system under which the boss is inevitable. The destruction of an individual boss is of little value. The people in their politics must establish a system which will eliminate not only an objectionable boss but the system of bossism. Representative government is made a mockery by the system of modern party conventions dominated by bosses and controlled by cliques. We demand the natural remedy of direct nominations by which the people not only elect, but which is far more important, select their representatives.

The Referendum.—We believe in the principle of the initiative and referendum, and we particularly demand that no franchise grant go into operation until the terms and conditions have been approved by popular vote in the locality interested.

Recall.—We demand for the people the right to recall public officials from the public service. The power to make officials reside in the people, and in them also should reside the power to unmake and remove from office any official who demonstrates his unfitness or betrays the public trust.

Election Corruption.—Of next importance in destroying the power of selfish special interests and the corrupt political bosses whom they control is to wrest from their hands their main weapon—the corruption fund. We demand severe and effective legislation against all forms of corrupt practice at the elections, and advocate prohibiting the use of any money at elections except for meetings, literature and the necessary travelling expenses of candidates. Bidding for votes, the Republican and Democratic candidates are making an outcry about publicity of contributions, although both the Republican and Democratic parties have for years consistently blocked every effort to pass a corrupt practices act. Publicity of contributions is desirable and should be required, but the main matter of importance is the use to which contributions are put. We believe that the dishonest use of money in the past, whether contributed by individuals or by corporations, has been chiefly responsible for the corruption which has undermined our system of popular government.

Economy.—We demand honest conduct of public office and businesslike and economical administration of public affairs, and we condemn the gross extravagance of Federal administration, and its appalling annual increase in appropriations. Unnecessary appropriations mean unnecessary taxes, and unnecessary taxes, whether direct or indirect, are paid by the people and add to the ever-increasing cost of living.

Overcapitalization.—We condemn the evil of overcapitalization. Modern industrial conditions make the corporation and stock company a necessity, but overcapitalization in corporations is as harmful and criminal as is personal dishonesty in an individual. Compelling the payment of dividends upon great sums that have never been invested, upon masses of watered stock not justified by the property, overcapitalization prevents the better wages, the better public service and the lower cost that should result from American inventive genius and that wide organization which is replacing costly individual competition. The collapse of dishonestly inflated enterprises robs investors, closes banks, destroys confidence and engenders panics. The Independence party advocates as a primary necessity for sounder business conditions and improved public service the enactment of laws, State and national, to prevent watering of stock, dishonest issues of bonds and other forms of corporation frauds.

Labor and Injunctions.—We denounce the so-called labor planks of the Republican and Democratic platforms as political buncombe and contemptible clap-trap unworthy of national parties claiming to be serious and sincere.

The Republican declaration that "no injunction or temporary restraining order should be issued without notice, except where irreparable injury would result from delay," is empty verbiage, for a showing of irreparable injury can always be made and is always made in ex parte affidavits.

The Democratic declaration that "injunctions should not be issued in any case in which injunctions should not issue if no industrial dispute were involved" is meaningless and worthless.

Such insincere and meaningless declarations place a low estimate upon the intelligence of the average American workingman and exhibit either ignorance of or indifference to the real interests of labor.

The Independence party condemns the arbitrary use of the writ of injunction and contempt proceedings as a violation of the fundamental American right of trial by jury.

From the foundation of our Government down to 1872 the Federal Judiciary act prohibited the issue of any injunction without reasonable notice until after a hearing. We assert that in all actions growing out of a dispute between employers and employees concerning terms or conditions of employment no injunction should issue until after a trial upon the merits, that such trial should be held before a jury and that in no case of alleged contempt should any person be deprived of liberty without a trial by jury.

The Independence party believes that the distribution of wealth is as important as the creation of wealth, and indorses these organizations among farmers and workers which tend to bring about a just distribution of wealth through good wages for workers and good prices for farmers, and which protect the employer and the consumer through equality of price for labor and for product, and we favor such legislation as will remove them from the operation of the Sherman anti-trust law.

We indorse the eight-hour work day, favor its application to all Government employees and demand the enactment of laws requiring that all work done for the Government, whether Federal or State, and whether done directly or indirectly through contractors or sub-contractors shall be done on an eight-hour basis.

We favor the enactment of a law defining as illegal any combination or conspiracy to black-list employees.

We demand protection for workmen through enforced use of standard safety appliances and provisions of hygienic conditions in the operation of factories, railways, mills, mines and all industrial undertakings.

We advocate State and Federal inspection of railways to secure a greater safety for railway employees and for the travelling public. We call for the enactment of stringent laws fixing employers' liabilities and a rigid prohibition of child labor through co-operation between the State governments and the National Government.

We condemn the manufacture and sale of prison made goods in the open market in competition with free labor manufactured goods. We demand that convicts shall be employed direct by the different States in the manufacture of products for use in State institutions and in making good roads, and in no case shall convicts be hired out to contractors or sub-contractors.

We favor the creation of a Department of Labor, including mines and mining, the head of which shall be a member of the President's Cabinet.

The great abuses of grain inspection, by which the producers are plundered, demand immediate and vigorous correction. To that end we favor Federal inspection under a strict civil service law.

A Central Bank.—The Independence party declares that the right to issue money is inherent in the Government, and it favors the establishment of a central governmental bank, through which the money so issued shall be put into general circulation.

The Tariff.—We demand a revision of the tariff, not by the friends of the tariff, but by the friends of the people, and declare for a gradual reduction of tariff duties, with just consideration for the rights of the consuming public and of established industry. There should be no protection for oppressive trusts which sell cheaply abroad and take advantage of the tariff at home to crush competition, raise prices, control production and limit work and wages.

The Railroads.—The railroads must be kept open to all upon exactly equal terms. Every form of rebate and discrimination in railroad rates is a crime against business and must be stamped out. We demand adequate railroad facilities and advocate a bill empowering shippers in time of need to compel railroads to provide sufficient cars for freight and passenger traffic and other railroad facilities through summary appeal to the courts. We favor the creation of an Interstate Commerce Court, whose sole function it shall be to review speedily and enforce summarily the orders of the Interstate Commerce Commission. The Interstate Commerce Commission has the power to initiate investigation into the reasonableness of rates and practices and no increase in rates should be put into effect until opportunity for such investigation is afforded. The Interstate Commerce Commission should proceed at once with a physical valuation of railroads engaged in interstate commerce.

Trusts.—We believe that legitimate organizations in business designed to secure an economy of operation and increased production are beneficial wherever the public participates in the advantages which result. We denounce all combinations for restraint of trade and for the establishment of monopoly in all products of labor, and declare that such combinations are not combinations for production, but for extortion, and that activity in this direction is not industry, but robbery.

In cases of infractions of the Anti-Trust law or of the Interstate Commerce act, we believe in the enforcement of a prison penalty against the guilty and responsible individuals controlling the management of the offending corporations, rather than a fine imposed upon stockholders.

Public Ownership.—We advocate the extension of the principle of public ownership of public utilities, including railroads, as rapidly as municipal, State or National Government shall demonstrate ability to conduct public utilities for the public benefit. We favor specifically government ownership of the telegraphs, such as prevails in every other civilized country in the world, and demand as an immediate measure that the Government shall purchase and operate the telegraphs in connection with the postal service.

Parcels Post; Postal Banks.—The parcels post system should be rapidly and widely extended and Government postal savings banks should be established, where the people's deposits will be secure, the money to be loaned to the people in the locality of the several banks and at a rate of interest to be fixed by the Government.

Good Roads.—We favor the immediate development of a national system of good roads connecting all States, and national aid to States in the construction and maintenance of post roads.

Postal Censorship.—We favor a court review of the censorship and arbitrary rulings of the Post-Office Department.

Statehood of Arizona and New Mexico.—We favor the admission of Arizona and New Mexico into separate Statehood.

Bucket Shop Suppression.—We advocate such legislation, both State and national, as will suppress the bucket shop and prohibit the fictitious selling of farm products for future delivery.

National Health Bureau.—We favor the creation of a national department of public health, to be presided over by a member of the medical profession, this department to exercise such authority over matters of public health, hygiene and sanitation which come properly within the jurisdiction of the National Government, and do not interfere with the right of States or municipalities.

Asiatic Exclusion.—We oppose Asiatic immigration which does not amalgamate with our population, creates race issues and un-American conditions, and which reduces wages and tends to lower the high standard of living and the high standard of morality which American civilization has established.

We demand the passage of an exclusion act which shall protect American workingmen, from competition with Asiatic cheap labor and which shall protect American civilization from the contamination of Asiatic conditions.

The Navy.—The Independence party declares for peace and against aggression and will promote the movement for the settlement of international disputes by arbitration.

We believe, however, that a small navy is poor economy and that a strong navy is the best protection in time of war and the best preventive of war. We, therefore, favor the speedy building of a navy sufficiently strong to protect at the same time both the Atlantic and Pacific coasts of the United States.

Waterways and Resources.—We rejoice in the adoption of both the Democratic and Republican platforms of the demand of the Independence party for improved national waterways and the Mississippi inland deep waterways project, to complete a ship canal from the Gulf to the Great Lakes. We favor the extension of this system to the tributaries of the Mississippi by means of which thirty States shall be served and 20,000 miles added to the coast line of the United States. The reclamation of arid lands should be continued and the irrigation programme now contemplated by the Government extended and steps taken for the conservation of the country's natural resources, which should be guarded not only against devastation and waste, but against falling into the control of the monopoly. The abuses growing out of the administration of our forest preserves must be corrected and provision should be made for free grazing from public lands outside of forest or other reservations. In behalf of the people residing in arid portions of our Western States we protest vigorously against the policy of the Federal Government in selling the exclusive use of water and electric light power derived from public works to private corporations, thus creating a monopoly and subjecting citizens living in those sections to exorbitant charges for light and power, and diverting enterprises originally started for public benefit into channels for corporate greed and oppression, and we demand that no more exclusive contracts be made.

Protection of Citizens Abroad.—American citizens abroad, whether native born or naturalized, and of whatever race or creed, must be secured in the enjoyment of all rights and privileges under our treaties, and wherever such rights are withheld by any country on the ground of race or religious faith, steps should be taken to secure the removal of such unjust discrimination.

Popular Election of Senators.—We advocate the popular election of United States Senators and of judges, both State and Federal, and favor a graduated income tax and any constitutional amendment necessary to these ends.

Equality and Opportunity.—Equality and opportunity, the largest measure of individual liberty consistent with equal rights, the overthrow of the rule of special interest and the restoration of government by the majority exercised for the benefit of the whole community; these are the purposes to which the Independence party is pledged, and we invite the co-operation of all patriotic and progressive citizens, irrespective of party, who are in sympathy with these principles and in favor of their practical enforcement.

PLATFORM OF THE SOCIALIST PARTY, ADOPTED AT CHICAGO, ILL., MAY 13, 1908.

The Socialist party, in national convention assembled, again declares itself as the party of the working class, and appeals for the support of all workers of the United States and of all citizens who sympathize with the great and just cause of labor.

We are at this moment in the midst of one of those industrial breakdowns that periodically paralyze the life of the nation. The much-boasted era of our national prosperity has been followed by one of general misery. Factories, mills, and mines are closed. Millions of men, ready, willing and able to provide the nation with all the necessaries and comforts of life are forced into idleness and starvation.

Within recent times the trusts and monopolies have attained an enormous and menacing development. They have acquired the power to dictate the terms upon which we shall be allowed to live. The trusts fix the prices of our bread, meat, and sugar, of our coal, oil, and clothing, of our raw material and machinery, of all the necessities of life.

The present desperate condition of the workers has been made the opportunity for a renewed onslaught on organized labor. The highest courts of the country have within the last year rendered decision after decision depriving the workers of rights which they had won by generations of struggle.

The attempt to destroy the Western Federation of Miners, although defeated by the solidarity of organized labor and the Socialist movement, revealed the existence of a far-reaching and unscrupulous conspiracy by the ruling class against the organizations of labor.

In their efforts to take the lives of the leaders of the miners the conspirators violated state laws and the Federal Constitution in a manner seldom equalled even in a country so completely dominated by the profit-seeking class as is the United States.

The Congress of the United States has shown its contempt for the interests of labor as plainly and unmistakably as have the other branches of government. The laws for which the labor organizations have continually petitioned have failed to pass. Laws ostensibly enacted for the benefit of labor have been distorted against labor.

The working class of the United States cannot expect any remedy for its wrongs from the present ruling class or from the dominant parties. So long as a small number of individuals are permitted to control the sources of the nation's wealth for their private profit in competition with each other and for the exploitation of their fellowmen, industrial depressions are bound to occur at certain intervals. No currency reforms or other legislative measures proposed by capitalist reformers can avail against these fatal results of utter anarchy in production.

Individual competition leads inevitably to combinations and trusts. No amount of Government regulation, or of publicity, or of restrictive legislation will arrest the natural course of modern industrial development.

While our courts, legislatures and executive offices remain in the hands of the ruling classes and their agents, the Government will be used in the interests of these classes as against the toilers.

Political parties are but the expression of economic class interests. The Republican, the Democratic, and the so-called "Independence" parties and all parties other than the Socialist party, are financed, directed, and controlled by the representatives of different groups of the ruling class.

In the maintenance of class government both the Democratic and Republican parties have been equally guilty. The Republican party has had control of the National Government and has been directly and actively responsible for these wrongs. The Democratic party, while saved from direct responsibility by its political impotence, has shown itself equally subservient to the aims of the capitalist class whenever and wherever it has been in power. The old chattel slave owning aristocracy of the South, which was the backbone of the Democratic party, has been supplanted by a child slave plutocracy. In the great cities of our country the Democratic party is allied with the criminal element of the slums as the Republican party is allied with the predatory criminals of the palace in maintaining the interest of the possessing class.

The various "reform" movements and parties which have sprung up within recent years are but the clumsy expression of widespread popular discontent. They are not based on an intelligent understanding of the historical development of civilization and of the economic and political needs of our time. They are bound to perish as the numerous middle class reform movements of the past have perished.

As measures calculated to strengthen the working class in its fight for the realization of this ultimate aim, and to increase its power of resistance against capitalist oppression, we advocate and pledge ourselves and our elected officers to the following programme.

General Demands. 1—The immediate Government relief for the unemployed workers by building schools, by reforesting of cutover and waste lands, by reclamation of arid tracts, and the building of canals, and by extending all other useful public works. All persons employed on such works shall be employed directly by the Government under an eight-hour work-day and at the prevailing union wages. The Government shall also loan money to States and municipalities without interest for the purpose of carrying on public works. It shall contribute to the funds of labor organizations for the purpose of assisting their unemployed members, and shall take such other measures within its power as will lessen the widespread misery of the workers caused by the misrule of the capitalist class.

2—The collective ownership of railroads, telegraphs, telephones, steamship lines and all other means of social transportation and communication, and all land.

3—The collective ownership of all industries which are organized on a national scale and in which competition has virtually ceased to exist.

4—The extension of the public domain to include mines, quarries, oil wells, forest, and water power.

5—The scientific reforestation of timber lands, and the reclamation of swamp lands. The land so reforested or reclaimed to be permanently retained as a part of the public domain.

6—The absolute freedom of press, speech and assemblage.

Industrial Demands. 7—The improvement of the industrial condition of the workers.

(a)—By shortening the workday in keeping with the increased productiveness of machinery.

(b)—By securing to every worker a rest period of not less than a day and a half in each week.

(c)—By securing a more effective inspection of workshops and factories.

(d)—By forbidding the employment of children under sixteen years of age.

(e)—By forbidding the interstate transportation of the products of child labor, of convict labor, and of all uninspected factories.

(f)—By abolishing official charity and substituting in its place compulsory insurance against unemployment, illness, accidents, invalidism, old age, and death.

Political Demands. 8—The extension of inheritance taxes, graduated in proportion to the nearness of kin.

9—A graduated income tax.

10—Unrestricted and equal suffrage for men and women, and we pledge ourselves to engage in an active campaign in that direction.

11—The initiative and referendum, proportional representation and the right of recall.

12—The abolition of the Senate.

13—The abolition of the power usurped by the Supreme Court of the United States to pass upon the constitutionality of legislation enacted by Congress. National laws to be repealed or abrogated only by act of Congress or by a referendum of the whole people.

14—That the Constitution be made amendable by majority vote.

15—The enactment of further measures for general education and for the conservation of health. The Bureau of Education to be made a department. The creation of a department of Public Health.

16—The separation of the present Bureau of Labor from the Department of Commerce and Labor, and the establishment of a Department of Labor.

17—That all judges be elected by the people for short terms, and that the power to issue injunctions shall be curbed by immediate legislation.

18—The free administration of justice.

Such measures of relief as we may be able to force from capitalism are but a preparation of the workers to seize the whole powers of Government, in order that they may thereby lay hold of the whole system of industry and thus come to their rightful inheritance.

PLATFORM OF THE SOCIALIST LABOR PARTY, ADOPTED AT NEW YORK, JULY, 1903.

The Socialist Labor party of America, in convention assembled, reasserts the inalienable right of man to life, liberty, and the pursuit of happiness.

We hold that the purpose of government is to secure to every citizen the enjoyment of this right; but, taught by experience, we hold furthermore that such right is illusory to the majority of the people, to wit, the working class, under the present system of economic inequality that is essentially destructive of their life, their liberty, and their happiness.

We hold that the true theory of politics is that the machinery of government must be controlled by the whole people; but again, taught by experience, we hold, furthermore, that the true theory of economics is that the means of production must likewise be owned, operated and controlled by the people in common. Man cannot exercise his right of life, liberty and the pursuit of happiness without the ownership of the land on and the tools with which to work. Deprived of these, his life, his liberty, and his fate fall into the hands of the class that owns those essentials for work and production.

We hold that the existing contradiction between the theory of democratic government and the fact of a despotic economic system—the private ownership of the natural and social opportunities—divides the people into two classes—the capitalist class and the working class; throws society into the convulsions of the class struggle, and perverts government to the exclusive benefit of the capitalist class.

Thus labor is robbed of the wealth which it alone produces, is denied the means of self-employment, and, by compulsory idleness in wage slavery, is even deprived of the necessaries of life.

Against such a system the Socialist Labor party raises the banner of revolt, and demands the unconditional surrender of the capitalist class.

The time is fast coming when, in the natural course of social evolution, this system, through the destructive action of its failures and crisis on the one hand, and the constructive tendencies of its trusts and other capitalist combinations on the other hand, will have worked out its own downfall.

We, therefore, call upon the wage-workers of America to organize under the banner of the Socialist Labor party into a class-conscious body, aware of its rights, and determined to conquer them.

And we also call upon all other intelligent citizens to place themselves squarely upon the ground of working-class interests, and join us in this mighty and noble work of human emancipation, so that we may put summary end to the existing barbarous class conflict by placing the land and all the means of production, transportation and distribution into the hands of the people as a collective body, and substituting the co-operative commonwealth for the present state of planless production, industrial war and social disorder—a commonwealth in which every worker shall have the free exercise and full benefit of his faculties, multiplied by all the modern factors of civilization.

PLATFORM OF THE PROHIBITION PARTY ADOPTED AT COLUMBUS, OHIO, JULY 16, 1908.

The Prohibition party of the United States, assembled in convention at Columbus, Ohio, July 15-16, 1908, expressing gratitude to almighty God for the victories of our principles in the past, for encouragement at present, and for confidence in early and triumphant success in the future, makes the following declaration of principles, and pledges their enactment into law when placed in power:

1. The submission by Congress to the several States, of an amendment to the Federal constitution prohibiting the manufacture, sale, importation, exportation, or transportation of alcoholic liquors for beverage purposes.
2. The immediate prohibition of the liquor traffic for beverage purposes in the District of Columbia, in the Territories and all places over which the National Government has jurisdiction; the repeal of the internal revenue tax on alcoholic liquors and the prohibition of interstate traffic therein.
3. The election of United States Senators by direct vote of the people.
4. Equitable graduated income and inheritance taxes.
5. The establishment of postal savings banks and the guaranty of deposits in banks.
6. The regulation of all corporations doing an interstate commerce business.
7. The creation of a permanent tariff commission.
8. The strict enforcement of law instead of official tolerance and practical license of the social evil which prevails in many of our cities, with its unspeakable traffic in girls.
9. Uniform marriage and divorce laws.
10. An equitable and constitutional employers' liability act.
11. Court review of post-office department decisions.
12. The prohibition of child labor in mines, workshops and factories.
13. Legislation basing suffrage only upon intelligence and ability to read and write the English language.
14. The preservation of the mineral and forest resources of the country, and the improvement of the highways and waterways.

Believing in the righteousness of our cause and the final triumph of our principles, and convinced of the unwillingness of the Republican and Democratic parties to deal with these issues, we invite to full party fellowship all citizens who are with us agreed

(*Revised December*, 1908, *at the New York Post-Office, for* THE WORLD ALMANAC.)

DOMESTIC RATES OF POSTAGE.

ALL mailable matter for transmission by the United States mails within the United States is divided into four classes, under the following regulations. (Domestic rates apply to Canada, Mexico, Cuba, Tutuila, Porto Rico, Guam, Hawaii, the Philippines, the "Canal Zone," the Republic of Panama, and Shanghai, China).

First-Class Matter.—This class includes letters, postal cards, "post cards," and anything sealed or otherwise closed against inspection, or anything containing writing not allowed as an accompaniment to printed matter under class three.

Rates of letter postage to any part of the United States, its possessions, or the above-named countries, *two cents per ounce or fraction thereof.*

Rates on local or drop letters at free delivery offices, two cents per ounce or fraction thereof. At offices where there is no free delivery by carriers, and the addressee cannot be served by rural free delivery carriers, one cent per ounce or fraction thereof.

Rates on **postal cards,** one cent (double or "reply" cards, two cents). Postal cards issued by the Post-Office Department may bear written, printed, or other additions as follows:

(*a*) The face of the card may be divided by a vertical line placed approximately one-third of the distance from the left end of the card; the space to the left of the line to be used for a message, etc., but the space to the right for the address only.

(*b*) Addresses upon postal cards may be either written, printed, or affixed thereto, at the option of the sender.

(*c*) Very thin sheets of paper may be attached to the card on condition that they completely adhere thereto. Such sheets may bear both writing and printing.

(*d*) Advertisements, illustrations, or writing may appear on the back of the card and on the left third of the face.

2. The addition to a postal card of matter other than as above authorized will subject the card, when sent in the mails, to postage according to the character of the message—at the letter rate if wholly or partly in writing or the third-class rate if entirely in print. In either case the postage value of the stamp impressed upon the card will not be impaired.

3. Postal cards must be treated in all respects as sealed letters, except that when undeliverable to the addressee they may not be returned to the sender.

4. Postal cards bearing particles of glass, metal, mica, sand, tinsel or other similar substances, are unmailable, except when inclosed in envelopes with proper postage attached, or when treated in such manner as will prevent the objectionable substances from being rubbed off or injuring persons handling the mails.

Cards that have been spoiled in printing or otherwise will be redeemed from *the original purchasers* at 75 per cent. of their face value if unmutilated.

POST CARDS—(Private Mailing Cards)—bearing written or printed messages are transmissible in the mails:

Private mailing cards ("post cards") in the domestic mails must conform to the following conditions:

(*a*) A "post card" must be an unfolded piece of cardboard not exceeding approximately 3 9-16 by 5 9-16 inches, nor less than approximately 2¾ by 4 inches.

(*b*) It must in form and in the quality and weight of paper be substantially like the Government postal card.

(*c*) It may be of any color not interfering with a legible address and postmark.

(*d*) It may or may not, at the option of the sender, bear near the top of the face the words "post card."

(*e*) The face of the card may be divided by a vertical line; the left half to be used for a message, etc., but that to the right for the address only.

(*f*) Very thin sheets of paper may be attached to the card, and then only on condition that they completely adhere thereto. Such sheets may bear both writing and printing.

(*g*) Advertisements and illustrations may appear on the back of the card and on the left half of the face.

2. Cards, without cover, conforming to the foregoing conditions are transmissible in the domestic mails (including the possessions of the United States) and to Cuba, Canada, Mexico, the Republic of Panama, and the United States postal agency at Shanghai, China, at the postage rate of 1 cent each.

3. When post cards are prepared by printers and stationers for sale, it is desirable that they bear in the upper right hand corner of the face an oblong diagram containing the words "Place postage stamp here," and at the bottom of the space to the right of the verticle dividing line, the words "This space for the address."

4. Cards which do not conform to the conditions prescribed by these regulations are, when sent in the mails, chargeable with postage according to the character of the message—at the letter rate, if wholly or partly in writing, or at the third-class rate, if entirely in print.

5. Cards bearing particles of glass, metal, mica, sand, tinsel, or other similar substances, are *unmailable*, except when inclosed in envelopes, or when treated in such manner as will prevent the objectionable substances from being rubbed off or injuring persons handling the mails.

Rates on special delivery letters, ten cents on each letter in *addition* to the regular postage. This entitles the letter to immediate delivery by special messenger. Special delivery stamps are sold at post-offices, and must be affixed to such letters. An ordinary ten-cent stamp affixed to a letter will entitle it to special delivery if the letter is marked "Special Delivery." The delivery, at carrier offices, extends to the limits of the carrier routes. At non-carrier offices it extends to one mile from the post-office. Postmasters are not obliged to deliver beyond these limits, and letters addressed to places beyond must await delivery in the usual way, notwithstanding the special delivery stamp.

Prepayment by stamps invariably required. Postage on all letters should be *fully* prepaid, but if prepaid one full rate and no more, they will be forwarded, and the amount of deficient postage collected on delivery; if wholly unpaid, or prepaid with less than one full rate and deposited at a post-office, the addressee will be notified to remit postage; and if he fails to do so, they will be sent to the Dead Letter Office; but they will be returned to the sender if he is located at the place of mailing, and if his address be printed or written upon them.

Letter rate is charged on all productions by the typewriter or manifold process, and on all printed imitations of typewriting or manuscript, unless such reproductions are presented at post-office windows in the minimum number of twenty identical copies separately addressed.

Letters and other matter prepaid at the letter rate—two cents an ounce or fraction thereof—(but no other class of mail matter) will be returned to the sender free, if a request to that effect is printed or written on the envelope or wrapper. The limit of weight is four pounds, except for a single book.

Prepaid letters will be forwarded from one post-office to another upon the written request of the person addressed, without additional charge for postage. The direction on forwarded letters may be changed as many times as may be necessary to reach the person addressed.

Second-Class Matter.—This class includes all newspapers and periodicals exclusively in print that have been "Entered as second-class matter," and are regularly issued at stated intervals as frequently as four times a year, from a known office of publication and mailed by the publishers or news-agents to actual subscribers or to news agents for sale, and newspapers and publications of this class mailed by persons other than publishers. Also periodical publications of benevolent and fraternal societies, organized under the lodge system and having a membership of a thousand persons, and the publications of strictly professional, literary, historical, and scientific societies, and incorporated institutions of learning, trade unions, etc., provided only that these be published at stated intervals not less than four times a year, and that they be printed on and be bound in paper. Publishers who wish to avail themselves of the privileges of the act are required to make formal application to the department through the postmaster at the place of publication, producing satisfactory evidence that the organizations, societies, and institutions represented come within the purview of the law, and that the object of the publications is to further the objects and purposes of the organizations.

Rates of postage to publishers, *one cent a pound or fractional part thereof*, prepaid in currency. Publications designed primarily for advertising or free circulation, or not having a legitimate list of subscribers, are excluded from the pound rate, and pay the third-class rate.

Publications sent to actual subscribers in the county where published are free, unless mailed for delivery at a letter-carrier office.

Rates of postage on second-class newspapers, magazines, or periodicals, mailed by others than the publishers or news agents, *one cent for each four ounces or fraction thereof*. It should be observed that the rate is one cent for each four ounces, not one cent for each paper contained in the same wrapper. This rate applies only when a complete copy is mailed. Parts of second-class publications or partial or incomplete copies are *third-class matter*. Second-class matter will be entitled to special delivery when special delivery stamps (or ten cents in ordinary stamps and the words "Special Delivery" placed on the wrapper) are affixed in addition to the regular postage.

Second-class matter must be so wrapped as to enable the postmaster to inspect it. The sender's name and address may be written in them or on the wrapper, also the words "sample copy," or "marked copy." Typographical errors in the text may be corrected, but any other writing subjects the matter to letter postage.

Third-Class Matter.—Mail matter of the third class includes printed books, pamphlets, engravings, circulars in print (or by the hectograph, electric-pen, or similar process when at least twenty identical copies, separately addressed, are mailed at post-office windows at one time), and other matter wholly in print, proof sheets, corrected proof sheets, and manuscript copy accompanying the same.

The rate on matter of this class is *one cent for each two ounces or fraction thereof* payable by stamps affixed, unless 2,000 or more identical pieces are mailed under special permit when the postage at that rate may be paid in money.

Manuscript unaccompanied by proof-sheets must pay letter rates.

Third-class matter must admit of easy inspection, otherwise it will be charged letter rates on delivery. It must be fully prepaid, or it will not be despatched. New postage must be prepaid for forwarding to a new address or returning to senders.

The limit of weight is four pounds, except single books in separate packages, on which the weight is not limited. It is entitled, like matter of the other classes, to special delivery when special delivery stamps are affixed in addition to the regular postage, or when ten cents in ordinary stamps are affixed in addition to the regular postage and the words "Special Delivery" are placed on the wrapper.

Upon matter of the third class, or upon the wrapper or envelope inclosing the same, or the tag or label attached thereto, the sender may write his own name, occupation, and residence or business address, preceded by the word "from," and may make marks other than by written words to call attention to any word or passage in the text, and may correct any typographical errors. There may be placed upon the blank leaves or cover of any book, or printed matter of the third-class, a simple manuscript dedication or inscription not of the nature of a personal correspondence. Upon the wrapper or envelope of third-class matter, or the tag or label attached thereto, may be printed any matter mailable as third-class, but there must be left on the address side a space sufficient for the legible address and necessary stamps.

Fourth-Class Matter.—Fourth-class matter is all mailable matter not included in the three preceding classes which is so prepared for mailing as to be easily withdrawn from the wrapper and examined. It embraces merchandise and samples of every description, and coin or specie.

Rate of postage, *one cent for each ounce or fraction thereof* (except seeds, roots, bulbs, cuttings, scions, and plants, the rate on which is *one cent for each two ounces or fraction thereof*). This matter must be fully prepaid, or it will not be despatched. Postage must be paid by stamps affixed, unless 2,000 or more identical pieces are mailed at one time when the postage at that rate may be paid in money. New postage must be prepaid for forwarding or returning. The affixing of special delivery ten-cent stamps in addition to the regular postage entitles fourth-class matter to special delivery. (See remarks under "first-class matter.")

Articles of this class that are liable to injure or deface the mails, such as glass, sugar, needles, nails, pens, etc., must be first wrapped in a bag, box, or open envelope and then secured in another outside tube or box, made of metal or hard wood, without sharp corners or edges, and having a sliding clasp or screw lid, thus securing the articles in a double package. The public should bear in mind that the first object of the department is to transport the mails safely, and every other interest is made subordinate.

Such articles as poisons, explosives, or inflammable articles, live or dead animals, insects, fruits or vegetable matter liable to decomposition, or substances exhaling a bad odor will not be forwarded in any case.

Firearms may only be sent when it is apparent that they are harmless.

The regulations respecting the mailing of liquids are as follows: Liquids, not ardent, vinous, spirituous, or malt, cocaine or derivatives thereof, and not liable to explosion, spontaneous combustion, or ignition by shock or jar, and not inflammable (such as kerosene, naphtha, or turpentine), may be admitted to the mails for transportation within the United States. Samples of altar or communion wine are mailable. When in glass bottles, such bottles must be very strong and must be inclosed in a metal, wooden or papier-mache block or tube, and there must be provided between the bottle and the block or tube a cushion of cotton, felt or other absorbent. The block or tube must be of sufficient strength to resist rough handling and support the weight of the mails piled in bags. If of wood, it must be at least three-sixteenths of an inch thick in the thinnest part; if of papier-mache it must be at least five-thirty seconds of an inch thick for bottles holding from two to four ounces, and at least one-eighth of an inch thick for bottles holding two ounces or less. The block or tube must be read-ered water-tight by an application of paraffine or other suitable substance, so that if the bottle be broken in transit the liquid will not escape or the tube become softened and allow the broken glass to be scattered in the mails. When inclosed in a tin cylinder, metal case, or tube, such cylinder, case, or tube should have a lid or cover so secured as to make the case or tube water tight, and should be securely fastened in a wooden or papier-mache block (open only at one end), and not less in thickness and strength than above described. Manufacturers or dealers intending to transmit articles or samples in considerable quantities should submit a sample package, showing their mode of packing, to the postmaster at the mailing office, who will see that the conditions of this section are carefully observed. The limit of admissible liquids and oils is not exceeding four ounces, liquid measure.

Limit of weight of fourth-class matter (excepting liquids and single books), four pounds.

The name and address of the sender, preceded by the word "from," also any marks, numbers, names, or letters for the purpose of description, such as prices, quantity etc., may be written on the wrapper of fourth-class matter without additional postage charge. A request to the delivering postmaster may also be written asking him to notify the sender in case the package is not delivered.

Third or Fourth Class Matter Mailable Without Stamps.—Under special permits postage may be paid in money for third or fourth class matter mailed in quantities of 2,000 or more *identical* pieces. For information concerning the regulations governing such mailings inquiry should be made of the postmaster.

Registration.—All kinds of postal matter may be registered at the rate of *eight cents for each package* in addition to the regular rates of postage, to be fully prepaid by stamps. Each package must bear the name and address of the sender, and a receipt will be returned from the person to whom addressed. Mail matter can be registered at all post-offices in the United States.

An indemnity—not to exceed $25 for any one registered piece, or the actual value of the piece, if it is less than $25—shall be paid for the loss of first-class registered matter mailed at and addressed to a United States post-office.

Domestic Money Orders.—Domestic money orders are issued by money-order post-offices for any amount up to $100, at the following rates:

For sums not exceeding $2.50, 3 cents; over $2.50 to $5, 5 cents; over $5 to $10, 8 cents; over $10 to $20, 10 cents; over $20 to $30, 12 cents; over $30 to $40, 15 cents; over $40 to $50, 18 cents; over $50 to $60, 20 cents; over $60 to $75, 25 cents; over $75 to $100, 30 cents.

Stamped Envelopes.—Embossed stamped envelopes and newspaper wrappers of several denominations, sizes, and colors are kept on sale at post-offices, singly or in quantities, at a small advance on the postage rate. Stamps cut from stamped envelopes are valueless; but postmasters are authorized to give good stamps for stamped envelopes or newspaper wrappers that may be spoiled in directing, if presented in a substantially whole condition.

All matter concerning lotteries, gift concerts, or schemes devised to defraud the public, or for the purpose of obtaining money under false pretences, is denied transmission in the mails.

Applications for the establishment of post-offices should be addressed to the First Assistant Postmaster-General, accompanied by a statement of the necessity therefor. Instructions will then be given and blanks furnished to enable the petitioners to provide the department with the necessary information.

The franking privilege was abolished July 1, 1873, but the following mail matter may be sent free by legislative saving clauses, viz.:

1. All public documents printed by order of Congress, the Congressional Record and speeches contained therein, franked by Members of Congress, or the Secretary of the Senate, or Clerk of the House.
2. Seeds transmitted by the Secretary of Agriculture, or by any Member of Congress, procured from that Department.
3. Letters and packages relating exclusively to the business of the Government of the United States, mailed only by officers of the same, and letters and parcels mailed by the Smithsonian Institution. All these must be covered by specially printed "penalty" envelopes or labels.
4. The Vice-President, Members and Members-elect and Delegates and Delegates-elect to Congress may frank any mail matter to any Government official or to any person correspondence, not over four ounces in weight, upon official or departmental business.

All communications to Government officers and to Members of Congress are required to be prepaid by stamps.

Suggestions to the Public (*from the United States Official Postal-Guide*).—Mail all letters, etc., as early as practicable, especially when sent in large numbers, as is frequently the case with newspapers and circulars.

All mail matter at large post-offices is necessarily handled in great haste and should therefore in all cases be so PLAINLY addressed as to leave NO ROOM FOR DOUBT AND NO EXCUSE FOR ERROR on the part of postal employés. Names of States should be written in full (or their abbreviations very distinctly written) in order to prevent errors which arise from the similarity of such abbreviations as Cal., Col.; Pa., Va., Vt.; Me., Mo., Md.; Ioa., Ind.; N. H., N. M., N. Y., N. J., N. C., D. C.; Miss., Minn., Mass.; Nev., Neb.; Penn., Tenn., etc., when hastily or carelessly written. This is especially necessary in addressing mail matter to places of which the names are borne by several post-offices in different States.

Avoid as much as possible using envelopes made of flimsy paper, especially where more than one sheet of paper, or any other article than paper, is inclosed. Being often handled, and even in the mail-bags subject to pressure, such envelopes not infrequently split open, giving cause of complaint.

Never send money or any other article of value through the mail except either by means of a money order or in a registered letter. Any person who sends money or jewelry in an unregistered letter not only runs a risk of losing his property, but exposes to temptation every one through whose hands his letter passes, and may be the means of ultimately bringing some clerk or letter-carrier to ruin.

See that every letter or package bears the full name and post-office address of the writer, in order to secure the return of the letter, if the person to whom it is directed cannot be found. A much larger portion of the undelivered letters could he returned if the names and addresses of the senders were always fully and plainly written or printed inside or on the envelopes. Persons who have large correspondence find it most convenient to use "special request envelopes;" but those who only mail an occasional letter can avoid much trouble by writing a request to "return if not delivered," etc., on the envelope.

When dropping a letter, newspaper, etc., into a street mailing-box, or into the receptacle at a post-office, always see that the packet falls into the box and does not stick in its passage, observe, also, particularly, whether the postage stamps remain securely in their places.

POSTAL INFORMATION—*Continued.*

Postage stamps should be placed on the upper right-hand corner of the address side of all mail matter.

The street and number (or box number) should form a part of the address of all mail matter directed to cities. In most cities there are many persons, and even firms, bearing the same name. Before depositing any package or other article for mailing, the sender should assure himself that it is wrapped and packed in the manner prescribed by postal regulations; that it does not contain *unmailable* matter nor exceed the limit of weight as fixed by law; and that it is fully prepaid and properly addressed.

It is unlawful to send an ordinary letter by express or otherwise outside of the mails unless it be inclosed in a Government-stamped envelope. It is also unlawful to inclose a letter in an express package unless it pertains wholly to the contents of the package.

It is forbidden by the regulations of the Post-Office Department for postmasters to give to any person information concerning the mail matter of another, or to disclose the name of a box-holder at a post-office.

Letters addressed to persons temporarily sojourning in a city where the Free Delivery System is in operation should be marked "Transient" or "General Delivery," if not addressed to a street and number or some other designated place of delivery.

Foreign books, etc., infringing United States copyright are *undeliverable* if received in foreign mails, or mailed here.

The foregoing rates, rules, and suggestions *apply to postal matters in the United States.*

Foreign Mails.

POSTAGE RATES AND CONDITIONS.

THE rates of postage to all foreign countries and colonies, including Newfoundland (except Canada, Cuba, Mexico, Panama, and Shanghai, China), are as follows:

Letters*	first ounce or less, 5 cents; each additional ounce	3 cents.
Postal cards, each		2 cents.
Newspapers and other printed matter, per 2 ounces		1 cent.
Commercial papers (such as legal and insurance papers, deeds, bills of lading, invoices, manuscript for publication, etc.)	Packets not in excess of 10 ounces	5 cents.
	Packets in excess of 10 ounces, for each 2 ounces or fraction thereof	1 cent.
Samples of merchandise.	Packets not in excess of 4 ounces	2 cents.
	Packets in excess of 4 ounces, for each 2 ounces or fraction thereof	1 cent.
Registration fee on letters or other articles		8 cents.

* Letter rate to Great Britain and Ireland is two cents an ounce, or fraction of an ounce.

On printed matter and commercial papers the limit of weight is 4 pounds 6 ounces, except that single volumes of books to Salvador, Canada, Mexico, Cuba, and Panama, are unrestricted as to weight. Size—The limit of size is 18 inches in any one direction, except that printed matter or commercial papers in rolls may be 30 inches long by 4 inches in diameter.

Ordinary letters for countries of the Postal Union (except Canada and Mexico) will be forwarded, whether any postage is prepaid on them or not. All other mailable matter must be prepaid at least partially. Domestic rates apply to Porto Rico, Guam, Philippine Islands, Cuba, "Canal Zone," Republic of Panama, Tutuila, and Hawaii and Shanghai City.

CANADA.

Letters, per ounce, prepayment compulsory	2 cents.
Postal cards, each	1 cent.
Newspapers, per 4 ounces	1 cent.
Merchandise (not exceeding 4 pounds 6 ounces), per ounce	1 cent.
Samples of merchandise, same as to other Postal Union countries.	
Commercial papers, same as to other Postal Union countries.	
Registration fee	8 cents.

Any article of correspondence may be registered. Packages of merchandise are subject to the regulations of either country to prevent violations of the revenue laws; must not be closed against inspection, and must be so wrapped and inclosed as to be easily examined. Samples must not exceed 12 ounces in weight. No sealed packages other than letters in their usual and ordinary form may be sent by mail to Canada.

U. S. NAVAL VESSELS.

Mail matter for officers or members of the crew of United States vessels of war stationed abroad is subject to domestic postage rates and conditions. Articles should be addressed "U. S. S. (name of vessel), care of Postmaster, New York, N. Y." and *be fully prepaid. Mail* so addressed will be forwarded to the vessels. ☞ *Express packages will not be received at the post-office unless they conform to the Postal Regulations and are placed in the mail with the postage properly prepaid.*

SHANGHAI, CHINA.

Domestic postage rates and conditions apply to articles addressed for delivery in the City of Shanghai, but for other places in China the Universal Postal Union (foreign) rates apply.

MEXICO.

Letters, newspapers, and printed matter are now carried between the United States and Mexico at same rates as in the United States. Samples, 2 cents for first 4 ounces, and 1 cent for each additional 2 ounces; limit of weight, 12 ounces. Merchandise other than samples should be sent by Parcels Post. No sealed packages other than letters in their usual and ordinary form may be sent by mail to Mexico, nor any package over 4 pounds 6 ounces in weight, except Parcels Post packages to certain cities. (See Parcels Post.)

SAMPLES.

Packets of samples of merchandise are admissible up to 12 ounces in weight, and the following dimensions apply to all Postal Union countries: 12 inches in length, 8 inches in width, and 4 inches in depth, or if they are in the form of a roll, 12 inches in length and 6 inches in diameter. Merchandise of salable value and goods not in execution of orders, or as gifts, must be paid at full letter rate, unless sent by Parcels Post to the countries with which Parcels Post exchange is maintained.

PARCELS POST.

Postage, 12 cents a pound or fraction thereof; greatest length (unless specially noted below), 3 feet 6 inches; greatest length and girth combined (unless specially noted below), 6 feet; limit of

FOREIGN MAILS—*Continued.*

weight (unless specially noted below), 11 pounds; value (unless specially noted below), not limited; registration fee, 8 cents.

Unsealed packages of mailable merchandise may be sent by Parcels Post to Bermuda, Jamaica, including Cayman Islands, Turks Islands, including Caicos Islands, Barbados (parcels cannot be registered), the Bahamas, British Honduras, Mexico (limit of size, 2 feet in length, 4 feet in girth; limit of weight for places named in "Postal Guide," 11 pounds; for other places, 4 pounds 6 ounces), Leeward Islands (Antigua, Anguilla, Barbuda, Dominica, Montserrat, Nevis, Redonda, St. Kitts and the Virgin Islands), Colombia (limit of size, 2 feet in length, 4 feet in girth), Costa Rica (limit of size, 2 feet in length, 4 feet in girth), Salvador, British Guiana, Danish West Indies (St. Croix, St. John and St. Thomas), and the Windward Islands (Grenada, Grenadines, St. Lucia, and St. Vincent), Trinidad, including Tobago; Venezuela (Bolivia, Ecuador, Peru and Chile, 20 cents per pound), Newfoundland, Honduras (Republic of), Germany, Italy, Netherlands, (parcels cannot be registered, and must not weigh over 4 pounds 6 ounces, or exceed $50 in value), New Zealand, including Cook and Fanning Islands; Nicaragua, Guatemala, Norway (Parcels must not weigh over 4 pounds 6 ounces or exceed $50 in value), Japan including Formosa, Karafuto (Japanese Saghalien) and Korea (parcels must not weigh over 4 pounds 6 ounces or exceed $50 in value), Hong Kong (parcels must not weigh over 4 pounds 6 ounces or exceed $50 in value), Belgium (Parcels must not weigh over 4 pounds 6 ounces or exceed $50 in value), Great Britain and Ireland (Parcels cannot be registered), Australia, including Tasmania) parcels must not weigh over 4 pounds 6 ounces or exceed $50 in value), Denmark (parcels must not weigh over 4 pounds 6 ounces or exceed $50 in value), Sweden (parcels must not weigh over 4 pounds 6 ounces or exceed $50 in value), China, the following places only: Amoy, Canton, Changsha, Cheefoo, Chinkiang, Foochow, Hangchow, Hankow, Hoihao (Hoihow), Hong Kong, Kiukiang, Liu Kung Tau, Nanking, Newchwang, Ningpo, Shanghai, Shanhaikwan, Shasi, Soochow, Swatow, Peking, Tien-Tsin, Tongku and Wuhu (parcels must not weigh over 4 pounds 6 ounces or exceed $50 in value); Manchuria, the following places only: Antoken (Antung), Choshun (Changchun), Dairen (Talien or Dalney), Daisekkio (Tashichiao), Daitoko (Tatungkou), Furanten (Fulantien), Gaibei (Kaiping), Giukaton (Newchwatun), Gwaboten (Wafangtien), Hishika (Pitzuwo), Honkeiko (Penhsihu), Hoten (Mukden), Howojo (Fenghuangcheng), Kaigen (Kaiyun), Kaijo (Haicheng), Kinshu (Chinchow), Koshurei (Kungchuling), Riojun (Port Arthur), Rioyo (Liaoyang), Riujuton (Liushutun), Senkinsai (Chienchinsai), Shiheigai (Supingchieh), Shinminfu (Singmingfu), Shoto (Changtu), Sokako (Tsaohokow), Sokaton (Suchiatun), Taikozan (Takushan), Tetsurei (Tiehling), Yendai (Yentai), Yugakujo (Hsiungyocheng) (parcels must not weigh over 4 pounds 6 ounces or exceed $50 in value) at the following postage rate: For a parcel not exceeding one pound in weight, 12 cents; for each additional pound or fraction thereof, 12 cents. The maximum weight allowed is eleven pounds—except that to certain places in Mexico and to all parts of Norway, Hong Kong, Japan, Belgium, and Australia, Denmark, Sweden, China (the places mentioned above), the limit is 4 pounds 6 ounces, and the value of parcels for these countries and Ecuador, Peru, must not exceed $50—the extreme dimensions allowed for Mexico, Costa Rica, and Colombia being two feet length by four feet girth, and for the other countries not more than three feet six inches in length, nor more than six feet in length and girth combined. Parcels must be wrapped so as to permit their contents to be easily examined by postmasters. The presence, in an unsealed parcel, of sealed receptacles containing mailable articles which cannot be safely transmitted in the unsealed receptacles, will not render the parcel unmailable, provided the contents of the sealed receptacles are plainly visible, or are unmistakably indicated by the method of packing or by a precise statement on the covers. But such sealed receptacles will not be admitted to the Parcels Post unless inclosed in an outside cover open to inspection. Any article absolutely prohibited admission to the regular mails for any country is also inadmissable to Parcels Post mails for that country; but no article is excluded from Parcels Post mails solely because it is dutiable in the country of destination. Liquids, poisonous, explosive, and inflammable substances are excluded. Parcels may be registered for 8 cents each to any of the above places, except Barbados and Great Britain and Ireland.

A Customs declaration (furnished on application at any post-office) must be attached to any Parcels Post package. Parcels for Salvador must have two declarations, and parcels for Venezuela three declarations attached. France—Two copies of the special declaration, "Form No. 2 Bis" (1402½), showing in addition to the usual entries the gross weight of the parcel and net weight of the contents, must be attached to parcels for France. One copy may be pasted to the package but the other copy must be affixed in such a manner that it can be readily removed at the exchange office where the mail is prepared for despatch to France. Parcels cannot be registered and must not weigh over 4 pounds 6 ounces.

GENERAL REGULATIONS RESPECTING FOREIGN MAILS.

Rates and conditions to countries not in the Universal Postal Union are now the same as those to Universal Postal Union countries.

Postage can be prepaid upon articles only by means of the postage stamps of the country *in* which the articles are mailed. Hence articles mailed in one country addressed to another country which bear postage stamps of the country to which they are addressed are treated as if they had no postage stamps attached to them.

Unpaid letters received from the Postal Union and insufficiently prepaid correspondence of all kinds is chargeable with double the amount of the deficient postage.

Matter to be sent in the mails at less than letter rates must be so wrapped that it can be readily examined at the office of delivery, as well as the mailing office, without destroying the wrapper.

Newspapers and periodicals sent in the mails to foreign countries other than those of the Postal Union should be wrapped singly. Those sent by publishers to regular subscribers in Canada, Cuba, Mexico, and Panama are transmissible as in domestic mails, except that packages addressed to Mexico, Cuba, and Panama must not exceed 4 pounds 6 ounces in weight.

The United States two-cent postal card should be used for card correspondence with foreign countries (except Canada, Cuba, Mexico, Panama, and Shanghai city, to which countries the one-cent card is transmissible), but where these cards cannot be obtained, it is allowable to use for this purpose the United States one-cent postal card with a one-cent United States adhesive postage stamp attached thereto. Private cards can now be used if conforming in size, etc., to Government cards, such cards should bear the words "post card."

Mail matter *of all kinds* received from any country of the Postal Union is required to be reforwarded at the request of the addressee, from one post-office to another, and in the case of articles other than Parcels Post packages, to any foreign country embraced in the Postal Union, without additional charge for postage.

All articles prohibited from domestic mails are also excluded from circulation in the mails to and

FOREIGN MAILS—*Continued.*

from foreign countries. Postal cards or letters addressed to go around the world will not be forwarded, being prohibited.

The act of March 3, 1883, imposes a duty of 25 per cent. ad valorem on all printed matter not therein otherwise provided for, without regard to mode of importation. Under said act all printed matter, *except newspapers and periodicals*, and except printed matter other than books imported in the mails for personal use, is subject to the regular duty of 25 per cent. ad valorem.

FOREIGN (INTERNATIONAL) MONEY ORDERS.

When payable in Switzerland, New Zealand, Belgium, Sweden, Norway, Japan, Denmark, Orange River Colony, Netherlands, Trinidad, Austria, Hungary, Bermuda, Luxemburg, Chile, Egypt, Bolivia, Mexico, Liberia, Costa Rica, Peru, Transvaal, Germany, Hong Kong, Portugal, and Apia, the charge is as follows:

For order not exceeding $10, 8 cents; over $10 and not exceeding $20, 10 cents; over $20 and not exceeding $30, 15 cents; over $30 and not exceeding $40, 20 cents; over $40 and not exceeding $50, 25 cents; over $50 and not exceeding $60, 30 cents; over $60 and not exceeding $70, 35 cents; over $70 and not exceeding $80, 40 cents; over $80 and not exceeding $90, 45 cents; over $90 and not exceeding $100, 50 cents.

When payable in any other foreign country, the charge is as follows: For order not exceeding $10, 10 cents; over $10 and not exceeding $20, 20 cents; over $20 and not exceeding $30, 30 cents; over $30 and not exceeding $40, 40 cents; over $40 and not exceeding $50, 50 cents; over $50 and not exceeding $60, 60 cents; over $60 and not exceeding $70, 70 cents; over $70 and not exceeding $80, 80 cents; over $80 and not exceeding $90, 90 cents; over $90 and not exceeding $100, $1.

The maximum amount for which a money order may be drawn payable in Cape Colony is $100. There is no limitation to the number of international orders that may be issued, in one day, to a remitter, in favor of the same payee.

Domestic rates and regulations apply to money orders for Canada, Cuba, Hawaii, Newfoundland, Porto Rico, and the Philippine Islands, also Windward Islands, Jamaica, and Leeward Islands, British Honduras, British Guiana, Canal Zone (Isthmus of Panama), Tutuila (Samoa), United States Postal Agency at Shanghai (China), Virgin Islands, Guam, and the Bahamas.

Distances and Postal Time from New York City.

TIME of transit of mails, as indicated by the Official Postal Guide, showing the time in transit from New York City between depot and depot. Subject to alteration consequent upon changes in time tables and connections.

Cities in United States.	Miles.	Hours.	Cities in United States.	Miles.	Hours.	Cities in United States.	Miles.	Hours.
Albany, N. Y.	142	3½	Detroit, Mich.	743	21	Portland, Ore.	3,181	114½
Atlanta, Ga.	882	24¼	Galveston, Tex.	1,789	56½	Prescott, Ariz.	2,724	94
Baltimore, Md.	188	6	Harrisburg, Pa.	182	6	Providence, R. I.	189	5
Bismarck, N. Dak.	1,738	60½	Hartford, Ct.	112	4	Richmond, Va.	344	11¼
Boisé, Idaho	2,736	93½	Helena, Mont.	2,423	89	St. Louis, Mo.	1,048	29
Boston, Mass.	217	6	Hot Springs, Ark.	1,367	55	St. Paul, Minn.	1,300	37
Buffalo, N. Y.	410	9½	Indianapolis, Ind.	808	23	Salt Lake City, Utah.	2,452	71½
Cape May, N. J.	172	5	Jacksonville, Fla.	1,077	30	San Francisco, Cal.	3,250	105
Carson City, Nev.	3,035	103¼	Kansas City, Mo.	1,302	38¼	Santa Fé, N. Mex.	2,173	82
Charleston, S. C.	804	21¼	Louisville, Ky.	854	30	Savannah, Ga.	905	26¼
Chattanooga, Tenn.	853	32	Memphis, Tenn.	1,163	40	Tacoma, Wash.	3,209	102
Cheyenne, Wyo.	1,899	54	Milwaukee, Wis.	985	29¼	Topeka, Kan.	1,370	48
Chicago, Ill.	900	23	Montgomery, Ala.	1,057	26	Trenton, N. J.	57	2
Cincinnati, O.	744	23	Montpelier, Vt.	327	10¼	Vicksburg, Miss.	1,288	50
Cleveland, O.	568	19½	New Orleans, La.	1,344	32	Vinita, Okla.	1,413	42
Columbus, O.	624	20	Omaha, Neb.	1,383	43	Washington, D. C.	228	6
Concord, N. H.	292	9½	Philadelphia, Pa.	90	3	Wheeling, W. Va.	496	14¼
Deadwood, S. Dak.	1,957	65½	Pittsburgh, Pa.	431	13	Wilmington, Del.	117	5
Denver, Col.	1,930	61½	Portland, Me.	325	12	Wilmington, N. C.	593	20
Des Moines, Ia.	1,257	87½						

DISTANCES AND MAIL TIME TO FOREIGN CITIES FROM THE CITY OF NEW YORK.

By Postal Route to—	Miles.	Days.	By Postal Route to—	Miles.	Days.
Adelaide, *via* San Francisco	12,845	34	Hong Kong, *via* San Francisco	10,590	25
Alexandria, *via* London	6,150	13	Honolulu, *via* San Francisco	5,645	13
Amsterdam, " "	3,985	9	Liverpool	3,540	8
Antwerp, " "	4,000	9	London	3,740	8
Athens, " "	5,055	12	Madrid, *via* London	4,925	9
Bahia, Brazil	5,870	21	Manila, *via* San Francisco	10,193	33
Bangkok, Siam, *via* San Francisco	12,990	43	Melbourne, *via* San Francisco	12,265	26
Bangkok, Siam, *via* London	13,125	41	Mexico City (railroad)	3,750	5
Batavia, Java, *via* London	12,800	34	Panama	2,355	6
Berlin	4,385	9	Paris	4,020	8
Bombay, *via* London	9,765	24	Rio de Janeiro	6,204	23
Bremen	4,235	8	Rome, *via* London	5,030	9
Buenos Ayres	8,045	29	Rotterdam, *via* London	3,985	9
Calcutta, *via* London	11,120	26	St. Petersburg, *via* London	5,370	10
Cape Town, *via* London	11,245	27	San Juan, Porto Rico	1,360	5
Constantinople, *via* London	5,810	11	Shanghai, *via* San Francisco	9,930	25
Florence, *via* London	4,800	10	Shanghai, *via* London	14,745	45
Glasgow	3,370	10	Stockholm, *via* London	4,975	10
Greytown, *via* New Orleans	2,815	7	Sydney, *via* San Francisco	11,570	21
Halifax, N. S.	645	2	Valparaiso, *via* Panama	5,915	37
Hamburg	4,820	9	Vienna	4,740	10
Havana	1,386	3	Yokohama, *via* San Francisco	7,848	20

Lumber Production of the United States.

(From Census Bulletin Issued July, 1908.)

THE Bureau of the Census, with the assistance of the Forest Service of the Department of Agriculture, has for some years collected statistics concerning the annual production of various forest products in the United States, and the preliminary totals for the cut of lumber, lath, and shingles for the year ending December 31, 1907, have been made public.

TOTAL LUMBER CUT.

Unusual importance is attached to the reports for 1907, which show that the aggregate cut of lumber in the United States increased from 37,551,000,000 feet, board measure, in 1906, to 40,256,000,000 feet in 1907—a gain of 2,705,000,000 feet, or 7.2 per cent. For lath and shingles the total production was 3,664,000,000 and 11,950,000,000, respectively, in 1907, as against 3,813,000,000 and 11,858,000,000, respectively, in 1906—a decrease of 149,000,000, or 3.9 per cent., in lath, and an increase of 92,000,000, or eight-tenths of 1 per cent., in shingles. The number of mills reporting in 1907 was 28,850, while in 1906 the cut of 22,398 mills was covered.

EFFECT OF THE PANIC OF 1907 AND OTHER INFLUENCES.

The substantial increase in the total production of lumber in 1907 as compared with 1906, in spite of the financial stringency which measurably affected most lines of manufacture during a part of the latter year, was remarkable, and especially so in view of certain well-known local causes which also operated during the whole or a part of the year to reduce the output of the regions affected. Aside from the car shortage, which necessitated a restriction of the cut in many localities during the earlier months of the year, the fact that the industry of lumber manufactured was practically suspended on the Pacific Coast early in the Fall, on account of the prospective raise in freight rates by the railroads which handle the product of the mills in this region, materially affected the amount of output. Furthermore, a steady decline from year to year is to be expected in the Lake States, because of the rapid exhaustion of their timber supply. In the Southern States, however—the principal producers of lumber during recent years—local conditions were substantially normal, but the effect of the business depression obtaining throughout the country during the latter part of 1907, while somewhat obscured, may nevertheless be discerned in the showing for that region.

THE CUT OF YELLOW PINE.

More than nine-tenths of the stand of yellow pine stumpage is in the Coast States, from Virginia to Texas, inclusive, and Arkansas. This group, together with Kentucky and Tennessee, reported a total lumber cut in 1907 of 17,694,218,000 feet by 11,395 mills, as against 15,096,110,000 feet by 8,143 mills in 1906—an increase of 17.2 per cent. in production and 39.9 per cent. in number of mills. Of this total output, the several species of yellow pine—long leaf, short leaf, loblolly, Cuban, etc.—contributed 12,816,790,000 feet, or 72.4 per cent., in 1907, and 11,298,014,000 feet, or 74.8 per cent., in 1906—an increase in the cut of this wood of 1,466,768,000 feet, or 13.4 per cent. Other woods showing important gains were: Oak, from 1,032,398,000 feet in 1906 to 1,405,763,000 feet in 1907; poplar, from 325,162,000 feet to 427,426,000 feet; red gum, from 286,696,000 feet to 472,754,000 feet; and tupelo, from 42,624,000 feet to 60,894,000 feet. Oak and poplar are the principal lumber trees of Kentucky and Tennessee. It is possible that the indicated increase in the cut of these woods was due, in part, to the substantially larger number of mills reported for these States in 1907.

PRODUCTION IN NEW YORK AND NEW ENGLAND.

In New York and New England, where the manufacture of lumber and allied products from standing timber still holds a relatively high place among the industries of the region, the totals were not materially changed from those of the preceding year; most of the States, however, showed gains, and in a few instances the relative increases were considerable. The total cut of New York and New England combined—3,617,482,000 feet for 1907—exceeding that of 1906 by 348,214,000 feet, an increase of 10.7 per cent. Such a showing is noteworthy in view of the waning timber supply in this region, and the adverse business conditions obtaining throughout a part of the period covered. Practically the entire output of the mills of this section—unlike that of the mills in the Lake States, the Southern States, and the Pacific Coast States—is marketed locally and is insufficient in quantity to satisfy the normal demand, a considerable percentage of the product consumed here being shipped in, chiefly from the South and from the Lake region. The falling off in the demand for lumber in these States during the latter part of 1907, therefore, while reflected sharply in the decreased shipments into them, apparently had little or no bearing on the output of the local mills, whose capacity was still short of the demand.

SPRUCE STILL A LEADING LUMBER TIMBER.

Although the wood pulp industry is making a heavy and increasing draft upon the supply of spruce, this tree still practically shares with white pine the place of first importance among the lumber timbers of this region. The cut of spruce reported in 1907 was 1,098,268,000 feet, an increase over 1906 of 75,914,000 feet, or 7.4 per cent. It formed 30.4 per cent. of the total output of all lumber in these States in 1907, while white pine contributed 31.8 per cent.

DECREASE IN WHITE PINE CUT OF THE LAKE STATES.

The total production of the Lake States was 5,491,680,000 feet in 1907 and 6,219,728,000 feet in 1906, a decrease of 728,048,000 feet, or 11.7 per cent. Among the various species the greatest loss was in pine, which decreased from 3,055,072,000 feet in 1906 to 2,497,505,000 feet in 1907, or 18.3 per cent.; while for hemlock, maple, and basswood the relative decreases were only 8.8, 5.6, and 9 per cent., respectively, and for birch there was an increase of 4.6 per cent. In these States, as a whole, pine still holds the place of first importance, though the history of lumbering in Michigan, where with the passing of pine the cut of the mills ran to hemlock and the hard woods, is being repeated in Wisconsin. In this State in 1907 the reported cut of pine for the first time fell below that of hemlock, the output of the latter exceeding that of the former by 10.7 per cent., while in 1906 the production of pine was greater than that of hemlock by 13.1 per cent. In Minnesota the cut of pine in 1907 formed 91.6 per cent. of the total lumber output of that State, and represented 60.9 per cent of the aggregate cut of this wood in all the Lake States.

THE Forest policy of the United States is of public interest for two principal reasons: First, it guarantees the perpetuation of forest resources having a capitalized value of $2,014,000,000; and second, it furnishes an object lesson in the conservation of natural resources in general. The movement to conserve for the use of the people the remaining forests on the public domain gave the final impetus to the wider movement to conserve all the natural resources of the land—forests, water, soils, and minerals.

The estimated total area of privately owned and National Forests in the United States is 600,000,000 acres, 32 per cent. of the total land area, exclusive of Alaska.

The lumber industry is fourth among the great industries of the United States. In 1907 between forty and forty-five billion board feet of lumber was produced, valued at from $675,000,000 to $750,000,000.

At the present rate of cutting the forest lands of the United States cannot long meet the enormous demands made upon them. The great pineries of the Lake States have been almost entirely eliminated, and great inroads have been made upon the supply of valuable timber throughout all parts of the country.

The heavy demands for timber have been rapidly pushing the great centres of lumber industry toward the South and West. In consequence the State of Washington has led for several years in lumber production, followed in order by Louisiana, Texas, Mississippi, Wisconsin and Arkansas. The annual production of yellow pine lumber now amounts to over 13,215 million feet; the increase in the cut of Douglas fir in the Northwest has brought that wood to second place, while white pine has fallen to third place.

A long step forward in the preservation of forests for purposes of permanent timber supply and the protection of watersheds and grazing lands was made, when, on February 1, 1905, the administration of the National Forests was transferred from the Department of the Interior to the Department of Agriculture. Under the present system the management of the National Forests, the total area of which on November 1, 1908, was 167,992,208 acres, is undertaken by the Forest Service, in the latter department.

A great saving has been effected to the naval stores industry by the introduction of the cup and gutter system of turpentining, instead of the old destructive system of boxing, by insuring a larger product of better quality, and prolonging the life of the longleaf pine forests upon which the industry depends.

In 1907, 3,963,000 cords of wood were used in the manufacture of paper, of which 925,373 cords were imported from Canada. The demand for pulpwood is making a severe drain on the spruce forests which furnish the principal supply, and investigations are under way to determine what woods, such as scrub pine, white fir, tupelo, and the like, can be successfully used to insure a continued supply of material. A larger drain upon our forest resources is made by the demand for railroad ties, of which 153,000,000, equivalent to five billion board feet, were used in 1907. White oak, hitherto the chief source of supply, is not plentiful enough to meet this demand indefinitely, and in many parts of the country the supply of chestnut, cedar, and cypress is dwindling; however, seasoning and treating methods are being found by which cheaper and more plentiful woods, such as lodgepole pine in the Northwest and loblolly pine in the South, are made fit for use as ties. Timber to the amount of two and one-half billion feet was used in 1907 for mine timbers.

THE FOREST SERVICE.

"Forest Service" has been the name sinee July 1, 1905, of that branch of the Department of Agriculture which was previously called the "Bureau of Forestry," and, earlier still, the "Division of Forestry."

Since February 1, 1905, the Forest Service has been charged, under the direction of the Secretary of Agriculture, with the administration of the National Forests. About the management of the National Forests, therefore, the work of the Service now centres. The forests, whose area in continental United States, excluding Alaska, on November 15, 1908, was 155,838,632 acres, and with Alaska, 167,992,208 acres are of vital importance for their timber and grass and for the conservation of stream flow. They are so managed as to develop their permanent value as a resource by use.

Beginning January 1, 1909, the organization of the Forest Service provides for a central force in Washington and six administrative district headquarters, located respectively at Portland, Ore., San Francisco, Cal.; Missoula, Mont.; Ogden, Utah; Denver, Col., and Albuquerque, New Mexico. Each of the field districts is in charge of a District Forester and an Assistant District Forester, and each of the different lines of Service work is directly under an officer in charge of this special line of work. Thus, by far the greater volume of Forest work is handled locally, and only larger questions of policy are referred to the Forester at Washington. The work in Washington is organized under five branches with fourteen offices, with the following branch and office chiefs in charge:

OFFICE OF THE FORESTER.

Administration—Gifford Pinchot, Forester; Overton W. Price, Associate Forester.

Inspection—R. E. Benedict, D. D. Bronson and E. S. Bruce, Inspectors; G. B. Sudworth, Dendrologist; Herbert A. Smith, Editor.

BRANCH OF OPERATION.

Administration—James B. Adams, C. S. Chapman, Assistant Foresters; H. B. Cramer, Fiscal Agent; G. G. Anderson, Assistant in Office Methods.

Office of Maintenance—R. K. Helphenstine, Jr., Chief.

Office of Accounts—E. A. Melzar, Chief and Fiscal Agent.

Office of Occupancy.—M. J. McVean, Chief.

Office of Geography—Fred G. Plummer, Chief.

BRANCH OF GRAZING.

Administration—A. F. Potter, Assistant Forester in Charge; L. E. Kneipp, Assistant.

Office of Control—Will C. Barnes, Chief.

Office of Development—W. C. Clos, Chief.

BRANCH OF SILVICULTURE.

Administration—William T. Cox, Assistant Forester in Charge; E. E. Carter, Assistant Forester; S. N. Spring.

Office of Silvics—R. Zon, Chief.

Office of Federal Co-operation—A. B. Patterson, Chief.

Office of State and Private Co-operation—J. G. Peters, Chief.

BRANCH OF PRODUCTS.

Administration—W. L. Hall, Assistant Forester in Charge; R. S. Kellogg, Assistant Forester.

Office of Wood Utilization—G. McGarvey Cline, Chief.

Office of Wood Preservation—W. F. Sherfesee, Chief.

Office of Publications—Findley Burns, Chief.

The following are in charge of the six field districts: DISTRICT 1—W. B. Greeley, District Forester; F. A. Silcox, Assistant District Forester. This district includes Montana, northeastern Washington, northern Idaho, northern Wyoming, and northwestern South Dakota.

DISTRICT 2—Smith Riley, District Forester; Paul G. Redington, Assistant District Forester. This district includes Colorado, southern Wyoming, South Dakota, northwestern Minnesota, Nebraska, western Kansas, and southeastern Utah.

DISTRICT 3—A. C. Ringland, District Forester; Earle H. Clapp, Assistant District Forester. This district includes Arizona, Arkansas, New Mexico, and Oklahoma.

DISTRICT 4—Clyde Leavitt, District Forester; F. W. Reed, Assistant District Forester. This district includes Utah, southern Idaho, western Wyoming, eastern Nevada, and northwestern Arizona.

DISTRICT 5—F. E. Olmsted, District Forester; Coert Du Bois, Assistant District Forester. This district includes California and southwestern Nevada.

DISTRICT 6—E. T. Allen, District Forester; Geo. H. Cecil, Assistant District Forester. This district includes Washington, Oregon, a small part of northern California, and Alaska.

The work of the dendrologist includes dendrological studies proper, direction of the Services, forest photograph collection, and charge of the forest exhibits prepared by the Service.

A leading branch of the dendrological studies is the making of an accurate forest map of the distribution of tree species in the United States, to show the extent, composition, and economic possibilities of our forest resources. Others of these studies concern the cedar forests of Texas, and important but little known trees indigenous to the United States, the growth of which may profitably extend to new localities for economic purposes. Prominent among the latter are the desert pines of California. An investigation is being made of the present and probable future supply of western tan bark oak, as well as of other trees the barks of which are used to adulterate tan bark, and the tannin contents of the barks are being determined by the Bureau of Chemistry. Included also is a study of basket willows. Experimental bolts are established on the Arlington Experimental Farm, near Washington, D. C. Attention is given especially to the conditions under which high-grade basket rods may be produced. Approved basket willow cuttings are distributed free each Spring to applicants interested in willow culture.

A series of important publications in course of preparation will describe and illustrate the tree species of the different regions of the United States. The first of these bulletins embraces the trees of the Pacific Coast.

The dendrologist also gives technical information about trees, in response to inquiries, including the identification of the wood, seeds, foliage, etc., of native and exotic trees. A large and growing correspondence evidences the public demand for such information.

The Government forest exhibits prepared for State, National, and international expositions explain what foresty is and show its application to the problems with which the Service is dealing. Through these displays much public interest is aroused and information given concerning our forests, their economic importance, and right and wrong methods of using them.

FOREST PLANTING.

The office of extension in the branch of silviculture, deals with all phases of forest planting within the National Forests. In the past two important problems have received special attention: (1) The reforesting of denuded watersheds where planting is needed in order to control and regulate the flow of streams directly supplying cities and towns; (2) planting within the treeless National Forests in the Middle West to provide for timber in the future and to serve as an object lesson to the people.

The trees used in planting are grown at nine Government nurseries in the following National Forests: Angeles, Gila, Nebraska, Pike, Wasatch, Pecos, Pocatello, Kansas and Helena. The combined area of seed and transplant beds at the nine stations is 11 acres. They now contain over 10,000,000 trees, from one to four years old. The seed sown in 1909 will produce not less than 6,000,000 trees.

The planting stations are so situated that in addition to providing plant material for local use they also serve as distributing points for other National Forests.

The preliminary stage of forest planting within the National Forests is now past, and several of the planting stations have this year produced trees of sufficient size to plant directly on the permanent site. About 700,000 trees were planted during the Winter and Spring of 1908, the greater part in the Nebraska, Kansas, Angeles, Santa Barbara, and Pike National Forests. In addition to planting, extensive broadcast seeding will be conducted on the National Forests in 1909. For this purpose over five tons of tree seeds were collected during the Fall of 1908. This amount will be sufficient to sow about ten square miles of denuded land. The largest single area to be sown is on the Black Hills National Forest, where one square mile will be seeded to Western yellow pine.

Any owner who wishes to learn whether forestry might be profitable to him may apply to the Forest Service for an examination of his lands. An agent of the Service is then sent to examine the forest. The cost of this examination is usually borne by the owner of the lands. In a few cases, however, where the results promise to be of unusual interest the examination is made entirely at the expense of the Forest Service. If the piece of woodland is small, as in farm wood lots, and management is practicable, a plan is outlined on the spot and carefully explained to the owner. In the case of large tracts the preparation of a working plan requires a more prolonged study on the ground. The agent sent to examine the tract therefore first finds out whether a sufficiently good opening for paying management exists to justify the outlay. His report is submitted to the owner, with an estimate of the cost of preparing the plan if a plan is found desirable.

If the owner desires the working plan, a force of men is sent to collect the necessary data. A thorough examination of the tract is made both from the Forester's and from the lumberman's points of view. The merchantable and immature trees upon sample strips are counted and their diameter measured, and from these data the stand on the whole tract is calculated. Volume and rate of growth are ascertained for the important species through tree analyses—that is, through measurements of felled trees and counts of their annual rings. Studies are made of reproduction, of the danger from fire, grazing, and insect attack, and of the best means of preventing such injuries. Market and transportation facilities are carefully investigated, and the yield of timber and the character and distribution of the forest are mapped.

When these facts have been collected they are worked up into the plan, which takes into account the special needs or purpose of the owner, as, for instance, to secure permanent supplies of mining timber, to maintain a game preserve, or to protect a watershed. The recommendations in the plan enable the owner to derive from the forest the fullest and most permanent revenue which is consistent with his special requirements.

Similar co-operation with private owners is carried on also in regard to Forest planting, either on denuded areas or to assist natural reproduction in reforesting the land.

FOREST PRESERVATION BY THE VARIOUS STATES.

New York has purchased and set aside 1,500,000 acres for a forest reserve. These lands are mainly in the Adirondacks, but partly in the Catskills. Patrol, to guard against theft of timber and especially against fire, is maintained under the Superintendent of Forests, who is the executive officer of the forest, fish and game commission. The planting of young trees on open places is now going forward at the rate of 500,000 seedlings annually.

Pennsylvania has recently been most active in taking measures for the preservation of its forests. In 1897, this State, to conserve the water supply, provided for the purchase of three forest reserves, of not less than 40,000 acres each, at the heads of the three principal river systems of the State. In accordance with this and other acts, land has been rapidly acquired, until, at the present time, the holdings of Pennsylvania amount to more than 700,000 acres. In 1901 Pennsylvania made its Bureau of Foresty a separate department. A school for forest wardens has been established at Mont Alto, and in connection with the protection and improvement of the forest reserves, the State is engaged in removing the mature timber.

Minnesota long took the lead in the excellence of a forest fire law, it being the first State to appoint a fire warden charged with responsibility for suppressing fires. New York, in 1900, also made provision for a chief fire warden. Maine and New Hampshire are other States possessing excellent fire laws. In 1899 Michigan appointed a commission to study the forest question, and to select land for a State forest reserve.

Under the supervision of a trained Forester, Wisconsin is selling mature timber from its forest reserve of 264,697 acres, which has been surveyed, mapped and placed under management. In co-operation with the office of Indian Affairs and the Forest Service the State Forester supervises the sale and cutting of timber on the Indian reservations in Wisconsin. On June 26, 1906, Congress passed a bill granting to Wisconsin, 20,000 acres of vacant Government lands.

Indiana took an important step forward when the State held forth encouragement to private owners to plant trees. Since 1904, Massachusetts has had a technically trained State Forester, who besides furnishing advice to landowners for the management of forest lands, delivers a course of lectures at the State agricultural college. In 1905, Maryland passed a law providing for a State Forester under much the same conditions.

California has manifested great interest in forest preservation. Under an appropriation of the Legislature of that State a study of its forest resources has been undertaken, and is now in progress in co-operation with the Forest Service. A State Forester has recently been appointed.

The States now having officers charged with the care of forest interests are: California, Connecticut, Indiana, Kansas, Louisiana, Maine, Maryland, Massachusetts, Michigan, Minnesota, New Hampshire, New Jersey, New York, North Carolina, North Dakota, Oregon, Pennsylvania, Rhode Island, Washington, West Virginia, and Wisconsin.

The Biltmore Forest School, at Biltmore, North Carolina, was established in 1898. Its director is Dr. C. A. Schenck, Forester to the Biltmore estate. The Yale Forest School, established in 1900, is a post-graduate school, whose head is Prof. Henry S. Graves. Harvard has had a forest school since 1903. The University of Michigan has a four-year undergraduate course in forestry. The lecturer is Prof. Filibert Roth.

THE AMERICAN FORESTRY ASSOCIATION.

The American Forestry Association whose headquarters are at 1417 G Street, N. W., Washington, D. C. was organized in 1882, and incorporated in January, 1897, with the following objects:

1. The promotion of a businesslike and conservative use and treatment of the forest resources of this country.

2. The advancement of legislation tending to this end both by the States and the Congress of the United States, the inauguration of forest administration by the Federal Government and by the States, and the extension of sound forestry by all proper methods.

3. The diffusion of knowledge regarding the conservation, management, and renewal of forests, the proper utilization of their products, methods of reforestation of waste lands, and the planting of trees.

The Association desires and needs as members all who are interested in promoting the objects for which it is organized—all who realize the importance of using the natural resources of the country in such a manner as not to exhaust them, or to work ruin to other interests. In particular it appeals to owners of woodlands, to lumbermen and Foresters, as well as to engineers, professional and business men who have to do with wood and its manifold uses, and to persons concerned in the conservation of water supplies for irrigation and other purposes.

The Association has over 5,000 members at the present time, residents of every State in the Union, Canada and foreign countries. The annual dues are two dollars; a magazine is published. The officers of the Association are:

President—Secretary of Agriculture, James Wilson; *Vice-Presidents-at-Large*—Dr. Edward Everett Hale, F. E. Weyerhaeuser, James W. Pinchot, Dr. B. E. Fernow; John L. Kaul; *Secretary*—————————Washington, D. C.; *Treasurer*—Otto Luebkert, Washington, D. C.

Local or State Forestry Associations have been formed in California, Colorado, Connecticut, Iowa, Kentucky, Massachusetts, Michigan, Minnesota, Nebraska, New Hampshire, New York, North Carolina, North Dakota, Ohio, Oregon, Pennsylvania, Tennessee, Utah, Washington and Wyoming.

ARBOR DAY.

Individual States and Territories have striven to encourage the preservation of trees by setting aside a certain day each year for the purpose of tree planting. Every State and Territory, with the exception of Delaware and the Indian Territory, have set apart such an Arbor Day. [See "Legal Holidays."]

NATIONAL PARKS.

The national parks were created during the period from 1872 to 1904. They have a total area of about 3,654,196 acres. The more important are the Yellowstone National Park in Wyoming and Montana; Sequoia National Park, General Grant National Park, and Yosemite National Park in California; Mt. Rainier National Park in Washington, and Crater Lake National Park in Oregon.

The reservation known as the Yellowstone National Park, set apart for public uses by an act of Congress passed in 1872, covers a tract of about sixty-five miles in length, from north to south, and about fifty-five miles in width, from east to west, lying chiefly in Northwestern Wyoming, and overlapping, to a small extent, the boundaries of Montana, on the north, and Idaho, on the west. This gives an area of 3,312 square miles, a tract that is nearly the area of the States of Rhode Island and Delaware combined, and nearly half as large as the State of Massachusetts. The Rocky Mountain chain crosses the southwestern portion in an irregular line, leaving by far the greater expanse on the eastern side. The least elevation of any of the narrow valleys is 6,000 feet, and some of them are from 1,000 to 2,000 feet higher. The mountain ranges which hem in these valleys are from 10,000 to upward of 11,000 feet in height, Electric Peak (in the northwest corner of the park, not far back of Mammoth Hot Springs) having an elevation of 11,155 feet, and Mount Langford and Turret Mountain (both in the Yellowstone Range) reaching the height of 11,155 and 11,142 feet respectively.

Game Laws of the

CLOSE SEASON FOR GAME

THE following table shows the close season for all game in the United States, with the exception of mountain sheep and goat and a few unimportant species. Where no dates are given kind of game does not exist, or close season at all times. Local laws, where operative, should be consulted.

		MAMMALS.				BIRDS.
		Deer.	Elk, Antelope, Moose, Caribou.	Squirrel.	Rabbit.	Quail.
1	Alabama	Jan. 1–Nov. 1 (6)	...	Jan. 1–Aug. 1 (22)	...	Mar. 1–Nov. 1
2	Alaska	Feb. 2–Apr. 1	Dec. 11–Aug. 20	...	...	...
3	Arizona	Dec. 1–Sept. 15 (a)	At all times	...	...	Mar. 1–Oct. 15
4	Arkansas	Feb. 1–Sept. 1	...	Dec. 1–May 1	...	Mar. 1–Nov. 1
5	California	Oct. 1–July 15 (a)	At all times	Jan. 1–Sept. 1	...	Feb. 15-Oct. 15
6	Colorado	Oct. 21–Oct. 1	To Oct. 15, 1911	...	...	To Oct. 1, 1920
7	Connecticut	To June 1, 1911	...	Dec. 1–Oct. 1	Dec. 1–Oct. 1	Dec. 1–Oct. 1
8	Delaware	...	...	Jan. 1–Nov. 15	Jan. 1–Nov. 15	Jan. 1–Nov. 15
9	Dist. of Col.	Jan. 1–Sept. 1	...	Feb. 1–Nov. 1	Feb. 1–Nov. 1	Mar. 15–Nov. 1
10	Florida	Feb. 1–Nov. 1	...	...	...	Mar. 1–Nov. 1
11	Georgia	Jan. 1–Sept. 1	...	...	...	Mar. 15-Nov. 1
12	Idaho	Jan. 1–Sept. 15	Jan. 1–Sept. 15 (1)	...	...	Dec. 1–Nov. 1
13	Illinois	To 1917 (11)	...	Nov. 16–July 1	...	Dec. 20–Nov. 11
14	Indiana	At all times (11)	...	Nov. 1–July 1	...	Jan. 1–Nov. 10
15	Long Island	4 days in Nov. (13)	...	Jan. 1–Nov. 1	Jan. 1–Nov. 1	Jan. 1–Nov. 1
16	Iowa	At all times	At all times	Jan. 1–Sept. 1	...	Dec. 15–Nov. 1
17	Kansas	...	...	At all times	...	Dec. 15–Nov. 15
18	Kentucky	Mar. 1–Sept. 1	...	Feb. 1–Nov. 15 (23)	Sept. 15–Nov. 15	Jan. 1–Nov. 15
19	Louisiana	Local Seasons	...	...	...	Mar. 1–Nov. 1
20	Maine	Dec. 16–Oct. 1 (12)	Dec. 1–Oct. 15 (2)	To May 1, 1911	April 1–Sept. 1	At all times
21	Maryland	Local laws	...	Dec. 1–Sept. 1	Dec. 25–Nov. 1	Dec. 25–Nov. 1
22	Massachusetts	To Nov. 1, 1910	...	To Oct. 1, 1910	Mar. 1–Oct. 1	Nov. 1–Oct. 1
23	Michigan	Dec. 1–Nov. 10 (12)	To 1913	Dec. 1–Oct. 15	...	Dec. 1–Oct. 15
24	Minnesota	Dec. 1–Nov. 10	Dec. 1–Nov. 10 (a)	...	...	Dec. 1–Oct. 1
25	Mississippi	Mar. 1–Nov. 15	...	...	...	Mar. 1–Nov. 1
26	Missouri	Jan. 1–Nov. 1	...	Jan. 1–June 1	...	Jan. 1–Nov. 1
27	Montana	Dec. 15–Sept. 1	Dec. 1–Sept. 1 (3)	...	...	At all times
28	Nebraska	At all times	At all times	At all times	...	Dec. 1–Nov. 15
29	Nevada	Nov. 15–Sept. 15 (a)	At all times (7)	...	...	Mar. 1–Sept. 15
30	New Hampshire	Dec. 15–Dec. 1 (17)	At all times	To Oct. 1, 1913	Mar. 1–Oct. 1	Dec. 15–Oct. 1
31	New Jersey	To Nov. 10, 1909	...	Jan. 1–Nov. 15 (24)	Jan. 1–Nov. 15 (24)	Jan. 1–Nov. 15 (24)
32	New Mexico	Dec. 1–Oct. 15 (a)	At all times	...	...	Feb. 1–Oct. 1
33	*New York	Nov. 1–Sept. 16*	At all times	Dec. 1–Oct. 1*	Dec. 1–Oct. 1*	Dec. 1–Nov. 1*
34	North Carolina	Feb. 1–Oct. 1	...	Local laws	...	Mar. 1–Nov. 1
35	North Dakota	Dec. 1–Nov. 10	At all times	...	...	Oct. 15–Sept. 1
36	Ohio	...	...	Oct. 31–Oct. 1	Dec. 5–Nov. 15	Dec. 5–Nov. 15
37	Oklahoma	At all times	At all times	...	...	Feb. 1–Oct. 15
38	Oregon	Nov. 1– July 15 (20)	...	Jan. 1–Oct. 1	...	Dec. 1–Oct. 1 (12)
39	Pennsylvania	Dec. 1–Nov. 15 (b)	...	Dec. 1–Oct. 1	Dec. 1–Oct. 15	Dec. 1–Nov. 1
40	Rhode Island	At all times (11)	...	Jan. 1–Nov. 1	Jan. 1–Nov. 1	Jan. 1–Nov. 1
41	South Carolina	Jan. 1–Sept. 1 (12)	...	...	...	Mar. 1–Nov. 15 (12)
42	South Dakota	Dec. 1–Nov. 1	To Jan. 1, 1911	...	...	Jan. 1–Sept. 1
43	Tennessee	To Oct. 1, 1911 (14)	...	Mar. 1–June 1 (12)	...	Mar. 1–Nov. 15
44	Texas	Jan. 1–Nov. 1 (a)	To July 1, 1912	...	...	Feb. 1–Nov. 1
45	Utah	Nov. 1–Oct. 1 (b)	At all times	...	...	At all times (12)
46	Vermont	Oct. 26–Oct. 31 (11)	At all times	Dec. 1–Sept. 15	May 1–Sept. 15	Dec. 1–Sept. 15
47	Virginia	Dec. 1–Sept. 1	...	Local laws	Feb. 1–Nov. 1	Feb. 1–Nov. 1 (12)
48	Washington	Dec. 15–Sept. 15	Nov. 1–Sept. 15 (a)	...	...	Jan. 1–Oct. 1
49	West Virginia	Dec. 16–Oct. 15	...	Jan. 1–Sept. 15	Jan. 1–Sept. 15	Dec. 20–Nov. 1
50	Wisconsin	Dec. 1–Nov. 11 (12)	At all times	Mar. 1–Sept. 1	Mar. 1–Sept. 1	To Oct. 1, 1915
51	Wyoming	Nov. 15–Sept. 15	Nov. 15–Sept. 15	...	...	At all times

1 Elk only. 2 Cow and calf moose and caribou, all year. 3 Moose, caribou, bison or Buffalo, all the year. 4 Prairie chicken—Massachusetts, closed season all year. Oklahoma, Jan. 1–Sept. 1. 5 Snipe—California, April 1–Oct. 15; Colorado, April 16–Sept. 10; New Hampshire, Dec. 1–Oct. 1. 6 Female protected all the year. 7 Antelope (males)—Nevada, Nov. 15–Sept. 15. 8 Rail—Connecticut, Jan. 1–Sept. 12. 10 Certain species. 11 Deer raised in inclosure may be killed at any time. 12 Local exceptions. 13 First two Wednesdays and first two Fridays after first Tuesday in November. 14 Except Fentress County, Jan. 1–Dec. 1. 15 In Suffolk County. 16 Plover—Missouri, Jan. 1–Aug. 1; Nebraska, Dec. 1–Sept. 15; 17 In Carroll and Coos counties, Dec. 1–Oct. 1; Grafton County, Dec. 15–Nov. 1. 18 Except July. 19 Except Mar. 1–April 21; Sundays and Mondays are also closed seasons for ducks and other waterfowl. 20 Female deer, Nov. 1–Sept. 1. 21 Swan, all year; Goose, May 1–Sept. 1. 22 Except May 15–June 15. 23 Except June 15–Sept. 15. 24 Southern Section, Northern Section, Dec. 2–Oct. 15. 25 Southern Section, Northern Section, Jan. 2–Oct. 15. Prohibitory laws against hunting doves and robins exist in nearly all States. Sale of game during close season is prohibited in most States. License fees from non-residents required in some States.

(a) Female deer and elk and deer without horns protected at all times. (b) Except deer without horns. Non-resident not permitted to kill.

*NEW YORK (Exceptions). DEER—Orange and Sullivan counties, Nov. 1–Oct. 16. Fawns at all times. Hunting with dogs, traps, or devices of any kind prohibited.

SQUIRREL—Exceptions. Richmond and Steuben counties all the year.

RABBIT, HARE—Exceptions, Clinton, Essex, Franklin, Fulton, Hamilton, Herkimer, Jefferson, Lewis, Saratoga, St. Lawrence, Warren and Washington counties, Jan. 3–Oct. 1.

QUAIL—Exception. Dutchess County, until 1910.

GROUSE—Exceptions. Steuben and Westchester counties, all the year.

PHEASANTS—Dutchess County, Jan. 1–Nov. 1.

WILD BIRDS—Catching, killing, or the possession of live or dead, and robbing of nests prohibited at all times—except English sparrow, crane, hawk, crow, owl, and blackbird.

Hunting and shooting on Sunday prohibited.

Export of game or birds taken in the State is prohibited.

FISH LAWS, NEW YORK STATE, OPEN SEASON.

Trout (Brook, Brown and Rainbow)—April 16 to August 31. Exceptions: Counties of Clinton, Essex, Franklin, Fulton, Hamilton, Lewis, Saratoga, St. Lawrence, Warren, Washington,

Several States, 1909.

IN THE UNITED STATES.

The first date of the close season and the first date of the open season are given. Open season may be found by reversing the dates.

Compiled and corrected to September 26, 1908.

BIRDS.

Grouse and Prairie Chicken.	Wild Turkey.	Pheasant.	Woodcock.	Duck, Goose, Swan.	Plover, Snipe, Rail.	
To Dec. 1, 1912	Apr. 1-Dec. 1 (6)	To Dec. 1, 1912	Mar. 15-Sept. 1	Mar. 15-Sept. 1	May 1-Nov. 1	1
Mar. 2-Sept. 1	....	....	....	Mar. 2-Sept. 1	Mar. 2-Sept. 1	2
Mar. 1-Oct. 15	Dec. 1-Sept. 15	Mar. 1-Oct. 15	....	....	Mar. 1-Oct. 15	3
Dec. 1-Oct. 31	May 1-Sept. 1	To Mar. 14, 1913	....	....	....	4
To Sept. 1, 1909	....	At all times	....	Feb. 15-Oct. 1	Feb. 15-Oct. 15 (5)	5
Oct. 2-Aug. 20	At all times	At all times	....	April 16-Sept. 10	Oct. 31-Aug. 1 (5)	6
Dec. 1-Oct. 1	....	Dec. 1-Oct. 1	Dec. 1-Oct. 1	Jan. 1-Sept. 1	Jan. 1-Sept. 1 (8)	7
....	....	Jan. 1-Nov. 15	....	Apr. 16-Oct. 1	Feb. 2-Sept. 1	8
Mar. 15-Sept. 1	Dec. 26-Nov. 1	Dec. 26-Nov. 1	Jan. 1-July 1	Apr. 1-Sept. 1	April 1-Sept. 1	9
....	Mar. 1-Nov. 1	....	....	April 1-Oct. 1	....	10
....	Mar. 15-Nov. 1	Mar. 15-Nov. 1	Feb. 1-Sept. 1	Feb. 1-Sept. 1 (10)	Mar. 15-Sept 1	11
Dec. 1-Aug. 15	....	Dec. 1-Sept. 1	....	Jan. 1-Sept. 15	Jan. 1-Sept. 15	12
To July 1, 1911	To July 1, 1913	To July 1, 1913	Dec. 1-Aug. 1	April 16-Sept. 1	May 2-Sept. 1	13
Jan. 1-Nov. 10	At all times	At all times	Jan. 1-July 1	April 1-Sept. 1	April 1-Sept. 1	14
Jan. 1-Nov. 1	....	Jan. 1-Nov. 1 (15)	Jan. 1-Nov. 1	Jan. 1-Oct. 1	Dec. 1-July 16	15
Dec. 1-Sept. 1	Dec. 15-Nov. 1	Dec. 15-Nov. 1	Jan. 1-July 10	April 15-Sept. 1	April 15-Sept. 1	16
Oct. 15-Sept. 15 (12)	....	To 1913	....	April 15-Sept. 1	Sept. 15-July 15	17
....	Feb. 1-Sept. 1	At all times	Feb. 1-June 20	April 1-Aug. 15	....	18
To Dec. 1, 1910	Apr. 15-Nov. 1 (6)	....	To Dec. 1, 1910	Mar. 1-Oct. 1	Mar. 1-Oct. 1	19
Dec. 1-Sept. 15	....	To 1913	Dec. 1-Sept. 15	Jan. 1-Sept. 1 (10)	May 1-Aug. 1	20
Dec. 25-Nov. 1	Dec. 25-Nov. 1	Dec. 25-Nov. 1	Dec. 25-Nov. 1 (18)	April 10-Nov 1	May 1-Aug. 15	21
Nov. 1-Oct. 1 (4)	....	At all times	Nov. 1-Oct. 1	Mar. 1-Sept. 1 (10)	Mar. 1-July 15	22
To 1910	To 1910	To 1910	Jan. 2-Sept. 1	Jan. 2-Sept. 1	Jan. 2-Sept. 1	23
Nov. 1-Sept. 1	....	To Jan. 1, 1910	Nov. 1-Sept. 1	Dec. 1-Sept. 1	Nov. 1-Sept. 1	24
....	May 1-Jan. 1 (6)	....	....	Mar. 1-Sept. 1	Mar. 1-Sept. 1	25
To Dec. 1, 1910	Feb. 1-Dec. 1	To Dec. 1, 1910	Jan. 1-Aug. 1	May 1-Sept. 15	May 1-Sept. 15 (16)	26
Dec. 1-Sept. 1	....	Dec. 1-Sept. 1	....	Dec. 1-Sept. 1	....	27
Dec. 1-Sept. 15	At all times.	At all times	....	April 11-Sept. 15	April 11-Sept. 15 (16)	28
Mar. 1-Sept. 15	....	....	Mar. 1-Sept. 15	Mar. 1-Sept. 15	Mar. 1-Sept. 15	29
Dec. 1-Oct. 1	....	....	Dec. 1-Oct. 1	Feb. 1-Oct. 1	Feb. 1-Oct. 1 (5)	30
Jan. 1-Nov. 15 (24)	Jan. 1-Nov. 15 (24)	Jan. 1-Nov. 15 (24)	Jan. 1-Nov. 15 (24)	Mar. 16-Nov. 1 (25)	Jan. 1-May 1	31
Jan. 1-Oct. 1	Jan. 1-Oct. 1	At all times	....	....	....	32
Dec. 1-Oct. 1*	....	To 1910*	Dec. 1-Oct. 1	Jan. 1-Sept. 16	Jan. 1-Sept. 16	33
....	Mar. 1-Nov. 1	....	Local laws	Local laws	....	34
Oct. 15-Sept. 1	....	Oct. 15-Sept. 1	Oct. 15-Sept. 1	May 1-Sept. 1	....	35
To Nov. 10, 1913	....	To Nov., 1913	Dec. 5-Sept. 1	Jan. 1-Sept. 1 (19)	Jan. 1-Sept. 1 (19)	36
At all times (4)	Jan. 1-Sept. 1	Jan. 1-Dec. 1	....	....	Jan. 1-Aug. 1	37
Dec. 1-Aug. 15	Dec. 1-Oct. 1	Dec. 1-Oct. 1	Dec. 1-Oct. 1	Feb. 1-Sept. 1	Jan. 1-Aug. 1	38
Dec. 1-Oct. 15	Dec. 1-Oct. 15	Dec. 1-Oct. 15	Dec. 1-Oct. 1	April 10-Sept. 1	Jan. 1-Sept. 1	39
Jan. 1-Nov. 1	....	To Oct. 1, 1910	Jan. 1-Nov. 1	April 1-Aug. 15	Jan. 1-Aug. 1	40
....	Mar. 1-Nov. 15 (12)	Mar. 1-Nov. 15 (12)	Mar. 1-Nov. 15 (12)	....	....	41
Jan. 1-Sept. 1	....	....	Jan. 1-Sept. 1	May 1-Sept. 1	May 15-Sept. 1	42
Mar. 1-Nov. 1	Mar. 1-Nov. 1 (12)	Jan. 1-Dec. 1	April 15-Oct. 1	April 15-Oct. 1	April 15-Oct. 1	43
To July 1, 1912	April 1-Nov. 1	To July 1, 1912	....	....	....	44
Dec. 1-Aug. 1	....	Dec. 1-Aug. 1	....	Jan. 1-Oct. 1	Jan. 1-Oct. 1	45
Dec. 1-Sept. 15	....	To Oct. 1, 1909	Dec. 1-Sept. 15	Jan. 1-Sept. 1	Dec. 1-Sept. 15	46
Feb. 1-Nov. 1 (12)	Feb. 1-Nov. 1 (12)	Feb. 1-Nov. 1 (12)	Feb. 1-Nov. 1 (12)	May 1-Oct. 15 (10)	Jan. 1-July 20	47
Jan. 1-Sept. 1	....	Jan. 1-Oct. 1	....	Mar. 1-Sept. 1 (12)	Mar. 1-Aug. 15	48
Dec. 15-Oct. 15	Dec. 15-Oct. 15	Dec. 15-Oct. 15	Nov. 2-July 15	April 1-Oct. 1	July 1-Mar. 1	49
Oct. 15-Oct. 1 (12)	....	To Oct. 1, 1915	Dec. 1-Sept. 1	Jan. 1-Sept. 1 (21)	Dec. 1-Sept. 1	50
Sept. 1-Aug. 1	....	To Sept. 1, 1912	....	May 1-Sept. 1	May 1-Sept. 1	51

and that portion of Herkimer County north of the Mohawk River, May 1 to August 31; counties of Allegany, Cattaraugus, Chautauqua, Cortland, Delaware, Livingston and Wyoming, April 16 to July 15; County of Chenango, April 16 to July 31; Genesee River in the County of Allegany, and Spring Brook in the County of Livingston, April 16 to August 31. Minimum length, six inches. Trout must not be sold. Not more than ten pounds of trout may be taken or transported by one person at one time. Trout must not be taken by any other method than angling.

Lake Trout and Whitefish.—May 1 to August 31. Exceptions: Lake Erie, Lake Ontario, and Otsego Lake, January 1 to October 31; counties of Ulster, Sullivan, Orange, Rockland, Westchester and Richmond (lake trout only), May 1 June 30; Lake Keuka (lake trout only), April 16 to August 31. Lake trout, minimum length, fifteen inches. Whitefish, minimum weight, two pounds in the round. Not more than twenty-five pounds of lake trout may be taken or transported by one person at one time.

Black Bass and Oswego Bass.—June 16 to December 31. Exceptions: Glen Lake, August 1 to October 31; Lake George and Schroon Lake, August 1 to December 15; town of Horicon and Trout Lake in the town of Bolton in Warren County, July 11 to December 31; Chautauqua and Cattaraugus counties, June 16 to October 15. Minimum length, ten inches. Limit per day to one person, twenty-four; to a boat, two or more persons, thirty-six; St. Lawrence River limit, twelve black bass to one person or twenty-four to one boat. Bass must not be taken by any other method than angling.

Pickerel and Pike.—May 1 to February 29. Exceptions: Lake George, June 16 to December 31; Glen Lake, June 16 to October 31. Pike, minimum length, ten inches. Pickerel, minimum length (St. Lawrence River), twenty inches.

Muscallonge.—June 1 to February 29. Exceptions: Chautauqua and Cattaraugus counties, June 16 to October 15. Minimum length, twenty-four inches.

Salmon.—March 1 to August 15.

(Long Island, Open Season.)

Trout.—Last Friday in March to August 30.

Lake Trout and Rainbow Trout.—April 1 to September 30.

Black Bass.—May 30 to December 31.

NOTE.—The State Fish and Game Laws apply where not in conflict with the Long Island provisions.

Lawn Tennis:

THE ranking of leading players as passed by the Executive Committee of the National Association, January 18, 1908, was as follows:

Class 1—Owe 2-6 of 15—W. A. Larned, B. C. Wright. Class 2 (scratch)—Karl H. Behr, R. D. Little. Class 3—1-6 of 15—Robert Le Roy, Clarence Hobart. Class 4—2-6 of 15—E. P. Larned, R. C. Seaver, Irving C. Wright, F. C. Colston, Henry Mollenhauer. Class 5—3-6 of 15—T. R. Pell, T. D. E. Jones, H. L. Westfall, F. C. Anderson, N. W. Niles, J. R. Carpenter, Jr., W. F. Johnson, Nat Emerson. Doubles ranking—Class 1—Handicap 2-6 of 15—Alexander and Hackett. Class 2 (scratch)—Larned and Clothier, Little and Hackett, B. Wright and Little. Class 3—1-2 of 15—Pell and Le Roy, Grant and Westfall, Leonard and Watson, Johnson and Johnson. Class 4—Receive 15—Neeley and Emerson, Thornton and Grant.

National Indoor Championships, New York, February 23-29. Singles—Wylie C. Grant, New York Tennis Club, defeated G. F. Touchard, 6—2, 6—8, 6—3, 6—4. F. B. Alexander and H. H. Hackett defeated W. B. Cragin, Jr., and M. S. Charlock, 6—3, 6—1, 6—4. Miss Marie Wagner won in the women's singles from Mrs. Frederick Schmitz, London, 6—3, 6—2, and in doubles Mrs. W. H. Pouch and Miss Elizabeth H. Moore defeated Mrs. A. H. MacCarthy and Miss Margaret Johnson, 13—11, 6—3.

All-Comers National Championship, out-door tournament, with 145 entries, Newport, August 18-28. Singles—Beals C. Wright defeated F. B. Alexander, 6—3, 6—3, 6—3, in the finals, but was defeated in the challenge round by W. A. Larned, title holder, 6—1, 6—2, 8—6. Champions in former years were: R. D. Sears, 1884-7; H. W. Slocum, 1888-9; O. S. Campbell, 1890-2; R. D. Wrenn, 1893-4 and 1896-7; F. H. Hovey, 1895; M. D. Whitman, 1898-0; W. A. Larned, 1901-2 and 1907-8; H. L. Doherty, 1903; H. Ward, 1904; B. C. Wright, 1905, and W. J. Clothier, 1906.

Important tennis contests, in chronological order, during the year were as follows:

Claud M. Butlin won the first international tournament in Mexico, April 19.

Women's Intercity, New York, April 25. Singles—Mrs. Barger-Wallach, New York, defeated Miss Edna Wildey, 6—3, 6—1. Doubles—Miss E. Sears and Miss M. Fenno, Boston, defeated Misses P. and D. Green, 7—5, 6—4. Mixed doubles—W. A. Larned and Mrs. A. H. MacCarthy defeated Miss J. A. Adee and R. Little, 6—3, 6—4. September 17, New York. Singles—Miss Emily W. Scott, New York, defeated Miss M. Johnson, 6—3, 3—6, 7—5.

Princeton defeated Columbia at Princeton, April 28, 5 matches to 4. Yale defeated Princeton at Princeton, May 9, 8 matches to 1. Harvard defeated Yale at New Haven, May 30, 5 matches to 4.

New England Championship at Hartford, June 10-13—H. L. Westfall, New York, defeated G. H. Nettleton, Yale, in the singles finals, 6—4, 6—1, 8—6, and T. R. Pell and and E. T. Gross defeated F. C. Inman and F. E. Howard in the doubles, 9—7, 6—2, 6—1. In the challenge round, T. R. Pell successfully defended his title against Westfall, 10—8, 6—3, 2—6, 8—6.

Metropolitan Championships, June 15. Singles—Ross Burchard defeated G. F. Touchard, 6—4, 9—7, 5—7, 6—1. Doubles—F. B. Alexander and H. H. Hackett defeated H. Torrance, Jr., and I. C. Wright, 6—2, 6—2, 6—2. Women's singles—Miss Elizabeth H. Moore defeated Miss Margaret Johnson, 6—2, 7—5. Doubles—Misses E. and N. Wildey defeated Misses E. Little and L. Hammond, 6—4, 2—6, 6—0. Mixed doubles—Mrs. A. G. Miles and S. C. Millett defeated Miss Elsie Little and I. C. Wright, 6—4, 9—7.

Women's National Championships, at Philadelphia, June 23-27. Singles—Mrs. Barger-Wallach, New York, defeated Miss Marie Wagner in the final round, 4—6, 6—1, 6—3. Challenge round, Mrs. Barger-Wallach defeated Miss Evelyn Sears, Boston, 6—2, 1—6, 6—3. Doubles—Miss M. Curtis and Miss E. Sears, Boston, defeated Miss C. Neely and Miss M. Stover, Chicago, 6—3, 5—7, 9—7. Mixed doubles—Miss E. Rotch and N. W. Niles defeated L. Hammond and R. D. Little, 6—4, 4—6, 6—4.

All-England Championship, Wimbledon, June 30—A. W. Gore defeated H. R. Barrett, 6—3, 6—2, 4—6, 3—6, 6—4. Norman E. Brooks did not defend the title. Mrs. Sterry won the women's singles, and in the absence of Miss May Sutton, of California, became champion of England. Olympic championships—J. G. Ritchie, England, won the gold medal for men and Mrs. Lambert Chambers, England, won the gold medal for women.

Gulf States Championship, New Orleans, June 25—Thornton and Grant, Atlanta, defeated Logan and Gardner, in doubles, 8—3, 6—3, 6—1, and Post won the singles. Southern Championship at Atlanta—Nat Thornton defeated Whitehead, of Virginia, in singles, 6—1, 6—2, 3—6, 7—5. Doubles—H. G. Whitehead and J. H. Winston, Norfolk, Va., defeated Grant and Thornton.

Middle States Championship, Orange L. T. C., New Jersey, July 3-4. Men's singles—Edward P. Larned, Orange L. T. C., defeated N. W. Niles, 6—1, 6—2, 6—3. Challenge round—W. A. Larned defaulted to E. P. Larned. Doubles—W. A. Larned and G. L. Wrenn defeated W. J. Clothier and E. W. Leonard, 6—4, 7—5, 10—8. Larned and Wrenn, challengers, defeated H. H. Hackett and R. D. Little, holders, 7—5, 7—5, 8—6. Women's singles—Miss Marie Wagner defeated Miss E. Scott in the finals, 6—1, 2—6, 8—6. Miss Carrie B. Neely retained her championship, as Miss Wagner forfeited because of accident. Doubles—Mrs. A. H. MacCarthy and Miss Johnson defeated Miss M. Wagner and Miss E. Marous, 6—8, 6—2, 6—2.

New York State Championships, N. Y. A. C. Courts, Travers Island, July 21-27—H. J. Mollenhauer defeated P. B. Hawk, in final round, 3—6, 6—2, 6—4, 7—5. Challenge round—H. H. Hackett defeated Mollenhauer, 6—3, 4—6, 6—3, 6—3, and this being his third successive Hackett gained permanent possession of the cup. Doubles—R. H. Palmer and G. F. Touchard defeated H. J. Mollenhauer and H. L. Westfall, 6—1, 6—4, 6—3.

Longwood and Eastern Doubles, Eighteenth Annual, Boston, July 27 to August 5. Singles—R. D. Little, New York, defeated B. C. Wright, Boston, in finals, 6—4, 2—6, 6—3, 6—1. W. A. Larned, Annapolis, defeated Little in challenge round, 6—4, 6—1, 6—8. Doubles—Wright and Little defeated Larned and G. L. Wrenn, 6—1, 4—6, 4—6, 6—2, 7—5. Preliminary doubles, rounds, at Crescent A. C., Brooklyn, August 13—Wright and Little defeated Whitehead and Winston, Virginia, 6—0, 6—3, 6—2. August 14—Wright and Little defeated Emerson and Waidner, Chicago, 7—5, 6—4, 6—3. Finals, Newport, August 18—H. H. Hackett and F. B. Alexander, New York, successfully defended their title against Wright and Little, 6—1, 7—5, 6—0.

Western Championship, Chicago, August 3. Singles—Nat Emerson defeated L. H. Waldner (challenger), 8—10, 6—0, 3—6, 6—1, 7—5. Doubles—Emerson and Waldner.

Lawn Tennis Cup, Southampton, L. I., August 11-15. Winners. Singles—W. J. Clothier. Doubles—W. A. Larned and R. D. Wrenn. Mixed doubles—Miss Edna Wildey and N. W. Niles.

Northwestern Championship, Minneapolis, August 8. Singles—N. Emerson, Cincinnati. Doubles—Waidner and Emerson forfeited to Graves and Adams, St. Paul.

National Association, Twenty-ninth Annual Tourney, 145 entries, Newport, August 18-28. Singles—Beals C. Wright defeated F. B. Alexander, 6—3, 6—3, 6—3. W. A. Larned defeated Wright in challenge round, 6—1, 6—2, 8—6.

Middle West Tournament, Omaha, August 21. Singles—C. S. Peters, Chicago. Doubles—C. D. Jones, St. Louis and A. Scribner, Omaha.

International, Twenty-second Annual, Niagara-on-the-Lake, Ont., August 24-27. Men's singles—Nat Niles, Boston, defeated Johnston, Philadelphia, 6—4, 6—4, 3—6, 8—6. Women's singles—Miss Wagner, New York, defeated Miss Moyes, Toronto, 6—3, 6—2. Miss May Sutton defaulted in challenge round.

Missouri Valley Championship, Kansas City, August 31. Singles—H. L. Brewster, St. Joseph. Doubles—Brewster and A. E. Sterling.

Tri-State Tourney, Cincinnati, August 31. Singles—Robert Le Roy, New York, defeated Nat Emerson (challenger), 6—0, 7—5, 6—4. R. C. Seaver, Boston, was the runner up. Emerson and W. P. Hunt won the doubles and Karl Little and Miss H. McLaughlin, the mixed doubles.

State Championships, Massachusetts. Singles—N. W. Niles defeated D. P. Rhodes but lost to R. C. Seaver in challenge round, 6—2, 6—3, 4—6, 5—7, 6—3. Central New Jersey. Singles—Dean Mathey defeated O. H. Hinck, 6—4, 6—3, 6—3. Doubles—Mathey and L. L. James defeated Aitken and Gordon, 6—0, 6—3, 6—4. Connecticut—Dr. P. B. Hawk defeated E. Q. Jackson (challenger), 6—2, 9—7, 6—1. Michigan—N. Bundy defeated H. G. Stevens. Ohio. Singles—E. B. Dewhurst defeated G. L. Wyeth (title holder). Doubles—P. Collins and H. C. Wick defeated Wyeth and H. F. Pattee. Wisconsin. Singles—R. J. Crozier, Philadelphia. Maine. Singles—D. P. Rhodes defeated H. Williston. Doubles—G. Bodman and D. P. Rhodes won. Maryland. Singles—Robert Le Roy defeated E. B. Dewhurst, 6—4, 6—3, 6—2. Doubles—J. A. C. Colston and Dewhurst defeated Le Roy and R. A. Holden. Pennsylvania. Singles—E. B. Dewhurst (challenger), defeated J. R. Carpenter, 6—0, 6—0, 9—7. New Jersey. Singles—R. H. Palmer. Women's singles—Miss Marie Wagner. Doubles—R. H. Palmer and H. C. Martin. Rhode Island. Singles—J. D. E. Jones. Doubles—T. Cross and E. N. Dana.

Metropolitan Lawn Tennis League, September 14—Won by the New York Lawn Tennis Club, T. R. Pell in singles and Pell and R. H. Palmer in doubles. Final standing of teams with games won and lost: New York L. T. C., 16—2; Crescent A. C., 12—6; Kings County L. T. C., 11—4; Montclair and Hamilton Grange L. T. C., 7—11; Knickerbocker F. C., 4—11; Brooklyn L. T. C., 3—15. Kings County and Knickerbocker forfeited a series.

International Series Boston, September 17-19—M. J. G. Ritchie, London, defeated Beals C. Wright, Boston, 6—1, 6—3, 6—2, and W. A. Larned, Summit, N. J., defeated John G. Parke, Dublin, 6—3, 6—3, 7—5. H. H. Hackett and F. B. Alexander defeated Ritchie and Parke in the only doubles match, 6—3, 2—6, 7—5, 6—1. Larned defeated Ritchie, 4—6, 6—3, 6—2, 6—3, and Wright defeated Parke, 8—10, 3—6, 6—4, 7—5, 6—2, in the final singles, earning the right to challenge for the Davis International Cup against Australia at Melbourne, December 5.

Pacific Coast Championships at Del Monte, Cal., September 12-18. Men's singles—M. Long, San Francisco, defeated W. F. Johnson, Philadelphia, 8—6, 6—2, 6—4. Long, challenger, defeated M. Loughlin for title. Women's singles—Miss May Sutton defeated Miss M. Hotchkiss and gained permanent possession of cup by defeating her sister, Miss Florence Sutton in challenge round. Men's doubles—Irving C. Wright and N. W. Niles defeated A. Bell and M. Freeman, but lost to M. McLoughlin and G. Janes in challenge round.

Philadelphia Women's Championship, September 26—Miss Rachel Harlan, Belmont Cricket Club, defeated Miss A. E. Wallace, Moorestown C. C., 6—2, 8—6.

Intercollegiate Championship, Merion C. C. Grounds, Philadelphia, October 5-9. Singles—N. W. Niles, Harvard, defeated A. S. Dabney, Harvard, 7—5, 6—1, 3—6, 6—2. Doubles—Tilden and Thayer, Pennsylvania, defeated Holden and Bundy, Yale, 6—2, 5—7, 8—6, 5—7, 6—6, 6—4, 11—9, 6—4.

Racquet and Court Tennis.

THE year furnished a number of unusually interesting competitions, the more important in their order of occurrence being as follows:

Intercity Doubles Racquet Match, Philadelphia and New York, January-February—Fincke and Clark, New York, defeated Brooke and Cassatt, Philadelphia, in the first series, 14—17, 15—10, 15—10, 12—15, 15—6. Second series—Waterbury and Whitney, New York, defeated Spencer and Rosegarten, Philadelphia, 15—6, 15—5, 15—11, 13—18, 15—8. In nine years New York has won eight matches.

National Amateur Racquet Championship, Singles, Boston, February 17-22—Quincy A. Shaw, Boston, defeated Percy D. Haughton in the finals, 9—15, 15—7, 15—3, 11—15, 15—5. Doubles, at Philadelphia—Scott and Boylston, Boston, defeated Clarke and Hewitt, New York, 15—12, 15—6, 1—15, 15—1, 15—1.

Gold Racquet Championship, C. H. Mackay Racquet, Tuxedo Park, N. Y., February-

RACQUET AND COURT TENNIS—*Continued.*

March—J. Gordon Douglas, New York, defeated F. F. Rolland, Montreal, Canadian champion, 15—8, 15—6, 18—16.

Eustace Miles, who came over for the open court tennis tournament in March with Peter Latham, the professional champion, played several exhibition matches. At Tuxedo Latham conceded Miles 15 and won, 6—2, 6—3, 6—5. The next day conceding Jay Gould the same odds. Gould defeated Latham, 4—6, 6—1, 6—2, 6—1.

National Amateur Court Tennis Championship, New York, April 8-12—E. H. Miles, England, defeated C. E. Sands, 6—2, 6—1, 6—3, and Payne Whitney defeated T. A. Havemeyer, 5—6, 6—4, 6—0, 6—0. Finals, Miles defeated Whitney, 6—4, 6—0, 6—1. Challenge round, Jay Gould defeated Miles, 6—2, 6—4, 1—6, 6—2.

Gold Racquet Championship for T. Suffern Tailer Emblem, Tuxedo, April 18-19—Pierre Lorillard, Jr., defeated Kingdon Gould, 6—4, 6—4, 6—2. Finals, Jay Gould defeated Lorillard, 6—0, 6—1, 6—0, and became permanent owner of the trophy.

World's Amateur Court Tennis Championship, London, May 9-16—Eustace Miles defeated V. H. Pennell in the finals, 4—6, 6—5, 6—1, 6—3. Challenge round, Jay Gould (title holder), defeated Miles, 6—0, 6—2, 1—6, 6—1.

Cecil (Punch) Fairs, world's professional champion at court tennis, who defeated E. Johnson for the title and $1.000 a side, July 4, winning seven of thirteen sets, was challenged by Jay Gould for a home-and-home series, in New York and London, in 1909.

Polo.

There being only one entry for the Club Championship of the Polo Association no game was played in 1908. In the Junior Championship at Van Cortlandt Park, September 5, the New Haven Polo Club (J. B. Thomas, Jr., H. Drury, L. E. Stoddard and J. Watson Webb) defeated Squadron A (Walter McClure, Louis Neilson, J. H. Hunt, and L. J. Hunt) 15 1-2 goals to 4 3-4.

Important cup events of the season with final games and scores follow:

Country Club Cups. Westchester—Meadow Brook defeated Country Club, Westchester, 10 1-4 goals to 6. Second Great Neck Challenge Cup—Meadow Brook defeated Rockaway, 10 1-2 goals to 9 1-2. Philadelphia Country Club Cups—Rockaway defeated New Haven, 15 1-2 goals to 10. Woodcrest Cups, Philadelphia Country Club—Meadow Brook defeated Rockaway, 13 1-2 goals to 9 1-4. Bryn Mawr Club Cups—Devon defeated Philadelphia Country Club, 11 1-2 goals to 9. Ladies' Challenge Cups, Bryn Mawr—Rockaway defeated New Haven, 15 1-2 goals to 10. Hempstead Cups, Meadow Brook—Meadow Brook defeated Great Neck, 9 goals to 2 3-4. Meadow Brook Club Cups—Meadow Brook defeated Rockaway, 13 goals to 9 3-4. Westbury Challenge Cups—Meadow Brook defeated Bryn Mawr, 12 goals to 3 1-2. Independence Cups, Rockaway Club—Great Neck defeated New Haven Freebooters, 9 goals to 3 1-4. Rockaway Hunting Club Cups—Meadow Brook defeated Rockaway, 11 1-4 goals to 8 1-4. Blizzard Cups, Rockaway Hunting Club—Squadron A defeated Meadow Brook II. Cedarhurst Challenge Cup, Rockaway—Meadow Brook defeated Rockaway, 16 goals to 5. Rumson Challenge Cups—Squadron A defeated Meadow Brook Freebooters, 15 1-2 goals to 4. Monmouth Challenge Cups—New Haven defeated Squadron A, 9 goals to 5 1-2. Narragansett Cups, Point Judith Country Club—Meadow Brook defeated Dedham, 8 goals to 4 1-2. Point Judith Cups—Meadow Brook, by default of Dedham. Newport Cups—New Haven defeated Westchester Leopards, 7 to 3. Westchester Cups at Newport—Meadow Brook defeated Bryn Mawr, 17 1-2 goals to 10. Freshmen Cups, Narragansett Pier—New Haven defeated Dedham, 8 1-2 to 1-2.

Fencing.

Tournaments held under the auspices of the Amateur Fencers' League of America during the year resulted as follows:

Three-Weapon Team Cup, January 4—Won by the New York Athletic Club; V. Curti, foils; W. D. Lyon, duelling sword; A. G. Anderson, sabre.

Novice Foil Competition, January 28—Won by A. C. Staley; A. S. Lyon, second; D. H. Smith, third.

Junior Championships, Foils, February 24—Won by G. K. Bainbridge, New York A. C.; G. H. Breed, Fencers' Club of New York, second; W. E. Harries, Cornell, third.

President Medals given by Dr. Graeme Hammond, March 18, five bouts, three weapons—Won by W. L. Bowman, New York A. C., 10 bouts; F. G. Byrne, New York A. C., 7 bouts, second; G. H. Breed, Fencers' Club, 6 bouts.

National Championships, April 23-24. Duelling Swords—Won by P. Benzenberg, New York Turn-Verein; S. McCullagh, New York A. C., second; G. H. Breed, Fencers' Club, third. Foils—W. L. Bowman, N. Y. A. C., won; V. P. Curti, N. Y. A. C., second; G. H. Breed, third. Sabres—G. W. Postgale, New York Turn-Verein, won; C. A. Bill, N. Y. A. C., second; F. J. Byrne, third.

Other important competitions of the year resulted as follows:

Colleges—West Point defeated Pennsylvania, 7 bouts to 2; Pennsylvania defeated Yale, 7 to 6; West Point defeated Columbia, 6 to 3; Columbia, defeated Pennsylvania, 5 to 4; Annapolis defeated Columbia, 5 to 4. Triangular meet—Columbia 8 vs. Pennsylvania 1; Yale 5 vs. Columbia 4; Yale 9 vs. Pennsylvania 0; West Point defeated Harvard, 9 to 0. Triangular meet—Annapolis, 16; Cornell, 7; Pennsylvania, 4. Intercollegiate Championship, March 28—West Point, 22; Annapolis, 21; Cornell, 15; Columbia, 15; Yale, 7; Massachusetts Technology, 1.

Saltus Cup and Medals—Won by Fencers' Club team, composed of Charles Tatham, W. Scott O'Connor, and G. H. Breed.

Women's Intercity Championship—Won by Philadelphia team, composed of Miss Bertha Pollock, Miss Emily Sailer, and Miss Helen Smith.

European Open-Air Championship at Nice—Won by M. Bernard Gravier; M. Duquet, second.

Curling.

ANNUAL events held under the auspices of the Grand National Curling Club of America, date and place of their occurrence in 1908, were as follows:

North vs. South of Scotland, Van Cortlandt Lake, New York, January 11. North—George Grieve, skip, 10; Alexander Fraser, skip, 12; Thomas T. Archibald, skip, 12; John Leslie, skip, 20. Total, 54. South—William Stewart, skip, 10; Robert Boyd, skip, 9; Thomas Nicholson, skip, 13, Thomas Wigley, skip, 4. Total, 36. George Grieve, Umpire. Won by North. Dalrymple Medal won by the North. Hoagland Flag won by John Leslie. Kirkpatrick Medal won by Alexander Fraser.

Mitchell Medal Match, Van Cortlandt, New York, January 28.—St. Andrew's, No. 1, J. F. Conley, Skip, 15 vs. Terrace City, S. A. Peene, skip, 10. St. Andrew's, No. 2, Bye. 2d Tie. February 18.—St. Andrew's, No. 1, J. F. Conley, skip, 15 vs. St. Andrew's, No. 2, John Leslie, skip, 12. Thomas J. Watt, Umpire. Medal won by James F. Conley.

Gordon Medal Match, Boston, Mass., January 30.—Thistle, N. Y., Thomas J. Watt, skip, 16 vs. St. Andrew's, Thomas Nicholson, skip, 12. Country Club, Brookline, G. H. Wendeler, skip, 10 vs. Caledonian, Thomas T. Archibald, skip, 17. Boston Curling Association, John McGaw, skip, 19 vs. Tuxedo, Dr. E. C. Rushmore, skip, 13. Brae Burn, Newton. Bye. 2d Tie.—Thistle, T. J. Watt, skip, 15 vs. Caledonian, T. T. Archibald, skip, 14. Boston Curling Association, John McGaw, skip, 18 vs. Brae Burn, G. H. Phelps, skip, 12. 3d Tie.—Thistle, T. J. Watt, skip, 18 vs. Boston Curling Association, John McGaw, skip, 9. Match won by Thistle Curling Club of New York, John McGaw, Umpire. Thomas J. Watt, skip.

International Two Rink Match for the Gordon Medal, at Montreal, February 7—Canada, Lachine Curling Club, W. O. Ryde, skip, 25; Caledonian, Montreal, Traid Lyall, skip, 24. Total, 49 vs. Grand National Curling Club, St. Andrew's, N. Y., John Leslie, skip, 11; Utica Curling Club, H. L. Ridings, skip, 17. Total, 28. Won by Canada.

Match for Silver Cup, presented by the Utica Curling Club, Van Cortlandt, New York, February 12—Terrace City, John Kellock, skip, 22 vs. Caledonian, No. 1, Thomas T. Archibald, skip, 13; St. Andrew's, No. 1, John Leslie, skip, 16 vs. Caledonian, No. 3, R. Dalglish, skip, 17; St. Andrew's, No. 3, Thomas Nicholson, skip, 8 vs. Van Cortlandt, Isiah Frazier, skip, 21; Thistle, Thomas J. Watt, skip, 9 vs. Caledonian, No. 2, J. Stalker, skip, 18; St. Andrew's, No. 2, Robert Boyd, skip, 26 vs. Yonkers, George Grieve, skip, 11; Empire, Manhattan Curling Club. Bye. 2d Tie.—Terrace City, John Kellock, skip, 19 vs. Caledonian, No. 2, J. Stalker, skip, 13; Van Cortlandt, Isiah Frazier, skip, 17 vs. Caledonian, No. 3, R. Dalglish, skip, 13; St. Andrew's No. 2, R. Boyd, skip, 10 vs. Empire, Manhattan, William Stewart, skip, 18. Terrace City. Bye. 3d Tie—Van Cortlandt, 13 vs. Empire, Manhattan, 11. Terrace City. Bye. 4th Tie.—Van Cortlandt, 16 vs. Terrace City, 15. Won by Van Cortlandt, Isiah Frazier, skip. James F. Conley, Umpire.

Scots vs. Americans, John Patterson Medal, Van Cortlandt, New York, February 22.—Scots, Forrest Macull, skip, 12; Robert Lauder, skip, 17; T. T. Archibald, skip, 20; R. Dalglish, skip, 13. Total, 62 vs. Americans—George Grieve, skip, 14; John Kellock, skip, 10; Edward Sheridan, skip, 13; Isiah Frazier, skip, 17. Total 54. Won by Scots. James F. Conley, Umpire.

Massachusetts vs. New York, Boston, Mass., January 31.—Massachusetts, Brae Burn, G. H. Phelps, skip, 11; Country Club, Brookline, Herbert Jaques, skip, 15; Boston Curling Association, John McGaw, skip, 14. Total 40 vs. New York, Caledonian, T. T. Archibald, skip, 6; Thistle, A. F. Dickson, skip, 9; St. Andrew's, Thomas Nicholson, skip, 14. Total 29. Won by Massachusetts.

CANADIAN RECORDS.

Important events held under the auspices of the Royal Caledonian Curling Club, Montreal, were as follows: Victorian Jubilee trophy and souvenir prize—Montreal Club, 30 vs. Ottawa Club, 25. Governor General's prize—Rideau Club, 36 vs. Caledonian Club, 35. Gordon International medal —Canada, 49 vs. United States, 28. Montreal A. A. A. trophy—Montreal Club, 153 vs. St. Lawrence Club, 112. Ladies R. C. C. trophy—Montreal Ladies' Club, 28 vs. St. Lawrence Ladies' Club, 16. Montreal C. C. Centenary Cup—won by Caledonian Club.

Quoits.

THE forty-second annual contest for the Bell medal, emblematic of the quoit championship of the United States, was held under the auspices of the Grand National Curling Club of America at Van Cortlandt Park, New York, September 17, and was won by Thomas Nicholson, St. Andrew's Curling Club. There were twelve competitors. John Pepper, holder of the emblem for 1908 did not enter. Nicholson was the runner up in 1907. The scores:

FIRST ROUND. Thomas Nicholson, St. Andrew's, 21, defeated Thomas Archibald, Caledonian, 5; E. Sheridan, Terrace City of Yonkers, 21, defeated John Leslie, St. Andrew's, 14; J. Thomson, Caledonian, 21, defeated John Rennie, St. Andrew's, 8; J. F. Conley, St. Andrew's, 21, defeated William Stewart, Empire-Manhattan, 9; H. Archibald, Caledonian, 21, defeated John Watt, Thistle, 13; F. McGregor, 21, defeated John McGregor, Empire-Manhattan, 11.

SECOND ROUND Thomas Nicholson, 21, defeated H. Archibald, 19; E. Sheridan, 21, defeated F. McGregor, 15; J. Thomas, 21, defeated J. F. Conley, 11.

THIRD ROUND. E. Sheridan, 21, defeated J. Thomson, 8; Thomas Nicholson, a bye.

FINAL ROUND. Thomas Nicholson—0, 0, 0, 0, 2, 0, 2, 1, 1, 2, 2, 0, 0, 2, 0, 0, 1, 1, 2, 1, 2, 2. Total, 21. E. Sheridan—1, 1, 1, 1, 0, 1, 1, 0, 0, 0, 0, 1, 2, 0, 1, 1, 0, 0, 1, 2. Total, 14.

Referee—Thomas Wigley, Terrace City Club of Yonkers.

Roque.

THE National Roque tournament was held at Norwich, Ct., August 17-25. Fourteen clubs were represented, two players coming from Topeka and Chicago. Officers elected were: President, J. H. McDonald, Chicago; First Vice-President, J. C. Kirk, Philadelphia; Second Vice-President, C. G. Williams, Washington; Third Vice-President, H. Bosworth, New London, Ct.; Secretary and Treasurer, N. L. Bishop, Norwich. First and second prizes were given in each of three divisions awarded on games won and lost as follows:

First Division—Edward Clark, Springfield, Mass., 12—2; Harold Bosworth, New London and J. F. Carleton, Springfield, 11—3 (Bosworth won the play-off).

Second Division—Harold Clark, Springfield, 11—1; Dr. B. Brooks, Philadelphia, 10—2.

Third Division—R. H. Steele, Springfield, 12—0; C. H. Goldey, Philadelphia, 8—1. E. Clark, who won the championship, is only 14 years of age. He made a record of fifteen minutes in one match.

prize winners with their points and standing were: W. Lemke, Rochester, N. Y., 110, twenty-eighth; G. Handelfinger, St. Louis, 109, thirtieth; J. Bissinger, New York, 108, thirty-first; M. Hess, Philadelphia, 104, thirty-ninth; G. E. Kern, St. Louis, 103, forty-first; H. Sexpel, Boston, 102, forty-third, and Ray Moore, New York, 100, forty-eighth.

Wrestling.

Two wrestling bouts among professionals of special interest to Americans was the defeat of Joe Rogers, of New York, by George Hackenschmidt, the "Russian Lion," in London, January 30, which Hackenschmidt won in two falls of 7m. 35s. and 6m. 45s., and the later defeat of Hackenschmidt in Chicago, April 3, by Frank Gotch. In the latter match after 1h. and 45m. without a fall for either man Hackenschmidt quit and Gotch became the world's champion heavyweight wrestler.

Intercollegiate bouts during the season resulted as follows: February—Princeton, 5 bouts, vs. Pennsylvania, 2; Yale, 5 vs. Princeton, 2; Cornell, 5 vs. Columbia, 2; Yale, 4 vs. Pennsylvania, 3; Princeton, 6 vs. Columbia, 1; Yale 6, vs. Princeton, 1. March—Yale, 6 vs. Cornell, 1; Princeton, 5 vs. Pennsylvania, 2; Yale, 7 vs. Columbia, 0; Princeton, 4 vs. Cornell 2. In a special match, R. Folwell, Pennsylvania, defeated R. B. Foster, Yale. The fourth annual Intercollegiate Championships were held at Pennsylvania University, March 20, and resulted as follows: Yale 10 points; Pennsylvania, 6; Princeton and Cornell, 3 each; Columbia, 0. Winners were: 115-pound class—Yerger, Pennsylvania; 125-pound class—L. Dole, Yale; 135-pound class—G. Dole, Yale; 145-pound class—Waite, Pennsylvania; 158-pound class, Parker, Yale; 175-pound class—Foster, Yale; heavyweight, Talbert, Cornell.

The National Championships of the A. A. U., in Madison Square Garden Concert Hall, New York, April 13, resulted as follows: 105-pound class—R. Schwartz, Boys' Club, New York; 115-pound class—George Mehnert, Newark Turn-Verein; 125-pound class—L. A. Dole, Yale; 135-pound class—G. S. Dole, Yale; 145-pound class—Max Weily, German-American A. C., New York; 158-pound class—C. Anderson, Swedish Gymnasium, Boston; heavyweight—J. Gunderson, Dovre Sporting Club, New York.

Skating.

LACK of good ice during the early season of 1907-8 carried all ice competitions over into February, results of important skating fixtures in their order being as follows:

Amateur Championships.—Montreal A. A. A. open air rink, February 3. Winners: One mile Junior—Russell Wheeler, Montreal, 3.14 1-5. 220 yds.—O. B. Bush, Vancouver, 20 4-5s. 880 yds., backwards—R. Wheeler, Montreal, 1.33 3-5. One mile—Fred Logan, Montreal, 3.22. 220-yd. hurdles—Fred. Robson, Toronto, 30s. 880 yds.—Edward Lamy, Saranac Lake, N. Y., 1.26 4-5. Three miles—E. Lamy, 9.53.

International Indoor Championship.—Duquesne Gardens, Pittsburgh, February 5-6. Winners in finals. Quarter-mile—E. Lamy, Saranac Lake, N. Y., 40s. Half-mile—Fred Robson, Toronto, 1.19 4-5. One mile—E. Lamy, 2.44 (old record 2.53). Two miles—E. Lamy, 6.11 4-5 (one heat in 5.48 3-5). Five miles—A. Anderson, Chicago, 15.07 3-5 (old record 15.09).

Eastern Amateur Championships.—Orange Lake, Newburgh, N. Y., February 12. Edward Lamy, the 17-year-old Saranac Lake skater, won the quarter-mile, half-mile, one-mile and five-mile events in respective times of 35 1-5s. (equalling record), 1.30, 3.19 1-5 and 17.06. A. R. Little, Newburgh, won the mile novice in 3.30 2-5.

National Championships.—Verona Lake, Montclair, N. J., February 22. One mile novice—G. V. Conniff, New York, 3.38. One mile championship—W. Sutphen, Brooklyn, 3.11 2-5. Three miles—W. Sutphen, 10.38. Two mile handicap—E. A. Leach, Newark (120 yds.), 6.32. Two mile relay (scratch), Verona Lake Skating Association team—(Sadeback, McCrowe, Williams and Palliser), 6.27 4-5.

Amateur Championships of Europe.—At Klagenfurt, Austria, February, 1908. 500 metres (546.8 yds.)—M. Oeholm, Stockholm, 47 1-5s. 1,500 metres (1,640.42 yds.)—Mathieson, Christiania, 2.29 2-5. 5,000 metres (3 miles 188 6-10 yds.)—Oeholm, 9.01 1-5. 10,000 metres—Oeholm, 18.24. International Championships—At Davos, Switzerland, February, 1908. 500 metres—Wikander, Helsingfors, 44 2-5s. (new world's record). 1,500 metres—O. Mathieson, Christiania, 2.20 4-5 (new world's record). This speed is about 11.6 yds. per second or 2.32 for the mile, a record for circular ice tracks. 5,000 metres—Mathieson, 8.55 3-5 (18 seconds slower than Eden's record in 1894 but Mathieson skated on ice covered with water.) 10,000 metres—Mathieson, 18.01 4-5.

Skating Records.—Revised, 1906, by a committee appointed by the National Amateur Skating Association, consisting of F. M. Clark, S. J. Montgomery and J. C. Hemment. 50 yards—6s., S. D. See and C. B. Davidson, Dec. 28, 1885. 75 yards—8 3-5s., S. D. See, Dec. 30, 1883. 100 yards—9 4-5s., J. S. Johnson, March 1, 1893. 150 yards—15⅞s., G. D. Phillips, Jan. 27, 1883. 150 yards (with wind)—14 1-5s., G. D. Phillips, Dec. 26, 1885. 200 yards—16 2-5s., J. C. Hemment, Jan. 24, 1895. 220 yards—19 4-5s., LeRoy A. See, Feb. 2, 1900. 300 yards—31 2-5s., G. D. Phillips, Dec. 30, 1883. 440 yards—35 1-5s., H. P. Mosher, Jan. 1, 1896. 600 yards—55¼s., O. Rudd, March 5, 1893. 880 yards—1m. 20 2-5s., J. Neilson, Feb. 1, 1896. 1,320 yards—2m. 13s., J. S. Johnson, Feb. 26, 1894. 1 mile—2m. 36s., J. Neilson, Feb. 2, 1895. 1 mile (straightaway, with wind)—2m. 12 3-5s., Tim Donoghue, February, 1887. 2 miles—5m. 42 3-5s., O. Rudd, Jan. 25, 1895. 3 miles—8m. 23s., J. F. Donoghue, Feb. 4, 1897. 4 miles—12m. ½s., J. Nilssen and A. Schiebe, Feb. 13, 1894. 5 miles—14m. 24s., O. Rudd, Feb. 20, 1896. 10 miles—31m. 11 1-5s., J. S. Johnson, Feb. 26, 1894. 30 miles—1h. 53m. 20s., J. F. Donoghue, Jan. 26, 1893. 40 miles—2h. 34m. 46s., J. F. Donoghue, Jan. 26, 1893. 50 miles—3h. 15m. 59 2-5s., J. F. Donoghue, Jan. 26, 1893. 60 miles—4h. 7m. 3-5s., J. F. Donoghue, Jan. 26, 1893. 70 miles—4h. 55m. 15 3-5s., J. F. Donoghue, Jan. 26, 1893. 80 miles—5h. 41m. 55s., J. F. Donoghue, Jan. 26, 1893. 90 miles—6h. 25m. 57 3-5s., J. F. Donoghue, Jan. 26, 1893. 100 miles—7h. 11m. 38 1-5s., J. F. Donoghue, Jan. 26, 1893. Best metre records.—500 metres (546.8 yards)—41 4-5s., J. S. Johnson, Jan. 24, 1895. 600 metres (656.17 yards)—59 3-5s., Morris Wood, Feb. 13, 1904. 1,000 metres (1,093.61 yards)—1m. 47s., J. K. McCulloch, Feb. 10, 1897. 1,500 metres (1,640.42 yards)—2m. 40 4-5s., J. K. McCulloch, Feb. 6, 1897. 5,000 metres (3 miles 188.06 yards)—9m. 25 2-5s., J. K. McCulloch, Feb. 10, 1897.

Hockey.

THE Hockey season in the East was the most brilliant of years, and while the championship in both the Amateur and Intercollegiate Hockey Leagues were won in straight victories the contests were full of exciting interest and far from being one sided. The Crescent Athletic Club won back the honors held two years previous, while Yale unexpectedly beat Harvard which had given promise of success. The standing:

AMATEUR HOCKEY LEAGUE	Games Won.	Games Lost.	Per Cent.	INTERCOLLEGIATE HOCKEY LEAGUE	Games Won.	Games Lost.	Per Cent.
Crescent Athletic Club.........	8	0	1.000	Yale............................	4	0	1.000
New York Athletic Club......	5	3	.625	Harvard........................	3	1	.750
St. Nicholas Hockey Club.....	5	3	.625	Columbia........................	1	3	.250
Hockey Club of New York....	2	6	.250	Princeton........................	1	3	.250
Wanderers Hockey Club.......	0	8	.000	Dartmouth........................	1	3	.250

Previous winners of the Amateur League Championship were: Brooklyn Skating Club, 1899; Crescent Athletic Club, 1900-3; Wanderers Hockey Club, 1904; Crescent Athletic Club, 1905-6; St. Nicholas Hockey Club, 1907.

The Interscholastic Championship of New York was won by the Brooklyn Polly Prep.

Toronto University Hockey team that won the intercollegiate championship of Canada, later defeating the Crescent A.C., in New York, March 14, 12 goals to 3. The Wanderers, of Montreal, that had won the Stanley cup, defeated the Shamrocks, of Montreal, in New York, March 17, by a score of 12 goals to 7. The Victoria team from Montreal, defeated the New York Athletic Club team, 8 goals to 6, in New York, March 24.

Hancock (Michigan) team won the championship of the Copper Country Amateur Hockey League, the teams, and games won and lost being as follows: Hancock, 18–6; Houghton, 16–8; Red Jacket, 5–19 and Laurium, 2–22. Hancock played a series of games with Duluth for the Championship of the Northwest which Hancock won.

Archery.

THE thirtieth annual meeting and tournament of the National Archery Association of the United States was held in Chicago, August 18, 19, 20, 21. Officers elected: President—Homer S. Taylor, 29 Wabash Avenue, Chicago. First Vice-President—H. B. Richardson, Boston. Second Vice President—J. M. Challiss, Atchison, Kan. Third Vice-President—E. H. Weston, Los Angeles, Cal. Secretary—H. W. Bishop, 315 Dearborn Street, Chicago. Treasurer—A. E. Spink, Chicago. Executive Committee, the above officers, and C. J. Strong, Cincinnati; L. F. Felt, Chicago; Dr. E. B. Weston, Chicago. The 1909 meeting is to be held in Chicago in August.

CHAMPIONSHIP AND LEADING SCORES.

DOUBLE YORK ROUND.

	100 yds. Hits. Scr.	80 yds. Hits. Scr.	60 yds. Hits. Scr.	Total. Hits. Scr.
Will H. Thompson, Seattle..............................	88–362	78–368	45–243	211–973
Homer S. Taylor, Chicago..............................	70–274	76–306	47–249	193–829
Col. Robt. Williams, Washington, D.C..............	73–309	68–274	44–236	185–819

Mr. Thompson won the York Round Championship.

DOUBLE AMERICAN ROUND.

	60 yds.	50 yds.	40 yds.	Total.
Col. Robt. Williams, Washington, D.C...............	52–282	58–336	59–389	169–1,007
Homer S. Taylor, Chicago..............................	57–247	60–334	60–357	177– 937
C. C. Beach, Battle Creek, Mich.......................	51–209	60–334	58–390	169– 933

Col. Williams won the American Round Championship.

DOUBLE NATIONAL ROUND.

	60 yds.	50 yds.	Total.
Miss Harriet Case, Chicago..	60–248	32–150	92–398
Mrs. Homer S. Taylor, Chicago....................................	21– 85	29–105	50–190

Miss Case won the National Round Championship.

DOUBLE COLUMBIA ROUND.

	50 yds.	40 yds.	30 yds.	Total.
Miss Harriet Case, Chicago..............................	29–127	38–132	45–237	112–546
Mrs. C. S. Woodruff, Chicago..............................	20– 84	35–169	43–213	98–466
Mrs. H. S. Taylor, Chicago..............................	22– 86	34–140	44–230	100–256

Miss Case won the Columbia Round Championship.

In addition to the championship contests there were several handicap shoots for which prizes were awarded.

Gymnastics.

GYMNASTS of the New York University team, intercollegiate champions for 1906 and 1907, and A. A. U. champions for 1907, made a clean sweep of the early season. The records show victories over Princeton, 33 to 15; over Yale, 33½ to 20½, and over Columbia, 32½ to 21½ points. J. Fernandez was the star of the winning team. Columbia defeated Yale in a dual meet 33 to 21 points.

Princeton made a remarkable showing in the tenth annual intercollegiate meet which the Tigers won with a total of 20 points. Columbia and New York University tied for second place with 10 points; Yale and Rutgers, 6; Harvard and Pennsylvania, 1, and Haverford, 0. For the individual championship, E. W. McCabe, Princeton, had 309.8 points; H. S. Schoonmaker, Columbia, 296, and H. L. Dowd, Princeton, 293.2.

Fred Steffens, National A. C., Brooklyn, won the all-around national championship of the A. A. U., scoring 50 points, while the point banner went to the West Side Y. M. C. A., with 20 points in eight events.

The International tournament was held at Frankfort-on-the-Main in July, and the all-around championship went to Mapler, of Munich, who made 120 out of a possible 150 points. The American

PHILADELPHIA cricketers who made a tour of Great Britain in July and August, 1908, as a visiting American team, had a very successful trip, winning seven of the fourteen games, one being a draw. In batting the team did not develop the strength expected, but the bowling far exceeded expectations, and J. B. King's record was the feature of the trip. For the first time in the history of American tours in England, the record of a hundred wickets captured was reached, the Belmont representative taking in all 115 wickets, at an average of over 10 runs a wicket. A. M. Wood was the most consistent scorer with the bat, making an average of 23 runs in 19 innings, with a high score of 132. The averages follow:

BATTING.

	Innings.	Not out.	High score.	Runs.	Av.
A. M. Wood	19	0	132	452	23.78
F. S. White	24	0	62	482	20.08
C. C. Morris	24	0	74	452	18.83
J. A. Lester	24	0	124	419	17.45
H. V. Hordern	24	4	55	334	16.70
N. Z. Graves, Jr.	24	1	76	381	16.56
J. B. King	24	0	53	386	16.08

BOWLING.

	Balls.	Mdns.	Runs.	Wkts.	Av.
J. B. King	2,704	141	1,206	115	10.48
J. A. Lester	426	11	224	15	14.93
H. V. Hordern	2,293	54	1,265	74	17.09
F. A. Greene	834	18	427	18	23.72
W. H. Sayen	474	10	303	10	30.30
E. M. Cregar	336	7	241	1	241.00

The thirty-fourth annual cricket match between All-Philadelphia, representing the United States and Canada, at Philadelphia, Sept. 14-15, ended in defeat for the visitors. The Canadians were all out for 116 runs in their second innings, while the Philadelphians scored 173 in their first innings.

At Philadelphia the New Jersey State League team was defeated by the All-Philadelphia eleven, which included J. B. King and A. M. Wood, 402 runs to 66.

In the Philadelphia Cricket League season, Merion Team A won the Halifax cup and the Philadelphia Club team won the Philadelphia cup.

METROPOLITAN DISTRICT LEAGUE CHAMPIONSHIP.

Columbia Oval for the first time won the championship of the Metropolitan District Cricket League in Class A, going through the season without defeat. In Section B the Manhattan Club also went through the season without defeat. The summaries:

SECTION A.

Club.	Played.	Won.	Lost.	Drn.	Per cent.
Columbia Oval	10	6	0	4	1,000
Brooklyn	10	5	1	4	.833
Manhattan	10	5	1	4	.833
Yonkers	10	3	5	2	.400
Kings County	10	2	6	2	.250
Bensonhurst	10	1	9	0	.100

SECTION B.

Club.	Played.	Won.	Lost.	Drn.	Per cent.
Manhattan	10	6	0	4	1,000
Brooklyn	10	5	2	3	.714
Bensonhurst	10	5	4	1	.555
Kings County	10	4	5	1	.444
Prospect Park	10	2	6	2	.250
Yonkers	10	2	7	1	.222

BATTING AVERAGES.

Section A.	Ins.	N.O.	H.S.	R.	Av.
A. Hoskings, Col. Oval	8	3	*122	318	63.66
F. J. Pr'd'gast, Man.	9	1	113	344	43.00
J. L. Foyer, Brooklyn	10	2	*78	319	39.57
D. G. Birkett, Col. O.	7	3	*71	156	39.00
H. A. Oxenham, Man.	9	2	76	185	26.43
J. P. Stuart, K. Co.	7	0	106	180	25.71
G. W. Hayman, Man.	9	1	77	186	23.25
H. Poyer, Brooklyn	9	0	71	197	21.90
F. F. Kelly, Man.	8	4	*23	84	21.00

* Not out.

Section B.	Ins.	N.O.	H.S.	R.	Av.
G. Wright, Man.	7	2	*42	155	31.11
E. Smith, Pros. Park.	9	0	50	205	22.77
E. E. Stevens, Man.	9	0	82	200	22.22
W. H. Williams, K. C.	10	1	*86	176	19.55
A. Baxter, Brooklyn	8	0	53	131	16.37
G. G. France, B'klyn.	7	1	47	96	16.00
G. Fitzgibbon, B'klyn.	8	5	17	46	15.33
E. O. Challenger, Bkn.	7	1	39	84	14.00
W. A. Huggins, Bh'st.	11	2	*23	114	12.66

* Not out.

BOWLING AVERAGES.

Section A.	Balls.	Mds.	R.	W.	Av.
H. A. Oxenham, Man.	638	15	267	48	5.56
A. Hoskings, Col. Oval	506	20	227	39	5.82
H. Poyer, Brooklyn	461	15	179	25	7.16
H. Rushton, Brooklyn.	633	31	204	28	7.28
J. L. Poyer, Brooklyn.	454	19	189	21	9.00

Section B.	Balls.	Mds.	R.	W.	Av.
F. Michaelouski, Ynks.	470	9	269	35	7.68
J. B. Barrow, Pros. P.	721	28	298	32	9.31
A. Corbin, Brooklyn	572	10	293	30	9.76
D. McArdle, Yonkers	558	12	335	25	13.40
J. Dixon, Manhattan	462	10	260	19	13.68

BEST SCORES IN CRICKET.

H. Livingstone, of the Pittsburgh Field Club, established a record for the United States by scoring three consecutive centuries in one week in a tournament held in Chicago during August, 1907. A similar feat was performed by H. N. R. Corbett in Canada in a tournament held in Vancouver, British Columbia, in August, 1906.

H. V. Hordern, of the University of Pennsylvania, established a record for the United States and Canada by securing 213 wickets during 1907.

A. C. MacLaren scored 424 for Lancashire vs. Somerset at Taunton, Eng., July, 1895, the record in a first-class match. A. E. J. Collins, playing at Clifton, June, 1899, for Clarke's House vs. North Town, scored 628 not out, the record in any match. Melbourne University scored 1,094 against Essendon at Melbourne, 1898, the highest authenticated record. In a match between A. E. Stottart's English team and New South Wales 1,739 runs were scored, a record in first-class cricket. The longest partnership on record was 623 by Captain Oates and Private Fitzgerald, First Royal Munster Fusiliers vs. Army Service Corps at Cunagh, 1895.

Best records in the United States and Canada are: G. S. Patterson's eleven, playing against A. M. Woods' eleven at Philadelphia, scored 689. J. B. King scored 344 not out for Belmont vs. Merion Team B in 1906. W. Robertson, 206 not out, and A. G. Sheath, 118 not out, scored 340 runs in partnership without the loss of a wicket at San Francisco in 1894. Smallest score was Americus, 0, vs. Roseville at Guttenburg, N. J., in 1897. Largest score in the Metropolitan District Cricket League Championship, New Jersey Athletic Club, 385 for five wickets, vs. Manhattan, at Bayonne, N. J., 1897. Smallest score in the same series, Crescent Athletic Club, 4, against the New Jersey Athletic Club, 1896. J. Wisden, bowling for George Parr's English eleven vs. United States and Canada's twenty-two, in 1859, at Rochester, secured six wickets in six consecutive balls.

Golf.

Low scoring feats were a feature of the golf season of 1908, the experts showing a marked improvement in scores over former years. Important tournaments of recent years, winners, and scores at 72 holes, and where held follow:

United States Open—1908, at Myopia, Fred McLeod, 322. 1907, at Philadelphia Cricket, Alexander Ross, 302. 1906, at Onwentsia, Alexander Smith, 295. 1905, at Myopia, W. Anderson, 314. 1904, at Glen View, W. Anderson, 303. 1903, at Baltusrol W. Anderson, 307. 1902, at Garden City, L. Auchterlonie, 307. 1901, at Myopia, W. Anderson, 331. 1900, at Chicago, H. H. Vardon, 313.

British Open—1908, at Prestwick, James Braid, 291. 1907, at Hoylake, A. Massy, 312. 1906, at Muirfield, J. Braid, 300. 1905, at St. Andrews, J. Braid, 318.

Western Open—1908, at St. Louis, W. Anderson, 299. 1907, Hinsdale, R. Stimpson, 307. 1906, at Homewood, Alexander Smith, 306. 1905, Cincinnati, Arthur Smith, 278.

Metropolitan Open—1908, at Baltusrol, Jack Hobens, 305. 1907, at Hollywood, G. Low, 294. 1906, at Fox Hills, W. Anderson, 300.

National—1908, at Garden City, J. D. Travers beat Max Behr, 8 up and 7 to play. 1907, at Euclid, J. D. Travers beat A. Graham, 6 up and 5 to play. 1906, E. M. Byers beat G. S. Lyon, 2 up. 1905, at Wheaton, H. Chandler Egan beat D. E. Sawyer, 6 up and 5 to play. Other winners—1904, H. Chandler Egan; 1903, W. J. Travis; 1902, L. N. James; 1901 and 1900, W. J. Travis.

Women's National—1908, at Washington, Miss Kate C. Harley. 1907, at Midlothian, Miss Margaret Curtis. 1906, at Brae Burn, Miss Harriet Curtis. 1905, at Morris County, Miss Pauline Mackay. 1904, at Merion C. C., Miss G. Bishop. 1903, at Wheaton, Miss B. Anthony. 1902-1, at Brookline and Baltusrol, Miss G. Hecker. 1900, at Shinnecock, Miss F. G. Griscom.

Important events of the year in their order were as follows:

Eighth Annual North and South Tournament. At Pinehurst, N. C., April 2—Allan Lard, Washington, defeated J. E. Porter, Allegheny County Club, 5 up and 4 to play. Miss Julia R. Mix, Edgewood, defeated Mrs. A. P. Chase, 1 up.

Williams defeated Princeton, 10 to 4, in their annual match at Princeton, May 22.

Metropolitan Championship. At Baltusrol, May 23—C. H. Seely, Wee Burn, defeated J. D. Travers, Garden City, 1 up, 38 holes.

British Amateur Championship, May 29—E. A. Lassen defeated H. F. Taylor, 7 up and 6 to play.

Middle Atlantic States Championship. At Washington, May 30—F. O. Korstman, Chevy Chase, defeated W. C. Harteris, 3 up and 2 to play.

Southern Championship. At Memphis, Tenn., May 30—Nelson Whitney, New Orleans, defeated H. Chandler Egan, Louisville, 4 up and 3 to play.

Women's Metropolitan Championship. At Orange, N. J., May 30—Miss Georgianna Bishop, Bridgeport, Ct., defeated Mrs. L. W. Callan, Englewood, 6 up and 5 to play.

New Jersey Championship, June 6—J. D. Travers defeated Max Behr, 11 up and 9 to play.

German Championship. At Berlin, June 8—Archie Gordon defeated A. Hinckley, 6 up and 5 to play.

Eastern Women's Tournament. At Watertown, Mass., June 10—Miss Fannie C. Osgood, Brookline, defeated Miss Mary B. Adams, 1 up. In the Women's Intercity Match Boston defeated Philadelphia, 11 to 4.

British Open "Pro." Championship, June 19—James Braid won for the fourth time since 1900; his score being 291 for four rounds, which is a record.

Western Open Championship. At St. Louis, June 19—W. Anderson, Onwentsia, Chicago, won with a score of 299.

French Championship. At Versailles, June 28—J. H. Taylor, England, defeated Arnaud Massey, making the four rounds in 300.

Massachusetts Championship. At Boston, July 2—Alexander Ross, West Newton, won in 290 strokes.

Connecticut Championship. At New Haven, July 11—B. T. Merrimann, Yale, defeated Roger Hovey, 8 up and 6 to play.

Olympic Cup Tournament. At Rock Island, Ill., July 12—Western Association team, Chicago, won, scoring 632 for 36 holes; Minnesota four, 651; Trans-Mississippi, 671; St. Louis, 672; Iowa, 728.

Western Amateur Championship. At Rock Island, July 18—Mason E. Phelps, Midlothian, Chicago and Yale, defeated H. W. Allen, St. Louis, 6 up and 5 to play.

Vermont Championship. At Manchester, August 9—Fred Herreshoff, Garden City, defeated F. A. Martin, Dartmoutn, 5 up and 4 to play.

U. S. Association, Fourteenth Annual Open Championship. At Myopia Links, Hamilton, Mass., August 29—W. Smith, Mexico, and Fred McLeod, Midlothian, Chicago, tied with 322 strokes for 72 holes. In the 18-hole play-off McLeod won, 77 to 83.

Irish Championship. At Newcastle, September 4—J. F. Mitchell, Edinburgh, defeated H. N. Cairnes, of Ireland, 3 up and 2 to go.

Greater N. Y. Championship. At Van Cortlandt Park, September 4—William Wallace, N. Y. Golf Club, defeated A. G. Lockwood, Boston, 3 up and 2 to play.

National Championship. At Garden City, L. I., September 19—J. D. Travers, Montclair, defeated Max Behr, Morris County, 8 up and 7 to play in 36-hole final.

Metropolitan Open Championship. At Baltusrol, September 25—Jack Hobens, Englewood, won with a score of 305 strokes.

Boston defeated Philadelphia and New York defeated Boston for the Robert Lesley Cup in the inter-city tournament at Garden City, October 3.

Intercollegiate Championship. At Brae Burn, Boston, October 6—Yale defeated Harvard in the finals, 14 points to 9. H. H. Wilder, Harvard, won the individual championship, defeating T. Briggs, 6 up and 5 to play.

Western Women's Championship. At St. Louis, October 9—Mrs. W. F. Anderson, Chicago, defeated Miss Grace Semple, St. Louis, 3 up and 2 to play. Winner made a new course record of 89 strokes.

Eastern Professional Championship. At Fox Hills, October 15—Won by Isaac Mackie, Fox Hills, 147 for 36 holes.

GOLF.—*Continued.*

Women's National Championship. At Chevy Chase, Washington, October 19—Miss Kate C. Harley, Fall River, Mass., defeated Mrs. T. H. Polhemus, Staten Island, 6 up and 5 to play.

Golf Records—In 1907 W. H. Horne, professional, at Beckenham, near London, drove the ball 381 yards. E. Blackwell, 1892, and with a gutta-percha ball, is credited with a drive of 366 yards from the seventeenth tee at St. Andrew's, Scotland, and Walter J. Travis, at Garden City, made a drive of 374 yards. Miss Margaret Curtis, Essex Country Club, Boston, made a women's record in America of 220 yards in the Women's National tournament on Midlothian Club links, Chicago, October 7, 1907.

Bowling.

THE second annual tournament of the National Bowling Association, representing Eastern bowlers, was held in Rochester, N. Y., March 2-14, 1908, with the following results: All events (nine games)—Larry Erdmann, Brooklyn, 1,956 pins. Previous winner: John Voorheis, Brooklyn, 1,965. Individual (3 games)—Fred Schwartje, Brooklyn, 697. Previous winner: F. Sauer, New York, 657. Two-Men-Team—McGuirk and Grady, Paterson, N. J., 1,318. Previous winners: Tuthill and Nelson, Brooklyn, 1,220. Five-Men Team—Brunswicks, New York, 2,893. Previous winners: Corinthians, New York, 2,814. Next tournament will be held in Madison Square Garden, New York, May 24 to June 5, 1909, with $50,000 in cash prizes, and on twenty-four B. B. C. alleys.

AMERICAN BOWLING CONGRESS TOURNAMENT.

The eighth annual tournament of the American Bowling Congress was held in Cincinnati, February 9-23, 1908. Next tournament in Pittsburgh in March, 1909. The winners; All Events (nine games)—R. Crable, East Liverpool, Ohio, 1,910. Previous winners: 1907, Harry Ellis, Grand Rapids, 1,767; 1906, J. T. Leacock, Indianapolis, 1,794; 1905, J. G. Reilly, Chicago, 1,791; 1904, Martin Kern, St. Louis, 1,804; 1903, Fred Strong, Chicago, 1,896; 1902, John Koster, New York, 1,841; 1901, Frank H. Brill, Chicago, 1,736. Individual—A. Wingler, Chicago, 699. Previous winners: 1907, Marshall B. Levy, Indianapolis, and R. F. Matak, St. Louis, tied on 624. In the roll-off Levy won—582 to 385. 1906, F. J. Favour, Oshkosh, Wis., 669; 1905, C. M. Anderson, St. Paul, 651; 1904, M. Kern, St. Louis, 647; 1903, D. A. Jones, Milwaukee, 683; 1902, Fred H. Strong, Chicago, 649; 1901 Frank H. Brill, Chicago, 648. Two-Men Teams—Kiene and Chalmers, Chicago, 1,254. Previous winners: 1907, E. C. Richter and E. M. Bigley, Louisville, 1,164; 1906, J. N. Reed, and E. Dresbach, Columbus, 1,247; 1905, R. Rolfe and E. Stretch, Chicago, 1,213; 1904, H. Krauss and C. H. Spiess, Washington, 1,184; 1903, A. Selbach and H. Collin, Columbus, 1,227; 1902, J. McClean and H. Steers, Chicago, 1,237; 1901, J. Voorheis and C. K. Starr, New York, 1,203. Five-Men Teams—Bonds, Columbus, 2,927. Previous winners: 1907, and tournament cities, Furniture Cities, Grand Rapids (St. Louis), 2,775; 1906, Centurys, Chicago (Louisville), 2,794; 1905, Gunthers No. 2, Chicago (Milwaukee), 2,795; 1904, Ansons, Chicago (Cleveland), 2,737; 1903, O'Learys, Chicago (Indianapolis), 2,819; 1902, Fidelias, New York (Buffalo), 2,792; 1901, Standards, Chicago (Chicago), 2,720.

CANADIAN B. A. TOURNAMENT.

The Canadian B. A. Tournament was held at Toronto, February 24 to March 2, 1908. Winners: Individual championship for the Evans trophy, George Doran, Toronto, 640. Open Singles—Jacob Cook, Sebring, Ohio, 660. Two-Men Team—Dewitt and Blouin, Chicago, 1,275. Five-Men Team—Hamiltons, Hamilton, Ont, 2,752. The Hamilton team won the international trophy presented by the Brunswick Balke-Collender Co., and valued at $500, their score being 2,752.

EVENING WORLD FREE HEADPIN TOURNAMENT.

The Evening World free headpin championship tournament was held at the White Elephant alleys, New York, February 3-24, 1908, and had the largest entry made in any bowling competition ever held in the world. Five hundred and eight five-men teams (2,540 bowlers) participated, and more than 260 watch fobs were given to competitors making scores of 100 pins and over. High scores were: Teams—Morris, New York, 529 pins; Park Row, New York, 523; Nonpareil, Brooklyn, 504; Elks, No. 324; New Brunswick, N. J., 502. Individual—C. Greenewald, Elks, New Brunswick, 115 (world's record in competition); Fred Stuhr, Midnight, New York, 114. Morris team received the Evening World trophy.

BEST SCORES IN TOURNAMENTS.

Big scores, tournaments, etc., mostly world records: Five-Men Teams—Howard's Majors, Chicago, May 8, 1906, 1,085, 1,207, 1,080. Total 3,372. Koenig and Kaiser, St. Louis, February 8, 1908, 1,074, 1,207, 1,083. Total, 3,364. Oxford team of Newark averaged 996 for twenty games in Bergman's tournament, New York, 1908. Three-Men Teams—Iroquois team (Noack, Blythe, Weiss), Newark, N. J., January 29, 1908, 612, 683, 679, 641, an average of 653. G. Riddell 238, M. Lindsey, 263 and A. Dunbar 256. Total 757, in competition at Wyman's, Columbia, New York. October 28, 1908. Two-Men Teams—Jimmy Smith and Harry Cohn, New York, in Milwaukee, September 28, 1907, rolled seven games in competition for a total of 3,086. Smith's average was 233 and Cohn's 218. Mrs. Bishop and Miss Littlefield rolled a total of 3,160 pins in nineteen games in a 12-hour endurance contest in Brooklyn, February 12, 1908. Individual—Seven 300 scores were made by bowlers in Greater New York tourneys in 1908. Charles Schaeder, in the Greater New York individual tournament, April, 1907, rolled six games of 236, 255, 269, 279, 268 and 233, an average of 256. John Koster, New York, 1907, averaged 283 for three games; 238 for thirteen games, and 240 for eight games. Lee Johns averaged 240 for eight games in the Greater New York tourney, April 22, 1908. Larry Staude, at Bergman's, New York, rolled three games of 300, 268 and 256 in a match, January 18, 1908. Duck Pins—Harry Fox made a world's record of 186 at Sievers & Laukenau's, New York, October 13, 1907. Red Raven Splits, at Baltimore, June 29, 1905, rolled 625 in competition. Candle Pins—Noddles, in Greater Boston League, March, 1908, made a five-men team score of 569. Headpin—Roseville, New Jersey, made a five-men team record of 541 pins in a tournament, while the Rosedales, New Jersey, rolled 543 in practice.

DUCK AND CANDLE PIN TOURNAMENT.

The second annual tournament of the National Duck and Candle Pin Association was held in Boston with the following winners and scores for three games: Duck Pins, Five-men team, Clancy's No. 3, Boston, 1,600; two-men, Beatty and Clancy, Boston, 701; individuals, P. F. Travers, Nashua, N. H., 382. Candle Pins. Five-men teams, Wildey Club, Boston, 1,615; two-men, Armstrong and Martell, Boston, 676; individuals, A. Lucia, Lynn, Mass., 325.

Rod and Reel Casting Records.

FLY-CASTING.

RECORDS made at the annual tournaments of the National Association of Scientific Angling Club (held August 14-15, 1908, at Washington Park, Chicago, and to be be held in 1909 under the auspices of the Angler's Club in New York) are as follows:

Salmon Casting—John Waddell and Perry Frazer tied, 114 feet (rod 15 foot). Washington Park, Chicago, August 14, 1908.

Long Distance Fly—Fred N. Peet, 110 feet. Washington Park, Chicago, August 14, 1908.

Delicacy and Accuracy Dry Fly—Fred N. Peet, 99 7-30 per cent. Racine, Wis., August 16, 1907.

Distance and Accuracy at Buoys—50, 55 and 60 feet—L. E. DeGarmo, 99 9-15 per cent. Washington Park, Chicago, August 14, 1908.

Dry Fly Accuracy at Buoys—20, 30, 40, 50 and 60 feet—I. H. Bellows, 99 per cent. Washington Park, Chicago, August 14, 1908.

* *One-Half Ounce Accuracy Bait at Buoys*—60, 70, 80, 90 and 100 feet—E. R. Letterman, 99 per cent., National Tournament. Racine, Wis., August 16, 1907.

One-Quarter Ounce Accuracy Bait at Buoys—60, 65, 70, 75 and 80 feet—Wm. Stanley, 99 1-15 per cent., National Tournament. Racine, Wis., August 16, 1907.

One-Half Ounce, Long Distance Bait on the Lawn—181 4-5 feet—R. J. Held. Washington Park, Chicago, August 15, 1908.

Salmon Casting (Professional)—John Enright, Ireland, 152 feet (rod 20 feet, 48 ounces). Central Park, New York, October 12, 1906; E. J. Mills, 140 feet (rod 15 feet). Central Park, New York, May 14, 1908. *Amateur*—W. M. Plevins, England, 129 feet (rod 15 feet). Central Park, New York, May 14, 1908.

Switch Fly-Casting—H. W. Hawes, 102 feet (rod 11 feet). Central Park, N. Y., 1887.

Light Rod Casting—Peter Cooper Hewitt, 100 feet 5½ inches (rods not to exceed 5¾ ounces). Madison Square Garden, 1887.

Fly-Casting for Black Bass—R. C. Leonard, 101 feet 6 inches. Madison Square Garden, 1897.

Light Rod Contest—Walter D. Mansfield, 129 feet 6 inches (rod 5 ounces). San Francisco, 1902.

Single-Handed Fly-Casting—Walter D. Mansfield, 134 feet (rod 11 feet; 10 ounces). San Francisco, 1902.

Single-Handed Fly-Casting—H. C. Golcher, 140 feet (rod 11 feet; 10¾ ounces). Golden Gate Park, San Francisco, 1902. At the same time T. W. Brotherton cast 137 feet in a heavy rod contest.

Dry Fly-Casting—For delicacy and accuracy at buoys 35, 40, and 45 feet. Fred N. Peet, 99 5-15 per cent., at Kalamazoo, Mich., August 3, 1906, in the International Tournament.

* Mr. Stanley's record was made from a platform, three casts at each buoy, weight dropping in a circle 30 inches in diameter. Every foot or fraction thereof from circle was scored as a demerit. The total of demerits divided by 15 and subtracted from 100, gave a score of 99 1-15 per cent.

WEIGHT-CASTING.

Striped Bass Casting (Light)—H. W. Hawes, 129 6-10 feet, average of five casts; sinker 1¼ ounces. Central Park, N. Y., 1884.

Striped Bass Casting (Heavy)—John A. Roosevelt, 204 feet 3 inches, average of five casts in lane 35 feet wide; rod 7 feet 5 inches; sinker 2¼ ounces. Central Park, N. Y., 1884.

Striped Bass Casting (Heavy)—W. H. Wood, 250 feet, longest single cast without lane; rod 9 feet; sinker 2¼ ounces. Central Park, N. Y., 1885.

Minnow Casting for Black Bass—E. C. Sturges, 140 feet 11 inches, average of five casts; sinker ½ ounce. Camp Lake, Wis., 1891.

Minnow Casting for Black Bass—F. B. Davidson, 167 1-5 feet, average of five casts; sinker ½ ounce. Chicago, 1894. Best single cast of 173 feet.

Long Distance Single-Handed Bait Cast—Dr. R. Johnson Held, 161 feet; ½ ounce weight, no limit to weight of rod or line, but free running reel. Central Park, N. Y., May 17, 1908.

Long Distance Single-Handed Bait Cast—Dr. R. J. Held, 205 feet (196⅓ feet average of five casts), ½ ounce weight. Central Park, N. Y., May 16, 1908.

Two-Handed Surf Cast for Distance—W. J. Wood, 250 feet, 1 inch, 2½ ounce weight, rod not less than 6 feet, free running reel and line of sufficient strength to lift a dead weight of 15 pounds 1 foot from ground. Polo Grounds, N. Y., 1887. W. J. Moran, 227 feet. Central Park, N. Y., May 16, 1908.

ENGLISH FLY AND BAIT-CASTING RECORDS.

Salmon Fly-Casting, Amateur—J. J. Hardy, 140 feet 3 inches (1895) (rod 18 feet), Wimbledon. John Enright, 147 feet (1896) (rod 20 feet), Wimbledon. Afterward, with the same rod, Mr. Enright made an exhibition cast before reliable witnesses of 151 feet 3 inches.

Salmon Fly-Casting, Scotch Professional—J. Stevens, 126 feet (1890), Twickenham.

Switch Salmon-Casting, Amateur—C. M. P. Burns, 108 feet (1888), Twickenham.

Trout Fly-Casting, Single-Handed Rod—P. D. Mallock, 92 feet (this distance was made by measuring the line after casting); R. B. Marston and Hyde Clark, tie, 74 feet; Reuben Wood (of Syracuse, N. Y.), 82 feet 6 inches.

Trout Fly-Casting, Two-Handed Rod—John Enright, 123 feet (1896), Wimbledon.

* *Thames Bait-Casting, Amateur*—R. Gillson, 191 feet 11 inches.

Longest Cast, Heavy (3 ounces lead)—Mr. Hobden, 216 feet.

† *Nottingham Bait-Casting, Amateur (2¼ ounces lead)*—J. T. Emery, 263 feet (1898).

Light Bait-Casting, Amateur (1¼ ounces lead)—J. T. Emery, 204 feet 6 inches (1896).

*In Thames casting the line is coiled at the feet of the caster.
†In Nottingham casting the cast is made from the reel.
Contributed by Fred. N. Peet, Chicago, Ill.

Squash.

THE National Championship in singles was held in Philadelphia, February 26-29, and was won by W. L. Freeland, Philadelphia, who defeated Dr. John A. Miskey, former champion, 15—7, 18—15. The American championship event was not held, Reginald Finck, New York Racquet and Tennis Club, having secured permanent possession of the trophy in the tournament of 1907, that being his third victory in consecutive **years.**

Rowing.

YALE VS. HARVARD—UNIVERSITY EIGHTS.

YALE and Harvard eights have rowed forty-two races, beginning in 1852 on Lake Winnipiseogee at two miles. In 1855 the course was changed to Springfield and lengthened to three miles. Lake Quinsigamond was the scene for nine years, and Lake Saltonsall for 1869. After an interval of seven years the crews in 1876-77 went to Springfield, Mass., when the four-mile course was inaugurated. In 1878 the crews changed again to New London, Ct. The records:

Date.	Won By.	Time. Winner.	Time. Loser.	Date.	Won By.	Time. Winner.	Time. Loser.
Aug. 3, 1852...	Harvard..	....	....	June 26, 1885....	Harvard..	25.15⅕	26.30
July 21, 1855....	Harvard..	....	....	July 2, 1886....	Yale......	20.41¼	21.05
July 26, 1857....	Harvard..	19.18	20.18	July 1, 1887....	Yale......	22.56	23.10¾
July 27, 1859....	Yale......	19.14	19.16	June 29, 1888....	Yale......	20.10	21.24⅕
July 24, 1860 ...	Harvard..	18.53	19.05	June 29, 1889 ...	Yale......	21.30	21.55
July 29, 1864....	Yale......	19.01	19.43½	June 27, 1890....	Yale......	21.29	21.40
July 28, 1865....	Yale......	17.42⅕	18.09	June 26, 1891...	Harvard..	21.23	21.57
July 27, 1866....	Harvard..	18.43	19.10	July 1, 1892....	Yale......	20.48	21.42⅕
July 19, 1867....	Harvard..	18.13	19.25⅕	June 3, 1893....	Yale......	25.01⅕	25.15
July 24, 1868....	Harvard..	17.48⅕	18.3-⅕	June 28, 1894....	Yale......	22.47	24.40
July 23, 1869....	Harvard..	18.02	18.11	June 28, 1895....	Yale......	21.30	22.05
July 22, 1870....	Harvard..	Foul.	Disq.	June 29, 1899....	Harvard..	20.52⅕	21.13
July 30, 1876....	Yale......	22.02	22.33	June 28, 1900....	Yale......	21.12 4-5	21.37 2-5
June 30, 1877....	Harvard..	24.36	24.44	June 27, 1901....	Yale......	23.37	23.45
June 28, 1878....	Harvard..	20.44¾	21.29	June 26, 1902....	Yale......	20.20	20.33
June 27, 1879....	Harvard..	22.15	23.58	June 25, 1903 ...	Yale......	20.19 4-5	20.29 3-5
July 1, 1880....	Yale......	24.27	25.09	June 30, 1904 ...	Yale......	21.40⅕	22.10
July 1, 1881....	Yale......	22.13	22.19	June 29, 1905....	Yale......	22.33	22.36
June 30, 1882....	Harvard..	20.47	20.50½	June 28, 1906....	Harvard..	23.02	23.11
June 28, 1883....	Harvard..	24.26	25.59	June 27, 1907 ...	Yale......	21.10	21.13
June 26, 1884 ...	Yale......	20.31	20.46	June 25, 1908 ...	Harvard..	24.10	27.45

Harvard crew: Faulkner, bow; E. C. Cutler, 2; Severance, 3; Lunt, 4; Waid, 5; E. C. Bacon, 6; Richardson, 7; Sargeant, 8; Blagden, coxswain. Average weight, 173; height, 5 ft. 11 1-2 in. Yale: Auchincloss, bow; Peyton, 2; Rice, 3; Hunt, 4; Dunkle, 5; Howe, 6; Ide, 7; Griswold, stroke; Cass, coxswain. Average weight, 178; height, 6 ft. 1-2 in.

'VARSITY FOUR-OARED—TWO MILES.

Yale 10.33 1-2; Harvard, 10.43 1-2. Yale crew: Odell, bow; Godley, 2; Miller, 3; Wallis, stroke. Average weight, 168; height, 5 ft. 9 in. Harvard crew: Ellis, bow; G. Bacon, 2; P. Withington, 3; Reece, stroke. Weight, 160; height, 5 ft. 10 1-2 in.

FRESHMAN EIGHT-OARED—TWO MILES.

Harvard, 9.38; Yale, 9.47 1-2. Harvard crew: Shillito, bow; Foster, 2; Whitney, 3; Waite, 4; L. Withington, 5; Eaton, 6; Hooper, 7; R. Cutler, stroke; Sales, coxswain. Weight, 166; height, 5 ft. 11 in. Yale crew: Thorne, bow; Jeffrey, 2; Van Blarcom, 3; Patterson, 4; Baker, 5; Frost, 6; Goodrich, 7; Livingstone, 8; Fearing, coxswain. Weight, 163; height, 6 ft.

INTERCOLLEGIATE 'VARSITY RACES.

Intercollegiate 'Varsity races of four miles, rowed at Poughkeepsie since 1900 have resulted as follows:

June 30, 1900.—Pennsylvania, 19.44 3-5; Wisconsin, 19.46 2-5; Cornell, 20.04 1-5; Columbia, 20.08 1-5; Georgetown, 20.19 1-5.

July 2, 1901.—Cornell, 18.53 1-5 (record); Columbia, 18.58; Wisconsin, 19.06 4-5; Georgetown, 19.21; Syracuse, 19.49; Pennsylvania, 19.58 1-5.

June 21, 1902.—Cornell, 19.05 3-5; Wisconsin, 19.13 3-5; Columbia, 19.18 3-5; Pennsylvania, 19.26; Syracuse, 19.31 2-5; Georgetown, 19.32.

June 26, 1903.—Cornell, 18.57; Georgetown, 19.27; Wisconsin, 19.29 2-5; Pennsylvania, 19.36 2-5; Columbia, 19.54 4-5.

June 28, 1904.—Syracuse, 20.22 3-5; Cornell, 20.31 1-2; Pennsylvania, 20.42; Columbia, 20.45 2-5; Georgetown, 20.52 2-5; Wisconsin, 21.01 1-5.

June 29, 1905.—Cornell, 20.29 2-5; Syracuse, 21.47 2-5; Georgetown, 21.49; Columbia, 21.53 4-5; Pennsylvania, 21.59 4-5; Wisconsin, 22.06 1-5.

June 23, 1906.—Cornell, 19.36 4-5; Pennsylvania, 19.43 4-5; Syracuse, 19.45 1-5; Wisconsin, 20.13 4-5; Columbia, 20.18 3-5; Georgetown, 20.36.

June 26, 1907.—Cornell, 20.02 3-5; Columbia, 20.04; Annapolis, 20.13 4-5; Pennsylvania, 20.33 2-5. Wisconsin, Georgetown, Syracuse.

June 28, 1908.—Syracuse, 19.34 1-5, Columbia, 19.35 1-5; Cornell, 19.39; Pennsylvania, 19.52 3-5; Wisconsin, 20.43 4-5. Winning crew: Dodge, bow; Shiner, 2; Roberts, 3; Duvall, 4; Hemenway, 5; Champlin, 6; Fisher, 7; Ten Eyck, stroke. Average weight of crew, 172; height, 5 ft. 11 in.

'VARSITY FOUR-OARED—TWO MILES.

Winners.—1900, Pennsylvania, 10.31 1-5; 1901, Cornell, 11.39 3-5; 1902, Cornell, 10.43 3-5; 1903, Cornell, 10.34; 1904, Cornell, 10.53 3-5; 1905, Syracuse, 10.15 2-5; 1906, Cornell, 10.35 1-5; 1907, Syracuse, 10.37 1-5; Cornell, 10.40; Pennsylvania, 10.49; Columbia, 10.59 3-5. 1908, Syracuse, 10.52 4-5; Columbia, 11.06 3-5; Pennsylvania, 10.57 4-5. Pennsylvania disqualified for fouling Columbia, latter being given second place.

FRESHMAN EIGHT-OARED—TWO MILES.

Winners.—1900, Wisconsin, 9.45 2-5; 1901, Pennsylvania, 10.20 1-5; 1902, Cornell, 9.39 4-5; 1903, Cornell, 9.18; 1904, Syracuse, 10.01; 1905, Cornell, 9.35 2-5; 1906, Syracuse, 9.51 3-5; 1907, Wisconsin, 9.58; Syracuse, 10.03; Pennsylvania, 10.04; Columbia, 10.05 2-5; Cornell,

ROWING—*Continued.*

10.07 4-5; 1908, Cornell, 9.29 2-5; Syracuse, 9.38 3-5; Columbia, 9.43; Wisconsin, 9.55 1-5; Pennsylvania, 10.42.

OTHER COLLEGE RACES IN 1908.

April 22.—Harvard 'Varsity eight defeated Annapolis on the two-mile course of the Severn River by half a length in a close race throughout. Harvard's time, 10.30; Annapolis, 10.31.

May 9.—Annapolis defeated Columbia crews in two races, each of two miles, on the Severn. Time, 'Varsity crews: Navy, 10.23 1-5; Columbia, 10.23 4-5. Second crews: Navy, 10.45 1-5; Columbia, 10.49 1-5.

May 16.—Columbia freshmen eight defeated Yale at Lake Whitney, New London. Time, 4.30.

May 21.—Pennsylvania 'Varsity eight defeated New York University on the Schuylkill course of one mile 500 yards in 6.51.

May 30.—Harvard 'Varsity eight defeated Cornell on the 1 7-8-mile Charles River course, Boston, by 10 lengths. Time, Harvard, 10.47; Cornell, 11.24.

IMPORTANT REGATTAS IN 1908.

May 23.—American Rowing Association at Philadelphia. Course 1 5-16 miles. Winning crews: Interscholastic eights, Georgetown Prep., Washington, 6.45 1-5. First fours, sculls—Nonpareil B. C., New York, 6.59 1-5. Second fours—Arundel B. C., Baltimore, 7.15 1-5. First singles—Durando Miller, New York A. C., 8.01 1-5. Second singles—W. Mehrhoff, Nassau B. C., New York, 8.13. First pair-oared shells—Doering-Campbell, West Philadelphia B. C., 8.03 2-5. First double sculls—Stewart-Quinn, New York A. C., 7.28 2-5. First four-oared shells—Bachelors Barge Club, Philadelphia, 7.07 3-5. First eight-oared shells, tie of University of Pennsylvania and New York A. C., 6.26 (new record). Second eights—Harvard freshmen, 6.23 4-5. Junior Collegiate eights, Yale, 6.27 (breaking course record of 6.34 made by Cornell in 1905).

May 30.—Harlem, forty-second annual regatta, New York. Junior singles—R. Vitacek, First Bohemian B. C., 7.46. Intermediate singles—F. Shea, Sheepshead Bay R. C. Senior singles—Durando Miller, New York A. C., 7.45. Association.. Junior doubles—Suchanek-Laznorsky, First Bohemian B. C. Intermediate singles—R. L. Smith, Vesper B. C., Philadelphia, 7.58. Doubles—Emerson-Corbett, Metropolitan B. C., 7.52 2-5. Senior doubles—Tie between Korvan-Fortune, Ravenswood B. C., and Stewart-Quinn, N. Y. A. C., 7.13. Junior four, gig—Wahnetah, Flushing. Junior centipede four—Union B. C. Senior centipede, N. Y. A. C. Intermediate four, gigs—Columbia University. Junior eights—Columbia, 6.27. Intermediate eights—Columbia, 6.23. Interscholastic eights—High School of Commerce. Senior eights—New York A. C. Races rowed in rain with rough water.

July 4.—New England A. R. A., twenty-second annual regatta, Charles River. Junior double—Lynch-Gibby, Boston A. A., 12.25. Centipede—Union B. C., New York, 9.40. Senior singles—P. C. Shields, Shawmut R. C., Boston, 11.50. Senior four—Riverside B. C., East Boston, 11.29. Junior singles—J. F. O'Neill, Shawmut R. C., Boston, 11.35. Senior doubles—Emerson-McEntee, Metropolitan B. C., New York, 11.25. Junior eights—Kalumet B. C., Worcester, 8.15. Intermediate fours—Riverside B. C. Senior eight—Riverside, 7.16.

July 4.—Peoples' Regatta, Philadelphia. Junior singles—J. Kernan, Ariel B. C., Baltimore, 11.47. Intermediate singles—J. A. Miller, New York A. C., 10.33. Senior singles—D. Miller, Jr., New York A. C., 10.37. Junior doubles—Brownell-Gordon, West Philadelphia B. C., 9.18 3-5. Senior doubles—Warnock-Bennett, Springfield B. C., 9.22. Intermediate doubles—Drinker-Thayer, University B. C., Philadelphia, 9.17 1-5. Junior four, gigs—Malta B. C., Philadelphia, 9.47 3-5. Intermediate four—Undine, Philadelphia, 9.42 1-5. Senior four, shells—Vesper B. C., Philadelphia. Junior quadruple—West Philadelphia B. C., 8.13. Junior eight, shells—Quaker City Barge Club, Philadelphia, 8.40 3-5. Intermediate eight—Malta, Philadelphia, 8.37. Senior eight, New York A. C., 7.48.

July 11.—Long Island Amateur R. A., twenty-third annual regatta, Flushing Bay. Junior singles—J. Hampton, Ravenswood B. C., 9.24. Senior singles—F. Shepheard, Seawanhaka B. C., 8.25. Junior doubles—Gollner-Conway, Metropolitan R. C., 8.24. Senior doubles—Rivas-Quinn, N. Y. A. C., 7.02 3-5. Junior four, gigs—Nassau B. C. Intermediate four, gigs—Wahnetah B. C., 7.53.

July 14.—Henley Regatta, England. Christ Church won the grand challenge cup, defeating Eaton in 7.10. A. G. McCulloch, Oxford, won the diamond sculls in 8.23. Magdalen College four won the Steward's cup in 7.27 1-2, which was the only new regatta record made.

August 8.—Canadian Henley, St. Catharines, Ont. Junior singles—C. J. Sheehan, Mutual B. C., Buffalo, 10.53. Intermediate singles—C. J. Sheehan, 10.40. Senior singles—H. Jacobs, Don R. C., 10.16. Intermediate doubles—Don R. C., 9.40. Senior doubles—Crawford-Laing, Don R. C., 10.17. Junior fours—Argonaut R. C., 9.12. Senior fours and senior eights—Winnipeg R. C.

August 14-15.—National Association of Amateur Oarsmen, thirty-sixth annual regatta, Springfield, Mass. Intermediate fours—Shells, Minnesota B. C., St. Paul, 9.37. Association singles—J. O'Neill, St. Mary's A. A., Halifax, 10.17 2-5. International senior fours—Straightaway, St. Mary's Halifax, 9.29. Senior doubles—Warnock-Bennett, Springfield B. C., 9.28 1-5. Intermediate doubles—West Philadelphia B. C., 9.43 4-5. Intermediate pairs—Nonpareil B. C., New York, 10.20. Intermediate eights, Minnesota B. C., St. Paul, 8.42. Senior fours—Vesper B. C., Philadelphia, 8.58 1-2. Senior eights—New York A. C., 8.44. Intermediate centipede, straightaway—Metropolitan B. C., New York, 9.13 3-5. Senior pairs—Hartman-De Baecke, Vesper B. C., Philadelphia, 10.00. Championship singles—Frank H. Greer, East Boston A. A., 9.53, won; J. O'Neill, Halifax, 10.08, second; H. S. Bennett, Springfield, third; Durando Miller, New York, fourth; F. Shepheard, New York, fifth. Intermediate singles—C. Faulkner, Riverside B. C., Cambridge, 10.17.

Middle States, seventeenth annual regatta, Potomac River, Washington, Sept. 7. Junior—Singles, G. W. Allison, West Philadelphia B. C., 6.22 3-5; doubles, New Rochelle R. C., New York, 5.54. Four-oared gigs—Pennsylvania B. C., 5.48 4-5. Octuple sculls—Malta B. C., Philadelphia, 5.50 1-5; eights, Potomac, Washington, 5.16. Association—Singles (senior), S. F. Gordon, West Philadelphia B. C., 6.12 2-5. Intermediate—Singles, T. J. Gorman, Potomac B. C., 6.38 2-5; doubles, New Rochelle B. C., 5.47; four-oared gigs, Malta B. C., 5.46 4-5; quadruple sculls, New Rochelle B. C., 5.22; eights, Potomac B. C.,

ROWING.—*Continued.*

5.22. Senior—Singles, Durando Miller, N. Y. A. C., 6.54; doubles, Brownwell-Gordon, West Philadelphia B. C., 5.32; four-oared shell, Vesper B. C.; Philadelphia, 5.11; quadruple, Nonpareil B. C., New York, 5.22; eights, N. Y. C. A., 4.58.

New England A. R. A., twentieth annual Fall regatta, Charles River, Boston, Sept. 7. Junior—Singles, W. Shayan, Shawmut R. C., Boston, 15.17; doubles, Fitzgerald-Bresnahan, Springfield B. C., 11.59; fours, East Boston A. A., 11.56; eights, Kalumet B. C., Worcester, 8.04. Senior—Singles, E. A. Pope, Boston A. A., 12.43; fours, St. Joseph A. A., 12.10 (others swamped). High wind and bad water.

Deaths of prominent oarsmen during the year included Edward Hanlan who rowed in over 200 races and lost only six, and John Hancon, a contemporary of Josh Ward in 1858.

February 25.—Webb defeated R. T. Ressider, by 2 1-2 lengths in New Zealand, retaining his professional sculling championship.

October 10.—Founders' Week and fiftieth anniversary Schuylkill Navy, Philadelphia. Mile events. Winners: Double scull—Fuessel-Shepheard, New York, 5.31 2-5. Four-oared shells—Hartman-De Baecke, Philadelphia, 5.26 3-5. Quadruple sculls—Fuessel-Shepheard, New York, 5.20. Senior singles—Durando Miller, New York; S. F. Gordon, Philadelphia, second; Lieut. von Gaza, Germany, third; 6.07 2-5. Eight-oared shells—Philadelphia, 5.05. Octuple shells—New York, 4.53 1-5.

October 12.—Ernest Barry, London, defeated George Towns, Australia, 1½ lengths in match race over Putney-Mortland course of 4¼ miles in England for the English championship. Barry's time, 21.12 1-5. The new champion is a brother of W. A. Barry, whom Towns beat for the title in 1897.

The Oxford-Cambridge Boat Races.

Year.	Date.	Winner.	Course.	Time. M.	Time. S.	Won by.
1897	April 3	Oxford	Putney to Mortlake	19	11 4-5	2⅓ lengths.
1898	March 26	Oxford	Putney to Mortlake	22	15	12 lengths.
1899	March 25	Cambridge	Putney to Mortlake	21	4	3¼ lengths.
1900	March 31	Cambridge	Putney to Mortlake	18	47	Won easily.
1901	March 30	Oxford	Putney to Mortlake	22	31	2-5 lengths.
1902	March 23	Cambridge	Putney to Mortlake	19	9	Won easily.
1903	April 1	Cambridge	Putney to Mortlake	19	32½	6 lengths.
1904	March 26	Cambridge	Putney to Mortlake	21	34	4½ lengths.
1905	April 1	Oxford	Putney to Mortlake	20	35	3 lengths.
1906	April 7	Cambridge	Putney to Mortlake	19	24	......
1907	March 16	Cambridge	Putney to Mortlake	20	26	4½ lengths.
1908	April 4	Cambridge	Putney to Mortlake	19	19	3 lengths.

The above table covers twelve years of the sixty-five in which the race has been rowed. The distance is about four miles, and the best time is 18.47, made by Oxford in 1893 and equalled by Cambridge in 1900.

Ice Yacht Club Races.

THE weather was unfavorable for good ice, although a number of important races were held on the Shrewsbury River and several records were broken. What was probably the fastest time ever made by an ice yacht was that of the Clarel, Capt. E. W. Price, of Long Branch, N. J., which covered a straightaway course of 1.2 miles in 31s., or at the rate of 2 1-3 miles per minute, or about 140 miles per hour. The wind was abeam and the boat was officially timed by several judges and spectators. The feat was performed in a leg of the Commodore's Cup Race, February 9, which event was won by the Eagle, which sailed the 15-mile course in 31.20s., also a new record for the Shrewsbury. Clarel was withdrawn after a fluke in the fourth leg of the race. Other races of the Shrewsbury Club were—Price Brothers' Cup, February 13; 15 miles—Won by the Drub in 42.31s.; Isabel, 43.30s., second. Pott's Cup, February 13; 15 miles—Won by Drub in 41.30s.

A unique match race for $1,000, between the Eagle of the Patchogue Scooter Club, Long Island, and the Windward of the Orange Lake Ice Yacht Club, was sailed on Orange Lake, Newburgh, N. Y., in three races, in February, and the Scooter easily won all three. By terms of the race the Scooter had to sail 10 miles to 20 for the ice yacht.

RACES FOR THE AMERICAN CHALLENGE PENNANT.

Date.	Name.	Owner.	Challenging Club.	Winning Club.	Course.	Miles	Time. H. M. S.	Wind.	Condition of Ice.
Feb. 14, 1887	Jack Frost	Arch'd Rogers	H.R.I.Y.C.	H.R.I.Y.C.	P.I.Y.C	16	0.43.40	Steady, S.	Hard
Mar. 8, 1888	Icicle	J. A. Roosevelt	N.S.I.Y.C.	H.R.I.Y.C.	H.R.I.Y.C.	12	0.36.59	Strong, N. W.	Soft
Feb. 25, 1889	Icicle	J. A. Roosevelt	N.S.I.Y.C.	H.R.I.Y.C.	H.R.I.Y.C.	16	0.51.41	Steady, N. W.	Hard
Feb. 5, 1892	Icicle	J. A. Roosevelt	N.S.I.Y.C.	H.R.I.Y.C.	H.R.I.Y.C.	20	0.46.19	Strong, N. W.	Hard
Feb. 9, 1898	Jack Frost	Arch'd Rogers	O.L.I.Y.C.	H.R.I.Y.C.	H.R.I.Y.C.	20	0.49.30	Steady, S. W.	Hard
Jan. 21, 1899	Icicle	J. A. Roosevelt	C.I.Y.C.	H.R.I.Y.C.	H.R.I.Y.C.	20	1.09.37	Steady, S.	Soft
Feb. 7, 1902	Jack Frost	Arch'd Rogers	N.S.I.Y.C.	H.R.I.Y.C.	H.R.I.Y.C.	20	1.02.21 2-5	Steady, S. S. E.	Hard
*Feb. 13, 1902	Jack Frost	Arch'd Rogers	N.S.I.Y.C.	H.R.I.Y.C.	H.R.I.Y.C.	20	0.53.24	Strong, N. W.	Hard

Abbreviations Explained.—P.I.Y.C., Poughkeepsie Ice Yacht Club; O.L.I.Y.C., Orange Lake Ice Yacht Club; H.R.I.Y.C., Hudson River Ice Yacht Club; C.I.Y.C., Carthage Ice Yacht Club. *Race under the new Deed of Gift. No races have been sailed since 1902, the club holding the trophy having received no challenge. Contributed to THE WORLD ALMANAC by John A. Roosevelt, Poughkeepsie, N. Y.

In the races at Gull Lake, Kalamazoo, Mich., in March, 1904, the Wolverine, owned by Commodore D. C. Olin, of the Kalamazoo Club, won the Stuart International Trophy. In the last heat over a 20-mile two-point course, the time of the Wolverine was 42 minutes.

At Kalamazoo, Mich., February 24, 1907, the Wolverine, owned by the Kalamazoo Ice Yacht Club, broke all world's records for a two-point course, sailing 20 miles in 39.50s. The boat was required to turn every two miles.

Yachting.

GENERAL financial depression in the early Spring had much to do in keeping many of the large yachts out of commission in 1908, although the season otherwise compared very favorably with any in the past decade. There were several Lipton cup races and the race weeks of New York clubs with the annual regattas were in every way successful. So, that while some of the larger boats, particularly the schooners, were not raced, as the season advanced the sport grew more interesting and the year closed with a bright outlook.

In accomplishing this result the Atlantic Yacht Club in holding a "Race Week" early in September revived interest among the yachtsmen on the Lower Bay by giving a similar impetus to the sport as the Larchmont Club on Long Island Sound. A special feature were the races for the Frederic Thompson Cups held under the auspices of the Atlantic Club which will be continued with greater interest in 1909.

IMPORTANT RACES SAILED IN 1908.

Marblehead to Bermuda race June 3-8, schooner Dervish, Commodore H. Morss, Corinthian Yacht Club, Marblehead—Won in class B, her elapsed time being 109h. 23m. 45s. Sloop Venona, E. J. Bliss, Eastern Yacht Club, Boston—Won in class C, her time being 100h. 16m.

New York to Block Island race for boats under 31 feet, 100 miles, June 20-21—sloop Frances, G. W. Robinson, Harlem Yacht Club—Won on time allowance in 14h. 3m. 10s. Sloop Nutmeg made the best time of 15½h.

Cape May ocean race, Brooklyn Yacht Club, for Lipton cup, 325 miles, July 4-7—schooner Shamrock, Frederic Thompson, Brooklyn Yacht Club, and sailed by Charles Barr—Won in 54h. 57m. 30s. elapsed time.

San Pedro, Cal., to Honolulu, ocean race, 2,500 miles, July 4-12—Won by Lurline, South Coast Yacht Club, Southern California, 13d. 21h. 31m. 43s.

Larchmont Yacht Club, race week, July 20-25—There were 548 entries for the week. Point winners; 57-footers, Aurora and Istalena, 3 each; 48-footer, Dorello; 27-footer, Seneca; 30-footer Alera.

Manhasset Bay Challenge Cup, July 28-29—Won by A. Hanan's 27-footer Seneca, Indian Harbor Yacht Club.

Astor and King Edward cup races, off Newport, R. I., August 8-10, Astor schooner cup—Won by Queen, J. Rogers Maxwell, N. Y., in 4h. 21m. 42s.; sloop and yawl cup—Won by sloop Avenger, R. W. Emmons, 2d, Boston, 4h. 5m. 23s. King's cup was won by Avenger in 5h. 52m. 24s. over a 38-mile course. F. F. Smith's sloop Effort won the King's cup in the first race of 1906 and Maxwell's schooner, Queen, won in 1907.

Rudder cup race, Hamilton, Ont., to Chaumont, N. Y., 165 miles—Won by Genesee, Rochester Yacht Club, in 31h. 50m. 55s.

Lipton cup race for 22-footers, at Chicago, August 15-20—Won by the Chicago, Chicago Yacht Club, in three races.

Dory race of the Amsterdam Yacht Club, Holland—Won by Tautog, George Gardiner Fry, American Yacht Club, New York.

Frederic Thompson $2,500 cup race for 22-footers, and Atlantic Yacht Club Race, week September 2-7—Cup for 22-footers—Won by F. T. Bedford's Eleanor, Bridgeport Yacht Club. Thompson $500 cup for schooner, yawl and sloop race around Fire Island Light Ship—Won by yawl Sakana Haviland Bros., Brooklyn Yacht Club. Elapsed time, 20h. 2m. 9s.

INTERNATIONAL RACES FOR THE AMERICA'S CUP.

DATE.	Course.	American Yacht.	Time. H. M. S.	English Yacht.	Time. H. M. S.	Result. M. S.
Aug. 22, 1851	Around Isle of Wight.....	America......	10.37.00	Aurora.......	10.55.00	Am. boat first home by 18.00.
Aug. 8, 1870	New York Y. C course....	Magic........	3.58.26 2-10	Cambria......	4.37.38 9-10	American boat won by 39.12.
Oct. 16, 1871	New York Y. C. course....	Columbia.....	6.19.41	Livonia......	6.46.45	American boat won by 27.04.
Oct. 18, 1871	20 m. windward and back.	Columbia.....	3.07.42	Livonia......	3.18.15	American boat won by 10.33.
Oct. 19, 1871	New York Y. C. course....	*Columbia....	4.17.35	Livonia......	4.02.25	* English boat won by 15.10.
Oct. 21, 1871	20 m. windward and back.	Sappho.......	5.39.02	Livonia......	6.09.23	American boat won by 30.21.
Oct. 23, 1871	New York Y. C. course....	Sappho.......	4.46.17	Livonia......	5.11.44	American boat won by 25.27.
Aug. 11, 1876	New York Y. C. course....	Madeleine....	5.23.54	Countess of Dufferin	5.34.53	American boat won by 10.59.
Aug. 12, 1876	20 m. windward and back.	Madeleine....	7.18.46	Countess of Dufferin	7.46.00	American boat won by 27.14.
Nov. 9, 1881	New York Y. C. course....	Mischief.....	4.17.09	Atalanta.....	4.45.39¼	American boat won by 28.30¼.
Nov. 10, 1881	16 m. leeward and back...	Mischief.....	4.54.53	Atalanta.....	5.33.47	American boat won by 38.54.
Sept. 14, 1885	New York Y. C. course....	Puritan......	6.06.05	Genesta......	6.22.24	American boat won by 16.19.
Sept. 16, 1885	20 m. leeward and back...	Puritan......	5.03.14	Genesta......	5.04.52	American boat won by 1.38.
Sept. 9, 1886	New York Y. C. course....	Mayflower....	5.26.41	Galatea......	5.38.43	American boat won by 12.02.
Sept. 11, 1886	20 m. leeward and back...	Mayflower....	6.49.00	Galatea......	7.18.09	American boat won by 29.09.
Sept. 27, 1887	New York Y. C. course....	Volunteer....	4.53.18	Thistle......	5.12.41¾	American boat won by 19.23¾.
Sept. 30, 1887	20 m. windward and back.	Volunteer....	5.42.56¼	Thistle......	5.54.45	American boat won by 11.48¾.
Oct. 7, 1893	15 m. windward and back.	Vigilant.....	4.05.47	Valkyrie II...	4.11.35	American boat won by 5.48.
Oct. 9, 1893	30 m. triangular course...	Vigilant.....	3.25.01	Valkyrie II...	3.35.36	American boat won by 10.35.
Oct. 13, 1893	15 m. windward and back.	Vigilant.....	3.24.39	Valkyrie II...	3.25.19	American boat won by .40.
Sept. 7, 1895	15 m. windward and back.	Defender.....	4.59.54 9-10	Valkyrie III..	5.08.44	American boat won by 8.49 1-10.
Sept. 10, 1895	30 m. triangular course....	Defender.....	3.55.56	Valkyrie III..	† disqualified	American boat won on foul.
Sept. 12, 1895	15 m. leeward and back...	Defender.....	4.43.43	Valkyrie III..	withdrew	American boat had walk over.
Oct. 16, 1899	15 m. windward and back.	Columbia.....	4.53.53	Shamrock I...	5.04.01	American boat won by 10.08.
Oct. 17, 1899	30 m. triangular course....	Columbia.....	3.27.00	Shamrock I...	disabled	American boat had walk over.
Oct. 20, 1899	15 m. leeward and back...	Columbia.....	3.38.09	Shamrock I...	3.44.43	American boat won by 6.34.
Sept. 28, 1901	15 m. windward and back.	Columbia.....	4.30.24	Shamrock II..	4. .	American boat won by 1.20.
Oct. 3, 1901	30 m. triangular course....	Columbia.....	3.12.35	Shamrock II..	3.	American boat won by 3.35.
Oct. 4, 1901	15 m. leeward and back...	Columbia.....	4.32.57	Shamrock II..	4. .	‡ American boat won by .41.
Aug. 22, 1903	15 m. windward and back.	Reliance.....	3.32.17	Shamrock III.	3.31.44	American boat won by 7.03.
Aug. 27, 1903	30 m. triangular course...	Reliance.....	3.14.54	Shamrock III.	3.[illegible]	American boat won by 1.19.
Sept. 3, 1903	15 m. leeward and back..	Reliance.....	4.28.06	Shamrock III.	......	English boat lost in fog.

* Columbia disabled, but finished race. † Valkyrie III. fouled Defender, and the race was awarded to American boat, though the challenger finished 47 secs. ahead in 3.55.09. ‡ Shamrock II. finished first, but lost race on time allowance of 43 secs. The Reliance allowed the Shamrock III. 1m. 57s. in all their races, Reliance measuring 108.41 ft. and Shamrock III. 104.37 ft. In the preliminary trials between Reliance, Constitution, and Columbia the Constitution won three races, although Reliance was selected as the Cup defender.

Motor Boats.

A REMARKABLE advance in speed, the installation of engines of extraordinarily high power in 40-foot hulls, and the successful defence of the British International Trophy marked the season of 1908 in motor boat building and racing. The record for speed previous to 1908 in this country was 25.622 nautical, or 29.504 statute, miles an hour. This was lifted to 31.09 nautical, or 35.8 statute, miles per hour during the year, an advance in speed of nearly 20 per cent. There were motor boat races during the season almost without number, and the field of activity extended from one extreme of the country to the other, and included not only the seacoast but every river and lake of consequence. The principal events were as follows:

Palm Beach, Fla., March 20—Dixie, owner, E. J. Schroeder, made a mile record of 2.18 3-5s. This is equal to 25.974 nautical, or 29.91 statute, miles an hour.

New York-Bermuda Ocean Race, June 6-8. Distance, approximately, 670 miles—Winner, Ailsa Craig; owner, James Craig; time, 66h. 32m. 30s. Second, Irene II.; owner, S. W. Granbery; actual time, 90h. 40m.; corrected time, 70h. 16m. 36s.

Seattle-Vancouver Race, June 29-30. Distance, 182 statute miles—Winner, Traveler; time, 17h. 57m. 59s.

Marblehead to New York Race, July 18-19. Distance, 272 nautical miles—Won by Irene II.; owner, S. W. Granbery; actual time, 32h. 33m.; corrected time, 27h. 03m. 20s. Second, Eronel; owner, Samuel Cochrane; actual time, 40h. 00m. 47s.; corrected time, 28h. 10m. 07s.

Chicago-Sturgeon Bay Race, July 18-20. Distance, 200 miles. Run in three sections, Chicago to Milwaukee, Milwaukee to Manitowoc, and Manitowoc to Sturgeon Bay—Class B, winner, Sacajawa; time, 21h. 17m. 46s.; second, Swastika, 21h. 55m. 49s. Class D, winner, Twister; actual time, 25h. 58m. 10s.; corrected time, 23h. 12m. 01s.

Race for the British International Trophy, Huntington Bay, August 3. Distance, 30 nautical miles—Winner, Dixie II. owner, E. J. Schroeder; time, 1h. 04m. 57s. Second, Wolseley-Siddeley; owner, Duke of Westminster; time, 1h. 05m. 46s.

Mile Record, Hempstead Bay, August 4—Dixie II., at the rate of 31.09 nautical, or 35.8 statute, miles.

Races for American Power Boat Association's Gold Challenge Cup, Chippewa Bay, St. Lawrence River, August 20-22. Distance, 30 statute miles:—First day, winner, Dixie II.; time, 1h. 01m. 37s.; second, Chip III.; time, 1h. 01m. 56s. Second day, winner, Dixie II.; time, 58m. 13s.; second, Chip III.; time, 58m. 19s. Third day, winner, Dixie II.; time, 1h. 00m. 25s.; second, Chip III.; time 1h. 00m. 58s. These races this year were run without time allowance.

Detroit Long Distance Race, August 22, 99 miles—Class R, speed boats, won on elapsed time by Gorning; actual time, 4h. 30m. 10s.; corrected time, 2h. 48m. 24s. Fastest actual time made by Scripps, 3h. 41m. 57s.

Toledo-Lake St. Clair Race, September 5. Distance, 190½ miles—Winner, Whim; time, 19h. 02m. 53s. Second, Delight; time, 21h. 46m. 37s.

National Motor Boat Carnival, Hudson River, September 21-26—International Championship Cup—Won by Dixie II.; owner, E. J. Schroeder; distance, 30 miles. Interstate Championship Cup—Won by Vim; owner, George F. Baker, Jr.; distance, 30 miles. Motor Yacht Championship—Won by Alabama; owner, J. H. Hoadley; distance, 20 miles. Cabin Launch Championship—Won by Eagle; owner, A. I. Piercy; distance, 20 miles. Long Distance Championship, 140 miles—Won by Vim; elapsed time, 5h. 49m. 44s.; corrected time, 3h. 47m. 59s. Long Distance Championship for Cruising Boats; distance, 60 miles—Won by Alabama; owner, J. H. Hoadley; time, 4h. 55m. 14s. Free for All Race; distance, 30 miles —Won by Dixie II.; time, 1h. 06m. 51s. Mile Championship—Won by Dixie II.; average of six trials, three with and three against the tide, equal to 28.772 knots, or 33.132 statute miles per hour

FOREIGN RECORDS.

A significant record made in foreign waters during the year was that by the Wolseley-Siddeley at Monaco, April 6. She covered a distance of 50 kilometres, equal to 31.07 statute miles in 56m. 17½s. This is at the rate of 28.76 nautical, or 33.12 statute miles an hour. On April 9, in the race over a 200-kilometre course for the Championship of the Sea, Panhard-Levassor finished in 3h. 45m. 02s., which gave her a speed almost the same as that made by Wolseley-Siddeley; 28.78 nautical, or 33.14 statute, miles an hour.

(Compiled by Charles P. Tower, Editor Motor Boat, 1133 Broadway, New York.)

Ski.

THE National Ski Association of America held its fourth annual championship tournament at Duluth, Minn., February 11-13, 1908. The American record of 103 ft., made by Carl Ek in 1902, has been steadily increased to 131 ft., made by John Evensen in the last tournament, this latter mark being within four feet of the world's record of 135 ft., made by Nels Gjestvang at Modum, Norway, February 9, 1902. In five tournaments of 1907-8 was the old mark of 114 feet made by Ole Mangseth, January 23, 1907, broken.

The National Association has a membership of thirty-five clubs and 3,500 active skiers. The present officers are: President, Carl Tellefsen, Ishpeming, Mich.; Vice-President, Alfred Munthe, St. Paul, Minn.; Secretary, Aksel H. Hotter, Ashland, Wis.; Treasurer, Dr. C. H. Mason, Superior, Wis. The fifth annual tournament will be held at Eau Claire, Wis., February 6-7, 1909.

Canoe Racing.

THE annual regatta of the American Canoe Association was held at Sugar Island, in the St. Lawrence River, August 7-21, with the following results, showing event, time and winners in the Record Series:

Combined, 3 miles—Everett V. Walker, 42.37s. Paddling, one-half mile—Everett V. Walker, 3.08s. Sailing, 3 miles—Herbert M. Moore, 48.14s.

A. C. A. Trophy, Decked Sailing, 9 miles—H. Lansing Quick. "Mab" Trophy, 7¼ miles—Matthias Ohlmeyer. Six-mile—George P. Douglas, 1h. 32m. 23s. Handicap, 4½ miles—William G. Harrison, 1h. 00m. 24s. Trial Race, 3 miles—George P. Douglas, 1h. 06m. 27s. Handicap, 3 miles—E. Howe Stockwell, 48m.

A. C. A. Trophy, first heat, 3 miles—George P. Douglas, 56.50s. Second heat—Herbert M. Moore, 45.12s. Third heat—Farnum F. Dorsey, 42.20s.

A. C. A. Trophy, Paddling, Racing Class, 1 mile—Walton Clark, Jr., 9m. Single blade, Single Racing Class, one-half mile—Robert C. Blackburn, 4.30⅘s. Tandem—Robert C. Blackburn and Arthur McNichol, 4.05 2-5s. Double blade, Single Racing Class, one-half mile—Walton Clark, Jr., 4.07 1-5s. Tandem—Walton Clark, Jr., and John R. Dickinson, 3.57 3-5s. Single blade, Single Cruising Class, one-half mile—Everett V. Walker, 5.20 2-5s. Tandem—Everett V. Walker and H. N. Wilson, 5.53 4-5s. Double blade, Tandem Cruising Class, one-half mile—William G. Sparrow, and Fred C. Pitcher, 5.05 1-5s. Tilting—W. G. Sparrow and H. M. Moore.

NEW YORK AND BROOKLYN RACES.

The regattas of the New York and Brooklyn Canoe Clubs resulted as follows:

New York. Percentages based upon season of five races—Austin M. Poole, .827; Oliver H. Sawyer, .782; C. A. Robinson, .655.

Brooklyn. Record 1908 Race; Winners. May 23, Decked Sailing Canoes—R. J. Wilkin. Open Sailing Canoes—T. O. Brown. Single Blade Paddling—H. A. Reitzenstein. Double Blade Paddling—H. A. Reitzenstein. June 20, Open Canoe Sailing—R. J. Wilkin. Single Blade Paddling—R. J. Wilkin. July 4, Decked Sailing Canoes—R. J. Wilkin. Single Blade Paddling—Arthur Knowlson. Mileage record for season, May 1 to September 19, won by W. S. Hallett, with 702 miles.

Basket Ball.

PENNSYLVANIA won the intercollegiate basket ball championship, playing eight games without defeat. The final standing, with games won and lost, was as follows: Pennsylvania, 8—0; Columbia and Yale, 5—3; Cornell and Princeton, 1—7. Previous winners were: Yale, 1902, 1903, 1907; Columbia, 1904, 1905; Pennsylvania, 1906.

Chicago University won in the Middle West, where the final standing was: Chicago and Wisconsin, 7—1; Minnesota, 2—6; Illinois, 4—4; Purdue, 0—8. In the play-off for first place Chicago defeated Wisconsin 18—16. Chicago and Pennsylvania played a home and home game for the national championship and Chicago won both contests.

Williams won the New England intercollegiate championship. Other important games of the college season resulted as follows: Yale, 16; Harvard, 12; Chicago, 28; Columbia, 13.

METROPOLITAN A. A. U. CHAMPIONSHIPS.

The Metropolitan A. A. U. championships, held at Newark, resulted as follows: National Turn Verein, 3—0; St. George A. C., 2—1; Alpha, 1—2; Tuxedo, 0—3.

PROTECTIVE LEAGUE CHAMPIONSHIPS.

The championship tournament of the Protective Athletic and Basket Ball Association, season 1907-'08, was divided into two classes—senior, average weight, 140 lbs., maximum individual weight, 155 lbs., and junior, average weight, 125 lbs., maximum individual weight, 135 lbs. Three tournaments to determine local championships and eligibility for the final or general championships of the East were held in Manhattan, Brooklyn, and Jersey City, with the following results:

Senior Championships—New York won by the Alerts; Brooklyn and Long Island won by the Emeralds; New Jersey and Long Island won by the Diamond Five. Junior Championships—New York won by the Metropolitans; Brooklyn and Long Island won by the Elgins; New Jersey and Long Island won by the Atlas. Final and General Eastern Championships—Senior: Won by Diamond Five of Jersey City; Emeralds of Brooklyn, second; Alerts of New York, third. Juniors: Won by Metropolitan Basket Ball Association of New York City; Elgin Team of Brooklyn, second, and Atlas Team of Jersey City, third.

Billiards and Pool.

BILLIARDS.

EXCITING contests, followed by several transfers of championship honors in billiards and pool, made the season of 1907-8 the most interesting of years. This great revival of interest in table games was manifested in the large attendance at tournaments and match games, both of amateur and professional, and in the demand for new equipment, all making the future outlook very bright. Aside from other interests at stake, the trophies in the events below mentioned were given by the Brunswick-Balke-Collender Company and are recognized as emblematic of the championship they represent.

World's Championship at 18.1 Balkline Billiards—Chicago, Dec. 2, 1907, Jacob Schaefer, defeated George Sutton, challenger, 500—88—11.63 to 486. Philadelphia, Jan. 23, 1908, Schaefer 500—59—7.69; defeated Albert G. Cutler, challenger, 476 -56—7.21. Chicago, March 11, Schaefer,

BILLIARDS AND POOL.—*Continued.*

500—95—14.29 defeated W. F. Hoppe, 423—59—12.15. Because of illness, Schaefer forfeited the emblem to Sutton in May, 1908.

World's Championship at 18.2 Balkline—Lenox Lyceum, New York, Jan. 27, 1908; George Sutton, champion, 500—93—7.46; defeated Ora C. Morningstar, challenger, 309—26; Madison Square Garden Concert Hall, New York, March 27, 1908, W. F. Hoppe, challenger, 500—99—20.83, defeated G. Sutton, 272—83. The week following Hoppe returned the emblem to the donors which, there being no challenging pending, brought this championship series to a close.

National Amateur Championship at 14.2 balkline—Chicago Athletic Association, March 14-23, 1908, final tournament of the series, was won by Calvin Demarest, who was already champion. Fifteen regular games and three ties, all 400 points up.

	Won.	H. R.	W. Av.	G. Av.		Won.	H. R.	W. Av.	G. Av.
Calvin Demarest	4	170	57.14	21.22	E. W. Gardner	2	75	13.80	11.01
H. A. Wright	4	133	30.08	16.14	J. F. Poggenburg	1	116	21.05	11.29
C. F. Conklin	4	141	15.39	12.11	Clarence Jackson	0	56	......	10.85

Conklin defeated Wright in the play-off, and Demarest both Conklin and Wright, against the latter running 202, which is high record for the series.

French Amateur Championship at du Monde at 18.2—Paris, April 3-10, 1908. First Tournament of new championship series. Fifteen regular games, 400 points up.

	Won.	H. R.	W. Av.	G. Av.		Won.	H. R.	W. Av.	G. Av.
Mortier	5	118	25	16.26	Darantiere	2	121	21.06	13.59
Rerolle	4	175	20	14.02	De Dree	1	79	7.55	7.94
Blanc	3	98	22.22	11.79	Labouret	0	58	......	6.37

The average of the tournament, 11.60, is high for its class at 18.2 as also is Rerolle's run of 175; but the highest winning average (Mortier's assumed 25) has been surpassed in both Paris and this city, in the latter of which his general average (assumed 16.26) has also been surpassed.

World's Amateur Championship at 18.2 Liederkranz Club, New York, April 28 to May 7, 1908. Ten regular games and two ties, all 400 points. Lucien Rerolle still French champion when he entered, represented France and Belgium, and Demarest and Conklin, and Poggenburg and Gardner stood for America. Rerolle won from Conklin in playing off and Gardner from Poggenburg. Rerolle's average of 16 surpassed his best record average at 18.2 in this country, and Gardner's 10.81 and 83 surpassed his prior 18.2 record both for average and for run.

	Won.	H. R.	W. Av.	G. Av.		Won	H. R.	W. Av.	G. Av.
Calvin Demarest	4	151	28.57	20.	J. F. Poggenburg	1	55	11.66	0.47
Lucien Rerolle	2	103	15.38	13.44	E. W. Gardner	1	62	10.54	8.50
C. F. Conklin	2	59	13.79	9.93					

Lambert Three-Cushion Championship of America, St. Louis, Mo., November and December, 1907. Harry P. Cline, tied with John Daly for first and second, won in playing off; John Horgan was third and Lloyd Jevne fourth; and Alfredo De Ora, Thomas Hueston and Chas. P. Day were tied for fifth, sixth and seventh, and H. B. Lean and Joseph Capron for eighth and ninth (last). There was no run of double figures, but Daly, without running more than 5, was credited with an average of 1.32 in defeating De Oro. Games were 50 points up. Same city, Feb. 6, 7, 8; 50 points a night, first match. Henry P. Cline, champion, 133; John Daly, challenger, 150—.66. Neither side ran above 6.

POOL.

World's Championship at Ball Pool.—St. Louis, Jan. 28-29, 1908. Thomas Hueston, champion, 600; Jerome Keogh, 584. Conferring upon Hueston permanent possession of the trophy; this closed the championship series. Chicago, February and March, 1908, new series instituted by a tournament in which Frank Sherman was first; Charles Weston, second; Alfredo De Oro, Thomas Weston and Edward Pelletier tied for third to fifth; Benjamin Allen, sixth; H. B. Lean, seventh, and Martin Fey, eighth and last. Philadelphia, May 18-20, 1908, first match, 200 balls a night, stake for this series having been raised to $250 a side in addition to the emblem. Frank Sherman, champion, 597; Alfredo De Oro, challenger, 600. Second match, four nights closing in St. Louis, Oct. 3, 1908, 200 balls a night, Alfredo De Oro, champion, 800; Benjamin Allen, challenger, 769.

THREE-CUSHION CAROMS.

World's Championship, Three-Cushion Billiards—St. Louis, 5-7, Thomas A. Hueston, challenger, defeated John Daly in 150-point match; Hueston 50—50—50; high run, 6; average, .57; Daly, 29—46—43; high run, 7; average, .50.

BEST RECORD AVERAGES.

Professionals.—100 points at 18.2, George Sutton, New York, 1906; 100 at 14.2 by Jacob Schaefer, New York, and F. C. Ives, Chicago, 1903; 40 at 8.2 by Jacob Schaefer, Chicago, 1883. Cushion Caroms—10 by Jacob Schaefer, New York, 1883 (4½x9 table), and at Chicago, 1887 (5x10 table). Champion's Game—37.97 by George F. Slosson, Paris, 1882.

Amateur.—57.14 at 14.2 by Calvin Demarest, Chicago, 1908; 33.33 at 18.2 by Lucien Rerolle, Paris, 1904.

BEST RECORD RUNS.

Professional.—307 at 18.2 by Willie Hoppe, Chicago, 1906; George Slosson ran 329 in academy exhibition with Cassignol, New York, March, 1908; 139 at 18.1 by Jacob Schaefer, 1899; 566 at 14.2 by Jacob Schaefer, New York, 1903; 246 at 8.2 by Maurice Vignaux, Chicago, 1883. Cushion Caroms—85 by F. C. Ives, Boston, 1896. Champion's Game—398 by George F. Slosson, Paris, 1882.

Amateur.—175 at 18.2 by Lucien Rerolle, Paris, 1908; 202 at 14.2 by Calvin Demarest, Chicago, 1908.

Miscellaneous.—Willie Hoppe made a run of 51 points "off the red" in a Paris academy, 1907; Thomas Bush, Elmira, N. Y., pocketed 88 balls from the "break," 1907; George Sutton, in practice for Schaefer at 18.1, ran 221 points. By use of the anchor cannon stroke (now barred) C. Dawson, in London, April, 1907, made an unfinished run of 23,769, remaining at the table six nights in a match with Lovejoy, who, by the irony of fate, claimed to have discovered the stroke. This run, however, has since been beaten.

Olympic Championships.

THE Olympic Championships were held in the Stadium, Shepherd's Bush, London, July 13-25, 1908. American athletes in track and field sports swept all before them, winning fifteen firsts to thirteen for all other nations, the points system showing 114 2-3 for America to 66 1-3 for the United Kingdom, second. Including aquatics, cycling and wrestling, in which America, not being fully represented, could hardly make a fair comparison, this country scored 131 points to 155 for the United Kingdom; Sweden had 31 points; Germany, 21, and France, 15 points.

The American team, consisting of about eighty men in charge of Trainer Mike Murphy of Pennsylvania, sailed from America June 26. Following their return a reception was given in New York on August 29 with a great military and civic parade, and the interest shown by President Roosevelt, Governor Hughes and city officials gave a national importance to the event in which the athletes received marked honors.

A recapitulation of the track and field events held in the Stadium is as follows:

RESULTS IN TRACK AND FIELD EVENTS AT OLYMPIAD.

EVENT.	Winner.	Second.	Third.	Time or Distance.	Previous Olympic Records.
100-Metre Run (109.3 yds.)	*e*Walker	*a*Rector	*c* Kerr	10 4-5s.	10 4-5s.
200-Metre Run (218.6 yds.)	*c*Kerr	*a* Cloughan	*a*Cartmell.	22 2-5s.	21 3-5s.
** 400-Metre Run (437.2 yds.)	*b*Halswelle	......	......	50s	49 1-5s.
800-Metre Run (874.4 yds.)	*a*Sheppard	*i* Lunghi	*g*Braun	1m. 52 4-5s.	1m. 56s.
1,500-Metre Run (1,639.5 yds.)	*a*Sheppard	*b* Wilson	*b*Hallows.	4m. 3 2-5s.	4m. 5 2-5s.
110-Metre Hurdle (120.2 yds.)	*a*Smithson	*a* Garrels	*a* Shaw	15s	15 2-5s.
400-Metre Hurdle (437.2 yds.)	*a* Bacon	*b* Hillman	*b*Treemer.	55s	57 3-5s.
3,200-Mtr.Ste'ple'e(3,497.6 yds.)	*b*Russell	*b*Robertson	*a*Eisele	10m. 47 4-5s.	......
5-Mile Run	*b*Voight	*b* Owen	*k*Svanberg	25m. 11 1-5s.	26m. 26 1-5s.
10-Mile Walk	*b*Larner	*b* Webb	*b* Spencer	*1h.15m.57 2-5s	1h.17m.38 4-5s.
Standing Broad Jump	*a*Ewry	*l*Tscilitiras	*a* Sheridan	10 ft. 11 1-2 in.	11 ft. 4 7-8 in.
Standing High Jump	*a*Ewry	*l*Tscilitiras *a* Biller	......	5 ft. 2 in.	5 ft. 5 in.
Running Broad Jump	*a*Irons	*a* Kelly	*c*Bricker	24 ft. 6 1-2 in	24 ft. 1 in.
Running High Jump	*a*Porter	*h* Somoty *b* Leahy *f* Andre	......	6 ft. 3 in	6 ft. 2 4-5 in.
Hop, Step and Jump	*b*Ahearne	*c*McDonald	*i*Larsen	48 ft. 11 1-4 in.	47 ft. 4 1-4 in.
Pole Vault	*a*Gilbert. *a*Cooke	*c* Jacobs *a* Campbell *b*Archibald	......	12 ft. 2 in.	11 ft. 6 in.
Hammer Throw	*a* Flanagan	*a*McGrath.	*c*Walsh	170 ft. 4 1-2 in.	168 ft. 1 in.
Shotput	*a* Rose	*b* Horgan	*a* Garrels	46 ft. 7 1-2 in.	48 ft. 7 in.
Discus Throw (free style)	*a* Sheridan.	*a* Giffin	*a*Horr	134 ft. 2 in.	136 ft. 1-3 in.
Discus Throw (Greek style)	*a* Sheridan.	*a* Horr	*r*Jarvinen.	124 ft. 8 in.	115 ft. 4 in.
Javelin Throw (free style)	*k*Lemming	*l* Doriza	*j* Halse	178 ft. 7 1-2 in.	175 ft. 6 in.
Javelin Throw (held in middle)	*k*Lemming	*j* Halse	*k* Nilsson	179 ft. 10 1-2 in	......
3-Mile Team Race	U. K.	U. S.	France	14m. 39 3-5s	......
Relay Race, 1,600 Mtr. (1,749.8 y.)	U. S.	Germany	Hungary	3m. 29 1-5s.	......
Tug of War	U. K.	U. K.	U. K.	......	......
Marathon Race (about 26 miles).	*a*Hayes	*e* Hefferon.	*a* Forshaw	2h. 55 m. 18s.	2h. 51m. 23 3-5s.
3,500-Metre Walk (3,825 yds.)	*b*Larner	*b* Webb	*c* Kerr.	*14m. 55s.	......

NOTE—Italic letters preceding names designate different countries the contestants represent, viz.: *a* United States, *b* United Kingdom, *c* Canada, *d* Australia, *e* So. Africa, *f* France, *g* Germany, *h* Hungary, *i* Italy, *j* Norway, *k* Sweden, *l* Greece, and *r* Finland.

** Carpenter, U. S., finished first but was disqualified for fouling; Robbins, U. S., second, and Halswelle, U. K., third. Declared void and ordered rerun. Americans withdrew, giving Halswelle walkover. Carpenter's time (unofficial) was 47 2-5s.

* World records.

RESULTS IN THE OTHER CONTESTS.

America won the rifle team match at Bisley, the total scores being as follows: Winder, Ohio, 429; Casey, Delaware, 423; Leushner, New York, 430; Benedict, Ohio, 412; Eastman, Ohio, 407. Grand total, 2,531. England, 2,496; Canada, 2,401; France, 2,272; Sweden, 2,213; Norway, 2,192; Greece, 1,986; Denmark, 1909. Gorman, 491; Calkins, 473; Dietz, 472 and Axtell, 418, won the revolver team match for America with a total of 1,914 against 1,868 for Belgium and 1,816 for England.

Jay Gould, of New York, defeated Eustace H. Mills, of England, in straight sets at court tennis, 6–5, 6–4, 6–4.

Winners in other competitions were as follows: 20-kilometre bicycle race (12.4 miles), Kingsbury, England, 34m. 13 2-5s.; 585-metre bicycle race (660 yards) Johnson, England, 51 1-5s.; 2,000-metre tandem cycle race (1.24 miles), Schell and Aufray, France, 3m. 7 3-5s.; 400-metre swim (437.2 yards), Taylor, England, 5m. 36 1-5s.; 100-metre back stroke, swimming (109.3 yards), Bieberstein, Germany, 1m. 24 3-5s.; gymnastic team contest, Sweden, 428 points; tug of war, London police; fancy diving, A. Zurner, Germany, 85.5 points; G. W. Zaidzik, America, 80.8 points, third; 5,000-metre bicycle (5,468 yards), Jones, England, 8m. 36 1-5s.; 100-kilometre bicycle (62 miles), Bartlett, England, 2h. 41m. 48 3-5s.; 200-metre breast stroke, swimming (218.6 yards), Holman,

England, 3m. 09 1-5s.; 100-metre swim (109.3 yards), C. M. Daniels, America, 1m. 5 3-5s.; 200-metre team swimming (218.6 yards), England, 2m. 55 1-5s., America third; high diving, Johansson, Sweden, 83.6 points; 1,500-metre swim (1,639.5 yards), Taylor, England, 22m. 8 2-5s.

Wrestling, catch-as-catch-can, 119 pounds, G. W. Mehnert, National Turn-Verein, America; featherweight, G. S. Dole, America; lightweight, Relwyskow, England; middleweight, Bacon, England; heavyweight, O'Kelly, England; Graeco-Roman, lightweight, Porro, Italy; middleweight, Martensson, Sweden; light heavyweight, Wakeman, Finland; heavyweight, Weisz, Hungary.

Fencing, Epee team, France; Sabre, Hungarian team; lawn tennis and covered courts, England, (J. G. Ritchie and Mrs. Lambert Chambers in singles); racquets, England; archery, England.

The Olympic regatta at Henley was a failure. No Americans entered, one reason being that the definition of an amateur by the English Stewards which barred all oarsmen who worked for a living was regarded as a slap at our scullers. H. T. Blackstaffe, Vesta Rowing Club, won the Wingfield Sculls which carries with it the English Amateur Championship and later defeated A. McCulloch, Leander Club, in the singles. Leander won the pair and eight oared, the latter from the Belgium crew, and Magdalen College defeated Leander in the four-oared race.

In the tryouts for the American team at Philadelphia, June 6, several new world and Olympic records were made. The results in these contests follow: 100-metre run, Lawson Robertson, Irish-American A. C.; 11s.; 110-metre hurdle, L. V. Howe, Yale, 15 4-5s.; 800-metre run, M. W. Sheppard, Irish American A. C. †1m. 54s.; Javelin, Platt Adams, New York A. C., 131 ft. 6 in.; 3,200-metre steeplechase, J. L. Eisele, New York A. C.; †10m. 47s.; Discus, free style, A. K. Dearborn, New York A. C., *139 ft. 11 in.; running high jump, H. F. Porter, New York A. C., 6 ft. 2 in.; 200-metre run. N. J. Cartmell, Pa., 21m. 4-5s.; 400-metre 3 feet hurdle, C. J. Bacon, Irish-American A. C., †55 4-5s.; shotput, W. W. Coe, Boston A. A., 45 ft. 10 1-2 in.; standing high Jump, R. C. Ewry, New York A. C., 5 ft.; 1,500-metre run, J. P. Halstead, Cornell, †4m. 1 1-5s.; running broad jump, E. T. Cook, Cornell, 23 ft. 2 1-2 in.; discus, Greek style, M. J. Sheridan, Irish-American A. C., 116 ft. 7 1-2 in.; 400-metre run, J. B. Tayler, Pa., 49 4-5s.; pole vault, A. C. Gilbert, Yale, *12 ft. 7 3-4 in.; hop, step and jump, Platt Adams, New York A. C., 46 ft. 11 in.; standing broad jump, R. C. Ewry, New York A. C., 11 ft. 1-2 in.; throwing the hammer, L. J. Talbot, Cornell, 166 ft. 9 in.; 5-mile run, F. G. Bellairs, New York A. C., 26m. 44s.

* World records. † Olympic records. J. A. Rector, University of Virginia, twice equalled the Olympic record of 10 4-5s. in trial and semi-final heats of the 100-metre run.

Best Athletic Records.

(Compiled by James E. Sullivan, President A. A. U., for The World Almanac.)

Best American records, including those made in 1908, for amateur athletics and at standard weights and distances, as accepted by the Amateur Athletic Union, are as follows:

Running—20 yards—2 4-5s., E. B. Bloss, Roxbury, Mass., February 22, 1892. 40 yards—4 2-5s., W. D. Eaton, Boston, February 11, 1905. 50 yards—5 2-5s., Victor S. Rice, Chicago, February 20, 1904; W. D. Eaton, New York, October 10, 1905; R. L. Murray, St. Louis, March 17, 1906. 75 yards—7 3-5s., L. H. Cary, Princeton, May 9, 1891; B. J. Wefers, Boston, January 25, 1896; Archie Hahn, Milwaukee, March 11, 1905. 100 yards—9 3-5s., Dan J. Kelly, Spokane, Wash., June 23, 1906; James Rector, Charlottesville, Va., May 16, 1908. 120 yards—11 4-5s., B. J. Wefers, Travers Island, September 26, 1896. 220 yards—21 95-100s. (electrical timing), H. Jewett, Montreal, September 24, 1892 (slight curve). Straightaway, 21 1-5s., B. J. Wefers, New York, May 30, 1896. Slight curve, 21 1-5s., Dan J. Kelly, Spokane, Wash., June 23, 1896. 440 yards, straightaway—47s., M. W. Long, Guttenburg Race Track, October 4, 1900. 880 yards—1m. 53 2-5s., C. H. Kilpatrick, New York, September 21, 1895. 900 yards—2m. 1 2-5s., Andrew Glarner, San Francisco, April 24, 1908. 1,000 yards—2m. 13s., L. E. Myers, New York, October 8, 1881. 1 mile—4m. 15 3-5s., T. P. Conneff, Travers Island, August 28, 1895. 2 miles—9m. 27 4-5s., Alex Grant, Travers Island, September 23, 1903. 3 miles—14m. 39s., W. D. Day, Bergen Point, N. J., May 30, 1890. 4 miles—20m. 11 1-5s., George V. Bonhag, New York, February 22, 1907. 5 miles—25m. 23 3-5s., E. C. Carter, New York, September 17, 1887. 6 miles—31m. 27 1-5s., E. C. Carter, Bergen Point, N. J., October 21, 1893. 7 miles—36m. 54s. 8 miles—42m. 19s., E. C. Carter, New York, November 6, 1886. 9 miles—47m. 41 4-5s., S. Thomas, Staten Island, October 26, 1889. 10 miles—52m. 33 2-5s., W. D. Day, Staten Island, October 26, 1889. 25 miles—2h. 52m. 24s., J. Gassman, Williamsburg, L. I., February 22, 1884. 50 miles—7h. 29m. 47s., P. Golden, Williamsburg, L. I., February 22, 1883. 100 miles—17h. 36m. 14s., J. Saunders, New York, February 21-22, 1882.

Walking—75 yards—12¼s. F. J. Mott, New York, April 18, 1878. ⅛ mile—36 3-5s., Wm. Young, Portland, Ore., August 3, 1905. ¼ mile—1m. 23s., H. L. Curtis, New York, September 26, 1891. ½ mile—3m. 2 2-5s., F. P. Murray, New York, October 22, 1883. ¾ mile—4m. 40½s., T. H. Armstrong, Jr., New York, October 26, 1877. 1 mile—6m. 29 3-5s., F. P. Murray, New York, October 27, 1883. 2 miles—13m. 48 3-5s., F. P. Murray, Williamsburg, L. I., May 30, 1884. 3 miles—21m. 9 1-5s., F. P. Murray, New York, November 6, 1883. 4 miles—29m. 40 4-5s., T. H. Armstrong, Jr., New York, November 6, 1877. 5 miles—38m. 00⅝s., W. H. Purdy, New York, May 22, 1880. 6 miles—45m. 28s., E. E. Merrill, Boston, October 5, 1880. 7 miles—54m. 7s., E. E. Merrill, Boston, October 5, 1880. 8 miles—1h. 2m. 8½s., J. B. Clark, New York, September 8, 1880. 9 miles—1h. 10m. 8s., E. E. Merrill, Boston, Mass., October 5, 1880. 10 miles—1h. 17m. 40¾s., E. E. Merrill, Boston, October 5, 1880. 15 miles—2h. 14m. 44s., W. O'Keefe, Williamsburg, L. I., December 31, 1880. 20 miles—3h. 8m. 10s.; 25 miles—4h. 3m. 35s., J. B. Clark, New York, December 5, 1879. 50 miles—9h. 29m. 22s.; 75 miles—15h. 00m. 15s.; 100 miles—21h. 00m. 42s., G. B. Gillie, New York, May 10-11, 1878. 100 miles—18h. 4m. 10 1-5s., T. E. Hammond, London, September 12, 1908; also 131 miles 880 yards in 24h. on public roads.

Hurdles—High, 3ft. 6in, 10 hurdles. 60 yards (5 hurdles)—8 1-5s., S. C. Northridge, New York, February 9, 1907. 120 yards—15s., A. B. Shaw, Chicago, September 12, 1908. 220 yards—27 3-5s., J. J. Eller, New York, October 11, 1908. 440 yards—60 3-5s., Charles Bacon, New York, October 11, 1908. Low, 2ft. 6in., 10 hurdles. 60 yards (5 hurdles)—

BEST ATHLETIC RECORDS—*Continued.*

8 1-5s., A. A. Jordan, New York, October 9, 1887. 120 yards—14 3-5s., A. F. Copeland, New York, October 20, 1888. 220 yards—24 4-5s. (around a turn), J. J. Eller, New York, September 19, 1908. 220 yards—23 3-5s. (straightaway), A. C. Kraenzlein, New York, May 28, 1898. 300 yards, 34 3-5s., H. L. Hillman, Travers Island, N. Y., September 23, 1905. 440 yards—54 3-5s., H. L. Hillman, Travers Island, N. Y., October 1, 1904. Metre races—110 metres (120.2 yds.), high hurdles—15s., Forest Smithson, Olympic games, 1908. Low hurdles—200 metres (218.6 yds.)—24 3-5s., H. L. Hillman, St. Louis, August 10, 1904. 400 metres (437.2 yds.)—55s. (3ft. hurdles), Charles Bacon, Olympic games, 1908.

Jumping—Standing high, without weights—5ft. 5¼in., Ray C. Ewry, Buffalo, N. Y., September 7, 1901. Running high, without weights—6ft. 6¾ in. Harry Porter, Bridgeport, Ct., September 5, 1908. Standing long, without weights—11ft. 4⅞in., Ray C. Ewry, St. Louis, August 29, 1904; with weights—12ft. 9½in., L. Hellwig, Williamsburg, L. I., November 30, 1884. Backward, with weights—9ft., J. J. Carpenter, Ann Arbor, Mich., November 8, 1884. Three standing—35ft. 8¾in., Ray C. Ewry, New York, September 7, 1903. Standing hop, step, and jump, without weights—30ft. 3in., J. Cosgrove, Albany, N. Y., April 25, 1894. With weights—31ft. 7in., W. W. Butler, Boston, June 18, 1886. Running hop, step, and jump, without weights—48ft. 6in., E. B. Bloss, Chicago, September 16, 1893. Running long, without weights—24ft. 7¼in., M. Prinstein, Philadelphia, April 28, 1900.

Vaulting—Fence vaulting—7ft. 3¾in., C. H. Atkinson, Cambridge, March 22, 1884. One-hand fence vaulting—5ft. 6½in., I. D. Webster, Philadelphia, April 6, 1886. Pole vaulting for height—12ft. 9½in., W. R. Dray, Danbury, Ct., June, 12, 1908. Pole vaulting for distance—28ft., Martin J. Sheridan, New York, October 25, 1907.

Hammer Throwing, 12-pound—190ft. 9in., L. J. Talbot, April 20, 1907. 16-pound—176ft. 1in., John Flanagan, Trenton, September 5, 1908; 177ft. 4in., M. J. McGrath, Bridgeport, Ct., September 5, 1908. 18-pound—161ft. ¼in., Ben Sherman, Boston, June 17, 1908. 21-pound—109ft. 1½in., Ben Sherman, Boston, June 17, 1908.

Shot Putting—8-pound—67ft. 7in.; 18-pound—43ft. 9½in.; 21-pound—40ft. 3⅝in.; 28-pound—34ft. 5¾in., all by Ralph Rose, at Travers Island, N. Y., September 14, 1907. 12-pound—57ft. 3in., Ralph Rose, New York, August 29, 1908. 14-pound—53ft. 4in., Ralph Rose, Trenton, September 5, 1908. 16-pound—50ft. 1¾in., Ralph Rose, Jersey City, September 26, 1908. 28-lb. weight, with follow—36ft. 3in., Dennis Horgan, Travers Island, September 29, 1906. 42lb. stone, with follow—26ft. 8¼in., J. S. Mitchel, New York, September 7, 1903. 56-lb. shot, with follow—23ft. ½in., W. Real, Boston, October 4, 1888.

Weight Throwing—14-pound, from shoulder, with follow—58ft. 2in., J. S. Mitchel, Boston, October 4, 1888. 56-pounds, one hand, without run or follow—28ft. 9in., J. S. Mitchel, New York, August 26, 1905; with two hands, without run or follow—31ft. 5in., John Flanagan, New York, August 26, 1905; two hands from a 7-foot circle, without follow—39ft. 1½in., John Flanagan, New York, September 19, 1908.; two hands, unlimited run and follow—40ft. 2in., John Flanagan, Long Island City, July 17, 1904; thrown for height—15ft. 6⅜in., J. S. Mitchel, Bayonne City, September 6, 1897; Irish style, one hand, with unlimited run and follow—38ft. 5in., J. S. Mitchel, New York, September 7, 1903.

Throwing the Discus—Free style—140ft. 5½in., Martin J. Sheridan, New York, October 4, 1908; 142ft. 7½in., M. F. Horr, Torrington, Ct., June 19, 1908 (questioned on technicality in measuring tape). Greek style—124ft. 8in., Martin J. Sheridan, Olympic games, 1908. In the Illinois University meet, October 24, 1907, Griffin, a freshman, threw the discus 150ft. 6in., but had no competition.

Throwing the Javelin—140ft. 2in., M. J. Sheridan, Long Island City, October 20, 1907. (American record).

Relay Racing—1,280 yards—2m. 28 4-5s., Georgetown University team (Edmunson, McCarthy, Reilly, Mulligan), St. Louis, March 26, 1904. 1,760 yards, for men, each to run 440 yards—3m. 21 2-5s., New York A. C. team (B. J. Wefers, M. W. Long, T. E. Burke, H. S. Lyons), New York, August 28, 1898; Harvard team (Schick, Lightner, Willis and Rust), Philadelphia, April 26, 1902. 2,400 yards, each man to run 600 yards—5m. 11 3-5s., Irish-American A. C. team (Odell, Riley, Bromilow, Sheppard), Long Island City, May 30, 1907. 2 miles—7m. 54 4-5s., N. Y. A. C. team (H. W. Cohn, J. A. Taylor, A. S. Macdonald, Joseph Bromilow), Travers Island, N. Y., June 10, 1905. 4 miles—17m. 58s., I.-A. A. C. team (J. P. Sullivan, G. V. Bonhag, H. W. Cohn, M. W. Sheppard), New York, February 3, 1906 (indoor); 18m. 10 2-5s., University of Michigan team (J. W. Maloney, H. P. Ramey, H. L. Coe, F. A. Rowe), Philadelphia, April 28, 1906 (outdoor).

Sack Racing—35 yards—5 3-5s., R. Mercer, Rochester, N. Y., March 15, 1901. 50 yards, over 4 hurdles, 1 foot high—9¾s., J. M. Nason, Buffalo, N. Y., December 6, 1890. 50 yards—7s., R. Mercer, Buffalo, N. Y., April 20, 1901. 75 yards—10 4-5s., R. Mercer, Buffalo, April 20, 1901. 75 yards, over 6 hurdles 1 foot high—16s., J. M. Nason, Buffalo, December 6, 1890. 100 yards—15 3-5s., J. M. Nason, Buffalo, July 11, 1891. 100 yards, over 10 hurdles 18in. high—21¼s., J. M. Nason, New York, September 29, 1882.

Hopping—50 yards—7 1-5s.; 80 yards—10 4-5s.; 100 yards—13 3-5s., S. D. See, Brooklyn, N. Y., October 15, 1885.

Running Backwards—50 yards—7 4-5s.; 75 yards—11 1-5s., S. S. Schuyler, New York, October 8, 1887. 100 yards—14s., A. Forrester, Toronto, Ont., June 23, 1888.

Three-Legged Races—50 yards—6s., H. L. Hillman, Jr., and Lawson Robertson, Brooklyn, November 11, 1905. 75 yards—8 2-5s., L. Pierce and G. Hall, New York, April 5, 1908. 100 yards—11 2-5s.; 120 yards—14s., Hillman and Robertson, Brooklyn, November 17, 1906. 220 yards—33s.; H. K. Zust and F. C. Puffer, New York, April 1, 1893.

Stone Gathering—8 stones, 2 yds. apart, a 5-yd. finish—31s., Charles J. P. Lucas, Medford, Mass., August 27, 1902. 10 stones, 5ft. interval, total distance 183 1-3 yds., with 19 rightabout turns—42s., Charles J. P. Lucas, St. Louis, October 12, 1904. 15 stones, 2yds. interval, total distance 480yds., with 29 rightabout turns—1m. 57¼s., E. P. Harris, Amherst, Mass., October 9, 1881. 25 stones, 1yd. interval, total distance 650yds., with 49 rightabout turns—2m. 39½s., M. Brewer, Williamstown, Mass., Oct. 18, 1879. 50 stones, 1yd. interval, total distance 1 mile 79 yds., with 99 rightabout turns—11m. 29s., G. R. Starke, Montreal, June 8, 1878.

Dumbbells—Holding one dumbbell in each hand at arm's length perpendicular above the head and dropped down to straight out from the shoulder horizontally, right hand,

79½lbs.; left hand, 57½lbs.—F. Winters, St. Louis, September 1, 1904. Pushing up slowly one dumbbell in each hand from the shoulder to arm's length, right hand, 100¼lbs.; left hand, 79½lbs.—F. Winters, St. Louis, September 1, 1904. Jerking up one dumbbell in each hand from the shoulder to arm's length, right hand, 100¼lbs.; left hand, 94¼lbs.—O. C. Osthoff, St. Louis, September 1, 1904. Tossing up one dumbbell with both hands from ground to shoulder, 215½lbs.—John Y. Smith, Boston, May 19, 1899. Pushing up one dumbbell with both hands five times from shoulder to full arm's length, 219lbs. 6oz., W. Stoessen, New York, December 17, 1897. Tossing up one dumbbell, weighing 201lbs., with one arm, six times, from shoulder to full arm's length—C. O. Breed, Boston, January 30, 1884. Pushing up one dumbbell, weighing 100lbs., 20 times, with one hand, from shoulder to full arm's length—G. N. Robinson, San Francisco, November 25, 1875. Pushing up one dumbbell, weighing 50lbs., 94 times, with one hand, from shoulder to full arm's length—A. A. Hylton, San Francisco, May 19, 1885. Pushing up one dumbbell, weighing 25lbs., 450 times, with one hand, from shoulder to full arm's length—G. W. W. Roche, San Francisco, November 25, 1875. Pushing up one dumbbell, weighing 12lbs., 14,000 times, with one hand, from shoulder to full arm's length—A. Corcoran, Chicago, October 4, 1873. Curling and putting up from shoulder to full arm's length above the shoulder two dumbbells at the same time, one in each hand, each weighing 100lbs.—W. B. Curtis, Chicago, September 10, 1859.

Lifting—With hands alone—1,384lbs., H. Leussing, Cincinnati, March 31, 1880. With harness—3,239lbs., W. B. Curtis, New York, December 20, 1868. Lifting the bar bell, 246lbs.—Periklès Kakousis, St. Louis, August 31, 1904.

Rope Climbing—Using both hands and feet—35ft. 8in. up, in 14 4-5s., C. E. Raynor, South Bethlehem, Pa., April 2, 1887. Using hands alone—18ft. up, 3 3-5s., Edward Kunath, Anchor A. C., Jersey City, March 25, 1902; bell 22ft. from the floor. 21ft. up, 6 3-5s., Kunath, New York, March 17, 1899; bell 35ft. above floor. 25ft. 6 2-5s., Kunath, New York, September 1, 1901.

Parallel Bars—Three successive arm-jumps, without swing—15ft., S. Strasburger, New York, November 10, 1873. With swings—19ft. 9in., A. A. Conger, New York, November 10, 1873. Push-ups, without swing—60 times; John N. Woodside, New York, September, 1908.

Kicking—Double kick—8ft. 1¾in., F. C. Crane, Aurora, Ill., November 20, 1901. Running hitch and kick—9ft. 1in., C. R. Wilburn, Annapolis, June 6, 1888. Running high kick—9ft. 8in., C. C. Lee, New Haven, Ct., March 19, 1887.

Jumping from Springboard—Running high jump—7ft. 7¼in., David Lane, Bridgeport, Ct., March 13, 1901. Running high dive—8ft. 6½in., Charles Stewart, San Francisco, Cal., September 19, 1893.

Pulling the Body Up by the Arms—Pulling the body up by the little finger of one hand—6 times; by one arm—12 times, A. Cutter, Louisville, Ky., September 18, 1878. By both arms—65 times, H. H. Seelye, Amherst, Mass., October, 1875.

Lacrosse.

HARVARD won the championship in the Northern and John Hopkins in the Southern division of the Intercollegiate Lacrosse League. The final standing with games won and lost by each team was: Northern Division—Harvard, 3—0; Cornell, 2—1; Hobart, 1—2; Columbia, 0—3. Southern Division—John Hopkins, 3—0; Swarthmore, 2—1; Lehigh, 1—2; Stevens, 0—3. Winners in former years since formation: Northern—Harvard, 1905; Cornell, 1906-7. Southern—Swarthmore, 1905; John Hopkins, 1905-6-7. Association officers are: President, W. S. Finlay, Cornell; Secretary-Treasurer, C. E. Marsters, Harvard, 502 Central Avenue, East Orange, N. J.

Tecumseh won the championship of the National Lacrosse Union of Canada in a very exciting finish. The final standing:

	Won.	Lost.	Pctge.
Tecumseh	8	*4	.666
Cornwall	7	5	.583
Capital	7	*5	.583
National	6	6	.500
Montreal	5	7	.416
Shamrock	4	8	.333
Toronto	4	8	.333

The Crescent A. C. lacrosse team, Brooklyn, maintained its previous good record by winning a number of important contests, among them the following: Defeated Mt. Washington at Baltimore, 6—2; lost to Toronto University at Brooklyn, 3—2; but a month later at Brooklyn defeated Toronto A. A. A., 4—3; defeated Brantford (Ont.) Club, 10—5, and the Montreal A. A. A. team, 9—1.

*Tecumsehs and Capitals were each charged with a forfeit for failing to play a championship match. Later in an exhibition match the Tecumsehs won by a score of 9 to 4.

Best I. C. A. A. A. A. Records.

100 yards—9 4-5s., B. J. Wefers, Georgetown University, New York, May 30, 1896. 220 yards—21 1-5s., B. J. Wefers, Georgetown University, New York, May 30, 1896. 440 yards—48 4-5s., J. B. Taylor, Pennsylvania, Cambridge, June 1, 1907. ½-mile—1m. 56s., E. B. Parsons, Yale, Philadelphia, May 27, 1905. 1 mile—4m. 20 3-5s., Guy Haskins, Pennsylvania, Cambridge, June 1, 1907. 2-mile run—9m. 34 4-5s., F. A. Rowe, Michigan, Cambridge, June 1, 1907. Running broad jump—24ft. 4½in., A. C. Kraenzlein, Pennsylvania, New York, May 27, 1899. Running high jump—6ft. 3¼in., T. Moffit, Pennsylvania, Cambridge, June 1, 1907. Putting 16lb. shot—46ft. 5½in., W. F. Krueger, Swarthmore, Cambridge, June 1, 1907. Throwing the hammer—164ft. 10in., J. R. DeWitt, Princeton, New York, May 31, 1902. Pole vault—12ft., Dray, Gilbert and Nelson, Yale, and Cook, Cornell, tied, Philadelphia, May 29, 1908. 120 yards high hurdle—15 1-5s., A. B. Shaw, Dartmouth, Philadelphia, May 29, 1908. 220 yards hurdle—23 3-5s., A. C. Kraenzlein, Pennsylvania, New York, May 28, 1898. 1-mile walk—6m. 45 2-5s., W. B. Fetterman, Jr., Pennsylvania, New York, May 28, 1898.

Best Interscholastic Records.

100 yards run—9 4-5s., E. E. Nelson, Volkmann School, at Cambridge, May 2, 1908. 220 yards run—21 3-5s., W. Schick, 1900-01; E. E. Nelson, at Cambridge, May 2, 1908. 440 yards run—50 1-5s., C. Long, 1901. 880 yards run—1m. 59 3-5s., H. E. Manvel, Princeton Interscholastic Meet, 1897. 1-mile run—4m. 28 3-5s., M. W. Sheppard, Ithaca, N. Y., May 13, 1905. 2-mile run—9m. 57 2-5s., M. W. Sheppard, Philadelphia, May 8, 1905. 120 yards hurdle—15 4-5s., R. G. Leavitt, 1903. 220 yards hurdle—25s., F. Scheuber, 1901. Running high jump—6ft. 2½in., J. S. Spraker, Princeton Meet, 1899. Running broad jump—23ft. 5in., E. T. Cook, Chillicothe, Ohio, May 25, 1906. Pole vault—12ft. 1½in., G. Mercer, Philadelphia, June 12, 1908. Putting 12-lb. shot—52ft. 8 2-5in., Ralph Rose, San Francisco, October 10, 1903. Putting 16lb. shot—45ft. 6¼in., Ralph Rose, San Francisco, May 2, 1903. Throwing 12lb. hammer—197ft. ½in., L. J. Talbot, Princeton, May 25, 1907. Throwing discus—126ft. 8½in., L. J. Talbot, Mercersburg, May 25, 1907. ½-mile relay—1m. 32 2-5s., Lewis Institute, at Northwestern University, May 2, 1903. 1-mile relay—3m. 30 1-5s., Centenary Collegiate Institute team, Middletown, Ct., May 26, 1906.

National A. A. U. Championships.

The national junior and senior championships of the Amateur Athletic Union were held at Travers Island, N. Y., September 18-19. The winners were as follows:

Junior Events. 100-yard dash—R. Cloughen, Irish-American A. C.; time, 10 1-5 sec. 880-yard run—H. Gissing, unattached; time, 1.56 4-5 sec. One-mile run—M. T. Norris, Brookline M. G. T. T.; time, 4.32 1-5 sec. 120-yard hurdles—G. W. Waller, N. Y. A. C.; time, 16 2-5 sec. 440-yard run—C. Cassassa, Irish-American A. C.; time, 51 2-5 sec. Five-mile run—M. P. Driscoll, Mercury A. C.; time, 26.23 2-5 sec. 220-yard dash—J. M. Rosenberger, Irish-American A. C.; time, 22 3-5 sec. 220-yard hurdles—J. Donohue, Irish-American A. C.; time, 26 3-5 sec. Putting 16-pound shot—H. B. Hill, Brookline M. G. T. T.; distance, 43 ft. 10½ in. Throwing 16-pound hammer—H. E. Kersberg, N. Y. A. C.; distance, 146 ft. 8½ in. Discus—Donald Cable, Swedish-American A. C.; distance, 120 ft. 2½ in. Pole vault—W. McLeod, Irish-American A. C., and J. L. Barr, N. Y. A. C., tied with 11 ft. 6 in. McLeod won jump-off, same distance. Running high jump—H. J. Grumpelt, N. Y. A. C., and E. Erickson, Mott Haven A. C., tied with 5 ft. 10½ in. Grumpelt won jump-off. Running broad jump—D. J. Ahearn, Irish-American A. C.; distance, 20 ft. 11½ in.

Point score—Irish-American A. C., 35; New York A. C., 31; Brookline (Mass.) M. G. T. T., 11; Montreal A. A. A., 9; Swedish-American A. C., 8; Pastime A. C., 7; Mercury A. C., 5; Chicago A. A. and Acorn A. A., 4.

Senior events: 100-yard dash—W. F. Hamilton, Chicago A. A.; time, 10 2-5 sec. 880-yard run—M. W. Sheppard, Irish-American A. C.; time, 1.55 3-5 sec. 120-yard high hurdles—A. B. Shaw, Chicago A. A.; time, 15 1-5 sec. 440-yard run—Harry Hillman, N. Y. A. C.; time, 49 3-5 sec. 220-yard run—W. F. Keating, Irish-American A. C.; time, 22 2-5 sec. 220-yard low hurdles—J. J. Eller, Irish-American A. C.; time, 24 4-5 sec. (New record.) Five-mile run—Fred Bellars, N. Y. A. C.; time, 26.14 4-5 sec. Putting 16-pound shot—Ralph Rose, Olympic A. C.; distance, 49 ft. ½ in. Pole vault—W. Hapenny, Montreal A. A.; distance, 11 ft. 9 in. Running high jump—H. F. Porter, Irish-American A. C.; distance, 5 ft. 11¼ in. Throwing 16-pound hammer—M. J. McGrath, N. Y. A. C.; distance, 173 ft. Discus—M. F. Horr, Irish-American A. C.; distance, 132 ft. 9 in. Running broad jump—Platt Adams, N. Y. A. C.; distance, 21 ft. 6½ in. 56-pound weight—J. J. Flanagan, Irish-American A. C.; distance, 37 ft. 1½ in. One-mile run—H. L. Trube, N. Y. A. C.; time, 4.25.

Irish-American A. C. won six of the events; New York A. C., five; Chicago A. A., two; and Olympic A. C., of San Francisco, and Montreal A. C., one each.

Athletic Championships.

CANADIAN A. A. U. CHAMPIONSHIPS.

The Canadian Amateur Athletic Union's twenty-fifth annual championships were held at Montreal, Oct. 3, the winners being as follows: 100-yard dash—C. G. Ekman, Acorn A. A., Brooklyn; time, 10 2-5 sec. 220-yard run—F. L. Lukeman, Montreal A. A. A.; time, 22 2-5 sec. 440-yard run—H. L. Hillman, N. Y. A. C.; time, 49 4-5 sec. 880-yard run—M. W. Sheppard, Irish-American A. C., New York; time, 155 3-5 sec. One-mile run—H. L. Trube, N. Y. A. C.; time 4.28 2-5 sec. Five-mile run—F. G. Bellars, N. Y. A. C.; time, 25.31 4-5 sec. (New record.) Two-mile junior run—B. Lee, Montreal A. A. A.; time, 10.46 2-5 sec. One-mile relay—New York A. C. (Spike, Sedley, Hillman, McEntee); time, 3.31 1-5 sec. 120-yard hurdles—F. L. Lukeman, Montreal A. A. A.; time, 16 2-5 sec. Running high jump—H. L. Porter, Irish-American A. C.; distance, 5 ft. 11 in. Running broad jump—F. L. Lukeman, Montreal A. A. A.; distance, 23 ft. 1¾ in. Pole vault—W. Hapenny, Montreal A. A. A.; distance, 11 ft. ½ in. Discus—M. J. McGrath, N. Y. A. C.; distance, 117 ft. 7½ in. Putting 16-pound shot—S. P. Gillies, N. Y. A. C.; distance, 39 ft. 9½ in. Throwing 16-pound hammer—M. J. McGrath, N. Y. A. C.; distance, 167 ft. 1 in. 56-pound weight—M. J. McGrath, N. Y. A. C.; distance, 35 ft. 11 in.

INTERCOLLEGIATE CHAMPIONSHIPS.

The thirty-third annual intercollegiate track and field championships were held at the University of Pennsylvania, May 29-30. The finals resulted as follows:

100-yard dash—N. J. Cartmell, Pennsylvania; time, 10 3-5 sec. One-mile run—J. P. Halsted, Cornell; time, 4.30. 440-yard run—J. B. Taylor, Pennsylvania; time, 52 1-5 sec. 120-yard high hurdles—A. B. Shaw, Dartmouth; time, 15 3-5 sec. Putting 16-pound shot—W. F. Krueger, Swarthmore; distance, 44 ft. Two-mile run—H. L. Trube, Cornell; time, 9.56. Running broad jump—E. T. Cook, Cornell; distance, 22 ft. 8½ in. Running high jump—E. P. Farmer, Dartmouth, and R. J. Harwood, Harvard, tied with 5 ft. 6½ in. 880-yard run—T. P. Jones, Pennsylvania; time, 2.02. Throwing 16-pound hammer—J. N. Pew, Cornell; distance, 155 ft. 2½ in. 220-yard hurdle—L. V. Howe, Yale; time, 24 3-5 sec. 220-yard dash—N. J. Cartmell, Pennsylvania; time, 22 sec. Pole vault—A. C. Gilbert, F. T. Nelson, W. R. Dray and C. S. Campbell, all Yale, tied at 11 ft.

Points—Cornell, 34; Pennsylvania, 29½; Yale, 22; Harvard, 17½; Dartmouth, 17; Michigan and Swarthmore, 6 each; Princeton, 4; Syracuse, 3; Columbia, 2. Rain and mud handicapped the athletes. In the preliminary trials, May 29, A. B. Shaw, in the 120-yard high hurdle, equalled the world's record of 15 1-5 seconds, made by Alvin Kraenzlein in 1898, and broke the intercollegiate record. Dray, Nelson, Gilbert and Cook cleared 12 ft. breaking the old intercollegiate mark of 11 ft. 11¾ in., made by Dray the previous year.

METROPOLITAN CHAMPIONSHIPS.

The Metropolitan junior and senior championships of the A. A. U., held, respectively, at Travers Island, July 11 and Sept. 12.

Junior Events: 100-yard dash—C. G. Ekman, Acorn A. A.; time, 10 1-5 sec. 880-yard run—C. L. Behn, Irish-American A. C.; time, 2:02. 120-yard hurdles—F. J. Sullivan, N. Y. A. C.; time, 17 sec. One-mile run—W. Berker, N. Y. A. C.; time, 4.33 3-5 sec. 440-yard run—R. W. Bacon; time, 53 sec. 220-yard run—G. J. Merz, N. Y. A. C.; time, 22 4-5 sec. 220-yard hurdles—W. R. Bursch, N. Y. A. C.; time, 26 4-5 sec. One-mile walk—A. F. Hunt, Pastime A. C.; time, 7.35. Three-mile run—M. P. Driscoll, Mercury A. C.; time, 15.12 4-5 sec. Putting 16-pound shot—H. A. Copp, N. Y. A. C.; distance, 41 ft. 5½ in. Throwing 16-pound hammer—H. F. Andrews, N. Y. A. C.; distance, 145 ft. 3 in. High jump—G. J. Fleming, N. Y. A. C.; distance, 5 ft. 10¾ in. Discus—Donald Cable, Swedish-American A. C.; distance, 111 ft. 6½ in.

Point score: New York A. C., 80; Irish-American A. C., 30; Pastime A. C., 17; Mercury A. C., 6.

Senior Events: 100-yard dash—W. F. Keating, Irish-American A. C.; time, 10 1-5 sec. 880-yard run—M. W. Sheppard, Irish-American A. C.; time, 1.57 4-5 sec. 120-yard high hurdles—J. J. Eller, Irish-American A. C.; time, 16 sec. 220-yard low hurdles—J. J. Eller, Irish-American A. C.; time 25 sec. (New record.) One-mile run—H. L. Trube, N. Y. A. C.; time, 4.29 1-5 sec. 440-yard dash—H. Hillman, N. Y. A. C.; time 50 1-5 sec. One-mile walk—S. Liebgold, Pastime A. C.; time, 7.46 2-5 sec. 220-yard dash—W. F. Keating, Irish-American A. C.; time, 22 3-5 sec. Three-mile run—M. P. Driscoll, Mercury A. C.; time, 15.03 4-5 sec. Pole vault—C. Allen, Irish-American A. C.; distance, 11 ft. 6 in. High jump—H. F. Porter, Irish-American A. C.; distance, 5 ft. 10 in. 16-pound hammer—J. J. Flanagan, Irish-American A. C.; distance, 172 ft. 10¾ in. 16-pound shot—M. F. Horr, Irish-American A. C.; distance, 44 ft. Broad jump—Platt Adams, N. Y. A. C.; distance, 21 ft. 11½ in. Discus—M. F. Horr, Irish-American A. C.; distance, 131 ft. 4½ in. 56-pound weight—J. J. Flanagan, Irish-American A. C.; distance 39 ft. 1½in.

Point score: Irish-American A. C., 89; New York A. C., 43; Pastime A. C. and Mercury A. C., five each; Acorn A. A. and Mott Haven A. C., one each.

COLLEGE MEETS AND CHAMPIONSHIPS.

The fourteenth annual relay carnival of the University of Pennsylvania was held in Philadelphia, April 25, with the following results in the more important events:

Special: 120-yard high hurdles—A. B. Shaw, Dartmouth, 15 1-5 sec. 100-yard dash—L. B. Stevens, Yale, 10 sec. Pole vault—W. R. Dray, Yale, 12 ft. 6½ in. (New record.) Running high jump—R. A. Riley, Yale, and L. Miller, Indiana, tied at 6 ft. Putting 16-pound shot—W. G. Burroughs, Illinois, 44 ft. 5 in. Throwing 16-pound hammer—M. F. Horr, Syracuse, 148 ft. 1 in. Running broad jump—E. T. Cook, Cornell, 22 ft. 1½ in. Discus—W. G. Burroughs, Illinois, 123 ft. 7 in. Relay championships. Two miles—Michigan (Bohusac, Rowe, Dull, Coe), 8.04 2-5 sec. One mile, preparatory school—Hill School, Pottstown, 3.34 3-5. One mile, high school—Brooklyn Manual Training (Cleman, Danielson, Lynch, Cozzens), 3.33 4-5 sec. (New record.) One mile—Pennsylvania (Haydock, Whitman, Taylor, Cartmell), 3.23 4-5 sec. Chicago University, second.

Western intercollegiate meet at Chicago, June 6. Winners. 100-yard dash—W. W. May, Illinois, 9 4-5 sec. 120-yard hurdles—F. J. Natwig, Wisconsin, 15 4-5 sec. Discus—J. Mesmer, Wisconsin, 121 ft. 1¾in. One-mile run—J. C. Blankenagle, Wisconsin, 4.28 1-5 sec. 440-yard run—N. A. Merriam, Chicago, 50 2-5 sec. Two-mile run—D. J. Carr, Michigan Agricultural, 9.56 1-5 sec. Running broad jump—H. Johnson, Indiana, 22 ft. 2¾ in. Throwing 16-pound hammer—D. P. Crawford, Leland Stanford, 138 ft. 4½ in. 220-yard dash—H. Huff, Grinnell, 22 1-5 sec. Putting 16-pound shot—O. P. Ostoff, Wisconsin, 42 ft. 1 in. 880-yard run—J. O. Miller, Leland Stanford, 1.58 2-5 sec. Running high jump—D. J. Martin, Leland Stanford, 5 ft. 10 in. Pole vault—C. S. Jacobs, Chicago, 12 ft.

Point score: Chicago, 24; Leland Stanford and Wisconsin, 20 each; Illinois, 18; Grinnell, 8.

Yale defeated Harvard in the dual meet at Cambridge, May 16, 60 1-5 points to 43 4-5. New records of the meet were: 120-yard hurdles—Robbins, Yale, 15 1-5 sec. Pole vault—A. C. Gilbert, Yale, 12 ft. 3¾ in. Shot put—Stephenson, Harvard, 43 ft. ½ in. Half-mile run—Witcher, Harvard, 1.58 3-5 sec. Results in other dual meets: Cornell, 80; Princeton, 37; Yale, 73; Princeton, 31. Harvard, 68; Dartmouth, 49.

New records of the college season: F. Smithson, New York A. C., made a new American record of 6 1-5 sec. in the 50-yard hurdle at Georgetown University indoor meet at Washington, March 7. Cornell defeated Columbia in the two-mile relay championship of the same meet. New England interscholastic meet, Boston, Feb. 29: 300-yard run—E. E. Nelson, Volkmann School, 35 sec. 1,000-yard run—H. Lee, Volkmann School, 2.25. Annual Interscholastic, Harvard A. A., Cambridge, May 2: 100-yard run in 9 4-5 sec. and 220-yard dash in 21 3-5 sec., both by E. E. Nelson, Volkmann School. Pole vault—W. R. Gardner, Andover, 11 ft. ¾ in. New England Association of the A. A. U. meet at Brookline, Mass., June 20: Pole vault—S. C. Lawrence, Boston A. A., 11 ft. 7¼ in. One-mile run—J. E. Ballard, Providence Technical High School, 4.31 2-5 sec. 440-yard run—W. C. Robbin, Cambridge Y. M. C. A., 50 1-5 sec. Putting 16-pound shot—W. W. Coe, Boston A. A., 46 ft. ¼ in. Throwing 16-pound hammer—B. F. Sherman, Harvard, 142 ft. 3 in. Western Interscholastic at Chicago, June 13: Pole vault—Schoolbinger, Harvard School, Chicago, 11 ft.

ATHLETIC CHAMPIONSHIPS—*Continued.*

8 in. 880-yard run—Percival Lake Forest, 1.59 2-5 sec. Pennsylvania freshmen's games: Mercer, George School, won the pole vault, making a new record of 12 ft. ½ in.; also the 440-yard dash in 50 4-5 sec., and the broad jump with 21 ft. 9 in.

MILITARY ATHLETIC CHAMPIONSHIPS.

Championship events of the Military Athletic League were held April 15 in the 22d Regt. Armory with the following results: 70-yard run—Lawson Robertson, 13th Regt., 7 2-5 sec. 880-yard run—M. W. Sheppard, 22d Regt., 2.01 4-5 sec. Sack race, 176 yards—T. MacMeekin, 23d Regt., 28 1-5 sec. Three-legged race—G. E. Hall and L. Pierce, 13th Regt., 8 2-5 sec. 220-yard hurdles—C. J. Bacon, 23d Regt., 28 2-5 sec. One-mile bicycle—W. Van den Dries, 22d Regt., 2.29 4-5 sec. 440-yard run—M. W. Sheppard, 22d Regt., 52 3-5 sec. One-mile run—J. P. Sullivan, 22d Regt., 4.29. (New record.) Tug-of-war—14th Regt. Two-mile bicycle race—W. Van den Dries, 22d Regt., 4.58 4-5 sec. (New record.) Obstacle race—J. J. McLoughlin, 22d Regt., 1.54. Two-mile run—Lawson Robertson, 13th Regt., 9.45 sec. One-mile relay—22d Regt. (Smith, McEntee, Frank, Koch and Sheppard), 3.22 1-5 sec.

WOMEN'S ATHLETIC RECORDS.

Winners in the annual field day games at Vassar College, May 9, 1908, with the best college records for these events follow:

50-yard dash—Amelia H. Ware, Topeka, '09, 6 4-5 sec. (best record, 6 1-5 sec., 1904). 100-yard dash—Margaret English, New Haven, '08, 13 3-5 sec. (13 sec., 1904). Basketball throw—Barbara Vandegrift, Wilmington, 67 ft. 7 in. (72 ft. 5½ in., 1902). Baseball throw—Inez Milholland, 180 ft. 4½ in. (195 ft. 3 in., 1904). Fence vault—Helen D. White, Germantown, '10, 4 ft. 6 5-8 in. (4 ft. 10¾ in., 1907). Running high jump—Helen D. Clark, Boston, '09, 4 ft. 2⅞ in. (New record). Running broad jump—Helen C. Dwight, Roselle, N. J., '09, 7 ft. 6 in. (14 ft. 6½ in., 1903). Standing broad jump—Adriana C. Feick, Newark, '09, 7 ft. 6 in. (7 ft. 8 in., 1906). Hop, step and jump—Theodora Wheeler, 27 ft. 2¾ in. (New record.) 8-pound shot—Inez Milholland, 31 ft. 8 in. (31 ft. 8⅞ in., 1907). Relay, 300 yards, team of 1908, 40 1-5 sec. (New record). 100-yard hurdles—No record in 1908; college record, 13 sec. in 1904.

Point score: Sophomores, 32 1-3; juniors, 30 2-3; seniors, 28 2-3; freshmen, 16 1-3.

Manual Training High School games for girls, held June 13, 1908, resulted as follows: 50-yard dash—A. Gubner, 6 3-5 sec. 100-yard dash—F. Deasy, 13 sec. 100-yard hurdles—M. McDonald, 15 3-5 sec. Grade relay, 110 yards each—Fourth grade, 59 2-5 sec. High jump (seniors)—L. Blix, 4 ft. 2 in. Running broad jump—F. Deasy, 13 ft. 3 in. Standing broad jump—E. McMahon, 6 ft. 10 in. Throwing baseball—A. Gubner, 189 ft. 7 in. Throwing basketball—A. Gubner, 71 ft. 2 in. All records in 1908 are new, excepting running broad jump (14 ft. 4 in.), and standing broad jump (7 ft. 2 in.), both held by E. McMahon.

In a tournament at Seattle, Sept. 22, Miss Frances Jacklin, a 16-year-old schoolgirl of that city, threw a baseball 192 ft. 6 in. She also circled the diamond in a base-running competition in 18¾ seconds. The distance is 120 yards.

BEST INDOOR RECORDS.

The A. A. U. does not recognize indoor records. The following list is compiled by George V. Bonhag:

Track Records—40-yard dash—W. D. Eaton, at Boston, Mass., 4 2-5 sec. 50-yard dash—W. D. Eaton, at Boston, Mass., 5 2-5 sec. 60-yard dash—F. L. Lukeman, at Montreal, March 30, 1908, 6 1-5 sec.; Washington Delgado, at New York, 6 2-5 sec. 65-yard dash—Lawson Robertson, at New York, Feb., 1908, 7 sec. 70-yard dash—William A. Schick, at New York, 7 1-5 sec. 100-yard dash—Bernard J. Wefers, at Brooklyn, 10 sec. 150-yard dash—Lawson Robertson, at New York, 16 1-5 sec. 220-yard dash—Lawson Robertson, at New York, 23 1-5 sec. 300-yard dash—Lawson Robertson, at New York, 33 1-5 sec. 440-yard dash—Harry Hillman, at Brooklyn, 50 4-5 sec. 600-yard dash—M. W. Sheppard, at New York, March 1908, 1.13 4-5 sec. 880-yard run—M. W. Sheppard, at New York, 1.58. 1,000-yard run—M. W. Sheppard, at New York, 2.17 4-5 sec. 1-mile run—Tad White, at New York, Jan., 1908, 4.23. 1½-mile run—D. C. Munson, at New York, 6.57 3-5 sec., Feb., 1905. 2-mile run—George V. Bonhag, at New York, 9.39 1-5 sec. 3-mile run—George V. Bonhag, Buffalo, 14.43 3-5 sec. 3¾-mile run—George V. Bonhag, at New York, 19 min. 1-5 sec., Feb. 22, 1907. 4-mile run—George V. Bonhag, at New York, 20.11 1-5 sec. 5-mile run—George V. Bonhag, at New York, 25.52 1-5 sec.

Hurdles—50 yards—High hurdles, Forest Smithson, at Portland, Ore., April 12, 1908, 6 2-5 sec. 60 yards—High hurdle, 3 ft. 6 in., 8 1-5 sec., S. C. Northbridge, New York, Feb. 9, 1907; Forest Smithson, at New York, Feb. 9, 1908. 70 yards, 5 hurdles, Forest Smithson, March 10, 1908, 8 4-5 sec. At Trenton, Feb. 28, 1908, Smithson was credited with 7 4-5 sec. for four hurdles, each 3 ft. 6 in. high, and at Washington, March 7, he cleared three hurdles of the same height in 6 1-5 sec. 100 yards, 8 hurdles, 2 ft. 6 in. high, 10 yards apart; first hurdle 20 yards from start, last hurdle 10 yards from finish, 12 1-5 sec.; J. S. Hill, Baltimore, Jan. 9, 1907. 100 yards—10 hurdles, 2 ft. 6 in. high, 12 1-5 sec.; S. C. Northbridge, Brooklyn, March 30, 1907. These records are also world's records. 220 yards, 10 hurdles, 3 ft. 6 in.—John J. Eller, at New York, 28 4-5 sec. 10 hurdles, 2 ft. 6 in.—Harry L. Hillman, at New York, 26 1-5 sec.

Shot Putting—12-pound—55 ft.; 16-pound—47 ft. 6½ in., W. W. Coe. 56-pound—M. J. Sheridan, at St. Louis, March 20, 1908, 15 ft. 6¾ in.

Pole vault for height—28 ft. 3 in., M. J. Sheridan.

High jump—H. F. Porter, at New York, Feb. 16, 1908, 6 ft. 3½ in.

Running high kick—H. B. Beebee, at Southboro, Mass., March 19, 1908, 9 ft. 8½ in.

Relay, 2,400 yards, Irish-American A. C. team (D. Meyer, H. Sedley, Tad White and C. Bacon), 23d Regt. meet, 1908, 5.06 4-5.

ALL-ROUND CHAMPIONSHIP.

John Bredemus, of Princeton University, won the national all-round championship of A. A. U. at the Celtic Park grounds of the Irish-American A. C., Long Island City,

ATHLETIC CHAMPIONSHIPS.—*Continued.*

September 7. He made a total of 5,809 points in the ten events, against 7,130 1-2, made by Martin Sheridan in 1907, which is a world's record. Sheridan did not compete in 1908, being in Ireland. J. Mahoney, New York A. C., was second with 6,321 points, and E. H. Clark, Boston A. A., third with 5,155. Events and records were: 100-yard run, won by Mahoney in 11 sec. (Bredemus fourth); half-mile walk, won by Clark in 3 min. 32 sec. (Bredemus second); running high jump, won by Mahoney, 5 ft. 11 in. (Bredemus third, 5 ft. 4 in.); 16-lb. hammer, won by E. J. Billar, 109 ft. 10 in. (Bredemus third, 106 ft. 7 in.); 120-yard high hurdles, won by J. J. McLaughlin, 17 sec. (Bredemus fourth); pole vault, won by Bredemus, 11 ft.; 56-lb. weight, won by Clark, 26 ft. 10 1-2 in. (Bredemus second, 20 ft. 11 in.); running broad jump, won by Mahoney, 20 ft. 3 1-2 in. (Bredemus fourth, 19 ft. 1½ in.); one-mile run, won by Dan Frank, 5 min. 41 sec. (Bredemus fourth); 16-lb. shot, won by Bredemus, 38 ft. 1-4 in.

Previous Winners—1884, W. E. Thompson, Montreal, P. Q.; 1885, M. W. Ford; 1886, M. W. Ford; 1887, A. A. Jordan; 1888, M. W. Ford; 1889, M. W. Ford; 1890, A. A. Jordan; 1891, A. A. Jordan; 1892, M. O'Sullivan; 1893, E. W. Goff; 1894, E. W. Goff; 1895, J. Cosgrove; 1896, L. P. Sheldon, N. Y. A. C.; 1897, E. H. Clark, B. A. A.; 1898, E. C. White, Cornell University; 1899, J. Fred Powers, St. Paul's Lyceum, Worcester, Mass.; 1900, H. Gill, Toronto, Y. M. C. A., Ont.; 1901, A. B. Gunn, Central Y. M. C. A.; 1902, Adam B. Gunn, Central Y. M. C. A.; 1903, Ellery H. Clark, Boston A. A.; 1904, Thomas F. Kiely, Carrick-on-Suir, Ireland; 1905, Martin J. Sheridan; 1906, Thomas F. Kiely, Ireland.

TEN-MILE RUN CHAMPIONSHIP.

The ten-mile run A. A. U. Championship was held at Celtic Park, Long Island City, N. Y., November 7, and was won by John T. Eisele, New York A. C., by six yards in 53.16 1-5 sec. The American record is 52.38 2-5 sec., made by Willie Day at Staten Island, October 26, 1889. Next to Eisele at the finish in their order were: W. Bailey, N. Y. A. C.; George V. Bonhag, Irish-American A. C.; James J. Lee, Boston A. A.; John J. Daly, Irish-American A. C., and S. Mellor, Mercury A. C. Lee led for seven miles, his time on each mile being 4.52 3-5 sec., 10.12 3-5 sec., 15.31 2-5 sec., 20.54, 26.21, 31.48 4-5 sec., and 37.13. Eisele's time in the last three miles were: 42.42 3-5 sec., 48.07, and 53.16 1-5 sec.

ENDURANCE RECORDS.

Long Distance Riding—Ten miles in 18.17 by Mme. Marantette (changing horses), Lansing, Mich., 1883. 50 miles in 1.50.03 (10 horses), Carl Pugh, San Barnardino, Cal., 1883. 200 miles in 8 hours (30 horses), N. H. Mowry, San Francisco, 1868. 1,071½ miles in 72 hours (changing horses, 12 hours daily), C. M. Anderson, San Francisco, 1884.

Military—Twenty-seven men of the Third Battery, National Guard, Brooklyn, rode from Nanuet, N. Y., to Brooklyn, 50 miles in 6 hours, August 27, 1908. Early stages of ride was in darkness and over mountain roads.

Swimming (Professional—20⅝ miles in 5.51.00, Fred Cavill, River Thames, 1876. 35 miles in 21.45.00, Dover to Calais, English Channel, Capt. Matthew Webb, 1875. 40 miles in 9.57.00, with tide, River Thames, England, 1878. Amateur—20 miles in 6.35.00, Jabez Wolff, England, 1906. 23 miles in 3.11.00, Miss Annette Kellerman, Vienna, 1906.

Walking (Professional)—100 miles 18.53.40, Dan O'Leary, Chicago, 1875. 200 miles in 40.46.30 and 531 miles in 144 hours, George Littlewood in 6-day race, England, 1882. Six-days, 12 hours per day, 363 miles, Joe Scott, England, 1888. American record, 363 miles, C. Faber, Pittsburgh, 1880. 4,000 quarter-miles in 4,000 consecutive periods of 10 minutes, W. Gale, England, 1877. 1,977½ miles in 1,000 consecutive hours, E. P. Weston, London, 1879. Greatest walk without a rest, 121¼ miles, C. A. Harriman, California, 1883. Portland, Me., to Chicago, 1,234 miles, 30 days 17 hours, E. P. Weston (28 years), 1867; same, in 1907 (68 years), in about 29 days.

Rowing—Thorsten and Arthur Stabell, South Norwalk, Ct., with W. A. Byxbee, coxswain and substitute, won the U. S. Volunteer Life Saving Corps race, Battery, N. Y., to Coney Island, 13¾ miles in 1¾ hours, September 13, 1908. Pair-oared dory boats.

Running (Professional—100 miles in 13.26.30, 300 miles in 58.17.06, Charles Rowell, New York, 1882. 623 miles in 144 hours, G. Littlewood, New York, 1888.

Skating (Amateur)—25 miles in 1.31.29, 50 miles in 3.15.59, 75 miles in 5.19.16, 100 miles in 7.11.38, all by J. F. Donoghue, Stamford, Ct., 1893.

NOTABLE ATHLETIC FEATS.

Throwing —Lacrosse ball—497 ft. 7½ in., B. Quinn, Ottawa, 1902. Baseball—135 yds. ½ in., Ed. Crane, 1884. 135 2-3 yds., Larry Twitchell (unofficial), 1889. Cricket ball—347 ft., J. Van Iffland, Kingston, Ont., 1883.

Football—Place kick, 200 ft. 8 in., W. P. Chadwick, Exeter, N. H., 1887. Drop kick, 189 ft. 11 in., P. O'Dea, Madison, Wis., 1898.

Boxing—Longest fight (bare knuckles), James Kelly and Jonathan Smith, 6¼ hours, Australia, 1855. Gloves—Andy Bowen and J. Burke, 7h. 19m. (110 rounds to a draw), New Orleans, 1893. Shortest fight with gloves—Battling Nelson knocked out W. Rossler, 3 secs., at Harvey, Ill., 1902. Largest number of rounds—Jack Jones defeated Patsy Tunney, 276 rounds, 4½ hours, England, 1825. Largest prize—Corbett and Sullivan, New Orleans, 1892; purse $25,000, stakes $10,000 a side). Largest side stake—$22,500, Jack Couper and W. Bendoff, South Africa, 1889.

Roller Skating.

CHAMPIONSHIPS of the Eastern Amateur Skating Association of the United States were held on the 14-lap St. Nicholas Rink, New York, Sept. 11-Oct. 2, and were won by Joseph Jordan. His times were: 440 yards, 45 4-5 sec.; 880 yards, 1.30; one mile, 3.03 1-5 sec.; three miles, 9.50 3-5 sec.; five miles, 18.02 4-5 sec. William Robinson, a Chicago amateur, is credited in October, 1908, with a mile in 2.24, three seconds better than Ollie Moore's professional record of 2.27. K. A. Skinner made a 5-mile professional record of 14.49 in Boston in 1886.

Trap Shooting.

THE highest yearly average of 1908 went to C. G. Spencer, who broke 94.9 ex 16,220 targets. This, however, did not equal the score of W. H. Heer, who finished in 1907 with 96.3. During 1908 Mr. Heer broke 98 per cent. of 3,935 targets, and also broke 100 straight 24 different times. The longest run in 1908 was made by George W. Maxwell, the one-armed champion, who broke 259 straight without a miss. Dropping his 260th bird and continuing the score, he broke 129 straight, which made his score 388 ex 389; a record which very few two-armed shooters have reached, and never before equalled by a one-armed shooter.

The five shoots given by the Interstate Association resulted as follows:

Southern Interstate Handicap, at Birmingham, Ala., in May. Preliminary Handicap—Won by A. S. Carrell; score, 91 ex 100. Southern Handicap—Won by George L. Lyon; score, 94 ex 100, and 18 ex 20 on shoot-off.

Grand American Handicap, at Chicago, in June. Preliminary Handicap—Won by C. H. Ditto; score, 95 ex 100. Grand American Handicap—Won by Fred Harlow; score, 92 ex 100, and 18 ex 20 on shoot-off. Amateur Championship—Won by George Roll; score, 183 ex 200, and 19 ex 20 on shoot-off. Highest general average at all targets—Won by George W. Maxwell; score, 499 ex 540. Professional Championship—Won by Fred Gilbert; score, 188 ex 200, and 20 straight on shoot-off.

Eastern Handicap, at Boston, in July. Preliminary Handicap—Won by H. E. Buckwalter; score, 88 ex 100. Eastern Handicap—Won by George L. Lyon; score, 91 ex 100.

Western Handicap, at Des Moines, Ia., in August. Preliminary Handicap—Won by M. Thompson; score, 93 ex 100, and 19 ex 20 on shoot-off. Western Handicap—Won by B. F. Elbert; score, 96 ex 100, and 19 ex 20 on shoot-off.

Rocky Mountain Handicap, at Denver, Col., in September. Preliminary Handicap—Won by J. H. Wilder; score, 94 ex 100. Rocky Mountain Handicap—Won by W. W. Shemwell; score, 94 ex 100.

STATE CHAMPIONSHIPS.

Washington—Won by B. Pleiss.
New Jersey—Won by A. P. Kinney.
Nebraska—Won by George W. Maxwell.
Iowa—Won by John Peterson.
Pennsylvania—Won by H. E. Buckwalter.
Illinois (amateur)—Won by Jesse Young.
Illinois (two-shot)—Won by Bert Waggoner.
Idaho N. C. T. Trophy—Won by B. Beane.
Arkansas—Won by E. A. Howell.
North Carolina—Won by R. Stokley.
Oklahoma—Won by L. E. Reed.
West Virginia—Won by Ed. O. Bower.
Wisconsin—Won by J. V. Winter.
Minnesota—Won by Mr. Chesterton.
New York—Won by John Martin.
Indiana—Won by W. N. Wise.
Texas—Won by W. S. Fowler.
Amateur Tri-State (Ohio, Indiana and Kentucky)—Won by George W. Waggoner.
Kentucky (at birds)—Won by W. F. Booker.
Ohio—Won by R. O. Heikes.
Kansas—Won by Charles Rankin.

OTHER TOURNAMENTS.

Sunny South Handicap, at Birds—Won by Fred King; score, 25 straight. Targets—Won by Otto Sens; score, 90 ex 100.

Grand Canadian Handicap, at Birds—Won by M. Mayhew; score, 26 straight. Targets—Won by W. H. Ewing; score, 47 ex 50, and 24 ex 25 on shoot-off.

Amateur Canadian Championship—Won by W. H. Ewing; score, 49 ex 50. Mr. Ewing won both the above with his favorite U. M. C. shells.

Olympic World's Target Championship—Won by W. H. Ewing.

Individual Championship of Metropolitan Clubs, at Montclair, N. J.—Won by G. K. Kouwenhoven; score, 95 ex 100.

Philadelphia Sportsmen's Show. Eastern Championship, at Birds—Won by Thomas Dando; score, 24 straight. Amateur Championship, at Targets—Won by George S. McCarty; score, 82 ex 100, at 21 yards.

State Team Event at the Grand American Handicap—Won by Illinois Team No. 1.

Grand American Handicap—Longest run, 196 straight, by C. M. Powers. Highest amateur and general averages, by C. M. Powers. Highest general average of all targets, by George W. Maxwell.

Canadian Indians Cup—Won by George L. Vivian; score, 360 ex 400.

American Indians Shoot—Won by W. R. Crosby; score, 670 ex 700.

Western Boosters Shoot—Won by F. G. Bills; score, 574 ex 600.

Westy Hogan Shoot, at Atlantic City, N. J., in September—Won by George S. McCarty; score, 499 ex 515. Westy Hogan Cup—Won by George E. Painter; score, 50 straight, and 24 ex 25 on shoot-off. Individual Championship, Lakes to the Gulf, at Greenville, Miss., October 13—Won by H. G. Gibbs; score, 93 ex 100. Pinehurst Mid-Winter Handicap, Pinehurst, N. C.—Won by C. W. Billings; score, 90 ex 100. Bergen Beach Cosmopolitan Cup—Won by John Hendrickson; score, 92 ex 100, and 24 ex 25 on shoot-off.

COLLEGE AND CLUB SHOOTS.

Boston A. A. defeated Yale at New Haven, February 28, teams of six men, 223 to 217. Crescent A. A. defeated Boston A. A. at Brooklyn, February 29, eight men teams, 100 targets, 580 to 543. Crescent A. A. defeated Yale at Brooklyn, five men, 100 targets, March 7, 402 to 387. Return match at New Haven, March 20, Yale won, 402 to 398. New York A. C. defeated Yale at Travers Island, March 28, six-men teams, 100 targets, 496 to 481. Return match at New Haven, N. Y. A. C. won, 508 to 489. Harvard defeated Princeton at Princeton, April 11, five-men teams, 193 to 190. Yale defeated Princeton at Princeton, May 16, five men teams, 100 targets, 416 to 410. Yale defeated Harvard at New Haven, May 25, 225 to 202. Yale won the Intercollegiate Tournament at Boston A. A. traps, May 9. Final scores: Yale, 415; Princeton, 373; Harvard, 371; Pennsylvania, 365.

Public Schools Athletic League.

THE good work accomplished by thousands of boys of the New York public schools in various meets held under the auspices of the Public Schools Athletic League has attracted attention all over the country because of the marked improvement of the competitors and growing interest of parents in manly sports.

Best records in all events follow:

ELEMENTARY SCHOOLS INDOOR RECORDS (weight classifications only).—50 yds. dash (80-lb. class)—6 4-5s.; H. Linicus, P. S. No. 9, Bronx; J. Mahon, P. S. No. 6, Manhattan, Dec. 15, 1906. 70 yds. (115-lb. class)—8 3-5s.; J. O. Hare, P. S. No. 18, Manhattan; D. Valentine, P. S. No. 3, Brooklyn; N. Patto, P. S. No. 30, Manhattan, Dec. 15, 1906; J. Nihill, P. S. No. 19, Manhattan, Feb. 22, 1908. 100 yds. (unlimited weight class)—11 2-5s.; C. Heller, P. S. No. 24, Manhattan, Feb. 22, 1908. 220 yds. (unlimited weight class)—26 1-5s.; F. Suarez, Jr., P. S. No. 3, Brooklyn, Dec. 15, 1906. 360 yds. relay (80-lb. class)—47 2-5s.; P. S. No. 77, Manhattan; P. S. No. 40, Manhattan; P. S. No. 3, Bronx, Nov. 23, 1907. 440 yds. relay (95-lb. class) 55s.; P. S. No. 40, Manhattan, Dec. 15, 1906. 440 yds. relay (115-lb. class)—54s.; P. S. No. 24, Manhattan, Feb. 22, 1908. 880 yds. relay (unlimited weight class)—1m. 49 2-5s.; P. S. No. 40, Manhattan, Feb. 22, 1908. Running high jump (80-lb. class)—4 ft. 4 in.; Simpson, P. S. No. 77, Manhattan, Feb. 22, 1908. Standing broad jump (80-lb. class)—7 ft. 8 in.; E. Lieb, P. S. No. 32, Bronx, Dec. 15, 1906; H. Spingarn, P. S. No. 10, Manhattan, Feb. 22, 1908. Running high jump (95-lb. class)—4 ft. 7 in.; Kessler, P. S. No. 77, Manhattan, Feb. 22, 1908. Standing broad jump (95-lb. class)—7 ft. 8 in.; F. Lee, P. S. No. 32, Bronx, Feb. 22, 1908. Putting 8-lb. shot (115-lb. class)—34 ft. 6 1-4 in.; F. Jeni, P. S. No. 127, Brooklyn, Feb. 22, 1908. Standing broad jump (115-lb. class)—8 ft. 9 1-2 in.; R. Bailin, P. S. No. 109, Brooklyn, Feb. 22, 1908. Running high jump (unlimited weight class)—5 ft. 1 in.; J. O'Brien, P. S. No. 10, Manhattan, Nov. 23, 1907. Putting 12-lb. shot (unlimited weight class)—37 ft. 1-2 in.; H. Clinton, P. S. No. 12, Bronx, Feb. 22, 1908.

HIGH SCHOOLS INDOOR RECORDS.—Juniors.—100 yds.—10 4-5s.; L. Perkins, H. S. Commerce, Jan. 6, 1906, Ottman, DeWitt Clinton, Jan. 6, 1906. 220 yds.—26s.; A. Cozzens, Manual Training, Dec. 15, 1906; B. Taylor, Boys' H. S., Jan. 25, 1908. Seniors—50 yds.—6s.; E. C. Jessup, Boys' H. S., Dec. 26, 1903. 100 yds.—10 3-5s.; E. C. Jessup, Boys' H. S., Dec. 17, 1904; A. B. Cozzens, Boys' H. S., Manual Training (in heat), Jan. 25, 1908. 220 yds.—25 3-5s.; George McNulty, Erasmus Hall (in heat), Jan. 25, 1908. 440 yds.—56 2-5s.; R. A. Geis, H. S. Commerce, Dec. 17, 1904; A. Clunan, Manual Training, Jan. 25, 1908. 880 yds.—2m. 6 3-5s.; D. Whitney, Erasmus Hall, Jan. 25, 1908. One mile—4m. 47 1-5s.; F. Youngs, Manual Training, Jan. 25, 1908. 100 yds. high hurdles—14 3-5s.; A. L. Goulden, Boys' H. S., Dec. 15, 1906. 440 yds. relay (100-lb. class)—53s.; Stuyvesant H. S. Jan. 25, 1908. 880 yds. relay (120-lb. class)—1m. 44 3-5s.; DeWitt Clinton, Jan. 25, 1908. 880 yds. midget relay—1m. 49 4-5s.; Morris H. S., Jan. 6, 1906. 1-mile relay championship—3m. 35s.; Manual Training (A. Clunan, A. Cozzens, F. Youngs, Danielson), March 7, 1908. Running high jump—5 ft. 4 1-2 in.; H. Rosenberg, Morris H. S., Jan. 25, 1908. Putting 12-lb. shot—42 ft. 8 1-4 in.; C. Hirschman, H. S. Commerce, Jan. 6, 1906.

SWIMMING—Tub race (20 yds.)—17 2-5s.; Guiteras, H. S. Commerce, Feb. 26, 1907. 50 yds.—33s.; M. Thompson, H. S. Commerce, Feb. 24, 1908. 75 yds.—57 3-5s.; M. Thompson, H. S. Commerce, Feb. 26, 1907. 100 yds.—1m. 15s.; N. Davis, Townsend Harris Hall H. S., Feb. 24, 1908. Relay race (160 yds.)—1m. 47 4-5s.; H. S. Commerce, Feb. 26, 1907.

SKATING—440 yds.—54 1-5s.; L. Crenim, DeWitt Clinton H. S., March 15, 1907. 880 yds.—1m. 56 4-5s.; L. Barnett, DeWitt Clinton H. S., March 15, 1907. 1-mile—3m. 59 2-5s.; L. Crenim, DeWitt Clinton H. S., March 15, 1907.

ELEMENTARY SCHOOLS OUTDOOR RECORDS—50 yds. (80 lbs.)—6 2-5s.; C. Sohneider, P. S. No. 77, Manhattan, June 15, 1907; H. Beebe, P. S. No. 144, Brooklyn, June 6, 1908. 100 yds. (unlimited weight)—11s.; D. Conklin, P. S. No. 25, Manhattan, June 16, 1906; J. O'Brien, P. S. No. 10, Manhattan, June 15, 1907. 220 yds—25s.; J. Weaver, P. S. No. 166, Manhattan, June 16, 1906. 360 yds. relay (80 lbs.)—44 4-5s.; P. S. No. 77, Manhattan, June 15, 1907. 440 yds. relay (95 lbs.)—52 3-5s.; P. S. No. 40, Manhattan, June 15, 1907. 440 yds. relay (115 lbs.)—50 2-5s.; P. S. No. 24, Manhattan, June 15, 1907. 880 yds. relay (115 lbs.)—1m. 48s.; P. S. No. 15, Brooklyn, June 15, 1906. 880 yds. relay (heavyweight)—1m. 41s.; P. S. No. 24, Manhattan, June 15, 1907. Running broad jump (80 lbs.)—17 ft.; J. Keller, P. S. No. 77, Manhattan, June 15, 1907. Running high jump (80 lbs.)—4 ft. 5 7-8 in.; W. Fisher, P. S. No. 40, Manhattan, June 15, 1907. Running broad jump (95 lbs.)—16 ft. 11 1-2 in.; C. Thompson, P. S. No. 144, Brooklyn, June 15, 1907. Running high jump (95 lbs.)—4 ft. 11 1-2 in.; R. Crowe, P. S. No. 32, Bronx, June 6, 1908. Putting 8-lb. shot (115 lbs.)—38 ft. 7 in.; J. Dobin, P. S. No. 10, Brooklyn, June 15, 1907. Running broad jump (115 lbs.)—18 ft. 8 1-4 in.; N. Sloane, P. S. No. 12, Bronx, June 15, 1907. Running high jump (115 lbs.)—F. Hanek, P. S. No. 23, Bronx, June 16, 1906. Putting 12-lb. shot (heavyweight)—39 ft. 7 1-2 in.; H. A. Clinton, P. S. No. 12, Bronx, June 6, 1908. Running high jump (heavyweight)—5 ft. 2 in.; J. Myer, P. S. No. 9, Brooklyn, June 15, 1907.

HIGH SCHOOLS OUTDOOR RECORDS—Junior—100 yds.—10 3-5s.; George McNulty, Erasmus Hall H. S., May 27, 1905. 220 yds.—23 3-5s.; George McNulty, Erasmus Hall H. S., May 27, 1905; B. Taylor, Boys' H. S., May 23, 1908. Senior—100 yds.—10 2-5s.; A. Cozzens, Manual Training H. S., May 25, 1907; May 23, 1908. 220 yds.—22 4-5s.; F. Tompkins, DeWitt Clinton H. S., May 27, 1905. 440 yds.—52 3-5s.; A. Cozzens, Manual Training H. S., May 23, 1908. 880 yds.—2m. 5 2-5s.; D. Whitney, Erasmus Hall H. S., May 18, 1907. 1-mile run—4m. 40 3-5s.; F. Youngs, Manual Training H. S., May 25, 1907. 120 yds. high hurdles—16 3-5s.; V. B. Havens, Boys' H. S., May 23, 1908. 220 yds. low hurdles—26 2-5s.; H. Starr, Boys' H. S., May 27, 1905. 1-mile schools relay—3m. 34 3-5s.; H. S. Commerce, May 13, 1905. 100-lb. relay (440 yds.)—51s.; H. S. Commerce, May 18, 1907. 120-lb. relay (880 yds.)—1m. 40 2-5s.; DeWitt Clinton H. S., May 26, 1906. 1-mile relay (heavyweight)—3m. 34 3-5s.; H. S. Commerce, May 13, 1905. Running high jump—5 ft. 9 in.; H. Rosenberg, Morris H. S., May 23, 1908. Running broad jump—21 ft.

PUBLIC SCHOOLS ATHLETIC LEAGUE.—*Continued.*

2 in.; H. Ludlam, H. S. Commerce, May 26, 1906. Pole vault—9 ft. 10 in.; M. F. Harmon, Boys' H. S., May 26, 1906. Putting 12-lb. shot—44 ft. 6 1-2 in.; H. Hirschman, H. S. Commerce, May 26, 1906. Throwing the discus (Greek style)—104 ft. 10 3-4 in.; D. Matthews, Erasmus Hall H. S., May 18, 1907.

ROWING—One mile (8-oared)—5m. 35s.; H. S. Commerce, May 30, 1907.

CROSS-COUNTRY CHAMPIONSHIP—Held on the Celtic Park Cross-Country Course, Dec. 7, 1907. Distance, about 2 3-4 miles. Won by F. Danielson, Manual Training H. S.; F. Youngs, Manual Training H. S., second; W. Jones, Erasmus Hall H. S., third. Team championship won by Manual Training H. S.. Team scores: Manual Training H. S., 45 points; H. S. Commerce, 90 points; DeWitt Clinton H. S. and Erasmus Hall H. S. tied for third place with 103 points each. Time of winner, 14m. 2 3-5s.

BASKETBALL, ELEMENTARY—Senior championship of the city won by P. S. 188, Manhattan. Junior championship won by P. S. 62, Manhattan. High School—Townsend Harris Hall won 9 and lost 1 game; DeWitt Clinton, 8—2; Erasmus and Stuyvesant tying with 7—3 each.

BASEBALL—Commercial H. S. won the championship with eight straight games.

SOCCER FOOTBALL IN 1907-8.

Elementary Schools.	Won.	Lost.	Tied.	Pts.
P. S. 109, Brooklyn	4	0	0	8
P. S. 24, Manhattan	3	1	0	6
P. S. 144, Brooklyn	1	2	2	4
P. S. 166, Manhattan	0	2	2	2
P. S. 22, Queens	0	3	1	1

High Schools.	Won.	Lost.	Tied.	Pts.
Manual Training	6	0	0	12
Morris	5	1	0	10
Commercial	4	2	0	8
Curtis	2	3	1	5
Boys'	2	4	0	4
DeWitt Clinton	1	4	1	3
Townsend Harris	0	5	0	0

TARGET SHOOTING.

The marksmanship shown by boys in the P. S. A. L. has been remarkable and of such an efficiency that were the country to requisition their services the League could furnish a regiment, trained with the use of a rifle, with three companies ready for service as marksmen, and one of sharpshooters. In the National Rifle Association invitation shoot in New York, Dec. 23, 1907, to Jan. 4, 1908, six boys from Morris High School in a sub-target gun match, five shots standing, made a score of 143, and for five shots prone 138, a total of 281. The twelfth team made a score of 254. In the school boy team match open to any public or private school in the United States not giving collegiate degrees—six in a team—10 shots each, standing and prone, Curtis H. S. scored 278 and 291, respectively, a total of 569, and the total score of the fourteenth team was 509. In rifle shooting—team and individual—the boys showed equal efficiency.

Rifle and Revolver Shooting.

SCORES made with rifle and revolver during the year of 1908, including those at the Olympic shoot at Bisley, England, were so remarkable as to attract universal attention.

OLYMPIC TEAM MATCH.

The International "Olympic" team match was held at Bisley, England, July 10 and 11 and was won by America; score, 2,531; Great Britain, second; score, 2,496; Canada, third; score, 2,439. The scores of other competitors were as follows: France, 2.272; Sweden, 2,213; Norway, 2,192; Greece, 1,986; Denmark, 1.909. Conditions of Match: teams of six, fifteen shots for record by each competitor, at 200, 500, 600, 800, 900, and 1,000 yards. Each team used the military arm of their country. Members of the American Team and their scores: Sergeant W. Leushner, N. G. N. Y., 430; Major W. B. Martin, N. G. N. J., 430; Major C. B. Winder, Ohio N. G., 429; Captain K. K. V. Casey, Delaware N. G., 423; Corporal A. Eastman, Ohio N. G., 412; Captain C. S. Benedict, Ohio N. G., 407.

NATIONAL MATCHES, 1908.

Team Match—Won by U. S. Infantry; score, 3,224. The other five prize winners were: U. S. Navy; score, 3,210; U. S. Cavalry, 3,180; U. S. Marine Corps, 3,117; Wisconsin, 3,073; Massachusetts, 3,056.

National Individual Match—Won by Lieut. A. D. Rothrock, Ohio N. G.; score, 300.

NATIONAL RIFLE ASSOCIATION OF AMERICA MATCHES.

Individual Military Championship for 1908—Won by Lieut. S. A. Harris, Fourteenth U. S. Infantry; score, 582.

Wimbledon Cup Match (1,000 yards Championship)—Won by Capt. K. K. V. Casey, Delaware N. G.; score, 97.

President's Match—Won by Sergeant A. Brest, Fifteenth U. S. Infantry; score, 304.

Leach Cup Match—Won by Capt. K. K. V. Casey, Delaware N. G.; score, 104.

Regimental Team Championship—Won by Sixth Massachusetts Infantry; score, 775.

Championship Regimental Skirmish Match—Won by Corps of Engineers, U. S. A.; score 440.

RIFLE AND REVOLVER SHOOTING.—*Continued.*

Championship Company Team Match—Won by U. S. Marine Corps; score, 453.
Press Match—Won by T. S. Van Gorder, Warren (Ohio) Chronicle; score, 43.
Life Members' Match—Won by Dr. W. G. Hudson; score, 68.
State Secretaries' Match—Won by H. W. McBride, Indiana; score, 47.
Inter-club Match—Won by Fourth N. J. Infantry Rifle Club; score, 222.
Individual (long range) Tyro Match—Won by Captain Holcomb, U. S. Marine Corps; score, 449.

INTERCOLLEGIATE AND INTERSCHOLASTIC MATCHES.

Intercollegiate Out-door Team (Championship for 1908)—Won by George Washington University, of Washington, D. C., at the Wakefield, Mass., range; score, 725.

Intercollegiate Indoor Championship—Won by Columbia College in New York City; score, 387.

Interscholastic Indoor Team Match (telegraph match)—Won by Culver Military School, Culver, Indiana; score, 925.

OTHER RIFLE RECORDS.

Dryden Trophy Match—Won by U. S. Marine Corps; score, 1,089.
Herrick Trophy Match—Won by U. S. Marine Corps; score, 1,647.
The McAlpin Trophy Match—Won by Ohio; score, 1,078.

In the Indoor 22-calibre Rifle League tournament at Rochester, January, 1908, R. Gute, Jeffersonville, N. Y., made a perfect bull's-eye at 75 ft. on a 4-in. cartoon. A. Hubalek, Brooklyn, won the National Championship with a score of 2,464, out of a possible 2,500. H. Harrison, Rochester, made a new world's record in the rapid-fire event, scoring 570 in 81 shots, in 60 seconds, all landing on the target.

Annie Oakley hit 1,016 brass discs 1½ in. in diameter, with rifle and single bullets, the discs being thrown in the air at a distance of 21 ft.

In the Olympic tryouts at Camp Perry, before sailing for England, Capt. K. K. V. Casey made 31 consecutive bull's-eyes; Corp. I. L. Eastman, Ohio National Guard, made a possible 75 at 900 yards, and the eight high men at 800, 900, and 1,000 yds., made a total of 1,716 out of a possible 1,800, or four points more than the Palma Trophy Team of 1907; all world's records.

THE NINTH ANNUAL U. S. R. A. TOURNAMENT.

The annual outdoor contests of the United States Revolver Association for 1908 were held contemporaneously at Bisbee, Ariz.; San Francisco, Chicago, New Orleans, Baltimore, Walnut Hill, Mass.; Springfield, Mass.; Portland, Me.; Sea Girt, N. J.; Paterson, N. J.; Portland, Ore.; New York City (Greenville, N. J.); Providence, R. I., and St. Louis, Mo. The entry of 150 contestants was the largest in the history of the association. The highest five contestants in each match received medals. Conditions and scores follow:

Match A. Any Revolver Championship. Open to all; distance, 50 yards; target, standard American; shots, 50; possible score, 500; weapon, any revolver within the rules; ammunition, any—Lieut. R. H. Sayre, New York, .38 S. & W. 8-in. bbl., 94, 92, 91, 93, 92. Total, 462. Charles Dominic, St. Louis, .38 S. & W., 89, 96, 89, 90, 90. Total, 454. Dr. I. R. Calkins, Springfield, .38 S. & W., 89, 88, 93, 92, 89. Total, 451. J. A. Dietz, New York, 90, 85, 89, 91, 93. Total, 448. S. E. Sears, St. Louis, Colt Off. Model, 86, 87, 90, 86, 96. Total, 445.

Match B. Pistol Championship. Weapon, any pistol within the rules. Other conditions as in Match A—J. E. Gorman, San Francisco, .22 S. & W. Total, 468. P. Hanford, New York, .22 S. & W. Total, 468. Dr. I. R. Calkins, Springfield, .22 S. & W. Total, 467. Walter H. Freeman, Mansfield, Mass., .22 S. & W. Total, 460. Lieut. R. H. Sayre, New York, .22 S. & W. Total, 460.

Match C. Military Revolver Championship. Weapon, military revolver or military magazine pistol; ammunition, strictly military; distance, 50 yards; target, standard American; shots, 75, fired in strings of five shots each; time limit, 15 seconds per string—C. F. G. Armstrong, San Francisco, .38 S. & W. Total, 568. Lieut. R. H. Sayre, New York, .38 S. & W. Total, 538. Thomas LeBoutillier, 2d., New York, .38 S. & W. Total, 532. W. G. Krieg, Chicago, .38 S. & W. Total, 529. Lieut.-Col. W. H. Whigham, Chicago, .38 S. & W. Total, 501.

Match D. Military Record Match. A re-entry match; shots, 25, fired in strings of five shots each. Other conditions as in Match C—C. F. G. Armstrong, San Francisco, .38 S. & W. Total, 194. Lieut. R. H. Sayre, New York, .38 S. & W. Military. Total, 192. W. G. Krieg, Chicago, .38 S. & W. Military. Total, 187. Thomas LeBoutillier, 2d., New York, .38 S. & W. Military. Total, 184. Charles Rie, Sergeant, Company C, Twenty-first Infantry, .38 Colt. Total, 155. A. L. A. Himmelwright, New York. Total, 97.

STATE CHAMPIONSHIPS.

Any Revolver Championship—Arizona, A. E. Mackenzie; California, J. E. Gorman; Illinois, W. G. Krieg; Louisiana, J. H. Wessels; Maine, S. B. Adams; Maryland, Capt. E. A. Smith; Massachusetts, Dr. I. R. Calkins; Missouri, Charles Dominic; New Jersey, R. M. Ryder; New York, Lieut. R. H. Sayre. Pistol Championship—Arizona, A. E. Mackenzie; California, J. E. Gorman; Illinois, W. G. Krieg; Louisiana, J. H. Wessels; Massachusetts, *Dr. I. R. Calkins; Maine, S. B. Adams; Missouri, M. R. Moore; New Jersey, T. P. Nicols; New Jersey, *P. Hanford; Oregon, J. T. Moore; Rhode Island, William Almy.

New U. S. R. A. Records. Revolver, 20 yards; 10 shots. November 15, 1907—C. C. Crossman, St. Louis, Mo., 100. Pistol, 20 yards; 50 shots; March 25, 1908—L. R. Hatch, Portland, Me., 462. Thirty shots, March 26, 1908—L. R. Hatch, Portland, Me., 279. Ten shots, May 18, 1908—F. L. Hayden, Portland, Me.

*National records take precedence.

The following records for 1907-8 were accepted by the Amateur Athletic Union at the annual meeting in November, 1908. They are not all world's records, however, such records being found under the separate head of "Best Athletic Records," on another page in this book.

65-yard run (indoor)—Lawson Robertson, I.-A. A. C., at 69th Regiment Armory, March 2. Time, 7s.

120-yard high hurdle—A. B. Shaw, Dartmouth College, at Intercollegiate games, Philadelphia, May 29. Time, 15 1/5s.

70-yard three-legged race (indoor)—G. E. Hall and Lyndon Pierce, April 15. Time, 8 3/5s.

220-yard low hurdle (2ft. 6in.), fifth of a mile track, around a turn—J. J. Eller, I.-A. A. C., at Travers Island, September 19. Time, 24 4/5s.

220-yard high hurdle (3ft. 6in.)—J. J. Eller, I.-A. A. C., at Celtic Park, October 11. Time, 27 3/5s.

440-yard high hurdle (3ft. 6in.)—Charles Bacon, I.-A. A. C., at Celtic Park, October 11. Time, 1m. 3/5s.

900-yard run—Andrew Glarner, San Francisco, April. Time, 2m. 1 3/5s.

16-lb. shot put—Ralph Rose, at Celtic Park, September 7. Distance, 49ft. 10in.

12-lb. shot put—Ralph Rose, at Celtic Park, August 29 (from 7ft. circle). Distance, 57ft. 8in.

Discus (7ft. circle)—M. F. Horr, I.-A. A. C., at Travers Island, September 19. Distance, 132ft. 10 in. (Weight, 4.4 lbs.)

Discus, Olympic style (8ft. 2½in. circle) (4lbs. 6½oz.)—Martin J. Sheridan, I.-A. A. C., at Pastime Oval, October 4. Distance, 140ft. 5½in.

16-lb. hammer—John Flanagan, I.-A. A. C., at Celtic Park, August 30 (9ft. circle). Distance, 179ft. 6¾in.

18-lb. hammer (including weight of head and wire handle)—B. F. Sherman, Boston, June 17. Distance, 131ft. ¼in.

21-lb. hammer (including weight of head and wire handle)—B. F. Sherman, Boston, June 17. Distance, 109ft. 1¼in.

Pole vault—Walter R. Dray, Yale, at Danbury, Ct., June 12. Height, 12ft. 9½in.

OLYMPIC RECORDS—TRY-OUTS, AT PHILADELPHIA, JUNE 6.

Greek discus—Martin J. Sheridan, I.-A. A. C. Distance, 116ft. 7½in.
100-metre run—J. A. Rector (equals record). Time, 10 4/5s.
800-metre run—M. W. Sheppard, I.-A. A. C. Time, 1m. 54s.
400-metre hurdle (3ft. high)—Charles Bacon. Time, 55 4/5s.
1,500-metre run—J. P. Halstead, N. Y. A. C. Time, 4m. 1 4/5s.
100-metre run—H. J. Huff, C. A. A., at Pittsburgh, June 20, equalled record of 10 4/5s.

Sunday World Field Days.

The Sunday World Public School Field Days were inaugurated in 1906. In the Spring of that year one hundred grammar schools in New York City held individual sets of field day games. This great series of athletic meets, in which nearly 20,000 boys took part, was planned by the Sunday World, which also gave the prizes. The games were under the direction of the New York Public Schools Athletic League. The programme of each meet consisted of individual and relay races, jumping, and weight throwing.

In the Spring of 1907 one hundred schools again had these field day meets. The boys then competed in classes according to their weight as follows: 80-pound class, 95-pound class, 115-pound class, unlimited (heavy) weight class.

In 1908, the third year of the Sunday World field days, the number of schools holding these games was increased to 114—35 in Manhattan, 38 in Brooklyn, 18 in Queens, 17 in the Bronx, and 6 in Richmond. The Sunday World All-City trophy was won by School No. 62, Manhattan. 1,027 boys took part in the games of this school at Seward Park on June 16.

In the three years of the Sunday World field days nearly 65,000 boys have competed in these meets. The percentage of boys entering the games was very large from many of the schools, exceeding 50 per cent. of the total enrolment of the school's grammar grades.

In the Fall of each year that the New York schools have held the Sunday World field days there has been a grand final meet of the entire series of the year's games, in which representatives of all the schools have participated. In 1908, this great meet was held on October 3, at the Curtis Athletic Field, New Brighton, S. I. Gold, silver and bronze medals were given as first, second and third prizes in each of the sixteen events on the programme. 1,400 boys competed in the games. Following are the winners of the gold medals:

50-yard dash, 80-pound class—Won by T. Hegarty, P. S. 49, Manhattan. Time, 6 3-5s.
70-yard dash, 80-pound class—Won by D. Crockett, P. S. 49, Manhattan. Time, 9s.
60-yard dash, 95-pound class—Won by H. Holzmacher, P. S. 123, Brooklyn. Time, 7 3-5s.
80-yard dash, 95-pound class—Won by L. Jackson, P. S. 89, Manhattan. Time, 9s.
70-yard dash, 115-pound class—Won by B. Lambert, P. S. 62, Manhattan. Time, 8 2-5s.
90-yard dash, 115-pound class—Won by M. Campbell, P. S. 110, Brooklyn. Time, 10 4-5s.
110-yard dash, heavy-weight class—Won by J. Nihill, P. S. 19, Manhattan. Time, 11s.
220-yard dash, heavy-weight class—Won by J. Robb, P. S. 69, Manhattan. Time, 26s.
360-yard relay, 80-pound class—Won by P. S. 144, Brooklyn (team: C. Reed, W. Palle, J. Steinberg, I. Sargol). Time, 47s.
440-yard relay, 95-pound class—Won by P. S. 26, Brooklyn (team: O. Tomell, E. Alpert, E. Riley, J. Keane). Time, 57s.
440-yard relay, 115-pound class—Won by P. S. 6, Manhattan (team: Leary, Leavy, O'Brien, Young). Time, 51s.

FIELD EVENTS.

Running broad jump, 80-pound class—Won by L. Roser, P. S. 110, Brooklyn, 15 ft. 1-2 in.
Running high jump, 95-pound class—Won by W. Fisher, P. S. 40, Manhattan, 4 ft. 10 in.
Running broad jump, 115-pound class—Won by G. Anderson, P. S. 82, Manhattan, 16 ft. 6 in.
Putting 12-pound shot, heavy-weight class—Won by J. Dailey, P. S. 12, Bronx, 31 ft. 10 1-2 in.
Running high jump, heavy-weight class—Won by L. Neice, P. S. 69, Manhattan, 5 ft. 3 in.

The Sunday World banner trophy, given to the school winning the greatest number of points in the final meet, was won by P. S. 69, Manhattan.

The American Turf.

THE season of 1908 for thoroughbred sport on the Metropolitan tracks about New York City had a dismal close quite in contrast to the very successful year which had preceded it and the promising opening of the Spring. This was due to the legislative enactment of the Agnew-Hart bills prohibiting betting, and the consequent lack of public interest. The meetings were continued at a heavy loss to the track owners, and the leading turfmen shipped many of their best horses to England.

James R. Keene, who in 1907 headed the list of winning horse owners with a world's record total of $403,016, closed the season of 1908 still in the lead but with only $281,965. Maskette, the champion filly of the season, was the greatest winner for Mr. Keene, her total being $56,000, Ballot $55,000, and Colin, third, $47,000. John E. Madden was the second largest winner, with $165,000, won by Sir Martin, the best two-year-old of the season, and Fayette. August Belmont won $94,000, and Harry Payne Whitney $75,000. Joe Notter, of the Keene stable, headed the list of winning jockeys, and E. Dugan was second.

The season abroad was made interesting through the entry in the English Derby of August Belmont's Norman III., the 6 to 1 favorite, and W. K. Vanderbilt's Seasick II. E. Ginistrelli's Italian bred filly Signorinetta won at 100 to 1. It was the first time an American bred horse was a favorite in this race. Signorinetta also won the Oaks (after Richard Croker's Rhodora fell), being the third filly to win this dual event. W. K. Vanderbilt's Seasick II. ran a dead heat for the French Derby, and his colt Northeast won the Grand Prix de Paris.

WINNERS OF IMPORTANT EVENTS.

KENTUCKY DERBY, LOUISVILLE.

(Distance, 1¼ miles.)

YEAR.	Owner, Winner, Second, and Third.	Time.	Value.
1903......	C. R. Ellison's Judge Himes, Early, Bourbon	2.09	$4,850
1904......	L. Durnell's Elwood, Ed. Tierney, Brancas	2.08½	4,850
1905......	S. S. Brown's Agile, Ram's Horn, Layson	2.10¾	4,850
1906......	George J. Long's Sir Huron, Lady Navarre, James Reddick	2.08⅘	4,850
1907......	J. H. Woodford's Pink Star, Zal, Overlands	2.12 3-5	4.850
1908......	C. E. Hamilton & Co.'s Stone Street. Sir Cleges	2.15 1-5	4,850

Record, 2.06¼, by Lieutenant Gibson in 1900.

METROPOLITAN HANDICAP, BELMONT PARK.

(Distance, 1 mile.)

YEAR.	Owner, Winner, Second, and Third.	Time.	Value.
1903......	H. P. Whitney's Gunfire, Old England, Lux Casta	*1.38½	$11.080
1904......	H. B. Duryea's Irish Lad, Toboggan, Beldame	1.40	10.880
1905†...	James R. Keene's Sysonby, O. L. Richard's Race King, } Colonial Girl	1.41 3-5	9,230
1906......	J. A. Drake's Grapple, Dandelion, Oxford	1.39	10,850
1907......	J. H. McCormick's Glorifier, Okenite, Roseben	1.40 4-5	10,570
1908......	B. Schreiber's Jack Atkin, Restigouche, Don Creole	1.38 3-5	9,620

† Dead heat.

CARTER HANDICAP, AQUEDUCT.

(Distance, 7 furlongs.)

YEAR.	Owner, Winner, Second, and Third.	Time.	Value.
1903......	J. A. Kyle's Ahumada, Yellow Tail, Illyria	1.33	$2,735
1904......	N. Bennington's Beldame, Peter Paul, Wotan	1.27	7,710
1905......	Sydney Paget's Ormonde's Right, Roseben, Little Em	1.26 4-5	7,100
1906......	D. C. Johnson's Roseben, Southern Cross, Red Knight	1.26 2-5	7,850
1907......	J. H. McCormick's Glorifier, Roseben, Don Diego	1.28 1-5	7,850
1908......	B. Schreiber's Jack Atkin, Red River, Chapultepec	1.27 4-5	6,850

EXCELSIOR HANDICAP, JAMAICA.

(Distance, 11-16 miles.)

YEAR.	Owner, Winner, Second, and Third.	Time.	Value.
1903......	W. C. Whitney's Blackstock, Heno, Yellow Tail	1.46 2-5	$8,730
1904......	F. R. Doctor's Rostand, Red Knight, Lord Badge	1.45 3-5	6,660
1905......	Albemarle Stables' Santa Catalina, Rapid Water, Sinister	1.46 2-5	6,450
1906......	Newcastle Stables' Merry Lark, Ormonde's Right, Eugenia Burch	1.47 1-5	7,350
1907......	T. D. Sullivan's Dr. Gardner, Glorifier, Cairngorm	1.48 1-5	7,350
1908......	Newcastle Stables' McCarter, Jack Atkin, Rifleman	1.46	6,850

THE AMERICAN TURF—*Continued.*

SARATOGA HANDICAP, SARATOGA.

(Distance, 1¼ miles.)

Year.	Owner, Winner, Second, and Third.	Time.	Value.
1903......	J. B. Haggin's Waterboy, Hunter Raine, Caughnawaga...............	2.05 3-5	$8,800
1904......	Aug. Belmont's Lord of the Vale, Bad News, Caughnawaga..........	2.05	8,800
1905......	J. Sanford's Caughnawaga, Water Light, Beldame......................	2.07	8,300
1906......	F. R. Hitchcock's Dandelion, Tangle, Gallavant............................	2.04 3-5	8,300
1907......	Newcastle Stables' McCarter, Running Water, Dandelion.............	2.05 3-5	8,300
1908......	Montpelier Stables' Monfort, Far West, Danoscara.....................	2.05 4-5	7,150

SUBURBAN HANDICAP, SHEEPSHEAD BAY.

(Distance, 1¼ miles.)

Year.	Owner, Winner, Second and Third.	Time.	Value.
1903......	Hampton Stable's Africander, Herbert, Hunter Raine................	2.10 2-5	$16,490
1904......	E. R. Thomas' Hermis, The Picket, Irish Lad..........................	*2.05	16,800
1905......	August Belmont's Beldame, Proper, First Mason......	2.05 3-5	16,800
1906......	A. Shield's Go-Between, Dandelion, Colonial Girl........................	2.05 1-5	16,800
1907......	C. E. Durnell's Nealon, Montgomery, Beacon Light....................	2.06 2-5	16,800
1908......	James R. Keene's Ballot, King James, Fair Play........................	2.03	19 750

BRIGHTON HANDICAP, BRIGHTON BEACH.

(Distance, 1¼ miles.)

Year.	Owner, Winner, Second, and Third.	Time.	Value.
1903......	J. B. Haggin's Waterboy, Roehampton, River Pirate......................	2.03 1-5	$8,000
1904......	Capt. S. S. Brown's Broomstick, Irish Lad, Highball........................	*2.02 4-5	21,750
1905......	H. P. Whitney's Artful, Ort Wells, Beldame....	2.04 4-5	21,750
1906......	W. S. Williams's Ram's Horn, First Mason, Tokalon......................	2.03 3-5	19,750
1907......	J. R. Keene's Peter Pan, McCarter, Montgomery..........................	2.03 2-5	19,750
1908......	Not run	....	....

THE FUTURITY, SHEEPSHEAD BAY.

(Distance, 6 furlongs.)

Year.	Owner, Winner, Second, and Third.	Time.	Value.
1903......	Sydney Paget's Hamburg Belle, Leonidas, The Minute Man..........	1.13	$35,930
1904......	H. B. Duryea's Artful, Tradition, Sysonby.................................	1.11 4-5	42,880
1905......	Ormondale Stables' Ormondale, Timber, Belmere.......................	1.11 4-5	38,680
1906......	W. Lakeland's Electioneer, Pope Joan, De Mund	1.13 3-5	37,270
1907......	J. R. Keene's Colin, Bar None, Chapultepec...............................	*1.11 1-5	24,830
1908......	James R. Keene's Maskette, Sir Martin, Helmet..........................	1.11 1-5	24,985

BROOKLYN HANDICAP, GRAVESEND.

(Distance, 1¼ miles.)

Year.	Owner, Winner, Second, and Third.	Time.	Value.
1903......	Westbury Stable's Irish Lad, Gunfire, Heno................................	*2.05 2-5	$14 950
1904......	Waldeck Stable's The Picket, Irish Lad, Proper..........................	2.06 3-5	15,800
1905......	J. R. Keene's Delhi, Ostrich, Graziallo..	2.06 2-5	15,800
1906......	J. W. Fuller's Tokalon, Dandelion, The Picket.............................	2.05 3-5	15 800
1907......	J. R. Keene's Superman, Beacon Light, Nealon,...........................	2.09	15,800
1908......	James R. Keene's Celt, Fair Play, Master Robert.........................	2.04 1-5	19,750

THE ENGLISH DERBY, EPSOM DOWNS—(ENGLISH TURF).

(Distance, about 1½ miles.)

Year.	Owner and Winner.	Sire.	Time.	Second.
1903..	Sir J. Miller's Rock Sand..............................	Sainfoin............	2.42 4-5	Vinicius.
1904...	Leopold de Rothschild's St. Amant............	St. Frusquin........	2.45 4-5	John O'Gaunt.
1905..	Lord Rosebery's Cicero..............................	Satire................	2.39 3-5	Jardy.
1906..	Maj. Loeder's Spearmint............................	Carbine............*	2.36 4-5	Picton.
1907..	Richard Croker's Orby...............................	Orme	2.44	Slieve Gallion.
1908..	E. Ginistrelli's Signorinetta........................	....	2.39 4-5	Primer.

* Record time for race.

THE AMERICAN TURF—*Continued.*

RECORD OF BEST PERFORMANCES ON THE RUNNING TURF.

Distance.	Name, Age, Weight, and Sire.	Place.	Date.	Time.
¼ mile	Bob Wade, 4	Butte, Mont.	Aug. 20, 1890	0.21¼
⅜ "	Atoka, aged, 103 lbs.	Butte, Mont.	Sept. 7, 1906	0.33½
3½ furlongs	Carmisa, 2, 102 lbs	Oakland (Cal.)	Feb. 21, 1908	0.40 2-5
½ mile	Geraldine, 4, 122 lbs	Morris Park (st. c.)	Aug. 30, 1889	0.46
	Bessie Macklin, 2, 100 lbs.	Dallas, Tex	Oct. 3, 1899	0.46½
4½ furlongs	Preceptor, 2, 112 lbs	Belmont Park (st. c.)	May 19, 1908	0.51
	Old England, 2, 108 lbs	Oakland (Cal. J. C.)	Dec. 18, 1901	0.53
⅝ mile	Maid Marian, 4, 111 lbs	Morris Park (st. c.)	Oct. 9, 1894	0.56¾
	Jack Nunnally, 3, 108 lbs	Oakland (Cal. J. C.)	Dec. 3, 1907	0.5 3
	Silver Stocking, 4, 102 lbs	Seattle, Wash'n	Aug. 17, 1908	0.5 3-5
5½ furlongs	Plater, 2, 107 lbs	Morris Park (st. c.)	Oct. 21, 1902	1.02½
	Fern L., 3, 92 lbs.	Seattle, Wash'n	Aug. 8, 1908	1.05
*Futurity c.	Kingston, aged, 139 lbs	Sheeps'd B. (C.I.J.C.)	June 22, 1891	1.08
6 furlongs	Artful, 2, 130 lbs	Morris Park (st. c.)	Oct. 15, 1904	1.08
	Nimbus, 3, 109 lbs	Yonkers, N. Y.	Aug. 18, 1908	1.11 1-
6½ furlongs	Lady Vera, 2, 90 lbs	Belm't P., L. I. (st. c.)	Oct. 19, 1906	1.16 3-
	Brookdale Nymph, 4, 124 lbs	Belmont Park, L. I.	Oct. 14, 1907	1.17 2-5
7 furlongs	Roseben, 5, 126 lbs	Belmont Park, L. I.	Oct. 16, 1906	1.22
	Colin, 2, 122 lbs	Belm't P., L. I. (st. c.)	Oct. 16, 1907	1.23
7½ furlongs	Restigouche, 3, 107 lbs	Belmont Park, L. I.	May 29, 1908	1.31 1-5
1 mile	Salvator, 4, 110 lbs.†	Monmouth P. (st. c.)	Aug 28, 1890	1.35½
	Kildeer, 4, 91 lbs	Monmouth P. (st. c.)	Aug. 13, 1892	1.37½
	Kiamesha, 3, 104 lbs	Belmont Park, L. I.	Oct. 9, 1905	1.37 2-5
	Dick Welles, 3, 112 lbs	Chicago (Harlem)	Aug. 14, 1903	1.37 2-5
	Fern, L., 3, 80 lbs	Seattle, Wash'n	Aug. 15, 1908	1.37 2-5
1 " 20 yds.	Macy, 4, 107 lbs	Chicago (Wash. Park)	July 2, 1898	1.40
	Maid Marian, 4, 106 lbs	Chicago (Wash. Park)	July 19, 1903	
	Six Shooter, 5, 111 lbs	Chicago (Wash. Park)	June 27, 1903	
1 " 40 yds.	Preen, 4, 104 lbs	Buffalo, N. Y	June 16, 1906	1.42
	Main Chance, 3, 114 lbs	Buffalo, N. Y	June 29, 1907	
1 " 50 yds.	Vox Populi, 4, 104 lbs	Seattle, Wash'n	Sept. 5, 1908	1.40 4-5
1 " 70 yds.	King's Daughter, 5, 124 lbs	Ft. Erie, Can	Aug. 25, 1908	1.42 2-5
1 " 100 yds.	Rapid Water, 6, 114 lbs	Oakland (Cal. J. C.)	Nov. 30, 1907	1.44 1-5
1 1-16 miles	Royal Tourist, 3, 104 lbs	Oakland, Cal	Nov. 11, 1908	1.44 1-5
	Green Seal, 4, 109 lbs	Seattle, Wash'n	Sept. 12, 1908	1.44 2-5
1⅛ "	Charles Edward, 3, 126 lbs	Brighton Beach	July 16, 1907	1.50 3-5
	Green Seal, 4, 107 lbs	Seattle, Wash'n	Aug. 20, 1908	1.50 3-5
1 3-16 "	Scintillant II., 6, 109 lbs	Chicago (Harlem)	Sept. 1, 1902	1.57 2-5
1¼ "	Broomstick, 3, 104 lbs	Brighton Beach	July 9, 1904	2.02 4-5
1 5-16 "	Ballot, 4, 126 lbs	Sheepsh'd Bay, (C.I.)	July 1, 1908	2.09 3-5
1 m. 500 yds	Swift Wing, 5, 100 lbs	Latonia, Ky	July 8, 1905	2.10 1-5
1⅜ miles	Irish Lad, 4, 126 lbs	Sheepsh'd Bay (C.I.)	June 25, 1904	2.17 3-5
1½ "	Goodrich, 3, 102 lbs	Chicago (Wash. Park)	July 16, 1898	2.30¼
1⅝ "	Africander, 3, 126 lbs	Sheepsh'd Bay (C.I.)	July 7, 1903	2.45 1-5
1¾ "	Major Daingerfield, 4, 120 lbs	Morris Park, N. Y.	Oct. 3, 1903	2.57
1⅞ "	Julius Cæsar, 5, 108 lbs	New Orleans, La.	Feb. 27, 1900	3.19
2 "	Judge Denny, 5, 105 lbs	Oakland (Cal. J. C.)	Feb. 12, 1898	3.26½
2 1-16 "	War Whoop, 4, 96 lbs	Ontario (Tor'to J. C.)	Sept. 23, 1905	3.34½
2⅛ "	Joe Murphy, 4, 99 lbs	Chicago (Harlem)	Aug. 30, 1894	3.42
2¼ "	Ethelbert, 4, 124 lbs	Brighton Beach, N. Y.	Aug. 4, 1900	3.49 1-5
2½ "	Kyrat, 3, 88 lbs	Newport, Ky	Nov. 18, 1899	4.24½
2⅝ "	Ten Broeck, 4, 104 lbs	Lexington, Ky	Sept. 16, 1876	4.58½
2¾ "	Hubbard, 4, 107 lbs	Saratoga, N. Y.	Aug. 9, 1873	4.58¾
3 "	Mamie Algol, 5, 108 lbs	New Orleans (City P.)	Feb. 16, 1907	5.19
4 "	Lucrezia Borgia, 4, 85 lbs.†	Oakland (Cal. J. C.)	May 20, 1897	7.11
	Big Bow, 6, 112 lbs	Oakland (Cal. J. C.)	Mar. 14, 1908	7.16

HEAT RACES.

Distance	Name	Place	Date	Time
¼ mile.	Sleepy Dick, aged	Kiowa, Kan	Oct. 19, 1888	0.21½ —0.22¼
⅜ "	Bob Wade, 4	Butte, Mont.	Aug. 16, 1890	0.36¼ —0.36¼
½ "	Eclipse, Jr., 4	Dallas, Tex	Nov. 1, 1890	0.48— 0.48— 0.48
	Bogus, aged, 113 lbs	Helena, Mont	Aug. 22, 1888	0.48 —0.48
	Bill Howard, 5, 122 lbs	Anaconda, Mont	Aug. 17, 1895	0.47½ —0.48½
⅝ "	Kittie Pease, 4, 82 lbs	Dallas, Tex	Nov. 2, 1887	1.00 —1.00
	Fox, 4, 113 lbs	San Francisco, Cal	Oct. 31, 1891	1.00 3-5—1.01 1-5
¾ "	Tom Hayes, 4, 107 lbs	Morris Park (st. c.)	June 17, 1892	1.10½ —1.12¾
	Lizzie S., 5, 118 lbs	Louisville	Sept. 28, 1883	1.13¼ —1.13¼
1 "	Guido, 4, 117 lbs	Chicago (Wash. Pk.)	July 11, 1891	1.41½ —1.41
1 (3 in 5)	L'Argentine, 5, 115 lbs	St. Louis	June 14, 1879	1.43—1.44—1.47¾
1 1-16 m.	Slipalong, 5, 115 lbs	Chicago (Wash. Pk.)	Sept. 2, 1885	1.51½ —1.48½
1⅛ mile.	What-er-Lou, 5, 119 lbs	San. Fran. (Ingleside)	Feb. 18, 1889	1.56 —1.54¾
1¼ "	Glenmore, 5, 114 lbs	Sheepshead Bay	Sept. 25, 1880	2.10 —2.14
1½ "	Patsy Duffy, aged, 115 lbs	Sacramento, Cal	Sept. 17, 1884	2.41¾ —2.41
2 "	Miss Woodford, 4, 107½ lbs	Sheepshead Bay	Sept. 20, 1884	3.33 —3.33¼
3 "	Norfolk, 4, 100 lbs	Sacramento, Cal.	Sept. 23, 1865	5.27½ —5.29½
4 "	Glenmore, 4, 108 lbs	Baltimore, Pimlico	Oct. 25, 1879	7.30½ —7.31

† Races against time. St. c., straight course. * 170 feet less than ¾ mile.

Compiled by Goodwin Bros. Turf Official Guide.

Harness Horse Racing.

THE six best performers of the year were as follows:

Trotters—Stallion: Allen Winter, 2.06½, b. h., by Ed. Winter, 2.12¾. Mare: Lillian R., 2.04½, b. m., by J. T., 2.12¼. Gelding: Highball, 2.03¾, b. g., by Dr. Hooker, 2.23¾.

Pacers—Stallion: Minor Heir, 1.59½ (race record, 2.00½), b. h., by Heir-at-Law, 2.05¾. Mare: Citation, 2.01¾, b. m., by Norvalson, 2.21¼. Gelding: The Eel, 2.02¼, g. g., by Gambolier, 2.22½.

FASTEST TROTTING RECORDS, 1908.

Yearlings—Lady Green Goods, 2.30, b. f., by Peter the Great, 2.07¼.

Two-year-olds—Colt: Robert C., 2.13¼, b. c., by Peter the Great, 2.07¼. Filly, Czarevna, 2.12¾, b. f., by Peter the Great, 2.07¼.

Three-year-olds—Colt: The Harvester, 2.08¾, br. c., by Walnut Hall, 2.08¼. Filly: The Leading Lady, 2.07, b. f., by Bingen, 2.06¼.

Four-year-olds—Colt: Aquin, 2.08½, b. c., by Aquilin, 2.19¾. Filly: Ruth Dillon, 2.06½, b. f., by Sidney Dillon. Gelding: Uhlan, 2.07¾, blk. g., by Bingen, 2.06¼.

Five-year-olds—Stallion: Allen Winter, 2.06½, b. h., by Ed. Winter, 2.12¾. Mare: Spanish Queen, 2.07, b. m., by Onward Silver, 2.05¼. Gelding: Red Cross, b. g., by Domineer, 2.20.

FASTEST NEW PERFORMER.

Stallion—Allen Winter, 2.06½, b. h., by Ed. Winter, 2.12¾. Mare—Spanish Queen, 2.07, b. m., by Onward Silver, 2.05¼.

HALF-MILE TRACK.

Stallion—Exalted, b. h., 2.09¾, by Expedition, 2.15¾. Mare—Happy F., 2.11¼, g. m., by Happy J., 2.14½. Gelding—Locust Jack, 2.09, g. g., by Keller Thomas, 2.12¾.

WORLD'S TROTTING RECORDS.

DISTANCE.	Name.	Place.	Date.	Time.		
1 mile (world's record)	Lou Dillon*	Memphis, Tenn.†	Oct. 24, 1905			1.58½
1 " in a race	Cresceus	Brighton Beach, N. Y.	Aug. 15, 1901			2.02¼
1 " on half-mile track.	George G*	Allentown, Pa.	Oct. 16, 1907			2.06¾
1 " by a stallion	Cresceus*	Columbus, Ohio	Aug. 2, 1901			2.02¼
1 " " gelding	Major Delmar*	Memphis, Tenn.†	Oct. 23, 1903			1.59¾
1 " " mare	Lou Dillon*	Memphis, Tenn.†	Oct. 24, 1903			1.58½
1 " (with runn'g mate)	Ayres P.*	Kirkwood, Del. (kite)	July 8, 1893			2.03½
1 " by a yearling	Pansy McGregor	Holton, Kan. (kite)	Nov. 18, 1893			2.23¾
	Adbell*	San José, Cal. (reg.)	Sept. 28, 1894			2.23
1 " ", two-year-old	Arion*	Stockton, Cal. (kite)	Nov. 10, 1891			2.10¾
	Trampfast	Lexington, Ky	Oct. 10, 1907			2.12¼
1 " " three-year-old	General Watts	Lexington, Ky	Oct. 17, 1907			2.06¾
	TheLe'di'gL'dy	Lexington, Ky	Oct. 15, 1908			2.07
1 " " four-year-old.	Directum	Nashville, Tenn. (reg.)	Oct. 18, 1893			2.05¼
	Fantasy*	Terre Haute, Ind. (reg.)	Sept. 13, 1894			2.06
1 " " five-year-old	Lou Dillon*	Memphis, Tenn.†	Oct. 24, 1903			1.58½
1 " " six-year-old	Lou Dillon*	Memphis, Tenn	Nov. 11, 1904			2.01
1 " to high wheel sulky	Major Delmar*	Memphis, Tenn	Oct. 26, 1904			2.07
Best 2 heats	Sweet Marie	Syracuse, N. Y	Sept. 12, 1906		2.04¾	2.02¾
" 3 "	Hamburg Belle	Hartford, Ct.	Sept. 7, 1908	2.05	2.06	2.04¾
2 miles.	Cresceus*	Memphis, Tenn.†	Oct. 22, 1902			4.17
3 "	Nightingale*	Nashville, Tenn. (reg.)	Oct. 20, 1893			6.55½
	Fairy Wood	Minneapolis, Minn.	July 1, 1895			7.16½
4 "	Bertie R	Blackpool, England†	Sept. 11, 1899			9.58
	Senator L.	San José, Cal. (reg.)	Nov. 2, 1894			10.12
5 "	Bishop Hero	Oakland, Cal. (reg.)	Oct. 14, 1893			12.30¾
10 "	Pascal*	New York, N. Y. (reg.)	Nov. 2, 1893			26.15
	Controller	San Francisco, Cal. (reg.)	Nov. 23, 1878			27.23¼
20 "	Capt. McGowan*	Boston, Mass. (reg.)	Oct. 31, 1865			58.25
30 "	Gen. Taylor*	San Francisco, Cal	Feb. 21, 1857			1.47.59
50 "	Ariel*	Albany, N. Y	May 5, 1846			3.55.40½
100 "	Conqueror*	Centreville, L. I.	Nov. 12, 1853			8.55.53

* Against time. † Paced by runner to sulky carrying wind or dust shield, runner preceding trotter.

Trotting—To Wagon.

Distance	Name	Place	Date	Time		
1 mile (against time)	Lou Dillon*	Memphis, Tenn.†	Oct. 23, 1903			2.00
1 " in a race	Lou Dillon	Memphis, Tenn	Oct. 21, 1903			2.04¾
Best 2 heats	Lou Dillon	Memphis, Tenn	Oct. 21, 1903	2.04¾		2.04¼
Best 3 heats	Hopeful	Chicago, Ill	Oct. 12, 1878	2.16½	2.17	2.17
2 miles	Ed. Bryan	Point Breeze, Phila	Sept. 1, 1907			4.43
3 "	Ed. Bryan	Point Breeze, Phila.	Nov. 8, 1905			7.30½
5 "	Fillmore	San Francisco, Cal	April 18, 1863			13.18
10 "	Julia Aldrich	San Francisco, Cal	June 15, 1858			29.04½
20 "	Controller	San Francisco, Cal	April 29, 1878			58.57

Trotting—By Teams.

Distance	Name	Place	Date	Time		
1 mile	The Monk*, Equity*	Memphis, Tenn	Oct. 21, 1904			2.07¾
1 " in a race	Rose Leaf, Sally Simmons.	Columbus, Ohio	Sept. 27, 1894			2.15¼
1 " road wagon	Maud S.*, Aldine*	Fleetwood Park, N. Y.	June 15, 1883			2.15½
Best 3 heats in a race	Arab, Conde	San Francisco, Cal.	Nov. 26, 1887	2.30½	2.23	2.18¾

*Against time. † Paced by runner to sulky carrying wind or dust shield, runner preceding trotter.

HARNESS HORSE RACING—*Continued.*

FASTEST PACING RECORDS, 1908.

Two-year-olds—Filly: Easter D., 2.13½, b. f., by Diablo, 2.09¼.

Three-year-olds—Colt: Ray o' Light, 2.08¼, b. c., by Searchlight, 2.03¼. Filly: Catherine Direct, 2.10¼, b. f., by Direct, 2.05½. Gelding: Billy Sam, 2.13¼, ro. g., by Red Sam.

Four-year-olds—Colt: Gordon Prince, Jr., 2.07¼, b. c., by Gordon Prince, 2.05½. Filly: Josephine, 2.07¼, b. f., by Zoloch, 2.05¼. Gelding: Washington W., 2.10¼, blk. g., by Ashland W. C., 2.19½.

Five-year-olds—Stallion: John Ward, 2.05¾, b. h., by Bingen, 2.06¼. Mare: Brenda Yorke, 2.04½, b. m., by Moko. Gelding: Gottett, 2.09¾, g. g., by Sam Twister, 2.13¼.

FASTEST NEW PERFORMER.

Stallion—Minor Heir, 1.59½ (race record, 2.00½), b. h., by Heir-at-Law, 2.05¾. Mare—Alcella, 2.07¾, b. m., by Gen. Forrest, 2.08. Gelding—The Eel, 2.02¼, g. g., by Gambolier, 2.22½.

HALF-MILE TRACK.

Stallion—Hedgewood Boy, 2.08¼, ch. h., by Chitwood, 2.22¼. Mare—Citation, 2.06¼, br. m., by Norvalson, 2.21¼. Gelding—Don Elmo, 2.06¾, b. g., by Stralsund.

WORLD'S PACING RECORDS.

Distance.	Name.	Place.	Date.	Time.		
1 mile (world's record)	Dan Patch*	St. Paul, Minn †	Sept. 8, 1906	......	......	1.55
1 " by a stallion	Dan Patch*	St. Paul, Minn †	Sept. 8, 1906	......	......	1.55
1 " by a gelding	Prince Alert*	New York, N. Y. †	Sept. 23, 1903	......	......	1.57
1 "	Dan Patch	Memphis, Tenn	Nov. 8, 1905	......	......	1.58
1 " by a mare	Dariel	Memphis, Tenn	Oct. 24, 1903	......	......	2.00¼
1 " (half mile track)	Dan Patch	Allentown, Pa	Sept. 21, 1905	......	......	2.02
1 " in a race	Star Pointer	Springfield, Ill	Oct. 1, 1897	......	......	2.00⅛
	Minor Heir	Lexington, Ky	Oct. 6, 1908	......	......	2.00½
1 " yearling filly	Belle Acton*	Lyons, Neb.	Oct. 14, 1892	......	......	2.20¾
1 " yearling colt	Manager H.	Springfield, Ill	....	......	......	2.20
1 " two-year-old	Directly*	Galesburg, Ill	Sept. 20, 1894	......	......	2.07¾
	Ecstacy	Lexington, Ky	Oct. 15, 1898	......	......	2.10½
1 " three-year-old	Klatawah	Louisville, Ky	Sept. 28, 1898	......	......	2.05½
1 " four-year-old	Ouline*	Sioux City, Iowa	Oct. 12, 1894	......	......	2.04
1 " high-wheel sulky	Dan Patch*	Macon, Ga. †	Nov. 30, 1903	......	......	2.04¾
½ mile	Dan Patch	Memphis, Tenn.	Oct. 27, 1903	......	......	.56
2 miles	Dan Patch*	Macon, Ga †	Nov. 30, 1903	......	......	4.17
3 "	Joe Jefferson*	Knoxville, Iowa (reg.)	Nov. 6, 1891	......	......	7.33¼
	James K. Polk	Centreville, L. I. (reg.)	Sept. 13, 1847	......	......	7.44
4 "	Joe Jefferson*	Knoxville, Iowa (reg.)	Nov. 13, 1891	......	......	10.10
5 "	Fisherman	San Francisco, Cal. (reg.)	Dec. 19, 1874	......	......	13.08½
Best 2 heats	Prince Alert	Memphis, Tenn	Oct. 26, 1901	......	2.02½	2.00¾

To Wagon.

Distance.	Name.	Place.	Date.	Time.		
1 mile (against time)	Dan Patch*	Memphis, Tenn.	Oct. 27, 1903	......	......	1.57¼
1 " in a race	Angus Pointer	Memphis, Tenn.	Oct. 20, 1904	......	......	2.04½
2 miles	Young America	....	....	......	......	4.58½
3 "	Longfellow	Sacramento, Cal	Sept. 7, 1869	......	......	7.53
4 "	Longfellow	San Francisco, Cal	Dec. 31, 1869	......	......	10.42½
5 "	Lady St. Clair	San Francisco, Cal	Dec. 11, 1874	......	......	12.54¾
Best 2 heats	Edith W	Memphis, Tenn	Oct. 22, 1902	......	2.05¾	2.05¾
Best 3 heats	Johnston	St. Paul, Minn	Sept. 16, 1887	2.16¼	2.15½	2.15¼

By a Team.

Distance.	Name.	Place.	Date.	Time.		
1 mile	Direct Hal* Prince Direct	Memphis, Tenn	Oct. 26, 1902	......	......	2.05½

*Against time. †Paced by runner to sulky carrying a wind or a dust shield, the runner preceding the pacer.

Records compiled by S. S. Toman, editor of The Trotter and Pacer.

Evolution of the Two-Minute Horse.

Yankee (2.59) was the first to trot a mile under three minutes. That was on June 5, 1806. Lady Suffolk was the first in the 2.30 list, she making a mark of 2.29½ at Beacon Course October 15, 1845. Flora Temple (2.19¾), at Kalamazoo, October 15, 1859, heralded the way for the 2.20 class. Dexter made a stallion record of 2.17¼ at Buffalo August 14, 1867. Smuggler, at Hartford, August 31, 1876, lowered this mark to 2.15¼. Rarus made a gelding record of 2.13¼ at Buffalo August 11, 1878. Goldsmith Maid made the first record below 2.15 by trotting a mile at Rochester August 12, 1874, in 2.14¾. Jay Eye See got a mark of 2.09¼ at Cleveland in 1884, and Maud S. the following year at Cleveland did a mile in 2.08¾. Later records were: Axtell, three-year-old stallion record of 2.12 at Terre Haute, October, 1889; Sunol, 2.08¼ at Stockton, Cal., October, 1891; Arion, two-year-old, 2.10¾, at Stockton, October, 1891; Nancy Hanks, 2.04 (bicycle-wheeled sulky), at Terre Haute, September, 1892; Directum, four-year-old, 2.05¼, at Nashville, October, 1893; Alix, 2.03¾, at Galesburg, Ill., September, 1894; The Abbott, 2.03¼, at Terre Haute, September, 1900; Cresceus, 2.02¾, at Cleveland, July, 1901; Major Delmar, 2.02¼, at Readville, August, 1903; Lou Dillon, 1.58½, at Memphis, October, 1903; Dan Patch, 1.55, at St. Paul, September, 1906.

Baseball.

The year of 1908 in baseball will go down into history as the greatest season of financial success and the most exciting finish in both the National League and American Association ever known in the great national game. Chicago won the national championship by only seven points over New York and Pittsburgh, tied for second place, while Detroit, in the American, won by four points over Cleveland, second, and nine over Chicago, in third place. The result was reached only in the final games of the season. Chicago and Detroit for the second successive year played off for the world's championship, the former winning in four of the five games played. The summaries:

At Detroit, October 10. Chicago—10 runs, 14 hits, 2 errors. Detroit—6 runs, 10 hits, 3 errors. Batteries—Chicago, Reulbach, Overall, Brown and Kling. Detroit, Killian, Summers and Schmidt.

At Chicago, October 11. Chicago—6 runs, 7 hits, 1 error. Detroit—1 run, 4 hits, 1 error. Batteries—Chicago, Overall and Kling. Detroit, Donovan and Schmidt.

At Chicago, October 12. Detroit—8 runs, 13 hits, 3 errors. Chicago—3 runs, 7 hits. Batteries—Detroit, Mullin and Thomas. Chicago, Pfeister, Reulbach and Kling.

At Detroit, October 13. Chicago—3 runs, 11 hits. Detroit—0 runs, 4 hits. Batteries—Chicago, Brown and Kling. Detroit, Summers, Winter and Schmidt.

At Detroit, October 14. Chicago—2 runs, 10 hits. Detroit—0 runs, 3 hits. Batteries—Chicago, Overall and Kling. Detroit, Donovan and Schmidt.

WORLD'S CHAMPIONSHIP SERIES AT A GLANCE.

CHICAGO.	G.	A.B.	R.	H.	S.O.	B.B.	2 B.	3 B.	H. R.	T. B.	P.C.	O.	A.	E.	P.C.
Sheckard, lf	5	21	2	5	3	2	2	0	0	7	.238	7	1	0	1,000
Evers, 2b	5	20	5	7	2	1	1	0	0	8	.350	5	21	0	1,000
Schulte, rf	5	18	4	7	1	2	0	1	0	9	.389	3	0	0	1,000
Chance, 1b	5	19	4	9	1	3	0	0	0	9	.474	65	1	1	.985
Steinfeldt, 3b	5	16	3	4	5	2	0	0	0	4	.250	4	11	1	.938
Hofman, cf	5	19	2	6	4	1	0	1	0	8	.316	10	2	0	1,000
Tinker, ss	5	19	2	5	2	0	0	0	1	8	.263	8	19	1	.964
Kling, c	5	16	2	4	2	2	1	0	0	5	.250	33	6	0	1,000
Reulbach, p	2	4	0	0	1	0	0	0	0	0	.000	0	5	0	1,000
Overall, p	3	6	0	2	1	0	0	0	0	2	.333	0	3	0	1,000
Brown, p	2	4	0	0	2	0	0	0	0	0	.000	0	6	0	1,000
Pfeister, p	1	2	0	0	2	0	0	0	0	0	.000	0	0	0	.000
Howard	1	1	0	0	0	0	0	0	0	0	.000	0	0	0	.000
Totals		165	24	49	26	13	4	2	1	60	.297	135	75	3	.986

DETROIT.	G.	A.B.	R.	H.	S.O.	B.B.	2 B.	3 B.	H. R.	T.B.	P.C.	O.	A.	E.	P.C.
McIntyre, lf	5	18	2	4	2	3	1	0	0	5	.222	10	0	1	.909
O'Leary, ss	5	19	2	5	[illegible]	0	0	0	0	5	.263	7	12	1	.950
Crawford, cf	5	21	2	5		1	1	0	0	6	.238	16	0	0	1,000
Cobb, rf	5	19	3	7		1	1	0	0	8	.368	3	0	0	1,000
Rossman, 1b	5	19	3	4		1	0	0	0	4	.211	47	5	1	.981
Schaefer, 3b-2b	5	16	0	2		1	0	0	0	2	.125	10	11	1	.955
Schmidt, c	4	14	0	1		0	0	0	0	1	.071	22	7	0	1,000
Thomas, c	2	4	0	2		1	1	0	0	3	.500	10	2	0	1,000
Downs, 2b	2	6	1	1		1	1	0	0	2	.167	2	8	1	.909
Coughlin, 3b	3	8	0	1		0	0	0	0	1	.125	2	4	1	.857
Killian, p	1	0	0	0		0	0	0	0	0	.000	0	1	0	1,000
Summers, p	2	5	0	1		0	0	0	0	1	.200	0	7	0	1,000
Donovan, p	2	4	0	0		1	0	0	0	0	.000	1	2	1	.750
Winter, p	2	0	0	0		0	0	0	0	0	.000	0	0	0	.000
Mullin, p	1	3	1	1		1	0	0	0	1	.333	0	2	0	1,000
Jones	3	2	1	0		1	0	0	0	0	.000	0	0	0	.000
Totals		158	15	34	26	12	5	0	0	39	.215	130	61	7	.964

Innings.	1.	2.	3.	4.	5.	6.	7.	8.	9.	Total.
Chicago Nationals	1	0	6	3	1	0	1	6	6.	—24
Detroit Americans	2	0	0	0	0	5	3	4	1.	—15

Runs batted in—Chicago: By Tinker, 4; Hofman, 4; Schulte, 3; Chance, 3; Steinfeldt, 3; Kling, 2; Sheckard, 1; Evers, 1. Detroit: By Cobb, 4; Rossman, 3; Crawford, 1; Thomas, 1; Coughlin, 1; Mullin, 1; Schmidt, 1; Downs, 1; Summers, 1. Runs scored on errors—Chicago, 3 (Rossman's wild throw, 1; Schaefer's fumble, 1; Donovan's wild pitch, 1); Detroit, 1 (Steinfeldt's error, 1). Sacrifice hits—Chicago, 9 (Steinfeldt, 3; Kling, Schulte, 2; Brown, Overall, Evers); Detroit, 4 (Schaefer, Cobb, Donovan, Coughlin). Stolen bases—Chicago, 12 (Steinfeldt, Hofman, 2; Tinker, 3; Schulte, 2; Sheckard, Evers, 3); Detroit, 5 (Donovan, Cobb, 2; Rossman, McIntyre). Left on bases—Chicago, 30; Detroit, 27. First base on errors—Chicago, 5; Detroit, 1. Double plays—Tinker and Chance; Evers and Chance; Hofman and Kling; Brown, Tinker and Chance; Downs, O'Leary and Rossman; Schaefer and Rossman; O'Leary, Schaefer and Rossman; Schmidt, Schaefer and Schmidt; O'Leary, Rossman and Coughlin. Wild pitches—Brown, 1; Overall, 1; Donovan, 1. Hit by pitcher—By Brown, 1 (McIntyre); by Reulbach, 1 (Coughlin). Hits—Off Overall, 7 in 18 1-3 innings; off Brown, 6 in 11 innings; off Reulbach, 9 in 7 2-3 innings; off Pfeister, 12 in 8 innings; off Summers, 19 in 14 2-3 innings; off Donovan, 17 in 17 innings; off Mullin, 7 in 9 innings; off Killian, 5 in 2 1-3 innings; off Winter, 1 in 1 inning. Struck out—By Overall, 15; by Reulbach, 5; by Brown, 5; by Pfeister, 1; by Donovan, 10; by Mullin, 8; by Summers, 7; by Killian, 1. Bases on balls—Off Overall, 7; off Pfeister, 3; off Reulbach, 1; off Brown, 1; off Summers, 4; off Donovan, 4; off Killian, 3; off Mullin, 1; off Winter, 1. Passed balls—Kling, 1; Schmidt, 1. Umpires—Messrs. Klem, Connolly, Sheridan and O'Day.

HOW THE MONEY IN THE SERIES WAS DIVIDED.

	Attendance.	Receipts.	Players' Share.	Club Owners' Share.	National Commission.
Detroit, First Game....	10,812	$16,473.00	$8,895.42	$5,930.28	$1,647.30
Chicago, Second Game.	17,760	26,927.00	14,540.58	9,693.72	2,692.70
Chicago, Third Game...	14,543	22,767.00	12,294.18	8,196.12	2,276.70
Detroit, Fourth Game..	12,907	19,231.00	10,384.74	6,923.16	1,923.10
Detroit, Fifth Game....	6,210	9,577.50	....	8,619.75	957.75
Totals...............	62,232	$94,975.50	$46,114.92	$39,363.03	$9,497.55

Chicago team received 60 per cent. of players' share—$27,668.95.
Detroit team received 40 per cent. of players' share—$18,445.97.
Owners of the two clubs divided $39,363.03 equally.

Previous series for the world's championship resulted as follows:

Year.	Contesting Teams.	Results of Series.					
1884.......	Providence *vs.* Metropolitan......	Providence....	3	Metropolitan..	0	Drawn.........	0
1885.......	Chicago *vs.* St. Louis...............	Chicago	3	St. Louis	3	Drawn.........	1
1886.......	Chicago *vs.* St. Louis...............	Chicago	2	St. Louis......	4	Drawn.........	0
1887.......	Detroit *vs.* St. Louis...............	Detroit	11	St. Louis......	4	Drawn.........	0
1888.......	New York *vs.* St. Louis.............	New York	6	St. Louis......	4	Drawn.........	0
1889.......	New York *vs.* Brooklyn..............	New York	6	Brooklyn......	3	Drawn.........	0
1890.......	Brooklyn *vs.* Louisville.............	Brooklyn.	3	Louisville.....	3	Drawn.........	1
1903.......	Boston *vs.* Pittsburgh...............	Boston	5	Pittsburgh	3	Drawn.........	0
1905.......	New York *vs.* Philadelphia........	New York	4	Philadelphia..	1	Drawn.........	0
1906.......	Chicago Am. *vs.* Chicago Nat......	Americans....	4	Nationals......	2	Drawn.........	0
1907.......	Chicago Nat. *vs.* Detroit Am.......	Chicago	4	Detroit.........	0	Drawn.........	1
1908.......	Chicago Nat. *vs.* Detroit Am.......	Chicago	4	Detroit.	1	Drawn.........	0

American League Record for 1908.

Clubs.	Detroit.	Cleveland.	Chicago.	St. Louis.	Boston.	Philadelp'a.	Washington	New York.	Games Won	Per Cent.
Detroit..................	..	9	13	12	11	14	16	15	90	.588
Cleveland...............	13	..	14	11	12	16	8	16	90	.584
Chicago..................	9	8	..	11	16	13	15	16	88	.579
St. Louis............. ..	10	11	10	..	7	13	15	17	83	.547
Boston...................	11	10	6	15	..	10	11	12	75	.487
Philadelphia...........	8	6	9	8	12	..	11	14	68	.444
Washington.............	5	14	6	7	11	11	..	13	67	.441
New York...............	7	6	6	5	10	8	9	..	51	.331
Games lost............	63	64	64	69	79	85	85	103	...	

National League Record for 1908.

Clubs.	*Chicago.	*New York.	Pittsburgh.	Philadelp'a.	Cincinnati.	Boston.	Brooklyn.	St. Louis.	Games Won	Per Cent.
*Chicago..................	..	11	10	9	16	16	18	19	99	.643
*New York...............	11	..	11	16	14	16	16	14	98	.636
Pittsburgh...............	12	11	..	13	14	15	13	20	98	.636
Philadelphia............	13	6	9	..	12	12	17	14	83	.539
Cincinnati.....	6	8	8	10	..	14	16	11	73	.473
Boston...................	6	6	7	10	8	..	12	14	63	.409
Brooklyn	4	6	9	5	6	10	..	13	53	.344
St. Louis................	3	8	2	8	11	8	9	..	49	.318
Games lost........	55	56	56	71	81	91	101	105	...	

*Because Merkle, of the New Yorks, neglected to touch second base after batting in the winning run with two out in a New York-Chicago game, at New York, September 23, in which New York scored two runs to one for Chicago, the game was protested by Chicago and ordered by the National Commission to be played over on October 8 at New York, when Chicago won, four runs to two.

PREVIOUS PENNANT WINNERS OF THE AMERICAN LEAGUE.

Year.	Champions.	Won.	Lost.	PerCent.	Year.	Champions.	Won.	Lost.	PerCent.
1900..	Chicago............	82	53	.607	1904..	Boston.............	95	59	.617
1901..	Chicago............	83	53	.610	1905..	Athletic...........	92	56	.621
1902..	Athletic............	83	53	.610	1906..	Chicago...........	93	58	.616
1903..	Boston..............	91	47	.659	1907..	Detroit............	92	58	.613

PREVIOUS PENNANT WINNERS OF THE NATIONAL LEAGUE.

Year.	Champions.	Won.	Lost.	PerCent.	Year.	Champions.	Won.	Lost.	PerCent.
1876..	Chicago............	52	14	.788	1892..	Boston........	102	48	.680
1877..	Boston..............	31	17	.648	1893..	Boston.............	86	44	.662
1878..	Boston..............	41	19	.707	1894..	Baltimore..........	89	39	.695
1879..	Providence.........	55	23	.705	1895..	Baltimore..........	87	43	.669
1880..	Chicago............	67	17	.798	1896...	Baltimore..........	90	39	.698
1881..	Chicago............	55	28	.667	1897..	Boston.............	93	39	.705
1882..	Chicago............	55	29	.655	1898...	Boston.............	102	47	.685
1883..	Boston..............	63	35	.643	1899..	Brooklyn...........	101	47	.682
1884..	Providence.........	84	28	.750	1900..	Brooklyn...........	82	54	.603
1885..	Chicago............	87	25	.770	1901..	Pittsburgh.........	90	49	.647
1886..	Chicago............	90	34	.725	1902..	Pittsburgh.........	103	36	.745
1887..	Detroit.............	79	45	.637	1903..	Pittsburgh.........	91	49	.650
1888..	New York..........	84	47	.641	1904..	New York..........	106	47	.693
1889..	New York..........	83	43	.659	1905..	New York..........	105	48	.686
1890..	Brooklyn...........	86	43	.667	1906..	Chicago............	116	36	.763
1891 .	Boston..............	87	51	.630	1907..	Chicago............	107	45	.704

FACTS WORTH REMEMBERING.

The total attendance at the world's championship games in 1907 was 78,086, and total receipts $101,767. Chicago players received $2,050 each, and Detroit $1,945.

Total attendance at National League and American Association games in 1907 was 6,136,557, or 300,000 more than in the previous best year of 1904. The National attendance in 1907 was 2,737,793, and the American, 3,398,764. Total attendance in 1908 was 7,069,122, of which the National had 3,514,285 and American 3,554,837. National League Club attendance at home and abroad was: Chicago, 619,807-601,704; New York, 880,700-670,300; Brooklyn, 272,900-308,320; Boston, 245,280-376,344; Philadelphia, 415,171-340,916; Pittsburgh, 366,427-567,871; Cincinnati, 365,111-376,157; St. Louis, 319,385-298,915. American—Detroit, 398,058-570,744; Philadelphia, 445,567-438,292; Boston, 464,987-414,697; Washington, 257,972-431,600; New York, 312,400-451,945; Chicago, 694,728-382,300; Cleveland, 414,730-481,700; St. Louis, 500,790-429,760.

Official baseball records made in field day events at Cincinnati, September 11, 1907, were: Long distance fungo hitting—Mike Mitchell, outfielder, Cincinnati, 413 ft. 8½ in. Running out a bunt to first base—Jack Thoney, Toronto; time, 3 1-5s. Long distance throw—Sheldon La Jeune, outfielder, Springfield, O., Central League, 399 ft. 10¾ in., 2 inches short of a throw by Hatfield in 1887. Third base circling contest—Clement, outfielder, Jersey City; time, 14 1-5s. At Providence, R. I., September 17, 1908, Phelan was credited with beating a bunt to first in 3s. flat. In field day games at Pittsburgh, October 7, 1908, Tom Leach, centre fielder, circled the bases in 14s. flat, and with slides to second and third, 16 1-5s.

Four series were played for the Temple Cup. In 1894 the New York Giants beat Baltimore four straight games. In 1895 Cleveland beat Baltimore four out of five. In 1896 Baltimore won four straight games from Cleveland. In 1897 Baltimore beat Boston four games to one.

Pitcher Wilhelm, Birmingham, Southern League, September 14, 1907, shut out Shreveport in both games of a double-header, and in fifty-nine consecutive innings of these two and other games not a hit was scored on him.

The first organized baseball club was the New York Knickerbockers in 1845. First match game was played in Hoboken in 1846. First championship team was in New York in 1858. First salaried team, Cincinnati, 1868.

Professional National Association was organized in 1871, National League in 1876, American Association in 1881 (disbanded in 1891), Players' League in 1890 (disbanded in 1892), and American League in 1894.

Glove first used on left hand by D. Allison, Cincinnati, 1886; mask invented by F. W. Thayer, Harvard, 1876.

Ted Sullivan's Waco team, Texas League, in 1903, made nine home runs in one game.

First Baseman Murch, Manchester team, in 1906; Paul Hines, at Providence, May 8, 1878; H. O'Hagan, Rochester, at Jersey City, Aug. 18, 1902, and L. Schlafly, Portland (Ore.) team, in 1905, made triple plays, unassisted.

Tom Jones, St. Louis, made 22 put-outs in one game at Boston, 1906. C. Shields, Seattle, in 1906, and the late C. Sweeney, in 1884, are each credited with striking out 19 men in one game.

Pitcher Reulbach, of the Chicago Nationals, shut out the Brooklyns in two games of a double-header, September 26, 1908. He allowed eight hits, passed two and struck out eleven men.

Owner Murphy, of the Chicago Nationals, in 1908, offered $50,000 for the release of Pitcher Christy Mathewson, which was refused by New York.

The largest attended games of 1908 were at the Pittsburgh-Chicago game in Chicago, October 3, and the Chicago-New York game in New York, October 8, each reaching over 30,000.

No-hit games in 1908: National League, July 4—Wiltse, New York, 1, vs. Philadelphia, 0. September 5—Rucker, Brooklyn, 6, vs. Boston, 0. American, June 30—Young, Boston, 8, vs. New York, 0. September 18—Rhoades, Cleveland, 2, vs. Boston, 1. September 20—Smith, Chicago, 1, vs. Philadelphia, 0. October 3—Joss, Cleveland, 1, vs. Chicago, 0.

At Jacksonville, Ill., September 3, 1908, The home team defeated the Ottumwas in a 20-inning contest, 4 to 1. Newark and Jersey City, Atlantic League, played a 19-inning tie game, 0 to 0, at Newark, July 5.

No-hit games, no runner reaching first base—John M. Ward, for Providence against Buffalo, in 1880, and Cy Young, for Boston, against Philadelphia Athletics, May 15, 1904.

Charles Radbourne pitched in 72 championship games for Providence in 1884 and won 56. He had 18 consecutive games and 26 out of 27.

Charles Street, catcher of the Washingtons, caught a ball dropped from the top of the Washington monument, 550 feet, Aug. 21, 1908.

Brooklyn and Pittsburgh played 16 innings in a game at Pittsburgh, August 22, 1908, without either side scoring; a new record in baseball.

Public School No. 9, Brooklyn, defeated Public School No. 24, of Manhattan, by a score of 4 to 3 in the final game for the city championship in 1908.

Pitcher Rucker, of Brooklyn, shut out Boston, September 5, 1908, without a hit or a run, allowed no bases on balls, and struck out 14 men. Rube Waddell, St. Louis, struck out 17 Washington and 16 Philadelphia players, a season's record.

Owen Keenan, a Youngstown pitcher, is credited with defeating Newcastle in two games, July 4, 1885, pitching right-handed in the morning and left-handed in the afternoon game.

The Linwoods, of Philadelphia, defeated the High Bridge team, of New York, 8 to 7 and 17 to 2, in two games for the intercity amateur championship in 1908.

The National Baseball League of Union Printers held its championship games at American League Park, New York, September 14-17, 1908, and Boston won. The scores: Pittsburgh, 13, vs. Cincinnati, 4; Boston, 28 vs. Philadelphia, 0; Chicago, 18 vs. St. Louis, 17; New York, 4, vs. Washington, 2; Pittsburgh, 15, vs. Chicago, 11; Boston, 9, vs. New York, 7; Boston, 5, vs. Pittsburgh, 1.

Detroit made 25 hits and beat Philadelphia, 21 to 2, at Philadelphia, July 17, 1908. Newark and Jersey City, Eastern League, July 5, played a 19-inning tie of 0 to 0, Newark

FACTS WORTH REMEMBERING—*Continued.*

got three hits and two bases on balls off Lafitte, and Jersey City got six hits and four bases on balls off Brockett. Each struck out 14 men.

Princeton defeated Yale, 4 to 2, and Harvard defeated Yale, 9 to 5, 1908, in the final games at the Polo Grounds, New York. Standing of college teams and games won and lost during the season was as follows: Princeton, 20-6; Yale, 17-10; Pennsylvania, 22-10; Holy Cross, 18-6; Annapolis, 19-3; Fordham, 17-2; Harvard, 11-12; Columbia, 6-5; Cornell, 9-10.

Cassidy, University of Rochester, pitched two successive no-hit, no-run games for Williamsville, Eastern Connecticut League, September, 1908, and struck out 33 men. Durham, of Indianapolis, won five double-headers in 1908, total runs against him being 8 and total hits 52. Willetts, of Wichita, Western Association, in 1906, struck out 30 men and allowed five hits in 18 innings. Lang, of Wausau, Wisconsin, Illinois League, won two games by score of 1 to 0, allowing four hits, one base on balls and striking out 18.

Six no-hit, no-run games were pitched in 1908: Young, Boston vs. New York; Rhoades, Cleveland vs. Boston; Smith, Chicago vs. Philadelphia; Joss, Cleveland vs. Chicago; Wiltse, New York vs. Philadelphia, and Rucker, Brooklyn vs. Boston. There is an official record of 47 such games since 1870, when Richmond (Worcester), shut out Cleveland.

At New York, May 23, 1906, in the New York-Chicago American League game, "Jiggs" Donahue, of Chicago, had but one chance at first base, and assist. June 18, 1907, the Kansas City Club of the American Association made a new record of 27 assists in a game with Toledo at Toledo.

In twelve consecutive years in the National League, Charles Bennett caught in 786 games and his grand average was .944. His batting average for the twelve years was .262. He led the league catchers in nine of the twelve years, was second twice, and sixth once.

James McCormick, in 1886, with the Chicago Nationals, pitched in 24 consecutive games without defeat, which is a record.

September 24, 1904, at Atlanta, Ga., the Shreveport and Atlanta teams, of the Southern League, played a full nine-inning game in 44 minutes.

In the thirteen years between 1877 and 1890, "Silver" Flint caught 835 out of 1,325 games played by his club, in most of which he never wore a mask or protector.

Adrian C. Anson, between 1876 and 1892, played in 1,582 ball games and made 2,252 hits. His batting average for the sixteen seasons was .344. Mike Kelley in 1,155 games, covering twelve consecutive seasons, had a batting average of .321. Dan Brouthers in 971 games in ten consecutive years had a grand average of .354. Roger Connors in 1,071 games in ten consecutive seasons had a grand average of .325.

Longest games, amateur—Brooklyn A. C., 4, vs. East End All-Stars, 1; 30 innings; Cleveland, O., July 4, 1907. Professional—Grand Forks vs. Fargo, 25 innings; score, 0 to 0; at Devils Lake, July 18, 1891. American League—Athletics, 4; Boston, 1; 24 innings; at Boston, September 1, 1906. National League—Cincinnati vs. Chicago; 20 innings; score, 7 to 7; at Cincinnati, July 30, 1902. Chicago, 2; Philadelphia, 1; 20 innings; at Philadelphia, August 24, 1905. Colleges—Wesleyan vs. Trinity; 19 innings; score, 2 to 2; at Hartford, June 6, 1907.

At Corry, Pa., July 25, 1908, the Corry's won a 23-inning game from the Falconer, N. Y., team by a score of 3 to 1. Bedient, of Falconer, struck out 42 men, a world's record, while Bickford, of Corry, retired 16. Pitcher Stoehr, of the Anderson, S. C., Club of the Carolina Association, broke the world's pitching record on August 6, when in his second game he held Charlotte without a hit until the thirteenth inning of a 15-inning game.

Greatest recorded feats in baseball. Most runs in a game—Chicago vs. Cleveland, July 24, 1882, 35-4. In most games—Barrett, Detroit, 162 games. At bat—Brown, Louisville, 1882, 658. Base hits—Keeler, Baltimore, 1897, 243. Chances accepted by catcher—Schreckengost, Atlantics, 1905, 899. By first baseman—Donohue, Chicago Americans, 1907, 986. By second baseman—Evers, Chicago Nationals, 1904, 899. By third baseman—Collins, Boston Nationals, 1899, 601. By shortstop—Allen, Philadelphia Nationals, 1892, 955. By a fielder—Slagle, Washington, 1899, 424. Games pitched—Hutchinson, Chicago, 1892, 70. Greatest number bases on balls given by pitcher—Rusie, New York, 1892, 261. Stolen bases—Stovey, Athletics, 1888, 156.

Greatest number championship games, one day—Three, September 1, 1890, Brooklyn vs. Pittsburgh. Scores, 10—9, 3—2, 8—4. Smallest number chances by first baseman—One assist by "Jiggs" Donohue, Chicago, at New York American League Park, May 23, 1906. Largest number consecutive games lost—26, Louisville Americans, 1889; 23 by Pittsburgh Nationals, 1890. Largest number won—20, Providence Nationals, 1884; Lancaster, Atlantic League, 1897. Shortest game—44 minutes, Atlanta vs. Shreveport, Southern League, September 24, 1904. Greatest number games won in one year—Chicago Nationals, 116, in 1906.

RECORDS OF THE MINOR LEAGUES FOR 1908.

American Association.

	Won.	Lost.	Pct.		Won.	Lost.	Pct.
Indianapolis.	92	61	.601	Minneapolis.	77	76	.504
Louisville...	88	65	.575	Milwaukee...	71	83	.461
Columbus....	86	68	.558	Kansas City.	70	83	.457
Toledo.......	81	72	.530	St. Paul......	48	105	.313

Arkansas State League.

	Won.	Lost.	Pct.		Won.	Lost.	Pct.
Hot Springs.	78	38	.672	Pine Bluff....	51	61	.455
Newport.......	65	44	.596	Argenta.......	49	68	.419
Helena........	67	48	.583	Brinkley.....	28	79	.262

Atlantic League.

	Won.	Lost.	Pct.		Won.	Lost.	Pct.
Allentown...	34	16	.680	Easton.......	26	24	.520
Shamokin...	31	17	.646	Mt. Carmel..	22	24	.478
Wilk's-Barre	30	22	.577	Pottsville....	17	29	.379
Hazleton.....	28	24	.538	Pittston......	5	37	.119

Blue Grass League.

	Won.	Lost.	Pct.		Won.	Lost.	Pct.
Frankfort....	47	23	.671	Lawrenceb'g	33	35	.483
Lexington...	37	31	.544	Shelbyville..	32	37	.464
Richmond...	36	34	.514	Winchester..	22	47	.319

Carolina Association.

	Won.	Lost.	Pct.		Won.	Lost.	Pct.
Greensboro..	51	38	.573	Winston-Sal.	41	48	.461
Greenville...	48	36	.571	Charlotte.....	40	47	.460
Spartanburg.	48	40	.545	Anderson....	33	52	.388

Central Association.

	Won.	Lost.	Pct.		Won.	Lost.	Pct.
Waterloo....	88	37	.704	Jacksonville.	56	69	.448
Burlington...	83	41	.669	Oskaloosa....	51	73	.411
Quincy	73	54	.575	Ottumwa....	47	78	.376
Keokuk.......	56	68	.452	Kewanee	46	79	.368

RECORDS OF THE MINOR LEAGUES—*Continued.*

CENTRAL LEAGUE.

	Won.	Lost.	Pct.		Won.	Lost.	Pct.
Evansville..	84	56	.600	Zanesville...	70	69	.503
South Bend.	80	60	.571	Gr'd Rapids.	66	73	.478
Dayton	77	63	.556	Terre Haute.	65	73	.471
Ft. Wayne .	75	65	.536	Wheeling....	40	98	.290

CONNECTICUT LEAGUE.

	Won.	Lost.	Pct.		Won.	Lost.	Pct.
Springfield..	84	41	.672	Holyoke.....	60	66	.473
Hartford	84	42	.667	Bridgeport ..	55	71	.437
New Haven.	63	63	.500	Meriden.....	54	72	.429
New Britain.	61	64	.488	Waterbury ..	42	84	.333

COTTON STATES LEAGUE.

	Won.	Lost.	Pct.		Won.	Lost.	Pct.
Jackson......	68	42	.618	Columbus....	57	57	.500
Vicksburg ...	66	49	.574	Meridian.....	47	67	.413
Gulfport.....	64	52	.552	Monroe.......	40	75	.348

*EASTERN-ILLINOIS LEAGUE.

	Won.	Lost.	Pct.		Won.	Lost.	Pct.
Staunton	23	9	.718	Shelbyville..	17	17	.500
Vincennes...	23	10	.690	Taylorville..	16	16	.500
Paris.........	17	15	.501	Linton.........	7	26	.212

* Disbanded August 25.

EASTERN LEAGUE.

	Won.	Lost.	Pct.		Won.	Lost.	Pct.
Baltimore....	83	57	.593	Montreal....	63	75	.457
Providence..	79	57	.581	Toronto......	60	77	.438
Newark......	79	58	.577	Jersey City..	58	79	.423
Buffalo.......	75	65	.536	Rochester ...	54	83	.394

EMPIRE STATE LEAGUE.

	Won.	Lost.	Pct.		Won.	Lost.	Pct.
Auburn......	32	24	.571	Carthage.....	26	25	.509
Watertown..	31	26	.544	Oswego.. ...	26	32	.448
Fulton.......	27	26	.509	Oneida.......	23	32	.418

INDIANA-ILLINOIS-IOWA LEAGUE.

	Won.	Lost.	Pct.		Won.	Lost.	Pct.
Springfield...	82	54	.603	Dubuque.....	67	69	.493
Decatur......	77	59	.566	Bloomington	64	73	.467
Cedar Rap's.	69	63	.523	Rock Island.	59	76	.437
Peoria	66	67	.496	Clinton	55	78	.414

NEW ENGLAND LEAGUE.

	Won.	Lost.	Pct.		Won.	Lost.	Pct.
Worcester...	80	44	.645	Lynn.........	54	70	.435
Lawrence....	75	49	.605	Fall River...	53	70	.431
Haverhill...	71	52	.577	Lowell	49	75	.395
Brockton....	66	56	.541	New Bedford	46	78	.371

NEW YORK STATE LEAGUE.

	Won.	Lost.	Pct.		Won.	Lost.	Pct.
Scranton.....	85	51	.625	Utica	74	64	.536
Binghamton.	79	61	.564	Albany	67	73	.479
Troy.	78	61	.561	Wilk's-Barre	60	78	.432
Syracuse.....	75	63	.543	Elmira	36	103	.259

NORTH WESTERN LEAGUE.

	Won.	Lost.	Pct.		Won.	Lost.	Pct.
Vancouver ..	85	62	.578	Spokane.....	72	75	.490
Tacoma......	74	66	.529	Butte	63	73	.463
Aberdeen....	73	69	.514	Seattle.......	65	87	.428

NORTHERN COPPER COUNTRY.

	Won.	Lost	Pct.		Won.	Lost.	Pct.
Brandon.....	50	31	.617	Duluth.......	45	45	.500
Winnipeg ...	47	33	.588	Fargo........	23	56	.291

OHIO-PENNSYLVANIA LEAGUE.

	Won.	Lost.	Pct.		Won.	Lost.	Pct.
Akron........	81	36	.693	Youngstown.	58	60	.492
E.Liverpool.	70	42	.626	New Castle..	47	70	.402
Canton.......	65	56	.537	McKeesport.	45	71	.388
Sharon.......	62	56	.525	Erie..........	42	79	.347

OHIO STATE LEAGUE.

	Won.	Lost.	Pct.		Won.	Lost.	Pct.
Lancaster,...	92	57	.617	Mansfield....	76	73	.510
Lima.........	80	67	.544	Newark	74	75	.497
Marion.......	78	71	.523	Portsmouth .	45	102	.306

OKLAHOMA-KANSAS LEAGUE.

	Won.	Lost.	Pct.		Won.	Lost.	Pct.
Tulsa	36	23	.610	Bartlesville..	30	29	.509
Independ'ce	34	25	.576	Muskogee ...	18	41	.305

PACIFIC COAST LEAGUE.

	Won.	Lost.	Pct.		Won.	Lost.	Pct.
Los Angeles.	110	78	.585	San Fran....	100	104	.490
Portland	95	90	.513	Oakland	83	116	.417

PENNSYLVANIA-WEST VIRGINIA LEAGUE.

	Won.	Lost.	Pct.		Won.	Lost.	Pct.
Uniontown. .	68	42	.618	Connellsville.	55	56	.495
Clarksburg ..	72	49	.595	Fairmount...	55	65	.456
Charleroi.....	57	54	.513	Grafton......	38	78	.328

SOUTH ATLANTIC LEAGUE.

	Won.	Lost.	Pct.		Won.	Lost.	Pct.
Jacksonv'le.	77	34	.694	Columbia.....	46	58	.442
Savannah...	64	45	.587	Macon.......	48	68	.412
Augusta.....	51	59	.464	Charleston..	44	66	.400

SOUTH CAROLINA STATE LEAGUE.

	Won.	Lost.	Pct.		Won.	Lost.	Pct.
Sumter.......	41	27	.603	Rock Hill....	28	40	.412
Chester......	40	30	.571	Orangeburg..	27	39	.409

SOUTHERN LEAGUE.

	Won.	Lost.	Pct.		Won.	Lost.	Pct.
Nashville....	75	56	.578	Mobile.......	67	68	.496
New Orleans	76	57	.571	Atlanta......	63	71	.470
Memphis...	72	62	.537	Little Rock..	62	77	.446
Montgomery	69	64	.519	Birmingham	53	82	.393

SOUTHERN MICHIGAN LEAGUE.

	Won.	Lost.	Pct.		Won.	Lost.	Pct.
Saginaw........	72	52	.581	Battle Creek	62	63	.496
Kalamazoo..	70	56	.556	Lansing......	60	65	.476
Jackson.....	68	57	.544	Flint.........	57	68	.456
Tecumseh....	64	62	.508	Bay City.....	48	78	.381

TEXAS STATE LEAGUE.

	Won.	Lost.	Pct.		Won.	Lost.	Pct.
San Antonio.	95	48	.664	Ft. Worth ...	68	74	.479
Dallas.	90	55	.621	Shreveport...	66	78	.458
Houston.....	77	67	.535	Galveston ...	57	86	.398
Waco........	70	73	.490	Austin........	49	95	.340

TRI-STATE LEAGUE.

	Won.	Lost.	Pct.		Won.	Lost.	Pct.
Williamsp't.	82	45	.646	Johnstown ..	64	63	.504
Harrisburg..	80	47	.630	Trenton	54	73	.425
Lancaster....	72	55	.567	Altoona......	49	78	.386
Reading.	67	60	.528	Wilmington.	40	87	.315

VIRGINIA STATE LEAGUE.

	Won.	Lost.	Pct.		Won.	Lost.	Pct.
Richmond...	87	41	.680	Portsmouth .	57	71	.445
Danville.......	74	52	.587	Lynchburg...	52	76	.406
Roanoke.....	63	67	.485	Norfolk......	52	78	.400

WESTERN ASSOCIATION.

	Won.	Lost.	Pct.		Won.	Lost.	Pct.
Topeka.......	89	50	.641	Hutchinson..	69	70	.497
Wichita......	87	53	.621	Webb City...	66	69	.489
Oklah. City..	81	58	.583	Springfield...	49	86	.363
Joplin........	71	66	.518	Enid..........	37	98	.274

WESTERN LEAGUE.

	Won.	Lost.	Pct.		Won.	Lost.	Pct.
Sioux City...	88	57	.607	Denver.......	69	75	.479
Omaha.......	86	59	.593	Pueblo.......	63	78	.447
Lincoln.....	74	73	.503	Des Moines.	54	94	.365

WISCONSIN—ILLINOIS LEAGUE.

	Won.	Lost.	Pct.		Won.	Lost.	Pct.
Wausau......	71	50	.587	Freeport.....	59	63	.484
Madison	68	54	.557	Fond du Lac.	57	67	.460
La Crosse....	67	57	.540	Oshkosh......	55	66	.455
Green Bay...	66	58	.532	Rockford.....	48	76	.387

[FOLLOWING ARE THE OFFICIAL BATTING AVERAGES OF THE AMERICAN LEAGUE PLAYERS WHO PARTICIPATED IN FIFTEEN OR MORE CHAMPIONSHIP GAMES FOR THE SEASON OF 1908.

Players and Clubs.	Games.	At Bat.	Runs.	1st Base.	2d Base.	3d Base.	H. Runs.	S. Hits.	St. Bases.	Per Cent.
Criss, St. Louis	64	82	15	28	6	0	0	0	1	.341
Cobb, Detroit	150	581	88	188	36	20	4	14	39	.324
Delehanty, Washington	83	287	33	91	11	4	1	9	16	.317
Crawford, Detroit	152	591	102	184	33	16	7	23	15	.311
Gessler, Boston	128	435	55	134	13	14	3	10	19	.308
Thomas, Detroit	40	101	6	31	1	0	0	1	0	.307
Thielman, Clevel'd & B.	14	23	4	7	2	1	0	3	1	.304
Hemphill, New York	142	505	62	150	12	9	0	14	42	.297
McIntyre, Detroit	151	569	105	168	24	13	0	13	20	.295
Rossman, Detroit	138	524	45	154	33	13	2	19	8	.294
Bush, Detroit	20	68	13	20	1	1	0	3	2	.294
Stovall, Cleveland	138	534	71	156	29	6	2	31	14	.292
Schweitzer, St. Louis	64	182	22	53	4	2	1	7	6	.291
Orth, New York	38	69	4	20	1	2	0	2	0	.290
Lajoie, Cleveland	157	581	77	168	32	6	2	30	15	.289
Unglaub, Bost'n & Wash.	144	542	46	155	21	8	1	15	14	.286
Blue, St. Louis & Phila.	17	42	4	12	1	2	0	1	0	.286
Stone, St. Louis	148	588	89	165	21	8	5	13	20	.281
McConnell, Boston	140	502	77	140	10	6	2	11	31	.279
Goode, Cleveland	46	154	23	43	1	3	1	4	7	.279
Dougherty, Chicago	138	482	68	134	11	6	0	19	47	.278
Collins, E., Philadelphia	102	330	39	90	18	7	1	15	8	.273
Ferris, St. Louis	148	555	54	150	26	7	2	30	6	.270
Cree, New York	21	78	5	21	0	2	0	1	1	.269
Tannehill, J., Wash.	27	45	1	12	1	0	0	0	0	.267
Murphy, Philadelphia	142	525	51	139	28	7	4	[illegible]	16	.265
Schmidt, Detroit	122	419	45	111	14	3	1	16	5	.265
Hartzell, St. Louis	115	422	41	112	5	6	2	23	24	.265
Keeler, New York	91	323	38	85	3	1	1	21	14	.263
Anderson, Chicago	123	355	36	93	17	1	0	13	21	.262
Schaefer, Detroit	153	584	96	151	20	10	3	43	40	.259
Lord, Boston	145	558	61	145	15	6	2	36	23	.259
Chase, New York	106	405	50	104	11	3	1	9	27	.257
Cravath, Boston	94	277	43	71	10	11	1	8	6	.256
Mullin, Detroit	55	125	13	32	2	2	1	3	2	.256
Delehanty, New York	87	125	12	32	1	2	0	1	9	.256
Thoney, Boston	109	416	58	106	5	9	2	9	16	.255
Coombs, Philadelphia	78	220	24	56	9	5	1	9	6	.255
Jones, F., Chicago	149	529	92	134	11	7	1	28	26	.253
Wallace, St. Louis	137	487	59	123	24	4	1	19	5	.253
Clymer, Washington	110	368	32	93	11	4	1	9	19	.253
Freeman, Washington	154	531	45	134	15	5	1	9	6	.252
Hahn, Chicago	122	447	58	112	12	8	0	13	11	.251
Hoffman, St. Louis	99	363	41	91	9	7	1	11	17	.251
O'Leary, Detroit	65	211	21	53	9	3	0	7	4	.251
Stahl, N. Y. & Boston	153	536	63	134	27	16	2	19	30	.250
Niles, N. Y. & Boston	113	394	47	98	14	6	5	14	21	.249
La Porte, Boston & N. Y.	101	301	21	75	4	8	0	8	6	.249
Jones, T., St. Louis	155	549	43	135	14	2	1	34	18	.248
Davis, H., Philadelphia	147	513	65	127	23	9	5	21	20	.248
Wagner, Boston	153	526	62	130	11	5	1	21	20	.247
Ball, New York	132	446	34	110	16	2	0	15	32	.247
Isbell, Chicago	84	320	31	79	15	3	1	17	18	.247
Burchell, Boston	32	69	6	17	0	0	0	3	0	.246
Bradley, Cleveland	148	548	70	133	24	7	1	60	18	.243
Hartsel, Philadelphia	129	460	73	112	16	6	4	8	15	.243
Clarke, J., Cleveland	131	492	70	119	8	4	1	9	37	.242
Clarke, N., Cleveland	97	290	34	70	8	6	1	7	6	.241
Warner, Washington	51	116	8	28	2	1	0	5	7	.241
Ganley, Washington	150	549	61	131	19	9	1	52	30	.239
Milan, Washington	130	485	55	116	10	12	1	10	29	.239
Turner, Cleveland	60	201	21	48	11	1	0	8	18	.239
Conroy, New York	141	531	44	126	22	3	1	22	23	.237
Sullivan, D., B'ton & Cl.	104	359	33	85	7	7	0	15	15	.237
Williams, St. Louis	148	539	63	127	20	7	4	22	7	.236
Moriarty, New York	101	348	25	82	12	1	0	8	22	.236
Powell, St. Louis	33	89	3	21	3	1	0	4	0	.236
Carrigan, Boston	57	149	13	35	5	2	0	8	1	.235
Hickman, Cleveland	65	197	16	46	6	1	2	2	2	.234
McBride, Washington	155	518	47	120	10	6	0	16	12	.232
Jones, C., St. Louis	74	263	37	61	11	2	0	6	14	.232
Hinchman, Cleveland	137	464	55	107	23	8	6	19	9	.231
O'Rourke, New York	34	108	5	25	1	0	0	3	4	.231
White, Chicago	51	109	12	25	1	0	0	9	4	.229
Cicotte, Boston	39	70	9	16	2	1	0	0	1	.229
Young, Boston	36	115	9	26	3	0	0	2	0	.226
Pickering, Washington	113	373	45	84	7	4	2	3	13	.225
Bemis, Cleveland	91	277	23	62	9	1	0	10	14	.224
McHale, Boston	21	67	9	15	2	2	0	4	4	.224
Barry, Philadelphia	40	135	13	30	4	3	0	2	5	.222
Rhoades, Cleveland	37	90	6	20	2	2	0	5	2	.222
Oldring, Philadelphia	116	464	38	96	14	2	1	19	13	.221
Altizer, Wash. & Clevel'd	93	291	30	65	2	3	0	24	15	.221
Downs, Detroit	84	289	29	64	10	3	1	8	2	.221
Schreck, Phila. & Chic.	77	223	17	49	7	1	0	8	1	.220

Players and Clubs.	Games.	At Bat.	Runs.	1st Base.	2d Base.	3d Base.	H. Runs.	S. Hits.	St. Bases.	Per Cent.
Speaker, Boston	31	118	12	26	2	3	0	9	2	.220
Bender, Philadelphia	20	50	5	11	1	0	0	1	1	.220
Davis, G., Chicago	128	419	41	91	14	1	0	30	22	.217
Collins, J., Philadelphia	115	433	34	94	14	3	0	13	5	.217
Nicholls, Philadelphia	150	550	58	119	17	3	4	31	14	.216
Tannehill, L., Chicago	141	482	44	104	15	3	0	21	6	.216
Perring, Cleveland	89	310	23	67	8	5	0	5	8	.216
Coughlin, Detroit	119	405	32	87	5	1	0	15	10	.215
Seybold, Philadelphia	48	130	5	28	2	0	0	3	2	.215
Heidrick, St. Louis	26	93	8	20	2	2	1	3	3	.215
Doyle, New York	12	14	1	3	0	0	0	2	0	.214
Birmingham, Cleveland	122	413	32	88	10	1	2	11	15	.213
McIlveen, New York	44	169	17	36	3	3	0	4	6	.213
Killifer, Detroit	28	75	9	16	1	0	0	6	4	.213
Gardner, New York	20	75	7	16	2	0	0	3	0	.213
Spencer, St. Louis	91	286	19	60	6	1	0	7	1	.210
Shipke, Washington	111	341	40	71	7	8	0	26	15	.208
McFarland, Boston	19	48	5	10	2	1	0	1	0	.208
Parent, Chicago	119	391	28	81	7	5	0	18	9	.207
Jones, D., Detroit	56	121	17	25	2	1	0	4	11	.207
Street, Washington	131	394	31	81	12	7	1	9	5	.206
Donahue, J., Chicago	93	304	22	62	8	2	0	8	14	.204
Altrock, Chicago	23	49	6	10	2	0	0	1	1	.204
Dineen, St. Louis	27	59	4	12	1	0	0	1	0	.203
Stephens, St. Louis	47	150	14	30	4	1	0	3	0	.200
Weaver, Chicago	15	35	1	7	1	0	0	1	0	.200
Donahue, Boston	35	86	8	17	2	0	1	2	0	.198
Smith, S., Phila. & St. L.	73	204	14	40	12	0	1	4	2	.196
Elberfeld, New York	19	56	11	11	3	0	0	2	1	.196
Schlitzer, Philadelphia	23	46	1	9	0	0	0	1	0	.196
Hughes, Washington	48	87	7	17	1	3	0	8	0	.195
Atz, Chicago	83	206	24	40	3	0	0	12	9	.194
Sullivan, W., Chicago	137	430	40	82	8	4	0	21	15	.191
Criger, Boston	84	237	12	45	4	2	0	7	1	.190
Blair, New York	76	211	9	40	5	1	1	6	4	.190
Smith, F., Chicago	48	106	15	20	7	0	0	6	1	.189
Lake, New York	44	112	6	21	4	1	1	1	2	.188
Edmonson, Washington	26	80	5	15	4	1	0	0	0	.188
Manning, New York	44	91	7	17	2	2	0	1	1	.187
Cates, Washington	40	59	5	11	1	1	0	5	0	.186
Kahoe, Washington	17	27	1	5	1	0	0	0	0	.185
Howell, St. Louis	41	120	10	22	7	0	1	3	0	.183
Falkenberg, Wash. & Cl.	25	44	6	8	0	0	0	1	0	.181
Powers, Philadelphia	62	172	8	31	6	1	0	6	1	.180
Chesbro, New York	44	100	8	18	2	1	0	3	0	.180
Plank, Philadelphia	36	89	4	16	4	0	0	1	1	.180
Owen, Chicago	25	50	3	9	3	0	0	1	1	.180
Liebhardt, Cleveland	38	80	4	14	4	1	0	10	0	.175
Walsh, Chicago	66	157	10	27	7	1	1	8	2	.172
Kleinow, New York	96	279	16	47	3	2	1	8	5	.168
Arellanes, Boston	12	30	1	5	0	2	0	0	0	.167
Seiver, Detroit	11	18	0	3	0	0	0	0	0	.167
Johnson, Washington	36	79	7	13	3	2	0	5	0	.165
Vickers, Philadelphia	53	106	4	17	3	0	0	4	0	.164
Willett, Detroit	30	67	4	11	1	0	0	2	0	.164
Winter, Bost'n & Detroit	29	67	4	11	1	0	0	2	0	.164
Newton, New York	23	25	3	4	1	0	0	1	0	.160
Donovan, Detroit	30	82	5	13	1	0	0	1	2	.159
Manush, Philadelphia	23	77	6	12	2	1	0	2	2	.156
Joss, Cleveland	42	97	6	15	3	2	0	3	3	.155
Moran, Philadelphia	19	59	4	9	0	0	0	2	1	.153
Burns, Washington	23	54	1	8	2	0	0	0	1	.148
Sweeney, New York	32	82	4	12	2	0	0	2	0	.146
Barr, Philadelphia	19	56	4	8	2	0	0	1	0	.143
Killian, Detroit	28	73	5	10	3	0	0	0	0	.137
Purtell, Chicago	26	69	3	9	2	0	0	6	2	.130
Morgan, Boston	20	63	4	8	1	0	0	5	0	.127
Summers, Detroit	40	113	6	14	2	0	0	4	0	.124
Smith, Washington	30	65	5	8	1	1	0	5	0	.123
Graham, St. Louis	21	42	0	5	0	0	0	2	0	.119
Pelty, St. Louis	21	42	3	5	0	0	0	4	0	.119
Pruitt, Boston & Cleve.	14	18	1	2	0	0	0	0	0	.111
Waddell, St. Louis	43	91	4	10	4	0	1	3	0	.110
Berger, Cleveland	29	74	8	8	3	0	0	5	0	.108
Check, Cleveland	27	48	5	5	1	0	0	3	0	.104
Keeley, Washington	31	49	3	5	0	0	0	6	1	.102
Carter, Philadelphia	14	20	1	2	0	0	0	0	0	.100
Hogg, New York	24	43	1	4	0	0	0	1	0	.093
Bailey, St. Louis	22	34	3	3	0	0	0	2	0	.088
Shaw, Chicago	22	49	0	4	1	0	0	1	0	.082
Dygert, Philadelphia	41	75	5	6	0	0	0	5	0	.080
Glaze, Boston	10	13	0	1	0	0	0	0	0	.077
Payne, Detroit	20	45	3	3	0	0	0	4	1	.067
Manuel, Chicago	17	15	0	1	0	0	0	1	0	.067
Steele, Boston	16	38	4	2	0	0	0	1	0	.053

OFFICIAL BATTING AVERAGES OF NATIONAL LEAGUE PLAYERS WHO PARTICIPATED IN FIFTEEN OR MORE CHAMPIONSHIP GAMES DURING THE SEASON OF 1908.

Players and Clubs.	Games.	At Bat.	Runs.	Base Hits.	Total Bases.	Home Runs.	Sac. Hits.	St. Bases.	Per Cent.	Players and Clubs.	Games.	At Bat.	Runs.	Base Hits.	Total Bases.	Home Runs.	Sac. Hits.	St. Bases.	Per Cent.
Wagner, Pittsburgh	151	568	100	201	308	10	14	53	.354	Crandall, New York	32	72	8	16	26	2	6	0	.222
Donlin, New York	155	593	71	198	268	6	33	30	.334	Jacklitsch, Philadelphia	30	86	6	19	22	0	4	3	.221
Doyle, New York	102	377	65	116	150	0	25	17	.308	Schlei, Cincinnati	88	300	31	66	83	1	13	2	.220
Bransfield, Philadelphia	143	527	53	160	208	3	16	30	.304	Mowrey, Cincinnati	68	227	17	50	61	0	11	5	.220
Evers, Chicago	123	416	83	125	156	0	22	36	.300	Lewis, Brooklyn	116	415	22	91	111	1	16	9	.219
Herzog, New York	59	160	38	48	58	0	10	16	.300	Knabe, Philadelphia	151	555	63	121	[illegible]	0	42	27	.218
Lobert, Cincinnati	155	570	71	167	232	4	32	47	.293	McLean, Cincinnati	98	309	24	67	87	1	8	2	.217
Zimmerman, Chicago	80	113	17	33	39	0	4	2	.292	Lumley, Brooklyn	116	440	36	95	144	4	16	4	.216
Titus, Philadelphia	149	539	75	154	194	2	41	27	.286	Pattee, Brooklyn	74	264	19	57	66	0	11	24	.216
Bridwell, New York	147	467	53	133	159	0	20	20	.285	Swacina, Pittsburgh	50	176	7	38	46	0	5	4	.216
McCormick, Phila. & N.Y.	70	274	31	78	100	0	7	6	.285	Shannon, N.Y. & Pitts.	106	395	44	85	96	1	12	18	.215
Magee, Philadelphia	142	508	79	144	212	2	19	40	.283	Sheehan, Brooklyn	145	468	45	100	122	0	26	9	.214
Bresnahan, New York	139	449	70	127	161	1	24	14	.283	Gilbert, St. Louis	89	276	12	59	66	0	8	6	.214
Murray, St. Louis	154	593	64	167	237	7	4	48	.282	John Kane, Cincinnati	127	455	61	97	131	3	26	30	.213
Howard, Chicago	89	315	42	88	104	1	11	11	.279	Bliss, St. Louis	43	136	9	29	36	1	5	3	.213
Stem, Boston	19	72	9	20	22	0	2	1	.278	Barry, St. Louis & N.Y.	102	335	29	71	84	0	12	10	.212
Kling, Chicago	125	424	51	117	162	4	13	16	.276	Richie, Philadelphia	25	52	0	11	[illegible]	0	0	0	.212
Graham, Boston	67	215	22	59	64	0	6	4	.274	Needham, New York	47	91	8	19	22	0	6	0	.209
Ritchey, Boston	120	421	44	115	137	2	21	7	.273	Brown, Chicago	44	121	5	25	[illegible]	0	5	2	.207
Chance, Chicago	126	452	65	123	164	2	16	27	.272	Egan, Cincinnati	18	68	8	14	19	0	6	7	.206
Bescher, Cincinnati	32	114	16	31	46	0	2	10	.272	Marshall, St. Louis & Ch.	15	34	4	7	9	0	1	0	.206
Merkle, New York	18	41	6	11	15	1	2	0	.268	Charles, St. Louis	119	454	39	93	116	1	20	15	.205
Seymour, New York	155	587	59	157	199	5	33	18	.267	Hannifin, N.Y. & Boston	80	259	30	53	69	2	11	7	.205
Osborn, Philadelphia	152	555	62	148	197	2	15	16	.267	McIntire, Brooklyn	40	100	5	20	25	0	1	0	.200
Beaumont, Boston	121	476	66	127	165	2	13	13	.267	Alperman, Brooklyn	57	213	17	42	50	1	9	2	.197
Tinker, Chicago	157	548	67	146	214	6	29	30	.266	Osteen, St. Louis	29	112	2	22	25	0	2	0	.196
Maddox, Pittsburgh	36	94	9	25	34	0	4	0	.266	Maloney, Brooklyn	107	359	31	70	98	3	14	14	.195
Clarke, Pittsburgh	151	551	83	146	200	2	[illegible]	24	.265	O'Rourke, St. Louis	53	164	8	32	40	0	8	2	.195
Shaw, St. Louis	96	367	40	97	121	1	8	9	.264	Spade, Cincinnati	35	87	9	17	19	0	3	0	.195
Moran, P., Chicago	45	150	12	39	46	0	8	6	.260	Ames, New York	18	36	5	7	7	0	4	0	.194
Leach, Pittsburgh	152	583	93	151	222	5	27	24	.259	Moeller, Pittsburgh	27	109	14	21	[illegible]	0	0	4	.193
Kelley, Boston	62	228	25	59	77	2	6	5	.259	Ritter, Brooklyn	37	99	6	19	23	0	2	0	.192
Bates, Boston	117	445	48	115	144	1	13	25	.258	Byrne, St. Louis	126	439	27	84	93	0	21	16	.191
Murdock, St. Louis	16	62	5	16	19	0	1	4	.258	Catterson, Brooklyn	[illegible]	68	5	13	19	1	2	0	.191
Tenney, New York	156	583	101	149	177	2	22	17	.256	Raymond, St. Louis	48	90	3	17	19	0	3	0	.189
Delahanty, St. Louis	138	499	37	127	168	1	15	11	.255	Starr, Pittsburgh	19	59	8	11	13	0	3	6	.186
Hoblitzell, Cincinnati	32	114	8	29	36	0	3	2	.254	Ludwig, St. Louis	62	187	15	34	40	0	4	3	.182
Devlin, New York	157	534	59	135	167	2	19	19	.252	Courtney, Philadelphia	42	160	14	29	32	0	5	1	.181
Storke, Pittsburgh	56	202	20	51	65	1	8	4	.252	McGinnity, New York	37	61	3	11	12	0	5	1	.180
Thomas, Phila. & Pitts	107	410	54	103	127	1	8	11	.251	Rucker, Brooklyn	42	117	3	21	25	0	1	1	.179
Abbaticchio, Pittsburgh	144	500	43	125	158	1	25	22	.250	Dorner, Boston	38	67	4	12	12	0	5	0	.179
Ganzel, Cincinnati	108	388	32	97	136	1	18	6	.250	Morris, St. Louis	23	73	1	13	16	0	4	1	.178
Konetchy, St. Louis	154	545	46	135	193	5	25	16	.248	Young, I., Boston, Pitts.	32	62	4	11	13	0	1	0	.177
Dooin, Philadelphia	132	435	28	108	133	0	12	20	.248	Lindaman, Boston	43	85	10	15	16	0	4	0	.176
Jordan, Brooklyn	146	515	58	127	191	12	11	9	.247	Bergen, Brooklyn	99	302	8	53	65	0	13	1	.175
Smith, Boston	38	130	13	32	41	1	4	2	.246	Moran, C., St. Louis	16	63	2	11	16	0	0	0	.175
Moren, Philadelphia	28	49	5	12	14	0	2	0	.245	Reilly, St. Louis	29	81	5	14	18	1	2	4	.173
Grant, Philadelphia	147	598	69	146	175	0	14	27	.244	Dunn, Brooklyn	20	64	3	11	14	0	2	0	.172
Sweeney, Boston	127	418	44	102	123	0	18	17	.244	Bell, Brooklyn	29	47	1	8	14	0	5	0	.170
Weimer, Cincinnati	15	45	7	11	12	0	2	1	.244	Lush, St. Louis	38	89	7	15	17	0	4	1	.169
Burch, Brooklyn	116	456	45	111	133	2	11	15	.243	Ferguson, Boston	37	65	8	11	14	0	3	0	.169
Hofman, Chicago	116	411	55	100	131	2	28	15	.243	Willis, Pittsburgh	41	103	9	17	18	0	4	0	.165
Paskert, Cincinnati	116	395	40	96	121	1	16	25	.243	Mathewson, New York	56	129	11	20	26	0	7	0	.155
Becker, Pitts. & Boston	60	236	17	57	64	0	2	9	.242	McQuillan, Philadelphia	48	119	4	18	19	0	6	0	.151
Hummell, Brooklyn	154	594	51	143	190	4	12	20	.241	Ewing, Cincinnati	37	94	5	14	17	0	4	2	.149
Steinfeldt, Chicago	150	539	63	130	165	1	32	12	.241	Lundgren, Chicago	23	47	2	7	7	0	5	0	.149
Kane, James, Pittsburgh	40	145	16	35	44	0	9	5	.241	Leever, Pittsburgh	38	61	5	9	11	0	2	1	.148
Karger, St. Louis	22	54	4	13	16	0	0	1	.241	McCarthy, Cin., Pit. & B.	17	41	4	6	7	0	4	0	.146
McGann, Boston	130	475	52	114	138	2	20	9	.240	Boultes, Boston	17	21	2	8	3	0	4	1	.143
Dahlen, Boston	144	524	50	125	161	3	21	10	.239	Flaherty, Boston	31	86	8	12	16	0	5	2	.140
Huggins, Cincinnati	135	498	65	119	143	0	28	30	.239	Fromme, St. Louis	20	36	2	5	5	0	2	0	.139
McMillan, Brooklyn	43	147	9	35	38	0	5	5	.238	Dubuc, Cincinnati	16	29	2	4	5	0	2	0	.138
Schulte, Chicago	102	386	42	91	118	1	29	15	.236	Higginbotham, St. Louis	19	38	3	5	5	0	1	0	.132
Wiltse, New York	44	110	9	26	28	0	7	[illegible]	.236	Overall, Chicago	37	70	3	9	12	0	8	1	.129
Doolan, Philadelphia	129	445	29	104	143	2	19	5	.234	Pastorius, Brooklyn	28	62	4	8	10	0	3	0	.129
Phelps, Pittsburgh	20	64	8	15	21	0	1	0	.234	Beebe, St. Louis	29	56	1	7	9	0	3	0	.125
Reulbach, Chicago	46	99	10	23	33	0	9	1	.232	Brain, Cincinnati & N.Y.	25	72	6	9	9	0	1	1	.125
Hostetter, St. Louis	45	155	10	36	45	0	10	1	.232	Corridon, Philadelphia	27	73	2	9	9	0	3	0	.123
Sheckard, Chicago	115	403	54	93	123	2	21	18	.231	Fraser, Chicago	26	50	3	6	7	0	5	1	.120
Taylor, New York	27	35	0	8	8	0	5	0	.229	Wilhelm, Brooklyn	42	111	4	12	12	0	5	0	.108
Gibson, Pittsburgh	140	486	37	111	144	2	10	4	.228	Pfiester, Chicago	33	79	2	8	9	0	4	1	.101
Browne, Boston	138	536	61	122	147	1	18	17	.228	Foxen, Philadelphia	22	53	0	5	5	0	1	1	.094
Hulswitt, Cincinnati	119	386	27	88	110	1	12	7	.228	Strang, New York	22	53	8	5	5	0	2	5	.094
Bowerman, Boston	74	254	16	58	71	1	4	4	.228	Coakley, Cin. & Chicago	36	82	3	7	8	0	5	0	.085
Wilson, Pittsburgh	144	529	47	120	151	3	19	12	.227	Camnitz, Pittsburgh	35	72	4	6	6	0	6	0	.083
Leifield, Pittsburgh	34	75	6	17	20	0	3	2	.227	Campbell, Cincinnati	35	72	1	6	8	0	6	0	.083
Bayless, Cincinnati	19	71	7	16	20	1	1	0	.225	McGlynn, St. Louis	16	26	0	2	2	0	1	0	.077
Gill, Pittsburgh	25	76	10	17	19	0	9	3	.224	Sparks, Philadelphia	33	77	1	4	4	0	11	0	.052
Mitchell, Cincinnati	119	406	41	90	114	1	14	18	.222	Sallee, St. Louis	25	41	2	2	2	0	1	0	.049
Slagle, Chicago	101	352	38	78	84	0	22	17	.222	Malarkey, New York	15	6	1	0	0	0	0	0	.000

OFFICIAL TEAM BATTING—AMERICAN LEAGUE.

CLUBS.	G.	A. B.	R.	1 B.	Pct.	CLUBS.	G.	A. B.	R.	1 B.	Pct.
Detroit	154	5113	646	1348	.264	New York	155	5084	459	1192	.234
Boston	155	5045	564	1248	.247	Washington	155	5037	479	1181	.234
St. Louis	155	5155	544	1264	.245	Chicago	156	503[illegible]	537	1131	.225
Cleveland	157	5114	568	1223	.239	Philadelphia	157	5066	486	1132	.22[illegible]

LEADING BATSMEN OF THE AMERICAN LEAGUE SINCE 1900.

Leading batsmen of the American League since 1900 have been: 1900, Ganzel, Kansas City, .391; 1901, Lajoie, Philadelphia, .422; 1902, Delehanty, Washington, .376; 1903, Farrell, Boston, .404; 1904, Lajoie, Cleveland, .381; 1905, Lajoie, Cleveland, .329; 1906, Stone, St. Louis, .358; 1907, Cobb, Detroit, .350; 1908, Criss, St. Louis, 341.

OFFICIAL TEAM BATTING—NATIONAL LEAGUE.

	G.	A. B.	R.	H.	T. B.	2 B.	3 B.	H. R.	S. H.	S. B.	Pct.		G.	A. B.	R.	H.	T. B.	2 B.	3 B.	H. R.	S. H.	S. B.	Pct.
New York	157	5006	651	1339	1667	182	43	20	250	181	.267	Boston	156	5131	537	1228	1502	137	43	17	194	134	.239
Chicago	158	5085	625	1267	1632	196	56	19	270	212	.249	Cincinnati	155	4879	488	1108	143[illegible]	129	77	14	214	196	.227
Pittsburgh	155	5109	585	1263	1696	162	[illegible]8	25	184	186	.247	St. Louis	154	4959	372	1105	1404	134	57	17	164	1[illegible]	.223
Philadelphia	155	5012	503	122[illegible]	1586	194	68	11	218	200	.244	Brooklyn	154	4897	375	1044	1258	110	60	28	166	11[illegible]	.213

Fly Ball Sacrifice Hits—New York, 49; Cincinnati, 47; Chicago, 47; Pittsburgh, 42; Boston, 41; Philadelphia, 28; St. Louis, 23; Brooklyn, 12.

Three Leading Fly Ball Sacrifice Hitters—Seymour, New York, 13; Donlin, New York, 10; Tinker, Chicago, 8.

LEADING BATSMEN—NATIONAL LEAGUE.

Leading batsmen of the National League since 1900 have been: 1900, Wagner, Pittsburgh, .380; 1901, Burkett, St. Louis, .382; 1902, Beaumont, Pittsburgh, .357; 1903, Wagner, Pittsburgh, .355; 1904, Wagner, Pittsburgh, .349; 1905, Seymour, Cincinnati, .377; 1906, Wagner, Pittsburgh, .339; 1907, Wagner, Pittsburgh, .350; 1908, Wagner, Pittsburgh, .354.

Aeronautic Records.

AEROSTATION.

FREE SPHERICAL BALLOONS.

WORLD'S record distance: Count Henry de la Vaulx and Comte Castillion de Saint Victor, Vincennes, France, to Korostychew, Russia, 1,925 kilometres (1,193 miles) in 35¾ hours, October 9-11, 1900.

United States record distance: Oscar Erbsloh and H. H. Clayton, St. Louis, Mo., to Bradley Beach, N. J., 872¼ miles, October 21-23, 1907, in 41 hours, winning the Gordon Bennett International Aeronautic Cup.

World's record duration in a race. Alfred Leblanc and Charles Levee, St. Louis to Herbertsville, N. J., 866.87 miles, in 44 hours and 5 minutes, October 21-23, 1907, in Gordon Bennett Cup Race.

World's record duration not in a race: 73 hours, made by Colonel Schaeck, a Swiss military officer, from Berlin, Germany, on October 11, 1908, in the Gordon Bennett International Balloon Race, landing in the sea off the coast of Norway. The old record of 52 hours was held by Drs. Kurt and Alfred Wegener.

World's record altitude: James Glaisher, September 5, 1862, claims to have reached 37,000 feet. This is now doubled. Professors Berson and Suring, of the Berliner Verein fur Luftschiffahrt, have reached an altitude of 34,000 feet.

DIRIGIBLES (STEERABLE BALLOONS).

World's record duration and distance: German military dirigible, "Gross II.," covered 800 kilometres in 13 hours 2 minutes, on September 11-12, 1908. Trip without a landing.

AVIATION.

World's record distance and duration: Wilbur Wright flew at Le Mans, France, on September 21, 1908, 1 hour 31 minutes 25 seconds in his aeroplane and covered 66.6 kilometres. He also holds record for flight with a passenger, as he flew on October 6, 1908, with one passenger, a distance of 70 kilometres in 1 hour 4 minutes 26 seconds.

AERONAUTIC TERMINOLOGY.

Aerostation—Transportation or locomotion through the air by means of using gas as a sustaining force.

Aviation—Transportation or locomotion through the air without gas as a sustaining force. Aviation is the art of mechanical or dynamic flight.

Spherical Balloon—Ordinary round balloon.

Dirigible (or dirigible balloon or steerable balloon)—An elongated gas bag equipped with a power plant and propellers.

Aeroplane—Commonly a machine having large surfaces, is held in the air by its planes being forced against air by a power plant and vertical propellers.

Helicopter—A "direct lift" machine, a machine with but a power plant and horizontal propellers. The propellers "screw" their way up into the air.

Ornithopter—A "flapping wing" machine, a close imitation of a bird.

AERO ORGANIZATIONS OF THE UNITED STATES.

Aero Club of America, New York.
†The Aeronautic Society, New York.
Aero Club of New England, Boston.
Aero Club of Hartford, Hartford, Ct.
*North Adams Aero Club, North Adams, Mass.
*Milwaukee Aero Club, Milwaukee, Wis.
*Pittsfield Aero Club, Pittsfield, Mass.
*Springfield Aero Club, Springfield, Mass.
*Aero Club of Philadelphia, Philadelphia, Pa.
*Philadelphia Aeronautical Recreation Society, Philadelphia, Pa.
*Ben Franklin Balloon Association, Philadelphia, Pa.
Other clubs are in process of formation.

NOTE.—*Has facilities for balloon ascensions in the same town. †Has grounds for experiments with flying machines.

Compiled by E. L. Jones, editor, Aeronautics, New York.

Bicycling.

THE season of 1908 in cycling showed a great revival of interest and many new records were established. This new interest, together with the fact that many new riders are coming to the front, speaks well for the future of the sport both as a pastime and in speed events on out and indoor tracks.

PROFESSIONAL MOTOR-PACED RECORDS IN COMPETITION.

Dist.	Time.	Holder.	Place.	Date.	Dist.	Time.	Holder.	Place.	Date.
1 m.	1.09 1-5	Hugh McLean.	Chas.Riv.Park	Aug. 27,1903	26 m.	29.22 3-5	R. A.Walthour	Chas.Riv.Park	May 31,1904
2 m.	2.19	Hugh McLean.	Chas.Riv.Park	Aug. 27,1903	27 m.	30.30 1-5	R. A.Walthour	Chas.Riv.Park	May 31,1904
3 m.	3.31 3-5	James Moran..	Chas.Riv.Park	June 28,1904	28 m.	31.37 2-5	R. A.Walthour	Chas.Riv.Park	May 31,1904
4 m.	4.43	H. Caldwell....	Chas.Riv.Park	Sept. 1,1903	29 m.	32.48	R. A.Walthour	Chas.Riv.Park	May 31,1904
4 m.	4.43	R. A.Walthour	Chas.Riv.Park	May 31,1904	30 m.	33.52 3-5	R. A.Walthour	Chas.Riv.Park	May 31,1904
5 m.	5.51	R. A.Walthour	Chas.Riv.Park	May 31,1904	31 m.	36.26	H. Caldwell...	Chas Riv.Park	Sept. 1,1903
6 m.	7.00 1-5	R. A.Walthour	Chas.Riv.Park	May 31,1904	32 m.	37.37 1-5	H. Caldwell...	Chas.Riv.Park	Sept. 1,1903
7 m.	8.07 3-5	R. A.Walthour	Chas.Riv.Park	May 31,1904	33 m.	38.48 4-5	H. Caldwell...	Chas.Riv.Park	Sept. 1,1903
8 m.	9.14 1-5	R. A.Walthour	Chas.Riv.Park	May 31,1904	34 m.	39.57 3-5	H. Caldwell...	Chas.Riv.Park	Sept. 1,1903
9 m.	10.22	R. A.Walthour	Chas.Riv.Park	May 31,1904	35 m.	41.07 3-5	H. Caldwell...	Chas.Riv.Park	Sept. 1,1903
10 m.	11.29 1-5	R. A.Walthour	Chas.Riv.Park	May 31,1904	36 m.	42.18 1-5	H. Caldwell...	Chas.Riv.Park	Sept. 1,1903
11 m.	12.36 1-5	R. A.Walthour	Chas.Riv.Park	May 31,1904	37 m.	43.28 1-5	H. Caldwell...	Chas.Riv.Park	Sept. 1,1903
12 m.	13.43	R. A.Walthour	Chas.Riv.Park	May 31,1904	38 m.	44.39 1-5	H. Caldwell...	Chas.Riv.Park	Sept. 1,1903
13 m.	14.50 2-5	R. A.Walthour	Chas.Riv.Park	May 31,1904	39 m.	45.49 2-5	H. Caldwell...	Chas.Riv.Park	Sept. 1,1903
14 m.	15.57 1-5	R. A.Walthour	Chas.Riv.Park	May 31,1904	40 m.	47.00	H. Caldwell...	Chas Riv.Park	Sept. 1,1903
15 m.	17.03 2-5	R. A.Walthour	Chas.Riv.Park	May 31,1904	41 m.	48.10 4-5	H. Caldwell...	Chas.Riv.Park	Sept. 1,1903
16 m.	18.10 3-5	R. A.Walthour	Chas.Riv.Park	May 31,1904	42 m.	49.21 1-5	H. Caldwell ..	Chas.Riv.Park	Sept. 1,1903
17 m.	19.17 2-5	R. A.Walthour	Chas.Riv.Park	May 31,1904	43 m.	50.31 1-5	H. Caldwell...	Chas.Riv.Park	Sept. 1,1903
18 m.	20 24 1-5	R. A.Walthour	Chas.Riv.Park	May 31,1904	44 m.	51.41 1-5	H. Caldwell...	Chas.Riv.Park	Sept. 1,1903
19 m.	21.30 4-5	R. A.Walthour	Chas.Riv.Park	May 31,1904	45 m.	52.50 4-5	H. Caldwell...	Chas.Riv.Park	Sept. 1,1903
20 m.	22.37 3-5	R. A.Walthour	Chas Riv.Park	May 31,1904	46 m.	54.23 4-5	H. Caldwell...	Chas.Riv.Park	Sept. 1,1903
21 m.	23.44 3-5	R. A.Walthour	Chas.Riv.Park	May 31,1904	47 m.	55.49 3-5	H. Caldwell...	Chas.Riv.Park	Sept. 1,1903
22 m.	24.51 4-5	R. A.Walthour	Chas.Riv.Park	May 31,1904	48 m.	57.21 1-5	H. Caldwell...	Chas.Riv.Park	Sept. 1,1903
23 m.	25.59	R. A.Walthour	Chas.Riv.Park	May 31,1904	49 m.	58.43 1-5	H. Caldwell...	Chas.Riv.Park	Sept. 1,1903
24 m.	27.07 3-5	R. A.Walthour	Chas.Riv.Park	May 31,1904	50 m.	59.59	H. Caldwell...	Chas.Riv.Park	Sept. 1,1903
25 m.	28.14 1-5	R. A.Walthour	Chas.Riv.Park	May 31,1904	100 m.	2.48.11 4-5	H. Caldwell...	Revere,Mass..	Sept. 8,1904

Fastest mile in competition, 1.06 1-5, R. A. Walthour, Charles River Park, Mass., May 31, 1904.

PROFESSIONAL AGAINST TIME–PACED RECORDS.

Dist.	Time.	Holder.	Place.	Date.	Dist.	Time.	Holder.	Place.	Date.
¼ m..	0.20	Major Taylor...	Chicago.......	Nov. 9,1899	2 m..	2.20 1-5	Joe Nelson.....	Chas.Riv.Park	Aug. 27,1903
⅓ m..	0.27 4-5	J. S. Johnson...	Nashville	Oct. 29,1896	3 m..	3.30 1-5	Joe Nelson.....	Chas. Riv. Park	Aug. 27,1903
½ m..	0.41	Major Taylor..	Chicago.......	Nov. 10,1899	4 m..	4.41 1-5	Joe Nelson.....	Chas. Riv.Park	Aug. 27,1903
⅔ m.	0.58 3-5	W.W. Hamilton	Coronado, Cal.	Mar. 2,1896	5 m..	5.51	Joe Nelson.....	Chas. Riv.Park	Aug. 27,1903
1 m..	1.06 1-5	R. A.Walthour.	Chas.Riv.Park	May 31,1904					

All competition records upward have eiased time tiials.

PROFESSIONAL AGAINST TIME–UNPACED RECORDS.

Dist.	Time.	Holder.	Place.	Date.	Dist.	Time.	Holder.	Place.	Date.
¼ m..	0.23 4-5	Iver Lawson...	Salt Lake City.	July 4,1906	4 m..	8.50	F. J. Titus.....	Woodside Park	July 2,1898
⅓ m..	0.34 1-5	W.W. Hamilton	Coronado, Cal.	Mar. 2,1896	5 m..	11.04 1-5	Alex. Peterson.	Dayton, Ohio..	Aug. 4,1902
½ m..	0.50 2-5	A. J. Clarke....	Saltair........	Aug. 24,1908	10 m..	23.09 2-5	W.W.Hamilton	Denver, Col...	July 9,1898
⅔ m..	1.14 1-5	W. C. Sanger..	Denver........	Nov. 16,1885	15 m..	35.03	W.W.Hamilton	Denver, Col...	July 9,1898
1 m..	1.53 2-5	W.M.Sam'lson.	Salt Lake City.	July 25,1901	20 m..	47.08 2-5	W.W.Hamilton	Denver, Col....	July 9,1898
2 m..	4.06 2-5	W.M.Sam'lson.	Salt Lake City.	July 21,1904	25 m..	59.13 2-5	W.W.Hamilton	Denver, Col....	July 9,1898
3 m..	5.32 4-5	F. J. Titus.....	Woodside Park	July 2,1898					

1 hour, 25 miles, 600 yards, W. W. Hamilton, Denver, July 9, 1898.

PROFESSIONAL HANDICAP RECORDS.

Distance.	Time.	Holder.	Handicapper.	Place.	Date.
¼ mile..............	00.28 2-5	F. L. Kramer...........	J. C. Wetmore..........	Vailsburg............	Sept. 5,1904
⅓ mile..............	.38	F. L. Kramer...........	R. F. Kelsey............	Vailsburg............	Aug. 16,1908
½ mile.	00.53 3-5	A. J. Clarke...........	F. E. Schefski..........	Salt Lake City.......	June 11,1907
⅔ mile..............	1.18	W. F. Sims............	W. Jose................	Washington..........	Aug. 15,1898
¾ mile..............	1.21	F. L. Kramer...........	F. E. Schefski	Salt Lake City.......	July 5,1907
1 mile..........	1.48 3-5	A. J. Clarke...........	F. E. Schefski..........	Ogden, Utah.........	July 17,1907
2 miles	3.41	Iver Lawson...........	F. E. Schefski..........	Salt Lake City	July 28,1906
3 miles.............	5.49	Iver Lawson...........	F. E. Schefski..........	Salt Lake City	June 22,1906
5 miles	10.15	W. S. Fenn...........	J. C. Wetmore..........	Vailsburg	Aug. 25,1901
10 miles............	21.53 1-5	W. S. Fenn............	J. C. Wetmore..........	Vailsburg	July 27,1902

PROFESSIONAL COMPETITION–UNPACED RECORDS.

Dist.	Time.	Holder.	Place.	Date.	Dist.	Time.	Holder.	Place.	Date.
¼ m.	0.28 1-5	F. L. Kramer.....	Vailsburg.....	May 4,1902	3 m..	5.35 3-5	Iver Lawson.....	Salt Lake City	July 25,1906
*⅓ m.	0.38	F. L. Kramer.....	Vailsburg.....	Aug. 16,1908	5 m..	9.48 1-5	Ernest A. Pye....	Ogden, Utah..	July 11,1906
*½ m.	0.51 1-5	A. J. Clarke......	Saltair, Utah..	Aug. 19,1908	10 m..	20.04 3-5	John Bedell	Park Sq., Bos.	Feb. 15,1908
*⅔ m.	1.18	W. F. Sims	Washington ..	Aug. 15,1898	15 m..	33.44	F. L. Kramer.....	Vailsburg.....	Sept. 22,1901
*¾ m.	1.21	F. L. Kramer.....	Salt Lake City	July 5,1907	20 m..	46.05 1-5	E. C. Hausman....	Mad-Sq.Gard.	Sept. 28,1901
*1 m.	1.48 3-5	A. J. Clarke......	Ogden, Utah..	July 17,1907	25 m..	57.26 3-5	F. L. Kramer.....	Vailsburg	Oct. 25,1908
*2 m.	3.41	Iver Lawson......	Salt Lake City	July 28,1906					

* Made in handicap.

A handicap record from scratch is recognized as competition record if the time made is better than has been made in any scratch race of the same distance.

One hour, 28 miles, 19 yards, W. Hedspeth, Dayton, O., July 31, 1902.

BICYCLING—*Continued.*

AMERICAN COMPETITION—PROFESSIONAL PACED HOUR RECORDS.

Hrs.	M.	Yds.	Holder.	Place.	Date.	Hrs.	M.	Yds.	Holder.	Place.	Date.
1....	50	3	Harry Caldwell..	Chas. Riv. Pk.	Sept. 1,1905	13....	335	1,540	W. F. King......	Salt LakeCity	Sept. 15,1901
2....	77	440	James Moran.....	Revere.......	Aug. 8,1903	14....	355		W. F. King......	Salt LakeCity	Sept. 15,1901
3....	106	900	Harry Caldwell..	Revere.......	Sept. 5,1904	15....	372		W. F. King......	Salt LakeCity	Sept. 15,1901
4....	137	275	Hugh McLean....	Revere.... ...	Sept. 5,1904	16....	397	220	W. F. King......	Salt LakeCity	Sept 15 1901
5....	168	910	James Moran.....	Revere......	Sept. 5,1904	17....	403	440	W. F. King......	Salt LakeCity	Sept. 15,1901
6....	197	220	James Moran.....	Revere... ...	Sept. 5,1904	18....	416		John Lawson.....	Los Angeles..	June 10,1900
7....	199	220	Chas. Turville....	Salt Lake City	Sept. 15,1901	19....	432		John Lawson.....	Los Angeles..	June 10,1900
8....	218	440	W. F. King......	Salt LakeCity	Sept. 15,1901	20....	450	1,540	John Lawson.....	Los Angeles..	June 10,1900
9....	246	440	W. F. King......	Salt LakeCity	Sept. 15,1901	21....	466	660	John Lawson.....	Los Angeles..	June 10,1900
10....	265		W. F. King......	Salt Lake City	Sept. 15,1901	22....	485	220	John Lawson.....	Los Angeles..	June 10,1900
11....	289		W. F. King.	Salt LakeCity	Sept. 15,1901	23....	507	1,320	John Lawson.....	Los Angeles..	June 10,1900
12....	312	880	B. W. Pierce......	Waltham.....	July 3,1899	24....	528	925	John Lawson.....	Los Angeles..	June 10,1900

PROFESSIONAL TANDEM COMPETITION—FLYING START.

1 m.	1.51	Kramer-Fogler..........	Vailsburg	June 28, 1908	5 m.	9.50 3-5	Mayer-Clarke..............	Saltair	June 28, 1908
2 m.	3.46 2-5	Kramer-Fogler..........	Vailsburg	Aug. 23, 1908					

AMATEUR HANDICAP RECORDS.

Distance.	Time.	Holder.	Handicapper.	Place.	Date.
¼ mile..............	0.29 3-5	M. L. Hurley..........	John C. Wetmore......	Vailsburg............	May 30,1902
⅓ mile..............	0.38 4-5	W. S. Fenn...........	R. F. Kelsey..........	Hartford............	Sept. 3,1900
½ mile..............	0.56 4-5	W. De Mara...........	F. E. Schefski.........	Salt Lake City........	Aug. 20,1907
⅔ mile..............	1.18	M. L. Hurley..........	R. F. Kelsey..........	Providence...........	July 1, 1901
¾ mile..............	1.24 4-5	W. De Mara...........	F. E. Schefski.	Ogden, Utah.........	July 21,1907
1 mile..............	1.55 3-5	J. B. Hume............	F. E. Schefski.........	Salt Lake City........	July 28,1906
2 miles.............	4.06 4-5	J. B. Hume............	F. E. Schefski.........	Salt Lake City........	Aug. 25,1905
3 miles.............	6.07	P. Lawrence...........	F. E. Schefski....... ..	Salt Lake City........	Aug. 15,1908
5 miles.............	10.36	J. B. Hume......	F. E. Schefski.........	Salt Lake City........	Aug. 4,1906

AMATEUR COMPETITION—UNPACED.

Dist.	Time.	Holder.	Place.	Date.	Dist.	Time.	Holder.	Place.	Date.
¼ m.	.28 2-5	M. L. Hurley...	Vailsburg.....	July 27,1902	10 m.	21.25	J. P. Linley....	New Haven....	May 30,1902
*⅓ m.	.38 4-5	W. S. Fenn.....	Hartford......	Sept. 3,1900	15 m.	35.32	G. H. Collett....	New York City.	May 30,1900
*½ m.	.56 4-5	W. De Mara ...	Salt Lake City.	Aug. 20,1907	20 m.	45.40 2-5	E. Snauder.	New Haven....	Aug. 5,1900
*⅔ m.	1.18	M. L. Hurley...	Providence...	July 1,1901	25 m.	1.00 39	Ed.W. Forres.	Vailsburg.....	July 28,1901
*¾ m.	1.24 4-5	W. De Mara....	Ogden, Utah ..	July 21,1907	30 m.	1.13.35.	J. P. Jacobson..	New York City	Aug. 25,1899
*1 m.	1.55 3-5	J. B. Hume.....	Salt Lake City.	July 28,1906	40 m.	1.39.56 3-5	J. P. Jacobson..	New York City	Aug. 25,1899
2 m.	3.53 2-5	P. Lawrence. ..	Saltair, Utah..	July 22,1908	50 m.	2.05.00 4-5	J. P. Jacobson..	New York City	Aug. 25,1899
3 m.	5.57 1-5	A. Carter.......	Ogden, Utah...	Aug. 3,1905	75 m.	3.30.36 1-5	W. Torrence....	New York City	Aug. 25,1899
4 m.	....	....	....	....	100 m.	4.57.24 2-5	W. Torrence....	New York City	Aug. 25,1899
5 m.	10.31	Hal McCormick	Salt Lake City.	July 17,1908					

* Made in handicap.

1 hour, 24 miles, 1,472 yards, George H. Collett, New York City, May 30, 1900.

AMATEUR AGAINST TIME—UNPACED.

Dist.	Time.	Holder.	Place.	Date.	Dist.	Time.	Holder.	Place.	Date.
¼ m..	.24 4-5	A. Crebs.........	Saltair, Utah..	Aug. 1,1908.	1 m..	1.55	Parley Giles.....	Saltair, Utah..	July 28, 1908
⅓ m..	.33 2-5	A. B. Simons.....	Deming.......	May 26,1896	2 m..	4.09	Parley Giles	Ogden, Utah..	July 8, 1908
½ m..	.53 1-5	P. Lawrence......	Salt Lake City.	Aug. 8,1908	3 m..	6.25 3-5	Parley Giles.....	Salt Lake City.	Aug. 4, 1908
⅔ m..	1.21 1-5	J. G. Hell	Denver	July 31,1897	4 m..	8.51 2-5	Parley Giles.....	Ogden, Utah..	Aug. 20,1908
¾ m..	1.23 3-5	P. Lawrence......	Saltair, Utah.	Aug. 19,1908	5 m..	11.00	Parley Giles.....	Ogden, Utah..	Aug. 20,1908

AMATEUR TANDEM COMPETITION.

1 m.	1.52 3-5	Hausman-Rutz. ...	....	....	3 m.	5.47 2-5	Wilcox-McCormack	Salt L.City	July 27,1905
2 m.	4.33	Wilcox-McCormack	SaltLakeCity	Aug. 1,1905	5 m.	10.15	Wilcox-McCormack	Salt L.City	June 13,1905

AMERICAN ROAD RECORDS—AMATEUR.

(Under N. C. A. Rules.)

Dist.	Time.	Made By	Place.	Dist.	Time.	Made By	Place.
1 m.	2.02	Henry Surman........ R. L. Guthbridge....... S. C. Haberles........	Westfield, N. J.....	15 m. 20 m. 25 m.	34.47 4-5 53.20 1.03.10	I. Lewin, C. R. C. Ass'n. J. M. Eifler............. Wm. F. Blum, Chicago..	Valley Stream, L. I. Valley Stream, L. I. Chicago, Ill.
2 m.	5.07 1-5	J. B. Hawkins, BrowerWh.	Valley Stream, L. I.	50 m.	2.21.18	R. Nelson, P. Wheelmen.	Atlantic City, N. J.
5 m.	12.28 2-5	J. B. Hawkins, BrowerWh.	Valley Stream, L. I.	60 m.	2.46.00	R. Nelson, P. Wheelmen.	Atlantic City, N. J.
10 m.	23.53	Archie Rawlings...... ...	Tampa, Fla........				

N. C. A. PROFESSIONAL SPRINT CHAMPIONSHIPS—NATIONAL CIRCUIT, 1908.

Rider.	1st.	2d.	3d.	4th.	Total Points.	Rider.	1st.	2d.	3d.	4th.	Total Points.
Frank L. Kramer	3	1	1	0	20	N. M. Anderson...	0	1	0	1	4
W. A. Bardgett.........	1	0	2	2	11	George Wiley...........	0	0	1	1	8
Jos. A. Fogler..........	0	3	0	0	9	A. J. Clarke.	0	0	1	0	2
John Bedell	1	0	0	0	5	Edw. Rupprecht........	0	0	0	1	1

Firsts count 5 points; Seconds, 3 points; Thirds, 2 points; Fourths, 1 point.

BICYCLING—Continued.

N. C. A. PROFESSIONAL PACED CHAMPIONSHIP, 1908.

Rider.	1st.	2d.	3d.	4th.	Total Points.	Rider.	1st.	2d.	3d.	4th.	Total Points.
Hugh McLean	18	3	1	0	110	S. H. Wilcox	1	1	1	0	10
James F. Moran	6	4	4	0	50	R. J. Walthour	2	0	0	0	10
George Wiley	5	5	2	1	44	F. A. MacFarland	0	3	0	0	9
Nat. Butler	4	7	0	0	41	Albert Champion	0	2	0	0	6
Elmer J. Collins	2	5	2	1	30	Menus Bedell	0	1	1	0	5
P. F. Logan	4	3	0	0	29	T. Jenkins	0	1	1	0	5
W. E. Samuelson	5	1	0	0	28	N. M. Anderson	0	1	0	0	3
E. F. Root	2	3	4	0	27	John King	0	1	0	0	3
John Bedell	2	4	2	0	26	Joe Nelson	0	1	0	0	3
Charles Vanoni	1	1	2	0	12	J. T. Halgin	0	0	1	0	2
Hardy K. Downing	1	2	0	0	11	Walter De Mara	0	0	0	1	1

Firsts count, 5 points; Seconds, 3 points; Thirds, 2 points; Fourths, 1 point.

N. C. A. AMATEUR CHAMPIONSHIPS, 1908.

Rider.	1st.	2d.	3d.	4th.	Total Points.	Rider.	1st.	2d.	3d.	4th.	Total Points.
Chas. H. Stein	2	2	0	1	17	Jerome Steinert	0	1	0	0	3
Fred. Hill	1	1	1	0	10	Edw. Seufert	0	0	1	0	2
George Cameron	1	0	1	1	8	Fred W. Jones	0	0	1	0	2
David Mackay	1	0	1	0	7	T. Connolly	0	0	1	0	2
James Zanes	1	0	0	0	5	Peter Drobach	0	0	0	1	1
H. Van den Dries	0	1	0	1	4	Charles Frank	0	0	0	1	1
Oscar Goerke	0	1	0	0	3	M. Van den Dries	0	0	0	1	1

Champions at various distances—¼ mile, James Zanes, Newark, N. J. ⅓ mile, Chas. H. Stein, Brooklyn, N. Y. ½ mile, George G. Cameron, New York. 1 mile, Chas. H. Stein, Brooklyn, N. Y. 2 miles, Fred. Hill, Boston, Mass. 5 miles, David Mackay, Newark, N. J.

IMPORTANT CYCLING EVENTS OF 1908.

George Lockner, Syracuse, N. Y., won the twentieth annual 25-mile Irvington-Milburn road race, June 6, 1908, from the 4½-minute mark; Herman Lind. 6 min., second; W. J. Klucrok, 3h. 30m., third. W. R. Stroud, Philadelphia, from 3-minute mark, finished fourth and also won first time prize in 1h. 10m. 31 2-5s.

F. Ryser won the 100-kilometre world's professional paced championship at Berlin, Germany, August 2, 1908; time 1h. 22m. 3s. A. E. Wills holds the record, made at Munich, Aug. 17, 1908, at 1h. 34s. Wills also holds 1-hour paced record made at Munich, Aug. 17, at 61 miles, 905 yards. Meredith won the amateur championship, same conditions, in 1h. 28m. 52s.

Arthur Van der Stuytt made 2-hour paced record at Leipsic, Germany, Oct. 11, 1908, at 106 miles. 1,498 yards.

Six-day race record held in Madison Square Garden, December, 1907: Rutt-Stohl, 2312-5 miles; Fogler-Moran, 2312-5 miles; Georget-Dupre, 2312-4 miles; Downing-Downey, 2312-4 miles; Galvin-Wiley, 2312-4 miles; Krebs-Vanderstuyft, 2312-3 miles; Logan-Bardgett, 2312-3 miles; Breton-Vanoni, 2312-1 miles.

Homing Pigeons.

Two new championship records for old birds were made during the season of 1908 when a bird owned by E. Edwin Atwood, Needham, Mass., flew 500 miles at a rate of 1705.62 yards per minute and another owned by Louis Gebfert, Fort Wayne, Ind., covered 1,004 miles in 5 days, 1 hour, 22 minutes.

CHAMPION RECORDS—OLD BIRDS.

Distances.	Speed. Yards per Minute.	Year	Owner.	Loft at—
100 miles	2511.87	1900	W. J. Lautz	Buffalo, N. Y.
200 "	1893.59	1897	C. H. Watchman	Baltimore, Md.
300 "	1848.00	1896	E. Rouff	Detroit, Mich.
400 "	1703.61	1905	Wm. Compa	Paterson, N. J.
500 "	1705.62	1908	E. Edwin Atwood	Needham, Mass.
600 "	1612.23	1907	Fred. May	Minneapolis, Minn.
700 "	1546.97	1898	W. J. Lautz	Buffalo, N. Y.
836 "	Finished second day	1902	Reuben Peters	Pittsburgh, Pa.
1,004 "	5d. 1h. 22m.	1905	Louis Gebfert	Ft. Wayne, Ind.

General average, 100, 200, 300, 400, 500 miles, 1394.63 yards; 1900, Harry Robertson, Brooklyn, N. Y. National general averages, 100, 200, 300, 400, 500, 600 miles, 1177.19 yards; 1899, Chas. Bang, Staten Island, N. Y. 1222.48 yards; 1905, F. C. Hersey, Jr., Wellesley, Mass. Average percentage nominated birds, 80 per cent.; 1906, Eli Moreton, Newark, N. J.

CHAMPION RECORDS—YOUNG BIRDS.

Distances.	Speed. Yards per Minute.	Year.	Owner.	Loft at—
100 miles	1597.75	1903	Wm. P. Betts	Buffalo, N. Y.
150 "	1800.95	1900	F. G. Thon	Rochester, N. Y.
200 "	1875.45	1894	P. G. Clark	Philadelphia, Pa.
300 "	1665.25	1905	F. P. Fetes	Buffalo, N. Y.
400 "	1060.97	1896	Jacob Eberle	Newark, N. J.
500 "	1191.30	1904	E. B. Walker	Buffalo, N. Y.
600 "	557.78	1897	G. W. Schaefer	Cream Ridge, N. J.

General average, 100, 150, 200 miles, 1356.73 yards; 1897, Adolph Busch, Staten Island, N. Y. National general averages, 1260.13 yards; 1904, Otto Kreger, Paterson, N. J. Average percentage nominated birds, 83⅓ per cent.; 1905, Paul F. Miller, Brooklyn, N. Y.

(Compiled by John Fischer, Secretary The International Federation of American Homing Pigeon Fanciers.)

Swimming.

The feature of the swimming season of 1908, as in most other sports, was the great reunion of champions at the Olympic games and the marked improvement that they showed. Charles M. Daniels, of the New York Athletic Club, did the best sprinting of the year, his records from 50 to 150 yards surpassing anything ever seen since the introduction of speed swimming. Henry Taylor, of England, excelled at the distances, his performances comparing favorably with even those of the late incomparable Kieran, of Australia.

CHAMPIONSHIP EVENTS OF 1908.

National Championships of the A. A. U. (open salt water). Seniors, at Travers Island, September 19, 440 yards—Won by C. M. Daniels, N. Y. A. C., in 5m. 54s.; J. H. Reilly, second; Karl Schmidt, third. September 5, 880 yards—Won by L. B. Goodwin, N. Y. A. C., in 13m. 23s.; J. H. Reilly, second; Karl Schmidt, third. One mile, at Sheepshead Bay, September 26—Won by C. M. Daniels, N. Y. A. C., in 27m. 20⅗s.; L. Manley, second; F. H. Jones, third. Five miles, at New Rochelle, August 24—L. B. Goodwin, N. Y. A. C., 2h. 10m. 25s.; E. E. Wenck, 2h. 19m. 23s., second. Junior events were not held.

National Championships of the A. A. U. (in baths). At New Illinois A. C., Chicago, March 17—Junior, 50 yards, breast stroke, D. T. Hammond, Chicago A. A., 33s.; Senior, 50 yards, M. Schwarz, Missouri A. C., 27⅗s.; Junior, fancy diving, D. T. Hammond, Chicago A. A., 231 points; Senior, 1,000 yards, L. B. Goodwin, N. Y. A. C., 14m. 13⅗s.; Junior, 50 yards, back stroke, H. J. Hebner, Illinois A. C., 32⅘s. At Chicago A. A., March 18—Senior, 150 yards, back stroke, A. M. Goessling, Missouri A. C., 2m. ⅕s.; Senior, 200 yards, breast stroke, A. M. Goessling, Missouri A. C., 2m. 46⅖s.; Senior, fancy diving, George Gaedzik, Chicago A. A., 182 points; Junior, 50 yards—George South, N. Y. A. C., 27⅕s. At East Liberty A. C., Pittsburgh, March 20—Senior, plunge, C. L. Brown, Illinois A. C., 74ft.; Senior, 220 yards, C. M. Daniels, N. Y. A. C., 2m. 36⅘s.; Junior, 100 yards, H. J. Hebner, Illinois A. C., 1m. 2s. At Oakland A. C., Pittsburgh, March 20—Junior, plunge, C. L. Brown, Illinois A. C., 73ft.; Senior, 500 yards, L. B. Goodwin, N. Y. A. C., 7m. 25s.; Junior, 220 yards, C. S. Sloan, East Liberty A. C., 2m. 47s. At New York A. C., March 27-28—Senior, 440-yard relay race, won by N. Y. A. C. team (G. South, L. B. Goodwin, C. D. Trubenbach and C. M. Daniels); University of Pennsylvania team (G. C. Sylvester, J. Graham, J. H. Dalrymple and J. K. Shyrock), second; time, 4m. 13⅗s. Senior, water polo—N. Y. A. C., 12, vs. Bath Beach S. C., 0; Chicago A. A., 7, vs. Columbia, 0; N. Y. A. C., 1, vs. Chicago A. A., 1. Chicago refused to play the extra period because of crippled men, and the game was awarded to New York A. C. Columbia (1) defeated Bath Beach S. C. (0) for third place. Junior, 500-yard swim, J. K. Shyrock, U. of Penn., 7m. 30⅘s.; Senior, 100-yard swim, C. M. Daniels, N. Y. A. C., 57⅕s.

Metropolitan A. A. U. Championships. Travers Island, August 15—440 yards, J. H. Reilly, Townsend Harris Hall School, 6m. 20s.; fancy diving, T. J. O'Callaghan, N. Y. A. C., 217 points. Travers Island, September 5—880 yards, L. B. Goodwin, N. Y. A. C., 13m. 23s.; 150 yards, back stroke, Bratton Cup, C. A. Ruberl, N. Y. A. C., 2m. 20s. Sheepshead Bay, September 7—One mile, L. B. Goodwin, N. Y. A. C., 28m. 37s.

Middle Atlantic A. A. U. Championships. At Philadelphia, August 22—Sackett Cup, 100 yards, J. H. Reilly, New York, 1m. 5⅘s.; 100 yards, T. G. Whitaker, Philadelphia, 1m. 14s.; half-mile, Dr. Robert Ferguson, Philadelphia, 15m. 39⅕s.; one mile, Dr. Ferguson, Philadelphia, 33m. 18⅖s.

Intercollegiate Championships—Because of a double tie in swimming and water polo an extra meet was held in College of the City of New York tank, April 12, with the following results: 800-foot relay, Sylvester, Graham, Dalrymple and Shyrock, Penn., won in 2m. 41⅗s.; fancy diving, Dalrymple, Penn., 182 points; 50-yard swim, Dennison, Princeton, 28s.; 220-yard, Shyrock, Penn., 3m. 16⅕s.; plunge for distance, Hopkinson, Penn., 67½ft.; 100-yard swim, Chambers, Princeton, 1m. 3⅗s. Points—Penn., 40; Princeton, 13. Water polo—Yale, 5; Penn., 0. The standing in meets won and lost up to this final meet was: Swimming—Pennsylvania and Princeton, 4-1; Harvard and Yale, 3-2; Columbia, 1-4; C. C. N. Y., 0-5. Water polo—Pennsylvania and Yale, 4-1; Columbia, 3-2; Princeton, 2-3; C. C. N. Y. and Harvard, 1-4.

NOTABLE EVENTS OF 1908.

New college records—50 yards, Dennison, Princeton, 26⅖s.; plunge for distance, Beatty, Yale, 72ft.; 800-foot relay, Pennsylvania, 2m. 40⅘s.; 100 yards, P. Withington, Harvard, 1m. 2⅖s.

New York Marathon, Battery to Coney Island, 13 miles, August 30—L. B. Goodwin, N. Y. A. C., 4h. 30m.; L. Manley, N. Y. A. C., 5h. 15m., second. Life Saving Marathon, same course, August 17—Won by John Forrester in 4h. 45m. 30s. Miss Clara T. Hurst, Staten Island, and Miss Augusta Gallup, New York, were among the six survivors.

Miss Elaine Golding, who made a record of 1m. 15s. for 100 yards at Huntington Bay, L. I., August 15, won the Women's Marathon across the Hudson, August 22, covering the three miles in 1h. 45m.

Ten-mile river swim, under the auspices of the Missouri A. C., September 7, at St. Louis—Won by H. J. Handy, I. A. C., 1h. 43m. 22⅕s.; R. B. Foster, C. A. A., second, 1h. 43m. 46⅘s. There were 64 entries in the 1908 event; 53 actual starters, 38 of whom finished. It is estimated that between 70,000 and 100,000 people saw the race. Handy gets a second leg on the Busch $1,000 Cup.

RECORDS OF 1908 ALLOWED BY THE A. A. U.

Sixty yards, bath, 2 turns, C. M. Daniels, December 19, 1907, Pittsburgh, 30s.; 75 yards,

SWIMMING—*Continued.*

C. M. Daniels, March 31, 1908, Pittsburgh, 40⅘s.; 80 yards, 5 turns, C. M. Daniels, March 15, New York, 43s.; 220 yards, 1 turn, C. M. Daniels, 2m. 40⅗s.; 330 yards, 2 turns, C. M. Daniels, 4m. 15s.; 440 yards, 3 turns, C. M. Daniels, 5m. 54⅕s., all open tidal water, at Travers Island, September 19; 200 yards, breast stroke, bath, 9 turns, A. M. Goessling, March 18, 2m. 46⅗s.; 150 yards, back stroke, bath, 5 turns, A. M. Goessling, March 18, 2m. ⅕s.; 400-yard relay, C. M. Daniels, C. D. Trubenbach, L. B. Goodwin and George South, New York, March 27, 4m. 13⅗s.; plunging (1m. time limit), 74ft., C. S. Brown, Chicago, March 21.

WORLD'S SWIMMING RECORDS.

Distance	Amateur Records.				Professional Records.	
	Made in Bath.		Made in Open Water.		*Open Water. Others made in baths.	
	Holder.	Time.	Holder.	Time.	Holder.	Time.
		H. M. S.		M. S.		M. S.
25 yards	C. M. Daniels (A.)...	11 3-5	....	....	....	....
50 yards	C. M. Daniels (A.)...	25	A. Wickham (Aus.)	24 3-5	....	....
60 yards	C. M. Daniels (A.)...	30	....	....	....	....
75 yards	C. M. Daniels (A.)...	40 1-5	....	....	....	....
100 yards	C. M. Daniels (A.)...	55 2-5	C. Healy (Aus.)...	57	J. Nuttall (E.)...	1.01⅕
120 yards	C. M. Daniels (A.)...	1.11 4-5	....	....	J. Nuttall (E.)...	1.18 2-5
150 yards	C. M. Daniels (A.)...	1.32 2-5	....	....	D. Billington (E.)	1.39
200 yards	B. Kieran (Aus.).....	2.13 2-5	....	....	D. Billington (E.)	2.18
220 yards	B. Kieran (Aus.).....	2.28 2-5	B. Kieran (Aus.)..	2.35	D. Billington (E.)	2.34 4-5
300 yards	B. Kieran (Aus.)....	3.31 4-5	....	....	D. Billington (E.)	3.32
350 yards	B. Kieran (Aus.).....	4.13 4-5	....	....	....	....
400 yards	B. Kieran (Aus.).....	4.51 1-5	....	....	D. Billington (E.)	5.03
440 yards	B. Kieran (Aus.).....	5.19	B. Kieran (Aus.)..	5.22 1-5	D. Billington (E.)	5.28
500 yards	B. Kieran (Aus.).....	6.07 1-5	....	....	D. Billington (E.)	6.18
600 yards	B. Kieran (Aus.).....	7.32 2-5	....	....	....	....
700 yards	B. Kieran (Aus.).....	8.54 1-5	....	....	....	....
800 yards	B. Kieran (Aus.).....	10.11 3-5	....	....	....	....
880 yards	B. Kieran (Aus.).....	11.11 3-5	H. Taylor (E.).....	11.25 2-5	D. Billington (E.)	11.35
900 yards	B. Kieran (Aus.).....	11.35 2-5	....	....	....	....
1,000 yards	B. Kieran (Aus.).....	12.52 2-5	D. Billington (E.).	13.34 4-5	D. Billington (E.)	13.16
1,100 yards	B. Kieran (Aus.).....	14.22 1-5	....	....	....	....
1,200 yards	B. Kieran (Aus.).....	15.44	....	....	....	....
1,300 yards	B. Kieran (Aus.).....	17.04 3-5	....	....	....	....
1,320 yards	W. Springfield (Aus.)	18.07 1-5	D. Billington (E.).	18.24	D. Billington (E.)	17.45 2-5
1,400 yards	B. Kieran (Aus.)....	18.23 2-5	....	....	....	....
1,500 yards	B. Kieran (Aus.).....	19.47 4-5	....	....	....	....
1,600 yards	B. Kieran (Aus.).....	21.09 2-5	....	....	....	....
1,700 yards	B. Kieran (Aus.).....	22.31 1-5	....	....	....	....
1 mile.....	B. Kieran (Aus.).....	23.16 4-5	W. Batterbee (E.).	24.33	J. Nuttall (E.).	26.08
2 miles....	Geo. Read (Aus.).....	54.54	....	....	....	....

RECORDS OF WOMEN.

		H. M. S.			H. M. S.
75 yards	Miss G. Smith (E.)........	57 4-5	200 yards	Miss E. McKay (E.).......	2.57
*100 yards	Miss E. Golding (A.).......	1.15	440 yards	Miss E. McKay (E.).......	6.51
100 yards	Miss J. Fletcher (E.)......	1.17	1 mile.....	Miss A. Kellerman (Aus.).	32.44

(A.) American. (Aus.) Australian. (E.) English. *With tide.

MISCELLANEOUS.

Swimming on the back—100 yards, C. Martin (E.), 1m. 13s.; 150 yards, C. Unwin (E.), 1m. 57⅘s.

Breast stroke—200 yards, A. M. Goessling (A.), 2m. 45⅗s.

Plunge for distance (one-minute time limit)—W. Taylor (E.), 82ft. 7in.

Under water swimming—E. P. Swateck (A.), 106yds. 2ft.

Five-men relay race—500 yards, Australian team (C. Healy, A. Wickham, J. Yartakorer, H. Baker, F. C. V. Lane), 5m. 4s.

Four-men relay race—200 yards, bath, New York A. C. team (C. D. Trubenbach, L. S. Crane, T. E. Kitching, C. M. Daniels), 1m. 48⅕s.; 200 yards, open water, New York A. C. team (C. M. Daniels, L. de B. Handley, Bud Goodwin, J. A. Ruddy), 1m. 54⅕s.

WATER POLO CHAMPIONSHIPS.

For the seventh year the water polo team of the New York A. C., coached by the great national expert, L. de B. Handley, showed its superiority over all comers, going through the season of 1908 without a defeat. The men who took part in the most important matches were Captain L. de B. Handley, Ogden M. Reid, Bud Goodwin, J. A. Ruddy, C. D. Trubenbach, James Steen, John Naething and Joseph Spencer.

Motorcycle.

In order to encourage practical construction and to eliminate "freaks" and machines of abnormal power and design, the governing body, the Federation of American Motorcyclists, does not recognize performances made on motorcycles having a greater piston displacement than 1,000 centimetres (61 cubic inches).

TRACK RECORDS.

Distance.	Style of Start.	Character of Record.	Holder.	Where Made.	Date.	Time.
½ mile	*F. S.	Competition	J. B. De Rosier	Cambridge, Mass.	Aug. 19, 1905	.38 4-5
1 mile	F. S.	Against time.	Fred Huyck	Detroit, Mich	Oct. 22, 1908	.54 2-5
1 mile	**S. S.	Against time.	Fred Huyck	Detroit, Mich	Oct. 22, 1908	1.03 3-5
1 mile	S. S.	Competition	P. K. C. Derkum	Los Angeles, Cal.	Feb. 22, 1908	1.04 1-5
2 miles	F. S.	Against time.	Walter Goerke	Detroit, Mich	Feb. 22, 1908	1.54
2 miles	S. S.	Against time.	Fred Huyck	Detroit, Mich	Feb. 22, 1908	2.06 4-5
2 miles	S. S.	Competition	P. K. C. Derkum	Los Angeles, Cal.	Feb. 22, 1903	2.04 2-5
3 miles	F. S.	Against time.	Walter Goerke	Detroit, Mich	Feb. 22, 1908	2.41 1-5
3 miles	S. S.	Against time.	Fred Huyck	Detroit, Mich	Oct. 22, 1908	3.03 3-5
3 miles	S. S.	Competition	P. K. C. Derkum	Los Angeles, Cal.	Feb. 22, 1908	3.03 2-5
4 miles	F. S.	Against time.	Walter Goerke	Detroit, Mich	Oct. 22, 1908	3.40 4-5
4 miles	S. S.	Against time.	Fred Huyck	Detroit, Mich	Oct. 22, 1908	4.00
4 miles	S. S.	Competition	P. K. C. Derkum	Los Angeles, Cal.	Feb. 22, 1908	4.01 2-5
5 miles	F. S.	Against time.	Walter Goerke	Detroit, Mich	Oct. 22, 1908	4.37 3-5
5 miles	S. S.	Against time.	Fred Huyck	Detroit, Mich	Oct. 22, 1908	4.56 2-5
5 miles	S. S.	Competition	P. K. C. Derkum	Los Angeles, Cal.	Feb. 22, 1908	4.58 1-5
6 miles	F. S.	Against time.	Walter Goerke	Detroit, Mich	Oct. 23, 1908	5.37
6 miles	S. S.	Against time.	Fred Huyck	Detroit, Mich	Oct. 22, 1908	5.53 3-5
7 miles	F. S.	Against time.	Walter Goerke	Detroit, Mich	Oct. 23, 1908	6.35
7 miles	S. S.	Against time.	Fred Huyck	Detroit, Mich	Oct. 22, 1908	6.52
8 miles	F. S.	Against time.	Walter Goerke	Detroit, Mich	Oct. 23, 1908	7.33 3-5
8 miles	S. S.	Against time.	Fred Huyck	Detroit, Mich	Oct. 22, 1908	7.47 4-5
9 miles	F. S.	Against time.	Fred Huyck	Detroit, Mich	Oct. 23, 1908	8.31 2-5
9 miles	S. S.	Against time.	Fred Huyck	Detroit, Mich	Oct. 22, 1908	8.45
10 miles	F. S.	Against time.	Fred Huyck	Detroit, Mich	Oct. 23, 1908	9.28 2-5
10 miles	S. S.	Against time.	Fred Huyck	Detroit, Mich	Oct. 22, 1908	9.42 2-5
10 miles	S. S.	Competition	F. C. Hoyt	Chicago, Ill	May 30, 1906	10.38
15 miles	F. S.	Against time.	Fred Huyck	Detroit, Mich	Oct. 23, 1908	14.19 3-5
15 miles	S. S.	Against time.	Fred Huyck	Detroit, Mich	Oct. 23, 1908	14.28 1-5
20 miles	S. S.	Against time.	Fred Huyck	Detroit, Mich	Oct. 22, 1908	18.15 3-5
20 miles	S. S.	Competition	F. C. Hoyt	Chicago, Ill	May 30, 1906	21.11 3-5
25 miles	S. S.	Against time.	Fred Huyck	Detroit, Mich	Oct. 22, 1908	24.00 3-5
25 miles	S. S.	Competition	M. J. Graves	Los Angeles, Cal.	June 28, 1908	26.38 3-5
30 miles	S. S.	Against time.	Fred Huyck	Detroit, Mich	Oct. 22, 1908	29.10 1-5
30 miles	S. S.	Competition	Walter Goerke	Philadelphia, Pa.	Oct. 5, 1907	35.07 3-5
35 miles	S. S.	Against time.	Fred Huyck	Detroit, Mich	Oct. 22, 1908	34.04 1-5
35 miles	S. S.	Competition	S. T. Kellogg	Philadelphia, Pa.	Oct. 5, 1907	41.49 3-5
40 miles	S. S.	Against time.	Fred Huyck	Detroit, Mich	Oct. 22, 1908	39.01 1-5
40 miles	S. S.	Competition	S. T. Kellogg	Philadelphia, Pa.	Oct. 5, 1907	48.06 2-5
45 miles	S. S.	Against time.	Fred Huyck	Detroit, Mich	Oct. 22, 1908	44.13 2-5
45 miles	S. S.	Competition	Walter Goerke	Philadelphia, Pa.	Oct. 5, 1907	54.55 1-5
48 m. 1570 yd	S. S.	Competition	Walter Goerke	Philadelphia, Pa.	Oct. 5, 1907	60.00
50 miles	S. S.	Against time.	Fred Huyck	Detroit, Mich	Oct. 22, 1908	49.02 3-5
55 miles	S. S.	Against time.	Fred Huyck	Detroit, Mich	Oct. 22, 1908	53.56 1-5
60 miles	S. S.	Against time.	Fred Huyck	Detroit, Mich	Oct. 22, 1908	48.49
61 1-5 miles	S. S.	Against time.	Fred Huyck	Detroit, Mich	Oct. 22, 1908	60.00
100 miles	S. S.	Competition	S. T. Kellogg	Philadelphia, Pa.	Oct. 10, 1908	2.05 4-5

*Flying start. **Standing start.

PROFESSIONAL AMERICAN RECORDS.

Distance.	Style of Start.	Character of Record.	Holder.	Where Made.	Date.	Time.
⅓ mile	F. S.	Against time.	J. B. De Rosier	Clifton, N. J.	Aug. 23, 1908	.13 1-5
½ mile	F. S.	Against time.	J. B. De Rosier	Clifton, N. J.	Aug. 23, 1908	.27 3-5
1 mile	F. S.	Against time.	J. B. De Bosier	Clifton, N. J.	July 5, 1908	.56
1 mile	S. S.	Against time.	J. B. De Rosier	Clifton, N. J.	July 26, 1908	1.02
2 miles	F. S.	Competition	J. B. De Rosier	Clifton, N. J.	July 26, 1908	2 05
3 miles	F. S.	Competition	J. B. De Rosier	Clifton, N. J.	Aug. 23, 1908	3.01 3-5
4 miles	F. S.	Competition	J. B. De Rosier	Clifton, N. J.	July 26, 1908	4.15
5 miles	F. S.	Competition	J. B. De Rosier	Clifton, N. J.	July 26, 1908	5.25
6 miles	F. S.	Competition	J. B. De Rosier	Clifton, N. J.	July 5, 1908	7 23
7 miles	F. S.	Competition	J. B. De Rosier	Clifton, N. J.	July 5, 1908	8.32
8 miles	F. S.	Competition	J. B. De Rosier	Clifton, N. J.	July 5, 1908	9.45
9 miles	F. S.	Competition	J. B. De Rosier	Clifton, N. J.	July 5, 1908	10.55 1-5
10 miles	F. S.	Competition	J. B. De Rosier	Clifton, N. J.	July 5, 1908	11.59

WORLD'S STRAIGHTAWAY RECORD.

Distance.	Style of Start.	Character of Record.	Holder.	Where Made.	Date.	Time.
1 mile	F. S.	Against time.	Glen H. Curtiss.	Ormond Beach, Fla.	Jan. 23, 1907	.46 2-5

MACHINES OVER 61 CU. IN. PISTON DISPLACEMENT, STRAIGHTAWAY.

Distance.	Style of Start.	Character of Record.	Holder.	Where Made.	Date.	Time.
1 mile	F. S.	Against time.	W. H. Wray	Ormond Beach, Fla.	Jan. 24, 1907	.44 2-5
1 mile	S. S.	Against time.	W. H. Wray	Ormond Beach, Fla.	Mch. 6, 1908	.50 2-5

NATIONAL CHAMPIONSHIPS.

The F. A. M. National Championship events were held at Morris Park, New York City, Nov. 3, 1908. The winners were: One mile—Fred Huyck, Chicago, 1m. 10 3-5s.; W. Goerke, Brooklyn; S. T. Kellogg, Springfield, Mass. Five miles—W. Goerke, 5m. 22 2-5s.; Fred Huyck; A. G. Chapple, New York. Ten miles—W. Goerke, 10m. 45 2-5s; S. T. Kellogg; A. G. Chapple. W. G. Collins, San Francisco, won the two-mile championship.

Chess.

Chess in this country and elsewhere flourished during 1908 and was not affected appreciably by the hard times. The year was noteworthy on account of the return to America of the Anglo-American Cable Match Trophy, donated by Sir George Newnes, and the Isaac L. Rice Intercollegiate Trophy, both of which were wrested from the British. The greatest event of the year was the world's championship match between Dr. E. Lasker and Dr. S. Tarrasch at Duesseldorf and Munich. Dr. Lasker won and retained his title. There were the usual international tournaments abroad, one of which, at Duesseldorf, was won by F. J. Marshall, of Brooklyn. Two famous masters of the game passed away—M. I. Tschigorin, of Russia, and H. E. Bird, of England. J. Mieses was the only foreign player to visit the United States. He made the circuit under the management of the American Chess Bulletin.

Sixteenth Intercollegiate Tourney—New York, December 21-24, 1907. Won by Columbia, with a team total of 9½ to 2½; Yale, 6½ to 5½; Princeton, 4½ to 7½; Harvard, 3½ to 8½. The winning team was L. J. Wolff, of Brooklyn, captain; H. Blumberg, of Brooklyn; H. C. Ramsdell and G. F. Comstock. Harvard has won the annual tournament 9 times, Columbia 6 and Yale once.

Ninth Triangular College Chess League Tournament—New York, December 26-28, 1907. Won by Cornell, with a team total of 5½ to 2½; Pennsylvania, 4 to 4; Brown, 2½ to 5½. Roy T. Black and Ernest H. Riedel, two Brooklyn students, played for Cornell. The tournament has been won 5 times by Cornell, 3 times by Pennsylvania and in 1906 there was a tie between Pennsylvania and Brown.

Marshall-Janowski Match—Played at Paris in January; score: Janowski, 5; Marshall, 2; drawn, 3.

New York State Meeting—February 22; championship tournament won by J. Finn; second and third, H. Helms and J. Rosenthal. General tournament won by J. Bernstein. New Jersey championship won by E. N. Olly.

Vienna Masters' Tournament—March 23-April 17. Winners: O. Duras, G. Maroczy and C. Schlechter (triple tie for first); 4, A. Rubinstein; 5, R. Teichmann; 6, R. Spielmann; 7. Dr. Perlis; 8, Tartakower; 9, 10 and 11 (triple tie), P. S. Leonhardt, F. J. Marshall and J. Mieses.

Anglo-American Cable Match—March 13 and 14.

Bds. America.		Great Britain.	
1. A. B. Hodges....	½	J. H. Blackburne....	½
2. H. G. Voight.....	½	H. E. Atkins........	½
3. H. Helms........	½	T. F. Lawrence......	½
4. E. Delmar........	½	G. W. Richmond....	½
5. S. L. Stadelman.	½	G. E. Wainwright...	½
6. C. S. Howell.....	½	W. Ward............	½
7. G. J. Schwietzer.	1	P. R. England.......	0
8. G. H. Wolbrecht.	1	R. P. Michell........	0
9. E. W. Libaire....	1	Rev. W. C. Palmer..	0
10. A. K. Robinson..	½	E. G. Sergeant......	½
Total	6½	Total	3½

The record: America, 6; Great Britain, 3; drawn, 1.

Intercollegiate Cable Match—March 21.

Bds. American.		British.	
1. W. H. Hughes...	0	N. J. Roughton.. ...	1
2. L. J. Wolff........	1	L. Illingworth.......	0
3. K. S. Johnson....	½	B. H. R. Stower.....	½
4. H. Blumberg.....	½	H. Lob...............	½
5. I. Ash............	½	C. G. Woodhouse....	½
6. C. Williams......	1	R. Petrie............	0
Total...............	3½	Total	2½

The record: American, 2; British, 3; drawn 3.

Women's United States Championship—Played in New York in February. Score: Mrs. S. R. Burgess, St. Louis, 4; Mrs. C. E. Nixdorff, Boston, 1.

Brooklyn C. C. Championship—Winner: Magnus Smith.

Manhattan C. C. Championship—Winner: Albert Pulvermacher.

Prague Masters' Tournament—May 18-June 12. Winners: O. Duras and C. Schlechter (tie for first); 3, M. Vidmar; 4, A. Rubinstein; 5, R. Teichmann; 6, G. Maroczy; 7, 8 and 9 (triple tie), P. S. Leonhardt, F. J. Marshall and H. Salwe; 10, D. Janowski.

Manhattan vs. Philadelphia—May 30. Score: Manhattan C. C., 10; Franklin C. C., 6.

Greater New York Chess League—Championship won by Dyker Heights Country Club, after a tie with the Lyceum Chess Club.

Crescent City Athletic Club—Championship won by Herbert M. Barrett. Team matches: May 28, N. Y. A. C., 5; Crescent A. C., 1. June 4, N. Y. A. C., 4½; Crescent A. C., 1½.

New York State C. A. Summer Meet—Trenton Falls, N. Y., July 20-25. Rice trophy won for Brooklyn Chess Club by C. S. Howell. General tournament won by E. R. Perry, of Manhattan.

Interscholastic Chess League—Won by Curtis High School, the team capturing the I. L. Rice trophy.

Duesseldorf Tournament—August 3-17. Winner: Frank J. Marshall, of Brooklyn; 2, H. Salwe; 3, R. Spielmann; 4, W. John; 5, J. Mieses; 6, H. Suechting; 7, Dr. Brody.

University of Pennsylvania vs. Oxford—Played in Oxford, July 27-30. Score: University of Pennsylvania, 11½; Oxford, 6½.

Curt-Smith Match—At the Brooklyn Chess Club, July 6 to August 9. Score: C. Curt, 4; M. Smith, 4; drawn, 7.

Western Championship—At Excelsior, Minn., August 17-25. Won by E. P. Elliott, St. Paul; 2 and 3 (tie), H. F. Lee and E. Michelsen, Chicago.

World's Championship—Duesseldorf and Munich, August 17-September 30. Score: Dr. E. Lasker, 8; Dr. S. Tarrasch, 3; drawn, 5.

Lodz Tournament—At Lodz, Russia, Sept. 20-Oct. 15. Won by A. Rubinstein, Lodz; 2, F. J. Marshall, Brooklyn; 3, H. Salwe, St. Petersburg.

(Compiled by Hermann Helms.)

American Whist.

THE LAWS OF WHIST ADOPTED BY THE AMERICAN WHIST CONGRESS AS REVISED AT THE THIRD CONGRESS, CHICAGO, JUNE 20-24, 1893, AND NOW IN FORCE.

THE GAME.

1. A game consists of seven points, each trick above six counting one. The value of the game is determined by deducting the losers' score from seven.

FORMING THE TABLE.

2. Those first in the room have the preference. If, by reason of two or more arriving at the same time, more than four assemble, the preference among the last comers is determined by cutting, a lower cut giving the preference over all cutting higher. A complete table consists of six; the four having the preference play. Partners are determined by cutting; the highest two play against the lowest two; the lowest deals and has the choice of seats and cards.

3. If two players cut intermediate cards of equal value, they cut again; the lower of the new cut plays with the original lowest.

4. If three players cut cards of equal value, they cut again. If the fourth has cut the highest card, the lowest two of the new cut are partners and the lowest deals. If the fourth has cut the lowest card, he deals and the highest two of the new cut are partners.

5. At the end of a game, if there are more than four belonging to the table; a sufficient number of the players retire to admit those awaiting their turn to play. In determining which players remain in, those who have played a less number of consecutive games have the preference over all who have played a greater number; between two or more who have played an equal number, the preference is determined by cutting, a lower cut giving the preference over all cutting higher.

6. To entitle one to enter a table, he must declare his intention to do so before any one of the players has cut for the purpose of commencing a new game or of cutting out.

CUTTING.

7. In cutting, the ace is the lowest card. All must cut from the same pack. If a player exposes more than one card, he must cut again. Drawing cards from the outspread pack may be resorted to in place of cutting.

SHUFFLING.

8. Before every deal the cards must be shuffled. When two packs are used the dealer's partner must collect and shuffle the cards for the ensuing deal and place them at his right hand. In all cases the dealer may shuffle last.

9. A pack must not be shuffled during the play of a hand, nor so as to expose the face of any card.

CUTTING TO THE DEALER.

10. The dealer must present the pack to his right-hand adversary to be cut; the adversary must take a portion from the top of the pack and place it toward the dealer; at least four cards must be left in each packet; the dealer must reunite the packets by placing the one not removed in cutting upon the other.

11. If, in cutting or in reuniting the separate packets, a card is exposed the pack must be reshuffled by the dealer and cut again; if there is any confusion of the cards or doubt as to the place where the pack was separated there must be a new cut.

12. If the dealer reshuffles the pack after it has been properly cut he loses his deal.

DEALING.

13. When the pack has been properly cut and reunited the dealer must distribute the cards, one at a time, to each player in regular rotation, beginning at his left. The last, which is the trump card, must be turned up before the dealer. At the end of the hand, or when the deal is lost, the deal passes to the player next to the dealer on his left and so on to each in turn.

14. There must be a new deal by the same dealer:

I. If any card except the last is faced in the pack.

II. If, during the deal or during the play of the hand, the pack is proved incorrect or imperfect; but any prior score made with that pack shall stand.

15. If, during the deal, a card is exposed the side not in fault may demand a new deal provided neither of that side has touched a card. If a new deal does not take place the exposed card is not liable to be called.

16. Any one dealing out of turn or with his adversaries' pack may be stopped before the trump card is turned, after which the deal is valid and the packs, if changed, so remain.

MISDEALING.

17. It is a misdeal:

I. If the dealer omits to have the pack cut and his adversaries discover the error before the trump card is turned and before looking at any of their cards.

II. If he deals a card incorrectly and fails to correct the error before dealing another.

III. If he counts the cards on the table or in the remainder of the pack.

IV. If, having a perfect pack, he does not deal to each player the proper number of cards and the error is discovered before all have played to the first trick.

V. If he looks at the trump card before the deal is completed.

VI. If he places the trump card face downward upon his own or any other player's cards.

A misdeal loses the deal, unless, during the deal, either of the adversaries touches a card or in any other manner interrupts the dealer.

AMERICAN WHIST.—*Continued.*

THE TRUMP CARD.

18. The dealer must leave the trump card face upward on the table until it is his turn to play to the first trick; if it is left on the table until after the second trick has been turned and quitted it is liable to be called. After it has been lawfully taken up, it must not be named, and any player naming it is liable to have his highest or his lowest trump called by either adversary. A player may, however, ask what the trump suit is.

IRREGULARITIES IN THE HANDS.

19. If, at any time after all have played to the first trick, the pack being perfect, a player is found to have either more or less than his correct number of cards and his adversaries have their right number, the latter, upon the discovery of such surplus or deficiency, may consult and shall have the choice:

I. To have a new deal; or

II. To have the hand played out, in which case the surplus or missing card or cards are not taken into account.

If either of the adversaries also has more or less than his correct number, there must be a new deal.

If any player has a surplus card by reason of an omission to play to a trick, his adversaries can exercise the foregoing privilege only after he has played to the trick following the one in which such omission occurred.

CARDS LIABLE TO BE CALLED.

20. The following cards are liable to be called by either adversary:

I. Every card faced upon the table otherwise than in the regular course of play, but not including a card led out of turn.

II. Every card thrown with the one led or played to the current trick. The player must indicate the one led or played.

III. Every card so held by a player that his partner sees any portion of its face.

IV. All the cards in a hand lowered or shown by a player so that his partner sees more than one card of it.

V. Every card named by the player holding it.

21. All cards liable to be called must be placed and left face upward on the table. A player must lead or play them when they are called, provided he can do so without revoking. The call may be repeated at each trick until the card is played. A player cannot be prevented from leading or playing a card liable to be called; if he can get rid of it in the course of play no penalty remains.

22. If a player leads a card better than any of his adversaries hold of the suit, and then leads one or more other cards without waiting for his partner to play, the latter may be called upon by either adversary to take the first trick, and the other cards thus improperly played are liable to be called; it makes no difference whether he plays them one after the other, or throws them all on the table together, after the first card is played, the others are liable to be called.

23. A player having a card liable to be called must not play another until the adversaries have stated whether or not they wish to call the card liable to the penalty. If he plays another card without awaiting the decision of the adversaries, such other card also is liable to be called.

LEADING OUT OF TURN.

24. If any player leads out of turn, a suit may be called from him or his partner the first time it is the turn of either of them to lead. The penalty can be enforced only by the adversary on the right of the player from whom a suit can lawfully be called.

If a player so called on to lead a suit has none of it, or if all have played to the false lead, no penalty can be enforced. If all have not played to the trick, the cards erroneously played to such false lead are not liable to be called, and must be taken back.

PLAYING OUT OF TURN.

25. If the third hand plays before the second, the fourth hand also may play before the second.

26. If the third hand has not played, and the fourth hand plays before the second, the latter may be called upon by the third hand to play his highest or lowest card of the suit led, or, if he has none, to trump or not to trump the trick.

ABANDONED HANDS.

27. If all four players throw their cards on the table, face upward, no further play of that hand is permitted. The result of the hand, as then claimed or admitted, is established, provided that, if a revoke is discovered, the revoke penalty attaches.

REVOKING.

28. A revoke is a renounce in error not corrected in time. A player renounces in error when, holding one or more cards of the suit led, he plays a card of a different suit.

A renounce in error may be corrected by the player making it, before the trick in which it occurs has been turned and quitted, unless either he or his partner, whether in his right turn or otherwise, has led or played to the following trick, or unless his partner has asked whether or not he has any of the suit renounced.

29. If a player corrects his mistake in time to save a revoke, the card improperly played by him is liable to be called; any player or players, who have played after him, may withdraw their cards and substitute others; the cards so withdrawn are not liable to be called.

30. The penalty for revoking is the transfer of two tricks from the revoking side to their adversaries; it can be enforced for as many revokes as occur during the hand. The

revoking side cannot win the game in that hand; if both sides revoke, neither can win the game in that hand.

31. The revoking player and his partner may require the hand in which the revoke has been made to be played out, and score all points made by them up to the score of six.

32. At the end of the hand the claimants of a revoke may search all the tricks. If the cards have been mixed, the claim may be urged and proved, if possible; but no proof is necessary, and the revoke is established, if, after it has been claimed, the accused player or his partner mixes the cards before they have been examined to the satisfaction of the adversaries.

33. The revoke can be claimed at any time before the cards have been presented and cut for the following deal, but not thereafter.

MISCELLANEOUS.

34. Any one, during the play of a trick and before the cards have been touched for the purpose of gathering them together, may demand that the players draw their cards.

35. If any one, prior to his partner playing, calls attention in any manner to the trick or to the score, the adversary last to play to the trick may require the offender's partner to play his highest or lowest of the suit led, or, if he has none, to trump or not to trump the trick.

36. If any player says: "I can win the rest," "The rest are ours," "We have the game," or words to that effect, his partner's cards must be laid upon the table and are liable to be called.

37. When a trick has been turned and quitted, it must not again be seen until after the hand has been played. A violation of this law subjects the offender's side to the same penalty as in the case of a lead out of turn.

38. If a player is lawfully called upon to play the highest or lowest of a suit, or to trump or not to trump a trick, or to lead a suit, and unnecessarily fails to comply, he is liable to the same penalty as if he had revoked.

39. In all cases where a penalty has been incurred, the offender must await the decision of the adversaries. If either of them, with or without his partner's consent, demands a penalty, to which they are entitled, such decision is final. If the wrong adversary demands a penalty or a wrong penalty is demanded, none can be enforced.

THE ETIQUETTE OF WHIST,

AS ADOPTED BY THE THIRD AMERICAN WHIST CONGRESS, CHICAGO, JUNE 20-24, 1893.

The following rules belong to the established code of Whist Etiquette. They are formulated with a view to discourage and repress certain improprieties of conduct, therein pointed out, which are not reached by the laws. The courtesy which marks the intercourse of gentlemen will regulate other more obvious cases:

I. No conversation should be indulged in during the play except such as is allowed by the laws of the game.

II. No player should in any manner whatsoever give any intimation as to the state of his hand or of the game, or of approval or disapproval of a play.

III. No player should lead until the preceding trick is turned and quitted.

IV. No player should, after having led a winning card, draw a card from his hand for another lead until his partner has played to the current trick.

V. No player should play a card in any manner so as to call particular attention to it, nor should he demand that the cards be placed in order to attract the attention of his partner.

VI. No player should purposely incur a penalty because he is willing to pay it, nor should he make a second revoke in order to conceal one previously made.

VII. No player should take advantage of information imparted by his partner through a breach of etiquette.

VIII. No player should object to referring a disputed question of fact to a bystander who professes himself uninterested in the result of the game and able to decide the question.

IX. Bystanders should not in any manner call attention to or give any intimation concerning the play or the state of the game, during the play of a hand. They should not look over the hand of a player without his permission; nor should they walk around the table to look at the different hands.

THE LAWS OF DUPLICATE WHIST,

AS ADOPTED BY THE AMERICAN WHIST LEAGUE JULY 14, 1900, AND AMENDED IN 1902, 1903, 1904, 1905 AND 1906.

DEFINITIONS.

The words and phrases used in these laws shall be construed in accordance with the following definitions, unless such construction is inconsistent with the context:

(a) The thirteen cards received by any one player are termed a "hand."

(b) The four hands into which the pack is distributed for play are termed a "deal"; the same term is also used to designate the act of distributing the cards to the players.

(c) A "tray" is a device for retaining the hands of a deal and indicating the order of playing them.

(d) The player who is entitled to the trump card is termed the "dealer," whether the cards have or have not been dealt by him.

(e) The first play of a deal is termed "the original play"; the second or any subsequent play of such deal, the "overplay."

(f) "Duplicate whist" is that form of the game of whist in which each deal is played once only by each player, and in which each deal is so overplayed as to bring the play of teams, pairs or individuals into comparison.

(g) A player "renounces" when he does not follow suit to the card led; he "renounces in error" when, although holding one or more cards of the suit led, he plays a card of a different suit; if such renounce in error is not lawfully corrected, it constitutes a "revoke."

(h) A card is "played" whenever, in the course of play, it is placed or dropped face upward on the table.

(i) A trick is "turned and quitted" when all four players have turned and quitted their respective cards.

LAW I.

SHUFFLING.

Section 1. Before the cards are dealt they must be shuffled in the presence of an adversary or the umpire.

Sec. 2. The pack must not be so shuffled as to expose the face of any card; if a card is so exposed the pack must be reshuffled.

LAW II.

CUTTING FOR THE TRUMP.

Section 1. The dealer must present the cards to his right hand adversary to be cut; such adversary must take from the top of the pack at least four cards and place them toward the dealer, leaving at least four cards in the remaining packet; the dealer must reunite the packets by placing the one not removed in cutting upon the other. If, in cutting or in reuniting the separate packets, a card is exposed the pack must be reshuffled and cut again; if there is any confusion of the cards or doubt as to the place where the pack was separated, there must be a new cut.

LAW III.

DEALING.

Section 1. When the pack has been properly cut and reunited, the cards must be dealt one at a time, face down, from the top of the pack, the first to the player at the left of the dealer and each successive card to the player at the left of the one to whom the last preceding card has been dealt. The last, which is the trump card, must be turned and placed face up on the tray, if one is used, otherwise, at the right of the dealer.

Sec. 2. There must be a new deal:

(a) If any card except the last is faced or exposed in any way in dealing.

(b) If the pack is proved incorrect or imperfect.

(c) If either more or less than thirteen cards are dealt to any player.

(d) If, after the first trick has been turned and quitted on the original play of a deal, one or more cards are found to have been left in the tray.

LAW IV.

THE TRUMP CARD.

Section 1. The trump card and the number of the deal must be recorded, before the play begins, on a slip provided for that purpose, and must not be elsewhere recorded. Such slip must be shown to an adversary then turned face down and placed in the tray, if one is used.

Sec. 2. The dealer must have the trump card face up until it is his turn to play to the first trick; he must take the trump card into his hand and turn down the trump slip before the second trick is turned and quitted.

Sec. 3 When a deal is taken up for overplay, the dealer must show the trump slip to an adversary, and thereafter the trump slip and trump card shall be treated as in the case of an original deal.

Sec. 4. After the trump card has been lawfully taken into the hand and the trump slip turned face down, the trump card must not be named nor the trump slip examined during the play of the deal; a player may, however, ask what trump suit is.

Sec. 5. If a player unlawfully looks at the trump slip his highest or lowest trump may be called; if a player unlawfully names the trump card or unlawfully shows the trump slip to his partner, his partner's highest or lowest trump may be called.

Sec. 6. These penalties can be inflicted by either adversary at any time during the play of the deal in which they are incurred before the player from whom the call can be made has played to the current trick; the call may be repeated at each or any trick until the card is played, but cannot be changed.

Sec. 7. When a deal has been played, the cards of the respective players, including the trump card, must be placed in the tray, face down, and the trump slip placed face up on top of the dealer's cards.

Sec. 8. If, on the overplay of a deal, the dealer turns a trump card other than the one recorded on the trump slip, and such error is discovered and corrected before the play of the deal is commenced, the card turned in error is liable to be called.

Sec. 9. If such error is not corrected until after the overplay has begun, and more than two tables are engaged in play, the players at that table shall take the average score for the deal; if less than three tables are in play there must be a new deal.

Sec. 10. Should a player record on the trump slip a different trump from the one turned in dealing, and the error is discovered at the next table, there must be a new deal. If the deal has been played at one or more tables with the wrong trump, the recorded trump must be taken as correct, and the players at the original tables take the average score for the deal; if less than three tables are in play there must be a new deal.

Sec. 11. By the unanimous consent of the players in any match a trump suit may be declared and no trump turned.

LAW V.

IRREGULARITIES IN THE HAND.

Section 1. If, on the overplay, a player is found to have more than his correct number of cards, or the trump card is not in the deck hand, or any card except the trump card is so faced as to expose any of the printing on its face, and less than three tables are engaged, there must be a new deal. If more than two tables are in play the hands must be rectified and then passed to the next table; the table at which the error was discovered must not overplay the deal, but shall take the average score.

Sec. 2. If, after the first trick has been turned and quitted on the overplay of a deal, a player is found to have less than his correct number of cards, and the others have their correct number, such player shall be answerable for the missing card or cards and for any revoke or revokes which he has made by reason of its or their absence.

LAW VI.

PLAYING, TURNING AND QUITTING THE CARDS.

Section 1. Each player, when it is his turn to play, must place his card face up before him and toward the centre of the table, and allow it to remain upon the table in this position until all have played to the trick, when he must turn it over and place it face down and nearer to himself, placing each successive card, as he turns it, so that it overlaps the last card played by him and with the ends toward the winners of the trick. After he has played his card, and, also after he has turned it, he must quit it by removing his hand.

Sec. 2. The cards must be left in the order in which they were played and quitted until the scores for the deal are recorded.

Sec. 3. During the play of a deal, a player must not pick up or turn another player's card.

Sec. 4. Before a trick is turned and quitted any player may require any of the other players to show the face of the card played to that trick.

Sec. 5. If a player names a card of a trick which has been turned or quitted, or turns or raises any such card so that any portion of its face can be seen by himself or his partner, he is liable to the same penalty as if he had led out of turn.

LAW VII.

CARDS LIABLE TO BE CALLED.

Section 1. The following cards are liable to be called:

(a) Every card so placed upon the table as to expose any of the printing on its face, except such cards as these laws specifically provide, shall not be so liable.

(b) Every card so held by a player as to expose any of the printing on its face to his partner or to both of his adversaries at the same time.

(c) Every card, except the trump card, named by the player holding it.

Sec. 2. If a player says, "I can win the rest," "The rest are ours," "It makes no difference how you play," or words to that effect, or if he plays or exposes his remaining cards before his partner has played to the current trick, his partner's cards must be laid face up on the table and are liable to be called.

Sec. 3. All cards liable to be called must be placed face up on the table and so left until played. A player must lead or play them when lawfully called, provided he can do so without revoking; the call may be repeated at each or any trick until the card is played. A player cannot, however, be prevented from leading or playing a card liable to be called; if he can get rid of it in the course of play no penalty remains.

Sec. 4. The holder of a card liable to be called can be required to play it only by the adversary on his right. If such adversary plays without calling it, the holder may play to that trick as he pleases. If the card becomes liable to be called after the adversary on his right has played to the current trick, it may be called to that trick. If it is the holder's turn to lead the card must be called before the preceding trick has been turned and quitted, or before the holder has led a different card; otherwise, he may lead as he pleases.

LAW VIII.

LEADING OUT OF TURN.

Section 1. If a player leads when it is the turn of an adversary to lead, and the error is discovered before all have played to such lead, a suit may be called from him as from his partner, as the case may be, the first time thereafter it is the right of either of them to lead. The penalty can be enforced only by the adversary on the right of the one from whom a lead can lawfully be called, and the right thereto is lost unless such adversary calls the suit he desires led before the first trick won by the offender or his partner, subsequent to the offence, is turned and quitted.

Sec. 2. If a player leads when it is his partner's turn, and the error is discovered before all have played to such lead, a suit may at once be called from the proper leader by his right hand adversary. Until the penalty has been exacted, waived or forfeited, the proper leader must not lead; should he so lead the card led by him is liable to be called.

Sec. 3. If a player when called on to lead a suit has none of it he may lead as he pleases.

Sec. 4. If all have not played to a lead out of turn when the error is discovered the card erroneously led and all cards played to such lead are not liable to be called, and must be taken into the hand.

LAW IX.

PLAYING OUT OF TURN.

Section 1. If the third hand plays before the second the fourth hand may also play before the second.

Sec. 2. If the third hand has not played, and the fourth hand plays before the second, the latter may be called upon by the third hand to play his highest or lowest card of the suit led, and if he has none of that suit, to trump or not to trump the trick; the penalty cannot be inflicted after the third hand has played to the trick. If the player liable to this penalty plays before it has been inflicted, waived or lost, the card so played is liable to be called.

LAW X.

Section 1. A renounce in error may be corrected by the player making it, except in the following cases, in which a revoke is established and the penalty therefore incurred:

(a) When the trick in which it occurs has been turned and quitted.

(b) When the renouncing player or his partner, whether in his right turn or otherwise, has led or played to the following trick.

Sec. 2. At any time before the trick is turned and quitted a player may ask an adversary if he has any of a suit to which such adversary has renounced in that trick, and can require the error to be corrected in case such adversary is found to have any of such suit.

Sec. 3. If a player who has renounced in error lawfully corrects his mistake, the card improperly played by him is liable to be called; any player who has played after him may withdraw his card and substitute another; a card so withdrawn is not liable to be called.

Sec. 4. The penalty for a revoke is the transfer of two tricks from the revoking side to their adversaries. If more than one revoke during the play of a deal is made by one side, the penalty for each additional revoke is the transfer of one trick only. It can be enforced for as many revokes as occur during the play of a deal, but is limited to the number of tricks won by the offending side; no pair, however, can score more than thirteen on the play of any one deal. The revoking players cannot score more, nor their adversaries less, than the average on the deal in which the revoke occurs.

In pair matches the score shall be recorded as made, independently of the revoke penalty, which shall be separately indicated as plus or minus revoke ("— R for the revoking side and + R" for their adversaries).

In such matches the penalty for a revoke shall not increase the score of the opponents of the revoking players above the maximum, as made at the other tables, on the deal in which the revoke occurs, nor shall the score of the revoking players be thereby reduced below the minimum, so made at the other tables, until the averages for the match and the relative scores of the other players have been determined; provided, however, that if the opponents win more tricks than such maximum, independently of the revoke penalty, the score shall stand as made. After the scores of the other players have been determined, the score of the revoking players shall, if necessary, be further reduced, so that in all cases they shall suffer the full penalty as provided in the first paragraph of this section.

Sec. 5. A revoke may be claimed at any time before the score of the deal has been agreed upon and recorded, but not thereafter.

Sec. 6. At the end of the play of a deal the claimants of a revoke can examine all the cards; if any hand has been shuffled the claim may be urged and proved if possible; but no proof is necessary, and the revoke is established, if, after it has been claimed, the accused player or his partner disturbs the order of the cards before they have been examined to the satisfaction of the adversaries.

LAW XI.

MISCELLANEOUS.

Section 1. If any one calls attention in any manner to the trick before his partner has played thereto, the adversary last to play to the trick may require the offender's partner to play his highest or lowest of the suit led, and if he has none of that suit to trump or not trump the trick.

Sec. 3. A player has the right to prevent his partner from committing any irregularity, and, for that purpose, may ask his partner whether or not he has a card of a suit to which he has renounced on a trick which has not been turned and quitted.

Sec. 4. If either of the adversaries, whether with or without his partner's consent, demands or waives a penalty to which they are entitled, such decision is final; if the wrong adversary demands a penalty, or a wrong penalty is demanded, none can be enforced.

Sec. 5. If a player is lawfully called upon to play the highest or lowest of a suit, to trump or not to trump a trick, to lead a suit, or to win a trick, and unnecessarily fails to comply, he is liable to the same penalty as if he had revoked.

Sec. 6. If any one leads or plays a card, and then, before his partner has played to the trick, leads one or more other cards, or plays two or more cards together, all of which are better than any his adversaries hold of the suit, his partner may be called upon by either adversary to win the first or any subsequent trick to which any of said cards are played, and the remaining cards so played are liable to be called.

Motorcycles.

THERE are probably in the neighborhood of 50,000 motorcycles in use in the United States. The tendencies in construction seem to be to increase power and to use two-cylinder motors and a magneto for the ignition current. The rules of the Federation of American Motorcyclists, the body controlling motor cycle contests, limit the size of motors to 61 cubic inches piston displacement, and the larger part of machines now being built have motors well up to this limit. Driving practice is about evenly divided between chains and belts. There is but one representative of the American industry equipped with gear drive, and this, too, is the only American machine with a four-cylinder motor. There are something like twenty-two active motor cycle manufacturers in this country.

FEDERATION OF AMERICAN MOTORCYCLISTS.

108 Park Row, New York City. Henry J. Wehman, Secretary.

Officers—President, E. L. Ovington, New York; Treasurer, G. B. Gibson, Westboro, Mass.; Vice-Presidents, for Eastern District, E. L. Buffington, Providence, R. I.; for Southern District, E. Y. White, San Antonio, Texas; for Western District, John R. Ball, Milwaukee, Wis.; for Pacific District, R. K. Holmes, Los Angeles, Cal.

Automobile Industry.

A conservative estimate of the total number of motor vehicles actually in use in the United States on November 1, 1908, is 150,000, with an original valuation of $245,400,000, or an average of $1,636 each. The total number produced in the United States in the ten years since the industry came into being (up to November 1, 1908), is not far from 211,000. The American cars in use ranged in price from $350 to $7,500, although more was paid in certain rare cases for cars fitted with special types of closed bodies. The foreign cars sold for from $4,500 to $12,000.

PRODUCTION IN THE UNITED STATES.

During the year 1908 approximately 65,000 cars were produced, which is a slight increase over the output for 1907. The cars produced in 1908 are valued at $122,000,000, and those produced in 1907 at $105,700,000. About 5,000 steam and electric vehicles were built in each year, the balance being those driven by gasoline motors. The value of the steam and electric vehicles produced in 1908 was probably $7,600,000. It is estimated that 60,000 hands (full capacity) are employed in building motor cars, and that the total capitalization of the 232 active and 50 not so active manufacturing companies is $95,000,000. It is also estimated that some 30,000 persons are employed in allied industries and that the total capital of the companies employing them is $37,000,000.

IMPORTS AND EXPORTS.

From October 1, 1907, to October 1, 1908, 1,543 cars were imported into the United States, having a valuation of $2,989,709. Of this number 156 were American cars re-imported, of the remainder 75 per cent. were of French manufacture, 17 per cent. Italian, and the remainder German and English. During the year ending with September 1, 1908, cars and parts to the value of $5,009,736 were exported. Of these the United Kingdom took $274,018, British North America $131,004, and France $68,197 worth. The remainder went to nearly all other parts of the world in smaller quantities. The fiscal year for the export records ends with July 1, and during that ending with July 1, 1908, 2,477 cars valued at $4,656,991 were exported. The figures for the preceding year are 2,862 cars valued at $4,890,886, showing a falling off in 1908 of 385 cars and $233,895.

IMPROVEMENTS AND PRICES.

The early production of new models for the season of 1909 is one of the features of the closing days of 1908. Practically all of the leading companies had their new models ready and on the road by the first of October. There is no radical change in general design, but the more general adoption of the magneto as a source of ignition current and the shaft drive by some of the more prominent concerns, who have hitherto been advocates of the double chain driving method, are noticeable. There is now, too, an unprecedented number of cars of the four-cylinder type of from 25 to 35 horse power selling for from $1,250 to $1,500. The motor buggy or high wheel type continues strong, especially in the middle West, where there are some twenty companies engaged exclusively in its manufacture.

COMMERCIAL VEHICLES.

There are about fifty companies engaged either exclusively or partially in the manufacture of motor vehicles for business purposes. A decided change is noticeable in the attitude of those who are using horses in their businesses toward the possible adoption of the motor. The failure of some of the earliest installations, owing largely to exorbitant claims made for them, somewhat retarded the development for a time, but the prejudice so born has been largely overcome, and with the much improved vehicle and the more rational demands as to what it should do, the machine is beginning steadily to replace the animal as it has in every field where they have come in conflict so far, and naturally always will. The much greater working capacity of the motor vehicle—owing to its speed and ability to work for indefinite periods of time—is its chief advantage. Economy of use usually results through this feature rather than through reduced cost of operation, although the relative value of the latter item increases rapidly in favor of the motor with the number of vehicles employed, it being capable of displacing a greater number of horse-drawn vehicles. It is generally conceded by those who should know that the best field for the electric commercial vehicle is in lines where the length of runs to be made is relatively short and the number of stops great. The gasoline vehicle is coming rapidly to the front in all other lines, and, in many cases, is doing well in this one, too. Very little has been done with steam, except that one company has built a number of ambulances, although it seems to have great possibilities.

TAXIMETER CABS.

No development has been more rapid since the manufacture of motor cars commenced than the use of motor cabs. During the past year about fifty companies were organized, with a total capitalization of $15,000,000, to operate them, and many of the independent cab men have forsaken the horse for the motor. It is estimated that 757 motor cabs were in operation in New York City on September 1, 1908, and that 515 were then on order. Services employing from 25 to 200 cabs have been started in nearly all the large cities.

GOOD ROADS AND LEGISLATION.

According to Federal statistics there are 2,151,570 miles of public roads in the United States. The total mileage of improved roads is 153,662, or 7.14 per cent.

The effort to put through the Federal bill for the regulation of motor vehicles has as yet not been successful. The American Automobile Association and other motoring bodies are working to bring about this much desired end in order that there may be greater uniformity in the matter of registration fees, licensing of operators, speed limits, etc. During the legislative season of 1908 the same conflict between the rural forces and the motorists, which has been seen each year since the first motor legislation was passed, was in evidence, and the general tendency in legislation of this sort seems to have been to impose heavier penalties for infractions of the law, and, in some cases, to have a more flexible maximum speed limit. Of those States which have automobile laws, the only ones which do not recognize, for a time at least, registrations in another State are Alabama, North Carolina, North Dakota, Oregon, Pennsylvania, Tennessee, Georgia, Maryland, Minnesota, New Jersey, Virginia. In Kansas, Kentucky, Montana, South Dakota, Texas and West Virginia there is no provision made for non-residents.

AUTOMOBILE SHOWS.

Much dissatisfaction was expressed last year by nearly every one concerned at the early date at which the shows were held throughout the country. Most manufacturers were not ready to exhibit and the public was not ready to buy. A return has been made to the old dates—shortly after the first of the year.

The first show of the year is that of the American Motor Car Manufacturers' Association, December 31 to January 7, in Grand Central Palace, New York, and the Importers' Automobile Salon exhibits at it. The Madison Square Garden show of the Association of Licensed Automobile Manufacturers will be held January 16 to 23. The Chicago show of the National Association of Automobile Manufacturers will be held February 6 to 13.

AMERICAN AUTOMOBILE ASSOCIATION.

437 Fifth Avenue, New York City, F. H. Elliott, Secretary.

Officers—President, William H. Hotchkiss, Automobile Club of Buffalo; First Vice-President, Lewis R. Speare, Bay State Automobile Association; Second Vice-President, Asa Paine, Florida East Coast Automobile Association; Third Vice-President, Ira M. Cobe, Chicago Automobile Club; Treasurer, George E. Farrington, Automobile Club of New Jersey; Secretary, Frederick H. Elliott; Executive Committee, Chairman, William H. Hotchkiss, Lewis R. Speare, George E. Farrington, Stanford L. Haynes, F. T. Sholes, Harry M. Rubey, L. E. Myers, Paul C. Wolff, Asa Paine, James T. Drought, F. H. Elliott, and the chairmen of the various boards as follows: Legislative, Charles T. Terry; Contest, Frank B. Hower; Good Roads, Robert P. Hooper; Racing, Jefferson DeMont Thompson; Publications, A. G. Batchelder; Touring Information and Maps, Powell Evans.

AUTOMOBILE EVENTS.

Two big road races were held in the United States in 1908, the Vanderbilt Cup contest, held over a course 23.46 miles long, on Long Island, of which the completed section of the new motor parkway formed a part, and the Grand Prize of the Automobile Club of America, held at Savannah. According to the terms of the agreement arrived at between the Automobile Club of America and the American Automobile Association, the national body, from which it had withdrawn and was in conflict for a time, the Vanderbilt cup is hereafter to be our "national" and the Grand Prize gold cup our "international" trophy. For the first time the Vanderbilt cup was won on October 24, 1908, by an American car, which averaged 64.3 miles per hour for the 258.06 miles. The entry list for the Grand Prize race, November 26, 1908, included the fastest cars in the world—six from Italy, five from France, five from Germany and seven from the United States—and the world's greatest racing drivers. The course at Savannah was 26.73 miles long and was covered fifteen times, making the total distance 400.95 miles. The 1908 international race conditions set a maximum cylinder bore of 155 m. m. for four-cylinder motors, or a total piston area not greater than that of a four-cylinder motor of the size given, and a minimum weight of 1,100 kilos or 2,424 pounds. The Vanderbilt 1908 conditions set only a minimum weight of 900 kilos, or 1,988.6 pounds, and a maximum weight of 1,200 kilos, or 2,644.8 pounds.

New track records were set during 1908 for the mile and five miles, the former, 51s., was made at Milwaukee by an Italian special racer, and the latter, 4m. 26s., at Providence by the same car. The 24-hour record for a single car was broken twice, both times at Brighton Beach, N. Y. The new record distance is 1,177 miles, and it was made by an American car. Throughout the country there were an unusually large number of road contests for both speed and endurance. The Glidden tour was held in July over a course running from Buffalo to Pittsburgh, Philadelphia, Albany, Boston, Portland, Me., and up through the White Mountains and down again to Saratoga. Fifty-six cars participated as contestants and non-contestants.

The trade is organized as follows:

NATIONAL ASSOCIATION OF AUTOMOBILE MANUFACTURERS, INC.

7 East Forty-second Street, New York City. S. A. Miles, General Manager.

Officers—President, Thomas Henderson; First Vice-President, S. D. Waldon, Second Vice-President, William E. Metzger; Third Vice-President, L. H. Kittridge; Secretary, C. C. Hildebrand; Treasurer, William R. Innis. Executive Committee—S. T. Davis, Jr., Locomobile Company of America, Bridgeport, Ct.; Windsor T. White, The White Company, Cleveland, O.; Charles Clifton, George N. Pierce Company, Buffalo, N. Y.; Thomas Henderson, Winton Motor Carriage Company, Cleveland, O.; William E. Metzger, Northern Motor Car Company, Detroit, Mich.; S. D. Weldon, Packard Motor Car Company, Detroit, Mich.; William R. Innis, Studebaker Bros. Manufacturing Company, South Bend, Ind.; C. C. Hildebrand, Stevens-Duryea Company, Chicopee Falls, Mass.; H. O. Smith, Premier Motor Manufacturing Company, Indianapolis, Ind.: Albert L. Pope, Pope Manufacturing Company, Hartford, Ct.; Benjamin Briscoe, Maxwell-Briscoe Motor Company, Tarrytown, N. Y.; L. H. Kittridge, Peerless Motor Car Company, Cleveland, O.; R. D. Chapin, Chalmers-Detroit Motor Company, Detroit, Mich.; William Mitchell Lewis, Mitchell Motor Car Company, Racine, Wis.; Angus Smith, Olds Motor Works, Lansing, Mich.

AMERICAN MOTOR CAR MANUFACTURERS' ASSOCIATION.

29 West Forty-second Street, New York City, Alfred Reeves, General Manager.

Committee of Management—Chairman, Benjamin Briscoe, Maxwell-Briscoe Motor Company; Vice-Chairman, R. E. Olds, Reo Motor Car Company; Treasurer, H. O. Smith,

AUTOMOBILE INDUSTRY.—*Continued.*

Premier Motor Manufacturing Company; Secretary, G. Vernor Rogers, Mitchell Motor Car Company; Auditor, W. H. Van Dervoort, Moline Automobile Company; Charles Lewis, Jackson Automobile Company; W. C. Marmon, Nordyke & Marmon Company; C. G. Stoddard, Dayton Motor Car Company; S. H. Mora, Mora Motor Car Company.

ASSOCIATION OF LICENSED AUTOMOBILE MANUFACTURERS.

7 East Forty-second Street, New York City. E. P. Chalfant, Assistant General Manager.

Officers—President, Charles Clinton, The George N. Pierce Company; Vice-President, Thomas Henderson, Winton Motor Carriage Company; Secretary, L. H. Kittridge, Peerless Motor Car Company; Treasurer, George Pope, Pope Manufacturing Company.

IMPORTERS' AUTOMOBILE SALON.

Bryant Park Building, New York City. Walter R. Lee, General Manager.

Officers—President, Andre Massenat; Vice-President, W. H. Barnard; Secretary, Paul LaCroix; Treasurer, Walter C. Allen.

ASSOCIATION PATENTS COMPANY.

7 East Forty-second Street, New York City.

Directors—President, Charles Clifton, The George N. Pierce Company; Vice-President, Thomas Henderson, Winton Motor Carriage Company; Secretary and Treasurer, E. P. Chalfant, A. L. A. M.; James H. Becker, Elmore Manufacturing Company; Elwood Haynes, The Haynes Automobile Company; George Pope, Pope Manufacturing Company; Marcus I. Brock, The Autocar Company.

MOTOR AND ACCESSORY MANUFACTURERS.

Officers—President, H. S. White, Shelby Steel Tube Company; First Vice-President, H. E. Raymond, The B. F. Goodrich Company; Second Vice-President, H. T. Dunn, Fisk Rubber Company; Third Vice-President, F. E. Castle, Gray & Davis; Treasurer, F. S. Gorton, Standard Welding Company; Secretary, P. S. Steenstrup, Hyatt Roller Bearing Company; Assistant Secretary, W. M. Sweep, Box 467, Newark, N. J.

NATIONAL ASSOCIATION OF ENGINE AND BOAT MANUFACTURERS.

314 Madison Avenue, New York City. Hugh S. Gambel, Secretary.

Officers—President, John J. Amory; First Vice-President, H. R. Sutphen; Second Vice-President, W. J. Reynolds; Third Vice-President, J. M. Pruscott; Treasurer, James Craig.

Automobiles.

THE year of 1908 in automobile sports marked the getting away to a considerable extent from track to road racing, which, with the Vanderbilt, Savannah, Briarcliff, Lowell and other similar events, clearly demonstrated that American manufacturers and American drivers are clearly able to hold their own with any other nation.

The completion of about ten miles of the Long Island Motor Parkway, over which a part of the Vanderbilt Cup race was run, has attracted wide public attention as a place where such events can be successfully conducted and the promises of its completion in 1909 has given a decided boom to auto road racing.

American Road Races of 1908.

SAVANNAH CHALLENGE TROPHY RACE, Savannah, Ga., March 19, 360 miles, for standard stock chassis, equipped with racing bodies and with engines limited to a maximum piston displacement of 575 cubic inches.

Place.	Machine.	H. P.	Driver.	Time.	Place.	Machine.	H. P.	Driver.	Time.
1.......	Isotta......	50	Strang......	6.21.30	3..	Acme......	50	Neustetter..	6.47.05
2.......	Apperson...	50	Lytle.......	6.44.37	4.......	Lozier......	45	Michener...	6.49.17

Winner's average, 50.70 miles per hour.

BRIARCLIFF TROPHY RACE, Westchester County, N. Y., April 24, 240 miles, for American or foreign stock chassis, with a total piston area not exceeding 103.87 square inches.

1.......	Isotta......	50	Strang......	5.14.13 1-5	4.......	Apperson...	50	Lytle.......	5.39.15 2-5
2.......	Fiat.... ...	60	Cedrino....	5.21.05 3-5	5.......	Bianchi.....	48	Sartori......	5.53.45 3 5
3.	Stearns.....	60	Vaughan....	5.28.29 2-5					

Winner's average, 46.15 miles per hour.

AMES TROPHY RACE, Lowell, Mass., Sept. 7, 254.4 miles, for standard stock chassis.

1.......	Isotta......	65	Strang......	4.42.34	3.......	Knox......	40	Bourque....	6.33.29
2.......	Berliet......	60	Grant......	6.14.58	4.......	Fiat........	60	Robertson..	6.38.32

Winner's average, 54 miles per hour.

FOUNDERS' WEEK CUP, Philadelphia, Pa., Oct. 10, 195 miles, for standard stock chassis.

1.......	Locomobile.	40	Robertson..	4.09.30	3.......	Lozier......	45	Michener...	4.17.26
2.......	Acme......	50	Patschke...	4.14.54	4.......	Peerless....	38	Maucher....	4.21.26

Winner's average, 48.25 miles per hour.

AUTOMOBILES—*Continued.*

VANDERBILT CUP RACE, Nassau County, Long Island, N. Y., Oct. 24, 258.06 miles, for racing cars.

1.......	Locomobile.	120	Robertson..	4.00.48 1-5	*3......	Locomobile.	120	Florida	4.28.10
2.......	Isotta......	60	Lytle.......	4.02.36 2-5	*4......	Mercedes...	120	Luttgen.....	4.30.35

Winner's average, 64.3 miles per hour.
*Unofficial time.

GRAND PRIZE OF AMERICA, Savannah, Ga., Nov. 26. Distance, 400 miles. Length of course, 26.73 miles, 18 turns. Cup given by the Automobile Club of America valued at $5,000 and $8,000 cash to drivers.

FOREIGN ROAD RACES.

GRAND PRIX, Dieppe, France, July 6, 478.1 miles, for racing cars limited to 155 mm. piston area.

1.......	Mercedes...	120	Lauten-schlager	6.55.43	3.......	Benz	110	Hanriot	7.05.13
2.......	Benz	110	Hemery....	7.04.24	4.......	Bayard-Clement	120	Rigal	7.30.36

Winner's average, 69.24 miles per hour.

FLORIO CUP, Bologna, Italy, Sept. 6, 328.2 miles, for racing cars limited to 155 mm. piston area.

1.......	Fiat........	123	Nazarro	4.25.21	4.......	Mors.......	120	Demogeot ..	4.57.11
2.......	De Dietrich.	123	Trucco	4.34.07	5.......	Fiat........	123	Lancia.....	4.08.51
3.......	Itala.......	115	Cagno......	4.56.12					

Winner's average, 74.3 miles per hour.

TOURISTS' TROPHY, otherwise known as the Four-Inch Race, Isle of Man, Sept. 24, 340 miles.

1.......	Hutton.....	....	Watson	6.43.05	3.......	Darracq....	....	George......	......
2.......	Darracq ...	....	Guinness...	......					

Winner's average, 50.25 miles per hour.

TRACK RECORDS.

HEAVYWEIGHT (1,432 TO 3,304 POUNDS) GASOLINE CARS.

Miles.	Time.	Driver.	H. P.	Machine.	Meet.	Date.
1..........	0.51	De Palma............	60	Fiat.............	St. Paul............	September 5, 1908
5..........	4.41	Chevrolet	90	Fiat.............	Empire City, N. Y....	June 26, 1905
10............	9.12 3-5	Oldfield............	60	Peerless..........	New York..........	October 29, 1904
25............	23.38 3-5	Oldfield............	60	Peerless..........	Fresno, Cal..........	December 13, 1904
50............	48.40 1-5	Oldfield..	60	Peerless..........	Fresno, Cal..	December 13, 1904
100..........	1.53.21 4-5	Clemens............	30	National..... ...	Indianapolis	November 4, 1905
500............	10.24.42	Vaughan	40	Decauville	Empire City, N. Y....	June 24, 1905
1000..........	21.58.00 4-5	Clemens-Merz........	30	National.........	Indianapolis	November 17, 1905
1094 3-16........	24 hours.	Clemens-Merz........	30	National.........	Indianapolis	November 17, 1905
1177.	24 hours.	Robertson-Lescault...	50	Simplex	Brighton Beach, N.Y..	October 2-3, 1908

MIDDLEWEIGHT (881 TO 1,432 POUNDS) GASOLINE CARS.

1................	0.56 2-5	Cedrino..............	24	Fiat........	Empire City, N. Y....	October 27, 1906
5................	5.00	Vaughan.............	40	Decauville........	Syracuse...........	September 18, 1905
10	* 9.47 1-5	Cedrino..............	24	Fiat..............	Empire City, N. Y....	May 30, 1907

LIGHTWEIGHT (551 TO 881 POUNDS) GASOLINE CARS.

1................	*0.55	Kulick...............	20	Ford..............	Empire City, N. Y....	November 8, 1904
5................	4.43 3-5	Kulick...............	20	Ford..............	Empire City, N. Y....	October 29, 1904

*Intermediate mile.

STEAM (ALL WEIGHTS).

1............ ...	0.54 4-5	Baldwin..............	40	Stanley	Readville, Mass......	September 14, 1907
5................	4.58	Webb Jay............	20	White	Empire City, N. Y....	June 26, 1905
10................	10.22 1-5	Webb Jay............	20	White............	Harlem Track, Chicago	May 27, 1905

STRAIGHTAWAY RECORDS.

FREE-FOR-ALL, GASOLINE.

1 kilo	0.19 2-5	Chevrolet............	200	Darracq..........	Ormond, Fla.........	January 25, 1906
1................	0.30 3-5	Chevrolet............	200	Darracq..........	Ormond, Fla.........	January 25, 1906
2................	0.58 2-5	Demogeot	...	Darracq..........	Ormond, Fla.........	January 29, 1906
5................	2.34	Hemery	200	Darracq..........	Ormond, Fla.........	January 24, 1906
10................	6.15	MacDonald	90	Napier.....	Ormond, Fla.........	January 24, 1906
100.	1.12.56 1-5	Bernin..............	60	Renault..........	Ormond, Fla.........	March 6, 1908
300................	3.53.44	Cedrino	60	Fiat.............	Ormond, Fla.........	March 5, 1908

FREE-FOR-ALL, STEAM.

1 kilo............	0.18 2-5	Marriott.............	..	Stanley..........	Ormond, Fla..........	January 25, 1906
1	0.28 1-5	Marriott.............	..	Stanley..........	Ormond, Fla..	January 25, 1906

Compiled by A. G. Batchelder, Editor of "The Automobile," New York.

Aeronautics in 1908.

MOTOR AEROPLANES.

THE year of 1908 marked an epoch in the history of aerial navigation, with the United States far ahead of all other nations in the matter of achievement. The motor-driven, heavier-than-air flying machine, although still crude, has been perfected to a point hardly dreamed of ten years ago, superseding in point of interest and scientific use the unwieldy balloon and out-distancing the tractable dirigible airship. Since the first aeroplane types of flying machines, designed by Maxim, Chanute and Lilienthal, the work of inventors has indicated steady progress, and this year, the greatest in the history of man's endeavor to conquer the air, stands out conspicuous because of the results obtained. There have been no new or radical ideas introduced, the wonderful flights witnessed having been the culmination of steady improvement following careful study and daring experiments.

During the year past scientists throughout the world, but more especially in France, have watched the practical demonstrations of the flying machine invented by Orville and Wilbur Wright with amazement. Simultaneously trials of the Wright aeroplanes were conducted at Le Mans, France, by Wilbur Wright, and at Fort Myer, near Washington, D. C., by his brother, Orville, early in September. The results exceeded the most sanguine expectations of aviators and scientists, with the exception of the Wright Brothers themselves, who three years ago asserted that they had solved the problem of aerial navigation with heavier-than-air machines.

The flights undertaken at Fort Myer by Orville Wright were brought to an abrupt end on September 17, when the aeroplane, which was being piloted by Wright, and who was accompanied by Lieut. Thomas E. Selfridge, of the United States Signal Corps, crashed to the ground from a height of 150 feet as a result of a propeller blade breaking. Lieutenant Selfridge was killed and Orville Wright seriously injured. At the time of the accident the aviator was conducting a series of experiments preliminary to undertaking the official tests prescribed by the United States Government. Under the Government specifications, the aeroplane must carry two persons having a combined weight of about 350 pounds, and sufficient fuel for a trip of 125 miles. The aeroplane must have a speed of at least 40 miles an hour in still air, but will be accepted at a speed of 36 miles an hour. Previous to the deplorable mishap Orville Wright, besides making many successful short trips in the aeroplane, had made two flights, each of about an hour's duration, during which time the machine was under perfect control.

At Le Mans, France, Wilbur Wright, with an aeroplane similar to the one operated by his brother at Fort Myer, carried on a long series of successful flights, breaking all world's records. On September 21, in the presence of the officials of the Aero Club of Sarthe, American Ambassador White, a large number of French and foreign officers and 10.000 spectators, the American aviator made a flight of 1 hour 31 minutes and 51 seconds, covering a distance of about 61 miles. Wright brought his machine to earth because of darkness, and said that he could easily have remained up another hour.

On October 6 Wilbur Wright remained in the air 1 hour 4 minutes and 26 seconds, and by so doing fulfilled the conditions of the contract signed by him and Lazare Weiller, who represented a French syndicate, in which he was to make two flights in one week, carrying a passenger or the equivalent in weight, over a distance of 50 kilometres each, or about 32 miles. The sum of $100,000 was paid to Wright for the patent rights for the aeroplane in France. Fifty aeroplanes were ordered at once. The best previous record of a flight with a passenger was made by Wilbur Wright a few days before, when he made a sustained flight of 55 minutes and 37 seconds.

The Wright aeroplane is 40 feet wide over all, its maximum height about 8 feet, and it weighs 800 pounds. Its propulsive force is furnished by a four-cylinder motor of about 30 horse power. The weight of the motor is 170 pounds without accessories. There are about 30 pounds of water for cooling the motor, which makes 1,400 revolutions a minute. The two propellers are geared for 500 revolutions a minute. Both propellers are placed behind the machine, the horizontal rudder is in front, and the vertical rudder behind. The surface of the aeroplane consists of 500 square feet of taut muslin.

Following the highly successful flights of the Wright machines here and abroad, the Navy Department of the United States Government adopted specifications for aeroplanes which, to be acceptable, must embody improvements not yet achieved by scientists. The conditions are as follows:

"Each machine is to carry two persons, one an observer, of an average weight of 175 pounds each, and a sufficient supply of fuel at the start for a flight of at least 200 miles, for a period of four hours, at an average speed of not less than 40 miles an hour, and to remain continuously in the air during the trial. The machines are to be so constructed as to be able to alight without damage, on land or water; to float on the latter, when at rest, without wetting any of the air-supporting or controlling areas, and to be able to rise therefrom without appreciable delay under their own power, without the aid of special starting apparatus."

Nothing daunted by the severity of these specifications, which were drawn up by Lieut. George C. Sweet, the Navy Department observer at the Fort Myer trials, the Wright Brothers, through the aid of capitalists, plan to erect an aeroplane factory in Detroit, Mich., where improved types of flying machines will be turned out, with the end in view of meeting the Navy requirements.

While far ahead of all competitors in solving the problem of the heavier-than-air machines, the Wright Brothers were not the only aviators to make signal achievements in 1908.

On January 13 Henry Farman won the Deutsche-Archdeacon prize of $10,000 by sailing a kilometre in a circle near Paris.

On May 27 Leon Delagrange made a flight of six miles before the King of Italy at Milan, and the following day made a record flight of ten miles.

On June 29 Louis Bleriot, in his monoplane, won the Aero Club's medal by flying 100 yards at Paris.

On July 4 Glenn H. Curtiss's aeroplane, the June Bug, made a mile flight and won the Scientific American Cup.

On July 7 Farman remained 20 minutes and 20 seconds in the air at Paris, winning Armongaud's $2,000 prize.

On September 2 two Cornell University students, John C. Buckhart and Oscar Trolicht, made a flight of three miles in five minutes in an aeroplane of their own making, near Ithaca, N. Y.

On September 6 Leon Delagrange, President of the Aviation Club of France, made a flight in his aeroplane at Issy, remaining in the air 29 minutes 54⅘ seconds, circled the field 15½ times, covering the distance of 15½ miles.

On October 28 A. M. Herring, with his American aeroplane, weighing only 200 pounds, made a short flight at Hempstead Plains, L. I. While attempting to make a turn, the machine pitched to the ground and was wrecked. Mr. Herring's aeroplane, which he will submit for a Government trial, is driven by an engine of 1,200 revolutions a minute. The planes are 20 feet long and 3 feet wide, less than half the size of those of the Wright aeroplane.

On October 30 Henry Farman drove his aeroplane from Mourmelon to Rheims, France, a distance of 20 miles, in a direct line, maintaining an elevation of from 150 to 300 feet. His speed was a mile a minute, but the aeroplane was aided by a strong wind blowing in the direction of flight.

On October 31 Louis Bleriot made a flight from Toury to a point near Artenay in his monoplane, a distance of 28 kilometres, landing, however, three times. His longest flight was that of 14 kilometres in ten minutes (nearly 9 miles).

On November 6 the first aeroplane society in England was formed at Claridge's Hotel, London, by Capt. W. G. Windham. The organization will be known as the Aeroplane Club.

On November 14 Wilbur Wright, at Le Mans, France, won the Aero Club's prize for the aeroplane first attaining a height of more than 30 metres (93 feet). Wright on his second flight went to a height of 60 metres (187 feet). For the first time since he has been conducting experiments in France, the American aviator succeeded in leaving ground in his aeroplane without the use of any outside mechanism.

Dr. Alexander Graham Bell has been conducting experiments on his tetrahedral, a kite form of airship, near Baddeck, N. S. So far no self-sustained flights have been accomplished.

Unusual interest has been manifested throughout the world during the past year in the development of the aeroplane. In the matter of prizes Europe is far ahead of the United States, over $200,000 having been offered for feats in the air. The Aerial League, in France, has offered a $10,000 cup for the aeroplanist covering 1,000 kilometres (621 miles) in less than 5 hours.

In this country the Aeronautic Society of New York, in September, leased the old Morris Park race track for a year, and issued a general invitation to all experimenters and inventors of aeroplanes, monoplanes, helicopters, gliders, wind wagons, all heavier-than-air machines, to hold trials. Trials have been held almost daily, but nothing notable has been accomplished. One of the experimenters was L. F. Leash, the Canadian aviator, who holds the world's record for long distance glides.

One machine, a monoplane, invented by C. W. Williams, of Richmond Hill, L. I., is built like an enormous parachute. The inventor asserts that in case of the motor breaking down during flight it will settle to earth slowly.

During the year the Aero Club was formed at Columbia University and a class in aeronautics instituted.

DIRIGIBLE BALLOONS.

Marked progress was made in the development of dirigible airships during the year 1908. The airship of the general type, first controlled in flight by Santos Dumont, has entered definitely into the military establishments of all of the great powers. It has been adopted by France, Germany, England, the United States Government, and is being contemplated by Russia. The three chief requirements of the airship—speed, endurance and control—have been attained in a measure sufficient to make them of use in military operations. In the military airships is foreseen the possibility of being able to pass over an enemy's country without effective opposition from its defenders. It will no longer be possible to maintain a position with troops disposed secretly. It will not be possible in the campaigns of the future to secretly move an army by day or night, as long as the air is infested with scouts. It is not known how far it may prove possible to employ airships in actual hostilities, but it is almost certain that the next great war will witness their use.

The British military airship, Mulli Secundus, the only one that has thus far been put through a course of tests by the British Government has not shown itself to be in the same class with the German and French productions. Its speed is about 21 miles an hour. During the past year, with a crew of three men, it has been driven over London and made many successful manoeuvres over the suburbs. The balloon is sausage-shaped, 100 feet long by 30 in diameter. It is driven by an engine fixed to a boat-like basket, constructed of aluminum and canvas.

The airships of the French Government, of which it owns several, are all descendants of the original Lebaudy dirigible, purchased from the Lebaudy Brothers, in 1905. The Lebaudy II. was the first airship owned by the Government. Three others were also built and delivered, but the Patrie, one of the most successful of the airships, escaped into the sky during the latter part of 1907 and was never found. There was no one on board at the time. The French dirigibles are all built with a gas bag about 200 feet long and 30 feet in diameter. The under side is lined with a flat, firm plate, which takes the place of the suspended framework of other types of airship. It gives stiffness to the elongated bag and prevents it from buckling in the wind. To this bottom piece is suspended a car, with a propeller on either side. The gas bag is equipped with side and rear fins to insure stability, and with a rudder in the rear.

The German Government has experimented with dirigible balloons of three types. The medium type corresponds more nearly to the approved French airship. The two extreme types are the flexible, represented by the airship of Major von Parseval, and the rigid, embodied in the production of Count von Zeppelin. The flexible airship aimed to attain the form most easily portable from place to place on the earth. The rigid type strove for size, lifting capacity and endurance. The Parseval type aimed to be a campaign balloon that could be depended on for service in the field. The Zeppelin device, of enormous size, was built to be as steady as a ship in the air. While the Parseval was able to ascend and descend frequently, the Zeppelin was built to stay in the air for days at a time.

Von Zeppelin's airship, the largest of its kind ever built, was purchased by the German Government. It is the greatest attempt at an airship of shiplike size that has ever been floated. The balloon is 420 feet long and 40 feet thick. This approaches more the shape of a lead pencil. The bag has a polygonal instead of a perfectly round surface, and the full thickness is carried almost to the ends.

The gas capacity of the Zeppelin dirigible, which is between 300,000 and 400,000 cubic feet, enables it to lift several tons. Two motors form part of this equipment. There is abundant buoyancy for all the fuel that need be stored for a thousand mile voyage.

On July 1, Count von Zeppelin broke all records for dirigibles by remaining in the air for twelve hours, making an extended trip over Northern Switzerland, at an average speed of 34 miles per hour. The airship moved with the greatest precision and was always under complete control. The aged inventor, who has spent his life and fortune in developing the Zeppelin, was given a tremendous ovation by his countrymen as a result of this feat.

On August 6, the Zeppelin airship while anchored at Echterdingen burst and was consumed by fire, leaving nothing but a twisted mass of wreckage. The blow prostrated Count von Zeppelin, for the mishap left him without funds to build another dirigible. The German people, however, raised by popular subscription nearly $1,000,000, and in a few weeks a new airship of the same pattern and size as the wrecked dirigible was sailing over Germany.

That flights in dirigibles can be made with practical safety was proven during the past year by the confidence shown in them by members of royalty, who, on several occasions, made ascents in the big German dirigibles. On August 21, Crown Prince Frederick Wilhelm made an ascension at Berlin in Major Parseval's semi-rigid dirigible. On October 27, Prince Henry of Prussia took an extended trip in Count von Zeppelin's new airship, remaining up several hours and part of the time himself guiding the huge airship.

In the development of dirigible airships in the United States aeronauts have made considerable progress, and the last year has witnessed the acceptance of a motor-driven airship for army use.

In July the United States Government offered a part of $75,000 as a prize for a practicable military means of dirigible, aerial navigation. The prize was competed for by Capt. Thomas Scott Baldwin, of California, at trials arranged at Fort Myer, near Washington, D. C. After exhaustive tests witnessed by prominent Government and Army officials the airship was accepted and instruction of army officers attached to the Signal Corps begun at once. The average speed made by the Baldwin dirigible during the tests was about 15 miles per hour.

On October 19, a contract for the construction of a dirigible balloon was awarded to Captain Baldwin by the Aerial Navigation Company, of Boston, which plans to carry on a freight and passenger line between Boston and New York, to start in May, 1909.

On August 23, Lambert, the Belgium inventor, made a successful ascent in a dirigible at Brussels. The airship at all times was under perfect control.

On September 10, a dirigible airship, with a semi-rigid frame resembling the French type, made a flight at St. Petersburgh, Russia, under the auspices of the St. Petersburgh Military Aero Club.

BALLOONING.

There were many balloon ascensions, as well as contests for endurance and distance, held in the United States and Europe during the year 1908. Several new records were established.

The principal event in the United States was the balloon race of the American Federation of Aero Clubs, held at Chicago on July 4, in which there were nine starters. The Fielding, of San Antonio, Texas, with E. H. Hunnewell as pilot and Dr. F. D. Fielding as assistant, landed at West Shefford, Quebec, a distance of 895 miles, beating the record of the German balloon Pommern, the winner of the James Gordon Bennett Cup last year, which travelled 876¾ miles.

Other entrants and the distances covered were: King Edward, Pilot, John Bennett; Assistant, Gerald Gregory; landed at Port Huron, a distance of 320 miles. Ville De Dieppe, Pilot, A. E. Mueller; Assistant, George Schoeneck; landed at Benton Harbor, Mich., a distance of 70 miles. The United States, Pilot, H. P. Shirley; Assistant, Horace Wilde, landed at East Pinkerton, Canada, a distance of 500 miles. The Cincinnati, Pilot, Leslie Haddock; Assistant, George Howard; landed at Covert, Mich., a distance of 320 miles. The American, Pilot, P. S. Hudson; Assistant, Lieut. J. J. Meade; landed at Carsonville, Mich., a distance of 300 miles. The Columbia, Pilot, C. H. Leichliter; Assistant, Martin Peterson; landed at Clinton, Ontario, a distance of 450 miles. The Illinois, Pilot, C. H. Pierrige; Assistant, J. B. Case; landed at Grand Island, Ontario, a distance of 545 miles. The Chicago, Pilot, C. A. Coey; Assistant, G. L. Bumbaugh; landed at Atwood, Ontario, a distance of 522 miles.

Three balloons engaged in a "point to point" race, the first contest of its kind undertaken, at North Adams, Mass., on August 14, and was won by the North Adams No. 1, which landed within five miles of its destination.

On June 29 the Swiss Aero Club balloon Cognac was successfully piloted across the Alps, the first time such a feat was ever accomplished.

The Grand Prix de l'Aero Club competition, in which there were eighteen entrants, was held at Paris, France, October 4. It was won by M. Georges Blanchet in the balloon Centaure, which landed near Alois on October 6, the balloon having been in the air 37 hours and 15 minutes, and travelled 550 kilometres.

AERONAUTICS IN 1908—*Continued.*

The principal event of the year was the third international balloon race for the James Gordon Bennett Cup, held at Berlin, Germany, on October 12, which resulted in the breaking of previous records, both for distance covered in a single flight and the time spent above the earth. The contest was won by the Swiss balloon Helvetia, piloted by Colonel Schaeck, with Lieutenant Missner as assistant. The balloon landed 40 kilometres north of Molde, in Norway, 1,250 kilometres (750 miles) from Berlin, the occupants having remained in the air 74 hours. Although the German Aero Club awarded the prize to the Helvetia, the decision has been contested by the British Aero Club, because Colonel Schaeck admitted that while over the sea, fishermen seized the trail rope and towed him to land, where he eventually anchored. The rules of the contest disqualifies any balloon which does not descend on dry land. The protest will come before a special meeting of the International Aeronautic Federation and a decision rendered early in the year. As it now stands, the Swiss Aero Club has the privilege of naming the next starting point of the race.

The cup was held by Germany, having been won by Herr Oscar Erbsloeh in the German balloon Pommern during the race held in St. Louis in 1907. Alfred Leblanc, in the French balloon Isle de France, who remained in the air 44 hours and 2 minutes, in the St. Louis race, held the record for time in the air. The Helvetia, winner of the Berlin race, also broke the record held by Leblanc in having remained in the air continuously for 74 hours.

In the Berlin race there were twenty-three starters, representing aeronauts from eight countries, as follows: United States, England, Germany, France, Italy, Spain, Belgium and Switzerland. Prior to the international race numerous contests were held for endurance, altitude and for skill in landing.

Misfortune pursued many of the aeronauts, and there were many narrow escapes from death. At the start the American built balloon Conqueror, having as pilot A. Holland Forbes, assisted by Augustus Post, after reaching an altitude of 4,000 feet, suddenly burst. Fortunately the collapsed balloon formed itself into a parachute, and the occupants in the basket reached the ground in safety. Many of the balloons were swept over the North Sea and descended in the water, the aeronauts being saved by sailors. In the ascension of the German balloon Busley, which left Berlin on October 11, the day before the big race, the pilot and his assistant, Dr. Niemeyer and Herr Heidemann, were unheard of for 96 hours. They were picked up by the sailors of a steam collier in the North Sea, 10 miles southwest of Heligoland.

The records of the landings of the other contestants in the race are as follows: The Banshee (British) landed at Huidding, Schleswig-Holstein, distance 435 kilometres; the Belgica (Belgium) near same place, distance 423 kilometres; Condor (French) landed at Tondern, distance 400 kilometres; the St. Louis (American) in the North Sea, distance about 384 kilometres; Isle de France (French) landed at Garding, distance of 365 kilometres; the Brise d'Automne (French) at same place; the Aetos (Italian) distance 355 kilometres; Utopie (Belgium) landed at Cuxhaven, distance of 350 kilometres; the Cognac (Swiss) landed near Coppel Neufeld, a distance of 352 kilometres; the Dusseldorf (German) landed at Mulsum, a distance of 346 kilometres; the Berlin (German) landed near Cuxhaven, a distance of 340 kilometres; the Britannia (British) landed near Bremen, a distance of 312 kilometres; the America II. (United States) landed at Mechlenburg, a distance of 200 kilometres. The English Aero Club, in disputing the decision of the German Club, asserts that the prize should be awarded to the Banshee, which sailed the greatest distance with the exception of the Helvetia. The first international race, which was held in Paris in 1906, was won by Lieutenant Lahm, U. S. A., by a flight of 402 miles.

Pugilism.

IMPORTANT RING FIGHTS IN 1908.

January 1.—San Francisco, Abe Attell and Owen Moran, 25 rounds. Draw.
January 3.—Los Angeles, Rudolph Unholz and George Memsic, 10 rounds. No decision.
January 8.—Peoria, Ill., Johnny Coulon defeated Kid Murphy, 10 rounds.
January 13.—Ogden, Utah, Battling Nelson knocked out Jack Clifford, 5 rounds.
January 14.—Reading, Pa., Willie Fitzgerald defeated Jim Bonner, 10 rounds.
January 14.—Boston, Packey McFarland defeated Bert Keyes, 12 rounds.
January 14.—Los Angeles, Sam Langford and Jim Barry, 10 rounds. No decision.
January 16.—Lymansville, R. I., Willie Fitzgerald defeated Jim Bonner, 10 rounds.
January 16.—Montreal, Mike Donovan defeated Joe Walcott, 10 rounds.
January 21.—Los Angeles, Joe Thomas and Jack Sullivan, 10 rounds. No decision.
January 21.—Albany, Jack Blackburn defeated Charley Hitte, 14 rounds.
January 21—Boston, Billy Papke defeated Walter Stanton, 4 rounds.
January 23.—New Haven, Harry Lewis defeated Frank Mantell, 3 rounds.
January 28.—Boston, Matty Baldwin and Kid Goodwin, 12 rounds. Draw.
January 29.—Peoria, Ill., Johnny Coulon defeated Kid Murphy, 10 rounds.
January 31.—San Francisco, Abe Attell defeated Frankie Neil, 13 rounds.
February 5.—Los Angeles, Battling Nelson and Rudolph Unholz, 10 rounds. No decision.
February 10.—London, Tommy Burns knocked out Jack Palmer, 4 rounds.
February 14.—Baltimore, Willie Fitzgerald and Fred Landers, 15 rounds. Draw.
February 20.—Peoria, Ill., Johnny Coulon knocked out Cooney Kelly, 9 rounds.
February 21.—Milwaukee, Packey McFarland defeated Freddie Welsh, 10 rounds.
February 22.—San Francisco, Stanley Ketchell knocked out Mike Sullivan, 1 round.
February 28.—San Francisco, Abe Attell knocked out Eddie Kelly, 7 rounds.
March 3.—Los Angeles, Battling Nelson and Jimmy Britt, 10 rounds. No decision.
March 3.—Boston, Sam Langford and Joe Jeannette, 12 rounds. Draw.
March 16.—Milwaukee, Billy Papke defeated Hugo Kelly, 10 rounds.
March 17.—Dublin, Tommy Burns knocked out Jem Roche, 1 round.
March 19.—Baltimore, Solly Weinrib defeated Kid Murphy, 8 rounds.
March 26.—Baltimore, Harry Lewis defeated Terry Martin, 15 rounds.
March 31.—San Francisco, Battling Nelson and Abe Attell, 15 rounds. Draw.
April 1.—Paris, Willie Lewis defeated Jeff Thorne, 10 rounds.

PUGILISM.—*Continued.*

April 7.—Boston, Sam Langford knocked out Jim Barry, 2 rounds.
April 9.—Baltimore, Johnny Summers knocked out Soldier Burns, 13 rounds.
April 11.—San Francisco, Packey McFarland defeated Jimmy Britt, 6 rounds.
April 18.—Paris, Tommy Burns knocked out Jewey Smith, 5 rounds.
April 20.—Boston, Harry Lewis knocked out Honey Mellody, 4 rounds.
April 23.—Los Angeles, Mike Sullivan defeated Jimmy Gardiner, 25 rounds.
April 27.—Augusta, Me., Harry Lewis knocked out Larry Conley, 3 rounds.
April 30.—San Francisco, Abe Attell defeated Tommy Sullivan, 4 rounds.
May 2.—Paris, Willie Lewis knocked out Walter Stanton, 5 rounds.
May 9.—Paris, Willie Lewis knocked out Jeff Thorne, 2 rounds.
May 9.—San Francisco, Stanley Ketchell knocked out Jack Sullivan, 20 rounds.
May 14.—San Francisco, Joe Gans defeated Rudolph Unholz, 11 rounds.
May 30.—San Francisco, Matty Baldwin defeated Grover Hayes, 12 rounds.
June 4.—Milwaukee, Stanley Ketchell defeated Billy Papke, 10 rounds.
June 13.—Paris, Tommy Burns knocked out Bill Squires, 8 rounds.
July 4.—San Francisco, Battling Nelson knocked out Joe Gans, 17 rounds.
July 4.—Los Angeles, Packey McFarland and Freddie Welsh, 25 rounds. No decision.
July 21.—New York, Sam Langford knocked out John Wille, 2 rounds.
July 24.—Los Angeles, Al Kaufmann defeated Battling Johnson, 7 rounds.
July 28.—Boston, Tommy Murphy defeated Rudolph Unholz, 10 rounds.
July 31.—San Francisco, Stanley Ketchell knocked out Hugo Kelly, 3 rounds.
August 19.—San Francisco, Stanley Ketchell knocked out Joe Thomas, 2 rounds.
August 24.—Australia, Tommy Burns knocked out Bill Squires, 13 rounds.
August 25.—Los Angeles, Al Kaufmann knocked out Jim Flynn, 9 rounds.
September 2.—New York, Tommy Murphy defeated Leach Cross, 6 rounds.
September 2.—New York, Sam Langford and Joe Jeannette, 6 rounds. No decision.
September 2.—Australia, Tommy Burns knocked out Bill Lang, 6 rounds.
September 7.—San Francisco, Abe Attell and Owen Moran, 23 rounds. Draw.
September 7.—Vernon, Cal., Billy Papke knocked out Stanley Ketchell, 12 rounds.
September 7.—Boston, Harry Lewis defeated Unk Russell, 12 rounds.
September 9.—Colma, Cal., Battling Nelson knocked out Joe Gans, 21 rounds.
September 29.—Boston, Tommy Murphy and Matty Baldwin, 12 rounds. Draw.
September 30.—San Francisco, Owen Moran defeated Eddie Hanlon, 20 rounds.
October 9.—New York, Al Kaufmann knocked out Fred Bradley, 4 rounds.
October 17.—New York, Kid McCoy defeated Jim Stewart, 6 rounds.
October 21.—New York, Packey McFarland defeated Leach Cross, 6 rounds.
October 30.—New York, Charley Griffin defeated Bert Keyes, 6 rounds.
November 2.—London, Jimmy Britt defeated Johnny Summers, 10 rounds.
November 2.—New York, Johnny Coulon and Young O'Leary, 6 rounds. No decision.
November 10.—Los Angeles, Al Kaufmann knocked out Terry Mustaine, 14 rounds.
November 18.—New York, Jem Driscoll defeated Matty Baldwin, 6 rounds.
November 18.—Philadelphia, Packey McFarland defeated Tommy Murphy, 6 rounds.
November 26.—San Francisco, Stanley Ketchell knocked out Billy Papke, 11 rounds.
November 26.—Los Angeles, Freddie Welsh defeated Abe Attell, 15 rounds.

A. A. U. CHAMPIONSHIPS.

The Amateur Athletic Union boxing championships were held in Boston, March 24-25, with the following winners in the final bouts: 105-pound class—Angus McDougall, Boston; 115-pound class—M. J. Carroll, New York; 125-pound class—Edward J. Walsh, New York; 135-pound class—J. Denning, New York; 145-pound class—William Rolfe, Boston; 158-pound class—Henry Hall, Boston; heavyweight class—Thomas Kennedy, New York.

IMPORTANT CHAMPIONSHIP CONTESTS.

John L. Sullivan—Defeated Paddy Ryan at Mississippi City, February 7, 1882, 9 rounds. Draw with Charlie Mitchell at Chantilly, France, March 10, 1888, 39 rounds. Defeated Jake Kilrain at Richburg, Miss., July 8, 1889, 75 rounds. All the above with bare knuckles.

James J. Corbett—Defeated Jake Kilrain at New Orleans, February 18, 1890, 6 rounds. Draw with Peter Jackson, San Francisco, May 21, 1891, 61 rounds. Defeated John L. Sullivan, New Orleans, September 7, 1892, 21 rounds. Defeated Charlie Mitchell, Jacksonville, January 25, 1894, 3 rounds.

Bob Fitzsimmons—Defeated Jack Dempsey, New Orleans, January 14, 1891, 13 rounds. Defeated Jim Corbett, Carson City, Nev., March 17, 1897, 14 rounds.

James J. Jeffries—Defeated Bob Fitzsimmons, Coney Island, N. Y., June 9, 1899, 11 rounds, and at San Francisco, July 25, 1902, 8 rounds. Defeated Tom Sharkey at Coney Island, November 3, 1899, 25 rounds. Defeated James J. Corbett at Coney Island, May 11, 1900, 23 rounds, and at San Francisco, August 14, 1903, 10 rounds. Retired and presented title to Marvin Hart at Reno, Nev., July 3, 1905, on the occasion of Hart's victory over Jack Root in 12 rounds.

Tommy Burns—Defeated Marvin Hart at Los Angeles, February 23, 1906, 20 rounds. Draw with Philadelphia Jack O'Brien, 20 rounds, at Los Angeles, November 28, 1906. Defeated O'Brien, 20 rounds, at Los Angeles, May 8, 1906. Knocked out Bill Squires, 1 round, Colma, Cal., July 4, 1907, and Gunner Moir in London, December 2, 1907, in 10 rounds.

LARGEST PURSES AND STAKES FOR FIGHTERS.

Date.	Winner.*	Loser.	Place.	Gate Receipts.	Date.	Winner.	Loser.	Place.	Gate Receipts.
Sept. 3, 1906.	Gans.......	Nelson	G'd'd.Nev	$69,715	July 25, 1902	Jeffries......	Fitzsimmons	San Fran.	$31,800
Nov. 3, 1899.	Jeffries.....	Sharkey.....	New York.	66,300	Mar. 17, 1897.	Fitzsimmons	Corbett......	Carson.	22,000
Aug. 14, 1903.	Jeffries.. ...	Corbett	San Fran.	63,340	Nov. 15, 1901.	Jeffries......	Ruhlin.	San Fran.	30,800
Aug. 30, 1900.	Corbett......	McCoy	New York.	56,750	Sept. 9, 1905	Nelson.......	Britt........	San Fran.	27,770
Dec. 20, 1904.	Nelson......	Britt	Colma,Cal	48,311	Oct. 31, 1904.	Britt	Gans........	San Fran.	21,765
Sept. 7, 1892.	Corbett	Sullivan.....	N.Orleans	*45,000	Dec. 19, 1903.	Jeffries......	Munroe	San Fran.	21,761
Mar. 8, 1893.	Fitzsimmons	Hall	N Orleans	40,000	Dec. 2, 1906.	Fitzsimmons.	Sharkey.....	San Fran.	21,000
Mar. 25, 1904.	Britt	Corbett	San Fran.	32,245	Mar. 31, 1903	Corbett......	McGovern...	San Fran.	20,880

*Purse $25,000 and $10,000 a side. See also Endurance Records.

Football.

FOOTBALL of 1908 reached its highest point of scientific development, was the most interesting and spectacular and the least injurious among players of any year since Rugby has been played in America. Attention given to the forward pass and onside kick, with other changes suggested by the new rules, brought into existence the "new football" with its more open plays and far superior to the gruelling line-bucking of former years. The attendance was the largest ever known.

SCORES OF LEADING EASTERN COLLEGES FOR 1908.*

AMHERST.

Opponent	Score
Fordham	0— 5
Vermont	0— 0
Tufts	6— 5
Trinity	6— 6
Dartmouth	0—17
Cornell	0— 6
Middlebury	51— 5
Williams	4— 0
	67—44

ANNAPOLIS.

Opponent	Score
Rutgers	18— 0
St. Johns	22— 0
Dickinson	22— 0
Md. Aggies	57— 0
Lehigh	16— 0
Harvard	6— 6
George Wash.	17— 0
Carlisle	6—16
Villanova	30— 6
Penn. State	5— 0
Virginia Poly	15— 4
West Point	4— 6
	218—38

BROWN.

Opponent	Score
New Hampshire	34— 0
Bates	34— 4
Colgate	6— 0
Bowdoin	12— 0
Pennsylvania	0—12
Lafayette	6— 8
Harvard	2— 6
Yale	10—10
Vermont	12— 0
	116—40

BUCKNELL.

Opponent	Score
Susquehanna	33— 0
Pennsylvania	0—16
Gettysburg	5— 6
Delaware	13— 0
Pittsburgh	0—22
Lafayette	6— 6
Penn. State	6—33
Dickinson	0— 6
Ursinus	17—11
	80—100

CARLISLE.

Opponent	Score
Conway Hall	53— 0
Lebanon Valley	39— 0
Villanova	10— 0
Penn. State	12— 5
Syracuse	12— 0
Pennsylvania	6— 6
Annapolis	16— 6
Harvard	0—17
Pittsburgh	6— 0
Minnesota	6—11
St. Louis	17— 0
	177—45

CORNELL.

Opponent	Score
Hamilton	11— 0
Oberlin	23—10
Colgate	9— 0
Vermont	9— 0
Penn. State	10— 4
Amherst	6— 0
Chicago	6— 6
Trinity	18— 6
Pennsylvania	4—17
	96—43

DARTMOUTH.

Opponent	Score
Vermont	11— 0
Mass. Aggies	23— 0
Tufts	18— 0
Williams	0— 0
Holy Cross	18— 5
Amherst	17— 0
Princeton	10— 6
Harvard	0— 6
	97—17

FORDHAM.

Opponent	Score
Amherst	5— 0
Jeff. Med.	45— 0
Princeton	0—17
Georgetown	22— 0
R. P. I.	22—12
Villanova	2— 0
	96—29

HARVARD.

Opponent	Score
Bowdoin	5— 0
Maine	16— 0
Bates	18— 0
Williams	10— 0
Springfield Tech.	44— 0
Annapolis	6— 6
Brown	6— 2
Carlisle	17— 0
Dartmouth	6— 0
Yale	4— 0
	132— 8

LAFAYETTE.

Opponent	Score
Wyoming	10— 0
State Normal	22— 0
Superba A. C.	4— 0
Princeton	0— 0
Medico-Chi.	23— 0
Brown	8— 6
Bucknell	6— 6
Pennsylvania	4—34
Lehigh	5—11
	82—57

PENN. STATE.

Opponent	Score
Bellefonte	5— 6
Grove City	30— 0
Carlisle	5—12
Pennsylvania	0— 6
Geneva State	51— 0
West Virginia	12— 0
Cornell	4—10
Bucknell	33— 6
Annapolis	0— 5
Pittsburgh	12— 6
	152—51

PENNSYLVANIA.

Opponent	Score
West Virginia	6— 0
Ursinus	30— 0
Bucknell	16— 0
Villanova	11— 0
Penn. State	6— 0
Gettysburg	23— 4
Brown	12— 0
Carlisle	6— 6
Carnegie Tech.	25— 0
Lafayette	34— 4
Michigan	29— 0
Cornell	17— 4
	215—18

PRINCETON.

Opponent	Score
Springfield Tech.	18— 0
Stevens	21— 0
Lafayette	0— 0
Villanova	6— 0
Virginia Poly	10— 4
Fordham	17— 0
Syracuse	0— 0
West Point	0— 0
Dartmouth	6—10
Yale	6—11
	84—25

SYRACUSE.

Opponent	Score
Hobart	51— 0
Hamilton	18— 0
Yale	0— 5
Carlisle	0—12
Rochester	23—12
Princeton	0— 0
Williams	23— 0
Colgate	0— 6
Tufts	28— 0
Michigan	28— 4
	171—39

WEST POINT.

Opponent	Score
Tufts	5— 0
Trinity	33— 0
Yale	0— 6
Colgate	6— 0
Princeton	0— 0
Springfield T. S.	6— 5
Wash. and Jeff.	6— 6
Villanova	25— 0
Annapolis	6— 4
	87—21

YALE.

Opponent	Score
Wesleyan	16— 0
Syracuse	5— 0
Holy Cross	18— 0
West Point	6— 0
Wash. and Jeff.	38— 0
Mass. Aggies	49— 0
Brown	10—10
Princeton	11— 6
Harvard	0— 4
	153—20

*In this, as in other tables, the first column of figures gives the score of the college whose name heads the series.

SCORES OF LEADING WESTERN COLLEGES FOR 1908.

Chicago won the championship among the Western colleges, the conference ranking of the "Big Eight" being: Chicago, Wisconsin, Illinois, Minnesota, Indiana, Purdue, Iowa and Northwestern. Michigan, while not in the conference, should be classed with the leaders on an excellent showing made. The All-Western team was: Schommer, Chicago, left end; Osthoff, Wisconsin, left tackle; Messmer, Wisconsin, left guard; Schulz, Michigan, centre; Van Hook, Illinois, right guard; Hoffman, Chicago, right tackle; Page, Chicago, right end; Steffen, Chicago, quarter; Allerdice, Michigan, left half; Kirk, Iowa, right half; Wilce, Wisconsin, fullback.

CHICAGO.

Opponent	Score
Purdue	39— 0
Indiana	29— 6
Illinois	11— 6
Minnesota	29— 0
Cornell	6— 6
Wisconsin	18—12
	132—30

ILLINOIS.

Opponent	Score
Monmouth	17— 6
Marquette	6— 6
Chicago	6—11
Indiana	10— 0
Iowa	22— 0
Purdue	15— 5
Northwestern	64— 8
	140—36

INDIANA.

Opponent	Score
De Pauw	16— 0
Chicago	6—29
Wisconsin	0—16
Illinois	0—10
Notre Dame	0—11
Purdue	10— 4
	32—69

IOWA.

Opponent	Score
Coe	0—92
Missouri	5—10
Nebraska	8—11
Illinois	0—22
Drake	6—12
Kansas	5—10
	24-157

MICHIGAN.	
Case School	16—6
M. A. C.	0—0
Notre Dame	12—6
O. S. U.	10—6
Vanderbilt	24—6
Kentucky	62—0
Pennsylvania	0—29
Syracuse	4—28
	128—81

MINNESOTA.	
Lawrence	6—0
Ames	17—12
Nebraska	0—0
Wisconsin	0—5
Chicago	0—29
Carlisle	11—6
	34—52

MISSOURI.	
Warrensburg	58—0
Rolla S. of M.	16—0
Iowa U.	10—5
Westminster	58—0
Iowa State	0—16
Drake	11—8
Washington	23—0
Kansas	4—10
	180—39

NEBRASKA.	
Peru	20—0
Doane	43—0
Grinnell	20—5
Minnesota	0—0
Haskell	10—0
Iowa	11—8
Ames	23—17
Kansas	5—20
Wabash	27—6
	159—56

OHIO STATE.	
Otterbein	18—0
Wooster	0—8
Denison	16—2
West. Reserve	0—18
Michigan	6—10
O. Wesleyan	20—9
Case School	8—18
Vanderbilt	17—6
Oberlin	14—12
Kenyon	10—9
	118—92

PURDUE.	
Chicago	0—39
Earlham	40—0
Monmouth	30—0
De Pauw	28—4
Northwestern	16—10
Illinois	5—15
Indiana	4—10
	123—78

ST. LOUIS U.	
Sch. Mines	18—0
State Normal	39—0
Arkansas	24—0
Wabash	4—0
W. U. of Penn.	0—13
Sewanee	6—6
Creighton	6—0
Carlisle	0—17
	97—36

WISCONSIN.	
Lawrence	35—0
Indiana	16—0
Marquette	9—6
Minnesota	5—0
Chicago	12—18
	77—24

SCORES OF THE LEADING SOUTHERN COLLEGES FOR 1908.

Southern colleges shared in the popular favor given to football over the entire country, the season in the South being one of financial success and marking a great advance in the game. The remarkable score of 420 points to 11 by Louisiana State was a feature of the season, although Virginia and Vanderbilt divided championship honors.

AUBURN, ALA.	
Gordon Inst.	43—0
Mercer	23—0
Sewanee	6—0
Louisiana	2—10
Georgia Tech.	44—0
Georgia U.	18—0
	136—10

GEORGIA TECH.	
Gordon Inst.	27—0
Mooney	30—0
Miss. A. & M.	23—0
Alabama	11—6
Tennessee	5—6
Auburn	0—44
Sewanee	0—6
Clemson	30—6
	126—68

LOUISIANA STATE.	
Y. M. C. G.	41—0
Army	81—5
Texas A. & M.	26—0
Auburn	10—2
S. P. U.	55—0
A. & M. Miss.	50—0
Baylor	89—0
Haskell	32—0
Arkansas	36—4
	420—11

SEWANEE.	
So. Military	5—0
Mooney	29—0
Castle Heights	32—5
Virginia	0—0
Auburn	0—6
Kentucky	12—0
St. Louis	6—6
Georgia Tech.	6—0
Vanderbilt	6—6
	96—23

TENNESSEE.	
N. Carolina	12—0
Maryville	39—5
Kentucky	7—0
Georgia	10—0
Georgia Tech.	6—5
Vanderbilt	9—16
Clemson	6—5
Chattanooga	35—6
Alabama	0—4
	124—41

VANDERBILT.	
S. P. U.	11—5
Maryville	32—0
Rose Poly	32—0
Clemson	41—0
Mississippi	29—0
Michigan	6—24
Tennessee	16—9
Ohio State	6—17
Washington U.	28—0
Sewanee	6—6
	207—61

VIRGINIA.	
Pennsylvania	0—6
St. Johns	18—9
Randolph	22—0
Davidson	12—0
Sewanee	0—0
A. & M. N. Car.	6—0
Georgetown	6—0
N. Carolina	31—0
	95—15

VIRGINIA POLY.	
Hampton-Sydney	50—0
Clemson	6—0
Princeton	4—10
V. M. I.	10—0
W. & L.	15—4
N. Carolina	10—0
G. Wash. U.	0—6
Annapolis	4—15
A. & M. N. Car.	5—6
	104—41

INTERCOLLEGIATE RECORDS.

YALE—HARVARD.

Yr.	Won by.	Score.
1883	Yale	24—4
1884	Yale	40—0
1885	No game.	
1886	Yale	30—4
1887	Yale	18—6
1888	No game.	
1889	Yale	6—0
1890	Harvard	12—6
1891	Yale	10—0
1892	Yale	6—0
1893	Yale	6—0
1894	Yale	12—4
1897	Tie	0—0
1898	Harvard	17—0
1899	Tie	0—0
1900	Yale	28—0
1901	Harvard	22—0
1902	Yale	23—0
1903	Yale	16—0
1904	Yale	12—0
1905	Yale	6—0
1906	Yale	6—0
1907	Yale	12—0
1908	Harvard	4—0

YALE—PRINCETON.

Yr.	Won by.	Score.
1883	Yale	6—0
1884	*Yale	6—4
1885	Princeton	6—5
1886	*Yale	4—0
1887	Yale	12—0
1888	Yale	12—0
1889	Princeton	10—0
1890	Yale	32—0
1891	Yale	20—0
1892	Yale	12—0
1893	Princeton	6—0
1894	Yale	24—0
1895	Yale	20—10
1896	Princeton	24—6
1897	Yale	6—0
1898	Princeton	6—0
1899	Princeton	11—10
1900	Yale	29—5
1901	Yale	12—0
1902	Yale	12—5
1903	Princeton	11—6
1904	Yale	12—0
1905	Yale	23—4
1906	Tie	0—0
1907	Yale	12—10
1908	Yale	11—6

*Unfinished games.

PENNSYLVANIA—CORNELL.

Yr.	Won by.	Score.
1893	Penn.	50—0
1894	Penn.	6—0
1895	Penn.	46—2
1896	Penn.	32—10
1897	Penn.	4—0
1898	Penn.	12—0
1899	Penn.	26—0
1900	Penn.	27—0
1901	Cornell	24—6
1902	Penn.	12—11
1903	Penn.	42—0
1904	Penn.	34—0
1905	Penn.	6—5
1906	Tie	0—0
1907	Penn.	12—4
1908	Penn.	17—4

ARMY—NAVY.

Yr.	Won by.	Score.
1890	Navy	24—0
1891	Army	32—16
1892	Navy	12—4
1893	Navy	6—4
1899	Army	17—5
1900	Navy	11—7
1901	Army	11—5
1902	Army	22—8
1903	Army	40—5
1904	Army	11—0
1905	Tie	6—6
1906	Navy	10—0
1907	Navy	6—0
1908	Army	6—4

CHICAGO—WISCONSIN.

Yr.	Won by.	Score.
1894	Wisconsin	30—0
1895	Chicago	22—12
1896	Wisconsin	24—0
1897	Wisconsin	23—8
1898	Chicago	6—0
1899	Chicago	17—0
1900	Wisconsin	39—5
1901	Wisconsin	35—0
1902	Chicago	11—0
1903	Chicago	15—6
1904	Chicago	18—11
1905	Chicago	4—0
1906-1907	No game.	
1908	Chicago	16—12

Cross Country and Marathons.

The Cross-Country season was one of great general interest and the sport seems to have secured a strong and continually improving place as one of the most healthful and pleasing of Spring and Fall out-of-door recreations. The more important events of 1908 follow:

Middle-States Championship, A. A. U., Fairmount Park, Philadelphia, 6½ miles, January 4. Won by Guy Haskins, University of Pennsylvania, in 31.23.

Metropolitan Association, A. A. U., Long Island City, N. Y., March 9, six miles. Won by W. Gould, Xavier A. A., in 31.10; B. Mann, Pastime A. C., second. Pastime A. C. won in team points—61.

St. Louis Marathon, 25 miles, May 2. Won by S. R. Hatch, Chicago, in 2h. 20m. 3-5s., breaking his own record by ten minutes, and five minutes behind Tom Longboat's world's record for the distance.

Y. M. C. A. Boys' Race, New York to Chicago, July 15-21. Distance, 1,092 miles; 1,250 relays and 1,131 boys. Actual running time 114 hours 46 minutes. Average miles per hour, 9.5; average time per mile, 6.19.

T. J. McAughey, Toronto Y. M. C. A., walked from that city to New York, July-August, 772 miles, in 11 days 22 hours.

Sergt. John Walsh, of Denver, 52 years old, walked from San Francisco to Boston, about 3,300 miles, in 79 days.

New Jersey A. A. Relay Marathon, 80 miles, Sea Girt to Newark, September 11. Seven teams of 15 men each. Elizabeth Y. M. C. A. team won in 7 hours 52 minutes.

Chicago Marathon, 25 miles, September 19. Won by A. L. Corey, in 2h. 57m. 30s.

Boston Marathon, Boston to Brockton, 25 miles, October 2. Won by James W. O'Mara in 2h. 35m. 24 3-5s.

Toronto Marathon, 19¼ miles, October 10. Won by Tom Longboat in 1h. 51m. 20s.

Los Angeles Marathon, 15 3-5 miles, September 9. Won by Edward Dietrick in 2h. 1m. 30s.

H. Siret, champion professional distance runner of France, covered the Olympic Marathon course of 26 miles, London, October 10, in 2h. 37m. 23s. John Hayes, of New York, won the Olympic race in 2h. 55m. 18s.

Newark Marathon, about 15 miles, October 21. Won by S. A. Mellor, Mercury A. C., Yonkers, in 1h. 21m. 3s.

Montreal Marathon, 15 miles, October 24. Won by Tom Longboat in 1h. 25m. 44s.

Annual junior and senior championships of the A. A. U. were held at Celtic Park, Long Island, November 14, 1908. Distance, 6¼ miles. Winners and first five men to finish were: Junior—James J. Lee, Boston A. A., 36.18; W. Kraemer, Acorn A. A., 36.37; M. Maloney, Trinity A. C., 36.49; G. J. Obermeyer, National A. C., 37.05; S. A. Mellor, Mercury A. C., 37.09. Winning team score—Trinity A. C., 78 points. Senior—Fred Bellars, New York A. C., 34.15; John J. Joyce, Irish-American A. C., 35.12; John J. Daly, Irish-American A. C., 35.30; Harvey Cohn, Irish-American A. C., 35.32; George V. Bonhag, Irish-American A. C., 35.40. The Irish-Americans took six of the seven first places.

College dual cross-country events in 1908—November 4, at New Haven, Cornell defeated Yale, 22 points to 37. Capt. Young, of Ithaca, finished first in 35.37, lowering the six-mile course record a full minute. Taylor, a team mate, being second in 36.00. November 12, over the six-mile Chestnut Hill course, Brookline, Mass., the Harvard team defeated Yale, 25 points to 30. Herbert Jacques, Harvard, finished first, in 36.48. November 14, over the Fairmount Park course of 5¾ miles, Carlisle team defeated Pennsylvania, 44 points to 61. The Indians won the first three places, Tewanina, ninth in the Olympic Marathon at London, being first, in 31.48; good time for the bad condition of the roads and sleet storm.

Hamilton, Ont., annual road race, November 9, was won by Holmer, of Halifax, in 1h. 51m. 16s. Record for the 19-mile course is 1h. 48m. 43s., held by S. A. Mellor.

Third annual interscholastic cross-country run under the auspices of Princeton University Track Association was held at Princeton, November 7, and was won by Newark High School team with 44 points. Brown Prep., Philadelphia and Mercersburg Academy tied for second place. Gallagher, Brown Prep., finished first in 17.21 for the 3½-mile course.

T. E. Hammond, London, on September 13, 1908, covered 100 miles on the road in 18h. 4m. 10½s., and also made a new 24-hour record of 131 miles 880 yards.

Intercollegiate Championship, at Princeton, N. J., November 21. Course 6 miles 300 yards. Seventy-two starters. H. C. Young, Cornell, finished first in 34.14; G. A. Dull, Michigan, second, in 34.16; H. Jacques, Harvard, third, in 34.20. Team score: Cornell, 29; Syracuse, 87; Harvard, 89; Yale, 90; Michigan, 105; Pennsylvania, 134; Columbia, 188. Princeton did not finish. Race was first held at Morris Park, 1890-1902; at Travers Island, 1903-1905, and since at Princeton. Individual winners—1890, J. F. Cregan, Princeton; 1900, Alex. Grant, Pennsylvania; 1901, D. W. Franchot, Yale; 1902, A. C. Bowen, Pennsylvania; 1903, W. E. Schutt, Cornell; 1904, E. T. Newman, Cornell; 1905, W. Hale, Yale; 1906, Lloyd Jones, Pennsylvania; 1907, Guy Haskins, Pennsylvania. Cornell has won team honors every year except in 1901, when its team was third and Yale first.

Marathon, Madison Square Garden, New York, November 25. Distance, 26 miles 380 yards. Dorando Pietri, Italy, defeated John J. Hayes, New York, leading in each mile and finishing in 2h. 44m. 20⅔s. Hayes' time, 2h. 45m. 5⅕s. Fastest mile, first, by Dorando, 5m. 27s. Track, ten laps. Fractional time—Five miles, 29m. 24s.; 10 miles, 1h. 6s.; 15 miles, 1h. 31m. 43s.; 20 miles, 2h. 4m. 23s.; 25 miles, 2h. 36m. 57s.

Interscholastic Cross-Country Championship, Fairmount Park, Philadelphia. November 26, 4¼ miles. Central H. S. team, Philadelphia, won with 68 points; Newark H. S., second, 82 points. Gallagher, Brown Prep., finished first and made a new course record of 22m. 10s.

New England Ten-Mile Cross-Country Championship, Cambridge, Nov. 26. W. S. Grassic, Boston, won in 57m. 28s.; J. E. Ballard, Providence, second, 58m. 23s.

Yonkers Marathon, 26 miles, at New York, November 26. (Rain and muddy roads.) J. T. Crowley, Irish-American A. C., won from 147 starters in 2h. 49m. 16⅗s.; S. A. Mellor, Mercury A. C., Yonkers, second, in 2h. 56m.; R. A. Fowler, Cambridge, Mass., third; Lewis Tewanina, Carlisle Indian School, fourth; E. Rykder, Oakdale A. A., Massachusetts, fifth; J. Clark, Xavier A. A., New York, sixth; Sidney Hatch, Illinois A. C., Chicago, seventh.

Sporting Addenda.

AUTOMOBILE.

Grand Prize Auto Race for Racing Cars (limited to 155 mm. piston area), Savannah, Ga., November 26. Distance, 402.8 miles (16 laps of 25.13 miles). Twenty starters. Order of finish and time: Louis Wagner, 120 h. p. Fiat, 6h. 10m. 31s.; Victor Hemery, 120 h. p. Benz, 6h. 11m. 27s.; Felice Nazarro, 120 h. p. Fiat, 6h. 18m. 47s.; Rene Hanriot, 120 h. p. Benz, 6h. 26m. 12s.; Lucien Hautvast, 120 h. p. Clement-Bayard, 6h. 34m. 6s.; Lewis Strang, 115 h. p. Renault, 6h. 34m. 37s. Wagner's average, 65.1 miles per hour, breaking previous best American road race record of 64.3, made by George Robertson in the Vanderbilt Cup race of 1908. Fastest lap, 21.08 (74 miles per hour), by Wagner in last lap. Besides the $5,000 gold cup won by Wagner, he received $4,000 in cash from the Automobile Club of America and $8,000 in other prizes.

International Light Car Race, Savannah, November 25. Distance, 196 miles (20 laps of 9.8 miles). Seventeen starters. Order of finish and time: W. M. Hilliard, Boston, 12-18 h. p. Lancia, 3h. 48m. 33s.; R. Burman, 18 h. p. Buick, 3h. 49m. 45s.; L. B. Larimer, 30 h. p. Chalmers, 3h. 53m. 55s.; E. A. Hearne, 18 h. p. Buick, 3h. 58m. 4s.; A. Poole, 10 h. p. Isotta, 4h. 11m. 22s. Hilliard's average, 52.56 miles per hour.

TURF.

Winning Owners and Jockeys Abroad.—Danny Maher headed the list of winning jockeys in England in 1908 with 169 winners, Wooton being second with 129. J. B. Joel was the largest winning owner in England with $131,230. August Belmont, $33,615, was fifteenth; Richard Croker, $31,985, sixteenth, and King Edward, $27,450, was seventeenth. In France W. K. Vanderbilt headed the winning owners with $263,640, of which Northeast, the best winning horse, won $81,380. M. Edmond Blanc won $142,235, and was second. G. Stern headed the list of winning jockeys with 141 firsts.

Leading winning stallions for the Eastern turf season of 1908 were: Hastings, $134,230; Ogden, $125,545; Disguise, $113,641; Voter, $84,945; Commando, $84,155. Fair Play, Priscillian and Field Mouse won for Hastings; Sir Martin and Fayette for Ogden; Maskette, Helmet and Melisande for Disguise; Ballot for Voter, and Colin and Celt for Commando.

Royal Tourist, with 104 pounds up, made a world's record of 1.44⅗ for 1 1-16 miles at Oakland, Cal., November 11.

Total cash distributed to horsemen on New York tracks in 1908 was $1,604,041, against $2,617,402 in 1907.

PUGILISM.

Champions at the various weights December 1, 1908, were: Heavyweight, Noah Brusso (Tommy Burns), Detroit; middleweight, Stanley Ketchell, Montana; welterweight, none. Harry Lewis knocked out William (Honey) Mellody, but not at the weight limit. Mellody has since retired. Lightweight, Battling Nelson, Chicago; featherweight, Abe Attell, California; bantam-weight, Johnny Coulon, Chicago.

BILLIARDS AND POOL.

World's Continuous Pool Championship—Thomas A. Hueston, St. Louis, defeated Alfredo De Oro, 600 to 436 points, three nights' play, St. Louis, November 10-12.

Three-Cushion Record—Charles Morin, Chicago, November 14, ran out a string of 50 points in 27 innings, a new world's record.

MOTORCYCLE.

100-Mile Record—Robert Stubbs rode 100 miles on a motorcycle at Birmingham, Ala., November 25, in 1h. 47m. 44s.

CHECKERS.

Charles F. Barker, Boston, defeated Joseph Drouillard, at Kansas City, Mo., November 13, in 43 out of 50 games for the championship and a side bet of $2,000. Barker won 10 and Drouillard 2 games, and 31 were drawn.

FOOTBALL.

Manhattan Interscholastic Championship was won by High School of Commerce, defeating De Witt-Clinton by a score of 17 to 0. Greater New York Championship was won by Poly. Prep., defeating Erasmus Hall, 13 to 0.

Canadian Intercollegiate Championship was won by University of Toronto, defeating Queen's University, 12 to 0. Canadian Rugby Championship—Tigers, of Hamilton, defeated University of Toronto Seniors, 21 to 17.

ROLLER SKATING.

World's record of 3 ft. 11 in. for high jump was made by John F. Davidson at New York, November 14. Frank Goldie, St. Louis, defeated Harry McDonald, at New York, November 12, for the mile Eastern professional championship, winning on a 17-lap track in 3m. 16⅗s.

RIFLE SHOOTING.

World's sub-target record for schoolboys of 268 out of a possible 280 was made by Manual Training High School, in competition for the Harry Payne Whitney trophy at New York, November 20. Team was composed of eight boys, and only two made perfect scores of 35.

SWIMMING.

Public Schools Athletic League records were made by Townsend Harris Hall boys at New York, November 27, as follows: Fifty yards in 33s., by H. Davis; 100 yards in 1m. 11⅕s., by N. Kohn, and plunge for distance, 46 ft., by H. Davis.

WHIST.

American Whist League Tournament—Held at New York, July 6-11. Brooklyn trophy, won by the New England W. A., with 2 matches plus 9 tricks. Hamilton trophy, won by the American W. C., Boston, defeating Pastime W. C., Boston, in final game. Winning team for second year was composed of H. H. Ward (captain), J. T. Slade, W. S. Kelly and P. G. Morey. Minneapolis Cup, won by Judge David Muhlfelder, Albany, and A. H. McCay, Baltimore. Associate Members' Cup, won by Miss M. H. Campbell, New York, and H. H. Ward, Boston. Next place of meeting, Niagara Falls.

Marriage and Divorce Laws.

(Revised to December 1, 1908.)

Marriage Licenses.—Required in all the States and Territories except Alaska, New Jersey (if residents, otherwise required), New Mexico and South Carolina. California requires man and woman to appear and be examined under oath.

Marriage, Prohibition of.—Marriages between whites and persons of negro descent are prohibited and punishable in Alabama, Arizona, Arkansas, California, Colorado, Delaware, Florida, Georgia, Idaho, Indiana, Kentucky, Louisiana, Maryland, Mississippi, Missouri, Nebraska, North Carolina, Oklahoma, Oregon South Carolina, Tennessee, Texas, Utah, Virginia, and West Virginia.

Marriages between whites and Indians are void in Arizona, North Carolina, Oregon, and South Carolina; and between whites and Chinese in Arizona, California, Mississippi, Oregon, and Utah.

Marriage between first cousins is forbidden in Alaska, Arizona, Arkansas, Illinois, Indiana, Kansas, Missouri, Nevada, New Hampshire, North Dakota, Ohio, Oklahoma, Oregon, Pennsylvania, South Dakota, Washington, and Wyoming, and in some of them is declared incestuous and void, and marriage with step-relatives is forbidden in all the States except Florida, Hawaiian Islands, Iowa, Kentucky, Minnesota, New York, Tennessee, Wisconsin.

Connecticut and Minnesota prohibit the marriage of an epileptic, imbecile, or feeble-minded woman under 45 years of age, or cohabitation by any male of this description with a woman under 45 years of age, and marriage of lunatics is void in the District of Columbia, Kentucky, Maine, Massachusetts, Nebraska; persons having sexual diseases in Michigan.

States.	Residence Required.	Causes for Absolute Divorce. *In addition to adultery, which is cause for divorce in all the States.* *
Alabama. . .	1 year.	Abandonment two years, crime against nature, habitual drunkenness, violence, pregnancy of wife by other than husband at marriage, physical incapacity, imprisonment for two years for felony.
Arizona.......	1 year.	Felony, physical incapacity, desertion one year, excesses, cruelty, neglect to provide one year, pregnancy of wife by other than husband at marriage, conviction of felony prior to marriage unknown to other party.
Arkansas.....	1 year.	Desertion one year, felony, habitual drunkenness one year, cruelty, former marriage existing, physical incapacity, permanent insanity.
California....	1 year.	Cruelty, desertion one year, neglect one year, habitual drunkenness one year, felony.
Colorado......	1 year.	Desertion one year, physical incapacity, cruelty, failure to provide one year, habitual drunkenness one year, felony, former marriage existing.
Connecticut..	3 years.	Fraudulent contract, wilful desertion three years with total neglect of duty, habitual drunkenness, cruelty, imprisonment for life, infamous crime involving violation of conjugal duty and punishable by imprisonment in State prison, seven years' absence without being heard from.
Delaware.....	......	Desertion three years, habitual drunkenness, physical incapacity, cruelty, felony—and at the discretion of the Court, fraud, want of age, neglect to provide three years.
D. of Columbia	2 years.	Marriages may be annulled for former existing marriage, lunacy, fraud, coercion, physical incapacity, and want of age at time of marriage.
Florida.......	2 years.	Cruelty, violent temper, habitual drunkenness, physical incapacity, desertion one year, former marriage existing, relationship within prohibited degrees.
Georgia.......	1 year.	Mental and physical incapacity, desertion three years, felony, cruelty, habitual drunkenness, force, duress, or fraud in obtaining marriage, pregnancy of wife by other than husband at marriage, relationship within prohibited degrees.
Idaho.........	6 mos.	Cruelty, desertion one year, neglect one year, habitual drunkenness one year, felony, insanity.
Illinois........	1 year.	Desertion two years, habitual drunkenness two years, former existing marriage, cruelty, felony, physical incapacity, attempt on life of other party, divorced party cannot marry for two years.
Indiana.......	2 years.	Abandonment two years, cruelty, habitual drunkenness, failure to provide two years, felony, physical incapacity.
Iowa..........	1 year.	Desertion two years, felony, habitual drunkenness, cruelty, pregnancy of wife by other than husband at marriage. The marriage may be annulled for the following causes existing at the time of the marriage: Insanity, physical incapacity, former existing marriage, consanguinity.
Kansas........	1 year.	Abandonment one year, cruelty, fraud, habitual drunkenness, gross neglect of duty, felony, physical incapacity, pregnancy of wife by other than husband at marriage, former existing marriage.
Kentucky....	1 year.	Separation five years, desertion one year, felony, physical incapacity, loathsome disease, habitual drunkenness one year, cruelty, force, fraud or duress in obtaining marriage, joining religious sect believing marriage unlawful, pregnancy of wife by other than husband at marriage or subsequent unchaste behavior, ungovernable temper.
Louisiana.....	......	Felony, habitual drunkenness, excesses, cruelty, public defamation of other party, abandonment, attempt on life of other party, fugitive from justice.
Maine.........	1 year.	Cruelty, desertion three years, physical incapacity, habits of intoxication by liquors, opium, or other drugs, neglect to provide, insanity under certain limitations.
Maryland	2 years.	Abandonment three years, unchastity of wife before marriage, physical incapacity, any cause which renders the marriage null and void *ab initio*.
Mass'chusetts	3-5 yrs.	Cruelty, desertion three years, habits of intoxication by liquors, opium or other drugs, neglect to provide, physical incapacity, imprisonment for felony, uniting for three years with religious sect believing marriage unlawful.
Michigan	1 year.	Felony, desertion two years, habitual drunkenness, physical incapacity, and in the discretion of the Court for cruelty or neglect to provide.

* Exclusive of South Carolina, which has no divorce law.

MARRIAGE AND DIVORCE LAWS—*Continued.*

STATES.	Residence Required.	Causes for Absolute Divorce. *In addition to adultery, which is cause for divorce in all the States.* *
Minnesota....	1 year.	Desertion one year, habitual drunkenness by liquors or opium, cruelty, physical incapacity, imprisonment for felony.
Mississippi....	1 year.	Felony, desertion two years, consanguinity, physical incapacity, habitual drunkenness by liquor, opium, or other drugs, cruelty, insanity at time of marriage, former existing marriage, pregnancy of wife by other than husband at marriage.
Missouri......	1 year.	Felony, absence one year, habitual drunkenness one year, cruelty, indignities, vagrancy, former existing marriage, physical incapacity, conviction of felony prior to marriage unknown to other party, wife pregnant by other than husband at marriage.
Montana......	1 year.	Cruelty, desertion, neglect one year, habitual drunkenness one year, felony, innocent party may not remarry within two years, and guilty party within three years of the divorce.
Nebraska.....	6 mos.	Abandonment two years, habitual drunkenness, physical incapacity, felony, failure to support two years, cruelty.
Nevada.......	6 mos.	Desertion one year, felony, habitual drunkenness, physical incapacity, cruelty, neglect to provide one year.
N.Hampshire	1 year.	Cruelty, felony, physical incapacity, absence three years, habitual drunkenness three years, failure to provide three years, treatment endangering health or reason, union with sect regarding marriage unlawful, wife separate without the State ten years, not claiming marital rights, husband absent from United States three years intending to become citizen of another country.
New Jersey..	(†)	Desertion two years, physical incapacity. No divorce may be obtained on grounds arising in another State unless they constituted ground for divorce in the State where they arose. The marriage may be annulled for the following causes existing at the time of the marriage: Want of legal age, former existing marriage, consanguinity, physical incapacity
New Mexico.	1 year.	Abandonment, cruelty, neglect to provide, habitual drunkenness, felony, physical incapacity, pregnancy of wife by other than husband at marriage.
New York....	(‡)	Adultery only. The marriage may be annulled for such causes as rendered the relationship void at its inception.
N. Carolina...	......	Pregnancy of wife by other than husband at marriage, physical incapacity; husband and wife living apart for ten years and having no issue.
North Dakota	1 year.	Cruelty, desertion one year, neglect one year, habitual drunkenness one year, felony. The marriage may be annulled for the following causes existing at the time of the marriage: Former existing marriage, insanity, physical incapacity, force or fraud inducing the marriage, or want of age.
Ohio...........	1 year.	Absence three years, cruelty, fraud, gross neglect of duty, habitual drunkenness three years, felony, former existing marriage; procurement of divorce without the State by one party, which continues marriage binding upon other party; physical incapacity.
Oklahoma...	1 year.	Abandonment one year, cruelty, fraud, habitual drunkenness, felony, gross neglect of duty, physical incapacity, former existing marriage, pregnancy of wife by other than husband at marriage.
Oregon........	1 year.	Felony, habitual drunkenness one year, physical incapacity, desertion one year, cruelty or personal indignities rendering life burdensome.
Pennsylvania	1 year.	Former existing marriage, desertion two years, personal abuse or conduct rendering life burdensome, felony, fraud, relationship within prohibited degrees, physical incapacity and lunacy.
Rhode Island.	2 years.	Cruelty, desertion five years, habitual drunkenness, excessive use of morphine, opium, or chloral, neglect to provide one year, gross misbehavior, living separate ten years, physical incapacity. Either party civilly dead for crime or prolonged absence. The marriage may be annulled for causes rendering the relationship originally void or voidable.
S. Carolina.....	......	No divorces granted.
South Dakota	1 year.	Cruelty, desertion one year, neglect one year, habitual drunkenness one year, felony. The marriage may be annulled for the following causes existing at the time of the marriage: Want of age, former existing marriage, insanity, physical incapacity, force or fraud inducing marriage.
Tennessee....	2 years.	Former existing marriage, desertion two years, felony, physical incapacity, attempt on life of other party, refusal of wife to live with husband in the State and absenting herself two years, pregnancy of wife by other than husband at marriage; at the discretion of the Court for cruelty, indignities, abandonment, or neglect to provide, habitual drunkenness.
Texas.........	6 mos.	Abandonment three years, physical incapacity, cruelty, excess, or outrages rendering life together insupportable, felony.
Utah.........	1 year.	Desertion one year, neglect to provide, physical incapacity, habitual drunkenness, felony, cruelty, permanent insanity.
Vermont.....	1 year.	Imprisonment three years, intolerable severity, desertion three years, neglect to provide.
Virginia......	1 year.	Insanity at marriage, felony, desertion three years, fugitive from justice two years, pregnancy of wife by other than husband at marriage, wife a prostitute, or either party convicted of felony before marriage unknown to other, physical incapacity.
Washington..	1 year.	Abandonment one year, fraud, habitual drunkenness, refusal to provide, felony, physical incapacity, incurable insanity, cruelty or indignities rendering life burdensome, other cause deemed sufficient by the Court.
West Virginia	1 year.	Desertion three years, felony, physical incapacity, pregnancy of wife by other than husband at marriage, husband a licentious character or wife a prostitute unknown to other party, either party convicted of felony before

* Exclusive of South Carolina, which has no divorce law. † Varies with cause. ‡ Actual residence.

MARRIAGE AND DIVORCE LAWS—*Continued.*

STATES.	Residence Required.	Causes for Absolute Divorce. *In addition to adultery, which is cause for divorce in all the States.**
West Virginia (cont.)		marriage unknown to other. The marriage may be annulled for the following causes existing at the time of the marriage: Former existing marriage, consanguinity, insanity, physical incapacity, miscegenation, want of age.
Wisconsin....	1 year.	Felony, desertion one year, cruelty, physical incapacity, habitual drunkenness one year, separation five years. Divorcee cannot marry for one year. The marriage may be annulled for the following causes existing at the time of the marriage: Want of age, or understanding, consanguinity, force or fraud inducing marriage, where marriage was contracted with former marriage existing, the second marriage is void without any divorce proceedings.
Wyoming.....	1 year.	Felony, desertion one year, habitual drunkenness, cruelty, neglect to provide one year, husband a vagrant, physical incapacity, indignities rendering condition intolerable, pregnancy of wife by other than husband at marriage, either party convicted of felony before marriage unknown to other. The marriage may be annulled for the following causes existing at the time of the marriage: Want of age, force or fraud. The marriage is void without divorce proceedings, consanguinity, insanity, former existing marriage.

*Exclusive of South Carolina, which has no divorce law.

(From Census Bulletin 96, Department of Commerce and Labor.)

THE Bureau of the Census has just completed a compilation of the statistics of marriage and divorce covering a period of twenty years from 1887 to 1906, inclusive. The total number of marriages recorded during the twenty years from 1887 to 1906, inclusive, was 12,832,044. The number annually reported increased from 483,069 in the year 1887 to 853,290 in the year 1906. The increase year by year was by no means uniform. The marriage rate is quickly responsive to changes in economic conditions. A small increase shown for 1893 and an actual decrease in the succeeding year reflect the influence of the panic of 1892, and normal conditions do not appear to have been restored in the matrimonial market until the year 1899. It is computed that if the average annual increase in marriages during the five years ending with 1892 had continued for the next six years, the aggregate number of marriages contracted during the latter period would have been greater than it was by 239,813. It is to be presumed that a considerable number of persons in this large total never contracted marriage.

The number of divorces reported for each State in each twenty-year period and the divorce rate in 1880 and 1900, based on a five-year average, were as follows:

STATE OR TERRITORY.	Total Divorces Granted. 1887 to 1906.	Total Divorces Granted. 1867 to 1886.	Divorce Rate Per 100,000 Population.* 1900.	Divorce Rate Per 100,000 Population.* 1880.
Continental United States	945,625	328,716	73	38
North Atlantic division	142,920	73,503	38	28
Maine	14,194	8,412	117	78
New Hampshire	8,617	4,979	112	85
Vermont	4,740	3,238	75	47
Massachusetts	22,940	9,853	47	30
Rhode Island	6,953	4,462	105	93
Connecticut	9,224	8,542	50	61
New York	29,125	15,355	23	16
New Jersey	7,441	2,642	23	13
Pennsylvania	30,686	16,020	35	21
South Atlantic division	58,603	16,357	33	13
Delaware	887	289	16	10
Maryland	7,920	2,185	40	12
Dist. of Columbia	2,325	1,105	58	31
Virginia	12,129	2,635	38	11
West Virginia	10,308	2,555	64	25
North Carolina	7,047	1,338	24	6
†South Carolina	....	163	..	1
Georgia	10,401	3,959	26	14
Florida	7,586	2,128	79	53
North Central division	434,476	162,830	96	55
Ohio	63,982	26,367	91	48
Indiana	60,721	25,193	142	70
Illinois	82,209	36,072	100	68
Michigan	42,371	18,433	104	72
Wisconsin	22,867	9,988	65	41
Minnesota	15,646	3,623	55	27
Iowa	34,874	16,564	93	60
Missouri	54,766	15,278	103	40
‡North Dakota	4,317	297	88	46
‡South Dakota	7,108	790	95	48
Nebraska	16,711	3,034	82	43
Kansas	28,904	7,191	100	44
South Central division	220,289	49,327	95	35
Kentucky	30,641	10,248	84	35
Tennessee	30,447	9,625	89	38
Alabama	22,807	5,204	69	27
Mississippi	19,903	5,040	74	30
Louisiana	9,785	1,697	41	10
Arkansas	29,541	6,041	136	53
Indian Territory	6,751	...	113	..
Oklahoma	7,669	...	129	..
Texas	62,055	11,472	131	49
Western division	89,337	26,699	129	89
Montana	6,454	822	167	125
Idaho	3,205	368	120	58
Wyoming	1,772	401	118	111
Colorado	15,844	3,687	158	138
New Mexico	2,437	255	73	12
Arizona	2,380	237	120	47
Utah	4,670	4,078	92	114
Nevada	1,045	1,128	111	106
Washington	16,215	906	184	75
Oregon	10,145	2,609	134	92
California	25,170	12,118	108	84

*Based on the annual average of divorce for the five-year period of which the census year is the median year. †All laws permitting divorce were repealed in 1878.

‡Organized from part of Dakota Territory, November 2, 1889. Divorces granted in the counties then comprising Dakota Territory are distributed between North Dakota and South Dakota, according as the counties are now located in one or the other of these States.

Wills.

A WILL OR TESTAMENT is a final disposition of a person's property to take effect after his death. A codicil is an addition or alteration in such disposition. All persons are competent to make a will except idiots, persons of unsound mind, and infants. In many States a will of an unmarried woman is deemed revoked by her subsequent marriage. A nuncupative or unwritten will is one made *orally* by a soldier in active service, or by a mariner while at sea.

In most of the States a will must be in writing, signed by the testator, or by some person in his presence, and by his direction, and attested by witnesses, who must subscribe their names thereto in the *presence* of the testator. The form of wording a will is immaterial as long as its intent is clear.

AGE at which persons may make wills is in most of the States 21 years. Males and females are competent to make wills at 18 years in the following States: California, Connecticut, Hawaiian Islands, Idaho, Montana, Nevada, North Dakota, Oklahoma, South Dakota, Utah; and in the following States only females at 18 years: Colorado, District of Columbia, Illinois, Maryland, Missouri, Washington, Wisconsin.

In the following States persons of 18 years may dispose of personal property only: Alabama, Arkansas, Missouri, Oregon, Rhode Island, Virginia, West Virginia; in Georgia any one over 14 years and in Louisiana any one over 16 years is competent to make a will. In Colorado persons of 17 years, and in New York males of 18 and females of 16 years may dispose of personalty. WITNESSES—Most of the States require two witnesses, except in Connecticut (3), District of Columbia (3), Maine (3), Massachusetts (3), New Hampshire (3), South Carolina (3), Vermont (3).

Acknowledgment of Deeds.

AN ACKNOWLEDGMENT is the act of declaring the execution of an instrument before an officer authorized to certify to such declaration. The officer certifies to the fact of such declaration, and to his knowledge of the person so declaring. Conveyances or deeds of land to be entitled to be recorded must first be acknowledged before a proper officer. Most of the States have forms of acknowledgments, which should be followed.

Acknowledgments may be taken in general by Notaries Public, Justices of the Peace, Judges or Clerks of Courts of the higher grades, Registers, Masters in Chancery, Court Commissioners, Town Clerks, Mayor and Clerks of incorporated cities, within their respective jurisdictions.

The requisites to a valid deed are the same in general as other contracts, but the appointment of an attorney to execute a deed for another person must in general be executed with the same formalities requisite to the deed itself.

SEALS or their equivalent (or whatever is intended as such) are necessary in Alaska, Connecticut, Delaware, District of Columbia, Florida, Idaho, Illinois, Maine, Maryland, Massachusetts, Michigan, Minnesota, Missouri, New Hampshire, New Jersey, New York, North Carolina, Oregon, Pennsylvania, South Carolina, Vermont, Virginia, West Virginia, Wisconsin, Wyoming. In almost all the States deeds by corporations must be under seal. FORMS are prescribed or indicated by the statutes of most of the States except Connecticut, Florida, Louisiana. SEPARATE ACKNOWLEDGMENT by wife is required in Alaska, Arkansas, Delaware, District of Columbia, Florida, Georgia, Idaho, Kentucky, Louisiana, Montana, Nevada, New Jersey, North Carolina, Oregon, Pennsylvania, South Carolina, Tennessee, Texas. ONE WITNESS to the execution of deeds is required in District of Columbia, Maine (customary), Maryland, Nebraska, New Jersey (usual), Oklahoma, Utah, Wyoming. TWO WITNESSES to the execution of deeds are required in Arkansas, Connecticut, Florida, Georgia, Louisiana, Michigan, Minnesota, New Hampshire, Ohio, Oregon, South Carolina, Texas, Vermont, Wisconsin.

Promissory Notes and Checks.

Negotiable instruments, the common forms of which are promissory notes, checks, or other bills of exchange, while having the same general requisites as other contracts, have certain distinct features. The purpose of the law is to facilitate as much as possible their free passing from hand to hand like currency. The assignment of an ordinary contract leaves the assignee in no different position for enforcing his rights than that of his assignor, but one who takes a negotiable instrument from a prior holder, without knowledge of any defences to it, before its maturity, and gives value for it, holds it free of any defences which might have been set up against his predecessors, except those defects that were inherent in the instrument itself.

To be negotiable an instrument must be in writing and signed by the maker (of a note) or drawer (of a bill or check).

It must contain an unconditional promise or order to pay a sum certain in money.

Must be payable on demand, or at a fixed future time.

Must be payable to order or to bearer.

In a bill of exchange (check) the party directed to pay must be reasonably certain.

Every negotiable instrument is presumed to have been issued for a valuable consideration, and want of consideration in the creation of the instrument is not a defence against a bona-fide holder.

An instrument is negotiated, that is completely transferred, so as to vest title in the purchaser, if payable to bearer, or indorsed simply with the name of the last holder, by mere delivery, if payable to order by the indorsement of the party to whom it is payable and delivery.

One who transfers an instrument by indorsement warrants to every subsequent holder that the instrument is genuine, that he has title to it, and that if not paid by the party primarily liable at maturity, he will pay it upon receiving due notice of non-payment.

To hold an indorser liable the holder upon its non-payment at maturity must give prompt notice of such non-payment to the indorser and that the holder looks to the indorser for payment. Such notice should be sent within twenty-four hours.

When an indorser is thus compelled to pay he may hold prior parties through whom he received the instrument liable to him by sending them prompt notice of non-payment upon receiving such notice from the holder.

One who transfers a negotiable instrument by delivery, without indorsing it, simply warrants that the instrument is genuine, that he has title to it, and knows of no defence to it, but does not agree to pay it if unpaid at maturity.

The maker of a note is liable to pay it if unpaid at maturity without any notice from the holder or indorser.

Notice to one of several partners is sufficient notice to all.

When a check is certified by a bank the bank becomes primarily liable to pay it without notice of its non-payment, and when the holder of a check thus obtains its certification by the bank, the drawer of the check and previous indorsers are released from liability, and the holder looks to the bank for payment.

A bona-fide holder of a negotiable instrument, that is, a party who takes an instrument regular on its face, before its maturity, pays value for it and has no knowledge of any defences to it, is entitled to hold the party primarily liable responsible for its payment, despite any defences he may have against the party to whom he gave it, except such as rendered the instrument void in its inception. Thus, if the maker of a note received no Value for it, or was induced to issue it through fraud or imposition, they do not defeat the right of a bona-fide holder to compel its payment from him.

The following States have enacted a similar Negotiable Instrument law: Colorado, Connecticut, District of Columbia, Florida, Maryland, Massachusetts, North Carolina, North Dakota, Pennsylvania, Oregon, Rhode Island, Utah, Virginia, Washington, Wisconsin, New York, and Tennessee—and the same general rules apply in all the States.

Distribution of Intestate's Personal Estate.

The following is a synopsis of the laws of the various States providing for the distribution of the personal estate of a deceased after the payment of funeral expenses and other debts where there is no will:

In many of the States the widow and children are entitled to receive a small portion of the estate, generally varying from $100 to $500, before the claims of creditors are paid. Aside from such exempt portion of the estate, the property to be distributed to the widow or relatives is that remaining after all creditors' claims have been satisfied.

The following is the plan of distribution of a male's property. The same rules apply to a female's estate, except in some States, where the rights of a husband in the estate of his deceased wife differ from those of a wife in the estate of her deceased husband, which will be shown in a separate table.

I. In all States where the deceased leaves a child or children, or descendants of any deceased child, and no widow, the children or descendants take the entire estate, to the exclusion of all other relatives. The children take equal shares, and in most States the descendants of a deceased child together take the share of their parent, except where the descendants are all in equal degree to the deceased (all grandchildren, no children surviving), when they share equally and do not take their proportionate share of their parent's interest.

No statement is given in this synopsis of the law of Louisiana, which, being founded on the provisions of the French code and Roman law instead of the English common law, which is the underlying principle in the other States, differs in many respects from the principles followed in the other States, especially on the question of the rights of a husband and wife in each other's property and in the property acquired by the husband and wife during their married life. The provisions of the law of Indiana are also not included, for the reason that for an accurate statement of its provisions a reading of the entire statute is necessary, together with the decisions of the Indiana courts construing its provisions, which would occupy too much space for a statement here.

II. (a) If deceased leaves a widow, and no children or descendants, the widow takes all. This is the rule in Alabama, Arizona, Colorado, Florida, Georgia, Illinois, Kansas, Minnesota, Mississippi, New Mexico, Ohio, Oregon, Tennessee, Texas, Washington, West Virginia, and Wisconsin.

(b) In the following States the widow takes one-half, the residue being taken by the other relatives in the manner and proportion in which they take the entire estate when the deceased leaves neither widow or descendants (given below): Arkansas, California, Delaware, District of Columbia, Idaho, Iowa, Kentucky, Maine, Maryland, Missouri, Montana, Nevada, New Jersey, North Carolina, Oklahoma, Pennsylvania, Rhode Island, South Carolina, South Dakota, and Virginia.

(c) In Massachusetts, North Dakota, and Utah the widow takes the entire estate up to $5,000 and one-half of the residue.

(d) In Connecticut and Vermont the widow takes the entire estate up to $2,000 and one-half the residue.

(e) In New York, in case deceased leaves a father surviving, the widow takes one-half; if no father surviving, the widow takes one-half and $2,000 in addition.

(f) In New Hampshire the widow takes $1,500, and, if the estate exceeds $3,000, one-half of the residue.

(g) In Wyoming the widow takes the entire estate up to $10,000 and three-fourths of the residue.

(h) In Nebraska the widow takes the use of the entire estate for her life.

(i) In Michigan the widow takes the entire estate up to $3,000 and one-half of the residue.

III. (a) When the deceased leaves a widow and children, or descendants, the widow takes one-third and the children share equally in the residue in the following States: Arizona, Arkansas, Connecticut, Delaware, District of Columbia, Illinois, Iowa, Maine, Maryland, Massachusetts, Minnesota, New Hampshire, New Jersey, New York, Ohio (one-half if less than $400), Pennsylvania, Rhode Island, South Carolina, Texas, Vermont, Virginia, and West Virginia.

(b) In the following States, if there be but one child, the widow takes one-half and the child one-half; if two or more children or their descendants, the widow takes one-third, as above, and the children or their descendants the residue: California, Florida, Idaho, Michigan, Montana, Nevada, North Dakota, Oklahoma, South Dakota, and Utah.

(c) In the following States the widow takes one-half and the children, or descendants, the residue: Colorado, Kansas, Kentucky, Oregon, Washington, and Wyoming.

(d) In the following States the widow takes the same share as each of the children: Mississippi, Missouri, Nebraska, Tennessee, and Wisconsin.

(e) In North Carolina, if there are less than three children, the widow takes one-third and the children the residue; if there are three or more children, the widow takes the same share as each of the children.

(f) In Alabama, if there is but one child, the widow takes one-half and the child one-half; if there are more than one child and less than five children, the widow takes the same share as each of the children; if there are five or more children, the widow takes one-fifth and the children or their descendants share equally in the residue.

(g) In Georgia, if there are less than five children, the widow takes the same share as each of the children; if there are five or more children, the widow takes one-fifth and the children or their descendants share equally in the residue.

(h) In New Mexico, the widow takes one-half of the estate acquired during marriage, otherwise than by gift (by purchase, for example) and the children or their descendants share equally in the residue; the widow also takes one-fourth of the estate acquired before marriage, or by gift or legacy during marriage, the children or their descendants taking the residue.

IV. (a) When the deceased leaves no widow, children or descendants, the parents take the entire estate in equal shares in the following States: Alabama, Arizona, California, Connecticut, Idaho, Iowa, Kansas, Kentucky, Maine, Massachusetts, Michigan, Minnesota, Montana, New Hampshire, New Mexico, Pennsylvania, Texas, Utah, Vermont, Washington, Wisconsin, and Wyoming.

In all of the States just mentioned, except Alabama, Arizona, Maine, and Texas, if one parent is dead, the surviving parent takes the entire estate, to the exclusion of brothers and sisters. In Alabama, Arizona, Maine, and Texas the surviving parent takes one-half and the brothers and sisters, or their descendants, take the residue.

In all of them, if both parents are dead, the brothers and sisters and their descendants take the entire estate.

(b) In the following States the father, if living, takes the entire estate; if the father is dead, then to the mother and brothers and sisters, or their descendants equally; and if both parents are dead, then to the brothers and sisters, or their descendants: Florida, Maryland, Nebraska, New Jersey, New York, Oklahoma, Oregon, Rhode Island, South Dakota, Tennessee, Virginia, and West Virginia.

(c) In the following States the father, if living, takes the entire estate; if the father is dead, then to the mother; and if both parents are dead, then to the brothers and sisters, or their descendants: Arkansas, Colorado, District of Columbia, Nevada, North Carolina, and North Dakota.

(d) In the following States the parents, if living, and the brothers and sisters, or their descendants, take the entire estate, sharing equally. Georgia, Illinois, Mississippi, Missouri, and South Carolina.

(e) In Delaware and Ohio the brothers and sisters, or their descendants, take the entire estate in preference to the parents, who only inherit if there are no brothers or sisters or lawful issue of any deceased brothers or sisters.

DISTRIBUTION OF FEMALE'S ESTATE.

In the following States, if the deceased was a married woman, the rights of her surviving husband in her personal estate differ from the rights of a widow in the estate of her deceased husband as shown in the above synopsis.

(a) In Delaware, District of Columbia, New Jersey, North Carolina, Rhode Island, and Virginia the husband takes the entire personal estate, whether there is any issue of the marriage or not.

(b) In New York, if there are no children or descendants of children, the husband takes the entire estate.

(c) In Florida, Georgia, and Pennsylvania, if there are no children or descendants, the husband takes the entire estate; if there are children, the husband takes the same share as each child.

(d) In Ohio the husband takes the entire estate if there are no children or descendants; if there are children or descendants, they take the entire estate.

(e) In Alabama the husband takes one-half of the estate, the children, or descendants, taking the residue.

Law Examinations in New York State.

To entitle an applicant to an examination as an attorney and counsellor he shall pay to the examiners a fee of $10, and he must prove (15 days in advance) to the satisfaction of the State Board of Law Examiners: 1. That he is a citizen of the State, twenty-one years of age, and that his residence for six months prior to the examination is actual and not constructive, which proof must be made by his own affidavit. 2. That he has studied law in the manner and according to the conditions prescribed for a period of three years, except that if the applicant is a graduate of any college or university his period of study may be two years instead of three; and except also that persons who have been admitted as attorneys in the highest court of original jurisdiction of another State or country, and have remained therein as practicing attorneys for at least one year, may be admitted to such examination after a period of law study of one year within this State. 3. That the applicant has passed the regents' examination or its equivalent must be proved by the production of a certified copy of the regents' certificate filed in the office of the Clerk of the Court of Appeals.

Address communications concerning law examinations to F. M. Danaher, Secretary, Albany, N. Y.

Law of Contracts.

A contract is an agreement of two or more parties, by which reciprocal rights and obligations are created. One party acquires a right, enforceable at law, to some act or forbearance from the other, who is under a corresponding obligation to thus act or forbear.

Generally speaking, all contracts which are made between two competent parties, for a proper consideration, without fraud and for a lawful purpose, are enforceable at law.

To the creation of a valid contract there must be:

1. Precise agreement. The offer of one party must be met by an acceptance by the other, according to the terms offered.
2. There must be a consideration. Something of value must either be received by one party or given up by the other.
3. The parties must have capacity to contract. The contracts of insane persons are not binding upon them. Married women are now generally permitted to contract as though single, and bind their

separate property. The contracts of an infant are generally not binding upon him, unless ratified after attaining his majority. The contracts of an infant for "necessaries" may be enforced against him to the extent of the reasonable value of the goods furnished. It is incumbent upon one seeking thus to hold an infant to show that the goods furnished were in fact necessary to the infant, and that he was not already supplied by his parents or guardians.

4. The party's consent must not be the result of fraud or imposition, or it may be avoided by the party imposed upon.

5. The purpose of the parties must be lawful. Agreements to defraud others, to violate statutes, or whose aim is against public policy, such as to create monopolies, or for the corrupt procurement of legislative or official action, are void, and cannot be enforced by any party thereto.

Contracts in general are equally valid, whether made orally or in writing, with the exception of certain classes of contracts, which in most of the States are required to be attested by a note or memorandum in writing, signed by the party or his agent sought to be held liable. Some of the provisions, which are adopted from the old **English Statute of Frauds,** vary in some of the States, but the following contracts very generally are required to be thus attested by some writing:

Contracts by their terms not to be performed within a year from the making thereof.

A promise to answer for the debt, default, or miscarriage of another person.

Contracts made in consideration of marriage, except mutual promises to marry.

Promise of an executor, or administrator, to pay debts of deceased out of his own property.

Contracts for the creation of any interest or estate in land, with the exception of leases for a short term, generally one year.

Contracts for the sale of goods above a certain value, unless a portion of the price is paid or part of the goods delivered. The required value of the goods sold varies in different States from $30 to $200. In a number of the States no such provision exists.

In many of the States declarations or conveyances of trust estates.

In many States representations as to the character, credit, or responsibility of another person.

Partial performance of the contract is generally held to dispense with the necessity for a writing.

If the damages liable to result from the breaking of a contract are uncertain, the parties may agree upon a sum to which either may be entitled as compensation for a breach, which will be upheld by the courts, but if the sum so fixed is not designed as a fair compensation to the party injured, but as a penalty to be inflicted, it will be disregarded.

A party is generally excused for the failure to perform what he has agreed only by the act of God or the public enemy. Except in cases involving a personal element in the work to be performed, such as the rendition of services, when the death or sickness of the party contracting to perform them is a valid excuse, or contracts for the performance of work upon a specified object, when its destruction without the fault of the party sought to be held liable is a sufficient excuse.

The Hudson-Fulton Celebration, 1909.

It is proposed to celebrate in the City and State of New York, during the eight days beginning on Saturday, September 25, 1909, the three hundredth anniversary of the discovery of the Hudson River by Henry Hudson in 1609, and the one hundredth anniversary of the first successful application of steam to the navigation of the river by Robert Fulton in 1807.

This Commission was formed by merging the Hudson-Tri-Centennial Association, formed in 1902, with Thomas Powell Fowler as President; the Hudson-Ter-Centenary Joint Committee, appointed by the Governor of the State and the Mayor of the City of New York in 1905, and of which the late Hon. Robert B. Roosevelt was Chairman, and the Fulton Centennial Celebration Committee, appointed by the Mayor of New York in 1905 upon the initiative of the New York Board of Trade and Transportation, and of which the Hon. William McCarroll was Chairman.

These were consolidated and incorporated by Chapter 325 of the Laws of 1906 under the title of the Hudson-Fulton Celebration Commission. It consists of 304 members, either named in the charter or appointed by the Governor of the State or the Mayor of the City of New York, including the Mayors of the 46 cities of the State and the Presidents of 38 incorporated villages on the Hudson River. Its officers and Executive Committee are as follows:

Gen. Stewart L. Woodford, 18 Wall Street, New York, President; Herman Ridder, Presiding Vice-President and Acting President; Andrew Carnegie, Hon. Joseph H. Choate, Rear-Admiral J. B. Coghlan (U. S. N.), Major-General F. D. Grant, Hon. Seth Low, J. Pierpont Morgan, Hon. Levi P. Morton, John E. Parsons, Gen. Horace Porter, Hon. Frederick W. Seward, Francis Lynde Stetson, Hon. Oscar S. Straus, William B. Van Rensselaer, Hon. Andrew D. White, Vice-Presidents; Isaac N. Seligman, 1 William Street, New York, Treasurer; Col. Henry W. Sackett, Tribune Building, New York, Secretary; Edward Hagaman Hall, Tribune Building, New York, Assistant Secretary.

Executive Committee—Gen. Stewart L. Woodford, 18 Wall Street, New York, Chairman; John E. Parsons, Vice-Chairman; Hon. James M. Beck, Tunis G. Bergen, Hon. William Berri, Andrew Carnegie, Hon. Joseph H. Choate, Sir Caspar Purdon Clarke, Rear-Admiral J. B. Coghlan (U. S. N.), William J. Curtis, Theodore Fitch, Major-General F. D. Grant, Edward Hagaman Hall, Col. William Jay, Dr. George F. Kunz, John La Farge, Hon. Seth Low, Hon. William McCarroll, Commandant Jacob W. Miller, Frank D. Millet, J. Pierpont Morgan, Hon. Levi P. Morton, Hon. Morgan J. O'Brien, Eben E. Olcott, Hon. George W. Perkins, Hon. N. Taylor Phillips, Gen. Horace Porter, Louis C. Raegener, Herman Ridder, Col. Henry W. Sackett, Isaac N. Seligman, Hon. Frederick W. Seward, J. Edward Simmons, Hon. John H. Starin, Francis Lynde Stetson, Hon. Oscar S. Straus, Spencer Trask, William B. Van Rensselaer, Lieut.-Commander Aaron Vanderbilt, Dr. Samuel B. Ward, Hon. Andrew D. White, Hon. William R. Willcox and Gen. James Grant Wilson.

There are about 45 other working committees.

PLAN OF CELEBRATION.

The following revised plan of celebration, submitted by the Committee on Plan and Scope, was adopted by the Commission, April 22, 1908:

RELIGIOUS SERVICE DAYS (SATURDAY, SEPTEMBER 25, and SUNDAY, SEPTEMBER 26, 1909).

Religious observances by those who are accustomed to worship on Saturday and Sunday.

RECEPTION DAY (MONDAY, SEPTEMBER 27, 1909).

General decoration of public and private buildings from New York to the head of the river.

Rendezvous of American and foreign vessels at New York.

Fac-simile of Hudson's Half Moon to enter the river, be formally received and take her place in line.

Fac-simile of Fulton's Clermont to start from original site with appropriate exercises and take position in line.

Visiting guests to disembark and be officially received.

Typical Indian Village at Inwood to be established by American Museum of Natural History.

In the evening a musical festival in New York City.

HISTORICAL DAY (TUESDAY, SEPTEMBER 28, 1909).

Commemorative exercises in Columbia University, New York University, College of City of New York, Cooper Union, University of St. John at Fordham, Hebrew University, Brooklyn Institute of Arts and Sciences, Public Schools, Historical Societies, and all the universities, colleges and institutions of learning throughout the State of New York; with free lectures for the people in New York City, under the auspices of the Board of Education.

Exhibits of paintings, prints, books, models, relics, etc., by Metropolitan Museum of Art, the American Museum of Natural History, the Hispanic Museum, the American Numismatic Society, the New York Public Library, the New York Historical Society, the New York Genealogical and Biographical Society, the American Geographical Society, Webb's School for Shipbuilders, the New York Yacht Club, and similar institutions throughout the State. If practicable, some of these exhibits may open earlier in the year and extend over a period of several months.

During the day visiting guests will be shown about the City of New York. (An Historical Pageant had been proposed for Tuesday and was under consideration November 17, 1908.)

In the evening the Official Literary Exercises will be held in the Metropolitan Opera House and Carnegie Hall.

MILITARY PARADE DAY (WEDNESDAY, SEPTEMBER 29, 1909).

Military parade, participated in by the United States Army, the United States Navy and Marine Corps, the National Guard and the Naval Militia.

In the evening reception to the official guests at the headquarters of the Department of the East on Governor's Island.

DEDICATION DAY (THURSDAY, SEPTEMBER 30, 1909).

Dedication of parks and memorials along the Hudson River. Efforts are being made to secure not only great memorials like Inwood Hill Park, the Hudson Memorial Bridge, the Verplanck's Point Park, the completion of the Palisades Drive, etc., but also the creation of parks, institutions or other public memorials in local communities along the Hudson.

The interest of historical and patriotic societies has been enlisted for the erection of monuments and tablets.

The programme for the day contemplates also:

Aquatic sports on the Hudson River, designed in the first instance for friendly competition between the crews of the naval vessels, but which may embrace motor boat races and such other amusements as may seem practicable and desirable.

A reception to Visiting guests at West Point during the day.

An official banquet in honor of distinguished guests in the City of New York in the evening.

HUDSON RIVER DAY (FRIDAY, OCTOBER 1, 1909).

Naval parade of the navy, merchant marine, excursion boats and pleasure craft from New York to Newburgh, taking with them the fac-similes of the Half Moon and Clermont.

Fetes champetres along the river-sides from New York to Newburgh.

Simultaneously with the advance of the Southern Hudson Division, a counter procession from Albany to Newburgh, the two divisions meeting and holding appropriate ceremonies at Newburgh. The delivery of the Half Moon and Clermont to the North Hudson Division will form a feature of these exercises.

CARNIVAL DAY (SATURDAY, OCTOBER 2, 1909).

Return of the two divisions of the naval parade to their respective starting points.

Children's fetes in public and private parks and playgrounds.

Grand carnival parade in New York City in the evening.

Illumination of the river from New York to Troy by signal fires and pyrotechnics on the mountain tops and other eligible points; illuminations of fleet in New York Harbor, and illuminations of streets and buildings in cities and Villages.

OLD HOME WEEK (SUNDAY, OCTOBER 3, TO SATURDAY, OCTOBER 9, 1909).

It has been suggested that the celebration be prolonged another week in order that communities along the Hudson River might have an opportunity for a series of "old home days," but this feature was not decided upon.

Soon after the Commission was formed a World's Fair at or near New York City was suggested. After giving several public hearings, the subject was referred to the Plan and Scope Committee, who, in their preliminary report, expressed the belief that the country had been surfeited with such temporary celebrations, and voiced the hope that the celebration of 1909 would be conducted on a plan which would leave monumental works of lasting benefit to the people.

Railroad Statistics.

MILEAGE, ASSETS, LIABILITIES, EARNINGS, EXPENDITURES, AND TRAFFIC OF SURFACE STEAM RAILROADS IN THE UNITED STATES.

This table was compiled from "Poor's Manual of Railroads of the United States for 1908."

Mileage of Railroads	224,382.19
Second Tracks and Sidings	99,651.19
Total Track	324,033.38
Steel Rails in Track	314,713.50
Iron Rails in Track	9,319.88
Locomotives	58,301
Cars, Passenger	35,321
" Baggage, Mail, etc.	11,952
" Freight	2,084,214
Total Revenue Cars	2,131,487
Liabilities.	
Capital Stock	$7,458,126,785
Bonded Debt§	9,043,286,284
Unfunded Debt	170,389,175
Current Accounts	857,734,167
Sinking and Other Funds	239,727,545
Total Liabilities	$17,769,263,956
Assets.	
Cost of Railroad and Equipment	$13,364,275,191
Other Investments	3,622,874,372
Sundry Assets	592,000,966
Current Accounts	979,730,908
Total Assets	$18,558,881,437
Excess of Assets over Liabilities	$789,617,481

Miles of Railroad Operated	225,227.23
Passenger Train Mileage	511,579,317
Freight " "	645,447,465
Mixed " "	27,211,527
Total	1,184,238,309
Passengers Carried	860,648,574
Passenger Mileage	28,166,116,577
Tons of Freight Moved	1,722,210,281
Freight Mileage	228,137,507,807
Traffic Earnings.	
Passengers	$574,718,578
Freight	1,825,061,858
Miscellaneous	202,977,067
Total Traffic Revenue	$2,602,757,503
Net Earnings	$833,839,600
Receipts from Other Sources	128,015,081
Total Available Revenue	$961,354,681
Payments.	
Interest on Bonds	$280,931,001
Other Interest	23,759,329
Dividends on Stock	247,258,219
Miscellaneous	75,176,725
Rentals—Interest	38,188,406
Dividends	31,087,374
Miscellaneous	18,127,456
Taxes	74,253,215
Total Payments	$788,781,755
Surplus	$172,572,926

§ Including, in 1907, 1906, 1905 and 1904, real estate mortgages, equipment, trust obligations, etc., previously included in item "unfunded debt."

COMPARATIVE STATISTICS OF RAILROADS IN THE UNITED STATES, 1897-1907.

Year.	Miles Operated.	Capital Stock.	Bonded Debt.	Gross Earnings.	Net Earnings.	Interest Paid.	Dividends Paid
1897	181,133	$5,453,782,046	$5,411,058,525	$1,132,866,626	$338,170,195	$231,046,819	$82,630,989
1898	184,194	5,581,522,858	5,635,363,594	1,249,558,724	389,666,474	237,133,099	94,937,526
1899	186,280	5,742,181,181	5,644,858,027	1,336,096,379	423,941,689	239,178,973	109,032,252
1900	191,511	5,804,346,250	5,758,592,754	1,501,695,378	483,247,526	244,447,806	140,343,653
1901	195,886	5,978,796,249	6,035,469,741	1,612,448,826	520,294,727	261,645,714	156,887,283
1902	197,381	6,078,290,596	6,465,290,839	1,720,814,900	560,026,277	263,237,451	178,200,752
1903	206,876	6,355,207,335	6,722,216,517	1,908,857,826	592,508,512	278,101,828	190,674,415
1904	211,074	6,477,045,374	7,475,840,203	1,977,638,713	639,240,027	275,800,200	211,522,166
1905	212,624	6,741,956,825	7,821,243,106	2,112,197,770	685,464,488	270,315,290	203,675,622
1906	218,476	7,106,408,976	7,851,107,778	2,346,640,286	790,187,712	309,538,574	253,340,925
1907	225,227	7,458,126,785	9,043,286,284	2,602,757,503	833,339,600	319,119,407	278,345,593

SUMMARY OF RAILWAY MILEAGE IN THE UNITED STATES.

(From Statistical Report of the Interstate Commerce Commission.)

Year.	Mileage on June 30, of Years Mentioned.				Miles of Line per 100 Sq. Miles.	Miles of Line per 10,000 Inhabitants.
	Official.	Unofficial.	Total.	Increase Over Preceding Year.		
1907	227,670.85	2,280.34	‡229,951.19	5,588.02	*7.74	†27.02
1906	222,571.52	1,791.65	224,363.17	6,262.13	7.55	26.78
1905	217,017.68	1,083.36	218,101.04	4,196.70	7.34	26.44
1904	212,577.57	1,326.77	213,904.34	5,927.12	7.20	26.34
1903	207,186.84	790.38	207,977.22	5,505.37	7.00	26.03
1902	201,672.83	799.02	202,471.85	5,234.41	6.82	25.76
1901	196,075.07	1,162.37	197,237.44	3,891.66	6.64	25.52
1900	192,940.67	405.11	193,345.78	4,051.12	6.51	25.44
1899	188,277.49	1,017.17	189,294.66	2,898.34	6.37	25.34
1898	185,370.77	1,025.55	186,396.32	1,967.85	6.28	25.40

* For 1900 and subsequent years on basis of 2,970,038 square miles, which covers "land surface" only, and excludes Alaska and Hawaii.

† On basis of 85,094,575 population for 1907, which is reached by adding to population of the United States in 1900, 75,994,575 (which excludes Alaska, Hawaii, and persons in the military and naval service stationed abroad), an estimated annual increase of 1,300,000 for each successive year. Averages for 1898 and 1899, based on an annual increase in population of 1,304,686, the population for 1890 being 62,947,714.

‡ Excludes mileage in Alaska (145.89) and Hawaii.

Principal Railroad Systems of United States and Canada

WITH A SYNOPSIS OF LAST ANNUAL REPORT OF INCOME AND EXPENDITURE AS SUBMITTED TO "THE WORLD ALMANAC" BY THE RAILROAD COMPANIES.

Systems, Location, and Financial Data.	Divisions, Mileage, and Operating Express.	General Officers.
Atchison, Topeka and Santa Fe Ry. System.—"Santa Fe." [Illinois, Iowa, Missouri, Kansas, Nebraska, Colorado, Texas, New Mexico, Arizona, California, Oklahoma, Louisiana, Nevada.] *For year ending June* 30, 1908. Total earnings......$90,617,796 Operating expenses 64,068,559 Net earnings......$26,549,237 Other income....... 671,910 Total net income.$27,221,147 Total payments...... 25,335,268 Surplus.......... $1,885,879	Atchison, Topeka and Santa Fé Ry., 5,629.91 m.; Coast Lines, 1,909.13 m.; Southern Kansas Ry. of Texas, 129.17 m.; Santa Fé, Prescott & Phœnix Ry., 125.07 m.; Eastern Ry. of New Mexico, 434.15 m. Total mileage, 9,745.61. Express Co.—Wells, Fargo & Co.	President, E. P. Ripley, Chicago, Ill.; Vice-Presidents, J. W. Kendrick, G. T. Nicholson and W. B. Jansen, Chicago, Ill.; General Managers, J. E. Hurley, Topeka, Kan.; A. G. Wells, Los Angeles, Cal.; F. G. Pettibone, Galveston, Texas; Freight Traffic Manager, J. E. Gorman, Chicago, Ill.; Passenger Traffic Manager, W. J. Black, Chicago, Ill.; Secretary, E. L. Copeland, Topeka, Kan.; Assistant Secretary, L. C. Deming, New York. General Offices, Chicago, Ill., and Topeka, Kan.; New York Offices, 5 Nassau St., 377 Broadway.
Atlantic Coast Line R. R. [Virginia, North Carolina, South Carolina, Georgia, Florida, Alabama.] *For year ending June* 30, 1908. Total earnings.....$26,029,052 Operating expenses 18,971,742 Net earnings.... . $7,057,310 Other income...... 3,146,376 Total net income.$10,203,686 Total payments.... 7,422,538 Surplus........... $2,781,148	Virginia, 139.06 m.; North Carolina, 1,014.38 m.; South Carolina, 872,57 m.; Georgia, 713.77 m.; Florida, 1,419.96 m.; Alabama, 246.89 m. Total mileage, 4,406.63. Express Co.—Southern.	President, T. M. Emerson; 1st Vice-President, Alex. Hamilton, Petersburg, Va.; 2d Vice-President, C. S. Gadsden, Charleston, S. C.; 3d Vice-President, J. R. Kenly; General Manager, W. N. Royall; Secretary, H. L. Borden, New York. General Offices, Wilmington, N. C.; New York Offices, 71, 407, and 1218 Broadway.
Baltimore & Ohio R. R. [New Jersey, Pennsylvania, Delaware, Maryland, District of Columbia, Virginia, West Virginia, Ohio, Illinois, Indiana, Kentucky, Missouri.] *For year ending June* 30, 1908. Total earnings......$73,608,781 Operating expenses 54,150,879 Net earnings.....$19 457,902 Other income...... 4,354,743 Total net income.$23 812,645 Total payments.... 13,655,857 Surplus...........$10,156,788	Lines included in income account, 4,006.32 m.; affiliated lines, 455.78 m. Total mileage, 4,462.10. Express Co.—United States.	President, O. G. Murray; 1st Vice-President, George F. Randolph; 2d Vice-President, H. L. Bond; 3d Vice-President, G. L. Potter; 4th Vice-President, J. V. McNeal; Secretary, C. W. Woolford; Manager Freight Traffic, C. S. Wight; Manager Passenger Traffic, D. B. Martin. General Offices, Baltimore, Md.; New York Offices, 2 Wall Street, 434 Broadway. General Offices B. & O. S. W. Div., Cincinnati, O.; New York Office, 2 Wall Street.
Bangor and Aroostook Railroad. [Maine.] *For year ending June* 30, 1908. Total earnings...... $2,844,082 Operating expenses 1,799,820 Net earnings..... $1,044,260 Total payments.... 1,034,382 Surplus.......... $9,878	Brownville to Caribou, 154 95 m.; Oldtown to Greenville, 76 m.; Fort Fairfield Junction to Fort Fairfield, 13.30 m.; Ashland Junction to Fort Kent, 94.89 m.; Caribou to Van Buren, 33.11 m.; Milo Junction to Katahdin Iron Works, 18.95 m.; Patten Junction to Patten, 5.67 m.; Caribou to Limestone, 15.72 m.; Spurs, 15.86 m.; South Lagrange to Searsport, 54.13 m.; Millinocket to East Millinocket, 8 m.; Medford Extension (new line), 29.45 m. Total mileage, 514.67. Express Co.—American.	President, F. W. Cram; Vice-President, Percy R. Todd. General Offices, Bangor, Me.
Boston and Albany R. R. [Massachusetts, New York.] *Earnings, expenses, etc., reported by New York Central and Hudson River R. R. Co., Lessee.*	Main Line, Boston, Mass., to Albany, N. Y., 200 m.; Ware River Br., 49 m.; Athol Br., 45 m.; Pittsfield and North Adams Br., 19 m.; Hudson and Chatham Br., 17 m.; Milford Br., 12 m.; Webster Br., 11 m.; other branches, 39 m. Total mileage, 392. Express Co.—American.	Vice-President and General Manager, A. H. Smith, New York, Assistant General Manager, J. H. Hustis, General Offices, Boston, Mass.

Systems, Location, and Financial Data.	Divisions, Mileage, and Operating Express.	General Officers.
Boston and Maine Railroad. [New York, Massachusetts, Vermont, New Hampshire, Maine, Quebec.] *For year ending June* 30, 1908. Total earnings.....$38,990,748 Operating expenses 29,354,196 Net earnings......$ 9,636,552 Other income ..... 757,799 Total net income. $10,394,351 Total payments ... 9,642,855 Surplus........... $ 751,496 Less Dividends, etc. 2,161,157 Deficit............ $1,409,661	Western Div. (Boston to Portland), 115.31 m.; Eastern Div. (Boston to Portland), 108.29 m.; Conway Jct., Me., to Intervale Jct., N.H., 73.37 m.; Worcester, Mass., to Portland, Me., 148.34 m.; Boston, Mass., to Groveton, N. H., 221.84 m.; Concord, N. H., to White River Jct., Vt., 69.50 m.; White River Jct., Vt., to Lennoxville, P. Q., 142.25 m.; N. Cambridge Jct. to Northampton, Mass., 95.69 m.; Springfield, Mass., to Keene, N.H., 74 m.; Boston to Rotterdam Jct. and Troy, 250.98 m.; Ashburnham Jct. to Bellows Falls, 53.85 m.; other branches, 934.10 m. Total mileage, 2,287.52. Express Co.—American.	President, Lucius Tuttle; 2d Vice-President and General Traffic Manager, W. F. Berry; 3d Vice-President and General Manager, Frank Barr; 4th Vice-President, W. J. Hobbs; Freight Traffic Manager, M. T. Donovan; Passenger Traffic Manager, D. J. Flanders; General Superintendent, C. E. Lee. General Offices, Boston, Mass.
Buffalo, Rochester and Pittsburgh Railway. [New York, Pennsylvania.] *For year ending June* 30, 1908. Total earnings..... $7,422,236 Operating expenses 5,154,217 Net earnings..... $2,268,018 Other income....... 617,263 Total net income $2,885,281 Total payments.... 1,849,089 Surplus........... $1,036,192	Main Line and branches, 347.86 m.; leased lines, 94.04 m.; trackage rights, 125.87 m. Total mileage, 567.77. Express Co.—American.	President, Arthur G. Yates, Rochester, N. Y.; Vice-President, Adrian Iselin, Jr., New York; General Manager, W. T. Noonan; Secretary, John H. Hocart, New York. General Offices, Rochester, N. Y.; New York Office, 36 Wall Street.
Canadian Northern Ry. [Manitoba, Saskatchewan, Alberta, Ontario, Minnesota.] *For year ending June* 30, 1908. Total earnings..... $9,709,462 Operating expenses 6,676,775 Net earnings..... $3,032,687 Total payments.... 2,353,757 Surplus........... $678,929	Total mileage, 2,894.9. Express Co.—Canadian Northern.	President, Wm. Mackenzie, Toronto, Ont.; Vice-President, D. D. Mann, Toronto, Ont.; 3d Vice-President, D. B. Hanna, Toronto, Ont.; Traffic Manager, Geo. H. Shaw, Winnipeg, Man.
Canadian Pacific Ry. [New Brunswick, Maine, Quebec, Ontario, Michigan, Manitoba, Assiniboia, Saskatchewan, Alberta, British Columbia.] *For year ending June* 30, 1908. Total earnings.....$71,884,173 Operating expenses 49,591,807 Net earnings.....$21,792,366 Other income...... 2,654,633 Total net income.$24,446,999 Total payments.... 18,867,283 Surplus.......... $5,579,715	Eastern Div., 1,275.5 m.; Ontario Div., 1,195.5 m.; Atlantic Div., 689.2 m.; Western Div., 1,833.4 m.; Pacific Div., 1,000.6 m.; Lake Superior Div., 981.7 m.; Central Div., 2,450.5 m. Total mileage, 9,426.4. Length of Main Line, Montreal to Vancouver, 2,908.4 m. Steamship lines: Vancouver, B. C., to Japan, China, Honolulu, H. I., Australia, Sydney, N. S. W.; Slocan Lake Line; Upper Lake Line; Lake Okanagan Line; Columbia and Kootenay Line; Atlantic Ocean—Liverpool to Montreal. Express Co.—Dominion.	Chairman of the Board, W. C. Van Horne; President, T. G. Shaughnessy; Vice-President, D. McNicoll; 2d Vice-President, Wm. Whyte, Winnipeg, Man.; 3d Vice-President, I. G. Ogden; 4th Vice-President, G. M. Bosworth; Secretary, W. R. Baker. General Offices, Montreal, Quebec; New York Offices, 31 Pine Street, 458 Broadway.
Central of Georgia Ry. [Georgia, Alabama, and Tennessee.] *For year ending June* 30, 1908 Total earnings......$11,383,013 Operating expenses. 8,504,207 Net earnings.......$2,878,806 Other income........ 440,637 Total net income..$3,319,443 Total payments..... 3,324,870 Deficit............. $5,427	Columbus-Andalusia, 138 m.; Griffin-Chattanooga, 198 m.; Macon-Athens, 105 m.; Savannah-Atlanta, 294 m.; Birmingham-Macon, 257 m.; Ft. Valley-Montgomery, 194 m.; Smithville-Lockhart, 178 m.; other branches, 551.9 m. Total mileage, 1,915.9. Express Co.—Southern.	President, J. F. Hanson, Macon, Ga.; 1st Vice-President, A. R. Lawton; 2d Vice-President, W. A. Winburn; General Manager, T. S. Moise; Secretary, C. C. Williams, Macon, Ga. General Offices, Savannah, Ga.; New York Office, 317 Broadway.
Central Railroad of New Jersey. [New York, New Jersey, Pennsylvania.] *For year ending June* 30, 1908 Total earnings.....$25,587,176 Operating expenses 15,466,638 Net earnings.....$10,120,538 Other receipts...... 1,432,539 Total net income. $11,553,077 Total payments... 6,429,604 Surplus.......... $5,123,473	New York to Scranton, 191.67 m.; Newark Br., 10.62 m.; South Br., 15.78 m.; Perth Amboy Br., 23.56 m.; High Bridge Br., 55.80 m.; sundry branches in New Jersey, 23.08 m.; sundry branches in Pennsylvania, 91.18 m.; New Jersey Southern Div., 174.24 m.; Freehold and Atlantic Highlands Div., 24.47 m.; New York and Long Branch R. R., 38.04 m. Total mileage, 648.44. Express Co.—United States. On New York and Long Branch R. R., Adams; United States.	President, George F. Baer; Vice-President, R. W. De Forest; Vice-President and General Manager, W. G. Besler; Secretary, G. O. Waterman. General Offices, 143 Liberty Street, New York.

Systems, Location, and Financial Data.	Divisions, Mileage, and Operating Express.	General Officers.
Central Vermont Ry. [Connecticut, Massachusetts, Vermont, Quebec.] *For year ending June* 30, 1908. Total earnings...... $3,740,760 Operating expenses. 2,932,658 Net earnings...... $808,102 Other income....... 13,840 Total net income. $821,942 Total payments..... 818,388 Surplus............ $3,554	Southern Div., 173.5 m.; Northern Div., 362.6 m. Total mileage, 537. Express Co.—American; Canadian; National.	President, Chas. M. Hays, Montreal, Can.; Vice-President, E. H. Fitzhugh; General Manager, G. C. Jones. General Offices, St. Albans, Vt.; New York Offices, 385 Broadway, 82 Wall Street.
Chesapeake & Ohio Ry. [Virginia, West Virginia, Kentucky, Ohio.] *For year ending June* 30, 1908. Total earnings...... $25,843,272 Operating expenses 17,186,747 Net earnings...... $8,656,525 Other income....... 762,832 Total net income. $9,419,357 Total payments..... 8,921,803 Surplus............ $497,554	Main Line, 664.9 m.; Louisville Line, 208.4 m.; James River Line, 229.9 m.; Washington Line, 94.5 m.; other branches, 643.6 m. Total mileage, 1,844.8. Express Co.—Adams.	President, Geo. W. Stevens; Vice-President, Decatur Axtell; Secretary, C. E. Wellford; General Manager, C. E. Doyle. General Offices, Richmond, Va.; New York Office, 362 Broadway.
Chicago and Alton R.R. [Illinois and Missouri.] *For year ending June* 30, 1908. Total earnings..... $12,087,734 Operating expenses 7,621,890 Net earnings...... $4,465,844 Other income....... 7,474 Total net income . $4,473,318 Total payments.. . 4,173,559 Surplus............ $299,759	Chicago to East St. Louis, 279.94 m.; Pequot Line, 26.91 m.; Dwight to Peoria, 81.95 m.; Verna to Lacon, 10.43 m.; Peoria to Springfield, 55.69 m.; Bloomington to Roodhouse, via Jacksonville, 110.41 m.; Iles to Murrayville, 34.34 m.; Roodhouse to Godfrey, 40.42 m.; Godfrey to Wann, 7.35 m.; Eldred to Barnett Junction, 48.62 m.; Roodhouse to Kansas City, 251.85 m.; Mexico to Cedar City, 50.12 m. Total mileage, 998.09. Express Co.—American; National.	President, T. P. Shonts, New York; Vice-President, George H. Ross; General Traffic Manager, W. L. Ross; Secretary, James S. Mackie, New York. General Offices, Chicago, Ill.; New York Office, 115 Broadway.
Chicago and Eastern Illinois Railroad. [Indiana and Illinois.] *For year ending June* 30, 1908. Total earnings..... $10,742,731 Operating expenses 7,256,900 Net earnings...... $3,485,831 Other income........ 891,607 Total net income.. $4,377,438 Total payments. .. 3,241,210 Surplus........... $1,136,228	Now part of "Frisco System."	President, H. I. Miller; 1st Vice-President, Robert Mather, New York; 3d Vice-President, W. B. Biddle; 4th Vice-President, C. W. Hillard, New York; Vice-President, E. L. Pollock; Secretary, J. S. Ford, Chicago. General Offices, Chicago, Ill.; New York Office, 115 Broadway.
Chicago and Northwestern Railway.—"The Northwestern Line." [Michigan, Illinois, Iowa, Wisconsin, Nebraska, Minnesota, North Dakota, South Dakota, Wyoming.] *For year ending June* 30, 1908.* Total earnings...... $63,219,344 Operating expenses 41,641,313 Net earnings...... $21,578,031 Other income....... 2,909,951 Total net income. $24,487,982 Total payments.... 19,613,561 Surplus........... $4,874,421	Wisconsin Div., 324.55 m.; Galena Div., 497.98 m.; Iowa Div., 569.46 m.; Madison Div., 510.80 m.; Minnesota and Dakota Div., 1,302.56 m.; Peninsula Div., 460.33 m.; Iowa and Minnesota Div., 323.11 m.; Northern Iowa Div., 383.57 m.; Ashland Div., 666.78 m.; Northern Wisconsin Div., 331.47 m.; Sioux City Div., 416.15 m.; Lake Shore Div., 386.71 m.; Nebraska & Wyoming Div., 1,458.76 m. Total mileage, 7,632.23; Chicago, St. Paul Minn. & O. Ry., 1,729.56. Express Co.—American.	President, Marvin Hughitt, Chicago, Ill.; Vice-President and Secretary, E. E. Osborn, New York City; Vice-Presidents, M. M. Kirkman, H. R. McCullough, J. M. Whitman, and William A. Gardner; General Manager, R. H. Aishton; Freight Traffic Manager, Marvin Hughitt, Jr.; Passenger Traffic Manager, W. B. Kniskern. General Offices, Chicago, Ill.; New York Offices, 111 Broadway.
Chicago, Burlington and Quincy Railroad.—"Burlington Route." [Illinois, Wisconsin, Minnesota, Iowa, Missouri, Nebraska, Kansas, Colorado, Wyoming, South Dakota, Montana.] *For year ending June* 30, 1908. Total earnings...... $78,459,063 Operating expenses 55,985,224 Net earnings...... $22,473,839 Other income ...... 15,194 Total net income. $22,489,033 Total payments.... 22,466,665 Surplus........... $22,368	Lines in Illinois, 1,680.20 m.; in Wisconsin, 223.10 m.; in Minnesota, 38.45 m.; in Iowa, 1,439.12 m.; in Missouri, 1,133.25 m.; in Nebraska, 2,865.48 m.; in Kansas, 260.14 m.; in Colorado, 429.35 m.; in Montana, 199.90 m.; in South Dakota, 283.37 m.; in Wyoming, 471.29 m. Total mileage, 9,023.65. Express Co.—Adams.	President, Geo. B. Harris; 1st Vice-President, Darius Miller; 2d Vice-President, Daniel Willard; 3d Vice-President and Secretary, T. S. Howland; Assistant Secretary, G. H. Earl, New York; Passenger Traffic Manager, P. S. Eustis; Freight Traffic Manager, G. H. Crosby. General Offices, Chicago, Ill.; New York Offices, 299, 379 Broadway. General Offices of lines west of the Missouri River at Omaha, Neb.

* Exclusive of Chicago, St. Paul, Minn. & O. Ry.

Systems, Location, and Financial Data.	Divisions, Mileage, and Operating Express.	General Officers.
Chicago Great Western Railway. [Illinois, Iowa, Minnesota, Missouri, Kansas, Nebraska.] Report for year ending June 30, 1908, not issued by Receivers when ALMANAC went to press.	Minneapolis to Chicago, 430 m.; Oelwein to Kansas City, 357 m.; Hayfield to Clarion, 100 m.; Oelwein to Omaha, 265 m.; De Kalb Br., 6 m.; Cedar Falls Br., 7 m.; Mantorville Br., 7 m.; Lehigh Br., 16 m.; Mankato-Osage Line, 210 m.; Winona-Rochester Line, 55 m. Total mileage, 1,453. EXPRESS Co.—Wells, Fargo & Co.	Receivers, A. B. Stickney, and C. H. F. Smith; President, A. B. Stickney; Vice-President, Ansel Oppenheim; General Manager, S. C. Stickney; General Traffic Manager, L. S. Cass; Secretary, R. C. Wight. General Offices, St. Paul, Minn.; New York Offices, 31 Nassau Street, 305 Broadway.
Chicago, Indianapolis and Louisville Ry. [Indiana, Illinois, Kentucky.] *For year ending June* 30, 1908. Total earnings..... $5,167,160 Operating expenses 4,003,458 Net earnings..... $1,163,702 Other income...... 272,423 Total net income. $1,436,125 Total payments... 1,073,762 Surplus........... $362,363	Chicago to Louisville, 325.3 m.; Monon to Indianapolis, 95.1 m.; Bloomfield Br., 40.3 m.; Michigan City Div., 60 m.; French Lick Br., 18 m. Total mileage, 537.9. EXPRESS Co.—American.	President, W. H. McDoel, Chicago, Ill.; Vice-President, M. F. Plant, New York; General Manager, B. E. Taylor, Chicago, Ill.; Secretary, J. A. Hilton, New York. General Offices, Chicago, Ill.; New York Office, 52 Broadway.
Chicago, Milwaukee and St. Paul Railway. [Illinois, Wisconsin, Michigan, Minnesota, Iowa, Missouri, South Dakota, North Dakota.] *For year ending June* 30, 1908. Total earnings...... $56,932,620 Operating expenses 37,163,368 Net earnings..... $19,769,252 Other income...... 1,052,662 Total net income. $20,821,914 Fixed charges...... 17,529,762 Surplus........... $3,292,152	Lines in Illinois, 412.62 m.; in Wisconsin, 1,731.75 m.; in Iowa, 1,871.13 m.; in Minnesota, 1,205.63 m.; in North Dakota, 153.31 m.; in South Dakota, 1,512.68 m.; in Missouri, 140.27 m.; in Michigan, 159.12 m. Total mileage, 7,186.69. EXPRESS Co.—United States.	Chairman, Roswell Miller, New York; President, A. J. Earling, Chicago, Ill.; 2d Vice-President, E. W. McKenna; 3d Vice-President, J. H. Hiland, Chicago; General Manager, W. J. Underwood, Chicago; Secretary, E. W. Adams, Milwaukee, Wis.; Assistant Secretary, J. M. McKinlay, New York. General Offices, Chicago, Ill., and Milwaukee, Wis.; New York Offices, 42 and 381 Broadway.
Chicago, Rock Island and Pacific Railway. [Illinois, Iowa, Minnesota, South Dakota, Missouri, Nebraska, Kansas, Oklahoma, Colorado, Tennessee, Arkansas, Louisiana.] *For year ending June* 30, 1908. Total earnings..... $58,484,196 Operating expenses 42,328,747 Net earnings..... $16,155,449 Other income...... 321,201 Total net income $16,476,650 Total payments... 15,688,332 Surplus........... $788,318	Chicago-Colorado Springs, 1,070.94 m.; Davenport-Terral, 830.11 m.; Herington-Texhoma, 323.34 m.; Keokuk-Des Moines, 162.40 m.; Des Moines-Sibley, 176.35 m.; Burlington-Minneapolis, 365.04 m.; Vinton-Watertown, 375.97 m.; Memphis-Texola, 649.40 m.; Haskell-Eunice, 302.92 m.; Kansas City-St. Louis, 298.50 m.; other lines and branches, 2,846.76 m. Total mileage, 7,401.73. Chicago, Rock Island and Gulf Railway, 470.65 m.; Chicago, Rock Island and El Paso Railway, 111.50 m.; EXPRESS Co.—U. S.; Wells, F. & Co.	President, B. L. Winchell; 1st Vice-President, R. A. Jackson; 2d Vice-President, H. U. Mudge; 3d Vice-President, W. B. Biddle; 4th Vice-President, C. W. Hillard; Vice-President, E. L. Pollock; Secretary, George H. Crosby. General Offices, Chicago, Ill.; New York Offices, 115 and 401 Broadway.
Cincinnati, Hamilton & Dayton Railway. [Ohio, Indiana, Illinois.] *For year ending June* 30, 1907. Total earnings..... $8,946,934 Operating expenses 6,782,125 Net earnings..... $2,164,809 Other income...... 101,924 Total net income $2,266,733 Total payments..... 3,128,086 Deficit........... $861,353	Main line and branches, 1,037.80 m. EXPRESS Co.—United States.	Receiver, Judson Harmon. President, F. D. Underwood, New York; Vice-President, George F. Brownell, New York; Secretary, Thos. J. Walsh, General Traffic Manager, C. L. Thomas. General Offices, Cincinnati, O.
Cleveland, Cincinnati, Chicago & St. Louis Ry. [Ohio, Indiana, Michigan, Illinois.] *For year ending Dec.* 31, 1907. Total earnings..... $26,447.804 Operating expenses 20,133,629 Net earnings..... $6,314,175 Other income...... 186,543 Total net income $6,500,718 Total payments.... 4,527,501 Surplus........... $1,973,217	Cleveland-Indianapolis Div., 341 m.; Mt. Gilead Short Line, 2 m.; Cincinnati-Sandusky Div., 369 m.; St. Louis Div., 309 m.; Chicago Div., 321 m.; Cairo Div., 270 m.; Peoria and Eastern Div., 352 m.; White Water Div., 70 m.; Michigan Div., 302 m.; Kankakee and Seneca Div., 42 m. Total mileage, 2,378. This Road is now part of New York Central System. EXPRESS Co.—American.	President, W. H. Newman; Vice-Presidents, E. V. W. Rossiter, W. C. Brown, C. F. Daly, A. H. Harris and John Carstensen, New York; C. E. Schaff, Chicago; General Manager, J. Q. Van Winkle; Secretary, D. W. Pardee, New York. General Offices, Cincinnati, O.; New York Office, Grand Central Station.

SYSTEMS, LOCATION, AND FINANCIAL DATA.	Divisions, Mileage, and Operating Express.	General Officers.
Colorado and Southern Railway.—"The Colorado Road." [Colorado, Wyoming, New Mexico.] *For year ending June* 30, 1908. Total earnings.....$14,280,535 Operating expenses 9,594,205 Net earnings..... $4,686,330 Other income...... 355,733 Total net income. $5,042,063 Total payments.... 3,550,159 Surplus....... $1,491 904	Pueblo Dist., 134.05 m.; Trinidad Dist., 113.98 m.; New Mexico Dist., 150.55 m.; Clear Creek Dist., 65.98 m.; Ft. Collins Dist., 182.90 m.; Platte Cañon Dist., 102.36 m.; Leadville Dist., 74.36 m.; Gunnison Dist., 164.51 m.; Wyoming Dist., 260.95 m. Total mileage, 1,249.64. Fort Worth and Denver City Ry., 454.49 m. EXPRESS Co.—Wells, Fargo & Co.	Chairman of the Board, G. M. Dodge, New York; President, Frank Trumbull, New York; Vice-President, A. D. Parker; Secretary, J. S. Mackie, New York. General Offices, Denver, Col.; New York Offices, 71 Broadway. Fort Worth and Denver City Ry.—President, Frank Trumbull, New York; Vice-President, D. B. Keeler, Fort Worth, Tex.; Secretary, W. O. Hamilton, Fort Worth, Tex. General Offices, Fort Worth, Tex.; New York Offices, 71 Broadway.
Colorado Midland Railway. [Colorado.] *For year ending June* 30, 1908. Total earnings...... $2,200,755 Operating expenses 1,773,925 Net earnings..... $426,830 Other income...... 57,915 Total net income $484,745 Total payments.... 462,427 Surplus.......... $22,318	Colorado Springs, Col., to Grand Junction, Col., 302 m.; Aspen Br., 18 m.; Jerome Park Br., 15 m. Total mileage, 335. EXPRESS Co.—Wells, Fargo & Co.	President, Frank Trumbull; Vice-President, C. H. Schlacks; General Manager, Geo. W. Vallery; Secretary, James S. Mackie, New York. General Offices, Denver, Col.; New York Offices, 71 and 195 Broadway.
Delaware and Hudson Railroad. [Pennsylvania, New York, Vermont.] *For year ending Dec.* 31, 1907. Total earnings.. ..$43,360,559 Operating expenses 33,787,774 Net earnings.... $9,572,785 Other income..... 1,468,995 Total net income $11,041,780 Total payments... 4,575,607 Surplus.......... $6,466,173	Pennsylvania Div., 130.09 m.; Saratoga Div.. 250.64 m.; Champlain Div., 230.69 m.; Albany and Susquehanna Div., 233.34 m. Total mileage, 844.76. EXPRESS Co.—National.	President, L. F. Loree; Vice-President, Chas. A. Peabody; 2d Vice-President, C. S. Sims, Albany N. Y.; 3d Vice-President, W. H. Williams; Secretary, F. M. Olyphant, New York. General Offices, 32 Nassau Street, New York.
Delaware, Lackawanna and Western Railroad. [New York, New Jersey, Pennsylvania.] *For year ending June* 30, 1908. Total earnings.... $33,810,253 Operating expenses 19,622,042 Net earnings.....$14,188,211 Other income....... 5,242,112 Total net income.$19,430,323 Total payments.... 15,782,597 Surplus $3,647,726	Main Line, Hoboken, N. J. to Buffalo, N. Y., 409.85 m.; Morristown Line., 34.46 m.; Sussex R. R. 30.55 m.; Bangor and Portland Ry. 38.38 m.; Bloomsburg Br., 79.66 m.; S. B. & N. Y. R. R.. 80.95 m.; Oswego & Syracuse Div, 34.98 m.; Utica Div., 105.51 m.; Ithaca Br., 34.41 m.; other branches 108.44 m. Total mileage, 957.19. EXPRESS Co.—United States.	President, W. H. Truesdale; Vice-Presidents, B. D. Caldwell, E. E. Loomis and W. S. Jenney; Secretary, A. D. Chambers. General Offices, 90 West Street, New York.
Denver and Rio Grande Railroad. [Colorado and New Mexico] *For year ending June* 30, 1908. Total earnings.....$20,386,431 Operating expenses 13,038,809 Net earnings .... $7,347,622 Other income ...... 597,148 Total net income. $7,944,770 Total payments.... 7,048,398 Surplus........... $896,372	Denver to Grand Junction, 449.88 m.; Salida to Grand Junction, 208.62 m.; Cuchara Junction to Silverton, 328.47 m.; Antonito to Santa Fé, 125.79 m.; Pueblo to Trinidad, 91.55 m.; Carbon Junction to Farmington, 47.66 m.; other branches, 576.87 m. Total mileage, 1,828.84. EXPRESS Co.—Globe; Wells Fargo & Co.	Chairman of the Board, George J. Gould, New York; President, Edward T. Jeffery, New York; Vice-President, Charles H. Schlacks, Denver, Col.; Secretary, Stephen Little, New York. General Offices, Denver, Col., and Salt Lake City, Utah; New York Offices, 195 and 335 Broadway.
Detroit and Mackinac Railway. [Michigan.] *For year ending June* 30, 1908. Total earnings..... $1,186,096 Operating expenses 807,365 Net earnings..... $378,731 Other income....... 18,314 Total net income. $397,045 Total payments.... 418,454 Deficit........... $21,409	Bay City to Cheboygan, 195.44 m.; Prescott Div., 11.8 m.; Rose City Div., 31.8 m.; Lincoln Br., 14.4 m.; Au Gres Br., 8.33 m.; logging branches, 81.49 m. Total mileage, 343.26. EXPRESS Co.—American.	President and General Manager, J. D. Hawks; Vice-President, G. M. Crocker; Secretary, C. B. Colebrook, New York. General Offices, Detroit, Mich.; New York Office, 40 Wall Street.

Systems, Location, and Financial Data.	Divisions, Mileage, and Operating Express.	General Officers.
Detroit, Toledo and Ironton Railway. [Michigan and Ohio.] *For year ending June 30*, 1908. Total earnings..... $1,186,096 Operating expenses 807,365 Net earnings..... $378,731 Other income...... 18,314 Total net income $397,045 Total payments... 418,454 Deficit........... $21,409	Detroit, Toledo & Ironton Ry., 436 m. Express Co.—American.	Receivers, G. K. Lowell, B. S. Warren, T. D. Rhodes. President, E. Zimmerman; Vice-President, F. A. Durban, Zanesville, O.; General Manager, Geo. K. Lowell. General Offices, Detroit, Mich.
Duluth, South Shore and Atlantic Railway. [Michigan, Wisconsin, Minnesota.] *For year ending June* 30, 1908. Total earnings .... $2,986,958 Operating expenses 2,252,786 Net earnings........ $734,172 Other income...... 30,405 Total net income. $764,577 Total payments.... 1,075,569 Deficit.............. $310,992	Main Line, 517.44 m.; other branches, 63.60 m. Total mileage, 581.04. Express Co.—Western. This road is now controlled by the Canadian Pacific Ry.	President and General Manager, W. F. Fitch, Marquette, Mich.; 1st Vice-President, Walter R. Baker, Montreal, Can.; 2d Vice-President, George H. Church, New York; Secretary, James Clarke, New York. General Offices, Marquette, Mich.; New York Office, 44 Wall Street.
Erie Railroad. [New York, New Jersey, Pennsylvania, Ohio, Indiana, Illinois.] *For year ending June* 30, 1908. Total earnings. ...$50,007,603 Operating expenses 41,089,032 Net earnings.....$ 8,918,571 Other income...... 2,750,467 Total net income $11,669,038 Total payments.... 13,868,265 Deficit........... $2,199,227	*Erie Division*. New York Div., 198 m.; Delaware Div., 104 m.; Susquehanna Div., 138 m.; Jefferson Div., 43 m.; Tioga Div., 65 m.; Rochester Div., 147 m.; Buffalo Div., 177 m.; Allegheny Div., 132 m.; Bradford Div., 84 m.; Wyoming Div., 100 m. *Ohio Division*: Meadville Div., 225 m.; Cincinnati Div., 204 m.; Mahoning Div., 167 m.; Lima Div., 127 m.; Chicago Div., 125 m. Greenwood Lake Div., 53 m.; Northern R.R. of New Jersey, 26 m. New Jersey & N. Y. R. R., 38 m. Total mileage of Erie R.R., 2,152. Express Co.—Wells, Fargo & Co.	President, F. D. Underwood; 1st Vice-President, G. F. Brownell; 2d Vice-President, G. A. Richardson; 3d Vice-President, H. B. Chamberlain; General Manager, J. C. Stuart; Secretary, David Bosman. General Offices, 50 Church Street, New York.
Florida East Coast Railway. [Florida.] Financial report of this company not made public.	Jacksonville to Homestead, 394 m., branch lines, 158 m. Total mileage, 552. Also connects with Steamship Lines from Miami to Key West, Havana, and Nassau. Express Co.—Southern.	President, H. M. Flagler, New York; Vice-President and General Manager, J. R. Parrott; 2d Vice-President, R. W. Parsons, New York; 3d Vice-President, J. E. Ingraham; Traffic Manager, J. P. Beckwith; Secretary, J. C. Salter, New York. General Offices, St. Augustine, Fla.; New York Office, 26 Broadway.
"Frisco System." [Illinois, Indiana, Missouri, Kansas, Arkansas, Oklahoma, Texas, Tennessee, Mississippi, Alabama.] *For year ending June* 30, 1907. (Exclusive of Chi. & E. Ill. R.R.) Total earnings.....$38,621,067 Operating expenses 24,872,579 Net earnings.....$13,748,488 Other income...... 1,540,866 Total net income.$15,289,354 Total payments. . 11,130,771 Surplus.... ...... $4,158,583	St. Louis & San Francisco R.R., 4,737 m.; Fort Worth & Rio Grande Ry., 195.88 m.; Chicago & Eastern Illinois R.R., 965.68 m.; St. Louis, San Francisco & Texas Ry., 124.61 m.; Paris & Great Northern R. R., 16.94 m. Total mileage, 6,022.10. Express Co.—Adams; Southern; Wells, Fargo & Co.	President, A. J. Davidson; 1st Vice-President, Robert Mather, New York; 2d Vice-President C. R. Gray; 3d Vice-President, W. B. Biddle; 4th Vice-President, A. Douglas; Secretary, F. H. Hamilton; Freight Traffic Manager, J. A. Middleton. General Offices, St. Louis, Mo.; New York Offices 115, 385, 401 Broadway
Georgia Railroad. [Georgia.] *For year ending June* 30, 1908. Total earnings. ... $2,923,277 Operating expenses 2,537,668 Net earnings..... $385,609 Other income...... 55,496 Total net income $441,105 Total payments.. . 692,083 Deficit........... $250,978.	Augusta, Ga., to Atlanta, Ga., 171 m.; Macon Br., 78 m.; Athens Br., 40 m.; Washington Br., 18 m. Total mileage, 307. Express Co.—Southern.	General Manager, Thos. K. Scott. General Offices, Augusta, Ga.; New York Office, 290 Broadway.

Systems, Location, and Financial Data.	Divisions, Mileage, and Operating Express.	General Officers.
Georgia Southern and Florida Ry. [Georgia and Florida.] *For year ending June* 30, 1907. Total earnings.... $2,273,345 Operating expenses 1,880,209 Net earnings..... $393,136 Other income...... 15,579 Total net income $408,715 Total payments.... 378,839 Surplus.......... $29,876	Macon, Ga., to Palatka, Fla., 285 m.; Valdosta, Ga., to Grand Crossing, Fla., 106.61 m. Total mileage, 391.61. Express Co.—Southern.	President, W. W. Finley, Washington, D. C.; Vice-President, J. B. Munson; Secretary, R. D. Lankford, New York. General Offices, Macon, Ga.
Grand Rapids and Indiana Railway. [Indiana and Michigan.] *For year ending Dec.* 31, 1907. Total earnings....... $4,149,694 Operating expenses 3,371,356 Net earnings...... $778,338 Other income....... 22,960 Total net income. $801,298 Total payments..... 740,334 Surplus $60,964	Richmond, Ind., to Mackinaw City, Mich., 460 m.; Traverse City Div., 26 m.; Muskegon Div., 37 m.; Harbor Springs Br., 6 m.; other branches, 61 m. Total mileage, 590. Express Co.—Adams.	President, Joseph Wood, Pittsburgh, Pa.; Vice-President, W. R. Shelby; General Manager, J. H. P. Hughart; Secretary, R. R. Metheany. General Offices, Grand Rapids, Mich.
Grand Trunk Railway. [Maine, New Hampshire, Vermont, Quebec, Ontario, Illinois, Indiana, Michigan.] *For 6 mos. ending June* 30, 1908 Total earnings..... £2,919,192 Operating expenses 2,137,287 Net earnings...... £781,905 Other income...... 123,766 Total net income £905,671 Total payments.... 609,710 Surplus........... £295,961	Eastern Div., 938 m.; Ottawa Div., 466 m.; Middle Div., 1,490.25 m.; Northern Div., 888.36 m.; Western Div., 859.73 m. Total mileage, 4,645. Express Co.—Canadian. On Grand Trunk Western Ry., National.	President, Chas. Rivers Wilson, London, Eng.; Vice-President, A. W. Smithers, London, Eng.; 2d Vice-President and General Manager, Chas. M. Hays; 3d Vice-President, E. H. Fitzhugh; 4th Vice-President, W. Wainwright. General Offices, Montreal, Quebec; New York Office, 290 Broadway.
Great Northern Railway. [Minnesota, North Dakota, South Dakota, Iowa, Nebraska, Montana, Idaho, Washington, Wisconsin.] *For year ending June* 30, 1908. Total earnings.... $54,429,632 Operating expenses 36,158,055 Net earnings.... $18,271,577 Other income...... 4,181,078 Total net income. $22,452,655 Total payments.... 19 983,823 Surplus $2,468,832	Great Northern Ry. Total mileage, 6,850.87. Express Co.—Great Northern.	President, L. W. Hill; 2d Vice-President, R. I. Farrington; 3d Vice-President and Secretary, E. T. Nichols, New York; General Manager, J. M. Gruber, General Offices, St. Paul, Minn.; New York Offices, 32 Nassau Street, 379 Broadway.
Hocking Valley Railway. [Ohio.] *For year ending June* 30, 1908 Total earnings...... $5,841,763 Operating expenses. 4,307,876 Net earnings...... $1,533,887 Other income....... 980,394 Total net income. $2,514,281 Total payments.... 2,291,354 Surplus.. .... $222,927	Toledo, O., to Pomeroy, O., 252.1 m.; Athens Br., 26.9 m.; Jackson Br., 17.5 m.; other branches, 50.5 m. Total mileage, 347. Express Co.—American North of Columbus, O.; Adams South of Columbus, O.	President, N. Monsarrat; 1st Vice-President, R. W. Hickox, Cleveland, O.; 2d Vice-President, J. H. Hoyt, Cleveland, O.; Secretary and Treasurer, W. N. Cott; Assistant Secretary and Treasurer, A. H. Gillard, New York. General Offices, Columbus O.
Houston and Texas Central Railroad. [Texas.] Financial report included in Southern Pacific Co.	Main Line, 337.98 m.; Western Br., 115 m.; Waco Br., 54.77 m.; Austin Div., 129.45 m.; Ft. Worth Br., 52.83 m.; Lancaster Br., 4.75 m. Nelleva-Mexia Cut-off, 94 m. Total mileage, 788.78. Express Co.—Wells, Fargo & Co.	President, R. S. Lovett; Vice-President, T. Fay; Secretary, W. H. Field. General Offices, Houston, Tex.; New York Office, 120 Broadway.

Systems, Location, and Financial Data.	Divisions, Mileage, and Operating Express.	General Officers.
Illinois Central Railroad. [Illinois, Indiana, Wisconsin, Iowa, Minnesota, South Dakota, Kentucky, Tennessee, Mississippi, Louisiana, Missouri, Alabama.] *For year ending June* 30, 1908. Total earnings..... $52,830,426 Operating expenses 37,893,478 Net earnings..... $14,936,948 Other income...... 4,357,229 Total net income. $19,294,177 Total payments.... 5,877,047 Surplus........... $13,417,130	Illinois Central R. R., 2,103.73 m.; Chicago, St. Louis and New Orleans R. R., 1,305.96 m.; Dubuque and Sioux City R. R., 759.88 m.; other branches, 424.24 m. Total mileage, 4,593.81. Yazoo and Miss. Val. R. R.. 1,370.66 m. Indianapolis Southern R. R., 179.26 m. Express Co.—American.	President, James T. Harahan; Vice-President, I. G. Rawn; Vice-President and Secretary, A. G. Hackstaff, New York; Assistant Secretaries, D. R. Burbank, New York, and B. A. Beck, Chicago, Ill. General Offices, Chicago, Ill.; New York Offices, 115 and 336 Broadway. General Offices Yazoo and Mississippi Valley R. R., Memphis, Tenn., and Chicago, Ill.
Intercolonial Railway. [Nova Scotia, New Brunswick, Quebec.] *For year ending Mar.* 31, 1908. Total earnings....... $9,173,558 Operating expenses. 9,157,435 Surplus.............. $16,123	Halifax and Montreal Line, 836.73 m.; St. John Br., 89.36 m.; Truro and Sydney Line, 214.17 m.; Oxford and Pictou Br., 69.10 m.; Canada Eastern Br., 125 m.; other branches, 114.26 m. Total mileage, 1,448.62. Express Co.—Canadian; Dominion.	General Manager, D. Pottinger. General Offices, Moncton, N. B.
International and Great Northern Railroad. [Texas.] No statement of earnings, etc., published by Receiver.	Gulf Div., 408.9 m.; Fort Worth Div., 372.7 m.; San Antonio Div., 422.9 m. Total mileage, 1,159.5. Express Co.—Pacific.	Receiver, Thomas J. Freeman; President, George J. Gould, New York; 1st Vice-President, Frank J. Gould, New York; 2d Vice-President and General Manager, H. W. Clark; Secretary, A. R. Howard; Assistant Secretary, H. B. Henson, New York. General Offices, Palestine, Tex.; New York Offices, 195 and 335 Broadway.
Iowa Central Railway. [Iowa and Illinois.] *For year ending June* 30, 1908. Total earnings..... $3,002,475 Operating expenses 2,215,831 Net earnings..... $786,644 Other income......... 30,747 Total net income. $817,391 Total payments... 599,260 Surplus. $218,131	Albia, Ia., to Albert Lea, Minn., 205.32 m.; Oskaloosa, Ia., to Peoria, Ill., 188.90 m.; other branches, 164.21 m. Total mileage, 558.43. Express Co.—Adams.	President, Edwin Hawley, New York; Vice-President, F. H. Davis, New York; Vice-President and General Manager, L. F. Day, Minneapolis, Minn.; Secretary, A. C. Doan, New York; Freight Traffic Manager, J. N. Tittemore, Minneapolis, Minn. General Offices, Minneapolis, Minn; New York Office, 25 Broad Street.
Kansas City Southern Railway. **Texarkana and Fort Smith Railway.** [Missouri, Kansas, Arkansas, Oklahoma, Louisiana, Texas.] *For year ending June* 30, 1908. Total earnings....... $8,758,928 Operating expenses 5,754,320 Net earnings..... $3,004,608 Other income...... 133,598 Total net income. $3,138,206 Total payments.... 2,364,934 Surplus........... $ 773,272	Kansas City, Mo., to Port Arthur, Tex., 788 m.; Fort Smith Br., 16 m.; Lake Charles Br., 23 m.; Air Line Branch, 6 m. Total mileage, 839. Express Co.—Wells, Fargo & Co.	Kansas City Southern Ry.—President, J. A. Edson; Vice-Presidents, E. F. Cost and R. J. McCarty; Secretary, R. B. Sperry, New York. General Offices, Kansas City, Mo. Texarkana and Fort Smith Ry.—President, J. A. Edson, Kansas City, Mo.; 1st Vice-President, W. L. Estes. General Offices, Texarkana, Tex.
Lake Erie and Western Railroad. [Ohio, Indiana, Illinois.] *For year ending Dec.* 31, 1907. Total earnings........ $5,066,939 Operating expenses. 3,854,744 Net earnings.. ...... $1,212,195 Other income....... 6,929 Total net income. $1,219,124 Total payments.... 975,460 Surplus............ $243,664	Main Line, 415.48 m.; Indianapolis and Michigan City Div., 160.25 m.; Fort Wayne and Connorsville Div., 108.57 m.; Rushville Br., 24.13 m.; Minster Br., 9.95 m.; Northern Ohio Ry., 161.75 m. Total mileage, 880.13. Express Co.—American. This road is controlled by Lake Shore & Mich. Southern Ry.	President, W. H. Newman; Vice-Presidents, W. C. Brown, E. V. W. Rossiter, J. Carstensen, C. F. Daly, A. H. Harris, New York; C. E. Schaff, Chicago, Ill.; Secretary, D. W. Pardee, New York; General Manager, D. C. Moon, Cleveland, O. General Offices, Grand Central Station, New York; Cleveland, O., and Indianapolis, Ind.

Systems, Location, and Financial Data.	Divisions, Mileage, and Operating Express.	General Officers.
Lake Shore and Michigan Southern Railway [New York, Pennsylvania, Ohio, Michigan, Indiana, Illinois.] *For year ending Dec.* 31, 1907. Total earnings.....$44,953,475 Operating expenses 34,538,461 Net earnings.....$10,415,014 Other income....... 5,716,419 Total net income $16,131,433 Total payments.... 8,745,717 Surplus........... $7,385,716	Eastern Div., 183 m.; Toledo Div., 190 m.; Michigan Div., 417 m.; Western Div., 101 m.; Franklin Div., 179 m.; Detroit Div., 160 m.; Lansing Div., 290 m. Total mileage, 1,520. Express Co.—United States; American.	Chairman of the Board, Chauncey M. Depew, New York; President, W. H. Newman, New York; Vice-Presidents, W. C. Brown, E. V. W. Rossiter, C. F. Daly, A. H. Harris and John Carstensen, New York; C. E. Schaff, Chicago, Ill.; Secretary, D. W. Pardee, New York; General Manager, D. C. Moon, Cleveland, O.; General Superintendent, J. J. Bernet, Cleveland, O. General Offices, Grand Central Station, New York, and Cleveland, O.
Lehigh Valley Railroad. [New York, New Jersey, Pennsylvania.] *For year ending June* 30, 1908. Total earnings.....$35,510,154 Operating expenses 22,203,704 Net earnings.....$13,306,450 Other income...... 1,521,017 Total net income.$14,827,467 Total payments.... 9,232,156 Surplus.... .... . $5,595,311	New Jersey and Lehigh Div., 217.82 m.; Mahanoy and Hazleton Divs., 206.42 m.; Wyoming Div., 318.09 m.; New York Div., 22.13 m.; Auburn Div., 302.30 m.; Buffalo Div., 331.94 m. Total mileage, 1,398.70. Express Co.—United States.	President, E. B. Thomas; 1st Vice-President, J. A. Middleton, New York; 2d Vice-President, T. N. Jarvis, New York; Secretary, D. G. Baird. General Offices, Philadelphia, Pa.; New York Office, 143 Liberty Street.
Long Island Railroad. [Long Island, New York.] *For year ending Dec.* 31, 1907. Total earnings.....$10,130,407 Operating expenses 8,526,584 Net earnings......$1,603,823 Other income........ 332,067 Total net income.$1,935,890 Total payments..... 2,794,720 Deficit............. $858,830	Main Line—Long Island City to Greenport, 94.74 m.; Long Island City to Montauk, 115.13 m.; branches owned, 106.48 m.; branches leased, 63.75 m.; New York and Rockaway Beach Ry, 11.74 m. Total mileage, 391.84. Express Co.—Long Island. This road is now controlled by the Pennsylvania R. R.	President and General Manager, Ralph Peters. General Offices, Long Island City, New York, and 128 Broadway, New York.
Louisville and Nashville Railroad. [Kentucky, Indiana, Illinois, Georgia, North Carolina, Virginia, Tennessee, Alabama, Florida, Louisiana, Mississippi.] *For year ending June* 30, 1908. Total earnings......$44,620,281 Operating expenses 33,594,291 Net earnings ....$11,025,990 Other income...... 1,320,668 Total net income $12,346,658 Total payments... 9,625,618 Surplus.......... $2,721,040	Cincinnati to Louisville, 114 m.; Louisville to Nashville, 187 m.; Nashville to New Orleans, 622 m.; Memphis Junction to Memphis, 260 m.; E. St. Louis to Edgefield Junction, 310 m.; Louisville to Lexington, 94 m.; Cincinnati to Atlanta, 485 m.; other branches, 2,293.20 m. Total mileage, 4,365.29. Express Co.—Adams; Southern.	President, Milton H. Smith; Chairman of Board, Henry Walters, New York; 1st Vice-President, W. L. Mapother; 2d Vice-President, A. W. Morriss, New York; 3d Vice-President, A. R. Smith; 4th Vice-President, G. E. Evans; Secretary, J. H. Ellis; General Manager, B. M. Starks; Traffic Manager, C. B. Compton. General Offices, Louisville, Ky.; New York Offices, 71 and 290 Broadway.
Maine Central Railroad. [Maine, New Hampshire, Vermont, Quebec.] *For year ending June* 30, 1908. Total earnings..... $8,514,256 Operating expenses 5,919,600 Net earnings..... $2,594,656 Other income....... 203,524 Total net income. $2,798,180 Total payments.... 2,787,812 Surplus. $10,368	Portland to Vanceboro, via Augusta, 250.90 m.; Cumberland Junction to Skowhegan, 91.20 m.; Bath to Lewiston and Farmington, 76.30 m.; Belfast Br., 33.13 m.; Dexter Br., 30.77 m.; Mt. Desert Br. (including Steam Ferry), 48.83 m.; Portland to Lunenburg, 109.10 m.; Quebec Junction to Lime Ridge, 108.18 m.; Bath to Rockland (including Steam Ferry), 49.09 m.; branches, 107.17 m. Total mileage, 931.40. Express Co.—American.	President, Lucius Tuttle; Vice-President and General Manager, Morris McDonald. General Offices, Portland, Me.
Michigan Central R.R. [New York, Ontario, Michigan, Ohio, Indiana, Illinois.] *For year ending Dec.* 31, 1907. Total earnings.....$28,547,109 Operating expenses 23,131,750 Net earnings..... $5,415,359 Other income...... 702,518 Total net income $6,117,877 Total payments.... 4,388,512 Surplus.......... $1,729,365	Main Line, Buffalo to Chicago, 536.4 m.; Toledo Div., 58.9 m.; St. Clair Div., 66.4 m.; Grand Rapids Div., 94.5 m.; Mackinaw Div., 182.3 m.; Air Line Div., 104.2 m.; Saginaw Div., 115.3 m.; Bay City Div., 108.9 m.; Saginaw Bay and N. W. Div., 27.4 m.; other branches, 481.5 m. Total mileage, 1,745.32. Express Co.—American.	Chairman of the Board, H. B. Ledyard, Detroit, Mich.; President, W. H. Newman, New York; Vice-Presidents, W. C. Brown, New York; C. E. Schaff, Chicago, Ill.; E. V. W. Rossiter, John Carstensen, C. F. Daly and A. H. Harris, New York; Secretary, D. W. Pardee, New York. General Offices, Grand Central Station, New York; Chicago, Ill.; Detroit, Mich.

Systems, Location, and Financial Data.	Divisions, Mileage, and Operating Express.	General Officers.
Minneapolis & St. Louis Railroad. — "Albert Lea Route." [Minnesota, Iowa, S. Dakota.] *For year ending June* 30, 1908. Total earnings...... $3,826,516 Operating expenses 2,816,345 Net earnings ... $1,010,170 Other income.. . 206,486 Total net income. $1,216,656 Total payments. .. 1,107,676 Surplus........... $108,980	St. Paul, Albert Lea and Southern Divs., 271.15 m.; Western and Pacific Divs., 217.52 m.; Southwestern Div., 153.50 m., Des Moines & Ft. Dodge Div., 156.72 m., M. D. & P. Div., 229.60 m. Total mileage, 1,028.49. Express Co.—Adams.	President, Edwin Hawley, New York; Vice-President and General Manager, L. F. Day; Secretary, A. C. Doan. General Offices, Minneapolis, Minn.; New York Office, 25 Broad Street.
Minneapolis, St. Paul and Sault Ste. Marie Railway—"Soo Line." [Michigan, Wisconsin, Minnesota, North Dakota, South Dakota.] *For year ending June* 30, 1908 Total earnings. . ..$11,509,857 Operating expenses 7,115,964 Net earnings. ... $4,393,893 Other income...... 669,111 Total net income $5,063,004 Total payments.... 3,062 135 Surplus........... $2,000,869	*Michigan*—Main Line, 208.18 m.; Br., 42.79 m.; *Wisconsin*—Main Line, 263.91 m., Br., 89.10 m.; *Minnesota*—Main Line, 231.28 m.; Br., 395.65 m.; *North Dakota*—Main Line, 361 m.; Br., 749.72 m.; *South Dakota*—Main Line, — m.; Branch Lines, 33.56 m. Total mileage, 2,375.19. Express Co.—Western.	President, Thomas Lowry; Vice-President and General Manager E. Pennington; Secretary, C. F. Clement. General Offices, Minneapolis, Minn.; New York Offices, 59 Wall Street, 458 Broadway.
Missouri, Kansas and Texas Railway.— [Missouri, Kansas, Oklahoma, Texas, Louisiana.] *For year ending June* 30, 1908. Total earnings.....$23,283,669 Operating expenses 16,432,107 Net earnings.... $6,851,562 Other income . 381,423 Total net income $7,232,985 Total payments 6,444,155 Surplus........... $788 830	Missouri, Kansas & Texas Ry., 1,725 m.; Missouri, Kansas & Texas Ry. of Texas, 1,245 m.; Galveston, Houston & Henderson R. R., 50 m.; Denison, Bonham & New Orleans R. R., 24 m., Wichita Falls Ry., 18 m.; Dallas, Cleburne & Southwestern R. R., 10 m. Total mileage, 3,072. Express Co.—American.	General Officers of the System—President, A. H. Joline, New York; Vice-President, Chas. G. Hedge, New York; Vice-President and General Manager, A. A. Allen, St. Louis, Mo.; Traffic Manager, C. Haile, St. Louis, Mo.; Secretary, C. N. Whitehead, New York. Officers of Missouri, Kansas & Texas Ry. Co. of Texas—President, A. H. Joline; Vice-President and General Manager, A. A. Allen; 2d Vice-President, J. N. Simpson, Dallas, Tex.; Secretary, C. S. Sherwin, Dallas, Tex. General Offices—St. Louis, Mo.; Parsons, Kan.; Dallas, Tex.; New York Offices, 49 Wall Street, 309 Broadway.
Missouri Pacific Ry. [Missouri, Kansas, Nebraska, Colorado, Oklahoma, Arkansas, Louisiana Tennessee, Illinois.] *For year ending June* 30, 1908 (Including Iron Mountain Line.) Total earnings . .$44,238,702 Operating expenses 31,646,287 Net earnings.....$12,592,415 Other income...... 2,875,297 Total net income $15,467,712 Total payments... 14,417,206 Surplus........... $1,050,506	Missouri Pacific Ry., 1,841 m.; Missouri Pacific Ry. Independent Br. Lines, 1,651 m.; St. Louis, Iron Mountain and Southern Ry., 2,594 m.; Central Br. Ry., 388 m. Total mileage, 6,474. Express Co.—Pacific.	President, George J. Gould, New York; Vice-Presidents, Frank Jay Gould, New York; Charles S. Clarke, St. Louis, Mo.; Alex. G. Cochran, St. Louis, Mo.; Secretary, A. H. Calef, New York. General Offices, St. Louis, Mo.; New York Offices, 195 Broadway.
Mobile and Ohio R.R. [Missouri, Illinois, Kentucky, Tennessee, Mississippi, Alabama.] *For year ending June* 30, 1908. Total earnings.... . $9,649,211 Operating expenses 6,818,003 Net earnings..... $2,831,208 Other income ...... 174,449 Total net income. $3,005,657 Total payments .. 2,690,433 Surplus........... $315,224	Main Line, St. Louis, Mo., to Mobile, Ala., 644.60 m.; Aberdeen Br., 9 m.; Starkville Br., 11 m.; Montgomery Div., 167.19 m.; Blocton Br., 11.82 m.; Columbus, Miss. Br., 14 m.; Warrior Southern R.R., 13.60 m.; Warrior Br., 9.51 m.; Millstadt Br., 7 m.; Mobile and Bay Shore Ry., 38.36 m. Total mileage, 926.08. Express Co.—Southern.	Chairman of the Board, W. Butler Duncan, New York; President, W. W. Finley, Washington, D. C.; 1st Vice-President, A. B. Andrews, Raleigh, N. C.; Vice-President, E. L. Russell, Mobile, Ala.; General Manager, R. V. Taylor, Mobile, Ala.; Secretary, Henry Tacon, Mobile, Ala. General Offices, Mobile, Ala.; St. Louis, Mo.; New York Office, 80 Broadway.

Systems, Location, and Financial Data.	Divisions, Mileage, and Operating Express.	General Officers.
Nashville, Chattanooga and St. Louis Railway.—"Lookout Mountain Route." [Georgia, Alabama, Tennessee, Kentucky.] *For year ending June* 30, 1908. Total earnings.....$10,738,252 Operating expenses. 8,182,099 Net earnings.... $2,556,153 Other income...... 310,641 Total net income $2,866,794 Total payments .... 2,577,003 Surplus $289,791	Main Line, 320.21 m.; McMinnville Br., 84.60 m.; Sequatchie Valley R. R., 68.10 m.; Tracy City Br., 31.17 m.; Centreville Br., 69.91 m.; Shelbyville Br., 8.01 m.; Lebanon Br., 29 21 m.: Western and Atlantic R. R., 136.82 m.; Rome R. R., 18.15 m.: Huntsville and Gadsden Line, 80.08 m.; Fayetteville and Columbia Br., 86 35 m.; Paducah and Memphis Div., 254.20 m.: Middle Tenn. and Ala. Div., 36.98 m.: West Nashville Br., 6.26 m. Total mileage. 1,230.05. Express Co.—Southern.	President and General Manager, J. W. Thomas, Jr.; Vice-President and Traffic Manager. H. F. Smith; Secretary, J. H. Ambrose. General Offices, Nashville, Tenn.; New York Office, 71 Broadway; General Offices of Western and Atlantic R. R., Atlanta, Ga.
New York Central and Hudson River R.R. [New York, New Jersey, Pennsylvania, Massachusetts.] *For year ending Dec.* 31, 1907. (For entire system east of Buffalo, except Dunkirk, Allegheny Valley and Pittsburgh R. R.) Total earnings.... $98,369,059 Operating expenses 75,803,333 Net earnings.....$22,565,726 Other income...... 11,476,051 Total net income.$34,041,777 Total payments... 22,957,948 Surplus...........$11,083,829	New York Central and Hudson River R.R., 806.66 m.; West Shore R. R., 478.97 m.; New York and Harlem R. R., 136.51 m.; Rome, Watertown and Ogdensburg R. R., 624.37 m.; Beech Creek R. R., 165.88 m.; Beech Creek Extension R.R., 126.46 m.; Mohawk and Malone Ry., 182.18 m.; Carthage and Adirondack Ry., 45.86 m.; New York and Putnam R. R., 58.88 m.; Fall Brook Ry., 91.51 m; Pine Creek Ry., 74.96 m.; Syracuse, Geneva and Corning Ry., 64.24 m.: Wallkill Valley R. R., 32.88 m.; other roads. 44.20 m.; New York & Ottawa Line 128.40 m.; St. Lawrence and Adirondack Ry., 65.07 m. Lines operated under trackage rights, 262.77 m.; Boston & Albany R. R., 392.49 m. Total mileage, 3,588. 82. Dunkirk. A. V. and P. R. R., 90.51 m. Express Co.—American. National Express on West Shore R. R.	Chairman of the Board, Chauncey M. Depew; President, William H. Newman; Senior Vice-President, W. C. Brown; Vice-Presidents, E. V. W. Rossiter; John Carstensen; Ira A. Place; Chas. F. Daly; Vice-President and General Manager. A. H. Smith; Secretary, D. W. Pardee. General Offices. Albany, N. Y. Operating Offices. Grand Central Station, Vanderbilt Avenue and Forty-second Street, New York.
New York, Chicago and St. Louis Railroad. [New York, Pennsylvania, Ohio, Indiana, Illinois.] *For year ending Dec.* 31, 1907. Total earnings.....$10,465,671 Operating expenses 7,761,899 Net earnings .... $2,703,772 Other income...... 19,213 Total net income. $2,722,985 Total payments.... 1,322,315 Surplus............ $1,400,670	Buffalo, N. Y., to Chicago, Ill., 523 m. Express Co.—National.	Chairman of the Board, Chauncey M. Depew. New York; President, W. H. Canniff, Cleveland, O.; Secretary, D. W. Pardee, New York. General Offices, Cleveland O.; New York Office, Grand Central Station.
New York, New Haven & Hartford Railroad. [Massachusetts, Rhode Island, Connecticut, New York.] *For year ending June* 30, 1908. Total earnings.....$53,050,147 Operating expenses 38,213,557 Net earnings.....$14,836,590 Other income...... 8,318,672 Total net income $23,155,262 Total payments.... 25,671,954 Deficit............ $2,516,692	New York Div., 115 m.; Hartford Div., 146 m.; Highland Div., 174 m.; Midland Div., 154 m.; Air Line-Northampton, 191 m.; Naugatuck Div., 61 m.; Berkshire Div., 181 m.; Worcester Div., 193 m.; Plymouth Div., 279 m.; Taunton Div., 231 m.; Providence Div., 82 m.; Shore Div., 195 m. Total mileage, 2,006. New England S. S. Co. is composed of the Fall River Line, Providence Line, Norwich Line, New London Line, New Bedford Line, New Haven Line, and Bridgeport Line. Express Co.—Adams.	President, Chas. S. Mellen; Vice-Presidents, T. E. Byrnes, Boston; H. M. Kochersperger; E. H. McHenry; E. G. Buckland, Providence, R. I.; B. Campbell; John F. Stevens; Secretary, J. G. Parker; General Manager, S. Higgins. General Offices, New Haven, Ct.; New York Offices, Grand Central Station.
New York, Susquehanna & Western Railroad. [New Jersey and New York.] *For year ending June* 30, 1908 Total earnings.... $3,268,642 Operating expenses 2,514,105 Net earnings..... $754,537 Other income .. .. 56,222 Total net income. $810,759 Total payments.... 895,066 Deficit............ $84,307	Main Line, Jersey City, N. J., to Stroudsburg, Pa., 101 m.; Wilkes-Barre and Eastern R. R., 64.69 m.; Middletown Div., 34.15 m. Total mileage 199.84. Express Co.—Wells, Fargo & Co. This road is now part of the Erie R. R. System.	President, F. D. Underwood; 1st Vice-President, G. F. Brownell; 2d Vice-President, G. A. Richardson; 3d Vice-President and General Traffic Manager. H. B. Chamberlain; General Manager, J. C. Stuart; Secretary, David Bosman. General Offices, 50 Church Street, New York.

Systems, Location, and Financial Data.	Divisions, Mileage, and Operating Express.	General Officers.
New York, Ontario and Western Railway. [New York, Pennsylvania.] *For year ending June* 30, 1907. Total earnings..... $8,121,494 Operating expenses 5,586,951 Net earnings..... $2,534,543 Other income...... 388,664 Total net income.. $2,923,207 Total payments.... 2,564,925 Surplus.......... $358,282 This road is controlled by the N.Y., N.H.& H.R.R.	Main Line, Cornwall, N. Y., to Oswego, N. Y., 271.75 m.; Delhi Br., 16.84 m.; Wharton Valley R.R., 6.80 m.; New Berlin Br., 22.38 m.; Utica Div., 31.30 m.; Rome Br., 12.78 m.; Scranton Div., 54.05 m.; Ellenville Br., 7.80 m.; Pecksport Ry., 3.69 m.; Weehawken, N. J., to Cornwall, N.Y. (trackage rights), 58.07 m.; Ellenville and Kingston R. R., 27.14 m.; Port Jervis, Mont. and Sum. R. R., 38.27 m. Total mileage, 545 87. EXPRESS CO.—Adams.	President, Thomas P. Fowler; Vice-President, J. B. Kerr; Vice-President and General Manager, J. E. Childs; Secretary, R. D. Rickard. General Offices, 56 Beaver Street, New York.
Norfolk and Western Railway. [Maryland, West Virginia, Virginia, North Carolina, Ohio.] *For year ending June* 30, 1908. Total earnings..... $28,962,217 Operating expenses 18,559,487 Net earnings..... $10,402,730 Other income...... 707,029 Total net income. $11,109,759 Total payments... 11,109,392 Surplus.......... $337	Norfolk to Columbus, O., 703.76 m.; Lynchburg to Durham, 115.43 m.; Roanoke to Hagerstown, 238.11 m.; Roanoke to Winston-Salem, 121.30 m.; Radford Junction to Bristol, 110.75 m.; North Carolina Junction to Fries, 43.49 m.; Graham to Norton, 100 40 m.; Portsmouth Junction to Cincinnati and Ivorydale, 105.92 m.; Columbus, Connecting and Terminal R. R., 3.51 m.; branches, 339 22 m. Total mileage, 1,881.89. EXPRESS CO.—Southern.	President, L. E. Johnson; 1st Vice-President, Wm. G. Macdowell, Philadelphia, Pa.; 2d Vice-President and General Manager, N. D. Maher; 3d Vice-President and Traffic Manager, T. S. Davant, Secretary, E. H. Alden, Philadelphia, Pa. General Offices, Roanoke, Va.; New York Offices, 40 Exchange Place and 398 Broadway.
Northern Pacific Ry.—"Yellowstone Park Line." [Wisconsin, Minnesota, North Dakota, Montana, Idaho, Washington, Oregon.] *For year ending June* 30, 1908. Total earnings..... $68,235,484 Operating expenses 42,582,518 Net earnings..... $25,652,966 Other income...... 4,748,415 Total net income. $30,401,381 Total payments .. 24,143,262 Surplus............ $6,258,119	St. Paul, Minn., to Portland, Ore., Tacoma and Seattle, Wash., 2,746.42 m.; other divisions and branches, 2,880.70 m. Total mileage, 5,627.12. This company connects with the Great Northern S. S. Co., Nippon Yusen Kaisha Ocean S. S. Co., China Mutual Steam Navigation Co., and Weir S. S. Lines from Seattle and Tacoma to China, Japan and Manila. EXPRESS CO.—Northern.	President, Howard Elliott; Vice-President, James N. Hill, New York; 2d Vice-President, J. M. Hannaford; 3d Vice-President, C. M. Levey; Secretary, G. H. Earl, New York. General Offices, St. Paul, Minn.; New York Offices, 34 Nassau Street and 319 Broadway.
Oregon Railroad and Navigation Co. [Oregon, Washington, Idaho.] This road is now part of the Union Pacific System.	Portland, Ore., to Huntington, Ore., 405 m.; Spokane Div., 245 m.; other branches, 614 m. Total mileage, 1,264. Steamer Lines: Portland to Astoria and Oregon City. EXPRESS CO.—Pacific.	President, E. H. Harriman, New York; Secretary, W. W. Cotton; Assistant Secretary, Alexander Millar, New York. General Offices, Portland, Ore.; New York Offices, 120 and 287 Broadway.
Oregon Short Line Railroad. [Utah, Wyoming, Idaho, Montana, Oregon.] This road is now part of the Union Pacific System.	Lines in Utah, 208.18 m.; in Wyoming, 119.51 m.; in Idaho, 958.94 m.; in Montana, 29.66 m.; in Oregon, 139.58 m. Total mileage, 1,455.87. EXPRESS CO.—Pacific.	President, Edward H. Harriman, New York; Vice-President and General Manager, W. H. Bancroft, Salt Lake City; Vice-President, Wm. D. Cornish, New York; Secretary, Alex. Millar, New York. General Offices, Salt Lake City, Utah; New York Office, 120 Broadway.
Pennsylvania Railroad. [New York, New Jersey, Pennsylvania, Delaware, Maryland, District of Columbia, Virginia, West Virginia, Michigan, Kentucky, Ohio, Indiana, Illinois.] Official report of earnings, operating expenses, etc., not available when ALMANAC was printed.	Eastern Pennsylvania Div., 1,226.30 m.; Western Pennsylvania Div., 669.97 m.; Philadelphia Terminal Div., 47.68 m.; New Jersey Div., 461.61 m.; Erie Div., 604.84 m.; Northern Central Ry. Div., 460.85 m.; Philadelphia, Baltimore and Washington R. R. Div., 694.15 m.; West Jersey and Sea Shore R. R. Div., 336.81 m.; Buffalo and Allegheny Valley Div., 791.84 m.; Baltimore, Chesapeake and Atlantic Ry., 87.66 m.; Barnegat R. R., 8.15 m.; Cherry Tree and Dixonville R.R., 36.57 m.; Cumberland Valley R. R. lines, 162.19 m.; Long Island R. R. lines, 391.75 m.; Maryland, Delaware & Virginia Ry., 78 33 m.; Monongahela R. R. lines, 57.49 m.; Pemberton & Heightstown R. R., 24 37 m.; other branches, 14.07 m. Total milenge lines east, 6,154.63. Pennsylvania lines west of Pittsburgh, 4,925.97 m. Total mileage 11,080.60. EXPRESS CO.—Adams.	President, James McCrea; 1st Vice-President, John P. Green; 2d Vice-President, Charles E. Pugh; 3d Vice-President, Samuel Rea; 4th Vice-President, John B. Thayer, Jr.; 5th Vice-President, Henry Tatnall; General Manager, W. W. Atterbury; Secretary, Lewis Neilson. General Offices, Broad Street Station, Philadelphia; New York Offices, 85 Cedar Street, 170, 1354 Broadway, and 263 Fifth Ave.

Systems, Location, and Financial Data.	Divisions, Mileage, and Operating Express.	General Officers.
Pere Marquette R.R. [Michigan, Ohio, Indiana, Illinois.] *For year ending June* 30, 1908. Total earnings.. .....$13,691,875 Operating expenses 10,426,790 Net earnings..... $3,265,085 Other income...... 445,282 Total net income $3,710,367 Total payments.... 4,104,034 Deficit........... $393,667	Grand Rapids Dist., 771,99 m.; Saginaw Dist., 1,035.02 m.; Detroit Dist., 188.34 m.; Lines to Canada (Buffalo Division) 365 02 m. Total mileage, 2,360.37. Express Co.—United States.	President and General Manager, William Cotter; Vice-President, J. L. Cramer; Secretary, J. E. Howard; General Traffic Manager, A. Patriarche. General Offices, Detroit, Mich.
Philadelphia and Reading Railway. [New Jersey, Pennsylvania, Delaware.] *For year ending June* 30, 1908 Total earnings......$42,664,595 Operating expenses 25,458,296 Net earnings.....$17,206,299 Total payments.... 10,860,659 Surplus......... $6,345,640	Reading Div., 349.67 m.; Philadelphia Div., 47.22 m.; New York Div., 152.41 m.; Harrisburg Div., 106.90 m.; Shamokin Div., 229.60 m.; Wilmington and Columbia Div., 118.09 m.; other lines operated separately, 487.52 m. Total mileage, 1,491.41. Express Co.—United States.	President, George F. Baer; Vice-President, Theodore Voorhees; Secretary, W. R. Taylor. General Offices, Philadelphia, Pa.
Queen and Crescent Route. (Ohio, Kentucky, Tennessee, Georgia, Alabama, Mississippi, Louisiana.] *For year ending June* 30, 1908. (Alabama Great Southern R. R.) Total earnings......$3,551,501 Operating expenses. 2,925,684 Net earnings ..... $625,817 Other income....... 258,131 Total net income. $883,948 Total payments..... 683,730 Surplus........... $210,218	Comprising the following lines: Cincinnati, New Orleans and Texas Pacific Ry., 338 m.; New Orleans and Northeastern R. R., 196 m.; Alabama and Vicksburg Ry., 142 m.; Vicksburg, Shreveport and Pacific Ry., 171 m.; Alabama Great Southern R. R., 309.41 m. Total mileage, 1,156.41. Express Co.—Southern.	C., N. O. & T. P. Ry.—President, W. W. Finley, Washington, D. C.; Vice-President, T. C. Powell, Cincinnati, O.; Secretary, R. D. Lankford, New York; General Manager, Horace Baker, Cincinnati, O. New York Office, 30 Church Street. Alabama Gt. So. R. R.—President, W. W. Finley, Washington, D. C.; 1st Vice-President, A. B. Andrews, Raleigh, N. C.; Vice-President, T. C. Powell, Cincinnati, O.; General Manager, Horace Baker, Cincinnati, O.
Rio Grande Western Railway. [Colorado and Utah.] Financial report included in Denver and Rio Grande R. R.	Grand Junction, Col., to Ogden, Utah, 328.12 m.; San Pete and Sevier Br., 132.51 m.; Tintic Br., 43.75 m.; Pleasant Valley Br., 21.54 m.; Bingham Br., 14.26 m.; Little Cottonwood Br., 10.16 m.; Provo Cañon Br., 26 m.; Sunnyside Br., 17.38 m.; Park City Br., 32.28 m.; San Pete Valley R. R., 49.68 m.; other branches, 99.02 m. Total mileage, 774.70. Express Co.—Globe; Wells, Fargo & Co.	Chairman of the Board, George J. Gould, New York; President, E. T. Jeffery, New York; Vice-President, Chas. H. Schlacks; Secretary, Stephen Little, New York. General Offices, Denver, Col.; New York Office, 195 Broadway.
Rutland Railroad. [Vermont and New York.] *For year ending Dec.* 31, 1907. Total earnings..... $3,058,087 Operating expenses 2,217,298 Net earnings...... $840,789 Other income....... 49,141 Total net income. $889,930 Total payments.... 746,758 Surplus.......... $143,172	White Creek, Vt., to Canada Line, Que., 161.42 m.; Chatham, N. Y., to Bennington, Vt., 57.21 m.; Bennington, Vt., to No. Bennington, 4.67 m.; Bellows Falls, Vt., to Rutland, Vt., 52.21 m.; Alburgh, Vt., to Ogdensburg, N. Y., 121.60 m.; Canada Line to Noyan Jct., Que., 3.39 m.; Leicester Jct., Vt., to Addison Jct., N. Y., 14 61 m. Total mileage, 415.11. Express Co.—American.	President, W. H. Newman, New York, General Manager, George T. Jarvis. General Offices, Rutland, Vt.
San Antonio and Aransas Pass Railway. [Texas.] *For year ending June* 30, 1908. Total earnings..... $3,157 928 Operating expenses 2,239,362 Net earnings..... $918,566 Other income... 21,376 Total net income.. $939,942 Total payments.... 1,103,564 Deficit........... $163,622	Houston, Tex., to San Antonio, Tex., 238 m.; Kenedy, Tex., to Corpus Christi, Tex., 88 m.; Rockport Br., 21 m.; Lockhart Br., 55 m.; Alice Br., 43 m.; Waco Br., 171 m.; Kerrville Br., 71 m.; Brownsville Br., 36.3 m. Total mileage, 723.7. Express Co.—Wells, Fargo & Co.	President, W. H. McIntyre; Vice-President and General Manager, W. M. Hobbs; 2d Vice-President, M. D. Monserrate; Secretary, Reagan Houston. General Offices, San Antonio, Tex.; New York Office, 120 Broadway.

Systems, Location, and Financial Data.	Divisions, Mileage, and Operating Express.	General Officers.
Seaboard Air Line Ry. [Virginia, North Carolina, South Carolina, Georgia, Florida, Alabama.] *For year ending June* 30, 1907. Total earnings.....$16,427,942 Operating expenses. 12,948,041 Net earnings..... $3,479,901 Other income....... 16,296 Total net income..$3,496,197 Fixed charges...... 3,954,497 Deficit.............. $458,300	First Div., 370.35 m.; Second Div., 386.51 m.; Third Div., 398.26 m.; Fourth Div., 534.24 m.; Fifth Div., 462.44 m.; Sixth Div., 459.17 m. Total mileage, 2,610.97. EXPRESS Co.—Southern.	Receivers, S. D. Warfield, R. L. Williams, and E. C. Duncan, Baltimore, Md.; Chief Executive Officer for Receivers, W. A. Garrett, Portsmouth, Va.; Vice-President, L. Sevier, Portsmouth, Va.; Secretary, D. C. Porteous, New York. General Offices, Portsmouth and Norfolk, Va.; New York Offices, 24 Broad Street, 387 and 1183 Broadway.
Southern Pacific Company.—"Sunset, Ogden and Shasta Routes." [Louisiana, Texas, New Mexico, Arizona, California, Nevada, Oregon, Utah.] *For year ending June* 30, 1907. (Including water lines also.) Total earnings...... $124,864,440 Operating expenses 82,578,907 Net receipts ...$42,285,533 Other income..... 3,665,365 Total net income $45,950,898 Total payments. 32,086,175 Surplus $13,864,723	Lines south of Portland and west of Ogden and Rio Grande River—Nevada and California Ry., 330.76 m.; Central Pacific Ry., 1,494.42 m.; Oregon & California R. R., 665.68 m.; South Pacific Coast Ry., 101.83 m.; Southern Pacific R. R., 3,264.09 m.; New Mexico and Arizona R. R. 88.19 m.; Sonora R. R., 263.45 m. Total mileage, 6,208.42. Sunset Central Lines — Morgan's Louisiana and Texas R. R. and Steamship Co., 350.95 m.; Iberia and Vermilion R. R., 21.00 m.; Louisiana Western R. R., 198.28 m.; Texas and New Orleans R. R., 448.48 m.; Galveston, Harrisburg and San Antonio Ry., 1,342.94 m.; Houston and Texas Central R. R., 789.01 m.; Houston, E. and W. Texas Ry., 190.94 m.; Houston and Shreveport R. R., 39.78 m. Total mileage, 3,381.38. EXPRESS Co.—Wells, Fargo & Co.	President, E. H. Harriman, New York; Vice-Presidents, W. D. Cornish, New York; J. C. Stubbs, Chicago, Ill.; J. Kruttschnitt, Chicago, Ill.; Vice-President and General Manager, E. E. Calvin; San Francisco, Cal.; Secretary, Alex. Millar, New York. General Offices, San Francisco, Cal.; New York Offices, 120 and 349 Broadway.
Southern Railway. [District of Columbia, Virginia, North Carolina, South Carolina, Georgia, Florida, Alabama, Mississippi, Tennessee, Kentucky, Illinois, Indiana, Missouri.] *For year ending June* 30, 1908. Total earnings.....$52,941,716 Operating expenses 39,854,722 Net earnings ....$13,086,994 Other income...... 2,441,391 Total net income.$15,528,385 Total payments.... 15,126,535 Surplus.......... $401,850	*Northern District:* Washington Div., 345.63 m.; Danville Div., 371.98 m.; Richmond Div., 279.15 m.; Norfolk Div., 427.18 m.; Durham Div., 241.25 m.; Winston-Salem Div., 379.01 m. Total, 1,802 95 m. *Middle District:* Knoxville Div., 359.02 m.; Murphy Div., 122.50 m.; Coster Div., 214.18 m.; Memphis Div., 332.13 m.; Asheville Div., 249 m. Total, 1,276.83 m. *Eastern District:* Charlotte Div., 462.14 m.; Columbia Div., 789.51 m.; Charleston Div., 446.57 m. Total, 1,698.22 m. *Western District:* Birmingham Div., 345.73 m.; Mobile Div., 568.47 m.; Atlanta Div., 508.27 m.; Columbus Div., 200.28 m. Total, 1,622.75 m. St. Louis-Louisville Line, 543.15 m. Southern Ry. in Miss., 268.92 m. Total mileage of system, 7,212.82. EXPRESS Co.—Southern.	President, W. W. Finley, Washington, D.C.; 1st Vice-President, A. B. Andrews, Raleigh, N. C.; 2d Vice-President, J. M. Culp, Washington, D.C.; Vice-President and General Manager, C. H. Ackert, Washington, D. C.; Vice-Presidents, H. B. Spencer, Washington, D. C.; T. C. Powell, St. Louis, Mo.; Fairfax Harrison, Washington, D. C.; Secretary, R. D. Lankford, New York. General Offices, Washington, D. C. New York Offices, Hudson Terminal and 299, 1200 Broadway.
St. Joseph and Grand Island Railway. [Missouri, Kansas, and Nebraska.] *For year ending June* 30, 1908. Total earnings..........$1,602,311 Operating expenses. 937,387 Net earnings...... $664,924 Other income....... 59,277 Total net income.. $724,201 Total payments .... 387,737 Surplus $336,464	Kansas City, Mo., to Grand Island, Neb., 313 m. EXPRESS Co.—Wells, Fargo & Co.	General Manager, J. Berlingett; Secretary, C. C. Tegethoff. General Offices, St. Joseph, Mo.

Systems, Location, and Financial Data.	Divisions, Mileage, and Operating Express.	General Officers.
St. Louis Southwestern Railway System.—"Cotton Belt Route." [Illinois, Missouri, Arkansas, Louisiana, Texas.] *For year ending June* 30, 1908. Total earnings..... $9,599,600 Operating expenses 7,502,594 Net earnings......$2,097,006 Other income....... 644,899 Total net income..$2,741,905 Total payments.... 2,422,080 Surplus............ $319,825	*St. Louis Southwestern Ry.:* Main Line, 428.9 m.; Stuttgart Br., 25.1 m., New Madrid Br., 6.1 m.; Little Rock Br., 44.4 m.; Shreveport Br.; 62.6 m.; Cairo Br., 57.7 m., Illinois Div. (joint track), 188.2 m. Total mileage, 773. *St. Louis Southwestern Ry. of Texas:* Main Line, 305.4 m.; Sherman Br., 52 3 m.; Fort Worth Br., 154.3 m.; Hillsboro Br., 40.2 m.; Lufkin Br., 130 9 m.; Dallas Br., 13.7 m. Total mileage, 696 8. Grand total mileage. 1,469 8. Express Co.—Pacific.	President, Edwin Gould, New York; Vice-President and General Manager, F. H. Britton, St. Louis, Mo.; Freight Traffic Manager, H. E. Farrell, St. Louis, Mo.; Secretary, A. J. Trussell, New York. General Offices, St. Louis, Mo., and 195 Broadway, New York. General Offices St. L. S. W. Ry. of Texas, Tyler, Tex.
Texas and Pacific Ry. [Louisiana, Arkansas, and Texas.] *For year ending June* 30, 1908. Total earnings.....$14,275,481 Operating expenses 10,911,201 Net earnings......$3,364,280 Fixed charges not reported by Company.	Eastern Div., 511 m.; Rio Grande Div., 620 m.; Louisiana Div., 356 m.; Port Allen Br., 102 m.; La Fourche Br., 28 m.; Texarkana Dist., 70 m.; Avoyelles Br., 56 m.; Natchitoches Br., 89 m.; Napoleonville Br., 16 m.; Bunkie and Gulf Extension, 37 m. Total mileage, 1,885. Express Co.—Pacific.	President, George J. Gould; Vice-President, Frank J. Gould, New York; Vice-President and General Manager, L. S. Thorne, Dallas, Tex.; Secretary, C. E. Satterlee, New York. General Offices, 195 Broadway, New York, and Dallas, Tex.
Toledo and Ohio Central Railway, and Kanawha and Michigan Ry. "Ohio Central Lines." [Ohio and West Virginia.] *For year ending June* 30, 1908. (Toledo and Ohio Cent. Ry.) Total earnings......$4,191,998 Operating expenses. 2,786,207 Net earnings......$1,405,791 Other income. ..... 176.893 Total net income. $1,582,684 Total payments...... 788,918 Surplus............. $793,766	Toledo to Bremen, 172.91 m.; New Lexington to Corning, 12.33 m.; Whitmore to Thurston, 145.57 m.; Roseland to Truro Junction, 4.20 m.; Peoria to St. Marys, 59.90 m.; trackage rights, 45.99 m. Total mileage, 440.90. Express Co.—United States.	Chairman of Board, Decatur Axtell, Richmond, Va.; President, N. Monsarrat, Columbus, O.; 1st Vice-President T. & O. C. Ry., Chas. G. Hickox, Cleveland, O.; 1st Vice-President K. & M. Ry., R. W. Hickox, Cleveland, O.; 2d Vice-President and Secretary, J. M. Ferris. General Offices, Toledo, O.
Toledo, St. Louis and Western Railroad.—"Clover Leaf Route." [Ohio, Indiana, Illinois, Missouri.] *For year ending June* 30, 1908. Total earnings.......$3,818,467 Operating expenses. 2,574,752 Net earnings......$1,243,715 Other income........ 418,943 Total net income. $1,662,658 Total payments..... 1,642,976 Surplus............ $19,682	Toledo, O., to St. Louis, Mo., 450.72 m. Express Co.—National.	President T. P. Shonts, New York; Vice-President, E. Hawley, New York; 2d Vice-President, Geo. H. Ross, Chicago, Ill.; General Traffic Manager, W. L. Ross, Chicago, Ill.; Secretary, James S. Mackie, New York.
Union Pacific Railroad.—"Overland Route." [Kansas, Nebraska, Iowa, Colorado, Wyoming, Utah, Missouri.] *For year ending June* 30, 1907. (Including Union Pacific, Oregon R. R. & Nav. Co., and Oregon Short Line.) Total earnings.....$76,040,727 Operating expenses 40,574,889 Net earnings.....$35,465,838 Other income...... 12,079,516 Total net income $47 545,354 Total payments... 36,392,189 Surplus..........$11,153,165	Nebraska Div., 799.54 m.; Kansas Div., 936.45 m.; Colorado Div., 752.97 m.; Wyoming Div., 461.03 m.; Utah Div., 350.93 m. Total mileage, 3,300.92. Express Co.—Pacific. This road also controls the Leavenworth, Kansas and Western Ry., Oregon R. R. and Nav. Co., and the Oregon Short Line.	President, E. H. Harriman, New York; Vice-President. Wm. D. Cornish, New York; Vice-President and General Manager, A. L. Mohler; Traffic Director, J. C. Stubbs, Chicago; Secretary, Alexander Millar, New York. General Offices, Omaha, Neb.; New York Office, 120 Broadway.

Systems, Location, and Financial Data.	Divisions, Mileage, and Operating Express.	General Officers.
Vandalia Railroad Co.—[Indiana, Illinois, Missouri.] *For year ending Dec.* 31, 1907. Total earnings.....$10,053,186 Operating expenses 7,947,472 Net earnings..... $2,105,714 Other income...... 27,772 Total net income $2,133,486 Total payments.... 1,053,540 Surplus........... $1,079,946	St. Louis Div., 243 m; Centre Point Br., 8 m.; Michigan Div., 275 m.; Vincennes Div., 117 m.; branches, 16 m; Terre Haute and Peoria R.R., 174 m. Total mileage, 832. Express Co.—Adams.	President, Joseph Wood; Vice-Presidents, J. J. Turner, D. T. McCabe and E. B. Taylor; General Manager, Benj. McKeen, St. Louis, Mo. General Offices, Pittsburgh, Pa.
Wabash Railroad. [Ontario, Canada, Ohio, Indiana, Michigan, Illinois, Missouri, Iowa.] *For year ending June* 30, 1908. Total earnings.....$25,740,074 Operating expenses 18,843,747 Net earnings..... $6,896,326 Other income...... 697,648 Total net income $7,593,974 Total payments.... 7,377,108 Surplus........... $216,866	Lines: In New York, 31 m.; in Canada, 244.3 m.; in Michigan, 105.6 m.; in Ohio, 170.2 m.; in Indiana, 357.4 m.; in Illinois, 745.2 m.; in Missouri, 654 m.; in Iowa, 208.9 m.; in Nebraska, .6 m. Total mileage, 2,517.2. Express Co.—Pacific.	President, F. A. Delano, Chicago, Ill.; Vice-Presidents, Edgar T. Welles, New York; W. H. Blodgett, and E. B. Pryor, St. Louis, Mo.; General Manager, Henry Miller, St. Louis, Mo.; Secretary, J. C. Otteson, New York. General Offices, St. Louis, Mo.; New York Offices, 195 and 387 Broadway.
Western Maryland Railroad. [Maryland, Pennsylvania, West Virginia.] *For year ending June* 30, 1907. Total earnings......$5,600,454 Operating expenses 3,729,978 Net earnings......$1,870,476 Other income........ 785,074 Total net income..$2,655,550 Total payments..... 2,644,586 Surplus............ $10,964	Main Line, 296 m. Total mileage, 543. Express Co.—Adams.	Receiver, B. F. Bush; Vice-President and General Manager, A. Robertson; Secretary, L. F. Timmerman, New York. General Offices, Baltimore, Md.
Wheeling and Lake Erie Railroad. [Ohio.] *For year ending June* 30, 1907. Total earnings......$6,124,206 Operating expenses. 4,125,369 Net earnings......$1,998,837 Other income....... 120,430 Total net income..$2,119,267 Total payments..... 1,592,335 Surplus............ $526,932	Toledo Div., 218 m.; Cleveland Div., 144 m.; Chagrin Falls Br., 8 m.; Ohio River Div., 13 m.; Huron Div., 13 m.; Carrollton Br., 45 m.; other branches, 47 m. Total mileage, 488. Express Co.—Pacific.	Receiver, B. A. Worthington; President, F. A. Delano, Chicago, Ill.; Vice-President, A. W. Krech, New York, Secretary, H. B. Henson, New York. General Offices, Cleveland, O.; New York Office, 195 Broadway.
Wisconsin Central Ry. [Illinois, Wisconsin, Michigan, Minnesota.] *For year ending June* 30, 1908. Total earnings......$7,307,311 Operating expenses. 5,130,643 Net earnings......$2,176,668 Other income....... 61,378 Total net income. $2,115,295 Total payments..... 1,764,285 Surplus............ $351,010	Chicago, Ill., to Trout Brook Junction, Minn., 452.02 m.; Abbotsford to Ashland, 132.56 m.; Portage Br., 70.75 m.; Moutello Br., 7.68 m.; Marshfield Br., 22.44 m.; Eau Claire Br., 9.84 m.; Manitowoc Div., 44.18 m.; Nekoosa Br., 32.61 m.; Ladysmith Br., 45.31 m; spurs to industries, 216.50 m.; other branches, 44.01 m. Total mileage, 1,077.90. Express Co.—National.	President, W. A. Bradford; Secretary, G. W. Webster, Milwaukee, Wis. General Offices, Chicago, Ill.; New York Offices, 17 Nassau St., 290 Broadway.

Railway Employes in the United States.

COMPARATIVE SUMMARY OF EMPLOYES AND AVERAGE DAILY COMPENSATION.
(From Statistical Report of the Interstate Commerce Commission.)

Class.	1907.		1906.		1905.		1904.		Average Daily Compensation.		
	Number.	Per 100 miles of line.	Number.	Per 100 miles of line.	Number.	Per 100 miles of line.	Number.	Per 100 miles of line.	1907.	1906.	1905.
General officers	6,407	3	6,090	3	5,536	2	5,165	2	11.93	11.81	11.74
Other officers	7,549	3	6,705	3	5,706	3	5,275	3	5.99	5.82	6.02
General office clerks	65,700	29	57,210	26	51,284	24	46,037	22	2.30	2.24	2.24
Station agents	35,649	16	34,940	16	35,245	16	34,918	16	2.05	1.94	1.93
Other stationmen	152,929	67	138,778	62	125,180	58	120,002	57	1.78	1.69	1.71
Enginemen	65,298	29	59,855	27	54,817	25	52,451	25	4.30	4.12	4.12
Firemen	69,384	31	62,678	28	57,892	27	53,004	26	2.54	2.42	2.38
Conductors	48,869	22	43,936	20	41,061	19	39,645	19	3.67	3.51	3.50
Other trainmen	134,257	59	119,087	53	111,405	51	106,734	50	2.54	2.35	2.31
Machinists	55,244	24	51,253	23	47,018	22	46,272	22	2.89	2.69	2.65
Carpenters	70,394	31	63,830	29	56,089	26	53,646	25	2.40	2.28	2.25
Other shopmen	221,656	97	199,940	90	176,348	81	159,472	75	2.06	1.92	1.92
Section foremen	41,391	18	40,463	18	38,217	18	37,609	18	1.90	1.80	1.79
Other trackmen	367,277	162	343,791	155	311,185	143	289,044	136	1.46	1.36	1.32
Switchtenders, watchmen	53,414	23	49,659	22	45,532	21	46,262	22	1.87	1.80	1.79
Tel. operators, despatchers	39,193	17	36,090	16	31,963	15	30,425	14	2.26	2.13	2.19
Emplo's—acc't float'g equip't.	9,139	4	8,314	4	8,753	4	7,495	3	2.27	2.10	2.17
All other emplo's and labor's.	228,324	100	198,736	89	178,965	82	160,565	76	1.92	1.83	1.83
Total	1,672,074	735	1,521,355	684	1,382,196	637	1,296,121	611			

Railway Accidents in the United States.

(From Statistical Report of the Interstate Commerce Commission.)

Year Ending June 30.	Employes.		Passengers.		Other Persons.		Total.	
	Killed.	Injured.	Killed.	Injured.	Killed.	Injured.	Killed.	Injured.
1897	1,693	27,667	222	2,795	4,522	6,269	6,437	36,731
1898	1,958	31,761	221	2,945	4,680	6,176	6,859	40,882
1899	2,210	34,923	239	3,442	4,674	6,255	7,123	44,620
1900	2,550	39,643	249	4,128	5,066	6,549	7,865	50,320
1901	2,675	41,142	282	4,988	5,498	7,209	8,455	53,339
1902	2,969	50,524	345	6,683	5,274	7,455	8,588	64,662
1903	3,606	60,481	355	8,231	5,879	7,841	9,840	76,553
1904	3,632	67,067	441	9,111	5,973	7,977	10,046	84,155
1905	3,361	66,833	537	10,457	5,805	8,718	9,703	86,008
1906	3,929	76,701	359	10,764	6,330	10,241	10,618	97,706
1907	4,534	87,644	610	13,041	6,695	10,331	11,839	111,016

The total number of passengers carried in 1907 was 873,905,133, as against in 1906, §797,946,116, 738,834,667 in 1905, 715,419,682 in 1904, 694,891,535 in 1903, 649,878,505 in 1902, 607,278,121 in 1901, 576,831,251 in 1900, 523,176,508 in 1899, 501,066,681 in 1898, and 489,445,198 in 1897. § Includes an estimate for certain roads, as their records for this item were destroyed in the San Francisco fire of April, 1906,

Kind of Accident.	Employes.		Passengers.		Other Persons.	
	Killed.	Injured.	Killed.	Injured.	Killed.	Injured.
Coupling or uncoupling	308	4,353	....	......	....	......
Collisions	572	4,724	214	4,294	63	706
Derailments	322	2,626	162	3,819	81	642
Parting of trains	14	451	1	54	5	25
Locomotives or cars breaking down	28	368	....	7	2	7
Falling from trains, locomotives, or cars	580	6,711	63	479	389	668
Jumping on or off trains, locomotives, or cars	225	6,387	88	1,552	507	1,498
Struck by trains, locomotives, or cars	1,648	2,589	39	134	5,288	4,742
Overhead obstructions	103	1,091	....	......	....	......
Other causes	424	19,696	27	2,312	321	1,695
Total	4,224	48,996	594	12,651	6,656	9,983

Three hundred and sixty-five persons were killed and 39,386 injured in handling traffic, tools, machinery, supplies, etc., and in getting on or off locomotives or cars at rest and from other causes.

National Association of Railroad Commissioners.

President, Martin S. Decker, Albany, N. Y. *First Vice-President*, R. Hudson Burr, Tallahassee, Fla. *Second Vice-President*, Charles F. Staples, St. Paul, Minn. *Secretary*, William H. Connolly, Interstate Commerce Commission, Washington, D. C.

Railroad Speed.

NOTABLE FAST RUNS OF PASSENGER TRAINS FOR LONG DISTANCES.

DATE.	Railroad.	Terminals.	Distance, Miles.	Inclusive. Time, H. M.	Inclusive. Miles per Hour.
May, 1848.	Great Western (England)	London—Didcot	53.25	0.47	68
July, 1885.	West Shore	East Buffalo—Frankfort	201.7	4.00	50.4
Aug., 1888.	London, N.W. & Caledonian	London—Edinburgh	400	7.38	52.4
Aug., 1894.	Plant System. Atlantic Coast Line	Jacksonville—Richmond	661.5	12.51	51.48
April, 1895.	Pennsylvania	Camden—Atlantic City	58.3	0.45¾	76.50
Aug., 1895.	London & Northwestern	London—Aberdeen	540	8.32	63.28*
Sept., 1895.	New York Central & H. R.	New York—Buffalo	436.50	6.47	64.33*
Sept., 1895.	N. Y. Central "World Flyer"	Albany—Syracuse	148	2.10	68.3
Feb., 1897.	Chicago, Burlington & Quincy	Chicago—Denver	1,025	18.52	58.74
April, 1897.	Lehigh Val., Black Diamond Exp.	Alpine, N. Y.—Geneva Junc., N. Y.	43.96	0.33	80
Aug., 1897.	Union Pacific	North Platte—Omaha	291	4.39	63.49
May, 1900.	Burlington Route	Burlington—Chicago	205.8	3.08½	65.5‡
Mar., 1902.	Burlington Route	Eckley—Wray	14.8	0.9	98.7
Aug., 1902.	"20th Century Ltd.," on L. Shore	Kendallville—Toledo	91	1.15	72.8
Mar., 1903.	Atlantic Coast Line	Jacksonville—Savannah	172	2.32	70.7
May, 1903.	"20th Century Ltd.," on L. Shore	Toledo—Elkhart	133.4	1.54	70.2
July, 1903.	Great Western (England)	London—Plymouth	246	3.54	63.13
April, 1904.	Michigan Central	Niagara Falls—Windsor	225.66	3 11½	70.74
July, 1904.	Great Western (England)	Paddington—Bristol	118.5	1.24	84.6
Nov., 1904.	Pennsylvania	Crestline—Fort Wayne	131	1.53	69.56
June, 1905.	Pennsylvania	Chicago—Pittsburgh	468	7.20	63.53*
June, 1905.	Lake Shore & Mich. Southern	Buffalo—Chicago	525	7.50	69.69‡
June, 1905.	Pennsylvania	New York—Chicago	897	16.3	56.07
June, 1905.	New York Central	Chicago—New York	960.52	15.56	60.28‡
July, 1905.	Pennsylvania	Washington, O.—Fort Wayne	81	1.4	75.84
Oct., 1905.	Pittsburgh, Ft. Wayne & C.	Crestline, O.—Clark Junc., Ind.	257.4	3.27	74.55

*Including stops. ‡Excluding stops.

FASTEST RECORDED RUNS FOR SHORT DISTANCES.

DATE.	Railroad.	Terminals.	Distance, Miles.	Time, M. S.	Miles per Hour.
May, 1893.	N. Y. Central & H. R.	Crittenden—"Empire State Exp."	1	0 32	112.5
Aug., 1895.	Pennsylvania	Landover—Anacosta	5.1	3.00	102
Jan., 1899.	Burlington Route	Siding—Arion	2.4	1.20	108
Mar., 1901.	Plant System	Run from Fleming to Jacksonville.	5	2.30	120
Jan., 1903.	N. Y. Central & H. R.	Palmyra—Macedon	7.29	4.00	109 35
April, 1904.	Michigan Central	Crisman—Lake	3.73	2.00	111.90
July, 1904.	Phila. & Reading	Egg Harbor—Brigantine Junction.	4.8	2.30	115.20
Oct., 1904.	N. Y. Central & H. R.	Croton—Ossining	3.51	2.00	105

The fastest time on record for a distance of over 440 miles was made by the Lake Shore and Michigan Southern R.R. from Buffalo to Chicago, in June, 1905, noted above. The fastest long-distance run less than 440 miles was on the New York Central R.R. September 11, 1895, from New York to Buffalo, 436 1-2 miles, in 407 minutes actual time. Average speed, 64 1-3 miles an hour, with two stops and 28 slow-ups, and on January 1, 1903, from Albany to Buffalo, 302 miles, in 295 minutes.

Among the fastest regular trains in the United States, for a shorter distance, are believed to be the New York Central "Empire State Express," between New York and Albany, 143 miles in 160 minutes, and the "Congressional Limited," on the Pennsylvania Railroad, which makes the run from Jersey City to Washington in 4 hours, 46 minutes, a distance of 227 miles.

On August 15, 1898, on P. & R. and C. R. R. of N. J., "Royal Blue Line," between Elizabeth, N. J., and Jenkintown, a distance of 69 miles, in 61 minutes, including 2 "slow-ups," some of the miles being traversed in 38 seconds.

The quickest run between Jersey City and Washington, 231 miles, was made on the Central Railroad of New Jersey, March 2, 1897 (by a special train, bearing Vice-President-elect Hobart and party), in 4 hours 8 minutes, making the running time, including "slow-ups" for taking water, changing engines, etc., 60 miles an hour. This beat the time of the "Aunt Jack" train, made by the Madison Square Theatre Company March 10, 1890, which was 4 hours 18 minutes, each way, going and returning.

The fastest long-distance foreign trains, including all stops, are, according to the "Railroad Gazette," as follows:

ROUTE.	Railways.	From	To	Miles.	Time—Hrs. Min.	Stops.	Inclusive Speed in Miles per Hour.
Sud Express	Orleans and Midi	Paris	Bayonne	486¼	8 59	6	54.13
East Coast	Gt. N. and N. E. Railways	London	Edinburgh	393⅛	7 45	3	50.77
West Coast	L. & N. W. and Caledonian Rys.	London	Glasgow	401½	8 00	3	50.18

Of long-distance runs in France one is made on the Northern Railway of France by the Paris-Calais express, which runs 185 miles in 184½ minutes, or a fraction over a mile a minute, allowing for a stoppage of 2½ minutes at Amiens.

Other notable long-distance fast runs: February 14-15, 1897—Pennsylvania Railroad and C., B. and Q., Jersey City to Denver, 1,937 miles, in 48 hours; average speed, 40.3 miles per hour. August 29-31, 1891—Canadian Pacific, Vancouver to Brockville, 2,802 miles, in 77 hours 9 minutes; average speed, 36.32 miles per hour.

The Jarrett and Palmer special theatrical train, Jersey City to Oakland (San Francisco), 3,311 miles, June, 1876, 83 hours 45 minutes; average speed, 39.53 miles per hour.

In October, 1905, the "Harriman Special" made the run from Oakland to Jersey City (3,239 miles) in 73 hours, 12 minutes, or 44.30 miles per hour. In May, 1906, the "Harriman Special" made the run from Oakland, Cal., to New York City in 71 hours, 27 minutes.

The "Scott Special" left Los Angeles, Cal., July 9, 1905, and arrived in Chicago (2,445.5 miles), July 11, having made the run in 44 hours 54 minutes, maintaining an average speed while in motion of 51 miles an hour.

On November 15, 1907, at Clayton, N. J., in a trial test on Pennsylvania R. R. between steam and electric locomotives, the steam engine made 93.6 miles an hour on a specially built seven-mile curved track, while the electric locomotive made but 90 miles an hour.

Railroad Traffic of the World.

Countries.	Miles of Railroad.	Cost of Roads and Equipments.	Passengers Carried.	Tons of Freight Carried.	Receipts.	Expenditures.
Europe	175,000	$20,100,000,000	2,700,000,000	1,145,000,000	$1,800,000,000	$1,040,000,000
America	250,000	15,800,000,000	700,000,000	1,250,000,000	1,800,000,000	1,300,000,000
Africa.........	12,500	760,000,000	36,000,000	11,000,000	65,000,000	34,000,000
Asia...........	37,500	1,500,000,000	248,000,000	42,000,000	120,000,000	60,500,000
Australia ...	15,000	760,000,000	62,000,000	13,500,000	55,000,000	33,000,000
Total	490,000	$38,920,000,000	3,746,000,000	2,461,500,000	$3,840,000,000	$2,427,500,000

These estimates are for 1900. Cost of roads and equipments in 1906 was estimated at $43,000,000,000, or an average of $76,000 per mile.

Railway Mileage in the United States.

(From Statistical Report of the Interstate Commerce Commission.)

State or Territory.	Mileage on June 30, 1907. Official.	Unofficial.	Total Mileage.	State or Territory.	Mileage on June 30, 1907. Official.	Unofficial.	Total Mileage.
Alabama..................	4,860.62	177.00	5,037.62	New Jersey..................	2,250.21	51.85	2,302.06
Alaska (See foot note)	.....	......	......	New Mexico..................	2,965.02	2.00	2,967.02
Arizona..................	1,928.48	2.50	1,930.98	New York..................	8,471.89	32.86	8,504.75
Arkansas..................	4,860.35	22.50	4,883.35	North Carolina..................	4,384.87	91.50	4,476.37
California..................	6,663.71	171.89	6,835.60	North Dakota..................	3,905.57	......	3,905.57
Colorado..................	5,295.12	.30	5,295.43	Ohio..................	9,260.60	13.85	9,274.45
Connecticut..................	1,015.61	......	1,015.61	Oklahoma..................	2,821.32	......	2,821.32
Delaware..................	335.98	......	335.98	Oregon..................	1,938.92	17.00	1,955.92
District of Columbia...	31.32	.80	32.12	Pennsylvania..................	11,258.66	99.11	11,357.77
Florida..................	3,970.49	40.33	4,010.82	Rhode Island..................	208.39	3.40	211.79
Georgia..................	6,786.33	82.50	6,868.83	South Carolina..................	3,270.91	53.50	3,324.41
Idaho..................	1,731.16	32.54	1,763.70	South Dakota..................	3,702.79	....	3,702.79
Illinois..................	12,137.10	68.98	12,206.08	Tennessee..................	3,725.27	35.50	3,760.77
Indiana..................	7,259.32	9.50	7,268.82	Texas..................	12,931.85	55.96	12,987.81
Indian Territory..................	2,667.05	90.30	2,757.35	Utah..................	1,956.59	29.50	1,986.09
Iowa..................	9,867.00	44.53	9,911.53	Vermont..................	1,071.47	22.76	1,094.23
Kansas..................	8,935.54	5.50	8,941.04	Virginia..................	4,055.66	131.14	4,186.80
Kentucky..................	3,441.19	42.95	3,484.14	Washington..................	3,766.82	39.80	3,806.62
Louisiana..................	4,557.70	180.20	4,737.90	West Virginia..................	3,264.02	91.42	3,355.44
Maine..................	2,093.46	57.46	2,150.92	Wisconsin..................	7,459.09	167.80	7,626.89
Maryland..................	1,431.94	36.88	1,468.82	Wyoming..................	1,525.59	......	1,525.59
Massachusetts..................	2,111.78	15.17	2,126.95				
Michigan..................	8,940.71	35.58	8,976.29	Grand total in U. S. 1907	237,670.85	2,280.34	*229,951.19
Minnesota..................	8,246.38	39.50	8,285.88	Grand total in U. S. 1906	222,571.52	1,791.65	224,363.17
Mississippi..................	4,081.11	88.00	4,169.11	Grand total in U. S. 1905	217,017.68	1,083.36	218,101.04
Missouri..................	8,038.52	63.48	8,101.95	Grand total in U. S. 1904	212,577.57	1,326.77	213,904.34
Montana..................	3,307.27	......	3,307.27	Grand total in U. S. 1903	207,186.84	790.38	207,977.22
Nebraska..................	5,931.61	33.10	5,964.71	Grand total in U. S. 1902	201,672.83	799.02	202,471.85
Nevada..................	1,699.68	......	1,699.68	Grand total in U. S. 1901	196,075.07	1,162.37	197,237.44
New Hampshire..................	1,248.30	......	1,248.30	Grand total in U. S. 1900	192,940.67	405.11	193,345.78

* Excludes mileage (145.89) in Alaska and Hawaii.

Wages of British Railway Employes.

A report on the number of railway employés in England, with the amount of wages paid by classes, recently published by the Amalgamated Society of Railway Servants, is the first complete one of the kind that has yet been issued. It was prepared by the secretary from reports called for last August, and may be accepted as correct. The report covers for the United Kingdom no less than 259,280 railway employés, who are always called in England, by law and usage, "railway servants." The fact is shown that over 100,000 of these are working at a wage of £1, or $4.86 per week, and are given in three several wage groups, as follows:

Group.	England and Wales.	Scotland.	Ireland.	United Kingdom.
$4.86 and under..................................	81,300	12,960	6,650	100,930
$5.10 to $7.29..................................	113,780	13,410	1,640	128,810
$7.35 and over..................................	26,610	2,320	810	29,540
Total	221,690	28,690	8,900	259,280

In these classifications the classes known as station masters, inspectors, clerks, laborers and mechanics in shops are not included, they not being under the care of the Amalgamated Society. If the pay of these several classes of railway workers were considered it would bring the general average up to $6.17, which figures are quoted by the Board of Trade as correct for 1906. In this calculation the amount paid for all overtime is taken into general wage account, which, under the rules governing railway labor, makes a considerable amount. This being deducted the general average of wage is about $5.75 per week for all and every class of labor employed in railway operation and maintenance. The classes not included by the Amalgamated Society number approximately 320,000, and on the basis afforded by its report the wage division shows 134,000 employés receiving $5.00 or less; 107,000, $5.00 to $7.50; and 78,000, $7.50 and over.—*Railway Age.*

UNITED STATES INTERSTATE COMMERCE COMMISSION.

WASHINGTON, D. C.

Martin A. Knapp, of New York, Chairman; Judson C. Clements, of Georgia; Charles A. Prouty, of Vermont; Francis M. Cockrell, of Missouri; Franklin K. Lane, of California; Edgar E. Clark, of Iowa; James S. Harlan, of Illinois. Edward A. Moseley, Secretary.

STATE RAILROAD COMMISSIONERS.

Alabama Railroad Commission—Montgomery. Chas. Henderson, President, Troy; W. D. Nesbitt, Birmingham; J. G. Harris, Montgomery; S. P. Kennedy, Secretary, Montgomery.

Arkansas Railroad Commission—Little Rock. R. P. Allen, Chairman; J. E. Hampton, J. W. Crockett; Wm. E. Floyd, Secretary.

California Railroad Commission—A. C. Irwin, President, Marysville, H. D. Loveland, San Francisco; Theo. Summerland, Los Angeles; Judson C. Brusie, Secretary, San Francisco.

Colorado State Board of Equalization—A. B. McGaffey, Secretary, Denver, Col.

Connecticut Board of Railroad Commissioners—Hartford. A. F. Gates, Chairman, Hartford; William O. Seymour, Ridgefield; O. R. Fyler, Torrington; Henry F. Billings, Clerk, Hartford.

Florida Railroad Commissioners—Tallahassee. R. Hudson Burr, Chairman; J. L. Morgan, White Springs; N. A. Blitch; Royal C. Dunn, Secretary.

Georgia Railroad Commission—S. G. McLendon, Chairman, Thomasville; H. W. Hill, Greenville; F. E. Callaway, La Grange; O. B. Stevens, Atlanta; George Hillyer, Atlanta; Geo. F. Montgomery, Secretary, Atlanta.

Idaho State Board of Equalization—Robt. S. Bragaw, State Auditor and Secretary, Boise City.

Illinois Railroad and Warehouse Commission—W. H. Boys, Chairman, Streator; B. A. Eckhart, Chicago; J. A. Willoughby, Belleville; Wm. Kilpatrick, Secretary, Springfield.

Indiana Railroad Commissioners—Indianapolis. Union B. Hunt, Chairman; Wm. J. Wood, C. V. McAdams, Chas. B. Ritey, Secretary.

Iowa Board of Railroad Commissioners—Des Moines. W. L. Eaton, Chairman; D. J. Palmer, N. S. Ketchum; D. N. Lewis, Secretary.

Kansas Railroad Commission—Topeka. G. W. Kanavel, Chairman; C. A. Ryker, F. J. Ryan; E. C. Shiner, Secretary.

Kentucky Railroad Commission—Frankfort. A. T. Siler, Chairman, Williamsburg; McD. Ferguson, La Center; L. P. Tarlton, Frankfort; D. B. Cornett, Secretary, Frankfort.

Louisiana Railroad Commission—Baton Rouge. C. L. de Fuentes, Chairman, New Orleans; Shelby Taylor, Crowley; J. J. Meredith; W. M. Barrow, Secretary.

Maine Railroad Commissioners—Augusta. Joseph B. Peaks, Chairman, Dover; Parker Spofford, Bucksport; Frank Keizer, Rockland; E. C. Farrington, Clerk, Augusta.

Maryland—State Tax Commissioner, Buchanan Schley, Annapolis.

Massachusetts Board of Railroad Commissioners—Boston. Walter P. Hall, Chairman, Fitchburg; Clinton White, Melrose; George W. Bishop, Newtonville; Charles E. Mann, Clerk, Malden.

Michigan Railroad Commission—Lansing. C. L. Glasgow, Chairman; G. W. Dickinson, James Scully; L. C. Cramton, Secretary.

Minnesota Railroad and Warehouse Commission—St. Paul. Ira B. Mills, Chairman; W. E. Young, C. F. Staples; A. C. Clausen, Secretary, St. Paul.

Mississippi Railroad Commission—Jackson. F. M. Lee, President; John A. Webb, W. R. Scott; T. R. Maxwell, Secretary.

Missouri Railroad and Warehouse Commission—Jefferson City. John A. Knott, Chairman; F. A. Wightman, Rube Oglesby; T. M. Bradbury, Secretary.

Montana Railroad Commission—Helena. B. T. Stanton, Chairman; N. Godfrey, E. A. Morley; H. K. Howey, Secretary.

Nebraska State Railway Commission—Lincoln. H. J. Winnett, Chairman; J. A. Williams, H. T. Clarke, Jr.; Clark Perkins, Sec.

Nevada—Carson City. H. F. Bartine, Chairman; Henry Thurtell, J. F. Shaughnessy; E. H. Walker, Secretary.

New Hampshire Railroad Commission—Concord. Henry M. Putney, Chairman, Manchester; Arthur G. Whittemore, Clerk, Dover.

New Jersey Railroad Commission—J. W. Congdon, Paterson; Edmund Wilson, Red Bank; B. D. Whiting, Newark; A. N. Barber, Secretary, Trenton.

New York Public Service Commission—First District—(Greater New York) New York City—Wm. R. Willcox, Chairman; Wm. McCarroll, Edward M. Bassett, Milo R. Maltbie, John E. Eustis. Second District—(all of State outside Greater New York) Albany, N. Y. Frank W. Stevens, Chairman; John B. Olmsted, Thos. M. Osborne, James E. Sague, Martin S. Decker.

North Carolina Corporation Commission—Raleigh. Franklin McNeill, Chairman; Sam. L. Rogers, E. C. Bedingfield; H. C. Brown, Secretary.

North Dakota Commissioners of Railroads—Bismarck. C. S. Deisem, President, La Moure; E. A. Stafne, Galchutt; S. Westby, Rugby; J. W. Foley, Secretary, Bismarck.

Ohio Railroad Commission—Columbus. J. C. Morris, Chairman; O. H. Hughes, O. P Gothlin; H. D. Manington, Secretary, Columbus.

Oklahoma Corporation Commission—Guthrie. J. E. Love, Chairman; A. P. Watson, J. J. McAlester; W. L. Chapman, Secretary.

Oregon Railroad Commission—Thos. K. Campbell, Chairman, Cottage Grove; Oswald West, Astoria; Clyde B. Aitchison, Portland; George O. Goodall, Secretary, Salem.

Pennsylvania State Railroad Commission—Harrisburg. Nathaniel Ewing, Chairman; John Y. Boyd, Chas. N. Mann; H. S. Calvert, Secretary.

Rhode Island Railroad Commissioner—Providence. J. P. Burlingame; D. J. White, Deputy.

South Carolina Railroad Commissioners—B. L. Caughman, Chairman, Columbia; J. H. Earle, Greenville; J. M. Sullivan, Anderson; T. B. Lumpkin, Secretary, Columbia.

South Dakota Railroad Commissioners—Sioux Falls. D. H. Smith, Chairman, Miller; W. G. Smith, Sturgis; George Rice, Flandreau; Wm. H. Stanley, Secretary, Sioux Falls.

Tennessee Railroad Commissioners—Nashville. B. A. Enloe, Chairman; Frank Avent, H. H. Hannah; Chas. H. Love, Secretary.

Texas Railroad Commission—Austin. Allison Mayfield, Chairman; O. B. Colquitt, L. J. Storey; E. R. McLean, Secretary.

Vermont State Railroad Commissioners—J. W. Redmond, Chairman, Newport; Eli H. Porter, Wilmington; S. H. Jackson, Barre; R. W. Spear, Clerk, Newport.

Virginia State Corporation Commission—Richmond. Robert R. Prentis, Chairman, Richmond; William F. Rhea, J. E. Willard; R. T. Wilson, Clerk.

Washington—H. A. Fairchild, Chairman, Olympia; J. C. Lawrence, Olympia; J. S. Jones; Olympia; O. O. Calderhead, Secretary.

West Virginia—State Auditor, Charleston.

Wisconsin Railroad Commission—Madison. B. H. Meyer, Halford Erickson, J. H. Roemer; John M. Winterbotham, Secretary.

Wyoming Board of Equalization—Cheyenne. Edward Gillette, President, Wm. R. Schnitger; Le Roy Grant, Secretary.

Railroad Equipment.

WEIGHT AND HORSE POWER OF DIFFERENT TYPES OF LOCOMOTIVES INCLUDING THE MODERN ELECTRIC TRACTOR, AND ALSO THE WEIGHT, SIZE AND COST OF FREIGHT CARS, ORDINARY COACHES, PARLOR AND SLEEPING CARS.

RECENT HEAVY LOCOMOTIVES.

Type.	Road.	Total Weight. (Pounds.)	Weight on Drivers. (Pounds.)	Diameter of Drivers. (Inches.)	Heating Surface. (Sq. Ft.)	Size of Cylinders. (Inches.)	Tractive Effort. (Pounds.)
Mallet Comp.	Erie	410,000	410,000	51	6,108	25 & 39x28	98,000
Mallet Comp.	Gt. Nor.	355,000	316,000	55	5,703	21½ & 33x32	71,600
Santa Fé	P. S. & N.	288,000	235,000	57	4,796	28x32	60,000
Decapod	B. R. & P.	275,000	248,000	52	3,536	24x28	55,350
Consolidation	B. & L. E.	250,300	225,200	54	3,805	24x32	63,800
Mogul	Vandalia	187,000	159,300	63	2,935	21x28	31,360
10-Wheel Switch	L. S. & M. S.	270,000	270,000	52	4,620	24x28	55,300
Pacific	Penna, L. W.	269,200	173,550	80	4,427	24x26	31,000
Prairie	A. T. & S. F.	248,200	174,700	69	4,020	17½ & 29x28	37,800
Atlantic	U. P.	209,000	110,000	81	2,655	16 & 27x28	24,281
10-Wheel	D. L. & W.	201,000	154,000	69	3,378	21½x26	35,100
American	C. R. R. of N. J.	161,300	111,300	69	2,006	19x26	23,120

The Erie Mallet Compound, particulars of which are given in the first line of the table, is the largest and most powerful locomotive ever built. If worked to its full capacity it could haul a train of 225 loaded freight cars of 50 tons capacity each on a level track at 15 miles an hour. Such a train would be 1¾ miles long, and the engine would be exerting 4,000 horse power. The Pacific type locomotive for the Pennsylvania Lines West is the heaviest passenger locomotive ever built, and is capable of hauling 15 passenger cars at 60 miles an hour on level track, at which speed it would have to exert nearly 5,000 horse power.

HEAVY ELECTRIC LOCOMOTIVES.

Road.	Weight on Drivers. (Pounds.)	Dia. of Drivers. (Inches.)	Type.*	Rated Horse Power.
B. & O.	160,000	42	D. C.	1,200
N. Y. C.	157,000	44	D. C.	2,200
N. Y., N. H. & H.	180,000	62	A. C.—D. C.	1,000
P. R. R. No. 1	175,100	56	D. C.	1,400
P. R. R. No. 2	195,200	56	D. C.	1,240

* D. C. signifies direct current, taken from third rail. A. C. signifies alternating current, taken from overhead trolley.

COST OF LOCOMOTIVES.

Type.	Service.	Average Weight. (Pounds.)	Cost.
Mogul	Freight.	160,000	$13,400
Consolidation	Freight.	200,000	16,500
Mallet Compound	Freight.	350,000	27,400
Atlantic	Pass.	185,000	17,000
Pacific	Pass.	225,000	18,700
Ten Wheel	Pass.	170,000	15,800

The average cost of locomotives in 1907 was about 8.2 cents per pound.

WEIGHT AND COST OF CARS.

Type.	Weight.	Capacity.	Length. (Inside Dimensions.)	Width. (Inside Dimensions.)	Height. (Inside Dimensions.)	Cost.
Wood Box	37,000 lbs.	80,000 lbs.	36 ft.	8 ft. 6 in.	8 ft.	$1,100
Steel Coal	42,000 lbs.	100,000 lbs	31 ft.	9 ft. 4 in.	7 ft. 6 in.	1,200
Flat	32,000 lbs.	80,000 lbs.	41 ft.	9 ft. 2 in.	....	950
Day Coach	85,000 lbs.	68 Pass.	60 ft.	8 ft. 10 in.	9 ft. 1 in.	9,000
Parlor Car	105,000 lbs.	34 Pass.	70 ft.	8 ft. 6 in.	9 ft. 4 in.	15,500
Sleeping Car	115,000 lbs.	27 Berths.	72 ft. 6 in.	8 ft. 6 in.	9 ft. 6 in.	19,000

Railways of America "Grouped" by Capitalists.

THE great railroad systems of the United States have been reduced to a few "groups" by means of consolidation and reconsolidation. The following is a list of these groups, which comprise three-quarters of all the railroad lines of the country:

Groups.	Mileage.	Stocks.	Bonds.
Vanderbilt	23,920	$611,304,000	$746,350,000
Pennsylvania	18,646	761,300,000	562,419,000
Harriman	27,529	976,702,000	1,225,816,000
Hill-Morgan	12,214	376,912,000	413,802,000
Morgan	12,568	560,719,000	532,908,000
Gould	20,520	528,170,000	803,710,000
Moore's	27,410	360,600,000	477,900,000
Rockefeller	15,900	248,310,000	304,512,000
Walters'	11,119	145,600,000	197,500,000
Independent	26,908	525,600,000	453,400,000
Total	196,734	$4,995,217,000	$5,718,317,000

Includes only regular passenger lines from New York.

Steamships.	Built. Year.	Built. Place.	Builders.	Gross Tonnage.	Indicated Horse Power.	Dimensions in Feet. Length.	Breadth.	Depth.
New York, Plymouth, Cherbourg and Southampton, Pier foot Fulton St., N. R.			American Line. (Office, 9 Broadway.)			Established 1892.		
St. Louis	1895	Philadelphia	Wm. Cramp & Sons	11629	20000	554	63	42
St. Paul	1895	Philadelphia	Wm. Cramp & Sons	11629	20000	554	63	42
Philadelphia	1901	Belfast	Harland & Wolff	10786	20000	560	63.3	42
New York	1888	Glasgow	J. & G. Thomson	10798	20000	560	63.3	42
New York and Glasgow, Pier foot W. 24th St.			Anchor Line. (Office, 17 Broadway.)			Established 1852.		
Furnessia	1880	Barrow	Barrow S. B. Co	5495	..	445	45	35
Astoria	1884	Dumbarton	Denny Bros	5200	..	440	46	35
Columbia	1901	Glasgow	D. & W. Henderson	8900	..	503	56	..
Caledonia	1904	Glasgow	D. & W. Henderson	9400	..	515	58	36 6
California	1907	Glasgow	D. & W. Henderson	9000	..	485	58	36.3
New York and London, Pier foot W. Houston St.			Atlantic Transport Line. (Office, 9 Broadway.)			Established 1892.		
Mesaba	1898	Belfast	Harland & Wolff	6833	772	482.1	52.2	31.6
Minneapolis	1900	Belfast	Harland & Wolff	13401	1224	600.7	65.5	43.3
Minnehaha	1900	Belfast	Harland & Wolff	13403	1227	600.7	65.5	43.3
Minnetonka	1902	Belfast	Harland & Wolff	13398	1227	600.7	65.5	43.3
Minnewaska	1908	Belfast	Harland & Wolff	14220	616	616	66	44
New York, Queenstown, and Liverpool, Pier foot Jane St.			Cunard Line. (Office, 21 State Street.)			Established 1840.		
Campania	1892	Fairfield	Fairfield Co	13000	30000	620	65.3	43
Lucania	1893	Fairfield	Fairfield Co	13000	30000	620	65.3	43
Etruria	1885	Fairfield	John Elder & Co	8200	14500	501.6	57.2	38.2
Umbria	1884	Fairfield	John Elder & Co	8200	14500	501.6	57.2	38.2
Mauretania	1906	Newcastle	Swan & Hunter	32500	70000	790	88	60.6
Lusitania	1906	Glasgow	J. Brown & Co	32500	70000	790	88	60.6
New York, Mediterranean-Adriatic Service, Pier ft. Jane St.			Cunard Line. (Office, 21 State Street.)			Established 1904.		
Carpathia	1903	Newcastle	Swan & Hunter	13600	..	540	64.5	..
Slavonia	1904	Glasgow	J. Brown & Co	10600	..	526	59	33
Pannonia	1904	Glasgow	J. Brown & Co	10000	..	501	59	35
Ultonia	1898	Newcastle	Swan & Hunter	10200	.	500	57.4	38.1
Caronia	1905	Glasgow	J. Brown & Co	20000	21000	676	72.6	44.9
Carmania	1905	Glasgow	J. Brown & Co	20000	21000	676	72.6	44.9
New York and Havre, Pier foot Morton St.			French Line (Office, 19 State Street.)			Established 1860.		
La Touraine	1890	St. Nazaire	CieGleTransatlantique	9778	12000	536	55	38
La Gascogne	1886	Toulon	Soc. des Forges, etc	7645	9000	508	52	38
La Bretagne	1886	St. Nazaire	CieGleTransatlantique	7315	9000	508	51	38
La Lorraine	1899	St. Nazaire	CieGleTransatlantique	15000	22000	580	60	40
La Savoie	1900	St. Nazaire	CieGleTransatlantique	15000	22000	580	60	40
La Provence	1904	St. Nazaire	CieGleTransatlantique	18400	30000	624	66	42
La Chicago	1907	St. Nazaire	CieGleTransatlantique	11103	9500	524	57	43
New York, Plymouth, Cherbourg, Southampton, Boulogne, Hamburg, Gibraltar, Naples, Genoa, and Alexandria, Pier foot 1st St., Hoboken.			Hamburg-American Line. (Office, 41 and 45 Broadway.)			Established 1847.		
Deutschland	1900	Stettin	Vulcan S. B. Co	16502	37800	686.6	67	44
Pennsylvania	1896	Belfast	Harland & Wolff	13333	5500	557.6	62	41
Pretoria	1898	Hamburg	Blohm & Voss	13234	5400	560	62	41
Graf Waldersee	1899	Hamburg	Blohm & Voss	13193	5500	560	62	41
Patricia	1897	Stettin	Vulcan S. B. Co	13273	6000	560	62	41
Bulgaria	1898	Hamburg	Blohm & Voss	11077	4000	501.6	62.2	34.6
Batavia	1899	Hamburg	Blohm & Voss	11464	4000	501	62.2	34.6
Moltke	1902	Hamburg	Blohm & Voss	12335	9500	525	62	39
Blücher	1901	Hamburg	Blohm & Voss	12334	9500	525.6	63.3	35.6
Hamburg	1900	Stettin	Vulcan S. B. Co	10532	9000	498	60.5	38
Amerika	1905	Belfast	Harland & Wolff	22225	15500	690	74	53
Kaiserin Auguste Victoria	1906	Stettin	Vulcan S.B. Co	24581	17500	700	77	54
President Lincoln	1907	Belfast	Harland & Wolff	18100	7500	615	68.1	52
President Grant	1907	Belfast	Harland & Wolff	18100	7500	615	68	52
Cleveland	1908	Hamburg	Blohm & Voss	18000	9300	600	65	55
Cincinnati	1908	Dantzig	Schichau Yards	18000	9300	600	65	55
New York, Boulogne, and Rotterdam, Piers foot 5th and 7th Sts., Hoboken.			Holland-America Line. Netherlands-American Line. (Office, 39 Broadway.)			Established 1872.		
Statendam	1898	Belfast	Harland & Wolff	10490	....	530	60	42.6
Potsdam	1899	Hamburg	Blohm & Voss	12606	....	570	62	43.6
Ryndam	1901	Belfast	Harland & Wolff	12540	....	570	62	43.6
Noordam	1902	Belfast	Harland & Wolff	12540	....	570	62	43.6
New Amsterdam	1905	Belfast	Harland & Wolff	17250	....	615	68½	48
Rotterdam	1908	Belfast	Harland & Wolff	24170	....	668	77	56

FLEET OF TRANSATLANTIC PASSENGER STEAMERS—*Continued.*

Steamships.	Built. Year.	Built. Place.	Builders.	Gross Tonnage.	Indicated Horse Power.	Dimensions in Feet. Length.	Dimensions in Feet. Breadth.	Dimensions in Feet. Depth.
New York, Plymouth, Cherbourg. Southampton, Bremen, Pier foot 2d St., Hoboken, N. J.			NORTH GERMAN LLOYD. (Office, 5 Broadway.)			Established 1857.		
Kaiser Wilhelm der Grosse	1897	Stettin	Vulcan S. B. Co.	14349	28000	649	66	43
Friedrich d. Grosse	1896	Stettin	Vulcan S. B. Co.	10568	7200	546	60	35
Bremen	1896	Danzig	F. Schichau	11570	8000	569	60	35
Grosser Kurfürst	1900	Danzig	F. Schichau	13182	9700	582	65	39
Rhein	1899	Hamburg	Blohm & Voss	10058	5500	520	58	40
Main	1900	Hamburg	Blohm & Voss	10067	5500	520	58	40
Prinz Fr. Wilhelm	1908	Geestemünde	J. C. Tecklenborg	17500	14000	613	68	42
Kronprinz Wilh'lm	1901	Stettin	Vulcan S. B. Co.	14908	35000	663	66	43
Neckar	1901	Geestemünde	J. C. Tecklenborg	9835	6000	520	58	37
Kaiser Wilhelm II.	1903	Stettin	Vulcan S. B. Co.	19500	40000	707	72	52.6
Prinzess Alice	1904	Stettin	Vulcan S. B. Co.	10911	9000	524	60	35
Kronprinzessin Cecilie	1907	Stettin	Vulcan S. B. Co.	20000	40000	707	72	52.6
George Washington	1908	Stettin	Vulcan S. B. Co.	27000	20000	723	78	54
New York, Gibraltar, Naples, and Genoa, Pier foot 2d Street, Hoboken, N. J.			NORTH GERMAN LLOYD. (Office, 5 Broadway.)			Established 1892.		
Prinzess Irene	1900	Stettin	Vulcan S. B. Co.	10881	9000	525	60	38
Königin Luise	1896	Stettin	Vulcan S. B. Co.	10711	7000	544	60	35
König Albert	1899	Stettin	Vulcan S. B. Co.	10643	9000	525	60	38
Barbarossa	1896	Hamburg	Blohm & Voss	10915	7000	546	60	35
Berlin	1908	Bremen	Weser Ship Bldg. Co.	19200	14000	612	70	32
New York and Antwerp, Pier foot Fulton St., N. R.			RED STAR LINE. (Office, 9 Broadway.)			Established 1873.		
Vaderland	1900	Glasgow	John Brown & Co.	11899	12000	580	60	42
Zeeland	1901	Glasgow	John Brown & Co.	11905	12000	580	60	42
Finland	1902	Philadelphia	Wm. Cramp & Sons	12000	10400	580	60	42
Kroonland	1902	Philadelphia	Wm. Cramp & Sons	12000	10400	580	60	42
Samland	1903	Camden	N. Y. Shipbuilding Co.	9710	..	490	58	31
Lapland	1908	Belfast	Harland & Wolff	18000	..	620	70	50
Gothland	1908	Belfast	Harland & Wolff	7660	4400	504	53	37
New York, Christiansand, Christiania, Copenhagen, Pier foot 17th Street, Hoboken.			SCANDINAVIAN-AMERICAN LINE. (Office, 1 Broadway.)			Established 1879.		
C. F. Tietgen	1897	Belfast	Harland & Wolff	8500	5500	485	53	42
Oscar II	1901	Glasgow	Stephen & Son	10000	8000	515	58	42
Hellig Olav	1902	Glasgow	Stephen & Son	10000	8000	515	58	42
United States	1903	Glasgow	Stephen & Son	10000	8000	515	58	42
New York, Queenstown, Liverpool, Plymouth, Cherbourg, and Southampton, Pier foot W. 11th St.			WHITE STAR LINE. (Office, 9 Broadway.)			Established 1870.		
Teutonic	1889	Belfast	Harland & Wolff	9984	16000	585	57	42
Majestic	1890	Belfast	Harland & Wolff	9965	16000	585	57	42
Oceanic	1899	Belfast	Harland & Wolff	17274	27000	704	68	49
Celtic	1901	Belfast	Harland & Wolff	20904	13000	700	75	49
Cedric	1902	Belfast	Harland & Wolff	21400	13000	700	75	49
Arabic	1903	Belfast	Harland & Wolff	15855	..	690	65	44
Baltic	1904	Belfast	Harland & Wolff	23876	13000	726	75	49
Adriatic	1907	Belfast	Harland & Wolff	24541	40000	726	75.6	52
Olympic (building)	..	Belfast	Harland & Wolff	..	45000	850	..	..
Titanic (building)	..	Belfast	Harland & Wolff	..	45000	850	..	..

DISPLACEMENT (TONS) OF SOME OCEAN LINERS.

CUNARD LINE.

Steamship.	Displacement (Tons).
Mauretania	45,000
Lusitania	45,000
Caronia	30,000
Carmania	30,000
Campania	18,000
Umbria	10,500

NORTH GERMAN LLOYD.

Steamship.	Displacement (Tons).
Kaiser Wilhelm II	26,000
Kaiser Wilhelm der Grosse	20,800

WHITE STAR LINE.

Steamship.	Displacement (Tons).
Adriatic	40,790
Baltic	40,740
Cedric	38,020
Celtic	37,870
Oceanic	31,500
Majestic	17,800
Teutonic	17,800

HAMBURG-AMERICAN LINE.

Steamship.	Displacement (Tons).
Kaiserin Aug. Victoria	43,000
Amerika	42,000
Deutschland	23,000

Fastest Atlantic Ocean Passages.

Route.	*Steamer.*	*Line.*	*Date.*	*D.*	*H.*	*M.*
Queenstown to New York	Lusitania	Cunard	Aug. 16-20, 1908	4	15	..
Queenstown to New York	Lucania	Cunard	Oct. 21-26, 1894	5	7	23
New York to Queenstown	Lusitania	Cunard	Nov. 16-21, 1907	4	22	50
New York to Queenstown	Lucania	Cunard	Sept. 8-14, 1894	5	8	38
Cherbourg to New York	Deutschland	Hamburg-Am.	Sept. 2-8, 1903	5	11	54
Southampton to New York	Kaiser Wilh. d. Gr'se.	No. Germ. Lloyd	Mar. 30-Apr. 5, 1898	5	20	..
New York to Southampton	Kaiser Wilh. d. Gr'se.	No. Germ. Lloyd	Nov. 23-29, 1897	5	17	8
Havre to New York	La Provence	French	Sept. 7-13, 1907	6	1	48
New York to Havre	La Provence	French	May 3-9, 1906	6	3	45
New York to Cherbourg	Kaiser Wilh. d. Gr'se.	No. Germ. Lloyd	Jan. 4-10, 1900	5	16	..
New York to Plymouth	Deutschland	Hamburg-Am.	Sept. 5-10, 1900	5	7	38
Plymouth to New York	Deutschland	Hamburg-Am.	July 7-12, 1900	5	15	46
New York to Naples	Deutschland	Hamburg-Am.	Jan. 20-28, 1904	7	16	44

Approximate Distances: Sandy Hook (Lightship), New York, to Queenstown (Roche's Point), 2,800 miles; to Plymouth (Eddystone), 2,962 miles; to Southampton (The Needles), 3,100 miles; to Havre, 3,170 miles; to Cherbourg (The Mole), 3,184 knots. The fastest day's run was made by the Lusitania, of the Cunard line, August, 1908—650 knots, or 25.66 knots per hour.

1905 record.—Allen line's turbine Steamer Virginian passed Cape Race June 13, 11 A. M., inward bound, having left Moville on the afternoon of June 9, thus crossing in less than four days.

Steamship development as shown in the relative proportions, speed, etc., of the Great Eastern and Mauretania:

Great Eastern.		Mauretania.	
Length	692 ft.	Length	790 ft.
Breadth	80 ft.	Breadth	88 ft.
Displacement	27,000 tons.	Displacement	45,000 tons.
Paddle, Screw and Sail: Speed	13 to 14 knots.	Quadruple Screws	27½ knots (trial speed).

THE RECORD-BREAKERS BETWEEN NEW YORK AND QUEENSTOWN—EAST OR WEST.

Date.	*Steamer.*	*D.*	*H.*	*M.*	*Date.*	*Steamer.*	*D.*	*H.*	*M.*
1856	Persia	9	1	45	1884	America	6	10	0
1866	Scotia	8	2	48	1887	Umbria	6	4	42
1869	City of Brussels	7	22	3	1888	Etruria	6	1	55
1873	Baltic	7	20	9	1891	Majestic	5	18	8
1875	City of Berlin	7	15	48	1891	Teutonic	5	16	31
1876	Germanic	7	11	37	1892	City of Paris	5	14	24
1877	Britannic	7	10	53	1893	Campania	5	12	7
1880	Arizona	7	7	23	1894	Lucania	5	7	23
1882	Alaska	6	18	37	1908	Lusitania	4	15	0
1884	Oregon	6	11	9					

Funnel Marks and Night Signals of Transatlantic Lines

Lines.	Funnel Marks.	Night Signals
American	Black, white band, black top.	Blue light forward, red light amidships, and blue light aft.
Anchor	Black	White lantern, then a red.
Atlantic Transp't	Red, with black top	Six ball roman candles, with green-white-red.
Cunard	Red, with black rings and black top	Blue light and two roman candles, each throwing out six blue balls.
French	Red, with black top	Blue light forward, white light amidships, and red light aft.
Hamburg-Amer.	Express service, buff; regular, black	Two red-white-blue lights, in quick succession, at stern.
Netherlands-Am.	Cream, white band, with green borders	Green light forward and aft, white light under the bridge.
Nor. Ger. Lloyd	Buff	Two blue-red lights, one forward, one aft.
Red Star	Black, white band, black top	Three red lights, one forward, one aft, and one amidships, simultaneously.
Scandinav.-Amer	Black, red, black	One white-red, followed by one red-white light.
White Star	Buff, with black top	Two green lights simultaneously.

House Flags of Transatlantic Lines.

Lines.	Flags.	Lines.	Flags.
American	White, with blue spreadeagle in centre.	Netherl'nds-Am	Green, white and green, N. A. S. M. in black letters in the white.
Anchor	White swallowtail flag, with red anchor.	North Ger. Lloyd	Key and anchor crossed in centre of a laurel wreath, in blue on a white field.
Atlantic Transp't	Red, white, and blue in horizontal bars, with stars.		
Cunard	Red flag, golden lion in centre.		
French	White flag, red ball in corner, with company's name.	Red Star	White swallowtail flag, red star.
Hamburg-Amer.	White and blue flag, diagonally quartered, with a black anchor and yellow shield in centre, bearing the letters H.A.P.A.G.	Scandinav.-Amer	Blue, with white Maltese cross.
		White Star	Red swallowtail flag, containing white star.

Immigration Into the United States, 1821=1908.

Year.	Total Alien Passengers.	Year.	Total Alien Passengers.	Year.	Total Immigrants.	Year.	Total Immigrants.
1821	9,127	1844	78,615	Fiscal year end'g June 30		1889	444,427
1822	6,911	1845	114,371	1867	298,967	1890	455,302
1823	6,354	1846	154,416	1868	282,189	1891	560,319
1824	7,912	1847	234,968	1869	352,569	1892	623,084
1825	10,199	1848	226,527	1870	387,203	1893	502,917
1826	10,837	1849	297,024	1871	321,350	1894	314,467
1827	18,875	1850	369,986	1872	404,806	1895	279,948
1828	27,382	1851	379,466	1873	459,803	1896	343,267
1829	22,520	1852	371,603	1874	313,339	1897	230,832
1830	23,322	1853	368,645	1875	227,498	1898	229,299
1831	22,633	1854	427,833	1876	169,986	1899	311,715
1832	60,482	1855	200,877	1877	141,857	1900	448,572
1833	58,640	1856	195,857	1878	138,469	1901	487,918
1834	65,365	1857	246,945	1879	177,826	1902	648,743
1835	45,374	1858	119,501	1880	457,257	1903	857,046
1836	76,242	1859	118,616	1881	669,431	1904	812,870
1837	79,340	1860	150,237	1882	788,992	1905	1,027,421
1838	38,914	1861	89,724	1883	603,322	1906	1,100,735
1839	68,069	1862	89,207	1884	518,592	1907	1,285,349
1840	84,066	1863	174,524	1885	395,346	1908	782,870
1841	80,289	1864	193,195	1886	334,203		
1842	104,565	1865	247,453	1887	490,109	Total	26,769,722
1843	52,496	1866	163,594	1888	546,889	1789 to 1820 est.	250,000

Of the whole number of immigrants in the fiscal year ending June 30, 1907, 1,004,756 came through the customs district of New York, 66,910 through Baltimore, 70,164 through Boston, 30,501 through Philadelphia, 3,539 through San Francisco, and 60,512 through other ports; also 48,967 through Canadian ports.

The reported occupations of immigrants arriving during the fiscal year 1907 were as follows: Laborers, 291,141; servants, 121,587; farm laborers, 323,854; tailors, 30,644; merchants and dealers, 14,470; carpenters, 20,656; shoemakers, 13,059; clerks, 11,980; mariners, 7,270; miners, 11,452. The number of professional immigrants (including 822 actors, 2,433 engineers, 1,114 musicians, and 1,673 teachers) was 12,600; of skilled laborers, 190,315; miscellaneous (including unskilled), 777,725; no occupation (including children), 304,709.

The total number of alien immigrants refused admission to the United States in the fiscal year ending 1907 was 13,064, of which 6,866 were paupers or persons likely to become public charges, 3,822 persons with loathsome or contagious diseases, 1,434 contract laborers, 189 insane, 29 idiots, 341 convicts, 18 prostitutes, 1 person who attempted to bring in prostitutes, 70 returned in one year after landing, 925 returned within three years because here in violation of law.

IMMIGRATION BY COUNTRIES IN FISCAL YEARS 1906 AND 1907.

Countries.	1907.	1908.	Countries.	1907.	1908.
Austria-Hungary	338,452	168,509	Wales	2,660	2,287
Belgium	6,396	4,162	Other Europe	107	97
Bulgaria, Servia and Montenegro	11,359	10,827	Total Europe	1,199,566	691,901
Denmark	7,243	4,954	China	961	1,397
France, including Corsica	9,731	8,788	Japan	30,226	15,803
German Empire	37,807	32,309	India	898	1,040
Greece	36,580	21,489	Turkey in Asia	8,053	9,753
Italy, inc. Sicily and Sardinia	285,731	128,503	Other Asia	386	372
Netherlands	6,637	5,946	Total Asia	40,524	28,365
Norway	22,133	12,412			
Portugal, inc. Cape Verde and Azore Islands	9,608	7,307	Africa	1,486	1,411
Roumania	4,384	5,228	Australia, Tasmania, and New Zealand	1,947	1,098
Russian Empire, and Finland	258,943	156,711	Pacific Islands, not specified	42	81
Spain, inc. Canary and Balearic Islands	5,784	3,899	British North America	19,918	38,510
			Central America	935	1,175
Sweden	20,589	12,809	Mexico	1,406	6,067
Switzerland	3,748	3,281	South America	2,779	2,315
Turkey in Europe	20,767	11,290	West Indies	16,189	11,888
England	56,637	47,031	Other countries	22	17
Ireland	34,530	30,556			
Scotland	19,740	13,506	Grand total	1,285,349	782,870

Owing to the great difficulty in obtaining accurate statements of the immigrants from the contiguous countries of Canada and Mexico, no statistics of immigration into the United States of citizens of those countries are gathered by the Bureau of Immigration and Naturalization. The constant ebb and flow of persons entering and leaving the United States from and to Mexico and Canada, at the numerous points where such movements can be conveniently made, renders accurate statements on this subject extremely difficult, and the Bureau of Immigration and Naturalization in its annual report for 1902 states that "the immigrants do not include arrivals from the neighboring countries of Mexico and Canada except such as come from abroad through ports in these countries for the avowed purpose of entering the United States." The fact, however, that the Census of 1900 shows the presence of 1,183,225 persons in the United States born in Canada and 103,445 persons born in Mexico proves that the number of arrivals from those countries, proper to be considered as immigrants, must be large.

BETWEEN NEW YORK CITY AND PLACES IN UNITED STATES AND CANADA.

EXPLANATION: Day rate, 40-3, means 40 cents for ten words and 3 cents for each additional word; night rate, 30-2, means 30 cents for ten words and 2 cents for each additional word. Address and signature are free. Rates given are Western Union rates.

Places.	Rate. Day.	Rate. Night.
ALABAMA	60-4	50-3
ALASKA:		
Eagle City	3.80-35	3.80-35
Juneau	2.60-23	2.60-23
Nome	4.80-45	4.80-45
St. Michael	4.30-40	4.30-40
Sitka	2.40-21	2.40-21
Skagway	2.90-26	2.90-26
Valdez	3.40-31	3.40-31
ARIZONA	1.00-7	1.00-7
ARKANSAS	60-4	50-3
BRITISH COLUMBIA: Grand Forks, Nanaimo, Nelson, New Westminster, Rossland, Vancouver, Victoria	1.00-7	1.00-7
Atlin	3.25-24	3.25-23
Port Simpson	2.75-19	2.75-18
CALIFORNIA	1.00-7	1.00-7
COLORADO	75-5	60-4
CONNECTICUT	25-2	25-1
DELAWARE	30-2	25-1
DISTRICT OF COLUMBIA	30-2	25-1
FLORIDA	60-4	50-3
GEORGIA	60-4	50-3
IDAHO	1.00-7	1.00-7
ILLINOIS	50-3	40-3
INDIANA	50-3	40-3
IOWA	60-4	50-3
KANSAS	60-4	50-3
KENTUCKY	50-3	40-3
KLONDIKE: See Alaska and Yukon.		
LOUISIANA	60-4	50-3
MAINE: Portland	35-2	25-1
All other places	40-3	30-2
MANITOBA: Winnipeg	75-5	60-4
MARYLAND: Annapolis, Baltimore, Frederick, Hagerstown	30-2	25-1
Cumberland	35-2	25-1
All other places	40-3	30-2
MASSACHUSETTS	25-2 to 30-2	25-1
MICHIGAN: Detroit, Mount Clemens, Port Huron	40-3	30-2
All other places	50-3 to 60-4	40-3 to 50-3
MINNESOTA	60-4	50-3
MISSISSIPPI	60-4	50-3
MISSOURI:		
St. Louis	50-3	40-3
All other places	60-4	50-3
MONTANA	75-5	60-4
NEBRASKA	60-4	50-3
NEVADA	1.00-7	1.00-7
NEW BRUNSWICK	50-3	40-3
NEWFOUNDLAND: St. John's	1.10-9	1.00-9
NEW HAMPSHIRE	35-2	25-1
NEW JERSEY	25-2	25-1
NEW MEXICO	75-5	60-4
NEW YORK:		
New York City	20-1	20-1
All other places	25-2 to 35-2	25-1
NORTH CAROLINA	50-3	40-3
NORTH DAKOTA	75-5	60-4
NOVA SCOTIA	50-3	40-3
OHIO	40-3	30-2
OKLAHOMA	75-5	60-4
ONTARIO:		
Niagara Falls	40-3	30-2
Sault Ste. Marie	60-4	50-3
All other places	50-3	40-3
OREGON	1.00-7	1.00-7
PENNSYLVANIA	25-2 to 40-3	25-1 to 30-2
PRINCE EDWARD ISLAND: Charlottetown	75-5	65-5
QUEBEC	50-3	40-3
RHODE ISLAND	30-2	25-1
SOUTH CAROLINA	60-4	50-3
SOUTH DAKOTA	75-5	60-4
TENNESSEE	50-3	40-3
TEXAS	75-5	60-4
UTAH	75-5	60-4
VERMONT	35-2	25-1
VIRGINIA	40-3 to 50-3	30-2 to 40-3
WASHINGTON	1.00-7	1.00-7
WEST VIRGINIA	40-3	30-2
WISCONSIN: Milwaukee	50-3	40-3
All other places	60-4	50-3
WYOMING	75-5	60-4
YUKON:		
Dawson	4.25-29	4.25-29

TELEGRAPH RATES TO FOREIGN COUNTRIES.

These rates are from New York City. The address and signature are included in the chargeable matter, and the length of words is limited to fifteen letters. When a word is composed of more than fifteen letters, every additional fifteen or the fraction of fifteen letters will be counted as a word.

	Per Word.
Abyssinia	$.80
Algeria	0.32
Alexandria (Egypt)	.50
Antigua	.81
Argentine Repub.	1.00
Austria	.32
Barbados	.91
Belgium	.25
Bermuda	.42
Bolivia	1.25
Brazil	.85 to 1.60
Bulgaria	.35
Burmah	.74
Callao (Peru)	1.25
Cairo (Egypt)	.50
Cape Colony (S. Af.)	.86
Ceylon	.76
Chile	1.25
China	1.22
Cochin China	1.19
Colon	.50
Cyprus	.50
Demerara	1.44
Denmark	$0.35
Ecuador	1.25
England	.25
France	.25
Germany	.25
Gibraltar	.43
Greece	.36
Guatemala	.55
Havana	.15
Hayti	1.05 to 1.55
Holland	.25
Honolulu	.47
Hungary	32
Iceland	.44
India	.74
Ireland	.25
Italy	.31
Jamaica	.48
Japan	1.33
Java	1.20
Korea (Seoul)	1.33
Malta	.35
Martinique	$1.00
Matanzas	.20
Melbourne, Vic.	0.66
Mexico City, $1.75, 10 wds.	
Nassau (Bahamas)	.35
Natal (So. Africa)	.86
New South Wales	.66
New Zealand	.66
Norway	.35
Orange River Col'y	.86
Panama	.50
Paraguay	1.00
Penang	1.11
Peru	1.25
Philippine Is. (Luzon, Manilla, etc.)	1.12
Other islands	1.27
Porto Rico	.75
Portugal	.39
Queensland	.66
Roumania	.34
Russia (Europe)	.43
Russia (Asia)	$.50
Santo Domingo	1.32
Scotland	.25
Servia	34
Sicily	.31
Siam	1.05
Singapore	1.11
Spain	.38
St. Thomas	.96
Sweden	.38
Switzerland	.30
Sydney (N. S. W.)	.66
Tangier	.45
Tasmania	.66
Transvaal	.86
Trinidad	.98
Turkey (Europe)	.37
Turkey (Asia)	.45
Uruguay	1.00
Venezuela	1.50 to 1.60
Vera Cruz, $1.75, 10 wds.	
Victoria (Aus.)	.66

TELEGRAPH RATES—*Continued.*

TELEGRAPH STATISTICS.

THE WESTERN UNION TELEGRAPH COMPANY:

Statement exhibiting the mileage of lines operated, number of offices, number of messages sent, receipts, expenses, and profits for 1870, 1875, 1880, and 1890, and each year from 1895 to 1908, inclusive:

YEAR.	Miles of Poles and Cables.	Miles of Wire.	Offices.	Messages.	Receipts.	Expenses.	Profits.
1870........	54,109	112,191	8,972	9,157,646	$7,138,737.96	$4,910,772.42	$2,227,965.54
1875........	72,833	179,496	6,565	17,153,710	9,564,574.60	6,335,414.77	3,229,157.83
1880........	85,645	233,534	9,077	29,215,509	12,782,894.53	6,948,956.74	5,833,937.79
1890........	183,917	678,997	19,382	55,878,762	22,387,028.91	15,074,303.81	7,312,725.10
1895........	189,714	802,651	21,360	58,307,315	22,218,019.18	16,076,629.97	6,141,389.21
1896........	189,918	825,929	21,725	58,760,444	22,612,736.28	16,714,756.10	5,897,980.18
1897........	190,614	841,002	21,769	58,151,684	22,638,859.16	16,906,656.03	5,732,203.13
1898........	189,847	874,420	22,210	62,173,749	23,915,732.78	17,825,581.52	6,090,151.26
1899........	189,856	904,633	22,285	61,398,157	23,954,312.05	18,085,579.19	5,868,732.86
1900........	192,705	933,153	22,900	63,167,783	24,758,569.55	18,593,205.87	6,165,363.68
1901........	193,589	972,766	23,238	65,657,049	26,354,150.85	19,668,902.68	6,685,248.17
1902........	196,115	1,029,984	23,567	69,374,883	28,073,095.10	20,780,766.21	7,292,328.89
1903........	196,517	1,089,212	23,120	*69,790,866	29,167,686.80	20,953,217.07	8,214,471.73
1904........	199,350	1,155,405	23,458	*67,909,973	29,249,390.44	21,361,915.46	7,887,474.98
1905........	200,224	1,184,557	23,815	*67,477,320	29,033,635.04	21,845,570.32	7,188,064.72
1906........	202,959	1,256,147	24,323	*71,487,082	30,675,655.00	23,605,072.00	7,070,583.00
1907........	205,646	1,321,199	24,760	*74,804,551	32,856,406.25	26,532,196.20	6,324,210.05
1908........	208,477	1,359,430	23,853	*62,371,287	28,582,212.09	25,179,215.33	3,402,996.76

* Not including messages sent over leased wires or under railroad contracts.

The capital stock is $97,370,000. Funded debt, $35,815,000.

The average toll per message in 1868 was 104.7; in 1890 was 32.4; in 1891 was 32.5; in 1892 was 31.6; in 1893 was 31.2; in 1894 was 30.5; in 1895 was 30.7; in 1896 was 30.9; in 1897 was 30.5; in 1898 was 30.1; in 1899 was 30.8; in 1900 was 30.8; in 1901 was 30.9; in 1902 was 31.0; in 1903 was 31.4; in 1904 was 31.7; in 1905 was 31.6; in 1906 was 31.6; in 1907 was 33.7; in 1908 was 33.7. The average cost per message to the company in 1868 was 63.4; in 1890 was 22.7; in 1891 was 23.2; in 1892 was 23.3; in 1893 was 22.7; in 1894 was 23.3; in 1895 was 23.3; in 1896 was 24.0; in 1897 was 24.8; in 1898 was 24.7; in 1899 was 25.1; in 1900 was 25.1; in 1901 was 25.1; in 1902 was 25.7; in 1903 was 25.6; in 1904 was 26.1; in 1905 was 27.3; in 1906 was 27.6; in 1907 was 30.2; in 1908 was 34.3.

The Postal Telegraph Cable Company also transacts business with the United States, and in 1908 operated 60,216 miles of poles and 350,127 miles of wire, by means of which it reached 25,507 places.

GROWTH OF THE TELEGRAPH SERVICE IN THE WORLD.

Number of messages, 1870: Norway, 466,700; Sweden, 590,300; Denmark, 513,623; Germany, 8,207,800; Netherlands, 1,837,800; Belgium, 1,998,800; France, 5,663,800; Switzerland, 1,629,235; Spain, 1,050,000; Italy, 2,189,000; Austria, 3,388,249; Hungary, 1,489,000; United States, 9,157,646; Great Britain and Ireland, 9,650,000.

Number of messages, 1905-06: Norway, 2,389,437; Sweden, 3,024,103; Denmark, 2,582,205; Germany, 50,837,325; Netherlands, 6,182,390; Belgium, 18,571,259; France, 53,555,880; Switzerland, 4,590,876; Spain, 4,047,761; Italy, 14,270,407; Austria, 18,247,444; Hungary, 17,759,447; Russia, 149,422,305; United States (1907), 90,000,000; Great Britain and Ireland, 89,478,000; Japan, 23,083,837; Australia, 11,369,139; New Zealand, 5,640,219; Argentine Republic, 2,121,543; India, 10,461,117; Mexico, 3,383,518; Canada, 5,963,247; Turkey, 6,057,473; Bulgaria, 1,525,112; Egypt, 1,925,051; Roumania, 2,389,073; Cape Colony, 2,952,643; Portugal, 3,343,738; Brazil, 1,638,140; Chile, 4,603,528; Greece, 1,304,573; Servia, 1,382,194; Guatemala, 1,281,419; Uruguay, 293,943; Colombia, 1,388,388; Persia, 216,171; Peru, 152,806; Paraguay, 103,820.

Messages, per capita: New Zealand, 5.05; Australia, 2.39; Belgium, 2.15; Great Britain and Ireland, 2.15; France, 1.25; Switzerland, 1.19; United States, 1.08; Netherlands, 1.04; Norway, 1.01; Germany, 0.68; Italy, 0.24; Spain, 0.28.

For statement regarding wireless telegraphy see article on "Electrical Progress in 1908."

MANUFACTURE OF TELEGRAPH AND TELEPHONE APPARATUS.

(From Census Bulletin No. 73 of 1907.)

An apparent falling off in the production of telegraph apparatus from $1,642,266 in 1900 to $1,111,194 in 1905 is accounted for in part by the growing custom among the larger telegraph systems of making and repairing their own apparatus. The value of the factory product in 1905 is distributed thus: 76,826 intelligence instruments (key, sounder, etc.), valued at $187,744; police, fire, district, and miscellaneous, valued at $592,070; wireless telegraph apparatus, valued at $114,050; and switchboards and parts and supplies, valued at $217,330. The most important recent improvements have been the introduction of printing telegraph systems and the development and extension of wireless telegraphy.

The total value of telephonic apparatus manufactured, as reported at the census of 1905, was $15,863,698, as compared with $10,512,412 for the census of 1900. Of this total value, $824,204 represented the value of 850,815 transmitters; $896,113, the value of 831,195 receivers; $6,483,418, the value of 887,447 complete sets of instruments; $68,826, the value of 4,560 interior systems complete without instruments; $5,154,447, the value of 4,283 central switchboards; $504,795, the value of 3,917 private exchange boards; and $2,071,895, the value of telephone parts and supplies (chiefly the signalling apparatus in magneto-telephone sets and the line protector fuses, etc.).

Illinois is the great centre of telephonic manufacturing industry in the United States, both as to number of factories and as to output. More than half the total product, or $8,357,521, was from this State. The output of New York was also large, but not quite half that of Illinois.

Recent inventions involving the use of telephonic apparatus are: A system of music production and distribution by means of electrical currents over the telephone circuits; the Poulsen telegraphone, the object of which is to furnish a record of the speech received over the telephone; a system of submarine signalling based on the use of the telephone; and the "telegraphone," an instrument used in connection with railway telegraph circuits.

The Submarine Cables of the World.

(From report issued by the Bureau International de l'Union Télégraphique.)

THE following table sets forth the entire system of submarine cables of the world, including those along the shores and in the bays, gulfs, and estuaries of rivers, but excepting those in lakes and the interior watercourses of continents. The list includes all cables operated by private companies, and in addition thereto under the name of each nation is given the list of cables operated by the government of that nation.

Companies.	Number of Cables.	Length of Cables in Nautical Miles.
Anglo-American Telegraph Co.	14	9,554
Transatlantic System—Valentia (Ireland) to Heart's Content (Newfoundland).		
Commercial Cable Co	12	15,450
Transatlantic System—Waterville (Ireland) to Canso (Nova Scotia).		
Canso, N. S., to New York.		
Canso, N. S., to Rockport, Mass.		
Commercial Pacific Cable Co.	6	10,004
San Francisco to Manila.		
Manila to Shanghai.		
De l'ils de Peel (Bouins) à Guam.		
Direct United States Cable Co.	2	3,095
Ballinskellig's Bay (Ireland) to Halifax (Nova Scotia).		
Halifax, N. S., to Rye Beach, N. H.		
Western Union Telegraph Co.	13	7,478
Transatlantic System—Sennen Cove, near Penzance, England, to Dover Bay, near Canso, N. S.		
Dover Bay, N. S., to New York.		
Gulf of Mexico System.		
Compagnie Française des Câbles Télégraphiques	32	12,102
Brest (France) to Cape Cod Mass.		
Brest (France) to St. Pierre-Miq		
St. Pierre to Cape Cod, Mass		
Cape Cod, Mass., to New York.		
African Direct Telegraph Co	11	3,029
Black Sea Telegraph Co	1	337
Western Telegraph Co.	28	18,759
Carcavellos, near Lisbon (Portugal), to Madeira, to St. Vincent (Cape Verde Island), to Pernambuco, Rio de Janeiro, Santos, Montevideo, Horta (Azores) to St. Vincent (Cape Verde Island).		
Central and South American Telegraph Co	18	7,500
Compania Telegrafico-Telefonica del Plata	1	28
Cuba Submarine Telegraph Co	10	1,143
Direct Spanish Telegraph Co	4	727
Direct West India Cable Co.	2	1,265
Bermuda-Turk's Island, and Turk's Island-Jamaica.		
Eastern and South African Telegraph Co	19	10,541
Eastern Extension Australasia and China Telegraph Co.	86	22,532
Eastern Telegraph Co.	98	40,911
Anglo-Spanish-Portuguese System.		
System West of Malta.		
Italo-Greek System.		
Austro-Greek System.		
Greek System.		
Turko-Greek System.		
Turkish System.		
Egypto-European System.		
Egyptian System.		
Egypto-Indian System.		
Cape Town to St. Helena.		
St. Helena to Ascension Island.		
Ascension Island to St. Vincent.		
Natal-Australia System.		
Europe and Azores Telegraph Co.	2	1,053
Compagnie Allemande des Câbles Transatlantiques	5	9,553
Borkum Island to Azores to Coney Island, N. Y.		
Borkum Island to Vigo, Spain.		
Grande Compagnie des Télégraphes du Nord	37	9,374
Cables in Europe and Asia.		
Deutsch-Niederlandische Telegraphen gesellschaft	3	3,416
Menado (Célèbes)—Japan (Caroline); Guam (Mariannes); Shanghai.		
Osteuropaische Telegraphengesells.	1	185
Kilios (Constantinople)—Constantza (Roumanie)		
Halifax and Bermuda Cable Co.	1	849
Indo-European Telegraph Co.	8	23
India Rubber, Gutta Percha, and Telegraph Works Co.	3	145
Mexican Telegraph Co.	3	1,528
River Plate Telegraph Co.	1	32
South American Cable Co.	2	2,049
United States and Hayti Telegraph and Cable Co.	1	1,391
West African Telegraph Co.	6	1,471
West Coast of America Telegraph Co.	7	1,979
West India & Panama Telegraph Co.	23	4,649
Grand total	405	203,052

CABLES OWNED BY NATIONS.

Nation	Number of Cables	Length of Cables in Nautical Miles
Austria	48	224
Belgium	3	77
Denmark	98	306
France	87	11,178
Germany	87	3,167
Great Britain and Ireland	191	2,304
Greece	46	54
Holland	36	248
Italy	41	1,073
Norway	626	970
Portugal	4	115
Russia	25	314
Russia in Asia	3	171
Spain	16	1,903
Sweden	13	209
Switzerland	3	16
Turkey	23	352
Argentine Republic and Brazil	41	105
Australia and New Zealand	46	439
Bahama Islands	1	213
British America	2	399
British India	8	1,993
Portuguese Possessions in Africa	2	26
Japan	137	4,364
Macao	1	2
Nouvelle Calédonie	1	1
Netherlands Indies	15	2,855
Sénegal, Africa	1	3
Siam	3	13
Indo-Chine Française	8	1,479
Pacific Cable Board (cables in the Pacific between British America and Australia)	5	7,837
Philippine Islands	33	1,313
United States (Alaska)	12	2,348
Total	1,651	46,066

Telephone Statistics.

THE following are the latest statistics made public by the American (Bell) Telephone and Telegraph Company. (See article on "Electrical Progress in 1908" in reference to other telephone companies.) The figures are for January 1 of each year:

	1906.	1907.	1908.		1906.	1907.	1908.
Exchanges and Branch offices	4,532	4,889	5,108	Miles of wire submarine	9,373	11,690	6,322
				Total miles of wire	4,514,682	6,007,732	6,946,511
Miles wire poles and Buildings	2,159,567	2,754,571	3,057,138	Total circuits	1,135,449	1,384,175	1,541,727
				Total employés	74,718	90,324	88,274
Miles underground	2,345,742	3,241,471	3,883,051	Total stations	2,241,367	2,727,289	3,035,533

In addition to the total number of stations given in the table there were on January 1, 1908, 755,316 stations belonging to independent companies connected by agreement to the Bell toll line system, so that, adding also the telephones employed for private line purposes, there was a total of 3,839,000 stations connected with the Bell system.

The number of instruments in the hands of licensees under rental at the beginning of 1908 was 7,544,105. The number of exchange connections daily in the United States is 18,130,803, or a total per year of about 5,838,100,000. The average number of daily calls per subscriber is six. The capital of the company is $179,595,255.

What are known as independent telephone companies, as distinguished from Bell companies, are nearly all represented in the International Independent Telephone Association. Of these there are about 9,000 companies operating an aggregate of over 3,500,000 instruments. The capital invested is approximately $350,000,000, the number of stockholders 500,000, and the income roughly is $105,000,000. During the last year the principal feature of the independent companies' activities was the extension of long-distance business. The Middle West has been best developed, and at present over independent lines continuous communication is possible throughout nearly all of the territory within the east and west limits of Philadelphia and Nebraska and Kansas, and the north and south limits of Minneapolis and Birmingham. The increase in business, according to locality, during 1907, varied from 10 to 40 per cent. and averaged between 15 and 20 per cent. (See also Electrical Progress in 1908).

Telephone messages per annum (latest reports): France, 205,685,374; Germany, 1,207,446,753; Great Britain and Ireland, 723,246,368; United States, 9,000,000,000; Austria, 166,474,183; Denmark, 108,750,035; Hungary, 82,909,800; Belgium, 53,977,696; Switzerland, 36,803,415; Netherlands, 31,470,095. In Italy and Spain the use of the telephone is very limited.

Canals.

STATEMENT showing the cost and date of construction, length, number of locks, and navigable depth of the principal canals of the United States used for commercial purposes.

CANALS. *And improvements.	Cost of Construction.*	When Completed	Len'h miles.	No. of Locks.	Depth feet.†	Location.
Albemarle and Chesapeake	$1,641,363	1860	44	1	7½	Norfolk, Va., to Currituck Sound, N. C.
Augusta	1,500,000	1847	9	...	11	Savannah River, Ga., to Augusta, Ga.
Black River	3,581,954	1849	35	109	4	Rome, N. Y., to Lyons Falls, N. Y.
Cayuga and Seneca	2,232,632	1839	25	11	7	Montezuma, N. Y., to Cayuga and Seneca Lakes, N. Y.
Champlain	4,044,000	1822	81	32	6	Whitehall, N. Y., to Watervliet, N. Y.
Chesapeake and Delaware	3,730,230	1829	14	3	9	Chesapeake City, Md., to Delaware City, Del.
Chesapeake and Ohio	11,290,327	1850	184	73	6	Cumberland, Md., to Washington, D. C.
Companys	90,000	1847	22	1	6	Mississippi River, La., to Bayou Black, La.
Delaware and Raritan	4,888,749	1838	66	14	8-9	New Brunswick, N. J., to Bordentown, N. J.
Delaware Division	2,433,350	1840	60	33	6	Easton, Pa., to Bristol, Pa.
Des Moines Rapids	4,582,009	1877	7½	3	5	At Des Moines Rapids, Mississippi River.
Dismal Swamp	2,800,000	1822	22	7	6	Connects Chesapeake Bay with Albemarle Sound.
Erie	52,540,800	1826	387	72	7	Albany, N. Y., to Buffalo, N. Y.
Fairfield	......	....	4½	None.	..	Alligator River to Lake Mattimuskeet, N. C.
Galveston and Brazos	340,000	1851	38	...	3½	Galveston, Tex., to Brazos River, Tex.
Hocking	975,481	1843	42	26	4	Carroll, O., to Nelsonville, O.
Illinois and Michigan	7,357,787	1848	102	15	6	Chicago, Ill., to La Salle, Ill.
Illinois and Mississippi	7,250,000	1895	75	3	7	Around lower rapids of Rock Riv., Ill. Connects with Miss. R.
Lehigh Coal and Navigation Co.	4,455,000	1821	108	57	6	Coalport, Pa., to Easton, Pa.
Louisville and Portland	5,578,631	1872	2½	2	..	At Falls of Ohio River, Louisville, Ky.
Miami and Erie	8,062,680	1835	274	93	5½	Cincinnati, O., to Toledo, O.
Morris	6,000,000	1836	103	33	5	Easton, Pa., to Jersey City, N. J.
Muscle Shoals and Elk R. Shoals	3,156,919	1889	16	11		Big Muscle Shoals, Tenn., to Elk River Shoals, Tenn.
Newberne and Beaufort	......	....	3	None.	..	Clubfoot Creek to Harlow Creek, N. C.
Ogeechee	407,810	1840	16	5	3	Savannah River, Ga., to Ogeechee River, Ga.
Ohio	4,695,204	1835	317	150	4	Cleveland, O., to Portsmouth, O.
Oswego	5,239,526	1828	38	18	7	Oswego, N. Y., to Syracuse, N. Y.
Pennsylvania	7,731,750	1839	193	71	6	Columbia, Northumberland, Wilkes-Barre, Huntingdon, Pa.
Portage Lake and Lake Super'r.	528,892	1873	25	None.	15	From Keweenaw Bay to Lake Superior.
Port Arthur	......	1899	7	...	26	Port Arthur, Tex., to Gulf of Mexico.
Santa Fe	70,000	1880	10	...	5	Waldo, Fla., to Melrose, Fla.
Sault Ste. Marie (ship canal)	4,000,000	1895	3	2	18	Connects Lakes Superior and Huron at St. Mary's River.
Schuylkill Navigation Company	12,461,600	1826	108	71	6¼	Mill Creek, Pa., to Philadelphia, Pa.
Sturgeon Bay and Lake Mich'n.	99,661	1881	1¼	None.	15	Between Green Bay and Lake Michigan.
St. Mary's Falls	7,909,667	1896	1⅓	1	21	Connects Lakes Superior and Huron at Sault Ste. Marie, Mich.
Susquehanna and Tidewater	4,931,345	1840	45	32	5½	Columbia, Pa., to Havre de Grace, Md.
Walhonding	607,269	1843	25	11	4	Rochester, O., to Roscoe, O.
Welland (ship canal)	26,080,366	1833	26¾	26	14	Connects Lake Ontario and Lake Erie.

The Harlem River Ship Canal, connecting the Hudson River and Long Island Sound, by way of Spuyten Duyvil Creek and Harlem River, was opened for traffic on June 17, 1895, and cost about $2,700,000. † Navigable depth.

FOREIGN SHIP CANALS.	Length, Miles.	Depth, Feet.	Bottom Width, Feet.	Cost.
Suez—Mediterranean and Red Seas	90	31	108	$100,000,000
Cronstadt—St. Petersburg	16	20½	....	10,000,000
Manchester Ship—Manchester and Liverpool	35½	26	120	75,000,000
Kaiser Wilhelm—Baltic and North Seas	61	29½	72	40,000,000
Elbe and Trave	41	10	72	6,000,000

The Stage.

BIRTHPLACES AND BIRTH YEARS OF LIVING DRAMATIC AND MUSICAL PEOPLE.

Name.	Birthplace.	Born.	Name.	Birthplace.	Born.
Abott, Bessie	Riverdale, N. Y	1885	Evesson, Isabel	St. Louis, Mo	1870
Adams, Maude	Salt Lake City, Utah	1872	Eytinge, Rose	Philadelphia, Pa	1837
Ade, George	Indiana, Ill	1866	Farnum, Dustin	Hampton Beach, N. H.	1876
Albam, Emma	Chambly, Canada	1852	Farrar, Geraldine	Melrose, Mass	1883
Alexander, George	Reading, England	1858	Faversham, William	England	1868
Allen, Viola	Alabama	1865	Fields, Lewis	New York	1867
Anderson, Mary	Sacramento, Cal	1859	Finney, James Lee	St. Louis, Mo	1863
Anglin, Margaret	Ottawa, Canada	1876	Fischer, Alice	Indiana	1875
Arden, Edwin	St. Louis, Mo	1864	Fiske, Minnie Maddern	New Orleans	1865
Arthur, Julia	Hamilton, Ont	1869	Fitch, Clyde	New York	1865
Ashley, Minnie	Fall River, Mass	1875	Fox, Della	St. Louis, Mo	1871
Ashwell, Lena	England	1872	Frohman, Chas	Sandusky, O	1858
Baird, Dorothea	England	1875	Frohman, Daniel	Sandusky, O	1850
Bancroft, Sir Squire B	England	1841	Galland, Bertha	New York	1877
Bancroft, Lady	England	1839	Garden, Mary	Scotland	1876
Bangs, Frank C	Alexandria, Va	1836	Genee, Mme	Aarhuus, Jutland, Den.	....
Barnabee, Henry Clay	Portsmouth, N. H	1833	George, Grace	New York City	1880
Barrymore, Ethel	Philadelphia, Pa	1880	Germon, Effie	Augusta, Ga	1845
Bateman, Isabel	Cincinnati, O	1854	Gerster, Etelka	Kaschau, Hungary	1857
Bateman, Kate	Baltimore, Md	1843	Gilbert, William S	London	1836
Bates, Blanche	Portland, Ore	1873	Gillette, William	Hartford, Ct	1856
Beere, Mrs. Bernard	Norfolk	1856	Gilman, Mabelle	New York City	1880
Belasco, David	San Francisco	1862	Glaser, Lulu	Allegheny, Pa	1874
Bell, Digby	Milwaukee, Wis	1851	Goodwin, Nat C	Boston, Mass	1857
Bellew, Kyrle	London	1855	Hackett, James K	Canada	1869
Bernard, Sam	Birmingham, Eng	1863	Hading, Jane	Marseilles, France	1859
Bernhardt, Sarah	Paris	1844	Hall, Pauline	Cincinnati, O	1865
Bingham, Amelia	Hickville, O	1869	Hammerstein, Oscar	Berlin, Germany	1847
Bispham, David	Philadelphia, Pa	1857	Hare, John	London	1844
Booth, Agnes	Australia	1843	Harned, Virginia	Boston, Mass	1868
Bourchier, Arthur	England	1863	Harrigan, Edward	New York City	1845
Brady, William A	San Francisco	1865	Harrison, Maud	England	1858
Buchanan, Virginia	Cincinnati, O	1846	Hauk, Minnie	New Orleans, La	1853
Burgess, Neil	Boston, Mass	1846	Hauptmann, Gerhard	Salzbrunn, Aust	1862
Burroughs, Marie	San Francisco	1866	Hawtrey, Charles	Eton, England	1853
Burke, Billie	Washington	1886	Held, Anna	Paris	1873
Byron, Oliver Doud	Baltimore, Md	1847	Herne, Chrystal	Boston, Mass	1883
Caine, Hall	Isle of Man	1853	Heron, Bijou	New York City	1863
Calve, Emma	Aveyron, France	1864	Herbert, Victor	Dublin, Ireland	1860
Campbell, Mrs. Patrick	London	1864	Hilliard, Robert S	Brooklyn	1860
Cawthorn, Joseph	New York	1868	Hitchcock, Raymond	Auburn, N. Y	1870
Carle, Richard	Somerville, Mass	1871	Hite, Mabel	Ashland, Ky	1885
Carey, Eleanor	Chile, S. A	1852	Holland, Edmund M	New York City	1848
Carr, Alexander	Russia	1880	Holland, Joseph Jefferson	New York City	1860
Carter, Mrs. Leslie	Lexington, Ky	1862	Hopper, De Wolf	New York City	1862
Carus, Emma	Berlin	1879	Hopper, Edna Wallace	San Francisco	1874
Chase, Pauline	Washington	1885	Illington, Margaret	Bloomington, Ill	1881
Clarke, Creston	Philadelphia	1865	Irish, Annie	England	1862
Clarke, Marguerite	Cincinnati	1887	Irving, H. B	London	1870
Claxton, Kate	New York City	1848	Irving, Isabel	Bridgeport, Ct	1870
Coghlan, Rose	Petersboro, England	1850	Irwin, May	Toronto, Canada	1862
Coghlan, Gertrude Evelyn	England	1876	James, Louis	Tremont, Ill	1842
Cohan, George M	Providence, R. I	1878	Janis, Elsie	Delaware, O	1889
Compton, Edward	London	1854	Jeffreys, Ellis	Ireland	1868
Conquest, Ida	Boston	1870	Jones, Henry Arthur	Grandsborough, England	1851
Conried, Heinrich	Bielitz, Aust	1855	Keim, Adelaide	New York	18[illegible]5
Coquelin, Benoit C	Boulogne, France	1841	Kendal, William H	London	1843
Courtleigh, William	Guelph, Ont	1867	Kendal, Mrs. W. H	Lincolnshire, England	1849
Courtenay, Wm. Leonard	Worcester, Mass	1875	Kelcey, Herbert H. L	London, England	1856
Coyne, Joseph	New York	1870	Kellogg, Clara Louise	Sumpterville, S. C	1842
Crabtree, Lotta	New York City	1847	Kidder, Kathryn	Newark	1868
Crane, William H	Leicester, Mass	1845	Labia, Mlle	Italy	1883
Crosman, Henrietta	Wheeling, W. Va	1865	Lackaye, Wilton	Virginia	1862
Daly, Arnold	New York	1875	Langtry, Lily	St. Saviour's, Jersey (E.)	1852
Damrosch, Walter J	Breslau, Prussia	1862	Lipman, Clara	Chicago	1869
Daniels, Frank	Boston, Mass	1860	Loftus, Cissie	Glasgow	1876
Davis, Fay	Boston, Mass	1872	Lorimer, Wright	Athol, Mass	1874
Dazie, Mlle	St. Louis, Mo	1884	Mack, Andrew	Boston, Mass	1863
Destinn, Emmy	Berlin	1878	Maeterlinck, Maurice	Belgium	1862
D'Arville, Camille	Holland	1863	Mann, Louis	New York City	1865
De Angelis, Jefferson	San Francisco	1859	Mannering, Mary	London	1876
De Belleville, Frederic	Belgium	1850	Mantell, Robert B	Ayrshire, Scotland	1854
De Koven, H. L. Reginald	Middletown, N. H	1859	Marlowe, Julia	Caldbeck, England	1865
De Merode, Cleo	Paris	1874	Martinot, Sadie	Yonkers, N. Y	1857
De Reszke, Edouard	Warsaw, Poland	1855	Mason, John	Orange, N. J	1857
De Reszke, Jean	Warsaw, Poland	1850	Matthison, Edith Wynne	England	1875
De Wolfe, Elsie	New York City	1865	Maude, Cyril	London	1862
Dixey, Henry E	Boston, Mass	1859	May, Edna	Syracuse	1877
Dodson, John E	London	1857	Melba, Nellie	Melbourne	1866
Donnelly, Dorothy Agnes	New York	1880	Miller, Henry	London	1859
Dorr, Dorothy	Boston, Mass	1867	Millward, Jessie	England	1861
Dressler, Marie	Canada	1869	Mitchell, Maggie	New York City	1832
Drew, John	Philadelphia, Pa	1853	Modjeska, Helena	Cracow, Poland	1844
Duse, Eleanora	Vigevano, Italy	1859	Mordaunt, Frank	Burlington, Vt	1841
Eames, Emma Hayden	Shanghai, China	1868	Morence, Bertha	Munich	1876
Earle, Virginia	Cincinnati	1875	Morris, Clara	Toronto, Canada	1846
Edeson, Robert	Baltimore, Md	1868	Mounet-Sully, Jean	Bergerac, France	1841
Elliott, Maxine	Rockland, Me	1871	Murphy, Joseph	Brooklyn, N. Y	1839
Ellsler, Effie	Philadelphia, Pa	1858	Nazimova, Mme	Yalta, Crimea, Russia	1879

Name.	Birthplace.	Born.
Nethersole, Olga	London	1863
Nielsen, Alice	Nashville, Tenn	1870
Nilsson, Christine	Wederslof, Sweden	1843
Nordica, Lillian	Farmington, Me	1858
Olcott, Chauncey	Providence, R. I	1862
O'Neill, James	Ireland	1849
O'Neill, Nance	Oakland, Cal	1875
Opp, Julie	New York	1871
Otero, Caroline	Spain	1868
Paderewski, Ignace J	Poland	1860
Patti, Adelina	Madrid	1843
Plympton, Eben	Boston, Mass	1850
Potter, Cora Urquhart	New Orleans	....
Powers, James T	New York City	1862
Priest, Janet	East Lowell, Me	1881
Prince, Adelaide	London	1866
Ravelle, Hamilton	Madrid	1869
Rehan, Ada	Limerick, Ireland	1860
Rejane, Gabrielle	Paris, France	1857
Reeve, Ada	London	1876
Richman, Charles	Chicago, Ill	1870
Ring, Blanche	Boston, Mass	1876
Ritchie, Adele	Philadelphia, Pa	1874
Roberts, Florence	New York City	1871
Robertson, J. Forbes	London	1853
Robson, Eleanor	England	1880
Robson, May	Ontario	1868
Russell, Annie	Liverpool	1864
Russell, Lillian	Clinton, Iowa	1860
Salvini, Tommaso	Milan, Italy	1880
Sanderson, Julia	Springfield, Mass	1887
Scheff, Fritzi	Vienna	1879
Schumann-Heink, Mme	Austria	1861
Scott, Cyril	Ireland	1866
Seabrooke, Thomas Q	Mt. Vernon, N. Y	1860
Sembrich, Marcella	Lemberg, Austria	1858
Shannon, Effie	Cambridge, Mass	1867
Shaw, Geo. Bernard	Dublin, Ireland	1856
Shaw, Mary	Wolfboro, N. H	1860
Skinner, Otis	Cambridgeport, Mass	1857
Sothern, Edward H.	England	1864
Sousa, John Philip	Washington	1854
Spong, Hilda	Australia	1875
Stanhope, Adelaide	Paris, France	1858
Stahl, Rose	Montreal	1875
Starr, Frances	Oneonta, N. Y	1886
Stevenson, Charles A	Dublin, Ireland	1850
Taliaferro, Mabel	New York	1887
Tearle, Osmond	Plymouth, England	1852
Tempest, Marie	London	1867
Templeton, Fay	Savannah	1861
Terry, Ellen	Coventry, England	1848
Tetrazzini, Mme	Italy	1874
Thompson, Denman	Girard, Pa	1833
Thursby, Emma	Brooklyn, N. Y	1857
Tree, Beerbohm	England	1853
Tyler, Odette	Savannah, Ga	1869
Tynan, Brandon	Dublin, Ireland	1879
Wainwright, Marie	Philadelphia	1853
Walcot, Charles	New York City	1840
Walsh, Blanche	New York City	1873
Ward, Genevieve	New York City	1838
Warfield, David	San Francisco, Cal	1866
Warde, Frederick	Warrington, England	1851
Warner, Charles	London	1846
Weber, Joseph	New York City	1867
Willard, Edward S	Brighton, England	1853
Wilson, Francis	Philadelphia, Pa	1854
Woodruff, Harry	Hartford, Ct	1869
Wyndham, Sir Charles	England	1837
Yeamans, Annie	Isle of Man	1836

PROFESSIONAL AND NON-PROFESSIONAL NAMES OF SOME ACTORS AND DRAMATISTS OF THE DAY AND OF EARLIER TIMES.

Professional Name.	Real Name.
Abingdon, Wm. L.	Lepper, Wm.
Abott, Bessie	Pickens, Miss Bessie.
Adams, Maude	Kiskadden, Maude.
Adams, Susanne	Stern, Mrs. Leo.
Albani, Mme.	Gye, Mrs. Ernest.
Alexander, George	Sampson, George.
Allen, Louise	Collier, Mrs. Wm.
Allen, Viola	Duryea, Mrs. Peter.
Anderson, Mary	Navarro, Mrs. A. F. de
Anderson, Sarah	Bearnstein, Mrs. Joseph.
Angelis, Aimee	Considine, Mrs. Geo.
Archer, Frank	Arnold, Frank B.
Armstrong, Sydney	Smyth, Mrs. W. G.
Arthur, Joseph	Smith, Arthur E.
Arthur, Julia	Cheney, Mrs. Benj. P.
Ashley, Minnie	Chanler, Mrs. Wm. A.
Atherton, Alice	Edouin, Mrs. Willie.
Baird, Dorothea	Irving, Mrs. Henry B.
Barry, Mrs. Thomas	Redmond, Mrs. Wm.
Barrymore, Maurice	Blythe, Herbert.
Bates, Blanche	Davis, Mrs. Milton F.
Beere, Mrs. Bernard	Olivier, Mrs. A. C. S.
Bentley, Irene	Smith, Mrs. Harry B.
Bergen, Nella	Hopper, Mrs. De Wolf.
Bernhardt, Sarah	Damala, Mme.
Bertram, Helen	Morgan, Mrs. E. J.
Bingham, Amelia	Bingham, Mrs. Lloyd.
Blair, Eugenie	Downing, Mrs. Eugenia.
Blanchard, Kitty	Rankin, Mrs. McKee.
Blauvelt, Lillian	Pendleton, Mrs. W. F.
Bonfanti, Mlle.	Hoffman, Mrs.
Bonehill, Bessie	Seeley, Mrs. Wm.
Bonita	Des Landes, Pauline L.
Booth, Agnes	Schoeffel, Mrs. John.
Booth, Rachel	Powers, Mrs. Jas. T.
Buffalo Bill	Cody, William F.
Burnett, Francis H.	Townsend, Mrs. S.
Burroughs, Marie	Macpherson, Mrs. R. B.
Burt, Laura	Stanford, Mrs. Hy. B.
Burton, Blanche	Standing, Mrs. Guy.
Busley, Jessie	Joy, Mrs. E. C.
Byron, Oliver	Doud, Oliver B.
Cahill, Marie	Arthur, Mrs. Daniel V.
Cameron, Beatrice	Mansfield, Mrs. Richd.
Cameron, Violet	De Bensaude, Mrs.
Carter, Mrs. Leslie	Payne, Mrs. Wm. L.
Carus, Emma	Everall, Mrs. Harry J.
Cavendish, Ada	Marshall, Mrs. Frank.
Cecil, Arthur	Blunt, Arthur Cecil.
Claude, Toby	Carleton, Mrs. W. T., Jr.
Claxton, Kate	Stevenson, Mrs. Chas.
Clayton, Bessie	Mitchell, Mrs. Julian.
Clayton, Estelle	Cooper, Mrs. S. E.
Clemmons, Katherine	Gould, Mrs. Howard.
Coe, Isabelle	McKee, Mrs. Frank.
Coghlan, Gertrude	Pitou, Jr., Mrs. A.
Coghlan, Rose	Sullivan, Mrs. John.
Cohan, Josephine	Niblo, Mrs. Frederick.
Compton, Miss	Carton, Mrs. R. C.
Comstock, Nannette	Burbeck, Mrs. Frank.
Conway, Minnie	Tearle, Mrs. Osmond.
Corinne	Flaherty, Corinne Kimball.
Courtleigh, William	Flynn, William.
Crosman, Henrietta	Campbell, Mrs. Maurice.
Dacre, Arthur	James, Arthur.
D'Arville, Camille	Crelin, Mrs. W. D.
Davis, Fay	Lawrence, Mrs. Gerald.
Davis, Phoebe	Grismer, Mrs. Jos. R.
Dazie, Mlle	Luescher, Mrs. M. A.
De Mar, Carrie	Hart, Mrs. Joseph.
De Silva, N.	Harvey, Mrs. Martin.
D'Orsay, Lawrence	Dorset, Wm. Lawrence.
Deutsch, Florence	Bernard, Mrs. Sam.
Dickson, Charles	Doblin, Charles.
Dillon, Louise	Dillon, Mrs. John.
Dockstader, Lew	Clapp, Geo. Alfred.
Dorr, Dorothy	Dam, Mrs. Hy. J. W.
Dressler, Marie	Kerber, Leila.
Durbin, Maud	Skinner, Mrs. Otis.
Duse, Eleanora	Cecci, Signora.
Elliot, Gertrude	Robertson, Mrs. J. Forbes.
Ellsler, Effie	Weston, Mrs. Frank.
Emerson, Billy	Redmond, William.
Emery, Winifred	Maude, Mrs. Cyril.
Erskine, James	Rosslyn, Earl of.
Ethel, Agnes	Tracy, Mrs.
Eytinge, Rose	Searle, Mrs. Cyril.
Faust, Lotta	Lang, Mrs. Richie.
Fenton, Mabel	Kelly, Mrs. Chas. J.
Fernandez, Bijou	Abingdon, Mrs. W. L.
Fetter, Selina	Royle, Mrs. Edwin Milton.
Filkins, Grace	Marix, Mrs. Adolph.
Firmin, Annie	Jack, Mrs. John.
Fisher, Alice	Harcourt, Mrs. Wm.
Fiske, Minnie Maddern	Fiske, Mrs. Harrison Gray.
Foy, Eddie	Fitzgerald, Edwin.

PROFESSIONAL AND NON-PROFESSIONAL NAMES—*Continued.*

Professional Name.	Real Name.
Fox, Della	Levy, Mrs.
Friganza, Trixie	O'Callahan, Delia Edna.
Gadski, Mme.	Tauscher, Mme.
George, Grace	Brady, Mrs. W. A.
Gerard, Florence	Abbey, Mrs. H. E.
Gerster, Etelka	Gardini, Mrs. Dr.
Gilman, Mabelle	Corey, Mrs. Ellis.
Glaser, Lulu	Herz, Mrs. R. C.
Goodrich, Edna	Goodwin, Mrs. Nat C.
Graham, Robert E.	McGee, Robert E.
Granger, Maude	Baxter, Mrs. W. R.
Granville, Gertie	Hart, Mrs. Tony.
Gray, Ada	Tingay, Mrs. Chas. T.
Grubb, Lillie	Hayman, Mrs. David.
Hading, Jane	Koning, Mme. Victor.
Hall, Pauline	White, Mrs. Frank.
Hanley, Emma	Allen, Mrs. Louise.
Hare, John	Fairs, John.
Harned, Virginia	Sothern, Mrs. Edw. H.
Harrison, Alice	Metz, Alice.
Harrison, Louis	Metz, Louis.
Hart, Senator Bob	Sutherland, J. M.
Hauk, Minnie	Wartegg, Frau von Hesse.
Heath, Caroline	Barrett, Mrs. Wilson
Heid, Anna	Ziegfeld, Mrs. Florence.
Henderson, Grace	Henderson, Mrs. D.
Herndon, Agnes	Jessel, Mrs. Jos. A.
Herne, James A.	Ahern, James.
Heron, Bijou	Miller, Mrs. Henry.
Heron, Matilda	Stoepel, Mrs. Robt.
Hite, Mabel	Donlin, Mrs. M. J.
Hodson, Henrietta	Labouchere, Mrs. Hy.
Hope, Eric	Yarmouth, Earl of.
Illington, Margaret	Frohman, Mrs. Daniel.
Irish, Annie	Dodson, Mrs. J. E.
Irving, Isabel	Thompson, Mrs. W. H.
Irwin, Beatrice	Simpson, Beatrice.
Irwin, May	Eisfeldt, Mrs. Kurt.
Janis, Elsie	Bierbower, Elsie Janis.
Janisch, Mme.	D'Arco, Countess.
Jansen, Marie	Key, Mrs. Barton.
Jeffreys-Lewis, Ida	Mainhall, Mrs. H.
Jeffreys, Ellis	Sleath, Mrs. Herbert.
Karl, Tom	Carroll, Thomas.
Keene, Laura	Taylor, Mrs.
Keene, Thomas W.	Eagleson, Thos. W.
Kellogg, Clara Louise	Strakosch, Mrs. C.
Kendal, William H.	Grimston, W. H.
Kendal, Mrs. W. H.	Grimston, Mrs. W. H.
Kimball, Grace	McGuire, Mrs. M. D.
Kimball, Jennie	Flaherty, Mrs. Jennie.
Kingdon, Edith	Gould, Mrs. Geo. J.
Langtry, Mrs.	De Bathe, Mrs. Hugo G.
Lee, Jennie	Burnett, Mrs. J. P.
Lehman, Lilli	Kalisch, Mme. Paul.
LeMoyne, Sarah Cowell	LeMoyne, Mrs. Wm. J.
Leslie, Elsie	Winter, Mrs. W. J.
Lewis, Ada	Parr, Mrs. John.
Lewis, Catherine	Robertson, Mrs. Donald.
Lewis, Lillian	Marston, Mrs. Laurence
Linthicum, Lotta	Strachan, Mrs. W. C.
Lipman, Clara	Mann, Mrs. Louis.
Loftus, Cecilia	McCarthy, Marie Cecilia
Logan, Celia	Connelly, Mrs. Jas. H.
Losee, Frank	Losee, Ira N.
Lotta	Crabtree, Charlotte.
MacLean, R. D.	Shepherd, Rezin D.
Maddern, Emma	Stevens, Mrs. R. E.
Mannering, Mary	Hackett, Mrs. J. K.
Mantelli, Mme. Eugenie	De Amicis, Mrs.
Mantell, Robert B.	Hudson, Robert.
Markham, Pauline	McMahon, Mrs.
Marlowe, Julia	Frost, Sarah.
Martinot, Sadie	Nethersole, Mrs. Louis.
Materna, Mme.	Friedrich, Mme.
May, Edna	Lewisohn, Mrs. O.
McDonald, Christie	Jefferson, Mrs. W. W.
Melba, Mme.	Armstrong, Mrs. N.
Millard, Evelyn	Coulter, Mrs. Robt. P.
Millward, Jessie	Glendenning, Mrs. J.
Miskel, Caroline	Hoyt, Mrs. Chas. (2)
Mitchell, Maggie	Abbott, Mrs. Chas.
Modjeska, Mme.	Chlapowski, Countess Chas. Bozenta.
Montague, Henry J.	Mann, Harry J.
Moore, Eva	Esmond, Mrs. H. V.
Moore, Mary	Albert, Mrs. James.
Mordaunt, Frank	Markyam, Francis.
Morris, Clara	Harriott, Mrs. F. C.
Murray, Alma	Forman, Mrs. Alfred.
Murska, Ilma di	Hill, Mrs.
Nazimova, Mme. Alla	Orleneff, Mrs. Paul N.
Neilson, Adelaide	Lee, Mrs. Philip H.
Neilson, Julia	Terry, Mrs. Frederick.
Neruda, Mme. Norman	Halle, Lady.
Nevada, Emma	Palmer, Mrs.
Nilsson, Christine	Miranda, Count. Casa.
Nobles, Miss Dolly	Nobles, Mrs. Milton.
Nordica, Mme.	Doime, Mme. Zoltan.
Olcott, Chauncey	Olcott, Chancellor J.
Opp, Julia	Faversham, Mrs. W. F.
O'Neil, Anne	Miner, Mrs. H. C.
Palmer, Minnie	Rogers, Mrs. John R.
Patti, Adelina	Cedarstrom, Baroness R.
Perugini, Signor	Chatterton, John.
Pitt, Fannie Addison	Pitt, Mrs. Henry M.
Pixley, Annie	Fulford, Mrs. Robt.
Potter, Mrs.	Potter, Cora Urquhart.
Prescott, Marie	Pertzel, Mrs.
Priest, Janet	Robb, Jr., Mrs. Thos.
Prince, Adelaide	Clarke, Mrs. Creston.
Raleigh, Cecil	Rowlands, Mr.
Rankin, Phyllis	Davenport, Mrs. Hy. L.
Raymond, John T.	O'Brien, John T.
Rehan, Ada	Crehan, Ada.
Rejane, Mme.	Porel, Mme. D. P. P.
Rice, Fannie	Purdy, Mrs. Dr.
Roberts, Florence	Morrison, Mrs. Lewis.
Robertson, Agnes	Boucicault, Mrs. Dion.
Robson, May	Brown, Mrs. Augustus.
Roosevelt, Blanche	Machetta, Mme.
Rorke, Kate	Gardner, Mrs. Jas.
Roselle, Amy	Dacre, Mrs. Arthur.
Ross, Chas. J.	Kelly, Chas. J.
Russell, Mme. Ella	Rhigini, Mme. de.
Russell, Lillian	Leonard, Helen Louise.
St. John, Florence	Marius, Mrs. Claude.
Sanderson, Julia	Sloane, Mrs. Tod.
Schumann-Heink, Mme.	Rapp, Mrs. Wm., Jr.
Sembrich, Mme.	Stengel, Mme. Guillaume.
Shannon, Effie	Kelcey, Mrs. Herbert
Shannon, Joseph W.	Sendelbach, J. W.
Shannon, Lavinia	Shine, Mrs. Giles.
Summerville, Amelia	Shaw, Amelia.
Spong, Hilda	Spong, Frances.
Stanhope, Adeline	Wheatcroft, Mrs. N.
Stahl, Rose	Bonnelli, Mrs. Wm.
Stirling, Mme. A.	Mackinlay, Mrs. J.
Stuart, Julia	Mackay, Mrs. Ed.
Stuart, Cosmo	Lennox, Cosmo C. G.
Stuart, Leslie	Barrett, T. A.
Sully, Daniel	Sullivan, Daniel.
Sutherland, Anne	Hartley, Mrs. Fred.
Taliaferro, Mabel	Thompson, Mrs. F.
Tempest, Marie	Stuart, Mrs. Cosmo.
Temple, Rose	Jones, Mrs. J. H.
Templeton, Fay	Patterson, Mrs.
Terriss, Ellaline	Hicks, Mrs. Seymour.
Terriss, William	Lewin, Arthur.
Terry, Ellen	Carew, Mrs. James.
Theo, Mme.	Piccolo, Cecile.
Tiffany, Annie Ward	Green, Mrs. Chas. H.
Tree, Henry Beerbohm	Birnbaum, Henry.
Truax, Sarah	Post, Mrs. Guy Bates.
Tyler, Odette	Shepherd, Mrs. R. D.
Ulmar, Geraldine	Carryll, Mrs. Ivan.
Valda, Mme. Giulia	Cameron, Mrs. Julia.
Vanbrugh, Violet	Bourchier, Mrs. Arthur.
Vane, Helen	Snyder, Mrs. Chas.
Vassar, Queenie	Cawthorn, Mrs. Jos.
Vaughn, Teresa	Mestayer, Mrs. W. A.
Vokes, Rosina	Clay, Mrs. Cecil.
Walker, Charlotte	Hayden, Mrs. John B.
Walsh, Blanche	Travers, Mrs. Wm.
Ward, Fannie	Lewis, Mrs. Joseph.
Ward, Genevieve	Guerbel, Countess.
Waring, Herbert	Rutty, Herbert W.
Warren, Lavinia	Stratton, Mrs. C. S.
Wiley, Dora	Golden, Mrs. Richard.
Wilton, Ellis	Doremus, Mrs. T. C.
Wynne-Matthison, Edith	Kennedy, Mrs
Yeamans, Lydia	Titus, Mrs. Fred. J.

The New York Public Service Act.

PUBLIC SERVICE COMMISSIONERS.

FIRST DISTRICT.

William R. Willcox, Chairman, Manhattan, New York; holds office until February 1, 1913
William McCarroll, Brooklyn; holds office until February 1, 1912.
Edward M. Bassett, Brooklyn; holds office until February 1, 1911.
Milo Roy Maltbie, Manhattan, New York; holds office until February 1, 1910
John E. Eustis, Manhattan, New York; holds office until February 1, 1909.

SECOND DISTRICT.

Frank W. Stevens, Chairman, Jamestown; holds office until February 1, 1913.
John B. Olmsted, Buffalo; holds office until February 1, 1912.
Thomas Mott Osborne, Auburn; holds office until February 1, 1911.
Martin S. Decker, New Paltz; holds office until February 1, 1910.
James E. Sagur, New Hamburg; holds office until February 1, 1909.

Chapter 429 of the Laws of 1907, "An Act to establish the Public Service Commissions and prescribing their powers and duties, and to provide for the regulation and control of certain public service corporations and making an appropriation therefor," became a law on June 6, 1907. Two Public Service Commissions of five members each were created by the Act, one with authority in the First District, which included the counties of New York, Kings, Queens and Richmond, and the other in the Second District, which included all the other counties of the State.

The Act abolished the existing State Board of Railroad Commissioners, the State Commission of Gas and Electricity, the State Inspector of Gas Meters, and the Board of Rapid Transit Commissioners of New York City. All the powers of the Railroad Commissioners, of the Commission of Gas and Electricity, and of the Inspector of Gas Meters were conferred upon the Public Service Commissions. All the powers and duties of the Board of Rapid Transit Railroad Commissioners of New York City were conferred upon the Public Service Commission of the First District. The first Commissioners appointed are to hold office, respectively, until February 1, 1909; February 1, 1910; February 1, 1911; February 1, 1912, and February 1, 1913. Each of their successors are to hold office for a period of five years. The Governor is authorized to remove any Commissioner for inefficiency, neglect of duty or misconduct in office, giving to him a copy of the charges against him, and an opportunity of being publicly heard in person or by counsel in his own defence.

The jurisdiction of the Public Service Commission of the First District extends to railroads and street railroads lying exclusively within that district, to any common carrier operating exclusively within that district, and to the manufacture, sale or distribution of gas and electricity for light, heat and power in that district. In addition the Commission of the First District is to exercise the powers heretofore conferred upon the Board of Rapid Transit Railroad Commissions. All jurisdiction not specifically granted to the Public Service Commission of the First District is granted to the Public Service Commission of the Second District. The annual salary of each Public Service Commissioner is to be $15,000; of their secretary, $6,000, and of their counsel, $10.000.

The Act provides that every railway corporation shall furnish with respect thereto such service or facilities as shall be safe and adequate, and in all respects just and reasonable; and, secondly, that all charges made or demanded by any such corporation, person or common carrier for the transportation of passengers, freight or property, for any service rendered, or to be rendered, in connection therewith, shall be just and reasonable, and not more than allowed by law or by order of the Public Service Commission having jurisdiction, and made as authorized by the Act. Every unjust or reasonable charge made or demanded for any such service or transportation of passengers, freight or property, or in connection therewith, or in excess of that allowed by law or by order of the Commission, is prohibited. A railroad corporation, upon the application of any shipper tendering traffic for transportation, must construct upon reasonable terms a switch connection. Every common carrier is to file with the Public Service Commission having jurisdiction, and print and keep open to public inspection, schedules showing the rates, fares and charges for the transportation of passengers and property within the State between each point upon its route and all other points thereon. The schedules are to plainly state the places between which property and passengers are to be carried, the classification of passengers, freight and property in force, all terminal charges, storage charges, icing charges, and all other charges which the Commission may require to be stated, all privileges or facilities granted or allowed, and any rules or regulations which may in any wise change, affect, or determine any part, or the aggregate of the rates, fares or charges, or the value of the service rendered to the passenger, shipper or consignee. Such schedules are to be plainly printed in large type; copies for the use of the public are to be kept posted in two public and conspicuous places in every depot, station and office of every common carrier where passengers or property are received for transportation in such manner as to be readily accessible to and conveniently inspected by the public. No common carrier, the Act says, "shall directly or indirectly by any special rate, rebate, drawback, or other device or method, charge, demand, collect or receive from any person or corporation a greater or less compensation for any service rendered or to be rendered in the transportation of passengers, freight or property, except as authorized in this Act, than it charges, demands, collects, or receives from any other person or corporation for doing a like and contemporaneous service in the transportation of a like kind of traffic under the same or substantially similar circumstances and conditions." The giving of free tickets, free passes, or free transportation for passengers or property, except to its employees and certain other specified classes, or in certain specified cases, is prohibited. No common carrier is to charge or receive any greater compensation in the aggregate for the transportation of passengers, or of a like kind or property, under substantially similar circumstances and conditions for a shorter than for a longer distance over the same line in the same direction, the shorter being included within the longer distance. Upon the application, however, of a common carrier the Public Service Commission may, by order, authorize it to charge less for a longer than for shorter distances for the transportation of passengers or property in special cases after investigation by the Commission. Every railroad corporation and street railway corporation is to have sufficient cars and motive power to meet all requirements for the transportation of passengers and property which may reasonably be anticipated. Every railroad corporation must furnish to all persons and corporations who apply therefor and offer freight for transportation sufficient and suitable cars for the transportation of such freight in car-load lots.

POWERS OF THE COMMISSIONS.

Each one of the Public Service Commissions is to have general supervision of all common carriers, railroads and street railroads, and is directed to keep informed as to their general condition, their capitalization, their franchises, and the manner in which their lines owned, leased, controlled or operated, are managed, conducted and operated, not only with respect to the adequacy, security and accommodation afforded by their service, but also with respect to their compliance with all provisions of law, orders of the Commission and Charter requirements. Each Commission is given power to examine all books, contracts, documents and papers of any person or corporation subject to its supervision, and by subpoena to compel production thereof. Each Commission is to prescribe the form of the annual reports required under the Act to be made by common carriers, railroad and street railroad corporations. Each Commission is to investigate the cause of all accidents on any railroad or street railroad within its district which result in loss of life or injury to persons or property, and which, in their judgment, require investigation. Whenever either Commission shall be of the opinion that the rates, fares or charges demanded by any common carrier, railroad corporation or street railroad corporation subject to its jurisdiction are unjust, unreasonable, unjustly discriminatory, or unduly preferential, or in anywise in violation of any provision of law, it shall determine the just and reasonable rates, fares and charges to be thereafter observed and in force as the maximum to be charged for the service to be performed. And whenever a Public Service Commission is of the opinion, after a hearing, that the equipment, appliances or service of any common carrier, railroad corporation or street railroad corporation is unsafe, its members are required to determine the safe equipment thereafter to be in force, and prescribe the same by an order to be served upon the common carrier, railroad corporation or street railway corporation concerned. The Commissions are granted power to require two or more common carriers owning a continuous line of transportation to establish joint rates, fares and charges. The Commissions may order repairs and improvements to be made to tracks, switches, terminals, and motive powers in order to promote the security or convenience of the public. If, in the judgment of the Commission having jurisdiction, any railroad corporation or street railroad corporation does not run trains enough or cars enough, or possess or operate motive power enough reasonably to accommodate the traffic, passengers and freight transported by it, or it does not run its trains or cars with sufficient frequency, such a Commission may make an order directing any such corporation to increase the number of its trains, or of its cars, or its motive power. A uniform system of accounts for railroad and street railway corporations is authorized. Without first having obtained the permission and approval of the proper Public Service Commission, no railroad corporation may begin the construction of a railroad or street railroad. The Commission within whose district such construction is to be made is authorized to grant its approval when, in its judgment, the exercise of the franchise or privilege is necessary or convenient for the public service. No franchise to own or operate a railroad or street railroad may be assigned, transferred or leased unless the assignment, transfer or lease is first approved by the proper Commission. No railroad corporation or street railroad corporation is to acquire the capital stock of any railroad corporation or street railroad corporation unless authorized to do so by one of the Commissions created by the Act. Every contract for a transfer of stock by or through any person or corporation to any corporation in violation of the Act, it is declared, shall be void. Common carriers, railroads, and street railroad corporations are authorized to issue stocks, bonds, notes and other evidences of indebtedness when necessary for the acquisition of property, provided, that they shall have secured from the proper Commission an order authorizing such an issue. For the purpose of enabling it to determine whether it should issue such an order, the Commission concerned is to make an inquiry, and examine such books or contracts as it may deem of importance in enabling it to reach a determination. The Act says that "any common carrier, railroad corporation or street railroad corporation which shall violate any provision of this Act, or which fails, omits, or neglects to obey, observe, or comply with any order, or any direction, or requirement of the Commission, shall forfeit to the people of the State of New York not to exceed the sum of $5,000 for each and every offence; every violation of any such order, or direction, or requirement, or of this Act, shall be a separate and distinct offence; and in case of a continuing violation, every day's continuance thereof shall be, and be deemed to be, a separate and distinct offence." It is also made a misdemeanor for the officer of a corporation to violate the Act, or to procure any violation by any such corporation. Summary proceedings in the courts are authorized in the case of offending corporations.

INTERSTATE TRAFFIC.

Either of the Commissions may investigate freight rates on interstate traffic on railroads within the State, and when such rates are, in the opinion of either Commissions, excessive or discriminatory, or are levied or laid in violation of the Interstate Commerce law, or in conflict with the rulings, orders or regulations of the Interstate Commerce Commission, the Commission concerned may apply by petition to the Interstate Commerce Commission for relief.

SUPERVISION OF GAS AND ELECTRICAL CORPORATIONS.

Each Commission within its jurisdiction is given general supervision of all persons and corporations having authority to maintain wires and pipes along or under the streets of a municipality for the purpose of furnishing or distributing gas, or of furnishing or transmitting electricity for light, heat or power. The Commissions may ascertain the quality of the gas supplied, examine the methods employed in manufacturing and supplying gas or electricity for light, heat or power, and order such improvements as will best promote the public interest, preserve the public health, and protect those using such gas or electricity. The Commissions also may fix the standard of illuminating power and purity of gas, not less than that prescribed by law, to be manufactured or sold by persons, corporations or municipalities for lighting, heating or power purposes; prescribe methods of regulation of the electric supply system as to the use for incandescent lighting; fix the initial efficiency of incandescent lamps furnished by the persons, corporations or municipalities generating and selling electric current for lighting, and by order require the gas so manufactured or sold to equal the standard so fixed by it, and, finally, establish the regulations as to pressure at which gas shall be delivered. The Commissions are authorized to determine by investigation whether or not the gas sold is of the purity and quality required. The Commissions may require the corporations manufacturing gas and electricity to keep uniform accounts. The Commission is to require every person and corporation under its supervision to submit to it an annual report showing in detail (1) the amount of its authorized capital stock and the amount thereof issued and outstanding; (2) The amount of its authorized bonded indebtedness, and the amount of its bonds, and other forms of evidence of indebtedness issued and outstanding; (3) its receipts and expenditures during the preceding year; (4) the amount paid as dividends upon its stock and as interest upon its bonds; (5) the name of, and the amount paid as salary, to each officer, and the amount paid as wages to its employees; (6) the location of its plant, or plants, and system, with a full description of its property and franchises, stating in detail how each franchise stated to be owned was acquired; and (7) such other facts pertaining to the operation and maintenance of the plant and system, and the affairs of such person or corporation as may be required by the Commission. Any corporation which shall neglect to make such a report is made liable to a penalty of $100, and an additional penalty of $100 for each day after the prescribed time for which it shall neglect to file the same. Every municipality engaged in operating any works or systems for the manufacture and supplying of gas or electricity is to be required to make an annual report to the Commission showing in detail (1) the amount of its authorized bonded indebtedness, and the amount of its bonds and other forms of evidence of indebtedness issued and outstanding for lighting purposes; (2) its receipts and expenditures during the preceding year; (3) the amount paid as interest upon its bonds and upon other forms of evidence of indebtedness; (4) the name of and the amount paid to each person receiving a yearly or monthly salary, and the amount paid as wages to employees; (5) the location of its plant and system, with a full description of the property; and (6) such other facts pertaining to the operation and maintenance of the plant and system as may be required by the Commission.

INSPECTION OF GAS AND ELECTRIC METERS.

Each Commission is to appoint inspectors of gas and electric meters, who are to inspect, examine, prove and ascertain the accuracy of any and all gas meters used or intended to be used for measuring, or ascertaining the quantity of illuminating or fuel gas or natural gas furnished by any gas corporation to or for the use of any person, and any and all electric meters used or intended to be used for measuring and ascertaining the quantity of electric current furnished for light, heat and power by any electrical corporation to or for the use of any person or persons. The law says that "No corporation or person shall furnish or put in use any gas meter which shall not have been inspected, proved and sealed, or any electric meter which shall not have been inspected, approved, stamped or marked by an inspector of the Commission." The law also says that "No gas corporation or electrical corporation incorporated under the laws of this or any other State shall begin construction, or exercise any right or privilege under any franchise hereafter granted, or under any franchise heretofore granted, but not heretofore actually exercised, without first having obtained the permission and approval of the proper Commission." The law further says: "No municipality shall build, maintain and operate for other than municipal purposes any works or system for the manufacture and supplying of gas or electricity for lighting purposes without a certificate of authority granted by the Commission."

American Society of International Law.

OFFICERS: President, Elihu Root; Vice-Presidents, Chief Justice Fuller, Justice William R. Day, Andrew Carnegie, John W. Foster, John W. Griggs, Richard Olney, Justice David J. Brewer, President-elect William H. Taft, Joseph H. Choate, Judge George Gray, W. W. Morrow, Secretary Oscar S. Straus; General Horace Porter; Recording Secretary, James B. Scott; Corresponding Secretary, Charles Henry Butler; Treasurer, Chandler P. Anderson.

Statistics of Principal Fraternal Organizations.

NOTICE—The following data concerning Fraternal Organizations is based upon the latest information obtainable, but is subject to the frequent changes incidental to the formation of these bodies.

American Benefit Society.—Founded 1893; sub-lodges, 140; members, 6,000; benefits disbursed since organization, $460,000; benefits disbursed last fiscal year, $67,250; President, W. H. Carberry, Boston, Mass.; Secretary, A. H. Bacon, Melrose, Mass.; Treasurer, William W. Towle, Boston, Mass. (Report of January 1, 1908.)

American Guild.—Founded 1890; subordinate chapters, 1,020; members, 25,000; benefits disbursed since organization, $1,726,179; benefits disbursed last fiscal year, $296,269; Governor, S. Galeski; Vice-Governor, B. T. Crump; Secretary, C. W. Kimpton; Treasurer, J. B. Montgomery. Headquarters, Richmond, Va. (Report of January 1, 1908).

Ben Hur, Tribe of.—Founded 1894; Supreme Temple, Crawfordsville, Ind.; subordinate courts, 1,200; members, 100,315; benefits disbursed since organization, $5,948,702; benefits disbursed last fiscal year, $883,968; Supreme Chief, D. W. Gerard, Crawfordsville, Ind.; Supreme Scribe, J. C. Snyder, Crawfordsville, Ind.; Supreme Keeper of Tribute, S. E. Voris, Crawfordsville, Ind.

B'nai B'rith, Independent Order of.—Founded 1843; grand lodges, 10; subordinate lodges, 396; members, 30,283; benefits disbursed last fiscal year, $395,408; President, Adolf Kraus, Chicago, Ill.; Vice-President, J. B. Klein, Bridgeport, Ct.; Treasurer, Jacob Furth, Cleveland, Ohio; Secretary, A. B. Seelenfreund, Chicago, Ill.

Brith Abraham Order.—Founded 1859; grand lodge, 1; sub-lodges, 334; members, 61,389; Grand Master, Samuel Dorf, New York; First Deputy Grand Master, A. Heller, Brooklyn, N. Y.; Secretary, Leonard Leisersohn, New York; Treasurer, M. S. Shill, New York.

Brotherhood of American Yeomen.—Founded 1897; subordinate homesteads, 1,475; members, 61,671; benefits disbursed since organization, $2,131,626; benefits disbursed last fiscal year, $466,232; President, William Koch; Secretary, W. E. Davy; Treasurer, G. M. Read. Address of officers, Des Moines, Iowa. (Report of January 1, 1908.)

Catholic Benevolent Legion.—Founded 1881; State councils, 6; subordinate councils, 385; members, 18,644; benefits disbursed since organization, $19,860,715; benefits disbursed last fiscal year, $824,053; President, R. B. Tippett, Baltimore, Md.; Secretary, J. D. Carroll, Brooklyn, N. Y.; Treasurer, John E. Dunn, Brooklyn, N. Y.

Catholic Knights of America.—Founded 1877; subordinate councils, 600; members, 20,000; benefits disbursed since organization, $16,000,000; benefits disbursed last fiscal year, $701,000; Supreme President, Felix Gaudin, New Orleans, La.; Supreme Vice-President, Hubert J. Crogban, Providence, R. I.; Supreme Secretary, Anthony Matre, St. Louis, Mo.; Supreme Treasurer, Charles E. Hannauer, St. Louis, Mo.

Catholic Mutual Benefit Association.—Founded 1876; grand State councils, 7; subordinate branches, 800; members, 59,442; benefits disbursed since organization, $19,164,829; benefits disbursed last fiscal year, $1,347,199; Supreme President, John J. Hynes, Buffalo, N. Y.; Supreme Recorder, Joseph Cameron, Hornell, N. Y.; Supreme Treasurer, William Muench, Syracuse, N. Y.

Court of Honor.—Founded 1895; grand courts, 1; district courts, 1,180; members, 65,000; benefits disbursed since organization, $5,588,303; benefits disbursed last fiscal year, $625,346; Chancellor, A. L. Hereford, Springfield, Ill.; Recorder, W. E. Robinson, Springfield, Ill.; Treasurer, B. F. Workman, Auburn, Ill.

Druids, United Ancient Order of.—Founded 1781 (in England), 1839 (in America); number of grand groves, 18; sub-groves, 528; total number of members (in America), 30,042; benefits disbursed in America, $6,267,371; benefits disbursed last fiscal year, $234,189; Supreme Arch, Julius S. Godeau, San Francisco, Cal. Supreme Secretary, H. Freudenthal, Albany, N. Y.; Supreme Treasurer, Louis Kraus, La Fayette, Ind.

Eagles, Order of.—Founded 1898; members, 311,159; benefits disbursed since organization, $3,920,532; benefits disbursed last fiscal year, $727,979; President, B. J. Monaghan, Philadelphia, Pa.; Vice-President, Frank E. Hering, South Bend, Ind.; Secretary, Conrad H. Mann, Kansas City, Mo.

Elks, Benevolent and Protective Order of.—Founded 1868; grand lodge, 1; sub-lodges 1,137; members in the United States, 284,321; benefits disbursed last fiscal year, $351,670; Grand Exalted Ruler, Rush L. Holland, Colorado Springs, Col.; Secretary, Fred. C. Robinson, Dubuque, Iowa; Treasurer, Edward Leach, N. Y. City.

Foresters, Ancient Order of.—Founded 1745; established in America 1836. The American branch is composed of 3 high courts and 420 subordinate courts, and has 40,992 members. Total membership throughout the world 1,275,080, as stated by the Foresters' Directory December 31, 1907. The surplus funds of the society amounted to $44,477,425, and its assets aggregated $83,500,000. Benefits disbursed since 1836, $135,950,000; benefits disbursed last fiscal year, over $4,950,000. Officers of the American branch are as follows: High Chief Ranger, Thomas Hollows, Lawrence, Mass.; High Sub-Chief Ranger, Charles Jacobson, New York City; High Court Treasurer, T. J. Scott, Summit, N. J.; Secretary, Robert A. Sibbald, Park Ridge, N. J.

Foresters, Independent Order of.—Founded 1874; high courts, 55; subordinate courts 5,000; members, 260,000; benefits disbursed since organization, $26,000,000; benefits disbursed last fiscal year, $2,757,118; Supreme Chief Ranger, E. G. Stevenson, Toronto, Ontario; Vice-Chief Ranger, J. D. Clark, Dayton, O.; Secretary, Robert Mathison, Toronto.

Foresters of America.—Is a distinct organization, not in affiliation with the above. Its present jurisdiction is limited to the United States. Founded 1864, reorganized 1889; grand courts, 18; sub-courts, 1,860; members, 235,441; benefits disbursed since organization, $22,821,912; benefits disbursed last fiscal year, $1,448,624; Supreme Chief Ranger, John J. O'Grady, New York; Supreme Sub-Chief Ranger, J. E. Lyddy, Bridgeport, Ct.; Supreme Treasurer, John J. Guerin, Philadelphia, Pa.; Supreme Secretary, E. M. McMurtry, Brooklyn, N. Y.; Supreme Recording Secretary, P. J. Brown, Worcester, Mass.

Fraternal Brotherhood.—Founded 1896; subordinate lodges, 450; members, 38,341; benefits disbursed since organization, $1,278,850; benefits disbursed last fiscal year, $253,309; President, J. A. Foshay; Vice-President, Emma R. Neidig; Secretary, H. V. Davis; Treasurer, William Mead. All in Los Angeles, Cal.

Fraternal Union of America.—Founded 1896; grand lodge, 1; local lodges, 620; members,

STATISTICS OF PRINCIPAL FRATERNAL ORGANIZATIONS—*Continued.*

28,627; benefits disbursed since organization, $1,940,474; benefits disbursed last fiscal year, $277,-346; President, F. F. Roose; Secretary, Samuel S. Baty. All in Denver, Col.

Free Sons of Israel, Independent Order of.—Founded 1849; grand lodges, 3; subordinate lodges, 102; members, 11,035; benefits disbursed since organization, $5,403,536; benefits disbursed last fiscal year, $298,013; Grand Master, M. S. Stern, 2013 Fifth Avenue, New York City; Secretary, Abraham Hafer, 21 West 124th Street, New York City; Treasurer, Louis Frankenthaler, New York City.

Golden Cross, United Order of.—Founded 1876; grand commanderies, 10; subordinate commanderies, 542; members, 19,656; benefits disbursed since organization, $9,630,604; benefits disbursed last fiscal year, $494,828; Supreme Commander, J. P. Burlingame, Providence, R. I.; Supreme Keeper of Records, W. R. Cooper, Knoxville, Tenn.; Supreme Treasurer, J. N. Ehle, Washington, D. C.

Heptasophs, Improved Order.—Founded 1878; conclaves, 826; members, 77,389; benefits disbursed since organization, $14,108,663; benefits disbursed last fiscal year, $1,317,597; Supreme Archon, M. G. Cohen, Pittsburgh, Pa.; Supreme Provost, Thos. B. Hicks, Richmond, Va.; Supreme Secretary, Samuel H. Tattersall, Baltimore, Md.; Supreme Treasurer, C. H. Ramsay, Boston.

Hibernians of America, Ancient Order of.—Founded 1836; State, Provincial and Territorial Boards, 50; divisions, 2,465; members, 217,000; benefits disbursed since organization, $27,892,750; benefits disbursed last fiscal year, $672,000; National President, Matthew Cummings, Boston, Mass.; National Vice-President, James J. Regan, St. Paul, Minn.; National Secretary, James T. Carroll, Columbus, O.; National Treasurer, John F. Quinn, Joliet, Ill. (Report of Jan. 1, 1908.)

Irish Catholic Benevolent Union.—Founded 1869; subordinate societies, 157; members, 15,000; benefits disbursed since organization, $2,491,413; benefits disbursed last fiscal years, $36,171; President, Daniel Duffy, Pottsville, Pa.; First Vice-President, T. J. Gilbool, Carbondale, Pa.; Treasurer, Martin P. Feeney, Providence, R. I.; Secretary, Frank P. McCue, Philadelphia.

Knights and Ladies of Honor.—Founded 1877; grand lodges, 16; sub-lodges, 1,400; members, 96,000; benefits disbursed since organization, $27,000,000; benefits disbursed last fiscal year, $1,505,000; Supreme Protector, S. B. Watts, Indianapolis, Ind.; Secretary, George D. Tait, Indianapolis, Ind.; Treasurer, George A. Byrd, Indianapolis, Ind.

Knights of Columbus.—Founded 1882; National council, 1; subordinate councils, 1,314; members, 210,078; benefits disbursed since organization, $3,669,597; benefits disbursed last fiscal year, $348,772; Supreme Knight, Edward L. Hearn, New Haven, Ct.; Deputy Supreme Knight, James A. Flaherty, Philadelphia, Pa.; National Secretary, Daniel Colwell, New Haven, Ct.; National Treasurer, P. J. Brady, Cleveland, O.

Knights of Honor.—Founded 1873; grand lodges, 36; subordinate lodges, 1,672; members, 40,126; benefits disbursed since organization, $86,692,268; benefits disbursed last fiscal year, $2,741,885; Supreme Dictator, J. C. Sheppard, Edgefield, S. C.; Supreme Reporter, Noah M. Givan, St. Louis, Mo.; Supreme Treasurer, Frank B. Sliger, St. Louis, Mo.

Knights of Malta, Ancient and Illustrious Order.—Founded in Jerusalem, 1048; grand commanderies, 5; sub-commanderies, 265; members, 30,000; benefits disbursed last fiscal year, $103,424; Supreme Commander, Geo. W. Welsh, York, Pa.; Supreme Recorder, Frank Gray, Philadelphia, Pa.; Supreme Treasurer, W. J. Rugh, Pittsburgh, Pa.

Knights of St. John and Malta.—Founded 1048; grand encampment, 1; subordinate encampments, 52; members, 4,000; benefits disbursed since organization, $843,239; benefits disbursed last fiscal year, $36,816; Grand Commander, Joseph G. Burrows, New York; Grand Chancellor, Henry C. Siegmann, New York; Grand Almoner, Jacob T. Ryder, Brooklyn, N. Y.

Knights of the Golden Eagle.—Founded 1873; grand castles, 15; sub-castles, 812; members, 71,960; benefits disbursed last fiscal year, $270,325; Supreme Chief, Dr. C. D. Krim, Columbus, O.; Master of Records, A. C. Lyttle, Philadelphia, Pa.; Keeper of the Exchequer, William Culbertson, Philadelphia, Pa.

Knights of the Maccabees of the World.—Founded 1883; great camps, 9; subordinate tents and hives, 4,847; members, 285,841; benefits disbursed since organization, $34,215,159; benefits disbursed last fiscal year, $3,422,752; Supreme Commander, D. P. Markey; Supreme Record Keeper, L. E. Sisler. Offices are located at Port Huron, Mich.

Knights of the Modern Maccabees (original order).—Founded in 1881; subordinate tents, 1,291; members, 112,846; total benefits paid, $13,362,150; benefits disbursed last fiscal year, $1,227,904; Great Commander, George S. Lovelace, Muskegon, Mich.; Great Record Keeper, A. M. Slay, Port Huron, Mich.

Ladies' Catholic Benevolent Association.—Founded 1890; subordinate branches, 1,049; members, 102,129; benefits disbursed since organization, $6,169,076; benefits disbursed last fiscal year, $740 024; Supreme President, Mrs. E. B. McGowan, Buffalo, N. Y.; Supreme Recorder, Mrs. J. A. Royer, Erie, Pa.; Supreme Treasurer, Mrs. Felice M. Girardot, Detroit, Mich.

Ladies of the Maccabees of the World.—Founded 1892; great hives, 3; subordinate hives, 2,727; members, 156,609, benefits disbursed since organization, $6,444,410; benefits disbursed last fiscal year, $783,850; Supreme Commander, Lillian M. Hollister, Detroit, Mich.; Record Keeper, Bina M. West, Port Huron, Mich.; Finance Keeper, Nellie C. V. Heppert, Akron, Ohio.

Loyal Americans of the Republic.—Founded 1896; subordinate assemblies, 681; members, 21,255; benefits disbursed since organization, $1,449,315; benefits disbursed last fiscal year, $217,-745; Supreme President, E. J. Dunn, Springfield, Ill.; Vice-President, Jesse M. Ott, Petersburg, Ill., Secretary, H. D. Cowan, Springfield, Ill.; Treasurer, A. F. Deicken, Springfield, Ill. (Report of Jan. 1, 1908.)

Mystic Circle, The Fraternal.—Founded 1884; grand rulings, 10; subordinate rulings, 1,320; members, 31,717; benefits disbursed since organization, $3,495,686; benefits disbursed last fiscal year, $384,103; Supreme Mystic Ruler, F. H. Duckwitz, Philadelphia, Pa.; Recorder, J. D. Myers, Philadelphia, Pa.; Treasurer, John Smiley, Philadelphia, Pa.

Mystic Workers of the World.—Founded 1896; grand lodge, 1; subordinate lodges, 805; members, 44 133; benefits disbursed since organization, $1,576,092; benefits disbursed last fiscal year, $318,112; Supreme Secretary, Edmund Jackson, Fulton, Ill.; Supreme Banker, A. F. Schoch, Ottawa, Ill. (Report of Jan. 1, 1908.)

National Provident Union.—Founded 1883; sub-councils, 41; members, 3,768; benefits disbursed since organization, $2,511,526; benefits disbursed last fiscal year, $92,250; President, David M. Evans, Brooklyn, N. Y.; Vice-President, Wm. H. Pond, Hartford, Ct.; Secretary, Frank E. Currier, Brooklyn, N. Y.; Treasurer, A. C. Jacobson, Brooklyn, N. Y.

National Union.—Founded 1881; councils, 850; members, 62,000; benefits disbursed since organization, $27,000,000; benefits disbursed last fiscal year, $1,991,485; President, H. E. Evans, Trenton, N. J.; Secretary, E. A. Myers, Toledo, O.; Treasurer, Charles O. Evarts, Cleveland, O.

New England Order of Protection.—Founded 1887; grand lodges, 6; sub-lodges, 404; members, 54,119; benefits disbursed since organization, $6,950,700; benefits disbursed last fiscal year, $774,300; Supreme Warden, F. T. Peabody, Melrose, Mass.; Supreme Secretary, D. M. Frye, Boston, Mass.; Supreme Treasurer, John P. Sanborn, Newport, R. I.

Order of Gleaners.—Founded 1894; subordinate lodges, 1,000; members, 56,000; benefits disbursed since organization, $744,521; benefits disbursed last fiscal year, $162,291; Supreme Chief Gleaner, Ara Collins, Charlotte, Mich.; Secretary, G. H. Slocum, Caro, Mich.; Treasurer, J. M. Ealy, Caro, Mich. (Report of Jan. 1, 1908.)

Owls, Order of.—Founded 1904; Grand nests, 1; subordinate nests, 469; members, 79,604. Supreme President, John W. Talbot; Supreme Vice-President, C. B. Crumpacker; Supreme Secretary, George D. Beroth; Supreme Treasurer, J. Lott Losey. Headquarters "Home Nest," South Bend, Indiana.

Pilgrim Fathers, United Order of.—Founded 1879; supreme colony, 1; subordinate colonies, 198; members, 19,634; benefits disbursed since organization, $6,862,880; benefits disbursed last fiscal year, $473,000; Supreme Governor, E. O. Foster, Salem, Mass.; Supreme Secretary, Nathan Crary, Lawrence, Mass.; Supreme Treasurer, A. V. Bugbee, Lawrence, Mass. (Report of Jan. 1, 1908.)

Protected Home Circle.—Founded 1886; grand councils, 10; sub-councils, 618; members, 65,273; benefits disbursed since organization, $4,349,674; benefits disbursed last fiscal year, $549,174; President, A. C. McLean; Vice-President, A. W. Williams; Secretary, W. S. Palmer; Treasurer, Alex. McDowell. Offices, Sharon, Pa.

Rechabites, Independent Order of.—Founded 1835 (in England), 1842 (in America); number of tents in America, 3; sub-tents, 1,182; members, 491,000; benefits disbursed since organization, $10,000,000; benefits disbursed last fiscal year in America, $220,000. High Chief Ruler, N. E. Vowles, Washington, D. C.; High Deputy Ruler, John Schombert, Midland, Md.; High Secretary, John C. Moore, Washington, D. C.; High Treasurer, Mrs. M. R. Mahoney, Washington, D. C.

Red Men, Improved Order of.—Founded 1763 and 1834; great councils, 46; tribes, 4,968; members, 471,661; benefits disbursed since organization, $23,918,007; benefits disbursed last fiscal year, $1,291,287; Great Incohonee, Joseph Farrar, Philadelphia, Pa.; Great Senior Sagamore, Geo. B. Griggs, Houston, Texas; Great Chief of Records, Wilson Brooks, Chicago, Ill.; Great Keeper of Wampum, Wm. Provin, Westfield, Mass.

Royal League.—Founded 1883; advisory councils, 10; subordinate councils, 220; members, 29,141; benefits disbursed since organization, $23,918,007; benefits disbursed last fiscal year, $539,204; Supreme Archon, W. E. Hyde, Chicago; Scribe, Charles E. Piper, Chicago; Treasurer, Holmes Hoge, Chicago, Ill.

Scottish Clans, Order of.—Founded 1878; grand clans, 1; subordinate clans, 133; members, 10,898; benefits disbursed since organization, $1,250,000; benefits disbursed last fiscal year, $98,500; Royal Chief, John Hill, St. Louis, Mo.; Royal Secretary, Peter Kerr, Boston, Mass.; Royal Treasurer, David King, New York City.

Shield of Honor.—Founded 1875; grand lodges, 6; sub-lodges, 111; members, 9,582; benefits disbursed since organization, $2,210,500; benefits disbursed last fiscal year, $155,250; Supreme Master, Chas. E. Siegmund, Baltimore, Md.; Secretary, Wm. T. Henry, Baltimore, Md.; Treasurer, John W. Meeks, Baltimore, Md.

Star of Bethlehem, Order of the.—Permanently established in America 1869; Eminent Grand Commandery of N. A. reorganized and incorporated in 1884; subordinate lodges, 280; members, 19,110; insurance auxiliary, The Eastern Star Benevolent Fund, 2,500 members; benefits paid since organization, $64,971; benefits disbursed last fiscal year, $8,057; Commander, F. C. Reichlin, Detroit, Mich.; Secretary, M. E. Crowe, 39 W. Elizabeth St., Detroit, Mich.; Treasurer, Thomas J. Crowe, Detroit, Mich. (Report of Jan. 1, 1908.)

Union Fraternal League.—Founded 1889; subordinate assemblies, 96; members, 3,052; benefits disbursed since organization, $194,245; benefits disbursed last fiscal year, $16,353 President, John Merrill, Boston; Vice-President, P. J. Tetrault, Holyoke, Mass.; Secretary, J. F. Reynolds, Boston; Treasurer, J. C. Barthelmes, Brookline, Mass.

United American Mechanics, Order of.—Founded 1845; State councils, 14; sub-councils, 559; members, 36,554; National Councilor, F. Z. Jones, Rome, N. Y.; National Secretary, John Server, Philadelphia, Pa.; National Treasurer, Joseph H. Shinn, Camden, N. J.

United American Mechanics, Junior Order of.—Founded 1853; State councils, 32; subcouncils, 1,9 8; members, 194,741; benefits disbursed since organization, $7,172,891; benefits disbursed last fiscal year, $664,915; National Councilor, H. C. Schaertzer, San Francisco, Cal.; Vice-Councilor, H. L. W. Taylor, Newport, Tenn.; Secretary, M. M. Woods, Philadelphia, Pa., Treasurer, Charles Reimer, Baltimore, Md.

United Workmen, Ancient Order of.—Founded 1868; grand lodges, 28; sub-lodges, 3,250; members, 219,729; benefits disbursed since organization, $163,445,905; benefits disbursed last fiscal year, $6,699,146; Master Workman, Will M. Narvis, Muscatine, Iowa; Recorder, M. W. Sackett, Meadville, Pa.; Receiver, Edwin F. Danforth.

Woodmen of America, Fraternity of Modern.—Founded 1884; head camp, 1; local camps, 12,099; members, 920,079; benefits disbursed since organization $64,561,733; benefits disbursed last fiscal year, $8,051,995; Head Consul, A. R. Talbot, Lincoln, Neb.; Head Clerk, C. W. Hawes, Rock Island, Ill.

Woodmen of the World.—Founded 1890; sovereign camps, 3; subordinate camps, 8,567; members, 529,023; benefits disbursed since organization, $40,876,456; benefits disbursed last fiscal year, $4,833,346; Sovereign Commander, Joseph Cullen Root, Omaha, Neb.; Clerk, John T. Yates, Omaha, Neb.; Adviser, W. A. Fraser, Dallas, Tex.

Yeomen of America.—Founded 1898; National council, 1; subordinate councils, 366; members, 15,587; benefits disbursed since organization, $348,391; President, Fred. B. Silsbee, Oregon, Ill.; Vice-President, C. D. Judd; Secretary, John L. Walker; Treasurer, William George. Headquarters, Aurora, Ill.

American Learned Societies.

Actuarial Society of America.—President, John K. Gore, Newark, N. J.; Vice-Presidents, Henry Moir, New York; Archibald A. Welch, Hartford, Ct.; Secretary, Arthur Hunter, 346 Broadway, New York City; Treasurer, David G. Alsop, Philadelphia, Pa.; Editor of the "Transactions," Clayton C. Hall, Baltimore, Md. The Actuarial Society of America was organized in 1889 for the purpose of promoting actuarial science. Applicants whose nominations are approved by the Council are admitted to membership on passing the requisite examinations. There are two classes of members; fellows, now numbering 131, and associates, 87. Besides including the actuaries of life insurance companies and consulting actuaries of the United States and Canada, the membership embraces leading actuaries in Europe and Australasia.

American Academy of Medicine.—President, Dr. Helene Putnam, Providence, R. I., Secretary and Treasurer, Dr. Charles McIntire, Easton, Pa.; Editor of the "Bulletin," Charles McIntire, Easton, Pa. Object—To associate physicians who are also alumni of academic (or scientific) colleges; to encourage intending physicians to pursue a regular course of study leading to a bachelor degree before entering upon the study of medicine; to investigate and discuss the various problems of "medical sociology." Entrance fee, $5; dues, $3 per annum. Present membership, 925. Organized 1876. Next annual meeting at Atlantic City, N. J. June 5-7, 1909.

American Academy of Political and Social Science.—President, L. S. Rowe, Ph. D., University of Pennsylvania; Secretary, Carl Kelsey, Ph. D., University of Pennsylvania; Editor of the Annals, Emory R. Johnson, Ph. D., University of Pennsylvania; Clerk, N. J. Smith-Fisher, West Philadelphia Station, Philadelphia. Founded in 1889 to promote the political and social sciences. Membership, 4,200, distributed among every State and 35 foreign countries. Annual fee, $5; fee for life members, $100. Annual meeting held in April.

American Antiquarian Society.—President, Waldo Lincoln, Worcester Mass.; Corresponding Secretaries—Foreign, Franklin B. Dexter, New Haven, Ct.; Domestic, Charles Francis Adams, Lincoln, Mass.; Recording Secretary, Andrew McF. Davis, Cambridge, Mass. Annual meeting is held at Worcester, Mass., the third Wednesday in October. Organized 1812. Domestic membership restricted to 175. Admission fee of United States members, $5; annual dues of New England members, $5.

American Anti-Tuberculosis League.—Secretary, Dr. W. H. Mayfield, St. Louis, Mo. Membership, 5,000.

American Asiatic Association. — President, Seth Low; Vice-President, Lowell Lincoln; Secretary, John Foord, P. O. Box 1500, New York. The purposes of the society are to foster and safeguard the trade and commercial interests of the citizens of the United States and others associated therewith in the Empires of China, Japan, and Korea, the Philippines, and elsewhere in Asia and Oceanica. Membership, 300. Organized 1898. Annual dues, $10. Auxiliary societies at Shanghai and Yokohama.

American Association for the Advancement of Science.—President, T. C. Chamberlin, University of Chicago; Permanent Secretary, L. O. Howard, Smithsonian Institution, Washington, D. C.; General Secretary, J. Paul Goode, University of Chicago; Secretary of the Council, Dayton C. Miller, Cleveland, O.; Treasurer, R. S. Woodward, Washington, D. C. The Association was chartered in 1874, being a continuation of the American Association of Geologists and Naturalists, organized in 1840. The membership is 6,000. Admission fee, $5; annual dues, $3.

American Association of Obstetricians and Gynecologists.—President, William H. Humiston, M. D., 536 Rose Building, Cleveland, O. Secretary, Wm. Warren Potter, M. D., 238 Delaware Ave., Buffalo, N. Y.

American Bar Association.—President, F. W. Lehmann, St. Louis, Mo.; Secretary, John Hinkley, 215 North Charles Street, Baltimore, Md.; Treasurer, Frederick E. Wadhams, Albany, N. Y. Each State and Territory is represented by one vice-president and one member of the General Council. Membership, about 3,500. This Association of lawyers of the United States was organized in 1878. The next annual meeting will be held in August, 1909.

American Chemical Society.—President, Marston T. Bogert, Columbia University, N. Y.; Secretary, Charles L. Parsons, Durham, N. H. The Society was organized in 1876 for "the advancement of chemistry and the promotion of chemical research." Publishes the "Journal of the American Chemical Society, monthly," and "Chemical Abstracts," semi-monthly; Editor, Wm. A. Noyes, Urbana, Ill., also "Journal of Industrial and Engineering Chemistry;" Editor, W. D. Richardson, Chicago, Ill. Annual dues, $10. Total membership, 4,000.

American Climatological Association.—President, Chas. E. Quimby, New York City; Secretary, Guy Hinsdale, M. D., Hot Springs, Va. Organized 1884. Next annual meeting, June 4-5, 1909, Fortress Monroe, Va.

American Dermatological Association.—President, T. Casper Gilchrist, Baltimore, Md.; Secretary, Grover W. Wende, M. D., 471 Delaware Avenue, Buffalo, N. Y.

American Dialect Society.—President, O. F. Emerson, Western Reserve University, Cleveland, Ohio; Secretary, W. E. Mead, Wesleyan University, Middletown, Ct., Treasurer, Prof. R. H. Fife, Wesleyan University, Middletown, Ct. Organized in 1889 for "the investigation of the spoken English of the United States and Canada, and incidentally of other non-aboriginal dialects in the same countries." Publishes "Dialect Notes" at irregular intervals. Annual fee, $1. Membership, about 300. Any person may become a member.

American Economic Association.—President, S. N. Patten, University of Pennsylvania; Secretary, W. M. Daniels, Princeton University, Princeton, N. J. Organized 1885. Has 1,000 members; annual dues, $3; life membership, $50; no other entrance fee. The objects of the Association are the encouragement of economic studies and the publication of papers thereon.

American Electro-Therapeutic Association.—President, Dr. Edward C. Titus, New York; Vice-Presidents, Dr. W. D. McFee, Haverhill, Mass.; Dr. T. D. Crothers, Hartford, Ct.; Secretary, Dr. J. Willard Travell, 27 E. 11th Street, New York, N. Y. Organized 1890. Membership, 280.

American Entomological Society.—President, Philip P. Calvert; Secretary, Henry Skinner, M. D., Philadelphia, Pa. Organized 1859. Object—The study of entomology. Membership, 140.

American Fisheries Society.—President, Tarelton H. Bean, Albany, N. Y.; Vice-President, Seymour Bower, Detroit, Mich.; Recording Secretary, George F. Peabody, Appleton, Wis.; Corresponding Secretary, Charles G. Atkins, East Orland, Me. Organized December, 1870. Annual dues, $2. Membership, about 400.

American Folklore Society.—President, R. B. Dixon, Harvard University, Cambridge, Mass.; Permanent Secretary, A. M. Tozzer, Harvard University, Cambridge, Mass. Organized in 1888 for "study of folklore in general, and in particular the collection and publication of folklore of North America." Membership fee, including a copy of "The Journal of American Folklore" (quarterly), $3 per annum.

AMERICAN LEARNED SOCIETIES—*Continued.*

American Forestry Association.—President, James Wilson, Secretary of Agriculture, Washington, D. C.; Secretary, Thomas E. Will, Office, 1417 G Street, N. W. Washington, D. C. Organized 1882. Membership, 7,000.

American Geographical Society.—President, Archer M. Huntington; Vice-Presidents, D. O. Mills, John Greenough; Corresponding Secretaries—Foreign, William Libbey; Domestic, Archibald D. Russell; Recording Secretary, Anton A. Raven. Offices of the Society, 15 West Eighty-first Street, New York City. The objects of the Society are to investigate and disseminate new geographical information; to establish in the chief maritime city of the country, for the benefit of commerce and navigaton, * * * a place where the means shall be afforded of obtaining accurate information for public use of every part of the globe. Organized in 1852; membership, 1,400. Annual dues, $10; no entrance fee.

American Gynæcological Society.—President, J. Riddle Goffe, M. D.. New York; Secretary, Le Roy Brown. M.D., 70 W. 82d St. New York. Organized 1876. Membership. 100.

American Historical Association.—President, Geo. F. Adams, New Haven, Ct. Secretary, A. Howard Clark, Smithsonian Institution. Washington, D. C.; Treasurer, Clarence W. Bowen, Ph.D. Association founded 1884, incorporated by Congress 1889. Object—The promotion of historical studies. Entrance fee, $3; annual dues, $3. Membership, 2,300.

American Institute of Architects.—Offices and library, The Octagon, Washington, D. C. President, Cass Gilbert, New York; Secretary and Treasurer, Glenn Brown, Washington. D. C. The Institute has 29 chapters, 323 fellows, 522 associates, 82 corresponding and 63 honorary members. Initiation fee is $5; yearly dues, fellows, $15, associates, $7.50. Organized 1857.

American Institute of Electrical Engineers.—President, Louis A. Ferguson; Secretary, Ralph W. Pope, at the executive offices, library, and reading-room, 33 West 39th St., New York. Entrance fee, $5; annual dues, associates, $10; members. $15. Monthly meetings, New York. Organized 1884. Prints its "Proceedings" monthly. Membership, 5,100.

American Institute of Homœopathy.—President, William E. Green. Little Rock; Secretary, Charles Gatchell, M. D., 100 State Street, Chicago, Ill. Organized in 1844, and is the oldest national medical organization in the United States. Has 2,100 members, representing every State in the Union, besides Canada.

American Institute of Mining Engineers.—President, John Hays, Hammond, N. Y.; Secretary, R. W. Raymond, 29 West 39th St., New York; Treasurer, Frank Lyman, New York. Membership, October 10, 1908, 4,272. Organized 1871. Incorporated 1905. Annual dues, $10.

American Laryngological Association.—President, Dr. A. Coolidge, Jr., Boston, Mass. Secretary, James E. Newcomb, M. D., 118 West Sixty-ninth Street, New York City. Organized 1878. Membership, 100.

American Laryngological, Rhinological and Otological Society.—President, Dr. Christian R. Holmes, 8 E. 8th St. Cincinnati, O. Secretary, Thomas J. Harris, M. D., 117 East Fortieth St.. New York City.

American Mathematical Society.—President, Henry S. White; Secretary, F. N. Cole, Columbia University, New York; Treasurer, J. H. Tanner; Librarian, D. E. Smith. Meetings held at Columbia University, New York. Society was reorganized as the American Mathematical Society, July, 1894. Object—To encourage and maintain an active interest in and to promote the advancement of mathematical science. Admission fee, $5; annual dues, $5; life membership, $50. Membership, 600. The Society publishes two journals, the "Bulletin" and the "Transactions."

American Medical Association.—President, Dr. Herbert L. Burrell, Boston Mass.; Secretary. Editor. Dr. George H. Simmons, 103 Dearborn Avenue, Chicago, Ill. Incorporated 1897 Next annual session at Atlantic City, N. J., June 8-11, 1909. Annual fee, $5. Membership, over 33,500.

American Medico-Psychological Association.—President, Dr. Wm. F Drewry, Va.; Secretary, Dr. Charles W. Peigrun, Poughkeepsie, N. Y. Next annual meeting at Atlantic City, May 1, 1909.

American Microscopical Society.—President, Prof Herbert Osborn, Columbus. Ohio; Secretary, Dr. Fred C. Zapffe, Chicago, Ill.: Treasurer, David L. Zook, Chicago, Ill.: Custodian, Magnus Pflaum. Pittsburgh, Pa. Organized 1878. Incorporated at Washington, D. C., 1891. Object—The encouragement of microscopical research. Initiation fee, $3; annual dues. $2. Membership, 450. Research funds, $2,530.

American Neurological Association.—President, S. Weir Mitchell, M D., Philadelphia, Pa. Secretary, G. M. Hammond, M. D., 60 West Fifty-fifth Street. New York City.

American Numismatic Association.—President. Farran Zerbe, Tyrone. Pa.; Vice-Presidents, J. M. Henderson, Columbus, Ohio; P. O. Tremblay, Montreal. Can; General Secretary. F. G. Duffield, Baltimore. Md.; Treasurer, D. A. Williams, Baltimore, Md. The society was founded in 1891 for the promotion of Numismatics. Membership, 600.

American Numismatic Society, Audubon Park, 156th Street, West of Broadway, New York —President, Archer M. Huntington; Recording Secretary, Bauman L. Belden; Corresponding Secretary, Henry Russell Drowne. Society founded in 1858 for the promotion of numismatics, etc., in the United States; possesses coin and medal collection and library. Total membership, 350.

American Ophthalmological Society.—President, S. B. St. John, Hartford, Ct.; Secretary, W. M. Sweet, 1205 Spruce Street, Philadelphia, Pa. Membership. 185.

American Oriental Society.—President, E. Washburn Hopkins, Yale University: Corresponding Secretary, A. V. W. Jackson, Columbia University, N. Y.; Recording Secretary, George F. Moore. Organized September 7, 1842, for the cultivation of learning in the Asiatic, African, and Polynesian languages, and the publication of works relating to these languages. Publishes an annual Journal. Annual fee, $5; fee for membership in section for Historical Study of Religions, $2; no admission fee. Membership, 328.

American Ornithologists' Union.—President, Charles F. Batchelder; Secretary, John H. Sage, Portland, Ct. Organized 1883. Object—The advancement of its members in ornithological science, the publication of a journal of ornithology and other works relating to that science, etc. Annual dues, fellows, $5; members, $4; associates, $3. Membership, 889.

American Orthopædic Association.—President. Ansel G Cook M. D., 179 Allyn St., Hartford, Ct.; Secretary, Robert B. Osgood, M D, 372 Marlborough Street, Boston Mass.

American Osteopathic Society.—President, Dr. Thomas L. Ray, Dallas, Tex. Secretary, Dr. H. L. Chiles, Auburn, N. Y. Founded 1897. Annual fee, $5. Membership, 2,200.

AMERICAN LEARNED SOCIETIES—*Continued.*

American Otological Society.—President, Dr. Frederick L. Jack, 215 Beacon Street, Boston, Mass.; Secretary, Dr. J. F. McKernon, 62 W. 52d Street, New York.

American Pediatric Society.—President, Chas. P. Putnam, M. D., Boston, Mass.; Secretary, Samuel S. Adams, M. D., 1 Dupont Circle, Washington, D.C. Next annual meeting at Lenox, Mass., May 27-28, 1909.

American Pharmaceutical Association.—President Oscar Oldberg, Chicago, Ill.; General Secretary, Chas. Caspari, Jr., Baltimore, Md.; Treasurer, H. M. Whelpley, St. Louis, Mo. Has 3,500 members. Organized 1852.

American Philological Association.—President, Prof. Charles E. Bennett, Cornell University; Vice-Presidents, Prof. Paul Shorey, University of Chicago, and Prof. John C. Rolfe, University of Pennsylvania; Secretary and Treasurer, Prof. Frank G. Moore, of Trinity College, Hartford, Ct. Initiation fee, $5; annual dues, $3. Total membership, about 600. The Association was organized in 1869. Its object is "the advancement and diffusion of philological knowledge."

American Philosophical Society.—President, William W. Keen; Vice-Presidents, Albert A. Michelson, William B. Scott, Simon Newcomb; Secretaries, I. Minis Hays, Arthur W. Goodspeed, James W. Holland, and Amos P. Brown. Office of Society, 104 South Fifth Street, Philadelphia, Pa. Object—For promoting useful knowledge. Founded in 1743.

American Physical Society.—President, Edward L. Nichols, Cornell University, Ithaca, N. Y. Secretary, Ernest Merritt, Cornell University, Ithaca, N. Y.

American Proctologic Society.—President, Geo. B. Evans, Dayton, Ohio; Secretary, Lewis H. Adler, Jr., M. D., 1610 Arch Street, Philadelphia, Pa.

American Psychological Association.—President, Henry Rutgers Marshall, New York City; Secretary and Treasurer, Prof. William Harper Davis, Lehigh University, Pennsylvania. Organized in 1892 for "the advancement of psychology as a science." Membership, 175. Annual dues, $1; no entrance fee.

American Public Health Association.—President, Dr. Gardner T. Swarts, Providence, R. I.; Secretary, Dr. Charles O. Probst, Columbus, Ohio. Meeting in Richmond, Va., October, 1909.

American Roentgen Ray Society.—President, P. M. Hickey, M D., Detroit, Mich.; Secretary, Geo. C. Johnston, M. D., 611 Fulton Building, Pittsburgh, Pa.

American Social Science Association.—President, John H. Finley, LL.D., College of City of New York; Treasurer, W. C. Le Gendre, 59 Wall Street, New York City; General Secretary, Isaac F. Russell, LL. D., 120 Broadway, New York. Annual fee, $5. The Association was founded in 1865. Incorporated by act of Congress, 1899. Membership, 1,000.

American Society of Curio Collectors.—President, Roy F. Greene, Arkansas City, Kan.; Secretary, F. May Tuttle, Osage, Iowa. A national society for naturalists, geologists, mineralogists, archæologists, numismatists, and antiquarians. Membership, 600.

American Society of Civil Engineers.—President, Charles Macdonald; Secretary, Charles Warren Hunt; Treasurer, Joseph M. Knap. Regular meetings first and third Wednesdays of each month (except July and August) at 8.30 P. M. at the Society's house, 220 West Fifty-seventh Street, New York City. Has 4,800 members. Instituted in 1852.

American Society of Mechanical Engineers.—President, M. L. Holman, New York; Secretary, Calvin W. Rice, 29 West Thirty-ninth Street, New York City. Society House, 29 West Thirty-ninth Street, New York City. Total membership, all grades, 3,511. Two annual meetings, in Spring and Autumn, the latter in New York City in December. Initiation fee, members and associates, $25; juniors, $15. Annual dues, members and associates, $15; juniors, $10. The Society was chartered in 1881. Membership is not limited in number.

American Society of Naturalists.—President, D. P. Penhallow, McGill University, Montreal, Can.; Secretary, H. McE. Knower, Johns Hopkins University; Treasurer, H. Von Schrenk, Missouri Botanic Garden, St. Louis, Mo. Organized 1883. Annual dues, $1. Membership, 232.

American Statistical Association.—President, Carroll D. Wright, Washington, D. C.; Vice-Presidents, Le Grand Powers, Frederick L. Hoffman, Walter F. Willcox, Henry Gannett, S. N. D. North; Secretary, C. W. Doten, 491 Boylston Street, Boston, Mass.; Treasurer, S. B. Pearmain. Membership, 340. Annual dues, $2. Association organized 1839.

American Surgical Association.—President, C. B. G. de Nancrede, 720 South University Ave., Ann Arbor, Mich.; Secretary, Robert G. Le Conte, 1530 Locust Street, Philadelphia, Pa. Number of members, 134.

American Therapeutic Society.—President, Frederic H. Gerrish, Portland, Me.; Secretary, Dr. Noble P. Barnes, 212 Maryland Avenue, Washington, D. C. Organized May 1, 1900.

American Urological Association.—President, Dr. W. T. Belfield, Chicago, Ill.; Secretary, Dr. Hugh Cabot, 87 Marlborough Street, Boston.

Archæological Institute of America (New York Society).—President, Prof. E. D. Perry, Columbia University; Secretary, Prof. Nelson G. McCrea, Columbia University. Organized 1879. Has 196 members. No entrance fee. Annual dues, $10.

Arctic Club.—President, Prof. W. H. Brewer, Yale University; Secretary, Capt. B. S. Osbon, 132 E. 23d Street, New York City. Organized 1894. Membership, 200.

Association of American Anatomists.—President, Prof. James P. McMurrich, Toronto University; Secretary-Treasurer, G. C. Huber, M. D., Ann Arbor, Mich. Has 240 members. Annual dues, $5.

Association of American Physicians.—President, Victor C. Vaughan, M. D., Ann Arbor, Mich.; Secretary, Geo. M. Kober, M. D., 1819 Q Street, N. W., Washington, D. C. Organized 1886. Membership limited to 135 active and 25 associate members.

Astronomical and Astrophysical Society of America.—President, Edward C. Pickering, Cambridge, Mass.; Secretary, W. J. Hussey, Ann Arbor, Mich. Organized 1898. Membership, 200.

Botanical Society of America.—President, W. F. Ganong, Northampton, Mass.; Secretary, Prof. D. S. Johnson, Baltimore, Md. Has 91 members, 41 associates. Founded 1893. Annual dues, $5. Enlarged by federation with the Society for Plant Morphology and Physiology and the American Mycological Society, 1906.

Geological Society of America.—President, Samuel Calvin, Iowa City, Iowa; Secretary, E. O. Hovey, American Museum of Natural History, New York; Treasurer, William Bullock Clark, Baltimore, Md.; Editor, J. Stanley-Brown. Society founded in 1888. Has 297 fellows. Entrance fee, $10; annual dues, $10.

Jewish Historical Society.—President, Dr. Cyrus Adler, Philadelphia, Pa.; Vice-Presidents, Simon W. Rosendale, Albany, N. Y.; Rev. Dr. David Philipson, Cincinnati, Ohio; Prof. Charles Gross, Cambridge, Mass., and Prof. Richard J. H. Gottheil, New York; Treasurer, N. Taylor

Phillips, New York City, N. Y.; Corresponding Secretary, Max J. Kohler, 42 Broadway, New York City, N. Y.; Recording Secretary, Dr. Isaac Friedenwald, New York.

Medical Association of the Southwest.—President, Jabez N. Jackson, M. D., Kansas City, Mo.; Secretary, F. H. Clark, M. D., El Reno, Okla.

Medico-Legal Society.—President, Clark Bell, 39 Broadway, New York City; Secretary, J. R. Abarbanell, 24 Vandewater Street, New York City. There are vice-presidents for each of the States and Territories and the principal foreign countries.

National Academy of Sciences.—President, Ira Remsen, Baltimore, Md.; Vice-President, Chas. D. Walcott, Washington, D.C.; Foreign Secretary, Simon Newcomb, Washington, D. C.; Home Secretary, Arnold Hague, Washington, D. C.; Treasurer, Samuel F. Emmons, Washington, D. C. The Academy, incorporated by act of Congress March 3, 1863, "shall, whenever called upon by any department of the Government, investigate, examine, experiment, and report upon any subject of science or art; the actual expense * * * to be paid from appropriations which may be made for the purpose." The Academy holds a stated session each year in the City of Washington on the third Tuesday in April. An Autumn meeting is held at such place and time as the Council shall determine. There are at present 107 members and 43 foreign associates.

National Association for the Study and Prevention of Tuberculosis (105 E. 22d Street, New York City).—President, Dr. Vincent Y. Bowditch; Hon. Vice-Presidents, Theodore Roosevelt, Dr. Wm. Osler; Executive Secretary, Dr. Livingston Ferrand.

National Association for the Study of Epilepsy.—President, Everett Flood, M. D., Palmer, Mass.; Secretary, J. F. Munson, M. D., Sonyea, N. Y.

National Geographic Society.—President, Willis L. Moore; Vice-President, Henry Gannett; Secretary, O. P. Austin; Editor, Gilbert H. Grosvenor. Headquarters at Washington, D. C. Its purpose is "the increase and diffusion of geographic knowledge." It publishes a monthly magazine. Organized 1888. Annual dues for members, $2. There are 36,000 members.

New York Zoological Society.—President, Levi P. Morton; Secretary, Madison Grant, 11 Wall Street, New York City; Treasurer, Percy R. Pyne, 30 Pine Street. William T. Hornaday, Director of the New York Zoological Park; Charles H. Townsend, Director of the Aquarium. Annual dues, $10; life membership, $200. The Zoological Park and the New York Aquarium are under the management of the Society.

Society for the Promotion of Agricultural Science.—President, Prof. Thomas F. Hunt, State College, Pa.; Secretary, Prof. F. Wm. Rane, State House, Boston, Mass. Organized 1882. Membership limited to 100 active and 100 associate members.

Society for the Promotion of Engineering Education.—President, Frederick E. Turneaure, University of Wisconsin, Madison, Wis.; Vice-Presidents, Mortimer E. Cooley, University of Michigan, Ann Arbor, Mich.; Olin H. Landreth, Union University, Schenectady, N. Y.; Secretary, A. L. Williston, Pratt Institute, Brooklyn, N. Y.; Treasurer, W. O. Wiley, No. 43 East 19th Street, New York, N. Y. 677 members (1908), from 107 engineering colleges, 19 manual training and trades schools; 106 members are practitioners and are not teachers. Founded in the Engineering Education Section of World's Engineering Congress, 1893, Chicago. Annual fee, $3.50.

Society of Chemical Industry (New York Section).—Chairman, Maximilian Tosh, Chemists' Club, New York City; Local Secretary, H. Schweitzer, 117 Hudson St., New York City. Membership, 1,584. The Society is international, while the New York branch is its American representative. The officers of the general society are: President, R. Meldola, London, W. E., England; Secretary Charles G. Cresswell, 9 Bridge Street, Westminster, London, S. W.

Society of Naval Architects and Marine Engineers.—President, Francis T. Bowles; Secretary-Treasurer, William J. Baxter, 29 West Thirty-ninth Street, New York City. Object—The promotion of the art of shipbuilding, commercial and naval. Headquarters, 29 West Thirty-ninth Street, New York City. Membership fee for members and associates, $10; annual dues, $10. Juniors, membership fee, $5; annual dues, $5. Has 801 members, associates and juniors.

Southern Medical Association.—President, Henry H. Martin, M. D., Savannah, Ga.; Secretary, Raymond Wallace, M. D., Chattanooga, Tenn.

Western Surgical and Gynecological Association.—President, W. W. Grant, M. D., Denver, Col.; Secretary, Arthur T. Mann, M. D., Donaldson Building, Minneapolis, Minn.

The Carnegie Institution of Washington.

THE Carnegie Institution of Washington was founded by Mr. Andrew Carnegie, January 28, 1902, when he gave to a board of trustees $10,000,000, in registered bonds, yielding 5 per cent. annual interest. In general terms, he stated that his purpose was to "found in the City of Washington an institution which, with the co-operation of institutions now or hereafter established, there or elsewhere, shall in the broadest and most liberal manner encourage investigation, research and discovery, show the application of knowledge to the improvement of mankind, and provide such buildings, laboratories, books, and apparatus as may be needed." Mr. Carnegie added $2,000,000 to his gift in 1907.

By an act of Congress, approved April 28, 1904, the institution was placed under the control of a board of twenty-four Trustees, all of whom had been members of the original board referred to above.

The Trustees meet annually, and during the intervals between such meetings the affairs of the Institution are conducted by an Executive Committee, chosen by and from the Board of Trustees, acting through the President of the Institution as chief executive officer.

The offices of the Institution are in the Bond Building, Fourteenth Street and New York Avenue, Washington, D. C.

Trustees of the Institution—Chairman, John S. Billings; *Vice-Chairman*, Elihu Root; *Secretary*, Cleveland H. Dodge; John D. Cadwalader, William N. Frew, Lyman J. Gage, Henry L. Higginson, E. A. Hitchcock, Charles L. Hutchinson, William Lindsay, Seth Low, D. O. Mills, S. Weir Mitchell, William W. Morrow, Henry S. Pritchett, William H. Taft, William H. Welch, Andrew D. White, Robert S. Woodward, Carroll D. Wright. (Two vacancies.)

President of the Institution—Robert S. Woodward.

Executive Committee—Chairman, Carroll D. Wright; John S. Billings, Cleveland H. Dodge, S. Weir Mitchell, Elihu Root, Charles D. Walcott, Robert S. Woodward. (One vacancy.)

New York Public Library, Astor, Lenox, and Tilden Foundations.

ESTABLISHED by consolidation of "The Trustees of the Astor Library," "The Trustees of the Lenox Library," and "The Tilden Trust," May 23, 1895, twenty-one Trustees being chosen from the Trustees of these corporations. The agreement of consolidation provided for the establishment and maintenance of a free public library and reading-room in the City of New York, with such branches as might be deemed advisable for the continued promotion of the objects and purposes of these several corporations.

The Trustees soon after the consolidation in 1895 determined to pursue a liberal policy and to create a great library system not only for the use of scholars, but for the people. The best permanent site for the future great library was considered to be in Bryant Park, on Fifth Avenue, between Fortieth and Forty-second Streets, on the site of the reservoir, which had become obsolete and was practically unused. On March 25, 1896, the Trustees made a formal address to the Mayor asking aid from the city in securing the site of the reservoir, and in May, 1896, the Legislature passed a law authorizing the removal of the reservoir and the lease by the land to the Library. On May 19, 1897, another act was passed providing for the construction by the city of a library building on the reservoir site, and for its lease to the Library, which act was amended in 1900, removing the limit of cost. On November 10 the architects were selected for the new building and on December 1 the plans were approved by the city. The style of architecture is Renaissance and the material used is white marble. The building fronts on Fifth Avenue, looking east. The greatest projection of the main façade of the building is seventy-five feet back of the Fifth Avenue building line. It is intended to make a terrace out of this seventy-five feet of foreground, serving as a grand approach to the main entrance. The terrace will be 455 feet long. There will be a hallway in the centre of the building eighty feet long and forty feet wide. The staircases which lead to the second and third floors will be of stone, twelve feet wide. The arches of the vestibule are thirty-five feet high and fifteen feet wide. The entrance to the stairs and the elevators will be found on the Fortieth Street side. The rooms for the circulation of books and the children's room will be on the basement floor, Forty-second Street side; on this floor will be also the rooms for newspapers, the binding and printing departments; the first floor will contain the offices of the business superintendent, superintendent of circulation, patents, and periodicals reading-rooms, and exhibition rooms; on the second floor will be the Trustees' room, the office of the Director, lecture and assembly rooms, cataloguing and accession departments, and various special reading-rooms; the third floor will contain the large general reading-rooms, the public catalogue, special reading-rooms for manuscripts, Americana, etc., the Stuart books and pictures, the print room, etc. There will be about 140 feet of ground between the west elevation of the building and the present park. The design of the building will be monumental in character, with classical proportions. After delays, owing to the inability of the city to appropriate funds for the work, the removal of the reservoir was begun on June 6, 1899. The entire building was under roof at the end of November, 1806.

On March 12, 1901, Mr. Andrew Carnegie offered to give $5,200,000 to the city for the construction and equipment of free circulating libraries upon condition that the city should provide the land and agree to maintain the libraries when built. This communication was submitted to the Mayor on March 15, and on April 26 an act was passed authorizing acceptance of the gift by the city upon the terms imposed by Mr. Carnegie. An agreement with the city was executed on July 17, the Library acting as agent for Mr. Carnegie, under which forty-two buildings are to be erected in Manhattan, the Bronx, and Richmond (later increased to fifty), on sites to be selected and purchased by the city with the approval of the Library, the buildings to be leased to the Library and to be under its control. The city agrees to provide adequate yearly maintenance, 10 per cent. of the cost of each building being agreed upon as a minimum.

On November 7, 1901, an agreement was made with three firms of architects in New York to prepare plans and specifications for these branch libraries. On June 6, 1902, an issue of bonds for $250,000 was authorized for purchase of sites. The first Carnegie building, known as the Yorkville branch, was opened December 13, 1902, at 222 East Seventy-ninth Street; the second, providing a new home for the Chatham Square branch, was opened November 2, 1903, at 31 East Broadway. By the end of 1908 thirty branches had been opened under this contract, and on two other sites buildings were going up, making a total of thirty-two sites. The Trustees of the Library are:

William W. Appleton,	John Murphy Farley,	J. Pierpont Morgan,	Chas. Howland Russell,
John Bigelow,	Samuel Greenbaum,	Morgan J. O'Brien,	Edward W. Sheldon,
John L. Cadwalader,	H. Van Ren. Kennedy,	Stephen H. Olin,	George W. Smith,
Andrew Carnegie,	John S. Kennedy,	Alexander E. Orr,	Frederick Sturges.
Cleveland H. Dodge.	Lewis Cass Ledyard,	George L. Rives,	Henry W. Taft.

Mayor of City of New York, *ex-officio*; Comptroller of the City of New York, *ex-officio*; President of the Board of Aldermen, *ex-officio*.

There is an advisory committee on circulation consisting of C. Scribner, W. W. Appleton, *Chairman;* Mark Ash, D. P. Ingraham, J. H McMahon, Cleveland H. Dodge, H. W. Taft.

BRANCHES—REFERENCE.—Astor Building, 425 Lafayette Street. Open week days 9 A. M. to 9 P. M. Lenox Building, 890 Fifth Avenue. Open from 9 A.M. to 6 P.M. week days.

BRANCHES—CIRCULATING.—33 E. Broadway (Chatham Sq.), 197 E. Broadway (Educational Alliance Building), 61 Rivington St., 66 Leroy St. (Hudson Park), 49 Bond St., 135 2d Ave. (Ottendorfer), 331 E. 10th St. (Tompkins Sq.), 251 W. 13th St. (Jackson Sq.), 228 E. 23d St., 209 W. 23d St. (Muhlenberg), 303 E. 36th St., 501 W. 40th St., 226 W. 42d St. (George Bruce), 123 E. 50th St. (Cathedral), 463 W. 51st St., 121 E. 58th St., 328 E. 67th St., 190 Amsterdam Ave. (Riverside and Travelling Libraries), 1465 Ave. A (Webster), 222 E. 79th St. (Yorkville), 444 Amsterdam Ave. (St. Agnes and Library for the Blind), 112 E. 96th St., 206 W. 100th St. (Bloomingdale), 174 E. 110th St. (Aguilar), 201 W. 115th St., 32 W. 123d St. (Harlem Library), 224 E. 125th St., 103 W. 135th St., 503 W. 145th St., 922 St. Nicholas Ave. (Washington Heights), 140th St. and Alexander Ave. (Mott Haven), 163th St. and Woodycrest Ave., 176th St. and Washington Ave. (Tremont), 3041 Kingsbridge Ave. (Kingsbridge); Stuyvesant and Hyatt Sts. (St. George); 12 Bennett St., Port Richmond; Canal and Brook Sts., Stapleton; Amboy Road, Tottenville. Branches open from 9 A. M. to 9 P. M. week days.

Statistics for year ended December 31, 1908: Volumes called for in reference branches, 941,155; number of readers using above volumes, 199,826; visitors to reference buildings, art galleries, exhibits, etc., 235,611; volumes given out for home use, 5,490,214; volumes in reference department, 724,894; pamphlets in reference department, 273,205; volumes in circulation department, 621,390.

The Library of Congress.

THE Library of Congress was established in 1800, destroyed in 1814 by the burning of the Capitol, afterward replenished by the purchase by Congress of the library of ex-President Jefferson, 6,760 volumes (cost, $23,950); in 1851, 35,000 volumes destroyed by fire; in 1852, partially replenished by an appropriation of $75,000; increased (1) by regular appropriations by Congress; (2) by deposits under the copyright law; (3) by gifts and exchanges; (4) by the exchanges of the Smithsonian Institution, the library of which (40,000 volumes) was, in 1866, deposited in the Library of Congress with the stipulation that future accessions should follow it. Sixty sets of Government publications are at the disposal of the Librarian of Congress for exchange, through the Smithsonian, with foreign governments, and this number may be increased up to 100. Other special accessions have been: The Peter Force collection (22,529 volumes, 37,000 pamphlets), purchased 1867, cost $100,000; the Count de Rochambeau collection (manuscript), purchased 1883, cost $20,000; the Toner collection (24 484 volumes (numerous pamphlets); gift in 1882 of Dr. Joseph M. Toner, the Hubbard collection (engravings); gift in 1898 of Mrs. Gardiner G. Hubbard.

The collection is now the largest in the Western Hemisphere, and third in the world. It comprised at the end of the fiscal year (June 30, 1908) about 1,535,008 printed books and pamphlets (including the law library of which, while a division of the Library of Congress, still remains at the Capitol), manuscripts, maps and charts, pieces of music, and photographs, prints, engravings, and lithographs. Of the printed books, probably one-sixth are duplicates not in use.

The collection is rich in history, political science, in official documents, National, State, and foreign, and in Americana, including important files of American newspapers and original manuscripts (colonial, revolutionary, and formative periods). Many of the rare books and manuscripts belonging to the Library are exhibited in show cases on the second floor.

The Smithsonian deposit is strong in scientific works, and includes the largest assemblage of the transactions of learned societies which exists in this country.

In 1897 the main collection was removed from the Capitol to the building erected for it under the acts of Congress approved April 15, 1886, October 2, 1888, and March 2, 1889, at a cost of $6,347,000 (limit by law, $6,500,000), exclusive of the land, which cost $585,000. The architects who furnished the original designs were John L. Smithmeyer and Paul J. Pelz. By the act of October 2, 1888, before the foundations were laid, Thomas L. Casey, Chief of Engineers of the Army, was placed in charge of the construction of the building, and the architectural details were worked out by Paul J. Pelz and Edward P. Casey. Upon the death of General Casey, in March, 1896, the entire charge of the construction devolved upon Bernard R. Green, General Casey's assistant, and under his superintendence the building was completed in February, 1897, opened to the public November, 1897. The building occupies three and three-quarter acres upon a site ten acres in extent at a distance of 1,270 feet east of the Capitol, and is the largest and most magnificent library building in the world. In the decorations some forty painters and sculptors are represented—all American citizens. The floor space is 326,195 square feet, or nearly 8 acres. The book stacks contain about 56 miles of shelving, affording space for 2,600,000 octavo volumes.

Plans have been adopted by Congress for covering in one of the interior courts to provide for needed increase of book space.

The Library is maintained by annual appropriations by Congress for various purposes, including the purchase of books.

Library Service.—Library proper, 236 employés; copyright, 70; distribution of cards, 25; law indexing, 5; disbursement and care of building and grounds, 127. Total, 463. By virtue of the act of 1897, employes in the Library proper are appointed by the Librarian of Congress "solely with reference to their fitness for their particular duties."

Copyright Office.—The Copyright Office is a distinct division of the Library of Congress, and is located on the ground floor, south side; open 9 to 4.30. It is under the immediate charge of the Register of Copyrights, who, by the act of February 19, 1897, is authorized "under the direction and supervision of the Librarian of Congress," to perform all the duties relating to copyrights. Copyright registration was transferred to the Librarian of Congress by the act of July 8, 1870. Of most articles copyrighted two copies, and of some one copy, must be deposited in the Library of Congress to perfect copyright.

Entitled by statute to draw books for home use are the following: The President, the Vice-President, Senators, Representatives, and Delegates in Congress (no books may be given out upon the orders of members in favor of those who are not members); Heads of Departments; the Justices, Reporter, and Clerk of the Supreme Court; the Judges and Clerk of the Court of Claims; Judges of the Court of Appeals of the District of Columbia and Judges of the Supreme Court of the District of Columbia; representatives at Washington of foreign governments; the Solicitor-General and Assistant Attorney-General; the Secretary of the Senate; the Clerk of the House of Representatives, the Solicitor of the Treasury, ex-Presidents of the United States; the Chaplains of the two Houses of Congress; the Secretary and Regents of the Smithsonian Institution; the members and Secretary of the Interstate Commerce Commission, and Chief of Engineers of the Army.

Inter-Library Loans.—While not a lending Library, but a reference Library, primarily and essentially, the Library of Congress maintains an inter-library loan system by which special service is rendered to scholarship by the lending of books to other libraries for the use of investigators, engaged in serious research, which it is not within the power or duty of the Library in question to supply, and which at the time, are not needed in Washington.

Hours.—The Library building is open to the public all days in the year excepting certain legal holidays. The hours are from 9 A.M. to 10 P.M. week days, and from 2 P.M. to 10 P.M. Sundays and holidays.

The Main Reading Room, and Periodical Reading Room are open to the public from 9 A.M. to 10 P.M. week days, and from 2 P.M. to 10 P.M. Sundays and holidays.

The Librarian's Office is open for the transaction of business from 9 A.M. to 4.30 P.M. week days, and from 2 P.M. to 6 P.M. Sundays and holidays.

The other administrative divisions of the Library, including the Copyright Office, are open for the transaction of business from 9 A.M. to 4.30 P.M. all days in the year, excepting legal holidays and Sundays.

Librarians Since the Inception of the Library.—1800-1814, the Clerk of the House of Representatives (for the time being); 1815-1829, George Watterston; 1829-1861, John S. Meehan; 1861-1864, John G. Stephenson; 1864-1897 (June 30), Ainsworth R. Spofford; 1897-January 17, 1899, John Russell Young; 1899 (April 5), Herbert Putnam.

General Administration.—Librarian of Congress, Herbert Putnam; Chief Assistant Librarian, Appelton P. C. Griffin; Chief Clerk, Allen R. Boyd.

Organizations for the Promotion of Education.

CHAUTAUQUA INSTITUTION.

Chancellor—John H. Vincent. *President*—George E. Vincent. *President of Trustees*—Clement Studebaker, Jr. *Secretary*—Ira M. Miller. *Treasurer*—Scott Brown. *Director*—Arthur E. Bestor. Located at Chautauqua, N. Y.

The Chautauqua Assembly, now *Chautauqua Institution*, was organized in 1874 as a result of the joint plan of Lewis Miller and John H. Vincent. It holds annual sessions during July and August at Chautauqua, N. Y. The plan includes Summer school courses of instruction in language, literature, science, and art, open lectures, concerts, and recitals, and various forms of platform entertainment and out-of-door recreation. Local assemblies patterned after the mother Chautauqua convene in different places throughout the United States and number over two hundred.

The Chautauqua Literary and Scientific Circle (Kate F. Kimball, Chautauqua, N. Y., Executive Secretary) was organized at Chautauqua in 1878, with the aim of continuing the influence of the Assembly throughout the year in all parts of the country. Since that time more than two hundred and sixty thousand members have been enrolled. The Circle aims to promote the habit of reading and study in history, literature, science, and art, in connection with the routine of daily life. Each year four books are specially published for the course, The Chautauquan Magazine (Frank Chapin Bray, Editor) and the membership book with review outlines. The essentials of the plan are: A definite course covering four years, each year complete in itself; specified volumes approved by the counsellors, allotment of time by the week and month, a monthly magazine with additional readings and notes, review outlines, and other aids. Individual readers may pursue the course alone, or local circles may be formed by three or four members. The time required is about one hour daily for nine months. Certificates are granted to those who complete the course. Seals are affixed to the certificates granted for collateral and advanced reading. Any one may become a member of the C. L. S. C. by sending an application, together with $5 for the unit (four books, membership book, and magazine for one year), to Chautauqua Institution, Chautauqua, N. Y.

THE PEABODY EDUCATION FUND.

In 1867 and 1869 George Peabody established a fund of $3,500,000, to be devoted to education in the Southern States of the Union. Of this amount $1,380,000 being in Mississippi and Florida bonds was not available, those of Mississippi, having been repudiated and those of Florida issued while it was a Territory, never having been recognized as legal by its authorities. The fund was placed in the charge and control of sixteen trustees, of whom Mr. Robert C. Winthrop, of Massachusetts, was the chairman. Mr. Peabody died in London in 1869. The trustees hold meetings annually, usually in New York. They fill vacancies caused by death or resignation. The present trustees are: Chief Justice Fuller, President of the Board; Joseph H. Choate, First Vice-President; Dr. Samuel A. Green, Secretary; J. Pierpont Morgan; President Theodore Roosevelt, of New York; Samuel A. Green, Richard Olney, and Right Rev. William Lawrence, of Massachusetts; James D. Porter, of Tennessee; Henderson M. Somerville, of New York; George Peabody Wetmore, of Rhode Island; Charles E. Fenner, of Louisiana; Hoke Smith, of Georgia, and Right Rev. William C. Doane. Prof. Wickliffe Rose is General Agent of the fund, with headquarters at 927 Stahlman Building, Nashville, Tenn., and has charge of the distribution of the fund in the several Southern States. In its earlier history the chief aim of the fund was to encourage and secure the establishment of public school systems for the free education of all children. That having been accomplished, the income of the fund is now used for the training of teachers through Normal Schools and Teachers' Institutes. In the year ending October 1, 1908, the amount distributed was $80,000. Power was conferred by the deed of trust on the trustees to distribute the fund at the expiration of thirty years, which period ended in 1897. In January, 1905, the trustees decided, by a vote of 11 to 2, to dissolve the trust. It was expected to take several years to wind it up. The corporation will then cease to exist.

THE JOHN F. SLATER FUND.

In 1882 Mr. John F. Slater, of Connecticut, placed in the hands of trustees the sum of $1,000,000, for the purpose of "uplifting the lately emancipated population of the Southern States and their posterity." For this patriotic and munificent gift the thanks of Congress were voted, and a medal was presented. Neither principal nor income is expended for land or buildings. Education in industries and the preparation of teachers are promoted in institutions believed to be on a permanent basis. The board consists of D. C. Gilman, of Johns Hopkins University, as President; Chief Justice Fuller, as Vice-President; Morris K. Jesup, as Treasurer, and Bishop Galloway, and Messrs. William A. Slater, John A. Stewart, Alexander E. Orr, Cleveland H. Dodge, Bishop Ellison Capers Seth Low, Wallace Buttrick, and C. C. Cuyler. The fund is at 2 Rector Street, New York. The fund is a potential agency in working out the problem of the education of the negro, and over half a million of dollars has already been expended. By the extraordinary fidelity and financial ability of the treasurer, the fund, while keeping up annual appropriations, has increased to $1,500,000. Schools established by States, denominations, and individuals are helped by annual donations. Among the most prominent are the Hampton Normal and Industrial, the Spelman, the Tuskegee, and schools at Orangeburg, S. C.; Tougaloo, Miss.; Marshall, Tex.; Raleigh, N. C.; New Orleans, etc.

THE GENERAL EDUCATION BOARD.

The General Education Board was organized in New York February 27, 1902, and incorporated by act of Congress, signed January 12, 1903. The following are members of the Board: Frederick T. Gates, Chairman; George Foster Peabody, Treasurer; Wallace Buttrick, Secretary; Charles W. Eliot, Andrew Carnegie, Robert C. Ogden, Walter H. Page, J. D. Rockefeller, Jr., Albert Shaw, Starr J. Murphy, Hugh H. Hanna, E. Benjamin Andrews, Edwin A. Alderman, Hollis B. Frissell, Harry Pratt Judson. The purposes of the Board are to promote education in the United States, without distinction of race, sex, or creed, and especially to promote, systematize, and make effective various forms of educational beneficence. Office, 2 Rector Street, New York City.

THE SOUTHERN EDUCATION BOARD.

The Southern Education Board of the Conference for Education in the South—the outcome of the Capon Springs and Winston-Salem Conferences—has been organized with these officers and members: *Chairman*, Robert C. Ogden, New York; *Treasurer*, George Foster Peabody, New York; *Secretary and Executive Secretary*, Edgar Gardner Murphy, Montgomery, Ala.; *Associate Secretary*, G. S. Dickerman, New Haven, Ct.; *Campaign Committee*, Edwin A. Alderman, *Chairman*; H. B. Frissell, Edgar Gardner Murphy, D. F. Houston, H. E. Fries, P. P. Claxton, S. J. Bowie, S. C. Mitchell, J. H. Kirkland, Wickliffe Rose, J. H. Dillard. The object of this organization is to awaken and inform public opinion and secure additional legislation and revenues for the betterment of the public schools, "the supreme public need of our time."

The Hall of Fame.

MARCH 5, 1900, the Council of New York University accepted a gift of $100,000, afterward increased to $250,000, from a donor, whose name was withheld, for the erection and completion on University Heights, New York City, of a building to be called "The Hall of Fame for Great Americans." A structure was accordingly built in the form of a semi-circle, 170 feet, connecting the University Hall of Philosophy with the Hall of Languages. On the ground floor is a museum 200 feet long by 40 feet wide, consisting of a corridor and six halls to contain mementoes of the names that are inscribed above. The colonnade over this is 400 feet long with provision for 150 panels, each about 2 feet by 6 feet, each to bear the name of a famous American.

Only persons who shall have been dead ten or more years are eligible to be chosen. Fifteen classes of citizens were recommended for consideration, to wit: Authors and editors, business men, educators, inventors, missionaries and explorers, philanthropists and reformers, preachers and theologians, scientists, engineers and architects, lawyers and judges, musicians, painters and sculptors, physicians and surgeons, rulers and statesmen, soldiers and sailors, distinguished men and women outside the above classes. Fifty names were to be inscribed on the tablets at the beginning, and five additional names every fifth year thereafter, until the year 2000, when the 150 inscriptions will be completed. In case of failure to fill all the panels allotted, the vacancies are to be filled in a following year.

In February, 1904, the plan was announced of an additional structure in the form of a loggia joining the colonnade on the north, having 30 panels for foreign born Americans, six to be filled in 1905, and beyond this of a Hall of Fame for Women, about 30 by 60 feet, with a museum on the ground floor and a main story above of 28 columns supporting a pedimented roof, with places for 60 tablets.

The rules prescribed that the Council should invite nominations from the public. Every nomination seconded by a member of the University Senate should be submitted to an electorate of one hundred eminent citizens selected by the Council.

In October, 1900, the University Senate received the ballots of the electors. Of the one hundred judges selected ninety-seven voted. The number of names which had been submitted to them was 252. Of these each judge returned a vote for fifty. The rule required that no candidate receiving less than fifty-one votes could be accepted. The returns showed that but twenty-nine candidates received the required number and were chosen. These were as follows: George Washington, Abraham Lincoln, Daniel Webster, Benjamin Franklin, Ulysses S. Grant, John Marshall, Thomas Jefferson, Ralph Waldo Emerson, Henry W. Longfellow, Robert Fulton, Washington Irving, Jonathan Edwards, Samuel F. B. Morse, David G. Farragut, Henry Clay, Nathaniel Hawthorne, George Peabody, Robert E. Lee, Peter Cooper, Eli Whitney, John J. Audubon, Horace Mann, Henry Ward Beecher, James Kent, Joseph Story, John Adams, William E. Channing, Gilbert Stuart, Asa Gray.

In October, 1905, under the rules named above, the Senate received the ballots of 95 Electors out of 101 appointed, of whom only 85 undertook to consider the names of women. A majority of 51 was demanded, but in the case of the names of women, a majority of only 47. The following persons were found to be duly chosen: John Quincy Adams, 59; James Russell Lowell, 58; William Tecumseh Sherman, 58; James Madison, 56; John Greenleaf Whittier, 53; Alexander Hamilton, 88; Louis Agassiz, 83; John Paul Jones, 54; Mary Lyon, 58; Emma Willard, 50; Maria Mitchell, 48.

Among the names which received less than a majority vote in the 1905 election were those of Oliver Wendell Holmes 48, Phillips Brooks 48, Bryant Parkman and Motley 46 each; Poe and Cooper 43 each; Bancroft and Greeley 39 each; Nathaniel Green and Mark Hopkins 38 each; Joseph Henry 32; Rufus Choate 31.

The Hall was dedicated May 30, 1901, when twenty-five or more national associations each unveiled one of the bronze tablets in the colonnade, and on May 30, 1907, the eleven new tablets were unveiled, orations being given by the Governors of New York and Massachusetts.

Since the Deed of Gift was amended to admit memorials to famous foreign born Americans, the roll of electors has been amended in like manner, Mr. Andrew Carnegie, a native of Scotland, succeeding to the place of Ex-President Grover Cleveland, deceased.

The Dickens Fellowship.

THE Dickens Fellowship is a worldwide league of English-speaking men and women whose purpose is to exemplify the teachings of Charles Dickens and to cultivate and diffuse the spirit which pervades his writings—the spirit of innocent festivity and mirth, of religion without bigotry, of charity without coldness, of universal philanthropy and human kinship. The society began its existence in London in October, 1902, and was designed by its founders not only to promote intellectual sociality but to serve as an agency for the performance of good works. The object and aims of the Fellowship are:

"To knit together in a common bond of friendship lovers of that great master of humor and pathos Charles Dickens. To spread the love of humanity, which is the keynote of all his work. To take such measures as may be expedient to remedy or ameliorate those existing social evils which would have appealed so strongly to the heart of Charles Dickens, and to help in every possible direction the cause of the poor and the oppressed. To assist in the preservation and purchase of buildings and objects associated with his name and mentioned in his works."

The Fellowship is open to all, without restriction as to class, creed or nationality. On the list of Vice-Presidents of the society are the following: Sir Francis C. Burnand, Sir Arthur Conan Doyle, the Rev. Canon Benham, Lady Florence Dixie, Hall Caine, Sir L. Alma-Tadema, J. Comyns Carr, T. P. O'Connor, M. P.; Miss Georgiana Hogarth, J. M. Barrie, Harry Furniss, W. S. Gilbert and Algernon Charles Swinburne. Branches of the Fellowship have been formed not only throughout Great Britain but on the Continent, in the United States and Canada, India, Ceylon, the Transvaal, Cape Town, Gold Coast of Africa, Australia, Egypt and the Persian Gulf, 15,000 members in all.

The officers of the Manhattan (New York) branch are: *President*—J. Woolsey Shepard. *Vice-Presidents*—Hon. H. A. Metz, H. M. Leipziger, Ph. D. *Corresponding Secretary*—Mrs. F. Foulke, 148 Putnam Avenue, Brooklyn, N. Y. *Recording Secretary*—A. Maerz. *Treasurer*—Paul Shotland. *Executive Council*—Dr. F. A. Lyons, Chairman, Mrs. F. A. Lyons, W. V. Hirsch, Mrs. W. V. Hirsch, Mrs. L. L. Levey, Mrs. Paul Shotland, Charles Ross Keen. Membership fees are $3 per annum. Secretary's office—71 Broadway, New York. Dickens entertainments are a feature. Meetings are held on or about the 7th of every month from October to May, inclusive, and each meeting is preceded by a dinner, which is served at 6.30 to 7 P. M., and ends at 8.15.

Smithsonian Institution.

FOR THE INCREASE AND DIFFUSION OF KNOWLEDGE AMONG MEN.

OFFICERS OF THE SMITHSONIAN INSTITUTION.

Ex-Officio Presiding Officer of the Institution, Theodore Roosevelt, President of the United States; *Chancellor of the Institution*, Melville W. Fuller, Chief Justice of the United States; *Secretary of the Institution*, Charles D. Walcott; *Assistant Secretary in Charge of United States National Museum*, Richard Rathbun; *Assistant Secretary in Charge of Library and Exchanges*, Cyrus Adler.

Board of Regents, Melville W. Fuller, Chief Justice of the United States, Chancellor; Charles W. Fairbanks, Vice-President of the United States; Shelby M. Cullom, Member of the Senate; Henry Cabot Lodge, Member of the Senate; A. O. Bacon, Member of the Senate; John Dalzell, Member of the House of Representatives; James R. Mann, Member of the House of Representatives; William M. Howard, Member of the House of Representatives; James B. Angell, citizen of Michigan; Andrew D. White, citizen of New York; John B. Henderson, citizen of Washington, D. C.; Alexander Graham Bell, citizen of Washington, D. C.; Richard Olney, citizen of Massachusetts; George Gray, citizen of Delaware.

The Institution at Washington, D. C., was established by statute in 1846, under the terms of the will of James Smithson, who bequeathed his fortune in 1826 to the United States for the "increase and diffusion of knowledge among men." From the income of the fund a building, known as the Smithsonian Building, was erected on land given by the United States. The Institution is legally an establishment having as its members the President of the United States, the Vice-President, the Chief Justice, and the President's Cabinet. It is governed by a Board of Regents consisting of the Vice-President, the Chief Justice, three members of the United States Senate, three members of the House of Representatives, and six citizens of the United States appointed by joint resolution of Congress. It is under the immediate direction of the Secretary of the Smithsonian Institution, who is the executive officer of the Board and the director of the Institution's activities.

For the increase of knowledge, the Institution aids investigators by making grants for research and exploration, supplying books, apparatus, laboratory accommodations, etc. It occasionally provides for lectures, which are published. It has initiated numerous scientific projects of national importance, some of which have been turned over to the Government and resulted in the creation of independent Government bureaus. It advises the Government in many matters of scientific importance, especially in those that have an international aspect. It co-operates with scientific bodies of national importance, like the National Academy of Sciences, the American Association for the Advancement of Science, the American Historical Association, etc. It issues three regular series of publications: Annual Reports, containing papers of general interest intended to keep the ordinary reader abreast of the progress of science; Contributions to Knowledge, the distinct feature of which is that each memoir constitutes an original contribution to knowledge; Miscellaneous Collections, which contain bibliographies, reports of expeditions, standard tables, and a scientific quarterly. All these publications are distributed gratuitously to important libraries throughout the world.

THE INSTITUTION LIBRARY.

The Institution maintains a library in co-operation with the Library of Congress, which numbers 250,000 volumes, and consists mainly of the transactions of learned societies and scientific periodicals. While the body of the library is deposited in the Library of Congress and accessible to all its readers, a working library is maintained at the Institution. Lists, bibliographies, rules for cataloguing and library work have been published. It supports a table at the Biological Station at Naples. All these and numerous other activities may be carried on solely from the income of the Smithsonian fund. The Regents are empowered to accept gifts without action of Congress, in furtherance of the purposes of the Institution, and to administer trusts in accord therewith.

The parent Institution has the administrative charge of several branches which grew out of its early activities and which are supported by Congressional appropriations. These are the National Museum, including the National Gallery of Art; the International Exchange Service, the Bureau of American Ethnology, the National Zoological Park, the Astrophysical Observatory, and the Regional Bureau for the International Catalogue of Scientific Literature.

THE UNITED STATES NATIONAL MUSEUM is the depository of the national collections. It is especially rich in the natural history, geology, paleontology, archaeology and ethnology of America, and has unique collections of American history, as well as many series relating to fine arts and the industrial arts. It is both an educational and a research museum, and issues numerous technical and popular scientific publications. The National Gallery of Art consists largely of the collections of etchings and engravings of George P. Marsh, the collections of Charles L. Freer, containing numerous paintings and etchings by Whistler, and examples of Chinese and Japanese art; the Harriet Lane Johnston collection, including a number of the greatest English portrait painters, and the collection of William T. Evans, of fifty paintings, representing some of the best work of American artists.

THE INTERNATIONAL EXCHANGES, carried on in accordance with the terms of a treaty entered into between the United States and various foreign nations, is for the free interchange of Governmental and scientific publications between the Government of the United States and foreign governments and institutions, and investigators in the United States and foreign lands. At present it has 56,314 correspondents, and since its establishment over 2,750,000 packages have been handled by it.

The Bureau of American Ethnology, a study of the North American Indian, the Astrophysical Observatory for the investigation of solar phenomena, the National Zoological Park at Washington, and the Regional Bureau for the collection and classification of the natural and physical sciences, are also departments of the work of the Institution,

Principal Universities and Colleges of the United States.

TABLE ONE.

THE statistics embraced in this table were communicated to THE WORLD ALMANAC by the Presidents of the respective institutions, and represent their condition at the close of 1908.

Persons writing to the different institutions for catalogues should inclose postage stamp for reply, and also indicate the reason for request.

Organized.	Colleges. For explanation of signs, see page 320.	Location.	Denominational Control.	President or Chairman of Faculty.	Instructors.*	Students.*	Volumes in Library
1896	Adelphi College†	Brooklyn, N. Y.	Non-Sect	C. H. Levermore, Ph.D.	30	500	12,000
1859	Adrian College†	Adrian, Mich	Meth. Prot.	Rev. B. W. Anthony, D. D.	25	200	7,000
1876	Ag.&Mech.Col.of Tex.	College Sta., Tex.	Non-Sect.	Robert T. Milner	46	626	6,212
1872	Alabama Poly. Inst.†	Auburn, Ala.	Non-Sect.	Chas. C. Thach, A.M., LL.D.	..	675	25,000
1856	Albany College†	Albany, Ore.	Presbyter'n	C. M. Crooks, A. B.	14	186	3,000
1861	Albion College†	Albion, Mich	Meth. Epis.	Samuel Dickie, LL. D.	28	450	18,500
1881	Albright College†	Myerstown, Pa.	Evangelical	Clellan A. Bowman, A. M.	19	209	7,000
1836	Alfred University†	Alfred, N. Y.	Non-Sect.	Rev. Boothe C. Davis, Ph. D.	25	273	21,250
1815	Allegheny College†	Meadville, Pa.	Meth. Epis.	William H. Crawford, D.D.	17	315	24,000
1886	Alma College†	Alma, Mich.	Presbyter'n	Rev. A. F. Bruske, M.S., D.D.	26	276	21,000
1884	Am. Intern'l Col.†	Springfield, Mass.	Non-Sect.	....	11	81	3,500
1893	American Univ.†	Harriman, Tenn.	....	Amos L. Edwards, B. L.	8	230	5,000
1893	American Univ.†	Washington, D. C.	Meth. Epis.	Rv. Frank'n Hamilton, Ph. D.	..	....	17,000
1821	Amherst College	Amherst, Mass.	Non-Sect.	George Harris, LL. D.	45	530	80,000
1853	Amity College†	College Springs, Ia	Non-Sect.	Rev. Ross T. Campbell, D. D.	10	181	1,500
1808	Andover The. Sem	Cambridge, Mass.	Congregat'l.	....	7	5	60,000
1853	Antioch College†	Yellow Springs, O.	Non-Sect.	S. D. Fess, LL. D.	10	234	9,000
1872	Arkansas College†	Batesville, Ark	Presbyter'n	Eugene R. Long, Ph.D.	8	153	4,800
1893	Armour Inst. Tech'y.	Chicago, Ill.	Non-Sect.	F. W. Gunsaulus, D.D., LL.D	100	1,805	25,000
1869	Atlanta University†§.	Atlanta, Ga.	Non-Sect.	Rev. Edward T. Ware, A. B	20	340	12,500
1820	Auburn Theol. Sem'y	Auburn, N. Y.	Presbyter'n	Rev. G. B. Stewart, D.D.	11	71	32,281
1869	Augsburg Seminary	Minneapolis, Minn	Lutheran	Sven Oftedal (Prof. Em.)	8	175	5,000
1860	Augustana College†	Rock Island, Ill.	Lutheran	Gustav A Andreen, Ph. D.	38	462	18,000
1858	Baker University†	Baldwin, Kan.	Meth. Epis.	Lemuel H. Murlin, D. D.	40	800	32,000
1855	Baldwin University†.	Berea, O.	Meth. Epis.	Robert L. Maggoner, A. M.	21	360	10,000
1889	Barnard College‡(*d*)	Manh'n Boro, N.Y.	Non-Sect.	Nich. M. Butler (Act. Dean)	70	580	3,000
1864	Bates College†	Lewiston, Me.	Non-Sect.	George C. Chase, D.D., LL.D.	21	450	31,875
1845	Baylor University†	Waco, Tex	Baptist	Samuel P. Brooks, LL. D.	90	725	21,000
1880	Bellevue College†	Bellevue, Neb.	Presbyter'n	Stephen W. Stookey, LL. D.	20	188	5,300
1846	Beloit College†	Beloit, Wis.	Non-Sect.	Edward Dwight Eaton, D.D.	35	481	41,300
1871	Benedict†§	Columbia, S. C.	Baptist	Rev. W. C. Osborn, D.D.	19	664	7,900
1855	Berea College†	Berea, Ky	Non-Sect	Wm. G. Frost, Ph. D., D. D.	65	1,150	24,000
1881	Bethany College†(*y*).	Lindsborg, Kan.	Lutheran	Rev. E. F. Pihlblad, A. M.	40	936	7,800
1840	Bethany College†	Bethany, W. Va.	Disciples	T. E. Cramblet, A. M., LL.D.	18	300	9,000
1864	Blackburn College†	Carlinville, Ill.	Presbyter'n	Walter H. Brady, Ph.D.	12	125	4,000
1863	Boston College(*y*)	Boston, Mass	R. Catholic.	Rev. Thos. I. Gasson, S. J.	25	525	40,000
1869	Boston University†	Boston, Mass	Meth. Epis.	W. E. Huntington, D. D.	150	1,459	60,000
1794	Bowdoin College	Brunswick, Me.	Undenom'l	Wm. De Witt Hyde, D.D.	57	428	91,546
1877	Brigham Young Col.†	Logan, Utah	Latter Day.	James H. Linford, B.S., B.D.	44	886	5,000
1764	Brown University (*k*).	Providence, R. I.	Non-Sect.	W. H. P. Faunce, D. D.	92	995	150,000
1885	Bryn Mawr Col.‡	Bryn Mawr, Pa.	Non-Sect.	M. C. Thomas, Ph. D., LL.D.	55	419	55,000
1872	Buchtel College†	Akron, O.	Univ'rsalist	Rv. A. B. Church, D.D., LL.D.	20	267	9,000
1846	Bucknell University†.	Lewisburg, Pa.	Baptist	John H. Harris, LL. D	55	771	30,000
1877	Buckner College†	Witcherville, Ark.	Baptist	J. V. Vermillion, A. B.	3	113	125
1855	Butler University†	Indianapolis, Ind.	Disciples	Thomas C. Howe	20	441	20,000
1870	Canisius College.	Buffalo, N. Y	R. Catholic.	Augustine A. Miller, S. J.	28	385	26,000
1866	Carleton College†	Northfield, Minn.	Non-Sect.	Herb't C. Wilson (Act. Dean)	21	328	23,000
1851	Carson & Newman C.†	Jeff. City, Tenn	Baptist	M. D. Jeffries, M. D., D. D.	23	529	2,500
1870	Carthage College†	Carthage, Ill	Lutheran.	Rev. Fred. L. Sigmund, D. D.	16	243	8,000
1881	Case Sc. Appl. Science	Cleveland, O	Non-Sect	Charles S. Howe, Ph. D.	37	434	5,000
1889	Catholic Univ. Am.(*f*).	Washington, D. C.	R. Catholic.	Rt. Rev. D. J. O'Connell	32	224	55,365
1894	Cedarville College†	Cedarville, O.	Ref. Presb.	Rev. D. McKinney, D. D.	11	105	2,500
1857	Central College†	Fayette, Mo.	Meth. Ep. S.	William A. Webb	12	181	11,000
1853	Central University†	Pella, Iowa	Baptist	L. A. Garrison, D. D.	13	189	5,000
1819	Central University.	Danville, Ky.	Presbyter'n	Rev. F. W. Hinitt, Ph.D., D.D.	87	751	22,000
1864	Central Wesleyan Col.†	Warrenton, Mo.	Meth. Epis.	Geo. B. Addicks, D. D., A. B.	31	302	8,000
1891	Charles City Col.†(*y*).	Charles City, Iowa.	Meth. Epis.	Rev. Frank E. Hirsch, D.D.	15	225	1,200
1785	Charleston College	Charleston, S. C.	Non-Sect.	Harrison Randolph, LL.D.	10	90	18,078
1853	Christian Univ.†	Canton, Mo	Christian Ch	Carl Johann, A. M., LL. D.	14	165	5,000
1869	Claflin Univ.†§(*y*)	Orangeburg, S. C.	Meth. Epis.	L. M. Dunton, A.M., D.D.	42	600	5,000
1902	Clark College	Worcester, Mass.	Non-Sect.	C. D. Wright, LL.D., Ph.D.	27	140	50,000
1870	Clark University §	Atlanta, Ga.	Meth. Epis.	W.H. Crogman, Litt. D.	25	532	3,000
1889	Clark University†	Worcester, Mass.	Non-Sect	G. Stanley Hall, Ph. D., LL.D	15	79	50,000
1896	Clarkson School Tech.	Potsdam, N. Y.	Non-Sect.	W. S. Aldrich, M.E.	9	92	2,856
1889	Clemson Agri. College	Clemson Col., S.C.	Non-Sect.	P. H. Mell, Ph. D., LL. D.	47	690	28,837
1881	Coe College†	Cedar Rapids, Ia.	Presbyter'n	....	19	297	6,000
1813	Colby College†	Waterville, Me	Non-Sect.	Arthur J. Roberts, A. M.	16	....	45,907
1819	Colgate University	Hamilton, N. Y.	Undenom'l.	Wm. H. Crawshaw (Act.)	47	482	51,406
1847	College City of N. Y.	Manh'n Boro, N.Y.	Non-Sect.	John H. Finley, LL. D.	221	4,383	39,000
1859	Col. of St. Elizabeth‡.	Convent Sta., N. J.	R. Catholic.	Sister Mary Pauline	34	365	20,000
1874	Colorado College†	Colorado Sp's, Col	Non-Sect	W. F. Slocum, LL. D., D. D.	50	598	43,000
1754	Columbia Univ. (*d*)	Manh'n Boro, N.Y.	Non-Sect	N. M. Butler, LL.D., Ph.D.	*d*614	*d*5,655	420,000
1839	Concordia College	Fort Wayne, Ind.	Lutheran	Rev. Martin Luecke	11	221	10,000
1890	Converse College‡	Spartanburg, S. C.	Non-Sect.	Robert P. Pell, Litt. D.	23	354	3,485

Organized.	Colleges—Table One For explanation of signs, see page 320.	Location.	Denominational Control.	President or Chairman of Faculty.	Instructors.*	Students*	Volumes in Library
1887	Cooper College†	Sterling, Kans	Un. Presb.	Rev. F. M. Spencer, D.D.	11	200	3,500
1853	Cornell College†	Mt. Vernon, Iowa	Meth. Epis.	James Elliott Harlan, LL.D	40	755	29,841
1868	Cornell University†	Ithaca, N. Y.	Non-Sect.	J. G. Schurman, LL.D., D.Sc.	548	4,465	353,638
1889	Cotner University†	Bethany, Neb.	Disciples	W. P. Aylsworth, LL. D.	52	377	2,500
1879	Creighton Univ. (*a*)	Omaha, Neb.	R. Catholic.	Rev. E. A. Magevney, S. J.	125	795	18,500
1842	Cumberland, Univ.†(*y*)	Lebanon, Tenn.	Presbyter'n	Vacant	21	216	20,000
1883	Dakota Wesley. Univ †	Mitchell, S. Dak.	Meth. Epis.	Samuel F. Kerfoot, D. D.	26	526	5,460
1769	Dartmouth College	Hanover, N. H.	Non-Sect.	Wm. J. Tucker, D.D., LL.D.	85	1,232	100,000
1837	Davidson College	Davidson, N. C.	Presbyter'n	Henry L. Smith, LL.D.	20	327	20,000
1902	Defiance College†	Defiance, O.	Christian	P. W. McReynolds, A.M.	20	345	4,000
1833	Delaware College	Newark, Del	Non-Sect.	Geo. A. Harter, M.A., Ph.D.	24	212	16,000
1831	Denison University†	Granville, O.	Baptist	Rev. Emory W. Hunt, D.D.	44	583	30,000
1837	De Pauw University†	Greencastle, Ind.	Methodist	Edwin H. Hughes, D. D.	33	1,001	9,780
1865	Des Moines Col.†	Des Moines, Iowa	Baptist	Loran D. Osborn, Ph.D.	16	244	6,000
1783	Dickinson College†	Carlisle, Pa.	Non-Sect.	Geo. E. Reed, S. T. D., LL.D.	33	550	36,000
1872	Doane College†	Crete, Neb	Congregat'l.	David B. Perry, A.M., D. D.	24	239	10,675
1881	Drake University†	Des Moines, Iowa	Independ't.	H. M. Bell, A. M.	120	1,846	16,000
1866	Drew Theol. Sem.	Madison, N. J	Meth. Epis.	Henry A. Butz, D. D.	8	175	104,121
1873	Drury College†	Springfield, Mo.	Non-Sect.	Joseph Henry George, D. D.	26	426	29,751
1847	Earlham College†	Richmond, Ind.	Friends	Robt. L. Kelly, Ph. M.	33	525	15,000
1855	Elmira College‡	Elmira, N. Y.	Presbyter'n	Rev. A. C. MacKenzie, D.D	19	292	6,204
1889	Elon College†	Elon College, N. C.	Christian	Emmett L. Moffitt, LL. D.	14	224	4,000
1836	Emory & Henry Col.†	Emory, Va.	Meth. Ep. S.	R. G. Waterhouse, M.A., D.D	11	230	12,000
1836	Emory College	Oxford, Ga.	Meth. Ep. S.	Rev. James E. Dickey, D.D.	14	265	31,000
1883	Emporia College†	Emporia, Kan.	Presbyter'n	Henry C. Culbertson, B.D.	22	399	8,000
1839	Erskine College†	Due West, S. C.	Ref. Presb.	James S. Moffatt, D. D.	10	184	10.000
1855	Eureka College†	Eureka, Ill.	Christian	Robert E. Hieronymus, A. M	16	210	8,000
1867	Ewing College†	Ewing, Ill.	Baptist	J. A. Leavitt, D. D.	19	350	8,000
1895	Fairmount College†	Wichita, Kan.	Congrega'l.	H. E. Thayer, D.D., B. D.	20	325	30,000
1888	Fargo College†	Fargo, N. Dak.	Congrega'l.	Edmund M. Vittum, D.D.	21	311	5,000
1882	Findlay College†	Findlay, O	Ch. of God	Rev. C. I. Brown, A.M., D.D.	17	400	2.000
1866	Fisk University† §	Nashville, Tenn.	Undenom'l.	Herbert H. Wright (Dean).	35	571	8,000
1841	Fordham University.	Fordham, N. Y. C.	R. Catholic.	Rev. David J. Quinn, S. J.	100	615	40,000
1881	Fort Worth Univ.†	Fort Worth, Tex.	Meth. Epis.	Wm. Fielder, D. D.	45	711	....
1906	Frank Hughes Coll'†.	Clifton, Tenn.	Undenom'l.	Rev. J. T. Baker, Ph. M.	12	246	1,000
1787	Franklin & Marshall.	Lancaster, Pa.	Ref. in U. S.	Rev. J. S. Stahr, LL.D., D.D.	23	394	45,000
1834	Franklin College† (*y*).	Franklin, Ind. (*y*).	Baptist	Elmer B. Bryan, LL.D.	21	300	17,000
1825	Franklin College†	New Athens, O.	Non-Sect.	A. M. Campbell	7	....	....
1851	Furman University	Greenville, S. C.	Baptist	E. M. Poteat, D. D., LL. D.	14	252	....
1864	Gallaudet College†	Washington, D. C.	Non-Sect.	Edw'd M. Gallaudet, LL.D.	16	105	6,000
1817	General Theol. Sem.	Manh'n Boro, N. Y.	Prot. Epis.	Rev. W. L. Robbins, Dean	15	115	44 227
1849	Geneva College† (*y*)	Beaver Falls, Pa (*y*)	Ref. Presb.	Rev. W. Henry George, A.B.	13	764	95,000
1829	Georgetown College†.	Georgetown, Ky.	Baptist	Arthur Yager	22	264	12,500
1789	Georgetown Univ.	Washington, D. C.	R. Catholic.	Rev. Joseph J. Hemmel, S.J.	149	855	98,000
1821	Geo. Washington Un.†	Washington, D.C.	Non-Sect.	Chas. W. Needham, LL. D.	215	1,258	37,000
1848	Girard College	Philadelphia, Pa.	Non-Sect.	A. H. Fetterolf, Ph.D., LL.D	70	1,707	16,556
1838	Greensboro Col. ‡	Greensboro, N. C.	Methodist	Mrs. Lucy H. Robertson	18	200	1,969
1890	Greer College† (*y*)	Hoopeston, Ill.	Non-Sect.	E. L. Bailey, B. S., M.S., B. O.	12	275	2,500
1876	Grove City Col.† (*y*)	Grove City, Pa.	Non-Sect.	Rev. I. C. Keller, Ph. D., D.D.	25	655	6,500
1837	Guilford College† (*y*).	Guilford Col., N. C.	Friends	Lewis L. Hobbs, A. B., A.M.	12	250	8,000
1862	Gustav. Adolph. C.†	St. Peter, Minn.	Lutheran	Peter A. Mattson, D.D., Ph.D	23	400	10,000
1812	Hamilton College	Clinton, N. Y.	Non-Sect.	M. W. Stryker, D.D., LL.D.	19	190	50,000
1854	Hamline Univ.†	St. Paul, Minn. (*x*).	Meth. Epis.	Rev. G. H. Bridgman, D.D.	26	365	10,000
1776	Hampden-Sidney Col.	Hamp.-Sidney, Va	Presbyter'n	W. H. Whiting, Jr. (Act. Pres)	8	127	15,000
1868	Hampton Inst.† (*j*) (*y*)	Hampton, Va.	Non-Sect.	Rev. H. B. Frissell, D. D.	124	1,295	22,186
1833	Hanover College†	Hanover, Ind.	Non-Sect.	Wm. A. Millis, LL. D.	16	200	20.000
1834	Hartford Theol Sem †	Hartford, Ct.	Congregat'l.	W. D. Mackenzie, D. D.	24	67	90,000
1636	Harvard Univ. (*l*)	Cambridge, Mass.	Non-Sect.	Charles Wm. Eliot, LL.D.	634	4,900	815,636
1882	Hastings College†	Hastings, Neb.	Presbyter'n	A. E. Turner, LL. D.	14	175	6,267
1833	Haverford College	Haverford, Pa.	Friends	Isaac Sharpless, Sc.D., LL.D	21	160	50,400
1855	Hedding College†	Abingdon, Ill.	Meth. Epis.	Wm. Pitt MacVey, A.B., B.D	16	210	5,000
1850	Heidelberg Univ.†	Tiffin, O.	Ref. in U.S.	Chas. E. Miller, A.M., D. D.	22	390	16,000
1884	Hendrix College	Conway, Ark.	Meth. Ep. S.	Stonewall Anderson, A. B.	13	246	1,300
1894	Henry Kendall C.†	Tulsa, Okla.	Presbyter'n	Levi H. Beeler, M. A.	14	125	5,000
1853	Hillsdale College†	Hillsdale, Mich.	Baptist	Jos. W. Mauck, A. M., LL.D	19	345	16,000
1867	Hiram College† (*y*)	Hiram, O.	Disciples	Miner Lee Bates, A.M., Ph.D	22	254	12,000
1849	Hiwassee College†	Hiwassee Col., T'n	Meth Ep. S.	Eugene Blake, D. D.	5	127	1,000
1822	Hobart College	Geneva, N. Y.	Non-Sect.	L. C. Stewardson, LL. D.	22	105	49,596
1843	Holy Cross College	Worcester, Mass.	R. Catholic.	Rev. Thos. E. Murphy, S.J.	38	415	35,000
1866	Hope College†	Holland, Mich.	Ref. of Am.	Gerrit J. Kollen, A.M., LL.D	24	311	15,000
1842	Howard College	Birmingham, Ala.	Baptist	A. P. Montague, LL. D.	10	200	2,000
1889	Howard Payne Col.†.	Brownwood, Tex.	Baptist		..	....	....
1867	Howard Univ.† (*c*)	Washington, D. C.	Undenom'l.	Wilbur P. Thirkield, LL. D.	100	1,000	46,000
1883	Huron College	Huron, S. Dak.	Presbyter'n	Rev. Calvin H. French, D.D.	18	415	6,000
1829	Illinois College†	Jacksonville, Ill.	Presbyter'n	C. H. Rammelkamp, Ph. D.	20	383	16,000
1850	Ill. Wesley. Univ.†	Bloomington, Ill.	Meth. Epis.	Rev. Theodore Kemp, D.D.	36	1,097	10,000
1902	Indiana Cent'l Univ.†	Indianapolis, Ind.	Un. Breth'n		10	102	1,500
1820	Indiana University†	Bloomington, Ind.	Non-Sect.	Wm. L. Bryan, Ph.D., LL. D	80	2,051	59,800
1902	Iowa Christian Col.†	Oskaloosa, Ia.	Non-Sect.	Charles J. Burton, D.D.	10	143	3,000
1847	Iowa College†	Grinnell, Iowa	Non-Sect.	J. H. T. Main	55	640	40,000
1869	Iowa State College†	Ames, Iowa	Non-Sect.	A. B. Storms, LL.D., D. D.	164	2,383	24,600
1842	Iowa Wesley. Univ.†	Mt. Pleasant, Iowa	Meth. Epis	Edwin A. Schell, Ph. D.	22	375	11,000
1901	James Millikin Univ.†	Decatur, Ill.	Presbyter'n	A. R. Taylor, Ph.D., LL. D.	50	937	6,000

Organized.	Colleges—Table One. For explanation of signs, see page 320.	Location.	Denominational Control.	President or Chairman of Faculty.	Instructors.*	Students.*	Volumes in Library
1887	John B. Stetson Un.†	De Land, Fla	Baptist	Lincoln Hulley, Ph.D., LL.D	49	520	14,500
1876	Johns Hopkins U. (*i*)	Baltimore, Md	Non-Sect	Ira Remsen, LL.D., Ph.D.	175	683	136,000
1876	Juniata College	Huntingdon, Pa	Baptist	M. G. Brumbaugh, LL.D.	32	408	28,000
1855	Kalamazoo College†	Kalmazoo, Mich	Baptist	A. G. Slocum	13	185	11,421
1886	Kansas City Univ.†	Kansas City, Kan	Meth. Prot.	D. S. Stepheus, D. D., Chan.	67	454	3,000
1858	Kansas Wesleyan U.†	Salina, Kan	Meth. Epis.	Rev. Robert P. Smith	40	1,249	7,500
1863	Ky. Wesleyan Col.†	Winchester, Ky	Meth. Ep. S.	H. K. Taylor	9	200	3,000
1824	Kenyon College	Gambier, O	Prot. Epis.	Rev. W. F. Peirce, M.A., LHD	15	112	35,000
1890	Keuka College†	Keuka Park, N. Y.	Disciples	Zephaniah A. Space, M.A.	15	150	4,000
1837	Knox College†	Galesburg, Ill	Undenom'l.	Thomas McClelland. D. D.	31	628	9,000
1875	Knoxville College†§	Knoxville, Tenn	United Pres.	Ralph W. McGranahan, D. D	32	507	2,500
1832	Lafayette College	Easton, Pa	Presbyter'n	Rev. E. D. Warfield, LL.D.	38	442	35,000
1856	Lake Erie College‡	Painesville, O	Non-Sect	Mary Evaus, A.M., Litt D.	21	163	9,500
1876	Lake Forest College †	Lake Forest, Ill	Undenom'l.	J. S. Scholte Nollen, Ph. D.	19	190	25,000
1872	Lander College ‡ (*y*)	Greenwood, S. C.	Meth. Ep. S.	Rev. John O Willson, D. D.	16	170	4,700
1829	Lane Theol. Seminary	Cincinnati, O	Presbyter'n	Wm. McKibbin, D. D., LL.D	5	29	25,000
1862	La Salle College	Philadelphia, Pa	R. Catholic	....	..	....	....
1847	Lawrence Univ.†	Appleton, Wis	Undenom'l.	Samuel Plantz, Ph.D., D.D.	37	610	24,100
1856	Leander Clark Col.†	Toledo, Ia	U. Brethren.	Franklin E. Brooks	17	312	6,000
1855	Lebanon†	Lebanon, O	Non-Sect	Rev. Floyd Poe	20	29[illegible]	10,000
1866	Lebanon Valley Col.†	Annville, Pa	U. Brethren.	Rev. Law. Keisler, A. B	23	319	6,000
1866	Lehigh University	S. Bethlehem, Pa	Non-Sect	Henry S. Drinker, LL.D	64	662	125,000
1891	Leland Stanford, Jr.†	Palo Alto, Cal	Non-Sect	David Starr Jordan, LL.D.	138	1,751	107,000
1869	Leland University §†	New Orleans, La	Non-Sect.	R. W. Perkins, M. A	64	1,975	4,000
1856	Lenox College†	Hopkinton, Iowa	Presbyter'n	Rev. E. E. Reed, M.A., D. D.	13	185	6,010
1874	Liberty College‡ (*y*)	Glasgow, Ky	Baptist	Robert E. Hatton, A. M.	19	225	3,500
1865	Lincoln College †	Lincoln, Ill	Presbyter'n	J. H. McMurray, A.M	15	334	7,000
1897	Lincoln Mem'l Un.†	Cu'b'd Gap, Tenn.	Non-Sect	Wm. L. Stooksbury	16	500	6,000
1851	Lombard College† (*y*)	Galesburg, Ill	Undenom'l.	Lewis B. Fisher, D.D., LL.D.	14	126	8,000
1860	Louisiana State Un†	Baton Rouge, La	Non-Sect	....	..	....	....
1852	Loyola College	Baltimore, Md	R. Catholic.	F. H. Brady, S. J	26	224	40,000
1861	Luther College	Decorah, Iowa	Lutheran	Rev. C. K. Kreus, B. A	14	167	15,215
1884	Macalester Col. †	St. Paul, Minn	Presbyter'n	T. M. Hodgman. A. B., LL.D.	25	250	10,200
1863	Manhattan College	Manh'n Boro, N.Y.	R. Catholic	Rev. Bro. Peter, F. S. C	18	252	11.257
1835	Marietta College†	Marietta, O	Non-Sect	Alfred T. Perry, A. M., D. D.	41	504	60,000
1864	Marquette Univers'ty	Milwaukee, Wis	R. Catholic	Rev. James McCabe, S. J	137	874	22,000
1819	Maryville College†	Maryville, Tenn	Presbyter'n	Samuel T. Wilson, D.D	32	631	13,000
1864	Mass. Agri. College†	Amherst, Mass	Non-Sect	Kenyon L. Butterfield	40	622	28,000
1864	Mass. Inst. Tech.†	Boston, Mass	Non-Sect	Richard C. MacLaurin	156	1,447	78,161
1829	McCormick Th. Se.	Chicago, Ill	Presbyter'n	Rev. J. G. K. McClure, D. D.	10	120	32,792
1828	McKendree College†	Lebanon, Ill	Meth. Epis.	John F. Harmon, D. D	11	226	10,000
1857	McMinnville College†	McMinnville, Ore.	Baptist	Rev. L. W. Riley, A.B	15	229	4,700
1809	Miami University†	Oxford, O	Non-Sect	Guy P. Benton, D.D., LL.D.	40	1,149	25,000
1857	Mich. Agri. College†	E. Lausing, Mich.	Non-Sect	J. L. Snyder, M. A., Ph. D.	96	1,350	30,000
1885	Mich. Col. of Mines	Houghton, Mich	Undenom'l.	F. W. McNair, B. S., D. Sc.	32	266	22,220
1800	Middlebury College†	Middlebury, Vt	Non-Sect	John M. Thomas, D.D	14	220	35,000
1887	Midland College†	Atchison, Kan	Lutheran	Rev. M. F. Troxell, A.M., D.D	15	205	8,000
1882	Milligan College†	Milligan, Tenn	Disciples	Freder'k D. Kershner, M.A.	12	178	4,000
1871	Mills Col. & Sem.‡ (*y*)	Seminary Park, Cal	Non-Sect.	Mrs. Cyrus T. Mills, Litt. D.	35	206	8,000
1891	Millsaps College	Jackson, Miss	Meth. Ep. S.	Wm. B. Murrah, D.D., LL.D.	12	300	10.000
1861	Milton College†	Milton, Wis	7th Day Bap	W. C. Daland. A. M., D. D	13	139	8,520
1878	Mississippi A. & M. C.	Agric'l Coll., Miss.	Non-Sect.	J. C. Hardy, A.M., LL.D	48	1,015	13,000
1826	Mississippi College	Clinton, Miss	Baptist	Rv. W. T. Lowrey, D.D., LL.D	13	330	3,000
1889	Missouri Val. Col.†	Marshall, Mo	Presbyter'n	William H. Black, D.D	13	279	14,500
1856	Monmouth College†	Monmouth, Ill	United Pres.	T. H. McMichael, A.M., D.D.	24	454	6,000
1854	Moore's Hill College†	Moore's Hill, Ind.	Meth. Epis.	Wm. S. Bovard, D. D	15	276	5,000
1894	Morningside Col.† (*y*)	Sioux City, Iowa	Methodist	W. S. Lewis, D.D., A.M.	37	480	5,200
1881	Morris Brown Col. †§	Atlanta, Ga	Methodist	E. W. Lee, A. M	28	940	3,000
1887	Mount Angel College.	Mount Angel, Ore.	R. Catholic	Rev. Bernard Murphy	25	..	....
1837	Mt. Holyoke College‡.	S. Hadley, Mass	Non-Sect	Mary E. Woolley, M. A	89	760	35,500
1808	Mt. St. Mary's College	Emmitsburg, Md.	R. Catholic.	Very Rev. D. J. Flynn, LL.D	30	350	12,000
1846	Mt. Union College†	Alliance, O	Non-Sect	Rev. W. H. McMaster	31	554	9,900
1867	Muhlenberg College	Allentown, Pa	Lutheran	John A. W. Haas, D. D.	15	124	15,000
1837	Muskingum College†	New Concord, O	United Pres.	Rev. J. K. Montgomery, D.D	20	400	4,000
1892	N.C. State Norl. & Ind.	Greenboro, N. C.	Non-Sect	J. I. Faust	55	545	6,000
1888	Neb. Wesleyan Un.†	University Pl, Neb	Meth. Epis.	Wm. J. Davidson	45	904	6,000
1856	Newberry College†	Newberry, S. C.	Lutheran	J. Henry Horms	13	241	11,000
1873	New Orleans Un.†	New Orleans, La	Meth. Epis.	John Wier, D. D	23	924	5,000
1825	Newton Theol. Inst.	Newton Cent. Mas	Baptist	Rev. George E. Horr, D. D.	8	53	30,000
1830	New York Univ. (*w*)	New York City (*w*)	Non-Sect	H. M. MacCracken, DD., LL.D	262	4,026	92,000
1856	Niagara University	Niagara Falls, N.Y	R. Catholic.	Rev. Edw'd J. Walsh, C. M.	28	260	20,000
1889	Nor. C. Ag. & M. Arts	West Raleigh, N.C.	Non-Sect.	Daniel Harvey Hill, A. M.	41	470	5,324
1870	Normal College‡	New York City	Non-Sect.	Geo. S. Davis, LL. D.	180	3,350	10,038
1861	Northwestern Col.†	Naperville, Ill	Evangelical.	H. J. Kiekhoefer, A.M., Ph.D.	22	483	10,000
1851	Northwestern Univ. †	Evanston, Ill. (*h*)	Non-Sect.	Abram W. Harris, LL. D	358	3,997	126,051
1865	Northwestern Univ.†	Watertown, Wis	Lutheran	A. F. Ernst, Ph.D	12	278	7,641
1819	Norwich University	Northfield, Vt	Non-Sect	Chas. H. Spooner, LL. D	14	180	13,000
1833	Oberlin College † (*y*)	Oberlin, O	Non-Sect	Henry C. King, D. D	129	1,848	177,070
1887	Occidental College †	Los Angeles, Cal.	Presbyter'n	John W. Baer, LL. D	33	400	7,000
1871	Ohio Northern Un.†	Ada, O	Meth. Epis.	Rev. Albert E. Smith, D.D.	30	1,643	5,000
1870	Ohio State Univ.†	Columbus, O	Non-Sect	W. O. Thompson, D.D., LL.D.	175	2,277	73,633
1804	Ohio University† (*y*)	Athens, O	Undenom'l.	Alston Ellis, Ph. D., LL.D.	55	1,386	27,500
1841	Ohio Wesleyan Univ.†	Delaware, O	Meth. Epis.	Rev. Herbert Welch, D. D.	124	1,286	55,000

Organized.	Colleges—Table One. For explanation of signs, see page 320.	Location.	Denominational Control.	President or Chairman of Faculty.	Instructors.*	Students*	Volumes in Library
1844	Olivet College†	Olivet, Mich.	Non-Sect.	E. G. Lancaster, Ph. D.	24	283	32,000
1885	Oregon Agri. Col.†	Corvallis, Ore	Non-Sect.	Wm. J. Kerr, D. Sc.	80	1,156	10,000
1903	Oriental College†	Alexandria, Va.	Non-Sect.	Helmut P. Holler, Ph. D.	40	120	3,000
1865	Ottawa Univ.†	Ottawa, Kan	Baptist	Rev. S. E. Price	20	434	5,000
1847	Otterbein Univers'y.†	Westerville, O.	U. Brethren.	L. Bookwalter, LL.D., D. D.	26	551	12,200
1886	Ouachita College†	Arkadelphia, Ark.	Baptist	Henry Sims Hartzog, LL. D.	30	400	9,500
1849	Pacific University†	Forest Grove, Ore.	Congregat'l.	Wm. N. Ferrin, A.M., LL.D	23	230	14,900
1875	Park College†	Parkville, Mo.	Presbyter'n	Lowell M. McAfee, LL. D.	25	420	15,000
1887	Parker College†	Winnebago, Minn.	Free Baptist	E. W. Van Aken, A. M.	9	....	3,500
1875	Parsons College†	Fairfield, Iowa	Presbyter'n	Willis E Parsons, D. D.	20	240	7,200
1874	Peabody Col.† (*g*)	Nashville, Tenn.	Non-Sect.	James D. Porter, LL.D.	32	587	20,000
1873	Penn College†	Oskaloosa, Iowa.	Friends	A. Rosenberger, A.B., LL.B.	18	221	4,800
1869	Pennsylvania College‡	Pittsburgh, Pa	Undenom'l.	H. D. Lindsay, D. D.	19	70	3,400
1832	Pennsylvania College†	Gettysburg, Pa.	Lutheran.	S. G. Hefelbower, D. D.	19	312	30,000
1858	Penna. Military Col.	Chester, Pa.	Non-Sect.	Charles E. Hyatt	14	138	2,000
1855	Penna. State College†.	State College, Pa.	Non-Sect.	Edwin E. Sparks	120	1,200	30,050
1877	Philander Smith Col.†	Little Rock, Ark.	Meth. Epis.	Rev. James M. Cox, D.D.	24	677	3,500
1854	Polytechnic Institute.	Brooklyn, N. Y.	Non-Sect.	Fred'k W. Atkinson, Ph. D.	38	815	8,500
1887	Pomona College†	Claremont, Cal.	Undenom'l.	Geo. A. Gates, D.D., LL. D.	38	507	11,000
1904	Potomac University†	Washington, D. C.	Undenom'l.	Ernest W. Porter, Ph.D.	18	210	5,000
1887	Pratt Institute†	Brooklyn, N. Y.	Non-Sect.	Charles M. Pratt, A. M.	134	3,688	92,000
1880	Presbyterian Col.†	Clinton, S. C.	Presbyter'n	Robert Adams, D. D.	8	117	2,000
1904	Presbyterian Col.†	Eustis, Fla.	Presbyter'n	Rev. A. H. Jolly	8	60	1,000
1812	Princeton Theol. Sem.	Princeton, N. J.	Presbyter'n	F. L. Patton, D.D., LL.D.	16	154	81,000
1746	Princeton University.	Princeton, N. J.	Non-Sect.	Woodrow Wilson, LL.D, LtD	163	1,301	342 000
1868	Pritchett College†	Glasgow, Mo.	Non-Sect.	U. S. Hall, A. B.	10	120	2,000
1871	Proseminar College	Elmhurst, Ill.	Evangelical	Rev. D. Irion, D. D.	8	137	2,056
1874	Purdue University†	Lafayette, Ind.	Non-Sect.	W. E. Stone, LL. D.	141	2,089	20,000
1879	Radcliffe College (*l*)	Cambridge, Mass.	Non-Sect.	Le Baron R. Briggs, LL. D.	113	427	22,671
1830	Randolph-Macon Col.	Ashland, Va.	Methodist.	R. E. Blackwell, A.M., LL.D.	15	140	12,000
1893	" Woman's Col.	Lynchburg, Va.	Ind'pd't Bd.	Wm. W. Smith, A.M., LL.D.	34	413	7,000
1824	Rensselaer Poly. Inst.	Troy, N. Y.	Non-Sect.	Palmer C. Ricketts, C. E.	42	651	8,300
1832	Richmond College†	Richmond, Va.	Baptist	F W Boatwright, M.A., LL.D.	18	321	16,121
1876	Rio Grande College†	Rio Grande, O.	Free Bapt.	Rev. J. M. Davis, D.D., Ph.D.	11	169	3,400
1850	Ripon College†	Ripon, Wis	Non-Sect.	R. C. Hughes, A.M., D.D.	23	279	18,169
1853	Roanoke College	Salem, Va.	Lutheran.	J. A. Morehead, A.M., D.D.	16	206	24,000
1885	Roch. A.& M. Inst† (*c*).	Rochester, N. Y.	Non-Sect.	L. P. Ross (Pres. Bd. Direct.).	60	3,348	2,010
1850	Rochester Theol. Sem.	Rochester, N. Y.	Baptist	Rev. A. H. Strong, D. D.	12	141	35,619
1856	Rock Hill College	Ellicott City, Md.	R. Catholic.	Rev. Bro. Abraham, F. S. C.	18	173	9,000
1847	Rockford College‡	Rockford, Ill.	Non-Sect.	Julia H. Gulliver, Ph. D.	30	211	5,000
1885	Rollins College†	Winter Park, Fla.	Non-Sect.	W. F. Blackman, Ph. D.	20	200	3,000
1883	Rose Poly. Inst.	Terre Haute, Ind.	Non-Sect.	C. Leo Mees, Ph.D.	21	230	12,000
1766	Rutgers College	N. Brunswick, N. J	Non-Sect.	Rev. W. H. S. Demarest D. D.	40	310	57,025
1880	Sacred Heart College	Pra. Du Chien, Wis	R. Catholic.	Rev. Jos. Spaeth, S. J.	22	136	13,000
1870	Scotia Seminary‡§	Concord, N. C.	Presbyter'n	Rev. D. J. Satterfield, D. D.	19	294	3,240
1856	Seton Hall College	South Orange, N. J.	R. Catholic.	Rev. James F. Mooney, D.D.	17	208	25,000
1865	Shaw University†§	Raleigh, N. C.	Baptist	Charles F. Meserve, LL. D.	33	516	5,040
1877	Shorter College‡	Rome, Ga.	Baptist	Thomas J. Simmons	30	250	5,000
1827	Shurtleff College†	Upper Alton, Ill.	Baptist.	J. D. S. Riggs, Ph.D., L.H.D.	15	175	13,000
1899	Simmons College‡	Boston, Mass.	Non-Sect.	H. Lefavour, Ph. D., LL. D.	63	565	8,600
1867	Simpson College† (*y*)	Indianola, Iowa	Meth. Epis.	Charles E. Shelton, A. M.	22	929	5,103
1875	Smith College‡	N'hampton, Mass.	Undenom'l.	L. Clark Seelye, D. D., LL.D.	117	1,567	27,500
1859	S'th'n Bap. Th. Sem.†.	Louisville, Ky.	Baptist	E. Y. Mullins, D.D., LL.D.	9	276	22,500
1856	Southern University†.	Greensboro', Ala.	Meth. Ep. S.	Rev. S. M. Hosmer, D. D.	12	180	8,500
1891	S'th'n N'm'l Uni.† (*y*)	Huntington, Tenn.	Non-Sect.	W. R. Richardson, A. M.	20	300	10,000
1875	Southwe'n Pres. Univ.	Clarksville, Tenn.	Presbyter'n	Wm. Dinwiddie (Vice-Chan)	12	118	8,000
1885	Southwest Kansas C.†	Winfield, Kan	Meth. Epis.	F. E. Mossman	30	505	4,000
1830	Spring Hill College (*y*)	Mobile, Ala.	R. Catholic.	F. X. Twellmeyer, S. J.	28	231	30,000
1865	State Univ. of Ky.†.	Lexington, Ky.	Non-Sect.	James K. Patterson, LL. D.	60	678	7,114
1847	State Univ. of Iowa†.	Iowa City, Iowa	Non-Sect.	George E. MacLean, LL.D.	160	2,815	65,000
1879	State Un. of Ky.†§	Louisville, Ky.	Baptist	Rev. Wm. T. Amiger, A.M.	47	288	1,000
1903	St. Angela College‡	New Rochelle, N. Y	R. Catholic.	Rev. M. C. O'Farrell, D.D.	..	290	3,500
1889	St. Anselm's College.	Manchester, N. H.	R. Catholic.	Rev. Hilary Pfraengle, D. D.	25	135	5,500
1891	St. Bede College (*y*)	Peru, Ill.	R. Catholic.	Rt. Rev. L. Schnerr, O. S. B.	16	176	8,000
1858	St. Benedict's College.	Atchison, Kan.	R. Catholic.	Rev. Innocent Wolf, O.S.B.	21	250	17,000
1848	St. Charles College	Ellicott City, Md.	R. Catholic.	Rev. F. X. McKenny, A.M.	18	200	15,000
1871	Stevens Inst. of Tech.	Hoboken, N. J.	Non-Sect.	A. C. Humphreys, Sc.D. LL.D	35	390	9,000
1847	St. Francis Xavier C.	Manh'n Boro. N. Y.	R. Catholic.	Rev. Thos. J. McCluskey, S. J	42	560	125,000
1784	St. John's College	Annapolis, Md.	Non-Sect.	Thomas Fell, Ph. D., LL.D.	13	180	10,000
1866	St. John's College	Washington, D. C.	R. Catholic.	Bro. Germanus, F. S. C.	12	140	5,000
1857	St. John's University.	Collegeville, Minn.	R. Catholic.	Rev. Peter Engel, Ph. D.	33	334	25,000
1858	St. Lawrence Univ.†	Canton, N. Y.	Non-Sect.	Rev. Almon Gunnison, D. D.	36	539	35,000
1818	St. Louis University	St. Louis, Mo.	R. Catholic.	John P. Frieden	180	954	59,000
1848	St. Mary's College	St. Mary's, Kan.	R. Catholic.	Rev. A. A. Breen, S. J.	43	426	21,000
1821	St. Mary's College	St. Mary, Ky.	R. Catholic.	Rev. M. Jaglowicz, C. R.	12	140	6,000
1874	St. Olaf College†	Northfield, Minn.	Lutheran	Rev. John N. Kildahl	29	532	6,800
1860	St. Stephen's College.	Annandale, N. Y.	Prot. Epis.	Geo. B. Hopson, D.D.	9	47	18,850
1865	St. Vincent's College.	Los Angeles, Cal.	R. Catholic.	Rev. Jos. S. Glass, D.D.	29	350	5,000
1858	Susquehanna Univ.†.	Selinsgrove, Pa.	Lutheran.	Rev. Chas. T. Aikens, A. M.	22	267	10,000
1869	Swarthmore Col.†	Swarthmore, Pa.	Friends	Joseph Swain, M.S., LL.D.	36	331	34,000
1870	Syracuse University†.	Syracuse, N. Y.	Non-Sect.	Rev. J. R. Day, S.T.D., LL.D.	220	3,300	90,000
1857	Tabor College†	Tabor, Iowa	Congregat'l.	....	13	130	14,650
1867	Talladega College† (*c*).	Talladega, Ala.	Congregat'l.	J. M. P. Metcalf	34	613	10,000

Organized.	Colleges—Table One. For explanation of signs, see page 320.	Location.	Denominational Control.	President or Chairman of Faculty.	Instructors.*	Students.*	Volumes in Library
1883	Tarkio College †	Tarkio, Mo	Un. Presb.	Rev. J. A. Thompson, D.D.	26	317	2,677
1846	Taylor University†	Upland, Ind	Meth. Epis.	Monroe Vayhinger, D.D.	17	177	6,000
1888	Teachers' College†	Manh'n Boro, N.Y.	Non-Sect.	Jas. E. Russell, Ph.D. (Dean)	d87	896	37,021
1884	Temple College†	Philadelphia, Pa.	Undenom'l.	Rus. H. Conwell, D.D., LL.D.	212	3,475	5,000
1893	Texas Christian Un. †	Waco, Tex	Disciples	Clinton Lockhart, A.M., PhD	31	400	5,000
1891	Throop Poly. Inst. †	Pasadena, Cal	Non-Sect.	James A. B. Scherer, Ph.D.	40	407	4,000
1894	Tome Institute†	Port Deposit, Md.	Non-Sect.	T. S. Baker, Ph. D.	45	532	11,877
1798	Transylvania Univ.	Lexington, Ky	Non-Sect.	Richard H. Crossfield	46	1,129	16,000
1823	Trinity College	Hartford, Ct	Non-Sect.	F. S. Luther, LL. D.	22	217	56,000
1900	Trinity College‡	Washington, D. C.	R. Catholic.	Sister Julia	25	120	13,700
1859	Trinity College †	Durham, N. C.	Meth. Ep. S.	John C. Kilgo, D. D., A. M.	36	430	40,000
1869	Trinity University†	Waxahachie, Tex.	Presbyter'n	Sam'l L. Thornbeak, LL. D.	16	230	2,500
1884	Tri-State College†(*p*).	Angola, Ind	Non-Sect.	C. M. Sniff, A. M.	23	1,000	4,000
1852	Tufts College†	Medford, Mass. (*e*)	Non-Sect.	F. W. Hamilton, D. D., LL. D	209	1,090	55,000
1845	Tulane Univ. †	New Orleans, La.	Non-Sect.	Edwin B. Craighead, LL. D.	163	1,782	49,360
1881	Tuskegee Institute†§.	Tuskegee, Ala	Non-Sect.	Booker T. Washington, A.M.	166	1,621	13,000
1859	Union Chris'n Col. †	Merom, Ind	Christian	O. B. Whitaker	13	148	3,000
1891	Union College†	College View, Neb.	Adventist	Chas. C. Lewis, M.S.	30	420	2,000
1795	Union College	Schenectady, N. Y.	Undenom'l.	Rev. G. Alexander, D. D.	31	322	39,840
1836	Union Theol. Sem. †	Manh'n Boro., N. Y	Non-Sect.	Francis Brown, D.D.	21	165	86,245
1845	Union University†	Jackson, Tenn	Baptist	John W. Conger, A.M., LL.D	18	278	9 000
1908	University College	Oak Hill, O.	Non-Sect.	Geo. J. Jones, D.D.	5	351	35,000
1831	Univ. of Alabama†	Tuscaloosa, Ala.‡‡	Non-Sect.	John W. Abercrombie, LL. D.	44	573	20,000
1891	Univ. of Arizona†	Tucson, Ariz.	Non-Sect.	K. C. Babcock, Ph. D., A. M.	35	237	13,000
1871	Univ. of Arkansas†	Fay'teville, Ark. (*g*	Non-Sect.	John N. Tillman, LL.D.	75	1,800	15,000
1860	Univ. of California†	Berkeley, Cal	Non-Sect.	Benj. Ide Wheeler, LL.D.	389	3,201	173,000
1867	Univ. of Chattanooga†	Ch't'n'ga, Tenn.††	Meth. Epis.	Rev. J. H. Race, D.D	58	632	9,500
1892	Univ. of Chicago†	Chicago, Ill.	Non-Sect. (*l*)	Harry P. Judson	303	5,038	473,175
1870	Univ. of Cin'nati† (*y*).	Cincinnati, O.	Non-Sect.	Chas. Wm. Dabney, LL.D.	135	1,374	100,000
1877	Univ. of Colorado†	Boulder, Col	Non-Sect.	Jas. H. Baker, M. A., LL. D.	133	1,150	45,000
1864	Univ. of Denver†	Univ. Park, Col.	Meth. Epis.	H. A. Buchtel, D. D., LL. D.	170	1,324	10,000
1905	Univ. of Florida	Gainesville, Fla.	Non-Sect.	Andrew Sledd, LL. D.	16	90	5,000
1785	Univ. of Georgia (*n*)	Athens, Ga	Non-Sect.	D. C. Barrow, A.M.	199	3,375	30,000
1892	Univ. of Idaho†	Moscow, Idaho	Non-Sect.	James A. MacLean, Ph. D.	46	400	12,696
1867	Univ. of Illinois† (*y*)	Urbana, Ill. (*r*)	Non-Sect.	E. J. James, Ph. D., LL. D.	430	4,600	101,481
1864	Univ. of Kansas†	Lawrence, Kan.	Non-Sect.	F. Strong, A. B., A.M., Ph. D.	117	2,250	60,000
1837	Univ. of Louisville†	Louisville, Ky	Non-Sect.	John Patterson, (*aa*)	160	900	5,000
1865	Univ. of Maine †	Orono, Me	Non-Sect.	G. E. Fellows, Ph. D., LL.D.	70	874	40,000
1837	Univ. of Michigan†	Ann Arbor, Mich.	Non-Sect.	James B. Angell, LL.D.	360	5,013	241,128
1869	Univ. of Minnesota†	Minneapolis, Minn	Non Sect.	Cyrus Northrop, LL.D.	345	4,600	118,000
1839	Univ. of Missouri†	Columbia, Mo. (*u*).	Non-Sect.	Albert R. Hill	202	2,536	88,063
1895	Univ. of Montana†	Missoula, Mont.	Non-Sect.	Clyde A. Duniway, Ph. D.	30	177	18,000
1785	Univ. of Nashville†	Nashville, Tenn.	Non-Sect.		66	1,457	20,000
1869	Univ. of Nebraska†	Lincoln, Neb	Non-Sect.		156	3,237	82,000
1886	Univ. of Nevada†	Reno, Nev	Non-Sect.	J. E. Stubbs, D.D., LL.D., M.A	30	276	15,038
1889	Univ. of N. Mexico†	Albuquerque, N.M	Non-Sect.	W. G. Tight, Ph.D.	16	158	8,000
1789	Univ. of N. Carolina	Chapel Hill, N. C.	Non-Sect.	Francis P. Venable, Ph. D.	94	790	50,000
1883	Univ. of N. Dakota †.	Grand Forks, N.D.	Undenom'l.	Webster Merrifield, M.A.	61	861	30,000
1840	Univ. of Notre Dame.	Notre Dame, Ind.	R. Catholic.	Rev. J. Cavanaugh, C.S.C.	80	920	55,000
1892	Univ. of Oklahoma†	Norman, Okla	Non-Sect.	Rev. A. G. Evans	57	790	20,000
1878	Univ. of Oregon†	Eugene, Ore	Non-Sect.	Prince L. Campbell, B. A.	v40	v512	20,000
1851	Univ. of the Pac. † (*y*)	San José, Cal	Meth. Epis.	M. S. Cross (Act. Pres.)	22	261	9,000
1740	Univ. of Penna. (*z*)	Philadelphia, Pa.	Non-Sect.	Chas. C. Harrison, LL.D.	435	4,500	285,000
1787	Univ. of Pittsburgh†.	Pittsburgh, Pa.	Non-Sect.	Sam'l B. McCormick, Chan.	150	1,138	10,000
1903	Univ. of Porto Rico† (*y*)	Rio Piedras, P. R.	Non-Sect.	E. G. Dexter, Ph. D. (Chan.)	18	419	3,000
1903	Univ. of Puget Sound.	Tacoma, Wash.	Meth. Epis.	L. L. Benbow, A. B	19	385	5,000
1850	Univ. of Rochester†	Rochester, N. Y.	Non-Sect.	Rush Rhees, D. D., LL.D.	24	380	50,500
1880	Univ. of S. Cal. †	Los Angeles, Cal.	Meth. Epis.	Geo. F. Bovard, A. M., D. D.	199	1,470	18,800
1805	Univ. of S. Carolina †	Columbia, S. C.	Undenom'l.	S. C. Mitchell, Ph.D., LL.D.	24	280	40,000
1882	Univ. of S. Dakota†	Vermillion, S. Dak.	Non-Sect.	Franklin B. Gault, Ph. D.	45	424	13,303
1868	Univ. of the South	Sewanee, Tenn.	Prot. Epis.	B. L. Wiggins, M. A., LL.D.	34	456	28,590
1794	Univ. of Tennessee† (*c*)	Knoxville, Tenn.	Non-Sect.	Brown Ayres, Ph.D., LL.D.	106	755	27,546
1883	Univ. of Texas†	Austin, Tex. (*s*)	Non-Sect.	Sidney E. Mezes, Ph.D.	85	2,462	63 445
1850	Univ. of Utah†	Salt Lake City, U.	Non-Sect.	J. T. Kingsbury, Ph.D., D.Sc	60	755	28,275
1791	Univ. of Vermont†	Burlington, Vt.	Non-Sect.	Mat. H. Buckham, D.D.	80	497	76,412
1825	Univ. of Virginia	Charlottesville, Va	Non-Sect.	E. A. Alderman, D.C.L. LL.D	72	788	70,000
1862	Univ. of Washington†	Seattle, Wash.	Non-Sect.	Thos. F. Kane, Ph. D.	103	1,703	36,387
1848	Univ. of Wisconsin†	Madison, Wis.	Non-Sect.	Chas. R. Van Hise, Ph.D.	395	4,500	135,000
1868	Univ. of Wooster†	Wooster, O.	Presbyter'n	Rev. Louis E. Holden, D. D.	38	661	29,000
1887	Univ. of Wyoming†	Laramie, Wyo.	Non-Sect.	Chas. O. Merica, LL.D.	40	230	32,000
1857	Upper Iowa Univ. †	Fayette, Iowa	Meth. Epis.		18	504	14,000
1893	Upsala College†	Kenilworth, N. J.	Lutheran	Rev. L. H. Beck, Ph. D.	9	69	1,500
1850	Urbana University†	Urbana, O.	N. Jerusa'm	Paul H. Seymour, (Act. Pres.	8	54	15,000
1869	Ursinus College†	Collegeville, Pa.	Non-Sect.	Rev. A. E. Keigwin, D.D.	20	183	14,000
1802	U. S. Mil. Academy.	West Point, N. Y.	Non-Sect.	Col. H. L. Scott, U.S.A. Supt.	90	533	72,438
1845	U. S. Naval Academy	Annapolis, Md.	Non-Sect.	Capt. C. J. Badger, U.S.N. S'pt	89	850	49,300
1890	Utah Agri. College †	Logan, Utah	Non-Sect.	John A. Widtsoe, A.M., Ph.D	50	882	15,920
1873	Valparaiso Univ. †	Valparaiso, Ind.	Non-Sect.	Henry B. Brown, A.M.	176	5,367	10,000
1872	Vanderbilt Univ. †	Nashville, Tenn.	Meth. Ep. S.	J. H. Kirkland, LL.D., D.C.L.	115	902	30,000
1861	Vassar College‡	Poughkeepsie, N.Y	Non-Sect.	Jas. M. Taylor, D.D., LL.D.	97	1,011	63,000
1842	Villanova.	Villanova, Pa.	R. Catholic.	Rev. L. A. Delurey, D. D.	24	375	10,000
1806	Vincennes Univ. †	Vincennes, Ind.	Non-Sect.	Horace Ellis, A. M., Ph. D.	16	318	2,200

Organized.	Colleges—Table One. For explanation of signs, see page 320.	Location.	Denominational Control.	President or Chairman of Faculty.	Instructors.*	Students*	Volumes in Library
1903	Virginia Chris. Col. †	Lynchburg, Va	Disciples	Josephus Hopwood, A.M	15	228	1,200
1839	Virginia Mil. Inst	Lexington, Va	Non-Sect	E. W. Nichols	21	340	15,000
1872	Virginia Poly. Inst.	Blacksburg, Va	Non-Sect	P. B. Barringer, M.D., LL.D.	56	553	10,000
1832	Wabash College	Crawf'rdsville, Ind	Non-Sect	G. L. Mackintosh, D. D	23	301	45,000
1833	Wake Forest College.	Wake Forest, N. C.	Baptist	Wm. L. Poteat, LL. D	32	371	19,000
1866	Walden Univ. §	Nashville, Tenn	Meth. Epis.	Rev. J. A. Kumler, A.M., D.D.	70	925	6,785
1865	Washburn College†	Topeka, Kan	Congregat'l,	Frank K. Sanders, D.D	98	711	15,000
1802	Wash. & Jefferson Col.	Washington, Pa	Non-Sect	Rev. Jas. D. Moffat, D. D	30	442	20,000
1749	Wash. & Lee Univ	Lexington, Va	Non-Sect.	Geo. H. Denny, LL. D., Ph.D.	36	560	50,000
1794	Wash. & Tusc'l'm Col. †	Greenville, Tenn	Presbyter'n	Rev. C. O. Gray, D. D	19	298	8,000
1782	Washington Col. †	Chestertown, Md.	Non-Sect.	James W. Cain. LL. D	11	138	3,000
1795	Washington College†.	Wash'n Col., Tenn	Non-Sect	Rev. Jas. T. Cooter, D. D	9	138	4,000
1890	Wash. State Col. †	Pullman, Wash	Non-Sect	Enoch A. Bryan, LL.D	97	1,446	17,500
1853	Washington Univ. †	St. Louis, Mo	Non-Sect	David F. Houston (Chan)	269	2,093	60,000
1850	Waynesburg College†	Waynesburg, Pa	Presbyter'n	Rev. Wm. M. Hudson, Ph.D.	21	301	5,000
1875	Wellesley College‡	Wellesley, Mass	Non-Sect.	Caroline Hazard, M.A., Lit. D	100	1,273	63,088
1868	Wells College‡	Aurora, N. Y	Non-Sect.	Rev. G. M. Ward, D.D., LL.D.	24	177	16,600
1836	Wesleyan Fem, Col(y)	Macon, Ga	Meth. Ep. S.	Du Pont Guerry	33	474	3,000
1831	Wesleyan Univ. †	Middletown, Ct.	Meth. Epis.	Wm. A. Shanklin, D. D	34	320	80,000
1855	West. Col. for Women	Oxford, O	Non-Sect	John G. Newman	26	245	13,606
1867	West. Maryland C. †	Westminster, Md.	Meth. Prot.	Rev. Thomas H. Lewis, D. D.	23	235	6,500
1826	West. Reserve Univ.(o	Cleveland, O	Non-Sect.	Charles F. Thwing, D. D	188	914	93,858
1825	Western Theol. Sem.	N. S. Pittsb'gh, Pa.	Presbyter'n	Rev. James A. Kelso, D.D.	10	64	34,000
1865	Westfield College†	Westfield, Ill	U. Brethren	Rev. B. F. Dougherty, A. M.	12	150	3,000
1900	West Lafayette Col. †	West Lafayette, O.	Meth. Prot.	James H. Straughn, A. M.	9	67	2,000
1849	Westminster College	Fulton, Mo	Presbyter'n	David R. Kerr, Ph. D., D. D.	13	183	6,375
1852	Westminster Col. †	N. Wilmington, Pa	United Pres.	Robert McW. Russell, D.D.	23	291	8,000
1867	West Virginia Univ. †	Morgant'n, W. Va	Non-Sect.	D. B. Purinton, Ph.D., LL.D.	78	1,208	35,644
1860	Wheaton College†	Wheaton, Ill	Congregat'l	Charles A. Blanchard, D. D.	20	280	4,500
1882	Whitman College†	Walla Walla, Wn.	Undenom'l.	Rev. S. B. L. Penrose, D. D.	37	370	15,255
1883	Whitworth College†	Tacoma, Wash	Presbyter'n.	Rev. B. H. Kroeze, A. M.	22	479	7,900
1856	Wilberforce Un. †§	Wilberforce, O	Meth. Epis.	Wm. S. Scarborough, LL. D.	32	350	10,000
1873	Wiley University†§	Marshall, Tex	Meth. Epis.	Rev. M. W. Dogan, Ph.D.	25	640	6,000
1844	Willamette Univ. †	Salem, Ore	Meth. Epis.	Fletcher Homan, A M., D.D.	45	420	3,500
1693	William & Mary C.	Williamsburg, Va.	Non-Sect	Lyon G. Tyler, M. A., LL. D.	22	238	20,000
1849	William Jewell Col.	Liberty, Mo	Baptist	John P. Greene, D. D., LL. D.	40	528	20,000
1793	Williams College	Williamst'n, Mass	Non-Sect	Harry A. Garfield, LL. D	57	485	62,080
1908	William Smith Col. ‡.	Geneva, N. Y	Non-Sect	L. C. Stewardson, LL. D	22	230	49,596
1875	Wilmington Col. †(y).	Wilmington, O	Friends	Albert J. Brown, A. M.	11	150	3,500
1869	Wilson College‡(y)	Chambersburg, Pa	Presbyter'n	M. H. Reaser, Ph.D., A. M.	35	344	8,000
1845	Wittenberg College †.	Springfield, O	Lutheran	Chas. G. Heckert, D.D.	38	525	16,000
1854	Wofford College	Spartanburg, S. C.	Luth. Meth.	Henry N. Snyder, M. A.	12	287	17,484
1885	Woman's College‡	Baltimore, Md	Meth. Epis.	Eugene A. Noble, S. T. D.	25	341	10,388
1865	Worcester Poly. Inst.	Worcester, Mass.	Non-Sect	E. A. Engler, Ph.D., LL.D	45	487	12,000
1701	Yale University	New Haven, Ct.	Non-Sect	Arthur T. Hadley, LL.D	400	3,450	550,000
1882	Yankton College†	Yankton, S. Dak.	Congregat'l.	Rev. Henry K. Warren, M.A.	24	382	8,000
1890	York College†	York, Neb	U. Brethren.	Wm. E. Schell, A. M., D. D.	17	564	2,000

TABLE TWO—COMMENCEMENT DAYS, GRADUATES, ETC.

Colleges. For explanation of signs, see page 320.	Commencement Day, 1909.	Graduates since Organization.*	Alumni Living.*	Earliest Graduates Living.	Graduated.	Present Addresses.
Adelphi College†	June 17	600	....	Rudolph Seldner	1897	Brooklyn, N. Y.
Ag. & Mech. Col. of T.	June 8	628	591	....	....	....
Alabama Poly. Inst. †	June	....	....	....	....	....
Albion College†	June 23	1,400	....	....	....	....
Alfred University†	June 10	884	....	Mrs. M. G. Stillman	1845	New London, Ct.
Allegheny College†	June 17	1,530	1,060	William Reynolds	1837	Meadville, Pa.
Alma College†	June 17	381	360	....	....	....
American Int'l Col. †	June	800	..	....	....	....
Amherst College	June 30	4,000	2,800	James L. Batchelder	1840	Chicago, Ill.
Andover Theo. Sem.	June 23	2,169	....	....	....	....
Antioch College†	June 16	262	210	John B. Weston	1857	Defiance, O.
Arkansas College†	June 8	164	146	Class of '76, 7 graduates living	by	last report.
Armour Inst. Tech.	May 27	435	429	Class of '97, all living by last	re	port.
Atlanta University†	May 27	590	517	Several of Class '76 living	by	last report.
Auburn Theol. Sem.	May 6	1,666	965	H. M. Lane	1843	Jersey City.
Augsburg Seminary	May 6	518	....	....	....	....
Augustana College †.	May 27	1,864	....	Dr. A. W. Dahlsten	1861	Lindsborg, Kan
Baker University†	June 5	600	580	....	....	....
Barnard College ‡	June 2	703	....	....	....	....
Bates College†	June 4	1,490	1,411	Joel S. Parsons	1867	Minneapolis, Minn.
Baylor University†	June 20	896	752	O. H. Leland	1856	McGregor, Tex.
Beloit College†	June 23	1,006	875	S. D. Peet	1851	Chicago.
Berea College†	June 9	....	....	George L. Pigg	1873	Wichita, Kan.
Bethany Col. (Kan.)†	May 27	974	....	Erick Glad	1892	Council Bluffs, Ia.
Bethany C. (W. Va.)†	June 9	11,000	8,000	J. W. McGarvey	1844	Lexington, Ky.
Blackburn College†	June 9	298	270	Rev. Harlan C. Carson	1870	Scotland, S. D.

COLLEGES—TABLE TWO. For explanation of signs, see page 320.	Commencement Day, 1909.	Graduates since Organization.*	Alumni Living.*	Earliest Graduates Living.	Graduated.	Present Addresses.
Boston College(u)	June 24	586	523	Class of '72, 6 graduates living	by	last report.
Boston University†	June 2	7,077	....	Rev. John B. Foote, D.D.	1850	Syracuse, N. Y.
Bowdoin College	June 24	5,654	2,728	Rev. Wm. W. Rand	1837	New York City.
Brigham Young Col.†	May 28	397	385	....	....	....
Brown University	June 16	6,100	3,500	Wm. H. Potter	1836	Kingston, R. I.
Bryn Mawr College‡	June 3	959	947	....	....	....
Buchtel College†	June 16	274	341	Mrs. S. C. Cole	1873	Akron, O.
Bucknell Univ. †	June 23	1,267	....	Rev. J. M. Lyons	1851	Philadelphia, Pa.
Butler College†	June 17	596	519	Mrs. A. M. Atkinson	1856	Indianapolis, Ind.
Canisius College	June 21	163	125	Rev. Dennis Reilly	1878	Buffalo, N. Y.
Carleton College†	June 9	662	611	James J. Dow	1874	Faribault, Minn.
Carson&N'man Col.†	May 27	....	....	W. W. Moody	1857	Sevierville, Tenn.
Carthage College†	May 27	246	226	Rev. J. M. Cromer, D. D.	1875	Kansas City, Mo.
Case Sc. Ap'l. Science	....	780	763	....	...	....
Cedarville College†	June 3	96	95	C. C. Morton	1897	Cedarville, Ohio.
Central Col. † (Mo.)	June 6-9	300	280	E. R. Barton	1861	Denver, Col.
Central Univ. † (Ia.)	....	200	....	Mrs. Frances G. B. Cutler	1863	Carthage, Ill.
Central Univ. (Ky.)	June 9	4,000	....	Rev. J. T. Lapsley	1839	Danville, Ky.
Cen. Wesleyan Col. †	June 6	525	489	Prof. J. H. Frick, A. M.	1870	Warrenton, Mo.
Charleston College	June 15	508	250	Chas. P. Bolles	1844	Washington, D. C.
Christian Univ. †	June 10	652	520	A. B. Chenoweth	1858	San Marcus, Tex.
Claflin Univ. †(u)	May 16	741	....	Dr. Wm. L. Bulkley	1882	Ridgefield Park, N. J.
Clemson Agri. Col	June 8	548	542	L. A. Sease	1896	Clemson Col., S. C.
Colby College†	June 30	1,589	1,131	William Mathews	1835	Boston, Mass.
Colgate University	June 24	5,011	1,310	....	....	....
College City of N. Y.	June 16	3,128	2,857	George W. Birdsall	1853	New York City, N. Y.
Col. of St. Elizabeth	June 15	200	180	Margaret Bogan	1865	Newark, N. J.
Colorado College†	June 16	378	369	F. W. Tuckerman, P. Hallack	1882	Los Angeles and N. Y.
Columbia University	June 2	20,869	16,874	T. B. Gilford	1835	New York City, N. Y.
Concordia College	Sept. 8	....	2,000	Rev. J. F. Biltz	1848	Concordia, Mo.
Cornell College†	June 17	1,305	1,198	Matthew Cavanagh	1858	Iowa City, Iowa.
Cornell University†	June 17	....	....	....	....	....
Cotner University†	June 10	298	....	Ellen B. Atwater	1891	St. Louis, Mo.
Creighton Univ	June 21	....	....	James C. Kinsler, LL. B.	1891	Omaha, Neb.
Cumberland Un.†(u)	June 4	3,519	398	Nathan Green	1845	Lebanon, Tenn.
Dakota Wesley. Un.†	June 10	402	498	Rev. O. E. Murray	1888	Murdo, S. Dak.
Dartmouth College	June 30	7,370	3,708	Rev. Jos. Munroe	1837	Bellingham, Mass.
Davidson College	May 26	2,000	1,400	Wm. P. Bynum	1842	Charlotte. N. C.
Delaware College	June 16	527	....	Henry S. Couden	1842	Aiken, Md.
Denison University†	June 17	797	540	Rev. Wm. Ashmore, D. D.	1845	Toledo, O.
DePauw University†	June 9	2,320	1,480	M. J. Durham	1844	Lexington, Ky.
Dickinson College†	June 9	4,907	2,277	Rev. John L. McKim	1830	Georgetown, Del.
Doane College†	June 30	286	270	Dan'l E. Tromble	1877	Collinsville, Ct.
Drake University†	June 16	3,200	3,100	James E. Denton	1882	Petaluma, Cal.
Drew Theol. Sem	May 20	1,400	....	James Boyd Brady	1869	Boston, Mass.
Drury College†	June 10	336	319	Mrs. Anna Conger	1875	Colorado City, Col.
Earlham College†	June 16	844	780	Luzena Thornburg	1862	Carthage, Ind.
Elmira College‡	June 9	639	....	....	....	....
Emory and H'y Col.	June 6-8	675	....	....	....	....
Emory College	June 9	1,532	....	Robert W. Lovett	1843	Georgia.
Emporia College†	....	233	224	William J. Coulson, LL. B.	1889	Fresno, Cal.
Erskine College †	June 1	786	541	J. F. Lee	1843	Anderson, S. C.
Fairmount College†	June 1	110	110	William S. Fleming, M. D.	1899	Arcada, Kan.
Fargo College†	June 16	64	64	Donald G. Colp	1896	Robbinsdale, Minn.
Findlay College †	June 17	102	95	Mrs. H. Van Kampen.	1889	Findlay, Ohio.
Fisk University†§	June 16	694	641	James D. Burrus	1875	Nashville, Tenn.
Fordham University	June 16	1,181	....	Augustine M. O'Neil	1849	New York City.
Franklin & Marshall	June 10	1,477	1,050	Rev. George L. Statey	1844	Green Village, Pa.
Franklin C. †(Ind.)(u)	June 14	....	....	*See note "h," on page 320.*		
General Theol. Sem	May 26	1,698	....	Rt. Rev. G. DeN. Gillespie, D.D	1840	Grand Rapids, Mich.
Georgetown College†	June 9	804	550	B. T. Blewitt, Andy Barnett	1846	Jennings, Mo., L'isv'le.
Georgetown Univ	June 3	4,833	....	Richard H. Clarke	1846	New York City.
Geo. Washington Un.	June 9	5,668	4,100	Francis M. Gunnell	1846	Washington, D. C.
Girard College	None	6,400	....	Rev. John T. Carpenter	1853	Philadelphia, Pa.
Greer College†(u)	July 30	319	300	C. E. Doty	1892	Charleston, Ill.
Grove City Col. †(u)	June 17	1,150	1,000	Rev. Samuel Dodds	1881	Grove City, Pa.
Guilford College†(u)	May 26	178	170	Jos. M. Dixon	1889	Missoula, Montana.
Gustavus Adolph†	May 27	759	750	Rev. L. P. Lundgren	1890	Hallock, Minn.
Hamline Univ†	June 9	....	....	Elizabeth A. Sorin	1859	Pasadena, Cal.
Hamilton College	June 24	2,858	1,543	Augustus L. Rhodes	1841	San Jose, Cal.
Hampton Inst†(c)(u)	....	1477	....	Class of '71, 4 graduates liv	ing	by last report.
Hanover College†	June 9	954	699	Edward W. Hawkins	1837	New Port, Ky.
Hartford The. Sem.†	May 26	644	450	Rev. S. F. Boem	1850	Philadelphia, Pa.
Harvard University	June 30	33,600	22,250	J. T. Coolidge	1881	Cambridge, Mass.
Haverford College	June 12	....	....	Anthony M. Kimber	1840	Germantown, Pa.
Hedding College†	June 17	268	240	M. Josephine Davis De Groot	1867	Macomb, Ill.
Heidelberg Univ. †	June 16	618	....	Rev. Geo. Z. Mechling, A. M.	1854	Hamilton, Ohio.
Hillsdale College†	June 17	1,142	800	Mrs. Eliza Scott Potter	1856	Los Angeles, Cal.
Hiram College†(u)	June 25	614	....	James M. Hurlburt	1869	Cleveland, Ohio.
Hiwassee College†	May 18	273	....	Wm. L. Eakin	1850	Chattanooga, Tenn.
Hobart College	June 16	1,530	807	Rev. Napoleon Barrows	1844	Short Hills, N. J.
Holy Cross College	June 17	1,091	905	Rev. P. F. Healy, G. H. Lloyd	1850	Philadelphia; Boston.

COLLEGES—TABLE TWO. For explanation of signs, see page 320.	Commencement Day, 1909.	Graduates since Organization.*	Alumni Living.*	Earliest Graduates Living.	Graduated.	Present Addresses.
Hope College†	June 16	390	....	William A. Shields	1866	Macomb, Ill.
Howard Univ.† (*d*)	May 26	2,587	2,587	James M. Gregory	1872	Bordentown, N. J.
Illinois College†	....	768	498	T. J. C. Fagg	1842	Louisiana, Mo.
Ill. Wesleyan Un.†	June 17	....	....	....	....	....
Indiana University †	June 23	4,187	3,215	Samuel C. Parks	1838	Kansas City, Mo.
Iowa College†	June 16	1,312	1,236	Class of '58, all living by last	rep	ort.
Iowa State Col.†	....	1,605	1,650	E. W. Stanton	1872	Ames, Iowa.
Iowa Wesley Un.†	June 17	771	580	Winfield Scott Maynes	1856	Council Bluffs, Iowa.
James Milliken Un.	June 15	78	62	Edward L. King	1905	Alton, Ill.
John B. Stetson U.†	June 1	....	....	....	....	....
Johns Hopkins Un(*g*)	June 8	2,179	2,115	....	....	....
Juniata College	June 17	523	....	Class of '79, 3 graduates liv	ing.	
Kansas Wesl. Univ.†	June 3	241	235	Rev. H. M. Mayo	1887	Denver, Col.
Kenyon College	June 23	....	1,200	Francis B. Meade	1834	Milwood, Va.
Knox College†	June 10	1,699	1,452	Wm. Barth; Geo. Bent	1849	S. Diego, Cal.; Chicago.
Knoxville College†§	June 10	340	....	W. J. Consler	1883	Knoxville, Tenn.
Lafayette Col. (Pa.)	June 24	2,380	1,916	Rev. Geo. D Stewart, D.D.	1845	Ft. Madison, Ia.
Lake Forest Univ.†	June 23	432	410	*See note "p," on page* 320.	1879	Los Angeles, Cal.
Lander College‡	June 1-2	186	171	Mrs. Ella C. Turner	1872	Greenwood, S. C.
Lawrence Univ.†	June 16	714	501	Rev. Henry Colman, D. D.	1857	Milwaukee, Wis.
Lebanon Valley Col.†	June 9	525	500	Mrs. M. W. Reitzel	1870	Chicago, Ill.
Lehigh University	June 9	1,817	1,695	Chas. E. Ronaldson, M. E.	1869	Philadelphia, Pa.
Leland Stanford, Jr.†	May 19	2,830	......	Several of class of '92		
Lenox College†	June 9	297	277	Ralph H. Kirk	1868	Cedar Rapids, Ia.
Liberty College‡(*u*)	June 4	....	....	....	....	....
Lincoln College	June 16	500	450	Serena Clay	1868	Lincoln, Ill.
Lincoln Mem'l Univ.	May 6	....	....	....	....	....
Lombard College†	June 3	450	350	W. W. Burrow	1856	Chicago, Ill.
Lou'na State Un.†(*u*)	June 3	412	....	Tilman L. Grimes	1869	Poland, La.
Loyola College	June 17	329	300	Edward F. Milholland, M. D.	1856	Baltimore, Md.
Manhattan College	June 15	815	723	Rev. J. P. McClancy, LL.D.	1866	Middletown, N. Y.
Marietta College†	June 9	940	600	George B. Bradley	1841	New Concord, O.
Marquette College	June 20	1058	970	Francis X. Bodden, A. M.	1888	Milwaukee, Wis.
Maryville Col.†	June 2	....	....	....	....	....
Mass. Agri. College†	June 23	700	650	Class of '71, 23 living by last	rep	ort.
Mass. Inst. Tech.†	June 8	4,127	3,945	Robert H. Richards	1868	Boston, Mass.
McKendree College†	June 10	754	....	Frederick Spier, A. M.	1845	St. Louis, Mo.
McMinnville Col.†	June 16	....	....	John H. Smith	1884	Astoria, Ore.
Miami University†	June 17	2,096	1,400	Chas. T. McCaughan, D.D.	1837	Winterset, Ia.
Mich. Agri. College†	June 23	....	....	A. F. Allen	1861	Vineland, Kan.
Middlebury College†	June 30	1,686	800	S. P. Giddings	1838	Washington, D. C.
Midland College†	June 2	250	100	Le Roy H. Kelsey	1891	St. Joseph, Mo.
Milligan College†	May 26	185	180	James A. Tate	1882	Shelbyville, Tenn.
Milton College†	June 17	317	278	Albert Salisbury	1870	Whitewater, Wis.
Miss. Ag. & Mech. Col.	May 29	....	....	....	....	....
Missouri Valley Col.†	May 27	609	......	May Caldwell (Mrs. C. J. Orr)	1890	St. Louis, Mo.
Monmouth College†	June 9	1,379	1,182	Mrs. Margaret F. Thompson.	1858	Monmouth, Ill.
Moore's Hill College†	June 17	400	360	Mrs. Jane Kahler	1858	San Fernando, Cal.
Morningside Col.†(*u*)	June 11	197	194	J. B. Trimble	1893	Kansas City, Mo.
Mt. Holyoke Col.‡	June 16	3,744	....	Mrs. W. S. Curtis	1839	Chicago, Ill.
Mt. St. Mary's Col.	June 18	1,500	....	Thomas E. Garvin	1844	Evansville, Ind.
Mt. Union College†	June 17	2,740	....	*See note "n," on page* 320.		
Muhlenberg College	June 15	658	605	Rev. John W. Rumple	1870	Brooklyn, N. Y.
Muskingum College†	June 17	600	480	A. M. Scott, Ph. D.	1851	New Concord, O.
Neb. Wesleyan Univ†	June 9	1,500	....	....	....	....
Newberry College†	June 10	......	....	Jas. E. Houseal	1869	Cedartown, Ga.
Newton Theol. Inst.	June 10	1,482	900	Rev. Jos. Monroe Rockwood.	1841	Bellingham, Mass.
New York Univ.	June 2	19,942	16,937	Henry B. Elliot, D. D.	1840	New York City, N. Y.
Niagara University	June 22	....	1,600	Rev. E. McCarty	1872	Brooklyn, N. Y.
N. Car. C. A. & M. Arts	May 26	424	415	....	....	....
Normal College ‡	June 24	12,000	....	....	....	....
Northwestern Col.†	June 17	664	631	B. Frank Dreisbach	1866	Circleville, Ohio.
Northw'n Un.† (Ill.)	....	10,000	9,000	....	....	....
Northw'n Un.†(Wis)	June 23	....	....	Rev. E. Tankow	1872	Caledonia, Minn.
Oberlin College†(*u*)	June 25	4,558	3,535	Samuel F. Porter	1836	Oberlin, Ohio.
Ohio Northern Uni.†	July 4	5,000	....	S. P. Grey	1874	Indianapolis, Ind.
Ohio State Univ.†(*u*)	June 24	2,159	....	Dr. Arthur Townshend	1878	New York City, N. Y.
Ohio University†	June 24	643	425	James M. Safford	1844	Dallas, Tex.
Ohio Wesleyan Un.†	June 17	3,695	3,119	William D. Godman	1846	Philadelphia, Pa
Olivet College†	June 16	700	625	Mrs. Griswold	1863	Vermontville, Mich.
Oregon Agri. Col.†	June 16	700	....	....	....	....
Oriental †	June 10	100	80	Rev. G. B. Riegel, D. D.	1906	E. Rochester, N. Y.
Ottawa Univ.† (*u*)	June 10	306	....	....	....	....
Otterbein Univ.†	June 9	796	....	Kate Winter Hanby	1857	Alhambra, Cal.
Ouachita College†	June 1	450	432	Frank P. Turner, A.B.	1888	Monticello, Ark.
Pacific University†	June 16	204	187	Harvey W. Scott	1863	Portland, Ore.
Park College†	June 24	666	631	Rev. W. T. Scott	1879	Cleone, Ore.
Parsons College†(*u*)	June 10	353	....	Class of '80, 11 graduates living	by	last report.
Penn College†	June 16	398	382	Linda Ninde Dorland	1875	Long Beach, Cal.
Pennsylvania Col.†	June 9	1,470	1,164	Rev. W. F. Eyster, D.D.	1839	Crete, Neb.
Penn. Col. for Wom'n	June 8	268	....	....	....	....
Penn. Military Col.	June 16	480	....	R. K. Carter	1867	Baltimore, Md.
Penn. State Col.†	June 16	1,174	1,131	John N. Banks	1861	Indiana, Pa.

Colleges—Table Two. For explanation of signs, see page 320	Commencement Day, 1909.	Graduates since Organization.*	Alumni Living.*	Earliest Graduates Living.	Graduated.	Present Addresses.
Philander Smith Col†	May 13	203	179	Rufus C. Childress	1888	Little Rock, Ark.
Polytechnic Inst.	June 6	....	...	....	....	....
Pomona College†	June 23	296	288	Class of '94, 11 graduates living	by	last report.
Princet'n Theol. Sem	May 3	5,550	3,095	Rev. J. Crowell	1835	East Orange, N. J.
Princeton University	June 16	10,229	a8,061	James C. Hepburn, M. D.	1832	East Orange, N. J.
Proseminar College	June 16	600	....	Rev. J. H. Dinkmeier	1873	Alhambra, Ill.
Purdue University†	June 9	3,222	2,899	Charles J. Bohrer	1876	La Fayette, Ind.
Radcliffe College‡	June 29	955	939	Mrs. Ward Clark	1883	Dover, N. H.
Randolph-Macon C.	June 10	700	500	Edward S. Brown	1843	Lynchburg, Va.
" Woman's Col	June 8	198	196	*See note "e," on page* 320.		
Rens'l'r Poly. In.	June 16	1,542	1,081	A. N. Haskin	1840	Petersburg, Va.
Richmond Col. (Va.).	June 16	....	....	Rev. P. S. Henson	1849	Boston, Mass.
Rio Grande College†.	June 17	....	85	Rev. Thomas D. Davis, A.M.	1883	Tecumseh, Neb
Ripon College†	June 16	375	...	Miss Luthera Harriet Adams	1867	Omro, Wis.
Roanoke College.	June 16	594	520	Rev. J. A. Snyder, D.D.	1856	Woodstock, Va.
Rochester A.&M. In †	June 10	618	....	....	....	....
Rochester Theo. Sem	May 12	960	700	Wm. Wallace Sawyer	1851	Milford, Ohio.
Rock Hill College	June 18	204	190	Thomas A. Whelan	1872	Baltimore, Md.
Rollins College†	June 3	400	350	Clara Louise Guild	1890	Sanford, Fla.
Rose Poly. Institute.	June 10	326	506	*See note "w," on page* 320.		
Rutgers College	June 23	2,338	1,334	Rev. John F. Mesick	1834	York, Pa.
Scotia Seminary ‡§.	May 26	716	....	....	....	....
Seton Hall College	June 16	476	350	Louis Edward Frith	1862	New York City, N. Y.
Shaw University†§	May 13	688	....	Rev. Cæsar Johnson	1878	Raleigh, N. C.
Shorter College.‡	June 2	413	381	Mary Darlington	1877	Washington, D. C.
Shurtleff College†	June 2	403	340	Hiram A. Gardiner	1842	Eaton, N. Y.
Simmons' College‡	June 16	141	141	....	....	....
Simpson College†(a).	June 11	449	421	Louise Anderson Burke	1870	Newkirk, Okla.
S'ern Bap. Th. S. (u)	May 26	3 000	....	....	....	....
Southern Univ.	June 9	516	465	J. V. Glass	1860	Birmingham, Ala.
Southwest Kan. Col.	June 3	194	192	Class of '89, 3 graduates living		
State Univ. of Iowa†	June 16	7,998	....	Dexter E. Smith	1858	Santa Ana, Cal.
State Univ. of Ky.†	June 3	738	712	William B. Munson, B. S.	1869	Denison, Tex.
Stevens Inst. Tech	June 3	1,282	1,192	J. Augustus Henderson	1873	State College, Pa.
St. Anselm's	June 24	91	86	John B. Peterson	1894	Brighton, Mass.
St. Francis Xavier C.	June 14	1,012	828	Henry A. Brann, D. D.	1857	New York City.
St. John's Col. (D.C.	June 16	159	....	John D. Coughlan	1873	Woodside, Md.
St. John's Col. (Md.)	June 16	730	560	Daniel Murray Thomas	1846	Baltimore, Md.
St. Lawrence Univ. †.	June 9	900	....	A. B. Hervey	1860	Bath, Me.
St. Louis University.	June 21	1,563	....	Rev. F. P. Garesche, S. J.	1843	Cincinnati, Ohio.
St. Mary's Col. (Kan.)	June 21	502	....	John J. Conroy, M. D.	1885	Chicago, Ill.
St. Mary's Col (Ky.)	June 17	....	....	John G. Mattingly	1840	St. Mary's, Ky.
St. Olaf College†	June 8	239	232	Dr. A. O. Sandbo	1890	Austin, Tex.
St. Vincent's College	June 17	....	....	Isidore B. Dockweiler, A. M.	1887	Los Angeles, Cal.
Swarthmore Col.†	June 9	862	816	*See note "f," on page* 320.		
Syracuse University†	June 9	5,000	....	Mrs. M. E. Nash Spence	1853	Fairgrove, Mich.
Tabor College†	June 10	258	242	Class of '70, 6 graduates living	by	last report.
Talladega College†	June 8	332	....	Rev. J. R. Sims	1876	Gadsden, Ala.
Tarkio College†	June 17	283	280	William R. Littell	1887	Tarkio, Mo.
Teachers' College	June 2	2,200	1,900	....	1894	....
Temple College†	June 12-14	2,483	....	T. T. Myers	....	....
Texas Christ. Univ.†	June 3	300	189	E. Milwee	1876	Mangum, Okla.
Throop Poly. Inst.†	June 8	492	484	Geo. F. Doty	1896	Spokane, Wash.
Tome Institute†	June 15	276	274	....	....	....
Trinity College (Ct.).	June 23	1,461	943	Dr. G. W. Russell	1834	Hartford, Ct.
Trinity Col. †(N. C.).	June 9	850	....	J. A. Edwards	1854	Hookerton, N. C.
Trinity University†	June 2	294	255	Rev. J. Sanford Groves	1871	Honey Grove, Tex.
Tri-State College†	Aug. 26	700	....	*See note "m," on page* 220.		
Tufts College†	June 16	2,832	2,629	Harvey Hersey, A. M.	1857	Barre, Vt.
Tulane University	May 19	....	....	....	....	....
Tuskegee Institute§	May 27	....	....	Class of '85, all living.		
Union Col†(Neb.)(u)	May 25	228	223	H. A. Owen; R. H. Biron	1894	Wichita; Minneapolis.
Union College (N. Y.)	June 9	5,349	2,425	Augustus A. Boyce	1832	Santa Barbara, Cal.
Union Theol. Sem	May 18	3,432	2,149	Henry B. Elliott	1843	N. Y. City.
Univ. of Alabama†	May 26	2,000	....	W. C. Richardson	1843	Tuscaloosa, Ala.
Univ. of Arizona†	June 2	60	57	Mrs. A. J. Gould	1895	Tucson, Ariz.
Univ. of Arkansas†	June 8	700	600	Charles McKinney	1875	St. Louis, Mo.
Univ. of California†	May 12	7,918	7,518	Rev. Albert F. Lyle	1864	Newark, N. J.
Univ. of Chattan'ga†	June 1	1,301	....	Rev. J. J. Manker	1871	Athens, Tenn.
Univ. of Chicago†	June 8	4,575	3,800	....	...	....
Univ. of Cincin'ti†(u)	June 1	4,479	....	....	...	....
Univ. of Colorado†	June 9	1,163	1,100	Oscar E. Jackson	1882	Denver, Col.
Univ. of Denver†	June 27	1,656	1,100	P. V. Carlin, M. D.	1882	Denver, Col.
Univ. of Georgia	June 16	...	....	Rev. Henry Newton	1841	Athens, Ga.
Univ. of Idaho†	June 16	214	209	Arthur P. Adair	1896	Boisé, Idaho.
Univ. of Illinois†(u)	June 10	5,987	5,500	James N. Matthews, M. D.	1872	Mason, Ill.
Univ. of Kansas†	June 9	3,200	3,003	L. D. L. Tosh	1873	Kansas City, Kan.
Univ. of Louisville†	June 10	10,000	....	....	..	....
Univ. of Maine†	June 9	1,320	1,251	Benj. Flint Gould	1872	Hollister, Cal.
Univ. of Michigan†	June 24	22,736	19,557	Theodore R. Palmer	1847	National City, Cal.
Univ. of Minnesota†	June 10	5,705	5,556	*See note "i," on page* 320.		
Univ. of Missouri†	June 2	....	....	....	....	....
Univ. of Montana†	June 10	144	143	*See note "l," on page* 320.		

COLLEGES—TABLE TWO. For explanation of signs, see page 320.	Commencement Day, 1909	Graduates since Organization.*	Alumni* Living.	Earliest Graduates Living.	Graduated.	Present Addresses.
Univ. of Nebraska†	June 10	8,375	3,299	Wm. H. Snell; Jas. S. Dales.	1873	Tacoma, W.; Linc'n, N.
Univ. of Nevada†	June 9	561	549	Frank H. Norcross	1891	Carson City, Nev.
Univ. of N. Carolina.	June 1	....	....	R. B. Creecy	1835	Elizabeth City, N. C.
Univ. of North Dak.†	June 17	627	614	....	....	....
Univ. of N. Mexico†	May 7	141	139	....	....	....
Univ. of Notre Dame.	June 17	2,000	1,000	*See note "k" on page* 320.		
Univ. of Oklahoma †.	June 10	250	244	C. R. Hume; R. P. Stoops	1898	Anadarko; N'man. Ok
Univ. of Oregon†	June 23	1,287	....	....	....	....
Univ. of Pittsburgh†.	....	3,500	2,000	William Waugh.	1842	Greenville, Pa.
Univ. of the Pac.†(*u*)	May 28	620	540	D. C. Vestal	1858	San Jose, Cal.
Univ. of Penn. **	June 16	23,340	15,000	....	....	....
Un. of Porto Rico.†(*u*)	June 19	42	42	Francisco Zuazaga	1903	Rio Piedras, P. R.
Univ. of Rochester†	June 16	1,629	1,377	A. A. Brooks	1851	Corpus Christi, Tex.
Univ. of S. California†	June 17	896	850	George F. Bovard	1884	Los Angeles, Cal.
Univ. of S. Carolina†	June 9	5,000	2,500	Major S. S. Tompkins	1840	Columbia, S. C.
Univ. of S. Dakota†	June 10	375	369	Clarence B. Antisdel	1888	....
Univ. of Tennessee†	June 1	....	....	Rev. James Park, D D	1840	Knoxville, Tenn.
Univ. of the South	June 24	780	736	James J. Hanna, C. E.	1873	New Orleans, La.
Univ. of Utah†	June 2	1,676	1,632	Wm. Bradford	1876	Salt Lake City, Utah.
Univ. of Vermont†	June 30	4,196	2,365	Wm. P. Pierson	1839	Onarga, Ill.
Univ. of Virginia	June 16	....	....	....	....	....
Univ. of Washingt'n†	June 2	1,011	974	Mrs. Clara McCarty Wilt	1876	Tacoma, Wash.
Univ. of Wisconsin†	June 23	7,194	....	Levi Booth	1854	Denver, Col.
Univ. of Wooster†	June 17	1,338	1,210	Rev. John C. Miller	1871	Orborne, Kan.
Univ. of Wyoming†	June 17	173	....	W. H. Bramel; F. V. Quinn.	1891	Salt L. City; L. Ang's.
Upper Iowa Univ.†	June 17	563	....	J. L. Paine; J. E. Clough	1862	Fayette, Iowa; Ind.
Upsala College†	May 29	106	103	David Magnusson	1894	San Francisco, Cal.
Ursinus College†	June 9	474	....	....	....	....
U. S. Mil. Academy.	June 12	4,749	....	Samuel G. French	1843	Freehold, N. J.
U. S. Naval Acad.	June 4	3,338	2,373	John H. Upshur	1847	Washington, D. C.
Utah Agri. College†.	June 1	123	120	John T. Carne, Jr	1894	Logan, Utah.
Valparaiso Univ.†	Aug. 5	12,600	12,000	Dr. Carl Ingerson	1875	St. Louis, Mo.
Vanderbilt Univ.†	June 15	....	4,500	Henry W. Morgan	1875	Nashville, Tenn.
Vassar College‡	June 9	3,162	2,982	....	....	....
Virginia Mil. Inst.	Sept. 16	2,011	2,011	Dr. O. M. Knight	1842	Oliveville, Va.
Virginia Poly. Inst.	June 16	737	697	Rev. A. Lloyd, D. D.	1875	New York City, N. Y.
Wabash College	June 16	1,033	815	John M. Cowan	1842	Springfield, Mo.
Wake Forest College	May 1	1,133	....	Dr. David R. Wallace	1850	Waco, Tex.
Walden Univ.†	May 13	1,453	1,125	J. M. Jamison, M.D.	1877	Topeka, Kan.
Washburn College†.	June 9	708	575	Julius B. Billard	1870	N. Topeka, Kan.
Wash. C.†(Tenn.)(*u*)	May 15	....	....	Judge O. P. Temple	1844	Knoxville, Tenn.
Wash. State Col.†	June 17	250	240	....	....	....
Washington Univ.†.	June 17	7,909	....	....	....	....
Wash. & Jeff. Col.	June 23	4,250	2,000	Levi Davis	1828	Alton, Ill.
Wash. & Lee Univ.	June 16	4,600	4,000	Wm. H. Ruffner, LL. D.	1841	Asheville, N. C.
Waynesburg College	June 24	700	400	Mrs. J. M. Howard	1854	Waynesburg, Pa.
Wellesley College‡	June 29	3,356	3,245	....	....	....
Wells College‡	June 9	356	340	Jeanette L. Daggett	1869	New York City, N. Y.
Wesleyan Univ.†(*u*).	June 3	2,300	1,500	Mrs. Catherine Benson	1840	Macon, Ga.
Wesleyan Univ. (Ct)†	June 30	2,714	1,910	Rev. B. Hawley, D. D	1838	Saratoga Spa, N. Y.
Western C. (Women)	June 9	753	620	Augusta M. Chapin	1856	Upper Alton, Ill.
West. Reserve Univ.	June 17	....	....	....	....	....
West. The. Sem. (*u*)	May 7	2,500	2,050	Thomas Mellon	....	....
West Va. Univ.†	June 16	1,032	900	M. H. Dent	1870	Grafton, W. Va.
Westfield College†	June 9	190	172	Rev. Jos. H. Snyder, D.D.	1870	Lecompton, Kan.
Westminster C. (Mo.)	June 10	340	286	Robert McPheeters	1856	Fulton, Mo.
Westmin'r Col. (Pa)†	June 10	1,500	940	Thomas Henderson Hanna	1856	Bloomington, Ind.
Wheaton College†	June 16	400	350	Rev. J. P. Stoddard	1860	Boston, Mass.
Whitman College†	June 16	142	141	*See note "z" on page* 320.		
Whitworth College†.	June 17	40	38	....	....	....
Wilberforce Univ.†	June 17	1,925	....	John T. Jenifer	1870	Baltimore, Md.
Wiley University†	May 12	147	123	William Wesley	1882	Terrell, Tex.
Williamette Univ.†	June 16	920	845	Mrs. E. J. Y. Moore	1859	Portland, Ore.
William Jewell Col.	June 16	600	500	De Witt C. Allen	1853	Liberty, Mo.
Williams College	June 23	4,963	2,417	William Rankin, LL. D	1831	Princeton, N. J.
Wittenberg College†.	June 3	1,246	1,049	W. H. Wynn, D. D.	1851	Tacoma, Wash.
Wofford College	June 14	737	646	Samuel Dibble, LL. D.	1856	Orangeburg, S. C.
Woman's Col. (Balt.)	June 9	772	759	Mrs. Walter Knipp	1892	Baltimore, Md.
Worcester Poly. Inst.	June 10	1,275	1,201	Henry P Armsby	1871	State College, Pa.
Yale University	June 30	24,660	14,806	Gurdon W. Russell	1837	Hartford, Ct.
Yankton College†	June 16	206	202	*See note "j," on page* 320.		
York College†	June 9	396	....	Mrs. Minnie B. Spore	1904	Canton, China.

The statistics embraced in this table were communicated to THE WORLD ALMANAC by the Presidents of the respective institutions, and represent their condition at the close of 1908.

Persons writing to the different institutions for catalogues should inclose postage stamp for reply, and also indicate the reason for request.

TABLE THREE—FINANCIAL STATISTICS OF UNIVERSITIES AND COLLEGES.

COST OF TUITION AND OTHER EXPENSES OF EDUCATION ITEMIZED, AND INCOME FROM PRODUCTIVE FUNDS AND BENEFACTIONS DURING THE LAST COLLEGE YEAR, COMMUNICATED TO "THE WORLD ALMANAC" BY THE COLLEGES.

COLLEGES. For explanation of signs, see page 320.	Tuition—Cost per Annum.	Living Expenses, Board, etc.	Other Expenses-Fees, Books, etc.	Productive Funds—Amount of.	Receipts from Benefactions.	Total Income, Including Tuition or Incidental Charges.
Adelphi College	$180	$273 up.	$20	....	....	....
Adrian College	15	144	50	$35,000	....	$25,000
Agri. & Mech. Col. (Tex.)	None.	137	58	209,000	....	243,365
Alabama Poly. Institute	(m)	135	50	30,000	$41,767	101,508
Albany College	50	117	15	4,000	2,800	7,800
Albion College	30	133-171	10-25	280,000	8,000	43,000
Albright College	50	200	......	135,000	....	§§1[illegible],000
Alfred University	50	125-200	25-50	377,500	7,020	33,571
Allegheny College	60	95-120	12-20	550,000	60,000	(c) 52,500
Alma College	32	170-200	10-15	292,920	38,812	65,965
Am. International Col.	40	135	11	....	....	....
American Un. (Tenn.)	50	100	15	None.	5,500	§§6,000
Amherst College	110	250	75	2,000,000	40,000	130,000
Andover Theol. Sem.	150	200-300	....	900,000	....	....
Antioch College	30	102	15-30	136,000	6,000	18,000
Armour Inst. Technology	125	144	25	....	....	....
Atlanta University	16	88	20	72,816	37,276	54,731
Auburn Theological Sem.	None.	150	None.	780,941	47,742	53,696
Augustana College	36	125 up.	....	92,175	28,650	70,719
Baker University	46-75	108-180	25-50	75,000	80,000	132,000
Baldwin University (j)	36	115	15	100,000	8,000	19,000
Barnard College‡	150	365 up.	5 up.	....	....	....
Bates College	50	96-148	50	646,622	65,382	(c) 52,908
Baylor University	50-60	180	20	55,600	....	93,335
Beloit College	80	150-200	50-150	876,297	2,480	76,869
Bellevue College	50	154	11-21	42,650	16,354	26,599
Berea College	None.	72	21-33	479,962	52,680	§§ 9,475
Bethany College (Kan.)	36-120	90 up.	....	58,500	3,462	67,000
Bethany College (W. Va.)	36	156	12	150,000	2,000	23,000
Blackburn College	50	150-175	20-40	100,000	25,000	(c) 8,500
Boston University	130	170 up.	50 up.	644,608	11,200	199,437
Bowdoin College	75	175	100	1,379,894	120,000	(c) 91,396
Brigham Young College	11	125-175	30-50	100,000	40,000	58,521
Brown University	153	300	100-200	3,500,000	....	213,000
Bryn Mawr College	200	125-275	10	1,128,494	51,000	§§ 80,709
Bucknell University	50	200	50	710,000	....	......
Butler College	48	180	15	450,000	....	....
Canisius College	50	220	30	....	....	....
Carleton College	40	150-200	10-25	350,000	2,500	40,000
Carson and Newman Col.	30-40	70-125	5-10	95,000	....	28,000
Carthage College	40	125-150	17-25	52,000	9,500	18,000
Case School Appl. Science	100	200-228	50	....	......	......
Catholic Univ. of Amer.	75	150	20	627,627	46,299	188,669
Cedarville College	28	140	10	60,000	12,000	15,200
Central College (Mo.)	50	150-200	40	172,000	5,500	29,000
Central Univ. of Iowa	43	117	25	100,000	25,000	(c) 13,000
Central Univ. of Ky	50	100-200	100-150	520,000	3,000	33,000
Central Wesleyan Col.	36	120	....	100,000	10,000	(c) 13,152
Charles City College (j)	38	150	20	53,000	....	9,000
Charleston College	40	125	10	293,700	8,776	22,104
Christian Univ. (Mo.)	40	120	10-20	20,000	2,500	....
Claflin University (a)	20	80	10	None	30,000	80,000
Clark College (Mass.)	50	150-200	....	1,300,000	......	64,000
Clark University (Ga.)	14	74	....	11,000	14,027	31,718
Clark University (Mass.)	100	200	....	3,700,000	......	....
Clarkson School Tech.	100	156-180	40-50	300,000	......	26,552
Clemson Agri. College	40	114	18	231,034	......	259,034
Coe College	40	200	12	400,000	14,791	33,900
Colby College	60	250	30	456,000	......	§§ 38.087
Colgate University	60	200	50	1,765,154	60,755	128,310
College of City of N. Y.	(m)	None.	None.	**	....	536,001
College of St. Elizabeth	200	100	....	None.	None.	....
Colorado College	50	300 up.	(y)	900,719	392.885	§§ 22,863
Columbia Univ. (b)	155-200	(f) 325	(f) 45	23,542,246	1,077,933	(c) 1,960,258
Concordia College	¶ 40	150	(i)	None.	....	......
Converse College‡	70	220	....	......	13,100	§§ 74.178
Cooper College	38	150-250	15	50,000	4,000	10.000
Cornell College (Iowa)	50	125-175	15-30	642,226	....	....
Cornell University (N. Y.)	100-150	....	....	8,875,676	233,486	1.356,498
Cotner University	30	150	....	....	....	§§ 17,426
Creighton University	(e)	500-640	....	....	....	....
Cumberland University (j)	75-100	90-150	40	100.000	......	....
Dakota Wesleyan Univ.	36	175	15	100,319	9,099	40,976
Dartmouth College	125	425-740	....	2,528,932	35,722	366,653
Davidson College	60	120-200	40-50	100,000	2,500	38,000
Delaware College	60	175-275	75 150	83,000	None.	52,000
Denison University	50	130	60	750,000	15,000	70,000

COLLEGES—TABLE THREE. For explanation of signs, see page 320.	Tuition—Cost per Annum.	Living Expenses, Board, etc.	Other Expenses—Fees, Books, etc.	Productive Funds—Amount of.	Receipts from Benefactions.	Total Income, including Tuition or Incidental Charges
De Pauw University	$50	$105-200	$25-60	$499,117	$24,273	$104,345
Des Moines College	42	144-180	20	101,500	5,000	(c) 10,000
Dickinson College	(ee)	226	35	378,808	14,375	91,705
Doane College	40	123	18	176,443	17,254	41,709
Drake University	50-100	150-250	25-75	407,843	42,000	136,051
Drew Theol. Seminary	115	(i)	50-55	550,000	11,850	36,500
Drury College	50	145 up.	....	200,000	....	37,600
Earlham College	77	163	5	340,000	15,000	44,000
Elmira College‡	150	275	35	75,000	....	51,396
Elon College	50	80-120	30-40	32,000	2,125	....
Emory and Henry Col	50	120-170	20-50	600	18,000	40,852
Emory College (j)	60	200 up.	None.	222,115	....	....
Emporia College	50	125	20-30	134,378	12,229	16,229
Erskine College	35	76-135	18-25	80,000	....	12,000
Eureka College	45	150	10-20	50,000	3,000	27,000
Ewing College	30	120	16	45,000	......	....
Fairmount College	40	135-162	100	82,000	2,000	14,000
Fargo College	32	150	25	86,000	38,000	58,000
Findlay College	38	100	15-20	100,000	5,000	31,926
Fisk University	17	94	25	52,000	22,000	41,000
Fordham University	100	300	20	....	....	....
Fort Worth Univ	50	144-153	18	....	....	51,684
Franklin College (Ind.) (i)	18	300	2 up.	400,000	....	17,000
Franklin Col. (Ohio)	40	104	15	None.	......	3,600
Franklin & Marshall Col.	None.	150	85	284,000	50,000	84,000
Furman University	50	90	30	176,000	....	17,087
Gen'l Theol. Sem. (P. E.)	None.	225	10	2,062,503	4,561	158,903
Geneva College	45	162	13	165,000	....	16,000
George Washington Univ.	150	200-350	25-50	265,954	20,622	157,526
Georgetown College	45	135-180	18	264,539	9,778	24,778
Georgetown Univ. (D. C.)	150	372	30	....	....	....
Girard College	None.	None.	None.	24,467,770	None.	1,337,445
Greensboro Female Col.	70	130	10-12	11,329	2,500	38,024
Greer College	48	168-192	25	2,500	....	....
Grove City College	60	115	25	50,000	8,120	(c) 29,000
Guilford College	60	120	15	175,000	2,000	45,927
Gustavus Adolphus Col.	34	150	....	50,000	9,000	18,000
Hamilton College	90	450-500	(y)	600,000	20,000	52,000
Hamline University	37	153	24	....	....	§§ 7,000
Hampden-Sidney College	50	150-250	50-60	168,000	375	17,053
Hanover College	None.	117-144	34	225,000	8,870	23,509
Hartford Theol. Sem	None.	175	25	....	......	....
Harvard University (j)	(k) 150	362-1,039	25 up.	21,011,574	693,065	2,129,563
Hastings College	50	140	12	101,070	53,399	(c) 7,202
Haverford College	150	175-350	30	1,280,000	31,000	110,000
Hedding College	51	108	20	60,000	2,500	13,000
Heidelberg University	60	108-144	20	205,000	7,000	24,000
Hendrix College	60	125-150	12-25	132,000	6,000	15,674
Henry Kendall College	37-50	144	10	190,000	6,000	18,000
Hillsdale College	27	75-130	30-75	230,314	6,075	20,884
Hiram College	50	110-160	15-25	160,000	....	....
Hiwassee College	18	72	10	None.	......	1,500
Hobart College	80	150-200	40-50	833,598	18,000	55,280
Holy Cross College	60	200	10-20	....	......	....
Hope College (Mich.)	24	125-156	38	287,705	2,250	31,339
Howard University (D. C.)	None.	115	12-25	216,997	....	103,463
Howard College	60	155	25	33,000	4,000	15,000
Howard Payne College (g)	50	200	10-15	....	....	145,108
Huron College	40	108	10	None.	47,000	60,000
Illinois College	50	110-225	10-20	294,000	106,240	30,191
Illinois Wesleyan Univ.	52	150-240	25	120,000	100,000	(c) 22,000
Indiana University	38	106	15	881,287	....	236,657
Indiana Central Univ.	38	106	15	71,000	7,000	9,000
Iowa College	55	144-189	25-50	813,616	16,772	(c) 91,057
Iowa State College	(m) 50	150-175	50-100	683,708	3,079	599,464
Iowa Wesleyan Univ.	45	120	5-25	61,000	15,000	23,000
James Millikin Univ.	40	240	6	230,000	30,000	74,838
John B. Stetson Univ.	72-60	173	10-20	284,143	80,000	152,299
Johns Hopkins Univ	150-200	160 up.	30 up.	4,500,000	11,000	327,000
Juniata College	60	150	25	215-121	....	81,600
Kansas City University	36	150	25	475,000	......	....
Kansas Wesleyan Univ.	40	110	15	35,000	25,000	§§ 7,850
Kentucky Wes. College	50	100	20	61,500	2,500	9,800
Kenyon College	75	120	30	505,823	9,380	47,231
Keuka College	36	114	40	....	6,623	16,899
Knox College	50	200-400	10-25	289,977	....	49,750
Knoxville College	10	75	25	10,000	20,000	20,500
Lafayette College (Pa.)	100	160-300	61	748,798	71,816	159,495
Lake Erie College	100	215	5 up.	85,000	7,390	43,295
Lake Forest College	50	174-215	17	748,927	143,194	(c) 60,717
Lawrence University	36	130-150	12	610,000	33,000	66,700
Lander College	38.50	130	37	1,200	2,650	21,760
Lane Theological Sem	None.	200	20	350,000	....	14,000

COLLEGES—TABLE THREE. For explanation of signs, see page 320.	Tuition—Cost per Annum.	Living Expenses, Board, etc.	Other Expenses—Fees, Books, etc.	Productive Funds—Amount of.	Receipts from Benefactions.	Total Income, Including Tuition or Incidental Charges.
Leander Clark College....	$36	$140	$15-25	$150,500	....	$19,000
Lebanon Valley College...	50	144 up.	18	9,500	$16,544	(c) 31,625
Lehigh University...........	60-150	250 350	50	1,178,000	....	....
Leland Stanford, Jr. Univ.	None.	300-450	(y)	24,525,922	......	854,812
Lenox College..................	30-50	140	10-25	102,097	3,510	14,366
Liberty College.............	50	150	25	....	....	12,000
Lincoln College.............	36	180	50	102,000	10,000	18,336
Lombard College............	36	110-150	30	200,000	....	15,000
Louisiana State Univ. (j)..	(m) 60	150-300	75	96,314	..	113,365
Macalester..................	32	126-162	12	42,000	120,074	130,000
Manhattan College............	75-100	250	10-35	None.	None.	42,686
Marietta College..............	30	175-225	20	235,000	11,308	34,000
Marquette College........	60	144-216	15-75	....	3,000	61,000
Maryville College...........	18	72	3	321,073	1,000	37,287
Mass. Agricultural Col....	(z) 120	225	20-40	240,666	None.	82,088
Mass. Inst. Technology...	250	300	30	2,730,409	92,332	755,944
McCormick Theol. Sem...	None.	200	30-40	1,800,000	10,000	67,000
McKendree College..........	45	125-200	10-20	133,180	....	10,585
McMinnville College.......	51	200-300	....	50,000	14,480	31,378
Miami University............	None.	105-180	5 up.	136,000	40,000	200,000
Michigan Agri. Col.......	(m) 15	(y) 200-300	(y)	1,173,000	None.	340,000
Mich. College of Mines....	(h) 25	330	100-150	None.	None.	102-382
Middlebury College..........	80	160	50	419,203	1,876	29,299
Midland College...............	40	100-125	15	40,000	7,000	14,000
Milligan College..............	40	100	20	40,000	12,000	§§ 9,000
Millsaps College (j)..........	30	100-150	20	200,000	50,000	(c) 18,000
Milton College.................	32-38	125-175	20-50	122,436	1,200	14,247
Mississippi College..........	40	150	15-30	110,000	30,000	....
Miss. Agri. & Mech. Col.....	(m) 30-50	125	25	.	....	145,195
Missouri Valley College...	51	126	......	185,044	....	26,696
Monmouth College..........	51	160 up.	18	273,952	54,280	92,782
Moore's Hill College.........	40	114	3	25,000	8,000	14,250
Morningside College (j)..	60	150 up.	40	219,000	204,400	228,962
Morris Brown College (a)	8.50	55.25	5-7	....	....	30,000
Mount Angel College.......	50	160	15 up.	...	....	......
Mount Holyoke College‡.	150	200	5 up.	809,233	2,874	235,613
Mount St. Mary's College	(i) 300	(i)	25	None.	None.	....
Mount Union College........	54	137	25	128,610	20,000	(c) 29,134
Muhlenberg College.........	75	175	15-25	256,614	82,113	108,745
Muskingum College.........	45	115	25	75,000	15,000	30,000
Nebraska Wesleyan Univ.	36	200-300	(y)	100,000	3,500	§§ 27,961
Newberry College.........	40	125	15-25	11,199	......	17,524
Newton Theol. Inst...........	None.	170	20 up.	895,183	32,228	46,866
New York University......	100-200	250-400	50	1,119,728	41,882	362,447
Niagara University...........	75	175	30	None.	12,000	88,000
Nor. Car. Ag. & Mech. Arts.	45	100	145	125,000	None.	173,047
Northwestern Col. (Ill.)..	54-60	175-250	30-50	300,000	....	30,000
Northwestern Univ. (Ill)..	100	250-350	50-75	243,490	130,333	943,495
Northwest'n Univ. (Wis.)	40	100	20	40,000	15,000	19,000
Norwich University......	65	135-200	20-40	110,000	100,000	315,000
Oberlin College (j)...........	50-75	130-275	20-40	1,650,668	142,264	290,539
Ohio Northern Univ......	45 up.	155	....	......	15,000	45,000
Ohio State University (j)	(x)	200-350	60-100	807,730	32,903	612,491
Ohio Univ. (Athens, O.)...	None.	125	75	90,000	....	175,000
Ohio Wesleyan Univ.........	* 60	(f) 135	(f) 45	300,000	90,700	252,200
Olivet College (j).............	50	(y) 150	....	200,000	11,600	43,500
Oregon Agri. College.....	None. (s)	175-250	18-25	125,000	None.	248,500
Ottawa University............	36	126-180	7-20	154,000	5,304	23,620
Otterbein University......	54	150	25	113,418	32,072	55,560
Ouachita College (j)..........	50	150	50	20,000	5,000	35,000
Pacific University (Ore.).	56	120-235	20-55	235,000	13,000	(c) 17,000
Park College.....................	20-30	75-200	1	343,016	3,423	25,008
Parker College............	30	100	12	71,396	1,240	10,175
Parsons College...............	41	65-75	36	230,000	....	19,609
Peabody College..........	* 30	300	50	††	††	50,000
Penn College (Iowa).........	44	150-250	10-15	85,000	7,580	33,245
Pennsylvania College........	30	125	45	200,000	8,912	33,401
Penna. College (Women).	125	275	20	....	....	......
Penna. Military Col.	550	(i)	....	......	......	......
Pennsylvania State Col....	(m) 100	175 up.	100	517,000	3,715	278,715
Philander Smith College..	16	72	7	None	372	16,000
Polytechnic Institute.......	200	....	....	......	50,999	200,442
Pomona College.............	90	200	20	270,000	40,000	56,000
Pratt Institute (j)............	6-75	225-288	20	2,152,783	500,000	234,270
Presbyterian Col. of S. C.	40	120	20	10,000	10,000	(c) 5,614
Princeton Theol. Sem......	None.	150	15	3,227,480	7,450	137,911
Princeton University.....	150-160	....	25 up.	3,739,200	1,004,270	(c) 411,910
Proseminar Elmhurst Col	150	(i)	15	5,000	4,816	28,714
Purdue University...........	(m) 25	200-250	75-100	340,000	None.	283,517
Radcliffe College‡............	200	258-500	35-60	460,000	84,000	§§ 72,854
Randolph-Macon College.	75	200	45-55	210,500	15,000	(c) 130,000
" " (Woman's)......	75	200	25	209,000	....	133,586
Rensselaer Poly. Inst......	200	220-375	43-80	1,612,000	....	....
Richmond College (Va.) (j)	70	120-175	30-50	380,000	23,000	(c) 47,620

COLLEGES—TABLE THREE. For explanation of signs, see page 320.	Tuition—Cost per Annum.	Living Expenses, Board, etc.	Other Expenses-Fees, Books, etc.	Productive Funds—Amount of.	Receipts from Benefactions.	Total Income, including Tuition or Incidental Charges.
Rio Grande College (*i*)	$28-32	$120	$10-30	$76,000	$105	$ 6,060
Ripon College	60	201	30	266,162	27,546	52,261
Roanoke College	50	125-150	20	129,000	32,000	(*c*) 21,400
Rochester A. & M. Inst.	75	216	15-50	366,408	14,698	111,927
Rochester Theol. Sem.	None.	150	75	1,638,562	6,048	69,062
Rock Hill College	260	200	40	.....	......	§§ 25,000
Rollins College (*j*)	34-52	138	25	215,000	45,000	52,000
Rose Polytechnic Inst.	100	165-210	35-50	550,000	......	50,000
Rutgers College	75	162-180	30-60	692,000	......	......
Scotia Seminary	None.	45	5 up.	12,000	10,500	19,283
Seton Hall College	(*i*) 380	(*i*)	15	None.	None.	......
Shorter College‡	70	205	10	41,000	......	52,750
Shurtleff College	34	150-200	30-40	155,564	5,517	26,487
Simmons College	100	260-300	10-25	2,858,827	....	139,204
Simpson College	40-67	117	10-30	100,000	40,000	(*c*) 48,171
Smith College	100	300	......	1,320,000	23,000	305,253
Southern Bapt. Theo. Sem.	None.	100	50	650,000	72,000	(*c*) 42,000
Southern University	50	120-150	7-10	60,000	4,000	23,247
Southwestern Col. (Kan.)	33-42	100-175	5-20	70,000	5,000	20,000
S. W. Presb. Un. (Tenn.) (*j*)	50	186	50	285,000	....	...
State Univ. of Kentucky	30-50	108-180	25	....	26,500	92,022
State Univ. of Iowa	20-50	175-250	15-50	240,320	....	572,478
State Univ. of Kentucky	25-40	126	25	..	None.	116,418
Stevens Institute Tech.	(*p*)	240-400	60	874,000	6,257	128,323
St. Angela College	120	320	25-30	....	....	......
St. Anselm's College	60	150	25-50	....	....	......
St. Bede College	200	(*i*)	10	None.	None.	......
St. Benedict's College	60	140	......	......	None.	......
St. Francis Xavier College	100	......	....	......	19,365	......
St. John's College (D. C.)	100	......	10	......	......	......
St. John's College (Md.)	75	160-170	20-30	...	20,000	36,000
St. Lawrence University	50	180	22	500,000	......	(*c*) 63,000
St. Louis University	60-150	125-300	5-250	20,000	2,000	49,000
St. Mary's College (Kan.)	260	200	8-40	None.	None.	102,657
St. Mary's College (Ky.)	40	160	15	None.	....	28,000
St. Olaf College	20	90	20	17,000	14,251	31,470
St. Stephen's College	120-130	(*i*)	3	107,234	11,285	31,016
St. Vincent's College	60	300	....	6,000	......	....
Susquehanna College	51	130	43	42,000	4,000	28,000
Swarthmore College	150	250	10-50	1,010,000	....	200,899
Syracuse University	75-125	162-266	15-50	1,500,000	410,227	1,100,261
Tabor College	45	144	75	70,000	...	14,000
Talladega College	90	...	150	162,213	7,461	13,213
Tarkio College	30	125-160	7-16	160,165	3,731	23,328
Taylor University	36	98	13	....	1,348	16,768
Teachers' Col. (N. Y. City)	150	235-422	20 up.	1,469,000	426,249	(*c*) 414,870
Temple College	10-150	....	....	20,000	1,995	124,766
Texas Christian Univ.	50	145-165	10	40,000	20,000	75,000
Throop Poly. Inst.	100	280-330	17	223,962	70,912	129,847
Tome Institute	(*i*) 700	......	20	......	....	....
Transylvania Univ.	36(*l*)	130-250	10-50	359,224	5,623	52,401
Trinity College	100	200-320	50	1,173,000	....	......
Trinity College (D. C.)	100	300-375	....	......	......	......
Trinity College (N. C.)	50	175	22	441,000	40,000	70,642
Trinity Univ. (Tex.)	72	132-150	50	42,256	1,401	18,522
Tufts College	100-150	150-200	150-200	1,550,000	42,511	223,371
Tulane University	85	215	70	2,049,378	5,587	300,074
Tuskegee Institute	None.	76.50	10	1,513,440	314,763	405,131
Union College (Ky.) (*j*)	40	90	15-20	278,000	....	..
Union College (Neb.)	40-50	150	20	....	None.	49,780
Union College (N. Y.)	75-120	200-300	35-75	669,671	26,317	80,325
Union Christian College	33	100	10	75,000	....	......
Union Theological Sem.	None.	150	....	......	....	....
Union University	60	125-150	15-25	150,000	....	....
Univ. of Alabama	(*o*)	125-175	40	1,073,641	2,500	134,701
Univ. of Arizona	(*m*) 20	150	125-200	10,500	10,000	108,000
Univ. of Arkansas	20	300	25	None.	None.	219,900
Univ. of California	(*v*)	....	....	4,121,805	906,896	1,182,419
Univ. of Chattanooga	(*oo*) 50	106	25	221,000	6,406	53,783
Univ. of Chicago	120-180	305-655	(*y*)	13,999,900	2,098,518	3,240,144
Univ. of Cincinnati	75-125	475-250	25-65	1,423,546	......	249,549
Univ. of Colorado	(*q*)	200-300	....	......	......	177,000
Univ. of Denver	45-100	150 up.	15 up.	380,000	58,000	115,000
Univ. of Georgia	(*ff*) 50	100-300	50-75	540,000	4,700	....
Univ. of Idaho	None.	150	100	415,000	None.	182,362
Univ. of Illinois (*j*)	50-110	180-250	120	638,694	None.	1,007,009
Univ. of Kansas	(*w*)	161	30	151,000	......	403,966
Univ. of Louisville	100	200	20	200,000	10,000	40,000
Univ. of Maine	30-40	200	45-55	218,300	None.	153,587
Univ. of Michigan	40-55	......	...	520,230	...	1,176,930
Univ. of Minnesota	20-150	300-700	15-100	1,500,000	20,000	645,000
Univ. of Missouri	None.	125-216	9	....	(*r*) 91,036	616,196
Univ. of Montana	None.	300	25-50	(*n*)	800	125,692

COLLEGES—TABLE THREE. For explanation of signs, see page 320.	Tuition—Cost per Annum.	Living Expenses, Board, etc.	Other Expenses—Fees, Books, etc.	Productive Funds—Amount of.	Receipts from Benefactions.	Total Income, Including Tuition or Incidental Charges.
Univ. of Nashville	$15 up.	$250	$15	....	$45,000	$49,500
Univ. of Nebraska	None ‡‡	....	50	$1,500,000	1,000	642,000
Univ. of Nevada	None.	162	12-18	(dd) 213,302	141,064	(c) 52,982
Univ. of New Mexico	(m)	180	11-20	None.	None.	32,000
Univ. of North Carolina	60	(f) 135	10-55	228,000	30,500	150,023
Univ. of North Dakota	(l)	131.25	26	....	......	136,909
Univ. of Notre Dame	100	300	25-30	None.	None.	......
Univ. of Oklahoma	None.	175-250	....	....	......	....
Univ. of Oregon	None.	150-250	15-55	125,000	....	90,000
Univ. of the Pacific (j)	50-70	200-230	40 up.	116,000	17,500	(c) 28,813
Univ. of Pennsylvania	150-200	365-565	15-55	5,337,796	509,435	§§540,624
Univ. of Pittsburgh	100-150	180-250	25-40	447,128	18,580	241,608
Univ. of Rochester	96	180-300	25-75	770,486	19,231	72,795
Univ. of the South	100	200-240	10-30	200,000	....	....
Univ. of South Carolina	40	107	100	None.	15,500	73,514
Univ. of South Dakota	12	130	10-25	......	None.	109,774
Univ. of S. California	70	166-240	12 up.	341,078	....	61,726
Univ. of State of Florida	(m) 20	120	30	158,300	......	40,2[illegible]0
Univ. of Tennessee	(bb)	162	90	399,000	50,000	143,023
Univ. of Texas	None.	(y) 300	(y)	1,998,963	....	259,233
Univ. of Utah	10-25	144-250	10-75	400,000	630	209,688
Univ. of Vermont	80	185-300	45-80	573,529	70,000	121,449
Univ. of Virginia	(d)	180 up.	40-90	779,420	14,928	§§78,957
Univ. of Washington	None.	200-300	50-100	1,500,000	None.	502,000
Univ. of Wisconsin	(m)	175-225	15-50	674,513	4,025	1,165,543
Univ. of Wooster	60	200	....	428,338	143,049	(c) 5[illegible],723
Univ. of Wyoming	None.	180	50	....	....	101,000
Upper Iowa University	48	120 up.	10-20	230,000	158,000	(c) 30,961
Upsala College	36-45	96	5-20	......	....	54,158
Urbana University	60	205 up.	20	100,000	....	7,000
Ursinus College	50	150	50-75	190,000	4,331	45,591
U.S. Military Academy	†	†	70	†	†	†
U.S. Naval Academy	§	§	§	§	§	§
Utah Agri. College	(aa)	130-190	20	121,282	......	146,203
Valparaiso University	50	172	28	1,000,000	None.	225,000
Vanderbilt University	100	150-200	50-100	1,550,000	None.	180,000
Vassar College‡	150	350	....	1,356,653	....	597,082
Vincennes University	30	120 up.	15	65,000	120,000	129,000
Virginia Christian College	45	100-125	25	..	500,000	(c) 10,000
Virginia Military Inst.	75	365	....	20,000	None.	150,000
Virginia Polytechnic Inst	50	276	....	760,000	None.	113,163
Wabash College	47	175-200	75-100	....	....	42,000
Wake Forest College	50	110-160	40	300,000	20,000	35,172
Walden University	12-50	87-130	4-16	35,050	250	43,670
Washburn College	50	162	25-30	145,000	23,000	61,000
Washington College (Md.)	50	148	20	10,000	None.	36,000
Wash'n Col. (Tenn.) (j)	18	75	5-10	75,000	5,000	(c) 6,500
Wash. State College	(m)	170	(y)	....	....	....
Wash'n & Jefferson Col.	60	150	50	513,938	8,150	54,750
Washington & Lee Univ.	50	160-240	25-75	850,000	85,000	(c) 80,000
Wash'n & Tusculum Col.	18-36	78	12	60,000	3,200	21,571
Washington University	100-150	....	....	6,375,000	....	471,900
Waynesburg College	45	150-200	25	7,700	3,100	10,700
Wellesley College‡	175	275	25	878,261	4,954	491,144
Wells College‡	150	350	....	360,000	....	115,000
Wesleyan University	85	120-300	50-70	1,506,919	84,626	134,327
West Lafayette College	36	100-150	5-10	....	....	......
Western Col. (Women)	100	200	20	77,511	478	73,658
Western Maryland Col.	45	180	20	None.	None.	......
Western Reserve Univ.	(gg) 100	200	40	1,805,812	272,153	510,031
Western Theol. Sem.	None.	130	25	731,550	6,154	44,172
Westfield College	30	150-200	2	25,000	3,000	9,000
Westminster Col. (Mo.)	60	140	30	242,878	21,213	42,669
Westminster Col. (Pa.)	60	300	30	150,000	30,000	43,000
West Virginia Univ.	25-50	150-210	(y)	115,904	None.	220,000
Wheaton College	50	100-200	20	88,189	14,124	31,424
Whitman College	50	166	(f) 100	232,000	5,240	71,000
Whitworth College	54	180	6	210,000	9,146	19,777
Wiley University	10	84	25	......	5,000	12,640
William & Mary College	35	135	16	154,000	....	57,798
William Jewell College	50	120	25	428,000	70,000	38,352
Willamette Univ.	60	125-175	15	150,000	50,000	(c) 16,620
Williams College	140	197-416	50	1,450,060	12,212	167,703
Wilmington Col. (Ohio) (j)	40	120	20	60,000	....	9,000
Wilson College (Women)	60	200	50	....	....	125,000
Wittenberg College	60	130	10	400,000	110,000	(c) 35,000
Wofford College	40	130-150	30	107,656	21,451	46,415
Woman's College (Balt.)	150	275	....	798,926	....	112,070
Worcester Poly. Inst.	150	250	20	....	....	....
Yale University	155 up.	(f) 325	(f) 45	9,497,102	1,088,496	(c) 1,157,686
Yankton College	36	108-126	10-15	183,537	5,211	24,745
York College	31.50	90-108	None.	4,150	6,740	13,070

Reference Marks Used in Preceding College Tables.

TABLE ONE.

* All departments. † Co-education of the sexes. ‡ Education of women only. § For the education of colored students. ‡‡ Medical Department at Mobile, Ala. †† At Athens, Tenn., also.

(*a*) Co-education excepting in Art Department.

(*b*) Co-education in Medicine and Law.

(*c*) No restriction as to color.

(*d*) Number of instructors and students given does not include the Horace Mann or Speyer schools.

(*e*) Branches at Tufts College and Boston.

(*f*) Confined strictly to post-graduate work. The national university of the church.

(*g*) Academic and Technical Departments at Fayetteville; Law and Medical Departments at Little Rock; Normal School (for negroes), Pine Bluff, Ark.

(*h*) And at Chicago.

(*i*) Co-education in graduate and Medicine Departments.

(*j*) For Indians and colored youths, both sexes.

(*k*) Separate Women's College.

(*l*) Radcliffe College is the women s college affiliated with Harvard University. The number of instructors and students shown at Radcliffe College are not included in the Harvard totals.

(*m*) Located in Pittsburgh and Allegheny.

(*n*) Both sexes are taught in separate colleges.

(*o*) Comprises Adelbert College for men, College for women and professional departments.

(*p*) Also Tri-State College of Engineering with 60 students, and College of Pharmacy with 40 students.

(*r*) Schools Pharmacy and Medicine at Chicago.

(*s*) Medical Department at Galveston.

(*t*) President and majority of Trustees are Baptists.

(*u*) School of Mines at Rolla, Mo.

(*v*) Outside of Law and Medicine.

(*w*) Co-education in Law, Pedagogy, Graduate, and Commerce, Accounts and Finance. The Undergraduate Schools are at University Heights. Bronx Borough, New York City; Law, Pedagogy, Graduate, and Commerce, Accounts and Finance at Washington Square; Medicine at East Twenty-sixth Street and First Avenue.

(*x*) College of Liberal Arts at St. Paul, Minn.; College Physicians and Surgeons at Minneapolis.

(*y*) Report at close of 1907.

(*z*) Women admitted to graduate, Law, Teacher's course, Biology and Music.

(*aa*) Dean of Medical College, T. C. Evans. Law College, W. O. Harris.

TABLE TWO.

* All departments. † Co-education of the sexes. ‡ Education of women only. § For the education of colored students. ** Co-education in law, graduate school and biology courses in the College.

(*a*) Including ex-members of the class.

(*c*) For colored and Indian students.

(*d*) No restriction as to color.

(*e*) Prof. Geo. P. Anderson, Seattle, Wash., and Christopher C. Gose, Walla Walla, Wash.; class of '86.

(*z*) Mrs. Emma Edith Reichmann, Troy, N. Y., and Mrs. Eva Matthews, Japan.

(*f*) Sarah A. Hillard, Salem, N. J.; Mrs. A. D. White, Ithaca, N. Y.; Elizabeth Holcomb, Charlestown, N. H.; Mrs. W. H. Appleton, Swarthmore, Pa.; Lowndes Taylor, Westchester, Pa.; all class of '73.

(*g*) Co-education in Graduate and Medical School.

(*h*) Timothy H. Ball, Crown Point, Ind., and Arthur Britton, Wyoming Valley, Wis.; both class of '50.

(*i*) Warren C. Eustis, Owatonna, Minn., and Henry M. Williamson, Portland, Ore.; both class of '73.

(*j*) Fred. B. Riggs, Santee, Neb.; G. G. Wenzloff, Springfield, S. Dak., and Benj. W. Burleigh, Hartington, Neb.; all class of '88.

(*k*) Robert W. Healy, Chattanooga, Tenn., and James O'Brien, Caledonia, Minn.; class of '59.

(*l*) Mrs. E. R. Glenny, Albia, Ia., and Miss E. Knowles, Missoula, Mont.; class of '98.

(*m*) Prof. Chas. Scaer, Winfield, Kan.; Prof. I. A. Melendy, Angola, Ind., and Mrs. D. R. Best, Angola, Ind.; all class of '87.

(*n*) J. W. Gillespie, Washington, D.C.; Samuel F. De Ford, Ottawa, O.; W. H. Dressler, Alliance O.; all class of '58.

(*p*) Rev. J. W. Chapman, Winona Lake, Ind.; B. F. Mills, Los Angeles, Cal.; class of '79.

(*u*) Report at close of 1907.

(*w*) S. S. Early, N. Easton, Mass.; Benj. McKeen, St. Louis; class of '85.

(*x*) Robt. S. Bean, Salem; Mrs. Ellen C. McCormack, and Matthew S. Wallis, Eugene, Ore.; all class of '78.

TABLE THREE.

* Free to teachers. ** Maintained by the city.

† At U. S. Military Academy tuition is free. Cadets are paid $709.50 per year each by the Government, out of which they pay their own expenses for board, clothing, etc.; living expenses average about $225 per annum. Total appropriations for tne support of Military Academy by Congress last college year, $1,929,703. †† Supported by Peabody Fund.

§ At U. S. Naval Academy tuition is free. Midshipmen are paid $500 per year each by the Government, out of which they pay their own expenses for board, clothing, etc.; living expenses average about $24 per month.

‡ Education of women only.

§§ Income from tuition, board, or incidental charges only.

¶ Free to those preparing for the ministry.

(*a*) For colored students.

(*b*) In making up the figures for Columbia University, Barnard College, Teachers' College, and the New York College of Pharmacy are included, because these institutions, although independent corporations financially, are integral parts of the educational system of Columbia University.

(*c*) Exclusive of benefactions.

(*d*) Average—academic, $75; engineering, $75; law, $100; medicine, $87.50.

(*e*) College of Arts, free; other departments average $100.

(*f*) Average.

(*g*) None, except law $40 and medicine $50.

(*h*) Non-residents, $150.

(*i*) Living expenses included in tuition charges.

(*j*) Report at close of 1907.

(*k*) Medical, Law and Pharmacy, $25; Engineering, $10.

(*l*) Law, $50; no charge in other branches.

(*m*) Free to State residents.

(*n*) 46,080 acres of land that cannot be sold for less than $10 per acre.

(*o*) Free in Academic and Engineering Depts.; $75 in Law School and Medical School.

(*p*) $150 for students residing in New Jersey; $225 for non-residents.

(*r*) State and Federal endowment.

(*s*) Registration fee, $5.

(*t*) Law, $50.

(*u*) Excluding Medical College in N. Y. City.

(*v*) Free for residents; Non-residents, $2.

(*w*) $10-$25 for residents; $20-$35 for non-residents.

(*x*) Free except in Law Dept., $60 a year.

(*y*) Charges for books, fees, etc., included in living expenses

(*z*) Free to citizens of United States.

(*aa*) $5 entrance fee.

(*bb*) 400 free State scholarships.

(*cc*) Total unclassed funds.

(*dd*) Endowment und.

(*ee*) Practically free.

(*ff*) Residents, $10.

(*gg*) Medical, $125; Dental, $150.

(*oo*) Law, $50; Medical, $65; Theological, free.

College Colors.

(Communicated to THE WORLD ALMANAC by the Presidents of the respective institutions.)

Adelphi College	Brown and Gold.
Alabama Polytechnic Institute	Orange and Blue.
Alfred University	Royal Purple and Old Gold.
Amherst College	Purple and White.
Armour Inst. of Technology	Yellow and Black.
Atlanta University	Steel Gray and Crimson.
Baker University	Burnt Orange.
Baldwin University	Old Gold and Seal Brown.
Barnard College	Light Blue and White.
Bates College	Garnet.
Baylor University	Green and Gold.
Berea College	Blue and White.
Boston University	Scarlet and White.
Bowdoin College	White.
Brigham Young College	Crimson and Gold.
Brown University	Brown and White.
Bryn Mawr College	Yellow and White.
Bucknell University	Orange and Blue.
Butler College	Blue and White.
Carleton College	Maize and Yale Blue.
Case School of Applied Science	Brown and White.
Catholic Univ. of America	Gold and White.
Central University (Ky.)	Cardinal and Blue.
Clemson Agricultural College	Purple and Orange.
College City of New York	Lavender.
College of St. Elizabeth	Blue and Gold.
Colorado College	Black and Old Gold.
Columbia University	Light Blue and White.
Cornell College (Iowa)	Royal Purple and White.
Cornell University	Carnelian and White.
Creighton University	Blue and White.
Dakota Wesleyan University	Royal Blue and White.
Dartmouth College	Green.
Denison University	Crimson.
De Pauw University	Old Gold.
Dickinson College	Red and White.
Drake University	Yale Blue and White.
Drury College	Scarlet and Gray.
Earlham College	Yellow and Cream.
Fordham University	Maroon.
Franklin and Marshall College	Blue and White.
Georgetown University (D. C.)	Blue and Gray.
George Washington University	Buff and Blue.
Girard College	Steel and Garnet.
Hamline University of Minn.	Red and Gray.
Harvard University	Crimson.
Heidelberg University	Black, Orange and Red.
Hillsdale College	Ultra-Marine (Blue).
Hobart College	Orange and Purple.
Howard University	Dark Blue and White.
Illinois Wesleyan University	Green and White.
Indiana University	Crimson and Cream.
Iowa College	Scarlet and Black.
Iowa State College	Cardinal and Gold.
Iowa Wesleyan University	White and Purple.
John B. Stetson University	Green and White.
Johns Hopkins University	Black and Old Gold.
Kansas City University	Purple and Orange.
Kansas Wesleyan University	Purple and Old Gold.
Lafayette College (Pa.)	Maroon and White.
Lake Forest University	Ruby Red and Black.
Lawrence University	White and Yale Blue.
Lebanon Valley College	Blue and White.
Leland University	Orange and Blue.
Leland Stanford, Jr., Univ	Cardinal.
Manhattan College	Green and White.
Marietta College	Navy Blue and White.
Marquette University	Blue and Gold.
Maryville College	Orange and Garnet.
Mass. Institute of Technology	Cardinal Red and Silver Gray.
Miami University	Scarlet and White.
Michigan Agricultural College	Green.
Mis. Agri. and Mech. College	Maroon and White.
Mount Holyoke College	Light Blue.
Mount Union College	Royal Purple.
Nebraska Wesleyan University	Yellow and Brown.
New York University	Violet.
Niagara University	Purple and White.
Normal College	Lavender and White.
Northwestern University (Ill.)	Royal Purple.
N. C. State Nor. and Ind. Col.	White and Gold.
Ohio Northern University	Orange and Black.
Ohio State University	Scarlet and Gray.
Ohio University	Orange Green and White.
Oregon Agricultural College	Orange.
Otterbein University	Cardinal and Tan.
Peabody College	Garnet and Baby Blue.
Pennsylvania State College	Navy Blue and White.
Polytechnic Inst. (Brooklyn)	Blue and Gray.
Pratt Institute (Brooklyn)	Cadmium Yellow.
Princeton University	Orange and Black.
Purdue University	Old Gold and Black.
Radcliffe College	Crimson and White.
Rensselaer Poly. Institute	Cherry and White.
Rutgers College	Scarlet.
Shaw University	Blue.
Shurtleff College	Garnet and Gold.
Simmons College	Blue and Gold.
Smith College	White.
Southwest Kansas College	Royal Purple.
State University of Ky.	Blue and White.
State University of Iowa	Old Gold.
Stevens Inst. of Technology	Silver Gray and Cardinal.
St. Francis Xavier College	Maroon and Blue.
St. Lawrence University	Scarlet and Brown.
St. Louis University	Blue and White.
Swarthmore College	Garnet.
Syracuse University	Orange.
Talladega College	Crimson and Azure.
Teachers' College (N. Y. City)	Blue and White.
Temple University	Cherry and White.
Texas Christian College	Royal Purple and White.
Throop Polytechnic Institute	Orange and White.
Trinity College (N. C.)	Navy Blue.
Tufts College	Brown and Blue.
University of Alabama	Crimson and White.
University of Arizona	Blue and Red.
University of Arkansas	Cardinal.
University of California	Blue and Gold.
University of Chattanooga	Old Gold and Blue
University of Chicago	Maroon.
University of Cincinnati	Red and Black.
University of Colorado	Silver and Gold.
University of Denver	Crimson and Gold.
University of Georgia	Red and Black.
University of Idaho	Silver and Gold.
University of Illinois	Orange and Blue.
University of Kansas	Crimson and Dark Blue
University of Louisville	Scarlet and Black.
University of Maine	Light Blue.
University of Michigan	Yellow and Blue.
University of Minnesota	Old Gold and Maroon.
University of Missouri	Black and Old Gold.
University of Montana	Copper, Gold, and Silver.
University of Nashville	Garnet and Blue.
University of Nevada	Royal Blue and Silver.
University of North Carolina	White and Blue.
University of North Dakota	Pink and Green.
University of Notre Dame	Old Gold and Marine Blue.
University of Oklahoma	Crimson and Cream.
University of Oregon	Green and Yellow.
University of Pennsylvania	Red and Blue.
University of Pittsburgh	Blue and Gold.
University of Porto Rico	White and Red.
University of Rochester	Dandelion Yellow.
University of South Carolina	Garnet and Black.
University of South Dakota	Vermilion.
University of Southern Cal.	Gold.
University of the South	Purple and Old Gold.
University of Tennessee	Orange and White.
University of Texas	Orange and White.
University of Utah	Crimson and Silver.
University of Vermont	Green and Gold.
University of Virginia	Orange and Dark Blue.
University of Washington	Purple and Gold.
University of Wisconsin	Cardinal.
University of Wooster	Black and Old Gold.
University of Wyoming	Brown and Gold.
U. S. Military Academy	Black, Gold, and Gray.
U. S. Naval Academy	Navy Blue and Gold.
Upper Iowa University	Peacock Blue and White.
Utah Agri. College	White and Blue.
Valparaiso University	Old Gold and Bright Brown.
Vanderbilt University	Black and Gold.
Vassar College	Rose and Gray.
Virginia Polytechnic Institute	Orange and Maroon.
Walden University	Black and Red.
Wake Forest College	Old Gold and Black.
Washburn College	Yale Blue.
Wash'n and Jefferson College	Red and Black.
Washington and Lee University	Blue and White
Washington State College	Crimson and Gray.
Washington University (Mo.)	Myrtle and Maroon.
Wellesley College	Deep Blue.
Wesleyan University	Cardinal and Black.
Western Reserve University	Crimson and White.
West Virginia University	Old Gold and Blue.
Whitman College	Cobalt Blue and Maize.
Wilberforce University	Green and Old Gold.
Willamette University	Cardinal and Old Gold.
Williams College	Royal Purple.
Woman's College of Balto.	Dark Blue and Old Gold.
Worcester Polytechnic Inst.	Crimson and Steel Gray.
Yale University	Blue.
Yankton College	Yellow and White.

American College Fraternities.

MEN'S GENERAL FRATERNITIES.

Fraternity.	Membership.	Active Chapters.	Inactive Chapters.	No. Houses.	Where and When Founded.	National Secretary.
Alpha Chi Rho	490	11	1	11	Trinity, 1895	James L. Robinson, New York City.
Alpha Delta Phi	11,274	23	6	23	Hamilton, 1832	Robert A. Gunn, New York City.
Alpha Tau Omega	7,850	59	22	45	Va. Military Inst., 1865.	L. W. Glazebrook, M. D., Wash., D. C.
Beta Theta Pi	15,698	70	20	59	Miami, 1839	Francis W. Shepardson, Chicago, Ill.
Chi Phi	5,193	18	30	18	Princeton, 1824	Theo. B. Appel, M. D., Lancaster, Pa.
Chi Psi	4,890	17	12	17	Union, 1841	Geo. P. Richardson, Newark, N. J.
Delta Kappa Epsilon	16,500	42	11	25	Yale, 1844	David B. Simpson, New York City.
Delta Phi	3,600	11	5	0	Union, 1827	Arthur G. Freeland, New York City.
Delta Psi	2,500	8	0	8	Columbia, 1847	(No National Secretary.)
Delta Sigma Phi	715	8	1	4	Coll. City of N. Y., 1901.	Meyer Boskey, New York City.
Delta Tau Delta	9,875	52	26	48	Bethany, 1859	Henry T. Bruck, Mt. Savage, Md.
Delta Upsilon	10,500	38	4	36	Williams, 1834	H. S. Smalley, Ann Arbor, Mich.
Kappa Alpha (North)	1,100	7	2	7	Union, 1825	Theo. Gilman, Jr., New York City.
Kappa Alpha (South)	9,280	48	10	30	Wash'ton and Lee, 1865	V. Otis Robertson, Jackson, Miss.
Kappa Sigma	9,057	74	15	48	University Va., 1869	Herbert M. Martin, Danville, Va.
Omega Pi Alpha	312	6	0	5	Coll. City of N. Y., 1901.	....
Phi Delta Theta	16,460	71	24	60	Miami, 1848	Samuel K. Ruick, Indianapolis, Ind.
Phi Gamma Delta	11,500	57	25	45	Wash. & Jefferson, 1848	Thomas L. Pogue, Cincinnati, O.
Phi Kappa Psi	10,500	43	20	34	Wash. & Jefferson, 1852	Henry H. McCorkle, New York City.
Phi Kappa Sigma	3,900	26	14	20	University Penn., 1850.	Herbert Stotesbury, Philadelphia, Pa.
Phi Sigma Kappa	3,000	23	0	23	Mass. Agr'l Coll., 1873.	Henry H. Dyersen, New York City.
Pi Kappa Alpha	5,000	30	6	10	University Va., 1868	Chas. W. Underwood, Atlanta, Ga.
Psi Upsilon	11,200	22	1	21	Union, 1833	George S. Coleman, New York City.
Sigma Alpha Epsilon	12,000	71	27	54	Univ. Alabama, 1856	Clar. W. Stowell, Providence, R. I.
Sigma Chi	9,280	57	21	51	Miami, 1855	Herbert C. Arms, Chicago, Ill.
Sigma Nu	8,000	59	14	48	Va. Military Inst., 1869.	Clarence E. Woods, Richmond, Ky.
Sigma Phi	1,425	9	2	8	Union, 1827	Alex. Duane, M. D., New York City.
Sigma Phi Epsilon	1,000	24	6	15	Richmond College, 1901	Wm. K. Phillips, Washington, D. C.
Sigma Pi	495	7	5	3	William and Mary, 1752	Robt. Geo. Patterson, Columbus, O.
Theta Chi	500	4	0	4	Norwich Univ., 1856	George H. Chapin, Jr., Boston, Mass.
Theta Delta Chi	5,000	26	16	19	Union, 1848	George N. Shaeffer, Lockport, N. Y.
Theta Xi (Eng., Scien.)	900	11	0	10	Rensselaer P. Inst., 1864	Frank R. Lanagan, Albany, N. Y.
Zeta Psi	5,500	22	9	15	N. Y. University, 1847	Robert B. Austin, New York City.
Total	215,494	1054	356	801		

WOMEN'S GENERAL FRATERNITIES.

Fraternity.	Membership.	Active Chapters.	Inactive Chapters.	No. Houses.	Where and When Founded.	National Secretary.
Alpha Chi Omega	1,270	14	1	8	De Pauw Univ., 1885	Helen Wright, Toulon, Ill.
Alpha Omicron Pi*	500	11	0	3	Barnard College, 1897	Elizabeth Toms, New York City.
Alpha Phi	1,800	14	0	3	Syracuse, Univ., 1872	Mrs. S. V. Balderston, Evanst'n, Ill.
Alpha Xi Delta	626	14	0	6	Lombard College, 1893	Mary E. Kay, Alliance, O.
Beta Sigma Omicron	600	10	6	3	Miss. State Univ., 1888.	Bernice Stall, Richmond, Va.
Chi Omega	1,400	22	1	2	Univ. Arkansas, 1895	Jessie Anna Parker, Olathe, Kan.
Delta Delta Delta	2,000	26	1	9	Boston University, 1883	Mrs. J. E. Rhodes, Minneapl's, Minn.
Delta Gamma	2,402	19	12	12	WarrenFemaleIn., 1873	Ruth Rosholt, Minneapolis, Minn.
Gamma Phi Beta	1,522	12	0	6	Syracuse Univ., 1874	Mabel E. Stone, Syracuse, N. Y.
Kappa Alpha Theta	3,860	29	7	14	De Pauw Univ., 1870	L. Pearle Green, Ithaca, N. Y.
Kappa Delta	820	13	2	0	Va. State Normal, 1897.	Mary S. Thomas, Columbia, S. C.
Kappa Kappa Gamma	6,000	33	10	16	Monmouth Col., 1870	Mrs. A. H. Roth, Erie, Pa.
Phi Mu	1,302	10	0	1	Wesleyan College, 1852	Bonita L. Hinton, New Orleans, La.
Pi Beta Phi	5,000	38	10	20	Monmouth Col., 1867	Elda L. Smith, Springfield, Ill.
Sigma Kappa	604	8	2	3	Colby College, 1874	Emma E. Kinne, Syracuse, N. Y.
Sigma Sigma Sigma	350	5	2	0	Va. State Normal, 1898.	Emma H. Moffett, Lebanon, Ky.
Zeta Tau Alpha	400	7	4	2	Va. State Normal, 1898.	Mrs. J. L. Bugg, Farmville, Va.
Total	30,456	285	58	105		

* Absorbed in January, 1908, the Delta Sigma fraternity founded at Brown University in 1901.

MEDICAL FRATERNITIES.

Fraternity.	Membership.	Active Chapters.	Inactive Chapters.	No. Houses.	Where and When Founded.	National Secretary.
Alpha Kappa Kappa*	3,000	34	0	0	Dartmouth, 1888.	Edw. L. Heintz, Chicago, Ill.
Alpha Mu Pi Omega	800	6	1	2	Univ. of Penn., 1890	J. Gurney Taylor, Philadelphia, Pa.
Alpha Omega Alpha†.	800	14	0	0	C. of Pys. & Sur., Cgo, 1902	Wm. W. Root, Losantville, Md.
Alpha Sigma	694	9	1	2	N.Y. Hom. Med Col, 1893	William H. Pine, Brooklyn, N. Y.
Delta Mu	650				Univ. of Vermont, 1884	E. H. Libby, Burlington, Vt.
Nu Sigma Nu‡	3,500	29	0	10	Un. Mich. Med. D't, 1882	Will. Walter, Chicago, Ill.
Omega Upsilon Phi	1,400	17	3	11	Univ. Buffalo, 1895	Maurice B. Uoff, Chicago, Ill.
Phi Alpha Gamma	2,200	12	1	9	N.Y. Hom. Med Col, 1894	Albert W. Greene, New York City.
Phi Alpha Sigma	800	5	0	4	Bellevue Med. Col., 1888	James H. Potter, New York City.
Phi Beta Pi	2,900	27	2	20	West'n Uv. of Pa., 1891	G. R. Pray, Jackson, Mich.
Phi Chi§	3,264	34	0	10	Univ. Vermont... 1886	Dunning S. Wilson, Louisville, Ky.
Phi Rho Sigma	2,000	21	1	17	N'thwest U. Med S., 1892	C. G. Goulee, Chicago, Ill.
Phi Theta Chi	160	1	0	1	Tufts Cl. Med. Sch, 1902	Frank E. Haskins, Boston, Mass.
Total	22,168	209	9	86		

AMERICAN COLLEGE FRATERNITIES—*Continued.*

LEGAL FRATERNITIES

Alpha Kappa Phi......	600	4	0	2	University, Miss., 1858	Olaf A. Olson, Chicago, Ill.
Delta Chi...............	2,642	20	2	18	Cornell University, 1890	W. W. Bride, Washington, D, C.
Phi Delta Phi..........	8,350	42	0	15	University, Mich., 1869	Geo. A. Katzenberger, Greenville, O.
Sigma Nu Phi..........	215	1	2	1	Law D'tN.U.W'sh., 1902	Wm. A. Lemmond, Washington, D.C.
Theta Lambda Phi......	2,000	9	0	3	Dick'son S. of Law, 1903	J. Ward Follette, New York City.
Total................	13,807	76	4	39		

* Absorbed in 1907 the Phi Sigma Psi fraternity organized at Starling Medical College in 1895.

† Membership is based exclusively on scholarship. It is the only medical college honour society in America and so admits women on the same basis as men, as does Phi Beta Kappa.

‡ Absorbed the Delta Epsilon Iota fraternity founded at Yale Medical School in 1889.

§ Originally two fraternities, the Northern founded at University of Vermont in 1867, and the Southern at Louisville Medical College in 1894; were combined in 1905.

UNITED CHAPTERS OF PHI BETA KAPPA.

The Phi Beta Kappa Society was founded at William and Mary College, Williamsburg, Va., December 5, 1776, and now consists of 71 chapters located in as many of the leading colleges and universities in the land. The total living membership is nearly 15,000. Until 1883 the growth of the Society was comparatively slow, but since the organization of the United Chapters the development has been rapid, 47 chapters having been organized. At the ninth triennial council, held September 12, 1907, at William and Mary College, eight charters were granted, as follows: Virginia, Michigan, Louisiana, Illinois and Ohio Wesleyan Universities, and Oberlin, Iowa and Franklin and Marshall Colleges. Women were first admitted in 1875, and the first charter to a woman's college, Vassar, was granted in 1898. Since then Smith, Wellesley, Mt. Holyoke and the Woman's College of Baltimore have received charters. At the recent Council President Mary E. Woolley, of Mt. Holyoke, was chosen to the Senate, the first woman to be thus honored. The officers for the term, 1907-1910 are: *President*, Prof. Edwin A. Grosvenor, LL.D., Amherst, Mass.; *Vice-President*, Hon. John J. McCook, LL.D., New York, N. Y.; *Secretary and Treasurer*, Rev. Oscar M. Voorhees, A.M., High Bridge, N. J.

Acacia Fraternity.—An intercollegiate organization for Master Masons founded at the University of Michigan in 1904, now has a membership of 654 and 14 active chapters. The *National Secretary* is Harry E. Kilmer, 728 Rialto Building, St. Louis, Mo.

The Professional Fraternities now number 52, with a membership exceeding 37,000. They are located in both technical and professional schools. With the exception of Theta Xi (Engineering Scientific), members of professional fraternities may also belong to the general college fraternities.

Local or "One-college" Fraternities exist in nearly all colleges, and some date back as early as 1825. Of the men's locals there are nearly 75, with a membership approximating 6,000. The women's local fraternities number about 50, with a total membership of about 1,200.

PROMINENT LIVING GRADUATE MEMBERS.

Alpha Chi Rho.—Joseph F. Johnson, Dean of New York University; William R. Shepherd, Professor of History, Columbia University.

Alpha Delta Phi.—Theodore Roosevelt, President of the United States; Joseph H. Choate, ex-Ambassador to England; Edward Everett Hale, Chaplain of the United States Senate; Hamilton W. Mable, author; James R. Garfield, Secretary of the Interior; Benjamin Ide Wheeler, President of the University of California; Charles W. Eliot, President of Harvard University; Timothy Dwight, ex-President of Yale University; Francis Lynde Stetson, railroad magnate; John D. Rockefeller, Jr.

Alpha Tau Omega.—Robert L. Owen, United States Senator from Oklahoma; Duncan C. Heyward, ex-Governor of South Carolina; Walter H. Page, editor and publisher; F. M. Simmons, United States Senator from North Carolina; Clifton R. Breckinridge, ex-Ambassador to Russia; Erskine M. Ross, United States Circuit Court Judge, California; A. I. Bacheller, author; Thomas F. Gailor, Episcopal Bishop of Tennessee; Theodore DuB. Bratton, Episcopal Bishop of Mississippi.

Beta Theta Pi.—John M. Harlan, Justice of the United States Supreme Court; David J. Brewer, Justice of the United States Supreme Court; General James A. Beaver, ex-Governor of Pennsylvania; Edward C. Stokes, ex-Governor of New Jersey; P. S. Grosscup, Judge of the United States Circuit Court; Rev. Frank W. Gunsaulus; Henry A. Buchtel, Governor of Colorado; Frank O. Lowden, Henry S. Boutell, Representative in Congress from Illinois.

Chi Phi.—Lee S. Overman, United States Senator from North Carolina; Franklin K. Lane, Interstate Commerce Commissioner; John B. Deaver, M. D.; Hugh H. Young, M. D.; Emory Speer, United States District Judge; Peter W. Meldim, of Savannah, Ga.; W. D. Jelks, ex-Governor of Alabama; W. K. Brooks, naturalist; F. R. Graves, Episcopal Bishop of Shanghai.

Chi Psi.—Elbridge T. Gerry; Melville W. Fuller, Chief Justice of the United States; Francis M. Scott, Justice New York Supreme Court; Clyde Fitch, playwright; Clinton Scollard, author; Don M. Dickinson, jurist; Frederick W. Whitridge, lawyer.

Delta Kappa Epsilon.—Theodore Roosevelt, President of the United States; Whitelaw Reid, Ambassador to Great Britain; Julian Hawthorne, author; Robert

E. Peary, Arctic explorer; Charles Waldstein, archaeologist; Arthur T. Hadley, President of Yale University.

Delta Psi.—H. D. Money, United States Senator from Mississippi; Gen. Stewart L. Woodford, ex-United States Minister to Spain; W. C. Doane, Episcopal Bishop of Albany; C. B. Galloway, Bishop of the Methodist Episcopal Church; Thomas Nelson Page, author; Luke E. Wright, United States Secretary of War; Stuyvesant Fish, ex-President Illinois Central Railroad; Willard Bartlett, Justice of the New York Supreme Court; Charles Cuthbert Hall, ex-President of Union Theological Seminary; J. Cleveland Cady, architect.

Delta Sigma Phi.—Arvid D. Anderson, Registrar of the College of the City of New York; William E. Waters, Professor of Greek, New York University.

Delta Tau Delta.—Albert J. Hopkins, United States Senator from Illinois; Champ Clark, Representative in Congress from Missouri; James A. Mann, Representative in Congress from Illinois; A. C. Humphreys, President of Stevens Institute of Technology; K. C. Babcock, President of University of Arizona; William Kent, M. E.; James E. Denton, M. E.; Will Carleton, writer; Frederick Palmer, war correspondent; Bion J. Arnold, electrical expert; William A. Lieb, Vice-President and General Manager Edison Electric Company; Rev. W. T. Manning, Rector of Trinity Church, New York City; Rev. C. E. Jefferson, Pastor Broadway Tabernacle, New York City; George Horton, Consul-General to Greece.

Delta Upsilon.—Charles E. Hughes, Governor of New York; William T. Jerome, District-Attorney of New York City; Fletcher D. Proctor, ex-Governor of Vermont; Frank H. Hitchcock, Chairman of the Republican National Committee; Sereno E. Payne, Representative in Congress from New York; M. Linn Bruce, Justice of the Supreme Court of New York; Edward M. Bassett, Public Service Commissioner of New York; David Starr Jordan, President Leland Stanford University; Flavel S. Luther, President of Trinity College, Hartford; William H. P. Faunce, President of Brown University.

Kappa Alpha (Northern).—Laurenus C. Seelye, President of Smith College; Edward H. Griffin, Dean of Johns Hopkins University; Francis E. Leupp, Commissioner of Indian Affairs; Frank H. Hiscock, Justice of the Supreme Court of New York; Hobart C. Chatfield-Taylor, author; Silas B. Brownell, Director of Princeton Theological Seminary; Horace White, Lieutenant-Governor-Elect of New York.

Kappa Alpha (Southern).—Joseph W. Folk Governor of Missouri; Morris Sheppard, Representative in Congress from Texas; John Temple Graves, editor; Thomas Dixon, author; John S. Candler, of Georgia, jurist; Edward Chambers Smith, lawyer; John S. Wise, lawyer.

Kappa Sigma.—William G. McAdoo, President of the Hudson Tunnels Company; Dr. John Covert Boyd, United States Navy; Rev. N. M. Waters, preacher; Dr. Lyon G. Tyler, President of William and Mary College; P. P. Campbell, Representative in Congress from Kansas.

Phi Delta Theta.—Adlai E. Stevenson, ex-Vice-President of the United States; William Allen White, author; Ray Stannard Baker, author; Brigadier-General Fred Funston, United States Army; John W. Foster, diplomatist; Malcolm R. Patterson, Governor of Tennessee; S. H. Elrod, Governor of South Dakota; Addison C. Harris, ex-Minister to Austria.

Phi Gamma Delta.—Charles W. Fairbanks, Vice-President of the United States; John W. Thomas, railroad president; Rev. James D. Moffat, President of Washington and Jefferson College; Charles W. Dabney, President of the University of Cincinnati; Joseph C. Hartzell and William F. McDowell, Bishops of the Methodist Episcopal Church.

Phi Kappa Psi.—Joseph B. Foraker, United States Senator from Ohio; James E. Watson, Representative in Congress from Indiana; Arthur L. Bates, Representative in Congress from Pennsylvania; H. L. Hadley, Governor-Elect of Missouri; P. H. Dugro, Justice of the Supreme Court of New York; David H. Greer, Bishop of New York; Frank S. Monette, ex-Attorney-General of Ohio; George E. Chamberlain, United States Senator-Elect from Oregon; Woodrow Wilson, President of Princeton University.

Phi Kappa Sigma.—Henry A. Du Pont, United States Senator from Delaware; Samuel D. McEnery, United States Senator from Louisiana; Claude A. Swanson, Governor of Virginia; Horatio C. King, lawyer and author; Charles I. Wilson, Brigadier-General United States Army; Colonel William Jay, of New York; E. A. Alderman, President of the University of Virginia; Daniel S. Tuttle, Episcopal Bishop of Missouri; Robert Strange, Episcopal Bishop of North Carolina; Frank M. Bristol, Bishop of the Methodist Episcopal Church.

Phi Sigma Kappa.—Charles S. Howe, President of the Case School of Applied Science; George B. Cortelyou, Secretary of the United States Treasury Department; Charles W. Needham, President of George Washington University; Charles S. Norton, Rear Admiral United States Navy.

Pi Kappa Alpha.—Rev. D. A. Blackburg, Pastor of Church of the Strangers, New York City; Dr. H. B. Arbuckle, educator; James Alston Cabell, lawyer and author.

Psi Upsilon.—William H. Taft, President-Elect of the United States; Andrew D. White, ex-Ambassador to England; Chauncey M. Depew, United States Senator from New York; John C. Spooner, ex-United States Senator from Wisconsin; William P. Frye, United States Senator from Maine; Nicholas Murray Butler, President Columbia University; J. Benjamin Dimmick, Mayor of Scranton, Pa.; Herbert L. Bridgman, journalist.

Sigma Alpha Epsilon.—John G. Carlisle, ex-Secretary of the Treasury; Jacob

M. Dickinson, of Chicago, jurist; John C. W. Beckham, ex-Governor of Kentucky; J. M. Dickinson, President of the American Bar Association; John G. Capers, United States Commissioner of Internal Revenue; James F. O'Neill, actor; Charles B. Howry, Justice United States Court of Claims; Thomas Watson, ex-Representative in Congress from Georgia.

Sigma Chi.—J. Taylor Ellyson, Lieutenant-Governor of Virginia; J. M. Hamilton, ex-Governor of Illinois; A. H. Lougino, ex-Governor of Mississippi; Robert S. McCormick, ex-Ambassador to France; James Deering, President of the International Harvester Company; George Ade, journalist and author; John M. Harris, President of Bucknell College; George H. Denny, President of Washington and Lee University; Booth Tarkington, author.

Sigma Nu.—H. D. Clayton, Representative in Congress from Alabama; Harvey Helm, Representative in Congress from Kentucky; Dr. Isadore Dyer, of New Orleans, leprosy expert; Rev. J. R. Sampey, D. D., theologian; Wade H. Ellis, Assistant Attorney-General of the United States.

Sigma Phi.—M. W. Stryker, President of Hamilton College; Andrew D. White, ex-President of Cornell University; Elihu Root, Secretary of State; Gerritt Smith, composer; Chester S. Lord, managing editor of the New York Sun; Charles E. Cheney, Bishop of the Reformed Episcopal Church; Bradley Martin, capitalist; Montgomery Schuyler, journalist; John E. Parsons, lawyer; John Bigelow, author, ex-Minister to France; James S. Sherman, Vice-President-Elect of the United States; Robert W. Patterson, editor, Chicago Tribune.

Sigma Pi.—William Jennings Bryan, editor; Richard Yates, ex-Governor of Illinois.

Theta Chi.—Charles F. Sayles, mechanical engineer; William R. Cutler, author and historian; General Edward B. Williston, Governor of Soldiers' Home, Washington, D. C.; George A. Converse, Rear-Admiral United States Navy; Major H. B. Hersey, Arctic explorer; Charles H. Spooner, President of Norwich University; De Witt C. Webb, mechanical engineer.

Theta Delta Chi.—F. W. Hamilton, President of Tufts College; Gonzalo de Quesada, Minister from Cuba; B. P. Lamberton, Rear-Admiral United States Navy; Cameron Mann, Episcopal Bishop of North Dakota; John W. Griggs, ex-Attorney-General of the United States; John B. McPherson, United States District Judge; A. M. Randolph, Episcopal Bishop of Southern Virginia; Charles R. Miller, editor of the New York Times; William D. Bloxham, ex-Governor of Florida.

Theta Xi.—David L. Hough, President New York Tunnel Company; Frederick H. Howland, editor Providence Tribune; Palmer C. Ricketts, President Rensselaer Polytechnic Institute; George Gibbs, electrical engineer; Sam Higgins, railroad manager; Henry Hodge, consulting bridge engineer; Rear-Admiral Mordecai T. Endicott, United States Navy.

Zeta Psi.—Rev. Almon Gunnison, President of St. Lawrence University; Daniel S. Goodschell, Bishop of the Methodist Episcopal Church; Nelson Dingley, ex-Representative in Congress from Maine; ex-Governor George D. Robinson, of Massachusetts; Rodney Welch and William H. McElroy, journalists; George M. Rose, ex-Speaker of the North Carolina House of Representatives.

Beginnings of Famous Universities.

THE University of Oxford has the reputation of having been founded by King Alfred in **872.**

The first college of the University of Cambridge was founded by Hugo, Bishop of Ely, in **1257.**

The University of Paris was founded by King Philip II. about **1200.**

The first university in the German Empire was at Prague, Bohemia, **1348.**

The Czar Alexander I. founded the Universities of St. Petersburg and Moscow in **1802.**

The oldest Spanish University is that of Salamanca, founded in **1240.**

The University of Copenhagen, Denmark, was founded in **1479.**

The University of Upsala, Sweden, was founded in **1477.**

The oldest Italian universities are Bologna, founded **1200**; Padua, **1222**; Naples, **1224**; Genoa, 1243; Perugia, 1276; Macerata, 1290. There were nine more founded between **1300** and **1550.** Italy was the greatest resort of students for the higher education in the Middle Ages.

Trinity College, Dublin, was incorporated by royal charter in **1591.**

The University of Edinburgh was founded in **1582** by a charter granted by King James VI, of Scotland.

Harvard University had its beginning at Newtown, afterward Cambridge, Mass., in **1636.**

Yale University had its beginning at Saybrook, Ct., in **1700**, and was removed to New Haven in 1716.

Columbia University was chartered as King's College in **1754.** The name was changed to Columbia College in 1784 and Columbia University in **1896.**

Princeton University, founded in 1746, was chartered as the College of New Jersey, and did not assume its present name officially until its one hundred and fiftieth anniversary in 1896.

William and Mary College (first steps taken toward establishing it in **1617**) erected at Williamsburg, Va., and charter granted in 1693.

The first common schools established by legislation in America were in Massachusetts, **1645**; but the first town school was opened at Hartford, Ct., prior to **1642.**

The University of Pennsylvania had its beginning at Philadelphia, Pa., in **1740.** It was chartered in 1753 as the Academy and Charitable School in the Province of Pennsylvania, and received a further charter as a college in **1755.** Its present title dates from **1791.**

The University of Jagielle, of Cracow, Poland, where Copernicus received his education, was founded in 1364 by the Polish King Kazimiers the Great, and endowed by a later Polish King, Jagielle, in **1400.**

The Common Schools of the United States.

States and Territories, 1906-1907.	Pupils Enrolled.	Per Cent. of Population Enrolled.	Average Daily Attendance.	Total No. of Teachers.*
N. Atlantic Div.				
Maine	131,671	18.34	98,437	6.755
N. Hampshire	65,210	14.95	49,663	2,916
Vermont	66,524	18.93	48,626	3,984
Massachusetts	508,816	16.72	415,508	14,166
Rhode Island	71,425	15.19	53,830	2,047
Connecticut	173,973	17.30	132,778	4,729
New York	1,343,379	16.02	1,033,070	41,197
New Jersey	394,060	17.53	276,095	10,011
Pennsylvania	1,225,388	17.42	933,441	33,449
S. Atlantic Div.				
Delaware	36,895	19.98	25,300	897
Maryland	234,085	18.15	134,951	5,290
Dis. of Columbia	51,992	16.89	41,185	1,484
Virginia	369,331	18.53	219,741	9,468
West Virginia	253,147	23.10	165,095	8,061
North Carolina	483,180	23.46	293,046	9,871
South Carolina	314,399	21.37	222,189	6,228
Georgia	499,103	21.08	311,489	10,360
Florida	130,465	20.93	88,825	3,289
S. Central Div.				
Kentucky	501,482	22.48	309,836	9,245
Tennessee	508,316	23.39	351,622	9,189
Alabama	400,000	20.14	210,000	5,400
Mississippi	482,208	27.80	285,047	9,499
Louisiana	225,008	14.37	160,472	5,615
Texas	705,305	19.90	473,276	17,553
Arkansas	340,182	23.62	220,621	8,113
Oklahoma	187,403	25.09	103,161	4,386
Indian Territ'y	104,125	15.05	61,450	2,740

States and Territories, 1906-1907.	Pupils Enrolled.	Per Cent. of Population Enrolled.	Average Daily Attendance.	Total No. of Teachers.*
N. Central Div.				
Ohio	827,414	18.40	627,780	26,517
Indiana	538,881	19.64	420,283	16,841
Illinois	983,921	17.83	770,020	28,083
Michigan	521,463	20.39	407,977	16,924
Wisconsin	465,490	20.30	327,975	14,491
Minnesota	429,012	20.71	321,599	13,928
Iowa	549,449	24.91	375,639	28,508
Missouri	741,745	21.78	493,418	17,847
North Dakota	124,000	25.42	72,000	6,109
South Dakota	110,094	23.63	68,249	5,090
Nebraska	279,532	26.16	184,647	9 639
Kansas	381,595	24.11	264,034	12,036
Western Div.				
Montana	48,744	16.05	34,738	1,741
Wyoming	19,795	18.76	14,032	787
Colorado	144,799	23.05	105,632	4,944
New Mexico	40,889	18.60	24,898	923
Arizona	24,962	16.96	15,352	626
Utah	77,947	24.64	60,018	1,892
Nevada	9,587	22.65	6,788	322
Idaho	66,699	31.31	48,417	1,897
Washington	188,989	29.96	130,750	6,209
Oregon	102,662	21.17	76,954	4,228
California	335,645	20.04	247,880	9,714
N. Atlantic Div.	3,980,446	16.80	3,041,448	119,254
S. Atlantic Div.	2,372,597	20.77	1,501,821	54,948
S. Central Div.	3,454,029	21.46	2,175,485	71,740
N. Central Div.	5,952,596	20.60	4,333,621	196,013
Western Div.	1,060,718	22.25	765,459	33,283
United States	16,820,386	19.82	11,817,834	475,238

* Males, 109,179. Females, 356,884.

Professional Schools in the United States.

Years.	Theological Schools.			Law Schools.			Medical Schools.* Regular.			Medical Schools.* Homœopathic.		
	Number.	Teachers.	Pupils.	Number.	Teachers.	Pupils.	Number.	Teachers.	Pupils.	Number.	Teachers.	Pupils.
1898-1899	163	996	8,261	96	966	11,874	122	3,562	21,401	21	636	1,802
1899-1900	154	994	8,009	96	1,004	12,516	121	3,545	22,752	22	735	1,909
1900-1901	150	988	7,567	100	1,106	13,642	123	3,876	24,199	21	639	1,812
1901-1902	148	1,034	7,348	102	1,155	13,912	123	4,084	24,447	20	649	1,551
1902-1903	153	1,031	7,372	99	1,158	14,057	118	4,025	24,847	19	666	1,462
1903-1904	153	1,055	7,392	95	1,167	14,302	122	4,253	24,694	19	666	1,289
1904-1905	156	1,094	7,411	96	1,190	14,714	120	4,532	24,012	18	640	1,129
1905-1906	150	1,103	7,968	98	1,274	15,411	123	4,877	24,927	18	703	1,083
1906-1907	162	1,236	9,178	101	1,209	16,700	124	5,642	22,022	18	654	1,102
	Dental Schools.			Schools of Pharmacy.			Nurse Training Schools.			Veterinary Schools.		
1898-1899	50	948	7,854	51	442	3,551	393	..	10,018	13	153	316
1899-1900	54	1,118	7,928	53	493	4,042	432	..	11,164	13	124	362
1900-1901	57	1 184	8,308	58	522	4,429	448	..	11,599	12	189	461
1901-1902	56	1,197	8,420	59	590	4,427	545	..	13,252	11	174	576
1902-1903	54	1,164	8,298	61	595	4,411	552	..	13,779	11	168	671
1903-1904	54	1 191	7,325	63	611	4,457	724	..	17,713	11	165	795
1904-1905	54	1,161	7,149	67	629	4,944	862	..	19,824	12	217	1,269
1905-1906	56	1,329	6,876	66	623	5,145	974	..	21,052	12	204	1,445
1906-1907	57	1,346	6,919	71	690	5,047	1,023	..	21,119	13	231	1,692

* There were also 10 Eclectic and Physiomedical Schools, with 330 instructors and 596 students in 1906-1907.

School and College Enrolment in 1907.

Grades.	Number of Pupils. Public.	Private.	Total.
Elementary (primary and grammar)	16,069,305	1,304,547	17,373,852
Secondary (high schools and academies)	771,687	190,099	961,786
Universities and colleges	53,623	96,077	149,700
Professional schools	11,517	51,739	63,256
Normal schools	62,428	8,011	70,439
City evening schools	315,093	.....	315,093
Business schools	......	137,364	137,364
Reform schools	35,231	......	35,231
Schools for deaf	11,701	533	12,234
Schools for blind	4,359	......	4,359

Grades.	Number of Pupils. Public.	Private.	Total.
Schools for feeble-minded	16,639	584	17,223
Government Indian schools	26,186	......	26,186
Indian schools (five civilized tribes)	......	4,307	4,307
Schools for natives in Alaska	2.639	.....	2,639
Schools for whites in Alaska	1,780	......	1,780
Orphan asylums and other benevolent institutions	......	15,000	15,000
Private kindergartens	......	105,932	105,932
Miscellaneous (art, music, etc.)	......	50,000	50,000
Total for United States	17,382,186	1,964,193	19,346,381

Statistics of Education.

UNIVERSITIES, COLLEGES AND TECHNOLOGICAL SCHOOLS IN THE UNITED STATES.

(Prepared for THE WORLD ALMANAC by the Statistician of the United States Bureau of Education.)

States and Territories, 1906-1907.	Income in 1906 1907				Libraries, Bound Volumes.	Value of Scientific Apparatus.	Value of Grounds and Buildings.	Value of Productive Funds.	Benefactions for Endowment.
	From Tuition Fees.	From Productive Funds.	From U. S. Government, State, or Municipal Appropriations.	Total Income.					
North Atlantic Division.									
Maine	$114,228	$83,896	$40,000	$349,973	$192,925	$160,704	$2,028,476	$1,911,627	$202,868
N. Hampshire	127,419	152,056	47,000	555,903	130,476	52,400	2,438,500	2,887,270	10,125
Vermont	50,396	52,848	33,130	221,804	120,222	105,500	1,254,000	983,691	16,297
Massachusetts	1,496,164	1,401,228	45,307	4,158,894	1,175,295	1,866,266	16,828,884	34,219,307	733,476
Rhode Island	138,778	148,855	47,000	520,897	172,102	221 679	1,839,219	3,217,522	57,344
Connecticut	491,271	532,037	38,500	1,889,322	636,560	721,230	7,978,388	10,269,797	749,277
New York	1,949,254	1,404,960	710,637	7,302,533	1,606,063	4,587,546	41,319,808	42,374,351	2,275,425
New Jersey	323,246	241,590	47,000	1,383,912	327,377	241,000	1,994,000	5,238,617	208,190
Pennsylvania	1,330,285	565,834	40,000	3,281,054	924,978	3,143,877	20,065,437	19,711,468	503,612
South Atlantic Division.									
Delaware	2,964	4,980	47,000	87,278	17,000	82,300	207,000	83,000	...
Maryland	172,607	210,775	45,000	756,866	297,526	397,460	10,998,089	4,526,381	109,134
D. of Columbia	234,030	26,140	103,700	682,266	219,087	124,006	5,610,567	1,545,588	22,500
Virginia	206,444	144,706	39,167	955,340	250,575	498,327	4,514,774	2,769,989	78,865
West Virginia	46,069	15,539	44,859	329,070	45,834	97,000	1,300,000	384,478	19,320
N. Carolina	178,055	106,768	47,000	733,579	167,415	292,120	2,975,114	1,700,013	63 000
S. Carolina	76,457	35,638	12,500	580,526	121,724	303,695	2,239,341	899,008	79,038
Georgia	98,293	56,522	18,667	420,352	109,000	169,700	2,139,200	1,032,689	11,500
Florida	28,085	28,378	12,500	190,842	26,000	80,967	569,143	609 968	40,000
South Central Division.									
Kentucky	136,680	120,179	21,375	519,959	104,642	372,159	2,265,932	2,280,985	20,879
Tennessee	241,469	159,203	53,250	862,927	186,511	368,146	4,492,124	3,036,300	61,596
Alabama	43,794	28,947	28,907	334,832	88,200	152,800	1,198,500	897,892	1,955
Mississippi	49,542	84,978	40,000	491,387	54,032	320,369	1,298,023	1,429,909	51,250
Louisiana	116,243	89,364	40,159	365,192	91,780	264,878	3,578,740	2,286,167	....
Texas	193,954	168,681	33,750	758,382	124,498	644,859	3,302,600	2,566,930	234
Arkansas	69,247	8,270	18,182	307,438	47,550	170,500	1,408,000	315,000	5,000
Oklahoma	18,940	27,908	44,500	355,996	34,251	294,700	1,187,500	1,520,000	100,000
Indian Ter.	6,500	....	....	6,500	4,500	10,000	200,000	....	15,180
North Central Division.									
Ohio	665,917	577,367	25,000	2,872,390	793,901	1,694,007	15,072,770	13,604,298	454,060
Indiana	291,247	134,147	25,000	1,103,790	317,234	942,156	5,502,400	3,352,616	124,073
Illinois	1,513,330	938,799	52,000	6,476,734	951,451	2,019,009	23,754,241	24,358,519	4,202,110
Michigan	381,416	155,568	48,692	1,534,431	371,951	1,191,396	4,465,998	3,176,069	20,022
Wisconsin	231,801	109,214	52,000	1,730,197	246,077	642,165	5,097,960	2,807,503	250,059
Minnesota	221,719	96,466	40,000	1,489,732	197,700	387,018	4,167,500	2,366,296	251,635
Iowa	372,900	153,526	61,128	2,021,621	282,528	1,236,239	6,874,224	3,844,940	634,608
Missouri	356,968	222,650	38,437	1,467,381	347,580	710,452	6,995,766	7,952,619	59,000
North Dakota	24,675	98,040	25,000	457,219	41,900	155,364	967,599	3,039,021	...
South Dakota	57,289	12,442	40,000	477,348	48,128	251,011	1,331,545	365,535	105,219
Nebraska	162,959	85,031	47,000	848,180	130,752	441,832	2,554,311	1,999,205	432,621
Kansas	267,724	64,717	40,000	1,110,358	247,543	560,840	3,810,575	1,521,985	124,10[illegible]
Western Division.									
Montana	5,719	22,000	47,000	295,485	31,664	179,760	585,000	1,343,385	....
Wyoming	1,070	7,508	47,500	85,992	22,010	105,757	225,000	400	....
Colorado	123,013	52,267	47,000	697,230	122,882	461,126	2,471,142	950,780	....
New Mexico	7,794	10,916	45,000	111,631	24,356	82,000	295,000	0	....
Arizona	3,744	....	25,000	116,845	11,000	49,661	182,499	0	....
Utah	30,362	27,854	40,000	416,750	49,555	201,854	1,031,544	160,000	....
Nevada	0	8,529	40,000	242,029	27,222	58,742	314,770	142,600	21,000
Idaho	0	24,336	47,000	125,086	8,200	34,436	207,500	310,128	....
Washington	72,780	18,293	47,000	689,377	81,300	295,270	1,798,000	509,500	19,500
Oregon	47,030	23,392	40,000	295,764	51,231	90,940	1,[illegible]38,750	677,514	131,200
California	308,106	1,027,614	47,000	2,352,817	394,742	674,619	10,302,929	30,018,144	189,932
N. Atlantic Div.	$6,024,041	$4,583,304	$1,048,574	19,064,292	5,285,998	11,100,202	95,746,712	120,813,650	4,756,614
S. Atlantic Div.	1,043,004	629,446	370,393	4,736,119	1,654,161	2,045,585	30,553,228	13,551,114	423,357
S. Central Div.	869,869	687,525	280,123	3,996,113	731,464	2,583,411	18,731,419	14,333,183	240,914
N. Central Div.	4,547,945	2,647,967	494,257	21,589,381	3,976,745	10,231,489	80,594,889	68,378,806	6,657,503
Western Div.	599,618	1,2[illegible]2,718	472,500	5,429,006	824,162	2,234,165	18,453,134	34,112,451	361,632
United States.	13,084,477	$9,770,960	$2,665,847	55,414,911	12472530	$28,194,852	244,078,382	251,189,204	12,440,020

Statistics of Education.

UNIVERSITIES, COLLEGES AND TECHNOLOGICAL SCHOOLS IN THE UNITED STATES.

(Prepared for THE WORLD ALMANAC by the Statistician of the United States Bureau of Education.)

States and Territories, 1904-1905.	Number of Institutions.	Professors and Instructors. Total Number.		Students. Preparatory Departments.		Collegiate Departments.		Graduate Departments.		Professional Departments.		Total Number.	
		Male.	Female.	Male.	Female.	Male.	Female.	Male.	Female.	Male.	Female.	Male.	Female.
North Atlantic Division.													
Maine	4	178	6	0	0	1,139	350	0	0	222	2	1,368	351
New Hampshire	3	135	0	71	0	1,270	14	28	0	62	0	1,513	14
Vermont	3	96	0	0	0	517	139	2	0	161	0	715	139
Massachusetts	13	1,414	17	506	10	6,347	511	575	57	2,276	109	9,884	624
Rhode Island	2	93	9	37	8	712	197	82	29	0	0	823	234
Connecticut	4	455	3	0	0	1,932	46	344	30	513	0	3,739	149
New York	26	2,276	134	5,541	487	7,814	2,504	1,097	443	3,900	96	21,146	5,243
New Jersey	6	267	5	341	26	2,051	1	116	0	0	0	2,518	27
Pennsylvania	33	1,456	116	1,783	926	8,803	1,148	431	85	2,860	42	15,933	3,845
South Atlantic Division.													
Delaware	2	27	2	35	26	153	29	3	0	0	0	191	55
Maryland	12	454	24	690	217	1,854	117	165	0	378	20	3,087	381
District of Columbia	6	483	19	449	63	589	249	161	13	1,717	27	3,016	492
Virginia	14	330	19	651	211	2,523	102	80	0	540	14	3,868	341
West Virginia	5	96	31	541	266	470	119	9	0	131	0	1,203	650
North Carolina	13	274	31	692	426	2,179	240	68	4	646	0	3,575	679
South Carolina	11	175	36	918	522	1,695	89	12	1	56	0	2,793	635
Georgia	11	156	58	895	605	1,308	101	8	0	171	1	2,510	754
Florida	4	57	34	270	308	144	60	6	3	37	2	457	373
South Central Division.													
Kentucky	11	262	83	870	463	1,175	361	13	1	877	9	3,768	1,116
Tennessee	15	483	79	1,526	979	1,517	724	44	7	1,892	6	4,980	1,826
Alabama	6	177	1	175	0	1,325	45	22	2	233	1	1,778	57
Mississippi	6	119	13	1,024	314	1,372	95	30	2	86	0	2,537	413
Louisiana	6	224	20	642	121	785	29	23	43	937	7	2,453	512
Texas	13	269	72	1,526	953	2,063	804	30	24	1,138	48	4,938	2,379
Arkansas	7	101	45	1,161	836	702	364	0	1	240	0	2,103	1,201
Oklahoma	6	115	40	560	347	387	266	3	1	118	4	1,640	876
Indian Territory	2	7	19	137	113	14	20	0	0	0	0	151	133
North Central Division.													
Ohio	34	1,065	263	2,531	1,355	3,951	3,002	135	62	1,203	16	10,004	6,717
Indiana	16	553	61	1,269	409	3,968	1,468	157	25	897	24	6,386	2,074
Illinois	31	1,506	312	5,619	2,720	5,419	2,900	444	193	3,118	150	15,912	8,102
Michigan	11	508	78	569	237	3,496	1,308	89	39	1,416	53	5,704	1,905
Wisconsin	10	507	58	848	184	3,236	1,314	157	46	454	4	4,635	1,775
Minnesota	9	445	70	1,135	423	1,721	1,326	69	43	1,118	27	4,404	2,199
Iowa	26	621	263	2,254	1,798	3,375	2,098	147	88	1,049	115	7,777	5,542
Missouri	16	670	115	2,369	1,095	2,522	794	133	31	1,219	16	6,282	2,383
North Dakota	4	97	25	793	445	195	96	8	6	151	3	1,243	865
South Dakota	7	119	53	598	638	381	213	21	9	67	2	1,245	1,038
Nebraska	9	481	90	1,111	386	1,777	1,621	70	60	743	20	3,729	2,558
Kansas	20	528	148	2,500	1,710	2,917	1,757	39	32	558	46	6,844	4,960
Western Division.													
Montana	3	50	15	182	116	236	163	5	7	0	0	493	346
Wyoming	1	17	9	13	35	53	21	17	19	0	0	107	157
Colorado	6	371	44	613	406	1,538	764	101	48	345	16	2,704	1,501
New Mexico	3	36	13	159	91	130	59	0	3	0	0	289	153
Arizona	1	18	7	76	66	47	23	0	3	0	0	123	92
Utah	3	126	35	855	649	433	303	11	4	45	1	1,322	1,037
Nevada	1	25	9	41	63	169	47	1	2	0	0	206	137
Idaho	1	27	6	92	40	156	75	0	0	0	0	248	115
Washington	6	210	38	532	297	1,110	762	33	20	194	23	2,172	1,429
Oregon	8	194	45	489	379	812	433	13	11	237	14	1,701	972
California	12	731	73	1,377	458	2,876	1,936	229	166	836	28	5,635	2,758
North Atlantic Division	94	6,370	290	8,279	1,457	30,585	4,910	2,675	644	9,994	249	57,639	10,626
South Atlantic Division	78	2,052	254	5,141	2,644	10,915	1,106	512	21	3,676	64	20,700	4,381
South Central Division	70	1,850	353	7,484	4,013	9,826	2,688	165	81	5,521	75	24,197	8,374
North Central Division	193	7,100	1,536	21,596	11,400	32,958	17,897	1,469	634	11,993	476	74,165	40,116
Western Division	45	1,805	294	4,429	2,600	7,560	4,586	410	283	1,657	82	15,000	8,697
United States	480	19,177	2,727	46,929	22,114	91,344	31,187	5,231	1,663	32,841	946	191,701	72,194

Women at Work in the United States.

(The Census Bureau issued in 1907 a report presenting statistics of Women at Work.)

In the United States the number of women at work as returned by the census of 1900 was almost five million. In continental United States—by which is meant the United States exclusive of Alaska, Hawaii and all other outlying territories or possessions—the exact number was 4,833,630.

RACE AND NATIVITY.

The total number includes 1,771,966 native white women whose parents also were natives; 1,090,744 native white women one or both of whose parents were immigrants; 840,011 white women who were themselves immigrants; 1,119,621 negro women, and 11,288 Indian and Mongolian women. Thus the native white women of native parentage constituted 36.7 per cent., or more than one-third, of the total number of women who were breadwinners, the other classes being represented by the following percentages: Native white of foreign parentage, 22.6; foreign born white, 17.4; negro, 23.2; Indian and Mongolian 2-10 of 1 per cent.

AGE.

Most of the women at work were young women; 68.4 per cent. of them were under 35 years of age, 44.2 per cent. were under 25, and 25.6 per cent. had not reached the age of 21. These figures are in marked contrast with those for the male sex. Of the men 16 years of age and over reported as workers or breadwinners, only 24.7 per cent. were under the age of 25, and only 12.7 per cent. were under 21. This contrast is indicative of the fact that large numbers of women who support themselves and others in early life cease to be breadwinners upon assuming the responsibilities of marriage and childbearing.

MARITAL CONDITION.

This conclusion is substantiated by the statistics of marital or conjugal condition. Almost two-thirds, or 65 per cent., of the total number of women at work were single, while 15.9 per cent. were married, 17.7 per cent. were widows and 1.3 per cent. were divorced.

PROPORTION OF WOMEN AT WORK.

The total number of women 16 years of age and over in continental United States in 1900 was 23,485,559. The number at work constituted 20.6 per cent. of this total. In other words, one woman in every five was a breadwinner, that term being used to designate persons reported by the Census as following a gainful occupation. Of the total male population of the same age—that is, 16 years and over—90.5 per cent. were breadwinners. This difference between the sexes as regards the percentage of breadwinners is probably not greater than would be anticipated. Men take up some occupation almost as a matter of course, and usually follow it the greater part of their lives. With women the adoption of an occupation, although by no means unusual, is far from being customary, and in the well-to-do classes of society is exceptional. Moreover, the pursuit of an occupation by women is probably more often temporary than permanent.

OCCUPATIONS OF WOMEN.

In the reports of the Twelfth Census (1900), the detailed classification of breadwinners with respect to the kind of work in which they were engaged distinguishes 303 occupations.

Notwithstanding the increasing diversity of employments for women, domestic service still remains the most important by far of the occupations in which they are engaged. Of the 4,833,630 women in continental United States reported as engaged in gainful occupations at the time of the Twelfth Census, 1,124,383, or almost one-fourth of the total number, were returned as servants. It may seem surprising that the next most important occupation for women is that of farm laborer, and that the number of women reported as following this occupation was 456,405, or almost half a million. The significance of the figures will be better understood if it is pointed out that 442,006, or 96.8 per cent. of these female farm laborers were reported from the Southern States, and that 361,804, or 79.3 per cent. of the total number, were of the negro race. Moreover, it appears that 277,727, or 60.9 per cent. of the total number, were members of the farmers' families, representing the wives and grown-up daughters, assisting in the work on the home farms. Next to these two leading occupations come four occupations not far apart in numerical importance, though widely different in character. They are the occupations of dressmaker, laundress, teacher and farmer. The largest of these occupations—that of dressmaker—employed 338,144 women, and the smallest—that of farmer—employed 307,706. Of teachers, there were 327,206; of laundresses, 328,935.

Three-fifths of the total number of women reported as breadwinners were found in the six occupations employing more than 300,000 women each, the aggregate number in these occupations being 2,882,779. The total number of women reported as textile mill operatives—231,458—makes this the seventh occupation group in numerical importance. The occupation next in rank is that of housekeepers and stewardesses. This comprised 146,929 women. The housekeepers here referred to are those working for wages, the housekeeping or housework done by women in their own homes not being treated by the Census as a gainful occupation, although it has, of course, a great economic importance, not to be overlooked in any attempt to estimate the social value of woman's work. If there are added to the occupation groups already mentioned the group of saleswomen, comprising 142,265 women, and that of seamstresses, comprising 138,724, the list includes the ten leading occupations for women, and accounts for 3,542,155, or 73.3 per cent. of the total number of women who are breadwinners.

Teaching is also an occupation in which women predominate. The occupation is one in which both sexes have long been competing on terms of approximate equality, and it is significant that it is also one in which the predominance of women is increasing. In 1880, the percentage of female teachers was 67.8; it advanced to 70.8 in 1890, and to 73.4 in 1900. In the group of textile mill operatives the two sexes were represented in about equal numbers. But in the remaining three of the ten leading occupations mentioned above, women, though numerous, were in the minority, constituting 24.1 per cent. of the total number of salesmen and saleswomen, 13.6 per cent. of the farm laborers and only 5.4 per cent. of the farmers.

Copyright Law of the United States.

DIRECTIONS FOR SECURING COPYRIGHT UNDER THE REVISED ACTS OF CONGRESS, INCLUDING THE PROVISIONS FOR FOREIGN COPYRIGHT, BY ACT OF MARCH 3, 1891.

SECTION 4,952 of the Revised Statutes of the United States, in force December 1, 1873, as amended by the act of June 18, 1874, as amended by the act of March 3, 1891, provides that the author, inventor, designer, or proprietor of any book, map, chart, dramatic or musical composition engraving, cut, print, or photograph or negative thereof, or of a painting, drawing, chromo, statuary, and of models or designs intended to be perfected as works of the fine arts, and the executors, administrators, or assigns of any such person, shall, upon complying with the provisions of this chapter, have the sole liberty of printing, reprinting, publishing, completing, copying, executing, finishing, and vending the same; and, in the case of a dramatic composition, of publicly performing or representing it, or causing it to be performed or represented by others. And authors or their assigns shall have exclusive right to dramatize or translate any of their works for which copyright shall have been obtained under the laws of the United States.

PRINTED TITLE REQUIRED.

A *printed* copy of the title of the book, map, chart, dramatic or musical composition, engraving, cut, print, photograph, or chromo, or a *description* of the painting, drawing, statue, statuary, or model or design, for a work of the fine arts, for which copyright is desired, must be delivered to the Librarian of Congress, or deposited in the mail, within the United States, *prepaid*, addressed "LIBRARIAN OF CONGRESS, WASHINGTON, D. C." This must be done on or before day of publication in this or any foreign country.

The *printed title* required may be a copy of the title-page of such publications as have title-pages. *In other cases, the title must be printed expressly for copyright entry*, with name of claimant of copyright. The style of type is immaterial, and the print of a typewriter will be accepted. But a separate title is required for each entry. The title of a *periodical* must include the date and number; and each number of a periodical requires a separate entry of copyright. Blank forms of application are furnished.

FEES.

The legal fee for *recording* each copyright claim is 50 cents, and for a *copy* of this record (or certificate of copyright) under seal of the office an additional fee of 50 cents is required, making $1 or $1.50, if certificate is wanted, which will be mailed as soon as reached in the records. No money is to be placed in any package of books, music, or other publications. A money order or express order avoids all risk. In the case of publications which are the production of persons not citizens or residents of the United States, but who are citizens or subjects of any country with which the United States has copyright agreement, the fee for recording title is $1, and 50 cents additional for a copy of the record. Certificates covering more than one entry in one certificate are not issued. Express orders, money orders, and currency only taken for fees. No postage stamps received.

DEPOSIT OF COPIES.

Not later than the day of publication in this country or abroad, two complete copies of the best edition of each book or other article must be delivered at the office of the Librarian of Congress, or deposited in the mail within the United States, addressed "LIBRARIAN OF CONGRESS, WASHINGTON, D. C.," to perfect the copyright.

The freight or postage must be prepaid. Books must be printed from type set in the United States or plates made therefrom; photographs from negatives made in the United States; chromos and lithographs from drawings on stone or transfers therefrom made in the United States. In the case of paintings, drawings, statuary, or models or designs for works of art, a photograph of the article is to be sent in lieu of the two copies. Without the deposit of copies required the copyright is void, and a penalty of $25 is incurred. No copy is required to be deposited elsewhere.

The law requires one copy of each new edition wherein any substantial changes are made to be deposited with the Librarian of Congress.

NOTICE OF COPYRIGHT.

No person shall maintain an action for the infringement of a copyright unless notice is given by inserting in every copy published, on the title-page or the page following, if it be a book; or if a map, chart, musical composition, print, cut, engraving, photograph, painting, drawing, chromo, statue, statuary, or model or design intended to be perfected as a work of the fine arts, by inscribing upon some visible portion thereof, or on the substance on which the same is mounted, the following words, viz.: "*Entered according to act of Congress, in the year ——, by ——, in the office of the Librarian of Congress, at Washington,*" or at the option of the person entering the copyright, the words: "*Copyright, 19—, by ——.*"

The law imposes a penalty of $100 upon any person who has not obtained copyright who shall insert the notice, "*Entered according to act of Congress,*" or "*Copyright,*" etc., or words of the same import, in or upon any book or other article, whether such article be subject to copyright or not.

TRANSLATIONS.

The copyright law secures to authors and their assigns the exclusive right to translate or to dramatize any of their works; no notice is required to enforce this right.

DURATION OF COPYRIGHT.

The original term of copyright runs for twenty-eight years. *Within six months before* the end of that time, the author or designer, or his widow or children, may secure a renewal for the further term of fourteen years, making forty-two in all.

RENEWALS.

Application for renewal must be accompanied by printed title and fee; and by explicit statement of ownership, in the case of the author, or of relationship, in the case of his widow or children, and must state definitely the date of the original copyright. Within two months from date of renewal the record thereof must be advertised in an American newspaper for four weeks.

TIME OF PUBLICATION.

The time of publication is not limited by any law or regulation, but the courts have held that it should take place "within a reasonable time." Registration of title may be secured for a projected as well as for a completed work. But the law provides for no *caveat* or notice of interference—only for actual entry of title.

ASSIGNMENTS.

Copyrights are assignable by any instrument of writing. Such assignment is to be recorded in the office of the Librarian of Congress within sixty days from execution, "in default of which it shall be void as against any subsequent purchaser or mortgagee for a valuable consideration, without notice." The fee for this record and certificate is $1, and for a certified copy of any record of assignment $1. A copy of the record (or duplicate certificate) of any copyright entry will be furnished, under seal of the office, at the rate of 50 cents each.

Statistics of the Press.

ROWELL'S American Newspaper Directory for **1908** reported the number of newspapers published in the United States and Canada as 22,487. Of these, 1,167 were Canadian publications. The following was the frequency of issue: Weekly, 16,067; monthly, 2,681; daily, 2,494; semi-monthly, 269; semi-weekly, 618; quarterly, 190; bi-weekly, 49; bi-monthly, 73; tri-weekly, 57—total, 22,487.

The following shows the number of papers printed in the States and Canada in 1907-08:

Alabama	237	Indiana	784	Nebraska	590	South Carolina	146
Alaska	23	Iowa	1,047	Nevada	58	South Dakota	353
Arizona	6	Kansas	732	New Hampshire	87	Tennessee	309
Arkansas	313	Kentucky	307	New Jersey	363	Texas	902
California	736	Louisiana	202	New Mexico	83	Utah	88
Canada	1,167	Maine	143	New York	1,835	Vermont	71
Colorado	370	Maryland	181	North Carolina	255	Virginia	245
Connecticut	159	Massachusetts	569	North Dakota	296	Washington	321
Delaware	30	Michigan	765	Ohio	1,119	West Virginia	217
Dis. of Columbia	63	Minnesota	739	Oklahoma	559	Wisconsin	687
Florida	157	Mississippi	212	Oregon	229	Wyoming	56
Georgia	373	Missouri	1,000	Pennsylvania	1,381		
Idaho	116	Montana	112	Rhode Island	48	Total	22,487
Illinois	1,619						

The total number of newspapers published in the world at present is estimated at about 60,000, distributed as follows: United States and Canada, 22,487; Germany, 8,049; Great Britain, 9,500; France, 6,681; Japan, 1,000; Italy, 2,757; Austria-Hungary, 2,958; Asia, exclusive of Japan, 1,000; Spain, 1,000; Russia, 1,000; Australia, 1,000; Greece, 130; Switzerland, 1,005; Holland, 980; Belgium, 956; all others, 1,000. Of these more than half are printed in the English language.

THE ASSOCIATED PRESS.

The following are the officers and directors of this organization: *President*—Frank B. Noyes. *First Vice-President*—Charles Hopkins Clark, Hartford *Courant*. *Second Vice-President*—Rufus N. Rhodes, Birmingham (Ala.) *News*. *Secretary*—Melville E. Stone. *Assistant Secretary*—Charles S. Diehl. *Treasurer*—Herman Ridder. *Executive Committee*—Adolph S. Ochs, Victor F. Lawson, Charles W. Knapp, Frank B. Noyes, and Charles H. Grasty. *Directors*—Adolph S. Ochs, New York *Times*; Clark Howell, Atlanta *Constitution*; W. L. McLean, Philadelphia *Bulletin*; Albert J. Barr, Pittsburgh *Post*; Charles W. Knapp, St. Louis *Republic*; Victor F. Lawson, Chicago *Daily News*; H. W. Scott, Portland *Oregonian*; Frank B. Noyes, Chicago *Record-Herald*; Thomas G. Rapier, New Orleans *Picayune*; Herman Ridder, New York *Staats-Zeitung*; M. H. De Young, San Francisco *Chronicle*; Charles H. Grasty, Baltimore *Evening News*; Gen. Charles H. Taylor, Boston (Mass.) *Globe*, and William R. Nelson, Kansas City *Star*.

INTERNATIONAL LEAGUE OF PRESS CLUBS.

Elected at the seventeenth annual convention, held in Birmingham, Ala., October 21-26, 1907: *President*—Daniel L. Hart, Wilkes-Barre (Pa.) *News*: *Vice-Presidents*—J. A. Rountree, Birmingham (Ala.), *Dixie Manufacturer*; Elden Small, Detroit *News*; Ada Tower Cable, Bradford (Pa.) *Herald*; George H. Hoffman, Philadelphia, *Nord Amerika*; Frank A. Burrelle, Burrelle's Bureau, N. Y.; *Secretary*—Lewis G. Early, Reading (Pa.) *Times*. *Treasurer*—Robert B. McIntyre, Brooklyn, *Item*. *Executive Committee*—T. J. Keenan, chairman, Pittsburgh (Pa.) *Publishers' Press*; Edward Keating, Denver, *News*; R. F. Johnston, Birmingham (Ala.) *Ledger*; C. Frank Rice, Boston Press Club; James A. Wood, Seattle, *Times*; Harry L. Hornberger, Philadelphia, Pen and Pencil Club; George H. Rowe, Brooklyn, *Times*; Giles H. Dickinson, Binghamton (N.Y.) *Republican*; H. B. Laufman, Pittsburgh, *Leader*; Victor F. Jagmetty, Atlantic City (N. J.) *Review*; Elizabeth A. Kelley, Denver, *Post*; Libbie Luttrell Morrow, Nashville, *Banner*; Harriet Hayden Finck, Philadelphia, Pennsylvania Woman's Press Association; Belva A. Lockwood, Washington (D. C.) *Peacemaker*. The eighteenth annual convention will be held in June, 1909.

United States Geographic Board.

Chairman, Henry Gannett, Geological Survey, Department of the Interior; *Secretary*, Charles S. Sloan, Bureau of the Census, Department of Commerce and Labor; Frank Bond, General Land Office, Department of the Interior; Andrew Braid, Coast and Geodetic Survey, Department of Commerce and Labor; Major Adolph von Haake, Post-Office Department; Arnold B. Johnson, Lighthouse Board, Department of Commerce and Labor; Lieut. Col. Thaddeus W. Jones, Department of War; Dr. C. Hart Merriam, Bureau of Biological Survey, Department of Agriculture; John S. Mills, Department of the Treasury; William McNeir, Chief of the Bureau of Rolls and Library, Department of State; Frank A. Kidd, Editor and Chief, Government Printing Office; Fred G. Plummer, Department of Agriculture; Charles W. Stewart, Department of the Navy; Com. A. G. Winterhalter, Hydrographer, Department of the Navy.

By Executive Order of August 10, 1906, the official title of the United States Board on Geographic Names was changed to United States Geographic Board, and its duties enlarged. The Board passes on all unsettled questions concerning geographic names which arise in the departments, as well as determining, changing, and fixing place names within the United States and its insular possessions, and all names hereafter suggested by any officer of the Government shall be referred to the Board before publication. The decisions of the Board are to be accepted by all the departments of the Government as standard authority. Advisory powers were granted the Board concerning the preparation of maps compiled, or to be compiled, in the various offices and bureaus of the Government, with a special view to the avoidance of unnecessary duplication of work; and for the unification and improvement of the scales of maps, of the symbols and conventions used upon them, and of the methods of representing relief. Hereafter, all such projects as are of importance shall be submitted to this Board for advice before being undertaken.

American Institute of Social Service.

ORGANIZED 1898 for social and industrial improvement, with the following officers: *President*—Josiah Strong. *Vice-President*—Warner Van Norden. *Director*—James Dangerfield. *Treasurer*—John T. Perkins. *Lecturer*—James H. Ecob. The Institute consists of forty men and women, who are its governing body. Each year one hundred distinguished students of social subjects may be elected collaborators for one year, and one hundred men and women who are distinguished for their public services, or who are known to be deeply interested in social and industrial betterment, may be elected for one year as associates. The Institute received the highest award (Grand Prix) in Social Economy, at the Paris Exposition, 1900; the St. Louis Exposition, 1904; Liege, 1905; Milan, 1906, and Paris, 1907. The headquarters of the Institute are at Bible House, Astor Place, New York.

The American Civic Alliance.

Chairman Executive Committee—N. Lafayette-Savay. *Chairman National Committee*—Rev. Thomas R. Slicer. *Chairman of the Council*—Robert Treat Paine. Office of the Executive, 43 Cedar Street, New York City.

The American Civic Alliance represents a movement for the unification of all the important interests of the country into one vast, organized effort to establish a great Civic Tribunal, founded on the Science of State, which is to be propagated amongst all men so that the truth may become a just arbitrator, and establish a balance between the conflicting interests for the good of all mankind.

With this object in view the Alliance proposes first of all to organize a national bureau of political research, devoted to the collection and systematization of political knowledge, and its arrangement into progressive courses to serve as a basis for scientific deductions and general edification.

Such bureau will be a part of the National Civic University for citizens, statesmen and diplomats, which will in the beginning carry on its work through special courses distributed throughout the country among the groups of students organized for that purpose; also by means of public press and lectures calculated to reach the public at large.

The Alliance Francaise.

THE Federation of French Alliances in the United States and Canada number 150 groups. The officers of the Federation are: *Honorary President*—J. J. Jusserand, French Ambassador. *President*—J. Le Roy White, Baltimore. *Vice-Presidents*—M. Alexander, T. Mason, New York; Z. P. Brosseau, Chicago, Ill.; L. R. Gregor, Montreal; A. Legallet, San Francisco, Cal. *Secretary*—M. Georges Lamouret, 1402 Broadway, New York. *Treasurer*—M. T. Tileston Wells. *Board of Directors*—Frederic R. Coudert, New York; James H. Hyde, New York; W. N. Sloan, New York; Paul Fuller, Louis Delamarre, Frank D. Pavey, Camille Thurwanger, and Samuel Boyle. Office, 1402 Broadway, New York City.

Actors' Fund of America.

President—Daniel Frohman. *Vice-President*—Joseph R. Grismer. *Treasurer*—Henry B. Harris. *Secretary*—Frank McKee. *Assistant Secretary*—Theodore Bromley.

The Actors' Fund was established in 1882 to provide assistance for disabled and needy members of the theatrical profession, and burial for such as leave no means therefor. The Actors' Fund Home, West New Brighton, Staten Island, under the direction of the Actors' Fund of America, was opened May 10, 1902. This is a home for aged and needy actors and actresses. There are 18 honorary members, and 220 life members. Office, 112-114 West Forty-second Street, New York.

Actors' Church Alliance of America.

NATIONAL COUNCIL.

President—Mrs. Mary Gibbs Spooner. *Vice-President*—Rev. Thomas H. Sill. *Secretary*—Miss Olinda D. Drescher. *Treasurer*—Miss Eliza B. Harris.

Additional Officers, 1909—Rev. H. Mottet, Miss Esther A. Rolph, Mr. J. C. Pumpelly, Rev. S. S. Mitchell, Miss Rose Rand, Mr. Damon Lyon, Mr. G. F. Sturgis, Miss Kizzie B. Masters. 1910—Rev. F. J. C. Moran, Mrs. J. A. Brown, Miss Ida Ackerman, Mr. N. M. Potts, Mrs. Wm. Walker, Mrs. C. E. Abbott, Mrs. M. Breyer, Mr. J. P. Collins, Mrs. Hudson Liston, Miss Isabelle Evesson.

The purpose of the Alliance is to establish closer relations between church and theatre, and ministering to members of the dramatic profession. It is established in 400 cities, and has on its rolls 1,200 chaplains. The calendars of church services of all denominations are posted in 600 theatres. The office of the General Secretary and headquarters is 133 West 44th Street.

American Society for the Prevention of Cruelty to Animals

President—Alfred Wagstaff. *Vice-President*—James Grant Wilson. *Secretary*—Richard Welling. *Treasurer*—Henry Bergh. *Board of Managers*—Henry Bergh, Horace W. Carpentier, George A. Plimpton, Charles S. Roe, Thomas Sturgis, Cortlandt S. Van Rensselaer, Francis E. Ward, Gordon Knox Bell, John D. Crimmins, George C. Holt, John H. Iselin, F. Aug. Schermerhorn, Evert Jansen Wendell, G. Howard Davison, Rush C. Hawkins, Jefferson Seligman, Alfred Wagstaff, Richard Welling, James Grant Wilson, Thomas F. McCarthy. *General Manager*, William K. Horton. *Superintendent*, Thomas F. Freel. Headquarters, Madison Avenue and Twenty-sixth Street, New York.

American Humane Association.

A FEDERATION of societies and individuals "for the prevention of cruelty, especially cruelty to children and animals." The officers are: *President*—Dr. William O. Stillman, Albany, N. Y. *Secretary*—N. J. Walker, Albany, N. Y. *Treasurer*—Edgar McDonald, Brooklyn, N. Y.

Religious Statistics.

NUMBERS IN THE WORLD ACCORDING TO CREED.

THE following estimates, by M. Fournier de Flaix, are the latest that have been made by a competent authority:

Creeds.	No. of Followers.	Creeds.	No. of Followers.
1 Christianity	477,080,158	5 Buddhism	147,900,000
2 Worship of Ancestors and Confucianism	256,000,000	6 Taoism	43,000,000
3 Hindooism	190,000,000	7 Shintoism	14,000,000
4 Mohammedanism	176,834,372	8 Judaism	7,186,000
		9 Polytheism	117,681,669

CHRISTIANITY.

Churches.	Total Followers.	Churches.	Total Followers.
Catholic Church	230,866,533	Armenian Church	1,690,000
Protestant Churches	143,237,625	Nestorians	80,000
Orthodox Greek Church	98,016,000	Jacobites	70,000
Church of Abyssinia	3,000,000		
Coptic Church	120,000	Total	477,080,158

DISTRIBUTION OF SEMITIC ARYAN RACES.

Geographical Divisions.	Christianity.			Mohammedanism.	Judaism.
	Catholic Church.	Protestant Churches.	Orthodox Churches.		
Europe	160,165,000	80,812,000	89,196,000	6,629,000	6,456,000
America	58,393,882	57,294,014	......	......	1,100,000
Oceanica	6,574,481	2,724,781	......	24,699,787	......
Africa	2,655,920	1,744,080	......	36,000,000	400,000
Asia	3,007,250	662,750	8,820,000	109,535,585	200,000
Total Followers	230,866,533	143,237,625	98,016,000	176,834,372	*8,156,000

RELIGIOUS DIVISIONS OF EUROPE.

Countries.	Catholic Church.	Protestant Churches.	Orthodox Churches.	Jews.	Mohammedans.	Unclassified
Russia	9,600,000	3,400,000	73,310,000	3,400,000	3,000,000	290,000
Germany	17,100,000	29,478,000	......	590,000	......	32,000
Austria-Hungary	31,100,000	3,900,000	3,100,000	1,700,000	......	100,000
France	35,387,000	580,000	......	49,000	......	84,000
United Kingdom	6,500,000	30,100,000	......	100,000	......	500,000
Italy	29,850,000	62,000	......	38,000	......	50,000
Spain	16,850,000	29,000	......	5,000	......	......
Belgium	5,880,000	15,000	......	3,000	......	2,000
Roumania	100,000	15,000	4,800,000	400,000	30,000	55,000
Ottoman Empire	320,000	11,000	1,700,000	60,000	2,708,000	70,000
Netherlands	1,545,000	2,756,000	......	83,000	......	16,000
Portugal	4,300,000	......	......	......	......	1,000
Sweden	1,000	4,698,000	......	2,000	......	1,000
Switzerland	1,172,000	1,710,000	......	8,000	......	10,000
Denmark	3,000	2,089,000	......	4,000	......	4,000
Greece	10,000	10,000	1,930,000	5,000	45,000	......
Servia	6,000	1,000	1,973,000	5,000	15,000	......
Bulgaria	29,000	......	1,393,000	......	571,000	......
Norway	1,000	1,958,000	......	......	......	1,000
Roumelia	30,000	......	700,000	4,000	240,000	2,000
Montenegro	5,000	......	290,000	......	......	1,000
Luxemburg	200,000	......	......	......	......	......
Malta	160,000	......	......	......	......	......
Gibraltar	16,000	......	......	......	......	......
Total Followers	160,165,000	80,812,000	89,196,000	6,456,000	6,629,000	1,219,000

The distinction between followers and actual communicants should be observed.

ENGLISH-SPEAKING RELIGIOUS COMMUNITIES OF THE WORLD.

Episcopalians	29,200,000	Free Thinkers	5,250,000
Methodists of all descriptions	18,650,000	Lutherans, etc	2,800,000
Roman Catholics	15,500,000	Unitarians	2,600,000
Presbyterians of all descriptions	12,250,000	Minor religious sects	5,500,000
Baptists of all descriptions	9,230,000	Of no particular religion	17,000,000
Congregationalists of all descriptions	6,150,000	English-speaking population	124,130,000

A very large number—more than 18,000,000—of Hindoos, Mohammedans, Buddhists, and others in the East also speak and read English.

The estimates in the last table were from Whitaker's (London) Almanack.

The "Encyclopedia Britannica," last edition, makes a rough estimate of numbers of Protestants in the world speaking all civilized languages, and places the Lutherans at the head, with over 42,000,000 members (mostly in Germany and Scandinavia), and the Anglican Church second, with about 20,000,000 members. * The American Jewish Year Book for 1907 estimated the number of Jews in the United States at 1,777,185 and in the world at 11,585,202 in 1907.

Religious Denominations in the United States.

Statistics of Ministers, Churches, and Communicants or Members, prepared by Dr. H. K. Carroll, late Special Agent of the United States Census Office, for *The Christian Advocate*, and published in 1908.

Denominations.	Ministers.	Churches.	Communicants.
Adventists:			
Evangelical	34	30	1,147
Advent Christians	912	610	26,500
Seventh-Day	488	1,750	64,332
Church of God	19	29	647
Life and Advent Union	60	28	3,800
Churches of God in Jesus Christ	56	97	2,872
Total Adventists	1,569	2,544	99,298
Baptists:			
Regular, North	7,998	9,595	1,155,422
Regular, South	13,412	21,216	1,981,749
Regular, Colored	12,201	17,721	1,778,824
Six Principle	8	12	858
Seventh-Day	98	84	8,509
Freewill	1,248	1,409	82,303
Original Freewill	120	167	12,000
General	475	535	29,347
Separate	113	103	6,479
United	25	204	13,209
Baptist Church of Christ	80	152	8,254
Primitive	2,130	3,530	126,000
Old Two Seed in the Spirit Predestinarian	300	473	12,851
Church of God and Saints of Christ	71	93	8,500
Total Baptists	38,279	55,294	5,224,305
Brethren (River):			
Brethren in Christ	146	65	3,500
Old Order, or Yorker	7	8	214
United Zion's Children	20	25	525
Total River Brethren	173	98	4,239
Brethren (Plymouth):			
Brethren (I.)	....	109	2,289
Brethren (II.)	....	88	2,419
Brethren (III.)	....	86	1,235
Brethren (IV.)	....	31	718
Total Plymouth Brethren	....	314	6,661
Buddhist (Chinese)	....	47	....
Buddhist and Shintoist (Japanese)	....	9	....
Catholics:			
Roman Catholic*	15,655	12,513	11,795,812
Maronite Catholic	10	10	35,000
Polish Catholic	33	43	42,850
Old Catholic	3	5	425
Reformed Catholic	6	4	1,750
Russian Orthodox	75	103	55,000
Greek Orthodox	43	42	100,000
Syrian Orthodox	13	21	30,000
Armenian	15	21	8,500
Total Catholics (c)	15,883	12,762	12,069,337
Catholic Apostolic	95	10	1,491
Christadelphians	....	63	1,277
Christian Connection	1,348	1,340	101,597
Christian Catholic (Dowie)	104	110	40,000
Christian Scientists	1,336	668	85,096
Christian Union	201	268	17,500
Church of God (Winnebrennarian)	499	590	41,475
Church of the New Jerusalem	139	144	8,200
Communistic Societies:			
Shakers	....	15	1,000
Amana	....	1	1,766
Harmony	....	1	8
Altruists	....	1	25
Church Triumphant (Koreshan Ecclesia)	....	3	205
Christian Commonwealth	....	1	80
Total Communists	....	22	3,084
Congregationalists	5,923	5,941	699,327
Disciples of Christ	6,673	11,307	1,285,123

Denominations.	Ministers.	Churches.	Communicants.
Dunkards:			
Conservatives	2,831	855	100,000
Old Order	230	75	4,000
Progressive	267	216	17,475
Seventh-Day (German)	9	13	230
Total Dunkards	3,337	1,159	121,705
Evangelical Bodies:			
Evangelical Association	950	1,652	103,525
United Evangelical Church	553	1,014	70,116
Total Evangelical	1,503	2,666	173,641
Friends:			
Orthodox	1,302	830	97,836
"Hicksite"	115	183	19,545
"Wilburite"	38	53	4,468
Primitive	11	9	232
Total Friends	1,466	1,075	122,081
Friends of the Temple	4	4	340
German Evangelical Protestant	100	155	20,000
German Evangelical Synod	974	1,262	237,321
Jews:			
Orthodox	135	340	62,000
Reformed	166	230	81,000
Total Jews (See Note a)	301	570	143,000
Latter-Day Saints:			
Utah Branch	752	775	350,000
Reorganized Branch	1,200	553	48,000
Total Mormons	1,952	1,328	398,000
Lutherans:			
(General Bodies):			
General Synod	1,322	1,734	265,469
United Synod, South	235	458	47,514
General Council	1,433	2,195	437,788
Synodical Conference	2,444	3,101	643,599
United Norwegian	480	1,335	154,055
(Independent Synods):			
Ohio	556	738	110,877
Buffalo	30	41	5,556
Hauge's	122	290	21,181
Eielsen's	6	26	1,200
Texas	15	23	2,200
Iowa	487	927	99,895
Norwegian	350	1,050	87,000
Michigan, etc.	37	54	7,933
Danish in America	61	117	11,737
Icelandic	9	43	4,451
Immanuel	17	11	3,250
Suomai, Finnish	24	110	13,201
Norwegian Free	148	340	42,738
Danish United	106	202	9,261
Slovakian	25	54	15,000
Finnish National	21	44	6,700
Finnish Apostolic	19	67	5,400
Church of the Lutheran Brethren (Norwegian)	10	14	1,600
Independent Congregations	83	200	25,000
Total Lutherans (b)	8,040	13,169	2,022,605
Swedish Evangelical Mission Covenant (Waldenstromians)	355	351	46,000
Mennonites:			
Mennonite	430	289	23,319
Bruederhoef	9	5	352
Amish	280	126	13,680
Old Amish	75	25	2,438
Apostolic	2	2	209
Reformed	43	34	1,680
General Conference	140	77	10,732
Church of God in Christ	18	18	449
Old (Wisler)	17	15	603
Bundes Conference	45	17	3,036
Defenceless	20	11	1,126
Brethren in Christ	161	82	4,066
Total Mennonites	1,240	701	61,690
Methodists:			
Methodist Episcopal	17,861	27,965	3,036,667
Union American M. E.	138	255	18,500
African Methodist Episcopal	6,070	6,815	850,000
African Union Meth. Protestant	200	125	4,000
African Methodist Episcopal Zion	3,912	3,241	578,310
Methodist Protestant	1,551	2,242	183,894

*Not including the Hawaiian and the Philippine Islands and Porto Rico.

RELIGIOUS DENOMINATIONS IN THE UNITED STATES—*Continued.*

Denominations.	Ministers.	Churches.	Communicants.
Methodists - Continued:			
Wesleyan Methodist	524	598	19,064
Methodist Episcopal, South	6,978	15,496	1,678,892
Congregational Methodist	415	425	24,000
Congregational Meth. (Colored)	5	5	319
New Congregational Methodist	238	417	4,022
Zion Union Apostolic	30	32	2,346
Colored Methodist Episcopal	2,673	2,619	214,739
Primitive	72	104	7,013
Free Methodist	1,126	1,117	31,435
Independent Methodist	8	15	2,569
Evangelist Missionary	92	47	5,014
Total Methodists	41,893	61,518	6,660,784
Moravians	129	119	17,199
Presbyterians:			
Northern	8,822	10,893	1,312,075
Cumberland	400	424	38,102
Cumberland (Colored)	588	558	42,000
Welsh Calvinistic	80	150	13,020
United	987	960	127,205
Southern	1,606	3,192	262,390
Associate	12	31	1,053
Associate Reformed, South	96	136	12,620
Reformed (Synod)	113	109	9,063
Reformed (General Synod)	23	28	8,500
Reformed (Covenanted)	1	1	40
Reformed in the U. S. & Canada	....	1	436
Total Presbyterians	12,723	16,478	1,821,504
Protestant Episcopal:			
Protestant Episcopal	5,115	7,705	821,240
Reformed Episcopal	82	74	9,419
Total Protestant Episcopal	5,197	7,779	830,659
Reformed:			
Reformed (Dutch)	719	667	121,210
Reformed (German)	1,164	1,754	284,073
Christian Reformed	116	175	25,175
Total Reformed	1,999	2,596	430,458
Salvation Army	4,765	1,016	28,000
Schwenkfeldians	6	8	740
Social Brethren	17	20	913
Society for Ethical Culture	10	5	2,142
Spiritualists	....	748	150,000
Theosophical Society	....	72	2,607
United Brethren:			
United Brethren	1,864	3,819	271,335
United Brethren (Old Constitution)	296	559	20,423
Total United Brethren	2,160	4,378	291,758
Unitarians	549	473	71,200
Universalists	728	910	52,621
Independent Congregations	54	156	14,126
Grand Total	161,715	210,249	33,409,104

The aggregate of 33,409,104 represents actual church membership, and includes all Catholics, but not all persons affiliated by family ties to Protestant bodies. The larger of the Protestant bodies may claim twice the number of their communicants as nominal adherents.—Editor of The Almanac.

Note.—(a) The American Jewish Year Book for 1908 estimates the number of the Jewish race in the United States in 1908 as 1,777,185. (b) The Lutheran Church Almanac gives the number of ministers as 7,483, churches or congregations 13,106, communicant members 1,785,799. (c) The official Directory of the Catholic Church in America, printed in Milwaukee, makes the following statement: Ministers 14,484, churches 11,814, population 12,651,944.—Editor of The Almanac.

Sunday-School Statistics of all Countries.

The following statistics of Sunday-schools were reported at the Twelfth International Sunday-School Convention, held at Louisville, Ky., June 18–23, 1908:

Countries.	Sunday Schools.	Teachers.	Scholars.
Europe:			
Great Britain and Ireland	46,399	684,342	7,450,374
Austria-Hungary	238	643	10,572
Belgium	132	348	6,600
Bulgaria	29	72	1,496
Denmark	1,000	5,000	80,000
Finland	7,611	12,928	165,140
France	1,200	7,000	67,000
Germany	8,073	28,356	855,114
Greece	6	8	200
Holland	2,020	5,092	206,000
Italy	350	1,500	16,000
Norway	325	2,000	26,000
Portugal	18	72	1,717
Russia	350	1,100	12,000
Spain	100	200	6,500
Sweden	4,455	18,025	320,000
Switzerland	1,762	7,490	122,567
Turkey in Europe	28	42	1,129
Asia:			
Persia	167	440	4,876
Siam	16	64	809
China	105	1,053	5,264
Japan	1,074	7,505	44,035
Turkey in Asia	516	4,250	25,833
Africa	4,246	8,455	161,394
North America:			
United States	140,519	1,451,855	11,329,253
Canada	10,750	85,6[illegible]	684,235
Newfoundland and Labrador	353	2,374	22,766
West Indies	2,306	10,769	111,335
Central America	231	577	5,741
Mexico	426	1,600	15,128
South America	350	3,000	150,000
Oceanica:			
Australasia	7,458	54,670	595,031
Fiji Islands	1,474	2,700	42,909
Hawaiian Islands	230	1,413	15,840
Other Islands	210	800	10,000
The World	244,528	2,411,373	22,572,858

The total number of teachers and scholars in the world, according to this report, was 25,432,936. The Thirteenth International Convention will be held at San Francisco, Cal., 1911.

The table does not include the schools of the Roman Catholic and Non-Evangelical Protestant churches. The number of scholars in Roman Catholic Sunday-schools in the United States is estimated at 1,000,000 by clerics.

The General Secretary of the International Sunday School Association is Marion Lawrance, 145 Dearborn Street, Chicago, Ill. The other officers are: Hon. John Stites, President, Louisville, Ky.; W. N. Hartshorn, Chairman of the Executive Committee, Boston, Mass.; Joseph Clark, Recording Secretary, Columbus, O.; Fred A. Wells, Treasurer, Chicago, Ill.; Vice-Presidents, Rev. H. H. Bell, D. D., San Francisco, Cal.; A. B. McCrillis, Providence, R. I.; Prof. Martin G. Brumbaugh, Ph. D., LL. D., Philadelphia, Pa.; Rev. Geo. W. Truett, D. D., Dallas, Tex.; E. H. Nichols, Chicago, Ill.; Prin. E. W. Sawyer, D. C. L., Summerland, B. C.; Bishop Geo. W. Clinton, D. D. (for the Negroes), Charlotte, N. C.; District Representatives, Judge Robert F. Raymond, Newton Centre, Mass.; Rev. Alexander Henry, D. D., Philadelphia, Pa.; George W. Watts, Durham, N. C.; Rev. W. N. Dresel, Evansville, Ind.; S. B. Harding, Waukesha, Wis.; I. W. Gill, Wichita, Kas.; W. N. Wiggins, Dallas, Tex.; A. L. Fellows, Denver, Col.; W. D. Wood, Seattle, Wash.; W. F. Cronemiller, Los Angeles, Cal.; Rev. Jenaro S. Paz, San Luis Potosi, Mex.

Roman Catholic Hierarchy of the United States.

APOSTOLIC DELEGATION.

Most Rev. Diomede Falconio, Archbishop of Larissa, Apostolic Delegate, Washington, D. C.

Very Rev. Bonaventure Cerretti, Auditor, Washington, D. C. | Secretary, Rev. W. F. Hughes.

ARCHBISHOPS.

See	Archbishop	Cons.
Baltimore, Maryland	James Gibbons, Cardinal	1868
Boston, Massachusetts	W. H. O'Connell	1901
Chicago, Illinois	James E. Quigley	1899
Cincinnati, Ohio	Henry Moeller	1904
Dubuque, Iowa	John J. Keane	1878
Milwaukee, Wisconsin	Sebastian G. Messmer	1892
New Orleans, Louisiana	James Blenk	1899
New York, New York	John M. Farley	1895
Portland, Oregon	Alexander Christie	1898
Philadelphia, Pennsylvania	Patrick J. Ryan	1872
St. Louis, Missouri	John Joseph Glennon	1896
St. Paul, Minnesota	John Ireland	1875
San Francisco, California	Patrick W. Riordan	1883
Santa Fe, New Mexico		

BISHOPS.

See	Bishop	Cons.
Albany, New York	Thos. M. Burke	1894
Alton, Illinois	James Ryan	1888
Altoona, Pennsylvania	Eugene A. Garvey	1901
Baker City, Oregon	Charles O'Reilly	1903
Belmont, North Carolina	Leo Haid, V. A.	1886
Belleville, Illinois	J. Janssen	1888
Boise, Idaho	A. J. Glorieux	1885
Boston, Massachusetts	John Brady (Auxiliary)	1891
Brooklyn, New York	C. E. McDonnell	1892
Brownsville, Texas	P. Verdagner, V. A.	1890
Buffalo, New York	Charles H. Colton	1903
Burlington, Vermont	J. S. Michaud	1893
Charleston, South Carolina	H. P. Northrop	1882
Cheyenne, Wyoming	John J. Keane	1902
Chicago, Illinois	A. J. McGavick (Auxiliary)	1899
Chicago, Illinois	P. Rode	..
Cleveland, Ohio		..
Columbus, Ohio	J. J. Hartley	1904
Concordia, Kansas	J. F. Cunningham	1898
Covington, Kentucky	C. P. Maes	1885
Dallas, Texas	Edward J. Dunne	1893
Davenport, Iowa	James Davis	1904
Denver, Colorado	N. C. Matz	1896
Detroit, Michigan	John S. Foley	1888
Duluth, Minnesota	James McGoldrick	1889
Erie, Pennsylvania	John F. Fitzmaurice	1897
Fall River, Massachusetts	Daniel F. Feehan	1907
Fargo, North Dakota	John Shanley	1889
Fort Wayne, Indiana	Herman Alerding	1900
Galveston, Texas	N. A. Gallagher	1882
Grand Rapids, Michigan	H. J. Ritchter	1883
Great Falls, Montana	M. Lenihan	1904
Green Bay, Wisconsin	Joseph J. Fox	1904
Harrisburg, Pennsylvania	John W. Shanahan	1899
Hartford, Connecticut		..
Helena, Montana	John P. Carroll	1904
Indianapolis, Indiana	F. S. Chatard	1878
Indianapolis, Indiana	D. O'Donaghue (Auxiliary)	1900
Kansas City, Missouri	John J. Hogan	1868
La Crosse, Wisconsin	James Schwebach	1893
Lead City, South Dakota	J. N. Stariha	1902
Leavenworth, Kansas	Thomas Lillis	1904
Lincoln, Nebraska	Thomas Bonacum	1887
Little Rock, Arkansas	John B. Morris	1906
Los Angeles, California	Thomas Conaty	1901
Louisville, Kentucky	William G. McCloskey	1868
Manchester, New Hampshire	G. A. Guertin	1907
Marquette, Michigan	Frederick Eis	1899
Mobile, Alabama	Edward P. Allen	1897
Nashville, Tennessee	Thomas S. Byrne	1894
Natchez, Mississippi	Thomas Heslin	1889
Natchitoches, Louisiana	Cornelius Van-de-Ven	1904
Newark, New Jersey	John J. O'Connor	1901
New York	Thomas F. Cusack (Auxil'y)	1904
Ogdensburg, New York	Henry Gabriels	1892
Oklahoma, Oklahoma	Theodore Meerschaert	1891
Omaha, Nebraska	Richard Scannell	1887
Peoria, Illinois	J. L. Spalding	1877
Peoria, Illinois	Peter J. O'Reilly (Auxiliary)	1900
Philadelphia, Pennsylvania	E. F. Prendergast (Auxiliary)	1897
Pittsburgh, Pennsylvania	Regis Canevin	1903
Portland, Maine	Louis S. Walsh	1906
Providence, Rhode Island	M. Harkins	1887
Richmond, Virginia	A. Van de Vyver	1889
Rochester, New York	B. J. McQuaid	1868
Rochester, New York	Thos. F. Hickey (Auxiliary)	1905
Rockford, Illinois	Peter J. Muldoon	..
St. Augustine, Florida	William J. Kenny	1902
St. Cloud, Minnesota	James Trobec	1897
St. Joseph, Missouri	M. F. Burke	1893
Sacramento, California	Thomas Grace	1896
Salt Lake City, Utah	Lawrence Scanlan	1887
San Antonio, Texas	J. A. Forest	1895
Santa Fe, New Mexico	J. B. Pitaval (Auxiliary)	1902
Savannah, Georgia	Benj. J. Keiley	1900
Seattle, Washington	Edward J. O'Dea	1896
Scranton, Pennsylvania	M. J. Hoban	1896
Sioux City, Iowa	Philip J. Garrigan	1902
Sioux Falls, South Dakota	Thomas O'Gorman	1896
Springfield, Massachusetts	Thomas D. Beaven	1892
Superior, Wisconsin	A. F. Schinner	1905
Syracuse, New York	P. A. Ludden	1887
Trenton, New Jersey	James A. McFaul	1894
Tucson, Arizona	Henry Granjon	1900
Wheeling, West Virginia	P. J. Donahue	1894
Wichita, Kansas	J. J. Hennessy	1888
Wilmington, Delaware	John J. Monaghan	1897
Winona, Minnesota	Joseph B. Cotter	1889

College of Cardinals.

Pope Pius X., born 1835; year of accession 1903.

CARDINAL BISHOPS.

Name	Office or Dignity.	Nation.	Age.	Cons.
Agliardi, Antonio	Vice-Chancellor	Italian	77	1896
Oreglia, L. S. S.	Dean Sac. Coll	Italian	81	1873
Satolli, Francesco	Pref. Cong. Studies	Italian	70	1895
Vannutelli, S.	Sub-Dean S. Coll	Italian	75	1887
Vannutelli, V.	Pref. Cong. Council	Italian	73	1869

CARDINAL PRIESTS.

Name	Office or Dignity.	Nation.	Age.	Cons.
Aguirre, G.	Abp. Burgos	Spaniard	74	1907
Andrieu, P	Bp. Marseilles	French	59	1907
Bacilieri, B.	Bp. Verona	Italian	67	1901
Boschi, Giulio	Abp. Ferrara	Italian	71	1901
Capecelatro, A.	Abp. Capua	Italian	85	1885
Cassetta, Francesco		Italian	68	1899
Cavalcanti, J.	Abp. Rio de Janeiro	Brazilian	69	1905
Cavallari, A	Patriarch Venice	Italian	60	1907
Cavicchioni, B.	Resident in Curia	Italian	73	1903
Coullie, Pierre	Abp. Lyons	French	80	1897
Cretoni, Serafino	Pref. Cong. Rites	Italian	76	1896
Di Pietro, Angelo	Pro-Pref. Datary	Italian	81	1893
Ferrari, Andrea	Abp. Milan	Italian	59	1894
Ferrata, D	Pref. Cong. Bishops	Italian	62	1896
Fischer, Anthony	Abp. Cologne	German	69	1903
Francica-Nava, G.	Abp. Catania	Italian	63	1899
Gasparri, P.	Tit. Abp. Cesarea	Italian	57	1907
Gennari, C.	Resident in Curia	Italian	70	1901
Gibbons, James	Abp. Baltimore	American	75	1886
Gotti, Gerolamo	Pref. Propaganda	Italian	75	1895
Gruscha, A. J.	Abp. Vienna	Austrian	89	1891
Herrera, Martin de	Abp. Compostella	Spanish	74	1897
Katschthaler, J.	Abp. Salzburg	Austrian	77	1903
Kopp, George	Abp. Breslau	German	72	1893
Lecot, Victor L	Abp. Bordeaux	French	78	1893
Logue, Michael	Abp. Armagh	Irish	69	1893
Lorenzelli, B.	Abp. Lucca	Italian	56	1907
Lualdi, A.	Abp. Palermo	Italian	51	1907
Lucon, L.	Abp. Rheims	French	68	1907
Maffi, P.	Abp. Pisa	Italian	51	1907
Martinelli, S	Resident in Curia	Italian	61	1901
Mercier, D.	Abp. Mechlin	Belgian	58	1907
Merry del Val, R.	Secretary of State	Spanish	44	1903
Moran, Patrick	Abp. Sydney	Irish	79	1885
Neto, G. Seb	Patriarch Lisbon	Port	67	1884
Prisco, Giuseppe	Abp. Naples	Italian	73	1896
Puzyna, K.	Bp. Cracow	Austrian	67	1901
Rampolla, M.	Apr. Vat. Basil	Italian	66	1887
Respighi, Pietro	Pope's Vicar-Gen.	Italian	66	1899
Richelmy, Agostino	Abp. Turin	Italian	59	1899
Rinaldini, A.	Nuncio Madrid	Italian	65	1907
Samass, J.	Abp. Agria (Eger)	Hungarian	81	1905
Sancha, C.	Abp. Toledo	Spanish	66	1894
Sanminiatelli, A.	Resident in Curia	Italian	69	1899
Skrbensky, Leo	Abp. Prague	Bohemian	46	1901
Vaszary, Claude	Abp. Strigonig	Hungarian	77	1893

COLLEGE OF CARDINALS—*Continued.*

CARDINAL DEACONS.

Name	Office	Nationality	Age	Created
Cagiano de Azevedo Bisletti	Major-Domo		66	1905
De Lai, G	Sec. Sac. Cong.	Italian	59	1907
Della Volpe, F.	Abg. Blogna	Italian	65	1899
Segna, F.	Pf. Vatican Archives.	Italian	73	1894
Vives y Tuto, G. C	Inquisitor	Spanish	55	1899

Bishops of Protestant Churches in the United States.

BISHOPS OF THE PROTESTANT EPISCOPAL CHURCH IN THE UNITED STATES.

Diocese.	*Cons.*
Alabama—Charles Minnegerode Beckwith, Selma.	1902
Alaska—Peter Trimble Rowe (missionary), Sitka.	1895
Arizona and New Mexico—J. M. Kendrick (miss.), Phœnix.	1889
Arkansas—William M. Brown, Little Rock	1897
California—William Ford Nichols, San Francisco	1890
" Sacramento: W. H. Moreland (missionary)	1899
" Los Angeles: Joseph H. Johnson, Pasadena	1896
Colorado—Charles Sanford Olmsted, Denver	1902
" Western—(vacant)	..
Connecticut—Chauncey B. Brewster, Hartford	1897
Dakota, N.—Cameron Mann (missionary), Fargo	1901
" S.—Wm. Hobart Hare (missionary), Sioux Falls	1873
" Frederick F. Johnson, assistant	1905
Delaware—Frederick J. Kinsman, Wilmington	1903
District of Columbia—Washington: Alfred Harding (elect)	..
Florida—Edwin Gardner Weed, Jacksonville.	1886
" Southern: William Crane Gray (miss.), Orlando	1892
Georgia—Frederick F. Reese, Savananh	1908
" Atlanta: C. Kinloch Nelson	1892
Idaho—James B. Funsten (missionary)	1899
Illinois—Chicago: Charles Palmerston Anderson	1900
" Quincy: M. Edward Fawcett	1904
" Springfield: Edward W. Osborne	1904
Indiana—Indianapolis: Joseph M. Francis	1899
" Michigan City: John H. White	1895
Iowa—Theodore N. Morrison, Davenport	1899
Kansas—Frank R. Millspaugh, Topeka	1895
" Salina: Sheldon Munson Griswold	1903
Kentucky—Charles Edward Woodcock, Louisville	1905
" Lexington: Lewis W. Burton	1896
Louisiana—Davis Sessums, New Orleans	1891
Maine—Robert Codman, Portland	1900
Maryland—William Paret, Baltimore	1885
" Easton: William Forbes Adams	1875
Massachusetts—William Lawrence, Cambridge	1893
" Western: Alex. H. Vinton, Springfield	1902
Michigan—Charles David Williams, Detroit	1906
" Marquette: Gershom M. Williams	1896
" Western: George D. Gillespie, Grand Rapids	1875
" John N. McCormick, Coadjutor, Grand Rapids.	1906
Minnesota—Samuel C. Edsall, Minneapolis	1899
" Duluth: James D. Morrison	1897
Mississippi—Theodore D. Bratton, Jackson	1903
Missouri—Daniel Sylvester Tuttle, St. Louis	1867
" Kansas City: Edward Robert Atwill	1890
Montana—Leigh R. Brewer, Helena	1880
Nebraska—A. L. Williams, Omaha	1899
" Kearney: Anson R. Graves (miss.)	1890
Nevada—Henry D. Robinson (miss.) Reno	1908
New Hampshire—William Woodruff Niles, Concord	1870
" Edward M. Parker, Coadjutor, Concord.	1906
New Jersey—John Scarborough, Trenton	1875
" Newark: Edwin S. Lines	1903
New York—David H. Greer, New York City	1904
New York—Central: Charles Tyler Olmsted, Utica	1902
" Western: William D. Walker, Buffalo	1883
" Albany: William Croswell Doane.	1869
" " Richard H. Nelson, Coadjutor	1904
" Long Island: Frederick Burgess, Garden City.	1902
North Carolina—Joseph Blount Cheshire, Raleigh	1893
" E. Carolina: Robert Strange, Wilmington	1904
" Asheville: J. M. Horner (missionary)	1898
Ohio—William Andrew Leonard, Cleveland	1889
" Southern: Boyd Vincent, Cincinnati	1889
Oklahoma and Indian Ter.—F. K. Brooke (miss.), Guthrie.	1893
Oregon—Charles Scalding, Portland	1906
" Eastern—Robert L. Paddock (miss.), Baker City	1907
Pennsylvania—Ozi William Whitaker, Philadelphia	1869
" A. Mackay-Smith, Coadjutor, Philadelphia	1902
" Pittsburgh: Cortlandt Whitehead	1882
" Central: Ethelbert Talbot, South Bethlehem.	1887
" Harrisburg: James H. Darlington	1905
Rhode Island—W. N. McVickar, Providence	1897
South Carolina—W. A. Guerry, Coadjutor, Columbia	1907
Tennessee—Thomas F. Gailor, Memphis	1893
Texas—George Herbert Kinsolving, Austin	1892
" Dallas: Alex. C. Garrett	1874
" West: James S. Johnston, San Antonio	1888
Utah—Franklin S. Spalding (missionary) Salt Lake	1904
Vermont—Arthur C. A. Hall, Burlington	1894
Virginia—Robert A. Gibson, Richmond	1897
" Southern: Alfred M. Randolph, Norfolk	1883
" " B. D. Tucker, Coadjutor, Lynchburg.	1906
West Virginia—George William Peterkin, Parkersburg	1878
" W. L. Gravatt, Coadjutor, Charlestown	1899
Wisconsin—Milwaukee: William Walter Webb	1906
" Fond du Lac: Charles C. Grafton	1889
" " " Reginald H. Weller, Coadjutor	1900
Washington—Olympia: Fred. W. Keator, Tacoma (miss.)	1902
" Spokane: Lemuel H. Wells (missionary)	1892
Wyoming—(Vacant)	..
Africa—Cape Palmas: S. D. Ferguson (miss.), Monrovia, Lib.	1885
Brazil—Lucien L. L. Kinsolving (missionary)	1899
China—Shanghai: Frederick R. Graves (missionary)	1893
" Hankow: Logan H. Roots (missionary)	1904
Cuba—Albion W. Knight (missionary)	1904
Japan—Tokio: John McKim (missionary)	1893
" Kyoto: S. C. Partridge (missionary)	1900
Hawaiian Islands—Honolulu: Henry B. Restarick (miss.)	1902
Mexico: Henry D. Aves (missionary)	1904
Philippine Islands—Charles H. Brent, Manila (miss.)	1901
Porto Rico—James H. Van Buren (missionary)	1902
Channing Moore Williams, late Bishop of China and Japan. Retired, Kyoto, Japan	1866
Thomas Augustus Jaggar, late Bishop of Southern Ohio. Retired, Boston, Mass.	1875
Charles C. Penick, late Bishop of Cape Palmas, Africa. Retired, Phœnix, Arizona	1877

BISHOPS OF THE METHODIST EPISCOPAL CHURCH.

	Residence.	*Elected.*
Thomas Bowman	East Orange, N J	1872
William F. Anderson	Chattanooga, Tenn	..
Henry W. Warren	Denver, Col	1880
Cyrus D. Foss	Philadelphia, Pa	1880
John M. Walden	Cincinnati, Ohio	1884
Willard F. Mallalieu	Auburndale, Mass	1884
John L. Nuelsen	Omaha, Neb	..
John H. Vincent	Indianapolis, Ind	1888
Daniel A. Goodsell	New York City	1888
James M. Thoburn	Miss. Bis. S. Asia (N.Y. City)	1888
Earl Cranston	Washington, D. C.	1896
Joseph C. Hartzell	Miss. Bis. Africa (Madeira)	1896
David H. Moore	Cincinnatti, Ohio	1900
John W. Hamilton	Boston, Mass	1900
Charles W. Smith	Portland, Ore	..
Wilson S. Lewis	Foochow, China	..
Edwin H. Hughes	San Francisco, Cal	..
Robert McIntyre	St. Paul, Minn	..
Frank M. Bristol	Argentina, S America	..
Frank W. Warne	Lucknow, India	..
William A. Quayle	Oklahoma City, Okla	..
Joseph F. Berry	Buffalo, N. Y	1904
Henry Spellmeyer	St. Louis, Mo	1904
William F. McDowell	Chicago, Ill	1904
James W. Bashford	Pekin, China	1904
William Burt	Zurich, Switzerland	1904
Luther B. Wilson	Philadelphia, Pa	1904
Thomas B. Neely	New Orleans, La	1904
Isaiah B. Scott	Miss. Bis. Afr. (Monrovia)	1904
William F. Oldham	Missionary Bishop, South Asia (Singapore)	1904
John E. Robinson	Missionary Bishop, Asia (Bombay)	1904
Merriman C. Harris	Mis. Bis. Seoul, Korea	1904

BISHOPS OF THE METHODIST EPISCOPAL CHURCH SOUTH.

	Residence	Elected
Alpheus W. Wilson	Baltimore, Md	1882
W. W. Duncan	Spartanburg, S. C.	1886
C. B. Galloway	Jackson, Miss	1886
E. R. Hendrix	Kansas City, Mo	1886
J. S. Key	Sherman, Tex	1886
O. P. Fitzgerald	Nashville, Tenn	1890
W. A. Candler	Atlanta, Ga	1898
H. C. Morrison	New Orleans, La	1898
E. E. Hoss	Monteagle, Tenn	1902
Seth Ward	Nashville, Tenn	1906
James Atkins	Waynesville, N. C	1906

(Continued on next page.)

BISHOPS OF PROTESTANT CHURCHES IN THE UNITED STATES—*Continued.*

BISHOPS OF THE AFRICAN METHODIST EPISCOPAL CHURCH.

H. M. Turner, Atlanta, Ga.	1880	Moses B. Salter, Charleston, S. C	1892
Wesley J. Gaines, Atlanta, Ga.	1888	Wm. B. Derrick, Flushing, N. Y.	1896
B. T. Tanner, Philadelphia, Pa.	1888	Evans Tyree, Nashville, Tenn.	1900
Abraham Grant, Indianapolis, Ind.	1888	C. T. Shaffer, Chicago, Ill.	1900
B. F. Lee, Wilberforce, Ohio.	1892	C. S. Smith, Cape Town, S. A.	1900
James A. Handy, Baltimore, Md.	1892	L. J. Coppin, Philadelphia, Pa.	1900

BISHOPS OF THE REFORMED EPISCOPAL CHURCH.

Charles Edward Cheney	Chicago, Ill.	Robert L. Rudolph	New York City.
Edward Cridge	Victoria, B. C.	William T. Sabine	New York City.
Samuel Fallows	Chicago, Ill.	Herman S. Hoffman	Philadelphia, Pa.
P. F. Stevens	Orangeburg, S. C.		

A. Kozlowski, Chicago, is Bishop of the Old Catholic Church, and S. Kaminski, Buffalo, of the Polish Catholic Church.

Bishops Sergius, of North America, and Innocent, of Alaska, represent the Greek Orthodox Church, and Archimandrite Raphael, New York, the Syrian Greek Orthodox Church.

The next triennial general convention of the Protestant Episcopal Church will be held in Cincinnati, Ohio in 1910.
The next general conference of the Methodist Episcopal Church, South, will be held May 5, 1910, at a place not yet determined.
The nineteenth general council of the Reformed Episcopal Church will be held at Toronto, Canada, May 19, 1909.

American Unitarian Association.

THIS Association was organized in Boston, Mass., May 25, 1825, and incorporated in 1847. Its objects, as defined in the report of the Committee on Organization, are as follows:

1. To collect and diffuse information respecting the state of Unitarian Christianity in our country.
2. To produce union, sympathy, and co-operation among liberal Christians.
3. To publish and distribute books and tracts, inculcating correct views of religion, in such form and at such price as shall afford all an opportunity of being acquainted with Christian truth.
4. To supply missionaries, especially in such parts of our country as are destitute of a stated ministry.
5. To adopt whatever other measures may hereafter seem expedient—such as contributions in behalf of clergymen with insufficient salaries, or in aid of building churches.

President—Rev. Sam'l A. Eliot, D.D., Boston, Mass. *Vice-Presidents*—Wallace Hackett, Portsmouth, N. H.; Eben S. Draper, Hopedale, Mass.; Emma C. Low, Brooklyn, N. Y.; Duncan U. Fletcher, Jacksonville, Fla.; Chas. W. Ames, St. Paul, Minn.; Horace Davis, San Francisco, Cal.; Horace Davis, LL. D., San Francisco, Cal.

Secretary—Rev. Lewis G. Wilson, Boston, Mass. *Assistant Secretary*—George W. Fox, Boston, Mass. *Treasurer*—Francis H. Lincoln, Boston, Mass.

The annual meeting will be held in Boston on Tuesday and Wednesday, May 25-26, 1909.

Universalist General Convention.

THE Universalist General Convention has jurisdiction over the ecclesiastical organizations of the Universalist Church in the United States and Canadian provinces. It meets biennially, the next meeting being ordered for October, 1909. The Convention is composed of the presidents, vice-presidents, and secretaries of the State conventions, and of clerical and lay delegates from the State conventions. All laws relating to fellowship, ordination, and discipline originate in the General Convention, and it is the final court of appeal in all cases of dispute or difficulty between State conventions. It has funds to the amount of over $380,000, the income of which, with the contributions of its constituency, is used for missionary and educational objects. The officers of the Convention are: *President*, C. L. Hutchinson, Chicago; *Vice-President*, George B. Wells, Philadelphia, Pa.; *Secretary*, Rev. I. M. Atwood, D. D., Rochester, N. Y.; *Treasurer*, Eugene F. Endicott, Boston, Mass.

The Young People's Christian Union of the Universalist Church was organized October 22, 1889, "to foster the religious life among the young people, to stimulate to all worthy endeavor, to train the young in the work of the Universalist Church, in the promulgation of its truth, and the increase of its power and influence." It has about 9,000 members, and its general officers and executive board are: *President*, Harry Russel Childs, New York City; *Secretary*, Robert W. Hill, 30 West Street, Boston, Mass.; *Treasurer*, Prof. Arthur W. Peirce, Franklin, Mass.; Rev. O. Howard Perkins, Brookline, Mass.; Miss Mabel A. Sammons, Joliet, Ill; Miss Mary Fosdick Jennings, Detroit, Mich.; Frank M. Bradley, Portland, Me.

The National Council of Congregational Churches

Is composed of delegates from Congregational conferences and associations, and was organized November 17, 1871. It meets once in three years, and the next triennial meeting will be held in Boston, Mass., October, 1910. The officers are: *Moderator*, T. C. MacMillan, Chicago, Ill.; *Secretary*, Rev. Asher Anderson, D. D., 614 Congregational House, Boston, Mass.; *Treasurer and Registrar*, Rev. Joel S. Ives, Hartford, Ct.

Reformed Church in America.*

OFFICERS of the General Synod of the Reformed Church in America: *President*, Rev. Wm. I. Chamberlain, D.D.; *Vice-President*, Rev. Albert Oltmans, D. D.; *Stated Clerk*, Rev. William H. De Hart, D. D., Raritan, N. J.; *Permanent Clerk*, Rev. Henry Lockwood.

The Treasurers are: Synod's Board of Direction, F. R. Van Nest; Foreign Missions, Rev. J. L. Amerman, D. D.; Domestic Missions, William T. Demarest; Education, John Berry; Publication, Abraham C. Holdrum. The Corresponding Secretaries of the Boards are: Foreign Missions, Rev. Henry N. Cobb, D. D.; Domestic Missions, Rev. J. Brownlee Voorhees; Education, Rev. John G. Gebhard, D. D.; Publication, Rev. Isaac W. Gowen, D. D.; Business Manager Board of Publication, Louis E. Turk. Denominational headquarters, 25 East Twenty-second Street, New York City.

* Known formerly as the Reformed Dutch Church.

The Encyclical on Modernism.

BY HIS HOLINESS POPE PIUS X.

The office divinely committed to us of feeding the Lord's flock has especially this duty assigned to it by Christ, namely, to guard with the greatest vigilance the deposit of the faith delivered to the saints, rejecting the profane novelties of words and oppositions of knowledge falsely so called. There has never been a time when this watchfulness of the supreme pastor was not necessary to the Catholic body; for, owing to the efforts of the enemy of the human race, there have never been lacking "men speaking perverse things" (Acts xx., 30), "vain talkers and seducers" (Tit. i., 10), "erring and driving into error" (II. Tim. iii, 13). Still, it must be confessed that the number of the enemies of the cross of Christ has in these last days increased exceedingly, who are striving, by arts entirely new and full of subtlety, to destroy the vital energy of the Church, and, if they can, to overthrow utterly Christ's kingdom itself. Wherefore we may no longer be silent, lest we should seem to fail in our most sacred duty, and lest the kindness that, in the hope of wiser counsels, we have hitherto shown them should be attributed to forgetfulness of our office.

GRAVITY OF THE SITUATION.

That we may make no delay in this matter is rendered necessary especially by the fact that the partisans of error are to be sought not only among the Church's open enemies; they lie hid, a thing to be deeply deplored and feared, in her very bosom and heart, and are the more mischievous the less conspicuously they appear.

We allude, venerable brethren, to many who belong to the Catholic laity, nay, and this is far more lamentable, to the ranks of the priesthood itself, who, feigning a love for the Church, lacking the firm protection of philosophy and theology, nay, more, thoroughly imbued with the poisonous doctrines taught by the enemies of the Church, and lost to all sense of modesty, vaunt themselves as reformers of the Church; and, forming more boldly into line of attack, assail all that is most sacred in the work of Christ, not sparing even the person of the Divine Redeemer, whom, with sacrilegious daring, they reduce to a simple, mere man.

ANALYSIS OF MODERNIST TEACHING.

To proceed in an orderly manner in this recondite subject, it must first of all be noted that every modernist sustains and comprises within himself many personalities; he is a philosopher, a believer, a theologian, an historian, a critic, an apologist, a reformer. These roles must be clearly distinguished from one another by all who would accurately know their system and thoroughly comprehend the principles and the consequences of their doctrines.

AGNOSTICISM ITS PHILOSOPHICAL FOUNDATION.

We begin, then, with the philosopher. Modernists place the foundation of religious philosophy in that doctrine which is usually called agnosticism. According to this teaching, human reason is confined entirely within the field of phenomena; that is to say, to things that are perceptible to the senses, and in the manner in which they are perceptible. It has no right and no power to transgress these limits. Hence it is incapable of lifting itself up to God and of recognizing His existence, even by means of visible things.

VITAL IMMANENCE.

However, this agnosticism is only the negative part of the system of the modernist: the positive side of it consists in what they call vital immanence. This is how they advance from one to the other. Religion, whether natural or supernatural, must, like every other fact, admit of some explanation. But when natural theology has been destroyed, the road to revelation closed through the rejection of the arguments of credibility, and all external revelation absolutely denied, it is clear that this explanation will be sought in vain outside man himself. It must, therefore, be looked for in man; and since religion is a form of life, the explanation must certainly be found in the life of man. Hence the principle of religious immanence is formulated.

DEFORMATION OF RELIGIOUS HISTORY THE CONSEQUENCE.

Therefore, the religious sentiment, which through the agency of vital immanence emerges from the lurking-places of the subconsciousness, is the germ of all religion, and the explanation of everything that has been or ever will be in any religion. This sentiment, which was at first only rudimentary and almost formless, gradually matured, under the influence of that mysterious principle from which it originated, with the progress of human life, of which, as has been said, it is a form. This, then, is the origin of all religion, even supernatural religion; it is only a development of this religious sentiment. Nor is the Catholic religion an exception; it is quite on a level with the rest, for it was engendered, by the process of vital immanence, in the consciousness of Christ, who was a man of the choicest nature, whose like has never been, nor will be.

THE ORIGIN OF DOGMAS.

Thus we have reached one of the principal points in the modernists' system, namely, the origin and the nature of dogma. For they place the origin of dogma in those primitive and simple formulas which, under a certain aspect, are necessary to faith; for revelation, to be truly such, requires the clear manifestation of God in the consciousness. But dogma itself, they apparently hold, is contained in the secondary formulas.

RELIGIOUS EXPERIENCE AND TRADITION.

By the modernists tradition is understood as a communication to others, through preaching, by means of the intellectual formula, of an original experience. To this formula, in addition to its representative value, they attribute a species of suggestive efficacy which acts both in the person who believes to stimulate the religious sentiment should it happen to have grown sluggish and to renew the experience once acquired, and in those who do not yet believe to awake for the first time the religious sentiment in them and to produce the experience. In this way is religious experience propagated among the peoples; and not merely among contemporaries by preaching, but among future generations both by books and by oral transmission from one to another.

FAITH AND SCIENCE.

Having reached this point, venerable brethren, we have sufficient material in hand to enable us to see the relations which modernists establish between faith and science, including history also under the name of science. And in the first place it is to be held that the object of the one is quite extraneous to and separate from the object of the other. For faith occupies itself solely with something which science declares to be unknowable for it. Hence each has a separate field assigned to it: science is entirely concerned with the reality of phenomena, into which faith does not enter at all; faith, on the contrary, concerns itself with the divine reality, which is entirely unknown to science. Thus the conclusion is reached that there can never be any dissension between faith and science, for if each keeps on its own ground they can never meet, and therefore never be in contradiction.

FAITH SUBJECT TO SCIENCE.

Yet it would be a great mistake to suppose that, given these theories, one is authorized to believe that faith and science are independent of one another. On the side of science the independence is indeed complete, but it is quite different with regard to faith, which is subject to science not on one, but on three grounds. For, in the first place, it must be observed that in every religious fact, when you take away the divine reality and the experience of it which the believer possesses, everything else, and especially the religious formulas of it, belongs to the sphere of phenomena, and therefore falls under the control of science. Let the believer leave the world if he will, but so long as he remains in it he must continue, whether he like it or not, to be subject to the laws, the observation, the judgments of science and of history. Further, when it is said that God is the object of faith alone, the statement refers only to the divine reality, not to the idea of God. The latter also is subject to science, which, while it philosophizes in what is called the logical order, soars also to the absolute and the ideal. It is therefore the right of philosophy and of science to form conclusions concerning the idea of God, to direct it in its evolution and to purify it of any extraneous elements which may become confused with it. Finally, man does not suffer a dualism to exist in him, and the believer therefore feels within him an impelling need so to harmonize faith with science that it may never oppose the general conception which science sets forth concerning the universe.

Thus it is evident that science is to be entirely independent of faith, while, on the other hand, and notwithstanding that they are supposed to be strangers to each other, faith is made subject to science.

THE MODERNIST AS THEOLOGIAN; HIS PRINCIPLES, IMMANENCE AND SYMBOLISM.

With the principle of immanence is connected another, which may be called the principle of divine permanence. It differs from the first in much the same way as the private experience differs from the experience transmitted by tradition. An example will illustrate what is meant, and this example is offered by the Church and the sacraments. The Church and the sacraments, they say, are not to be regarded as having been instituted by Christ Himself.

MODERNISM AND ALL THE HERESIES.

And now can anybody who takes a survey of the whole system be surprised that we should define it as the synthesis of all heresies? Were one to attempt the task of collecting together all the errors that have been broached against the faith and to concentrate the sap and substance of them all into one, he could not better succeed than the modernists have done. Nay, they have done more than this, for, as we have already intimated, their system means the destruction not of the Catholic religion alone, but of all religion. With good reason do the rationalists applaud them, for the most sincere and the frankest among the rationalists warmly welcome the modernists as their most valuable allies.

THE CAUSE OF MODERNISM.

To penetrate still deeper into modernism, and to find a suitable remedy for such a deep sore, it behooves us, venerable brethren, to investigate the causes which have engendered it and which foster its growth. That the proximate and immediate cause consists in a perversion of the mind cannot be open to doubt. The remote causes seem to us to be reduced to two: curiosity and pride. Curiosity by itself, if not prudently regulated, suffices to explain all errors. Such is the opinion of our predecessor, Gregory XVI., who wrote: "A lamentable spectacle is that presented by the aberrations of human reason when it yields to the spirit of novelty, when, against the warnings of the apostle, it seeks to know beyond what it is meant to know; and when relying too much on itself it thinks it can find the truth outside the Church, wherein truth is found without the slightest shadow of error." (Ep. Encycl. Singulari nos 7 Kal., July, 1834.)

But it is pride which exercises an incomparably greater sway over the soul to blind it and plunge it into error; and pride sits in modernism as in its own house, finding sustenance everywhere in its doctrines and an occasion to flaunt itself in all its aspects. It is pride which fills modernists with that confidence in themselves and leads them to hold themselves up as the rule for all, pride which puffs them up with that vainglory which allows them to regard themselves as the sole possessors of knowledge and makes them say, inflated with presumption, "We are not as the rest of men," and which, to make them really not as other men, leads them to embrace all kinds of the most absurd novelties. It is pride which rouses in them the spirit of disobedience, and causes them to demand a compromise between authority and liberty; it is pride that makes of them the reformers of others, while they forget to reform themselves, and which begets their absolute want of respect for authority, not excepting the supreme authority. No, truly, there is no road which leads so directly and so quickly to modernism as pride. When a Catholic layman or a priest forgets that precept of the Christian life which obliges us to renounce ourselves if we would follow Jesus Christ, and neglects to tear pride from his heart, ah! but he is a fully ripe subject for the errors of modernism. Hence, venerable brethren, it will be your first duty to thwart such proud men, to employ them only in the lowest and obscurest offices: the higher they try to rise, the lower let them be placed, so that their lowly position may deprive them of the power of causing damage. Sound your young clerics, too, most carefully, by yourselves and by the directors of your seminaries, and when you find the spirit of pride among any of them, reject them without compunction from the priesthood. Would to God that this had always been done with the proper vigilance and constancy!

If we pass from the moral to the intellectual causes of modernism, the first which presents itself, and the chief one, is ignorance. Yes, these very modernists who pose as doctors of the Church, who puff out their cheeks when they speak of modern philosophy, and show such contempt for scholasticism, have embraced the one with all its false glamour because their ignorance of the other has left them without the means of being able to recognize confusion of thought, and to refute sophistry. Their whole system, with all its errors, has been born of the alliance between faith and false philosophy.

Given at St. Peter's, Rome, on the 8th day of September, 1907, the fifth year of our pontificate.

PIUS X., POPE.

The Emmanuel Movement.

BY THE REV. SAMUEL M'COMB, D.D.
ASSOCIATE DIRECTOR OF THE EMMANUEL MOVEMENT.

THE second century of our era witnessed a remarkable outburst of spiritual and intellectual life. The old gods and cults lost their attractions and new divinities claimed the homage of the Roman world. Theosophic speculation imported from the East revealed to the prosaic Roman unsuspected psychical energies, and out of this revelation new worships arose.

Our own time is witnessing also a spiritual revival. The materialism which threatened belief in the soul thirty years ago is now dead. The spirit is coming to its rights, and the philosophy that is attracting the best minds is idealistic. Psychology is revealing to us the wonders of personality, is showing us a self within a self, is giving us a vision of potentialities which we may hope, under the new environment that awaits us beyond the grave, will develop into abiding actualities. It has also demonstrated the profound unity of soul and body, the solidarity of brain and mind; so that every process of consciousness, whether it be a sensation, a feeling, or an idea, has its counterpart in the physical organism.

In the sphere of religion, too, men are conscious of a new atmosphere. The tide of faith is returning. The great critical movement of the nineteenth century has done its work, and Christianity is being reduced to its simplest and most intelligible form, and everywhere there is the feeling that in the religion of Christ, thus freed from all the accretions that have gathered round it through its history, there are healing and reconciling forces. Many are convinced that religion is something grander and simpler and more vital than had been suspected. There is a return to the great idea of Christ and of the Apostolic Age, that the whole kingdom of evil, of which disease forms a part, is opposed to the Divine Will, and that God is on the side of health, mental, moral and physical.

One of the most notable manifestations of the new spirit is to be seen in the extraordinary growth of mental healing cults. These cults for the most part rest on a very precarious metaphysic, know little or nothing of the Bible as the trained scholar knows it, and regard medical science as little better than an elaborate illusion. Their essence is a kind of crazy idealism, which defies the obvious facts of experience and conceives of the body as lying plastic at the will of the spirit. In spite, however, of their theological and metaphysical sins, these movements have done great service in recalling both physicians and sufferers to such facts as these: that many persons are sick because they and their friends think that they are sick; that many others are sick because they violate law moral and law physiological; that the idea of sickness has a tendency to realize itself and to create an atmosphere in which the sickness is perpetuated. Nor can any one doubt that these healing cults effect many cures; do, as a matter of fact, dissipate fear, worry, anger; uplift the soul above the things that harass it; and put upon their feet, morally and physically, many who have been a burden to themselves and to their families.

Now, the Emmanuel Movement, while having a point of contact with these systems in that it utilizes consciously what they utilize unconsciously, yet in all essential features stands over against them by way of contrast. The fundamental idea underlying it may be expressed thus: It is an effort to unite in friendly alliance a simple New Testament Christianity as modern Biblical scholarship corroborates it and the proved conclusions of modern medicine, and more especially of modern psychological medicine, in the interests of suffering humanity. It imposes no new dogma, philosophical or theological. It claims to be the possessor of no new revelation except that which is the product on the one hand of the growing Christian consciousness, and that which on the other hand comes through the revelation God makes of Himself in the discoveries of science. Its great aim is to give to faith the things of faith and to science the things of science. Because scientific, it distinguishes between those forms or types of nervous suffering which are functional in character and those which are organic. This distinction, it is true, cannot be in the ultimate resort defended, but for all practical purposes it is valid and well recognized. Hence, one of the fundamental principles of the Emmanuel plan, and one which distinguishes it sharply from all systems of metaphysical healing—Christian Science, Mental Science, Faith Healing, etc.—is that there is first of all a thorough medical examination of the patient before any psychic treatment is entered upon. This examination is necessary not only in order to rule out any organic disease or distinctly organic complications of a seemingly pure functional disorder, but also in order to obtain an intelligent comprehension of the functional disorder itself, if functional disorder it be. From another point of view, the same necessity becomes obvious. Patients, for example, have come to us who have been treated by physicians for organic diseases by means of drugs and special diet, and upon examination it has been found that the disorders were purely functional in character. Now, of these functional disorders the nomenclature is constantly changing, but, roughly speaking, we may say that they fall under the following five great groups:

1. Neurasthenia, or, as it is popularly called, nervous prostration, which has an infinite number of shades from a slight sense of depression or fatigue to the profoundest exhaustion of the nervous system.
2. Hysteria. This is an abnormal disposition of the nervous system, in which the sufferer is peculiarly amenable to suggestion and self-suggestion.
3. Hypochrondia. The main feature of this disorder is fear of disease.
4. Psychasthenia. This word is only two years old and is used to cover the large group of nervous troubles in which the psychical element is predominant.
5. Drug addictions. Here we have those moral slaveries, such as alcoholism, cocainism, morphinism, which, while they affect profoundly physiological processes, are now recognized as rooted in psychical and moral tendencies.

The Emmanuel Movement believes that minister and doctor should unite their forces, should come to a common understanding and should thus solve the difficulty presented by so many semi-moral and semi-nervous disorders by attacking them simultaneously from the spiritual as well as from the physical side. Hence, the remedies applied in the Emmanuel clinic are mainly psychological, moral and religious, but not without regard to any physical needs that may be evident. The psychic remedies are those which have been used for some time past with singular success in the great psycho-therapeutic clinics of Europe and to a much less extent in some of the hospitals of this country. We have taken advantage of the fruitful union which has been consummated between medicine and psychology.

Presbyterian Assemblies.

OFFICERS OF THE LAST GENERAL ASSEMBLY OF THE PRESBYTERIAN CHURCH IN THE UNITED STATES OF AMERICA.

Moderator—Rev. Baxter P. Fullerton, D.D., LL.D., St. Louis, Mo.

Stated Clerk—Rev. W. H. Roberts, D.D., LL.D., 1319 Walnut Street, Philadelphia, Pa.

TRUSTEES.

President—John H. Converse, LL.D., Philadelphia. | *Treasurer*—Charles B. Adamson, Philadelphia.

AGENCIES OF THE CHURCH.

The following may be addressed at 156 Fifth Avenue, New York City, viz.: The Board of Home Missions, the Board of Foreign Missions, the Board of Church Erection, and the College Board.

The following are located at 1319 Walnut Street, Philadelphia, Pa., viz.: The Trustees of the General Assembly, the Board of Education, the Board of Publication and Sabbath-school Work, and the Board of Ministerial Relief.

The Board of Missions for Freedmen is located at Bessemer Building, Sixth Street, Pittsburgh, Pa.

The Church magazine, *The Assembly Herald*, has its office at 1328 Chestnut Street, Philadelphia, Pa.

OFFICERS OF THE LAST GENERAL ASSEMBLY OF THE PRESBYTERIAN CHURCH IN THE UNITED STATES.*

Moderator—Rev. W. W. Moore, D.D., LL.D., Richmond, Va.

Stated Clerk—Rev. W. A. Alexander, D.D., 501 College St., Clarksville, Tenn.

TRUSTEES.

President—George E. Wilson, Esq., Charlotte, N. C.

Secretary and Treasurer—John R. Pharr, Esq., Charlotte, N. C.

SECRETARIES.

Foreign Missions—Rev. S. H. Chester, D.D., Nashville, Tenn.

Home Missions—Rev. S. L. Morris, D.D., Atlanta, Ga.

Publication—R. E. Magill, Esq., Richmond, Va.

Ministerial Education and Relief—Rev. H. H. Sweets, 232 Fourth Avenue, Louisville, Ky.

Colored Evangelization—Rev. James G. Snedecor, LL.D., Tuscaloosa, Ala.

* Commonly known as the Southern Presbyterian Church.

Alliance of the Reformed Churches

THROUGHOUT THE WORLD HOLDING THE PRESBYTERIAN SYSTEM.

THIS organization represents nine Reformed and Presbyterian Churches in the United States, with a constituency of 6,500,000; the Presbyterian Church in Canada, with a constituency of 600,000, and more than 80 different denominations on the five continents other than North America, with a constituency of at least 25,000,000 persons. The American Secretary is the Rev. W. H. Roberts, D.D., LL.D., Philadelphia, Pa. The following are the organizations in the United States, Canada, and Mexico which are members of the Alliance:

PRESBYTERIAN CHURCH IN THE UNITED STATES OF AMERICA, COMMONLY KNOWN AS THE PRESBYTERIAN CHURCH, NORTH.

Stated Clerk—Rev. W. H. Roberts, D.D., LL.D., 1319 Walnut Street, Philadelphia, Pa.
Next meeting of General Assembly, Denver, Col., May 20, 1909. (Communicants, 1,300,329.)

PRESBYTERIAN CHURCH IN THE UNITED STATES, COMMONLY KNOWN AS THE PRESBYTERIAN CHURCH, SOUTH.

Stated Clerk—Rev. W. A. Alexander, D.D., 501 College Street, Clarksville, Tenn.
Next meeting of General Assembly, Savannah, Ga., May 20, 1909. (Communicants, 268,733.)

UNITED PRESBYTERIAN CHURCH OF NORTH AMERICA.

Stated Clerk—Rev. D. F. McGill, D.D., 1508 Chartiers Street, Allegheny, Pa.
Next meeting of General Assembly, Knoxville, Tenn., May 26, 1909. (Communicants, 153,956)

REFORMED (DUTCH) CHURCH IN AMERICA.

Stated Clerk—Rev. Wm. H. De Hart, D.D., Raritan, N. J.
Next meeting of General Synod, Place to be fixed. (Communicants, 117,139.)

REFORMED (GERMAN) CHURCH IN THE UNITED STATES.

Stated Clerk—Rev. John Ph. Stein, D.D., Reading, Pa.
Next meeting of the General Synod, Canton, Ohio, May 16, 1909. (Communicants, 248,271.)

REFORMED PRESBYTERIAN CHURCH, GENERAL SYNOD.

Stated Clerk—Rev. James Y. Boice, D.D., 4020 Spruce Street, Philadelphia, Pa.
Next meeting of the General Synod, Philadelphia, Pa., May 19, 1909. (Communicants, 3,500.)

ASSOCIATE REFORMED SYNOD OF THE SOUTH.

Stated Clerk—Rev. James Boyce, Due West S. C. (Communicants, 13,368)

SYNOD OF THE REFORMED PRESBYTERIAN CHURCH OF NORTH AMERICA.

Stated Clerk—Rev. J. W. Sproull, D.D., 2325 Perrysville Avenue, Allegheny, Pa.
Next meeting of the Synod, Chicago, Ill., May 25, 1909. (Communicants, 9,404.)

WELSH PRESBYTERIAN CHURCH.

Stated Clerk—Rev. William E. Evans, Mankato, Minn.
Next meeting of General Assembly, Cotter, Ia., September 18, 1910. (Communicants, 14,000.)

THE PRESBYTERIAN CHURCH IN CANADA.

Stated Clerk—Rev. Frederick Duval, D.D., Winnipeg, Canada.
Next meeting of General Assembly, Hamilton, June 2, 1909. (Communicants, 264,999.)

PRESBYTERIAN CHURCH OF MEXICO, GENERAL SYNOD.

Stated Clerk—Rev. William Wallace, Saltillo, Mexico.
Next meeting of the Synod, July, 1909. (Communicants, 8,000.)

Christian Science.

THE Christian Science Publication Committee, for the State of New York, contributes the following statement:

There are many institutes for teaching Christian Science, and upward of 4.000 practitioners of Christian Science mind-healing. Organizations can now be found in almost every city in the United States, and there are branches in Canada, Nova Scotia, British Columbia, Mexico, the Bahamas, British West Indies, the Hawaiian Islands, Cuba, Philippine Islands, Sandwich Islands, British Isles, France, Germany, Norway, Switzerland, Italy, Australia, New South Wales, India, China, South Africa, and many other countries.

All Christian Science churches, other than the Mother Church in Boston, are branches of that church. In all of these the Sunday services are uniform, and consist of correlative passages read from the Bible and the Christian Science text-book, "Science and Health, with Key to the Scriptures," by Mary Baker G. Eddy. The selections comprising the lesson sermon are compiled by a central committee, and are published by the Christian Science Publishing Society in Boston, in a pamphlet known as "The Christian Science Quarterly." The church services are conducted by two readers, generally a man and a woman. On Wednesday evening a meeting is held in every church of this denomination. Testimonies of healing and remarks on Christian Science are given by the members of the congregation at these meetings.

Mrs. Eddy says in her book, "Retrospection and Introspection:" "I claim for healing scientifically the following advantages: 1. It does away with all material medicines and recognizes the antidote for all sickness, as well as sin, in the immortal mind; and mortal mind is the source of all the ills which befall mortals. 2. It is more effectual than drugs, and cures when they fail, or only relieve, thus proving the superiority of metaphysics over physics. 3. A person healed by Christian Science is not only healed of his disease, but he is advanced morally and spiritually. The mortal body being but the objective state of the mortal mind, this mind must be renovated to improve the body." The absence of creed and dogma in the Christian Science Church, its freedom from materialism, mysticism, and superstition, also the simplicity, uniformity, and impersonality of its form of worship and organization, are among the distinguishing features which characterize this modern religious movement. Hypnotism, mesmerism, spiritualism, theosophy, faith-cure, and kindred systems are foreign to true Christian Science. Those practising these beliefs are denied admission to the Christian Science Church.

The Theosophical Society.

MR. WELLER VAN HOOK, General Secretary of the American section, contributes the following statement:

The Theosophical Society was founded in New York City on November 17, 1875, by Mme. H. P. Blavatsky and Col. Henry S. Olcott, but its headquarters were removed in 1879 to Adyar, Madras, India. Its objects are three: (*a*) To form a nucleus of the Universal Brotherhood of Humanity, without distinction of race, creed, sex, caste, or color; (*b*) to encourage the study of comparative religion, philosophy, and science; (*c*) to investigate unexplained laws of nature and the powers latent in man. It has spread into almost all countries, and has now eleven territorial sections, each presided over by a general secretary: America, Great Britain, India, Scandinavia, Holland, Hungary, France, Italy, Germany, Australia, and New Zealand. During the 33 years of its existence it has admitted about 28,000 members and chartered over 750 branches. The membership at present of the American section is about 2,500; there are 85 branches. The society holds forth no doctrines and enjoins none, but Theosophy is the natural study of its members, and a large and increasing number of theosophical treatises is poured out by students. Reincarnation and Karma are the basic stones of the Theosophical system. The president, Mrs. Annie Besant, resides at the Adyar headquarters; the general secretary of the American section is Weller Van Hook, 103 State Street, Chicago, Ill. Some organizations using the name "Theosophical" have been formed since 1875, but they are distinct from and unaffiliated with the original Theosophical Society.

The Society appeals for support and encouragement to all who truly love their fellow men and desire the eradication of the evils caused by the barriers raised by race, creed or color, which have so long impeded human progress; to all scholars, to all sincere lovers of TRUTH, *wheresoever it may be found*, and to all philosophers, alike in the East and in the West; and lastly to all who aspire to higher and better things than the mere pleasures and interests of a worldly life, and are prepared to make the sacrifices by which alone a knowledge of them can be attained.

The Universal Brotherhood and Theosophical Society.

MR. J. H. FUSSELL, Secretary of the Universal Brotherhood and Theosophical Society, Point Loma, Cal., contributes the following statement:

The Universal Brotherhood and Theosophical Society, founded by Mme. H. P. Blavatsky in New York, 1875, continued after her death under the leadership of the co-founder, William Q. Judge, and now under the leadership of their successor, Katherine Tingley, has its International Headquarters at the World's Theosophical Centre, Point Loma, California.

This organization declares that brotherhood is a fact in nature. The principal purpose of the organization is to teach brotherhood, demonstrate that it is a fact in nature, and make it a living power in the life of humanity, establishing Raja Yoga schools throughout the world, and creating a new literature. Its subsidiary purpose is to study ancient and modern religion, science, philosophy, and art, to investigate the laws of nature and the latent divine powers in man. It declares in its constitution that every member has a right to believe or disbelieve in any religious system or philosophy, each being required to show that tolerance for the opinions of others which he expects for his own. The head of this organization is Katherine Tingley, and the secretary-general is Frank M. Pierce. The headquarters are at Point Loma, Cal.

The Salvation Army.

THE following statement is contributed to THE WORLD ALMANAC by direction of the Commander:

The Salvation Army is a religious body organized on military principles, with a view of reaching the non-churchgoers of the world. It was first started in July, 1865. in the East End of London as a Christian mission. Thirteen years later, on Christmas, 1878, it received the name of the Salvation Army. Since then its growth throughout the world has been increasing.

The father and founder, Gen. William Booth, was born in Nottingham, England, on April 10, 1829. In 1852 he entered the ministry of the Methodist Church, and became a powerful evangelist, attracting immense crowds and witnessing thousands of conversions. Finding, however, that the churchless masses could not be reached by ordinary methods, he resigned his pastorate and established the Army.

As a temperance movement it is stated that the Salvation Army has been the means of converting hundreds of thousands of confirmed drunkards. Total abstinence is a condition of membership. The International headquarters are at 101 Victoria Street, London, England. Its world-wide operations are carried on in 54 countries and colonies. embracing 8,055 posts, under the charge of 21,025 officers and employés, with 51,161 local officers, 19,683 brass bandsmen, and about 50,000 musicians. 69 periodicals are published in 24 languages, with a weekly circulation of about 1,013,292. There are 786 Social Relief Institutions in the world, under the charge of 2,334 officers and employés. About 6,292 fallen women annually pass through the 115 rescue homes, and from 80 to 90 per cent. of these are permanently restored to lives of virtue. There are 137 slum settlements in the slum districts of great cities, the worst dives, saloons, and tenements being regularly visited. The number of annual conversions in connection with the spiritual work has averaged from 200,000 to 250,000 during the past ten years, making a total of over 2,000,000, of whom not less than 200,000 were converted from lives of drunkenness.

The real estate owned by the Army amounts to about $4,021,980, its personal property over $753,664, and its annual trade turnover to more than $378,594. The Salvation Army is incorporated in the State of New York. For the developments of its trade a special incorporation has been formed, the Reliance Trading Company, while the Salvation Army Industrial Homes Company has been incorporated for the extension of its rapidly growing industrial homes for the unemployed. Training colleges for cadets have been established for the training of officers in New York and Chicago, with a small branch in San Francisco.

The headquarters of the Salvation Army in America are at 120 West Fourteenth Street, New York City, where information may be obtained.

The Volunteers of America.

THE following statement of the purposes of the position and this organization has been prepared for THE WORLD ALMANAC in the othee of Gen. Ballington Booth:

This organization is a philanthropic, social, and religions movement. It was inaugurated by Gen. and Mrs. Ballington Booth, in March, 1896, and incorporated November 6, 1896, in response to a number of requests on the part of American citizens. It is organized in military style, having as its model the United States Army, but in conjunction with military discipline and methods of work it possesses a thoroughly democratic form of government, having a constitution, and its by-laws being framed by a Grand Field Council that meets annually and is thoroughly representative. Though only twelve years old the Volunteers have representatives and branches of their benevolent work in almost all the principal cities of the United States. Its field is divided into regiments or sections, which come under the control and oversight of thirty principal staff officers, its chief centres being New York, Philadelphia, Boston, Pittsburgh, Denver, Chicago, Indianapolis, Cleveland, and San Francisco. It has philanthropic institutions in Chicago, Joliet, Austin, Fort Dodge, Kansas City, Pueblo, Boston, Lynn, Malden, Minneapolis, Erie, Pittsburgh, Buffalo, Newcastle, Philadelphia, Newark, Orangeburg, New York City and other centres.

In addition to the Volunteer reading rooms, thousands of copies of Christian literature are circulated in State prisons, jails, hospitals, soldiers' homes, and children's homes. In connection with the Volunteers, there are also sewing classes; hospital nurses; temporary financial relief departments; boys' fresh-air camps; Thanksgiving and Christmas dinners, and many other worthy undertakings.

The National Spiritualists' Association

OF THE UNITED STATES OF AMERICA.

PRESIDENT WARNE makes the following statement regarding this Association:

Organized September 28, 1893; incorporated November 1, 1893, at Washington, D. C. Objects: The objects of said Association shall be the organization of the various Spiritualist Societies of the United States into one general association for the purpose of mutual aid and co-operation in benevolent, charitable, educational, literary, musical, scientific, religious, and missionary purposes and enterprises germane to the phenomena, science, philosophy, and religion of spiritualism.

Active Working Local Societies, 437; State associations, 22; Other local societies meeting at irregular intervals, 216; Public meetings not organized as societies, 225; Camp meeting associations, 32; academy for liberal education, 1; churches and temples, 120; membership of avowed spiritualists, 75,000; unidentified with organized societies, but believers in the philosophy and phenomena, and frequent attendants upon public services, 1,500,000 to 2,000,000. A host of people from every walk in life, impossible of exact enumeration, are investigating psychic truths through mediums. Number of public mediums, 1,500; private mediums, many thousands; ordained ministers, 370; total valuation of church, temple, and camp meeting property, $2,000,000.

Officers for the year ending in October, 1909: Dr. George B. Warne, 4203 Evans Ave., Chicago, President; Charles Schirm, Baltimore, Vice-President; George W. Kates, Washington, D. C., Secretary; Cassius L. Stevens, Pittsburgh, Pa., Treasurer; Illtyd C. I. Evans, Washington, D. C.; Thomas Grimshaw, St. Louis, Mo. J. S. Maxwell, Minneapolis, Minn.; Miss Elizabeth Harlow, Haydenville, Mass.; A. W. Belden, San Diego, Cal., Trustees.

Headquarters of National Spiritualists' Association, 600 Pennsylvania Ave., Washington, D. C. The Seventeenth Annual Convention of the National Spiritualists' Association will be held in Rochester, N. Y., in October, 1909.

Young People's Society of Christian Endeavor.

OFFICERS OF THE UNITED SOCIETY OF CHRISTIAN ENDEAVOR.—Office, Tremont Temple, Boston, Mass. *President*, Rev. Francis E. Clark, D. D., LL.D., *Treasurer*, Hiram N. Lathrop; *General Secretary*, William Shaw.

Each society is in some local church, and in no sense outside. It exists simply to make the young people loyal and efficient members of the Church of Christ. It is the Church training the young. Its motto is, "For Christ and the Church." In November, 1908, there were 70,761 societies, with a membership of 3,500,000, chiefly in the United States and Canada, and in Australia, Great Britain, China, India, Japan, and in all missionary lands. It is found in about the same proportions in all the great evangelical denominations and in all their subdivisions.

The United Society is simply the bureau of information for all the societies. It prints the literature, supports one general secretary, and is the general headquarters of the work. It levies no taxes, however, and assumes no authority, but every society manages its own affairs in its own way. It is supported by the sales of its literature, badges, etc. It is managed by a board of trustees, representing the great evangelical denominations, the President being Francis E. Clark, D. D., LL.D., the founder of the society; General Secretary, William Shaw; Treasurer, Hiram N. Lathrop. The executive committee of the board of trustees meets quarterly to consult concerning the best interests of the society.

American Board of Commissioners for Foreign Missions.

THE head office of the American Board of Commissioners for Foreign Missions is at the Congregational House, 14 Beacon Street, Boston, Mass. There are three district offices: (1) at the United Charities Building, Twenty-second Street and Fourth Avenue, New York City, Rev. C. C. Creegan, D.D., District Secretary; (2) 153 La Salle Street, Chicago, Ill., Rev. A. N. Hitchcock, Ph. D., District Secretary; (3) Berkeley, California, Barker Block, Rev. H. M. Tenney, District Secretary. Its officers are: *President*, Samuel B. Capen, LL.D., Boston, Mass.; *Vice-President*, Henry C. King, D. D., Oberlin, O.; *Corresponding Secretaries*, James L. Barton, D. D., Cornelius H. Patton, D. D.; *Treasurer*, Frank H. Wiggin; *Editorial Secretaries*, E. E. Strong, D. D., Rev. William E. Strong; *Associate Secretary*, Harry Wade Hicks; *Recording Secretary*, Henry A. Stimson, D.D.; *Prudential Committee*, Hon. Arthur H. Wellman, Francis O. Winslow, Prof. Arthur L. Gillett, D. D., Col. Charles A. Hopkins, Herbert A. Wilder, Rev. Edward M. Noyes, Rev. John H. Denison, Rev. Albert P. Fitch, Henry H. Proctor, Rev. Geo. A. Hall, Arthur Perry, Rev. Lucius H. Thayer; *Publishing and Purchasing Agent*, John G. Hosmer.

The American Board, which is the oldest foreign missionary society in the United States, was organized June 29, 1810. During the past ninety-eight years of its history it has sent out over 2,500 missionaries, of whom 569 are now in service. Into the 600 churches which have been organized by these missionaries there have been received from the first nearly 200,000 members. The total receipts from the beginning have been over $38,500,000.

The mission fields now occupied by the Board are: Mexico; Micronesian Islands; Philippine Islands; Japan; North China; Shansi, in Northwestern China; Foochow and Hong Kong, in Southern China; Ceylon; Madura, in Southern India; the Marathi field of Western India; East Central Africa; Southern Africa; West Central Africa; European and Asiatic Turkey; Austria, and Spain.

United Society of Free Baptist Young People.

A GENERAL society representing the local societies of young people of the Free Baptist Denomination. The officers are as follows: *President*, E. P. Metcalf, Providence, R. I.; *Vice-President*, Rev. J. H. Wolfe, Tecumseh, Neb.; *Recording Secretary*, Miss Agnes Collins, South Danville, N. H.; *General Secretary*, Harry S. Myers, 156 Fifth Ave.; *Treasurer*, Rev. Arthur Given, D.D., Providence, R. I. There are 400 societies, with a membership of 15,000.

Baptist Young People's Union of America.

THE Union is a federation of young people's societies connected with Baptist churches in all the States and Canada. The following are the International officers: *President*, E. Y. Mullins, D.D., Louisville, Ky.; *Vice-Presidents*, Geo. W. Truett, D.D., Dallas, Tex.; Charles Senior, Toronto, Ont.; W. J. Williamson, D.D., St. Louis, Mo.; *General Secretary*, George T. Webb, 324 Dearborn Street, Chicago, Ill.; *Recording Secretary*, Rev. H. W. Reed, Ph. D., Rock Island, Ill.; *Treasurer*, H.B. Osgood, Chicago, Ill. The Union was organized July 7 and 8, 1891. It holds annual meetings. Next meeting will be held at Saratoga Springs, N. Y., July, 1909.

The Brotherhood of St. Andrew.

THE following was prepared for THE WORLD ALMANAC by the General Secretary:

"The Brotherhood of St. Andrew is an organization of men in the Protestant Episcopal Church. Its sole object is the spread of Christ's kingdom among men. It works under two rules, known as (1) The Rule of Prayer: To pray daily for the spread of Christ's kingdom among men, especially young men, and for God's blessing upon the labors of the Brotherhood, and (2) The Rule of Service: To make at least one earnest effort each week to lead some man nearer to Christ through His church." There are now 1,300 active chapters with a membership of about fifteen thousand men.

The Brotherhood idea has also taken root in Canada, and the Brotherhood of St. Andrew in the Church of England in the Dominion of Canada has been formed, with four hundred chapters and thirty-eight hundred men. A similar organization has been formed in the Scottish Episcopal Church. In the West Indies there is a membership of 1,000 men, and there is also a national organization in Japan. June 12, 1896, the Brotherhood of St. Andrew in the Church of England was formed.

The Brotherhood in the United States includes a Junior Department to train young men and elder boys for Christian work. It has 500 chapters in the United States, with about six thousand members.

The officers are: *President*, Robert H. Gardiner; *Editor* of *St. Andrew's Cross* and *General Secretary*, Hubert Carleton, Broad Exchange Building, Boston, Mass.; *Associate Secretary*, George H. Randall. The Secretaries will furnish information and literature to any one who may be interested in the work.

Young Men's Christian Associations.

OFFICERS OF THE INTERNATIONAL COMMITTEE.—Office, No. 124 East Twenty-eighth Street, New York. *Chairman*, Lucien C. Warner; *Treasurer*, Frederick B. Schenck; *General Secretary*, Richard C. Morse. *Board of Trustees—Treasurer*, Jas. G. Cannon, New York City. The International Committee is the general executive of the Associations of North America. It consists of 54 representative Christian laymen, and employs a force of 67 secretaries in the home and 78 in the foreign fields.

OFFICERS OF THE WORLD'S COMMITTEE.—Headquarters, No. 3 Général Dufour, Geneva, Switzerland. *Chairman*, R. Sarasin Warnery; *Secretary*, Louis Perrot; *Treasurer*, Paul Des Gouttes; *General Secretaries*, Charles Fermaud and Christian Phildius. The committee is composed of members representing America, Austria-Hungary, Belgium, Brazil, Denmark, Great Britain, France, Germany, Italy, Netherlands, Norway, Portugal, Russia, Spain, South Africa, Sweden, Switzerland, China, Korea, Ceylon, Japan, and India.

OFFICERS OF THE STATE EXECUTIVE COMMITTEE OF THE YOUNG MEN'S CHRISTIAN ASSOCIATIONS OF THE STATE OF NEW YORK.—General office, No. 215 West 23d Street, New York. *Chairman*, Edmund P. Platt; *Treasurer*, Samuel Woolverton; *State Secretary*, John W. Cook. This committee was incorporated under the laws of New York April 14, 1886, having for its object "the establishing and assisting Young Men's Christian Associations, and generally to provide for the spiritual, intellectual, physical, and social well-being of young men in accordance with the aims and methods of Young Men's Christian Associations of the State of New York." The membership in the State is 54,511, divided as follows: General, 30,639; Railroad, 9,756; Student, 3,313; Boys' Departments, 9,065; County and Small Town, 729. A biennial meeting of the State Association, comprising the 187 Associations in the State, is held in February, the even years.

OFFICERS OF THE YOUNG MEN'S CHRISTIAN ASSOCIATION OF THE CITY OF NEW YORK.—General office, No. 215 West Twenty-third Street, New York. *President*, W. Fellowes Morgan; *Treasurer*, Samuel Sloan, Jr.; *General Secretary*, Henry M. Orne.

There are 7,942 associations in the world, of which 1,939 are in North America. The total membership of these American associations is 446,032; they occupy 630 buildings of their own, valued at $39,138,411, and have 784 libraries, containing 519,772 volumes. They have 44,831 young men as students in evening educational classes, and 187,110 in their physical departments. They employ 2,544 general secretaries and other paid officials, and expended last year for current expenses—local, State, and international—$6,992,294.

The World's Young Women's Christian Association.

THE World's Young Women's Christian Association was formed in 1894. Seventeen National Associations are now affiliated: Great Britain, United States, Canada, Germany, Italy, France, Australasia, Finland, Holland, Japan, Portugal, South Africa, Sweden, India, Denmark, and Hungary. The headquarters are in London. Office, 26 George Street, Hanover Square, West. The Executive Committee is composed of a resident membership in London and two representatives from America and other countries. Miss Morley is President; Miss Clarissa Spencer, General Secretary. The Third World's Conference was held in Paris, France, 1906.

The Young Women's Christian Association of the United States of America was formed in December, 1906, the object being stated thus: "To unite in one body the Young Women's Christian Association of the United States; to establish, develop and unify such associations; to advance the physical, social, intellectual, moral and spiritual interests of young women; to participate in the work of the World's Young Women's Christian Association." The national convention occurs biennially; in the interim the work of the organization is carried on by the National Board of thirty members. One hundred and eighty city associations and 557 student associations are members of the national organization. There are twenty-four territorial and State organizations. Each year nine Summer conferences are held to train volunteer workers in Bible study and Association work. The National Training School to prepare young women for executive positions is located at 3 Gramercy Park, New York, and there are ten training centres in different parts of the United States. The official organ is *The Association Monthly*. The national organization is a member of the World's Association; the Student Department is a member of the World's Student Christian Federation, and is connected with the Student Volunteer Movement. National headquarters, 125 East Twenty-seventh Street, New York. *President of National Board*, Grace H. Dodge; *Executive for Home Department*, Mabel Cratty; *Executive for Foreign Department*, Harriet Taylor.

American Tract Society.

THE Society was founded in 1825. Its work is interdenominational and international in scope, and is commended by all the evangelical churches. It has published the Gospel message in 174 languages, dialects and characters. Its total issues of books, tracts, and periodicals at the Home Office amount to 767,844,534 copies. It has made foreign cash appropriations to the value of $768,713.25, by means of which millions of books and tracts have been published at mission stations abroad. Its colporters have made 16,643 358 family visits, largely among the immigrants, and have circulated 16,812,645 volumes. The grand total of its gratuitous distribution has been to the value of $2,472,126.05. The society depends upon donations and legacies for the support of its work. Offices, 150 Nassau Street, New York. *President*, William Phillips Hall; *General Secretary*, Judson Swift, D.D.

American Bible Society.

THE American Bible Society was founded in 1816. It is a charitable institution, whose sole object is to encourage a wider circulation of the Scriptures without note or comment. It invites the contribution and co-operation of "all who accept the Bible as their rule of life and believe that every human being is entitled to know what it teaches concerning truth and duty." The officers are a president, and twenty-six vice-presidents, headed by J. L. Chamberlain, Maine. Among the others are Gen. O. O. Howard, Vermont; Frank E. Spooner, Illinois; John W. Foster, District of Columbia; T. A. Brouwer, New York; Cyrus Northrop, Minnesota; James H. Carlisle, South Carolina; Howard Van Epps, Georgia; E. E. Beard, Tennessee; William J. Northen, Georgia; William A. Robinson, Kentucky; John B. Smith, New Hampshire; W. P. Dillingham, Vermont; David J. Brewer, District of Columbia; James A. Beaver, Pennsylvania; Elbert A. Brinckerhoff, New Jersey, and John L. Williams, Virginia. There are thirty-six managers, divided into four classes as to terms of office. The Corresponding Secretaries are: Rev. John Fox, D. D., and Rev. W. I. Haven, D. D.; Recording Secretary, Rev. H. O. Dwight, LL. D. The Treasurer is William Foulke. The issues for the year ending March 31, 1908, were 1,895,941 copies, and for the ninety-two years of the existence of the Society, 82,316,323 copies. This includes Bibles in many foreign tongues, and the languages of several American Indian tribes. (The British and Foreign Bible Society, established in 1804, has distributed to March 31, 1908, 209,000,000 copies.) The offices of the Society are at the Bible House, Fourth Avenue, New York.

The Vedanta Society.

THE following statement of the purposes of this Society has been prepared by the Secretary, Mrs. C. G. Kelley:

The Vedanta Society of New York was established in 1884 by Swami Vivekananda of India, delegate to the Parliament of Religions at Chicago, and was regularly incorporated in 1898 by Swami Abhedananda, now at its head. The object of the Society is not to form a new sect or creed, or to make proselytes, but to explain through logic and reason the spiritual laws that govern our lives; to show that the True Religion of the Soul is not antagonistic to, but in harmony with, philosophy and science; to establish that Universal Religion which underlies all the various sects and creeds of special religions; to propagate the principles taught by great seers of Truth and religious leaders of different countries and illustrated by their lives; and to help mankind in the practical application of those principles in their spiritual, moral, intellectual and physical needs.

The present headquarters of the Society with its Circulating Library, Reading Room and Chapel, are at 135 West Eightieth Street, New York City. Here throughout the Winter season a service with lecture by Swami Abhedananda is held every Sunday morning at 11, and a class lecture on Tuesday evening at 8. There are Yoga classes for practical training in the Science of Breathing, in Concentration, Meditation and Self-Control every Thursday evening at 8, and on Saturday morning at 10.30. Besides these there is also a correspondence class for non-resident members in which the same instructions are given in writing by the Swami. An associate membership exists for those who do not wish regular instruction but who desire to be affiliated with the Society. Among the honorary members are Rev. R. Heber Newton, D.D.; Charles R. Lanman, Ph. D., LL.D., Professor of Sanskrit at Harvard University; Hiram Corson, A.M., LL.D., Litt. D., Professor of English Literature Emeritus at Cornell University; Professor Franklin W. Hooper, M. A., Director of the Brooklyn Institute of Arts and Sciences.

The officers of the Society are: *President*—Professor Herschel C. Parker. *Vice-President*—————————*Secretary*—Mrs. Christina G. Kelley. *Treasurer*—Charles Baumann.

The Society has a large publishing department and issues a catalogue containing nearly forty titles of works on the Philosophy and Religion of Vedanta. Within the last five years it has sent out from its headquarters 39,876 books and pamphlets written by Swamis of India. It also issues a monthly Bulletin. The Vedanta Society of New York has a Summer school called the "Vedanta Ashrama" It is situated in West Cornwall, Ct., on a farm of 250 acres. There are also centres in Pittsburgh, San Francisco and Los Angeles, besides a Peace Retreat in the mountains of Santa Clara County, Cal. These organizations in America are affiliated with hundreds of Vedanta Societies throughout India and Ceylon.

The Latter-Day Saints.

THE Mormons, or Church of Jesus Christ of Latter-Day Saints, were organized April 6, 1830, with six members, by Joseph Smith, at Fayette, Seneca County, N. Y. After being driven by mobs from various places in Missouri, Ohio, and Illinois, they settled at Great Salt Lake, Utah, under the leadership of Brigham Young, in 1847. The total church membership is 300,000, and the number of elders, 1,700. The present First President of the Church is Joseph Fielding Smith.

The following statement of the doctrines of the Church was issued with the approval of Prophet Joseph Smith:

1. We believe in God, the Eternal Father, and in his Son, Jesus Christ, and in the Holy Ghost.
2. We believe that men will be punished for their own sins, and not for Adam's transgression.
3. We believe that through the atonement of Christ all mankind may be saved, by obedience to the laws and ordinances of the Gospel.
4. We believe that these ordinances are: First. Faith in the Lord Jesus Christ; second, Repentance; third, Baptism by immersion for the remission of sins; fourth, Laying on of hands for the Gift of the Holy Ghost.
5. We believe that a man must be called of God, by "Prophecy, and by the laying on of hands," by those who are in authority to preach the Gospel and administer in the ordinances thereof.
6. We believe in the same organization that existed in the Primitive Church, viz.: Apostles, prophets, pastors, teachers, evangelists, etc.
7. We believe in the gift of tongues, prophecy, revelation, visions, healing, interpretation of tongues, etc.
8. We believe the Bible to be the word of God, as far as it is translated correctly; we also believe the Book of Mormon to be the word of God.
9. We believe all that God has revealed, all that He does now reveal, and we believe that He will yet reveal many great and important things pertaining to the Kingdom of God.
10. We believe in the literal gathering of Israel and in the restoration of the Ten Tribes; that Zion will be built upon this continent; that Christ will reign personally upon the earth, and that the earth will be renewed and receive its paradisic glory.
11. We claim the privilege of worshiping Almighty God according to the dictates of our conscience, and allow all men the same privilege, let them worship how, where or what they may.
12. We believe in being honest, true, chaste, benevolent, virtuous, and in doing good to all men; indeed, we may say that we follow the admonition of Paul. "We believe all things, we hope all things," we have endured many things, and hope to be able to endure all things. If there is anything virtuous, lovely, or of good report, or praiseworthy, we seek after these things.

The Reorganized Church of Jesus Christ of Latter-Day Saints is a separate body, having its headquarters at Lamoni, Iowa. It was organized in 1851, and is presided over by Joseph Smith, Independence, Mo., son of the Prophet. Membership 60,000. It has 1,600 active ministers and a Sunday-school membership of 25,000. The Brooklyn, N. Y., branch is at Park Place and Schenectady Avenue. B. R. McGuire, Pastor.

American Sunday-School Union.

THE American Sunday-School Union is the offspring of the old First Day Society, which was founded in Philadelphia in 1791. In 1817 this organization became the Philadelphia Sunday and Adult School Union, and in 1824 it assumed its present title. Its objects are to "concentrate the efforts of Sabbath-school societies in different portions of our country to disseminate useful information; to circulate moral and religious publications in every part of the land, and endeavor to plant a Sunday-School wherever there is a population."

Some idea of the Society's work and growth may be obtained from the following facts: The Philadelphia Union began with one juvenile book in 1817, and with one missionary in 1821. Now the American Sunday-School Union's publications are numbered by the thousands, and it has distributed over $10,000,000 worth of religions literature; it maintains more than 150 permanent missionaries and it has organized an average of more than 1,300 new Sabbath-schools a year—nearly four a day for every day of the last eighty years. Its present officers are: *President*——————— *Vice-Presidents*—John H. Converse, William N. Ashman and Isaac Sharpless. *Recording Secretary*—J. M. Andrews. The headquarters of the Society are at No. 1816 Chestnut Street, Philadelphia, Pa.

National Woman's Christian Temperance Union.

THE following statement of the purposes of the society was prepared for THE WORLD ALMANAC by an officer of the Union:

The National W. C. T. U. was organized in Cleveland, Ohio, in 1874, and is the sober second thought of the great woman's crusade. It is now regularly organized in every State of the Union.

There are about 10,000 local unions, with a membership and following, including the children's societies, of about half a million. The W. C. T. U. has forty distinct departments of work, presided over by as many women experts, in the National Society, and in nearly every State. All the States in the Republic have laws requiring the study of scientific temperance in the public schools, and all these laws were secured by the W. C. T. U.; also the laws forbidding the sale of tobacco to minors. The first police matrons and most industrial homes for girls were secured through the efforts of this society, as were the refuges for erring women. Laws raising the age of consent and providing for better protection for women and girls have been enacted by many Legislatures through the influence of the Union.

The World's W. C. T. U. was founded through the influence of Frances E. Willard in 1883, and already has auxiliaries in more than fifty countries and provinces. The white ribbon is the badge of all the W. C. T. U. members, and is now a familiar emblem in every civilized country.

The headquarters of the National organization is The Willard Rest Cottage, Evanston, Ill. The following are the officers: *President*, Mrs. Lillian M. N. Stevens, Portland, Me.; *Vice-President-at-Large*, Miss Anna A. Gordon, Evanston, Ill.; *Corresponding Secretary*, Mrs. Frances P. Parks, Evanston, Ill.; *Recording Secretary*, Mrs. Elizabeth Preston Anderson, Valley City, N. D.; *Assistant Recording Secretary*, Mrs. Sara H. Hoge, Lincoln, Va.; *Treasurer*, Mrs. Elizabeth P. Hutchinson, Evanston, Ill.

Church Temperance Society.

GENERAL OFFICERS.—*President*, Rt. Rev. Daniel Sylvester Tuttle, S. T. D., Bishop of Missouri; *Vice-Presidents*, sixty Bishops of the Protestant Episcopal Church; *Chairman*, Rt. Rev. Frederick Courtney D.D.; *Vice-Chairman*, Rev. D. Parker Morgan, D.D., of New York; *Treasurer*, Irving Grinnell; *General Secretary*, Robert Graham. The Society was organized within the Protestant Episcopal Church in 1881. Its adult membership combines those who temperately use and those who totally abstain from intoxicating liquors as beverages. It works on the lines of moral as well as of legal suasion, and its practical objects are: 1. Training the young in habits of temperance. 2. Rescue of the drunkard. 3. Restriction of the saloon by legislation. 4. Counteractive agencies, such as iced water fountains, lunch wagons, coachmen's and firemen's coffee vans, coffee-houses, workingmen's clubs, reading-rooms, and other attractive wholesome resorts. The Church Temperance Legion (comprising the Knights of Temperance, Young Crusaders, and Veteran Knights) deals with boys, seeking to induce them to keep sober, pure, and reverent from the earliest years of manhood, and it endeavors to perpetuate those habits in men. Headquarters, the Church Mission House, New York.

Society of St. Vincent de Paul.

THIS great Roman Catholic organization, founded in Paris, France, in which its head othee is located, has branches in every part of the civilized world. Its principal mission is the care of the poor in their homes to the end that the unity of the family may be preserved, but it conducts many other works of charity, such as free employment bureaus, Summer homes, boys' clubs, hospital and prison visitation committees, etc.

The local or parish branches of the Society are known as conferences; these conferences are grouped in sections under the jurisdiction of Particular and Central Councils, and the latter, in the United States, are under the jurisdiction of three Superior Councils. The office of the Superior Council of New York is located at No. 375 Lafayette Street, New York City. New Orleans, La., and St. Louis, Mo., also have Superior Councils.

The officers of the Superior Council are as follows: *Spiritual Director*, The Rt. Rev. Denis J. McMahon, D. D.; *President*, Thomas M. Mulry; *Secretary*, Edmond J. Butler; *Treasurer*, Michael J. Scanlan.

Christian and Missionary Alliance.

OFFICERS.—*President and General Superintendent*, Rev. A. B. Simpson, 692 Eighth Avenue, New York City; *Secretary*, A. E. Funk; *Treasurer*, David Crear.

The Christian Alliance was founded in 1887. It combined with the International Missionary Alliance in 1897, and the present title was adopted. Membership consists of all professing Christians who shall subscribe to the principles of the order and enroll their names. The objects of the Alliance are stated to be "Wide diffusion of the Gospel in its fulness, the promotion of a deeper and higher Christian life, and the work of evangelization, especially among the neglected classes in distant and especially in heathen countries." Its income in 1906-7 was over a quarter of a million dollars. State auxiliary and local branches are being rapidly formed. Connected with the Alliance are the Missionary Training Institute, Institute for the Training of Home Workers, Berachah Home. The headquarters of the Alliance are at 690 Eighth Avenue, New York City.

The Young People's Christian Endeavor Union.

THE Union was organized June 5, 1890. It is a union of all forms of young people's societies within the Church, uniting them for the purpose of denominational direction. There are now 2,215 societies, of which 575 are junior societies. The total membership is 83,652. Each conference is called a Branch and holds its annual conventions, when a review of the year's work is made and new plans are laid. At present there are about forty Branches or Districts, and nearly every one is doing something special in missions, either at home or abroad. The General Union holds its convention every two years. *The Watchword* is the organ of the Union. Single subscription, $1.00; club rates, 75 cents. Its circulation is nearly 42,000. H. F. Shupe, D. D., New Madison, Ohio, is editor. Last year, 1908, $1,600 were raised for a boys' home in Africa. The Junior work is one of the strong departments, superintended by Mrs. G. W. Kitzmiller, Dayton, Ohio. Rev. J. E. Shannon, Marion, Ind., is Superintendent of Bible Study. J. E. Kuhn and Lyda B. Wiggin are Superintendents of Missions; Rev. J. S. Kendall, Cleveland, Ohio, is Superintendent of Christian Stewardship. The principal officers are: *President*, Rev. J. G. Huber, D. D., Dayton, Ohio; *Corresponding Secretary*, H. F. Shupe, Dayton, Ohio; *Treasurer*, E. Jay Rogers, Dayton, Ohio.

The Brotherhood of Andrew and Philip.

THIS organization, founded in 1888, held its first federal convention in the City of New York in 1893. It is composed of members of twenty-four evangelical denominations—the Reformed Church in America, the Reformed Church in the United States, the Congregational, Presbyterian (North, South, Canadian, and United), Methodist Episcopal, Methodist Protestant, Baptist, United Brethren, Lutheran, Reformed Episcopal, Church of Christ, Progressive Brethren, Friends, United Evangelical, Free Baptist, Federal, African Methodist Episcopal, and Evangelical Association. It has chapters in Australia and Japan, China and England. Its objects are embodied in the statement that "Any man can belong to the Brotherhood who will promise to pray daily for the spread of the kingdom of Christ among men, and to make an earnest effort each week to bring at least one man within the hearing of the Gospel." The number of chapters of the Brotherhood in the United States is 1,130, and the membership 42,670. The Rev. Dr. Rufus W. Miller, the founder, 1308 Arch Street, Philadelphia, Pa., is President of the Federal Council, and Rev. Wm. H. Pheley, Ph. D., Fifteenth and Race Streets, Philadelphia, Pa., General Secretary.

The Daughters of the King.

THE Order of the Daughters of the King was organized on Easter Evening, 1885. It is desired by its promoters that a careful distinction shall be made between the Daughters of the King and the King's Daughters. This is the older society, and differs from the King's Daughters in many important particulars. In the first place, it is more of an order than a society, and is distinctively Episcopal. Its work is definite, and is "for the spread of Christ's kingdom among young women," and the "active support of the rector's plans in the parish in which the particular chapter may be located." Its badge is a cross of silver, a Greek cross fleury, and its mottoes are "Magnanimeter Crucem Sustine" and "For His Sake." Its colors are white and blue—white, the old royal color of Israel, and blue, the color of the Virgin Mary, the "blessed daughter of Israel's King, the Mother of the King of Kings." Its constitution is framed, as far as is possible, in the terms of that of the Brotherhood of St. Andrew, the work of the two organizations being similar. The officers of the Council are: *President*, Mrs. E. A. Bradley; *General Secretary*, Miss Elizabeth L. Ryerson. Office of the Council, Church Missions House, 281 Fourth Avenue, New York.

International Order of The King's Daughters and Sons.

HEADQUARTERS, 156 5th Ave., New York City. Officers: President, Miss Kate Bond; Secretary and Treasurer, Mrs. Mary Lowe Dickinson.

The Order is an interdenominational, religious and philanthropic society, working locally in Circles, County and City Unions, Chapters, State and National organizations. Branches are established in twenty-nine States, and in nine Canadian provinces.

The objects of the Order are "the development of spiritual life and the stimulation of Christian activities." Its membership is very large and extends all over the world. The Order has established or supported several hundred institutions of different kinds in different localities. The badge is a small silver cross, which is also the corporate seal of the society. A monthly magazine, "The Silver Cross," is the official organ of the Order.

Luther League of America.

President—William C. Stoever, Philadelphia, Pa. *General Secretary*—Luther M. Kuhns, Omaha, Neb. *Chairman National Executive Committee*, Mr. E. F. Eilert, New York.

The first National Convention of the Luther League of America was held at Pittsburgh, Pa., October 30 and 31, 1895. The League is a Lutheran organization, linking together the Lutheran young people who are laboring for the good of the Church by means of many individual societies of various names and styles of organization, each within its own immediate church. The constitution declares that its objects shall be "to encourage the formation of the young people's societies in all Lutheran congregations in America, to urge their affiliation with their respective State or Territorial leagues, and with this league to stimulate the various young people's societies to greater Christian activity and to foster the spirit of loyalty to the Church." The fundamental principles are federation and co-operation. The aggregate enrolled membership of the various local organizations represented in the national organization is over 100,000 These are comprised in twenty-five States, fourteen of which already have permanent State organizations. The first local organization adopting the title of "The Luther League" was organized by delegates of six Lutheran Church societies in the City of New York, April 19, 1888.

The Epworth League.

OFFICERS OF THE EPWORTH LEAGUE OF THE METHODIST EPISCOPAL CHURCH.—*President*—Bishop W. A. Quayle, Oklahoma City, Okla., *General Secretary*—Edwin M. Randall, D.D., 57 Washington Street, Chicago, Ill. *Treasurer*—Rev. Paul C. Curnick, D.D., South Bend, Ind. The Central Office of the Epworth League is located at 57 Washington Street, Chicago, Ill.

The Epworth League was organized at Cleveland, Ohio, May, 1889, by the union of five societies then existing in the Methodist Episcopal Church. These several societies held under their jurisdiction 1,500 local societies, with a membership of about 6,000. It spread rapidly throughout the denomination until it is now organized in nearly every church, and has become the largest denominational society of young people in the world. Its official organ, the *Epworth Herald*, has a circulation of 100,000.

OFFICERS OF THE EPWORTH LEAGUE OF THE METHODIST EPISCOPAL CHURCH SOUTH.—*President*—Bishop W. A. Candler, D.D., LL.D. *General Secretary*—Rev. H. M. Du Bose, D.D. *Assistant Secretary and Treasurer*—Rev. F. S. Parker, D.D., Nashville, Tenn. The general organ of the League is the *Epworth Era*, published weekly by the book agents of the Methodist Episcopal Church South, Nashville, Tenn., and Dallas, Texas; H. M. Du Bose, Editor; F. S. Parker, Assistant Editor. The League in the Methodist Episcopal Church South was provided for by the General Conference of 1890, and in January of the following year its organization was effected. It came under the supervision of the Sunday-School Board. The General Conference of 1894 created it a separate connectional board and elected a General Secretary. It has now 3,569 chapters, with a total membership of 123,325.

The Federal Council of the Churches of Christ

IN AMERICA.

FIVE hundred officially appointed delegates of thirty denominations at Carnegie Hall, New York City, met in November, 1905, and recommended a Plan of Federation, which has since been adopted by the official action of National Assemblies of Churches, representing an aggregate membership of about fifteen millions:

"II. The following Christian bodies are represented in this Federal Council: Baptist Churches (North), Free Baptist Churches, Negro Baptist Churches, Christian Connection, Congregational Churches, Disciples of Christ, Evangelical Association, Evangelical Synod, Friends, Evangelical Lutheran Church, General Synod, Methodist Episcopal Church, Methodist Episcopal Church (South), Primitive Methodist Church, Colored Methodist Episcopal Church of America, Methodist Protestant Church, African Methodist Episcopal Church, African Methodist Episcopal Zion Church, Mennonite Church, Moravian Church, Presbyterian Church in the U. S. A., Cumberland Presbyterian Church, Welsh Presbyterian Church, Reformed Presbyterian Church, United Presbyterian Church, Protestant Episcopal Church, Reformed Church in America, Reformed Church in the U. S. A., Reformed Episcopal Church, Seventh Day Baptist Churches, United Brethren in Christ, United Evangelical Church.

"III. The object of this Federal Council is: (1) To express the fellowship and catholic unity of the Christian Church. (2) To bring the Christian bodies of America into united service for Christ and the world. (3) To encourage devotional fellowship and mutual counsel concerning the spiritual life and religions activities of the Churches. (4) To secure a larger combined influence for the Churches of Christ in all matters affecting the moral and social condition of the people, so as to promote the application of the law of Christ in every relation of human life. (5) To assist in the organization of local branches of the Federal Council to promote its aims in their communities.

"IV. This Federal Council has no authority over the constituent bodies adhering to it; but its province is limited to the expression of its counsel and the recommending of a course of action in matters of common interest to the churches, local councils and individual Christians. It has no authority to draw up a common creed, or form of government or of worship, or in any way to limit the full autonomy of the Christian bodies adhering to it."

The first meeting of the Federal Council was held in Philadelphia, Dec. 2-8, 1908. Upward of four hundred delegates were in attendance.

The officers of the Executive Committee are: *Chairman*, William H. Roberts, D. D. *Secretary*, E. B. Sanford, D. D. Office, 81 Bible House, New York.

Religious Education Association.

THE Religious Education Association was organized on February 12, 1903, at the close of a three days' convention held in Chicago, called to consider the improvement of moral and religious education.

Its service is fourfold: Arousing the public mind to a sense of the need of religious education, and knowledge of the right methods therein; uniting the forces for religious education; promoting investigation in religious education; providing a forum and a clearing-house for religious education. It now enrolls over 2,000 members, including laymen, college presidents and professors, pastors, teachers and parents, interested in the problem of reverent, scientific, effective character training. It holds great conventions and smaller conferences, publishes annual volumes and a journal, and renders service to thousands of churches, Sunday-schools, colleges and individuals. It knows no sectarian lines. It has no theological platform. It invites to membership all who sympathize with its purpose.

The officers are: *President*, Francis Greenwood Peabody, Cambridge, Mass.; *First Vice-President*, Benjamin Ide Wheeler, Berkeley, Cal.; *Chairman Executive Board*, Loring Wilbur Messer, Chicago, Ill.; *Vice-Chairman Executive Board*, Jesse A. Baldwin, Chicago, Ill.; *Treasurer*, Charles L. Hutchinson, Chicago, Ill.; *Recording Secretary*, William Pierson Merrill, Chicago, Ill.; *General Secretary*, Henry Frederick Cope, 153 La Salle Street, Chicago, Ill.

Brotherhood of the Red Diamond.

BROTHERHOOD of the Red Diamond (organized 1898). Organizations for boys in churches, twelve to fifteen years; inter-denominational. National headquarters, No. 137 E. 25th Street, New York City. William Alberti Whiting, General Superintendent.

National Purity Federation.

THE following statement is contributed to THE WORLD ALMANAC by B. S. Steadwell, president of the Federation:

The object of this Federation is to unite in national co-operation all those forces in America that are striving to promote purity in the life of the individual and in social relations through preventive, educational, reformatory, rescue, law enforcement, legislative and sanitary lines of effort. It is in every sense non-sectarian, and is open to all who are sincerely and seriously striving to promote its object. Many of the leaders in religious, philanthropic and reform movements in the United States are officially connected with this Federation. Each year a largely attended national purity congress is held under the auspices of the Federation.

The officers are: *President*, B. S. Steadwell, La Crosse, Wis.; *First Vice-President*, Dr. Howard A. Kelly, Baltimore, Md.; *Second Vice-President*, Judge B. B. Lindsey, Denver, Col.; *Recording Secretary*, Mrs. Ida B. Wise, Des Moines, Iowa; *Corresponding Secretary*, Miss Julia E. Morrow, Cincinnati, Ohio; *Treasurer*, Charles A. Mitchell, Cherokee, Okla.

Medal of Honor Legion.

THE Legion is composed of officers and enlisted men of the United States army and navy who have been awarded medals of honor for most distinguished gallantry in action during any war in which the United States has been engaged. At the present time it has 458 such members. At the last reunion, held at Winsted, Ct., September 24-25, 1906, the following officers were elected: *Commander*—P. DeLacy, Scranton, Pa. *Senior Vice-Commander*—S. B. Horne, Winsted, Ct. *Junior Vice-Commander*—William Search, Boston, Mass. *Quartermaster*—N. D. Preston, Philadelphia, Pa. *Chaplain*—Rev. Dr. William Hubbell, New York City. *Adjutant*—John C. Hunterson, Philadelphia, Pa. *Judge Advocate*—Walter Thorn, Brooklyn, N. Y. *Inspector*—Charles H. Houghton, Newark, N. J. *Surgeon-in-Chief*—Gabriel Grant, M. D., New York City. *Historian*—St. Clair A. Mulholland, Philadelphia, Pa.

Naval Order of the United States.

THE Naval Order of the United States is composed of a General Commandery and commanderies in the States of Massachusetts, Pennsylvania, New York, California, and Illinois, and in the District of Columbia. The General Commandery meets triennially on October 5, and the State Commanderies meet annually in the month of November. The Massachusetts Commandery is the parent Commandery, and was organized at Boston on July 4, 1890. The General Commandery was established three years later, on June 19, 1893. The Companions of the Order are officers and the descendants of officers who served in the navy and marine corps in any war or in any battle in which the said naval forces of the United States have participated. The membership clause, as adopted at the triennial congress held at Boston, October 5, 1895, provides for two classes of members: First, veteran officers and their male descendants; and, second, enlisted men who have received the United States naval medal of honor for bravery in the face of the enemy.

The officers of the General Commandery elected at the triennial meeting October 5, 1907, are: *General Commander*—Admiral George Dewey, U. S. N., Washington, D. C. *Vice-General Commanders*—Rear-Admiral Joseph B. Coghlan, U. S. N., New York; Rear-Admiral H. W. Lyon, U. S. N., Massachusetts; Rear-Admiral James H. Dayton, U. S. N., Illinois. *Assistant General Recorder*—William H. Stayton (late U. S. N.), 170 Broadway, New York. *General Registrar*—H. M. M. Richards (late U. S. N.), Pennsylvania. *General Treasurer*—George De Forest Barton (late U. S. N.), New York. *General Historian*—Charles P. Welch, U. S. N., California. *General Chaplain*—George Williamson Smith, D. D. (late U. S. N.), New York. *General Judge Advocate*—M. B. Field (late U. S. N.), New York.

Army and Navy Union.

National Commander—J. Edwin Browne, Baltimore, Md. *Senior Vice-National Commander*—Bernard A. Flood, New York City. *Junior Vice-National Commander*—J. E. B. Stuart, Virginia. *Adjutant-General*—E. J. Bonner, Baltimore, Md. *Inspector-General*—S. E. Adams, Jersey City, N. J. *Paymaster-General*—J. R. McCullough, New York. *Judge Advocate-General*—R. McKinlay Power, New York. *Surgeon-General*—J. E. Hendricksen, Virginia. *National Chaplain*—Rev. John P. Chidwick, Brooklyn, N. Y.

The Army and Navy Union was organized at Cincinnati and incorporated under the laws of Ohio in March, 1888. The national organization (called the National Corps) was organized in August, 1890. The Union admits to its ranks any man who possesses an honorable discharge from the United States service, either regular or volunteer army and navy or marine corps, whether said service was before, during, or since any war at home or abroad. There are twelve garrisons in Greater New York.

The Navy League of the United States.

THE Navy League of the United States was incorporated under the laws of the State of New York on January 2, 1903. Its declared object being "to acquire and spread before the citizens of the United States, through branch organizations and otherwise, information as to the condition of the Naval forces and equipment of the United States, and to awaken public interest and co-operation in all matters tending to aid, improve, and develop their efficiency." It is strictly non-partisan. Men, women and children are eligible to membership. The button of the League is of silver gilt and blue enamel, with letters in white, and anchor of gold, and is worn by members. The membership fee is one dollar annually. There are eighty-three sections in the United States, and sections in England, France, Canada, Colombia, and two in Italy. Five or more citizens may sign an application for a charter to form a section of the League. The headquarters of the League are at 1808 I Street, N. W., Washington, D. C.

The General Officers are: *President*—Gen. Horace Porter; *Vice-President*, William McAdoo; *Secretary*, Henry H. Ward; *Treasurer*, Clinton E. Braine; *Recorder*, Robert S. Sloan; *General Counsel*, Herbert L. Satterlee; *Assistant Secretary*, C. W. Metcalf. *Honorary Members*—President Theodore Roosevelt, and Secretary of the Navy Charles J. Bonaparte. *Directors*—Captain J. W. Miller, W. H. Stayton, A. Noel Blakeman, C. W. Poor, Louis A. Osborne, George C. Sargent, Robert S. Sloan, George De Forest Barton, W. De W. Dimock, J. Frederic Tams, Aaron Vanderbilt, Francis B. Allen, General Horace Porter, William McAdoo, Herbert L. Satterlee, C. J. Parsons.

National Association of Naval Veterans.

Commodore Commanding—Alex. S. McWilliams, 85 Marston Avenue, W., Detroit, Mich. *Fleet Captain*—William H. Egbert, Newark, N. J. *Fleet Commander and Chief of Staff*—Robert McWilliams, Detroit, Mich. *Fleet Lieutenant-Commander*—Samuel Smith, Detroit, Mich. *Fleet Lieutenant*—John Giles, New Haven, Ct. *Fleet Paymaster*—Henry F. McCollum, New Haven, Ct. *Fleet Surgeon*—Henry J. Brewer, M. D., Brooklyn, N. Y. *Fleet Chaplain*—Isaac K. Archer, Philadelphia, Pa. *Fleet Judge Advocate*—Frederick E. Haskins, Brooklyn, N. Y. *Fleet Historian*—Daniel F. Kelly, Philadelphia, Pa. *Fleet Boatswain*—George Wright, Hartford, Ct. *Fleet Secretary*—James Reid, Detroit, Mich. Organized 1887. 5,000 members. 1,500 contributing members. 25 associations in all the principal cities of the United States.

Military Order of the Loyal Legion.

Commander-in-Chief—Major-Gen. Grenville M. Dodge. *Senior Vice-Commander-in-Chief*—Rear-Admiral John C. Watson. *Junior Vice-Commander-in-Chief*—Lient.-Gen. John C. Bates. *Recorder-in-Chief*—Brevet Lieut.-Col. John P. Nicholson. *Registrar-in-Chief*—Major William P. Huxford. *Treasurer-in-Chief*—Paymaster George De F. Barton. *Chancellor-in-Chief*—Brevet Capt. J O. Foering. *Chaplain-in-Chief*—Brevet Major Henry S. Burrage, D. D. *Council-in-Chief*—Brevet Major Henry L. Swords, Brevet Major A. M. Van Dyke, Captain John C. Currier, First Lieut. and Adjt. Lewis H. Chamberlain, Brevet Major Charles B. Amory.

The Military Order of the Loyal Legion of the United States was organized by officers and ex-officers of the army, navy, and marine corps of the United States who took part in the War of 1861-65. Membership descends to the eldest direct male lineal descendant, according to the rules of primogeniture. There are 21 commanderies, each representing a State, and one commandery representing the District of Columbia. The total membership of the Loyal Legion is 8,880.

ROLL OF COMMANDERIES.

No.	Commandery of the—	Headquarters.	Instituted.	Recorders.	Address.
1	State of Pa.....	Philadelphia.	Apr. 15, 1865	Brev. Lieut.-Col. J. P. Nicholson.	Flander's Bldg., Phila.
2	State of N. Y..	N. Y. City....	Jan. 17, 1866	Asst. Paymaster A. N. Blakeman	140 Nassau St., New York
3	State of Maine.	Portland.....	Apr. 25, 1866	Brevet Major Henry S. Burrage.	Togus, Me.
4	State of Mass..	Boston.......	Mar. 4, 1868	First Lieut. Charles H. Porter...	18 Central St., Boston.
5	State of Cal....	San Francisco	Apr. 12, 1871	Lieut.-Col. W. R. Smedburg......	San Francisco, Cal.
6	State of Wis...	Milwaukee ..	May 15, 1874	First Lieut. A. R. Houston........	P. O. Box 28, Milwaukee.
7	State of Illinois	Chicago......	May 8, 1879	Capt. Roswell H. Mason...........	320 Ashland B., Chicago.
8	District of Col..	Washington .	Feb. 1, 1882	Major Wm. P. Huxford..........	Kellogg Bldg., Wash.
9	State of Ohio...	Cincinnati ...	May 3, 1882	Major W. R. Thrall............	Cincinnati.
10	State of Mich..	Detroit.......	Feb. 4, 1885	Brevet Brig.-Gen. F. W. Swift...	Detroit.
11	State of Minn..	St. Paul......	May 6, 1885	Lieut. David L. Kingsbury......	St Paul
12	State of Oregon	Portland.....	May 6, 1885	Capt. Gavin E. Cankin............	Portland, Ore.
13	State of Mo....	St. Louis	Oct. 21, 1885	Capt. William R. Hodges.........	Laclede Bldg., St. Louis.
14	State of Neb...	Omaha.......	Oct. 21, 1885	First Lieut. F. B. Bryant........	Omaha.
15	State of Kansas	Leavenworth	Apr. 22, 1886	Lient.-Col. Ezra B. Fuller........	Fort Leavenworth.
16	State of Iowa..	Des Moines ..	Oct. 20, 1886	First Lieut and Adj. J. W. Muffly	Des Moines.
17	State of Col....	Denver	June 1, 1887	Lieut. Austin W. Hogle..........	Denver.
18	State of Ind....	Indianapolis.	Oct. 17, 1888	Major W. W. Daugherty.........	Indianapolis.
19	State of Wash.	Tacoma......	Jan. 14, 1891	Mr. Walter R. Beals.............	Seattle.
20	State of Vt.....	Burlington...	Oct. 14, 1891	Brevet Capt. H. O. Wheeler.....	Burlington.
21	State of Md....	Baltimore....	Dec. 8, 1904	Lieut. Joseph J. Janney.........	Baltimore, Md.

Instituted October 21, 1885. Brevet Lieut.-Col. John P. Nicholson, 1535 Chestnut Street, Philadelphia, *Recorder-in-Chief.*

Societies of the Union Army of 1861-65.

SOCIETY OF THE ARMY OF THE TENNESSEE.

President—Gen. Grenville M. Dodge, Iowa. *Vice-Presidents*—Major Leo Rassieur, Missouri; Col. Gilbert D. Munson, California; Capt. W. T. Rigby, Vicksburg, Miss.; Mrs. Andrew Hickenlooper, Ohio; Gen. Joseph R. Smith, U. S. A., Pennsylvania; Capt. Syl. T. Smith, Illinois; Capt. J. R. Dunlap, Indiana; Col. H. C. Warmoth, Louisiana; Mr. P. T. Sherman, New York; Gen. James H. Wilson, Delaware; Col. Fred Welker, Iowa; Gen. L. F. Hubbard, Minnesota. *Corresponding Secretary*—Major W. H. Chamberlin, Cincinnati, O. *Treasurer*—Major Augustus M. Van Dyke, Cincinnati, O. *Recording Secretary*—Col. Cornelius Cadle, Cincinnati, O. The Society was organized at Raleigh, N. C., April 14, 1865. The headquarters are at Cincinnati.

ARMY OF THE TENNESSEE ASSOCIATION.

President—H. L. Deam. *Secretary*—Byron W. Bonney, 624 C Street, N. E., Washington, D. C. *Treasurer*—James S. Roy. Organized at Washington, D. C., Angust, 1902. All who served in that army eligible to membership.

SOCIETY OF THE ARMY OF THE CUMBERLAND.

President—Gen. Gates P. Thruston, Nashville, Tenn. *Corresponding Secretary*—Private O. A. Somers, Kokomo, Ind. *Treasurer*—Gen. E. A. Carman, Washington. D. C. *Recording Secretary*—Lieut. John E. Stivers, Chattanooga, Tenn. *Historian*—Col. G. C. Kniffin. *Executive Committee*—Gen. James Barnett, Chairman; Gen. C. H. Grosvenor, Gen. Frank G. Smith, Capt. H. S. Chamberlain, Capt. J. W. Foley, Sergt. D. M. Steward, Gen. Smith D. Atkins, Major W. J. Colburn, officers of the Society, *ex-officio.* The Society was organized in February, 1868, and its present membership is 350.

SOCIETY OF THE ARMY OF THE POTOMAC.

President—Capt. Charles Curie. *Vice-Presidents*—Col. Albert Clark, Major Charles Lyman, Sergeant-Major Wm. H. Cloutman, Gen. Henry E. Tremain, Lieut. John Tregaskis, Gen. Newton M. Curtis, Gen. Vanhartness Bukey, Sergeant-Major George W. States, Col. George H. Patrick, Capt. George B. Fox, Capt. W. A. Howe, Gen. Howard L. Porter, Gen. Nicholas W. Day, Major James H. Reeve, Gen. William Birney, Gen. Horatio C. Gibson, Col. John J. McCook, Gen. George L. Gillespie, Sergeant Charles D. Marcy. *Treasurer*—Charles A. Shaw. *Recording Secretary*—Gen. Horatio C. King. *Corresponding Secretary*—Col. William F. Fox, Albany, N. Y. The Society was organized in 1868. The present membership is over 2,000.

ASSOCIATION OF THE THIRTEENTH ARMY CORPS.

President—Gen. E. A. Carr, U. S. A., retired. *Treasurer*—Capt. E. C. Dougherty. *Secretary*—Fletcher White, 1410 Euclid Street, N. W., Washington, D. C. The Association was organized at Milwaukee, August, 1889.

The Forty Immortals of the French Academy *

	Year Elected.	Name.	Born.	Predecessor.
1	1870....	Emile Ollivier	Marseilles, 1825	De Lamartine.
2	1874....	Alfred Jean François Mezières	Paris, 1826	St. Marc-Girardin.
3	1886....	Othénin P. de Cléron Comte d'Haussonville.	Gurey, 1843	Caro.
4	1888....	Jules Arnaud Arsène Claretie	Limoges, 1840	Cuvillier-Fleury.
5	1888....	Eugène Marie Melchior, Vicomte de Vogué.	Nice, 1848	Désiré Nisard.
6	1890....	Charles Louis de Saulses de Freycinet	Foix, 1828	Emile Augier.
7	1891....	Louis Marie Jullen Viaud (Pierre Loti)	Rochefort, 1850	Octave Feuillet.
8	1892....	Ernest Lavisse	Nouvien, 1842	Jurien de la Gravière.
9	1893....	Paul Louis Thureau-Dangin	Paris, 1837	Rousset.
10	1894....	Paul Bourget	Amiens, 1852	Maxime Du Camp.
11	1894....	Henri Houssaye	Paris, 1858	Leconte de Lisle.
12	1895....	Jules Lemaitre	Orleans, 1853	Jean Victor Duruy.
13	1896 ...	Jacques Anatole Thibault (Anatole France).	Paris, 1844	Comte de Lesseps.
14	1896 ...	Marquis Marie C. A. Costa de Beauregard ..	Nyotte, Savoy, 1839.	Camille C. Doucet.
15	1896....	Louis Jules Albert Comte Vandal	Paris, 1861	Léon Say.
16	1897....	Albert Comte de Mun	Lumigny, 1841	Jules Simon.
17	1897....	Gabriel Hanotaux	Beaurevoir, 1853	Challemel-Lacour.
18	1899....	Henri Leon Emile Lavedan	Orleans, 1859	Henri Meilhac.
19	1899....	Paul Deschanel	Brussels, 1856	Hervé.
20	1900 ...	Paul Hervieu	Neuilly, 1857	Pailleron.
21	1900....	Auguste Emile Faguet	La Roche, 1847	Cherbuliez.
22	1901....	Charles Jean Melchior, Marquis de Vogué..	Paris, 1829	Duc de Broglie.
23	1901...	Edmond Rostand	Marseilles, 1868	Bornier.
24	1903....	Frederic Masson	Paris, 1847	Gaston Paris.
25	1903....	René Bazin	Angeres, 1863	Legouve.
26	1905....	Etienne Lamy	Jura, 1849	Gerárd.
27	1906....	Alexandre Felix Joseph Ribot	St. Omer, 1842	D'Andiffret Pasquier.
28	1906....	Maurice Barrès	Charmes, 1862	De Hérédia.
29	1907....	Marquis de Segur	Paris, 1853	Rousse.
30	1907....	Maurice Donnay	Paris, 1860	Sorel.
31	1907....	Maitre André Barboux	Chateauroux, 1834..	Brunetiere.
32	1908....	Jules Henri Poincaré	Nancy, 1854	Prudhomme.
33	1908 ...	Jean Richepin	Medea, Algeria, 1848	Theuriet.
34	1908....	Frances Charmes	Aurillac, 1848	Berthelot.
35	....	Vacant	....	Boissier.
36	....	Vacant	....	Sardou.
37	....	Vacant	....	Coppée.
38	....	Vacant	....	Halévy.
39	....	Vacant	....	Mathieu.
40	....	Vacant	....	Prevost.

* The French Academy is one of five academies, and the most eminent, constituting the Institute of France. It was founded in 1635 by Cardinal Richelieu, and reorganized in 1816. It is composed of 40 members, elected for life, after personal application and the submission of their nomination to the head of the State. It meets twice weekly, at the Palace Mazarin, 23 Quai Conti, Paris, and is "the highest authority on everything appertaining to the niceties of the French language, to grammar, rhetoric, and poetry, and the publication of the French classics." The chief officer is the secretary, who has a life tenure of his position. The present permanent secretary is Marie L. A. G. Boissier, who was elected an Academician in 1876. A chair in the Academy is the highest ambition of most literary Frenchmen.

The other academies of the Institute of France are: The Academy of Inscriptions and Belles-Lettres, with 40 members; Academy of Sciences, with 68 members; Academy of Fine Arts, with 40 members (as follows: Painting, 14; sculpture, 8; architecture, 8; engraving, 4; musical composition, 6), and Academy of Moral and Political Science, with 40 members. All members are elected for life.

The Carnegie Hero Fund.

In April, 1904, Andrew Carnegie created a fund of $5,000,000 for the benefit of the dependents of those losing their lives in heroic effort to save their fellow men, or for the heroes themselves if injured only. Provision was also made for medals to be given in commemoration of heroic acts.

The endowment known as "The Hero Fund" was placed in the hands of a commission composed of twenty-one persons, residents of Pittsburgh, Pa., of which Charles L. Taylor is President, and F. M. Wilmot, Secretary, and Manager of the fund.

In his letter to the Hero Fund Commission Mr. Carnegie outlined the general scheme of the fund thus: "To place those following peaceful vocations who have been injured in heroic effort to save human life, in somewhat better positions pecuniarily than before, until able to work again. In case of death, the widow and children or other dependents are to be provided for until she remarries, and the children until they reach a self-supporting age. For exceptional children, exceptional grants may be made for exceptional education. Grants of sums of money may also be made to heroes or heroines as the commission thinks advisable—each case to be judged on its merits."

The fund applies only to acts performed within the United States of America, the Dominion of Canada, the Colony of Newfoundland, and the waters thereof, and such acts must have been performed on or after April 15, 1904.

The Commission has awarded two hundred and twenty medals: one hundred and eight bronze, ninety-nine silver, and thirteen gold. In addition to the medals, $148,702 has been awarded for disablement benefits, and special purposes, and for the dependents of heroes who lost their lives, including payments made to December 31, 1908, on monthly allowances. On that date the amount of monthly allowances in effect was $9,660 annually. The Commission has also awarded $124,462 for relief of sufferers from disasters: at Brockton, Mass., $10,000; from the California earthquake, $54,462; at Monongah Mines, Monongah, W. Va., $35,000, and at Darr Mine, Jacobs Creek, Pa., $25,000.

Carnegie Libraries.

Andrew Carnegie has given approximately 1,700 library buildings in the United States and abroad.

The Lambeth Encyclical.

(In part only.)

RESOLUTIONS FORMALLY ADOPTED BY THE EPISCOPAL CONFERENCE OF 1908.

With regard to ministries of healing, this Conference, confident that God has infinite blessings and powers in store for those who seek them by prayer, communion, and strong endeavor, and conscious that the clergy and laity of the Church have too often failed to turn to God with such complete trust as will draw those powers into full service, desires solemnly to affirm that the strongest and most immediate call to the Church is to the deepening and renewal of her spiritual life, and to urge upon the clergy of the Church so to set forth to the people Christ, the Incarnate Son of God, and the truth of His abiding Presence in the Church and in Christian souls by the Holy Spirit, that all may realize and lay hold of the power of the indwelling Spirit to sanctify both soul and body, and thus, through a harmony of man's will with God's Will, to gain a fuller control over temptation, pain and disease, whether for themselves or others, with a firmer serenity and a more confident hope.

With a view to resisting dangerous tendencies in contemporary thought, the Conference urges the clergy in their dealings with the sick to teach as clearly as possible the privilege of those who are called, through sickness and pain, to enter especially into the fellowship of Christ's sufferings, and to follow the example of His patience.

The Conference recommends the provision for use in pastoral visitation of some additional prayers for the restoration of health more hopeful and direct than those contained in the present Office for the Visitation of the Sick, and refers this recommendation to the committee to be appointed by the president under the resolution on the subject of Prayerbook enrichment.

The growing prevalence of disregard of the sanctity of marriage calls for the active and determined co-operation of all right-thinking and clean-living men and women, in all ranks of life, in defence of the family life and the social order, which rest upon the sanctity of the marriage tie.

The influence of all good women in all ranks of life should be specially applied to the remedying of the terrible evils which have grown up from the creation of facilities for divorce.

This Conference reaffirms the resolution of the Conference of 1888 as follows:

"(a) That, inasmuch as our Lord's words expressly forbid divorce, except in case of fornication or adultery, the Christian Church cannot recognize divorce in any other than the excepted case, or give any sanction to the marriage of any person who has been divorced contrary to this law, during the life of the other party.

"(b) That under no circumstances ought the guilty party, in the case of a divorce for fornication or adultery, to be regarded, during the lifetime of the innocent party, as a fit recipient of the blessing of the Church on marriage.

"(c) That, recognizing the fact that there always has been a difference of opinion in the Church on the question whether our Lord meant to forbid marriage to the innocent party in a divorce for adultery, the Conference recommends that the clergy should not be instructed to refuse the sacraments or other privileges of the Church to those who, under civil sanction, are thus married."

When an innocent person has, by means of a court of law, divorced a spouse for adultery, and desires to enter into another contract of marriage, it is undesirable that such a contract should receive the blessing of the Church.

The Conference regards with alarm the growing practice of the artificial restriction of the family, and earnestly calls upon all Christian people to discountenance the use of all artificial means of restriction as demoralizing to character and hostile to national welfare.

The Conference affirms that deliberate tampering with nascent life is repugnant to Christian morality.

The Conference expresses most cordial appreciation of the services rendered by those medical men who have borne courageous testimony against the injurious practices spoken of, and appeals with confidence to them and to their medical colleagues to co-operate in creating and maintaining a wholesome public opinion on behalf of the reverent use of the married state.

The social mission and social principles of religion should be given a more prominent place in the study and teaching of the Church, both for the clergy and the laity.

The ministry of the laity requires to be more widely recognized, side by side with the ministry of the clergy, in the work, the administration, and the discipline of the Church.

A committee or organization for social service should be part of the equipment of every diocese, and, as far as practicable, of every parish.

The Church should teach that the Christian who is an owner of property should recognize the governing principle that, like all our gifts, our powers, and our time, property is a trust held for the benefit of the community, and its right use should be insisted upon as a religious duty.

The Conference urges upon members of the Church practical recognition of the moral responsibility involved in their investments. This moral responsibility extends to:

(a) The character and general social effect of any business or enterprise in which their money is invested;

(b) The treatment of the persons employed in that business or enterprise;

(c) The due observance of the requirements of the law relating thereto;

(d) The payment of a just wage to those who are employed therein.

The existing Central Consultative Body shall be reconstructed on representative lines as follows:

(a) It shall consist of the Archbishop of Canterbury (ex-officio) and of representative Bishops appointed as follows: Province of Canterbury 2, Province of York 1, the Church of Ireland 1, the Episcopal Church in Scotland 1, the Protestant Episcopal Church in the United States of America 4, the Church of England in Canada 1, the Church of England in the Dioceses of Australia and Tasmania 1, the Church of the Province of New Zealand 1, the Province of the West Indies 1, the Church of the Province of South Africa 1, the Province of India and Ceylon 1, the Dioceses of China and Korea and the Church of Japan 1, the missionary and other extra-provincial Bishops under the jurisdiction of the Archbishop of Canterbury 1. Total 18.

(b) The foregoing scheme of representation shall be open to revision from time to time by the Lambeth Conference.

(c) The mode of appointing these representative Bishops shall be left to the churches that appoint. A representative Bishop may be appointed for one year or for any number of years, and need not be a member of the body which appoints him. Each member shall retain office until the election of his successor has been duly notified to the Archbishop of Canterbury.

(d) For the purpose of appointing the Bishop who is to represent the body of missionary and other extra-provincial Bishops under the jurisdiction of the Archbishop of Canterbury, each of those Bishops shall be requested by the Archbishop of Canterbury to nominate a Bishop to him. The list of Bishops so nominated shall be then sent to all the Bishops entitled to vote, and each of them shall, if he thinks fit to vote, send to the Archbishop the name of the one in that list for whom he votes. The largest number of votes shall carry the election.

The Central Consultative Body shall be prepared to receive consultative communications from any Bishop, but shall, in considering them, have careful regard to any limitations upon such references which may be imposed by provincial regulation.

This Conference reaffirms the resolution of the Conference of 1897 that "Every opportunity should be taken to emphasize the Divine purpose of visible unity amongst Christians as a fact of revelation." It desires further to affirm that in all partial projects of reunion and intercommunion the final attainment of the Divine purpose should be kept in view as our object; and that care should be taken to do what will advance the reunion of the whole of Christendom, and to abstain from doing anything that will retard or prevent it.

The Conference is of opinion that it should be the recognized practice of the Churches of our Communion (1) at all times to baptize the children of members of any church of the Orthodox Eastern Communion in cases of emergency, provided that there is a clear understanding that baptism should not be again administered to those so baptized; (2) at all times to admit members of any Church of the Orthodox Eastern Communion to communicate in our churches, when they are deprived of the ministrations of a priest of their own communion, provided that (a) they are at that time admissible to communion in their own churches, and (b) are not under any disqualifications so far as our own rules of discipline are concerned.

The Conference would welcome any steps that might be taken to ascertain the precise doctrinal position of the ancient separate Churches of the East with a view to possible inter-communion.

We desire earnestly to warn members of our communion against contracting marriages with Roman Catholics under the conditions imposed by the modern Roman canon law, especially as these conditions involve the performance of the marriage ceremony without any prayer or invocation of the Divine blessing, and also a promise to have their children brought up in a religious system which they cannot themselves accept.

This Conference receives with thankfulness and hope the report of its Committee on Reunion and Intercommunion, and is of opinion that, in the welcome event of any project of reunion between any Church of the Anglican Communion and any Presbyterian or other non-episcopal Church which, while preserving the faith in its integrity and purity, has also exhibited care as to the form and intention of ordination to the ministry, reaching the stage of responsible official negotiation, it might be possible to make an approach to reunion on the basis of consecrations to the Episcopate on lines suggested by such precedents as those of 1610. Further, in the opinion of the Conference, it might be possible to authorize arrangements (for the period of transition toward full union on the basis of Episcopal ordination) which would respect the convictions of those who had not received Episcopal Orders, without involving any surrender of our part of the principle of Church order laid down in the Preface to the Ordinal attached to the Book of Common Prayer.

Every opportunity should be welcomed of co-operation between members of different communions in all matters pertaining to the social and moral welfare of the people.

The members of the Anglican Communion should take pains to study the doctrines and position of those who are separated from it and to promote a cordial mutual understanding; and, as a means toward this end, the Conference suggests that private meetings of ministers and laymen of different Christian bodies for common study, discussion and prayer should be frequently held in convenient centres.

The constituted authorities of the various Churches of the Anglican Communion should, as opportunity offers, arrange conferences with representatives of other Christian Churches, and meetings for common acknowledgment of the sins of division, and for intercession for the growth of unity.

Catholic Summer School of America.

A Roman Catholic Chautauqua or Summer School was opened at New London, Ct., in the Summer of 1892 under the auspices of distinguished clergymen and laymen, and the first meetings were held from July 30 to August 14. The association has since acquired a site at Cliff Haven, near Plattsburg, N. Y., on Lake Champlain, upon which the necessary buildings have been erected, and here the Summer School is held annually from July to September. The work of the institution is continued throughout the year by means of reading circles and study clubs on the University Extension plan. The President is the Rev. John Talbot Smith, LL. D., New York, and the Secretary, Charles Murray, 7 East Forty-second Street, New York.

Benefactions of 1908.

DESPITE the financial depression, beginning in October, 1907, and extending until the recent Presidential election, the benefactions of the American people for 1908 amounted to $57,980,600, thus exceeding those of the previous year, when the total sum reached was $50,000,000.

A significant phase of the bequests is that, with the exception of Andrew Carnegie, the donors have been men and women whose names are not well known and whose fortunes are of the more moderate variety.

Andrew Carnegie heads the list of givers for 1908 with $21,350,000. Of this sum $2,000,000 was given to the Carnegie Institute in Washington, D. C. (Mr. Carnegie previously gave $10,000,000 worth of United States Steel bonds to this institution five years ago); $3,000,000 to the technical schools of Pittsburgh, Pa., provided the city purchase ground adjoining the present site of the schools; $1,250,000 to Scotland to establish a Hero Fund similar to the one so successfully maintained in America; $5,000,000 additional to the Carnegie Foundation for the advancement of teaching; $200,000 to Berea College (which sum is the largest given by Mr. Carnegie at one time for individual college purposes); $10,000,000 for a proposed consolidation of six Chicago educational institutions; and $100,000 in various bequests to libraries, churches and institutions in sums ranging from $1,000 to $20,000 each.

Frederick Cooper Hewitt, of Oswego, N. Y. (died September, 1908), left over $7,500,000 to various charities. Of this sum $2,000,000 goes to the New York Post Graduate Medical School and Hospital; $1,500,000 to the Metropolitan Museum of Art, which is also named as the residuary legatee of Mr. Hewitt's estate, which, it is believed, will amount to $3,000,000; $500,000 to Yale University; $100,000 to the Sheltering Arms Society of New York; $100,000 to the Free Industrial School for Crippled Children; $200,000 to the Little Missionary Day Nursery, New York; $100,000 to The Netherwood (New Jersey) Fresh Air Home; $10,000 to the Society for the Prevention of Cruelty to Animals; $3,000 to the Temperance Industrial Institute of Claremont, Va., and $30,000 to the Geburn Free Library of Oswego, N. Y.

George F. Parkman, of Boston, Mass. (died September, 1908), made Boston his residuary legatee, leaving his estate of $8,000,000—$4,000,000 to establish a fund for the perpetual maintenance and care of Boston Common and other Boston parks. In addition the will provides for bequests of hundreds of thousands of dollars to Boston and other educational and charitable institutions; $50,000 each to the Massachusetts General Hospital, Harvard University, Home for Aged Men, Boston Athenaeum, Children's Hospital, McClane Insane Asylum, Perkins Institute, Massachusetts School for the Blind, besides other public bequests. If Boston refuses the residue of the estate, provisional bequests are made of $100,000 to the Massachusetts Institute of Technology and $20,000 each to the New England Hospital for Women and Children, Massachusetts Charitable Eye and Ear Infirmary, and The Industrial School for Girls, the remainder to be given to the Public Library of Boston.

Benjamin Rose, of Cleveland, O. (died in London, July, 1908), left his entire fortune of $5,000,000 for institutions for the aged and for deformed children in his native city. The buildings are to be erected on the twenty-acre Rose estate, on Lake Shore Boulevard, and are to be named "The Albert," in honor of a son of Mr. Rose who was drowned.

Henry J. Baker, senior member of the firm of H. J. Baker & Brothers, Importers, New York City (died in Plymouth, England, August, 1908), left $1,500,000 to philanthropic work. One million dollars is to be applied to the establishment of a home for aged people and $500,000 to Tufts College, Massachusetts.

Morris K. Jesup, of New York City (died January, 1908), bequeathed to New York City institutions $1,115,500. The American Museum of Natural History in New York City receives $1,000,000 of this amount; The Brick Presbyterian Church of New York, $100,000; the Congregational Church at Westport, Conn., $8,000; Library at Westport, Conn., $5,000; and the Congregational Church at Lenox, Mass., $2,500. Mr. Jesup's bequest to the Museum of Natural History was the last of a long series of gifts to this institution. He financied the Putnam anthropological expedition in 1907, costing $150,000, and gave collections valued at $30,000 during the same year.

John Stewart Kennedy, a retired banker, of New York City, celebrated his golden wedding anniversary with a donation of $1,000,000 to the Presbyterian Hospital of New York, of which institution Mr. Kennedy is President. Mr. Kennedy's benefactions are many and varied, but his name is usually withheld on the request of their donor.

Mrs. Russell Sage, of New York, leads in the class of benefactors between the half and million dollar mark. Amounts contributed by her, although less than in the year 1907, total for 1908 $910,000. The American Bible Society receives from Mrs. Sage $500,000 toward a permanent endowment fund; while Princeton is given $250,000 for the erection of a new dormitory for freshmen. Mrs. Sage contributed $150,000 to the United States Government for the purchase of Constitution Island, to be used as an accessory to the West Point Military Academy, and the remaining $10,000 goes to hospitals for endowing beds.

Mrs. Sarah Conley (widow of W. H. Conley, of the Riter-Conley Manufacturing Company, of Pittsburgh, Pa.), at her death in September, 1908, left her estate of $500,000 to be divided by two Pittsburgh charities—The Beulah Home and the Pittsburgh Bible Institute.

Bloodgood Cutter, the deceased farmer-poet of Long Island, N. Y., left $500,000 to the American Bible Society of New York.

Henry Phipps, of Pittsburgh and New York, who five years ago founded the Phipps Institute for Tuberculosis Research in Philadelphia, gave $500,000 to the Johns Hopkins Hospital of Baltimore for the Scientific Inquiry of Mental Abnormalities. This gift is said to have been suggested by the development of mental conditions brought forward in the case of Harry Thaw. It is interesting to note, in connection with Mr. Phipps's gift, that medical research received no attention whatever from our philanthropists prior to ten years ago, since which time this important work has been enriched by gifts amounting to $33,000,000.

John D. Rockefeller made a provisional bequest of $600,000 to the Memorial Library to the late President Harper, of the University of Chicago. Mr. Rockefeller agreed to contribute $3 for every $1 secured up to $200,000, and this sum is so nearly subscribed that Mr. Rockefeller's donation seems safe to go in with the year's bequest.

George H. F. Schrader, a wealthy manufacturer and inventor of New York City, presented $500,000 in cash and securities to The New York Association for Improving the Condition of the Poor. By the terms of Mr. Schrader's gift $105,000 of his half million is to be used for a Convalescent Home for Mothers and Children at Hartsdale, N. Y., to be known as the Caroline Rest. This gift is in memory of Mr. Schrader's mother.

Why Archibald Henry Blout, of Orlenton Manor, Hertfordshire, England, left the residuary of his estate to Yale University still remains a mystery. It amounted to $450,000, but England collected $62,000 as inheritance tax, and legal and other fees connected with the settling of the estate reduced Yale's share to $328,000.

Miss Amy Sheldon, of New York and Newport (died February, 1908), bequeathed $316,000 to charities. Harvard University received $300,000 for the rebuilding of the library building known as Gore Hall; Newport Hospital received $5,000, and the Newport and Redwood Libraries $6,000; Trinity Church, of Newport, and Grace Church, of New York receive $2,500 each for the purpose of providing free pews.

Miss Alice Byington, of Stockbridge, Mass. (died February, 1908), left by will $300,000 to the following institutions: The Hampton Institute, of Hampton, Va., which receives $160,000; The Normal and Agricultural School, of the same place, $50,000; The Normal and Industrial Institute of Tuskegee, Ala., $50,000; The Mount Hermon School for Boys, at East Northfield, Mass., $25,000; The Massachusetts Society for the Prevention of Cruelty to Animals, $2,000; The Laurel Hill Association, of Stockbridge, Mass., $10,000, and the town of Stockbridge, $2,000.

Charles E. Wood, of Washington, D. C. (died February, 1908), left $300,000 to establish a sanitarium at Atlantic City, N. J., to be modeled on the lines of the Kellogg Sanitarium at Battle Creek, Mich.

Clarence H. Mackay, of the Postal Telegraph Company, New York, gave $300,000 for the Mackay School of Mines, including $30,000 for the John W. Mackay Statue, and $50,000 for campus improvement at the University of Nevada. In addition to these bequests, Mr. Mackay announces an annual contribution of $6,000 for the maintenance of this school. This amount at 5 per cent. interest represents a gift of $120,000.

Joseph Fuller Barton, of Utica, N. Y., at his death remembered the afflicted in his own city and New York by bequeathing $280,000 for philanthropic purposes. Of this sum New York City receives $20,000 for the American Home Missionary Society, and $20,000 for the American Female Guardian Society and Home of the Friendless; Utica receives $40,000 for the Home for Aged Men and Couples; $40,000 for the Home of the Friendless; $40,000 for the House of the Good Shepherd; $40,000 to St. Luke's Hospital; $40,000 to St. Elizabeth Hospital and $40,000 to the Utica Orphan Asylum.

James R. Sayre, Jr., of Newark, N. J., the largest manufacturer of brick in the United States (died September, 1908), bequeathed $250,000 to various public charities and religious institutions of Newark and Sayreville. Mr. Sayre's beneficences range in sums from $18,000 to $50,000 to each institution.

Walter T. Griffen, of Brooklyn, N. Y., formerly Consul to Limoges, France, left by will $250,000 to various charities. Mr. Griffen's fortune was made from his invention to replace coal with peat. No mention is made of the objects for which the bequest is to be used other than that it be applied to philanthropic purposes as directed by Dr. James A. Blake, of Brooklyn, N. Y.

William Kent, of Chicago, Ill., made a gift to the Government as public spirited as Mrs. Sage's presentation of Constitution Island. He deeded to the United States 295 acres of primeval redwood forest, six miles from San Francisco. The gift is to be named the "Muir Woods," after John Muir, the noted naturalist. The money value of Mr. Kent's bequest represents $150,000.

James A. Patten, of Chicago, Ill., presented $150,000 to the Northwestern University to be used in constructing a new gymnasium.

J. D. Hooker, of Los Angeles, Cal., has given the largest telescope in the world, to be placed in the Mount Wilson Observatory at Mount Wilson, Cal. The instrument is to be made in France and will cost Mr. Hooker $150,000.

Mrs. Jane A. Townsend, of New York, widow of Randolf W. Townsend (died September, 1908), left $150,000 to various Presbyterian institutions and Yale University, Yale to receive $50,000.

Mrs. Grace M. Kuhn, widow of Hartman Kuhn, of Philadelphia, but a resident of Boston and Lenox (died October, 1908), left $185,000 to be distributed as follows: $175,000 to Harvard University for a department of Biological Chemistry, and $10,000 for the Massachusetts General Hospital.

Mrs. Emma A. Tillotson, of New York, widow of Luther G. Tillotson, the railroad pioneer, at her death bequeathed $150,000 to various educational and charitable institutions of the City of New York, $5,000 being given to most of them.

Dr. John Ordronaux, who died at Glen Head, L. I., January 20, 1908, left $150,000 to various churches, colleges and charities. Harvard, Dr. Ordonaux's alma mater, receives the largest single bequest of $30,000, the others varying from $5,000 to $10,000. Dr. Ordronaux showed no denominational prejudices, remembering Methodist, Presbyterian, Episcopal and Catholic churches equally.

Mrs. Oliver, of Pittsburgh, Pa., presented $150,000 to Yale for the Daniel Leet Oliver Memorial Hall, in memory of her son.

Mr. Leopold Vilsack, millionaire banker and brewer of Pittsburgh, Pa., left by will $105,000 to twenty-five Catholic charitable institutions.

Rosine M. Parmentier, of Brooklyn, N. Y. (died January, 1908), left $100,000 to Catholic institutions.

The children of the late Orlando Harriman made a bequest to Columbia University of $100,000. This sum to found the Orlando Harriman Fund to support a chair in the Department of English.

Mrs. Martha Potter, of Ossining, N. Y., daughter of the late Congressman Orlando B. Potter (died May, 1908), left $100,000 to be distributed among the various churches and charities of her native place

James Willis, of New York, donated $100,000 to Cooper Union of New York, the money to be applied to the improvement of the Tompkins Market property.

William Waldorf Astor (living in London), gave $100,000 to Oxford University, England.

Miss Clemence L. Stephens, of New York (died April, 1908), left $115,000 to various New York charities.

An unknown donor presented Columbia University with $100,000. This gift was to establish a Chair in Humanity, a departure heretofore unknown in colleges.

BENEFACTIONS OF 1908—*Continued.*

Other bequests to colleges that are not included above are: John E. Firch, of Oakland, Cal., gave $100,000 to Gettysburg College, Gettysburg, Pa.

New York Alumni of Michigan University subscribed $300,000 for a dormitory and "Commons" at Ann Arbor, Mich.

Berea College, Kentucky (exclusive of Carnegie's gift of $200,000), announces $80,000 for general college use.

An unknown donor presented Vassar with $75,000 to be used for the construction of a new chemistry building.

Washington University, of St. Louis, Mo., has received $100,000 from William Barr, of West Orange, N. J.

Columbia University is enriched by the gift of Edward Hall Cole, amounting to $100,000, and other gifts amounting to $68,000; total, $168,000.

Wellesley announces the Alice Freeman Palmer endowment of $50,000 to be now completed, and an additional gift of $2,500 from Miss Bancroft, of Wellesley, Mass.; total, $52,500.

Oden Evenson, of West Salem, Wis., by his will divided $40,000 among several Norwegian Lutheran colleges, to be used in the education of farmer boys of poor parents.

The Moody educational institutions announce bequests of $60,000.

Yale University announces gifts for the year amounting to $1,374,600, including the Laura Carrier bequest of $100,000, D. Willis James's of $97,250, and the F. K. Vanderbilt gift of $50,000.

Harvard University is the recipient of $624,000.

Additional private bequests to charitable institutions and religious bodies below the $100,000 mark in sums varying from $2,000 to $88,000, total $952,500, bringing the year's beneficences up to $57,980,600.

Esperanto.

AN INTERNATIONAL LANGUAGE.

Esperanto is an artificial language invented by the Russian, Dr. L. L. Zamenhof, of Warsaw, Poland. It has only one object in view, namely, to serve as an international auxiliary language; it is not in the least intended to replace the national languages. The first book in the new language was published in 1887.

The new language, having met with the approval of such authorities as Professor Max Muller, Count Tolstoi and Sir William Ramsey, gradually spread over many countries. Its grammar has been translated into some twenty-eight languages and dialects, and nearly thirty monthly Journals are devoted to its propaganda.

Interest in Esperanto began in 1905 in the United States, and its progress here has been facilitated principally by a succession of strong articles in its favor in the North American Review, edited by Colonel George Harvey. Societies for the study and propagation of Esperanto were formed in Boston, New York, Philadelphia and other cities. The New York Society, of which Dr. Max Talmey and Andrew Kangas were the organizers, began its work in July, 1905. A National Esperanto Society was founded, with Colonel Harvey as President.

In November, 1908, it was announced that the New York Society for the Study of Esperanto had decided to abandon it for a more simplified form of artificial language. The reason given was that Esperanto had been found, after experience in its use, to be too full of logical defects for endurance and universal ultimate acceptance.

ILO AS A SUBSTITUTE.

The following statement of the position taken by the New York Society in this matter has been prepared for THE WORLD ALMANAC by Andrew Kangas:

"Esperanto was invented in 1887 by Dr. L. Zamenhof, of Warsaw, Poland, to serve as an international auxiliary language, i. e., a means of communication between persons whose native tongues are not the same. It is an artificial language resembling, to some extent, a Latin dialect, but also containing chords of Anglo-German origin, as well as a large percentage of frequently occurring 'arbitrary' words, i. e., ones not borrowed from or resembling living languages. Its pronunciation is strictly phonetic. The success of Esperanto, which is now known over the entire world, and the comparative facility with which it can be mastered, are chiefly due to its system of prefixes and suffixes and methods of word-combination, by means of which its rather limited vocabulary is considerably amplified.

"The international language offers an immediate advantage by laying open to its possessor the whole world. It breaks down the barriers of speech, and procures for one in every land a multitude of persons who understand one's language and are ready to exchange ideas and service with him. If one wishes to correspond with people of different nations, with whose language he is not conversant, for the purpose of commerce, science, information or amusement, this can be easily accomplished by the help of the "Linguo Internacione." Where travellers of different nations may only with difficulty understand each other by means of a few written Latin words, the pronunciation of Latin being different in different nations, with the international language they would be able to speak together and help one another.

"The Delegation for the Adoption of an Auxiliary International Language, founded in 1901, having received the adhesion of 310 societies of all countries and the approval of 1,250 members of academies and universities, elected in 1907 an International Committee, consisting of eminent scientists, Esperantists and linguists, who, after examining all past and present schemes for an international language, adopted Esperanto with a few alterations, so calculated as to preserve the principles and essential qualities of the language invented by Dr. Zamenhof, while applying those principles more consistently and doing away with unnecessary complications. The following are the chief alterations effected:

"Suppression of all accented letters (making it possible to print the language anywhere, while preserving phonetic spelling and often restoring the international orthography; suppression of adjectival declension and accusative (very troublesome for most nations, and chiefly for people with little knowledge of grammar); regularization of word-building, (thus preventing the influx of national idioms and giving a solid basis to the scientific and technical vocabulary, without which the international language cannot obtain a footing in the world of science); enrichment of the vocabulary by adoption of new roots selected according to the principle of the 'maximum internationality,' i. e., roots found in most European languages; rejection of all arbitrary forms, unpronounceable sounds, etc. The resultant, called Simplified Esperanto, or 'Ilo,' (Internaelone Linguo), is a language understood without previous study by every fairly educated man, owing to its being the quintessence of European languages. It is a marvel of simplicity and regularity—no unnecessary rules, no exceptions. It is learned by reading; when you can read it, you can write it; when you can write it, you can speak it. And experience has proven that people from the most different countries pronounce it so nearly alike as to make any differences as trifling and as little troublesome as dialects of English in this country—less so, in fact.) It has already won the approval and hearty support of the best and oldest Primitive-Esperantists, and, thanks to the help of the scientists in the delegation and on the committee, is likely to be some day adopted by all governments and introduced into the schools of all civilized countries. Judging from past success, this possibility no longer seems remote.

"The New York Esperanto Society, Inc., the pioneer group for the propagation of the international language in this country, was formed to promote the study of Esperanto with its eventual modifications, and to enable students to acquire a thorough knowledge of same, as well as the ability to converse freely in it. This society has adopted 'Simplified Esperanto' as the best solution of the problem of a universal tongue, at the same time assuming the new title of 'The New York Ilo Society.' Its official organ is 'Progreso,' published monthly in the interests of the international language. Text-books and literature, in any civilized language, can be had through the society, the dues, of which are $3 a year; non-residents, $1.50, including subscription to 'Progreso.' Instruction is free to members. Further information can be obtained from the Secretary, Andrew Kangas, on enclosing stamp for reply.

"The following are the officers of the New York Ilo Society: Andrew Kangas, President and Corresponding Secretary, 920 Longwood avenue, New York; Alexander Smith, Vice-President; Dr. Max Talmey, Treasurer; John Ed. Hearn, Recording Secretary; J. W. Phoebus and E. Gilbert, Counselors."

THE ESPERANTO MOVEMENT ACTIVE.

The advocates of Esperanto in the United States, however, continue an active propaganda. Colonel George Harvey, President of the National Esperanto Society, has made the following statement in reference to the defection of the New York local society:

"I know nothing about the local society. But the National Esperanto movement is constantly growing. The National Society has 2,000 members, and the North American Review's Society has 2,000 more. I should judge there were about 6,000 other Esperantists scattered through the country. The North American will certainly continue to advocate Esperanto. The International Esperanto Congress will be held here next year."

The Production of Books.

American Publications, 1907 (including new editions)—Fiction, **1,171**; theology and religion, 876; law, 707; physical and mathematical science, 706; poetry and the drama, 697; biography, correspondence, 603; Juvenile, 603; literature and collected works, 644; medical, hygiene, 461; political and social science, 521; description, geography, travel, 482; education, 465; history, 415; useful arts, 351; fine arts, illustrated gift books, 323; domestic and rural, 162; humor and satire, 204; philosophy, 163; sports and amusements, 97; works of reference, 69. Total 1907, 9,620; total 1906, 7,139; total 1905, 8,112; total 1904, 8,291; total 1903, 7,856; total 1902, 7,833; total 1901, 8,141; total 1900, 6,356; total 1899, 5,321; total 1898, 4,886; total 1897, 4,928. Of the production of 1907, there were 6,517 books by American authors.

British Publications, 1907 (including new editions)—Theology, sermons, 850; educational, classical, 697; novels and Juvenile works, 2,782; law, 243; political and social economy, trade, 763; arts, sciences, and illustrated works, 1209; travels, geographical research, 464; history, biography, 873; poetry and the drama, 527; year-books and serials, 465; medicine, surgery, 342; belles-lettres, essays, 336; miscellaneous, 363. Total 1907, 9,914; total 1906, 8,603; total, 1905, 8,252; total 1904, 8,334; total 1903, 8,381; total 1902, 7,381.

German Publications, 1907—Bibliography, encyclopaedias, 623; theology, 2,549; law and political science, 2,922; medicine, 1,849; natural sciences, mathematics, 1,556; philosophy and theosophy, 743; education, books for the young, 4,210; language and literature, 1,953; history, 1,269; geography, 1,555; military science, 693; commerce, industrial arts, 2,014; architecture and engineering, 1,001; domestic economy, agriculture, 932; drama and popular literature, 4,195; art, 869; year-books, 616; miscellaneous, 525. Total 1907, 30,073; total 1906, 28,703; total 1905, 28,886; total 1904, 28,378; total 1903, 27,606; total 1902, 26,906; total 1901, 25,331. These statistics include many pamphlets which in other countries are not classed as books.

French Publications, 1907—Religion, 579; law, 526; philosophy, 168; mysticism, 36; political and social science, 147; military and naval science, 374; mathematics, 61; natural sciences, 205; medicine, surgery, 950; agriculture, 295; industrial arts, 222; domestic economy, 191; history, biography, 1,257; geography, travels, 229; belles-lettres, fiction, 1808; literature (foreign), 248; literature (ancient), 32; fine arts, 101; education, 1,091; popular science, 115, miscellaneous, 109. Total 1907, 10,785; total 1906, 10,898; total 1905, 12,416; total 1904, 12,139; total 1903, 12,264; total 1902, 12,199; total 1901, 13,053; total 1900, 13,362.

The book productions in the Netherlands in 1905 were 3,290; Switzerland in 1903, 7,816; Belgium in 1904, 2,995; Denmark in 1903, 1,544; Roumania in 1901, 1,739, Spain and Portugal in 1897, 1,200; Austria-Hungary in 1899, 5,000; Japan in 1899, 21,255; Russia in 1901, 5,935; British India in 1891, 7,700; Turkey in 1890, 940; Norway in 1903, 712; Sweden in 1900, 1,683; Poland in 1903, 934; Italy in 1907, 7,040. The total book publications of the world annually approximate 150,000. Paul Otlet, the Secretary of the Brussels International Bibliographic Institute, estimates the number of printed books since the invention of printing to January, 1900, at 12,163,000 separate works, and the number of periodicals at between fifteen and eighteen millions.

Mr. A. Growoll, editor of "The Publishers' Weekly," has furnished the statistics from which the above figures have been compiled.

Literature in 1908.

NOTABLE BOOKS OF THE YEAR.

The viewpoint of this survey must not be overlooked. It does not claim to be a critical literary estimate of the literature of 1908. It aims to give the average reader looking for authoritative information the names of books that were popular "sellers" and the chief books bearing upon the events of the period covered. It is put together from the popular and "news" view of the subject. Next year will be a year of literary centennials. Anniversaries of Edgar Allen Poe, Alfred Tennyson, Oliver Wendell Holmes, Charles Darwin, William Ewart Gladstone and Abraham Lincoln are to be celebrated. Milton's third centenary has just been observed (December 9). There have been between 7,000 and 8,000 books, and at the time of writing almost another thousand are on the way.

FICTION.

The "big sellers" of the year were Winston Churchill's "Mr. Crewe's Career" (a thoroughly American railroad story of systems of "management" and "reform"); John Fox, Jr.'s, "The Trail of the Lonesome Pine" (bitter family feuds, raiding of illicit whiskey, booming of real estate, on the borders of Kentucky and Virginia); Mary Johnston's "Lewis Rand" (romance of the days of Thomas Jefferson and Aaron Burr, her principal character a Virginia lawyer); Maurice Hewlett's "Half Way House" (social life in London of to-day); Mrs. Humphry Ward's "The Testing of Diana Mallory" (heroine suffers for her mother's sin and is deserted by her politically ambitious lover; English social and political life); Robert Herrick's "Together" (married life in the United States to-day, inside view of railroad trusts, specialist physicians, vast hotels, given in boldest language); Rex E. Beach's "The Barrier" (supposed illegitimate birth and Indian blood in the heroine in Alaskan mining town); Francis Hopkinson Smith's "Peter" (a novel of which Peter is not the hero—stock-broking methods in Wall Street); Edward C. Booth's "The Post Girl" (a Yorkshire story, the hero musician and composer like the author); William F. De Morgan's "Somehow Good" (remarkable tale of complete suspension of memory); David G. Phillips's "Old Wives for New" (realistic story of New York married life, divorce, etc.); Marion Crawford's "The Prima Donna," sequel to "Fair Margaret" (now completed by "The Diva's Ruby"); Harold MacGrath's "The Lure of the Mask" (a masked singer with rich European possessions); Esther and Lucia Chamberlin's "The Coast of Chance" (San Francisco story of theft of valuable ring and consequent detective work); Louis J. Vance's "The Black Bag" (bag of jewels and many complications); Mary Roberts Rinehart's "The Circular Staircase" (murder and circumstantial evidence, much humor); Meredith Nicholson's "The Little Brown Jug of Kildare" (pure adventure, introducing the Governors of North and South Carolina); Robert W. Chambers's "The Firing Line" (scene Florida, life of the rich and idle); George Barr McCutcheon's "The Husbands of Edith" (a highly humorous story); and same author's "Man from Brodny's" (clever lawyer's work in breaking absurd will on imaginary island); Edward Phillips Oppenheim's "The Great Secret" (imaginary international conspiracy. Germany to crush England. American multi-millionaires to furnish funds); Ellen Glasgow's "The Ancient Law" (heredity); Alice Brown's "Rose McLeod" (heroine arrives as brother's widow in typical New England family; her father social agitator); Mrs. Mary Stewart Cutting's "The Wayfarers" (business man in charge rebels against fraudulent methods and almost starves with wife and children); Elizabeth Ellis's "Fair Moon of Bath" (the famous English watering-place in the "Pretender's" days); and Mr. and Mrs. Williamson's "The Chauffeur and the Chaperon" (motor-boat trip through waters of Holland).

The appalling extravagance and extreme poverty of present day, the wild craze for excitement of the idle rich, the looseness of the ties of matrimony, and the looseness of business honor, found expression in books reflecting American conditions, many of which led to much discussion. In this category fall Herrick's "Together" and Chambers's "The Firing Line," already mentioned as "big sellers." Upton Sinclair brought out two volumes of a trilogy he is writing on society of the hour, "The Metropolis" and "The Money Changers," to be followed by "The Machine." The first deals with the mad extravagance of spending in New York and almost grotesque ways of seeking amusement; the second with many of same characters deals with the trusts and railroads and gives plan of panic of 1907; the third will relate to politics and "machine" government. "A Little Brother to the Rich," by Joseph Medill Patterson, a Western man of social, financial and political position, has a message to make the idle rich pause and think; his hero lets money become his sole thought. "The Flame Dancer," by Frances Aymar Mathews (unflattering picture of fashionable New York); "Altars to Mammon," by Elizabeth Neff (clergyman faces problem of "tainted money" owned by man upright in private life, unscrupulous in business); "The Distributors," by Anthony Partridge (rich modern society with morbid thirst for new sensations and relaxed moral fibre), and "Katherine Trevelyan," by Louise Mounsell Field (realistic picture of New York frivolous society). "The Bond," by Neith Boyce, gives analysis of the marriage bond in its entirely modern aspect; "The Broken Snare," by Ludwig Lewisohn (psychological study of the marriage relation); "The Dissolving Circle" (men and women waiting to get divorces in South Dakota and how they kill time). In line are "The Master Influence," by Thomas McKean (social conditions of modern people. Governor Hughes supposed to be hero); "The Reaping," by Mary Imlay Taylor (political and fashionable life in Washington); "Get Rich Quick Wallingford," by Chester G. Randolph (financier and promoter, works from carpet tacks to control of wheat market).

Of interest to owners of automobiles are "The Car and the Lady," by Percy F. Megargel and Grace Sartwell Mason ($50,000 bet on race from New York to Portland. Oregon); "The Lady in the Car" (gentlemanly thief travels by automobile through various parts of Europe in pursuit of business); and the "big seller," "Chauffeur and Chaperon." Technically description, but reading like fiction, are Henry Cottrell Rowland's "Across Europe in a Motor Boat" (7,000 miles from the Seine to the Black Sea); "British Highways and Byways from a Motor Car," by Thomas Dowler Murphy (5,000-mile tour in the British Isles); "Through Persia in a Motor Car," by Claude Anet (ten people, over Caucasus into Persia); "Motor Flight Through France," by Mrs. Edith Wharton (old towns, Gothic cathedrals); "Motoring Abroad," by Frank Presbrey (out-of-the-way places of France and British Isles); and "Motor Days in England," by John M. Dillon.

Among the best detective stories were: Edward Frederic Benson's "The Blotting Book;" Edgar Wallace's "Angel Esquire;" Houghton Townley's "The Bishop's Emeralds;"

Arthur Hornblow's "The Profligate;" Mrs. Walton's "The Lost Clue;" Henry Kitchell Webster's "The Whispering Man;" Gaston Le Roux's "Mystery of the Yellow Room;" "The Four-Pools Mystery;" The Clutch of Circumstance, by James Barnes; Charles Edmonds Walk's "The Silver Blade;" Jacques Futrelle's "The Thinking Machine" (clever story of omniscience); Samuel Hopkins Adams's "The Flying Death" (mystery of Long Island fishing village). The negro question is treated in Robert Lee Durham's "The Call of the South" (hero Harvard graduate with tinge of negro blood); and Katherine Evans Blake's "The Stuff of a Man" (much of existing horrible conditions traced to the white man). All kinds of visionary schemes for the future of society and political conditions were treated in "The Statue," by Eden Phillpotts and Arnold Bennett (international intrigue, mystery and murder); "The Vanishing Fleet," by Roy Norton (forecast of possibilities of électricity, invention of airship); "The War in the Air," by Herbert G. Wells (German airships attack United States, every nation involved); "The Mad Scientist," by Raymond McDonald (new powers of nature, houses, battleships sail through air; cipher of fifty words, prize for solution); "Evacuation of England," by Louis Pope Gratacap (Isthmus of Panama sinks; all climates ard geologies change); "The Man Who Ended War," by Hollis Godfrey (by means of a mysterious invention a man destroyed all the battleships of the world). The transcendental supernatural ideas of the day were worked into William H. Mallock's "An Immortal Soul" (heroine possesses double personality); "Vera the Medium," by Richard Harding Davis (spirit called to influence the making of a will); "The Shadow World." by Hamlin Garland (describes marvellous phenomena in psychics for which author vouches); "Some Ladies in Haste," by Robert W. Chambers (mental suggestion cures smoking habit); "The Vigil," by Harold Bagbie (Oxford student becomes social revivalist); "Lord of the World," by Father Benson (modernism, materialism and "psycho-fads"). Historical fiction was almost crowded out this year by society and psychological fiction. "Sir Richard Escombe," by Max Pemberton (social practices in time of George II.), ran side by side in competition for a prize with Mrs. Wilkins-Freeman's "Shoulders of Atlas" (New England story with bewildering mystery), in a New York daily paper, and Mr. Pemberton won. Humor was furnished by "The Letters of Jennie Allen," by Grace Donworth (bright, unselfish, unspelled letters full of wit and pathos); and "Bridget," by Mrs. Herman Bosch (the servant question of the hour told by the greenhorn, who shows the weaknesses of the parlor, also). Volumes of excellent short stories were a feature of the year.

BIOGRAPHY.

The coming Lincoln centennial called out an edition of his works in nine volumes edited by Marion Mills, "The Lincoln Centennial Medal," presenting the medal of Abraham Lincoln by Jules Edward Roine, with papers on the medal and a reproduction in full size, embedded in pasteboard to show both sides, besides about twenty-five other volumes by and about Lincoln. Biographies of actors were a feature of the year. They include "Who's Who on the Stage, 1908," edited by Walter Browne and E. Le Roy Koch; "Impressions of Henry Irving," by Walter Hernès Pollock; "Life of Henry Irving," in two volumes, by Brereton; "Richard Mansfield, the Man and the Actor," by Paul Wilstach; "Story of My Life," autobiography of Ellen Terry; and William Winter's "Other Days," chronicles and memories covering two generations by the art critic of The Tribune. Musicians were covered in "Stokes's Encyclopedia of Music and Musicians;" "Musical Memories," by George Putnam Upton; "Claude Achille Debussy," by Louise Liebich, composer of "Pelleas et Melisande;" "Personal Recollections of Wagner," translated from Angelo Neumann, one of the greatest producers of Wagner's music dramas; "The Operas of Wagner," plots, music and history and much biographical material by J. Cuthbert Hadden; "Johannes Brahms," by H. C. Colles. Two books on Whistler: "The Life of James Whistler," by Mr. and Mrs. Pennell, and "With Whistler in Venice," by Otto Henry Bacher. Biographies of American public men were very numerous. "Men of America" is a biographical dictionary of contemporaries in every walk of life, and separate biographies include De Wolfe Howe's "The Life and Letters of George Bancroft;" Kerr's "John Sherman;" "Letters and Literary Memories of Samuel Jones Tilden," edited by John Bigelow; Francis Arthur Jones's "Thomas Alva Edison;" William Bayard Hale's "Week in the White House with Theodore Roosevelt" (same author who was to publish his interview with Kaiser William which was suppressed); Pendleton's Greenslett's "Thomas Bailey Aldrich;" Gould's "Concerning Lafcadio Hearn," which raised great discussion; Macy's "Edgar A. Poe," in Beacon Biographies; Kitton's "Charles Dickens;" Ingleby's "Oscar Wilde;" Gosse's "Henrik Ibsen," and Montrose J. Moses's "Ibsen; the Man and His Plays." George Herbert Palmer's "Life of Alice Freeman Palmer," his wife, for years president of Wellesley College, was a book much talked of among literary people. Among other biographies of interest are Spears's "Story of the New England Whalers;" Robert Collyer's "Memories;" the third volume Carl Schurz's "Autobiography," completed from material left by Schurz; and "Who is Who in Insurance," an international biographical dictionary, edited by Isidor Singer, chief editor of the "Jewish Encyclopedia."

POLITICAL AND SOCIAL.

One of the great questions the United States must face in early future is the race question as brought before it in the negro problem and in the problem of immigration. On the first question came "Race Adjustment," essays on the negro in America by Kelly Miller; "Some Phases of the Negro Question," by Charles W. Melick; Alfred Holt Stone's "Studies in the American Race Question;" Dubois's "Economic Co-operation Among Negro Americans," and Montgomery's "Vital American Problems." Immigration found exploitation in "Watson's Addresses on Immigration" and Josiah Royce's "Race Questions, Provincialism and Other American Problems." Books Americans should study before another election are Stimson's "American Constitution" (the national powers, the rights of States); Gauss's "American Government;" Woodrow Wilson's "Constitutional Government in the United States;" Fuller's "Government by the People" (laws and government regulating the election system and control of political parties in the United States); "Governor Hughes's Addresses and Papers, with President Schurman's Estimate of the Governor's Public Career;" "Present Day Problems," by William Howard Taft, President-elect of the United States; Andrew Carnegie's "Problems of To-day" (wealth, labor, socialism); "The American Executive and Executive Methods," by President Finlay, of

New York College; "The American As He Is," by Murray Butler, of Columbia University; Merriam's "Primary Elections:" Marriot's "Uncle Sam's Business;" Senator Beveridge's "Americans of To-day and To-morrow" (a vision of political conditions fifteen year's hence); and Rowe's "Problems of City Government." The panic of last year brought up many writings on the question of finances and modes of living. Launey's "The World's Gold" (its geology, extraction and political economy); Henry's "How to Invest Money;" Lownhaupt's "Investment Bonds;" John C. Van Dyke's "The Money God" (business methods in American life); Chapman's "Work and Wages;" Shaw's "Current Issues" (trusts, tariff); Henry Wood's "Money Hunger" (commercial immorality in United States); and Byron Mathews's "Our Irrational Distribution of Wealth" (advocates public ownership). Other notable books in this department are: Mahan's "Naval Administration and Warfare" (Monroe Doctrine, value of Pacific cruise of 1908); Franklin Matthews's "With the Battle Fleet" (cruise of battleships, 1908); Spears's "History of United States Navy;" Harry Perry Robinson's "Twentieth Century American" (comparative study of the two great Anglo-Saxon nations); Frederic Harrison's "National and Social Problems;" Galsworthy's "A Commentary" (an indictment of modern social conditions); Lawrence Lowell's "Government of England;" Graham Brooks's "As Others See Us;" Harvey's "Women" (duty to charm, right to vote); Wells's "New Words for Old" (socialism); Stevens's "Liberators" (public ownership of railroads). There are also Artman's "Legalized Outlaws" (liquor traffic); Travis's "The Young Malefactor" (child criminals); Kelly's "Elimination of the Tramp" (advocating a labor colony system as in Holland, Switzerland, etc.); "The Cry of the Children" (child labor); and Beatrice Sands's "Weepers in Playtime" (orphan homes and institutions for children).

LITERATURE.

Books about books and collected essays of well-known living writers were a feature of the year. Horne's "Technique of the Novel;" Hamilton's "Materials and Methods of Fiction;" Scott-James's "Modernism and Romance" explained and criticised the most popular form of literature—the novel. Gaige and Harcourt, in "Books and Reading," gave "humanity essays" on what books stand for in life of the world); Henry M. Alden, editor of Harper's Magazine, in "Magazine Writing and the New Literature," cleverly and authoritatively sums up the literature of the day; and Bliss Perry, editor of The Atlantic Monthly, in "Park Street Papers," gives a history of that old periodical and its influence. Volumes of essays, all dealing extensively with books, included: Arthur C. Benson's "At Large" (full of sage, restful humor); Chesterton's "All Things Considered;" Frederic Harrison's "Realities and Ideals" (social, political, literary, artistic); Hinds's "Diary of a Looker-On" (arranged under days of the month); E. S. Martin's "In a New Century;" Agnes Repplier's "A Happy Half Century" (books and spirit of leisure of end of eighteenth and first quarter of nineteenth century), and Henry D. Sedgwick's "New American Type" (mob-spirit in literature; Mark Twain, Mrs. Wharton).

RELIGION AND SPECULATION.

A feature of the year, and now at it's height, was the curing of disease by various forms of religion and the triumph of mind over matter. Christian Science received more than its usual attention, and there were three biographies of Mrs. Eddy. The "Emmanuel Movement" was started by Dr. Elwood Worcester in the Protestant Episcopal Emmanuel Church, Boston. Dr. Worcester wrote "Religion and Medicine" (the moral control of nervous disorders and description of the "movement"), and "The New Life;" and literature on the subject now includes Achorn's "Some Physical Disorders Having Mental Origin;" Cabot's "Psychotherapy in Its Relation to Religion;" Coriat's "Some Familiar Forms of Nervousness;" Lawrence's "A Letter of Hope" (moral victory over physical woes); McComb's "The Healing Ministry of the Church;" Macomber's "History of the Emmanuel Movement from Standpoint of a Patient;" Macdonald's "Mind, Religion and Health" (appreciation of Emmanuel Movement); Josiah Royce's "Some Social Aspects of Social Therapeutics" (author is of Harvard University); and W. J. Mann's "The Emmanuel Summer School." Other forms of healing are covered by Dresser's "A Physician to the Soul" (refutes Christian Science); Horace Fletcher's "Optimism, a Real Remedy" (thorough mastication of food); Dr. Quackenbos's "Hypnotic Therapeutics in Theory and Practice" ("suggestion" the cure); Bishop Fallows's "Health and Happiness" ("Movement" now going on in St. Paul's Church, Chicago); Henry Wood's "The New Old Healing" ("suggestion"); Charles S. Minot's "Problem of Age, Growth and Death" and Metchnikoff's "Prolongation of Life" were much studied. Speculation on the supernatural brought Fournier d'Albe's "New Light on Immortality" (author Secretary of Dublin Society for Psychical Research); Bruce's "Riddle of Personality;" Chesterton's "Orthodoxy," sequel to "Heretics;" Sir Oliver Lodge's "Science and Immortality" (articles from Hibbert Journal and Contemporary Review); Podmore's "Naturalization of the Supernatural," and Herbert G. Wells's "First and Last Things" (serious confession of faith and rule of life). Leading physicians and clergymen have given serious consideration to these books during the year.

MISCELLANEOUS.

A few books on subjects just now receiving great attention are William I. Hull's "The Two Hague Conferences," and "Texts of the Peace Conferences at the Hague, 1899—1907," edited by James Brown Scott; "The Ocean Carrier," by Russell Smith (rates of ocean transportation and commercial history of many ships); James O. Fagan's "Confessions of a Railroad Signalman" (specially dwells on frightful ratio of accidents in United States; book brought him Government position); "Submarine Telegraphs; Their History, Construction and Working" (appendix on "Wireless"); A. I. H. Harper's "Woman Suffrage Throughout the World," and many pamphlets on both sides of question (anti side predominates); "The Niagara River" (its immense commercial future); separation of Church and State in France treated in Sabatier's "Open Letter to Cardinal Gibbons," and Newman Smyth's "Passing Protestantism and Coming Catholicism." Educational problems handled in Dr. Eliot's "University Administration" (describes forty years' presidency of Harvard University, from which author is now retiring); "Moral Instruction and Training in Schools" (report of an international inquiry; fine bibliographies of subject); Flexner's "The American College" (points out weaknesses after long study of educational systems.

Painting and Sculpture.

NATIONAL ACADEMY OF DESIGN.

NATIONAL ACADEMICIANS.

Elected.
1902. Abbey, Edwin, Fairford, England.
1899. Adams, Herbert, 131 West 11th Street.
1902. Alexander, J. W., 123 East 63d Street.
1899. Barse, George F., Jr., Katonah, N. Y.
1902. Beaux, Cecelia, East Gloucester, Mass.
— — Beckwith, J. Carroll, 58 West 57th Street.
1905. Benson, Frank W., Salem, Mass.
1888. Blashfield, Edwin H., 48 West 59th Street.
1903. Bitter, Karl, Weehawken, N. J.
1863. Brevoort, J. R., Yonkers, N. Y
1881. Bridgman, Frederick A., Paris.
1875. Bristol, John B., 120 East 23d Street.
1863. Brown, J. G., 51 West 10th Street.
1906. Brush, George De Forest, Dublin, N. H.
1907. Bunce, William Gedney, Hartford, Ct.
1899. Butler, Howard Russell, 35 Wall Street.
1875. Calverley, Charles, Caldwell, N. J.
1906. Carlsen, Emil, 43 East 59th Street.
1908. Cass, Gilbert, 11 East 24th Street.
1890. Chase, William M., 303 Fifth Avenue.
1885. Church, F. S., Carnegie Hall.
1898. Clinedinst, B. West, 1000 Madison Avenue.
1908. Cole, Timothy, Abroad.
1862. Colman, Samuel, 267 Central Park West.
1903. Cox, Kenyon, 145 West 55th Street.
1901. Crane, Bruce, P. O. Box 1692, N. Y. City.
1904. Curran, C. C., 16 West 61st Street.
1906. Daingerfield, Elliott, 145 West 55th Street.
1863. Dana, W. P. W., 57 Onslow Gardens, London.
1906. Davis, C. H., Mystic, Ct.
1906. Dearth, H. G., Carnegie Hall.
1898. De Forest, Lockwood, 7 East 10th Street.
1906. Dessar, Louis Paul, 27 West 67th Street.
1907. Dewey, Charles Melville (elect), 218 West 23d Street
1888. Dewing, Thos. W., 51 West 10th Street.
1883. Dielman, Frederick, 51 West 10th Street.
1907. Dougherty, Paul (elect), 27 West 67th Street.
1906. Du Mond, Frank V., 27 West 67th Street.
1906. Duveneck, Frank (elect), Cincinnati.
1902. Eakins, Thomas, Philadelphia, Pa.
1904. Foster, Ben., 253 West 42d Street.
1899. Fowler, Frank, 106 West 55th Street.
1901. French, Daniel Chester, 125 West 11th Street.
1882. Gaul, Gilbert, Nashville, Tenn.
1907. Gay, Edward, Mount Vernon, N. Y.
1905. Grafly, Charles, Philadelphia, Pa.
1867. Griswold, C. C., 262 West 12th Street.
1867. Guy, Seymour Joseph, 51 West 10th Street.
1868. Hall, George Henry, 96 Fifth Avenue.
1889. Hamilton, Hamilton, Peekskill, N. Y.
1901. Harrison, Alexander, 118 East 40th Street.
1891. Hartley, J. S., 145 West 55th Street.
190[illegible]. Hassam, Childe, 27 West 67th Street.
1863. Hennessy, W. J., London, England.
1906. Henri, Robert, 58 West 57th Street.
1869. Henry, E. L., 7 West 43d Street.
1865. Homer, Winslow, Scarboro, Me.
1897. Howe, Wm. H., Bronxville, N. Y.
1882. Howland, Alfred C., Pasadena, Cal.
1899. Inness, George, Jr.
1906. Isham, Samuel, 80 West 40th Street.
1894. Jones, Francis C., 33 West 67th Street.
1883. Jones, H. Bolton, 33 West 67th Street.
1905. Kendall, William Sergeant, 26 West 8th Street.
1906. Kost, F. W., 146 West 55th Street.
1869. La Farge, John, 51 West 10th Street.
1907. Lathrop, W. L., New Hope, Pa.
1897. Lippincott, William H., 7 West 43d Street.
1906. Loeb, Louis, 58 West 47th Street.

Elected.
1890. Low, Will. H., Bronxville, N. Y.
1906. MacMonnies, Frederick W. (elect), France.
1906. MacNeil, Hermon A., College Point, N.Y.
1876. Magrath, William, 11 East 14th Street.
1885. Maynard, George W., 7 West 48d Street.
1907. McKim, Charles F., 160 Fifth Avenue.
1906. Melchers, Gari, 80 West 40th Street.
1875. Miller, Charles H., Queens, L. I.
1885. Millet, F. D., 6 East 23d Street.
1895. Moeller, Louis, Wakefield, N. Y.
1906. Mora, F. Luis, 142 East 18th Street.
1884. Moran, Thomas, 24 West 22d Street.
1891. Mowbray, H. Siddons, 66 West 11th Street.
1887. Murphy, J. Francis, 222 West 23d Street.
1870. Nehlig, Victor, abroad.
1885. Nicoll, J. C., 51 West 10th Street.
1906. Niehaus, Charles H., 148 West 36th Street.
1904. Ochtman, Leonard, Cos Cob, Ct.
1897. Palmer, Walter L., Albany, N. Y.
1906. Parrish, Maxfield, Windsor, Vt.
1884. Parton, Arthur, 318 West 57th Street.
1869. Perry, E. Wood, 333 Fourth Avenue.
1908. Post, George B., 347 Fifth Avenue.
1906. Potter, Edward C., Greenwich, Ct.
1906. Potthast, Edward H., 318 West 57th Street.
1904. Proctor, A. Phimister, 855 Pelham Avenue.
1907. Pyle, Howard, Wilmington, Del.
1906. Ranger, Henry W., 228 West 44th Street.
1906. Redfield, Edward W., Centre Bridge, Pa.
1906. Reid, Robert, 142 East 33d Street.
1908. Rehn, F. K. M., 222 West 23d Street.
1906. Roth, Fred'k G. R., White Plains, N. Y.
1906. Ryder, Albert P., 308 West 15th Street.
1897. Sargent, John S., London, England.
1907. Schofield, W. Elmer, Philadelphia, Pa.
1875. Sellstedt, L. G., Buffalo, N. Y.
1861. Shattuck, Aaron D., Granby, Ct.
1888. Shirlaw, Walter, 39 West 25th Street.
1890. Shurtleff, R. M., 44 West 22d Street.
1905. Smedley, Wm. T., Carnegie Hall.
1882. Smillie, George H., 156 East 36th Street.
1876. Smillie, James D., 156 East 36th Street.
1906. Snell, Henry B., 116 West 41st Street.
1906. Tarbell, Edmund C., Boston, Mass.
1901. Thayer, Abbott H., Monadnock, N. H.
1880. Tiffany, Louis C., 27 East 72d Street.
1891. Tryon, D. W., 226 West 59th Street.
1886. Turner, C. Y., 35 West 14th Street.
1907. Van Boskerck, Robert W., 58 West 57th Street.
1865. Vedder, Elihu, abroad.
1891. Vinton, Frederic P., Boston, Mass.
1899. Volk, Douglas, 215 West 57th Street.
1906. Vonnoh, Robert W., 25 West 67th Street.
1902. Walker, Henry O., Lakewood, N. J.
1891. Walker, Horatio, 372 Fifth Avenue.
1883. Ward, Edgar M., 51 West 10th Street.
1863. Ward, J. Q. A., 119 West 52d Street.
1895. Watrous, Harry W., 58 West 57th Street.
1886. Weir, J. Alden, 51 West 10th Street.
1866. Weir, John F., New Haven, Ct.
1897. Weldon, C. D., 51 West 10th Street.
1861. Whittredge, Worthington, Summit, N. J.
1906. Wiggins, J. Carleton, 1079 Dean Street, Brooklyn.
1897. Wiles, Irving R., 106 West 55th Street.
1873. Wilmarth, Lemuel E., 352 Adelphi Street, Brooklyn.
1908. Wolf, Henry, 110 East 91st Street.
1907. Woodbury, Charles H., Boston, Mass.
1880. Yewell, George H., 51 West 10th Street.

ASSOCIATE NATIONAL ACADEMICIANS.

Allen, Thomas, Boston, Mass.
Armstrong, D. Maitland, 61 Washington Square, South.
Bacher, Otto H., Bronxville, N. Y.
Ballard, Frederick William, 152 West 55th Street.
Ballin, Hugo, 146 West 55th Street.
Beal, Gifford, 27 West 67th Street
Bell, E. A., 226 Central Park South.
Birney, William Verplanck, 58 West 57th Street.
Bogert, George H., 204 West 55th Street.
Boston, Joseph H., 203 Montague Street, Brooklyn, N. Y.
Brandegee, Robert B., Farmington, Ct.
Bridges, Miss Fidelia, Canaan, Ct.
Burroughs, Bryson, 50 East 86th Street.
Calder, Alexander S., Oracle, Arizona.
Chapman, Carlton T., 58 West 57th Street.
Chase, Adelaide Cole, Boston, Mass.
Clark, Walter, New Rochelle, N. Y.
Clarke, Thomas Shields, 50 Riverside Drive.
Coffin, William A., 58 West 57th Street.
Coleman, C. C., abroad.
Cook, Walter, 135 East 37th Street.
Cooper, Colin Campbell, 58 West 57th Street.
Couse, E. Irving, 58 West 57th Street.
Cox, Louise, 75 West 55th Street
Craig, Thomas B., Rutherford, N. J.
Crowninshield, Frederick, 314 West End Avenue.
Cushing, Howard Gardiner.
Day, Francis, 27 West 67th Street.
DeHaven, F., 23 West 24th Street.
DeLuce, Percival, 114 East 23d Street.
Drake, W. H., 37 West 22d Street.
Earle, L. C., Montclair, N. J.
Eaton, C. Warren, 318 West 57th Street.
Faxon, Wm. Bailey, 152 West 57th Street.
Ferguson, Henry A., 226 West 78th Street.
Flagg, Montague, 253 West 42d Street.
Franzen, August, Carnegie Hall.
Frazier, Kenneth, 58 East 78th Street.

Fuller, Henry Brown, Windsor, Vt.
Fuller, Lucia Fairchild, Windsor, Vt.
Gaugengigl, I. M., Boston, Mass.
Ganley, Robert David, 938 Eighth Avenue.
Genth, Lillian M., Philadelphia.
Glackens, Wm. J., 58 West 57th Street.
Granville-Smith, W., 96 Fifth Avenue.
Green, Frank Russell, 211 West 85th Street.
Groll, Albert L.
Harper, William St. John, 166 West 107th Street.
Harrison, Birge, 7 West 43d Street.
Hastings, Thomas, 225 Fifth Avenue.
Hawthorne, Chas. W., 145 East 23d Street.
Herter, Albert, 578 Fifth Avenue.
Hills, Laura C., Boston, Mass.
Hubbell, Henry S., Paris.
Hyde, William H., 105 East 61st Street.
Jongers, Alphonse, 58 West 57th Street.
Keith, Dora Wheeler, 33 West 67th Street.
Kline, William Fair, 244 West 14th Street.
Konti, Isadore, 32 West 67th Street.
Lathrop, Francis, 29 Washington Square.
Lawson, Ernest, 9 East 42d Street.
Loop, Mrs. Henry A., Saratoga Springs, N. Y.
Lockwood, Wilton, Boston, Mass.
Loomis, Chester, Englewood, N. J.
Lyman, Joseph, Century Club.
MacEwen, Walter, Paris, France.
MacMonnies, Mary F., Eure, France.
Marsh, Fred. Dana, Nutley, N. J.
Martiny, Philip, 80 Washington Square.
Mayer, Constant, abroad.
McCord, George H., 114 East 23d Street.
Mielatz, C. F. W., 135 East 15th Street.
Moschowitz, Paul, 114 East 23d Street.
Niemeyer, John Henry, New Haven, Ct.
Nettleton, Walter, Stockbridge, Mass.
O'Donovan, W. R., 31 St. Nicholas Place.
Parsons, Charles, Boonton, N. J.
Pearce, Charles Sprague, France.
Pennell, Joseph, London.
Platt, Charles A., 16 Gramercy Park.
Poore, H. R., Orange, N. J.
Prellwitz, Edith Mitchell, 247 West 71st Street.
Prellwitz, Henry, Wilmington, Del.
Remington, Frederic, New Rochelle, N. Y.
Rice, William M. J., 55 West 33d Street.
Robinson, Will. S., 202 West 74th Street.
Root, Edward F., Old Lyme, Ct.
Sartain, William, 152 West 57th Street.
Schreyvogel, Charles, Hoboken, N. J.
Sewell, Amanda Brewster, 25 West 67th Street.
Sewell, R. V. V., 25 West 67th Street.
Shannon, J. J., London.
Sherwood, Rosina Emmet, 251 Lexington Avenue.
Story, George H., 230 West 59th Street.
Story, Julian, Philadelphia, Pa.
Thorne, William, 58 West 57th Street.
Van Laer, A. T., 30 East 57th Street.
Vonnoh, Bessie Potter, 33 West 67th Street.
Walcott, H. M., Rutherford, N. J.
Webb, J. Louis, abroad.
Weinman, Adolph A., 97 Sixth Avenue.
Whittemore, Wm. J., 318 West 57th Street.
Yates, Cullen, 939 Eighth Avenue.

COUNCIL, 1908-1909.

President, Frederick Dielman; *Vice-President*, Herbert Adams; *Corresponding Secretary*, H. W. Watrous; *Recording Secretary*, Kenyon Cox; *Treasurer*, Francis C. Jones; W. Sergeant Kendall, Will. H. Low, H. B. Snell, J. Alden Weir, Louis Loeb, J. W. Oleandy.

The addresses given in the list refer to the City of New York when not otherwise specified. The National Academy was founded in 1826. The schools of the National Academy are open from the first Monday in October to the middle of May. Circulars containing rules and other details may be had on application at the Academy, corner Amsterdam Avenue and West 109th Street.

NATIONAL SCULPTURE SOCIETY.

The National Sculpture Society, with headquarters at New York, was incorporated in 1896. It is composed of lay and sculptor members, and has for its object the spreading of the knowledge of good sculpture, the fostering of the taste for ideal sculpture and its production, both for the household and museums; the promotion of the decoration of public and other buildings, squares, and parks with sculpture of a high class; the improvement of the quality of the sculptor's art as applied to industries, and the providing, from time to time, for exhibitions of sculpture and objects of industrial art in which sculpture enters. The officers are as follows:

Honorary President—John Q. A. Ward. *President*—Herbert Adams. *Vice-Presidents*—Thomas Hastings, H. A. MacNeil. *Secretary*—J. Scott Hartley. *Treasurer*—I. Wyman Drummond. *Council*—Class expiring January 1, 1909: Karl Bitter, Thomas Hastings, J. Scott Hartley, Arnold W. Brunner, Harvey Wiley Corbett, I. Wyman Drummond. Class expiring January 1, 1910: Herbert Adams, Edward P. Casey, Albert Jaegers, H. A. MacNeil, A. A. Weinman, John De Witt Warner. Class expiring January 1, 1911: Chester Beach, John M. Carrere, Isadore Konti, Richard E. Brooks, Daniel Chester French, Artillio Piccirilli.

ROYAL ACADEMY.

President—Sir Edward John Poynter, Bart. *Keeper*—E. Crofts. *Treasurer*—T. G. Jackson. *Librarian*—W. F. Yeames. *Secretary*—Frederick A. Eaton. *Registrar*—E. F. Dixon.

ROYAL ACADEMICIANS.

1898 Abbey, Edwin Austin.
1898 Aitchison, George.
1879 Alma-Tadema, Sir Lawrence, O. M.
1891 Brock, Thomas.
1897 Crofts, Ernest.
1877 Davis, Henry Wm. Banks.
1891 Dicksee, Frank.
1887 Fildes, Sir Luke.
1902 Frampton, Sir George J.
1892 Gilbert, Alfred, M. V. O.
1891 Gow, Andrew C.
1881 Graham, Peter.
1898 Gregory, Edward John.
1890 Herkomer, Sir Hubert von, C. V. O.
1897 Jackson, Thomas Graham.
1898 Leader, Benj. Williams.
1876 Leslie, George Dunlop.
1898 Lucas, John Seymour.
1903 Macbeth, Robert Walker.
1893 MacWhirter, John.
1905 Murray, David.
1877 Orchardson, Sir W. Quiller.
1881 Onless, Walter William.
1876 Poynter, Sir Edward John, Bart.
1881 Rivière, Briton.
1895 Richmond, Sir Wm. Blake, K.C.B.
1869 Sant, James.
1897 Sargent, John Singer.
1877 Shaw, Richard Norman.
1906 Solomon, J. Solomon.
1887 Stone, Marcus.
1905 Swan, John MacAllan.
1888 Thornycroft, Wm. Hamo.
1895 Waterhouse, John Wm.
1903 Waterlow, Sir E. Albert.
1903 Webb, Sir Aston.
1893 Woods, Henry.
1907 Wyllie, William Lionel.
1878 Yeames, Wm. Frederick.

Honorary Retired Academician: 1853, William Powell Frith, C. V. O.

ASSOCIATES.

Bacon, John H. F.
Belcher, John.
Blomfield, Reginald.
Bramley, Frank.
Brangwyn, Frank.
Brown, J. A. Arnesby.
Clausen, George (R. A. elect).
Colton, William Robert.
Cope, Arthur Stockdale.
Cowper, F. Cadogan.
Crowe, Eyre.
Drury, E. A. B.
East, Alfred.
Farquharson, Joseph.
Forbes, Stanhope A.
Hacker, Arthur.
Hemy, Charles N.
Henry, George.
John, Wm. Goscombe.
La Thangue, Henry H.
North, John W.
Parsons, Alfred.
Pegram, Henry A.
Pomeroy, F. W.
Shannon, James J.
Short, Frank.
Sims, Charles.
Smythe, Lionel P.
Storey, George Adolphus.
Stott, Edward.
Strang, William.
Tuke, Henry S.

Review of Scientific Progress in 1908.

ARCHAEOLOGY.

CENTRAL ASIA has been the field of extensive exploration work during 1908. Many temples and cities have been found which were built by highly civilized races. Grunwedel and Le Coq, under the auspices of the German Government, explored Turfan and Lop-Nor in Chinese Turkestan, and returned with 200 cases of pottery, coins and other relics. Another explorer, Stein, visited the region south of Lop-Nor, where he found numerous manuscripts in Chinese, Sanscrit and an unknown Iranian tongue, besides documents with impressions of Roman seals of the third century A. D. Three hundred miles to the east, near Sa Chow, he discovered the remains of the Great China Wall, constructed by the Emperor Wu-li in the second century B. C., and followed it for 140 miles.

In Greece several new discoveries have been made, and work is being actively pushed on rebuilding some of the old temples. At Phigala the Greek Archaeological Society has nearly rebuilt a large temple; the doors are already in place and the raising of the columns begun. At Lindus a Danish expedition found about 600 stone inscriptions, and near the southern extremity of Rhodes a necropolis and two ancient temples of an unknown city.

The recent excavations for the foundation of the new building for the Ministry of Agriculture, Industry and Commerce in Rome brought to light blocks of tufa belonging to a wall built during the Servian Age. Architectural fragments of terra cotta and marble were found close by, and also three male torsos and part of an inscription in large letters, which was evidently from a public monument.

Work will begin early in 1909 on excavating the city of Memphis, Egypt. The Egyptian Research Account announces that it will cost $15,000 a year for fifteen years to excavate the temple site alone.

A party headed by W. R. Moorehead and Dr. C. Peabody were sent by the Phillips Academy, Andover, Mass., during May, 1908, to explore the Ozark Mountains, Arkansas. Traces were found that showed the mountains were at one time inhabited by a primitive race. Stone and bone implements of good workmanship were numerous, but the pottery was rare and crude.

The Sawtell Avenue Mound, the last of the mounds in Cleveland, O., has been removed. Its original dimensions were 63 feet north and south, 75 feet east and west, by 10 feet high. The mound was of red gravel and clay, the same as the surrounding soil, but no bones or other objects were found in the mound itself. Trenches about five feet deep were dug, and six skeletons were unearthed, besides copper beads and flint arrow points, which are now on exhibition at the Western Reserve Historical Society.

The Metropolitan Museum, of New York, has acquired many noteworthy additions. Mr. J. P. Morgan presented a series of fifteenth century tapestries from Burgundy, and the Salter estate eighteen paintings of various schools. Other accessions include a set of armor for man and horse of the seventeenth century, a bronze bust of Pope Innocent X., attributed to Alessando Algardi, and two large painted windows, probably made shortly after 1500, which illustrate the German school at the close of the mediaeval period.

ASTRONOMY.

A new comet was discovered by Mr. Morehouse, at Yerkes Observatory, Williams Bay, Wis., September 1, 1908. The notable feature about the comet was the brightness and the form of the tail, which changed from night to night, on some nights being very bright and extending 8 to 10 degrees from the head, and on others very faint. It approached the sun until December 25, when it was at perihelion, and at one time was within 100,000,000 miles of the earth. The comet will be visible to observers in the southern hemisphere during February, March and April, 1909.

The most favorable land view of the partial solar eclipse June 28, 1908, was in Florida, where for nearly four minutes the annular phase was visible over a pathway eighty-six miles wide. Peculiar distortions were noticed at the moon's limb, and, although the sun was almost at its least diameter, yet the moon was not sufficient to cover it.

Halley's comet, first observed by Halley in 1682, one of the most remarkable comets known to astronomers, is coming toward the earth on its regular visit once every seventy-five years. It is about 150 miles in diameter, and will not be visible to the naked eye until July or August, 1909. It is estimated that there is one chance in 286,000,000 of its striking the earth. As it approaches the sun metallic vapors of iron and magnesium are given off.

Mr. Mellotte, of the Greenwich Observatory, Greenwich, England, after many observations of an object near the planet Jupiter, confirmed the supposition held by many astronomers that Jupiter had eight satellites. The new satellite is not so bright as the others, but has been photographed at the Lick Observatory and by Dr. Wolff, of Heidelberg, Germany.

On August 20, 1908, members of the Department of Meridian Astrometry of the Carnegie Institute, in charge of Prof. L. Boss, of the Dudley Observatory, Albany, N. Y., sailed for the Argentine Republic to establish a branch observatory. The site chosen is at San Luis, 500 miles west of Buenos Ayres. The chief object of the observatory is to gather data for making a general catalogue of about 25,000 stars, with their positions and motions accurately computed. The department has already completed a catalogue of 6,188 stars, from the North to the South Pole, that can be seen without a telescope.

A great red spot on Jupiter, which evidently influences the other markings on the planet, has attracted the attention of astronomers. The results of recent observations seem to show that portions of the disturbed area are accelerated as they approach the red spot, and that at previous conjunctions the dark matter seemed to be passing around the south side of it.

Many tests have been made with the new telescope of the Carnegie Solar Observatory,

Mount Wilson, Cal. The telescope is mounted on the top of a steel tower 65 feet high, and has mirrors that receive the rays of the sun and reflect them to an object glass 12 inches in diameter. The glass has a focal length of 60 feet, and forms an image of the sun 6½ inches in diameter. In connection with the mirrors is a spectroscope 30 feet long for examining any peculiar disturbances in the sun, as sun spots and flames near its edge.

Harvard University completed the mounting of a five-foot reflecting telescope, one of the largest in the world, purchased by the estate of A. A. Common. It has been assigned to photometric work, and will be able to show stars of the seventeenth and eighteenth magnitude.

CHEMISTRY.

By the Food and Drug Act many companies were stopped from selling their products under the names given to them. Flour made from wheat containing 15 per cent. of durum wheat and branded as manufactured from the finest hard spring wheat was declared to be misbranded. A product labelled Canadian Rye Whiskey, found on examination to consist of practically neutral spirits artificially colored in imitation of aged whiskey, was held to be adulterated and misbranded.

The German law forbids the importation of meat preserved with boric acid or its salts.

Considerable anxiety was felt by the chemical trade over the threatened exhaustion of the nitrate beds in Chile if the present annual exportation of 2,000,000 tons continued. New beds have been recently discovered in the provinces of Antofagasta and Atacama, with estimated deposits of 1,500,000,000 tons, which with the present supply makes a total of 1,600,000,000 tons available. Assuming the world's consumption will increase to 5,000,000 tons per annum, there will be enough to last for over 300 years.

The metal tungsten has proved to be particularly well adapted for filaments in incandescent lamps. A 40-watt tungsten lamp, compared to other lamps, saves its first cost four times over, and large sizes even more. One million American-made tungsten lamps are in use, and nearly 75,000 are manufactured every day.

A new method for making pure hydrogen, devised by Mauricheau-Beaupre, of Paris, France, depends upon the decomposition of water by especially prepared aluminum. To aluminum filings are added mercuric chloride and potassium cyanide, which produces great heat. If the mixture is treated with water in such a way as to keep it about 70 degrees, a steady evolution of pure hydrogen takes place. This is a simple method of preparing hydrogen for balloons.

Prof. K. Onnes, of Leiden, Germany, in his laboratory, on July 10, 1908, made liquid helium, which boils at 4.3 degrees absolute temperature.

F. Bordas, a French chemist, has succeeded in changing the color of sapphires so they pass successively through the stages of red, violet, blue, green and yellow. A bluish sapphire exposed to radium bromide of activity 1,800,000 goes through the series of changes from blue to yellow, while a red stone similarly exposed goes through the complete series.

Professor Thorpe, of England, after working two years extracting radium from a quantity of Joachimstahl pitchblende to determine its atomic weight, found it to be 226.8, which is very close to that previously determined by Madame Curie of 226.18.

A new instrument—the Shore Schleroscope—for comparing the hardness of different materials—will have a wide field of usefulness. The instrument is very simple, consisting of a pointed steel hammer that falls on the material to be tested, and the rebound of the hammer is measured. According to the readings of the scale on the side, the hardness of gold to glass is as 14 to 130.

H. Henriet claims that the ozone in the air is formed by the action of the ultra-violet rays from the sun upon oxygen in the higher regions of the atmosphere. He further claims carbon dioxide has its sole origin in combustion on the earth and its varying quantities are due entirely to atmospheric causes.

The following are a few of the chemicals manufactured in the United States by the aid of electricity: Sodium, caustic soda, hydrochloric acid, potassium chlorate and bromine.

GEOLOGY.

Copper is now being extensively mined on the Kasaan Peninsula, in the southeastern part of Alaska. The peninsula is about 18 miles long, 3 to 6 miles wide, and has an area of 60 square miles. The average contents per ton of ore mined is 48 pounds of copper, .035 ounces of gold and .27 ounces of silver, having a total value of $10 a ton. It is estimated that over 8,000,000 pounds of copper were shipped away during 1908.

The recent experiments of the coal testing plant of the United States Geological Survey at St. Louis, Mo., have added a new interest to lignite. The experiments have shown that a gas of higher quality can be obtained from lignite than from bituminous coal, and one ton of lignite used in a gas producer plant will yield as much power as the best Pennsylvania or West Virginia bituminous coals burned under a boiler. Brown lignite, on which te ts were made, is found in North Dakota, Texas and other States west of the Mississippi River.

The manufacture of cement has had a wonderful growth, and cement mills are superseding those of iron and steel in Lehigh and Northampton Counties, Pennsylvania. An enormous belt of cement material extends through these counties, making the manufacture of cement a very profitable industry.

From the results of observations by Dr. J. Melne, of England, on earthquakes, their strength and direction are better understood. He noted that small earthquakes only have a duration of a few seconds near the origin, and at places 50 to 100 miles away they may not be even recordable. With large earthquakes this loss of strength during transmission is not appreciable, and the duration near the antipodes may be as great as near the origin.

The maximum is about 90 degrees from the origin. He also noted that large earthquakes travel furthest in a certain direction. Out of 79 with well-known origins south of the Caucasus Mountains, north of India, and to the east and south of Japan, they have travelled further to the west than to the east, and only a small percentage have gone south across the equator.

A paper read before the Royal Society of London by R. M. Deeley proves that the movements of glaciers are such as would result if ice obeyed the laws of viscous flow.

The relation of the wind to the topography of coastal drift sands has been thoroughly investigated by P. O. Seffu, of Mexico City, Mexico. He calls attention to the sand dunes in Brittany, that have moved on an average 27 feet a year for the past 200 years, and to those at Norfolk, England, facing the North Sea, 150 feet to 180 feet a year.

On the island of Cebu, one of the Philippine Islands, there have recently been found indications of the presence of several million tons of coal. The lack of suitable timber to support a weak roof, and the high inclination of the coal beds, offer difficulties which may prevent it from being profitably mined.

ENGINEERING.

Steam turbines for electric railway and lighting purposes are rapidly replacing reciprocating engines. A large number of direct connected turbines and dynamos have been installed in the past year, and a 6,000 K. W. unit is not an uncommon size. One of 12,000 h. p. has been shipped to the central electric light station at Buenos Ayres, Argentine Republic, by Signor Tosi, of Legnano, Italy. Turbines are sometimes used for power purposes in preference to engines. A mammoth 24,000 h. p. turbine is being built at the Mannheim works of Brown, Boveri & Co. for the Krupp steel plant at Rheinhausen.

Reinforced concrete is coming into use more and more for large engineering undertakings. Thousands of tons of concrete will be required in building the new water system for New York. The Olive Bridge Dam (of the Ashokan Reservoir, the main source of the supply) will be a mass of concrete 240 feet high, 25 feet at the top, 190 feet at the base and 1,000 feet long, and the Catskill Aqueduct, extending from the reservoir to New York, a distance of 80 miles, will also be of concrete, reinforced with steel rods.

The railroad from Miami to Key West, belonging to the Florida East Coast Railroad, is nearly completed. The railroad extends from key to key, and in one place over two miles of reinforced concrete viaduct was necessary. The tracks average thirty feet above the water, and the viaducts are strong enough to resist any storm that might arise.

Cars for railroads run by gasoline have been experimented on, and for certain localities have proved to be very successful. At the front of the car is the gasoline engine, connected to a dynamo, which generates electricity for the motors on the trucks. Storage batteries assist the dynamos when an extra heavy load is being carried. In some cars the dynamos and motors are omitted, the engine being geared to the wheels.

At Gary, Ind., the new city built by the United States Steel Corporation, five large gas engines have been erected at the steel works. The engines are of the horizontal, twin cylinder, four-cycle type, and at 75 revolutions per minute develop 3,000 brake horse power.

Several steel rolling mills are now driven by electricity. The 30-inch plate mill of the Illinois Steel Company is driven by two 2,000 h. p. direct-current shunt-wound motors mounted on a common shaft. The speed varies from zero to 150 revolutions per minute and the mill can be reversed in four to six seconds.

Steel belts, instead of leather and cotton, have been successfully tried in Germany for driving machinery in shops and power houses. The advantages claimed for them are smaller pulleys, no adjusting after once set up, and true running.

The Fish Street Station of the Chicago Edison Company has four 7,000 h. p. and six 11,500 h. p. Curtis turbines, making a total of nearly 100,000 h. p. This is one of the largest power stations in the world.

Geographical Research in 1908.

AFRICA.

A large tract of 3,500 square miles of unexplored country in Southern Nigeria has been opened up and brought under Government control. Lieutenant E. A. Steel, of the Royal Artillery, England, has written a comprehensive and exhaustive report on the country and the inhabitants, having spent four years' travelling through parts where no white man had ever been before.

The perplexing question of the relationship between the Hottentots and the Bushmen has again been discussed and a satisfactory conclusion appears to be reached. It is now believed that both were of one stock, which had its origin in Central Africa, from where they migrated at long intervals to their present abode south of Zambesi. The Bushmen arrived first and were followed several years after by the Hottentots. In the meantime the latter had advanced from the hunter to the pastoral stage, and perhaps by the infusion of Hamitic blood may be attributed their increased stature and loss of alertness that so distinguished the original Bushmen.

Sir Harry Johnston gives the credit of the discovery of the Ubangi River to Mr. Greenfell, who also explored the Falls of Mobangi, between Zanzo and Mokoangai.

Attempts made to establish the cattle industry in the interior have met with very poor results. Three trading companies started agencies at Nkama on the Nkisi hills. None of them were successful, as a large percentage of the cattle died before they were sent to Stanley Pool or Noki. It was difficult to account for the great mortality among them. The coarse grass was unsuitable; but the chief cause was probably due to the tsetse fly.

GEOGRAPHICAL RESEARCH IN 1908—*Continued.*

Railroad construction in Africa is rapidly progressing. Jebba has been made an important centre, and roads are being built north and south. At the same time, the High Commission of Northern Nigeria is building a road from Baro, on the Nigel, to Zaria and Kano. When completed the system will be over 800 miles long.

The Trans-Saharan postal service is nearing completion, and will be in operation by May or June, 1909, or even before. A telegraph service will doubtless be extended across the desert in the near future.

A thorough survey and report have been compiled by Major A. F. Andrade on the rich deposits of sulphate of copper in the Mbembe Valley. He mentions that in some places there are thick veins of almost pure malachite. The last United States Consular Report also refers to the above deposits and confirms Major Andrade's statements.

In the past year the people of Uganda excelled all others in Africa in the cultivation of cotton and the growing of rubber trees.

A representative from Liberia visited the United States with the hope of inducing many of the negroes to return. The following advantages of the country were given, viz.: A popular form of government, good schools and a pleasant and healthy climate.

The Congo States, long dominated by King Leopold, of Belgium, have passed out of his control. The many atrocities that have been committed in the past to secure rubber and ivory from the natives will be stopped.

ASIA.

Parties under Dr. Kaznakoff and Captain Kosloff examined the western shore of Oring Nor, and determined, astronomically, the geographical latitude of the point where the Yellow River flows out of Oring Nor. They also explored Eastern Thibet and Kam, making a special study of the N'golohs and the rovings of the principal N'goloh caravan. The N'golohs numbe. over 50,000 families, divided into tribes governed by independent chieftains, but all important matters are referred to a council of seven elected from among their number.

Great value is attached to the report of Professor Obrucheff on his explorations in the mountains of Chinese Dzemgaria. He explored many ranges and has furnished a detailed geological account of their structure.

An interesting trip was made by Captain Toussaint, in the German gunboat Vaterland, on the Yangtse River, above the middle rapids, almost to the foot of the Thibetan Highlands. A large number of soundings were made, so accurate maps could be drawn, to assist steamers in navigating the river.

Several explorers have returned from different parts of Thibet, and from their reports a good knowledge has been obtained on an almost unknown country. Dr. Sven Hedin suffered not only from cold and hunger, but also from treacherous wandering tribes, from whom he was obliged to disguise his identity. He explored chiefly the mountains bounding Brahmaputra Valley, which he crossed several times, once by way of the Samyela Pass, at an altitude of 18,000 feet. The Chino-Thibetan frontier was explored by M. Bacot, who reported great restlessness on the part of the tribes along the borders. One of the tribes, the Lamas, showed great ferocity, not only against the Chinese but also the French missionaries, four of whom they murdered. The experiences of R. F. Johnston were different from either Hedin or Bacot. He visited the principalities in Eastern Thibet and followed the Su-ham railroad, which was completed in 1908. Everywhere he was treated cordially and courteously, even in the town of Liang Shan, where the late Mrs. Bishop was mobbed.

Two prominent scientists, Doctors Zurick and Treub, noted marvellous growths of new flora at Krakatan, on the Straits of Sunda. During the volcanic eruption of 1883 every vestige of plant life was destroyed. At the present time, the southeastern side from shore to summit is covered with green plants and shrubs, of which over 130 different specimens have been collected.

M. Cordier explored the land of the Lolos and has written a complete description of their origin, language and mode of living. Captain D'Ollene, on another expedition, found several Lolos books, and also Miaotse manuscripts with a key to their interpretation. A Chinese professor of the University of Yumian-sen, to whom they were shown, recognized them as a cursive form of Chinese characters of about 300 B. C.

EUROPE.

Remarkable progress has been made by the province of Luneburger Heide, Germany, in cattle raising. Only a few years ago the country was an uninterrupted expanse of heath, but, with the building of a railroad and the discovery of the Kieselgue beds, new life has been awakened in the people.

Wonderful reports of vineyard culture come from the section of Lower Languedoc, from Aude to the Rhone River. In the department of Herault vines now cover 470,000 acres, from which during the past year 310,000,000 gallons of wine were made.

Improvements to the mouth of the Danube River at Sulina have made the river one of the busiest in Europe, besides developing Sulina into a thriving town.

The Royal Geographical Society of England has published a series of articles entitled, "The Story of London Maps."

The topography of Northwestern Greece has been made a special study by Rev. C. M. Church and Professor J. S. Myers.

The British Museum will celebrate the 150th anniversary of its foundation in 1909.

Reports on two expeditions to Iceland confirm the information that Iceland is a home of refinement and art, with an excellent educational system. Professor Herman writes about the high moral standing and the cleanliness of the people.

The Tenth International Geographical Congress will convene in Rome in 1911.

Laws have been passed in Germany that municipal authorities should have powers to readjust and rearrange plots of land belonging to private individuals. This has led to the making of wider streets and more open spaces in many of the large cities, as Frankfort, Berlin, etc.

The improvements to the port of Havre, France, undertaken in 1896, were completed in 1908. Their total cost, including the breakwater and the piers, was $11,500,000.

Forestry work, while comparatively new in America, has been studied for years in Europe. In Switzerland it is so successful in protecting the fertile valleys from floods that the methods adopted by the Government have a high reputation, and the schools where they are taught are attended by students from all over the world.

AMERICA.

The United States Geological Survey has completed an investigation of the water in the Great Lakes. Three million three hundred and fifty thousand pounds of dissolved minerals pass out of Lake Ontario into the St. Lawrence River and then into the Atlantic Ocean every year. Of this amount 441,000 pounds comes from Lake Superior, 666,000 from Lake Michigan, 913,000 from Lake Huron, 840,000 from Lake Erie and 490,000 from Lake Ontario.

Dr. L. A. Bauer presented to the National Academy of Science the results of the Magnetic Survey of the United States. Great attention has been paid to the elimination of instrumental errors and the multiplication of stations, thus increasing the accuracy of the work.

Recent borings and soundings in Niagara River, above and below the falls, revealed the fact that immediately below the falls is a basin 192 feet deep, and further down, at the Cantilever Bridge, it is only 86 feet.

The Canadian Government is proceeding with the survey of the route of the Georgian Bay Canal. The Government contemplates building a ship canal 22 feet deep from Georgian Bay to Montreal, a distance of 440 miles. This undertaking in some respects even surpasses the Panama Canal, and will bring Montreal into prominence as a shipping port. An important feature of the Georgian Canal is the trémendous water-power that can be developed all along the route. The completion of the canal will result in the possible development of at least 1,000,000 horse-power. The estimated cost of the canal is $100,000,000.

The Geographical Board of Canada has named the canyon below the Grand Falls of Hamilton River McLean's Canyon, in honor of John McLean, one of the early officers of the Hudson Bay Company, who discovered the falls and canyon in 1839.

Work is now in progress on the construction of a telegraphic line through the western part of the State of Matto Grosso, Brazil.

The Alberta Irrigation project of the Canadian Pacific Railway is one of the largest ever undertaken in America. It consists in irrigating about 1,400,000 acres of land in Southern Alberta, Canada, directly east of the Bow River. The surveys that have been made indicate that about 51 miles of main canals and 2,850 miles of secondary canals and ditches will have to be built, necessitating the removal of 27,750,000 cubic yards of material. The cost will be about $8,000,000.

The Salt River project in Salt River Valley, Arizona, is another large irrigation undertaking. Over 180,000 acres will be served and it will develop land that heretofore has been worthless. The project is 67 per cent. completed.

Work on the Panama Canal has progressed favorably during 1908. The Panama Railroad, which, owing to its poor construction, was of little use in carrying freight, has been rebuilt and the sanitary conditions of the camps improved. The men employed are of a better class than at first, and, by adopting a systematic organization, more work is being done than ever before.

On February 26, 1908, President Roosevelt transmitted to Congress a preliminary report of the Inland Waterways Commission which he appointed in 1907. The report outlined a statement of principles and made several recommendations in regard to improving inland navigation.

POLAR RESEARCH.

A party of whalers came across McClure's ship, the Investigator, which was abandoned by him in the Winter of 1853 when icebound on the north side of Banks' Land. The ship is reported to be in a remarkably well preserved state.

Numerous experiments have been made to determine the direction of the polar currents, by casting casks adrift at various latitudes.

Mr. Shackleton's Antarctic Expedition met with considerable difficulty endeavoring to find a place to land. Their ship, the Nimrod, was blown out to sea in a terrific blizzard, and the party suffered many hardships. Winter quarters were finally established at Cape Royds, near Mt. Erebus, where the Nimrod left the party, but will return in the Spring of 1909.

Commander Peary sent a wireless telegram from Sidney, Cape Breton, on July 17, 1908. He intends proceeding to Smith Sound, and will make his Winter quarters at Grant Land. He has with him special sounding apparatus, and will endeavor to obtain a line of soundings from Grant Land to the Pole. He expects to be gone two years, and is in hopes this time of reaching the North Pole.

The Royal Scottish Geographical Society, by the approval of the King of England, has conferred a royal medal on the Prince of Monaco for his scientific explorations in the Polar regions. His last trip to Prince Charles-foreland, and the account of it by W. S. Bruce, as well as the carefully detailed map he published of certain portions of the Arctic country, with the shapes and positions of the glaciers and hills, are valuable additions to Arctic literature.

Dr. Charcot will sail early in 1909 from Havre, France, to explore the Antarctic regions. His ship, named the "Pourquoi Pas," is 141 feet long by 29 feet wide, and will carry 250 tons of coal and 100 tons of supplies. He intends to explore Alexander Land, and will not return before 1911.

Electrical Progress in 1908.

PROGRESS in electrical lines as in all others during the first half of 1908 was retarded by the hold-over of the depression that marked the close of 1907, and its influence was felt throughout the year. At the time of going to press it is impossible to state accurately the total of electrical earnings for the year in all fields, but judging by previous years, and allowing for the depression, it seems safe to say it reached $1,500,000,000, including the sale of machinery and apparatus of all kinds and the revenue from street railways, lighting, telephone, telegraphs and cables, &c. The sale of current suffered least, the increase of business and the building of central stations comparing favorably with that of the previous year. Electric exports were only about 72 per cent. of what they were in 1907, based on the first nine months of the two years. The last three months of the year saw some improvement. One good effect of the lessened business done on account of the depression was more time for experimental work and scientific research, and the year was notable in the amount of this work done in all lines.

In the central stations' desire to increase the sale of current much was done to promote the use of electrical household utilities. Electrically heated contrivances, and notably flat irons, were more than ever used. There is not much cooking by electricity yet, but an evidence that some of the obviously practical appliances will be made use of increasingly from now on. Heating by electricity, although greatly improved in the last fifteen years, has not reached the point where it would be adopted if expense was a consideration. At present it costs many times as much as steam heat and is justified only for intermittent and temporary heating or for convenience, safety or other consideration, as in electric cars. So much can be done by electricity that sufficiently cheap current is all that determines how extensively it is used. Near water powers considerable heating is done by electricity, although that is one of its least economical applications. The use of electricity in construction work for operating contractors' machinery in place of the usual portable steam boiler outfit is becoming common in the larger cities, notably New York. Its greater convenience makes it a real economy where local electric companies are in position to supply the current at reasonable rates.

The International Conference on Electrical Units and Standards held in London last Fall proposed international standards for the ohm, ampere, volt and watt. It is highly desirable that all countries agree on these recommendations, so that the slight disparity now existing between their standards may be eliminated. Another proposal in line with these standards is one from France for an international standard of candle power.

TELEGRAPHY AND TELEPHONY.

Increase in numbers of wireless telegraph stations was one of the most marked features of electrical progress in 1908, notably where there were not already wire telegraphs because of prohibitive expense of line construction. In Canada, for example, the Government has been improving the telephone systems and installing wireless telegraph systems, so that soon all the principal parts will have some means of communication. Wireless apparatus was installed at Nome and Fort Gilbert, Alaska, last year by the United States army signal officers. The Navy Department decided to construct a powerful long distance wireless station at Washington with a mast 350 to 400 feet high, having a range of 3,000 miles. Two wireless ship equipments with a radius of 1,000 miles are also to be ordered. Strange as it may seem, the most generally known systems of wireless telegraphy are not those used by the United States Government. The inventor, an American, Shoemaker by name, has equipped over forty land stations and over thirty war vessels with his system.

Wireless communication was established between San Francisco and Hawaii, a distance of over 2,000 miles. A movement was also started to connect nearly all the groups of islands in the South Pacific by systems of wireless telegraphs. A distance of 2,900 miles was made in one wireless transmission reported from the Pacific Coast.

A De Forest wireless telegraph system established on the Caribbean coast is operated by the United Fruit Company and gives service to Central America. The latest use of the Eiffel Tower in Paris is as a mast for wireless telegraph antennae. The station being erected here will be so powerful that it is hoped to get direct communication with New York. The wireless telegraph system on the Great Lakes, inaugurated in 1907, connecting the largest lake ports, was an important factor in last season's shipping, giving control almost as complete as could be had of goods handled by rail.

Although the Glace Bay (Nova Scotia) Marconi wireless telegraph station, which was only put into experimental operation a little over a year ago, is declared to be very successful and averaging between 5,000 and 6,000 words daily, the promise of continuous and cheap communication between Great Britain and Canada does not appear to have been made good, since the British and Canadian governments are about to lay a cable from Ireland to Nova Scotia, a link in the British Empire plan for a "red line around the world." The rate to the public is to be fivepence (10 cents) per word instead of the present shilling (25 cents) rate. A cable is projected from Germany to Brazil by the Deutsch-Atlantische Telegraphen-Gesellschaft, via Teneriffe, with branches to Liberia and the German colonies on the west coast of Africa. Some additional short cables have been laid on the east and west coasts of Africa.

Evidently the limit is about reached in perfecting the telephone (except the wireless). Although more are working on it than ever, little that is new has been brought out for two years. A new party line telephone, known as the harmonic telephone, connects four to eight parties on the same circuit, and any one may be called selectively. A new loud-speaking instrument capable of amplifying ordinary sounds is intended principally to supply music to subscribers. The formation of a company to handle long-distance telephone and telegraph business over the wires of the independent telephone companies of the United States was definitely decided upon. The same wires will be used for both services. This was probably the biggest event of the year in the independent telephone field. Several local independent telephones were organized and much work was done on the Pacific coast. The automatic and semi-automatic systems operated by many of these companies are gaining in popularity. The Bell Company now sells its instruments so that any one can buy and install them.

The American Railway Association has approved the use of the telephone in place of the telegraph for the operation of railroad trains, asserting that it is as safe and more expeditious than the telegraph. This is regarded as an important announcement which will mean considerable business to the makers of instruments, and the indorsement of so conservative a body is equivalent to an assurance that the substitution will be made. The Chicago, Milwaukee and St. Paul Railroad experimented with a telephone train despatching system in place of the old telegraph. It was also reported that telephones will be used to transact the railway business of the Missouri Pacific Railway with the exception of train orders.

Submarine telephone cables were recently introduced in Germany. One connects that country with Denmark, Fehmarn and Holland and is twelve miles long, to say nothing of the remainder of its circuit. The cable is insulated with paper and an air space and finally covered with two waterproof, seamless lead coatings and iron wire, jute and bituminous compound.

De Forest and Poulsen have made some headway in the matter of wireless telephony. The former had an opportunity to put some apparatus to test on vessels in the United States Navy, which are stated to have given success. According to a despatch from Rome, Prof. Maiorana has succeeded in tests of wireless telephony between Rome and Magdalena Island, Sardinia, 250 miles.

ELECTRIC LIGHTING.

Last year this field saw not so much that was new as more common use of the newer forms of lamps and improvements in the methods of manufacturing them. Tungsten lamps are now regularly on the market and are being extensively advertised. While they cost more than carbon filament lamps, they are of much higher efficiency and longer life and have a color more nearly that of sunlight. The recent reductions in their price will have much to do with hastening their more extended use. The 25-watt tungsten lamp was the latest improvement in lamps of its character, and came out toward the end of the year. Tungsten and tantalum lamps were both more used than before, and it is evident that those two forms at least among all the newer metallic filament lamps brought out in the last two years are destined to extensive adoption. A former difficulty with the metallic filament lamps was their inability to burn in any position. The latest improvements in nearly all cases have removed this objection.

Metallic filament lamps are much more used abroad than in this country—roughly ten times more, and they seem to be gaining steadily in popularity.

The flaming arc light is also more in evidence abroad, particularly in Germany, where it originated. Unquestionably it has a field as an advertising means. It has a striking color, very intense brilliance and is remarkably efficient. It is practically limited, however, to out-of-doors illumination, and even for street lighting has its faults. Most of its light is thrown downward, making close spacing necessary for uniform distribution. The luminous arc lamps of the magnetite and titanium forms are superior for street lighting on account of their better lateral distribution. They also have faults, but these will probably be overcome when they receive the attention they deserve because of their low current consumption relative to the light given.

ELECTRO-CHEMISTRY AND ELECTRO-METALLURGY.

In 1908 perhaps the most measurable progress was made in electro-chemistry, a field the possibilities of which cannot yet begin to be estimated, so wide is its scope. Electro-chemical industries are growing more numerous every year, notable among them being those producing compounds of nitrogen used for fertilizer and in various arts, phosphorus, carbon and silicon products, &c.

An event was the announcement of Sherard Cowper-Coles's centrifugal process for the direct electrolytic production of copper tubes, sheets and wire. In an industry of such magnitude as that of the refining of copper by electrolysis, producing over 400,000 tons annually, this process will doubtless mean much, as it is claimed to overcome many of the former difficulties. The cathode is revolved during the deposition of the copper, which has the effect of agitating the electrolyte, rubbing down each particle of copper as deposited, preventing foreign matter and air bubbles from being occluded, and insuring an even deposition. The plates can be rolled and the tubes and wire drawn. Plates are formed around large drums, tubes on smaller mandrels and wire as a spiral on a large drum, being formed to circular cross section by drawing through dies as it is uncoiled from the drum. With the changing over of the equipment of the United States mint at San Francisco all of the Government's plants for refining gold, silver and copper are now operating on the electrolytic process, it having been found the cheapest and the one giving the purest metal for coins. A new electrolytic process for treating the tailings from silver mines operating under the Baker-Burwell patents was satisfactorily tested at Elkhorn, Mont., and a 100-ton plant is now being built in which it will be employed.

The electric furnace in iron and steel work commanded much attention last year. The manufacture of ferro alloys by its use is becoming very important. Near water powers, where current can be generated cheaply, the electric furnace is especially attractive for metallurgical work. It was predicted by The Iron Age that before many years the "baby" Bessemer furnace will be completely overshadowed by the electric furnace in the steel foundry. As compared with all other means it most nearly perfectly controls the chemical composition of the steel produced. A new electric furnace invented by Paul Girod was announced, which differs from older of the inventor's designs in being not simply a resistance furnace, but a combined arc and resistance heating type. It is intended for making high grade steels.

The Patent Office is something of an indication of the trend of the times. There were granted last year about 280 patents on electro-chemical subjects and over forty on electric furnaces in the United States alone.

ELECTRIC RAILWAYS.

Electrification of steam roads was the most conspicuous work done in electric traction last year. It will naturally be very gradual if ever complete. Branches for local service will come first, and eventually these may merge into a single continuous system. Difficulties in operating long-distance electric trains no longer exist, and it is largely a matter of the expense of making a change that now controls the situation. Statistics show a much lower cost of operating for electric lines than for steam lines per car mile. The Pennsylvania Railroad awarded the contract for the electrification of its New York and New Jersey terminals. It will amount to at least $5,000,000, and will include 100 locomotives. The first electrified section will be from Harrison, N. J., to Jamaica, L. I., including the tunnels under the rivers. The locomotives used will be of a new type having seven-feet driving wheels, and will be the most powerful ever constructed. One already tested made over ninety miles an hour and promises 120. To operate the system 250,000 horse-power will be required. The Illinois Central Railroad voted to proceed with the electrification of its Chicago terminal. The electrification of the Erie Railroad is also under consideration. The New York Central Railroad increased its equipment by the purchase of twelve more electric locomotives. The New York, New Haven and Hartford Railroad also extended its electric service, installing additional single phase equipment, indicating that the original equipment has fulfilled expectations. The New Canaan branch is the latest to be electrified by this system, but it had been operated on direct current for the previous seven years. A pressure of 11,000 volts is used and the trolley wire is an overhead single catenary line instead of a double catenary as used on the main line. In Italy 1,000 miles of steam railroad lines are now in process of conversion to electrical operation with hydro-electric power. The country has water-power resources for twenty times the present requirements. Tests in Sweden were completed satisfactorily which will result probably in the electrification of the entire State railroad system. Hydro-electric plants will furnish the power. The electric operation of all steam trains in Switzerland is now under consideration, and extensive investigations and reports have been made by experts giving recommendations as to the carrying out of the project.

A feature of the year was the headway made by the single-phase system, which is advocated very strongly because of its economy. Wherever applied to interurban work it seems to have fulfilled requirements very satisfactorily. Single-phase locomotives were installed last year to operate trains through the St. Clair tunnel of the Grand Trunk Railway, replacing steam locomotives. It is said to be the heaviest railway service handled by electricity in the world. The Great Northern Railway's adoption of three-phase electric locomotives was of especial interest, since it was the first time in this country. Three-phase systems have given satisfaction abroad, but they have been slower of adoption in this country. The simpler overhead work for the other two systems has done much to hold back the introduction of the three-phase system. The Windsor, Essex and Lake Shore Rapid Railway Company was the first in Canada to adopt single-phase equipment. It is reported to be giving splendid success. The Spokane and Inland Empire Electric Railroad, a single-phase system located in Washington and Idaho, is 225 miles long and is in all respects the equivalent of a steam road, handling freight as well as passengers. Last year the total earnings were over a million, and more than one and one-half million was expended in improvements and extensions, including a power plant with two 5,000-horse-power units.

Nearly all large cities made some extensions to their lines during the year or added new equipment in power plants or rolling stock. This, in spite of the times, indicates what is to be expected—that during depressions street railways are likely to suffer as little as any industry. In the tunnels of the Hudson and Manhattan Railroad under the Hudson River, opened last year, is the latest in block signalling and interlocking and automatic train stopping. It is much the same system as that used on the Boston Elevated Railroad and in the New York Subway, but improved to the point of even greater safety. A mono-rail road was planned by the Interborough Rapid Transit Company of New York to be in operation this Spring. The Northwestern Elevated Railway of Chicago opened a new branch last year.

POWER AND POWER TRANSMISSION.

With regard to prime movers the situation remains about the same, though, perhaps, the lines are drawn more clearly between the three principal types, steam engines, steam turbines and gas engines. The exact advantages and disadvantages are better defined, and each still has its special place. Turbines are especially good for electrical work because they have a large overload capacity on good efficiency, good speed regulation, small space, &c., but they are not equal to either steam or gas reciprocating engines in thermal efficiency or economy. The gas engine has the honors in that direction, and is growing more popular each year. Producer gas plants are being applied quite extensively now in electric work. One of the pioneer installations is that of an interurban Wisconsin line which compares favorably with all other forms of artificial power central stations. Nothing yet available is as economical as water-power.

News of large hydro-electric developments came from all parts of the world. The Great Western Power Company, California, finished an enormous plant to have 80,000 kilowatts under one roof. The water wheels and generators are the largest of their types. The company owns water rights in Northern California representing 420,000 horse-power and will develop them as rapidly as a demand for current arises. It was estimated that the available water-power of the United States, if proper water storage was provided, would supply all present requirements. Measures were taken in many European countries to further the development of their water-powers. An elaborate hydro-electric plant was started in Simla, British India, a vicinity where large water-powers are available. One of the largest hydro-electric stations in South America was completed on the Piabanha River, Brazil. Its present capacity is 15,000 horse-power and its ultimate capacity will be 50,000 horse-power. A tidal power plant was reported as to be undertaken at Cuxhaven near the mouth of the Elbe in Germany to supply the local and nearby towns with electric light and power. Its capacity is to be 14,000 horse-power.

The first section of the 60,000-volt transmission line, twenty-eight miles long, supplying Niagara current (Ontario Power Company) to the Buffalo, Lockport and Rochester Railway, was built last year. The suspended insulator has grown in favor during the past year as a partial solution of some of the difficulties attending high voltage transmission lines. It has the advantage of large vertical space on the poles, so that towers alone seem suitable for supporting them.

Society of Tammany, or Columbian Order.

Grand Sachem—Daniel F. Cohalan. *Sachems*—Louis F. Haffen, Thomas F. McAvoy, Thomas E. Rush, John J. Scannell, Charles F. Murphy, Julius Harburger, John F. Ahern, Asa Bird Gardiner, George W. Plunkitt, Timothy D. Sullivan, John Fox, William Dalton *Secretary*—Thomas F. Smith. *Treasurer*—Joseph P. Day. *Sagamore*—Bryan P. Henry. *Wiskinkie*—John A. Boyle.

This organization was formed in 1789, being the effect of a popular movement in New York having primarily in view a counterweight to the so-called "aristocratic" Society of the Cincinnati. It was essentially anti-Federalist or democratic in its character, and its chief founder was William Mooney, an upholsterer and a native-born American of Irish extraction. It took its first title from a noted ancient, wise and friendly chief of the Delaware tribe of Indians, named Tammany, who had, for the want of a better subject, been canonized by the soldiers of the Revolution as the American patron saint. The first meeting was held May 12, 1789. The act of incorporation was passed in 1805. The Grand Sachem and thirteen Sachems were designed to typify the President and the Governors of the thirteen original States. William Mooney was the first Grand Sachem. The Society is nominally a charitable and social organization, and is distinct from the General Committee of the Tammany Democracy, which is a political organization, and cannot use Tammany Hall without the consent of the Society.

Military Order of Foreign Wars.

THE Military Order of Foreign Wars of the United States was instituted in the City of New York December 27, 1894, by veterans and descendants of veterans of one or more of the five foreign wars which the United States had been engaged in, to wit: The War of the Revolution, the War with Tripoli, the War of 1812, the Mexican War, and the War with Spain, "to perpetuate the names and memory of brave and loyal men who took part in establishing and maintaining the principles of the Government" in said wars, and "to preserve records and documents relating to said wars, and to celebrate the anniversaries of historic events connected therewith." Since the establishment of the order the United States has fought its fifth foreign war. By an amendment to the constitution all American officers who participated in the War with Spain, or any future foreign campaign recognized by the United States Government as "war," are rendered eligible to membership as veteran companions.

Members are entitled "companions," and are either "veteran companions" or "hereditary companions." The former are commissioned officers of the army, navy, or marine corps of the United States who participated in any of the foreign wars of the United States. The latter are direct lineal descendants, in the male line only, of commissioned officers who served honorably in any of the said wars. Commanderies may be established in each of the States, and State commanderies now exist in the States of New York, Pennsylvania, Connecticut, Illinois, California, Massachusetts, Maryland, Ohio, Missouri, Vermont, Virginia, Rhode Island, Louisiana, Indiana, Wisconsin, Michigan, Texas, Georgia, Colorado, New Jersey, and the District of Columbia.

The National Commandery was instituted March 11, 1896, by the officers of the New York, Pennsylvania, and Connecticut commanderies. The following are the officers of the National Commandery: *Commander-General*—Major-Gen. Alexander S. Webb, U. S. A. *Secretary-General*—James H. Morgan, New York. *Treasurer-General*—Col. Oliver C. Bosbyshell. *Registrar-General*—Rev. Henry N. Wayne. *Judge-Advocate-General*—Frank Montgomery Avery. Present membership, over 1,800 companions. There are Vice-Commanders-General representing each State commandery.

Regular U. S. Army and Navy Union.

A PATRIOTIC, fraternal, and beneficial organization, chartered under act of Congress, for soldiers' and sailors' rights and benefits.

National Commander—James B. Morton, Washington, D. C. *National Senior Vice-Commander*—James P. Lockwood, Chicago, Ill. *National Junior Vice-Commander*—Dr. John H. Grant, Buffalo, N. Y. *Adjutant-General*—Michael J. Hackett, headquarters, 4 Warder Street, N. W., Washington, D. C. Membership is confined to regulars of the United States Army, Navy, or Marine Corps, whether discharged, retired, or in the service.

Society of Veterans of Indian Wars

OF THE UNITED STATES.

Commander—Brig.-Gen. Judson D. Bingham, U. S. A., retired, *Historian*—Brig.-Gen. Charles King, U. S. A. *Assistant Recorder*—Major G. A. Bingham, U. S. A., Philadelphia, Pa. This society was instituted by officers of the United States Army at Philadelphia, April 23, 1896.

The objects are "to perpetuate the faithful services, heroism, and privations of the officers and soldiers of the Army of the United States of America, as well as of the auxiliary forces of the several States of the Union, in their successive campaigns conducted against a savage foe on our frontiers, in the interests of civilizati n and for the settlement and defence of our Territories, at different periods in the history of our common country since the close of the War of the Revolution; and also to collect and preserve for publication a record of these services and other historical data relating thereto, as well as to unite in a fraternal bond of union all those who are entitled to membership therein."

Order of Indian Wars of the United States.

Commander—Major-General Alfred E. Bates, U. S. A., retired, Metropolitan Club, Washington, D. C. *Recorder and Treasurer*—Major Lloyd M. Brett, 1st U. S. Cavalry, Washington, D. C. *Historian*—Brig.-Gen. Charles King, U. S. A.

This order was organized at Chicago, Ill., June 10, 1896, and received its charter from the State of Illinois. The order consists of two classes of companions: First, commissioned officers of the army, navy and marine corps, and of State and Territorial organizations, which have been, or may hereafter be, engaged in conflicts, battles or actual field service against hostile Indians in the United States; second, sons of living members of the first class. The object of the Association is to perpetuate the history of the services rendered by the American military forces in their conflicts and wars within the territory of the United States, and to collect and secure for publication historical data relating to the instances of brave deeds and personal devotion by which Indian warfare has been illustrated.

Society of the Cincinnati.

GENERAL OFFICERS.

President-General................Hon. Winslow Warren, Mass.
Vice-President-General............Hon. James Simons, LL.D., S. C.
Secretary-General...............Hon. Asa Bird Gardiner, LL.D., L.H.D., R.I.
Assistant Secretary-General......Mr. John Collins Daves, N. C.
Treasurer-General...............Vacant.
Assistant Treasurer-General.....Mr. Charles Isham, New York.

The historic and patriotic Order of the Cincinnati was founded by the American and French officers at the cantonments of the Continental army on the Hudson at the close of hostilities in the War of the Revolution for American Independence, May 10, 1783.

In forming the society it was declared that, "To perpetuate, therefore, as well the remembrance of this vast event as the mutual friendships which have been formed under the pressure of common danger, and, in many instances, cemented by the blood of the parties, the officers of the American army do hereby, in the most solemn manner, associate, constitute, and combine themselves into one Society of Friends, to endure as long as they shall endure, or any of their eldest male posterity, and in failure thereof the collateral branches who may be judged worthy of becoming its supporters and members."

For convenience, thirteen State societies were formed, and one in France, under the direct patronage of Louis XVI. Upon the roll of original members appeared the names of all the great historic military and naval characters of the Revolution, and upon the roll of honorary members, elected for their own lives only, appeared many of the signers of the Declaration of Independence.

THE RIGHT TO MEMBERSHIP.

All Continental officers who had served with honor and resigned after three years' service as officers, or who had been rendered supernumerary and honorably discharged, in one of the several reductions of the American army, or who had continued to the end of the war, and all French officers who had served in the co-operating army under Count d'Estaing, or auxiliary army under Count de Rochambeau, and held or attained the rank of colonel for such services, or who had commanded a French fleet or ship of war on the American coast, were entitled to become original members, and upon doing so were required to contribute a month's pay.

STATE SOCIETIES.

The Cincinnati is organically *one* society in membership, but for convenience in admission of members and in its charitable and patriotic objects is subdivided into State societies, there being thirteen, and the one in France, which was dispersed at the Reign of Terror in 1793, but is being re-established. Four dormant societies were restored to membership at the triennial meeting of 1902.

Membership descends to the eldest lineal male descendant, if judged worthy, and, in failure of direct male descent, to male descendants through intervening female descendants.

The general society when legislating for the good of the Order is composed of the general officers and five delegates from each State society, and meets triennially. In 1854 it ruled that proper descendants of Revolutionary officers who were entitled to original membership, but who never could avail themselves of it, are qualified for hereditary membership, if found worthy, on due application.

GENERAL OFFICERS SINCE ORGANIZATION.

The following have been the principal general officers:

PRESIDENTS-GENERAL.

1783..Gen. George Washington, LL.D., Va.
1800..Major-Gen. Alexander Hamilton, LL.D., N. Y.
1805..Major-Gen. Charles Cotesworth Pinckney, LL.D., S. C.
1825..Major-Gen. Thomas Pinckney, A.M., S. C.
1829..Major-Gen. Aaron Ogden, LL.D., N. J.
1839..Major-Gen. Morgan Lewis, A.M., N. Y.
1844..Brevet Major William Popham, N. Y.
1848..Brig.-Gen. H. A. Scammell Dearborn, A.M., Mass.
1854..Hon. Hamilton Fish, LL.D., N. Y.
1896..Hon. William Wayne, A.M., Pa.
1902..Hon. Winslow Warren, A.M., Mass.

VICE-PRESIDENTS-GENERAL.

1784..Major-Gen. Horatio Gates, LL.D., Va.
1787..Major-Gen. Thomas Mifflin, A.M., Pa.
1799..Major-Gen. Alexander Hamilton, LL.D., N. Y.
1800..Major-Gen. Charles Cotesworth Pinckney, LL.D., S. C.
1805..Major-Gen. Henry Knox, A.M., Mass.
1811..Brig.-Gen. John Brooks, M.D., LL.D., Mass.
1825..Major-Gen. Aaron Ogden, LL.D., N. J.
1829..Major-Gen. Morgan Lewis, A.M., N. Y.
1839..Major the Hon. William Shute, N. J.
1844..Hon. Horace Binney, LL.D., Pa.
1848..Hon. Hamilton Fish, LL.D., N. Y.
1854..Hon. Charles Stewart Davies, LL.D., Mass.
1866..Mr. James Warren Sever, A.M., Mass.
1872..Hon. James Simons, A.M., S. C.
1881..William Armstrong Irvine, M.D., Pa.
1887..Hon. Robert Milligan McLane, Md.
1896..Hon. Winslow Warren, A.M., Mass.
1902..Hon. James Simons, Jr., LL.D., S. C.

SECRETARIES-GENERAL.

1783..Major-Gen. Henry Knox, A.M., Mass.
1799..Major the Hon. William Jackson, Pa.
1829..Mr. Alexander W. Johnston, Pa.
1857..Mr. Thomas McEwen, A.M., M.D., Pa.
1875..Mr. George Washington Harris, Pa.
1884..Hon. Asa Bird Gardiner, LL.D., L.H.D., R.I.

The last triennial meeting of the general society was held at Charleston, S. C., in April, 1908. The next triennial meeting will be held at Newport, R. I., in May, 1911.

The office of the Secretary-General is at 24 Stone Street, New York City.

The number of living hereditary members of the Society of the Cincinnati, as reported at the triennial meeting April, 1908, was 842. The limited list of honorary members of the Order includes President Roosevelt, Admiral Dewey, Lieut.-Generals Miles and Chaffee, and ex-President Loubet, of France. Presidents Andrew Jackson, Zachary Taylor, James Buchanan, Ulysses S. Grant, Benjamin Harrison, Grover Cleveland, and William McKinley, were also honorary members.

President James Monroe was an original member like Washington, and President Pierce was an hereditary member.

SOCIETY OF THE CINCINNATI—*Continued.*

The following are the presidents, vice-presidents, and secretaries of the several State societies:

STATES.	Presidents.	Vice-Presidents.	Secretaries
New Hampshire	Henry Oakes Kent	Stephen Moody Crosby	Francis Coffin Martin.
Massachusetts.	Winslow Warren	Thornton K. Lothrop	David Greene Haskins.
Rhode Island	Asa Bird Gardiner	Charles Warren Lippitt	George W. Olney.
Connecticut	Vacant	Henry Larcom Abbott	Morris Woodruff Seymour.
New York	Talbot Olyphant	Francis Key Pendleton	Francis Burrall Hoffman.
New Jersey	James W. S. Campbell	William Pennington	Wessel T. B. S. Imlay.
Pennsylvania	Richard Dale	Francis Marinus Caldwell	Wm. Macpherson Hornor.
Delaware	John Patten Wales	Philip Howell White	John O. Platt.
Maryland	Oswald Tilghman	Henry Randall Webb	Thomas E. Sears.
Virginia	Windham R. Meredith	William Gordon McCabe	Heth Lorton.
North Carolina.	Wilson Gray Lamb	John Collins Daves	M. De Lancey Haywood.
South Carolina.	James Simous	Daniel E. Huger Smith	Henry M. Tucker, Jr.
Georgia	Walter Glasco Charlton.	William Hall Milton	George Francis Tennile.

Sons of the Revolution.

General President—Ex-Gov. John Lee Carroll, Md.
General Vice-President—Edmund Wetmore, N. Y.
Second General Vice-President—W. G. Harvey, S. C.
General Treasurer—R. M. Cadwalader, Pa.
Assistant General Treasurer—Henry Cadle, Mo.
General Secretary—J. M. Montgomery, N. Y.
Assistant General Secretary—Wm. Libbey, N. J.
General Registrar—Walter Gilman Page, Mass.
General Historian—Capt. William G. McCabe, Va.
General Chaplain—Rev. Edward E. Hale, D. C.

The society of the "Sons of the Revolution" was originated in New York in 1875 by John Austin Stevens, in conjunction with other patriotic gentlemen of Revolutionary ancestry. The New York Society was instituted February 22, 1876; reorganized December 3, 1883, and incorporated May 3, 1884, to "keep alive among ourselves and our descendants the patriotic spirit of the men who, in military, naval, or civil service, by their acts or counsel, achieved American independence; to collect and secure for preservation the manuscript rolls, records, and other documents relating to the War of the Revolution, and to promote intercourse and good feeling among its members now and hereafter." Eligibility to membership is confined to male descendants, above the age of twenty-one years, from an ancestor who as either a military, naval, or marine officer, soldier, sailor, or marine, or official in the service of any one of the thirteen original Colonies or States, or of the National Government, representing or composed of those Colonies or States, assisted in establishing American independence during the War of the Revolution between the 19th day of April, 1775, when hostilities commenced, and the 19th day of April, 1783, when they were ordered to cease. The next triennial meeting of the general society will be held in the City of Washington, April 19, 1911.

The officers of the New York Society Sons of the Revolution are as follows: *President*—Edmund Wetmore. *Vice-Presidents*—Robert Olyphant, Joseph Tompkins Low, William Graves Bates. *Secretary*—Henry Russell Drowne, Fraunces' Tavern, corner Broad and Pearl Streets, New York. *Treasurer*—Arthur Melvin Hatch. *Registrar*—Prof. Henry Phelps Johnston.

There are thirty State societies and a society in the District of Columbia. The aggregate membership is 7,560, that of the New York Society being over 2,000, and the Pennsylvania Society over 1,000.

Sons of the American Revolution.

President-General—Henry Stockbridge, Md.
Vice-Pres.-Gen.—George W. Bates, Mich.
Vice-Pres.-Gen.—William J. Van Patten, Vt.
Vice-Pres.-Gen.—John R. Webster, Neb.
Vice-Pres.-Gen.—Clarkson N. Guyer, Col
Treasurer-General—Willard Secor, Iowa.
Registrar-General and Secretary-General—A. Howard Clark, D. C.
Historian-General—Walter K. Watkins, Mass.
Chaplain-General—Rev. Frank O. Hall, N. Y.

The National Society of "Sons of the American Revolution" was organized in New York April 30, 1889, and chartered in Connecticut in 1890. Its purposes are the same as those of the older organization, the "Sons of the Revolution." State societies exist in thirty-eight States, the District of Columbia and Hawaii. A California society of descendants of Revolutionary patriots, entitled "Sons of Revolutionary Sires," organized July 4, 1875, having reorganized and changed its name in 1889, has been admitted to membership. A formal movement by this society and the "Sons of the Revolution" toward a union was attempted in 1892, and again in 1897, but was not successful. The total membership of the organization is about 11,000.

The New York or Empire State Society was organized February 11, 1890. The following are the officers: *President*—C. A. Pugsley. *Secretary*—Louis Annin Ames, 239 Broadway, New York. *Registrar*—Teunis D. Huntting. *Historian*—Josiah C. Pumpelly.

Aztec Club of 1847.

President—Col. Augustus S. Nicholson, U. S. M. C., Hamilton, Va. *Vice-President*—Gen. Simon B. Buckner, Munfordville, Ky. *Secretary*—William M. Sweeny, Astoria, N. Y. *Treasurer*—William Turnbull, New York City. *Vice-Treasurer*—Edward H. Floyd-Jones, New York City.

This society, originally composed of officers of the United States Army who served in the war with Mexico, was formed in the City of Mexico in 1847, and has been continued, "with a view to cherish the memories and keep alive the traditions that cluster about the names of those officers who took part in the Mexican War." Membership is confined to officers of the army, navy, and marine corps who served in the war, or their male blood relatives. Each primary member may nominate as his successor his son or a male blood relative, who during the life of the primary member is known as associate-member, and on the death of the former is entitled, as his representative, to full membership. There are 226 members.

Wars of the United States.

STATEMENT OF THE NUMBER OF UNITED STATES TROOPS ENGAGED.

Wars.	From—	To—	Regulars.	Militia and Volunteers.	Total*
War of the Revolution	April 19, 1775	April 11, 1783	130,711	164,080	309,781
Northwestern Indian Wars	Sept. 19, 1790	Aug. 3, 1795	....	....	8.983
War with France	July 9, 1798	Sept. 30, 1800	....	....	†4,593
War with Tripoli	June 10, 1801	June 4, 1805	....	....	†3,330
Creek Indian War	July 27, 1813	Aug. 9, 1814	600	13,181	13,781
War of 1812 with Great Britain	June 18, 1812	Feb. 17, 1815	85,000	471,622	576.622
Seminole Indian War	Nov. 20, 1817	Oct. 21, 1818	1,000	6,911	7,911
Black Hawk Indian War	April 21, 1831	Sept. 30. 1832	1,339	5,126	6,465
Cherokee disturbance or removal	1836	1837	....	9,494	9.494
Creek Indian War or disturbance	May 5, 1836	Sept. 30, 183[illegible]	935	12,483	13,418
Florida Indian War	Dec. 23, 1835	Aug. 14, 1843	11,16[illegible]	29,953	41,122
Aroostook distnrbance	1836	1839	....	1,500	1,500
War with Mexico	April 24, 1846	July 4, 1848	30,954	73,776	112,230
Apache, Navajo, and Utah War	1849	1855	1,500	1,061	2,501
Seminole Indian War	1856	1858	....	3,687	3.687
Civil War‡	1861	1865	....	....	2.772.408
Spanish-American War	April 21, 1898	Aug. 12, 1898	....	....	§274,717
Philippine Insurrection	1899	1900	....	....	60.000

* Including all branches of the service. † Naval forces engaged. ‡ The number of troops on the Confederate side was about 750,000. § Troops actually engaged, about 60,000.

THE GREAT BATTLES OF THE CIVIL WAR.

(From "Regimental Losses in the American Civil War," by William F. Fox, Lieutenant-Colonel, U. S. V.)

As to the loss in the Union armies, the greatest battles in the war were:

Date.	Battle.	Killed.	Wounded*	Missing.	Aggregate.
July 1-3, 1863	Gettysburg	3,070	14,497	5,434	23,001
May 8-18, 1864	Spottsylvania	2,725	13,413	2,258	18,396
May 5-7, 1864	Wilderness	2.246	12,037	3,383	17,666
September 17, 1862	Antietam†	2.108	9.549	753	12,410
May 1-3, 1863	Chancellorsville	1,606	9,762	5,919	17,287
September 19-20, 1863	Chickamauga	1,656	9,749	4,774	16,179
June 1-4, 1864	Cold Harbor	1,844	9,077	1,816	12,737
December 11-14, 1862	Fredericksburg	1,284	9.600	1,769	12,653
August 28-30, 1862	Manassas‡	1,747	8,452	4,263	14,462
April 6-7, 1862	Shiloh	1,754	8,408	2,855	13,047
December 31, 1862	Stone River§	1,730	7,802	3,717	13,249
June 15-19, 1864	Petersburg (assault)	1,688	8,513	1,185	11,386

* Wounded in these and the following returns includes mortally wounded.
† Not including South Mountain or Crampton's Gap.
‡ Including Chantilly, Rappahannock, Bristol Station, and Bull Run Bridge.
§ Including Knob Gap and losses on January 1 and 2, 1863.

The Union losses at Bull Run (first Manassas) July 21, 1861, were: Killed, 470; wounded, 1,071; captured and missing, 1,793; aggregate, 3,334.

The Confederate losses in particular engagements were as follows: Bull Run (first Manassas), July 21, 1861, killed, 387; wounded, 1,582; captured and missing, 13; aggregate, 1,982. Fort Donelson, Tenn., February 14-16, 1862, killed, 466; wounded, 1,534; captured and missing, 13,829; aggregate, 15,829. Shiloh, Tenn., April 6-7, 1862, killed, 1,723; wounded, 8,012; captured and missing, 959; aggregate, 10,694. Seven Days' Battle, Virginia, June 25-July 1, 1862, killed, 3,478; wounded, 16,261; captured and missing, 875; aggregate, 20,614. Second Manassas, August 21-September 2, 1862, killed, 1,481; wounded and missing, 7,627; captured and missing, 89; aggregate, 9,197. Antietam campaign, September 12-20, 1862, killed, 1,886; wounded, 9,348; captured and missing, 1,367; aggregate, 12,601. Fredericksburg, December 13, 1862, killed, 596; wounded, 4,068; captured and missing, 651; aggregate, 5,315. Stone River, Tenn., December 31, 1862, killed, 1,294; wounded, 7,945; captured and missing, 1,027; aggregate, 10,266. Chancellorsville, May 1-4, 1863, killed, 1,665; wounded, 9,081; captured and missing, 2,018; aggregate, 12,764. Gettysburg, July 1-3, 1863, killed, 2,592; wounded, 12,706; captured and missing, 5,150; aggregate, 20,448. Chickamauga, September 19-20, 1863, killed, 2,268; wounded, 13,613; captured and missing, 1,090; aggregate, 16,971.

Gettysburg was the greatest battle of the war. Antietam the bloodiest. The largest army was assembled by the Confederates at the seven days' fight; by the Unionists at the Wilderness.

The number of casualties in the volunteer and regular armies of the United States, during the war of 1861-65, according to a statement prepared by the Adjutant-General's office, was as follows: Killed in battle, 67,058; died of wounds, 43.012; died of disease, 199,720; other causes, such as accidents, murder, Confederate prisons, etc., 40,154; total died, 349,944; total deserted, 199,105. Number of soldiers in the Confederate service who died of wounds or disease (partial statement), 133,821; deserted (partial statement), 104,428. Number of United States troops captured dnring the war, 212,608; Confederate troops captured, 476,169. Number of United States troops paroled on the field, 16,431; Confederate troops paroled on the field, 248,599. Number of United States troops who died while prisoners, 30,156; Confederate troops who died while prisoners, 30,152.

Societies of the War of 1812.

THE VETERAN CORPS OF ARTILLERY OF THE STATE OF NEW YORK, CONSTITUTING THE MILITARY SOCIETY OF THE WAR OF 1812.

INSTITUTED as a military society by the officers of the War of 1812 on January 3, 1826, in the City of New York, and incorporated under the laws of the State of New York by the surviving veteran members, January 8, 1892. Consolidated January 8, 1848, with the Veteran Corps of Artillery (instituted by officers of the Revolutionary War November 25, 1790). Hiram Cronk, last surviving Veteran member War of 1812, born April 29, 1800, died May 13, 1905.

The officers are: *Vice-Commandant and Acting Commandant*—Asa Bird Gardiner, LL. D., L. H. D. *Adjutant*—Howland Pell, 7 Pine Street, New York. *Paymaster*—Charles Isham. *Quartermaster*—Chas. Augustus Schermerhorn. *Commissary*—Clarence H. Eagle. *Chaplain*—F. Landon Humphreys, S. T. D.

The original members comprise those who actually served in the military or naval forces of the United States during the War of 1812, or on vessels other than merchant ships which sailed under commissions of letters of marque and reprisal from the United States in that war.

Eligibility to hereditary membership is confined by law to descendants of those who actually served in the War of 1812, and to descendants of former members.

THE GENERAL SOCIETY OF THE WAR OF 1812.

Composed of federated State societies, in Pennsylvania, Maryland, Massachusetts, Connecticut, Ohio, Illinois, District of Columbia, New York, New Jersey, and Delaware, the members of each of which State Societies are borne upon the membership roll of the General Society. Any male person above the age of twenty-one years who participated in, or who is a lineal descendant of one who served during the War of 1812-14 in the army, navy, revenue marine, or privateer service of the United States, offering satisfactory proof to the State Society to which he makes application, and is of good moral character and reputation, may become a member. In case of failure of lineal descendants of an actual participant in said war, one collateral representative who is deemed worthy may be admitted to membership. *President-General*—John Cadwalader, Pennsylvania. *Secretary-General*—Calvin Lord, 141 Purchase Street, Boston, Mass. *Assistant Secretary-General*—John Mason Dulany, Baltimore, Md. *Treasurer-General*—George H. Richards Orange, N. J. *Assistant Treasurer-General*—James Malcolm Henry, Washington, D. C. *Surgeon-General*—George Horace Burgin, M. D., Pennsylvania. *Judge-Advocate-General*—John Biddle Porter, Pennsylvania. *Chaplain-General*—Rev. Henry Branch, Maryland.

The American Flag Association.

President—Col. Ralph E. Prime, Yonkers, N. Y. *Secretary*—Theodore Fitch, 120 Broadway, New York; *Treasurer*, A. Noel Blakeman, 140 Nassau Street, New York. The American Flag Association was organized February 17, 1898, its motto being, "One Flag, One Country, God over all." Its object is to secure National and State legislation for the protection of the flag from degrading and desecrating uses, and to secure a general observance of June 14 as "Flag Day," because on that day in 1777 Congress adopted the United States flag. The Association is composed of individual members and also the members of the Flag Committees of patriotic societies for the purpose of fostering public sentiment in favor of honoring the flag of our country and preserving it from desecration. It aims to co-ordinate the efforts of all flag committees.

Women's Patriotic Societies.

COLONIAL DAMES OF AMERICA.

OFFICERS.

President—Mrs. Edward King. *First Vice-President*—Mrs. Paul Dana. *Second Vice-President*—Miss J. J. Boudinot. *Treasurer*—Mrs. George Augustus Lung. *Secretary*—Mrs. Timothy Matlack Cheesman, 109 University Place, New York City. *Historian*—Miss Julia Livingston Delafield. *Advisory Council*—Franklin Bartlett, Louis V. Bright.

The Society of the Colonial Dames of America was organized in the City of New York May 23, 1890, and was the first society of women for this patriotic purpose founded in this country. It was incorporated April 23, 1891. The Society is purely patriotic and educational in its objects, which are: (1) To collect and preserve relics, manuscripts, traditions, and mementoes of the founders and builders of the thirteen original States of the Union, and of the heroes of the War of Independence, that the memory of their deeds and achievements may be perpetuated. (2) To promote celebrations of great historic events of National importance, to diffuse information on all subjects concerning American history, particularly among the young, and to cultivate the spirit of patriotism and reverence for the founders of American constitutional history. This Society has already a large membership and chapters in many States. It is a distinct organization from that which follows.

COLONIAL DAMES OF AMERICA.

OFFICERS OF THE NATIONAL SOCIETY.

Honorary President—Mrs. Howard Townsend. *President*—Mrs. William Ruffin Cox, Virginia. *Vice-Presidents*—Mrs. Alexander F. Jamieson, New Jersey; Mrs. Henry F. Le Hunte Lyster, Michigan; Mrs. Barrett Wendell, Massachusetts. *Secretary*—Mrs. Joseph Lamar, Augusta, Georgia. *Assistant Secretary*—Mrs. John Y. Taylor, Washington, D. C. *Treasurer*—Mrs. Alexander J. Cassatt, Haverford, Pa. *Registrar*—Mrs. Nathaniel Terry Bacon, Peace Dale, R. I. *Historian*—Miss Alice French, Davenport, Iowa.

This society is a distinct organization from the one described in the first paragraph.

The National Society is composed of delegates from the State societies. These exist in the thirteen original States and in twenty-one other States and the District of Columbia, and are all incorporated. The aggregate membership is over 5,000.

Under the constitution of the National Society it is prescribed that the members shall be women "who are descended in their own right from some ancestor of worthy life who came to reside in an American Colony prior to 1750, which ancestor, or some one of his descendants, being a lineal ascendant of the applicant, shall have rendered efficient service to his country during the Colonial period, either in the founding of a commonwealth or of an institution which has survived and developed into importance, or who shall have held an important position in the Colonial Government, and who, by distinguished services, shall have contributed to the founding of this great and powerful nation." Services rendered after 1776 do not entitle to membership, but are accepted for supplemental applications. There is no admission except through Colonial ancestry.

DAUGHTERS OF THE AMERICAN REVOLUTION.

OFFICERS OF THE NATIONAL SOCIETY.

President-General—Mrs. Donald McLean, 186 Lenox Avenue, New York City. *Vice-President-General* (of organization of chapters)—Mrs. Charlotte Emerson Main. *Vice-Presidents-General*—Mrs. Charles H. Deere, Ill.; Mrs. J. Moyan Smith, Ala.; Mrs. Wallace Delafield, Mo.; Mrs. Alexander Ennis Patton, Pa.; Mrs. Charles H. Terry, N. Y.; Mrs. Wm. A. Smoot, Va.; Mrs. Ira Yale Sage, Ga.; Mrs. A. A. Kendall, Me.; Mrs. Ellen Spencer Mussey, Washington, D. C.; Mrs. Baldwin Day Spilman, W. Va.; Mrs. John T. Sterling, Ct.; Mrs. Wm. E. Stanley, Kan.; Mrs. Egbert R. Jones, Miss.; Mrs. Erastus G. Putnam, N. J.; Mrs. Truman H. Newberry, Mich.; Mrs. Theodore C. Bates, Mass.; Mrs. H. S. Chamberlain, Tenn.; Mrs. Lindsay Patterson, N. C.; Mrs. Drayton W. Bushnell, Ia.; Mrs. Sallie Marshall Hardy, Ky. *Chaplain-General*—Mrs. Esther Frothingham Noble, D. C. *Recording Secretary-General*—Miss Elisabeth F. Pierce, D. C. *Registrar-General*—Mrs. Amos G. Draper, D. C. *Historian-General*—Mrs. J. Eakin Gadsby, D. C. *Corresponding Secretary-General*—Mrs. John Paul Earnest, D. C. *Treasurer-General*—Mrs. Mabel G. Swormstedt, D. C. *Assistant Historian-General*—Mrs. Henry S. Bowron, D. C. *Librarian-General*—Mrs. H. H. Boynton, D. C.

The Society was organized in the City of Washington, D. C., October 11, 1890. The headquarters are in Washington. Its present membership is reported by the Secretary-General to be 55,780. 600 State chapters exist in forty-five States and Territories and the District of Columbia, presided over by regents. Chapter regents have been appointed for England, Cuba, and the Philippines.

Any woman may be eligible for membership who is of the age of eighteen years, and who is descended from an ancestor who, "with unfailing loyalty, rendered material aid to the cause of independence as a recognized patriot, as soldier or sailor, or as a civil officer in one of the several Colonies or States, or of the United Colonies or States," provided that the applicant shall be acceptable to the Society. Every application for membership must be indorsed by at least one member of the National Society, and is then submitted to the Registrars-General, who report on the question of eligibility to the Board of Management, and upon its approval the applicant is enrolled as a member.

DAUGHTERS OF THE REVOLUTION.

OFFICERS OF THE GENERAL SOCIETY.

President-General—Mrs. Frank E. Fitz, Mass. *Recording Secretary-General*—Mrs. John A. Heath, Mass. *Corresponding Secretary-General*—Mrs. Josephine Wandell, N. Y. *Treasurer-General*—Mrs. Peter T. Austin, N. Y. *Registrar-General*—Mrs. J. J. Casey, N. Y. *Historian-General*—Mrs. Arthur H. Pray, Mass. *Librarian-General*—Mrs. John C. Montgomery, Col. *Board of Managers*—Mrs. James L. Chapman, Miss Mary Ellen Butterick, Mrs. Fred A. Dreer, Mrs. Geo. H. Plummer, Miss K. J. C. Carville, Mrs. Theresa Voss Smith, Mrs. Sara E. Schaumberg, Mrs. Chas. W. Dayton, Mrs. John R. Weeks, Mrs. Henry W. Helfer, Mrs. S. M. Buckman, Mrs. D. Phœnix Ingraham, Mrs. Frank P. Whiting, Mrs. Frederick J. Park, Mrs. O. La Forest Perry, Mrs. V. Gilpin Robinson, Mrs. Treadwell L. Ireland, Mrs. Clarence L. Bleakley, Mrs. Clinton Viles, and Mrs. Ashbel P. Fitch.

The General Society was organized in the City of New York August 20, 1891. Eligibility to membership is restricted to "women who are lineal descendants of an ancestor who was a military or naval or marine officer, soldier, sailor, or marine in actual service under the authority of any of the thirteen Colonies or States, or of the Continental Congress, and remained always loyal to such authority, or descendants of one who signed the Declaration of Independence, or of one who as a member of the Continental Congress or of the Congress of any of the Colonies or States, or as an official appointed by or under the authority of any such representative bodies, actually assisted in the establishment of American independence by service rendered during the War of the Revolution, becoming thereby liable to conviction of treason against the Government of Great Britain, but remaining always loyal to the authority of the Colonies or States." State societies exist in a large number of States. The office of the General Society is 156 Fifth Avenue, New York.

DAMES OF THE REVOLUTION.

THE Society of Dames of the Revolution was organized in 1896. The regulation as to membership is that the Society shall be composed entirely of women above the age of eighteen years, of good moral character, who are descended in their own right from an ancestor who, either as a military, naval, or marine officer, or official in the service of any one of the thirteen original Colonies or States, or of the National Government representing or composed of those Colonies or States, assisted in establishing American independence during the War of the Revolution, April 19, 1775, when hostilities commenced, and April 19, 1783, when they were ordered to cease. Local chapters may be organized when authorized by the Board of Managers of the Society. The president is Mrs. Montgomery Schuyler, 250 Wingah Avenue, New Rochelle, N. Y. Secretary, Miss R. C. C. Carville, 257 Webster Avenue, New Rochelle.

UNITED STATES DAUGHTERS OF 1812.

OFFICERS OF THE NATIONAL SOCIETY

President-National—Mrs. William Gerry Slade, New York. *Vice-Presidents-National*—Mrs. B. L. Whitney, Michigan; Mrs. Robert Hall Niles, Illinois; Mrs. George H. Wilson, Kentucky. *Recording Secretary*—Mrs. S. P. S. Mitchell. *Corresponding Secretary*—Mrs. Frank Wheaton. The office of the National Society is at 332 West Eighty-seventh Street, New York.

Membership Qualifications—Any woman over eighteen years of age of good character and a lineal descendant of an ancestor who rendered civil, military, or naval service during the War of 1812, or the period of the causes which led to that war (subsequent to the War of the Revolution), may be eligible to membership, provided the applicant be acceptable to the Society. In all the States the initiation fee is $1. The President of the New York State Society is Mrs. William Gerry Slade; the Corresponding Secretary is Mrs. George B. Wallis, Jr.

WASHINGTON HEADQUARTERS ASSOCIATION.

President—Mrs. Samuel J. Kramer. *Recording Secretary*—Mrs. Edwin R. Fay. *Corresponding Secretary*—Mrs. Robert Dhu Macdonald, No. 32 West 70th Street, New York City. The purpose of the Association is to preserve the old mansion on 160th Street, near Amsterdam Avenue, New York City, which was at one time, in the War of the Revolution, the headquarters of Washington. The property is owned by the city and is under the care and direction of the Knickerbocker, Mary Washington, Colonial and Manhattan Chapters of the Daughters of the American Revolution. It is open daily to the public.

Grand Army of the Republic.

Commander-in-Chief....................Henry M. Nevius, Red Bank, N. J.

Senior Vice-Commander. J. K. Hamilton, Toledo, O. | *Surgeon-General*.. Dr. G. L. Taneyhill, Balt., Md.
Junior Vice-Commander..Chas. C. Royce, Chico, Cal. | *Chaplain-in-Chief*. Rev. J. F. Spence, Knoxv., Tenn.

OFFICIAL STAFF.

Adjutant-Gen'l..Frank O. Cole, Jersey City, N. J. | *Inspector-General*. W. H. Hornaday, Lawton, Okla.
Quartermaster-Gen'l, C. D. R. Stowits, Buffalo, N. Y. | *Judge-Advocate-General*, A. B. Beers, Bridgep't, Ct.

The National Council of Administration has 45 members, each department having one member.

Departments. (45.)	Department Commanders.*		Assistant Adjutants-General.		Members.
Alabama	W. M. Campbell	Florence	C. C. Chapin	Birmingham	125
Arizona			P. P. Parker	Phœnix	130
Arkansas	J. M. McClincock	Devall Bluff	Geo. W. Clarke	Little Rock	352
Calif. & Nevada	G. E. Adams	San Francisco	J. M. Quinn	Los Angeles	5,756
Colo. & Wyom.	John C. Kennedy	Denver, Col.	W. C. Thomas	Greeley, Col.	2,554
Connecticut	Virgil F. McNeil	New Haven	William E. Morgan	New Haven	3,619
Delaware	Wm. Mondenhall	Wilmington	J. S. Litzenberg	Wilmington	564
Florida	William James	Jacksonville	F. A. Curtis	Orlando	315
Georgia	Alex. Mattison	Atlanta	S. C. Brown	Fitzgerald	357
Idaho	John H. Ironton	Boise	George Hoskins	Payette	471
Illinois	Thos. W. Scott	Fairfield	Charles A. Partridge	Chicago	18,024
Indiana	Wm. H. Armstrong	Indianapolis	John R. Fesler	Indianapolis	14,045
Iowa	E. J. Conner	Washington	George A. Newman	Des Moines	10,974
Kansas	J. R. Baird	Spearville	Chas. Harris	Topeka	11,029
Kentucky	C. C. Degman	Springdale	Lewis Sandlin	Berea	2,036
La. & Mississippi	Alfred Mitchell	New Orleans	E. K. Russ	New Orleans	1,067
Maine	Chas. W. Skillings	Portland	Wm. H. Halston	Cumbl'd Mills	5,235
Maryland	C. A. E. Spaemer	Baltimore	Lewis M. Zimmerman	Baltimore	1,916
Massachusetts	Daniel Gleason	Natick	Wilford A. Wetherbee	Boston	14,786
Michigan	Sam. J. Lawrence	Northville	Fayette Wyckoff	Lansing	10,688
Minnesota	P. G. Woodward	Anoka	Orton S. Clark	Minneapolis	5,477
Missouri	Frank M. Sterrett	St. Louis	Thomas B. Rodgers	St. Louis	7,309
Montana	Jesse P. Stevens	Butte	A. N. Bull	Bozeman	440
Nebraska	J. H. Culver	Milford	A. M. Trimble	Lincoln	4,552
N. Hampshire	D. F. Healey	Manchester	Frank Battles	Concord	2,568
New Jersey	George Barrett	Camden	A. T. Connett	Flemington	4,393
New Mexico	Sam. A. Simpson	Taos	Jacob Weltner	Sante Fe	237
New York	James Owens	New York City	Wm. S. Bull	Albany	25,214
North Dakota	P. H. Cummings	Fargo	E. C. Geary	Fargo	344
Ohio	Jos. W. O'Neall	Lebanon	T. T. Smith	Columbus	21,752
Oklahoma	Thos. Prothero	El Reno	T. H. Soward	Pawnee	2,008
Oregon	Jas. S. Nelson	Oregon City	C. A. Williams	Portland	1,873
Pennsylvania	Wm. J. Patterson	Pittsburg	Chas. A. Suydam	Philadelphia	22,892
Potomac	James A. Allen	Washington, D. C.	O. H. Oldroyd	Washington	2,161
Rhode Island	Chas. R. Brayton	Providence	Philip S. Chase	Providence	1,374
South Dakota	Chas. Barrett	Sioux Falls	A. M. English	Yankton	1,455
Tennessee	A. J. Gahagan	Chattanooga	Sylvanus Hersey	Knoxville	1,299
Texas	J. C. Bonnell	Houston	W. O Kretsinger	Denison	462
Utah	N. D. Corser	Salt Lake City	Alfred Kent	Salt Lake City	281
Vermont	Chas. H. Cota	St. Albans	C. D. Williams	Burlington	2,707
Va. & No. Caro.	James E. Fuller	Norfolk	A. A. Hager	Sold'r's Home	611
Wash. & Alaska	R. J. Chase	Seattle	J. R. D. Conger	Tacoma	3,231
West Virginia	D. Mayer	Charlestown	John B. McNally	Ravenswood	1,191
Wisconsin	Phil. Cheek	Baraboo	J. A. Watrous	Whitewater	7,311

Total, December 31, 1907....................225,157

* New post officers are elected December, 1908, and installed in January, 1909.

The number of Grand Army posts December 31, 1907, was 6,057. Losses by death during the preceding year, ending December 31, 1907, were 10,242.

The first post of the Grand Army was organized at Decatur, Ill., April 6, 1866. The first National Encampment was held at Indianapolis, November 20, 1866. The next Encampment will be at Salt Lake City, Utah, in 1909.

NATIONAL ENCAMPMENTS AND COMMANDERS-IN-CHIEF.

1866—Indianapolis......Stephen A. Hurlbut, Ill.
1868—Philadelphia......John A. Logan, Ill.
1869—Cincinnati......John A. Logan, Ill.
1870—Washington......John A. Logan, Ill.
1871—Boston......A. E. Burnside, Rhode Is.
1872—Cleveland......A. E. Burnside, Rhode Is.
1873—New Haven......Charles Devens, Jr., Mass.
1874—Harrisburg......Charles Devens, Jr., Mass.
1875—Chicago......John F. Hartranft, Pa.
1876—Philadelphia......John F. Hartranft, Pa.
1877—Providence......J. C. Robinson, New York.
1878—Springfield......J. C. Robinson, New York.
1879—Albany......William Earnshaw, Ohio.
1880—Dayton......Louis Wagner, Pa.
1881—Indianapolis......George S. Merrill, Mass.
1882—Baltimore......Paul Van Der Voort, Neb.
1883—Denver......Robert B. Beath, Pa.
1884—Minneapolis......John S. Kountz, Ohio.
1885—Portland, Me......S. S. Burdette, D. C.
1886—San Francisco......Lucius Fairchild, Wis.
1887—St. Louis......John P. Rea, Minn.
1888—Columbus......William Warner, Mo.
1889—Milwaukee......Russell A. Alger, Mich.
1890—Boston......Wheelock G. Veazey, Vt.
1891—Detroit......John Palmer, New York.
1892—Washington......A. G. Weissert, Wis.
1893—Indianapolis......John G. B. Adams, Mass.
1894—Pittsburgh......Thos. G. Lawler, Ill.
1895—Louisville......Ivan N. Walker, Ind.
1896—St. Paul......Thaddeus S. Clarkson, Neb.
1897—Buffalo......John P. S. Gobin, Pa.
1898—Cincinnati......*James A. Sexton, Ill.
1898—Cincinnati......† W. C. Johnson, Ohio.
1899—Philadelphia......Albert D. Shaw, N. Y.
1900—Chicago......Leo Rassieur, Mo.
1901—Cleveland......Eli Torrance, Minn.
1902—Washington, D. C. Thos. J. Stewart, Pa.
1903—San Francisco......John C. Black, Ill.
1904—Boston......* W. W. Blackmar, Mass.
1905—Boston......† John R. King, D. C.
1905—Denver......James Tanner, N. Y.
1906—Minneapolis......R. B. Brown, Ohio.
1907—Saratoga......Charles G. Burton, Mo.

* Died while in office. † After the death of the Commander-in-Chief, the Senior Vice-Commander succeeded him.

Woman's Relief Corps.

AUXILIARY TO THE GRAND ARMY OF THE REPUBLIC.

National President—Mrs. Kate E. Jones, Ilion, N. Y. *National Secretary*—Mrs. Eliza Brown Daggett, Ilion, N. Y. This organization was created by the mothers, wives, daughters, and sisters of Union soldiers of the civil war of 1861-65, for the purpose of aiding and assisting the Grand Army of the Republic, and to "perpetuate the memory of their heroic dead," to "extend needful aid to the widows and orphans," to "cherish and emulate the deeds of our army nurses," and to "inculcate lessons of patriotism and love of country among our children and in the communities in which we live." The organization is composed of 35 departments, which are subdivided into corps, as well as detached corps in several States where no departments exist. The year ending June, 1908, there were 3,119 corps and 158,366 members.

Sons of Veterans, U. S. A.

Commander-in-Chief—Edgar Allan, Jr., Richmond, Va. *Senior Vice-Commander-in-Chief*—A. I. Vescelius, Paterson, N. J. *Junior Vice-Commander-in-Chief*—L. M. Alexander, Buffalo, N. Y. *Chief of Staff*—Edwin M. Amies, Altoona, Pa. *National Secretary*—Horace H. Hammer, Reading, Pa. *National Treasurer*—James Lewis Rake, Reading, Pa. *National Inspector*—A. J. Boutwell, Concord, N. H.

Camp No. 1, Sons of Veterans, U. S. A., was organized in the City of Philadelphia September 29, 1879. The organization is composed of lineal descendants, over eighteen years of age, of honorably discharged soldiers, sailors, or marines who served in the late civil war. There are now about one thousand Camps, with a membership of fifty thousand, distributed among twenty-five Divisions, corresponding to States, the general society or national body constituting the Commandery-in-Chief. Each Camp has its own officers, the head officer being the Commander. The principal officer of the Division is the Division Commander.

The Sons of Veterans Auxiliary is an association of women auxiliary to the above organization. Miss Molly Donaldson, 148 Madison St., Paterson, N. J., is National President, and Miss Mary L. Tredo, Paterson, N. J., National Secretary.

Societies of Spanish War Veterans.

Astor Battery Association.—*President*—Otto Koenig, New York City. *Vice-President*—Charles E. Callan, New York City. *Treasurer*—John N. Ostrander, New York City. *Secretary*—George S. Geis, 449 South Spring Street, Los Angeles, Cal. Organized December, 1904. Composed of original members of the Astor Battery, which served in the Philippines campaign of 1898. Meets annually, August 13, anniversary of the capture of Manila, at Reunion-Army of the Philippines, and at the annual national encampment of the United Spanish War Veterans.

Naval and Military Order of the Spanish-American War.—Instituted February 2, 1899. Officers of the National Commandery.—*Commander-in-Chief*—Lieut-Col. Charles Dick, Akron, O. *Senior Vice-Commander-in-Chief*—Lieut. John S. Muckle, Philadelphia, Pa. *Junior Vice-Commander-in-Chief*—Ensign William E. Edgar, Fall River, Mass. *Recorder-in-Chief*—Major Frank Keck, 78 Broad Street, New York. *Registrar-in-Chief*—Major Samuel T. Armstrong, New York. *Deputy Registrar-in-Chief*—Capt. William E. English, Indianapolis, Ind. *Treasurer-in-Chief*—Major George F. Shiels, New York. *Chaplain-in-Chief*—Major Edw. J. Vattmann, Ill. The Commander of the New York Commandery is Brig.-Gen. John W. Clous. Membership is composed of persons who served on the active list or performed active duty as commissioned officers, regular or volunteer, during the war with Spain, or who participated in the war as naval or military cadets. Membership descends to the eldest male descendant in the order of primogeniture.

Society of the Army of the Philippines.—*Commander-in-Chief*—Captain H. A. Crow, Connellsville, Pa. *Vice-Commander-in-Chief*—Major B. J. H. Farrell, Chicago, Ill. *Junior Commander-in-Chief*—Major-General J. Franklin Bell, U. S. A. *Paymaster-General*—Lieut. Charles B. Lewis, Denver, Colo. *Judge Advocate General*—J. H. Fraine, Grafton, N. Dak. The next annual meeting will be held at Galesburg, Ill., in August, 1908.

Society of the Army of Santiago de Cuba.—Organized in the Governor's Palace at Santiago de Cuba July 31, 1898. *President*—Major-Gen. J. Ford Kent. *First Vice-President*—Major-Gen. H. S. Hawkins. *Second Vice-President*—Lieut.-Col. Charles Dick. *Third Vice-President*—Major-Gen. S. S. Sumner. *Fourth Vice-President*—Brig.-Gen. Chambers McKibbin. *Secretary and Treasurer*—Lieut.-Col. Alfred C. Sharpe. *Historian*—Major G. Creighton Webb. *Registrar-General*—Col. Philip Reade. Annual dues $1, life membership $25. No initiation fee. There are branch societies in Massachusetts, New York, Ohio, Michigan, Illinois, California, and the District of Columbia.

United Spanish War Veterans.—National Encampment United Spanish War Veterans—Organized April 18, 1904, by the consolidation of the National Army and Navy Spanish War Veterans, National Association of Spanish-American War Veterans, and the Society of the Service Men of the Spanish War. *Commander-in-Chief*—Charles W. Newton, Connecticut. *Adjutant-General*—Henry H. Saunders, Hartford, Ct. *Quartermaster-General*—Joseph E. Jette, Montana. *Senior Vice-Commander*—Charles E. Stroud, Ohio. *Junior Vice-Commander*—Moses R. Doyon, Indiana. *Judge-Advocate General*—Edward H. White, Illinois. *Surgeon-General*—J. O'Donoghue, Roxbury, Mass. *Chaplain-in-Chief*—Rev. W. H. I. Reany, Brooklyn, N. Y. *Commissary-General*—Henry C. Schoenler, New York. *Paymaster-General*—S. D. C. Hays, Colorado. *Chief of Engineers*—S. R. Cohen, Ky. *Chief Signal Officer*—Isadore Weill, New York. *Chief of Ordnance*—J. J. Helberg, Wisconsin. *Chief of Artillery*—Adna G. Clarke, Kansas. *Chief Mustering Officer*—William D. Wild, New York. *National Historian*—J. Walter Mitchell, Washington, D. C. Soldiers and sailors of the regular and volunteer army, navy, and marine corps who served honorably during the war with Spain or the insurrection in the Philippines are eligible to membership.

United Volunteer Association.—All white soldiers and sailors who served honorably in the military or naval service of the United States during the war with Spain or the incident insurrection in the Philippines are eligible to membership. This society was organized at Chattanooga, Tenn., August 17, 1899, and has a membership of nearly 38,000. It is national in scope and character. Officers: *President*—Col. William J. Fife, California. *First Vice-President*—Capt. G. A. Wheatley, Texas. *Second Vice-President*—Major E. R. DuMont, Mississippi. *Third Vice-President*—Major Clay C. MacDonald. *Secretary*—Col. William C. Liller, 23 Irving Place, New York City. *Treasurer*—Joseph H. Stiner, New York City.

Union Veteran Legion.

National Commander—Thomas J. Shannon. *Senior Vice-National Commander*—W. B. Tracy, Bradford, Pa. *Junior Vice-National Commander*—Jacob B. Smith, Wilmington, Del. *Quartermaster-General*—J. M. Keyser, Pittsburgh, Pa. *Judge-Advocate-General*—Levi Bird Duff, Pittsburgh, Pa. *Inspector-General*—Hiram McCalmsat, Mansfield, O. *Chief-of-Staff*—W. P. Madden, Xenia, O. *Adjutant-General*—O. P. Hallam; headquarters: 326 Fifth Street, S. E., Washington, D. C.

The Union Veteran Legion was organized at Pittsburgh, Pa., March, 1884, and the National Organization was perfected November 17, 1886. Encampments are now organized in 21 States and the District of Columbia, numbering 152 encampments. The membership is over 20,000. To become a member, the applicant must have been an officer, soldier, sailor, or marine of the Union army, navy, or marine corps during the late civil war, who volunteered prior to July 1, 1863, for a term of three years, and was honorably discharged for any cause, after a service of at least two continuous years; or was, at any time, discharged by reason of wounds received in the line of duty; also those who volunteered for a term of two years prior to July 22, 1861, and served their full term of enlistment, unless discharged for wounds received in the line of duty; but no drafted person, nor substitute, nor any one who has at any time borne arms against the United States, is eligible. A statement by the Adjutant-General of the Legion says: "It is believed that those who entered the service prior to July, 1863, had but one object in view, and that was the preservation of the Union. There were no bounties prior to that date, nor were there any fears of a draft; consequently, those who shouldered a musket or wielded a sabre felt that it was a sacred duty to offer their lives in defence of their country's honor." Next National Encampment meets at Washington, D. C., on the second Wednesday in September, 1909.

The American Continentals.

Commandant—Col. Henry D. Tyler. *Chief-of-Staff*—Major-General O. O. Howard, U. S. A. *Engineer*—Col. W. DeH. Washington. *Inspector-General*—Brig-Gen. Philip Reade, U. S. A. *Judge Advocate*—Col. Homer Lee. *Historian*—Major L. G. Tyler. *Paymaster*—Capt. Albert J. Squier. *Commissary*—Capt. G. H. Warren. *Adjutant*—Capt. Louis H. Cornish.

The American Continentals is a uniformed patriotic corps composed of descendants of officers and soldiers of the War of the Revolution. The staff headquarters and office of the Adjutant are Room 61, Drexel Building, Wall and Broad Streets, New York.

Colonial Society of America.

President—Stephen M. Newman, A.M., D.D. *Honorary President*—Gen. Henry E. Tremain. *Vice-Presidents*—Herman W. Booth and Charles S. Goodrich. *Treasurer*—Benjamin F. Buck. *Secretary*—Theodore W. Compton, No. 160 Fifth Avenue, New York. *Advisory Committee*—Edward Everett Hale, D. D., LL.D.; Levi P. Morton, Gen. Benjamin F. Tracy, George G. DeWitt, Charles W. Drayton, Gen. Henry E. Tremain.

The object of this Society is to advance historic research, and particularly to arouse and sustain widespread interest in the perpetuation of the memory of the chief historic events, places and scenes in the colonial and revolutionary periods of our country.

The Society consists of members, patrons and fellows. They are persons interested in American history and the preservation of the memory of historic scenes and places in the colonial and revolutionary periods.

The Society prepares each year etchings of historic scenes, buildings and places of America, and India proofs printed from the etching plates, signed by the artist, are sent to all members, patrons and fellows of the Society, together with the Memorial Book of the Society, which contains a complete history of the subjects represented in the etchings. It also issues reproductions of rare documents, relics, etc., of historic value pertaining to the period.

The American Cross of Honor.

THIS life-saving order was organized A. D. 1898, and is composed of persons upon whom the United States Government has conferred the life-saving medal of honor. May 1, 1906, Congress incorporated the order, and the following officers were elected: Thomas H. Herndon, President; John J. Delaney, Vice-President; Harry A. George, Secretary, and Richard Stockton, Treasurer. All persons who have received the life-saving medal of honor under any act of Congress are eligible to membership in the order. No membership fees or annual dues are collected from any member of this order, only voluntary contributions being received to assist in paying the current expenses.

The cross of the order will be conferred annually upon the person who has rendered the most heroic services in saving life and who, also, has received the medal of honor of the United States Government.

Interstate National Guard Association.

THIS association is composed of representatives of the Organized Militia of the States of the Union, and its purpose is to conserve the interests of that body of troops. The last annual meeting was held at Columbia, S. C. The next will be held at Boston, Mass., in March, 1908. The following are the officers:

President—Major-General Charles Dick, of Ohio. *Vice-Presidents*—Brigadier-General Thomas J. Stewart, of Pennsylvania; Brigadier-General J. Clifford R. Foster, of Florida; Brigadier-General W. T. McGurrin, of Michigan; Brigadier-General W. H. Thrift, of Iowa; Brigadier-General Ortis Hamilton, of Washington; Brigadier-General F. B. Wood, of Minnesota; Brigadier-General N. H. Henry, of New York; Brigadier-General J. B. Lauck, of California; Brigadier-General Lawrason Riggs, of Maryland; Brigadier-General J. F. Armfield, of North Carolina; Brigadier-General G. M. Cole, of Connecticut; Brigadier-General Roger D. Williams, of Kentucky. *Secretary*—Brigadier-General J. W. F. Hughes, of Nebraska. *Treasurer*—Brigadier-General C. J. Anderson, of Virginia.

United Confederate Veterans.

Commander—Gen. Clement A. Evans, Atlanta, Ga. *Adjutant-General and Chief of Staff*—Major-Gen. William E. Mickie, New Orleans, La.

Army of Northern Virginia Department—*Commander*—Lieut.-Gen. C. Irvine Walker, Charleston, S. C. *Adjutant-General*—Brig.-Gen. Richard B. Davis, Petersburg, Va.

Army of Tennessee Department—*Commander*—Lieut.-Gen. Geo. W. Gordon, Memphis, Tenn. *Adjutant-General*—Brig.-Gen. E. T. Sykes, Columbus, Miss.

Trans-Mississippi Department—*Commander*—Lieut.-Gen. W. L. Cabell, Dallas, Tex. *Adjutant-General*—Brig.-Gen. A. T. Watts, Beaumont, Tex.

The *Confederate Veteran*, Nashville, Tenn., established by S. A. Cunningham, is the official organ.

This Association was organized at New Orleans, June 10, 1889. Its avowed purpose is strictly social, literary, historical, and benevolent. Its constitution says that it "will endeavor to unite in a general federation all associations of Confederate veterans, soldiers, and sailors now in existence or hereafter to be formed; to gather authentic data for an impartial history of the war between the States; to preserve relics or mementoes of the same; to cherish the ties of friendship that should exist among men who have shared common dangers, common sufferings, and privations; to care for the disabled and extend a helping hand to the needy; to protect the widows and the orphans, and to make and preserve a record of the resources of every member, and, as far as possible, of those of our comrades who have preceded us in eternity." State organizations are authorized, and are called Divisions. The permanent headquarters of the Association are at New Orleans, La. Number of Camps, 1,690. Number of members, according to last report, about 75,000. The last reunion of the veterans was at Birmingham, Ala., June 9-11, 1908; and the next will be held at Memphis, Tenn., at a date not yet named.

United Sons of Confederate Veterans.

THE general society of this organization, which is composed of representatives of local camps throughout the United States, held its last reunion May 30—June 3, 1907, at Richmond, Va. The following is the official roster:

Commander-in-Chief—John W. Apperson, Memphis, Tenn. *Adjutant-General and Chief of Staff*—Nathan Bedford Forrest, Memphis, Tenn. *Inspector-General*—Robert L. Cook, Bessemer, Ala. *Quartermaster-General*—Edwin A. Taylor, Memphis, Tenn. *Commissary-General*—Fontaine W. Mahood, Washington, D. C. *Judge-Advocate-General*—Harry L. Seay, Dallas, Tex. *Surgeon-General*—Dr. C. M. Brown, Huntington, West Virginia. *Chaplain-General*—Rev. Wm. E. Thompson, Memphis, Tenn.

United Daughters of the Confederacy.

President—Mrs. Cornelia Branch Stone, Galveston, Tex. *First Vice-President*—Mrs. Martin S. Willard, Wilmington, Del. *Second Vice-President*—Mrs. John P. Poe, Baltimore, Md. *Recording Secretary*—Mrs. L. E. Williams, Anchorage, Ky. *Corresponding Secretary*—Mrs. R. C. Cooley, Jacksonville, Fla. *Treasurer*—Mrs. Andrew L. Dowdell, Opelika, Ala. Mrs. Stonewall Jackson, of Charlotte, N. C.; Mrs. M. C. Goodlett, of Nashville, Tenn.; Mrs. Clement C. Clopton, Alabama; Mrs. Albert Sidney Johnston Pritchard, of California; Mrs. Braxton Bragg, New Orleans, La.; Mrs. L. H. Raines, Savannah, Ga.; Mrs. John H. Reagan, Texas; Mrs. John S. Williams, Louisville, Ky.; Mrs. Magnus Thompson, Washington, D. C., are honorary presidents for life.

The United Daughters of the Confederacy was organized at Nashville, Tenn., September 10, 1894. It is composed of the widows, wives, mothers, sisters, and lineal female descendants of men who served honorably in the army and navy of the Confederate States, or who served in the civil service of the Confederate States or one of the Southern States, or who gave personal services to the Confederate cause. There are local federations, governed by State divisions, which in turn are subordinate to the general organization. The objects of the United Daughters of the Confederacy, as stated in the constitution of the society, are "social, literary, historical, monumental, benevolent, and honorable in every degree, without any political signification whatever." It will endeavor: (1) To unite in the federation all bodies of Southern women now organized or that may hereafter be formed. (2) To cultivate ties of friendship among our women whose fathers, brothers, sons, and, in numberless cases, mothers, shared common dangers, sufferings, and privations; and to perpetuate honor, integrity, valor, and other noble attributes of true Southern character. (3) To instruct and instill into the descendants of the people of the South a proper respect for and pride in the glorious war history, with a veneration and love for the deeds of their forefathers which have created such a monument of military renown, and to perpetuate a truthful record of the noble and chivalric achievements of their ancestors. All with the view of furnishing authentic information from which a conscientious historian will be enabled to write a correct and impartial history of the Confederate side during the struggle for Southern independence. The organization now has 900 chapters in the United States, North and South, with 40,000 members.

Society of the Army and Navy of the Confederate States

IN THE STATE OF MARYLAND.

President—Capt. George W. Booth. *Vice-President*—Major W. Stuart Symington. *Secretary*—Capt. William L. Ritter, 541 Carrollton Avenue, Baltimore, Md. *Treasurer*—Capt. F. M. Colston. There are twelve vice-presidents and an executive committee of seven members. The Society of the Army and Navy of the Confederate States in the State of Maryland was organized in 1871, "to collect and preserve the material for a truthful history of the late war between the Confederate States and the United States of America; to honor the memory of our comrades who have fallen; to cherish the ties of friendship among those who survive, and to fulfil the duties of sacred charity toward those who may stand in need of them." The membership is 925.

American National Red Cross.

INCORPORATED by Congress, 1905. National Headquarters, Room 341, War Department, Washington, D. C. *President*—William H. Taft. *Treasurer*—Beekman Winthrop. *Counsellor*—Alford W. Cooley. *Secretary*—Charles L. Magee. *Chairman of Central Committee*—Maj.-General Geo. W. Davis, U. S. A., Ret. *Board of Consultation*—Brig.-General Robert M. O'Reilly, Surgeon-General, U. S. A.; Rear-Admiral Presley M. Rixey, Surgeon-General, U. S. N.; Surgeon-General Walter Wyman, U. S. Public Health and Marine Hospital Service.

General Society of Mayflower Descendants.

THE Society of Mayflower Descendants was organized in the City of New York December 22, 1894, by lineal descendants of the Mayflower pilgrims, "to preserve their memory, their records, their history, and all facts relating to them, their ancestors, and their posterity." Every lineal descendant over eighteen years of age, male or female, of any passenger of the voyage of the Mayflower which terminated at Plymouth, Mass., December, 1620, including all signers of "The Compact," are eligible to membership. The initiation fee is $10 and the annual dues are $5. The Triennial Congress is held in September at Plymouth, Mass. Societies have been organized in New York, Connecticut, Massachusetts, Pennsylvania, Illinois, District of Columbia, Ohio, New Jersey, Wisconsin, Rhode Island, Michigan, Minnesota, Maine, Colorado, and California. The officers of the General Society are: *Governor-General*, Samuel B. Capen; *Deputy Governors-General*, Richard Henry Greene, Charles E. Gross, Chas. A. Hopkins, J. Granville Leach, Frederick M. Steele, Solomon E. Faunce, Charles D. Standish, William Howard Doane, Archie Lee Talbot, George Corlis Nightingale; *Secretary-General*, Clarence Ettienne Leonard, 443 E. 23d St., New York; *Treasurer-General*, James M. Rhodes; *Historian-General*, Edward H. Whorf; *Elder-General*, Rev. John Lewis Ewell; *Captain-General*, Miles Standish, M. D.; *Surgeon-General* Dr. Abiel W. Nelson; *Assistants-General*, Howland Davis, Edwin S. Crandon, Herbert Jenney, William Waldo Hyde, Walter M. Howland, and George C. Mason.

The Huguenot Society of America.

THIS Society was organized April 13, 1883, and has its office in New York at No. 105 East Twenty-second Street. *President*, Col. William Jay; *Vice-Presidents*, Oscar B. Ireland, Theodore M. Banta, Henry M. Lester, A. T. Clearwater, Nathaniel Thayer, Richard Olney, William Ely, James W. Hunter, Herbert Du Puy, Prof. Allan Marquand, Col. Henry A. Dupont, Rev. Robert Wilson; *Treasurer*, T. J. Oakley Rhinelander; *Secretary*, Mrs. James M. Lawton; *Executive Committee*, the officers of the society, the chairmen of the committees on pedigrees, publication, library, and finance, and Bayard Dominick, William Mitchell, Edward O. Flagg, William D. Dutton, Samuel R. Thayer; *Chaplain*—Rt. Rev. Bishop J. H. Darlington. Descent from Huguenot ancestors is the qualification necessary for membership.

Society of Colonial Wars.

Governor-General—Arthur J. C. Sowdon, Boston. *Vice-Governor-General*—Howland Pell, New York. *Secretary-General*—Clarence Storm, Room 62, 45 William Street, N. Y. *Deputy Secretary-General*—Samuel V. Hoffman. *Treasurer-General*—Wm. Macpherson Hornor, Philadelphia, Pa.; *Registrar-General*—George Norbury Mackenzie, Baltimore. *Historian General*—T. J. Oakley Rhinelander, N. Y. *Chaplain-General*—Rt. Rev. Daniel S. Tuttle, St. Louis. *Surgeon-General*—Dr. Justin E. Emerson, Detroit. *Chancellor-General*—Henry Stockbridge, Baltimore.

The Society of Colonial Wars was instituted in 1892 to "perpetuate the memory of these events and of the men who, in military, naval, and civil positions of high trust and responsibility, by their acts or counsel assisted in the establishment, defence, and preservation of the American Colonies, and were in truth the founders of this nation. With this end in view it seeks to collect and preserve manuscripts, rolls, and records; to provide suitable commemorations or memorials relating to the American Colonial period, and to inspire in its members the paternal and patriotic spirit of their forefathers, and in the community respect and reverence for those whose public services made our freedom and unity possible." Eligibility is confined to an adult male descendant of an ancestor who fought in battle under Colonial authority, from the settlement of Jamestown, Va., in 1607, to the battle of Lexington, in 1775, or who served as Governor, Deputy-Governor, Lieutenant-Governor, Member of the Council, or as a military, naval, or marine officer in the service of the Colonies, or under the banner of Great Britain, or was conspicuous in military, official, or legislative life during that period.

Mount Vernon Ladies' Association.

THE Washington Estate at Mount Vernon, Va., is under the care and direction of the Mount Vernon Ladies' Association of the Union. The founder of the Association in 1854 was Miss Ann Pamela Cunningham, of South Carolina. She was the first Regent, and her successors have been Mrs. Lily M. Berghman, 1874, and Mrs. Justine Van Rensselaer Townsend, 1893, the present Regent. There are Vice-Regents for thirty States.

The present officers are: *Regent*—Mrs. Justine Van Rensselaer Townsend. *Secretary*—Mrs. Jennie Meeker Ward, Washington, D.C. *Treasurer*—E. Francis Riggs, D. C. *Resident Superintendent*—Harrison H. Dodge. *Assistant Superintendent*—James Young. *Advisory Committee*—Lewis Cass Ledyard, N. Y.

The Order of the Founders and Patriots of America.

Governor-General—Col. Rollin Simmons Woodruff, New Haven, Ct. *Deputy Governor-General*—Gen. Edward Franc Jones, Binghamton, N. Y. *Chaplain-General*—Joseph F. Falsom, D. D., Newark, N. J. *Secretary-General*—Clarence E. Leonard, New York. *Treasurer-General*—William Alexander N. Doreland, M. D., Philadelphia, Pa. *Attorney-General*—Robert Hinckley, Philadelphia, Pa. *Registrar-General*—Wm. Edward Fitch, M. D., New York. *Genealogist-General*—George Franklin Newcomb, New Haven, Ct. *Historian-General*—Wm. White Knapp, Flushing, N. Y.

The Order was founded in 1896, its object being "to bring together and associate congenial men whose ancestors struggled together for life and liberty, home and happiness, in the land when it was a new and unknown country, and whose line of descent from them comes through patriots who sustained the Colonies in the struggle for independence in the Revolutionary War; to teach reverent regard for the names and history, character and perseverance, deeds and heroism of the founders of this country and their patriot descendants; to teach that the purpose of the founders could have had no lasting result but for their patriot sons; to inculcate patriotism; to discover, collect, and preserve records, documents, manuscripts, monuments, and history relating to the first colonists and their ancestors and their descendants, and to commemorate and celebrate events in the history of the Colonies and the Republic." Eligibility—Any man above the age of twenty-one years, of good moral character and reputation, and a citizen of the United States, who is lineally descended, in the male line of either parent, from an ancestor who settled in any of the Colonies now included in the United States of America prior to May 13, 1657, and whose intermediate ancestors in the same line during the Revolutionary period adhered as patriots to the cause of the Colonies, shall be eligible for membership. There are State Societies in New York, Connecticut, New Jersey, and Pennsylvania. The Governor of the New York Society is Edward Hagaman Hall, Tribune Building, New York. The Secretary is William White Knapp, Flushing, New York.

Principal Battleships of Naval Powers.

(Compiled from the latest authentic sources of official information. Only the principal and more modern battleships are given. Most of the principal powers possess powerful armored cruisers equal to or in greater number than battleships, and in addition many vessels of smaller and older types.)

Following Great Britain, the first naval power, the United States now ranks second; Germany and Japan tie for third place, while France has sunk to fifth; Russia, once the third naval power, has now declined to the eighth place.

GREAT BRITAIN.

Name.	Displacement. Tons.	Draught. Feet.	Indicated Horse-Power.	Keel Laid	Date of Completion.	Cost.	Armament. Guns.	Armament. Torpedo Tubes.	Speed. Knots.	Complement.
Collingwood (1)	19,250	..	24,500	1908	1910	....	....	..	..	..
Foudroyant (1)	....	..	....	..	..	....	....	..	..	..
St. Vincent (1)	19,250	..	24,500	1907	1910	....	....	..	..	..
Vanguard (1)	19,250	..	24,500	1908	1910	....	....	..	..	..
Bellerophon (1)	18,600	29	23,000	1906	1909	....	10 12-in., — 4 in...	5	21	800
Téméraire (1)	18,600	29	23,000	1907	1909	....	" ..	5	21	800
Superb (1)	18,600	29	23,000	1907	1909	....	" ..	5	21	800
Dreadnought	17,900	31	23,000	1905	1906	$9,065,500	10 12-in., 27 12-pdr..	5	21	800
Lord Nelson	16,600	27	20,000	1904	1907	8,040,410	4 12-in., 10 9-in., 15 12-pdr., 16 3-pdr., 6 Pompons, 2 M...	5	18	865
Agamemnon	16,600	27	20,000	1904	1907	8,025,325	" ..	5	18	865
King Edward	16,350	27	18,000	1902	1905	7,366,225	4 12-in., 4 9-in., 10 6-in., 12 12-pdr., 14 3-pdr., 2 Max......	5	18	777
Commonwealth	16,350	27	18,538	1902	1905	6,962,055	4 12-in., 4 9-in., 10 6-in., 14 12-pdr., 16 3-pdr...............	4	18	777
Dominion	16,350	27	18,438	1902	1905	6,828,950	" ..	4	18	777
Hindustan	16,350	27	18,521	1902	1905	7,272,630	" ..	4	19	777
New Zealand	16,350	27	18,440	1903	1905	7,121,875	" ..	4	19	777
Africa	16,350	27	18,698	1901	1906	7,307,145	" ..	4	19	777
Britannia	16,350	27	18,698	1901	1906	7,253,785	" ..	4	19	777
Hibernia	16,350	27	18,698	1901	1906	7,224,140	" ..	4	19	777
Queen	15,000	29	15,000	1901	1904	5,274,995	4 12-in., 12 6-in., 18 12-pdr., 6 3-pdr....	4	18	900
Prince of Wales	15,000	29	15,000	1901	1904	5,570,395	" ..	4	18	900
Hood	14,150	28	13,000	..	1[illegible]93	5,162,045	4 13-in., 10 6-in., 10 6-pdr., 12 3-pdr...	3	17	730
Formidable	15,000	27	15,000	1898	1901	5,113,525	4 12-in., 12 6-in., 18 12 pdr., 8 3-pdr....	4	18	750
Irresistible	15,000	27	15,000	1898	1902	5,240,680	" ..	4	18	750
Implacable	15,000	27	15,000	1898	1902	4,945,580	" ..	4	18	750
London	15,000	29	15,345	189[illegible]	1902	5,189,975	4 12-in., 12 6-in., 16 12-pdr., 8 3-pdr....	4	18	755
Venerable	15,000	29	15,345	1899	1902	5,463,765	" ..	4	18	755
Bulwark	15,800	29	15,345	1899	1902	4,889,230	" ..	4	18	755
Magnificent	14,900	28	12,000	1893	1895	4,543,9[illegible]5	4 12-in., 12 6-in., 16 12-pdr., 12 3-pdr..	5	17	757
Majestic	14,900	28	12,000	1894	1895	4,581,910	" ..	5	17	757
Prince George	14,900	28	12,000	1894	1896	4,477,520	" ..	5	17	757
Victorious	14,900	28	12,000	1894	1897	4,426,060	" ..	5	17	757
Cæsar	14,900	28	12,000	1895	1898	3,540,848	" ..	5	17	757
Hannibal	14,900	28	12,000	1894	1897	4,533,995	" ..	5	17	757
Illustrious	14,900	28	12,000	1895	1898	4,472,925	" ..	5	17	757
Jupiter	14,900	28	12,000	1894	1897	4,510,055	" ..	5	17	757
Mars	14,900	28	12,000	1894	1897	4,512,010	" ..	5	17	757
Royal Sovereign	14,150	28	13,312	1899	1902	4,195,680	4 13-in., 10 6-in., 16 6-pdr., 12 3-pdr....	3	17	712
Ramillies	14,150	28	13,312	1889	1893	4,513,000	" ..	3	17	730
Empress of India	14,150	28	13,312	1890	1893	4,231,605	" ..	3	17	730
Resolution	14,150	28	13,312	1891	1893	4,377,610	" ..	3	17	730
Royal Oak	14,150	28	13,312	1892	1894	4,496,360	" ..	3	17	730
Repulse	14,150	28	13,312	1889	1904	3,405,896	" ..	3	17	730
Revenge	14,150	28	13,312	1889	1895	4,[illegible]80,505	" ..	3	17	730
Albemarle	14,000	27	18,296	1900	1903	5,049,175	4 12-in., 12 6-in., 12 12-pdr., 8 3-pdr...	4	18	750
Cornwallis	14,000	27	18,296	1899	1904	5,115,735	" ..	4	18	750
Duncan	14,000	27	18,296	1899	1903	5,115,735	" ..	4	18	750
Exmouth	14,000	27	18,296	1899	1903	5,162,045	" ..	4	18	750
Russell	14,000	27	18,296	1899	1903	5,189,975	" ..	4	18	750
Canopus	12,950	26	13,500	1897	1900	3,466,064	4 12-in., 12 6-in., 12 12-pdr., 8 3-pdr....	4	18	700
Ocean	12,950	26	13,500	1897	1900	3,635,102	" ..	4	18	700
Goliath	12,950	26	13,500	1897	1900	3,364,054	" ..	4	18	700
Glory	12,950	26	13,500	1896	1901	3,364,056	" ..	4	18	700
Albion	12,950	26	13,500	1896	1902	3,434,980	" ..	4	18	700
Vengeance	12,950	26	13,500	1897	1901	3,345,668	" ..	4	18	700

UNITED STATES.

A full statement of the battleships of United States Navy will be found on other pages. See Index.

NAME.	Displacement. Tons.	Draught. Feet.	Indicated Horse-Power.	Keel Laid	Date of Completion.	Cost.	ARMAMENT. Guns.	Torpedo Tubes.	Speed Knots.	Complement.
GREAT BRITAIN—*Continued.*										
Swiftsure	11,800	25	12,500	1902	1904	4,225,180	4 10-in., 14 7-in., 14 14-pdr., 12 12-pdr., 12 6-pdr.	2	19	700
Triumph	11,800	25	12,500	1902	1904	4,227,395	"	2	19	700
Barfleur (2)	10,500	26	13,163	1890	1894	2,913,025	4 10-in., 10 6-in., 2 9-pdr., 8 6-pdr., 9 3-pdr., 12 6-pdr.	3	18	625
Centurion (2)	10,500	26	13,163	1891	1893	2,965,220	"	3	18	625
GERMANY.										
Ersatz-Sachsen (1)	17,710	26	24,000	1906	1909	....	10 11-in., 16 24-pdr.	6	19	860
Ersatz-Baden (1)	19,000	26	24,000	1907	1910	....	"	6	19	860
Ersatz-Württemb'g (1)	19,000	26	24,000	1907	1910	....	"	6	19	860
Ersatz-Beowulf (1)	19,000	26	24,000	1907	1910	....	"	6	19	860
Ersatz-Oldenburg (1)	19,000	26	24,000	1907	1910	....	"	6	19	860
Ersatz-Frithjof (1)	19,000	26	24,000	1907	1910	....	"	6	19	860
Nassau (1)	17,710	26	24,000	1907	1909	....	"	6	19	860
Deutschland	13,200	25	16,000	1903	1906	6,070,000	4 11-in., 14 6-in., 20 24-pdr., 4 1-pdr.	6	18	729
Hannover	13,200	25	16,000	1904	1907	6,070,000	"	6	18	729
Schleswig-Holstein (1)	13,200	25	16,000	1904	1908	6,070,000	"	6	18	729
Pommern	13,200	25	16,000	1904	1907	6,070,000	"	6	18	729
Schlesien (1)	13,200	25	16,000	1904	1908	6,070,000	"	6	18	729
Braunschweig	13,200	26	16,000	1901	1904	5,787,500	4-11 in., 14 6-in., 20 24-pdrs., 12 1-pdr., 8 M.	6	18	691
Hessen	13,200	26	16,000	1902	1905	5,787,500	"	6	18	691
Elsass	13,200	26	16,000	1901	1904	5,787,500	"	6	18	691
Preussen	13,200	26	16,000	1902	1905	5,787,500	"	6	18	691
Lothringen	13,200	26	16,000	1902	1906	5,787,500	"	6	18	691
Wittelsbach	11,830	28	15,000	1898	1902	5,500,000	4 9-in., 18 6-in., 12 15-pdr., 12 1-pdr., 8 M.	6	18	650
Wettin	11,830	28	15,000	1899	1902	5,500,000	"	6	18	650
Zahringen	11,830	28	15,000	1899	1902	5,500,000	"	6	18	650
Schwaben	11,830	28	15,000	1900	1903	5,500,000	"	6	18	650
Mecklenburg	11,830	28	15,000	1900	1903	5,500,000	"	6	18	650
Kaiser Frederick III	11,150	28	14,000	1895	1898	4,812,500	"	6	18	660
K. Wilhelm der Grosse	11,150	28	14,000	1898	1901	4,812,500	"	6	18	660
K. Wilhelm II	11,150	28	14,000	1896	1900	4,812,500	"	6	18	660
K. Karl der Grosse	11,150	28	14,000	1898	1901	4,812,500	"	6	18	660
K. Barbarossa	11,150	28	14,000	1898	1901	4,812,500	"	6	18	660
Brandenburg	10,060	26	10,000	1890	1894	3,720,000	6 11-in., 8 4-in., 8 15-pdr., 12 1-pdr., 4 M	3	17	568
Weissenburg	10,060	26	10,000	1890	1894	3,720,000	"	3	17	568
Worth	10,060	26	10,000	1890	1894	3,720,000	"	3	17	568
Kurfurst Friedrich Wilhelm	10,060	26	10,000	1890	1894	3,720,000	"	3	17	568
COAST SERVICE BATTLESHIPS.										
Siegfried	4,150	18	5,100	(8)	(9)	(10)	3 9-in., 10 15-pdr., 6 1-pdr.	4	15	297
Hildebrand	4,150	18	5,100	(8)	(9)	(10)	"	4	15	297
Beowulf	4,150	18	5,100	(8)	(9)	(10)	3 9-in., 10 15-pdr., 6 1-pdr.	4	15	297
Hagen	4,150	18	5,100	(8)	(9)	(10)		4	15	297
Frithjof	4,150	18	5,100	(8)	(9)	(10)	"	4	15	297
Odin	4,150	18	5,100	(8)	(9)	(10)	"	4	15	297
Heimdall	4,150	18	5,100	(8)	(9)	(10)	"	4	15	297
Aegir	4,150	18	5,100	(8)	(9)	(10)	"	4	15	297
JAPAN.										
No. 1 (1)	20,750	28	26,500	1906	1910	....	14 12-in., 10 6-in., 12 4-in.	5	20	....
No. 2 (1)	20,750	28	26,500	1907	1910	....	"	5	20	....
Satsuma (1)	19,250	29	27,000	1906	1908	....	4 12-in., 12 10-in., 12 6-in.	5	20	....
Aki (1)	18,800	29	27,000	1905	1908	....	"	5	20	....
Kashima	16,400	27	17,000	1904	1906	....	4 12-in., 4 10-in., 12 6-in., 12 14-pdr., 3 3-pdr.	5	18	980
Katori	16,400	27	17,000	1904	1906	....	"	5	18	980
Mikasa	15,200	28	15,000	1899	1902	....	4 12-in., 14 6-in., 20 12-pdr., 8 3-pdr., 4 2-pdr.	4	18	935
Shikishima	15,000	28	14,500	1897	1900	....	"	5	18	741
Asahi	15,000	28	14,500	1897	1901	....	4 12-in., 14 6-in., 20 12-pdr., 8 3-pdr., 6 2-pdr.	5	18	741
Iwami (3)	13,566	26	16,500	1900	1904	....	4 12-in., 6 8-in., 20 12-pdr., 20 3-pdr., 8 1-pddr.	4	18	750
Hizen (4)	12,700	25	16,000	1898	1902	$5,000,000	4 12-in., 12 6-in., 20 12-pdr., 20 3-pdr.	4	18	750

Name.	Displacement. Tons.	Draught. Feet.	Indicated Horse-Power.	Keel Laid.	Date of Completion.	Cost.	Armament. Guns.	Armament. Torpedo Tubes.	Speed. Knots.	Complement.
JAPAN—*Continued.*										
Suwo (5)	12,674	27	14,500	1898	1902	5,000,000	4 10-in., 11 6-in., 20 12-pdr.	4	19	732
Sagami (6)	12,674	27	14,500	1895	1901	5,000,000	"	4	19	732
Fuji	12,300	29	13,690	1894	1897	5,500,000	4 12-in., 10 6-in., 16 12-pdr.	5	18	600
Tango (7)	11,000	28	9,000	1892	1898	5,500,000	4 12-in., 12 6-in., 16 3-pdr.	4	16	750
FRANCE.										
Danton (1)	18,400	27	22,500	1906	1910	$8,006,120	4 12-in., 12 9-in., 16 12-pdr., 10 3-pdr.	2	19	681
Mirabeau (1)	17,710	27	22,500	1906	1910	9,016,120	"	2	19	681
Diderot (1)	17,710	27	22,500	1907	1911	10,004,120	"	2	19	681
Condorcet (1)	17,710	27	22,500	1907	1911	10,004,120	"	2	19	681
Vergniaud (1)	17,710	27	22,500	1907	1912	10,004,120	"	2	19	681
Voltaire (1)	17,710	27	22,500	1907	1912	10,004,120	"	2	19	681
Démocratie	14,635	28	18,000	1903	1907	4,892,720	4 12-in., 10 7-in., 13 9-pdr., 10 3-pdr.	2	18	793
Justice	14,635	28	18,000	1903	1907	8,351,925	"	2	18	793
Liberté	14,635	28	18,000	1903	1907	8,262,180	"	2	18	793
Verité (G)	14,635	28	18,000	1903	1908	8,307,055	"	2	18	793
Republique	14,865	28	19,626	1901	1906	7,615,680	4 12-in., 18 6-in., 26 3-pdr., 2 1-pdr.	2	19	793
Patrie	14,865	28	19,626	1902	1906	8,374,350	"	2	19	793
Suffren	12,527	28	16,500	1899	1903	5,977,820	4 12-in., 10 6-in., 8 3-in., 20 ⅛-in.	2	18	615
Charlemagne	11,105	28	14,500	1894	1899	5,482,160	4 12-in., 10 5-in., 8 4-in., 20 3-pdr.	2	18	632
St. Louis	11,105	28	14,500	1895	1900	5,404,985	"	2	18	632
Gaulois	11,105	28	14,500	1896	1899	5,464,625	"	2	18	632
Bouvet	12,007	28	14,000	1893	1898	5,503,850	2 12-in., 2 10-in., 8 5-in.	2	18	621
Massena	11,735	27	13,500	1892	1898	5,502,000	"	2	17	642
Charles Martel	11,693	28	14,996	1891	1896	5,464,150	"	2	18	632
Carnot	11,954	27	16,300	1891	1896	5,350,440	"	2	17	625
Jauréguiberry	11,637	28	15,800	1891	1896	5,347,680	"	2	18	625
Brennus	11,190	26	14,000	1889	1895	4,958,835	3 13-in., 10 6-in., 4 9-pdr., 14 3 pdr.	6	17	696
Henri IV	8,948	23	11,500	1897	1903	4,006,240	2 10-in., 7 5-in.	2	17	464
Bouvines	6,691	23	8,400	1890	1894	2,973,200	2 12-in., 8 4-in.	2	16	323
Tréhouart	6,691	23	8,400	1890	1896	2,965,500	"	2	16	323
Jemmappes	6,474	22	9,250	1889	1895	2,625,000	2 13-in., 4 4-in.	2	16	334
Valmy	6,474	23	8,954	1889	1895	2,894,785	"	2	16	297
Furieux (2)	5,925	22	5,033	1883	1905	1,323,200	2 9-in., 4 9-pdr., 8 3-pdr.	2	14	248
Indomptable (2)	7,105	23	6,605	1883	1903	....	2 10-in., 6 4-in., 10 3-pdr.	2	14	332
Caiman (2)	7,050	25	6,000	1885	1903	....	"	2	14	332
Requin (2)	7,078	25	7,000	1885	1903	....	"	2	14	332
ITALY.										
Vittorio Emanuele	12,625	26	20,000	1901	1907	$5,600,000	2 12-in., 12 8-in., 12 12-pdr.	4	22	715
Regina Elena	12,625	26	20,000	1901	1907	5,600,000	"	4	22	715
Napoli (1)	12,625	26	20,000	1903	1908	5,600,000	"	4	22	715
Roma (1)	12,625	26	20,000	1903	1908	5,600,000	"	4	22	715
Benedetto	13,427	27	14,000	1898	1904	5,750,000	4 12-in. 4 8-in., 12 6-in., 16 12-pdr., 8 6-pdr.	4	18	720
Regina Margherita	13,427	27	14,000	1898	1904	5,750,000	"	4	18	720
Ammiraglio di St. Bon.	9,800	26	9,000	1897	1901	3,500,000	4 10-in., 8 6-in., 8 4-in., 8 6-pdr.	4	16	542
Emanuele Filiberto	9,800	26	9,000	1897	1902	3,500,000	4 10-in., 8 6-in., 8 4-in., 6 12-pdr., 6 3-pdr.	4	16	542
Varese	7,400	25	13,500	1898	1901	3,000,000	1 10-in., 2 8-in., 14 6-in.	4	20	517
Giuseppe Garibaldi	7,400	25	13,500	1898	1901	3,000,000	"	4	20	517
Francesco Ferrusio	7,400	25	13,500	1899	1904	3,000,000	"	4	20	517
No. 1 (1)	19,000	28	30,000	1907	1912	....	8 12-in., 12 4-in.	..	24	..
San Giorgo (1)	9,830	25	20,000	1904	1909	....	4 10-in., 8 8-in., 16 12-pdr., 8 3-pdr.	..	24	550
San Marco (1)	9,830	25	20,000	1905	1910	....	"	..	24	550
Pisa (1)	9,830	25	20,000	1906	1908	....	"	..	24	550
Amalfi (1)	9,830	25	20,000	1906	1908	....	"	..	24	550
AUSTRO-HUNGARY.										
Ersatz Teggethoff (1)	14,500	....	....	1907	1910	....	4 12-in., 8 9-in.	....	20	....
Stefanie (1)	14,500	....	....	1907	1911	....	"	....	20	....
Rudolf (1)	14,500	....	....	1907	1912	....	"	....	20	....

AUSTRO-HUNGARY—*Continued.*

Name.	Displacement. Tons.	Draught. Feet.	Indicated Horse-Power.	Keel Laid	Date of Completion.	Cost.	Armament. Guns.	Armament. Torpedo Tubes.	Speed Knots.	Complement.
Erzherzog Karl	10,000	25	14,000	1901	1905	$3,650,000	4 9-in., 12 7-in., 14 12-pdr	2	19	700
" Friedrich	10,000	28	14,000	1902	1906	,650.000	"	2	19	700
" Max	10,000	25	14,000	1903	1907	.650.000	"	2	19	700
Habsburg	8,340	25	11,900	1899	1903	3,504,000	12 6-in., 3 9-in., 10 12-pdr	2	18	638
Arpad	8,340	25	11,900	1899	1903	2, 40,000	"	2	18	638
Babenburg	8,3·0	25	11,900	1900	1904	2,640,000	"	2	18	638
Erzherzog Ferd'nd (1)	14,500	26	20,000	....	....	....	4 12-in., 8 9-in., 20 4-in	2	20	..
Radetzky (1)	14,500	26	14,500	....	....	....	"	2	..	..
Wien	5,600	21	8,480	1893	1896	1,980,000	4 9-in., 6 6-in., 14 3-pdr	4	16	460
Monarch	5,600	21	8,480	1893	1896	2,000,000	"	4	16	460
Budapest	5,600	21	8,480	1893	1896	2,000,000	"	4	16	460

RUSSIA.

Name.	Displacement. Tons.	Draught. Feet.	Indicated Horse-Power.	Keel Laid	Date of Completion.	Cost.	Armament. Guns.	Armament. Torpedo Tubes.	Speed Knots.	Complement.
Imperator Pavel (1)	17,400	27	17,600	1903	1909	$6,000,000	4 12-in., 12 8-in., 20 4-in	6	18	....
AndreiPervoswanni (1)	17,400	27	17,600	1903	1909	6,000,000	"	6	18	....
Slava	13,566	26	16,500	1902	1905	7,500,000	4 12-in., 12 6-in., 20 12-pdr., 20 3-pdr	4	18	750
Tsessarevitch	13,380	28	16,300	1899	1904	6,000,000	4 12-in., 12 6-in., 20 12 pdr., 2 9-pdr., 20 3-pdr		18	732
Pantelimon	12,480	27	10,600	1898	1902	5,000,000	4 12-in., 16 6-in., 14 3-in		17	636
Ievstafi (1)	12,733	27	10,600	1905	....	....	4 12-in., 16 6-in., 14 3-in	4	16	731
Zlatoust (1)	12,733	27	10,600	1905	....	....	"	3	16	731
Trisvititelia	13,318	27	10,600	1893	1896	6,000,000	4 12-in., 8 6-in., 4 4-in	6	18	582
Rostislav	8,880	24	8,500	1896	1899	4,250,000	4 10-in., 8 5-in	6	16	624
Georgi Pobiedoncsetz	10,280	26	10,600	1892	1896	2,155,000	6 12-in., 7 6-in	7	16	500
Sinope	10,180	27	13,000	1887	1890	4,500,000	"	7	16	325

SWEDEN.

Name.	Displacement. Tons.	Draught. Feet.	Indicated Horse-Power.	Keel Laid	Date of Completion.	Cost.	Armament. Guns.	Armament. Torpedo Tubes.	Speed Knots.	Complement.
Oscar II	4,275	16	8,500	1905	1907	....	2 8-in., 8 6-in., 10 6-pdr	2	18	326
Aran	3,650	16	6,500	1901	1902	....	2 8-in., 6 6-in., 10 3-pdr., 2 1-pdr	2	17	250
Vasa	3,650	16	6,500	1893	1901	....	"	2	17	250
Tapperheten	3,650	16	6,500	1901	1904	....	"	2	17	250
Dristigheten	3,500	16	5,570	1900	1901	....	2 8-in., 6 6-in., 10 6-pdr., 2 1-pdr	2	16	250

NORWAY.

Name.	Displacement. Tons.	Draught. Feet.	Indicated Horse-Power.	Keel Laid	Date of Completion.	Cost.	Armament. Guns.	Armament. Torpedo Tubes.	Speed Knots.	Complement.
Norge	3,800	16	4,850	1898	1901	$1,750,000	2 8-in., 6 6-in., 8 12-pdr	2	17	250
Eidsvold	3,800	16	4,850	1898	1901	1,750,000	"	2	17	250
Haarfagre	3,400	19	3,700	1896	1898	1,500,000	2 8-in., 6 4-in., 6 12-pdr., 6 1-pdr	2	17	220
Tordenskjold	3,400	19	3,700	1897	1899	1,500,000	"	2	17	220

DENMARK.

Name.	Displacement. Tons.	Draught. Feet.	Indicated Horse-Power.	Keel Laid	Date of Completion.	Cost.	Armament. Guns.	Armament. Torpedo Tubes.	Speed Knots.	Complement.
Herluf Trolle	3,470	16	4,200	1896	1901	....	2 9-in., 1 6-in., 10 6-pdr	3	16	250
Olfert Fischer	3,470	16	4,200	1896	1901	....	"	3	16	250
Peder Skram (1)	3,470	16	4,200	..	..	....	"	3	16	250
Skjold	2,160	17	2,200	1893	1899	....	1 9-in., 3 4-in., 4 3-pdr., 2 1-pdr	4	13	210
Hvitfeldt	3,200	..	5,000	1886	1889	1,000,000	2 10-in., 10-6 pdr., 2 Mach	4	15	298

THE NETHERLANDS.

Name.	Displacement. Tons.	Draught. Feet.	Indicated Horse-Power.	Keel Laid	Date of Completion.	Cost.	Armament. Guns.	Armament. Torpedo Tubes.	Speed Knots.	Complement.
Tromp	5,300	18	6,000	1904	1906	1,737,500	2 9-in., 4 6-in., 10 12-pdr	3	16	344
Koningin Regentes	4,950	18	5,300	1898	1902	1,737,500	2 9-in., 4 6-in., 8 12-pdr	3	16	320
De Ruyter	4,950	18	5,300	1900	1904	1,737,500	"	3	16	320
Hertog Hendrik	4,950	18	5,300	1899	1903	1,737,500	"	3	16	320
Gelderland	3,950	17	10,000	1895	1900	....	2 6-in., 6 4-in., 4 12-pdr., 8 1-pdr	4	20	333
Noordbrabant	3,950	17	10,000	1897	1900	....	"	4	20	333
Utrecht	3,950	17	10,000	1897	1900	....	"	4	20	333
Heemskerck (1)	5,130	17	6,600	1908	..	1,700,000	2 9-in., 6 6-in., 6 12-pdr	2	17	441

Name.	Displacement. Tons.	Draught. Feet.	Indicated Horse-Power.	Keel Laid	Date of Completion.	Cost.	Armament. Guns.	Armament. Torpedo Tubes.	Speed Knots.	Complement.
SPAIN.										
Pelayo	9,950	28	8,000	1887	1890	....	2 12-in., 2 11-in., 9 5-in., 12 2-pdr., 9 1-pdr., 1 M.	7	16	621
Emperador Carlos V	9,200	29	15,000	1893	1898	3,600,000	2 9-in., 8 5-in., 4 4-in., 2 12-pdr., 8 6-pdr.	6	19	600
Princesa de Asturias	7,000	25	10,000	1896	..	3,000,000	2 9-in., 8 5-in., 2 12-pdr., 8 6-pdr.	2	18	497
Cataluna	7,000	25	10,000	1900	..	3,000,000	" ..	2	18	497
Reina Regente	5,372	19	15,0[illegible]0	1899	1906	....	10 6-in., 12 6-pdr., 2 1-pdr.	3	21	497
PORTUGAL.										
Vasco da Gama	3,100	20	6,000	1875	1902	660,000	2 8-in., 1 6-in., 1 12-pdr., 6 3-pdr.	2	15	218
Don Carlos I	4,100	17	12,500	1898	1899	....	4 6-in., 8 4-in., 12 3-pdr., 10 1-pdr.	5	20	473
TURKEY.										
Messoudieh	10,000	27	11,000	1874	1876	....	2 9-in., 12 6-in., 14 12-pdr., 10 6-pdr., 2 3-pdr., 2 field	..	16	600
Assar-I-Tewfik	5,000	25	3,560	1903	1907	....	3 6-in., 7 4-in., 6 6-pdr.	..	13	320
GREECE.										
Hydra	5,000	24	6,700	1889	1891	....	3 10-in., 5 6-in., 1 4-in., 8 9-pdr., 4 3-pdr., 12 1-pdr.	3	17	440
Spetsai	5,000	24	6,700	1889	1891	....	" ..	3	17	440
Psara	5,000	24	6,700	1890	1892	....	" ..	3	17	440
Pisa (2)	9,830	23	18,000	1906	1909	....	4 10-in., 8 8-in., 16 12-pdr.	3	22	550
ARGENTINE REPUBLIC.										
Independencia	2,336	13	2,780	1891	1893	880,000	2 9-in., 4 4-in., 4 3-pdr., 2 1-pdr.	2	14	225
Libertad	2,336	13	2,780	1890	1892	880,000	2 9-in., 4 4-in., 4 3-pdr., 2 1-pdr.	2	14	225
Almirante Brown (2)	4,267	22	4,500	1880	1897	....	10 6-in., 4 4-in., 8 3-pdr	2	14	380
BRAZIL.										
Minas Geraes (1)	18,000	25	24,500	1907	1910	....	12 12-in., 22 4-in.	4	21	....
Sao Paulo (1)	18,000	25	24,500	1907	1910	....	" ..	4	21	....
Rio de Janeiro (1)	18,000	25	24,500	1907	1911	....	" ..	4	21	....
Riachuelo	5,700	22	7,000	1883	1895	1,825,000	4 9-in., 6 4-in., 6 3-pdr., 15 M.	5	16	390
Deodoro	3,162	15	3,400	1896	1901	....	2 9-in., 4 4-in., 2 12-pdr., 4 6-pdr.	2	14	200
Floriano	3,162	15	3,400	1896	1901	....	" ..	2	14	200
CHILE.										
O'Higgins	8,500	22	10,000	1896	1898	3,500,000	4 8-in., 10 6-in., 4 4-in., 10 12-pdr., 10 6-pdr., 4 Mach.	5	19	420
Capitan Prat	6,901	26	12,000	1888	1893	1,955,000	4 9-in., 8 4-in., 6 6-pdr., 4 3-pdr., 10 1-pdr., 5 Max.	4	18	480
Almirante Cochrane (2)	3,500	22	2,920	..	1900	....	6 8-in., 1 13-pdr., 4 6-pdr., 4 1-pdr.	4	12	242

NOTES—1. Building. 2. Reconstructed. 3. Formerly the Russian Oriel, captured 1905. 4. Formerly the Russian Retvizan, scuttled at Port Arthur and raised September, 1905. 5. Formerly the Russian Pobieda, scuttled during war and salved 1905. 6. Formerly the Russian Peresviet, scuttled during war and salved 1905. 7. Formerly the Russian Poltava, sunk during war and salved 1905. 8. Keels laid from 1838 to 1892. 9. Completed from 1899 to 1903. 10. Cost from $850,000 to $1,167,500.

Sovereigns of Europe.

ARRANGED ACCORDING TO THE DATES OF THEIR ACCESSION.

Sovereigns.	Accession.	Age at Accession.
Francis Joseph, Emperor of Austria	1848	19
Ernest, Duke of Saxe-Altenburg	1853	27
John II., Prince of Lichtenstein	1858	19
Nicholas, Prince of Montenegro	1860	20
George I., King of the Hellenes	1863	18
Leopold II., King of the Belgians	1865	31
Charles, King of Roumania	1866	27
George II., Duke of Saxe-Meiningen	1866	41
Henry XIV., Prince of Reuss (younger line)	1867	36
Abdul Hamid, Sultan of Turkey	1876	34
Charles, Prince of Schwarzburg-Sondershausen	1880	50
Alphonso XIII., King of Spain	1886	..
Otto I., King of Bavaria	1886	39
Ferdinand, Prince of Bulgaria	1887	27
William II., German Emperor	1888	30
Albert, Prince of Monaco	1889	42
Gunther, Pr. of Schwarzburg-Rudolstadt	1890	39
Wilhelmina, Queen of Netherlands	1890	11
William, King of Württemberg	1891	44
Ernest Louis, Grand Duke of Hesse	1892	24
Frederick, Prince of Waldeck	1893	29
George, Prince of Schaumburg-Lippe	1893	46
Nicholas II., Emperor of Russia	1894	27
Frederick IV., Grand Duke of Mecklenburg-Schwerin	1897	16
Fred'k Augustus, Grand Duke, Oldenburg	1900	48
Victor Emmanuel III., King of Italy	1900	31
Charles Edward, Duke of Saxe-Coburg-Gotha	1900	17
William Ernest, G'd Duke Saxe-Weimar	1901	25
Edward VII., King of Great Britain, etc.	1901	60
Henry XXIV., Pr. of Reuss (elder line)	1902	23
Peter, King of Servia	1903	59
Pius X., Pope	1903	69
Frederick, Duke of Anhalt	1904	48
Adolphus Frederick, Duke of Mecklenburg-Strelitz	1904	56
Augustus III., King of Saxony	1904	39
William, Grand Duke of Luxembourg	1905	53
Haakon VII., King of Norway	1905	33
Frederick VIII., King of Denmark	1906	63
Frederick II., Grand Duke of Baden	1907	50
Gustaf V., King of Sweden	1907	49
Manuel II, King of Portugal	1908	19

ARRANGED ACCORDING TO THEIR RESPECTIVE AGES.

Sovereigns.	Yr. of Birth	Age Jan. 1, 1909. y.	m.	d.
George II., Duke of Saxe-Meiningen	1826	82	8	28
Ernest, Duke of Saxe-Altenburg	1826	82	3	14
Charles, Prince of Schwarzburg-Sondershausen	1830	78	4	24
Francis Joseph, Emperor of Austria	1830	78	4	13
Henry XIV., Pr. of Reuss (y'nger line)	1832	76	7	3
Leopold II., King of the Belgians	1835	73	8	21
Pius X., Pope	1835	73	6	30
Charles, King of Roumania	1839	69	8	19
John II., Prince of Lichtenstein	1840	68	2	26
Nicholas, Prince of Montenegro	1841	67	2	23
Edward VII., King of G't Britain, etc.	1841	67	1	23
Abdul Hamid, Sultan of Turkey	1842	66	3	8
Frederick VIII., King of Denmark	1843	65	6	28
Peter, King of Servia	1844	64	..	..
George I., King of the Hellenes	1845	63	6	7
George, Pr. of Schaumburg-Lippe	1846	62	7	24
William, King of Württemberg	1848	60	10	3
Otto, King of Bavaria	1848	60	8	4
Adolphus Frederick, Grand Duke of Mecklenburg-Strelitz	1848	60	5	9
Albert, Prince of Monaco	1848	60	1	19
William, Grand Duke of Luxembourg	1852	56	8	10
Gunther, Pr. of Schwarzb'g-Rudolstadt	1852	56	4	9
F'k Augustus, Grand Duke of Oldenburg	1852	56	6	28
Frederick, Duke of Anhalt	1856	52	4	13
Frederick II., Grand Duke of Baden	1857	51	5	23
Gustaf V., King of Sweden	1858	50	6	14
William II., German Emperor	1859	49	11	4
Ferdinand, Prince of Bulgaria	1861	47	10	6
Frederick, Prince of Waldeck	1865	43	11	11
Augustus III., King of Saxony	1865	43	7	7
Nicholas II., Emperor of Russia	1868	40	7	14
Ernest Louis, Grand Duke of Hesse	1868	40	1	6
Victor Emmanuel III., King of Italy	1869	39	8	19
Haakon VII., King of Norway	1872	36	8	29
William Ernest, G'd D'k Saxe-Weimar	1876	32	6	22
Henry XXIV., Pr. of Reuss (eld. line)	1878	30	9	12
Wilhelmina, Queen of Netherlands	1880	28	4	1
Frederick IV., Grand Duke of Mecklenburg-Schwerin	1882	26	0	1
Charles Edward, Duke of Saxe-Coburg-Gotha	1884	24	0	11
Alphonso XIII., King of Spain	1886	22	7	14
Manuel II., King of Portugal	1889	19	11	15

COST OF THE BRITISH ROYAL FAMILY.

The annuities paid by the British people to the royal family for its support are as follows: The King and Queen, $2,350,000; Prince of Wales, $100,000; Princess of Wales, $50,000; Princess Christian, $30,000; Princess Louise (Duchess of Argyll) $30,000; Duke of Connaught, $125,000; Princess Beatrice, $30,000; Duchess of Albany, $30,000; Duchess of Mecklenburg-Strelitz, $15,000; Trustees for the King's Daughters, $90,000; Total, $2,910,000. The King also receives the revenues of the Duchy of Lancaster. During recent years these have amounted to about $500,000 per annum. The Prince of Wales has an income also from the revenues of the Duchy of Cornwall, amounting to about $300,000 per annum. When the royal children marry dowries are usually provided for them. The last of the children of the late Queen Victoria to marry, Princess Beatrice, received $150,000 as dowry from the British people by Parliamentary grant.

THE RULERS OF FRANCE FROM THE REVOLUTION OF 1792.

(Whitaker's Almanack.)

The First Republic.

The National Convention first sat....Sept. 21, 1792
The Directory nominated..............Nov. 1, 1795

The Consulate.

Bonaparte, Cambacérô, and Lebrun..Dec. 24, 1799
Bonaparte, Consul for 10 years.........May 6, 1802
Bonaparte, Consul for life.............Aug. 2, 1802

The Empire.

Napoleon I. decreed Emperor.........May 18, 1804
Napoleon II. (never reigned).....died July 22, 1832

The Restoration.

Louis XVIII. re-entered Paris.......May 3, 1814
Charles X. (dep. July 30, 1830, d. Nov. 6, 1836) 1824

The House of Orleans.

Louis Philippe, King of the French............1830
(Abdicated Feb. 24, 1848; died Aug. 26, 1850).

The Second Republic.

Provisional Government formed......Feb. 22, 1848
Louis Napoleon elected President....Dec. 19, 1848

The Second Empire.

Napoleon III. elected Emperor.......Nov. 22, 1852
(Deposed Sept. 4, 1870, died Jan. 9, 1873.)

The Third Republic.

Committee of Public Defence.........Sept. 4, 1870
L. A. Thiers elected President.........Aug. 31, 1871
Marshal MacMahon elected President. May 24, 1873
Jules Grévy elected President........Jan. 30, 1879
Marie F. S. Carnot elected President..Dec. 3, 1887
(Assassinated at Lyons June 24, 1894.)
Jean Casimir Perier elected President. June 27, 1894
Felix François Faure elected Pres't..Jan. 17, 1895
Emile Loubet elected President.......Feb. 18, 1899
Armand Fallières elected President..Jan. 17, 1906

Heads of the Governments of the World.

DECEMBER 31, 1908.

Country.	Official Head.	Title.	Born.	Acceded.
Abyssinia	Menelik II	Emperor	1843	March 12, 1889
Afghanistan	Habibulla Khan	Ameer	1872	Oct. 3, 1901
Annam	Duy Tan	King	1899	Oct., 1907
Argentine Republic	José Figueroa Alcorta	President	....	Mar. 12, 1906
Austria-Hungary	Francis Joseph	Emperor	Aug. 18, 1830	Dec. 2, 1848
Baluchistan	Mir Mahmud	Khan	....	Aug., 1893
Belgium	Leopold II	King	April 9, 1835	Dec., 10, 1865
Bokhara	Seid Abdul Ahad	Ameer	1864	Nov. 12, 1885
Bolivia	Ismael Montes	President	....	Oct. 24, 1904
Brazil	Alphonso Penna	President	....	Nov. 15, 1906
Bulgaria	Ferdinand	Czar	Feb. 26, 1861	Aug. 11, 1887
Chile	Pedro Montt	President	....	1906
China	Pu-yi (Hsuantung)	Emperor	Feb. 11, 1906	1908
Colombia	General Rafael Reyes	President	....	1904
Congo Free State	Leopold (King of the Belgians)	Sovereign	April 9, 1835	April 30, 1885
Costa Rica	G. Gonzalez Viquez	President	....	1906
Cuba	José Miguel Gomez	President	1853	Jan. 1909
Denmark	Frederick VIII	King	June 3, 1843	Jan. 29, 1906
Dominican Republic	Ramon Caceres	President	....	Jan. 1906
Ecuador	Eloy Alfaro	President	....	1906
Egypt	Abbas Pacha	Khédive	July 14, 1874	Jan. 7, 1892
France	Armand Fallières	President	1841	Jan. 17, 1906
Germany	William II	Emperor	Jan. 27, 1859	June 15, 1888
Prussia	William II	King		
Bavaria	Otto	King	April 27, 1848	June 13, 1886
Saxony	Frederick Augustus III	King	May 25, 1865	Oct. 15, 1904
Württemberg	William II	King	Feb. 25, 1848	Oct. 6, 1891
Baden	Frederick II	Grand Duke	July 9, 1857	Sept. 28, 1907
Hesse	Ernst Louis V	Grand Duke	Nov. 25, 1868	March 13, 1892
Anhalt	Frederick	Duke	Aug. 19, 1856	Jan. 24, 1904
Mecklenburg-Schwerin	Frederick Francis IV	Grand Duke	April 9, 1882	April 10, 1897
Mecklenburg-Strelitz	Adolphus Frederick	Grand Duke	July 22, 1848	May 30, 1904
Oldenburg	Frederick Augustus	Grand Duke	Nov. 16, 1852	June 13, 1900
Saxe-Altenburg	Ernest	Duke	Sept. 16, 1826	Aug. 3, 1853
Saxe-Coburg and Gotha	Charles Edward	Duke	July 19, 1884	July 30, 1900
Saxe-Meiningen	George II	Duke	April 2, 1826	Sept. 20, 1868
Saxe-Weimar	William Ernest	Grand Duke	June 10, 1876	Jan. 5, 1901
Waldeck-Pyrmont	Frederick	Prince	Jan. 20, 1865	May 12, 1893
Brunswick	Johann Albrecht	Regent	....	May 28, 1907
Great Britain and Ireland	Edward VII	King	Nov. 9, 1841	Jan. 22, 1901
Greece	George	King	Dec. 24, 1845	Oct. 31, 1863
Guatemala	Manuel Estrada Cabrera	President	Dec. 24, 1856	Sept. 25, 1898
Hayti	Antoine Simon	President	....	Dec. 17, 1908
Honduras	Miguel R. Davila	President	....	April 18, 1907
India, Empire of	Edward	Emperor	Nov. 9, 1841	Jan. 22, 1901
Italy	Victor Emmanuel III	King	Nov. 11, 1869	July 29, 1900
Japan	Mutsuhito	Mikado	Nov. 3, 1852	Feb. 13, 1867
Khiva	Seid Mahomed Rahim	Kahn	1845	1865
Korea	Yi-Syck	Emperor	....	July 19, 1907
Liberia	Arthur Barclay	President	1854	May, 1907
Luxembourg	William	Grand Duke	April 22, 1852	Nov. 19, 1905
Mexico	General Porfirio Diaz	President	Sept. 30, 1830	Dec. 1, 1884
Monaco	Albert	Prince	Nov. 13, 1848	Sept. 10, 1889
Montenegro	Nicholas	Prince	Oct. 7, 1841	Aug. 14, 1860
Morocco	Muley Hafid	Sultan	1873	1908
Nepal	Surendra Bikram Shamsher Jang	Maharaja	Aug. 8, 1875	May 17, 1881
Netherlands	Wilhelmina	Queen	Aug. 31, 1880	Sept. 5, 1898
Nicaragua	General José S. Zelaya	President	1852	1893
Norway	Haakon VII	King	Aug. 3, 1872	Nov. 18, 1905
Oman	Seyyid Feysal bin Turkee	Sultan	....	June 4, 1888
Panama	José D. de Obaldia	President	1845	1908
Paraguay	E. Gonzalez Navero	President	....	1908
Persia	Mohammed Ali Mirza	Shah	June 21, 1872	Jan. 9, 1907
Peru	A. B. Leguia	President	....	1908
Portugal	Manuel II	King	Nov. 15, 1889	Feb. 1, 1908
Roumania	Charles	King	April 20, 1839	March 26, 1881
Russia	Nicholas II	Emperor	May 18, 1868	Nov. 2, 1894
Salvador	Fernando Figueroa	President	....	Jan., 1907
Servia	Peter (Karageorgevitch)	King	1844	June 15, 1903
Siam	Khoulalonkorn	King	Sept. 21, 1853	Oct. 1, 1868
Spain	Alphonso XIII	King	May 17, 1886	May 17, 1886
Sweden	Gustaf V	King	June 16, 1858	Dec., 8, 1907
Switzerland	T. Zemp	President	....	1909
Tunis	Mohamed en Nasir	Bey	....	1908
Turkey	Abdul Hamid II	Sultan	Sept. 22, 1842	Aug. 31, 1876
United States of America	Theodore Roosevelt*	President	Oct. 27 1858	Sept. 14, 1901
Uruguay	Claudio Williman	President	....	March 1, 1907
Venezuela	Juan Vicente Gomez	President	....	Dec., 1908
Zanzibar	Seyyid Ali	Sultan	1856	1902

DECEMBER 1, 1908.

AUSTRIA-HUNGARY.

(After a prolonged cabinet crisis, seeing the impossibility of the parliamentary parties agreeing on the nomination of a political ministry, the Emperor named six high officials ad interim ministers, and appointed only a Premier, a Minister of Defences and three Ministers representing the three nationalities.)

EMPIRE.

Minister Foreign Affairs—Baron A. L. von Aehrenthal
Minister Finance—Herr von Burian.
Minister War—F. Z. M. von Schonaich.
Minister Navy—Adm. Count R. Montecuccoli.

AUSTRIA.

Premier—Baron Richard Bienerth.
Minister Interior—Baron von Haerdtl.
Minister Defences—F. M. L. Friedrich von Georgi.
Minister Railways—Dr. von Forster.
Minister Public Instruction—Ritter von Kanera.
Minister Finance—Baron von Torkasch-Koch.
Minister Justice—Dr. Holzknecht von Hort.
Minister Agriculture—Herr von Pop.
Minister Commerce—Dr. Mataja.
Minister Labor Department—Dr. Count Wickenburg.
Minister German National—Dr. Schreiner.
Minister Czech National—Dr. Zaczek.
Minister Polish National—Ritter David von Abrahamovic.

HUNGARY.

Premier and Finances—Dr. Alexander Wekerle.
Minister Defences—F. Z. M. von Zekelfalussy.
Minister Commerce—Franz Kossuth.
Minister Education & Worship—Count Alb. Appony.
Minister Interior—Count Julius Andrassy.
Minister Agriculture—Baron Artur Feilitsch.
Minister Justice—Dr. Guenther.
Minister for Croatia—Count Theo. Pejacsevich.

BELGIUM.

Premier and Minister of the Interior and Agriculture—M. Schollaert.
Minister of Justice—M. De Lantsheere
Minister of Foreign Affairs—M. Julien Davignon.
Minister of Finance—M. Julien Liebaert.
Min. of Sciences and Arts—M. le Baron Descamps.
Minister of Industry and Labor—M. Armand Hubert.
Minister of Public Works—M. Auguste Delbeke.
Minister of Railways, Posts and Telegraphs—M. Georges Helleputte.
Minister of War—M. le Lieut.-General Hellebaut.
Minister of the Colonies (Congo)—M. Renkin.

FRANCE.

President of the Council and Minister of the Interior—M. Clemenceau.
Minister Foreign Affairs—M. Pichon.
Minister War—General Picquart.
Minister Marine—M. Alfred Picard.
Minister Justice—M. Guyot-Dessaigne.
Minister Finance—M. Caillaux.
Minister Agriculture—M. Ruau.
Minister Commerce—M. Doumergue.
Minister Public Instruction and Fine Arts—M. Briand.
Minister Colonies—M. Millies-Lacroix.
Minister Public Works—M. Barthou.
Minister of Labor and Public Health—M. Viviani

GERMANY.

Chancellor of the Empire—Prince Bernard v. Bülow.
Minister Foreign Affairs—Herr von Schoen.
Minister Interior—Herr von Betmann-Holweg.
Minister Marine—Admiral von Tirpitz.
Minister Justice—Dr. Nieberding.
Minister Finance—Herr von Sydow.
Minister Post-Office—Herr Kraetke.
Minister Railroads—General von Breitenbach.

ITALY.

President and Minister Interior—Signor Giolitti.
Minister Foreign Affairs—Signor Tittoni.
Minister Justice—Signor Orlando.
Minister War—Signor Casana.
Minister Marine—Rear-Admiral Mirabello.
Minister Instruction—Signor Rava.
Minister Finance—Signor Lacava.
Minister Treasury—Signor Carcano.
Minister Agriculture—Signor Cocco-Ortu.
Minister Public Works—Signor Bertolini.
Minister Posts and Telegraphs—Signor Schanzer.

NETHERLANDS.

Premier and Minister Finance—M. Kolkman.
Minister Foreign Affairs—M. de Marees van Sinderen.
Minister Colonies—M. Idenburg.
Minister War—M. Sabron.
Minister Interior—M. Heemskerk.
Minister Marine—M. Wentholt.
Minister Water (Waterstaat)—M. Bevers.
Min. Agriculture, Industry and Commerce—M. Talma.

NORWAY.

President Council—G. Knudsen.
Minister Foreign Affairs—W. Christophersen.
Minister Defence—Col. H. D. Lowzow.
Minister Justice and Police—J. Castberg.
Minister Public Works—N. Ihlen.
Minister Religion and Instruction—K. Seip.
Minister of Agriculture—H. K. H. Foosnäs.
Min. Commerce, Navig. and Ind.—L. Abrahamsen.
Minister Finance and Customs—G. Knudsen.
Minister Public Accounts—H. K. H. Foosnäs.

RUSSIA.

President of the Council and Minister Interior—M. Stolypin.
Minister Foreign Affairs—M. Isvolsky.
Minister Finance—M. Kokowzew.
Minister Instruction and Religion—M. Schwartz.
Minister Imperial Household—Baron Fredericks.
Min. Im. Domains and Agriculture—M. Wassiltschikow
Minister War—General Rödiger.
Minister Marine—Vice-Admiral Diekow.
Minister Justice—M. Shcheglovitoff.
Minister Public Works and Communications—General Schaffhausen.

SPAIN.

President of Council—Senor Maura.
Minister War—Marshal Primo de Rivera.
Minister Marine—Admiral Ferrandis.
Minister Interior—Senor Lacierva.
Minister Finance—Senor Gonzalez Besada.
Minister Justice—Marques de Figueroa.
Minister Foreign Affairs—Senor Allendesalazar.
Minister Instruction—Senor Rodriguez San Pedro.
Minister Public Works—Senor Sanchez Guerra.

SWEDEN.

Premier—S. A. A. Lindman.
Minister Foreign Affairs—E. Trolle.
Minister Justice—G. A. Petersson.
Minister War—M. O. B. Malm, Major-General.
Minister Marine—Com. Count C. A. Ehrensvärd.
Minister Interior—Count H. E. G. Hamilton.
Minister Finance—C. J. G. Swartz.
Minister Instruction—A. H. Hammarskjold.
Minister Agriculture—A. Petersson.
Ministers without portfolios—C. F. W. Hederstierna, G. W. A. Roos.

Reigning Families

OF THE PRINCIPAL EUROPEAN COUNTRIES.

AUSTRIA-HUNGARY.

Francis Joseph I., the Emperor of Austria and King of Hungary, was born August 18, 1830, and was proclaimed Emperor of Austria after the abdication of his uncle, Ferdinand I., on December 2, 1848. He was crowned King of Hungary June 8, 1867. He married, in 1854, Elizabeth, a daughter of Duke Maximilian of Bavaria. She died by the hand of an Anarchist in Geneva, September 10, 1898. They had issue:

1. Archduchess Gisela, born 1856; married to Leopold, son of the Regent Luitpold of Bavaria. Issue, two daughters and two sons.
2. Archduke Rudolph, late heir apparent, born 1858; died by suicide, 1889. He married, 1881, Stephanie, daughter of the present King of the Belgians, and had issue one daughter, the Archduchess Elizabeth, born 1883; married, 1902, Prince Otto Windischgrätz. The widowed Crown Princess Stephanie married, March, 1900, Count Elémer Lonyay.
3. Archduchess Marie Valerie, born 1868; married, 1890, Archduke Francis-Salvator of Tuscany.

On the death of the Crown Prince, in 1889, the right of succession to the throne passed to the Emperor's eldest brother, the Archduke Charles Louis, who was born 1833, and died 1896; he married, 1862 (second marriage), the Princess Annunciata, daughter of King Ferdinand II. of Naples, and had issue the Archduke Francis Ferd'nand, born 1863, who is the heir presumptive to the throne (married, morganatically, 1900, Countess Sophie Chotek, and renounced the claim of his issue by her to the throne); the Archduke Otto, born 1865, died 1906, married to the Princess Marie Josefa of Saxony, had two sons (Archdukes Charles, born 1887, and Maximilian, born 1895); the Archduke Ferdinand, born 1868, and unmarried, and the Archduchess Margaret Sophia, born 1870, died 1902; she married in 1893 Albert, Duke of Württemberg. By a third marriage, the Archduke Charles Louis had two daughters.

The Emperor has a second brother, the Archduke Louis Victor, born 1842, who is unmarried, and a sister-in-law, Empress Carlotta of Mexico, the widow of his brother Maximilian, executed at Queretaro in 1867. She is insane, and lives in Belgium with the King, her brother.

There are over seventy other archdukes and archduchesses of Austria, cousins of the Emperor, collateral relatives of the reigning house and members of the formerly reigning branches of Tuscany and Modena. The family is descended from Count Rudolph of Hapsburg, who was elected Emperor of Germany in 1273.

BAVARIA.

Otto, King of Bavaria, was born April 27, 1848, and succeeded his brother, Ludwig II., June 13, 1886, when that mad monarch committed suicide by drowning himself in the Starnberg Lake. Otto is also crazy, is shut up in one of his châteaux, and the kingdom is governed by Prince Luitpold, his uncle, as regent. The latter is also the heir apparent to the throne; was born in 1821; married, 1844, the Austrian Archduchess Augusta of Tuscany, who is dead, and has four children:

1. Prince Louis, born 1845; married the Austrian Archduchess Maria Theresa, and has six daughters and four sons, the eldest of the latter being Prince Rupert, born 1869, and married, 1900, his cousin, Duchess Marie Gabrielle of Bavaria; has two suns, Luitpold and Albrecht.
2. Prince Leopold, born 1846; married to the Austrian Archduchess Gisela, daughter of the Emperor Francis Joseph I. There are two daughters and two sons.
3. Princess Theresa, born 1850; prioress of a convent in Munich.
4. Prince Arnulf, 1852, married the Princess Theresia of Lichtenstein, and died 1907, leaving a son, Prince Henry.

King Otto has five cousins who bear princely titles, children of his dead uncle, Adalbert.

The royal house of Bavaria comes from the Counts of Wittelsbach of the twelfth century, one of whose descendants was elevated to the rank of Elector, and a later one made King by Napoleon I.

BELGIUM

Leopold II., King of the Belgians, was born April 9, 1835, and was a son of Leopold I., Prince of Saxe-Coburg-Gotha (uncle of Queen Victoria), who was elected King of the Belgians in 1831, and Princess Louise, daughter of King Louis Philippe of France. The present King, who ascended the throne in 1865, was married, in 1853, to the Austrian Archduchess Marie Henriette (died 1902), and has the following children:

1. Princess Louise, born 1858; married to Prince Philippe of Saxe-Coburg-Gotha. (Divorced.)
2. Princess Stephanie, born 1864; married, 1881, to the late Crown Prince Rudolph of Austria, and has one daughter. Princess Stephanie married, 1900, Elémer, Count Lonyay of Nagy-Lonyay and Vasoras-Nameny, Chamberlain to the Emperor of Austria.
3. Princess Clementine, born 1872.

The King's brother was Prince Philippe, Count of Flanders, born in 1837; married to the Hohenzollern Princess Marie, and died in 1905. His son, Prince Albert, is the present heir apparent, born in 1875, and married, in 1900, the Princess Elizabeth (daughter of Duke Charles Theodore of Bavaria). They have two sons, Prince Leopold, born in 1901, and Charles Theodore, born in 1903, and a daughter, Princess Marie Jose, born 1906. Prince Philippe had also two daughters, Henriette, born 1870; married, 1896, the Duke of Vendome; and Josephine, born 1872; married, 1894, Prince Charles of Hohenzollern-Sigmaringen.

The sister of the King is the hapless ex-Empress Carlotta of Mexico, widow of Maximilian. She was born in 1840, widowed in 1867, has no children, and is now insane.

DENMARK.

Frederick VIII., King of Denmark, succeeded to the throne of Denmark by virtue of the law of the Danish succession on the death of his father, King Christian IX., in 1906. He was born 1843; married the Princess Louise of Sweden in 1869, and has three daughters and four sons, the eldest of the latter being Crown Prince Christian, born in 1870, and married, 1898, Princess Alexandrina of Mecklenburg-Schwerin, and has two sons; and the second, Prince Charles, born 1872, and married, 1896, Princess Maud, third daughter of King Edward VII., and elected King of Norway in 1905, as Haakon VII. The eldest daughter is married to Prince Charles of Sweden.

The King's brothers and sisters are:

1. The Queen of Great Britain and Ireland (Alexandra), born 1844; married 1863, and has four living children.
2. The King of the Hellenes (George I.), born 1845; married to the Grand Duchess Olga of Russia, and has one daughter and five sons, the eldest of the latter being Prince Constantine.
3. The Dowager Empress of Russia (Dagmar), born 1847; married the late Czar Alexander III. in 1866, and has four children, one being the present Czar.
4. The Duchess of Cumberland (Thyra), born 1853; married the present Duke of Cumberland (English title), son of the ex-King of Hanover, in 1878, and has two sons and three daughters.

5. Prince Waldemar, born 1858; married, 1885, the Princess Marie of Orleans, daughter of the Duke of Chartres, and has four sons and a daughter. He was offered the crown of Bulgaria in 1886, but declined.

GERMANY.

William II., German Emperor and King of Prussia, was born January 27, 1859; succeeded his father, the Emperor Frederick III., June 15, 1888. He married the Princess Victoria of Schleswig-Holstein-Sonderburg-Augustenburg (born 1858), and has had issue:

1. Frederick William, Crown Prince, born 1882, married, June 6, 1905, to Duchess Cecilie of Mecklenburg-Schwerin, and has two sons, William Frederick, born July 4, 1906, and Louis Ferdinand, born November 9, 1907; 2. William Eitel-Frederick, born 1883, married, February 27, 1906, Princess Sophie Charlotte of Oldenburg; 3. Adalbert, born 1884; 4. August, born 1887, married his cousin, Princess Victoria of Schleswig-Sonderburg, 1908; 5. Oscar, born 1888; 6. Joachim, born 1890; 7. Victoria Louise, born 1892.

The Emperor's brother is Prince Henry, born 1862, and married, 1888, to his cousin, Princess Irene of Hesse, daughter of the late Princess Alice of England, and has two sons; and the Emperor has four sisters, all the children of the late Emperor Frederick and the Princess Victoria of England (the Dowager Empress Frederick, who died in 1901). The sisters are:

1. Princess Charlotte, born 1860; married, 1878, to George, hereditary Prince of Saxe-Meiningen, and has one daughter.
2. Princess Victoria, born 1866; married, 1890, to Prince Adolph of Schaumburg-Lippe.
3. Princess Sophia, born 1870; married, 1889, to Constantine, Crown Prince of Greece, and has three sons and a daughter.
4. Princess Margaret, born 1872; married, 1893, to Prince Frederick Charles of Hesse, and has five sons.

The Emperor has an aunt, the Princess Louise, born 1838, widow of the late Grand Duke of Baden; and he has a number of cousins, descendants of the brothers and sisters of the Emperor William I. One of these is Princess Margaret, daughter of the late Prince Frederick Charles and wife of the British Duke of Connaught, son of Queen Victoria. The reigning family is descended from Frederick of Hohenzollern, a German count in 980, and Frederick William, the Elector of Brandenburg, 1640-88, whose son became King of Prussia.

GREECE.

George I., King of the Hellenes, born December 24, 1845, elected King in 1863. He is the brother of the present King of Denmark, Frederick VIII., and brother of the Queen of Great Britain and the Dowager Empress of Russia. He married, 1867, the Grand Duchess Olga, eldest daughter of the Grand Duke Constantine of Russia, grand uncle to the present Emperor. They have had six living children, five sons and one daughter. The eldest son is:

Prince Constantine, born 1868; married, 1889, the Princess Sophia, sister of the present German Emperor, and has three sons—Prince George, born 1890; Prince Alexander, born 1893, and Prince Paul, born 1901—and a daughter, Princess Helen, born 1896.

The King's eldest daughter, Alexandra, married, in 1889, the Grand Duke Paul, uncle of the present Emperor of Russia, and died September 24, 1891, leaving a daughter and a son.

ITALY.

Victor Emmanuel III., King of Italy, was born November 11, 1869, and is the only son of Humbert I., second King of United Italy, murdered by the Anarchist Bresci at Monza, July 29, 1900. He married, in 1896, Princess Helene, fourth daughter of Nicholas, Prince of Montenegro, and has four children—Princess Iolande, born June 1, 1901; Princess Mafalda, born November 10, 1902; Prince Humbert (heir apparent), born September 15, 1904, and Princess Giovanna, born November 13, 1907.

Emmanuel, Duke of Aosta, born 1869, is eldest son of the late Prince Amadeus, uncle of present King (and ex-King of Spain); married, 1895, Princess Helene of Orleans, daughter of the late Count of Paris, and they have had issue two children—Amadeus, born 1898, and Aimone, born 1900. The three remaining sons of the late Prince Amadeus are Victor, Count of Turin, born 1870; Louis, Duke of Abruzzi, born 1873, and Humbert, Count of Salemi, born in 1889 of his second marriage with his niece, Princess Letitia, daughter of Prince Napoleon Bonaparte and the Princess Clotilde.

The mother of the King is Queen Margherita, daughter of the late Prince Ferdinand of Savoy. She was born 1851, and married the late King 1868.

The following are the aunts of the King:

1. Princess Clotilde, born 1843; married, 1859, to Prince Napoleon Jerome Bonaparte, the late head of the Bonaparte family, and has issue two sons and a daughter, Letitia. (See "Bonapartists.")
2. Dowager Queen Maria Pia of Portugal, born 1847, and married, 1862, to the late King Louis of Portugal, and has one son.

The King's great aunt by marriage, the Princess Elizabeth, widow of the Duke of Genoa, has a son (Prince Thomas, Duke of Genoa, married, 1883, Princess Isabella, daughter of Prince Adelbert of Bavaria, and has three sons and two daughters) and a daughter, the latter being the late King Humbert's wife. The family is descended from the Counts of Savoy, who flourished in the Eleventh Century.

NETHERLANDS.

Wilhelmina, Queen of the Netherlands and Princess of Orange-Nassau, born August 31, 1880, daughter of the late King William III. and Emma, daughter of Prince George Victor of Waldeck-Pyrmont. She married, February 7, 1901, Duke Henry of Mecklenburg-Schwerin.

The Queen's mother is the late Regent Queen Emma, whose regency lasted from the death of the late King, her husband, November 23, 1890, until the end of the minority of her daughter, August 31, 1898. The Queen's aunt is the Princess Sophia, married to the Grand Duke of Saxe-Weimar. She has a son, Prince Charles, born 1844, and two daughters. This family, known as the House of Orange, is descended from the Princes of Orange, stadtholders during the Dutch Republic.

NORWAY.

Haakon VII., King of Norway, was before his election to the crown by the Norwegian people, in 1905, Prince Charles of Denmark. He is the second son of King Frederick VIII. of Denmark; was born 1872; married, 1896, Princess Maud, third daughter of King Edward VII. of Great Britain, and has one son, Olav Alexander Edward Christian Frederick, born July 2, 1903.

PORTUGAL.

Manuel II., King of Portugal, born in 1899, son of King Charles and Queen Amelie of Orleans, ascended the throne on the 1st of February, 1908, after the tragic and terrible assassination that day in Lisbon of his father and elder brother, Prince Louis Philippe. He is unmarried. The King has an uncle, Prince Infante Alfonso, Duke of Oporto, born in 1865, and unmarried.

The reigning family belongs to the House of Braganza, whose founder was an illegitimate son of King John I. (A. D. 1400) of the old line of Portuguese kings.

RUSSIA.

Nicholas II., Emperor of Russia, was born May 18, 1868, and succeeded his father, the late Emperor Alexander III., November 1, 1894. He is married to the Princess Alice (Alix) of Hesse-Darmstadt, daughter of the Princess Alice of Great Britain, and has four daughters and one son—Olga, born in 1895; Tatjana, born in 1897; Marie, born in 1899; Anastasia, born in 1901, and Alexis (the Czarevitch), born August 12, 1904.

The late Emperor Alexander III., born in 1845, married, in 1866, the Princess Dagmar, sister of the present King of Denmark, had issue three sons: 1. Nicholas, the present Emperor; 2. Grand Duke George (the late Czarevitch), born 1871, died 1899; 3. Grand Duke Michael, born December 4, 1878, and two daughters: 1. Grand Duchess Xenia, born April 6, 1875; married, August 6, 1894, her cousin, the Grand Duke Alexander, has four sons and two daughters; and, 2. Grand Duchess Olga, born June 13, 1882, married to Prince Peter of Oldenburg. The uncles and aunts of the Emperor are:

1. Grand Duke Vladimir, born 1847; married, 1874, the Princess Marie of Mecklenburg-Schwerin, and has three sons and one daughter; Grand Duke Cyril, born in 1876; married, 1905, Melita, second daughter of the late Duke of Coburg and divorced wife of the Grand Duke of Hesse. Grand Duke Boris, who was in America in 1902, is the second son and was born in 1877.

2. Grand Duke Alexis, High Admiral, born 1850. He was unmarried. Died Paris, November 14, 1908.

3. Grand Duchess Marie, born 1853; married the late Duke of Edinburgh, and has had one son (deceased) and four daughters.

4. Grand Duke Sergius, born 1857; married, 1884, Princess Elizabeth of Hesse-Darmstadt, daughter of Princess Alice of England. Assassinated in 1905. He left no issue.

5. Grand Duke Paul, born 1860; married, 1889, Princess Alexandra, daughter of the King of the Hellenes. She died September 24, 1891, leaving a son, the Grand Duke Demetrius, and a daughter. In 1902 he contracted a morganatic marriage with Olga Pistolkohrs, now Countess Hohenfelsen.

The Emperor has one grand uncle (son of the Emperor Nicholas I.), Grand Duke Michael, born 1832, field marshal in the Russian Army; married, 1857, Princess Cecelia of Baden, and has issue six living children, the eldest daughter, Anastasia, born 1860, being the widow of the Grand Duke of Mecklenburg-Schwerin and mother of the German Crown Princess.

A grand uncle, the Grand Duke Constantine, born 1827; died January 12, 1892; married, 1848, Princess Alexandra of Saxe-Altenburg, and had issue five children, the Grand Duke Nicholas, born 1850, being the eldest, and the Grand Duchess Olga, born 1851, the eldest daughter, being married to the King of the Hellenes.

A third grand uncle, the Grand Duke Nicholas, born 1831, field marshal in the Russian Army, died in 1891; married, in 1856, the Princess Alexandra of Oldenburg, and had issue two sons, Grand Duke Nicholas, born 1856, married, 1907, Anastasia, daughter of the present Prince of Montenegro, and sister of Queen Helene, of Italy, and Grand Duke Peter, married, in 1889, Militsa, sister of the preceding.

The Russian reigning family is descended from Michael Romanoff, elected Czar in 1613. The members of the family for over two centuries, however, have married so generally into the German royal houses that the present Romanoffs are practically, by blood, Germans; as much so as their kinsman, the head of the German Empire.

SAXONY.

Frederick August, King of Saxony, born May 25, 1865, succeeded his father, King George, October 15, 1904. He married in 1891 Archduchess Louise of Austria (from whom he was separated in 1903). The King has three daughters and three sons, the Crown Prince being George, born 1893.

The King has two sisters, Mathilde, born 1863, unmarried, and Maria Josepha, born 1867, married to the late Archduke Otto of Austria, and two brothers, Johann Georg, born 1869, married first to Duchess Isabella of Württemberg (died 1904), and in 1906 to Princess Maria Immaculata of Bourbon, and Max, born 1870, a priest in Holy Orders.

A great aunt of the King, Princess Elizabeth, born 1830, married Prince Ferdinand of Sardinia, and after his death in 1856 Marchese Rapallo, who died in 1882.

The royal house of Saxony is one of the oldest in Europe, having given an emperor to Germany as early as the beginning of the Tenth Century. The Elector of Saxony assumed the title of King in 1806, and was confirmed therein in 1815.

SPAIN.

Alphonso XIII., King of Spain, born May 17, 1886, nearly six months after the death of his father, Alphonso XII. His mother is Maria Christina, an Austrian princess. He married in 1906 the English Princess Victoria Eugenie, daughter of Princess Henry of Battenberg, youngest sister, of King Edward VII. He has two sons, Alphonso, Prince of the Asturias, heir to the Spanish throne, born the 10th of May, 1907, and Prince Jaime, born at La Granja Palace, near Madrid, on the 22d of July, 1908.

The King's only surviving sister, the Infanta Maria Teresa, born in 1882, is married to her cousin the Infante Ferdinand, of Bavaria, son of Prince Louis of Bavaria. They have one son, the Infante Alfonso Luis Fernando, born in 1906.

The King's aunts are the Infantas Isabella, widow of the Count de Girgenti; Maria, wife of Prince Louis of Bavaria, and Eulalie, wife of Prince Antonio of Orleans (separated from him by deed of separation), who visited the United States and the World's Fair in 1893.

The King's grandmother, ex-Queen Isabella, born in 1830, crowned 1833, abdicated 1870, died April 9, 1904. Her husband, the Infante Francis d'Assisi, born 1822, died in 1902.

The King's grand aunt, the Infanta Louisa, widow of the Duke of Montpensier (son of King Louis Philippe of France), now dead, was the mother of a son and three daughters: 1. The wife of the late Count of Paris and mother of the French pretender, the Duke of Orleans; 2. The late Queen Mercedes, wife of Alphonso XII., deceased; 3. The Infanta Christina, also deceased.

A second cousin of the King is Don Carlos, born in 1848, and a pretender to the Spanish throne, who is married, and has four daughters and a son, Prince Jaime, born in 1870.

The Spanish reigning family are Bourbons, descendants of King Louis XIV. of France.

SERVIA.

Peter I., King of Servia, born in Belgrade, 1846, son of Alexander Karageorgevic, Prince of Servia from 1842 to 1858. Was proclaimed King on the night of June 10-11, 1903, by the officers of the Servian Army after they had murdered King Alexander and Queen Draga, and was crowned in October, 1904. King Peter I. was married in 1883 to Princess Zorka of Montenegro, who died in 1890. He has two sons and a daughter—George, Alexander and Helen.

King Peter is descended from Karageorge, a peasant, who was the leader of the insurrection against Turkey in 1804. He reigned as Prince of Servia from 1804 to 1813, when he was supplanted by the Obrenovic during a second insurrection.

SWEDEN.

Gustaf V., King of Sweden, born June 16, 1858; son of Oscar II., and great-grandson of Marshal Bernadotte. He married, 1881, the Princess Victoria of Baden, and has had three sons, the eldest of whom is the Crown Prince Gustavus Adolphus, who married in 1905 Princess Margaret of Connaught, and has two sons, born 1906 and 1907. The King's other sons are: Prince Wilhelm, born 1884, and married, 1908, the Grand Duchess Maria Pawlowna of Russia, and Prince Eric, born 1889. The King has three brothers: Prince Oscar, born 1859, married Lady Ebba Munck, one of his mother's maids of honor, and relinquished his rights to the throne; Prince Carl, born 1861, and married, 1897, Princess Ingeborg, second daughter of the King of Denmark, and Prince Eugene, born 1865. The King has a niece, Louise, married to the King of Denmark. The royal family comes from Napoleon's Marshal Bernadotte, a Frenchman, who was elected heir-apparent to the crown of Sweden in 1810 and became King in 1818.

WÜRTTEMBERG.

William II., King of Württemberg, born February 25, 1848, succeeded his uncle, King Charles I., October 6, 1891. He married, 1877, Princess Marie of Waldeck, who died leaving a daughter, Pauline, born 1877, and married, 1898, Prince Frederick of Wied. The King married, second, Princess Charlotte of Schaumburg-Lippe, by whom he has no children. As the King has no male descendants, the heir presumptive is his distant kinsman, Duke Albert, born 1865, married to the Archduchess Margareta, niece of the Emperor of Austria, who died in 1902, and has three sons and three daughters.

The French Pretenders.

BONAPARTIST.

Of the Emperor Napoleon I. and his brothers Joseph and Louis, male issue is now extinct. The Emperor's brothers Lucien and Jerôme are represented by the following living descendants, and they constitute the present Imperialist house of France:

Prince Victor Napoleon (of the house of Jerôme), born July 18, 1862, is the son of the late Prince Napoleon (who died March 18, 1891) and the Princess Clotilde, sister of the late King Humbert of Italy. The Prince has been recognized by his party as the undisputed head of the Bonaparte family. He lives in Brussels and is morganatically married, and has had three children. His only brother, Prince Louis Napoleon, born 1864, is a general in the Russian Army, and is unmarried. His sister, Princess Letitia, born 1866, is the widow of Prince Amadeus of Italy, her own uncle, by whom she had a son, Prince Humbert, born 1889.

The late aunt of Prince Victor Napoleon, the Princess Mathilde, born 1820; married, 1840, Prince Demidoff of Russia; died in 1904 without children.

Prince Charles Napoleon, brother of the late Cardinal Bonaparte, who died February 12, 1899, was the last representative of the eldest son of Napoleon's brother Lucien, in the male line. He was born 1839; was married and had two daughters—Marie, wife of Lieutenant Gotti, of the Italian Army, and Eugénie, unmarried. He had three sisters, married respectively to the Marquis of Roccagivoine, Count Primoli and Prince Gabrelli, who have descendants.

Prince Roland Bonaparte is the only living male cousin of Prince Charles Napoleon. He is a son of the late Prince Pierre Napoleon Bonaparte; was born 1858; married, 1880, the daughter of Blanc, one of the proprietors of the Monte Carlo gambling-hell. His wife died in 1882, leaving him a daughter and a fortune. He has one sister, Jeanne, born 1861, and married to the Marquis de Villeneuve.

Ex-Empress Eugénie, widow of Emperor Napoleon III., was a daughter of Count Cyprien de Montijo, a Spanish grandee, and was born May 5, 1826. She married 1853. Became a widow, 1873. Her only son, Prince Louis Napoleon, was killed in Zululand in 1879.

BOURBON—ORLEANIST.

Philippe, Duke of Orleans, born 1869, succeeded his father, the late Count of Paris, in 1894, as the head of the royal family of France. He married, in 1896, the Archduchess Marie-Dorothea, daughter of the Archduke Joseph, cousin of the Emperor of Austria. His mother (still living) was the Spanish Infanta Louise of Montpeusier, and he has one brother, the Duke of Montpensier, and four sisters—Princess Amelie, married to the King of Portugal; Helena, married to the Duke of Aosta, nephew of the late King Humbert of Italy; Isabel, married to the Duke of Guise, son of the Duke of Chartres, and Louise, married to Prince Charles of Bourbon, grandson of King Ferdinand II., of Naples.

The only uncle of the Duke of Orleans is the Duke of Chartres, born 1840, and married to a daughter of the Prince of Joinville. The issue are two daughters and two sons, the eldest son being Prince Henry, born 1867 (died at Saigon, Cochin-China, in 1901); the second, the Duke of Guise; the eldest daughter, Princess Marie, being married to Prince Waldemar of Denmark, and the second daughter, Princess Marguerite, being married (in 1896) to Patrice MacMahon, Duke of Magenta.

The grand uncles of the Duke of Orleans (who were the sons of King Louis Philippe) are all dead. They were the Prince of Joinville, born 1818, died 1900, married to a daughter of Pedro I. of Brazil, and had one daughter and one son, the Duke of Penthièvre, born 1845; Henry, Duke of Aumale, born 1822, died (childless) 1897; Anthony, Duke of Montpensier, born 1824, died 1890 (married, 1852, a sister of Queen Isabella of Spain, and had a daughter, the wife of the Count of Paris, and a son, Prince Anthony, born 1866, who married, 1888, his cousin, the Infanta Eulalie of Spain), and Louis, Duke of Nemours, born 1814, died 1896. He was the father of two daughters, the Princess Czartoryska, deceased, and Princess Blanche of Orleans, and two sons, the eldest being the Count of Eu, born 1842, married to a daughter of Pedro II. of Brazil, and having three children, and the second the Duke of Alençon, born 1844, and married to a Bavarian princess (who was burned in the Paris bazaar fire in 1897), and having two children.

By the death of the Count of Chambord, in 1883, the elder line of the Bourbons of France became extinct, and the right of succession merged in the Count of Paris, grandson of King Louis Philippe, representative of the younger, or Orleans, line.

The British Empire.

THE UNITED KINGDOM.

Countries.	Area in Square Miles.	How Acquired by England.	Date.	Population.
England } Wales ... }	58,324	Conquest	1282	32,527,843
Scotland	30,405	Union	1603	4,472,103
Ireland	32,360	Conquest	1172	4,458,775
Islands	302		....	150,370
Total	121,391			41,976,827

COLONIES AND DEPENDENCIES.

Countries.	Area in Square Miles.	How Acquired by England.	Date.	Population.
EUROPE:				
Gibraltar	2	Conquest	1704	27,460
Malta, etc	122	Treaty cession	1814	188,141
ASIA:				
India (including Burmah)	1,800,258	{ Conquest. { Transfer from E. India Co.	Begun 1757 } 1858 }	294,360,356
Ceylon	25,365	Treaty cession	1801	3,578,333
Cyprus	3,584	Convention with Turkey	1878	237,022
Aden and Socotra	3,070	(Aden) conquest	1839	44,000
Straits Settlements	1,500	Treaty cession	1785-1824	272,249
Hong Kong	30½	Treaty cession	1841	386,159
Labuan	31	Treaty cession	1846	8,411
British North Borneo	31,000	Cession to Company	1877	175,000
AFRICA:				
Cape Colony	276,800	Treaty cession	1588, 1814	2,433,000
Natal and Zululand	29,200	Annexation	1843	925,118
St. Helena	47	Conquest	1673	3,342
Ascension	38	Annexation	1815	380
Sierra Leone	4,000	Settlement	1787	76,655
British Guinea, Gold Coast, etc.	339,900	Treaty cession	1872	23,455,000
Mauritius, etc	1,063	Conquest and cession	1810, 1814	392,500
British South and East Africa	1,989,247	Conquest and cession	1870-1890	14,911,000
Transvaal	119,139	Conquest	1900	1,091,156
Orange River Colony	48,326	Conquest	1900	207,503
AMERICA:				
Ontario and Quebec	612,735	Conquest	1759-60 }	} 5,371,315
New Brunswick	27,985	Treaty cession	1763 }	
Nova Scotia	21,428	Conquest	1627 }	
Manitoba	73,732	Settlement	1813 }	
British Columbia, etc	372,630	Transfer to Crown	1858 }	
Northwest Territories	2,634,880	Charter to Company	1670 }	
Prince Edward Island	2,184	Conquest	1745 }	
Newfoundland	42,200	Treaty cession	1713	217,037
British Guiana	104,000	Conquest and cession	1803-1814	294,000
British Honduras	7,562	Conquest	1798	37,479
Jamaica	4,193	Conquest	1655	771,900
Trinidad and Tobago	1,754	Conquest	1797	279,700
Barbados	166	Settlement	1605	195,600
Bahamas	5,794	Settlement	1629	54,358
Bermuda	19	Settlement	1612	17,536
Other Islands	8,742		......	255,000
AUSTRALASIA:				
New South Wales	310,700	Settlement	1788	1,379,700
Victoria	87,884	Settlement	1832	1,208,710
South Australia	903,690	Settlement	1836	364,800
Queensland	668,497	Settlement	1824	510,520
Western Australia	975,876	Settlement	1828	194,800
Tasmania	26,215	Settlement	1803	174,230
New Zealand	104,032	Purchase	1845	787,660
Fiji	7,423	Cession from the natives	1874	120,950
New Guinea (British)	88,460	Annexation	1884	350,000

Estimates of area and present population are by Whitaker, and in some cases by the "Statesman's Year-Book," except for British Africa and the late accessions there, which are corrected by Ravenstein's figures. The entire population of the empire, according to the estimates of the "Statesman's Year-Book," is 392,846,835, and the total area, 11,433,283. The East Indian possessions extend over a territory larger than the continent of Europe without Russia; but the North American possessions are greater still, and, inclusive of Hudson's Bay and the great lakes, have a larger area than the whole of Europe. British Africa and Australasia are the next possessions in size.

POPULATION OF THE UNITED KINGDOM BY SUCCESSIVE CENSUSES.

	1831.	1841.	1851.	1861.	1871.	1881.	1891.	1901.
England	13,090,523	15,002,443	16,921,888	18,954,444	21,495,131	24,613,926	27,499,984	} 32,527,843
Wales	806,274	911,705	1,005,721	1,111,780	1,217,135	1,360,513	1,501,034	}
Scotland	2,364,386	2,620,184	2,888,742	3,062,294	3,360,018	3,735,573	4,033,103	4,472,103
Ireland	7,767,401	8,196,597	6,574,278	5,798,967	5,412,377	5,174,836	4,706,448	4,458,775
Total	24,028,584	26,730,929	27,390,629	28,927,485	31,484,661	34,884,848	*37,888,439	†41,976,827

* Including 147,870 inhabitants of islands in the United Kingdom. † Including 150,370 in islands, but not including 367,736 army, navy and merchant seamen abroad.

The British Royal Family.

DECEMBER 1, 1908.

EDWARD VII., "by the grace of God of the United Kingdom of Great Britain and Ireland and of the British Dominions Beyond the Seas, King, Defender of the Faith, Emperor of India," was born November 9, 1841, and succeeded his mother January 22, 1901. He was married to the Princess Alexandra of Denmark (born December 1, 1844), March 10, 1863. In the following table their children and grandchildren are enumerated: [Children in SMALL CAPS. Their children follow.]

NAME.	Born	Died.	Married.	Date.
1. ALBERT VICTOR, DUKE OF CLARENCE	1864	1892		
2. GEORGE FREDERICK, PRINCE OF WALES	1865	......	Princess Victoria Mary of Teck	1893
Edward Albert	1894	......		
Albert Frederick	1895	......		
Victoria Alexandra	1897	......		
Henry William	1900	......		
George Edward	1902	......		
John Charles	1905	......		
3. LOUISE VICTORIA, DUCHESS OF FIFE	1867	......	Duke of Fife	1889
Alexandra Victoria	1891	......		
Maud Alexandra	1893	......		
4. VICTORIA ALEXANDRA	1868	......		
5. MAUD, QUEEN OF NORWAY	1869	......	King Haakon VII. of Norway	1896
Olaf Alexander Edward	1903	......		
6. ALEXANDER	1871	1871		

OTHER DESCENDANTS OF THE LATE QUEEN VICTORIA.*

NAME.	Born	Died.	Married.	Date.
1. VICTORIA ADELAIDE, PRINCESS ROYAL	1840	1901	Crown Prince of Prussia (succ. as German Emperor, March, 1888. Died June, 1888)	1858
Frederick William (succ. as German Emperor, June, 1888). (*Issue*, 6 sons, 1 daughter)	1859	......	Princess Augusta of Schleswig-Holstein	1881
Charlotte. (*Issue*, 1 daughter)	1860	......	Prince of Saxe-Meiningen	1878
Henry. (*Issue*, 2 sons)	1862	......	Princess Irene of Hesse	1888
Sigismund	1864	1866		
Victoria	1866	......	Prince Adolphus of Schaumburg-Lippe	1890
Joachim	1868	1879		
Sophia Dorothea. (*Issue*, 3 sons, 2 dau.)	1870	......	Duke of Sparta, son of King of Greece	1889
Margaret. (*Issue*, 6 sons)	1872	......	Prince Frederick Charles of Hesse	1893
3. ALICE MAUD MARY, GRAND DUCHESS OF HESSE	1843	1878	Louis IV., Grand Duke of Hesse (died March 13, 1892)	1862
Victoria Alberta. (*Issue*, 2 sons, 1 daughter)	1863	......	Prince Louis of Battenberg	1884
Elizabeth	1864	......	Grand Duke Sergius of Russia	1884
Irene Marie. (*Issue*, 2 sons)	1866	......	Prince Henry of Prussia	1888
Ernest Louis, Grand Duke of Hesse. (*Issue*, 1 son, 1 daughter)	1868	......	Princess Victoria of Saxe-Coburg-Gotha	1894
Frederick William	1870	1873		
Alice Victoria. (*Issue*, 1 son 4 dau.)	1872	......	Emperor Nicholas II. of Russia	1894
Mary Victoria	1874	1878		
4. ALFRED, DUKE OF SAXE-COBURG-GOTHA, DUKE OF EDINBURGH	1844	1900	Grand Duchess Marie, daughter of Alexander II., Emperor of Russia	1874
Alfred Alexander	1874	1899		
Marie Alexandra Victoria. (*Issue*, 2 sons, 2 daughters)	1875	......	Ferdinand, Crown Prince of Roumania	1893
Victoria Melita. (*Issue*, 1 son, 1 dau.)	1876	......	(†) Grand Duke Cyril of Russia	1905
Alexandra Louise. (*Issue*, 1 son, 3 daughters).	1878	......	Hereditary Prince of Hohenlohe-Langenberg	1896
Beatrice	1884	......		
5. HELENA, PRINCESS CHRISTIAN	1846	......	Pr. Fred. Chris. of Schleswig-Holstein	1866
Christian Victor	1867	1900		
Albert John	1869	......		
Victoria Louise	1870	......		
Louise Augusta	1872	......	‡ Prince Aribert of Anhalt-Dessau	1891
Harold	1876	1876		
6. LOUISE, DUCHESS OF ARGYLL	1848	......	Duke of Argyll	1871
7. ARTHUR, DUKE OF CONNAUGHT	1850	......	Princess Louise of Prussia	1879
Margaret. (*Issue*, 1 son)	1882	......	Prince Gustavus Adolphus of Sweden	1905
Arthur Patrick	1883	......		
Victoria Patricia	1886	......		
8. LEOPOLD, DUKE OF ALBANY	1853	1884	Princess Helena of Waldeck-Pyrmont	1882
Alice Mary. (*Issue*, 1 daughter)	1883	......	Prince Alexander of Teck	1904
Leopold, 2d Duke of Albany, Duke of Saxe-Coburg-Gotha (*Issue*, 1 son)	1884	......	Princess Victoria of Schleswig-Holstein-Glücksburg	1905
9. BEATRICE MARY VICTORIA FEODORE	1857	......	Prince Henry of Battenberg (died 1896)	1885
Alexander Albert	1886	......		
Victoria Ena (*Issue*, 2 sons)	1887	......	King Alphonso XIII. of Spain	1906
Leopold Arthur Louis	1889	......		
Maurice Victor Donald	1891	......		

First cousins of the late Queen Victoria in the paternal line were the Duke of Cambridge, born 1819, died 1904; Augusta, Duchess of Mecklenburg-Strelitz, born 1822, and Mary Adelaide, Duchess of Teck, born 1822, died 1897. The Queen also had a large number of cousins through her mother, the Duchess of Kent. Whitaker's Peerage has a list of over 240 living blood relatives of the late Queen. *[Children in SMALL CAPS. Their children follow.] †Second marriage; her first husband was Ernest Louis, Grand Duke of Hesse, married 1894, from whom she was divorced. The children are by first husband. ‡ Marriage dissolved in 1900.

Order of Succession to the British Throne.

The following is the order of succession to the British throne (January, 1908) to the last of the living descendants of George III. Failing all these the succession would fall to the other descendants of the preceding British kings going backward in regular order. Every future new birth among the descendants of Victoria and George III. in the line below takes its relative place therein.

DESCENDANTS OF KING EDWARD VII.

1 Prince of Wales, son.
2 Prince Edward of Wales, grandson.
3 Prince Albert of Wales, grandson.
4 Prince Henry of Wales, grandson.
5 Prince George Edward of Wales, grandson.
6 Prince John of Wales, grandson.
7 Princess Victoria of Wales, granddaughter.
8 The Princess Royal, Duchess of Fife, daughter.
9 Princess Alexandra (Duff) granddaughter.
10 Princess Maud (Duff) granddaughter.
11 Princess Victoria of United Kingdom, daughter.
12 Queen of Norway, daughter.
13 Crown Prince of Norway, grandson.

DESCENDANTS OF QUEEN VICTORIA.

14 Grand Duchess Cyril of Russia, granddaughter.
15 Hereditary Princess of Hohenlohe-Langenburg, granddaughter.
16 Prince Gottfried of Hohenlohe-Langenburg, great grandson.
17 Princess Maria of Hohenlohe-Langenburg, great-granddaughter.
18 Princess Alexandra of Hohenlohe-Langenburg, great-granddaughter.
19 Princess Irma of Hohenlohe-Langenburg, great-granddaughter.
20 Princess Beatrice of Saxe-Coburg, granddaughter.
21 The Duke of Connaught, son.
22 Prince Arthur of Connaught, grandson.
23 Princess Gustavus of Sweden, granddaughter.
24 Prince Gustavus Adolphus of Sweden, great-grandson.
25 Princess Patricia of Connaught, granddaughter.
26 The Duke of Saxe-Coburg-Gotha, grandson.
27 Prince Johann Leopold of Saxe-Coburg-Gotha, great-grandson.
28 Princess Alice of Teck, granddaughter.
29 Princess May Helen of Teck, great-granddaughter.
30 The German Emperor, grandson.
31 The Crown Prince of Germany, great-grandson.
32 Prince Wilhelm of Germany, great-great-grandson.
33 Prince Wilhelm Friedrich, great-grandson.
34 Prince Eitel-Frederick of Prussia, great grandson.
35 Prince Adalbert of Prussia, great-grandson.
36 Prince Augustus of Prussia, great-grandson.
37 Prince Oscar of Prussia, great-grandson.
38 Prince Joachim of Prussia, great-grandson.
39 Princess Victoria of Prussia, great-granddaughter.
40 Prince Henry of Prussia, grandson.
41 Prince Waldemar of Prussia, great-grandson.
42 Prince Sigismund of Prussia, great-grandson.
43 Hereditary Princess of Saxe-Meiningen, granddaughter.
44 Princess Heinrich of Reuss, great-granddaughter.
45 Princess Adolphus of Schomburg-Lippe, granddaughter.
46 Crown Princess of Greece, granddaughter.
47 Prince George of Greece, great-grandson.
48 Prince Alexander of Greece, great grandson.
49 Prince Paul of Greece, great-grandson.
50 Princess Helena of Greece, great-granddaughter.
51 Princess Eirene of Greece, great-granddaughter.
52 Princess Frederick Charles of Hesse, granddaughter.
53 Prince Frederick Wilhelm of Hesse, great-grandson.
54 Prince Maximilian of Hesse, great-grandson.
55 Prince Philip of Hesse, great-grandson.
56 Prince Wolfgang of Hesse, great-grandson.
57 Prince Richard of Hesse, great-grandson.
58 Prince Christoph of Hesse, great-grandson.
59 Grand Duke of Hesse, grandson.
60 Prince (Son of No. 59), great-grandson.
61 Princess Louise of Battenberg, granddaughter.
62 Prince George of Battenberg, great-grandson.
63 Prince Louis of Battenberg, grandson.
64 Princess Andrew of Greece, great-granddaughter.
65 Princess Margaret of Greece, great-great-granddaughter.
66 Princess Louisa of Battenberg, great-granddaughter.
67 Grand Duchess Sergius of Prussia, granddaughter.
68 Princess Henry of Prussia (Wife of No. 40), granddaughter.
69 The Empress of Russia, granddaughter.
70 The Tsarevitch, great-grandson.
71 The Grand Duchess Olga of Russia, great-granddaughter.
72 The Grand Duchess Tatiana of Russia, great-granddaughter.
73 The Grand Duchess Marie of Russia, great-granddaughter.
74 The Grand Duchess Anastasia of Russia, great-granddaughter.
75 Princess Christian of Schleswig-Holstein, daughter.
76 Prince Albert of Schleswig-Holstein, grandson.
77 Princess Victoria of Schleswig-Holstein, granddaughter.
78 Princess Louise of Schleswig-Holstein, granddaughter.
79 Princess Louise, Duchess of Argyll, daughter.
80 Princess Henry of Battenberg, daughter.
81 Prince Alexander of Battenberg, grandson.
82 Prince Leopold of Battenberg, grandson.
83 Prince Maurice of Battenberg, grandson.
84 The Queen of Spain, granddaughter.
85 The Prince of the Asturias, Alphonso, great-grandson.

DESCENDANTS OF KING GEORGE III

86 The Duke of Cumberland, great-grandson.
87 Prince George of Cumberland, great-great-grandson.
88 Prince Ernest of Cumberland, great-great-grandson.
89 Princess Maximilian of Baden, great-great-granddaughter.
90 Princess Marie of Baden, great-great-great-granddaughter.
91 Grand Duchess of Mecklenburg-Schwerin, great-great-granddaughter.
92 Princess Olga of Cumberland, great-great-granddaughter.
93 Baroness von Pawel Rammingen, great-granddaughter.
94 Dowager Grand Duchess of Mecklenburg-Strelitz, granddaughter.
95 The Grand Duke of Mecklenburg-Strelitz, great-grandson.
96 Hereditary Grand Duke of Mecklenburg-Strelitz, great-great-grandson.
97 Duke Charles of Mecklenburg-Strelitz, great-great-grandson.
98 Duchess Marie of Mecklenburg-Strelitz (Countess Jametel), great-great-granddaughter.
99 Son of No. 98, great-great-great-grandson.
100 Duchess August (Princess Militza of Montenegro), great-great-granddaughter.
101 The Duke of Teck, great-grandson.
102 Prince George of Teck, great-great-grandson.
103 Princess Victoria of Teck, great-great-granddaughter.
104 Princess Helena of Teck, great-great-granddaughter.
105 Prince Francis of Teck, great-grandson.
106 Prince Alexander of Teck (Husband of No. 28), great grandson.
107 Prince Rupert of Teck, great-great-grandson.
108 Princess May of Teck, great-great-granddaughter.
109 Princess of Wales.

PRECEDING SUCCESSION TO THE THRONE.

In the year 1066, Harold, the last of the Saxon kings, being slain in battle, William the Conqueror, as he was afterward called, seized the throne by right of conquest, and the succession passed from him to his second son, William, and then to his third son, Henry I. On the death of the latter a war ensued between his granddaughter Matilda and his nephew Stephen, which resulted in favor of the latter. On Stephen's death the crown reverted to Matilda's son, Henry II., who was succeeded by his second son, Richard I. He dying without children, Henry's fourth son, John, succeeded, who was followed by his son, Henry III. He in turn was followed by his eldest son, Edward I., who was in succession followed by his son and grandson, Edward II. and Edward III. The son of Edward III. dying in his father's lifetime, a grandson, Richard II., succeeded, and in his reign were sown the seeds of the Wars of the Roses, which were afterward to bear such ill fruit.

Richard II. was deposed by Henry IV., who was the eldest son of a younger brother of his father. Henry IV. was succeeded by his son, Henry V., and he by his son, Henry VI., who was deposed by Edward IV., who claimed the throne by right of descent from Lionel, third son of Edward III., and who was an elder brother of John of Gaunt, the father of Henry IV. Edward IV. was succeeded by his son, Edward V., who died an infant, and then by his brother, Richard III., who was slain in the battle of Bosworth Field, fought between him and Henry Tudor, great-great-grandson of John of Gaunt by his third wife, Katherine Swynford. Henry ascended the throne under the title of Henry VII., and married Elizabeth, the daughter of Edward IV., and thus united the two houses of York and Lancaster and put an end to the Wars of the Roses.

Henry VII. was followed by his son, Henry VIII., who was succeeded in turn by his three children, Edward VI., Mary I., and Elizabeth, at whose death the crown fell to James VI. of Scotland, great-grandson of Margaret, eldest daughter of Henry VII. of England, who ascended the throne of England under the title of James I. On his death his third son ascended as Charles I., but he was beheaded in 1649 by Cromwell, who was made Protector until his death in 1660, when the eldest son of Charles came to the throne as Charles II. and he was followed by his brother, James II. The latter abdicated in 1688, and was succeeded by a nephew, who had married the eldest daughter of James, and the two reigned under their joint names as William III. and Mary II.

On their death James II.'s second daughter, Anne, ascended, and she dying childless the crown fell to the Elector of Hanover, who was grandson of Elizabeth, daughter of James I. of England. This Prince, George I., was succeeded by his son, George II., who was succeeded by his grandson, George III. After a longer reign than any previous English monarch, this king was succeeded by his eldest son, George IV., and by his third son, William IV., both of whom dying childless the crown fell to Victoria, only child of Edward, fourth son of George III., who ascended the throne in 1837, and she was succeeded on her death by her eldest son, the present sovereign.

TITLE AND OATH OF THE KING.

The Royal Titles Act, which received the Royal Assent on August 17, 1901, enacted that—

"It shall be lawful for His Most Gracious Majesty, with a view to the recognition of His Majesty's Dominions beyond the seas, by His Royal Proclamation under the Great Seal of the United Kingdom, issued within six months after the passing of this act, to make such addition to the style and titles at present appertaining to the Imperial Crown of the United Kingdom and its dependencies as to His Majesty may seem fit."

Mr. Chamberlain, the Secretary for the Colonies, sent the following telegram to Colonial Governors, asking them which title for the King they preferred. No. 3 was generally approved.

"King Edward's accession offers an opportunity of considering the titles of the Monarch, and I am desirous that the separate and greatly increased importance of the Colonies should be recognized, if possible.

"The following suggestions have been made:—

"First.—'King of Great Britain and Ireland, Emperor of India, and King (or Sovereign) of Canada, Australasia, and all British Dominions beyond the Seas.'

"Second.—Addition to present title of the words, 'Sovereign Lord (or King) of the British Realms beyond the Seas.'

"Third.—Addition to present title of the words, 'King of all the British Dominions beyond the Seas', without specifying any particular Colony.

"On the whole, I prefer the third suggestion."

On November 4, 1901, the title assumed by His Majesty was "*Edward VII., by the Grace of God of the United Kingdom of Great Britain and Ireland, and of the British Dominions beyond the Seas, King, Defender of the Faith, Emperor of India.*"

THE KING'S ACCESSION OATH.

The Accession Oath taken by King Edward, to which so much exception was taken, is as follows:—

"I, Edward, do solemnly and sincerely, in the presence of God, profess, testify, and declare, that I do believe that in the Sacrament of the Lord's Supper there is not any transubstantiation of the elements of bread and wine into the body and blood of Christ at or after the consecration thereof by any person whatsoever; and that the invocation or adoration of the Virgin Mary or any other Saint, and the sacrifice of the Mass, as they are now used in the Church of Rome, are superstitious and idolatrous, and I do solemnly, in the presence of God, profess, testify and declare, that I do make this declaration, and every part thereof, in the plain and ordinary sense of the words read unto me as they are commonly understood by English Protestants, without any evasion, equivocation, or mental reservation whatsoever, and without any dispensation already granted me for this purpose by the Pope or any other authority or person whatsoever, or without any hope of any such dispensation from any person or authority whatsoever, or without thinking that I am or can be acquitted before God or man, or absolved of this declaration or any part thereof, although the Pope or any other person or persons or power whatsoever should dispense with or annul the same, or declare that it was null and void from the beginning."

The *revised form of oath* which the Select Committee of the House of Lords suggested for the King's Accession Oath ran thus:—

"I, A. B., by the Grace of God, King (or Queen) of Great Britain and Ireland, Defender of the Faith, do solemnly and sincerely, in the presence of God, profess and testify, and declare that I do believe, that in the Sacrament of the Lord's Supper there is not any transubstantiation of the elements of bread and wine into the body and blood of Christ, at or after the consecration thereof by any person whatsoever. And I do believe that the invocation or adoration of the Virgin Mary or any other Saint, and the sacrifice of the Mass, as they are now used in the Church of Rome, are contrary to the Protestant Religion. And I do solemnly, in the presence of God, profess, testify and declare that I do make this declaration and every part thereof unreservedly."

But this amendment was so much criticised that it was withdrawn.

BRITISH PREMIERS SINCE THE ACCESSION OF GEORGE III.

1760—Duke of Newcastle.
1762—Earl of Bute.
1763—George Grenville.
1765—Marquis of Rockingham.
1766—Earl of Chatham.
1767—Duke of Grafton.
1770—Lord North.
1782—Marquis of Rockingham.
1782—Earl of Shelbourne.
1783—William Pitt.
1801—Henry Addington.
1804—William Pitt.
1806—Lord Grenville.
1807—Duke of Portland.
1809—Spencer Perceval.
1812—Earl of Liverpool.
1827—George Canning.
1827—Viscount Goderich.
1828—Duke of Wellington.
1830—Earl Grey.
1834—Viscount Melbourne.
1834—Sir Robert Peel.
1835—Viscount Melbourne.
1841—Sir Robert Peel.
1846—Lord John Russell.
1851—Earl of Derby.
1852—Earl of Aberdeen.
1855—Lord Palmerston.
1858—Earl of Derby.
1859—Lord Palmerston.
1865—Lord John Russell.
1866—Earl of Derby.
1868—Benjamin Disraeli.
1868—William E. Gladstone.
1874—Benjamin Disraeli.
1880—William E. Gladstone.
1885—Marquis of Salisbury.
1886—William E. Gladstone.
1886—Marquis of Salisbury.
1892—William E. Gladstone.
1894—Earl of Rosebery.
1895—Marquis of Salisbury.
1902—Arthur J. Balfour.
1905—H. Campbell-Bannerman.
1908—Herbert Hy. Asquith.

The British Government.

THE MINISTRY.

The Present Liberal Ministry.	December 1, 1908.	The Late Unionist Ministry.
Herbert Henry Asquith.........	*Prime Minister. First Lord of the Treasury.*	Arthur J. Balfour.
Earl of Crewe......................	*Lord Privy Seal.*	Marquis of Salisbury.
Sir Edward Grey, Bart............	*Foreign Secretary.*	Marquis of Lansdowne.
Lord Loreburn......................	*Lord High Chancellor.*	Earl of Halsbury.
Viscount of Wolverhampton......	*President of the Council.*	Marquis of Londonderry.
David Lloyd George.............	*Chancellor of the Exchequer.*	Austen Chamberlain.
Herbert John Gladstone..	*Home Secretary.*	Aretas Akers Douglas.
Earl of Crewe......................	*Colonial Secretary.*	Hon. Alfred Lyttelton.
Richard Burdon Haldane.........	*Secretary for War.*	Hugh O. Arnold Forster.
Viscount Morley of Blackburne..	*Secretary for India.*	Hon. St. John Brodrick.
John Sinclair..........................	*Secretary for Scotland.*	Marquis of Linlithgow.
Reginald McKenna.................	*First Lord of the Admiralty.*	Earl Cawdor.
Winston Spencer Churchill........	*President Board of Trade.*	Marquis of Salisbury.
John Burns.........	*Pres. Local Government Board.*	Gerald William Balfour.
Walter Runciman..................	*President Board of Education.*	Marquis of Londonderry.
Lord Fitzmaurice......................	*Chancellor Duchy Lancaster.*	Sir W. H. Walrond.
Sydney C. Buxton............... .	*Postmaster-General.*	Lord Stanley.
Augustine Birrell, K.C............	*Chief Secretary for Ireland.*	Walter Hume Long.
Sir Samuel Walker, Bart..........	*Lord Chancellor for Ireland.*	Lord Ashbourne.
Earl Carrington........................	*President Board of Agriculture.*	Hon. Ailwyn Fellowes.
Lewis Vernon Harcourt..........	*First Commissioner of Works.*	....
John Henry Whitley..........	*Lords Commissioners of the Treasury.*	Hon. Edmund Talbot.
John Herbert Lewes......		H. W. Forster.
Cecil William Norton...........		Lord Balcarres.
Chas. E. Hy. Hobhouse.........	*Joint Secs. Treasury.*	Sir A. Acland Hood.
Joseph Albert Pease.......... ...		Victor Cavendish.
Richard Knight Causton..........	*Paymaster-General.*	Sir Savile Crossley, Bart.
Herbert Louis Samuel............	*Political Secretary Home Office.*	Hon. Thomas Cochrane.
Thos. McK. Wood.................	*Political Secretary Foreign Office.*	Earl Percy.
Lt.-Col. J. E. B. Seely, D.S.O.....	*Political Secretary Colonial Office.*	Duke of Marlborough.
Thos. R. Buchanan.................	*Political Secretary India Office.*	Marquis of Bath.
Lord Lucas...........................	*Political Secretary War Office.*	Earl of Donoughmore.
Sir W. S. Robson, K.C.	*Attorney-General.*	Sir Robert B. Finlay, K. C.
Sir S. Thos. Evans, K.C.	*Solicitor-General.*	Sir Edward Carson, K. C.

HOUSEHOLD OFFICIALS.

Earl Beauchamp....................	*Lord Steward.*	Earl of Pembroke.
Viscount Althorp..................	*Lord Chamberlain.*	Earl of Clarendon.
....	*Master of the Horse.*	Duke of Portland.

SCOTLAND.

John Sinclair	*Secretary and Keeper of Great Seal.*	Marquis of Linlithgow.
Lord Dunedin..........................	*Lord Justice-General.*	Lord Kinross.
Thomas Shaw, K.C..................	*Lord Advocate.*	Charles Scott Dickson, K. C.
....	*Keeper of the Privy Seal.*	Earl of Leven and Melville.
Lord Kingsburgh.....................	*Lord Justice Clerk.*	Lord Kingsburgh (Macdonald)
....	*Lord Clerk Register.*	Duke of Montrose.
Alexander Ure, K. C..................	*Solicitor-General.*	James Avon Clyde, K. C.

IRELAND.

Earl of Aberdeen....................	*Lord-Lieutenant.*	Earl Dudley (not in the Cabinet)
Augustine Birrell, K. C...........	*Chief Secretary.*	W. H. Long (in the Cabinet).
Sir J. B. Dougherty.................	*Under-Secretary.*	Sir Antony Patrick MacDonnell.
Sir Samuel Walker, Bart..........	*Lord Chancellor.*	Lord Ashbourne.
Richard Robert Cherry, K.C......	*Attorney-General.*	John Atkinson, K. C.

COURTS OF LAW.

House of Lords—*Lord High Chancellor*, Lord Loreburn, and such peers of Parliament as are holding or have held high judicial office.

Lords of Appeal in Ordinary—Lords Macnaghten, Robertson, Atkinson and Collins.

Court of Appeal—*Ex-Officio Judges*, The Lord High Chancellor, the Lord Chief Justice of England, the Master of the Rolls, and the President of the Probate, Divorce, and Admiralty Division. *Master of the Rolls*, Sir Herbert Hardy Cozens-Hardy. *Lords Justices*, Sir Roland Vaughan Williams, Sir John Fletcher Moulton, Sir George Farwell, Sir H. Burton Buckley, Sir Wm. Raun Kennedy.

High Court of Justice, Chancery Division—*President*, The Lord High Chancellor. *Justices*, Sir Matthew Ingle Joyce, Sir C. Swinfen Eady, Sir T. Rolls Warrington, Sir Ralph Neville, Sir Robert John Parker, Sir Harry T. Eve.

High Court of Justice, King's Bench Division—*Lord Chief Justice of England*, Lord Alverstone. *Justices*, Sir William Grantham, Sir John Compton Lawrance, Sir Edward Ridley, Sir John C. Bigham, Sir Charles John Darling, Sir Arthur M. Channel, Sir Walter Phillimore, Bart., Sir Thomas T. Bucknill, Sir Joseph Walton, Sir Arthur Richard Jelf, Sir Reginald More Bray, Sir Alfred T. Lawrence, Sir Henry Sutton, Sir William Pickford, Lord Coleridge.

High Court of Justice, Probate, Divorce, and Admiralty Division—*President*, Sir John Gorell Barnes. *Justice*, Sir Henry Bargrave Deane.

Court of Arches—*Judge*, Sir Lewis Tonna Dibdin.

Bankruptcy Court—*Judge*, Sir J. C. Bigham. *Registrars*, H. S. Giffard, John E. Linklater, Herbert J. Hope, Henry J. Hood.

This and the following pages of information about the British Empire have been revised for The World Almanac for 1909 by the Editor of Whitaker's Almanack, London.

THE BRITISH GOVERNMENT—*Continued.*

ARMY.

COUNCIL.

Secretary of State for War..Rt. Hon. R. B. Haldane, K. C., M. P.

Chief of the General Staff—Gen. Sir W. G. Nicholson, G. C. B.
Adjutant-General—Lieut.-Gen. Sir C. W. H. Douglas, K. C. B.
Quartermaster-General—Maj.-Gen. Sir H. S. G. Miles, K. C. B.
Master-General of the Ordnance—Maj.-Gen. C. F. Hadden, K. C. B.
Civil Member—Lord Lucas.
Finance Member—F. D. Acland, M. P.
Secretary—Col. Sir E. W. D. Ward, K. C. B.

FIELD MARSHALS.

Sir Frederick Paul Haines, Royal Scots Fusiliers.
Viscount Wolseley, Colonel Royal Irish Regiment.
Earl Roberts, V. C., Colonel Irish Guards.
H. M. German Emperor, Col. 1st (Royal) Drag.
H. R. H. Duke of Connaught.
Sir Evelyn Wood, V. C., Colonel Royal Horse Guards.
Sir George White, V. C., Col. Gordon Highlanders.
Lord Grenfell.
Sir C. H. Brownlow, G. C. B.
H. I. M. Emperor of Austria-Hungary.

GENERALS—ACTIVE LIST.

H. R. H. Prince Christian of Schleswig-Holstein.
H. R. H. Duke of Cumberland.
Viscount Kitchener of Khartoum, G. C. B.
H. R. H. Prince of Wales, K. G.
Sir F. W. Forestier-Walker.
C. H. Scafe.
Sir Edward Stedman, K. C. B.
Lord Methuen, G. C. B.
H. M. King of Spain.
Sir Archibald Hunter, K. C. B.
Hon Sir Neville Lyttelton, G. C. B.
Sir Alfred Gaselee, G. C. I. E.
Christopher S. S. Fagan, R. M. L. I.
Sir W. G. Nicholson, K. C. B.
Sir J. D. P. French.
Sir I. S. M. Hamilton.

NAVY.

LORDS COMMISSIONERS OF THE ADMIRALTY.—*First Lord*, Rt. Hon. Reginald McKenna, M. P.; *Senior Naval Lord*, Admiral of the Fleet Sir John Fisher; *Second Naval Lord*, Vice-Admiral Sir Wm. Henry May, K. C. B.; *Third Naval Lord and Controller*, Rear-Admiral Sir J. R. Jellicoe, K. C. V. O.; *Junior Naval Lord*, Rear-Admiral A. S. Winstol; *Civil Lord*, George Lambert.

ADMIRALS OF THE FLEET.—Sir James Elphinstone Erskine, Sir Charles F. Hotham, Lord Walter Talbot Kerr, Sir Edward Hobart Seymour, Sir John Fisher, Sir Arthur K. Wilson, V. C. *Honorary Admirals of the Fleet.*—H. I. M. William II., German Emperor; H. I. M. Nicholas II., Emperor of Russia.

ADMIRALS.—Sir Harry Rawson, Sir Gerard Henry Uctred Noel, Sir Arthur Dalrymple Fanshawe, Sir Lewis A. Beaumont, Lord Charles Beresford, Sir James A. T. Bruce, H. R. H. the Prince of Wales, Sir Arthur W. Moore, Sir W. A. Dyke Acland, B. C.; Sir C. C. Drury, Sir R. N. Custance, R. W. Craigie, Sir W. H. Fawkes. *Honorary Admirals*—H. R. H. Prince Henry of Prussia, H. M. King of the Hellenes, H. M. King of Sweden, H. M. King of Norway.

VICE-ADMIRALS.—Sir G. L. Atkinson-Willes, Sir W. H. May, Sir R. F. H. Henderson, Hon. Sir A. G. Curzon-Howe, Angus MacLeod, Sir Edmund Samuel Poë, Arthur Charles B. Bromley, John Durnford, Charles J. Barlow, Hon. Sir Hedworth Lambton, Sir Francis C. B. Bridgeman, Sir Richard Poore, B. T.; George A. Giffard, Charles G. Robinson, W. H. B. Graham, R. F. O. Foote, E. H. Gamble, Sir A. B. Milne, Bart.; G. F. King-Hall, H. S. H. Prince Louis of Battenberg, Sir H. D. Barry, G. Neville.

FLAG-OFFICERS IN COMMISSION.

Nore, *Adm.* Sir Gerard H. U. Noel, K. C. B.
Portsmouth, *Adm.* Sir A. D. Fanshawe, K. C. B.
Plymouth, *Adm.* Sir Wilmot H. Fawkes, K. C. B.
Queenstown, Ireland, *Rear-Adm.* Sir A. W. Paget, K. C. M. G.
Channel Fleet, *Adm.* Lord Charles Beresford, G. C. V. O., K. C. B.
Battle Squadron, *Vice-Adm*, Sir A. B. Milne, Bart., K. C. V. O. (Second in Command).
First Cruiser Squadron, *Rear-Adm.* Chas. H. Adair.
Atlantic Fleet, *Vice-Adm.* Hon. Sir Asseton G. Curzon-Howe, K. C. B.
Mediterranean, *Adm.* Sir Charles C. Drury, G. C. V. O.
N. Am. and W. Indies and Particular Service Squadron, *Vice-Adm.* Frederick S. Inglefield.
Eastern Fleet, *Vice-Adm.* Hon. Sir Hedworth Lambton, K. C. B., K. C. V. O.
Cape of Good Hope, *Rear-Adm.* G. Le C. Egerton, C. B.

THE ESTABLISHED CHURCH OF ENGLAND.

ENGLISH ARCHBISHOPS.

Trans.
1903. *Canterbury*, Randall T. Davidson, *b.* 1848.
1909. *York*, Cosmo Gordon Lang, *b.* 1864.

ENGLISH BISHOPS.

App.
1901. *London*, Arthur Foley W. Ingram, *b.* 1858.
1901. *Durham*, Handley Carr Glyn Moule, D. D., *b.* 1841.
1903. *Winchester*, Herbert Edward Ryle, *b.* 1856.
1898. *Bangor*, W. H. Williams, D. D., *b.* 184 .
1894. *Bath and Wells*, G. W. Kennion, *b.* 1846.
1904. *Birmingham*, Charles Gore, D. D., *b.* 1853.
1897. *Bristol*, George Forrest Browne, *b.* 1833.
1904. *Carlisle*, J. W. Diggle, *b.* 1847.
1888. *Chester*, Francis John Jayne, *b.* 1845.
1907. *Chichester*, C. J. Ridgeway, D. D., *b*, 1842.
1895. *Ely*, Frederick Henry Chase.
1903. *Exeter*, Archibald Robertson, *b.* 1853.
1905. *Gloucester*, E. C. Sumner Gibson, *b.* 1848.
1895. *Hereford*, John Percival, *b.* 1835.
1891. *Lichfield*, Hon. Augustus Legge, *b.* 1839.
1885. *Lincoln*, Edward King, *b.* 1829.
1900. *Liverpool*, Francis James Chavasse, *b.* 1846.

App.
1883. *Llandaff*, J. P. Hughes.
1903. *Manchester*, Edward A. Knox, *b.* 1854.
1907. *Newcastle*, Norman D. J. Straton, *b.* 1840.
1893. *Norwich*, John Sheepshanks, *b.* 1834.
1901. *Oxford*, Francis Paget, *b.* 1851.
1896. *Peterborough*, Hon. Edwd. Carr Glyn, *b.* 1843.
1884. *Ripon*, William Boyd Carpenter, *b.* 1841.
1905. *Rochester*, John R. Harmer, *b.* 1857.
1903. *St. Albans*, Edgar Jacob, *b.* 1844.
1889. *St. Asaph*, Alfred George Edwards, *b.* 1848.
1897. *St. David's*, John Owen, *b.* 1853.
1885. *Salisbury*, John Wordsworth, *b.* 1843.
1907. *Sodor and Man*, Thos. Wortley Drury, *b.* 1848
1905. *Southwark*, E. S. Talbot, *b.* 1844.
1904. *Southwell*, Edward Hoskyns, *b.* 1861.
1891. *Truro*, Charles Wm. Stubbs, *b.* 1845.
1897. *Wakefield*, George Rodney Eden, *b.* 1853.
1901. *Worcester*, H. W. Yeatman-Biggs, *b.* 1845.

THE BRITISH GOVERNMENT—*Continued.*

DIPLOMATIC INTERCOURSE.

Countries.	British Representatives Abroad.	Foreign Representatives in England.
Argentine Republic	Walter B. Townley	Don F. L. Dominguez.
Austria-Hungary	Rt. Hon. Sir F. L. Cartwright, K. C. M. G.	Count Dietrichstein.
Belgium	Sir A. H. Hardinge, K. C. B.	Comte de Lalaing.
Brazil	Sir William H. D. Haggard, K. C. B.	Regis de Oliveira.
Chile	H. G. O. Bax-Ironside	Domingo Gana.
China	Sir J. N. Jordan, K. C. M. G.	Li Chiu-fong.
Denmark	Hon. Sir Alan Johnstone, K. C. V. O.	M. F. E. de Bille.
Ecuador	C. L. des Graz	Don Celso Nevares.
Egypt	Sir Eldon Gorst, K. C. B.	(None.)
France	Rt. Hon. Sir F. L. Bertie, G. C. M. G.	M. Paul Cambon.
German Empire	Rt. Hon. Sir W. E. Goschen, G. C. V. O.	Count P. Wolff-Metternich.
Greece	Sir F. E. H. Elliott, G. C. V. O.	Athos Romanos.
Guatemala	L. E. Gresley Carden	(Vacant.)
Italy	Rt. Hon. Sir Rennell Rodd, G. C. V. O.	Marq. di San Giuliano.
Japan	Sir Claude M. Macdonald, G. C. M. G.	Takaski Kato.
Mexico	Reginald Thomas Tower, C. V. O.	Miguel Covarrubias.
Morocco	Hon. Reginald Lister, C. V. O.	(None.)
Netherlands	Sir George Buchanan, K. C. V. O.	Baron Gericke van Herwijnen.
Norway	Arthur James Herbert, K. C. V. O.	J. Irgens.
Persia	Sir G. H. Barclay, K. C. M. G.	Muktasham-es-Saltaneh.
Peru	C. L. des Graz	Don Carlos G. Candamo.
Portugal	Hon. Sir Francis Hyde Villiers, K. C. M. G.	Marquis de Soveral, G. C. M. G.
Russia	Sir Arthur Nicholson, Bart., G. C. B.	Count Benckendorff.
Servia	James B. Whitehead	(Vacant).
Siam	Ralph Paget, C. M. G.	Phya Wismto Kosa.
Spain	Rt. Hon. Sir M. W. E. de Bunsen, G. C. V. O.	Señor Villa Urrutia.
Sweden	Sir C. A. Spring Rice, K. C. M. G.	Count H. Wrangel.
Switzerland	Sir Geo. F. Bonham, Bart.	Gaston Carlin.
Turkey	Rt. Hon. Sir G. A. Lowther, G. C. M. G.	Rifaat Bey.
United States	Rt. Hon. James Bryce, O. M.	Whitelaw Reid.
Uruguay	Robert J. Kennedy, C. M. G.	Daniel Muñoz.

COLONIAL GOVERNORS.

Commonwealth of Australia.—Earl of Dudley, G. C. M. G.
New South Wales.—Admiral Sir H. H. Rawson, G. C. B.
Victoria.—Sir T. D. G. Carmichael, Bart.
South Australia.—Sir George R. Le Hunte.
Queensland.—Lord Chelmsford.
West Australia.—Admiral Sir F. G. D. Bedford.
Tasmania.—Sir Gerald Strickland.
New Zealand.—Lord Plunket.
South Africa.—Earl of Selborne, *High Com'r.*
Cape Colony.—Hon. Sir Walt. F. Hely-Hutchinson.
Natal.—Col. Sir Matthew Nathan, K. C. M. G.
Orange River Colony.—Sir H. J. Goold-Adams, K. C. M. G.
Malta.—Lt.-Gen. H. F. Grant, C. B.
Canada.—Earl Grey.
Newfoundland.—Sir William MacGregor.
Jamaica.—Sir Sydney H. Olivier, K. C. M. G.
Barbados.—Sir G. T. Carter.
Bahamas.—Sir W. Grey Wilson.
Bermudas.—Lt.-Gen. F. W. Kitchener, C. B.
Trinidad.—(Vacant.)
British Guiana.—Sir F. M. Hodgson.
Hong Kong.—Col. Sir F. J. D. Lugard, K. C. M. G.
Ceylon.—Col. Sir Henry E. McCallum, G. C. M. G.
Fiji.—Sir Everard F. im Thurn.
Sierra Leone.—Sir Leslie Probyn, K. C. V. O.
Straits Settlements.—Sir J. Anderson.
Windward Islands.—Sir R. C. Williams, K. C. M. G.
Leeward Islands.—Sir E. B. Sweet-Escott.
Falkland Islands.—William L. Allardyce.
Mauritius.—Sir C. Boyle.
Gold Coast Colony.—Sir J. P. Rodger.
British Honduras.—Br.-Gen. E. J. E. Swayne, C. B.
Lagos and Nigeria, Southern.—Sir Walter Egerton, K. C. M. G.
Gambia (West Africa)—Sir G. C. Denton, K. C. M. G.
Nigeria, Northern.—Lt.-Col. Sir Percy Girouerd, K. C. M. G.
British East Africa.—Lt.-Col. J. H. Sadler, C. B.
Uganda.—Sir H. H. J. Bell, K. C. M. G.

GOVERNMENT OF INDIA.

Viceroy and Governor-General.......The Rt. Hon. Earl of Minto, G. M. S. I., G. M. I. E.
Governor of Madras.......Sir Arthur Lawley, G. C. I. E.
Governor of Bombay.......Col. Sir George S. Clarke, G. C. M. G.
Lieutenant-Governor of Bengal.......Edw. N. Baker, C. S. I.

SECRETARIES TO THE GOVERNMENT OF INDIA.

LEGISLATIVE.—J. M. Macpherson, C. S. I.
HOME.—Sir H. H. Risley, K. C. I. E.
REVENUE AND AGRICULTURE.—J. Wilson, C. S. I.
FINANCE.—J. S. Meston; W. S. Meyer, C. I. E.
FOREIGN.—S. H. Butler, C. I. E.
ARMY DEPARTMENT.—Major-Gen. A. W. L. Bayly, C. B.
MILITARY SUPPLY.—Col. E. W. Maconchy, D. S. O.
COMMERCE AND INDUSTRY.—B. Robertson, C. I. E.
PUBLIC WORKS.—L. M. Jacob, C. S. I.

Agents to Governor-General: Central India, Maj. H. Daly, C. S. I.; *Rajputana*, E. G. Colvin, C. S. I.; *Baluchistan*, Col. Sir A. H. McMahon, K. C. I. E. *Khorassan*, Major P. M. Sykes, C. M. G.
Residents: Hyderabad, C. S. Bayley, C. S. I.; *Mysore*, S. M. Fraser, C. I. E.; *Cashmere*, Maj. Sir F. E. Younghusband, K. C. I. E.; *Baroda*, Lieut.-Col. M. J. Meade; *Nepal*, Major J. Mauners Smith, C. I. E., V. C.; *Gwalior*, Lieut.-Col. A. F. Pinhey, C. I. E.; *Indore*, Maj. J. L. Kaye; *Jaipur*, Lieut. Col. C. Herbert, C. I. E.; *Udaipur*, C. H. A. Hill, C. I. E.

MILITARY ESTABLISHMENT.

COMMANDER-IN-CHIEF IN INDIA.—H. E. Gen. Viscount Kitchener of Khartoum, G. C. B.
Chief of Staff, Lieut.-Gen. Sir Beauchamp Duff, K. C. B.
Adjutant-General, Major-Gen. R. I. Scallon, C. B.
Quartermaster-General, Major-Gen. A. C. Sclater, C. B.

GENERALS OFFICERS COMMANDING THE FORCES.

NORTHERN ARMY.—Lieut.-Gen. Sir Josceline H. Wodehouse, K. C. B.
SOUTHERN ARMY.—Lieut.-Gen. Sir E. C. Barrow, K. C. B.

The British Parliament.

The supreme legislative power of the British Empire is, by its constitution, vested in Parliament. This body consists of two houses, the Lords and the Commons.

THE HOUSE OF LORDS.

The House of Lords is composed of the whole Peerage of England and of the United Kingdom, and of certain representatives of the peerages of Scotland and Ireland, but many members of these latter have also English titles which give them seats in the House. The Duke of Buccleuch sits as Earl of Doncaster, and the Duke of Leinster as Viscount Leinster. The House at present consists of 3 Princes of the Blood, 2 Archbishops, 22 Dukes, 23 Marquises, 124 Earls, 40 Viscounts, 24 Bishops, 335 Barons, 16 Scottish Representative Peers elected for each Parliament, and 28 Irish Representative Peers elected for life—in all, 617 members.

The Lord Chancellor of England is always the Speaker of the House of Lords.

A TABLE OF BRITISH DUKES.

Created.	Title.	Name.	Born.	Succeeded	Heir to Title.
1868	Abercorn*	James Hamilton, 2nd Duke	1838	1885	Marq. of Hamilton M. P., s.
1881	Albany†	H. R. H. Leopold, 2nd Duke (*l*)	1884	1884	H. R. H. Prince Johann of Saxe-Coburg, s.
1701	Argyll	John Douglas Sutherland Campbell, 9th Duke (*k*)	1845	1900	Lord A. Campbell, b.
1703	Atholl‡	John J. H. H. Stewart-Murray, 7th Duke	1840	1864	Marq. Tullibardine, s.
1682	Beaufort	H. A. W. Fitzroy Somerset, 9th Duke	1847	1899	Marq. of Worcester, s.
1694	Bedford	Herbrand Arthur Russell, 11th Duke	1858	1893	Marq. of Tavistock, s.
1673	Buccleuch & (1684) Queensberry‡	Wm. H. W. Montagu-Douglas-Scott, 6th Duke (*a*)	1831	1884	Earl of Dalkeith, s.
1874	Connaught†	H. R. H. Arthur William Patrick, 1st Duke	1850	....	Prince Arthur, s.
1337	Cornwall & (1892) York†	H. R. H. George, Prince of Wales	1865	....	Prince Edward, s.
1799	Cumberland†	H. R. H. Ernest Augustus, 3rd Duke (*b*)	1845	1878	Earl of Armagh, s.
1694	Devonshire	Victor C. W. Cavendish, 9th duke	1868	1908	Marq. of Hartington, s.
1889	Fife	Alex. William George Duff, 1st Duke (*c*)	1849	...	Lady Alex. Duff, d.
1675	Grafton	Aug. Charles Lennox Fitzroy, 7th Duke (*d*)	1821	1882	Earl of Euston, s.
1643	Hamilton‡ and Brandon	Alfred D. Douglas-Hamilton, 13th Duke	1862	1895	Percy D. Hamilton, c.
1694	Leeds	George Godolphin Osborne, 10th Duke	1862	1895	Marq of Carmarthen, s.
1766	Leinster*	Maurice Fitzgerald, 6th Duke (minor)	1887	1893	Lord D. Fitzgerald, b.
1719	Manchester	William Augustus Drogo Montagu (*e*)	1877	1892	Viscount Mandeville, s.
1702	Marlborough	Chas. R. J. Spencer-Churchill, 9th Duke (*f*)	1871	1892	Marq. of Blandford, s.
1707	Montrose‡	Douglas B. M. R. Graham, 5th Duke	1852	1874	Marq. of Graham, s.
1756	Newcastle	Henry P. A. Pelham-Clinton, 7th Duke	1864	1879	Lord H. Pelham-Clinton-Hope, b.
1438	Norfolk	Henry Fitzalan Howard, 15th Duke (*g*)	1847	1860	Earl Arundel & S., s.
1766	Northumberland	Henry George Percy, 7th Duke	1846	1899	Earl Percy, M. P., s.
1716	Portland	W. J. A. Cavendish-Bentinck, 6th Duke	1857	1879	Marq. of Titchfield, s.
1675	Richmond & (1876) Gordon & (1675) Lennox‡	Charles H. Gordon-Lennox, 7th Duke (*h*)	1845	1903	Earl of March, s.
1707	Roxburghe‡	Henry John Innes-Ker, 8th Duke (*m*)	1876	1892	Lord A. R. Innes-Ker, b.
1703	Rutland	Henry John Brinsley Manners, 8th Duke	1852	1906	Marq. of Granby, s.
1684	St. Albans	Charles V. de Vere Beauclerk, 11th Duke (*i*)	1870	1898	Ld Osborne Beauclerk, b
1547	Somerset	Algernon St. Maur, 15th Duke	1846	1894	Lord Ernest St. Maur, b.
1833	Sutherland	Crom. Sutherland-Leveson-Gower, 4th Duke	1851	1892	Marq. of Stafford, s.
1814	Wellington	Arthur Charles Wellesley, 4th Duke (*j*)	1849	1900	Marq. of Douro, s.
1874	Westminster	Hugh Richard Arthur Grosvenor, 2nd Duke	1879	1899	Lord A. Grosvenor, u.

s, son; b, brother; c, cousin; n, nephew; u, uncle.

* Irish Dukes. † Royal Dukes. ‡ Scottish Dukes. (*a*) Eighth Duke of Queensberry, descendant of the Duke of Monmouth, son of King Charles II. (*b*) Son of King George V., of Hanover. (*c*) Husband of the Princess Louise, eldest daughter of the Prince of Wales. (*d*) Descendant of Henry Fitzroy, first Duke, son of King Charles II. and Barbara Villiers. (*e*) His mother was Miss Yznaga, of New York. His wife (whom he married November 14, 1900) was Miss Helena Zimmerman, of Cincinnati, Ohio. (*f*) His wife was Miss Consuelo Vanderbilt, daughter of William K. Vanderbilt, of New York. (*g*) Premier Duke. (*h*) Descendant of Charles Lennox, first Duke, son of King Charles II. and Louise-Renée de Queronailles. (*i*) Descendant of Charles Beauclerk, first Duke, son of King Charles II. and Nell Gwynne. (*j*) Grandson of the great Duke of Wellington, the victor of Waterloo. (*k*) Husband of Princess Louise, sixth child of Queen Victoria. (*l*) Duke of Saxe-Coburg-Gotha. (*m*) His wife (1903) was Miss Goelet, of New York.

THE HOUSE OF COMMONS.

The present House of Commons consists of 670 members—465 for England, 30 for Wales, 72 for Scotland, and 103 for Ireland.

The division of parties in the House of Commons, returned in the general elections of January and February, 1906, was as follows: Conservatives and Liberal-Unionists, 158; Liberals, 387; Nationalists, 84, and 41 Independent Labor members; the ministerial majority being 354.

The Speaker of the House is the Rt. Hon. James William Lowther, M. P. for Penrith.

Population of Great Britain and Ireland.

CENSUS OF 1901.

ENGLAND.

COUNTIES.	Population.	COUNTIES.	Population.	COUNTIES.	Population.	COUNTIES.	Population.
Bedford	171,249	Essex	1,085,576	Monmouth	292,327	Suffolk	384,198
Berks	254,931	Gloucester	634,666	Norfolk	460,040	Surrey	2,008,923
Bucks	195,534	Hampshire	798,756	Northampton	338,064	Sussex	605,052
Cambridge	190,687	Hereford	114,401	Northumberland	602,859	Warwick	897,678
Chester	814,555	Hertford	250,530	Nottingham	514,537	Westmoreland	64,305
Cornwall	322,957	Huntingdon	57,773	Oxford	182,768	Wiltshire	273,845
Cumberland	266,921	Kent	1,351,849	Rutland	19,708	Worcester	488,401
Derby	620,196	Lancaster	4,406,787	Shropshire	239,321	York	3,585,122
Devon	660,444	Leicester	433,994	Somerset	508,104	Total	30,805,466
Dorset	202,962	Lincoln	498,781	Stafford	1,234,382		
Durham	1,187,324	Middlesex	3,585,139				

SCOTLAND.

Aberdeen	303,889	Edinburgh	437,553	Linlithgow	64,787	Selkirk	23,339
Argyll	73,166	Elgin	44,757	Nairn	9,291	Shetland	27,755
Ayr	254,133	Fife	218,350	Orkney	27,723	Stirling	141,894
Banff	61,439	Forfar	283,729	Peebles	15,066	Sutherland	21,389
Berwick	30,785	Haddington	38,653	Perth	123,255	Wigtown	32,591
Bute	18,659	Inverness	89,901	Renfrew	268,418	Shipping population	9,583
Caithness	33,619	Kincardine	40,891	Ross and Cromarty	76,149	Total	4,471,957
Clackmannan	31,991	Kinross	6,980	Roxburgh	48,793		
Dumbarton	113,660	Kirkcudbright	39,359				
Dumfries	72,562	Lanark	1,337,848				

WALES.

Anglesey	50,590	Carnarvon	126,885	Merioneth	49,130	Radnor	23,263
Brecon	59,906	Denbigh	129,935	Montgomery	54,892		
Cardigan	60,237	Flint	81,727	Pembroke	88,749	Total	1,720,609
Carmarthen	135,325	Glamorgan	860,022				

IRELAND.

LEINSTER.		Westmeath	61,527	ULSTER.		CONNAUGHT.	
Carlow	37,723	Wexford	103,860	Antrim	461,240	Galway	192,146
Dublin	447,266	Wicklow	60,679	Armagh	125,238	Leitrim	69,201
Kildare	63,469	MUNSTER.		Cavan	97,368	Mayo	202,627
Kilkenny	78,821	Clare	112,129	Donegal	173,625	Roscommon	101,639
King's	60,129	Cork	404,813	Down	289,335	Sligo	84,022
Longford	46,581	Kerry	165,231	Fermanagh	65,243		
Louth	65,741	Limerick	146,018	Londonderry	144,329	Total	4,456,546
Meath	67,463	Tipperary	159,754	Monaghan	74,505		
Queen's	57,226	Waterford	87,030	Tyrone	150,468		

The population returns are from the official census of Great Britain and Ireland taken in March, 1901. The total population, excluding army, navy, and merchant seamen abroad, is 41,454,578.

The City of London.

Lord Mayor.	*Ald.*	*Shff.*	*Mayor*
Sir George Wyatt Truscott, Kt.	1895	1902	1908
Aldermen.			
Sir John Whittaker Ellis, Bart.	1872	1874	1881
Sir Henry Edmund Knight, Kt.	1874	1875	1882
Sir Joseph Savory, Bart.	1883	1882	1890
Sir Walter Henry Wilkin, K.C.M.G.	1888	1894	1895
Sir George Faudel Faudel-Phillips, Bart., G.C.I.E.	1888	1884	1896
Col. Sir H. D. Davies, K.C.M.G.	1889	1887	1897
Sir Alfred James Newton, Bart.	1890	1888	1899
Sir Marcus Samuel, Bart.	1891	1894	1902
Sir James Thomson Ritchie, Bart.	1891	1896	1903
Sir John Pound, Bart.	1892	1895	1904
Sir Walter Vaughan Morgan, Bart.	1892	1900	1905
Sir William Purdie Treloar, Bart.	1892	1899	1906
Sir John Charles Bell, Bart.	1894	1901	1907
All the above have passed the Civic Chair.			
Sir John C. Knill, Bart.	1897	1903	....
Sir Thomas Vesey Strong, Kt.	1897	1904	....
Sir Henry George Smallman, Kt.	1898	1905	....
Sir Thomas Boor Crosby, Kt., M.D.	1898	1906	....
Sir David Burnett, Kt.	1902	1907	....
W. C. Simmons	1903	....	....
W. Murray Guthrie	1903	....	....
Francis Stanhope Hanson	1905	1908	....
Francis Howse	1906	....	....
Sir T. Vansittart Bowater, Kt.	1907	1906	....
Charles Johnston	1907	....	....
Sir Charles C. Wakefield	1908	1907	....

The Lord Mayor has an annual salary of £10,000, or $50,000.

Population of London.

LONDON WITHIN VARIOUS BOUNDARIES.	Area in Statute Acres.	POPULATION. 1881.	1891.	1901.
Within the Registrar-General's Tables of Mortality		3,815,544		
Within the Limits of the County of London	74,672	3,834,194	4,228,317	4,536,063
London School Board District		3,834,194		
City of London within Municipal and Parliamentary Limits	671	50,658	37,705	26,897
Metropolitan Parliamentary Boroughs (including the City)	75,442	3,834,194	4,232,118	4,542,725
Metropolitan and City Police Districts	443,421	4,766,661	5,633,806	6,580,616

The German Government.

(For the Ministry, see Index.)

POLITICAL DIVISIONS IN THE REICHSTAG.

PARTIES.	Number of Members.	PARTIES.	Number of Members.
German Conservatives	59	Free Conservatives	24
Centre (Clericals)	109	Radicals	42
Poles	20	South German Radicals	8
National Liberals	57	Anti-Semites	11
Social Democrats	43	Agrarians	8
Alsatian (meaning Anti-German)	3	Total	397
Independent (unclassified)	13		

The largest group, the Clericals or Centre, represents mainly the Rhine districts and South Germany. The Conservatives, though sometimes in opposition, especially on agrarian questions, are regarded as the ministerial party, and with them are allied the National Liberals and some smaller groups, insuring the Government a majority.

THE ARMY.

The Commander-in-Chief is the Emperor.

Field-Marshal-Generals—Baron von Loë, von Hahnke, Prince Leopold of Bavaria, Count von Haeseler.

General Staff, Chief—General von Moltke.

Corps Commanders—*First Corps*, Eastern Prussia, Königsberg, General von Kluck; *Second Corps*, Pomerania, Stettin, Lieutenant-General von Heeringen; *Third Corps*, Berlin, General von Bülow; *Fourth Corps*, Magdeburg, General von Beneckendorff u. von Hindenburg; *Fifth Corps*, Posen, General Kirchbach; *Sixth Corps*, Breslau, General von Woyrsch; *Seventh Corps*, Münster, General Baron von Bernhardi; *Eighth Corps*, Coblenz, General von Ploetz; *Ninth Corps*, Altona, Lieutenant-General von Vietinghoff; *Tenth Corps*, Hanover, General von Löwenfeld; *Eleventh Corps*, Cassel, General Scheffer-Boyadel; *Twelfth Corps*, Dresden, General von Broizem; *Thirteenth Corps*, Stuttgart, General Duke Albrecht von Württemberg; *Fourteenth Corps*, Carlsruhe, General von Hoiningen; *Fifteenth Corps*, Strassburg, General Rit er Hentschel von Gilgenheimb; *Sixteenth Corps*, Metz, General von Prittevitz und Gaffron; *Seventeenth Corps*, Dantzic, General von Mackensen; *Eighteenth Corps*, Frankfort-on-Main, General von Eichhorn; *Nineteenth Corps*, Leipsic, General von Kirchbach; *First Bavarian Army Corps*, Munich, General Prince Rupprecht of Bavaria; *Second Bavarian Army Corps*, Würzburg, General Reichlin von Meldegg; *Third Bavarian*, General Baron von Taun-Rathsamhausen. *Commander of the Guards*—General von Kessel.

The French Government.

(For the Ministry, see Index.)

President..ARMAND FALLIERES.

The annual allowance to the President of the Republic is 600,000 francs, with a further allowance of 600,000 francs for his expenses.

NATIONAL ASSEMBLY.

SENATE.—*President*, Antonin Dubost; *Vice-Presidents*, MM. Guerin, Leydet, Monis, Lourties; *Secretary-General*, M. Dupre.

CHAMBER OF DEPUTIES.—*President*, M. Henri Brisson; *Vice-Presidents*, MM. Etienne Berteaux, Rabier, vacancy; *Secretary-General*, M. Launoy.

The number of Senators is 300, and they are at present politically divided into about 270 Republicans and 30 representatives of the various shades of the opposition.

The Deputies number 591, and are divided into the following groups: 246 Radicals, allied to the "Socialist-Radical" group; 79 Advanced Republicans, 8 Dissident Radicals, 23 Independent Socialists, 53 United Socialists, 64 Progressists (Moderate Republicans), 118 Members of Composite Opposition ("Right"; they include Royalists, Bonapartists, members of the "Liberal Action Party" and 23 "Nationalists.")

THE ARMY.

Supreme Commander—General de Lacroix. Conseil Superieur de la Guerre, Generals Duchesne, Voyron, Dodds, Michal, Burnez, Ceigne, Desbordes, de Lacroix, Davignon.

Military Governor of Paris—General Dalstein.

Commanders of Corps d'Armee—*First Corps*, Lille, General Davignon; *Second Corps*, Amiens, General Debatisse; *Third Corps*, Rouen, General de Torcy; *Fourth Corps*, Le Mans, General Oudri; *Fifth Corps*, Orleans, General Millet; *Sixth Corps*, Chalons-sur-Marne, General Durand; *Seventh Corps*, Besançon, General Robert; *Eighth Corps*, Bourges, General Plagnol; *Ninth Corps*, Tours, General Trémeau; *Tenth Corps*, Rennes, General Passerieu; *Eleventh Corps*, Nantes, General Peloux; *Twelfth Corps*, Limoges, General Tournier; *Thirteenth Corps*, Clermont-Ferrand, General Durand; *Fourteenth Corps*, Lyons, General Gallieni; *Fifteenth Corps*, Marseilles, General Mathis; *Sixteenth Corps*, Montpellier, General Marion; *Seventeenth Corps*, Toulouse, General Rouvray; *Eighteenth Corps*, Bordeaux, General Oudard; *Nineteenth Corps*, Algiers, General Bailloud; *Twentieth Corps*, Nancy, General Pau; *Commander-General of Colonial Corps d'Armee*, General Archinard (Paris).

THE NAVY.

Commanders of Squadrons and Divisions of Squadrons.—Squadrons of the Western Mediterranean and Levant, Vice-Admiral Germinet (flagship Suffren), Commander-in-Chief; Northern Squadron, Vice-Admiral Jauréguiberry (flagship Massena), Commander-in-Chief; Squadron of Extreme Orient, Vice-Admiral Boisse (flagship Montcalm), Commander-in-Chief; Naval Division of the Atlantic, Rear-Admiral Thierry (flagship Kléber); Naval Division of the Pacific, Captain Buchard; Naval Division of the Indian Ocean, Commander Lormier.

The Russian Government.

(For the Ministry, see Index.)

COUNCIL OF THE EMPIRE.

President..............................His Imperial Highness the Grand Duke Michael Nicolaëvitch.

THE ARMY.

The Commander-in-Chief is the Emperor.

Commanders of Military Conscriptions—First Conscription, St. Petersburg, H. I. H. the Grand Duke Nicholas Nicolaevitch. *Second Conscription*, Vilna, General Krszivicki. *Third Conscription*, Warsaw, General Skalon. *Fourth Conscription*, Kiew, General Suchomlinow. *Fifth Conscription*, Odessa, General Kaulbars. *Sixth Conscription*, Moscow, G. M. Hörschelmann. *Seventh Conscription*, Kazan, General of Infantry Sandezki. *Eighth Conscription*, Don, General Samsonoff. *Ninth Conscription*, Caucasus, General of Infantry Prince Woronzow-Daschkow. *Tenth Conscription*, Turkestan, Lieutenant-General Mistchenko. *Eleventh Conscription*, Western Siberia, General of Cavalry Lieutenant-General Schmidt. *Twelfth Conscription*, Irkutsk, General Selivanoff. *Thirteenth Conscription*, Amoor, General Unterberger.

THE NAVY.

Commander-in-Chief, Vice-Admiral Eberhardt.

The Italian Government.

(For the Ministry, see Index.)

PARLIAMENT.

President of the Senate—Signor Manfredi. *President of the Chamber of Deputies*—Signor Marcora.

THE ARMY.

Chief of Staff—General Pollio.

Corps Commanders—Turin, Lieutenant-General Barbieri; Alessandria, Lieutenant-General Goiran; Milan, Lieutenant-General Mainoni; Genoa, Lieutenant-General Pedotti; Verona, Lieutenant-General Gobbo; Bologna, Lieutenant-General Ponza di S. Martino; Ancona, Lieutenant-General Asinari di Bernezzo; Florence, Lieutenant-General Vigano; Rome, Lieutenant-General Fecia di Cossato; Naples, Lieutenant-General Duke of Aosta; Bari, Lieutenant-General Marritelli; Palermo, Lieutenant-General Mazza.

COMMANDERS OF MILITARY DIVISIONS.

1. Turin, Lieutenant-General Frugoni; 2. Novara, Lieutenant-General Valcamonica; 3. Alessandria, Lieutenant-General Moni; 4. Cuneo, Lieutenant-General Crema; 5. Milan, Lieutenant-General Costantini; 6. Brescia, Lieutenant-General Bellini; 7. Piacenza, Lieutenant-General Sapelli di Capriglio; 8. Genoa, Lieutenant-General Massone; 9. Verona, Lieutenant-General Caneva; 10. Padua, Lieutenant-General Incisa di Camerana; 11. Bologna, Lieutenant-General Vacquer Paderi; 12. Ravenna, Lieutenant-General Grandi; 13. Ancona, Lieutenant-General Gastinelli; 14. Chieti, Lieutenant-General Goggia; 15. Florence, Lieutenant-General Della Noce; 16. Livorno, Lieutenant-General Zuccari; 17. Rome, Lieutenant-General Brusati Roberto; 18. Perugia, Lieutenant-General Marini; 19. Cagliari, Lieutenant-General D. Majo; 20. Naples, Lieutenant-General Cadorna; 21. Salerno, Lieutenant-General Toselli Lazzarini; 22. Bari, Lieutenant-General Tommasi; 23. Catanzaro, Lieutenant-General D'Ottone; 24. Palermo, Lieutenant-General Corticelli; 25. Messina, Lieutenant-General Del Rosso.

THE NAVY.

Admiral—H. R. H. Prince Thomas, Duke of Genoa. *Commanders of Squadrons—Active*, Vice-Admiral Morin; *Instruction*, Rear-Admiral Grenet.

The Austrian-Hungarian Government.

(For the Ministry, see Index.)

THE AUSTRIAN REICHSRATH.

President of the House of Lords—Prince Alfred Windischgrätz. *Vice-Presidents*—Prince Karl Auersperg and Prince Schoenburg. *President of the House of Deputies*—Dr. Richard Weiskirchner.

THE HUNGARIAN REICHSTAG.

President of the House of Magnates—Count Albin Csaky. *President of the House of Representatives*—Dr. Julius V. Justh.

THE ARMY.

The Commander-in-Chief is the Emperor.

Inspectors-General of Troops—F. Z. M. Eugen Barn Albori; G. d. C. Archduke Eugene; F. Z. M. Ferdinand Fiedler.

Commander-in-Chief of the Imperial and Royal Austrian Reserves (Landwehr)—F. Z. M. Archduke Friedrich.

Commander-in-Chief of the Royal Hungarian Reserves (Honved)—G. d. C. Wilhelm Klobucar.

Corps Commanders—First Corps, Cracow, F. Z. M. Moritz von Steinsberg; *Second Corps*, Vienna, F. Z. M. Mansuet Ritter von Versbach; *Third Corps*, Graz, F. Z. M. Oscar Potiorek; *Fourth Corps*, Buda-Pesth, F. Z. M. Hubert Baron Czibulka; *Fifth Corps*, Presburg, F. Z. M. Baron von Steininger; *Sixth Corps*, Kaschaie, F. Z. M. Joh. Mörk von Mörkenstein; *Seventh Corps*, Temesvar, F. M. L. Liborius Frank; *Eighth Corps*, Prague, F. Z. M. Albert von Koller; *Ninth Corps*, Josefstadt, F. M. L. Adolf von Rummer; *Tenth Corps*, Przemysl, F. Z. M. Arthur von Pino; *Eleventh Corps*, Lemberg, F. M. L. Count Karl Auersperg; *Twelfth Corps*, Hermannstadt, G. d. C. Josef von Gaudernak; *Thirteenth Corps*, Agram, F. M. L. Raimund Gerba; *Fourteenth Corps*, Innsbruck, F. M. L. Joh. Edler von Schemua; *Fifteenth Corps*, Sarajewo, G. d. C. Anton Edler von Winzor; *Dalmatia*, Zara, F. Z. M. Marian Varesanin von Vares. *Inspector-General of Cavalry*—G. d. C. von Brudermann. *Inspector-General of Artillery*—F. Z. M. Archduke Leopold Salvator. *Inspector of Engineering*—F. M. L. Ernest Baron Leithner. *Inspector of Military Instruction*—F. M. L. Siegler von Eberswald.

NOTE—G. d. C., General of Cavalry; F. Z. M., Feldzeugmeister; F. M. L., Field Marshal-Lieutenant.

Dominion of Canada.

Governor-General (Salary, $50,000)..Earl Grey.

Ministry.

The salary of each member of the Dominion Cabinet holding a portfolio is $7,000 per annum, except the Premier, who receives $12,000. The leader of the Opposition, Mr. R. L. Borden, receives $7,000. The present ministry was sworn into office July 11, 1896. It is liberal in politics.

Premier and President of the Privy Council—Rt. Hon. Sir Wilfred Laurier, G. C. M. G.
Secretary of State—Hon. Charles Murphy.
Minister of Trade and Commerce—Rt. Hon. Sir Richard Cartwright, G. C. M. G.
Minister of Justice—Hon. A. B. Aylesworth, K. C.
Minister of Marine and Fisheries—Hon. Louis P. Brodeur.
Minister of Militia and Defence—Hon. Sir Fred. W. Borden, K. C. M. G.
Postmaster-General—Hon. Rodolphe Lemieux.
Minister of Agriculture—Hon. Sydney A. Fisher.
Minister of Public Works—Hon. William Pugsley.
Minister of Finance—Hon. William S. Fielding.
Minister of Railways and Canals—Hon. George P. Graham.
Minister of the Interior—Hon. Frank Oliver.
Minister of Customs—Hon. William Paterson.
Minister of Inland Revenue—Hon. W. Templeman.

The Senate (Dominion Parliament) is composed of 87 members, Hon. Raoul Dandurand, Speaker, whose salary is $4,000. Each Senator receives a sessional indemnity of $2,500 and mileage. The House of Commons is composed of 221 members, Hon. Robert Franklin Sutherland, Speaker, whose salary is $4,000. Each member of the House receives a sessional indemnity of $2,500. The members of the House of Commons are elected under the several provincial franchises, in accordance with a federal act passed in 1898. The Senators are appointed for life by the Crown on the nomination of the Governor in Council.

Area, Population and Seats of Government, and Lieutenant-Governors of the Provinces.

Provinces.	Area, Square Miles.*	Population, 1901.	Seats of Government.	Lieutenant-Governors.	Appointed.
Alberta†	253,540	72,841	Edmonton	Hon. G. H. V. Bulyea	1905
British Columbia	357,600	178,657	Victoria	Hon. James Dunsmuir	1906
Manitoba	73,732	255,211	Winnipeg	Hon. Sir D. H. McMillan, K. C. M. G.	1907
New Brunswick	27,985	331,120	Fredericton	Hon. L. J. Tweedie	1902
Nova Scotia	21,428	459,574	Halifax	Hon. Duncan C. Fraser	1906
Ontario	260,862	2,182,947	Toronto	Hon. J. M. Gibson	1908
Prince Edward Island	2,184	103,259	Charlottetown	Hon. D. A. Mackinnon, K. C.	1904
Quebec	351,873	1,648,898	Quebec	Hon. L. P. Pelletier	1908
Saskatchewan†	250,650	91,460	Regina	Hon. A. E. Forget	1905
Mackenzie, Ungava, & Franklin, N. W. T.	1,922,735	18,875	Regina	....	....
Keewatin, N. W. Ter.	516,571	‡	Winnipeg	Alexander Henderson, Com'r.	1907
Yukon Territory	196,976	27,219	Dawson	Frederick White, Com'r.	1905
Total	3,729,665	5,371,315			

*Land and water included in area. †Alberta and Saskatchewan were erected into provinces in 1905. Mackenzie, Ungava, Franklin, Keewatin and Northwest Territories are territorial districts. ‡Included in Mackenzie, Ungava and Franklin.

High Commissioner in London, England, Lord Strathcona and Mount Royal, G. C. M. G. Salary, $10,000.

The Dominion of Canada has an area of 3,729,665 square miles (excluding the Hudson Bay, the Gulf of St. Lawrence and all tidal waters) and comprises one-sixteenth of the land surface of the globe. It is the largest of all the British possessions, Australia, the next in size, containing 2,946,691 square miles. The Government of Canada is federal, centred at Ottawa, which city is the capital of the Dominion, while the provinces have their respective local Legislatures. The head of the Federal Government is the Governor-General, appointed by the King of Great Britain, and holding office for five years, his salary being paid by the Dominion Government.

The Lieutenant-Governors of the several provinces are appointed by the Federal Government for a term of five years. The Legislatures are elected by the people of each province. The highest Court in the Dominion is the Supreme Court, composed of a Chief Justice and five Judges, each of whom receives a salary of $9,000 per annum, except the Chief Justice, who is paid an additional $1,000. From the decisions of this Court the only tribunal to which appeal can be made is to the Judicial Committee of the Imperial Privy Council of Great Britain. The only other Federal Court is the Exchequer Court, presided over by a single Judge, for trying cases connected with the revenue. Salary $8,000. All others are of a provincial character, limited to jurisdiction in their respective provinces only.

Finances.

Revenue (financial year ending March 31, 1907, 9 months*), $67,999,328, of which $39,760,173 was from customs, $11,805,413 from excise, $5,061,728 from post-office, $16,839,586 from public works, including government railways; miscellaneous, $4,532,428. The revenue in 1906 amounted to $80,139,360, and in 1908 the revenue was $96,054,506.

*Change in fiscal year.

DOMINION OF CANADA—*Continued.*

The expenditure on account of consolidated fund (9 months*) was $51,542,161, of which $6,712,771 was for interest; $1,487,495 for civil government; $867,798 for administration of justice; $1,322,075 for legislation; $2,026,642 for light-house and coast service; $1,128,-877 for mail subsidies and steamship subventions; $940,680 for Indians; $693,685 for fisheries; $94,984 for geological survey and observatories; $625,812 for arts, agriculture, quarantine, and statistics; $3,347,038 for militia and defence; $5,520,571 for public works; $6,745,134 for subsidies to provinces; $3,979,557 for post-office; $7,011,858 for railways and canals; $1,222,949 for collecting customs revenue; $679,155 for ocean and river service; $611,201 for immigration; $647,836 for mounted police.

National Debt.

The gross public debt of Canada on March 31, 1907 (9 months*), amounted to $379,-966,826. The total assets counted against gross public debt amounted to $116,294,966.

Militia.

Under the new establishments the total strength of the Canadian active militia, June 30, 1906, was as follows:

Cavalry, 18 regiments and 10 independent companies; field artillery, 10 brigades and 3 independent batteries; garrison artillery, 7 regiments and 1 independent company; engineers, 4 companies and 1 telegraph section; infantry, 91 regiments (of various strength) and 10 independent companies; army service corps, 12 companies; medical corps, 18 field ambulances.

Total of all ranks, approximately, 51,280. There are 475 rifle clubs; 135 cadet corps. Attached to the military schools and colleges there are 1,075 men.

Trade.

Exports (domestic and foreign) (1907-1908): To British Empire, $147,720,018; United States, $96,920,138; Germany, $2,374,607; France and possessions, $1,836,140; Belgium, $3,377,479; China, $955,718; Japan, $740,958; Holland, $855,085. Total exports, $280,-006,606, of which goods not the produce of Canada, $33,045,638.

Imports (1907-1908): From British Empire, $111,240,895; United States, $210,652,825; Germany, $8,163,047; France and possessions, $9,922,616; Belgium, $2,380,649; Japan, $2,177,244; China, $728,054; Cuba, $471,017; South America, $1,759,704; Italy, $781,-497; Switzerland, $2,734,779; Holland, $1,426,335. Total imports, $358,428,616. Of the merchandise imported, $218,160,047 was dutiable, and $140,268,569 free.

Imports of coin and bullion, $6,548,661, and the exports $16,637,654.

Banks.

Chartered banks (December 31, 1907): Capital paid up, $95,953,732; reserve fund, $69,-806,892; making total banking capital, $165,760,624; circulation redemption fund, $4,304,524. Total assets, $945,685,708; total liabilities, $769,026,924; notes in circulation, $75,784,482; deposits, $654,839,711; loans and discounts, $709,975,274.

Deposits in savings banks (1907): Government, $62,541,802; special, $28,520,547. Total, $91,062,349.

Railways.

Canada has a network of steam railways, the total mileage of which at the end of March, 1907, was 22,452 miles.

Fisheries.

The following is a statement of the money value of the fisheries within the Dominion of Canada, 1873-1907 inclusive:

Year	Value	Year	Value	Year	Value
1873	$10,547,402.44	1885	$17,722,973.18	1897	$22,783,546.00
1874	11,681,886.20	1886	18,672,288.00	1898	19,667,127.00
1875	10,350,385.29	1887	18,386,103.00	1899	21,891,706.00
1876	11,117,000.00	1888	17,418,510.00	1900	21,557,639.00
1877	12,005,934.00	1389	17,655,256.00	1901	25,737,154.00
1878	13,215,686.00	1890	17,725,000.00	1902	21,959,433.00
1879	13,529,153.00	1891	18,979,000.00	1903	23,101,878.00
1880	14,499,980.00	1892	18,942,000.00	1904	23,516,439.00
1881	15,817,163.00	1893	20,686,661.00	1905	29,479,562.00
1882	16,824,092.00	1894	20,719,573.00	1906	26,279,485.00
1883	16,958,192.00	1895	20,185,298.00	1907	25,504,000.00
1884	17,776,404.24	1896	20,407,424.00		

General Statistics.

Post-offices (year ended March 31, 1907, 9 months*), 11,377; number of letters and post-cards mailed, 301,341,000. In 1907 (9 months*) tonnage of sea-going vessels entered and cleared, 13,904,874 tons register; tonnage of shipping engaged in the coasting trade, 46,-324,062 tons; tonnage of shipping engaged in the Great Lakes carrying between Canada and the United States, 17,888,743 tons registered; vessels built and registered, 361; tonnage, 49,928; lighthouses, 901.

Population of Cities, Census of 1901.

Montreal, 267,730; Toronto, 208,040; Quebec, 68,840; Ottawa, 59,928; Hamilton, 52,634; Winnipeg, 90,204; Halifax, 40,832; St. John, 40,711; London, 37,981; Vancouver, 26,133; Victoria, 20,816; Kingston, 17,961; Brantford, 16,619; Hull, 13,993; Charlottetown, 12,080; Valleyfield, 11,055; Sherbrooke, 11,765; Sydney, 9,909; Moncton, 9,026. In 1906 Brandon, 10,411; Calgarry, 11,967; Edmonton, 11,163; Winnipeg, 90,204; Regina, 6,169; Moosejaw, 6,251.

* Change in fiscal year.

These pages of Canadian statistics were revised for THE WORLD ALMANAC for 1907 in the office of Census and Statistics of the Department of Agriculture, Dominion of Canada.

Mexico.

President (Salary, $50,000)........................ ... .GENERAL PORFIRIO DIAZ.
Vice-President..SEÑOR DON RAMON CORRAL.

MINISTRY.

The salary of each member of the Cabinet is $15,000.

Secretary of Foreign Affairs—Señor Don Ignacio Mariscal.
Secretary of the Interior—Señor Don Ramon Corral.
Secretary of Justice—Señor Don Justino Fernandez.
Secretary of Improvements—Señor Don Olegario Molina.
Secretary of Finances—Señor Don José Ives Limantour.
Secretary of War and Navy—Señor General Manuel Gonzalez Cosio.
Secretary of Communications and Public Works—Señor Don Leandro Fernandez.
Secretary of Public Instruction—Señor Don Justo Sierra.

AREA, POPULATION, CONSTITUTION, AND GOVERNMENT.

States and Territories.	Area Square Miles.	Population, 1900.	Capitals.	States and Territories.	Area Square Miles.	Population, 1900.	Capitals.
Aguas Calientes.	2,951	101,910	Aguas Calientes.	Queretaro........	3,558	228,489	Queretaro.
Campeche	18,091	84,281	Campeche.	San Luis Potosi..	25,323	582,486	San Luis Potosi.
Chiapas	27,230	363,607	San Cristobal.	Sinaloa...........	33,681	296,109	Culiacan.
Chihuahua.......	87,828	327,004	Chihuahua.	Sonora	76,922	220,553	Hermosillo.
Coahuila.........	62,375	280,899	Saltillo.	Tabasco	10,075	158,107	S. Juan Bautista.
Colima...........	2,273	65,026	Colima.	Tamaulipas......	32,585	218,948	Ciudad Victoria.
Durango	38,020	371,274	Durango.	Tepic (Ter.).....	11,279	149,677	Tepic.
Guanajuato......	11,374	1,065,317	Guanajuato.	Tlaxcala	1,595	172,217	Tlaxcala.
Guerrero	25,003	474,594	Chilpancingo.	Vera Cruz........	29,210	960,570	Jalapa.
Hidalgo	8,920	603,074	Pachuca.	Yucatán	35,214	312,264	Merida.
Jalisco...........	31,855	1,137,311	Guadalajara.	Zacatecas	24.764	462,886	Zacatecas.
Mexico............	9,250	934,457	Toluca.	L.California(Ter)	58,345	48,624	La Paz.
Michoacan.......	22,881	935,849	Morelia.	Federal District.	463	541,516	City of Mexico.
Morelos..........	2,774	161,697	Cuernavaca.	Islands...........	1,561	.....	......
Nuevo Leon.....	24,324	326,940	Monterey.	Quintana Roo *.	..	....	......
Oaxaca...........	35,392	947,910	Oaxaca.				
Puebla	12,207	1,024,446	Puebla.	Total...........	767,259	13,607,259	

*The area and population of the newly created Territory of Quintana Roo is included in Yucatan in the table.

The present Constitution of Mexico bears date February 5, 1857, with subsequent amendments. By its terms Mexico is considered a Federative Republic, divided into States, nineteen at the outset, but at present twenty-seven in number, with three Territories and one Federal District, each having a right to manage its own local affairs, while the whole are bound together in one body politic by fundamental and constitutional laws. The powers of the Federal Government are divided into three branches—the legislative, executive, and judicial. The legislative power is vested in a Congress, consisting of a House of Representatives and a Senate; the executive in a President, and the judicial in Federal Courts. Representatives elected by the suffrage of all male adults, at the rate of one member for 40,000 inhabitants, hold their places for two years. The qualifications requisite are to be twenty-five years of age and a resident in the State. The Senate con[illegible]f two members from each State, of at least thirty years of age, who hold their places for [illegible] years. Senators are elected indirectly, half of them being renewed every two years. The members of both Houses receive salaries of $3,000 each a year.

The President is elected by electors popularly chosen in a general election and holds office for six years. According to the last Amendment of the Constitution, it does not prohibit his re-election. In case of his sudden disability, the Vice-President, who is also permanent President of the Senate, officiates in his place. Congress has to meet annually, from September 16 to December 15, and from April 1 to May 31, and a permanent committee of both Houses sits during the recesses.

FINANCE AND COMMERCE.

The Federal revenues collected during the fiscal year ended June 30, 1906, were $101,972,624; disbursements were $79,466,912; value of imports year ended June 30, 1905 (gold valuation), $86,122,293; value of exports, $208,520,451 (in silver).

ARMY AND NAVY.

The army consists of infantry, 26,000; engineers, 766; artillery, 2,304; cavalry, 8,454; rural guards of police, 2,365; gendarmerie, 250; total, 37,103. There are over 3,000 officers.

There are six gunboats of from 1,000 to 1,300 tons, armed with rapid-firing four-inch guns and with rapid-firing six pounders; a transport of 1,600 tons, armed with 57 mm. guns; another transport of 900 tons; two training ships, one of steam, 1,300 tons, armed with 12 cm. and 57 mm., and the other, a sailing ship of 700 tons. There are, also, several small revenue cutters watching the coast on both oceans; a naval school, a navy-yard, and a floating dock at Vera Cruz, and a shipyard at Guaymas. The Military School is at Chapultepec.

NATIONAL DEBT.

The national debt is $138,838,900 gold, and $142,116,950 payable in silver.

INTERNAL IMPROVEMENTS.

Miles of railway in operation, 19,000; miles of telegraph line, 45,000; post-offices, 2,207.

This information about Mexico was compiled mainly from the bulletins of the Bureau of American Republics, Washington, D. C., and was corrected to date for the WORLD ALMANAC at the Office of the Mexican Embassy at Washington.

Central and South American Trade.

TOTAL IMPORTS AND EXPORTS, 1907.

COUNTRIES.	Imports.	Exports.	COUNTRIES.	Imports.	Exports.
Argentine Republic	$285,860,683	$296,204,369	Hayti	$4,000,000	$7,000,000
Bolivia	23,000,000	32,000,000	Honduras	2,331,517	2,012,409
Brazil	224,000,000	270,000,000	Mexico	116,215,000	123,513,000
Chile	107,193,877	102,229,466	Nicaragua	3,500,000	4,500,000
Colombia	13,000,000	13,000,000	Panama*	23,032,809	1,960,665
Costa Rica	7,555,000	9,350,000	Paraguay	7,000,000	3,707,000
Cuba	104,460,935	104,069,037	Peru	24,000,000	26,000,000
Dominican Republic	4,948,961	7,638,356	Salvador	4,250,000	7,000,000
Ecuador	8,500,000	11,750,000	Uruguay	34,425,204	35,150,937
Guatemala	7,316,574	10,174,486	Venezuela	10,335,817	16,203,972

* Includes Canal Zone.

For trade with the United States see Index. For population of Latin-American Republics see Index.

The above returns were compiled from the reports of the International Bureau of American Republics.

The Bureau was established at Washington under the recommendation of the Pan-American Conference of 1890, for the purpose of maintaining closer relations of commerce and friendship between the American Republics. At the Pan-American Conference at Mexico in 1901, its scope was enlarged, while at the Third Pan-American Conference held at Rio de Janeiro in 1906 a resolution was passed for its reorganization upon broader lines, so that it should become a world-recognized and practical institution for the development of Pan-American commerce and comity. For statement of its general purposes see page 99.

The list of Directors who have administered the affairs of the Bureau since it was organized is as follows: William E. Curtis, 1890-1893; Clinton Furbish, 1893-1897; Joseph P. Smith, 1897-1898; Frederic Emory, 1898-1899; W. W. Rockhill, 1899-1905; William C. Fox, 1905-1907; John Barrett, 1907.

Work has begun on the new building of the Bureau, located on the Van Ness Park site, Seventeenth and B Streets, Washington, for which Mr. Andrew Carnegie gave $750,000 and the different republics $250,000, making a total of $1,000,000 available for the new home and grounds of the Bureau.

TRADE OF THE LATIN-AMERICAN REPUBLICS, 1907.

	WITH THE WORLD.			WITH THE UNITED STATES.		
	Total Exports.	Total Imports.	Total Foreign Trade.	Total Exports.	Total Imports.	Total Trade.
South America	$806,245,744	$737,315,581	$1,543,561,325	$141,220,693	$96,976,896	$238,197,589
Panama	1,960,665	23,032,809	24,993,474	1,680,953	18,665,323	20,346,276
Central America	33,036,895	24,953,091	57,989,986	13,728,203	10,095,800	23,824,003
Mexico	123,513,000	116,215,000	239,728,000	87,904,000	73,188,000	161,092,000
Island Republics	118,707,393	113,409,896	232,117,289	95,323,663	57,318,850	152,642,513
Grand Totals	$1,083,463,697	$1,014,926,377	$2,098,390,074	$339,857,512	$256,244,869	$596,102,381

Division of Africa

AMONG THE EUROPEAN POWERS.

	Area.	Population.		Area.	Population.
BRITISH AFRICA: Basutoland, Bechuanaland Protectorate, Cape Colony, Central Africa, East Africa Protectorate, Uganda Protectorate, Zanzibar Protectorate, Mauritius, Natal, Niger Coast Protectorate, Territory of the Royal Niger Co., South Africa, West Africa, Zululand and Islands, and the Boer colonies*	2,807,760	43,495,754	GERMAN AFRICA: Togoland, Cameroons, South West Africa, East Africa	920,920	10,200,000
			ITALIAN AFRICA: Eritrea, Somaliland	278,500	850,000
			PORTUGUESE AFRICA: Angola, the Congo, Guinea, East Africa and Islands	735,304	4,431,970
			SPANISH AFRICA: Rio de Oro, Adrar, Fernando Po and Islands	243,877	136,000
			TURKISH AFRICA: Tripoli and the Mediterranean Coast, Egypt*	798,738	8,117,265
FRENCH AFRICA: Algeria, Senegal, French Soudan and the Niger, Gaboon and Guinea Coast, Congo Region, Somali Coast, Madagascar and Islands	1,232,454	18,073,890	BELGIAN AFRICA: The Congo State	900,000	30,000,000
			Total	8,087,553	117,104,871

* Egypt and the Egyptian Soudan, although nominally under the suzerainty of Turkey, are really controlled by Great Britain, and it is only a matter of time as to when they will be incorporated into the British Empire. Adding Egypt and the Soudan to the Empire would increase the figures above given to 3,207,700 square miles and 50,316,019 population.

The remaining territory of Africa unoccupied is a part of the great Desert of Sahara and the Independent States of Abyssinia and Liberia. Even this territory, except the last, is destined to pass under the power of the Europeans. The tabular figures are from "The Statesman's Year-Book."

Largest Cities of the Earth.

POPULATION ACCORDING TO THE LATEST OFFICIAL CENSUSES.

Cities.	Census Year.	Population.	Cities.	Census Year.	Population.	Cities.	Census Year.	Population.
London*	1901	4,536,541	Hong Kong	1901	283,905	Johannesburg	1904	158,580
New York	1905	4,014,304	Newark	1905	283,289	Colombo, Ceylon	1901	158,228
Paris	1901	2,714,068	Teheran	est.	280,000	Howrah	1901	157,594
Tokio, Japan	1908	2,085,160	Bradford	1901	279,809	Barmen	1905	156,080
Berlin	1906	2,040,148	Washington	1900	278,718	Poona	1901	153,320
Chicago	1900	1,698,575	Bucharest	1900	276,178	Bologna	1901	152,009
Vienna	1901	1,674,957	Havana	1902	275,000	Venice	1901	151 840
Canton	est.	1,600,000	Montreal	1901	267,730	Toulouse	1901	149,841
Peking	est.	1,600,000	West Ham, England	1901	267,308	Messina	1901	149,778
St. Petersburg	1905	1,429,000	Lucknow	1901	264,049	Catania	1901	149,2[illegible]5
Philadelphia	1900	1,293,697	Bordeaux	1901	257,638	Seville	1900	148,315
Constantinople	est.	1,125,000	Riga	1897	256,197	Soerabaya, Java	1900	146,944
Osaka	1908	1,117,151	Dusseldorf	1905	253,274	Sunderland	1901	146,565
Calcutta †	1901	1,026,987	Hanover, Germany	1905	250,024	St. Etienne	1901	146,559
Moscow	1902	1,092,360	Tunis	est.	250,000	Bagdad	est.	145,000
Buenos Ayres	1905	1,000,250	Stuttgart	1905	249,286	Aachen	1905	144,095
Rio de Janeiro	1906	811,265	Newcastle	1901	247,025	Valparaiso	1904	143,769
Hamburg	1906	802,793	Chemnitz	1905	244,927	Aberdeen	1901	143,722
Bombay	1901	776,006	The Hague	1905	242,054	Kazan	1900	143,707
Warsaw	1901	756,426	Magdeburg	1905	240,633	Roubaix	1901	142,365
Glasgow	1901	735,906	Hull	1901	240,618	Fez, Morocco	est.	140,000
Buda-Pesth	1901	732,324	Nottingham	1901	239,753	Algiers †	1901	138,709
Liverpool	1901	702,247	Charlottenburg, Prussia	1905	239,559	Gratz	1901	138,080
Brussels †	1905	612,401	Rangoon	1901	234,881	Oldham, England	1901	137,238
Bangkok	est.	600,000	Genoa	1901	231,710	Saratvo	1897	137,147
Manchester, England	1901	606,751	Jersey City	1905	232,699	Posen	1905	136,808
Boston	1905	595,083	Essen, Germany	1905	231,360	Brunswick, Germany	1905	136,397
St. Louis	1900	575,238	Christiania	1900	227,626	Yekaterinoslav	1897	135,532
Cairo, Egypt	1897	570,062	Damascus	est.	225,000	Patna	1901	134,785
Naplec	1901	563,541	Stettin	1905	224,119	Croydon, England	1901	133,885
Amsterdam	1905	557,614	Konigsberg	1905	223,770	Denver	1900	133,8[illegible]9
Madrid	1900	539,835	Salford	1901	220,956	Goteborg	1902	133,625
Munich	1905	538,983	Manila	1904	219,928	Nantes	1901	132,990
Barcelona	1900	533,090	Bremen	1905	214,861	Toledo, Ohio	1900	131,822
Birmingham, England	1901	522,182	Valencia	1900	213,530	Bareilly	1901	131,208
Dresden	1905	516,996	Leicester	1901	211,574	Lima	1903	130,2[illegible]3
Madras	1901	509,346	Lille	1901	210,696	Havre	1901	130,196
Baltimore	1900	508,957	Benares	1901	209,331	Malaga	1900	130.109
Leipzig	1905	503,672	Delhi	1901	208,575	Allegheny	1900	129,896
Melbourne †	1901	496,079	Toronto	1901	208,040	Blackburn	1901	129,216
Milan	1901	491,460	Florence	1901	205,589	Worcester, Mass.	1905	128,135
Marseilles	1901	491,161	Louisville	1900	204,731	Nagpur	1901	127,734
Sydney †	1901	481,830	Lahore	1901	202,964	Aleppo	est.	127,150
Copenhagen †	1901	476,806	Minneapolis	1900	202,718	Kishinev	1897	125,787
Breslau	1905	470,904	Prague	1901	201,589	Columbus	1900	125,560
Rome	1901	462,783	Smyrna	est.	201,000	Basle	1904	124.392
Lyons	1901	459,099	Providence	1905	198,635	Brighton, England	1901	123,478
Odessa	1900	449,673	Cawnpore	1901	197,170	Srinagar	1901	122,618
Haidarabad †	1901	448,466	Seoul, Korea	1902	196,646	Liege	1905	122,207
Leeds	1901	428,953	Portsmouth, England	1901	189,160	Rosario, Argentina	1903	122,156
Cologne	1905	428,722	Agra	1901	188,022	Astrakhan	1897	121,580
Sheffield	1901	409,070	Ahmadabad	1901	185,889	Heroshima	1903	121.196
Cleveland	1900	381,768	Mandelay	1901	183,816	Kassel, Germany	1905	120,267
Kioto	1903	380,568	Rochester	1905	181,672	Bogota	1886	120,000
Shanghai	est.	380,000	Tabriz	1881	180,000	Rostov-on-Don	1897	119,889
Buffalo	1905	376,618	Trieste	1901	178,559	Surat	1901	119,306
Rotterdam	1905	370,390	Dortmund	1905	175,577	Beirut	est.	118,800
Lisbon	1900	356,009	Zurich	1904	175,083	Meerut	1901	118,129
Lodz	1897	351,570	Bahia	1890	174,412	Syracuse	1905	117,498
Belfast	1901	349,180	Kharkov	1897	173,989	Rouen	1901	116,316
Kobe, Japan	1908	345,952	Allahabad	1901	172,032	Karachi	1901	116,163
Mexico City	1900	344,721	Nagasaki	1908	169,941	Batavia	1900	115,887
San Francisco	1900	342,782	Halle-on-Salle	1905	169,916	Derby	1901	114,848
Bristol, England	1901	339,042	Indianapolis	1900	169,164	Utrecht	1905	114,321
Turin	1901	335,656	Altona, Germany	1905	168,320	Preston	1901	112,982
Frankfort-on-Main	1905	334,978	Bolton	1901	168,205	Geneva	1904	112,736
Santiago, Chile	1904	334,538	Oporto	1900	167,955	Norwich, England	1901	111,728
Yokohama	1903	326,035	Strasburg	1905	167,678	Helsingfors	1904	111,654
Cincinnati	1900	325,902	Cardiff	1901	164,420	Pernambuco	1890	111,556
Pittsburgh	1900	321,616	Kiel, Germany	1905	163,772	Murcia, Spain	1900	111,539
Alexandria, Egypt	1897	319,766	Kansas City, Mo.	1900	163,752	Paterson, N. J.	1905	111,529
Kiev	1897	319,000	Manheim	1905	163,693	Athens	1896	111,486
Stockholm	1905	317,964	Adelaide †	1901	163,430	Birkenhead	1901	110,915
Edinburgh	1901	316,479	St. Paul	1900	163,065	Krefeld	1905	110,344
Palermo	1901	309,694	Elberfeld	1905	162,853	Gateshead	1901	109,887
Montevideo	1904	298,127	Vilna	1897	162,633	Tula	1897	109,352
Nuremberg	1905	294,426	Ghent	1905	162,482	Brunn	1901	109,346
Antwerp	1905	291,949	Amritsar	1901	162,429	Reims	1901	108,385
Dublin	1901	290,638	Dundee	1901	160,871	New Haven	1900	108,027
Nagoya	1903	288,639	Jaipur	1901	160,167	Plymouth, England	1901	107,509
New Orleans	1900	287,104	Lemberg	1901	159,877	Madura	1901	105,984
Detroit	1900	285,704	Dantzig	1905	159,648	Fall River, Mass	1905	105,762
Milwaukee	1900	285,315	Bangalore	1901	159,046	Nice, France	1901	105,109

* Population of Greater London (metropolitan and city police districts), 6,581,372. † With suburbs.

NOTE.—The population of Chinese cities other than Cauton, Peking, and Shanghai is omitted, because reports respecting it are utterly untrustworthy. There are forty or more Chinese cities whose inhabitants are numbered by rumor at from 200,000 to 1,000,000 each, but no official censuses have ever been taken; and setting aside consideration of the Oriental tendency to exaggeration, there is reason to believe that the estimates of population in many instances covered districts of country bearing the same names as the cities, instead of definite municipalities.

Population of the United States,

AT EACH CENSUS FROM 1790 TO 1900.

STATES AND TERRITORIES.	1820.	1830.	1840.	1850.	1860.	1870.	1880.	1890.	1900.
Alabama	127,901	309,527	590,756	771,623	964,201	996,992	1,262,595	1,513,017	1,828,697
Alaska	....	....	....	....	....	....	*	*	63,592
Arizona	....	....	....	....	....	9,658	40,440	59,620	122,931
Arkansas	14,255	30,388	97,574	209,897	435,450	484,471	802,525	1,128,179	1,311,564
California	....	....	....	92,597	379,994	560,247	864,694	1,208,130	1,485,053
Colorado	....	....	....	....	34,277	39,864	194,327	419,198	539 700
Connecticut	275,148	297,675	309,978	370,792	460,147	537,454	622,700	746,258	908,420
Dakota	....	....	....	....	4,837	14,181	135,177	....	....
Delaware	72,749	76,748	78,085	91,532	112,216	125,015	146,608	168,493	184,735
D. of Columbia	32,039	39,834	43,712	51,687	75,080	131,700	177,624	230,392	278,718
Florida	....	34,730	54,477	87,445	140,424	187,748	269,493	391,422	528,542
Georgia	340,985	516,823	691,392	906,185	1,057,286	1,184,109	1,542,180	1,837,353	2,216,331
Hawaii	....	....	....	....	....	....	....	....	154,001
Idaho	....	....	....	....	....	14,999	32,610	84,385	161,772
Illinois	55,162	157,445	476,183	851,470	1,711,951	2,539,891	3,077,871	3,826,351	4,821,550
Indiana	147,178	343,031	685,866	988,416	1,350,428	1,680,637	1,978,301	2,192,404	2,516,462
Indian Territory	....	....	....	....	....	....	....	*	392,060
Iowa	....	....	43,112	192,214	674,913	1,194,020	1,624,615	1,911,896	2,231,853
Kansas	....	....	....	....	107,206	364,399	996,096	1,427,096	1,470,495
Kentucky	564,135	687,917	779,828	982,405	1,155,684	1,321,011	1,648,690	1,858,635	2,147,174
Louisiana	152,923	215,739	352,411	517,762	708,002	726,915	939,946	1,118,587	1,381,625
Maine	298,269	399,455	501,793	583,169	628,279	626,915	648,936	661,086	694,466
Maryland	407,350	447,040	470,019	583,034	687,049	780,894	934,943	1,042,390	1,188,044
Massachusetts	523,159	610,408	737,699	994,514	1,231,066	1,457,351	1,783,085	2,238,943	2,805,346
Michigan	8,765	31,639	212,267	397,654	749,113	1,184,059	1,636,937	2,093,889	2,420,982
Minnesota	....	....	....	6,077	172,023	439,706	780,773	1,301,826	1,751,394
Mississippi	75,448	136,621	375,651	606,526	791,305	827,922	1,131,597	1,289,600	1,551,270
Missouri	66,557	140,455	383,702	682,044	1,182,012	1,721,295	2,168,380	2,679,184	3,106,665
Montana	....	....	....	....	....	20,595	39,159	132,159	243,329
Nebraska	....	....	....	....	28,841	122,993	452,402	1,058,910	1,066,300
Nevada	....	....	....	....	6,857	42,491	62,266	45,761	42,335
New Hampshire	244,022	269,328	284,574	317,976	326,073	318,300	346,991	376,530	411,588
New Jersey	277,426	320,823	373,306	489,555	672,035	906,096	1,131,116	1,444,933	1,883,669
New Mexico	....	....	....	61,547	93,516	91,874	119,565	153,593	195,310
New York	1,372,111	1,918,608	2,428,921	3,097,394	3,880,735	4,382,759	5,082,871	5,997,853	7,268,894
North Carolina	638,829	737,987	753,419	869,039	992,622	1,071,361	1,399,750	1,617,947	1,893,810
North Dakota	....	....	....	....	....	....	....	182,719	319,146
Ohio	581,295	937,903	1,519,467	1,980,329	2,339,511	2,665,260	3,198,062	3,672,316	4,157,545
Oklahoma	....	....	....	....	....	....	....	61,834	398,331
Oregon	....	....	....	13,294	52,465	90,923	174,768	313,767	413,536
Pennsylvania	1,047,507	1,348,233	1,724,033	2,311,786	2,906,215	3,521,951	4,282,891	5,258,014	6,302,115
Rhode Island	83,015	97,199	108,830	147,545	174,620	217,353	276,531	345,506	428,556
South Carolina	502,741	581,185	594,398	668,507	703,708	705,606	995,577	1,151,149	1,340,316
South Dakota	....	....	....	....	....	....	....	328,808	401,570
Tennessee	422,771	681,904	829,210	1,002,717	1,109,801	1,258,520	1,542,359	1,767,518	2,020,616
Texas	....	....	....	212,592	604,215	818,579	1,591,749	2,235,523	3,048,710
Utah	....	....	....	11,380	40,273	86,786	143,963	207,905	276 749
Vermont	235,966	280,652	291,948	314,120	315,098	330,551	332,286	332,422	343,641
Virginia	1,065,116	1,211,405	1,239,797	1,421,661	1,596,318	1,225,163	1,512,565	1,655,980	1,854,184
Washington	....	....	....	....	11,594	23,955	75,116	349,390	518,103
West Virginia	....	....	....	....	....	442,014	618,457	762,704	958,800
Wisconsin	....	....	30,945	305,391	775,881	1,054,670	1,315,497	1,686,880	2,069,042
Wyoming	....	....	....	....	....	9,118	20,789	60,705	92,531
Total	9,633,822	12,866,020	17,069,453	23,191,876	31,443,321	38,558,371	50,155,783	62,622,250	†76,303,387

Population Continental United States (including Alaska), 76,149,386 (1900); Philippines (1903), 7,635,426; Porto Rico, 953,243; Hawaii, 154,001; Guam, 8,661; American Samoa, 5,800. Total population, 85,271,093. Population 1909, estimating Continental United States, about 96,250,000. For population of States by State Censuses of 1905, consult index.

*The inhabitants of Alaska and the Indian Territory are not included in the enumeration of 1890. The population of Alaska in 1890 was 30,329; of the Indian Territory, 179,321. Total population of the United States in 1890, 62,831,900. The inhabitants of Alaska were not included in the enumeration of 1880. The population was 33,426. Total population of the United States in 1880. 50,189,209.

† Includes 91,219 persons in the military and naval service of the United States.

POPULATION: CENSUS OF 1790.—Connecticut, 237,946; Delaware, 59,096; Georgia, 82,548; Kentucky, 73,677; Maine,‡ 96,540; Maryland, 319,728; Massachusetts, 378,787; New Hampshire, 141,885; New Jersey, 184,139; New York, 340,120; North Carolina, 393,751; Pennsylvania, 434,373; Rhode Island, 68,825; South Carolina, 249,073; Tennessee, 35,691; Vermont, 85,425; Virginia, 747.610. Total U. S., 3,929,214.

POPULATION: CENSUS OF 1800.—Connecticut, 251,002; Delaware, 64.273; District of Columbia, 14,093; Georgia, 162.686; Indiana, 5,641; Kentucky, 220.955; Maine,‡ 151,719; Maryland, 341,548; Massachusetts, 422,845; Mississippi, 8,850; New Hampshire, 183,858; New Jersey, 211,149; New York, 589,051; North Carolina, 478,103; Ohio, 45,365; Pennsylvania, 602,365; Rhode Island, 69,122; South Carolina, 345,591; Tennessee, 105,602; Vermont, 154,465; Virginia, 880.200. Total U. S., 5,308,483.

POPULATION: CENSUS OF 1810.—Connecticut, 261.942; Delaware, 72.674; District of Columbia, 24,-023; Georgia, 252.433; Illinois, 12,282; Indiana. 24.520; Kentucky, 406.511; Louisiana, 76.556; Maine,‡ 228.705; Maryland. 380.546; Massachusetts, 472,040; Michigan, 4,762; Mississippi, 40,352; Missouri, 20,845; New Hampshire, 214.460; New Jersey, 245.562; New York, 959,049; North Carolina. 555,500; Ohio. 230,760; Pennsylvania, 810,091; Rhode Island. 76,931; South Carolina. 415.115; Tennessee, 261,727; Vermont, 217,-895; Virginia, 974,600. Total U. S., 7,239,881. ‡ Maine a part of Massachusetts until admitted in 1820.

POPULATION PRIOR TO 1790 (according to Bancroft): 1688, 200,000; 1714, 434,600; 1727, 580,000; 1750, 1,260,000; 1754, 1,425,000; 1760, 1,695,000; 1770, 2,312,000; 1780, 2,945,000 (2,383,000 white, 562,000 colored).

Population of the United States.

BY STATE CENSUSES TAKEN IN 1905.

TEN States took enumerations of their population in the year 1905. The following were the totals of each. (For details of several States see ALMANAC of 1906, pages 404 and 405).

STATES.	Total Population, 1905.	STATES.	Total Population, 1905.	STATES.	Total Population, 1905.
Florida............	625,200	New Jersey.......	2,144,134	South Dakota.....	464,288
Iowa.............	2,216,068	New York.........	8,066,672	Wisconsin.........	2,228,949
Massachusetts....	3,003,636	Rhode Island.....	480,082	Wyoming.........	101 816
Michigan..........	2,655,463				

PROPORTION OF SEXES IN THE UNITED STATES.

(Extracts from Census Bulletin No. 14.)

MORE MALES THAN FEMALES IN THE UNITED STATES.

The whole population of continental United States was first counted with distinction of sex in 1820. During the seventy years from 1830 to 1900 the absolute excess of males was greater at each census than at any preceding census with one exception—that of 1870—when the excess of males was less than in 1850 and 1860.

This reduction of the excess of males between 1860 and 1870, by about 300,000, was doubtless due to the deaths in the Civil War and the diminished immigration during the decade.

The greatest relative excess of males was in 1890, when in each 10,000 people there were 242 more males than females.

By 1900 this excess had decreased to 216 in 10,000, less than the relative excess in 1890 and 1860, but greater than that at each other census.

In continental United States there are 1,638,321 more males than females, or about two in each 100 people.

Probably in the population of the world, as a whole, and certainly in that half of it which has been counted with distinction of sex, there are several millions more males than females.

In continental United States, however, the relative excess of males is greater than the average for all countries.

Europe has an excess of females; every other continent, so far as known, has an excess of males.

The divisions of continental United States with the smallest proportion of males are the District of Columbia (47.4 per cent.), Massachusetts (48.7 per cent.), and Rhode Island (49.1 per cent.); those with the largest are Wyoming (62.9 per cent.), and Montana (61.6 per cent.

As a rule sparsely settled regions have an excess of males and densely settled regions an excess of females.

CITIES HAVE MORE FEMALES THAN MALES.

American cities as a rule have more females than males. In the 1,861 cities, each having in 1900 at least 2,500 inhabitants, there were 201,959 more females than males, and this notwithstanding the many western cities which contained more males than females, and the enormous number of foreign-born in the country, five-ninths of them male, and a large proportion of them living in the cities.

This tendency of American cities to develop a population having a majority of females had increased since 1890, when, in the 1,490 cities, each having at least 2,500 inhabitants, there were 6,929 more males than females.

While the excess of 6,929 males in American cities in 1890 became an excess of 210,959 females in American cities in 1900, the excess of 1,519,559 males in country districts in 1890 became an excess of 1,840,280 males in 1900.

Or, expressing the facts in ratios, of each 1,000 inhabitants of such cities in 1890, 500 were males and in 1900, 497 were males; of each 1,000 inhabitants living outside these cities in 1890, 519 were males, and in 1900 520 were males. The difference thus in the number of males or of females between an average thousand of city and of country population in 1890 was 19, and in 1900, 23.

WOMEN LIVE LONGER THAN MEN.

Notwithstanding the great excess of males in the total population of the United States, there are two periods of life at which the reported number of females is greater. One, extending from about eighty-three years of age to the end of life, is probably due mainly to the longer average life of woman; the other, from sixteen to twenty-five, is probably apparent rather than real, and due mainly to the greater number of women who claim, erroneously, to belong to this age period.

In 1900, among the 13,367,147 persons attending school, 499 in each 1,000 were male and 501 female; in 1890, in the same class, 510 per 1,000 were male and 490 female.

INCREASING PROPORTION OF GIRLS AMONG SCHOOL CHILDREN.

In all races and in all parts of the country there has been a decided increase since 1890 in the proportion of females among persons attending school. This increase is due mainly to the increase in the proportion of young women among persons at least fifteen years of age attending school, the increase at this age period being nearly five times as great as at any other, and more than three times as great as the average increase for all ages.

DEATH RATE HIGHER FOR MALES THAN FEMALES.

The death rate of males in the registration area of the United States in 1900 was 19.0 per 1,000, and that of females 16.6 per 1,000, the former having a death rate higher by about one-seventh than the latter. In the 346 registration cities the death rate of males was 20.0, and that of females 17.2 per 1,000, the male rate exceeding the female by one-sixth. In the rest of the registration area the male death rate was 15.8 and that of females 15.0 per 1,000, the male rate exceeding the female by one-nineteenth.

Population of the United States,

ACCORDING TO SEX, NATIVITY, AND COLOR.

(Compiled from the Reports of the Census of 1900.)

States and Territories.	Males.	Females.	Native Born.	Foreign Born.	Whites.	Negroes.*	Chinese.	Japanese.	Indians.†
Alabama	916,764	911,933	1,814,105	14,592	1,001,152	827,307	58	3	177
Alaska	45,872	17,720	50,931	12,661	30,507	168	3,116	265	29,536
Arizona	71,795	51,136	98,698	24,233	92,903	1,848	1,419	281	26,480
Arkansas	675,312	636,252	1,297,275	14,289	944,580	366 866	62	....	66
California	820,531	664,522	1,117,813	367,240	1,402,727	11,045	45,753	10,151	15,377
Colorado	295,332	244,368	448,545	91,155	529,046	8,570	599	48	1,437
Connecticut	454,294	454,126	670,210	238,210	892,424	15,226	599	18	153
Delaware	94,158	90,577	170,925	13,810	153,977	30,697	51	1	9
District of Columbia	132,004	146,714	258,599	20,119	191,532	86,702	455	7	22
Florida	275,246	253,296	504,710	23,882	297,333	230,730	120	1	358
Georgia	1,103,201	1,113,130	2,203,928	12,403	1,181,294	1,034,813	204	1	19
Hawaii	106,369	47,632	63,221	90,780	66,890	233	25,767	61,111	....
Idaho	93,367	68,405	137,168	24,604	154,495	293	1,467	1,291	4,226
Illinois	2,472,782	2,348,768	3,854,803	966,747	4,734,873	85,078	1,503	80	16
Indiana	1,285,404	1,231,058	2,374,341	142,121	2,458,502	57,505	207	5	243
Indian Territory	208,952	183,108	387,202	4,858	302,680	36,853	27	....	52,500
Iowa	1,156,849	1,075,004	1,925,933	305,920	2,218,667	12,693	104	7	382
Kansas	768,716	701,779	1,343,810	126,685	1,416,319	52,003	39	4	2,130
Kentucky	1,090,227	1,056,947	2,096,925	50,249	1,862,309	284,706	57	....	102
Louisiana	694,733	686,892	1,328,722	52,903	729,612	650,804	599	17	593
Maine	350,995	343,471	601,136	93,330	692,226	1,319	119	4	798
Maryland	589,275	598,769	1,094,110	93,934	952,424	235,064	544	9	3
Massachusetts	1,367,474	1,437,872	1,959,[illegible]22	846,324	2,769,764	31,974	2,968	53	587
Michigan	1,248,905	1,172,077	1,879,329	541,653	2,398,563	15 816	240	9	6,354
Minnesota	932,490	818,904	1,246,076	505,318	1,737,036	4,959	166	51	9,182
Mississippi	781,451	769,819	1,543,289	7,981	641,200	907,630	237	....	2,203
Missouri	1,595,710	1,510,955	2,890,286	216,379	2,944,843	161,234	449	9	130
Montana	149,842	93,487	176,262	67,067	226,283	1,523	1,739	2,441	11,343
Nebraska	564,592	501,708	888,593	177,347	1,056,526	6,269	180	3	3.322
Nevada	25,603	16,732	32,242	10,093	35,405	134	1,352	228	5,216
New Hampshire	205,379	206,209	323,481	88,107	410,791	662	112	1	22
New Jersey	941,760	941,909	1,451,785	431,884	1,812,317	69,844	1,393	52	63
New Mexico	104,228	91,082	181,685	13,625	180,207	1,610	341	8	13,144
New York	3,614,780	3,654,114	5,368,469	1,900,425	7,156 881	99,232	7,170	354	5,257
North Carolina	938,677	955,133	1,889,318	4,492	1,263,603	624,469	51	....	5,687
North Dakota	177,493	141,653	206,055	113,091	311,712	286	32	148	6,968
Ohio	2,102,655	2,054,890	3,698,811	458,734	4,060,204	96,901	371	27	42
Oklahoma	214,359	183,972	382,651	15,680	367,524	18,831	31	....	11,945
Oregon	232,985	180,551	347,788	65,748	394,582	1,105	10,397	2,501	4,951
Pennsylvania	3,204,541	3,097,574	5,316,865	985,250	6,141,664	156,845	1,927	40	1,639
Rhode Island	210,516	218,040	294,037	134,519	419,050	9,092	366	13	35
South Carolina	664,895	675,421	1,334,788	5,528	557,807	782,321	67	....	121
South Dakota	216,164	185,406	313,062	88,508	380,714	465	165	1	20,225
Tennessee	1,021,224	999,392	2,002,870	17,746	1,540,186	480,243	75	4	108
Texas	,578,900	1,469,810	2,869,353	179,357	2,426,669	620,722	836	13	470
Utah	141,687	135,062	222,972	53,777	272,465	672	572	417	2,623
Vermont	175,138	168,503	298,894	44,747	342,771	826	39	....	5
Virginia	925,897	928,287	1,834,723	19,461	1,192,855	660,722	243	10	354
Washington	304,178	213,925	406,739	111,364	496,304	2,514	3,629	5,617	10,039
West Virginia	499,242	459,558	936,349	22,451	915,233	43,499	56	....	12
Wisconsin	1,067,562	1,001,480	1,553,071	515,971	2,057,911	2,542	212	5	8,372
Wyoming	58,184	34,347	75,116	17,415	89,051	940	461	393	1,686
Total	39,059,242	37,244,145	65,843,302	10,460,085	66,990,802	8,840,789	119,050	85,986	266,760

* Including all persons of negro descent. † Including Indians taxed and not taxed.

TABLE SHOWING INCREASE IN SEX, NATIVITY, AND COLOR 1890 TO 1900.

	Aggregates.		Per Cent.		Increase.	
	1900.	1890.	1900.	1890.	Number.	Per Cent.
Total population	76,303,387	63,069,756	100.0	100.0	13,233,631	21.0
Males	39,059,242	32,315,063	51.2	51.2	6,744,179	20.9
Females	37,244,145	30,754,693	48.8	48.8	6,489,452	21.1
Native born	65,843,302	53,761,665	86.3	85.2	12,081,637	22.5
Foreign born	10,460,085	9,308,091	13.7	14.8	1,151,994	12.4
White	66,990,802	55,166,184	87.8	87.5	11,824,618	21.4
Colored	9,312,585	7,903,572	12.2	12.5	1,409,013	17.8
Native white	56,740,739	46,030,105	74.4	73.0	10,710,634	23.3
Native parents	41,053,417	34,514,450	53.8	54.7	6,538,967	18.9
Foreign parents	15,687,322	11,515,655	20.6	18.3	4,171,667	36.2
Foreign white	10,250,063	9,136,079	13.4	14.5	1,113,984	12.2
Negro	8,840,789	7,488,788	11.6	11.9	1,352,001	18.1
Chinese	119,050	126,778	0.2	0.2	§7,728	§6.1
Japanese	85,986	14,399	0.1	(‖)	71,587	497.2
Indian	266,760	273,607	0.3	0.4	§6,847	§2.5

§ Decrease. ‖ Less than one-tenth of 1 per cent.

Population of the United States,

DWELLINGS, FAMILIES, HOMES, AND DENSITY.

(Compiled from the Reports of the Census of 1900.)

States and Territories.	Total Dwellings.	Total Families.*	Homes.					Density of Population.	
			Owned.†			Hired.	Unknown.		
			Free.	Mortgaged.	Uknown.			1890.	1900.
Alabama	362,295	374,765	94,692	20,549	7,208	231,180	17,351	29.4	35.5
Alaska	10,565	13,459	7,190	22	....	1,644	3,327	....	0.1
Arizona	28,763	29,875	13,259	1,009	1,049	10,545	1,955	0.8	1.1
Arkansas	259,004	265,238	95,510	16,469	7,848	130,411	12,183	21.3	24.7
California	313,217	341,781	100,228	40,216	6,550	162,275	15,421	7.8	9.5
Colorado	120,364	127,459	39,000	12,923	3,042	61,386	5,998	4.0	5.2
Connecticut	159,677	203,424	37,930	37,496	1,429	119,094	4,691	154.0	187.5
Delaware	38,191	39,446	7,759	5,115	767	23,835	1,531	86.0	94.3
District of Columbia.	49,385	56,678	8,441	4,261	296	40,753	1,714	3,839.9	4,645.3
Florida	113,594	117,001	40,810	5,469	4,651	55,920	6,779	7.2	9.7
Georgia	436,153	455,557	101,114	17,603	10,950	291,447	29,598	31.2	37.6
Hawaii	32,366	36,922	5,172	438	711	21,086	2,356	....	23.9
Idaho	36,487	37,491	20,163	3,215	992	9,218	2,231	1.1	1.9
Illinois	845,836	1,036,158	273,594	161,615	16,388	547,369	25,223	68.3	86.1
Indiana	552,495	571,513	200,035	103,643	8,605	242,588	12,201	61.1	70.1
Indian Territory	75,539	76,701	17,809	463	6,259	47,746	3,740	5.8	12.6
Iowa	468,682	480,878	163,640	112,877	6,243	183,053	10,897	34.5	40.2
Kansas	314,375	321,947	116,784	61,504	4,998	126,240	9,896	17.5	18.0
Kentucky	413,974	437,054	172,042	35,034	11,066	204,009	12,077	46.5	53.7
Louisiana	269,395	284,875	64,861	12,204	6,510	181,577	16,297	24.6	30.4
Maine	148,507	163,344	75,262	24,296	2,979	55,028	4,023	22.1	23.2
Maryland	221,706	242,331	58,577	27,108	5,017	135,353	13,782	105.7	120.5
Massachusetts	451,362	613,659	108,766	93,502	3,859	379,696	19,050	278.5	348.9
Michigan	521,648	548,094	191,863	128,939	9,474	198,078	14,004	36.5	42.2
Minnesota	317,037	342,658	126,181	74,654	7,354	118,034	11,061	16.5	22.1
Mississippi	310,963	318,948	73,159	23,517	5,969	194,637	18,832	27.8	33.5
Missouri	593,528	654,333	193,229	118,742	10,273	307,492	17,136	39.0	45.2
Montana	53,779	55,889	23,656	3,398	1,509	20,556	3,006	1.0	1.7
Nebraska	213 972	220,947	71,133	44,242	5,330	90,711	6,574	13.8	13.9
Nevada	10,960	11,190	5,636	543	332	3,134	827	0.4	0.4
New Hampshire	86,635	97,902	35,839	12,989	1,765	42,840	3,101	41.8	45.7
New Jersey	321,032	415,222	61,755	69,804	4,496	259,848	13,090	193.8	250.3
New Mexico	44,903	46,355	26,652	632	1,939	13,118	3,169	1.3	1.6
New York	1,035,180	1,634,523	277,767	230,870	12,900	1,048,800	42,833	126.1	152.6
North Carolina	360,491	370,072	130,650	24,735	9,837	188,162	14,181	33.3	39.0
North Dakota	63,319	64,690	33,409	13,710	2,044	11,863	2,334	2.7	4.5
Ohio	857,636	944,433	317,012	149,376	15,204	431,301	21,781	90.1	102.0
Oklahoma	85,309	86,908	50,246	6,532	2,984	23,157	3,010	2.0	10.3
Oregon	87,525	91,214	37,284	10.771	2,119	33,745	3,626	3.4	4.4
Pennsylvania	1,236,238	1,320,025	326,687	174,920	22,236	742,385	36,946	116.9	140.1
Rhode Island	67,816	94,179	14,506	10,780	723	64,362	2,364	318.4	407.0
South Carolina	259,302	269,864	57,138	13,994	5,922	174,448	16,357	38.2	44.4
South Dakota	81,863	83,536	37,153	17,115	2,517	22,610	2,895	4.5	5.2
Tennessee	385,588	402,536	146,763	20,995	11,417	206,077	13,765	42.3	48.4
Texas	575,734	589,291	196,165	50,160	15,608	299,312	20,810	8.5	11.6
Utah	53,490	56,196	31,344	4,292	1,088	17,012	1,472	2.6	3.4
Vermont	75,021	81,462	26,712	19,662	1,377	31,014	1,794	36.4	37.6
Virginia	347,159	364,517	133,836	26,530	10,208	177,087	13,088	41.3	46.2
Washington	106,622	113,086	44,681	10,421	2,102	45,113	4,854	5.3	7.7
West Virginia	180,715	186,291	77,972	14.831	5,666	80,759	4,552	31.0	38.9
Wisconsin	398,017	426,063	161,059	104,966	7,985	137,009	9,308	31.1	38.0
Wyoming	19,664	20,116	7,779	1,078	817	7,388	1.570	0.6	0.9
Total	14,474,777	16,239,797	4,739,914	2,180,229	298,612	8,246,747	540,935	21.2	25.6

*The average size of families was 4.7 persons in 1900, against 5 in 1880 and 5.6 in 1850. Of the 15,963,965 private families in 1900, 14,042,546 had male heads and 1,921,419 female heads.

†Of 7,218,755 persons owning their homes in 1900, 5,064,848 were native whites, 1,730,970 were foreign whites, 372,444 were negroes, 48,219 were Indians, and 2,274 Chinese and Japanese.

The density of population is obtained by dividing the population of each State and Territory and of the United States by its total land area in square miles at each census. In computing density of population for the United States, the areas and population of Alaska and Hawaii in 1900, of Alaska in 1890, and of Indian Terrritory in 1860, 1870, and 1880 are not considered. The area of Indian reservations, outside of Indian Territory, is included in the area of the States and Territories in which they are severally situated, and in that of the United States, prior to 1890, although the population of these Indian reservations was not ascertained, and, for this reason, cannot be considered in figuring density of population at the censuses prior to 1890.

The density of population of the United States, exclusive of Alaska and Hawaii, according to the Census of 1900, is 25.6—that is, there were in the United States in 1900, on the average, 25.6 inhabitants to the square mile, using land surface only. At the Census of 1790 there were less than 5 inhabitants to the square mile, so that the density of the population of the country has increased in 110 years more than fivefold, although the land area of the country in 1900, exclusive of Alaska and Hawaii, was more than three and one-half times what it was in 1790.

Population of the United States.

(Compiled from the Reports of the Census of 1900.)

POPULATION ACCORDING TO AGE.

Months.	Number.	Years.	Number.	Years.	Number.	Years.	Number.	Years.	Number.
Under 1.	153,474	15......	1,533,018	37......	899,682	59......	380,233	81..............	49,725
1 to 2....	332,330	16......	1,561,503	38......	1,037,433	60......	548,144	82..............	44,826
3 to 5....	496,121	17......	1,489,146	39......	959,098	61......	287,645	83..............	35,944
6 to 8....	476,031	18......	1,534,070	40......	1,196,762	62......	331,577	84..............	32,133
9 to 11...	458,936	19......	1,438,352	41......	733.459	63......	323.026	85..............	29,022
		20......	1,531,494	42......	844,453	64......	300,971	86..............	19,695
Years.		21......	1,426,849	43......	738,418	65......	354.279	87..............	16,741
		22......	1,485,923	44......	734,074	66......	265,241	88..............	13,189
1........	1,768,078	23......	1,436,297	45......	880,796	67......	249,924	89..............	9,953
2........	1,830,332	24......	1,454,453	46......	651,391	68......	225,985	90..............	11,401
3........	1,824,312	25......	1,476,860	47......	632,388	69......	207,497	91..............	4,382
4........	1,831,014	26......	1,312,957	48......	663,877	70......	273,449	92..............	3,627
5........	1,808,569	27......	1,282.976	49......	626.160	71......	152 639	93..............	2,592
6........	1,832,613	28......	1,311,166	50......	862,051	72......	171 447	94..............	1,990
7........	1,782,918	29......	1,145,482	51......	510,652	73......	148,699	95..............	2,293
8........	1,780,445	30......	1,465,256	52......	572,186	74......	137,607	96..............	1,291
9........	1,669,578	31......	956,575	53......	495,521	75......	155,236	97..............	895
10........	1,740,628	32......	1,102,117	54......	502.419	76......	110,605	98..............	1,021
11........	1,583.131	33......	1,030,812	55......	569,826	77......	93,510	99..............	766
12........	1,637.509	34......	1.001.279	56......	464,794	78......	86,687	100 and over...	3,504
13........	1,550,402	35......	1,136,406	57......	399,636	79......	73,819	All ages.......	75,994,575
14........	1,568,564	36......	932 162	58......	396,683	80......	88,884	Age unknown	200,584

POPULATION ACCORDING TO CONJUGAL CONDITION.

Sex and Conjugal Condition.	Number.	Per Cent.	Sex and Conjugal Condition.	Number.	Per Cent.	Sex and Conjugal Condition.	Number.	Per Cent.
Both sexes......	76,303,387	100.0	Males...........	39,059,242	100.0	Females........	37,244,145	100.0
Single	44,187 155	57.9	Single.........	23,666,836	60.6	Single	20.520,319	55.1
Married.......	27,849,761	36.5	Married.......	14,003,798	35 9	Married.......	13,845,963	37.2
Widowed.....	3,903,857	5.1	Widowed.....	1,182,293	3.0	Widowed.....	2,721,564	7.3
Divorced......	199,868	0.3	Divorced	84,903	0.2	Divorced......	114,965	0.3
Unknown.....	162,746	0.2	Unknown.....	121.412	0.3	Unknown	41,334	0.1

NOTE.—The figures relating to conjugal condition are not absolute, as the statements as to those married and unmarried are apt to be incorrectly reported, partly through unintentional misstatement and partly through a desire to conceal the facts. For instance, an incorrect return may be made through lack of knowledge, in the case of boarders and lodgers (particularly men) who are reported as single when in fact they are or have been married; or from motives of concealment, in the case of divorced persons who report themselves as single, of couples who have separated but are not legally divorced, or of persons who are not lawfully married.

POPULATION ACCORDING TO ILLITERACY.

General Nativity and Color.	Aggregate.	Can Read but Cannot Write.		Can Neither Read Nor Write.		General Nativity and Color.	Aggregate.	Can Read but Cannot Write.		Can Neither Read Nor Write.	
		Number.	Per C't	Number.	Per C't			Number.	Per C't	Number.	Per C't
Aggregate........	6,180,069	955 843	15.5	5,224,226	84.5	Colored (total)...	2,979,323	309,884	10.4	2,669,439	89.6
White (total)....	3.200,746	645,959	20.2	2,554,787	79.8	Persons of					
Native white...	1,913,611	445,263	23.3	1,468,348	76.7	negro descent	2,853,194	306,303	10.7	2,546.891	89.3
Native parents	1,734,764	410,013	23.6	1,324,751	76.4	Chinese.........	25,396	1,024	4.0	24,372	96.0
For'gn parents	178,847	35,250	19.7	143,597	80.3	Japanese.......	4,386	137	3.1	4,249	96.9
Foreign white.	1,287 135	200,696	15.6	1,086,439	84.4	Indian	96,347	2,420	2.5	93,927	97.5

These returns do not apply to the literacy of persons of less than ten years of age.

For enumeration of Illiterates by States, see table of "Population According to School Age and Voting Age."

POPULATION WHICH CANNOT SPEAK ENGLISH.

General Nativity and Color.	Both Sexes.		Males.		Females.		General Nativity and Color.	Both Sexes.		Males.		Females.	
	Number.	Per C't	Number.	Per C't	Number.	Per C't		Number.	Per Cent	Number.	Per Cent	Number.	Per Cent
Native white—foreign parents.....	65,008	4.6	28,164	4.2	36,844	5.0	Japanese	14.843	1.1	14,448	2.2	395	0.1
Foreign white.....	1,217,280	86.7	563,982	84.2	653,298	89.1	Indian.......	72,583	5.2	32,309	4.8	40,274	5.5
Chinese...........	33,498	2.4	31,191	4.6	2,307	0.3	Aggregate.......	1,403,212	100.0	670,094	100.0	733,118	100.0

These returns embrace only persons of ten years of age and over.

Population of the United States,

ACCORDING TO SCHOOL AGE AND VOTING AGE.

(Compiled from the Reports of the Census of 1900.)

States and Territories.	School Age. Five to Twenty Years.			Voting Age.					
	Total.	Whites.	Negroes. †	Total.	Native Born.	Foreign Born.	Whites.	Negroes. †	Illiterates.
Alabama	733,222	394,152	338,980	413,862	405 598	8,264	232,294	181,471	139,649
Alaska	11,408	1,718	10	37,956	26,489	11,467	25,953	141	10,735
Arizona	38,868	28,371	365	44,081	30,306	13,775	34,911	1,084	10,523
Arkansas	529,375	380,815	148,534	313,836	305,464	8,372	226,597	87,157	62,615
California	420,081	405,868	3,225	544,087	318,817	225,270	489,545	3,711	33,508
Colorado	160,531	157,752	2,043	185,708	133,935	51,773	181,616	3,215	7,689
Connecticut	257,101	252,760	4,272	280,340	173,248	107,092	275,126	4,576	18,984
Delaware	59,635	48,782	10,849	54,018	47,202	6,816	45,592	8,374	7,538
District of Columbia	77,291	51,212	26,046	83,823	73,722	10,101	60,318	23,072	7,052
Florida	197,600	110,537	86,908	139,601	127,865	11,736	77,962	61,417	30,849
Georgia	885,725	457,958	427,741	500,752	493,740	7,012	277,496	223,073	158,247
Hawaii	33,774	23,827	79	79,607	13,064	66,543	19,576	93	27,363
Idaho	54,964	53,261	69	53,932	38,185	15,747	50,328	130	2,936
Illinois	1,589,915	1,565,606	24,238	1,401,456	932,574	468,882	1,370,209	29,762	67,481
Indiana	843,885	825,394	18,389	720,206	646,889	73,317	701,761	18,186	40,016
Indian Territory	159,125	121,420	14,882	97,361	94,361	3,000	77,865	9,146	15,482
Iowa	767,870	763,785	3,912	635,298	477,273	158,025	630,665	4,441	17,061
Kansas	527,560	507,611	18,878	413,786	346,761	67,025	398,552	14,695	14,214
Kentucky	798,027	693,455	104,512	543,996	518,772	25,224	469,206	74,728	102,528
Louisiana	538,267	276,563	261,453	325 943	299,772	26,171	177,878	147,348	122,638
Maine	199,153	198,519	369	217,663	178,931	38,732	216,856	445	13,952
Maryland	403,026	318,052	84,946	321,903	279,216	42,687	260,979	60,406	40,352
Massachusetts	778,110	769,710	7,996	843,465	495,734	347,731	830,049	10,456	53,694
Michigan	790,275	783,220	4,814	719,478	457,353	262,125	712,245	5,193	39,230
Minnesota	612,990	608,547	1,063	506,794	245,768	261,026	502,384	2,168	20,785
Mississippi	633,026	253 153	378,923	349,177	344,151	5,026	150,530	197,936	118,057
Missouri	1,105,258	1,049,414	55,767	856,684	743,659	113,025	809,797	46,418	60,327
Montana	65,871	61,032	289	101,931	58,237	43,694	94,873	711	5,900
Nebraska	386,384	383,229	1,781	301,091	209,961	91,130	297,817	2,298	7,388
Nevada	11,399	9,703	18	17,710	10,523	7,187	14,652	70	2,271
New Hampshire	110,895	110,708	172	130,987	96,099	34,888	130,648	230	10,295
New Jersey	572,938	553,230	19,585	555,608	357,447	198,161	532,750	21,474	38,305
New Mexico	69,712	64,137	401	55,067	47,482	7,585	50,804	775	15,585
New York	2,146,764	2,119,156	25,476	2,184,965	1,346,829	838,136	2,145,057	31,425	130,004
North Carolina	753,826	490,782	260,755	417,578	415,048	2,530	289,263	127,114	122,658
North Dakota	112,789	110,193	97	95,217	39,344	55,873	93 237	115	5,158
Ohio	1,338,345	1,308,510	29,804	1,212,222	985,969	226,254	1,180,599	31,235	58,698
Oklahoma	147,656	135,960	7,106	109,191	100,528	8,663	101,543	4,827	6,479
Oregon	131,687	129,875	201	144,446	101,923	42,523	131,261	560	6,978
Pennsylvania	2,031,171	1,986,430	43,394	1,817,239	1,330,099	487,140	1,763,433	51,668	139,982
Rhode Island	124,646	122,223	2,403	127,144	72,820	54,324	124 001	2,765	11,675
South Carolina	560,773	218,323	342,401	283,325	280,221	3,104	130,375	152,860	99,516
South Dakota	147,165	140,461	134	112,681	67,079	45,602	107,353	184	5,442
Tennessee	780,421	589,451	190,925	487,380	477,739	9,641	375,046	112,236	105,851
Texas	1,215,634	955,906	259,491	737,768	650,599	87,169	599,961	136,875	113,788
Utah	106,513	105,378	136	67,172	41,939	25,233	65,205	358	2,470
Vermont	98,614	98,357	255	108,356	87,465	20,891	108,027	289	8,544
Virginia	704,771	435,612	268,962	447,815	436,389	11,426	301,379	146,122	113,353
Washington	158,245	153,180	528	195,572	126,190	69,382	183,999	1,230	6,635
West Virginia	356,471	341,637	14,823	247,970	235,036	12,934	233,129	14,786	32,066
Wisconsin	730,685	726,950	661	570,715	313 188	257,527	567,218	1,006	31,136
Wyoming	37.500	26,607	215	37,898	26,563	11,335	36,262	481	1,636
Total *	26,110,788	22,490,211	3,500,194	21,329 819	16,227,285	5,102,534	19,036,148	2,065,989	2,326,295

* Including all persons in the military and naval service of the United States. † Including all persons of negro descent.

The whole number of persons of school age—that is, from 5 to 20 years of age, inclusive—in 1900 is 26,110,788, of whom 21,573,492 are from 5 to 17 years of age and 4,537,296 from 18 to 20 years of age. These figures include, however, 217,523 persons of school age reported in Alaska, Hawaii, Indian Territory, and on Indian reservations. Eliminating the latter from the account there are native born, 24,689,118; foreign born, 1,204,147; native white (native parents), 14,775,476; native white (foreign parents), 6,371,221; foreign white, 1,193,443; colored, 3,553,125; persons of negro descent, 3,485,188; males, 12,972,994; females, 12,920,271.

The number of males of voting age is 21,329,819, of which there are native born, 16,227,285; foreign born, 5,102,534; native white (native parents), 10,636,898; native white (foreign parents), 3,466,721; foreign white, 4,932,524; colored, 2,293,676; persons of negro descent, 2,065,589.

The ratio of population to males of voting age in the entire country is 3.6. This ratio varies, however, for the several elements of the population, the ratio of negro population to negro males of voting age being 4.8.

AREA.—According to the Census of 1900, the largest county in the United States is Custer County, Montana, which has 20,400 square miles. The smallest is Bristol County, Rhode Island, which has 25 square miles.

Population of the United States.

(Compiled from the Reports of the Census of 1900.)

FOREIGN POPULATION ACCORDING TO COUNTRY OF BIRTH.

Country	Number	Country	Number	Country	Number
Africa	2,577	France	104,534	Poland (unknown)	20,436
Asia*	11,927	Germany	2,669,164	Portugal	37,144
Atlantic islands	10,955	Greece	8,655	Roumania	15,043
Australia	7,041	Holland	105,098	Russia	424,372
Austria	276,702	Hungary	145,815	Scotland	234,699
Belgium	29,848	India	2,069	South America	4,814
Bohemia	156,999	Ireland	1,619,469	Spain	7,284
Canada (English)†	787,798	Italy	484,703	Sweden	574,625
Canada (French)†	395,427	Japan	81,590	Switzerland	115,959
Central America	3,911	Luxembourg	3,042	Turkey	9,949
China	106,659	Mexico	103,445	Wales	93,744
Cuba	11,159	Norway	338,426	West Indies‖	14,468
Denmark	154,616	Pacific islands§	2,659	Other countries	2,587
England	843,491	Poland (Austrian)	58,503	Born at sea	8,310
Europe‡	2,272	Poland (German)	150,232		
Finland	63,440	Poland (Russian)	154,424	Total foreign born	10,460,085

*Except China, Japan, and India. †Includes Newfoundland. ‡Not otherwise specified. §Except Philippine Islands. ‖Except Cuba and Porto Rico.

POPULATION OF FOREIGN PARENTAGE.

Specified Countries.	Total.	Having Both Parents Born as Specified.	Having One Parent Born as Specified and One Parent Native.	Specified Countries.	Total.	Having Both Parents Born as Specified.	Having One Parent Born as Specified and One Parent Native.
Austria	434,728	408,195	26,533	Poland	687,711	668,536	19,175
Bohemia	356,865	325,400	31,465	Russia	685,360	669,810	15,550
Canada, English	1,319,141	683,440	635,701	Scotland	623,350	421,192	202,158
Canada, French	812,621	635,972	176,649	Sweden	1,084,842	998,538	86,304
Denmark	308,488	266,752	41,736	Switzerland	255,278	187,924	67,354
England	2,146,271	1,364,159	782,112	Wales	246,596	173,416	73,180
France	267,257	171,347	95,910	Other countries	1,079,366	912,055	167,311
Germany	7,832,681	6,244,799	1,587,882	Of mixed foreign parentage	1,340,678	1,340,678	......
Hungary	216,402	210,307	6,095				
Ireland	4,981,047	4,001,461	979,586				
Italy	732,421	706,598	25,823	All classes	26,198,939	21,074,679	5,124,260
Norway	787,836	684,100	103,736				

These returns embrace persons born in foreign countries as well as native born persons having one or both parents born in foreign countries.

NUMBER OF INHABITANTS JUNE 1, 1900, TO EACH VOTE CAST NOVEMBER 6, 1900.

City	Ratio	City	Ratio	City	Ratio	City	Ratio
Salt Lake City, Utah	2.73	Rochester, N. Y.	4.60	Buffalo, N. Y.	5.17	Boston, Mass.	6.70
Dayton, Ohio	3.79	St. Louis, Mo.	4.60	Minneapolis, Minn.	5.24	Lawrence, Mass.	6.75
Albany, N. Y.	3.82	Toledo, Ohio	4.64	Hartford, Ct.	5.27	Portland, Ore.	7.11
Columbus, Ohio	3.89	New Haven, Ct.	4.72	San Francisco, Cal.	5.42	Lowell, Mass.	7.14
Grand Rapids, Mich.	4.03	Kansas City, Kan.	4.75	Philadelphia, Pa.	5.51	St. Joseph, Mo.	7.71
Cincinnati, Ohio	4.22	Elizabeth, N. J.	4.90	New York, N. Y.	5.66	Somerville, Mass.	7.88
Syracuse, N. Y.	4.29	Milwaukee, Wis.	4.90	Manchester, N. H.	5.84	Providence, R. I.	7.99
Camden, N. J.	4.30	Omaha, Neb.	4.94	Hoboken, N. J.	5.92	Cambridge, Mass.	8.09
Kansas City, Mo.	4.33	Cleveland, Ohio	4.95	Springfield, Mass.	6.14	Richmond, Va.	8.57
Des Moines, Iowa	4.35	Louisville, Ky.	4.95	Duluth, Minn.	6.15	New Bedford, Mass.	8.92
Utica, N. Y.	4.36	Newark, N. J.	4.97	Lynn, Mass.	6.22	Fall River, Mass.	9.27
Trenton, N. J.	4.37	Paterson, N. J.	4.99	Portland, Me.	6.30	New Orleans, La.	12.64
Baltimore, Md.	4.50	Jersey City, N. J.	5.05	Seattle, Wash.	6.30	Savannah, Ga.	16.18
Wilmington, Del.	4.57	Bridgeport, Ct.	5.11	St. Paul, Minn.	6.40	Atlanta, Ga.	17.61
Chicago, Ill.	4.58	Detroit, Mich.	5.16	Worcester, Mass.	6.50		

This table shows how very wide of the mark in nearly all of these cities would be an estimate of the population made by multiplying the vote cast by any single ratio, and that this method of estimating a city's population is without foundation.

DISTRIBUTION OF POPULATION BY TOPOGRAPHIC DIVISIONS.

Division	Population	Division	Population	Division	Population
Prairie region	13,300,970	Appalachian valley	4,499,072	Great plains	1,052,719
New England hills	10,260,153	Coastal plain (west of Mississippi River)	1,974,677	Pacific valley	995,363
Lake region	9,571,215	Coast lowlands	1,865,952	Rocky Mountain	592,972
Interior timbered region	8,129,760	Mississippi alluvial region	1,227,094	Great basin	375,345
Piedmont region	6,809,103	Ozark hills	1,203,880	Columbian mesas	356,758
Coastal plain (east of Mississippi River)	6,427,635	Coast ranges	1,079,992	Plateau region	201,669
Allegheny plateau	6,070,246			Continental U. S.	75,994,575

This table shows that the Prairie region and the New England hills include over three-tenths (31 per cent), and with the Lake region and the Interior timbered region over one-half (54.8 per cent.) of the population of the country.

Negro Population of the United States.

COMPILED FROM BULLETIN NO. 8 OF THE BUREAU OF THE CENSUS.

(For negro population of the United States by States in 1900, see Index.

States and Territories.	Per Cent. of Negroes to Total Population.	Per Cent. of Total Negro Population in Each State.†	Per Cent. of Mulattoes to Total Negro Population, 1890.*	Per Cent. of Illiterate in Negro Population, 1900.	Per Cent. of Illiterate in Negro Population, 1890.	Per Cent. of Negroes 10 to 14 Years of Age Attending School.	States and Territories.	Per Cent. of Negroes to Total Population.	Per Cent. of Total Negro Population in Each State.†	Per Cent. of Mulattoes to Total Negro Population, 1890.*	Per Cent. of Illiterate in Negro Population, 1900.	Per Cent. of Illiterate in Negro Population, 1890.	Per Cent. of Negroes 10 to 14 Years of Age Attending School.
Alabama	45.2	09.4	11.4	57.4	69.1	41.4	Nebraska	00.6	00.1	31.7	11.8	19.1	85.5
Arizona	01.5	‡	31.3	12.7	19.2	..	Nevada	00.3	‡	..	..	..	..
Arkansas	28.0	04.2	12.8	43.0	53.6	54.4	New Hampshire	00.2	‡	..	11.9	22.5	..
California	00.7	00.1	42.2	13.4	26.5	86.2	New Jersey	03.7	00.8	15.1	17.2	28.1	76.7
Colorado	01.6	00.1	34.7	13.0	17.6	86.5	New Mexico	00.8	‡	50.4	19.1	45.8	78.4
Connecticut	01.7	00.2	25.0	11.5	15.3	86.6	New York	01.4	01.1	21.7	10.8	17.1	82.5
Delaware	16.6	00.3	12.5	38.1	49.5	62.4	North Carolina	33.0	07.1	13.8	47.6	60.1	55.1
Dist. of Columbia	31.1	01.0	26.2	24.3	35.0	80.5	North Dakota	00.1	‡	..	..	..	..
Florida	43.7	02.6	11.9	38.4	50.5	62.4	Ohio	02.3	01.1	42.5	17.8	25.4	88.5
Georgia	46.7	11.7	09.9	52.4	67.3	45.6	Oklahoma	04.7	00.2	27.5	26.0	39.0	76.8
Idaho	00.2	‡	..	..	..	..	Oregon	00.3	‡	53.0	08.8	17.1	..
Illinois	01.8	01.0	29.3	18.1	26.8	79.4	Pennsylvania	02.5	01.8	23.9	15.1	23.2	80.8
Indiana	02.3	00.6	30.2	22.6	32.3	88.4	Rhode Island	02.1	00.1	27.0	14.1	18.1	90.5
Indian Territory	09.4	00.4	..	42.8	..	35.7	South Carolina	58.4	08.9	09.7	52.8	64.1	44.7
Iowa	00.6	00.1	29.8	18.5	26.1	80.4	South Dakota	00.1	‡	..	..	..	..
Kansas	03.5	00.6	26.5	22.3	32.8	86.5	Tennessee	23.8	05.4	17.3	41.6	54.2	56.5
Kentucky	13.3	03.2	19.4	40.1	55.9	68.1	Texas	20.4	07.0	13.5	38.2	52.5	67.6
Louisiana	47.1	07.4	16.3	61.1	72.1	34.7	Utah	00.2	‡	..	06.3	26.6	..
Maine	00.2	‡	57.4	14.2	15.9	77.9	Vermont	00.2	‡	..	14.6	20.4	..
Maryland	19.8	02.7	15.9	35.1	50.1	63.5	Virginia	35.6	07.5	19.3	44.6	57.2	57.2
Massachusetts	01.1	00.4	36.3	10.7	14.3	89.3	Washington	00.5	‡	34.8	11.6	17.7	84.4
Michigan	00.7	00.2	53.8	10.9	18.9	89.5	West Virginia	04.5	00.5	28.6	32.3	44.5	67.6
Minnesota	00.3	00.1	46.2	07.9	12.1	83.7	Wisconsin	00.1	‡	58.8	11.4	20.6	81.3
Mississippi	58.5	10.3	11.5	49.1	60.8	52.5	Wyoming	01.0	‡	..	17.2	17.8	..
Missouri	05.2	01.8	23.6	28.1	41.7	73.3							
Montana	00.6	‡	27.1	11.4	11.0	..	Total U. S.	11.6	100.0	15.2	44.5	57.5	53.8

* No enumeration of mulattoes was taken in 1900. The returns of 1890 include quadroons and octoroons. † The whole United States being 100 per cent., the ratios show what proportion of the whole resides in each specified State. ‡ Less than one-tenth of one per cent.

The ten counties in the United States having the largest negro population are, in percentages, Isaquena, Miss., 94.0; Tensas, La., 93.5; Madison, La., 92.7; East Carroll, La., 91.6; Beaufort, S. C., 90.5; Tunica, Miss., 90.5; Washington, Miss., 89.7; Coahoma, Miss., 88.2; Leflore, Miss., 88.2; Bolivar, Miss., 88.1.

The negro population of cities having the largest number of negroes in 1900 was: Washington, D. C., 86,702; Baltimore, Md., 79,258; New Orleans, La., 77,714; Philadelphia, Pa., 62,613; New York City, 60,666; Memphis, Tenn., 49,910; Louisville, Ky., 39,139; Atlanta, Ga., 35,727; St. Louis, Mo., 35,516; Richmond, Va., 32,230; Charleston, S. C., 31,522; Chicago, Ill., 30,150; Nashville, Tenn., 30,044; Savannah, Ga., 28,090.

More than three-fourths (77.3 per cent.) of the negroes live in the country districts.

Illiteracy among negroes is about seven times as common as among whites.

There are 3,992,337 negroes in Continental United States engaged in gainful occupations.

The death rate of negroes in the registration area in 1900 was 30.2 per cent.; that of whites in the same area was 17.3 per cent.

The proportion of negro children to negro women 15 to 49 years of age was largest in 1880 and smallest in 1900. There has been uniformly a larger proportion of negro children than of white children. That difference more than doubled between 1860 and 1880, but in 1900 it was less than half what it was in 1880 and less than at any other census except 1860.

Though the negroes have a larger proportion of children than the whites, it has been noticed that the whites of the South have a larger proportion than the whites in other sections of the country.

At the two censuses preceding the Civil War, the proportion of children for the two races at the South was substantially the same. The immediate effect of the Civil War and Reconstruction, if the figures of 1870 may be trusted to that extent, was to reduce the proportion of children among Southern whites by about one-eighth, and among negroes by about one twenty-fifth. The following decade saw an increase in the proportion for each race, but as the decrease among the negroes, 1860 to 18.0, has been less, so was the increase, 1870 to 1880, greater. But between 1880 and 1900 there was a decrease of 160 in the number of negro children at the South to 1,000 negro women, and a decrease of only 75 white children to 1,000 white women. As a result, in 1900 there were for the first time more white children than negro children at the South to 1,000 women.

NEGRO SLAVES IN THE UNITED STATES IN 1790.

New Hampshire, 158; Vermont, 17; Rhode Island, 952; Connecticut, 2,759; New York, 21,324; New Jersey, 11,423; Pennsylvania, 3,737; Delaware, 8,887; Maryland, 103,036; Virginia, 293,427; North Carolina, 100,572; South Carolina, 107,097; Georgia, 29,264; Tennessee, 3,417; Kentucky, 11,830. Total slaves, 697,897. Total population, 3,929,214.

Present Population of the United States.

(JANUARY 1, 1909.)

ACCORDING TO ESTIMATES MADE FOR "THE WORLD ALMANAC" BY THE GOVERNORS OF THE STATES AND TERRITORIES.

THE Governors were requested to make estimates of the present population of their respective States and Territories for THE WORLD ALMANAC for 1909. Where the executives failed to respond in time the estimates were made by other State officials, as indicated in the table.

STATES AND TERRITORIES.	Estimated Population.	STATES AND TERRITORIES.	Estimated Population.
Alabama	2,100,000	Montana	(e) 300,000
Alaska	(c) 32,000	Nebraska	1,350,000
Arizona	200,000	Nevada	132,000
Arkansas	(a) 1,445,793	New Hampshire	440,000
California	1,800,000	New Jersey	2,500,000
Colorado	800,000	New Mexico	500,000
Connecticut	1,100,000	New York	8,546,356
Delaware	200,000	North Carolina	2,500,000
District of Columbia	(b) 340,000	North Dakota	600,000
Florida	683,000	Ohio	4,615,000
Georgia	2,675,000	Oklahoma	1,950,000
Idaho	350,000	Oregon	650,000
Illinois	5,391,300	Pennsylvania	7,450,000
Indiana	2,775,000	Rhode Island	511,000
Iowa	2,232,000	South Carolina	1,496,724
Kansas	1,700,000	South Dakota	500,000
Kentucky	2,250,000	Tennessee	(a) 2,220,000
Louisiana	1,681,625	Texas	4,000,000
Maine	756,000	Utah	340,000
Maryland	1,188,044	Vermont	350,000
Massachusetts	(d) 3,258,422	Virginia	2,100,000
Michigan	2,875,000	Washington	1,250,000
Minnesota	2,125,000	West Virginia	1,200,000
Mississippi	200,000	Wisconsin	2,410,000
Missouri	3,575,862	Wyoming	125,000
Grand Total, January 1, 1909			89,770,126

(a) Report of January 1, 1908. (b) By the Secretary of the Board of District Commissioners. (c) White population. (d) By Labor Bureau of Statistics. (e) By State Bureau of Agriculture, Labor and Industry.

Voting Population of the United States.

(CENSUS REPORT OF 1900.)

GENERAL NATIVITY AND COLOR.	MALES OF VOTING AGE.				
	Total Number.	LITERATE.		ILLITERATE.	
		Number.	Per Cent.	Number.	Per Cent.
Aggregate	21,329,819	19,002,279	89.1	2,327,540	10.9
Native born	16,277,285	14,519,747	89.5	1,707,538	10.5
Foreign born	5,102,534	4,482,532	87.8	620,002	12.2
Native white—native parents	10,636,898	10,017,232	94.2	619,666	5.8
Native white—foreign parents	3,466,721	3,397,637	98.0	69,084	2.0
Foreign white	4,932,524	4,366,987	88.5	565,537	11.5
Colored	2,293,676	1,220,423	53.2	1,073,253	46.8
Persons of negro descent	2,065,989	1,088,940	52.7	977,049	47.3
Chinese	103,006	70,804	68.7	32,202	31.3
Japanese	59,054	39,031	66.1	20,023	33.9
Indian	65,627	21,648	33.0	43,979	67.0

The above summary shows that of the 21,329,819 males of voting age in 1900, 19,002,279, or 89.1 per cent. were literate, and 2,327,540, or 10.9 per cent., were illiterate. By "illiterate" is meant all persons who can neither read nor write, or who can read but not write. There is a very large percentage of illiterates among each of the several classes of colored males of voting age, and a considerable proportion also among foreign white males of voting age. Of the two classes of native white males of voting age much the larger proportion of illiterates is found among those of native parentage, 5.8 per cent. of this class of voters being illiterate as compared with 2 per cent. for native white males of voting age who are of foreign parentage.

Occupations in the United States.

NUMBER OF PERSONS ENGAGED IN PRINCIPAL SPECIFIED OCCUPATIONS.

(Census of 1900.)

All occupations	29,285,922
Agricultural pursuits	10,438,219
Agricultural laborers	4,459,346
Dairymen and dairywomen	10,931
Farmers, planters, and overseers	5,681,257
Gardeners, florists, nurserymen, etc	62,418
Lumbermen and raftsmen	72,190
Stock raisers, herders, and drovers	85,469
Turpentine farmers and laborers	24,737
Wood choppers	36,265
Other agricultural pursuits	5,606
Professional service	1,264,737
Actors, professional showmen, etc	34,923
Architects, designers, draughtsmen, etc	29,580
Artists and teachers of art	24,902
Authors and scientists	6,058
Chemists, assayers, and metallurgists	8,887
Clergymen	111,942
Dentists	29,683
Electricians	50,782
Engineers (civil)	20,153
Engineers (mechanical and electrical)	14,440
Engineers (mining)	2,908
Journalists	30,098
Lawyers	114,703
Musicians and teachers of music	92,264
Officials, National *	40,595
Officials, State	4,345
Officials, county and city	45,350
Physicians and surgeons	140,415
Surveyors	6,034
Teachers and professors in colleges, etc	445,797
Not specified	5,714
Domestic and personal service	5,691,746
Barbers and hairdressers	131,383
Bartenders	88,977
Boarding and lodging house keepers	71,371
Bootblacks	8,248
Firemen (Fire Department)	14,876
Hotel-keepers	54,981
Housekeepers and stewards	155,524
Hunters, trappers, guides, and scouts	11,340
Janitors	51,226
Laborers (not specified)	2,619,488
Longshoremen	20,934
Launderers and laundresses	387,018
Nurses and midwives	121,269
Policemen, watchmen, and detectives	116,615
Restaurant-keepers	34,023
Saloon-keepers	83,875
Servants and waiters	1,565,440
Sextons	5,714
Soldiers (U. S.)	103,902
Sailors and marines (U. S.)	22,842
Not specified	28,422
Trade and transportation	4,778,233
Agents, insurance, real estate, etc	241,333
Auctioneers	2,813
Bankers and brokers	73,384
Bookkeepers and accountants	255,526
Clerks and copyists	603,721
Commercial travellers	92,938
Decorators, drapers, and window dressers	3,053
Foremen and overseers, stable, railroad, etc	55,503
Hostlers	65,381
Hucksters and peddlers	76,872
Livery-stable keepers	33,680
Mail letter carriers	28,378
Merchants and dealers (retail)	792,887
Drugs and medicines	57,346
Dry goods, fancy goods, and notions	45,840
Groceries	156,557
Liquors and wines	13,119
Boots and shoes	15,289
Cigars and tobacco	15,367
Clothing and men's furnishings	18,097
Coal and wood	20,866
General store	33,031
Lumber	16,774
Produce and provisions	34,194
Not specified	366,457
Merchants and dealers (wholesale)	42,310
Messengers and errand and office boys	71,695
Newspaper carriers and newsboys	6,904
Officials of banks and companies	74,246
Packers and shippers	59,769
Porters and helpers (in stores, etc.)	54,274
Salesmen and saleswomen	611,787
Sailors, boatmen, pilots	80,024
Steam railroad employes	582,471
Stenographers and typewriters	112,464
Street railway employes	68,936
Telegraph and telephone linemen	14,765
Telegraph and telephone operators	75,080
Undertakers	16,200
Weighers, gaugers, and measurers	6,670
Not specified	34,056
Manufacturing and mechanical pursuits	7,112,987
BUILDING TRADES.	
Carpenters and joiners (including ship carpenters)	602,741
Masons (brick and stone)	161,048
Painters, glaziers, and varnishers	277,990
Paper-hangers	22,004
Plasterers	35,706
Plumbers and gas and steam fitters	97,884
Roofers and slaters	9,068
Mechanics (not otherwise specified)	9,487
CHEMICALS AND ALLIED PRODUCTS.	
Oil well and oil works employes	24,626
Other chemical workers	14,814
CLAY, GLASS, AND STONE PRODUCTS.	
Brick and tile makers, etc	49,934
Glass workers	49,999
Marble and stone cutters	54,525
Potters	16,140
FISHING AND MINING.	
Fishermen and oystermen	73,810
Miners (coal)	344,292
Miners (gold and silver)	59,095
Miners (not otherwise specified)	133,010
Quarrymen	24,598
FOOD AND KINDRED PRODUCTS.	
Bakers	79,407
Butchers	114,212
Butter and cheese makers	19,261
Confectioners	31,249
Meat packers, curers, and picklers	18,776
Millers	40,576
Other food preparers	13,666
IRON AND STEEL AND THEIR PRODUCTS.	
Blacksmiths	227,076
Iron and steel workers	290,797
Machinists	283,432
Steam boilermakers	33,087
Stove, furnace, and grate makers	12,473
Tool and cutlery makers	28,122
Wheelwrights	13,539
Wireworkers	18,487
LEATHER AND ITS FINISHED PRODUCTS.	
Boot and shoe makers and repairers	209,056
Harness and saddle makers and repairers	40,193
Leather curriers and tanners	42,684
Trunk and leather-case makers, etc	7,051
LIQUORS AND BEVERAGES.	
Bottlers and soda-water makers, etc	10,546
Brewers and maltsters	20,984
Distillers and rectifiers	3,145
LUMBER AND ITS MANUFACTURES.	
Cabinet makers and furniture manufacturing employes	58,719
Coopers	37,226
Piano and organ makers	6,220
Saw and planing mill employes	161,687
Other woodworkers	82,390
METALS AND METAL PRODUCTS OTHER THAN IRON AND STEEL.	
Brass workers	26,760
Clock and watch makers and repairers	24,188
Copper workers	8,188
Gold and silver workers	26,146
Gunsmiths, locksmiths, and bellhangers	7,452
Tinplate and tinware makers	70,613
Other metal workers	40,988

*Including army and navy officers.

(Continued on next page.)

OCCUPATIONS IN THE UNITED STATES—*Continued.*

Occupation	Number	Occupation	Number
Paper and Printing.		Seamstresses	151,379
Bookbinders	30,286	Shirt, collar, and cuff makers	39,432
Compositors	38,849	Tailors and tailoresses	230,277
Engravers	11,150	Other textile workers	30,046
Paper and pulp mill operatives	36,329	**Miscellaneous Industries.**	
Printers, lithographers, and pressmen	116,484	Broom and brush makers	10,222
Textiles.		Builders and contractors	56,935
Artificial-flower makers	2,775	Candle, soap, and tallow makers	4,022
Bleachery and dye works operatives	22,289	Engineers and firemen (not locomotive)	224,546
Carpet factory operatives	19,388	Gas works employes	6,955
Cotton ginners	1,395	Glove makers	12,276
Cotton mill operatives	246,004	Manufacturers and officials, etc	158,123
Hosiery and knitting mill operatives	47,120	Officials of mining and quarrying companies	17,935
Silk mill operatives	54,460	Photographers	27,029
Woollen mill operatives	73,196	Publishers of books, maps, and newspapers	10,970
Other textile mill operatives	104,619	Rubber factory operatives	21,866
Dressmakers	347,076	Tobacco and cigar factory operatives	131,464
Hat and cap makers	22,733	Upholsterers	30,839
Milliners	87,881	Other miscellaneous industries	507,521

URBAN POPULATION.

Geographical Divisions.	Total Population.		Urban Population.		Increase in Total Population.		Increase in Urban Population.	
	1900.	1890.	1900.	1890.	Number.	Per Cent.	Number.	Per Cent.
North Atlantic division	21,046,695	17,406,969	13,613,736	10,071,957	3,639,726	20.9	3,541,779	35.2
South Atlantic division	10,443,480	8,557,922	2,049,520	1,554,190	1,585,558	17.9	495,330	31.9
North Central division	26,333,004	22,410,417	9,343,213	6,744,936	3,922,587	17.5	2,598,277	38.5
South Central division	14,080,047	11,170,137	1,896,655	1,339,232	2,909,910	26.1	557,423	41.6
Western division	4,091,349	3,102,269	1,469,268	1,035,659	989,080	31.9	433,609	41.9
Hawaii	154,001	89,990	39,306	22,907	64,011	71.1	16,399	71.6
Total	76,148,576	63,037,704	28,411,698	20,768,881	13,110,872	20.8	7,642,817	36.8

Ratio of Urban to Total Population: 1900—31.1 per cent.; 1890—29.1 per cent.; 1860—16.1 per cent.; 1850—12.5 per cent.; 1820—4.9 per cent.; 1790—3.4 per cent.

CENTRE OF POPULATION IN THE UNITED STATES.

Date.	Position of Centre of Population.					Westward Movement During Preceding Decade.
	N. Latitude		W. Longitude		Approximate Location by Important Towns.	
	°	′	°	′		Miles.
1790	39	16.5	76	11.2	23 miles east of Baltimore, Md.	......
1800	39	16.1	76	56.5	18 miles west of Baltimore, Md	41
1810	39	11.5	77	37.2	40 miles northwest by west of Washington, D. C	36
1820	39	5.7	78	33.0	16 miles north of Woodstock, Va	50
1830	38	57.9	79	16.9	19 miles W.S.W. of Moorefield, in the present State of W. Va	39
1840	39	2.0	80	18.0	16 miles south of Clarksburg, in the present State of W. Va.	55
1850	38	59.0	81	19.0	23 miles S.E. of Parkersburg, in the present State of W. Va.	55
1860	39	0.4	82	48.8	20 miles south of Chillicothe, Ohio	81
1870	39	12.0	83	35.7	48 miles east by north of Cincinnati, Ohio	42
1880	39	4.1	84	39.7	8 miles west by south of Cincinnati, Ohio	58
1890	39	11.9	85	32.9	20 miles east of Columbus, Ind	48
1900	39	9.5	85	48.9	6 miles southeast of Columbus, Ind	14
					Total	519

This table was prepared by the Census Office. The centre of the negro population in 1890 was near Rome, Ga., and was travelling Gulfward.

The centre of area of the United States, excluding Alaska and Hawaii and other recent accessions, is in Northern Kansas, in approximate latitude 39° 55′, and approximate longitude 98° 50′. The centre of population is therefore about three-fourths of a degree south and more than thirteen degrees east of the centre of area.

RANK OF STATES ACCORDING TO POPULATION.

Rank.	States and Territories.	Population.	Rank.	States and Territories.	Population.	Rank.	States and Territories.	Population.
1	New York	7,268,894	19	Minnesota	1,751,394	36	New Hampshire	411,588
2	Pennsylvania	6,302,115	20	Mississippi	1,551,270	37	South Dakota	401,570
3	Illinois	4,821,550	21	California	1,485,053	38	Oklahoma	398,331
4	Ohio	4,157,545	22	Kansas	1,470,495	39	Indian Territory	392,060
5	Missouri	3,106,665	23	Louisiana	1,381,625	40	Vermont	343,641
6	Texas	3,048,710	24	South Carolina	1,340,316	41	North Dakota	319,146
7	Massachusetts	2,805,346	25	Arkansas	1,311,564	42	Dist. of Columbia	278,718
8	Indiana	2,516,462	26	Maryland	1,188,044	43	Utah	276,749
9	Michigan	2,420,982	27	Nebraska	1,066,300	44	Montana	243,329
10	Iowa	2,231,853	28	West Virginia	958,800	45	New Mexico	195,310
11	Georgia	2,216,331	29	Connecticut	908,420	46	Delaware	184,735
12	Kentucky	2,147,174	30	Maine	694,466	47	Idaho	161,772
13	Wisconsin	2,069,042	31	Colorado	539,700	48	Hawaii	154,001
14	Tennessee	2,020,616	32	Florida	528,542	49	Arizona	122,931
15	North Carolina	1,893,810	33	Washington	518,103	50	Wyoming	92,531
16	New Jersey	1,883,669	34	Rhode Island	428,556	51	Alaska	63,592
17	Virginia	1,854,184	35	Oregon	413,536	52	Nevada	42,335
18	Alabama	1,828,697						

Population of Incorporated Places; Census of 1900.*

ONE HUNDRED LARGEST CITIES.

Cities.	Population.	Cities.	Population.	Cities.	Population.	Cities.	Population.
New York, N. Y	3,437,202	Toledo, Ohio	131,822	Wilmington, Del	76,508	Kansas City, Kan	51.418
Chicago, Ill	1,698,575	Allegheny, Pa	129,896	Camden, N. J	75,935	Harrisburg, Pa	50,167
Philadelphia, Pa	1,293,697	Columbus, Ohio	125,560	Trenton, N. J	73,307	Portland, Me	50,145
St. Louis, Mo	575,238	Worcester, Mass	118,421	Troy, N. Y	75,057	Yonkers, N. Y	47,931
Boston, Mass	560,892	Syracuse, N. Y	108,374	Bridgeport, Ct	70,996	Norfolk, Va	46.624
Baltimore, Md	508,957	New Haven, Ct	108,027	Lynn, Mass	68,513	Waterbury, Ct	45,859
Cleveland, Ohio	381,768	Paterson, N. J	105,171	Oakland, Cal	66,960	Holyoke, Mass	45,712
Buffalo, N. Y	352,387	Fall River, Mass	104,863	Lawrence, Mass	62,559	Fort Wayne, Ind	45.115
San Francisco, Cal	342,782	St. Joseph, Mo	102,979	New Bedford, Mass.	62,442	Youngstown, Ohio	44,885
Cincinnati, Ohio	325,902	Omaha, Neb	102,555	Des Moines, Iowa	62,139	Houston, Tex	44,633
Pittsburgh, Pa	321,616	Los Angeles, Cal	102.479	Springfield, Mass	62,059	Covington, Ky	42,938
New Orleans, La	287.104	Memphis, Tenn	102,320	Somerville, Mass	61,643	Akron, Ohio	42,728
Detroit, Mich	285,704	Scranton, Pa	102.026	Hoboken, N. J	59,364	Dallas, Tex	42,638
Milwaukee, Wis	285,315	Lowell, Mass	94,969	Evansville, Ind	59,007	Saginaw, Mich	42,345
Washington, D. C	278.718	Albany, N. Y	94,151	Manchester, N. H	56,987	Lancaster, Pa	41,459
Newark, N. J	246,070	Cambridge, Mass	91,886	Utica, N. Y	56,383	Lincoln, Neb	40,169
Jersey City, N. J	206,433	Portland, Ore	90,426	Peoria, Ill	56,100	Brockton, Mass	40,063
Louisville, Ky	204,731	Atlanta, Ga	89,872	Charleston, S. C	55.807	Binghamton, N. Y	39,647
Minneapolis, Minn	202,718	Grand Rapids, Mich.	87,565	Savannah, Ga	54.244	Augusta, Ga	39.441
Providence, R. I	175,597	Dayton, Ohio	85.333	Salt Lake City, Utah	53,531	Honolulu, Hawaii	39,306
Indianapolis, Ind	169,164	Richmond, Va	85,050	San Antonio, Tex	53,321	Pawtucket, R. I	39,231
Kansas City, Mo	163,752	Nashville, Tenn	80.865	Duluth, Minn	52,969	Altoona, Pa	38,973
St. Paul, Minn	163,065	Seattle, Wash	80,671	Erie, Pa	52,733	Wheeling, W. Va	38,878
Rochester, N. Y	162,608	Hartford, Ct	79,850	Elizabeth, N. J	52,130	Mobile, Ala	38,469
Denver, Col	133,859	Reading, Pa	78,961	Wilkes-Barre, Pa	51,721	Birmingham, Ala	38,415

INCORPORATED PLACES HAVING 5,000 INHABITANTS OR MORE.

Adrian, Mich	9,654	Bayonne, N. J	32,722	Cadillac, Mich	5,997	Columbus, Miss	6,484
Akron, Ohio	42,728	Beatrice, Neb	7,875	Cairo, Ill	12,566	Columbus, Ohio	125,560
Alameda, Cal	16,464	Beaumont, Tex	9,427	Calais, Me	7,655	Concord, N. H	19,632
Albany, N.Y.	94,151	Beaverdam, Wis	5,128	Cambridge, Md	5,747	Concord, N. C	7,910
Albuquerque, N.M.	6,238	Beaver Falls, Pa	10,054	Cambridge, Mass.	91,886	Conneaut, Ohio	7,133
Alexandria, Ind	7,221	Bedford, Ind	6.115	Cambridge, Ohio	8,241	Connellsville, Pa	7,160
Alexandria, La	5,648	Bellaire, Ohio	9,912	Camden, N. J	75,935	Connersville, Ind	6,836
Alexandria, Va	14,528	Bellefontaine, Ohio.	6,649	Canal Dover, Ohio	5,422	Conshohocken, Pa	5,762
Allegheny, Pa	129,896	Belleville, Ill	17,484	Canandaigua, N. Y.	6,151	Corning, N.Y	11,061
Allentown, Pa	35,416	Bellevue, Ky	6,332	Canton, Ill	6,564	Corry, Pa	5,369
Alliance, Ohio	8,974	Beloit, Wis	10,436	Canton, Ohio	30,667	Corsicana, Tex	9,313
Alpena, Mich	11,802	Belvidere, N. J	6,937	Carbondale, Pa	13,536	Cortland, N.Y	9,014
Alton, Ill	14,210	Bennington, Vt	5,656	Carlisle, Pa	9,626	Coshocton, Ohio	6,473
Altoona, Pa	38,973	Benton Harbor, M'h.	6,562	Carnegie, Pa	7,330	Council Bluffs, Iowa	25,802
Americus, Ga	7,674	Berkeley, Cal	13,214	Carthage, Mo	9,416	Covington, Ky	42,938
Amsterdam, N. Y	20,929	Berlin, N. H	8,886	Catskill, N. Y	5,484	Crawfordsville, Ind.	6,640
Anaconda, Mont	9,453	Bessemer, Ala	6,358	Cedar Falls, Iowa	5.319	Creston, Iowa	7,752
Anderson, Ind	20,178	Bethlehem, Pa	7,293	Cedar Rapids, Iowa	25,656	Cripple Creek, Col	10,147
Anderson, S. C	5,498	Beverly, Mass	13,884	Centreville, Iowa	5,256	Crookston, Mich	5,359
Annapolis, Md	8.525	Biddeford, Me	16,145	Central Falls, R. I	18,167	Cumberland, Md	17,128
Ann Arbor, Mich	14,509	Biloxi, Miss	5,467	Centralia, Ill	6,721	Dallas, Tex	42,638
Anniston, Ala	9,695	Binghamton, N. Y.	39,647	Chambersburg, Pa	8.864	Danbury, Ct	16,537
Ansonia, Ct	12,681	Birmingham, Ala	38,415	Champaign, Ill	9,098	Danville, Ill	16,354
Antigo, Wis	5,145	Bloomfield, N. J	9,668	Charleroi, Pa	5,930	Danville, Pa	8,042
Appleton, Wis	15.085	Bloomington, Ill	23,286	Charleston, Ill	5,488	Danville, Va	16,520
Archbald, Pa	5,396	Bloomington, Ind	6,460	Charleston, S. C	55,807	Davenport, Iowa	35,254
Ardmore, I. T	5,681	Bloomsburg, Pa	6,170	Charleston, W. Va	11,099	Dayton, Ky	6,104
Argentine, Kan	5,878	Blue Island, Ill	6,114	Charlotte, N. C	18,091	Dayton, Ohio	85.333
Arkansas City, Kan.	6,140	Boise, Idaho	5,957	Charlottesville, Va.	6,449	Decatur, Ill	20,754
Asheville, N. C	14,694	Bonham, Tex	5,042	Chattanooga. Tenn.	30,154	Defiance, Ohio	7,579
Ashland, Ky	6,800	Boone, Iowa	8,880	Cheboygan, Mich	6,489	De Kalb, Ill	5,904
Ashland, Pa	6,438	Boston, Mass	560,892	Chelsea, Mass	34,072	Delaware, Ohio	7,940
Ashland, Wis	13,074	Boulder, Col	6,150	Chester, Pa	33.988	Denison, Tex	11,807
Ashtabula, Ohio	12,949	Bowling Green, Ky.	8,226	Cheyenne, Wyo	14,087	Denver, Col	133,859
Astoria, Ore	8,381	Bowling Green, O.	5,067	Chicopee, Mass	19,167	Derby, Ct	7,930
Atchison, Kan	15,722	Braddock, Pa	15,654	Chicago, Ill	1,698.575	Des Moines, Iowa	62,139
Athens, Ga	10,245	Bradford, Pa	15,029	Chicago Heights, Ill	5,100	De Soto, Mo	5,611
Atlanta, Ga	89,872	Brainerd, Minn	7,524	Chillicothe, Mo	6.905	Detroit, Mich	285,704
Atlantic City, Iowa	5,046	Brattleboro, Vt	5.297	Chillicothe, Ohio	12,976	Dixon, Ill	7,917
Atlantic City, N. J.	27,838	Brazil, Ind	7,786	Chippewa Falls, Wis	8,094	Dover, N. H	13,207
Auburn, Me	12,951	Brenham, Tex	5,968	Cincinnati, Ohio	325,902	Dover, N. J	5,938
Auburn, N. Y	30,345	Bridgeport, Ct	70,936	Circleville, Ohio	6,991	Dubois, Pa	9,375
Augusta, Ga	39,441	Bridgeton, N. J	13,913	Clarksville, Tenn.	9,431	Dubuque, Iowa	36.297
Augusta, Me	11,683	Bristol, Ct	6,268	Clearfield, Pa	5,081	Duluth, Minn	52,969
Aurora, Ill	24,147	Bristol, Pa	7,104	Cleburne, Tex	7.493	Dunkirk, N.Y	11,616
Aurora, Mo	6,191	Bristol, Tenn	5,271	Cleveland, Ohio	381.768	Dunmore, Pa	12,583
Austin, Minn	5,474	Brockton, Mass	40,063	Clinton, Iowa	22,698	Duquesne, Pa	9,036
Austin, Tex	22,258	Brookfield, Mo	5,484	Clinton, Mo	5,061	Durham, N. C	6,679
Baker City, Ore	6,663	Brownsville, Tex	6,305	Coatesville, Pa	5,721	East Liverpool, Ohio	16,485
Baltimore, Md	508,957	Brunswick, Ga	9,081	Cohoes, N. Y	23,910	Easton, Pa	25,238
Bangor, Me	21,850	Brunswick, Me	5,210	Coldwater, Mich	6.216	East Orange, N. J	21,506
Baraboo, Wis	5,751	Bucyrus, O	6,560	Colo. Springs, Col	21,085	Eastport, Me	5,311
Barre, Vt	8.448	Buffalo, N. Y	352,387	Columbia, Mo	5.651	East St. Louis, Ill	29,655
Batavia, N. Y	9,180	Burlington, Iowa	23,201	Columbia, Pa	12,316	Eau Claire, Wis	17,517
Bath, Me	10,477	Burlington, N. J	7,392	Columbia, S. C	21,108	Edwardsville, Pa	5,165
Baton Rouge, La	11,269	Burlington, Vt	18,640	Columbia, Tenn	6.052	Elgin, Ill	22,433
Battle Creek, Mich.	18,563	Butler, Pa	10,853	Columbus, Ga	17,614	Elizabeth, N. J	52,130
Bay City, Mich	27,628	Butte, Mont	30,470	Columbus, Ind	8,130	Elizabeth, N. C	6,348

*As reported by the U. S. Census Office. Unincorporated towns and townships were not considered. For population of some of the cities in this list, by later State censuses Index.

INCORPORATED PLACES HAVING 5,000 INHABITANTS OR MORE—*Continued.*

Cities.	Population.	Cities.	Population.	Cities.	Population.	Cities.	Population.
Elkhart, Ind.	15,184	Haverstraw, N. Y.	5,935	Lima, Ohio	21,723	Mt. Vernon, Ind.	5,132
Elmira, N.Y.	35,672	Hazelton, Pa.	14,230	Lincoln, Ill.	8,962	Mt. Vernon, N.Y.	21,228
El Paso, Tex.	15,906	Helena, Ark.	5,550	Lincoln, Neb.	40,169	Mt. Vernon, Ohio	6,633
Elwood, Ind.	12,950	Helena, Mont.	10,770	Litchfield, Ill.	5,918	Muncie, Ind.	20,942
Elyria, Ohio	8,791	Henderson, Ky.	10,272	Little Falls, Minn.	5,774	Murphysboro, Ill.	6,463
Emporia, Kan.	8,223	Herkimer, N. Y.	5,555	Little Falls, N. Y.	10,381	Muscatine, Iowa	14,073
Englewood, N. J.	6,253	Hillsboro, Tex.	5,346	Little Rock, Ark.	38,307	Muskegon, Mich.	20,818
Erie, Pa.	52,733	Hoboken, N. J.	59,364	Lock Haven, Pa.	7,210	Nanticoke, Pa.	12,116
Escanaba, Mich.	9,549	Holland, Mich.	7,790	Lockport, N. Y.	16,581	Nashua, N. H.	23,898
Etna, Pa.	5,384	Holyoke, Mass.	45,712	Logan, Utah	5,451	Nashville, Tenn.	80,865
Eureka, Cal.	7,327	Homestead, Pa.	12,154	Logansport, Ind.	16,204	Natchez, Miss.	12,210
Evanston, Ill.	19,259	Honolulu, Hawaii	39,306	Long Branch, N. J.	8,872	Naugatuck, Ct.	10,541
Evansville, Ind.	59,007	Hoosick Falls, N.Y.	5,671	Lorain, Ohio	16,028	Nebraska City, Neb.	7,380
Everett, Mass.	24,336	Hopkinsville, Ky.	7,280	Los Angeles, Cal.	102,479	Neenah, Wis.	5,954
Everett, Wash.	7,838	Hornellsville, N. Y.	11,918	Louisiana City, Mo.	5,131	Negaunee, Mich.	6,935
Fairmont, W. Va.	5,655	Hot Springs, Ark.	9,973	Louisville, Ky.	204,731	Nelsonville, Ohio	5,421
Fall River, Mass.	104,863	Houston, Tex.	44,633	Lowell, Mass.	94,969	Nevada, Mo.	7,461
Fargo, N. Dak.	9,589	Hudson, N. Y.	9,528	Ludington, Mich.	7,166	New Albany, Ind.	20,628
Faribault, Minn.	7,868	Huntingdon, Pa.	6,053	Lynchburg, Va.	18,891	Newark, N. J.	246,070
Fergus Falls, Minn.	6,072	Huntington, Ind.	9,491	Lynn, Mass.	68,513	Newark, Ohio	18,157
Findlay, Ohio	17,613	Huntington, W. Va.	11,923	McKeesport, Pa.	34,227	New Bedford, Mass.	62,442
Fitchburg, Mass.	31,531	Huntsville, Ala.	8,068	McKee's Rocks, Pa.	6,352	Newbern, N. C.	9,090
Flint City, Mich.	13,103	Hutchinson, Kan.	9,379	Macomb, Ill.	5,375	New Brighton, Pa.	6,820
Florence, Ala.	6,478	Ilion, N. Y.	5,138	Macon, Ga.	23,272	New Britain, Ct.	25,998
Fond du Lac, Wis.	15,110	Independence, Mo.	6,974	Madison, Ind.	7,835	N. Brunswick, N. J.	20,006
Fort Dodge, Iowa	12,162	Indianapolis, Ind.	169,164	Madison, Wis.	19,164	Newburgh, N. Y.	24,943
Fort Madison, Iowa.	9,278	Iola, Kan.	5,791	Mahanoy, Pa.	13,504	Newburgh, Ohio	5,909
Fort Scott, Kan.	10,322	Ionia City, Mich.	5,209	Malden, Mass.	33,664	Newburyport, Mass.	14,478
Fort Smith, Ark.	11,587	Iowa City, Iowa	7,987	Malone, N.Y.	5,935	Newcastle, Pa.	28,339
Fort Wayne, Ind.	45,115	Iron Mountain, M'h.	9,242	Manchester, N. H.	56,987	New Haven, Ct.	108,027
Fort Worth, Tex.	26,688	Ironton, Ohio	11,868	Manchester, Va.	9,715	New Iberia, La.	6,815
Fostoria, Ohio	7,730	Ironwood, Mich.	9,705	Manistee, Mich.	14,260	New London, Ct.	17,548
Frankfort, Ind.	7,100	Irvington, N. J.	5,255	Manitowoc, Wis.	11,786	New Orleans, La.	287,104
Frankfort, Ky.	9,487	Ishpeming, Mich.	13,255	Mankato, Minn.	10,599	N. Philadelphia, O.	6,213
Franklin, N. H.	5,846	Ithaca, N. Y.	13,136	Mansfield, Ohio	17,640	Newport, Ky.	28,301
Franklin City, Pa.	7,317	Jackson, Mich.	25,180	Marietta, Ohio	13,348	Newport, R. I.	22,034
Frederick, Md.	9,296	Jackson, Miss.	7,816	Marinette, Wis.	16,195	Newport News, Va.	19,635
Fredericksburg, Va.	5,068	Jackson, Tenn.	14,511	Marion, Ind.	17,337	New Rochelle, N. Y.	14,720
Freeland, Pa.	5,254	Jacksonville, Fla.	28,429	Marion, Ohio	11,862	Newton, Kan.	6,208
Freeport, Ill.	13,258	Jacksonville, Ill.	15,078	Marlboro, Mass.	13,609	Newton, Mass.	33,587
Fremont, Neb.	7,241	Jamestown, N. Y.	22,892	Marquette, Mich.	10,058	New Ulm, Minn.	5,403
Fremont, Ohio.	8.439	Janesville, Wis.	13,185	Marshall, Mo.	5,086	N. Whatcom, Wash.	6,834
Fresno, Cal.	12,470	Jeannette, Pa.	5,865	Marshall, Tex.	7,855	New York, N. Y.	3,437,202
Frostburg, Md.	5,274	Jefferson, Mo.	9,664	Marshalltown, Iowa	11,544	Niagara Falls, N.Y.	19,457
Fulton, N. Y.	5,281	Jeffersonville, Ind.	10,774	Marshfield, Wis.	5,240	Niles, Ohio	7,468
Gainesville, Tex.	7,874	Jersey City, N. J.	206,433	Martinsburg, W.Va.	7,564	Nome, Alaska *	12,488
Galena, Ill.	5.005	Johnstown, N. Y.	10,130	Martin's Ferry, Ohio	7,760	Norfolk, Va.	46,624
Galena, Kan.	10.155	Johnstown, Pa.	35,936	Mason City, Iowa	6,746	Norristown, Pa.	22,265
Galesburg, Ill.	18,607	Joliet, Ill.	29,353	Massillon, Ohio	11,944	North Adams, Mass.	24,200
Galion, Ohio	7,282	Joplin, Mo.	26,023	Matawan, N.Y.	5,807	Northampton, Mass.	18,643
Gallipolis, Ohio	5,432	Kalamazoo, Mich.	24,404	Mattoon, Ill.	9,622	North Braddock, Pa.	6,535
Galveston, Tex.	37,789	Kane, Pa.	5,296	Maysville, Ky.	6,423	N'h Plainfield, N. J.	5,009
Gardiner, Me.	5,501	Kankakee, Ill.	13,595	Meadville, Pa.	10,291	N. Tonawanda, N.Y.	9,069
Geneva, N. Y.	10,433	Kansas City, Kan.	51,418	Medford, Mass.	18,244	Norwalk, Ct.	6,125
Glens Falls, N. Y.	12,613	Kansas City, Mo.	163,752	Melrose, Mass.	12,962	Norwalk, Ohio	7,074
Glenville, Ohio	5,588	Kaukauna, Wis.	5,115	Memphis, Tenn.	102,320	Norwich, Ct.	17,251
Gloucester, Mass.	26,121	Kearney, Neb.	5,634	Menasha, Wis.	5,589	Norwich, N. Y.	5,766
Gloucester, N. J.	6,840	Kearny, N. J.	10,896	Menominee, Mich.	12,818	Norwood, Ohio	6,480
Gloversville, N. Y.	18,349	Keene, N. H.	9,165	Menominee, Wis.	5,655	Oakland, Cal.	66,960
Goldsboro, N. C.	5,877	Kenosha, Wis.	11,606	Meriden, Ct.	24,296	Oconto, Wis.	5,646
Goshen, Ind.	7,810	Kenton, Ohio	6,852	Meridian, Miss.	14,050	Oelwein, Iowa	5,142
Grafton, W. Va.	5,650	Keokuk, Iowa	14,641	Merrill, Wis.	8,537	Ogden, Utah	16,313
Grand Forks, N. D.	7,652	Kewanee, Ill.	8,382	Mexico, Mo.	5,099	Ogdensburg, N. Y.	12,633
Grand Island, Neb.	7,554	Key West, Fla.	17,114	Michigan City, Ind.	14,850	Oil City, Pa.	13,264
G'd Rapids, Mich.	87,565	Kingston, N. Y.	24,535	Middletown, Ct.	9,589	Oklahoma City, Okla	10,037
Great Falls, Mont.	14,930	Kirksville, Mo.	5,966	Middletown, N.Y.	14,522	Old Forge, Pa.	5,630
Green Bay, Wis.	18,684	Knoxville, Tenn.	32,637	Middletown, Ohio	9,215	Oldtown, Me.	5,763
Greensboro, N. C.	10,035	Kokomo, Ind.	10,609	Middletown, Pa.	5,608	Olean, N. Y.	9,462
Greensburg, Ind.	5,034	Laconia, N. H.	8,042	Millvale, Pa.	6,736	Olyphant, Pa.	6,180
Greensburg, Pa.	6,508	Lacrosse, Wis.	28,895	Millville, N. J.	10,583	Omaha, Neb.	102,555
Greenville, Miss.	7,642	Lafayette, Ind.	18,116	Milton, Pa.	6,175	Oneida, N. Y.	6,364
Greenville, Ohio.	5,501	Lake Charles, La.	6,680	Milwaukee, Wis.	285,315	Oneonta, N. Y.	7,147
Greenville, S. C.	11,860	Lancaster, Ohio	8,991	Minneapolis, Minn.	202,718	Orange City, N. J.	24,141
Greenville, Tex.	6,860	Lancaster, Pa.	41,459	Mishawaka, Ind.	5,560	Oshkosh, Wis.	28,284
Griffin, Ga.	6,857	Lansing, Mich.	16,485	Moberly, Mo.	8,012	Oskaloosa, Iowa	9,212
Guthrie, Okla.	10,006	Lansingburg, N.Y.	12,595	Mobile, Ala.	38,469	Ossining, N. Y.	7,939
Hackensack, N. J.	9,443	Laporte, Ind.	7,113	Moline, Ill.	17,248	Oswego, N. Y.	22,199
Hagerstown, Md.	13,591	Laramie, Wyo.	8,207	Monmouth, Ill.	7,460	Ottawa, Ill.	10,588
Hamilton, Ohio	23,914	Laredo, Tex.	13,429	Monongahela, Pa.	5,173	Ottawa, Kan.	6,934
Hammond, Ind.	12,376	La Salle, Ill.	10,446	Monroe, La.	5,4[illegible]	Ottumwa, Iowa	18,197
Hannibal, Mo.	12,780	Laurium, Mich.	5,643	Monroe, Mich.	5,043	Owatonna, Minn.	5,561
Hanover, Pa.	5,302	Lawrence, Kan.	10,862	Montclair, N. J.	13,962	Owego, N. Y.	5,039
Harrisburg, Pa.	50,167	Lawrence, Mass.	62,559	Montgomery, Ala.	30,346	Owensboro, Ky.	13,189
Harrison, N. J.	10.596	Lead, S. Dak.	6,210	Montpelier, Vt.	6,266	Owosso, Mich.	8,696
Hartford, Ct.	79,850	Leadville, Col.	12,445	Morristown, N. J.	11,267	Paducah, Ky.	19,446
Hartford, Ind.	5,912	Leavenworth, Kan.	20,735	Moundsville, W.Va.	5,362	Painesville, Ohio	5,024
Harvey, Ill.	5,395	Lebanon, Pa.	17,628	Mt. Carmel, Pa.	13.179	Palestine, Tex.	8,297
Hastings, Neb.	7,188	Lewiston, Me.	23,761	Mt. Clemens, Mich.	6,576	Pana, Ill.	5,530
Haverhill, Mass.	37,175	Lexington, Ky.	26,369	Mt. Vernon, Ill.	5,216	Paris, Ill.	6,105

INCORPORATED PLACES HAVING 5,000 INHABITANTS OR MORE—*Continued.*

Cities.	Population.	Cities.	Population.	Cities.	Population.	Cities.	Population.
Paris, Tex.	9,358	Rochester, N. Y.	162,608	South Bethlehem, Pa.	13,241	Vicksburg, Miss.	14,834
Parkersburg, W. Va.	11,703	Rockford, Ill.	31,051	South Norwalk, Ct.	6,591	Vincennes, Ind.	10,249
Parsons, Kan.	7,682	Rock Hill, S. C.	5,485	South Omaha, Neb.	26,001	Wabash, Ind.	8,618
Pasadena, Cal.	9,117	Rock Island, Ill.	19,493	South Portland, Me.	6,287	Waco, Tex.	20,686
Passaic, N. J.	27,777	Rockland, Me.	8,150	Spartanburg, S. C.	11,395	Walla Walla, Wash.	10,049
Paterson, N. J.	105,171	Rockville, Ct.	7,287	Spokane, Wash.	36,848	Wallingford, Ct.	6,737
Pawtucket, R. I.	39,231	Rome, Ga.	7,291	Springfield, Ill.	34,159	Waltham, Mass.	23,481
Peekskill, N. Y.	10,358	Rome, N. Y.	15,343	Springfield, Mass.	62,059	Warren, Ohio	8,529
Pekin, Ill.	8,420	Rutland, Vt.	11,499	Springfield, Mo.	23,267	Warren, Pa.	8,043
Pensacola, Fla.	17,747	Saco, Me.	6,122	Springfield, Ohio	38,253	Washington, D.C.	278,718
Peoria, Ill.	56,100	Sacramento, Cal.	29,282	Spring Valley, Ill.	6,214	Washington, Ind.	8,551
Perth Amboy, N. J.	17,699	Saginaw, Mich.	42,345	Stamford, Ct.	15,997	Washington, Pa.	7,670
Peru, Ill.	6,863	St. Albans, Vt.	6,239	Staunton, Va.	7,289	Washington C.H., O.	5,751
Peru, Ind.	8,463	St. Charles, Mo.	7,982	Steelton, Pa.	12,086	Waterbury, Ct.	45,859
Petersburg, Va.	21,810	St. Cloud, Minn.	8,663	Sterling, Ill.	6,309	Waterloo, Iowa	12,580
Petoskey, Mich.	5,285	St. Johnsbury, Vt.	5,666	Steubenville, Ohio	14,349	Watertown, N. Y.	21,696
Philadelphia, Pa.	1,293,697	St. Joseph, Mich.	5,155	Stevens Point, Wis.	9,524	Watertown, Wis.	8,437
Phillipsburg, N. J.	10,052	St. Joseph, Mo.	102,979	Stillwater, Minn.	12,318	Waterville, Me.	9,477
Phœnix, Ariz.	5,544	St. Louis, Mo.	575,238	Stockton, Cal.	17,506	Watervliet, N. Y.	14,321
Phœnixville, Pa.	9,196	St. Mary's, Ohio	5,359	Streator, Ill.	14,079	Waukegan, Ill.	9,426
Pine Bluff, Ark.	11,496	St. Paul, Minn.	163,065	Summit, N. J.	5,302	Waukesha, Wis.	7,419
Piqua, Ohio	12,172	Salem, Mass.	35,956	Sumter, S. C.	5,673	Wausau, Wis.	12,354
Pittsburgh, Kan.	10,112	Salem, N. J.	5,811	Sunbury, Pa.	9,810	Waycross, Ga.	5,919
Pittsburgh, Pa.	321,616	Salem, Ohio	7,582	Superior, Wis.	31,091	Waynesboro, Pa.	5,396
Pittsfield, Mass.	21,766	Salina, Kan.	6,074	Syracuse, N. Y.	108,374	Webb City, Mo.	9,201
Pittston, Pa.	12,556	Salisbury, N. C.	6,277	Tacoma, Wash.	37,714	Wellston, Ohio	8,045
Plainfield, N. J.*	15,369	Salt Lake, Utah	53,531	Talladega, Ala.	5,056	Wellsville, Ohio	6,146
Plattsburg, N. Y.	8,434	San Antonio, Tex.	53,321	Tamaqua, Pa.	7,267	W. Bay City, Mich.	13,119
Plymouth, Pa.	13,649	San Bernardino, Cal.	6,150	Tampa, Fla.	15,839	Westbrook, Me.	7,283
Pomono, Cal.	5,626	San Diego, Cal.	17,700	Tarentum, Pa.	5,472	West Chester, Pa.	9,524
Pontiac, Mich.	9,769	Sandusky, Ohio	19,664	Taunton, Mass.	31,036	West Haven, Ct.	5,247
Portage, Wis.	5,459	San Francisco, Cal.	342,782	Temple, Tex.	7,065	West Hoboken, N.J.	23,094
Port Chester, N. Y.	7,440	San Jose, Cal.	21,500	Terre Haute, Ind.	36,673	West New York, N.J.	5,267
Port Huron, Mich.	19,158	Santa Barbara, Cal.	6,587	Terrell, Tex.	6,330	West Orange, N. J.	6,889
Port Jervis, N. Y.	9,385	Santa Cruz, Cal.	5,659	Texarkana, Tex.†	5,256	West Pittston, Pa.	5,846
Portland, Me.	50,145	Santa Fe, N. M.	5,603	Thomasville, Ga.	5,322	Wheeling, W. Va.	38,878
Portland, Ore.	90,426	Santa Rosa, Cal.	6,673	Tiffin, Ohio	10,989	White Plains, N. Y.	7,899
Portsmouth, N. H.	10,637	Saratoga Sp's, N.Y.	12,409	Titusville, Pa.	8,244	Wichita, Kan.	24,671
Portsmouth, Ohio	17,870	Sault Ste. Marie, Mh.	10,538	Toledo, Ohio	131,822	Wilkes-Barre, Pa.	51,721
Portsmouth, Va.	17,427	Savannah, Ga.	54,244	Tonawanda, N. Y.	7,421	Wilkinsburg, Pa.	11,886
Pottstown, Pa.	13,696	Sayre, Pa.	5,243	Topeka, Kan.	33,608	Williamsport, Pa.	28,757
Pottsville, Pa.	15,710	Schenectady, N. Y.	31,682	Torrington, Ct.	8,360	Willimantic, Ct.	8,937
Poughkeepsie, N.Y.	24,029	Scranton, Pa.	102,026	Traverse City, Mich.	9,407	Wilmington, Del.	76,508
Princeton, Ind.	6,041	Seattle, Wash.	80,671	Trenton, Mo.	5,396	Wilmington, N. C.	20,976
Providence, R. I.	175,597	Sedalia, Mo.	15,231	Trenton, N. J.	73,307	Winchester, Ky.	5,964
Provo, Utah	6,185	Selma, Ala.	8,713	Trinidad, Col.	5,345	Winchester, Va.	5,161
Pueblo, Col.	28,157	Seneca Falls, N. Y.	6,519	Troy, N. Y.	60,651	Winfield, Kan.	5,554
Putnam, Ct.	6,667	Seymour, Ind.	6,445	Troy, Ohio	5,881	Winona, Minn.	19,714
Quincy, Ill.	36,252	Shamokin, Pa.	18,202	Tucson, Ariz.	7,531	Winsted, Ct.	6,804
Quincy, Mass.	23,899	Sharon, Pa.	8,916	Tuscaloosa, Ala.	5,094	Winston-Sal'm, N.C.‡	13,650
Racine, Wis.	29,102	Sharpsburg, Pa.	6,842	Tyler, Tex.	8,069	Woburn, Mass.	14,254
Rahway, N. J.	7,935	Sheboygan, Wis.	22,962	Tyrone, Pa.	5,847	Woonsocket, R. I.	28,204
Raleigh, N. C.	13,643	Shelbyville, Ind.	7,169	Union, N. J.	15,187	Wooster, Ohio	6,063
Reading, Pa.	78,961	Shenandoah, Pa.	20,321	Union, S. C.	5,400	Worcester, Mass.	118,421
Red Bank, N. J.	5,428	Sherman, Tex.	10,243	Uniontown, Pa.	7,344	Wyandotte, Kan.	5,152
Red Wing, Minn.	7,525	Shreveport, La.	16,013	Urbana, Ill.	5,728	Xenia, Ohio	8,696
Rensselaer, N. Y.	7,466	Sidney, Ohio	5,688	Urbana, Ohio	6,808	Yonkers, N. Y.	47,931
Richmond, Ind.	18,226	Sioux City, Iowa	33,111	Utica, N. Y.	56,383	York, Neb.	5,132
Richmond, Va.	85,050	Sioux Falls, S. Dak.	10,266	Valdosta, Ga.	5,613	York, Pa.	33,708
Riverside, Cal.	7,973	Somersworth, N. H.	7,023	Vallejo, Cal.	7,965	Youngstown, Ohio	44,885
Roanoke, Va.	21,495	Somerville, Mass.	61,643	Valparaiso, Ind.	6,280	Ypsilanti, Mich.	7,378
Rochester, Minn.	6,843	South Amboy, N. J.	6,349	Van Wert, Ohio	6,422	Zanesville, Ohio	23,538
Rochester, N. H.	8,466	South Bend, Ind.	35,999				

* Not incorporated. † Texarkana, Tex., has 5,256; Texarkana, Ark., a separate incorporation, 4,914. ‡ Winston, 10,008; Salem, 3,642—separate places, but practically one town, having only one post-office, Winston-Salem.

POPULATION OF NEW ENGLAND TOWNS NOT INCLUDED IN THE ABOVE TABULATION.

Towns.	Population.	Towns.	Population.	Towns.	Population.	Towns.	Population.
CONNECTICUT.		Brookline	19,935	Montague	6,150	Wellesley	5,072
Branford	5,706	Bridgewater	5,806	Natick	9,488	Westboro	5,400
East Hartford	6,406	Clinton	13,667	North Attleboro	7,253	Westfield	12,310
Greenwich	12,172	Concord	5,652	Northbridge	7,036	West Springfield	7,105
Groton	5,962	Danvers	8,542	Norwood	5,480	Weymouth	11,324
Killingly	6,885	Dedham	7,457	Orange	5,520	Whitman	6,155
Manchester	10,601	Easthampton	6,603	Palmer	7,801	Williamstown	5,013
Orange	6,995	Framingham	11,302	Peabody	11,523	Winchendon	5,001
Southington	5,890	Franklin	5,017	Plymouth	9,592	Winchester	7,248
Stonington	8,540	Gardner	10,813	Revere	10,395	Winthrop	6,058
MASSACHUSETTS.		Great Barrington	5,854	Rockland	5,327		
Adams	11,134	Greenfield	7,927	Saugus	5,084	RHODE ISLAND.	
Amesbury	9,473	Hingham	5,059	Southbridge	10,025	Bristol	6,901
Amherst	5,028	Hudson	5,454	Spencer	7,627	Burrillville	6,317
Andover	6,813	Hyde Park	13,244	Stoneham	6,197	Coventry	5,279
Arlington	8,603	Leominster	12,392	Stoughton	5,442	East Providence	12,138
Athol	7,061	Marblehead	7,582	Wakefield	9,290	Lincoln	8,937
Attleboro	11,335	Methuen	7,512	Ware	8,263	Warren	5,108
Blackstone	5,721	Middleboro	6,885	Watertown	9,706	Warwick	21,316
Braintree	5,981	Milford	11,376	Webster	8,804	Westerly	7,541
		Milton	6,578				

Foreign-Born Population of Largest Cities

OF THE UNITED STATES—CENSUS OF 1900.

Principal Countries of Birth.	Baltimore.		Boston.		Buffalo.		Chicago.		Cincinnati.		Cleveland.		Detroit.	
	Number.	Per Ct.	Number.	Per Ct.	Number.	Per Ct.	Number.	Per Ct.	Number.	Per Ct.	Number.	Per Ct.	Number.	Per Ct.
Total	68,600	100	197,129	100	104,252	100	587,112	100	57,961	100	124,631	100	96,503	100
Austria	1,356	2.0	1,115	0.6	776	0.8	11,815	2.0	654	1.1	4,630	3.7	471	0.5
Bohemia	2,321	3.4	93	*	39	*	36,362	6.2	94	0.2	13,599	10.9	612	0.6
Canada (English)†	629	0.9	47,374	24.0	16,509	15.8	29,472	5.0	928	1.6	7,839	6.3	25,403	26.3
Canada (French)†	51	0.1	2,908	1.5	733	0.7	5,307	0.9	103	0.2	772	0.6	3,541	3.7
Denmark	107	0.2	675	0.3	148	0.1	10,166	1.7	49	0.1	373	0.3	231	0.2
England	2,841	4.1	13,174	6.7	6,908	6.6	29,308	5.0	2,201	3.8	10,621	8.5	6,347	6.6
France	369	0.5	1,003	0.5	791	0.8	2,989	0.5	748	1.3	485	0.4	589	0.6
Germany	33,208	48.4	10,523	5.3	36,720	35.2	170,738	29.1	38,219	65.9	40,648	32.6	32,027	33.2
Holland	98	0.1	391	0.2	311	0.3	18,555	3.2	369	0.6	804	0.6	397	0.4
Hungary	155	0.2	330	0.2	215	0.2	4,946	0.8	208	0.4	9,558	7.7	91	0.1
Ireland	9,690	14.1	70,147	35.6	11,292	10.8	73,912	12.6	9,114	15.7	13,120	10.5	6,412	6.7
Italy	2,042	3.0	13,738	7.0	5,669	5.4	16,008	2.7	917	1.6	3,065	2.5	905	0.9
Mexico	12	*	13	*	8	*	102	*	18	*	9	*	8	*
Norway	188	0.3	1,145	0.6	185	0.2	22,011	3.8	12	*	249	0.2	75	0.1
Poland (Austrian)	139	0.2	61	*	2,643	2.5	9,499	1.6	4	*	752	0.6	1,074	1.1
Poland (German)	733	1.1	216	0.1	13,092	12.6	32,995	5.6	89	0.2	3,577	2.9	10,703	11.1
Poland (Russian)	1,694	2.5	3,375	1.7	2,811	2.7	15,026	2.6	344	0.6	4,119	3.3	1,738	1.8
Poland (unknown)	245	0.4	180	0.1	284	0.3	2,193	0.4	34	0.1	144	0.1	116	0.1
Russia	10,493	15.3	14,995	7.6	1,199	1.2	24,178	4.1	1,976	3.4	3,607	2.9	1,332	1.4
Scotland	594	0.9	4,473	2.3	1,868	1.8	10,347	1.8	461	0.8	2,179	1.8	2,496	2.6
Sweden	236	0.3	5,541	2.8	743	0.7	48,836	8.3	111	0.2	1,000	0.8	267	0.3
Switzerland	186	0.3	400	0.2	590	0.6	3,251	0.6	657	1.1	1,288	1.0	491	0.5
Wales	92	0.1	308	0.2	153	0.2	1,818	0.3	240	0.4	1,490	1.2	101	0.1
Other countries	1,121	1.6	4,951	2.5	565	0.5	7,278	1.2	411	0.7	703	0.6	1,076	1.1

Principal Countries of Birth.	Milwaukee.		New Orleans		New York.		Philadelphia.		Pittsburgh.		St. Louis.		San Francisco.	
	Number.	Per Ct.	Number.	Per. Ct.	Number.	Per Ct.	Number.	Per Ct.	Number.	Per Ct.	Number.	Per Ct.	Number.	Per Ct.
Total	88,919	100	30,325	100	1,270,080	100	295,340	100	84,878	100	111,356	100	116,885	100
Austria	1,616	1.8	391	1.3	71,427	5.6	5,154	1.8	3,553	4.2	2,563	2.3	1,841	1.6
Bohemia	1,719	1.9	17	0.1	15,055	1.2	270	0.1	75	0.1	2,590	2.3	197	0.2
Canada, (Eng.)†	1,687	1.9	310	1.0	19,399	1.5	2,989	1.0	994	1.2	2,151	1.9	4,770	4.1
Canada (French)†	217	0.2	85	0.3	2,527	0.2	294	0.1	79	0.1	339	0.3	429	0.4
Denmark	514	0.6	92	0.3	5,621	0.4	934	0.3	38	*	390	0.4	2,171	1.8
England	2,134	2.4	1,262	4.2	68,836	5.4	36,752	12.4	8,902	10.5	5,800	5.2	8,956	7.7
France	263	0.3	4,428	14.6	14,755	1.2	2,521	0.9	573	0.7	1,462	1.3	4,870	4.2
Germany	53,854	60.5	8,733	28.8	322,343	25.4	71,319	24.2	21,222	25.0	58,781	52.8	35,194	30.1
Holland	606	0.7	47	0.2	2,608	0.2	258	0.1	62	0.1	368	0.3	244	0.2
Hungary	381	0.4	68	0.2	31,516	2.5	2,785	0.9	2,124	2.5	561	0.5	315	0.3
Ireland	2,653	3.0	5,398	17.8	275,102	21.7	98,427	33.3	18,620	21.9	19,421	17.4	15,963	13.6
Italy	726	0.8	5,866	19.3	145,433	11.5	17,830	6.0	5,709	6.7	2,227	2.0	7,508	6.4
Mexico	6	*	299	1.0	282	*	63	*	5	*	76	0.1	1,459	1.2
Norway	1,702	1.9	95	0.3	11,387	0.9	692	0.2	63	0.1	172	0.2	2,172	1.8
Poland (Austrian)	627	0.7	1	*	3,995	0.3	970	0.3	1,023	1.2	322	0.3	29	*
Poland (German)	15,115	17.0	10	*	1,881	0.1	1,728	0.6	3,515	4.1	1,192	1.1	109	0.1
Poland (Russian)	1,245	1.4	29	0.1	25,231	2.0	4,163	1.4	6,243	7.4	1,248	1.1	538	0.5
Poland, (unkn'n)	46	0.1	15	0.1	1,766	0.1	693	0.2	403	0.5	95	0.1	110	0.1
Russia	1,135	1.3	439	1.4	155,201	12.2	28,951	9.8	4,107	4.8	4,785	4.3	1,511	1.3
Scotland	667	0.8	218	0.7	19,836	1.6	8,479	2.9	2,264	2.7	1,264	1.1	3,000	2.6
Sweden	659	0.7	170	0.6	28,320	2.2	2,143	0.7	1,072	1.3	1,116	1.0	5,248	4.5
Switzerland	653	0.7	314	1.0	8,371	0.7	1,707	0.6	544	0.6	2,752	2.6	2,085	1.8
Wales	307	0.4	35	0.1	1,686	0.1	1,033	0.4	2,539	3.0	238	0.2	386	0.3
Other countries	459	0.5	2,003	6.6	37,502	3.0	5,185	1.8	1,149	1.3	1,443	0.3	17,780	15.2

*** Less than one-tenth of 1 per cent. † Includes Newfoundland.**

Total foreign-born population of Allegheny, Pa., 30,216; Atlanta, Ga., 2,531; Charleston, S. C., 2,592; Columbus, O., 12,328; Denver, Col., 25,301; Fall River, Mass., 50,042; Hartford, Ct., 23,758; Indianapolis, Ind., 17,122; Jersey City, N. J., 58,424; Kansas City, Mo., 18,410; Louisville, Ky., 21,427; Lowell, Mass., 40,974; Memphis, Tenn., 5,110; Minneapolis, Minn., 61,021; Newark; N. J., 71,363; New Haven, Ct., 30,802; Paterson, N. J., 38,791; Providence, R. I., 55,855; Rochester, N. Y., 40,748; St. Paul, Minn., 46,819; Washington, D. C., 20,119; Worcester, Mass., 37,652.

The City of New York contains (1900) 786,435 persons of German parentage, wholly or in part; 725,511 of Irish parentage; 245,525 of Russian; 218,918 of Italian; 204,109 of English and Scotch; 113,237 of Austrian; 53,469 of Polish; 52,430 of Hungarian; 29,441 of French; 44,798 of Swedish; 170,084 of other foreign countries. Total, 2,643,957.

Ninety-four per cent. of the foreign-born population is resident in the Northern and 6 per cent. in the Southern States.

Of the population in the United States, in 1900, 34.3 per cent. was of wholly or partial foreign parentage. This includes 13.7 per cent. of foreign born.

Manufacture of Chemicals in the United States.

THE Bureau of the Census published in 1908 a bulletin on Chemicals and Allied Products. It was prepared under the supervision of William M. Steuart, Chief Statistician for Manufactures, by Charles E. Munroe, Professor of Chemistry at George Washington University, and forms a part of the census of manufactures of 1905.

The data presented indicate a most flourishing condition for the industry as a whole. In 1905, 1,786 establishments, with a capital of $323,997,131, were engaged in the manufacture of chemicals valued at $282,169,216. These plants furnished employment for 70,345 persons and paid them $44,529,881 in salaries and wages.

In 1900 the number of establishments was 1,691; the capital, $238,471,290, and the value of products $202,506,076. The salaried officials and wage-earners employed numbered 55,302, and were paid $33,122,930.

At the last census, therefore, as compared with the census of 1900, the capital had increased $85,525,841, or 35.9 per cent.; the value of products, $79,663,140, or 39.3 per cent.; the number of employees, 15,043, or 27.2 per cent., and the amount paid the employees $11,406,951, or 34.4 per cent. Every principal item reported for the industry increased except the number of children employed, which was reduced one-tenth. The wages paid to the children, however, increased about one-twentieth.

The bulletin discussed nineteen classes of products. Paints and varnishes formed the most important class, with products valued at $91,487,326. Fertilizers were second in rank, with a value of $56,632,853; while explosives were third, with a value of $29,602,884. Sodas, fine chemicals, and acids were valued at more than $10,000,000 and less than $20,000,000, while wood distillates, electro-chemicals, tanning materials, dyestuffs and alums ranged in value between $5,000,000 and $10,000,000. The remaining classes with products valued at over $1,000,000 were plastics, compressed and liquefied gases, and essential oils.

PAINTS AND VARNISHES.

A great variety of products is included under the classification "paints and varnishes." The number of establishments manufacturing these products increased from 615 in 1900 to 664 in 1905, their capital from $60,834,921 to $77,149,357, and the value of products from $69,922,022 to $91,487,326, while the number of employees increased from 13,513 to 16,288, and their salaries and wages from $10,011,998 to $12,094,708. The increases of $16,314,436 in capital and $21,565,304 in value of products are particularly noteworthy.

OVER 3,000,000 TONS OF FERTILIZERS MANUFACTURED.

In 1905, 400 establishments were engaged primarily in manufacturing fertilizers of various kinds, and their products were valued at $56,632,853, a gain of 26.8 per cent. over the value of products for 1900.

The States leading in the number of plants producing fertilizers were Georgia, Pennsylvania, Maryland, Virginia, New York, North Carolina and New Jersey. For the first time these products were reported for Alaska, Colorado, Nevada, Wisconsin and Wyoming.

The total production of fertilizers, including the output manufactured as subsidiary, as well as that produced as primary product, amounted to 3,591,771 tons, valued at $56,973,634.

130,920,829 POUNDS OF DYNAMITE.

Considerably more than 1,000 varieties of explosives are in existence. Cartridges, detonators, fuses and other devices containing explosives for use in guns and in blasting are classed as "ammunition," and colored fires, rockets, railroad torpedoes, signal lights and other devices of this nature are classed as "fireworks;" consequently this report discusses only gunpowder, nitroglycerin and similar explosives. Such products to the value of $29,602,884 were produced during the last census year in 124 establishments engaged primarily in their manufacture. Since in 1900 such products were valued at only $17,125,418, the increase amounted to $12,477,466, or 72.9 per cent.

The number of employees engaged in the production of explosives increased from 5,270 to 7,089 and the amount paid them from $3,298,203 to $5,105,824.

In 1905, 130,920,829 pounds of dynamite manufactured as principal or secondary product were valued at $12,900,193; 51,579,270 pounds of nitroglycerin, at $7,730,175; 205,436,200 pounds of blasting powder, at $7,377,077; 7,009,720 pounds of smokeless powder, at $4,406,477; 5,905,953 pounds of gun cotton, at $2,435,805; and 10,383,944 pounds of gunpowder, at $1,541,483.

About half of the States of the country were engaged in the manufacture of explosives, although more than half of the establishments were in the States of Pennsylvania, Ohio and New Jersey.

SODA ASH.

The output of the establishments manufacturing soda products as reported at the census of 1905 was valued at $18,466,504. The capital invested amounted to $22,728,369. The increase in capital as well as that in value of products in 1905 as compared with 1900 amounted to over $7,000,000.

The soda ash produced was valued at $8,204,545; the caustic soda, at $3,185,959; and the bicarbonate of soda, at $1,135,610.

Seven establishments reported a combined output of 41,764,000 pounds of borax, valued at $2,122,808, and this production does not include the borax that was consumed in further manufacture in the establishments in which it was produced.

SULPHURIC ACID.

The general class of acids is divided into two sub-classes. The first includes sulphuric, nitric and mixed acids, and is of special importance, because of the extensive use of sulphuric acid in the manufacture of other chemical products. The value of products made for sale in the 82 establishments engaged primarily in the manufacture of these acids was $9,052,646. Of this amount, $2,097,568 was attributed to other products than the specified acids.

The value of sulphuric acid reported either as primary or as subsidiary product and of that consumed in further manufacture in the establishment in which it was produced, amounted to $15,174,886, the quantity being 1,042,262 tons. Of the States manufacturing this acid, Georgia was first in rank in number of establishments, while other prominent States were Pennsylvania, New Jersey, South Carolina and New York.

The total production of nitric acid was 108,380,387 pounds, valued at $5,232,527, and the States leading in number of establishments engaged in this manufacture were New Jersey, California, Pennsylvania and New York.

Of acids produced by mixing sulphuric and nitric acids, 140,668,950 pounds, valued at $4,142,147, were manufactured.

A capital of $4,857,350 was invested in the production of all other acids, the value of which amounted to $2,726,487.

CHEMICALS PRODUCED BY THE AID OF ELECTRICITY.

In the comparatively short time that has elapsed since electricity was first practically employed in the manufacture of chemicals, many new and advantageous processes have been found, which have resulted not only in the more economical production of substances already obtained by other methods, but also in the addition of some substances hitherto unknown to commerce.

The data for 1905 show that the production of electro-chemicals was valued at over $7,000,000.

Niagara Falls is the chief seat of the electro-chemical industry, and it has held this rank since the industry was introduced into this country.

One of the principal results of the application of electricity to the production of chemicals has been the cheapening of carbon tetrachloride to such an extent that it can be applied to common uses. One important use is that of a cleansing agent, for which it is very valuable, as it does not injure the most delicate color or fabric.

A recent development of scientific interest is the use of the electric furnace in melting quartz or rock crystal. Other developments worthy of special note are found in the electric smelting of iron ore, and in the manufacture of phosphorus, graphite, barium hydroxide and silicide.

TANNING MATERIALS.

The output of tanning materials was valued at $5,615,590 at the census of 1905. Since the value of such products was only $1,713,284 in 1900 the gain has been remarkable, amounting to $3,902,306, or 227.8 per cent. The principal increase in the industry has occurred in the Southern States. The decrease in New Jersey and Pennsylvania has been due to the growing remoteness of natural raw material.

PRINT WORKS MANUFACTURING DYESTUFFS.

Dyestuffs to the value of $5,277,523 were manufactured in establishments in which they formed the primary products. This is a decrease of $359,941, or 6.4 per cent., from the value reported at the census of 1900. Since the dyeing and printing industries have prospered and should therefore consume more rather than less dyestuffs, it is evident that the dye and print works have manufactured a large part of the dyestuffs which they have consumed in the manufacture of their finished products in place of purchasing them from other manufacturers as formerly.

MANUFACTURE OF ALUMS.

The alum industry was in a flourishing condition at the census of 1905. The value of the alums manufactured increased from $2,882,421 in 1900 to $5,058,305 in 1905. During this period the capital more than doubled. The States leading in the number of establishments engaged in this industry in 1905 were Pennsylvania, Massachusetts and Illinois.

The Lincoln Centennial.

THE one hundredth anniversary of the birth of Abraham Lincoln will be commemorated in various forms, both national and local, in 1909. Mr. Lincoln was born near Hodgenville, Larue County, Ky., February 12, 1809.

THE GETTYSBURG SPEECH.

(*Address at the Dedication of Gettysburg Cemetery, November* 19, 1863.)

Fourscore and seven years ago our fathers brought forth upon this continent a new nation, conceived in liberty, and dedicated to the proposition that all men are created equal.

Now we are engaged in a great civil war, testing whether that nation, or any nation so conceived and so dedicated, can long endure. We are met on a great battlefield of that war. We are met to dedicate a portion of it as the final resting-place of those who here gave their lives that that nation might live. It is altogether fitting and proper that we should do this.

But in a larger sense we cannot dedicate, we cannot consecrate, we cannot hallow this ground. The brave men, living and dead, who struggled here have consecrated it far above our power to add or detract. The world will little note nor long remember what we say here, but it can never forget what they did here. It is for us, the living, rather to be dedicated here to the unfinished work that they have thus far so nobly carried on. It is rather for us to be here dedicated to the great task remaining before us; that from these honored dead we take increased devotion to the cause for which they here gave the last full measure of devotion; that we here highly resolve that the dead shall not have died in vain; that the nation shall, under God, have a new birth of freedom, and that government of the people, by the people, and for the people, shall not perish from the earth.

National Municipal and Civic Organizations.

NATIONAL MUNICIPAL LEAGUE.

President—Charles J. Bonaparte, Baltimore, Md. *First Vice-President*—Charles Richardson, Philadelphia. *Second Vice-President*—Thomas N. Strong, Portland, Ore. *Third Vice-President*—Hon. Henry L. McCune, Kansas City, Missouri; *Fourth Vice-President*—Walter L. Fisher, Chicago, Ill. *Fifth Vice-President*—George W. Guthrie, Pittsburgh. *Secretary*—Clinton Rogers Woodruff, 121 South Broad Street, Philadelphia. *Treasurer*—George Burnham, Jr., Philadelphia. *Executive Committee*—Chairman, Horace E. Deming, New York; Albert Bushnell Hart, Cambridge, Mass.; Robert Treat Paine, Jr., Boston; Charles S. De Forest, New Haven, Ct.; Dudley Tibbets, Troy; George Haven Putnam, New York; James P. Baxter, Portland, Me.; E. H. Prentice, New York; Norman Hapgood, New York; H. D. W. English, Pittsburgh; Charles H. Ingersoll, New York; William G. Low, New York; Frederick Almy, Buffalo; Clarence L. Harper, Philadelphia; Thomas Raeburn White, Philadelphia; J. Horace McFarland, Harrisburg, Pa.; Oliver McClintock, Pittsburgh; W. P. Bancroft, Wilmington, Del.; H. B. F. Macfarland, Washington; Elliott Hunt Pendleton, Cincinnati; Morton D. Hull, Chicago; J. L. Hudson, Detroit; John A. Butler, Milwaukee; David P. Jones, Minneapolis; Dwight F. Davis, St. Louis; Frank N. Hartwell, Louisville; E. O. Kontz, Atlanta; James H. Causey, Denver; Frank J. Symmes, Berkeley; Charles D. Willard, Los Angeles; Harvey S. Chase, Boston, and the officers. The League is composed of associations formed in cities of the United States, and having as an object the improvement of municipal government. It has no connection with State or national parties or issues, and confines itself strictly to municipal affairs. Any association belonging to the League may withdraw at any time.

LEAGUE OF AMERICAN MUNICIPALITIES.

President—Silas Cook, E. St. Louis, Ill.; *First Vice-President*—David Heineman, Detroit, Mich.; *Second Vice-President*—William G. Taylor, Wilmington, Del.; *Third Vice-President*—L. A. Lapointe, Montreal, Can.; *Fourth Vice-President*—R. J. Duvant, Savannah, Ga.; *Secretary-Treasurer*—John MacVicar, Des Moines. *Trustees*—Wm. H. Baker, Lockport, N.Y.; William M. O'Bryan, Owensboro, Ky.; M. F. Funkhouser, Omaha, Neb.; William J. Hosey, Fort Wayne, Ind.; John R. Cronin, Joliet, Ill.; T. J. McCarty, Charleston, S. C.; Thomas T. Crittenden, Jr., Kansas City, Mo.

The objects of the League of American Municipalities are as follows—The general improvement and facilitation of every branch of municipal administration by the following means: First—The perpetuation of the organization as an agency for the co-operation of American cities in the practical study of all questions pertaining to municipal administration. Second—The holding of annual conventions for the discussion of contemporaneous municipal affairs. Third—The establishment and maintenance of a central bureau of information for the collection, compilation, and dissemination of statistics, reports, and all kinds of information relative to municipal government. The membership of the League includes nearly all of the important cities in this country and Canada.

NATIONAL GOOD ROADS ASSOCIATION.

President—Arthur C. Jackson, Chicago, Ill.; *Vice-President and Treasurer*—Martin Dodge, Washington, D. C. *Secretary*—James C. Barthoif, Chicago, Ill. This Association was organized by delegates from thirty-eight States in national convention at Chicago November 21, 1900, and an extensive campaign for good roads all over the Union is in progress. Headquarters, Chicago, Ill.; annual membership fee, $1.

AMERICAN CIVIC ASSOCIATION.

President—J. Horace McFarland, Harrisburg, Pa. *First Vice-President and Secretary*—Clinton Rogers Woodruff, North American Building, Philadelphia. *Vice-Presidents*—George B. Leighton, Monadnock, N. H.; Robert Watchorn, New York; David P. Jones, Minneapolis; Mrs. Edward W. Biddle, Carlisle, Pa.; Fielding J. Stilson, Los Angeles. *Executive Board*—Mrs. M. F. Johnston, Richmond, Ind.; Miss Mary M. Butler, Yonkers, N. Y.; Frederick L. Ford, Hartford, Ct.; Outdoor Art, Warren H. Manning, Boston; Press, R. B. Watrous, Milwaukee; Parks and Public Reservations, Henry A. Barker, Providence; Public Nuisances, Harlan P. Kelsey, Salem, Mass.; Railroad Improvement, Mrs. A. E. McCrea, Chicago; Mrs. Edwin F. Moulton, Warren, O.; John Nolen, Cambridge, Mass.; John Quincy Adams, City Hall, N. Y.; Kenyon L. Butterfield, Amherst, Mass.; Mrs. Caroline Bartlett Crane, Kalamazoo, Mich. Social Settlements—Graham Romeyn Taylor, Chicago; *Treasurer*—William B. Howland, New York.

The American Civic Association was formed by merger of the American League for Civic Improvement and the American Park and Outdoor Art Association, June 10, 1904. The Association seeks to combine and make efficient the country-wide effort for civic betterment. It has led in the effort to prevent the destruction of Niagara Falls for power purposes; it advocates rational forest treatment; it is inaugurating a campaign for the restraint and reduction of objectionable outdoor advertising as a defacement of nature, and it urges community beauty. It fosters parks, playgrounds, and outdoor recreation; it arouses communities, and leads them toward betterment. A lantern-slide service is maintained, and many bulletins are issued.

SOCIETY OF BUILDING COMMISSIONERS AND INSPECTORS.

President—James G. Houghton, Commissioner of Buildings, Minneapolis, Minn.; *Asst. Secretary*—William T. Miller, Washington, D. C. The International Society of State and Municipal Building Commissioners and Inspectors is an association of the chiefs of the Building Departments of the United States, Canada and Mexico, the principal cities of Europe, Australia and China, to promote the "improvement of building methods; the revision and perfecting of building ordinances and securing their more thorough enforcement; the lessening of our appalling fire losses; mutual assistance, the interchange of ideas, and the binding in closer union of the building bureaus of the several cities with the view of ultimate uniformity of building laws."

INTERNATIONAL REFORM BUREAU.

International Reform Bureau, 206 Pennsylvania Avenue, S. E., Washington, D. C. *President*—Henry W. Blair, *Secretary*—Rev. F. D. Power, D.D. *Superintendent and Treasurer*—Dr. Wilbur F. Crafts. Devoted to the repression of intemperance, impurity, Sabbath-breaking, gambling, and kindred evils, by lectures, letters, legislation, and literature. The Bureau has drawn twelve laws that have passed Congress.

The Public Lands of the United States.

(Prepared for THE WORLD ALMANAC by the General Land Office.)

TABULAR statement showing area of public lands vacant and subject to entry and settlement in the public land States and Territories, July 1, 1908:

State or Territory.	Area Unappropriated and Unreserved.		
	Surveyed.	Unsurveyed.	Total.
	Acres.	Acres.	Acres
Alabama	129,713	......	129,713
Alaska	......	*368,021,509	368,021,509
Arizona	12,905,121	29,864,081	42,769,202
Arkansas	1,061,185	......	1,061,185
California	23,232,284	6,640,209	29.872,493
Colorado	21,498,272	2,198,425	23,696,697
Florida	353,294	61,648	414,942
Idaho	7,308,958	19,476,044	26,785,002
Illinois	......	......	......
Indiana	......	......	......
Iowa	......	......	......
Kansas	171,446	......	171,446
Louisiana	116,249	......	116,249
Michigan	135,551	......	235,551
Minnesota	1,523,205	265,500	1,788,705
Mississippi	42,791	......	42.791
Missouri	27,480	......	27,480
Montana	20,570,256	25,962,184	46,532,440
Nebraska	3,074,658	......	3,074,658
Nevada	33,339,460	27,837,590	61,177,050
New Mexico	31,566,999	13,210,906	44,777,905
North Dakota	2,189,300	132,850	2,322,150
Ohio	......	......	......
Oklahoma	86,339	......	86,339
Oregon	12,188,457	4,769,456	16,957,913
South Dakota	6,414,049	147,246	6,561,295
Utah	11,901,823	24,677,175	36,578,998
Washington	2,347,825	2,287,176	4,635,001
Wisconsin	13,280	......	13,280
Wyoming	34,492,943	2,652,359	37,145,302
Total	226,690,938	528,204,358	754,895,296

*The unreserved lands in Alaska are mostly unsurveyed and unappropriated.

Cash receipts of the General Land Office during the fiscal year ended June 30, 1908: From the disposal of public lands $11,492,453.76; from the disposal of Indian lands, $997,972.52; from sales of reclamation town lots and water rights, $75,843.57; from depredations on public lands, $110,611.43; from sales of government property (office furniture, etc.), $720.37; for furnishing copies of records and plats, $37,418.81; from sales of timber, $689.00. Total receipts, $12,715,709.46.

The total number of entries made, acres sold and amount received therefor under the Timber and Stone acts of June 3, 1878, and August 4, 1892, were: From June 3, 1878, to June 30, 1908: Entries, 88,545; acres, 11,833,121.88, amount, $29,601,285.31.

UNITED STATES LAND OFFICES.

State or Territory.	Land Office.	State or Territory.	Land Office.	State or Territory.	Land Office.
Alabama	Montgomery.	Kansas	Dodge City.	No. Dakota	Minot.
Alaska	Fairbanks.	"	Topeka.	"	Williston.
"	Juneau.	Louisiana	Natchitoches.	Oklahoma	El Reno.
"	Nome.	"	New Orleans.	"	Guthrie.
Arizona	Phœnix.	Michigan	Marquette.	"	Lawton.
Arkansas	Camden.	Minnesota	Cass Lake.	"	Woodward.
"	Dardanelle.	"	Crookston.	Oregon	Burns.
"	Harrison.	"	Duluth.	"	La Grande.
"	Little Rock.	Mississippi	Jackson.	"	Lakeview.
California	Eureka.	Missouri	Springfield.	"	Portland.
"	Independence.	Montana	Billings.	"	Roseburg.
"	Los Angeles.	"	Bozeman.	"	The Dalles.
"	Oakland.	"	Glasgow.	So. Dakota	Aberdeen.
"	Redding.	"	Great Falls.	"	Chamberlain.
"	Sacramento.	"	Helena.	"	Lemmon.
"	Susanville.	"	Kalispell.	"	Mitchell.
"	Visalia.	"	Lewistown.	"	Pierre.
Colorado	Del Norte.	"	Miles City.	"	Rapid City.
"	Denver.	"	Missoula.	Utah	Salt Lake City.
"	Durango.	Nebraska	Alliance.	"	Vernal.
"	Glenwood Springs.	"	Broken Bow.	Washington	North Yakima.
"	Hugo.	"	Lincoln.	"	Olympia.
"	Lamar.	"	North Platte.	"	Seattle.
"	Leadville.	"	O'Neill.	"	Spokane.
"	Montrose.	"	Valentine.	"	Vancouver.
"	Pueblo.	Nevada	Carson City.	"	Walla Walla.
"	Sterling.	New Mexico	Clayton.	"	Waterville.
Florida	Gainesville.	"	Las Cruces.	Wisconsin	Wausau.
Idaho	Blackfoot.	"	Roswell.	Wyoming	Buffalo.
"	Boisé.	"	Santa Fé.	"	Cheyenne.
"	Cœur d'Alene.	No. Dakota	Tucumcari.	"	Douglas.
"	Hailey.	"	Bismarck.	"	Evanston.
"	Lewiston.	"	Devil's Lake.	"	Lander.
Iowa	Des Moines.	"	Dickinson.	"	Sundance.
Kansas	Colby.	"	Fargo.		

American and Japanese Agreement.

FOR THE PRESERVATION OF THE STATUS QUO IN THE REGIONS OF THE PACIFIC OCEAN AND THE CHINESE EMPIRE.

NOTES between the Governments of the United States and Japan were exchanged at Washington, November 30, 1908, concerning the preservation of the existing status quo in the regions of the Pacific Ocean and the Chinese Empire. They were as follows:

THE JAPANESE AMBASSADOR TO THE SECRETARY OF STATE.

Embassy of Japan,
Washington, D. C., November 30, 1908.

Sir: The exchange of views between us which has taken place at the several interviews which I have recently had the honor of holding with you has shown that, Japan and the United States holding important outlying insular possessions in the region of the Pacific Ocean, the Governments of the two countries are animated by a common aim, policy and intention in that region.

Believing that a frank avowal of that aim, policy and intention would not only tend to strengthen the relations of friendship and good neighborhood which have immemorably existed between Japan and the United States, but would materially contribute to the preservation of the general peace, the Imperial Government have authorized me to present to you an outline of their understanding of that common aim, policy and intention:

1. It is the wish of the two Governments to encourage the free and peaceful development of their commerce on the Pacific Ocean.

2. The policy of both Governments, uninfluenced by any aggressive tendencies, is directed to the maintenance of the existing status quo in the region above mentioned, and to the defense of the principle of equal opportunity for commerce and industry in China.

3. They are accordingly firmly resolved reciprocally to respect the territorial possessions belonging to each other in said region.

4. They are also determined to preserve the common interests of all powers in China by supporting by all pacific means at their disposal the independence and integrity of China and the principle of equal opportunity for commerce and industry of all nations in that Empire.

5. Should any event occur threatening the status quo as above described or the principle of equal opportunity as above defined, it remains for the two Governments to communicate with each other in order to arrive at an understanding as to what measures they may consider it useful to take.

If the foregoing outline accords with the view of the Government of the United States, I shall be gratified to receive your confirmation. I take this opportunity to renew to your Excellency the assurance of my highest consideration.

K. TAKAHIRA.

Hon. Elihu Root, Secretary of State.

THE SECRETARY OF STATE TO THE JAPANESE AMBASSADOR.

Department of State,
Washington, November 30, 1908.

Excellency: I have the honor of acknowledging the receipt of your note of to-day setting forth the result of views between us in our recent interviews defining the understanding of the two Governments in regard to their policy in the region of the Pacific Ocean.

It is a pleasure to inform you that this expression of mutual understanding is welcome to the Government of the United States as appropriate to the happy relations of the two countries and as occasion for a concise mutual affirmation of that accordant policy respecting the Far East which the two Governments have so frequently declared in the past.

I am happy to be able to confirm to your Excellency on behalf of the United States the declaration of the two Governments embodied in the following words:

[Here follow the five articles of the declaration.]

Accept, Excellency, the renewed assurance of my highest consideration.

ELIHU ROOT.

His Excellency Baron Korogo Takahira, Japanese Ambassador.

STATEMENT BY THE JAPANESE AMBASSADOR.

Baron Takahira on December 1 gave out the following statement:

"The notes exchanged explain themselves fully, and I do not think I need add anything to what is therein contained. As will be seen in their wording, the notes are in the form of a declaration and are not a treaty or agreement. They are simply a re-affirmation of what was declared by the two Governments years ago, or a definition of the understanding already existing.

"It is, however, to be noted that the notes which are exchanged between Governments of such great moral standing as the United States and Japan will have a great importance in the carrying out of their common policy. Japan has entire confidence in the great moral strength of the United States Government, and the latter fully trusts in the strong good faith of the Japanese Government, as has been amply proved by past experiences.

"In this respect it is something like a transaction between trusted friends, and it is sincerely to be hoped that the people of each country will have the same confidence as their own Governments in respect to the declaration of the other. In doing so there will be everything to gain and nothing to lose, and friendly intercourse and commercial relations will be fully developed."

THE conditions under and the manner in which an alien may be admitted to become a citizen of the United States are prescribed by Sections 2,165-74 of the Revised Statutes of the United States, as amended by Chapter 3592 of the Acts of the First Session of the 59th Congress. (See Index for Citizen's Expatriation Act.)

DECLARATION OF INTENTIONS.

The alien must declare upon oath before a circuit or district court of the United States or a district or supreme court of the Territories, or a court of record of any of the States having common law jurisdiction and a seal and clerk, of which he is a resident, two years at least prior to his admission, that it is, *bona fide*, his intention to become a citizen of the United States, and to renounce forever all allegiance and fidelity to any foreign prince or State, and particularly to the one of which he may be at the time a citizen or subject.

PETITION ON APPLICATION FOR ADMISSION.

At the time of his application for admission, which must be not less than two years nor more than seven years after such declaration of intention, he shall make and file a petition in writing, signed by himself (and duly verified by the affidavits of two credible witnesses who are citizens of the United States, and who shall state that they have personally known him to be a resident of the United States at least five years continuously, and of the State or district at least one year previously), in one of the courts above specified, that it is his intention to become a citizen and reside permanently in the United States, that he is not a disbeliever in organized government or a believer in polygamy, and that he absolutely and forever renounces all allegiance and fidelity to any foreign country of which he may at the time of filing his petition be a citizen or subject.

CONDITIONS FOR CITIZENSHIP.

He shall, before his final admission to citizenship, declare on oath in open court that he will support the Constitution of the United States, and that he absolutely and entirely renounces all foreign allegiance. If it shall appear to the satisfaction of the court that immediately preceding the date of his application he has resided continuously within the United States five years at least, and within the State or Territory where such court is held one year at least, and that during that time he has behaved as a man of good moral character, attached to the principles of the Constitution of the United States and well disposed to the good order and happiness of the same, he may be admitted to citizenship. If the applicant has borne any hereditary title or order of nobility he must make an express renunciation of the same. No person who believes in or is affiliated with any organization teaching opposition to organized government or who advocates or teaches the duty of unlawfully assaulting or killing any officer of any organized government because of his official character, shall be naturalized. No alien shall be naturalized who cannot speak the English language. An alien soldier of the United States Army of good character may be admitted to citizenship on one year's previous residence. Any alien in the United States navy or marine corps, who has served five consecutive years in the United States navy or one enlistment in the United States marine corps, and honorably discharged, shall be admitted to citizenship upon his petition, without any previous declaration of his intention to become a citizen.

MINORS.

An alien minor may take out his first papers on attaining the age of eighteen years, but he can only become a citizen after having his first papers at least two years, and having resided within the United States five years, and after having attained the age of twenty-one years.

The children of persons who have been duly naturalized, being under the age of twenty-one years at the time of the naturalization of their parents, shall, if dwelling in the United States, be considered as citizens thereof.

CITIZENS' CHILDREN WHO ARE BORN ABROAD.

The children of persons who now are or have been citizens of the United States are, though born out of the limits and jurisdiction of the United States, considered as citizens thereof. (See Index for Citizen's Expatriation Act, Section 6.)

CHINESE.

The naturalization of Chinamen is expressly prohibited by Sec. 14, Chap. 126, Laws of 1882.

PROTECTION ABROAD TO NATURALIZED CITIZENS.

Section 2,000 of the Revised Statutes of the United States declares that "all naturalized citizens of the United States while in foreign countries are entitled to and shall receive from this Government the same protection of persons and property which is accorded to native-born citizens. But when a naturalized citizen shall have resided for two years in the foreign State from which he came, it shall be presumed that he has ceased to be an American citizen, and his place of general abode shall be deemed his place of residence during the said years. It is provided that such a presumption may be overcome on the presentation of satisfactory evidence before a diplomatic or consular officer of the United States."

THE RIGHT OF SUFFRAGE.

The right to vote comes from the State, and is a State gift. Naturalization is a Federal right and is a gift of the Union, not of any one State. In nearly one-half of the Union aliens (who have declared intentions) vote and have the right to vote equally with naturalized or native-born citizens. In the other half only actual citizens may vote. (See Table of Qualifications for Voting in each State, on another page.) The Federal naturalization laws apply to the whole Union alike, and provide that no alien may be naturalized until after five years' residence. Even after five years' residence and due naturalization he is not entitled to vote unless the laws of the State confer the privilege upon him, and he may vote in several States six months after landing, if he has declared his intention, under United States law, to become a citizen.

INHABITANTS OF THE NEW INSULAR POSSESSIONS.

The inhabitants of Hawaii were declared to be citizens of the United States under the act of 1900 creating Hawaii a Territory. Under the United States Supreme Court decision in the insular cases, in May, 1901, the inhabitants of the Philippines and Porto Rico are entitled to full protection under the Constitution, but not to the privileges of United States citizenship until Congress so decrees, by admitting the countries as States or organizing them as Territories.

Qualifications for Voting in Each State of the Union.

(Communicated to The World Almanac and corrected to date by the Attorneys-General of the respective States.)

In all the States except Colorado, Idaho, Utah, and Wyoming the right to vote at general elections is restricted to males of 21 years of age and upward. (See also "New York," next page.) Women are entitled to vote at school elections in several States. They are entitled by law to full suffrage in the States of Colorado, Idaho, Utah, and Wyoming. (See article entitled "Woman Suffrage.")

States.	Requirements as to Citizenship.	Previous Residence Required. In State.	In County.	In Town.	In Precinct.	Persons Excluded from Suffrage.
Alabama*	Citizen of United States or alien who has declared intention (j)	2 yrs.	1 yr.	3 mo.	3 mo.	Convicted of treason or other felonies, idiots, or insane.
Arizona T.*	Citizen of U. S. by nativity or naturalization (a) (b) (h).	1 yr.	30 dys	....	30 dys	Idiot, insane, felon, under guardianship.
Arkansas*	Citizen of United States or alien who has declared intention.	1 yr.	6 mo.	30 dys	30 dys	Idiots, insane, convicted of felony, failure to pay poll-tax, U. S. soldiers, or mariners.
Calif'rnia*	Citizen by nativity, naturalization (90 days prior to election), or treaty of Queretaro.	1 yr.	90 dys	....	30 dys	Chinese, idiots, insane, embezzlers of public moneys, convicted of infamous crime.†
Colorado*.	Citizen, native or naturalized, male or female, who is duly registered.	1 yr.	90 dys	....	10 dys	While confined in public prison, under guardianship, *non compos mentis*, insane.
Conn.*	Citizen of United States who can read English language.	1 yr.	....	6 mo.	....	Convicted of heinous crime, unless pardoned.
Delaware*	Citizen of the United States.	1 yr.	3 mo.	....	30 dys	Insane, paupers or persons convicted of felony unpardoned.
Dis. of Col.	See foot note on following page.					
Florida*	Citizen of the United States.	1 yr.	6 mo.	....	....	Idiots, duellists, convicted of felony or any infamous crime.
Georgia (i)	Citizen of the U. S. who has paid all his taxes since 1877.	1 yr.	6 mo.	....	....	Convicted of felony, bribery, or larceny, unless pardoned, idiots, and insane.
Idaho*	Citizen of the United States, male or female.	6 mo.	30 dys	....	....	Idiots, insane, convicted of felony, bigamists, polygamists, under guardianship (n).
Illinois*	Citizen of the United States (b).	1 yr.	90 dys	30 dys	30 dys	Convicted of felony or bribery in elections, unless restored to citizenship (h).
Indiana*	Citizen or alien who has declared intention and resided 1 year in United States.	6 mo.	....	60 dys	30 dys	United States soldiers, sailors, and marines, and persons convicted of infamous crime (l).
Iowa*	Citizen of the United States.	6 mo.	60 dys	....	....	Idiots, insane, convicted of infamous crime, U.S. soldiers (h).
Kansas*	Citizen of United States or alien who has declared intention (b)	6 mo.	30 dys	30 dys	10 dys	Convicted of treason or felony, insane, under guardianship (d).
Kent'ky*.	Citizen of the United States (b)	1 yr.	6 mo.	60 dys	60 dys	Convicted of treason, felony, or bribery in an election, idiots, and insane (h) (m).
Louisia'a* Those able their name, o	Citizen of United States....... to read and write, or who own $300 w r whose father or grandfather was en	2 yrs. orth of titled to	1 yr. propert vote o	.... y asse n Jan. 1	6 mo. ssed in , 1867.	Idiots, insane, felons, under indictment, inmates of prison or charitable institution except soldiers' home.
Maine*	Citizen of the United States	3 mo.	3 mo.	3 mo.	3 mo.	Paupers and Indians not taxed, under guardianship.†
Maryla'd*	Citizen of the United States	1 yr.	6 mo.	6 mo.	1 day.	Felons not pardoned, lunatics, *non compos mentis*, bribery.
Mass.*	Citizen who can read and write (b).	1 yr.	6 mo.	6 mo.	6 mo.	Paupers and persons under guardianship.
Michigan*	Citizen of the United States or alien who declared intention 2 years and 6 months prior to November 8, 1894 (b).	6 mo.	20 dys	20 dys	20 dys	Indians with tribal relations, duellists and accessories.
Minn.*	Citizen of United States who has been such for 3 months preceding election (b).	6 mo.	30 dys	30 dys	30 dys	Convicted of treason or felony, unpardoned, under guardianship, insane, Indians lacking customs of civilization.
Miss.*	Citizen of the United States who can read or understand Constitution.	2 yrs.	1 yr.	1 yr.	1 yr (c)	Insane, idiots, Indians not taxed, felons, persons who have not paid taxes, bigamists.
Missouri*	Citizen of United States or alien who has declared intention not less than 1 year or more than 5 before election.	1 yr.	60 dys	60 dys	20 dys	Persons in poorhouses or asylums at public expense, those in prison, or convicted of infamous crimes (k).
Montana*.	Citizen of the United States (b)	1 yr.	30 dys	....	....	Felons not pardoned, idiots, insane, Indians (j).
Nebraska*	Citizen of United States or alien who has declared intention 30 days before election (b).	6 mo.	40 dys	30 dys	10 dys	Convicted of treason or felony, unless restored to civil rights, persons *non compos mentis* (h).

* Australian Ballot law or a modification of it in force. † Or a person unable to read the Constitution in English and to write his name. (a) Or citizens of Mexico who desire to become citizens under treaties of 1848 and 1854. (b) Women can vote in school elections. (c) Clergymen are qualified after six months' residence in precinct. (d) Also public embezzlers, persons guilty of bribery, or dishonorably discharged soldiers from U. S. service, unless reinstated. (g) Also soldiers, sailors, and marines in U. S. service. (h) No soldier, seaman, or marine deemed a resident because stationed in the State. (i) The Australian system sometimes prevails in municipal primaries in Georgia, but same is made applicable by rule of party ordering primary and not by the law. (j) Poll-taxes must be paid to date, by Feb. 1, preceding election. (k) Also soldiers (except those living in soldiers' homes), sailors and marines in U. S. Service. (l) During term fixed by court. (m) Widows and spinsters owning property or having ward of school age may vote in school elections. (n) Also inmates of houses of ill fame.

QUALIFICATIONS FOR VOTING—*Continued.*

States.	Requirements as to Citizenship.	Previous Residence Required. In State.	In County.	In Town.	In Precinct.	Persons Excluded from Suffrage.
Nevada*..	Citizen of the United States.....	6 mo.	30 dys	30 dys	30 dys	Idiots, insane, unpardoned convicts. Indians, Chinese.
N.Hamp.*	Citizen of the United States (*a*)	6 mo.	6 mo..	6 mo..	6 mo..	Paupers (*h*).
N. Jersey*	Citizen of the United States....	1 yr...	5 mo..	....	....	Idiots, paupers, insane, convicted of certain crime, unless pardoned or restored by law (*j*).
N. M. Ter.	Citizen of the United States......	6 mo..	3 mo..	30 dys	30 dys	Convicted of felony, unless pardoned. U. S. soldier, sailor, or camp follower, Indians.
N. York*..	Citizen who shall have been a citizen for ninety days prior to election.	1yr(*k*)	4 mo..	(*l*)	(*l*)	Offenders against elective franchise rights, guilty of bribery, betting on elections, and persons convicted of bribery or infamous crime and not restored to citizenship by the Executive. Convicts in House of Refuge or Reformatory not disqualified.
Woman otherwise qualified but for sex may vote at village elections or town meetings to raise money by tax or assessment if she owns property in village or town. Elector of town not entitled to vote on proposition for raising of money or incurring town liability unless he or his wife own property in town assessed on last assessment roll.						
N. Car......	Citizen of the United States...	2 yrs..	6 mo..	....	4 mo..	Convicted of felony or infamous crime, idiots, lunatics (*o*).
N. Dak.*..	Citizen of the United States and civilized Indian † (*a*).	1 yr....	6 mo..	....	90 dys	Under guardianship, persons *non compos mentis*, or convicted of felony and treason, unless restored to civil rights.
Ohio*.	Citizen of the United States (*a*)	1 yr...	30 dys	20 dys	20 dys	Idiots, insane, and felons, persons in U.S. military and naval service on duty in Ohio.
Okla.*.....	Citizen of United States (*a*) †....	1 yr..	6 mo..	None.	30 dys	Felons, idiots, insane, paupers.
Oregon*...	Citizen of U. S. or alien who has declared intention more than 1 year prior to election (*a*).	6 mo.	No (*n*)	None.	None.	Idiots, insane, convicted of felony, Chinese.
Penna.*....	Citizen of the United States at least one month, and if 22 years old or more must have paid tax within two years.	1 yr..	....	....	2 mo.	Convicted of perjury and fraud as election officers, or bribery of voters.
Rhode I.*	Citizen of the United States.. ...	2yr	....	6 mo..	....	Paupers, lunatics (*g*).
S. Car........	Citizen of the United States (*e*)	2yr(*c*)	1 yr...	4 mo..	4 mo..	Felons, bribery unless pardoned, insane, paupers.
S. Dak.*...	Citizen of the United States or alien who has declared intention, Indian who has severed tribal relations (*a*).	6 mo §	30 dys	10 dys	10 dys	Under guardianship, insane, convicted of treason or felony, unless pardoned, U.S. soldiers, seamen, and marines.
Tenn.*	Citizen of the U. S. who has paid poll-tax of preceding year.	1 yr...	6 mo.	....	....	Convicted of bribery or other infamous offence.
Texas*......	Citizen of the U. S. or alien who has declared intention six months prior to election.	1 yr...	6 mo..	6 mo..	(*d*)	Idiots, lunatics, paupers, felons unless pardoned or restored, U. S. soldiers, marines, and seamen (*m*).
Utah*,......	Citizen of the United States, male or female	1 yr....	4 mo..	....	60 dys	Idiots, insane, convicted of treason or crime against elective franchise, unless pardoned (*j*).
Vermont*	Citizen of the United States......	1 yr...	3 mo..	3 mo..	3 mo.	Those who have not obtained the approbation of the local board of civil authority.
Virginia*	See note at foot of page.........	2 yrs..	1 yr...	1 yr...	30 dys	Idiots, lunatics, paupers (*f*) (*j*).
Wash'n* ..	Citizen of the United States and all residents of Territory prior to Statehood (*a*).	1 yr...	90 dys	30 dys	30 dys	Idiots, lunatics, convicted of infamous crimes, Indians not taxed.
West Va.*	Citizen of the State....................	1 yr...	60 dys	6 mo..	(*d*)	Paupers, idiots, lunatics, convicted of treason, felony, or bribery at elections.
Wis.*.......	Citizen of United States or alien who has declared intention, and civilized Indians † (*a*).	1 yr...	10 dys	10 dys	10 dys	Under guardianship, insane, convicted of crime or treason, betting on elections.
Wyom.*...	Citizen of the United States, male or female.	1 yr...	60 dys	10 dys	10 dys	Idiots, insane, felons, unable to read State Constitution in the English language.

* Australian Ballot law or a modification of it in force. † Indian must have severed tribal relations. § One year's residence in the United States prior to election required. (a) Women can vote in school elections. (c) Ministers in charge of an organized church and teachers of public schools are entitled to vote after six months' residence in the State. (d) Actual residence in the precinct or district required. (e) Who has paid six months before election any poll-tax then due, and can read and write any section of the State Constitution, or can show that he owns and has paid all taxes due the previous year on property in the State assessed at $300 or more. (f) Or convicted of bribery, embezzlement of public funds, treason, forgery, perjury, felony, and petty larceny, duellists and abettors, unless pardoned by Legislature. (g) Or persons non compos mentis, sentence to State Prison for one year or more takes away right to vote until restored by General Assembly, under guardianship. (h) Also persons excused from paying taxes at their own request, and those unable to read the State Constitution in English, or write. (j) No soldier, seaman, or marine deemed a resident because stationed in the State. (k) Inhabitance not residence. (l) Thirty days in election district. (m) And any person subject to poll-tax who failed to pay same prior to Feb. 1 of year in which he offers to vote. (n) Must be resident of County to vote for County officers. (o) All persons unable to read and write, and whose ancestor was not entitled to vote prior to Jan. 1, 1867.

In Virginia.—Voting qualifications. All persons who six months before the election have paid their State poll-taxes for the three preceding years. Also any person who served in time of war in the army or navy of the United States, of the Confederate States, or of any State of the United States or of the Confederate States.

Residents of the District of Columbia never had the right to vote therein for national officers, or on other matters of national concern, after the Territory embraced in it was ceded to the United States and became the seat of the general government.

Requirements Regarding Registration of Voters.

(Continuation of "Qualifications for Voting," on preceding pages.)

THE registration of voters is required in the States of Alabama, California, Colorado, Connecticut, Delaware, Florida, Georgia, Idaho, Louisiana, Maine, Maryland, Massachusetts, Michigan, Minnesota, Mississippi (four months before election), Montana, Nevada, New Jersey, New York, North Carolina, Oregon, South Carolina, Tennessee, Utah, Vermont, Virginia, Washington, West Virginia, Wisconsin, Wyoming, and the Territories of Arizona and New Mexico.

In Pennsylvania voters are registered by the assessors. If any voter is missed by assessors and not registered he can swear in his vote.

In Ohio it is required in cities of 11,800 to 100,000 population in presidential years; annually in cities of 100,000 or over.

In Illinois registration of voters is required by law, and in Cook County, where Chicago is located, persons not registered are not entitled to vote; but outside of Cook County generally they can vote if not registered by swearing in their votes, and producing one witness, a householder and registered voter of the voting district, as to their qualifications as electors severally.

In Iowa in cities having 3,500 inhabitants. In Nebraska in cities of over 7,000 inhabitants.

In Kentucky in all cities of the first, second, third and fourth classes, in Kansas in cities of the first and second classes, in North Dakota in cities and villages of 800 inhabitants and over, in Ohio in cities of the first and second classes.

In Missouri it is required in cities of 25,000 inhabitants and over.

In Oklahoma it is required in all cities of the first class.

In Rhode Island non-taxpayers are required to register yearly before June 30. In South Dakota registration is required prior to general biennial elections.

The registration of voters is not required in Arkansas, Indiana, New Hampshire or Texas.

Woman Suffrage.

IN the United States there are four States where women have the same political rights as men and where they may vote at all elections upon the same terms, viz.: Wyoming (established 1869), Colorado (established 1893), Idaho (established 1896), Utah (established 1896).

School suffrage for women prevails in some form in twenty-nine States, as follows: Arizona, Colorado, Connecticut, Delaware, Florida, Iowa, Illinois, Indiana, Idaho, Kentucky, Kansas, Michigan, Massachusetts, Minnesota, Mississippi, Montana, Nebraska, New Hampshire, New Jersey, New York, North Dakota, Oklahoma, Ohio, South Dakota, Utah, Vermont, Washington, Wyoming and Wisconsin.

In 1887 Montana gave tax-paying women the right to vote upon all questions submitted to taxpayers; in 1894 bond suffrage was given to women in Iowa; in 1898 the women of Minnesota were given the right to vote for library trustees, and in the same year Louisiana gave women taxpayers the right to vote in person or by proxy on all questions of taxation.

Women in Kansas have municipal suffrage (established in 1887) and bond suffrage (established in 1903.)

In 1901 New York gave tax-paying women in all towns and villages of the State the right to vote on questions of local taxation.

In 1908 Michigan adopted a constitutional amendment providing for tax-paying suffrage for women taxpayers.

In Great Britain women have suffrage on the same terms as men except in Parliamentary elections.

Women have full suffrage in Australia and New Zealand, the Isle of Man, Finland and Norway. Twenty-five women were elected members of the Finnish Parliament in 1908.

Women have municipal suffrage in Ontario, Nova Scotia, Manitoba, Quebec, British Columbia and the Northwest Territory, in Iceland, Denmark and Sweden. In France women engaged in commerce have the right to vote for Judges of the Tribunal of Commerce.

Women have some voting privileges in Cape Colony, in parts of India and even in Russia.

At the present time the storm centre of the movement is Great Britain. The International Woman Suffrage Alliance will meet in convention in London in the Spring of 1909.

The International Woman Suffrage Alliance is composed of National Woman Suffrage Associations representing 16 countries. Its officers are as follows: Mrs. Carrie Chapman Catt, New York City, President; Dr. Anita Augsburg, Hamburg, Germany, First Vice-President; Mrs. Millicent Garrett Fawcett, London, England, Second Vice-President; Mrs. Rachel Foster Avery, Swarthmore, Pa., Secretary; Mrs. Stanton Coit, London, England, Treasurer.

The officers of the National American Woman Suffrage Association are, Rev. Anna Howard Shaw, Moylan, Pa., President; Rachel Foster Avery, Swarthmore, Pa., First Vice-President; Mrs. Florence Kelley, New York City, Second Vice-President; Miss Kate M. Gordon, New Orleans, La., Corresponding Secretary; Miss Alice Stone Blackwell, Boston, Mass., Recording Secretary; Mrs. Harriet Taylor Upton, Warren, Ohio, Treasurer; Miss Laura Clay, Lexington, Ky., First Auditor. National Headquarters, Warren, Ohio.

The New York State Association Opposed to Woman Suffrage has its central office in New York City. Its officers are as follows: Mrs. Francis N. Scott, President; Mrs. Arthur M. Dodge, First Vice-President; Mrs. Elihu Root, Mrs. Richard Watson Gilder, Mrs. William A. Putnam, Mrs. Robert McVickar, Mrs. George D. Miller, and Mrs. William P. Northrup, Vice-Presidents; Mrs. Francis S. Bangs, Treasurer; Mrs. George Phillips, Secretary, Room 819, Engineering Societies Building, 29 West 39th St., New York City. There are also organizations in Massachusetts, Illinois, Oregon, Iowa and Washington. These are founded with the object of testifying to legislative committees and through the medium of the public press that the opposition to woman suffrage is based upon what is claimed to be "the intelligent conviction of the majority of representative women in all lines of social, industrial, and domestic progress." Pamphlets with information as to the objects of the Association may be had from the Secretary.

Democratic National and State Committees.

DEMOCRATIC NATIONAL COMMITTEE.

Appointed by the Democratic National Convention at Denver, Col., July, 1908.

Chairman	NORMAN E. MACK	Buffalo, N. Y.
Secretary	Urey Woodson	Owensboro, Ky.
Alabama	John W. Tomlinson	Birmingham.
Alaska	A. J. Daly	Nome,
Arizona	S. J. Michelson	Phœnix.
Arkansas	Guy B. Tucker	Little Rock.
California	Nathan Cole, Jr.	Los Angeles.
Colorado	Alva Adams	Pueblo.
Connecticut	H. S. Cummings	Stamford.
Delaware	Willard Saulsbury	Wilmington.
Dist. of Col	Edwin A. Newman	Washington.
Florida	T. Albert Jennings	Pensacola.
Georgia	Clark Howell	Atlanta.
Hawaii	Gilbert J. Waller	Honolulu.
Idaho	Simon P. Donnelly	Lake View.
Illinois	Roger C. Sullivan	Chicago.
Indiana	Thomas Taggart	French Lick.
Iowa	Martin J. Wade	Iowa City.
Kansas	John H. Atwood	Leavenworth.
Kentucky	Urey Woodson	Owensboro.
Louisiana	Robert Ewing	New Orleans.
Maine	E. L. Jones	Waterville.
Maryland	J. F. C. Talbott	Lutherville.
Massachusetts	John W. Coughlin	Fall River,
Michigan	Edwin O. Wood	Flint.
Minnesota	F. B. Lynch	St. Paul.
Mississippi	C. H. Williams	Yazoo City.
Missouri	Wm. A. Rothwell	Moberly.
Montana	J. Bruce Kremer	Butte.
Nebraska	P. L. Hall	Lincoln.
Nevada	John Sunderland	Reno.
New Hampshire	Eugene E. Reed	Manchester.
New Jersey	Rob't S. Hudspeth	Jersey City.
New Mexico	A. A. Jones	Las Vegas.
New York	N. E. Mack	Buffalo.
North Carolina	Josephus Daniels	Raleigh.
North Dakota	William Collins	Bottineau.
Ohio	Harvey C. Garber	Cleveland.
Oklahoma	W. T. Brady	Tulsa.
Oregon	M. A. Miller	Lebanon.
Pennsylvania	James Kerr†	Clearfield.
Porto Rico	D. M. Field	Guayama.
Rhode Island	G. W. Greene	Woonsocket.
South Carolina	B. R. Tillman	Trenton.
South Dakota	E. S. Johnson	Rapid City.
Tennessee	R. E. Mountcastle	Nashville.
Texas	R. M. Johnston	Houston.
Utah	Frank K. Nebeker	Salt Lake City.
Vermont	Thos. H. Brown	Rutland.
Virginia	J. Taylor Ellyson	Richmond.
Washington	W. H. Dunphy	Walla Walla.
West Virginia	John T. McGraw	Grafton.
Wisconsin	T. E. Ryan	Waukesha.
Wyoming	J. E. Osborne	Rawlins.

DEMOCRATIC STATE COMMITTEES.

STATES.	Chairmen.	Post-Offices.	Secretaries.	Post-Offices.
Alabama	Frank S. White	Birmingham	E. W. Pettus, Jr.	Selma.
Arkansas	R. F. Millwee	Clarendon	Bruce T. Bullion	Conway.
California	John E. Raker	Alturas	John F. Murray	San Francisco.
Colorado	Chas. B. Ward	Boulder	Rob. M. Van Deusen	Hahn's Peak.
Connecticut	Chas. W. Comstock	Norwich	E. S. Thomas	New Haven.
Delaware	Thos. F. Bayard	Wilmington	James Lord	Dover.
Florida*	Duncan U. Fletcher	Jacksonville	Herbert L. Dodd	Lake City.
Georgia	Hewlitt A. Hall	Newnan	B. M. Blackburn	Atlanta.
Idaho*	H. W. Lockhart	Pocatello	Chas. E. Arney	Boisé.
Illinois*	Chas. Boeschenstein	Edwardsville	D. J. Hogan	Geneva.
Indiana	W. S. Jackson	Greenfield	Jos. L. Reiley	Indianapolis.
Iowa	C. L. Price	Indianola	John F. Dalton	Manson.
Kansas	H. S. Martin	Marion	W. H. L. Pepperell	Concordia.
Kentucky	Henry R. Prewitt	Mt. Sterling	R. G. Phillips	Elizabethtown.
Louisiana	Albert Estopinal	St. Bernard La.	Robert S. Landry	New Orleans.
Maine	Fred. Emery Beane	Hallowell	Wm. F. Curran	Bangor.
Maryland	Murray Vandiver	Havré de Grace	Lloyd Wilkinson	Baltimore.
Massachusetts *	John P. Feeney	Woburn	Geo. T. McLaughlin	Sandwich.
Michigan*	John T. Winship	Saginaw	A. R. Canfield	Clare.
Minnesota	Frank A. Day	St. Paul	Ed. A. Stevens	Minneapolis.
Mississippi*	C. L. Lomax	Greenwood	L. P. Haley	Okolona.
Missouri*	W. N. Evans	West Plains	R. W. Napier	Hamilton.
Montana*	David G. Browne	Fort Benton	Harvey Bliss	Big Timber.
Nebraska	T. S. Allen	Lincoln	C. M. Gruenther	Columbus.
Nevada*	J. L. Considine	Reno	J. G. Driscoll	Reno.
New Hampshire	John B. Jameson	Antrim	Guy H. Cutter	Joffrey.
New Jersey	James R. Nugent	Newark	William K. Devereux	Asbury Park.
New Mexico*	James G. Fitch	Socorro	Summers Burkhart	Albuquerque.
New York*	Wm. J. Conners	Buffalo	John W. Potter	Marcy.
North Carolina	A. H. Eller	Winston-Salem	Alex. J. Feild	Raleigh.
North Dakota	J. L. Cashel	Grafton	E. A. McCann	Stillwater.
Ohio	William L. Finley	Kenton	Chas. C. Marshall	Sidney.
Oklahoma	J. B. Thompson	Pauls Valley	J. D. Burke	Guthrie.
Oregon	Alex. Sweek	Portland	J. B. Ryan	Portland.
Pennsylvania	G. W. Dimeling	Clearfield	P. Gray Meek	Bellefonte.
Rhode Island	F. E. Fitzsimmons	Lonsdale	Peter J. Gaskin	Valley Falls.
South Carolina *	Willie Jones	Columbia	....	....
South Dakota	R. F. Lyons	Vermillion	H. E. Hitchcock	Mitchell.
Tennessee	Austin Peay	Clarksville	T. D. Lawler	Memphis.
Texas	A. B. Storey	Lockhart	J. C. McNealus	Dallas.
Utah*	Lyman R. Martineau	Salt Lake City	John E. Clark	Salt Lake City.
Vermont	Emory S. Harris	Bennington	Henry Conlin	Winooski.
Virginia	J. Taylor Ellyson	Richmond	J. N. Brenaman	Richmond.
Washington*	A. R. Titlow	Tacoma	Carl Eshelman	Tacoma.
West Virginia	W. G. Bennett	Weston	Alfred E. Kenny	Parkersburg.
Wisconsin	H. H. Manson	Wausau	W. C. Brawley	Wausau.
Wyoming *	F. D. Hammond	Casper	Warren Galvin	Rawlins.

* Committees subject to revision in States marked *. † Deceased.

Republican National and State Committees.

REPUBLICAN NATIONAL COMMITTEE.

Appointed by the Republican National Convention at Chicago, June, 1908.

Chairman	F. H. HITCHCOCK	Wash'ton, D.C.
Secretary	William Hayward.	
Treasurer	George R. Sheldon	New York.
Alabama	P. D. Barker	Mobile.
Alaska	L. P. Shackelford	Juneau.
Arizona	W. S. Sturgis	Tucson.
Arkansas	Powell Clayton	Eureka Springs
California	George A. Knight	San Francisco.
Colorado	Chas. E. Cavender	Leadville.
Connecticut	Chas. F. Brooker	Ansonia.
Delaware	T. C. du Pont	Wilmington.
Dist. Columbia	Sidney Bieber	Washington.
Florida	J. N. Coombs	Apalachicola.
Georgia	Henry Blun, Jr	Savannah.
Hawaii	A. G. M. Robertson	Honolulu.
Idaho	W. E. Borah	Boise.
Illinois	Frank O. Lowden	Oregon.
Indiana	Harry S. New	Indianapolis.
Iowa	Ernest E. Hart	Council Bluffs.
Kansas	David W. Mulvane	Topeka.
Kentucky	A. R. Burnam	Richmond.
Louisiana	Pearl Wight	New Orleans.
Maine	John F. Hill	Augusta.
Maryland	Wm. P. Jackson	Salisbury.
Massachusetts	W. Murray Crane	Dalton.
Michigan	John W. Blodgett	Grand Rapids.
Minnesota	Frank B. Kellogg	St. Paul.
Mississippi	L. B. Moseley	Jackson.
Missouri	Charles Nagel	St. Louis.
Montana	Thos. C. Marshall	Missoula.
Nebraska	Victor Rosewater	Omaha.
Nevada	P. L. Flanigan	Reno.
New Hampshire	F. W. Estabrook	Nashua.
New Jersey	Franklin Murphy	Newark.
New Mexico	Solomon Luna	Los Lunas.
New York	Wm. L. Ward	Port Chester.
North Carolina	E. C. Duncan	Raleigh.
North Dakota	James Kennedy	Fargo.
Ohio	A. I. Vorys	Lancaster.
Oklahoma	C. M. Cade	Shawnee.
Oregon	R. E. Williams	Dallas.
Pennsylvania	Boies Penrose	Philadelphia.
Philippines	Henry B. McCoy	Manila.
Porto Rico	R. H. Todd	San Juan.
Rhode Island	Charles R. Brayton	Providence.
South Carolina	John G. Capers	Greenville.
South Dakota	Thomas Thorson	Canton.
Tennessee	Nathan W. Hale	Knoxville.
Texas	Cecil A. Lyon	Sherman.
Utah	C. E. Loose	Provo City.
Vermont	James W. Brock	Montpelier.
Virginia	Alvah H. Martin	Portsmouth.
Washington	R. L. McCormick	Tacoma.
West Virginia	N. B. Scott	Wheeling.
Wisconsin	Alfred T. Rogers	Madison.
Wyoming	Geo. E. Pexton	Evanston.

REPUBLICAN STATE COMMITTEES.

STATES.	Chairmen.	Post-Offices.	Secretaries.	Post-Offices.
Alabama*	Jos. O. Thompson	Birmingham	N. L. Steele	Birmingham.
Arkansas	F. W. Tucker	Little Rock	N. S. Bratton	Little Rock.
California	P. S. Teller	San Francisco	W. H. Davis	San Francisco.
Colorado*	John F. Vivian	Denver	....	....
Connecticut	Michael Kenealy	Stamford	George E. Hinman	Willimantic.
Delaware	T. O. Du Pont	Wilmington	Frank L. Speakman	Wilmington.
Florida	Henry S. Chubb	Gainesville	Joseph E. Lee	Jacksonville.
Georgia	W. H. Johnson	Atlanta	John H. Deveaux	Savannah.
Illinois	Roy O. West	Chicago	Edward St. Clair	Chicago.
Indiana	James P. Goodrich	Indianapolis	Carl W. Riddick	Winamac.
Iowa*	F. P. Woods	Estherville	C. F. Franke	Parkersburg.
Kansas	J. W. Dolly	Maple Hill	W. T. Beck	Holton.
Kentucky	Robert H. Winn	Mt. Sterling	Alvis S. Bennett	Louisville.
Louisiana	F. B. Williams	Patterson	M. J. McFarlane	New Orleans.
Maine	Byron Boyd	Augusta	Frank H. Briggs	Auburn.
Maryland*	John B. Hanna	Bel Air	John C. Simering	Baltimore.
Massachusetts*	Geo. H. Doty	Boston	Wm. M. Flanders	Boston.
Michigan	Gerrit J. Diekema	Holland	D. E. Alward	Clare.
Minnesota	A. D. Brown	Madison	J. A. Martin	St. Paul.
Mississippi	Fred. W. Collins	Summit	T. V. McAllister	Vicksburg.
Missouri*	Thos. K. Niedringhaus	St. Louis	Joseph McCoy	St. Louis.
Montana*	Fletcher Maddox	Great Falls	Chas. E. Wight	Anaconda.
Nebraska	J. W. Kiefer, Jr	Bostwick	J. M. O'Neal	Lincoln.
Nevada*	H. J. Humphreys	Reno	A. N. Salisbury	Reno.
New Hampshire	Oscar L. Young	Laconia	Harry J. Brown	Concord.
New Jersey*	Frank O. Briggs	Trenton	J. Herbert Potts	Jersey City.
New Mexico	H. O. Bursum	Socorro	James W. Raynolds	Sante Fé.
New York	Timothy L. Woodruff	New York City	Lafayette B. Gleason	New York City.
North Carolina	S. B. Adams	Greensboro	T. J. Haskins	Asheville.
North Dakota	James Johnson	Minot	M. H. Jewell	Bismarck.
Ohio	Henry A. Williams	Columbus	W. H. Phipps	Paulding.
Oklahoma*	Jake L. Harmon	Lawton	V. W. Whiting	Enid.
Oregon*	G. A. Westgate	Albany	S. C. Spencer	Portland.
Pennsylvania	W. R. Andrews	Meadville	John R. Williams	Scranton.
Rhode Island*	Geo. R. Lawton	Tiverton	Nathan M. Wright	Providence.
South Carolina	Edmund H. Deas	Darlington	W. F. Myers	Columbia.
South Dakota	W. O. Cook	Sioux Falls	J. S. Wingfield	Mitchell.
Tennessee	Newell Sanders	Chattanooga	H. A. Luck	Nashville.
Texas	Cecil A. Lyon	Sherman	Bart Marshall	Sherman.
Utah	C. E. Loose	Provo City	George B. Squires	Salt Lake City.
Vermont	F. C. Williams	Newport	Earle S. Kinsley	Ruthland.
Virginia	C. B. Slemp	Big Stone Gap	Geo. L. Hart	Roanoke.
Washington	Ellis de Bruler	Seattle	J. W. Lysons	Seattle.
West Virginia	Samuel V. Matthews	Charleston	Virgil L. Highland	Clarksburg.
Wisconsin	E. A. Edmonds	Appleton	A. H. Lambeck	Milwaukee.
Wyoming	Chas. W. Burdick	Cheyenne	Robert P. Fuller	Cheyenne.

* Committees subject to revision in States marked *.

Prohibition Party National Committee.

Chairman .... CHARLES R. JONES, Chicago, Ill.
Vice-Chairman .... A. G. WOLFENBARGER, Lincoln, Neb.
Secretary .... W. G. CALDERWOOD, Minneapolis, Minn.
Treasurer .... FELIX T. MCWHIRTER, Indianapolis, Ind.

Arizona—Frank J. Sibley, Tucson; Dr. John Wix Thomas, Phœnix. Arkansas—Henry Hatton, Beebe; H. Brady, Beebe. California—T. K. Beard, Modesto; Wiley J. Phillips, Los Angeles. Colorado—A. B. Taynton, Denver; John W. Carpenter, Greely. Connecticut—Frederick G. Platt, New Britain; William N. Taft, W. Goshen. Delaware—Geo. W. Todd, Wilmington; Lewis T. Brosius, Wilmington. Florida—John P. Coffin, Eustis; Francis Trueblood, Bradentown. Georgia—Geo. Gordon, Atlanta; W. S. Witham, Atlanta. Illinois—Oliver W. Stewart, Chicago; A. E. Wilson, Chicago. Indiana—Felix T. McWhirter, Indianapolis; Charles Eckhart, Auburn. Iowa—O. D. Ellett, Marshalltown; K. W. Brown, Ames. Kansas—Earle R. De Lay, Emporia; J. N. Wood, Ottawa. Kentucky—Mrs. Frances E. Beauchamp, Louisville; T. B. Demaree, Wilmore. Louisiana—E. E. Israel, Baton Rouge. Maine—Nathan F. Woodbury, Auburn; Lyman B. Merritt, Houlton. Maryland—Finley C. Hendrickson, Cumberland; Geo. R. Gorsuch, Baltimore. Massachusetts—John M. Fisher, Attleboro; J. B. Lewis, Boston. Michigan—Samuel Dickey, Albion; Fred W. Corbett, Adrian. Minnesota—W. G. Calderwood, Minneapolis; Geo. W. Higgins, Minneapolis. Missouri— H. P. Faris, Clinton; Charles E. Stokes, Kansas City. Montana—Mrs. Kate M. Hamilton, Butte. Nebraska—A. G. Wolfenbarger, Lincoln; D. B. Gilbert, Fremont. New Hampshire—A. H. Morrill, Laconia; John S. Blanchard, Concord. New Jersey—Geo. J. Haven, Camden; Joel C. VanCise, Summit. New York—Clarence E. Pitts, Oswego; Geo. E. Stockwell, Fort Plain. North Carolina—J. M. Templeton, Cary; Thos. P. Johnson, Salisbury. North Dakota—Theo. E. Ostlund, Hillsboro; M. H. Kiff, Tower City. Ohio—F. M. Mecartney, Columbus; J. B. Martin, Cincinnati. Oklahoma—Charles Brown, Carmen; Rev. J. M. Monroe, Oklahoma City. Oregon—F. McKercher, Portland; W. P. Elmore, Brownsville. Pennsylvania—A. A. Stevens, Tyrone; David P. McCalmont, Franklin. Rhode Island—C. H. Tilley, Providence; Bernon E. Helme, Kingston. South Dakota—W. T. Raffety, Miller; Quincy Lee Morrow, Brookings. Tennessee—A. D. Reynolds, Bristol; J. B. Stinespring, Sandford. Texas—J. B. Cranfill, Dallas; Walter C. Swengel, Dallas. Vermont—H. S. Eldred, Sheldon; Dr. Hausen, Montpelier. Virginia—G. M. Smithdeal, Richmond; James W. Bodley, Staunton. Washington—Guy Posson, Seattle; R. E. Dunlop, Seattle. West Virginia—Edward W. Mills, Fairmont; U. A. Clayton, Fairmont. Wisconsin—W. D. Cox, Milwaukee. B. E. Van Keuren, Oshkosh. Wyoming—Lemuel L. Laughlin, Laramie; C. J. Sawyer, Laramie.

People's Party National Committee.

Chairman .... JAMES H. FERRISS, Joliet, Ill.
Vice-Chairman .... W. S. MORGAN, Hardy, Ark.
Secretary .... CHARLES Q. DE FRANCE, Lincoln, Neb.
Treasurer .... GEORGE F. WASHBURN, Boston, Mass.

Socialist Labor Party National Committee.

PAUL AUGUSTINE, National Secretary, 28 City Hall Place, New York City. The National Executive Committee is composed of Olive M. Johnson, Fruitvale, Cal.; Joseph Marek, New Haven, Conn.; G. A. Jenning, E. St. Louis, Ill.; Joseph Matz, Indianapolis, Ind.; J. H. Arnold, Louisville, Ky.; Arthur E. Reimer, So. Boston, Mass.; Herman Richter, Hamtramck, Mich.; J. W. Billings, Colorado; G. H. Campbell, Minnesota; Julius Eck, Hoboken, N. J.; C. F. Meier, Missouri; John Kircher, Cleveland, O.; Boris Reinstein, New York; A. S. Dowler, El Paso, Texas; Steve Brearcliff, Seattle, Wash.; Albert Schnabel, Wisconsin; J. E. Schmidt, Roanoke, Va.; J. A. McConnell, Pennsylvania.

The party is organized in local organizations known as "sections," such sections existing in thirty States. Any seven persons in any city or town of the United States may form a section, providing they acknowledge the platform and constitution of the Socialist Labor party and do not belong to any other political party. In places where no section exists, or where none can be formed, any person complying with the aforesaid provisions may become a member-at-large upon application to the National Executive Committee. Sections are not permitted to charge initiation fees. All questions of importance arising within the party are decided by general vote. At each meeting of the section a chairman is elected, and the same rule holds good with all standing committees.

Socialist Party National Committee.

J. MAHLON BARNES, National Secretary, 180 Washington Street, Chicago. This organization, known nationally as the Socialist Party, is officially known as the Social Democratic Party in Wisconsin, and the Public Ownership Party in Minnesota, to conform to the election laws in those States. The National Executive Committee is composed of seven men, elected by a national referendum of party members. The national secretary is elected in like manner. The term of office is one year The following are the members of the National Executive Committee: Victor L. Berger, Milwaukee, Wis. A. H. Floaten, Denver, Colo.; John M. Work, Des Moines, Ia.; Morris Hillquit, New York, N. Y.; A. M. Simons, Chicago, Ill.; Carl D. Thompson, Milwaukee; J. G. Phelps Stokes, Stamford, Ct. The National Committee is composed of representatives from each organized State or Territory, of which there are thirty-nine. Representation is as follows: "Each State or Territory shall be represented on the National Committee by one member and by an additional member for every one thousand members or major fraction thereof in good standing in the party." The apportionment is made by the national secretary at the beginning of each year, based upon the dues received from the respective States.

The Presidential Election of 1912.

THE next Presidential election will take place on Tuesday, November 5, 1912.

The President and Vice-President of the United States are chosen by officials termed "Electors" in each State, who are, under existing State laws, chosen by the qualified voters thereof by ballot, on the first Tuesday after the first Monday of November in every fourth year preceding the year in which the Presidential term expires.

The Constitution of the United States prescribes that each State shall "appoint," in such manner as the Legislature thereof may direct, a number of electors equal to the whole number of Senators and Representatives to which the State may be entitled in Congress; but no Senator or Representative or person holding an office of trust or profit under the United States shall be an elector. The Constitution requires that the day when electors are chosen shall be the same throughout the United States. At the beginning of our Government most of the electors were chosen by the Legislatures of their respective States, the people having no direct participation in their choice; and one State, South Carolina, continued that practice down to the breaking out of the civil war. But in all the States now the electors are, under the direction of State laws, chosen by the people on a general State ticket.

The manner in which the chosen electors meet and ballot for a President and Vice-President of the United States is provided for in Article XII. of the Constitution, and is as follows:

The electors shall meet in their respective States, and vote by ballot for President and Vice-President, one of whom, at least, shall not be an inhabitant of the same State with themselves; they shall name in their ballots the person voted for as President, and in distinct ballots the person voted for as Vice-President; and they shall make distinct lists of all persons voted for as President, and of all persons voted for as Vice-President, and of the number of votes for each, which lists they shall sign and certify, and transmit, sealed, to the seat of government of the United States, directed to the President of the Senate.

The same article then prescribes the mode in which the Congress shall count the ballots of the electors, and announce the result thereof, which is as follows:

The President of the Senate shall, in the presence of the Senate and House of Representatives, open all the certificates, and the votes shall then be counted; the person having the greatest number of votes for President shall be President, if such number be a majority of the whole number of electors appointed; and if no person have such majority, then from the persons having the highest numbers, not exceeding three, on the list of those voted for as President, the House of Representatives shall choose immediately, by ballot, the President. But in choosing the President the votes shall be taken by States, the representation from each State having one vote; a quorum for this purpose shall consist of a member or members from two-thirds of the States, and a majority of all the States shall be necessary to a choice. And if the House of Representatives shall not choose a President, whenever the right of choice shall devolve upon them, before the fourth day of March next following, then the Vice-President shall act as President, as in the case of the death or other constitutional disability of the President. The person having the greatest number of votes as Vice-President shall be the Vice-President, if such number be a majority of the whole number of electors appointed; and if no person have a majority, then from the two highest numbers on the list the Senate shall choose the Vice-President; a quorum for the purpose shall consist of two-thirds of the whole number of Senators, and a majority of the whole number shall be necessary to a choice.

The procedure of the two houses, in case the returns of the election of electors from any State are disputed, is provided in the "Electoral Count" act, passed by the Forty-ninth Congress. The act directs that the Presidential electors shall meet and give their votes on the second Monday in January next following their election. It fixes the time when Congress shall be in session to count the ballots as the second Wednesday in February succeeding the meeting of the electors.

The Constitution also defines who is eligible for President of the United States, as follows:

No person except a natural-born citizen or a citizen of the United States at the time of the adoption of this Constitution shall be eligible to the office of President; neither shall any person be eligible to that office who shall not have attained to the age of thirty-five years.

The qualifications for Vice-President are the same.

The Electoral Vote.

THE following was the electoral vote of the States in 1908 as based upon the Apportionment act of 1900:

STATES.	Electoral Votes.	STATES.	Electoral Votes.	STATES.	Electoral Votes.
Alabama	11	Maryland	8	Oregon	4
Arkansas	9	Massachusetts	16	Pennsylvania	34
California	10	Michigan	14	Rhode Island	4
Colorado	5	Minnesota	11	South Carolina	9
Connecticut	7	Mississippi	10	South Dakota	4
Delaware	3	Missouri	18	Tennessee	12
Florida	5	Montana	3	Texas	18
Georgia	13	Nebraska	8	Utah	3
Idaho	3	Nevada	3	Vermont	4
Illinois	27	New Hampshire	4	Virginia	12
Indiana	15	New Jersey	12	Washington	5
Iowa	13	New York	39	West Virginia	7
Kansas	10	North Carolina	12	Wisconsin	13
Kentucky	13	North Dakota	4	Wyoming	3
Louisiana	9	Ohio	23	Total	483
Maine	6	Oklahoma	7		

Electoral votes necessary to a choice 242

Oklahoma has been admitted to the Union since the last Presidential election with seven electoral votes, which are included in the above enumeration. Arizona having at the election of 1906 rejected joint statehood with New Mexico under the permissory act of Congress, neither will attain statehood before the presidential election of 1908, unless the Sixtieth Congress admits them separately during the year, in which case each will have three electoral votes, making 489 electoral votes in all, or 245 electoral votes necessary to a choice.

The States in the Presidential Elections, 1864 to 1908.

STATES.	1864	1868	1872	1876	1880	1884	1888	1892	1896	1900	1904	1908
Alabama	No vote	Rep.	Rep.	Dem.	Dem.	Dem.	Dem.	Dem.	Dem.	Dem.	Dem.	Dem.
Arkansas	No vote	Rep.	Rep.	Dem.	Dem.	Dem.	Dem.	Dem.	Dem.	Dem.	Dem.	Dem.
California	Rep.	Rep.	Rep.	Rep.	Split *g*	Rep.	Rep.	Split *h*	Split	Rep.	Rep.	Rep.
Colorado	......	......	......	Rep. *a*	Rep.	Rep.	Rep.	Pop.	Dem.	Dem.	Rep.	Dem.
Connecticut	Rep.	Rep.	Rep.	Dem.	Rep.	Dem.	Dem.	Dem.	Rep.	Rep.	Rep.	Rep.
Delaware	Dem.	Dem.	Rep.	Dem.	Dem.	Dem.	Dem.	Dem.	Rep.	Rep.	Rep.	Rep.
Florida	No vote	Dem. *a*	Rep.	Rep.	Dem.	Dem.	Dem.	Dem.	Dem.	Dem.	Dem.	Dem.
Georgia	No vote	Dem.	Dem.	Dem.	Dem.	Dem.	Dem.	Dem.	Dem.	Dem.	Dem.	Dem.
Idaho	......	......	......	......	......	......	......	Pop.	Dem.	Dem.	Rep.	Rep.
Illinois	Rep.	Rep.	Rep.	Rep.	Rep.	Rep.	Rep.	Dem.	Rep.	Rep.	Rep.	Rep.
Indiana	Rep.	Rep.	Rep.	Dem.	Rep.	Dem.	Rep.	Dem.	Rep.	Rep.	Rep.	Rep.
Iowa	Rep.	Rep.	Rep.	Rep.	Rep.	Rep.	Rep.	Rep.	Rep.	Rep.	Rep.	Rep.
Kansas	Rep.	Rep.	Rep.	Rep.	Rep.	Rep.	Rep.	Pop.	Dem.	Rep.	Rep.	Rep.
Kentucky	Dem.	Dem.	Dem.	Dem.	Dem.	Dem.	Dem.	Dem.	Split *b*	Dem.	Dem.	Dem.
Louisiana	No vote	Dem.	Rep.	Rep.	Dem.	Dem.	Dem.	Dem.	Dem.	Dem.	Dem.	Dem.
Maine	Rep.	Rep.	Rep.	Rep.	Rep.	Rep.	Rep.	Rep.	Rep.	Rep.	Rep.	Rep.
Maryland	Rep.	Dem.	Dem.	Dem.	Dem	Dem.	Dem.	Dem.	Rep.	Rep.	Split *j*	Split *k*
Massachusetts	Rep.	Rep.	Rep.	Rep.	Rep.	Rep.	Rep.	Rep.	Rep.	Rep.	Rep.	Rep.
Michigan	Rep.	Rep.	Rep.	Rep.	Rep.	Rep.	Rep.	Split *c*	Rep.	Rep.	Rep.	Rep.
Minnesota	Rep.	Rep.	Rep.	Rep.	Rep.	Rep.	Rep.	Rep.	Rep.	Rep.	Rep.	Rep.
Mississippi	No vote	No vote	Rep.	Dem.	Dem.	Dem.	Dem.	Dem.	Dem.	Dem.	Dem.	Dem.
Missouri	Rep.	Rep.	Dem.	Dem.	Dem.	Dem.	Dem.	Dem.	Dem.	Dem.	Rep.	Dem.
Montana	......	......	......	......	......	......	......	Rep.	Dem.	Dem.	Rep.	Rep.
Nebraska	......	Rep.	Rep.	Rep.	Rep.	Rep.	Rep.	Rep.	Dem.	Rep.	Rep.	Dem.
Nevada	Rep.	Rep.	Rep.	Rep.	Dem.	Rep.	Rep.	Pop.	Dem.	Dem.	Rep.	Rep.
New Hampshire	Rep.	Rep.	Rep.	Rep.	Rep.	Rep.	Rep.	Rep.	Rep.	Rep.	Rep.	Rep.
New Jersey	Dem.	Dem.	Rep.	Dem.	Dem.	Dem.	Dem.	Dem.	Rep.	Rep.	Rep.	Rep.
New York	Dem.	Dem.	Rep.	Dem.	Rep.	Dem.	Rep.	Dem.	Rep.	Rep.	Rep.	Rep.
North Carolina	Rep.	Rep.	Rep.	Dem.	Dem.	Dem.	Dem.	Dem.	Dem.	Dem.	Dem.	Dem.
North Dakota	......	......	......	......	......	......	......	Split *d*	Rep.	Rep.	Rep.	Dem.
Ohio	Rep.	Rep.	Rep.	Rep.	Rep.	Rep.	Rep.	Split *e*	Rep.	Rep.	Rep.	Rep.
Oklahoma	......	......	......	......	......	......	......	......	......	......	......	Dem.
Oregon	Rep.	Dem.	Rep.	Rep.	Rep.	Rep.	Rep.	Split *f*	Rep.	Rep.	Rep.	Rep.
Pennsylvania	Rep.	Rep.	Rep.	Rep.	Rep.	Rep.	Rep.	Rep.	Rep.	Rep.	Rep.	Rep.
Rhode Island	Rep.	Rep.	Rep.	Rep.	Rep.	Rep.	Rep.	Rep.	Rep.	Rep.	Rep.	Rep.
South Carolina	No vote	Rep.	Rep.	Rep.	Dem.	Dem.	Dem.	Dem.	Dem.	Dem.	Dem.	Dem.
South Dakota	......	......	......	......	......	......	......	Rep.	Dem.	Rep.	Rep.	Rep.
Tennessee	No vote	Rep.	Dem.	Dem.	Dem.	Dem.	Dem.	Dem.	Dem.	Dem.	Dem.	Dem.
Texas	No vote	No vote	Dem.	Dem.	Dem.	Dem.	Dem.	Dem.	Dem.	Dem.	Dem.	Dem.
Utah	......	......	......	......	......	......	......	......	Dem.	Rep.	Rep.	Rep.
Vermont	Rep.	Rep.	Rep.	Rep.	Rep.	Rep.	Rep.	Rep.	Rep.	Rep.	Rep.	Rep.
Virginia	No vote	No vote	Rep.	Dem.	Dem.	Dem.	Dem.	Dem.	Dem.	Dem	Dem.	Dem.
Washington	......	......	......	......	......	......	......	Rep.	Dem.	Rep.	Rep.	Rep.
West Virginia	Rep.	Rep.	Rep.	Dem.	Dem.	Dem.	Dem.	Dem.	Rep.	Rep.	Rep.	Rep.
Wisconsin	Rep.	Rep.	Rep.	Rep.	Rep.	Rep.	Rep.	Dem.	Rep.	Rep.	Rep.	Rep.
Wyoming	......	......	......	......	......	......	......	Rep.	Dem.	Rep.	Rep.	Rep.

a Electors chosen by the Legislature. *b* Rep., 12; Dem., 1. *c* Rep., 9; Dem., 5. *d* Rep., 1; Dem., 1. *e* Rep., 22; Dem., 1. *f* Rep., 3; People, 1. *g* Dem., 5; Rep., 1. *h* Dem., 8; Rep., 1. *i* Dem., 1; Rep., 8. *j* Dem., 7; Rep. 1. *k* Dem. 5; Rep. 3.

SALARY OF THE PRESIDENT.

The salary of the President of the United States was the cause of discussion in the First Congress, in view of the fact that the Constitution declared that the President should receive compensation for his services. Washington had notified his fellow citizens that he desired no salary. The limits suggested in Congress ranged from $15,000 to $70,000. The salary was finally placed at $25,000 and this remained the compensation until President Grant's second term (March 3, 1873), when it was increased to $50,000, the present sum. Chapter 2918 of the Laws of the Second Session of the Fifty-ninth Congress, Approved March 4, 1907, appropriated "for travelling expenses of the President of the United States, to be expended at his discretion and accounted for by his certificate solely, $25,000." This will probably be continued in the future. The appropriation for the care of the White House and its stable and greenhouses was in 1907, $50,000.

REFERENCE NOTES TO THE TWO FOLLOWING PAGES.

* The candidates starred were elected. (a) The first Republican Party is claimed by the present Democratic Party as its progenitor. (b) No candidate having a majority of the electoral vote, the House of Representatives elected Adams. (c) Candidate of the Anti-Masonic Party. (d) There being no choice, the Senate elected Johnson. (e) Eleven Southern States, being within the belligerent territory, did not vote. (f) Three Southern States disfranchised. (g) Horace Greeley died after election, and Democratic electors scattered their votes. (h) There being a dispute over the electoral vote of Florida, Louisiana, Oregon, and South Carolina, they were referred by Congress to an electoral commission composed of eight Republicans and seven Democrats, which, by a strict party vote, awarded 185 electoral votes to Hayes and 184 to Tilden. (i) Free Democrat. (j) Free Silver Prohibition Party. (k) In Massachusetts. There was also a Native American ticket in that State, which received 184 votes. (m) Middle of the Road or Anti-Fusion People's Party. (n) United Christian Party. (o) Union Reform Party.

For popular and electoral vote by States in 1900, 1904 and 1908 consult Index.

Presidential Elections

FROM 1789 TO 1908.

AGGREGATE POPULAR VOTE AND ELECTORAL VOTE FOR CANDIDATES FOR PRESIDENT AND VICE-PRESIDENT AT EACH ELECTION.

NOTE.—There is, properly speaking, no popular vote for President and Vice-President; the people vote for electors, and those chosen in each State meet therein and vote for the candidates for President and Vice-President. The record of any popular vote for electors prior to 1824 is so meagre and imperfect that a compilation would be useless. In most of the States, for more than a quarter century following the establishment of the Government, the State Legislatures "appointed" the Presidential electors, and the people therefore voted only indirectly for them, their choice being expressed by their votes for members of the Legislature. In this tabulation only the aggregate electoral votes for candidates for President and Vice-President in the first nine quadrennial elections appear.

ELECTORAL VOTES.

1789. Previous to 1804, each elector voted for two candidates for President. The one who received the largest number of votes was declared President, and the one who received the next largest number of votes was declared Vice-President. The electoral votes for the first President of the United States were: George Washington, 69; John Adams, of Massachusetts, 34; John Jay, of New York, 9; R. H. Harrison, of Maryland, 6; John Rutledge, of South Carolina, 6; John Hancock, of Massachusetts, 4; George Clinton, of New York, 3; Samuel Huntingdon, of Connecticut, 2; John Milton, of Georgia, 2; James Armstrong, of Georgia; Benjamin Lincoln, of Massachusetts, and Edward Telfair, of Georgia, 1 vote each. Vacancies (votes not cast), 4. George Washington was chosen President and John Adams Vice-President.

1792. George Washington, Federalist, received 132 votes; John Adams, Federalist, 77; George Clinton, of New York, Republican (a), 50; Thomas Jefferson, of Virginia, Republican, 4; Aaron Burr, of New York, Republican, 1 vote. Vacancies, 3. George Washington was chosen President and John Adams Vice-President.

1796. John Adams, Federalist, 71; Thomas Jefferson, Republican, 68; Thomas Pinckney, of South Carolina, Federalist, 59; Aaron Burr, of New York, Republican, 30; Samuel Adams, of Massachusetts, Republican, 15; Oliver Ellsworth, of Connecticut, Independent, 11; George Clinton, of New York, Republican, 7; John Jay, of New York, Federalist, 5; James Iredell, of North Carolina, Federalist, 3; George Washington, of Virginia; John Henry, of Maryland, and S. Johnson, of North Carolina, all Federalists, 2 votes each; Charles Cotesworth Pinckney, of South Carolina, Federalist, 1 vote. John Adams was chosen President and Thomas Jefferson Vice-President.

1800. Thomas Jefferson, Republican, 73; Aaron Burr, Republican, 73; John Adams, Federalist, 65; Charles C. Pinckney, Federalist, 64; John Jay, Federalist, 1 vote. There being a tie vote for Jefferson and Burr, the choice devolved upon the House of Representatives. Jefferson received the votes of ten States, which, being the largest vote cast for a candidate, elected him President. Burr received the votes of four States, which, being the next largest vote, elected him Vice-President. There were 2 blank votes.

1804. The Constitution of the United States having been amended, the electors at this election voted for a President and a Vice-President, instead of for two candidates for President. The result was as follows: For President, Thomas Jefferson, Republican, 162; Charles C. Pinckney, Federalist, 14. For Vice-President, George Clinton, Republican, 162; Rufus King, of New York, Federalist, 14. Jefferson was chosen President and Clinton Vice-President.

1808. For President: James Madison, of Virginia, Republican, 122; Charles C. Pinckney, of South Carolina, Federalist, 47; George Clinton, of New York, Republican, 6. For Vice-President, George Clinton, Republican, 113; Rufus King, of New York, Federalist, 47; John Langdon, of New Hampshire, 9; James Madison, 3; James Monroe, 3. Vacancy, 1. Madison was chosen President and Clinton Vice-President.

1812. For President, James Madison, Republican, 128; De Witt Clinton, of New York, Federalist, 89. For Vice-President, Elbridge Gerry, of Massachusetts, 131; Jared Ingersoll, of Pennsylvania, Federalist, 86. Vacancy, 1. Madison was chosen President and Gerry Vice-President.

1816. For President, James Monroe, of Virginia, Republican, 183; Rufus King, of New York, Federalist, 34. For Vice-President, Daniel D. Tompkins, of New York, Republican, 183; John Eager Howard, of Maryland, Federalist, 22; James Ross, of Pennsylvania, 5; John Marshall, of Virginia, 4; Robert G. Harper, of Maryland, 3. Vacancies, 4. Monroe was chosen President and Tompkins Vice-President.

1820. For President, James Monroe, of Virginia, Republican, 231; John Q. Adams, of Massachusetts, Republican, 1. For Vice-President, Daniel D. Tompkins, Republican, 218; Richard Stockton, of New Jersey, 8; Daniel Rodney, of Delaware, 4; Robert G. Harper, of Maryland, and Richard Rush, of Pennsylvania, 1 vote each. Vacancies, 3. James Monroe was chosen President and Daniel D. Tompkins Vice-President.

ELECTORAL AND POPULAR VOTES.

Year of Election.	Candidates for President.	States.	Political Party.	Popular Vote.	Plurality.	Electoral Vote.	Candidates for Vice-President.	States.	Political Party.	Electoral Vote.
1824	Andrew Jackson	Tenn.	Rep	155,872	50,551	(b) 99	John C. Calhoun*	S. C.	Rep	182
	John Q. Adams*	Mass.	Rep	105,321	....	84	Nathan Sanford	N. Y.	Rep	30
	Henry Clay	Ky	Rep	46,587	....	37	Nathaniel Macon	N. C.	Rep	24
	Wm. H. Crawford	Ga	Rep	44,282	....	41	Andrew Jackson	Tenn.	Rep	13
							M. Van Buren	N. Y.	Rep	9
							Henry Clay	Ky	Rep	2
1828	Andrew Jackson*	Tenn.	Dem	647,231	138,134	178	John C. Calhoun*	S. C.	Dem	171
	John Q. Adams	Mass.	Nat. R.	509,097	....	83	Richard Rush	Pa	Nat. R.	83
							William Smith	S. C.	Dem	7
1832	Andrew Jackson*	Tenn.	Dem	687,502	157,313	219	M. Van Buren*	N. Y.	Dem	189
	Henry Clay	Ky	Nat. R.	530,189	....	49	John Sergeant	Pa	Nat. R.	49
	John Floyd	Ga	Ind	} 33,108	....	11	Henry Lee	Mass	Ind	11
	William Wirt (c)	Md	Anti-M			7	Amos Ellmaker (c)	Pa	Anti-M	7
							Wm. Wilkins	Pa	Dem	30
1836	Martin Van Buren*	N. Y.	Dem	761,549	24,893	170	R. M. Johnson (d)*	Ky	Dem	147
	W. H. Harrison	O	Whig	} 736,656	....	73	Francis Granger	N. Y.	Whig	77
	Hugh L. White	Tenn.	Whig			26	John Tyler	Va	Whig	47
	Daniel Webster	Mass	Whig			14	William Smith	Ala	Dem	23
	Willie P. Mangum	N. C.	Whig			11				
1840	W. H. Harrison*	O	Whig	1,275,017	146,315	234	John Tyler*	Va	Whig	234
	Martin Van Buren	N. Y.	Dem	1,128,702	....	60	R. M. Johnson	Ky	Dem	48
	James G. Birney	N. Y.	Lib	7,059	....	..	L. W. Tazewell	Va	Dem	11
							James K. Polk	Tenn.	Dem	1
							Thomas Earle	Pa	Lib	..
1844	James K. Polk*	Tenn.	Dem	1,337,243	38,175	170	George M. Dallas*	Pa	Dem	170
	Henry Clay	Ky	Whig	1,299,068	....	105	T. Frelinghuysen	N. J.	Whig	105
	James G. Birney	N. Y.	Lib	62,300	....	..	Thomas Morris	O	Lib	..

Year of Election.	Candidates for President.	States.	Political Party.	Popular Vote.	Plurality.	Electoral Vote.	Candidates for Vice-President.	States.	Political Party.	Electoral Vote.
1848	Zachary Taylor*	La	Whig	1,360,101	139,557	163	Millard Fillmore*	N. Y.	Whig	163
	Lewis Cass	Mich	Dem	1,220,544	....	127	William O. Butler	Ky	Dem	127
	Martin Van Buren	N. Y.	F. Soil.	291,263	....	..	Charles F. Adams	Mass	F. Soil.	..
1852	Franklin Pierce*	N. H.	Dem	1,601,474	220,896	254	William R. King*	Ala	Dem	254
	Winfield Scott	N. J.	Whig	1,380,576	....	42	William A. Graham	N. C.	Whig	42
	John P. Hale	N. H.	F.D. (i)	156,149	....	..	George W. Julian	Ind	F. D.	..
	Daniel Webster (k)	Mass	Whig	1,670	....	..				
1856	James Buchanan*	Pa	Dem	1,838,169	496,905	174	J. C. Breckinridge*	Ky	Dem	174
	John C. Fremont	Cal	Rep	1,341,264	...	114	William L. Dayton	N. J.	Rep	114
	Millard Fillmore	N. Y.	Amer.	874,538	....	8	A. J. Donelson	Tenn	Amer.	8
1860	Abraham Lincoln*	Ill	Rep	1,866,352	491,195	180	Hannibal Hamlin*	Me	Rep	180
	Stephen A. Douglas	Ill	Dem	1,375,157	....	12	H. V. Johnson	Ga	Dem	12
	J. C. Breckinridge	Ky	Dem	845,763	....	72	Joseph Lane	Ore	Dem	72
	John Bell	Tenn	Union	589,581	....	39	Edward Everett	Mass	Union	39
1864	Abraham Lincoln*	Ill	Rep	2,216,067	407,342	e 212	Andrew Johnson*	Tenn	Rep	212
	George B. McClellan	N. J.	Dem	1,808,725	....	21	George H. Pendleton	O	Dem	21
1868	Ulysses S. Grant*	Ill	Rep	3,015,071	305,456	f 214	Schuyler Colfax*	Ind	Rep	214
	Horatio Seymour	N. Y.	Dem	2,709,615	....	80	F. P. Blair, Jr	Mo	Dem	80
1872	Ulysses S. Grant*	Ill	Rep	3,597,070	762,991	286	Henry Wilson*	Mass	Rep	286
	Horace Greeley	N. Y.	D. & L.	2,834,079	....	g ..	B. Gratz Brown	Mo	D. & L.	47
	Charles O'Conor	N. Y.	Dem	29,408	....	..	John Q. Adams	Mass	Dem	..
	James Black	Pa	Temp.	5,608	....	..	John Russell	Mich	Temp.	..
	Thomas A. Hendricks	Ind	Dem	....	....	42	George W. Julian	Ind	Lib.	5
	B. Gratz Brown	Mo	Dem	....	....	18	A. H. Colquitt	Ga	Dem	5
	Charles J. Jenkins	Ga	Dem	....	....	2	John M. Palmer	Ill	Dem	3
	David Davis	Ill	Ind.	....	....	1	T. E. Bramlette	Ky	Dem	3
							W. S. Groesbeck	O	Dem	1
							Willis B. Machen	Ky	Dem	1
							N. P. Banks	Mass	Lib.	1
1876	Samuel J. Tilden	N. Y.	Dem	4,284,885	250,935	184	T. A. Hendricks	Ind	Dem	184
	Rutherford B. Hayes*	O	Rep	4,033,950	....	h 185	William A. Wheeler*	N. Y.	Rep	185
	Peter Cooper	N. Y.	Gre'nb	81,740	....	..	Samuel F. Cary	O	Gre'nb	..
	Green Clay Smith	Ky	Pro	9,522	....	..	Gideon T. Stewart	O	Pro.	..
	James B. Walker	Ill	Amer.	2,636	....	..	D. Kirkpatrick	N. Y.	Amer.	..
1880	James A. Garfield*	O	Rep	4,449,053	7,018	214	Chester A. Arthur*	N. Y.	Rep	214
	W. S. Hancock	Pa	Dem	4,442,035	....	155	William H. English	Ind	Dem	155
	James B. Weaver	Iowa	Gre'nb	307,306	....	..	B. J. Chambers	Tex	Gre'nb	..
	Neal Dow	Me	Pro	10,305	....	..	H. A. Thompson	O	Pro.	..
	John W. Phelps	Vt	Amer.	707	....	..	S. C. Pomeroy	Kan	Amer.	..
1884	Grover Cleveland*	N. Y.	Dem	4,911,017	62,683	219	T. A. Hendricks*	Ind	Dem	219
	James G. Blaine	Me	Rep	4,848,334	....	182	John A. Logan	Ill	Rep	182
	John P. St. John	Kan	Pro	151,809	....	..	William Daniel	Md	Pro.	..
	Benjamin F. Butler	Mass	Gre'nb	133,825	....	..	A. M. West	Miss.	Gre'nb	..
	P. D. Wigginton	Cal	Amer.	....	....	..				
1888	Grover Cleveland	N. Y.	Dem	5,538,233	98,017	168	Allen G. Thurman	O	Dem	168
	Benjamin Harrison*	Ind	Rep	5,440,216	....	233	Levi P. Morton*	N. Y.	Rep	233
	Clinton B. Fisk	N. J.	Pro	249,907	....	..	John A. Brooks	Mo	Pro.	..
	Alson J. Streeter	Ill	U. L.	148,105	....	..	C. E. Cunningham	Ark	U. L.	..
	R. H. Cowdry	Ill	U'd L.	2,808	....	..	W. H. T. Wakefield	Kan	U'd L.	..
	James L. Curtis	N. Y.	Amer.	1,591	....	..	James B. Greer	Tenn	Amer.	..
1892	Grover Cleveland*	N. Y.	Dem	5,556,918	380,810	277	Adlai E. Stevenson*	Ill	Dem	277
	Benjamin Harrison	Ind	Rep	5,176,108	....	145	Whitelaw Reid	N. Y.	Rep	145
	James B. Weaver	Iowa	Peop	1,041,028	....	22	James G. Field	Va	Peop	22
	John Bidwell	Cal	Pro	264,133	....	..	James B. Cranfill	Tex	Pro.	..
	Simon Wing	Mass	Soc L.	21,164	....	..	Charles H. Matchett	N. Y.	Soc. L.	..
1896	William McKinley*	O	Rep	7,104,779	601,854	271	Garret A. Hobart*	N. J.	Rep.	271
	William J. Bryan	Neb	Dem. }	6,502,925	{	176	Arthur Sewall	Me	Dem	149
	William J. Bryan	Neb	Peop }		{	..	Thomas E. Watson	Ga	Peop	27
	Joshua Levering	Md	Pro	132,007	....	..	Hale Johnson	Ill	Pro	..
	John M. Palmer	Ill	N. Dem	133,148	....	..	Simon B. Buckner	Ky	N. Dem	..
	Charles H. Matchett	N. Y.	Soc. L.	36,274	....	..	Matthew Maguire	N. J.	Soc. L.	..
	Charles E. Bentley	Neb	Nat. (j)	13,969	....	..	James H. Southgate	N. C.	Nat. (j)	..
1900	William McKinley*	O	Rep	7,207,923	849,790	292	Theodore Roosevelt*	N. Y.	Rep	292
	William J. Bryan	Neb	Dem. P	6,358,133	....	155	Adlai E. Stevenson	Ill	Dem. P	155
	John G. Woolley	Ill	Pro	208,914	....	..	Henry B. Metcalf	O	Pro	..
	Wharton Barker	Pa	MP(m)	50,373	....	..	Ignatius Donnelly	Minn	MP(m)	..
	Eugene V. Debs	Ind	Soc. D.	87,814	....	..	Job Harriman	Cal	Soc. D.	..
	Jos. F. Malloney	Mass	Soc. L.	39,739	....	..	Valentine Remmel	Pa	Soc. L.	..
	J. F. R. Leonard	Ia	U C (n)	1,059	....	..	John G. Woolley	Ill	U C (n)	..
	Seth H. Ellis	O	U R (o)	5,698	....	..	Samuel T. Nicholson	Pa	U R (o)	..
1904	Theodore Roosevelt*	N. Y.	Rep	7,623,486	2,545,515	336	Charles W. Fairbanks*	Ind	Rep	336
	Alton B. Parker	N. Y.	Dem	5,077,971	....	140	Henry G. Davis	W. Va.	Dem	140
	Eugene V. Debs	Ind	Soc	402,283	....	..	Benjamin Hanford	N. Y.	Soc	..
	Silas C. Swallow	Pa	Pro	258,536	....	..	George W. Carroll	Tex	Pro	..
	Thomas E. Watson	Ga	Peop	117,183	....	..	Thomas H. Tibbles	Neb	Peop	..
	Charles H. Corrigan	N. Y.	Soc. L.	31,249	....	..	William W. Cox	Ill.	Soc. L.	..
1908†	William H. Taft*	O	Rep	7,061,875	1,045,715	303	James S. Sherman	N. Y.	Rep	321
	William J. Bryan	Neb	Dem	6,015,160	....	180	John W. Kern	Ind	Dem	162
	Eugene V. Debs	Ind	Soc	482,000	....	..	Benjamin Hanford	N. Y.	Soc	..
	Eugene W. Chafin	...	Pro.	260,000	....	..	Aaron S. Watkins	..	Pro	..
	Thos. E. Watson	Ga	Peo	90,000	....	..	Samuel Williams	Ind	Peo	..
	August Gillhaus	N. Y.	Soc. L.	32,000	....	..	Donald L. Munro	Va	Soc. L.	.
	Thos. L. Hisgen	Mass	Ind	....	....	..	John Temple Graves	Ga	Ind	..

* The candidates starred were elected. † Estimated vote.

THE PRESIDENTS OF THE UNITED STATES—THEIR BIOGRAPHIES IN BRIEF.

(Compiled for THE WORLD ALMANAC from published memoirs, newspaper records, and personal correspondence with the families of the ex-Presidents. The references will be found on second following page.)

No.	Full Name.	Paternal Ancestry.	Parentage—Father.	Father's Vocation.	Parentage—Mother.
1..	George Washington	English	Augustine Washington	Planter	Mary Ball.
2..	John [illegible]ms	English	John Adams	Farmer	Susanna Boylston.
3..	Thomas Jefferson	Welsh	Peter Jefferson	Planter	Jane Randolph.
4..	James Madison	English	James Madison	[illegible]er	Nelly Conway.
5..	James Monroe	Scotch	Spence Monroe	Planter	Eliza Jones.
6..	John Quincy Adams	English	John Adams	Lawyer	Abigail [illegible]ith.
7..	Andrew Jackson	Scotch-Irish	[illegible] Jackson	Farmer	Elizabeth Hutchinson.
8..	Martin Van Buren	Dutch	Abraham Van Buren	Farmer	Maria Hoes.
9..	William [illegible]ry Harrison	English	Benjamin Harrison	Statesman	Elizabeth [illegible]ett.
10..	John Tyler	English	John Tyler	Jurist	Mary Armistead.
11..	James Knox Polk	Scotch-Irish	Samuel Polk	Farmer	Jane Knox.
12..	Zachary Taylor	English	Richard Taylor	Planter	Sarah Strother.
13..	Millard Fillmore	English	Nathaniel Fillmore	Farmer	[illegible]be Millard.
14..	Franklin Pierce	English	Benjamin Pierce	Farmer	Anna Kendrick.
15..	James Buchanan	Scotch-Irish	James Buchanan	Merchant	Elizabeth Speer.
16..	Abraham Lincoln	English	[illegible]as Lincoln	Farmer	Nancy Hanks.
17..	Andrew Johnson	English	Jacob Johnson	Sexton and Constable	Mary McDonough.
18..	Ulysses Simpson Grant	Scotch	Jesse Root Grant	[illegible]er	Harriet Simpson.
19..	Rutherford [illegible]d Hayes	Scotch	Rutherford Hayes	Merchant	[illegible]ia Birchard.
20..	James Abram Garfield	English	Abram Garfield	Farmer	Eliza Ballou.
21..	Chester Alan Arthur	Scotch-Irish	William Arthur	Clergyman	Malvina Stone.
22, 24..	Grover Cleveland	English	Richard Falley Cleveland	Clergyman	Anna Neal.
23..	Benjamin Harrison	English	[illegible]n Scott Harrison	Farmer	Elizabeth F. Irwin.
25..	William McKinley	Scotch-Irish	[illegible]	Iron Manufacturer	Nancy C. [illegible]in.
26..	Theodore Roosevelt	Dutch	Theodore Roosevelt	Merchant	[illegible]ha Bullock.
27..	William Howard Taft (elect.)	English	Alphonso Taft	Lawyer	Louise M. Torrey.

No.	President.	Birth. (Time.)	Birth. (Place).	Vocation. In Early Life.	Vocation. When Elected.	College.	Year of Grad.‡
1..	Washington..	February 22, 1732	[illegible]ar Bridges Creek, Westmoreland Co., Va.	Surveyor	Planter	None	....
2..	J. Adams	[illegible]er 30, 1735	[illegible]y, Norfolk [illegible], Mass	Teacher	Lawyer	Harvard	1755
3..	Jefferson	April 13, [illegible]3	Shadwell, Albemarle [illegible], Va.	Lawyer	Lawyer	William and Mary.	1762
4..	Madison	March 16, 1751	Port [illegible], King George [illegible], Va.	Lawyer	Lawyer	Princeton	1771
5..	Monroe	April 28, 1758	Head of Monroe's [illegible], Westmoreland Co., Va	Lawyer	St'sman*	William and Mary	1776
6..	J. Q. Adams.	July 11, 1767	[illegible]y, Norfolk County, Mass	Lawyer	Lawyer	Harvard	1787
7..	Jackson	March 15, 1767	Near Cureton's Pond, Union [illegible], N. C.†	Lawyer	Lawyer	None	....
8..	Van Buren	December 5, 1782	Kinderhook, [illegible], N. Y	Lawyer	Lawyer	None	....
9..	Harrison	February 9, [illegible]3	Berkeley, [illegible]es City [illegible], Va	Soldier	Farmer	Hampden-Sydney.	1790
10..	Tyler	March 29, [illegible]0	Greenway, Charles City [illegible], Va	Lawyer	Lawyer	William and Mary.	1807
11..	Polk	[illegible] 2, 1795	Near Pineville, Mecklenburg Co., N. C.	Lawyer	Lawyer	Uni. of N. Carolina	1818
12..	Taylor	November 24, 1784	[illegible] C. H., Orange [illegible], Va.	Soldier	Soldier	None	....
13..	Fillmore	January 7, 1800	Summerhill, [illegible]ga County, N. Y	Tailor	Lawyer	[illegible]	....
14..	Pierce	November 23, 1804	Hillsborough, Hillsborough [illegible], N. H.	Lawyer	[illegible]	Bowdoin	1824
15..	Buchanan	April 23, 1791	[illegible] Gap, Franklin [illegible], Pa	Lawyer	Lawyer	Dickinson	1809
16..	Lincoln	[illegible]ary 12, [illegible]09	Near Hodgenville, Larue [illegible], Ky	F'm-ha'd	Lawyer	None	....
17..	Johnson	[illegible]ber 29, 1808	Raleigh, Wake County, N. C.	Tailor	St'sman	None	....
18..	Grant	April 27, 1822	Point Pleasant, Clermont [illegible], O	Soldier	Soldier	West Point	1843
19..	Hayes	October 4, 1822	Delaware, Del ware County, O.	Lawyer	Lawyer	Kenyon	1842
20..	Garfield	[illegible]er 19, 1831	Orange [illegible], Cuyahoga [illegible], O.	Teacher	Lawyer	[illegible]s	1856
21..	Arthur	[illegible] 5, 1830	Fairfield, Franklin [illegible], Vt.	Teacher	Lawyer	Union	1848
22, 24..	Cleveland	March 18, 1837	Caldwell, Essex County, N. J	Teacher	Lawyer	[illegible]one	....
23..	B Harrison	A[illegible]ust 20, 1833	North Bend, Hamilton [illegible], O.	Lawyer	Lawyer	Miami University.	1853
25..	McKinley	January 29, 1843	Niles, Trumbull [illegible], O.	Lawyer	Lawyer	None	....
26..	Roosevelt	[illegible]er 27, 1858	28 E 20th St., [illegible] City, N. Y	Publicist	Pub. offi'l	Harvard	1880
27..	Taft (elect.)	September 15, 1857	Cincinnati, Ohio	[illegible]	Lawyer	Yale	1878

THE PRESIDENTS OF THE UNITED STATES—*Continued.*

No.	PRESIDENT.	Married.	Wife's Name.	Wife Born.	Wife Died.	Sons.	Dau.	Home When Elected.	Politics.	Inaug.	Age	Years.
1..	Washington....	1759....	Martha (Dandridge) Custis§	1732......	1802......	..	..	Mount Vernon, Va.......	Federalist	1789	57	7 y. 10 mo. 4 d.
2..	J. Adams	1764....	Abigail Smith	1744......	1818......	3	2	Quincy, Mass.............	Federalist.........	1797	61	4
3..	Jefferson.......	1772....	Martha (Wayles) Skelton§	1748......	1782......	1	5	Monticello, Va.........	Republican (a)...	1801	57	8
4..	Madison	1794....	Dolly (Payne) Todd§	1772......	1849......	..	..	Montpelier, Va.........	Republican.......	1809	57	8
5..	Monroe	1786....	Eliza Kortwright	1768......	1830......	..	2	Oak Hill, Va...........	Republican........	1817	58	8
6..	J. Q. Adams....	1797....	Louisa Catherine Johnson	1775......	1852......	3	1	Quincy, Mass............	Republican (b)...	1825	57	4
7..	Jackson........	1791	Rachel (Donelson) Robards‖	1767......	1828......	..	..	Hermitage, Tenn........	Democrat.........	1829	61	8
8..	Van Buren.....	1807....	Hannah Hoes	1783......	1819......	4	..	Kinderhook, N. Y.......	Democrat.........	1837	54	4
9..	Harrison........	1795....	Anna Symmes	1775......	1864......	6	4	North Bend, O..........	Whig	1841	68	1 mo.
10..	Tyler	1813....	Letitia Christian	1790......	1842......	3	4	Williamsburg, Va........	Democrat.	1841	51	3 y. 11 mo.
		1844....	Julia Gardiner	1820......	1889......	5	2					
11..	Polk	1824....	Sarah Childress	1803......	1891......	..	..	Nashville, Tenn	Democrat..........	1845	49	4
12..	Taylor..........	1810....	Margaret Smith	1788......	1852......	1	3	Baton Rouge, La..........	Whig..............	1849	64	1 y. 4 mo. 5 d.
13..	Fillmore	1826....	Abigail Powers	1798......	1853......	1	1	Buffalo, N. Y............	Whig..............	1850	50	2 y. 7 mo. 26 d.
		1858....	Caroline (Carmichael) McIntosh§	1813	1881......	..	..					
14..	Pierce..........	1834....	Jane Means Appleton	1806......	1863......	3	..	Concord, N. H............	Democrat..........	1853	48	4
15..	Buchanan......	....	....	......	......	..	..	Wheatland, Pa............	Democrat..........	1857	65	4
16..	Lincoln	1842....	Mary Todd	1818......	1882......	4	..	Springfield, Ill...........	Republican........	1861	52	4 y. 1 mo. 11 d.
17..	Johnson	1827....	Eliza McCardle	1810......	1876......	3	2	Greenville, Tenn..........	Republican........	1865	56	3 y. 10 mo. 19 d.
18..	Grant..........	1848....	Julia Dent	1826......	1902......	3	1	Washington, D. C.........	Republican........	1869	46	8
19..	Hayes..........	1852....	Lucy Ware Webb	1831......	1889......	7	1	Fremont, O...............	Republican........	1877	54	4
20..	Garfield	1858....	Lucretia Rudolph	1832......	......	4	1	Mentor, O	Republican........	1881	49	6½ mo.
21..	Arthur.........	1859....	Ellen Lewis Herndon	1837......	1880......	1	1	New York City	Republican........	1881	50	3 y. 5½ mo.
22..	Cleveland	1886....	Frances Folsom	1864......	......	1	3	Buffalo, N. Y............	Democrat..........	1885	47	4
23..	B. Harrison....	1853....	Caroline Lavinia Scott	1832......	1892......	1	1	Indianapolis, Ind........	Republican........	1889	55	4
		1896....	Mary Scott (Lord) Dimmick§	1858......	......	..	1					
24..	Cleveland......	....	(See above.)	......	......	..	..	New York City	Democrat..........	1893	56	4
25..	McKinley......	1871....	Ida Saxton	1844......	1907......	..	2	Canton, O	Republican........	1897	53	7 y. 6 mo. 10 d.
26..	Roosevelt......	1883....	Alice Lee	......	1884......	..	1	Oyster Bay, N. Y.........	Republican........	1901	42	......
		1886....	Edith Kermit Garow	......	......	4	1					
27..	Taft (elect.)...	1886....	Helen Herron	......	......	2	1	Cincinnati, O.............	Republican........	1909	51	......

No.	PRESIDENT.	Time of Death.	Age.	Cause of Death.	Place of Death.	Place of Burial.	Religious Connection.
1..	Washington....	December 14, 1799..	67	Pneumonia	Mount Vernon, Va.	Mount Vernon, Va.	Episcopalian.
2..	J. Adams	July 4, 1826	90	Debility	Quincy, Mass.	First Congregational Church, Quincy, Mass.	Congregationalist.
3..	Jefferson	July 4, 1826	83	Chronic Diarrhœa	Monticello, Va.	Monticello, Albemarle Co., Va.	Liberal (c).
4..	Madison.......	June 28, 1836	85	Debility	Montpelier, Va.	Montpelier, Hanover Co., Va.	Episcopalian.
5..	Monroe........	July 4, 1831	73	Debility	New York City	Hollywood Cemetery, Richmond, Va.	Episcopalian.
6..	J. Q. Adams....	February 23, 1848..	80	Paralysis	Washington, D. C.	First Congregational Church, Quincy, Mass.	Congregationalist.
7..	Jackson	June 8, 1845	78	Consumption	Hermitage, Tenn.	Hermitage, near Nashville, Tenn.	Presbyterian.
8..	Van Buren	July 24, 1862	79	Asthmatic Catarrh	Lindenwold, N. Y.	Cemetery, Kinderhook, N. Y.	Reformed Dutch.
9..	Harrison	April 4, 1841	68	Bilious Pleurisy	Washington, D. C.	North Bend, Hamilton Co., O.	Episcopalian.
10..	Tyler	January 17, 1862	71	Bilious Attack	Richmond, Va.	Hollywood Cemetery, Richmond, Va.	Episcopalian.
11..	Polk	June 15, 1849	53	Chronic Diarrhœa	Nashville, Tenn.	Polk Place, Nashville, Tenn.	Presbyterian.
12..	Taylor	July 9, 1850	65	Bilious Fever	Washington, D. C.	Springfield, 5 miles from Louisville, Ky.	Episcopalian.
13..	Fillmore	March 9, 1874	74	Debility	Buffalo, N. Y.	Forest Lawn Cemetery, Buffalo, N. Y.	Unitarian.
14..	Pierce..........	October 8, 1869	64	Inflammation of Stomach	Concord, N. H.	Minot Lot, Old Cemetery, Concord, N. H.	Episcopalian.
15..	Buchanan	June 1, 1868	77	Rheumatic Gout	Wheatland, Pa.	Woodward Hill Cemetery, Lancaster, Pa.	Presbyterian.
16..	Lincoln	April 15, 1865	56	Assassination	Washington, D. C.	Oak Ridge Cemetery, Springfield, Ill.	Presbyterian.
17..	Johnson........	July 31, 1875	66	Paralysis	Carter's Depot, Tenn.	Greenville, Greene Co., Tenn.	Methodist (d).
18..	Grant..........	July 23, 1885	63	Cancer	Mt. McGregor, N. Y.	Riverside Park, New York City	Methodist.
19..	Hayes..........	January 17, 1893	70	Paralysis of the Heart	Fremont, O.	Cemetery, Fremont, O.	Methodist.
20..	Garfield	September 19, 1881..	49	Assassination	Long Branch, N. J.	Lake View Cemetery, Cleveland, O.	Disciples.
21..	Arthur	November 17, 1886..	56	Bright's Disease	New York City	Rural Cemetery, Albany, N. Y.	Episcopalian.
22, 24..	Cleveland	June 24, 1908	71	Debility	Princeton, N. J.	Cemetery, Princeton, N. J.	Presbyterian.
23..	B. Harrison	March 13, 1901	67	Pneumonia	Indianapolis, Ind.	Crown Hill Cemetery, Indianapolis, Ind.	Presbyterian.
25..	McKinley	September 14, 1901..	57	Assassination	Buffalo, N. Y.	Cemetery, Canton, O.	Methodist.
26..	Roosevelt	....	..	....	....	....	Reformed Dutch.
27..	Taft (elect.)....	....	..	....	....	....	Unitarian..........

NOTES TO THE TABLES OF THE PRESIDENTS, ON THE TWO PRECEDING PAGES.

* Monroe abandoned the profession of law when a young man, and was afterward, and until his election, always holding public office. † Jackson called himself a South Carolinian, and his biographer, Kendall, recorded his birthplace in Lancaster Co., S. C.; but Parton has published documentary evidence to show that Jackson was born in Union Co., N. C., less than a quarter mile from the South Carolina line. ‡ Or of departure from college.

§ Widows. Their maiden names are in parentheses. ‖ She was the divorced wife of Captain Robards. (*a*) The Democratic party of to-day claims lineal descent from the first Republican party, and President Jefferson as its founder. (*b*) Political parties were disorganized at the time of the election of John Quincy Adams. He claimed to be a Republican, but his doctrines were decidedly Federalistic. The opposition to his Administration took the name of Democrats, and elected Jackson President. (*c*) Randall, the biographer of Jefferson, declares that he was a believer in Christianity, although not a sectarian. (*d*) While President Johnson was not a church-member, he was a Christian believer. His wife was a Methodist.

Washington's first inauguration was in New York, and his second in Philadelphia. Adams was inaugurated in Philadelphia, and Jefferson and the Presidents following elected by the people, in the City of Washington. Arthur took the Presidential oath of office first in New York City. John Adams and Jefferson died on the same day, the Fourth of July, 1826, and Monroe died on the Fourth of July five years later. John Quincy Adams was a Representative and Andrew Johnson a Senator in Congress after the expiration of their Presidential terms, and both died while holding those offices. Tyler was a Representative in the Confederate Congress from Virginia, and died in office

Lincoln, Garfield and McKinley were assassinated while in office. Lincoln at Ford's Theatre, Washington, D. C., April 14, 1865, from a pistol shot fired by John Wilkes Booth, who was killed near Fredericksburg, Va., April 26, 1865, by Sergeant Boston Corbett. Garfield was shot in the Pennsylvania Railroad Depot, Washington, D. C., July 2, 1881, and died at Elberon, Long Branch, N. J., September 19, 1881. The assassin was Charles Jules Guiteau, who was hanged at Washington, D. C., June 30, 1882. McKinley was shot twice September 6, 1901, while in the Temple of Music of the Pan-American Exposition, Buffalo, N. Y., and died from his wounds at the home of John G. Milburn, Buffalo, September 14, 1901. The assassin was Louis Czolgosz, who was electrocuted at Auburn State Prison, New York, October 29, 1901.

Jackson was shot at in the Capitol at Washington, D. C., January 29, 1835, by a house painter named Richard Lawrence, escaping because the pistol of the assassin missed fire.

Cleveland after taking the oath as President, kissed the open bible, his lips touching Psalm CXII, verses 5-10, inclusive. Garfield's first act after taking the oath was to kiss his mother.

The sixth President was the son of the second President, and the twenty-third President was the grandson of the ninth President. William Henry Harrison was the eighth and Benjamin Harrison the tenth in descent from Pocahontas and John Rolfe. Lincoln was the first President wearing a full beard, Grant the first wearing a mustache. Buchanan and Cleveland were bachelors when they entered the White House as Presidents, but Cleveland surrendered during his first term. Washington, Madison, Monroe, Pierce and Hayes were born on Friday. J. Q. Adams, Pierce, Garfield and McKinley (second term), were inaugurated on Friday. Tyler, Polk, Pierce and Arthur died on Friday. Lincoln was assassinated on Friday.

There were remarkable coincidences in the lives of Abraham Lincoln and Jefferson Davis. Both were born in Kentucky; Lincoln in 1809, Davis in 1808. Both removed from their native State in childhood, Lincoln to the Northwest, Davis to the Southwest. Lincoln was a Captain of Volunteers and Davis a Second Lieutenant of Regulars in the Black Hawk War of 1832. They began their political careers the same year, 1844, Lincoln being a Presidential Elector for Clay, and Davis for Polk. They were elected to Congress about the same time, 1845 and 1846. They were called to preside over their respective governments the same year and within a few days; Davis, February 8, 1861, Lincoln, March 4, 1861.

Washington, Monroe, and Jackson were soldiers in the Revolutionary War; Jackson, W. H. Harrison, Tyler, Taylor, and Buchanan in the War of 1812-15; Lincoln in the Black Hawk War; Taylor, Pierce, and Grant in the Mexican War; Grant, Hayes, Garfield, Arthur, B. Harrison, and McKinley in the Civil War, and Roosevelt was in the War with Spain. Adams and Jefferson were signers of the Declaration of Independence, and Washington and Madison of the Constitution.

Grant was christened Hiram Ulysses and Cleveland Stephen Grover. W. H. Harrison was the oldest man elected to the Presidency, and Grant the youngest, but Roosevelt was the youngest to become President. Cleveland was the only President married in the White House, and his second daughter the only President's child born therein. Grant's daughter (Mrs. Sartoris), and Roosevelt's daughter (Mrs. Longworth), were the only children of Presidents married therein. Wives of Tyler and Benjamin Harrison died in the White House. W. H. Harrison was father of the largest family, six sons and four daughters.

THE PRESIDENTIAL SUCCESSION.

The Presidential succession is fixed by chapter 4 of the acts of the Forty-ninth Congress, first session. In case of the removal, death, resignation, or inability of both the President and Vice-President, then the Secretary of State shall act as President until the disability of the President or Vice-President is removed or a President is elected. If there be no Secretary of State, then the Secretary of the Treasury will act; and the remainder of the order of succession is as follows: The Secretary of War, Attorney-General, Postmaster-General, Secretary of the Navy, and Secretary of the Interior. The Secretary of Agriculture and Secretary of Commerce and Labor were added by subsequent enactment. The acting President must, upon taking office, convene Congress, if not at the time in session, in extraordinary session, giving twenty days' notice. This act applies only to such Cabinet officers as shall have been confirmed by the Senate and are eligible under the Constitution to the Presidency.

Vice-Presidents of the United States.

	Name.	Birthplace.	Year.	Paternal Ancestry.	Residence.	Qualified.	Politics.	Place of Death.	Year.	Age at Death.
1	John Adams	Quincy, Mass	1735	English	Mass.	1789	Fed	Quincy, Mass	1826	90
2	Thomas Jefferson	Shadwell, Va	1743	Welsh	Va	1797	Rep	Monticello, Va	1826	83
3	Aaron Burr	Newark, N. J	1756	English	N. Y.	1801	Rep	Staten Island, N. Y.	1836	80
4	George Clinton	Ulster Co., N. Y	1739	English	N. Y.	1805	Rep	Washington, D. C.	1812	73
5	Elbridge Gerry	Marblehead, Mass	1744	English	Mass.	1813	Rep	Washington, D. C.	1814	70
6	Daniel D. Tompkins	Scarsdale, N. Y	1774	English	N. Y.	1817	Rep	Staten Island, N. Y.	1825	51
7	John C. Calhoun	Abbeville, S. C.	1782	Scotch-Irish	S. C.	1825	Rep	Washington, D. C.	1850	68
8	Martin Van Buren	Kinderhook, N. Y.	1782	Dutch	N. Y.	1833	Dem.	Kinderhook, N. Y.	1862	79
9	Richard M. Johnson	Louisville, Ky	1780	English	Ky	1837	Dem.	Frankfort, Ky	1850	70
10	John Tyler	Greenway, Va	1790	English	Va	1841	Dem.	Richmond, Va	1862	72
11	George M. Dallas	Philadelphia, Pa	1792	English	Pa	1845	Dem.	Philadelphia, Pa	1864	72
12	Millard Fillmore	Summerhill, N. Y.	1800	English	N. Y.	1849	Whig.	Buffalo, N. Y	1874	74
13	William R. King	Sampson Co., N. C.	1786	English	Ala.	1853	Dem.	Dallas Co., Ala	1853	67
14	John C. Breckinridge	Lexington, Ky	1821	Scotch	Ky	1857	Dem.	Lexington, Ky	1875	54
15	Hannibal Hamlin	Paris, Me	1809	English	Me	1861	Rep	Bangor, Me.	1891	81
16	Andrew Johnson	Raleigh, N. C	1808	English	Tenn.	1865	Rep	Carter Co., Tenn	1875	66
17	Schuyler Colfax	New York City, N. Y.	1823	English	Ind.	1869	Rep	Mankato, Minn	1885	62
18	Henry Wilson	Farmington, N. H.	1812	English	Mass.	1873	Rep	Washington, D. C.	1875	63
19	William A. Wheeler	Malone, N. Y	1819	English	N. Y.	1877	Rep	Malone, N. Y.	1887	68
20	Chester A. Arthur	Fairfield, Vt	1830	Scotch-Irish	N. Y.	1881	Rep	New York City, N.Y.	1886	56
21	Thos. A. Hendricks	Muskingum Co., O.	1819	Scotch-Irish	Ind.	1885	Dem.	Indianapolis, Ind	1885	66
22	Levi P. Morton	Shoreham, Vt	1824	Scotch	N. Y.	1889	Rep	....	....	..
23	Adlai E. Stevenson	Christian Co., Ky	1835	Scotch-Irish	Ill.	1893	Dem.	....	....	..
24	Garret A. Hobart	Long Branch, N. J	1841	English	N. J.	1897	Rep	Paterson, N. J	1899	55
25	Theodore Roosevelt	New York City, N. Y.	1858	Dutch	N. Y.	1901	Rep	....	....	..
26	Charles W. Fairbanks	Unionville Center, O.	1852	English	Ind.	1905	Rep	....	....	..
27	James S. Sherman (elect)	Utica, N. Y	1855	English	N. Y.	1909	Rep	....	....	..

Presidents pro tempore of the United States Senate.

Congress.	Years.	Name.	State.	Born.	Died.	Congress.	Years.	Name.	State.	Born.	Died.
1, 2	1789-92	John Langdon	N. H.	1739	1819	19, 20	1826-28	Nathaniel Macon	N. C.	1757	1837
2	1792	Richard H. Lee	Va	1732	1794	20-22	1828-32	Samuel Smith	Md	1752	1839
2, 3	1792-94	John Langdon	N. H.	1739	1819	22	1832	L. W. Tazewell	Va	1774	1860
3	1794-95	Ralph Izard	S. C.	1742	1804	22, 23	1832-34	Hugh L. White	Tenn.	1773	1840
3, 4	1795-96	Henry Tazewell	Va	1753	1799	23	1834-35	George Poindexter	Miss.	1779	1853
4	1796-97	Samuel Livermore	N. H.	1732	1803	24	1835-36	John Tyler	Va	1790	1862
4, 5	1797	William Bingham	Pa	1751	1804	24-26	1836-41	William R. King	Ala.	1786	1853
5	1797	William Bradford	R. I.	1729	1808	26, 27	1841-42	Saml. L. Southard	N. J.	1787	1842
5	1797-98	Jacob Read	S. C.	1752	1816	27-29	1842-46	W. P. Mangum	N. C.	1792	1861
5	1798	Theo. Sedgwick	Mass.	1746	1813	29, 30	1846-49	D. R. Atchison	Mo	1807	1886
5	1798-99	John Laurence	N. Y.	1750	1810	31, 32	1850-52	William R. King	Ala.	1786	1853
5	1799	James Ross	Pa	1762	1847	32, 33	1852-54	D. R. Atchison	Mo.	1807	1886
6	1799-1800	Samuel Livermore	N. H.	1732	1808	33, 34	1854-57	Jesse D. Bright	Ind.	1812	1875
6	1800	Uriah Tracy	Ct.	1755	1807	34	1857	James M. Mason	Va	1798	1871
6	1800-1801	John E. Howard	Md	1752	1827	35, 36	1857-61	Benj. Fitzpatrick	Ala.	1802	1869
6	1801	James Hillhouse	Ct.	1754	1832	36-38	1861-64	Solomon Foot	Vt.	1802	1866
7	1801-02	Abraham Baldwin	Ga	1754	1807	38	1864-65	Daniel Clark	N. H.	1809	1891
7	1802-03	Stephen R. Bradley	Vt	1754	1830	39	1865-67	Lafayette S. Foster	Ct.	1806	1880
8	1803-04	John Brown	Ky	1757	1837	40	1867-69	Benjamin F. Wade	Ohio	1800	1878
8	1804-05	Jesse Franklin	N. C.	1758	1823	41, 42	1869-73	Henry B. Anthony	R. I.	1815	1884
8	1805	Joseph Anderson	Tenn.	1757	1837	43	1873-75	M. H. Carpenter	Wis.	1824	1881
9, 10	1805-08	Samuel Smith	Md.	1752	1839	44, 45	1875-79	Thomas W. Ferry	Mich.	1827	1896
10	1808-09	Stephen R. Bradley	Vt	1754	1830	46	1879-81	A. G. Thurman	Ohio	1813	1895
10, 11	1809	John Milledge	Ga.	1757	1818	47	1881	Thomas F. Bayard	Del.	1828	1898
11	1809-10	Andrew Gregg	Pa	1755	1835	47	1881-83	David Davis	Ill.	1815	1886
11	1810-11	John Gaillard	S. C.	1765	1826	48	1883-85	Geo. F. Edmunds	Vt	1828	....
11, 12	1811-12	John Pope	Ky	1770	1845	49	1885-87	John Sherman	Ohio.	1823	1900
12, 13	1812-13	Wm. H. Crawford	Ga.	1772	1834	49-51	1887-91	John J. Ingalls	Kan.	1833	1900
13	1813-14	Joseph B. Varnum	Mass.	1750	1821	52	1891-93	C. F. Manderson	Neb.	1837	....
13-15	1814-18	John Gaillard	S. C.	1765	1826	53	1893-95	Isham G. Harris	Tenn.	1818	1897
15, 16	1818-19	James Barbour	Va	1775	1842	54-60	1895-	William P. Frye	Me	1831	....
16-19	1820-26	John Gaillard	S. C.	1765	1826						

Speakers of the U. S. House of Representatives.

Congress.	Years.	Name.	State.	Born.	Died.	Congress.	Years.	Name.	State.	Born.	Died
1	1789-91	F. A. Muhlenburg	Pa	1750	1801	29	1845-47	John W. Davis	Ind.	1799	1850
2	1791-93	Jonathan Trumbull	Ct.	1740	1809	30	1847-49	Robert C. Winthrop	Mass.	1809	1894
3	1793-95	F. A. Muhlenburg	Pa	1750	1801	31	1849-51	Howell Cobb	Ga	1815	1868
4, 5	1795-99	Jonathan Dayton	N. J.	1760	1824	32, 33	1851-55	Linn Boyd	Ky	1800	1859
6	1799-1801	Theo. Sedgwick	Mass.	1746	1813	34	1855-57	Nathaniel P. Banks	Mass.	1816	1894
7-9	1801-07	Nathaniel Macon	N. C.	1757	1837	35	1857-59	James L. Orr	S. C.	1822	1873
10, 11	1807-11	Joseph B. Varnum	Mass.	1750	1821	36	1859-61	Wm. Pennington	N. J.	1796	1862
12, 13	1811-14	Henry Clay	Ky	1777	1852	37	1861-63	Galusha A. Grow	Pa	1823	1907
13	1814-15	Langdon Cheves	S. C.	1776	1857	38-40	1863-69	Schuyler Colfax	Ind.	1823	1885
14-16	1815-20	Henry Clay	Ky	1777	1852	41-43	1869-75	James G. Blaine	Me	1830	1893
16	1820-21	John W. Taylor	N. Y.	1784	1854	44	1875-76	Michael C. Kerr	Ind.	1827	1876
17	1821-23	Philip P. Barbour	Va	1783	1841	44-46	1876-81	Samuel J. Randall	Pa	1828	1890
18	1823-25	Henry Clay	Ky	1777	1852	47	1881-83	John W. Keifer	Ohio	1836	....
19	1825-27	John W. Taylor	N. Y.	1784	1854	48-50	1883-89	John G. Carlisle	Ky	1835	....
20-23	1827-34	Andrew Stevenson	Va	1784	1857	51	1889-91	Thomas B. Reed	Me	1839	1902
23	1834-35	John Bell	Tenn.	1797	1869	52, 53	1891-95	Charles F. Crisp	Ga.	1845	1896
24, 25	1835-39	James K. Polk	Tenn.	1795	1849	54, 55	1895-99	Thomas B. Reed	Me	1839	1902
26	1839-41	R. M. T. Hunter	Va	1809	1887	56, 57	1899-1903	David B. Henderson	Ia	1840	1906
27	1841-43	John White	Ky	1805	1845	58-60	1903-	Joseph G. Cannon	Ill.	1836	....
28	1843-45	John W. Jones	Va	1805	1848						

SECRETARIES OF STATE.

Presidents.	Cabinet Officers.	Residences.	Date of Appointment.	Presidents.	Cabinet Officers.	Residences.	Date of Appointment.
Washington	Thomas Jefferson	Va	1789	Fillmore	Daniel Webster	Mass	1850
"	Edmund Randolph	"	1794	"	Edward Everett	"	1852
"	Timothy Pickering	Mass	1795	Pierce	William L. Marcy	N. Y.	1853
Adams	"	"	1797	Buchanan	Lewis Cass	Mich	1857
"	John Marshall	Va	1800	"	Jeremiah S. Black	Pa	1860
Jefferson	James Madison	"	1801	Lincoln	William H. Seward	N. Y.	1861
Madison	Robert Smith	Md	1809	Johnson	"	"	1865
"	James Monroe	Va	1811	Grant	Elihu B. Washburn	Ill	1869
Monroe	John Quincy Adams	Mass	1817	"	Hamilton Fish	N. Y.	1869
J. Q. Adams	Henry Clay	Ky	1825	Hayes	William M. Evarts	"	1877
Jackson	Martin Van Buren	N. Y.	1829	Garfield	James G. Blaine	Me	1881
"	Edward Livingston	La	1831	Arthur	F. T. Frelinghuysen	N. J.	1881
"	Louis McLane	Del	1833	Cleveland	Thomas F. Bayard	Del	1885
"	John Forsyth	Ga	1834	B. Harrison	James G. Blaine	Me	1889
Van Buren	"	"	1837	"	John W. Foster	Ind	1892
Harrison	Daniel Webster	Mass	1841	Cleveland	Walter Q. Gresham	Ill	1893
Tyler	"	"	1841	"	Richard Olney	Mass	1895
"	Hugh S. Legaré	S. C.	1843	McKinley	John Sherman	Ohio	1897
"	Abel P. Upshur	Va	1843	"	William R. Day	"	1897
"	John C. Calhoun	S. C.	1844	"	John Hay	"	1898
Polk	James Buchanan	Pa	1845	Roosevelt	"	"	1901
Taylor	John M. Clayton	Del	1849	"	Elihu Root	N. Y.	1905

SECRETARIES OF THE TREASURY.

Presidents.	Cabinet Officers.	Residences.	Date of Appointment.	Presidents.	Cabinet Officers.	Residences.	Date of Appointment.
Washington	Alexander Hamilton	N. Y.	1789	Pierce	James Guthrie	Ky	1853
"	Oliver Wolcott	Ct	1795	Buchanan	Howell Cobb	Ga	1857
Adams	"	"	1797	"	Philip F. Thomas	Md	1860
"	Samuel Dexter	Mass	1801	"	John A. Dix	N. Y.	1861
Jefferson	"	"	1801	Lincoln	Salmon P. Chase	Ohio	1861
"	Albert Gallatin	Pa	1801	"	William P. Fessenden	Me	1864
Madison	"	"	1809	"	Hugh McCulloch	Ind	1865
"	George W. Campbell	Tenn	1814	Johnson	"	"	1865
"	Alexander J. Dallas	Pa	1814	Grant	George S. Boutwell	Mass	1869
"	William H. Crawford	Ga	1816	"	Wm. A. Richardson	"	1873
Monroe	"	"	1817	"	Benjamin H. Bristow	Ky	1874
J. Q. Adams	Richard Rush	Pa	1825	"	Lot M. Morrill	Me	1876
Jackson	Samuel D. Ingham	"	1829	Hayes	John Sherman	Ohio	1877
"	Louis McLane	Del	1831	Garfield	William Windom	Minn	1881
"	William J. Duane	Pa	1833	Arthur	Charles J. Folger	N. Y.	1881
"	Roger B. Taney	Md	1833	"	Walter Q. Gresham	Ind	1884
"	Levi Woodbury	N. H.	1834	"	Hugh McCulloch	"	1884
Van Buren	"	"	1837	Cleveland	Daniel Manning	N. Y.	1885
Harrison	Thomas Ewing	Ohio	1841	"	Charles S. Fairchild	"	1887
Tyler	"	"	1841	B. Harrison	William Windom	Minn	1889
"	Walter Forward	Pa	1841	"	Charles Foster	Ohio	1891
"	John C. Spencer	N. Y.	1843	Cleveland	John G. Carlisle	Ky	1893
"	George M. Bibb	Ky	1844	McKinley	Lyman J. Gage	Ill.	1897
Polk	Robert J. Walker	Miss	1845	Roosevelt	"	"	1901
Taylor	William M. Meredith	Pa	1849	"	Leslie M. Shaw	Ia.	1901
Fillmore	Thomas Corwin	Ohio	1850	"	George B. Cortelyou	N. Y.	1907

SECRETARIES OF WAR.

Presidents.	Cabinet Officers.	Residences.	Date of Appointment.	Presidents.	Cabinet Officers.	Residences.	Date of Appointment.
Washington	Henry Knox	Mass	1789	Taylor	Edward Bates	Mo	1850
"	Timothy Pickering	"	1795	Fillmore	Charles M. Conrad	La	1850
"	James McHenry	Md	1796	Pierce	Jefferson Davis	Miss	1853
Adams	"	"	1797	Buchanan	John B. Floyd	Va	1857
"	John Marshall	Va	1800	"	Joseph Holt	Ky	1861
"	Samuel Dexter	Mass	1800	Lincoln	Simon Cameron	Pa	1861
"	Roger Griswold	Ct	1801	"	Edwin M. Stanton	Ohio	1862
Jefferson	Henry Dearborn	Mass	1801	Johnson	"	"	1865
Madison	William Eustis	"	1809	"	U. S. Grant *(ad. in.)*	Ill	1867
"	John Armstrong	N. Y.	1813	"	Lor. Thomas *(ad. in.)*		1868
"	James Monroe	Va	1814	"	John M. Schofield	N. Y.	1868
"	William H. Crawford	Ga	1815	Grant	John A. Rawlins	Ill	1869
Monroe	Isaac Shelby	Ky	1817	"	William T. Sherman	Ohio	1869
"	Geo. Graham *(ad. in.)*	Va	1817	"	William W. Belknap	Ia	1869
"	John C. Calhoun	S. C.	1817	"	Alphonso Taft	Ohio	1876
J. Q. Adams	James Barbour	Va	1825	"	James Don. Cameron	Pa	1876
"	Peter B. Porter	N. Y.	1828	Hayes	George W. McCrary	Ia	1877
Jackson	John H. Eaton	Tenn	1829	"	Alexander Ramsey	Minn	1879
"	Lewis Cass	Ohio	1831	Garfield	Robert T. Lincoln	Ill	1881
"	Benjamin F. Butler	N. Y.	1837	Arthur	"	"	1881
Van Buren	Joel R. Poinsett	S. C.	1837	Cleveland	William C. Endicott	Mass	1885
Harrison	John Bell	Tenn	1841	B. Harrison	Redfield Proctor	Vt	1889
Tyler	"	"	1841	"	Stephen B. Elkins	W. Va.	1891
"	John McLean	Ohio	1841	Cleveland	Daniel S. Lamont	N. Y.	1893
"	John C. Spencer	N. Y.	1841	McKinley	Russell A. Alger	Mich	1897
"	James M. Porter	Pa	1843	"	Elihu Root	N. Y.	1899
"	William Wilkins	"	1844	Roosevelt	"	"	1901
Polk	William L. Marcy	N. Y.	1845	"	William H. Taft	Ohio	1904
Taylor	George W. Crawford	Ga	1849	"	Luke E. Wright	Tenn	1908

SECRETARIES OF THE INTERIOR.

Presidents.	Cabinet Officers.	Residences.	Date of Appointment.	Presidents.	Cabinet Officers.	Residences.	Date of Appointment.
Taylor	Thomas Ewing	Ohio	1849	Grant	Zachariah Chandler	Mich	1875
Fillmore	James A. Pearce	Md	1850	Hayes	Carl Schurz	Mo	1877
"	Thos. M. T. McKennan	Pa	1850	Garfield	Samuel J. Kirkwood	Iowa	1881
"	Alexander H. H. Stuart	Va	1850	Arthur	Henry M. Teller	Col	1882
Pierce	Robert McClelland	Mich	1853	Cleveland	Lucius Q. C. Lamar	Miss	1885
Buchanan	Jacob Thompson	Miss	1857	"	William F. Vilas	Wis	1888
Lincoln	Caleb B. Smith	Ind	1861	B. Harrison	John W. Noble	Mo	1889
"	John P. Usher	"	1863	Cleveland	Hoke Smith	Ga	1893
Johnson	"	"	1865	"	David R. Francis	Mo	1896
"	James Harlan	Iowa	1865	McKinley	Cornelius N. Bliss	N. Y	1897
"	Orville H. Browning	Ill	1866	"	Ethan A. Hitchcock	Mo	1899
Grant	Jacob D. Cox	Ohio	1869	Roosevelt	"	"	1901
"	Columbus Delano	"	1870	"	James R. Garfield	Ohio	1907

SECRETARIES OF THE NAVY.

Presidents.	Cabinet Officers.	Residences.	Date of Appointment.	Presidents.	Cabinet Officers.	Residences.	Date of Appointment.
Jefferson	Benjamin Stoddert	Md	1801	Taylor	William B. Preston	Va	1849
"	Robert Smith	"	1801	Fillmore	William A. Graham	N. C	1850
"	Jacob Crowninshield	Mass	1805	"	John P. Kennedy	Md	1852
Madison	Paul Hamilton	S. C	1809	Pierce	James C. Dobbin	N. C	1853
"	William Jones	Pa	1813	Buchanan	Isaac Toucey	Ct	1857
"	B. W. Crowninshield	Mass	1814	Lincoln	Gideon Welles	"	1861
Monroe	"	"	1817	Johnson	"	"	1865
"	Smith Thompson	N. Y	1818	Grant	Adolph E. Borie	Pa	1869
"	Samuel L. Southard	N. J	1823	"	George M. Robeson	N. J	1869
J. Q. Adams	"	"	1825	Hayes	Richard W. Thompson	Ind	1877
Jackson	John Branch	N. C	1829	"	Nathan Goff, Jr	W. Va	1881
"	Levi Woodbury	N. H	1831	Garfield	William H. Hunt	La	1881
"	Mahlon Dickerson	N. J	1834	Arthur	William E. Chandler	N. H	1882
Van Buren	"	"	1837	Cleveland	William C. Whitney	N. Y	1885
"	James K. Paulding	N. Y	1838	B. Harrison	Benjamin F. Tracy	"	1889
Harrison	George E. Badger	N. C	1841	Cleveland	Hilary A. Herbert	Ala	1893
Tyler	"	"	1841	McKinley	John D. Long	Mass	1897
"	Abel P. Upshur	Va	1841	Roosevelt	"	"	1901
"	David Henshaw	Mass	1843	"	William H. Moody	"	1902
"	Thomas W. Gilmer	Va	1844	"	Paul Morton	Ill	1904
"	John Y. Mason	"	1844	"	Charles J. Bonaparte	Md	1905
Polk	George Bancroft	Mass	1845	"	Victor H. Metcalf	Cal	1907
"	John Y. Mason	Va	1846	"	Truman H. Newberry	Mich	1908

SECRETARIES OF AGRICULTURE.

Presidents.	Cabinet Officers.	Residences.	Date of Appointment.	Presidents.	Cabinet Officers.	Residences.	Date of Appointment.
Cleveland	Norman J. Colman	Mo	1889	McKinley	James Wilson	Ia	1897
B. Harrison	Jeremiah M. Rusk	Wis	1889	Roosevelt	"	"	1901
Cleveland	J. Sterling Morton	Neb	1893				

POSTMASTERS-GENERAL.†

Presidents.	Cabinet Officers.	Residences.	Date of Appointment.	Presidents.	Cabinet Officers.	Residences.	Date of Appointment.
Washington	Samuel Osgood	Mass	1789	Lincoln	Montgomery Blair	Md	1861
"	Timothy Pickering	"	1791	"	William Dennison	Ohio	1864
"	Joseph Habersham	Ga	1795	Johnson	"	"	1865
Adams	"	"	1797	"	Alexander W. Randall	Wis	1866
Jefferson	"	"	1801	Grant	John A. J. Cresswell	Md	1869
"	Gideon Granger	Ct	1801	"	James W. Marshall	Va	1874
Madison	"	"	1809	"	Marshall Jewell	Ct	1874
"	Return J. Meigs, Jr.	Ohio	1814	"	James N. Tyner	Ind	1876
Monroe	"	"	1817	Hayes	David McK. Key	Tenn	1877
"	John McLean	"	1823	"	Horace Maynard	"	1880
J. Q. Adams	"	"	1825	Garfield	Thomas L. James	N. Y	1881
Jackson	William T. Barry	Ky	1829	Arthur	Timothy O. Howe	Wis	1881
"	Amos Kendall	"	1835	"	Walter Q. Gresham	Ind	1883
Van Buren	"	"	1837	"	Frank Hatton	Ia	1884
"	John M. Niles	Ct	1840	Cleveland	William F. Vilas	Wis	1885
Harrison	Francis Granger	N. Y	1841	"	Don M. Dickinson	Mich	1888
Tyler	"	"	1841	B. Harrison	John Wanamaker	Pa	1889
"	Charles A. Wickliffe	Ky	1841	Cleveland	Wilson S. Bissell	N. Y	1893
Polk	Cave Johnson	Tenn	1845	"	William L. Wilson	W. Va	1895
Taylor	Jacob Collamer	Vt	1849	McKinley	James A. Gary	Md	1897
Fillmore	Nathan K. Hall	N. Y	1850	"	Charles Emory Smith	Pa	1898
"	Samuel D. Hubbard	Ct	1852	Roosevelt	"	"	1901
Pierce	James Campbell	Pa	1853	"	Henry C. Payne	Wis	1901
Buchanan	Aaron V. Brown	Tenn	1857	"	Robert J. Wynne	Pa	1904
"	Joseph Holt	Ky	1859	"	George B. Cortelyou	N. Y	1905
"	Horatio King	Me	1861	"	George von L. Meyer	Mass	1907

† The Postmaster-General was not considered a Cabinet officer until 1829.

ATTORNEYS-GENERAL.

Presidents.	Cabinet Officers.	Residences.	Date of Appointment.	Presidents.	Cabinet Officers.	Residences.	Date of Appointment.
Washington	Edmund Randolph	Va	1789	Jefferson	Cæsar A. Rodney	Del	1807
"	William Bradford	Pa	1794	Madison	"	"	1809
"	Charles Lee	Va	1795	"	William Pinkney	Md	1811
Adams	"	"	1797	"	Richard Rush	Pa	1814
"	Theophilus Parsons	Mass	1801	Monroe	"	"	1817
Jefferson	Levi Lincoln	"	1801	"	William Wirt	Va	1817
"	Robert Smith	Md	1805	J. Q. Adams	"	"	1825
"	John Breckinridge	Ky	1805	Jackson	John McP. Berrien	Ga	1829

ATTORNEYS-GENERAL—*Continued.*

Presidents.	Cabinet Officers.	Residences.	Date of Appointment.	Presidents.	Cabinet Officers.	Residences.	Date of Appointment.
Jackson	Roger B. Taney	Md	1831	Johnson	Henry Stanbery	Ohio	1866
"	Benjamin F. Butler	N. Y	1833	"	William M. Evarts	N. Y	1868
Van Buren	"	"	1837	Grant	Ebenezer R. Hoar	Mass	1869
"	Felix Grundy	Tenn	1838	"	Amos T. Ackerman	Ga	1870
"	Henry D. Gilpin	Pa	1840	"	George H. Williams	Ore	1871
Harrison	John J. Crittenden	Ky	1841	"	Edwards Pierrepont	N. Y	1875
Tyler	"	"	1841	"	Alphonso Taft	Ohio	1876
"	Hugh S. Legare	S. C	1841	Hayes	Charles Devens	Mass	1877
"	John Nelson	Md	1843	Garfield	Wayne MacVeagh	Pa	1881
Polk	John Y. Mason	Va	1845	Arthur	Benjamin H. Brewster	Pa	1881
"	Nathan Clifford	Me	1846	Cleveland	Augustus H. Garland	Ark	1885
"	Isaac Toucey	Ct	1848	B. Harrison	William H. H. Miller	Ind	1889
Taylor	Reverdy Johnson	Md	1849	Cleveland	Richard Olney	Mass	1893
Fillmore	John J. Crittenden	Ky	1850	"	Judson Harmon	Ohio	1895
Pierce	Caleb Cushing	Mass	1853	McKinley	Joseph McKenna	Cal	1897
Buchanan	Jeremiah S. Black	Pa	1857	"	John W. Griggs	N. J	1897
"	Edwin M. Stanton	Ohio	1860	"	Philander C. Knox	Pa	1901
Lincoln	Edward Bates	Mo	1861	Roosevelt	"	"	1901
"	Titian J. Coffey (*ad. in.*)	Pa	1863	"	William H. Moody	Mass	1904
"	James Speed	Ky	1864	"	Charles J. Bonaparte	Md	1907
Johnson	"	"	1865				

SECRETARIES OF COMMERCE AND LABOR.

Roosevelt	George B. Cortelyou	N. Y	1903	Roosevelt	Oscar S. Straus	N. Y	1907
"	Victor H. Metcalf	Cal	1904				

* Should changes occur while the ALMANAC is passing through the press they will be found noted on the page of "Occurrences During Printing."

NOTE.—The individual States have been represented the following number of times in Cabinet positions: New York, 34; Massachusetts, 33; Pennsylvania, 28; Ohio, 24; Virginia, 22; Maryland, 18; Kentucky, 15; Connecticut, 9; Indiana, 9; Georgia, 8; Tennessee, 8; Illinois, 8; Missouri, 7; Maine, 6; South Carolina, 6; Wisconsin, 6; Delaware, 5; Iowa, 5; Michigan, 5; New Jersey, 5; Mississippi, 4; North Carolina, 4; Louisiana, 3; Minnesota, 3; New Hampshire, 3; West Virginia, 3; Vermont, 2; California, 3; Alabama, 1; Arkansas, 1; Colorado, 1; Nebraska, 1; Oregon, 1.

Justices of the United States Supreme Court.

(Names of the Chief Justices in italics.)

Name.	Service. Term.	Yrs.	Born.	Died.	Name.	Service. Term.	Yrs.	Born.	Died.
John Jay, N. Y	1789-1795	6	1745	1829	Levi Woodbury, N. H	1845-1851	6	1789	1851
John Rutledge, S. C	1789-1791	2	1739	1800	Robert C. Grier, Pa	1846-1870	23	1794	1870
William Cushing, Mass	1789-1810	21	1733	1810	Benj. R. Curtis, Mass	1851-1857	6	1809	1874
James Wilson, Pa	1789-1798	9	1742	1798	John A. Campbell, Ala	1853-1861	8	1811	1889
John Blair, Va	1789-1796	7	1732	1800	Nathan Clifford, Me	1858-1881	23	1803	1881
Robert H. Harrison, Md	1789-1790	1	1745	1790	Noah H. Swayne, Ohio	1861-1881	20	1804	1884
James Iredell, N. C	1790-1799	9	1751	1799	Samuel F. Miller, Iowa	1862-1890	28	1816	1890
Thomas Johnson, Md	1791-1793	2	1732	1819	David Davis, Ill	1862-1877	15	1815	1886
William Paterson, N. J	1793-1806	13	1745	1806	Stephen J. Field, Cal	1863-1897	34	1816	1899
John Rutledge, S. C	1795-1795	...	1739	1800	*Salmon P. Chase*, Ohio	1864-1873	9	1808	1873
Samuel Chase, Md	1796-1811	15	1741	1811	William Strong, Pa	1870-1880	10	1808	1895
Oliver Ellsworth, Ct	1796-1800	4	1745	1807	Joseph P. Bradley, N. J	1870-1892	22	1813	1892
Bushrod Washington, Va	1798-1829	31	1762	1829	Ward Hunt, N. Y	1872-1882	10	1811	1886
Alfred Moore, N. C	1799-1804	5	1755	1810	*Morrison R. Waite*, Ohio	1874-1888	14	1816	1888
John Marshall, Va	1801-1835	34	1755	1835	John M. Harlan, Ky	1877-	...	1833	......
William Johnson, S. C	1804-1834	30	1771	1834	William B. Woods, Ga	1880-1887	7	1824	1887
Brock. Livingston, N. Y	1806-1823	17	1757	1823	Stanley Matthews, Ohio	1881-1889	8	1824	1889
Thomas Todd, Ky	1807-1826	19	1765	1826	Horace Gray, Mass	1881-1902	21	1828	1902
Joseph Story, Mass	1811-1845	34	1779	1845	Samuel Blatchford, N. Y	1882-1893	11	1820	1893
Gabriel Duval, Md	1811-1836	25	1752	1844	Lucius Q. C. Lamar, Miss	1888-1893	5	1825	1893
Smith Thompson, N. Y	1823-1843	20	1767	1843	*Melville W. Fuller*, Ill	1888-	...	1833	......
Robert Trimble, Ky	1826-1828	2	1777	1828	David J. Brewer, Kan	1889-	...	1837	......
John McLean, Ohio	1829-1861	32	1785	1861	Henry B. Brown, Mich	1890-1906	6	1836	......
Henry Baldwin, Pa	1830-1844	14	1779	1844	George Shiras, Jr., Pa	1892-1903	11	1832	......
James M. Wayne, Ga	1835-1867	32	1790	1867	Howell E. Jackson, Tenn	1893-1895	2	1832	1895
Roger B. Taney, Md	1836-1864	28	1777	1864	Edward D. White, La	1893-	...	1845	......
Philip P. Barbour, Va	1836-1841	5	1783	1841	Rufus W. Peckham, N. Y	1895-	...	1838	....
John Catron, Tenn	1837-1865	28	1786	1865	Joseph McKenna, Cal	1898-	...	1843	....
John McKinley, Ala	1837-1852	15	1780	1852	Oliver W. Holmes, Mass	1902-	...	1841	....
Peter V. Daniel, Va	1841-1860	19	1785	1860	William R. Day, Ohio	1903-	...	1849	....
Samuel Nelson, N. Y	1845-1872	27	1792	1873	William H. Moody, Mass	1906-	...	1853	....

United States Department Officials.

COMMISSIONERS OF PENSIONS.

Year.	Commissioners.	Year.	Commissioners.	Year.	Commissioners.
1861-68	Joseph H. Barrett	1876-81	John A. Bentley	1893-96	William Lochren
1868-69	Christopher C. Cox	1881-84	William W. Dudley	1896-97	Dominic I. Murphy
1869-71	H. Van Aernam	1884-85	Otis P. G. Clarke	1897-1902	Henry C. Evans
1871-75	James H. Baker	1885-89	John C. Black	1902-04	Eugene F. Ware
1875-76	H. M. Atkinson	1889	James Tanner	1905	Vespasian Warner
1876	Charles R. Gill	1889-93	Green B. Raum		

COMMISSIONERS OF PATENTS.

1836	Henry L. Ellsworth	1868	Elisha Foote	1885	M. V. Montgomery
1845	Edmund Burke	1869	Samuel S. Fisher	1887	Benton J. Hall
1849	Thomas Ewbank	1871	Mortimer D. Leggett	1889	Charles E. Mitchell
1852	Silas H. Hodges	1874	John M. Thacher	1891	William E. Simonds
1853	Charles Mason	1875	Rodolphus H. Duell	1893	John S. Seymour
1857	Joseph Holt	1877	Ellis Spear	1897	Benj. Butterworth
1859	William D. Bishop	1878	Halbert E. Paine	1898	Charles H. Duell
1860	Phillip F. Thomas	1880	Edgar M. Marble	1901	Frederick I. Allen
1861	David P. Holloway	1883	Benj. Butterworth	1907	E. B. Moore
1865	Thomas C. Theaker				

DIRECTORS OF THE MINT.

1792-95	David Rittenhouse	1853	Thomas M. Pettit	1879-84	Horatio C. Burchard
1795	Henry W. Desaussure	1853-61	James R. Snowden	1885-88	James P. Kimball
1795-1805	Elias Boudinot	1861-66	James Pollock	1889-93	Edward O. Leech
1806-24	Robert Patterson	1867-69	Henry R. Linderman	1893-98	Robert E. Preston
1824-35	Samuel Moore	1869-73	James Pollock	1898	George E. Roberts
1835-51	Robert M. Patterson	1873-79	Henry Linderman	1908	Frank A. Leach
1851-53	George N. Eckert				

Diplomatic Intercourse.

ALL representatives not otherwise designated bore the title of minister plenipotentiary or envoy extraordinary or both.

RUSSIA.

UNITED STATES MINISTERS AND AMBASSADORS TO RUSSIA.

Presidents.	Ministers.	States.	Date.*	Presidents.	Ministers.	States.	Date.*
Madison	John Quincy Adams	Mass.	1809	Grant	Andrew G. Curtin	Pa.	1869
"	Levett Harris, ch. d'aff	Pa.	1814	"	James L. Orr	S. C.	1872
"	William Pinkney	Md.	1816	"	Marshall Jewell	Ct.	1873
Monroe	George W. Campbell	Tenn.	1818	"	Eugene Schuyler, ch. d'aff	N. Y.	1874
"	Henry Middleton	S. C.	1820	"	George H. Boker	Pa.	1875
J. Q. Adams	" "	"	1820	Hayes	E. W. Stoughton	N. Y.	1878
Jackson	John Randolph	Va.	1830	"	Wickham Hoffman, ch. d'aff	"	1879
"	James Buchanan	Pa.	1832	"	John W. Foster	Ind.	1880
"	John R. Clay, ch. d'aff	"	1833	Garfield	" "	"	1880
"	William Wilkins	"	1834	Arthur	Wickham Hoffman, ch. d'aff.	N. Y.	1881
"	John R. Clay, ch. d'aff	"	1835	"	William H. Hunt	La.	1882
Van Buren	George M. Dallas	"	1837	"	Alphonso Taft	Ohio	1884
"	W. W. Chew, ch. d'aff	"	1839	Cleveland	George V. M. Lothrop	Mich.	1885
"	Churchill C. Cambreleng	N. Y.	1840	"	Lambert Tree	Ill.	1888
Tyler	Charles S. Todd	Ky.	1841	B. Harrison	George W. Wurts, ch. d'aff	Pa.	1889
Polk	Ralph J. Ingersoll	Ct.	1846	"	Charles Emory Smith	"	1890
"	Arthur P. Bagby	Ala.	1848	"	Andrew D. White	N. Y.	1892
Fillmore	Neil S. Brown	Tenn.	1850	Cleveland	Clifton R. Breckinridge	Ark.	1894
Pierce	Thomas H. Seymour	Ct.	1853	McKinley	Ethan A. Hitchcock	Mo.	1897
Buchanan	Francis W. Pickens	S. C.	1858	"	" " amb.	"	1898
"	John Appleton	Me.	1860	"	Charlemagne Tower, amb.	Pa.	1899
Lincoln	Cassius M. Clay	Ky.	1861	Roosevelt	" "	"	1899
"	Simon Cameron	Pa.	1862	"	Robert S. McCormick, amb.	Ill.	1902
"	Bayard Taylor	N. Y.	1862	"	George von L. Meyer, amb	Mass.	1905
"	Cassius M. Clay	Ky.	1863	"	John W. Riddle. amb	Mass.	1907

RUSSIAN MINISTERS AND AMBASSADORS TO THE UNITED STATES.

Emperors.	Ministers.	Date.*	Emperors.	Ministers.	Date.*
Alexander I.	Andre de Daschkoff, ch. d'aff	1809	Alex. II	Alexander Gorloff, ch. d'aff	1871
"	Count Theodore de Pahlen	1810	"	Baron Henri d'Offenberg	1872
"	Andre de Daschkoff	1811	"	Nicholas de Voigt, ch. d'aff	1874
"	Chevalier Pierra de Poletica	1819	"	Nicholas Shishkin	1875
"	George Ellisen, ch. d'aff	1822	"	Michel Bartholomei	1880
"	Baron de Tuyll	1823	Alex. III.	Charles de Struve	1882
Nicholas I.	Baron de Maltitz, ch. d'aff	1826	"	Baron Gustave Schilling, ch. d'aff	1892
"	Baron de Krudener	1827	"	Prince Cantacuzene	1893
"	George Krehmer, ch. d'aff	1838	Nicholas II	" "	1893
"	Alexander de Bodisco	1838	"	E. de Kotzebue	1896
Alex. II	Edward de Stoeckl	1854	"	Count Cassini, ambassador	1898
"	Waldemar Bodisco, ch. d'aff	1868	"	Baron Rosen, ambassador	1905
"	Constantine Catacazy	1869			

* Date of Commission.

GREAT BRITAIN.

UNITED STATES MINISTERS AND AMBASSADORS TO GREAT BRITAIN.

Presidents.	Representatives.	States.	Date.
Washington	Thomas Pinckney	S. C.	1792
"	Rufus King	N. Y.	1796
John Adams	" "	"	1796
Jefferson	James Monroe*	Va.	1803
	William Pinkney	Md.	1806
Madison	Jonathan Russell, ch. d'aff.	R. I.	1811
"	John Quincy Adams	Mass.	1815
Monroe	J. Adams Smith, ch. d'aff.	"	1817
"	Richard Rush	Pa.	1817
J. Q. Adams	Rufus King	N. Y.	1825
"	Albert Gallatin	Pa.	1826
"	W. B. Lawrence, ch. d'aff.	N. Y.	1827
"	James Barbour	Va.	1828
Jackson	Louis McLane	Del.	1829
"	Washington Irving, ch. d'aff.	N. Y.	1831
"	Martin Van Buren	"	1831
"	Aaron Vail, ch. d'aff.	"	1832
"	Andrew Stevenson	Va.	1836
Tyler	Edward Everett	Mass.	1841
Polk	Louis McLane	Md.	1845
"	George Bancroft	N. Y.	1846
Taylor	J. C. B. Davis, ch. d'aff.	Mass.	1849
"	Abbott Lawrence	"	1849
Fillmore	Joseph R. Ingersoll	Pa.	1852
Pierce	James Buchanan	"	1853
"	George M. Dallas	"	1856
Buchanan	" " "	"	1856
Lincoln	Charles Francis Adams	Mass.	1861
Johnson	" " "	"	1861
"	Reverdy Johnson	Md.	1868
Grant	John Lothrop Motley	Mass.	1869
"	Robert C. Schenck	Ohio	1870
"	Edwards Pierrepont	N. Y.	1876
Hayes	John Welsh	Pa.	1877
"	Wm. J. Hoppin, ch. d'aff.	N. Y.	1879
"	James Russell Lowell	Mass.	1880
Garfield	" " "	"	1880
Arthur	" " "	"	1880
Cleveland	Edward J. Phelps	Vt.	1885
B. Harrison	Robert T. Lincoln	Ill.	1889
Cleveland	Thos. F. Bayard, ambassador.	Del.	1893
McKinley	John Hay, ambassador	Ohio	1897
"	Henry White, ch. d'aff.	R. I.	1898
"	Joseph H. Choate, ambassador	N. Y.	1899
Roosevelt	" " "	"	1899
"	Whitelaw Reid, ambassador	"	1905

BRITISH MINISTERS AND AMBASSADORS TO THE UNITED STATES.

Sovereigns.	Representatives.	Date.
George III	George Hammond	1791
"	Phineas Bond, ch. d'aff	1795
"	Robert Liston	1796
"	Edward Thornton, ch. d'aff	1800
"	Anthony Merry	1803
"	David M. Erskine	1806
"	Francis James Jackson	1809
"	John Philip Morier, ch. d'aff	1810
"	Augustus John Foster	1811
"	Anthony St. John Baker, ch. d'aff	1815
"	Charles Bagot	1816
George IV	Gibbs Crawford Antrobus, ch. d'aff	1819
"	Sir Stratford Canning	1820
"	Henry Unwin Addington, ch. d'aff	1823
"	Charles Richard Vaughan	1825
William IV	" " "	1825
"	Charles Bankhead, ch. d'aff	1835
Victoria	Henry Stephen Fox	1836
"	Richard Pakenham	1844
Victoria	John F. T. Crampton, ch. d'aff	1847
"	Sir Henry Lytton Bulwer	1849
"	John F. T. Crampton, ch. d'aff	1851
"	" " " envoy and min.	1852
"	Philip Griffith, ch. d'aff	1853
"	John Savile Lumley, ch. d'aff	1855
"	Lord Napier	1857
"	Lord Lyons	1859
"	Joseph Hume Burnley, ch. d'aff	1864
"	Sir Frederick W. A. Bruce	1865
"	Francis Clark Ford, ch. d'aff	1867
"	Sir Edward Thornton	1868
"	Lionel S. Sackville West	1881
"	Sir Julian Pauncefote†	1889
"	" " " ambassador	1893
Edward VII	" " " "	1893
"	Hon. Sir Michael H. Herbert, amb.	1902
"	Sir Henry Mortimer Durand, amb.	1903
"	James Bryce, ambassador	1907

*Monroe was appointed alone in 1803, and then jointly with Pinkney in 1806. †Later Lord Pauncefote.

AUSTRIA AND AUSTRIA-HUNGARY.

UNITED STATES MINISTERS AND AMBASSADORS TO AUSTRIA.

Presidents.	Representatives.	States.	Date.
Van Buren	Henry A. Muhlenberg	Pa	1838
"	J. R. Clay, ch. d'aff	"	1840
Tyler	Daniel Jenifer	Md.	1841
Polk	Wm. H. Stiles, ch. d'aff	Ga.	1845
Taylor	J. Watson Webb, ch. d'aff	N. Y.	1849
Fillmore	C. J. McCurdy, ch. d'aff	Ct.	1850
"	T. M. Foote, ch. d'aff	N. Y.	1852
Pierce	H. R. Jackson, min. res.	Ga	1853
Buchanan	J. Glancy Jones	Pa.	1858
Lincoln	Anson Burlingame	Mass.	1861
"	John Lothrop Motley	"	1861
Johnson	George W. Lippitt, ch. d'aff.	R. I.	1867
"	John Hay, ch. d'aff	Ill.	1867
"	Henry M. Watts	Pa.	1868
Grant	John Jay	N. Y.	1869
"	Godlove S. Orth	Ind	1875
Grant	Edward F. Beale	D. C.	1876
Hayes	John A. Kasson	Ia.	1877
Garfield	William Walter Phelps	N. J.	1881
Arthur	Alphonso Taft	Ohio	1882
"	John M. Francis	N. Y	1884
Cleveland	A. M. Kiely	Va.	1885
"	James Fenner Lee, ch. d'aff	Md.	1885
"	Alexander R. Lawton	Ga.	1887
B. Harrison	Frederick D. Grant	N. Y.	1889
Cleveland	Bartlett Tripp	S. Dak.	1893
McKinley	Charlemagne Tower	Pa.	1897
"	Addison C. Harris	Ind	1899
"	Robert S. McCormick	Ill	1901
Roosevelt	" "	"	1901
"	Bellamy Storer, ambassador	Ohio	1902
"	Charles S. Francis, amb	N. Y.	1906

AUSTRIAN MINISTERS AND AMBASSADORS TO THE UNITED STATES.

Emperors.	Representatives.	Date.
Ferdinand I.	Baron de Mareschal	1838
"	Chevalier Hulsemann, ch. d'aff	1841
Franz Joseph.	" " "	1841
"	" " min. res.	1855
"	Count Nicholas Giorgi, min. res.	1863
"	Count Wydenbruck	1865
"	Baron de Frankenstein, ch. d'aff	1867
"	Baron Charles de Lederer	1868
"	Baron von Schwarz Senborn	1874
Franz Joseph.	Count Ladislaus Hoyos	1875
"	Chevalier E. S. von Tavera, ch. d'aff.	1877
"	Baron Ernest von Mayr	1879
"	Count Lippe-Weissenfeld, ch. d'aff.	1881
"	Baron Ignatz von Schaeffer	1882
"	Count Lippe-Weissenfeld, ch. d'aff.	1885
"	Chevalier E. S. von Tavera	1887
"	L. Hengelmuller von Hengervar	1895
"	" " amb.	1902

FRANCE.

UNITED STATES MINISTERS AND AMBASSADORS TO FRANCE.

Presidents.	Representatives.	States.	Date.	Presidents.	Representatives.	States.	Date.
Confederation	Thomas Jefferson	Va.	....	Tyler	Henry Ledyard, ch. d'aff.	Mich.	1842
Washington	William Short, ch. d'aff.	"	1790	"	William R. King	Ala.	1844
"	Gouverneur Morris	N. Y.	1792	Polk	J. L. Martin, ch. d'aff.	N. C.	1846
"	James Monroe	Va.	1794	"	Richard Rush	Pa.	1847
"	Charles C. Pinckney	S. C.	1796	Taylor	William C. Rives	Va.	1849
John Adams	Charles C. Pinckney	"	1797	Fillmore	" "	"	1849
John Adams	John Marshall	Va.	1797	Pierce	Henry S. Sanford, ch. d'aff.	Ct.	1853
John Adams	Elbridge Gerry	Mass.	1797	"	John Y. Mason	Va.	1853
"	Oliver Ellsworth	Ct.	1799	Buchanan	W. R. Calhoun, ch. d'aff.	S. C.	1859
"	William Vans Murray	Md.	1799	"	Charles J. Faulkner	Va.	1860
"	William R. Davie	N. C.	1799	Lincoln	William L. Dayton	N. J.	1861
Jefferson	Robert R. Livingston	N. Y.	1801	"	John Bigelow	N. Y.	1864
"	John Armstrong	"	1804	Johnson	John Hay, ch. d'aff.	Ill.	1866
Madison	Jonathan Russell, ch. d'aff.	R. I.	1810	"	John A. Dix	N. Y.	1866
"	Joel Barlow	Ct.	1811	Grant	Elihu B. Washburne	Ill.	1869
"	William H. Crawford	Ga.	1813	Hayes	Edward F. Noyes	Ohio	1877
"	Henry Jackson, ch. d'aff.	Ky.	1815	Garfield	Levi P. Morton	N. Y.	1881
"	Albert Gallatin	Pa.	1816	Arthur	" "	"	1881
Monroe	James Brown	La.	1823	Cleveland	Robert M. McLane	Md.	1885
Jackson	William C. Rives	Va.	1829	B. Harrison	Whitelaw Reid	N. Y.	1889
"	Nathaniel Niles, ch. d'aff.	Vt.	1832	"	T. Jefferson Coolidge	Mass.	1892
"	Edward Livingston	La.	1833	Cleveland	James B. Eustis, ambassador	La.	1893
"	Thomas P. Barton, ch. d'aff.	Pa.	1835	McKinley	Horace Porter, ambassador	N. Y.	1897
"	Lewis Cass	Ohio	1836	Roosevelt	" " "	"	1897
Van Buren	" "	"	1836	"	Robert S. McCormick, amb.	Ill.	1905
Tyler	Lewis Cass	Ohio	1836	"	Henry White, ambassador	R. I.	1907

FRENCH MINISTERS AND AMBASSADORS TO THE UNITED STATES.

Government.	Representatives.	Date.	Government.	Representatives.	Date.
Louis XVI	Count de Moustier	1788	Napoleon III	Count de Sartiges	1851
"	M. Otto, ch. d'aff.	1789	"	Viscount Jules Treilhard, ch. d'aff.	1859
"	Colonel Ternant	1791	"	Henri Mercier	1860
Convention	Edmond C. Genet	1793	"	Viscount Jules Treilhard, ch. d'aff.	1863
Directory	Joseph Fauchet	1794	"	Louis de Geofroy, ch. d'aff.	1864
"	Pierre Auguste Adet	1795	"	Marquis de Montholon	1865
Consulate	" " "	1795	"	Jules Berthemy	1866
"	L. A. Pichon, ch. d'aff.	1801	"	Count de Faverney, ch. d'aff.	1869
Napoleon I	General Turreau	1805	"	Prevost Paradol	1870
"	M. Serurier	1811	"	Jules Berthemy	1870
Louis XVIII	"	1811	Nat. Defence	Viscount Jules Treilhard	1870
"	G. Hyde de Neuville	1816	Pres. Thiers	Henry de Bellonnet, ch. d'aff.	1871
"	Count de Menou, ch. d'aff.	1822	"	Marquis de Noailles	1872
Charles X	Baron de Mareuil	1824	Pr. MacMahon	A. Bartholdi	1874
"	Count de Menou, ch. d'aff.	1827	"	F. de Vaugelas, ch. d'aff.	1876
"	Roux de Rochelle	1830	"	Mamime Outrey	1877
L. Philippe	M. Serurier	1831	"	Theodore J. D. Roustan	1882
"	Alphonse Pageot, ch. d'aff.	1835	Pres. Grevy	J. Patenotre	1891
"	Edouard Pontois	1837	Pres. Carnot	"	1891
"	Alphonse Pageot, ch. d'aff.	1839	"	" ambassador	1893
"	L. Adolph Aime Fourier de Bacourt	1840	Pres. Faure	" "	1893
"	Alphonse Joseph Yver Pageot	1842	"	Jules Cambon, ambassador	1898
L. Napoleon	Guillaume Tell Lavallee Poussin	1848	Pres. Loubet	" "	1898
"	E. A. Olivier Sain de Boislecomte	1850	"	Jean J. Jusserand, ambassador	1902

GERMANY.

UNITED STATES MINISTERS AND AMBASSADORS TO THE GERMAN EMPIRE.

Presidents.	Representatives.	States.	Date.	Presidents.	Representatives.	States.	Date.
Grant	George Bancroft	N. Y.	1871	Arthur	John A. Kasson	Ia.	1884
"	Nicholas Fish, ch. d'aff.	"	1874	Cleveland	George H. Pendleton	Ohio	1885
"	J. C. Bancroft Davis	"	1874	B. Harrison	William Walter Phelps	N. J.	1889
Hayes	H. Sidney Everett, ch. d'aff.	Mass.	1877	Cleveland	Theodore Runyon, amb.	"	1893
"	Bayard Taylor	Pa.	1878	"	Edwin F. Uhl, ambassador	Mich.	1896
"	H. Sidney Everett, ch. d'aff.	Mass.	1878	McKinley	Andrew D. White, amb.	N. Y.	1897
"	Andrew D. White	N. Y.	1879	Roosevelt	" "	"	1897
Garfield	H. Sidney Everett, ch. d'aff.	Mass.	1881	"	Charlemagne Tower, amb.	Pa.	1902
Arthur	A. A. Sargent	Cal.	1882	"	David J. Hill, amb.	N. Y.	1907

GERMAN MINISTERS AND AMBASSADORS TO THE UNITED STATES.

Emperors.	Representatives.	Date.	Emperors.	Representatives.	Date.
William I	Kurd von Schlozer	1871	William II	Theodore von Holleben	1892
"	Count von Beust, ch. d'aff.	1882	"	Baron von Saurma-Jeltsch, amb.	1893
"	Karl von Eisendecher	1883	"	Baron Max von Thielmann, amb.	1895
"	H. von Alvensleben	1884	"	Herr von Holleben, ambassador	1898
William II	Count Arco Valley	1888	"	Baron Speck von Sternburg, amb.	1904
"	A. von Mumm, ch. d'aff.	1891	"	Johann Heinrich von Bernstorff, amb.	1908

ITALY.

UNITED STATES MINISTERS AND AMBASSADORS TO ITALY.

Presidents.	Representatives.	States.	Date.	Presidents.	Representatives.	States.	Date.
Lincoln	George P. Marsh	Vt.	1861	B. Harrison	William Potter	Pa.	1892
Johnson	" "	"	1861	Cleveland	J. J. Van Alen, ambassador*	R. I.	1893
Grant	" "	"	1861	"	Wayne MacVeagh, amb.	Pa.	1893
Hayes	" "	"	1861	McKinley	William F. Draper, amb.	Mass.	1897
Garfield	" "	"	1861	"	George Von L. Meyer, amb.	"	1901
Arthur	" "	"	1861	Roosevelt	" " " "	"	1901
"	William Waldorf Astor	N. Y.	1882	"	Henry White, ambassador	R. I.	1905
Cleveland	John B. Stallo	Ohio	1885	"	Lloyd C. Griscom, amb	Pa.	1907
B. Harrison	Albert G. Porter	Ind	1889				

* Mr. Van Alen was confirmed by the Senate but declined, and Mr. MacVeagh was appointed.

ITALIAN MINISTERS AND AMBASSADORS TO THE UNITED STATES.

Kings.	Representatives.	Date.	Kings.	Representatives.	Date.
V. Emmanuel	Chevalier Joseph Bertinatti	1861	Humbert	Prince Camporeale, ch. d'aff.	1880
"	Romeo Cantagalli, ch. d'aff	1866	"	Baron de Fava	1881
"	Chevalier Marcello Cerruti	1867	"	Marquis Imperiali, ch. d'aff	1891
"	Count Luigi Colobiano, ch. d'aff	1869	"	Baron de Fava	1892
"	Count Luigi Corti	1870	"	" " " ambassador	1893
"	Count Litta, ch. d'aff	1874	V. Emman. II.	" " " "	1893
"	Baron Alberto Blanc	1875	"	E. Mayor des Planches, ambassador	1901

SPAIN.

UNITED STATES MINISTERS TO SPAIN.

Presidents.	Ministers.	States.	Date.	Presidents.	Ministers.	States.	Date.
Washington	W. Carmichael, ch. d'aff.	Md.	1790	Lincoln	H. J. Perry, ch. d'aff.	N. H.	1864
"	William Short, min. res.	Va.	1794	"	John P. Hale	"	1865
"	Thomas Pinckney	S. C.	1794	Grant	Daniel E. Sickles	N. Y.	1869
"	David Humphreys	Ct.	1796	"	Alvey A. Adee, ch. d'aff.	"	1873
Jefferson	Charles Pinckney	S. C.	1801	"	Caleb Cushing	Mass.	1874
"	G. W. Erving, ch. d'aff.	Mass.	1805	Hayes	James Russell Lowell	"	1877
	Official relations with Spain were broken off from 1808 to 1814.			"	Lucius Fairchild	Wis.	1880
				Garfield	" "	"	1880
				Arthur	Hannibal Hamlin	Me.	1881
Madison	G. W. Erving	Mass.	1814	"	John W. Foster	Ind	1883
Monroe	John Forsyth	Ga.	1819	Cleveland	Jabez L. M. Curry	Va.	1885
"	Hugh Nelson	Va.	1823	"	Perry Belmont	N. Y.	1889
J. Q. Adams	Alexander H. Everett	Mass.	1825	B. Harrison	Thomas W. Palmer	Mich.	1889
Jackson	Cornelius P. Van Ness	Vt.	1829	"	E. Burd Grubb	N. J.	1890
"	A. Middleton, Jr., ch. d'aff.	S. C.	1836	"	A. Loudon Snowden	Pa.	1892
Van Buren	John H. Eaton	Tenn.	1837	Cleveland	Hannis Taylor	Ala.	1893
"	Aaron Vail, ch. d'aff.	N. Y.	1840	McKinley	Stewart L. Woodford	N. Y.	1897
Tyler	Washington Irving	"	1842		Official relations with Spain were broken off, April, 1898, to April, 1899.		
Polk	Romulus M. Saunders	N. C.	1846				
Taylor	Daniel M. Barringer	"	1849				
Pierce	Pierre Soule	La.	1853	"	Bellamy Storer	Ohio	1899
"	Augustus C. Dodge	Ia.	1855	Roosevelt	" "	"	1899
Buchanan	William Preston	Ky.	1858	"	Arthur S. Hardy	N. H.	1902
Lincoln	Carl Schurz	Wis.	1861	"	William M. Collier	N. Y.	1906
"	Gustavus Koerner	Ill.	1862				

SPANISH MINISTERS TO THE UNITED STATES.

Sovereigns.	Ministers.	Date.	Sovereigns.	Ministers.	Date.
Carlos IV	Jose Ignacio de Viar, ch. d'aff.	1789	Provis. Gov.	Mauricio Lopez Roberts	1869
"	Jose Ignacio de Viar, } joint		Amadeo I	Admiral Don Jose Polo de Bernabe	1872
"	Jose de Jaudenes, } ch. d'aff.	1791	Pr. Figueras	" " " " "	1872
"	Carlos M. de Irujo	1796	" Castelar	" " " " "	1872
"	Valentin de Foronda, ch. d'aff.	1807	" Serrano	Antonio Mantilla	1874
	Official relations with Spain were broken off from 1808 to 1814.		Alphonso XII.	Jose Brunetti, ch. d'aff.	1878
			"	Felipe Mendez de Vigo y Osorio	1879
Fernan. VII	Luis de Onis	1809	"	Francisco Barca del Corral	1881
"	Mateo de la Serna, ch. d'aff.	1819	"	Enrique Dupuy de Lome, ch. d'aff.	1883
"	Francisco Dionisio Vives	1820	"	Juan Valera y Alcala Galiano	1884
"	Joaquin de Anduaga	1821	Alph. XIII	Emilio de Muruaga	1886
"	F. P. Rivas y Salmon, ch. d'aff.	1823	"	Miguel Suarez Guanes	1890
"	Francisco Tacon	1827	"	Jose Felipe Segario, ch. d'aff.	1891
M. Christina	" "	1827	"	Enrique Dupuy de Lome	1892
Isabella II	Angel Calderon de la Barca	1835	"	Emilio de Muruaga	1893
"	Pedro Alcantara Argaiz	1839	"	Enrique Dupuy de Lome	1896
"	Fidencio Bourman, ch. d'aff.	1844	"	Louis Polo y Bernabe	1898
"	Angel Calderon de la Barca, min. res.	1844		Diplomatic intercourse broken off by the war.	
"	Jose Maria Magallon, ch. d'aff.	1853			
"	Leopoldo Augusto de Cueto	1854	"	Jose Brunetti, Duke of Arcos	1899
"	Alfonso Escalante	1855	"	Emilio de Ojeda	1902
"	Gabriel Garcia y Tassara	1857	"	Bernardo J. de Cologan	1906
"	Facundo Goni	1867	"	Ramon Pina	1907

Governors of New York.

COLONIAL.

GOVERNORS.	Terms.	GOVERNORS.	Terms.	GOVERNORS.	Terms.
Adrian Joris	1623-1624	John Nanfan, Lt.-Gov.	1699-1700	James De Lancey, Lt.-	
Cornelius Jacobzen Mey.	1624-1625	Earl of Bellomont	1700-1701	Gov.	1755
William Verhulst	1625-1626	Col. William Smith	1701	Sir Charles Hardy	1755-1757
Peter Minuit	1626-1633	Col. Abraham De Peyster		James De Lancey, Lt.-	
Wouter Van Twiller	1633-1638	Col. Peter Schuyler		Gov.	1757-1760
William Kieft	1638-1647	John Nanfan, Lt.-Gov.	1701-1702	Cadwallader Colden,	
Petrus Stuyvesant	1647-1664	Lord Cornbury	1702-1708	President	1760-1761
Richard Nicolls	1664-1668	Lord Lovelace	1708-1709	Cadwallader Colden,	
Francis Lovelace	1668-1673	Peter Schuyler, Pres.	1709	Lt.-Gov.	1761
Anthony Colve	1673-1674	Richard Ingoldsby, Lt.-		Robert Monckton	1761
Edmond Andros	1674-1677	Gov.	1709	Cadwallader Colden,	
Anthony Brockholles,		Peter Schuyler, Pres.	1709	Lt.-Gov.	1761-1762
Com.-in-Chief	1677-1678	Richard Ingoldsby, Lt.-		Robert Monckton	1762-1763
Sir Edmond Andros	1678-1681	Gov.	1709	Cadwallader Colden,	
Anthony Brockholles,		Gerardus Beekman,		Lt.-Gov.	1763-1765
Com.-in-Chief	1681-1683	President	1710	Sir Henry Moore	1765-1769
Thomas Dongan	1683-1688	Robert Hunter	1710-1719	Cadwallader Colden,	
Sir Edmond Andros	1688	Peter Schuyler, Pres.	1719-1720	Lt.-Gov.	1769-1770
Francis Nicholson	1688-1689	William Burnet	1720-1728	Earl of Dunmore	1770-1771
Jacob Leisler	1689-1691	John Montgomerie	1728-1731	William Tryon	1771-1774
Henry Sloughter	1691	Rip Van Dam, President	1731-1732	Cadwallader Colden,	
Richard Ingoldsby,		William Cosby	1732-1736	Lt.-Gov.	1774-1775
Com.-in-Chief	1691-1692	George Clark, Lt.-Gov.	1736-1743	William Tryon	1775-1780
Benjamin Fletcher	1692-1698	George Clinton	1743-1753	James Robertson	1780-1783
Earl of Bellomont	1698-1699	Sir Danvers Osborne	1753-1755	Andrew Elliott, L.-Gov.	1783

STATE.

1	George Clinton	1777-1795	14	William H. Seward	1839-1842	27	John A. Dix	1873-1874
2	John Jay	1795-1801	15	William C. Bouck	1843-1844	28	Samuel J. Tilden	1875-1876
3	George Clinton	1801-1804	16	Silas Wright	1845-1846	29	Lucius Robinson	1877-1880
4	Morgan Lewis	1804-1807	17	John Young	1847-1848	30	Alonzo B. Cornell	1880-1882
5	Daniel D. Tompkins	1807-1817	18	Hamilton Fish	1849-1851	31	Grover Cleveland	1883-1884
6	John Taylor	1817	19	Washington Hunt	1851-1852	32	David B. Hill	1885-1891
7	De Witt Clinton	1817-1822	20	Horatio Seymour	1853-1854	33	Roswell P. Flower	1892-1894
8	Joseph C. Yates	1822-1824	21	Myron H. Clark	1855-1856	34	Levi P. Morton	1895-1896
9	De Witt Clinton	1824-1826	22	John A. King	1857-1858	35	Frank S. Black	1897-1898
10	Nathaniel Pitcher	1828	23	Edwin D. Morgan	1859-1862	36	Theodore Roosevelt	1899-1900
11	Martin Van Buren	1828-1829	24	Horatio Seymour	1863-1864	37	Benjamin B. Odell, Jr.	1901-1904
12	Enos T. Throop	1829-1832	25	Reuben E. Fenton	1865-1868	38	Francis W. Higgins	1905-1906
13	William L. Marcy	1833-1839	26	John T. Hoffman	1869-1872	39	Charles E. Hughes	1907-1910

Mayors of the City of New York.

BEFORE the Revolution the Mayor was appointed by the Governor of the Province; and from 1784 to 1820 by the Appointing Board of the State of New York, of which the Governor was the chief member. From 1820 to the amendment of the Charter, in 1830, the Mayor was appointed by the Common Council. In 1898 the term of the first Mayor of Greater New York (Van Wyck) began.

	MAYORS.	Terms.		MAYORS.	Terms.		MAYORS.	Terms.
1	Thomas Willett	1665	33	Robert Walters	1720-1725	64	James Harper	1844-1845
2	Thomas Delavall	1666	34	Johannes Jansen	1725-1726	65	Wm. F. Havemeyer	1845-1846
3	Thomas Willett	1667	35	Robert Lurting	1726-1735	66	Andrew H. Mickle	1846-1847
4	Cornelis Steenwyck	1668-1670	36	Paul Richard	1735-1739	67	William V. Brady	1847-1848
5	Thomas Delavall	1671	37	John Cruger, Sr	1739-1744	68	Wm. F. Havemeyer	1848-1849
6	Matthias Nicolls	1672	38	Stephen Bayard	1744-1747	69	Caleb S. Woodhull	1849-1851
7	John Lawrence	1673	39	Edward Holland	1747-1757	70	Ambrose C. Kingsland	1851-1853
8	William Dervall	1675	40	John Cruger, Jr.	1757-1766	71	Jacob A. Westervelt	1853-1855
9	Nicholas de Meyer	1676	41	Whitehead Hicks	1766-1776	72	Fernando Wood	1855-1858
10	S. van Cortlandt	1677	42	David Matthews, Tory	1776-1784	73	Daniel F. Tiemann	1858-1860
11	Thomas Delavall	1678	43	James Duane	1784-1789	74	Fernando Wood	1860-1862
12	Francis Rombouts	1679	44	Richard Varick	1789-1801	75	George Opdyke	1862-1864
13	William Dyre	1680-1681	45	Edward Livingston	1801-1803	76	C. Godfrey Gunther	1864-1866
14	Cornelis Steenwyck	1682-1683	46	De Witt Clinton	1803-1807	77	John T. Hoffman	1866-1868
15	Gabriel Minville	1684	47	Marinus Willett	1807-1808	78	T. Coman (act'g Mayor)	1868
16	Nicholas Bayard	1685	48	De Witt Clinton	1808-1810	79	A. Oakey Hall	1869-1872
17	S. van Cortlandt	1686-1687	49	Jacob Radcliff	1810-1811	80	Wm. F. Havemeyer	1873-1874
18	Peter Delanoy	1689-1690	50	De Witt Clinton	1811-1815	81	S. B. H. Vance (Acting)	1874
19	John Lawrence	1691	51	John Ferguson	1815	82	William H. Wickham	1875-1876
20	Abraham De Peyster	1692-1695	52	Jacob Radcliff	1815-1818	83	Smith Ely	1877-1878
21	William Merritt	1695-1698	53	Cadwallader D. Colden	1818-1821	84	Edward Cooper	1879-1880
22	Johannes De Peyster	1698-1699	54	Stephen Allen	1821-1824	85	William R. Grace	1881-1882
23	David Provost	1699-1700	55	William Paulding	1825-1826	86	Franklin Edson	1883-1884
24	Isaac de Riemer	1700-1701	56	Philip Hone	1826-1827	87	William R. Grace	1885-1886
25	Thomas Noell	1701-1702	57	William Paulding	1827-1829	88	Abram S. Hewitt	1887-1888
26	Philip French	1702-1703	58	Walter Bowne	1829-1833	89	Hugh J. Grant	1889-1892
27	William Peartree	1703-1707	59	Gideon Lee	1833-1834	90	Thomas F. Gilroy	1893-1894
28	Ebenezer Wilson	1707-1710	60	Cornelius W Lawrence	1834-1837	91	William L. Strong	1895-1897
29	Jacobus van Cortlandt	1710-1711	61	Aaron Clark	1837-1839	92	Robert A. Van Wyck	1898-1901
30	Caleb Heathcote	1711-1714	62	Isaac L. Varian	1839-1841	93	Seth Low	1902-1903
31	John Johnson	1714-1719	63	Robert H. Morris	1841-1844	94	George B. McClellan	1904-1909
32	Jacobus van Cortlandt	1719-1720						

The Panama Canal.

PROGRESS OF THE WORK IN 1908.

In April, 1907, President Roosevelt put the construction work of the Canal in charge of Army engineers, and during the twelve months ended November 1, 1908, 35,016,024 cubic yards were excavated. From May 1, 1904, to November 1, 1907, the excavation amounted to but 18,714,931 yards.

The work has progressed speedily, the present efficiency having been attained early in the year. In December, 1907, it was decided to increase the width of the locks from 100 to 110 feet, the increase being made necessary by the construction of larger commercial and war ships. The change was suggested by the construction of officers of the navy when they let the contracts for the battleships Delaware and North Dakota.

But one change in the Commission took place during 1908: Jackson Smith, in charge of the Department of Labor, Supplies and Quarters, resigned on September 15, and was succeeded by Lieut.-Col. H. F. Hodges, U. S. A., another army engineer, so that now Hon. J. C. S. Blackburn, of Kentucky, is the only civilian member of the Commission.

The Canal Commission consists of the following persons

Lieut.-Col. George W. Goethals, salary $15,000, Chairman and Chief Engineer; Major D. D. Gaillard, U. S. A., salary $14,000; Major William L. Sibert, U. S. A., salary $14,000; H. H. Rosseau, Civil Engineer, U. S. N., salary $14,000; Hon. Joseph C. S. Blackburn, of Kentucky, salary $14,000; Col. W. C. Gorgas, U. S. A., salary $14,000; Lieut.-Col. H. F. Hodges, salary $14,000; Joseph Bucklin Bishop, Secretary, salary $10,000. Each member of the Commission is provided with a furnished house and is allowed all expenses while in the United States on official business.

Lieutenant-Colonel Goethals is in charge of Construction and Engineering; Major D. D. Gaillard has charge of the Department of Excavation and Dredging; Major William L. Sibert, Department of Locks and Dam Construction; H. H. Rosseau, in charge of Department of Municipal Engineering, Motive Power and Machinery, and Building Construction; Hon. Joseph C. S. Blackburn, in charge of Civil Administration; Col. W. C. Gorgas, Chief of the Department of Sanitation, and Lieut.-Col. H. F. Hodges, in charge of the Department of Labor, Quarters and Subsistence.

During a visit to Washington in July, 1908, Lieutenant-Colonel Goethals made an unofficial estimate as to the time required for completing the Canal by predicting that ships would pass through the waterway on January 1, 1915. He did that chiefly with a view to warn those interested against what to him seemed the too optimistic estimates of those who noted the speed with which he was "making the dirt fly." The optimists, taking the rate of excavation in the three months preceding, estimated that the Canal would be dug by the Fall of 1911. They overlooked the fact that the Canal is a V-shaped ditch, and the deeper the steam shovels go the fewer of them can be used, because there will not be room for them in the cut.

It is the impression of men connected with the work that the lieutenant-colonel, in making this estimate, leaned to the side of conservatism as far as the others bent to that of radicalism.

THE DIMENSIONS OF THE WORK.

The Canal will have a summit elevation of 85 feet above the sea, to be reached by a flight of three locks located at Gatun, on the Atlantic side, and by one lock at Pedro Miguel and a flight of two at Miraflores, on the Pacific side; all these locks to be in duplicate—that is, to have two chambers, side by side. Each lock will have a usable length of 1,000 feet and a width of 110 feet. The summit level will be maintained by a large dam at Gatun and a small one at Pedro Miguel, making the great Gatun Lake, which will have an area of 164.23 square miles. A small lake, about two square miles in area, with a surface elevation of 55 feet, will be formed on the Pacific side, between Pedro Miguel and Miraflores, the valley of the Rio Grande being closed by a small dam and the locks at Miraflores.

The Canal is to be about 50 miles in length, from deep water in the Caribbean Sea to deep water in the Pacific Ocean. The distance from deep water to the shore line in Limon Bay is about 4½ miles, and from the Pacific shore line to deep water is about 5 miles; hence the length of the Canal from shore to shore will be approximately 40½ miles.

The bottom width of the Canal will vary from 200 feet in Culebra Cut to an indefinite width in the deep waters of the lakes. The approaches from deep water to land on both sides of the Canal are to be 500 feet wide, and the cuts in the shallow parts of the lakes from 500 to 1,000 feet wide. The Canal will have a minimum depth of 41 feet.

The amount of material excavated by the old and new Panama Canal Companies was 81,548,000 cubic yards.

It was estimated in the report of the Commission for 1901 that 36,689,965 cubic yards of the prism excavated by the French would be useful in the main line of the new Canal, to which must be added the prism excavated by the company since the date of that report, 3,510,231 cubic yards, making a total of 40,200,196 cubic yards. This amount will be reduced by the submergence of the channel between Gatun and Bohio, which would have been utilized by the plan of the Commission of 1901, but not in the present project.

The following is the total estimated excavation required, May 1, 1904, based on the present working plans:

	Cubic yards.
In Canal prism	106,931,849
Excavation for locks, regulating works and diversion channel	10,363,400
Dredging entrance to old Canal at Colon for wharf purposes, and to aid in construction of Gatun works; and at Panama to keep channel open to La Boca	7,039,607
Total	124,334,856

(To this amount should be added the additional excavation necessitated by the recently adopted plan changing the location of the locks at La Boca to Miraflores and constructing

THE PANAMA CANAL.—*Continued.*

a sea level channel between those points, estimated at 18,000,000 cubic yards—exact figures not yet available.)

For purpose of comparison, it may be stated that the estimated amount of excavation required in the Canal prism for a sea level canal, as recommended by the majority of the Board of Consulting Engineers, was 231,026,477 cubic yards.

MATERIAL EXCAVATED BY THE UNITED STATES.

The amount of material excavated since American occupation is as follows:

Year and Month.	Atlantic Division.		Central Division.*	Pacific Division.		Total.
	Steam shovels.	Dredges.	Steam shovels.	Steam shovels.	Dredges.	
1904.	Cubic yds.	Cubic yds.	Cubic yds.	Cubic yds.	Cubic yds.	Cubic yds.
May	....	....	27,556	....	....	27,556
June	....	....	32,551	....	....	32,551
July	....	....	31,599	....	....	31,599
August	....	....	35,056	....	....	35,056
September	....	....	25,220	....	....	25,220
October	....	....	19,695	....	....	19,695
November	....	....	28,860	....	....	28,860
December	....	....	42,935	....	....	42,935
Totals	....	....	243,472	....	....	243,472
1905.						
January	....	....	70,650	....	....	70,650
February	....	....	75,200	....	....	75,200
March	....	....	132,840	....	....	132,840
April	....	....	126,749	....	....	126,749
May	....	....	75,935	....	....	75,935
June	....	60,700	76,905	....	50,676	188,281
July	....	58,950	78,570	....	41,333	178,153
August	....	53,183	49,210	....	54,530	156,923
September	....	48,837	44,085	....	114,308	207,230
October	....	48,800	52,940	....	81,836	183,576
November	....	38,000	60,540	....	71,176	169,716
December	....	92,250	70,630	....	71,094	233,974
Totals	....	399,820	914,254	....	485,153	1,799,227
1906.						
January	....	90,700	120,990	....	95,940	307,630
February	....	105,500	168,410	....	95,940	369,850
March	....	126,650	239,178	....	116,820	482,648
April	....	87,200	213,177	....	110,700	411,077
May	....	64,875	196,209	....	112,340	373,424
June	....	73,500	212,623	....	62,697	348,820
July	....	69,000	159,789	....	98,400	327,189
August	....	54,000	244,823	....	111,930	410,753
September	....	128,540	291,452	....	105,780	520,772
October	3,055	111,020	327,009	....	97,170	538,254
November	11,517	68,260	221,642	....	92,988	389,407
December	12,056	58,400	307,689	....	90,528	468,673
Totals	26,628	1,027,645	2,702,991	....	1,191,233	4,948,497
1907.						
January	47,539	111,100	566,750	....	94,710	820,099
February	70,177	110,002	639,112	....	93,480	912,771
March	100,151	84,145	816,270	3,905	92,319	1,096,790
April	103,450	69,889	879,527	1,756	104,855	1,159,480
May	70,528	133,847	690,365	762	122,157	1,017,659
June	75,013	124,118	624,586	4,907	133,575	962,199
July	74,890	100,922	770,570	13,772	108,336	1,067,498
August	120,480	194,297	780,706	15,865	168,384	1,288,692
September	152,575	420,842	775,014	12,806	153,975	1,516,212
October	218,091	431,770	860,126	7,220	357,122	1,874,329
November	202,625	427,572	884,676	9,525	305,423	1,830,821
December	277,496	442,835	1,124,137	7,715	349,551	2,201,734
Totals	1,513,030	2,660,339	9,369,899	78,233	2,143,789	15,765,290
1908.						
January	354,990	400,701	1,006,460	7,203	469,259	2,709,613
February	348,420	497,728	1,448,410	30,046	668,519	2,927,123
March	456,448	546,886	1,615,118	85,554	783,281	3,487,287
April	440,892	496,366	1,572,057	110,243	676,539	3,296,097
May	321,080	564,380	1,196,742	90,228	530,466	2,702,897
June	270,979	572,749	1,456,177	96,340	656,821	3,050,069
July	236,874	625,497	1,467,022	130,727	696,176	3,156,350
August	204,571	638,217	1,540,610	131,334	737,774	3,252,506
September	178,102	624,770	1,469,808	136,120	750,080	3,158,886
October	216,961	505,260	1,598,981	137,560	765,876	3,224,638
Grand total	4,574,978	10,580,804	27,902,070	1,042,792	10,540,754	53,730,955

53,730,955 cubic yards excavated up to November 1, 1908; 35,016,024 cubic yards were excavated in the last twelve months.

	Cubic yards.
Total approximate amount of excavation required on May 1, 1904, as shown on preceding page, (estimated)	142,000,000
Amount excavated to November 1, 1908	53,730,955
Amount remaining to be excavated November 1, 1908	88,269,045

*Including Culebra Cut.

There are now on the Isthmus forty-eight 95-ton, forty-two 70-ton, ten 45-ton and one 38-ton steam shovels, or a total of one hundred and one steam shovels.

FORCE EMPLOYED.

In the month of September, 1908, there were approximately 45,000 employees on the Isthmus on the rolls of the Commission and of the Panama Railroad; about 6,000 of whom were Americans. There were actually at work on September 2, 1908, 31,869 men—25,985 men for the Commission and 5,884 for the Panama Railroad Company. Of the 25,985 men working for the Commission, 4,377 were on the gold roll, which comprises those paid in United States currency, and 21,608 men on the silver roll, which comprises those paid on the basis of Panaman currency or its equivalent. Those on the gold roll include mechanics, skilled artisans of all classes, clerks and higher officials, most of whom are Americans; those on the silver roll include principally the common laborers, who are practically all foreigners. Of the 5,884 Panama Railroad employees, 791 were on the gold roll.

FINANCES OF THE CANAL.

The following is a statement of the appropriations and expenditures down to June 30, 1908, exclusive of the $50,000,000 appropriated and paid for the rights of way and franchises:

APPROPRIATIONS.

Construction of Canal, June 28, 1902		$10,000,000.00
Construction of Canal, December 21, 1905		11,000,000.00
Construction of Canal, February 27, 1906		5,990,786.00
Construction of Canal, June 30, 1906		25,456,415.08
Expenses in the United States	$368,242.69	
Construction, engineering and administration	21,018,537.24	
Civil Administration	968,200.00	
Sanitation and hospitals	2,101,435.15	
Re-equipment of Panama Railroad	1,000,000.00	
Construction of Canal, March 4, 1907		27,161,367.50
Expenses in the United States	$253,000.00	
Construction, engineering and administration	20,366,000.00	
Civil Administration	825,000.00	
Sanitation and hospitals	2,034,000.00	
Re-equipment of Panama Railroad	1,385,000.00	
Purchase of Panama Railroad bonds	2,298,367.50	
Construction of Canal, February 15, 1908		12,178,900.00
Expenses in the United States	$18,600.00	
Construction, engineering and administration	11,990,400.00	
Sanitation and hospitals	169,900.00	
		$91,787,468.58
Miscellaneous—Collections account sale of Government property, etc.		3,140,103.05
Balance due individuals and companies, account collections from employees		3,828.35
Total receipts		$94,931,399.98
In addition to appropriations above set forth, the act of May 27, 1908, appropriated, to continue the construction of the Canal		$29,177,000.00
Made up of the following items:		
Expenses in the United States	$176,000.00	
Construction, engineering and administration	23,450,000.00	
Civil Administration	241,000.00	
Sanitation and hospitals	1,575,000.00	
Re-equipment of Panama Railroad	1,100,000.00	
Purchase of two ships for Panama Railroad Company	1,550,000.00	
Re-location of Panama Railroad	1,085,000.00	
Total appropriations to June 30, 1908		$120,964,468.58
Total, including franchise		170,964,468.58

THE PANAMA CANAL—*Continued.*

DISBURSEMENTS.

Classified expenditures			$76,047,062.72
Department of Civil Administration		$2,146,996.77	
Department of Sanitation		6,925,910.77	
Department of Construction and Engineering		35,874,846.14	
Canal construction	$30,104,095.27		
Municipal improvements on Zone	3,533,618.70		
Municipal improvements in Panama and Colon	2,237,132.17		
Cost of plant		31,099,309.04	
Rights of way and franchises			40,168,651.28
Rights acquired from Republic of Panama		$10,000,000.00	
Rights acquired from New Panama Canal Company		39,168,651.28	
Payment to New Panama Canal Company	$40,000,000.00		
Less value of French material sold or used in construction	831,348.72		
Panama Railroad Company stock purchased			157,118.24
Loans to Panama Railroad Company for re-equipment and redemption of bonds			4,382,264.24
Paid into United States Treasury for sale of Government property, etc			3,136,232.27
Services rendered and material sold to individuals and companies			2,327,343.24
Unclassified expenditures			4,137,247.94
Material and supplies on hand		$3,916,075.22	
Payments to Panama Railroad Company		195,843.30	
Other unclassified items		25,329.42	
Advances to laborers for their transportation			31,728.61
Total			$139,387,648.54
Less amounts included above, but unpaid on June 30, 1908			1,678,417.72
Salaries and wages unpaid on pay rolls, prior to June 1, 1908		$190,636.84	
Pay rolls for the month of June, 1908		1,487,780.88	
Total disbursements to June 30, 1908			$137,709,230.82
Balances available June 30, 1908			7,222,169.16
Congressional appropriations		$7,214,470.03	
Collections account sales of Government property, etc		3,870.78	
Collections from employees account individuals and companies		3,828.35	
Total			$144,931,399.98

State Legislation Regulating Railroad Rates.

No important railroad rate legislation was enacted in 1908, it being the "off year" in which Legislatures of only twelve States were in session. Special sessions were held in several States, but only North Carolina and Mississippi dealt with the rate question. North Carolina passed a 2½-cent rate bill which deprives the State Railroad Commission of authority to fix rates. The Mississippi Legislature refused to pass the 2-cent rate urged by the Governor.

Railroads in the South effected a truce in the warfare of 1907 by agreement in several of the States to try a 2½-cent rate for a year. The Railroad Commission of Ohio, the pioneer State in regulating rates, reported that Ohio roads have prospered under the Ohio 2-cent rate law.

The Courts, State and Federal, were kept busy with litigation over the rate laws of 1907. The most far-reaching decisions were those in the Minnesota and North Carolina cases, handed down by the United States Supreme Court on March 23, 1908. These decisions held the North Carolina 2-cent rate law confiscatory and therefore unconstitutional, and the Minnesota freight rate act invalid for the same reason. Two mooted questions were settled, viz: (1) Enjoining a State official is not suing the State, and (2) A Federal Court may test the validity of a State rate law. Subsequently, the "injunction-proof" features of the Alabama, Arkansas, Missouri and Mississippi railroad acts, forbidding transfer of suits from State to Federal courts under penalty of fine or forfeiture of charter, were declared unconstitutional. Oklahoma's similar provision, under which the charter of the St. Louis and San Francisco road was ordered annulled, is being attacked on the same ground.

The important legislative and judicial acts of the year follow:

ALABAMA—"Injunction-proof" provision overthrown by Federal Circuit Court and enforcement of 2¼-cent passenger rate and freight act affecting 110 commodities en-

STATE LEGISLATION REGULATING RAILROAD RATES.—*Continued.*

joined permanently. State Commission filed protest with Interstate Commerce Commission against advance of freight rates; matter pending.

ARKANSAS—Inhibition of appeal to Federal courts declared unconstitutional; Railroad Commission refused to recede from strict enforcement of 2-cent rate law, which railroads combined to fight; enforcement of act enjoined by Federal Circuit Court; matter pending; Commission will ask Legislature for large appropriation to continue legal fight.

COLORADO—Railroad Commission resumed work, which it had suspended pending decision of the Colorado Supreme Court, which upheld constitutionality of law creating the Commission.

GEORGIA—"Little Joe" Brown, who was a "conservative" member of the State Railroad Commission, was elected Governor largely on the issue of his attitude toward the railroads; United States Circuit Court enjoined enforcement of higher freight rate schedule, but put railroads under $100,000 bond each to refund to shippers in event of adverse ruling in litigation now pending.

ILLINOIS—An injunction was issued against the Illinois Railroad Commission enforcing its switching rate order, as a means of testing the Commission's authority to make rates.

KANSAS—The State Supreme Court upheld the Kansas demurrage act; the State Railroad Commission ordered a reduction of freight rates and was enjoined by the Federal Circuit Court from enforcing the order.

KENTUCKY—The State appealed to the United States Supreme Court from the decision of the Federal Circuit Court declaring unconstitutional the law empowering the Kentucky Railroad Commission to fix rates; pending.

LOUISIANA—A special session of the Louisiana Legislature passed an act prohibiting foreign corporations transferring suits from the State to Federal courts, and, under this act, late in 1908, had the Texas and Pacific enjoined from transferring a suit, which will be made a test case. The Louisiana Railroad Commission was one of the most active in ordering reductions of rates.

MINNESOTA—The United States Supreme Court declared confiscatory and unconstitutional the Minnesota freight act.

MISSISSIPPI—A special session of the Legislature refused by a large majority to pass a 2-cent rate law. The railroads resisted orders of the State Railroad Commission reducing rates on export cotton; were defeated in the lower courts and are taking an appeal to the United States Supreme Court. The State act penalizing transferring suits to Federal jurisdiction was declared unconstitutional.

MISSOURI—The State Supreme Court declared unconstitutional the act compelling the granting of free passes to shippers of live stock, on the ground of discrimination; the State's inhibition of appeal to Federal courts was declared unconstitutional; enforcement of the State freight rate act was enjoined; case pending.

NEBRASKA—The Gould roads applied to the State Railroad Commission for permission to increase passenger rates from 2 to 3 cents a mile and freight rates by 15 per cent.; preparations were made to test the 2-cent fare act.

NEW HAMPSHIRE—The Attorney-General brought suit against the Boston and Maine for raising freight rates.

NEW YORK—The Attorney-General brought suit against seven coal carrying roads for maintaining an alleged coal monopoly in violation of the State Anti-Monopoly law.

NEVADA—The State Railroad Commission is still tied up with litigation to test its authority.

NORTH CAROLINA—Following Governor Glenn's recession from his defiance of the Federal courts in 1907 a special session of the Legislature passed a 2½-cent rate bill, superseding the 2-cent fare bill which the United States Supreme Court declared unconstitutional. The new law does not give the State Commission power to fix rates.

OKLAHOMA—Constitutionality of the Oklahoma prohibition of appeal to Federal courts is being attacked; the State Railroad Commission, in spite of the constitutional rate of 2 cents a mile, excepted certain short roads from its provisions.

OREGON—The Southern Pacific Company attacked the law creating the State Railroad Commission.

PENNSYLVANIA—The State Supreme Court, four to three, declared the State 2-cent rate law confiscatory and unconstitutional.

TEXAS—The State Commission withdrew its 2½-cent rate order against the H. & T. C. and the Harriman lines in Texas abandoned their fight against the Commission. The M. K. & T. issued the first 2-cent mileage in Texas. The State's reciprocal demurrage law was overthrown.

VIRGINIA—The 500-mile 2-cent mileage act was declared unconstitutional on the ground of confiscation.

WASHINGTON—The Federal District Court decided that the State Railroad Commission has no authority to fix rates; that this power belongs to the Legislature and cannot be delegated.

WEST VIRGINIA—Injunction proceedings to prevent enforcement of the State 2-cent rate law were commenced.

WISCONSIN—The Wisconsin Railroad Commission act was upheld by the State Supreme Court.

Regulation of Railroad Rates.

THE following are the clauses of the act approved June 29, 1906, to amend the act of 1887 and other acts amendatory thereof entitled "An Act to Regulate Commerce," which specifically relate to the construction of switches, filing of schedules of rates and fares, prohibition of discriminations and rebates and hearing of complaints and remedial action thereon by the Interstate Commerce Commission.

FURNISHING SWITCHES AND TRANSPORTATION.

Any common carrier subject to the provisions of this act, upon application of any lateral, branch line of railroad, or of any shipper tendering interstate traffic for transportation, shall construct, maintain, and operate upon reasonable terms a switch connection with any such lateral, branch line of railroad, or private side track which may be constructed to connect with its railroad, where such connection is reasonably practicable and can be put in with safety and will furnish sufficient business to justify the construction and maintenance of the same; and shall furnish cars for the movement of such traffic to the best of its ability, without discrimination in favor of or against any such shipper.

FILING OF SCHEDULES OF RATES.

Every common carrier subject to the provisions of this act shall file with the commission created by this act and print and keep open to public inspection schedules showing all the rates, fares and charges for transportation between different points on its own route and between points on its own route and points on the route of any carrier by railroad, by pipe line, or by water when a through route and joint rate have been established. If no joint rate over the through route has been established, the several carriers in such through route shall file, print and keep open to public inspection as aforesaid, the separately established rates, fares and charges applied to the through transportation. The schedules printed as aforesaid by any such common carrier shall plainly state the places between which property and passengers will be carried, and shall contain the classification of freight in force, and shall also state separately all terminal charges, storage charges, icing charges, and all other charges which the commission may require, all privileges or facilities granted or allowed, and any rules or regulations which in anywise change, affect, or determine any part of the aggregate of such aforesaid rates, fares and charges, or the value of the service rendered to the passenger, shipper, or consignee.

DISCRIMINATION FORBIDDEN.

No carrier, unless otherwise provided by this act, shall engage or participate in the transportation of passengers or property, as defined in this act, unless the rates, fares, and charges upon which the same are transported by said carrier have been filed and published in accordance with the provisions of this act; nor shall any carrier charge or demand or collect or receive a greater or less or different compensation for such transportation of passengers or property, or for any service in connection therewith, between the points named in such tariffs than the rates, fares, and charges which are specified in the tariff filed and in effect at the time; nor shall any carrier refund or remit in any manner or by any device any portion of the rates, fares, and charges so specified, nor extend to any shipper or person any privileges or facilities in the transportation of passengers or property, except such as are specified in such tariffs.

REBATES.

Any person, corporation, or company who shall deliver property for interstate transportation to any common carrier, subject to the provisions of this act, or for whom as consignor or consignee, any such carrier shall transport property from one State, Territory, or the District of Columbia to any other State, Territory, or the District of Columbia or foreign country, who shall knowingly by employé, agent, officer, or otherwise, directly or indirectly, by or through any means or device whatsoever, receive or accept from such common carrier any sum of money or any other valuable consideration as a rebate or offset against the regular charges for transportation of such property, as fixed by the schedules of rate provided for in this act, shall in addition to any penalty provided by this act forfeit to the United States a sum of money three times the amount of money so received or accepted, and three times the value of any other consideration so received or accepted, to be ascertained by the trial court; and the Attorney-General of the United States is authorized and directed, whenever he has reasonable grounds to believe that any such person, corporation, or company has knowingly received or accepted from any such common carrier any sum of money or other valuable consideration as a rebate or offset as aforesaid, to institute in any court of the United States of competent jurisdiction, a civil action to collect the said sum or sums so forfeited as aforesaid; and in the trial of said action all such rebates or other considerations so received or accepted for a period of six years prior to the commencement of the action, may be included therein, and the amount recovered shall be three times the total amount of money, or three times the total value of such consideration, so received or accepted, or both, as the case may be.

HEARING OF COMPLAINTS.

The commission is authorized and empowered, and it shall be its duty, whenever, after full hearing upon a complaint made as provided in section thirteen of this act, or upon complaint of any common carrier, it shall be of the opinion that any of the rates, or charges whatsoever, demanded, charged, or collected by any common carrier or carriers, subject to the provisions of this act, for the transportation of persons or property as defined in the first section of this act, or that any regulations or practices whatsoever of such carrier or carriers affecting such rates, are unjust and unreasonable, or unjustly discriminatory, or unduly preferential or prejudicial, or otherwise in violation of any of the provisions of this act, to determine and prescribe what will be the just and reasonable rate or rates, charge or charges, to be thereafter observed in such case as the maximum to be charged; and what regulation or practice in respect to such transportation is just, fair, and reasonable to be thereafter followed; and to make an order that the carrier shall cease and desist from such violation, to the extent to which the commission find the same to exist, and shall not thereafter publish, demand, or collect any rate or charge for such transportation in excess of the maximum rate or charge so prescribed. All shall conform to the regulation or pratice so prescribed.

ESTABLISHMENT OF ROUTES AND RATES.

The commission may also, after hearing on a complaint, establish through routes and joint rates as the maximum to be charged, and prescribe the division of such rates as hereinbefore provided, and the terms and conditions under which such through routes shall be operated, when that may be necessary to give effect to any provision of this act, and the carriers complained of have refused or neglected to voluntarily establish such through routes and joint rates, provided no reasonable or satisfactory through route exists, and this provision shall apply when one of the connecting carriers is a water line.

Prosecutions Under the Anti-Rebate Laws.

INDICTMENTS were brought against forty-three persons (natural and corporate) during the year 1908, under the provisions of the act to regulate commerce and the Elkins act, forbidding the giving or acceptance of rebates or discriminations. The indictments brought during 1908 and their status on November 10, 1908, were as follows:

United States vs. Max Agal and Simon Levin (District of Vermont). February 29, 1908, indictment returned, charging mis-billing of freight. May 26, 1908, plea of guilty. June 26, 1908, fined $50.

United States vs. American News Company (Southern District of New York). October 13, 1908, indictment returned, charging mis-billing of freight. Case pending.

United States vs. P. H. Barteman (District of Maryland). September 29, 1908, indictment returned, charging unlawful use of interstate pass. Case pending.

United States vs. California Pine Box and Lumber Company (Northern District of California). June 26, 1908, indictment returned, charging acceptance of rebates from Southern Pacific Company. Case pending.

United States vs. Chapman & Dewey Lumber Company (Eastern District of Missouri). March 3, 1908, indictment returned, charging acceptance of rebates from St. Louis and San Francisco Railroad Company. March 10, 1908, plea of guilty, fined $18,000.

United States vs. Chesapeake and Ohio Railway (Eastern District of Virginia). June 9, 1908, two indictments returned, charging rebating. Cases pending.

United States vs. Chicago, Rock Island and Pacific Railway (Northern District of Illinois). July 18, 1908, indictment returned, charging issuance of illegal passes.

United States vs. L. J. Clark (District of South Carolina). April 21, 1908, indictment returned, charging misuse of passes. Plea of guilty, fined $100.

United States vs. A. J. Fischlowitz (Southern District of New York). October 13, 1908, indictment returned, charging mis-billing of freight. Case pending.

United States vs. F. Konigsberg and Leon (Southern District of New York). October 13, 1908, indictment returned, charging mis-billing of freight. Case pending.

United States vs. A. P. Gilbert, Assistant General Freight Agent, Chesapeake and Ohio Railway (Eastern District of Virginia). June 9, 1908, indictment returned, granting rebates. Case pending.

United States vs. Harry Gore and Max Robinavitz (Northern District of West Virginia). January 21, 1908, indictment returned, charging false billing of freight. June 9, 1908, plea of guilty. Fined $100.

United States vs. Hannacher & Schlemmer Company (Southern District of New York). October 13, 1908, indictment returned, charging false billing of freight. Case pending.

United States vs. Herrmann, Aukam & Co. (Southern District of New York). June —, 1908, indictment returned, charging false billing of freight. Case pending.

United States vs. Illinois Central Railroad Company (Eastern District of Louisiana). May 16, 1908, indictment returned, granting rebates. Case pending.

United States vs. Illinois Terminal Railroad Company (Southern District of Illinois). September 12, 1908, indictment returned, charging failure to file rates. Case pending.

United States vs. Illinois Glass Company and Illinois Terminal Railroad Company (Southern District of Illinois). September 12, 1908, indictment returned, charging acceptance of rebates. Case pending.

United States vs. Illinois Central Railroad Company (Northern District of Illinois). July 23, 1908, indictment returned, charging illegal issuance of passes.

United States vs. W. R. Johnson (Eastern District of Virginia). June 9, 1908, indictment returned, charging acceptance of rebates. Case pending.

United States vs. Manhattan Brass Company (Southern District of New York). October 13, 1908, indictment returned, charging false billing of freight. Case pending.

United States vs. Missouri, Kansas and Texas Railway Company (Western District of Missouri). May 5, 1908, indictment returned, charging rebating. Case pending.

United States vs. Missouri Pacific Railway Company (District of Arkansas). April 14, 1908, indictment returned, charging rebating. Case pending.

United States vs. St. Louis, Iron Mountain and Southern Railway Company (District of Arkansas). April 14, 1908, indictment returned, charging rebating. Case pending.

United States vs. W. C. Stith, Traffic Manager, Missouri Pacific Railway Company (District of Arkansas). April 14, 1908, indictment returned, charging rebating.

United States vs. T. H. Bunch (District of Arkansas). April 14, 1908, indictment returned, charging acceptance of rebates. Case pending.

United States vs. Warner Moore & Co. (Eastern District of Virginia). June 12, 1908, indictment returned, charging acceptance of rebates. Case pending.

United States vs. Nastas (Western District of Missouri). May 9, 1908, indictment returned, charging misuse of passes. Case pending.

United States vs. Nick Nastas, Samuel C. Clark and Louis Agnes (Western District of Missouri). May 9, 1908, indictment returned, charging conspiracy to evade anti-pass law.

United States vs. L. M. Neiberg (District of Vermont). February 29, 1908, indictment returned, charging false billing of freight. May 19, 1908, plea of guilty, fined $250.

United States vs. Dan Pounds (Northern District of Alabama). September 19, 1908, indictment returned, charging misuse of free passes. Case pending.

United States vs. Penn Fruit Company (Southern District of California). July 10, 1908, indictment returned, charging acceptance of rebates. Case pending.

United States vs. St. Louis and San Francisco Railroad Company (Eastern District of Missouri). March 3, 1908, indictment returned, charging rebating. March 10, 1908, plea of guilty. Fined $18,000.

United States vs. Siff & Cohen (Southern District of New York). October 13, 1908, indictment returned, charging false billing of freight. Case pending.

United States vs. James Solsky (Western District of Michigan). July 8, 1908, indictment returned, charging false billing of freight. July 9, 1908, defendant acquitted.

United States vs. Southern Pacific Company, three indictments (Southern District of California). June 1, 1908, indictments returned, charging rebating. Cases pending.

United States vs. Southern Pacific Company, three indictments (Northern District of California). June 30, 1908, indictments, charging rebating. Cases pending.

United States vs. Tom Williams (Northern District of Alabama). March 7, 1908, indictment returned, charging violation of anti-pass law. Plea of guilty, fined $100.

Cuban Occupation in 1908.

THE military occupation of Cuba by the United States, which began in 1906, continued throughout 1908, but terminates on January 28, 1909, in accordance with the President's announcement on January 14, 1908, that the government would be restored to the Cubans not later than February 1, 1909. Gov. Charles E. Magoon remained at the head of the Government, which administered the affairs of the republic under the constitution of Cuba for the benefit of the Cuban people, having at his command about 5,000 American troops, which at no time, however, were called upon for any service other than that pertaining to their enlistment in the Army of the United States.

The most important work of the year was the nomination of candidates for President and Vice-President under the electoral laws prepared by a commission of twelve members, representing all parties in the republic, as well as the Americans in the provisional government. The nominating elections held in the late Summer of 1908 passed without disturbance. The general election was held on November 14, and resulted in the Liberals carrying every province, thus assuring the electoral vote of the whole republic for Major-General Jose Miguel Gomez for President and Dr. Alfredo Zayas, leader of one of the factions that made the administration of President Palma a failure, for Vice-President.

The Liberals also carried all the provinces for Senatorial electors. The Cuban system provides for the choosing of Senators by colleges of electors chosen in the way in which Presidential electors are selected in the United States. But it also provides for proportional representation in the House of Representatives. The administration of President Gomez, therefore, will have to meet a small but determined minority in the popular branch of the law-making body.

The census taken in 1907 showed a population of 1,572,845. That result of the compilation showed the gross frauds committed by the Moderate party during the campaign in 1906, which led to the state of affairs compelling intervention by the United States. Although the Liberals refused to present themselves for registration for the election of 1906, yet the Moderates, in charge of the election machinery, reported that 432,313 voters had voluntarily presented themselves for registration.

The census taken by the intervening government showed that there were but 419,342 men of all parties on the island entitled to vote, and that considerably more than a year after the registration for the election in 1906.

Governor Magoon's administration has been one, the benefits of which will endure for generations in Cuba. Its most lasting monument and the most grateful to the farmer of the country will be the network of roads constructed under American supervision. Cuba is dependent upon its agriculture for the production of wealth, and has been subject to great economic waste by reason of lack and cost of inland transportation. The products of Cuba are hauled to market over trails that are barely passable during the dry season and absolutely impassable during the rainy season. Realizing the necessities of the situation, the provisional government gave its best efforts to supplying the remedy. A comprehensive plan of road improvements was adopted, and in all parts of the island trunk roads and local roads were constructed and are now under construction. On September 29, 1906, when the provisional government began, there were but 366 miles of macadamized highway in Cuba, many of which had been constructed under the American military government. On May 1, 1908, the mileage had been increased by the provisional administration to 537 miles, and there were 457 miles of road under construction.

Other public works were provided in all parts of the island. Harbors were dredged, lighthouses were built, hospitals, asylums courthouses and other public buildings were erected and repaired, bridges provided and waterworks furnished the principal towns. All these important works, as well as the road work, were paid for out of current funds.

To meet the demand for legislative action, and in pursuance of the plan of the Peace Commission, an advisory commission was created, composed of twelve members, nine of whom were prominent Cubans, all political parties being represented, and three Americans, who had had experience with Spanish law. The Commission on organizing was charged with the drafting of five laws—an electoral law, a municipal law, a provincial law, a judiciary law and a civil service law. To these were added a law organizing the armed forces, a military code, a law organizing the national executive departments, a general telephone law, a notarial law, and the revision of portions of mortgage law. Numerous minor degrees were reported by the Commission, and the lack of adequate legislation obliged the Commission to draft a municipal accounting law and a municipal tax law in connection with the organic municipal law.

In addition, a Commission was convened constituted by prominent Cuban judges and lawyers, for the revision of the harsh and antiquated Penal Code and the Code of Criminal Procedure.

Much attention was given to the matter of sanitation, which, in Cuba, is not only of vital importance to the health of the inhabitants, but has also a direct bearing upon the development and commerce of the country, for vessels will not enter a port of the island if all other ports of the world are quarantined against Cuba. The matter is also one of serious moment to the people and commerce of the Southern States of the United States. Yellow fever has been stamped out in Cuba during the American military government, but reappeared. Indefatigable work on the part of the provisional administration again suppressed it. In view of the special importance of sanitation in Cuba a law was promulgated which nationalized the sanitary service of the island and provided a National Board of Sanitation, charged with the responsibility of securing proper sanitation throughout the island and invested with the authority necessary for obtaining that result.

COMPARATIVELY few prosecutions under the terms of the Sherman Anti-Trust law were begun during the year 1908. The energies of those members of the Attorney-General's staff engaged in that work and the closely related prosecutions under the rebate section of the Interstate Commerce law were absorbed in the trial of the cases against the Standard Oil combination, the Tobacco Trust and the Du Pont Powder Company.

The Standard held first place in the thoughts of the trust-breaking staff. There are twenty-one cases against it under the rebate section pending in the courts, the chief of which is the $29,240,000 fine case. That fine, imposed on August 3, 1907, is unpaid. On July 22, 1908, the Circuit Court of Appeals for the Seventh Circuit reversed the case and remanded it to the District Court for further proceedings in accordance with the views of the Appellate Court expressed in the opinion delivered by Judge Peter Grosscup.

The Government, as soon as possible, filed an application for a rehearing of the case by the Circuit Court of Appeals. That application was denied November 10, 1908. Thereupon Attorney-General Bonaparte announced that a petition to have the case reviewed by the Supreme Court would be filed on November 30. Such a course is necessary because the jurisdiction of the Circuit Court of Appeals is conclusive in criminal actions such as this one. There are twenty-one other criminal actions against the Standard and its subsidiaries still pending.

The civil case against it under the Sherman act is being prepared for hearing before the Circuit Court at St. Louis. A record bound in fifteen enormous volumes has been made. The end is not in sight.

The Government achieved its most notable victory since the Northern Securities case on November 7, when the Circuit Court at New York decided that the American Tobacco Company and its subsidiaries, except the Imperial Tobacco Company and the United Cigar Stores Company, constitute a restraint in trade between the States and foreign nations within the meaning of the Sherman law.

The Court, in this case, issued an injunction which is suspended during appeal to the Supreme Court of the United States, forbidding the tobacco trust to ship goods in interstate commerce while the illegal combination remains in force. That order differs from the usual order in trust cases in that it places the burden of proving that the illegal practices have ceased upon the defendants. Heretofore, the burden has been on the Government to show that the order of the court has not been obeyed, and that the defendant or defendants should be punished for contempt. The tobacco combination, should the Supreme Court sustain the lower tribunal, will be compelled to satisfy the court that it had complied with the law ere it might ship any of its products from one State to another.

The following cases have been begun under the Sherman law since the 1908 edition of the ALMANAC went to press.

CIVIL SUITS.

United States vs. One Hundred and Seventy-five Cases of Cigarettes—October 28, 1907. Information filed in the District Court for the Eastern District of Virginia covering the seizure of 175 cases of cigarettes under Section 6 of the Sherman Anti-Trust act. Case pending.

United States vs. Union Pacific Railroad Company et al—February 1, 1908, a bill in equity was filed in the Circuit Court of the United States for the District of Utah, charging a combination and conspiracy in violation of the Sherman act. Case pending.

United States vs. New York, New Haven and Hartford Railroad Company et al—May 22, 1908, a bill in equity was filed in the Circuit Court of the United States for the District of Massachusetts charging the New Haven company with combining and attempting to combine under one common control the various railroad and electric railway systems in New England, in violation of the Sherman act. Case pending.

CRIMINAL ACTIONS.

United States vs. H. D. Corbett Stationery Company et al—November 1, 1907, indictment returned in the District Court for the District of Arizona charging a combination in restraint of trade. November 4, 1907, demurrer filed. November 14, 1907, demurrers sustained and defendants referred to next grand jury.

United States vs. Union Pacific Coal Company et al—November 20, 1907, indictment returned in the District Court for the District of Utah, charging a conspiracy to violate and for a violation of the Sherman act. January 6, 1908, demurrer filed. March 2, 1908, demurrer sustained as to first count and overruled as to second count. Case pending.

United States vs. Charles L. Simmons et al—January 20, 1908, indictment returned in the District Court for the Southern District of Alabama charging a combination in restraint of trade and commerce in the matter of the manufacture and sale of plumbers' supplies. Pending.

United States vs. E. J. Ray et al—February 14, 1908, indictment returned in the Circuit Court for the Eastern District of Louisiana against seventy-two laborers charging a combination and conspiracy in restraint of foreign trade and commerce, in violation of the Sherman act. Case pending.

United States vs. E. J. Ray et al—February 15, 1908, indictment returned in the Circuit Court for the Eastern District of Louisiana against seventy-two laborers charging a combination and conspiracy in restraint of interstate trade and commerce, in violation of the Sherman act. Case pending.

United States vs. Joseph Stiefvater et al—February 15, 1908, indictment returned in the United States Circuit Court for the Eastern District of Louisiana, charging a combination in restraint of trade and commerce in the matter of the manufacture and sale of plumbers' supplies. Case pending.

United States vs. American Naval Stores Company et al—April 11, 1908, indictment returned in the United States Circuit Court for the Southern District of Georgia, charging a combination in restraint of trade and commerce in the matter of the manufacture and sale of turpentine. Case pending.

United States vs. John H. Parks et al—June 16, 1908, indictment returned in the Circuit Court of the United States for the Southern District of New York, charging a combination in restraint of trade in the matter of the manufacture and sale of paper. June 19, 1908, defendants pleaded guilty and sentenced to pay fines aggregating $50,000, which were paid. Case against John H. Parks pending.

Record of Events in 1908.

Jan. 1. In Georgia the law prohibiting the sale of alcoholic beverages became effective.

Jan. 4. George A. Pettibone was acquitted of the murder of ex-Gov. Steunenburg.

Jan. 9. The East River Tunnel from the Battery, Manhattan, to Brooklyn, was opened.

Jan. 12. American battleship fleet arrived at Rio de Janeiro and was enthusiastically welcomed.

Jan. 13. In a theatre fire at Boyerstown, Pa., nearly 200 persons perished.

Jan. 13. Henry Farnam made a successful ascent in a heavier than air machine at Paris, and won a prize of $10,000.

Jan. 13. The New York Clearing House voted to admit trust companies to membership.

Jan. 15. The Senate passed joint resolution remitting to China about $13,000,000 of the Boxer indemnity.

Jan. 16. The French defeated the Moors near Settal, Morocco.

Jan. 18. John R. Walsh was found guilty of misapplying funds of the Chicago National Bank.

Jan. 20. The Pennsylvania two-cent railroad fare law was declared unconstitutional by the Pennsylvania Supreme Court.

Jan. 21. The claim of the French Government against the Panama Canal Company and Colombia was compromised by the payment of $1,600,000.

Jan. 22. Morris K. Jesup left $1,000,000 to the American Museum of Natural History.

Jan. 27. The law prohibiting discrimination against members of labor organizations was declared unconstitutional by the United States Supreme Court.

Feb. 1. Harry K. Thaw, acquitted of the murder of Stanford White on the ground of insanity, was removed to the insane asylum at Matteawan.

Feb. 1. King Carlos of Portugal and the Crown Prince were assassinated.

Feb. 2. Manuel II. was proclaimed King of Portugal.

Feb. 6. Sir Harry MacLean was liberated by Raisuli.

Feb. 10. An Arbitration Treaty with France was signed at Washington.

Feb. 12. The New York to Paris automobile race started with six entries.

Feb. 14. Deputy Fire Chief Krueger, of New York, was killed at a fire.

Feb. 17. The Turkish reserves were called out and moved to the Persian frontier.

Feb. 20. The American battleship fleet arrived at Callao, Peru.

Feb. 20. General Stoessel, the Russian commander at Port Arthur, was found guilty and condemned to death. Sentence was commuted to ten years' imprisonment.

Feb. 23. Father Leo Heinrichs, a Catholic priest, was shot, and killed in Denver by Giuseppe Alio, an Anarchist.

Feb. 25. The first of the tunnels under the Hudson between New York and New Jersey was opened.

Feb. 26. The New York State Senate refused to remove Otto Kelsey, State Superintendent of Insurance.

Feb. 28. The Women's Enfranchisement bill was passed on first reading by the British House of Commons.

Feb. 29. Japan demanded of China an apology and indemnity for the seizure of the Tatsu Maru. China immediately surrendered the vessel.

March 4. Senator Redfield Proctor, of Vermont, died.

March 4. In a schoolhouse fire at North Collinwood, near Cleveland, O., 167 children were burned to death.

March 12. The American battleship fleet arrived at Magdalena Bay, Mexico.

March 13. In the Pennsylvania capitol fraud four defendants were found guilty.

March 13. Harry Orchard was sentenced to death by Judge Wood, of Boise, Idaho, who, however, recommended leniency to the Governor.

March 23. Durham W. Stevens, an American, member of the Japanese Council in Korea, was killed by a Korean in San Francisco.

March 23. The United States Supreme Court declared the railroad rate laws of Minnesota and North Carolina unconstitutional.

March 26. The Knickerbocker Trust Company, of New York, reopened for business.

March 28. At Hanna, Wyo., over sixty miners were entombed by an explosion in the Union Pacific Coal Company's mine.

March 29. The German Emperor withdrew his objections to the appointment of David J. Hill as Ambassador.

April 2. The Czar dissolved the Finnish Diet for expressed sympathy with the Terrorists.

April 2. The British torpedo boat destroyer Tiger was cut in two and sunk off the Isle of Wight with the loss of thirty-four men.

April 4. The Fifth Avenue Hotel, of New York, closed its doors.

April 5. Sir Henry Campbell-Bannerman resigned as Premier of Great Britain, and was succeeded (April 8) by H. H. Asquith.

April 12. A fire at Chelsea, Mass., caused a loss of $6,000,000.

April 22. Sir Henry Campbell-Bannerman, ex-Premier of Great Britain, died.

April 29. Rev. Morgan Dix, rector of Trinity parish, New York, died.

May 13. The Conference of Governors on the Conservation of National Resources met at the White House, Washington, and continued in session until May 15.

May 14. The Franco-British Exposition was opened in London by the Prince of Wales.

May 14. The new buildings of the College of the City of New York were formally opened.

May 15. Admiral Sperry took command of the Atlantic fleet at San Francisco.

May 15. The Omaha Packing Company's plant, at South Omaha, was destroyed by fire with a loss of $1,250,000.

May 21. Governor Hughes, of New York, signed the Bucket Shop bill.

May 27. A complete agreement on Morocco was reached by France and Germany.

May 29. The International Polar Congress met at Brussels, twelve countries being represented.

May 30. M. Delagrange made an aerial record near Rome, Italy, covering 12,750 metres in 15 minutes 26 seconds with his aeroplane.

May 30. The body of George Clinton, first Governor of New York, was removed from Washington to Kingston, N. Y., with ceremonies in the City of New York.

May 31. Eight newly chosen Bishops of the Methodist Episcopal Church were consecrated at Baltimore.

May 31. The city of Kingston, N. Y., celebrated the 250th anniversary of its settlement.

June 3. The body of M. Zola was moved from Montmartre to the Pantheon; during the ceremonies Major Alfred Dreyfus was wounded by Gregori, a military writer.

June 4. The jury disagreed on the fourth trial of Caleb Powers for murdering Gov. Goebel, of Kentucky.

June 5. An explosion on the cruiser Tennessee killed five men.

June 8. President Roosevelt appointed a National Commission of fifty-seven on the Conservation of National Resources.

June 11. Governor Hughes signed the Anti-Race Track Gambling bills.

June 13. Ten thousand Suffragettes marched

RECORD OF EVENTS IN 1908—*Continued.*

as a demonstration from the Victoria Embankment to Albert Hall, London.

June 16. The Pan-Anglican Church Congress convened in London.

June 23. The Secretary of the American Legation left Caracas, Venezuela, and (July 9) the Venezuelan chargé left Washington, thus severing diplomatic relations.

June 24. Ex-President Grover Cleveland died.

June 30. The New York Mayoralty contest ended with an instructed verdict finding McClellan to have been elected by a plurality of 2,791, a net gain of 863 for Hearst.

June 30. William H. Taft resigned as Secretary of War.

July 1. The Norfolk and Southern Railroad Company went into the hands of a receiver.

July 6. The Roosevelt, Commander Peary's ship, started on a Polar expedition.

July 7. Mme. Anna Gould married Prince Helie de Sagan, in London.

July 11. The battleship South Carolina was launched at Philadelphia.

July 12. Senor Jose Domingo Obaldia was elected President of Panama.

July 16. The American battleship fleet reached Honolulu.

July 22. The $29,400,000 fine against the Standard Oil Company was set aside by the United States Circuit Court of Appeals, and immediate steps were taken for a retrial.

July 22. The Quebec Tercentenary began, the Prince of Wales and Vice-President Fairbanks making addresses.

July 22. President Castro expelled M. de Reus, the Minister of the Netherlands at Caracas, Venezuela.

July 24. The Sultan of Turkey proclaimed the restoration of the Constitution of 1876, and four days later took the oath of allegiance to it.

July 24. The Marathon race was won in London by Hayes, an American.

Aug —. Race riots, accompanied by lynching of negroes and wrecking of property, occurred at Springfield, Ill.

Aug. 4. William B. Allison, of Iowa, died.

Aug. 4. Extensive forest fires raged in Kootenay Valley, B. C., destroying three towns and over $6,000,000 of property.

Aug. 5. Count Zeppelin's airship was destroyed by fire.

Aug. 8. The American battleship fleet arrived at Auckland Harbor, New Zealand.

Aug. 18. Persia appointed diplomatic representatives at Athens, Greece, for the first time in 2,399 years.

Aug. 19. The American battleship fleet arrived at Sydney, N. S. W.

Aug. 20. The Belgian Chamber of Deputies passed the Congo annexation treaty. It passed the Senate September 9.

Aug. 23. Baron Speck Von Sternburg, German Ambassador to the United States, died in Germany.

Aug. 24. Richard L. Hand reported to the Governor that the charges against District-Attorney Jerome were unfounded.

Aug. 26. The British steamer Dunearn foundered off the Japanese coast with a loss of fifty-two lives.

Aug. 30. A fire in New Orleans destroyed $1,500,000 of property.

Sept. 2. The French defeated 15,000 Moorish tribesmen, at Boudenib, on the Algerian frontier.

Sept. 4. The American battleship fleet left Melbourne.

Sept. 10. Count Tolstoi's eightieth birthday was celebrated.

Sept. 13. At the Eucharistic Congress, in session at London, a procession of the Papal legate and prelates was held—without ceremonial features.

Sept. 17. An accident to Orville Wright's aeroplane at Fort Myer, Va., caused the death of Lieut. Thomas E. Selfridge, and serious injuries to Mr. Wright.

Sept. 17. W. R. Hearst made public correspondence showing Senator Foraker's connection with the Standard Oil Company.

Sept. 20. Governor Hoke Smith, of Georgia, signed a bill terminating the convict-lease system in that State.

Sept. 22. On the New York Stock Exchange 1,490,000 shares of stock changed hands—a record for the year.

Sept. 27. The 250th anniversary of Pittsburgh was celebrated.

Oct. 1. The two-cent postage rate between the United States and Great Britain went into effect.

Oct. 2. The American battleship fleet arrived at Manila.

Oct. 5. Bulgaria was declared independent at Tirnova by Prince Ferdinand. France, England and Russia agreed on united action to prevent war.

Oct. 7. Harry A. Garfield was inaugurated president of Williams College.

Oct. 8. A treaty of arbitration with China was signed at Washington.

Oct. 12. The Servian Assembly voted to support the Government against Austrian aggression. The Montenegrin Assembly followed with a credit of $3,200,000 to its War Ministry.

Oct. 20-25. The American battleship fleet was received with honors by the Japanese.

Oct. 26. In the Canadian elections the Liberals were retained in power.

Oct. 28. The London Telegraph published an authorized interview of the German Emperor with an Englishman in which he commented freely on international affairs. It created protests in Germany.

Oct. 29. The American battleship fleet arrived at Amoy, China.

Nov. 3. The Presidential election.

Nov. 4. President Eliot, of Harvard University, resigned.

Nov. 5. Charles W. Morse and Alfred H. Curtis were found guilty of fraudulent banking practices.

Nov. 6. General Antoine Simon assumed the provisional Presidency of Hayti.

Nov. 9. Ex-United States Senator Carmack, of Tennessee, was shot dead as the result of a political feud.

Nov. 10. The battleship North Dakota was launched at Quincy, Mass.

Nov. 12. In an explosion in the Radbod Mine, near Hamm, Westphalia, 339 miners were killed.

Nov. 13. An attempt to assassinate Francis J. Heney, the prosecutor of the San Francisco grafters, was made in the courtroom in that city.

Nov. 13. Secretary of the Navy Metcalf resigned.

Nov. 14. General Jose Miguel Gomez, the candidate of the Liberal party, was elected President of Cuba.

Nov. 14-15. The deaths of the Emperor and the Dowager Empress of China were announced.

Nov. 17. The Emperor of Germany assented that foreign affairs would in future be carried on through the Foreign Office.

Nov. 21. The Yale-Harvard football game was won by Harvard.

Nov. 23. Riots occurred in and around Perth Amboy, N. J., among the pottery employees. The militia were finally called out.

Nov. 28. The Marianna Mine at Monongahela, Pa., was wrecked by an explosion that entombed over a hundred miners.

Nov. 30. An agreement between the United States and Japan on Pacific Ocean affairs was announced.

Dec. 2. Nord Alexis, President of Hayti, fled from Port au Prince.

Death Roll of 1908.

Age at death is given in parentheses; vocation, place, cause, and time of death when known follow.

Abbott, Edward (Rev.) (67), journalist, Boston, April 12.
Ackley, Seth M. (62), Rear-Admiral U. S. N. (retired), Washington, Feb. 8.
Alden, William Livingston (71), journalist and author, Buffalo, N. Y., Jan. 14.
Alexis, Grand Duke of Russia (58), uncle of the Czar, former Commander of the Russian Navy, Paris, pneumonia, Nov. 11.
Allen, Philip Loring (30), journalist, New York, typhoid fever, May 26.
Allen, Theodore or "The" (75), gambling-house keeper, New York, locomotor ataxia, May 12.
Allison, William Boyd (79), statesman, U. S. Senator from Iowa, Dubuque, heart disease, Aug. 4.
Amicis, Edmondo de (62), author, Bordighera, Italy, congestion of the brain, March 11.
Anthony, William A. (73), electrical engineer, New York, heart disease, May 29.
Astor, Mrs. William (78), social leader, New York, heart disease, Oct. 30.
Backus, Truman Jay (66), President of the Packer Collegiate Institute of Brooklyn, N. Y., Brooklyn, March 24.
Balch, George Beall (87), Read-Admiral U. S. N. (retired), Baltimore, Md., pneumonia, April 16.
Baily, Elisha L. (84), Brigadier-General U. S. A. (retired), San Francisco, March 24.
Bangs, Frank C. (72), actor, Atlantic City, N. J., accident, June 12.
Bannerman, Sir Henry Campbell (72), ex-Premier of the British Ministry, London, heart failure, April 22.
Barnes, Oliver Weldon (88), civil engineer, New York, pneumonia, Nov. 14.
Bartlett, George Alonzo, Professor of German and Regent of Harvard University, Cambridge, Mass., Nov. 25.
Batcheller, George Sherman (72), Judge of International Tribunal of Egypt, Paris, cancer of the mouth, July 2.
Belmont, Oliver Hazard Perry (50), Hempstead, L. I., septic poisoning, June 10.
Berry, Albert Seaton (73), jurist, ex-Representative in Congress, Newport, Ky., pneumonia, Jan. 7.
Bingham, Hiram (77), Congregational clergyman, Baltimore, Md., Oct. 25.
Boissier, Marie Louis Gaston (85), historian and archaeologist, Secretary of the French Academy, Paris, June 10
Bonner, Hugh (60), Fire Commissioner of New York, New York, March 13.
Bourgade, Peter (63), Roman Catholic Archbishop of Santa Fe, Chicago, heart failure, May 17.
Bourne, Edward Gaylord (48), professor of history, Yale University, New Haven, Conn., Feb. 24.
Brick, Abraham Lincoln (48), Representative in Congress from Indiana, Indianapolis, Ind., Bright's disease, April 7.
Bryan, Joseph (63), proprietor of the Richmond Times-Despatch, Richmond, Va., Nov. 20.
Bryan, William James, (31), U. S. Senator for Florida, Washington, typhoid fever, March 23.
Budd, James H. (58), ex-Governor of California, Stockton, Cal., rheumatism, July 30.
Buller, Sir Redvers (69), Lieutenant General British Army, London, June 2.
Burchard, Horatio Chapin (83), former director of the United States Mint, Freeport, Ill., May 14.
Burden, Mrs. William Proudfit (Natica Belmont Rives) (22), social leader, New York, gas poisoning, Feb. 21.
Caddagan, John P., hotel manager, New York, cirrhosis of the liver, Oct. 29.
Camden, Johnson N. (80), ex-United States Senator from West Virginia, Baltimore, Md., Bright's disease, April 25.
Capers, Ellison (71), Bishop Protestant Episcopal Church, Diocese of South Carolina, Columbia, S. C., April 22.
Carmack, Edward W. (50), ex-United States Senator from Tennessee, Nashville, Tenn., killed by Robert J. Cooper in street fight, Nov. 9.
Carroll, Henry (70), Brigadier General U. S. A. (retired), Colorado Springs, Col., Feb. 18.
Cedrino, Emanuel, autoist, Baltimore, Md., automobile accident, May 29.
Chadwick, Henry (84), the "Father of Baseball," newspaper reporter, Brooklyn, April 20.
Chase, George L (80), President of the Hartford Fire Insurance Company, Hartford, Conn., debility, Jan 7.
China, Dowager Empress of—Tsi-An (74), Pekin, Nov. 15.
China, Emperor of—Kuan Hgsu—(36), Pekin, neurasthenia, Nov. 8.
Clark, Charles Dickson (61), U. S. District Judge, Chattanooga, Tenn., March 15.
Cleveland, Grover (71), ex-President of the United States, Princeton, N. J., June 24.
Clous, John Walter (71), ex-Judge Advocate General United States Army, New York, Sept. 1.
Coghlan, Joseph Bullock (64), Rear-Admiral U. S N. (retired), New Rochelle, N. Y., heart disease, Dec. 5.
Cogswell, James Kelsey (61), Rear-Admiral U. S. N. (retired), Jacksonville, Fla., internal hemorrhage, Aug. 12.
Coppee, Francois (67), poet and dramatist, Paris, France, May 23.
Corliss, Augustus W. (71), Brigadier-General U. S. A. (retired), Denver, Col., Sept. 4.
Cornish, William D., vice-president of the Union Pacific Railroad, Chicago, Ill., Nov. 6.
Crickmore, Henry G. (69), turf reporter, New York, pneumonia, Nov. 3.
Crowninshield, Arent Schuyler (65), Rear-Admiral U. S. N. (retired), Philadelphia, May 27.
Curtis, Alfred A. (77), Vicar-General of the Roman Catholic Archdiocese of Baltimore, Baltimore, cancer of the stomach, July 11.
Cutcheon, Byron M. (72), ex-Representative in Congress from Michigan, Ypsilanti, Mich., April 12.
Dailey, Peter F. (40), actor, Chicago, pneumonia, May 23.
Dameron, Charles Emile (60), landscape painter, Paris, Jan. 22.
Daniels, George H. (66), railroad man, Lake Placid, N. Y., hardening of the arteries, July 1.
Darlington, Joseph G (65), merchant, Philadelphia, March 18.
De Chaulnes, Duke—Emenuel de Luynes—(30), married Miss Shonts, Paris, embolism of the heart, April 23.
Derby, Earl of—Frederick Arthur Stanley—(67), former Governor-General of Canada, London, June 14.
Devonshire, Duke of—Spencer Compton Cavendish—(75), statesman, Cannes, France, heart disease, March 24.
De Witt, Calvin (68), retired, Brigadier-General United States Army, Wyoming, heart disease, Sept. 3.

Dix, Morgan (81), rector of Trinity Parish, New York, New York, chronic asthma, April 29.

Dodge, Francis S. (66), Brigadier-General U. S. A., retired, Washington, Feb. 19.

Doremus, Mrs. Sarah Hall (104), oldest woman in New Jersey, Newark, N. J., July 16.

Douglas, Stephen A. (58), lawyer, Chicago, Ill., Oct. 8.

Drachmann, Holger Henrik, Herboldt (62), poet and author, Hornback, Denmark, Jan. 13.

Duncan, William W. (69), Bishop of the Methodist Episcopal Church South, Spartanburg, S. C., March 2.

Durborrow, Allen C. (51), ex-Representative in Congress from Illinois, Chicago, March 11.

Dyas, Ada (68), actress, Seaton, England, March 12.

Edgren, John Alexis (69), theological writer, Oakland, Cal., heart disease, Jan. 26.

Edouin, Willie (68), actor, London, England, April 14.

Eidlitz, Leopold (84), architect, New York, March 22.

Ely, William Davis (93), oldest alumnus of Yale University, manufacturer, Providence, R. I., June 11.

Emerson, Edwin (82), educator, Yokohama, Japan, Nov. 4.

Ewing, Samuel Currier (77), Presbyterian clergyman, oldest missionary in the world in age and service, Cairo, Egypt, April 5.

Farwell, John V. (83), merchant and capitalist, Chicago, Aug. 21.

Fax, Reuben (44), actor, New York, heart disease, Aug. 14.

Fergusson, Arthur W. (49), Secretary to the Philippine Commission, Manila, heart disease, Jan. 29.

Fessenden, Samuel (61), political manager, Stamford, Ct., heart disease, Jan. 7.

Finerty, John Frederick (62), journalist, Chicago, disease of the liver, June 10.

Fithian, Edwin (87), Rear-Admiral U. S. N. (retired), Bridgeton, N. J., Aug. 29.

Fitzgerald, Gen. Louis (70), ex-President of Mercantile Trust Company of New York, Garrisons's, N. Y., Oct. 6.

Fowler, Charles Henry (71), Bishop of the Methodist Episcopal Church, New York, heart disease, March 20.

Franchot, Stanislaus P. (57), State Senator of New York, Montreal, Canada, paralysis, March 24.

Frank, Royal Thaxter (75), Brigadier-General U. S. A. (retired), Washington, March 15.

Gerschunin, Gregory Androwitch (40), Russian revolutionist, Switzerland, March 18.

Gilman, Daniel Coit (77), educator, former President of Johns Hopkins University, Norwich, Ct., heart disease, Oct.13.

Gilmore, Edward G. (69), theatrical manager, New York, peritonitis, Nov. 6.

Glass, Henry (64), Rear-Admiral U. S. N. (retired), Paso Robles, Cal., heart failure, Sept. 1.

Guachalla, Fernando, President-elect of Bolivia, La Paz, July 24.

Hague, James Duncan (72), mining engineer, Stockbridge, Mass., heart disease, Aug. 4.

Halevy, Ludovic (74), dramatist and novelist, Paris, May 8.

Hall, Charles Cuthbert, President of the Union Theological Seminary, New York, New York, disease of the liver, March 25.

Hall, John A. (67),President of the Massachusetts Mutual Life Insurance Company of Springfield, Mass., London, England, Sept. 3.

Halstead, Murat (79), journalist, Cincinnati, O., cerebral hemorrhage, July 2.

Harris, Joel Chandler, "Uncle Remus" (60), author and journalist, Atlanta, Ga., cirrhosis of the liver, July 3.

Hartsuff, Albert, Brigadier-General U. S. A. (retired), Chicago, heart disease, June 21.

Haskell, Harry Leland (68), Brigadier-General U. S. A. (retired), San Diego, Cal., Oct. 25.

Haven, Franklin (71), financier, President of the Merchants' National Bank of Boston, Boston, April 7.

Haven, George Griswold (73), financier, New York, March 18.

Henderson, David (55), journalist and theatrical manager, Chicago, May 27.

Hewitt, Frederick C. (69), banker and millionaire, Owego, N. Y., apoplexy, Aug. 31.

Hopkins, Henry (70), educator, ex-President of Williams College, Rotterdam, Holland, pneumonia, Aug. 13.

Horstmann, Ignatius Frederick (68), Roman Catholic Bishop of Cleveland, Canton, O., heart disease, May 13.

Hosmer, Harriet G. (77), sculptor, Feb. 21.

Hough, Alfred Lacey (82), Brigadier General U. S. A. (retired), Princeton, N. J., April 28.

Howard, Bronson (66), dramatist, Avon, N. J., heart disease, Aug. 4.

Howard, Joseph, Jr. (74), journalist, New York, Bright's disease, March 31.

Hunton, Eppa (86), Brigadier General in the Confederate Army, ex-Representative in Congress, Richmond, Va., Oct. 11.

Jefferson, Charles Burke (58), theatrical manager, eldest son of Joseph Jefferson, New York, June 23.

Jepson, Eugene, actor, Cleveland, O., heart disease, June 1.

Jesup, Morris Ketchum (78), merchant, ex-President New York Chamber of Commerce, New York, heart disease, Jan. 22.

Jones, James K. (69), ex-United States Senator from Arkansas, Washington, heart failure, June 1.

Jordan, Thomas D. (66), ex-Controller of the Equitable Life Assurance Society, New York, heart disease, July 14.

Kane, Theodore F. (67), Rear-Admiral U. S. N. (retired), New York, heart disease, March 14.

King, Edward (75), banker, New York, Nov. 20.

Kline, Jacob (68), Brigadier-General U. S. A. (retired), Baltimore, Md., Bright's disease, March 23.

Knight, Edward J. (45), Bishop of the Protestant Episcopal Diocese of Western Colorado, Clearfield, Cal., mountain fever, Nov. 17.

Knowles, Sir James (77), architect, founder of the Nineteenth Century Magazine, London, England, Feb. 13.

Laidlaw, Alexander Hamilton (80), physician, New York, July 29.

Lanham, Samuel W. T. (62), ex-Governor of Texas, Weatherford, Tex., July 29.

Larocque, Joseph (78), lawyer, New York, pneumonia, June 10.

Latimer, Asbury C. (57), United States Senator from South Carolina, Washington, peritonitis, Feb. 20.

Lawler, Thomas G. (64), former Commander-in-Chief of the Grand Army of the Republic, Rockford, Ill., Feb. 3.

Leeds, William Bateman (47), financier, Paris, France, June 23.

Lee, Leslie A. (56), educator, professor of geology in Bowdoin College, Portland, Me., May 20.

Lee, Stephen D. (75), Lieutenant-General in the Confederate Army, Commander-in-Chief of the United Confederate Veterans, Vicksburg, Miss., cerebral hemorrhage, May 28.

Lie, Jonas L. (75), poet and novelist, Christiania, Norway, July 5.

Linevitch, Nicolai P. (70), Lieutenant-General Russian Army, commander of the Russian forces in Asia in the war with Japan, St. Petersburg, pneumonia, April 23.

Linlithgow, Marquis of—John Adrian Louis Hope—ex-Governor-General of Australia, Secretary for Scotland, Paris, France, March 1.
Lippe, Prince of—Leopold—(37), reigning Prince, Heidelberg, Jan. 28.
Lucca, Baroness Pauline Wallhofen (67), singer, Vienna, Austria, cancer, Feb. 28.
MacDowell, Edward (47), composer and pianist, New York, Jan. 24.
Mackay, Donald Sage (45), clergyman of the Reformed Church, New York, heart disease, Aug. 27.
Maignan, Albert Pierre Rene (64), historical painter, France, Sept. 29.
Malet, Sir Edward Baldwin (71), diplomatist, London, June 29.
Mandel, Emanuel (64), Chicago merchant, Basle, Switzerland, accident, Sept. 5.
Mathieu, Francois Desire (69), Cardinal, former Archbishop of Toulouse, France, London, Oct. 26.
McElmell, Jackson (74), Rear-Admiral U. S. N. (retired), May 31.
Mellon, Thomas (94), millionaire banker, Pittsburgh, Pa., Feb. 3.
Menocal, Aniceto G. (69), civil engineer, New York, July 20.
Merriam, Greenlief A. (58), Captain U. S. N., Commandant of the Portsmouth Navy Yard, Portsmouth, N. H., appendicitis, Sept. 2.
Merrill, George E. (62), President of Colgate University, Hamilton, N. Y., June 11.
Merrian, Homer (95), publisher of Webster's Dictionary, Pasadena, Cal., May 25.
Meyer, Adolph (65), Representative in Congress from Louisiana, New Orleans, heart disease, March 8.
Miles, Evan (70), Brigadier-General U. S. A. (retired), San Francisco, Cal., May 24.
Miller, James M. (61), Rear-Admiral U. S. N., Governor of the United States Naval Home, Philadelphia, Philadelphia, Pa., Nov. 11.
Miller, John (65), ex-Governor of North Dakota, Duluth, Minn., Oct. 26.
Moulton, Louise Chandler (73), author, Boston, Bright's disease, Aug. 10.
Murphy, Nathan O. (59), ex-Governor of Arizona, San Diego, Cal., hemorrhage of the stomach, Aug. 23.
Nelson, Henry Loomis (60), Professor of Political Science at Williams College, New York, heart failure, Feb. 29.
Nichols, Othneil Foster (62), civil engineer, Brooklyn, N. Y., Feb. 5.
Nodzu, Field Marshal (68), Japanese commander in the war with Russia, Oct. 18.
Norton, Charles Eliot (81), educator, author, professor of history of art at Harvard University, Cambridge, Mass., Oct. 21.
Novello, Clara (90), singer, March 16.
Oliver, James H. (85), plough manufacturer, South Bend, Ind, March 2.
Olney, Clarence C. (65), railroad official Atlantic Coast Line, Charleston, S. C., heart disease, March .
"Ouida"—Louise de la Ramee—(63), novelist, Viareggio, Italy, asthma complicated with heart disease, Jan. 25.
Palma, Tomas Estrada (73), first President of the Republic of Cuba, Santiago, Nov. 4.
Parker, Charles Henry (92), oldest Harvard alumnus, Boston, Mass., April 9.
Parker, William H. (61), Representative in Congress from South Dakota, Deadwood, S. D., dropsy, June 26.
Parkhurst, Henry Martyn (83), astronomer, Brooklyn, N. Y., pneumonia, Jan. 20.
Pastor, Antonio—"Tony"—(71), comic singer and theatrical manager, Elmhurst, N. Y., Aug. 26.
Perry, David (67), Brigadier-General U. S. A. (retired), Washington, May 18.
Portugal, Crown Prince of—Louis Philippe—(20), assassinated, Lisbon, Feb. 1.
Portugal, King of—Charles I.—(43), Lisbon, assassinated, Feb. 1.
Potter, Henry Codman (74), Protestant Episcopal Bishop of the Diocese of New York, Cooperstown, N. Y., embolism of the leg, July 21.
Powers, Lewellyn (69), Representative in Congress from Maine, ex-Governor, Houlton, Me., July 28.
Proctor, Redfield (77), United States Senator from Vermont, ex-Secretary of War, Washington, pneumonia, March 4.
Rae, Charles W. (61), Rear-Admiral, Engineer-in-Chief of the United States Navy, Washington, May 13.
Randall, James Ryder (65), poet and journalist, author of "Maryland, My Maryland," Augusta, Ga., pneumonia, Jan. 14.
Reid, Sir Robert (65), railroad builder and capitalist, Montreal, Canada, June 3.
Rich, Isaac B. (81), theatrical manager, Boston, diabetes, June 10.
Richard, Francois Marie B. (89), Cardinal, Archbishop of Paris, Paris, pneumonia, Jan. 28.
Rockwell, Charles H. (68), Rear-Admiral U. S. N. (retired), Chatham, Mass., July 1.
Roehrig, Frederic Louis Otto (89), Orientalist, philologist and composer, Pasadena, Cal., July 15.
Rogers, "Gus" (39), comedian, New York, intestinal hemorrhage, Oct. 19.
Roosa, Daniel B. St. John (70), physician, New York, March 7.
Rouxel, Gustave Augustine (68), Roman Catholic Auxiliary Bishop of the Archdiocese of New Orleans, New Orleans, La., March 17.
Rowell, George P. (70), advertisement manager, Poland Springs, Me., Aug. 28.
Rudini, Marquise de (69), former Premier of Italy, Aug. 7.
Russell, Alexander W. (84), Rear-Admiral U. S. N. (retired), Philadelphia, heart failure, Nov. 26.
Sackville, Baron—Lionel Sackville West—(81), former British Minister to the United States, Sevenoaks, England, Sept 3.
Samuels, Samuel (83), former clipper ship commander, Brooklyn, N. Y., May 18.
Sanford, George Bliss (66), Colonel U. S. A. (retired), President of the Connecticut Society of the Cincinnati, New York, cancer of the tongue, July 13.
Sankey, Ira D. (68), evangelist and singer, Brooklyn, heart disease, Aug. 13.
Sardou, Victorien (77), dramatist, Paris, France, pneumonia, Nov. 8.
Sargent, Frank P. (54), U. S. Immigration Commissioner, Washington, stomach disease, Sept. 4.
Sass, George Herbert (63), poet, journalist, Charleston, S. C., Feb. 10.
Satterlee, Henry Yates (65), Protestant Episcopal Bishop of the Diocese of Washington, Washington, D. C., pneumonia, Feb. 22.
Satterlee, Walter (65), artist, New York, May 28.
Sawyer, Charles H. (68), ex-Governor of New Hampshire, Dover, N. H., Jan. 18.
Saxe-Altenburg, Prince Ernest of (82), Reigning Duke, Berlin, Feb. 6.
Saxton, Rufus (84), Brigadier-General U. S. A. (retired), Washington, D. C., Feb. 2.
Searles, John Ennis (68), American financier, London, England, heart disease, Oct. 23.
Sears, Joshua M. (83), millionaire Boston real estate owner, Providence, R. I., automobile accident, Aug. 12.
Semple, Eugene (68), ex-Governor of Washington Territory, San Diego, Cal., pneumonia, Aug. 28.
Senner, Joseph H. (62), journalist, New York, apoplexy, Sept. 28.
Senn, Nicholas (64), surgeon, Chicago, Ill., heart disease, Jan. 2.

Shipley, Samuel R. (80), financier, Philadelphia, April 22.
Shipman, John Henry (84), journalist, Brooklyn, N. Y., July 21.
Smith, Charles Emory (66), journalist, former Minister to Russia and Postmaster-General, Philadelphia, heart disease, Jan. 19.
Soto, Marco Aurelio (61), ex-President of the Republic of Honduras, Paris, France, Feb. 24.
Sparks, John (65), Governor of Nevada, Reno, Nev., Bright's disease, May 22.
Spofford, Ainsworth R. (83), former Librarian of Congress, Holderness, N. H., paralysis, Aug. 11.
Stedman, Edmund Clarence (74), poet, banker, New York, heart disease, Jan. 18.
Sternburg, Baron Speck von, German Ambassador to the United States, Heidelberg, inflammation of the lungs, Aug. 23.
Stevens, Durham White (56), diplomatist, adviser to the Korean Government, San Francisco, Cal., assassinated, March 25.
Stevens, Benjamin F. (85), President of the New England Mutual Life Insurance Company, Boston, April 14.
Stewart, Alexander P. (87), Lieutenant-General in the Confederate Army, Biloxi, Miss., Aug. 30.
Stickney, Albert (68), lawyer, New York, April 30.
Stone, Col. William Leete (73), historical author, Mount Vernon, N. Y., June 11.
Strobel, Edward H. (53), diplomatist, General Adviser to the Government of Siam, Bangkok, Siam, blood poisoning, Jan. 15.
Sullivan, Thomas C. (75), Brigadier-General U. S. A. (retired), Fortress Monroe, Va., heart failure, March 12.
Thomas, Charles M. (62), Rear-Admiral U. S. N. (retired), Del Monte, Cal., heart disease, July 3.
Thompson, Lydia (72), actress, London, England, Nov. 17.
Tierney, Michael (68), Roman Catholic Bishop of the Diocese of Hartford Ct., Hartford, apoplexy, Oct. 5.
Totten, Charles A. L. (57), scientist, Milford, Ct., April 12.
Troup, Alexander (68), Connecticut politician and journalist, New York, apoplexy, Sept. 5.
Turr, Stephen (83), Garabaldian General, Budapest, Hungary, May 2.
Tuscany, Archduke Ferdinand IV., Grand Duke of (73), Salzburg, Austria, Jan. 17.
Tyler, Sir Henry Whatley (81), railroad magnate, London, Jan. 30.
Ulrich, Charles F. (50), painter, New York, May —.
Urquhart, Isabelle (43), actress, Rochester, N. Y., internal hemorrhage, Feb. 7.
Vilas, William F. (68), ex-Postmaster-General and Secretary of the Interior, Madison, Wis., paralysis, Aug. 27.
Walton, Sir John Lawson (56), Attorney-General in the British Ministry, London, pneumonia, Jan. 18.
Wanamaker, Thomas B. (47), merchant, Paris, nervous prostration, March 2.
Watterson, Harvey (30), lawyer, New York, accident, Nov. 11.
Wheelock, Joseph, Sr. (69), actor, Long Branch, N. J., heart disease, Sept. 28.
Whittier, Charles A. (63), Brigadier-General U. S. A. (retired), at sea on steamship Mauretania, May 14.
Whyte, William Pinckney (84), United States Senator from Maryland, Baltimore, erysipelas, March 17.
Wiggins, Thomas (60), "Blind Tom," musical prodigy, Hoboken, N. J., apoplexy, June 13.
Wiley, Ariosto Appling (57), Representative in Congress from Alabama, Hot Springs, Va., inflammatory rheumatism, June 17.
Wilson, Edward (88), Bishop of the Reformed Episcopal Church, Metuchen, N. J., June 3.
Wilson, George West (49), journalist, Jacksonville, Fla., June 2.
Wilson, Mrs. Richard T. (77), social leader, New York, heart disease, May 30.
Wise, George D. (77), ex-Representative in Congress from Virginia, Richmond, Va., Feb. 4.
Wister, Annis Lee (78), translator of German novels, Wallingford, Pa., Nov. 15.
Wormeley, Katherine Prescott (79), author, Jackson, N. H., Aug. 5.
Worthington, George (68), Protestant Episcopal Bishop of the Diocese of Nebraska, Mentone, France, heart disease, Jan. 7.
Wright, John H. (56), Professor of Greek at Harvard University and Dean of the Graduate School, Cambridge, Mass., heart disease, Nov. 25.
Wyckoff, Walter Augustus (48), sociologist, Princeton, N. J., May 15.
Yeaman, George Helm (79), lawyer, former Minister to Denmark, Jersey City, N. J., Feb. 23.
Young, Charles Augustus (73), astronomer, Hanover, N. H., pneumonia, Jan. 4.

American Federation of Catholic Societies.

THE American Federation of Catholic Societies was founded in 1901. It is composed of fourteen national organizations, many State and county federations and parishes. Total membership about 2,000,000. Its objects are the cementing of the bonds of fraternal union among the Catholic laity, and the fostering and protection of Catholic interests. The Federation has the approval and blessing of eighty archbishops and bishops, and of Pope Pius X. National headquarters are at 3871 Utah Place, St. Louis, Mo. The officers are as follows: *President*—Edward Feeney, Brooklyn, N. Y. *First Vice-President*—J. B. Oelkers, Newark, N. J. *Secretary*—Anthony Matre, St. Louis, Mo. *Treasurer*—Mrs. Elizabeth Rodgers, Chicago, Ill.

American Sociological Society.

President—William Graham Sumner, Yale University, New Haven, Ct. *Vice-Presidents*—Prof. Franklin H. Giddings, Columbia University, New York City, and Prof. Albion W. Small, University of Chicago. *Secretary and Treasurer*—Prof. C. W. A. Veditz, George Washington University, Washington, D. C. Organized in 1905 to encourage the scientific study of society. Membership about 250. Holds annual meetings. Publishes an annual volume of "Papers," and the "American Journal of Sociology." Annual dues, $3.00.

The Famous Old People of 1909.

Age. (Age at the last birthday is given. The list was made up for January 1, 1909.)

92. Sir Theodore Martin, author.
91. Sir Joseph Hooker, botanist; John Bigelow, journalist and diplomatist.
90. Bishop Thomas Bowman.
89. Julia Ward Howe, President Palmer, of the Northwestern Mutual Life Insurance Company. Bishop Gillespie, of Western Michigan.
88. John Tenniel, cartoonist; Florence Nightingale, Baron Strathcona.
87. Sir Charles Tupper.
86. Edward Everett Hale, Prof. Alfred R. Wallace, Donald G. Mitchell, Rev. Dr. Theodore L. Cuyler.
85. Thomas Wentworth Higginson, Prof. Goldwin Smith, Rev. Dr. Robert Collyer, ex-Senator Henry G. Davis, of West Virginia, Bishop McQuaid.
84. Professor Huggins, astronomer; ex-Vice-President Levi P. Morton.
83. Sir William Aitken, pathologist; Professor March, philologist; D. O. Mills, financier; Emile Ollivier, French academician; General Daniel E. Sickles.
82. Ex-Empress Eugenie.
81. Pere Hyacinthe, Marquis of Ripon, Lord Lister.
80. Sir Henry James, lawyer; De Freycinet, French statesman; ex-Senator Edmunds, ex-President Dwight, of Yale; Count Tolstoi, Clara Barton, George Meredith, James B. Angell.
79. General Booth, Salvation Army leader; Senator Cullom, Viscount Peel.
78. President Diaz, of Mexico; Emperor Francis Joseph, J. Q. A. Ward, sculptor; Salvini, tragedian; ex-Secretary Tracy, Gen. Oliver O. Howard, Bishop Doane, ex-Senator Jones, of Nevada; Senator Teller, Justin McCarthy, Henry M. Flagler.
77. General Galliffet, French soldier; ex-President Gilman, of Johns Hopkins; Frederic Harrison, positivist; Henry Labouchère, journalist; Henri Rochefort, Senator Frye, Sir George Nares, Arctic explorer; Joseph H. Choate.
76. Field Marshal Lord Roberts, British Army; Maggie Mitchell, actress; Professor Vambery, Andrew D. White, ex-Justice Shiras, Prof. William Crookes, G. W. Custis Lee.
75. Chief Justice Fuller, Field Marshal Lord Wolseley, Denman Thompson, actor; Justice Harlan, President Amador, of Panama; ex-Secretary Bliss, Senator Platt, of New York; Professor Koch, George W. Smalley, journalist; Colonel J. S. Mosby, ex-Congressman Grosvenor of Ohio.
74. Senator Depew, President Eliot, of Harvard University; Sir John Lubbock (Lord Avebury), Ludovic Halévy, Cardinal Gibbons.
73. Pope Pius X., Leopold II., King of the Belgians; Rev. Lyman Abbott, Alexander Agassiz, ex-Secretary Carlisle, "Mark Twain," Charles Francis Adams, Alfred Austin, poet; Richard Olney, ex-Vice-President Stevenson, Gen. Stewart L. Woodford, ex-Prime Minister Combes, of France; Hetty Green, Andrew Carnegie, Secretary of Agriculture Wilson, Manton Marble, journalist.
72. Sir Edward J. Poynter, President of the Royal Academy; Prof. C. F. Chandler, Alma-Tadema, painter; W. S. Gilbert, dramatist; General Merritt, Joseph Chamberlain, William Winter, dramatic critic; Lord Brassey, Edward Dicey, Sir Norman Lockyer, Speaker Joseph G. Cannon, Senator Hale, Henry M. Alden.
71. Whitelaw Reid, Gen. Horace Porter, W. D. Howells, novelist; J. Pierpont Morgan, Archbishop Ireland, Sir Michael Hicks-Beach, Justices Brewer and Peckham, Miss Braddon, Swinburne, poet; Admiral Dewey, Bishop Tuttle.
70. Prof. James Bryce, ex-Queen Liliuokalani, John Morley, John Wanamaker, ex-President Loubet. Generals Brooke and E. S. Otis, F. Hopkinson Smith, Senator Bacon, Cardinal Satolli.
69. Rear-Admiral Schley, Cardinal Logue, General Miles, Senator Clark, of Montana; Bishop Keane, Asa Bird Gardiner, John D. Rockefeller, King Charles of Roumania.
68. Capt. A. T. Mahan, Henry Watterson, ex-Labor Commissioner Wright, Clemenceau, Palmer Cox, Sir Hiram S. Maxim, Austin Dobson, poet; Thomas Hardy, novelist; General Kelly-Kenney, Lord Reay, President of the British Academy; Gen. S. B. M. Young, Justice Oliver Wendell Holmes.
67. King Edward VII., Senator Aldrich, Rear-Admiral Melville, James Gordon Bennett, Sir Wilfred Laurier, Coquelin, Marquis Ito, Japanese statesman; Sir Charles Wyndham, Mounet-Sully, William Rockefeller, President Fallieres, of France, Senator Elkins.
66. Abdul Hamid, Sultan of Turkey; Anna Dickinson, General Corbin, General Chaffee, Cardinal Rampolla, Senator Daniel, of Virginia; Lord Alverstone, Flammarion, astronomer; Robert T. Lincoln, Joaquin Miller, Charles Warren Stoddard, author; Francois Coppée.
65. Justice McKenna, Christine Nilsson, Adelina Patti, Senators Dillingham and Nelson, David B. Hill, Henry James, Jr., novelist; Sir Charles Dilke, Sereno E. Payne, King Frederick VIII. of Denmark.

---

64. Sarah Bernhardt, Queen Alexandra, General Greely, John Hare, comedian; Modjeska, King Peter of Servia, Clark Russell, novelist; Rev. Dr. W. H. Roberts, George W. Cable, Richard Watson Gilder, Andrew Lang, Viscount Aoki, Japanese statesman.
63. King George of Greece, Justice White, U. S. Supreme Court; Kyrle Bellew, actor; William H. Crane, actor; Duke of Argyle, General MacArthur, Elihu Root, Rear Admiral Sigsbee, Alexander Graham Bell, scientist.
62. Rear-Admiral Evans, Lord Charles Beresford, Senators Foraker, Wetmore and Hopkins, Hamilton W. Mabie, Col. William F. Cody; Millet, painter; Charles H. Taylor, journalist; George Westinghouse, Julian Hawthorne, Princess Christian of England, William Waldorf Astor.
61. Thomas A. Edison, Senator Tillman, Lotta Crabtree, Oscar Hammerstein, Rear Admiral Goodrich, Bishop Hall, of Vermont, John D. Archbold, Arthur J. Balfour, statesman; Kate Claxton, King William of Wurtemberg, King Otto of Bavaria.
60. Associate Justice Day, of the Supreme Court; Frances Hodgson Burnett, author; William T. Stead, journalist.

At what age does one become "old"? Five centuries ago a man was old at fifty. But the hale and hearty gentleman of to-day who has just turned sixty would probably protest against being classed among old people, even if famous. That his susceptibilities may not be wounded, therefore, a separating dash has been discreetly introduced after age sixty-five.

The American Multi-Millionaires.

THE VANDERBILTS.

DESCENDANTS OF COMMODORE CORNELIUS VANDERBILT.

Born on Staten Island, N. Y., 1794; married, 1st, Sophia Johnson, 1813; 2d, Frances Crawford, 1869; died 1877.

Children.	Grandchildren.	Great-Grandchildren.	Great-Great-Grandchildren.
1. Phebe Jane Vanderbilt, b. 1815; m. James M. Cross, 1841; d. 1853.	1. Cornelius Vanderbilt Cross, b. 1834; m. Emma Eldert; d. 1902.		
	2. Ethelinda Cross; m. Burrett Wilson Horton.		
	3. Norman Cross, b. 1842; d. 1907.		
2. Ethelinda Vanderbilt, b. 1818; m. Daniel B. Allen, 1839; d. 1888.	1. Vanderbilt Allen, b. 1840; m. 1st. Helena Mount, 1861; 2d, Edith De Silvier, 1873; 3d, Edith Mott, 1890; d. 1898.	1. Marie Fatimeh Allen, b. 1870; m. John C. Wilmerding, Jr., 1892.	
		2. Ethel Gladys De Silvier Allen, b. 1875.	
	2. William Barton Allen, b. 1844; m. Mary Sutton; d. 1890.	1. W. S. Vanderbilt Allen, b. 1861.	
		2. Ethelinda Allen, b. 1863; m. James H. Ward, 1892; d. 1899.	1. Vanderbilt B. Ward, b. 1893. 2. Mildred S. Ward, b. 1896.
	3. Franklin Allen.		
	4. Harry Allen, d. 1899.		
	5. Annie Allen, b. 1869; m. 1888, John Wallace; d. (killed) 1896.	1. Allen Wallace, b. 1889.	
3. William Henry Vanderbilt, b. 1821; m. Maria Louise Kissam, 1840; d. 1885.	1. Cornelius Vanderbilt, b. 1843; m. Alice Gwynne, 1867; d. 1899.	1. William H. Vanderbilt, b. 1871; d. 1892.	
		2. Cornelius Vanderbilt, b. 1873; m. Grace Wilson, 1896.	1. Cornelius Vanderbilt, b. 1898. 2. Grace Vanderbilt, b. 1899.
		3. Gertrude Vanderbilt, b. 1876; m. Harry Payne Whitney, 1896.	1. Flora Payne Vanderbilt Whitney, b. 1897. 2. Vanderbilt Whitney, b. 1899.
		4. Alfred Gwynne Vanderbilt, b. 1877; m. Elsie French, Jan. 11, 1901; div. 1908.	1. William Henry Vanderbilt, b. Nov. 24, 1901.
		5. Reginald C. Vanderbilt, b. 1880; m. Cathleen G. Neilson, 1903.	1. Kathleen, b. 1904.
		6. Gladys M. Vanderbilt, b. 1885; m. Count Laszlo Szechenyi, 1908.	1. A daughter, b. Oct. 27, 1908.
	2. Margaret Louisa Vanderbilt; m. Elliot F. Shepard, 1870.	1. Maria Louisa Shepard, b. 1870; m. William Jay Schieffelin, 1891.	1. William Jay Schieffelin, Jr., b. 1891. 2. Margaret Louisa Schieffelin, b. 1893. 3. Mary Jay Schieffelin, II., b. 1896. 4. John Jay Schieffelin, b. 1897. 5. Louise Vanderbilt Schieffelin, b. 1901.
		2. Edith Shepard, b. 1872; m. Ernesto G. Fabbri, 1896.	1. Teresa Fabbri, b. 1897. 2. Ernesto G. Fabbri, Jr., b. 1900.
		3. Margaret Shepard, b. 1875; d. 1892.	
		4. Alice Shepard, b. 1874; m. Dave Hennen Morris, 1895.	1. Dave H. Morris, Jr., b. 1900. 2. Louise Morris, b. 1901.
		5. Elliot F. Shepard, b. 1877; m. Mrs. Esther Potter, 1897.	
	3. William K. Vanderbilt, b. 1849; m. Alva Murray Smith, 1874 (now Mrs. O. H. P. Belmont); 2d, 1903, Mrs. Ann Harriman (Sands) Rutherfurd.	1. Consuelo Vanderbilt, b. 1877; m. Duke of Marlborough, 1895.	1. John, Marquis of Blandford, b. 1897. 2. Lord Ivor Charles Spencer-Churchill, b. 1898.
		2. William K. Vanderbilt, b. 1878; m. Virginia Fair, 1899.	1. Muriel Vanderbilt, b. 1900. 2. Consuelo Vanderbilt, b. 1903. 3. A son, b. 1907.
		3. Harold S. Vanderbilt, b. 1884.	
	4. Emily T. Vanderbilt; m. William D. Sloane, 1874.	1. Florence A. Sloane, b. 1875; m. James A. Burden, Jr., 1895.	1. James A. Burden, b. 1897.
		2. Emily Vanderbilt Sloane, b. 1877; m. J. H. Hammond.	
		3. Lila Vanderbilt Sloane, b. 1879; m. Wm. B. Osgood Field, 1902.	
		4. Malcolm D. Sloane, b. 1881.	
	5. Frederick W. Vanderbilt, b. 1858; m. Mrs. Alfred Torrance (nee Anthony), 1880.		

NOTE.—In the pedigrees of the Vanderbilts and Astors the dates in some instances, particularly of the older branches and of branches residing abroad, are subject to correction. The above table and that of the Astors were submitted to members of the respective families and were revised by them to the best of their knowledge.

THE VANDERBILTS—Continued.

Children.	Grandchildren.	Great-Grandchildren.	Great-Great-Grandchildren.
3. William Henry Vanderbilt (Continued).	6. Florence Adele Vanderbilt; m. H. McKown Twombly, 1877.	1. Ruth Twombly, b. 1878; d.	
		2. Florence Twombly, b. 1880, m. William A. M. Burden, 1904.	
		3. H. McKown Twombly, b. 1883, d. 1906.	
		4. Alice Twombly, b. 1886, d. '96	
	7. Eliza Osgood Vanderbilt; m. William Seward Webb, 1881.	1. James Watson Webb, b. 1884.	
		2. William Seward Webb, b. 1887.	
		3. Frederica Webb, m. Ralph Pulitzer, 1905.	1. Ralph Pulitzer, Jr., b. 1906.
		4. Vanderbilt Webb.	
	8. George Washington Vanderbilt, b. 1862; m. Edith Stuyvesant Dresser, 1898.	1. Cornelia Stuyvesant Vanderbilt, b. 1900.	
4. Emily Vanderbilt, b. 1823; m. William K. Thorn, 1849; d. 1896.	1. William K. Thorn, b. 1851.		
	2. Emily Thorn, b. 1853; m. 1st, Daniel King, 1869; 2d, James C. Parrish, 1873.	1. Louise Alice King, b. 1870; m. Alexander Baring.	
	3. —— Thorn, b. 1858; m. Gustav Kissell, 1881.		
5. Cornelius Jeremiah Vanderbilt, b. 1825; d. 1882.			
6. Eliza Vanderbilt, b. 1828; m. George A. Osgood, 1849; d. 1895.			
7. Sophia Vanderbilt, b. 1830; m. Daniel Torrance, 1849.	1. Alfred Torrance, b. 1850; m. Bertha Anthony, 1872; d. 1885. She married, 1880, Frederick W. Vanderbilt.		
	2. Marie Torrance, b. 1852; m. John Hadden, Jr., 1873.	1. John Hadden, b. 1874.	
8. Maria Alicia Vanderbilt, b. 1831; m. 1st, Nicholas La Bau, 1847.	1. Bertha V. La Bau; m. George M. Browne.		
	2. Edith La Bau; m. Tiffany Dyer.		
	3. Lillian La Bau; m. 1st, Eugene Blois; 2d, Jose Aymar, 1897.		
9. Catherine Vanderbilt, b. 1834; m. 1st, Smith Barker, 1850; 2d, Gustave Lafitte, 1861; d. 1887.	1. Clarence Johnson Barker, b. 1853; d. 1896.		
	2. Catherine Barker, b. 1857.		
	3. Morris Lafitte, b. 1863.		
10. Marie Louise Vanderbilt, b. 1835; m. 1st, Horace Clark, 1851; 2d, Robert Niven, 1860; d. 1891.	1. Louise Clark, b. 1853; m. 1st, Clarence L. Collins, 1874; 2d, Capt. Barty Midford; 3d, Count M. L. Suberville, d. 1895.	1. Edith Lyman Collins, b. 1876; m. Count Czaykowski (Rechid Bey), 1897.	
	2. Charlotte E. Niven; m. Count de Sers.		
11. Frances Vanderbilt, b. 18[illegible]; d. 1866.			
12. George W. Vanderbilt, b. 1841; d. 1866.			

THE GOULDS

DESCENDANTS OF JAY GOULD.

Born May 27, 1836; married Helen Day Miller, 1863; died 1892.

Children.	Grandchildren.	Great-Grandchildren.	Great-Great-Grandchildren.
1. George Jay Gould, b. 1864; m. Edith Kingdon, 1886.	1. Kingdon Gould, b. 1887.		
	2. Jay Gould, b. 1888.		
	3. Marjorie Gwynne Gould, b. 1890.		
	4. Helen Vivian Gould, b. 1892.		
	5. George Jay Gould, Jr., b. 1896.		
	6. Edith K. Gould, b. 1901. 7. Gloria Anna, b. 190[illegible].		
2. Edwin Gould, b. 1866; m. Sarah Shrady, 1892.	1. Edwin Gould, b. 1893.		
	2. Frank Miller Gould, b. 1899.		
3. Helen Miller Gould, b. 1868.			
4. Howard Gould, b. 1871; m. Katherine Clemmons, 1898.			
5. Anna Gould, b. 1875; m. Count Paul Marie Boniface de Castellane, 1895; div. 1906; m. Prince de Sagan, 1908.	1. Boniface de Castellane, b. 1897.		
	2. George de Castellane, b. 1898.		
	3. Jay de Castellane, b. 1902.		
6. Frank Jay Gould, b. 1877; m. Helen Margaret Kelly, 1901.	1. Helen Margaret Gould, b. 1902.		
	2. Dorothy Gould, b. 1904.		

THE ASTORS.

DESCENDANTS OF JOHN JACOB ASTOR.

Born at Waldorf, Germany, 1763; married Sarah Todd, cousin of Henry Brevoort, in New York, 1785; died 1848.

CHILDREN.	Grandchildren.	Great-Grandchildren.	Great-Great-Grandchildren.
1. Magdalen Astor, b. 1786; m. 1st, Gov. Adrien B. Bentzen, of Santa Cruz, 1807; 2d, Rev. John Bristed, 1819; d. 1854.	1. Charles Astor Bristed, b. October 6, 1820; m. 1st, Laura Brevoort, 1847; 2d, Grace A. Sedgwick, 1867; d. January 15, 1874.	1. John Jacob Astor Bristed, b. 1848; d. 1880.	
		2. Charles Astor Bristed, b. 1869; m. Mary Rosa Donnelly, 1894.	1. Mary Symphorosa Bristed. 2. Katharine Elizabeth Grace Bristed.
2. John Jacob Astor, b. 1788; d. 1834.			
3. Eliza Astor, b. 1790; m. Count Rumpff, 1825; d. 1836.			
4. William Backhouse Astor, b. 1792; m. Margaret Alida Armstrong, 1818; d. 1875.	1. Emily Astor, b. 1819; m. Samuel Ward, 1838; d. 1841.	1. Margaret Astor Ward, b. 1838; m. John Winthrop Chanler, 1856; d. 1875.	1. John Armstrong Chanler, b. 1862; m. Amelie Rives, 1888. 2. Winthrop Astor Chanler, b. 1868; m. Margaret Terry, 1882, and had issue: 1. Laura Astor Chanler; 2. John Winthrop Chanler, d. 1894; 3. Margaret Astor Chanler; 4. Beatrice Chanler, b. 1891; 5. Hester Chanler; 6, a son; 7. Theo. Ward, b. 1902. 3. Elizabeth Astor Chanler; m. John J. Chapman, 1898, and had issue: Chanler Chapman, b. 1901. 4. Wm. Astor Chanler, b. 1867; m. Minnie Ashley, 1903; issue 1904, Wm. Astor Chanler, Jr. 5. Robert Winthrop Chanler; m. Julia Remington Chamberlain, 1893, and had issue: Dorothy Chanler. 6. Margaret Livingston Chanler; m. Richard Aldrich. 1906. 7. Alida Beekman Chanler; m. Temple Emmet, 1896, and had issue: 1. Elizabeth Emmet; 2. Margaret Emmet; 3. Alida Emmet; 4. Temple Emmet, Jr. 8. Lewis Stuyvesant Chanler, b. 1869; m. Alice Chamberlain, 1890, had issue: 1. Lewis Stuyvesant Chanler, Jr., b. 1891; 2. Alida Chanler, b. 1894; 3. Wm. Astor Chanler, b. 1895; 4. a daughter, 1907.
	2. John Jacob Astor, b. 1822; m. Charlotte Augusta Gibbes, 1846; d. 1890.	1. William Waldorf Astor, b. 1847; m. Mary Dahlgren Paul, 1878; she died 1895.	1. William Waldorf Astor, b. 1879; m. Nannie Langhorne Shaw, 1906; issue, 1907, son. 2. Pauline Astor, b. 1880; m. Capt. H. Spender Clay, 1904; issue 1905, a daughter. 3. John Jacob Astor, b. 1886. 4. Gwendolin, b. 1889; d. 1902.
	3. Laura Astor, b. 1824; m. Franklin Delano, 1841; d. 1902.		
	4. Mary Alida Astor, b. 1826; m. John Carey, 1850; d. 1881.	1. Arthur Astor Carey; m. Agnes Whiteside, 1889.	1. Reginald Carey, b. 1890. 2. Arthur Graham Carey, b. 1892. 3. Alida Carey, b. 1893. 4. Frances, b. 1898.
		2. Henry Astor Carey; d. 1893.	
		3. Margaret Laura Carey; m. 1st, Baron de Steurs; 2d, Elliot Zborowsky.	1. Margaret Eugenia Victorine de Steurs. 2. John Herbert Eugene Francois de Steurs. 3. Hubert Victor Arthur de Steurs.
	5. William Astor, b. 1830, d. 1892; m. Caroline Webster Schermerhorn, 1853; d. 1908.	1. Emily Astor, b. 1854; m. James J. Van Alen, 1876; d. 1881.	1. Mary Van Alen, b. 1876. 2. James Laurens Van Alen, b. 1878; m. 1900, Margaret Louise Post, and had issue: James Henry Van Alen, b. 1902. 3. Sarah Steward Van Alen, b. 1881; m. 1902, Robert J. F. Collier.
		2. Helen Astor, b. 1855; m. James Roosevelt Roosevelt, 1878; d. 1893.	1. James Roosevelt Roosevelt, Jr., b. 1879. 2. Helen Rebecca Roosevelt, b. 1881.

THE ASTORS—Continued.

Children.	Grandchildren.	Great-Grandchildren.	Great-Great-Grandchildren.
4. William Backhouse Astor (Continued).	5. William Astor (Continued).	3. Charlotte Augusta Astor, b. 1858; m. 1st, J. Coleman Drayton, 1879; 2d, George Ogilvy Haig, 1896.	1. Caroline Astor Drayton, b. 1880. 2. Henry Coleman Drayton, b. 1883; m. Constance Knower, 1905. 3. Wm. Astor Drayton, b. 1888. 4. Alida Livingston Drayton, b. 1890; d. 1898.
		4. John Jacob Astor, b. 1865; m. Ava Lowle Willing, 1891.	1. William Vincent Astor, b. 1891. 2. Ava Alice Muriel Astor, b. 1902.
		5. Caroline Schermerhorn Astor, b. 1861; m. Marshall Orme Wilson, 1884.	1. Marshall Orme Wilson, Jr., b. 1885. 2. Richard Thornton Wilson, b. 1886.
	6. Henry Astor, b. 1832; m. Malvina Dykeman, 1852.		
5. Henry Astor, b. 1794; d. 1808.			
6. Dorothea Astor, b. 1795; m. Walter Langdon, 1812; d. 1853.	1. Sarah Langdon, b. 1813; m. Francis R. Boreel, 1834; d. 1897.	1. William Walter Astor Boreel, b. 1838; m. Mary Emily Milbank; d. 1892.	1. Robert John Ralph Boreel; m. Miss Ives.
		2. Eliza Boreel; m. Baron H. W. Pallandt; d.	
		3. Alfred Boreel; m. daughter of Baron de Mydrecht.	
		4. Robert Boreel; d. 1896.	
		5. Daughter; m. Baron Otto Groenice.	
		6. Daughter, unmarried; d.	
	2. John J. A. Langdon, b. 1814; d. 1837.		
	3. Eliza Langdon, b. 1816; m. Matthew Wilks, 1842; d. 1899.	1. Eliza Wilks; m. Byam K. Stevens, 1869.	
		2. Alice Wilks; m. William N. Keefer, M. D.	1. Matthew Wilks Keefer. 2. Petrena Keefer. 3. Eliza Christine Keefer.
		3. Langdon Wilks, b. 1855; m. Pauline Kingsmill, 1891.	
		4. Matthew Astor Wilks.	
		5. Katherine Langdon Wilks.	
	4. Louisa Langdon, b. 1819; m. Delancey Kane, 1841.	1. Walter Langdon Kane; b. 1851; m. Mary Hunter, 1877; d. 1896.	1. Carolyn Hunter Kane, b. 1880; m. Edgar Morris Phelps, 1900, and had issue: 1 Walter Kane Phelps, b. 1901; 2. Henry Delafield Phelps, b. 1902. 2. Helen Dorothy Kane.
		2. Delancey Astor Kane, b. 1844; m. Eleanor Iselin, 1872.	1. Delancey Iselin Kane.
		3. John Innes Kane, b. 1855; m. Annie Schermerhorn, 1878.	
		4. Louisa Langdon Kane.	
		5. Emily Astor Kane; m. Augustus Jay, 1876.	1. Delancey Kane Jay. 2. Peter Augustus.
		6. Sybil Kent Kane.	
		7. Woodbury Kane; m. Mrs. Sallie Hargous Elliott, 1905; d. 1905.	
		8. Samuel Nicholson Kane; d. 1906.	
	5. Walter Langdon, b. 1821; m. Catherine Livingston, 1847; d. 1893.	1. A son; d.	
	6. Woodbury Langdon, b. 1824; m. Helen Colford Jones, 1847; d. 1892.	1. Woodbury Gersdorf Langdon, b. 1850; m. Sophia E. Montgomery, 1882.	1. Sophie E. Langdon, b. 1883. 2. Woodbury G. Langdon, Jr. 3. } 4. } Three younger children. 5. }
	7. Cecelia Langdon, b. 1827; m. Jean de Notbeck, 1849.	1. Eugenia de Notbeck, b. 1852.	
		2. Cecelia de Notbeck, b. 1856.	
		3. A daughter.	
		4. A son.	
	8. Eugene Langdon, b. 1832; m. Harriet Lowndes, 1859; d. 1868.	1. Marion Langdon, b. 1864; m. Royal Phelps Carroll, 1891.	1. Marion Dorothea Carroll.
		2. Anne L. Langdon, b. 1865; m. Howard Townsend, 1894.	1. Sophie W. Townsend. 2. Anne Langdon Townsend. 3. Howard Van Rensselaer Townsend. 4. Eugene Langdon Townsend.

THE ROCKEFELLERS.

DESCENDANTS OF WILLIAM A. ROCKEFELLER.

Born 1810; married Eliza Davison.

CHILDREN.	Grandchildren.	Great-Grandchildren.	Great-Great-Grandchildren.
1. John D. Rockefeller, b. 1839; m. Laura C. Spelman, 1864.	1. Bessie Rockefeller, b. 1866; m. Prof. Charles A. Strong. 1889; d. 1906.		
	2. Alta Rockefeller, b. 1871; m. 1901, E Parmalee Prentice.	1. Son, deceased. 2. Son, b. Nov. 29, 1907.	
	3. Edith Rockefeller, b. 1872; m. Harold F. McCormick, 1895.	1. John Rockefeller McCormick, b. 1897; d. 1901. 2. Fowler McCormick, b. 1899. 3. Harold McCormick, Jr. 4. Daughter, b. 1903. 5. Muriel McCormick, b. 1904.	
	4. John D. Rockefeller, Jr., b. 1874; m. Abby Greene Aldrich, 1901.	1. Daughter, b. Nov. 10, 190[illegible]. 2. John D. Rockefeller, 3rd, b. 1906.	
2. William Rockefeller, b. 1841; m. Almira Geraldine Goodsell, 1864.	1. William G. Rockefeller, b. 1870; m. Elsie Stillman, 1896.		
	2. Emma Rockefeller, b. 1868; m. Dr. David Hunter McAlpin, 1896.		
	3. Percy Avery Rockefeller, b. 1878; m. Isabel G. Stillman, 1901.	1. Isabella Rockefeller, b. 1902.	
	4. Ethel Geraldine Rockefeller, b. 1882; m. 1907, Marcellus Hartley Dodge.		

THE MORGANS.

DESCENDANTS OF JUNIUS SPENCER MORGAN.

Born 1813; married, 1836, Juliet Pierpont; died 1890.

CHILDREN.	Grandchildren.	Great-Grandchildren.	Great-Great-Grandchildren.
1. John Pierpont Morgan, b. 1837; m. 1st, Amelia Sturges; 2d, 1865, Frances Louise Tracy.	1. Louisa Pierpont Morgan, b. 1866; m. 1900, Herbert Livingston Satterlee.	1. Mabel Morgan Satterlee. 2. Eleanor Morgan Satterlee.	
	2. John Pierpont Morgan, Jr., b. 1867; m. 1890, Jane Norton Grew.	1. Junius Spencer Morgan, b. 1892. 2. Jane Norton Morgan. 3. Frances Tracy Morgan. 4. Henry Sturgis Morgan.	
	3. Juliet Pierpont Morgan, b. 1870; m. 1894, William Pierson Hamilton.	1. Helen Morgan Hamilton. 2. Pierpont Morgan Hamilton. 3. Laurens Morgan Hamilton. 4. Alexander Hamilton.	
	4. Anne Tracy Morgan, b. 1873.		
2. Sarah Spencer Morgan, b. 1839; m. 1866, George Hale Morgan; d. 1896.	1. Junius Spencer Morgan; m. Josephine Adams Perry.	1. Sarah Spencer Morgan. 2. Alexander Perry Morgan.	
	2. Caroline Lucy Morgan.		
	3. George D. Morgan.		
3. Mary Lyman Morgan, b. 1844; m. 1867, Walter Haynes Burns; he died 1897.	1. William Burns; died an infant.		
	2. Walter Spencer Morgan Burns.		
	3. Mary Burns; m. 1901, Lewis Vernon Harcourt.	1. Doris Vernon Harcourt. 2. Olivia Harcourt. 3. Daughter.	
4. Junius Spencer Morgan, b. 1846; d. 1858; unmarried.			
5. Juliet Pierpont Morgan, b. 1847; m. 1867, Rev. John B. Morgan.	1. Ursula Junius Morgan. 2. John Junius Morgan.		

THE MACKAYS.

DESCENDANTS OF JOHN W. MACKAY.

Born at Dublin, Ireland, 1831; m. Marie Louise Hungerford-Bryant (w.) 1867; died July 20, 1902.

CHILDREN.	Grandchildren.	Great-Grandchildren.	Great-Great-Grandchildren.
Eva Bryant Mackay (adopted); m. 1885 Poince de Galatro-Colonna (afterward Prince di Stigliano).	1. Andrea Galatro-Colonna. 2. Bianca Galatro-Colonna. 3. Marco Galatro-Colonna.		
1. John W. Mackay, Jr., b. Aug. 12, 1870; d. Paris, Oct. 18, 1895 (unmarried).			
2. Clarence H. Mackay; b. April 17, 1874; m. 1898 Katherine Duer.	1. Katherine Duer Mackay. 2. Ellin Duer Mackay.		

THE HAVEMEYERS.

DESCENDANTS OF WILLIAM FREDERICK HAVEMEYER.

Born in New York, 1804; married Sarah Agnes Craig, 1828; died November 30, 1874.

Children.	Grandchildren.	Great-Grandchildren.	Great-Great-Grandchildren.
1. William Havemeyer, b. 18—; d. 1834.			
2. Sarah Chandler Havemeyer; m. Hector Armstrong, 1856.	1. William F. H. Armstrong; m. Jennie Herrman.		
3. John Craig Havemeyer. b. New York, 1833; m. Alice Alide Francis, 1872.	1. Harriet Francis Havemeyer.		
	2. John Francis Havemeyer; m. Mary Hayward Mitchell, 1899.	1. Helen Mitchell Havemeyer.	
		2. John Francis Havemeyer.	
	3. Alice Louise Havemeyer.		
4. Henry Havemeyer, b. —; m. Mary J. Moller, 1864; d. 1886.	1. William Moller Havemeyer; d. 1900.		
	2. William F. Havemeyer 2d. d. 1904.		
	3. J. Blanche Havemeyer; m. Adair Campbell.	4 children living in Scotland.	
	4. Edythe Havemeyer.		
	5. Agnes J. Havemeyer; m. — Burnham; d. 1893.		
	6. Harry Havemeyer, d. —.		
5. Hector Craig Havemeyer; d. December, 1889.			
6. James Havemeyer; m. Delia Conklin, 1870.	1. James Craig Havemeyer; m. Adah Bryant.		
	2. Agnes Havemeyer; m. John V. A. Cattus.		
7. Laura Amelia Havemeyer; m. Nov. 30, 1869, Isaac Walker Maclay.	1. Julia Havemeyer Maclay; m. Charles Ward Hall.	1. Charles W. Hall.	
		2. Archibald Maclay Hall.	
		3. Hector Craig Hall.	
	2. Agnes Craig Maclay.		
	3. William Frederick Maclay.		
	4. Henry Havemeyer Maclay.		
	5. Archibald Maclay.		
	6. Laura Grace Maclay.		
8. Charles W. Havemeyer; m. Julia Loomis, 1874, d. 1895.	1. Julia Loomis Havemeyer.		
	2. Loomis Havemeyer.		
9. William Frederick Havemeyer, b. March 31, 1850; m. Josephine Harmon, 1877.	1. Hector H. Havemeyer, b. 1878; m. Ray M. Russell, 1902.	1 child.	
	2. Martha J. Havemeyer, b. 1879; m. William R. Willcox, 1903.	1 child.	
	3. Arthur Havemeyer, b. 1882.		
	4. Raymond Havemeyer, b. 1884.		

THE HAVEMEYERS.

DESCENDANTS OF FREDERICK CHRISTIAN HAVEMEYER.

Born in New York, February 5, 1807; married Sarah Osborne Townsend, 1831; died July 28, 1891.

Children.	Grandchildren.	Great-Grandchildren.	Great-Great-Grandchildren.
1. Frederick Christian Havemeyer; married.			
2. Charles O. Havemeyer; died in infancy.			
3. Mary O. Havemeyer; m. J. Lawrence Elder; d. 1864.	1. Frederick H. Elder; died unmarried, 1884.		
	2. Minnie H. Elder; m. McCoskey Butt.	1. Robert McCoskey Butt.	
		2. Laurence H. Butt.	
4. George W. Havemeyer; d. 1861; unmarried.			
5. Kate B. Havemeyer; m. Louis J. Belloni.	1. Mary Louise H. Belloni.		
	2. Kate H. Belloni; m. Laurence Griffith.	1. Louie Belloni Griffith.	
	3. Sadie H. Belloni.		
	4. George (Miss) H. Belloni; m. Dr. George E. McLaughlin.	1. Katherine Havemeyer McLaughlin.	

THE HAVEMEYERS—Continued.

CHILDREN.	Grandchildren.	Great-Grandchildren.	Great-Great-Grandchildren.
6. Theodore Augustus Havemeyer, b. New York, May 17, 1839; m. October 12, 1863, Emily De Loosey; d. April 28, 1897.	1. Natalie Ida Blanche Havemeyer, b. New York, 1864; m. John Mayer, August 1884; d. Mahwah, N. J., 1900.	1. Emily A. Mayer, b. 1885; m. M. G. Willis, 1906.	1. M. G. Willis, Jr., b. 1907.
		2. John Ed. Mayer, b. 1887.	
		3. Rowland Mayer, b. 1890.	
		4. Joseph Mayer, b. Rome, Italy, 1900.	
	2. Emily Blanche Havemeyer, b. Westchester, N. Y., 1865; m. Ed. Clarkson Potter, January, 1885.	1. Ed. C. Potter, Jr., b. December, 1885; m. Lisa B. Marshall, 1905.	1. Catharine Potter, b. 1906.
		2. Dorothea Havemeyer Potter, b. 1887.	
		3. Emily De Loosey Potter, b. 1889.	
		4. Thomas Wyndeart Potter, b. 1891.	
		5. Marie Blanche Potter, b. 1892.	
		6. Theodore Havemeyer Potter, b. 1893.	
		7. Charles Robert Potter, b. 1895.	
		8. Julia Blachford Potter, b. 1896.	
		9. Lillian Fredericka Potter, b. 1899.	
		10. Richard Milford B. Potter, b. 1900.	
		11. Eleanor May Potter, b. 1902.	
	3. Charles Frederick Havemeyer, b. New York, 1867; m. Camilla Morse, 1890; d. 1898.	1. Theodore A. Havemeyer, 3d, b. 1892.	
		2. Charles Frederick Havemeyer, b. 1898.	
	4. Theodore A. Havemeyer, Jr., b. 1868; m. Katherine Aymer Sands, 1891.		
	5. Blanche Maximilian Havemeyer, b. Vienna, 1871; m. William Butler Duncan, Jr., 1891.	1. Natalie Duncan, b. 1892.	
		2. David Duncan, b. 1893.	
		3. Dorothy Duncan, b. 1900.	
		4. William B. Duncan, 3d, b. 1903.	
	6. Marie Ida Pauline Havemeyer, b. 1872; m. Perry Tiffany, 1894.	1. Marion Tiffany, b. 1895.	
		2. Theodore Perry Tiffany, b. 1897; m. H. F. Godfrey, 1906.	
	7. Henry Osborne Havemeyer, Jr., b. 1876; m. Charlotte Whiting, 1900.	1. Carlotta Havemeyer, b. 1901.	
		2. Henry Osborn Havemeyer, 3d, b. 1903.	
		3. Florence Havemeyer, b. 1905.	
	8. Theodora Havemeyer, b. 1878; m. Lieut-Com. Cameron McCrea Winslow, U. S. N., 1899.	1. Natalie Emily Winslow, b. 1900.	
		2. Henry Cameron McCrea Winslow, b. 1901.	
		3. Theodora Winslow, b. 1903.	
		4. Emily Winslow, b. 1904.	
	9. Frederick Christian Havemeyer, 3d, b. 1880; m. Lillie Harriman Travis, 1906.		
7. Henry O. Havemeyer, b. New York, Oct. 18, 1847; d. 1908, m. Louisine Waldron Elder, 1883; d. Dec. 4, 1907.	1. Adaline Havemeyer.		
	2. Horace Havemeyer.		
	3. Electra Havemeyer.		
8. Sarah Louise Havemeyer; m. Frederick Wendell Jackson.	1. Charles F. H. Jackson.		
	2. Louise A. Jackson.		

THE FIELDS.

DESCENDANTS OF MARSHALL FIELD.

Born in Conway, Mass., 1835; m. 1st, Nannie D. Scott, 1863; 2d, Delia Spencer-Caton, 1905, d. 1906.

CHILDREN.	Grandchildren.	Great-Grandchildren.	Great-Great-Grandchildren.
1. Marshall Field, Jr., b. 1868; m. 1890, Albertine Huck; d. Nov. 27, 1905.	1. Marshall Field III., b. 1893.		
	2. Henry Field, b. 1895.		
	3. Gwendolyn Field, b. 1902.		
2. Ethel Field, b. 1873; m. 1st, Arthur Tree, 1891; 2d, Capt. David Beatty, D. S. O., 1901.	1. Ronald Lambert Field Tree, b. 1897.		
	2. David Field Beatty, b. 1905.		

THE BELMONTS.

DESCENDANTS OF AUGUST BELMONT.

Born at Alzy, Germany, Dec. 6, 1816; married, 1849, Caroline Slidell Perry; died Nov. 24, 1890.

CHILDREN.	Grandchildren.	Great-Grandchildren.	Great-Great-Grandchildren.
1. Perry Belmont, b. 1851; m. 1899, Jessie Robbins.			
2. August Belmont, b. 1853; m. Elizabeth Hamilton Morgan; she died 1898.	1. August Belmont, Jr., b. 1882; m. Alice W. de Goicouria, 1906	1. Jessie Morgan Belmont, b. 1907.	
	2. Raymond Belmont, b. 1888.		
	3. Morgan Belmont, b. 1892.		
3. Oliver H. P. Belmont, b. 1858; d. 1908; m. 1st, Sara Swan Whiting, 1883; 2d, Alva E. Smith (Vanderbilt), 1896.	1. Natica, b. 1884; m. Wm. Proudfit Burden, April 17 1907; d. Feb. 21, 1908.		
4. Frederika, b. 1854; m. 1877, Samuel S. Howland; d. 1902.			
5. Raymond Belmont, b. 1866; d. 1887.			
6. Jennie Belmont; d. 1875.			

THE WHITNEYS.

DESCENDANTS OF WILLIAM COLLINS WHITNEY.

Born in Conway, Franklin Co., Mass., July 5, 1841; married, 1st, 1869, Flora B. Payne, daughter of Henry B. Payne, of Ohio, who died Feb. 4, 1893; 2d, Sept. 28, 1896, Mrs. Edith Sybil Randolph, who died May 6, 1899. He died Feb. 2, 1904.

CHILDREN.	Grandchildren.	Great-Grandchildren.	Great-Great-Grandchildren.
1. Harry Payne Whitney, b. in New York, April 29, 1872; m. Gertrude Vanderbilt, 1896.	1. Flora Payne Whitney, b. 1897.		
	2. Vanderbilt Whitney, b. 1899.		
2. Pauline Whitney; m. Almeric Hugh Paget, 1895.	1. Pauline Paget, b. 1896.		
	2. Flora Payne Paget; d.		
	3. Alice Paget, b. 1899.		
3. Payne Whitney; m. Helen Hay, 1902.	1. Daughter, b. Feb. 5, 1903.		
	2. Son, b. Aug. 17, 1904.		
4. Dorothy Payne Whitney.			
5. Child; d. Feb. 3, 1883.			

THE LEITERS.

DESCENDANTS OF LEVI ZEIGLER LEITER.

Born at Leitersberg, Washington Co., Md., 1834; married Mary Theresa Carver, October 18, 1866; died at Bar Harbor, Me., June 6, 1904.

CHILDREN.	Grandchildren.	Great-Grandchildren.	Great-Great-Grandchildren.
1. Joseph Leiter, b. in Chicago, December 4, 1868; m. June 10, 1908, Juliette Williams.			
2. Mary Victoria Leiter, b. May 27, 1870; m. April 22, 1895, Rt. Hon. George Nathaniel Curzon, now Lord Curzon of Kedleston, ex-Viceroy of India; d. 1906.	1. The Hon. Mary Irene Curzon.		
	2. The Hon. Cynthia Blanche Curzon.		
	3. The Hon. Alexandria N. Curzon.		
3. Nancy Lathrop Carver Leiter; m. November 29, 1904, Major Colin Powys Campbell.	1. Colin Campbell, b. 1907. 2. Mary Campbell, b. 1908.		
4. Marguerite Hyde Leiter; m. Dec. 26, 1904, Henry Molyneux Paget Howard, Earl of Suffolk	1. Charles Henry George Howard, Lord Andover, b. 1906. 2. Cecil, b. 1908.		

THE GOELETS.

DESCENDANTS OF ROBERT GOELET.

Born in New York, 1809; married Sarah Ogden; died 1879.

CHILDREN.	Grandchildren.	Great-Grandchildren.	Great-Great-Grandchildren.
1. Robert Goelet, b. New York, Sept. 29, 1841; m. Henrietta Louise Warren, 1879; d. April 27, 1899.	1. Robert Walton Goelet, b. March 19, 1880.		
	2. Beatrice Goelet; d. 1897.		
2. Ogden Goelet, b. June 11, 1846; m. May R. Wilson, 1877; d. Aug. 27, 1897.	1. Robert Goelet; m. Elsie Whelen, 1904.	Ogden Goelet, b. Jan. 17, 1907.	
	2. May Goelet; m. the Duke of Roxburghe, 1903.		

THE LORILLARDS.

DESCENDANTS OF PETER LORILLARD.

Born March 17, 1796; married Catherine Griswold; died 1867.

Children.	Grandchildren.	Great-Grandchildren.	Great-Great-Grandchildren.
1. Pierre Lorillard, b. 1833; m. Emily Taylor, 1858; d. 1901.	1. Emily Lorillard, b. 1858; m. William Kent, 1881.	1. William Kent, Jr., b. April 14, 1882.	
		2. Emily L. Kent, b. Oct. 23, 1884.	
		3. Peter L. Kent, b. March 3, 1887.	
		4. Richard Kent, b. Feb. 5, 1904.	
	2. Pierre Lorillard, Jr., b. 1860; m. Caroline J. Hamilton, 1881.	1. Pierre Lorillard, 3rd, b. March 10, 1882.	
		2. Griswold Lorillard, b. June, 1885.	
	3. Griswold N. Lorillard, b. 1863; d. 1888, unmarried.		
	4. Maude Louise Lorillard, b. 1873; m. Thomas Suffern Tailer, 1893; 2d, Cecil Baring, London, England, Nov. 8, 1902.	1. Lorillard Tailer, b. Dec. 25, 1897.	
		2. Daphne Baring, b. Feb., 1904.	
		3. Daughter b. Oct., 1905.	
2. George L. Lorillard, married.	No issue.		
3. Louis L. Lorillard; m. Katherine Beekman.	1. Louis L. Lorillard, Jr.		
	2. George L. Lorillard.		
	3. Beeckman Lorillard; m. 1903, Kathleen Doyle.		
4. Jacob Lorillard; m. Frances A. Uhlhorn.	1. Augusta Lorillard; m. William H. Sands.	1. Harold A. Sands.	
		2. Anita L. Sands.	
	2. Ernest E. Lorillard; m. Elizabeth K. Screven.	1. Mary V. R. Lorillard.	
	3. Jacob Lorillard, Jr.		
5. Eva Lorillard; m. Col. Lawrence Kip, 1867.	1. Lorillard Kip; d. 1898.		
	2. Eva Maria Kip; d. 1870.		
	3. Edith Kip; m. Richard McCreery.	1. Lawrence McCreery.	
6. Mary Lorillard; m. Henry I. Barbey.	1. Henry G. Barbey.		
	2. Mary L. Barbey; m. Alfred Seton, Jr.	1. Marie Seton.	
		2. Helen Seton.	
		3. Henry Seton.	
	3. Ethel Lynde Barbey; m. 1895, A. Lanfear Norrie.	1. Lanfear Norrie.	
		2. Emily Rita Norrie.	
		3. Valerie Norrie.	
	4. Helene Barbey; m. Count Hermann de Pourtales.	1. Irene Pourtales.	
		2. Alex. Pourtales.	
		3. Jacquelin Pourtales.	
	5. Eva Barbey; m. Baron Andre de Neuflize.	1. Marie Madeline de Neuflize.	
	6. Rita Barbey.		
	7. Pierre L. Barbey.		
7. Catherine Lorillard; m. James P. Kernochan.	1. James Lorillard Kernochan; m. Eloise Stevenson; d. 1903.		
	2. Catherine Lorillard Kernochan; m. Herbert C. Pell.	1. Herbert C. Pell, Jr.	
		2. Clarence C. Pell.	

THE CARNEGIES.

DESCENDANT OF ANDREW CARNEGIE.

Born at Dumfermline, Scotland, Nov. 25, 1835; married, 1887, Louise Whitfield.

Children.	Grandchildren.	Great-Grandchildren.	Great-Great-Grandchildren.
Margaret Carnegie, b. 1897.			

There are relatives of Mr. Carnegie residing in the United States, including the family of his late brother Thomas at Pittsburgh, Pa., but Andrew Carnegie is alone the founder of the American multi-millionaire family.

THE ARMOURS.

DESCENDANTS OF PHILIP DANFORTH ARMOUR.

Born in Stockbridge, N.Y., May 16, 1832; married, 1862, Malvina Belle Ogden; died Jan. 6, 1901.

Children.	Grandchildren.	Great-Grandchildren.	Great-Great-Grandchildren.
1. Jonathan Ogden Armour, b. 1863; m. Lolita Sheldon.	1. Lolita, b. 1896.		
2. Philip Danforth Armour, Jr., b. 1869; m. 1890; d. 1900.	1. Philip Danforth Armour, 3d, b. 1894.		
	2. Lester Armour, b. 1896.		

United States Steamboat Inspection Service.

THE Steamboat Inspection Service, by act of Congress approved February 14, 1903, was transferred from the Treasury Department to the Department of Commerce and Labor. The transfer went into effect July 1, 1903. The Supervising Inspector-General of the Steamboat Inspection Service, George Uhler, reported to the Secretary of Commerce and Labor for the fiscal year ended June 30, 1908: Number of annual certificates of inspection issued to domestic steam, motor, sail vessels, and barges, 7,738; number of certificates issued to foreign steamers, 452; total number of annual certificates of inspection issued to domestic and foreign, 8,190. Decrease in number of certificates to domestic vessels over previous year, 105; increase of number of certificates to foreign vessels over previous year, 33; decrease in number of certificates of all kinds of vessels over previous year, 72. Gross tonnage of domestic vessels, all kinds, inspected, 4,428,723; gross tonnage of foreign steamers inspected, 2,916,272. Increase in gross tonnage of foreign steam vessels inspected over previous year, 492,968. Increase in tonnage of all kinds domestic vessels inspected over previous year, 199,156. Number of officers' licenses issued, 26,056. Number of new life-preservers inspected, 183,800, of which number 2,146 were rejected. Decrease in number of new preservers inspected from previous year, 29,649. Increase in number of life-preservers rejected over previous year, 1,104. Number of marine boiler plates inspected at the mills by assistant inspectors, 3,691, being a decrease in number inspected from previous year of 2,133. Number of applicants examined for color blindness, 843, of which number 52 were found color-blind and rejected, and 791 were passed. Decrease in number of applicants passed from previous year, 647.

CAUSES.	Number of Accidents.	Number of Lives Lost.	CAUSES.	Number of Accidents.	Number of Lives Lost.
Fire	8	12	Accidents to machinery	..	..
Collisions	24	129	Snags, wrecks, and sinking	21	71
Explosions or accidental escape of steam	3	6	Accidental drowning	..	106
Breaking of steam pipes, mud drums, etc	1	2	Miscellaneous	7	59
			Total	64	385

Of the total number of 385 lives lost, 106 were from accidents for which the victims were entirely responsible, and 59 from suicide and other causes beyond the power of the Service to avert. This leaves 220 lives lost that can be fairly charged to accident, collision, or foundering, not a very large number when it is considered how many millions of persons travel upon vessels subject to the inspection rules of this Service.

During the year ended December 31, 1907, 372,847,379 passengers were carried on steamers which are required by law to make report, an increase of 14,552,788 over the previous calendar year.

Increase in number of accidents over previous year, 9. Decrease in number of lives lost over previous year, 120.

The Rhodes Scholarship at Oxford University.

CECIL RHODES, statesman, who died at Cape Town, South Africa, March 26, 1902, directed in his will dated July 1, 1899, that a part of his fortune, estimated at $10,000,000, should be applied to the creation of a fund for the support of a certain number of scholarships covering a three-years' course at the University of Oxford. He directed that the selection of the recipients of this gift should be made two from each State and Territory of the United States, or one hundred in all, fifteen from Germany and from one to nine from each of the British Colonies. The scholarships are awarded on marks only, three-tenths whereof shall be given to a candidate for his "Literary and Scholastic" attainments, the remainder being for his love of outdoor athletics and sports, for strong, manly qualities such as courage, generosity and kindness, and for high moral character, and especially for ambition to serve and lead in large public affairs.

The agencies for final selection vary a good deal. Scholars from Cape Colony are chosen by the individual schools to which the scholarships are especially assigned. In several of the Canadian provinces and in a few States of the American Union it has been decided that an appointment shall be made in rotation by the leading universities. Under this system the field of selection each year is somewhat narrowed, but it is possible to carry out more closely than otherwise the suggestions made by Mr. Rhodes, who appears to have had in his mind selection by a single institution. The five German students for whom annual provision is made are nominated, according to the terms of the will, by the Emperor himself. In the great majority of the States of the Union, in outlying colonies like Bermuda, Jamaica and Newfoundland, in four provinces of Canada, in New Zealand and the States of Australia, the final choice of the scholar is left in the hands of a Committee of Selection. Great care has been taken in the constitution of these committees, as it has been felt that on the wise and impartial exercise of their judgment depends more than upon anything else the full success of the scheme.

In most of the States the selection is made by a committee appointed by representatives of the colleges; in some the appointments are made in rotation by the leading colleges.

The conditions regulating the award of scholarships in the American States provide that the candidates shall have satisfactorily completed the work of at least two years in some college of liberal arts and sciences. Except under extraordinary circumstances the upper age limit must be twenty-four years at the time of entering upon the scholarship at Oxford. To be eligible the candidate must be a citizen of the United States, or the son of a citizen, and must be unmarried. Each student receives an allowance of £300 a year, which is equivalent to $1,500, payable in quarterly instalments, which is just enough to enable him to pay his college fees and necessary expenses. As the first instalment is not available until some time after the arrival of the student, he should go abroad with one or two hundred dollars in his possession.

At the beginning of Michaelmas term, October, 1904, there entered Oxford seventy-two Rhodes scholars; forty-three were Americans, twenty-four colonials and five Germans. In 1906, the full number, 190 in all, were in residence, and thereafter this number will be maintained, the vacancies being filled as men complete their three-years' course. The last examination in the United States took place in January, 1908. There will be examinations also in 1910, 1911, 1913, 1914, and so on, omitting every third year. The examinations are not competitive, but qualifying. Inquiries as to particulars by intending candidates may be addressed to any college. Information about Oxford, its colleges and course of studies, should be addressed to F. J. Wylie, the Oxford agent of the Rhodes trustees, Oxford, England.

Value of Foreign Coins in United States Money.

(Proclaimed by the Secretary of the Treasury October 1, 1908.*)

Country.	Standard.	Monetary Unit.	Value in U. S. Gold Dollar.	Coins.
Argent. R.	Gold	Peso	$0.96,5	Gold: argentine ($4.82,4) and ½ argentine. Silver: peso and divisions.
Austria-H.	Gold	Crown	.20,3	Gold: 10 and 20 crowns. Silver: 1 and 5 crowns.
Belgium	Gold	Franc	.19,3	Gold: 10 and 20 francs. Silver: 5 francs.
Bolivia	Silver	Boliviano	.38,2	Silver: boliviano and divisions.
Brazil	Gold	Milreis	.54,6	Gold: 5, 10, and 20 milreis. Silver: ½, 1, and 2 milreis.
Canada	Gold	Dollar	1.00	
Cent. Am.	Silver	Peso†	.46,5	Silver: peso and divisions.
Chile	Gold	Peso	.36,5	Gold: escudo ($1.82,5), doubloon ($3.65), and condor ($7.30). Silver: peso and divisions.
China	Silver	Tael: Shanghai	.57,2	
		Tael: Haikwan	.63,7	
		Tael: Canton	.62,4	
Colombia	Gold	Dollar	1.00	Gold: condor ($9.64,7) and double-condor. Silver: peso.
Costa Rica	Gold	Colon	.46,5	Gold: 2, 5, 10, and 20 colons ($9.30,7). Silver: 5, 10, 25, and 50 centimos.
Denmark	Gold	Crown	.26,8	Gold: 10 and 20 crowns.
Ecuador	Gold	Sucre	.48,7	Gold: 10 sucres ($4.86,65). Silver: sucre and divisions.
Egypt	Gold	Pound (100 piasters)	4.94,3	Gold: pound (100 piasters), 5, 10, 20, and 50 piasters. Silver: 1, 2, 5, 10, and 20 piasters.
France	Gold	Franc	.19,3	Gold: 5, 10, 20, 50, and 100 frs. Silver: 5 frs.
Germany	Gold	Mark	.23,8	Gold: 5, 10, and 20 marks.
Gt. Britain	Gold	Pound sterling	4.86,6½	Gold: sovereign (pound sterling) and ½ sov'gn.
Greece	Gold	Drachma	.19,3	Gold: 5, 10, 20, 50, and 100 drachmas. Silver: 5 drachmas.
Hayti	Gold	Gourde	.96,5	Gold: 1, 2, 5, and 10 gourdes. Silver: gourde and divisions.
India	Gold	Pound sterling §	4.86,6½	Gold: sov. ($4.86,65). Sil.: rupee and div'ns.
Italy	Gold	Lira	.19,3	Gold: 5, 10, 20, 50, and 100 lire. Silver: 5 lire.
Japan	Gold	Yen	.49,8	Gold: 5, 10, and 20 yen. Silver: 10, 20, and 50 sen.
Mexico	Gold	Peso ¶	.49,8	Gold: 5 and 10 pesos. Silver: dollar (or peso)** and divisions.
Neth'lands	Gold	Florin	.40,2	Gold: 10 florins. Silver: 1, and 2½ florins.
N'foundl'd	Gold	Dollar	1.01,4	Gold: 2 dollars ($2.02,8).
Norway	Gold	Crown	.26,8	Gold: 10 and 20 crowns.
Panama	Gold	Balboa	1.00,0	Gold: 1, 2½, 5, 10, and 20 balboas. Silver: peso and divisions.
Peru	Gold	Libra	4.86,6½	Gold: ½ and 1 libra. Sil.: sol and divisions.
Portugal	Gold	Milreis	1.08	Gold: 1, 2, 5, and 10 milreis.
Russia	Gold	Ruble	.51,5	Gold: 5, 7½, 10, and 15 rubles. Silver: 5, 10, 15, 20, 25, 50, and 100 copeks.
Spain	Gold	Peseta	.19,3	Gold: 25 pesetas. Silver: 5 pesetas.
Sweden	Gold	Crown	.26,8	Gold: 10 and 20 crowns.
Switz'land	Gold	Franc	.19,3	Gold: 5, 10, 20, 50, & 100 francs. Silver: 5 fr's.
Turkey	Gold	Piaster	.04,4	Gold: 25, 50, 100, 250, and 500 piasters.
Uruguay	Gold	Peso	1.03,4	Gold: peso. Silver: peso and divisions.
Venezuela	Gold	Bolivar	.19,3	Gold: 5, 10, 20, 50, and 100 bolivars. Silver: 5 bolivars.

* The coins of silver-standard countries are valued by their pure silver contents, at the average market price of silver for the three months preceding the date of this circular. † Not including Costa Rica. § The sovereign is the standard coin of India, but the rupee ($0.3244) is the money of account, current at 15 to the sovereign. ‖ Customs. ¶ Seventy-five centigrams fine gold. ** Value in Mexico 49.8.

TABLE SHOWING THE VALUE OF FOREIGN COINS AND PAPER NOTES IN AMERICAN MONEY BASED UPON THE VALUES EXPRESSED IN THE ABOVE TABLE.

Number.	British £ Sterling	German Mark.	French Franc, Italian Lira.	Chinese Tael (Haikwan.)	Dutch Florin.	Jap. Yen, Mex. Peso.	Russian Gold Ruble.	Austrian Crown.
1	$4.86,6½	$0.23,8	$0.19,3	$0.57,2	$0.40,2	$0.49,8	$0.51,5	$0.20,3
2	9.73,3	0.47,6	0.38,6	1.14,4	0.80,4	0.99,6	1.03	0.40,6
3	14.59,9½	0.71,4	0.57,9	1.71,6	1.20,6	1.49,4	1.54,5	0.60,9
4	19.46,6	0.95,2	0.77,2	2.28,8	1.60,8	1.99,2	2.06	0.81,2
5	24.33,2½	1.19	0.96,5	2.86,0	2.01	2.49,0	2.57,5	1.01,5
6	29.19,9	1.42,8	1.15,8	3.43,2	2.41,2	2.98,8	3.09	1.21,8
7	34.06,5½	1.66,6	1.35,1	4.00,4	2.81,4	3.48,6	3.60,5	1.42,1
8	38.93,2	1.90,4	1.54,4	4.57,6	3.21,6	3.98,4	4.12	1.62,4
9	43.79,8½	2.14,2	1.73,7	5.14,8	3.61,8	4.48,2	4.63,5	1.82,7
10	48.66,5	2.38	1.93	5.72,0	4.02	4.98,0	5.15	2.03
20	97.33	4.76	3.86	11.44,0	8.04	9.96,0	10.30	4.06
30	145.99,5	7.14	5.79	17.16,0	12.06	14.94,0	15.45	6.09
40	194.66	9.52	7.72	22.88,0	16.08	19.92,0	20.60	8.12
50	243.32,5	11.90	9.65	28.60,0	20.10	24.90,0	25.75	10.15
100	486.65	23.80	19.30	57.20,0	40.20	49.80,0	51.50	20.30

Insular Possessions of the United States.

THE PHILIPPINES.

THE Philippine group, lying off the southern coast of Asia, between longitude 120 and 130 and latitude 5 and 20 approximately, number about 2,000 islands, great and small, in a land and sea area of 1,200 miles of latitude and 2,400 miles of longitude. The actual land area is about 140,000 miles. The six New England States, New York, and New Jersey have about an equivalent area. The island of Luzon, on which the capital city (Manila) is situated, is the largest member of the group, being about the size of the State of New York. Mindanao is nearly as large, but its population is very much smaller. The latest estimates of areas of the largest islands are: Luzon, 44,400; Mindanao, 34,-000; Samar, 4,800; Panay, 4,700; Mindoro, 4,000; Leyte, 3,800; Negros, 3,300; Cebu, 2,400.

A census of the Philippines was taken by the United States Government in 1903 under the auspices of the Census Office. The population returned was 7,635,426. Of this number almost seven million are more or less civilized. The wild tribes form about 9 per cent. of the entire population. Racially the inhabitants are principally Malays. The civilized tribes are practically all adherents of the Catholic Church, the religion being that introduced into the country by the Spaniards when they took possession of the islands in 1565. The Church has since then been a strong ruling power and the priesthood numerous. The Moros are Mohammedans and the other wild peoples have no recognized religious beliefs. The total number of non-Christian peoples is 647,740.

The density of population in the Philippines is 67 per square mile. In Continental United States it is 26 per square mile. Foreigners number about 50,000, of whom nearly three-fourths are Chinese. Exclusive of the Army there are 8,135 Americans in the islands, nearly one-half being located in the municipalities. There are thirty different races in the islands, all speaking distinct dialects, the largest tribe being the Visayans, who form nearly one-fourth of the entire civilized population. The Tagalogs, occupying the provinces in the vicinity of Manila, rank second in numbers, and the Ilocanos the third. Education has been practically reorganized by the Americans. The number of persons attending school is 811,715. Six thousand teachers are employed, four-fifths of whom are Filipinos. English is very generally taught, and the next generation of Filipinos will probably speak that tongue. Pauperism is almost unknown in the islands. In 1902 there were only 1,668 paupers maintained at public charge. The average normal death rate in the Philippines is 32 per thousand. The birth rate is 48 per thousand. There were in 1902 41 newspapers published, 12 being in English, 24 in Spanish, 4 in native dialects, and 1 in Chinese. The estimated real estate property value is 469,527,058 pesos, and the personal property 152,718,661 pesos. The reported value of church buildings, mostly Catholic, is 41,698,710 pesos. While there are four towns with more than 10,000 population Manila is the only incorporated city. Its inhabitants numbered 219,928 in 1902.

The climate is one of the best in the tropics. The islands extend from 5° to 21° north latitude, and Manila is in 14° 35′. The thermometer during July and August rarely goes below 79° or above 85°. The extreme ranges in a year are said to be 61° and 97°, and the annual mean 81°.

AGRICULTURE.

Although agriculture is the chief occupation of the Filipinos, yet only one-ninth of the surface is under cultivation. The soil is very fertile, and even after deducting the mountainous areas it is probable that the area of cultivation can be very largely extended and that the islands can support population equal to that of Japan (42,000,000).

The chief products are hemp, rice, corn, sugar, tobacco, cocoanuts, and cacao, hemp being the most important commercial product and constituting two-thirds of the value of all exports. Coffee and cotton were formerly produced in large quantities—the former for export and the latter for home consumption; but the coffee plant has been almost exterminated by insects and the home-made cotton cloths have been driven out by the competition of those imported from England. The rice and corn are principally produced in Luzon and Mindoro and are consumed in the islands. The cacao is raised in the southern islands, the best quality of it at Mindanao. The sugar cane is raised in the Visayas. The hemp is produced in Southern Luzon, Mindoro, the Visayas, and Mindanao. It is nearly all exported in bales. Tobacco is raised in all the islands.

IMPORTS AND EXPORTS.

In the year ending December 31, 1908, the exports of merchandise from the United States to the Philippines were $11,455,707, and the total imports from the Philippines for the same period were $10,164,223.

The imports of merchandise from foreign countries, year ending December 31, 1907, were $23,-630,496, and the exports were $21,634,153. The principal foreign countries trading with the Philippines are Great Britain, French East Indies, China, and Spain.

CIVIL GOVERNMENT FOR THE PHILIPPINES.

On July 1, 1902, Congress passed (chapter 1369) "An act temporarily to provide for the administration of the affairs of civil government in the Philippine Islands and for other purposes." Under this act complete civil government was established in the Archipelago and the office of Military Governor with military rule was terminated. William H. Taft was appointed Governor by the President. Governor Taft was succeeded by Luke E. Wright in December, 1903, by Henry Clay Ide in 1905, and James F. Smith, the present Governor, in 1906. The government was composed of a civil Governor and seven commissioners, of whom four were Americans and three Filipinos. By act of Congress approved May 11, 1908, the Commission was increased by one member, to be appointed by the President, making the Commission nine members in all, including the Governor. There were four executive departments—Interior Finance, and Justice, Commerce and Police, and Public Instruction. There are thirty-nine provinces, each with a Governor, a Supreme Court with seven judges, and fourteen judicial districts. In March, 1907, the President, in accordance with the act of Congress, directed the Commission to call a general election of delegates to a Philippine Assembly. The new Assembly was chosen July 20, and was opened October 16 by Secretary of War Taft. It is politically divided as follows: Nacionalists, 31; Progresistas, 16; Independents, 19; Immediatistas, 7; Independistas, 4; Nacional Independiente, 1; Catolico, 1. The total vote recorded at the election for delegates was 97,803, which is only 1.4 per cent. of the population.

PORTO RICO.

The island of Porto Rico, over which the flag of the United States was raised in token of formal possession on October 18, 1898, is the most eastern of the Greater Antilles in the West Indies and is separated on the east from the Danish island of St. Thomas by a distance of about fifty miles, and from Hayti on the west by the Mona passage, seventy miles wide. Distances from San Juan, the capital, to important points are as follows: New York, 1,411 miles; Charleston, S. C., 1,200 miles; Key West, Fla., 1,050 miles; Havana, 1,000 miles.

The island is a parallelogram in general outline, 108 miles from the east to the west, and from 37 to 43 miles across, the area being about 3,600 square miles, or somewhat less than half that of the State of New Jersey (Delaware has 2,050 square miles and Connecticut 4,990 square miles). The

INSULAR POSSESSIONS OF THE UNITED STATES—*Continued.*

population according to an enumeration made by the United States Government in 1900 showed a population of 953,243, of whom 589,426 are white and 363,817 are colored. The density was 26.4 to the square mile; 83.2 per cent. of the population cannot read.

Porto Rico is unusually fertile, and its dominant industries are agriculture and lumbering. In elevated regions the vegetation of the temperate zone is not unknown. There are more than 500 varieties of trees found in the forests, and the plains are full of palm, orange, and other trees. The principal crops are sugar, coffee, tobacco, and maize, but oranges, bananas, rice, pineapples, and many other fruits are important products. The largest article of export from Porto Rico is sugar. The next largest is tobacco. The other exports in order of amount are coffee, fruits, molasses, cattle, timber, and hides.

The principal minerals found in Porto Rico are gold, carbonates, and sulphides of copper and magnetic oxide of iron in large quantities. Lignite is found at Utuado and Moca, and also yellow amber. A large variety of marbles, limestones, and other building stones are deposited on the island, but these resources are very undeveloped. There are salt works at Guanica and Salina on the south coast, and at Cape Rojo on the west, and these constitute the principal mineral industry in Porto Rico.

The principal cities are Mayaguez, with 15,187, Ponce, 27,952 inhabitants; and San Juan, the capital, with 32,048. The shipments of domestic merchandise from the United States to Porto Rico, year ending December 31, 1908, were $22,360,366. The exports of domestic merchandise to the United States were $25,885,776. The foreign trade, year ending December 31, 1907, was: Imports, $3,580,887; exports, $4,899,372.

An act providing for a civil government for Porto Rico was passed by the Fifty-sixth Congress and received the assent of the President April 12, 1900. A statement of its provisions was printed in THE WORLD ALMANAC for 1901, pages 92 and 93. President Roosevelt in his message to Congress in December, 1906, recommended the granting of United States citizenship to the Porto Ricans.

Under this act a civil government was established, which went into effect May 1, 1900. There are two legislative chambers, the Executive Council, or "Upper House," composed of the Government Secretary, Attorney-General, Treasurer, Auditor, Commissioner of the Interior, and Commissioner of Education, and five citizens appointed by the President, and the House of Delegates, or "Lower House," consisting of 35 members, elected by the people. The island is represented near the Congress of the United States by a Resident Commissioner.

GUAM.

The island of Guam, the largest of the Marianne or Ladrone Archipelago, was ceded by Spain to the United States by Article 2 of the Treaty of Peace, concluded at Paris December 10, 1898. It lies in a direct line from San Francisco to the southern part of the Philippines, and is 5,200 miles from San Francisco and 900 miles from Manila. It is about 32 miles long and 100 miles in circumference, and has a population of about 8,661, of whom 5,249 are in Agana, the capital. The inhabitants are mostly immigrants or descendants of immigrants from the Philippines, the original race of the Ladrone Islands being extinct. The prevailing language is Spanish. Nine-tenths of the islanders can read and write. The island is thickly wooded, well watered, and fertile, and possesses an excellent harbor. The productions are tropical fruits, cacao, rice, corn, tobacco, and sugar cane.

Commander Taussig, of the United States gunboat Bennington, took possession of the island and raised the United States flag over Fort Santa Cruz on February 1, 1899.

TUTUILA.

Tutuila, the Samoan island which, with its attendant islets of Tau, Olesinga, and Ofu, became a possession of the United States by virtue of the tri-partite treaty with Great Britain and Germany in 1899, covers, according to the Bureau of Statistics of the Treasury Department, fifty-four square miles, and has 5,800 inhabitants. It possesses the most valuable island harbor, Pago-Pago, in the South Pacific, and perhaps in the entire Pacific Ocean. Commercially the island is unimportant at present, but is extremely valuable in its relations to the commerce of any nation desiring to cultivate transpacific commerce.

Ex-Chief Justice Chambers, of Samoa, says of Pago-Pago that "The harbor could hold the entire naval force of the United States, and is so perfectly arranged that only two vessels can enter at the same time. The coaling station, being surrounded by high bluffs, cannot be reached by shells from outside." The Government is increasing the capacity to 10,000 tons.

The Samoan Islands, in the South Pacific, are fourteen in number, and lie in a direct line drawn from San Francisco to Auckland, New Zealand. They are 4,000 miles from San Francisco, 2,200 miles from Hawaii, 1,900 miles from Auckland, 2,000 miles from Sydney, and 4,200 miles from Manila. Germany governs all the group except the part owned by the United States. The inhabitants are native Polynesians and Christians of different denominations.

WAKE AND OTHER ISLANDS.

The United States flag was hoisted over Wake Island in January, 1899, by Commander Taussig, of the Bennington, while proceeding to Guam. It is a small island in the direct route from Hawaii to Hong Kong, about 2,000 miles from the first and 3,000 miles from the second.

The United States possesses a number of scattered small islands in the Pacific Ocean, some hardly more than rocks or coral reefs, over which the flag has been hoisted from time to time. They are of little present value and mostly uninhabited. The largest are Christmas, Gallego, Starbuck, Penrhyn, Phœnix, Palmyra, Howland, Baker, Johnston, Gardner, Midway, Morell, and Marcus islands. The Midway Islands are occupied by a colony of telegraphers in charge of the relay in the cable line connecting the Philippines with the United States and a camp of United States marines, in all about forty persons.

The Santa Barbara group is a part of California and the Aleutian chain, extending from the peninsula of Kamchatka in Asiatic Russia to the promontory in North America which separates Bering Sea from the North Pacific, a part of Alaska.

HAWAII.

Hawaii was annexed to the United States by joint resolution of Congress July 7, 1898. A bill to create Hawaii a Territory of the United States was passed by Congress and approved April 30, 1900.

The area of the several islands of the Hawaiian group is as follows: Hawaii, 4,210 square miles; Maui, 760; Oahu, 600; Kauai, 590; Molokai, 270; Lanai, 150; Niihau, 97; Kahoolawe, 63. Total, 6,740 square miles.

At the time of the discovery of the islands by Captain Cook in 1778 the native population was about 200,000. This has steadily decreased, so that at the last census the natives numbered but 31,019,

INSULAR POSSESSIONS OF THE UNITED STATES—*Continued.*

which was less than that of the Japanese and Chinese immigrants settled in the islands. A census taken early in 1897 revealed a total population of 109,020, distributed according to race as follows:

	Males.	Females.	Total.		Males.	Females.	Total.
Hawaiians	16,399	14,620	31,019	Portuguese	8,202	6,898	15,100
Part Hawaiians	4,249	4,236	8,485	Americans	1,975	1,111	3,086
Japanese	19,212	5,195	24,407	British	1,406	844	2,250
Chinese	19,167	2,449	21,616				

The remainder were Germans, French, Norwegians, South Sea Islanders, and representatives of other nationalities. The American population was 2.73 per cent. of the whole. The American population has increased since annexation.

The first United States census of the islands was taken in 1900 with the following result: Hawaii Island, 46,843; Kauai Island. 20.562; Niihau Island, 172; Maui Island. 25.416; Molokai Island and Lanai Island, 2.504; Oahu Island, 58,504. Total of the Territory, 154,001. The population of the City of Honolulu is 39,306.

The exports from Hawaii to the United States in the twelve months ending December 31, 1908, were valued at $41,595,708. The imports into Hawaii from the United States for the same period were valued at $14,638,717. The imports from foreign countries for the same period were $4,682,399, exports $587,205.

The new Territorial Government was inaugurated at Honolulu June 14, 1900, and the first Territorial Legislature began its sessions at Honolulu February 20. 1901. The Legislature is composed of two houses—the Senate of fifteen members. holding office four years, and the House of Representatives of thirty members, holding office two years. The Legislature meets biennially, and sessions are limited to sixty days.

The Executive power is lodged in a Governor, a Secretary, both appointed by the President, and hold office four years, and the following officials appointed by the Governor, by and with the consent of the Senate of Hawaii. An Attorney-General, Treasurer, Commissioner of Public Lands, Commissioner of Agriculture and Forestry, Superintendent of Public Works, Superintendent of Public Instruction. Auditor and Deputy, Surveyor, High Sheriff, and members of the Boards of Health, Public Instruction, Prison Inspectors, etc. They hold office for four years, and must be citizens of Hawaii.

The Judiciary of the Territory is composed of the Supreme Court, with three Judges, the Circuit Court, and such inferior courts as the Legislature may establish. The Judges are appointed by the President. The Territory is a Federal Judicial District, with a District Judge, District-Attorney, and Marshal, all appointed by the President. The District Judge has all the powers of a Circuit Judge.

The Territory is represented in Congress by a delegate, who is elected biennially by the people.

Provision is made in the act creating the Territory for the residence of Chinese in the Territory, and prohibition as laborers to enter the United States.

Territorial Expansion of the United States.

THERE have been thirteen additions to the original territory of the Union, including Alaska the Hawaiian, Philippine, and Samoan Islands and Guam, in the Pacific, and Porto Rico and Pine Islands, in the West Indies, and the Panama Canal zone; and the total area of the United States, including the noncontiguous territory, is now fully five times that of the original thirteen colonies.

The additions to the territory of the United States subsequent to the peace treaty with Great Britain of 1783 are shown by the following table, prepared by the United States General Land Office:

ADDITIONS TO THE TERRITORY OF THE UNITED STATES FROM 1800 TO 1900.

Territorial Division.	Year.	Area Added.	Purchase Price.	Territorial Division.	Year.	Area Added.	Purchase Price.
		S. Miles.	Dollars.			S. Miles.	Dollars.
Louisiana purchase	1803	875,025	15,000,000	Porto Rico	1898	3,600	....
Florida	1819	70,107	5,499,768	Pine Islands (W. Indies)	1898	882	......
Texas	1845	389,795	....	Guam	1898	175	......
Oregon Territory	1846	288,689	....	Philippine Islands	1899	143,000	20,000,000
Mexican cession	1848	523,802	*18,250,000	Samoan Islands	1899	73	....
Purchase from Texas	1850	†	10,000,000	Additional Philippines	1901	68	100,000
Gadsden purchase	1853	36,211	10,000,000				
Alaska	1867	599,446	7,200,000	Total	..	2,937,613	87,039,768
Hawaiian Islands	1897	6,740	......				

* Of which $3,250,000 was in payment of claims of American citizens against Mexico. † Area purchased from Texas amounting to 123,784 square miles is not included in the column of area added, because it became a part of the area of the United States with the admission of Texas.

ACQUISITION OF THE PANAMA CANAL ZONE IN 1904.

Article 2 of the treaty between the United States and the Republic of Panama, ratified by the United States Senate February 23, 1904, treaty in effect February 26, 1904, provided for the cession, in perpetuity, by Panama, of a strip of territory adjacent to the canal, as follows:

"The Republic of Panama grants to the United States in perpetuity the use, occupation, and control of the zone of land and land under water for the construction, maintenance, operation, sanitation, and protection of said canal of the width of ten miles, extending to the distance of five miles on each side of the centre line of the route of the canal to be constructed; the said zone beginning in the Caribbean Sea, three marine miles from mean low-water mark, and extending to and across the Isthmus of Panama into the Pacific Ocean to a distance of three marine miles from mean low-water mark, with the proviso that the cities of Panama and Colon and the harbors adjacent to said cities, which are included within the boundaries of the zone above described, shall not be included within this grant. The Republic of Panama further grants to the United States in perpetuity the use, occupation, and control of any other lands and waters outside of the zone above described which may be necessary and convenient for the construction, maintenance, operation, sanitation, and protection of the said canal or of any auxiliary canals or other work necessary and convenient for the construction, maintenance, operation, sanitation, and protection of the said enterprise. The Republic of Panama further grants to the United States in perpetuity the use, occupation, and control of all islands within the limits of the zone above described, and in addition thereto the group of small islands in the Bay of Panama named Perico, Naos, Culebra, and Flamingo."

Polar Research in 1908.

BY WALTER WELLMAN.

Commander Robert E. Peary sailed from New York in July in the Arctic ship Roosevelt, and made good progress to Cape Sabine and Etah, Greenland, there taking on board Esquimaux, dogs and walrus meat, and steaming northward late in August, after sending back his coal ship, the Erik. Nothing has since been heard from the Roosevelt, but if Commander Peary has been successful in escaping the perils of ice navigation through Robeson and Kennedy Channels he is wintering on the north shore of Grant Land, at or near his old station, Cape Sheridan, about 500 statute miles from the North Pole. From this point Commander Peary expects to set out for the Pole about March 1, 1909, sledging over the sea ice. Before leaving America he announced that he should this time try to leave the land considerably to the west of Cape Sheridan, as he believes the ice will not be so much broken up there as directly north of his headquarters. It will be remembered that Mr. Peary was prevented attaining the Pole in his former expedition, when he did establish the record for the "Farthest North," by an open channel or "lead" in the ice which he could not cross without a fatal delay. The channel of open water which blocked his progress was only a mile or two in width, and other Arctic travellers have expressed surprise that Mr. Peary carried with him no boat or canoe with which the crossing could be effected. All others who have attempted sledging to the Pole over the uncertain, shifting sea ice, which is never at rest, not even in the coldest weather, have carried light canoes or kyaks or tarpaulins with which sledges could be converted into rafts. Whether or not Mr. Peary has included such within his present equipment he did not announce before leaving America. Inasmuch as such channels of water are likely to be met at any time, and in any part of the Arctic Sea, it is presumed that this time Mr. Peary has gone prepared to cross them. That some such craft or makeshift is an absolute essential to success is now considered axiomatic by Arctic travellers, because in "a dash for the Pole" time is a vital factor. The favorable season for sledging is limited to about 110 days, and provisions for men and dogs are carried for this period only. A delay of a week waiting beside an open channel which could be crossed with a boat or canoe in a few hours may be fatal to the chances of the pole-seeker, as it was to Mr. Peary in 1906. Mr. Peary announced before sailing that this time he was prepared, if necessary, to remain three years in the Arctic regions, and that if he does not gain the Pole in 1909 he will renew the effort in 1910.

There are now three distinct methods by which it is believed it is possible to reach the Pole. The first is the "dash" with dogs and sledges, which Mr. Peary adheres to, and with which he has made a nearer approach to the Pole than any other explorer. This method is also employed by Dr. Frederick A. Cook, who sailed north in June, 1907, as head of the "Bradley Polar Expedition," wintered at Etah, and in February, 1908, set out for the Pole with a few Esquimaux, intending to follow the western route, via Ellesmere Land, so fully explored by Captain Sverdrup a few years ago. Dr. Cook had not returned to Etah in August, and fear as to his safety has been entertained, though his friends do not share in it because he is travelling in a country filled with game and no doubt can take care of himself through another Winter. His chances for reaching the Pole are not considered very good, as he had more than 300 miles to travel to reach the Arctic Sea, or that much greater distance than Peary will have to go if the latter establishes his base, as before, on the north coast of Grant Land.

The second method is the drift method employed by Frithjof Nansen, and now to be renewed by another Norwegian, Roald Amundsen, who achieved the Northwest Passage with the sloop Gjoa. Captain Amundsen announced in November that in the Summer of 1910 he would sail from San Francisco in the Fram, the famous ice-ship used by Nansen and Sverdrup, intending to thrust her within the ice-pack northwest of Behring Strait, and to "drift" for three or four years through the Arctic Ocean. In the Nansen voyage the Fram started farther west, and two years later the drift had carried her to the 86th parallel of latitude, or within 390 statute miles of the Pole. Dr. Nansen and other Arctic students have believed that if the Fram could start farther east the current may carry her across the Pole itself.

The third method is travel through the air. Andree tried this with an ordinary balloon, without motive power or steering means, and lost his life. In November it was reported his grave had been found in Labrador, but the report lacked confirmation, and it is believed the grave was that of a fisherman or sailor. There is now little doubt that Andree's balloon came down in the Barentz Sea, east of Spitzbergen and southwest of Franz Josef Land, a few days after the start from Dane's Island, July, 1897.

The Wellman plan to reach the Pole by a modern airship, carrying a total weight of 19,000 pounds, and driven by powerful engines at a rate of 20 miles per hour, is an effort to make the greatest possible use of scientific and mechanical progress in geographical exploration. In 1906 the airship headquarters, comprising balloon house, machine shops, gas apparatus, etc., was established at Dane's Island, Spitzbergen. In 1907 a start for the Pole was prevented by an exceptionally unfavorable season, but the airship was thoroughly tested and found efficient in a trial voyage, though too late in the year to start for the Pole. This airship, the second largest yet built, has been repaired and improved, the headquarters have been maintained, and the expedition is to be renewed in the near future. In view of the success of the Zeppelin and other airships during the year confidence in the ultimate success of the Wellman plan is increasing.

August 15 the ship Denmark, of the Danish expedition to the east coast of Greenland, arrived at Bergen, Norway, bringing news that Mylius Ericsen, leader of the expedition, had perished in a snowstorm, along with Lieutenants Hagen and Broenlund, in November, 1907. The object of the expedition was to explore the northeast coast of Greenland, north of Cape Bismarck. The three men had left the ship and worked their way northward. Owing to the unusual severity of the weather in that region during the Summer of 1907, they were unable to start on their return before the Autumn, and while traversing the high inland ice were caught in a storm. A relief party

POLAR RESEARCH IN 1908.—*Continued.*

found the body of Lieutenant Broenlund in a crevice, not far from a depot. Beside it were sketches showing the work done by the party, and his diary, in which was the following entry:

"Perished at 79 degrees, under a trial return over inland ice, in November. Arrived here under a decreasing moon, and cannot go on, owing to frozen feet and darkness. The corpses of the others are in the middle of the fiord. Hagen died November 15, and Mylius some ten days later. (Signed) JOERGEN BROENLUND."

The relief party was unable to find the bodies of Ericsen and Hagen, on account of the heavy snow. The expedition was successful in roughly charting nearly all of the coast of Northeast Greenland, and discovered many large islands.

Dr. Jean Charcot, of Paris, sailed from Havre, August 15, in a new ship built to his order, named the Pourquoi Pas (Why Not?), en route for the Antarctic regions. He hopes to explore the continent which is believed to surround the South Pole. Dr. Charcot was favored with a gift of $120,000 from the French Government, and this sum was more than doubled by the Rothschilds and other patriotic and wealthy Frenchmen. The expedition is outfitted for three years. The Pourquoi Pas called at South American points in the Autumn and sailed for Alexander Land, which lies southeast of Patagonia.

Lieutenant Shackleton, the English explorer, is at work in Victoria Land, south of New Zealand, having in his equipment both horses and automobiles, with either or both of which he hopes to make extensive journeys over the "glacial continent." The mystery of the Antarctic regions is attracting more and more attention. Scottish, German and Belgian expeditions to that region are now under contemplation.

The International Polar Congress met at Brussels, Belgium, in May. The objects of the Congress are to create an international association for the study of the Polar regions; to obtain an international agreement upon questions relating to Polar geography; to organize a concerted international effort to reach the North Pole; to organize expeditions for the extension of Polar research in all directions, and to prepare a programme of scientific work for all such expeditions.

National Conventions of Political Parties in 1908.

PEOPLE'S PARTY NATIONAL CONVENTION—April 2 and 3. Held at St. Louis, Mo. Thomas E. Watson, of Georgia, was nominated for President and Samuel W. Williams, of Indiana, for Vice-President unanimously on the first ballots.

SOCIALIST PARTY NATIONAL CONVENTION—May 10-17. Held at Chicago, Ill. Nominations of candidates for President and Vice-President were made May 14. Eugene V. Debs, of Indiana, was nominated for President on the first ballot, the vote being: Eugene V. Debs, 152; James F. Carey, of Massachusetts, 17; Carl D. Thompson, of Wisconsin, 16; A. M. Simons, of Illinois, 2. Ben Hanford, of New York, was nominated for Vice-President on the first ballot, the vote being: Ben Hanford, 106; Seymour Stedman, of Illinois, 43; May Wood Simons, of Illinois, 20; John W. Slayton, of Pennsylvania, 12; scattering, 2.

REPUBLICAN PARTY NATIONAL CONVENTION—June 16-19. Held at Chicago, Ill. Nominations of candidates were made June 18. William H. Taft, of Ohio, was nominated for President on the first ballot, the vote being: William H. Taft, 702; Philander C. Knox, of Pennsylvania, 68; Charles E. Hughes, of New York, 67; Joseph G. Cannon, of Illinois, 58; Charles W. Fairbanks, of Indiana, 40; Robert M. La Follette, of Wisconsin, 25; Joseph B. Foraker, of Ohio, 16; Theodore Roosevelt, of New York, 3. James S. Sherman, of New York, was nominated for Vice-President on the first ballot, the vote being: James S. Sherman, 816; Franklin Murphy, of New Jersey, 77; Curtis Guild, Jr., of Massachusetts, 75; George L. Sheldon, of Nebraska, 10; Charles W. Fairbanks, of Indiana, 1.

SOCIALIST LABOR PARTY NATIONAL CONVENTION—July 4. Held at New York City. Martin R. Preston, of Nevada, was nominated for President unanimously. Donald M. Munro, of Virginia, was nominated for Vice-President, Arthur S. Dower, of Texas, being the other candidate. As Preston is a convict in the Nevada Penitentiary and under the Constitutional age he was ineligible for President, and the party subsequently nominated August Gillhaus, of New York, in his place as "candidate by proxy."

DEMOCRATIC PARTY NATIONAL CONVENTION—July 7-10. Held at Denver, Col. Nominations of candidates were made July 10. William J. Bryan, of Nebraska, was nominated for President on the first ballot, the vote being 892½; John A. Johnson, of Minnesota, 46. John W. Kern, of Indiana, was nominated for Vice-President unanimously, other candidates having been withdrawn prior to a ballot.

PROHIBITION PARTY NATIONAL CONVENTION—July 15-16. Held at Columbus, O. Nominations of candidates were made July 16. Eugene W. Chafin, of Illinois, was nominated for President on the third ballot, receiving 636 votes, against 451 for William B. Palmore, of Missouri, and other candidates. Aaron S. Watkins, of Ohio, was nominated for Vice-President on the first ballot by a large majority, the other candidates, T. B. Demaree, of Kentucky, and Charles S. Holler, of Indiana, receiving a few votes.

INDEPENDENCE PARTY NATIONAL CONVENTION—July 29. Held at Chicago, Ill. Thomas L. Hisgen, of Massachusetts, was nominated for President on the third ballot, the vote being: Thomas L. Hisgen, 831; Milford W. Howard, of Alabama, 38; John Temple Graves, of Georgia, 7; William R. Hearst, of New York, 2. For Vice-President, John Temple Graves was nominated on the first ballot.

United States Internal Revenue Receipts.

SUMMARY OF INTERNAL REVENUE RECEIPTS FROM 1881 TO 1908, INCLUSIVE.

Fiscal Years.	Spirits.	Tobacco.	Fermented Liquors.	Banks and Bankers.	Miscellaneous.	Adhesive Stamps.	Collections Under Repealed Laws.
1881	$67,153,975	$42,854,991	$13,700,241	$3,762,208	$231,078	$7,924,708	$152,163
1882	69,873,408	47,391,989	16,153,920	5,253,458	199,830	7,570,109	78,559
1883	74,368,775	42,104,250	16,900,616	3,748,995	305,803	7,053,053	71,852
1884	76,905,385	26,062,400	18,084,954	....	289,144	....	265,068
1885	67,511,209	26,407,088	18,230,782	....	222,681	....	49,361
1886	69,092,266	27,907,363	19,676,731	....	194,422	....	32,087
1887	65,829,322	30,108,067	21,922,188	4,288	219,058	....	29,283
1888	69,306,166	30,662,432	23,324,218	4,203	154,970	....	9,548
1889	74,312,206	31,866,861	23,723,835	6,179	83,898	....	....
1890	81,687,375	33,958,991	26,008,535	69	135,555	....	....
1891	83,335,964	32,796,271	28,565,130	....	256,214	....	....
1892	91,309,984	31,000,493	30,037,453	....	239,532	....	....
1893	94,720,261	31,889,712	32,548,983	....	166,915	....	....
1894	85,259,252	28,617,899	31,414,788	2	1,876,509	....	....
1895	79,862,627	29,704,908	31,640,618	....	1,960,794	....	....
1896	80,670 071	30,711,629	33,784,235	135	1,664,545	....	....
1897	82 008,543	30,710,297	32,472,162	85	1 426 506	....	....
1898	92,547,000	36 230,522	39,515,421	1,180	2,572,696	794,418	....
1899	99,283,534	52,493,208	68,644,558	....	9,225,453	43,837,819	....
1900	109 868,817	59,355 084	73,550,754	1,461	11,575,626	40,964 365	....
1901	116,027,980	62,481,907	75,669,908	1,918	13,448 921	39,241,036	....
1902	121,138,013	51,937,925	71,988,902	228	13,360,130	12,442 792	....
1903	131,953,472	43,514,810	47,547,856	899	7,723,345	....	....
1904	135,810,015	44,655,809	49,083,459	....	3,354,722	....	....
1905	135,958,513	45,659,910	50,360,553	....	2,209,000	....	....
1906	143,394,055	48,422,997	55,641,859	....	1,644,027	....	....
1907	156,326,902	51,811,070	59,567,818	....	1,948,232	....	....
1908	140,158,807	49,862,754	59,807,617	....	1,836,772	....	....

Of the receipts in 1908 classed as "Miscellaneous," $954,304 was from oleomargarine, $459,860 from playing cards, and $241,680 from penalties.

RECEIPTS BY STATES AND TERRITORIES.

FISCAL YEAR ENDED JUNE 30, 1908.

States and Territories.	Aggregate Collections	States and Territories.	Aggregate Collections.
Alabama (a)	$310,904.43	Nebraska	$2,124,035.80
Arkansas	105,511.18	New Hampshire, Maine, Vermont.	483,144.64
California and Nevada	6,444,353.40	New Jersey	6,969,893.42
Colorado and Wyoming	685,424.34	New Mexico and Arizona	105,209.31
Connecticut and Rhode Island	1,834,346 69	New York	30,359,597.81
Florida	1,058,036.75	North Carolina	5,081,091.21
Georgia	419,269.59	North and South Dakota	172,400.40
Hawaii	56,878 14	Ohio	19,599,646.84
Illinois	46,122 844.97	Oregon	550,401.55
Indiana	26,546,753.39	Pennsylvania	21,250,640.91
Iowa	933,725.05	South Carolina	214,409.99
Kansas and Oklahoma	323,725 20	Tennessee	2,402,660.91
Kentucky	26,874,585.54	Texas	773,857.94
Louisiana (b)	5,206,645.98	Virginia	4,561,521.30
Maryland, Del., D.C., and 2 Va. Dists.	7,045,596 41	Washington and Alaska	1,064,875.96
Massachusetts	4,311,892.39	West Virginia	1,456,021.05
Michigan	6,184,500 85	Wisconsin	8,239,331.45
Minnesota	1,812,788.97		
Missouri	9,334,561.62	Total	$251,665,950.04
Montana, Idaho and Utah	644,864.66		

(a) Including Mississippi after June 1, 1908. (b) Including Mississippi to May 31, 1908.

WITHDRAWALS FOR CONSUMPTION.

The quantities of distilled spirits, fermented liquors, manufactured tobacco, snuff, cigars, cigarettes, and oleomargarine on which tax was paid during the last two fiscal years are as follows:

Articles Taxed.	Fiscal years ended June 30— 1907.	1908.	Increase.	Decrease.
Spirits distilled from apples, peaches, grapes, pears, pineapples, oranges, apricots, berries, prunes, figs and cherries....gals..	1,993,688	1,670,031	......	323,657
Spirits distilled from materials other than apples, peaches, grapes, pears, pineapples, oranges, apricots, berries, prunes, etc...gals..	134,142,074	119,808,402	......	14,333,672
Wine made in imitation of champagne, etc....bottles..no..	......	69	69	......
Fermented liquors....bbls..	58,546,111	58,747,680	201,569	......
Cigars, weighing more than 3 pounds per thousand....no..	7,490,144,793	6,904,758,783	......	585,386,010
Cigars, weighing not more than 3 pounds per thousand....no..	1,152,133,426	1,009,352,296	......	142,781,130
Cigarettes, weighing not more than 3 pounds per thousand....no..	5,151,862,180	5,383,204,680	231,342,500	......
Cigarettes, weighing more than 3 pounds per thousand....no..	15,159,227	19,131,483	3,972,256	......
Snuff....lbs..	23,401,196	22,547,762	......	853,434
Tobacco, chewing and smoking....lbs..	369,186,303	364,109,395	......	5,076,908
Oleomargarine....lbs..	68,988,850	79,107,302	10,118,452	......
Adulterated butter....lbs..	68,586	177,123	108,537	......
Process or renovated butter....lbs..	63,751,640	50,240,708	.....	13,510,932

Note.—The quantity of mixed flour withdrawn cannot be stated, owing to the variable number of pounds taxed.

United States Internal Revenue Taxes.

SCHEDULE OF ARTICLES AND OCCUPATIONS SUBJECT TO TAX.

SPECIAL TAXES AND RATES.

Rectifiers of less than 500 barrels a year, $100; rectifiers of 500 barrels or more a year, $200.
Wholesale liquor dealers, $100; retail liquor dealers, $25.
Wholesale dealers in malt liquors, $50; retail dealers in malt liquors, $20.
Manufacturers of stills, $50; and for stills or worms, manufactured, each, $20.
Brewers: Annual manufacture less than 500 barrels, $50; annual manufacture 500 barrels or more, $100.

Manufactures of filled cheese, $400; wholesale dealers in filled cheese, $250; retail dealers in filled cheese, $12.

Manufacturers of oleomargarine, $600; wholesale dealers in oleomargarine artifically colored in imitation of butter, $480; wholesale dealers in oleomargarine free from artificial coloration, $200; retail dealers in oleomargarine artificially colored in imitation of butter, $48: retail dealers in oleomargarine free from artificial coloration, $6.

Manufacturers of adulterated butter, $600; wholesale dealers in adulterated butter, $480; retail dealers in adulterated butter, $48; manufacturers of process or renovated butter, $50; manufacturers, packers or repackers of mixed flour, $12.

DISTILLED SPIRITS, ETC.

Distilled spirits, per gallon, $1.10; stamps for distilled spirits intended for export, each, 10 cents; except when affixed to packages containing two or more 5-gallon cans for export, 5 cents.

Case stamps for spirits bottled in bond, 10 cents.

Wines, liquors, or compounds known or denominated as wine, and made in imitation of sparkling wine or champagne, but not made from grapes grown in the United States, and liquors not made from grapes, currants, rhubarb or berries grown in the United States, but produced by being rectified or mixed with distilled spirits or by the infusion of any matter in spirits, to be sold as wine, or as a substitute for wine, in bottles containing not more than 1 pint per bottle or package, 10 cents; same, in bottles, containing more than 1 pint, and not more than 1 quart, per bottle or package, 20 cents (and at the same rate for any larger quantity of such merchandise, however put up or whatever may be the package).

Grape brandy used in the fortification of pure, sweet wine under an act approved June 7, 1906 (to be assessed), per gallon, 3 cents.

FERMENTED LIQUORS.

Fermented liquors per barrel, containing not more than 31 gallons, $1 (and at a proportionate rate for halves, thirds, quarters, sixths and eighths of barrels); more than one barrel of 31 gallons, and not more than 63 gallons, in one package, $2.

TOBACCO AND SNUFF.

Tobacco, however prepared, manufactured and sold, or removed for consumption or sale, per lb., 6 cents; snuff, however prepared, manufactured and sold, or removed for consumption or sale, per lb., 6 cents.

CIGARS AND CIGARETTES.

Cigars of all descriptions made of tobacco, or any substitute therefor, and weighing more than 3 lbs. per thousand, $3; cigars of all descriptions made of tobacco, or any substitute therefor, and weighing not more than 3 lbs. per thousand, 18 cents per lb., 54 cents; cigarettes weighing not more than 3 lbs. per thousand and of a wholesale value or price of more than $2 per thousand, 36 cents per lb., $1.08; cigarettes weighing not more than 3 lbs. per thousand and of a wholesale value or price of not more than $2 per thousand, 18 cents per lb., 54 cents; cigarettes weighing more than 3 lbs. per thousand, $3.

OLEOMARGARINE.

Oleomargarine, domestic, artificially colored to look like butter, of any shade of yellow, per lb., 10 cents; oleomargarine, free from coloration that causes it to look like butter, of any shade of yellow, per lb., ¼ of one cent; oleomargarine imported from foreign countries, per lb., 15 cents.

ADULTERATED BUTTER AND PROCESS OR RENOVATED BUTTER.

Adulterated butter, per lb., 10 cents; process or renovoted butter, per lb., ¼ of one cent.

FILLED CHEESE.

Filled cheese, per lb., 1 cent; same, imported, per lb., 8 cents.

OPIUM.

Prepared smoking opium, per lb., $10.

MIXED FLOUR.

Mixed flour, per barrel of 196 lbs., or more than 98 lbs., 4 cents; half barrel of 98 lbs., or more than 49 lbs., 2 cents; quarter barrel of 49 lbs., or more than 24½ lbs., 1 cent; eighth barrel of 24½ lbs. or less, ½ of one cent. (Mixed flour imported from foreign countries, in addition to import duties, must pay internal revenue tax as above.)

CIRCULATION OF AND NOTES PAID OUT BY BANKS AND BANKERS.

Circulation issued by any bank, etc., or person (except a national bank taxed under Section 5214, Revised Statues, and Section 13, Act March 14, 1900), per month, 1-12 of 1 per cent.

Circulation (except national banks) exceeding 90 per cent. of capital, in addition, per month, 1-6 of 1 per cent.

Banks, etc., on amount of notes of any person, State bank, or State banking association, used for circulation and paid out, 10 per cent.

Banks, etc., bankers, or associations, on amount of notes of any town, city, or municipal corporation paid out by them, 10 per cent.

Every person, firm, association, other than national bank associations, and every corporation, State bank, or State banking association, on the amount of *their own notes* used for circulation and paid out by them, 10 per cent.

Every such person, firm, association, corporation, State bank, or State banking association, and also every national banking association, on the amount of notes of any person, firm, association, other than a national banking association, or of any corporation, State bank or State banking association, or of any town, city, or municipal corporation, used for circulation, and paid out by them, 10 per cent.

PLAYING CARDS.

Playing cards, per pack, containing not more than 54 cards, 2 cents.

TAXES NOT PAYABLE BY STAMPS.

Tax on deficiencies in production of spirits—On excess of materials used in production of spirits; on circulation of banks and bankers; on notes paid out by banks and others; on brandy used in the fortification of wine. Penalties of 50 per cent. and 100 per cent.

Receipts and Expenditures U. S. Government, 1878=1908.

REVENUE BY FISCAL YEARS.

Years. Ending June 30.	Customs.	Internal Revenue.	Direct Tax.	Sales of Public Lands.	Miscellaneous Sources. Premiums on Loans & Sales of Gold Coin.	Miscellaneous Sources. Other Miscellaneous Items.	Total Revenue.	Excess of Revenue over Ordinary Expenditures.
1878	$130,170,680	$110,581,625	....	$1,079,743	$317,102	$15,614,728	$257,763,879	$20,799,552
1879	137,250,048	113,561,611	....	924,781	1,505,048	20,585,697	273,827,184	6,879,301
1880	186,522,065	124,009,374	$31	1,016,507	110	21,978,525	333,526,611	65,883,653
1881	198,159,676	135,264,386	1,517	2,201,863	....	25,154,851	360,782,293	100,069,405
1882	220,410,730	146,497,595	160,142	4,753,140	....	31,703,643	403,525,250	145,543,811
1883	214,706,497	144,720,369	108,157	7,955,864	....	30,796,695	398,287,582	132,879,444
1884	195,067,490	121,586,073	70,721	9,810,705	....	21,984,882	348,519,870	104,392,626
1885	181,471,939	112,498,726	....	5,705,986	....	24,014,055	323,690,706	63,463,771
1886	192,905,023	116,805,936	108,240	5,630,999	....	20,989,528	336,439,727	93,956,589
1887	217,286,893	118,823,391	32,892	9,254,286	....	26,005,815	371,403,278	103,471,098
1888	219,091,174	124,296,872	1,566	11,202,017	....	24,674,446	379,266,065	111,341,274
1889	223,832,742	130,881,514	....	8,038,652	....	24,297,151	387,050,059	87,761,081
1890	229,668,585	142,606,706	....	6,358,273	....	24,447,420	403,080,983	85,040,272
1891	219,522,205	145,686,249	....	4,029,535	....	23,374,457	392,612,447	26,838,542
1892	177,452,964	153,971,072	....	3,261,876	....	20,251,872	354,937,784	9,914,454
1893	203,355,017	160,296,130	....	3,182,090	....	18,253,898	385,818,629	2,341,674
1894	131,818,531	147,111,232	....	1,673,637	....	17,118,618	297,722,019	*69,803,261
1895	152,158,617	143,421,672	....	1,103,347	....	16,706,438	313,390,075	*42,805,223
1896	160,021,752	146,762,865	....	1,005,523	....	19,186,061	326,976,200	*25,203,246
1897	176,554,126	146,688,774	....	864,581	....	23,614,422	347,721,905	*18,052,254
1898	149,819,594	169,943,040	....	1,243,129	....	84,845,631	405,321,335	*38,047,247
1899	206,141,225	272,486,648	....	3,070,137	....	33,324,840	515,652,666	*89,898,657
1900	233,164,871	295,327,927	....	2,836,883	....	35,911,171	567,240,852	79,527,060
1901	238,585,456	307,180,664	....	2,965,120	....	38,954,098	587,685,338	77,717,984
1902	254,444,709	271,880,122	....	6,261,927	....	29,891,476	562,478,233	91,287,376
1903	284,479,582	230,810,124	....	11,024,744	....	34,082,224	560,396,674	54,297,667
1904	261,274,565	232,904,119	....	9,283,342	....	37,169,723	540,631,749	*41,770,572
1905	261,798,857	234,095,741	....	7,017,011	....	41,363,076	544,274,685	*23,004,229
1906	300,657,413	249,063,868	....	7,585,524	....	37,607,910	594,914,715	26,187,141
1907	333,230,126	270,309,388	....	11,553,178	....	50,213,442	665,306,134	86,945,543
1908	285,680,653	250,714,008	....	12,715,709	....	587,180,054	599,895,763	*59,656,361

EXPENDITURES BY FISCAL YEARS.

Years. Ending June 30.	Premium on Loans and Purchase of Bonds, etc.	Other Civil and Miscellan'ous Items.	War Department.	Navy Department.	Indians.	Pensions.	Interest on Public Debt.	Total Ordinary Expenditures.
1878	....	$53,177,704	$32,154,148	$17,365,301	$4,629,280	$27,137,019	$102,500,875	$236,964,327
1879	....	65,741,555	40,425,661	15,125,127	5,206,109	35,121,482	105,327,949	266,947,883
1880	....	54,713,530	38,116,916	13,536,985	5,945,457	56,777,174	95,757,575	267,642,958
1881	$2,795,320	64,416,325	40,466,461	15,686,672	6,514,161	50,059,280	82,508,741	260,712,888
1882	1,061,249	57,219,751	43,570,494	15,032,046	9,736,747	61,345,194	71,077,207	257,981,440
1883	....	68,678,022	48,911,383	15,283,437	7,362,590	66,012,574	59,160,131	265,408,138
1884	....	70,920,434	39,429,603	17,292,601	6,475,999	55,429,228	54,578,378	244,126,244
1885	....	87,494,258	42,670,578	16,021,080	6,552,495	56,102,267	51,386,256	260,226,935
1886	....	74,166,930	34,324,153	13,907,888	6,099,158	63,404,864	50,580,146	242,483,138
1887	....	85,264,826	38,561,026	15,141,127	6,194,523	75,029,102	47,741,577	267,932,180
1888	....	72,952,261	38,522,436	16,926,438	6,249,308	80,288,509	44,715,007	267,924,801
1889	8,270,842	80,664,064	44,435,271	21,378,809	6,892,208	87,624,779	41,001,484	299,288,978
1890	17,292,363	81,403,256	44,582,838	22,006,206	6,708,047	106,936,855	36,099,284	318,040,711
1891	20,304,244	110,048,167	48,720,065	26,113,896	8,527,469	124,415,951	37,547,135	365,773,905
1892	10,401,221	99,841,988	46,895,456	29,174,139	11,150,578	134,583,053	23,378,116	345,023,330
1893	....	103,732,799	49,641,773	30,136,084	13,345,347	159,357,558	27,264,392	383,477,954
1894	....	102,165,471	54,567,930	31,701,294	10,293,482	141,177,285	27,841,406	367,746,867
1895	....	93,279,730	51,804,759	28,797,796	9,939,754	141,395,229	30,978,030	356,195,298
1896	....	87,216,235	50,830,921	27,147,732	12,165,528	139,434,001	35,385,029	352,179,446
1897	....	90,401,267	48,950,267	34,561,546	13,016 802	141,053,164	37,791,110	365,774,159
1898	....	96,520,505	91,992,000	58,823,985	10,994,668	147,452,369	37,585,056	443,368,583
1899	....	119,191,256	229,841,254	63,942,104	12,805,711	139,394,929	39,896,925	605,072,180
1900	....	105,773,190	134,774,768	55,953,078	10,175,107	140,877,316	40,160,333	487,713,792
1901	....	122,282,003	144,615,697	60,506,978	10,896,073	139,323,622	32,342,979	509,967,353
1902	....	113,469,324	112,272,216	67,803,128	10,049,585	138,488,560	29,108,045	471,190,858
1903	....	124,944,290	118,619,520	82,618,034	12,935,168	138,425,646	28,556,385	506,099,007
1904	....	186,766,703	115,035,411	102,956,102	10,438,350	142,550,266	24,646,490	582,402,321
1905	....	146,952,549	122,175,074	117,550,308	14,236,074	141,773,964	24,590,944	567,278,913
1906	....	120,000,627	93,659,462	110,956,167	12,746,512	141,034,081	24,310,326	568,727,565
1907	....	124,117,119	101,671 881	97,606,595	15,140,292	139,290,910	24,482,524	578,360,592
1908	....	146,898,930	110,284,864	118,726,347	14,550,758	153,887,995	21,424,990	659,552,125

The total receipts of the United States from the beginning of the Government, 1789, to 1908 have been: From customs, $10,623,877,484; internal revenue, $7,794,728,092; direct tax, $328,131,944; public lands, $391,960,383; miscellaneous, $1,781,736,077; total, excluding loans, $20,741,630,749.

The total expenditures of the United States from the beginning of the Government, 1789, to 1908 have been: For civil and miscellaneous, $4,252,721,996; war, $6,364,523,657; navy, $2,327,207,151; Indians, $469,338,140; pensions, $3,893,433,740; interest, $3,191,817,866; total, $20,825,050,821.

*Expenditures in excess of revenue.

American and Foreign Shipping.

UNITED STATES VESSELS. 1908.

Class.	Engaged in Foreign Trade.		Engaged in Coastwise Trade.	
	Number.	Tonnage.	Number.	Tonnage.
Steamers	469	595,147	9,952	4,099,045
Sailing vessels, Canal-boats, Barges	1,084	335,266	12,499	2,272,817
Total	1,553	930,413	22,451	6,371,862

The entire number of documented vessels was 25,425, of which 10,926 were steamers and 14,499 were vessels other than steamers, all aggregating 7,365,445 tons.

The estimated value of the whole amount of floating property under the flag, according to the census of 1890, was $215,069,296. The value according to the census of 1900 has not yet been reported. The statistics of the above table are for the fiscal year ending June 30, 1908.

SHIPBUILDING IN THE UNITED STATES.

The following table shows the class, number, and tonnage of the documented vessels built in this country during the last four years reported:

Class.	1905.		1906.		1907.		1908.	
	Number.	Tons.	Number.	Tons.	Number.	Tons.	Number.	Tons.
Sailing vessels	310	79,418	229	35,209	147	24,907	134	31,981
Steam vessels	560	197,702	650	315,707	674	365,405	923	481,624
Canal-boats	30	3,248	83	8,832	62	6,577	46	4,970
Barges	202	49,948	259	58,997	274	74,443	354	95,641
Total	1,102	330,316	1,221	418,745	1,157	471,323	1,457	614,216

IRON AND STEEL TONNAGE BUILT IN THE UNITED STATES, 1876-1908.

Years.	Sailing Vessels and Barges.	Steam Vessels.	Total.	Years.	Sailing Vessels and Barges.	Steam Vessels.	Total.
1876	......	21,346	21,346	1893	13,104	81,428	94,532
1877	......	5,927	5,927	1894	4,649	46,821	51,470
1878	......	26,960	26,960	1895	5,975	42,619	48,594
1879	......	22,007	22,007	1896	16,832	96,388	113,220
1880	44	25,538	25,582	1897	46,158	78,236	124,394
1882	......	40,096	40,096	1898	13,765	48,501	62,266
1883	2,033	37,613	39,646	1899	28,361	103,018	131,379
1884	4,432	31,200	35,632	1900	28,903	167,948	196,851
1885	731	43,297	44,028	1901	26,571	236,128	262,699
1888	692	14,215	14,907	1902	9,430	270,932	280,362
1887	92	34,261	34,353	1903	18,112	240,107	258,219
1888	746	35,972	36,718	1904	18,773	222,307	241,080
1889	33	53,479	53,512	1905	12,336	170,304	182,640
1890	4,975	75,402	80,377	1906	8,276	289,094	297,370
1891	6,309	99,309	105,618	1907	15,039	333,516	348,555
1892	5,282	46,092	51,374	1908	7,392	442,625	450,017

*COMPARATIVE GROWTH OF THE TONNAGE OF THE MERCHANT NAVIES OF THE UNITED STATES AND OF THE PRINCIPAL MARITIME COUNTRIES OF EUROPE FROM 1860 TO 1907.

Countries.	1860.	1870.	1880.	1890.	1895.	1903.	1904.	1905.	1906.	1907.
American	5,299,175	4,194,740	4,068,034	4,424,497	4,635,960	6,087,345	6,291,535	6,456,543	6,674,969	6,938,794
British	5,710,968	7,149,134	8,447,171	11,597,106	13,424,146	16,006,374	16,969,418	16,831,938	17,555,867	18,325,628
French	996,124	1,072,048	919,298	1,045,102	1,154,783	1,622,016	1,760,609	1,739,077	1,751,724	1,779,214
Norwegian	558,927	1,022,515	1,518,655	1,584,355	1,713,611	1,653,740	1,779,991	1,799,852	1,902,980	1,960,589
Swedish	.....	346,862	542,642	475,984	515,010	721,116	791,627	834,582	883,506	921,024
Danish	......	178,646	249,466	280,065	366,585	581,247	632,972	648,536	690,165	750,404
German	......	982,355	1,182,097	1,569,311	1,865,490	3,283,247	3,393,140	3,525,744	3,932,109	4,076,175
Dutch	433,922	389,614	328,281	378,784	469,695	658,845	722,193	734,879	768,688	883,633
Belgian	33,111	30,149	75,666	110,571	116,331	157,047	156,231	165,524	167,204	185,630
Italian	......	1,012,164	999,196	816,567	838,101	1,180,335	1,259,122	1,141,502	1,262,174	1,321,131
Austro-Hungarian	.....	329,377	290,971	269,648	306,119	578,697	574,976	576,472	619,866	674,960
Greek	263,075	404,0[illegible]	.....	307,[illegible]	381,180	378,199	517,307	499,164	533,329	572,748

Tonnage of the United States in 1908, 7,365,445.

The above tables have been compiled from the report of the Commissioner of Navigation of the United States. Russia in 1907-8 had a tonnage of 1,350,365, and Spain of 766,192.

*From Bureau Veritas.

Express Business in the United States.

(Special Census Report.)

THE Bureau of the Census in December, 1908, issued a report giving the results of a second census of the express business in the United States. The statistics presented cover the fiscal year ending June 30, 1907. The following is a summary:

In 1907 there were 34 express companies, as compared with 18 in 1890. Only 10 of the companies reporting in 1890 were in existence under the same name in 1907; the remaining 8 companies have gone out of business, have been absorbed by other companies, or are operating under other names.

The total express mileage increased from 174,059 miles to 235,903 miles, a gain of 35.5 per cent. Both the mileage operated over railroads and that operated over water lines showed large gains, the former having increased from 160,122 to 216,973, or 35.5 per cent., and the latter, from 10,882 to 17,796, or 63.5 per cent. A large part of the gain in steamboat mileage is attributable to the extension of the express business into Alaska.

Ninety-one per cent. of the total mileage in 1907 was operated over steam railroads, 7.5 over steamboat lines, nine-tenths of 1 per cent. over electric roads, and five-tenths of 1 per cent. over stage lines. Fourteen companies reported the use of electric roads for express transportation, and of these five, operating 205.30 miles, use such roads exclusively.

THE LEADING COMPANIES.

In 1907, as in 1890, the express business was dominated by the following six companies: Adams, American, Pacific, Southern, United States and Wells, Fargo & Co. The last mentioned leads in the amount of mileage operated, with the American Express Company a close second. These six leading companies operated 92.7 per cent. of the total mileage in 1890, and 87.5 per cent. in 1907. The decrease in the percentage is accounted for by the increase in the number, and consequently in the mileage, of smaller companies and departments of railroads, and by the inclusion at the present census of mileage operated in Alaska and Porto Rico, territories which have been opened to the express business since 1890.

Of the 34 companies operating in 1907, 19 operated in only 1 State; of the remaining 15, only 9 operated in more than five States and only the six leading companies in more than ten.

EMPLOYEES, SALARIES AND WAGES.

Among the companies reporting in 1907, seven departments of railways (operating 480.57 miles) could not segregate the data for employees and wages from the general accounts of the railroad. The 27 remaining companies reported the following officers and employees, with their compensation: 138 general officers, with salaries of $939,820; 528 other officers, $1,000,097; 3,796 general-office clerks, $2,762,508; 29,388 local agents, $9,395,848; 12,530 local-office clerks, $8,326,446; 14,521 drivers and delivery men, $7,872,271; 9,416 other local employees, $4,652,018; and 8,967 messengers, helpers and guards, $4,542,024. The total number of employees in 1907 was 79,284, or 73.4 per cent. greater than in 1890, and the total wages or salaries paid, $39,491,032, or 144.1 per cent. greater.

EXPRESS MONEY ORDERS.

The issuing of financial paper was a comparatively new extension of the express business in 1890. At that time there were six companies issuing money orders, as compared with thirteen in 1907. The number of money orders issued has increased from 4,598,567 to 14,014,960, a gain of 204.8 per cent.

In addition to the money orders issued in 1907, which had a total value of $147,346,656, express companies issued 792,737 travellers' checks and letters of credit, of a value of $20,828,932. The total value of financial paper issued by express companies, $168,175,588, is 29.8 per cent. of the value of domestic and international money orders issued by the United States Post-Office Department. The value of all kinds of financial paper reported by the American Express Company was $81,018,641, or nearly half of the total for all companies.

ORGANIZATION, RECEIPTS AND EXPENDITURES.

Of the 34 express companies represented at the census of 1907, 16 are corporations, 12 are departments of railways, 4 are unincorporated associations, 1 is owned by a partnership and 1 by an individual.

The total receipts of all the express companies amount to $128,117,176, of which 97 per cent. is receipts from operation and 3 per cent. receipts from other sources. Over 90 per cent. of the total receipts represents the receipts of the six leading companies. The proportion of the total business transacted by these companies remains about the same, although the total number of companies in the express business and the total volume of business have about doubled.

The two important items of expense in the express business are the amounts paid to steam roads and the salaries and wages, which in 1907 were $56,378,349 and $39,531,754, respectively, and together constituted, as in 1890, over 80 per cent. of the reported operating expenses.

National Republican League of the United States.

THE National Republican League of the United States was organized in Chickering Hall, New York City, December 15-17, 1887, by delegates from about 350 Republican clubs of the United States, assembled in national convention, pursuant to a call issued by the Republican Club of New York City. It is composed of the Republican clubs of the United States, organized by States and united in a national organization. Its purpose is "Organization and Education." It aims to enlist recruits for the Republican party, particularly the younger men and the "first voters." National conventions have since been held at Baltimore, 1889; Nashville, 1890; Cincinnati, 1891; Buffalo, 1892; Louisville, 1893; Denver, 1894; Cleveland, 1895; Milwaukee, 1896; Detroit, 1897; Omaha, 1898 (biennial sessions afterward); St. Paul, 1900; Chicago, 1902; Indianapolis, 1904; Philadelphia, 1906, Cincinnati, 1908. At the close of the campaign of 1908, the League, including the Taft campaign clubs, comprised approximately 4,000 clubs, with a membership of 1,500,000. *Officers*—President, **John Hays Hammond, Gloucester, Mass.; Secretary, Snell Smith, Hotel Astor, New York City.**

Foreign Trade of the United States.

(Compiled from the Report of the Bureau of Statistics of the Department of Commerce and Labor.)

EXPORTS.

Merchandise and Specie Exported from the United States During the Fiscal Year Ended June 30, 1908.

Articles.	Quantities.	Values.
Domestic Merchandise.		
Agricultural Implements	....	$24,344,398
Aluminum and Manufactures of	....	290,016
Animals	....	34,101,289
Books, Maps, Engravings, and other Printed Matter	....	6,107,058
Brass, and Manufactures of	....	3,701,871
Breadstuffs: Corn ... bush.	52,445,800	33,942,197
" Oats ... bush.	1,158,622	624,569
" Wheat ... bush.	100,371,057	99,736,767
" Wheat Flour ... bbls.	13,927,247	64,170,508
Cars, Carriages, and other Vehicles and Parts of	....	22,072,902
Chemicals, Drugs, Dyes, and Medicines	....	20,873,155
Clocks and Watches and Parts of	....	2,848,725
Coal: Anthracite ... tons	2,837,778	13,839,397
" Bituminous ... tons	9,944,957	25,518,362
Copper Ore ... tons	81,465	1,808,131
" Manufactures of	....	104,064,530
Cotton, Unmanufactured ... lbs.	3,816,998,693	437,788,202
" Manufactures of	....	25,177,758
Earthen, Stone, and China Ware	....	1,145,670
Fertilizers	....	10,970,931
Fibres, Vegetable, and Textile Grasses, Manufactures of	....	7,225,798
Fish	....	5,685,916
Fruits, Apples, Green or Ripe ... bbls.	1,049,545	3,660,854
Fruits and Nuts, all other	....	10,678,000
Furs and Fur Skins	....	7,712,890
Glass and Glassware	....	2,505,417
Glucose or Grape Sugar	....	2,540,640
Gunpowder and other Explosives	....	3,705,517
Hay ... tons	77,281	1,463,010
Hops ... lbs.	22,920,480	2,963,167
India Rubber Manufactures	....	7,573,570
Instruments for Scientific Purposes	....	11,578,010
Iron and Steel, Manufactures of	....	183,982,182
Leather, and Manufactures of	....	40,688,619
Malt Liquors	....	1,020,172
Marble, Stone, and Manufactures of	....	1,248,996

Articles.	Quantities.	Values.
Domestic Merchandise.		
Musical Instruments	....	$3,371,521
Naval Stores	....	21,6[illegible]1,599
Nickel, Nickel Oxide and Matte	....	2,948,058
Oil Cake, Oil Cake Meal ... lbs.	1,691,550,533	21,866,761
Oils: Animal ... galls.	1,205,298	612,336
" Mineral, Crude ... galls.	135,223,575	6,465,114
" Mineral, Refined or Manuf'd.	....	97,651,326
" Vegetable	....	19,633,967
Paints, Pigments, and Colors	....	4,001,824
Paper, and Manufactures of	....	8,064,706
Paraffine, Paraffine Wax ... lbs.	178,709,676	8,740,929
Provisions: Beef Products ... lbs.	363,824,146	31,526,421
" Hog Products ... lbs.	1,291,062,480	124,806,125
" Oleomargarine	215,479,332	19,578,222
" Other Meat Products	....	9,852,847
" Dairy Products	....	4,955,201
Seeds: Clover ... lbs.	3,547,747	579,100
" All other	....	8,104,588
Soap	....	3,407,220
Spirits, Distilled ... proof galls.	1,507,237	1,816,287
Starch ... lbs.	48,125,851	1,142,054
Molasses, and Syrup ... galls.	16,501,514	2,387,427
Sugar ... lbs.	25,511,003	974,184
Tobacco, Unmanufactured ... lbs.	330,812,658	34,727,157
" Manufactures of	....	4,736,522
Vegetables	....	3,895,294
Wood, and Manufactures of	....	83,349,575
Wool, and Manufactures of	....	2,219,815
All other Articles	....	73,550,945
Total Exports, Domestic Mdse	....	$1,834,786,357
Exports, Foreign Merchandise	....	25,986,989
Total Exports, Domestic & Foreign	....	$1,860,773,246
Specie: Gold	....	$72,432,924
" Silver	....	57,921,202
Total Exports, Domestic & F'r'gn	....	$1,991,127.472

IMPORTS.

Merchandise and Specie Imported into the United States During the Fiscal Year Ended June 30, 1908.

Articles.	Quantities.	Values.
Merchandise.		
Animals	....	$4,777,459
Art Works	....	4,310,767
Books, Maps, Engravings, etc.	....	6,036,693
Bristles	....	2,097,777
Cement, Portland, Hydraulic ... lbs.	573,437,777	1,973,472
Chemicals, Drugs, Dyes, and Medicines	....	73,237,033
Clocks and Watches, and Parts of	....	2,922,142
Coal, Bituminous ... tons	1,981,467	5,123,862
Cocoa, Crude, and Shells of ... lbs.	82,831,242	14,257,250
Coffee ... lbs.	890,640,057	67,688,106
Copper and Manufactures of (not ore)	....	24,361,902
Cork Wood, and Manufactures of	....	4,249,006
Cotton, Unmanufactured ... lbs.	71,072,855	14,172,241
" Manufactures of	....	68,379,781
Earthen, Stone, and China Ware	....	13,427,969
Feathers, Flowers, etc.	....	10,755,954
Fertilizers	....	4,965,316
Fibres, Vegetable, Unmanufactured	....	35,493,313
" Vegetable, Manufactures of	....	54,467,572
Fruits and Nuts	....	37,354,742
Furs, and Manufactures of	....	15,918,149
Glass and Glassware	....	6,570,123
Hair Unmanufactured	....	2,770,658
Hats, Bonnets, and Materials for	....	4,852,548
Hides and Skins, other than Fur ... lbs.	282,764,925	54,770,130
India Rubber and Gutta-Percha, Crude ... lbs.	85,225,073	37,753,266
Iron and Steel, and Manufactures of	....	27,607,909
Jewelry and Precious Stones	....	17,388,327
Lead, Ore and Base Bullion ... lbs.	187,667,734	4,167,142

Articles.	Quantities.	Values.
Merchandise.		
Leather, and Manufactures of	....	$14,127,238
Malt Liquors ... galls.	7,519,106	3,464,671
Meats and Dairy Products	....	8,768,816
Oils	....	18,292,393
Paper, and Manufactures of	....	12,223,058
" Stock, Crude	....	8,675,926
Rice ... lbs.	212,803,392	4,798,553
Silk, Unmanufactured	....	64,546,903
" Manufactures of	....	32,717,668
Spices	....	3,591,537
Spirits, Distilled	....	6,560,606
Sugar ... lbs.	3,371,997,112	80,258,147
Tea ... lbs.	94,149,564	16,309,670
Tin, in Bars, Blocks, or Pigs ... lbs.	77,739,059	25,295,061
Tobacco, Unmanufactured ... lbs.	32,056,049	22,870,328
" Manufactures of	....	4,397,585
Toys	....	7,206,423
Vegetables	....	8,289,068
Wines	....	10,746,527
Wood, and Manufactures of	....	43,527,174
Wool, Unmanufactured ... lbs.	125,980,524	23,664,938
" Manufactures of	....	19,387,978
All other Articles	....	135,537,711
Total Merchandise	....	1,194,341,792
Specie: Gold	....	148,337,321
" Silver	....	44,658,097
Total Imports	....	1,387,337,210

FOREIGN TRADE OF THE UNITED STATES—*Continued.*

VALUE OF IMPORTS AND EXPORTS OF MERCHANDISE, 1882-1908.

Year Ending June 30.	Exports.		Total Exports.	Imports.	Total Exports and Imports.	Excess of Exports.	Excess of Imports.
	Domestic.	Foreign.					
1882	$733,239,732	$17,302,525	$750,542,257	$724,639,574	$1,475,181,831	$25,902,683	....
1883	804,223,632	19,615,770	823,839,402	723,180,914	1,547,020,316	100,658,488	....
1884	724,964,852	15,548,757	740,513,609	667,697,693	1,408,211,302	72,815,916	....
1885	726,682,946	15,506,809	742,189,755	577,527,329	1,319,717,084	164,662,426	....
1886	665,964,529	13,560,301	679,524,830	635,436,136	1,314,960,966	44,088,694	....
1887	703,022,923	13,160,288	716,183,211	692,319,768	1,408,502,979	23,863,443	$28,002,607
1888	683,862,104	12,092,403	695,954,507	723,957,114	1,419,911,621	....	2,730,277
1889	730,282,609	12,118,766	742,401,375	745,131,652	1,487,533,027	....	....
1890	845,293,828	12,534,856	857,828,684	789,310,409	1,647,139,093	68,518,275	....
1891	872,270,283	12,210,527	884,480,810	844,916,196	1,729,397,006	39,564,614	....
1892	1,015,732,011	14,546,137	1,030,278,148	827,402,462	1,857,680,610	202,875,686	18,735,728
1893	831,030,785	16,634,409	847,665,194	866,400,922	1,714,066,116	....	....
1894	869,204,937	22,935,635	892,140,572	654,994,622	1,547,135,194	237,145,950	....
1895	793,392,599	14,145,566	807,538,165	731,969,965	1,539,508,130	75,568,200	....
1896	863,200,487	19,406,451	882,606,938	779,724,674	1,662,331,612	102,882,264	....
1897	1,032,007,603	18,985,953	1,050,993,556	764,730,412	1,815,723,968	286,263,144	....
1898	1,210,291,913	21,190,417	1,231,482,330	616,049,654	1,847,532,984	615,432,676	....
1899	1,203,931,222	23,092,080	1,227,023,302	697,148,489	1,924,171,791	529,874,813	....
1900	1,370,763,571	23,719,511	1,394,483,082	849,941,184	2,244,424,266	544,541,898	....
1901	1,460,462,806	27,302,185	1,487,764,991	823,172,165	2,310,937,156	664,592,826	....
1902	1,355,481,861	26,237,540	1,381,719,401	903,320,948	2,285,040,349	478,398,453	....
1903	1,392,231,302	27,910,377	1,420,141,679	1,025,719,237	2,445,860,916	394,422,442	....
1904	1,435,179,017	25,648,254	1,460,827,271	991,087,371	2,451,914,642	469,739,900	....
1905	1,491,744,641	26,817,025	1,518,561,666	1,117,513,071	2,636,074,737	401,048,595	....
1906	1,717,953,382	25,911,118	1,743,864,500	1,226,563,843	2,970,428,343	517,300,657	....
1907	1,853,718,034	27,133,044	1,880,851,078	1,434,421,425	3,315,272,503	446,429,653	....
1908	1,834,786,357	25,986,989	1,860,773,346	1,194,341,792	3,055,115,038	666,431,554	....

The imports and exports of specie are not included in the above table.

VALUE OF IMPORTS INTO AND EXPORTS FROM THE UNITED STATES OF MERCHANDISE BY COUNTRIES, YEAR ENDED JUNE 30, 1908.

Countries.	Imports.	Exports.	Countries.	Imports.	Exports.
Austria-Hungary	$15,425,659	$16,174,738	Colombia	$6,380,755	$3,452,375
Azores and Madeira Islands	34,531	211,921	Ecuador	2,401,188	1,909,126
Belgium	19,895,677	52,948,582	Guianas:		
Denmark	1,272,938	21,543,628	British	230,828	1,988,385
France	101,999,541	116,123,468	Dutch	780,369	645,417
Germany	142,935,547	276,910,223	French	33,136	834,174
Gibraltar	11,048	371,365	Paraguay	14,645	100,568
Greece	3,019,666	1,290,804	Peru	6,670,616	6,959,579
Greenland, Iceland, etc.	56,774	22,908	Uruguay	1,264,796	3,866,661
Italy	44,844,174	54,217,394	Venezuela	6,725,184	2,555,863
Malta, Gozo, etc	4,584	548,859	Aden	1,615,261	1,097,277
Netherlands	20,305,864	102,218,050	Chinese Empire	26,020,922	22,843,671
Norway	3,668,909	6,841,626	British China	28,169	7,641
Portugal	4,967,922	3,086,072	French China	14,400	....
Roumania	11,135	447,759	German China	536,329	470,731
Russia in Europe	11,113,421	16,342,377	Japanese China	....	8,198,896
Servia	52,353	3,806	British East Indies	61,489,287	11,886,858
Spain	14,152,712	21,906,379	Dutch East Indies	14,095,364	2,181,952
Sweden	4,633,672	9,671,810	French East Indies	....	602,169
Switzerland	24,698,036	646,840	Hong Kong	2,129,256	8,975,161
Turkey in Europe	4,554,509	1,418,024	Japan	68,107,545	41,432,327
Great Britain and Ireland	190,355,475	580,663,522	Korea	3,045	1,563,113
Bermuda	455,546	957,066	Persia	529,492	3,885
British Honduras	737,389	1,299,145	Russia, Asiatic	341,627	2,072,915
British North America:	75,131,666	167,035,947	Siam	51,858	392,663
Newfoundland and Labrador	1,169,050	3,587,748	Turkey in Asia	6,205,061	555,376
Central American States:			All other Asia	....	211
Costa Rica	4,405,165	2,696,744	British Australasia	11,186,668	28,280,661
Guatemala	2,390,167	1,750,700	New Zealand, etc	3,040,168	6,502,362
Honduras	2,268,070	1,768,395	French Oceanica	543,193	346,504
Nicaragua	1,160,832	1,574,879	German Oceanica	54,406	56,212
Panama	1,469,344	18,232,666	Philippine Islands	10,164,223	11,481,732
Salvador	981,715	1,357,297	British West Africa	91,271	2,055,046
Mexico	46,945,690	55,509,604	British South Africa	1,760,350	7,847,045
Miquelon, Langley, etc	137	45,687	British East Africa	655,534	354,637
West Indies:			Canary Islands	83,521	685,591
British	12,129,350	12,475,324	French Africa	498,045	1,545,145
Cuba	83,284,692	47,161,306	German Africa	....	120,064
Danish	592,292	727,193	Liberia	1,035	58,432
Dutch	361,966	706,210	Madagascar	1,907	15,979
French	60,111	1,455,701	Morocco	262,396	8,468
Hayti	689,045	3,649,172	Portuguese Africa	67,935	5,463,949
San Domingo	4,583,661	2,703,276	Spanish Africa	....	9,139
Argentine Republic	11,024,098	31,858,155	Turkey in Africa—Egypt	12,863,051	2,126,383
Bolivia	384	1,226,238	Tripoli	1,614	3,010
Brazil	74,577,844	19,490,122			
Chile	14,777,811	9,194,650	Total	$1,194,341,792	$1,860,773,346

FOREIGN TRADE OF THE UNITED STATES—*Continued.*

IMPORTS AND EXPORTS AT PRINCIPAL PORTS OF THE UNITED STATES.

Customs Districts.	Year Ending June 30. Imports.		Exports.		Customs Districts.	Year Ending June 30. Imports.		Exports.	
	1907.	1908.	1907.	1908.		1907.	1908.	1907.	1908.
Baltimore....	$37,774,305	$29,477,101	$104,808,952	$80,988,505	New York...	$853,696,952	$658,215,938	$627,949,857	$701,062,913
Boston and Charlestown	124,432,977	93,678,716	100,872,147	96,051,668	Norfolk and Portsm'th.	945,678	1,096,563	8,359,445	12,534,632
Brunswick...	39,393	65,961	11,225,477	12,397,838	Pensacola...	606,908	687,484	19,218,433	20,333,978
Charleston...	3,528,553	3,375,997	1,082,466	2,510,965	Philadelphia	79,869,942	63,432,007	94,832,48[illegible]	109,261,436
Detroit	6,252,034	7,982,642	40,485,134	37,158,424	Portl'd, Me..	1,101,308	1,100,157	14,86[illegible]	11,093,000
Galveston....	7,029,186	5,693,609	237,308,494	161,352,201	Puget Sound	25,353,373	22,208,814	43,659,[illegible]	44,082,767
Mobile.......	3,950,360	4,538,698	24,468,719	27,983,997	San Fran....	54,094,570	48,251,476	33,026,66[illegible]	28,000,000
New Orleans.	46,046,772	42,785,646	170,562,428	159,455,773	Savannah...	2,203,867	2,203,867	63,039,824	61,695,330
N'wp'rt News	2,945,919	1,627,045	14,932,671	8,365,885	Wilm'n, NC.	812,876	879,060	18,566,468	30,291,681

GROWTH OF UNITED STATES EXPORTS.

Fiscal Year Ending June 30.	Europe.	North America.	South America.	Asia and Oceanica.	Africa and Other Countries.	Total.
1898	$973,806,245	$139,627,841	$33,821,701	$66,710,813	$17,515,730	$1,231,482,330
1899	936,602,093	157,931,707	35,659,902	78,235,176	18,594,424	1,227,023,302
1900	1,040,167,763	187,594,625	38,945,763	108,305,082	19,469,849	1,394,483,082
1901	1,136,504,605	196,534,460	44,400,195	84,783,113	25,542,618	1,487,764,991
1902	1,008,033,981	203,971,080	38,043,617	98,202,118	33,468,605	1,381,719,401
1903	1,029,256,657	215,482,769	41,137,872	95,827,528	38,436,853	1,420,141,679
1904	1,057,930,131	234,909,959	50,755,027	93,002,028	24,230,126	1,460,827,271
1905	1,020,972,641	260,570,235	56,894,131	161,584,056	18,540,603	1,518,561,666
1906	1,200,166,036	308,382,982	75,159,781	140,593,361	19,562,340	1,743,864,500
1907	1,298,452,380	249,840,641	82,157,174	133,889,857	16,511,026	1,880,851,078
1908	1,283,600,155	324,674,660	83,583,919	148,574,047	20,340,565	1,860,773,346

DOMESTIC EXPORTS OF THE UNITED STATES BY GREAT CLASSES.

Fiscal Year Ending June 30.	Agriculture.		Mining.		Manufactures.		Total Exports of Domestic Merchandise.
	Values.	Per Cent.	Values.	Per Cent.	Values.	Per Cent.	Values.
1860	$256,560,972	81.13	$999,465	.31	$40,345,892	12.76	$316,242,423
1870	361,188,483	79.35	5,026,111	1.10	68,279,764	15.00	455,208,341
1880	685,961,091	83.25	5,863,232	.71	102,856,015	12.48	823,946,353
1885	530,172,966	72.96	15,797,885	2.18	147,187,527	20.25	726,682,946
1889	532,141,490	72.87	19,947,513	2.73	138,675,507	18.99	730,282,609
1890	629,820,808	74.51	22,297,755	2.64	151,102,376	17.87	845,293,828
1891	642,751,344	73.69	22,054,970	2.53	168,927,315	19.37	872,270,283
1892	798,328,232	78.60	20,692,885	2.04	159,510,937	15.70	1,015,732,011
1893	615,382,986	74.05	20,020,026	2.41	158,023,118	19.02	831,030,785
1894	628,363,038	72.28	20,449,598	2.35	183,728,808	21.14	869,204,937
1895	553,210,026	69.73	18,509,814	2.33	183,595,743	23.14	793,392,599
1896	569,879,297	66.02	20,045,654	2.32	228,571,178	26.48	863,200,487
1897	683,471,139	66.23	20,804,573	2.01	277,285,391	26.87	1,032,007,603
1898	853,683,570	70.54	19,410,707	1.60	290,697,354	24.02	1,210,291,913
1899	784,776,142	65.19	28,156,174	2.34	339,592,146	28.21	1,203,931,222
1900	835,858,123	60.98	37,843,742	2.76	433,851,756	31.65	1,370,763,571
1901	943,811,020	64.62	39,207,875	2.68	410,932,524	28.14	1,460,462,806
1902	851,465,622	62.83	39,216,112	2.90	403,641,401	29.77	1,355,481,861
1903	873,322,882	62.73	39,311,239	2.81	407,526,159	29.28	1,392,231,302
1904	853,643,073	59.48	45,981,213	3.20	452,415,921	31.52	1,435,179,017
1905	820,863,405	55.03	50,968,052	3.42	543,607,975	36.44	1,491,744,641
1906	969,457,306	56.43	53,055,261	3.09	603,227,836	35.11	1,717,953,382

COMMERCE WITH CUBA, PORTO RICO, HAWAII, AND THE PHILIPPINES.

Fiscal Year Ending June 30.	Exports from the United States to— Cuba.	Porto Rico.	Hawaii.	Philippines.	Imports into the United States from— Cuba.	Porto Rico.	Hawaii.	Philippines.
1893	$24,157,698	$2,510,607	$2,827,663	$154,378	$78,706,506	$4,008,623	$9,146,767	$9,159,857
1894	20,125,321	2,720,508	3,306,187	145,466	75,678,261	3,135,634	10,066,317	7,008,342
1895	12,807,661	1,833,544	3,723,057	119,255	52,871,259	1,506,512	7,888,961	4,731,366
1896	7,530,880	2,102,094	3,985,707	162,466	40,017,730	2,296,653	11,757,704	4,982,857
1897	8,259,776	1,988,888	4,690,075	94,597	18,406,815	2,181,024	13,687,799	4,383,740
1898	9,561,656	1,505,946	5,907,155	127,804	15,232,477	2,414,356	17,187,380	3,830,415
1899	18,619,377	2,685,848	9,305,470	404,193	25,408,828	3,179,827	17,831,463	4,409,774
1900	26,513,400	4,640,449	13,509,148	2,640,449	31,371,704	3,078,648	20,707,903	5,971,208
1901	25,964,801	6,861,917	No data.	4,027,064	43,423,088	5,883,892	27,903,058	4,420,912
1902	26,623,500	10,882,653	No data.	5,258,470	34,694,684	8,378,766	24,730,060	6,612,700
1903	21,761,638	12,245,845	10,943,061	4,038,909	62,942,790	11,051,195	26,242,869	11,372,584
1904	27,377,465	11,210,060	11,683,393	4,832,900	76,983,418	11,722,826	25,157,255	12,066,934
1905	38,380,601	13,974,070	11,753,180	6,200,620	86,304,259	15,633,145	36,112,055	12,657,904
1906	47,763,688	19,224,881	12,036,675	5,459,414	84,979,831	19,142,461	26,882,199	12,337,927
1907	49,305,274	25,686,285	14,435,725	8,661,424	97,441,690	22,070,133	29,071,813	11,510,438
1908	47,161,306	22,677,376	15,038,155	11,461,732	83,284,692	25,891,261	41,640,505	10,164,223

Countries Excelling in Production

OF THE PRINCIPAL STAPLES, AND THE RESPECTIVE QUANTITIES PRODUCED THEREIN.

(Compiled in the Bureau of Statistics of the Department of Commerce and Labor from latest available official data.)

Commodity.	Year.	Unit.	Countries of Maximum Production.		Countries Holding Second Place.	
			Country.	Quantity.	Country.	Quantity.
Corn	1907	Bushels	United States	2,592,320,000	Austria-Hungary	196,622,000
Wheat	1907	"	" "	634,087,000	Russia	511,000,000
Rye	1907	"	Russia	828,000,000	Germany	384,150,000
Oats	1907	"	"	905,797,000	United States	754,443,000
Rice	1906	1,000 lbs	British India	68 104,000	China	*a*
Sugar	1907-8	Tons 2,240 lbs	Germany	2,102,200	British India	2,051,900
Tea	1907	Pounds	China	*b* 214,683,000	" "	248,020,000
Coffee	1907-8	Bags, 132 lbs.	Brazil	11,349,271	Venezuela	*b* 750,000
Cocoa	1907	Pounds	"	54,074,000	St. Thome	53,336,000
Tobacco	1906	"	United States	682,429,000	British India	*c* 450,000,000
Cotton	1907	Bales, 500 lbs.	" "	10,882,385	" "	2,444,800
Wool	1907	Pounds	Australia	*b* 657,393,105	Argentina	*b* 341,294,000
Silk	1906	"	China	*d*	Japan	24,120,000
Coal	1907	Tons 2,240 lbs	United States	428,895,914	United Kingdom	267,830,962
Petroleum	1907	Bls. 42 gal	" "	166,095,335	Russia	61,850,734
Pig iron	1907	Tous 2,240 lbs	" "	25,781,361	Germany	12,671,700
Steel	1907	Tons 2,240 lbs	" "	23,362,594	"	11,873,000
Copper	1907	Pounds	" "	868,996,500	Mexico	126,764,500
Tin	1907	"	Federated Malay States.	108,484,800	Bolivia	*e* 34,720,000
Gold	1907	Ounces fine Dollars	Transvaal	6,451,384 133,361,943	United States	4,374,827 90,435,700
Silver	1907	Ounces fine Dollars	Mexico	61,141,203 40,357,200	" "	56,514,700 37,299,700

a Actual production unknown; roughly estimated at 50-60,000 million pounds. *b* Figures of domestic exports; no data for production. *c* Unofficial estimate. *d* Production unknown; exports of raw silk from China during calendar year 1907, 15,495,000 lbs. *e* Arrivals in Europe of Bolivian tin.

The Twelve Greatest Seaports.

THE following table, prepared by the Bureau of Statistics, Department of Commerce and Labor, shows the relative rank in tonnage movement of the principal ports of the world. Figures of coastwise trade are not included:

Port.	Year.	Entered. Tons.	Cleared. Tons.	Port.	Year.	Entered. Tons.	Cleared. Tons.
New York	*1906	10,476,993	9,913,960	Shanghai	1905	7,195,006	7,149,156
Antwerp	1905	9,861,528	9,800,149	Rotterdam	1904	7,181,374	6,764,960
† Hong Kong-Victoria	1904	9,680,642	9,652,454	‡ Singapore	1904	6,175,905	6,155,848
Hamburg	1905	9,417,449	9,525,418	Cardiff	1905	4,337,720	7,476,879
London	1905	10,814,115	7,913,115	Colombo	1905	5,179,045	5,139,749
Liverpool	1905	7,806,844	6,932,687	Marseilles	1904	5,061,912	4,645,467

* Fiscal year. † Exclusive of Chinese junks engaged in the foreign trade. The tonnage of these vessels entered in 1904 was 1,524,874. ‡ Exclusive of warships, transports, native craft, and vessels under fifty tons, but inclusive of vessels engaged in trade between the Straits Settlements.

Imports and Exports of Principal Countries.

(Compiled by the Bureau of Statistics, Department of Commerce and Labor, from the official records of the various countries).

(Years ending December 31, unless stated otherwise; imports for consumption and exports of domestic merchandise, unless stated otherwise; gold and silver bullion and coin not included, unless stated otherwise).

Countries.	Yrs.	Imports.	Exports.	Countries.	Yrs.	Imports.	Exports.
Argentina *a*	1907	$275,855,555	$285,837,216	India, British *a e*	1907	$442,822,376	$562,525,863
Australian Commonwealth	1907	243,603,310	288,276,826	Italy	1907	532,774,686	357,337,405
Austria-Hungary	1907	475,808,863	473,160,653	Japan *d*	1907	245,584,575	213,394,963
Belgium	1907	661,718,835	515,700,825	Mexico *f*	1908	110,324,925	120,883,976
British S. Africa *c*	1907	133,746,224	231,900,283	Netherlands	1907	1,068,823,000	883,926,000
Bulgaria	1907	24,055,344	24,239,777	Norway *d*	1907	103,369,690	58,952,442
Canada *b*	1908	351,879,955	246,960,968	Portugal	1906	65,545,000	31,396,000
Chile *a*	1907	107,193,877	102,521,466	Russia *a*	1906	412,355,271	563 866,338
China	1907	328,957,082	208,860,751	Spain *a*	1906	172,490,612	152,593,410
Denmark	1906	149,899,904	105,461,216	Sweden *a*	1906	171,076,242	135,146,654
Egypt *d*	1907	128,445,224	138,468,981	Switzerland	1907	311,659,190	222,509,951
France	1907	1,167,196,064	1,069,611,790	United Kingdom *d*	1907	3,143,292,673	2,074,124,666
Germany	1907	2,046,187,150	1,634,803,436	United States *g*	1908	1,183,120,665	1,834,786,357
Greece *h*	1907	28,639,886	22,397,531	Uruguay *a h*	1907	35,595,662	36,346,069
				Venezuela *a h*	1907	10,335,817	16,203,972

a General trade. *b* Fiscal year ending March 31. *c* Includes gold and silver bullion and parcels post. Imports include articles for colonial governments. *d* General imports. *e* Fiscal year beginning April 1. Government stores are included in imports but not in exports. *f* Fiscal year ending June 30. Gold and silver bullion and coin are included. *g* Fiscal year ending June 30. *h* Includes gold and silver.

Statistics of Manufactures in the United States.

(CENSUS OF 1905.)

THE census of manufactures of 1905, which covered the calendar year 1904 and included continental United States and Alaska, was the first in which the canvass was confined to establishments conducted under what is known as the factory system, thus excluding the neighborhood industries and hand trades. The statistics for these mechanical trades have been a confusing element in the census of manufactures, and their omission confines the data to a presentation of the true manufacturing industries of the country. To secure comparable figures for 1900, which included neighboring industries, hand trades, and educational, eleemosynary, and penal institutions, it was therefore necessary to revise the published reports of the Twelfth Census. In comparing the results of the present census with those of former censuses, the different methods should be considered.

The revision of the published statistics for 1900, necessary for purposes of comparison, involved considerable difficulty. Certain industries, such as custom millinery, custom tailoring, dressmaking, taxidermy, cobbling, carpentering, and custom grist and saw mills were wholly omitted. But the only available information on which to base the elimination of nonfactory establishments for industries, which included factories as well as local establishments, was that contained in the original reports from these establishments, and those reports were not collected with such segregation in view. It was found that some establishments, which in 1900 did little real manufacturing, had in the five years developed into true factories. On the other hand, in certain establishments the strictly manufacturing operations conducted in 1900 had later been discontinued, although the establishments were still in business doing custom or repair work only. The latter class, however, was composed mainly of small establishments, and, except as to the number reported, their inclusion or omission has little effect on the statistics.

Reports were not secured from small establishments in which manufacturing was incidental to mercantile or other business; or from establishments in which the value of the products for the year amounted to less than $500; or from educational, eleemosynary and penal institutions; or from governmental establishments. The census of 1905, however, was not confined to an enumeration of large factories.

The statistics for the manufacturing industries of the country under the revised conditions, for the censuses of 1900 and 1905 are summarized in the following table:

	1905.	1900.	Per ct. of increase.		1905.	1900.	Per ct. of increase.
Number of establishments	216,262	207,562	4.2	Women 16 years and over	1,065,884	918.511	16.0
Capital	$12,686,265,673	$8,978,825,200	41.3	Wages	$317,279,008	$248,814,074	27.5
Salaried officials, clerks, &c., number	519,751	364,202	42.7	Children under 16 years	159,899	161,276	20.9
Salaries	$574,761,231	$380,889,091	50.9	Wages	$27,988,207	$24,574,541	13.9
Wage-earners, average number	5,470,321	4,715,023	16.0	Miscellaneous expenses	$1,455,019,473	$905,600,225	60.7
Total wages	$2,611,540,532	$2,009,735,799	29.9	Cost of materials used	$8,503,949,756	$6,577,614,074	29.3
Men 16 years and over	4,244,538	3,635,236	16.8				
Wages	$2,266,273,317	$1,736,347,184	30.5	Value of products including custom work and repairing	$14,802,147,087	$11,411,121,122	29.7

MANUFACTURES BY STATES.

States and Territories.	Capital Employed.	Wage-Earners.	Wages Paid	Value of Products.	States and Territories.	Capital Employed.	Wage-Earners.	Wages Paid	Value of Products.
Alabama.	$105,382,859	62,173	$21,878,451	$109,169,922	Montana.	$52,589,810	8,957	$8,652,217	$66,415,452
Alaska...	10,684,799	1,938	1,095,579	8,244,524	Nebraska	80,235,310	20,260	11,022,149	154,918,220
Arizona.	14,395,654	4,793	3,969,248	28,083,192	Nevada..	2,891,997	802	693,407	3,096,274
Arkansas	46,306,116	33,089	14,543,635	53,864,394	N. Hamp	109,495,072	65,366	27,693,203	123,610,904
California	282,647,201	100,355	64,656,686	367,218,494	N. Jersey	715,060,174	266,336	128,168,801	774,369,025
Colorado.	107,663,500	21,813	15,100,365	100,143,999	N. Mex'o.	4,638,248	3,478	2,153,068	5,705,880
Conn'cut.	373,283,580	181,605	87,942,628	369,082,091	New Y'k.	2,031,459,515	856,947	430,014,851	2,488,345,579
Delaware	50,925,630	18 475	8,158,203	41,160,276	N. C'lina	141,000,639	85,339	21,375,294	142,520,776
Dis. Col..	20,199,783	6,299	3,658,370	18,359,159	N. Dak'ta	5,703,837	1,755	1,031,307	10,217,914
Florida...	32,971,982	42,091	15,767,182	50 298,290	Ohio.....	856,988,830	364,298	182,429,425	960,811.857
Georgia...	135,211,551	92,749	27,392,442	151,040,455	Okla'ma.	11,107,763	3,199	1,655,324	16,549 656
Idaho......	9,689,445	3,061	2,059,391	8,768,743	Oregon ..	44,023,548	18,523	11,443,512	55,525,123
Illinois...	975,844,799	379,436	208,405,468	1,410,342,129	P'vania..	1,995,836,988	763,282	367,960,890	1,955,551,332
Indiana..	312,071,234	154,174	72,058,099	393,954,405	Rhode Isl	215,901,375	97,318	43,112,637	202,109,583
Indian T.	5,016,654	2,257	1.144,078	7,909,451	S. C'lina.	113,422,224	59,441	13,868,950	79,376,262
Iowa.....	111,427,429	49,481	22,997,053	160,572,313	S. Dakota	7,585,142	2,492	1,421,680	13,085,333
Kansas...	88,680,117	35,570	18,883,071	198,244,992	Tenn'see	102,439,481	60,572	22,805,628	137,960,476
Kentuc'y	147,282,478	59,794	24,438,684	159,753,968	Texas....	115,664,871	49,066	24,468,942	150,528,389
Louisiana	150,810,608	55,859	25,315,750	186,379,592	Utah.....	26,004,011	8,052	5,157,400	38,926,464
Maine ...	143,707,750	74,958	32,691,759	144,020,197	Vermont	62,658,741	33,106	15,221,059	63,083,611
Maryland	201,877,966	94,174	36,144,244	243,375,996	Virginia.	147,989,182	80,285	27,943,058	148,856,525
Mass.....	965,948,887	488,399	232,388,946	1,124,092,051	Wash'n.	96,952,621	45,199	30,087,287	128,821,667
Michigan	337,894,102	175,229	81,278,837	429,120,060	West Va.	86,820,823	43,758	21,153,042	99,040,676
Min'sota.	184,903,271	69,636	35,843,145	307,858,073	W'consin	412,647,051	151,391	71,471,805	411,139,681
Missi'pi..	50,256,309	38,690	14,819,034	57,451,445	W'ming.	2,695,889	1,834	1,261,122	3,523,260
Missouri.	379,368,827	133,167	66,644,126	439.548,957					

For the United States the totals are: Capital, $12,686,265,673; number of wage-earners, 5,470,321; wages paid, $2,611,540,532; value of products, $14,802,147,087.

STATISTICS OF MANUFACTURES IN THE UNITED STATES—*Continued.*

TOTALS FOR GROUPS OF INDUSTRIES.

GROUP.	No. Establishments.	Capital Employed.	Salaried Officials, Clerks, etc.		Wage-Earners.		Total Cost of Materials.	Value of Products.
			Number.	Salaries.	Average Number.	Total Wages.		
United States	216,262	$12,686,265,673	519,751	$574,761,231	5,470,321	$2,611,540,532	$8,503,949,756	$14,802,147,087
Food & kindred products	45,790	1,173,151,276	53,224	51,456,814	354,054	164,601,803	2,304,416,564	2,845,234,900
Textiles.......	17,042	1,744,169,234	61,907	69,281,415	1,156,305	419,841,630	1,246,562,061	2,147,441,418
Iron and steel and their products....	14,239	2,331,498,157	82,112	100,444,686	857,298	482,357,503	1,179,981,458	2,176,739,726
Lumber and its remanufactures.....	32,726	1,013,827,138	45,555	48,571,861	735,945	336,058,173	518,908,150	1,223,730,336
Leather and its finished products....	4,945	440,777,194	17,233	18,372,722	255,368	116,694,140	471,112,921	705,747,470
Paper and printing....	30,787	798,758,312	80,009	81,808,311	350,205	185,547,791	308,269,655	857,112,256
Liquors and beverages..	6,381	659,547,620	12,647	21,421,353	68,340	45,146,285	139,854,147	501,266,605
Chemicals and allied products........	9,680	1,504,728,510	45,071	49,864,233	210,165	93,965,248	609,351,160	1,031,965,263
Clay, glass and stone products.........	10,775	553,846,682	18,768	21,555,724	285,365	148,471,903	123,124,392	391,230,422
Metals & metal products, other than iron & steel.	6,310	598,340,758	19,471	24,854,590	211,706	117,599,837	644,367,583	922,262,456
Tobacco......	16,828	323,983,501	9,236	8,800,434	159,408	62,640,303	126,088,608	331,117,681
Vehicles for land transportation....	7,285	447,697,020	24,632	24,334,118	384,577	221,860,517	334,244,377	643,924,442
Shipbuilding..	1,097	121,623,700	2,480	3,339,741	50,754	29,241,087	37,463,179	82,769,239
Miscellaneous industries...	12,377	974,316,571	47,406	50,655,229	390,831	187,514,312	460,205,501	941,604,873

VALUES OF PRINCIPAL ARTICLES OF DOMESTIC MANUFACTURES EXPORTED FROM THE UNITED STATES FROM 1880 TO 1907.

NOTE.—These nine groups form about 80 per cent. of the total value of manufactures exported.

YEAR ENDING JUNE 30.	Iron and Steel Manufactures.	Copper Manufactures.	Agricultural Implements.	Wood Manufactures.	Mineral Oils, Refined.	Chemicals, Drugs, Dyes, etc.	Leather, and Manufactures of.	Cotton Manufactures.	Paper, and Manufactures of.
1880..............	$14,716,524	$793,455	$2,245,742	$3,975,694	$34,291,418	$4,174,070	$6,760,186	$10,467,651	$1,201,143
1885..............	16,592,155	5,447,423	2,561,602	4,780,495	44,354,114	4,806,193	9,692,408	11,836,591	972,493
1890..............	25,542,208	2,349,392	3,859,184	6,509,645	44,658,854	5,424,279	12,428,847	9,999,277	1,226,686
1892..............	28,800,930	7,226,392	3,794,983	6,062,789	39,704,152	4,691,582	12,084,781	13,226,277	1,382,251
1893..............	30,106,482	4,525,573	4,657,333	6,058,896	37,574,667	5,766,425	11,912,154	11,809,355	1,540,886
1894..............	29,220,264	19,697,140	5,027,915	6,773,724	37,083,891	6,537,401	14,283,429	14,340,886	1,906,634
1895..............	32,000,989	14,468,703	5,413,075	6,249,807	41,498,372	7,130,324	15,614,407	13,789,810	2,185,257
1896..............	41,160,877	19,720,104	5,176,775	7,426,475	56,261,567	8,138,789	20,242,756	16,837,396	2,713,875
1897..............	57,497,872	31,621,125	5,240,686	8,592,416	56,463,185	8,792,545	19,161,446	21,037,678	3,333,163
1898..............	70,406,885	32,180,872	7,609,732	9,0[illegible]8,219	51,782,316	8,655,418	21,113,640	17,024,092	5,494,564
1899..............	93,716,031	35,983,529	12,432,197	9,765,285	51,070,276	10,042,916	23,466,985	23,566,914	5,477,884
1900..............	121,913,548	57,852,960	16,099,149	11,232,838	68,247,588	12,132,373	27,293,010	24,003,087	6,215,833
1901..............	117,319,320	43,267,021	16,313,434	11,099,643	64,425,859	13,660,346	27,923,653	20,272,418	7,438,901
1902..............	98,552,562	41,218,373	16,286,740	11,617,690	66,218,004	12,141,011	29,798,323	32,108,362	7,312,030
1903..............	96,642,467	39,667,196	21,006,622	13,071,251	60,923,634	12,581,471	31,617,389	32,216,304	7,180,014
1904..............	111,948,586	57,142,079	22,749,635	12,980,112	72,487,415	14,480,323	33,980,615	22,403,713	7,543,728
1905..............	134,727,921	86,225,291	20,721,741	12,560,935	73,433,787	15,859,422	37,936,745	49,666,080	8,236,088
1906..............	160,984,985	81,282,664	24,554,427	13,718,752	77,025,196	18,331,974	40,642,858	52,944,033	9,536,065
1907..............	181,530,871	94,762,110	26,936,456	13,533,500	78,228,819	20,373,036	45,476,969	32,305,412	9,856,733

For 1907 the value of paraffin and paraffin wax exported was $8,808,245. Manufactures constituted 35.11 per cent. of total exports from the United States in 1906.

PRODUCTION IN THE GREAT MANUFACTURING COUNTRIES.

(Compiled by the Chief of the Bureau of Statistics, Department of Commerce and Labor.)

COUNTRIES.	1888.	1900.	Increase.	
			Amount.	Per Cent.
United Kingdom.......................	$3,990,000,000	$5,000,000,000	$1,010,000,000	25
Germany...............................	2,837,000,000	4,600,000,000	1,763,000,000	62
France..................................	2,360,000,000	3,450,000,000	1,090,000,000	46
Total..................................	$9,187,000,000	$13,030,000,000	$3,863,000,000	42
United States..........................	$7,022,000,000	$13,004,000,000	$5,982,600,000	85

These figures are in all cases estimates, except those of the United States Census of 1900, which are for gross production. The figures for 1888 are Mulhall's.

Public Debt of the United States.

OFFICIAL STATEMENT OF NOVEMBER 1, 1908.

Interest-bearing Debt.

Consols of 1930, 2 per cent	$646,250,150.00
Loan of 1908-1918, 3 per cent	63,945,460.00
Loan of 1925, 4 per cent	118,489,900.00
Panama Canal loan	54,631,980.00
Certificates of Indebtedness	13,936,500.00
Aggregate of interest-bearing debt	$897,253,990.00

Debt on which Interest has Ceased since Maturity.

Aggregate debt on which interest has ceased since maturity	$3,738,235.26

Debt Bearing No Interest.

United States notes	$346,681,016.00
Old demand notes	53,282.50
National bank notes: Redemption account	39,069,430.00
Fractional currency	6,861,924.28
Aggregate of debt bearing no interest	$392,665,652.78

Certificates and Notes Issued on Deposits of Coin and Silver Bullion.

Gold certificates	$850,817,869.00
Silver certificates	488,793,000.00
Treasury notes of 1890	4,705,000.00
Aggregate of certificates and Treasury notes, offset by cash in the Treasury	$1,344,315,869.00

Classification of Debt November 1, 1908.

Interest-bearing debt		$897,253,990.00
Debt on which interest has ceased since maturity		3,738,235.26
Debt bearing no interest		392,665,652.78
Aggregate of interest and non-interest bearing debt		$1,293,657,878.04
Certificates and Treasury notes offset by an equal amount of cash in the Treasury		1,344.315,869.00
Aggregate of debt, including certificates and Treasury notes		$2,637,973,747.04

Cash in the Treasury.

Gold certificates	$850,817,869.00	
Silver certificates	488,793,000.00	
Treasury notes of 1890	4,705,000.00	
		1,344,315,869.00
National bank 5 per cent. fund	$23,400,117.40	
Outstanding checks and warrants	11,009,147.08	
Disbursing officers' balances	68,561,127.36	
Post-Office Department account	3,573,193,11	
Miscellaneous items	2,761,975.58	
		109,305,560.53
Reserve fund	$150,000,000.00	
Available cash balance	166,882,253.18	
		316,882,253.18
Total		$1,770,503,682.71
Cash balance in the Treasury November 1, 1908, exclusive of reserve and trust funds		$166,882,253.18

Principal of the Public Debt.

Statement of outstanding Principal of the Public Debt of the United States on January 1 of each year from 1792 to 1842, inclusive; on July 1 of each year from 1843 to 1886, inclusive; on December 1 of each year from 1887 to 1892, inclusive; on November 1, from 1893 to 1907, inclusive, except December 1, 1906.

Year		Amount	Year		Amount	Year		Amount
1792	Jan. 1	$77,217,924.66	1831	Jan. 1	$39,123,191.68	1870	July 1	$2,480,672,427.81
1793	"	80,352,634.04	1832	"	24,322,235.18	1871	"	2,353,211,332.32
1794	"	78,427,404.77	1833	"	7,001,698.83	1872	"	2,253,251,328.78
1795	"	80,747,587.39	1834	"	4,760,082.08	1873	"	2,234,482,993.20
1796	"	83,762,172.07	1835	"	37,513.05	1874	"	2,251,690,468.43
1797	"	82,064,479.33	1836	"	336,957.83	1875	"	2,232,284,531.95
1798	"	79,228,529.12	1837	"	3,308,124.07	1876	"	2,180,395,067.15
1799	"	78,408,669.77	1838	"	10,434,221.14	1877	"	2,205,301,392.10
1800	"	82,976,294.35	1839	"	3,573,343.82	1878	"	2,256,205,892.53
1801	"	83,038,050.80	1840	"	5,250,875.54	1879	"	2,340,567,232.04
1802	"	86,712,632.25	1841	"	13,594,480.73	1880	"	2,128,791,054.63
1803	"	77,054,686.30	1842	"	26,601,226.28	1881	"	2,077,389,253.58
1804	"	86,427,120.88	1843	July 1	32,742,922.00	1882	"	1,926,688,678.03
1805	"	82,312,150.50	1844	"	23,461,652.50	1883	"	1,892,547,412.07
1806	"	75,723,270.66	1845	"	15,925,303.01	1884	"	1,838,904,607.57
1807	"	69,218,398.64	1846	"	15,550,202.97	1885	"	1,872,340,557.14
1808	"	65,196,317.97	1847	"	38,826,534.77	1886	"	1,783,438,697.78
1809	"	57,023,192.09	1848	"	47,044,862.23	1887	Dec. 1	1,664,461,536.38
1810	"	53,173,217.52	1849	"	63,061,858.69	1888	"	1,680,917,706.23
1811	"	48,005,587.76	1850	"	63,452,773.55	1889	"	1,617,372,419.53
1812	"	45,209,737.90	1851	"	68,304,796.02	1890	"	1,549,206,126.48
1813	"	55,962,827.57	1852	"	66,199,341.71	1891	"	1,546,961,695.61
1814	"	81,487,846.24	1853	"	59,803,117.70	1892	"	1,563,612,455.63
1815	"	99,833,660.15	1854	"	42,242,222.42	1893	Nov. 1	1,549,556,353.63
1816	"	127,334,933.74	1855	"	35,586,858.56	1894	"	1,626,154,037.68
1817	"	123,491,965.16	1856	"	31,972,537.90	1895	"	1,717,481,779.90
1818	"	103,466,633.83	1857	"	28,699,831.85	1896	"	1,785,412,640.00
1819	"	95,529,648.28	1858	"	44,911,881.03	1897	"	1,808,777,643.40
1820	"	91,015,566.15	1859	"	58,496,837.88	1898	"	1,964,837,130.90
1821	"	89,987,427.66	1860	"	64,842,287.88	1899	"	2,092,686,024.42
1822	"	93,546,676.98	1861	"	90,580,873.72	1900	"	2,132,373,031.17
1823	"	90,875,877.28	1862	"	524,176,412.13	1901	"	2,151,585,743.89
1824	"	90,269,777.77	1863	"	1,119,772,138.63	1902	"	2,175,246,168.89
1825	"	83,788,432.71	1864	"	1,815,784,370.57	1903	"	2,218,883,772.89
1826	"	81,054,059.99	1865	"	2,680,647,869.74	1904	"	2,304,697,418.64
1827	"	73,987,357.20	1866	"	2,773,236,173.69	1905	"	2,293,846,382.34
1828	"	67,475,043.87	1867	"	2,678,126,103.87	1906	Dec. 1	2,429,370,043.54
1829	"	58,421,413.67	1868	"	2,611,687,851.19	1907	Nov. 1	2,492,231,518.54
1830	"	48,565,406.50	1869	"	2,588,452,213.94	1908	Nov. 1	2,637,973,747.04

Public Debt of the States, Cities, Counties,

AND MINOR CIVIL DIVISIONS IN THE UNITED STATES.

(Statement by the Bureau of The Census, 1906.)

State or Territory.	Indebtedness Less Sinking Fund Assets.							
	Total.					Per capita.		
	1902			1890.	1880.	1902.	1890.	1880.
	Aggregate Debts.	Debts of States.*	Debts of Cities Counties and Minor Civil Divisions.					
North Atlantic Div.	$946,604,780	$82,777,688	$863,827,092	$470,078,913	$540,840,297	$43.36	$27 02	$37.28
Maine	15,046 819	2,785,383	12,261,436	15,772,146	23,235,980	21.46	23.86	35.81
New Hampshire	11,413,234	1,551,148	9,862,086	8,148,362	10,792,583	27.27	21.64	31.10
Vermont	5,216 774	362,946	4,853,828	3,785,373	4,499,188	15.08	11.39	13.54
Massachusetts	209,762,910	65,964,005	143,798,905	84,094,876	91,909 651	72.72	37.56	51.55
Rhode Island	28,150,226	2,619,928	25,530,298	12,998,661	12,971,063	62.67	37.62	46.91
Connecticut	31,887,835	1,677,964	30,209,871	23,724,510	22,001,661	33.89	31.79	35.33
New York	436,683,365	7,498,239	429,185,126	201,255,570	218,845,804	57.55	33.55	43.06
New Jersey	81,147,209	156,550	81,203,759	49.257,740	49,382,675	40.82	34.09	43.66
Pennsylvania	127,296,408	374,625	126,921,783	71,041,675	107,201,692	19.55	13.51	25.03
South Atlantic Div.	159,834,215	52,270,418	107,563,797	166,685,368	167,919,910	14.85	18.82	22.10
Delaware	4,144,634	762,092	3,382,542	2,919,084	2,371,296	22.04	17.32	16.17
Maryland	30,643,317	4,942,394	25,700,923	41,898,651	41,429,179	25.18	40.20	44.31
Dist. of Columbia	14,540,191	....	14,540,191	19,781,050	22,498,323	50.42	85.86	126.66
Virginia	48,106,325	24,171,863	23,934,462	52,222,126	45,518,776	25.40	31.54	30.09
West Virginia	4,767,776	....	4,767,776	2,532,460	1,640.935	4.78	3.32	2.65
North Carolina	15,348,108	6,754,928	8,593,180	11,123,638	17,962,535	7.88	6.87	12.83
South Carolina	15,751,327	6,730,439	9,020,888	13,659,645	14,185,060	11.43	11.87	14.25
Georgia	21,285,731	7,876,202	13,409,529	20,272,095	19,648,265	9.29	11.03	12.74
Florida	5,246,806	1,032,500	4,214,306	2,276,619	2,665,541	9.36	5.81	9.89
North Central Div.	468,862,168	28,831,190	440,030,978	320,934,194	246,058,507	17.34	14.35	14.17
Ohio	117,230,101	4,685,016	112,545,085	70,927,147	53,044,175	27.55	19.32	16.59
Indiana	34,827,941	2,913,767	31,914,164	24,471.528	18,352,649	13.49	11.16	9.28
Illinois	80,715,039	2,155,122	78,559,937	42,468,138	46,388,888	16.08	11.10	15.07
Michigan	34,838,727	6,566,366	28,272,361	16,941,928	12,055,902	14.07	8.09	7.36
Wisconsin	22,347,683	2,278,068	20,069,615	10,420,731	12,085,984	10.48	6.18	9.19
Minnesota	40,683,737	1,755,033	38,928,704	26,237,825	11,328,433	22.07	20.15	14.51
Iowa	17,439,904	49,589	17,390,375	11,275,319	8,137,767	7.84	5.90	5.01
Missouri	50,396,922	4,365 635	46,031,287	51,557,568	60,263,761	15.79	19.24	27.79
North Dakota	5,608,158	968,330	4,639,828	3,854,514	131,726	15.31	21.10	3.57
South Dakota	6,584,351	457,263	6,127,088	6,613,702	867,134	15.56	20.11	8.82
Nebraska	22,415,041	2,005,001	20,410,040	15,536 772	7,489,974	21.01	14.67	16.56
Kansas	35,774,494	632,000	35,142,494	40,629,022	15,912,114	24.42	28.47	15.97
South Central Div.	173,776,068	55,073,705	118,702,363	135,153,789	143,982,958	11.86	12.32	16.14
Kentucky	22,748,773	2,198,482	20,550,291	19,432,885	14,982,449	10.32	10.46	9.09
Tennessee	32,717,130	17,984,468	14.732,662	29,543,843	40,750,137	15.79	16.71	26.42
Alabama	27,092,343	12,726,569	14,365,774	18,956,149	18,007,774	14.32	12.53	14.26
Mississippi	8,403,920	2,877,124	5,526,796	6,192,927	4,955,789	5.24	4.81	4.38
Louisiana	37,777,047	13,592,795	24,184,252	33,335,497	42,865,471	26,34	29.80	45.60
Arkansas	4,225,715	1,191,382	3,034,333	7,599,835	10,733,140	3 13	6.73	13.37
Indian Territory	665,129	....	665,129	....	....	1.53	....	....
Oklahoma	3,696,326	509,766	3,186,560	....	....	7.99	....	....
Texas	36,449,685	3.993,119	32,456,566	20,092,653	11,688,198	11.35	8.99	7.34
Western Division	115,118,595	15,361,189	99,757,406	45,066,604	24,476,975	26 84	14.88	13.85
Montana	8,920,689	1,203,769	7,716,920	2,926,268	765,248	33.87	22.15	19.54
Idaho	3,883,823	324,174	3,559,649	1,594,333	229,882	22.02	18.89	7.05
Wyoming	2.566,260	300,530	2,265,730	1,647,381	205,462	26.66	27.14	9.88
Colorado	22,066,653	3,797,329	18,269,324	9,458,331	3,627,742	39.06	22.95	18.67
New Mexico	4,579,516	998,923	3,580,593	2,831,538	84,872	23.64	18.44	0.71
Arizona	6,591,834	3,099,333	3,492,501	2,937,971	377,501	50.75	49.28	9.33
Utah	6,612,568	974,492	5,638 076	1,217,501	116,251	22 81	5.85	0.81
Nevada	1,184,189	243,904	940,285	985,165	1,399,765	27.97	21.52	22.48
Washington	29,556,734	1,271,391	28,285,343	3,418.798	239,311	53.71	9.78	3.19
Oregon	11,302,400	236.267	11,066,133	2,479,859	848,502	26,11	7.90	4.86
California	17,853,929	2,911,077	14,942,852	15,569,459	16.582,439	11.60	12.89	19.18
Continental United States	1,864,195,826	234,314,190	1,629,881,636	1,137,918,868	1,123,278,647	23.72	18.17	22.40

Minor civil divisions included in the third column above embrace villages, towns, townships, precincts, fire districts, irrigation districts, poor districts, school districts, etc.

* Combined funded and floating debt in 1902.

SINKING FUND ASSETS OF STATES, 1902.—The following States in 1902 maintained sinking funds to the amounts attached: Massachusetts, $18,304.730; Rhode Island. $444,452; New York, $2,545,116; New Jersey, $172,550; Pennsylvania, $4.432,024; Delaware. $7,658; Maryland, $1.974,587; Virginia, $3,176,040; South Carolina, $517,648; Florida, $160,200; Ohio, $254,569; Indiana, $61; Michigan, $86,237; Minnesota, $365,966; Missouri, $520,204; North Dakota, $1,116; South Dakota, $46,737; Kentucky, $324,548; Arkansas, $65,580; Montana, $111,483; Idaho, $431,306; Colorado, $164,953; New Mexico, $123,277; Arizona, $1,002; Nevada, $18,494; California, $419,630. Total, $34,670,265.

Indebtedness and Finances of Nations.

(From Summary prepared by the Bureau of Statistics, Department of Commerce and Labor.)

Countries.	Revenue and Expenditures.			Debt.			
	Year.	Revenue.	Expenditure.	Year.	Total.	Interest Per Cent.	Interest and other Annual Charges.
Argentina	1906	$101,915,035	$98,379,638	1906–7	$444,440,067	4½–5	$30,221,928
Australasia:							
Australia, Commonwealth of	....	a	a	....	....	....	....
Australia, States	1904–5	165,748,231	164,971,284	1905	1,128,632,767	3 –5	44,122,954
New Zealand	1905–6	37,229,202	34,660,858	1906	306,059,246	3 –5	10,157,379
Austria-Hungary	1906	72,008,078	72,008,078	1906	1,092,863,255	3 –4	48,214,724
Austria	1906	369,865,472	369,265,569	1906	818,096,120	3 –5½	42,157,238
Hungary	1906	261,981,691	262,995,860	1905	1,102,742,776	3 –4½	44,366,029
Belgium	1906	107,860,738	109,366,961	1906	621,640,286	2½–3	24,925,698
Bolivia	1906	4,963,773	5,575,441	1906	2,977,924	d	d
Brazil	1906	118,388,586	113,427,944	1906	542,213,359	4 –6	34,787,569
Bulgaria	1966	22,764,900	22,764,000	1906	73,452,805	5 –6	6,187,650
Canada	1905–6	78,006,599	54,061,325	1907	253,997,742	2½–4	13,145,047
Central America							
Costa Rica	1905–6	3,401,391	3,401,391	1906	20,962,242	2½–5	403,281
Guatemala	1905	2,673,290	3,562,935	1906	14,148,366	4 –8	1,960,022
Honduras	1905	1,420,875	1,436,842	1905–6	104,335,589	5 –10	162,164
Nicaragua	1905	1,632,800	1,342,600	1905	6,330,739	4 –6	191,539
Salvador	1905	3,764,571	4,430,027	1906	4,609,361	4 –5	1,696,440
Chile	1906	56,549,978	56,549,978	1905	95,720,654	4½–5	5,113,942
China	1905	25,841,699	25,841,699	1906	597,192,000	4 –7	30,912,000
Colombia	1906	10,632,389	10,632,389	1905–6	19,541,567	3 –10	827,993
Cuba	1905–6	29,609,746	18,997,663	1907	47,695,350	5 –6	2,581,721
Denmark	1906–7	22,919,541	23,018,117	1906	64,231,718	3 –4	2,127,120
Ecuador	1906	5,931,300	6,417,500	1906	14,737,291	4 –7	1,439,200
Egypt	1906	67,382,304	64,886,665	1906	468,314,391	3 –4¼	22,745,783
France	1906	715,074,344	715,874,069	1906	5,655,134,825	3 –3½	237,855,497
Algeria	1906	18,440,642	18,421,431	1905	6,313,838	3	737,440
Tunis	1906	14,948,227	14,929,509	1907	46,263,300	3 –3½	1,524,677
French East Indies	1905–6	24,603,417	24,603,417	....	....	....	....
German Empire	1906–7	570,563,137	572,600,260	1905	855,963,454	3 –3½	30,358,300
States	1903–4	b1,081,271,985	c1,014,632,056	1905	2,957,356,846	3 –4	120,537,100
Colonies	1906–7	3,138,700	3,424,300	....	....	....	....
Greece	1906	19,743,277	19,540,468	1906	167,052,145	2½–5	5,317,795
Hayti	1905–6	4,278,860	4,214,415	1906	24,810,673	2½–6	2,250,363
India (British)	1905–6	412,825,000	404,260,000	1905	1,127,923,363	2½–4½	37,599,616
Italy	1905–6	470,565,700	440,503,700	1905	2,767,911,949	3 –5	130,803,281
Japan	1906–7	246,362,944	246,362,944	1906	932,445,798	4 –6	72,752,294
Formosa	1906–7	12,833,510	12,833,510	....	....	....	....
Congo Free State	1906	5,684,376	6,610,404	....	....	....	....
Korea	1906	3,727,388	3,967,759	....	....	....	....
Luxemburg	1906–7	3,283,690	3,375,257	1906	2,316,000	3½	160,893
Mexico	1905–6	51,269,008	48,314,646	1906	222,058,181	3 –5	12,577,739
Netherlands	1906–7	71,451,788	74,760,449	1907	458,069,211	2½–3	14,718,505
Dutch East Indies	1906	61,109,136	64,957,870	....	....	....	....
Dutch possessions in America	1906	1,720,158	2,261,250	....	....	....	....
Norway	1905–6	26,821,673	26,911,111	1906	91,764,945	3 –3½	3,758,975
Paraguay	1906	2,126,746	1,873,304	1906	12,303,592	3	156,952
Persia	1904–5	7,056,000	7,056,000	1906	16,737,500	5	900,000
Peru	1906	12,197,327	12,555,720	1905	15,266,000	1	129,478
Portugal	1905–6	62,064,000	63,096,000	1906	864,701,627	3 –4½	21,369,000
Portuguese Colonies	1905–6	10,165,000	10,242,000	....	....	....	....
Roumania	1906–7	46,110,834	45,883,673	1906	278,247,239	3½–7½	16,086,604
Russia	1905	1,451,308,000	1,650,448,000	1906	4,038,199,722	3 –6	172,385,884
Finland	1905	20,660,819	23,246,364	1906	27,073,900	3 –3½	1,205,734
Santo Domingo	1905	2,427,802	2,399,811	1906	30,236,731	2¾–4	1,056,734
Servia	1905–6	17,216,965	17,208,864	1905	88,971,135	4 –5	5,564,999
Siam	1905–6	16,085,871	15,861,925	1906	4,866,500	4½	218,993
Spain	1906	172,767,678	165,674,506	1906	1,829,265,995	2½–5	69,356,706
Sweden	1906–7	51,826,000	51,826,000	1906	102,059,288	3 –3⅝	3,684,862
Switzerland	1905	24,955,530	22,526,223	1906	e19,787,648	3½	1,037,642
Turkey	1905–6	14,212,326	14,212,326	1906	458,603,213	3½–5	9,492,450
United Kingdom	1905–6	700,666,869	683,801,430	1906	3,839,620,745	2½–2¾	150,295,210
British Colonies	1905–6	143,722,000	153,566,228	1906	f612,510,084	2½–6	23,802,418
Uruguay	1906–7	18,931,770	18,819,027	1906	125,585,243	3½–5	6,857,312
Venezuela	1904	10,721,363	10,214,626	1906	45,160,402	3	2,756,000
Total	....	$8,971,287,021	$8,988,727,487	....	36,548,455,489	....	$1,550,433,038

(a) Included in budgets of States. (b) Exclusive of $134,771,300 contributed to the Imperial Treasury. (c) Exclusive of $131,466,154 transferred by the Imperial Treasury to the various States. (d) Internal debt only; the foreign debt has been taken over by Chile. (e) Exclusive of the railroad debt. (f) A part of which is guaranteed by the home government.

WEALTH OF NATIONS.

These are the latest estimates:

United States	$116,000,000,000	Italy (Nitti)	$13,000,000,000
Great Britain and Ireland	62,200,000,000	Belgium	6,800,000,000
France (Turgnam)	42,800,000,000	Spain	5,400,000,000
Germany	42,000,000,000	Netherlands	5,000,000,000
Russia	35,000,000,000	Portugal	2,500,000,000
Austria-Hungary	20,000,000,000	Switzerland	2,400,000,000

Bonded Debts and Assessed Valuations of States.

States and Territories.	Valuation Realty Property.	Valuation Personal Property.	Total Assessed Valuation.	Per. Ct. Actual Value.	Tax Rate Per $1,000.	Bonded Debt.
Alabama	$255,301,787	$195,397,886	$450,529,553	60	$6.50	$16,194,000
Arizona	....	....	80,637,541	40	7.50	1,012,000
Arkansas	199,378,648	102,802,915	302,181,563	50	6.75	1,250,500
California	431,754,444	275,481,764	1,994,511,229	100	4.00	(s) 1,726,500
Colorado (d)	....	....	465,000,000	....	4.50	2,300,000
Connecticut	452,000,000	313,000,000	(x) 791,769,979	Full.	....	876,100
Delaware	....	....	(c) 76,000,000	....	....	756,785
Dist. of Columbia	247,306,494	31,507,929	278,814,423	67	15.00	11,103,750
Florida	....	....	(a) 142,018,871	....	7.50	601,567
Georgia	339,143,931	(r) 360,392,948	699,536,879	65	5.00	7,136,000
Idaho	....	....	115,680,056	....	4.34	1,364,000
Illinois	785,861,540	340,801,617	1,126,663,157	Full.	5.00	None.
Indiana	1,096,600,950	671,214,537	1,767,815,487	60	3.36	1,389,615
Iowa	475,893,422	123,492,167	599,385,589	25	4.00	None.
Kansas	1,573,048,790	880,643,069	2,453,691,859	90-100	.90	623,000
Kentucky (b)	487,835,250	143,313,606	644,489,000	....	5.00	26,000
Louisiana (a)	....	....	459,271,270	....	5.00	11,108,0[illegible]0
Maine (b)	292,464,911	74,049,103	366,514,014	Full.	2.50	(u) 1,095,000
Maryland	....	....	765,109,228	....	1.60	(v) 5,978,926
Massachusetts (a)	2,746,005,835	1,757,420,786	4,503,426,621	....	....	105,796,662
Michigan (a)	1,290,164,227	364,207,665	1,654,371,892	80	2.41	None.
Minnesota	873,585,056	163,432,357	1,037,017,413	50	....	550,000
Mississippi (d)	131,315,281	63,236,476	222,847,525	....	6.00	2,887,026
Missouri	1,040,252,288	(r) 581,518,925	1,621,771,213	33⅓	1.70	None.
Montana	124,117,983	(r) 127,732,877	251,850,860	100	2.50	None.
Nebraska	255,484,621	136,250,843	391,735,464	20	6.25	None.
Nevada (a)	32,241,372	12,223,625	44,464,997	....	....	613,000
New Hampshire	....	....	244,972,264	100	....	706,700
New Jersey (d)	....	....	918,418,741	....	....	....
New Mexico (a)	19,780,671	23,462,076	43,242,746	20	14.00	965,123
New York	8,553,298,187	620,268,058	9,173,566,245	....	8.64	26,230,660
North Carolina (a)	287,245,762	(r) 288,124,551	575,370,313	75	4.30	6,880,950
North Dakota	146,000,000	(r) 81,000,000	227,000,000	20	5.20	692,000
Ohio (e)	1,451,067,020	662,739,148	2,113,806,168	60	1.35	None.
Oklahoma (a)	52,365,888	44,259,716	96,625,604	25	6.50	None.
Oregon (b)	104,956,302	83,101,939	188,058,281	33⅓	5.45	None.
Pennsylvania	4,665,263,899	1,104,513,428	5,769,777,327	....	....	(w) 72,234
Rhode Island	373,981,711	114,996,396	488,978,107	75	1.80	3,650,000
South Carolina (a)	132,273,168	(r) 135,164,869	267,438,037	40	4.50	6,685,774
South Dakota	202,180,542	51,721,950	283,696,268	....	3.00	(e) 250,000
Tennessee (a)	344,519,946	(r) 130,346,703	474,866,649	100	3.50	14,236,767
Texas (b)	743,559,216	395,463,514	1,139,022,730	....	3.80	3,989,400
Utah (a)	....	....	146,204,050	60	5.00	900,000
Vermont	139,749,702	44,138,368	183,888,070	Full.	1.30	(b) 135,500
Virginia (d)	316,563,279	107,270,401	423,842,680	....	4.00	24,363,795
Washington	471,712,181	101,358,347	573,070,528	60	6.70	1,000,000
West Virginia	475,000,000	375,000,000	850,000,000	80	.85	None.
Wisconsin (b)	1,146,813,692	237,767,063	1,384,580,755	75	11.27	2,251,000
Wyoming	....	....	67,580,051	25	6.20	182,000

The returns are for the fiscal year 1908, except when otherwise indicated. (a) Fiscal year 1907. (b) Fiscal year 1905. (c) Fiscal year 1903. (d) Fiscal year 1902. (e) Floating indebtedness. (r) Including railroads. (s) Floating indebtedness, $230,660. (u) October 10, 1906. (v) Net debt, $562,901. (w) Net debt. (x) Exclusive of railroad, telephone and telegraph property.

List of Appropriations by Congress, 1903-1909.

	1903.	1904.	1905.	1906.	1907.	1908.	1909.
Deficiencies	$24,944,124.77	$19,651,968.25	$25,083,395.78	28,998,961.98	$28,165,777.03	$10,509,311.42	$42,662,723.93
Legislative, Executive and Judicial	25,396,683.20	27,598,653.66	28,558,258.22	29,136,752.06	29,684,919.30	32,126,333.80	32,832,913.50
Sundry Civil	54,394,601.63	61,763,709.11	49,968,011.34	56,269,468.66	80,789,470.28	103,046,481.30	94,115,143.22
Support of the Army	91,730,136.41	77,888,752.83	77,070,300.88	70,396,631.64	71,817,165.08	78,634,582.75	95,382,247.61
Naval Service	78,856,363.13	81,876,791.43	97,505,140.94	100,336,679.94	102,071,670.27	98,958,507.50	122,662,485.47
Indian Service	8,986,028.10	8,540,406.77	9,447,961.40	7,923,814.34	9,260,549.98	10,123,188.05	9,253,347.87
Rivers and Harbors	32,540,199.50	20,228,150.99	10,872,200.00	26,561,281.75	17,254,050.04	43,310,813.00	18,092,945.00
Forts and Fortifications	7,298,955.00	7,188,416.22	7,518,192.00	6,747,893.00	5,053,993.00	6,898,011.00	9,316,745.00
Military Academy	2,627,324.42	652,748.67	973,947.26	673,713.38	1,664,707.67	1,929,703.42	845,634.87
Post-Office Department	Indefinite.	Indefinite.	Indefinite.	Indefinite.	Indefinite.	Indefinite.	Indefinite.
Pensions	139,842,230.00	139,847,600.00	138,360,700.00	138,250,100.00	140,245,500.00	146,143,000.00	163,053,000.00
Consular and Diplomatic	1,987,483.31	1,968,250.69	2,020,100.69	2,123,047.72	3,091,094.17	3,092,333.72	3,538,852.72
Agricultural Department	5,208,960.00	5,978,160.00	5,902,040.00	6,882,690.00	9,930,440.00	9,447,290.00	11,672,106.00
District of Columbia	8,544,469.97	8,638,097.00	11,018,540.00	9,801,197.62	10,232,102.16	10,440,598.63	10,001,888.85
Miscellaneous	4,081,747.24	3,025,064.95	2,860,828.52	5,139,545.21	40,172,757.57	1,079,989.19	14,086,212.78
Totals	486,439,306.68	464,846,770.57	467,159,617.03	489,241,777.30	549,434,246.55	555,739,443.78	627,516,246.83

Fisheries of the United States.

(Compiled by the United States Bureau of Fisheries.)

Sections.	Vessels Employed.		Persons Employed.	Capital Invested.	Value of Products.
	No.	Tons.			
South Atlantic States (1902)	526	5,740	23,452	$2,991,149	$2,839,633
Gulf States (1902)	714	9,221	18,029	4,707,460	3,494,196
Middle Atlantic States (1904)	3,583	54,540	83,103	26,673,521	18,963,976
New England States (1905)	1,447	45,668	37,339	22,530,720	14,184,205
Great Lakes (1903)	206	3,846	9,333	7,474,422	2,745,501
Mississippi River and Tributaries (1903)	5	138	13,377	3,555,540	1,841,168
Minor Interior Waters (chiefly for 1900, 1902, and 1903)	1	22	2,491	266,050	425,929
Pacific Coast States (1904)	226	10,382	19,658	12,839,949	6,680,866
Alaska Territory (1906)	223	68,965	12,357	12,835,458	8,801,865
Total	6,931	198,522	219,139	$93,874,269	$59,977,339

VALUE OF FOREIGN FISHERIES.

Belgium	$ 1,000,000	Norway	$ 8,000,000
Canada	46,000,000	Portugal	4,000,000
Denmark	3,000,000	Spain	8,000,000
Italy	3,000,000	Great Britain	46,000,000
Japan	13,000,000	The World including the U. S.	192,000,000

UNITED STATES BUREAU OF FISHERIES.

DEPARTMENT OF COMMERCE AND LABOR.

The work of the Bureau of Fisheries comprises (1) the propagation of useful food fishes, including lobsters, oysters and other shellfish, and their distribution to suitable waters; (2) the inquiry into the causes of decrease of food fishes in the lakes, rivers and coast waters of the United States, the study of the waters of the coast and interior in the interest of fish-culture, and the investigation of the fishing grounds of the Atlantic, Gulf and Pacific coasts, with the view of determining their food resources and the development of the commercial fisheries; (3) the collection and compilation of the statistics of the fisheries and the study of their methods and relations. Office, Sixth and B Streets, Washington, D. C. The official force of the Bureau is as follows: *Commissioner*, George M. Bowers; *Deputy Commissioner*, Hugh M. Smith; *Chief Clerk*, I. H. Dunlap. *Assistants in Charge of Division; Inquiry Respecting Food Fishes*, B. W. Everman; *Fish Culture*, John W. Titcomb; *Statistics and Methods*, A. B. Alexander; *Architect and Engineer*, Hector von Bayer.

National Democratic League.

The National Democratic League is a permanent organization, federation or league of Democratic clubs organized throughout the country, to which every regularly organized Democratic club or association is entitled to membership.

The objects of the League are to encourage and assist in the formation of permanent Democratic clubs and State leagues, to unite such clubs and leagues for effective and organized work, and generally to advance the principles of the Democratic party. *Chairman*—Col. William C. Liller, Lancaster, Pa. *Secretary*—Lorenzo G. Warfield, Washington, D. C. *Treasurer*—Capt. Joseph P. Watkins, Richmond, Va. Headquarters of the League, 511 Fourteenth Street, N. W., Washington, D. C.

Silver Bay Association.

President—William D. Murray. *Vice-President*—J. S. Cushman. *Treasurer*—D. H. McAlpin. *General Secretary*—C. M. Willis. *Recording Secretary*—R. L. Wensley, 125 East Twenty-seventh Street, New York.

The Silver Bay Association is incorporated under the New York Legislature, and holds the property on Lake George for the use of Summer Christian conferences. The property consists of 1,400 acres, including a large main building, fifteen cottages, auditorium and athletic field.

Cost of Maintaining Armies and Navies.

The net cost of the British Army and its operations, according to estimates for 1908-09, will amount to $138,800,000, while the cost of maintaining the Navy will approximate $170,000,000. The United States Army budget for the past fiscal year amounted to over $103,000,000, and for the Navy nearly $104,000,000. The military expenditure of the German Empire entered in the budget for 1908-09 amounted in all to $206,000,000, while the estimate for the Navy was $83,000,000. The estimated cost of maintaining the French Army in 1907 is $189,000,000, and the Navy $64,000,000. Italy, during the present fiscal year, expects to spend $29,000,000 on her Navy, and a still larger sum on the Army. The Russian Navy estimates for 1908-09 ou nearly $49,000,000, and those of Austro-Hungary nearly $12,000,000. Previous to the war with Russia the military expenditure of Japan was less than $25,000,000. The expenditure during the war from October, 1903, to May, 1905, amounted to $500,000,000 for the Army and $90,000,000 for the Navy. The total naval estimate for Japan for 1908-09 amounts to $10,000,000.

Monetary Statistics.

(Compiled from the Report of the Director of the Mint.)

MONETARY SYSTEMS AND APPROXIMATE STOCKS OF MONEY IN THE AGGREGATE AND PER CAPITA IN THE PRINCIPAL COUNTRIES OF THE WORLD JAN. 1, 1907.

Countries.	Estimated Population.	Stock of Gold.	Stock of Silver.			Uncovered Paper.	Per Capita.			
			Full Tender.	Limited Tender.	Total.		Gold.	Silver.	Paper.	Total.
United States....	$85,400,000	$1,593,300,000	$571,300,000	$127,400,000	$698,700,000	$610,800,000	$18.66	$8.18	$7.15	$33.99
Austria-Hungary	49,400,000	306,400,000	......	105,300,000	105,300,000	119,300,000	6.20	2.13	2.41	10.74
Belgium	7,200,000	31,100,000	15,000,000	9,700,000	24,700,000	125,800,000	4.32	3.43	17.47	25.22
British Empire:										
Australasia.....	4,800,000	125,000,000	......	10,000,000	10,000,000	......	26.04	2.08	....	28.12
Canada........	5,800,000	62,400,000	......	6,700,000	6,700,000	72,500,000	10.76	1.15	12.50	24.41
Unit'd K'gd'm	44,100,000	486,700,000	......	116,800,000	116,800,000	116,800,000	11.03	2.65	2.65	16.33
India	295,200,000	337,300,000	603,800,000	......	603,800,000	38,900,000	1.14	2.05	.13	3.32
South Africa..	7,700,000	61,400,000	......	20,000,000	20,000,000	......	7.97	2.60	....	10.57
Str's Settlem'ts	5,400,000	600,000	42,000,000	7,000,000	49,000,000	22,200,000	.11	9.07	4.11	13.29
Bulgaria.........	4,000,000	7,200,000	1,000,000	2,200,000	3,200,000	2,900,000	.180	.80	.73	3.23
Cuba	1,600,000	38,200,000	......	5,000,000	5,000,000	......	23.88	3.12	....	27.00
Denmark........	2,600,000	22,600,000	......	6,100,000	6,100,000	10,700,000	8.69	2.35	4.11	15.15
Egypt...........	11,200,000	140,000,000	......	15,000,000	15,000,000	......	12.50	1.34	....	13.84
Finland	2,800,000	5,100,000	......	400,000	400,000	12,700,000	1.82	.14	4.54	6.50
France..........	39,300,000	926,400,000	347,400,000	63,700,000	411,100,000	269,200,000	23.57	10.46	6.85	40.88
Germany	60,600,000	1,030,300,000	......	219,700,000	219,700,000	267,100,000	17.00	3.62	4.41	25.03
Greece	2,400,000	5,600,000	100,000	......	100,000	42,600,000	2.33	.04	17.75	20.12
Hayti...........	1,400,000	1,000,000	1,000,000	1,500,000	2,500,000	7,600,000	.71	1.79	5.43	7.93
Italy	33,700,000	215,500,000	28,300,000	3,400,000	31,700,000	150,600,000	6.39	.94	4.47	11.80
Japan	51,700,000	80,100,000	......	48,200,000	48,200,000	96,900,000	1.55	.93	1.87	4.35
Mexico	13,600,000	40,000,000	52,800,000	4,000,000	56,800,000	51,[illegible]00,000	2.94	4.18	3.76	10.88
Netherlands	5,600,000	45,900,000	48,000,000	4,600,000	52,600,000	57,800,000	8.20	9.39	10.32	27.91
Norway	2,300,000	8,300,000	......	3,100,000	3,100,000	7,000,000	3.61	1.35	3.04	8.00
Portugal.........	5,400,000	8,600,000	......	33,400,000	33,400,000	61,200,000	1.59	6.19	11.33	19.11
Roumania........	6,600,000	20,700,000	......	600,000	600,000	27,600,000	3.14	.09	4.18	7.41
Russia...........	143,400,000	939,400,000	......	77,900,000	77,900,000	......	6.55	.54	....	7.09
Servia...	2,700,000	2,200,000	......	3,200,000	3,200,000	1,500,000	.81	1.19	.55	2.55
Siam	6,100,000	......	44,500,000	......	44,500,000	1,100,000	....	7.29	.18	7.47
Spain	18,800,000	90,900,000	......	173,700,000	173,700,000	97,100,000	4.84	9.24	5.16	19.24
Sweden..........	5,300,000	22,600,000	......	7,700,000	7,700,000	34,800,000	4.26	1.45	6.57	12.28
Switzerland......	3,300,000	29,000,000	......	11,600,000	11,600,000	24,600,000	8.79	3.51	7.45	19.75
Turkey..........	24,000,000	50,000,000	30,000,000	10,000,000	40,000,000	......	2.07	1.66	....	3.73
Cent. Am. States	4,700,000	2,000,000	......	7,400,000	7,400,000	62,900,000	.43	1.57	13.38	15.38
China	330,100,000	......	350,000,000	......	350,000,000	......	....	1.06	....	1.06
Total.........	1,330,100,000	$6,888,900,000	$2,139,000,000	$1,121,200,000	$3,260,200,000	$4,132,000,000	$5.18	$2.45	$3.10	$10.73

NOTE.—The value of the monetary stock of silver-standard countries has been changed to conform to the decline in silver values. The monetary stock of Mexico and other countries where the Mexican dollar circulates is given in Mexican dollars at bullion value.

WORLD'S PRODUCTION OF GOLD AND SILVER FOR THE CALENDAR YEAR, 1906.

Countries.	Gold.		Silver.		Countries.	Gold.		Silver.	
	Oz., fine.	Value.	Oz., fine.	Com. Val.		Oz., fine.	Value.	Oz., fine.	Com. Val.
United States...	4,565,333	$94,373,800	56,517,900	$38,256,400	Chile........ ...	45,886	$948,500	397,853	$269,300
Mexico.........	896,615	18,534,700	55,225,268	37,381,400	Colombia.	105,982	2,190,800	763,335	516,700
Canada..........	581,657	12,023,900	8,568,665	5,800,000	Ecuador........	14,233	294,200	13,592	9,200
Africa..........	6,553,484	135,472,500	702,464	475,500	Brazil	116,243	2,403,000	......	......
Australasia.	3,985,684	82,391,400	14,237,246	9,637,000	Venezuela	1,223	25,300	......	......
Russia..........	943,056	19,494,700	166,183	112,500	British Guiana..	77,770	1,607,700	......	......
Austria-Hungary	123,617	2,255,400	1,692,119	1,145,400	French Guiana..	89,955	1,859,700	......	......
Germany........	3,590	80,400	5,696,433	3,855,900	Peru...........	40,102	829,000	7,404,238	5,011,900
Italy	1,993	41,200	672,449	455,200	Central America.	92,432	1,910,700	1,670,159	1,130,500
Spain...........	......	......	4,064,532	2,751,200	Japan..........	156,016	3,225,100	2,451,357	1,659,300
Greece	......	......	829,025	561,200	China	88,961	1,839,000	......	......
Turkey	289	6,000	37,874	25,600	Korea....	108,844	2,250,000	......	......
France..........	......	......	890,555	602,800	India	584,744	12,087,700	......	......
Great Britain....	1,414	29,200	137,216	92,900	Brit. East Indies	....	......	......	......
Argentina	268	5,500	14,440	9,800					
Bolivia.........	912	18,800	3,096,998	2,096,300	Total, (inc. o'rs)	19,361,864	$400,245,300	165,840,840	$112,120,500

Production 1907: Gold, fine ounces, 19,854,875; Value $410,436,600; Silver, fine ounces, 184,948,867, Value $122,090,000.

COINAGE OF NATIONS IN 1907.

Countries.	Gold.	Silver.	Countries.	Gold.	Silver.	Countries.	Gold.	Silver.
United States...	$131,907,490	$13,178,436	France	$75,261,788	$1,[illegible]02,130	Russia.........	$280	$5,660,338
Philippine Isls..	......	6,730,260	Indo-China.....	......	14,061,745	Siam...........	......	1,342,891
Austria-Hung'y.	4,605,184	3,458,435	Tunis	266	77,551	Sweden.........	......	714,428
Brazil...	40,962	4,340,900	Germany	15,925,915	20,216,679	Switzerland.....	579,000	653,305
Australasia.	52,772,229	......	Italy...........	......	2,115,806	Turkey......	10,036,231	1,323,756
Canada...... ..	......	1,194,000	Japan	8,944,080	9,586,999	Other Countries	90,867	21,015,041
Great Britain...	100,011,442	9,924,740	Mexico	10,632,152	9,651,451			
India	......	84,630,837	Netherlands....	......	1,819,200	Total......	$411,803,902	$222,976,131
China..........	......	5,316,439	Dutch E. Indies.	......	1,869,300			
Egypt..........	......	2,224,350	Peru.	996,016	415,527			

MONETARY STATISTICS—*Continued.*

COMMERCIAL RATIO OF SILVER TO GOLD.

Year	Ratio	Year	Ratio	Year	Ratio	Year	Ratio	Year	Ratio
1700	14.81	1868	15.59	1878	17.94	1888	21.99	1898	35.03
1750	14.55	1869	15.60	1879	18.40	1889	22.09	1899	34.36
1800	15.68	1870	15.57	1880	18.05	1890	19.76	1900	33.33
1850	15.70	1871	15.57	1881	18.16	1891	20.92	1901	34.68
1860	15.29	1872	15.63	1882	18.19	1892	23.72	1902	39.15
1863	15.37	1873	15.92	1883	18.64	1893	26.49	1903	38.10
1864	15.37	1874	16.17	1884	18.57	1894	32.56	1904	35.70
1865	15.44	1875	16.59	1885	19.41	1895	31.60	1905	33.87
1866	15.43	1876	17.88	1886	20.78	1896	30.66	1906	30.54
1867	15.57	1877	17.22	1887	21.13	1897	34.28	1907	31.24

BULLION VALUE OF 371¼ GRAINS OF PURE SILVER AT THE ANNUAL AVERAGE PRICE OF SILVER.

Year.	Value.	Year.	Value.	Year.	Value.	Year.	Value.	Year.	Value.
1850	$1.018	1880	$0.886	1887	$0.757	1894	$0.491	1901	.461
1865	1.035	1881	.876	1888	.727	1895	.506	1902	.408
1870	1.027	1882	.878	1889	.723	1896	.522	1903	.443
1875	.964	1883	.858	1890	.809	1897	.467	1904	.447
1877	.929	1884	.859	1891	.764	1898	.456	1905	.472
1878	.891	1885	.823	1892	.674	1899	.465	1906	.523
1879	.868	1886	.769	1893	.603	1900	.479	1907	.725

PURCHASES OF SILVER BY THE UNITED STATES.

Act Authorizing.	Fine Ounces.	Cost.	Average Price
February 12, 1873	5,434.282	$7,152,564	$1.314
January 14, 1875	31.603.906	37,571,148	1.189
February 28, 1878	291,292,019	308,199,262	1.058
July 14, 1890 (to November 1, 1893, date of the repeal of the purchasing clause of the act of July 14, 1890)	168.674,682	155,931,002	.924
Section 3526 Revised Statutes	6.924.286	4,694,566	0.6101
Total	503,929,175	$513,548,542	$1.015

SOURCES OF GOLD AND SILVER PRODUCT OF THE UNITED STATES.

The following table, compiled from reports made by the United States Geological Survey as to the sources of production for the calendar year 1907, shows the distribution among the various gold and silver producing States and Territories of the amount of gold and silver extracted from quartz, the amount of gold obtained from placer, and the amount of silver obtained from lead ores and copper ores as by-product.

States and Territories.	Gold. Quartz.	Gold. Placer.	Silver. Quartz.	Silver. Lead Ores.	Silver. Copper Ores.
	Fine Ozs.	Fine Ozs.	Fine Ozs.	Fine Ozs.	Fine Ozs.
Alabama	1,255	....	189	....	250
Alaska	138,292	727,722	97,729	....	52,055
Arizona	124,141	2,172	976,965	113,442	1,421,490
California	478,?95	330,919	448,179	82,353	608,326
Colorado	1,002,590	4,878	7,411,905	3,576,386	241,485
Georgia	2,003	1,133	84	....	780
Idaho	43,48?	17,265	846,595	7,03?,?29	536,007
Michigan	....	....	....	....	299,764
Missouri	....	....	....	25,692	....
Montana	142,104	16,867	1,699,954	328,385	7,289,266
Nevada	552,637	2,874	6,479,370	318,286	285,947
N. Hmpsre	....	....	....	174	....
N. Mexico	15,027	935	542,425	47,796	115,323
N. Car'lina	3,590	476	775	....	20,892
Oregon	38,596	16,032	85,871	....	847
S. Carolina	2,605	45	124	....	....
S. Dakota	200,140	45	93,895	....	....
Tennessee	185	....	....	....	58,358
Texas	1	....	303,688	....	....
Utah	247,321	438	131,693	7,354,407	3,503,976
Vermont	2	....	....	....	3,814
Virginia	395	5	148	....	73
Wash'gton	11,475	1,057	45,184	7,205	2,970
Wyoming	256	195	77	....	3,638
Total	3,0?4,609	1,192,890	19,164,850	18,886,955	14,445,261

RATIO OF SOURCES OF SILVER PRODUCT OF THE UNITED STATES.

Source.	1903.	1904.	1905.	1906.	1907.
	Per cent.	Per cent.	Per cent.	Per cent.	Per cent.
Quartz mills	29.9	26.2	24.9	29.6	36.6
Lead bullion	45.6	46.8	44.8	30.8	36.0
Copper bullion	24.5	27.0	30.3	39.6	27.5
Total	100.0	100.0	100.0	100.0	100.0

APPROXIMATE DISTRIBUTION BY PRODUCING STATES AND TERRITORIES OF THE PRODUCT OF GOLD AND SILVER IN THE UNITED STATES FOR THE CALENDAR YEAR 1907.

States and Territories.	Gold, Value.	Silver, Commercial Value.	Total Value. (Silver at Commercial Value.)
Alabama	$27,400	$400	$27,800
Alaska	18,489,400	118,300	19,188,600
Arizona	2,661,000	1,916,000	4,580,000
California	16,853,500	1,049,400	17,902,900
Colorado	20,897,600	7,587,000	28,486,500
Georgia	64,800	500	64,300
Idaho	1,258,900	5,208,300	6,887,700
Michigan	....	218,700	216,700
Missouri	....	16,700	16,700
Montana	3,472,600	7,345,500	10,818,100
Nevada	15,411,000	5,465,100	20,879,100
New Mexico	330,000	395,700	683,900
North Carolina	$78,700	$16,600	$95,300
Oregon	1,222,200	63,400	1,285,600
South Carolina	58,100	100	58,200
South Dakota	4,138,200	70,400	4,103,700
Tennessee	3,800	38,500	41,500
Texas	1,000	201,500	202,500
Utah	5,121,600	7,528,500	12,398,800
Washington	262,300	55,400	317,700
Wyoming	9,400	1,100	4,100
Other States	74,200	4,700	155,600
Total	$90,435,700	$37,299,700	$127,737,300

MONETARY STATISTICS—*Continued.*

PRODUCT OF GOLD AND SILVER FROM MINES IN THE UNITED STATES, 1868-1907.

Year.	Gold.		Silver.	
	Fine Ounces.	Value.	Fine Ounces.	Commercial Value.
1868	2,322,000	$48,000,000	9,281,200	$12,306,900
1869	2,394,562	49,500,000	9,281,200	12,297,600
1870	2,418,750	50,000,000	12,375,000	16,434,000
1871	2,104,312	43,500,000	17,789,100	23,588,300
1872	1,741,500	36,000,000	22,236,300	29,396,400
1873	1,741,500	36,000,000	27,630,400	35,881,600
1874	1,620,122	33,490,900	28,868,200	36,917,500
1875	1,619,009	33,467,900	24,539,300	30,485,900
1876	1,931,575	39,929,200	29,996,200	34,919,800
1877	2,268,662	46,897,400	30,777,800	36,991,500
1878	2,477,109	51,206,400	35,022,300	40,401,000
1879	1,881,787	38,900,000	31,565,500	35,477,100
1880	1,741,500	36,000,000	30,318,700	34,717,000
1881	1,678,612	34,700,000	33,257,800	37,657,500
1882	1,572,187	32,500,000	36,196,900	41,105,900
1883	1,451,250	30,000,000	35,732,800	39,618,400
1884	1,489,950	30,800,000	37,743,800	41,921,300
1885	1,538,373	31,801,000	39,909,400	42,503,500
1886	1,686,788	34,869,000	39,694,000	39,482,400
1887	1,603,049	33,136,000	41,721,600	40,887,200
1888	1,604,478	33,167,500	45,792,700	43,045,100
1889	1,594,775	32,967,000	50,094,500	46,838,400
1890	1,588,877	32,845,000	54,516,300	57,242,100
1891	1,604,840	33,175,000	58,330,000	57,630,000
1892	1,597,098	33,015,000	63,500,000	55,662,500
1893	1,739,323	35,955,000	60,000,000	46,800,000
1894	1,910,813	39,500,000	49,500,000	31,422,100
1895	2,254,760	46,610,000	55,727,000	36,445,500
1896	2,568,132	53,088,000	58,834,800	39,654,600
1897	2,774,935	57,363,000	53,860,000	32,316,000
1898	3,118,398	64,463,000	54,438,000	32,118,400
1899	3,437,210	71,053,400	54,764,500	32,858,700
1900	3,829,897	79,171,000	57,647,000	35,741,100
1901	3,805,500	78,666,700	55,214,000	33,128,400
1902	3,870,000	80,000,000	55,500,000	29,415,000
1903	3,560,000	73,591,700	54,300,000	29,322,000
1904	3,892,480	80,464,700	57,682,806	33,456,000
1905	4,178,592	86,337,700	58,938,355	35,952,397
1906	4,565,333	94,373,800	56,517,900	38,256,400
1907	4,374,287	90,435,700	56,514,700	37,299,700

Total product from 1792 to 1907 inclusive: Gold, fine ounces, 143,638,148; value, $2,969,227,000. Silver, fine ounces, 1,733,544,955; commercial value, $1,511,673,897. The estimate prior to 1873 was by Rossiter W. Raymond.

PRODUCTION OF THE PRECIOUS METALS SINCE THE DISCOVERY OF AMERICA.

Years.	Gold.	Silver-Coining Value.	Ratio.	Years.	Gold.	Silver-Coining Value.	Ratio.
1492-1520	$107,931,000	$54,703,000	10.75	1892	146,298,000	198,014,400	23.72
1521-1560	204,697,000	297,226,000	11.30	1893	157,494,800	213,944,400	26.49
1561-1600	189,012,000	597,244,000	11.80	1894	181,175,600	212,829,600	32.56
1601-1640	223,572,000	678,800,000	14.00	1895	198,763,600	216,566,900	31.60
1641-1680	239,655,000	584,691,000	15.00	1896	202,251,600	203,069,200	30.66
1681-1720	313,491,000	579,869,000	15.21	1897	236,073,700	207,413,000	34.28
1721-1760	580,727,000	801,712,000	14.75	1898	286,879,700	218,576,800	35.03
1761-1800	511,675,000	1,273,468,000	15.09	1899	306,724,100	217,648,200	34.36
1801-1810	118,152,000	371,677,000	15.61	1900	254,576,300	224,441,200	33.33
1811-1820	76,063,000	224,786,000	15.51	1901	262,273,300	223,691,300	34.68
1821-1830	94,479,000	191,444,000	15.80	1902	296,737,600	210,441,900	39.15
1831-1840	134,841,000	247,930,000	15.75	1903	325,961,500	217,131,800	38.10
1841-1850	363,928,000	324,400,000	15.83	1904	346,892,200	217,716,700	35.70
1851-1860	1,332,981,000	372,261,000	15.29	1905	380,288,700	222,794,500	33.87
1861-1870	1,263,015,000	507,174,000	15.56	1906	401,973,200	213,827,600	30.54
1871-1880	1,150,814,000	918,578,000	18.05	1907	410,436,600	239,172,300	31.24
1881-1890	1,059,892,000	1,298,820,000	19.76				
1891	130,650,000	177,352,000	20.92	Total	$12,491,839,300	$12,953,697,200	..

WORLD'S CONSUMPTION OF GOLD AND SILVER IN THE ARTS, 1907.

Country.	Gold.	Silver.	Country.	Gold.	Silver.
		Fine ounces.			Fine ounces.
United States	$33,549,500	22,137,200	Russia	$5,700,500	8,915,300
Great Britain	14,500,000	7,500,000	Austria-Hungary	3,358,800	1,923,700
France	15,850,700	8,252,900	Netherlands and Belgium	1,500,000	1,000,000
Germany	11,000,000	6,500,000	India (British)	35,796,200	34,848,500
Switzerland	7,310,600	2,218,300	Other countries	3,480,200	2,272,400
Italy	3,000,000	2,000,000	Total	$135,046,500	92,568,300

MONETARY STATISTICS—*Continued.*

PRESENT MONETARY SYSTEM OF THE UNITED STATES ILLUSTRATED.

	Gold Coin.	Standard Silver Dollars.	Subsidiary Silver Coin.	Minor Coin.
Weight........	25.8 grains to the dollar.	412.5 grains.	385.8 grains to the dollar.	5c. piece: 77.16 grains, 75 p. c. copper, 25 p. c. nickel.
Fineness......	900-1000.	900-1000.	900-1000.	1c. piece: 48 grains, 95 p. c. copper, 5 p. c. tin and zinc.
Ratio to gold..	....	15.988 to 1.	14.953 to 1.	
Limit of issue.	Unlimited.	Coinage ceased in 1905.	Needs of the people.	Needs of the people.
Denominations	$20, $10, $5, $2½.	$1.	50 cents, 25 cents, 10 cents.	5 cents, 1 cent.
Legal tender..	Unlimited.	Unlimited, unless otherwise contracted,	Not to exceed $10.	Not to exceed 25 cents.
Receivable	For all public dues.	For all public dues.	For all dues up to $10.	For all dues up to 25 cents.
Exchangeable.	For gold certificates, as below, and subsidiary and minor coin.	For silver certificates and smaller coin.	For minor coin.	....
Redeemable ...	....	....	In "lawful money" at the Treasury in sums or multiples of $20.	In "lawful money" at the Treasury in sums or multiples of $20.

	Gold Certificates.	Silver Certificates.	United States Notes.	Treasury Notes of 1890.	National Bank Notes.
Limit of issue.	Unlimited for gold coin unless gold reserve falls below $100,000,000.	Quantity of silver dollars coined, $562,178,530.	$346,681,016.	No further issues; volume steadily diminishing by redemption with silver dollars.	Not to exceed capital and surplus of banks.
Denominations	$10,000, $5,000, $1,000, $500, $100, $50, $20, $10.	$100, $50, $20, $10, $5, $2, $1.	$1,000, $500, $100, $50, $20, $10, $5, $2, $1.	$1,000, $100, $50, $20, $10, $5, $2, $1.	$1,000, $500, $100, $50, $20, $10, $5.
Legal tender..	Not a tender.	Not a tender.	For all debts, public and private, except customs and interest on public debt.	Unlimited, unless otherwise contracted.	Not a tender.
Receivable....	For all public dues.	For all public dues.	For all public dues.	For all public dues.	For all public dues except customs.
Exchangeable..	For subsidiary and minor coin.	For silver and minor coin.	For subsidiary and minor coin.	For silver and minor coin.	For subsidiary silver and minor coin.
Redeemable...	In gold coin at the Treasury.	In silver dollars at the Treasury.	In gold at the Treasury.	In gold at the Treasury.	In "lawful money" at the Treasury, or at bank of issue.

"Lawful money" includes gold coin, silver dollars, United States notes, and Treasury notes. United States notes are by regulation receivable for customs so long as they continue redeemable in coin. There are still in use small amounts of $1 and $2 national bank notes; also $500 and $1,000 silver certificates. Treasury notes were issued for purchases of silver bullion, which was coined into dollars wherewith the notes are being redeemed as rapidly as practicable. The issue of national bank notes is practically dependent upon the market price of United States bonds; when the premium is high it is not profitable to issue notes. "Emergency" issues based upon other bonds and upon commercial paper are authorized under certain conditions.

The above table was prepared for THE WORLD ALMANAC by Maurice L. Muhleman, former Deputy Assistant United States Treasurer, New York.

COINAGE OF THE MINTS OF THE UNITED STATES FROM THEIR ORGANIZATION, 1792, TO DECEMBER 31, 1907.

DENOMINATION.	Pieces.	Values.	DENOMINATION.	Pieces.	Values.
GOLD.			Dimes..........	1,355,000	$271,000.00
Double eagles..........	104,188,140	$2,083,762,800.00	Half dimes (coinage discontinued, act of February 12, 1873).....	1,118,552,562	55,927,628.10
Eagles..........	43,054,780	430,540,780.00	Three-cent pieces (coinage discontinued, act of Feb. 12, 1873)....	42,736,240	1,282,087.20
Half eagles..........	64,410,753	322,053,765.00	Total silver..........	2,481,363,686	$941,224,0[illegible].95
Three-dollar pieces (coinage discontinued under act of September 26, 1890)..........	539,792	1,619,376.00	MINOR.		
Quarter eagles..........	12,964,502	32,411,255 00	Five-cent pieces, nickel.........	591,171,564	$29,558,578.20
Dollars (coinage discontinued under act of September 26, 1890)..........	19,499,337	19,499,337.00	Three-cent pieces, nickel (coinage discontinued, act of September 26, 1890)..........	31,378,316	941,349.48
Dollars, Louisiana Purchase Exposition (act of June 28, 1902).	250,258	250,258.00	Two-cent pieces, bronze (coinage discontinued, act of September 26, 1890)..........	45,601,000	912,020.00
Dollars, Lewis & Clark exposition	60,069	60,069.00	One-cent pieces, copper (coinage discontinued, act of February 21, 1857)..........	156,288,744	1,562,887.44
Total gold..........	244,967,631	$2,890,198,640.00	One-cent pieces, nickel (coinage discontinued, act of April 22, 1864)..........	200,772,000	2,007,720.00
SILVER.			One-cent pieces, bronze.........	1,64[illegible],804,368	16,428,043.68
Dollars (coinage discontinued, act of Feb. 12, 1873, resumed act of Feb. 28, 1878)..........	578,303,848	$578,303,848.00	Half-cent pieces, copper (coinage discontinued, act of February 21, 1857)..........	798,522,200	39,926.11
Trade dollars (discontinued, act of Feb. 19, 1887)..........	35,965,924	35,965,924.00	Total minor..........	3,466,538,192	$51,450,524.91
Dollars (Lafayette souvenir, act of March 3, 1899)..........	50,000	50,000.00	Total coinage..........	6,19[illegible],869,509	$3,882,873,247.86
Half dollars..........	348,773,393	174,386,696.50			
Half dollars (Columb'n souvenir)	5,000,000	2,500,000.00			
Quarter dollars..........	350,586,719	87,646,679.75			
Quarter dollars (Colb'n souvenir)	40,000	10,000.00			
Twenty-cent pieces (coinage discontinued, act of May 2, 1878)					

Silver-dollar coinage under acts of April 2, 1792, $8,031,238; February 28, 1878, $378,166,793; July 14, 1890, $36,087,285; June 12, 1898, $42,139,872; June 13, 1898, $108,800,188; March 3, 1891, $5,078,472; total, $579,085,260.

The Potentiality of the United States.

President James W. Van Cleve, of the National Association of Manufacturers, makes the following estimate of the productive power of the United States, compared with that of the entire world:

	United States.	The World.	U.S. P.C.
Population, 1900	76,000,000	1,500,000,000	.05
Wheat, bushels, 1905	693,000,000	3,337,000,000	.20
Coal, tons, 1905	350,000,000	1,000,000,000	.35
Gold, 1906, value	$96,000,000	$400,000,000	.24
Manufacturings, value of products, 1905	$15,000,000,000	$43,000,000,000	.35
Silver, 1905, value	$38,000,000	$100,000,000	.38
Pig iron, tons, 1905	23,000,000	57,000,000	.40
Steel, tons, 1905	20,000,000	48,000,000	.42
Petroleum, gallons, 1905	6,000,000,000	11,000,000,000	.55
Copper, tons, 1905	403,000,000	735,000,000	.55
Cotton, bales, 1906	12,000,000	17,000,000	.70
Corn, bushels, 1906	2,927,000,000	3,700,000,000	.79

WEALTH OF THE UNITED STATES.

An estimate of the wealth of the United States in 1907 is given on another page as $116,000,000,000. A Census Office report issued in 1907 presented the following classification of the forms in which the national wealth is divided, with their valuations. The calculations were for the year 1904:

Real property and improvements taxed	$55,510,228,057
Real property and improvements exempt	6,831,244,570
Live stock	4,073,791,736
Farm implements and machinery	844,989,863
Manufacturing machinery, tools, and implements	3,297,754,180
Gold and silver coin and bullion	1,998,603,303
Railroads and their equipment	11,244,752,000
Street railways	2,219,966,000
Telegraph systems	227,400,000
Telephone systems	585,840,000
Pullman and private cars	123,000,000
Shipping and canals	846,489,804
Privately owned waterworks	275,000,000
Privately owned central electric light and power stations	562,851,105
Agricultural products	1,899,379,652
Manufactured products	7,409,291,668
Imported merchandise	495,543,685
Mining products	408,066,787
Clothing and personal adornments	2,500,000,000
Furniture, carriages and kindred property	5,750,000,000

The Lake Mohonk Conference.

ON THE INDIANS AND OTHER DEPENDENT PEOPLES.

The twenty-fifth annual session of the Lake Mohonk Conference, at Lake Mohonk, N. Y., held in 1907, adopted the following platform in reference to the Porto Ricans, Hawaiians, and Filipinos:

1. We urge that our Government shall steadfastly adhere to the principle that a moral responsibilty, which we cannot neglect, and which is higher than all commercial considerations, requires us to legislate and to administer so as to promote the highest welfare of the people of these islands.

2. We urge that Congress shall without delay legislate so as to effect a radical reduction of the duties now collected on products of the Philippine Islands.

3. We advise that the greatest educational emphasis be put upon the primary schools and the preparation of teachers therefor, and that such instruction shall have special reference to industrial training. The utmost effort should be made to secure the enrolment and attendance of all children. We maintain that it is the duty of Congress to provide adequately for such education, even if the necessary money were to come from direct appropriation.

4. Education in the duties of citizenship is an essential element in social and political progress. So fast as the Filipinos demonstrate their political capacity, powers of self-government should be granted and enlarged.

5. We recommend Congressional enactment to enable a large number of persons in the Philippine Islands to be naturalized as citizens of said islands. We believe that provision should be made by Congress whereby educated and duly qualified Porto Ricans may become citizens of the United States.

6. We urge upon Congress immediate legislation to protect the inhabitants of our insular possessions against the great evils of the opium traffic and the opium habit, which already threaten them.

7. We recommend that the application of the coastwise shipping act be permanently suspended with reference to the Philippines, and that Congress give serious attention to legislation necessary to relieve Hawaii from the disadvantages which this law imposes, and encourage the industrial development of Porto Rico.

8. With clear recognition of the ability shown in the administration of affairs in the Philippines, and the conviction that we have a body of competent men trained in colonial administration, it still seems to us that the Bureau of Insular Affairs, whose functions are essentially civil, should be ultimately committed to some other department than the Department of War.

Banking Statistics.

THE NATIONAL BANKS OF THE UNITED STATES.

(From the annual report of the Comptroller of the Currency.)

Year Ending Sept. 1.	No. of Banks.	Capital.	Surplus.	Total Dividends.	Total Net Earnings.	Ratio of Dividends to Capital.	Ratio of Dividends to Capital and Surplus.	Ratio of Earnings to Capital and Surplus.
1880..	2,072	$454,215,062	$120,145,649.00	$36,111,473.00	$45,186,034.00	8.02	6.35	7.88
1890..	3,353	625,089,645	208,707,786.00	51,158,883.33	72,055,563.52	8.19	6.14	8.65
1894..	3,755	672,951,450	246,001,328.00	45,333,270.00	41,955,248.00	6.07	4.09	4.05
1895..	3,716	660,287,065	247,466,002.00	45,969,663.00	46,866,557.00	6.96	5.06	5.15
1896..	3,682	652,725,750	248,235,323.00	45,525,947.00	49,742,318.00	6.97	5.05	5.52
1897..	3,620	633,173,895	249,044,948.00	42,394,241.00	44,273,314.00	6.64	4.78	4.99
1898..	3,581	615,818,725	244,281,879.00	44,291,971.00	50,032,972.00	7.17	5.15	5.82
1899..	3,561	608,674,895	247,930,970.00	46,691,502.00	54,346,692.00	7.67	5.45	6.34
1900..	3,604	608,754,600	251,950,843.42	48,033,094.39	87,276,836.60	7.88	5.58	10.14
1901..	3,969	635,511,286	268,451,548.00	51,699,779.00	81,853,797.00	9.05	5.72	8.15
1902..	4,269	673,763,767	302,513,154.55	68,199,493.62	106,581,476.85	10.92	6.99	10.12
1903..	4,700	722,797,806	353,105,524.91	63,565,848.10	109,881,530.97	8.79	5.91	10.21
1904..	5,134	761,682,495	390,452,345.00	75,588,889.00	112,936,426.00	9.92	6.56	9.80
1905..	5,505	776,175,576	407,643,159.00	73,138,174.00	105,909,385.00	8.95	6.18	9.42
1906..	5,876	801,326,590	440,616,689.50	89,264,850.00	127,526,836.00	11.14	7.18	10.26
1907..	6,043	842,685,939	522,382,747.59	99,728,239.00	152,235,434.00	11.90	7.30	11.20
*1908	6,751	893,932,010	548,850,476.00	97,336,282.00	131,333,288.00	10.89	6.75	9.10

* To July 1; abstract period changed.

The circulation outstanding Sept. 23, 1908, was $613,726,155; individual deposits, $4,548,135,165; principal resources, loans and discounts, $4,750,612,731; United States bonds on deposit to secure circulation, $628,073,040; United States bonds on hand and with the Treasurer to secure public deposits, $89,033,690; specie, $680,185,555; legal tender notes, $188,238,515; aggregate resources, $9,027,260,485.

RESOURCES AND LIABILITIES OF STATE BANKS, LOAN AND TRUST COMPANIES, SAVINGS AND PRIVATE BANKS, 1908.

Classification.	State Banks. 11,220 Banks.	Loan and Trust Companies. 842 Companies.	Savings Banks. 1,453 Banks.	Private Banks. 1,007 Banks.	Total. 14,522 Banks.
Resources.					
Loans on real estate	$188,352,185	$153,727,485	$1,440,061,503	$19,610,740	$1,801,751,913
Loans on other collateral security	127,270,669	821,341,681	66,624,785	7,521,699	1,022,758,834
Other loans and discounts	2,090,944,681	404,412,308	364,362,059	80,226,816	2,939,945 864
Overdrafts	29,447,901	860,744	1,050,343	1,796,144	33,155,132
United States bonds	2,888,514	555,303	13,860,545	297,157	17,601,519
State, county, and municipal bonds	3,729,479	89,639,659	587,155,390	1,100,443	681,624,971
Railroad bonds and stocks	2,698,260	29,576,312	618,193,415	550,901	651,018,888
Bank stocks	184,385	4,805,843	24,265,271	205,348	29,460,847
Other stocks, bonds and securities	492,935,533	651,298,154	343,465,167	5,821,879	1,493,520,733
Due from other banks and bankers	549,297,603	391,578,223	163,616,708	27,298,378	1,131,785,912
Real estate, furniture and fixtures	136,146,988	97,112,461	57,010,988	6,448,497	296,718,934
Checks and other cash items	71,251,438	5,878,676	779,228	1,529,589	79,438,931
Cash on hand	308,736,342	118,398,874	43,483,533	8,497,540	479,116,289
Other resources	28,754,507	96,452,153	85,604,217	636,349	211,447,226
Total	$4,032,638,485	$2,865,632,876	$3,809,533,152	$161,541,480	10,869,345,993
Liabilities.					
Capital stock	$502,513,303	$278,408,759	$36,013,455	$21,122,836	$838,058,353
Surplus fund	217,112,085	370,145,308	244,711,501	5,556,229	837,525,433
Other undivided profits	86,503,972	45,894,591	39,412,250	3,475,238	175,286,051
Dividends unpaid	682,749	467,115	......	35,160	1,185,024
Individual deposits	2,937,129,598	1,866,964,314	3,479,192,891	126,673,158	8,409,959,961
Due to other banks and bankers	207,432,987	163,014,678	3,187,417	1,561,453	375,196,535
All other liabilities	81,263,791	140,738,111	7,015,338	3,117,396	232,134,636
Total	$4,032,638,485	$2,865,632,876	$3,809,533,152	$161,541,480	$10,869,345,993

STATEMENT SHOWING THE AMOUNTS OF GOLD AND SILVER COINS AND CERTIFICATES, UNITED STATES NOTES, AND NATIONAL BANK NOTES IN CIRCULATION NOVEMBER 2, 1908.

	General Stock Nov. 2, 1908.	In Treasury Nov. 2, 1908.†	Amount in Circulation Nov. 2, 1908.	Amount in Circulation Nov. 1, 1907.
Gold Coin (including bullion in Treas'y)	$1,649,358,744	$188,480,313	$610,060,562	$574,459,086
Gold Certificates*	....	43,571,480	807,246,389	677,295,909
Standard Silver Dollars	563,554,812	21,567	74,740,245	88,822,959
Silver Certificates*	4,893,158	483,899,842	464,349,568	....
Subsidiary Silver	150,935,970	19,272,269	131,663,701	127,461,2[illegible]9
Treasury Notes of 1890	4,705,000	13,775	4,691,225	5,601,926
United States Notes	346,681,016	3,686,960	342,994,056	343,254,153
National Bank Notes	665,844,192	22,642,191	643,202,001	595,123,866
Total	$3,381,079,734	$282,581,713	$3,098,498,021	$2,876,368,696

Population of the United States November 2, 1908, estimated at 87,971,000; circulation per capita, $35.22.

* For redemption of outstanding certificates an exact equivalent in amount of the appropriate kinds of money is held in the Treasury, and is not included in the account of money held as assets of the Government.

† This statement of money held in the Treasury as assets of the Government does not include deposits of public money in National Bank depositaries to the credit of the Treasurer of the United States, amounting to $120,279,145.98.

For a full statement of assets see Public Debt Statement.

BANKING STATISTICS—*Continued.*

BANKING STATISTICS OF EUROPE.

CAPITAL, SPECIE, CIRCULATION, ETC., OF THE PRINCIPAL FOREIGN BANKS, JUNE 30, 1907.
[Expressed in Millions of Dollars.]

EUROPEAN BANKS.	Capital.	Gold.	Silver.	Total Specie.	Circulation.	Deposits and Current Accounts.	Loans.
Imperial Bank of Germany........	28.9	......	......	184.3	456.1	152.4	412.3
Banks of Issue of Germany................	15.8	......	......	16.1	37.5	18.1	47.6
Bank of Austria-Hungary................	41.9	226.6	60.8	......	393.9	......	178.4
National Bank of Belgium................	9.6	......	......	......	141.0	17.5	118.5
National Bank of Bulgaria...	....	5.5	2.0	......	8.6	17.0	11.9
National Bank of Denmark................	....	27.2	......	......	34.9	.8	13.7
Bank of Spain..........................	28.9	77.8	129.0	......	311.0	102.4	198.1
Bank of Finland..........................	1.9	4.9	.3	......	18.2	4.2	11.7
Bank of France..........................	35.2	510.6	190.1	......	916.2	140.2	142.8
National Bank of Greece.................	3.9	......	......	.4	23.1	22.9	21.6
Bank of Italy............................	28.9	......	......	......	224.5	35.0	127.5
Bank of Naples..........................	11.6	29.8	3.0	......	66.6	16.1	3 .5
Bank of Sicily..........................	....	8.6	.4	......	14.8	10.6	10.9
Bank of Norway..........................	3.5	8.0	......	......	21.4	1.9	12.0
Bank of Netherlands.........	....	......	......	......	110.6	2.5	62.0
Bank of Portugal..............	14.6	5.6	5.1	......	74.5	29.3	26.5
National Bank of Roumania...............	2.9	14.6	.4	......	43.1	......	25.2
Imperial Bank of Russia.................	27.5	458.5	30.3	......	582.2	235.6	224.2
National Bank of Servia.................	1.1	2.7	1.9	......	6.6	.6	2.3
Royal Bank of Sweden............	86.5	20.1	10.3	......	52.8	276.3	381.5
Banks of Issue of Switzerland.	44.9	......	......	24.6	46.8	340.0	324.5
Imperial Ottoman Bank...................	24.0	......	......	12.3	6.1	58.0	35.4
Bank of Algiers..........................	....	......	......	12.1	22.9	2.2	26.7
Bank of Japan.........	15.0	10.8	......	41.7	170.8	200.8	83.3
Banks of Mexico	162.6	48.6	17.7	......	117.5	381.5	338.7
Banks of Central and South America......	128.6	......	......	......	29.2	373.0	342.2
United Kingdom (including Colonial and Foreign Joint Stock Banks with London offices)	1,008.9	......	......	......	306.1	7,691.0	6,651.1
Bank of Australasia...........	102.6	......	......	142.3	30.8	674.6	557.7
Bank of Canada	95.7	... .	......	24.1	79.5	650.5	718.3
Total..................................	1,925.1	1,459.9	454.3	457.9	4,347.3	11,455.0	11,161.1

TRANSACTIONS OF THE NEW YORK CLEARING-HOUSE.

YEAR ENDING SEPT. 30.	No. of Banks.	Capital.	Clearings.	Balances Paid in Money.	Average Daily Clearings.	Average Daily Balances Paid in Money.	Balances to Clearings
1893.......	65	$60,922,700	$34,421,380,870	$1,696,207,176	$113,978,082	$5,616,580	4.9
1894.......	66	61.622,700	24,230,145,368	1,585,241,634	79,704,426	5,214,611	6.5
1895.......	67	62,622,700	28,264,379,126	1,896,574,349	92,670,095	6,218,276	6.7
1896.......	66	60,622,700	29,350,894,884	1,843,289,239	96,232,442	6,043,571	6.2
1897.......	66	59,022,700	31,337,760,948	1,908,901,898	103,424,954	6,300,006	6.0
1898.......	65	58,272,700	39,853,413,948	2,338,529,016	131,529,419	7,717,918	5.87
1899.......	64	58,922,700	57,368,230,771	3,085,971,370	189,961,029	10,218,448	5.37
1900.......	64	74,222,700	51,964,588,564	2,730,441,810	170,936,147	8,981,716	5.25
1901.......	62	81,722,700	77,020,672,464	3,515,037,741	254,193,639	11,600,785	4.56
1902.......	60	100,672,700	74,753,189,435	3,377,504,072	245,898,649	11,110,210	4.51
1903.......	57	113,072,700	70,833,655,940	3,315,516,487	233,005,447	10,906,304	4.68
1904.......	54	115,972,700	59,672,796,804	3,105,858,576	195,648,514	10,183,143	5.20
1905.......	54	115,972,700	91,879,318,369	3,953,875,975	302,234,600	13,006,171	4.33
1906.......	55	118,150,000	103,754,100,091	3,832,621,023	342,422,772	12,648,914	3.69
1907.......	53	129,400,000	95,315,421,238	3,813,926,108	313,357,569	12,545,809	4.00
1908......	50	126,350,000	73,630,971,913	3,409,632,271	241,413,022	11,179,122	4.63

EXCHANGES OF CLEARING-HOUSES OF UNITED STATES CITIES.

CLEARING-HOUSE AT—	EXCHANGES FOR YEARS ENDED SEPTEMBER 30—				
	1908.	1907.	1906.	1905.	1904.
New York...	$73,630,971,913	$95,315,421,238	$103,754,100,091	$91,879,318,369	$59,672,796,804
Boston.......	7,096,412,351	8,548,822,227	8,149,377,513	7,469,812,036	6,410,272,150
Chicago	11,425,304,804	12,265,923,407	10,873,546,251	9,821,718,562	8,808,093,268
Philadelp'ia	6,528,291,691	7,508,096,431	7,553,273,999	6,766,147,857	5,491,236,568
St. Louis.....	3,020,989,964	3,180,598,102	2,934,576,620	2,907,886,282	2,682,218,323
San Franc'co	1,711,329,602	2,299,411,061	1,875,314,042	1,753,010,570	1,513,927,257
Baltimore...	1,265,049,236	1,499,394,515	1,432,070,248	1,249,411,909	1,097,603,459
Pittsburgh...	2,190,479,976	2,761,441,799	2,630,996,408	2,431,366,780	1,986,720,497
Cincinnati...	1,202,794,250	1,399,770,100	1,291,921,250	1,192,662,600	1,196,854,400
Kansas City	1,733,550,111	1,605,752,939	1,184,893,262	1,167,294,894	1,096,400,926
New Orleans	815,937,419	1,030,268,162	984,264,235	953,995,496	961,992,245
Minneapolis.	1,077,894,272	1,120,680,545	976,122,113	901,693,286	793,558,708
Detroit.......	667,397,268	726,744,655	650,042,094	575,309,586	516,588,762
Louisville....	562,448,145	670,752,450	640,362,310	594,392,208	539,702,428
Cleveland...	766,518,416	914,658,049	812,973,376	754,739,346	700,078,208
Other cities..	12,543,324,980	13,814,779,578	12,005,495,101	10,083,082,176	8,673,269,979
Total.....	126,238,694,398	154,662,515,258	157,749,328,913	140,501,841,957	102,150,313,982

Clearing-House returns prepared for THE WORLD ALMANAC by Assistant Manager W. J. Gilpin, of New York Clearing-House.

Statistics of Savings Banks.

NUMBER OF DEPOSITORS, AMOUNT OF DEPOSITS, AND AVERAGE TO EACH DEPOSITOR, 1907-1908.

STATES AND TERRITORIES.	Number of Depositors.	Amount of Deposits.	Average to Each Depositor.
Maine	*a* 235,346	$85,502,202	$379.43
N. Hampshire	186,610	81,639,166	437.49
Vermont	159,841	60,493,727	378.46
Massachusetts	1,971,644	706,940,596	358.55
Rhode Island	121,561	66,590,142	547.79
Connecticut	539,873	256,372,062	473.75
N. Eng. States	3,204,875	$1,257,537,895	$392.38
New York	2,719,598	1,378,232,780	506.78
New Jersey	282,014	92,631,487	328.46
Pennsylvania	452,638	160,638,670	354.89
Delaware	31,396	8,830,296	281.25
Maryland	213,524	78,469,584	367.50
Dis. of Columbia	46,871	6,054,480	129.17
East'n States	3,746,041	$1,724,857,297	$460.45
West Virginia	4,858	1,099,489	226.32
North Carolina	*b* 36,492	5,760,337	157.85
South Carolina	*b* 21,698	7,891,789	363.71

STATES AND TERRITORIES.	Number of Depositors.	Amount of Deposits.	Average to Each Depositor.
Florida	*b* 4,209	$844,632	$200.00
S'thern States	67,257	$15,506,247	$231.89
Ohio	99,668	52,930,291	541.10
Indiana	31,393	11,431,050	364.13
Illinois	617,782	181,361,054	293.57
Wisconsin	5,799	1,085,014	187.10
Minnesota	91,718	21,799,456	237.68
Iowa	*b* 364,523	132,748,558	364.17
Middle States.	1,210,853	$402,355,423	$332.28
Nebraska	14,862	2,160,715	145.32
Colorado	*b* 10,775	3,351,285	311.00
West'n States	25,637	$5,512,000	$215.00
Calif'nia (Total)			
Pacific States.	*b* 451,155	254,695,083	564.54
United States.	8,705,848	$3,660,553,945	$420.47

Whole number of banks, 1,453.

No returns for 1904-1905 from the following States, and returns for previous years are given: Alabama, 1893-94; depositors, 2,500; amount of deposits, $102,347. New Mexico, 1894-95; depositors, 217; amount of deposits, $37,951. Washington, 1894-95; depositors, 5,512; amount of deposits, $1,148,104. Oregon, 1895-96; depositors, 1,631; amount of deposits, $972,298. Georgia, 1896-97; depositors, 5,384; amount of deposits, $288,010. Florida, 1899-1900, depositors, 877; amount of deposits, $255,395. Louisiana, 1899-1900, depositors, 10,518; amount of deposits, $3,284,892. Texas, 1899-1900; depositors, 2,986; amount, $584,424. Tennessee, 1900-1901; depositors, 19,823; amount, $3,519,333.

a Oct. 27, 1907. *b* Partially estimated.

SAVINGS BANKS, DEPOSITORS, AND DEPOSITS IN THE UNITED STATES EVERY TEN YEARS FROM 1830 TO 1890 AND ANNUALLY SINCE 1895.

YEAR.	Number of Banks.	Number of Depositors.	Deposits.	YEAR.	Number of Banks.	Number of Depositors.	Deposits.
1830	36	38,085	$6,973,304	1899	942	5,687,818	$2,230,366,954
1840	61	78,701	14,051,520	1900	1,002	6,107,083	2,449,547,885
1850	108	251,354	43,431,130	1901	1,007	6,358,723	2,597,094,580
1860	278	693,870	149,277,504	1902	1,036	6,666,672	2,750,177,290
1870	517	1,630,846	549,874,358	1903	1,078	7,035,228	2,935,204,845
1880	629	2,335,582	819,106,973	1904	1,157	7,305,443	3,060,178,611
1890	921	4,258,893	1,524,844,506	1905	1,237	7,696,229	3,261,236,119
1895	1,017	4,875,519	1,810,597,023	1906	1,319	8,027,192	3,482,137,198
1897	980	5,201,132	1,939,376,035	1907	1,415	8,588,811	3,690,078,945
1898	979	5,385,746	2,065,631,298	1908	1,453	8,705,848	3,660,553,945

The above and following tables were compiled from the report of the Comptroller of the Currency.

NUMBER OF DEPOSITORS AND AMOUNT OF DEPOSITS IN FOREIGN COUNTRIES.
(Latest reports received by the Comptroller of the Currency.)

COUNTRIES.	Date of Reports.	Number of Depositors.	Deposits.	Average Deposit Account.	Average Deposit Per Inhabitant.
Austria	1905-6	5,685,547	$1,086,797,635	$191.15	$39.95
Belgium	1906	2,419,740	156,733,934	64.77	21.65
Bulgaria	1904	124,007	2,723,182	21.95	.68
Chile	1908	198,419	22,876,142	115.29	6.73
Denmark	1906	1,352,490	223,628,544	165.35	86.01
Egypt	1907	74,179	1,928,749	26.00	.17
France	1906	12,462,900	921,150,000	73.91	23.46
Germany	1905	17,947,538	3,016,719,512	168.09	49.88
Hungary	1906	1,632,450	391,666,881	239.93	19.13
Italy	1907	6,953,078	667,645,797	96.02	19.69
Japan	1906-8	14,471,560	99,289,016	6.86	2.01
Luxemburg	1906	57,491	9,372,493	163.03	37.99
Netherlands	1905-6	1,658,985	93,214,669	56.19	16.43
Norway	1906	826,873	108,124,517	130.76	46.59
Roumania	1904	157,099	8,038,960	51.17	1.28
Russia (including Asiatic part)	1908	6,376,996	595,598,312	93.40	4.07
Spain	1907	469,491	53,553,238	114.07	2.74
Sweden	1907	1,988,336	187,233,225	94.17	35.08
Switzerland	1900	1,300,000	193,000,000	148.46	62.26
United Kingdom	1907	12,471,755	1,020,271,823	81.81	23.14
Total Foreign Countries	....	92,520,410	$9,297,682,919	$100.49	$11.55

The Bankruptcy Law.

EXTRACTS FROM THE UNITED STATES BANKRUPTCY ACT OF JULY 1, 1898.

SEC. 4. WHO MAY BECOME BANKRUPTS.—(*a*) Any person who owes debts, except a corporation, shall be entitled to the benefits of this act as a voluntary bankrupt.

(*b*) Any natural person (except a wage-earner or a person engaged chiefly in farming or the tillage of the soil), any unincorporated company, and any corporation engaged principally in manufacturing, trading, printing, publishing, or mercantile pursuits, owing debts to the amount of one thousand dollars or over, may be adjudged an involuntary bankrupt upon default or an impartial trial, and shall be subject to the provisions and entitled to the benefits of this act. Private bankers, but not national banks or banks incorporated under State or Territorial laws, may be adjudged involuntary bankrupts.

SEC. 7. DUTIES OF BANKRUPTS.—(*a*) The bankrupt shall (1) attend the first meeting of his creditors, if directed by the court or a judge thereof to do so, and the hearing upon his application for a discharge, if filed; (2) comply with all lawful orders of the court; (3) examine the correctness of all proofs of claims filed against his estate; (4) execute and deliver such papers as shall be ordered by the court; (5) execute to his trustee transfers of all his property in foreign countries; (6) immediately inform his trustee of any attempt, by his creditors or other persons, to evade the provisions of this act, coming to his knowledge; (7) in case of any person having to his knowledge proved a false claim against his estate, disclose that fact immediately to his trustee; (8) prepare, make oath to, and file in court within ten days, unless further time is granted, after the adjudication if an involuntary bankrupt, and with the petition if a voluntary bankrupt, a schedule of his property, showing the amount and kind of property, the location thereof, its money value in detail, and a list of his creditors, showing their residences, if known (if unknown that fact to be stated), the amount due each of them, the consideration thereof, the security held by them, if any, and a claim for such exemptions as he may be entitled to, all in triplicate, one copy of each for the clerk, one for the referee, and one for the trustee; and (9) when present at the first meeting of his creditors, and at such other times as the court shall order, submit to an examination concerning the conducting of his business, the cause of his bankruptcy, his dealings with his creditors and other persons, the amount, kind, and whereabouts of his property, and, in addition, all matters which may affect the administration and settlement of his estate; but no testimony given by him shall be offered in evidence against him in any criminal proceedings.

Provided, however, that he shall not be required to attend a meeting of his creditors, or at or for an examination at a place more than one hundred and fifty miles distant from his home or principal place of business, or to examine claims except when presented to him, unless ordered by the court, or a judge thereof, for cause shown, and the bankrupt shall be paid his actual expenses from the estate when examined or required to attend at any place other than the city, town, or village of his residence.

FAILURES IN THE UNITED STATES.

	NUMBER.*		LIABILITIES.*		YEARLY FAILURES.		
	1908.	1907.	1908.	1907.	Year.	No.	Liabilities.
					1864....	520	$8,579,000
					1865....	530	17,625,000
MANUFACTURERS.					1866....	1,505	53,783,000
Iron, foundries, and nails..........	56	42	$2,101,173	$4,100,213	1867....	2,780	96,666,000
Machinery and tools..............	199	117	6,640,136	13,109,530	1868....	2,608	63,694,000
Woollens, carpets, and knit goods.	26	17	1,495,213	1,280,747	1869....	2,799	75,054,054
Cottons, lace, and hosiery..........	23	21	639,233	2,153,659	1870....	3,546	88,242,000
Lumber, carpenters, and coopers..	414	282	14,994,299	15,262,140	1871....	2,915	85,252,000
Clothing and millinery............	422	274	3,978,980	3,746,241	1872....	4,069	121,056,000
Hats, gloves, and furs..............	47	27	648,055	312,704	1873....	5,183	228,499,900
Chemicals, drugs, and paints......	58	21	3,489,492	490,269	1874....	5,830	155,239,000
Printing and engraving............	175	120	3,974,940	1,235,863	1875....	7,740	201,000,000
Milling and bakers..................	229	139	10,357,190	1,698,073	1876....	9,092	191,117,000
Leather, shoes, and harness........	70	50	2,223,917	774,700	1877....	8,872	190,669,936
Liquors and tobacco................	110	72	1,857,416	1,863,178	1878....	10,478	234,383,132
Glass, earthenware, and bricks....	119	58	3,119,687	2,007,575	1879....	6,658	98,149,053
All other.	1,015	714	23,620,700	14,749,065	1880....	4,735	65,752,000
					1881....	5,582	81,155,932
Total manufacturing.............	2,963	1,954	$79,140,431	$62,783,957	1882....	6,738	101,547,564
					1883....	9,184	172,874,172
					1884....	10,968	226,343,427
TRADERS.					1885....	10,637	124,220,321
General stores........................	1,401	936	$10,244,836	$6,529,527	1886....	9,834	114,644,119
Groceries, meats, and fish..........	2,130	1,611	14,588,872	5,60_278	1887....	9,634	167,560,944
Hotels and restaurants............	461	298	2,710,618	3,466,634	1888....	10,679	123,829,973
Liquors and tobacco................	834	571	4,234,875	2,301,706	1889....	10,882	148,784,337
Clothing and furnishing............	792	470	6,642,002	4,568,174	1890....	10,907	189,856,964
Dry goods and carpets..............	527	330	5,926,143	3,795,583	1891....	12,273	189,868,638
Shoes, rubbers, and trunks.........	318	176	2,283,659	850,404	1892....	10,344	114,044,167
Furniture and crockery...........	249	161	2,663,899	1,621,371	1893....	15,242	346,779,889
Hardware, stoves, and tools.......	313	221	3,144,354	1,810,196	1894....	13,885	172,992,856
Drugs and paints....................	381	243	2,443,173	1,498,161	1895....	13,197	173,196,060
Jewelry and clocks.................	261	131	4,159,542	1,111,947	1896....	15,088	226,096,834
Books and papers....................	69	55	564,629	301,258	1897....	13,351	154,332,071
Hats, furs, and gloves..............	39	18	506,501	126,701	1898....	12,186	130,662,899
All other............................	974	657	12,697,124	6,306,987	1899....	9,337	90,879,889
					1900....	10,774	138,495,673
Total trading......................	8,749	5,878	$72,810,227	$39,893,927	1901....	11,002	113,092,876
					1902....	11,615	117,476,769
Brokers and transporters...	454	258	27,726,865	13,358,464	1903....	12,069	155,444,185
					1904....	12,199	144,202,311
Total commercial................	12,166	8,090	$179,677,523	$116,036,348	1905....	11,520	102,676,172
					1906....	10,682	119,201,515
Banking............................	147	29	$116,108,661	$12,945,669	1907....	11,725	197,385,225

* Nine months to September 30. Other years calendar years. These statistics were prepared for THE WORLD ALMANAC by R. G. Dun & Co.

Stock List and Prices of Leading Stocks in 1908.

OUTSTANDING STOCK AND BONDED INDEBTEDNESS.

HIGHEST AND LOWEST PRICES ON THE NEW YORK STOCK EXCHANGE IN 1907 AND 1908

STOCKS.	Stock Outstanding.	Bonds Outstanding.	Rate Per Ct. Last Div.	Date Payment Last Dividend Declared.	Highest and Lowest. 1907.		Highest and Lowest. 1908 (b)	
Adams Express	$12,000,000	$36,000,000	4	Dec. 1, 1908	330	150	200	164
Allis-Chalmers	19,820,000	10,456,000	..	....	16⅞	4	14⅞	5
Allis-Chalmers pfd	16,150,000		1¾	Feb. 1, 1904	43¾	14	50	14
Amalgamated Copper (a)	153,887,900	....	50c.	Nov. 30, 1908	121⅞	41¾	88⅜	45⅛
American Agricultural Chemical	17,114,100	....	..	....	25⅝	10	35	13
American Agricultural Chemical pfd	18,382,000		3	Oct. 15, 1908	95	75	96	78½
American Beet Sugar (a)	15,000,000	....	..	....	23½	7¾	24⅞	9½
American Beet Sugar pfd. (a)	4,090,000		1½	Oct. 1, 1908	80	75	80	65
American Can	41,233,300	....	..	....	7½	3	10¼	4
American Can pfd	41,233,300		1¼	Oct. 1, 1908	60½	34	76⅞	44
American Car & Foundry	30,000,000	....	½	Oct. 1, 1908	45⅛	24⅜	47¾	25½
American Car & Foundry pfd	30,000,000	....	1¾	Oct. 1, 1908	103	78	108	84¼
American Cotton Oil	20,237,100	5,000,000	3	Dec. 1, 1908	36½	21	44¾	24¾
American Cotton Oil pfd	10,198,600		3	Dec. 1, 1908	92½	70	97	80
American Express	18,000,000	....	3	Jan. 2, 1909	247	175	210	170
American Hide & Leather	11,274,100	7,194,000	..	....	6¼	2½	6¼	2¾
American Hide & Leather pfd	12,548,300		1	Aug. 15, 1905	30½	9	29¾	12½
American Ice Securities	19,037,700	2,897,080	1¾	July 20, 1907	88	8⅛	31⅞	12½
American Linseed (a)	16,750,000	....	..	....	19¼	6⅜	15	5⅞
American Linseed pfd (a)	16,750,000		1¾	Sept. 15, 1900	36	16½	32	17
American Locomotive	25,000,000	....	1¼	Aug. 26, 1908	75¾	32¼	59⅝	31⅜
American Locomotive pfd.	25,000,000		1¾	Oct. 21, 1908	112	83	110⅞	85½
American Malt Corp	5,896,000	....	..	....	7½	2½	8⅝	3
American Malt Corp. pfd.	8,952,800		2½	Nov. 3, 1908	40	17	51⅛	21
American Smelters Securities pfd B.	30,000,000	....	1¼	Dec. 1, 1908	93⅛	60	84⅛	70
American Smelting & Refining	50,000,000	349,000	1	Oct. 15, 1908	155	58¼	107	55½
American Smelting & Refining pfd.	50,000,000		1¾	Oct. 1, 1908	117⅜	81¾	110⅜	87¾
American Snuff	11,001,700	....	4	Oct. 1, 1908	205	150	200	125
American Snuff pfd	12,000,000		1½	Oct. 1, 1908	102	70	97½	80
American Steel Foundries, new	14,247,400	3,500,000	..	....	..	..	41	28
American Steel Foundries pfd	1,415,800		1	Aug. 1, 1904	47½	20	42⅝	26⅛
American Sugar Refining (a)	45,000,000	....	1¾	Jan. 2, 1909	137½	93¾	137¾	98¾
American Sugar Refining pfd. (a)	45,000,000	....	1¾	Jan. 2, 1909	131¾	103	131	105
American Telephone & Telegraph	180,587,000	153,000,000	2	Oct. 15, 1908	133	89¾	132⅝	101
American Tobacco pfd	78,689,100	107,933,100	1½	Oct. 1, 1908	98⅛	60	97½	72½
American Woollen (a)	29,501,100	....	..	....	36½	12⅛	31⅞	15½
American Woollen pfd. (a)	35,000,000		1¾	Oct. 15, 1908	102⅞	68	97	78¼
Anaconda Copper (a)	30,000,000	....	50c.	Oct. 14, 1908	75⅝	25⅛	53½	27½
Atchison, Topeka & Santa Fé	102,956,500	310,227,550	2½	Dec. 1, 1908	108⅛	66⅝	98⅜	66
Atchison, Topeka & Santa Fé pfd	114,173,730		2½	Aug. 1, 1908	101⅝	78	100⅜	83⅜
Atlantic Coast Line	48,537,600	47,322,000	2½	Jan. 11, 1909	133⅜	58	110¾	59½
Baltimore & Ohio	152,175,829	255,532,430	3	Sept. 1, 1908	122	75⅝	109¾	76½
Baltimore & Ohio pfd	60,000,000		2	Sept. 1, 1908	94½	75	90½	80
Bethlehem Steel	14,862,000	19,146,000	..	....	20½	8	27¼	12
Bethlehem Steel pfd	14,908,000		¾	Feb. 1, 1907	65	23	57	35
Brooklyn Rapid Transit (a)	45,000,000	85,226,000	..	....	83⅝	26¾	57½	88⅜
Brooklyn Union Gas	15,000,000	18,000,000	3	Oct. 1, 1908	125	80	150	85
Buffalo, Rochester & Pittsburgh	10,500,000	21,065,000	2	Aug. 15, 1908	115	68	98	75½
Buffalo, Rochester & Pittsburgh pfd	6,000,000		3	Aug. 15, 1908	139¾	90	105	105
Canada Southern	15,000,000	20,000,000	1¼	Aug. 1, 1908	65¼	52	68	54
Canadian Pacific	121,680,000	40,238,086	3½	Sept. 30, 1908	195¼	138	180⅛	140
Central Leather	38,409,952	34,526,600	..	....	40	11⅞	30⅜	15½
Central Leather pfd	31,061,500		1¾	Oct. 1, 1908	102	68	101¼	75¾
Chesapeake & Ohio	62,799,100	101,781,354	1	Dec. 22, 1908	56	23¼	48¾	25½
Chicago, Burlington & Quincy	110,839,100	183,064,000	2	July 1, 1908	228	200	..	..
Chicago Great Western	44,465,195	....	..	....	18	6⅞	14⅝	3⅛
Chicago Great Western deb	28,127,000	....	..	July 15, 1907	79	46	68¼	33½
Chicago Great Western pfd. "A"	11,336,900	....	2½	Apr. 1, 1907	71¾	21	39	15½
Chicago Great Western pfd. "B"	23,049,606	....	..	....	26⅛	8¼	17⅛	5
Chicago, Milwaukee & St. Paul	83,377,900	122,176,500	3½	Oct. 20, 1908	157½	93½	150	103⅜
Chicago, Milwaukee & St. Paul pfd	49,976,400		3½		165½	130	163	138
Chic., Mil. & St. Paul com., ctfs	......	....	..	....	141	85	144⅞	98
Chic., Mil. & St. Paul pfd., ctfs	......	....	..	....	149	111	160	125⅝
Chicago, Rock Island & Pacific	74,859,600	174,332,000	1¾	Oct. 1, 1908	..	..	..	..
Chicago, St. P., Minn. & Omaha	11,256,800	28,459,000	3½	Aug. 20, 1908	170	106	153	114
Chicago, St. P., Minn. & Omaha pfd	18,556,200		3½	Aug. 20, 1908	165	137½	170	137
Chicago Union Traction	20,000,000	25,993,000	..	....	6¼	1¾	4½	1
Chicago Union Traction pfd	12,000,000		1¼	Oct. 25, 1900	19⅜	3	14¾	4
Chicago & Alton	19,542,800	59,350,000	1	Aug. 15, 1908	27½	8⅛	48	10
Chicago & Alton pfd	20,423,300		2	July 15, 1908	69	48	71	47
Chicago & Northwestern	99,609,600	147,089,000	3½	July 1, 1908	205	126	177	135½
Chicago & Northwestern pfd	22,395,000		2	Oct. 1, 1908	234	183	216	185
Cleveland, Cincinnati, Chic. & St. L.	47,056,300	64,612,727	1	Mar. 2, 1908	92⅞	48	69¾	47½
Cleveland, Cincinnati, Chic. & St. L. pfd.	10,000,000		1¼	Oct. 20, 1908	108⅝	85	100	85⅛

STOCK LIST AND PRICES OF LEADING STOCKS IN 1908—*Continued.*

STOCKS.	Stock Outstanding.	Bonds Outstanding.	Rate Per Ct. Last Div.	Date Payment Last Dividend Declared.	Highest and Lowest, 1907.		Highest and Lowest, 1908.(b)	
Cleveland, Lorain & Wheeling	$8,000,000	$9,893,000	2½	Mar. 2, 1908	90	85	102	100
Cleveland, Lorain & Wheeling pfd	5,000,000		2½	Apr. 1, 1908	115	92	115	115
Cleveland & Pittsburgh	19,521,643	9,782,000	1¾	Dec. 1, 1908	175	160½	172	165
Colorado & Southern	31,000,000		2	Dec, 15, 1908	38⅞	17	48½	21
Colorado & Southern 1st pfd	8,500,000	38,431,207	2	Oct. 1, 1908	69½	41	70¾	50⅜
Colorado & Southern 2d pfd	8,500,000		2	Oct. 1, 1908	58½	29½	64½	39¾
Columbus & Hocking Coal	7,000,000	1,132,000	1½	Oct. 1, 1907	28⅜	14	24	14¾
Consolidated Coal	10,250,000	5,155,000	1½	July 31, 1908	99½	80	90	87½
Consolidated Gas	80,235,000	20,859,100	1	Dec. 15, 1908	140¼	74	159½	96
Corn Products Refining	49,716,100	2,204 000	..	....	24¾	8	20½	10¾
Corn Products Refining pfd	29,774,400		1	Oct. 10, 1908	88	46	80	56
Delaware, Lackawanna & Western	26,200,000	....	12½	Dec. 15, 1908	510	369½	575	420
Delaware & Hudson	42,400,000	43,536,000	2¼	Sept. 15, 1908	227½	123	178¼	141½
Denver & Rio Grande	38,000,000	49,134,500	..	....	42⅞	16	35¼	14¼
Denver & Rio Grande pfd	45,761,400		2½	July 15, 1908	83⅞	53	78	39¼
Des Moines & Fort Dodge	4,283,100	3,672,000	..	....	18	5¼	17	5
Diamond Match	16,000,000	....	2½	Dec. 15, 1908	130	113	..	..
Distillers Securities Company (*a*)	30,726,538	13,990,568	½	Oct. 31, 1908	78	25	38½	27¼
Duluth, South Shore & Atlantic (*a*)	12,000,000	20,000,000			19½	6¼	18¾	6
Duluth, South Shore & Atlantic pfd (*a*)	10,000,000		..	....	39	10	33¾	11¾
Erie	12,378,900		..	....	44½	12¼	36	12
Erie 1st pfd	47,892,400	194,334,900	2	Feb, 28, 1907	75⅞	28	50	24⅜
Erie 2d pfd	16,000,000		2	Apr. 9, 1907	67	20	40½	16
Evansville & Terre Haute pfd	1,284,000	6,627,000	2½	Oct. 15, 1908	93	90	85	79
Federal Mining & Smelting	6,000,000	....	1½	Dec. 16, 1907	163	50	94	72½
Federal Mining & Smelting pfd	12,000,000	....	1¾	Dec. 15, 1908	97	55	89	59
Federal Sugar	6,677,200	....	..	...	62½	42	68½	55
Federal Sugar pfd	3,322,800	....	1½	Nov. 2, 1908	100	76	100	73½
Fort Worth & Denver City (*a*)	9,375,000	8,176,000	1	Oct. 15, 1908	..	...	..	..
General Chemical	7,410,300	....	1	Dec. 1, 1908	75½	50	65	50
General Chemical pfd	11,000,000	....	1½	Oct. 1, 1908	103	82	99½	89
General Electric	65,174,700	14,968,000	2	Jan. 15, 1909	163	89½	158	111
Granby Consol.	13,500,000	....	$2	Dec. 15, 1908	152	60	109½	78¾
Great Northern pfd	209,713,700	....	1¾	Nov. 2, 1908	189¾	107½	141⅝	113¼
Great Northern pfd receipts	60,000,000	....	..	....	130¾	98	126⅜	114
Great Northern tem. ore ctfs (*a*)	....	....	$1	Mar. 16, 1908	85	37	75⅛	48½
Hocking Valley Receipts	1,000,000	19,912,000	2	July 13, 1908	115	63	95	62
Hocking Valley pfd	15,000,000		2	July 13, 1908	94	64	89½	69
Homestake Mining	21,840,000	....	75	Nov. 26, 1908	85	54	96½	67
H. B. Claflin	3,829,100	....	2	Oct. 15, 1908	106	99¾	..	..
Illinois Central	107,348,000	127,638,275	3½	Sept. 1, 1908	172	116	149¾	122¼
Interborough-Metropolitan	93,262,192	67,825,600	...	....	39	4⅞	15½	6¾
Interborough-Metropolitan pfd	45,740,000		1¼	July 1, 1907	75½	14	38¼	17⅛
International Harvester	60,000,000	....	..	....	..	..	67½	52
International Harvester pfd	60,000,000	....	1¾	Dec. 1, 1908	..	..	110¼	99
International Mercantile Marine	49,931,735	72,406,129	..	....	8⅛	4¼	9½	5⅞
International Mercantile Marine pfd	51,730,971	....	..	....	24	10	24	16
International Paper	17,442,800	17,560,000	1	July 1, 1899	18½	7½	13¼	8
International Paper pfd	22,406,700		½	Oct. 15, 1908	81	51	65	47
International Power (*a*)	5,048,000	....	1	Jan. 25, 1906	50¾	35	35	29
International Steam Pump	17,762,500	3,500,000	½	Apr. 1, 1905	41	8	34⅛	13
International Steam Pump pfd	11,350,000		1½	Nov. 2, 1908	81	50	83½	65
Iowa Central	8,524,683	9,720,000	..	....	28⅞	9½	30¾	10
Iowa Central pfd	5,674,771		1½	Mar. 1, 1900	51	29	48¾	27½
Kansas City Southern	30,000,000	30,000,000	..	....	30¾	18	31¾	18
Kansas City Southern pfd	21,000,000		1	Oct. 15, 1908	61¾	48	65½	46
Keokuk & Des Moines	2,600,400	2,750,000	..	....	11	4	10	3¾
Keokuk & Des Moines pfd	1,524,600		1¼	Aug. 1, 1908	37½	37½	26	20
Lake Erie & Western	11,840,000	10,875,090	..	....	28½	11	25	12
Lake Erie & Western pfd	11,840,000		1	Jan. 15, 1908	67½	39¾	55	36
Lake Shore	50,000,000	135,000,000	6	July 29, 1908	300	300	330	274
Long Island	12,000,000	43,168,702	1	Nov. 2, 1896	67½	26	55	28½
Louisville & Nashville	60,000,000	130,116,500	2½	Aug. 10, 1908	145⅛	85½	122¾	87¼
Mackay Companies	41,380,400	....	1	Jan. 1, 1909	75¼	40	77⅛	52
Mackay Companies pfd	50,000,000	....	1	Jan. 1, 1909	71	50	71	59⅞
Manhattan Railway	60,000,000	40,561,000	1¾	Oct. 1, 1908	146	100⅞	146½	120
Maryland Coal pfd	1,885,005	....	2½	June 30, 1908	..	..	90	90
Mergenthaler Linotype	10,996,000	....	2½	Sept. 30, 1908	213	197½	200	191
Metropolitan Street Railway (*a*)	52,000,000	40,854,000	1¾	July 1, 1907	107	23	43	15
Mexican Central	59,127,100	138,584,738	..	....	27⅝	12¾	20½	14½
Michigan Central	18,738,000	26,765,000	3	July 29, 1908	125	125	165	165
Minneapolis, St. Paul & Sault Ste. Marie	16,800,000	55,295,000	3	Oct. 15, 1908	140¼	60	135	79¾
Minneap., St. Paul & Sault Ste. Marie pfd	8,400,000		3½	Oct. 15, 1908	168	110	149½	123½
Minneapolis & St. Louis	6,000,000	19,795,900	2½	Jan. 15, 1904	59	23½	52	20
Minneapolis & St. L. pfd	4,000,000		2½	July 15, 1908	90	62½	85	61
Missouri, Kansas & Texas	63,300,300	76,300,300	..	....	44½	20¾	38¼	17½
Missouri, Kansas & Texas pfd	13,000,000		2	Nov. 10, 1908	72¾	53	71½	46
Missouri Pacific	79,753,985	92,525,000	2½	Jan. 30, 1908	92¾	44⅜	64½	28½
Morris & Essex	15,000,000	30,277,000	3½	July 1, 1908	179	155	184	169

STOCK LIST AND PRICES OF LEADING STOCKS IN 1908—*Continued.*

Stocks.	Stock Outstanding	Bonds Outstanding.	Rate Per Ct. Last Div.	Date Payment Last Dividend Declared.	Highest and Lowest, 1907.		Highest and Lowest, 1908.(b)	
Nashville, Chattanooga & St. Louis	$10,000,000	$16,005,000	2½	Aug. 3, 1908	147	97	120	97¾
National Biscuit (a)	29,236,000	856,424	1¼	Jan. 15, 1909	86¼	58½	92½	68
National Biscuit pfd. (a)	24,804,500		1¾	Nov. 30, 1908	117½	90	120	102
National Lead (a)	20,655,400	....	1¼	Jan. 2, 1909	76¼	33	92	36
National Lead pfd. (a)	24,367,600	....	1¾	Dec. 15, 1908	103	80	106⅜	87½
New Central Coal	1,000,000	....	2	Nov. 2, 1908	25	25	50	30
New Jersey Central	27,436,800	52,851,000	2	Nov. 2, 1908	220	144	211¾	160
New York Air Brake (a)	10,000,000	3,000,000	2	Oct. 22, 1907	141½	47½	98	50
New York Central & Hudson River	178,632,000	230,414,845	1¼	Oct. 15, 1908	134⅞	89	118¼	90⅛
New York, Chicago & St. Louis	14,000,000		..	....	63½	19¾	52¼	24½
New York, Chicago & St. Louis 1st pfd	5,000,000	22,397,000	5	Mar. 2, 1908	110	85	105	85
New York, Chicago & St. Louis 2d pfd	11,000,000		5	Mar. 2, 1908	91¾	41	81½	59⅞
New York Dock	7,000,000	11,800,000	..	....	42	25	30	28
New York Dock pfd	10,000,000		2	Oct. 15, 1908	71	67¼	74⅞	70
New York, Lackawanna & Western	10,000,000	22,000,000	1¼	Oct. 1, 1908	124½	124½	..	..
New York, New Haven & Hartford	97,088,900	36,829,000	2	Sept. 30, 1908	189½	127⅜	161	128⅜
New York, Ontario & Western	58,113,982	23,948,000	2	Aug. 3, 1908	48⅝	28	44⅞	29⅛
New York & Harlem	10,000,000	12,000,000	2	Oct. 1, 1908	365	365	335	335
Norfolk & Western	64,469,200	87,852,500	2	Dec. 18, 1908	92¼	56	84¾	58
Norfolk & Western pfd	22,991,700		2	Aug. 18, 1908	90½	70	87⅜	74
North American	29,793,300	....	1¼	Sept. 2, 1907	89¾	37	77¼	42⅛
Northern Central	19,342,500	6,822,000	4	July 15, 1908	194	157	..	..
Northern Pacific	155,000,000	186,703,376	†1¾	Nov. 2, 1908	189½	100½	157¾	116⅞
Northern Pacific rects, 87½ per cent. paid	....	....	..	....	134	91½	145	103
Ontario Mining	15,000,000	....	30c.	Dec. 20, 1902	8⅝	2⅛	6	2
Pacific Coast	7,000,000		1	Nov. 2, 1908	124⅛	56	93½	65
Pacific Coast 1st pfd	1,525,000	5,000,000	1¼	Nov. 2, 1908	78	65	90	90
Pacific Coast 2d pfd	4,000,000		1	Nov. 2, 1908	124½	80	97	79
Pacific Mail	20,000,000	....	1½	Dec. 1, 1899	41½	19	33½	24
Pennsylvania R. R.	314,594,650	§308,292,610	3	Nov. 30, 1908	141⅜	103½	131½	108¾
Pittsburgh, Cincinnati, Chicago & St. Louis	29,176,864	56,314,000	2	Aug. 15, 1908	78	51	88	59
Pittsburgh, Cincinnati, Chicago & St. L. pfd	27,468,227		2½	July 15, 1908	105½	69½	108¾	81
Pittsburgh Coal	32,000,000	21,180,000	..	....	16⅞	7	14⅜	8½
Pittsburgh Coal pfd	32,000,000		1¾	Apr. 25, 1905	60⅝	37	49⅜	37
Pittsburgh, Ft. Wayne & Chicago	59,759,100	5,565,500	1¾	Oct. 1, 1908	168	163	164¼	164
Pressed Steel Car	12,500,000	1,500,000	1	Aug. 30, 1904	57	15⅝	41	17¼
Pressed Steel Car pfd	12,500,000		1¾	Nov. 26, 1908	100	64	99¾	69½
Pullman	100,000,000	....	2	Nov. 16, 1908	181⅛	135¼	174	147
Quicksilver	5,708,700	....	..	....	1⅛	¾	⅝	½
Quicksilver pfd	4,291,300		½	June 1, 1903	1¾	1⅝	1½	1½
Railway Steel Spring (a)	13,500,000	. .	2	Apr. 22, 1908	57½	21½	46⅜	23¾
Railway Steel Spring pfd. (a)	13,500,000		1¾	Dec. 21, 1908	99½	72	101	75
Reading	70,000,000		2	Aug. 1, 1908	139⅛	70½	141⅜	92⅛
Reading 1st pfd	28,000,000	74,962,000	2	Sept. 10, 1908	92	73	90	78
Reading 2d pfd	49,148,100		2	Nov. 10, 1908	94	67	89½	76
Rensselaer & Saratoga	10,000,000	2,000,000	4	July 1, 1908	205	185	..	..
Republic Iron & Steel	27,191,000	8,496,000	..	....	41¼	12	29	14¾
Republic Iron & Steel pfd	20,416,900		1¾	Apr. 1, 1908	100	60½	89½	63
Rock Island	89,747,200	....	..	....	30⅛	11¼	24	10½
Rock Island pfd	49,148,700	....	1	Nov. 1, 1905	64½	26½	51	20¾
Rome, Watertown & Ogdensburg	10,000,000	9,576,000	1¼	Nov. 15, 1908	125	107	119½	114¼
Rutland pfd	9,057,600	11,570,000	1½	Jan. 15, 1908	35	24½	30	24
St. Joseph & Grand Island	4,600,000		..	....	19	19	18½	13
St. Joseph & Grand Island 1st pfd	5,498,500	4,000,000	2½	July 15, 1902	..	..	53	34
St. Joseph & Grand Island 2d pfd	3,500,000		..	....	..	..	27¾	16
St. Lawrence & Adirondack	1,615,000	1,200,000	5	Dec. 31, 1907	..	..	..	..
St. Louis & San Francisco 1st pfd	5,000,000		1	Nov. 2, 1908	70	58	62	43
St. Louis & San Francisco 2d pfd	16,000,000	134,624,997	1	Dec. 1, 1905	48⅜	24	35	19¼
St. L. & S. F., C. & E. Ill. new stock ctfs	10,445,000		1½	July 1, 1908	71	60	66¾	49
St. Louis Southwestern	16,500,000	46,239,250	..	....	26⅜	11	22	10
St. Louis Southwestern pfd	20,000,000		..	....	62½	25	54⅝	24½
Sloss-Sheffield Steel & Iron	10,000,000	4,000,000	1	Dec. 1, 1908	77¾	26	81¾	36
Sloss-Sheffield Steel & Iron pfd	6,700,000		1¾	Oct. 1, 1908	105	80	109¾	87½
Southern Pacific	197,849,259	39,457,500	1½	Jan. 2, 1909	96¼	63¼	120½	66¼
Southern Pacific pfd	74,866,538		3½	Jan. 15, 1909	118⅛	100	125½	106⅜
Southern	120,000,000		..	....	34	10	26¾	9⅛
Southern pfd	60,000,000	202,349,800	1½	Oct. 17, 1907	94½	29½	61	25½
Southern, Mob. & Ohio tr. ctfs	5,670,200		2	Oct. 1, 1907	97	85	82	60
Tennessee Copper	5,000,000	400,000	*$1.25	Sept. 30, 1908	53½	17	52¼	25½
Texas Pacific Land Trust	6,206,275	....	..	....	85	45	76	45
Texas & Pacific	38,763,810	54,970,000	..	....	37⅛	17½	33	12¾
Third Avenue	16,000,000	40,000,000	1½	July 31, 1907	123	15	47	15½
Toledo, Peoria & Western	4,076,900	4,895,000	..	....	17¼	17¼	..	..
Toledo Railway & Light	13,875,000	13,258,000	1	May 1, 1907	29	9	15¼	6¼
Toledo, St. Louis & Western	10,000,000	28,027,000	..	....	33¾	16	38¾	12
Toledo, St. Louis & Western pfd	10,000,000		2	Oct. 15, 1908	54⅞	30	62½	33
Twin City Rapid Transit	20,100,000	17,900,000	1¼	Nov. 14, 1908	109	68¾	95½	78¼
Twin City Rapid Transit pfd	3,000,000		1¾	Oct. 1, 1908	115	100	124	120

STOCK LIST AND PRICES OF LEADING STOCKS IN 1908—*Continued.*

Stocks.	Stocks Outstanding.	Bonds Outstanding.	Rate Per Ct. Last Div.	Date Payment Last Dividend Declared.	Highest and Lowest, 1907.		Highest and Lowest, 1908.(b)	
Union Bag & Paper	$16,000,000	$2,169,000	..	....	8⅛	4	9¾	4
Union Bag & Paper pfd	11,000,000		1	Oct. 15, 1908	61	39⅝	66¾	44⅞
Union Pacific	195,489,900	225,000,000	2½	Jan. 2, 1909	183	100	184⅞	110½
Union Pacific pfd	99,569,300		2	Oct. 1, 1908	96	75	98	79¼
United Fruit Co	21,303,800	106,000	2	Oct. 15, 1908	120	101½	151½	115
United Railways Investment	19,400,000	18,150,000	..	....	62	10⅛	34¾	15
United Railways Investment pfd	15,000,000		*2½	Jan. 2, 1907	71⅛	20	50	27⅞
United States Cast Iron Pipe	12,106,300	1,194,000	1	Dec. 2, 1907	49½	17	30¼	18⅝
United States Cast Iron Pipe pfd	12,106,300		1¾	Sept. 1, 1908	89	49	78⅞	56⅝
United States Express	10,000,000	....	2	Nov. 16, 1908	117	70	90	70
United States Leather (a)	62,882,300	4,680,000	..	....	12	13	..	..
United States Leather pfd. (a)	62,282,300		1½	Oct. 1, 1908	114	87	118	95
United States Realty & Imp. Co	16,162,800	13,284,000	1	Nov. 2, 1908	90½	36	64	36¼
United States Reduction & Refining (a)	5,918,800	1,879,000	1	July 1, 1903	30¼	5½	15¼	4
United States Reduction & Ref. pfd. (a)	3,945,800		1½	Oct. 1, 1907	68	18¼	39	16
United States Rubber	25,000,000	....	1	Apr. 30, 1900	52½	13½	37½	17½
United States Rubber 1st pfd	36,263,000	....	2	Oct. 31, 1908	109⅞	61¼	106¾	76
United States Rubber 2d pfd	9,965,000	....	1½	Oct. 31, 1908	78⅛	39	75¾	42
United States Steel	508,302,500	601,791,341	½	Dec. 30, 1908	50⅜	21⅞	58¾	25¾
United States Steel pfd	360,281,100		1¾	Nov. 30, 1908	107¾	79⅝	114⅝	87¼
Utah Copper	6,597,500	1,500,000	50c.	Dec. 31, 1908	39½	13	52¾	20
Virginia Iron, Coal & Coke	9,073,680	5,377,000	b5	Oct. 1, 1907	97	31	68	43
Wabash	52,427,673	118,029,000	..	....	18½	8	15⅝	6¾
Wabash pfd	38,427,673		..	....	38½	14⅛	36⅝	13
Wells-Fargo	8,000,000	....	5	July 15, 1908	300	250	325	250
Western Maryland	15,685,400	58,718,000	..	....	30½	6	16	5
Western Union Telegraph	99,550,800	38,615,000	½	Oct. 15, 1908	84½	54	70	41
Westinghouse Electric & Mfg	21,663,000	....	2½	Oct. 10, 1907	154	32	94	38
Westinghouse Electric & Mfg. 1st pfd	3,998,700		2½	Oct. 10, 1907	160	60	125	59½
Wheeling & Lake Erie	20,000,000	15,000,000	..	....	16¾	6	11¾	4½
Wheeling & Lake Erie 1st pfd	4,986,900		..	....	37¾	13	24¼	12⅛
Wheeling & Lake Erie 2d pfd	11,993,500		..	....	21	8	15¾	6
Wisconsin Central	16,147,900	34,450,105	..	....	25⅞	11	31¾	13¼
Wisconsin Central pfd	11,267,100		..	....	51½	28	64	33

(a) Unlisted stocks. (b) Report of prices in 1908 is to December 1.

THE WORLD ALMANAC is indebted to "Bradstreet's" for the stock list and prices of stocks.

American Battle Dates.

The following are the dates of the more important of the conflicts of the French and Indian Wars, the Revolutionary War, and the War of 1812:

FRENCH AND INDIAN WARS.

1754—May 28........Great Meadows, Pa.
1755—July 9.........Braddock's Field.
1755—September 8..Lake George.
1756—August 11.....Oswego, N. Y.
1756—September 8..Kittanning, Pa.
1757—July 6..........Fort William Henry.
1758—July 6..........Ticonderoga.
1758—August 27.....Fort Frontenac.
1758—November 25..Fort Du Quesne.

REVOLUTIONARY WAR.

1775—April 19.......Lexington and Concord.
1775—May 10........Ticonderoga.
1775—June 17........Bunker Hill.
1775—December 31..Quebec.
1776—June 28........Fort Moultrie.
1776—August 27.....Long Island.
1776—October 28.....White Plains, N. Y.
1776—November 16..Fort Washington, N. Y.
1776—December 26..Trenton.
1777—January 3......Princeton.
1777—August 6.......Oriskany.
1777—August 16.....Bennington.
1777—September 11..Brandywine.
1777—September 19..Bemis Heights.
1777—October 4......Germantown.
1777—October 7......Saratoga.
1777—October 17.....Burgoyne's surrender.
1778—June 28........Monmouth.
1778—July 3..........Wyoming massacre.
1778—August 29.....Rhode Island.
1778—December 29..Savannah.
1779—July 15........Stony Point, N. Y.
1779—October 8......Savannah.
1780—May 12.........Charleston captured.
1780—May 29.........Waxhaw.
1780—June 23........Springfield, N. J.
1780—August 16.....Camden, S. C.
1780—October 7......King's Mountain.
1781—January 17.....Cowpens.
1781—March 15......Guilford Court House.
1781—September 8...Eutaw Springs.
1781—October 17.....Yorktown.

WAR OF 1812.

1812—August 16.....Detroit (surrendered).
1812—October 13....Queenstown.
1813—April 27.......York (Toronto).
1813—May 9..........Fort Meigs.
1813—May 27.........Fort George.
1813—October 5......The Thames.
1813—November 11..Chrystler's Field.
1814—July 5..........Chippewa.
1814—July 25........Lundy's Lane.
1814—August 15.....Fort Erie.
1814—August 24.....Bladensburg, Md.
1814—September 11..Plattsburg, N. Y.
1814—September 13..Fort McHenry, Md.
1814—October 19.....Lyons's Creek.
1815—January 8......New Orleans.

United States Post-Office Statistics.

Fiscal Years.	Number of Post-Offices.	Extent of Post Routes in Miles.	Revenue of the Department.	Expenditure of the Department.	Amount Paid for Compensation to Postmasters.	Amount Paid for Transportation of the Mail.
1880......	42,989	343,888	$33,315,479	$36,542,804	$7,701,418	$22,255,984
1881......	44,512	344,006	36,785,398	39,251,736	8,298,743	23,196,032
1882......	46,231	343,618	41,876,410	40,039,635	8,964,677	22,846,112
1883......	47,863	353,166	45,508,693	42,816,700	10,319,441	23,067,323
1884......	50,017	359,530	43,338,127	46,404,960	11,283,831	25,359,816
1885......	51,252	365,251	42,560,844	49,533,150	11,431,305	27,765,124
1886......	53,614	366,667	43,948,423	50,839,435	11,348,178	27,553,239
1887......	55,157	373,142	48,837,610	52,391,678	11,929,481	28,135,769
1888......	57,281	403,977	52,695,176	55,795,358	12,600,186	29,151,168
1889......	58,999	416,159	56,175,611	61,376,847	13,171,382	31,893,359
1890......	62,401	427,991	60,882,097	65,930,717	13,753,096	33,885,978
1891......	64,329	439,027	65,931,786	71,662,463	14,527,000	36,805,621
1892......	67,119	447,591	70,930,475	76,323,762	15,249,565	38,837,236
1893......	68,403	453,832	75,896,933	81,074,104	15,862,621	41,179,054
1894......	69,805	454,746	75,080,479	84,324,414	15,899,709	45,375,359
1895......	70,064	456,026	76,983,128	86,790,172	16,079,508	46,336,326
1896......	70,360	463,313	82,499,208	90,626,296	16,576,674	47,993,067
1897......	71,022	470,032	82,665,462	94,077,242	16,917,621	49,918,193
1898......	73,570	480,462	89,012,618	98,033,523	17,460,621	52,204,382
1899......	75,000	496,948	95,021,384	101,632,160	18,223,506	53,797,752
1900......	76,688	500,982	102,354,579	107,740,268	19,112,097	56,236,196
1901......	76,945	511,808	111,631,193	115,554,920	19,949,514	58,151,210
1902......	76,215	507,540	121,848,047	124,785,697	20,783,919	61,000,441
1903......	74,169	506,268	34,224,443	138,784,488	21,631,724	65,186,715
1904......	71,131	406,818	143,582,624	152,362,117	22,273,344	69,724,853
1905......	68,131	486,805	152,826,585	167,399,169	22,743,342	72,756,392
1906......	65,600	478,711	167,932,782	178,449,778	23,548,988	75,981,551
1907......	62,663	463,406	183,585,005	190,238,288	24,575,696	80,460,767
1908......	61,158	450,738	191,478,663.41	208,351,886.15	25,599,397.52	81,157,720

Of the whole number of post-offices at the close of the fiscal year, June 30, 1908, 6,846 were Presidential offices and 54,312 were fourth class offices.

The number of pieces of postal matter of all kinds which passed through the mails of the United States in the fiscal year was 13,173,340,329. The annual aggregate number of letters transmitted through the post-offices of the world may be estimated at 30,000,000,000, and of newspapers, 15,000,000,000.

DOMESTIC MONEY-ORDERS ISSUED IN 1908.

States and Territories.	Amount.	States and Territories.	Amount.	States and Territories.	Amount.
Alabama	$6,778,836.77	Maine	$5,332,462.71	Porto Rico	$2,361,088.07
Alaska	1,560,742.85	Maryland	3,679,812.06	Rhode Island	2,838,177.17
Arizona	3,059,551.97	Massachusetts	16,548,449.86	South Carolina	3,181,895.11
Arkansas	5,981,658.47	Michigan	20,149,661.16	South Dakota	4,144,808.56
California	28,934,583.81	Minnesota	13,143,312.58	Tennessee	5,235,953.04
Colorado	9,312,393.63	Mississippi	5,640,504.51	Texas	19,665,029.22
Connecticut	6,963,704.36	Missouri	13,669,593.99	Utah	3,402,039.35
Delaware	603,979.12	Montana	5,258,255.98	Vermont	2,728,924.32
District of Columbia	2,130,053.20	Nebraska	8,840,830.50	Virginia	6,057,184.13
Florida	4,345,822.93	Nevada	3,275,511.62	Washington	13,440,543.79
Georgia	7,334,022.53	New Hampshire	2,840,744.41	West Virginia	6,011,391.09
Hawaii	2,140,240.16	New Jersey	8,947,158.21	Wisconsin	14,125,682.73
Idaho	4,225,940.12	New Mexico	1,955,967.29	Wyoming	2,197,314.32
Illinois	29,956,949.61	New York	42,283,196.46		
Indiana	14,566,618.30	North Carolina	4,025,173.32	Tutuila	18,020.96
Indian Territory	3,047,569.55	North Dakota	5,143,189.36	Shanghai U.S. Postal Ag'cy	64,721.69
Iowa	12,718,299.39	Ohio	23,473,536.51	Guam	52,591.02
Kansas	11,273,915.40	Oklahoma	4,749,018.25	Supt. M. O. System	166,423.79
Kentucky	3,950,650.31	Oregon	6,964,598.10		
Louisiana	5,389,195.76	Pennsylvania	41,090,633.14	Total	$486,478,146.65

The number of domestic money-orders issued in the fiscal year 1908 was 65,345,395; number of international money-orders, 3,230,815; amount, $81,502,011.

National Association of Postmasters

OF FIRST CLASS OFFICES.

The National Association of Postmasters of First Class Offices was organized at Detroit, Mich., October 8, 1898.

The Association consists of postmasters and assistant postmasters of the first class post-offices in the United States, and presidents and first vice-presidents of State associations of postmasters. Heads of the Post-Office Department and Chiefs of Bureaus at Washington are honorary members.

Article 3 of the Constitution declares that: "The object of this Association is to aid in the improvement of the Postal Service of the United States through the mutual interchange of ideas of members of the Association and officials of the Post-Office Department."

The annual meetings are attended by the heads of Departments and Chiefs of Bureaus of the Post-Office Department, who address the conventions and answer questions pertaining to the practical work of the post-office.

The following are the officers and executive committee for 1908-09: *President*—Henry Blun, Jr., Savannah, Ga. *First Vice-President*—E. M. Morgan, New York. *Second Vice-President*—F. G. Withoft, Dayton, Ohio. *Third Vice-President*—Edward R. Sizer, Lincoln, Neb. *Fourth Vice-President*—Isador Sobel, Erie, Pa. *Fifth Vice-President*—R. E. Woods, Louisville, Ky. *Treasurer*—D. C. Owen, Milwaukee. *Secretary*—Frank J. Zaiser, Burlington, Iowa.

Postal Statistics of the World.

Countries.	Yr.	Letters and Postal Cards	News-papers.	Other Printed Matter.	Parcels.	Postal Matter of all Kinds.	Number of Post-Offices	Money Orders Issued.	
		Number.	Number.	Pieces.	Number.	Pieces.		Number.	Value.
Argentine Republic	1904	......	......	......	......	450,556,888	2,282	......	......
Austria-Hungary	1904	1,507,243,060	253,727,100	162,972,771	65,506,970	......	12,979	57,834,422	......
Australia	1904	288,782,268	121,011,846	......	......	......	6,595	......	......
Belgium	1905	294,576,265	147,756,316	185,420,949	......	......	1,308	......	......
Brazil	1905	24,730,000	......	*62,845,000	......	......	2,871	......	......
Canada	1905	315,482,000	......	......	......	......	10,879	1,924,130	$32,349,475
Cape of Good Hope	1905	45,792,384	8,470,000	7,452,720	536,800	......	1,043	......	......
Chile	1904	......	......	......	......	68,866,394	1,010	......	......
Denmark	1905	134,341,084	......	111,825,174	......	......	972	......	......
France	1904	1,291,135,000	......	*1,640,344,000	......	......	11,869	......	......
Germany	1905	3,745,274,510	1,715,765,814	1,385,671,180	85,918,680	......	39,052	......	......
Gt. Britain & Ireland	1905	3,507,500,000	1,854,000,000	......	101,700,000	......	23,283	13,596,153	44,612,785
Greece	1904	17,571,000	......	12,794,000	......	......	592	......	......
India—British	1906	665,423,360	40,200,838	43,719,063	4,955,379	......	53,882	......	......
Italy	1904	399,266,000	......	*606,922,000	......	......	8,817	......	......
Japan	1906	972,265,400	200,845,276	23,978,475	13,885,058	......	6,822	......	......
Mexico	1906	......	......	.....	......	184,000,000	2,638	......	......
Netherlands	1905	208,719,799	232,313,000	......	6,206,684	......	....	535,528	......
Norway	1905	82,846,000	69,233,500	9,501,200	1,442,800	......	....	......	......
Portugal	1904	......	......	......	......	91,076,000	3,061	......	......
Russia	1904	790,962,150	367,561,843	134,504,802	8,569,734	......	....	18,643,799	......
Spain	1905	220,532,000	.....	*201,444,000	......	......	3,902	......	......
Sweden	1904	......	......	......	......	387,559,180	3,419	......	......
Switzerland	1905	220,522,701	145,946,953	59,882,484	5,265,192	......	1,677	......	......
Turkey	1904	28,489,000	......	6,888,000	......	......	1,407	......	......
United States	1907	......	......	......	......	12,255,666,367	62,665	62,530,408	486,478,146
Victoria	1905	119,689,073	42,290,841	......	......	......	1,673	......	......
Western Australia	1905	22,106,829	10,074,035	......	......	......	295	......	......

* Including newspapers.

The United States Light-House Establishment.

THE following are the members of the Light-House Board:
Oscar S. Straus, Secretary of Commerce and Labor and *ex-officio* President of the Board.
Rear-Admiral Adolph Marix, U. S. N., Chairman, Washington, D. C.
Col. Walter S. Franklin, Baltimore, Md.
Dr. Henry S. Pritchett, Carnegie Foundation, New York.
Col. Daniel W. Lockwood, Corps of Engineers, U. S. A., New York.
Capt. Samuel P. Comly, U. S. N., Washington, D. C.
Maj. James B. Cavanaugh, Corps of Engineers, U. S. A., Washington, D. C.
Capt. H. T. Mayo, U. S. N., Naval Secretary, Washington, D. C.
Lieut.-Col. Thomas L. Casey, Corps of Engineers, U. S. A., Engineer Secretary, Washington, D. C.

The establishment is divided into sixteen districts, each in charge of an inspector and engineer, the former being navy and the latter army officers. The Board has supervision of all administrative duties relating to the construction and maintenance of light-houses, light-vessels, beacons, fog-signals, buoys, and their appendages, and has charge of all records and property appertaining to the establishment.

The United States Government Printing Office.

The Public Printer has charge of all business relating to the public printing and binding. He appoints the officers and employees of the Government Printing Office, and purchases all necessary machinery and material. The foreman of printing has charge of all matter which is to be printed. His department consists of the following divisions: The document, job, specification, press, folding, stereotype, and Congressional Record rooms, as well as the various branch offices. The Superintendent of Documents has general supervision of the distribution of all public documents, excepting those printed for the use of the two Houses of Congress and the Executive Departments. He is required to prepare a comprehensive index of public documents and consolidated index of Congressional documents, and is authorized to sell at cost any public document in his charge the distribution of which is not specifically directed. The following are the official heads of the several departments: Public Printer, Samuel B. Donnelly; Secretary to the Public Printer, William J. Dow; Attorney, Frank E. Elder; Deputy Public Printer, Henry T. Brian; Congressional Clerk, William A. Smith; Superintendent of Work, John R. Berg; Superintendent of Documents, William L. Post.

United States Secret Service.

The Secret Service Division of the Treasury Department is under the direction of John E. Wilkie, chief of the division. The service is principally engaged in detecting and prosecuting makers and dealers in counterfeit paper money and coin, although its operations include the detection of all violations of the laws of the United States. Details are also furnished for the protection of the President of the United States, and in the frequent journeyings of the present President he is always accompanied by one or more secret service men.

The arrests of counterfeiters number about 400 annually; other arrests are for bribery, impersonating United States Government officers, perjury, and violating Sections 5,392, 5,414, 5,415, 5,424, 5,432, 5,438, 5,440, 5,459 and 5,479 of the United States Revised Statutes.

Building and Loan Associations.

THE following statistics of local Building and Loan Associations in the United States were reported at the last annual meeting of the United States League of Local Building and Loan-Associations, held at New Orleans, February 28-2 , 1908. The returns are for 1907-08:

STATES.	No. of Associations.	Total Membership.	Total Assets.	STATES.	No. of Associations.	Total Membership.	Total Assets.
Pennsylvania	1,400	374,950	$146,915,600	Kansas	48	16,343	$5,118,842
Ohio	644	321,780	132,714,147	Iowa †	56	15,950	4,577,214
New Jersey	415	143,886	67,802,407	Wisconsin	52	12,200	4,490,486
Illinois	502	100,680	50,074,144	West Virginia	39	10,495	3,834,544
Massachusetts	135	114,705	47,220,074	Maine	35	9,345	3,676,453
New York	240	107,450	37,633,163	Tennessee	15	4,658	2,590,204
Indiana	334	117,974	34,040,117	New Hampshire	16	7,110	1,915,187
California	110	33,565	19,522,896	Connecticut	13	4,731	1,804,857
Michigan	55	39,958	14,157,529	Minnesota †	18	,085	1,433,990
Nebraska	66	39,898	11,422,890	North Dakota	7	2,200	1,286,681
Louisiana	50	25,437	10,328,307	Other States	975	292,625	114,753,275
Missouri	118	20,625	8,839,903				
North Carolina	81	21,469	5,355,536	Total	5,424	1,839,119	$731,508,446

The following was the statement of receipts and expenditures by local associations in 1906:

Receipts: Weekly dues, $176,941,728; paid-up stock, $15,697,056; deposits, $44,070,000; loans repaid, $143,264,112; interest, $39,692,832; premium, $2,652,336; fines, $477,312; pass books and initiation, $748,512; borrowed money, $51,153,744; real estate sold, $6,286,416; miscellaneous receipts, $12,581,696; total, $518,409,648.

Disbursements: Pass book loans, $12,882,000; mortgage loans, $209,925,072; stock withdrawals, $145,254,720; paid-up stock withdrawals, $19,336,560; deposit withdrawals, $37,539,504; expenses, $5,239,584; borrowed money, $49,352,976; interest, $1,312,608; real estate purchased, $2,533,008; miscellaneous, $12,995,904; cash on hand, January 1st, 1908, $22,037,712; total, $518,404,648.

The officers of the League, elected at the annual meeting of 1908, are as follows: President, W. G. Weeks, New Iberia, La.; First Vice-President, B. H. Jones, Boston, Mass.; Second Vice-President, Jay W. Sutton, Sault Ste. Marie, Mich.; Third Vice-President, James M. McKay, Youngstown, O. Treasurer, Joseph K. Gamble, Philadelphia, Pa.; Secretary, H. F. Cellarius, Cincinnati, Ohio; Assistant Secretary, Addison B. Burk, Philadelphia, Pa.

In 1893 there were 240 national building and loan associations in the United States, with total assets of $37,020,366. Since that date this class of associations has greatly decreased in numbers. On Jan. 1, 1908, they were approximately 35 in number, with estimated assets of $14,500,000.

Production of Coal.

AREA OF THE WORLD'S COAL-FIELDS, IN SQUARE MILES.

CHINA and Japan, 200,000; United States, 194,000; India, 35,000; Russia, 27,000; Great Britain, 9,000; Germany, 3,600; France, 1,800; Belgium, Spain, and other countries, 1,400. Total, 471,800.

The coal-fields of China, Japan, Great Britain, Germany, Russia, and India contain apparently 303,000,000,000 tons, which is enough for 450 years at present rate of consumption. If to the above be added the coal-fields in the United States, Canada, and other countries, the supply will be found ample for 1,000 years. Improved machinery has greatly increased the yield per miner, and thus produced a fall in price to the advantage of all industries.

The production of the principal countries in 1907 in metric tons of 2,205 pounds was: United States 430,430,183; United Kingdom, 267,828,276; Germany, (*a*) 205,342,688; Austria-Hungary, (*a*) 39,876,511; France, 37,022,556; Belgium, 23,824,499; Russia, 17,800,000; Japan, 12,890,000; Australasia, 10,534,000; India, 10,694,891; Canada, 10,510,961; Spain, (*a*) 3,250,000; Sweden, 305,308; So. Africa, (*b*) 3,945,043; Italy, (*a*)(*b*) 225,000; all other countries, (*b*) 3,475,780; total, partly estimated, 1,078,155,696 metric tons. (*a*) Including lignite. (*b*) Estimated.

COAL PRODUCTION IN THE UNITED STATES 1907 (TONS OF 2,000 POUNDS).

STATES.	Tons.	Value at Mine.		STATES.	Tons.	Value at Mine.	
		Total.	Per Ton.			Total.	Per Ton.
Bituminous.				*Bituminous.*			
Alabama	14,417,863	$19,608,294	$1.36	Tennessee	6,760,017	$8,179,621	$1.21
Arkansas	1,930,400	2,606,040	1.35	Texas	1,300,000	2,080,000	1.60
California	29,800	50,660	1.70	Utah	1,967,621	3,364,632	1.71
Colorado	10,920,527	15,179,533	1.39	Virginia	4,570,341	8,244,614	1.80
Georgia and N. Carol.	365,300	423,748	1.16	Washington	3,713,824	7,427,648	2.00
Illinois	*a* 51,317,146	54,396,175	1.06	West Virginia	47,205,965	46,733,905	.99
Indiana	11,692,072	12,276,676	1.05	Wyoming	6,218,859	10,883,003	1.75
Indian Territory (*f*)	3,450,000	6,486,000	1.88	Alaska and Nevada	15,500	60,450	3.90
Iowa	(*f*) 7,568,424	11,882,426	1.57				
Kansas	6,137,040	9,328,301	1.52	Total bituminous	388,222,868	$463,654,776	$1.20
Kentucky	10,207,060	11,431,907	1.12				
Maryland	5,529,663	6,617,354	1.20	*Anthracite.*			
Michigan	(*b*) 1,898,446	3,758,928	1.98	Colorado	45,113	$145,264	$3.22
Missouri	4,350,000	6,916,500	1.59	New Mexico	17,000	64,600	3.80
Montana	1,810,000	3,348,500	1.85	Pennsylvania	86,279,719	198,443,354	2.30
New Mexico (*f*)	(*f*) 2,302,062	3,729,340	1.62				
North Dakota	268,300	563,430	2.10	Total anthracite	86,341,832	$198,653,218	$2.30
Ohio	32,465,949	35,712,244	1.10				
Oregon	51,600	141,900	2.75	Total Coal } Sh. Tons	474,564,700	$662,307,994	$1.40
Pennsylvania	149,759,089	172,222,952	1.15	Total Coal } Metric Tons	430,430,183	......	1.54

(*a*) Figures reported by the U. S. Geological Survey. (*b*) For the 12 months ending Nov. 30, 1907. (*c*) Estimated. (*f*) Fiscal year ending June 30. Imports of coal into the United States for the calendar year 1907 amounted to 2,116,122 short tons, of which 9,896 tons were classed as anthracite.

Production of Crude Petroleum in the United States.

Year Ending June 30	Production.*		Exportation Mineral Refined, or Manufactured.†				Total. (Including Residuum.‡)	
	Barrels (of 42 gallons).	Gallons.	Mineral, Crude. Gallons.	Naphthas, Benzine, Gasoline. Gallons.	Illuminating. Gallons.	Lubricating (Heavy Paraffine, etc.) Gallons.	Gallons.	Value.
1894	48,412,666	2,033,331,972	121,926,849	15,555,754	730,368,626	40,190,577	908,252,314	$41,499,806
1895	49,344,516	2,072,469,622	111,285,264	14,801,224	714,859,144	43,418,942	884,502,082	46,660,082
1896	52,892,276	2,221,475,592	110,923,620	12,349,319	716,455,565	50,525,520	890,458,994	62,383,403
1897	60,960,361	2,560,335,162	131,726,243	14,249,028	771,350,626	50,199,345	973,514,946	62,635,037
1898	60,475,516	2,539,971,672	113,297,397	16,252,929	824,426,581	60,299,365	1,034,249,876	56,125,578
1899	55,364,233	2,325,297,786	114,088,060	16,252,785	722,279,480	67,424,393	999,713,706	56,273,168
1900	57,070,850	2,396,975,700	133,023,656	21,988,093	721,027,637	74,583,769	967,252,341	75,611,750
1901	63,363,929	2,661,284,933	138,445,430	17,834,254	781,207,105	71,457,605	1,034,643,890	71,112,788
1902	69,389,194	2,914,346,148	133,536,800	23,498,479	842,829,070	76,035,611	1,106,208,470	72,302,822
1903	88,290,725	3,728,210,472	134,892,170	13,149,228	699,810,892	93,314,566	941,699,749	67,253,533
1904	100,461,337	4,219,376,154	114,573,946	16,910,071	741,567,086	88,809,242	984,424,767	79,060,469
1905	117,090,772	4,917,812,456	123,059,010	30,816,655	823,021,953	97,487,196	1,123,334,584	79,793,222
1906	134,717,572	5,658,138,360	139,688,615	32,756,694	864,361,210	146,110,702	1,257,949,042	84,041,327
1907	126,493,936	5,312,745,312	128,175,737	26,357,054	894,529,432	136,140,226	1,185,202,449	84,855,715

* Production is for calendar year preceding the fiscal year. † Export statistics for the fiscal years ending June 30. ‡ Residuum—tar, pitch, and all other from which the light bodies have been distilled. In 1898 this amounted to 19,973,604 gallons, in 1899 to 30,668,988 gallons, in 1900 to 16,629,186 gallons, in 1901 to 25,696,596 gallons, in 1902 to 30,309,510 gallons, in 1903 to 21,715,720 gallons, in 1904 to 22,560,570 gallons, in 1905 to 75,031,821 gallons, in 1906 to 65,228,009 gallons.

The above is compiled from the Report of the Bureau of Statistics of the Treasury Department.

Over 262,000,000 barrels (of 42 gallons) of petroleum, according to the office of the Geological Survey, are now produced annually in the world. Of this amount 166,000,000 barrels are produced in the United States, 61,000,000 in Russia, and the remainder is distributed among a dozen countries, Austria producing 8,300,000; Sumatra, Java and Borneo, 8,700,000; Roumania, 8,100,000; Canada, 780,000; Germany, 756,000.

Production of Copper, Tin, and Zinc.

THE production of copper in the world in 1907, stated in metric tons of 2204.6 lbs., was as follows: United States, 398,736; Spain and Portugal, 50,470; Chile, 27,112; Japan, 49,718; Germany, 20,818; Mexico, 61,127; Australasia, 41,910; South Africa, 6,838; Canada, 21,022; other localities, 46,056; total of the world, 723,807.

The copper production of the United States in 1907 was distributed as follows (figures are in tons of 2,000 lbs.): Alaska, 3,305; Arizona, 128,433; California, 17,199.4; Colorado, 6,672; Idaho, 5,735.5; Michigan, 110,158.5; Montana, 113,145.4; New Mexico, 4,326.4; Utah, 34,166.5; Wyoming, 1,459.5; Southern States, 11,204.3; other States, 3,814.3; total productions, 439,620.8.

The production of tin in the world in 1907, in long tons, was: England, 4,406.6; Straits Settlements, 55,660; Banka and Billiton, 13,493; Australasia, 6,612; Bolivia, 15,500; United States, none; total of the world, 99,965.

The production of zinc in the world in 1907, in metric tons, was as follows: Austria, 11,359; Belgium, 152,370; France, (c) 49,733; Germany, 208,195; Holland, 14,990; Italy, (d); Russia, 9,738; Spain, (c) 6,000; United Kingdom, 55,595; United States, 226,398; total of the world, 736,500

(c) An approximate separation of the total which is reported for France and Spain. (d) Included in Austria.

The statistics of Production of Coal, Copper, Tin and Zinc, and those of Pig Iron and Steel, which follow, were compiled for THE WORLD ALMANAC by "The Mineral Industry" and the "Engineering and Mining Journal."

Production of Pig Iron and Steel

IN PRINCIPAL COUNTRIES IN METRIC TONS.

Year.	Austria-Hungary.		Belgium.		Canada.	France.		Germany.	
	Pig Iron.	Steel.	Pig Iron.	Steel.	Pig Iron.	Pig Iron.	Steel.	Pig Iron.	Steel.
1902......	1,335,000	1,443,900	1,102,910	776,875	325,075	2,427,427	1,635,300	8,402,660	7,780,682
1903......	1,355,000	1,146,000	1,299,211	981,740	269,665	2,827,668	1,854,620	10,085,634	8,801,515
1904......	1,369,500	1,195,000	1,307,399	1,069,880	274,777	2,999,787	2,080,354	10,103,941	8,930,291
1905......	1,372,300	1,188,000	1,310,290	1,023,000	475,491	3,077,000	2,110,000	10,987,623	10,066,553
1906......	1,403,500	1,195,000	1,431,160	1,440,860	550,618	3,319,032	2,371,377	12,478,067	11,135,085
1907......	1,405,000	1,195,500	1,406,980	1,466,710	590,444	3,588,949	2,677,805	13,045,760	12,063,632

Year.	Italy.		Russia.		Spain.		Sweden.	
	Pig Iron.	Steel.	Pig Iron.	Steel.	Pig Iron.	Steel.	Pig Iron.	Steel.
1902............	24,500	119,500	2,597,435	2,183,409	330,747	163,564	524,400	283,500
1903............	28,250	116,000	2,486,610	2,410,938	380,284	199,642	506,825	317,107
1904............	27,600	113,800	2,978,325	2,811,948	375,250	196,000	528,525	333,522
1905............	31,300	117,800	2,125,000	1,650,000	383,100	237,864	531,200	340,000
1906............	30,450	109,000	2,350,000	1,763,000	387,500	251,600	552,250	397,525
1907............	32,000	115,000	2,768,220	2,076,000	385,000	247,100	615,778	420,216

Year.	United Kingdom.		United States.		All Other Countries.		Totals.	
	Pig Iron.	Steel.	Pig Iron.	Steel.	Pig Iron.*	Steel.* †	Pig Iron.	Steel.
1902............	8,653,976	5,102,420	18,003,448	15,186,406	615,000	596,950	44,342,579	34,972,487
1903............	8,952,183	5,114,647	18,297,400	14,756,691	625,000	599,514	47,113,730	36,298,414
1904............	8,699,661	5,107,309	16,760,986	13,746,051	633,000	566,165	46,058,751	36,150,320
1905............	9,746,221	5,983,691	23,340,258	20,354,291	655,000	426,000	54,054,783	43,900,648
1906............	10,346,802	6,565,670	25,706,882	23,772,506	650,000	420,000	59,207,761	49,421,623
1907............	10,276,109	6,627,112	26,193,863	23,733,391	625,000	405,000	60,932,108	51,027,466

* Estimated. † Not including Canada, which in 1905 produced 403,449 tons; in 1906, 515,200 tons; and in 1907, 516,300 tons.

Mineral Products of the United States.

ORES AND MINERALS.

PRODUCTS.	Measures.	1906. Quantity.	1906. Value.	1907. Quantity.	1907. Value.
Antimony ore	Sh. T.	295	$44,250	210	$28,432
Asbestos	Sh. T.	1,695	20,565	950	11,700
Asphaltum (*u*)	Sh. T.	116,653	1,066,019	223,861	2,826,489
Barytes	Sh. T.	63,486	252,719	65,579	251,308
Bauxite	L. T.	78,331	352,490	(*u*) 97,776	(*u*) 480,330
Borax	Sh. T.	58,173	1,182,410	......	......
Chrome ore	L. T.	180	1,800	335	5,620
Coal, anthracite	Sh. T.	72,209,566	166,307,002	86,341,832	193,653,218
Coal, bituminous	Sh. T.	341,612,837	401,717,090	388,222,868	463,654,776
Diatomaceous earth (*u*)	Sh. T.	8,099	72,108	......	104,406
Emery	Sh. T.	2,147	22,780	(*u*) 1,069	(*u*) 12,294
Feldspar (*u*)	Sh. T.	72,656	401,531	92,799	558,944
Flint	Sh. T.	(*u*) 66,697	*u*) 243,012	75,561	407,699
Fluorspar	Sh. T.	34,683	201,481	36,350	202,736
Fuller's earth	Sh. T.	28,000	237,950	34,039	323,275
Garnet	Sh. T.	5,404	179,548	6,723	209,895
Graphite, amorphous (*u*)	Sh. T.	16,853	102,175	26,962	138,381
Graphite, crystalline	Lb.	4,894,483	170,866	4,586,149	149,548
Gypsum (*u*)	Sh. T.	1,540,585	3,837,975	1,751,748	4,942,264
Iron ore	L. T.	49,237,129	107,091,574	52,955,070	117,560,255
Limestone flux	L. T.	15,486,139	7,339,125	15,722,801	7,480,121
Magnesite	Sh. T.	(*e*) 4,000	240,000	......	......
Manganese ore (*u*) (*d*)	L. T.	6,921	88,132	5,604	63,369
Mica, sheet (*u*)	Lb.	1,423,100	252,248	1,060,182	349,311
Mica, scrap (*u*)	Sh. T.	1,489	22,742	3,025	42,800
Monazite (*u*)	Lb.	846,175	152,812	547,948	65,754
Petroleum, crude	Bbl. (*i*)	131,771,505	80,277,279	164,347,930	123,260,948
Phosphate rock	L. T.	2,052,742	8,464,535	2,251,459	10,450,522
Pumice (*u*)	Sh. T.	12,200	16,750	8,112	33,818
Pyrites	L. T.	225,045	767,866	261,871	851,346
Quartz, crystalline (*u*)	Sh. T.	24,082	121,671	22,977	157,094
Salt (*u*)	Bbl. (*k*)	28,172,380	6,658,350	29,704,128	7,439,551
Sand, glass	Sh. T.	1,089,430	1,208,788	1,187,296	1,250,067
Slate, roofing (*u*)	Squares (*f*)	......	5,668,346	1,277,554	4,817,769
Sulphur	L. T.	294,000	6,247,500	307,806	6,427,025
Talc, common (*u*)	Sh. T.	58,972	874,356	......	......
Talc, fibrous	Sh. T.	64,200	541,600	59,000	501,500
Tin ore	Sh. T.	10	3,044	63	15,209
Tungsten ore	Sh. T.	1,096	442,784	1,468	715,031
Whetstones and Oilstones (*u*)	......	......	268,070	......	264,188
Zinc ore	Sh. T.	905,175	17,250,420	902,923	......
Total enumerated	......	......	$820,411,263	......	*$949,706,993

* Does not include the value of zinc ore, the figures for which are not available.

SECONDARY MINERALS AND CHEMICALS.

PRODUCTS.	Measures.	1906. Quantity.	1906. Value.	1907. Quantity.	1907. Value.
Alundum	Lb.	4,331,233	$303,186	6,751,444	$405,086
Ammonium sulphate	Sh. T.	75,000	4,674,750	89,000	5,511,770
Arsenic	Lb.	1,663,000	83,150	2,020,000	101,000
Bromine	Lb.	1,229,000	184,350	1,062,000	138,060
Calcium chloride	Sh. T.	(*w*)	......	45,000	450,000
Carborundum	Lb.	6,225,280	435,770	7,532,670	451,960
Cement, nat. hyd (*u*)	Bbl. (*g*)	3,935,151	2,362,140	2,887,700	1,467,302
Cement, Portland (*u*)	Bbl. (*h*)	46,610,822	51,240,652	48,785,390	53,992,551
Cement, slag (*u*)	Bbl. (*t*)	481,224	412,912	557,252	443,998
Coke	Sh. T.	33,333,039	88,582,079	36,993,622	99,055,150
Copper sulphate (*c*)	Lb.	50,925,932	3,157,408	44,867,650	2,804,228
Copperas	Sh. T.	22,839	228,390	26,771	294,481
Crushed steel	Lb.	837,000	58,590	840,000	58,800
Graphite, artificial	Lb.	4,868,000	312,764	6,924,000	483,717
Lead, white	Sh. T.	123,640	15,234,297	111,409	12,254,990
Lead, sublimed white	Sh. T.	7,988	798,880	8,700	1,026,600
Lead, red	Sh. T.	13,693	1,874,448	13,370	1,778,717
Lead, orange mineral	Sh. T.	2,927	421,488	815	123,917
Litharge	Sh. T.	13,816	1,890,050	14,769	1,624,553
Mineral wool	Sh. T.	5,357	55,550	9,008	81,769
Zinc oxide (*m*)	Sh. T.	77,800	6,257,361	85,390	7,731,100
Total	......	......	$178,568,215	......	$190,279,749

MINERAL PRODUCTS OF THE UNITED STATES—*Continued.*

METALS.

Products.	Measures.	1906.		1907.	
		Quantity.	Value.	Quantity.	Value.
Aluminum	Lb.	14,350,000	$5,166,000	26,000,000	$10,920,000
Antimony	Lb.	5,916,000	1,283,772	5,794,000	859,830
Copper	Lb.	917,620,000	180,000,339	879,241,766	181,660,141
Ferromanganese (*q*)	L. T.	305,642	16,810,310	339,348	21,887,946
Gold (fine)	Troy oz.	4,565,333	94,373,800	4,314,742	89,191,726
Iron (pig)	L. T.	25,001,549	480,279,756	25,442,013	580,077,896
Lead	Sh. T.	345,529	39,093,151	350,130	37,288,845
Nickel (*s*)	Sh. T.	7,150	6,360,640	8,750	7,875,000
Platinum	Troy oz.	(*e*)400	8,800	....	....
Quicksilver	Flasks.(*o*)	28,293	1,157,184	20,932	780,506
Silver (fine)	Troy oz.	56,517,900	37,748,757	58,850,550	38,445,181
Tin (*u*)	Sh. T.	(*w*)	....	(*v*)1,662	914,404
Zinc	Sh. T.	225,494	27,961,256	249,612	29,763,735
Total metals	......	......	$890,243,765	......	$999,665,210
Total ores and minerals	......	......	820,411,263	......	*949,706,993
Secondary products	......	......	178,568,215	......	190,279,749
Grand total enumerated	......	......	$1,889,223,243	......	$2,139,651,952

*Not including the value of zinc ore.

(*c*) Includes sulphate made from metallic copper. (*d*) Does not include manganiferous iron ore. (*e*) Estimated. (*f*) One "square" covers 100 square feet. (*g*) Barrels of 265 lbs. (*h*) Barrels of 380 lbs. (*i*) Barrels of 42 gallons. (*k*) Includes salt used in manufacture of alkali; the barrel of salt weighs 280 lbs. (*m*) Includes a small quantity made from spelter. (*o*) Flasks of 75 lbs. (*q*) Includes spiegeleisen, although the value is given as for ferromanganese. (*s*) Includes nickel from Canadian ores smelted in the United States. (*t*) Barrels of 330 lbs. (*u*) Figures reported by the United States Geological Survey. (*v*) Recovered from scrap metal. (*w*) Statistics not collected.

The foregoing statistics of "Mineral Products of the United States" were compiled by the New York periodical, "The Mineral Industry," and "The Engineering and Mining Journal."

Production of Tobacco.

RETURNS FOR 1906 TO THE DEPARTMENT OF AGRICULTURE.

States.	Product.	Acreage.	Farm Value.	States.	Product.	Acreage.	Farm Value.
	Pounds.	Acres.			Pounds.	Acres.	
Kentucky	252,300,000	290,000	$19,427,100	Maryland	17,724,000	29,540	$17,724,000
Ohio	74,200,000	70,000	8,533,000	Indiana	10,980,000	12,000	10,980,000
Virginia	73,555,425	108,971	6,031,545	New York	8,842,500	7,074	1,220,265
North Carolina	69,807,640	120,358	6,980,764	Massachusetts	8,246,000	4,712	1,525,510
Wisconsin	49,725,000	39,000	6,712,875	Other States	21,814,565	29,829	3,919,164
Pennsylvania	35,750,000	26,000	4,897,750				
Tennessee	34,069,000	43,400	2,555,175				
Connecticut	24,532,900	14,140	4,415,922	Total U.S.	682,428,560	796,099	$68,232,647

The imports of tobacco, fiscal year 1907, were 39,540,321 pounds, valued at $26,055,248. Of these importations 20,333,264 pounds, valued at $13,527,863, were from Cuba. The exports were 340,742,864 pounds, valued at $33,377,398.

STATISTICS OF TOBACCO-GROWING COUNTRIES.

Countries.	Year.	Production.	Total Consumption.	Total Revenue (Customs and Excise).	Per Capita Consumption.	Per Capita Tax.	Tax per Pound Consumed.
		Pounds.	Pounds.	Dollars.	Pounds.	Dollars.	Cents
United States	1904	660,461,000	440,000,000	65,832,102	5.40	0.80	15.0
Germany	1903-4	72,911,000	201,783,000	16,567,000	3.44	.28	8.2
Russia	1902	232,767,000	150,244,000	21,254,000	1.10	.18	16.1
France	1902	54,610,000	84,393,000	81,063,000	2.16	2.08	96.1
United Kingdom	1904	....	83,378,000	63,806,000	1.95	1.49	76.5
Austria	1902	15,895,000	78,755,000	27,443,000 44,633,000	3.02	1.04 1.69	34.9 56.7
Hungary	1903	134,567,000	47,905,000	14,264,000 22,484,000	2.42	.72 1.14	29.8 47.0

Production of other countries in pounds in 1904: Cuba, 45,748,000; Brazil, 55,000,000; Belgium, 13,983,000; British India, 441,000; Java, 49,100,000; Sumatra, 46,500,000; Japan, 105,853,000; Turkey, 90,000,000; Philippines, 33,100,000. Total world, 2,046,817,000.

Reciprocity Treaties and Agreements.

(List of reciprocity treaties between the United States and foreign countries since 1850)

Countries with Which Reciprocity Treaties and Agreements Have Been Made.	Signed.	Took Effect.	Terminated.
British North American Possessions (treaty)	June 5, 1854	March 16, 1855	March 17, 1866.
Hawaiian Islands (treaty)	January 30, 1875	September 9, 1876	April 30, 1900.
Brazil (agreement)	January 31, 1891	April 1, 1891	
Santo Domingo (agreement)	June 4, 1891	September 1, 1891	
Great Britain:			
Barbados (agreement)	February 1, 1892	February 1, 1892	
Jamaica (agreement)	February 1, 1892	February 1, 1892	
Leeward Islands (agreement)	February 1, 1892	February 1, 1892	
Trinidad (including Tobago) (agreement)	February 1, 1892	February 1, 1892	
Windward Islands (excepting Grenada) (agreement)	February 1, 1892	February 1, 1892	August 27, 1894.
British Guiana (agreement)	February 1, 1892	April 1, 1892	
Salvador (agreement)	December 30, 1891	February 1, 1892 (provisional)	
Nicaragua (agreement)	March 11, 1892	March 12, 1892	
Honduras (agreement)	April 29, 1892	May 25, 1892 (provisional)	
Guatemala (agreement)	December 30, 1891	May 30, 1892	
Spain, for Cuba and Porto Rico (agreement)	June 16, 1891	September 1, 1891 (provisional)	
Austria-Hungary (agreement)	May 25, 1892	May 26, 1892	
France (agreement)	May 28, 1898	June 1, 1898	Still in force.
Germany (agreement)	January 30, 1892	February 1, 1892	August 24, 1894.
Portugal and Azores and Madeira Islands (agreement)	May 22, 1900	June 12, 1900	Still in force.
Italy (agreement)	February 8, 1900	July 18, 1900	Still in force.
Switzerland (treaty of 1850)	....	June 1, 1898	March 23, 1900.
Switzerland	....	January 1, 1906	Still in force.
Cuba (agreement)	December 17, 1903	December 27, 1903	Still in force.
Spain (agreement)	August 27, 1906	September 1, 1906	Still in force.
Bulgaria (agreement)	September 15, 1906	September 15, 1906	Still in force.
Germany (ageeement)	April 22, 1907	July 1, 1907	Still in force.
Great Britain	November 19, 1907	December 5, 1907	Still in force.
France (additional articles)	January 28, 1908	January 28, 1908	Still in force.
Netherlands	May 16, 1907	August 12, 1908	Still in force.

Additional list of Reciprocity treaties—Argentine Republic, took effect April 9, 1855. Bolivia, took effect January 8, 1863. China, took effect January 13, 1904. Costa Rica, took effect May 26, 1852. Hayti, took effect July 6, 1865. Japan, took effect March 21, 1895. Liberia, took effect March 18, 1863. Paraguay, took effect March 12, 1860. Servia, took effect December 27, 1882. All the above treaties are still in force.

The treaty with Cuba, which went into operation December 27, 1903, gives a reduction of 20 per cent. duty on all dutiable articles from Cuba entering the United States, and a reduction ranging from 20 to 40 per cent. on articles from the United States entering Cuba.

Arbitration Treaties.

The United States Senate, Sixtieth Congress, ratified twelve arbitration Conventions, the countries being Denmark, France, Great Britain, Italy, Japan, Mexico, Netherlands, Norway, Portugal, Spain, Sweden and Switzerland. An arbitration treaty between China and the United States was signed at the State Department, Washington, October 8, 1908, and an arbitration treaty between Peru and the United States, December 5th.

The Senate on January 28, 1905, ratified a treaty with Guatemala, San Salvador, Peru and Honduras providing for the submission to arbitration at the Permanent Court of the Hague of "all claims for pecuniary loss or damage which may be presented by their respective citizens and which cannot be amicably adjusted through diplomatic channels, and when said claims are of sufficient importance to warrant the expenses of arbitration," the treaty to remain in force five years from the date of its ratification by the last signatory government (the United States).

The Monroe Doctrine.

"The Monroe doctrine" was enunciated in the following words in President Monroe's message to Congress December 2, 1823:

"In the discussions to which this interest has given rise, and in the arrangements by which they may terminate, the occasion has been deemed proper for asserting, as a principle in which rights and interests of the United States are involved, that the American continents, by the free and independent condition which they have assumed and maintain, are henceforth not to be considered as subjects for future colonization by any European power. * * * We owe it, therefore, to candor and to the amicable relations existing between the United States and those powers to declare that we should consider any attempt on their part to extend their system to any portion of this hemisphere as dangerous to our peace and safety. With the existing colonies or dependencies of any European power we have not interfered and shall not interfere. But with the governments who have declared their independence and maintain it, and whose independence we have, on great consideration and on just principles, acknowledged, we could not view any interposition for the purpose of oppressing them or controlling in any other manner their destiny by any European power in any other light than as the manifestation of an unfriendly disposition toward the United States."

Secretary of State Olney in his despatch of July 20, 1895, on the Venezuelan Boundary Dispute, said:

"It (the Monroe doctrine) does not establish any general protectorate by the United States over other American States. It does not relieve any American State from its obligations as fixed by international law, nor prevent any European power directly interested from enforcing such obligations or from inflicting merited punishment for the breach of them."

President Roosevelt in a speech in 1902 upon the results of the Spanish-American war, said:

"The Monroe doctrine is simply a statement of our very firm belief that the nations now existing on this continent must be left to work out their own destinies among themselves, and that this continent is no longer to be regarded as the colonizing ground of any European power. The one power on the continent that can make the power effective is, of course, ourselves; for in the world as it is, a nation which advances a given doctrine, likely to interfere in any way with other nations, must possess the power to back it up, if it wishes the doctrine to be respected."

Grain Statistics.

GRAIN PRODUCTION OF THE UNITED STATES.

UNITED STATES Census reports of the production of the principal cereals in the several census years to 1890, with the reports of the Department of Agriculture for 1892-1907.

YEARS.	Indian Corn.	Wheat.	Oats.	Barley.	Rye.	Buckwheat.
	Bushels.	Bushels.	Bushels.	Bushels.	Bushels.	Bushels.
1870	760,944,549	287,745,626	282,107,157	29,761,305	16,918,795	9,821,721
1880	1,754,861,535	459,479,503	407,858,900	44,113,495	19,831,595	11,817,327
1890	1,489,970,000	399,262,000	523,621,000	67,168,344	25,807,472	12,432,831
1892	1,628,464,000	515,949,000	661,035,000	80,096,762	27,978,824	12,143,185
1893	1,619,496,131	396,131,725	638,854,850	69,869,495	26,555,446	12,132,311
1894	1,212,770,052	460,267,416	662,086,928	61,400,465	26,727,615	12,668,200
1895	2,151,139,000	467,103,000	824,444,000	87,373,000	27,210,000	15,341,000
1896	2,283,875,000	427,684,000	707,346,000	69,695,000	24,369,000	14,090,000
1897	1,902,967,933	530,149,168	698,737,809	66,685,127	27,363,324	14,997,451
1898	1,924,185,000	675,149,000	730,905,000	55,792,000	25,657,000	11,722,000
1899	2,078,143,933	547,303,846	796,177,713	73,381,563	23,961,741	11,094,471
1900	2,105,102,516	522,229,505	809,125,989	58,925,833	23,995,927	9,566,966
1901	1,522,519,891	748,460,218	736,808,724	109,932,924	30,344,830	15,125,939
1902	2,523,648,312	670,063,008	987,842,712	134,954,023	33,630,592	14,529,770
1903	2,244,176,925	637,821,835	784,094,199	131,861,391	29,363,416	14,243,644
1904	2,467,480,934	552,399,517	894,595,552	130,748,958	27,241,515	15,008,336
1905	2,707,993,540	692,979,489	953,216,197	136,651,020	28,485,952	14,585,082
1906	2,927,416,091	735,260,970	964,904,522	178,916,484	33,374,833	14,641,937
1907	2,592,320,000	634,087,000	754,443,000	153,597,000	31,566,000	14,290,000

Indications of crops for 1908 in bushels: Indian corn, 2,642,687,000; wheat, 660,020,000; oats, 789,161,000; barley, 167,482,000; rye, 30,921,000; buckwheat, 15,648,000.

THE WHEAT CROP OF THE WORLD, IN BUSHELS, 1907.*

COUNTRIES.	Bushels.	COUNTRIES.	Bushels.	COUNTRIES.	Bushels.
United States	634,087,000	Spain	100,331,000	Australasia	73,967,000
Canada	96,606,000	France	369,970,000	Mexico	10,000,000
Argentina	155,993,000	Germany	127,843,000	Russia in Asia	56,000,000
Chile	15,776,000	Belgium	12,000,000	Turkey in Asia	35,000,000
Austria	52,069,000	Great Britain	56,950,000	Croatia-Slavonia	10,200,000
Hungary proper	120,508,000	Portugal	6,000,000	Servia	8,375,000
Roumania	42,237,000	Russia in Europe	455,000,000	Japan	22,932,000
Turkey in Europe	16,000,000	British India	315,386,000	Other countries	64,633,000
Bulgaria	30,000,000	Egypt	12,000,000		
Italy	177,543,000	Algeria	31,120,000	The world	3,108,526,000

* Report of the United States Department of Agriculture.

The rye crop of principal countries in 1907 was (in bushels): United States, 31,566,000; Germany, 384,150,000; Austria-Hungary, 129,234,000; Russia in Europe, 776,000,000; France, 58,578,000; Sweden, 21,597,000; the world, 1,545,621,000.

The barley crop of the world in 1907 (in bushels) was 1,267,814,000; oats crop, 3,582,041,000.

PRICES OF WHEAT (CHICAGO MARKET), 1863-1908.*

YEARS.	Months of Lowest Price.	Yearly Range of Prices.	Months of Highest Price.	YEARS.	Months of Lowest Price.	Yearly Range of Prices.	Months of Highest Price.
1863	August	80 @1.12½	December.	1886	October	69⅜@ 84¾	January.
1864	March	1.07 @2.26	June.	1887	August	66⅝@ 94¾	June.
1865	December	85 @1.55	January.	1888	April	71⅛@2.00	September. †
1866	February	77 @2.03	November.	1889	June	75½@1.08¾	February.
1867	August	1.55 @2.85	May.	1890	February	74¼@1.08¼	August.
1868	November	1.04½@2.20	July.	1891	July	85 @1.16	April.
1869	December	76½@1.46	August.	1892	October	69⅛@ 91¾	February.
1870	April	73¼@1.31½	July. [Sept.	1893	July	54⅜@ 88	April.
1871	August	99½@1.32	Feb., April, and	1894	Septe'ber	50 @ 65¼	April.
1872	November	1.01 @1.61	August.	1895	January	48¾@ 85⅜	May.
1873	September	89 @1.46	July.	1896	June	53⅝@ 94⅜	November.
1874	October	81½@1.28	April.	1897	April	64⅛@1.09	December.
1875	February	83¼@1.30½	August.	1898	October	62 @1.85	May. ‡
1876	July	83 @1.26¾	December.	1899	December	64 @ 79½	May.
1877	August	1.01½@1.76½	May.	1900	January	61½@ 87½	June.
1878	October	77 @1.14	April.	1901	July	63⅛@ 79½	December.
1879	January	81⅝@1.33½	December.	1902	October	67½@ 95	September.
1880	August	86½@1.32	January.	1903	March	70¼@ 93	September.
1881	January	95⅜@1.43¼	October.	1904	January	81¼@1.22	October.
1882	December	91⅛@1.40	April and May.	1905	August	77⅞@1.24	February.
1883	October	90 @1.13½	June.	1906	Aug.-Sep.	69⅛@ 94¾	April.
1884	December	69½@ 96	February.	1907	January	71 @1.05¼	October.
1885	March	73⅜@ 91¾	April.	1908	July	84½@1.11	May.

* No. 2 cash wheat. † The Hutchinson "corner" figure; $1.04⅛@1.05¼ the following day. ‡ The Leiter "corner" figure.

The above table was compiled by Charles B. Murray, editor of the Cincinnati *Price Current.*

Principal Cereal Crops in the United States.

PRODUCTION BY STATES IN 1907. (Preliminary Estimate.)

(Compiled from the Annual Report of the Department of Agriculture.)

States and Territories.	Oats, Bushels.	Corn, Bushels.	Wheat, Bushels.	States and Territories.	Oats, Bushels.	Corn, Bushels.	Wheat, Bushels.
Maine	4,266,000	444,000	210,000	Kansas	16,380,000	155,142,000	65,609,000
NewH'mpshire	423,000	910,000	......	Kentucky	3,379,000	93,060,000	8,808,000
Vermont	2,652,000	1,980,000	23,000	Tennessee	3,058,000	78,364,000	7,400,000
Massachusetts	245,000	1,584,000	......	Alabama	3,850,000	45,896,000	890,000
Rhode Island	59,000	312,000	......	Mississippi	1,611,000	42,500,000	22,000
Connecticut	315,000	1,848,000	......	Louisiana	406,000	28,000,000	......
New York	37,086,000	16,200,000	7,197,000	Texas	9,500,000	155,589,000	2,812,000
New Jersey	1,770,000	8,757,000	1,998,000	Oklahoma	6,270,000	113,265,000	8,631,000
Pennsylvania	29,689,000	45,922,000	30,095,000	Arkansas	3,412,000	43,430,000	1,463,000
Delaware	120,000	5,308,000	2,460,000	Montana	11,760,000	90,000	4,003,000
Maryland	825,000	22,196,000	14,763,000	Wyoming	2,220,000	75,000	855,000
Virginia	2,862,000	46,025,000	8,188,000	Colorado	5,890,000	2,608,000	8,497,000
West Virginia	1,834,000	21,280,000	4,477,000	New Mexico	462,000	1,218,000	1,104,000
North Carolina	2,995,000	45,078,000	5,320,000	Arizona	116,000	300,000	388,000
South Carolina	3,900,000	29,807,000	2,669,000	Utah	2,025,000	280,000	4,637,000
Georgia	5,010,000	57,538,000	2,673,000	Nevada	301,000	......	960,000
Florida	411,000	7,017,000	......	Idaho	5,706,000	150,000	8,639,000
Ohio	36,480,000	117,640,000	30,677,000	Washington	10,545,000	324,000	35,045,000
Indiana	36,683,000	168,840,000	34,013,000	Oregon	9,765,000	440,000	15,265,000
Illinois	101,675,000	342,756,000	40,104,000	California	4,556,000	1,836,000	20,520,000
Michigan	30,534,000	57,190,000	12,731,000				
Wisconsin	51,700,000	46,688,000	2,955,000	Total bushels	754,443,000	2,592,320,000	634,087,000
Minnesota	61,985,000	43,605,000	67,600,000	Total acres	31,837,000	99,931,000	45,211,000
Iowa	108,900,000	270,220,000	7,653,000	Total Farm			
Missouri	14,254,000	241,025,000	29,212,000	Value, Dec. 1.	$334,568,000	$1,336,901,000	$554,437,000
North Dakota	32,340,000	3,080,000	55,130,000	Yield per acre.	23.7	25.9	14.0
South Dakota	32,728,000	47,175,000	32,480,000	Farm price	44.3	51.6	87.4
Nebraska	51,490,000	179,328,000	45,911,000				

Farm Productions in the United States.

Crop.	Year.	Unit of Measure	Quantity.	Value.	Crop.	Year.	Unit of Measure	Quantity.	Value.
Animals	1907	Number	204,131,992	$4,423,697,853	Molasses	Census.	Gallons	6,312,809	$788,990
Apples	Census.	Bush...	175,397,600	(a)	Nursery prod'ts.	Census.	....	......	10,123,873
Apricots	Census.	Bush...	2,642,128	(a)	Nuts (f)	Census.	....	......	1,949,931
Beans, Castor	Census.	Bush...	143,388	134,084	Onions	Census.	Bush...	11,790,974	6,637,413
Beans, Dry	Census.	Bush...	5,064,490	7,633,636	Orchard prod'ts.	Census.	Bush...	212,365,600	(g) 83,750,961
Bees	Census.	Swarms	4,109,626	10,186,513	Peaches & Nect.	Census.	Bush...	15,432,603	(a)
Broom Corn	Census.	Pounds.	90,947,370	3,588,414	Peanuts	Census.	Bush...	11,964,109	7,270,515
Butter	1905	Pounds.	531,478,141	113,189,452	Pears	Census.	Bush...	6,625,417	(a)
Cereals (b) (l)	1906	Bush...	4,854,514,837	h2,065,886,900	Peas, dry	Census.	Bush...	9,440,210	7,903,966
Cheese	1905	Pounds.	317,144,872	28,611,760	Plums & Prunes	Census.	Bush...	8,764,032	(a)
Chicory	Census.	Pounds.	21,495,870	73,627	Potatoes, Irish	1907	Bush...	207,942,000	183,880,000
Cider	Census.	Barrels.	1,754,927	(a)	Potatoes, Sweet	Census.	Bush...	42,517,412	19,869,840
Cotton	1907	Pounds.	5,302,940,000	551,506,696	Rice [cleaned]	1907	Pounds.	18,738,000	16,081,000
Cotton Seed	1905	Tons...	5,060,205	(c) 75,564,041	Seeds, Clover	Census.	Bush...	1,349,209	5,359,578
Flaxseed	1907	Bush...	25,851,000	24,713,000	Seeds, Flax	Census.	Bush...	19,979,492	19,624,901
Flowers, Plants.	Census.	....	......	18,758,864	Seeds, Grass	Census.	Bush...	3,515,869	2,868,839
Forest products.	Census.	....	......	109,864,774	Sugar, Beet	1906	Pounds.	967,223,040	(k) 23,895,781
Fruits, small	Census.	....	......	25,029,757	Sugar, Cane	1906	Pounds.	544,320,000	(k) 28,804,608
" sub-trop'l	Census.	....	......	8,227,838	Sugar, Maple	Census.	Pounds.	11,928,770	1,074,260
Grapes	Census.	Cental..	13,009,841	(d) 14,090,234	Syrup, Cane	Census.	Gallons	12,293,032	4,293,475
Hay	1907	Tons...	63,677,000	743,507,000	Syrup, Maple	Census.	Gallons	2,056,611	1,562,451
Hemp	Census.	Pounds.	11,750,630	546,338	Syrup, Sorghum	Census.	Gallons	16,972,783	5,288,083
Honey (e)	Census.	Pounds.	62,862,885	6,656,611	Tobacco	1907	Pounds.	608,125,000	76,234,000
Hops	Census.	Pounds.	49,209,704	4,081,929	Vegetables, Mis.	Census.	....	......	113,644,398
Milk (i)	Census.	Gallons	7,265,804,304	.....	Wool	1906	Pounds.	298,915,130	129,410,942

(a) Included in orchard products. (b) Not including rice. (c) Based on average price paid by crushers. (d) Including value of raisins, wine, etc. (e) Including wax. (f) Not including peanuts. (g) Including value of cider, vinegar, etc. (i) $472,276,783, was the aggregate value of milk, butter and cheese by the Census of 1900. (k) Value of product in 1905, based on the export value of refined. (l) Estimated 1907 corn crop 2,553,732,000 bushels.

The Census of 1900 gave the following farm statistics for the United States: Farms, total number, 5,739,657; value of farm property, $20,514,001,838; land and improvements, $13,114,492,056; buildings, $3,660,198,191; implements and machinery, $761,261,550; live stock, $3,078,050,041; expenditures in 1899 for labor, $365,305,921; for fertilizers, $54,783,757; number of farms operated by owners, 3,713,371; by cash tenants, 752,920; by share tenants, 1,273,366; by white persons, 4,970,129; by negroes, 746,717. Value of farm products in 1907, estimated by Commissioner of Agriculture, $7,412,000,000.

DOMESTIC ANIMALS IN THE UNITED STATES. CENSUS OF 1900.

Domestic Animals.	Total.		On Farms and Ranges.		Not on Farms or Ranges.	
	Number.	Value.	Number.	Value.	Number.	Est. Value.
All domestic animals	....	$3,193,856,459	....	$2,979,197,586	....	$214,658,873
Neat cattle, cows, bulls, &c.	69,335,832	$1,516,307,270	67,719,410	$1,475,204,633	1,616,422	$41,102,637
Horses and colts	21,203,901	1,050,526,967	18,267,020	896,513,217	2,936,881	154,013,750
Mules	3,438,523	207,274,557	3,264,615	196,222,053	173,908	11,052,504
Asses and burros	110,012	6,776,583	94,165	5,811,184	15,847	965,399
Sheep and lambs	61,735,014	170,881,743	61,503,713	170,203,119	231,301	678,624
Swine	64,686,155	238,686,872	62,868,041	231,978,031	1,818,114	6,708,841
Goats	1,948,952	3,402,467	1,870,599	3,265,349	78,353	137,118

1908: Number of horses, 19,992,000; mules, 3,869,000; milch cows, 21,194,000; other cattle, 50,073,000.

The Cotton Supply.

CROP OF THE UNITED STATES FOR SEVENTY-EIGHT YEARS.

THE following statements are furnished by the New York "Commercial and Financial Chronicle:"

YEAR.	Bales.	YEAR.	Bales.	YEAR.	Bales.	YEAR.	Bales.
1830	976,845	1849	2,728,596	1871	4,352,317	1890	7,313,726
1831	1,038,848	1850	2,096,706	1872	2,974,351	1891	8,655,518
1832	987,487	1851	2,355,257	1873	3,930,508	1892	9,038,707
1833	1,070,438	1852	3,015,029	1874	4,170,388	1893	6,717,142
1834	1,205,324	1853	3,262,882	1875	3,832,991	1894	7,527,211
1835	1,254,328	1854	2,930,027	1876	4,669,288	1895	9,892,766
1836	1,360,752	1855	2,847,339	1877	4,485,423	1896	7,162,473
1837	1,422,930	1856	3,527,845	1878	4,811,265	1897	8,714,011
1838	1,801,497	1857	2,939,519	1879	5,073,531	1898	11,180,960
1839	1,360,532	1858	3,113,962	1880	5,757,397	1899	11,235,383
1840	2,177,835	1859	3,851,481	1881	6,589,329	1900	9,439,559
1841	1,634,945	1860	4,669,770	1882	5,435,845	1901	10,425,141
1842	1,683,574	1861	3,656,006	1883	6,992,234	1902	10,701,453
1843	2,378,875	1862-1865	No record	1884	5,714,052	1903	10,758,326
1844	2,030,409	1866	2,193,987	1885	5,669,021	1904	10,123,686
1845	2,394,503	1867	2,019,774	1886	6,550,215	1905	13,556,841
1846	2,100,537	1868	2,593,993	1887	6,513,624	1906	11,319,860
1847	1,778,651	1869	2,439,039	1888	7,017,707	1907	13,550,760
1848	2,347,634	1870	3,154,946	1889	6,935,082	1908	11,581,829

The returns are for the years ending September 1. The average net weight, per bale, for 1908 is 487 pounds.

EXPORTS AND DOMESTIC CONSUMPTION OF AMERICAN COTTON.

	1907-1908.	1906-07.	1905-1906.	1904-1905.	1903-1904.	1902-1903.	1901-1902.	1900-1901.
	Bales.	Bales.	Bales.	Bales.	Bales.	Bales.	Bales.	Bales.
Export to Europe	7,275,973	8,144,301	6,448,430	8,333,556	5,941,602	6,482,849	6,440,787	6,415,477
Consumption, United States, Canada, etc.	4,677,988	5,578,677	5,120,273	4,963,348	4,257,369	4,471,305	4,539,018	4,071,030
Total	11,953,961	13,722,978	11,568,703	13,296,904	10,198,971	10,954,154	10,979,805	10,486,507

COTTON CONSUMPTION OF THE WORLD.

CONSUMPTION, BALES, 500 LBS.	Great Britain.	Continent.	United States.	India.	All Others.	Total World.
1890-91	3,384,000	3,631,000	2,367,000	924,000	195,000	10,511,000
1891-92	3,181,000	3,640,000	2,576,000	914,000	275,000	10,586,000
1892-93	2,866,000	3,692,000	2,551,000	918,000	395,000	10,422,000
1893-94	3,233,000	3,848,000	2,264,000	959,000	297,000	10,601,000
1894-95	3,250,050	4,030,000	2,743,000	1,074,000	446,000	11,543,000
1895-96	3,276,050	4,160,000	2,572,000	1,105,000	492,000	11,605,000
1896-97	3,224,000	4,368,000	2,738,000	1,004,000	546,000	11,880,000
1897-98	3,432,000	4,628,000	2,962,000	1,141,000	725,000	12,888,000
1898-99	3,519,000	4,784,000	3,553,000	1,314,000	845,000	14,015,000
1899-1900	3,334,000	4,576,000	3,856,000	1,139,000	868,000	13,773,000
1900-1901	3,269,000	4,576,000	3,727,000	1,060,000	784,000	13,416,000
1901-1902	3,253,000	4,836,000	4,037,000	1,384,000	905,000	14,415,000
1902-1903	3,185,000	5,148,000	4,015,000	1,364,000	766,000	14,478,000
1903-1904	3,017,000	5,148,000	3,909,000	1,368,000	869,000	14,311,000
1904-1905	3,620,000	5,148,000	4,310,000	1,474,000	990,000	15,542,000
1905-1906	3,774,000	5,252,000	4,726,000	1,586,000	1,047,000	16,385,000
1906-1907	3,892,000	5,460,000	4,950,000	1,552,000	1,078,000	16,932,000
1907-1908	3,690,000	5,720,000	4,227,000	1,500,000	992,000	16,129,000

SOURCES OF COTTON SUPPLY, 1907-1908.

The following shows the actual requirements in 1907-1908 and the estimate of Ellison & Co. for 1908-1909:

	1907-1908.	1906-1907.	1905-1906.	1904-1905.	1903-1904.
	Total Actual Bales.	Total Actual Bales.	Total Actual Bales.	Total Actual Bales.	Total Actual Bales.
America	12,117,000	12,432,000	11,967,000	11,768,000	10,273,000
East Indies	1,068,000	1,299,000	1,288,000	872,000	1,300,000
Other countries	876,000	1,292,000	1,274,000	1,020,000	1,063,000
Total	14,307,000	15,023,000	14,529,000	13,660,000	12,636,000
Average weight	488.8	489.3	484.3	495.2	485.1
Bales of 500 lbs	13,987,000	14,702,000	14,072,000	13,528,000	12,259,000

SPINDLES IN OPERATION.

	1908.	1907.	1906.	1905.	1904.	1903.
Great Britain	54,600,000	52,000,000	50,000,000	48,500,000	47,500,000	47,100,000
Continent	37,000,000	35,800,000	35,500,000	35,000,000	34,600,000	34,300,000
United States	26,752,000	25,924,000	24,781,000	24,073,000	23,214,000	22,240,000
East Indies	5,400,000	5,400,000	5,200,000	5,250,000	5,200,000	5,100,000
Total	123,752,000	119,124,000	115,481,000	112,823,000	110,514,000	108,740,000

THE COTTON CROP OF THE UNITED STATES BY STATES.

States.	1901-02.	1902-03.	1903-04.	1904-05.	1905-06.	1906-07	1907-1908.
	Bales.	Bales.	Bales.	Bales.	Bales.	Bales.	Bales
North Carolina.....	426,000	504,000	490,000	728,000	711,000	644,000	675,000
South Carolina.....	948,000	955,000	845,000	1,160,000	1,140,000	941,000	1,205,000
Georgia	1,493,000	1,498,000	1,405,000	1,955,000	1,900,000	1,728,000	1,920,000
Florida.	56,000	60,000	55,000	90,000	82,000	66,000	62,000
Alabama	1,287,000	1,065,000	1,040,000	1,470,000	1,374,000	1,332,000	1,202,000
Mississippi..........	1,460,000	1,418,000	1,385,000	1,730,000	1,275,000	1,548,000	1,495,000
Louisiana....	851,000	864,000	832,000	1,110,000	595,000	980,000	700,000
Texas.	2,682,000	2,575,000	2,446,000	3,235,000	2,525,000	4,073,000	2,309,000
Arkansas...........	771,000	938,000	855,000	915,000	640,000	915,000	775,000
Tennessee...........	229,000	303,000	255,000	320,000	300,000	317,000	290,000
All others..	498,000	578,000	516,000	864,000	778,000	1,007,000	949,000
Total crop.. . ..	10,701,000	10,758,000	10,124,000	13,557,000	11,320,000	13,551,000	11,582,000

HIGHEST AND LOWEST PRICES

IN NEW YORK FOR MIDDLING UPLANDS COTTON FROM JANUARY 1 TO DECEMBER 31 OF THE YEARS NAMED.

Year.	Highest.	Lowest.	Year.	Highest.	Lowest.	Year.	Highest.	Lowest.	Year.	Highest.	Lowest.
1835....	25	15	1870....	25¾	15	1883....	11⅛	10	1896....	8⅞	7 1-16
1840....	10	8	1871....	21¼	14¾	1884....	11 15-16	9¾	1897....	8¼	5 13-16
1850....	14	11	1872....	27⅞	18⅝	1885 ...	11½	9 3-16	1898....	6 9-16	5 5-16
1860....	11⅝	10	1873....	21⅜	13⅝	1886....	9 9-16	8 13-16	1899...	7 13-16	5⅞
1861....	38	11½	1874....	18⅞	14¾	1887....	11 7-16	9 7-16	1900....	11	7 9-16
1862....	69½	20	1875....	17⅛	13 1-16	1888....	11⅜	9⅝	1901....	12	7 13-16
1863....	93	51	1876....	13⅝	10⅞	1889....	11½	9¾	1902....	9⅞	8 3-16
1864 ...	190	72	1877....	13 5-16	10 15-16	1890....	12¾	9 3-16	1903....	14.10	8.85
1865....	120	35	1878....	13 3-16	8 13-16	1891....	9½	7¾	1904....	17.25	6.85
1866....	52	32	1879....	13¾	9¼	1892....	10	6 11-16	1905....	12.60	7.00
1867....	36	15½	1880....	13¼	10 15-16	1893....	9 15-16	7¼	1906....	12.25	9.60
1868....	33	16	1881....	13	10 7-16	1894....	8 5-16	5 9-16	1907....	13.55	10.70
1869....	35	25	1882....	13 1-16	10¼	1895....	9⅜	5 9-16	1908*...	12.25	9.00

* To November 6.

EXPORTS OF COTTON FROM THE UNITED STATES.

(From Census Bulletin No. 90.)

The exports of domestic cotton from the United States during the year ending August 31, 1907, amounted to 9,036,434 bales of 500 pounds each. Of this amount 3,966,119, or 44 per cent., went to the United Kingdom; 2,315,651, or 26 per cent., to Germany, and 1,006,633, or 11 per cent., to France. During the twenty-six years from 1880 to 1906 the exports to the United Kingdom increased 45 per cent.; those to Germany nearly 400 per cent., and those to France 82 per cent. The exports to Italy increased from 75,145 bales in 1880 to 567,916 bales in 1906, or nearly sevenfold. Exports to Japan are noteworthy because of the remarkable variations in the quantities for the different years, as well as for the growth in these exports since 1890, which is the first year for which they are presented in the report. In 1906 they amounted to 262,283 bales, while for 1904 they were 336,575 bales. The exports to Russia decreased, a fact which may be partially explained by the increased production of cotton in Russian territory, by the importation of Persian cotton, and by the recent unsettled conditions in that country.

Exports of sea-island cotton formed about one-third of the 57,550 bales reported by the ginners as produced in 1906. In 1905 about 36 per cent. of the sea-island crop was exported. The United Kingdom takes about three-fourths of the amount exported, while most of the remainder goes to France.

EXPORTS OF COTTON MANUFACTURES.

The total value of exports of cotton goods of domestic manufacture was $32,305,412, of which $11,496,734, or 36 per cent., was for unbleached cloths; $2,240,431, or 7 per cent., for bleached cloths, and $7,502,082, or 23 per cent., for dyed, colored, or printed cloths. Of the total value of cotton manufactures exported $4,425,035, or 14 per cent., went to Europe; $14,821,264, or 46 per cent., to North and South America; $12,325,874, or 38 per cent., to Asia, and the remainder to Africa. The export of American yarns to the Far East is insignificant, as that market is controlled by British India and Japan.

IMPORTS OF COTTON MANUFACTURES.

Imports of cotton manufactures during the year ending June 30, 1907, were valued at $73,704,636, more than one-half of which consisted of laces and embroideries. Switzerland leads in the export of laces to this country with $13,979,808, or about one-third of the total. France was second with $12,484,906. Of the bleached, dyed, or printed cloths imported 79 per cent. came from the United Kingdom, which country also supplied more than three-fourths of the thread, yarn, and warps imported. Practically all of the imports of hosiery and knit goods, amounting in value to $8,671,848, came from Germany.

THE UNITED STATES SUPPLIES TWO-THIRDS OF THE COTTON.

The number of cotton spindles in the world, as shown by the report, is 123,332,971. As nearly as it can be determined, the amount of cotton consumed was 19,493,441 bales, a weekly consumption of 374,874 bales. This is not, however, the total consumption for the world, as in a number of Eastern countries and in South and Central America large quantities of cotton are grown and consumed which do not enter into commercial channels, and therefore cannot be estimated with any certainty. The figures indicate, however, that the United States furnished two-thirds of the supply of the world.

Statistics of Wool in the United States.

Fiscal Year.	Total Imports.	Exports, Domestic and Foreign.	Net Imports. Classes I. and II.	Net Imports. Class III.	Production Preceding Year.	Retained for Consumption.	Fine Wool. Retained for Consumption.	Fine Wool. Per Cent. of Foreign.
	Pounds.	Pounds.	Pounds.	Pounds.	Pounds.	Pounds.	Pounds.	
1894-95....	206,081,890	6,622,190	98,388,318	105,402,507	325,210,712	524,722,428	419,319,921	23.46
1895-96.....	230,911,473	12,972,217	126,966,355	97,918,882	294,296,726	512,235 982	414,317,100	30.64
1896-97.....	350,852,026	8,700,598	235,282,735	112,141,457	272,474,708	614,627,365	502,485 908	46.84
1897-98....	132,795,302	2,625,971	47,480,033	82,810,437	259,153,251	389,322,582	306,512,145	15.50
1898-99	76,736,209	14,095,335	3,349,870	60,947,423	266,720,674	329,361 558	268,387,135	1.25
1899-1900...	155,918,455	7,912,557	44,680,424	105,525,783	272,191,330	420,197,228	314,671,445	14.20
1900-01.....	103,583,505	3,790,067	32,865,844	67,127,159	288,636,621	388,430,059	321,502,465	10.10
1901-02.....	166,576,966	3,227,941	69,315,286	93,842,199	302,502,382	465,851,407	371,694,390	18.65
1902-03.....	177,137,796	3,511,914	54,747,533	119,397,268	316,341,032	489,966,914	370,569,646	14 63
1903-04.....	173,742,834	3,182,803	55,999,545	114,880,236	287,450,000	458,010,031	345,129,795	16.22
1904-05.....	249,135,746	2,561,648	131,407,321	112,292,726	291,783,032	538,357,130	426,066,402	31.54
1905-06.....	201,688,668	5,642,859	98,336,137	97,902,153	295,488,438	491,534,247	393,632,094	24.99
1906-07.....	203,847,545	3,446,748	91,726,655	108,888,982	298,715,130	499,115,927	390,226,945	23.50
1907-08.....	125,980,524	5,626,463	57,846,442	62,690,077	298,294,750	418,648,811	346,141,192	16.71

The wool statistics on this page were prepared by W. J. Battison, of Boston, for the National Association of Wool Manufacturers.

THE WORLD'S PRODUCTION OF WOOL.

Countries.	Pounds.	Countries.	Pounds.	Countries.	Pounds.
North America:		Europe:		Asia—*Continued:*	
United States†	291.783,032	Great Britain and		Asiatic Turkey	33 000.000
British Provinces	12.000.000	Ireland†	133,124,762	China	35,000,000
Mexico	10,000,000	France	91,000,000	All other Asia	15,000,000
		Spain	102,600,000		
Total	313.783.032	Portugal	13,410,000	Total	274,000,000
		Germany	49.590,000		
		Italy†	21.451.000	Africa:	
Central America and West Indies	5.000.000	Austria-Hungary	64,300,000	Algeria and Tunis	30,425,000
		Russia, inc. Poland	361,100,000	Cape Colony, Natal,	
		Sweden & Norway	8,200,000	Orange Free State	100,000.000
South America:		Turkey and Balkan		Egypt	3.000.000
Argentina	370,000.000	Peninsula	67,500,000	All other Africa	1,000,000
Brazil	1,500.000	All other Europe	14,000,000		
Chile	7.500.000			Total	134.425,000
Uruguay	96.000.000	Total	926.275,762		
Venezuela	15,000,000			Australasia	480,000,000
All other South		Asia:		Oceanica	50,000
America	20,000,000	Russia	60,000,000		
		Central Asia	46.000,000	Grand total	2,643,533,794
Total	510,000,000	British India	85,000,000		

* These are the latest complete returns, and are for 1904-05. Those of the United States for 1908, washed and unwashed are 298,294,750 pounds. In Great Britain and Ireland the production for 1907 was 130,176,546 pounds. In most European countries the production has fallen off considerably, but statistics are not available. The production for Australasia for the season of 1907-08 is estimated at 656,810,010 pounds. † Fleece washed.

WOOL MANUFACTURES.

(From Census Bulletin No. 74.)

The period intervening between the censuses of 1900 and 1905 was an unusually prosperous season for the industries which use wool as chief raw material, namely: Woollen goods, worsted goods, carpets and rugs, other than rag; felt goods, and wool hats. The 1,213 establishments engaged in wool manufacture in 1905 were distributed thus: Woollen goods, 792; worsted goods, 226; carpets and rugs, 139; felt goods, 39, and wool hats, 17. The total capital invested was $370,861,691. There was an increase in every industry except wool hat manufacture, where there was a decrease of 19.7 per cent. The average number of wage-earners in the several industries was 179,976. Materials used in the wool manufacture cost $242,561,096.

The total value of products, $380,934,003, is made up of the output of woollen mills, $142,196,658; of worsted goods factories, $165,745,052; of carpet and rug factories, $61,586,433; of felt goods factories, $8,948,594, and of wool hat factories, $2,457,266.

Massachusetts held first rank in the total value of products of all branches, and in value of worsted goods and woollen goods; Pennsylvania was first in the manufacture of carpets and rugs, and New York led in the manufacture of felt goods and wool hats. The cities of Philadelphia, Pa.; Lawrence, Mass., and Providence, R. I., are still the leading centres of wool manufacture.

In 1905 the worsted manufacture exceeded that of woollen goods in capital, cost of materials, and value of products. An indication of the change of fashion from woollen to worsted goods is the decrease in woollen yarn purchased from 38,903,178 pounds in 1900 to 38,141,488 pounds in 1905, coincident with an increase in worsted yarn from 34,377,736 pounds in 1900 to 43,403,705 in 1905. The quantity of scoured wool consumed in the woollen manufacture was 282,194,618 pounds, and the total quantity of yarns purchased was 203,079,791 pounds, costing $59,904,637. Cotton, either alone or mixed with wool, has largely supplanted wool as the material of a great number of fabrics. There are important increases in the silk yarn used and in the yarn of jute, ramie, and other vegetable fibres.

The principal machinery was 5,968 cards, 1,549 combing machines, 4,021,098 spindles, and 77,985 looms.

Sugar Production.

MULHALL gives the following estimates of the production of cane and beet sugar in the world in English tons from 1840 to 1898; and Willett & Gray, New York, for the years following:

Years.	Cane.	Beet.	Total.	Years.	Cane.	Beet.	Total.	Years.	Cane.	Beet.	Total.
	Tons.	Tons.	Tons.		Tons.	Tons.	Tons.		Tons.	Tons.	Tons.
1840...	1,100,000	50,000	1,150,000	1898...	2,850.000	4,650,000	7,500,000	1904...	4,618,289	4,918,480	9,536,769
1850...	1,200,000	200,000	1,400,000	1900...	2,839,500	5,608,544	8,448,044	1905...	4,906,082	7,237,717	12,143,799
1860...	1,830,000	400,000	2,230,000	1901...	3,657,416	6,066,939	9,724,355	1906...	6,733,626	7,217,366	13,950,992
1870...	1,850,000	900,000	2,750,000	1902...	4,070,282	6,923.487	10,993,769	1907...	7,343,444	7,143,818	14,487,262
1880...	1,860,000	1,810.000	3,670,000	1903...	4,163,941	5,756,720	9,920,661	1908...	7,218,000	6,980,000	14,198,000
1890...	2,580,000	2,780,000	5,360,000								

The production of sugar in 1907-1908 by sugar-growing countries, in tons of 2,240 pounds, as reported by Willett & Gray, was:

Countries.	Cane Sugar.	Countries.	Cane Sugar.	Countries.	Beet Sugar.
Louisiana	335,000	Java	1,156,477	United States	440,200
Porto Rico	194,000	Hawaii	460,000	Germany	2,127,000
Cuba	961,958	Queensland	188,307	Austria	1,425,000
British West Indies	101,340	Mauritius	170,000	France	728,000
Hayti and S. Domingo.	50,000	Demerara	105,000	Russia	1,410,000
Peru	150,000	Argentina	109,445	Belgium	232,000
Brazil	180,000	Philippines	125,000	Holland	175,000

Beet sugar production in the United States in 1907-08, by States, in tons of 2.240 pounds: Wisconsin, 13,571; Michigan, 76,078; Colorado, 183,345; Utah, 39,720; Idaho, 27,715; California, 63,847; all others, 35,924. Total, 440,200.

CONSUMPTION OF SUGAR.

Licht's estimate of consumption of sugar of all kinds in various countries in 1907 per capita in pounds was: Germany, 41; Austria, 24; France, 36; Spain, 11; England, 94; Switzerland, 55; United States, (W&G) 78; Russia, 21; Netherlands, 41; Denmark, 74; Italy, 8; Belgium, 30; Turkey, 12.

The consumption of sugar in the United States in the calendar year 1907, estimated by Willett & Gray, of New York, was:

Imported (including 418,102 tons Hawaiian, 212,853 Porto Rican, and 10,700 Philippine sugar)	2,337,352	Domestic Maple	10,000
Domestic, manufactured from imported molasses	6,249	Domestic Beet	375,410
Domestic Cane	264,968	Domestic Total	656,627
		Total product consumed in the U. S.	2,993,979
		or 77.54 pounds per capita.	

Tea, Coffee and Cocoa.

(From Report of the Bureau of Statistics of the Department of Commerce and Labor.)

Coffee.—Sources of supply in 1904. Exports from coffee-growing countries in pounds.

Brazil	1,600,000,000	Haiti and Santo Domingo	71,000,000
Colombia, Venezuela, Ecuador, Peru, and Chile	200,000,000	British West Indies	11,000,000
Central America	165,000,000	British East Indies	58,000,000
Mexico	35,000,000	Dutch East Indies	135,000,000
Cuba and Porto Rico	18,000,000	Total	2,299,000,000

Consumption of leading countries in 1904, in pounds.

United States	960,879,000	Austria-Hungary	108,687,000
Germany	396,205,000	Holland	28,930,000
France	167,552,000	Great Britain and Iréland	28,783,000
Belgium	125,411,000	Canada	6,188,000

Imports of coffee in the United States, year ending June 30, 1907, were: From Brazil, 778,559,591 pounds, value $57,559,591. Other South America, 105,281,077 pounds; value $9,289,554. Central America, 64,432,202 pounds; value $7,304,606. The remainder in smaller quantities from other countries.

Tea.—Sources of supply in 1904: Exports from principal tea-growing countries in pounds.

British India	208,049,000	Japan	68,359,000
China	193,467,000	Java	23,595,000
Ceylon (1903)	149,227,000		

Figures of total production in each of these countries exceed total exports, except China, about whose consumption there are no available statistics.

Consumption of leading countries in 1904, in pounds.

Great Britain and Ireland	256,660,000	Canada (1903)	23,969,000
Russia	120,829,000	Netherlands	8,778,000
United States	109,623,000	Germany	6,903,000
Australia (1900)	29,266,000	France	2,440,000

The number of pounds of tea consumed per capita was: Great Britain and Ireland, 6.09; United States, 1.34; Russia, 0.95; Australia, 6.93; Canada, 5.60; France, 0.06; Germany, 0.12.

The imports of tea in the United States in the fiscal year 1907 were 86,362,490 pounds, valued at $13,915,544. Of this 37,411,053 pounds were imported from Japan and 31,233,259 pounds from China.

Cocoa.—World's production of cocoa, 1903, in pounds: Ecuador, 46,500,000; San Thomé (Portuguese Africa), 45,000,000; Brazil, 43,000,000; Trinidad, 29,000,000; Venezuela, 25,000,000; Santo Domingo, 15,000,000; Grenada, 13,000,000; all others, 37,500,000. Total production, 260,000,000.

World's consumption of cocoa, 1903, in pounds: United States, 63,000,000; Germany, 43,000,000; France, 41,000,000; Great Britain, 35,000,000; Netherlands, 33,000,000; Spain, 12,500,000; all others, 33,000,000.

The importation of raw cocoa into the United States in the fiscal year 1907 was 92,249,819 pounds, and of chocolate 3,541,961 pounds. There has been an immense increase in the importation of cocoa in the past ten years.

The American Hog.

HOGS PACKED AND MARKETED, YEAR ENDING MARCH 1, 1908.

CITIES.	Number of Hogs.	CITIES.	Number of Hogs.	CITIES.	Number of Hogs.
Chicago	6,29[illegible],410	Cedar Rapids	647,750	Other Places East	1,061,000
Kansas City	3,574,835	Cleveland	757,976	Receipts at New York, Philadelphia and Baltimore	3,219,000
Omaha	2,261,626	Louisville	241,150		
St. Louis	1,853,279	Sioux City	1,107,450		
St. Joseph	1,873,917	St. Paul	930,621		
Indianapolis	1,755,669	Nebraska City	198,412		
Milwaukee	1,424,461	Other Places West	3,667,034	Total 1908	34,400,000
Cincinnati	695,375	Boston	1,270,000	" 1907	30,978,000
Ottumwa	696,029	Buffalo	869,000	" 1906	31,273,000

DISTRIBUTION OF HOG PRODUCTS EXPORTED FROM THE UNITED STATES IN 1908.*

COUNTRIES.	LARD.		HAMS.		BACON.		PORK.	
	Quantities, Pounds.	Values.	Quantities, Pounds.	Values.	Quantities, Pounds.	Values.	Quantities, Pounds.	Values.
United Kingdom	205,788,762	$18,604,631	195,779,646	$22,080,500	192,931,564	$20,643,223	67,447,8[illegible]1	$[illegible],504,129
Belgium	29,541,290	2,744,441	11,299,280	1,245,722	10,339,456	1,010,550	1,818,250	153,480
France	17,405,487	1,606,305	....	....	4,033,078	407,763	....	....
Germany	184,722,4[illegible]0	16,451,254	82,525	8,873	535,245	54,311	3,785,487	32[illegible],189
Netherlands	55,975,847	5,043,167	163,707	17,539	4,670,659	460,088	4,311,035	364,491
Other Europe	31,371,427	2,830,682	1,450,801	155,718	19,293,660	1,864,448	27,893,117	2,329,983
British North America	12,612,843	1,154,108	3,548,799	430,784	1,541,515	210,040	19,855,365	1,629,690
Total †	603,413,770	$54,789,748	221,769,634	$25,167,059	241,189,929	$25,481,246	149,505,937	$13,332,654

* Fiscal year ending June 30, 1908. † Total, including all other countries.

Production of Poultry and Eggs.

THE Census of 1900 gave the production of poultry in the Census year in the United States as 250,623,114. The enumeration covered chickens, guinea fowls, turkeys, geese and ducks three months old and over. The largest production was in Iowa, 20,043,343, and the next largest, Illinois, 17,737,262.

The production of eggs in the Census year 1900 in the United States was 1,293,662,433 dozen. The leading production by States was Iowa, 99,621,920 dozen; Ohio, 91,766,630; Illinois, 86,402,670; Missouri, 85,203,290; Kansas, 73,190,390; Indiana, 70,782,200; Pennsylvania, 67,038,180. New York, 62,096,690; Texas, 58,040,810; Michigan, 54,318,410; all in dozens.

The report of the Census of 1900 showed 3.29 poultry per capita, and 17 dozen eggs per capita per annum for the United States.

Dairy Products.

THE Twelfth Census (Bulletin 189) presented the following condensed analysis of the dairy industry of the United States for the Census year 1900:

Cows kept for milk on farms	number..	17,139,674
Cows kept for milk not on farms	"	973,033
Total number of cows kept for milk		18,112,707
Milk produced on farms	gallons..	7,266,392,674
Milk produced not on farms	"	*462,190,676
Total gallons of milk produced		7,728,583,350
Butter made on farms	pounds	1,071,745,127
Butter made in factory creameries	"	420,126,546
Butter made in urban dairy establishments	"	827,470
Total pounds of butter made		1,492,699,143
Cheese made on farms	pounds..	16,372,330
Cheese made in factories	"	281,972,324
Cheese made in urban dairy establishments	"	662,164
Total pounds of cheese made		299,006,818
Condensed milk produced	pounds..	186,921,787

* Estimated.

Wine Production of the World.

THE following table shows estimates of wine production in gallons by the principal wine-producing countries according to the French publication *Moniteur Vinicole*, and is for the year 1905.

COUNTRIES.	Gallons.	COUNTRIES.	Gallons.	COUNTRIES.	Gallons.
France (inc. Algeria and Tunis)	1,710,900,000	Roumania	52,840,000	Brazil	5,600,000
Italy	856,520,000	Argentine Repub.	34,350,000	Cape Colony	4,490,000
Spain	428,000,000	Turkey	34,350,000	Azores, Canary and Madeira Islands	3,830,000
Austria-Hungary	192,800,000	United States	34,000,000	Uruguay	2,780,000
Portugal	108,320,000	Bulgaria	29,100,000	Peru	2,400,000
Germany	79,600,000	Switzerland	22,190,000	Bolivia	610,000
Russia	76,620,000	Australasia	7,925,000		
Chile	74,200,000	Servia	6,605,000		
		Oceanica	6,605,000	Total	3,775,060,000

Production of Liquors and Wines in the United States.

PRODUCTION OF FERMENTED LIQUORS AND DISTILLED SPIRITS.

Year Ending June 30.	Fermented Liquors.	Production of Distilled Spirits, Exclusive of Brandy Distilled from Fruit.						Production of Fruit Braudy.†	Total Production of Distilled Spirits.‡
		Bourbon Whiskey.	Rye Whiskey.	Alcohol.	Rum.	Gin.	Pure Neutral Spirits.		
	Barrels.*	Gallons.	Gallons.	Gallons.	Gallons.	Gallons.	Gallons.	Gallons.	Gallons.
1896......	35,859,255	16,935,862	9,153,066	9,960,301	1,490,288	1,098,376	25,564,738	3,403,832	89,992,555
1897......	34,462,822	6,113,726	4,269,220	9,503,533	1,294,157	1,159,314	16,877,306	1,813,427	64,279,075
1898......	37,529,339	13,439,459	8,818,240	11,672,795	1,340,547	1,267,580	20,613,205	2,906,108	83,668,411
1899......	36,697,634	17,256,331	10,792,565	11,974,354	1,494,379	1,266,823	25,876,229	3,097,769	100,162,334
1900......	39,471,593	19,411,829	14,296,568	10,735,771	1,614,514	1,597,081	24,173,671	3,760,487	109,245,187
1901......	40,614,258	26,209,804	18,263,709	10,775,117	1,724,582	1,636,200	30,228,804	4,047,602	128,568,201
1902......	44,550,127	20,336,250	21,587,221	11,483,305	2,202,047	1,752,251	37,429,734	4,220,400	103,401,447
1903......	46,720,179	26,068,555	22,407,053	12,034,127	2,247,907	1,913,404	54,620,400	6,430,673	112,905,399
1904......	48,265,168	20,247,089	18,371,343	11,486,082	1,801,179	2,110,216	57,997,506	5,193,262	139,505,211
1905......	49,522,029	26,742,168	20,410,422	11,610,799	1,791,987	2,187,709	60,944,811	5,448,584	153,259,378
1906......	54,724 553	24,968,943	21,469,720	11,173,614	1,730,102	2,323,289	59,626,733	4,444,072	150,110,197
1907......	55,622,002	33 090,791	23,550,196	16,123,379	2,022,407	2,947,688	60,802,852	6,138,305	174,712,218

*Of not more than 31 gallons. †Including apple, peach, and grape. ‡Including also high wines and miscellaneous spirits.

The production of wines in the United States in 1900 was 24,306,905 gallons, of which California produced 14,620,000, New York 2,528,250, and Ohio 1,934,838 gallons. The total production in 1902 was 29,058,700 gallons.

Importation of Spirits, Malt Liquors, and Wines

INTO THE UNITED STATES, IN QUANTITIES.

	1905.	1906.	1907.	1908.
Malt Liquors, in bottles or jugs, gallons	1,362,069	1,582,619	2,041,688	1,954,333
" not in bottles or jugs, gallons	3,836,487	4,395,033	5,165,929	5,564,773
Spirits, Distilled and Spirituous Compounds, Brandy, proof gallons	403,386	470,433	629,333	592,382
Spirits, Distilled and Spirituous Compounds, all other, proof gallons	2,368,366	2,639,680	3,270,226	3,216,228
Spirits, domestic manufacture, returned, gallons	316,469	177,499	162,072	148,298
Wines, Still Wines in casks, gallons	3,973,919	4,482,499	5,213,458	5,443,782
" Still Wines in bottles, dozen	488,773	546,688	636,938	628,428
" Champagne and other sparkling, dozen	372,811	415,394	419,403	366,669

VALUES.

	1905.	1906.	1907.	1908.
Malt Liquors	$2,405,314	$2,738,855	$3,408,763	$3,464,677
Spirits, Distilled and Compounds	5,005,058	5,524,767	6,886,691	6,400,167
Wines	10,241,921	10,993,968	11,808,781	10,746,527

Consumption of Spirits, Malt Liquors, and Wines

IN THE UNITED STATES, IN GALLONS.

Year Ending June 30.	Distilled Spirits Consumed.			Wines Consumed.		Malt Liquors Consumed.		Total Consumption.
	Domestic Spirits.		Imported Spirits.	Domestic Wines.	Imported Wines.	Domestic Malt Liquors.	Imported Malt Liquors	
	From Fruit.	All Other.						
1895.....	1,102,703	75,228,928	1,496,860	16,582,657	3,054,392	1,040,259,039	3,033,067	1,140,764,716
1896.....	1,440,810	68,069,563	1,541,504	14,599,757	4,101,649	1,077,325,634	3,300,531	1,170,379,448
1897.....	1,146,131	69,789,991	2,230,711	33,940,319	4,647,988	1,066,307,704	3,002,558	1,181,065,402
1898......	1,411,448	79,207,887	916,549	17,453,684	3,118,633	1,161,769,114	2,457,848	1,266,281,366
1899.....	1,306,218	84,614,652	1,389,358	22,835,587	3,525,109	1,132,723,202	2,797,427	1,249,191,553
1900.....	1,386,361	94,156,023	1,705,998	26,492,491	3,935,000	1,218,183,252	3,316,908	1,349,176,033
1901....	1,509,271	100,066,821	1,941,629	24,002,439	4,388,140	1,254,653,009	3,596,382	1,390,127,379
1902.....	1,403,204	104,110,194	2,245,239	44,737,244	5,020,066	1,378,168,215	3,707,222	1,539,081,991
1903.....	1,515,072	113,598,545	2,439,535	32,631,154	5,601,425	1,445,675,414	4,204,538	1,605,851,455
1904.....	1,637,303	116,808,978	2,655,716	37,538,709	5,517,568	1,489,354,250	4,837,075	1,658,609,958
1905.....	1,595,021	116,544,822	2,730,425	29,369,408	6,002,309	1,532,949,602	5,201,168	1,694,392,765
1906.....	1,781,643	122,961,612	3,011,289	39,847,044	6,638,179	1,694,021,375	5,964,267	1,874,225,409
1907.....	1,993,688	134,308,693	3,782,055	50,079,283	7,659,565	1,814,695,785	7,171,842	2,019,690,911

Consumption of Beer, Wine, and Alcohol

IN PRINCIPAL COUNTRIES, IN GALLONS.

Countries.	Malt Liquors.	Wines.	Alcohol.	Countries.	Malt Liquors.	Wines.	Alcohol.
United States.........	1,821,861,627	57,138,848	†140,084,436	Belgium..............	395,285,258	8,948,200	9,805,000
United Kingdom......	1,500,709,000	16,646,933	58,318,373	Italy....	6,725,000	1,045,961,000	11,150,400
Russia..............	151,633,892	*25,000,000	172,550,500	Austria-Hungary......	545,674,043	119,218,000	*120,000,000
Germany..............	1,782,778,000	113,583,000	124,313,300	Denmark.	63,213,000	......	*4,000,000
France...............	289,103,000	1,342,830,600	97,177,968	Sweden...............	44,410,000	898,200	10,730,500
Spain................	*20,000,000	321,816,000	......	Portugal..............	......	87,142,000	......

*Estimated. Returns are for 1903, except United States, 1907, and United Kingdom, 1904; France, malt, 1904; Russia and Austria-Hungary, 1901; Italy, wine, 1902; Sweden, wine, 1907. †Distilled spirits.

Alabama—Prohibition.
Alaska—Prohibition under acts of Congress.
Arizona—Local option, quarterly fee, United States license $25 annually. County and Territorial $300 annually.
Arkansas—Local option, fee $800.
California—Local option, fee by authorities.
Colorado—Local option, fee $500 up.
Connecticut—Local option, fee $150—$450.
Delaware—New Castle County and City of Wilmington, licensed. Kent and Sussex Counties, local option, fee $200—$300.
District of Columbia—License by excise board on the written consent of the majority of the owners of real estate, and of the residents on the front of the square on which the saloon is to be located, and of the owners of real estate and of the residents of the confronting side of the opposite square, fee $800.
Florida—Local option, fee $1,250.
Georgia—Prohibition.
Idaho—Annual license by authorities, fee $750.
Illinois—Local option license by city council or village or county board, fee not less than $500.
Indiana—County local option. Whenever 20 per cent. of the voters of the county petition the county commissioners the latter shall be a "yes" or "no" vote as to prohibiting the sale of intoxicants by saloons within the county.
Iowa—License by petition of voters, fee $600 up.
Kansas—Prohibition.
Kentucky—County local option, except cities of the first, second and third classes may vote separately; fee $150.
Louisiana—State and local license, $100 up.
Maine—Prohibition.
Maryland—Local option, fee $18—$450.
Massachusetts—Local option, fee not less than $1,000; number limited, one to one thousand inhabitants; in Boston, one to five hundred.
Michigan—Local option, fee $500—$800.
Minnesota—License fee, $500—$1,000.
Mississippi—Prohibition.
Missouri—The counties may, by majority vote, pass the local option law, and if this is not done the county courts may grant a license and fix a tax of not less than $200, nor more than $400 per year, for State and not less than $500, nor more than $800 for county purposes.
Montana—Semi-annual fee $150—$300.
Nebraska—Local option, fee $500—$1,000.
Nevada—State license $50 per annum; wholesale $100 per annum; retail drug store $12 per annum.
New Hampshire—License by majority of voters, fees based on population, maximum $1,200.
New Jersey—Local option, fee $100—$800.
New Mexico—License by county commissioners, fee $100—$400.
New York—Local option in towns, fee $150—$1,200, according to population.
North Carolina—Prohibition.
North Dakota—Prohibition.
Ohio—Local option, fee $1,000.
Oklahoma—Constitutional prohibition.
Oregon—Local option, fee $400.
Pennsylvania—License under control of courts, fee $100—$1,100.
Rhode Island—Local option, fee $300—$1,000.
South Carolina—County control, State regulation.
South Dakota—License by local authorities, fee $400—$600.
Tennessee—License issued by local authorities, fee $500.
Texas—License issued by county clerk, fee $750.
Utah—License granted by local authorities, fee $400—$1,200.
Vermont—License local option act was adopted February 3, 1903, and took effect March 3, 1903.
Virginia—Control of local courts, fee $450 (wholesale or retail); local option provided for.
Washington—License issued by local authorities, fee $300—$1,000.
West Virginia—License by courts and local authorities, fee retail $600; wholesale $750.
Wisconsin—Local option, fee $100—$200, with power in voters to increase from $200—$500.
Wyoming—License issued by local authorities, fee $100—$300.

LIQUOR TRAFFIC IN NEW YORK CITY.

Comparative table showing the number of licenses issued and net receipts under excise boards for year ending April 30, 1896 (old law), also number of liquor tax certificates in force, net revenue, State's share net revenue, boroughs' share net revenue, benefit to boroughs by diminished State tax, together with total benefit to each borough comprising the City of New York, for the year ending April 30, 1908 (new law).

Boroughs.	Number of Licenses Issued, 1895-96 (Old Law).	Number of Certificates in Force April 30, 1908 (New Law).	Net Receipts Under Excise Boards, 1895-96 (Old Law).	Net Revenue Year Ending April 30, 1908 (New Law).	State's Share Net Revenue Year Ending April 30, 1908 (New Law).	Boroughs' Share Net Revenue Year Ending April 30, 1908 (New Law).	Benefit to Boroughs by Diminished State Tax Year Ending April 30, 1908 (New Law).	Total Benefit to Each Borough Year Ending April 30, 1908 (New Law).
Manhattan and Bronx..	8,906	6,868	$1,056,013.10	$7,563,391.91	$3,781,696.07	$3,781,695.84	$5,064,609.36	$8,846,305.20
Brooklyn.....	4,702	3,771	599,115.89	3,480,453.14	1,740,228.03	1,740,225.11	1,240,813.66	2,981,038.77
Queens........	1,206	1,380	43,424.61	496,736.87	248,368.54	248,368.33	222,851.64	471,219.97
Richmond....	543	491	38,364.83	179,526.88	89,763.52	89,763.36	54,908.14	144,671.50
Total.	15,357	12,510	$1,736,918.43	$11,720,108.80	$5,860,056.16	$5,860,052.64	$6,583,182.80	$12,443,235.44

Table showing the number of liquor tax certificates (covering hotels, saloons, clubs, etc.) in force April 30, 1908, by boroughs, in the City of New York.

Boroughs.	Hotels.	Saloons, Clubs, etc.	Boroughs.	Hotels.	Saloons, Clubs, etc.
Manhattan and the Bronx	822	5,011	Richmond	156	293
Brooklyn	335	2,948			
Queens..............	276	967	Total New York City................	1,589	9,219

When to Serve Beverages.

(From Osborn's Vintage and Production of Wines and Liquors.)

Appetizer—Dry Pale Sherry plain or with a dash of bitters, Vermouth plain or a Cocktail.
With Oysters—Rhine Wine, Moselle, Dry Sauternes, or Capri; cool.
With Soup—Sherry or Madeira; cool.
With Fish—Sauternes, Rhine Wine, Moselle, or Capri; cool.
With Entrées—Claret or Chianti; temperature of room.
With Roast—Claret, Burgundy, or Chianti; temperature of room.
With Game—Champagne (cold), Old Vintage Champagne; cool.
With Pastry—Madeira; cool.
With Cheese—Port; temperature of room.
With Fruit—Tokay, Malaga, or Muscat; temperature of room.
With Coffee—Brandy or Cordial; temperature of room.

The Prohibition Movement.

THE Associated Prohibition Press of Chicago thus sketches the status of the Prohibition movement in America on January 1, 1909, as compared with the situation five years ago, in 1904:

In five years the Prohibition reform has commanded the interest of the American people as perhaps no other cause in half a century.

In five years' time five new Prohibition States, with an aggregate population of 10,000,000, have been added to three already won. The eight now under Prohibition are Maine, Kansas, North Dakota, Georgia, Oklahoma, Alabama, Mississippi and North Carolina.

Aroused public sentiment in the three old Prohibition States have substituted efficient and successful law-enforcement for nullification and spasmodic law and order.

In addition to that, State Prohibition has been made the dominant issue in thirteen other States, and in the Presidential campaign just closed, for the first time since 1888, has overshadowed and eclipsed the old issues of the politicians in practically every State in the Union.

In 1904 the National Liquor League of the United States was organized at Cincinnati, January 7 and 8, to put the "lid" on the apparent beginnings of a Prohibition renaissance. In 1904 the liquor trade, through its National Protective Bureau, announced it had circulated within twelve months over 4,000,000 specially prepared leaflets attacking the Prohibition argument. Since that time, at a low estimate, 20,000,000 of these leaflets have been distributed broadcast and in the most carefully selected fashion.

Despite the five years of the "National Liquor League of the United States," 20,000,000 people have been added to the territory which has outlawed the saloon, including 150 new Prohibition cities, five new Prohibition States, hundreds of new Prohibition counties, and thousands of new Prohibition towns and villages in all the rest of the country.

Nearly two-thirds of the territory and nearly one-half of the people are under some form of Prohibition protection

Seventeen million people in the South under Prohibition in 1904.

Twenty-five million people in the South under Prohibition in 1909.

There are to-day 300 Prohibition cities in the United States, having a population of over 5,000 each, with a total population of nearly 4,000,000.

In 1904 there were scarcely 100 Prohibition cities of 5,000 or over; there are now 90 Prohibition cities of 10,000 or over.

The Prohibition Party is now organized and aggressively at work in nearly every State of the Union.

One of the most striking contrasts between 1904 and 1909 is seen in the transformation which has been wrought in the attitude of the daily and secular press toward the Prohibition question. Since 1904 leading daily papers in all parts of the country have begun to exclude liquor advertising from their columns.

The daily press of America to-day is giving more attention to and far more friendly treatment of the Prohibition issue than was the case in 1904.

STATE.	1904.	1909.
Alabama.......	20 Prohibition counties. 11 Dispensaries. 35 License.	State Prohibition (in effect December 31, 1908).
Arizona........	No Prohibition territory.	2 Prohibition districts. Phoenix, State Capital, gave majority for Prohibition (two-thirds required). State Prohibition asked for when admitted.
Arkansas......	44 Prohibition counties. 29 License. 2 Partially license.	57 Prohibition counties. State Prohibition probable in 1909.
California......	175 Prohibition towns.	250 Prohibition towns. Large part of Southern California saloon-free.
Colorado.......	Few Prohibition towns. No local option law.	Nearly 100 Prohibition towns. State local option law 1907. Denver half Prohibition.
Connecticut....	Half of State local Prohibition.	Increase in Prohibition vote. State Prohibition campaign.
Delaware......	Few small Prohibition towns.	Two-thirds of State under Prohibition. State campaign on.
District of Columbia....	Apathy dominant.	Prohibition campaign on, urged by Prohibition forces of nation, aided by many local societies.
Florida........	30 Prohibition counties.	37 Prohibition counties. State Prohibition campaign.
Georgia........	104 Prohibition counties out of 134. Large cities all licensed.	State Prohibition since January 1, 1908. Crime cut in two; drunkenness reduced two-thirds.
Idaho..........	No Prohibition territory. "Wide open" State.	No license in many towns. Law enforcement throughout State. Sunday saloon-closing by State law 1907.
Illinois.........	8 Prohibition counties. 500 Prohibition towns "Wide open" Sundays.	36 Prohibition counties. 2,500 Prohibition towns. Only 2 counties which wholly license. Strict Sunday closing except in Chicago.

THE PROHIBITION MOVEMENT—*Continued.*

STATE.	1904.	1909.
Indiana........	140 Prohibition townships.	900 Prohibition townships. Two-thirds of State population in Prohibition territory. County option law passed October, 1908.
Iowa..........	25 Licensed counties. Lax enforcement of law.	25 Licensed counties. Strict enforcement. Prohibition State campaign.
Kansas........	State Prohibition. Law enforcement. Law enforcement crusade at Kansas City, Kas., a failure.	State Prohibition. Strict enforcement. Prohibition enforcement success in Kansas City.
Kentucky......	47 Prohibition counties. Legislature defeated very moderate local option bill.	92 Prohibition counties. Only 4 wholly licensed counties. State Prohibition campaign.
Louisiana......	20 Prohibition parishes out of 54.	37 Prohibition parishes. State Prohibition narrowly defeated in first legislative skirmish.
Maine..........	State Prohibition. Lax enforcement.	State Prohibition. Strict enforcement.
Maryland......	15 Prohibition counties.	Same. Strict Sunday closing of saloons.
Massachusetts.	250 Prohibition towns and cities.	360 Prohibition towns and cities. 18,000 State majority against license. Worcester largest Prohibition city in the world.
Michigan......	2 Prohibition counties. 400 Prohibition towns.	11 Prohibition counties. 700 Prohibition towns. Strict law enforcement.
Minnesota......	400 Prohibition towns.	1,611 Prohibition towns. Strict law enforcement. 3 Party Prohibitionists in Legislature.
Mississippi.....	65 Prohibition counties. Legislature defeated State Prohibition amendment.	State Prohibition (December 31, 1908).
Missouri.......	3 Prohibition counties 1905.	77 Prohibition counties. State Prohibition campaign. Strict Sunday closing.
Montana.......	No Prohibition territory.	1 Prohibition county. Local gains.
Nebraska......	200 Prohibition towns.	600 Prohibition towns. 22 Prohibition counties. State Prohibition campaign.
Nevada........	No Prohibition territory.	Local gains.
New Hampshire	State Prohibition repealed 1903.	144 Prohibition towns 1904; 183 Prohibition towns 1908. Campaign on for resubmission of Prohibition.
New Jersey....	"Wide open" State.	Sunday closing and vigorous law enforcement. State-wide agitation for county option.
New Mexico....	Nothing.	State Prohibition asked for when admitted.
New York......	285 Prohibition towns. Cities all licensed by State law.	Some local gains.
North Carolina.	Local option bill passed 1903. Raleigh, State Capital, had dispensary run by church deacons and elders.	State Prohibition carried May 26 by 40,000.
North Dakota..	State Prohibition. Lax enforcement in some sections.	State Prohibition. State-wide enforcement.
Ohio...........	145 Prohibition towns. First State local option law passed.	1,621 Prohibition towns. County Prohibition law. 47 counties voted dry in first sixty days of law. 80 Prohibition counties predicted within two years.
Oklahoma......	Few Prohibition towns.	State Prohibition.
Oregon.........	No Prohibition territory. No local option law.	State county option law. 21 Prohibition counties out of 34.
Pennsylvania...	Prohibition sentiment apathetic.	State-wide movement for county Prohibition.
Rhode Island...	20 Prohibition towns.	Some local gains. New State enforcement law.
South Carolina.	State dispensary.	State dispensary abolished (1907). 18 Prohibition counties. State Prohibition campaign.
South Dakota..	Scattering Prohibition towns.	13 Prohibition counties.
Tennessee......	8 Licensed cities. Liquor men threatened repeal of Adams local option law.	152 Prohibition counties. State Prohibition campaign on; referendum vote promised.
Utah..........	No Prohibition territory.	County Prohibition campaign sweeping the State.
Vermont.......	Prohibition repealed 1903.	138 Prohibition towns out of 240 in 1904. 216 Prohibition towns 1908. State Prohibition campaign.
Virginia.......	Local option law passed 1903.	66 Prohibition counties.
Washington....	Few Prohibition towns.	General local gains. County option likely in 1909.
West Virginia..	40 out of 54 counties dry.	State campaign on.
Wisconsin......	300 Prohibition towns.	789 Prohibition towns. State campaign for county Prohibition.
Wyoming......	No Prohibition territory.	Some local gains.

The Defective Classes.

The Insane.—The total number of insane in the United States on June 1, 1890 (Census of the United States), was 106,485, of whom 74,028 were in hospitals. In the collection of statistics of the insane in 1903 (Census Special Report issued August, 1906), only the insane in hospitals were considered. These had increased to 150,151 on December 31, 1906. The number of hospitals for the insane had increased in thirteen years from 162 in 1890 to 328 in 1903.

In 1903 the number of insane males in hospitals was 78,523, and insane females 71,628. In proportion to population there were more white than negro insane. None of the insane in hospitals were under twelve years of age. The maximum concentration occurred between ages twenty-five and thirty-five years. Female insane live longer than male insane, and white insane than negro insane.

More than one-fourth, 27.8 per cent. of the hospital insane had been inmates less than one year, less than one-sixteenth per cent. had been in hospitals at least twenty years. 41.6 per cent. had been employed as laborers and servants before becoming inmates, 22.5 per cent. had been occupied in agriculture, transportation and other outdoor pursuits, and 16 per cent. in manufacturing and mechanical industries. Of the 328 hospitals for the insane, 226 were public and 102 private in character. The annual cost of maintenance of insane in public hospitals approximated $21,000,000.

The Feeble-Minded.—The number of feeble-minded in institutions on December 31, 1903, was 14,347. The Census estimate of the number of feeble-minded in the general population is not less than 150,000. Of the feeble-minded in institutions 58 per cent. were under twenty years of age, and 85 per cent. were under thirty years of age. Three-fifths of the inmates were epileptics.

The Deaf and Dumb.—The total number of deaf mutes in the United States on June 1, 1890 (the latest Census returns on the subject), was 40,592—whites, 37,447; negroes, 3,115; others, 30; males, 22,429; females, 18,163; native-born whites, 33,278; foreign-born whites, 4,169.

The number of persons so deaf as to be unable to hear loud conversation on June 1, 1890, was 121,178, of whom 80,611 were able to speak. The latter were 49,278 males, 31,338 females, 77,308 whites, 3,308 negroes.

The Blind.—The total number of blind in the United States on June 1, 1890, was 50,568—whites, 43,351; negroes, 7,060; others, 157; males, 28,080; females, 22,488; native-born whites, 34,205; foreign-born whites, 9,146. The number of blind in one eye only was 93,988.

The number of insane persons in Great Britain and Ireland in 1896, according to Mulhall, was 128,896, or 328 per 100,000 population; Austria (1890), 51,880; Hungary (1890), 28,158. The number of insane in Germany in 1884 was 108,100; France, 93,900; Russia, 80,000.

Suicides.

In European cities the number of suicides per 100,000 inhabitants is as follows: Paris, 42; Lyons, 29; St. Petersburg, 7; Moscow, 11; Berlin, 36; Vienna, 28; London, 23; Rome, 8; Milan, 6; Madrid, 3; Genoa, 31; Brussels, 15; Amsterdam, 14; Lisbon, 2; Christiania, 25; Stockholm, 27; Constantinople, 12; Geneva, 11; Dresden, 51. Madrid and Lisbon show the lowest, Dresden the highest figure.

The average annual suicide rate in countries of the world per 100,000 persons living is given by Barker as follows: Saxony, 31.1; Denmark, 25.8; Schleswig-Holstein, 24.0; Austria, 21.2; Switzerland, 20.2; France, 15.7; German Empire, 14.3; Hanover, 14.0; Queensland, 13.5; Prussia, 13.3; Victoria, 11.5; New South Wales, 9.3; Bavaria, 9.1; New Zealand, 9.0; South Australia, 8.9; Sweden, 8.1; Norway, 7.5; Belgium, 6.9; England and Wales, 6.9; Tasmania, 5.3; Hungary, 5.2; Scotland, 4.0; Italy, 3.7; Netherlands, 3.6; United States, 3.5; Russia, 2.9; Ireland, 1.7; Spain, 1.4. A later enumeration of suicides in France gives 8,926 as the number in 1900, or 23.6 per cent.

The causes of suicide in European countries are reported as follows: Of 100 suicides: Madness, delirium, 18 per cent.; alcoholism, 11; vice, crime, 19; different diseases, 2; moral sufferings, 6; family matters, 4; poverty, want, 4; loss of intellect, 14; consequence of crimes, 3; unknown reasons, 19.

The number of suicides in the United States in the Census year 1900 was 5,498. The number of suicides in States and cities of the United States which have laws requiring the registration of deaths in the five years 1900 to 1904, inclusive, as reported in the Special Mortality Report of the Census Office, published in 1906, was 20,834. The methods of death by suicide in numbers, were: By poison, 6,946; firearms, 4,938; hanging, 3,232; asphyxia, 1,487; cutting, 1,171; drowning, 1,059; jumping from high places, 252; crushing, 87; other methods, 1,662. Insanity is the principal cause of suicide. The largest proportion of deaths by suicide, according to age, is from forty to forty-nine years. Summer appears to be the favorite season.

The number of suicides in fifty American cities in ten years, 1895 to 1905, inclusive, according to Frederick L. Hoffmann statistician of the Prudential Insurance Company of New Jersey, was 26,079. The ten cities having the highest rate per 100,000 of the population were: San Francisco, 52.2; Hoboken, 30.2; St. Louis, 27.4; Oakland, 24.9; Chicago, 22.7; New York (Manhattan and Bronx), 22.2; Milwaukee, 21.8; Newark, 21.6; Cincinnati, 20.6; Indianapolis, 17.6. The average of fifty cities was 17.8. The number of suicides in New York (Manhattan and Bronx) in 1906 was 442 and in Chicago 385.

Statistics of Births.

The Statesman's Year Book gives the following returns of births in 1900, in principal European countries. The birth registration, except in Germany, is not full. The Census returns of the United States for 1900 have not yet been published.

Countries.	Total Number of Births.	Number of Illegitimate Births.	Countries.	Total Number of Births.	Number of Illegitimate Births.
Austria	995,537	135,933	Germany	2,045,286	183,504
Hungary	768,673	70,921	Italy	1,003,970	63,406
England and Wales	926,304	36,814	Norway	67,013	4,949
Scotland	131,355	8,503	Sweden	136,523	15,641
Ireland	101,459	2,702	Russia (1898)	5,769,218	....
France	827,297	73,121	Spain	627,848	....

In "Statisque Humaine de la France," M. J. Bertillon presents the following table, showing that the French are the least prolific and the Germans the most prolific people of Europe: Number of children born alive annually per 1,000 women of 15 to 50 years: France, 102; Ireland, 114; Belgium, 127; England, 136; Netherlands, 137; Spain, 141; Prussia, 150; Bavaria, 156. The number of children born in France in 1904 was 818,229, the smallest number registered in late years. In August, 1906, Hanaw Kailua, in Hilo, Hawaii, gave birth to seven children; Mrs. Snell, of Malad, Idaho, on September, 19, 1889, gave birth to six children.

Mortality Statistics.

The Census Office published in 1906 a report of Mortality Statistics of States and cities which have laws or ordinances requiring the registration of deaths. It covered the years 1900 to 1904, inclusive, and in 1904 represented a population of 32,996.989. The total number of deaths reported was 551,354, the rate per 1,000 of the population being 16.7. But ten States and the District of Columbia with certain cities were included in the Registration Area. The Census enumeration of 1900, which follows, covered the whole United States so far as returns could be obtained.

DEATHS IN THE UNITED STATES IN CENSUS YEAR 1900.

(Compiled from the Report of the Census Office.)

States and Territories.	Total.	Male.	Female.	White, Total.	White, Native.	White, Foreign.	Colored, Total.
The United States	1.039,094	551,611	487,483	892,092	694,736	175.252	147,002
Registration record	512,669	272,819	239,850	475,640	337,288	126,465	37,029
Registration States	301,670	157,745	143,925	292,618	210,918	78,077	9,052
Cities in registration States	191,667	100,041	91,626	184,408	124,490	58.096	7,259
Rural part of registration States.	110,003	57,704	52,299	108,210	86.428	19,981	1,793
Registration cities in other States	210,999	115,074	95,925	183,022	126.370	48,388	27,977
Non-registration	526,425	278,792	247,633	416.452	357,448	48,787	109,973
Alabama	25,699	12.970	12,729	12,937	12,308	341	12,762
Arizona	1,223	750	473	947	681	219	276
Arkansas	22,518	11.813	10,705	16,372	15.804	280	6,146
California	22,506	13,998	8.508	21,081	13,687	6.874	1,425
Colorado	7,428	4,471	2,957	7,210	4,856	1,233	218
Connecticut	15,422	7.902	7,520	15,048	10.800	3,941	374
Delaware	3.075	1.644	1,431	2,490	2,134	236	585
District of Columbia	6,364	3,274	3.090	3,660	2,989	616	2.704
Florida	6.482	3,520	2,962	3,408	2,943	381	3.074
Georgia	26,941	13,321	13,620	13.094	12,637	257	13,847
Idaho	1,242	762	480	1.075	850	189	167
Illinois	61,229	33,641	27.588	59,618	42.545	16,052	1.611
Indiana	33,586	17.454	16.132	32,312	28.307	3,247	1.274
Indian Territory	5,286	2.795	2,491	3,936	3.863	37	1,350
Iowa	19,573	10,612	8,961	19,362	14.089	4.240	211
Kansas	16,261	8,978	7,283	15.209	11,691	1,720	1,052
Kentucky	27,091	13,843	13,248	22.035	19.047	1,221	5,056
Louisiana	20,955	10,971	9.984	10.250	8,465	1,670	10,705
Maine	12,148	6,292	5,856	12,112	10,497	1,487	36
Maryland	20,422	10,526	9,896	15,341	12,177	2.391	5,081
Massachusetts	49,756	25,352	24,404	49,061	34,952	13,645	695
Michigan	33,572	18,084	15,488	33.205	24.068	8,752	367
Minnesota	17,005	9.354	7.651	16.816	10,318	6,285	189
Mississippi	20,251	10,299	9,952	7,444	7,120	150	12,807
Missouri	38.084	20,480	17,604	34.959	29.383	4,771	3,125
Montana	2.188	1,387	801	1,930	1.069	534	258
Nebraska	8,[illegible]64	4,480	3,784	8,015	6,042	1,737	249
Nevada	438	290	148	349	201	137	89
New Hampshire	7,400	3,663	3,737	7,388	5.848	1.077	12
New Jersey	32,735	17,462	15,273	31,069	22,829	7,915	1,666
New Mexico	2,674	1,455	1,219	2.398	2,228	116	276
New York	130,268	68,648	61,620	127,332	88,479	37,505	2,936
North Carolina	21,068	10,427	10,641	13,217	12,805	63	7,851
North Dakota	2,287	1,159	1,128	2,046	1.291	715	241
Ohio	53,362	28,648	24,714	51.481	40,219	9,356	1,881
Oklahoma	3,181	1,741	1,440	2,704	2,563	113	477
Oregon	3.396	2.019	1,377	3,176	2,412	632	220
Pennsylvania	90,199	49.150	41,049	86,653	67.229	16,354	3,546
Rhode Island	8,176	4.132	4,044	7,939	5.571	2,295	237
South Carolina	17,166	8,461	8.705	5.808	5,605	144	11,358
South Dakota	3,088	1,654	1.434	2,448	1,672	751	640
Tennessee	30,572	15,354	15.218	21,629	20,257	511	9,543
Texas	34,160	18,045	16,115	26.216	23.526	2,136	7,944
Utah	3,079	1,821	1.258	2,972	1,934	983	107
Vermont	5,829	2,936	2,893	5.804	4,885	844	25
Virginia	25,252	13,112	12,140	14.070	13,472	439	11,182
Washington	4,910	3,148	1,762	4,594	3,065	1,211	316
West Virginia	9,588	5,046	4,542	9,074	8.651	338	514
Wisconsin	24,928	13,815	11,113	24,747	15,298	8,974	181
Wyoming	767	452	315	651	474	137	116

The Census year ended May 31, 1900.

In the summaries of the results the data are classed as "registration" and "non-registration," according to the source from which the original returns were obtained. The non-registration class includes the areas in which the deaths were reported by the enumerators, and those areas in which registration was too defective to be accepted.

The average age at death in 1890 was 31.1 years; in 1900 it was 35.2 years.

MORTALITY STATISTICS—*Continued.*

The cities with a population above 100,000 showed the following death rates for 1900 and 1890:

	1900.	1890.		1900.	1890.		1900.	1890.		1900.	1890.
Washington	22.8	23.7	Rochester, N.Y.	15.0	17.3	Louisville	20.0	20.1	Cleveland	17.1	20.2
Boston	20.1	23.4	Syracuse, N.Y.	13.8	19.6	New Orleans	28.9	26.3	Columbus	15.8	14.7
Fall River	22.4	23.2	Providence	19.9	21.1	Baltimore	21.0	22.9	Toledo	16.0	18.9
Worcester, Mass.	15.5	18.0	Los Angeles, Cal.	18.1	20.0	Minneapolis	10.8	13.5	Allegheny, Pa.	18.4	18.2
Detroit	17.1	18.7	San Francisco	20.5	22.5	St. Paul	9.7	14.9	Philadelphia	21.2	21.3
Jersey City	20.7	25.6	Denver	18.6	23.0	Kansas City	17.4	17.3	Pittsburgh	20.0	20.1
Newark, N.J.	19.8	27.4	Chicago	16.2	19.1	St. Joseph	9.1	—	Scranton, Pa.	20.7	21.8
Paterson, N.J.	19.0	22.2	New York	20.4	*25.3	St. Louis	17.9	17.4	Memphis	25.1	25.3
Buffalo, N.Y.	14.8	18.4	Indianapolis	16.7	17.3	Cincinnati	19.1	21.0	Milwaukee	15.9	18.8

* Estimated.

St. Joseph, Mo., with a death rate of 9.1 per 1,000, showed the lowest mortality, and Shreveport, La., with 45.5 the highest.

CAUSES OF DEATH IN THE CENSUS YEAR 1900.

NUMBER OF DEATHS FROM CERTAIN CAUSES, WITH PROPORTION FROM EACH CAUSE PER 100,000 FROM ALL CAUSES, IN 1900 AND 1890.

CAUSES OF DEATH.	1900.		1890.		CAUSES OF DEATH.	1900.		1890.	
	Number.	Proportion.	Number.	Proportion.		Number.	Proportion.	Number.	Proportion.
Consumption*	111,079	10,688	102,199	12,146	Diseases of the stomach¶	13,484	1,298	8,080	960
Pneumonia	105,971	10,198	76,496	9,091	Measles	12,866	1,238	9,256	1,100
Heart disease†	69,315	6,671	44,959	5,343	Croup	12,484	1,201	13,862	1,647
Diarrhœal diseases‡	46,907	4,514	47,201	5,610	Diseases of the liver**	12,249	1,179	9,460	1,124
Unknown causes	40,539	3,901	34,286	4,074	Diseases of the brain	11,479	1,104	12,322	1,464
Diseases of the kidneys §	36,724	3,534	19,457	2,312	Inanition	11,382	1,095	6,995	831
Typhoid fever	35,379	3,405	27,058	3,216	Dropsy	11,264	1,084	10,070	1,197
Cancer	29,475	2,837	18,536	2,203	Whooping cough	9,958	958	8,432	1,002
Old age	29,222	2,812	16,591	1,972	Peritonitis	7,501	722	4,995	594
Apoplexy	26,901	2,589	14,999	1,783	Railroad accidents	6,930	667	5,756	684
Inflammation of the brain and meningitis	25,664	2,470	17,775	2,113	Septicæmia	6,776	652	3,748	445
Cholera infantum	25,576	2,461	27,510	3,269	Burns and scalds	6,772	652	3,850	458
Paralysis‖	23,865	2,297	16,570	1,969	Scarlet fever	6,333	609	5,969	709
Bronchitis	20,223	1,946	21,422	2,546	Suicide	5,498	529	3,932	467
Debility and atrophy	17,282	1,663	25,536	3,035	Drowning	5,387	518	5,104	607
Influenza	16,645	1,602	12,957	1,540	Appendicitis	5,111	492	....	....
Diphtheria	16,475	1,586	27,815	3,306	Rheumatism	5,067	488	4,508	536
Convulsions	15,505	1,492	16,598	1,973	Diabetes	4,672	450	2,407	286
Malarial fever	14,874	1,431	18,594	2,210	Hydrocephalus	4,302	414	4,338	516
Premature birth	14,720	1,417	7,635	908	Cerebro-spinal fever	4,174	402	3,333	396
					Gunshot wounds	4,060	391	2,552	303

* Including general tuberculosis. † Including pericarditis. ‡ Including cholera morbus, colitis, diarrhœa, dysentery, and enteritis. § Including Bright's disease. ‖ Including general paralysis of the insane. ¶ Including gastritis. ** Including jaundice, and inflammation and abscess of the liver.

This table serves only to indicate the relative frequency of deaths from the specified causes, as reported. It should be considered in connection with the following table, which gives the number of deaths due to the same causes in the registration area, with the death rates per 100,000 of population.

DEATHS FROM CERTAIN CAUSES IN THE REGISTRATION AREA IN 1900 AND 1890, WITH DEATH RATES DUE TO EACH CAUSE, PER 100,000 OF POPULATION.

CAUSES OF DEATH.	1900.		1890.		CAUSES OF DEATH.	1900.		1890.	
	Number.	Rate.	Number.	Rate.		Number.	Rate.	Number.	Rate.
Pneumonia	55,296	191.9	38,752	186.9	Diseases of the stomach**	5,743	20.0	3,565	18.1
Consumption*	54,898	190.5	48,236	245.4	Diseases of the brain	5,357	18.6	6,055	30.9
Heart disease†	38,608	134.0	23,939	121.8	Peritonitis	5,028	17.5	3,419	17.4
Diarrhœal diseases‡	24,509	85.1	20,457	104.1	Unknown causes	4,849	16.8	4,827	24.6
Diseases of the kidneys§	24,124	83.7	11,736	59.7	Measles	3,801	13.2	2,662	13.5
Apoplexy	19,173	66.6	9,631	49.0	Railroad accidents	3,792	13.2	2,761	14.0
Cancer	17,296	60.0	9,410	47.9	Whooping cough	3,669	12.7	3,098	15.8
Old age	15,558	54.0	8,823	44.9	Suicide	3,400	11.8	2,027	10.3
Bronchitis	13,903	48.3	14,632	74.4	Scarlet fever	3,327	11.5	2,682	13.6
Cholera infantum	13,758	47.8	15,659	79.7	Hydrocephalus	3,173	11.0	3,033	15.4
Debility and atrophy	13,108	45.5	17,427	88.6	Drowning	3,152	11.0	2,543	12.9
Inflammation of the brain and meningitis	12,026	41.8	9,666	49.1	Septicæmia	2,867	10.0	1,517	7.7
Diphtheria	10,201	35.4	13,786	70.1	Appendicitis	2,858	9.9	....	....
Typhoid fever	9,749	33.8	9,097	46.3	Croup	2,830	9.8	5,432	27.6
Premature birth	9,690	33.7	4,948	25.2	Diabetes	2,693	9.4	1,089	5.5
Convulsions	9,522	33.1	11,050	56.3	Burns and scalds	2,545	8.8	1,081	5.5
Paralysis‖	9,450	32.8	6,980	35.5	Malarial fever	2,526	8.8	3,773	19.2
Inanition	7,859	27.3	5,445	27.7	Cerebro-spinal fever	2,039	7.1	1,241	6.3
Influenza	6,882	23.9	1,215	6.2	Dropsy	1,979	6.9	2,034	10.3
Diseases of the liver ¶	6,514	22.7	4,742	24.2	Rheumatism	1,951	6.8	1,587	8.1
					Gunshot wounds	1,103	3.8	479	2.4

* Including general tuberculosis. † Including pericarditis. ‡ Including cholera morbus, colitis, diarrhœa, dysentery, and enteritis. § Including Bright's disease. ‖ Including general paralysis of the insane. ¶ Including jaundice, and inflammation and abscess of the liver. ** Including gastritis.

The following was the death rate per thousand in various countries in 1900: Austria, 25.4; Belgium, 19.3; Denmark, 16.9; England and Wales, 18.2; France, 21.9; German Empire, 22.1; Hungary, 26.9; Ireland, 19.6; Italy, 23.8; Netherlands, 17.8; Norway, 15.9; Scotland, 18.5; Spain, 28.9; Sweden, 16.8; Switzerland, 19.3; United States (registration area), 17.6.

Statistics of Homicide.

In the Independent of April 11, 1907, James Edgar Bisun contributed the following statistics of homicide in principal countries of the world:

Josiah Strong's "Social Progress" for 1906 gives the following table of homicides and the annual average:

	Tried.	Con-victed.		Tried.	Con-victed.		Tried.	Con-victed.
Italy	3,606	2,805	England	318	151	Hungary	...	625
Austria	689	499	Ireland	129	54	Holland	35	28
France	847	580	Scotland	60	21	Germany	567	476
Belgium	132	101	Spain	1,584	1,085			

The average number of murders in the United States annually during the past twenty years, from 1885 to 1904, was 6,597. In 1896 the murders reached high-water mark, 10,662, and in 1895 there were 10,500. In Germany the convictions equalled 95 per cent. and a fraction; in the United States, 1.3 per cent.

In this connection, the nationalities of the homicides in the United States will be of interest. August Drahm gives the following: Native white, 42.94 per cent.; foreign born, 16.50 per cent.; negroes, 37.12 per cent.; Chinese and Japs, 1.28 per cent.; civilized Indians, 1.21 per cent.

Capital Punishment.

In Italy there is no capital punishment, and it has been abolished in the States of Maine, Michigan, Wisconsin, Rhode Island, and Kansas; Colorado and Iowa have both restored it after brief periods of abolition. As to the methods of carrying out death sentences; the guillotine is employed publicly in France, Belgium, Denmark, Hanover and two cantons of Switzerland, and privately in Bavaria, Saxony, and also in two cantons of Switzerland. The gallows is used publicly in Austria, Portugal and Russia; and privately in Great Britain and the United States, except in New York and New Jersey, where the electric chair has been substituted. Death by the sword obtains in fifteen cantons in Switzerland, in China and Russia, publicly, and in Prussia privately. Ecuador, Oldenburg and Russia have adopted the musket publicly; while in China they have strangulation by the cord, and in Spain the garrote, both public; and in Brunswick, death by the axe.

The Anti-Saloon League.

President—Bishop Luther B. Wilson, Chattanooga, Tenn. *Recording Secretary*—Rev. S. E. Nicholson, Harrisburg, Pa. *Corresponding Secretary*—James L. Ewin, 900 F Street, N. W., Washington, D. C. *Treasurer*—Foster Copeland, Columbus, Ohio.

The Anti-Saloon League was founded in 1890, and is installed in practically every State of the union.

The League throughout the nation employs 500 persons, who give their entire time to the work of this institution, and it has over 100 offices from which were distributed during the year 100,000,000 pages of anti-saloon literature. The annual income is about $400,000.

Prisoners' Commutation Table.

The following table shows the time subtracted for uniformly good conduct from the terms to which prisoners are sentenced under the regulations in force in the State prisons of New York:

Sentence.	Commutation.			Remaining Short Term.			Sentence.	Commutation.			Remaining Short Term.		
	Years.	Months.	Days.	Years.	Months.	Days.		Years.	Months.	Days.	Years.	Months.	Days.
Years.							Years.						
1	..	2	..	..	10	..	11	3	11	..	7	1	..
1½........	..	3	..	1	3	..	11½......	4	1	15	7	4	15
2	..	4	..	1	8	..	12	4	4	..	7	8	..
2½........	..	6	..	2	..	..	12½......	4	6	15	7	11	15
3	..	8	..	2	4	..	13	4	9	..	8	3	..
3½........	..	10	..	2	8	..	13½......	4	11	15	8	6	15
4	1	..	..	3	..	..	14	5	2	..	8	10	..
4½........	1	2	15	3	3	15	14½......	5	4	15	9	1	15
5	1	5	..	3	7	..	15	5	7	..	9	5	..
5½........	1	7	15	3	10	15	15½......	5	9	15	9	8	15
6	1	10	..	4	2	..	16	6	..	..	10	..	..
6½........	2	..	15	4	5	15	16½......	6	2	15	10	3	15
7	2	3	..	4	9	..	17	6	5	..	10	7	..
7½........	2	5	15	5	..	15	17½......	6	7	15	10	10	15
8	2	8	..	5	4	..	18	6	10	..	11	2	..
8½........	2	10	15	5	7	15	18½......	7	..	15	11	5	15
9	3	1	..	5	11	..	19	7	3	..	11	9	..
9½........	3	3	15	6	2	15	19½......	7	5	15	12	..	15
10	3	6	..	6	6	..	20	7	8	..	12	4	..
10½........	3	8	15	6	9	15	30	11	10	..	18	2	..

2 months off first year, 2 months off second year, 4 months off third year, 4 months off fourth year, 5 months off fifth year and 5 months off each subsequent year after five years.

American Institute of Civics.

FOUNDED 1885, INCORPORATED UNDER THE LAWS OF CONGRESS.

Chairman of the Corporation, Melville W. Fuller, Chief Justice of the Supreme Court; Vice-Chairman, Henry Wade Rogers, Dean of Yale University Law School; President of the Institute, Henry Randall Waite, Ph. D.; Secretary and Editor of Citizenship, Bouck White; Auditor and Chairman of Executive Committee, General George Clinton Batcheller; Treasurer, William H. Trafton.

MEMBERS OF THE CORPORATION.

Hon. E. B. Sherman, Chicago, Ill.; Hon. Henry Wade Rogers, LL. D., Yale University; General Oliver O. Howard, United States Army; Merrill E. Gates, Washington, D. C.; William J. Coombs, Brooklyn, N. Y., Edward A. Mosely, Washington, D. C.; General Henry B. Carrington, United States Army; Mrs. Mary S. Lockwood, Washington, D. C.; Alden Freeman, East Orange, N. J; Rev. Adolph Roeder, Orange, N. J.; Chief Justice Melville W. Fuller, Washington, D. C.; ex-Governor John G. McCullough, North Bennington, Vt.; General George Clinton Batcheller, New York City; Adam H. Fetterolf, President Girard College, Philadelphia; John Elderkin, New York City; Louis Annin Ames, New York City; William H. Douglas, New York City; B. Frank Mebane, Spray, N. C.; Colonel John Wellington Faxon, Chattanooga, Tenn.; Otto M. Eidlitz, New York City; Henry Randall Waite, East Orange, N. J.; William H. Trafton, New York City; General Joseph C. Breckinridge, United States Army; Clinton R. Woodruff, Philadelphia, Pa.; Colonel Albert A. Pope, Boston, Mass.; Rastus S. Ransom, New York City; George F. Seward, New York City; Arthur L. Wyman, Libertyville, Ill.; Rev. W. F. Slocum, Colorado Springs, Col.; General Horatio C. King, Brooklyn, N. Y; Crammond Kennedy, Washington, D. C.

The purposes of the American Institute of Civics are to promote the intelligence as to affairs of citizenship and government, the patriotism, vigilance, and other qualities of citizenship, which are essential to the common weal under the rule of the people. To this end it seeks to bring into effective co-operation home influences, educational efficiencies, the press, the pulpit, the platform and other available agencies, irrespective of parties, sects or classes.

It seeks especially to promote the education of American youths for the intelligent and conscientious discharge of their duties at the primary and the ballot box. In brief, it applies to the cure of the civic evils, which everywhere menace the common weal, the sure process of "formation" rather than inefficient attempts in the way of "reformation."

The membership includes citizens in every State whose high character, commanding influence, and subordination of selfish considerations to the public good, qualify them for the high services in which the Institute seeks to enlist them. These citizens constitute what is known as the Institute's National Body of Councillors. Applications for membership in this body may be addressed to the president.

Funds for the defrayal of expenses are derived from, annual dues (for members generally, $3; for teachers and ministers, $2) and from voluntary contributions.

The publications of the Institute, including "Citizenship," its official organ, are sent to contributing members free of charge. Address all communications to American Institute of Civics, Fulton Chambers, 102 Fulton Street, New York City.

Area of the Great Lakes of the United States.

	Superior.	Michigan.	Huron.	Erie.	Ontario.
Greatest length in miles	890	345	270	250	190
Greatest breadth in miles	160	84	105	60	52
Greatest depth in feet	900	1,800	1,000	204	412
Area in square miles	32,000	22,400	23,000	10,000	6,700
Drainage in square miles	85,000	70,040	74,000	39,680	29,760
Height above sea-level in feet	600	578	574	564	234
Latitude, degrees north	46° 45'	41° 15'	43° 20'	41° 20'	43° 10'
	48° 50'	45° 55'	46° 10'	42° 50'	44° 10'
Longitude, degrees west	84° 30'	84° 40'	80° 10'	78° 35'	76° 20'
	92° 15'	87° 08'	84° 30'	83° 10'	79° 50'
Boundary line in miles	390	None	220	200	160
United States shore line in miles	955	1,320	510	370	230

Casualty Insurance in the United States.

INSURANCE in force January 1, 1908.—Personal Accident and Health, $3,800,000,000; Steam Boiler, $750,000,000; Plate Glass, $100,000,000; Employers' Liability (estimated), $1,800,000,000; Fidelity, $1,000,000,000; Surety, $1,000,000,000; Credit, $40,000,000; Burglary, $50,000,000.

CASUALTY AND SURETY INSURANCE BUSINESS IN 1907.

The following was the business transacted in the United States in 1907 by the thirty-seven companies transacting a miscellaneous insurance business:

Class of Business.	Prem. Received	Losses Paid.	P.C.	Class of Business.	Prem. Received	Losses Paid.	P.C.
Burglary	$2,295,538	$796,909	34.7	Personal Accident	$18,865,102	$8,101,101	42.9
Credit	2,072,014	710,939	34.3	Plate Glass	2,845,950	1,198,476	42.1
Fidelity and Surety	11,129,940	4,319,406	38.8	Steam Boiler	2,062,289	170,425	8.2
Health	3,872,936	1,579,534	40.8	Sprinkler	158,440	28,947	18.3
Liability	22,759,060	10,999,586	48.3				

Ocean Marine Insurance.

Fifteen marine insurance companies reporting to the New York State Insurance Department had on January 1, 1907, assets of $23,204,275, net surplus of $7,660,025, and risks in force of $301,288,072.

International Polar Commission.

ORGANIZED at Brussels, Belgium, May 29, 1908. *President*—Capt. Umberto Cagni, R. N., Italy. *Vice-President*—Dr. Otto Nordenskjold, Sweden. *Secretary*—Prof. Georges Lecointe, Uccle, Belgium.

MEMBERS—S. E. Moreno, Argentina; Capt. R. Muirhead Collins (active), Australia; Dr. Prof. De Kovesligethy (active), Hungary; Adrian De Gerlache de Gomery and Georges Lecointe (active), Belgium; Henri Arctowski and Capt. J. Melaerts (associate), Belgium; Capt. Holm and Dr. A. J. C. Steenstrup (active), Denmark; Herbert L. Bridgman (active), United States; Capt. Umberto Cagni and Dr. Guido Cora (active), Italy; W. Pember Reeves (active), New Zealand; Capt. Lamie and Dr. J. P. Van Der Stok (active), Holland; Captain Phaff and Dr. E. Van Everdingen (associate), Holland; Prof. S. Mehedinit and E. G. Racovitza (active), Roumanie; Maj. Gens. Andre Wilkitsky and Jules De Shokalsky (active), Russia; Prof. Otto Nordenskjold and Prof. B. G. De Geer (active), Sweden; Prof. Joh. G. Anderson (associate), Sweden; Carsten E. Borchgrevink (associate), Norway.

The American Bonapartes.

Prince Jerome Bonaparte (King of Westphalia). born Ajaccio, Corsica, November 15, 1784; died at Ville Genis, near Paris, June 24, 1860. Married, first, at Baltimore, Md., December 24, 1803, Elizabeth, daughter of William Patterson, Esq. She was born at Baltimore February 6, 1785, and died in that city April 4, 1879. The issue of the marriage was:

Jerome Napoleon Bonaparte, born at Camberwell, England, July 7, 1805; died at Baltimore, Md., June 17, 1870. Married, November 3, 1829, Susan May, daughter of Benjamin Williams, of Roxbury, Mass. She was born April 2, 1812, and died September 15, 1881. The issue of the marriage was:

(1) Jerome Napoleon Bonaparte, born at Baltimore, Md., November 5, 1830; died at Beverly, Mass., September 3, 1893. He was educated at and graduated from West Point Military Academy, and served as a colonel in the French army in the Franco-Prussian war. He was married September 7, 1871, to Catherine Le Roy, daughter of Samuel Appleton and widow of Newbold Edgar. The issue of the marriage was:

(1) Louise Eugenie Bonaparte, born February 7, 1873. Married December 29, 1896, Comte Adam de Moltke-Huitfeldt, of Denmark, and has issue: (1) Marie Louise Caroline, born November 7, 1897; (2) Leon Charles Joseph, born November 14, 1898; (3) Jerome Eugene Otto, born January 14, 1902; (4) Adam Nicolas, born May 17, 1908.

(2) Jerome Napoleon Bonaparte, born Paris, France, February 26, 1878, Harvard B. A. and Georgetown University. A banker in Washington, D. C. Unmarried.

(2) Charles Joseph Bonaparte, born at Baltimore, Md., June 9, 1851. Married September 1, 1875, Ellen Channing, daughter of Thomas Mills Day, of Newport, R. I. No issue. Mr. Bonaparte is a Harvard B. A., 1871; LL. B., 1878; a lawyer; was Secretary of the Navy 1905-07, and is now Attorney-General of the United States.

Brussels Universal and International Exhibition of 1910.

A Universal and International Exhibition will open at Brussels, Belgium, in the month of April, 1910, and continue six months. Its palaces and halls will be erected in the new quarter of the Avenue Louise, in the Bois de la Cambre, a favorite resort of the Brussels people.

The exhibition will include, in broad lines, artistic, scientific, industrial, commercial and colonial sections. The artistic section will consist of an international saloon of fine arts. The scientific section will embrace, with the various degrees of education, the instruments and general methods connected with letters, sciences, and arts. The industrial section will be made up of all the products, methods and materials, both industrial and agricultural. Steps will be taken to render fully complete the special groups connected with fancy trades, mines, metallurgy, machinery, electricity, arm manufacturing and mechanical locomotion. The programme further contains special exhibitions, temporary agricultural and horticultural shows, congresses, conferences, artistic and sportive fetes.

The Executive Committee also proposes to organize during the exhibition popular games and competitions. Furthermore, like other exhibitions, national compartments will be formed wherein the works and productions of a same country will be divided into groups and classes, according to a system of general classification. The exhibition will cover a total area of about two hundred acres, a large portion of which will be reserved to the foreign sections. The installations will be connected with the Belgian State Railway, so as to bring all exhibits up to the required spot on rail tracks laid down in the halls and grounds.

An international jury of awards will be instituted, to operate under the control of the Commissioner-General of the Belgian Government. The members of the jury will be designated by the Government of their respective countries. Foreign Governments have been advised of the organization of the Brussels Universal and International Exhibition, in which they will be invited to take part and to be officially represented by accredited Commissioners; these Commissioners, representing their respective nationalities and having the charge of their interests, will arrange with the Executive Committee of the exhibition company, through the Government Commissioner-General, all questions relating to the distribution of space reserved to their respective country and installation of each national section.

Although an undertaking solely due to private initiative, the Brussels Exhibition has insured the effective co-operation of the Belgian Government, and also the support of the city of Brussels and province of Brabant. It is placed under the high patronage of His Majesty the King of the Belgians and under the honorary presidency of His Royal Highness Prince Albert of Belgium. The Duke d'Ursel has been invested with the functions of Government Commissioner-General to the Brussels Exhibition, and M. J. Gody, has been appointed Deputy Commissioner-General.

All communications connected with the exhibition are to be addressed by prepaid letter to the President of the Executive Committee, 34 Rue des XII Apotres, Brussels.

Tampa Isthmian Canal Exposition of 1910.

An Exposition of the industrial arts will be held at Tampa, Florida, from January to May, 1910, inclusive, to commemorate the progress of the work on the Panama Canal. It was originally purposed to hold this Exposition in 1908, but the time has been postponed to 1910, with the concurrence of Congress. The head of the Exposition project is Thomas J. L. Brown, President of the Florida Mid-Winter Fair Association, Tampa, Florida.

Congress on June 30, 1906, adopted the following joint resolutions:

"Whereas, it is fitting that the commencement of the work on the Panama Canal should be celebrated in a suitable manner to the end that the importance of this great isthmian waterway may be accentuated and the sentiment in favor of its early completion fostered and kept alive; and

"Whereas, the City of Tampa, in the State of Florida, by reason of its being further to the southward and nearer to said canal than any other city in the country, having a deep and commodious harbor, reached by ample railroad facilities, as also on account of its salubrious climate and the spirit of American progress among its citizens, manifest in the rapid growth and development of the city and her commerce, affords a suitable place for such an Exhibition; and

"Whereas, it has been determined to hold such an Exposition at Tampa, Florida, during the months of January, February, March, April and May, A.D., 1908, and

"Whereas, his Excellency Napoleon B. Broward, Governor of the State of Florida, did on December 30, 1905, issue his proclamation calling an Isthmian Exposition to be held in the City of Tampa, commencing in the month of January, A. D., 1908, for the purpose aforesaid, and inviting the Governors of the several States comprising the United States of America, as well as the Governors of the Territories of the United States, to secure the co-operation of their State Legislatures in aid of said Exposition by participating therein and sending exhibits of their resources to said Exposition; therefore be it

"Resolved, that the President be, and he is hereby, requested to hold a naval review in Tampa Bay at such time during the progress of said Exposition as he may deem best.

"Resolved further, that the President of the United States be, and he is hereby, requested to cause to be made such display of the Army of the United States at said Exposition as he may deem advisable.

"Resolved further, that nothing contained in this concurrent resolution shall be construed as committing the United States to any obligation hereafter to appropriate money for expenses or liabilities of any kind or character made or incurred by any one for the entertainment of the guests of such Exposition, or in connection with such celebration and Exhibition."

Baltimore Exposition in 1914.

It is proposed to hold an International Exposition on the water front at Baltimore in 1914, that being the one hundredth anniversary of both the climax of the war of 1812 and the birth of the "Star Spangled Banner." The idea originated with the Baltimore "American," in which the national song was first published from Francis Barton Key's manuscript and received the general approval of citizens. The City Council has taken steps toward an organization and the Maryland State authorities have promised co-operation.

The Japanese National Exposition of 1917.

The following statement has been prepared for THE WORLD ALMANAC by the Japanese Embassy at Washington:

The Exposition which will be held in 1917 in Tokio is a national exposition, and is to be maintained and administered by the Imperial Government of Japan. It was planned to have the exposition held during the year 1912, but early in 1908 it was decided that owing to world wide financial disturbances during 1907 it would be advisable to postpone the exposition until 1917. That will be the fiftieth anniversary of the accession of the present Emperor during whose reign Japan has made such wonderful strides in commerce, manufactures and, in fact, in every field of human endeavor. While it is a national exposition, the participation of the governments and peoples of foreign countries is cordially invited and the Japanese Government will make the plan on such a scale as not only to render it the largest exposition ever held in Japan, but give it a positively international character. This has been communicated to several countries, and many of them, appreciating the desire of the Japanese Government, have already shown their readiness to render their assistance.

It is expected that the national appropriation alone in connection with the projected exposition will amount to about $5,000,000. Added to this, the local government and municipality of Tokio, as well as the various local governments throughout the Empire of Japan and the Government of Formosa, and so forth, will make appropriations in their respective budgets so that the total governmental and municipal appropriation covering the direct expenditures of the exposition will aggregate at least more than $10,000,000.

The grounds of the exposition will occupy about 250 acres of land, of which about thirty acres will be covered by buildings already decided upon. Special buildings will be set apart for exhibits representative of arts and science, including those relating to education and also of machineries and electrical appliances.

The period during which the exposition is to be held is determined to be from April 1 to October 31, so as to include both the cherry blossom and the chrysanthemum seasons, of which so much has been written by writers on Japan, and talked of by foreign visitors who have been there.

From these facts it can be easily seen that the Japanese Government desires to offer an unexcelled opportunity for foreigners to take a trip to Japan and to be entertained with attractions and amusements which even the natives may not often witness except on such an occasion.

Being a national exposition, the primary object of the enterprise is to widen the knowledge of the Japanese people as regards the industrial development attained within their own country as well as in the whole world; but, nevertheless, no better opportunity will be found in the near future than this exposition for one who entertains the desire to know the Japanese people better and to study deeper the natural and industrial resources of the country, no less than the present state of civilization and industrial achievement of her people.

Alaska-Yukon-Pacific Exposition of 1909.

From June 1 to October 16, 1909, there will be held at Seattle, Wash., an international exposition, the Alaska-Yukon-Pacific Exposition.

The primary purpose of the Exposition is to exploit the resources of the Alaska and Yukon territories in the United States and the Dominion of Canada and to make known and foster the vast importance of the trade of the Pacific Ocean and of the countries bordering thereon. In addition it will demonstrate the marvellous progress of Western America.

It is the aim of the Exposition to correct the common impression that Alaska and Yukon are nothing but countries of cold and gold and to place the Territories in their true light before the eyes of the world. Another object of the Exposition is to increase the trade of the nations that are lapped by its waters.

The Exposition complete represents an expenditure of approximately $10,000,000. It occupies 250 acres of the campus of the University of Washington, adjoining one of the many beautiful residence districts of Seattle, on the gentle slopes and terraces overlooking Puget Sound, Lake Washington and Lake Union. The lakes are natural, fresh water bodies, Washington having an area of 38½ square miles and Union an area of 1⅓ square miles. The unsurpassed stretches of water front on both lakes afford great opportunities for aquatic features, the like of which no other exposition ever possessed.

The grounds are twenty minutes' ride by five double-tracked electric car lines from the business centre of Seattle and are scenically one of the finest exposition sites ever laid out. The snow-clad Olympic and Cascade ranges of mountains are in plain view from all points of the grounds. Mount Rainier, the highest peak in the United States, rises to a height of 14,526 feet, and Mount Baker, another formidable peak of the Cascades, towers 11,000 feet.

Twelve large exhibit buildings form the nucleus of the Exposition. Around these cluster the State, Territorial and Concessions buildings, foreign pavilions, the Administration group and smaller exhibit structures.

The main exhibit buildings are: (1) United States Government, (2) Alaska, (3) Yukon, (4) Manufactures, Liberal Arts and Education, (5) Agriculture, (6) Machinery, (7) Forestry, (8) Fine Arts, (9) Fisheries, (10) Mines, (11) Hawaii and the Philippines, (12) Foreign.

On June 1, 1907, just two years prior to opening day, before a crowd of 15,000 persons, the first spadeful of earth was turned and work begun on the Exposition. The exercises, which were held in the natural amphitheatre and participated in by governors, mayors and other prominent people of the Pacific Coast, were preceded by a large military parade in the city. The day, which was a holiday in Seattle, was made a memorable one in the history of the Pacific Northwest. Hon. John Barrett, director of the International Bureau of American Republics, represented President Roosevelt.

Work on the grounds since then has progressed rapidly. Eight buildings were completed by the 1st of November, 1908, and the others will be ready for their exhibits on April 1, 1909. The management claims that it will be the first fair in history that will be complete in every detail on the opening date.

The United States Government is participating on a large scale. The last session of Congress appropriated $600,000. In addition to the main Government building, Alaska, Hawaii and the Philippine Islands have separate structures.

The preliminary funds for the Exposition were raised by the people of Seattle. The capital stock was placed at $500,000 and a day set aside for the sale of the stock. In the one day the amount was oversubscribed $150,000, and the capital stock was increased to $800,000, all of which was sold in Seattle.

Last October the Exposition management offered $350,000 worth of Exposition bonds, and the entire amount was sold in Seattle in ten days, making the total amount subscribed to the Exposition by the people of Seattle $1,150,000.

The States of Washington, Oregon, California, Montana, Colorado, Nevada, Utah, Wyoming, North Dakota, Wisconsin, Michigan, Minnesota, Kansas, Illinois, Indiana, North Carolina, Ohio, Pennsylvania, New York, Texas and Arizona have all arranged to show their resources.

In the foreign exhibits will be featured the products of the countries bordering on the Pacific. The following countries are represented in this display: Australia, Canada, Chile, China, Colombia, Costa Rica, Ecuador, Formosa, Korea, French East Indies, German Colonies, Guatemala, Honduras, British India, Japan, Mexico, Dutch East Indies, Nicaragua, New Zealand, Panama, Peru, Siam and Salvador.

In addition to the foregoing, the United States, Great Britain, France, Germany, Russia and the Netherlands will make exhibits representative of their interest in Pacific trade development.

Official Roster: J. E. Chilberg, President; John H. McGraw, Vice-President; R. A. Ballinger, Vice-President; A. S. Kerry, Vice-President; William M. Sheffield, Secretary; C. R. Collins, Treasurer; I. A. Nadeau, Director-General; James A. Wood, Director of Exploitation; Welford Beaton, Chief of Publicity; Frank P. Allen, Jr., Director of Works; Henry E. Dosch, Director of Exhibits; A. W. Lewis, Director of Concessions.

Freemasonry.

MASONIC GRAND LODGES IN THE UNITED STATES AND BRITISH AMERICA.

Grand Lodges.	No. Members, 1908.	Grand Secretaries.	Grand Lodges.	No. Members, 1908.	Grand Secretaries.
Alabama...	19,966	G. A. Beauchamp, Montg'y.	Nevada......	1,241	C. N. Noteware, Carson.
Arizona....	1,394	G. J. Roskruge, Tucson.	N. Brunswick*	2,482	J. Twining Hartt, St. John.
Arkansas*..	18,293	F. Hempstead, Little Rock.	N. Hampshire	9,727	F. D. Woodbury, Concord.
Brit. Col....	3,258	R. E. Brett, Victoria.	New Jersey..	28,475	Benj. F. Wakefield, Trent.
California..	36,126	G. Johnson, San Francisco.	New Mexico.	*	A. A. Keen, Albuquerque.
Canada.....	39,795	Ralph L. Gunn, Hamilton.	New York....	152,008	E. M. L. Ehlers, N. Y. City.
Colorado...	12,226	C. H. Jacobson, Denver.	N. Carolina..	16,835	John C. Drewry, Raleigh.
Connecticut	20,752	John H. Barlow, Hartford.	North Dakota	5,915	F. J. Thompson, Fargo.
Delaware...	2,888	Virginius V. Harrison,	Nova Scotia..	5,020	Thomas Mowbray, Halifax.
		Wilmington.	Ohio..........	68,679	J. H. Bromwell, Cincin'ti.
Dist. of Col..	7,999	Arvine W. Johnston, Wash.	Oklahoma...	15,518	J. S. Hunt, Guthrie.
Florida.....	7,228	W. P. Webster, Jacksonville.	Oregon.......	8,085	Jas. F. Robinson, Portland.
Georgia.....	28,420	W. A. Wolihin, Macon.	Pennsylvania	75,273	Wm. A. Sinn, Philadelphia.
Idaho.......	2,395	Theop. W. Randall, Boisé.	Pr. Ed. Island	635	N. MacKelvie, Summerside
Illinois.....	85,583	Isaac Cutter, Coup Point.	Quebec.......	5,488	Will. H. Whyte, Montreal.
Indiana....	47,353	C. W. Prather, Indianapolis.	Rhode Island	6,719	S. P. Williams, Providence.
Iowa........	37,838	N. R. Parvin, Cedar Rapids.	S. Carolina..	10,403	Jacob T. Barron, Columbia.
Kansas.....	28,764	Albert K. Wilson, Topeka.	South Dakota	6,675	G. A. Pettigrew, Sioux Falls
Kentucky..	30,600	H. B. Grant, Louisville.	Tennessee...	20,986	John B. Garrett, Nashville.
Louisiana..	10,584	R. Lambert, New Orleans.	Texas........	41,736	John Watson, Waco.
Maine......	26,530	Stephen Berry, Portland.	Utah.........	1,343	C. Diehl, Salt Lake City.
Manitoba...	13,871	James A. Ovas, Winnipeg.	Vermont.....	12,078	H. H. Ross, Burlington.
Maryland..	12,310	Wm. M. Isaac, Baltimore.	Virginia......	17,644	G. W. Carrington, Richm'd.
Mass........	*	S. D. Nickerson, Boston.	Washington.	10,903	Horace W. Tyler, Tacoma.
Michigan....	56,010	L. B. Winsor, Reed City.	W. Virginia..	11,778	H. R. Howard, Pt. Pleasant.
Minnesota.	22,014	John Fishel, St. Paul.	Wisconsin....	22,974	Wm. W. Perry, Milwaukee.
Mississippi.	14,371	F. Speed, Vicksburg.	Wyoming....	2,102	W. L. Kuykendall, Saratoga
Missouri...	45,348	J. R. Parson, St. Louis.			
Montana...	4,421	Cornelius Hedges, Jr., Hel.	Total......	1,288,562	
Nebraska....	15,728	Francis E. White, Omaha.			

* Total membership not officially reported.

The returns of the Grand Lodges of the United States and British America for 1905-1906 were as follows: Whole number of members, 1,062,425; raised, 81,386; admissions and restorations, 28,155; withdrawals, 22,008; expulsions and suspensions, 659; suspensions for non-payment of dues, 12,760; deaths, 16,123. Gain in membership over preceding year, 58,177. Membership in 1906, 1,129,001; gain over the preceding year of 66,576.

These Grand Lodges are in full affiliation with the English Grand Lodge, of which the Duke of Connaught is Grand Master, and the Grand Lodges of Ireland, Scotland, Cuba, Peru, South Australia, New South Wales, Victoria, and also with the Masons of Germany and Austria. They are not in affiliation and do not correspond with the Masons under the jurisdiction of the Grand Orient of France; they, however, affiliate with and recognize Masons under the jurisdiction of the Supreme Council. Freemasonry is under the ban of the Church in Spain, Italy, and other Catholic countries, and the membership is small and scattered.

ANCIENT ACCEPTED SCOTTISH RITE MASONS.

Supreme Council of Sovereign Grand Inspectors-General of the Thirty-third and Last Degree.

The officers of the Northern Jurisdiction are: *M. P. Sovereign Grand Commander*, Henry L. Palmer, Wis. *P. G. Lieutenant-Commander*, Samuel C. Lawrence, Mass. *Grand Treasurer-General*, Newton D. Arnold, R. I. *Grand Minister of State*, John C. Smith, Ill. *Grand Secretary-General*, James H. Codding; office, 299 Broadway, New York.

The officers of the Southern Jurisdiction are: *M. P. Sovereign Grand Commander*, James D. Richardson, Tenn. *Secretary-General*, Dr. A. B. Chamberlin, 433 Third Street, N. W., Washington, D. C. These grand bodies are in relations of amity with the Supreme Councils for France, England, Scotland, Ireland, Belgium, Brazil, the Argentine Republic, Uruguay, Paraguay, Peru, Portugal, Italy, Mexico, Colombia, Chile, Central America, Greece, Canada, Cuba, Switzerland, Egypt, Tunis, and Spain.

Supreme Council of Sovereign Grand Inspectors-General of the Thirty-third and Last Degree of the Ancient and Accepted Scottish Rite, as Organized by Joseph Cerneau, Thirty-third Degree, in the Year 1807.

M. P. Sovereign Grand Commander, Andrew J. Provost, N. Y. *Grand Secretary-General*, Alfred C. Dupont, M. D., N. Y. The Sovereign Grand Consistory has had a continuous existence of one hundred and one years, with its Grand Orient at New York, where, under the ægis of the Grand Orient of France, it was organized by M. ·. I. ·. Joseph Cerneau, thirty-third degree. The Supreme Council has fraternal relations with the Supreme Councils of Great Britain and Ireland, Canada, Italy, Egypt, Cuba, Argentina, Australia, New Zealand, Mexico, Belgium, Germany, and Switzerland, Greece, Austria-Hungary, and other Grand Orients. It has jurisdiction over seventy-three subordinate Consistories of Sublime Princes of the Royal Secret, which are subdivided into Lodges of Perfection, Councils of Princes of Jerusalem, Chapters of Rose Croix, and Consistories, with a membership of many thousands. The two Consistories in Manhattan are Cerneau, No. 1, with over a thousand Sublime Princes, and Giordano Bruno, No. 66, working in the Italian language. Official address, No. 320 Temple Court, Beekman Street, New York.

Ancient Accepted Scottish Rite.

The Supreme Council of Sovereign Grand Inspectors-General, thirty-third and last degree of the Ancient Accepted Scottish Rite of Freemasonry for the United States of America, their Territories and Dependencies, Orient of New York. Officers—*Sovereign Grand Commander*, M. W. Bayliss, Washington, D. C. *Lieutenant-Grand Commander*, C. W. Edwards, Albany, N. Y. *Minister of State*, George Gibson, Washington, D. C. *Treasurer-General*, Holden O. Hill, Providence, R. I. *Secretary-General*, M. W. Morton, Providence, R. I. This Supreme Council was organized in the City of New York on October 28, 1807, and exercises jurisdiction over the whole of the United States.

FREEMASONRY—*Continued.*

ROYAL ARCH MASONS.

OFFICERS OF THE GENERAL GRAND CHAPTER.

General Grand High Priest—Joseph E. Dyas, Paris, Ill.
Dep. Gen. Grand High Priest—William C. Swain, Milwaukee, Wis.
Gen. Grand King—Nathan Kingsley, Austin, Minn.
Gen. Grand Scribe—Bernard G. Witt, Henderson, Ky.
Gen. Grand Treasurer—John M. Carter, Baltimore, Md.
Gen. Grand Secretary—Christopher G. Fox, Buffalo, N. Y.
Gen. Grand Captain of the Host—George E. Corson, Washington, D. C.
Gen. Grand Principal Sojourner—Frederick W. Craig, Des Moines, Iowa.
Gen. Grand Royal Arch Captain—William F. Kuhn, Farmington, Mo.
Gen. Grand Master 3d Vail—Bestor G. Brown, Topeka, Kan.
Gen. Grand Master 2d Vail—Charles N. Rix, Hot Springs, Ark.
Gen. Grand Master 1st Vail—J. Albert Blake, Boston, Mass.

The office of the General Grand Secretary is at Buffalo, N. Y.

The number of grand chapters, each representing a State or Territory (except Pennsylvania and Virginia), is 44, and the number of enrolled subordinate chapters is 2,683, exclusive of 28 subordinate chapters in the Territories of the United States, the Sandwich Islands, Porto Rico, Chile, and the Chinese Empire, which are under the immediate jurisdiction of the General Grand Chapter.

The total membership of the enrolled subordinate chapters is 266,919. The degrees conferred in Chapters are Mark Master, Past Master, Most Excellent Master, and Royal Arch Mason. The next triennial meeting will be held in 1909, at Savannah, Ga.

KNIGHTS TEMPLAR.

OFFICERS OF THE GRAND ENCAMPMENT OF THE UNITED STATES OF AMERICA.

Grand Master—Henry W. Rugg, Providence, R. I.
Deputy Grand Master—W. B. Melish, Cincinnati, O.
Grand Generalissimo—A. MacArthur, Troy, N. Y.
Grand Captain-General—W. F. Pierce, San F'n'sco.
Grand Senior Warden—L. S. Smith, Pittsburgh, Pa.
Grand Junior Warden—J. K. Orr, Atlanta, Ga.
Grand Treasurer—H. Wales Lines, Ct.
Grand Recorder—John A. Gerow, Detroit, Mich.

The office of the Grand Recorder is at Detroit, Mich.

The number of grand commanderies in the United States and Territories, each representing individual States or Territories (except that Massachusetts and Rhode Island are combined), is 46. Commanderies subordinate to Grand Commanderies, 1,201, with a membership of 171,204. Commanderies subordinate to Grand Encampment, 8; membership, 1,045; total number of commanderies, 1,209; total membership, 172,149. The next triennial conclave will be held in Chicago, Ill., August, 1910. The orders conferred in a Commandery of Knights Templar are Red Cross, Knight Templar, and Knight of Malta. A Mason, to obtain these orders, must be a Master Mason and Royal Arch Mason in good standing, and a member of both Lodge and Chapter.

COLORED MASONIC BODIES.

There are thirty-eight grand lodges in as many different States of the United States and one in Canada. The Prince Hall Grand Lodge, of Massachusetts, is the oldest lodge, having been organized in the year 1808. It was the outgrowth of African Lodge, No. 459, the warrant for which was granted to Prince Hall and fifteen other colored Masons September 24, 1784. The number of colored Masons in the United States and Canada is 150,000; Royal Arch, 14,000; Knights Templar, 12,000; Nobles of the Mystic Shrine, 2,000; Ancient Accepted Scottish Rite Masons, 5,712. The Grand Lodge of New York, organized in 1848, has jurisdiction over thirty lodges, located in different parts of the State. The total membership is about 2,000. H. A. Spencer, Grand Master, Rochester, N. Y.; Benj. Myers, Grand Secretary.

SOVEREIGN SANCTUARY OF ANCIENT AND PRIMITIVE FREEMASONRY.

RITE OF MEMPHIS—IN AND FOR THE CONTINENT OF AMERICA.

M. I. Grand Master-General...H. G. Goodale, 96°
V. I. Grand Administrator-General. W. F. Ford, 95°
V. I. Grand Chancellor-General..J. S. Phillips, 95°
V. I. Grand Secretary-General..E. T. Stewart, 95°

Official address, German Masonic Temple, 220 East Fifteenth Street, New York City. M. I. Sovereign Grand Master Harvey G. Goodale, 96°, Jamaica, Long Island, N. Y. J. Adelphi Gottlieb, M. D., M. A., LL. D., Legate of the M. I. Sovereign Grand Master and Sovereign Sanctuary Embassy, 225 West 106th Street, New York City, U. S. A.

The Sovereign Sanctuary is composed of Masons who have received the 95th degree of Patriarch Grand Conservator of the Rite; and has jurisdiction over the continent of America. It was formally instituted in the United States in the year 1856. The American body is in affiliation with the various Masonic powers of the world and has a regular exchange of Representatives with England, Ireland, New Zealand, Italy, Spain, Roumania, Egypt, etc. The Degrees of the Rite, which are ninety of instruction and seven official, are conferred in the subordinate bodies of the Rite thus: Fourth to 18th degree in a Chapter Rose Croix; 19th to 42d degree in a Senate of Hermetic Philosophers; 43d to 90th degree in a Council of Sublime Masters of the Great Work.

Nobles of the Mystic Shrine.

THE Ancient Arabic Order of the Nobles of the Mystic Shrine is not a regular Masonic body, but its membership is composed strictly of Masons who have reached the 32d degree, A. A. S. Rite (18th degree in England), or Knights Templar in good standing. There are 113 temples in the United States, and a total membership of about 128,000.

The following are the imperial officers for the United States for 1908-09: *Imperial Potentate,* Edwin I. Alderman, Cedar Rapids, Ia.; *Imperial Deputy Potentate,* George L. Street, Richmond, Va.; *Imperial Chief Rabban,* Fred. A. Hines, Los Angeles, Cal.; *Imperial Assistant Rabban,* J. Frank Treat, Fargo, N. Dak.; *Imperial High Priest and Prophet,* William J. Cunningham, Baltimore, Md.; *Imperial Oriental Guide,* William W. Irwin, Wheeling, W. Va.; *Imperial Treasurer,* William S. Brown, 523 Wood Street, Pittsburgh, Pa.; *Imperial Recorder,* Benjamin W. Rowell, 206 Masonic Temple, Boston, Mass.; *Imperial First Ceremonial Master,* Jacob T. Barron, Columbia, S. C.; *Imperial Second Ceremonial Master,* Frederick R. Smith, Rochester, N. Y.; *Imperial Marshal,* J. Putnam Stevens, Portland, Me.; *Imperial Captain of the Guard,* Henry F. Neidringhaus, Jr., St. Louis, Mo.; *Imperial Outer Guard,* Charles E. Ovenshire, Minneapolis, Minn.

Odd Fellowship.

SOVEREIGN GRAND LODGE OF THE INDEPENDENT ORDER OF ODD FELLOWS.

OFFICERS.

Grand Sire—John L. Nolen, Nashville, Tenn.
D. Grand Sire—W. L. Kuykendall, Saratoga, Wyo.
Grand Secretary—John B. Goodwin, Baltimore. Md.
Assistant Grand Secretary—J. Edward Kroh, Baltimore, Md.
Grand Treasurer—M. R. Muckle, Philadelphia, Pa.
Gd. Chaplain—Rev. W. I. Canter, Fairmont, W. Va.
Grand Marshal—E. L. Pilsbury, Charlestown, Mass.
Grand Guardian—W. O. Carbis, Salt Lake City, Utah.
Grand Messenger—Will A. Steidley, Leesville, La.

GRAND LODGES AND MEMBERSHIP IN SUBORDINATE LODGES.
(Reported to the Annual Communication in 1908.)

Jurisdiction.	No. of Members	Jurisdiction.	No. of Members	Jurisdiction.	No. of Members
Alabama	22,698	Maine	24,507	Oklahoma	26,714
Alberta	2,426	Manitoba	5,970	Ontario	37,699
Arizona	1,811	Maritime Provinces	8,039	Oregon	14,398
Arkansas	26,414	Maryland	8,996	Pennsylvania	140,900
British Columbia	4,211	Massachusetts	57,656	Quebec	3,931
California	42,308	Michigan	48,064	Rhode Island	6,185
Colorado	12,601	Minnesota	19,324	South Carolina	4,816
Connecticut	19,513	Mississippi	4,195	South Dakota	8,032
Delaware	2,772	Missouri	58,768	Tennessee	35,023
District of Columbia	1,936	Montana	4,943	Texas	30,718
Florida	3,902	Nebraska	20,718	Utah	2,788
Georgia	30,010	Nevada	1,477	Vermont	6,992
Idaho	7,044	New Hampshire	15,025	Virginia	28,602
Illinois	83,332	New Jersey	28,568	Washington	19,662
Indiana	74,919	New Mexico	1,685	West Virginia	20,515
Iowa	55,147	New York	113,602	Wisconsin	18,275
Kansas	40,813	North Carolina	15,418	Wyoming	2,313
Kentucky	26,057	North Dakota	5,467		
Louisiana	3,791	Ohio	82,733	Total*	1,396,319

The membership of the Independent Order of Odd Fellows, which includes the Grand Lodges of Australasia, Germany, Denmark, Sweden, Switzerland, and the Netherlands, is 1.442.758, female members not included. The American organization is not in affiliation with an English order entitled the Manchester Unity of Odd Fellows. *Including Saskatchewan, 1,843 members.

The Encampment branch of the Independent Order of Odd Fellows numbers 208,437 members; Rebekah lodges, sisters, 371,687; brothers, 199,513; Chevaliers of the Patriarchs Militant, 21,524. The next meeting of the Sovereign Grand Lodge will be at Seattle, Washington, Sept. 20-25, 1909.

The total relief paid by the Independent Order of Odd Fellows, year ending December 31, 1907, was $5,112,993.75; brothers relieved, 137,368; widowed families relieved, 6,832; paid for relief of brothers, $3,278,922.62; for widowed families, $173,570.80; education and relief of orphans, $149,845.10; burying the dead, $1,006,253.74.

INDEPENDENT ORDER OF ODD FELLOWS, MANCHESTER UNITY.

Officers of New York District: J. B. Riddell, Prov. G. M.; D. E. McHenry, Deputy Prov. G. M.; J. R. Harley, Prov. Treasurer; Alex. Lawson, Prov. C. S., 118 West 139th St., New York City.

This Order was founded in 1800 and is represented throughout the United States, Canada, Great Britain and Ireland, South Africa, Australia, and New Zealand by 434 districts, 5,032 lodges, and over 1,000,000 members, with a capital of $65,000,000.

GRAND UNITED ORDER OF ODD FELLOWS OF AMERICA.

OFFICERS.

Grand Master—W. L. Houston, Washington, D. C.
Deputy Grand Master—L. N. Porter, L. Rock, Ark.
Grand Treasurer—B. J. Davis, Atlanta, Ga.
Grand Secretary—J. F. Needham, 602 Spruce St., Philadelphia, Pa.
Grand Directors—G. H. Mays, Jacksonville, Fla.; J. C. Johnson, Baltimore, Md.; A. T. Shirley, Herndon, Va.; T. P. Woodland, New Orleans; W. W. Lawrence, Newbern, N. C.

This organization is composed of colored Odd Fellows, subordinate to G. U. O. O. F. Friendly Society, Manchester, England. The following is the statistical report for the year ending August 31, 1908: Lodges enrolled, 5,303; households, 3,328; P. G. M. Councils, 306; Patriarchies, 156; D. G. Lodges, 39; juvenile societies, 560; district households, 27. Total number of branches, 9,719. Total membership, 384,618.

Order of Good Templars.

THE INTERNATIONAL SUPREME LODGE.

Int. Chief Templar — Edward Wavrinsky, M. P., Stockholm.
Int. P. Chief Templar—Jos. Malins, Birmingham, Eng.
Int. Counselor —Geo. F. Cotterill, Seattle, Wash.
Int. Vice-Templar — Mrs. G. Buason, Winnipeg, Manitoba, Canada.
Int. Supt. of Juvenile Work—J. W. Hopkins, Gloucester, England.
Int. Electoral Supt.—Guy Hayler, Bulnear-York, England.
Int. Secretary—Tom Honeyman, Glasgow, Scotland
Int. Asst. Secretary—Oscar S. Ohlander, Chicago, Ill.
Int. Treasurer—Herman Blume, Hamburg.
Int. Chaplain—Rev. H. Greensmith, Oswego, N. Y.
Int. Marshal—G. A. Murray, Allahabad, India.
Int. Dept. Marshal — Mrs. F. Natts, Australia.
Int. Messenger—Mrs. N. Larson Ledet, Aarhus, Denmark.
Int. Guard—Rev. A. R. Edwards, Tallahassee, Fla.
Int. Sentinel—D. Fenton, Transvaal, Africa.

The last report of the International Secretary returned the number of grand lodges in the world as 70, and the membership as 419,749. The membership of the juvenile branch was 239,586. The Good Templars, which is a beneficial order, based on total abstinence, are organized in nearly every State of the Union, England, Ireland, Scotland, Wales, Germany, Denmark, Sweden, and Norway, Canada, West Indies, East, West, and South Africa, Australia, New Zealand, British India, Iceland, and other countries. The International Supreme Lodge will hold its next meeting at Hamburg, Germany, in 1911.

Order of the Sons of Temperance.

NATIONAL DIVISION OF NORTH AMERICA.

M. W. Patriarch—J. O. McCarthy, Toronto, Ont.
M. W. Associate—Rev. Alfred Noon, Boston, Mass.
M. W. Scribe—Ross Slack, 118 Rose Street, Trenton, N. J.
M. W. Treasurer—M. M. Eavenson, Philadelphia.
M. W. Chaplain—Rev. N. J. Kirby, Gagetown, N. B.
M. W. Conductor—Edwin F. Marvin, Bridgeport, Ct.
M. W. Sentinel—Herbert Blessing, Camden, N. J.
M. W. Supt. Y. P. Work—Rev. Robert A. Spence, Philadelphia, Pa.

The Order of the Sons of Temperance was organized in the City of New York September 29, 1842, It is composed of subordinate, Grand, and National Divisions. It has five National Divisions—one for North America, one for Great Britain and Ireland, two for Australia, and one for New Zealand. In the course of its existence it has had nearly four million members on its rolls. Its present membership in North America is 34,879, of whom 13,537 are in the United States. Its fundamental principle is total abstinence from all intoxicating liquors.

The 65th annual session of the National Division of North America will be held at Worcester, Mass., July, 1909.

The Royal Arcanum.

SUPREME COUNCIL.

Supreme Regent—Robert Van Sands, Illinois.
Supreme Vice-Regent—C. H. Bowen, Rhode Island.
Supreme Orator—F. T. McFaden, Virginia.
Past Supreme Regent—H. C. Wiggins, New York.
Supreme Secretary—A. T. Turner, Massachusetts.
Supreme Treasurer—E. A. Skinner, New York.
Supreme Auditor—Wm. F. McConnell, New York.
Supreme Chaplain—W. H. Druckemiller, Pennsylvania.
Supreme Warden—D. R. Benedict, Colorado.

The membership of the Order October 31, 1908, was 240,850; the number of grand councils, 30, and subordinate councils, 1,989. The Supreme Council was organized at Boston June 23, 1877, and incorporated under the laws of Massachusetts. Number of deaths to October 31, 1908, 44,336. Benefits paid to October 31, 1908, $120,504,779.98. Emergency fund, October 31, 1908, $4,731,883.25.

Knights of Pythias.

SUPREME LODGE.

Supreme Chancellor—Henry P. Brown, Cleburne, Texas.
Supreme Vice-Chancellor—George M. Hansom, Calais, Maine.
Supreme Prelate—DeWitt C. Cobb, New Jersey.
Supreme Keeper of Records and Seal—R. L. C. White, Nashville, Tenn.
Supreme Master of Exchequer—Thos. D. Meares, Wilmington, N. C.
Supreme Master at Arms—Samuel H. Davis, Davis, Okla.
Supreme Inner Guard—E. A. Powers, Montreal.
Supreme Outer Guard—W. D. Cameron, Meridian, Miss.
President Board of Control, Insurance Dept.—Union B. Hunt, Chicago, Ill.
Major-General Military Dept.—Arthur J. Stoddard, St. Paul, Minn.

MEMBERSHIP, JANUARY 1, 1909.

Alabama	11,535	Illinois	2,475	Minnesota	8,565	Ohio	80,829	Vermont	2,365
Arizona	1,626	Indiana	57,789	Mississippi	10,102	Oklahoma	71,574	Virginia	5,958
Arkansas	6,975	Iowa	24,012	Missouri	27,504	Ontario	2,484	Washington	8,065
Br. Columbia	3,114	Kansas	12,460	Montana	2,980	Oregon	5,805	W. Virginia	13,046
California	18,457	Kentucky	13,062	Nebraska	6,781	Pennsylv'nia	52,569	Wisconsin	10,391
Colorado	8,050	Louisiana	7,727	Nevada	1,429	Quebec	405	Wyoming	1,238
Connecticut	7,938	Maine	16,270	New Hamp.	6,915	Rhode Island	3,032	Subordinate lodges	1,070
Delaware	1,460	Manitoba	1,539	New Jersey	14,236	S. Carolina	11,802		
Dis. of Col.	1,591	Mar. Prov's.	2,103	New Mexico	1,418	S. Dakota	2,929		
Florida	6,534	Maryland	9,938	New York	24,903	Tennessee	12,526	Total	698,536
Georgia	13,792	Massach'tts	23,067	N. Carolina	8,854	Texas	24,717		
Idaho	2,475	Michigan	17,557	N. Dakota	3,211	Utah	1,762		

Membership of the Insurance Department (Life Insurance), 79,469, representing an aggregate insurance of $123,321,000. Membership of the military department, 24,965. The office of the Supreme Keeper of Records and Seal is at Nashville, Tenn. The next biennial convention of the Supreme Lodge will be held at Milwaukee, Wis., beginning August 2, 1910.

Membership of Fraternal Organizations.

ACCORDING to the last reports of the supreme bodies of these organizations to THE WORLD ALMANAC, the membership of the principal fraternal organizations in the United States and Canada is as follows:

Odd Fellows	1,396,319	Tribe of Ben Hur	100,315
Freemasons	1,288,562	Knights and Ladies of Honor	96,000
Modern Woodmen of America	920,079	Improved Order of Heptasophs	77,389
Knights of Pythias	698,536	Knights of the Golden Eagle	71,960
Independent Order of Rechabites	491,000	National Union	62,000
Woodmen of the World	529,023	Brotherhood of American Yeomen	61,671
Improved Order of Red Men	471,661	Protected Home Circle	65,273
Knights of the Maccabees	285,841	Catholic Mutual Benefit Association	59,442
Royal Arcanum	240,850	Order of Gleaners	56,000
Ancient Order of United Workmen	219,729	Court of Honor	65,000
Independent Order of Foresters	260,000	Brith Abraham Order	61,389
Order of Eagles	311,159	New England Order of Protection	54,119
Foresters of America	235,441	Knights of Honor	40,126
Benevolent and Protective Order of Elks	284,321	Ancient Order of Foresters	40,992
Ancient Order of Hibernians	217,000	United Order of American Mechanics	36,554
Knights of Columbus	210,078	Sons of Temperance	34,879
Junior Order of United Amer. Mechanics	194,741	Independent Order of B'nai B'rith	30,283
Ladies of the Maccabees	156,609	Knights of Malta	30,000
Knights of the Modern Maccabees	112,846	Smaller organizations	536,642
Ladies' Catholic Benevolent Association	102,129	Total	10,175,976

Statistics of the Countries of the World.

Countries.	Population.	Sq. Miles.	Capitals.
China	432,000,000	4,277,170	Peking.
British Empire*	392,846,535	11,435,283	London.
Russian Empire	14[illegible],796,600	8,660,395	St. Petersburg
United States†	87,971,000	3,602,990	Washington.
United States and Islands‡	96,250,000	3,756,884	Washington.
Philippines	7,635,426	122,000	Manila.
Porto Rico	953,243	3,606	San Juan.
Hawaii	154,001	6,449	Honolulu.
Tutuila, Samoa	5,800	54	....
Guam	8,661	200	....
France and Colonies	92,531,325	4,296,130	Paris.
France	38,961,945	207,054	Paris.
Colonies	53,412,840	4,089,076	....
Algeria	4,739,558	184,474	Algiers.
Senegal, etc	4,523,000	806,000	St. Louis.
Tunis	1,900,000	51,000	Tunis.
Cayenne	32,908	30,500	Cayenne.
Cambodia	1,500,000	37,400	Saigon.
Cochin-China	2,968,529	22,000	....
Tonquin	7,000,000	46,400	Hanoi.
New Caledonia	51,514	7,650	Noumea.
Tahiti	10,300	600	....
Sahara	2,550,000	1,544,000	....
Madagascar	2,505,000	227,000	Antanauarivo
German Empire, in Europe	60,641,278	208,830	Berlin.
Prussia	37,293,324	134,603	Berlin.
Bavaria	6,524,372	29,282	Munich.
Saxony	4,508,601	5,787	Dresden.
Wurttemberg	2,302,179	7,528	Stuttgart.
Baden	2,010,728	5,821	Karlsruhe.
Alsace-Lorraine	1,814,564	5,600	Strasburg.
Hesse	1,209,175	2,965	Darmstadt.
Mecklenburg-Schwerin	625,045	5,135	Schwerin.
Hamburg	874,878	158	....
Brunswick	485,958	1,424	Brunswick.
Oldenburg	438,856	2,479	Oldenburg.
Saxe-Weimar	388,095	1,388	Weimar.
Anhalt	328,029	906	Dessau.
Saxe-Meiningen	268,916	953	Meiningen.
Saxe-Coburg-Gotha	242,432	755	Gotha.
Bremen	263,440	99	....
Saxe-Altenburg	206,508	511	Altenburg.
Lippe	145,577	469	Detmold.
Reuss (younger line)	144,584	319	Gera.
Mecklenburg-Strelitz	103,451	1,131	Neu Strelitz.
Schwarzburg-Rudolstadt	96,835	363	Rudolstadt.
Schwarzburg-Sonderh'n.	85,152	333	S'ndershausen
Lubeck	105,857	115	....
Waldeck	59,127	433	Arolsen.
Reuss (elder line)	70,603	122	Greiz.
Schaumburg-Lippe	44,992	131	Buckeburg.
German Africa	12,210,000	931,460	....
Austro-Hungarian Empire	46,973,359	261,035	Vienna.
Japan (with Formosa)	49,732,952	147,655	Tokio.
Netherlands	5,591,701	12,648	Amsterdam.
Netherlands and Colonies	41,347,182	795,648	Amsterdam.
Borneo	1,129,889	212,737	....
Celebes	1,878,473	71,470	....
Java	28,746,688	50,554	Batavia.
Moluccas	410,190	43,864	Amboyna.
New Guinea	200,000	151,789	....
Sumatra	3,168,312	161,612	....
Surinam	70,007	46,060	Paramaribo.
Turkish Empire	41,049,720	1,622,080	Constantin'ple
European Turkey	6,130,200	65,350	....
Asiatic Turkey	17,683,500	693,610	....
Tripoli	1,000,000	398,000	Tripoli.
Bulgaria	3,744,300	37,200	Sofia.
Egypt	9,821,100	400,000	Cairo.
Italy	32,475,253	110,550	Rome.
Italy and Colonies	36,825,253	449,050	Rome.
Abyssinia	3,500,000	150,000	....
Eritrea	450,000	88,500	....
Somal Coast	400,000	100,000	....
Spain	18,891,574	194,783	Madrid.
Spanish Africa	273,709	258,580	....
Spanish Islands	127,172	1,957	....
Brazil	17,371,069	3,218,130	Rio Janeiro.
Mexico	13,607,259	767,005	City of Mexico
Korea	10,519,000	82,000	Seoul.
Congo State	30,000,000	900,000	....
Persia	7,653,000	628,000	Teheran.
Portugal	5,423,132	35,490	Lisbon.
Portugal and Colonies	14,582,084	838,442	Lisbon.
Portuguese Africa	8,248,527	793,980	....
Portuguese Asia	910,425	8,972	....
Sweden	5,294,885	172,876	Stockholm.
Norway	2,240,032	124,129	Kristiania.
Morocco	5,000,000	219,000	Fez.
Belgium	7,074,910	11,373	Brussels.
Siam	7,000,000	220,000	Bangkok.
Roumania	5,912,520	50,720	Bucharest.
Argentine Republic	5,974,771	1,135,840	Buenos Ayres.
Colombia	4,500,000	438,436	Bogota.
Afghanistan	4,000,000	215,400	Cabul.
Chile	5,000,000	291,544	Santiago.
Peru	2,971,844	697,640	Lima.
Switzerland	3,315,443	15,976	Berne.
Bolivia	2,267,935	709,000	La Paz.
Greece	2,433,806	25,014	Athens.
Denmark	2,605,268	15,388	Copenhagen.
Denmark and Colonies	2,585,660	102,022	Copenhagen.
Iceland	78,470	39,756	Rejkjavik.
Greenland	11,893	46,740	Godthaab.
West Indies	30,527	138	....
Venezuela	2,323,527	593,943	Caracas.
Servia	2,493,770	18,630	Belgrade.
Liberia	2,060,000	35,000	Monrovia.
Nepaul	4,000,000	54,000	Khatmandu.
Cuba	1,722,953	45,883	Havana.
Oman	1,500,000	82,000	Muscat.
Guatemala	1,842,134	48,290	N. Guatemala.
Ecuador	1,500,000	429,000	Quito.
Hayti	1,400,000	10,204	Port au Prince
Salvador	1,006,848	7,225	San Salvador.
Uruguay	1,111,758	72,210	Montevideo.
Khiva	800,000	22,320	Khiva.
Paraguay	635,571	196,349	Asuncion.
Honduras	500,114	46,250	Tegucigalpa.
Nicaragua	428,191	49,200	Managua.
Dominican Republic	610,000	18,045	San Domingo.
Costa Rica	341,590	18,400	San Jose.
Panama	361,000	32,380	Panama.
Montenegro	228,000	3,630	Cettinje.

* These estimates of the population and area of the British Empire include the recently acquired possessions in Africa. For statistics in detail see tabular page entitled "The British Empire." † Estimated for 1909 by the United States Comptroller of the Currency. ‡ Estimated for January 1, 1909. The population and area of the Latin American nations are those reported by the Bureau of American Republics for 1907–8.

Civil Lists of European Sovereigns.

Austria-Hungary, Emperor of, $3,875,000.

Bavaria, King of, $1,350,616

Belgium, King of, $660,000.

Denmark, King of, $227,775; and Crown Prince, $28,800.

Greece, King of, $260,000.

Great Britain and Ireland, the King and Queen receive $2,350,000 and the remainder of the Royal family are allowed $560,000. The King also receives the revenues of the Duchy of Lancaster, $600,000 per annum, and the Prince of Wales those of the Duchy of Cornwall, about $300,000.

Italy, King of, $3,010,000, of which $360,000 for family.

Netherlands, Queen of, $250,000; also a large revenue from domains, and $62,500 for royal family, courts, and palaces.

Portugal, King of, $567,000.

Prussia, King of, $3,846,121; also a vast amount of private property, castles, forests, and estates, out of which the court expenditure and royal family are paid.

Roumania, King of, $201,482.

Russia, Czar of, had private estates of more than 1,000,000 square miles of cultivated land and forests, besides gold and other mines in Siberia. The annual income was estimated at about $12,000,000. In consequence of the unsettled condition of the empire this is much reduced at present.

Saxony, King of, $852,000.

Servia, King of, $204,000.

Spain, King of, $1,765,000, besides $600,000 for family.

Turkey—The Sultan's income is derived from the revenue of the Crown domains, estimated at about $7,500,000.

Würtemberg, King of, $500,000.

Life Insurance Statistics.

CONDITION OF REGULAR LEGAL RESERVE COMPANIES JANUARY 1, 1908, AND BUSINESS THE PRECEDING YEAR.*

No. of Cos.	Assets.	Premiums Received.	Total Income.	Payments to Policyholders (Losses, Dividends, Surrenders, &c.)	Total Expenditures.	New Policies Issued.		Policies in Force.	
						No.	Amount.	No.	Amount.
138	$3,052,732,353	$533,077,447	$678,656,595	$309,696,977	$439,787,411	4,902,829	$1,921,350,782	24,787,535	$14,063,362,639

CONDITION AND BUSINESS OF ASSESSMENT COMPANIES AND ORDERS.

No. of Cos.	Assets.	Assessments Collected.	Total Income.	Payments to Policyholders	Total Expenditures.	New Policies Issued.		Insurance in Force.	
						No.	Amount.	No. of Members.	Amount.
667	$85,544,461	$107,031,073	$128,274,413	$88,760,082	$105,851,829	†1,550,000	$1,382,747,458	7,970,839	$8,766,909,295

* Including industrial policies. † Estimated.

The returns of life insurance in the first three tables were compiled from "The Insurance Year-Book," published by The Spectator Company.

INCOME AND DISBURSEMENTS FOR TWENTY YEARS.

The following table shows the receipts and disbursements of the "old-line" life insurance companies reporting to the New York Insurance Department for twenty years:

Year Ending Dec. 31.	No. of Companies.	Total Income.	Total Payments for Losses, Endowments, and Annuities.	Total Payments for Lapsed, Surrendered, and Purchased Policies.	Total Dividends to Policyholders.	Total Payments to Policyholders.	Taxes, Commissions, and other Expenses.	Total Disbursements.
1887....	29	$130,657,526	$42,827,054	$10,413,379	$14,852,624	$68,003,557	$25,031,101	$93,447,289
1888....	30	147,024,431	48,569,964	11,234,569	14,324,827	74,129,360	27,905,878	103,369,145
1889....	30	168,184,699	53,081,834	12,240,142	13,951,069	79,273,667	34,898,168	114,503,360
1890....	30	187,424,959	58,606,615	13,827,225	14,271,501	86,707,341	39,616,782	126,653,530
1891....	29	201,931,425	62,731,497	16,230,891	13,991,236	92,953,614	42,350,372	135,792,048
1892....	31	223,024,998	72,576,866	15,658,759	14,386,195	102,621,820	49,665,730	152,890,333
1893....	32	236,683,206	75,903,820	19,839,418	14,823,176	110,566,414	55,205,336	166,512,254
1894....	33	256,624,478	78,313,162	23,164,108	14,577,455	116,054,725	61,073,545	177,863,333
1895....	35	266,897,200	84,791,622	22,889,493	15,297,604	122,978,718	62,052,872	185,772,902
1896....	36	279,373,107	90,146,264	26,368,039	17,083,169	134,219,515	64,160,732	199,173,299
1897....	35	301,268,179	92,688,307	26,431,312	18,425,197	137,544,815	67,582,025	205,866,394
1898....	35	320,306,169	98,465,681	26,436,307	19,694,634	144,566,622	72,667,590	218,063,363
1899....	37	355,946,005	111,788,691	23,080,965	20,917,143	155,786,799	86,622,697	243,154,558
1900....	40	392,358,741	120,945,587	22,190,804	22,568,261	165,704,652	94,782,023	261,467,238
1901....	38	437,935,470	135,674,468	23,907,412	23,811,649	183,393,529	103,051,203	287,181,045
1902....	39	488,736,272	142,777,004	26,346,122	26,589,715	195,712,841	116,474,384	312,931,556
1903....	42	534,161,859	158,131,967	31,497,758	30,617,368	220,247,094	128,440,557	349,453,708
1904....	42	580,743,959	171,804,278	35,916,236	33,334,133	241,054,647	138,202,722	380,049,676
1905....	43	614,712,082	179,795,591	42,366,560	35,795,581	257,957,732	134,986,906	393,743,139
1906....	43	632,446,618	183,626,623	55,178,177	39,782,313	278,587,113	124,797,879	404,215,088
1907....	37	625,718,823	191,854,912	55,441,688	45,109,125	292,405,725	107,942,425	401,089,735

ASSETS OF AND AMOUNT INSURED BY THE PRINCIPAL AMERICAN COMPANIES JANUARY 1, 1908.

Companies.	Insurance in Force.	Gross Assets.	Companies.	Insurance in Force.	Gross Assets.
New York Life, N. Y.	$2,005,341,184	$516,762,763	Connecticut Mutual........	$174,716,005	$66,762,350
Metropolitan, N. Y.......	1,804,946,581	209,825,777	National Life, Vt...........	151,779,282	40,692,155
Mutual Life, N. Y.........	1,452,752,408	510,579,976	State Mutual, Mass...........	121,725,794	30,618,011
Equitable Life, N. Y.....	1,340,126,354	460,788,026	Fidelity Mutual, Pa.........	119,452,264	15,404,601
Prudential, N. J..	1,337,367,045	151,047,694	Germania, N. Y.............	114,589,963	39,622,162
Northwestern Mut., Wis..	881,563,592	236,035,222	Phœnix Mutual, Ct.........	103,080,718	23,891,147
Mutual Benefit, N. J......	440,742,990	112,497,404	Home Life, N. Y............	86,193,297	20,669,963
Penn Mutual, Pa..........	425,956,270	92,049,382	Manhattan Life, N. Y......	69,066,914	20,421,876
Jno. Hancock Mut., Mass..	273,116,166	49,421,304	Berkshire Life, Mass........	64,910,790	16,443,588
Ætna Life, Ct.............	271,027,574	86,703,239	Union Mutual, Me..........	62,842,507	13,771,872
Union Central, Ohio	256,564,566	62,264,653	Washington Life, N. Y.....	57,859,321	19,118,046
Massachusetts Mutual....	213,475,260	46,751,608	Security Mutual, N. Y.....	48,473,969	4,921,779
Provident Life & Trust, Pa.	191,986,786	60,964,095	Connecticut General........	36,427,869	7,332,210
Travelers' (Life Dept.)....	180,335,420	46,151,632	Columbian National.........	35,500,886	4,284,832
New England Mutual.....	178,872,320	44,454,097	United States, N. Y........	35,018,078	8,826,777

LIFE INSURANCE IN VARIOUS COUNTRIES.

Insurance in force, United States (including assessment insurance), $20,809,015,450; Great Britain, $4,426,124,000; Germany, $1,400,000,000; France, $727,673,358; Austria, $370,621,530; Scandinavia, $150,402,801; Switzerland, $144,412,854; Russia, $62,839,902.

LIFE INSURANCE STATISTICS—*Continued.*

RECEIPTS AND DISBURSEMENTS IN 1907 OF COMPANIES REPORTING TO THE NEW YORK INSURANCE DEPARTMENT.

Companies.	Receipts.			Disbursements.				
	Premiums Received.	Interest Received.	Total Income.	Death Claims Paid.	Matured Endowments.	Lapsed and Surrendered.	Dividends to Policyholders.	Total Paid Policyholders.
Ætna Life	$10,256,271	$3,256,432	$13,788,479	$3,510,372	$2,129,394	$922,406	$918,364	$7,491,778
Berkshire	2,503,836	665,839	3,275,127	784,243	117,929	562,431	343,060	1,807,663
Connecticut Mutual	5,588,922	2,597,095	8,722,880	4,395,792	236,764	683,897	1,196,187	6,508,741
Equitable, New York	54,431,248	17,995,064	74,758,157	18,992,080	4,704,119	12,814,159	7,508,776	45,161,364
Fidelity Mutual	4,351,515	645,076	5,220,777	1,318,424	......	300,740	70,777	1,692,311
Germania	4,955,823	1,537,246	6,891,393	1,533,212	1,221,755	499,707	309,843	3,603,[illegible]86
Hartford Life	2,126,453	142,454	2,288,994	1,404,506	......	47,839	47,090	1,499,435
Home Life	3,352,579	824,815	4,334,269	1,089,337	294,319	378,341	301,672	2,109,558
Illinois Life	1,426,510	255,109	1,761,879	486,616	21,407	252,287	34,660	796,770
John Hancock	17,410,728	1,779,159	19,507,831	5,122,998	129,040	698,348	1,364,197	7,314,583
Life Ins. Co. of Virginia	2,320,494	138,497	2,479,878	701,529	572	39,618	27,737	770,086
Manhattan	2,299,472	702,763	3,330,240	1,287,353	185,695	313,014	57,018	1,854,491
Massachusetts Mutual	7,542,253	1,939,879	9,673,142	2,259,777	279,663	639,273	1,151,014	4,329,727
Metropolitan	64,046,983	7,387,540	72,738,733	17,912,807	320,562	1,036,896	3,694,876	23,098,151
Michigan Mutual	1,581,026	485,229	2,079,862	644,960	282,109	186,690	31,809	1,145,568
Mutual Benefit	16,664,430	4,869,841	21,667,692	5,407,700	1,405,051	1,915,032	2,239,455	11,135,673
Mutual, New York	56,639,200	21,166,019	80,023,493	23,294,033	5,075,597	8,147,995	4,321,493	43,651,121
National, U. S. A	1,908,351	379,072	2,310,056	361,870	707	117,535	5,193	487,915
National, Vermont	5,922,753	1,710,022	7,675,465	1,634,689	643,212	763,238	222,386	3,356,954
New England Mutual	6,814,552	1,796,029	8,913,847	2,368,482	435,331	702,070	899,777	4,405,660
New York Life	79,940,309	20,367,225	101,950,798	22,761,594	5,802,737	11,832,697	5,877,354	48,048,866
Northwestern Mutual	33,441,810	9,735,106	43,595,422	7,909,316	2,021,404	5,538,530	7,911,285	23,448,481
Pacific Mutual	3,718,881	576,793	4,398,615	881,683	33,841	373,206	253,587	1,553,314
Penn Mutual	15,700,452	4,085,814	20,278,824	4,608,313	1,331,728	1,365,189	1,361,086	8,921,992
Phœnix Mutual	3,946,145	1,076,854	5,084,703	1,215,396	195,249	397,726	414,569	2,234,248
Provident Life and Trust	7,669,604	2,681,351	10,736,501	2,131,909	2,415,618	742,812	1,060,634	6,423,324
Prudential	50,861,532	4,910,888	56,782,017	14,016,756	230,720	2,028,301	703,874	18,040,216
Security Mutual, N. Y.	1,575,820	158,769	1,798,864	575,318	......	95,301	28,374	698,286
State Life	2,624,316	214,728	2,941,802	528,246	......	255,665	88,345	873,256
State Mutual	4,528,762	1,208,315	5,919,338	1,344,746	497,576	546,362	584,728	2,979,642
Travelers	5,932,318	1,964,998	8,605,968	1,852,512	603,637	321,323	53,439	2,916,044
Union Central	9,466,664	3,347,572	12,923,476	2,013,342	738,129	695,890	1,081,462	4,553,213
Union Mutual	2,214,038	493,643	2,922,027	757,701	156,763	242,200	105,799	1,264,855
United States	1,116,708	416,989	1,584,329	656,321	107,812	398,630	79,289	1,260,201
Washington	2,228,450	560,611	3,167,426	913,573	758,785	414,713	112,777	2,234,405

DISBURSEMENTS.—Continued.

Companies.	Commissions Paid.	Salaries Paid.	All Other Expenses.	Dividends to Stockholders.	Taxes.	Profit and Loss.	Total Expenses.	Total Disbursements.
Ætna Life	$950,199	$257,908	$316,780	$200,000	$380,978	......	$2,138,025	$9,629,803
Berkshire	214,463	62,168	103,613	1,785	42,499	......	441,218	2,248,881
Connecticut Mutual	518,617	170,558	393,334	......	217,501	......	1,439,637	8,020,378
Equitable, New York	5,736,831	1,405,898	1,662,904	7,000	670,859	......	9,953,523	55,114,887
Fidelity Mutual	600,236	176,892	229,492	......	74,116	$2,606	1,136,311	2,828,622
Germania	724,356	164,506	224,519	24,000	60,241	1,241	1,234,340	4,833,126
Hartford Life	157,606	76,695	68,531	50,000	24,482	19,443	406,965	1,906,400
Home Life	389,407	124,843	143,933	15,000	56,525	......	753,298	2,862,856
Illinois Life	304,452	95,017	107,720	7,000	14,971	51,200	607,473	1,404,243
John Hancock	4,046,896	513,630	874,217	......	204,120	2,076	5,721,166	13,035,749
Life Ins. Co. of Virginia	694,298	130,171	171,335	24,000	48,421	1,880	1,071,923	1,842,009
Manhattan	230,826	122,716	240,873	26,000	44,160	......	733,771	2,588,262
Massachusetts Mutual	764,063	189,947	213,092	......	132,770	45,426	1,451,130	5,780,857
Metropolitan	13,350,173	2,510,912	3,288,473	140,000	935,523	165,610	20,566,065	43,664,216
Michigan Mutual	251,628	63,255	71,478	25,000	32,967	8,316	459,419	1,604,987
Mutual Benefit	1,674,678	384,573	512,974	......	427,178	126,418	3,171,123	14,306,796
Mutual, New York	3,905,267	1,200,790	2,323,241	......	768,616	79,703	8,950,308	52,601,429
National, U. S. A	402,010	87,139	100,377	50,000	30,585	44,213	728,518	1,216,433
National, Vermont	664,361	131,939	217,750	......	151,395	9,503	1,188,186	4,545,140
New England Mutual	640,791	193,187	239,714	......	112,845	......	1,235,118	5,640,778
New York Life	6,627,429	1,345,542	2,075,405	......	970,125	......	11,379,533	59,428,399
Northwestern Mutual	3,712,623	636,341	798,248	......	762,820	217,706	6,292,233	29,740,713
Pacific Mutual	714,833	130,413	499,528	70,000	46,028	......	1,176,304	2,729,618
Penn Mutual	1,796,946	337,282	499,649	......	456,925	6,923	3,286,917	12,208,909
Phœnix Mutual	495,565	121,225	114,500	......	109,743	......	854,964	3,089,212
Provident Life and Trust	695,009	318,196	285,413	......	115,164	......	1,508,616	7,940,940
Prudential	10,561,402	1,675,954	2,409,864	200,000	1,069,579	176,713	16,377,057	34,417,273
Security Mutual, N. Y.	291,306	77,965	96,182	......	30,784	23,590	527,799	1,226,085
State Life	684,399	116,931	102,689	......	49,667	5,142	982,112	1,855,368
State Mutual	462,185	84,141	149,832	......	81,216	14,155	817,594	3,797,236
Travelers	727,280	141,506	320,995	......	81,554	......	1,585,406	4,501,450
Union Central	1,056,026	224,178	511,575	10,000	158,981	......	2,004,960	6,558,173
Union Mutual	205,148	80,649	83,132	......	46,432	173	432,255	1,697,110
United States	115,747	65,730	84,834	30,800	16,496	94,565	422,605	1,682,806
Washington	203,780	95,447	171,263	......	34,398	2,856	570,453	2,804,863

Fire Insurance Statistics.

CONDITION AND TRANSACTIONS OF COMPANIES DOING BUSINESS IN THE UNITED STATES, YEAR ENDING JANUARY 1, 1908.

Number of Companies.	Capital.	Assets Exclusive of Premium Notes.	Net Surplus.	Cash Premiums Received during Year.	Total Cash Income during Year.
347 Stock*....... 271 Mutual......	$88,560,679	$565,677,747	$175,726,623	$316,810,104	$342,268,242

Number of Companies.	Paid for Losses during Year.	Paid for Dividends during Year.	Expenses other than Losses and Dividends during Year.	Total Disbursements during Year.	Risks Written during Year.
347 Stock*....... 271 Mutual......	$147,089,344	$26,009,878	$108,688,988	$281,788,210	†$32,000,000,000

* Including 36 Lloyds. † Approximation. These statistics of fire insurance business in the United States are, with the exception of the estimate of risks written during the year, compiled from "The Insurance Year-Book," published by The Spectator Company. They do not include the returns of a few stock companies and some 500 mutuals and town and county mutuals, whose transactions are purely local and individually of small volume.

CONDITION OF THE PRINCIPAL JOINT-STOCK COMPANIES DOING BUSINESS IN THE UNITED STATES JANUARY 1, 1908.*

Companies.	Admitted Assets.	Capital.	Net Surplus.	Companies.	Admitted Assets.	Capital.	Net Surplus.
Home, New York.......	$20,862,698	$3,000,000	$6,703,211	Glens Falls, N. Y.....	$4,267,271	$200,000	$2,020,893
Hartford, Ct............	18,882,806	2,000,000	3,189,005	Globe & Rutgers, N.Y.	4,153,182	400,000	1,098,732
Continental, New York.	16,399,452	1,000,000	7,503,591	Hanover Fire, N. Y..	4,114,164	1,000,000	854,091
Ætna, Ct................	14,884,569	4,000,000	3,529,539	Munich, Germany.....	3,893,267	†200,000	1,225,594
German-American, N. Y	13,508,038	1,500,000	4,415,353	Sun, England..........	3,790,767	†200,000	1,051,989
Liverp., London & Globe	12,560,211	†200,000	4,401,167	Westchester Fire, N.Y.	3,625,089	300,000	907,460
Royal, England..........	11,894,083	†200,000	3,094,131	London, England.....	3,261,453	†200,000	783,636
Ins. Co. of N. America.	11,221,740	3,000,000	976,343	Phœnix, England.....	3,071,445	†200,000	903,571
Phenix, New York......	8,719,795	1,500,000	849,462	Palatine, England....	3,063,759	†200,000	1,049,547
Phœnix, Ct..............	7,965,454	2,000,000	1,425,837	Norwich Union, Eng..	2,987,740	†200,000	538,461
Fire Association, Pa.....	7,840,675	750,000	1,786,785	Milwau. Mechanics'...	2,773,583	500,000	497,295
National, Ct.............	7,453,965	1,000,000	1,168,273	Rossia, Russia..........	2,736,235	†200,000	389 576
American, N. J.	7,230,738	750,000	1,601,615	Agricultural, N. Y....	2,717,477	500,000	511.617
Springfield F. & M........	7.204,959	2,000,000	862,399	Providence-Wash., R.I	2,632,185	500,000	174,178
Queen, New York.......	6,844,560	1,000,000	1,961,539	Franklin, Pa............	2,569,478	400,000	413,649
N. British & Mercantile.	6,832,711	†200,000	2,698,689	London Assurance.....	2,435,172	†200,000	618,474
Commercial Union, Eng.	6,744,997	†200,000	1,885,166	Girard F. & M., Pa....	2,246,339	500,000	305,410
Pennsylvania Fire.......	6,462,117	750,000	1,615,284	Western Assur., Can.	2,313,222	†200,000	584,137
Fireman's Fund..........	5,938,085	1,600,000	603,221	Spring Garden, Pa....	2,230,820	400,000	126,576
Connecticut Fire..........	5,817,424	1,000,000	1,042,596	Orient, Ct.............	2,222,546	500,000	338,275
Germania, N. Y..........	5,185,650	1,000,000	949,261	Williamsb'rgh C., N.Y.	2,146,618	250,000	455,686
American Central, Mo....	5,039,623	2,000,000	817,793	Royal Exchange, Eng.	2,110,754	†200,000	796,200
St. Paul F. & M., Minn....	4,994,843	500,000	1,048,519	Federal, N. J.........	2,092,812	1,000,000	332,889
Boston, Mass............	4,804,570	1,000,000	1,964,842	Security, Ct...........	2,075,660	500,000	236,392
Firemen's, N. J..........	4,701,069	1,000,000	2,148,371	Atlas, England........	2,021,223	†200,000	587,590
Scottish Union & Nat'l..	4,663,344	†200,000	2,347,685	United Firemen's, Pa	1,995,419	400,000	88,677
Northern, England......	4,592,631	†200,000	1,335,196	Hamburg-Bremen....	1,987,693	†200,000	392,048
Northwestern Nat'l, Wis	4,533,883	1,000,000	1,153,694	Caledonian, Scotland.	1,840,817	†200,000	466,658
New Hampshire Fire....	4,500,404	1,100,000	1,314,363	Delaware, Pa..........	1,787,038	400,000	145,255
Niagara Fire, N. Y.......	4,326,789	750,000	785,090				

* Annual statements of the fire insurance companies are rendered to the insurance departments during the month of January; therefore the statistics of condition January 1, 1909, were not ready when this publication went to press.

† The New York law requires a deposit of $200,000 from foreign companies with the insurance department. This is treated by the department as "deposit capital," and the surplus stated in the next column is "surplus beyond deposit capital" and other liabilities.

ANNUAL PROPERTY LOSSES IN THE UNITED STATES BY FIRES—1877-1908.

Years.	Property Loss.	Insurance Loss.	Years.	Property Loss.	Insurance Loss.
1877..................	$68,265,800	$37,398,900	1894..................	$140,006,484	$89,574,699
1878..................	64,315,900	36,575,900	1895..................	142,110,233	84,689,030
1879..................	77,703,700	44,464,700	1896..................	118,737,420	73,903,800
1880..................	74,643,400	42,525,000	1897..................	116,354 570	66,722,140
1881..................	81,280,900	44,641,900	1898..................	130,593 905	73,796,080
1882..................	84,505,024	48,875,131	1899..................	153,597,830	92,683,715
1883..................	100,149,228	54,808,664	1900..................	160,929,805	95.403,650
1884..................	110,008,611	60,679,818	1901..................	174,160,680	106,680,590
1885..................	102,818,796	57,430,789	1902..................	161,488,355	94,775,045
1886..................	104,924,750	60,506,567	1903..................	145,302,155	87,900,000
1887..................	120,283,055	69,659,508	1904..................	230,520,131	138,314,212
1888..................	110,885,665	63,965,724	1905..................	165,221,650	109,236,420
1889..................	123,046,833	73,679,465	1906..................	444,326,124	276,732,270
1890..................	108,993,792	65,015,465	1907..................	215,671,250	114,646,335
1891..................	143,764,967	90,576,918	1908..................	* 237,000,000	* 135,000 000
1892..................	151,516,098	93,511,936			
1893..................	167,544,370	105,994,577	Total 32 years...	$4,595,301,970	$2,723,945,365

* Estimated.

The New Thought.

The "New Thought" is said by its leaders to be "a science, a philosophy, a religion." Their theory of the universe—which they hold to be real—is that it is composed of two essential elements—one, the Creator (spirit), and the created (matter); that the creative force consists or is manifested in vibrations of a "Spiritual Ion," which acts and reacts upon the objects of the material world; that these creative Spiritual Ions pervade everything, and that man can so grade the vibrations of his being as to draw different qualities and use different degrees from the storehouse (as it is called) of "Spiritual Ion."

Faith they regard as one of the chief instruments through which the Ions of the individual can be brought to a condition where they may draw most largely and of the best from the Universal Storehouse. Other instrumentalities are reason, illumination and emanation. They recognize the dual character of the mind and define the so-called subjective mind—the subconscious intelligence—as the home in man of the Spiritual Ion. Whatever, then, is done to increase the efficiency of the subjective mind is of benefit to the individual, as he can thereby draw more largely upon the inexhaustible reservoir of the Creative Spiritual Ion.

The doctrines are those of a progress toward perfection through the instrumentalities above suggested, and others. They believe in the power of the Creative Spirit to cure disease, and in the last analysis to cure without drugs or surgery. They do not, however, put this extreme of belief in practise, but restrict their efforts to cases that are curable through the instrumentality of the subconscious mentality of the subject. The movement differs from Christian Science in that it carries no negation of matter nor of pain, but affirms that that which is can be cured through the progression of the individual toward perfection. The system of cure, as practised, does not essentially differ from that adopted by the Christian Scientists, and within the sphere of their self-imposed limitations, by Dr. Worcester and the practitioners of the Emmanuel Movement, and consists largely of putting the patient into a receptive or a hypnotic condition, and while he is in such condition controlling the functional reactions by suggestion or auto-suggestion.

The leaders of New Thought use the word God as synonymous with the "Creative Spiritual Ion," the "Great First Cause," "Universal Intelligence," "Absolute Substance," "Cosmic Consciousness;" the Bible they accept as a history of the spiritual man, of individuals, and of the nations whom it depicts. They do not allow its inspiration, nor to Jesus Christ divinity. The New Thought has "churches" in Boston, New York, Newark, Buffalo and in many other centres. Schools for the advancement of its propaganda are also to be found in these cities, and a quite extensive literature sets forth its theories and its claims.

The Alfred B. Nobel Prizes.

THE Swedish scientist, Alfred B. Nobel, the inventor of dynamite, died in 1896, bequeathing his fortune, estimated at $9,000,000, to the founding of a fund, the interest of which should yearly be distributed to those who had mostly contributed to "the good of humanity." The interest is divided in five equal shares, given away, "One to the person who in the domain of physics has made the most important discovery or invention, one to the person who has made the most important chemical discovery or invention, one to the person who has made the most important discovery in the domain of medicine or physiology, one to the person who in literature has provided the most excellent work of an idealistic tendency, and one to the person who has worked most or best for the fraternization of nations, and the abolition or reduction of standing armies, and the calling in and propagating of peace congresses."

The prizes for physics and chemistry are awarded by the Swedish Academy of Science, that for physiological or medical work by the Caroline Institute (the faculty of medicine in Stockholm), that for literature by the Swedish Academy in Stockholm, and the peace prize is awarded by a committee of five persons, elected by the Norwegian Storthing.

In accordance with these statutes the awarders of the prizes (the four above named institutions) elect fifteen deputies for two consecutive years, the Academy of Science electing six, and the other prize awarders three each. These deputies elect for two consecutive years four members of the Board of Directors of the Nobel Institute, which Board, exclusively consisting of Swedes, must reside in Stockholm. A fifth member, the President of the Board, is nominated by the Government. The Board of Directors has in its care the funds of the institution, and hands yearly over to the awarders of the prizes the amount to be given away. The value of each prize is on an average $40,000. The distribution of the prizes takes place every year on December 10, the anniversary of Mr. Nobel's death. Full information can be obtained from "Nobelstiftelsens Styrelse" (The Board of Directors of the Nobel Institute), Stockholm, Sweden.

The awards made until now have been: Physics, 1901, W. C. Röntgen, German; 1902, H. A. Lorentz and P. Zeeman, Hollanders; 1903, H. A. Becquerel, P. Curie, and Marie Curie, all French; 1904, Lord Rayleigh, English; 1905, Prof. Philipp Leonard, of Kiel University, German; 1906, Prof. J. J. Thomson, of the University of Cambridge, English; 1907, Prof. Albert A. Michelson, of the University of Chicago, American; 1908, Professor Gabriel Lippman, University of Paris, France.

Chemistry: 1901, J. H. van Hoff, Professor of the Berlin University, Hollander; 1902, E. Fischer, German; 1903, S. A. Arrhenius, Swede, 1904, Sir William Ramsay, English; 1905, Adolph von Boeyer, German; 1906, Prof. Henri Moissan, French; 1907, Prof Edouard Buchner, of the Berlin University, German; Sir William Crookes, English; 1908, Professor Ernest Rutherford, University of Manchester, English.

Medicine: 1901, E. A. von Behring, German; 1902, R. Ross, English; 1903, N. R. Finsen, Dane; 1904, Pavloff, Russian; 1905, Prof. Robert Koch, German; 1906, Prof. Ramon y Cajal, Spanish; Professor Golgi, French; 1907, Dr. Laveran, of Paris, French; 1908, Dr. Paul Ehrlich, of Berlin, German; and Professor Elie Metschnikoff, Pasteur Institute, Paris, Russian.

Literature: 1901, R. F. A. Sully-Prudhomme, French; 1902, Th. Mommsen, German; 1903, Björnstierne Björnson, Norwegian; 1904, Frederic Mistral, French, and José Echagray, Spaniard; 1905, Henry Stenkiewicz, Pole; 1906, Professor Carducci, Italian; 1907, Rudyard Kipling, English; 1908, Professor Rudolf Eucken, Jena University, German.

Peace: 1901, Henri Dunant, Swiss, and Fr. Passy, French; 1902, E. Ducommun and A. Gobat, both Swiss; 1903, W. R. Cremer, English; 1904, The Institution of International Law, the first award to an institution; 1905, Baroness von Suttner, Austrian; 1906, President Theodore Roosevelt, American; 1907, Ernesto Teodoro Moneta, Italian, and Louis Renault, French; 1908, K. P. Arnoldson, Swede; and M. F. Bajer, Dane,

Cities.	Area in Square Miles.	Estimated Population Jan. 1, 1909	Net Public Debt.	Assessed Valuation of § All Taxable Property.	Per Cent. of Actual Val.*	Tax Rate†	Mayors.	Terms Expire.
Albany, N. Y.	11¼	98,537	$3,035,114	$80,143,725	100	$1.94	Henry F. Snyder	Dec. 31, 1909
Atlanta, Ga.	13	150,000	2,891,364	90,783,850	60	1.25	ROBERT F. MADDOX	Jan. 4, 1911
Baltimore, Md.	31½	650,000	19,881,929	624,482,590	100	2.16	*J. Barry Mahool*	May 21, 1911
Binghamton, N. Y.	10	47,000	811,500	32,593,990	80	*b*1.90	Clarence M. Slauson	Dec. 31, 1909
Boston, Mass.	42⅔	622,010	60,071,349	1,327,662	100	1.65	George A. Hibbard.	Jan. 1, 1910
Bridgeport, Ct.	13.4	100,000	1,541,654	74,508,171	100	1.56	Henry Lee	Nov. 2, 1909
Brooklyn Boro., N.Y.	77⅔	1,492,970	(*a*)	1,418,312,907	100 *g*	1.67	*Incorp'd in City of*	*New York.*
Buffalo, N. Y.	42	400,000	20,040,216	298,176,669	100	1.84	*James N. Adam*	Jan. 1, 1910
Cambridge, Mass.	6½	99,832	7,992,392	106,711,200	100	2.01	W. C. WARDWELL	Jan. 4, 1909
Camden, N. J.	9	100,000	4,494,230	53,330,783	100	1.89	Chas. H. Ellis	Dec. 31, 1910
Charleston, S. C.	5⅓	62,000	3,788,200	18,960,821	50	2.88	*R. G. Rhett*	Dec. 12, 1911
Chattanooga, Tenn.	6	84,000	2,241,000	22,959,191	60	1.65	*W. R. Crabtree*	Oct. 8, 1909
Chicago, Ill.	190½	2,572,835	24,771,000	477,921,976	2[illegible]	[illegible].35	Fred. A. Busse	Apr. 4, 1911
Cincinnati, O.	43⅓	475,000	10,891,641	247,886,470	60	2.96	Leopold Markbreit	Jan. 1, 1910
Cleveland, O.	45	525,000	30,309,261	240,262,315	35	3.22	*Tom L. Johnson*	Dec. 31, 1909
Cohoes, N. Y.	8	25,000	*q* 855,823	11,470,219	100	*b*1.60	Merritt D. Hanson	Dec. 31, 1909
Columbus, O.	16	180,000	11,330,425	87,307,905	66⅔	3.19	Chas. A. Bond	Jan. 1, 1910
Council Bluffs, Iowa	16¼	35,000	221,531	4,212,815	25	9.35	*Thomas Maloney*	Apr. 1, 1910
Covington, Ky.	3¼	58,250	2,044,500	23,221,463	75	1.70	John J. Craig	Jan. 1, 1912
Dallas, Tex.	15	90,000	*c* 2,408,750	60,449,976	60	1.75	S. J. HAYS	May 1, 1909
Davenport, Iowa	10	50,000	175,000	22,897,625	50	1.80	*George W. Scott*	Apr. 18, 1910
Dayton, O.	11	130,000	3,353,000	57,000,000	60	2.96	*Edward E. Burkhart.*	Dec. 31, 1909
Denver, Col.	59¼	200,000	1,221,096	121,799,315	60	3.40	*Robert W. Speer*	June 1, 1912
Des Moines, Iowa	54	95,000	741,000	74,041,360	25	8.20	A. J. MATHIS	Apr. 1, 1910
Detroit, Mich.	36	400,000	6,450,686	305,656,900	100	1.47	*Wm. B. Thompson*	Jan. 8, 1909
District of Columbia	See	below	and at W	ashington,	D.C.	and	foot-note next	page.
Dubuque, Iowa	13	50,000	800,000	24,560,940	80	1.20	*H. A. Schunk*	Apr. 2, 1910
Duluth, Minn.	67⅓	88,000	2,391,000	35,403,388	33⅓	3.37	Roland D. Haven	Feb. 28, 1910
Elizabeth, N. J.	9¾	70,000	2,941,000	52,065,175	100	1.46	Victor Mravlag	Dec. 31, 1910
Elmira, N. Y.	8¼	42,000	1,085,500	20,131,790	80	2.56	*Daniel Sheehan*	Jan. 1, 1909
Erie, Pa.	7	68,000	365,164	25,699,080	40	2.50	*M. Liebel, Jr.*	Apr. 4, 1911
Fall River, Mass.	41	115,000	3,940,941	86,275,484	100	1.92	*John T. Coughlin*	Jan. 5, 1910
Fort Wayne, Ind.	8⅓	65,000	589,800	30,581,530	60	1.10	*Wm. J. Hosey*	Jan. 1, 1910
Galveston, Tex.	7¾	39,000	3,915,983	25,595,372	60	1.83	*H. A. Landes*	May 11, 1909
Grand Rapids, Mich.	17½	114,000	3,034,200	80,046,002	100	1.96	George E. Ellis	May 1, 1910
Harrisburg, Pa.	7	80,000	1,172,291	40,000,000	60	1.95	Edward Z. Gross	Apr. 1, 1910
Hartford, Ct.	17¼	105,000	4,231,634	103,074,585	75	2.20	Edward W. Hooker.	Apr. 5, 1910
Haverhill, Mass.	32	42,000	1,465,404	29,580,320	100	1.90	Edwin H. Moulton	Jan. 1, 1910
Hoboken, N. J.	1¾	75,000	1,706,663	65,429,204	100	1.51	*George H. Steil*	Jan. 1, 1910
Holyoke, Mass.	16¼	54,000	1,145,004	45,889,500	100	1.70	Nathan P. Avery	Jan. 7, 1909
Houston, Tex.	16	90,000	3,919,000	51,700,000	33⅓	1.80	*H. B. Rice*	Apr. 12, 1909
Indianapolis, Ind.	31	243,460	2,771,800	176,825,075	66⅔	2.18	Chas. A Bookwalter.	Jan. 1, 1910
Jacksonville, Fla.	9	62,000	1,768,000	24,000,000	50	1.61	*Wm. H. Sebring*	June 18, 1909
Jersey City, N. J.	19.2	251,084	11,422,763	232,769,781	100	1.92	*H. Otto Wittpenn*	Jan. 1, 1910
Kalamazoo, Mich.	8½	45,000	762,464	19,834,585	100	1.00	*Frank H. Milham*	May 1, 1909
Kansas City, Mo.	26	300,000	4,011,721	131,318,585	40	1.25	*Thos. T. Crittenden, Jr.*	Apr. 18, 1910
Lawrence, Mass.	7	76,616	1,389,164	56,473,458	85	1.68	William P. White	Jan. —, 1910
Little Rock, Ark.	8½	60,000	178,585	19,063,176	40	2.87	*W. R. Duley*	Apr. 11, 1909
Los Angeles, Cal.	61	300,000	9,612,425	265,570,272	50	1.25	*A. C. Harper*	Jan. 1, 1910
Louisville, Ky.	21	275,000	11,000,000	166,000,000	80	1.75	James F. Grimstead.	Nov. 16, 1909
Lowell, Mass.	14	100,000	2,851,814	75,445,738	100	1.94	George H. Brown	Jan. —, 1910
Lynn, Mass.	11⅓	88,000	*c* 4,441,700	68,399,271	80	2.00	*J. E. Rich*	Dec. 31, 1910
Manchester, N. H.	33¾	65,000	1,655,000	37,746,708	100	1.86	*Eugene E. Reed*	Dec. 31, 1910
Memphis, Tenn.	16	175,000	2,784,000	80,381,311	60	1.91	*James H. Malone*	Jan. 1, 1910
Milwaukee, Wis.	22¾	400,000	8,907,000	223,040,800	60	2.59	*David S. Rose*	Apr. —, 1910
Minneapolis, Minn.	53¼	310,000	8,641,304	175,447,951	60	2.65	*James C. Haynes*	Jan. 1, 1911
Mobile, Ala.	15	65,000	3,806,000	27,116,000	25	2.35	*Pat. J. Lyons*	Oct. 1, 1910
Nashville, Tenn.	9¾	135,000	*c* 4,789,600	69,459,393	80	1.50	*James S. Brown*	Oct. 15, 1909
Newark, N. J.	23	320,000	16,350,141	295,780,793	100	1.63	*Jacob Haussling*	Jan. 1, 1910
New Bedford, Mass.	19⅓	100,000	1,495,797	75,400,973	80	1.76	WM. J. BULLOCK	Jan. 3, 1910
New Brunswick, N. J.	2	25,000	700,000	11,213,682	66⅔	1.90	*W. Edwin Florance*	Jan. 1, 1910
New Haven, Ct.	22½	130,000	3,957,286	119,434,462	100	1.47	*James B. Martin*	Jan. 1, 1910
New Orleans, La.	192	375,000	23,867,020	228,745,936	100	2.20	*Martin Behrman*	Dec. —, 1912

Cities.	Realty.	Personalty.	Cities.	Realty.	Personalty.
Albany	$74,759,575	$5,384,150	Milwaukee	$170,279,840	$52,760,960
Baltimore	325,723,818	298,758,772	Minneapolis	126,833,505	48,614,446
Boston	1,082,405	245,257,038	Newark, N. J.	254,865,056	40,915,737
Buffalo‡	269,469,620	7,345,500	New Haven	102,554,813	13,369,501
Chicago	346,843,590	121,078,386	New Orleans	151,357,465	77,388,471
Cincinnati	192,392,530	55,493,940	New York City, see next page.		
Cleveland	176,819,230	63,443,085	Philadelphia	1,248,894,400	(*f*) 1,793,886
Denver	94,095,215	27,704,100	Pittsburgh	698,671,156	5,600,167
Detroit	212,315,460	93,341,440	Providence	174,559,260	58,037,640
District of Columbia	276,590,774	35,000,000	San Francisco (q)	327,504,907	102,361,702
Indianapolis (q)	131,674,400	45,150,675	St. Louis	487,856,020	88,486,280
Los Angeles	241,954,985	22,823,187	Seattle	149,279,822	28,856,896
Louisville	103,016,724	54,862,760			

Democrats in *italics;* Republicans in Roman; others in SMALL CAPS.

* Percentage of assessment upon actual valuation. † Tax on each $100 of assessed valuation for all purposes. ‡ Special Franchise $21,361,549. § Realty. (*a*) See "New York City," next page. (*b*) City tax. (*c*) Bonded debt. (*d*) After April 1, 1908, five Commissioners will assume executive control of city affairs. (*e*) Funded debt. (*f*) Assessed valuation of horses and cattle only. (*g*) Realty, about 78 per cent. (*q*) Report of December 1, 1907.

Cities.	Area in Square Miles.	Estimated Population Jan. 1, 1909	Net Public Debt.	Assessed Valuation of all Taxable Property.	Per Cent. of Actual Val.*	Tax Rate†	Mayors.	Terms Expire.
Newport, R. I.	6½	25,000	$1,206,000	$49,433,800	80	$1.30	*Patrick Boyle*	Jan. —,1910
Newton, Mass.	18	39,000	4,042,009	68,933,800	100	1.82	George Hutchinson	Jan. 10,1910
New York City‡	‡326¾	4,422,685	See note *j*	‡7,158,190,400	100 *i*	§	*Gco. B. McClellan*	Jan. 1,1910
Omaha, Neb	24	145,000	5,670,000	26,479,148	20	5.73	*James C. Dahlman*	May 21,1909
Paterson, N. J.	8⅓	120,000	4,226,634	92,466,059	100	1.76	*Andrew F. McBride*	Dec. 31,1939
Peoria, Ill	8½	75,000	497,500	11,375,291	20	7.64	*A. B. Tolson*	May 4,1909
Philadelphia, Pa	129½	1,491,161	61,695,320	*e*1,683,852,278	100	1.50	John E. Reyburn	Apr. 1,1911
Pittsburgh, Pa	38	565,000	25,368,463	*e* 704,271,323	80	1.45	*George W. Guthrie*	Apr. 6,1909
Portland, Me	17½	65,000	1,284,241	57,077,625	100	1.96	Adam P. Leighton	Dec. 7,1909
Portland, Ore	44	250,000	....	215,579,945	75	4.60	*Harry Lane*	July 1,1909
Poughkeepsie, N. Y.	3½	26,000	1,610,000	13,556,130	80	2.64	*John K. Sague*	Dec. 31,1910
Providence, R. I.	18¼	211,000	13,861,551	(*e*)232,596,900	100	1.65	Henry Fletcher	Jan. 3,1910
Quincy, Ill	5 3-5	40,000	689,000	5,920,267	20	7.64	John H. Best	May 1,1909
Reading, Pa	6.2	100,000	1,184,116	52,724,600	70	1.70	William Rick	May 1,1911
Richmond, Va	10	114,050	7,049,597	105,811,707	70 *h*	1.75	*D. C. Richardson*	Sept. 1,1912
Rochester, N. Y.	13	200,000	12,036,998	149,764,385	82	1.89	Hiram H. Edgerton	Dec. 31,1909
Sacramento, Cal	8⅓	46,000	1,118,600	28,500,000	50	1.60	C. L. White	Jan. 1,1910
Saginaw, Mich	16	55,000	1,868,067	25,032,733	85	2.00	Geo. W. Stewart	Dec. 31,1910
San Antonio, Tex	36	100,000	2,098,000	54,660,000	70	1.60	*Bryan Callaghan*	June 1,1909
San Diego, Cal	76	45,000	1,900,000	27,804,000	66⅔	1.48	John F. Forward	May 2,1909
San Francisco, Cal	44	400,000	6,816,600	(*e*)454,332,820	60	1.90	*Edward R. Taylor*	Jan. 8,1912
Savannah, Ga	6¼	80,000	3,078,000	47,391,051	60	1.25	*G. W. Tiedeman*	Jan. 21,1909
Schenectady, N. Y.	7¾	77,000	2,203,888	45,431,706	78	1.72	Horace S. Van Voost	Dec. 31,1909
Scranton, Pa	19	130,000	2,029,799	77,435,085	80	2.00	J. Benj. Dimmick	Apr. 5,1909
Seattle, Wash	54	300,000	6,081,706	(*e*)178,136,718	60	3.08	John F. Miller	Mar. 16,1910
Sioux City, Iowa	45	62,000	1,209,427	32,291,852	25	8.40	*W. G. Sears*	Mar. 30,1910
Somerville, Mass	4¼	75,000	1,508,000	63,158,400	100	1.84	J. M. Woods	Jan. 3,1910
Springfield, Ill (q)	7½	68,000	862,000	8,616,572	20	7.92	Roy R. Reece	May 1,1909
Salt Lake City, Utah	8¼	100,000	3,798,000	48,940,038	70	1.30	JNO. S. BRANSFORD	Jan. 3,1910
Springfield, Mass	38½	82,347	2,649,126	97,098,308	90	1.55	Wm. E. Sanderson	Jan. 3,1910
Springfield, O.	10	60,000	1,500,000	23,000,000	66⅔	2.75	*Wm. R. Burnett*	Jan. 1,1910
St. Joseph, Mo.	9¾	123,000	997,589	29,435,825	60	1.30	*Alvah P. Clayton*	Apr. —,1910
St. Louis, Mo.	61⅓	704,593	19,427,178	(*e*)526,342,200	70	2.22	*Rolla Wells*	Apr. 12,1909
St. Paul, Minn	55½	235,000	8,816,000	104,864,241	50	2.95	*Daniel W. Lawler*	June 1,1910
Syracuse, N. Y.	15	130,000	8,496,700	97,734,311	100	1.93	Alan C. Fobes	Dec. 31,1909
Tacoma, Wash	32	110,000	3,822,000	53,925,693	60	3.61	John W. Linck	Apr. 20,1910
Taunton, Mass. (q)	50	30,967	1,534,671	21,842,382	100	1.86	Edgar L. Crossman	Jan. 1,1910
Toledo, O.	28½	193,303	7,207,288	78,984,230	60	2.67	BRAND WHITLOCK	Dec. 31,1909
Topeka, Kan	8	50,000	1,748,100	43,293,020	100	1.65	William Green	Apr. 9,1909
Trenton, N. J.	9	100,000	(*q*)3,419,591	(*q*) 70,054,408	100	1.62	*Walter Madden*	Jan. 1,1910
Troy, N. Y.	9½	76,910	3,808,251	55,981,974	100	1.69	Elias P. Mann	Dec. 31,1909
Utica, N. Y.	9	72,000	1,594,343	48,511,897	66⅔	1.78	Thomas Wheeler	Dec. 31,1909
Washington, D. C.	69¼	340,000	13,767,564	(*e*)311,590,774	66⅔	1.50	See foot of page.	
Williamsport, Pa	7.2	39,000	537,346	14,043,522	75	3.00	Chas. D. Wolfe	Apr. 3,1911
Wilmington, Del	10	90,000	2,881,150	49,238,867	80	2.15	Horace Wilson	June 30,1909
Worcester, Mass	38½	148,320	6,318,251	129,323,426	100	1.70	James Logan	Jan. —,1910
Yonkers, N. Y.	21	73,000	5,188,966	63,977,310	70	2.32	Nathan A. Warren	Dec. 31,1909

Democrats in *italics*; Republicans in Roman; others in SMALL CAPS.

* This is the percentage of assessment upon actual valuation. † Tax on each $100 of assessed valuation for all purposes. ‡ Population of New York City as follows: Manhattan, 2,292,894; Bronx, 327,553; Brooklyn, 1,492,970; Queens, 232,580; Richmond, 76,688. Area in square miles—Manhattan, 21.93; Bronx, 40.65; Brooklyn, 77.62; Queens, 129.50; Richmond, 57.19. Taxable valuations—all boroughs—Realty, $6,722,415,789; personalty, $435,774,611. Manhattan—Realty, $4,584,536,431; personalty, $327,810,632. Bronx—Realty, $441,228,718; personalty, $11,539,630. Brooklyn—Realty, $1,334,864,835; personalty, $83,448,072. Queens—Realty, $296,458,980; personalty, $9,908,830. Richmond—Realty, $65,326,825; personalty $3,067,397. § Tax rate, Manhattan and Bronx, $1.61; Brooklyn, $1.67; Queens, $1.66; Richmond, $1.71. (*a*) Land 66⅔, personal, 50 per cent. (*b*) State and county, $1.00; school, .60; city, $1.40. (*c*) Bonded debt. (*d*) Municipal taxes. (*e*) For division of realty and personalty see preceding page. (*h*) Personal 100 per cent. (*i*) Realty about 78 per cent. (*j*) Net funded debt, including schools, $596,204,494. (*q*) Report of December 1, 1907.

GOVERNMENT OF THE DISTRICT OF COLUMBIA.

The municipal government of the District of Columbia is vested by act of Congress approved June 11, 1878, in three Commissioners, two of whom are appointed by the President from citizens of the District having had three years' residence therein immediately preceding that appointment, and confirmed by the Senate. The other Commissioner is detailed by the President of the United States from the Corps of Engineers of the United States Army, and must have lineal rank senior to Captain, or be a Captain who has served at least fifteen years in the Corps of Engineers of the Army. The Commissioners appoint the subordinate official service of said government, except the Board of Education, which is appointed by the Supreme Court of the District of Columbia. The present Commissioners are H. B. F. Macfarland (Republican), President, whose term will expire May 5, 1909; Henry L. West (Democrat), whose term will expire February 1, 1909; Major Jay J. Morrow (non-partisan), Corps of Engineers, United States Army, detailed during the pleasure of the President of the United States, Secretary William Tindall. Offices of Commissioners, 464 Louisiana Ave., N. W., Washington, D. C.

Three separate local governments existed in the District of Columbia from its establishment until 1871, namely: the City of Washington, the Town of Georgetown, and the Levy Court. The latter had jurisdiction over the portion of the District of Columbia outside of the city and town mentioned. All three of these governments were abolished by an act of Congress approved February 21, 1871, which provided a territorial form of government for the entire District of Columbia, with a Governor, Secretary, Board of Public Works, and Council, appointed by the President of the United tates, and a House of Delegates and a delegate in Congress elected by the citizens of said district.

The United States Revenue Cutter Service.

THE United States Revenue Cutter Service is a military arm of the Government attached to and under the direction of the Treasury Department. The Service was organized in 1790 and constituted the original naval force of the country. There being at that time no Navy Department, the Service was placed under the Treasury Department, where it has remained ever since. It is charged with the enforcement of the navigation and customs laws of the United States, the assistance of vessels in distress, the protection of the sealing industry in Alaska, the enforcement of the quarantine laws, and numerous other duties appropriate to its class of vessels. Each Winter, by direction of the President, a number of the cutters patrol the coast for the special purpose of assisting vessels in distress. The Service co-operates with the Navy when directed by the President and has so co-operated in every war in which the United States has been engaged. The officers of the Service are commissioned by the President and hold rank by law with officers of the Army and Navy as follows:

Captain-Commandant with Colonel in the Army and Captain in the Navy; Senior Captains and Engineer-in-Chief with Lieutenant-Colonels in the Army and Commanders in the Navy; Captains with Majors in the Army and Lieutenant-Commanders in the Navy; First Lieutenants with Captains in the Army and Lieutenants in the Navy; Second Lieutenants with First Lieutenants in the Army and Lieutenants (Junior Grade) in the Navy; Third Lieutenants with Second Lieutenants in the Army and Ensigns in the Navy.

There are now in the Service 238 commissioned officers and cadets on the active list, and 1,500 petty officers and enlisted men. The officers are: 1 Captain-Commandant, 6 Senior Captains, 31 Captains, 37 First Lieutenants, 35 Second Lieutenants, 46 Cadets of the line, 1 Engineer-in-Chief, 6 Captains of Engineers, 28 First Lieutenants of Engineers, 22 Second Lieutenants of Engineers, 11 Third Lieutenants of Engineers, 12 Cadet Engineers and 2 Constructors.

Commissioned officers of the line are appointed from Cadet graduates of the School of Instruction at South Baltimore, Md. The Cadet course covers three years and embraces professional and academic subjects. Cadets are appointed after competitive examinations, conducted by boards of commissioned officers of the Revenue Cutter Service. Candidates must be not less than eighteen nor more than twenty-four years of age.

Appointments to the Engineer Corps are made after competitive examination, and successful candidates are appointed Cadet Engineers for a period of six months prior to being commissioned Second Assistant Engineers in the Service. Candidates for the Engineer Corps must be not less than twenty-one nor more than twenty-six years of age.

The present Commandant of the Service is Captain-Commandant Worth G. Ross, U. S. R. C. S., and Engineer-in-Chief Chas. A. McAllister, U. S. R. C. S., is head of the Engineer Corps.

LIST OF VESSELS OF THE REVENUE CUTTER SERVICE.

NAME.	Headquarters.	Displacement.	Guns.	NAME.	Headquarters.	Displacement.	Guns.
(First Class.)				(Second Class.)			
Algonquin	San Juan, P. R.	936	5	Perry	Seattle, Wash.	451	1
Apache	Baltimore, Md.	664	1	Windom	Galveston, Tex.	528	4
Bear	San Francisco, Cal.	1,200	3	Winona	Gulfport, Miss.	340	1
Gresham	Boston, Mass.	936	4	Woodbury	Portland, Me.	500	1
Itasca	Practice Ship.	839	10	(Third Class.)			
Manning	Honolulu, T. H.	962	4	Arcata	Port Townsend, Wash.	130	..
McCulloch	San Francisco, Cal.	1,280	6	Calumet	New York, N. Y.	169	..
Mohawk	New York, N. Y.	980	2	Davey	New Orleans, La.	153	..
Onondaga	Philadelphia, Pa.	936	2	Golden Gate	San Francisco, Cal.	220	..
Rush	Sitka, Alaska.	550	3	Guthrie	Baltimore, Md.	126	..
Seminole	Wilmington, N. C.	785	3	Hartley	San Francisco, Cal.	48	..
Seneca	New York, N. Y.	1,480	4	Hudson	New York, N. Y.	174	..
Thetis	San Francisco, Cal.	1,200	1	Mackinac	Sault Ste. Marie, Mich.	220	..
Tuscarora	Milwaukee, Wis.	670	1	Manhattan	New York, N. Y.	174	..
(First Class Sea-going Tugs.)				Winnisimmet	Boston, Mass.	174	..
				Wissahickon	Philadelphia, Pa.	174	..
Acushnet	New Bedford, Mass.	769	2	(Launches.)			
Snohomish	Neah Bay, Wash.	795	2	Alert	Mobile, Ala.	17	..
(Second Class.)				Guard	Port Townsend, Wash.	30	..
Chase	Practice Ship.	520	7	Guide	New York, N. Y.	32	..
Colfax	Station Ship.	486	1	Patrol	Chicago, Ill.	...	..
Forward	Key West, Fla.	435	1	Penrose	Pensacola, Fla.	30	..
Morrill	Detroit, Mich.	397	1	Scout	Port Townsend, Wash.	30	..
Pamlico	Newbern, N. C.	408	2	Tybee	Savannah, Ga.	40	..

The following vessels, with their displacements, are under construction: Tahoma, 1,050, and Yamacraw, 1,006.

The Life-Saving Service.

THE ocean and lake coasts of the United States are picketed with the stations of the Life-Saving Service attached to the United States Treasury Department. Sumner I. Kimball is general superintendent, with headquarters at Washington, and there is a corps of inspectors, superintendents, station keepers, and crews, extending over the entire coast line, together with a Board on Life-Saving Appliances, composed of experts selected from the Revenue Cutter Service, the Army, the Life-Saving Service, and civilians.

At the close of the last fiscal year the life-saving establishment embraced 280 stations, 201 being on the Atlantic Coast, 60 on the lakes, 18 on the Pacific Coast, and 1 at the falls of the Ohio, Louisville, Ky. In the following table are the statistics of the service:

	Year Ending June 30, 1908.	Since Introduction of Life-Saving System in 1871, to June 30, 1908.		Year Ending June 30, 1908.	Since Introduction of Life-Saving System in 1871, to June 30, 1908.
Disasters	386	18,411	Shipwrecked persons succored at stations	421	21,285
Value property involved	$12,911,915	$265,046,509	Days' succor afforded	848	49,870
Value property saved	$11,056,805	$211,124,032	Vessels totally lost on U. S. coasts	52	......
Value property lost	$1,855,110	$53,922,477			
Persons involved	3,749	127,395			
Persons lost	16	1,194			

In addition to the foregoing there were 708 casualties to smaller craft, such as sailboats, rowboats, etc., on which there were 1963 persons, of whom 6 were lost. The cost of the maintenance of the service during the year was $1,962,524.99.

The States and the Union.

THE THIRTEEN ORIGINAL STATES.

	STATES.	Ratified the Constitution.		STATES.	Ratified the Constitution.
1	Delaware	1787, December 7.	8	South Carolina	1788, May 23.
2	Pennsylvania	1787, December 12.	9	New Hampshire	1788, June 21.
3	New Jersey	1787, December 18.	10	Virginia	1788, June 26.
4	Georgia	1788, January 2.	11	New York	1788, July 26.
5	Connecticut	1788, January 9.	12	North Carolina	1789, November 21.
6	Massachusetts	1788, February 6.	13	Rhode Island	1790, May 29.
7	Maryland	1788, April 28.			

STATES ADMITTED TO THE UNION.

	STATES.	Admitted.*		STATES.	Admitted.*
1	Vermont	1791, March 4.	18	California	1850, September 9.
2	Kentucky	1792, June 1.	19	Minnesota	1858, May 11.
3	Tennessee	1796, June 1.	20	Oregon	1859, February 14.
4	Ohio	1803, February 19.	21	Kansas	1861, January 29.
5	Louisiana	1812, April 30.	22	West Virginia	1863, June 19.
6	Indiana	1816, December 11.	23	Nevada	1864, October 31.
7	Mississippi	1817, December 10.	24	Nebraska	1867, March 1.
8	Illinois	1818, December 3.	25	Colorado	1876, August 1.
9	Alabama	1819, December 14.	26	North Dakota	1889, November 2.
10	Maine	1820, March 15.	27	South Dakota	1889, November 2.
11	Missouri	1821, August 10.	28	Montana	1889, November 8.
12	Arkansas	1836, June 15.	29	Washington	1889, November 11.
13	Michigan	1837, January 26.	30	Idaho	1890, July 3.
14	Florida	1845, March 3.	31	Wyoming	1890, July 11.
15	Texas	1845, December 29.	32	Utah	1896, January 4.
16	Iowa	1846, December 28.	33	Oklahoma	1907, November 16.
17	Wisconsin	1848, May 29.			

The Territories.

TERRITORIES.	Organized.	TERRITORIES.	Organized.
New Mexico	September 9, 1850.	District of Alaska	July 27, 1868.
Arizona	February 24, 1863.	Hawaii	June 14, 1900.
District of Columbia	July 16, 1790—Mar. 3, '91		

* Date when admission took effect is given from U. S. Census reports. In many instances the act of admission by Congress was passed on a previous date.

NEW POSSESSIONS.—A government for Porto Rico was established by the Fifty-sixth Congress. The Philippines are under a provisional civil government, Guam, and Tutuila, under Governors, and the Isthmian Canal Zone under a Commission, all appointed by the President.

State and Territorial Statistics.

STATES AND TERRITORIES.	Gross Area in Square Miles.*	Extreme Breadth, Miles.†	Extreme Length, Miles.	Capitals.	STATES AND TERRITORIES.	Gross Area in Square Miles.*	Extreme Breadth, Miles.†	Extreme Length, Miles.	Capitals.
Alabama	52,250	200	330	Montgomery	Nebraska	77,510	415	205	Lincoln.
Alaska Ter.	590,884	800	1,100	Juneau.	Nevada	110,700	315	485	Carson City.
Arizona Ter.	113,020	335	390	Phœnix.	New Hamp	9,305	90	185	Concord.
Arkansas	53,850	275	240	Little Rock.	New Jersey	7,815	70	160	Trenton.
California	158,360	375	770	Sacramento.	N. Mexico T.	122,580	350	390	Santa Fé.
Colorado	103,925	390	270	Denver.	New York	49,170	320	310	Albany.
Connecticut	4,990	90	75	Hartford.	N. Carolina	52,250	520	200	Raleigh.
Delaware	2,050	35	110	Dover.	N. Dakota	70,795	360	210	Bismarck.
Dist. of Col.	70	9	10	Washington.	Ohio	41,060	230	205	Columbus.
Florida	58,680	400	460	Tallahassee.	Oklahoma	70,057	585	210	Guthrie.
Georgia	59,475	250	315	Atlanta.	Oregon	96,030	375	290	Salem.
Idaho	84,800	305	490	Boisé.	Pennsylvania	45,215	300	180	Harrisburg.
Illinois	56,650	205	380	Springfield.	Rhode Island.	1,250	35	50	Providence.
Indiana	36,350	160	265	Indianapolis.	S. Carolina	30,570	235	215	Columbia.
Iowa	56,025	300	210	Des Moines.	South Dakota.	77,650	380	245	Pierre.
Kansas	82,080	400	200	Topeka.	Tennessee	42,050	430	120	Nashville.
Kentucky	40,400	350	175	Frankfort.	Texas	265,780	760	620	Austin.
Louisiana	48,720	280	275	Baton Rouge	Utah	84,970	275	345	Salt Lake C'y
Maine	33,040	205	235	Augusta.	Vermont	9,565	90	155	Montpelier.
Maryland	12,210	200	120	Annapolis.	Virginia	42,450	425	205	Richmond.
Massachus'tts	8,315	190	110	Boston.	Washington	69,180	340	230	Olympia.
Michigan	58,915	310	400	Lansing.	W. Virginia	24,780	200	225	Charleston.
Minnesota	83,365	350	400	St. Paul.	Wisconsin	56,040	290	300	Madison.
Mississippi	46,810	180	340	Jackson.	Wyoming	97,890	365	275	Cheyenne.
Missouri	69,415	300	280	Jefferson C'y	Total U. S.	3,616,484	‡2,720	‡1,600	
Montana	146,080	580	315	Helena.					

Areas of the new possessions: Philippines, 115,026 square miles; Porto Rico, 3,435; Hawaii, 6,449; Tutuila and islets, 77; Guam, 210; Panama Canal strip, 474. * Gross area includes water as well as land surface. These areas are those published by the United States Census Office in 1900. † Breadth is from east to west. Length is from north to south. ‡ Breadth from Quoddy Head, in Maine, to Cape Flattery, in Washington; length from the 49th parallel to Brownsville, on the Rio Grande. This is exclusive of Alaska.

States and Territories.	Governors. Names.	Salaries	L'gth Term, Years.	Terms Expire.	Legislatures. Next Session Begins.	Ann. or Bien.	Limit of Session.	Time of Next State or Territorial Election.
Alabama	*Braxton B. Comer*	$5,000	4	Jan. —,1911	Jan. 10,1911	Quad	50 dys	Nov. 8,1910
Alaska	Wilford B. Hoggatt*	5,000	4	Mar.21,1910	....	....	....	....
Arizona	Joseph H. Kibbey*	3,000	4	Feb.27,1909	Jan. 18,1909	Bien.	60 dys	Nov. 2,1910
Arkansas	*George W. Donaghey*	3,000	2	Jan. —,1911	Jan. 11,1909	Bien.	60 dys	Sept.14,1910
California	James N. Gillett	6,000	4	Jan. —,1911	Jan. 4,1909	Bien.	90 dys	Nov. —,1910
Colorado	*John F. Shafroth*	5,000	2	Jan. —,1911	Jan 6,1909	Bien.	90 dys	Nov. —,1910
Connecticut	George L. Lilley	4,000	2	Jan. —,1911	Jan. 4,1911	Bien.	None.	Nov. —,1910
Delaware	Simeon S. Pennewill	4,000	4	Jan. 21,1913	Jan. 5,1909	Bien.	60 dys	Nov. 4,1910
Florida	*Albert W. Gilchrist*	5,000	4	Jan. —,1913	Jan. 5,1909	Bien.	60 dys	Nov. 8,1910
Georgia	*Hoke Smith.*†	5,000	2	July 1,1909	June —,1909	Ann.	50 dys	Oct. 7,1911
Hawaii	Walter F. Frear*	5,000	4	June28,1911	Jan. 5,1909	Bien.	90 dys	Nov. —,1911
Idaho	James H. Brady	5,000	2	Jan. 7,1911	Jan. 4,1909	Bien.	60 dys	Nov. 3,1910
Illinois	Charles S. Deneen	12,000	4	Jan. —,1913	Jan. 6,1909	Bien.	None.	Nov. —,1910
Indiana	*Thomas R. Marshall*	8,000	4	Jan. —,1913	Jan. 7,1909	Bien.	60 dys	Nov. —,1910
Iowa	B. F. Carroll	5,000	2	Jan. —,1911	Jan. 11,1909	Bien.	None.	Nov. 5,1910
Kansas	Walter R Stubbs	5,000	2	Jan. 10,1911	Jan. 12,1909	Bien.	50 dys	Nov. 10,1910
Kentucky	Augustus E. Willson	6,500	4	Dec. —,1911	Jan. —,1910	Bien.	60 dys	Nov. 6,1911
Louisiana	*Jared Y. Sanders*	5,000	4	May —,1912	May —,1910	Bien.	60 dys	Apr. —,1912
Maine	Bert M. Fernald	3,000	2	Jan. —,1911	Jan. 5,1909	Bien.	None.	Sept. 11,1911
Maryland	*Austin L. Crothers*	4,500	4	Jan. 13,1912	Jan. 1,1910	Bien.	90 dys	Nov. 8,1910
Massachusetts	Eben S. Draper	8,000	1	Jan. —,1910	Jan. 1,1909	Ann.	None.	Nov. 6,1909
Michigan	Fred. M. Warner	5,000	2	Jan. —,1911	Jan. 6,1909	Bien.	None.	Nov. 8,1910
Minnesota	*John A. Johnson*	7,000	2	Jan. 1,1911	Jan. 5,1909	Bien.	90 dys	Nov. 8,1910
Mississippi	*Edmond F. Noel*	4,500	4	Jan. 18,1912	Jan. 4,1910	Bien.	None.	Nov. 7,1911
Missouri	Herbert S. Hadley	5,000	4	Jan. —,1913	Jan. 6,1909	Bien.	90 dys	Nov. —,1910
Montana	*Edwin L. Norris*	5,000	4	Jan. —,1913	Jan. 4,1909	Bien.	60 dys	Nov. —,1910
Nebraska	*A. C. Shallenberger*	2,500	2	Jan. —,1911	Jan. 5,1909	Bien.	60 dys	Nov. 1,1910
Nevada	*D. S. Dickerson*	4,000	4	Dec.31,1910	Jan. 16,1909	Bien.	60 dys	Nov. —,1910
N. Hampshire	Henry B. Quinby	3,000	2	Jan. —,1911	Jan. 6,1909	Bien.	None	Nov. —,1910
New Jersey	John Franklin Fort	10,000	3	Jan. 17,1911	Jan. 12,1909	Ann.	None	Nov. —,1910
New Mexico	George Curry*	3,000	4	Jan. 22,1912	Jan. 18,1909	Bien.	60 dys	Nov. —,1910
New York	Charles E. Hughes	10,000	2	Dec.31,1910	Jan. 6,1909	Ann.	None.	Nov. 2,1909
N. Carolina	*W. W. Kitchin*	4,000	4	Jan. —,1913	Jan. 6,1909	Bien.	60 dys	Nov. 5,1912
North Dakota	*John Burke*	3,000	2	Jan. —,1911	Jan. 5,1909	Bien.	60 dys	Nov. 8,1910
Ohio	*Judson Harmon*	10,000	2	Jan. 8,1910	Jan. 4,1909	Bien.	None.	Nov. —,1910
Oklahoma	*Charles N. Haskell*	4,500	4	Jan. —,1911	Jan. 5,1909	Bien.	60 dys	Nov. —,1910
Oregon	*George E. Chamberlain*‡	5,000	4	Jan. 11,1911	Jan. 11,1909	Bien.	40 dys	Nov. —,1910
Pennsylvania	Edwin S. Stuart	10,000	4	Jan. 17,1911	Jan. 5,1909	Bien	None.	Nov. 2,1909
Porto Rico	Regis H. Post*	8,000	4	Mar. 6,1911	Jan. 8,1909	Ann.	60 dys	....
Rhode Island	Aram J. Pothier	3,000	1	Jan. —, 1910	Jan. 5,1909	Ann.	None.	Nov. 2,1909
S. Carolina	*Martin F. Ansel*	3,000	2	Jan. —,1910	Jan. 11,1909	Ann.	40 dys	Nov. 8,1911
South Dakota	R. S. Vessey	3,000	2	Jan. —,1911	Jan. 5,1909	Bien.	60 dys	Nov. —,1910
Tennessee	*Malcom R. Patterson*	4,000	2	Jan. —,1911	Jan. 4,1909	Bien.	75 dys	Nov. 3,1910
Texas	*Thomas M. Campbell*	4,000	2	Jan. —,1911	Jan. 12,1909	Bien.	None.	Nov. 7,1910
Utah	William Spry	4,000	4	Jan. —,1913	Jan. 11,1909	Bien.	60 dys	Nov. —,1912
Vermont	George H. Prouty	1,500	2	Oct. —,1910	Oct. 5,1910	Bien.	None.	Sept. 6,1910
Virginia	*Claude A. Swanson*	5,000	4	Feb. 1,1910	Jan. 12,1910	Bien.	60 dys	Nov. 2,1909
Washington	Samuel G. Cosgrove	6,000	4	Jan. —,1913	Jan. 11,1909	Bien.	60 dys	Nov. —,1913
West Virginia	Wm. E. Glasscock	5,000	4	Mar. —,1913	Jan. 13,1909	Bien.	45 dys	Nov. 2,1909
Wisconsin	James O. Davidson	5,000	2	Jan. —,1911	Jan. 6,1909	Bien.	None.	Nov. 1,1910
Wyoming	Bryant B. Brooks	2,500	4	Jan. —,1911	Jan. 12,1909	Bien.	40 dys	Nov. —,1910

Democrats in italics. Republicans in Roman. †To be succeeded on July 1, 1909, by Joseph M. Brown. ‡In event of Governor Chamberlain's election as United States Senator the Secretary of State Frank W. Benson, Republican, would succeed him upon his resignation as Governor. * Territorial Governors are appointed by the President.

PAY AND TERMS OF MEMBERS OF LEGISLATURES.

States and Territories.	Salaries of Members, Annual or Per Diem, while in Session.	Terms of Members, Years. Senators.	Representatives	States and Territories.	Salaries of Members, Annual or Per Diem, while in Session.	Terms of Members, Years. Senators.	Representatives	States and Territories.	Salaries of Members, Annual or Per Diem, while in Session.	Terms of Members, Years. Senators.	Representatives
Alabama	$4 per diem	4	4	Maine	$300 ann.	2	2	Oklah'ma	$6 per diem	4	2
Arizona	$4 "	—	—	Maryland	$5 per diem	4	2	Oregon	$3 "	4	2
Arkansas	$6 "	4	2	Mass.	$750 ann.	1	1	Penna.	$1,500 ses'n.	4	2
California	$8 "	4	2	Michigan	$800 ann.	2	2	Porto Rico	$5 per diem	—	—
Colorado	$7 "	4	2	Minn.	$500 ann.	4	2	R. Island	$5 "	1	1
Connec't.	$300 ann.	2	2	Miss'sippi	$400 ses'n.	4	4	S. Carol'a.	$200 ann.	4	2
Delaware	$5 per diem	4	2	Missouri	$5 per diem	4	2	S. Dakota	$5 per diem	2	2
Florida	$6 "	4	2	Montana	$6 "	4	2	Tenn.	$4 "	2	2
Georgia	$4 "	2	2	Nebraska	$5 "	2	2	Texas	$5 "	4	2
Hawaii	$400 ann.	—	—	Nevada	$10 "	4	2	Utah	$4 "	4	2
Idaho	$5 per diem	—	2	N. Hamp.	$200 ann.	2	2	Vermont	$3 "	2	2
Illinois	$1,000 ann.	4	2	N. Jersey	$500 "	3	1	Virginia	$500 ses'n.	4	2
Indiana	$6 per diem	4	2	N. Mexico	$4 per diem	2	2	Wash'ton	$5 per diem	4	4
Iowa	$550 ses'n.	4	2	N. York	$1,500 ann.	2	1	W. Va.	$4 "	4	2
Kansas	$150 ann.	4	2	N. Caro'la.	$4 per diem	2	2	Wisc'nsin	$500 ann.	4	2
Kent'cky	$5 per diem	4	2	N. Dak.	$5 "	4	2	Wyoming	$5 per diem	4	2
Louisiana	$5 "	4	4	Ohio	$1,000 ann.	2	2				

All of the States and Territories pay mileage also, except New Hampshire and New Jersey, but free transportation is accorded in the latter by all railroads to members by law.

The Federal Government.

President ‡..................THEODORE ROOSEVELT, of New York,* ....Salary, $50,000.
Vice-President ‡...........CHARLES WARREN FAIRBANKS, of Indiana, " 12,000.

THE CABINET.

Arranged in the order of succession for the Presidency declared by Chapter 4, Acts of 49th Congress, 1st Session, and Subsequent acts.

Secretary of State—Elihu Root, of New York.
Secretary of the Treasury—Geo. B. Cortelyou, of N.Y.
Secretary of War—Luke E. Wright, of Tenn.
Attorney-General—Charles J. Bonaparte, of Md.
Postmaster-General—George von L. Meyer, of Mass.
Secretary of the Navy—Truman H. Newberry, of Mich.
Secretary of Interior—James R. Garfield, of Ohio.
Secretary of Agriculture—James Wilson, of Iowa.
Secretary of Commerce and Labor—Oscar S. Straus, of New York.

The salaries of the Cabinet officers are $12,000 each.

THE DEPARTMENTS.

STATE DEPARTMENT.

Assistant Secretary—Robert Bacon, N. Y. $5,000
Second Ass't Secretary—A. A. Adee, D.C. 4,500
Third Ass't Sect'y—Huntington Wilson, Ill. .. 4,500
Chief Clerk—Wilbur J. Carr, D.C. 3,000
Ass't Solicitors { Joshua R. Clark, Jr., Utah. 3,000
{ William C. Dennis, Ind. 3,000
Ch. Diplomatic Bureau—S. Y. Smith, D. C. ... 2,250
Ch. Consular Bureau—Herbert C. Hengstler .. $2,250
Ch. Indexes & Archives—John R. Buck 2,100
Ch. Bureau Accounts—Thos. Morrison, N. Y. 2,100
Ch. Bureau Rolls & Lib'y—William McNeir .. 2,100
Ch. Bureau Trade Relations—John B. Osborne 2,100
Ch. Bureau Appointments—Vacant 2,100
Ch. Bureau Passports— 2,100

TREASURY DEPARTMENT.

Assistant Secretary—Beekman Winthrop, N. Y. $5,000
Assistant Secretary—James B. Reynolds, Mass 5,000
Assistant Secretary—Louis A. Coolidge, Mass.. 4,500
Chief Clerk—Walter W. Ludlow, Minn. 3,000
Chief Appointment Div.—Chas. Lyman, Ct. 3,000
Ch. Bookkeeping Div.—W. F. MacLennan, N. Y. 3,500
Chief Public Moneys Div.—E. B. Daskam, Ct.. 3,000
Chief Customs Div.—C. P. Montgomery, N. Y. 3,000
Ch. Loans & Cur. Div—A. T. Huntington, Mass. 3,000
Ch. Stationery & Pr'g Div.—G. Simmons, D. C.. 2,500
Chief Mails and Files Div.—S. M. Gaines, Ky.. 2,500
Ch. Revenue Cutter Service—Worth G. Ross.... .....
Director of Mint—Frank A. Leach, Cal. 4,500
Government Actuary—Joseph S. McCoy, N. J. 1,800
Superv. Surgeon-Gen.—Walter Wyman, Mo... 4,000
Ch. Bur. Eng. & Printing—Jos. E. Ralph, Ill. .. 5,000
Supervising Architect—James K. Taylor, Pa.. 5,000
Compt. of Treasury—Robt. J. Tracewell, Ind. 5,500
Gen. Supt. Life Saving Ser.—S. I. Kimball, Me. $4,500
Auditor for Treasury—Wm. E. Andrews, Neb. 4,000
Auditor for War Dept.—Benj. F. Harper, Ind. 4,000
Auditor for Int. Dept.—R. S. Person, S. D.... 4,000
Auditor for Navy Dept.—Ralph W. Tyler..... 4,000
Auditor for State, etc.—Caleb R. Layton, Del. 4,000
Auditor for P. O. Dept.—M. O. Chance, Ill.... 4,000
Treasurer of U. S.—Chas. H. Treat, N. Y..... 6,000
Assistant Treasurer—G. C. Bantz, Md. 3,600
Register Treasury—Wm. T. Vernon, Kan.... 4,000
Deputy Register—Cyrus F. Adams, Ill 2,250
Comp'r of Currency—L. O. Murray, N. Y.... 5,000
Commis. Internal Rev.—John G. Capers, S. C. 6,000
Dep. Com. Internal Rev.—R. Williams, Jr., La. 4,000
Dep. Com. Internal Rev.—J. C. Wheeler, Mich. 3,600
Solicitor Internal Rev.—Flet. Maddox, Mont.. 4,500
Solicitor of Treasury—M. D. O'Connell, Iowa. 4,500
Chief Secret Service—Jno. E. Wilkie, Ill....... 4,000

WAR DEPARTMENT.

Ass't Secretary—Robert Shaw Oliver, N. Y.. $5,000
Ass't and Chief Clerk—John C. Scofield, Ga... 4,000
Chief of Staff—Major-Gen. J. F. Bell.......... 8,000
Chief Clerk—Nathaniel Hershler, Ill......... 2,000
Mil. Secretary—Maj.-Gen. F. C. Ainsworth... 8,000
Chief Clerk—Jacob Frech, D. C. 2,000
Insp.-Gen.—Brig.-Gen. E. A. Garlington 6,000
Chief Clerk—Warren H. Orcutt, Me. 1,800
Judge-Adv.-Gen.—Brig.-Gen. Geo. B. Davis.. 6,000
Chief Clerk and Solicitor—L. W. Call, Kan.... 2,250
Q'rmaster-Gen.—Brig.-Gen. Jas. B. Aleshire. 6,000
Chief Clerk—Henry D. Saxton, Mass. 2,000
Commissary-Gen.—Brig.-Gen. H. G. Sharpe. 6,000
Chief Clerk—Emmet Hamilton, Minn. 2,000
Surgeon-Gen.—Brig.-Gen. R. M. O'Reilly.... 6,000
Chief Clerk—John Wilson, N. J. $2,000
Paymaster-Gen.—Brig.-Gen. C. H. Whipple... 6,000
Chief Clerk—R. O. Kloeber, Va. 2,000
Ch. of Engineers—Brig.-Gen. W. L. Marshall. 6,000
Chief Clerk—Phineas J. Dempsey, Va. 2,000
Chief of Ordnance—Brig.-Gen. Wm. Crozier... 6,000
Chief Clerk—John J. Cook, D. C. 2,000
Chief Signal Officer—Brig.-Gen. James Allen. 6,000
Chief Clerk—Herbert S. Flynn................ 2,000
Ch. Bu. In. Aff.—Brig.-Gen. C. R. Edwards 6,000
Chief Clerk—A. D. Wilcox, Pa. 2,000
Officer Charge Pub. Bldgs.—Col. C. S. Bromwell 4,000
Chief Clerk—E. F. Concklin, N. Y. 2,400
Landscape Gardener—George H. Brown, D. C.. 2,400

NAVY DEPARTMENT.

Ass't Secretary—Herbert L. Satterlee........ $4,500
Chief Clerk—Frank S. Curtis.................. 3,000
Pres. General Board—Admiral George Dewey. 13,500
Chief Yards and Docks—Civil Engineer Richard C. Hollyday† 5,500
Chief Ordnance—R.-Adm. N. E. Mason. 5,500
Chief Supplies and Accounts—Paymaster-Gen. E. B. Rogers. 5,500
Chief Medicine—Sur.-Gen. Presley M. Rixey† 5,500
Chief Equipment—R.-Adm. W. S. Cowles... 5,500
Chief Construction—Naval Constructor Washington L. Capps† 5,500
Chief Navigation—R.-Adm. J. E. Pillsbury... $7,500
Engineer-in-Chief—R.-Adm. J. K. Barton... 5,500
Judge-Adv.-Gen.—Capt. E. H. Campbell...... 4,500
Pres. Naval Exam. Board—Rear-Admiral J. N. Hemphill 6,375
Pres. Naval Retiring Board—Captain J. N. Hemphill.................................. 6,375
Ch. Intellig. Office—R.-Adm. R. P. Rodgers.. 4,165
Supt. Naval Obs.—R-Adm. W. J. Barnette .. 4,165
Director Nautical Alm.—Prof. M. Updegraff.. 2,700
Hydrographer—Com. A. G. Winterhalter.... 3,570
Comdt. Marine Corps—Brig.-Gen. G. F. Elliott.. 7,500

* Secretary to the President, William Loeb, Jr.
† Rank and title of Rear-Admiral while holding said office.
‡ On March 4, 1909, William H. Taft of Ohio and James S. Sherman of New York, will become respectively President and Vice-President of the United States.

POST-OFFICE DEPARTMENT.

Chief Clerk—Charles A. Conrad, Ky $3,000
Ass't Chief Clerk—Geo. G. Thomson, Mich... 2,000
First Ass't P. M. G.—Chas. P. Grandfield, Mo. 5,000
Second Ass't P. M. G.—Joseph Stewart, Mo.... 5,000
Third Ass't P. M. G.—A. L. Lawshe, Ind...... 5,000
Fourth Ass't P. M. G.—P. V. DeGraw, Pa...... 5,000
Assistant Attorney-Gen.—Russell P. Goodwin. 5,000
Purchasing Agent—W. E. Cochran, Col........ 4,000
Appointment Clerk—George S. Paull, Ohio.... $2,000
Supt. Div. of Foreign Mails—Basil Miles, Pa... 3,000
Supt. Div. of Money-Orders—E. F. Kimball, Mass 3,500
Gen. Supt. Div. of Ry. M. S.—Alex. Grant, Mich 4,000
Supt. Div. of Dead Letters—James R. Young, Pa. 2,750
Chief Inspector—Frank E. McMillin, Mass... 4,000
Disbursing Clerk—W. M. Mooney, Ohio...... 2,250

INTERIOR DEPARTMENT.

First Ass't Secretary—Frank Pierce, Utah...... $5,000
Assistant Secretary—Jesse E. Wilson, Ind...... 4,500
Chief Clerk—Edward M. Dawson, Md.......... 3,000
Ass't Atty.-Gen.—George W. Woodruff, Pa.. 5,000
Commis. Land Office—Fred Dennett, N. D.... 5,000
Ass't Commis.—Samuel V. Proudfit, Ia...... 3,500
Commis. Pensions—Vespasian Warner, Ill.... 5,000
First Deputy Com. of Pensions—Jas. L. Davenport, N. H. 3,600
Sec. Dep. Com. of Pen.—Leverett M. Kelley, Ill. 3,600
Commis. Education—Elmer E. Brown, Cal...$4,500
Chief Clerk—Lovick Pierce, Ga................ 2,000
Com. Indian Affairs—Francis E. Leupp, D.C. 5,000
Ass't Commis.—Charles F. Larrabee, Me...... 3,000
Commis. Patents—Edward B. Moore, Mich... 5,000
Ass't Commis.—Cornelius C. Billings, Vt..... 3,500
Direc. Geol. Surv.—George Otis Smith, Me... 6,000
Chief Clerk Geol. Survey—Henry C. Rizer, Kan. 2,500
Direc. Reclamation Service—F. H. Newell, Pa..7,000

DEPARTMENT OF JUSTICE.

Solicitor-Gen.—Henry M. Hoyt, Pa..........$7,500
Ass't to Atty.-Gen.—Wade H. Ellis, Ohio..... 7,000
Ass't Atty.-Gen.—John G. Thompson, Ill..... 5,000
Ass't Atty.-Gen.—John I. Thompson, Kan.... 5,000
Ass't Atty.-Gen.—Chas. W. Russell, W. Va... 5,000
Ass't Atty.-Gen.—James A. Fowler, Tenn ... 5,000
Ass't Atty.-Gen.—William W. Brown, Pa... 5,000
Ass't Atty.-Gen.—Geo. W. Woodruff, Pa..... 5,000
Solicitor State Dept.—Jas. B. Scott, Cal........$4,500
Solicitor Dept. Com. & Labor—Chas. Earl, Md. 5,000
Solicitor of the Treasury—Maurice D. O'Connell, Ia.............................. 5,000
Chief Clerk—O. J. Field, Kan................ 3,000
Appointment Clerk—Chas. B. Sornborger, Md. 2,000
Atty. for Pardons—James A. Finch, N. Y.... 2,750
Disbursing Clerk—Alex. C. Caine, Ohio....... 2,750

DEPARTMENT OF AGRICULTURE.

Ass't Secretary—Willett H. Hays, Minn......$5,000
Chief Clerk—S. R. Burch, Kan................ 3,000
Appointment Clerk—Joseph B. Bennett, Wis.. 2,000
Chief Weather Bureau—Willis L. Moore, Ill. 5,000
Chief Bur. Animal Indust.—Dr. A. D. Melvin, Ill. 5,000
Director Experiment Stations—A. C. True, Ct... 3,500
Chief Div. Publications—Geo. Wm. Hill, Minn. 3,000
Chief Div. Accounts—A. Zappone, D. C....... 3,250
Chief Bureau Soils—Milton Whitney, Md.... 3,500
Chief Forest Service—Gifford Pinchot, N. Y.... 5,000
Statistician—V. H. Olmstead, N. C. $3,500
Entomologist—L. O. Howard, N. Y........... 4,000
Chemist—H. W. Wiley, Ind................. 5,000
Chief Bur. Biological Survey—C. H. Merriam, N. Y.............................. 3,000
Direct. Public Roads—Prof. L. W. Page, Mass... 2,750
Statistical Scientist—G. K. Holmes, D. C...... 3,000
Chief Bureau of Plant Industry—B. T. Galloway, Mo.............................. 5.000
Librarian—Miss C. R. Barnett, Ohio............ 2,000

DEPARTMENT OF COMMERCE AND LABOR.

Assistant Sec'y.—William R. Wheeler, Cal...$5,000
Chief Clerk—Frank H. Bowen, Mass.......... 3,000
Disbursing Clerk—Wm. L. Soleau, Md....... 2,750
Commis. Corporations—H. K. Smith, Ct....... 5,000
Commis. Manufacturers—John M. Carson, Pa. 4,000
Commissioner of Labor—C. P. Neill, D.C....... 5,000
Chair. Lt.-H. Bd.—Rear-Adm. Adolph Marix. 6,000
Director Census—S. N. D. North, Mass....... 6,000
Sup. Coast & Geod. Survey—O. H. Tittmann, Mo. 6,000
Ch. Bureau Statistics—Oscar P. Austin, D. C. 4,000
Sup. Insp.-Gen. Stbt. Serv.—Geo. Uhler, Pa.. 4,000
Commissioner Fisheries—G. M. Bowers, W. Va. $6,000
Commis. Navigation—E. T. Chamberlain, N. Y. 4,000
Commis.-Gen. Immigration—Daniel J. Keefe, Mich.............................. 5,000
Director Bur. Standards—S. W. Stratton, Ill.. 5,000
Ch. Div. Appointments—G. W. Leadley, N. Y. 2,250
Ch. Div. Printing—G. C. Havenner, D. C...... 2,000
Ch. Div. Naturalization—R. K. Campbell, Va. 3,500
Ch. Div. Inform. Immigration—T. V. Powderly, Pa.............................. 3,500
Ch. Div. Supplies—W. W. Fowler, Mass...... 2,000

Civil Service Commis.—John C. Black, Ill.... $4,500
Civil Service Commis.—J. A. McIlhenny, La.. 4,000
Civil Service Commis.—H. F. Greene, Minn.. 4,000
Chief Examiner Civ. Ser.— 3,000
Secretary Civil Service—John T. Doyle, N. Y.. 2,500
Public Printer—Samuel B. Donnelly, N. Y....5,500
Librarian of Congress—Herbert Putnam, Mass. 6,000
Assistant Librarian— 4,000
Director Bureau of American Republics—John Barrett, Ore..............................$5,000
Chief Clerk Bureau Amer. Rep.—William C. Wells.............................. 2,500
Secretary—Francisco J. Yanes.................. 3,000
Sec. Smithsonian Institute—Chas. D. Walcott.. 3,000
Dir. Bureau Amer. Ethnology—W. H. Holmes. —

INTERSTATE COMMERCE COMMISSION.

Martin A. Knapp, N. Y., Chairman.......$10.000
Judson C. Clements, Ga...................... 10,000
Charles A. Prouty, Vt........................ 10,000
Francis M. Cockrell, Mo...................... 10,000
Franklin K. Lane, Cal..........................$10,000
Edgar E. Clark, Iowa.......................... 10,000
James S. Harlan, Ill.......................... 10,000
Edward A. Moseley, Mass., Secretary..... 5,000

SPANISH TREATY CLAIMS COMMISSION.

James Perry Wood, Ohio......................$5,000
William A. Maury, D. C...................... 5,000
William L. Chambers, Ala.................... 5,000
Harry K. Daugherty, Pa........................$5,000
Roswell P. Bishop, Mich...................... 5,000

BOARD OF INDIAN COMMISSIONERS.

Chairman—Darwin R. James, N. Y.
Secretary—Merrill E. Gates, Washington, D. C.
Albert K. Smiley, N. Y.
E. Whittlesey, D. C.
William D. Walker, N. Y.
Joseph T. Jacobs, Mich.
Patrick J. Ryan, Pa.
Andrew S. Draper, Ill.
George Vaux, Jr., Pa.
Michael Bannin, N. Y.
The board serves without salary.

UNITED STATES PENSION AGENTS.*

Augusta, Me............Selden Connor.
Boston, Mass............Augustus J. Hoitt.
Buffalo, N. Y............Charles A. Orr.
Chicago, Ill............Charles Bent.
Columbus, Ohio.........W. R. Warnock.
Concord, N. H............Joab N. Patterson
Des Moines, Iowa.......William V. Willcox.
Detroit, Mich............Oscar A. Janes.
Indianapolis, Ind.......Albert O Marsh.
Knoxville, Tenn........William Rule.
Louisville, Ky..........Andrew T. Wood.
Milwaukee, Wis........Frederick H. Magdeburg.
New York City, N. Y..Michael Kerwin.
Philadelphia, Pa........St. Clair A. Mulholland.
Pittsburgh, Pa...........Daniel Ashworth.
San Francisco, Cal......Jesse B. Fuller.
Topeka, Kan............Wilder S. Metcalf.
Washington, D. C......John R. King.

* Salaries of Pension Agents, $4,000.

UNITED STATES ASSISTANT TREASURERS.

Sub-Treasuries.	*Assistant Treasurers.*
Baltimore	Clarence C. Pusey.
Boston	Edwin U. Curtis.
Chicago	William Boldenweck.
Cincinnati	Charles A. Bosworth.
New Orleans	Clarence S. Hebert.
New York	George S. Terry
Philadelphia	Joseph Bosler.
St. Louis	Thomas J. Akins.
San Francisco	William C. Ralston.

SUPERINTENDENTS OF MINTS.

Carson City..(Equipped as Assay Office), Roswell K. Colcord, Assayer in charge.
New Orleans....Hugh S. Suthon.
Philadelphia....John H. Landis.
San Francisco....Edward Sweeny.
Denver....F. M. Downer.

COLLECTORS OF CUSTOMS.

Houlton, Me., William M. Sewell.
Bangor, Me., Albert R. Day.
Bath, Me., Elwell S. Crosby.
Belfast, Me., Samuel W. Johnson.
Castine, Me., John M. Vogell.
Ellsworth, Me., Henry Whiting.
Machias, Me., Frank L. Shaw.
Kennebunk, Me., George E. Cousens.
Eastport, Me., Jacob C. Pike.
Portland, Me., Charles M. Moses.
Saco, Me., William L. Gerrish.
Waldoboro, Me., Fred. W. Wight.
Wiscasset, Me., Daniel H. Moody.
York, Me., Herbert D. Philbrick.
Portsmouth, N. H., Sherman T. Newton.
Bristol, R. I., Charles A. Barbour.
Newport, R. I., Robert S. Burlingame.
Providence, R. I., George W. Gardiner.
Burlington, Vt., Charles H. Darling.
Newport, Vt., Curtis S. Emory.
Bridgeport, Ct., Fred. Enos.
Hartford, Ct., Frank S. Kellogg.
New Haven, Ct., J. Rice Winchell.
New London, Ct., Thomas O. Thompson.
Stonington, Ct., Charles T. Stanton.
Barnstable, Mass., Thacher T. Hallet.
Boston, Mass., George H. Lyman.
Edgartown, Mass., Charles H. Marchant.
Fall River, Mass., James Brady.
Gloucester, Mass., William H. Jordan.
Marblehead, Mass., Luke B. Colbert.
Nantucket, Mass., Obed G. Smith.
New Bedford, Mass., Rufus A. Soule.
Plymouth, Mass., Herbert Morissey.
Salem, Mass., David M. Little.
Buffalo, N. Y., Frederick O. Murray.
Cape Vincent, N. Y., William J. Grant.
Plattsburg, N. Y., John F. O'Brien.
Dunkirk, N. Y., John Bourne.
Rochester, N. Y., Geo. F. Roth.
New York, N. Y., Edward S. Fowler.
Niagara Falls, N. Y., John A. Merritt.
Ogdensburg, N. Y., Wm. H. Daniels.
Oswego, N. Y., James H. Cooper.
Sag Harbor, N. Y., Peter Dippel.
Jersey City, N. J., John Doscher, Asst. Col.
Bridgeton, N. J., William B. Boone.
Burlington, N. J., Reginald Branch.
Somers Point, N. J., Walter Fifield.
Newark, N. J., George L. Smith.
Perth Amboy, N. J., Robert Carson.
Tuckerton, N. J., Frank W. Leach.
Camden, N. J., F. F. Patterson, Asst. Col.
Philadelphia, Pa., Chester W. Hill.
Erie, Pa., Benjamin B. Brown.
Wilmington, Del., David S. Clark.
Washington, D. C., Howard S. Nyman.
Annapolis, Md., Lawrence Bailliere.
Baltimore, Md., William F. Stone.
Crisfield, Md., Lincoln A. Dryden.
Alexandria, Va., Lewis McK. Bell.
Cape Charles, Va., C. G. Smithers.
Norfolk, Va., Floyd Hughes.
Petersburg, Va., William Mahone.
Tappahannock, Va., John Rosler.
Newport News, Va., J. E. B. Stuart.
Richmond, Va., Joseph B. Stewart.
Beaufort, N. C., Christopher D. Jones.
Newbern, N. C., Daniel W. Patrick.
Elizabeth City, N. C., D. O. Newberry.
Wilmington, N. C., Benjamin F. Keith.
Beaufort, S. C., Robert Smalls.
Charleston, S. C., Wm. D. Crum.
Georgetown, S. C., Isaiah J. McCottrie.
Brunswick, Ga., Henry T. Dunn.
Savannah, Ga., John H. Deveaux.
St. Mary's, Ga., John M. Holzendorf.
Mobile, Ala., William F. Tebbetts.
Gulfport, Miss., Frederick W. Collins.
Natchez, Miss., Cyrus G. Engle.
Vicksburg, Miss., William L. Short.
Apalachicola, Fla., Antoine J. Murat.
Cedar Keys, Fla., Fred. C. Cubberly.
Fernandina, Fla., John W. Howell.
Jacksonville, Fla., William H. Lucas.
Key West, Fla., George W. Allen.
St. Augustine, Fla., Frank J. Howatt.
Tampa, Fla., Matthew B. Macfarlane.
Pensacola, Fla., John E. Stillman.
New Orleans, La., Henry McCall.
Brashear, La., John A. Thornton.
Brownsville, Tex., Vacant.
Corpus Christi, Tex., James J. Haynes.
Eagle Pass, Tex., Robert W. Dowe.
El Paso, Tex., Alfred L. Sharpe.
Galveston, Tex., Francis L. Lee.
Port Arthur, Tex., Russell H. Dunn.
Cleveland, O., Charles F. Leach.
Sandusky, O., Charles A. Judson.
Toledo, O., Joseph C. Bonner.
Detroit, Mich., John B. Whelan.
Grand Haven, Mich., Walter I. Lillie.
Marquette, Mich., Gad Smith.
Port Huron, Mich., Vacant.
Chicago, Ill., John C. Ames.
St. Paul, Minn., John Peterson.
Duluth, Minn., Levi M. Willcuts.
Milwaukee, Wis., William H De Vos.
Great Falls, Mont., Charles M. Webster.
San Francisco, Cal., Fred'k S. Stratton.
San Diego, Cal., Frank W. Barnes.
Los Angeles, Cal., Cornelius W. Pendleton.
Eureka, Cal., Sterling A. Campbell.
Astoria, Ore., William F. McGregor.
Coos Bay, Ore., Morton Tower.
Portland, Ore., Philip S. Malcolm.
Yaquina, Ore., Charles B. Crosno.
Port Townsend, Wash., Fred. C. Harper.
Juneau, Alaska, Clarence L. Hobart.
Nogales, Ariz., Cornelius O'Keefe.
Pembina, N. D., Judson La Moure.
Honolulu, H. I., E. R. Stackable.
San Juan, P. R., James H. Causten.

SURVEYORS OF CUSTOMS.

Portland, Me., Joshua L. Chamberlain.
Boston, Mass., Jeremiah J. McCarthy.
Springfield, Mass., Henry L. Hines.
Albany, N. Y., William Barnes, Jr.
Greenport, N. Y., John A. Bassarear.
New York, N. Y., James S. Clarkson.
Patchogue, N. Y., Sidney O. Weeks.
Port Jefferson, N. Y., Arthur N. Randall.
Syracuse, N. Y., Ernest I. Edgecomb.
Philadelphia, Pa., Perry M. Lytle.
Pittsburgh, Pa., Mahlon M. Garland.
Baltimore, Md., Robert A. Ravenscroft.
Wheeling, W. Va., Charles T. Reed.
Atlanta, Ga., Marcellus O. Markham.
New Orleans, La., Fenton W. Gibson.
Louisville, Ky., J. Frank Taylor.
Paducah, Ky., John R. Puryear.
Memphis, Tenn., Joseph T. Spence.
Chattanooga, Tenn., Charles L. Peacock.
Nashville, Tenn., John J. Gore.
Knoxville, Tenn., Thomas B. McLemore.
Kansas City, Mo., Charles W. Clark.
St. Joseph, Mo., John Albus, Jr.
St. Louis, Mo., Charles F. Gallenkamp.
Cincinnati, O., Amor Smith, Jr.
Columbus, O., William C. Kennedy.
Dayton, O., Oscar I. Robbins.
Evansville, Ind., Frank B. Posey.
Indianapolis, Ind., Leopold G. Rothschild.
Michigan City, Ind., Charles J. Robb.
Cairo, Ill., Thomas C. Elliott.
Galena, Ill., William Vincent.
Peoria, Ill., Julius S. Starr.
Rock Island, Ill., Robert G. Pearce.
Burlington, Ia., George H. Ludde.
Council Bluffs, Ia., Leander M. Shubert.
Des Moines, Ia., Geo. L. Godfrey.
Dubuque, Ia., John M. Lenihan.
Sioux City, Ia., James H. Bolton.
Denver, Col., Winfield S. Boynton.
Lincoln, Neb., Henry C. M. Burgess.
Omaha, Neb., Benjamin H. Barrows.
La Crosse, Wis., Robert Calvert.
Grand Rapids, Mich., Sheridan F. Master.
San Francisco, Cal., Edward F. Woodward.
Salt Lake City, Utah, Jac. J. Greenwald.
Houston, Tex., Samuel L. Hain.

NAVAL OFFICERS OF CUSTOMS.

Boston, Mass., James O. Lyford.
New York, N. Y., Frederick J. H. Kracke.
Chicago, Ill., Thomas N. Jamieson.
New Orleans, La., Elmer E. Wood.
Baltimore, Md., J. Stuart McDonald.
San Francisco, Cal., John P. Irish.
Philadelphia, Pa., Walter T. Merrick.

POSTMASTERS OF PRINCIPAL CITIES OF THE UNITED STATES.

New York, Edward M. Morgan, 1907.
Chicago, Ill., Daniel A. Campbell, 1907.
Brooklyn, N.Y., Geo. H. Roberts, Jr., 1905.
St. Louis, Mo., Frank Wyman, 1903.
Boston, Mass., E. C. Mansfield, 1907.
Baltimore, Md., Wm. Hall Harris, 1905.
San Francisco, Cal., Arthur G. Fisk, 1908.
Cincinnati, O., Elias R. Monfort, 1907.
Cleveland, O., Charles C. Dewstoe, 1905.
Buffalo, N. Y., Fred. Greiner, 1905.
Pittsburgh, Pa., Wm. H. Davis, 1906.
Washington, D. C., Benj. F. Barnes, 1906.
Detroit, Mich., Homer Warren, 1906.
Milwaukee, Wis., David C. Owen, 1906.
Newark, N. J., James L. Hays, 1908.
Minneapolis, Minn., William D. Hale, 1906.
Jersey City, N. J., Peter F. Wanser, 1906.
Louisville, Ky., Robert E. Woods, 1906.
Omaha, Neb., Benj. T. Thomas, 1908.
Rochester, N. Y., Wm. S. Whittlesey, 1907.
St. Paul, Minn., Edward Yanish, 1907.
Providence, R. I., Clinton D. Sellew, 1906.
Denver, Col., Paul J. Sours, 1908.
Indianapolis, Ind., Rob't H. Bryson, 1908.
Allegheny, Pa., Wm. J. Kopp, 1907.
Albany, N. Y., Jas. B. McEwan, 1908.
Columbus, Ohio, Harry W. Krumm, 1906.
Syracuse, N. Y., Vacant.
Worcester, Mass., James W. Hunt, 1907.
Toledo, O., William H. Tucker, 1907.
Richmond, Va., Royal E. Cabell, 1906.
New Haven, Ct., Jas. A. Howarth, 1906.
Lowell, Mass., Albert G. Thompson, 1906.
Nashville, Tenn., Andrew W. Wills, 1906.
Scranton, Pa., Ezra H. Ripple, 1906.
Fall River, Mass., Geo. T. Durfee, 1907.
Memphis, Tenn., L. W. Dutro, 1908.
Dayton, O., Frederick G. Withoft, 1908.
Troy, N. Y., Albert E. Bonesteel, 1906.
Grand Rapids, Mich., L. K. Bishop, 1906.
Reading, Pa., Augustus M. High, 1907.
Camden, N. J., Robert L. Barber, 1907.
Trenton, N. J., Alexander C. Yard, 1906.
Lynn, Mass., Wm. F. Craig, 1905.
Atlanta, Ga., Edwin F. Blodgett, 1906.
Wilmington, Del., Henry C. Conrad, 1906.
New Orleans, La., T. J. Woodward, 1905.
Kansas City, Mo., Joseph H. Harris, 1906.
Philadelphia, Pa., Rich'd L. Ashhurst, 1906.
Charleston, S. C., Wilmot L. Harris, 1908.

THE FEDERAL GOVERNMENT—*Continued.*

THE JUDICIARY.

SUPREME COURT OF THE UNITED STATES.

Chief Justice of the United States—Melville W. Fuller, of Illinois, born 1833, appointed 1888.

		Born.	App.
Asso. Justice—	John M. Harlan, Ky.	1833	1877
" "	David J. Brewer, Kan.	1837	1889
" "	Edward D. White, La.	1845	1894
" "	Rufus W. Peckham, N. Y.	1838	1895
Asso. Justice—	Joseph McKenna, Cal.	1843	1898
" "	Oliver W. Holmes, Mass.	1841	1902
" "	William R. Day, Ohio	1849	1903
" "	William H. Moody, Mass.	1853	1906

Reporter—Charles H. Butler, N. Y. *Clerk*—J. H. McKenney, D. C. *Marshal*—John M. Wright, Ky.

The salary of the Chief Justice of the United States is $13,000; Associate Justices, $12,500 each.

CIRCUIT COURTS OF THE UNITED STATES.

Cir.	Judges.	App.
1.	Le Baron B. Colt, R. I.	1884
	William L. Putnam, Me.	1892
	Francis C. Lowell, Mass.	1905
2.	E. Henry Lacombe, N. Y.	1887
	Alfred C. Coxe, N. Y.	1902
	Henry G. Ward, N. Y.	1907
	Walter C. Noyes, Ct.	1907
3.	George M. Dallas, Pa.	1892
	George Gray, Del.	1899
	Joseph Buffington, Pa.	1906
4.	Nathan Goff, W. Va.	1892
	Jeter C. Pritchard, N. C.	1904
5.	Don A. Pardee, Ga.	1881
	A. P. McCormick, Tex.	1892
	David D. Shelby, Ala.	1899
6.	Horace H. Lurton, Tenn.	1893
	Henry F. Severens, Mich.	1900
	John K. Richards, Ohio	1903
7.	Peter S. Grosscup, Ill.	1899
	Francis E. Baker, Ind.	1902
	William H. Seaman, Wis.	1905
	Christian C. Kohlsaat, Ill.	1905
8.	Walter H. Sanborn, Minn.	1892
	Willis Van Devanter, Wyo.	1903
	William C. Hook, Kan.	1903
	Elmer B. Adams, Mo.	1905
9.	William B. Gilbert, Ore.	1892
	Erskine M. Ross, Cal.	1895
	William W. Morrow, Cal.	1897

Salaries, $7,000 each. The judges of each circuit and the justice of the Supreme Court for the circuit constitute a Circuit Court of Appeals. The FIRST CIRCUIT consists of Maine, Massachusetts, New Hampshire, Rhode Island. SECOND—Connecticut, New York, Vermont. THIRD—Delaware, New Jersey, Pennsylvania. FOURTH—Maryland, North Carolina, South Carolina, Virginia, West Virginia. FIFTH—Alabama, Florida, Georgia, Louisiana, Mississippi, Texas. SIXTH—Kentucky, Michigan, Ohio, Tennessee. SEVENTH—Illinois, Indiana, Wisconsin. EIGHTH—Arkansas, Colorado, Oklahoma, Iowa, Kansas, Minnesota, Missouri, Nebraska, New Mexico, North Dakota, South Dakota, Utah, Wyoming. NINTH—Alaska, Arizona, California Idaho, Montana, Nevada, Oregon, Washington, Hawaii.

UNITED STATES COURT OF CLAIMS.

Chief Justice—Stanton J. Peelle, Ind. *Associate Judges*—Charles B. Howry, Miss.; Fenton W. Booth, Ill.; Geo. W. Atkinson, W. Va.; Samuel S. Barney, Wis. Salaries, Chief Justice, $6,500; Justices, $6,000.

DISTRICT COURTS OF THE UNITED STATES.

Districts.	Judges.	Addresses.	App.
Ala.: N. & M.	Thomas G. Jones	Montgomery	1901
" N.	Oscar R. Hundley	Birmingham	1908
" S. D.	H. T. Toulmin	Mobile	1887
Alaska	R. A. Gunnison	Juneau	1904
"	Alfred S. Moore	Nome	1906
"	Silas H. Reid	Fairbanks	1908
Ark.: E. D.	Jacob Trieber	Little Rock	1901
" W. D.	John H. Rogers	Fort Smith	1896
Cal.: N. D.	John J. DeHaven	San Francisco	1897
"	Wm. C. VanFleet	San Francisco	1907
" S. D.	Olin Wellborn	Los Angeles	1895
Colorado	Robert E. Lewis	Denver	1906
Connecticut	James P. Platt	Hartford	1902
Delaware	Ed. G. Bradford	Wilmington	1897
Fla.: N. D.	W. B. Sheppard	Pensacola	1908
" S. D.	James W. Locke	Jacksonville	1872
Ga.: N. D.	Wm. T. Newman	Atlanta	1886
" S. D.	Emory Speer	Macon	1885
Hawaii	Sanford B. Dole	Honolulu	1903
Idaho	Frank S. Dietrich	Boisé	1907
Ill.: N. D.	Sol. H. Bethea	Chicago	1905
	Ken. M. Landis	Chicago	1905
" S. D.	J. O. Humphrey	Springfield	1901
" E.	F. M. Wright	Urbana	1905
Indiana	A. B. Anderson	Indianapolis	1902
Iowa: N. D.	Henry T. Reed	Cresco	1904
" S. D.	S. McPherson	Red Oak	1900
Kansas	John C. Pollock	Topeka	1903
Ky.: W. D.	Walter Evans	Louisville	1899
" E. D.	A. M. J. Cochran	Maysville	1901
La.: E. D.	Eug. D. Saunders	New Orleans	1907
" W. D.	Aleck Boarman	Shreveport	1881
Maine	Clarence Hale	Portland	1902
Maryland	Thomas J. Morris	Baltimore	1879
Mass	Frederic Dodge	Boston	1905
Mich.: E. D.	Henry H. Swan	Detroit	1891
" W. D.	L. E. Knappen	Grand Rapids	1906
Minnesota	Milton D. Purdy	Minneapolis	1908
"	Page Morris	Duluth	1903
Miss.: N. & S.	Henry C. Niles	Kosciusko	1892
Montana	Wm. H. Hunt	Helena	1904
Mo.: E. D.	David P. Dyer	St. Louis	1907
" W. D.	John F. Philips	Kansas City	1888
Nebraska	Wm. H. Munger	Omaha	1897
"	Thos. C. Munger	Lincoln	1907
Nevada	E. S. Farrington	Carson	1907
N. Hamp.	Edgar Aldrich	Littleton	1891
New Jersey	W. M. Lanning	Trenton	1904
"	Joseph Cross	Elizabeth	1905
N. Y.: N. D.	George W. Ray	Norwich	1902
" W. D.	John R. Hazel	Buffalo	1900
" S. D.	Geo. B. Adams	N. Y. City	1901
"	George C. Holt	N. Y. City	1903
"	Chas. M. Hough	N. Y. City	1906
" E. D.	T. I. Chatfield	Brooklyn	1907
N. C.: E. D.	Thos. R. Purnell	Raleigh	1897
" W. D.	James E. Boyd	Greensboro	1901
N. Dakota	Chas. F. Amidon	Fargo	1897
Ohio: N. D.	R. W. Tayler	Cleveland	1905
" S. D.	A. C. Thompson	Cincinnati	1898
" S. D.	John E. Slater	Columbus	1908
Okla.: E. D.	R. E. Campbell	Muskogee	1908
" W. D.	John H. Cotteral	Guthrie	1908
Oregon	C. E. Wolverton	Portland	1906
Pa.: E. D.	J. B. McPherson	Philadelphia	1899
" "	Jas. B. Holland	Philadelphia	1904
" M. D.	R. W. Archbald	Scranton	1901
" W. D.	Jas. S. Young	Pittsburgh	1908
Porto Rico	Bern'd S. Rodey	San Juan	1906
R. Island	A. L. Brown	Providence	1896
S. Carolina	W. H. Brawley	Charleston	1894
S. Dakota	John E. Carland	Sioux Falls	1896
Tenn.: E. & M.	Ed. T. Sanford	Knoxville	1908
" W. D.	John E. McCall	Memphis	1905
Tex.: E. D.	D. E. Bryant	Sherman	1890
" W. D.	Thos. S. Maxey	Austin	1888
" N. D.	Edw. R. Meek	Dallas	1899
" S. D.	W. T. Burns	Houston	1902
Utah	J. A. Marshall	Salt Lake C.	1896
Vermont	James L. Martin	Brattleboro	1906
Va.: E. D.	E. Waddill, Jr.	Richmond	1898
" W. D.	H. C. McDowell	Lynchburg	1901
Wash.: W. D.	C. H. Hanford	Seattle	1890
" E. D.	Edw. Whitson	Spokane	1905
W. Va.: N. D.	A. G. Dayton	Phillippi	1905
" S. D.	B. F. Keller	Bramwell	1901
Wis.: E. D.	Jos. V. Quarles	Milwaukee	1905
" W. D.	A. L. Sanborn	Madison	1905
Wyoming	John A. Riner	Cheyenne	1890

Salaries of District Judges, $6,000 each.

United States District-Attorneys and Marshals.

Districts.	District-Attorneys. Names.	Official Address.	Dates Appointed.	Marshals. Names.	Official Address.	Dates Appointed.
Alabama, N.	Oliver D. Street	Birmingham	Jan. 14, 1908	Pope M. Long	Birmingham	Jan. 14, 1906
" M.	Erastus J. Parsons	Montgomery	Feb. 8, 1906	James H. Judkins	Montgomery	Jan. 31, 1906
" S.	Wm. H. Armbrecht	Mobile	Feb. 2, 1908	Gilbert B. Deans	Mobile	Jan. 14, 1908
Alaska, 1st Div.	J. J. Boyce	Juneau	Feb. 18, 1907	James M. Shoup	Juneau	June 6, 1908
" 2d Div.	Geo. B. Grigsby	Nome	Mar. 24, 1908	Thomas C. Powell	Nome	Jan. 24, 1905
" 3d Div.	James J. Crossley	Fairbanks	May 18, 1908	Henry K. Love	Fairbanks	Oct. 9, 1908
Arizona	Jos. L. B. Alexander	Phœnix	Dec. 12, 1905	Benj. F. Daniels	Tucson	Apr. 25, 1906
Arkansas, E.	Wm. G. Whipple	Little Rock	Feb. 23, 1905	Harmon L. Remmel	Little Rock	May 8, 1906
" W.	James K. Barnes	Fort Smith	May 29, 1906	John F. Mayes	Fort Smith	Mar. 6, 1906
California, N.	Robt. T. Devlin	San Francisco	Mar. 8, 1905	Charles T. Elliott	San Francisco	June 22, 1906
" S.	Oscar Lawler	Los Angeles	Dec. 19, 1905	L. V. Youngworth	Los Angeles	June 22, 1906
Colorado	Thomas Ward, Jr.	Denver	Feb. 17, 1908	Dewey C. Bailey	Denver	Feb. 26, 1907
Connecticut	John T. Robinson	Hartford	Apr. 2, 1908	Edson S. Bishop	Hartford	Dec. 18, 1906
Delaware	John P. Nields	Wilmington	Dec. 10, 1907	William R. Flinn	Wilmington	Dec. 10, 1907
Dist. of Columbia	Daniel W. Baker	Washington	Dec. 19, 1905	Aulick Palmer	Washington	Jan. 9, 1906
Florida, N.	Emmet Wilson	Pensacola	Oct. 12, 1907	T. F. McGourin	Pensacola	Feb. 27, 1907
" S.	John M. Cheney	Jacksonville	Jan. 23, 1906	John F. Horr	Jacksonville	Feb. 18, 1906
Georgia, N.	Farish C. Tate	Atlanta	Dec. 18, 1905	W. H. Johnson	Atlanta	Dec. 18, 1905
" S.	Marion Erwin	Macon	Dec. 19, 1905	Geo. F. White	Macon	Dec. 13, 1904
Hawaii (trm 6 y)	Robt. W. Breckons	Honolulu	Feb. 10, 1908	E. R. Hendry	Honolulu	Feb. 10, 1908
Idaho	C. H. Lingenfelter	Boise	June 15, 1908	Shadrach L. Hodgin	Boise	June 15, 1908
Illinois, N.	Edwin W. Sims	Chicago	Sept. 1, 1906	Luman T. Hoy	Chicago	June 28, 1905
" E.	Wm. E. Trautmann	Danville	Dec. 19, 1905	Charles P. Hitch	Danville	Dec. 19, 1905
" S.	Wm. A. Northcott	Springfield	Dec. 19, 1905	Leon A. Townsend	Springfield	Dec. 19, 1905
Indiana	Joseph B. Kealing	Indianapolis	Dec. 12, 1905	H. C. Pettit	Indianapolis	Dec. 12, 1905
Iowa, N.	Frederick F. Fayville	StormLake (P.O.)	Dec. 10, 1907	Edward Knott	Dubuque	Dec. 10, 1907
" S.	Marcellus L. Temple	Osceola (P.O.)	Dec. 17, 1907	Frank B. Clark	Des Moines	Dec. 10, 1907
Kansas	Harry J. Bone	Topeka	Dec. 18, 1905	Wm. H. Mackey, Jr.	Topeka	Jan. 8, 1907
Kentucky, W.	George Du Relle	Louisville	June 22, 1906	George W. Long	Louisville	Dec. 17, 1905
" E.	J. H. Tinsley	Covington	Apr. 17, 1905	S. G. Sharp	Covington	Jan. 16, 1905
Louisiana, E.	Rufus E. Foster	New Orleans	Jan. 1, 1908	Victor Loisel	New Orleans	Mar. 19, 1908
" W.	Milton C. Elstner	Shreveport	Feb. 18, 1903	Cornelius C. Duson	Shreveport	Feb. 10, 1908
Maine	Robt. T. Whitehouse	Portland	Jan. 16, 1906	Henry W. Mayo	Portland	Dec. 10, 1907
Maryland	John C. Rose	Baltimore	June 28, 1906	J. F. Langhammer	Baltimore	July 17, 1906
Massachusetts	Asa P. French	Boston	Jan. 9, 1906	Guy Murchie	Boston	Apr. 28, 1908
Michigan, E.	Frank H. Watson	Detroit	May 2, 1906	Milo D. Campbell	Detroit	May 2, 1906
" W.	George G. Covell	Grand Rapids	Feb. 15, 1906	Frank W. Wait	Grand Rapids	Jan. 19, 1907
Minnesota	Charles C. Haupt	St. Paul	June 3, 1906	W. H. Grimshaw	St. Paul	Dec. 19, 1907
Mississippi, N.	William D. Frazee	Oxford	Dec. 19, 1905	Aaron M. Storer	Oxford	Apr. 28, 1908
" S.	Robert C. Lee	Jackson	Jan. 20, 1906	Edgar S. Wilson	Jackson	Feb. 6, 1906
Missouri, E.	Henry W. Blodgett	St. Louis	Dec. 17, 1907	Wm. L. Morsey	St. Louis	June 11, 1906
" W.	A. S. VanValkenburgh	Kansas City	Dec. 12, 1905	E. R. Durham	Kansas City	July 1, 1906
Montana	James W. Freeman	Helena	June 1, 1908	Arthur W. Merrifield	Helena	Dec. 18, 1906
Nebraska	Charles A. Goss	Omaha	Jan. 29, 1906	William P. Warner	Omaha	Dec. 20, 1905
Nevada	Samuel Platt	Carson City	Jan. 13, 1906	Robert Grimmon	Carson City	Dec. 13, 1904
New Hampshire	Charles W. Hoitt	Nashua (P.O.)	Feb. 12, 1907	Eugene P. Nute	Concord	Dec. 19, 1907
New Jersey	John B. Vreeland	Morristown	Dec. 10, 1907	Thomas J. Alcott	Trenton	Dec. 20, 1905
New Mexico	David J. Leahy	Las Vegas	Dec. 16, 1907	C. M. Foraker	Albuquerque	Dec. 19, 1905
New York, N.	George B. Curtiss	Binghamton	June 5, 1904	C. D. McDougall	Auburn	Jan. 10, 1905
" S.	Henry L. Stimson	New York	Jan. 16, 1906	William Henkel	New York	Jan. 17, 1906
" E.	W. J. Youngs	Brooklyn	Dec. 20, 1906	Chas. J. Haubert	Brooklyn	Apr. 22, 1906
" W.	Lyman M. Bass	Buffalo	Dec. 23, 1906	Wm. R. Compton	Elmira	June 5, 1904
N. Carolina, E.	Henry Skinner	Greenville	Feb. 1, 1906	Claudius Dockery	Raleigh	Mar. 7, 1906
" W.	Alfred E. Holton	Winston	Mar. 20, 1906	James M. Milliken	Greensboro	Feb. 13, 1906
North Dakota	Patrick H. Rourke	Fargo	Dec. 11, 1906	James F. Shea	Fargo	Dec. 18, 1905
Ohio, N.	William A. Day	Cleveland	Feb. 28, 1908	Frank M. Chandler	Cleveland	Jan. 18, 1905
" S.	S. T. McPherson	Cincinnati	Dec. 10, 1907	Eugene L. Lewis	Cincinnati	Dec. 13, 1906
Oklahoma, E.	Wm. J. Gregg	Muskogee	Jan. 13, 1908	Samuel G. Victor	Muskogee	Mar. 31, 1908
" W.	John Embry	Guthrie	Feb. 19, 1908	John R. Abernathy	Guthrie	Jan. 13, 1908
Oregon	John McCourt	Portland	Mar. 17, 1908	Chas. J. Reed	Portland	Jan. 16, 1906
P'nsylvania, E.	J. Whitaker Thompson	Philadelphia	Apr. 29, 1908	John B. Robinson	Philadelphia	Jan. 10, 1905
" M.	Chas. B. Witmer	Sunbury	Dec. 10, 1907	James M. Yeager	Scranton	Dec. 21, 1907
" W.	John W. Dunkle	Pittsburgh	Mar. 18, 1905	S. P. Stone	Pittsburgh	Dec. 19, 1905
Porto Rico	Jose R. F. Savage	San Juan	Dec. 19, 1906	Samuel C. Bothwell	San Juan	July 5, 1900
Rhode Island	Charles A. Wilson	Providence	Jan. 21, 1906	Daniel R. Ballou	Providence	Feb. 20, 1906
South Carolina	Ernest F. Cochran	Charleston	Feb. 1, 1906	J. Duncan Adams	Charleston	Mar. 1, 1907
South Dakota	Edward E. Wagner	Sioux Falls	May 30, 1908	Seth Bullock	Sioux Falls	Jan. 13, 1906
Tennessee, E.	James R. Penland	Knoxville	Dec. 20, 1905	William A. Dunlap	Knoxville	Dec. 20, 1905
" M.	A. M. Tillman	Nashville	Feb. 1, 1906	John W. Overall	Nashville	Mar. 9, 1906
" W.	George Randolph	Memphis	June 8, 1906	Frank S. Elgin	Memphis	June 28, 1906
Texas, N.	Wm. H. Atwell	Dallas	June 19, 1906	George H. Green	Dallas	Mar. 2, 1907
" S.	Lock McDaniel	Houston	Jan. 16, 1907	Calvin G. Brewster	Galveston	June 27, 1906
" E.	James W. Ownby	Beaumont	July 1, 1906	A. J. Houston	Paris	May 26, 1908
" W.	Charles A. Boynton	Waco	June 1, 1906	Eugene Nolte	San Antonio	Mar. 4, 1906
Utah	Hiram E. Booth	Salt Lake City	June 27, 1906	Lucien H. Smyth	Salt Lake City	Oct. 21, 1908
Vermont	Alexander Dunnett	St. Johnsbury	Dec. 11, 1906	Horace W. Bailey	Rutland	Dec. 10, 1907
Virginia, E.	Lunsford L. Lewis	Richmond	Jan. 9, 1906	Morgan Treat	Richmond	Dec. 19, 1905
" W.	Thomas Lee Moore	Christians'g P.O.	Feb. 1, 1906	S. Brown Allen	Staunton (P.O.)	Mar. 20, 1906
Washington, E.	A. Geo. Avery	Spokane	Dec. 12, 1905	Geo. H. Baker	Spokane	Dec. 12, 1905
" W.	Elmer Ely Todd	Seattle	Dec. 10, 1907	Chas. B. Hopkins	Tacoma	Mar. 7, 1906
W. Virginia, N.	R. Blizzard	Parkersburg	Dec. 18, 1905	C. D. Elliott	Parkersburg	Dec. 18, 1905
" S.	Elliott Northcott	Huntington	Dec. 12, 1905	Frank H. Tyree	Huntington	Dec. 17, 1905
Wisconsin, E.	H. K. Butterfield	Milwaukee	Apr. 22, 1905	Harry A. Weil	Milwaukee	Feb. 11, 1907
" W.	Wm. G. Wheeler	Madison	Jan. 23, 1905	Rockwell J. Flint	Madison	Feb. 10, 1908
Wyoming	Timothy F. Burke	Cheyenne	Dec. 10, 1907	Louis G. Davis	Cheyenne	Feb. 28, 1907

N., Northern; S., Southern; E., Eastern; W., Western; M., Middle; C., Central.

The Army.

GENERAL STAFF OF THE ARMY.

Major-General J. Franklin Bell, Chief of Staff.
Major-General William P. Duvall. Brigadier-General Arthur Murray.
Brigadier-General William W. Wotherspoon.

COLONELS.

Stephen C. Mills, Inspector General.
George S. Anderson, 1st Cavalry.
Joseph W. Duncan, 6th Infantry.
Montgomery M. Macomb, 6th Field Artillery.

LIEUTENANT-COLONELS.

Robert K. Evans, 5th Infantry.
Thaddeus W. Jones, 3d Cavalry.
William P. Evans, 11th Infantry.
Erasmus M. Weaver, Coast Artillery Corps.
Millard F. Waltz, 27th Infantry.
Walter L. Finley, 13th Cavalry.

MAJORS.

Eben Swift, 9th Cavalry.
John T. Knight, Quartermaster's Department.
Henry L. Ripley, 8th Cavalry.
Daniel H. Boughton, 11th Cavalry.
Francis J. Kernan, 25th Infantry.
Robert L. Hirst, 29th Infantry.
John F. Morrison, 20th Infantry.
Henry C. Cabell, 14th Infantry.
Wm. P. Burnham, 7th Infantry.
Samuel D. Sturgis, 1st Field Artillery.

MAJORS—*Continued.*

Cornélis De W. Willcox, Coast Artillery Corps.
Henry D. Todd, Jr., Coast Artillery Corps.

CAPTAINS.

Walter H. Gordon, 18th Infantry.
Marcus D. Cronin, 25th Infantry.
Julius A. Penn, 7th Infantry.
Michael J. Lenihan, 25th Infantry.
Peter C. Harris, 9th Infantry.
George W. Read, 9th Cavalry.
Fred W. Sladen, 14th Infantry.
Henry G. Learnard, 14th Infantry.
P. D. Lochridge, 13th Cavalry.
Milton F. Davis, 10th Cavalry.
John W. Furlong, 6th Cavalry.
Ralph H. Van Deman, 21st Infantry.
Frank S. Cocheu, 12th Infantry.
William Chamberlaine, Coast Artillery Corps.
Joseph P. Tracy, Coast Artillery Corps.
Johnson Hagood, Coast Artillery Corps.
Samuel C. Vestal, Coast Artillery Corps.
Fox Conner, 1st Field Artillery.
Thomas E. Merrill, 1st Field Artillery.
Sherwood A. Cheney, Corps of Engineers.

GENERAL OFFICERS OF THE LINE.

Rank	Name	Command	Station
Lieutenant-General	Arthur MacArthur		Milwaukee, Wis.
Major-General	Leonard Wood	Department of the East	New York City.
"	John F. Weston	Department of California	San Francisco, Cal.
"	Frederick D. Grant	Department of the Lakes	Chicago, Ill.
"	J. Franklin Bell	Chief of Staff	Washington, D. C.
"	William P. Duvall	Assistant to Chief of Staff	Washington, D. C.
"	Thomas H. Barry	Army of Cuban Pacification	Havana, Cuba.
Brigadier-General	Frederick Funston	Army School of the Line	Fort Leavenworth, Kan.
"	William H. Carter	Department of the Missouri	Omaha, Neb.
"	Tasker H. Bliss	Div. of the Philippines (tem'y)	Manila, P. I.
"	Albert L. Mills	Department of Luzon	Manila, P. I.
"	Winfield S. Edgerly	Department of Dakota	St. Paul, Minn.
"	John J. Pershing	Ft. Wm. McKinley	Manila, P. I.
"	Arthur Murray	Chief of Coast Artillery	Washington, D. C.
"	Albert L. Myer	Department of Texas	San Antonio, Tex.
"	Earl D. Thomas	Department of the Colorado	Denver, Col.
"	Charles Morton	Fort D. A. Russel	Wyoming.
"	Charles L. Hodges	Department of the Visayas	Manila, P. I.
"	Wm. W. Wotherspoon	President Army War College	Washington, D. C.
"	Ramsay D. Potts	Department of the Gulf	Atlanta, Ga.
"	Daniel H. Brush	Department of the Columbia	Vancouver Bks., Wash'n.
"	John B. Kerr	Mounted Service School	Fort Riley, Kansas.
"	Fredk. A. Smith	Unassigned (temporarily)	

CHIEFS OF STAFF CORPS AND BUREAUS OF THE WAR DEPARTMENT.

Rank	Name	Office	Station
Major-General	Fred. C. Ainsworth	The Adjutant-General	Washington, D. C.
Brigadier-General	William P. Hall	Adjutant-General	Washington, D. C.
"	Ernest A. Garlington	Inspector-General	Washington, D. C.
"	George B. Davis	Judge-Advocate-General	Washington, D. C.
"	James B. Aleshire	Quartermaster-General	Washington, D. C.
"	Henry G. Sharpe	Commissary-General	Washington, D. C.
"	Robert M. O'Reilly	Surgeon-General	Washington, D. C.
"	Charles H. Whipple	Paymaster-General	Washington, D. C.
"	Wm. L. Marshall	Chief of Engineers	Washington, D. C.
"	William Crozier	Chief of Ordnance	Washington, D. C.
"	James Allen	Chief Signal Officer	Washington, D. C.

RETIREMENTS OF GENERALS ON THE ACTIVE LIST.

The following are the dates of the future retirements of Generals on the active list: Brigadier-General Surgeon-General Robert M. O'Reilly, January 14, 1909; Lieutenant-General Arthur MacArthur, June 2, 1909; Major-General John F. Weston, November 13, 1909; Brigadier-General Charles Morton, March 18, 1910; Brigadier-General Winfield S. Edgerly, May 29, 1910; Chief of Engineers William L. Marshall, June 11, 1910; Brigadier-General Albert L. Myer, November 14, 1910; Brigadier-General Earl D. Thomas, January 4, 1911; Brigadier-General John B. Kerr, March 12, 1911; Major-General William P. Duvall, January 13, 1911; Judge-Advocate-General George B. Davis, February 14, 1911; Brigadier-General Charles L. Hodges, March 13, 1911; Brigadier-General Daniel H. Brush, May 9, 1912; Brigadier-General William P. Hall, June 11, 1912; Chief Signal Officer James Allen, February 13, 1913; Brigadier-General Frederick A. Smith, May 15, 1913; Major-General Frederick D. Grant, May 30, 1914; Brigadier-General Ramsay D. Potts, September 1, 1914; Brigadier-General William W. Wotherspoon, November 16, 1914; Chief of Artillery Arthur Murray, April 29, 1915; Brigadier-General William H. Carter, November 19, 1915; The Adjutant-General, Fred. C. Ainsworth, September 11, 1916; Inspector-General Ernest A. Garlington, February 20, 1917;

RETIREMENTS OF GENERALS ON THE ACTIVE LIST—*Continued.*

Brigadier-General Tasker H. Bliss, December 31, 1917; Brigadier-General Albert L. Mills, May 7, 1918; Chief of Ordnance William Crozier, February 19, 1919; Major-General Thomas H. Barry, October 13, 1919; Major-General J. Franklin Bell, January 9, 1920; Quartermaster-General James B. Aleshire, October 31, 1920; Commissary-General Henry G. Sharpe, April 30, 1922; Brigadier-General John J. Pershing, September 13, 1924; Major-General Leonard Wood, October 9, 1924; Brigadier-General Frederick Funston, November 9, 1929

GENERAL OFFICERS ON THE RETIRED LIST AND YEAR OF RETIREMENT.

Abbot, Henry L.....1895..B. G..Cambridge, Mass.
Adams, Henry M..1908.. " ..Buffalo, N. Y.
Alexander, Chas. T..1897.. " ..Washington, D. C.
Alexander, W. L....1905.. " ..Pasadena, Cal.
Allen, Charles J....1904.. " ..Washington, D.C.
Anderson, Harry R.1907.. " ..Baltimore, Md.
Anderson, Thos. M..1899.. " ..Philadelphia, Pa.
Andrews, Geo. L...1892.. " ..Washington, D. C.
Andruss, E. Van A..1902.. " ..Brooklyn, N. Y.
Atwood, Edwin B..1903.. " ..Chicago, Ill.
Auman, William...1902.. " ..Buffalo, N. Y.
Babcock, John B....1903.. " ..London, England.
Bailey, Clarence M..1899.. " ..Chicago, Ill.
Baldwin, Frank D..1906.. " ..Denver, Col.
Baldwin, Theo. A..1903.. " ..Catoosa Sp'gs, Ga.
Barlow, John W...1901... " ...New London, Ct.
Barr, Thomas F....1901.. " ...Boston, Mass.
Bates, Alfred E.....1904..M.G...Washington, D. C
Bates, John C.......1906..L.G..Washington, D. C.
Beck, William H...1905..B.G...Washington, D. C.
Bell, James M......1901.. " ..New York City.
Biddle, James.......1896.. " ..Santa Barbara, Cal.
Bingham, Judson D.1895.. " ..Philadelphia, Pa.
Bingham, Theo. A..1904.. " ..New York City.
Bird, Charles........1902.. " ..Wilmington, Del.
Birkhimer, Wm. E..1906.. " ..Washington, D. C.
Bisbee, William H..1902.. " . Boston, Mass.
Borden, George P..1907.. " ..New York City.
Bowman, A. H......1903.. " ...Washington, D. C.
Bradley, Luther P..1886.. " ..Tacoma, Wash.
Breck, Samuel......1897.. " ...Brookline, Mass.
Breckinridge, J. C...1903...M.G..Annapolis, Md.
Brooke, John R.....1902.. " ...Paris, France.
Brown, Justus M..1903..B. G...Hackensack, N. J.
Bubb, John W......1907.. " ..Portland, Oregon.
Buchanan, Jas. A...1906.. " ..Washington, D. C.
Buffington, A. R....1901.. " ..Madison, N. J.
Bullis, John L......1905.. " ..San Antonio, Tex.
Burbank, James B..1902.. " ..New York City.
Burke, Daniel W.....1899.. " ..Portland, Ore.
Burt, Andrew S... 1902.. " ...Washington, D. C.
Burton, George H..1906.. " ..Los Angeles, Cal.
Butler, John G......1904.. " ..Washington, D. C.
Byrne, Charles C....1901.. " ..Rome, Italy.
Califf, Joseph M.....1906.. " ..Towanda, Pa.
Carey, Asa B.........1899.. " ..Boston, Mass.
Carlton, Caleb H....1897.. " ..Washington, D. C.
Carpenter, L. H....1899.. " ..Philadelphia, Pa.
Carr, Camillo C. C..1906.. " ..London, England.
Carr, Eugene A......1893.. " ...Washington, D. C.
Carrington, H. B....1870.. " ...Hyde Park, Mass.
Catlin, Isaac S.......1870.. " ..Owego, N. Y.
Caziarc, Louis V....1906.. " ..Luzerne, Switz'd.
Chaffee, Adna R....1906..L. G..Los Angeles, Cal.
Chance, Jesse C. ...1903..B. G..Fremont, Ohio.
Chandler, John G...1894.. " ...Los Angeles, Cal.
Cleary, Peter J. A...1903.. " ..Chattan'ga, Tenn.
Closson, H. W.......1896.. " ..Washington, D. C.
Coates, Edwin M...1900.. " ..Washington, D.C.
Compton, Chas. E...1899.. " ..Washington, D. C.
Comstock, Cyrus B..1895.. " ..New York City.
Cook, Henry C......1898.. " ..Fall River, Mass.
Cooke, Lorenzo W..1906.. " ..Lemon Grove, Cal.
Coolidge, Chas. A...1903.. " ..Detroit, Mich.
Cooney, Michael.....1899.. " ..Washington, D. C.
Cooper, Charles L...1903.. " ...Denver, Col.
Coppinger, J. J.... 1898.. " ...Washington, D. C.
Corbin, Henry C....1906..L. G..Chevy Chase, D. C.
Coxe, Frank M.....1904.. " ..San Francisco, Cal.
Craighill, W. P.......1897.. " ...Charlest'wn, W. Va
Craigie, David J.....1903., " ...Washington, D. C.
Crawford, M.........1908..B. G..Washington, D. C.
Daggett, Aaron S.. 1901.. " ...Washington, D. C.
Davis, Chas. E. L. B.1908.. " ..Washington, D.C.
Davis, Charles L....1903.. " ...Schenectady, N. Y.
Davis, Edward.......1905.. " ..Honolulu, H. I.
Davis, George W...1903..M.G..Washington, D. C.
Davis, John M. K..1908..B. G..Hartford, Ct.
Davis, Wirt.........1901...B.G..Washington, D. C.
De Russy, I. D.....1902.. " ...New York City.
Dimmick, Eug. D...1903.. " ...Washington, D. C.
Dougherty, Wm. E..1904.. " ..Fruitvale, Cal.
Drum, R. C.........1889.. " ...Bethesda, Md.
Dudley, N. A. M...1889.. " ..Roxbury, Mass.
Duggan, Walter T..1907.. " ..Fort Bayard, N. M.
Dunwoody, H. H. C..1904.. " ..Washington, D. C.
Eagan, Charles P....1900 . " ..New York City.
Ennis, William.....1905... " ..Newport, R. I.
Ernst, Oswald H....1906.. " ..Washington, D.C.
Ewers, Ezra P.......1801.. " ..Owenton, Ky.
Farley, Joseph P....1903.. " ..Fort Monroe, Va.
Forbes, Theodore F..1903.. " ..Washington, D. C.
Forwood, Wm. H..1902.. " ...Washington, D.C.
Fountain, S. W.....1905.. " ...Devon, Pa.
Freeman, Henry B..1901.. " ...Douglas, Wyo.
Furey, John V......1903.. " ...Brooklyn, N. Y.
Gibson, Horatio G..1891.. " ..Washington, D. C.
Gillespie, George L...1905..M.G..Washington, D. C.
Gilmore, John C...1901..B.G..Washington, D. C.
Girard, Alfred C... 1905... " ..Chicago, Ill.
Godfrey, Edward S.1907.. " ..Tucson, Ariz.
Goodale, G. A........1903.. " ...Wakefield, Mass.
Gordon, David S....1896.. " ..Piedmont, Cal.
Graham, W. M.. ...1898.... " ..Washington, D. C.
Greely, A. W........1908..M.G ..Washington, D. C.
Greenleaf, Chas. R..1902..B. G..Berkeley, Cal.
Grierson, B. H.......1890.. " ...Jacksonville, Ill.
Grimes, George S...1907.. " ..Washington, D. C.
Guenther, F. L.......1902.. " ..New York City.
Hains, Peter C.......1904.. " ...Washington, D. C.
Hall, Charles B.....1908..M.G..Paris, France.
Hall, Robert H.....1901..B. G...Buffalo, N. Y.
Harbach, Abram A.1902.. " ..Rochester, N. Y.
Hardin, M. D.......1870.. " ..Chicago, Ill.
Hasbrouck, H. C....1903.. " ..Newburgh, N. Y.
Haskin, William L.1903.. " ..Elmira, N. Y.
Hathaway, F. H.....1904.. " ..Portland, Ore.
Hawkins, H. S......1898.. " ..Washington, D. C.
Hawkins, John P..1894.. " ..Indianapolis, Ind.
Hayes, Edward M.1903.. " ..Dover, Del.
Heap, David P......1905.. " ..Pasadena, Cal.
Hennisee, A. G......1903.. " ..Los Angeles, Cal.
Hobbs, Charles W..1903.. " ..Washington, D. C.
Hodges, Henry C...1895.. " ..Buffalo, N. Y.
Hood, Charles C....1902.. " ..Philadelphia, Pa.
Hooton, Mott........1902.. " ..Portland, Me.
Howard, Oliver O..1894..M. G..Burlington, Vt.
Hoxie, Richard L..1908..B. G..Washington, D. C.
Hubbell, Henry W.1905.. " ..Warrenton, Va.
Huggins, Eli L.....1903.. " ..San Diego, Cal.
Hughes, Robert P.1903..M. G..New Haven, Ct.
Humphrey, Chas. F.1907.. " ..Washington, D. C.
Hyde, John McE...1904..B. G..Brookline, Mass.
Irwin, B. J. D......1894.. " ..Ontario, Canada.
Jackson, Henry....1901.. " ..Leavenworth, Kan.
Jocelyn, Stephen P.1907.. " ..Burlington, Vt.
Jones, Wm. A.......1905.. " ..Plainfield, N. J.
Kellogg, Edgar R...1899.. " ..Toledo, Ohio.
Kent, Jacob F.......1898.. " ..Watervliet, N. Y.
Kimball, Amos S..1902.. " ..Washington, D. C.
Kobbe, William A..1904..M. G..Pasadena, Cal.
Kress, John A......1903..B. G..St. Louis, Mo.
Langdon, Loomis L.1894.. " ..Brooklyn, N. Y.
Lazelle, Henry M. 1894.. " ..Geo'ville, Canada.
Leary, Peter, Jr... 1904.. " ..Baltimore, Md.
Lebo, Thomas C....1904.. " ..Paris, France.
Lee, James G. C....1900.. " ..Columbia, S. C.
Lee, Jesse M........1907..M. G..Ft. Sm H'st'n, Tex.
Lieber, G. Norman..1901.. " ..Washington, D. C.
Lincoln, Sumner H.1902.. " ..Fern Bank, Ohio.
Lockwood, Benj. C 1907..B. G..Detroit, Mich.
Lodor, Richard......1896 ..M. G..New York City.
Long, Oscar F......1904..B. G..Piedmont, Cal.
Ludington, M. I.....1903..M. G..Skaneateles, N. Y
Lydecker, Garrett J.1907..B. G..Detroit, Mich.
McCaskey, Wm. S..1907..M. G..San Diego, Cal.

GENERAL OFFICERS ON THE RETIRED LIST AND YEAR OF RETIREMENT—*Continued.*

Name	Year	Rank	Residence
McClellan, John	1906	M.G.	Washington, D. C.
McCrea, Tully	1903	"	Washington, D. C.
McGinness, John R.	1904	B.G.	Norfolk, Va.
McGregor, Thomas	1901	"	Benicia, Cal.
Mackenzie, Alex	1908	M.G.	Washington, D. C.
McKibbin, Cham	1902	"	Washington, D. C.
Macklin, Jas. E.	1906	B.G.	Ft. Bayard, N. Mex.
Magruder, D. L.	1889	"	Bryn Mawr, Pa.
Mansfield, S. M.	1903	"	Boston, Mass.
Markley, Alfred C.	1907	B.G.	Radnor, Pa.
Matile, Leon A.	1903	"	Washington, D. C.
Merriam, Henry C.	1903	M.G.	Washington, D. C.
Merrill, Abner H.	1906	B.G.	Montclair, N. J.
Merritt, Wesley	1900	M.G.	Washington, D. C.
Miles, Nelson A.	1903	L.G.	Washington, D. C.
Miller, Crosby P.	1906	B.G.	Washington, D. C.
Miller, James	1903	"	Temple, N. H.
Mills, Anson	1897	"	Washington, D. C.
Miner, Charles W.	1903	"	Columbus, Ohio.
Mizner, Henry R.	1891	"	Detroit, Mich.
Moale, Edward	1902	"	San Francisco, Cal.
Moore, Francis	1905	"	New York City.
Mordecai, Alfred	1904	"	Washington, D. C.
Morgan, M. R.	1897	"	St. Paul, Minn.
Morris, Charles	1908	"	Portland, Me.
Moseley, Edward B.	1907	"	Philadelphia, Pa.
Muhlenberg, J. C.	1908	"	San Francisco, Cal.
Murray, Robert	1886	"	Chestnut Hill, Pa.
Myrick, John R.	1903	"	New York City.
Noble, Charles H.	1906	"	Indianapolis, Ind.
Noyes, Henry E.	1901	"	San Francisco, Cal.
O'Connell, John J.	1904	"	Washington, D. C.
Osgood, Henry B.	1907	"	Stephentown, N. Y.
Osterhaus, Peter J.	1905	"	Duisburg, Ger.
Otis, Elwell S.	1902	M.G.	Rochester, N. Y.
Ovenshine, S.	1899	B.G.	Washington, D. C.
Page, John H.	1903	"	Washington, D. C.
Parker, Daingerfi'd	1896	"	Washington, D. C.
Patterson, J. H.	1899	"	Albany, N. Y.
Penney, Chas. G.	1903	"	Nordhoff, Cal.
Pennington, A. C. M.	1899	"	New York City.
Pennypacker, Gal.	1883	"	Philadelphia, Pa.
Perry, Alex. J.	1892	"	Washington, D. C.
Phipps, Frank H.	1907	"	Springfield, Mass.
Pitman, John	1906	"	O. Orange, N. J.
Pratt, Richard H.	1903	"	Philadelphia, Pa.
Pratt, Sedgwick	1906	"	Pasadena, Cal.
Price, Butler D.	1906	"	Washington, D. C.
Quinton, William	1902	"	New York City.
Randall, George M.	1905	M.G.	Cheyenne, Wyo.
Randolph, Wal. F.	1904	"	Washington, D. C.
Rawles, Jacob B.	1903	B.G.	San Francisco, Cal.
Ray, P. Henry	1906	"	Youngstown, N. Y.
Raymond, Chas. W.	1904	"	New York City.
Reade, Philip	1908	"	Lowell, Mass.
Reed, Henry A.	1906	"	Washington, D. C.
Reilly, James W.	1903	"	Washington, D. C.
Robe, Charles F.	1903	"	San Diego, Cal.
Robert, Henry M.	1901	"	Oswego, N. Y.
Roberts, Benj. K.	1905	"	Washington, D. C.
Roberts, Cyrus S.	1903	"	Lakeville, Conn.
Robinson, Frank U.	1905	"	Cairo, Egypt.
Rochester, W. B.	1890	"	Washington, D. C.
Rodenbough, T. F.	1870	"	New York City.
Rodgers, John I.	1902	"	Brooklyn, N. Y.
Rodney, George B.	1903	"	Hollywood, Cal.
Rogers, William P.	1903	"	Washington, D. C.
Rucker, D. H.	1882	"	Washington, D. C.
Sanger, Joseph P.	1904	M.G.	Washington, D. C.
Sawtelle, C. G.	1897	M.G.	Washington, D. C.
Schwan, Theodore	1901	"	Washington, D. C.
Scully, James W.	1900	"	Atlanta, Ga.
Sears, Clinton B.	1908	B.G.	Newton Ctr., Mass.
Shaler, Charles	1905	M.G.	Indianapolis, Ind.
Sheridan, M. V.	1902	"	Washington, D. C.
Sickles, Daniel E.	1869	"	New York City.
Simpson, John	1902	B.G.	Philadelphia, Pa.
Simpson, M. D. L.	1888	"	Riverside, Ill.
Smith, Allen	1905	"	Spokane, Wash.
Smith, Charles S.	1907	"	Washington, D. C.
Smith, Frank G.	1903	"	Washington, D. C.
Smith, Jacob H.	1902	"	London, Eng.
Smith, Jared A.	1903	"	Cleveland, Ohio.
Smith, Joseph R.	1895	"	Philadelphia, Pa.
Smith, Rodney	1893	"	St. Paul, Minn.
Smith, William	1895	"	P'lh'm M'n'r, N. Y.
Sniffen, Culver C.	1908	"	Washington, D. C.
Snyder, Simon	1902	"	Reading, Pa.
Stanton, William	1906	"	London, Eng.
Sternberg, Geo. M.	1902	"	Washington, D. C.
Stickney, Amos	1907	"	New York City.
Story, John P.	1905	"	Los Angeles, Cal.
Sumner, E. V.	1899	"	Syracuse, N. Y.
Sumner, Samuel S.	1906	M.G.	Syracuse, N. Y.
Suter, Chas. R.	1905	B.G.	Brookline, Mass.
Taylor, Asher C.	1903	"	Manila, P. I.
Taylor, Frank	1905	"	Seattle, Wash.
Thompson, J. M.	1903	"	Salt L. City, Utah.
Thorp, Frank	1906	"	Washington, D. C.
Tiernon, John L.	1903	"	Buffalo, N. Y.
Tilford, Joseph G.	1891	"	Washington, D. C.
Tompkins, Chas. H.	1894	"	Washington, D. C.
Townsend, E. F.	1895	"	Washington, D. C.
True, Theo. E.	1904	"	Los Angeles, Cal.
Van Horne, W. M.	1901	"	Austin, Ill.
Van Voast, James	1883	"	Cincinnati, Ohio.
Viele, Charles D.	1900	"	Los Angeles, Cal.
Vincent, Thos. M.	1896	"	Washington, D. C.
Vogdes, Anthony W.	1904	"	San Diego, Cal.
Vroom, Peter D.	1903	"	New York City.
Wade, James F.	1907	M.G.	Jefferson, Ohio.
Wallace, Wm. M.	1906	B.G.	Chevy Chase, Md.
Ward, H. C.	1906	"	Louisville, Ky.
Ward, Thomas	1902	"	Rochester, N. Y.
Wells, Almond B.	1903	"	Geneva, N. Y.
Wessells, H. W., Jr.	1901	"	Washington, D. C.
Wheaton, Loyd	1902	M.G.	Chicago, Ill.
Wheelan, James N.	1901	B.G.	Paris, France.
Wheeler, Dan'l D.	1903	"	Fredericksb'g, Va.
Wherry, Wm. M.	1899	"	Cincinnati, Ohio.
Whitall, S. R.	1906	"	Grosse Isle, Mich.
Whittemore, J. M.	1900	"	New Haven, Ct.
Wilcox, Timothy E.	1904	"	Washington, D. C.
Williams, Constant	1907	"	St. Paul, Minn.
Williston, Edw. B.	1900	"	Portland, Ore.
Wilson, Chas. I.	1901	"	New York City.
Wilson, James H.	1901	"	Wilmington, Del.
Wilson, John M.	1901	"	Washington, D. C.
Wood, Henry C.	1896	"	New York City.
Wood, Oliver E.	1906	"	Washington, D. C.
Wood, Palmer G.	1906	"	Los Angeles, Cal.
Woodhull, A. A.	1901	"	Princeton, N. J.
Woodruff, Carle A.	1903	"	Raleigh, N. C.
Woodruff, Chas. A.	1903	"	Berkeley, Cal.
Woodward, G. A.	1879	"	Washington, D. C.
Woodward, S. L.	1904	"	St. Louis, Mo.
Young, S. B. M.	1904	L.G.	Y'l'st'ne, Pk, Wyo.

ORGANIZATION OF THE ARMY.*

The army in active service as now organized under the acts of Congress of February 2, 1901, January 25, 1907, and April 23, 1908, comprises 15 regiments of cavalry, 765 officers and 13,266 enlisted men; 6 regiments of field artillery, 220 officers and 5,245 enlisted men; a coast artillery corps, 170 companies, 628 officers and 19,321 enlisted men; 30 regiments of infantry, 1,530 officers and 26,616 enlisted men; 3 battalions of engineers, 2,002 enlisted men, commanded by officers detailed from the corps of engineers; the Porto Rico Regiment of Infantry, 31 officers and 576 enlisted men; staff corps, Military Academy, Indian scouts, recruits, etc., 8,900 enlisted men, and a provisional force of 50 companies of native scouts in the Philippines, 166 officers and 5,508 enlisted men. The total number of commissioned officers, staff and line, on the active list, is 4,477, (including 191 first lieutenants Medical Reserve Corps on active duty), and the total enlisted strength, staff and line, is 77,743, exclusive of the provisional force and the hospital corps. The law provides that the total enlisted strength of the army shall not exceed at any one time 100,000.

* For Military Divisions and Departments, see Index.

RELATIVE RANK OF THE SUPERIOR OFFICERS OF THE REGULAR ARMY.

No.	Name, Rank, and Date of Commission. November 1, 1908.	Corps or Regiment and Corps.
	LIEUTENANT-GENERAL.	
1	MacArthur, Arthur, Sept. 15, 1906	general officer
	MAJOR-GENERALS.	
1	Wood, Leonard ... Aug. 8, 1903	general officer
2	Ainsworth, Fred. C. Apr. 23, 1894	the adjt. gen.
3	Weston, John F..... Oct. 8, 1906	general officer
4	Grant, Fred. D ...... Feb. 6, 1906	general officer
5	Greely, Adolphus W Feb. 10, 1906	general officer
6	Bell, J. Franklin... Jan. 8, 1907	general officer
7	Duvall, Wm. P..... Oct. 2, 1907	general officer
8	Barry, Thomas H.. Apr. 29, 1908	general officer
	BRIGADIER-GENERALS.	
1	Funston, Frederick. Apr. 1, 1901	general officer
2	Davis, George B.... May 24, 1901	j. a. g. dept.
3	Crozier, William .. Nov. 22, 1901	ord. dept.
4	Carter, William H.. July 15, 1902	general officer
5	Bliss, Tasker H..... July 21, 1902	general officer
6	O'Reilly, Robert M. Sept. 7, 1902	med. dept.
7	Hall, William P.... Apr. 23, 1904	a. g. dept.
8	Mills, Albert L..... May 7, 1904	general officer
9	Edgerly, Winfield S. June 23, 1905	general officer
10	Sharpe, Henry G... Oct. 12, 1905	sub. dept.
11	Allen, James....... Feb. 10, 1906	sig. corps.
12	Edwards, C. R..... June 30, 1906	chf. bu. ins. af.
13	Pershing, John J... Sept. 20, 1906	general officer
14	Murray, Arthur... Oct. 1, 1906	ch. coast art.
15	Garlington, E. A... Oct. 1, 1906	ins. gen. dept.
16	Myer, Albert L...... Mar. 23, 1907	general officer
17	Thomas, Earl D.... Apr. 18, 1907	general officer
18	Morton, Charles.... Apr. 19, 1907	general officer
19	Hodges, Charles L.. Apr. 30, 1907	general officer
(*)	Bandholtz, H. H... June 30, 1907	ch. Phil. const†
20	Aleshire, James B.. July 1, 1907	qm. dept.
21	Wotherspoon, W. W. Oct. 3, 1907	general officer
22	Whipple, Chas. H.. Jan. 1, 1908	pay dept.
23	Potts, Ramsay D... Jan. 31, 1908	general officer
24	Brush, Daniel H... Feb. 17, 1908	general officer
25	Kerr, John B....... Apr. 13, 1908	general officer
26	Marshall, Wm. L.. July 2, 1908	corps of eng.
27	Smith, Fred'k A... Oct. 24, 1908	general officer
	COLONELS.	
1	Larned, Charles W. Aug. 14, 1886	prof. m. a.
2	Tillman, Samuel E.. Dec. 31, 1890	prof. m. a.
3	Augur, Jacob A..... June 9, 1902	10 cavalry.
4	Heistand, H. O. S.. July 22, 1902	a. g. dept.
5	Girard, Joseph B.... Sept. 7, 1902	med. corps.
6	Wood, Edward E... Oct. 5, 1902	prof. m. a.
7	Sweet, Owen J ..... Feb. 18, 1903	28 infantry.
8	Greenough, Geo. G.. Feb. 21, 1903	coast artillery
9	McCauley, C. A. H. Feb. 24, 1903	qm. dept.
10	Hatfield, C. A. P ... Mar. 2, 1903	13 cavalry.
11	Gorgas, William C.. Mar. 9, 1903	med. corps.
12	Mills, Stephen C..... Apr. 12, 1903	ins. gen. dept.
13	Dorst, Joseph H.... Apr. 15, 1903	3 cavalry.
14	Crowder, Enoch H.. Apr. 16, 1903	j. a. g. dept.
15	Anderson, Geo. S... Apr. 18, 1903	9 cavalry.
16	Harvey, Philip F... Aug. 6, 1903	med. corps.
17	Andrews, George... Aug. 7, 1903	a. g. dept.
18	Cornman, Daniel... Aug. 8, 1903	7 infantry.
19	Byrne, Charles B. .. Aug. 9, 1903	med. corps.
20	Duncan, Joseph W. Aug. 9, 1903	6 infantry.
21	Mansfield, F. W..... Aug. 12, 1903	2 infantry.
22	Van Orsdale, John T. Aug. 14, 1903	17 infantry.
23	Clem, John L........ Aug. 15, 1903	qm. dept.
24	Huston, Joseph F... Aug 15, 1903	19 infantry.
25	Patten, William S.. Aug. 17, 1903	qm. dept.
26	Steever, Edgar Z... Aug. 17, 1903	4 cavalry.
(*)	Harbord, James G.. Aug. 17, 1903	Philip. const.†
27	Simpson, Wm. A... Aug. 18, 1903	a. g. dept.
28	Dudley, Edgar S.... Nov. 22, 1903	j. a. g. dept.
29	Hoyt, Ralph W..... Dec. 3, 1903	25 infantry.
30	Williams, Chas. A. Jan. 23, 1904	21 infantry.
31	Maus, Marion P..... Jan. 24, 1904	20 infantry.
32	Woodbury, Thos. C. Mar. 29, 1904	3 infantry.
33	Adams, Milton B.. Apr. 23, 1904	corps of eng.
34	McCain, Henry P.. Apr. 23, 1904	a. g. dept.
35	Havard, Valery.... Apr. 26, 1904	med. corps.
36	Howe, Walter....... May 20, 1904	coast artillery
(*)	Bromwell, Chas. S. June 1, 1904	chg. pub. bldgs.
37	Pullman, John W.. June 25, 1904	qm. dept.
	COLONELS—*Continued.*	
38	Chamberlain, J. L.. Nov. 21, 1904	ins. gen. dept.
39	Pratt, Edward B... Dec. 16, 1904	30 infantry.
40	Hoff, John Van R.. Jan 19, 1905	med. corps.
41	Adair, George W... April 6, 1905	med. corps.
42	Cowles, Calvin D... April 11, 1905	5 infantry.
43	Kerr, James T..... June 17, 1905	a. g. dept.
44	Taylor, Sydney W. June 20, 1905	2 field art.
45	Ward, Frederick K. June 23, 1905	7 cavalry.
46	Dravo, Edward E... Oct. 6, 1905	sub. dept.
47	Smith, Abiel L...... Oct. 13, 1905	sub. dept.
48	Scott, Walter S..... Oct. 30, 1905	15 infantry.
49	Gardener, Cornelius. Dec. 26, 1905	16 infantry.
50	Thompson, Rich. E. Feb. 10, 1906	sig. corps.
51	Reynolds, Alfred.. Feb. 17, 1906	22 infantry.
52	Rodgers, Alex...... Mar. 7, 1906	6 cavalry.
53	Patterson, Robt. H. Apr. 1, 1906	coast artillery
54	Fiebeger, Gustav J. May 26, 1906	prof. m. a.
55	Pitcher, Wm. L.... June 15, 1906	27 infantry.
56	Hoskins, John D. C. June 22, 1906	coast artillery
57	Blunt, Stanhope E. June 25 1906	ord. dept.
58	Heath, Frank....... June 25 1906	ord. dept.
59	Lockwood, Dan'l W. June 27, 1906	corps of eng.
60	Dent, John C....... July 2, 1906	14 infantry.
61	McGunnegle, G. K.. July 3, 1906	1 infantry.
62	Schuyler, Walter S. Aug. 20, 1906	5 cavalry.
63	Kingsbury, H. P... Aug. 31, 1906	8 cavalry.
(*)	Scott, Hugh L...... Aug. 31, 1906	supt. m. a.
64	Ruffner, Ernest H.. Sept. 9, 1906	corps of eng.
65	Comegys, Wm. H.. Sept. 13, 1906	pay dept.
66	West, Frank........ Oct. 1, 1906	2 cavalry.
67	Harris Henry L..... Oct. 1, 1906	coast artillery
68	Chase, Geo. F....... Oct. 2, 1906	ins. gen. dept.
69	Lundeen, John A... Oct. 2, 1906	coast artillery
70	Greene, Henry A... Oct. 20, 1906	10 infantry.
(*)	Rivers, Wm. C..... Oct. 26, 1906	Philip. const.†
(*)	Hersey, Mark L.... Oct. 27, 1906	Philip. const.†
71	Bolton, Edwin B.... Dec. 2, 1906	4 infantry.
72	Whistler, G. N...... Jan. 25, 1907	coast artillery
73	Dyer, Alexander B.. Jan. 25, 1907	4 field art.
74	Andrews, Henry M.. Jan. 25, 1907	1 field art.
75	Parkhurst, Chas. D.. Jan. 25, 1907	coast artillery
76	Pope, James W..... Feb. 16, 1907	qm. dept.
77	Knight, John G. D.. Mar. 2, 1907	corps of eng.
78	Loughbor'h, R. H. R. Mar. 7, 1907	13 infantry.
79	Yeatman, R. T..... Mar. 26, 1907	11 infantry.
80	Lyle, David A...... Mar. 26 1907	ord. dept.
81	Macomb, M. M..... Apr. 5, 1907	6 field art.
82	Davis, Thomas F... Apr. 11, 1907	18 infantry.
83	Tucker, Wm. F..... Apr. 15 1907	pay dept.
84	Parker, James...... Apr. 18, 1907	11 cavalry.
85	Garrard, Joseph.... Apr. 20, 1907	15 cavalry.
86	Maus, Louis M .... May 10, 1907	med. corps.
87	Wisser, John P....... May 27, 1907	coast artillery
(*)	Hall, Herman........ July 3, 1907	Philip. const.†
88	Rockwell, James... Aug. 9, 1907	ord. dept.
89	Niles, Lotus......... Aug. 12, 1907	3 field art.
90	Booth, Charles A.... Oct. 1, 1907	26 infantry.
91	Birnie, Rogers....... Oct. 10, 1907	ord. dept.
92	Allison, James N... Oct. 13, 1907	sub. dept.
93	Crane, Charles J..... Oct. 25, 1907	9 infantry.
94	Harrison, Geo. F. E.. Oct. 29, 1907	coast artillery
95	Bailey, Hobart K... Dec. 23, 1907	29 infantry.
96	Williams, John R.. Jan. 20, 1908	coast artillery
97	Bixby, William H.. Feb. 14, 1908	corps of eng.
98	Ruhlen, George..... Feb. 25, 1908	qm. dept.
99	Brown, Edward T.. Feb. 25 1908	5 field art.
100	Rossell, William T.. Feb. 28, 1908	corps of eng.
101	Paulding, William. Mar. 8, 1908	24 infantry.
102	Baker, Frank........ Mar. 17, 1908	ord. dept.
103	Taylor, Blair D..... Mar. 31, 1908	med. corps.
104	Smith, George R.... Apr. 7, 1908	pay dept.
105	Dodd, George A..... Apr. 14, 1908	12 cavalry.
106	Torney, George H. Apr. 23, 1908	med. corps.
107	Crampton, Louis W. Apr. 23, 1908	med. corps.
108	Sharpe, Alfred C.... May 9, 1908	23 infantry.
109	Leach, Smith S...... June 2, 1908	corps of eng.
110	Bowen, Wm. H. C.. July 1, 1908	12 infantry.
111	Kingman, Dan. C... July 6, 1908	corps of eng.
112	Anderson, George L. July 10, 1908	coast artillery
113	Black, William M.. July 28, 1908	corps of eng.

(*) Holds rank specified, temporarily, under special assignment. † Philippines Constabulary.

RELATIVE RANK OF THE SUPERIOR OFFICERS OF THE REGULAR ARMY—*Continued.*

No.	Name, Rank, and Date of Commission. November 1, 1908.	Corps or Regiment and Corps.
	COLONELS—*Continued.*	
114	Fisk, Walter L....... Aug. 7, 1908	corps of eng.
115	Coffin, William H.. Sept. 1, 1908	coast artillery
116	Todd, Albert........ Oct. 10, 1908	coast artillery
117	Mason, Charles W... Oct. 28, 1908	8 infantry.
118	Hickey, James B... Nov. 15, 1908	14 cavalry.
119	McClernand, Edw. J. Nov. 20, 1908	1 cavalry.
	LIEUTENANT-COLONELS.	
1	Gordon, Wm. B...... Mar. 27, 1901	prof. m. a.
2	Carbaugh, Harvey C Dec. 18, 1902	j. a. g. dept.
3	Hull, John A....... Apr. 16, 1903	j. a. g. dept.
4	Miller, Wm. H..... Aug. 15, 1903	qm. dept.
5	Jones, Samuel R.... Aug. 17, 1903	qm. dept.
6	Dunn, George M.... Nov. 22, 1903	j. a. g. dept.
7	Robinson, W. W., Jr. Jan. 20, 1904	qm. dept.
8	Echols, Charles P... June 29, 1904	prof. m. a.
9	Scriven, George P.. July 6, 1904	sig. corps.
10	Von Schrader, F.... July 9, 1904	qm. dept.
11	Sawyer, J. Estcourt. July 10, 1904	qm. dept.
12	Appel, Daniel M.... Aug. 3, 1904	med. corps.
13	Perley, Harry O.... Aug. 14, 1904	med. corps.
14	Williams, Arthur ... Dec. 16, 1904	15 infantry.
15	Davis, William B. ... Jan. 19, 1905	med. corps.
16	Gray, William W.... Apr. 6, 1905	med. corps.
17	Hunt, Levi P........ Apr. 7, 1905	2 cavalry.
18	Murray, Cunliffe H.. Apr. 8, 1905	11 cavalry.
19	Irons, James A...... Apr. 9, 1905	14 infantry.
20	Lovering, Leon'd A. Apr. 11, 1905	4 infantry.
21	Evans, Robert K .... Apr. 14, 1905	5 infantry.
22	Brodie, Alexander O. June 10, 1905	a. g. dept.
(*)	Howze, Robert L... June 15, 1905	com. of cadets
23	Alvord, Benjamin... June 17, 1905	a. g. dept.
24	Brechemin, Louis... July 1, 1905	med. corps.
25	Cooke, George F....... July 28, 1905	22 infantry.
26	Brainard, David L .. Aug. 8, 1905	sub. dept.
27	Davis, George B..... Oct. 6, 1905	sub. dept.
28	Chubb, Charles St. J. Oct. 11, 1905	2 infantry.
29	Jones, Thaddeus W. Oct. 20, 1905	3 cavalry.
30	Stevens, Robert R.. Dec. 15, 1905	qm. dept.
31	Wood, William T.. Feb. 3, 1906	ins. gen. dept.
32	Glassford, Wm. A. Feb. 10, 1906	sig. corps.
33	Evans, Wm. P....... Feb. 17, 1906	11 infantry.
34	Hardie, Francis H. Mar. 7, 1906	15 cavalry.
35	La Garde, Louis A... Mar. 17, 1906	med. corps.
36	Banister, John M.. Mar. 29, 1906	med. corps.
37	Hodgson, Fred'k G. Mar. 31, 1906	qm. dept.
38	Roessler, Sol. W... Apr. 2, 1906	corps of eng.
39	Wilson, Rich. H..... Apr. 5, 1906	16 infantry.
40	Kniskern, Albert D. Apr. 24, 1906	sub. dept.
41	Febiger, Lea.. ...... May 5, 1906	3 infantry.
42	French, F. H....... June 25, 1906	ins. gen. dept.
43	Mitcham, Oren B.. June 25, 1906	ord. dept.
44	Bruff, Lawrence L. June 25, 1906	ord. dept.
45	Hunter, George K.. June 30, 1906	5 cavalry.
46	McClure, Charles... July 3, 1906	a. g. dept.*
47	Wolf, Silas A....... July 13, 1906	28 infantry.
48	O'Connor, Chas. M. Aug. 20, 1906	8 cavalry.
49	Abbot, Frederic V.. Sept. 9, 1906	corps of eng.
50	Wilder, Wilber E.. Sept. 13, 1906	ins. gen. dept.
(*)	Winn, Frank L .... Sept. 18, 1906	sec. lt. gen.
51	Casey, Thomas L.. Sept. 26, 1906	corps of eng.
52	Guilfoyle, John F..... Oct. 1, 1906	7 cavalry.
53	Watts, Charles H ... Oct. 1, 1906	9 cavalry.
54	Edwards, Frank A... Oct. 2, 1906	12 cavalry.
55	Buttler, Wm. C.... Oct. 6, 1906	9 infantry.
56	Rogers, James S. .... Oct. 20, 1906	1 infantry.
57	Young, George S.... Oct. 30, 1906	21 infantry.
58	Bullard, Robert L... Oct. 31, 1906	8 infantry.
59	Clark, Charles H.... Nov. 12, 1906	ord. dept.
60	Moon, Henry B....... Dec. 2, 1906	20 infantry.
61	Glenn, Edwin F...... Jan. 1, 1907	23 infantry.
62	Townsend, C. McD... Jan. 11, 1907	corps of eng.
63	Day, Matthias W.... Jan. 19, 1907	6 cavalry.
64	Slaker, Adam........ Jan. 25, 1907	coast art.
65	Ludlow, Henry H... Jan. 25, 1907	coast art.
66	Hamilton, Wm. R... Jan. 25, 1907	coast art.
67	Foster, Charles W.... Jan. 25, 1907	2 field art.
68	Deems, Clarence ... Jan. 25, 1907	coast art.
69	White, John V...... Jan. 25, 1907	coast art.
70	Weaver, Erasmus M. Jan. 25, 1907	coast art.

No.	Name, Rank, and Date of Commission. November 1, 1908.	Corps or Regiment and Corps.
	LIEUT.-COLONELS—*Continued.*	
71	Hoyle, Eli D......... Jan. 25, 1907	6 field art.
72	Adams, Granger..... Jan. 25, 1907	5 field art.
73	Marsh, Frederick.... Jan. 25, 1907	coast art.
74	Woodward, Chas. G. Jan. 25, 1907	coast art.
75	Cecil, George R...... Jan. 31, 1907	10 infantry.
76	Bellinger, John B... Feb. 16, 1907	qm. dept.
77	Goethals, George W Mar. 2, 1907	corps of eng.
78	Ladd, Eugene F...... Mar. 2, 1907	a. g. dept.
79	Mann, Wm. A........ Mar 7, 1907	6 infantry.
80	Waltz, Millard F.... Mar. 26, 1907	27 infantry.
81	Hobbs, Frank E...... Mar. 26, 1907	ord. dept.
82	Gayle, Edward E.... Apr. 5, 1907	4 field art.
83	Allen, Samuel E..... Apr. 11, 1907	coast art.
84	Rogers, Harry L..... Apr. 15, 1907	pay dept.
85	Finley, Walter L.... Apr. 18, 1907	13 cavalry.
86	Ames, Robert F...... May 6, 1907	12 infantry.
87	Appel, Aaron H..... May 10, 1907	med. corps.
88	Strong, Frederick S. May 27, 1907	a. g. dept.
89	Millis, John............ June 7, 1907	corps of eng.
90	Biddle, John.......... June 9, 1907	corps of eng.
91	Gresham, John C.... July 24, 1907	14 cavalry.
92	Benét J. Walker .... Aug. 9, 1907	ord. dept.
93	Greble, Edwin St. J. Aug. 12, 1907	3 field art.
94	Hodges, Harry F... Aug. 27, 1907	corps of eng.
95	Vinson, Webster.... Sept. 4, 1907	pay dept.
96	Gibson, Wm. W..... Sept. 19, 1907	ord. dept.
97	Getty, Robert N..... Oct. 1, 1907	7 infantry.
98	Jones, Frank B...., Oct. 4, 1907	a. g. dept.
99	Babbitt, Edwin B... Oct. 10, 1907	ord. dept.
100	Eastman, Frank F.. Oct. 13, 1907	sub. dept.
101	Blunt, Albert C... . Oct. 29, 1907	coast art.
102	Gale, George H. G. . Oct. 31, 1907	10 cavalry.
103	Warren, James G... Nov. 15, 1907	corps of eng.
104	Abercrombie, W. R. Dec. 23, 1907	25 infantry.
105	Wallace, H. S...... Jan. 1, 1908	pay dept.
106	Rafferty, Wm. C... Jan. 20, 1908	coast art.
107	Burr, Edward...... Feb. 14, 1908	corps of eng.
108	Rumbough, David J. Feb. 25, 1908	1 field art.
109	Beach, Lansing H... Feb. 28, 1908	corps of eng.
110	Lissak, Ormond M. Feb. 29, 1908	ord. dept.
111	Nichols, William A. Mar. 8, 1908	13 infantry.
112	Terrett, Colville P.. Mar. 14, 1908	17 infantry.
113	Dunn, Beverly W.. Mar. 17, 1908	ord. dept.
114	Littell, Isaac W.... Mar. 19, 1908	qm. dept.
115	Payson, Francis L. Apr. 7, 1908	pay dept.
116	Richard, Charles... Apr. 10, 1908	med. corps.
117	Ebert, Rudolph G.. Apr. 23, 1908	med. corps.
118	Arthur, William H. Apr. 23, 1908	med. corps.
119	Bushnell, George E. Apr. 23, 1908	med. corps.
120	Birmingham, H. P. Apr. 23, 1908	med. corps.
121	Carter, Edward C.. Apr. 23, 1908	med. corps.
122	Stephenson, Wm.... May 1, 1908	med. corps.
123	Newcomb, W. P.... May 1, 1908	coast art.
124	Taylor, Charles W.. May 6, 1908	a. g. dept.
125	Zinn, George A...... May 8, 1908	corps of eng.
126	Phister, Nat. P...... May 9, 1908	30 infantry.
127	Langfitt, Wm. C.... June 2, 1908	corps of eng.
128	Paxton, Alexis R.. June 25, 1908	24 infantry.
129	Torrey, Zerah W.... July 1, 1908	18 infantry.
130	Sanford, James C.. July 6, 1908	corps of eng.
131	Phillips, Charles L.. July 10, 1908	coast art.
132	Jackson, James B... July 18, 1908	26 infantry.
133	Chittenden, H. M.. July 28, 1908	corps of eng.
134	Fitch, Graham D... Aug. 7, 1908	corps of eng.
(*)	Ruggles, C. L. H... Aug. 21, 1908	prof. m. a.
135	Bailey, Charles J... Sept. 1, 1908	coast art.
136	Townsley, Chas. P.. Oct. 10, 1908	coast art.
137	Beach, William D.. Nov. 15, 1908	4 cavalry.
138	Shunk, William A.. Nov. 20, 1908	1 cavalry.
	MAJORS.	
1	Carter, W. Fitzhugh Nov. 30, 1897	med. corps.
2	Gibson, Robert J.... Apr. 23, 1898	med. corps.
3	Johnson, R. W...... Nov. 6, 1899	med. corps.
4	Phillips, John L.... Oct. 8, 1900	med. corps.
5	Borden, William C. Feb. 2, 1901	med. corps.
6	Mearns, Edgar A... Feb. 2, 1901	med. corps.
7	Edie, Guy L......... Feb. 2, 1901	med. corps.
8	Crosby, William D.. Feb. 2, 1901	med. corps.
9	Gandy, Charles M.. Feb. 2, 1901	med. corps.

* Temporary rank of Lieutenant-Colonel.

RELATIVE RANK OF THE SUPERIOR OFFICERS OF THE REGULAR ARMY—*Continued.*

No.	Name, Rank, and Date of Commission. November 1, 1908.	Corps or Regiment and Corps.
	MAJORS—*Continued.*	
10	Ewing, Charles B...Feb. 2,1901	med. corps.
11	McCaw, Walter D..Feb. 2,1901	med. corps.
12	Kean, Jefferson R...Feb. 2,1901	med. corps.
13	Raymond, Henry I. Feb. 2,1901	med. corps.
14	Kendall, Wm. P... Feb. 2,1901	med. corps.
15	Morris, Edward R..Feb. 2,1901	med. corps.
16	Downey, George F..Feb. 2,1901	pay dept.
17	Harris, H. S. T.....Feb. 4,1901	med. corps.
18	Banister, Wm. B...Apr. 2,1901	med. corps.
19	Krauthoff, Chas. R. Apr. 8,1901	sub. dept.
20	Woodruff, Chas. E. Apr. 13,1901	med. corps.
21	Goodman, Thos. C..May 3,1901	pay dept.
22	Houston, James B..May 3,1901	pay dept.
23	Dodds, Frank L.....May 22,1901	j. a. g. dept.
24	Porter, John B......May 27,1901	j. a. g. dept.
25	Shillock, Paul ......June 7,1901	med. corps.
26	Goodier, Lewis E...June 18,1901	j. a. g. dept.
27	Rafferty, Ogden.....Oct. 24,1901	med. corps.
28	Bingham, G. S......Oct. 26,1901	qm. dept.
29	Ray, Beecher B.....Nov. 12,1901	pay dept.
30	Mason, Charles F...Dec. 9,1901	med. corps.
31	Glennan, James D..Jan. 1,1902	med. corps.
32	Bradley, Alfred E..Jan. 1,1902	med. corps.
33	Lord, Herbert M...Feb. 20,1902	pay dept.
34	Tillson, John C. F..Mar. 12,1902	4 infantry.
35	Browne, Edward H. Mar. 28,1902	2 infantry.
36	Willcox, Charles....Apr. 7,1902	med. corps.
37	Ducat, Arthur C....Apr. 14,1902	7 infantry.
38	Devol, Carroll A....May 5,1902	qm. dept.
39	Liggett, Hunter.....May 5,1902	13 infantry.
40	Kennon, L. W. V....May 28,1902	10 infantry.
41	Lassiter, William...May 28,1902	a. g. dept.
42	Morton, Charles G..May 28,1902	ins. gen. dept.
43	Pickering, Abner...June 9,1902	22 infantry.
44	Frick, Euclid B.....June 28,1902	med. corps.
45	Maney, James A...June 28,1902	17 infantry.
46	Bailey, Harry L....June 28,1902	2 infantry.
47	Keefer, Frank R....June 30,1902	med. corps.
48	Cruse, Thomas......July 5,1902	qm. dept.
49	Bishop, Hoel S......July 8,1902	14 cavalry.
50	Mallory, John S....July 8,1902	12 infantry.
51	Andrus, Edwin P..July 15,1902	3 cavalry.
52	Rochester, W. B., Jr. July 24,1902	pay dept.
53	Sibley, Fred'k W..July 30,1902	2 cavalry.
54	Miller, Samuel W..July 30,1902	ins. gen. dept
55	Raymond, Thos. U..Aug. 12,1902	med. corps.
56	Snyder, Henry D...Sept. 7,1902	med. corps.
57	Cheever, Benj. H...Sept. 13,1902	13 cavalry.
58	McCarthy, Dan'l E. Oct. 2,1902	qm. dept.
59	Van Vliet, Rob't C..Oct. 3,1902	10 infantry.
60	Buck, William L...Oct. 11,1902	10 infantry.
61	Wales, Philip G....Oct. 27,1902	med. corps.
62	Wheeler, Homer W. Oct. 29,1902	11 cavalry.
63	Smith, Allen M....Nov. 23,1902	med. corps.
64	Clark, Wallis O. ...Nov. 28,1902	5 infantry.
65	Chynoweth, Edw...Dec. 5,1902	17 infantry.
66	Plummer, Edw. H. Dec. 31,1902	3 infantry.
67	Read, Robt. D......Jan. 16,1903	10 cavalry.
68	Swift, Eben..........Jan. 24,1903	9 cavalry.
69	Morrow, Henry M. Jan. 27,1903	j. a. g. dept.
70	Lockett, James.....Jan. 30,1903	4 cavalry.
71	Kirby, Henry.......Feb. 4,1903	18 infantry.
72	Howe, Edgar W....Feb. 10,1903	27 infantry.
73	Clarke, Joseph T...Feb. 13,1903	med corps.
74	Blocksom, Aug. P. Feb. 17,1903	ins. gen. dept.
75	Smith, Robert S....Feb. 19,1903	pay dept.
76	Gaston, Joseph A..Feb. 22,1903	1 cavalry.
77	Knight, John T.....Feb. 24,1903	qm. dept.
78	Scott, Hugh L......Feb. 25,1903	14 cavalry.
79	Greene, Frank.......Mar. 2,1903	sig. corps.
80	Reber, Samuel .....Mar. 2,1903	sig. corps.
81	Squier, George O...Mar. 2,1903	sig. corps.
82	Dunning, Sam'l W..Mar. 19,1903	20 infantry.
83	Carson, John M., Jr. Apr. 12,1903	qm. dept.
84	McCormick, Loyd S. Apr. 15,1903	ins. gen. dept.
85	Ripley, Henry L....Apr. 15,1903	8 cavalry.
86	Partello, Jos. M. T..Apr. 17,1903	25 infantry.
87	Galbraith, Jacob G. Apr. 18,1903	ins. gen. dept.
88	Erwin, James B....Apr. 22,1903	ins. gen. dept.
89	Morgan, George H. Apr. 27,1903	a. g. dept.
90	Boughton, Dan'l H. May 25,1903	11 cavalry.
	MAJORS—*Continued.*	
91	Truitt, Charles M...June 23,1903	a. g. dept.
92	Bethel, Walter A...July 15,1903	j. a. g. dept.
93	Sickel, Horatio G...July 16,1903	12 cavalry.
94	Bell, George, Jr. ......July 26,1903	ins. gen. dept.
95	Hart, William H....July 27,1903	sub. dept.
96	Clarke, Charles J. T. July 29,1903	26 infantry.
97	Parke, John S., Jr..July 31,1903	14 infantry.
98	Ireland, Marritte W Aug. 3,1903	med. corps.
99	McCoy, Frank B....Aug. 8,1903	17 infantry.
100	Fisher, Henry C.....Aug. 9,1903	med. corps.
101	Noyes, Charles R....Aug. 12,1903	9 infantry.
102	Blatchford, R. M...Aug. 13,1903	11 infantry.
103	Beacom, John H...Aug. 14,1903	6 infantry.
104	May, Willis T.......Aug. 14,1903	15 infantry.
105	Baxter, John E....Aug. 15,1903	qm. dept.
106	Hearn, Lawrence J. Aug. 15,1903	21 infantry.
107	Johnson, F. O......Aug. 16,1903	2 cavalry.
108	Zalinski, Moses G..Aug. 17,1903	qm. dept.
109	Slocum, Herbert J. Aug. 26,1903	7 cavalry.
110	Wright, Walter K. Aug. 26,1903	8 infantry.
111	Pendleton, Edw. P. Aug. 26,1903	29 infantry.
112	Shaw, Henry A....Sept. 22,1903	med. corps.
113	Penrose, Chas. W..Oct. 15,1903	25 infantry.
114	Howell, Daniel L...Nov. 24,1903	18 infantry.
115	Holloway, Geo. T...Nov. 30,1903	pay dept.
116	Winship, Blanton..Jan. 4,1904	j. a. g. dept.
117	Kernan, Francis J..Jan. 20,1904	25 infantry.
118	Wood, Winthrop S. Jan. 20,1904	qm. dept.
119	Baker, Chauncey B. Jan. 22,1904	qm. dept.
120	Gambrill, Wm. G...Jan. 23,1904	pay dept.
121	Kennedy, Chase W. Jan. 24,1904	a. g. dept.
122	Keleher, T. D........Jan. 25,1904	pay dept.
123	Davis, Alex. M.....Mar. 17,1904	sub. dept.
124	Griffith, Thos. W...Mar. 29,1904	28 infantry.
125	McIver, George W. Mar. 29,1904	20 infantry.
126	Richardson, W. P..Apr. 7,1904	13 infantry.
127	Barth, Charles H...Apr. 7,1904	12 infantry.
128	Gaillard, D. du B...Apr. 23,1904	corps of eng.
129	Taylor, Harry.......Apr. 23,1904	corps of eng.
130	Sibert, William L...Apr. 23,1904	corps of eng.
131	Kuhn, Joseph E....Apr. 23,1904	corps of eng.
132	Craighill, Wm. E..Apr. 23,1904	corps of eng.
133	Newcomer, H. C...Apr. 23,1904	corps of eng.
134	Patrick, Mason M..Apr. 23,1904	corps of eng.
135	Nicholson, Wm. J...May 13,1904	7 cavalry.
136	Riché, Charles S....June 11,1904	corps of eng.
137	Swift, Henry........June 14,1904	chaplain.
138	Williamson, G. McK. June 25,1904	qm. dept.
139	Russel, Edgar.......July 6,1904	sig. corps.
140	Foster, Fred. W.....July 8,1904	5 cavalry.
141	Slavens, Thos. H...July 9,1904	qm. dept.
142	Stanley, David S...July 10,1904	qm. dept.
143	Rees, Thomas H...July 11,1904	corps of eng.
144	Bundy, Omar.......July 12,1904	ins. gen. dept.
145	Brown, William C..July 28,1904	3 cavalry.
146	Winter, Francis A..Aug. 3,1904	med. corps.
147	Purviance, Wm. E. Aug. 14,1904	med. corps.
148	Pickett, George E..Sept. 6,1904	pay dept.
149	Potter, Charles L...Sept. 14,1904	corps of eng.
150	Brewer, Edwin P..Sept. 15,1904	7 cavalry.
151	Hatch, Everard E..Oct. 20,1904	26 infantry.
152	Shanks, David C....Nov. 5,1904	4 infantry.
153	Allaire, Wm. H....Nov. 5,1904	23 infantry.
154	Deshon, George D...Dec. 5,1904	med. corps.
155	Stamper, Willson Y. Dec. 16,1904	3 infantry.
156	McCulloch, C. C., Jr. Jan. 19,1905	med. corps.
157	Gallagher, Hugh J..Jan. 19,1905	sub. dept.
158	Shunk, Francis R...Feb. 16,1905	corps of eng.
(*)	Duncan, George B..Feb. 28,1905	Phil. scouts.
(*)	Mearns, Robert W..Feb. 28,1905	Phil. scouts.
(*)	Rockenbach, S. D..Feb. 28,1905	Phil. scouts.
(*)	Hutton, Franklin S. Feb. 28,1905	Phil. scouts.
159	Brett, Lloyd M......Mar. 30,1905	1 cavalry.
160	Reynolds, Fred'k P. Mar. 31,1905	med. corps.
161	Woodson, Robert S..Apr. 6,1905	med. corps.
162	Goldman, Henry J..Apr. 8,1905	12 cavalry.
163	Blauvelt, Wm. F...Apr. 9,1905	pay dept.
164	Macomb, Aug. C....Apr. 10,1905	9 cavalry.
165	Lewis, Thos. J......Apr 22,1905	13 cavalry.
166	Mercer, Wm. A.....June 26,1905	11 cavalry.
167	Barney, Geo. F.....June 30,1905	coast art.

* Rank of Major temporarily.

RELATIVE RANK OF THE SUPERIOR OFFICERS OF THE REGULAR ARMY—*Continued.*

No.	Name, Rank, and Date of Commission. November 1, 1908.	Corps or Regiment and Corps.
	MAJORS—*Continued*	
168	Hodges, H. C., Jr....July 15, 1905	1 infantry.
169	Hirst, Robert L......July 20, 1905	29 infantry.
170	Roberts, Harris L...July 28, 1905	26 infantry.
171	Grierson, Charles H. Aug. 2, 1905	10 cavalry.
172	Dawes, James W.... Aug. 12, 1905	pay dept.
173	Chatfield, Walter H. Aug. 15, 1905	27 infantry.
174	Fechét, Eugene O....Aug. 22, 1905	sig. corps.
175	Ruthers, George W. Aug. 28, 1905	sub. dept.
176	Canby, James........Oct. 4, 1905	pay dept.
177	Morrison, John F....Oct. 6, 1905	20 infantry.
178	Wilkins, Harry E...Oct. 6, 1905	sub. dept.
179	Rowan, Andrew S. Oct. 11, 1905	15 infantry.
180	Jervey, Henry.......Oct. 15, 1905	corps of eng.
181	Benson, Harry C....Oct. 20, 1905	5 cavalry.
182	Sands, George H ....Oct. 20, 1905	10 cavalry.
183	Harmon, Millard F. Nov. 7, 1903	coast art.
184	Cronkhite, A..........Nov. 24, 1905	coast art.
185	Schofield, R. McA.. Dec. 15, 1905	qm. dept.
186	McKinstry, Chas. H Jan. 1, 1906	corps of eng
187	Saltzman, C. McK..Feb. 10, 1906	sig. corps.
188	Hunter, Chas. H ...Feb. 16, 1906	coast art.
189	Steedman, Rich. R..Feb. 17, 1906	6 infantry.
190	Treat, Charles G....Feb. 19, 1906	3 field art.
191	Trippe, Percy E ....Feb. 21, 1906	3 cavalry.
192	Foote, Stephen M...Feb. 24, 1906	coast art.
193	Judson, Wm. V......Mar. 2, 1906	corps of eng.
194	Cotter, John.........Mar. 3, 1906	9 infantry.
195	Van Deusen, Geo. W. Mar. 3, 1906	2 field art.
196	Dickman, Jos. T ....Mar. 7, 1906	13 cavalry.
197	Brooks, John C. W..Mar. 16, 1906	coast art.
198	Straub, Paul F ......Mar. 17, 1906	med. corps.
199	Sage, William H....Mar. 23, 1906	a. g. dept.
200	Bartlett, George T..Mar. 26 1906	coast art.
201	Stark, Alex. N ......Mar. 29, 1906	med. corps.
202	Yates, Arthur W....Mar. 31, 1906	qm. dept.
203	Bennett, Chas. A....Apr. 1, 1906	coast art.
204	Lynch, Charles......Apr. 2, 1906	med. corps.
205	Winslow, E. Evel'h..Apr. 2, 1906	corps. of eng.
206	Goodin, James A....Apr. 5, 1906	7 infantry.
207	Millar, Edward A...Apr. 14, 1906	5 field art.
208	Stivers, Charles P...Apr. 24, 1906	sub. dept.
209	Flagler, Clem't A. F. May 5, 1906	corps of eng.
210	Root, Edwin A......May 25, 1906	19 infantry.
211	Kulp, John S.........May 26, 1906	med. corps.
212	Hale, Harry C.......June 15, 1906	a. g. dept.
213	Davis, Henry C.....June 22, 1906	coast art.
214	Thompson, John T. June 25, 1906	ord. dept.
215	Taggart, Elmore F..June 25, 1906	24 infantry.
216	Wheeler, Charles B. June 25, 1906	ord. dept.
217	Peirce, William S...June 25, 1906	ord. dept.
218	Burr, George W.....June 25, 1906	ord. dept.
219	Ruggles, C. L' H. ....June 25, 1906	ord. dept.
220	Horney, Odus C.....June 25, 1906	ord. dept.
221	Montgomery, Geo..June 25, 1906	ord. dept.
222	Dickson, Tracy C....June 25, 1906	ord. dept.
223	Jamieson, Chas. C...June 25, 1906	ord. dept.
224	Joyes, John W......June 25, 1906	ord. dept.
225	Hoffer, Jay E........June 25, 1906	ord. dept.
226	Harding, Chester....June 27, 1906	corps of eng.
227	Landis, J. F. R.......June 30, 1906	6 cavalry
228	Faison, Samson L..June 30, 1906	24 infantry.
229	Ridgway, Thomas..June 30, 1906	coast art.
230	Ruckman, John W. June 30, 1906	coast art.
(*)	Howland, Harry S..June 30, 1906	Phil. scouts.
231	Hasbrouck, Alfred. July 2, 1906	14 infantry.
232	Kreps, Jacob F......July 3, 1906	22 infantry.
233	Munson, Edward L. July 11, 1906	med. corps.
234	Cabell, Henry C.....July 13, 1906	14 infantry.
235	Perkins, Frederick. Aug. 7, 1906	a. g. dept.
236	West, Parker W....Aug. 20, 1906	14 cavalry.
237	Burnham, Wm. P..Aug. 20, 1906	7 infantry.
238	Harts, Wm. W......Sept. 9, 1906	corps of eng.
239	Arrasmith, Jas. M..Sept. 11, 1906	15 infantry.
240	Foltz, Fred'k S. ....Sept. 13, 1906	15 cavalry.
241	Gardner, John H...Sept. 13, 1906	1 cavalry.
242	Lynch, John R.......Sept. 13, 1906	pay dept.
243	Jadwin, Edgar......Sept. 26, 1906	corps of eng.
244	Stone, William P...Sept. 30, 1906	coast artillery
245	Stevens, Charles J..Oct. 1, 1906	5 cavalry.
246	Haynes, Ira A.......Oct. 1, 1906	a. g. dept.
	MAJORS—*Continued.*	
247	Walke, Willoughby. Oct. 1, 1906	coast artillery
248	Carleton, Guy.......Oct. 2, 1906	4 cavalry.
249	Conklin, John.......Oct. 3, 1906	2 field art.
250	Johnston, Wm. H...Oct. 6, 1906	16 infantry.
251	Atkinson, Benj. W..Oct. 20, 1906	4 infantry.
252	Dugan, Thomas B..Oct. 28, 1906	12 cavalry.
253	Beall, Fielder M. M. Oct. 31, 1906	28 infantry.
254	Morton, Kenneth...Nov. 12, 1906	ord. dept.
255	Nichols, Maury.....Dec 2 1906	3 infantry.
(*)	Munro, James N....Dec. 5 1906	Philip. scouts
256	Keller, Charles......Jan. 11, 1907	corps of eng.
257	McDonald, John B. Jan. 19, 1907	15 cavalry.
258	Lewis, Isaac N.......Jan. 25, 1907	coast artillery
259	Sturgis, Samuel D..Jan. 25, 1907	1 field art.
260	Benton, Elisha S....Jan. 25, 1907	coast artillery
261	Hawthorne, H. L...Jan, 25, 1907	coast artillery
262	Willcox, C. DeW...Jan. 25, 1907	coast artillery
263	Barrette, John D....Jan. 25, 1907	coast artillery
264	Hubbard, Elmer W. Jan. 25, 1907	coast artillery
265	Cree, John K.........Jan. 25, 1907	coast artillery
266	Berry, Lucien G.....Jan. 25, 1907	3 field art.
267	McMahon, John E..Jan. 25, 1907	6 field art.
268	Menoher, Charles T. Jan. 25, 1907	1 field art.
269	Mott, T. Bentley.....Jan. 25, 1907	4 field art.
270	Stevens, G. W. S....Jan. 25, 1907	coast artillery
271	Davis, Richmond P..Jan. 25, 1907	coast artillery
272	Hinds, Ernest.......Jan. 25, 1907	a. g. dept.
273	Robinson, Wirt.....Jan. 25, 1907	coast artillery
274	Landers, George F..Jan. 25, 1907	coast artillery
275	Gatchell, George W..Jan. 25, 1907	coast artillery
276	Straub, Oscar I......Jan. 25, 1907	coast artillery
277	Schumm, H. C......Jan. 25, 1907	coast artillery
278	Hunter, Alfred M...Jan. 25, 1907	coast artillery
279	Hayden, John L....Jan. 25, 1907	coast artillery
280	March, Peter C......Jan. 25, 1907	6 field art.
281	Wilson, Eugene T..Jan. 25, 1907	coast artillery
282	Blake, Edmund M..Jan. 25, 1907	coast artillery
283	Ellis, Wilmot E.....Jan. 25, 1907	coast artillery
284	O'Neil, John P......Jan. 31, 1907	30 infantry.
285	Deakyne, Herbert..Mar. 2, 1907	corps of eng.
286	Simpson, Wendell L. Mar. 7, 1907	19 infantry.
287	Dentler, C. E.......Mar. 12, 1907	23 infantry.
288	Kennedy, James M. Mar. 20, 1907	med. corps.
289	Thompson, J. K....Mar. 26, 1907	16 infantry.
290	Williams, C. C......Mar. 26, 1907	ord. dept.
291	Kenly, William L...Apr. 5, 1907	5 field art.
292	Haan, William G...Apr. 9, 1907	coast artillery
293	Jordan, Sidney S...Apr. 11, 1907	a. g. dept.
294	Barroll, Morris K...Apr. 13, 1907	coast artillery
295	Stanton, Charles E..Apr. 15, 1907	pay dept.
296	Rivers, Tyree R....Apr. 18, 1907	4 cavalry.
297	Allen, Henry T. ...Apr. 20, 1907	8 cavalry.
298	Howard, Deane C..Apr. 24, 1907	med. corps.
299	Styer, Henry D.....May 6, 1907	29 infantry.
300	Fremont, F. P......May 25, 1903	5 infantry.
301	Wilson, William H..May 10, 1907	med. corps.
302	Skerrett, Delamere..May 27, 1907	pay dept.
303	Bromwell, Chas. S..June 7, 1907	corps of eng.
304	Cosby, Spencer. ....June 9, 1907	corps of eng.
(*)	Foster, Arthur B...June 15, 1907	Phil. scouts.
(*)	McMaster, Geo. H..June 30, 1907	Phil. scouts.
305	Kimball, Amos W..July 3, 1907	qm. dept.
306	Stevens, Pierre C....July 23, 1907	pay dept.
307	Freeman, Samuel D. July 24, 1907	9 cavalry.
308	Hof, Samuel ....Aug. 9, 1907	ord. dept.
309	McGlachlin, E. F...Aug. 12, 1907	4 field art.
310	Anderson, Wm. T..Aug. 29, 1907	chaplain.
311	Slaughter, B. D.....Sept. 4, 1907	pay dept.
312	Tschappat, Wm. H..Sept. 19, 1907	ord. dept.
313	Ayer, Waldo E......Oct. 1, 1907	9 infantry.
314	Noble, Robert H....Oct. 4, 1907	1 infantry.
315	Rice, John H........Oct. 10, 1907	ord. dept.
316	Cole, Henry G.......Oct. 13, 1907	sub. dept.
317	Morse, Benj. C......Oct. 20, 1907	27 infantry.
318	Finley, John P......Oct. 23, 1907	28 infantry.
319	Day, Frederick R....Oct. 25, 1907	30 infantry.
320	Campbell, A.........Oct. 29, 1907	coast artillery
321	Heard, John W.....Oct. 31, 1907	6 cavalry.
322	Reichmann, Carl...Nov. 8, 1907	24 infantry.
323	McIndoe, James T..Nov. 15, 1907	corps of eng.

* Rank of Major temporarily.

RELATIVE RANK OF THE SUPERIOR OFFICERS OF THE REGULAR ARMY—*Continued.*

No.	Name, Rank, and Date of Commission. November 1, 1908.	Corps or Regiment and Corps.
	MAJORS—*Continued.*	
324	Edwards, Arthur M. Dec. 6, 1907	sub. dept.
325	Fitz-Gerald, E. H.. Dec. 14, 1907	chaplain.
326	Roudiez, Leon S.... Dec. 23, 1907	30 infantry.
327	Hains, John P....... Dec. 27, 1907	pay dept.
328	Wren, William C... Jan. 1, 1908	12 infantry.
329	Bateman, Cephas C. Jan. 17, 1908	chaplain.
330	Todd, Henry D., Jr. Jan. 20, 1908	coast art.
331	Winston, Thos. W. Jan. 21, 1908	coast art.
332	Buffington, Abr. P. Jan. 27, 1908	21 infantry.
333	Morrow, Jay J...... Jan. 31, 1908	corps of eng.
334	Walkley, Charles S. Feb. 6, 1908	chaplain.
335	Beckurts, Chas. L.. Feb. 13, 1908	5 infantry.
336	Cavanaugh, J. B.... Feb. 14, 1908	corps of eng.
337	Horton, William E. Feb. 25, 1908	qm. dept.
338	Lassiter, William.. Feb. 25, 1908	ins. gen. dept.
339	Jervey, James P... Feb. 28, 1908	corps of eng.
340	King, David M..... Feb. 29, 1908	ord. dept.
341	Moore, Tredwell W. Mar. 8, 1908	1 infantry.
342	Wright, Wm. M... Mar. 14, 1908	8 infantry.
343	Brewster, André W. Mar. 15, 1908	19 infantry.
344	Cheatham, B. F.... Mar. 17, 1908	qm. dept.
345	Ames, Thales L.... Mar. 17, 1908	ord. dept.
346	Bailey, George G... Mar. 19, 1908	qm. dept.
347	Muir, Charles H.... Mar. 24, 1908	23 infantry.
348	Groves, Leslie R.... Mar. 25, 1908	chaplain.
349	Lewis, William F... Apr. 10, 1908	med. corps.
350	Slocum, S. L' H..... Apr. 14, 1908	2 cavalry.
351	Bratton, Thomas S. Apr. 15, 1908	med. corps.
352	Kirkpatrick, T. J.. Apr. 22, 1908	med. corps.
353	Stone, John H. .... Apr. 23, 1908	med. corps.
354	Rand, Irving W.... Apr. 23, 1908	med. corps.
355	Fauntleroy, P. C... Apr. 23, 1908	med. corps.
356	Wilson, James S.... Apr. 23, 1908	med. corps.
357	Dutcher, Basil H... Apr. 23, 1908	med. corps.
358	Fuller, Leigh A.... Apr. 23, 1908	med. corps.
359	Skinner, George A. Apr. 23, 1908	med. corps.
360	Darnall, Carl R..... Apr. 23, 1908	med. corps.
361	Page, Henry........ Apr. 23, 1908	med. corps.
362	Ashford, Bailey K. Apr. 23, 1908	med. corps.
363	Webber, Henry A. Apr. 23, 1908	med. corps.
364	Clayton, Jere B.... Apr. 23, 1908	med. corps.
365	Chamberlain, W. P. Apr. 23, 1908	med. corps.
366	Schreiner, E. R.... Apr. 23, 1908	med. corps.
367	Shimer, Ira A...... Apr. 23, 1908	med. corps.
368	Hartsock, F. M.... Apr. 23, 1908	med. corps.
369	Duval, Douglas F.. Apr. 23, 1908	med. corps.
370	Manly, Clarence J.. Apr. 23, 1908	med. corps.
371	Baker, David....... Apr. 23, 1908	med. corps.
372	Parmerter, A. L.... Apr. 24, 1908	21 infantry.
373	Davidson, Joseph T. Apr. 25, 1908	qm. dept.
374	Truby, Albert E.... May 1, 1908	med. corps.
375	Church, James R... May 1, 1908	med. corps.
376	Hearn, Clint C...... May 1, 1908	coast art.
377	Forsyth, William W. May 6, 1908	6 cavalry.
378	Howell, George P.. May 8, 1908	corps of eng.
379	Smiley, Samuel E.. May 9, 1908	2 infantry.
380	Devore, Daniel B... May 15, 1908	11 infantry.
381	Ford, Joseph H..... May 20, 1908	med. corps.
382	Kutz, Charles W.... June 2, 1908	corps of eng.
383	Ashburn, Percy M. June 24, 1908	med. corps.
384	Buck, Beaumont B. June 25, 1908	16 infantry.
385	Martin, William F. June 30, 1908	18 infantry.
386	Johnson, E. M., jr. July 3, 1908	6 infantry.
387	Walker, M.......... July 6, 1908	corps of eng.
388	Davis, William C... July 10, 1908	coast artillery
389	McIntyre, Frank... July 18, 1908	8 infantry.
390	Baker, David J., jr. July 18, 1908	11 infantry.
391	Shelton, George H.. July 24, 1908	bu. ins. af.
392	Raymond, Robert R. July 28, 1908	corps of eng.
393	Ladue, William B.. Aug. 7, 1908	corps of eng.
394	Mauldin, Frank G.. Sept. 1, 1908	coast art.
395	Ketcham, Daniel W. Oct. 10, 1908	coast art.
(*)	Hancock, Wm. F... Oct. 3, 1906	coast art.
(*)	McFarland, M. C.... Oct. 12, 1908	P. R. inf.
396	Morrow, William M. Oct. 12, 1908	P. R. inf.
397	Poore, Benjamin A. Oct. 28, 1908	22 infantry.
398	McRae, James H.... Oct. 31, 1908	13 infantry.
399	O'Hern, Edward P. Oct. 31, 1908	ord. dept.
(*)	Heiberg, Elvin R... Nov. 10, 1908	Phil. scouts.
400	Flynn, William F.. Nov. 15, 1908	15 cavalry.
401	Irwin, Francis G.... Nov. 20, 1908	8 cavalry.

FIELD OFFICERS OF REGIMENTS AND OF THE ARTILLERY CORPS.

First Cavalry.
Col. E. J. McClernand.
Lt.-Col. Wm. A. Shunk.
Maj. Joseph A. Gaston.
Maj. Lloyd M. Brett.
Maj. John H. Gardner.

Second Cavalry.
Col. Frank West.
Lt.-Col. Levi P. Hunt.
Maj. Fred'k W. Sibley.
Maj. F. O. Johnson.
Maj. S. L' H. Slocum.

Third Cavalry.
Col. Jos. H. Dorst.
Lt.-Col. T. W. Jones.
Maj. Edwin P. Andrus.
Maj. William C. Brown.
Maj. Percy E. Trippe.

Fourth Cavalry.
Col. Edgar Z. Steever.
Lt.-Col. Wm D. Beach.
Maj. James Lockett.
Maj. Guy Carleton.
Maj. Tyree R. Rivers.

Fifth Cavalry.
Col. Walter S. Schuyler.
Lt.-Col. Geo. K. Hunter.
Maj. Fred. W. Foster.
Maj. Harry C Benson.
Maj. Charles J. Stevens.

Sixth Cavalry.
Col. Alexander Rodgers.
Lt.-Col. Matthias W. Day
Maj. J. F. R. Landis.
Maj. John W. Heard.
Maj. Wm. W. Forsyth.

Seventh Cavalry.
Col. Frederick K. Ward.
Lt.-Col. J. F. Guilfoyle.
Maj. Herbert J. Slocum.
Maj. Wm. J. Nicholson.
Maj. Edwin P. Brewer.

Eighth Cavalry.
Col. H. P. Kingsbury.
Lt.-Col. C. M. O'Connor.
Maj. Henry L. Ripley.
Maj. Henry T. Allen.
Maj. Francis G. Irwin.

Ninth Cavalry.
Col. George S. Anderson.
Lt.-Col. Chas. H. Watts.
Maj. Eben Swift.
Maj. Aug. C. Macomb.
Maj. Sam'l D. Freeman.

Tenth Cavalry.
Col. Jacob A. Augur.
Lt.-Col. Geo. H. G. Gale.
Maj. Robert D. Reed.
Maj. C. H. Grierson.
Maj. George H. Sands.

Eleventh Cavalry.
Col. James Parker.
Lt.-Col. C. H. Murray.
Maj. Homer W. Wheeler
Maj. D. H. Boughton.
Maj. William A. Mercer.

Twelfth Cavalry.
Col. George A. Dodd.
Lt.-Col. F. A. Edwards.
Maj. Horatio G. Sickel.
Maj. H. J. Goldman.
Maj. Thomas B. Dugan.

Thirteenth Cavalry.
Col. Chas. A. P. Hatfield.
Lt.-Col. Walter L. Finley
Maj. Ben. H. Cheever.
Maj. Thomas J. Lewis.
Maj. Joseph T. Dickman.

Fourteenth Cavalry.
Col. James B. Hickey.
Lt.-Col. Jno. C. Gresham.
Maj. Hoel S. Bishop.
Maj. Hugh L. Scott.
Maj. Parker W. West.

Fifteenth Cavalry.
Col. Joseph Garrard.
Lt.-Col. F. H. Hardie.
Maj. William F. Flynn.
Maj. Frederick S. Foltz.
Maj. John B. McDonald.

First Field Artillery.
Col. Henry M. Andrews.
Lt.-Col. D. J. Rumbough.
Maj. Samuel D. Sturgis.
Maj. Charles T. Menoher

Second Field Artillery.
Col. Sydney W. Taylor.
Lt.-Col. Chas. W. Foster.
Maj. G. W. Van Deusen.
Maj. John Conklin.

Third Field Artillery.
Col. Lotus Niles.
Lt.-Col. E. St. J. Greble.
Maj. Lucien G. Berry.
Maj. Charles G. Treat.

Fourth Field Artillery.
Col. Alexander B. Dyer.
Lt.-Col. Edward E. Gayle
Maj. T. Bentley Mott.
Maj. E. F. McGlachlin, Jr.

Fifth Field Artillery.
Col. Edward T. Brown.
Lt.-Col. Granger Adams.
Maj. Edward A. Millar.
Maj. William L. Kenly.

Sixth Field Artillery.
Col. M. M. Macomb.
Lt.-Col. Eli D. Hoyle.
Maj. John E. McMahon.
Maj. Peyton C. March.

Artillery Corps.

Colonels.

G. G. Greenough.
W. Howe.
R. H. Patterson.
J. D. C. Hoskins.
H. L. Harris.
J. A. Lundeen.
G. N. Whistler.
C. D. Parkhurst.
J. P. Wisser.
G. F. E. Harrison.
J. R. Williams.
G. L. Anderson.
W. H. Coffin.
A. Todd.

Lieutenant-Colonels.

A. Slaker.
H. H. Ludlow.
W. R. Hamilton.
C. Deems.
J. V. White.
E. M. Weaver.
F. Marsh.
S. E. Allen.
A. C. Blunt.

FIELD OFFICERS OF REGIMENTS AND OF THE ARTILLERY CORPS—*Continued.*

Lieut.-Col.—*Continued.*
W. C. Rafferty.
W. P. Newcomb.
C. L. Phillips.
C. J. Bailey.
C. P. Townsley.

Majors.

G. F. Barney.
M. F. Harmon.
A. Cronkhite.
C. H. Hunter.
S. M. Foote.
J. C. W. Brooks.
G. T. Bartlett.
C. A. Bennett.
H. C. Davis.
T. Ridgway.
J. W. Ruckman.
W. P. Stone.
W. Walke.
I. N. Lewis.
E. S. Benton.
H. L. Hawthorne.
C. De W. Willcox.
J. D. Barrette.
E. W. Hubbard.
J. K. Cree.
G. W. S. Stevens.
R. P. Davis.
W. Robinson.
G. F. Landers.
G. W. Gatchell.
O. I. Straub.
H. C. Schumm.
A. M. Hunter.
J. L. Hayden.
E. T. Wilson.
E. M. Blake.
W. E. Ellis.
W. G. Haan.
M. K. Barroll.
A. Campbell.
H. D. Todd, jr.
T. W. Winston.
C. C. Hearn.
W. C. Davis.
F. G. Mauldin.
D. W. Ketcham.
W. F. Hancock.

First Infantry.

Col. Geo. K. McGunnegle.
Lt.-Col. James S. Rogers
Maj. H. C. Hodges, Jr.
Maj. Robert H. Noble.
Maj. Tredwell W. Moore.

Second Infantry.

Col. F. W. Mansfield.
Lt.-Col. C. St. J. Chubb.
Maj. Edward H. Browne.
Maj. Harry L. Bailey.
Maj. Samuel E. Smiley.

Third Infantry.

Col. Thos. C. Woodbury.
Lt.-Col. Lea Febiger.
Maj. Edw. H. Plummer
Maj. Wilson Y. Stamper.
Maj. Maury Nichols.

Fourth Infantry.

Col. Edwin B. Bolton.
Lt.-Col. L. A. Lovering.
Maj. John C. F. Tillson.
Maj. David C. Shanks.
Maj. Benj. W. Atkinson.

Fifth Infantry.

Col. Calvin D. Cowles.
Lt.-Col. Robert K. Evans.
Maj. Wallis O. Clark.
Maj. Francis P. Fremont.
Maj. Chas. L. Beckurts.

Sixth Infantry.

Col. Joseph W. Duncan.
Lt.-Col. Wm. A. Mann.
Maj. John H. Beacom.
Maj. R. R. Steedman.
Maj. E. M. Johnson, Jr.

Seventh Infantry.

Col. Daniel Cornman.
Lt.-Col. Robert N. Getty.
Maj. Arthur C. Ducat.
Maj. James A. Goodin.
Maj. Wm. P. Burnham.

Eighth Infantry.

Col. Charles W. Mason.
Lt.-Col. R. L. Bullard
Maj. Walter K. Wright.
Maj. Wm. M. Wright.
Maj. Frank McIntyre.

Ninth Infantry.

Col. Charles J. Crane.
Lt.-Col. Wm. C. Buttler.
Maj. Chas. R. Noyes.
Maj. John Cotter.
Maj. Waldo E. Ayer.

Tenth Infantry.

Col. Henry A. Greene.
Lt.-Col. George R. Cecil.
Maj. L. W. V. Kennon.
Maj. Robert C. Van Vliet.
Maj. William L. Buck.

Eleventh Infantry.

Col. Richard T. Yeatman.
Lt.-Col. Wm. P. Evans.
Maj. Rich. M. Blatchford
Maj Daniel B. Devore.
Maj. David Baker, Jr.

Twelfth Infantry.

Col. Wm. H. C. Bowen.
Lt.-Col. Robert F. Ames.
Maj. John S. Mallory.
Maj. Charles H. Barth.
Maj. Wm. C. Wren.

Thirteenth Infantry.

Col. Robert H. R. Loughborough.
Lt.-Col. Wm. A. Nichols.
Maj. Hunter Liggett.
Maj. Wilds P. Richardson
Maj. James H. McRae.

Fourteenth Infantry.

Col. John C. Dent.
Lt.-Col. James A. Irons.
Maj. John S. Parke.
Maj. Alfred Hasbrouck.
Maj. Henry C. Cabell.

Fifteenth Infantry.

Col. Walter S. Scott.
Lt.-Col. Arthur Williams.
Maj. Willis T. May.
Maj. A. S. Rowan.
Maj. J. M. Arrasmith.

Sixteenth Infantry.

Col. Cornelius Gardener.
Lt.-Col. R. H. Wilson.
Maj. Wm. H. Johnston.
Maj. Jas. K. Thompson.
Maj. Beaumont B. Buck.

Seventeenth Infantry.

Col. John T. Van Orsdale.
Lt.-Col. Colville P. Terrett
Maj. James A. Maney.
Maj. Edw. Chynoweth.
Maj. Frank B. McCoy.

Eighteenth Infantry.

Col. Thomas F. Davis.
Lt.-Col. Zera W. Torrey.
Maj. Henry Kirby.
Maj. Daniel L. Howell.
Maj. William F. Martin.

Nineteenth Infantry.

Col. Jos. F. Huston.
Lt.-Col. D. A. Frederick.
Maj. Edwin A. Root.
Maj. W. L. Simpson.
Maj. André W. Brewster.

Twentieth Infantry.

Col. Marion P. Maus.
Lt.-Col. Henry B. Moon.
Maj. S. W. Dunning.
Maj. George W. McIver.
Maj. John F. Morrison.

Twenty-first Infantry.

Col. Chas. A. Williams.
Lt.-Col. Geo. S. Young.
Maj. Lawrence J. Hearn.
Maj. A. P. Buffington.
Maj. A. L. Parmerter.

Twenty-second Infantry.

Col. Alfred Reynolds.
Lt.-Col. George F. Cooke.
Maj. Abner Pickering.
Maj. Jacob F. Kreps.
Maj. Benjamin A. Poore.

Twenty-third Infantry.

Col. Alfred Sharpe.
Lt.-Col. Edwin F. Glenn.
Maj. Wm. H. Allaire.
Maj. Clarence E. Dentler.
Maj. Charles H. Muir.

Twenty-fourth Infantry.

Col. William Paulding.
Lt.-Col. Alexis R. Paxton
Maj. Elmore F. Taggart.
Maj. Samson L. Faison.
Maj. Carl Reichmann.

Twenty-fifth Infantry.

Col. Ralph W. Hoyt.
L.-C'l W. R. Abercrombie
Maj. Jos. M. T. Partello.
Maj. Chas. W. Penrose.
Maj. Francis J. Kernan.

Twenty-sixth Infantry.

Col. Chas. A. Booth.
Lt.-Col. J. B. Jackson.
Maj. Charles J. T. Clarke.
Maj. E. E. Hatch.
Maj. Harris L. Roberts.

Twenty-seventh Infantry.

Col. Wm. L. Pitcher.
Lt.-Col. Millard F. Waltz.
Maj. Edgar W. Howe.
Maj. W. H. Chatfield.
Maj. Benj. C. Morse.

Twenty-eighth Infantry.

Col. Owen J. Sweet.
Lt.-Col. Silas A. Wolf.
Maj. Thos. W. Griffith.
Maj. F. M. M. Beall.
Maj. John P. Finley.

Twenty-ninth Infantry.

Col. Hobart K. Bailey.
Lt.-Col. R. B. Turner.
Maj. Edwin P. Pendleton.
Maj. Robert L. Hirst.
Maj. Henry D. Styer.

Thirtieth Infantry.

Col. Edward B. Pratt.
Lt.-Col. Nat. P. Phister.
Maj. Leon S. Roudiez.
Maj. Joseph P. O'Neil.
Maj. Frederick R. Day.

MILITARY DIVISIONS AND DEPARTMENTS.

DEPARTMENT OF THE EAST.—New England, New York, New Jersey, Pennsylvania, Delaware, Maryland, District of Columbia, West Virginia, Virginia, Porto Rico and islands and keys adjacent thereto; headquarters, Governor's Island, N. Y. Commander, Maj.-Gen. Leonard Wood.

DEPARTMENT OF THE GULF.—North Carolina, South Carolina, Tennessee, Georgia, Florida, Alabama, Louisiana and Mississippi; headquarters, Atlanta, Ga. Commander, Brig.-Gen. Ramsay D. Potts.

DEPARTMENT OF THE LAKES.—Wisconsin, Michigan, Illinois, Indiana, Ohio and Kentucky; headquarters, Chicago, Ill. Commander, Maj.-Gen. Fred'k D. Grant.

DEPARTMENT OF THE MISSOURI.—Missouri, Iowa, Nebraska, South Dakota, Wyoming (except Yellowstone National Park) and Kansas; headquarters, Omaha, Neb. Commander (temporarily), Brig.-Gen. William H. Carter.

DEPARTMENT OF DAKOTA.—Minnesota, North Dakota, Montana, and the Yellowstone National Park; headquarters, St. Paul, Minn. Commander, Brig.-Gen. W. S. Edgerly.

DEPARTMENT OF TEXAS.—Texas, Arkansas and Oklahoma; headquarters, San Antonio, Tex. Commander, Brig.-Gen. A. L. Myer.

DEPARTMENT OF THE COLORADO.—Colorado, Utah, Arizona and New Mexico; headquarters, Denver, Col. Commander, Brig.-Gen. Earl D. Thomas.

DEPARTMENT OF CALIFORNIA.—California, Nevada and Hawaii; headquarters, San Francisco, Cal. Commander, Maj.-Gen. John F. Weston.

MILITARY DIVISIONS AND DEPARTMENTS—*Continued.*

DEPARTMENT OF THE COLUMBIA.—Washington, Oregon, Idaho (excepting the Yellowstone National Park) and Alaska; headquarters, Vancouver Barracks, Wash. Commander, Brig.-Gen. Daniel H. Brush.

ARMY OF CUBAN PACIFICATION.—Headquarters, Havana, Cuba. Commander, Brig.-Gen. T. H. Barry.

PHILIPPINES DIVISION.—Embracing Departments of Luzon, Visayas and Mindanao; headquarters, Manila, P.I. Commander, Brig.-Gen. Tasker H. Bliss (temporarily).

DEPARTMENT OF LUZON.—Headquarters, Manila, P.I. Commander, Brig.-Gen. A. L. Mills.

DEPARTMENT OF THE VISAYAS.—Headquarters Iloilo, P.I. Commander, Brig.-Gen. C. L. Hodges.

DEPARTMENT OF MINDANAO.—Headquarters Zamboanga, P.I. Commander, Brig.-Gen. ——.

ARMY PAY TABLE.

GRADE.	Pay of Officers in Active Service. Yearly Pay.					Pay of Retired Officers. Yearly Pay.				
	First 5 years' Service.	After 5 years' Service.	After 10 years' Service.	After 15 years' Service.	After 20 years' Service.	First 5 years' Service.	After 5 years' Service.	After 10 years' Service.	After 15 years' Service.	After 20 years' Service.
		10 *p. c.*	20 *p. c.*	30 *p. c.*	40 *p. c.* *a*					
Lieutenant-General	$11,000	....	....	....	....	$8,250	......	....	......	....
Major-General	8,000	....	....	....	....	6,000	......	....	......	....
Brigadier-General	6,000	....	....	....	....	4,500	......	....	......	....
Colonel (*b*)	4,000	$4,400	$4,800	$5,000	$5,000	3,000	$3,300.00	$3,600	$3,750.00	$3,750
Lieutenant-Colonel (*b*)	3,500	3,850	4,200	4,500	4,500	2,625	2,887.50	3,150	3,375.00	3,375
Major (*b*)	3,000	3,300	3,600	3,900	4,000	2,250	2,475.00	2,700	2,924.40	3,000
Captain	2,400	2,640	2,880	3,120	3,360	1,800	1,980.00	2,160	2,340.00	2,520
First Lieutenant	2,000	2,200	2,400	2,600	2,800	1,500	1,650.00	1,800	1,950.00	2,100
Second Lieutenant	1,700	1,870	2,040	2,210	2,380	1,275	1,402.50	1,530	1,657.44	1,785

Chaplains have the rank and pay of major, captain and first lieutenant, respectively.

(*a*) Service increase of pay of officers below rank of brigadier-general cannot exceed 40 per cent. in all.

(*b*) The maximum pay of a colonel is $5,000, of a lieutenant-colonel $4,500, and of a major $4,000.

The pay of non-commissioned officers is from $21 to $99 per month, and of privates from $15 to $25 per month.

Service outside the United States, except in Porto Rico and Hawaii, 10 per cent. additional for officers and 20 per cent. for enlisted men.

Naval Militia.

THE Naval Militia is now organized in eighteen States and the District of Columbia, as follows:

STATE.	Commissioned Officers.	Enlis'd Men.	Total.	Commanding Officer.	STATE.	Commissioned Officers.	Enlis'd Men.	Total.	Commanding Officer.
California	49	509	558	Capt. Geo. W. Bauer.	Missouri	110	120	131	Com. W. F. Roberts.
Connecticut	22	220	242	Com. F. S. Cornwell.	New Jersey	27	301	328	Com. E. McC. Peters. Com. A. De Unger.
D. Columbia	14	187	201	Com. S. W. Stratton.	New York	52	741	793	Capt. J. W. Miller.
Georgia	10	107	117	Com. H. S. Colding.	N. Carolina	44	343	387	Capt. T. C. Daniels.
Illinois	50	669	719	Capt. W. F. Purdy.	Ohio	19	183	202	Lieut.-Com. A. Nicklett. Lieut.-Com. F. R. Semon.
Louisiana	48	577	625	Capt. J. W. Bostick.	Pennsylvania	8	87	95	Com. C. W. Ruschenberger.
Maine	4	60	64	Lieut. E. G. Scully.	Rhode Island	19	212	231	Com. Wm. C. Bliss.
Maryland	21	172	293	Com. F. H. Wagner.	S. Carolina	21	185	206	Lieut.-Com. C. L. Du Bos.
Mass	43	496	539	Lieut.-Com. J. H. Dillaway.					
Michigan	40	356	396	Capt. F. D. Standish.					
Minnesota	13	162	175	Com. Guy A. Eaton.					
Total						515	5687	6202	

All matters relating to the Naval Militia come under the cognizance of the Assistant Secretary of the Navy, who transacts all business with the Naval Militia through the Governors and Adjutants-General (or Quartermasters-General) of the States. The officer in the Navy Department, Washington, having charge of Naval Militia matters is Captain A. E. Culver, U. S. N.

FOR UNITED STATES NAVAL ENLISTMENT, SEE PAGE 580.

The Organized and Unorganized Militia of the U. S.

COMPILED for THE WORLD ALMANAC from the latest official reports.

The Militia law of January 21, 1903, provides; "That the militia shall consist of every able bodied male citizen of the respective States * * * and shall be divided into two classes—the organized militia, to be known as the National Guard * * * or by such other designations as may be given them by the laws of the respective States or Territories, and the remainder to be known as the reserve militia."

States and Territories.	Official Designation of the Organized Militia.	Gen'l and Gen'l Staff Officers.	Regimen'l and Comp. Officers.	Total Commis-sion-d.	Enlisted Men.	Tot'l Com-mis'd and Enlisted (Org'ized Militia).	Reserve Militia (Unorgan-ized).
Alabama	Alabama National Guard	42	174	216	3,010	3,226	350,000
Arizona	National Guard of Arizona	1	32	33	340	373	40,000
Arkansas	Arkansas National Guard	34	88	122	1,174	1,296	310,000
California	National Guard of California	41	152	193	2,082	2,275	284,385
Colorado	National Guard of Colorado	16	53	69	644	713	125,136
Connecticut	Connecticut National Guard	27	154	181	2,526	2,707	116,117
Delaware	Organized Militia of Delaware	6	33	39	349	388	32,000
District of Columbia	National Guard of District of Columbia	14	118	132	1,203	1,335	62,634
Florida	Florida State Troops	24	70	94	1,160	1,254	239,760
Georgia	National Guard of Georgia	27	185	212	2,806	3,018	500,000
Hawaii	National Guard of Hawaii	14	26	40	452	492	8,000
Idaho	National Guard of Idaho	8	53	61	469	530	50,000
Illinois	Illinois National Guard	82	418	500	5,813	6,313	1,031,175
Indiana	Indiana National Guard	33	153	186	2,121	2,307	636,738
Iowa	Iowa National Guard	20	182	202	2,455	2,657	333,135
Kansas	Kansas National Guard	22	106	128	1,275	1,403	369,894
Kentucky	Kentucky State Guard	26	124	150	1,590	1,740	500,000
Louisiana	Louisiana State National Guard	26	80	106	1,142	1,248	250,000
Maine	National Guard of the State of Maine	13	95	108	1,174	1,282	103,043
Maryland	Maryland National Guard	14	149	163	1,741	1,904	180,000
Massachusetts	Massachusetts Volunteer Militia	78	346	424	5,102	5,526	516,446
Michigan	Michigan National Guard	50	163	213	2,648	2,861	700,000
Minnesota	National Guard of Minnesota	35	161	196	2,612	2,808	218,000
Mississippi	Mississippi National Guard	34	85	119	1,083	1,202	420,053
Missouri	National Guard of Missouri	30	178	208	2,811	3,019	500,000
Montana	National Guard of Montana	7	29	36	386	422	75,000
Nebraska	Nebraska National Guard	20	88	108	1,299	1,407	128,000
Nevada (a)	Nevada National Guard	....	....	....	....	....	15,000
New Hampshire	New Hampshire National Guard	27	98	125	1,443	1,568	40,000
New Jersey	National Guard of New Jersey	98	253	351	3,982	4,333	514,998
New Mexico	National Guard of New Mexico	7	24	31	243	274	46,000
New York	National Guard of New York	215	731	946	13,800	14,746	1,422,019
North Carolina	North Carolina National Guard	49	155	204	1,835	2,039	200,000
North Dakota	North Dakota National Guard	12	52	64	639	703	75,000
Ohio	Ohio National Guard	55	391	446	5,099	5,545	1,085,110
Oklahoma	Oklahoma National Guard	8	45	53	660	713	125,000
Oregon	Oregon National Guard	16	85	101	1,343	1,444	110,000
Pennsylvania	National Guard Pennsylvania	97	606	703	9,345	10,048	1,062,425
Rhode Island	Rhode Island National Guard	33	83	116	961	1,077	90,000
South Carolina	National Guard of South Carolina	16	159	175	1,714	1,889	207,171
South Dakota	South Dakota National Guard	14	50	64	562	626	65,000
Tennessee	National Guard of Tennessee	7	104	111	1,430	1,531	390,000
Texas	Texas National Guard	41	161	202	2,032	2,234	425,000
Utah	National Guard of Utah	4	33	37	330	367	28,000
Vermont	National Guard of Vermont	8	55	63	781	844	46,500
Virginia	Virginia Volunteers	29	134	163	1,803	1,966	250,000
Washington	National Guard of Washington	12	44	56	639	695	170,000
West Virginia	West Virginia National Guard	23	75	98	986	1,084	140,000
Wisconsin	Wisconsin National Guard	23	171	194	2,825	3,019	438,472
Wyoming	Wyoming National Guard	9	32	41	439	480	1,800
Total		1,547	7,036	8,583	102,358	110,941	14,987,011

(a) No organized militia.

Alaska has no militia, though provision is made for such if need arises. Guam and Samoa have each a small provisional force, used more for police purposes than for military. The Philippines have a constabulary force which can be used either for police or war purposes, provided the latter is on the islands. Porto Rico has a regiment of eight companies of infantry which is a part of the army. The enlisted men of this regiment are natives of Porto Rico. The reserve militia in the Southern States is assumed to include negroes capable of bearing arms.

DISTANCE PROJECTILES HAVE BEEN THROWN FROM WARSHIPS OR COAST-DEFENSE GUNS.

THE following table will show the range of guns on board warships at an elevation of 15 degrees, which is, on board ship, the highest projectile range:

Size of Gun.	Distance projectile will be thrown.	Size of Gun.	Distance projectile will be thrown.
3 inch	4.80 miles	7 inch	7.70 miles
4 inch	6.00 miles	8 inch	10 00 miles
5 inch	6.25 miles	10 inch	10.80 miles
6 inch	6.80 miles	12 inch	12.00 miles

All these guns have been fired, and, in a number of instances, the projectile has gone slightly farther than indicated above.

The 16-inch gun at Sandy Hook, which is the largest and, in fact, the only gun of this character in the Army, has a muzzle velocity of 2,150 feet per second. It throws a projectile weighing 2,400 pounds a distance of about 21 miles.

The 12-inch rifle of the Army has a muzzle velocity of 2,250 feet per second, and will throw a projectile weighing 1,046 pounds about 15,000 yards at the extreme range permitted by the carriage.

The Navy.

FLAG OFFICERS.

ADMIRAL.

Rank.	*Name.*	*Duty.*	*Where Stationed.*
Admiral	George Dewey	Senior Member General Board	Washington, D. C.

REAR-ADMIRALS.

Rank.	*Name.*	*Duty.*	*Where Stationed*
Rear-Admiral	Caspar F. Goodrich	Commandant Navy Yard, New York	New York, N. Y.
"	Charles S. Sperry	Commanding Atlantic Fleet	Flagship Connecticut.
"	Wm. T. Swinburne	Commanding Pacific Fleet	Flagship West Virginia.
"	Joseph N. Hemphill	President Naval Ex. and Ret. B'ds.	Washington, D. C.
"	William H. Emory	En route home from Asiatic Station	——
"	Eugene H. C. Leutze	Commandant Navy Yard, Washington	Washington, D. C.
"	Uriel Sebree	Comdg. 2d Div. 1st Sq. Pacific Fleet	Flagship Tennessee.
"	Edwin C. Pendleton	Comdt. 4th Naval Dist. and Navy Yard, Philadelphia	Philadelphia, Pa.
"	William Swift	Commandant Navy Yard, Boston	Boston, Mass.
"	Conway H. Arnold	Commanding 3d Sq. Atlantic Fleet	Flagship Dolphin.
"	Edward D. Taussig	Com 5th Nav. Dist. and N. Yd., Norfolk	Norfolk, Va.
"	John E. Pillsbury	Chief Bureau of Navigation	Washington, D. C.
"	Adolph Marix	Member Light House Board	Washington, D. C.
"	Raymond P. Rodgers	Chief Office Naval Intelligence	Washington, D. C.
"	Royal R. Ingersoll	Member General Board	Washington, D. C.
"	Seaton Schroeder	Com. 3d Div. 2d Sq. Atlantic Fleet	Flagship Louisiana.
"	Richard Wainwright	Comdg. 2d Div. 1st Sq. Atlantic Fleet	Flagship Georgia.
"	Thomas C. McLean	Pres. Board Inspection and Survey	Washington, D. C.
"	William J. Barnette	Supt. Naval Observatory	Washington, D. C.
"	Edwin K. Moore	Commandant 1st Naval District and Navy Yard	Portsmouth, N. H.
"	John A. Rodgers	Commandant Navy Yard	Puget Sonnd, Wash.
"	James D. Adams	Navy Yard (Court Martial Duty)	New York, N. Y.
"	Gottfried Blocklinger	Member Naval Ex. and Ret. Boards	Washington, D. C.
"	William P. Potter	Comdg. 4th Div., U. S. Atlantic Fleet	Flagship Wisconsin.
"	Nathan E. Niles	Comdg. Receiving Ship Hancock	New York, N. Y.
"	Giles B. Harber	Comdg. 3d Squadron U. S. Pacific Fleet	Flagship Rainbow.
"	Newton E. Mason	Chief Bureau Ordnance	Washington, D. C.

RETIRED LIST.

Rank.	*Name.*	*Residence.*
Rear-Ad.	Cipriano Andrade	New York, N. Y.
"	George W. Baird	Washington, D. C.
"	Charles J. Barclay	Brookline, Mass.
"	Albert S. Barker	Washington, D. C.
"	Alexander B. Bates	Binghamton, N. Y.
"	Robert M. Berry	Detroit, Mich.
"	Warner B. Bayley	Washington, D. C.
"	George A. Bicknell	New Albany, Ind.
"	John V. B. Bleecker	Morristown, N. J.
"	George M. Book	San Antonio, Tex.
"	Royal B Bradford	Washington, D. C.
"	George Brown	Indianapolis, Ind.
"	Willard H. Brownson	Washington, D. C.
"	William G. Buehler	Philadelphia, Pa.
"	William T. Burwell	Coronado, Cal.
"	Silas Casey	Washington, D. C.
"	French E. Chadwick	Newport, R. I.
"	Colby M. Chester	B. Equip., W'n, D. C.
"	Charles E. Clark	Greenfield, Mass.
"	Richardson Clover	Napa, Cal.
"	Geo. P. Colvocoresses	Litchfield, Ct.
"	George A. Converse	Pres. Bd. on Constr.
"	Francis A. Cook	Northampton, Mass
"	Philip H. Cooper	Morristown, N. J.
"	Charles S. Cotton	Leave abroad.
"	Albert R. Couden	Bd. Nav. Ordnance.
"	Joseph E. Craig	Washington, D. C.
"	Bartlett J. Cromwell	Washington, D. C.
"	William S. Cowles	Chf. Bu. Equipm't.
"	Charles H. Davis	Washington, D. C.
"	Benjamin F. Day	Glasgow, Va.
"	William P. Day	Leave abroad.
"	James H. Dayton	South Bend, Ind.
"	Francis H. Delano	Portsmouth, N. H.
"	Francis W. Dickins	Washington, D. C.
"	Franklin J. Drake	Del. Wtr. Gap, N. Y.
"	Andrew Dunlap	Washington, D. C.
"	Nehemiah M. Dyer	Melrose, Mass.
"	Joseph G. Eaton	Boston, Mass.
"	James Entwistle	Paterson, N. J.
"	Henry Erben	New York, N. Y.
"	Robley D. Evans	Washington, D. C.
"	William H. Everett	Newport, R. I.
"	Oscar W. Farenholt	San Francisco, Cal.
"	Wells L. Field	Bennington, Vt.
"	William M. Folger	Windsor, Vt.
Rear-Ad.	John D. Ford	Baltimore, Md.
"	Charles T. Forse	Pittsburgh, Pa.
"	James M. Forsyth	Shamokin, Pa.
"	Samuel R. Franklin	Washington, D. C.
"	Perry Garst	Boone, Iowa.
"	Edward H. Gheen	Washington, D. C.
"	William C. Gibson	Brooklyn, N. Y.
"	James G. Green	Edenton, N. C.
"	Franklin Hanford	Scottsville, N. Y.
"	D. B Harmony	Washington, D. C.
"	P. F. Harrington	Riverdale, N. Y.
"	John M. Hawley	Washington, D. C.
"	Francis J. Higginson	Cold Spring, N. Y.
"	John A. Howell	Warrenton, Va.
"	Henry L. Howison	Yonkers, N. Y.
"	John J. Hunker	New York, N. Y.
"	Charles T. Hutchins	Washington, D. C.
"	George E. Ide	New York, N. Y.
"	Richard Inch	Washington, D. C.
"	Theodore F. Jewell	Washington, D. C.
"	Mortimer L. Johnson	Portsmouth, N. H.
"	Louis Kempff	San Francisco, Cal.
"	Harry Knox	Annapolis, Md.
"	Ben. P. Lamberton	Washington, D. C.
"	Edwin Longnecker	Wernersville, Pa.
"	Leavitt C. Logan	Jamestown, N. Y.
"	John Lowe	Washington, D. C.
"	Stephen P. Luce	Newport, R. I.
"	Nicoll Ludlow	New York, N. Y.
"	Henry W. Lyon	Paris, Me.
"	M. R. S. Mackenzie	Morristown, N. J.
"	Alfred T. Mahan	Quogue, L. I.
"	Washburn Maynard	Narragansett, R. I.
"	Henry N. Manney	Washington, D. C.
"	Henry B. Mansfield	Brooklyn, N. Y.
"	Ed. O. Matthews	Cambridge, Mass.
"	Alex. H. McCormick	Annapolis, Md.
"	Bowman H. McCalla	Santa Barbara, Cal.
"	John McGowan	Washington, D. C.
"	William W. Mead	Leave abroad.
"	John P. Merrill	Pres. Nav. War Col.
"	John F. Merry	Somerville, Mass.
"	Joseph N. Miller	East Orange, N. J.
"	Merrill Miller	Berkeley, Cal.
"	Robert W. Milligan	Annapolis, Md.
"	Chas. S. Norton	Westfield, N. J.

Rank.	Name.	Residence.
Rear-Ad.	Charles O'Neil	Washington, D. C.
"	Thomas Perry	Port Deposit, Md.
"	George W. Pigman	Oakland, Md.
"	Ebenezer S. Prime	Huntington, N. Y.
"	Francis M. Ramsay	Washington, D. C.
"	John J. Read	Mt. Holly, N. J.
"	Allen V. Reed	Washington, D. C.
"	William H. Reeder	Leave abroad.
"	George C. Reiter	Leave abroad.
"	George C. Remey	Washington, D. C.
"	Henry B. Robeson	Walpole, N. H.
"	Frederick Rodgers	Washington, D. C.
"	Charles R. Roelker	Washington, D. C.
"	Albert Ross	North Chicago, Ill.
"	James H. Sands	Wilton, N. H.
"	Winfield S. Schley	Washington, D. C.
"	Charles D. Sigsbee	Washington, D. C.
"	John Schouler	Annapolis, Md.
"	Thos. O. Selfridge	Washington, D. C.
"	Frederic Singer	New Orleans, La.
"	John A. B. Smith	Atlantic City, N. J.
"	Albert S. Snow	Brookline, Mass.
"	Arthur B. Speyers	New York, N. Y.
Rear-Ad.	Oscar F. Stanton	New London, Ct.
"	Thomas H. Stevens	Washington, D. C.
"	Yates Stirling	Baltimore, Md.
"	Charles H. Stockton	Washington, D. C.
"	Edward T. Strong	Andover, Mass.
"	George W. Sumner	Patchogue, L. I.
"	Fred'k M. Symonds	Galesville, Wis.
"	Silas W. Terry	Washington, D. C.
"	Chapman C. Todd	Lexington, Ky.
"	Joseph Trilley	San Francisco, Cal.
"	John H. Upshur	Washington, D. C.
"	Samuel W. Very	Newton, Mass.
"	Asa Walker	Annapolis, Md.
"	George H. Wadleigh	Dover, N. H.
"	Eugene W. Watson	Washington, D. C.
"	John C. Watson	Louisville, Ky.
"	Aaron W. Weaver	Washington, D. C.
"	Harrie Webster	Richmond, Va.
"	Clifford H. West	Brooklyn, N. Y.
"	William H. Whiting	New York, N. Y.
"	George F. F. Wilde	North Easton, Mass.
"	William C. Wise	San Francisco, Cal.

COMMODORES.*
RETIRED LIST.

Rank.	Name.	Residence.
Commodore	Charles W. Bartlett	Annapolis, Md.
"	William H. Beehler	Key West, Fla
"	Charles G. Bowman	Delphi, Ind.
"	James H. Bull	Leave abroad.
"	R. G. Davenport	Washington, D.C.
"	Robt. G. Denig	Insp. (Bu. St. Eng).
"	Geo. L. Dyer	Com. Nav. Yd. Cha'ston.
"	William C. Eaton	New York, N. Y.
"	Rogers H. Galt	Norfolk, Va.
"	James H. Gillis	Kane, Pa.
"	W. S. Moore	Duxbury, Mass.
"	Henry Morrell	Brooklyn, N. Y.
"	J. A. H. Nickels	Richmond, Va.
Commodore	Nathaniel J. K. Patch	Boston, Mass.
"	Geo. H. Peters	Leave abroad.
"	Chas. P. Perkins	Com. Pac. Nav. Dist.
"	Theodoric Porter	Annapolis, Md.
"	R. L. Phythian	Annapolis, Md.
"	John M. Robinson	Washington, D. C.
"	Karl Rohrer	Naval Sta., San Juan.
"	Frank E. Sawyer	Newtonville, Mass.
"	H. N. Stevenson	Pittsfield, Mass.
"	W. H. Turner	Cincinnati, O.
"	A. V. Wadhams	Wadhams Mills, N. Y.
"	Rush R. Wallace	Washington, D. C.

*The grade of Commodore on the active list has been abolished.

The following are the dates of future retirements of Rear-Admirals (named in the order of their rank) now on the active list, for age limit, under the law: Caspar F. Goodrich, January 7, 1909; Charles S. Sperry, September 3, 1909; William T. Swinburne, August 24, 1909; Joseph N. Hemphill, June 18, 1909; William H. Emory, December 17, 1908; Eugene H. C. Leutze, November 16, 1909; Uriel Sebree, February 20, 1910; Edwin C. Pendleton, May 27, 1909; William Swift, March 17, 1910; Conway H. Arnold, November 14, 1910; Edward D. Taussig, November 20, 1909; John E. Pillsbury, December 15, 1908; Adolph Marix, May 10, 1910; Raymond P. Rodgers, December 20, 1911; Royal R. Ingersoll, December 4, 1909; Seaton Schroeder, August 17, 1911; Richard Wainwright, December 17, 1911; Thomas C. McLean, October 25, 1909; William J. Barnette, February 2, 1909; Edwin K. Moore, July 24, 1909; John A. Rodgers, July 26, 1910; James D. Adams, May 4, 1910; Gottfried Blocklinger, October 23, 1909; William P. Potter, May 10, 1912; Nathan E. Niles, December 27, 1909; Giles B. Harber, September 24, 1911; Newton E. Mason, October 14, 1912.

THE NAVY.

The active list of the Navy comprises 1,771 commissioned and 597 warrant officers on the active list, and 878 commissioned and 84 warrant officers on the retired list. The enlisted strength allowed by law is 44,500 men and apprentice seamen.

MARINE CORPS.

The United States Marine Corps consists of a force of 267 officers and 9,313 men. Major-General George P. Elliott is commandant.

The origin of the Navy Department may be said to date from October 13, 1775, when Congress authorized the equipment of two cruisers, mounting respectively 10 and 14 guns. Before the end of that year 15 more vessels of from 20 to 36 guns were authorized. The affairs of the Navy were at that time intrusted to a "Marine Committee." In 1798 the present department was formally created, and Benjamin Stoddart appointed the first Secretary.

CAPTAINS OF THE NAVY—ACTIVE LIST—NOVEMBER 30, 1908.

Name.	Present Duty.	Commission	Name.	Present Duty.	Commission
Arthur P. Nazro	Com. Wabash	Dec. 28, 1904	Corwin P. Rees	Com. Nav. Sta., Honolulu.	Sept. 30, 1905
William W. Kimball	Naval Exam. Board.	Jan. 12, 1905	Lewis C. Heilner	Com. 8th Naval Dist.	Jan. 7, 1906
Uriah R. Harris	Com. Naval Sta., Cav'te.	Feb. 21, 1905	Joseph B. Murdock	Com. Rhode Island	Jan. 22, 1906
Edward B. Barry	Supervisor Naval Auxil.	Mar. 31, 1905	Hugo Osterhaus	Com. Connecticut	Feb. 19, 1906
Herbert Winslow	Navy Yard, Boston	Apr. 22, 1905	Albert C. Dillingham	Com. Franklin	Feb. 19, 1906
Albert G. Berry	Com. Lancaster	June 16, 1905	John B. Collins	Com. Indiana	Feb. 28, 1906
Thomas S. Phelps	Com. Mare Island N. Y'd	June 26, 1905	Charles E. Vreeland	Com. Kansas	Apl. 13, 1906
Daniel D. V. Stuart	Navy Yard, Norfolk	July 1, 1905	John B. Milton	Com. Independence	June 6, 1906
Kossuth Niles	Com. Louisiana	July 1, 1905	Aaron Ward	Supervisor N. Y. Harbor.	June 6, 1906
Dennis H. Mahan	Navy Yard, Puget Sound.	July 1, 1905	Sidney A. Staunton	Member General Board	June 12, 1906
Albert F. Dixon	Gen'l Insp. Machinery	July 1, 1905	Chauncey Thomas	Insp. 3d L. H. Dist.	July 1, 1906
Samuel P. Comly	Light House Board	July 1, 1905	William A. Marshall	Com. No. Carolina	July 1, 1906
John Hubbard	Com. Minnesota	July 8, 1905	Edward F. Qualtrough	Com. Georgia	July 1, 1906
Alexander McCrackin	Com. West Virginia	Sept. 8, 1905	Lucien Young	Navy Yard, Mare Island.	July 1, 1906

CAPTAINS OF THE NAVY—ACTIVE LIST—*Continued.*

Name.	Present Duty.	Commission	Name.	Present Duty.	Commission
Wm. H. H. Southerland	Com. New Jersey	July 22,1906	Cameron McR. Winslow	Com. New Hampshire	Jan. 28,1908
Charles E. Fox	Nav. Hosp., Mare Island	Aug. 5,1906	Isaac S. K. Reeves	Mem. B'd Insp. & Survey	Jan. 30,1908
John C. Fremont	Com. Mississippi	Oct. 10,1906	Alexander Sharp	Com. Virginia	Apr. 23,1908
Albert Mertz	Com. L. H. Vessels	Nov. 2,1906	Nathaniel R. Usher	Asst. to Bu. Navigation.	Apr. 23,1908
Vincendon L. Cottman	Com. California	Feb. 8,1907	Frank F. Fletcher	En Route to At. Fleet	May 15,1908
Thomas B. Howard	Com. Ohio	Feb. 24,1907	Frank E. Beatty	Com. Wisconsin	July 1,1908
Walter C. Cowles	Com. Kentucky	Mar. 19,1907	Moses L. Wood	Com. Maryland	July 1,1908
Austin M. Knight	Com. Washington	July 1,1907	Robert M. Doyle	Com. Missouri	July 1,1908
Charles J. Badger	Supt. Naval Academy	July 1,1907	Wythe M Parks	Navy Yard, New York	July 1,1908
Samuel W. B. Diehl	Waiting orders	July 1,1907	Frank H. Bailey	Navy Yard, New York	July 1,1908
Reginald F. Nicholson	Com. Nebraska	July 1,1907	William B. Caperton	Com. Maine	July 1,1908
Edmund B. Underwood	Com. Colorado	July 1,1907	James T. Smith	Com. South Dakota	July 1,1908
Frank A. Wilner	Com. Pennsylvania	July 1,1907	George S. Willits	Navy Yard, Puget Sound,	July 1,1908
Charles B. T. Moore	Navy Yard, Philadelphia	July 1,1907	Walter F. Worthington	Naval Academy	July 1,1908
Ten Eyck D. W. Veeder	Com. Alabama	July 1,1907	William N. Little	Insp. Duty, Bu. St. Eng.	July 1,1908
Alfred Reynolds	Com. Montana	July 1,1907	Frank H. Eldridge	Mem. Nav. Exam. Board	July 4,1908
John K. Barton	Chief Bureau of St. Eng.	July 8,1907	Henry C. Gearing	Naval Station, Olongapo.	July 11,1908
Bradley A. Fiske	Com. Tennessee	Aug. 28,1907	Templin M. Potts	Navy Yard, Wash., D.C.	July 19,1908
Hamilton Hutchins	Com. Kearsarge	Oct. 13,1907	Burns T. Walling	Com. Birmingham	July 20,1908
John M. Bowyer	Com. Illinois	Nov. 8,1907	Clifford J. Boush	Navy Yard, Portsmouth.	Aug. 1,1908
George B. Ransom	Insp. duty, Bu. St. Eng.	Nov. 8,1907	James H. Sears	Com. Concord	Sept. 3,1908
Abraham V. Zane	Navy Yard, Portsmouth.	Dec. 6,1907	Abraham E. Culver	Special Duty, Navy Dept.	Sept. 7,1908
John R. Edwards	Insp. Machinery, Cramps	Jan. 3,1908	Henry T. Mayo	Nav. Secy. L.H.Board	Oct. 25,1908
Stacy Potts	Sick leave	Jan. 28,1908	Charles C. Rogers	Com. Milwaukee	Oct. 30,1908
James M. Helm	Com. Idaho	Jan. 28,1908	John T. Newton	Gen. Insp. Equipment	Nov. 12,1908
Albert B. Willits	Insp. Mach. Camden, N.J.	Jan. 28,1908	Benjamin Tappan	Bd. of Insp. and Survey	Nov. 12,1908

COMMANDERS OF THE NAVY—ACTIVE LIST—NOVEMBER 30, 1908.

Name.	Present Duty.	Commission	Name.	Present Duty.	Commission
Charles F. Pond	Ins. 3d L. H. Dist	Mar. 31,1905	Frederic C. Bowers	Bureau of Steam Eng	Feb. 24,1907
Walter McLean	Com. Cleveland	Mar. 31,1905	George R. Salisbury	Com. Naval Base, Culebra	Mar. 19,1907
Washington I. Chambers	Asst. to Bu. of Ordnance.	Apr. 22,1905	John L. Purcell	Waiting orders	Mar. 19,1907
James C. Gillmore	Chg. Nav. Rec. Sta., N. Y.	Apr. 30,1905	Robert F. Lopez	Ins. 12th L. H. Dist	July 1,1907
Charles A. Gove	Naval Academy	May 6,1905	Frank W. Kellogg	Navy Yard, New York	July 1,1907
De Witt Coffman	Chg. Nav. Mag. Ft. Mifflin	June 16,1905	Reuben O. Bitler	Navy Yard, Norfolk	July 1,1907
Thomas D. Griffin	Com. Paducah	June 26,1905	Harry Phelps	Waiting orders	July 1,1907
Richard T. Mulligan	Bureau of Navigation	June 28,1905	Albert A. Ackerman	Com. Prairie	July 1,1907
Wm. Braunersreuther	Chg. Nav. Mag., Iona Is.	June 30,1905	Leo D. Miner	Navy Yard, Mare Island.	July 1,1907
Francis H. Sherman	Com. Philadelphia	July 1,1905	Albert P. Niblack	Com. Hartford	July 1,1907
William S. Hogg	Com. Glacier	July 1,1905	Edward Simpson	Com. Montgomery	July 1,1607
Reynold T. Hall	Eng. Off. Newport News.	July 1,1905	Thomas W. Kinkaid	Insp. duty, Bu. St'm. Eng.	July 1,1907
William F. Fullam	Com. Nav. Tr. St. Newport	July 1,1905	William S. Sims	Insp. Target Practice	July, 1,1907
Albert G. Winterhalter	Hydrographer	July 1,1905	Louis S. Van Duzer	Ex. Off. Connecticut	July 1,1907
John M. Orchard	Naval Station, Cavite	July 1,1905	Wilson W. Buchanan	Ex. Off. Ohio	July 1,1907
Augustus F. Fechteler	Bd. of Insp. and Survey.	July 1,1905	William J. Maxwell	Com. Marietta	July 1,1907
Edward E. Wright	Com. Chattanooga	July 1,1905	William S. Smith	Bureau of Steam Eng	July 1,1907
Albert Gleaves	Com. St. Louis	July 1,1905	John F. Luby	Navy Yard, Boston	July 1,1907
James P. Parker	Com. Denver	July 1,1905	Hugh Rodman	Ins. 6th L. H. Dist	July 1,1907
Ben W. Hodges	Naval Observatory	July 1,1905	John A. Hoogewerff	Nav. Sta. Olongapo	July 6,1907
Herbert O. Dunn	Nav. Rec. Sta., Baltimore	July 1,1905	Edward E. Capehart	Ex. Off. Louisiana	July 8,1907
Albert W. Grant	Chf. of Staff, At. Fleet	July 1,1905	Henry B. Wilson	Com. Chester	July 12,1907
Valentine S. Nelson	Com. Panther	July 1,1905	Gustav Kaemmerling	Bureau of Steam Eng	July 26,1907
William S. Benson	Com. Albany	July 1,1905	Emil Theiss	Insp. duty Quincy, Mass.	Aug. 28,1907
Frank M. Bostwick	Com. Buffalo	July 1,1905	Spencer S. Wood	Ex. Off. Idaho	Oct. 16,1907
Harry M. Dombaugh	Com. Arkansas	July 1,1905	Guy W. Brown	Ex. Off. No. Carolina	Nov. 8,1907
Thomas S. Rodgers	Navy Yard, Philadelphia	July 1,1905	William B. Fletcher	Naval War College Staff.	Nov. 18,1907
John G. Quinby	Navy Yard, Norfolk	July 1,1905	Marbury Johnston	Com. Galveston	Dec. 6,1907
James H. Glennon	Com. Yorktown	July 8,1905	Edwin A. Anderson	Navy Yard, Mare Island.	Dec. 6,1907
William R. Rush	Com. Ranger	Sept. 9,1905	Joseph L. Jayne	General Board	Jan. 3,1908
Harry S. Knapp	Com. Charleston	Sept. 30,1905	Albert L. Key	Com. Salem	Jan. 28,1908
William L. Rodgers	Naval War College	Dec. 27,1905	William L. Howard	Ex. Off. Mississippi	Jan. 28,1908
Harry McL. P. Huse	Com. Celtic	Feb. 25,1907	Robert B. Higgins	Navy Yard, New York	Jan. 30,1908
Roy C. Smith	Naval War College	Jan. 7,1906	John C. Leonard	Insp. duty, Bu. Ordnance	Apr. 22,1908
George W. McElroy	Insp. duty, Bu. St. Eng.	Jan. 7,1906	John M. Ellicott	Com. Solace	May 15,1908
Robert S. Griffin	Asst. to Bu. St. Eng	Jan. 22,1906	Charles W. Dyson	Bureau of Steam Eng	July 1,1908
Edward Lloyd, Jr.	Com. Wilmington	Feb. 19,1906	Harry George	Navy Yard, New York	July 1,1908
Richard M. Hughes	Com. Helena	Feb. 28,1906	Frederick L. Chapin	Nav. At. Paris & S. Ptsb'rg	July 1,1908
Frank W. Bartlett	Naval Academy	Apr. 13,1906	William C. Herbert	Nav. Sta. Cavite	July 1,1908
Frederick C. Bieg	Bureau of Steam Engin'g	May 13,1906	Alexander S. Halstead	Inspector Bu. Ordnance	July 1,1908
George R. Clark	Naval Academy	June 6,1906	Harry A. Field	Ex. Off. Tennessee	July 1,1908
William P. White	Com. Wolverine	June 6,1906	Chester M. Knepper	Bureau of Ordnance	July 1,1908
George E. Burd	Navy Yard, Boston	June 12,1906	Clarence S. Williams	General Board	July 1,1908
John H. Shipley	Com. Des Moines	June 29,1906	Frank K. Hill	General Board	July 1,1908
James H. Oliver	Ch. of Staff Pacific Fleet	June 30,1906	Roger Wells	Ex. Off. New Hampshire.	July 1,1908
John E. Craven	Com. Dubuque	July 1,1906	John D. McDonald	Com. Castine	July 1,1908
John J. Knapp	Com. Wyoming	July 1,1906	Hilary P. Jones, jr.	Navy Yard, Washington	July 1,1908
John Hood	Com. Tacoma	July 1,1906	William R. Shoemaker	Bureau of Navigation	July 1,1908
Edward E. Hayden	Naval Observatory	July 1,1906	Charles M. Fahs	Ins. 1st L. H. Dist	July 1,1908
Benjamin C. Bryan	Navy Yard, Philadelphia	July 1,1906	Charles P. Plunkett	Insp. duty, Fore Riv. Mass	July, 1,1908
Charles C. Marsh	Com. Yankee	July 1,1906	Volney O. Chase	Bureau of Ordnance	July 4,1908
Charles H. Harlow	Com. Na. St. Guantanamo.	July 1,1906	Patrick W. Hourigan	Ex. Off. New Jersey	July 11,1908
Clarence A. Carr	Navy Yard, Mare Island.	July 22,1906	George R. Slocum	Puget Sound Navy Yard.	July 19,1908
William A. Gill	Com. Rainbow	Aug. 5,1906	William G. Miller	Ex. Off. Minnesota	July 20,1908
Harold P. Norton	Bureau of Steam Engin'g	Oct. 10,1906	George W. Kline	Ex. Off. Georgia	Aug. 1,1908
Frank M. Bennett	Ins. 7th L. H. Dist	Nov. 2,1906	Joseph Strauss	Ex. Off. Montana	Sept. 3,1908
John A. Dougherty	Naval Attache, Tokio	Dec. 11,1906	Robert L. Russell	Ins. 5th L. H. Dist	Sept. 7,1908
John H. Gibbons	Naval Attache, London	Dec. 25,1906	Harrison A. Bispham	Ins. 4th L. H. Dist	Oct. 25,1908
Thomas Snowden	Com. Mayflower	Feb. 8,1907	Armistead Rust	Chg. Surveying Expedi'n	Oct. 30,1908
Thomas F. Carter	Insp. duty Pittsburg	Feb. 18,1907	George R. Evans	Bd. Insp. and Survey	Nov. 12,1908

Abbreviations: Bu.—Bureau; Ch.—Chief; Com.—Commanding; Eng.—Engineer or Engineering; Ex.—Executive; Insp.—Inspector or Inspection; Nav.—Naval; Off.—Officer; Sta.—Station; St.—Steam.

THE NAVY—*Continued.*

VESSELS OF THE UNITED STATES NAVY.

Name.	Class.	Keel Laid.	Displacement, Tons.	Speed, Knots.	Horse-Power.	Cost.	Batteries. Main.	Batteries. Secondary.
Armored Vessels.								
Seagoing Battle-ships.								
Alabama	B S	1896	11,552	17	11,207	$2,650,000	4 13-in. B L R, 14 6-in. R F guns.	16 6-pdr. R F, 2 1-pdr. R F, 2, 3-in. F.
Connecticut	B S	1903	16,000	19	16,500	4,600,000	4 12-in. B L R, 8 8-in. B L R, 12 7-in. B L R.	20 3-in. R F, 12 3-pdr. semi-auto., 4 1-pdr. auto., 2 3-in. field, 6 30-cal. a., 2 30-cal m.
Delaware*	B S	1907	20.000	21	25,000	3,987,000	10 12-in. B L R, 14 5-in. R F.	4 3-pdr. s. a., 4 1-pdr. s. a., 2 3-in. F., 2 30-cal. m.
Florida ‡	B S	....	....	......	....	....	....	....
Georgia	B S	1901	14,948	19	19,000	3,590,000	4 12-in. B L R, 8 8-in. B L R, 12 6-in. R F guns.	12 3-in. R F, 12 3-pdr. R F, 2 3-in. field, 6 30-cal. a., 2 30-cal. m.
Idaho	B S	1904	13,000	17	10,000	2,999,500	4 12-in. B L R, 8 8-in. B L R, 8 7-in. B L R.	12 3-in. R F G, 6 3-pdr. S-A., 2 1-pdr. R F, 2 3-in. field, 6 30-cal. a.
Illinois	B S	1897	11,552	17	12,757	2,595,000	4 13-in. B L R, 14 6-in. R F guns.	16 6-pdr. R F, 2 1-pdr. R F, 2 3-in. F, 4 30-cal. a.
Indiana	B S	1891	10,288	15	9,607	3,063,000	4 13-in. B L R, 8 8-in. B L R, 4 6-in. R F guns.	20 6-pdr. R F, 2 1-pdr. R F, 1 3-in. F, 2 30-cal. a.
Iowa	B S	1893	11,346	17	11,933	3,010,000	4 12-in. B L R, 8 8-in. B L R, 4 4-in. R F guns.	22 6-pdr. R F, 4 1-pdr. R F, 2 3-in. F, 4 30-cal. a.
Kansas	B S	1904	16,000	18	19,545	4,165,000	4 12-in. B L R, 8 8-in. B L R, 12 7-in. B L R.	20 3-in. R F, 12 3-pdr. semi-auto., 2 1-pdr. auto., 2 3-in. field, 2 30-cal. a.
Kearsarge	B S	1896	11,520	17	11,788	2,250,000	4 13-in. B L R, 4 8-in. B L R, 14 5-in. R F guns.	12 6-pdr. R F, 2 1-pdr., 2 3-in. F, 4 30-cal. a.
Kentucky	B S	1896	11,250	17	12,179	2,250,000	4 13-in. B L R, 4 8-in. B L R, 14 5-in. R F guns.	20 6-pdr. R F, 4 1-pdr. R F, 2 3-in. F, 4 30-cal. a.
Louisiana	B S	1903	16,000	19	20,748	3,990,000	4 12-in. B L R, 8 8-in. B L R, 12 7-in. B L R.	20 3-in. R F, 12 3-pdr. semi-automatic, 2 1-pdr. automatic, 2 3-in. field, 6 30-cal. a., 2 30-cal. m.
Maine	B S	1899	12,500	18	15,603	2,885,000	4 12-in. B L R, 16 6-in. R F guns.	6 3-in. R F, 8 3-pdr. R F, 2 1-pdr. R F, 2 3-in. F, 2 30-cal. a.
Massachusetts	B S	1891	10,288	16	10,240	3,063,000	4 13-in. B L R, 8 8-in. B L R.	20 6-pdr. R F, 2 1-pdr. R F, 1 3-in. F, 2 30-cal. a.
Michigan*	B S	1906	16,000	18	16,500	3,585,000	8-12-in. B L R........	22 3-in. semi-auto., 2 3-pdr. s.a., 8 1-pdr. s a., 2 3-in. F, 2 30-cal. a., 2 30 cal. m.
Minnesota	B S	1903	16,000	19	20,235	4,110,000	4 12-in. B L R, 8 8-in. B L R, 12 7-in. B L R.	20 3-in. R F, 12 3-pdr. semi-auto., 2 1-pdr. auto., 2 3-in. field, 2 30-cal. m.
Mississippi	B S	1904	13,000	17	10,000	2,999,500	4 12-in. B L R, 8 8-in. B L R, 8 7-in. B L R.	12 3-in. R F G, 6 3-pdr. S A, 2 1-pdr. R F, 2 3-in. field, 6 [illegible] a.
Missouri	B S	1900	12,500	18	15,845	2,885,000	4 12-in. B L R, 16 6-in. R F guns.	6 3-in. R F, 8 3-pdr. R F, 4 1-pdr. R F, 2 3-in F.
Nebraska	B S	1902	14,948	19	21,283	3,733,600	4 12-in. B L R, 8 8-in. B L R, 12 6-in. R F gns.	12 3-in. R F, 12 3-pdr. R F, 2 3-in. F, 6 30-cal. a., 2 30-cal. m.
New Hampshire	B S	1905	16,000	18	16,500	3,748,000	4 12-in. B L R, 8 8-in. B L R, 12 7-in. B L R.	20 3-in. R F, 12 3-pdr. S A, 2 1-pdr. S A, 2 3-in. field, 6 30-cal. a., 2 30-cal. m.
New Jersey	B S	1902	14,948	19	23,089	3,405,000	4 12-in. B L R, 8 8-in. B L R, 12 6-in. R F guns.	12 3-in. R F, 12 3-pdr. R F, 2 1-pdr. R F, 2 3-in. field, 4 30-cal. a., 2 30-cal. m.
North Dakota*	B S	1907	20,000	21	25,000	4,377,000	10 12-in. B L R, 14 5-in. R F.	4 3-pdr. s. a., 4 1-pdr. s. a., 2 3-in. F., 2 30-cal. m.
Ohio	B S	1899	12,500	18	16,220	2,899,000	4 12-in. B L R, 16 6-in. R F guns.	6 3-in. R F, 8 3-pdr. R F, 6 1-pdr. R F, 2 3-in. F, 2 30-cal. a.
Oregon	B S	1891	10,288	17	11,037	3,222,810	4 13-in. B L R, 8 8-in. B L R.	20 6-pdr. R F, 2 1-pdr. R F, 4 30-cal. a.
Rhode Island	B S	1902	14,948	19	20,310	3,405,000	4 12-in. B L R, 8 8-in. B L R, 12 6-in. R F guns.	12 3-in. R F, 12 3-pdr. R F, 2 1-pdr. R F, 2 3-in. F, 4 30-cal. a., 2 30-cal. m.
South Carolina	B S	1906	16,000	18	16,500	3,540,000	8 12-in. B L R........	22 3-in. semi-automatic, 2 3-pdr. S-A, 8 1-pdr. S-A, 2 3-in. F, 2 30-cal. a., 2 30-cal. m.
Texas	B S	1889	6,315	17	8,507	2,500,000	2 12-in. B L R, 6 6-in. R F guns.	12 6-pdr. R F, 4 1-pdr. R F, 4 37-mm. H R C, 2 Colts.
Utah ‡	B S	....	....	......	....	....	....	....
Vermont	B S	1904	16,000	18	17,982	4,179,000	4 12-in. B L R, 8 8-in. B L R, 12 7-in. B L R.	20 3-in. R F, 12 3-pdr. semi-automatic, 4 1-pdr. automatic, 2 3-in. field, 6 30-cal. a., 2 30-cal. m.
Virginia	B S	1902	14,948	19	22,841	3,590,000	4 12-in. B L R, 8 8-in. B L R, 12 6-in. R F guns.	12 3-in. R F, 12 3-pdr. R F, 2 3-in F, 6 30-cal. a., 2 30-cal. m.
Wisconsin	B S	1897	11,552	17	12,452	2,674,950	4 13-in. B L R, 14 6-in. R F guns.	16 6-pdr. R F, 6 1-pdr. R F, 2 3-in. F, 4 30-cal. a.

* Under construction. ‡ Not yet building or contracted for.

THE NAVY—*Continued.*

VESSELS OF THE UNITED STATES NAVY.—Continued.

Name.	Class.	Keel Laid.	Displacement, Tons.	Speed, Knots.	Horse-Power.	Cost.	Batteries. Main.	Batteries. Secondary.
ARMORED CRUISERS.								
Brooklyn	A C	1893	9,215	22	18,425	$2,986,000	8 8-in. B L R, 12 5-in. R F guns.	12 6-pdr. R F, 4 1-pdr. R F, 2 3-in. R F field, 4 30-cal. a., 1 30-cal. m.
California	A C	1902	13,680	22	29,000	3,800,000	4 8-in. B L R, 14 6-in. R F guns.	18 3-in. R F, 12 3-pdr. S A R F, 2 1-pdr. R F, 2 3-in. R F field, 4 30-cal. a., 2 30-cal. m.
Colorado	A C	1901	13,680	22	26,837	3,780,000	4 8-in. B L R, 14 6-in. R F guns.	18 3-in. R F, 12 3 pdr. S A R F, 2 1-pdr. R F, 2 3-in. R F field, 2 machine, 6 a. guns, Colts.
Maryland	A C	1901	13,680	22	28,059	3,775,000	4 8-in. B L R, 14 6-in. R F guns.	18 3-in. R F, 12 3-pdr. S A R F, 2 1-pdr. R F, 2 3-in. R F field, 2 machine, 6 a. guns, Colts.
Montana	A C	1905	14,500	22	23,000	4,400,000	4 10-in. B L R, 16 6-in. R F.	22 3-in. R F, 12 3-pdr. S A, 2 3-in. field, 2 30-cal. machine, 2 30-cal. automatic.
New York	A C	1890	8,150	21	17,075	2,985,000	4 8-in. B L R, 10 5-in. R F guns.	8 3-in. R F, 4 3-pdr. R F.
North Carolina	A C	1905	14,500	22	23,000	4,400,000	4 10-in. B L R, 16 6-in. R F.	22 3-in. R F, 12 3-pdr. S A, 4 1-pdr. S A, 2 3-in. field, 2 30-cal. machine, 2 30-cal. automatic.
Pennsylvania	A C	1901	13,680	22	28,600	3,890,000	4 8-in. B L R, 14 6-in. R. F. G.	18 3-in. R F, 12 3-pdr. S A, 2 1-pdr. R F, 2 3-in. field, 2 machine, 6 automatic.
South Dakota	A C	1902	13,680	22	28,543	3,750,000	4 8-in. B L R, 14 6-in. R. F guns.	18 3-in. R F, 12 3-pdr S A, 2 1-pdr. R F, 2 3-in. R F field, 4 30-cal. a, 2 30-cal. m.
Tennessee	A C	1903	14,500	22	26,963	4,035,000	4 10-in. B L R, 16 6-in. R F guns.	22 3-in. R F, 12 3-pdr. S A, 2 1-pdr. R F, 2 3-in. R F, 6 automatic.
Washington	A C	1903	14,500	22	27,152	4,035,000	4 10-in. B L R, 16 6-in. R F guns.	22 3-in. R F, 12 3-pdr. S A, 2 1-pdr. R F, 2 3-in. R F, 2 machine, 2 automatic.
West Virginia	A C	1901	13,680	22	26,135	3,885,000	4 8-in. B L R, 14 6-in. R F guns.	18 3-in. R F, 12 3-pdr. S A, 8 1-pdr. R F, 2 3-in. R F field, 2 machine, 2 automatic.
RAM.								
Katahdin	R	1891	2,150	16.11	5,014	930,000	4 6-pdr. R F guns.	....
DBL. TURRET MONITORS.								
Amphitrite	C D	1874	3,990	10.5	1,600	†	4 10-in. B L R, 2 4-in. R F guns.	2 6-pdr. R F, 2 3-pdr. R F, 5 1 pdr. R F, 1 3-in. F, 1 30-cal. a, 2 37-in. mm. R C.
Miantonomoh	C D	1874	3,990	10.5	1,426	†	4 10-in. B L R.	2 6-pdr. R F, 2 3-pdr. R F, 4 1-pdr. R F, 1 Colt.
Monadnock	C D	1875	3,990	12	3,000	†	4 10-in. B L R, 2 4-in. R F guns.	4 6-pdr. R F, 4 1 pdr. R F.
Monterey	C D	1889	4,084	13.6	5,104	1,628,950	2 12-in. B L R, 2 10-in. B L R.	6 6-pdr. R F, 4 1-pdr. R F, 2 Colts.
Puritan	C D	1875	6,060	12.4	3,700	†	4 12-in. B L R, 6 4-in. R F guns.	6 6-pdr. R F G, 2 1-pdr. R F G, 2 Colt automatic, 2 machine.
Terror	C D	1874	3,990	10.5	1,600	†	4 10-in. B L R, 4 4-in. R F guns.	2 6-pdr. R F, 2 3-pdr. R F, 2 37 mm. H R C, 2 1-pdr. R F.
SIN. TURRET MONITORS								
Arkansas	C D	1899	3,225	12.03	1,739	960,000	2 12-in. B L R, 4 4-in. R F guns.	3 6-pdr. S A, 4 1-pdr. a., 4 1-pdr. R F, 2 30-cal. a.
Florida ‡	C D	1899	3,225	12.40	2,336	925,000	2 12-in. B L R, 4 4-in. R F guns.	3 6-pdr. S A, 4 1-pdr. a., 4 1-pdr. R F, 2 30-cal. a.
Nevada	C D	1899	3,225	13.04	1,970	962,000	2 12-in. B L R, 4 4-in. R F guns.	3 6-pdr. S A, 4 1-pdr. a., 4 1-pdr., R F, 2 30-cal. a.
Wyoming	C D	1899	3,225	11.80	2,359	975,000	2 12-in. B L R, 4 4-in. R F guns.	3 6-pdr. S A, 4 1-pdr. a., 4 1-pdr. R F, 2 30-cal. a.
UNARMORED STEEL VESSELS								
Albany	P C	....	3,430	20.5	7,400	....	10 5-in. R F guns.	10 3-pdr. S A, 2 1-pdr. R F, 1 3-in. F, 2 Colts.
Atlanta	P C	1883	3,000	15.60	3,500	617,000	6 6-in. R F, 2 8-in. B L R.	6 6-pdr. R F, 4 1-pdr. R F, 2 Colts, 1 3-in. R F field.
Baltimore	P C	1887	4,413	20.09	8,778	1,325,000	12 6-in. R F guns.	6 3-pdr. R F, 6 3-in. R F, 4 1-pdr. R F, 4 automatic, 1 3-in. R F field, 4 30-cal. a.
Boston	P C	1883	3,035	15.60	4,300	619,000	6 6-in. R F, 2 8-in. B L R.	6 6-pdr. R F, 2 1-pdr. R F, 2 Colts, 1 3-in. R F field. 2 30-cal. a
Charleston	P C	1902	9,700	22	27,200	2,740,000	14 6-in. R F.	18 3-in. R F, 12 3-pdr. S A, 8 1-pdr. automatic, 8 1-pdr. R F, 2 30-cal. machine, 4 30-cal. automatic, 2 3-in. field.
Chattanooga	P C	1900	3,200	16.5	5,303	1,039,966	10 5-in. R F guns.	8 6-pdr. R F, 2 1-pdr. R F, 4 Colt automatic, 1 3-in. field.
Chicago	P C	1883	4,500	18	9,000	889,000	4 8-in. B L R, 14 5-in. R F guns.	9 6-pdr. R F, 2 1-pdr. R F, 2 Colts, 1 3-in. R F field.
Cincinnati	P C	1890	3,183	19	8,290	1,100,000	11 5-in. R F guns.	8 6-pdr. R F, 2 1-pdr. R F, 2 Colts, 1 3-in. R F field.
Cleveland	P C	1900	3,200	16.5	4,640	1,041,650	10 5-in. R F guns.	8 6-pdr. S A, 2 1-pdr. R F, 4 Colt automatic, 1 3-in. field.
Columbia	P C	1890	7,375	22.8	18,269	2,725,000	1 8-in. B L R, 2 6-in. R F, 8 4-in. R F guns.	12 6-pdr. R F, 2 1-pdr. R F, 2 Colts, 1 3-in. R F field.

† Appropriation to complete Amphitrite, Miantonomoh, Monadnock, Puritan and Terror, $3,178,046. ‡ Name to be changed.

THE NAVY—*Continued.*

VESSELS OF THE UNITED STATES NAVY.—Continued

Name.	Class.	Keel Laid.	Displacement, Tons.	Speed, Knots.	Horse-Power.	Cost.	Batteries. Main.	Batteries. Secondary.
Denver	P C	1900	3,191	16.75	6,135	$1,080,000	10 5-in. R F guns.	8 6-pdr. S A, 2 1-pdr. R F, 4 Colt automatic, 1 3-in. field.
Des Moines	P C	1900	3,200	16.5	5,340	1,065,000	10 5-in. R F guns.	8 6-pdr. R F, 2 1-pdr. R F, 4 Colt automatic, 1 3-in. field.
Detroit	C	1890	2,072	19	5,207	612,500	10 5-in. R F guns.	6 6 pdr. R F, 2 1-pdr. R F, 2 Colts, 1 3-in. R F field.
Galveston	P C	1901	3,200	16.5	5,073	1,027,000	10 5-in. R F guns.	8 6-pdr. S A, 2 1-pdr. R F, 4 Colt automatic, 1 3-in. field.
Marblehead	C	1890	2,072	18.4	4,937	674,000	10 5-in. R F guns.	6 6-pdr. R F, 2 1-pdr. R F, 2 Colts, 1 3-in. field.
Milwaukee	P C	1902	9,700	22	24,000	2,825,000	14 6-in. R F guns.	18 3-in. R F, 12 3-pdr. S A, 4 1-pdr. automatic, 8 1-pdr. R F, 2 .30 cal. machine, 8 .30 cal. automatic, 2 3-in. field.
Minneapolis	P C	1891	7,350	23.073	20,544	2,690,000	1 8-in. B L R, 2 6-in. R F, 8 4-in. R F guns.	12 6-pdr. R F, 2 1-pdr. R F, 2 Colts, 1 3-in. R F field.
Montgomery	C	1890	2,072	19.05	5,580	612,500	10 5-in. R F guns.	4 6-pdr. R F.
Newark	P C	1888	4,083	19	8,727	1,248,000	12 6-in. R F guns.	6 3-in R F, 6 3-pdr. S. A, 4 1-pdr. R F, 1 3-in. field, 4 .30 cal. a.
New Orleans	P C	....	3,430	20	7,500	....	10 5-in. R F.	10 3-pdr. S A, 2 1-pdr. R F, 2 .30 cal. automatic, 1 3-in. field.
Olympia	P C	1891	5,865	21.686	17,080	1,796,000	10 5-in. R F guns, 4 8-in. B L R, 11 5-in. R.	14 6-pdr. R F, 4 1-pdr. R F, 2 Colts.
Philadelphia	P C	1888	4,410	19.678	8,653	1,350,000	....	Housed over.
Raleigh	P C	1889	3,183	19	8,500	1,100,000	11 5-in. R F guns.	8 6-pdr. R F, 2 1-pdr. R F, 2 Colts, 1 3-in. field.
Reina Mercedes‡	C	....	2,835	17	....	....	....	Housed over.
San Francisco	P C	1888	4,083	19.525	9,761	1,428,000	12 6-in. R F.	Housed over.
St. Louis	P C	1902	9,700	22	27,264	2,740,000	14 6-in. R F guns.	18 3-in. R F, 12 3-pdr. S A, 4 1-pdr. automatic, 8 1-pdr. R F, 2 .30 cal. machine, 8 .30 cal. automatic, 2 3-in. field.
Tacoma	P C	1900	3,200	16.58	5,287	1,041,900	10 5-in. R F guns.	8 6-pdr. S A, 2 1-pdr. R F, 4 Colt automatic, 1 3-in. field.
UNARMORED STEEL VESSELS, SCOUT CRUISERS.								
Birmingham	S C	1905	3,750	24	16,000	1,556,000	2 5-in. R F, 6 3-in. R F.	2 torpedo tubes.
Chester	S C	1905	3,750	24	16,000	1,688,000	2 5-in. R F, 6 3-in. R F.	2 torpedo tubes.
Salem	S C	....	3,750	24	16,000	1,556,000	2 5-in. R F, 6 3-in. R F.	2 torpedo tubes.
GUNBOATS.								
Bennington	G B	1888	1,710	17.5	3,380	490,000	6 6-in. R F.	4 6-pdr. R F, 2 .30 cal. Colts, 4 1-pdr. R F.
Castine	G B	1891	1,177	16	2,180	318,500	8 4-in. R F guns.	4 6-pdr. R F, 2 1-pdr. R F, 1 Colt, a.
Concord	G B	1888	1,710	16.8	3,359	490,000	6 6-in. R F.	4 3-pdr. S A, 2 1-pdr. R F, 2 .30 cal. Colts.
Don Juan de Austria‡	G B	....	1,130	12	1,500	180,000	6 3-in. R F guns.	4 6-pdr. R F, 2 1-pdr. R F, 2 Colts.
General Alava‡	G B	....	1,115	10	770	....	....	2 6-pdr., 2 1-pdr., R F.
Helena	G B	1894	1,397	13	1,988	280,000	8 4-in. R F guns.	4 6-pdr. R F, 2 Colts.
Isla de Cuba‡	G B	....	1,030	13	2,700	215,000	6 3-in. R F guns.	4 6-pdr. R F, 4 Colts.
Isla de Luzon‡	G B	....	1,030	11	2,700	215,000	4 4-in. R F guns.	4 6-pdr. R F, 4 Colts.
Machias	G B	1891	1,177	15.46	2,046	318,500	8 4-in. R F guns.	4 6-pdr. R F, 2 1-pdr. R F, 2 Colts.
Nashville	G B	1894	1,371	16.	2,536	280,000	8 4-in. R F guns.	4 6-pdr. R F, 2 1-pdr. R F, 2 Colts.
Petrel	G B	1887	890	11.79	1,095	247,000	4 6-in. R F.	2 3-pdr. R F, 2 1-pdr. R F, 2 Colts, a.
Wilmington	G B	1894	1,397	15.08	1,894	280,000	8 4-in. R F guns.	4 6-pdr. R F, 4 1-pdr. R F, 4 Colts.
Yorktown	G B	1887	1,740	16	3,392	455,000	6 6-in. R F guns.	4 3-pdr. R F, 4 1-pdr. R F, 2 Colts.
Annapolis	C G B	1896	1,010	13	1,227	227,700	6 4-in. R F guns.	4 6-pdr. R F, 2 1-pdr. R F, 2 Colts.
Dubuque	C G B	1903	1,085	12	1,193	295,000	6 4-in. R F guns.	4 6-pdr. R F, 2 1-pdr. R F, 2 Colts.
Marietta	C G B	1896	1,990	13	1,054	223,000	6 4-in. R F guns.	4 6-pdr. R F, 2 1-pdr. R F, 1 Colt.
Newport	C G B	1896	1,010	12	1,008	229,400	6 4-in. R F guns.	4 6-pdr. R F, 2 1-pdr. R F, 1 Colt.
Paducah	C G B	1903	1,085	12	1,200	355,000	6 4-in. R F guns.	4 6-pdr. R F, 2 1-pdr. R F, 2 Colts.
Princeton	C G B	1896	1,010	10.64	835	230,000	6 4-in. R F guns.	4 6-pdr. R F, 2 1-pdr. R F, 2 Colts.
Vicksburg	C G B	1895	1,010	13	1,118	229,400	6 4-in. R F guns.	4 6-pdr. R F, 2 1-pdr. R F, 2 Colts.
Wheeling	C G B	1896	990	12	1,081	219,000	6 4-in. R F guns.	4 6-pdr. R F, 2 1-pdr. R F, 1 Colt.
SPECIAL CLASS.								
Dolphin	D B	1883	1,486	16	2,253	315,000	2 4-in. R F guns.	3 6-pdr. R F, 4 3-pdr. R F, 2 Colts.
Vesuvius	D G B	1904	929	21	3,795	350,000	3 15-in. dynamite guns.	1 3-pdr. R F.
Cumberland	T S	1904	1,800	..	....	410,000	6 4-in. R F guns.	4 6-pdr. R F guns, 2 1-pdr. R F guns, 2 Colts.
Intrepid	T S	1904	1,800	..	....	410,000	6 4-in. R F guns.	4 6-pdr. R F guns, 2 1-pdr. R F guns, 2 Colts.
Boxer	T B	1904	345	.	....	50,000	....	....
Severn	T S	1895	1,175	..	....	112,600	6 4-in. R F guns.	4 6-pdr. R F guns, 2 1-pdr. R F guns, 2 Colts.
AUXILIARY CRUISERS.								
Buffalo	S C	1892	6,000	14.5	3,600	575,000	2 5-in., 4 4-in. R F guns.	2 6-mm. Colts, 6 6-pdr.
Dixie	S C	1893	6,114	14	3,800	575,000	8 5-in. R F guns.	4 6 & 4 1-pdr., 2 Colts, 1 3 in. f.
Panther	I C	1889	3,380	13	....	375,000	6 5-in., 2 4-in. R F guns	6 3-pdr., 1 Colt, 1 3-in. field
Prairie	I C	1890	6,620	14.5	3,800	575,000	8 6-in. R F guns.	6 6-pdr., 4 3-pdr., 2 Colts, 4 1-pdr.
Yankee	I C	1892	6,225	12.5	3,800	575,000	8 5-in. R F guns.	6 6-pdr., 2 1-pdr., 2 Colts.

* Under construction. ‡ Captured from Spain.

THE NAVY—*Continued.*

VESSELS OF THE UNITED STATES NAVY.—Continued.

Name.	Class.	Keel Laid.	Displacement, Tons.	Speed, Knots.	Horse Power.	Cost.	Batteries. Main.	Batteries. Secondary.
Torpedo Boats.								
Bagley	T B	1900	175	29	4,200	$161,000	....	3 1-pdr. R F, 3 18-in. W T.
Bailey	T B	1898	280	30	5,600	210,000	....	4 6-pdr. R F, 2 18-in. W T.
Barcelo‡	T B	....	66	17	600	....	....	....
Barney	T B	1900	175	29	4,200	161,000	....	3 1-pdr. R F, 3 18-in. W T.
Biddle	T B	1900	175	28	4,200	161,000	....	3 1-pdr. R F, 3 18-in. W T.
Blakeley	T B	1899	196	26	3,000	159,400	....	3 1-pdr. R F, 3 18-in. W T.
Cushing	T B	1888	105	22.5	1,720	82,750	....	3 1-pdr. R F, 3 18-in. W T.
Dahlgren	T B	1897	146	30	4,200	194,000	....	4 1-pdr. R F, 2 18-in. W T.
Davis	T B	1897	154	23	1,750	81,546	....	3 1-pdr. R F, 3 18-in. W T.
De Long	T B	1899	196	26	3,000	159,400	....	3 1-pdr. R F, 3 18-in. W T.
Du Pont	T B	1896	165	28	....	144,000	....	4 1-pdr. R F, 3 18-in. W T.
Ericsson	T B	1892	120	24	1,800	113,500	....	4 1-pdr. R F, 3 18-in. W T.
Farragut	T B	1897	279	30	5,878	227,500	....	4 6-pdr. R F, 2 18-in. W T.
Foote	T B	1896	142	24	2,000	97,500	....	3 1-pdr. R F, 3 18-in. W T.
Fox	T B	1897	154	23	1,750	81,546	....	3 1-pdr. R F, 3 18-in. W T.
Goldsborough	T B	1898	255	30	6,000	214,500	....	4 6-pdr. R F, 2 18-in. W T.
Gwin	T B	1897	45	20	850	39,000	....	1 1-pdr. R F, 2 18-in. W T.
MacKenzie	T B	1897	65	20	850	48,500	....	1 1-pdr. R F, 2 18-in. W T.
Manly	T B	...	....	19	850	24,250	....	2 1-pdr. R F, 2 18-in. W T.
McKee	T B	1897	65	..	850	45,000	....	2 1-pdr. R F, 2 18-in. W T.
Morris	T B	1897	104	24	1,750	85,000	....	4 1-pdr. R F, 3 18-in. W T.
Nicholson*	T B	1898	218	26	....	165,000	....	3 1-pdr. R F, 3 18-in. W T.
O'Brien	T B	1898	219	26	....	165,000	....	3 1-pdr. R F, 3 18-in. W T.
Porter	T B	1896	165	28	....	144,000	....	4 1-pdr. R F, 3 18-in. W T.
Rodgers	T B	1896	143	24	2,295	97,500	....	3 1-pdr. R F, 3 18-in. W T.
Rowan	T B	1896	210	27	3,200	160,000	....	4 1-pdr. R F, 3 18-in. W T.
Shubrick	T B	1899	200	26	3,375	129,750	....	3 1-pdr. R F, 3 18-in. W T.
Somers	T B	....	150	17	1,900	72,997	....	4 1-pdr. R F, 3 18-in. W T.
Stiletto	T B	1888	318	18	359	25,000	....	....
Stockton	T B	1899	200	26	3,275	129,750	....	3 1-pdr. R F, 3 18-in. W T.
Stringham	T B	1898	340	30	7,200	236,000	....	4 6-pdr. R F, 2 18-in. W T.
T. A. M. Craven	T B	1897	146	30	4,200	194,000	....	4 1 pdr. R F. 2 18-in. W T.
Talbot	T B	1897	46	21	850	39,000	....	1 1-pdr. R F, 2 18-in. W T.
Thornton	T B	1899	200	25	3,000	129,750	....	3 1-pdr. R F, 3 18-in. W T.
Tingey	T B	1899	165	25	3,000	168,000	....	3 1-pdr. R F, 3 18-in. W T.
Wilkes	T B	1899	165	26	3,495	146,000	....	3 1-pdr. R F, 3 18-in. W T.
Winslow	T B	1896	142	24	2,000	97,500	....	3 1-pdr. R F, 3 18-in. W T.
								....
Submarine.								....
Adder	S T B	1900	120	8	160	170,000	....	1 torpedo tube, 3 W T.
Bonita*	......	....	....	....	....	....	....	....
Cuttlefish	S T B	....	....	....	....	....	....	....
Grampus	S T B	1900	120	8	160	170,000	....	1 torpedo tube, 3 W T.
Grayling*	......	....	....	....	....	....	....	....
Holland	S T B	....	74	8	45	150,000	....	1 torpedo tube, 3 W T.
Moccasin	S T B	1900	120	8	160	170,000	....	1 torpedo tube, 3 W T.
Norwhal*	......	....	....	....	....	....	....	....
Octopus	S T B	....	....	....	....	....	....	....
Pike	S T B	1900	120	8	160	170,000	....	1 torpedo tube, 3 W T.
Plunger	S T B	1901	168	8	160	170,000	....	2 W T.
Porpoise	S T B	1900	120	8	160	170,000	....	1 torpedo tube, 3 W T.
Salmon*	......	....	....	....	....	....	....	....
Snapper*	......	....	....	....	....	....	....	....
Stingray*	......	....	....	....	....	....	....	....
Shark	S T B	1901	120	8	160	170,000	....	1 torpedo tube, 3 W T.
Tarpon*	......	....	....	....	....	....	....	....
Tarantula	S T B	....	....	....	....	....	....	....
Viper	S T B	....	....	....	....	....	....	....
Tor.-Boat Destroyers.								
Bainbridge	T D	1899	420	29	8,000	283,000	....	2 3-in. & 5 6-pd. R F, 2 18-in. W T.
Burrows*	......	....	....	....	....	....	....	....
Barry	T D	1899	420	29	8,000	283,000	....	2 3-in. R F, 5 6-pdr. R F, 2 18-in. W T.
Chauncey	T D	....	420	29	8,000	283,000	....	2 3-in. R F, 5 6-pdr. R F, 2 18-in. W T.
Dale	T B D	1899	420	28	8,000	260,000	....	2 18-in. W T, 2 3-in. R F, and 5 6-pdr. R F.
Decatur	T B D	1899	420	28.10	8,000	260,000	....	2 18-in. W T, 2 3-in. R F, and 5 6-pdr. R F.
Drayton*	......	....	....	....	....	....	....	....
Flusser*	......	....	....	....	....	....	....	....
Hopkins	T B D	1899	408	29.02	7,200	291,000	....	2 18-in. W T. 2 3-in. R F, and 5 6-pdr. R F.
Hull	T B D	1899	408	28.04	7,200	291,000	....	2 18-in. W T, 2 3-in. R F, and 5 6-pdr. R F.
Lamson*	......	....	....	....	....	....	....	....
Lawrence	T B D	1899	446	28.41	6,375	281,000	....	2 18-in. W T, 2 3-in. R F. and 5 6-pdr. R F.
Macdonough	T B D	1899	430	28.03	6,125	281,000	....	2 18-in. W T, 7 6-pdr. S-A.
Mayrant*	......	....	....	....	....	....	....	....
McCall*	......	....	....	....	....	....	....	....
Paulding*	......	....	....	....	....	....	....	....

* Under construction or contracted for.

THE NAVY—*Continued.*

VESSELS OF THE UNITED STATES NAVY.—Continued.

Name	Class.	Keel Laid.	Dis-placement, Tons.	Speed, Knots	Horse Power.	Cost.	Batteries. Main.	Batteries. Secondary.
Paul Jones	T B D	1899	480	28.91	7,980	$285,000	....	2 18-in. W T, 2 3-in. R F, and 5 6-pdr. R F.
Perkins*	......	....	....	....	....	....	....	....
Perry	T B D	1899	480	28.32	9,100	285,000	....	2 18-in. W T, 2 3-in. R F, and 5 6-pdr. R F.
Preble	T B D	1899	480	28.03	7,600	285,000	....	2 18-in. W T, 2 3-in. R F, and 5 6-pdr. R F.
Preston*	......	....	....	....	....	....	....	....
Reid*	......	....	....	....	....	....	....	....
Roe*	......	....	....	....	....	....	....	....
Smith*	......	....	....	....	....	....	....	....
Sterrett*	......	....	....	....	....	....	....	....
Stewart	T B D	1900	420	29.69	8,000	282,000	....	2 18-in. W T, 2 3-in. R F, and 5 6-pdr. R F.
Terry*	......	....	....	....	....	....	....	....
Truxton	T B D	1899	433	29.58	8,300	286,000	....	2 18-in. W T, 2 3-in. R F, and 6 6-pdr. R F.
Warrington*	......	....	....	....	....	....	....	....
Whipple	T B D	1899	433	28.24	8,300	286,000	....	2 18-in. W T, 2 3-in. R F, and 6 6-pdr. R F.
Worden	T B D	1899	433	29.86	8,300	286,000	....	2 18-in. W T, 2 3-in. R F, and 6 6-pdr. R F.

Under construction or contracted for.

VESSELS OF THE NAVY IN COMMISSION.

CORRECTED TO NOVEMBER 10, 1908.

ATLANTIC FLEET.

FIRST SQUADRON.

Rear-Admiral Charles S. Sperry, Commander.

FIRST DIVISION.

Connecticut, 1st C. B. S. (Flagship of Rear-Admiral Sperry), Capt. Hugo Osterhaus.
Kansas, 1st C. B. S.. Capt. C. E. Vreeland.
Vermont, 1st C. B. S., Capt. Frauk F. Fletcher.
Minnesota, 1st C. B. S. Capt. J. Hubbard.

SECOND DIVISION.

Rear-Admiral Richard Wainwright, Commander.

Georgia, 1st C. B. S. (Flagship of Rear-Admiral Wainwright), Capt. Edward F. Qualtrough.
Nebraska, 1st C.B.S.. Capt. R. F. Nicholson.
New Jersey, 1st C. B. S., Capt. Wm. H. H. Southerland.
Rhode Island, 1st C. B. S., Capt. Joseph P. Murdock.

SECOND SQUADRON.

THIRD DIVISION.

Rear-Admiral Seaton Schroeder, Commander.

Louisiana, 1st C. B. S. (Flagship of Rear-Admiral Schroeder), Capt. Kossuth Niles.
Virginia, 1st C.B S., Capt. Alexander Sharp.
Ohio, 1st C. B. S., Capt. Thos. B. Howard.
Missouri, 1st C. B. S., Capt. Robert M. Doyle

VESSELS ON SPECIAL SERVICE OR UNASSIGNED.

Abarenda (col.), mer. com., W. C. Fincke, Master.
Alabama, 1st C. B. S.. Capt. Ten Eyck D. W. Veeder.
Albany, P. C...Com. William S. Benson.
Arkansas, M..Com. Harry M. Dombaugh.
Birmingham (scout cruiser), Capt. Burns T. Walling.
Brutus (col.), mer. com., Charles O. Tilton, Master.
Buffalo, C.C....Com. Frank M. Bostwick.
Cæsar (col.), mer. com., Richard J. Easton.
Chester (scout cruiser), Com. Henry B. Wilson.
Chicago, P. C.....Com. Albert P. Niblack.
Des Moines. P. C..Com. John H. Shipley.
Dubuque, G.......Com. John E. Craven.
Eagle, C. G..Lieut.-Com. G. R. Marvell.
Fortune (tug).....Lieut. Edwin H. Dodd.
Grampus (submarine), Lieut. Edwin H. Dodd.
Hannibal (collier), mer. com., Albert B. Randall, Master.
Hist (surveying ship), Com. Armistead Rust.
Indiana, 1st C.B.S. Capt. John B. Collins.
Iroquois (tug)....Lieut.-Com. S. E. Moses.
Lebanon (collier), merchant complement, Jeremiah Merithew, Master.
Marietta, G....Com. William J. Maxwell.
Mayflower (despatch boat), Com. Thomas Snowdon.
Montgomery (torpedo experimental ship), Com. Edward Simpson.
Nero (collier), mer. com., William R. Kennedy, Master.
Nevada, M....Com. Harry M. Dombaugh.
Olympia, P. C....Com. Albert P. Niblack.
Osceola (tug). Chief Btsn. Arthur Smith.
Paduach, G.....Com. Thomas D. Griffin.
Peoria............Btsn. Harold S. Olsen.
Pike (submarine), Lieut. Kirby B. Crittenden.
Potomac (tug), Chief Btsn. Ernest V. Sandstrom.
Prairie, C. C...Com. Albert A. Ackerman.
Ranger..........Com. William R. Rush.
Rocket (tug)...Chief Btsn. John Mahony.
Salem (scout cruiser), Com. Albert L. Key.
Scorpion, G., Lieut.-Com. Geo. W. Logan. Station ship at Constantinople.
Sterling (collier), mer. com., Gustav E. Peterson, Master.
Sylph, C. G.......Lieut. Roger Williams.
Tacoma, P. C..........Com. John Hood.
Triton (tug), Chief Btsn. August Ohmsen.
Uncas (tug), Chief Btsn. August Wohltman.
Wolverine, C....Com. William P. White.
Wyoming, M.......Com. John J. Knapp.
Yankee, C. C.....Com. Charles C. Marsh.
Yorktown, G....Com. James H. Glennon. At Mare Island, Cal.

THIRD TORPEDO FLOTILLA.

Lieut. Willis G. Mitchell, Flotilla Commander.

Stringham (torpedo boat), Lieut. Willis G. Mitchell.
Barney (torpedo boat). Ensign George C. Pegram.
Tingey (torpedo boat), Lieut. James O. Richardson.
De Long (torpedo boat), Lieut. Frank H. Sadler.
Thornton (torpedo boat), Lieut. Charles A. Blakeley.

Abbreviations. 1st C. B. S.—First-class battleship. A. C.—Armored cruiser. P. C.—Protected cruiser. C. C.—Converted cruiser. C.—Cruiser. C. G.—Converted gunboat. Col.—Collier. Dest.—Destroyer. G.—Gunboat. M.—Monitor. Mer. Com.—Merchant complement. T. B.—Torpedo boat. Sta. ship—Station ship. R. S.—Receiving ship.

THE NAVY—*Continued.*

FOURTH DIVISION.

Rear-Admiral William P. Potter, Commander.

Wisconsin, 1st C. B. S. (Flagship of Rear-Admiral Potter), Capt. Frank E. Beatty.
Illinois, 1st C. B. S..Capt. J. M. Bowyer.
Kentucky, 1st C. B. S., Capt. Walter C. Cowles.
Kearsarge, 1st C. B. S., Capt. Hamilton Hutchins.

THIRD SQUADRON.

Rear-Admiral Conway H. Arnold, Commander.

FIFTH DIVISION.

Dolphin,* Despatch Boat, Lieut.-Com., Thomas Washington.
Idaho, 1st C. B.S...Capt. James M. Helm.
Maine,† 1st C. B. S., Capt. William B. Caperton.
Mississippi, 1st C. B. S., Capt. John C. Fremont.
Montana, A. C. ..Capt. Alfred Reynolds.
New Hampshire, 1st C. B. S., Capt. Cameron McR. Winslow.
North Carolina, A. C., Capt. William A. Marshall.

* When the Maine becomes flagship the Dolphin will be assigned to special service.
† The Maine has been designated as the flagship of the Third Squadron, Atlantic Fleet.

FLEET AUXILIARIES.

Ajax (collier), mer. com., Joseph S. Hutchinson, Master.
Celtic (supply ship), Commander Harry McL. P. Huse.
Culgoa (supply ship), Lieut.-Com. John B. Patton.
Panther (repair ship), Com. Valentine S. Nelson.
Yankton (tender), Lieut.-Commander Charles B. McVay.

PACIFIC FLEET.

Rear-Admiral William T. Swinburne, Commander-in-Chief.

Send mail for war vessels stationed at points in the Pacific addressed to the person, with the name of the ship and "Pacific Station, via San Francisco, Cal."

FIRST SQUADRON.

FIRST DIVISION.

West Virginia, A. C. (Flagship of Rear-Admiral Swinburne), Capt. Alexander McCrackin.
Colorado, A. C., Capt. Edmund B. Underwood.
Maryland, A.C......Capt. Moses L. Wood.
Pennsylvania, A. C., Capt. Frank A. Wilner.

SECOND DIVISION.

Rear-Admiral Uriel Sebree, Commander.

Tennessee, A. C. (Flagship of Rear-Admiral Uriel Sebree), Capt. Bradley A. Fiske.
California, A. C., Capt. Vincendon L. Cottman.
South Dakota, A. C., Lieut.-Com. Herman O. Stickney.
Washington, A. C., Capt. Austin M. Knight.

SECOND SQUADRON.

THIRD DIVISION.

Milwaukee, P. C....................Com. Charles C. Rogers
St. Louis, P. C..........................Com. Albert Gleaves.

FOURTH DIVISION.

There are at present no vessels assigned to this division.

THIRD SQUADRON.

Rear-Admiral Giles B. Harber, Commander.

FIRST DIVISION.

Rainbow (Flagship of Rear-Admiral Harber), Lieut.-Com. Irvin V. Gillis.
Charleston, P. C..Com. Harry S. Knapp.
Chattanooga, P. C...Com. Ed. E. Wright.
Cleveland, P. C...Com. Walter McLean.
Denver, P. C. ....Com. John M. Orchard.
Galveston, P. C. Com. Maubury Johnston.

SECOND DIVISION.

Concord, G..........Com. James H. Sears.
Wilmington, G..Com. Edward Lloyd, Jr.
Helena, G......Com. Richard M. Hughes.
Villalobos, G....Lieut. James H. Comfort.
Callao, G...........Lieut. Guy Whitlock.
Samar. ....Ensign Reed M. Fawell.

UNITED STATES NAVAL ENLISTMENT.

The term of enlistment of all enlisted men of the Navy is four years. Minors over the age of eighteen may be enlisted without consent of parents or guardians, but minors under, but claiming to be over eighteen years of age, are liable; if enlisted, to punishment for fraudulent enlistment. Only such persons shall be enlisted as can reasonably be expected to remain in the service. Every person, before being enlisted, must pass the physical examination prescribed in the medical instructions. Applicants for enlistment must be American citizens, able to read and write English, and when enlisted must take the oath of allegiance. No person under the age of seventeen can be enlisted

Information regarding rates and pay can be obtained by writing BUREAU OF NAVIGATION, NAVY DEPARTMENT. The following is a list of permanent central Navy Recruiting Stations:

Boston, Mass., 66 Hanover St.; New York, N. Y., 87 South St.; Philadelphia, Pa., 1413 Filbert St.; Baltimore, Md., 15 South Gay St.; Pittsburgh, Pa., 417 Fourth Ave.; Buffalo, N. Y., P. O. Bldg.; Erie, Pa., U. S. S. WOLVERINE, foot of State St.; Cincinnati, O., P. O. Bldg.; Indianapolis, Ind., P. O. Bldg.; Cleveland, O., 227 Euclid Ave.; Detroit, Mich., Hamlet Bldg.; Chicago, Ill., 100 Lake St.; Minneapolis, P. O. Bldg.; St. Louis, Mo., P. O. Bldg.; Chattanooga, Tenn., 916½ Market St.; New Orleans, La., 730 Common St.; Omaha, Neb., P. O. Bldg.; Kansas City, Mo., P. O. Bldg.; Oklahoma City, Okla., 220 W. Grand Ave.; Dallas, Tex., P. O. Bldg.; Denver, Col., Alamo Bldg., 17th and Market Sts.; Los Angeles, Cal., San Fernando Bldg., 4th and Main Sts.

RELATIVE RANK IN THE UNITED STATES ARMY AND NAVY.

Section 1466 of the Revised Statutes of the United States.

Generals rank with Admirals.
Lieutenant-Generals rank with Vice-Admirals.
Major-Generals rank with first nine Rear-Admirals.
Brigadier-Generals rank with Rear-Admirals after the first nine and Commodores.
Colonels rank with Captains.
Lieutenant-Colonels rank with Commanders.
Majors rank with Lieutenant-Commanders.
Captains rank with Lieutenants.
First Lieutenants rank with Lieutenants Junior Grade.
Second Lieutenants rank with Ensigns.
Cadets rank with Midshipmen.

THE NAVY—*Continued.*

DIMENSIONS, COAL SUPPLY, ARMOR, AND COMPLEMENT.

Vessels.	Length on Load Water Line.		Extreme Breadth.		Mean Draught.		Normal Coal Supply.	Bunker Capacity.	Number of Torpedo Tubes.	Armor.			Protective Deck.		Complement.		Type of Engines.
										Sides.	Turrets.	Barbette.	Ends.	Amidship.	Officers.	Men.	
	Ft.	In.	Ft.	In.	Ft.	In.	Tons.	Tons.		In.	In.	In.	In.	In.			
Alabama	368	0	72	2	23	8	800	1,286	4–18	16.5	14	15	3to4	2¾	34	647	T. S., V. T. E.
Albany	346	0	43	9	18	0	512	747	..	..	7½	..	..	3	19	333	T. S., V. T. E.
Amphitrite	259	3	56	6	14	2	250	271	..	9	7	11.5	..	1¾	23	172	T. S., I. E.
Annapolis	168	0	36	0	12	5	100	225	..	..	..	..	..	..	11	136	S. S., V. T. E.
Arkansas	252	0	50	0	12	2	344	344	..	11	10	11	..	1.5	13	155	T. S., V. T. E.
Atlanta	277	3	42	1	16	10	382	573	..	..	..	..	1.5	1.5	19	285	S. S., H. C.
Baltimore	327	6	48	7	20	0	709	1,064	..	..	..	..	4	2.5	30	353	T. S., H. T. E.
Bennington	230	0	36	0	13	8	200	373	..	..	..	..	⅜	⅜	11	176	T. S., H. T. E.
Birmingham	420	0	47	1	16	9	..	1,250	2–21	..	..	..	..	..	16	340	T. S., V. T. E.
Boston	277	3	42	1	17	0	380	456	..	..	..	..	1.5	1.5	22	260	S. S., H. E.
California	502	0	69	6	24	1	900	2,024	2–18	5to6	6½	6	4	1.5	41	787	T. S., V. T. E.
Castine	204	0	32	1	12	0	125	280	..	..	..	..	⅜	5–16	11	143	T. S., V. T. E.
Charleston	424	0	66	0	22	6	650	1,500	..	..	..	..	3	2	36	634	T. S., V. T. E.
Chattanooga	292	0	44	0	15	9	467	703	..	..	..	..	2 &1	½	19	308	T. S., V. T. E.
Chester	420	0	47	1	16	9	..	1,250	2–21	..	..	..	..	..	16	340	4-Screw Turbine.
Chicago	325	0	48	2	20	4	593	890	..	..	..	..	1.5	1.5	32	445	T. S., H. T. E
Cincinnati	300	0	42	0	18	0	384	577	..	..	..	..	2.5	1	20	341	T. S., V. T. E.
Cleveland	292	0	44	0	15	9	467	703	..	..	..	..	2 &1	½	19	308	T. S., V. T. E.
Colorado	502	0	69	6	24	1	900	1,828	2–18	5to6	6	6	4	1.5	41	787	T. S., V. T. E.
Columbia	412	0	58	2	22	6	750	1,525	..	..	..	..	4	2.5	28	465	T. S., V. T. E.
Concord	230	0	36	0	13	5	200	381	..	..	..	..	⅜	⅜	10	191	T. S., H. T. E.
Connecticut	450	0	76	10	24	6	900	2,200	4–21	11	12	15	3	3	41	815	T. S., V. T. E.
Cumberland	176	0	45	8	16	5	..	100	..	..	..	..	..	..	16	320	Sail Power.
Delaware*	510	0	85	2	26	11	..	2,500	2–21	..	..	..	..	..	55	878	T. S., V. T. E.
Denver	292	0	44	0	15	9	467	703	..	..	..	..	2 &1	½	19	308	T. S., V. T. E.
Des Moines	292	0	44	0	15	9	467	703	..	..	..	..	2 &1	½	19	308	T. S., V. T. E.
Detroit	257	0	37	0	14	8	200	368	..	..	..	..	7–16	5–16	12	263	T. S., V. T. E.
Dolphin	240	0	32	0	14	0	..	265	1–18 1–21	..	..	..	..	..	7	129	S. S., V. C.
Don Juan de Austria	210	0	32	0	12	6	..	210	..	..	..	..	..	..	..	129	S. S.
Dubuque	174	0	35	0	12	3	100	200	..	..	..	..	..	..	9	149	T. S., V. T. E.
Florida †	252	0	50	0	12	2	355	355	..	11	10	11	..	1.5	13	158	T. S., V. T. E.
Galveston	292	0	44	0	15	9	467	703	..	..	..	..	2 &1	½	19	308	T. S., V. T. E.
General Alara	212	6	29	9	11	0	..	240	..	..	..	..	..	..	8	80	S. S., T. E.
Georgia	435	0	76	2	23	9	900	1,705	4–21	11	12	10	3	3	40	772	T. S., V. T. E.
Helena	250	0	40	0	9	0	100	300	..	..	..	..	⅜	5–16	10	173	T. S., V. T. E.
Idaho	368	0	77	0	24	8	600	1,750	2–18	9	12	10	3	3	34	691	T. S., V. T. E.
Illinois	380	0	72	2	24	0	800	1,270	1–18	16	14	15	4	2¾	34	647	T. S., V. T. E.
Indiana	348	0	69	3	23	10	400	1,475	1–18	18	15	17	3	2¾	26	610	T. S., V. T. E.
Intrepid	176	0	45	8	16	5	..	100	..	..	..	..	..	..	16	320	Sail Power.
Iowa	360	0	72	2	23	10	625	1,660	4–14	14	17	15	3	2¾	35	546	T. S., V. T. E.
Isla de Cuba	192	0	30	0	12	3	159	195	..	..	..	..	2.5	1.5	8	136	T. S., H. T. E.
Isla de Luzon	192	0	30	0	12	3	159	195	..	..	..	..	2.5	1.5	8	134	T. S., H. T. E
Kansas	450	0	76	10	24	6	900	2,200	4–21	9	12	10	3	3	41	815	T. S., V. T. E.
Katahdin	259	0	43	5	15	0	175	193	..	6	..	..	6	2	7	90	T. S., H. T. E.
Kearsarge	368	0	72	2	23	10	410	1,503	1–18	16.5	17	15	5	2¾	39	618	T. S., V. T. E.
Kentucky	368	0	72	2	23	10	410	1,503	1–18	16.5	17	15	5	2¾	35	616	T. S., V. T. E.
Louisiana	450	0	76	10	24	6	900	2,200	4–21	11	12	10	3	3	41	815	T. S., V. T. E.
Machias	204	0	32	1	12	0	125	280	..	..	..	..	⅜	5–16	10	143	T. S., V. T. E.
Maine	388	0	72	2	24	3	1,000	1,867	2–18	11	12	12	4	2	41	772	T. S., V. T. E.
Marblehead	257	0	37	0	14	7	200	335	..	..	..	..	7–16	5–16	13	258	T. S., V. T. E.
Marietta	174	0	34	0	12	2	120	241	..	..	..	..	..	..	11	134	T. S., V. T. E.
Maryland	502	0	69	6	24	1	900	2,024	2–18	6	6.5	6	4	1.5	41	787	T. S., V. T. E.
Massachusetts	348	0	69	3	23	10	400	1,475	3–18	18	15	17	3	2¾	26	560	T. S., V. T. E.
Miantonomoh	259	0	55	6	14	6	250	260	..	7	11.5	..	..	1¾	16	164	T. S., I. C.
Michigan	450	0	80	2	24	6	900	2,200	2–18	11	12	10	3	3	51	818	T. S., V. T. E.
Milwaukee	424	0	66	0	22	6	650	1,650	..	..	..	..	3	2	36	684	T. S., V. T. E.
Minneapolis	412	0	58	2	22	6	750	1,400	..	..	..	..	4	2.5	33	500	T. S., V. T. E.
Minnesota	450	0	76	10	24	6	900	2,200	4–21	9	12	10	3	3	41	815	T. S., V. T. E.
Missouri	388	0	72	2	23	8	1,000	1,837	2–18	11	12	12	4	2.5	40	739	T. S., V. T. E.
Mississippi	375	0	77	0	24	8	600	1,750	2–21	9	12	10	3	3	34	691	T. S., V. T. E.
Monadnock	259	6	55	6	14	7	250	386	..	9	7.5	11.5	..	1¾	14	210	T. S., H. T. E.
Montana	502	0	72	10	25	0	900	2,014	4–21	5	9	8	4	2	40	821	T. S., V. T. E.
Monterey	256	0	59	0	14	10	200	233	..	13	8	13	..	3	19	215	T. S., V. T. E.
Montgomery	257	0	37	0	14	7	200	340	6	..	..	..	7–16	5–16	20	232	T. S., V. T. E.
Nashville	220	0	38	1	11	0	150	400	..	..	..	..	⅜	5–16	11	167	T. S., Q. T. E.
Nebraska	435	0	76	2	23	9	900	1,705	4–21	11	12	10	3	3	40	772	T. S., V. T. E.
Nevada	252	0	50	0	12	5	338	388	..	11	10	11	..	1.5	13	158	T. S., V. T. E.
Newark	311	5	49	2	19	9	400	882	..	..	..	..	3	2	35	396	T. S., H. T. E.
New Hampshire	450	0	76	10	24	6	900	2,314	4–21	9	12	11	3	3	41	841	T. S., V. T. E.
New Jersey	435	0	76	2	23	9	900	1,705	4–21	11	12	10	3	3	40	772	T. S., V. T. E.
New Orleans	346	0	43	9	18	0	750	767	..	..	..	..	3	1¼	24	342	S. S., V. T. E.
Newport	168	0	36	0	12	2	100	237	..	..	..	..	..	..	11	108	T. S., V. T. E.
New York	380	6	64	10	23	3	750	1,334	2	4	5	10	6	3	25	473	T. S., V. T. E.
North Carolina	502	0	72	10	25	0	900	2,014	4–21	5	9	8	4	2	40	821	T. S., V. T. E.
North Dakota*	510	0	85	2	26	11	..	2,500	2–21	..	..	..	..	..	55	878	Twin screw Tur.
Ohio	388	0	72	2	23	7	1,000	2,000	2–18	11	12	12	4	2.5	41	779	T. S., V. T. E.
Olympia	340	0	53	0	21	6	400	1,136	..	..	..	..	4¾	2	30	454	T. S., V. T. E.
Oregon	348	1	69	3	24	6	400	1,449	3–18	18	15	17	3	2¾	35	505	T. S., V. T. E.

* Under construction. † Monitor. Name will be changed when Battleship Florida is completed.

THE NAVY—*Continued.*

DIMENSIONS, COAL SUPPLY, ARMOR, AND COMPLEMENT.

Vessels.	Length on Load Water Line.		Extreme Breadth.		Mean Draught.		Normal Coal Supply.	Bunker Capacity.	Number of Torpedo Tubes.	Armor.			Protective Deck.		Complement.		Type of Engines.
										Sides.	Turrets.	Barbette.	Ends.	Amidship.	Officers.	Men.	
	Ft.	In.	Ft.	In	Ft.	In	Tons.	Tons.		In.	In.	In.	In.	In.			
Paducah	174	0	35	0	12	3	100	246	..	..	..	..	..	..	9	149	T. S., V. T. E.
Pennsylvania	502	0	69	6	24	1	900	1,828	2–18	6	6.5	6	4	1.5	41	787	T. S., V T. E.
Petrel	181	0	31	0	11	6	100	213	..	..	..	..	⅜	5–16	8	126	T. S., H. T. E.
Philadelphia	327	6	48	7	19	6	400	1.074	..	..	..	..	4	2.5	34	359	T. S., H. T. E.
Princeton	168	0	36	0	12	9	100	239	..	..	..	..	..	..	11	130	S. S., V. T. E.
Puritan	290	3	60	1	18	0	307	314	..	14	8	14	..	2	22	248	T. S., H. C.
Raleigh	300	0	42	0	18	0	575	571	..	..	..	..	2.5	1	20	297	T. S., V. T. E.
Reina Mercedes	292	0	43	3	16	9	..	240	..	..	..	..	..	..	15	560	....
Rhode Island	435	0	76	2	23	9	900	1.705	4–21	11	12	10	3	3	40	772	T. S., V. T. E.
Salem	420	0	47	1	16	9	..	1,250	2–21	..	..	..	..	..	16	240	2 screw Turbine.
San Francisco	310	0	49	3	20	4	350	678	..	..	..	..	3	2	24	319	T. S., H. T. E.
Severn	175	0	37	0	16	0	..	43	..	..	..	..	..	..	..	256	Sail Power.
South Carolina	450	0	80	2	24	6	900	2,200	2–21	11	12	10	3	3	51	818	T. S., V. T. E.
South Dakota	502	0	69	6	24	1	900	2,024	2–18	6	6.5	6	4	1.5	41	787	T. S., V. T. E.
St. Louis	424	0	66	0	22	6	650	1,500	..	..	..	..	3	2	26	634	T. S., V. T. E.
Tacoma	292	0	44	1	15	9	467	703	..	..	..	..	2 &1	½	19	308	T. S., V. T. E.
Tennessee	502	0	72	10	25	0	910	1,762	4–21	5	9	7	3	1.5	40	816	T. S., V. T. E.
Terror	259	6	55	6	14	6	250	285	..	7	11.5	..	..	1¾	14	164	T. S., I. C.
Texas	301	4	64	1	22	6	500	845	..	12	12	..	3	2	30	398	T. S., V. T. E.
Topeka	250	0	35	0	17	9	273	410	..	..	..	..	..	..	21	131	T. S., H. C.
Utah‡	...		....		....		..	..	..	..	..	..	..	..	..	....	......
Vermont	450	0	76	10	24	6	900	2,200	4–21	9	12	10	3	3	41	815	T. S., V. T. E.
Vesuvius	252	0	26	0	10	0	..	132	2–18 1–21	..	..	..	..	..	4	47	T. S., V. T. E.
Vicksburg	168	0	36	0	12	1	100	239	..	..	..	..	..	..	11	128	S. S., V. T. E.
Virginia	435	0	76	2	23	9	900	1,705	4–21	11	12	10	3	3	40	772	T. S., V. T. E.
Washington	502	0	72	10	25	0	900	1,762	4–21	5	9	7	4	1.5	40	816	T. S., V. T. E.
West Virginia	502	0	69	6	24	1	900	2,024	2–18	6	6.5	6	4	1.5	41	787	T. S., V. T. E.
Wheeling	174	0	34	0	12	3	120	241	..	..	..	..	..	..	9	129	T. S., V. T. E.
Wilmington	250	9	40	0	9	0	100	300	..	..	..	..	⅜	5–16	10	189	T. S., V. T. E.
Wisconsin	368	0	72	2	23	8	800	1,245	1–18	16.5	14	15	4	2¾	34	647	T. S., T. V. E.
Wyoming	252	0	50	0	12	4	381	381	..	11	10	11	..	1.5	13	158	T. S., V. T. E.
Yorktown	230	0	36	0	14	2	200	381	..	..	..	..	⅜	⅜	14	182	S. S., H. T. E.

NAVY-YARDS.

1. Brooklyn Navy-Yard, Brooklyn, N. Y.
2. Charlestown Navy-Yard, Boston, Mass.
3. Portsmouth Navy-Yard, near Norfolk, Va.
4. Kittery Navy-Yard, opposite Portsmouth, N. H.
5. Philadelphia Navy-Yard, Philadelphia, Pa.
6. Mare Island Navy-Yard, near San Francisco, Cal.
7. Washington City Navy-Yard, Washington, D. C.
8. Puget Sound Navy Yard, Bremerton, Wash.

There are naval stations at Port Royal, S. C.; Charleston, S. C.; Key West, Fla.; Pensacola, Fla.; Algiers, La.; Great Lakes, North Chicago, Ill.; a torpedo and training station at Newport, R. I., and a training station on Yerba Buena Island, Cal., and the Naval War College, Newport, R. I.

Naval stations have been established at Tutuila, Samoa; Island of Guam; San Juan, Porto Rico; Culebra, W. I.; Guantanamo, Cuba; Honolulu, H. I., and Cavite, Philippine Islands. The latter has become an important naval base for the Asiatic squadron.

OLD VESSELS.

There are in the Navy a small number of old vessels which are unserviceable for war purposes. Ten of these vessels are in service as receiving ships at the principal navy yards.

TUGS.

There are 42 tugs in the Naval Service, of which the Potomac has a displacement of 785 tons, and the two smallest, the Chickasaw and Rapido, 100 tons. These vessels are distributed among the various naval stations in the United States and the Philippine Islands. Two new sea-going tugs, Patapsco and Patuxent, of 755 tons each, are in course of construction.

VESSELS USED BY NAVAL MILITIA.

The following vessels have been assigned to the various naval militia: Aileen, Aleit, Alvarado, Don Juan de Austria, Dorothea, Elfrida, Essex, Gopher, Hawk, Huntress, Inca, Isla de Cuba, Newark, Oneida, Pinta, Portsmouth, Puritan, Sandoval, Shearwater, Stranger, Sylvia, and Yantic.

SUMMARY OF THE UNITED STATES NAVY.

Battleships (first and second class), 27; Armored Cruisers, 10; Cruisers, first class, 5; Cruisers, second class, 7; Cruisers, third class, 16; Torpedo Boat Destroyers, 16; Torpedo Boats, 36, Submarines, 12; Monitors, 10; Wooden Cruisers, 4; Gunboats, 38; Transports, 7; Supply Ships, 7; Hospital Ship, 1, Colliers, 15; Converted Yachts, 24; Tugs, 42; Training Sailing Ships, 5, Receiving Ships, 9; Unserviceable for sea-going purposes, 10. Under construction or authorized: Battleships, first-class, 6; Torpedo Boat Destroyers, 15; Submarines, 15; Gunboat, 1; Colliers, 7; Tugs, 2.

THE NAVY—*Continued.*

UNITED STATES NAVY PAY TABLE.

Rank.	At Sea.	On Shore Duty.	On Leave or Waiting Orders.
Admiral	$14,850	$13,500	*....
Rear-Admirals, first nine	8,800	8,000	....
Rear-Admirals, second nine	6,600	6,000	....
Brigadier-General, Commandant Marine Corps	6,600	6,000	....
Captains	4,400	4,000	....
Commanders	3,850	3,500	....
Lieutenant-Commanders	3,300	3,000	....
Lieutenants	2,640	2,400	....
Lieutenants (Junior Grade)	2,200	2,000	....
Ensigns	1,870	1,700	....
Chief Boatswains, Chief Gunners, Chief Carpenters, Chief Sailmakers	1,870	1,700	....
Midshipmen (At Nav. Acad)	600	600	....
Midshipmen (After Grad'n)	1,400	1,400	....
Mates	1,500	1,125	....

Rank.	At Sea.	On Shore Duty.	On Leave or Waiting Orders.
Medical and Pay Directors and Inspectors having the same rank at sea	$4,400	$4,000	*....
Fleet-Surgeons and Fleet-Paymasters	4,400	4,000	....
Surgeons and Paymasters	3,300	3,000	....
Chaplains	2,200 to 4,400	2,000 to 4,000	....
Professors and Civil Engineers	2,640 to 4,400	2,400 to 4,000	....
Naval Constructors	2,640 to 4,400	2,400 to 4,000	....

*Generally one-half sea pay. Officers paid under old navy pay lose one half pay for each day not performing active duty. Officers receiving army pay are allowed 30 days' leave per year with full shore pay.

All officers paid under this table, below the rank of Rear-Admiral, are entitled to 10 per cent. increase upon the full yearly pay of their grades for each and every period of five years' service as "longevity pay," computed upon their total actual service in the Navy or Marine Corps, provided that the total amount of such increase shall not exceed 40 per cent. upon the full yearly pay of their grade.

Officers of the line, medical and pay corps, commissioned prior to July 1, 1899, are entitled to receive pay according to the then existing law whenever it is in excess of the pay of officers of corresponding rank in the Army.

All officers on sea duty and all officers on shore duty beyond the continental limits of the United States shall while so serving receive ten per centum additional of their salaries and increase as above provided, and such increase shall commence from reporting for duty on board ship or the date of sailing from the United States for shore duty beyond seas or to join a ship in foreign waters.

Warrant officers (boatswains, gunners, carpenters, sailmakers, pharmacists, warrant machinists and pay clerks) are paid from $1,125 to $2,250 a year.

Commandants' clerks receive from $1,000 to $1,800 a year.

Petty officers (masters-at-arms, boatswains' mates, gunners' mates, gun captains, quartermasters, machinists, hospital stewards, yeomen, bandmasters, first musicians, coxswains, electricians, boiler-makers, coppersmiths, blacksmiths, plumbers and fitters, sailmakers' mates, carpenters' mates, oilers, printers, painters, water tenders, and hospital apprentices (first class) receive from $396 to $924 a year.

The pay of first-class seamen per month is $26; seamen gunners, $28; firemen, first class, $38; musicians, first class, $34.

The pay of second-class seamen per month is: Ordinary seamen, $21; firemen, second class, $33; shipwrights, $27; musicians, second class, $33.

The pay of third-class seamen per month is: Landsmen, for training, $17; coal passers, $24; apprentices, third class, $10.

The United States Battleship Fleet (Return Schedule),

WHICH DEPARTED FOR THE PACIFIC COAST DECEMBER 16, 1907.

Rear-Admiral Charles S. Sperry, Commander-in-Chief.

1. The mail address of all vessels of the first four divisions and of the Panther, Culgoa and Yankton is "In care of Postmaster, New York City."

Fleet Itinerary.—Manila to United States: Leave Manila December 1; arrive Colombo December 14; leave Colombo December 20; arrive Suez January 5.

Pass through canal and coal at Port Said as expeditiously as possible, and as soon as ships are coaled they will proceed to Mediterranean ports as follows, dates of arrival at these ports being approximate and dependent upon the rapidity with which the ships can pass through the canal and coal at Port Said:

Connecticut—Vermont, arrive Villefranche January 14, leave January 27; Minnesota—Kansas, arrive Marseilles January 14, leave January 27; Georgia—Nebraska—Kentucky, arrive Genoa January 15, leave January 27; Rhode Island—New Jersey, arrive Leghorn January 15, leave January 27; Louisiana—Virginia, arrive Malta January 15, leave January 19; Louisiana—Virginia, arrive Algiers January 22, leave January 30; Ohio—Missouri, arrive Athens January 13, leave January 25; Wisconsin—Illinois—Kearsarge, arrive Naples January 17, leave January 27. After leaving the above ports—First Division arrive Negro Bay January 31, leave February 3; First Division, arrive Gibraltar February 3, leave February 6; Second, Third and Fourth Divisions, arrive Negro Bay February 1, leave February 1; fleet reassemble off Gibraltar and proceed to United States, arrive February 22, at Hampton Roads, Virginia.

2. The Commander-in-Chief will make all arrangements for the forwarding of mail addressed as above to the vessels of the fleet.

3. Mail sent in care of the Postmaster, New York city, must be prepaid, with domestic postage, and must bear the name of the ship for which it is intended.

4. Express packages must not be sent to the above addresses, as there is no way of forwarding them, and they will simply be returned to the sender at his expense.

Diplomatic and Consular Service.

AMBASSADORS EXTRAORDINARY AND PLENIPOTENTIARY.

Country.	*Name and State.*	*Salary.*
Aust.-Hungary	Charles S. Francis, N. Y.	$17,500
Brazil	Irving B. Dudley, Cal.	17,500
France	Henry White, R. I.	17,500
Germany	David J. Hill, N. Y.	17 500
Great Britain	Whitelaw Reid, N. Y.	17,500
Italy	Lloyd C. Griscom, Pa.	$17,500
Japan	Thomas J. O'Brien, Mich.	17,500
Mexico	David E. Thompson, Neb.	17.500
Russia	John W. Riddle, Minn.	17,500
Turkey	John G. A. Leishman, Pa.	17.500

ENVOYS EXTRAORDINARY AND MINISTERS PLENIPOTENTIARY.

Country.	*Name and State.*	*Salary.*
Argentine Rep.	Spencer S. Eddy, Ill.	$12,000
Belgium	Henry Lane Wilson, Wash.	12,000
Bolivia	James F. Stutesman, Ind.	10,000
Chile	John Hicks, Wis.	12,000
China	W. W. Rockhill, D. C.	12,000
Colombia	Thomas C. Dawson, Iowa	10,000
Cuba	Edwin V. Morgan, N. Y.	12,000
Denmark	Maurice Francis Egan, D. C.	10,000
Ecuador	Williams C. Fox, N. J.	10,000
Greece	Richmond Pearson, N. C. ††	10,000
Guatemala	William Helmke, Kansas	10,000
Hayti	Henry W. Furniss, Ind.	10,000
Honduras	Philip M. Brown	10,000
Morocco	Samuel R. Gummere, N. J.	10,000
Netherlands	Arthur M. Beaupré, Ill. **	12,000
Nicaragua	John G. Coolidge, Mass.	$10,000
Norway	Herbert H. D. Peirce, Mass.	10,000
Panama	Herbert G. Squiers, N. Y.	10.000
Paraguay	Edward C. O'Brien, N. Y. ‡	10,000
Persia	John B. Jackson, N. J.	10,000
Peru	Leslie Combs, Ky.	10,000
Portugal	Charles Page Bryan, Ill.	10,000
Roumania	Horace G. Knowles, Del.	10,000
Salvador	H. Percival Dodge, Mass.	10,000
Servia	Horace G. Knowles, Del. *	10,000
Siam	Hamilton King, Mich.	10.000
Spain	William M. Collier, N. Y.	12,000
Sweden	Charles H. Graves, Minn.	10,000
Switzerland	Brutus J. Clay, Ky.	10,000
Venezuela		10,000

MINISTERS RESIDENT AND CONSULS-GENERAL.

Country.	*Name and State.*	*Salary.*
Dominican Rep.	Fenton R. McCreery, Mich.	10,000
Liberia	Ernest Lyon, Md.	$5,000

SECRETARIES OF EMBASSIES AND LEGATIONS.

Country.	*Name and State.*	*Salary.*
Argentine Rep.	Charles S. Wilson, Me.	$2,625
Aust.-Hungary	George B. Rives, N. Y.	3,000
Aust.-Hungary	N. O'Shaughnessy, N. Y. (2d)	2,000
Brazil	Henry L. Janes, Wis.	3,000
Belgium	Robert W. Bliss, N. Y.	2,625
Chile	U. Grant Smith, Pa.	2,625
China	Henry R. Fletcher, Pa.	2,625
China	F. M. Dearing, Mo. (2d Sec.)	1,800
Colombia	Paxton Hibben, Ind.	2,000
Cuba	G. Cornell Tarler, N. Y. (2d)	1,800
France	Henry Vignaud, La.	3,000
France	A. B. Blanchard, La. (2d Sec.)	2,000
France	W. Blumenthal, N. Y. (3d)	1,200
Germany	R. S. R. Hitt, Ill.	3,000
Germany	Jos. C. Grew, Mass. (2d Sec.)	2,000
Germany	Arthur Orr, Ill. (3d Sec).	1,200
Great Britain	John R. Carter, Md.	3,000
Great Britain	C. W. Wadsw'th, N. Y. (2d Sec)	2,000
Great Britain		1,200
Guatemala	Algernon Sartoris, D. C.	2,000
Italy	John W. Garrett, Md.	3,000
Italy	R. M. Winthrop, Mass. (2d)	2,000
Japan	Peter A. Jay, R. I.	3,000
Japan	George P. Wheeler, Wash.	2,000
Mexico	William F. Sands, D. C.	$3,000
Mexico	A. Campbell Turner, Mo. (2d)	2,000
Morocco		2,000
Netherlands	Charles D. White, N. J.	2,625
Nicaragua	John H. Gregory, Jr., La.	2,000
Norway	M. M. Langhorne, Va.	2,000
Panama	Geo. T. Weitzel, Mo.	2,000
Paraguay	Har Bowsley, Jr., N. J.	2,000
Persia	Fredyric O. de Biller, N. J.	2,000
Peru	Richard R. Neill, Pa.	2,000
Portugal	Geo. L. Lorillard, R. I.	2,000
Roumania	Norman Hutchinson, Cal.	2,000
Russia	M. Schuyler, Jr., N. Y. (1st)	3,000
Russia	J. Van A. MacMurray, N. J. (2d	2,000
Salvador	Arthur H. Frazier, Pa.	2,000
Servia	Norman Hutchinson, Cal.	2,000
Siam		2,000
Spain	William H. Buckler, Md.	2,625
Sweden	James G. Bailey, Ky.	2,000
Switzerland	Jacob Sleeper, Mass.	2,000
Turkey	Lewis Einstein, N. Y.	3,000
Turkey	(2d Sec.)	2,000
Venezuela		2,000

CONSULAR SERVICE.

C. G., Consul-General; C., Consul; V. C., Vice-Consul; D. C., Deputy Consul; C. A., Consular Assistant; Agt., Consular Agent.

There are about 1,100 consular representatives of the United States of the several grades abroad. Those at the principal places in the world are given here. Where there are a cousul and vice or deputy consul at the same place only the consul is given. Consular officers are *ex-officio* notaries for all the States of the United States.

CONSULS-GENERAL AT LARGE.

Albert R. Morawetz, Ariz.; Alfred L. M. Gottschalk, N. Y.; George H. Murphy, N. C.; Fleming D. Cheshire, N. Y. Salaries $5,000 each.

	Argentine Republic.	
Buenos Ayres	Alban G. Snyder, W. Va.	$4,500
Rosario	Thos. B. Van Horne, Ohio, C.	2,500
	Austria-Hungary.	
Buda-Pesth	Paul Nash, N. Y., C.	3 500
Carlsbad	John S. Twells, Pa., C.	3,000
Prague	Joseph I. Brittain, Ohio, C.	3,500
Reichenberg	Charles B. Harris, Ind., C.	4,000
Trieste	Geo. M. Hotschick, Wis., C.	3,000
Vienna	W. A. Rublee, Wis., C. G.	6,000
	Belgium.	
Antwerp	H. W. Diedrich, C. G.	5,500
Brussels	Ethelbert Watts, Pa., C. G.	5,500
Ghent	William P. Atwell, C.	3,000
Liege	Henry A. Johnson, C.	3,000
	Brazil.	
Bahia	Pierre P. Demers, N. H., C.	4,000
Para	Geo. H. Pickerell, Ohio, C.	4,000
Pernambuco	G. A. Chamberlain, N. J., C.	4,000
Rio de Janeiro	Geo. E. Anderson, Ill., C. G.	8,000
Santos	John W. O'Hara, Ind., C.	4,000
	Chile.	
Iquique	Rea Hanna, Cal., C.	$3,000
Valparaiso	Alfred A. Winslow, Ind., C.	4,500
	China.	
Amoy	Julian H. Arnold, Cal., C.	4,500
Canton	Leo A. Bergholz, N. Y., C. G.	5,500
Chefoo	John Fowler, Mass., C.	4,500
Foochow	Samuel L. Gracey, Mass., C.	4.500
Hankau	William Martin, N. Y., C. G.	4,500
Nankin	James C. McNally, Pa., C.	4,000
Niuchwang	Thos. E. Heenan, Minn., C.	4,500
Shanghai	Charles Denby, Ind., C. G.	8,000
Tientsin	Edw. T. Williams, Ohio, C. G.	5,500
	Colombia.	
Barranquilla	Chas. C. Eberhardt, Kan. C.	3,500
Bogotá	Jay White, Mich., C. G.	3,500
Cartagena	Isaac A. Manning, Ore., C.	2,000
	Costa Rica.	
San José	John C. Caldwell, Kan., C.	3,000

* Also accredited to Roumania and Bulgaria. ‡ Also to Costa Rica. ** Also to Luxembourg. †† Also to Montenegro. ‡ Also to Uruguay.

DIPLOMATIC AND CONSULAR SERVICE—*Continued.*

Post	Officer	Salary
	Cuba.	
Cienfuegos	Max J. Baehr, Neb., C.	$4,500
Havana	James L. Rodgers, Ohio, C.G.	8,000
Santiago	Ross E. Holaday, Ohio, C.	4,500
	Denmark and Dominions.	
Copenhagen	Frank R. Mowrer, Ohio, C.G.	3,000
St. Thomas	Chris. H. Payne, W. Va., C.	3,000
	Dominican Republic.	
Puerto Plata	Ralph J. Totten, Tenn., C.	2,000
Samana	F. Lample, A.	Fees.
San Domingo	Fen. R. McCreery, Mich., C.G.	....
	Ecuador.	
Guayaquil	Her. R. Dietrich, Mo., C. G.	4,500
	France and Dominions.	
Algiers, Africa	James Johnson, N. J., C.	2,500
Bordeaux	D. I. Murphy, D. C., C.	4,000
Boulogne-sur-Mer	Wm. Whitman, Agt.	....
Brest	A. Pitel, Agt.	....
Calais	James B. Milner, Ind., C.	3,000
Cannes	Jean B. Cognet, Fr., Agt.	....
Cette	Carl D. Hagelin, Fr., Agt.	....
Cherbourg	Octave Canuet, France, Agt.	....
Dieppe	W. P. Palmer-Samborne, Agt	....
Dijon	Nicolas Chapuis, Agt.	....
Gorée - Dakar, Africa		2,000
Grenoble	Charles P.H. Nason, C.	2,000
Guadel'pe, W.I.	Jos. M. Authier, R. I.	2,000
Havre	Alphonse Ganlin, C.	5,000
Honfleur	John N. Bourke, Agt.	....
La Rochelle	George H. Jackson, Ct., C.	2,500
Lille	Chris. J. King, R. I., Agt.	....
Limoges	Eugene L. Belisle, Mass., C.	2,500
Lyons	John C. Covert, Ohio, C.	5,000
Marseilles	H. L. Washington, D.C., C.G.	5,500
Mart'que, W.I.	Geo. B. Anderson, D.C., C.	2,500
Mentone	Achille Isuard, Agt.	....
Nantes	Louis Goldschmidt, N.H., C.	3,000
Nice	William D. Hunter, Minn., C.	2,500
Paris	Frank H. Mason, Ohio, C.G.	12,000
Paris	Hanson C. Coxe, N.Y., D.C.G.	....
Paris	D. B. Mason, O., V. & D.C.G.	....
Paris	Elw'd A. Weldon, Pa., D.C.G.	....
Rennes	Ernest Folliard, France, Agt.	....
Rheims	William Bardell, N. Y., C.	3,500
Roubaix	Chapman Colman, Ky., C.	2,500
Rouen	Oscar Malmros, C.	2,000
St. Etienne	William H. Hunt, N. Y.	2,500
St. Pierre	Douglass Jenkins, S. C., C.	2,000
Tahiti, Soc. Isl.	Julius D. Dreher, S. C.	2,000
Tamatave, Madagascar	James G. Carter, Ga., C	2,500
Toulon	Benj. A. Jouve, France, Agt.	....
	Germany.	
Aix la Chapelle	Pendleton King, C.	3,000
Annaberg	George N. Ifft, Ind., N.Y., C.	3,000
Apia, Samoa	Leon Mitchell, N. Y., C.	3,500
Bamberg	William Bardel, N. Y., C.A.	2,500
Barmen	Geo. Eugene Eager, Ill., C.	3,500
Berlin	A. M. Thackara, Pa., C.G.	8,000
Bremen	William T. Fee, Ohio, C.	5,000
Breslau	Herman L. Spahr, S. C., C.	2,500
Brunswick	Talbot J. Albert, Md., C.	2,500
Chemnitz	Thomas H. Norton, Ohio, C.	3,500
Coburg	Frank Dillingham, Cal., C.G.	4,500
Cologne	Hiram J. Dunlap, Ill., C.	3,500
Crefeld	Joseph E. Haven, Ill., C.	2,500
Dantzic	Ernest A. Claaszen, Ger., Agt.	....
Dresden	T. St. J. Gaffney, N. Y., C. G.	4,500
Düsseldorf	Peter Lieber, Ind., C.	3,000
Frankfort	Richard Guenther, Wis., C.G	5,500
Freiburg, Baden	E. Theophilus Liefeld, Ct., C.	3,000
Glauchau	Geo. A. Bucklin, Jr., Okla., C.	2,000
Hamburg	Rob. P. Skinner, Ohio, C.G.	8,000
Hanover	Rob't J. Thompson, Ill., C.	3,000
Kehl	William J. Pike, Pa., C.	3,000
Leipsic	S. P. Warner, Md., C.	4,000
Magdeburg	Frank S. Hannah, Ill., C.	2,500
Mainz	Robert S.S. Bergh, N. Dak., C.	3,000
Mannheim	Samuel H. Shank, Ind., C.	3,500
Munich	Thos. W. Peters, D.C., C.G.	4,500
Nuremberg	Heaton W. Harris, Ohio, C.	4,000
Plauen	Carl B. Hurst, D. C., C.	4,000
Stettin		$2,500
Stuttgart	Edward Higgins, Mass., C.	4,000
Weimar	Will L. Lowry, Ill., C.	2,500
Zittau	Clarence R. Slocum, N.Y., C.	2,500
	Great Britain and Dominions.	
Aberdeen	Wm. P. Quann, Minn., Agt.	....
Aden, Arabia	Geo. M. Gordon, Ara., V. C.	....
Adelaide	George H. Prosser, Agt.	..
Antigua, W. I.	Geo. B. Anderson, C.	2,000
Auckland, N.Z.	Wm. A. Prickitt, N.J., C.G.	4,500
Barbados, W.I.	Chester W. Martin, Mich., C.	3,000
Belfast, Ire.	S. S. Knabenshue, Ohio, C.	5,000
Belize, Hond.	William L. Avery, Mont., C.	2,500
Belleville, Ont.	Mich'l J. Hendrick, N.Y., C.	2,000
Birmingham	Albert Halstead, D. C., C.	4,500
Bloemfontein	A. E. Fichardt, S. Africa	....
Bombay, India	E. H. Dennison, Ohio, C.	4,000
Bradford, Eng.	Erastus Sheldon Day, Ct., C.	3,500
Brisbane	J. Asbury Caldwell, Ill., Agt	....
Bristol, Eng.	J. Perry Worden, Mich., C.	2,000
Calcutta, India	Wm. H. Michal, Neb., C. G.	6,000
Campb't'n, N.B.	Theodosius Botkin, U., C.A.	2,000
Cape Town	Julius G. Lay, D. C., C.G.	6,000
Cardiff, Wales	Lorin A. Lathrop, Cal., C.	2,500
Ceylon	Wm. C. Teichmann, Mo., C.	3,000
Charlottetown, P. E. I.	Franklin D. Hale, Vt., C.	2,000
Coaticook, Que.	Franklin D. Hale, Vt., C.	2,000
Collingwood, Ont.	Augustus G. Seyfert, Pa., C.	2,500
Cork, Queenst.	Henry S. Culver, Ohio, C.	2,500
Dawson, N. W. Ter.	George C. Cole, W.V., C.	5,000
Demerara	George H. Moulton, Col., C.	3,000
Dover	Francis W. Prescott, Agt.	....
Dublin	Alfred K. Moe, N. J., C.	4,000
Dundee	John C. Higgins, Del., C.	4,000
Dunfermline	Maxwell Blake, Mo., C.	3,000
Durban, Natal	E. S. Cunningham, Tenn., C.	3,500
Edinburgh	Rufus Fleming, Ohio, C.	3,500
Fort Erie, Ont.	Horace J. Harvey, N. Y., C.	2,000
Gaspé Basin, Que.	Almar F. Dickson, Mass., C.	2,000
Georgetown, Guiana	Arthur J. Clare, D. C., C.	3,500
Gibraltar	Richard L. Sprague, C.	2,500
Glasgow	John N. McCunn, Wis., C.	4,500
Halifax, N.S.	David F. Wilber, N.Y., C.G.	4,500
Hamilton, Ber.	W. Maxwell Greene, R.I., C.	2,500
Hamilton, Ont.	Jas. M. Shepard, Mich., C.	3,000
Hobart, Tasm.	Henry D. Baker, Ill., C.	2,000
Hong Kong	Amos P. Wilder, Wis., C.G.	8,000
Huddersfield	Fred. I. Bright, Ohio, C.	3,000
Hull, Eng.	Walter C. Hamm, Pa., C.	2,500
Kimberley, S.A.	A. F. Williams, Agt., Cal.	....
Kingston, Jam.	Fred'ick Van Dyne, N.Y., C.	4,500
Kingston, Ont.	H. D. Van Sant, N. J., C.	2,500
Leeds	Lewis Dexter, R. I., C.	2,500
Liverpool	John L. Griffiths, Ind., C.	8,000
Londonderry	Phil. O'Hagan, Ireland, Agt.	....
Limerick	Edmund Ludlow, Agt.	....
London	Robert J. Wynne, Pa., C.G.	12,000
London	R. Westacott, Mass., V.C. G.	....
London	F. W. Frigout, Eng., D. C. G.	....
Madras	Nathaniel B. Stewart, Ga., C.	3,000
Malta	William H. Gale, Va., C.	2,500
Manchester	Church Howe, Neb., C.	6,000
Melbourne	John F. Jewell, Ill., C.	3,000
Moncton, N. B.	M. J. Hendrick, N. Y., C.	2,000
Montreal	William H. Bradley, Ill., C.G.	6,000
Nassau, N.P.	Julian Potter, N. Y., C.	3,000
Newcastle-on-Tyne	Horace W. Metcalf, Me., C.	3,000
Newcastle, N. S. W.	Geo. B. Killmaster, Mich., C.	3,000
Niagara Falls, Ont.	W. H. H. Webster, N.Y., C.	2,000
Nottingham	Frank W. Mahin, Iowa, C.	4,500
Ottawa, Ont.	John G. Foster, Vt., C. G.	6,000
Plymouth	Joseph G. Stephens, Ind., C.	2,500
Port Hope, Ont.	Harry P. Dill, Me., C.	2,500
Port Louis, Mauritius	Samuel C. Reat, Ill., C.	2,000
Pt. Sarnia, Ont.	Neal McMillan, Mich., C.	2,500
Portsmouth	Joseph G. Stephens, Ind., C.	2,500

DIPLOMATIC AND CONSULAR SERVICE—*Continued.*

Post	Officer	Salary
Pt. Stanley, F.I.	John E. Rowen, Iowa, C.	$2,000
Prescott, Ont.	Martin R. Sackett, N. Y., C.	2,500
Quebec	William W. Henry, Vt., C.	3,500
St. John, N. B.	Gebhard Willrich, Wis. C.	2,000
St. John's, N.F.	James S. Benedict, N. Y., C.	2,500
St. John's, Que.	Charles Deal, N.Y., C.	2,000
St. Steph'n, N.B.	Chas. A. McCullough, Me., C.	2,000
Sheffield	Charles N. Daniels, Ct., C.	3,000
Sherbr'ke, Que.	Paul Lang, N. H., C.	3,500
Sierra Leone	William J. Yerby, Tenn., C.	2,000
Singapore	T. Haynes, S. C., C. G.	4,500
Southampton	Albert W. Swalm, Iowa, C.	4,500
St. Lucia, W. I.	William Peter, Agt.	....
St. Vincent, W.I.	Ernest A. Richards, Agt.	....
Suva, Fiji	Leslie E. Brown, Suva, V. C.	Fees.
Swansea, Wales	Jesse H. Johnson, Tex., C.	3,000
Sydney, N. S.	John E. Kehl, Ohio, C.	3,000
Sydney, N.S.W.	John P. Bray, N. Dak., C. G.	5,500
Toronto, Ont.	Robert S. Chilton, Jr., C.	4,000
Trinidad, W. I.	Vacant	3,000
Turks Island	Joseph A. Howells, Ohio, C.	2,000
Vancouver, B.C.	George N. West, D. C., C. G.	4,500
Victoria, B. C.	Abraham E. Smith, Ill., C.	4,000
Wellingt'n, N.Z.	John Duncan, Agt.	....
Windsor, Ont.	Harry A. Conant, Mich., C.	2,500
Winnipeg, Man.	John E. Jones, D. C., C. G.	4,500
Yarmouth, N.S.	Alfred J. Fleming, Mo., C.	2,500

Greece.

Post	Officer	Salary
Athens	George Horton, Ill., C.	3,000
Patras	Edward I. Nathan, Pa., C.	2,000

Guatemala.

Post	Officer	Salary
Guatemala	William P. Kent, Va., C. G.	3,500

Hayti.

Post	Officer	Salary
Aux Cayes	Adolph Strohm, Agt.	....
Cape Haytien	Lem. W. Livingston, Fla., C.	2,000
Jacmel	Louis Vital, Agt.	....
Port au Prince	John B. Terres, N. Y., C.	3,000

Honduras.

Post	Officer	Salary
Tegucigalpa	Wm. E. Alger, Mass., C.	2,500

Italy.

Post	Officer	Salary
Bologna	Carlo Gardini, Italy, Agt.	....
Florence	Jerome A. Quay, Pa. C.	3,000
Genoa	James A. Smith, Vt.	4,500
Leghorn	Ernest A. Man, Fla., C.	3,000
Messina	Arthur S. Cheney, Conn., C.	2,000
Milan	James E. Dunning, Me., C.	4,000
Naples	C. S. Crowninshield, D. C., C	4,000
Palermo	William H. Bishop, C.	3,500
Rome	Chapman Coleman, Ky., C.	3,500
San Remo	Albert Ameglio, Agt.	....
Turin	A. H. Michelson, Mass., C.	2,000
Venice	James V. Long, Pa., C.	2,000

Japan.

Post	Officer	Salary
Nagasaki	Geo. H. Scidmore, Wis., C.	3,500
Kobe	J. H. Snodgrass, W. Va., C.	5,000
Tamsui, Formo.	Carl F. Deichman, Mo., C.	3,000
Yokohama	Harry B. Miller, C. G.	6,000
Dalny	Roger S. Greene, Mass., C.	3,500
Seoul	T. Sammons, Wash., C. G.	5,500

Liberia.

Post	Officer	Salary
Monrovia	Ernest Lyon, Md., C. G.	....

Mexico.

Post	Officer	Salary
Acapulco	Maxwell Moorhead, Pa., C.	2,500
Chihuahua	Lewis A. Martin, W. Va., C.	2,500
Ciudad Porfirio Diaz	Luther T. Ellsworth, O., C.	2,500
Ensenada	Everett E. Bailey, Ill., C.	2,000
Durango	Chas. M. Freeman, N. H., C.	2,000
Matamoras	Clarence A. Miller, Mo., C.	2,000
Mazatlan	Louis Kaiser, Ill., C.	2,500
Mexico	M. C. Piquette, V. & D. C. G.	...
Monterey	Philip C. Hanna, Iowa, C. G.	3,500
Nuevo Laredo	Alonzo B. Garrett, W. Va., C.	2,500
Tampico	P. Meriell Griffith, O., C.	3,000
Vera Cruz	William W. Canada, Ind., C.	4,500

Morocco.

Post	Officer	Salary
Tangier		$3,500

Netherlands and Dominions.

Post	Officer	Salary
Amsterdam	Henry H. Morgan, La., C.	5,000
Batavia, Java	B. S. Rairden, Me., C.	3,000
Curaçao, W. I.	Elias H. Cheney, N. H., C.	2,500
Rotterdam	Soren Listoe, Minn., C. G.	5,500

Nicaragua.

Post	Officer	Salary
Managua	Jose de Olivares, Mo., C.	3,000

Norway.

Post	Officer	Salary
Bergen	Felix S. S. Johnson, N. J., C.	2,500
Christiania	H. Bordewich, Minn., C. G.	3,000

Panama.

Post	Officer	Salary
Colon	James C. Kellogg, La., C.	4,000
Panama	Arnold Shanklim, C. G.	5,500

Paraguay.

Post	Officer	Salary
Asuncion	Edward J. Norton, Tenn., C.	2,000

Persia.

Post	Officer	Salary
Tabriz	William F. Doty, N. J., C.	3,000

Peru.

Post	Officer	Salary
Callao	Samuel M. Taylor, O., C. G.	4,500

Portugal and Dominions.

Post	Officer	Salary
Fayal	M. Benarus, Azores, Agt.	....
Lisbon	Louis H. Ayme, Ill., C. G.	3,500
Oporto	William H. Stuve, Agt.	....
St. Michael's	Edw. A. Creevey, Conn., C.	3,000

Roumania.

Post	Officer	Salary
Bucharest	Nor. Hutchinson, Cal., C. G.	....

Russia.

Post	Officer	Salary
Batum	Alex. Heingartner, Ohio, C.	2,500
Cronstadt	Peter Wigius, Agt.	....
Moscow	Hunter Sharp, N. C., C. G.	5,500
Odessa	John H. Grout, Mass., C.	3,500
Riga	Hernando de Soto, Cal., C.	3,000
St. Petersburg	James W. Ragsdale, Cal., C.	5,500
Vladivostok	Lester Maynard, Cal., C.	3,500
Warsaw	George N. Ifft, Idaho, C.	4,000

Salvador.

Post	Officer	Salary
San Salvador	Arthur H. Frazier, Pa., C. G.	....

Servia.

Post	Officer	Salary
Belgrade	R. S. S Bergh, N. Dak., C.	3,000

Spain and Dominions.

Post	Officer	Salary
Barcelona	Frank D. Hill, Minn., C. G.	5,500
Cadiz	James Sanderson, Agt.	....
Carthagena	Alexander J. Marks	Fees.
Madrid	R. M. Bartleman, Mass., C.	2,500
Malaga	Charles M. Caughy, Md., C.	3,000
Seville	L. J. Rosenberg, Mich., C.	3,000
Teneriffe	Solomon Berliner, N. Y., C.	2,500
Valencia	Chas. S. Winans, Mich., C.	2,500

Sweden.

Post	Officer	Salary
Gothenburg	Wm. H. Robertson, Va., C.	2,500
Stockholm	Edw. L. Adams, N. Y., C. G.	3,500

Switzerland.

Post	Officer	Salary
Basel	George Gifford, Me., C.	3,500
Berne	George Heimrod, Neb., C.	3,500
Geneva	Francis B. Keene, Wis., C.	3,500
St. Gall	Robt. E. Mansfield, Ind., C.	4,500
Zurich	H. de Castro, N. Y., C. G.	4,500

Turkey and Dominions.

Post	Officer	Salary
Alexandretta	John T. Peristiany, Agt.	....
Alexandria	David R. Birch, Pa., C.	3,500
Beirut, Syria	G. B. Ravndal, S. Dak., C. G.	4,500
Cairo	Lewis M. Iddings, C. G.	....
Constantinople	Ed. H. Osmun, Minn., C. G.	6,000
Jerusalem	Thomas R. Wallace, Ia., C.	3,000
Port Said	Harry Broadbent, Agt.	....
Smyrna	Ernest L. Harris, Ill., C. G.	3,500
Suez	Frederick T. Peake, Agt.	....
Trebizond	Milo A. Jewett, Mass., C.	2,500

Uruguay.

Post	Officer	Salary
Montevideo	Frederic W. Goding, Ill., C.	3,500

Venezuela.

Post	Officer	Salary
Caracas	John Brewer, Md., Agt.	....
La Guayra	Thomas P. Moffat, C.	3,000
Maracaibo	E. H. Plumacher, Tenn., C.	2,500
Puerto Cabello	James W. Johnson, N. Y., C.	2,000

Zanzibar.

Post	Officer	Salary
Zanzibar	Arthur Garrels, Mo., C.	2,500

It is not necessary to address a consul by name if the business is of an official nature. "Official business" should be written on the envelope.

Foreign Embassies and Legations in the United States.

COUNTRY.	REPRESENTATIVES.	RANK.
Argentine Republic	Senor Don Epifanio Portela	Envoy Extraordinary and Minister Plenipotentiary.
"	Senor Don Alberto P. Costa	First Secretary of Legation.
Austria-Hungary	Mr. L. Hengelmuller von Hengervar	Envoy Extraordinary and Minister Plenipotentiary.
"	Baron Louis Ambrozy	Counselor of Embassy.
"	Baron F. Haymerle	Secretary.
Belgium	Baron Ludovic Moncheur	Envoy Extraordinary and Minister Plenipotentiary.
"	Mr. E. de Cartier de Marchienne	Counselor of Legation.
Bolivia	Senor Don Ignacio Calderon	Envoy Extraordinary and Minister Plenipotentiary.
"	Senor Don Jorge E. Zalles	Secretary of Legation.
Brazil	Senhor Joaquin Nabuco	Ambassador Extraordinary and Plenipotentiary.
"	Senhor Sylvino G. de Amaral	First Secretary.
"	Senhor E. L. Chermont	Second Secretary.
Chile	Senor Don Anibal Cruz	Envoy Extraordinary and Minister Plenipotentiary.
"	Senor Don Alberto Yoacham	First Secretary of Legation.
China	Dr. Wu Ting-fang	Envoy Extraordinary and Minister Plenipotentiary.
"	Mr. Ou Shou-tchun	First Secretary of Legation.
Colombia	Senor Don Enrique Cortes	Envoy Extraordinary and Minister Plenipotentiary.
Costa Rica	Senor Don Joaquin Barnardo Calvo	Envoy Extraordinary and Minister Plenipotentiary.
Cuba	Senor Don Gonzalo de Quesada	Envoy Extraordinary and Minister Plenipotentiary.
"	Senor Don Arturo Padro y Almeida	First Secretary.
Denmark	Count Moltke	Envoy Extraordinary and Minister Plenipotentiary.
Dominican Republic	Senor Don Emilio C. Joubert	Minister Resident.
" "	Senor Don Arturo L. Fiallo	Secretary of Legation.
Ecuador	Senor Don Luis Felipe Carbo	Envoy Extraordinary and Minister Plenipotentiary.
"	Senor Don Luis Alberto Carbo	Secretary of Legation.
France	M. J. J. Jusserand	Ambassador Extraordinary and Plenipotentiary.
"	M. des Portes de la Fosse	Counselor of the Embassy.
"	Major Fournier	Military Attache.
"	Vicomte Charles de Chambrun	Secretary.
"	Lieut.-Com. de Beaupre	Naval Attache.
"	Vicomte de Martel	Third Secretary.
German Empire	Count Johann Heinrich von Bernstorff	Ambassador Extraordinary and Plenipotentiary.
"	Count Hermann von Hatzfeldt-Wildeuburg	Counselor of Legation and First Secretary of Embassy.
"	Baron Hartmann von Richthofen	Second Secretary.
"	Mr. von Stumm	Third Secretary.
"	Commander Reitzmann	Naval Attache.
"	Major von Livonius	Military Attache.
Great Britain	Right Hon. James Bryce	Ambassador Extraordinary and Plenipotentiary.
"	Mr. Alfred Mitchell Innes	Counselor of Embassy.
"	Mr. G. Young	First Secretary.
"	Mr. W. H. Kinnaird	Second Secretary.
"	Mr. Esmond Ovey	Third Secretary.
"	Mr. H. Beresford-Hope	Attache.
"	Lieut.-Col. B. R. James	Military Attache.
Guatemala	Senor Dr. Luis Toledo Herrarte	Envoy Extraordinary and Minister Plenipotentiary.
Hayti	Mr. J. N. Leger	Envoy Extraordinary and Minister Plenipotentiary.
Honduras	Dr. Luis Lazo	Envoy Extraordinary and Minister Plenipotentiary.
Italy	Signor Edmondo Mayor des Planches	Ambassador Extraordinary and Plenipotentiary.
"	Signor Roberto Centaro	Second Secretary.
"	Signor Giuliano Cora	Attache.
"	Lieut. Filippo Camperio	Naval Attache.
Japan	Mr. Kogoro Takahira	Ambassador Extraordinary and Plenipotentiary.
"	Mr. Masanas Hanihara	Second Secretary.
"	Mr. Matsuzo Nagai	Third Secretary.
Mexico	Senor Don Enrique C. Creel	Ambassador Extraordinary and Plenipotentiary.
"	Senor Don Jose F. Godoy	Minister Plenipotentiary.
"	Senor Don Julio W. Baz	Second Secretary.
Netherlands	Jonkheer J. Loudon	Envoy Extraordinary and Minister Plenipotentiary.
"	Mr. W. A. Royaards	Counselor of Legation.
Nicaragua	Senor Don Luis F. Corea	Envoy Extraordinary and Minister Plenipotentiary.
Norway	Mr. O. Gude	Envoy Extraordinary and Minister Plenipotentiary.
Panama	Senor Don J. Augustin Arango	Envoy Extraordinary and Minister Plenipotentiary.
Persia	Gen. Morteza Kahn	Envoy Extraordinary and Minister Plenipotentiary.
Peru	Mr. Filipe Pardo	Envoy Extraordinary and Minister Plenipotentiary.
"	Senor Manuel de F. y Santander	Secretary.
Portugal	Visconde de Alte	Envoy Extraordinary and Minister Plenipotentiary.
Russia	Baron Rosen	Ambassador Extraordinary and Plenipotentiary.
"	M. Kroupensky	Counselor of Embassy.
"	Prince Nicolas Koudacheff	First Secretary of Embassy.
"	Colonel Baron de Bode	Military Attache.
"	Commander Nebolsine	Naval Attache.
Salvador	Senor Don Frederico Mejia	Envoy Extraordinary and Minister Plenipotentiary.
Siam	Phya Akharaz Varadhara	Envoy Extraordinary and Minister Plenipotentiary.
"	Mr. Edward H. Loftus	Counselor of Legation.
Spain	Senor Don Ramon Pina	Envoy Extraordinary and Minister Plenipotentiary.
"	Senor Don Luis Pastor	First Secretary of Legation.
"	Senor Don Manuel Walls y Merino	Second Secretary of Legation.
"	Lieut.-Col. Don Nicolas Urculla y Cervijo	Military Attache.
Sweden	Mr. Herman de Lagercrantz	Envoy Extraordinary and Minister Plenipotentiary.
Switzerland	Mr. Leo Vogel	Envoy Extraordinary and Minister Plenipotentiary.
"	Mr. Henri Martin	Secretary of Legation.
Turkey	Munji Bey	Consul-General in Charge.
"	Djelal Munif Bey	First Secretary of Legation.
Uruguay	Dr. Luis M. Lafinur	Envoy Extraordinary and Minister Plenipotentiary.

Foreign Consuls in the United States.

(In Principal Places. For Foreign Consuls in the City of New York consult Index.)

C. G., Consul-General; C., Consul; V. C., Vice-Consul; C. A., Consular Agent; A. C., Acting Consul; P. C., Pro-Consul.

ARGENTINE REPUBLIC.

Ala., Mobile, Manuel S. Macias, V. C.
Cal., San Francisco,
Fla., { Fernandina, Thomas C. Borden, V. C.
{ Pensacola, J. Harris Pierpont, V. C.
Ga., Savannah, Andrés E. Moynelo, V. C.
Ill., Chicago, Eduardo Oldendorff, V. C.
La., New Orleans, Alfred Le Blanc, V. C.
Me., Portland, Clarence W. Small, V. C.
Md., Baltimore, James F. Ferguson, V. C.
Mass., Boston, Guillermo McKissock, V. C.
Pa., Philadelphia, Guillermo P. Wilson, V. C.
Va., Norfolk, Guillermo Klyver, V. C.

AUSTRIA-HUNGARY.

Ala., Mobile, Siegfried Kissler, C.
Cal., San Francisco, Karl Ruiz de Roxas, A. C.
Fla., Pensacola, H. Baars, V. C.
Ga., Savannah, Edward Karow, C.
Ill., Chicago, Alexander Nuber von Pereked, C.G.
La., New Orleans, Franz Hindermann, C.
Md., Baltimore, G. Louis Hester, C.
Mass., Boston, Arthur Donner, C.
Mo., St. Louis, Ferdinand Diehm, C
Pa., Hazleton, Vacant, C. A.
Pa., Philadelphia, T. von Schutzenburg, C.
Pa., Pittsburgh, Julius Von Bornemisza, C.
P. I., Manila, Peter Krafft, C.
Tex., Galveston, John Reymershoffer, C.
Wis., Milwaukee,

BELGIUM.

Ala., Mobile, Robert B. du Mont, C.
Cal., { San Francisco, F. Wodon, C. G.
{ Los Angeles, V. Ponet, V. C.
Col., Denver, J. Mignolet, C.
Fla., Jacksonville, Joseph Buttgenbach, V. C.
Ga., Atlanta, Laurent de Give, C.
Ill., Chicago, Ch. Henrotin, C.
Ky., Louisville, St. De Ridder, C.
La., New Orleans, Ch. de Waepenaert, C. G.
Mass., Boston, E. S. Mansfield, C.
Mich., Detroit, Théophile François, C.
Mo., St. Louis, L. Seguenot, C.
Pa., Philadelphia, Paul Hagemans, C. G.
P. I., Manila, Ch. Le Vionnois, C.
S. C., Charleston, B. Rutledge, C.
Va., { Norfolk and Newport News, J. P. André Mottu, C. A.
{ Richmond, W. O. Nolting, C.

BOLIVIA.

Cal., { San Diego, Philip Morse, C.
{ San Francisco, Gabriel V. Calle, C. G.
Ill., Chicago, Frederick Harnwell, C.
Mo., Kansas City, E. R. Heath, Hon. C.
Pa., Philadelphia, Wilfred H. Schoff, Hon. C.

BRAZIL.

Cal., San Francisco, Archibald Barnard, V. C.
La., New Orleans, Charles Dittman, V. C.
Md., Baltimore, Leonce Rabillon, V. C.
Mo., St. Louis, Affonso de Figueiredo, V. C.
Pa., Philadelphia, Napoleon Bonaparte Kelly, V. C.

CHILE.

Cal., San Francisco, Juan Searle, C.
Ill., Chicago, M. J. Steffens, V. C.
Md., Baltimore, R. G. Leupold, C.
Mass., Boston, Horacio N. Fisher, C.
Pa., Philadelphia, Dudley Bartlett, C.

CHINA.

Cal., San Francisco, Hsu Ping-chen, C. G.
Hawaii, Honolulu, Tseng Hai, C.
Mass., Boston, Stephen W. Nickerson, Hon. C.
P. I., Manila, Su Yu-Tchu, C. G.

COLOMBIA.

Ill., Chicago, Erskine M. Phelps, C.
Mass., Boston, Jorge Vargas Heredia, C.
Mo., St. Louis, J. Arbuckle, C.

COSTA RICA.

Cal., San Francisco, José Maria Tinoco, C. G.
Ill., Chicago, Berthold Singer, C.
La., New Orleans, Lamar C. Quintero, C. G.
Md., Baltimore, William A. Riordan, C.
Mass., Boston, Guillermo Figueroa, C.
Pa., Philadelphia, Gustavo Niederlein, C.

DENMARK.

Ala., Mobile, Louis Donald, V. C. for Alabama.
Cal., San Francisco, H. H. Birkholm, C.
Ga., Savannah, J. B. Holst, V. C.
Hawaii, Honolulu, H. R. Macfarlane, C.
Ill., Chicago, Christian H. Hansson, C.
Kan., Kansas City, Jep Hansen Malland, V. C.
Ky., Louisville, Charles E. Currie, C.
La., New Orleans, Thyge Soegaard, V. C.
Md., Baltimore, Holger A. Koppel, V. C.
Mass., Boston, Gustaf Lundberg, C.
Mich., Detroit, Peter Sörensen, V. C.
Minn., St. Paul, John C. Nelson, V. C.
Mo., St. Louis, V. C.
Neb., Omaha.
O., Cleveland, Mark L. Thomsen, V. C.
Ore., Portland, V. C
Pa., Philadelphia, J. N. Wallem, V. C.
P. I., Manila, R. H. Wood, C.

DOMINICAN REPUBLIC.

Ill., Chicago, F. W. Job, V. C.
Md., Baltimore, William A. Riordan, V. C.
N. C., Wilmington, Andrew J. Howell, Jr., V. C.
Porto Rico, San Juan, J. E. Medina y Cortes, C. G.

ECUADOR.

Cal., { Los Angeles, Thomas Duqué, Hon. C. G.
{ San Francisco, Dr. D. P. Arcentales, C. G.
Ill., Chicago, Luis Millet, C.
Mass., Boston, Gustavo Preston, C.
Pa., Philadelphia, Cassius A. Green, C.

FRANCE.

Ala., Mobile, G. A. Rivière, C. A.
Alaska, Nome City, Albert Schneider, C. A.
Cal., San Francisco, Henri Aoine Joseph Mérou, C.
Col., Denver, A. Bourquin, C. A.
Ga., Savannah, Alexis Nicolas, C. A.
Hawaii, Honolulu, R. Etienne C. Menant, V. C.
Ill., Chicago, L. E. Houssin de Saint Laurent, C.
Ky., Louisville, Michel Hermann, C. A.
La., New Orleans, Marie P. V. Dejaux, C.
Md., Baltimore, Léonce Rabillon, C. A.
Mass., Boston, Joseph J. Flamand, C. A.
Mich., Detroit, Joseph Belanger, C. A.
Minn., St. Paul, François Célestin Boucher, C. A.
Mo., St. Louis, Louis Seguenot, C. A.
O., Cincinnati, Eugene C. Pociey, C. A.
Ore., Portland, Charles Henri Labbé, C. A.
Pa., Philadelphia, Raymond de Lobel-Mahy, V. C.
P. I., Manila, Jean B. G. Bertrand, C.
P. R., San Juan, Paul C. M. Robin, C.
Tex., Galveston, Chas. J. Z. M. M. de Peillon, V. C.
Wash., Seattle, P. J. B. Joujou-Roche, C. A.

GERMANY.

Ala., Mobile, E. Holzborn, C.
Cal., San Francisco, Franz Bopp, C.
Col., Denver, Georg Plehn, C.
D. C., Washington, Gustave Dittmar, C. A.
Ga., Atlanta, Dr. Erich Zoepffel, C.
Hawaii, Honolulu, W. Pfotenhauer, C.
Ill., Chicago, Walther Wever, C. G.
La., New Orleans, F. von Nordenflycht, C.
Md., Baltimore, Carl A. Luderitz, C.
Mass., Boston, Wilhelm T. Reincke, C.
Mo., St. Louis, Maximillian von Loehr, C.
N. C., Wilmington, James Sprunt, C.
O., Cincinnati, Joseph Lettenbaur, C.
Ore., Portland,
Pa., Philadelphia, Werner Hagen, C.
P. I., Manila, Franz Grunenwald, C.
P. R., Ponce, Julius Umbach, V. C.
S. C., Charleston, Emil Jahnz, C.
Tex., Galveston, Otto Scheidt, C.
Va., Richmond, Carl E. Victor, C.
Wash., Tacoma, Otto Richter, V. C.

GREAT BRITAIN.

Ala., Mobile, Edmund J. Seiders, V. C.
Cal., San Francisco, Walter Risley Hearn, C. G.
Col., Denver, Alfred Cribben, V. C.
Fla., Jacksonville, John W. Morris, V. C.
Fla., Key West, W. J. H. Taylor, V. C.
Ga., Savannah, James A. Donnelly, C.
Hawaii, Honolulu, Alfred E. Wileman, C.
Ill., Chicago, Alexander Finn, C. G.

FOREIGN CONSULS IN THE UNITED STATES—*Continued.*

La., New Orleans, H. T. Carew-Hunt, C.
Me., Portland, John Bernard Keating, V. C.
Md., Baltimore, Gilbert Fraser, C.
Mass., Boston, William Wyndham, C.
Miss., Biloxi, J. J. Lemon, V. C.
Mo., St. Louis, Thomas E. Erskine, C.
Mo., Kansas City, Herbert W. Mackirdy, V. C.
Neb., Omaha, Mathew Alexander Hall, V. C.
N. C., Wilmington, James Sprunt, V. C.
Ore., Portland, James Laidlaw, C.
Pa., Philadelphia, Wilfred Powell, C.
P. I., Manila, R. de B. M. Layard, C. G.
P. I., Cebu, Charles Augustin Fulcher, V. C.
Porto Rico, San Juan, Wm. B. Churchward, C.
R. I., Providence, George A. Stockwell, V. C.
S. C., Charleston, Alexander Harkness, V. C.
Tex., Galveston, Horace Dickinson Nugent, C.
Va., Richmond, Arthur Ponsonby Wilmer, V. C.
Wash., Seattle, Bernard Pelly, V. C.

GREECE.

Cal., San Francisco, Richard de Fontana, C.
Ill., Chicago, Nikolaos Sallopoulos, C.
Mass., Boston, Anthony L. Benachi, C.
Mo., St. Louis, H. M. Pesmazoglow, in charge.
Pa., Philadelphia, S. Edwin Megargee, C.

GUATEMALA.

Cal., San Francisco, Felipe Galicia, C. G.
Ill., Chicago, A. C. Garsia, Hon. C.
Mass., Boston, Benjamin Preston Clark, Hon. C.
Mo., St. Louis, L. D. Kingsland, Hon. C. G.

HAYTI.

Ga., Savannah, T. B. Harris, V. C.
Ill., Chicago, Cuthbert Singleton, C.
Mass., Boston, Benjamin C. Clark, C.

HONDURAS.

Cal., San Francisco, Vacant.
Ill., Chicago, George F. Stone, C. G.
La., New Orleans, J. Ernesto Alvarado, C. G.
Md., Baltimore, C. Morton Stewart, Jr., C. G.

ITALY.

Ala., Mobile, Giovanni Ivulich, C. A.
Cal., San Francisco, Salvatore L. Rocca, C. G.
Ct., New Haven, Michele Riccio, C. A.
Ga., Savannah, Mose Cafiero, C. A.
Hawaii, Honolulu, F. A. Schaefer, C.
Ill., Chicago, Guido Sabetta, C.
La., New Orleans, Luigi A. Marescotti, C.
Md., Baltimore, Prospero Schiaffino, C. A.
Mich., Detroit, C. Pietro di Antonio, C. A.
Mass., Boston, Marquis A. Faa di Bruno, C.
Mo., St. Louis, Domenico Ginocchio, C. A.
O., Cleveland, Nicola Cerri, C. A.
Ore., Portland, F. C. d'Olivola, C. A.
Pa., Philadelphia, G. F. Fornie, C.
Pa., Pittsburgh, Giulio Ricciardi, V. C.
S. C., Charleston, Giovanni Sottile, C. A.
Tex., Galveston, C. Nicolini, C. A.
Va., Norfolk, Arturo Parati, C. A.
Wash., Seattle, Augusto J. Ghiglione, C. A.

JAPAN.

Ala., Mobile, Wm. P. Hutchison, Hon. C.
Cal., San Francisco, Chozo Koike, C. G.
Hawaii, Honolulu, Miki Saitow, C. G.
Ill., Chicago, K. Matsubara, in charge.
La., New Orleans, John Walker Phillips, Hon. C.
Ore., Portland, Jokichi Iwava, C. A.
Pa., Philadelphia, J. F. McFadden, Hon. C.
Wash., Seattle, Tokichi Tanaka, C.

LIBERIA.

Mass., Boston, Charles Hall Adams, C. G.
Pa., Philadelphia, Thomas J. Hunt, C.

MEXICO.

Ala., Mobile, Alphonso Jimenez, V. C.
Cal., San Francisco, Dr. Plutarco Ornelas, C. G.
Ill., Chicago, Augustin Pina, C.
La., New Orleans, Fernando Baz, Jr., C.
Md., Baltimore, Regelio F. Guel, C.
Mass., Boston, Arturo P. Cushing, C.
Mo., St. Louis, Miguel E. Diebold, C.
O., Cincinnati, Hugo Fromman, V. C.
Pa., Philadelphia, M. Torres y Sagaseta, C.
Tex., Galveston, Manuel N. Velarde, C.
Va., Norfolk, Juan B. Didapp, C.

NETHERLANDS.

Cal., San Francisco, G. J. G. Marsily, C.
Ill., Chicago, G. Birkhoff, Jr., C. G.
La., New Orleans, W. J. Hammond, C.
Md., Baltimore, R. H. Mottu, C.
Mass., Boston, C. V. Dasey, C.
Mo., St. Louis, G. H. ten Brock, C.
Pa., Philadelphia, Arnold Katz, C.

NICARAGUA.

Cal., San Francisco, Dr. F. R. Mayorga, C. G.
Ill., Chicago, B. Singer, C.
La., New Orleans, Gustavo A. Bonilla, C.

NORWAY.

Ill., Chicago, Frederick Herman Gade, C.
Iowa, Decorah, Johannes B. Wist, V. C.
Mass., Boston, Peter Justin Paasche, V. C.
Minn., St. Paul, Engebreth H. Hobe, C.
Neb., Omaha, A. L. Undeland, V. C.
Ohio, Cleveland, Ole M. Friestad, V. C.
Wis., Milwaukee, Olof J. Rove, V. C.

PARAGUAY.

D. C., Washington, Clifford S. Walton, C. G.

PERU.

Cal., San Francisco, Enrique Grau, C.
Pa., Philadelphia, Wilfredo H. Schoff, Hon. C.

PORTUGAL.

Cal., San Francisco, Ig. R. da Costa Duarte, C. G.
Ill., Chicago, A. de Q. Ribeiro, C.
La., New Orleans, Maurice Generelly, V. C.
Md., Baltimore, Adelbert W. Means, V. C.
Mass., Boston, Viscount de Valle da Costa, C.
Pa., Philadelphia, John Mason, V. C.

RUSSIA.

Ala., Mobile, Murray Wheeler, V. C.
Cal., San Francisco, Paul Kozakévitch, C.
Ga., Savannah, W. W. Williamson, V. C.
Ill., Chicago, Baron E. de Schilling, C.
Md., Baltimore, Charles Nitze, V. C.
Mass., Boston, T. Quincy Browne, V. C.
Ore., Portland,
Pa., Philadelphia, William R. Tucker, V. C.

SALVADOR.

Cal., San Francisco, Encarnacion Mejia, C. G.
Mass., Boston, Geo. A. Lewis, Hon. C.

SPAIN.

Ala., Mobile, Luis Marty Moragues, Hon. V. C.
Cal., San Francisco, José M. L. de Espinosa, C.
Ill., Chicago, Berthold Singer, Hon. V. C.
La., New Orleans, José Texidor y Jugo, C.
Md., Baltimore, Prospero Schiaffino, Hon. V. C.
Mo., St. Louis, James Arbuckle, V. C.
Pa., Philadelphia, Horatio C. Newcomb, Hon. V. C.
P. I., Manila, Arturo Baldasano y Topete, C. G.
Porto Rico, San Juan, Joaquin Carsi y Rivera, C.
Va., Norfolk, Carlos C. Richardson, Hon. V. C.

SWEDEN.

Ala., Mobile, Robert H. Smith, V. C.
Cal., San Francisco, William Matson, C.
Col., Denver, Hjalmar R. Sahlgaard, V. C.
Ill., Chicago, J. R. Lindgren, V. C.
La., New Orleans, Pearl Wight, V. C.
Mass., Boston, Birger G. Adolf Rosentwist, V. C.
Minn., St. Paul, J. A. Jackson, in charge of V. C.
Mo., St. Louis, Charles A. A. Ekstromer, V. C.
Pa., Philadelphia, Marcel Alonzo Viti, V. C.

SWITZERLAND.

Cal., San Francisco, Antoine Borel, C.
Ill., Chicago, Arnold Holinger, C.
Mo., St. Louis, Jacques Buff, C.
Pa., Philadelphia, Gustav A. Walther, C.

TURKEY.

Cal., San Francisco, George E. Hall, C. G.
D. C., Washington, Dr. Schoenfeld, C. G.
Ill., Chicago, Charles Henrotin, C. G.
Mass., Boston, Frank G. Macomber, Hon. C. G.

URUGUAY.

Ill., Chicago, Juan Moffit, C.
Mass., Boston, W. Allen Taft, Jr., Prov. V. C.
Pa., Philadelphia, Johan N. Wallem, C.

VENEZUELA.

Cal., San Francisco, J. L. Eastland, C.
Ill., Chicago, José M. Alvizua, C.
Pa., Philadelphia, W. P. Wilson, C.

Apportionment of Congressional Representation.

Ratios under Constitution and at Each Census, 1790 to 1900, by States.

STATE.	RATIOS UNDER CONSTITUTION AND CENSUSES.												
	Constitution.	1790	1800	1810	1820	1830	1840	1850	1860	1870	1880	1890	1900
	30,000.	33,000.	33,000.	35,000.	40,000.	47,700.	70,680.	93,423.	127,381.	131,425.	151,911.	173,901.	194,182.
	Representation.												
Alabama	....	....	....	1	3	5	7	7	6	8	8	9	9
Arkansas	....	....	....	....	....	1	1	2	3	4	5	6	7
California	....	....	....	....	....	....	2	2	3	4	6	7	8
Colorado	....	....	....	....	....	....	....	....	....	1	1	2	3
Connecticut	5	7	7	7	6	6	4	4	4	4	4	4	5
Delaware	1	1	1	2	1	1	1	1	1	1	1	1	1
Florida	....	....	....	....	....	....	1	1	1	2	2	2	2
Georgia	3	2	4	6	7	9	8	8	7	9	10	11	11
Idaho	....	....	....	....	....	....	....	....	....	....	1	1	1
Illinois	....	....	....	1	1	3	7	9	14	19	20	22	25
Indiana	....	....	....	1	3	7	10	11	11	13	13	13	13
Iowa	....	....	....	....	....	....	2	2	6	9	11	11	11
Kansas	....	....	....	....	....	....	....	....	1	3	7	8	8
Kentucky	....	2	6	10	12	13	10	10	9	10	11	11	11
Louisiana	....	....	....	1	3	3	4	4	5	6	6	6	7
Maine	....	....	....	*7	7	8	7	6	5	5	4	4	4
Maryland	6	8	9	9	9	8	6	6	5	6	6	6	6
Massachusetts	8	14	17	13	13	12	10	11	10	11	12	13	14
Michigan	....	....	....	....	....	1	3	4	6	9	11	12	12
Minnesota	....	....	....	....	....	....	....	2	2	3	5	7	9
Mississippi	....	....	....	1	1	2	4	5	5	6	7	7	8
Missouri	....	....	....	....	1	2	5	7	9	13	14	15	16
Montana	....	....	....	....	....	....	....	....	....	....	1	1	1
Nebraska	....	....	....	....	....	....	....	....	1	1	3	6	6
Nevada	....	....	....	....	....	....	....	....	1	1	1	1	1
New Hampshire	3	4	5	6	6	5	4	3	3	3	2	2	2
New Jersey	4	5	6	6	6	6	5	5	5	7	7	8	10
New York	6	10	17	27	34	40	34	33	31	33	34	34	37
North Carolina	5	10	12	13	13	13	9	8	7	8	9	9	10
North Dakota	....	....	....	....	....	....	....	....	....	....	1	1	2
Ohio	....	....	1	6	14	19	21	21	19	20	21	21	21
Oregon	....	....	....	....	....	....	....	1	1	1	1	2	2
Pennsylvania	8	13	18	23	26	28	24	25	24	27	28	30	32
Rhode Island	1	2	2	2	2	2	2	2	2	2	2	2	2
South Carolina	5	6	8	9	9	9	7	6	4	5	7	7	7
South Dakota	....	....	....	....	....	....	....	....	....	....	2	2	2
Tennessee	....	1	3	6	9	13	11	10	8	10	10	10	10
Texas	....	....	....	....	....	....	2	2	4	6	11	13	16
Utah	....	....	....	....	....	....	....	....	....	....	....	1	1
Vermont	....	2	4	6	5	5	4	3	3	3	2	2	2
Virginia	10	19	22	23	22	21	15	13	11	9	10	10	10
Washington	....	....	....	....	....	....	....	....	....	....	1	2	3
West Virginia	....	....	....	....	....	....	....	....	....	3	4	4	5
Wisconsin	..	....	....	....	....	....	2	3	6	8	9	10	11
Wyoming	....	....	....	....	....	....	....	....	....	....	1	1	1
Total	65	106	142	186	213	242	232	237	243	293	332	357	386

* Included in the 20 members originally assigned to Massachusetts, but credited to Maine after its admission as a State March 15, 1820.

NOTE.—The following representation included in the table was added after the several census apportionments indicated: First—Tennessee, 1. Second—Ohio, 1. Third—Alabama, 1; Illinois, 1; Indiana, 1; Louisiana, 1; Maine, 7; Mississipi, 1. Fifth—Arkansas, 1; Michigan 1. Sixth—California, 2; Florida, 1; Iowa, 2; Texas, 2; Wisconsin, 2. Seventh—Massachusetts, 1; Minnesota, 2; Oregon, 1. Eighth—Illinois, 1; Iowa, 1; Kentucky, 1; Minnesota, 1; Nebraska, 1; Nevada, 1; Ohio, 1; Pennsylvania, 1; Rhode Island, 1; Vermont, 1. Ninth—Colorado, 1. Tenth—Idaho, 1; Montana, 1; North Dakota, 1; South Dakota, 2; Washington, 1; Wyoming, 1. Eleventh—Utah, 1.

Party Divisions

IN THE HOUSE OF REPRESENTATIVES, 60TH AND 61ST CONGRESSES.

States.	Sixtieth Congress.*		Sixty-first Congress.*		States.	Sixtieth Congress.*		Sixty-first Congress.*	
	Dem.	Rep.	Dem.	Rep.		Dem.	Rep.	Dem.	Rep.
Alabama	9	..	9	..	Nevada	1	..	1	..
Arkansas	7	..	7	..	New Hampshire	..	2	..	2
California	..	8	..	8	New Jersey	4	6	3	7
Colorado	..	3	3	..	New York	12	25	11	26
Connecticut	..	5	..	5	North Carolina	10	..	7	3
Delaware	..	1	..	1	North Dakota	..	2	..	2
Florida	3	..	3	..	Ohio	5	16	8	13
Georgia	11	..	11	..	Oklahoma	..	..	2	3
Idaho	..	1	..	1	Oregon	..	2	..	2
Illinois	5	20	6	19	Pennsylvania	7	25	5	27
Indiana	4	9	11	2	Rhode Island	1	1	..	2
Iowa	1	10	1	10	South Carolina	7	..	7	..
Kansas	..	8	..	8	South Dakota	..	2	..	2
Kentucky	7	4	8	3	Tennessee	8	2	8	2
Louisiana	7	..	7	..	Texas	16	..	16	..
Maine	..	4	..	4	Utah	..	1	..	1
Maryland	3	3	3	3	Vermont	..	2	..	2
Massachusetts	3	11	3	11	Virginia	9	1	9	1
Michigan	..	12	..	12	Washington	..	3	..	3
Minnesota	1	8	1	8	West Virginia	..	5	..	5
Mississippi	8	..	8	..	Wisconsin	2	9	1	10
Missouri	12	4	10	6	Wyoming	..	1	..	1
Montana	..	1	..	1					
Nebraska	1	5	3	3	Total	164	222	172	219

* As constituted at the beginning of the Congress.

PARTY DIVISIONS IN CONGRESS SINCE THE FORMATION OF THE REPUBLICAN PARTY IN 1859.

Congresses.	Years.	Senate.					House of Representatives.				
		Dem.	Rep.	Amer.	Union.	Ind.	Dem.	Rep.	Amer.	Union.	Ind.
XXXVI	1859-1861	38	26	2	..	..	101	113	23	..	..
XXXVII	1861-1863*	10	31	..	2	..	42	106	..	28	..
XXXVIII	1863-1865*	9	36	..	5	..	75	102	..	..	9
XXXIX	1865-1867	11	41	..	..	..	40	145	..	..	..
XL	1867-1869	11	42	..	..	..	49	143	..	..	..
XLI	1869-1871	11	58	..	..	..	78	151	..	..	..
XLII	1871-1873	17	57	..	..	..	103	138	..	..	5 †
XLIII	1873-1875	20	47	..	..	7 †	92	194	..	..	14
XLIV	1875-1877	29	43	..	..	2 †	168	107	..	..	..
XLV	1877-1879	39	36	..	..	1 †	151	142	..	..	..
XLVI	1879-1881	44	32	..	..	..	148	129	..	..	16 ‡
XLVII	1881-1883	38	37	..	..	1 §	138	146	..	..	10 ‡
XLVIII	1883-1885	36	40‖	..	..	..	198	124	..	..	1 ‡
XLIX	1885-1887	34	42	..	..	..	204	120	..	..	1 ‡
L	1887-1889	37	39	..	..	..	168	153	..	..	4
LI	1889-1891	37	39	..	..	..	159	166	..	..	..
LII	1891-1893	39	47	..	..	2 ¶	236	88	..	..	8 ¶
LIII.**	1893-1895	44	38	..	..	3 ¶	220	126	..	..	8 ¶
LIV	1895-1897	39	42	..	..	5 ¶	104	246	..	..	7 ¶
LV	1897-1899	34	46	..	..	10‡‡	134§§	206	..	..	16¶¶
LVI	1899-1901	26	53	..	..	11 ¶¶¶	163	185	..	..	9‡‡‡
LVII	1901-1903	29	56	..	..	3 §§§	153	198	..	..	5‖‖‖
LVIII	1903-1905	32	58	..	..	..	174	206	..	..	2***
LVIX	1905-1907	32	58	..	..	..	136	250	..	..	..
LX	1907-1909	31	61	..	..	..	164	222	..	..	..
LXI	1909-1911	32	60	..	..	..	172	219	..	..	..

Parties as constituted at the beginning of each Congress are given. These figures were liable to change by contests for seats, etc.

* During the Civil War most of the Southern States were unrepresented in Congress.

† Liberal Republicans. ‡ Greenbackers. § David Davis, Independent, of Illinois.

‖ Two Virginia Senators were Readjusters, and voted with the Republicans.

¶ People's party, except that in the House of Representatives of the Fifty-fourth Congress one member is classed as Silver party.

** Three Senate seats were vacant (and continued so) and two Representative seats were unfilled (Rhode Island had not yet effected a choice) when the session began. Rhode Island subsequently elected two Republicans.

‡‡ Five Populists, two Silver party, three Independents. §§ Including fifteen members classed as Fusionists. ¶¶ Including three members classed as Silver party. There was one vacancy.

‡‡‡ Six Populists, three Silver party.

¶¶¶ Five Populists, one Silver party, two Independents, and three vacancies.

‖‖‖ Three Populists, one Silver party, one Fusion party, one vacancy.

§§§ One Populist, one Silver party, one Fusionist, two vacancies.

*** Two Union Labor and two vacancies—one Democratic, one Republican.

The Sixtieth Congress.

BEGAN MARCH 4, 1907, AND ENDS MARCH 4, 1909.

SENATE.

President..Charles W. Fairbanks, R., of Indiana.

Terms Expire.	Senators.	P. O. Address.
	ALABAMA.	
1915	Joseph F. Johnston, D.	Birmingham.
1913	John H. Bankhead, D.	Fayette.
	ARKANSAS.	
1909	James P. Clarke, D.	Little Rock.
1913	Jefferson Davis, D.	Little Rock.
	CALIFORNIA.	
1909	George C. Perkins, R.	Oakland.
1911	Frank P. Flint, R.	Los Angeles.
	COLORADO.	
1909	Henry M. Teller, D.	Denver.
1913	Simon Guggenheim, R.	Denver.
	CONNECTICUT.	
1909	Frank B. Brandegee, R.	New London.
1911	Morgan G. Bulkeley, R.	Hartford.
	DELAWARE.	
1911	Henry A. Du Pont, R.	Wilmington.
1913	H. A. Richardson, R.	Dover.
	FLORIDA.	
1909	William H. Milton, D.	Marianna.
1911	James P. Taliaferro, D.	Jacksonville.
	GEORGIA.	
1909	Alexander S. Clay, D.	Marietta.
1913	Augustus O. Bacon, D.	Maçon.
	IDAHO.	
1909	Weldon B. Heyburn, R.	Wallace.
1913	William E. Borah, R.	Boise.
	ILLINOIS.	
1909	Albert J. Hopkins, R.	Aurora.
1913	Shelby M. Cullom, R.	Springfield.
	INDIANA.	
1909	James A. Hemenway, R.	Boonville.
1911	Albert J. Beveridge, R.	Indianapolis.
	IOWA.	
1915	Albert B. Cummins, R.	Des Moines.
1913	Jona. P. Dolliver, R.	Fort Dodge.
	KANSAS.	
1909	Chester I. Long, R.	MedicineLodge
1913	Charles Curtis, R.	Topeka.
	KENTUCKY.	
1909	James B. McCreary, D.	Richmond.
1913	T. H. Paynter, D.	Frankfort.
	LOUISIANA.	
1909	Samuel D. McEnery, D.	New Orleans.
1913	Murphy J. Foster, D.	Franklin.
	MAINE.	
1911	Eugene Hale, R.	Ellsworth.
1913	William P. Frye, R.	Lewiston.
	MARYLAND.	
1909	John W. Smith, D.	Snow Hill.
1911	Isidor Rayner, D.	Baltimore.
	MASSACHUSETTS.	
1911	Henry Cabot Lodge, R.	Nahant.
1913	Winthrop M. Crane, R.	Dalton.
	MICHIGAN.	
1911	Julius C. Burrows, R.	Kalamazoo.
1913	William A. Smith, R.	Grand Rapids.
	MINNESOTA.	
1911	Moses E. Clapp, R.	St. Paul.
1913	Knute Nelson, R.	Alexandria.
	MISSISSIPPI.	
1911	Hernando D. Money, D.	Miss'ippi City.
1913	Anselm J. McLaurin, D.	Brandon.
	MISSOURI.	
1909	William J. Stone, D.	Jefferson City.
1911	William Warner, R.	Kansas City.
	MONTANA.	
1911	Thomas H. Carter, R.	Helena.
1913	Joseph M. Dixon, R.	Missoula.
	NEBRASKA.	
1911	Elmer J. Burkett, R.	Lincoln.
1913	Norris Brown, R.	Kearney.
	NEVADA.	
1909	Francis G. Newlands, D.	Reno.
1911	George S. Nixon, R.	Winnemucca.
	NEW HAMPSHIRE.	
1909	Jacob H. Gallinger, R.	Concord.
1913	Henry E. Burnham, R.	Manchester.
	NEW JERSEY.	
1911	John Kean, R.	Elizabeth.
1913	Frank O. Briggs, R.	Trenton.
	NEW YORK.	
1909	Thomas C. Platt, R.	New York.
1911	Chauncey M. Depew, R.	New York.
	NORTH CAROLINA.	
1909	Lee S. Overman, D.	Salisbury.
1913	Fernifold M. Simmons, D.	Raleigh.
	NORTH DAKOTA.	
1909	H. C. Hansbrough, R.	Devil's Lake.
1911	Porter J. McCumber, R.	Wahpeton.
	OHIO.	
1909	Joseph B. Foraker, R.	Cincinnati.
1911	Charles Dick, R.	Akron.
	OKLAHOMA.	
1913	Robert L. Owen, D.	Muskogee.
1915	Thomas P. Gore, D.	Lawton.
	OREGON.	
1909	Charles W. Fulton, R.	Astoria.
1913	Jonathan Bourne, Jr., R.	Portland.
	PENNSYLVANIA.	
1909	Boies Penrose, R.	Philadelphia.
1911	Philander C. Knox, R.	Pittsburgh.
	RHODE ISLAND.	
1911	Nelson W. Aldrich, R.	Providence.
1913	George P. Wetmore, R.	Newport.
	SOUTH CAROLINA.	
1909	Frank B. Gary, D.	Abbeville.
1913	Benjamin R. Tillman, D.	Trenton.
	SOUTH DAKOTA.	
1909	Albert B. Kittridge, R.	Sioux Falls.
1913	Robert J. Gamble, R.	Yankton.
	TENNESSEE.	
1911	James B. Frazier, D.	Chattanooga.
1913	Robert L. Taylor, D.	Nashville.
	TEXAS.	
1911	Charles A. Culberson, D.	Dallas.
1913	Joseph W. Bailey, D.	Gainesville.
	UTAH.	
1909	Reed Smoot, R.	Provo City.
1911	George Sutherland, R.	Salt Lake City.
	VERMONT.	
1909	William P. Dillingham, R.	Montpelier.
1911	Redfield Proctor, R.	Proctor.
	VIRGINIA.	
1911	John W. Daniel, D.	Lynchburg.
1913	Thomas S. Martin, D.	Scottsville.
	WASHINGTON.	
1909	Levi Ankeny, R.	Walla Walla.
1911	Samuel H. Piles, R.	Seattle.
	WEST VIRGINIA.	
1911	Nathan B. Scott, R.	Wheeling.
1913	Stephen B. Elkins, R.	Elkins.
	WISCONSIN.	
1909	Isaac Stephenson, R.	Marinette.
1911	Robert M. La Follette, R.	Madison.
	WYOMING.	
1911	Clarence D. Clark, R.	Evanston.
1913	Francis E. Warren, R.	Cheyenne.

D., Democrats, 31; R., Republicans, 61.

HOUSE OF REPRESENTATIVES.

ALABAMA.

Dist.	*Representative.*	*Politics.*	*P. O. Address.*
1	George W. Taylor*	Dem	Demopolis.
2	O. C. Wiley*	Dem	Montgomery.
3	Henry D. Clayton*	Dem	Eufaula.
4	William B. Craig	Dem	Selma.
5	J. Thomas Heflin*	Dem	Lafayette.
6	Richmond P. Hobson	Dem	Fayette.
7	John L. Burnett*	Dem	Gadsden.
8	William Richardson*	Dem	Huntsville.
9	Oscar W. Underwood*	Dem	Birmingham.

ARKANSAS.

Dist.	*Representative.*	*Politics.*	*P. O. Address.*
1	R. Bruce Macon*	Dem	Helena.
2	S. Brundidge, Jr.*	Dem	Searcy.
3	John C. Floyd*	Dem	Yellville.
4	W. B. Cravens	Dem	Fort Smith.
5	Charles C. Reid*	Dem	Morrillton.
6	Joseph T. Robinson*	Dem	Lonoke.
7	Robert M. Wallace.*	Dem	Magnolia.

CALIFORNIA.

Dist.	*Representative.*	*Politics.*	*P. O. Address.*
1	W. F. Englebright*	Rep	Nevada City.
2	Duncan E. McKinlay*	Rep	Santa Rosa.
3	Joseph R. Knowland*	Rep	Alameda.
4	Julius Kahn*	Rep	San Francisco.
5	Everis A. Hayes*	Rep	San Jose.
6	James C. Needham*	Rep	Modesta.
7	James McLachlan*	Rep	Pasadena.
8	Sylvester C. Smith*	Rep	Bakersfield.

COLORADO.

At Large.

Dist.	*Representative.*	*Politics.*	*P. O. Address.*
	George W. Cook	Rep	Denver.
1	Robert W. Bonynge*	Rep	Denver.
2	Warren A. Haggott	Rep	Idaho Springs

CONNECTICUT.

At Large.

Dist.	*Representative.*	*Politics.*	*P. O. Address.*
	George L. Lilley*	Rep	Waterbury.
1	E. Stevens Henry*	Rep	Rockville.
2	Nehemiah D. Sperry*	Rep	New Haven.
3	Edwin W. Higgins*	Rep	Norwich.
4	Ebenezer J. Hill*	Rep	Norwalk.

DELAWARE.

At Large.

Dist.	*Representative.*	*Politics.*	*P. O. Address.*
	Hiram R. Burton*	Rep	Lewes.

FLORIDA.

Dist.	*Representative.*	*Politics.*	*P. O. Address.*
1	Stephen M. Sparkman*	Dem	Tampa.
2	Frank Clark*	Dem	Gainesville.
3	William B. Lamar*	Dem	Tallahassee.

GEORGIA.

Dist.	*Representative.*	*Politics.*	*P. O. Address.*
1	Charles G. Edwards	Dem	Savannah.
2	James M. Griggs*	Dem	Dawson.
3	Elijah B. Lewis*	Dem	Montezuma.
4	Wm. C. Adamson*	Dem	Carrollton.
5	L. F. Livingston*	Dem	Covington.
6	Charles L. Bartlett*	Dem	Macon.
7	Gordon Lee*	Dem	Chickamauga.
8	William M. Howard*	Dem	Lexington.
9	Thomas M. Bell*	Dem	Gainesville.
10	Thos. W. Hardwick*	Dem	Sandersville.
11	Wm. G. Brantley*	Dem	Brunswick.

IDAHO.

Dist.	*Representative.*	*Politics.*	*P. O. Address.*
	Burton L. French*	Rep	Moscow.

ILLINOIS.

Dist.	*Representative.*	*Politics.*	*P. O. Address.*
1	Martin B. Madden*	Rep	Chicago.
2	James R. Mann*	Rep	Chicago.
3	William W. Wilson*	Rep	Chicago.
4	James T. McDermott	Dem	Chicago.
5	A. J. Sabath	Dem	Chicago.
6	William Lorimer*	Rep	Chicago.
7	Philip Knopf*	Rep	Chicago.
8	Charles McGavin.*	Rep	Chicago.
9	Henry S. Boutell*	Rep	Chicago.
10	George E. Foss*	Rep	Chicago.
11	Howard M. Snapp*	Rep	Joliet.
12	Charles E. Fuller*	Rep	Belvidere.
13	Frank O. Lowden	Rep	Oregon.

ILLINOIS—*Continued.*

Dist.	*Representative.*	*Politics.*	*P. O. Address.*
14	James McKinney*	Rep	Aledo.
15	George W. Prince*	Rep	Galesburg.
16	Joseph V. Graff*	Rep	Peoria.
17	John A. Sterling*	Rep	Bloomington.
18	Joseph G. Cannon*	Rep	Danville.
19	William B. McKinley*	Rep	Champaign.
20	Henry T. Rainey*	Dem	Carrollton.
21	Ben. F. Caldwell†	Dem	Chatham.
22	Wm. A. Rodenberg*	Rep	East St. Louis.
23	Martin D. Foster	Dem	Olney.
24	Pleasant T. Chapman*	Rep	Vienna.
25	N. B. Thistlewood	Rep	Cairo.

INDIANA.

Dist.	*Representative.*	*Politics.*	*P. O. Address.*
1	John H. Foster*	Rep	Evansville.
2	John C. Chaney*	Rep	Sullivan.
3	W. E. Cox	Dem	Jasper.
4	Lincoln Dixon*	Dem	North Vernon.
5	Elias S. Holliday*	Rep	Brazil.
6	James E. Watson*	Rep	Rushville.
7	Jesse Overstreet*	Rep	Indianapolis.
8	John A. M. Adair	Dem	Portland.
9	Charles B. Landis*	Rep	Delphi.
10	E. D. Crumpacker*	Rep	Valparaiso.
11	George W. Rauch	Dem	Marion.
12	Clarence C. Gilhams*	Rep	La Grange.
13	Henry A. Barnhart	Dem	Rochester.

IOWA.

Dist.	*Representative.*	*Politics.*	*P. O. Address.*
1	C. A. Kennedy	Rep	Montrose.
2	Albert F. Dawson*	Rep	Preston.
3	Benj. P. Birdsall*	Rep	Clarion.
4	Gilbert N. Haugen*	Rep	Northwood.
5	Robert G. Cousins*	Rep	Tipton.
6	Daniel W. Hamilton	Dem	Sigourney.
7	John A. T. Hull*	Rep	Des Moines.
8	William P. Hepburn*	Rep	Clarinda.
9	Walter I. Smith*	Rep	Council Bluffs.
10	James P. Conner*	Rep	Denison.
11	Elbert H. Hubbard*	Rep	Sioux City.

KANSAS.

Dist.	*Representative.*	*Politics.*	*P. O. Address.*
1	D. R. Anthony, Jr.	Rep	Leavenworth.
2	Charles F. Scott*	Rep	Iola.
3	Philip P. Campbell*	Rep	Pittsburgh.
4	James M. Miller*	Rep	Council Grove.
5	Wm. A. Calderhead*	Rep	Marysville.
6	William A. Reeder*	Rep	Logan.
7	E. H. Madison	Rep	Dodge City.
8	Victor Murdock*	Rep	Wichita.

KENTUCKY.

Dist.	*Representative.*	*Politics.*	*P. O. Address.*
1	Ollie James*	Dem	Marion.
2	Augustus O. Stanley*	Dem	Henderson.
3	A. D. James	Rep	Penrod.
4	Ben. Johnson	Dem	Bardstown.
5	Swagar Sherley*	Dem	Louisville.
6	Joseph L. Rhinock*	Dem	Covington.
7	W. P. Kimball	Dem	Lexington.
8	Harvey Helm	Dem	Stanford.
9	James B. Bennett*	Rep	Greenup.
10	John W. Langley	Rep	Prestonburg.
11	Don C. Edwards*	Rep	London.

LOUISIANA.

Dist.	*Representative.*	*Politics.*	*P. O. Address.*
1	Albert Estopinal	Dem	St. Bernard.
2	Robert C. Davey*	Dem	New Orleans.
3	Robert F. Broussard*	Dem	New Iberia.
4	John T. Watkins*	Dem	Minden.
5	Joseph E. Ransdell*	Dem	Lake Providence.
6	George K. Favrot	Dem	Baton Rouge.
7	Arsené P. Pujo*	Dem	Lake Charles.

MAINE.

Dist.	*Representative.*	*Politics.*	*P. O. Address.*
1	Amos L. Allen*	Rep	Alfred.
2	John P. Swasey	Rep	Canton.
3	Edwin C. Burleigh*	Rep	Augusta.
4	Frank E. Guernsey	Rep	Dover.

MARYLAND.

Dist.	Representative.	Politics.	P. O. Address.
1	W. H. Jackson†	Rep.	Salisbury.
2	J. F. C. Talbott*	Dem.	Lutherville.
3	Harry B. Wolf	Dem.	Baltimore.
4	John Gill, Jr*	Dem.	Baltimore.
5	Sydney E. Mudd*	Rep.	La Plata.
6	George A. Pearre*	Rep.	Cumberland.

MASSACHUSETTS.

Dist.	Representative.	Politics.	P. O. Address.
1	George P. Lawrence*	Rep.	North Adams.
2	Frederick H. Gillett*	Rep.	Springfield.
3	Charles G. Washburn*	Rep.	Worcester.
4	Charles Q. Tirrell*	Rep.	Natick.
5	Butler Ames*	Rep.	Lowell.
6	Aug. P. Gardner*	Rep.	Hamilton.
7	Ernest W. Roberts*	Rep.	Chelsea.
8	Samuel W. McCall*	Rep.	Winchester.
9	John A. Keliher*	Dem.	Boston.
10	Joseph F. O'Connell	Dem.	Boston.
11	Andrew J. Peters	Dem.	Boston.
12	John W. Weeks*	Rep.	Newton.
13	William S. Greene*	Rep.	Fall River.
14	William C. Lovering*	Rep.	Taunton.

MICHIGAN.

Dist.	Representative.	Politics.	P. O. Address.
1	Edwin Denby*	Rep.	Detroit.
2	Chas. E. Townsend*	Rep.	Jackson.
3	Washington Gardner*	Rep.	Albion.
4	Edw. L. Hamilton*	Rep.	Niles.
5	Gerrit J. Diekema	Rep.	Holland.
6	Samuel W. Smith*	Rep.	Pontiac.
7	Henry McMorran*	Rep.	Port Huron.
8	Joseph W. Fordney*	Rep.	Saginaw.
9	James C. McLaughlin	Rep.	Muskegon.
10	George A. Loud*	Rep.	Au Sable.
11	Arch. B. Darragh*	Rep.	St. Louis.
12	H. Olin Young*	Rep.	Ishpeming.

MINNESOTA.

Dist.	Representative.	Politics.	P. O. Address.
1	James A. Tawney*	Rep.	Winona.
2	W. S. Hammond	Dem.	St. James.
3	Charles R. Davis*	Rep.	St. Peter.
4	Frederick C. Stevens*	Rep.	St Paul.
5	Frank M. Nye	Rep.	Minneapolis.
6	Charles A. Lindbergh	Rep.	Little Falls.
7	Andrew J. Volstead*	Rep.	Granite Falls.
8	J. Adam Bede*	Rep.	Pine City.
9	Halvor Steenerson*	Rep.	Crookston.

MISSISSIPPI.

Dist.	Representative.	Politics.	P. O. Address.
1	E. S. Candler, Jr.*	Dem.	Corinth.
2	Thomas Spight*	Dem.	Ripley.
3	B. G. Humphreys*	Dem.	Greenville.
4	Wilson S. Hill*	Dem.	Winona.
5	Adam M. Byrd*	Dem.	Philadelphia.
6	Eaton J. Bowers*	Dem.	Bay St. Louis.
7	Frank A. McLain*	Dem.	Gloster.
8	John Sharp Williams*	Dem.	Yazoo City.

MISSOURI.

Dist.	Representative.	Politics.	P. O. Address.
1	James T. Lloyd*	Dem.	Shelbyville.
2	William W. Rucker*	Dem.	Keytesville.
3	Joshua W. Alexander	Dem.	Gallatin.
4	Charles F. Booher	Dem.	Savannah.
5	Edgar C. Ellis*	Rep.	Kansas City.
6	D. A. De Armond*	Dem.	Butler.
7	Courtney W. Hamlin†	Dem.	Springfield.
8	D. W. Shackleford*	Dem.	Jefferson City.
9	Champ Clark*	Dem.	Bowling Green.
10	Richard Bartholdt*	Rep.	St. Louis.
11	Henry S. Caulfield	Rep.	St. Louis.
12	Harry M. Coudrey*	Rep.	St. Louis
13	Madison R. Smith	Dem.	Farmington.
14	Joseph J. Russell	Dem.	Charleston.
15	Thomas Hackney	Dem.	Carthage.
16	Robert Lamar†	Dem.	Houston.

MONTANA.

At Large.

Dist.	Representative.	Politics.	P. O. Address.
	Charles N. Pray	Rep.	Fort Benton.

NEBRASKA.

Dist.	Representative.	Politics.	P. O. Address.
1	Ernest M. Pollard*	Rep.	Nehawka.
2	Gilbert M. Hitchcock†	Dem.	Omaha.
3	John F. Boyd	Rep.	Neligh.
4	Edmund H. Hinshaw*	Rep.	Fairbury.
5	George W. Norris*	Rep.	McCook.
6	Moses P. Kinkaid*	Rep.	O'Neill.

NEVADA.

At Large.

Dist.	Representative.	Politics.	P. O. Address.
	George A. Bartlett	Dem.	Tonopah.

NEW HAMPSHIRE.

Dist.	Representative.	Politics.	P. O. Address.
1	Cyrus A. Sulloway*	Rep.	Manchester.
2	Frank D. Currier*	Rep.	Canaan.

NEW JERSEY.

Dist.	Representative.	Politics.	P. O. Address.
1	H. C. Loudenslager*	Rep.	Paulsboro.
2	John J. Gardner*	Rep.	Atlantic City.
3	Benjamin F. Howell*	Rep.	New Brunswick.
4	Ira W. Wood*	Rep.	Trenton.
5	Charles N. Fowler*	Rep.	Elizabeth.
6	William Hughes†	Dem.	Paterson.
7	R. Wayne Parker*	Rep.	Newark.
8	Le Gage Pratt	Dem.	East Orange.
9	Eugene W. Leake	Dem.	Jersey City.
10	James A. Hamill	Dem.	Jersey City.

NEW YORK.

Dist.	Representative.	Politics.	P. O. Address.
1	William W. Cocks*	Rep.	Old Westbury.
2	George H. Lindsay*	Dem.	Brooklyn.
3	Otto G. Foelker	Rep.	Brooklyn.
4	Charles B. Law*	Rep.	Brooklyn.
5	George E. Waldo*	Rep.	Brooklyn.
6	William M. Calder*	Rep.	Brooklyn.
7	John J. Fitzgerald*	Dem.	Brooklyn.
8	Daniel J. Riordan*	Dem.	New York.
9	Henry M. Goldfogle*	Dem.	New York.
10	William Sulzer*	Dem.	New York.
11	Charles V. Fornes	Dem.	New York.
12	W. Bourke Cockran*	Dem.	New York.
13	Herbert Parsons*	Rep.	New York.
14	William Willett, Jr.	Dem.	Far Rockaway.
15	J. Van Vechten Olcott*	Rep.	New York.
16	Francis B. Harrison†	Dem.	New York.
17	William S. Bennet*	Rep.	New York.
18	Joseph A. Goulden*	Dem.	New York.
19	John E. Andrus*	Rep.	Yonkers.
20	Thomas W. Bradley*	Rep.	Walden.
21	Samuel McMillan	Rep.	Lake Mahopac.
22	William H. Draper*	Rep.	Troy.
23	George N. Southwick*	Rep.	Albany.
24	George W. Fairchild	Rep.	Oneonta.
25	Cyrus Durey	Rep.	Johnstown.
26	George R. Malby	Rep.	Ogdensburg.
27	James S. Sherman*	Rep.	Utica.
28	Charles L. Knapp*	Rep.	Loweville.
29	Michael E. Driscoll*	Rep.	Syracuse.
30	John W. Dwight*	Rep.	Dryden.
31	Sereno E. Payne*	Rep.	Auburn.
32	James Breck Perkins*	Rep.	Rochester.
33	J. Sloat Fassett*	Rep.	Elmira.
34	Peter A. Porter	Rep.	Niagara Falls.
35	William H. Ryan*	Dem.	Buffalo.
36	De A. S. Alexander*	Rep.	Buffalo.
37	Edw. B. Vreeland*	Rep.	Salamanca.

NORTH CAROLINA.

Dist.	Representative.	Politics.	P. O. Address.
1	John H. Small*	Dem.	Washington.
2	Claude Kitchin*	Dem.	Scotland Neck.
3	Charles R. Thomas*	Dem.	Newbern.
4	Edward W. Pou*	Dem.	Smithfield.
5	William W. Kitchin*	Dem.	Roxboro.
6	H. P. Godwin	Dem.	Dunn.
7	Robert N. Page*	Dem.	Biscoe.
8	Richard N. Hackett	Dem.	Wilkesboro.
9	Edwin Y. Webb*	Dem.	Shelby.
10	W. T. Crawford†	Dem.	Waynesville.

NORTH DAKOTA.

At Large.

Dist.	Representative.	Politics.	P. O. Address.
	Thomas F. Marshall*	Rep.	Oakes.
	Asle J. Gronna*	Rep.	Lakota.

OHIO.

Dist.	Representative.	Politics.	P. O. Address.
1	Nicholas Longworth*	Rep.	Cincinnati.
2	Herman P. Goebel*	Rep.	Cincinnati.
3	John E. Harding	Rep.	Middletown.
4	W. E. Tou Velle	Dem.	Celina.
5	T. T. Ansberry	Dem.	Defiance.
6	M. R. Denver	Dem.	Wilmington.
7	J. Warren Keifer*	Rep.	Springfield.
8	Ralph D. Cole*	Rep.	Findlay.
9	Isaac R. Sherwood†	Dem.	Toledo.
10	Henry T. Bannon*	Rep.	Portsmouth.

OHIO—*Continued.*

Dist.	*Representative.*	*Politics.*	*P. O. Address.*
11	Albert Douglas	Rep.	Chillicothe.
12	Edward L. Taylor, Jr.*	Rep.	Columbus.
13	Grant E. Mouser*	Rep.	Marion.
14	Jay F. Laning	Rep.	Norwalk.
15	Beman G. Dawes*	Rep.	Marietta.
16	Capell L. Weems*	Rep.	St. Clairsville.
17	W. A. Ashbrook	Dem.	Johnstown.
18	James Kennedy*	Rep.	Youngstown.
19	W. Aubrey Thomas*	Rep.	Niles.
20	Paul Howland	Rep.	Cleveland.
21	Theo. E. Burton*	Rep.	Cleveland.

OKLAHOMA.

1	Bird S. McGuire*	Rep.	Pawnee.
2	Elmer L. Fulton	Dem.	Oklahoma City.
3	James S. Davenport	Dem.	Vinita.
4	C. D. Carter	Dem.	Ardmore.
5	Scott Ferris	Dem.	Lawton.

OREGON.

1	W. C. Hawley	Rep.	Salem.
2	W. R. Ellis†	Rep.	Pendleton.

PENNSYLVANIA.

1	Henry H. Bingham*	Rep.	Philadelphia.
2	Joel Cook	Rep.	Philadelphia.
3	J. Hampton Moore*	Rep.	Philadelphia.
4	Reuben O. Moon*	Rep.	Philadelphia.
5	W. W. Foulkrod	Rep.	Philadelphia.
6	George D. McCreary*	Rep.	Philadelphia.
7	Thomas S. Butler*	Rep.	West Chester.
8	Irving P. Wanger*	Rep.	Norristown.
9	H. Burd Cassel*	Rep.	Marietta.
10	T. D. Nicholls	Dem.	Scranton.
11	John T. Lenahan	Dem.	Wilkes-Barre.
12	Charles N. Brumm†	Rep.	Minersville.
13	John H. Rothermel	Dem.	Reading.
14	George W. Kipp	Dem.	Towanda.
15	William B. Wilson	Dem.	Blossburg.
16	John G. McHenry	Dem.	Benton.
17	Benjamin K. Focht	Rep.	Lewisburg.
18	Marlin E. Olmsted*	Rep.	Harrisburg.
19	John M. Reynolds*	Rep.	Bedtord.
20	Daniel F. Lafean*	Rep.	York.
21	Charles F. Barclay	Rep.	Sinnemahoning.
22	George F. Huff*	Rep.	Greensburg.
23	Allen F. Cooper*	Rep.	Uniontown.
24	Ernest F. Acheson*	Rep.	Washington.
25	Arthur L. Bates*	Rep.	Meadville.
26	J. Davis Brodhead	Dem.	South Bethlehem.
27	Joseph G. Beale	Rep.	Leechburg.
28	Nelson P. Wheeler	Rep.	Endeavor.
29	William H. Graham*	Rep.	Allegheny.
30	John Dalzell*	Rep.	Pittsburgh.
31	James Francis Burke*	Rep.	Pittsburgh.
32	Andrew J. Barchfeld*	Rep.	Pittsburgh.

RHODE ISLAND.

1	D. L. D. Granger*	Dem.	Providence.
2	Adin B. Capron*	Rep.	Smithfield.

SOUTH CAROLINA.

1	George S. Legare*	Dem.	Charleston.
2	James O. Patterson*	Dem.	Barnwell
3	Wyatt Aiken*	Dem.	Abbeville.
4	Joseph T. Johnson*	Dem.	Spartanburg.
5	David E. Finley*	Dem.	Yorkville.
6	J. Edwin Ellerbe*	Dem.	Sellers.
7	Asbury F. Lever*	Dem.	Lexington.

SOUTH DAKOTA.

At Large.

	Philo Hall	Rep.	Brookings.
	Eben W. Martin†	Rep.	Deadwood.

TENNESSEE.

1	Walter P. Brownlow*	Rep.	Jonesboro.
2	Nathan W. Hale*	Rep.	Knoxville.
3	John A. Moon*	Dem.	Chattanooga.
4	Cordell Hull	Dem.	Crossville.
5	William C. Houston*	Dem.	Woodbury.
6	John W. Gaines*	Dem.	Nashville.
7	Lemuel P. Padgett*	Dem.	Columbia.
8	Thetus W. Sims*	Dem.	Linden.

TENNESSEE.—*Continued.*

Dist.	*Representative.*	*Politics.*	*P. O. Address.*
9	Finis J. Garrett*	Dem.	Dresden.
10	George W. Gordon	Dem.	Memphis.

TEXAS.

1	Morris Sheppard*	Dem.	Texarkana.
2	Sam. B. Cooper†	Dem.	Beaumont.
3	Gordon Russell*	Dem.	Tyler.
4	Choice B. Randell*	Dem.	Sherman.
5	Jack Beall*	Dem.	Waxahachie.
6	Rufus Hardy	Dem.	Corsicana.
7	Alex. W. Gregg*	Dem.	Palestine.
8	John M. Moore*	Dem.	Richmond.
9	George F. Burgess*	Dem.	Gonzales.
10	Albert S. Burleson*	Dem.	Austin.
11	Robert L. Henry*	Dem.	Waco.
12	O. W. Gillespie*	Dem.	Fort Worth.
13	John H. Stephens*	Dem.	Vernon.
14	James L. Slayden*	Dem.	San Antonio.
15	John N. Garner*	Dem.	Uvalde.
16	William R. Smith*	Dem.	Colorado.

UTAH.

At Large.

	Joseph Howell*	Rep.	Logan.

VERMONT.

1	David J. Foster*	Rep.	Burlington.
2	Kittridge Haskins*	Rep.	Brattleboro.

VIRGINIA.

1	William A. Jones*	Dem.	Warsaw.
2	Harry L. Maynard*	Dem.	Portsmouth.
3	John Lamb*	Dem.	Richmond.
4	Francis R. Lassiter†	Dem.	Petersburg.
5	E. W. Saunders*	Dem.	Rocky Mount.
6	Carter Glass*	Dem.	Lynchburg.
7	James Hay*	Dem.	Madison.
8	Charles C. Carlin	Dem.	Alexandria.
9	C. Bascom Slemp	Rep.	Big Stone Gap.
10	Henry D. Flood*	Dem.	W. Appomattox.

WASHINGTON.

At Large.

	Wesley L. Jones*	Rep.	North Yakima.
	Francis W. Cushman*	Rep.	Tacoma.
	Wm. E. Humphrey*	Rep.	Seattle.

WEST VIRGINIA.

1	W. P. Hubbard	Rep.	Wheeling.
2	George C. Sturgiss	Rep.	Morgantown.
3	Joseph Holt Gaines*	Rep.	Charleston.
4	Harry C. Woodyard*	Rep.	Spencer.
5	James A. Hughes*	Rep.	Huntington.

WISCONSIN.

1	Henry A. Cooper*	Rep.	Racine.
2	John M. Nelson	Rep.	Madison.
3	James W. Murphy	Dem.	Plattville.
4	William J. Cary	Rep.	Milwaukee.
5	Wm. H. Stafford*	Rep.	Milwaukee.
6	Charles H. Weisse*	Dem.	Sheboygan Falls.
7	John J. Esch*	Rep.	La Crosse.
8	James H. Davidson*	Rep.	Oshkosh.
9	Gustave Kuestermann	Rep.	Green Bay.
10	E. A. Morse	Rep.	Antigo.
11	John J. Jenkins*	Rep.	Chippewa Falls.

WYOMING.

1	Frank W. Mondell*	Rep.	Newcastle.

ALASKA.

	Thomas Cale	Rep.	Fairbanks.

ARIZONA.

	Marcus A. Smith*	Dem.	Tucson.

NEW MEXICO.

	William H. Andrews*	Rep.	Albuquerque.

HAWAII.

	Jonah K. Kalanianole*	Rep.	Honolulu.

PORTO RICO.

	Tulio Larrinaga*	Rep.	Commissioner. San Juan.

PHILIPPINE ISLANDS.

	Benito Legarda	Rep.	Commissioner. Manila.
	Pablo O. de Leon	Rep.	Commissioner. Manila.

Republicans, 223; Democrats, 168; whole number, 391.
*Served in the Fifty-ninth Congress. †Served in a previous Congress.
The salaries of Representatives are $7,500 per annum and a mileage of 20 cents per mile each way. Salary of the Speaker $12,000.

The Sixty-first Congress.

BEGINS MARCH 4, 1909, AND ENDS MARCH 4, 1911.

SENATE.

President.....................................James S. Sherman, R., of New York.
Secretary.....................................Charles G. Bennett, R., of New York.

Terms Expire.	Senators.	P. O. Address.
	ALABAMA.	
1915	Joseph F. Johnston, D.	Birmingham.
1913	John H. Bankhead, D.	Fayette.
	ARKANSAS.	
1915	James P. Clarke, D.	Little Rock.
1913	Jefferson Davis, D.	Little Rock.
	CALIFORNIA.	
1915	George C. Perkins, R.	Oakland.
1911	Frank P. Flint, R.	Los Angeles.
	COLORADO.	
1915	A Democrat	
1913	Simon Guggenheim, R.	Denver.
	CONNECTICUT.	
1915	Frank B. Brandegee, R.	New London.
1911	Morgan G. Bulkeley, R.	Hartford.
	DELAWARE.	
1911	Henry A. DuPont, R.	Wilmington.
1913	H. A. Richardson, R.	Dover.
	FLORIDA.	
1915	D. U. Fletcher, D.	
1911	James P. Taliaferro, D.	Jacksonville.
	GEORGIA.	
1915	Alexander S. Clay, D.	Marietta.
1913	Augustus O. Bacon, D.	Macon
	IDAHO.	
1915	Weldon B. Heyburn, R.	Wallace.
1913	William E. Borah, R.	Boisé
	ILLINOIS.	
1915	Albert J. Hopkins, R.	Aurora.
1913	Shelby M. Cullom, R.	Springfield.
	INDIANA.	
1915	A Democrat	
1911	Albert J. Beveridge, R.	Indianapolis.
	IOWA.	
1915	Albert B. Cummins, R.	Des Moines.
1913	Jona P. Dolliver, R.	Fort Dodge.
	KANSAS.	
1915	Joseph L. Bristow, R.	
1913	Charles Curtis, R.	Topeka.
	KENTUCKY.	
1915	William O. Bradley, R.	Frankfort.
1913	T. H. Paynter, D.	Frankfort.
	LOUISIANA.	
1915	Samuel D. McEnery, D.	New Orleans.
1913	Murphy J. Foster, D.	Franklin.
	MAINE.	
1911	Eugene Hale, R.	Ellsworth.
1913	William P. Frye, R.	Lewiston.
	MARYLAND.	
1915	John W. Smith, D.	Snow Hill.
1911	Isador Rayner, D.	Baltimore.
	MASSACHUSETTS.	
1911	Henry Cabot Lodge, R.	Nahant.
1913	Winthrop M. Crane, R.	Dalton.
	MICHIGAN.	
1911	Julius C. Burrows, R.	Kalamazoo.
1913	William A. Smith, R.	Grand Rapids.
	MINNESOTA.	
1911	Moses E. Clapp, R.	St. Paul.
1913	Knute Nelson, R.	Alexandria.
	MISSISSIPPI.	
1911	Hernando D. Money, D.	Missi'ppi City
1913	Anselm J. McLaurin, D	Brandon.
	MISSOURI.	
1915	William J. Stone, D.	Jefferson City.
1911	William Warner, R.	Kansas City.
	MONTANA.	
1911	Thomas H. Carter, R.	Helena.
1913	Joseph M. Dixon, R.	Missoula.
	NEBRASKA.	
1911	Elmer J. Burkett, R.	Lincoln.
1913	Norris Brown, R.	Kearney.
	NEVADA.	
1915	Francis G. Newlands, D.	Reno.
1911	George S. Nixon, R.	Winnemucca
	NEW HAMPSHIRE.	
1915	Jacob H. Gallinger, R.	Concord.
1913	H. E. Burnham, R.	Manchester.
	NEW JERSEY.	
1911	John Kean, R.	Elizabeth.
1913	Frank O. Briggs, R.	Trenton.
	NEW YORK.	
1915	A Republican	New York.
1911	Chauncey M. Depew, R.	New York.
	NORTH CAROLINA.	
1915	Lee S. Overman, D.	Salisbury.
1913	F. M. Simmons, D.	Raleigh.
	NORTH DAKOTA.	
1915	M. N. Johnson, R.	
1911	Peter J. McCumber, R.	Wahpeton.
	OHIO.	
1909	Joseph B. Foraker, R.	Cincinnati.
1911	Charles Dick, R.	Akron.
	OKLAHOMA.	
1913	Robert L Owen, D.	Muskogee.
1915	Thomas P. Gore, D.	Lawton.
	OREGON.	
1915	Geo. E. Chamberlain, D.	
1913	Jonathan Bourne, Jr., R.	Portland.
	PENNSYLVANIA.	
1915	Boies Penrose, R.	Philadelphia.
1911	Philander C. Knox, R.	Pittsburgh.
	RHODE ISLAND.	
1911	Nelson W. Aldrich, R.	Providence
1913	George P. Wetmore, R.	Newport.
	SOUTH CAROLINA.	
1915	E. D. Smith, D.	
1913	Benj. R. Tillman, D.	Trenton.
	SOUTH DAKOTA.	
1915	George I. Crawford, R.	
1913	Robert J. Gamble, R.	Yankton.
	TENNESSEE.	
1911	James B. Frazier, D.	Chattanooga.
1913	Robert L. Taylor, D.	Nashville.
	TEXAS.	
1911	Charles A. Culberson, D.	Dallas.
1913	Joseph W. Bailey, D.	Gainesville.
	UTAH.	
1915	Reed Smoot, R.	Provo.
1911	George Sutherland, R.	Salt Lake City
	VERMONT.	
1915	William P. Dillingham, R.	Montpelier.
1911	Carroll S. Page, R.	Hyde Park.
	VIRGINIA.	
1911	John W. Daniel, D.	Lynchburg.
1913	Thomas S. Martin, D.	Scottsville.
	WASHINGTON.	
1915	Wesley L. Jones, R.	
1911	Samuel H. Piles, R.	Seattle.
	WEST VIRGINIA.	
1911	Nathan B. Scott, R.	Wheeling.
1913	Stephen B. Elkins, R.	Elkins.
	WISCONSIN.	
1915	Isaac Stephenson, R.	Marinette.
1911	Robert M. La Follette, R.	Madison.
	WYOMING.	
1911	Clarence D. Clark, R.	Evanston.
1913	Francis E. Warren, R.	Cheyenne.

Total number of Senators, 92, of whom 60 will be Republicans and 32 Democrats. The Senatorial vacancies will be filled by the Legislatures meeting in 1909. The salary of a Senator is $7,500 per annum and 20 cents per mile for travelling from and to the Seat of Government.

HOUSE OF REPRESENTATIVES—ELECT.

ALABAMA.

Dist. Representative. Politics. P. O. Address.

1 George W. Taylor*.....Dem..Demopolis.
2 S. H. Dent, Jr...........Dem..Montgomery.
3 Henry D. Clayton*....Dem..Eufaula.
4 William B. Craig.........Dem..Selma.
5 J. Thomas Heflin*......Dem..Lafayette.
6 Richmond P. Hobson ..Dem..Fayette.
7 John L. Burnett*........Dem..Gadsden.
8 William Richardson*..Dem..Huntsville.
9 Oscar W. Underwood*.Dem..Birmingham.

ARKANSAS.

1 Robert Bruce Macon*...Dem..Helena.
2 W. A. Oldfield............Dem..Batesville.
3 John C. Floyd* ....Dem..Yellville.
4 Ben Cravens*..............Dem..Fort Smith.
5 Charles C. Reid*.........Dem..Morrillton.
6 Joseph T. Robinson*...Dem..Lonoke.
7 Robert M. Wallace*....Dem..Magnolia.

CALIFORNIA.

1 W. F. Englebright*....Rep...Nevada City.
2 Duncan E. McKinlay*.Rep...Santa Rosa.
3 Joseph R. Knowland*...Rep...Alameda.
4 Julius Kahn*...............Rep...San Francisco.
5 Everis A. Hayes*........Rep...San José.
6 James C. Needham*....Rep...Modesta.
7 James McLachlan*.....Rep...Pasadena.
8 Sylvester C. Smith*....Rep...Bakersfield.

COLORADO.

At Large.

Edward T. Taylor......Dem..Glenwood Springs
1 Atterson W. Rucker...Dem..Rucker Ridge.
2 John A. Martin.........Dem..Pueblo.

CONNECTICUT.

At Large.

John Q. Tilson..........Rep...New Haven.
1 E. Stevens Henry*......Rep...Rockville.
2 Nehemiah D. Sperry*..Rep...New Haven.
3 Edwin W. Higgins*.....Rep...Norwich.
4 Ebenezer J. Hill*.......Rep...Norwalk.

DELAWARE.

At Large.

William H. Heald......Rep...Wilmington.

FLORIDA.

1 Stephen M. Sparkman*.Dem..Tampa.
2 Frank Clark*............Dem..Gainesville.
3 J. Walter Kehoe......Dem..Pensacola.

GEORGIA.

1 Charles G. Edwards...Dem..Savannah.
2 James M. Griggs*.......Dem..Dawson.
3 Dudley M. Hughes.....Dem..Danville.
4 William C. Adamson*..Dem..Carrollton.
5 Leonidas F. Livingston*Dem..Covington.
6 Charles L. Bartlett*....Dem..Macon.
7 Gordon Lee*..............Dem..Chickamauga.
8 William M. Howard*...Dem..Lexington.
9 Thomas M. Bell*........Dem..Gainesville.
10 Thomas W. Hardwick*.Dem..Sandersville.
11 William G. Brantley*..Dem..Brunswick.

IDAHO.

Thomas R. Hamer.....Rep...Stanton.

ILLINOIS.

1 Martin B. Madden*.....Rep...Chicago.
2 James R. Mann*........Rep...Chicago.
3 William W. Wilson*....Rep...Chicago.
4 James T. McDermott*.Dem..Chicago.
5 A. J. Sabath*.............Dem..Chicago.
6 William Lorimer*......Rep...Chicago.
7 Fred Lundin...............Rep...Chicago.
8 Thomas Gallagher.....Dem..Chicago.
9 Henry S. Boutell* .....Rep...Chicago.
10 George Edmund Foss*..Rep...Chicago.
11 Howard M. Snapp*.....Rep...Joliet.
12 Charles E. Fuller*.....Rep...Belvidere.
13 Frank O. Lowden* .....Rep...Oregon.
14 James McKinney*.....Rep...Aledo.
15 George W. Prince*......Rep...Galesburg.
16 Joseph V. Graff*.........Rep...Peoria.

ILLINOIS—Continued.

Dist. Representative. Politics. P. O. Address.

17 John A. Sterling*......Rep...Bloomington.
18 Joseph G. Cannon*......Rep...Danville.
19 William B. McKinley*.Rep...Champaign.
20 Henry T. Rainey*......Dem..Carrollton.
21 James M. Graham.....Dem..Springfield.
22 Wm. A. Rodenberg*....Rep...East St. Louis.
23 Martin D. Foster*......Dem..Olney.
24 Pleasant T. Chapman*..Rep...Vienna.
25 N. B. Thistlewood*.....Rep...Cairo.

INDIANA.

1 John W. Boehne ....Dem..Evansville.
2 William Cullop..........Dem..Vincennes.
3 W. E Cox*...............Dem..Jasper.
4 Lincoln Dixon*..........Dem..North Vernon.
5 Ralph W. Moss..........Dem..Brazil.
6 W. O. Barnard............Rep...Newcastle.
7 Charles A Korbly......Dem...Indianapolis.
8 John A. M. Adair*.....Dem..Portland.
9 Martin A. Morrison.....Dem..Frankfort.
10 Edgar D. Crumpacker*.Rep...Valparaiso.
11 George W. Rauch*......Dem..Marion.
12 Cyrus Kline...............Dem..Angola.
13 Henry A. Barnhart.....Dem..Rochester.

IOWA.

1 C. A. Kennedy*.........Rep...Montrose.
2 Albert F. Dawson*.....Rep...Preston.
3 Charles Pickett.........Rep...Waterloo.
4 Gilbert N. Haugen*....Rep...Northwood.
5 James W. Good.........Rep...Cedar Rapids.
6 N. E. Kendall............Rep...Albia.
7 John A. T. Hull*........Rep...Des Moines.
8 W. D. Jamieson........Dem..Shenandoah.
9 Walter I. Smith*.......Rep...Council Bluffs.
10 Frank P. Woods........Rep...Estherville.
11 E. H. Hubbard*........Rep...Sioux City.

KANSAS.

1 Dan'l R. Anthony, Jr.*Rep...Leavenworth.
2 Charles F. Scott*.......Rep...Iola.
3 Philip P. Campbell*...Rep...Pittsburgh.
4 James M. Miller*.......Rep...Council Grove.
5 William A. Calderhead*Rep...Marysville.
6 William A. Reeder*....Rep...Logan.
7 E. H. Madison*.........Rep...Dodge City.
8 Victor Murdock*........Rep...Wichita.

KENTUCKY.

1 Ollie M. James*.........Dem..Marion.
2 Augustus O. Stanley*..Dem..Henderson.
3 R. Y. Thomas ....Dem..Central City.
4 Ben Johnson*............Dem..Bardstown.
5 Swagar Sherley*........Dem..Louisville.
6 Joseph L. Rhinock*....Dem..Covington.
7 J. Campbell Cantrill...Dem..
8 Harvey Helm*............Dem..Stanford.
9 Joseph B. Bennett* ....Rep...Greenup.
10 John W. Langley*......Rep...Prestonburg.
11 Don C. Edwards*.......Rep...London.

LOUISIANA.

1 Albert Estopinal.......Dem..New Orleans.
2 Robert C. Davey*.......Dem..New Orleans.
3 Robert F. Broussard*..Dem..New Iberia.
4 John T. Watkins*......Dem..Minden.
5 Joseph E. Ransdell*....Dem..Lake Providence
6 Robert C. Wickliffe.....Dem..St. Francesville.
7 Arsené P. Pujo*.........Dem..Lake Charles.

MAINE.

1 Amos L. Allen*.........Rep...Alfred.
2 John P. Swasey........ Rep...Canton.
3 Edwin C. Burleigh*....Rep...Augusta.
4 Frank E. Guernsey.....Rep...Dover.

MARYLAND.

1 J. Harry Covington.....Dem..Easton.
2 Joshua F. C. Talbott*..Dem..Lutherville.
3 John Kronmiller.......Rep...Baltimore.
4 John Gill, Jr.*..........Dem..Baltimore.
5 Sydney E Mudd*.......Rep...La Plata.
6 George A. Pearre*......Rep...Cumberland.

MASSACHUSETTS.

Dist.	Representative.	Politics	P. O. Address.
1	George P. Lawrence*	Rep.	North Adams.
2	Frederick H. Gillett*	Rep.	Springfield.
3	Charles G. Washburn*	Rep.	Worcester.
4	Charles Q. Tirrell*	Rep.	Natick.
5	Butler Ames*	Rep.	Lowell.
6	Augustus P. Gardner*	Rep.	Hamilton.
7	Ernest W. Roberts*	Rep.	Chelsea.
8	Samuel W. McCall*	Rep.	Winchester.
9	John A. Keliher*	Dem.	Boston.
10	Joseph F. O'Connell*	Dem.	Boston.
11	Andrew J. Peters*	Dem.	Boston.
12	John W. Weeks*	Rep.	Newton.
13	William S. Greene*	Rep.	Fall River.
14	William C. Lovering*	Rep.	Taunton.

MICHIGAN.

Dist.	Representative.	Politics	P. O. Address.
1	Edwin Denby*	Rep.	Detroit.
2	Charles E. Townsend*	Rep.	Jackson.
3	Washington Gardner*	Rep.	Albion.
4	Edward L. Hamilton*	Rep.	Niles.
5	Gerrit J. Diekema*	Rep.	Holland.
6	Samuel W. Smith*	Rep.	Pontiac.
7	Henry McMorran*	Rep.	Port Huron.
8	Joseph W. Fordney*	Rep.	Saginaw.
9	James C. McLaughlin*	Rep.	Muskegon.
10	George A. Loud*	Rep.	Au Sable.
11	Francis H. Dodds	Rep.	Mt. Pleasant.
12	H. Olin Young*	Rep.	Ishpeming.

MINNESOTA.

Dist.	Representative.	Politics	P. O. Address.
1	James A. Tawney*	Rep.	Winona.
2	W. S. Hammond*	Dem.	St. James.
3	Charles R. Davis*	Rep.	St. Peter.
4	Fred. C. Stevens*	Rep.	St. Paul.
5	Frank M. Nye	Rep.	Minneapolis.
6	Charles A. Lindbergh*	Rep.	Little Falls.
7	Andrew J. Volstead*	Rep.	Granite Falls.
8	Clarence B. Miller	Rep.	Duluth.
9	Halvor Steenerson*	Rep.	Crookston.

MISSISSIPPI.

Dist.	Representative.	Politics	P. O. Address.
1	Ezekiel S. Candler, Jr.*	Dem.	Corinth.
2	Thomas Spight*	Dem.	Ripley.
3	Benj. G Humphreys*	Dem.	Greenville.
4	T. U. Sisson	Dem.	
5	Adam M. Byrd*	Dem.	Philadelphia.
6	Eaton J. Bowers*	Dem.	Bay St. Louis.
7	W. J. Dickson	Dem.	
8	J. W. Collier	Dem.	Warren.

MISSOURI.

Dist.	Representative.	Politics	P. O. Address.
1	James T. Lloyd*	Dem.	Shelbyville.
2	William W. Rucker*	Dem.	Keytesville.
3	Joshua W. Alexander*	Dem.	Gallatin.
4	Charles F. Booher*	Dem.	Savannah.
5	William P. Borland*	Dem.	Kansas City.
6	David A. De Armond*	Dem.	Butler.
7	Courtney W. Hamlin*	Dem.*	Springfield.
8	Dorsey W. Shackleford*	Dem.	Jefferson City.
9	Champ Clark*	Dem.	Bowling Green.
10	Richard Bartholdt*	Rep.	St. Louis.
11	Patrick F. Gill	Dem.	St. Louis.
12	Harry M. Coudrey*	Rep.	St. Louis.
13	Politte Elvins	Rep.	Elvins
14	Charles A. Crow	Rep.	Caruthersville.
15	Charles H. Morgan†	Rep.	Joplin.
16	Arthur P. Murphy†	Rep.	Rolla.

MONTANA.

At Large.

Dist.	Representative.	Politics	P. O. Address.
	Charles N. Pray*	Rep.	Fort Benton.

NEBRASKA.

Dist.	Representative.	Politics	P. O. Address.
1	John A. Maguire	Dem.	Lincoln.
2	Gilbert M. Hitchcock*	Dem.	Omaha.
3	James P. Latta	Dem.	Tekamah.
4	Edmund H. Hinshaw*	Rep.	Fairbury.
5	George W. Norris*	Rep.	McCook.
6	Moses P. Kinkaid*	Rep.	O'Neill.

NEVADA.

At Large.

Dist.	Representative.	Politics	P. O. Address.
	George A. Bartlett*	Dem.	Tonopah.

NEW HAMPSHIRE.

Dist.	Representative.	Politics	P. O. Address.
1	Cyrus A. Sulloway*	Rep.	Manchester.
2	Frank D. Currier*	Rep.	Canaan.

NEW JERSEY.

Dist.	Representative.	Politics	P. O. Address.
1	Henry C. Loudenslager*	Rep.	Paulsboro.
2	John J. Gardner*	Rep.	Atlantic City.
3	Benjamin F. Howell*	Rep.	New Brunswick.
4	Ira W. Wood*	Rep.	Trenton.
5	Charles N. Fowler*	Rep.	Elizabeth.
6	William Hughes*	Dem.	Paterson.
7	Richard Wayne Parker*	Rep.	Newark.
8	William H. Wiley†	Rep.	East Orange.
9	Eugene F. Kinkead	Dem.	Jersey City.
10	James A. Hamill*	Dem.	Jersey City.

NEW YORK.

Dist.	Representative.	Politics	P. O. Address.
1	William W. Cocks*	Rep.	Old Westbury.
2	George H. Lindsay*	Dem.	Brooklyn.
3	Otto G. Foelker	Rep.	Brooklyn.
4	Charles B. Law*	Rep.	Brooklyn.
5	Richard Young	Rep.	Brooklyn.
6	William M. Calder*	Rep.	Brooklyn.
7	John J. Fitzgerald*	Dem.	Brooklyn.
8	Daniel J. Riordan*	Dem.	New York.
9	Henry M. Goldfogle*	Dem.	New York.
10	William Sulzer*	Dem.	New York.
11	Charles V. Fornes*	Dem.	New York.
12	Michael F. Conroy	Dem.	New York.
13	Herbert Parsons*	Rep.	New York.
14	William Willett, Jr*	Dem.	Far Rockaway.
15	J. Van Vechten Olcott*	Rep.	New York.
16	Francis B. Harrison*	Dem.	New York.
17	William S. Bennet*	Rep.	New York.
18	Joseph A. Goulden*	Dem.	New York.
19	John E. Andrus*	Rep.	Yonkers.
20	Thomas W. Bradley*	Rep.	Walden.
21	Hamilton Fish	Rep.	Garrison.
22	William H. Draper*	Rep.	Troy.
23	George N. Southwick*	Rep.	Albany.
24	George W. Fairchild*	Rep.	Oneonta.
25	Cyrus Durey*	Rep.	Johnstown.
26	George R. Malby*	Rep.	Ogdensburg.
27	Charles S. Millington	Rep.	Herkimer.
28	Charles L. Knapp*	Rep.	Lowville.
29	Michael E. Driscoll*	Rep.	Syracuse.
30	John W. Dwight*	Rep.	Dryden.
31	Sereno E. Payne*	Rep.	Auburn.
32	James Breck Perkins*	Rep.	Rochester.
33	J. Sloat Fassett*	Rep.	Elmira.
34	James S. Simmons	Rep.	Niagara Falls
35	Daniel A. Driscoll	Dem.	Buffalo.
36	De Alva S. Alexander*	Rep.	Buffalo.
37	Edward B. Vreeland*	Rep.	Salamanca.

NORTH CAROLINA.

Dist.	Representative.	Politics	P. O. Address.
1	John H. Small*	Dem.	Washington.
2	Claude Kitchin*	Dem.	Scotland Neck.
3	Charles R. Thomas*	Dem.	Newbern.
4	Edward W. Pou*	Dem.	Smithfield.
5	J. M. Morehead	Rep.	Greensboro.
6	H. L. Godwin*	Dem.	Dunn.
7	Robert N. Page*	Dem	Biscoe.
8	Charles H. Cowles	Rep.	Wilkesboro.
9	Edwin Y. Webb*	Dem.	Shelby.
10	J. G. Grant	Rep.	Hendersonville.

NORTH DAKOTA.

At Large.

Dist.	Representative.	Politics	P. O. Address.
	L. B. Hanna	Rep.	Fargo.
	Asle J. Gronna	Rep.	Lakota.

OHIO.

Dist.	Representative.	Politics	P. O. Address.
1	Nicholas Longworth*	Rep.	Cincinnati.
2	Herman P. Goebel	Rep.	Cincinnati.
3	James M. Cox	Dem.	Dayton.
4	W. E. Tou Velle*	Dem.	Celina.
5	T. T. Ansberry*	Dem.	Defiance.
6	M. R. Denver*	Dem.	Wilmington.
7	J. Warren Keifer*	Rep.	Springfield.
8	Ralph D. Cole*	Rep.	Findlay.
9	Isaac R. Sherwood*	Dem.	Toledo.
10	A. R. Johnson	Rep.	Ironton.
11	Albert Douglas*	Rep.	Chillicothe.
12	Edward L. Taylor, Jr.*	Rep.	Columbus.
13	Carl Anderson	Dem.	Fostoria.
14	William G. Sharpe	Dem.	Elyria.
15	James Joyce	Rep.	Cambridge.
16	D. A. Hollingsworth	Rep.	Cadiz.

OHIO.—Continued.

Dist.	Representative.	Politics.	P. O. Address.
17	W. A. Ashbrook*	Dem.	Johnstown.
18	James Kennedy*	Rep.	Youngstown.
19	W. Aubrey Thomas*	Rep.	Niles.
20	Paul Howland*	Rep.	Cleveland.
21	Theodore E. Burton*	Rep.	Cleveland.

OKLAHOMA.

Dist.	Representative.	Politics.	P. O. Address.
1	Bird S. McGuire*	Rep.	Pawnee.
2	Richard T. Morgan	Rep.	Woodward.
3	C. E. Creager	Rep.	Muskogee.
4	Charles D. Carter*	Dem.	Ardmore.
5	Scott Ferris*	Dem.	Lawton.

OREGON.

Dist.	Representative.	Politics.	P. O. Address.
1	W. C. Hawley*	Rep.	Salem.
2	W. R. Ellis*	Rep.	Pendleton.

PENNSYLVANIA.

Dist.	Representative.	Politics.	P. O. Address.
1	Henry H. Bingham*	Rep.	Philadelphia.
2	Joel Cook*	Rep.	Philadelphia.
3	J. Hampton Moore*	Rep.	Philadelphia.
4	Reuben O. Moon*	Rep.	Philadelphia.
5	W. W. Foulkrod*	Rep.	Philadelphia.
6	George D. McCreary*	Rep.	Philadelphia.
7	Thomas S. Butler*	Rep.	West Chester.
8	Irving P. Wanger*	Rep.	Norristown.
9	William W. Griest	Rep.	Lancaster.
10	T. D. Nicholls *	Dem.	Scranton.
11	Henry W. Palmer†	Rep.	Wilkes-Barre.
12	Alfred B. Garner	Rep.	Ashland.
13	John H Rothermel*	Dem.	Reading.
14	Charles C Pratt	Rep.	New Milford.
15	William B. Wilson*	Dem.	Blossburg.
16	John G. McHenry*	Dem.	Benton.
17	Benjamin K. Focht*	Rep.	Lewisburg.
18	Marlin E. Olmsted*	Rep.	Harrisburg.
19	John M. Reynolds*	Rep.	Bedford
20	Daniel F. Lafean*	Rep.	York.
21	Charles F. Barclay*	Rep.	Sinnemahoning.
22	George F. Huff*	Rep.	Greensburg.
23	Allen F. Cooper*	Rep.	Uniontown.
24	John K. Tener	Rep.	Charleroi.
25	Arthur L. Bates*	Rep.	Meadville.
26	A. Mitchell Palmer	Dem.	Stroudsburg.
27	J. N. Langham	Rep.	Indiana.
28	Nelson P. Wheeler*	Rep.	Endeavor.
29	William H. Graham*	Rep.	Allegheny.
30	John Dalzell*	Rep.	Pittsburgh.
31	James Francis Burke*	Rep.	Pittsburgh.
32	Andrew J. Barchfeld*	Rep.	Pittsburgh.

RHODE ISLAND.

Dist.	Representative.	Politics.	P. O. Address.
1	William P. Sheffield	Rep.	Newport.
2	Adin B. Capron*	Rep.	Smithfield.

SOUTH CAROLINA.

Dist.	Representative.	Politics.	P. O. Address.
1	George S. Legare*	Dem.	Charleston.
2	James O. Patterson*	Rep.	Barnwell.
3	Wyatt Aiken*	Dem.	Abbeville.
4	Joseph T. Johnson*	Dem.	Spartanburg.
5	David E. Finley*	Dem.	Yorkville.
6	J. Edwin Ellerbe*	Dem.	Sellers.
7	Asbury F. Lever*	Dem.	Lexington.

SOUTH DAKOTA.

At Large.

Dist.	Representative.	Politics.	P. O. Address.
	Charles H. Burke†	Rep.	Pierre.
	Eben W. Martin†	Rep.	Deadwood.

TENNESSEE.

Dist.	Representative.	Politics.	P. O. Address.
1	Walter P. Brownlow*	Rep.	Jonesboro.
2	R. W. Austin	Rep.	Knoxville.
3	John A. Moon*	Dem.	Chattanooga.
4	Cordell Hull*	Dem.	Crossville.
5	William C. Houston*	Dem.	Woodbury.
6	J. W. Byrnes	Dem.	Nashville.
7	Lemuel P. Padgett*	Dem.	Columbia.
8	Thetus W. Sims*	Dem.	Linden.
9	Finis J. Garrett*	Dem.	Dresden.
10	George W. Gordon	Dem.	Memphis.

TEXAS.

Dist.	Representative.	Politics.	P. O. Address.
1	Morris Sheppard*	Dem.	Texarkana.
2	Martin Dies	Dem.	
3	Gordon Russell*	Dem.	Tyler.
4	Choice B. Randell.*	Dem.	Sherman.
5	Jack Beall*	Dem.	Waxahachie.
6	Rufus Hardy*	Dem.	Corsicana.
7	Alexander W. Gregg*	Dem.	Palestine.
8	John M. Moore *	Dem.	Richmond.
9	George F. Burgess*	Dem.	Gonzales.
10	Albert S. Burleson*	Dem.	Austin.
11	Robert L. Henry*	Dem.	Waco.
12	Oscar W. Gillespie*	Dem.	Fort Worth.
13	John H. Stephens*	Dem.	Vernon.
14	James L. Slayden*	Dem.	San Antonio.
15	John N. Garner*	Dem.	Uvalde.
16	William R. Smith*	Dem.	Colorado

UTAH.

At Large.

Dist.	Representative.	Politics.	P. O. Address.
	Joseph Howell*	Rep.	Logan.

VERMONT.

Dist.	Representative.	Politics.	P. O. Address.
1	David J. Foster*	Rep.	Burlington.
2	Frank H. Plumly	Rep.	Northfield.

VIRGINIA.

Dist.	Representative.	Politics.	P. O. Address.
1	William A. Jones*	Dem.	Warsaw.
2	Harry L. Maynard*	Dem.	Portsmouth.
3	John Lamb*	Dem.	Richmond.
4	Francis R. Lassiter*	Dem.	Petersburg.
5	E. W. Saunders*	Dem.	Rocky Mount.
6	Carter Glass*	Dem.	Lynchburg.
7	James Hay*	Dem.	Madison.
8	Charles C. Carlin*	Dem.	Alexandria.
9	C. Bascom Slemp*	Rep.	Big Stone Gap.
10	Henry D. Flood*	Dem.	W. Appomattox.

WASHINGTON.

Dist.	Representative.	Politics.	P. O. Address.
	Wm. E. Humphrey*	Rep.	Seattle.
	Francis W. Cushman*	Rep.	Tacoma.
	Miles Poindexter*	Rep.	Spokane.

WEST VIRGINIA.

Dist.	Representative.	Politics.	P. O. Address.
1	W. P. Hubbard*	Rep.	Wheeling.
2	George G. Sturgiss*	Rep.	Morgantown.
3	Joseph Holt Gaines*	Rep.	Charleston.
4	Harry C. Woodyard*	Rep.	Spencer.
5	James A. Hughes*	Rep.	Huntington.

WISCONSIN.

Dist.	Representative.	Politics.	P. O. Address.
1	Henry A. Cooper*	Rep.	Racine.
2	John M. Nelson*	Rep.	Madison.
3	A. W. Kopp	Rep.	Plattville.
4	William J. Cary*	Rep.	Milwaukee.
5	William H. Stafford*	Rep.	Milwaukee.
6	Charles H. Weisse*	Dem.	Sheboygan Falls.
7	John J. Esch*	Rep.	La Crosse.
8	James H. Davidson*	Rep.	Oshkosh.
9	Gustave Kustermann*	Rep.	Green Bay.
10	E. A. Morse*	Rep.	Antigo.
11	Irvine L. Lenroot	Rep.	Superior.

WYOMING.

Dist.	Representative.	Politics.	P. O. Address.
1	Frank W. Mondell*	Rep.	Newcastle.

DELEGATES FROM THE TERRITORIES.

ALASKA.

James Wickersham.. .Rep...Fairbanks.

ARIZONA.

Ralph H. Cameron......Rep...Flagstaff.

NEW MEXICO.

William H. Andrews*..Rep...Albuquerque.

HAWAII.

Jonah K. Kalanianaole*Rep...Honolulu.

PORTO RICO.

Tulio Larrinaga*...Rep. Commissioner, San Juan.

PHILIPPINE ISLANDS.

Benito Legarda.......Rep..Commissioner, Manila.
P. Ocampo de Leon...Rep..Commissioner, Manila.

Republicans, 219; Democrats, 172; whole number, 391.

* Served in the Sixtieth Congress. † Served in a previous Congress.

LIBRARY OF CONGRESS.—The Library building is open to the public all days in the year excepting legal holidays. The hours are from 9 A. M. to 10 P. M. week days, and from 2 P. M. to 10 P. M. Sundays.

New York State Government.

(JANUARY 1. 1909.)

Office	Name	Term	Salary
Governor	Chas. E. Hughes, New York	Term ex. Dec. 31, 1910	Salary, $10,000 and mansion.
Lieutenant-Governor	Horace White, Syracuse	" " " 1910	" 5,000.
Sec'y to Governor	Robert H. Fuller, New York.	....	" 4,000.

Office	Name	Term	Salary
Secretary of State	Samuel S. Koenig, New York	Term ex. Dec. 31, 1910	Salary, $5,000
Comptroller	Charles H. Gaus, Albany	" " " 1910	" 6,000
State Treasurer	Thomas B. Dunn, Rochester	" " " 1910	" 5,000
Attorney-General	Edward R. O'Malley, Buffalo	" " " 1910	" 5,000
State Engineer and Surveyor	Frank M. Williams, Madison	" " " 1910	" 5,000
Commissioner of Education	Andrew S. Draper, Albany	" " April, 1910	" 7,500
Superintendent of Insurance	Otto Kelsey, Geneseo	" " Feb. 11, 1909	" 7,000
Superintendent Banking Dept.	Clark Williams, New York	" " May 9, 1911	" 7,000
Superintendent State Prisons	Cornelius V. Collins, Troy	" " April 17, 1913	" 6,000
Superintendent Public Works	Frederick C. Stevens, Attica	" " Dec. 31, 1908	" 6,000

Deputy Secretary of State—James L. Whalen.
Deputy Supt. of Insurance (1st)—Henry D. Appleton.
Deputy Supt. of Insurance (2d)—Daniel F. Gordon. *Examiner and Acting Second Deputy Supt.*

First Assistant Commissioner of Education—Augustus F. Downing.

Tax Commissioner—Benj. E. Hall, Dec. 31, 1909.
" " Frank E. Perley, Dec. 31, 1910.
" " E. E. Woodbury, Dec. 31, 1908.
Salaries, $5,000 each.

CANAL BOARD.

Lieutenant-Governor Horace White.
Secretary of State Samuel S. Koenig.
Comptroller Charles H. Gaus.
State Treasurer Thomas B. Dunn.
Attorney-General Edward R. O'Malley.
State Engineer and Surveyor Frank W. Williams.
Superintendent Public Works Fred'k C. Stevens.

PUBLIC SERVICE COMMISSIONERS.

First District—William R. Willcox, Feb. 1, 1913; William McCarroll, Feb. 1, 1912; Edward M. Bassett, Feb. 1, 1911; Milo Roy Maltbie, Feb. 1, 1910; John E. Eustis, Feb. 1, 1909.

Second District—Frank W. Stevens, Feb. 1, 1913; Thomas Mott Osborne, Feb. 1, 1911; John B. Olmsted, Feb. 1, 1912; James F. Sague, Feb. 1, 1909; Martin S. Decker, Feb. 1, 1910.

STATE ARCHITECT.

Franklin B. Ware, New York. Salary, $7,500.

COMMISSIONERS OF CANAL FUND.

Lieutenant-Governor, Secretary of State, Comptroller, State Treasurer, Attorney-General.

CIVIL SERVICE COMMISSIONERS.

Roscoe C. E. Brown, Brooklyn.
Charles F. Milliken, Canandaigua.
John E. Kraft, Kingston.
Charles S. Fowler, Albany, *Chief Examiner*.
Salaries of Commissioners, $3,000 each.

STATE BOARD OF ARBITRATION AND MEDIATION.

John Williams. Dec. 31, 1911. Salary, $5,000.
John Lundrigan. Salary, $3,000.
M. J. Reagan $2,500.
John J. Bealin $1,400.

INDUSTRIAL MEDIATOR.

Michael J. Reagan.

FOREST, FISH, AND GAME COMMISSIONER.

James Spencer Whipple, Salamanca. Salary, $5,000.

STATE HISTORIAN.

Victor H. Paltsits. Term expires April 25, 1911. Salary, $4,500.

FISCAL SUPERVISOR OF STATE CHARITIES.

Charles M. Bissell. Term expires June 9, 1912. Salary $6,000.

STATE COMMISSIONER OF EXCISE.

Maynard N. Clement, Canandaigua. Term expires April 1, 1911. Salary, $7,000.

THE GOVERNOR'S STAFF.*

Adjutant-General—Brig.-Gen. Nelson H. Henry.
Military Secretary—Col. George Curtis Treadwell.
Aides-de-Camp—Col. Selden E. Marvin, Major G. Barrett Rich, Jr., Major Frederick M. Crossett, Major Frederic P. Moore, Commander Robert P. Forshew, Lieut.-Col. Charles E. Davis, Major Charles J. Wolf, Major Albert H. Dyett, Major Oliver D. Bridgman, Capt. Charles A. Simmons, Capt. Charles Healy, Major Elliot Bigelow, Jr., Capt. William R. Fearn, Capt. John H. Ingraham, Capt. Edwin H. Tracy, Capt. Howard K. Brown.

COURT OF CLAIMS.

Theodore H. Swift, Potsdam.
Chas. H. Murray, New York.
A. J. Rodenbeck, Rochester.
} Salaries, $8,000 each

COMMISSIONER OF AGRICULTURE.

Raymond A. Pearson. Term expires April 29, 1911.

QUARANTINE COMMISSIONERS.

Smith Pine, New York.
Frederick H. Schroeder, Brooklyn.
} $2,500 each.

STATE COMMISSIONER OF HEALTH.

Eugene H. Porter, M. D., New York. Salary, $3,500.

COMMISSIONER OF LABOR.

John Williams, Dec. 31, 1911. Salary, $5,000.
First Deputy, W. W. Walling. Salary, $3,000.
Second Deputy, John Lundrigan. Salary, $3,000.

STATE SUPERINTENDENT OF PUBLIC BUILDINGS.

Daniel W. Cahill, Watertown. Salary, $5,000.

STATE SEALER OF WEIGHTS AND MEASURES.

Fritz Reichmann, Troy.

STATE FISH CULTURIST.

Tarleton H. Bean. Salary, $3,000.

STATE COMMISSION IN LUNACY.

Albert W. Ferris, M. D., $7,500; William L. Parkhurst, $5,000; Shelden T. Viele, $5,000.

WATER SUPPLY COMMISSION.

Henry H. Persons, East Aurora; Charles Davis, Kingston; John A. Sleicher, New York; Ernest J. Lederle, New York; Milo M. Acker, Hornell.

ADVISORY BOARD OF CONSULTING ENGINEERS FOR THE NEW CANAL.

Edward A. Bond, Watertown; Thomas W. Symons, Buffalo; William A. Brackenridge, Niagara Falls; Mortimer G. Barnes, New York; Alfred B. Fry, New York.

STATE RACING COMMISSION.

James W. Wadsworth, Geneseo; John Sanford, Amsterdam; Harry K. Knapp, New York.

REGENTS OF THE UNIVERSITY.

Chancellor, Whitelaw Reid; *Vice-Chancellor*, St. Clair McKelway; Daniel Beach, Pliny T. Sexton, T. Guilford Smith, Albert Vander Veer, William Nottingham, Charles A. Gardiner, Lucian L. Shedden, Edward Lauterbach, Eugene A. Philbin.

*Under the new Military Code the Governor must drop four civilians whose names appear in list of Governor's Staff, but the change had not been made when ALMANAC was printed. Changes, if any, in above lists will be announced in later edition.

Legislature of the State of New York

SESSION OF 1909.

SENATE.

President, Lieutenant-Governor Horace White, Rep., of Syracuse.

Dist.	*Names of Senators.*	*Politics.*	*P. O. Address.*
1	Orlando Hubbs	Rep	Central Islip.
2	Dennis J. Harte*	Dem.	Long Island City
3	Thomas H. Cullen*	Dem	Brooklyn.
4	Reuben L. Gledhill	Rep	Brooklyn.
5	Barth S. Cronin	Dem	Brooklyn.
6	Eugene M. Travis*	Rep	Brooklyn.
7	Patrick H. McCarren*	Dem	Brooklyn.
8	Alvah W. Burlingame, Jr.	Rep	Brooklyn.
9	John Kissel	Rep	Brooklyn.
10	Charles Alt	Rep	Brooklyn.
11	Christopher D. Sullivan*	Dem	New York City.
12	Timothy D. Sullivan	Dem	New York City.
13	William J. A. Caffrey	Dem	New York City.
14	Thomas F. Grady*	Dem	New York City.
15	Thomas J. McManus*	Dem	New York City.
16	Robert F. Wagner	Dem	New York City.
17	George B. Agnew*	Rep	New York City.
18	Alexander Brough	Rep	New York City.
19	Josiah T. Newcomb	Rep	New York City.
20	James J. Frawley*	Dem	New York City.
21	Stephen J. Stilwell	Dem	New York City.
22	George M. S. Schultz	Dem	New york City.
23	Howard R. Bain	Dem	N. Brighton, S.I.
24	J. M. Wainwright	Rep	Rye.
25	John B. Rose	Rep	Roseton.
26	John F. Schlosser	Rep	Fishkill L'ding.
27	John N. Cordts*	Rep	Kingston.
28	William J. Grattan*	Rep	Cohoes.
29	Victor M. Allen	Rep	Troy.
30	Edgar T. Brackett	Rep	Saratoga Spr'gs.
31	William A. Gardner	Dem	Amsterdam.
32	Seth G. Heacock*	Rep	Ilion.
33	James A. Emerson*	Rep	Warrensburgh.
34	William T. O'Neil*	Rep	St Regis Falls.
35	George H. Cobb*	Rep	Watertown.
36	Frederick M. Davenport	Rep	Clinton.
37	Jotham P. Allds*	Rep	Norwich.
38	Hendrick S. Holden	Rep	Syracuse.
39	Harvey D. Hinman*	Rep	Binghamton.
40	Charles J. Hewitt	Rep	Locke
41	Benn Conger	Rep	Groton.
42	John Raines*	Rep	Canandaigua.
43	Frank C. Platt	Bep	Painted Post.
44	George H. Witter	Rep	Wellsville.
45	George L. Meade	Rep	Rochester.
46	Charles J. White	Rep	Brockport.
47	James P Mackenzie	Rep	N. Tonawanda.
48	Henry W. Hill*	Rep	Buffalo.
49	Samuel J. Ramsperger*	Dem	Buffalo.
50	George A. Davis*	Rep	Buffalo.
51	Charles M. Hamilton	Rep	Ripley.

Republicans	35
Democrats	16
Total	51

* Members of the last Senate. Senators are elected for two years. The terms of the above expire December 31, 1910. Salary, $1.500 and mileage.

ASSEMBLY.

Dist.	*Names of Members.*	*Politics.*	*P. O. Address.*
	ALBANY.		
1	J. Newton Fiero	Rep	Albany.
2	William W. Nolan*	Rep	Albany.
3	Robert B. Waters*	Rep	Green Island.
	ALLEGANY.		
	Jesse S. Phillips*	Rep	Andover.
	BROOME.		
	Harry C. Perkins*	Rep	Binghamton.
	CATTARAUGUS.		
	Ellsworth J. Cheney	Rep	Sandusky.
	CAYUGA.		
	William B. Reed	Rep.	Sterling.
	CHAUTAUQUA.		
1	Augustus F. Allen*	Rep	Jamestown.
2	John L. Sullivan	Rep	Dunkirk.
	CHEMUNG.		
	Seymour Lowman	Rep	Elmira
	CHENANGO.		
	Julien C. Scott*	Rep	Bainbridge.
	CLINTON.		
	Wm. R. Weaver	Rep	Peru.
	COLUMBIA.		
	Albert S. Callon	Rep	Valatie.
	CORTLAND.		
	Charles F. Brown*	Rep	Cortland.
	DELAWARE.		
	Henry J. Williams*1	Rep	Downsville.
	DUTCHESS.		
1	Myron T. Smith*	Rep	Millbrook.
2	Everitt H. Travis	Rep	Poughkeepsie.
	ERIE.		
1	Orson J. Weimert*	Rep	Buffalo.
2	John Lord O'Brian*	Rep	Buffalo.
3	Leo. J. Neupert	Dem	Buffalo.
4	Edward D. Jackson	Dem	Buffalo.
	ERIE—*Continued.*		
5	Edward P. Costello	Dem	Buffalo.
6	James M. Rogan	Dem	Buffalo.
7	Gottfried H. Wende	Dem	Buffalo.
8	Clarence MacGregor*	Rep	Buffalo.
9	Frank B. Thorn*	Rep	Orchard Park.
	ESSEX.		
	James Shea*	Rep	Lake Placid.
	FRANKLIN.		
	Harry H. Hawley*	Rep	Malone.
	FULTON AND HAMILTON.		
	Scott Partridge	Dem	Northville.
	GENESEE.		
	Fred B. Parker*	Rep	Elba.
	GREENE.		
	William C. Brady*	Rep	Athens.
	HERKIMER.		
	Charles L. Fellows	Rep	Newport.
	JEFFERSON.		
1	A. D. Lowe*	Rep	Depauville.
2	Gary H. Wood*	Rep	Antwerp.
	KINGS.		
1	Henry S. Goodspeed	Rep	Brooklyn.
2	William J. Gillin	Dem	Brooklyn.
3	Michael A. O'Neil	Dem	Brooklyn.
4	Geo. W. Brown	Rep	Brooklyn.
5	Charles J. Weber*	Rep	Brooklyn.
6	Thomas J. Surpless*	Rep	Brooklyn.
7	Thomas J. Geoghegan*	Dem	Brooklyn.
8	John J McKeon	Dem	Brooklyn.
9	George A. Voss*	Rep	Brooklyn.
10	Charles F. Murphy*	Rep	Brooklyn.
11	William W. Colne*	Rep	Brooklyn.
12	George A. Green*	Rep	Brooklyn.
13	John H. Donnelly*	Dem	Brooklyn.
14	James F. Fay*	Dem	Brooklyn.
15	John J. Schutta	Dem	Brooklyn.

ASSEMBLY—*Continued.*

KINGS—*Continued.*

Dist. Names of Members. Politics. P. O. Address.
16 Robert H. Clarke..........Rep...Brooklyn.
17 John R. Farrar*..........Rep...Brooklyn.
18 Warren I. Lee*.......... Rep...Brooklyn.
19 Felix J. Sanner..........Dem..Brooklyn.
20 Harrison C. Glore*......Rep...Brooklyn.
21 Samuel A. Gluck*........Dem..Brooklyn.
22 Albert Lachman..........Rep...Brooklyn.
23 Isaac Sargent*..........Rep....Brooklyn.

LEWIS.
C. Fred. Boshart*........Rep...Lowville.

LIVINGSTON.
Jas. W. Wadsworth, Jr*.Rep...Mt. Morris.

MADISON.
Orlando W. Burhyte*...Rep...Brookfield.

MONROE.
1 Edward H. White.......Rep...Rochester Jc.
2 James L. Whitley*......Rep...Rochester.
3 Louis E. Lazarus.........Rep....Rochester.
4 Cyrus W. Phillips.........Rep...Rochester.
5 John J. McInerney........Rep...Brockport.

MONTGOMERY.
T. Romeyn Staley*......Rep...Amsterdam.

NASSAU.
William G. Miller*......Rep...Freeport.

NEW YORK.
1 Thomas B. Caughlan*...Dem..New York City.
2 Alfred E. Smith*........Dem..New York City.
3 James Oliver*............Dem..New York City.
4 Aaron J. Levy............Dem...New York City.
5 John T. Eagleton*........Dem..New York City.
6 Adolph Stern*..........Dem..New York City.
7 Peter P. McElligott......Dem .New York City.
8 Moritz Graubard*........Dem..New York City.
9 John C. Hackett*........Dem..New York City.
10 Harold Spielberg.........Dem..New York City.
11 Owen W. Bohan..........Dem..New York City.
12 James A. Foley*.........Dem..New York City.
13 James J. Hoey*..........Dem..New York City.
14 John J. Herrick*.........Dem..New York City.
15 William M. Bennett*....Rep. .New York City.
16 Martin G. McCue*........Dem..New York City.
17 Frederick R. Toombs....Rep...New York City.
18 Mark Goldberg*..........Dem..New York City.
19 Andrew F. Murray.......Rep...New York City.
20 Patrick J. McGrath*.... .Dem..New York City.
21 Robert S. Conklin*.......Rep...New York City.
22 George W. Baumann.....Dem..New York City.
23 James A. Francis*......Rep...New York City.
24 Thomas A. Brennan.....Dem..New York City.
25 Artemas Ward, Jr*.....Rep...New York City.
26 Irving J. Joseph.........Dem..New York City.
27 Beverley R. Robinson*..Rep....New York City.
28 Jacob Levy................Dem..New York City.
29 Lindon Bates, Jr.........Rep...New York City.
30 Louis A. Cuvillier*.......Dem..New York City.
31 Samuel Marks.......... ...Rep...New York City.
32 Jesse Silberman*.........Dem...New York City.
33 Philip J. Schmidt*........Dem..New York City.
34 Charles Stein..............Dem..New York City.
35 John V. Sheridan*........Dem..New York City.

NIAGARA.
1 Joseph A. Jordan........Dem..N. Tonawanda.
2 W. Levell Draper*.......Rep...Wilson.

ONEIDA.
1 John W. Manley...........Dem..Utica.
2 Ladd J. Lewis*...........Rep...Sauquoit.
3 C. Robert Edwards.......Rep...Rome.

ONONDAGA.
1 John C. McLaughlin*.. Rep....Jordan.
2 Fred. W. Hammond*...Rep...Syracuse.
3 J. Henry Walters*.......Rep...Syracuse.

ONTARIO.
George B. Hemenway*.. Rep...Naples.

ORANGE.

Dist. Names of Members. Politics. P. O. Address.
1 Caleb H. Baumes.........Rep...Newburgh.
2 Charles A. Evans ....Dem..Howells.

ORLEANS.
Frank J. Murphy..........Rep...Morton.

OSWEGO.
Frank L. Smith............Rep...Phoenix.

OTSEGO.
Charles Smith*............Rep...Oneonta.

PUTNAM.
John R. Yale*.............Rep...Brewster.

QUEENS.
1 Thomas H. Todd*........Dem..L. I. City.
2 William Klein*..........Dem..College Point.
3 Conrad Garbe*...........Dem..Woodhaven.
4 William A. DeGroot*....Rep...Richmo'd Hill.

RENSSELAER.
1 Frederick C. Filley*......Rep...Troy.
2 Bradford R. Lansing*....Rep...Rensselaer.

RICHMOND.
Thomas J. Lanahan .....Dem.Mariner's H'bor.

ROCKLAND.
Rutledge I Odell..........Rep...Tompkins Cove.

ST. LAWRENCE.
1 Fred. J. Gray*.............Rep...Ogdensburg.
2 Edwin A. Merritt, Jr.*..Rep...Potsdam.

SARATOGA.
George H. Whitney*....Rep...Mechanicsville.

SCHENECTADY.
Loren H. White..........Dem..Delanson.

SCHOHARIE.
Daniel D. Frisbee.........Dem..Middleburgh.

SCHUYLER.
W. E. Leffingwell.........Dem..Watkins.

SENECA.
Alexander C. Martin... Rep...Seneca Falls.

STEUBEN.
1 John L. Miller............Rep...Corning.
2 Charles K. Marlatt*.... Rep...Troupsburg.

SUFFOLK.
1 John M. Lupton*.........Rep...Mattituck, L. I.
2 George L. Thompson. ...Rep...Kings Park.

SULLIVAN.
Calvin Millen.............Rep....Bethel.

TIOGA.
Frank L. Howard*.......Rep...Waverly.

TOMPKINS.
Wm. R. Gunderman*.....Rep...Ithaca.

ULSTER.
1 Joseph M. Fowler*.......Rep...Kingston.
2 Edward Young............Rep...Milton.

WARREN.
William R. Waddell*...Rep...North Creek.

WASHINGTON.
James S. Parker*.........Rep...Salem.

WAYNE.
Edson W. Hamn*........Rep....Lyons.

WESTCHESTER.
1 Harry W. Hains*.........Rep...Yonkers.
2 Holland S. Duell.........Rep...New Rochelle.
3 Frank L. Young..........Rep...Ossining.
4 George W. Mead.........Rep...Lake Waccabuc.

WYOMING.
Robert M. McFarlane*..Rep...Eagle.

YATES.
Llewellyn J. Barden......Rep...Gage.

* Members of the last Assembly. Assemblymen are elected for one year. Salary, $1,500 and mileage.

Republicans.. 99
Democrats.. 15

Judiciary of the State of New York.

JUDGES OF THE COURT OF APPEALS OF NEW YORK.

JUDGES.	Residences.	Counties.	Salaries.	Politics.	Terms Expire.
Edgar M. Cullen, Chief Judge.........	Albany.......	Albany.......	$14,200	Dem.....	Dec. 31, 1918
Albert Haight, Associate Judge......	Buffalo........	Erie..........	13,700	Rep....	" 31, 1912
John Clinton Gray, "	New York....	New York....	13,700	Dem.....	" 31, 1913
Irving G. Vann, "	Syracuse......	Onondaga....	13,700	Rep. ...	" 31, 1910
Edward T. Bartlett, "	New York....	New York....	13,700	Rep. ...	" 31, 1911
William E. Werner, "	Rochester.....	Monroe.......	13,700	Rep. ...	" 31, 1918
Frank H. Hiscock, "	Syracuse......	Onondaga....	13,700	Rep....	" 31, 1910
Emory A. Chase, "	Catskill.......	Greene........	13,700	Rep....	" 31, 1910
Willard Bartlett, "	Brooklyn.	Kings	13,700	Dem	" 31, 1917

JUDGES OF THE APPELLATE DIVISION OF THE SUPREME COURT.

DEPARTMENT.	Justices.	Residences.	Politics.	Designations Expire.
1st. The county of New York.	John Proctor Clarke...	New York........	Rep.....	Oct. 4, 1910
	Edward Patterson.....	"	Dem.....	" 31, 1909
	George L. Ingraham..	"	Dem.....	" 31, 1910
	Chester B. McLaughlin	Port Henry	Rep.....	" 31, 1909
	Frank C. Laughlin.....	Buffalo...........	Rep.	Dec. 31, 1909
	James W. Houghton..	Saratoga Springs.	Rep.	Oct. 25, 1910
	Francis M. Scott......	New York........	Dem.....	Dec. 4, 1911
2d. Kings, Queens, Nassau, Richmond, Suffolk, Rockland, Westchester, Putnam, Orange, Dutchess.	Michael H. Hirschberg	Newburgh........	Rep.....	" 31, 1910
	William J. Gaynor....	Brooklyn.........	Dem.....	" 31, 1912
	John Woodward.	Jamestown.......	Rep.	" 31, 1910
	Almet F. Jenks........	Brooklyn.........	Dem.....	April 4, 1910
	Warren B. Hooker....	Fredonia.........	Rep.	Dec. 31, 1908
	Adelbert P. Rich......	Auburn...........	Rep.	Temporary.
	Nathan L. Miller......	Cortland..........	Rep.	Temporary.
3d. Sullivan, Ulster, Greene, Columbia, Schoharie, Albany, Rensselaer, Fulton, Schenectady, Montgomery, Saratoga, Washington, Warren, Hamilton, Essex, Clinton, Franklin, St. Lawrence, Delaware, Otsego, Broome, Chenango, Madison, Cortland, Tioga, Tompkins, Schuyler, Chemung.	A. V. S. Cochrane.....	Hudson...........	Rep.	Jan. 8, 1911
	Walter Lloyd Smith...	Elmira............	Rep.	Dec. 31, 1916
	Alden Chester.........	Albany...........	Rep.	Dec. 31, 1909
	John M. Kellogg......	Ogdensburg......	Rep.	Nov. 13, 1910
	Albert H. Sewell.......	Walton............	Rep.	Dec. 31, 1911
4th. Herkimer, Oneida, Lewis, Jefferson, Oswego, Onondaga, Cayuga, Seneca, Wayne, Ontario, Yates, Steuben, Livingston, Monroe, Allegany, Wyoming, Genesee, Orleans, Niagara, Erie, Cattaraugus, Chautauqua.	Peter B. McLennan...	Syracuse..........	Rep.	Dec. 31, 1920
	Alfred Spring.........	Franklinville	Rep.	Jan. 9, 1909
	Pardon C. Williams...	Watertown.......	Rep.	" 15, 1910
	Frederick W. Kruse..	Olean........	Rep.	" 3, 1911
	James A. Robson.........	Canandaigua.....	Rep.	" 7, 1912

JUSTICES OF THE SUPREME COURT.

The salaries of Justices of the Supreme Court are: First and Second Districts, $17,500; remaining Districts, $7,200; but non-resident Justices, sitting in the Appellate Divisions of the First and Second Departments, receive the same compensation as the Justices in those Departments; if assigned to duty in the First and Second Districts, other than in the Appellate Division, their additional compensation is $10 per day.

DISTRICTS.	Justices.	Residences.	Politics.	Terms Expire.
1st. The city and county of New York.	Edward Patterson.....	New York........	Dem.....	Dec. 31, 1909
	Samuel Greenbaum ...	"	Dem.....	" 31, 1915
	George L. Ingraham..	"	Dem.....	" 31, 1919
	Francis M. Scott.......	"	Dem	" 31, 1911
	Joseph E. Newburger.	"	Dem	" 31, 1919
	Charles H. Truax......	"	Dem.....	" 31, 1909
	James A. Blanchard..	"	Rep.	" 31, 1915
	Charles F. MacLean...	"	Dem.....	" 31, 1909
	Vernon M. Davis......	"	Dem.....	" 31, 1916
	Philip H. Dugro........	"	Dem.....	" 31, 1914
	Victor J. Dowling......	"	Dem.....	" 31, 1918
	Edward E. McCall.....	"	Dem.....	" 31, 1916
	H. A. Gildersleeve....	"	Dem.....	" 31, 1919
	James Fitzgerald......	"	Dem.....	" 31, 1912
	James A. O'Gorman..	"	Dem.....	" 31, 1913
	Henry Bischoff, Jr.....	"	Dem.....	" 31, 1917
	Irving Lehman........	"	Dem.....	" 31, 1922
	Leonard A. Giegerich..	"	Dem.....	" 31, 1920

JUDICIARY OF THE STATE OF NEW YORK—*Continued.*

Districts.	Justices.	Residences.	Politics.	Terms Expire.
1st. The city and county of New York.	Edward B. Amend	New York	Dem.	Dec. 31, 1916
	John Proctor Clarke	"	Rep	" 31, 1915
	John W. Goff	"	Dem.	" 31, 1920
	Samuel Seabury	"	Ind. L.	" 31, 1920
	M. Warley Platzek	"	Dem.	" 31, 1920
	Peter A. Hendrick	"	Dem.	" 31, 1920
	John Ford	"	Ind. L.	" 31, 1920
	Mitchell L. Erlanger	"	Dem.	" 31, 1920
	Charles W. Dayton	"	Dem.	" 31, 1920
	Charles L. Guy	"	Dem.	" 31, 1920
	John J. Brady	"	Dem.	" 31 1920
	James W. Gerard	"	Rep.	" 31, 1921
2d. Kings, Queens, Nassau, Richmond, and Suffolk.	William J. Gaynor	Brooklyn	Dem.	" 31, 1921
	Joseph A. Burr	"	Rep.	" 31, 1919
	Luke D. Stapleton	"	Dem.	" 31, 1922
	William D. Dickey	"	Rep	" 31, 1909
	Josiah T. Marean	Brooklyn	Dem.	" 31, 1912
	Almet F. Jenks	"	Dem.	" 31, 1912
	Garret J. Garretson	Elmhurst	Rep	" 31, 1910
	William J. Kelly	Brooklyn	Dem.	" 31, 1916
	Samuel T. Maddox	"	Rep	" 31, 1910
	Edward B. Thomas	"	Rep	" 31, 1920
	Walter H. Jaycox	Patchogue	Rep	" 31, 1920
	Joseph Aspinall	Brooklyn	Rep	" 31, 1920
	Frederick E. Crane	"	Rep	" 31, 1920
	Lester W. Clark	New Brighton	Rep	" 31, 1920
	Abel E. Blackmar	Brooklyn	Rep	" 31, 1922
	William J. Carr	"	Dem.	" 31, 1920
	Townsend Scudder	Glen Head	Dem.	" 31, 1920
3d. Columbia, Rensselaer, Sullivan, Ulster, Albany, Greene, and Schoharie counties.	George H. Fitts	Albany	Rep.	" 31, 1919
	Wesley O. Howard	Troy	Rep	" 31, 1916
	A. V. S. Cochrane	Hudson	Rep	" 31, 1915
	Alden Chester	Albany	Rep.	" 31 1909
	Emory A. Chase	Catskill	Dem.	" 31, 1910
	James A. Betts	Kingston	Rep.	" 31, 1912
4th. Warren, Saratoga, St. Lawrence, Washington, Essex, Franklin, Clinton, Montgomery, Hamilton, Fulton, and Schenectady counties	John M. Kellogg	Ogdensburg	Rep.	" 31, 1917
	Edgar A. Spencer	Gloversville	Rep.	" 31, 1915
	James W. Houghton	Saratoga Springs.	Rep.	" 31, 1914
	Charles C. Van Kirk	Whitehall	Rep.	" 31, 1907
	Henry T. Kellogg	Plattsburg	Rep	" 31, 1917
	Chester B. McLaughlin	Port Henry	Rep.	" 31, 1909
5th. Onondaga, Jefferson, Oneida, Oswego, Herkimer, and Lewis counties.	William S. Andrews	Syracuse	Rep.	" 31, 1913
	Watson M. Rogers	Watertown	Rep.	" 31, 1914
	P. C. J. DeAngelis	Utica	Rep.	" 31, 1920
	Irving L. Devendorf	Herkimer	Rep.	" 31, 1919
	Frank H. Hiscock	Syracuse	Rep.	" 31, 1910
	Pardon C. Williams	Watertown	Rep.	" 31, 1911
	Peter B. McLennan	Syracuse	Rep.	" 31, 1920
	William E. Scripture	Rome	Rep.	" 31, 1909
6th. Otsego, Delaware, Madison, Chenango, Tompkins, Broome, Chemung, Schuyler, Tioga, and Cortland counties.	Albert F. Gladding	Norwich	Rep.	" 31, 1920
	Albert H. Sewell	Walton	Rep.	" 31, 1913
	Nathan L. Miller	Cortland	Rep.	" 31, 1918
	Henry B. Coman	Morrisville	Rep.	" 31, 1920
	Walter Lloyd Smith	Elmira	Rep.	" 31, 1916
	George F. Lyon	Binghamton	Rep.	" 31, 1909
7th. Livingston, Ontario, Wayne, Yates, Steuben, Seneca, Cayuga, and Monroe counties.	James A. Robson	Canandaigua	Rep	" 31, 1918
	Adelbert P. Rich	Auburn	Rep	" 31, 1914
	Nathaniel Foote	Rochester	Rep.	" 31, 1919
	William W. Clark	Wayland	Rep.	" 31, 1920
	Arthur E. Sutherland	Rochester	Rep.	" 31, 1919
	George A. Benton	Spencerport	Rep.	" 31, 1920
	Samuel N. Sawyer	Palmyra	Rep.	" 31 1921
8th. Erie, Chautauqua, Cattaraugus, Orleans, Niagara, Genesee, Allegany, and Wyoming counties.	John S. Lambert	Fredonia	Rep.	" 31, 1917
	Warren B. Hooker	"	Rep.	" 31, 1913
	Alfred Spring	Franklinville	Rep.	" 31, 1909
	Frank C. Laughlin	Buffalo	Rep.	" 31, 1909
	Truman C. White	"	Rep.	" 31, 1910
	Frederick W. Kruse	Olean	Rep.	" 31, 1914
	John Woodward	Jamestown	Rep.	" 31, 1910
	Cuthbert W. Pound	Lockport	Rep.	" 31, 1920
	Edward K. Emery	Buffalo	Rep.	" 31 1920
	Louis W. Marcus	"	Rep.	" 31, 1920
	Charles H. Brown	Belmont	Rep.	" 31, 1920
	Charles B. Wheeler	Buffalo	Rep.	" 31, 1921
9th. Westchester, Putnam, Dutchess, Orange and Rockland counties	Isaac N. Mills	Mt. Vernon	Rep.	" 31, 1920
	Arthur S. Tompkins	Nyack	Rep.	" 31, 1920
	Joseph Morschauser	Poughkeepsie	Rep	" 31, 1920
	Michael H. Hirschberg	Newburgh	Rep	" 31, 1910
	Martin J. Keogh	New Rochelle	Dem.	" 31, 1909

New York Counties.

SHOWING POLITICAL AND JUDICIAL DIVISIONS OF WHICH THEY ARE UNITS.

COUNTIES.	Senatorial Districts.	Congressional Districts.	Supreme Court Districts.	Appellate Div. Supreme Court Departments.
Albany	28	23	3	3
Allegany	44	37	8	4
Broome	39	30	6	3
Cattaraugus	51	37	8	4
Cayuga	40	31	7	4
Chautauqua	51	37	8	4
Chemung	41	33	6	3
Chenango	37	30	6	3
Clinton	33	26	4	3
Columbia	26	21	3	3
Cortland	40	30	6	3
Delaware	39	24	6	3
Dutchess	26	21	9	2
Erie	48, 49, 50	35, 36	8	4
Essex	33	26	4	3
Franklin	34	26	4	3
Fulton and Hamilton	32	25	4	3
Genesee	44	34	8	4
Greene	27	21	3	3
Herkimer	32	27	5	4
Jefferson	35	28	5	4
Kings	3 to 10	2 to 7	2	2
Lewis	32	28	5	4
Livingston	43	34	7	4
Madison	37	29	6	3
Monroe	45, 46	32	7	4
Montgomery	31	25	4	3
Nassau	1	1	2	2
New York	11 to 22	8 to 18	1	1
Niagara	47	34	8	4
Oneida	36	27	5	4
Onondaga	38	29	5	4
Ontario	42	31	7	4
Orange	25	20	9	2
Orleans	47	34	8	4
Oswego	35	28	5	4
Otsego	37	24	6	3
Putnam	26	21	9	2
Queens	2	1	2	2
Rensselaer	29	22	3	3
Richmond	23	8	2	2
Rockland	23	20	9	2
St. Lawrence	34	26	4	3
Saratoga	30	25	4	3
Schenectady	31	23	4	3
Schoharie	31	24	3	3
Schuyler	41	33	6	3
Seneca	40	33	7	4
Steuben	43	33	7	4
Suffolk	1	1	2	2
Sullivan	25	20	3	3
Tioga	41	30	6	3
Tompkins	41	30	6	3
Ulster	27	24	3	3
Warren	33	25	4	3
Washington	30	22	4	3
Wayne	42	31	7	4
Westchester	24	19	9	2
Wyoming	44	34	8	4
Yates	42	31	7	4

COUNTIES IN THE ORDER OF THEIR CREATION.

No. County.	Formed from	Date of Creat'n
1—Albany	(Original)	Nov. 1, 1683
2—Dutchess	(Original)	Nov. 1, 1683
3—Kings	(Original)	Nov. 1, 1683
4—New York	(Original)	Nov. 1, 1683
5—Orange	(Original)	Nov. 1, 1683
6—Queens	(Original)	Nov. 1, 1683
7—Richmond	(Original)	Nov. 1, 1683
8—Suffolk	(Original)	Nov. 1, 1683
9—Ulster	(Original)	Nov. 1, 1683
10—Westchester	(Original)	Nov. 1, 1683
11—Montgomery	Albany	March 12, 1772
12—Washington	Albany	March 12, 1772
13—Columbia	Albany	April 4, 1786
14—Clinton	Washington	March 7, 1788
15—Ontario	Montgomery	Jan. 27, 1789
16—Rensselaer	Albany	Feb. 7, 1791
17—Saratoga	Albany	Feb. 7, 1791
18—Herkimer	Montgomery	Feb. 16, 1791
19—Otsego	Montgomery	Feb. 16, 1791
20—Tioga	Montgomery	Feb. 16, 1791
21—Onondaga	Herkimer	March 5, 1794
22—Schoharie	Albany and Otsego	April 6, 1795
23—Steuben	Ontario	March 18, 1796
24—Delaware	Ulster and Otsego	March 10, 1797
25—Rockland	Orange	Feb. 23, 1798
26—Chenango	Tioga and Herkimer	March 15, 1798
27—Oneida	Herkimer	March 15, 1798
28—Essex	Clinton	March 1, 1799
29—Cayuga	Onondaga	March 8, 1799
30—Greene	Albany and Ulster	March 25, 1800
31—St. Lawrence	Clinton	March 3, 1802
32—Genesee	Ontario	March 30, 1802
33—Seneca	Cayuga	March 24, 1804
34—Jefferson	Oneida	March 28, 1805
35—Lewis	Oneida	March 28, 1805
36—Madison	Chenango	March 21, 1806
37—Broome	Tioga	March 28, 1806
38—Allegany	Genesee	April 7, 1806
39—Cattaraugus	Genesee	March 11, 1808
40—Chautauqua	Genesee	March 11, 1808
41—Franklin	Clinton	March 11, 1808
42—Niagara	Genesee	March 11, 1808
43—Cortland	Onondaga	April 8, 1808
44—Schenectady	Albany	March 7, 1809
45—Sullivan	Ulster	March 27, 1809
46—Putnam	Dutchess	June 12, 1812
47—Warren	Washington	March 12, 1813
48—Oswego	Oneida and Onondaga	March 1, 1816
49—Hamilton	Montgomery	April 12, 1816
50—Tompkins	Cayuga and Seneca	April 7, 1817
51—Livingston	Genesee and Ontario	Feb. 23, 1821
52—Monroe	Genesee and Ontario	Feb. 23, 1821
53—Erie	Niagara	April 2, 1821
54—Yates	Ontario	Feb. 5, 1823
55—Wayne	Ontario and Seneca	April 11, 1823
56—Orleans	Genesee	Nov. 12, 1824
57—Chemung	Tioga	March 29, 1836
58—Fulton	Montgomery	April 18, 1838
59—Wyoming	Genesee	May 14, 1841
60—Schuyler	Chemung, Steuben & Tompkins	April 17, 1854
61 Nassau	Queens	Jan. 1, 1899

Soldiers' Homes.

NATIONAL HOME FOR DISABLED VOLUNTEER SOLDIERS.

President of the Board of Managers... Maj. James W. Wadsworth, 346 Broadway, New York City, N.Y.
Secretary.......................................Col. W. P. Brownlow, Jonesboro, Tenn.

There are branches of the National Home at Dayton, O.; Milwaukee, Wis.; Togus, Me.; Hampton, Va.; Leavenworth, Kan.; Santa Monica, Cal.; Marion, Ind., Danville, Ill., Johnson City, Tenn., and Hot Springs, S. Dak. The aggregate number of members cared for is about 35,000.

REQUIREMENTS FOR ADMISSION.

1. An honorable discharge from the United States service during a war in which it was engaged.
2. Disability which prevents the applicant from earning his living by labor.
3. Applicants for admission will be required to stipulate and agree to abide by all the rules and regulations made by the Board of Managers, or by its order; to perform all duties required of them, and to obey all the lawful orders of the officers of the Home. Attention is called to the fact that by the law establishing the Home the members are made subject to the Rules and Articles of War, and will be governed thereby in the same manner as if they were in the Army of the United States.
4. A soldier or sailor must forward with his application for admission his Discharge Paper, and when he is a pensioner, his Pension Certificate, which papers will be retained at the branch to which the applicant is admitted, to be kept there for him, and returned to him when he is discharged. This rule is adopted to prevent the loss of such papers and certificates, and to hinder fraudulent practices; and no application will be considered unless these papers are sent with it. If the original discharge does not exist, a copy of discharge, certified by the War or Navy Department, or by the Adjutant-General of the State, must accompany the application.

There are State Homes for disabled volunteer soldiers provided by the States of California, Colorado, Connecticut, Idaho, Illinois, Indiana, Iowa, Kansas, Massachusetts, Michigan, Minnesota, Missouri, Montana, Nebraska, New Hampshire, New Jersey, New York, North Dakota, Ohio, Oregon, Pennsylvania, Rhode Island, South Dakota, Vermont, Washington, Wisconsin, and Wyoming.

STATE HOMES FOR DISABLED VOLUNTEER SOLDIERS.

STATES.	Location.	STATES.	Location.	STATES.	Location.
California......	Yountville.	Minnesota.....	Minnehaha.	North Dakota..	Lisbon.
Colorado........	Monte Vista.	Missouri	St. James.	Ohio............	Sandusky.
Connecticut	Noroton Heights	Montana........	Columbus Falls	Oregon	Roseburg.
Idaho	Boisé.	Nebraska	Grand Island.	Pennsylvania..	Erie.
Illinois	Quincy.	Nebraska	Milford.	Rhode Island..	Bristol.
Indiana	Lafayette.	N. Hampshire.	Tilton.	South Dakota..	Hot Springs.
Iowa............	Marshalltown.	New Jersey....	Kearny.	Vermont	Bennington.
Kansas	Fort Dodge.	New Jersey....	Vineland.	Washington ...	Orting.
Massachusetts..	Chelsea.	New York.....	Bath.	Wisconsin	Waupaca.
Michigan.	Grand Rapids.	New York.....	Oxford.	Wyoming......	Cheyenne.

UNITED STATES HOME FOR REGULAR ARMY SOLDIERS.

The United States Soldiers' Home in the District of Columbia receives and maintains discharged soldiers of the *regular* army. All soldiers who have served twenty years as enlisted men in the army (including volunteer service, if any), and all soldiers of less than twenty years' service who have incurred such disability, by wounds, disease, or injuries *in the line of duty while in the regular army*, as unfits them for further service, are entitled to the benefits of the Home.

A pensioner who enters the Home may assign his pension, or any part of it, to his child, wife, or parent, by filing written notice with the agent who pays him. If not so assigned, it is drawn by the treasurer of the Home and held in trust for the pensioner, to whom it is paid in such sums as the commissioners deem proper while he is an inmate of the Home, the balance being paid in full when he takes his discharge and leaves the Home.

Inmates are subject to the Rules and Articles of War, the same as soldiers in the army. They are comfortably lodged, fed, and clothed, and receive medical attendance and medicine, all without cost to them. There are 1,250 men now receiving the benefits of the Home.

Applications for admission to the Home may be addressed to the "Board of Commissioners, Soldiers' Home, War Department, Washington City, D. C.," and must give date of enlistment and date of discharge, with letter of company and number of regiment for each and every term of service, and rate of pension, if any, and must be accompanied by a medical certificate showing nature and degree of disability if any exists.

National Cemeteries.

NATIONAL Cemeteries in which the soldiers of the civil and Spanish wars are interred are located at the following places:

Alexandria, La.; Alexandria, Va.; Andersonville, Ga.; Annapolis, Md.; Antietam, Md.; Arlington, Va.; Balls Bluff, Va.; Barrancas, Fla.; Baton Rouge, La.; Battle-Ground, D. C.; Beaufort, S. C.; Beverly, N. J.; Brownsville, Tex.; Camp Butler, Ill.; Camp Nelson, Ky.; Cave Hill, Ky.; Chalmette, La.; Chattanooga, Tenn.; City Point, Va.; Cold Harbor, Va.; Corinth, Miss.; Crown Hill, Ind.; Culpepper, Va.; Custer Battlefield, Mont.; Cypress Hills, N. Y.; Danville, Ky.; Danville, Va.; Fayetteville, Ark.; Finns Point, N. J.; Florence, S. C.; Fort Donelson, Tenn.; Fort Gibson, Okla.; Fort Harrison, Va.; Fort Leavenworth, Kan.; Fort McPherson, Neb.; Fort Scott, Kan.; Fort Smith, Ark.; Fredericksburg, Va.; Gettysburg, Pa.; Glendale, Va.; Grafton, W. Va.; Hampton, Va.; Jefferson Barracks, Mo.; Jefferson City, Mo.; Keokuk, Ia.; Knoxville, Tenn.; Lebanon, Ky.; Lexington, Ky.; Little Rock, Ark.; Loudon Park, Md.; Marietta, Ga.; Memphis, Tenn.; Mexico City, Mex.; Mill Springs, Ky.; Mobile, Ala.; Mound City, Ill.; Nashville, Tenn.; Natchez, Miss.; New Albany, Ind.; New Berne, N. C.; Philadelphia, Pa.; Poplar Grove, Va.; Port Hudson, La.; Quincey, Ill.; Raleigh, N. C.; Richmond, Va.; Rock Island, Ill.; St. Augustine, Fla.; Salisbury, N. C.; San Antonio, Tex.; San Francisco, Cal.; Santa Fé, N. M.; Seven Pines, Va.; Shiloh, Tenn.; Soldiers' Home, D. C.; Springfield, Mo.; Staunton, Va.; Stone River, Tenn.; Vicksburg, Miss.; Wilmington, N. C.; Winchester, Va.; Woodlawn, N. Y.; Yorktown, Va.

Administration of Deceased Persons' Estates.

INHERITANCE TAX LAWS.

THE following is a synopsis of several of the laws of the various States affecting the administration of the estate of a deceased person:

1. Who to Administer.—(a) If the deceased leave a will, the duty of administration falls upon the executor. If no executor is named, or in the event of the death or refusal of the executor to act, the Court will grant administration under the will to some suitable person, generally selected from those most largely interested under the provisions of the will, such as the residuary legatees, if any. (b) If the deceased died intestate, letters of administration are granted to the following persons in practically all the States:

First—To the surviving husband or widow.

Second—To one or more of the next of kin entitled to share in the estate.

Third—If none of the above consent to act, to one of the creditors of the estate, except in localities where there is provided by law a Public Administrator, who is preferred to creditors.

In practically all the States an administrator is required to give bond for the faithful performance of his duties in double the value of the estate to be administered.

In most of the States, if so provided by the will, no bond is required of an executor, except that in some States an executor is required to give a bond to cover the probable amount of the debts of the estate, and in practically all the States, in the discretion of the Court, for cause shown, an executor may be required to give a bond.

2. Claims of Creditors.—The procedure in the several States in presenting creditors' claims against the estate varies very considerably. In the majority of the States the executor or administrator is required promptly to give public notice to creditors to present their claims to him, and the creditors are required so to present their claims supported by an affidavit that the same are justly due and owing from the estate, above any offsets or counter claims, within a period limited generally to six months or a year. The law of each State should be consulted for more specific details.

3. The following table contains an analysis of the laws of the several States, covering:

(1) The time provided for accounting to the Court by executors and administrators on their administration.

(2) The inheritance or succession tax upon property received either by intestate laws, last will, or by gift or transfer, designed to take effect at death.

(3) The various classes of estate obligations given priority over other claims in case of the insolvency of the estate.

State.	Accounting.	Inheritance Tax.	Preferred Obligations.
Alabama......	Annual accounts. Final account in one year if condition of estate permits.	None.	1. Funeral expenses. 2. Administration expenses. 3. Expenses of last sickness. 4. Taxes. 5. Wages of servants or employees.
Arizona.......	As directed by the Court.	None.	No statutory provision.
Arkansas......	Annual accounts. Final accounting in three years.	Five per cent. tax on property passing to collateral relatives (other than lineal descendants or ancestors).	1. Funeral expenses. 2. Expenses of last sickness. 3. Wages of servants. 4. Judgments which are liens on land of deceased.
California.....	Must file account in ten months.	On estates less than $25,000 in value the tax rate varies from 1% to 5%, governed by the relationship to deceased, the nearer the relationship the smaller the rate of tax. On larger estates the above rate is increased from 1½ to 3 times. The tax exempt inheritances vary from $10,000 to a widow or minor child to $500 passing to remote relatives or strangers.	1. Funeral expenses. 2. Expenses of last sickness. 3. Debts preferred by U. S. laws. 4. Wages due within sixty days. 5. Judgments, mortgages and other liens.
Colorado......	Account in one year.	Property passing to parents, husband or wife, child, brother or sister, wife or widow of son, husband of daughter, lineal descendant, or adopted child, or child acknowledged as such for ten years, is taxable at 2%, except estates less than $10,000 are exempt to above persons. To uncle, aunt, nephew or niece or their descendants tax of 3%, no exemption. To all others above $500: On $500 to $10,000, tax is 3%; $10,000 to $20,000, 4%; $20,000 to $50,000, 5%; above $50,000, 6%.	1. Moneys held by deceased as trustee or executor. 2. Expenses of funeral and last sickness.

State.	Accounting.	Inheritance Tax.	Preferred Obligations.
Connecticut...	Account in one year.	All estates exempt up to $10,000. Tax on excess as follows: To parents, husband or wife, or lineal descendants, ½%; to others 3%.	1. Funeral and administration expenses. 2. Expenses of last sickness. 3. Taxes. 4. Other preferred claims by State laws.
Delaware......	Account in one year.	Property passing to parents, wife, children or descendants exempt. To others, tax of 5%; estates exempt up to $500.	1. Funeral expenses. 2. Expenses of last sickness. 3. Wages, to servants and laborers. 4. Rent (not over one year). 5. Judgments. 6. Obligations of record. 7. Obligations under seal. 8. Contracts for payment of money or delivery of goods.
District of Columbia....	Account in fifteen months.	None.	1. Judgments or decree of Court. 2. Other debts.
Florida........	Annual accounts.	None.	1. Administration expenses. 2. Funeral expenses. 3. Expenses of last sickness. 4. Judgments and debts due to State.
Georgia.......	Annual accounts.	None.	1. Year's support of family. 2. Expenses of funeral and last sickness. 3. Administration expenses. 4. Taxes. 5. Fiduciary obligations. 6. Judgments, mortgages and other liens. 7. Rent. 8. Liquidated demands.
Idaho.........	First account in three months. Future accounts as directed by the Court.	Tax on estates less than $25,000 at following rates: (a) To husband or wife, lineal issue or ancestor, 1%; exempt to widow or minor child, $10,000; to others of Class A, exempt $4,000. (b) To brother or sister, or their descendants, or wife or widow of son, or husband of daughter, 1½%; exempt, $2,000. (c) To uncles, aunts or descendants, 3%; exempt, $1,500. (d) To great-uncles, great-aunts or descendants, 4%; exempt, $1,000. (e) To more distant relatives or strangers in blood, 5%; exempt, $500. On larger estates than $25,000 the above rates are multiplied as follows: $25,000 to $50,000, 1½ times above; $50,000 to $100,000, 2 times above; $100,000 to $500,000, 2½ times above; $500,000 and upward, 3 times above.	1. Funeral expenses. 2. Expenses of last sickness. 3. Debts preferred by U. S. laws. 4. Judgments and mortgages.
Illinois........	Inventory in three months. Accounts as directed by the Court.	On property passing to parents, husband or wife, wife or widow of son, husband of daughter, lineal descendants, or one to whom deceased stood in relation of parent, tax 1%; exempt up to $20,000.	1. Funeral and administration expenses. 2. Allowance to widow and children. 3. Expenses of last sickness, except doctor's bill and

State.	Accounting.	Inheritance Tax.	Preferred Obligations.
Illinois—(Continued)..		To uncle, aunt, niece or nephew or descendants, 2%; exempt, $2,000. All other cases as follows: On less than $10,000, 3%; $10,000 to $20,000, 4%; $20,000 to $50,000, 5%; above $50,000, 6%. All estates less than $500 exempt.	wages to servants. 4. Debts to common school or township funds. 5. Doctor's bill, last sickness. 6. Money owed in fiduciary capacity.
Indiana.......	Accounts as directed by Court.	None.	1. Administration expenses. 2. Funeral expenses. 3. Expenses of last sickness. 4. Taxes. 5. Debts secured by liens on real estate. 6. Wages, not over $50.
Iowa..........	First account in six months. Annually thereafter. Final account in three years.	Property passing to parents, husband or wife, lineal descendants, adopted child or issue thereof is exempt. To others 5% tax above $1,000. To alien non-residents of the State tax is 20%, unless alien is brother or sister, when tax is 10%.	1. Debts preferred by U. S. laws. 2. Public rates and taxes. 3. Claims filed within six months after notice.
Kansas........	Annual accounts.	None.	1. Funeral expenses. 2. Expenses of last sickness. Administration expenses. Wages of servants. 3. Debts due to State. 4. Judgments. 5. All demands presented within one year after letters of administration. 6. Demands presented after one year and before two years. 7. Demands presented after two years and before three years.
Kentucky.....	As directed by Court.	Tax of 5% on all estates over $500 except to parents, husband or wife, lawful issue, husband of daughter, wife or widow of son, lineal descendants or adopted child, which are exempt.	1. Funeral expenses. 2. Administration expenses. 3. Moneys due in fiduciary capacity.
Louisiana.....	Annual accounts.	Exempt to $10,000 to parents or lineal ancestors, children or descendants; excess taxable at 2%; to others 5%.	1. Funeral expenses. 2. Legal expenses. 3. Expenses of last sickness. 4. Servants' wages within one year. 5. Debts for food and supplies within six months. 6. Salaries, clerks.
Maine.........	As directed by the Court.	Exempt to parents, husband or wife, lineal descendants, adopted child, or descendants, wife or widow of son, husband of daughter; to others, 4% above $500.	1. Funeral and administration expenses. 2. Allowance to husband, widow or children. 3. Expenses of last sickness. 4. Debts preferred under U. S. laws. 5. Taxes.
Maryland.....	Account in one year. Thereafter every six months till closed.	Exempt to parents, husband or wife, children, or lineal descendants; to others, 2½%.	1. Taxes. 2. Arrears of rent. 3. Judgments or decrees of Court.
Massachusetts.	Annual accounts.	(a) To husband or wife, lineal ancestor, lineal descendants, adopted child or descendants thereof, wife or widow of son, husband of daughter, taxable as follows: Under $1,000, exempt; $1,000 to $50,000, 1%; $50,000 to $100,000,	1. Debts preferred by U. S. laws. 2. Public rates and taxes. 3. Wages, not over $100.

State.	Accounting.	Inheritance Tax.	Preferred Obligations.
Massachusetts—(Continued)		1½%; above $100,000, 2%. (b) To brother, sister, nephew or niece: Up to $25,000, 3%; $25,000 to $100,000, 4%; above $100,000, 5%. To all other persons, 5%.	
Michigan	Eighteen months allowed to close estate. More may be granted by Court up to four years.	Tax of 1% to parents, husband or wife, child, brother or sister, wife or widow of son, husband of daughter, lineal descendants, adopted child, or one to whom deceased stood in relation of parent, exempt to $2,000. To others, 5% over $100.	1. Administration expenses. 2. Funeral expenses. 3. Expenses of last sickness. 4. Debts preferred by U. S. laws.
Minnesota	Eighteen months to settle estate, though further time may be allowed.	All inheritances above $10,000 are taxable as follows: $10,000 to $50,000, 1½%; $50,000 to $100,000, 3%; above $100,000, 5%. Estates below $10,000 exempt.	1. Administration expenses. 2. Funeral expenses. 3. Expenses of last sickness. 4. Debts preferred by U. S. laws. 5. Taxes.
Mississippi	Annual accounts.	None.	No statutory preference.
Missouri	Annual accounts. Final settlement after two years.	All inheritances taxable at 5% except to parents, husband or wife, or lineal descendants, which are exempt.	1. Funeral expenses. 2. Expenses of last sickness; wages of servants. 3. Taxes and public debts. 4. Judgments. 5. All demands presented within one year after letters. 6. All demands exhibited after one and before two years.
Montana	One year allowed for settlement of estate.	Tax of 1% to parents, husband or wife, lawful issue, brother or sister, or adopted child, exempt to $7,500. To all others, 5%.	1. Funeral expenses. 2. Expenses of last sickness. 3. Debts preferred under U. S. laws. 4. Judgments and mortgages.
Nebraska	Final account in three years.	Taxable at 1% to parents, husband or wife, child, brother or sister, wife or widow of son, husband of daughter, adopted child, or where deceased stood in relation of parent, and lineal descendants in lawful wedlock, exempt to $10,000. To uncle, aunt, nephew or niece, or descendants, 2%; exempt to $2,000. To others, above $500 as follows: $500 to $5,000, 2%; $5,000 to $10,000, 3%; $10,000 to $20,000, 4%; $20,000 to $50,000, 5%; above $50,000, 6%.	1. Funeral expenses. 2. Expenses of last sickness. 3. Debts preferred by U. S. laws.
Nevada	First account after three months. Thereafter as directed by Court.	None.	1. Funeral expenses. 2. Expenses of last sickness. 3. Debts preferred by U. S. laws. 4. Judgments and mortgages.
N.Hampshire	Two years allowed for settlement of estate.	Exempt to parents, husband or wife, lineal descendants, brother, sister, adopted child, wife or widow of son, husband of daughter. To all others, 5%.	1. Administration expenses. 2. Funeral expenses. 3. Allowance to widow. 4. Taxes and expenses of last sickness.
New Jersey	Account in one year.	Exempt to parents, husband or wife, children, lineal descendants, brother or sister, husband of daughter, wife or widow of son. To all others, 5%.	1. Expenses of last sickness. 2. Funeral expenses. 3. Judgments and decrees.

State.	Accounting.	Inheritance Tax.	Preferred Obligations.
New Mexico...	First account in one year. Yearly thereafter.	None.	1. Administration expenses. 2. Funeral and last sickness expenses. 3. Allowance for widow and minor children. 4. Debts preferred by U. S. or territory laws. 5. Taxes.
New York.....	Account in one year.	(a) Taxable at 1% to parents, husband or wife, child, step-child, brother, sister, wife or widow of son, husband of daughter, lawful issue and descendants, or one to whom deceased stood in relation of parents; exempt to $10,000. (b) To others, 5% above $500.	1. Funeral and administration expenses. 2. Debts preferred under U. S. laws. 3. Taxes. 4. Judgments and decrees.
N. Carolina...	Annual accounts. Final account in two years.	Exempt to husband or wife. (1) To lineal ancestors, or descendants, brothers or sisters, or where mutual relation of parents and child existed ¾%; exempt to $2,000. (2) Descendants of brother or sister, 1½%. (3) Uncles or aunts, or descendants, 3%. (4) Great-uncles, great-aunts, or descendants, 4%. (5) To all others: $2,000 to $5,000, 5%; $5,000 to $10,000, 7½%; $10,000 to $25,000, 10%; $25,000 to $50,000, 12½%; above $50,000, 15%.	1. Debts secured by liens on property of deceased. 2. Funeral expenses. 3. Taxes. 4. Debts due U. S. or State. 5. Judgments. 6. Wages within one year. Medical attendance within one year.
N. Dakota.....	As directed by Court.	Exempt to parents, husband or wife, lineal descendants, adopted child, or descendants thereof. To others, 2% above $25,000.	1. Administration expenses. 2. Funeral and last sickness expenses. 3. Allowance to family. 4. Debts preferred by U. S. laws. 5. Debts secured by liens on property of deceased
Ohio..........	First account in 18 months. Annually thereafter.	Exempt to parents, husband or wife, brother, sister, nephew, niece, lineal descendant, adopted child, person legally designated as heir, and descendants thereof, wife widow of son, husband of daughter. To others, 5% above $200.	1. Administration, funeral and last sickness expenses. 2. Allowance to widow and children for twelve months. 3. Debts preferred by U. S. laws. 4. Public rates and taxes. 5. Wages, within a year. Not over $150 to one person.
Oklahoma.....	Accounts as required by the Court.	A graduated tax is imposed, determined by varying relationship to deceased and the amount of property passing to each person.	1. Funeral expenses. 2. Expenses of last sickness. 3. Support of family for ninety days. 4. Taxes to U. S. or State. 5. Debts preferred by U. S. or State laws. 6. Judgments or mortgages. 7. Other claims presented to administrator within six months.
Oregon........	Semi-annual accounts.	Estates less than $10,000 are exempt. (a) Tax of 1% to parents, husband or wife, child, brother or sister, wife or widow of son, husband of daughter, adopted child, one to whom deceased	1. Funeral expenses. 2. Taxes due U. S. 3. Expenses of last sickness. 4. Public rates and taxes.

State.	Accounting.	Inheritance Tax.	Preferred Obligations.
Oregon—(Continued)..		bore relation of parent, or lineal descendant in lawful wedlock, upon the amount received by each person above $5,000. (b) Tax of 2% to uncle, aunt, niece, nephew or descendants on amount received by each above $2,000. In all other cases above $500: $500 to $10,000, 3%; $10,000 to $20,000, 4%; $20,000 to $50,000, 5%; above $50,000, 6%.	5. Debts preferred by U. S. laws. 6. Debts secured by liens on property of deceased. 7. Wages within ninety days.
Pennsylvania..	Account in one year.	Estates less than $250 exempt. Exempt to parents, husband or wife, children, or lineal descendants, stepchildren, wife or widow of son. To all others, 5%.	1. Funeral and last sickness expenses. Wages due household servants within one year. 2. Rent, within one year.
Rhode Island..	Estate to be settled in two years.	None.	1. Funeral expenses. 2. Expenses of last sickness. 3. Debts due to U. S. 4. Debts due to State, and State and town taxes. 5. Wages within six months, not exceeding $100 to one person. 6. Other claims presented within six months.
S. Carolina....	Annual accounts.	None.	1. Funeral, last sickness, probate and administration expenses. 2. Debts due to public. 3. Judgments, mortgages and executions. 4. Rent. 5. Bonds, contract debts.
S. Dakota....	Account in one year.	A tax is imposed, graduated by varying relationships to deceased and amounts of property passing to each person.	1. Funeral expenses. 2. Expenses of last sickness. 3. Administration expenses. 4. Wages for 60 days. 5. Debts preferred by U. S. laws. 6. Debts secured by liens on property of deceased.
Tennessee....	Estate to be settled in two years.	Exempt to parents, husband or wife, children and lineal descendants. To others, 5% over $250	No priority.
Texas.........	Annual accounts.	None.	1. Expenses of funeral and last sickness if presented within sixty days. 2. Administration expenses, including allowance for support of widow and children for one year. 3. Debts secured by mortgage or other lien. 4. Other debts presented within twelve months.
Utah..........	First account in six months.	Tax of 5% on all estates over $10,000.	1. Funeral expenses. 2. Expenses of last sickness and administration.

State.	Accounting.	Inheritance Tax.	Preferred Obligations.
Utah—(Continued)..			3. Wages, within sixty days, not over $100 to one person. 4. Debts preferred by U. S. or State laws. 5. Debts secured by liens.
Vermont......	Account in one year.	Exempt to parents, husband or wife, lineal descendants, adopted child, or lineal descendant thereof, wife or widow of son, husband of daughter. To all others, 5% above $2,000.	1. Funeral expenses. 2. Expenses of last sickness. 3. Taxes. 4. Debts due to State. 5. Debts due to U. S.
Virginia.......	Account in 18 months. Annually thereafter.	Exempt to lineal ancestors or lineal descendants, husband or wife, brother or sister. To all others, 5%.	1. Funeral and administration expenses. 2. Expenses of last sickness, not exceeding $50, doctor or druggist. 3. Taxes. 4. Money owing as trustee or in fiduciary capacity.
Washington...	Account in one year.	(a) Tax of 1% above $10,000 to parents, husband or wife, lineal descendants, adopted child, or lineal descendant thereof. (b) To collaterals, including the third degree of relationship, 3% up to $50,000, 4½% from $50,000 to $100,000, and 6% from $100,000 upward. (c) To those further removed, 6% up to $50,000, 9% up to $100,000, 12% above $100,000. (d) On all sums to collaterals who are aliens not residing in U. S., tax of 25%.	1. Funeral expenses. 2. Expenses of last sickness. 3. Debts preferred by U. S. laws. 4. Wages, within ninety days. 5. Taxes. 6. Judgments and mortgages.
W. Virginia...	Account in 18 months. Annually thereafter.	Tax of 1% to parents, husband or wife, children or lineal descendants, above $20,000. To brother or sister, 3%. To grandfather or grandmother, 5%. To all others, 7½%.	1. Debts due to U. S. 2. Taxes. 3. Moneys due as fiduciary. 4. Voluntary obligations.
Wisconsin.....	Accounts as required by Court.	(1) Tax of 1% to husband, wife, lineal descendants, lineal ancestors, adopted child, one to whom deceased bore relationship of parent, and lineal issue thereof. (2) To brothers, sisters and descendants, wife or widow of son, or husband of daughter, 1½%. (3) To uncles, aunts or descendants, 3%. (4) To great-uncles, great-aunts and descendants, 4%. (5) To all others, 5%. When the estate is above $25,000 the above rates are multiplied as follows: $25,000 to $50,000, 1½ times on excess; $50,000 to $100,000, 2 times on excess; $100,000 to $500,000, 2½ times on excess; above $500,000, 3 times on excess.	1. Last sickness and funeral expenses. 2. Debts preferred by U. S. laws.
Wyoming.....	Accounts every six months.	Tax of 2% on amount above $10,000 to parents, husband or wife, child, brother, sister, lineal descendants, wife or widow of son, husband of daughter, adopted or acknowledged child for ten years. Except that to husband, wife or child resident of the State $25,000 to each is exempt. To others than above, tax of 5%.	1. Funeral and administration expenses. 2. Expenses of last sickness and sixty days' wages. 3. Medicine and medical attendance of last sickness. 4. Judgments and mortgages. 5. All claims presented within six months. 6. All claims presented within one year.

The Armed Strength of the World.

COMPILED from the latest available data. For the Army and Navy of the United States, see pages devoted thereto. [Consult Index.]

LAND FORCES OF THE PRINCIPAL STATES OF EUROPE, AND OF JAPAN; ALSO OF THE SECONDARY STATES OF EUROPE, ASIA AND AMERICA.

COUNTRIES.	Available for Active Service.	Reserves*	Total War Strength.	Available for Duty Unorg.†	COUNTRIES.	Available for Active Service.	Reserves*	Total War Strength.	Available for Duty Unorg.†
Germany....	617,000	1,223,000	1,840,000	1,900,000	Switzerland..	159,000*h*	96,000*h*	235,000	....
France........	529,000*a*	761,000	1,200,000	1,000,000	Turkey........	350,000	450,000	800,000	800,000
Russia........	1,100,000	700,000	1,800,000	5,200,000	Greece........	25,000*i*	25,000	50,000	100,000
Austria-					China........	60,000	500,000	560,000	....
Hungary..	409,000	381,000	790,000	1,600,000	Mexico........	26,600	82,000	108,600	700,000
Italy..........	240,000	390,000	630,000	1,200,000	Brazil........	25,000	20,000	45,000	1,000,000
Great Britain.	250,000*b*	489,000*c*	739,000	1,700,000	Argentine....	19,000	120,000	139,000	300,000
Japan.........	225,000	375,000	600,000	2,000,000	Chile........	5,000	75,000	80,000	175,000
Spain.........	100,000	200,000	300,000	780,000	Peru..........	4,000	10,000	14,000	....
Belgium......	45,000	80,000	125,000	350,000	Venezuela....	9,600	....	9,600	125,000
Netherlands..	40,000*d*	100,000*e*	140,000	200,000	Bolivia........	3,000	18,000	21,000	100,000
Denmark.....	14,000	36,000	40,000	125,000	Colombia......	5,000	....	5,000	200,000
Sweden.......	62,000	284,000	346,000	....	Guatemala....	7,000	50,000	57,000	50,000
Norway.......	30,000	95,000	125,000	....	Ecuador......	4,300	....	4,300	90,000
Portugal......	30,000*f*	125,000	155,000	200,000	Salvador......	3,000	18,000	21,000	40,000
Bulgaria *g*....	52,500*c*	322,500	375,000	60,000	Nicaragua....	4,000	36,000	40,000	....
Servia........	35,000	140,000	175,000	....	Uruguay......	5,200	30,000	35,200	30,000
Roumania....	135,000	35,000	170,000	175,000	Haiti.........	6,800	....	6,800	40,000

*Except as to some of the principal and a few of the minor States, it is doubtful whether the numbers given of the reserves or auxiliary forces could be mobilized and made effective within a considerable period of time. †These figures are based on estimated male population of military age, deducting "total war strength." In some States, all men of military age are enrolled in national militia and are partly trained. *a* Exclusive of Colonial troops. *b* Including regular forces at home, in the Colonies, and 76,000 men in India and excluding the native Indian army of 160,000. *c* Includes "army reserve," organized militia and volunteers. *d* Exclusive of Colonial army of 36,000. *e* Estimated. *f* Exclusive of troops in Colonies. *g* Nominally subject to Turkey. *h* Trained National militia. *i* Army is being reorganized.

NAVIES OF THE WORLD.

POWERS.	Modern Batt'eships.	Older Battleships.	Armored Cruisers.	First Class Cruisers.	Second Class Cruisers.	Third Class Cruisers.	Scout Ships.	Torpedo Gunboats.	Torpedo Boat Destroyers.	Torpedo Boats.	Submarines.	Monitors.	Unprotected Cruisers.	Personnel. Officers and Men.
Great Britain........	55	2	38	19	32	14	9	17	158	167	61	..	..	*99,679
United States........	25	4	8	5	7	16	3	40	16	36	19	10	10	47,750
Germany..............	24	4	14	..	11	10	..	21	93	47	4	..	..	†33,500
Japan................	14	5	13	3	12	2	2	..	62	95	16	..	..	‡36,480
France...............	25	3	22	8	8	3	..	..	76	331	61	..	..	25,500
Italy................	9	4	..	7	3	13	..	10	29	110	13	..	..	27,789
Austria-Hungary......	9	..	5	..	..	4	..	7	12	44	2	..	..	11,993
Russia...............	11	2	5	6	8	2	..	8	80	55	35	..	..	60,000
Sweden...............	5	7	1	..	..	..	..	5	6	56	..	11	..	4,000
Norway...............	4	..	..	..	..	..	4	4	3	29	..	..	..	1,130
Denmark..............	4	3	..	..	1	4	..	..	..	24	..	..	..	4,000
Netherlands..........	6	2	..	..	7	1	..	26	..	90	1	..	..	8,600
Spain................	..	5	..	..	1	3	..	5	5	9	..	..	..	5,000
Portugal.............	2	..	..	..	..	4	..	..	..	10	1	..	..	6,000
Greece...............	..	3	..	..	..	..	..	8	..	12	..	..	..	4,000
Turkey...............	..	5	..	..	2	..	..	3	5	38	..	..	..	30,800
Argentine............	3	1	4	1	2	2	..	2	4	8	..	..	..	5,000
Brazil...............	3	1	..	1	1	3	..	5	..	..	..	..	..	8,000
Chile................	2	1	..	1	3	1	..	2	6	14	..	..	..	8,000
China................	..	..	..	1	3	..	10	..	..	..	..	..	..	..
Siam.................	..	..	..	..	1	..	..	..	..	..	..	..	..	§5,110
Mexico...............	..	..	..	..	..	5	..	2	..	..	..	..	..	1,160

* Naval reserve; seamen number 23,000. † Reserve of 110,000 men. ‡ Reserve of 114,000 men. § Reserve of 20,000 men.

THE MARINE CORPS.

The Commandant of the Marine Corps is responsible to the Secretary of the Navy for the general efficiency and discipline of the corps; make such distribution of officers and men for duty at the several shore stations as shall appear to him to be most advantageous for the interest of the service, furnishes guards for vessels of the Navy, according to the standard scale of allowance, under the direction of the Secretary of the Navy, issues orders for the movement of officers and troops, and such other orders and instructions for their guidance as may be necessary, and has charge and exercises general supervision and control of the recruiting service of the corps and of the necessary expenses thereof, including the establishment of recruiting officers.

United States Military Academy at West Point.

EACH Senator, Congressional District, and Territory—also the District of Columbia, Porto Rico Alaska, and Hawaii—is entitled to have one cadet at the Academy. There are also forty appointments at large, specially conferred by the President of the United States. The number of students is thus limited to 529.

Appointments are usually made one year in advance of date of admission, by the Secretary of War, upon the nomination of the Senator or Representative. These nominations may either be made after competitive examination or given direct, at the option of the Representative. The Representative may nominate two legally qualified second candidates, to be designated alternates. The alternates will receive from the War Department a letter of appointment, and will be examined with the regular appointee, and the best qualified will be admitted to the Academy in the event of the failure of the principal to pass the prescribed preliminary examinations. Appointees to the Military Academy must be between seventeen and twenty-two years of age, free from any infirmity which may render them unfit for military service, and able to pass a careful examination in English grammar, English composition, English literature, arithmetic, algebra through quadratic equations, plane geometry, descriptive geography and the elements of physical geography, especially the geography of the United States, United States history, the outlines of general history. The Secretary of War is authorized to permit not exceeding four Filipinos, to be designated, one for each class, by the Philippine Commission, to receive instruction at the United States Military Academy at West Point; Provided, That the Filipinos undergoing instruction, shall receive the same pay, allowances, and emoluments as are authorized by law for cadets at the Military Academy appointed from the United States, to be paid out of the same appropriations; And provided further, That said Filipinos undergoing instruction on graduation shall be eligible only to commissions in the Philippine Scouts. And the provisions of Section 1321, Revised Statutes; are modified in the case of the Filipinos undergoing instruction, so as to require them to engage to serve for eight years, unless sooner discharged, in the Philippine Scouts.

The course of instruction, which is quite thorough, requires four years, and is largely mathematical and professional. The principal subjects taught are mathematics, English, French, drawing, drill regulations of all arms of the service, natural and experimental philosophy, chemistry, chemical physics, mineralogy, geology, electricity, history, international, constitutional, and military law, Spanish, civil and military engineering, art and science of war, and ordnance and gunnery. About one-fourth of those appointed usually fail to pass the preliminary examinations, and but little over one-half the remainder are finally graduated. The discipline is very strict—even more so than in the army—and the enforcement of penalties for offences is inflexible rather than severe. Academic duties begin September 1 and continue until June 1. Examinations are held in each December and June, and cadets found proficient in studies and correct in conduct are given the particular standing in their class to which their merits entitle them, while those cadets deficient in either conduct or studies are discharged.

From about the middle of June to the end of August cadets live in camp, engaged only in military duties and receiving practical military instruction. Cadets are allowed but one leave of absence during the four years' course, and this is granted at the expiration of the first two years. The pay of a cadet is $709.50 per year, and, with proper economy, is sufficient for his support. The number of students at the Academy is usually about four hundred and seventy.

Upon graduating cadets are commissioned as second lieutenants in the United States Army. The whole number of graduates from 1802 to 1908, inclusive, has been 4,749. It is virtually absolutely necessary for a person seeking an appointment to apply to his Senator or Member of Congress. The appointments by the President are usually restricted to sons of officers of the army and navy, who, by reason of their shifting residence, due to the necessities of the service, find it next to impossible to obtain an appointment otherwise. The Superintendent is Colonel Hugh L. Scott, U. S. A., and the military and academic staff consists of 101 persons. Capt. Joseph S. Herron, 2d Cavalry, is adjutant.

United States Naval Academy at Annapolis.

THE students of the Naval Academy are called Midshipmen. Two Midshipmen are allowed for each Senator, Representative, and Delegate in Congress, two for the District of Columbia, and five each year from the United States at large. The appointments from the District of Columbia and five each year at large are made by the President. One Midshipman is allowed from Porto Rico, who must be a native of that island. The appointment is made by the President, on the recommendation of the Governor of Porto Rico. The Congressional appointments are equitably distributed, so that as soon as practicable each Senator, Representative, and Delegate in Congress may appoint one Midshipman during each Congress. The course for Midshipmen is six years—four years at the Academy, when the succeeding appointment is made, and two years at sea, at the expiration of which time the examination for graduation takes place. Midshipmen who pass the examination for final graduation are appointed to fill vacancies in the lower grade of the Line of the Navy, in the order of merit as determined by the Academic Board of the Naval Academy. The act of June 29, 1906, prescribes that the Secretary of the Navy shall as soon as possible after June 1 of each year preceding the graduation of Midshipmen in the succeeding year, notify in writing each Senator, Representative, and Delegate in Congress of any vacancy that will exist at the Naval Academy because of such graduation, and which he shall be entitled to fill by nomination of a candidate and one or more alternates therefor. The nomination of a candidate and alternate or alternates to fill said vacancy shall be made upon the recommendation of the Senator, Representative, or Delegate, if such recommendation is made by March 4 of the year following that in which said notice in writing is given, but if it is not made by that time the Secretary of the Navy shall fill the vacancy by appointment of an actual resident of the State, Congressional District, or Territory, as the case may be, in which the vacancy will exist, who shall have been for at least two years immediately preceding the date of his appointment an actual and bona fide resident of the State, Congressional District, or Territory in which the vacancy will exist, and of the legal qualification under the law as now provided. Candidates allowed for Congressional Districts, for Territories, and for the District of Columbia must be actual residents. Candidates at the time of their examination must be physically sound, well formed, and of robust constitution. Attention will also be paid to the stature of the candidate, and no one *manifestly* under size for his age will be received at the Academy. The height of candidates for admission shall not be less than 5 feet 2 inches between the ages of 16 and 18 years, and not less than 5 feet 4 inches between the ages of 18 and 20 years; and the minimum weight at 16 years of age shall be 100 pounds, with an increase of not less than 5 pounds for each additional year or fraction of a year over one-half. Any marked deviation in the relative height and weight to the age of a candidate will add materially to the consideration for rejection. Candidates must be unmarried, and any Midshipman who shall marry, or who shall be found to be married, before his graduation, shall be dismissed from the service, and no Midshipman may marry between the date of his graduation from the Naval Academy and his final graduation after two years' service at sea, except by permission of the Secretary of the Navy. All candidates must, at the time of their examination for admission, be between the ages of 16 and 20 years. The pay of a Midshipman is $600, beginning at the date of admission. The regulations regarding places and times of examinations and subjects of examinations may be obtained by addressing the Chief of the Bureau of Navigation, Navy Dept., Washington, D. C.

Interest Laws and Statutes of Limitations.

States and Territories.	Interest Laws.		Statutes of Limitations.		
	Legal Rate.	Rate Allowed by Contract.	Judg'ents, Years.	Notes, Years.	Open Accounts, Years.
	Per ct.	Per ct.			
Alabama	8	8	20	6	3
Arkansas	6	10	10	5	3
Arizona	6	Any rate.	5	4	3
California	7	Any rate.	5	4	4
Colorado	8	Any rate.	20	6	6
Connecticut	6	6	(o)	(e)	6
Delaware	6	6	10	6‖	3
D. of Columbia	6	10	12	3	3
Florida	8	10	20	5‖	2
Georgia	7	8	7	6‖	4
Idaho	7	12	6	5	4
Illinois	5	7	20	10	5
Indiana	6	8	20	10	6
Iowa	6	8	20(d)	10	5
Kansas	6	10	5	5	3
Kentucky	6	6	15	15	5(a)
Louisiana	5	8	10	5	3
Maine	6	Any rate.	20	6(c)	6§§
Maryland	6	6	12	3	3
Massachusetts	6	Any rate.	20	6	6
Michigan	5	7	10	6	6
Minnesota	7	10	10	6	6
Mississippi	6	10	7	6	3
Missouri	6	8	10	10	5
Montana	8	Any rate.	10(b)	8	5
Nebraska	7	10	5‡‡	5	4
Nevada	7	Any rate.	6	4	4
N. Hampshire	6	6	20	6	6
New Jersey	6	6	20	6	6
New Mexico	6	12	7	6	4
New York	6	6††	20(n)	6	6§§
North Carolina	6	6	10	3*	3
North Dakota	7	12	10	6	6§§
Ohio	6	8	15(p)	15	6
Oklahoma	6	10	5(h)	5	3
Oregon	6	10	10	6	6
Pennsylvania	6	6	5(f)	6‖	6
Rhode Island	6§	Any rate.	20	6	6
South Carolina	7	8	20	6	6
South Dakota	7	12	10(l)	6	6
Tennessee	6	6	10	6	6
Texas	6	10	10‡‡	4	2
Utah	8	12	8	6	4
Vermont	6	6	8	6	6§§
Virginia	6	6	20	5*	2¶
Washington	6	12	6	6	3
West Virginia	6	6	10	10	5
Wisconsin	6	10	20(n)	6	6
Wyoming	8	12	21	5	8

* Under seal, 10 years. † If made in State; if outside, 2 years. § Unless a different rate is expressly stipulated. ‖ Under seal, 20 years. ¶ Store accounts; other accounts 3 years; accounts between merchants 5 years. †† New York has by a recent law legalized any rate of interest on call loans of $5,000 or upward, on collateral security. ‡‡ Becomes dormant, but may be revived. §§ Six years from last item. (a) Accounts between merchants 2 years. (b) In courts not of record 5 years. (c) Witnessed 20 years. (d) Twenty years in Courts of Record; in Justice's Court 10 years. (e) Negotiable notes 6 years, non-negotiable 17 years. (f) Ceases to be a lien after that period. (h) On foreign judgments 1 year. (i) Is a lien on real estate for only 10 years. (k) And indefinitely by having execution issue every 5 years. (l) Ten years foreign, 20 years domestic. (n) Not of record 6 years. (o) No limit. (p) Foreign. Domestic 6 years.

Penalties for usury differ in the various States.

Arizona, California, Colorado, Maine, Massachusetts (except on loans of less than $1,000), Montana, Nevada, Rhode Island and Wyoming have no provisions on the subject.

Loss of *principal and interest* is the penalty in Arkansas and New York.

Loss of principal in Delaware and Oregon.

Loss of interest in Alabama, Alaska, District of Columbia, Florida, Idaho, Illinois, Iowa, Louisiana, Michigan, Minnesota, Mississippi, Nebraska, New Jersey, North Carolina (double amount if paid), North Dakota (double amount if paid), Oklahoma, South Carolina, South Dakota, Texas, Virginia, Washington (double amount if paid), Wisconsin, and Hawaii.

Loss of excess of interest in Connecticut, Georgia, Indiana, Kansas, Kentucky, Maryland, Missouri, New Hampshire (three times), New Mexico, Ohio, Pennsylvania, Tennessee, Vermont, and West Virginia.

State Flowers.

THE following are "State Flowers," as adopted in most instances by the vote of the public school scholars of the respective States:

Alabama ....†Golden Rod
Arkansas ....Apple Blossom
California ....California Poppy (Eschscholtzia)
Colorado ....Columbine
Connecticut ....Mountain Laurel
Delaware ....Peach Blossom
Idaho ....Syringa
Illinois ....Violet
Indiana ....Corn
Iowa ....*Wild Rose
Kansas ....Sunflower
Louisiana ....Magnolia
Maine ....*Pine Cone and Tassel
Maryland ....Golden Rod
Michigan ....Apple Blossom
Minnesota ....Moccasin
Mississippi ....Magnolia
Missouri ....Golden Rod
Montana ....Bitter Root
Nebraska ....Golden Rod
New York ....Rose
North Dakota ....Wild Rose
Ohio ....Carnation
Oklahoma ....Crimson Rambler
Oregon ....Golden Rod
Rhode Island ....Violet
South Dakota ....Anemone
Texas ....Blue Bonnet
Utah ....Sego Lily
Vermont ....Red Clover
Washington ....Rhododendron
West Virginia ....Rhododendron

In other States the scholars or State Legislatures have not yet taken action.

* Adopted by State Legislature, not by public school scholars. † Adopted by public school scholars.

In England the primrose is worn on the birthday of Lord Beaconsfield. On the anniversary of Parnell's death his followers wear a sprig of ivy. The Jacobites wear white roses on June 10. In France the Orleanists wear white daisies and the Bonapartists the violet.

Popular and Electoral Vote for President in 1908.

States.	Popular Vote.								Electoral Vote	
	Bryan, Dem.	Taft, Rep.	Debs, Soc.	Chafin, Pro.	Gillhaus, Soc. L.	Watson, Pop.	Hisgen, Ind.	Plurality.	Bryan, Dem.	Taft Rep.
Alabama	74,374	41,692	1,399	622	...	1,568	495	32.682 D	11	...
Arkansas	87,015	56,624	5.750	1,121	...	1,121	313	30,391 D	9	...
California	127,492	214,398	28,659	11,770	...	...	4,278	86,906 R	...	10
Colorado	126.772	123,732	7,960	5,538	..	..	..	3.040 D	5	...
Connecticut	68,255	112.815	5,113	2.380	..	..	650	44,560 R	...	7
Delaware	22.071	25.014	240	670	...	...	28	1.943 R	...	3
Florida	31.104	9.923	3,747	1,356	...	1.948	553	21.181 D	5	...
Georgia	72,350	41,692	584	1,059	...	16,958	77	30.658 D	13	...
Idaho	36.080	52.606	6,243	1.740	..	..	210	16.526 R	...	3
Illinois	450,810	629,932	34,711	29.364	1,675	601	7,648	179 122 R	...	27
Indiana	338,262	348,903	13,476	18,045	643	1,193	514	10.641 R	...	15
Iowa	266,358	275.210	8,937	9.837	...	251	404	8 852 R	...	13
Kansas	161,209	197,216	12,420	5,033	...	..	301	36,007 R	...	10
Kentucky	244.092	235.711	4,037	5,887	342	324	77	8.381 D	13	...
Louisiana	63,568	8,958	2,538	...	...	..	82	54,510 D	9	...
Maine	35.403	65,987	1,758	1.487	...	...	652	30.584 R	...	6
Maryland	115.908	113,803	2,323	3,302	...	..	485	21.105 D	6	2
Massachusetts	155,543	265,966	10,779	4.374	952	..	19,175	110 423 R	...	16
Michigan	175,771	335,580	11,586	16.974	1,096	..	760	160,409 R	...	14
Minnesota	69,594	155,416	10.021	8,658	..	..	420	98,729 R	...	11
Mississippi	60.876	4.505	1,048	...	...	1,309	..	85,812 D	10	...
Missouri	346.754	347,203	15,381	4.191	867	1,165	397	629 R	...	18
Montana	29.431	32,375	5.991	1,486	..	..	1,200	2,944 R	...	3
Nebraska	131,099	126,997	3,524	5,179	...	..	..	4,002 D	8	...
Nevada	11,212	10,777	2,203	...	...	..	415	435 D	3	...
New Hampshire	33,655	53,149	1,299	905	...	..	584	19.484 R	...	4
New Jersey	182.522	265.298	1,196	4.930	1,196	..	2,916	82.776 R	...	12
New York	667,100	870.070	38,448	22,654	3,877	..	35,785	202.970 R	...	39
North Carolina	136.928	114,887	..	..	...	..	..	22 041 D	12	...
North Dakota	32,909	57.771	2,411	..	...	..	38	24.862 R	...	4
Ohio	502,721	572 312	33,795	11,402	721	162	439	69.591 R	...	23
Oklahoma	122.406	110.558	21,729	..	..	434	244	11.848 D	7	..
Oregon	38.049	62.530	7.339	2.682	...	..	289	24.481 R	...	4
Pennsylvania	448,785	572.312	33.913	36.684	1,222	..	1,057	123.537 R	...	34
Rhode Island	24,706	43,952	1,295	996	207	..	814	19,246 R	...	4
South Carolina	62.283	3.963	101	...	...	..	45	58,320 D	9	...
South Dakota	40.223	67,352	2.846	4,039	...	..	88	27,129 R	...	4
Tennessee	135.819	118.519	1 878	268	...	1,081	232	17.300 D	12	...
Texas	216,737	65.602	7.870	1,634	176	994	115	151.135 D	18	...
Utah	42,601	61.015	4,895	...	...	...	87	18.414 R	...	3
Vermont	11,496	39.552	..	799	...	...	804	28,056 R	...	4
Virginia	82.916	52,573	256	1,111	25	225	51	30,333 D	12	...
Washington	58,691	102.062	4,700	14,177	..	..	248	43 371 R	...	5
West Virginia	111,418	137.869	3,679	5.139	...	..	46	26.451 R	...	7
Wisconsin	166.632	247,747	28.164	11.564	..	..	..	81,115 R	...	13
Wyoming	14,918	20.846	1,715	66	..	...	64	5,928 R	...	3
Total	6,393,182	7,637,676	448,453	241,252	15,421	83,871	83,183	...	162	321

Popular Vote, Taft over Bryan **1,233,494**
Popular Vote, Taft over all **411,314**
Electoral Vote, Taft over Bryan **159**
Total Popular Vote, all candidates **14,852,841**
Total Popular Vote, including scattering votes **14,833,711**

The above was compiled from the highest vote received by the electors.

Total Vote for President, 1904 and 1908.

States.	1908.	1904.	States.	1908.	1904.	States.	1908.	1904.
Alabama	90,115	109.684	Maryland	235,821	224,224	Oregon	110,889	90,184
Arkansas	151,944	116,411	Massachusetts	457,789	445,104	Pennsylvania	1,068,244	1,231,170
California	386,597	331.545	Michigan	541,230	520.437	Rhode Island	71,970	68.656
Colorado	261,228	243,693	Minnesota	244.109	297,592	South Carolina	66.392	56,912
Connecticut	189.213	191,116	Mississippi	77,738	58.383	South Dakota	114,547	101.995
Delaware	48.013	42.873	Missouri	716,458	643,861	Tennessee	257 797	242,756
Florida	48.591	39.302	Montana	70.483	64.444	Texas	292.028	234,008
Georgia	142.720	138,198	Nebraska	266.799	224,702	Utah	108.598	101,624
Idaho	96,879	72 578	Nevada	24,607	36.154	Vermont	52.651	51.887
Illinois	1,144.741	1,068,944	N. Hampshire	89,592	90,089	Virginia	137,157	130,544
Indiana	721,036	682.185	New Jersey	455.862	432.547	Washington	179,878	128,713
Iowa	460 997	485.703	New York	1,637,984	1,617.770	West Virginia	258.151	239.780
Kansas	376,179	324.588	North Carolina	251 815	207,867	Wisconsin	454.107	443.014
Kentucky	491,470	435,765	North Dakota	93 129	70.175	Wyoming	37,608	30,655
Louisiana	76.146	53.908	Ohio	1,121.852	1,004,393			
Maine	106,087	96.027	Oklahoma	255,371	...			

Total vote, including scattering vote, 1900, 13,961,566; 1904, 13,528,979; 1908, 14,852,841.

Popular and Electoral Vote for President, 1888-1908.

States.	1908. Popular Vote. Bryan, Dem.	Taft, Rep.	Debs, Soc.	Chafin, Pro.	Gillhaus, Soc.L.	Watson, Pop.	Hisgen, Ind.	Pluralities.	1904. Electoral Vote. Parker, Dem.	Roosevelt, Rep.	1900. Electoral Vote. Bryan Dem.	McKinley Rep.	1896. Electoral Vote. Bryan, Dem.	McKinley Rep.	1892. Electoral Vote. Cleveland, Dem.	Harrison, Rep.	Weaver, Pop.	1888. Electoral Vote. Cleveland, Dem.	Harrison, Rep.
[illegible]a.	74,374	41,692	1,399	622	....	1,568	495	82,682 D	11	..	11	..	11	..	11	..	..	10	..
Arkansas	87,015	56,624	5,750	1,121	....	1,121	313	30,391 D	9	..	8	..	8	..	8	..	..	7	..
California	127,492	214,398	28,659	11,770	....	....	4,278	86,906 R	..	10	..	9	1	8	8	1	..	..	8
Colorado	126,772	123,732	7,960	5,538	....	....	..	3,040 D	..	5	4	..	4	..	..	..	4	..	3
Connecticut	68,255	112,815	5,113	2,380	....	....	650	44,560 R	..	7	..	6	..	6	6	..	..	6	..
[illegible]e	22,071	25,014	240	670	....	....	28	1,943 R	..	3	..	3	..	3	3	..	..	3	..
Florida	31,104	9,923	3,747	1,356	....	1,948	553	21,181 D	5	..	4	..	4	..	4	..	..	4	..
Georgia	72,350	41,692	584	1,059	....	16,958	77	30,658 D	13	..	13	..	13	..	13	..	..	12	..
Idaho	36,080	52,606	6,243	1,740	....	....	210	16,526 R	..	3	3	..	3	..	..	..	3	..	..
[illegible]s.	450,810	629,932	34,711	29,364	1,675	601	7,648	179,122 R	..	27	..	24	..	24	24	..	..	..	22
Indiana	338,262	348,903	13,476	18,045	643	1,193	514	10,641 R	..	15	..	15	..	15	15	..	..	..	15
Iowa	266,358	275,210	8,937	9,837	....	251	404	8,852 R	..	13	..	13	..	13	..	13	..	..	13
Kansas	161,209	197 216	12,420	5,033	....	....	301	36,007 R	..	10	..	10	10	..	..	..	10	..	9
Kentucky	244,092	235,711	4,037	5,887	342	321	77	8,381 D	13	..	13	..	1	12	13	..	..	13	..
Louisiana	63,568	8,958	2,538	....	....	....	82	54,510 D	9	..	8	..	8	..	8	..	..	8	..
Maine	35,403	65,987	1,758	1,487	....	....	652	30,584 R	..	6	..	6	..	6	..	6	..	..	6
Maryland	115,908	113 803	2,323	3,302	....	....	485	21,105 D	7	1	..	8	..	8	8	..	..	8	..
Massachusetts	155,543	265,966	10.779	4,374	952	....	19,175	110,423 R	..	16	..	15	..	15	..	15	..	..	14
Michigan	175,771	335,580	11,586	16,974	1,096	....	760	160,409 R	..	14	..	14	..	14	5	9	..	..	13
Minnesota	69,594	155,416	10,021	8,658	....	....	420	98,729 R	..	11	..	9	..	9	..	9	..	..	7
Mississippi	60,876	4,505	1 048	....	....	1,309	..	85,812 D	10	..	9	..	9	..	9	..	..	9	..
Missouri	346,754	347,203	15,381	4,191	867	1,165	397	629 R	..	18	17	..	17	..	17	..	..	16	..
Montana	29,431	32,375	5,991	1,486	....	....	1,200	2,944 R	..	3	3	..	3	..	..	3	..	..	..
Nebraska	131,099	126,997	3,524	5,179	....	....	..	4,002 D	..	8	..	8	8	..	..	8	..	..	5
Nevada	11,212	10,777	2,203	......	....	....	415	435 D	..	3	3	..	3	..	..	..	3	..	3
New Hampshire	33,655	53,149	1,299	905	....	....	584	19,484 R	..	4	..	4	..	4	..	4	..	..	4
New Jersey	182.522	265,298	1,196	4,930	1,196	....	2,916	82,776 R	..	12	..	10	..	10	10	..	..	9	..
New York	667,100	870,070	38,448	22,654	3,877	....	35,785	202,970 R	..	39	..	36	..	36	36	..	..	..	36
North Carolina	136,928	114,887	....	....	....	....	..	22,041 D	12	..	11	..	11	..	11	..	..	11	..
North Dakota	33,909	57,771	2.411	......	....	....	38	24,862 R	..	4	..	3	..	3	1	1	1	..	..
Ohio	502,721	572,312	33,795	11,402	721	162	439	69,591 R	..	23	..	23	..	23	1	22	..	..	23
Oklahoma	122,406	110,558	21,729	...	....	434	244	11,848 D	...	..	..	..	..	...	..	..	..	..	..
Oregon	38,049	62,530	7,339	2,682	....	....	289	24,481 R	..	4	..	4	..	4	..	3	1	..	3
Pennsylvania	448,785	572,312	33,913	36,684	1,222	....	1,067	133,537 R	..	34	..	32	..	32	..	32	..	..	30
Rhode Island	24,706	43,952	1,295	996	207	....	814	19,246 R	..	4	..	4	..	4	..	4	..	..	4
South Carolina	62,283	3,963	101	....	....	....	45	58,320 D	9	..	9	..	9	..	9	..	..	9	..
South Dakota	40,223	67,352	2.846	4,039	....	....	88	27,129 R	..	4	..	4	4	..	..	4	..	..	..
Tennessee	135,819	118,519	1.878	268	....	1,081	232	17,300 D	12	..	12	..	12	..	12	..	..	12	..
[illegible]s	216,737	65,602	7,870	1,634	176	994	115	151,135 D	18	..	15	..	15	..	15	..	..	13	..
Utah	42,601	61,015	4,895	....	....	.. .	87	18,414 R	..	3	..	3	3	..	..	..	..	..	..
[illegible]ont.	11,496	39,552	....	799	....	....	804	28,056 R	..	4	..	4	..	4	..	4	..	..	4
Virginia	82,916	52,573	256	1,111	25	225	51	30,333 D	12	..	12	..	12	..	12	..	..	12	..
Washington	58,691	102,062	4,700	14,177	....	....	248	43,371 R	..	5	..	4	4	..	..	4	..	..	..
W. Virginia	111,418	137,869	3.679	5,139	....	....	46	26,451 R	...	7	..	6	..	6	6	..	..	6	..
Wisconsin	166,632	247,747	28,164	11,564	....	....	..	81,115 R	..	13	..	12	..	12	12	..	..	..	11
Wyoming	14,918	20,846	1,715	66	....	....	64	5,928 R	...	3	..	3	3	..	..	3	..	..	..
Total	6,393,182	7,637.676	448,453	241,252	21	33,871	83,183	....	140	336	155	292	176	271	277	145	22	168	233
Plurality	......	1,233,494	....	....	....	....	..	....	....	....	....	....	....	....	....	....	....	....	....

Election Returns.

BY STATES, COUNTIES, AND CONGRESSIONAL DISTRICTS.

ALABAMA.

Counties (66.)	President, 1908.				Governor, 1906.	
	Bryan, Dem.	Taft, Rep.	Watson, Pop.	Debs, Soc.	Comer, Dem.	Stratton, Rep.
Autauga	655	97	..	..	810	21
Baldwin	439	107	..	62	265	4
Barbour	1,303	43	34	6	969	4
Bibb	670	139	16	77	570	30
Blount	1,133	973	23	..	1,147	577
Bullock	782	10	..	..	433	0
Butler	727	137	19	9	810	1
Calhoun	1,438	570	26	9	1,376	96
Chambers	1,025	50	15	9	1,002	12
Cherokee	712	602	26	46	1,205	110
Chilton	656	891	37	27	754	828
Choctaw	590	44	9	9	418	..
Clarke	1,169	56	5	4	720	4
Clay	863	594	26	2	1,092	454
Cleburne	278	344	2	..	1,242	91
Coffee	1,305	341	196	13	1,750	9
Colbert	849	353	..	46	534	56
Conecuh	651	111	11	8	457	5
Coosa	717	447	7	..	870	228
Covington	1,054	315	74	17	909	53
Crenshaw	1,100	311	38	15	946	12
Cullman	1,239	1,521	53	10	1,490	737
Dale	921	346	30	4	900	39
Dallas	1,420	28	4	4	736	2
De Kalb	1,395	1,104	18	18	1,344	617
Elmore	1,063	138	6	4	879	43
Escambia	614	112	..	25	402	6
Etowah	1,309	996	17	44	1,434	500
Fayette	731	678	45	9	968	334
Franklin	650	652	10	42	736	416
Geneva	854	501	126	4	904	63
Greene	423	12	4	..	373	3
Hale	714	13	..	1	522	..
Henry	723	79	72	8	514	4
Houston	965	242	28	10	715	4
Jackson	1,404	469	19	3	847	91
Jefferson	7,803	2,182	28	367	6,874	273
Lamar	839	163	2	..	845	175
Lauderdale	1,177	427	4	14	858	28
Lawrence	602	344	17	14	576	55
Lee	1,126	..	..	..	658	17
Limestone	1,188	238	2	6	774	13
Lowndes	633	36	..	..	539	6
Macon	482	38	5	4	301	5
Madison	2,168	277	1	17	1,309	21
Marengo	1,333	78	20	..	726	2
Marion	1,100	589	1	2	851	195
Marshall	1,313	925	51	10	1,458	476
Mobile	2,423	447	8	52	967	59
Monroe	856	18	5	1	470	5
Montgomery	2,621	79	1	9	1,365	21
Morgan	1,548	494	21	92	976	37
Perry	775	12	4	..	457	1
Pickens	816	69	23	20	723	9
Pike	1,507	39	15	..	847	23
Randolph	799	395	3	5	580	79
Russell	516	33	2	16	338	3
Shelby	1,011	1,231	215	23	1,012	758
St. Clair	820	781	107	6	983	416
Sumter	719	3	..	1	535	..
Talladega	1,016	351	10	2	829	50
Tallapoosa	1,343	104	6	8	1,031	17
Tuscaloosa	1,729	168	8	78	1,319	16
Walker	1,632	1,367	..	43	2,047	1,015
Washington	464	40	2	10	312	6
Wilcox	1,027	2	..	..	612	..
Winston	443	949	10	2	556	767
Total	74,374	25,305	1,565	1,347	62,771	10,002
Plurality	49,069	..	..	..	52,769	..
Per cent.	71.92	22.54	1.542	1,336	85.79	14.21
Scattering		....			389	
Whole vote		103,399			73,162	

ALABAMA—*Continued.*

For President in 1908 Chafin, Pro., received 662 votes; Hisgen, Ind., received 146 votes.

For President in 1904 Swallow, Pro., received 612 votes.

The vote for Governor in 1902 was: Jelks, Dem., 67,763; Smith, Rep., 24,431.

For President in 1900 Barker, Pop., received 4,178 votes, and Woolley, Pro., 2,762 votes.

Bryan's Democratic vote in 1896 was 105,390, and the Populist vote 24,917. The scattering vote: Palmer, N. D., 6,462; Levering, Pro., 2,147.

VOTE FOR REPRESENTATIVES IN CONGRESS, 1908.

Districts.

I. Counties of Choctaw, Clarke, Marengo, Mobile, Monroe, and Washington. G. W. Taylor, Dem., 7,457.

II. Counties of Baldwin, Butler, Conecuh, Covington, Crenshaw, Escambia, Montgomery, Pike, and Wilcox. S. H. Dent, Jr., Dem., 10,754.

III. Counties of Barbour, Bullock, Coffee, Dale, Geneva, Henry, Lee, and Russell. Henry D. Clayton, Dem., 9,993.

IV. Counties of Calhoun, Chilton, Cleburne, Dallas, Shelby, and Talladega. W. B. D. Craig, Dem., 6,239.

V. Counties of Autauga, Chambers, Clay, Coosa, Elmore, Lowndes, Macon, Randolph, and Tallapoosa. J. T. Heflin, Dem., 8,024; W. W. Wadsworth, Rep., 1,543.

VI. Counties of Fayette, Greene, Lamar, Marion, Pickens, Sumter, Tuscaloosa, and Walker. Richmond P. Hobson, Dem., 9,211.

VII. Counties of Cherokee, Cullman, De Kalb, Etowah, Franklin, Marshall, St. Clair, and Winston. John L. Burnett, Dem., 8,972; W. H. Freeman, Rep., 2,926. Burnett's plurality, 7,046.

VIII. Counties of Colbert, Jackson, Lauderdale, Lawrence, Limestone, Madison, and Morgan. Wm. Richardson, Dem., 9,691; Jeremiah Murphy, Rep., 2,028. Richardson's majority, 7,663.

IX. Counties of Bibb, Blount, Hale, Perry, and Jefferson. O. W. Underwood, Dem., 11,288; J. B. Sloan, Rep., 2,567; Scattering, 359; Underwood's plurality, 8,611.

PRESENT STATE GOVERNMENT.

Governor, B. B. Comer; Lieutenant-Governor, Henry B. Gray; Secretary of State, Frank N. Julian; Auditor, W. W. Brandon; Adjutant-General, Bibb Graves; Attorney-General, A. M. Garber; Treasurer, W. D. Seed; Superintendent of Education, H. C. Gunnells; Commissioner of Agriculture, J. A. Wilkinson; ex officio Commissioner of Insurance, A. C. Sexton; Commissioner of Public Lands, Frank N. Julian—all Democrats.

JUDICIARY.

Supreme Court: Chief Justice, John R. Tyson; Associate Justices, Jonathan Haralson, N. D. Denson, John C. Anderson, R. T. Simpson, James R. Dowdell, and Thomas McClellan; Clerk, R. F. Ligon, Jr.—all Democrats.

STATE LEGISLATURE, 1909.

	Senate.	*House.*	*Joint Ballot.*
Democrats	35	69	104
Republicans	..	.	1
Populists	...	1	..
Democratic majority	35	67	103

ALABAMA—*Continued.*

VOTE OF THE STATE SINCE 1872.

		Dem.	Rep.	Gr.	Pro.	Plu.
1872.	President	79,229	90,272	....	....	*10,974 R
1876.	President	102,002	68,230	....	....	*33,772 D
1880.	President	90,687	56,178	4,642	....	34,509 D
1882.	Governor	100,391	46,386	....	....	*54,199 D
1884.	President	92,973	59,144	762	....	33,829 D
1886.	Governor	144,821	37,116	....	576	107,621 D
1888.	Governor	155,973	44,770	....	343	111,203 D
1888.	President	117,320	56,197	....	583	61,123 D
1890.	Governor	139,910	42,440	....	1,380	97,470 D
				Pop.		
1892.	Governor	126,959	....	115,522	....	*11,437 D
1892.	President	138,138	9,197	85,181	239	52,957 D
			R.& Pop.			
1896.	Governor	128,541	89,290	....	....	*39,251 D
			Rep.	*N. D.*		
1896.	President	130,307	54,737	6,462	2,147	75,570 D
1898.	Governor	111,936	52,164	....	....	*59,772 D
				Pop.		
1900.	Governor	115,167	28,291	17,543	1,301	86,876 D
1902.	Governor	67,763	24,421	....	....	*43,342 D
1904.	President	79,857	22,472	5,057	612	57,385 D
1906.	Governor	62,771	....	10,002	....	52,769 D
1908.	President	74,374	25,305	1 542	622	49,069 D

* Majority.

ARIZONA.

Counties. (13.)	Congress, 1908.			Congress, 1904.		
	Smith, Dem.	Cameron, Rep.	Cannon, Soc.	Smith Dem.	Fowler, Rep.	Gibson, Pro.
Apache	195	263	..	209	301	2
Cochise	2,233	2,526	356	2,001	1,374	13
Coconino	396	570	49	496	567	10
Gila	976	945	404	752	383	2
Graham	1,423	1,146	169	1,111	793	..
Maricopa	1,995	2,224	179	1,731	1,974	55
Mohave	361	195	53	344	213	..
Navajo	204	395	38	290	331	1
Pima	1,260	1,296	116	893	1,027	6
Pinal	349	357	28	369	206	..
Santa Cruz	342	308	27	239	309	1
Yavapai	1,326	1,532	332	1,492	1,608	24
Yuma	567	578	161	467	435	1
Total	11,727	12,435	1,912	10,494	9,521	108
Plurality	..	708	..	973	..	..
Per cent	44.49	47.10	7.17	49.01	44.51	0.55
Scattering		282			53	
Whole vote		26,356			19,667	

PRESENT TERRITORIAL GOVERNMENT.

Governor, Jos. H. Kibbey; Secretary, John H. Page; Treasurer, E. E. Kirkland; Auditor, John H. Page; Adjutant-General, J. H. McClintock; Attorney-General, E. S. Clark; Superintendent of Education, R. L. Long—all Republicans.

JUDICIARY.

Supreme Court: Chief Justice, Edward Kent; Associate Justices, Richard E. Sloan, Fletcher M. Doan, John H. Campbell, Fredk. S. Nare; Clerk, Shelby M. Collum—all Republicans.

TERRITORIAL LEGISLATURE, 1909.

	Council.	House.	Joint Ballot.
Democrats	10	17	27
Republicans	2	7	9
Democratic majority	8	10	18

VOTE OF THE TERRITORY SINCE 1890.

	Dem.	Rep.	Pop.	Ind.	Maj.
1890	6,137	4,941	....	....	1,196 D
1892	7,152	5,171	....	....	1,981 D
1894	4,773	5,648	3,006	....	*875 R
1896	6,065	4,090	3,895	....	*1,975 D
1898	8,212	7,384	....	....	828 D
1900	8,664	7,664	....	....	1,000 D
1902	9,716	9,239	....	....	477 D
1904	10,494	9,521	....	....	973 D
			Soc.		
1906	11,101	8,909	2,078	....	2,192 D
1908	11,727	12,435	1,912	...	708 R

* Plurality.

ARKANSAS.

Counties. (75.)	President, 1908.				Governor, 1908.	
	Bryan, Dem.	Taft, Rep.	Chafin Pro.	Debs, Soc.	Donaghey Dem.	W'rthington Rep.
Arkansas	937	673	161	42	1,332	485
Ashley	1,100	822	1	45	1,779	264
Baxter	607	302	7	64	758	289
Benton	3,067	1,532	76	155	3,227	1,350
Boone	1,149	682	10	64	1,389	908
Bradley	906	316	9	30	1,116	222
Calhoun	554	233	2	8	667	105
Carroll	1,295	1,051	21	72	1,347	1,205
Chicot	428	644	1	2	1,213	448
Clark	1,206	1,007	13	27	1,155	329
Clay	1,527	1,010	11	106	1,772	829
Cleburne	506	297	19	55	873	280
Cleveland	771	426	2	1	951	299
Columbia	1,614	817	3	9	1,356	431
Conway	2,533	824	6	45	2,935	487
Craighead	1,647	711	31	165	2,106	532
Crawford	1,261	1,339	16	67	1,606	1,275
Crittenden	428	383	6	6	1,057	64
Cross	719	564	2	59	1,273	413
Dallas	724	636	4	33	886	417
Desha	519	266	1	6	534	286
Drew	1,124	680	4	40	1,181	428
Faulkner	1,772	752	26	93	2,719	740
Franklin	1,308	567	18	119	1,575	573
Fulton	741	367	3	63	924	373
Garland	1,340	1,105	17	105	2,728	1,407
Grant	524	160	1	16	754	154
Greene	1,606	550	11	82	1,709	437
Hempstead	1,779	1,351	15	27	2,277	1,029
Hot Springs	834	687	6	23	1,468	565
Howard	968	611	10	83	1,030	371
Independence	159	948	14	109	2,003	972
Izard	873	392	14	53	1,027	343
Jackson	1,055	864	13	101	1,626	875
Jefferson	1,585	1,386	11	125	2,667	851
Johnson	1,155	554	12	140	1,278	543
Lafayette	743	552	2	..	648	175
Lawrence	1,188	583	20	59	1,649	479
Lee	1,182	354	1	29	1,294	205
Lincoln	389	159	5	16	963	32
Little River	663	435	12	105	683	196
Logan	1,716	1,151	19	88	2,009	1,005
Lonoke	1,385	592	17	30	1,593	353
Madison	1,441	1,542	6	69	1,549	1,438
Marion	705	371	8	81	913	475
Miller	1,038	727	3	36	1,276	308
Mississippi	930	1,180	11	155	1,599	695
Monroe	912	1,023	26	41	1,061	422
Montgomery	553	522	15	87	922	524
Nevada	890	784	9	47	1,367	476
Newton	377	584	3	36	545	977
Ouachita	1,156	1,505	5	14	1,367	1,266
Perry	608	445	..	..	887	417
Phillips	1,194	394	1	3	1,360	168
Pike	568	602	6	21	774	582
Poinsett	845	462	..	2	1,359	339
Polk	825	628	21	165	1,446	544
Pope	1,664	814	7	78	1,620	611
Prairie	1,003	812	11	41	1,169	471
Pulaski	3,893	3,545	25	228	5,375	2,018
Randolph	1,348	517	6	28	1,708	447
Saline	899	369	7	53	1,088	244
Scott	893	483	14	75	1,298	523
Searcy	597	636	14	141	960	1,069
Sebastian	3,635	2,052	65	620	3,763	1,615
Sevier	1,073	526	19	199	1,329	344
Sharp	940	317	6	78	1,011	262
St. Francis	619	755	14	80	1,302	528
Stone	496	267	..	33	719	326
Union	1,407	558	2	11	1,808	207
Van Buren	798	670	40	39	1,190	802
Washington	2,748	2,734	58	185	2,890	1,873
White	1,718	687	75	92	1,977	826
Woodruff	1,049	756	7	51	1,115	428
Yell	1,743	1,040	14	194	1,949	908
Total	87,015	56,624	1,121	5,750	111478	45,409
Plurality	30,391	..	..	..	66,096	..
Per cent	57.92	36.62	.73	3.78	..	..
Whole vote		151,944			163,674	

ARKANSAS—*Continued.*

For President in 1908 Watson, Pop., received 1,121 votes; Hisgen, Ind., 313.

The vote for President in 1904 was: Parker, Dem., 64,434; Roosevelt, Rep., 46,860; Parker's plurality, 17,574.

VOTE FOR REPRESENTATIVES IN CONGRESS, 1908.

Districts.

I. Counties of Clay, Greene, Craighead, Mississippi, Crittenden, Cross, Poinsett, St. Francis, Lee, Phillips, and Woodruff. R. B. Macon, Dem., 13,057; Bloodworth, Rep., 6,534. Macon's majority, 6,523.

II. Counties of Stone, Sharp, Randolph, Lawrence, Fulton, Izard, Independence, White, Cleburne, Jackson, Prairie, and Monroe. W. A. Oldfield, Dem., 12,416; Myers, Rep., 6,785. Oldfield's majority, 5,631.

III. Counties of Washington, Benton, Madison, Carroll, Newton, Boone, Searcy, Baxter, Marion, and Van Buren. J. C. Floyd, Dem., 13,708; Mills, Rep., 8,984. Floyd's majority, 4,724.

IV. Counties of Crawford, Logan, Sebastian, Scott, Polk, Sevier, Howard, Pike, Little River, Montgomery, and Miller. Craven, Dem., 13,554; Meacham, Rep., 9,112. Craven's majority, 4,442.

V. Counties of Franklin, Johnson, Pope, Yell, Conway, Faulkner, Perry, and Pulaski. C. C. Reid, Dem., 15,341; Caron, Rep., 7,849. Reid's majority, 7,492.

VI. Counties of Garland, Hot Springs, Saline, Dallas, Grant, Desha, Cleveland, Lincoln, Drew, Jefferson, Arkansas, and Lonoke. J. T. Robinson, Dem., unopposed, 17,384.

VII. Counties of Hempstead, Clark, Nevada, Columbia, Union, Ouachita, Lafayette, Calhoun, Bradley, Ashley, and Chicot. R. M. Wallace, Dem., 12,349; Young, Rep., 8,318. Wallace's majority, 4,013.

PRESENT STATE GOVERNMENT.

Governor, George W. Donaghey; Lieutenant-Governor, X. O. Pindall; Secretary of State, O. C. Ludwig; Treasurer, James L. Yates; Auditor, J. R. Jobe; Attorney-General, Wm. F. Kirby; Superintendent of Education, Geo. B. Cook; Commissioner of Agriculture, Guy B. Tucker; Commissioner of Insurance, A. E. Moore; Commissioner of Public Lands, L. L. Coffman—all Democrats.

JUDICIARY.

Supreme Court: Chief Justice, Joseph M. Hill; Justices, Edgar A. McCulloch, C. D. Wood, Burrill B. Battle, and Jesse C. Hart; Clerk of the Court, P. D. English—all Democrats.

STATE LEGISLATURE, 1908.

	Senate.	*House.*	*Joint Ballot.*
Democrats	35	95	130
Republicans	..	5	5
Democratic majority.	35	90	125

VOTE OF THE STATE SINCE 1876.

	Dem.	*Rep.*	*Gr.*	*Wheel.*	*Maj.*
1876. Pres...	58,083	38,669	....	....	19,414 D
1880. Pres...	60,865	42,549	4,079	....	*18,316 D
1884. Pres...	72,927	50,895	1,847	....	*22 032 D
1886. Gov....	90,650	54,070	....	19,169	*36,580 D
			U. Lab.	*Pro.*	
1888. Gov....	99,229	....	84,223	....	15,006 D
1888. Pres...	85,962	58,752	10,613	641	*27,210 D
1890. Gov....	106,267	....	85,181	....	21,086 D
			Pop.		
1892. Pres...	87,834	46,884	11,831	113	*40,950 D
1894. Gov....	91,114	35,836	13,990	851	*55,278 D
1896. Gov....	74,809	26,055	24,541	1,551	*48,724 D
1896. Pres...	110,103	37,512	....	839	*72,591 D
1900. Gov....	88,637	44,701	3,641	....	*43,936 D
1900. Pres...	81,142	44,800	972	....	*36,342 D
1902. Gov....	77,354	29,251	8,345	4,791	48,103 D
			Soc.		
1904. Pres...	64,434	46,860	2,318	1 816	17,574 D
1906. Gov...	102,749	40,965	2,169	3,274	61,784 D
1908. Pres...	87,015	56,624	5,750	1,121	22,056 D

* Plurality.

CALIFORNIA.

COUNTIES. (57.)	PRESIDENT, 1908. Bryan, Dem.	Taft, Rep.	Chafin, Pro.	Debs, Soc.	PRESIDENT, 1904. Parker, Dem.	Roosevelt, Rep.
Alameda	7,110	21,380	608	3,462	4,386	19,065
Alpine	11	75	..	..	9	74
Amador	874	1,035	25	38	915	1,279
Butte	2,746	3,094	199	384	1,574	2,739
Calaveras	833	1,323	17	167	844	1,571
Colusa	1,064	730	23	52	900	885
Contra Costa	1,599	3,336	71	438	1,257	2,833
Del Norte	711	450	28	19	187	429
El Dorado	202	986	28	71	865	1,248
Fresno	1,019	6,384	22	148	2,815	4,929
Glenn	4,743	618	508	863	725	765
Humboldt	1,206	4,221	138	865	1,249	4,930
Imperial	675	909	102	204	..	..
Inyo	618	583	37	158	231	452
Kern	2,215	2,270	57	380	1,724	2,359
Kings	859	1,198	70	112	595	1,110
Lake	628	625	64	110	594	641
Lassen	361	551	9	81	301	573
Los Angeles	22,076	41,483	4,033	4,702	10,030	32,507
Madera	574	596	21	121	610	784
Marin	983	2,732	28	219	772	2,199
Mariposa	480	352	14	86	487	461
Mendocino	1,752	2,746	88	293	1,489	2,904
Merced	1,100	1,107	104	152	863	972
Modoc	574	620	12	24	444	559
Mono	121	224	..	25	82	245
Monterey	1,616	2,486	265	211	1,415	2,453
Napa	1,336	2,405	100	206	1,135	2,425
Nevada	1,368	1,825	76	296	1,167	2,249
Orange	1,911	3,244	451	375	1,034	2,665
Placer	1,491	1,865	69	171	1,023	2,050
Plumas	395	659	12	59	347	707
Riverside	1,374	3,229	427	565	678	2,638
Sacramento	4,533	6,515	106	608	2,384	6,666
San Benito	681	937	52	63	643	888
S. Bernardino	2,685	4,729	618	777	1,573	3,884
San Diego	2,393	5,412	212	1,342	1,398	4,303
San Francisco	21,260	33,184	406	4,523	18,027	39,816
San Joaquin	3,331	4,470	167	547	2,293	4,498
S. Luis Obispo	1,381	2,008	154	370	1,167	2,015
San Mateo	1,314	2,867	29	301	851	2,146
Santa Barbara	1,640	2,713	104	376	1,152	2,676
Santa Clara	3,836	7,950	696	883	3,100	8,274
Santa Cruz	1,643	2,886	237	540	1,105	2,626
Shasta	1,389	1,891	69	577	935	1,891
Sierra	410	600	11	54	376	791
Siskiyou	1,657	1,813	39	264	1,219	2,104
Solano	2,083	3,115	102	402	1,555	3,176
Sonoma	3,168	5,427	285	483	2,816	5,269
Stanislaus	1,390	1,663	315	182	1,110	1,437
Sutter	652	896	28	45	488	872
Tehama	894	1,064	62	204	720	1,234
Trinity	331	393	14	130	308	467
Tulare	2,329	2,742	143	466	1,643	2,221
Tuolumne	878	943	72	187	1,006	1,280
Ventura	1,181	1,864	48	158	840	1,995
Yolo	1,553	1,707	74	127	1,301	1,702
Yuba	902	1,270	11	78	633	1,235
Total	127492	214398	11,770	28,659	89,404	205226
Plurality	..	86,906	..	..	..	115822
Per cent	32.97	55.66	3.04	7.10	26.96	61.89
Scattering		4,278				36,915
Whole vote		386,597				331,545

For Governor in 1906 Blanchard, Pro., received 8,141 votes.

For President in 1904 Swallow, Pro., received 7,380 votes; Debs, Soc., 29,535.

The vote for Governor in 1902 was: Lane, Dem., 143,782; Pardee, Rep., 145,332; Brower, Soc., 9,582; Knouse, Pro., 4,636; scattering, 14,488.

VOTE FOR REPRESENTATIVES IN CONGRESS, 1908.

Districts.

I. Counties of Del Norte, Humboldt, Lassen, Marin, Modoc, Plumas, Shasta, Sierra, Siskiyou, Tehama, Alpine, Calaveras, Mariposa, Nevada, El Dorado, Amador, Tuolumne, and Trinity. Holland, Dem., 14,031; Englebright, Rep., 20,624; Cunningham, Soc., 2,898; Fassett, Pro., 546.

CALIFORNIA—*Continued.*

II. Counties of Mendocino, Glenn, Colusa, Butte, Sutter, Yuba, Sacramento, Yolo, Lake, Napa, Sonoma, and Marin. Hays, Dem., 19,193; McKinlay, Rep., 28,627; Gaylord, Soc., 2,003.

III. Counties of Alameda, Contra Costa, and Solano. Peckham, Dem., 9,889; Knowland, Rep., 27,857; Sands, Ind. L., 9,230; Philbrick, Soc., 4,052; Montgomery, Pro., 717.

IV. County of San Francisco (part). McGnire, Dem., 7,497; Kahn, Rep., 9,202; Doyle, Soc., 699; Meserve, Pro., 60.

V. Counties of San Francisco (part), San Mateo, and Santa Clara. Tracy, Dem., 24,531; Hayes, Rep., 28,127; Mesner, Soc., 3,640; Vail, Pro., 1,045.

VI. Counties of Santa Cruz, Monterey, San Benito, Fresno, Kings, Madera, Merced, Stanislaus, and San Joaquin. Feliz, Dem., 15,868; Needham, Rep., 21,323; Pattison, Soc., 2,288; Webb, Pro., 1,509.

VII. County of Los Angeles. Rush, Dem., 25,445; McLachlan, Rep., 37,244; Hentig, Ind. L., 791; Holston, Soc., 4,432; Atwood, Pro., 5,899.

VIII. Counties of San Luis Obispo, Santa Barbara, Ventura, Kern, Tulare, Inyo, San Bernardino, Orange, Riverside, and San Diego. Shepherd, Dem., 18,245; Smith, Rep., 29,305; Richardson, Soc., 5,025.

PRESENT STATE GOVERNMENT.

Governor, Jas. N. Gillett; Lieutenant-Governor, Warren Porter; Secretary of State, C. F. Curry; Treasurer, W. R. Williams; Comptroller, A. B. Nye; Adjutant-General, J. B. Lauck; Attorney-General, V. S. Webb; Superintendent of Education, Ed. Hyatt; Commissioner of Insurance, E. Myron Wolfe; Commissioner of Lands, W. S. Kingsbury—all Republicans.

JUDICIARY.

Supreme Court: Chief Justice, W. H. Beatty; Associate Justices, H. Melvin, Lucien Shaw, F. M. Angellotti, Lucien Sloss, F. W. Henshaw, W. G. Lorigan; Clerk, F. L. Caughey—all Republicans.

STATE LEGISLATURE, 1908.

	Senate.	*House.*	*Joint Ballot.*
Republicans	30	60	90
Democrats	10	20	30
Labor Union	..	18	...
Republican majority	20	40	60

VOTE OF THE STATE SINCE 1872.

	Dem.	*Rep.*	*Amer.*	*Pro.*	*Gr.*	*Maj.*
1872. Pres.	40,749	54,044	....	....	....	13,295 R
1876. Pres.	76,464	79,264	....	....	....	2,800 R
1880. Pres.	80,472	80,370	....	....	3,404	*102 D
1884. Pres.	89,288	102,416	....	2,920	2,017	*13,128 R
1886. Gov.	84,970	84,318	7,347	6,432	12,227	*652 D
1888. Pres.	117,729	124,816	1,591	5,761	....	*7,087 R
1890. Gov.	117,184	125,129	10,073	....	....	*7,945 R
			Pop.		*Ind.*	
1892. †Pres	118,293	118,149	25,352	8,129	....	*144 D
1894. Gov.	111,944	110,738	51,304	10,561	....	1,206 D
1894. Sec.	86,443	126,541	49,734	8,262	2,405	40,098 R
			N. D.			
1896. Pres.	143,373	146,170	2,006	2,573	....	*2,797 R
			Soc. L.			
1898. Gov.	129,261	148,354	5,143	4,297	....	19,093 R
			Soc. D.			
1900. Pres.	124,985	164,755	7,554	5,024	....	39,770 R
1902. Gov.	143,782	145,332	5,992	4,636	....	1,550 R
1904. Pres.	89,294	205,226	29,535	7,380	......	115,932 R
1906. Gov.	117,590	12.589	16,030	8,141	....	8,299 R
1908. Pres.	127,492	214,398	28,659	11 770	....	86,906 R

*Plurality. †8 Democratic and 1 Republican electors were chosen.

COLORADO.

COUNTIES. (59.)	PRESIDENT, 1908.				GOVERNOR, 1908.	
	Bryan, Dem.	Taft, Rep.	Chafin Pro.	Debs, Soc.	Shafroth, Dem.	McDonald, Rep.
Adams	1,281	1,221	..	..	1,280	1 227
Arapahoe	1,514	1,341	..	..	1,390	1,457
Archuleta	503	513	..	..	493	489
Baca	216	179	..	.	170	222
Bent	920	824	..	..	863	881
Boulder	4,856	5,772	..	..	5,776	4,697
Chaffee	1,230	1,691	..	..	1,696	1,222
Cheyenne	445	331	..	..	325	441
Clear Creek	872	1,706	..	..	1,677	887
Conejos	1,736	1,365	...	..	1,203	1,635
Costilla	1,051	560	..	..	565	1,040
Custer	500	555	..	..	554	500
Delta	1,843	2,006	..	..	2,112	1,707
Denver	33,141	30,218	..	..	34,034	27,632
Dolores	69	185	..	..	185	63
Douglas	780	630	..	..	631	772
Eagle	521	832	..	..	838	519
Elbert	973	787	..	..	781	964
El Paso	8,002	6,005	..	..	6 062	7,833
Fremont	3,060	3,135	..	..	3 288	2,967
Garfield	1,514	1,900	..	..	1,906	1,494
Gilpin	844	1,187	..	..	1,202	823
Grand	527	487	..	..	522	488
Gunnison	894	1,481	..	..	1,504	859
Hinsdale	156	217	..	..	228	160
Huerfano	3,077	776	..	..	774	3,068
Jefferson	2,630	2,583	..	..	2,692	2,512
Kiowa	473	405	..	..	409	465
Kit Carson	985	752	..	..	746	980
Lake	1,919	2,646	..	..	2,602	2,005
La Plata	1,383	1,991	..	..	1,951	1,396
Larimer	4,489	3,629	..	..	3,673	4,481
Las Animas	5,722	4,212	..	..	4,285	5,598
Lincoln	794	577	..	..	577	779
Logan	1,054	952	..	..	978	1,025
Mesa	3,049	2,824	..	..	2,824	3,020
Mineral	218	496	..	..	490	215
Montezuma	442	951	..	..	943	450
Montrose	1,195	1,461	..	..	1,498	1,129
Morgan	1,672	1,208	..	..	1,271	1,639
Otero	3,242	3,554	..	..	3,625	3,118
Ouray	542	1,085	..	..	1,072	555
Park	464	807	..	..	806	470
Phillips	504	401	..	..	400	504
Pitkin	533	1,262	..	..	1,250	11528
Prowers	1,439	1,027	..	...	1,048	1,370
Pueblo	7,353	8,098	..	..	8,443	6,918
Rio Blanco	380	467	..	..	450	390
Rio Grande	1,132	1,144	..	..	1,187	1,681
Routt	1,157	1,345	..	..	1,407	1,102
Saguache	815	824	..	..	823	812
San Juan	549	773	..	..	796	533
San Miguel	882	927	..	..	966	842
Sedgwick	544	278	..	..	289	540
Summit	367	747	..	..	726	884
Teller	3,105	4,192	..	..	4,268	3,059
Washington	599	424	..	..	573	439
Weld	5,544	4,650	..	..	4,624	5,486
Yuma	1,061	1,148	..	..	1,207	1,011
Total	126772	123732	5,538	7,960	123898	118832
Plurality	..	3,040	..	..	11,066	..
Per cent	45.45	49.38	2.12	3.05	51.89	48.11
Whole vote	261,228				247,730	

For President in 1904: Watson, Pop., received 824 votes; Corrigan, Soc. L., 335; scattering, 8,901.

For Governor in 1904 Chamberlain, Pro., received 2,066 votes.

VOTE FOR REPRESENTATIVES IN CONGRESS, 1908.

At Large—Taylor, Dem., 126,953; Burger, Rep., 121,273; McCarthy, Pro., 6,183; Brown, Soc., 8,151.

Districts.

I. Counties of Arapahoe, Boulder, Jefferson, Lake, Larimer, Logan, Morgan, Park, Phillips, Sedgwick, Washington, Weld, and Yuma: A. W. Rucker, Dem., 60,650; Bouynge, Rep., 56,664; Greer, Soc., 3,356.

COLORADO—*Continued.*

II. Counties of Archuleta, Baca, Bent, Chaffee, Cheyenne, Clear Creek, Conejos, Costilla, Custer, Delta, Dolores, Douglas, Eagle, Elbert, El Paso, Fremont, Garfield, Gilpin, Grand, Gunnison, Hinsdale, Huerfano, Kiowa, Kit Carson, La Plata, Las Animas, Lincoln, Mesa, Montezuma, Mineral, Montrose, Otero, Ouray, Pitkin, Prowers, Pueblo, Rio Blanco, Rio Grande, Routt, Saguache, San Juan, San Miguel, and Summit. J. A. Martin, Dem., 66,942; Haggott, Rep., 64,434; Ashbourne, Soc., 4,771.

PRESENT STATE GOVERNMENT.

Governor, John H. Shafroth; Lieutenant-Governor, Stephen R. Fitzgarrald; Secretary of State, James B. Pearce; Treasurer, Wm. J. Galligan; Auditor, Roady Kenehan; Attorney-General, Jno. T. Barnett; Superintendent of Public Instruction, Katherine M. Cook—all Democrats.

JUDICIARY.

Supreme Court: Chief Justice, Robert W. Steele, Dem.; Justices, John Campbell, Rep.; Luther M. Goddard, Rep.; S. M. White, Dem.; W. A. Hill, Dem.; M. S. Bailey; Dem.; Wm. H. Gabbert, Rep.; G. W. Musser, Dem.; Clerk, H. G. Clark, Rep.

STATE LEGISLATURE, 1908.

	Senate.	*House.*	*Joint Ballot.*
Democrats	20	53	73
Republicans	15	12	27
Democratic majority.	5	41	46

VOTE OF THE STATE SINCE ITS ADMISSION.

		Dem.	*Rep.*	*Gr.*	*Pro.*	*Maj.*
1876.	Governor	13,316	14,154	....	....	838 R
1880.	President	24,647	27,450	1,435	....	*2,803 R
1884.	President	27,723	36,290	1,958	....	*8,567 R
1888.	President	37,567	50,774	....	1,266	*13,207 R
		Fusion.†				
1892.	President	53,585	38,620	....	1,638	*14,964 F
		Fusion.		*Pop.*		
1896.	President	161,153	26,271	....	1,717	134,882 F
1900.	Governor	121,995	93,245	....	3,786	28,750 F
1900.	President	122,733	93,072	....	3,790	29,661 F
				Soc.		
1904.	President	101,103	134,687	4,304	3,438	34,582 R
1906.	Governor	74,512	92,646	16,938	....	18,134 R
1908.	President	128,898	118,832	7,960	5,538	3,040 D

* Plurality. † Fusion of Pops. and Silver Dems.

CONNECTICUT.

COUNTIES. (8.)	PRESIDENT, 1908.				GOVERNOR, 1908.	
	Bryan, Dem.	Taft, Rep.	Chafin Pro.	Debs, Soc.	Thayer Dem.	Lilley, Rep.
Hartford	12,967	24,781	891	1,252	16,553	21,040
New Haven	22,394	32,204	441	2,087	27,459	27,085
New London	6,549	9,941	154	240	7,247	9,187
Fairfield	14,917	24,064	347	1,020	16,555	22,205
Windham	2,623	4,960	152	53	3,073	4,434
Litchfield	4,128	8,978	204	161	5,893	7,170
Middlesex	2,935	5,071	114	55	3,518	4,476
Tolland	1,742	2,816	77	245	1,962	2,582
Total	68,255	112815	2,380	5,113	82,260	98,179
Plurality	..	44,560	..	..	..	15,819
Per cent	35.94	59.64	1.25	2.67	43.43	46.65
Scattering	1,340				4	
Whole vote	189,903				189,085	

For President in 1904 Parker, Dem., received 72,909; Roosevelt, Rep., 111,089; Corrigan, Soc. Lab., 575; scattering, 11 votes.

The vote for Governor in 1904 was: Robertson, Dem., 79,164; Roberts, Rep., 104,736; Sheldon, Pop., 481; Beard, Pro., 1,498; Sweetland, Soc., 4,390; Sullivan, Soc. Lab., 562.

VOTE FOR REPRESENTATIVES IN CONGRESS, 1908.

At Large—Avery, Dem., 70,039; Tilson, Rep., 111,557; scattering, 8,663.

CONNECTICUT—*Continued.*

Districts.

I. Counties of Hartford and Tolland. Gerth, Dem., 15,595; E. S. Henry, Rep., 26,829; scattering, 2,646.

II. Counties of Middlesex and New Haven. Riley, Dem., 26,832; N. D. Sperry, Rep., 36,083; scattering, 2,674.

III. Counties of New London and Windham. Hunter, Dem., 9,190; E. W. Higgins, Rep., 14,935; scattering, 606.

IV. Counties of Fairfield and Litchfield. Wilson, Dem., 19,423; E. J. Hill, Rep., 32,843; scattering, 1,910.

PRESENT STATE GOVERNMENT.

Governor, George L. Lilley; Lieutenant-Governor, Frank B. Weeks; Secretary of State, Matthew H. Rogers; Treasurer, Freeman F. Patten; Comptroller, Thos. D. Bradstreet; Attorney-General, Marcus H. Holcomb; Adjutant-General, George M. Cole; Commissioner of Insurance, Theodore H. Macdonald—all Republicans.

JUDICIARY.

Supreme Court: Chief Justice, Simeon E. Baldwin, Dem.; Associate Justices, S. O. Prentice, Rep.; F. B. Hall, Rep.; John M. Thayer, Dem.; Alberto T. Roraback, Rep.; Clerk, Geo. A. Conant.

STATE LEGISLATURE, 1908.

	Senate.	*House.*	*Joint Ballot*
Republicans	26	191	215
Democrats	9	64	73
Republican majority.	17	127	142

VOTE OF THE STATE SINCE 1872.

		Dem.	*Rep.*	*Gr.-Lab.*	*Pro.*	*Plu.*
1872.	Pres.	45,866	50,626	....	....	4,760 R
1876.	Pres.	61,934	59,084	774	378	2,850 D
1880.	Pres.	64,415	67,071	868	409	2,656 R
1884.	Pres.	67,167	65,893	1,684	2,489	1,284 D
1888.	Pres.	74,920	74,584	240	4,234	336 D
				Pop		
1892.	Pres.	82,395	77,030	806	4,026	5,365 D
				Nat. Dem.		
1896.	Pres.	56,740	110,285	4,334	1,808	53,545 R
1898.	Gov.	64,277	81,015	....	1,460	16,738 R
				Soc. D.		
1900.	Pres.	73,997	102,567	1,029	1,617	28,570 R
				Soc.		
1902.	Gov.	69,330	85,338	2,804	1,436	16,008 R
1904	Pres.	72,909	111,089	4,543	1,506	38,180 R
1906.	Gov.	67,776	88,384	2,932	1,820	20,608 R
1908.	Pres.	68,255	112,815	5,113	2,380	44,560 R

DELAWARE.

COUNTIES. (3.)	PRESIDENT, 1908.			PRESIDENT, 1904.	
	Bryan, Dem.	Taft, Rep.	Chafin, Pro.	Parker Dem.	Roosevelt, Rep.
Kent	4,098	4,159	103	3,780	4,601
New Castle	12,963	14,987	437	11,170	13,198
Sussex	5,013	5,870	133	4,410	5,915
Total	22,071	25,014	670	19,360	23,714
Plurality	...	2,943	..	...	4,354
Per cent	45.75	52.10	1.33	44.12	54.04
Scattering	....			197	
Whole vote	48,024			43,878	

For President, 1908, Debs, Soc., received 239 votes; Hisgen, Ind., 30.

The vote for Governor in 1904 was: Pennewill, Dem., 19,780; Lea, Rep., 22,532; Chandler, Reg. Rep., 802. Lea's plurality, 2,752.

VOTE FOR REPRESENTATIVE IN CONGRESS, 1908.

The total vote for each candidate for Congress, 1908, was: Levin I. Handy, Dem., 22,515; William H. Heald, Rep., 24,314; Hawkins, Pro., 330; Houck, Soc., 228; Cresson, Ind., 10.

DELAWARE—*Continued.*

PRESENT STATE GOVERNMENT.

Governor, Simeon H. Pennewill; Lieutenant-Governor, John M. Mendinhall; Secretary of State, to be named; Treasurer, David O. Morse; Auditor, Theo. F. Clark; Attorney-General, Andrew C. Gray: Adjutant-General, to be named; Commissioner of Insurance, Chas. H. Maull—all Republicans, except Gray, Dem.

JUDICIARY.

Supreme Court: Chancellor, John R. Nicholson, Dem.; Chief Justice, Chas. B. Lore, Dem.; Associate Justices, Ignatius C. Grubb, Dem.; W. C. Spruance, Rep.; James Pennewill, Rep.; William H. Boyce, Dem.; Clerk, Walter Pardoe, Rep.

STATE LEGISLATURE, 1908.

	Senate.	*House.*	*Joint Ballot.*
Republicans	11	17	28
Democrats	6	18	24
Majority	5R	1D	4R

VOTE OF THE STATE SINCE 1872.

		Dem.	*Rep.*	*N. D.*	*Pro.*	*Maj.*
1872.	President	10,206	11,115	....	....	909 R
1876.	President	13,381	10,740	....	....	2,641 D
1880.	President	15,183	14,150	....	....	1,033 D
1884.	President	16,976	13,053	...	....	3,923 D
						Plu.
1888.	President	16,414	12,973	....	400	3,441 D
1892.	President	18,581	18,083	....	565	498 D
1896.	President	13,424	16,804	877	355	3,630 R
				Soc. D.		
1900.	Governor	18,808	22,421	59	584	3,613 R
1900.	President	18,858	22,529	57	538	3,671 R
1902.	Treasurer	16,602	20,705	....	575	4,103 R
1904.	President	19,360	23,714	....	607	4,354 R
1908.	President	22,071	25,014	239	670	2,004 R

FLORIDA.

Counties. (45.)	President, 1908.				President, 1904.	
	Bryan, Dem.	Taft, Rep.	Chafin Pro.	Debs, Soc.	Parker Dem.	Roosevelt, Rep.
Alachua	1,239	686	88	25	1,277	543
Baker	152	104	7	51	207	120
Bradford	729	180	38	19	553	125
Brevard	294	225	1	50	633	124
Calhoun	241	339	2	12	162	160
Citrus	371	33	6	26	369	21
Clay	355	122	38	22	247	50
Columbia	465	279	23	61	595	317
Dade	961	275	53	160	887	307
De Soto	992	224	44	112	721	188
Duval	2,381	641	100	233	2,011	671
Escambia	1,887	718	101	351	1,573	497
Franklin	283	112	9	56	336	144
Gadsden	563	89	12	34	471	54
Hamilton	452	116	17	84	455	155
Hernando	260	57	3	14	172	12
Hillsborough	2,703	367	146	366	1,976	516
Holmes	438	337	8	40	284	140
Jackson	1,122	353	10	134	1,186	354
Jefferson	565	149	21	23	471	123
La Fayette	487	90	44	15	275	122
Lake	487	200	45	62	529	148
Lee	266	72	74	109	266	84
Leon	698	143	25	44	649	84
Levy	411	189	11	64	426	151
Liberty	176	69	4	11	143	50
Madison	511	32	7	23	595	66
Manatee	644	93	28	104	592	91
Marion	1,352	482	116	120	1,091	230
Monroe	630	227	31	289	680	287
Nassau	466	92	16	20	509	161
Orange	952	485	26	63	874	315
Osceola	193	81	1	12	271	65
Pasco	436	81	15	21	453	96
Polk	1,251	290	41	154	869	125
Putnam	79[illegible]	454	32	105	562	219
St. John's	758	344	32	116	550	204
St. Lucie	280	63	7	38	..	..
Santa Rosa	[illegible]	212	10	35	403	73
Sumter	[illegible]	62	22	[illegible]	[illegible]	61
Suwanee	597	150	19	220	581	125
Taylor	250	160	12	41	163	119
Volusia	736	444	28	41	654	263
Wakulla	239	56	6	31	233	39
Walton	504	369	13	46	354	322
Washington	652	288	14	82	414	202
Total	31,104	9,923	1,356	3,747	27,046	8,314
Plurality	21,181	..	..	..	18,732	..
Per cent	64.70	20.65	2.80	7.07	69.82	21.47
Scattering	...				27	
Whole vote	48,076				39,329	

Vote for Governor in 1908 was: Gilchrist, Dem., 33,036; Cheney, Rep., 6,453; Pettigrew, Soc., 2,427.

In 1908, Watson, Pop., for President received 1,946 Votes; Hisgen, Ind., 553.

VOTE FOR REPRESENTATIVES IN CONGRESS, 1908.

Districts.

I. Taylor, La Fayette, Levy, Marion, Citrus, Sumter, Hernando, Pasco, Hillsborough, Polk, Manatee, De Soto, Lee, Monroe, Lake. S. M. Sparkman, Dem., 9,971; G. W. Allen, Rep., 1,990; C. C. Allen, Soc., 1,297.

II. Hamilton, Suwanee, Columbia, Baker, Bradford, Nassau, Duval, Clay, Putnam, St. John, Volusia, Osceola, Orange; Brevard, Dade, Alachua. Frank Clark, Dem., 10,7[illegible]; W. R. O'Neal, Rep., 2,552; A. N. Jackson, Soc., 862.

III. Escambia, Santa Rosa, Walton, Holmes, Washington, Jackson, Calhoun, Franklin, Liberty, Gadsden, Leon, Wakulla, Jefferson, Madison. D. H. Mays, Dem., 9,304; W. H. Northrup, Rep., 1,712.

PRESENT STATE GOVERNMENT.

Governor, Albert W. Gilchrist; Secretary of State, H. C. Crawford; Treasurer, W. V. Knott; Comptroller, A. C. Croom; Attorney-General, Park M. Trammell; Auditor, Ernest Amos; Adjutant-General, J. C. R. Foster; Superintendent of Public Instruction, W. M. Holloway; Commissioner of Agriculture, B. E. McLin—all Democrats.

JUDICIARY.

Supreme Court: Chief Justice, T. M. Shackelford; Associate Justices, W. A. Hocker, R. F. Taylor, J. B. Whitefield, Chas. B. Parkhill and R. S. Cockrell; Clerk, Milton H. Mabey—all Democrats.

STATE LEGISLATURE, 1908.

The Legislature is: Senate, Dems., 32; House, Dems. 68, Socialist 1.

VOTE OF THE STATE SINCE 1872.

		Dem.	*Rep.*	*N. D.*	*Pro.*	*Maj.*
1872.	President	15,428	17,765	....	....	2,337 R
1876.	President	24,440	24,350	....	....	90 D
1880.	President	27,954	23,654	....	....	4,310 D
1884.	President	31,769	28,031	....	....	3,738 D
1888.	President	39,561	26,657	....	423	*12,904 D
			Pop.			*Plu.*
1892.	President	30,143	4,843	....	475	25,300 D
		D. & Pop.	*Rep.*			
1896.	President	32,736	11,288	654	1,778	21,444 D
		Dem.		*Pop.*		
1900.	Governor	29,251	6,238	631	....	23,013 D
1900.	President	28,007	7,314	1,070	1,039	20,683 D
1902.	Sec. State	16,428	....	....	....	16,428 D
					Soc.	
1904.	President	27,046	8,314	1,605	1,742	18,732 D
1908.	President	31,104	9,923	1,946	3,747	21,181 D

*Plurality.

GEORGIA.

Counties.	President, 1908.				President, 1904.	
	Bryan, Dem.	Taft, Rep.	Chafin Pro.	Watson, Pop.	Parker Dem.	Roosevelt, Rep.
Appling	249	250	..	244	354	237
Baker	149	36	..	29	496	16
Baldwin	417	201	8	74	637	62
Banks	211	221	1	147	424	204
Bartow	726	780	11	73	791	406
Ben Hill	407	412	104	49	..	..
Berrien	595	212	19	64	889	68
Bibb	1,945	565	14	51	2,117	236
Brooks	472	362	4	103	429	102
Bryan	..	..	..	..	259	125
Bullock	756	116	..	218	596	54

GEORGIA—*Continued.*

Counties.	President, 1908. Bryan, Dem.	Taft, Rep.	Chafin Pro.	Watson, Pop.	President, 1904. Parker Dem.	Roosevelt, Rep.
Burke	519	193	..	70	657	52
Butts	348	167	5	131	531	80
Calhoun	272	106	..	33	369	19
Camden	181	233	4	1	380	321
Campbell	210	140	..	116	308	40
Carroll	917	505	4	336	1.187	400
Catoosa	317	213	3	4	256	120
Charlton	124	58	6	2	207	31
Chatham	3,305	1,209	18	17	2,645	363
Chattaho'ch'e	111	118	..	17	107	62
Chattooga	437	716	9	28	472	378
Cherokee	826	665	6	100	622	242
Clarke	720	207	2	96	773	118
Clay	242	161	2	42	270	47
Clayton	248	223	11	99	333	59
Clinch	202	157	1	11	285	144
Cobb	889	548	18	174	1,170	220
Coffee	534	382	2	54	571	267
Colquitt	390	125	..	327	446	62
Columbia	144	12	1	185	189	2
Coweta	1,032	220	1	19	1,072	160
Crawford	285	24	..	32	314	4
Crisp	452	206	..	36	..	..
Dade	228	72	..	7	217	37
Dawson	125	219	5	5	207	260
Decatur	782	537	4	131	996	182
De Kalb	740	356	43	218	815	219
Dodge	544	177	1	44	678	98
Dooly	507	271	2	87	1,050	107
Dougherty	583	158	..	6	462	49
Douglas	152	181	4	187	231	133
Early	375	173	3	136	466	12
Echols	140	15	..	..	159	12
Effingham	302	89	1	55	370	47
Elbert	714	103	15	305	878	6
Emmanuel	549	530	8	473	519	94
Fannin	420	681	..	..	456	504
Fayette	338	162	..	151	260	59
Floyd	1,204	677	25	138	1,799	478
Forsyth	150	345	1	79	455	357
Franklin	379	253	9	329	486	207
Fulton	4,790	2,906	165	190	5,781	1,766
Gilmer	360	519	8	4	550	617
Glascock	63	52	4	264	117	11
Glynn	467	298	2	12	701	316
Gordon	476	615	1	97	525	323
Grady	463	238	33	215	..	..
Greene	412	428	25	201	451	201
Gwinnett	677	541	38	392	1,219	132
Habersham	364	230	17	77	681	183
Hall	707	634	33	94	1,204	195
Hancock	457	80	2	71	482	31
Haralson	252	506	23	106	349	477
Harris	556	94	1	77	649	80
Hart	408	192	5	200	452	93
Heard	203	5	..	34	368	14
Henry	369	194	51	27	461	64
Houston	855	27	166	..	736	78
Irwin	388	174	..	30	658	342
Jackson	735	406	12	323	964	33
Jasper	557	155	..	28	613	59
Jeff Davis	172	156	..	11	...	..
Jefferson	373	361	4	..	379	489
Jenkins	188	53	..	76	..	..
Johnson	135	162	3	355	257	59
Jones	385	332	..	28	498	29
Laurens	957	730	..	594	878	390
Lee	337	252	..	7	285	63
Liberty	219	412	1	160	242	245
Lincoln	157	1	5	249	195	.
Lowndes	681	154	31	58	888	289
Lumpkin	261	218	..	..	525	253
Macon	350	196	3	131	465	180
Madison	560	170	..	89	733	49
Marion	217	155	..	89	247	51
McDuffie	157	25	5	323	196	4
McIntosh	147	161	..	..	142	2
Meriwether	683	211	4	115	765	98
Miller	161	23	..	44	174	1
Milton	182	120	2	50	283	248
Mitchell	555	196	1	205	511	135
Monroe	456	162	..	217	278	21
Montgomery	414	254	..	213	693	241
Morgan	462	187	2	66	316	67
Murray	312	539	..	20	270	252
Muscogee	1,599	459	...	10	1,522	164
Newton	648	303	11	48	928	354
Oconee	136	51	..	240	198	99
Oglethorpe	495	67	..	112	720	6
Paulding	256	630	3	188	402	341
Pickens	187	731	4	3	347	810
Pierce	295	150	..	72	354	73
Pike	727	230	..	121	662	92
Polk	492	901	10	74	653	689
Pulaski	651	107	..	64	605	29
Putnam	410	20	..	16	550	3
Quitman	87	81	1	66	119	35
Rabun	283	171	..	13	353	131
Randolph	522	366	..	83	551	87
Richmond	1,727	267	..	345	1,706	169
Rockdale	352	172	..	87	434	133
Schley	219	173	2	04	343	35
Screven	355	428	9	357	430	25
Spalding	725	199	22	29	925	112
Stephens	306	261	..	27	..	..
Stewart	415	241	..	23	429	155
Sumter	876	476	4	36	918	159
Talbot	408	129	5	44	493	74
Taliaferro	235	216	..	130	377	184
Tattnall	584	283	18	432	621	171
Taylor	253	159	..	163	409	63
Telfair	613	29	227	..	739	50
Terrell	528	142	..	53	630	77
Thomas	765	723	7	308	862	374
Tift	450	99	..	104	..	..
Toombs	282	200	3	98	..	..
Towns	196	291	..	2	338	411
Troup	714	45	2	287	892	20
Turner	276	105	22	137	..	..
Twiggs	301	73	..	21	378	30
Union	344	418	..	5	419	466
Upson	369	145	..	249	468	77
Walker	754	925	6	32	864	501
Walton	727	389	6	225	870	240
Ware	771	190	16	12	635	158
Warren	158	166	4	257	220	68
Washington	630	267	..	479	975	195
Wayne	394	144	30	34	417	89
Webster	114	117	..	26	163	53
White	121	183	..	36	297	179
Whitfield	586	775	6	26	569	427
Wilcox	380	120	1	22	591	194
Wilkes	557	65	12	216	622	6
Wilkinson	280	55	1	55	534	37
Worth	457	237	..	251	520	572
Total	72,350	41,692	1,059	16,965	83,472	24,003
Plurality	30,658	..	...	..	59,469	..
Per cent	55.34	31.57	0.29	12.80	64.40	18.47
Scattering	....				1,042	
Whole vote	132,727				138,198	

The vote for Governor in 1906 was Hoke Smith, Dem., 94,223; Osborne, Soc., 98.

For President in 1904 Debs, Soc., received 197; Swallow, Pro., 845 votes.

For President in 1908 Debs, Soc., received 584 votes; Hisgen, Ind., 77.

The vote for Governor in 1904 was: Terrell, Dem., 67,523. No opposition.

VOTE FOR REPRESENTATIVES IN CONGRESS, 1908.

Districts.

I. Counties of Bryan, Bullock, Burke, Chatham, Effingham, Emmanuel, Liberty, McIntosh, Screven, Tattnall and Toombs. Charles G. Edwards, Dem., 9,845; James M. Elders, Rep., 427.

II. Counties of Baker, Berrien, Calhoun, Clay, Colquitt, Decatur, Dougherty, Early, Grady, Miller, Mitchell, Quitman, Randolph, Terrell, Thomas, Tift, Turner and Worth. James M. Griggs, Dem., 9,273.

GEORGIA—*Continued.*

III. Counties of Ben Hill, Crawford, Crisp, Dooly, Houston, Lee, Macon, Pulaski, Schley, Stewart, Sumter, Taylor, Twiggs, Webster and Wilcox. Dudley M. Hughes, Dem., 7,627; F. G, Boatright, Rep., 25.

IV. Counties of Carroll, Chattahoochee, Coweta, Harris, Heard, Marion, Meriwether, Muscogee, Talbot, and Troup. W. C. Adamson, Dem., 7,242.

V. Counties of Campbell, Clayton, De Kalb, Douglas, Fulton, Newton, Rockdale, and Walton. Leonidas F. Livingston, Dem., 8,909.

VI. Counties of Baldwin, Bibb, Butts, Fayette, Henry, Jones, Monroe, Pike, Spalding, and Upson. Chester L. Bartlett, Dem., 6,575.

VII. Counties of Bartow, Catoosa, Chattooga, Cobb, Dade, Floyd, Gordon, Haralson, Murray, Paulding, Polk, Walker, and Whitfield. Gordon Lee, Dem., 11.396.

VIII. Counties of Clark, Elbert, Franklin, Greene, Hart, Jasper, Madison, Morgan, Oconee, Oglethorpe, Putnam, and Wilkes. W. M. Howard, Dem., 7.112.

IX. Counties of Banks, Cherokee, Dawson, Fannin, Forsyth, Gilmer, Gwinnett, Habersham, Hall, Jackson, Lumpkin, Milton, Pickens, Rabun, Towns, Union, and White. Thomas M. Bell, Dem., 11,653.

X. Counties of Columbia, Glascock, Hancock, Jefferson, Lincoln, McDuffie, Richmond, Taliaferro, Warren, Washington, and Wilkinson. Thomas W. Hardwick, Dem., 6,853.

XI. Counties of Appling, Brooks, Camden, Charlton, Clinch, Coffee, Dodge, Echols, Glynn, Irwin, Jeff Davis, Johnson, Laurens, Lowndes, Montgomery, Pierce, Telfair, Wayne and Ware. W. G. Brantley, Dem., 9,741.

PRESENT STATE GOVERNMENT.

Governor, Hoke Smith; Secretary of State and ex-officio Com'r of Public Lands, Philip Cook; Treasurer, R. E. Park; Comptroller and ex-officio Com. of Insurance, W. A. Wright; Adjutant-General, A. J. Scott; Attorney-General, John C. Hart; State School Commissioner, Jessie M. Pound; Commissioner of Agriculture, Thos. G. Hudson—all Democrats.

JUDICIARY.

Supreme Court: Chief Justice, Wm. H. Fish; Associate Justices, Horace M. Holden, J. H. Lumpkin, M. W. Beck, Beverly D. Evans and Samuel C. Atkinson; Clerk, Z. D. Harrison—all Democrats.

STATE LEGISLATURE, 1908.

	Senate.	*House.*	*Joint Ballot.*
Democrats	44	181	225
Republicans	..	..	..
Democratic majority	44	181	225

VOTE OF THE STATE SINCE 1872.

	Dem.	*Rep.*	*Pro.*	*Maj.*
1872. President	76,278	62,715	....	13,563 D
1876. President	130,088	50,416	....	79.642 D
1880. President	102,470	54,086	....	48.384 D
1884. President	94,567	47,603	168	46.964 D
1888. President	100,499	40,496	1,808	60,203 D

	Dem.	*Rep.*	*Pop.*	*Pro.*	*Plu.*
1892. President	129,361	48,305	42,937	988	81,056 D

	Dem.	*Rep.*	*Nat. D.*	*Pop.*	*Pro.*	*Plu.*
1896. Gov'nor	120,827	....	....	85,832	....	*34,995 D
1896. Presid't.	94,232	60,091	2.708	....	5,613	34,141 D
1898. Gov'nor	118 557	51,580	....	....	....	66,977 D
1900. Gov'nor	90,448	....	....	23,235	....	*67,213 D
1900. Presid't	81,700	35,035	....	4,584	1,396	48,665 D
1902. Gov'nor	81,548	......	......	5,566	.....	*75,982 D
1904. Presid't	88,331	25,335	....	23,490	....	62,996 D
			Soc.			
1906. Gov'nor	94,223	......	98	....	....	94,125 D
1908. Presid't.	72,350	41,692	584	16,965	1,059	30,658 D

* Majority.

IDAHO.

COUNTIES. (21.)	PRESIDENT, 1908. Bryan Dem.	Taft, Rep.	Chafin, Pro.	Debs, Soc.	PRESIDENT, 1904. Parker Dem.	Roosevelt, Rep.
Ada	..	..	.	..	1,466	4,536
Bannock	..	..	..	..	1,063	2,826
Bear Lake	..	..	..	..	769	1,538
Bingham	..	..	..	..	890	3,186
Blaine	..	..	..	..	775	1,225
Boisé	..	..	..	..	639	1,053
Canyon	..	..	..	..	1,025	3,172
Cassia	..	..	..	..	346	1,105
Custer	..	..	..	..	429	496
Elmore	..	..	..	..	433	593
Fremont	..	..	..	..	1,278	3,869
Idaho	..	..	..	..	1,381	2,731
Kootenai	..	..	..	..	1,178	4,165
Latah	..	..	..	..	940	3,267
Lemhi	..	..	..	..	564	786
Lincoln	..	..	..	..	262	688
Nez Perce	..	..	..	..	1,696	3,956
Oneida	..	..	..	..	906	2,339
Owyhee	..	..	..	..	393	663
Shoshone	..	..	..	..	1,116	3,695
Washington	..	..	..	..	931	1,894
Total	36,080	52,606	1,740	6,243	18,480	47,783
Plurality	..	16,526	..	..	..	29,303
Per cent	37.27	54.33	1.77	6.23	25.33	65.85
Scattering	210				6,315	
Whole vote	96,879				72,578	

For President in 1904 Swallow, Pro., received 1,013 votes; Debs, Soc., 4,949; Watson, Pop., 353.

The vote for Governor in 1904 was: Heitfield, Dem., 24,192; Gooding, Rep., 41,877; Shaw, Soc., 4,000; Headly, Pro., 990; Bartley, Pop., 179.

VOTE FOR REPRESENTATIVE IN CONGRESS, 1908.

Exact vote unavailable as ALMANAC went to press. Thomas R. Hamer, Rep., elected by large plurality.

PRESENT STATE GOVERNMENT.

Governor, James H. Brady; Lieutenant-Governor, Lewis H. Sweetzer; Secretary of State, Robert Lansdon; Treasurer, Charles A. Hastings; Auditor, S. D. Taylor; Attorney-General, D. C. McDougal; Superintendent of Education, S. Belle Chamberlain; Inspector of Mines, to be appointed; Superintendent of Agriculture, to be appointed—all Republicans.

JUDICIARY.

Supreme Court: Chief Justice, James F. Ailshie, Rep.; Associate Justices, Isaac N. Sullivan, Rep.; George H. Stewart, Rep.; Clerk, I. W. Hart, Dem.

STATE LEGISLATURE, 1909.

	Senate.	*House.*	*Joint Ballot*
Republicans	15	39	54
Dem.-Fus	6	12	18
Republican majority.	9	27	36

VOTE OF THE TERRITORY AND STATE SINCE 1880.

	Dem.	*Rep.*			*Maj.*
1880. Congress	3,604	2,090	....	....	1,514 D
1884. Congress	1,547	741	....	....	786 D
1888. Congress	6,404	9,609	....	....	3,203 R
1890. Governor	7,948	10,262	....	....	2,314 R
			Pro.	*Pop.*	*Plu.*
1892. President	....	8,599	288	10,520	1,921 P
1892. Governor	6,769	8,178	264	4,865	1,409 R
1894. Governor	7,057	10,208	....	7,121	3,087 R
	Dem.	*Rep.*	*Pro.*	*Pop.*	*Plu.*
1896. President	23,192	6,324	179	....	16,868 D
1898. Governor	19,407	13,794	1,175	....	5,613 F
1900. Governor	28,628	26,466	1,031	....	2,227 F
1900. President	26,414	29,997	857	213	2,216 D
				Soc.	
1902. Governor	26,091	31,874	636	1,737	5,833 R
1904. President	18,480	47,783	1,013	4,949	29,303 R
1906. Governor	29,496	38,386	1,037	4,650	8,900 R
1908. President	36,080	52,606	1,740	6,243	16,526 R

ILLINOIS.

COUNTIES. (102.)	PRESIDENT, 1908.				GOVERNOR, 1908.	
	Bryan Dem.	Taft, Rep.	Chafin, Pro.	Debs, Soc.	Stevenson Dem.	Deneen, Rep.
Adams	8,294	7,233	242	496	..	..
Alexander	2,027	3,790	54	56	..	..
Bond	1,465	2,143	289	84	..	..
Boone	587	2,805	155	127	..	..
Brown	1,609	947	64	11	..	..
Bureau	2,871	5,280	534	424	..	..
Calhoun	905	735	76	8	..	..
Carroll	1,129	2,875	223	67	..	..
Cass	2,434	1,878	90	14	..	..
Champaign	4,836	7,162	472	42	..	..
Christian	4,156	3,686	324	260	..	..
Clark	2,793	3,158	159	18	..	..
Clay	2,152	2,250	96	42	..	..
Clinton	3,016	2,104	61	181	..	..
Coles	3,957	4,388	206	58	..	..
Cook	152990	230400	5,96[illegible]	18,8[illegible]2	..	..
Crawford	2,890	3,090	207	42	..	..
Cumberland	1,810	1,739	81	13	..	..
De Kalb	1,732	5,866	341	97	..	..
De Witt	2,155	2,628	188	15	..	..
Douglas	1,917	2,656	192	11	..	..
Du Page	1,975	4,530	449	77	..	..
Edgar	3,433	3,757	189	50	..	..
Edwards	747	1,614	120	14	..	..
Effingham	2,826	1,877	91	29	..	..
Fayette	3,193	3,261	203	31	..	..
Ford	1,164	2,617	178	10	..	..
Franklin	2,401	2,539	121	152	..	..
Fulton	4,906	6,077	405	568	..	..
Gallatin	1,845	1,411	81	34	..	..
Greene	3,159	2,004	166	49	..	..
Grundy	1,359	3,127	190	207	..	..
Hamilton	2,128	1,809	110	30	..	..
Hancock	4,260	3,781	226	38	..	..
Hardin	680	813	45	9	..	..
Henderson	820	1,547	102	12	..	..
Henry	2,499	6,387	478	438	..	..
Iroquois	2,966	4,855	314	67	..	..
Jackson	3,149	4,016	234	145	..	..
Jasper	2,317	1,860	131	7	..	..
Jefferson	3,377	3,210	133	83	..	..
Jersey	1,818	1,460	71	26	..	..
Jo Daviess	2,310	3,132	184	94	..	..
Johnson	1,055	1,913	81	20	..	..
Kane	4,360	12,840	613	311	..	..
Kankakee	2,461	5,999	184	74	..	..
Kendall	556	1,948	116	11	..	..
Knox	3,277	7,084	381	320	..	..
Lake	2,264	6,392	352	237	..	..
La Salle	7,589	11,159	454	705	..	..
Lawrence	2,253	2,197	192	14	..	..
Lee	2,144	4,255	232	37	..	..
Livingston	3,778	5,358	347	73	..	..
Logan	3,546	3,451	172	81	..	..
Macon	4,615	6,643	399	170	..	..
Macoupin	5,775	4,988	340	511	..	..
Madison	7,812	9,463	351	814	..	..
Marion	4,001	3,455	201	270	..	..
Marshall	1,714	1,893	113	48	..	..
Mason	2,264	1,924	204	24	..	..
Massac	652	2,084	85	7	..	..
McDonough	3,112	3,733	374	84	..	..
McHenry	1,887	5,331	194	51	..	..
McLean	5,982	8,953	840	197	..	..
Menard	1,748	1,600	135	19	..	..
Mercer	1,777	2,871	231	85	..	..
Monroe	1,512	1,733	15	9	..	..
Montgomery	3,909	3,782	318	242	..	..
Morgan	3,993	4,019	204	116	..	..
Moultrie	1,695	1,704	93	19	..	..
Ogle	1,761	4,348	338	28	..	..
Peoria	8,898	10,828	299	515	..	..
Perry	2,482	2,392	192	67	..	..
Piatt	1,530	2,349	153	12	..	..
Pike	3,859	2,932	257	185	..	..
Pope	748	1,706	58	6	..	..
Pulaski	1,080	2,185	56	19	..	..
Putnam	413	834	51	16	..	..
Randolph	3,172	3,045	151	101	..	..
Richland	1,938	1,684	122	67	..	..

ILLINOIS—*Continued.*

COUNTIES.	PRESIDENT, 1908.				GOVERNOR, 1904.	
	Bryan Dem.	Taft, Rep.	Chafin, Pro.	Debs, Soc.	Stevenson Dem.	Deneen, Rep.
Rock Island	4,739	8,196	344	1,072	..	..
Saline	2,471	3,125	124	249	..	..
Sangamon	9,351	10,422	626	458	..	..
Schuyler	1,876	1,622	216	18	..	..
Scott	1,376	1,101	71	20	..	..
Shelby	4,065	3,312	380	40	..	..
Stark	738	1,635	71	22	..	..
St. Clair	11,342	12,619	344	1,517	..	..
Stephenson	4,076	4,605	254	84	..	..
Tazewell	3,786	3,767	237	119	..	..
Union	2,690	1,695	127	12	..	..
Vermilion	6,320	11,726	824	385	..	..
Wabash	1,814	1,511	158	22	..	..
Warren	2,327	3,283	257	175	..	..
Washington	1,830	2,355	111	64	..	..
Wayne	2,791	2,946	160	26	..	..
White	2,934	2,436	147	61	..	..
Whiteside	2,140	5,257	498	64	..	..
Will	5,693	10,358	316	425	..	..
Williamson	3,513	4,786	272	484	..	..
Winnebago	2,163	8,919	531	747	..	..
Woodford	2,156	2,204	203	54	..	..
Total	450810	629932	29,364	34,711	526912	550076
Plurality	....	179122	....	....	..	23,164
Per cent	39.89	53.67	2.54	3.00	48.88	51.12
Scattering					..	
Whole vote	....	1,155,254			1,154,612	

For President in 1908, Hisgen, Ind., received 7,724 votes; Watson, Pop., 633; Turney, United Christian, 400.

For State Treasurer in 1906. Allin, Pro., received 38,393 votes; McDermott, Soc., 42,002; Francis, Soc. L., 3,757.

For President in 1904, Corrigan, Soc. L., 4,698; Watson, Pop., 6,725; Holcomb, Cont., 830.

The vote for Governor in 1904 was: Sturger, Dem, 334,880; Deneen, Rep., 634,029; Patton, Pro., 35,390; Collins, Soc. Dem., 59,062; Veal, Soc. L., 4,379; Hogan, Peo., 4,364; Speht, Cont., 780.

VOTE FOR REPRESENTATIVES IN CONGRESS, 1908

Districts.

I. County of Cook. M. L. Mandable, Dem., 13,692; M. B. Madden, Rep., 23,370; J. H. Greer, Soc., 825.

II. County of Cook. John T. Donahoe, Dem., 14,351; J. R. Mann, Rep., 32,024; F. B. Irish, Pro., 991; B. Berlyn, Soc., 2,082.

III. County of Cook. F. J. Crowley, Dem., 15,995; W. W. Wilson, Rep., 24,979; C. F. Woerner, Soc., 1,696.

IV. County of Cook. James T. McDermott, Dem., 16,606; Chas. S. Wharton, Rep., 12,196; J. P. Baldwin, Pro., 253; Wellman, Soc., 1,015.

V. County of Cook. Adolph J. Sabath, Dem., 12,927; Anthony Michalek, Rep., 9,876; C. C. Graff, Pro., 221; Siskins, Soc., 1,285.

VI. County of Cook. Frank C. Wood, Dem., 17,093; William Lorimer, Rep., 32,540; J. A. Jarvis, Soc., 1,646; Clark, Pro., 1,255.

VII. County of Cook. Frank Buchanan, Dem., 20,088; Fred Lundin, Rep., 31,513, O. R. Jenks, Pro., 1,343; George Koop, Soc., 4,183.

VIII. County of Cook. Thomas Gallagher, Dem., 15,963; P. M. Ksycki, Rep., 1[illegible],660; Thomas McLean, Soc., 1,407.

IX. County of Cook. Chas. C. Stillwell, Dem., 13,544; H. S. Boutell, Rep., 21,110; J. O. Johnson, Pro., 618; J. M. Barnes, Soc., 1,761.

X. Counties of Cook (part) and Lake. Western Starr, Dem., 14,840; Geo. E. Foss, Rep., 31,130; C. O. Boring, Pro., 1,294; A. M. Simons, Soc., 2,010; L. W. Hardy, Soc., 2,777.

XI. Counties of Du Page, Kane, McHenry and Will. C. McNaughton, Dem 15,875; H. M. Snapp, Rep., 29,821; F. Farmilo Pro., 2,227; F. L. Raymond, Soc., 776.

ILLINOIS—*Continued.*

XII. Counties of Boone, De Kalb, Grundy, Kendall, La Salle, and Winnebago, M. N. Armstrong, Dem., 13,794; Chas. E. Fuller, Rep., 33,340; C. L. Logan, Pro., 2,026; Joseph McCabe, Soc., 1,833.

XIII. Counties of Carroll, Jo Daviess, Lee, Ogle, Stephenson, and Whiteside. W. C. Green, Dem., 13,273; Frank O. Lowden, Rep., 24,797; F. W. Emerson, Pro., 1,952; G. W. Ashford, Soc., 356.

XIV. Counties of Hancock, Henderson, McDonough, Mercer, Rock Island, and Warren. M. J. McEniry, Dem., 14,745; James McKinney, Rep., 23,394; W. L. Clark, Pro., 1,573; H. Strom, Soc., 1,393.

XV. Counties of Adam, Fulton Henry, Knox, and Schuyler. W. E. Lancaster, Dem., 22,410; George W. Prince, Rep., 26,770; W. W. Vose, Pro., 1,775; E. L. Switzer, Soc., 1,731.

XVI. Counties of Bureau, Marshall, Peoria, Putnam, Stark, and Tazewell. James W. Hill, Dem., 18,557; J. V. Graff, Rep., 23,880; G. W. Warner, Pro., 1,363; J. T. White, Soc., 1,038.

XVII. Counties of Ford, Livingston, Logan, McLean, and Woodford. C. S. Schneider, Dem., 16,737; J. A. Sterling, Rep., 22,014; W. P. Allen, Pro., 2,228.

XVIII. Counties of Clark, Cumberland, Edgar, Iroquois, Kankakee, and Vermilion. Henry C. Bell, Dem., 21,795; Joseph G. Cannon, Rep., 29,170; G. B. Winter, Pro., 1,727; C. V. Walls, Soc., 490.

XIX. Counties of Champaign, Coles, De Witt, Douglas, Macon, Moultrie, Shelby, and Piatt. F. B. Hammil, Dem., 24,913; Wm. B. McKinley, Rep., 30,588; G. N. Baker, Pro., 1,985; L. Williams, Soc., 325.

XX. Counties of Brown, Calhoun, Cass, Greene, Jersey, Mason, Menard, Morgan, Pike, and Scott. Henry T. Rainey, Dem., 24,023; J. H. Danskin, Rep., 17,726; J. E. Vertrees, Pro., 1,230; W. L. Heberling, Soc., 451.

XXI. Counties of Christian, Macoupin, Montgomery, and Sangamon. Jas, M. Graham, Dem., 23,433; H. K. Wilson, Rep., 21,716; Wm. Brandon, Pro., 2,364; Koenig Kraemer, Soc., 1,442.

XXII. Counties of Bond, Madison, Monroe, St. Clair, and Washington. Chas. A. Karch, Dem., 24,341; W. A. Rodenberg, Rep., 27,858; A. J. Meek, Pro., 1,098; J. W. Taunt, Soc., 2,184.

XXIII. Counties of Clinton, Crawford, Effingham, Fayette, Jasper, Jefferson, Lawrence, Marion, Richland, and Wabash. Martin D. Foster, Dem., 28,184; Frank L. Dickson, Rep., 23,772; H. T. Davis, Soc., 646.

XXIV. Counties of Clay, Edwards, Gallatin, Hamilton, Hardin, Johnson, Massac, Pope, Saline, Wayne, and White. J. Q. A. Ledbetter, Dem., 18,333; Pleasant T. Chapman, Rep., 21,833; Montgomery, Pro., 1,070.

XXV. Counties of Alexander, Franklin, Jackson, Perry, Pulaski, Randolph, Union, and Williamson. L. R. Spilman, Dem., 20,537; N. B. Thistlewood, Rep., 24,319; P. E. Michaels, Pro., 1,262; D. W. Boone, Soc., 987.

PRESENT STATE GOVERNMENT.

Governor, Chas S. Deneen; Lieutenant-Governor, L. Y. Sherman; Secretary of State, James A. Rose; Treasurer, Andrew Russell: Auditor, J. S. McCullough; Attorney-General, W. H. Stead; Adjutant-General, to be named; Superintendent of Insurance, to be named, Superintendent of Public Instruction, Francis G. Blair—all Republicans.

JUDICIARY.

Supreme Court: Chief Justice, Jas. H. Cartright, Rep.; Associate Justices, Wm. M. Farmer, Dem.; John P. Hand, Rep.; Frank K. Dunn, Rep.; Guy C. Scott, Dem.: Alonzo K. Vickers, Rep.; Orrin N. Carter, Rep. Clerk of the Court, C. Mamer, Rep.

ILLINOIS—*Continued.*

STATE LEGISLATURE, 1909.

	Senate.	*House.*	*Joint Ballot.*
Republicans	38	89	127
Democrats	13	64	77
Republican majority.	25	25	50

VOTE OF THE STATE SINCE 1872.

		Dem.	*Rep.*	*Gr.*	*Pro.*	*Plu.*
1872.	President.	184,772	241,237	....	....	*56,445 R
1876.	President.	258,601	278,232	17,207	....	19,631 R
1880.	President.	277,321	318,037	26,358	440	40,716 R
1884.	President.	312,351	337,469	10,776	12,074	25,118 R
				Labor.		
1888.	President.	348,371	370,473	7,090	21,695	22,102 R
				Pop.		
1892.	President.	426,281	399,288	22,207	25,870	26,993 D
		D. & Pop.		*N. D.*		
1896.	President.	464,632	607,130	6,390	9,796	142,498 R
		Dem.		*Pop.*		
1898.	Treasurer.	405,490	448,940	7,886	11,753	43,450 R
				S. D.		
1900.	Governor.	518,966	580,198	8,617	15,643	61,232 R
1900.	President.	503,061	597,985	9,687	17,623	94,924 R
1902.	Treasurer.	360,925	450,695	20,167	18,434	89,770 R
1904.	President.	327,606	632,645	69,225	34,770	305,039 R
1906.	Sec. State.	271,984	417,544	42,002	88,393	145,560 R
				Soc.		
1908	President.	450,810	629,932	34,711	29,364	179,112 R

* Majority.

INDIANA.

COUNTIES. (92.)	PRESIDENT, 1908.				GOVERNOR, 1908.	
	Bryan, Dem.	Taft, Rep.	Chafin Pro.	Debs, Soc.	Marshall, Dem.	Watson, Rep.
Adams	3,404	1,726	141	13	3,311	1,743
Allen	12,145	9,468	340	494	12,983	8,447
Bartholomew	3,637	3,306	151	59	3,798	3,191
Benton	1,566	1,936	103	15	1,664	1,800
Blackford	2,214	1,835	166	42	2,261	1,775
Boone	3,525	3,471	166	11	3,557	3,439
Brown	1,177	653	68	5	1,127	642
Carroll	2,590	2,546	152	68	2,598	2,517
Cass	5,234	4,700	349	38	5,397	4,507
Clark	4,085	3,706	82	68	4,097	3,648
Clay	4,204	3,766	110	499	4,222	3,661
Clinton	3,680	3,626	281	78	3,666	3,571
Crawford	1,539	1,403	126	82	1,507	1,390
Daviess	3,253	3,424	134	204	3,183	3,413
Dearborn	3,365	2,520	94	41	3,401	2,405
Decatur	2,564	2,838	159	39	2,562	2,777
De Kalb	3,684	2,991	287	63	3,742	2,869
Delaware	5,725	7,014	475	316	6,150	6,568
Dubois	3,344	1,397	36	58	3,334	1,378
Elkhart	5,697	6,245	596	400	5,974	6,222
Fayette	1,700	2,394	114	81	1,789	2,312
Floyd	4,064	3,431	94	226	4,108	3,283
Fountain	2,846	2,894	122	45	2,860	2,791
Franklin	2,616	1,670	74	7	2,592	1,633
Fulton	2,350	2,426	125	13	2,346	2,425
Gibson	3,656	3,753	241	86	3,682	3,695
Grant	5,819	7,181	1,140	339	6,021	6,916
Greene	4,172	4,145	84	930	4,152	4,071
Hamilton	2,947	4,421	435	24	2,997	4,320
Hancock	3,040	2,472	146	22	3,027	2,441
Harrison	2,646	2,419	100	67	2,579	2,396
Hendricks	2,571	3,231	146	..	2,562	3,188
Henry	3,197	4,358	332	61	3,337	4,168
Howard	3,497	4,423	550	255	3,628	4,291
Huntington	3,712	3,973	405	241	3,762	3,918
Jackson	3,783	2,631	140	30	3,697	2,596
Jasper	1,495	1,939	70	7	1,520	1,847
Jay	3,370	3,256	426	53	3,379	3,189
Jefferson	2,708	2,995	176	97	2,745	2,879
Jennings	1,871	2,100	101	21	1,900	2,064
Johnson	3,268	2,519	193	9	3,241	2,493
Knox	5,116	4,247	199	375	5,196	4,108
Kosciusko	3,362	4,377	233	54	3,409	4,315
La Grange	1,414	2,351	133	10	1,461	2,280
Lake	5,502	9,499	125	303	6,022	8,539
Laporte	5,680	5,824	126	103	5,872	5,538
Lawrence	3,118	3,884	93	119	3,103	3,824
Madison	8,296	7,481	497	894	8,507	7,237
Marion	34,078	34,351	839	1,075	36,674	31,967

INDIANA—*Continued.*

Counties.	President, 1908.				Governor, 1908.	
	Bryan, Dem.	Taft, Rep.	Chafin Pro.	Debs, Soc.	Marshall, Dem.	Watson, Rep.
Marshall	3,287	2,947	199	55	3,261	2,911
Martin	1,733	1.667	34	11	1,720	1,637
Miami	4,176	3,820	233	187	4,293	3,683
Monroe	2.780	3,051	77	14	2,718	2,992
Montgomery	4.227	4,457	195	44	4,401	4,306
Morgan	2.789	3.074	121	44	2 807	3,032
Newton	1.190	1.645	65	8	1,299	1,531
Noble	3,239	3,507	120	29	3,374	3,368
Ohio	622	619	16	3	623	609
Orange	1.961	2,423	70	44	1,991	2,373
Owen	2,023	1,726	61	51	2,010	1,704
Parke	2,707	3,026	315	204	2,676	2,963
Perry	2.356	1,903	34	37	2.357	1,827
Pike	2,360	2,359	59	131	2,314	2,354
Porter	1,789	2,940	78	59	1.872	2,72[illegible]
Posey	3,084	2.444	147	69	3,121	2,33[illegible]
Pulaski	1,832	1,561	110	14	1,845	1,545
Putnam	3.131	2.626	121	36	3,086	2,611
Randolph	2,600	4,792	388	87	2,742	4,570
Ripley	2.749	2,660	88	76	2.803	2,583
Rush	2,544	3.102	191	13	2.563	3,070
Scott	1,243	979	51	3	1,220	976
Shelby	4,035	3,529	252	95	4,101	3,420
Spencer	2,662	2.920	61	18	2,635	2,876
Starke	1,305	1.521	43	39	1,315	1,475
Steuben	1,453	2,704	182	13	1,515	2,614
St. Joseph	8,562	11,222	272	705	9,289	10,370
Sullivan	4,659	2,942	225	398	4,497	2,905
Switzerland	1,537	1,444	58	14	1,519	1,446
Tippecanoe	4,984	6,164	289	65	5,295	5,768
Tipton	2,556	2,395	183	13	2,547	2,396
Union	808	1.066	73	18	808	1,046
Vanderburgh	8,033	9,116	135	1,034	8,775	8.469
Vermillion	1.844	2.568	217	407	1,841	2.483
Vigo	10.685	10,223	257	690	11,902	9,202
Wabash	3,116	4,091	337	87	3,219	3,991
Warren	1.045	2,092	70	3	1,061	1,994
Warrick	2,782	2,839	138	101	2,783	2,798
Washington	2.573	1,976	74	12	2,488	1,951
Wayne	4,503	6,731	179	308	5,276	5,840
Wells	3.345	2,185	482	65	3,312	2,129
White	2,326	2,423	144	19	2,337	2,387
Whitley	2,493	2,302	134	13	2 535	2,241
Total	338262	348993	18,045	13,476	348493	334040
Plurality	..	10.731	..	..	14.353	..
Per cent	47.06	48.55	2.51	1.73	50.91	49.09
Whole vote	718,776				682,533	

For President in 1904, Parker, Dem., received 274,345 votes: Roosevelt, Rep., 368,289; Swallow, Pro., 23,496; Debs, Soc., 12,013; Watson, Pop., 2,444; Corrigan, Soc. L., 1,598.

The vote for Governor in 1904 was: Kern, Dem., 274,998; Hanly, Rep., 359,362; McWhirter, Pro., 22,690; Templeton, Peo., 2,065; Hallenberger, Soc., 10,991; Dillon, Soc. Lab., 1,437. Hanly's plurality, 84,364.

VOTE FOR REPRESENTATIVES IN CONGRESS, 1908.

Districts.

I. Counties of Gibson, Posey, Pike, Spencer, Vanderburgh, and Warrick. Bohne, Dem., 23,054; Foster, Rep., 22,965; Hull. Pro., 475; Strong, Soc., 1,199. Bohne's plurality, 89.

II. Counties of Daviess, Greene, Monroe, Owen. Sullivan, Knox. Lawrence, and Martin. Cullup, Dem., 27,172; John C. Chaney, Rep., 24,609; Rome, Pro., 684; Lackey, Soc., 1,821. Cullup's plurality, 2,563.

III. Counties of Clark, Floyd, Harrison. Dubois, Orange, Crawford, Perry, Scott, and Washington. Cox, Dem., 24,139; Lewis, Rep., 18,966; Hannagan, Pro., 559; Schwartz, Soc., 314. Cox's plurality, 5,173.

IV. Counties of Dearborn, Decatur, Jackson, Brown, Bartholomew, Jennings, Jefferson, Ohio, Ripley, and Switzerland. Lincoln Dixon, Dem., 25,231; Cox, Rep., 20,726; Bigney, Pro., 901; Bumper, Soc., 261. Dixon's plurality, 4 505.

V. Counties of Clay, Parke, Vermillion, Vigo, Hendricks, Morgan, and Putnam. Ralph W. Morse, Dem., 28.844; Maxwell, Rep., 27,361; Woodward, Pro., 1.200; Van Horne, Soc., 1,548. Morse's plurality, 1,483.

VI. Counties of Fayette, Henry, Hancock, Franklin, Shelby, Union, Rush and Wayne, Kuhn, Dem., 26,065; W. C. Barnard, Rep., 26,893; Worth, Pro., 1,441; Cox, Soc., 544. Barnard's plurality, 828.

VII. Counties of Marion and Johnson. Korbly, Dem., 34,686; Jesse Overstreet, Rep., 34,003; Lemon, Pro., 87; Gabriel, Soc., 1,014. Korbly's plurality, 683.

VIII. Counties of Adams, Blackford, Delaware, Jay, Madison, Randolph, and Wells. Adair, Dem., 29,259; Nathan B. Hawkins, Rep., 23,890; Bartlett Pro., 4,322; Watles, Soc., 1,157. Adair's plurality, 5,369.

IX. Counties of Boone, Clinton, Fountain, Carroll, Hamilton, Montgomery, and Tipton. Martin A. Morrison, Dem., 27,540; C. B. Landis, Rep., 26,449; Kirkpatrick, Pro., 1,878; Sharpe, Soc., 1,157. Morrison's plurality, 1,091.

X. Counties of Benton, Laporte, Jasper, Tippecanoe, Warren, Lake, Newton, Porter, and White. Darroch, Dem., 26,742; Edgar D. Crumpacker, Rep., 32,954; Wade, Pro., 843. Crumpacker's plurality, 6,212.

XI Counties of Howard, Cass, Grant, Huntington, Miami, and Wabash. Rauch, Dem., 25,526; Charles H. Gard, Rep., 24,313; Outland, Pro., 2,327; Nix, Soc., 762. Rauch's plurality, 1,213.

XII. Counties of Allen, De Kalb, La Grange, Noble, Steuben, and Whitley. Cyrus Cline, Dem., 25,051; Gilhaus, Rep., 22,706; Eckhar , Pro., 1,062; Brunskill, Soc., 561. Cline's plurality, 2,345.

XIII. Counties of Elkhart, Kosciusko, Fulton, Pulaski, Marshall, St. Joseph, and Starke, Henry A. Barnhart, Dem., 23,509; Chas. W. Miller, Rep., 28,229; Neuman, Pro., 1,257; Dunbar, Soc., 1,128. Barnhart's plurality, 280.

PRESENT STATE GOVERNMENT.

Governor, James R. Marshall; Lieutenant-Governor, Frank J. Hall; Secretary of State, Fred A. Sims; Treasurer, Oscar Hadley; Auditor, John C. Billheimer; Attorney-General, James Bingham; Adjutant-General, Oran Perry; Superintendent of Education, F. A. Cotton; Commissioner of Insurance, Auditor *ex officio*—all Republicans except Marshall and Hall, Democrats.

JUDICIARY.

Supreme Court: Chief Justice, John H. Gillette. Justices, John V. Hadley. James H. Jordan, Leander J. Monks, Oscar H. Montgomery; Clerk of the Court, Edward V. Fitzpatrick—all Republicans.

STATE LEGISLATURE, 1909.

	Senate.	*House.*	*Joint Ballot.*
Republicans	27	40	67
Democrats	23	60	83
Majority	4 R	20 D	16 D

INDIANA—*Continued.*

VOTE OF THE STATE SINCE 1876.

	Dem.	*Rep.*	*Gr.*	*Pro.*	*Plu.*
1876. President	213.526	208.011	9,533	....	5,515 D
1880. President	225,528	232.164	12.986	...	6.641 R
1884. President	244,992	238,480	8,293	3,028	6,512 D
			U. Lab.		
1888. President	261,013	263,361	2,694	9,881	2,348 R
			Pop.		
1892. President	262,740	255,615	22,208	13,050	7.125 D
1896. President	305,573	323,754	....	3,056	18.181 R
1900. Governor	306,368	331.531	....	13.451	25.163 R
1900. President	309,584	333,063	....	13.718	26,470 R
			Soc.	*Pro.*	
1902. Sec. State	263,265	298,819	7.134	17,765	35,554 R
1904. President	274,345	368,289	12,013	23,496	93,944 R
1906. Sec. State	263,526	294,351	7,824	20,785	30,825 R
1908. President	338,262	348.993	13,476	18,045	10,731 R

IOWA.

Counties. (99.)	President, 1908.				Governor, 1908.	
	Bryan, Dem.	Taft, Rep.	Chafin Pro.	Debs. Soc.	White, Dem.	Carroll Rep.
Adair	1,322	2,185	45	24	1,323	2,015
Adams	1,325	1,595	57	30	1,319	1,524
Allamakee	1.725	2,521	40	7	1,654	2,349
Appanoose	2,167	3,161	80	322	2,140	3.008
Audubon	1,050	1,701	33	9	1,050	1,588
Benton	2,418	3,180	76	34	2,492	3,098
Blackhawk	3,127	5,437	293	244	3,118	5,318
Boone	1,958	3,368	151	350	1.839	3,129
Bremer	1,925	1,656	56	14	1.899	1.511
Buchanan	1,889	2.552	118	16	1,837	2.407
Buena Vista	1,054	2,337	86	66	924	2,185
Butler	994	2,467	79	15	945	2,160
Calhoun	1,152	2,353	152	64	1,085	2,137
Carroll	2,510	1,865	58	12	2,616	1,632
Cass	1,655	2.799	47	64	1,651	2,581
Cedar	1,986	2,455	67	22	1,993	1.976
Cerro Gordo	1.520	2,990	98	60	1.350	2,673
Cherokee	1,084	2,300	68	24	1,007	2,132
Chickasaw	1,877	1.571	35	15	1,899	1,507
Clarke	1,134	1,624	37	3	1,086	1,557
Clay	778	1,921	41	16	729	1,759
Clayton	3,026	2,773	61	30	2,972	2,515
Clinton	4,821	4,836	80	191	5.033	4.055
Crawford	2,322	2,169	69	22	2,398	1,935
Dallas	1,871	3,133	142	78	1,751	3,045
Davis	1,749	1,484	40	20	1,684	1.490
Decatur	1,809	2,149	56	58	1,771	2,079
Delaware	1,471	2,396	65	36	1,395	2,432
Des Moines	3,975	4,153	103	233	4,165	3,623
Dickinson	503	1,109	26	25	744	1,045
Dubuque	6,645	4,708	53	427	6,857	3,779
Emmet	522	1,401	24	38	486	1,354
Fayette	2,281	3,369	179	86	2,200	3,113
Floyd	1,250	2.462	48	15	1,152	2,247
Franklin	737	2,154	50	5	659	2,038
Fremont	1,979	1,949	59	21	1,906	1,856
Greene	1,152	2,574	84	16	1,143	2,453
Grundy	1,105	1,861	45	1	1,036	1,755
Guthrie	1,532	2,560	60	11	1,472	2,427
Hamilton	1,145	2,765	109	34	1,179	2,474
Hancock	804	1,750	49	3	705	1,588
Hardin	1,187	3,123	146	19	1,133	2,883
Harrison	2,425	2,914	111	108	2,308	2,838
Henry	1,606	2,653	82	11	1,474	2,480
Howard	1,408	1,530	57	55	1,337	1,465
Humboldt	587	1,818	54	9	571	1,677
Ida	1,181	1,367	19	12	1,210	1,231
Iowa	1,907	2,230	83	19	1,942	2,122
Jackson	2,545	2,542	35	109	2.559	2.334
Jasper	2,889	3,543	152	91	2.825	3,312
Jefferson	1,439	2,271	166	17	1,406	2,166
Johnson	3,314	2,758	50	14	3,154	2,661
Jones	2.176	2,453	52	23	2,115	2,349
Keokuk	2,459	2,728	151	40	2,440	2,585
Kossuth	1,826	2,612	35	9	1,758	2,493
Lee	4,706	4,262	73	86	4,528	4,082
Linn	5.493	6,938	213	121	5,002	6,558
Louisa	978	2,025	46	19	928	1,952
Lucas	1,267	1,757	109	35	1,161	1,715
Lyon	1,064	1,650	29	56	1,123	1,495
Madison	1,404	2,425	182	56	2,608	2,489
Mahaska	3,035	3,326	395	92	2,901	3,201
Marion	2,739	2,625	160	154	2,608	2,498
Marshall	1,941	3,887	309	195	1,790	3,436
Mills	1,522	1,959	55	17	1,423	1,891
Mitchell	988	1.932	36	9	915	1,820
Monona	1,732	1,977	35	15	1,671	1,897
Monroe	1,979	2,686	112	418	1,871	2,556
Montgomery	1,282	2,553	74	49	1,172	2.398
Muscatine	3,038	3,523	85	475	3,144	3,240
O'Brien	1,326	1,912	36	36	1,343	1,780
Osceola	777	1,000	18	11	767	885
Page	1,726	3,141	196	101	1,552	3,023
Palo Alto	1,340	1,639	59	61	1,120	1,300
Plymouth	2,168	2,622	99	39	2,323	2,191
Pocahontas	1,315	1,857	35	22	1,323	1,691
Polk	7,924	12,555	527	601	7,706	12,903
Pottawat'mie	5,520	6,137	169	162	5,340	5,850
Poweshiek	1,661	2,794	184	33	1,586	2,666
Ringgold	1,092	1,940	83	15	1,022	1,891
Sac	1,230	2,366	74	21	1,176	2,188
Scott	5,845	6,845	71	667	7,035	5.435
Shelby	1,935	1,973	53	33	1,947	1.876
Sioux	1,891	2,697	32	22	1,759	2,432
Story	1,195	3,790	293	52	1,049	3,506
Tama	2,550	2,774	151	38	2,477	2,635
Taylor	1,585	2,460	94	46	1,437	2,380
Union	1,843	2,207	124	37	1,712	2,186
Van Buren	1,730	2,133	77	17	1,693	2,084
Wapello	3,124	4,541	124	551	3,693	4.361
Warren	1,645	2,589	163	19	1,585	2.593
Washington	2,119	2,631	122	17	2.034	2.534
Wayne	1,756	2,092	119	45	1,694	2,001
Webster	2,374	3,658	241	192	2,316	3,274
Winnebago	489	1,710	40	9	410	1,590
Winneshiek	2,008	2,767	65	29	1,919	2,588
Woodbury	5,222	6,587	256	230	5,035	6,049
Worth	449	1,433	30	16	388	1.362
Wright	866	2,498	77	10	772	2,312
Total	266358	275210	9,837	8,287	195855	303443
Plurality	..	8,852	..	..	..	107588
Per cent	47.53	49.28	1.75	1.44	39.23	60.77
Scattering		665			....	
Whole vote		560,337			499,298	

For President in 1904 Parker, Dem., received 149,141 votes; Roosevelt, Rep., 307,907.

For President in 1904 Swallow, Pro., received 11,601 votes; Debs, Soc., 14,847; Watson, Pop., 2,207 votes.

The vote for Governor in 1903 was: Sullivan, Dem., 159,708; Cummins, Rep., 238,798; Hanson, Pro., 12,378; Work, Soc., 6,479; Weller, Peo., 589.

VOTE FOR REPRESENTATIVES IN CONGRESS, 1908.

Districts.

I. Counties of Des Moines, Henry, Jefferson, Lee, Louisa, Van Buren, and Washington. George S. Tracey, Dem., 16,965; Charles A. Kennedy, Rep., 18,318; Chas. H. Schick, Soc., 278; Geo. W. Holmes, Pro., 470. Kennedy's plurality, 1,623.

II. Counties of Clinton, Iowa, Jackson, Johnson, Muscatine, and Scott. Mark A. Walsh, Dem., 21,050; A. F. Dawson, Rep., 22,915; Kennedy, Soc., 750; Whitlock, Pro., 202. Dawson's plurality, 1,865.

III. Counties of Blackhawk, Bremer, Buchanan, Butler, Delaware, Dubuque, Franklin, Hardin and Wright. Chas. Elliott, Dem., 17,362; Chas E. Pickett, Rep., 25,530; Garwick, Soc., 684; Britnell, Pro., 734. Pickett's plurality, 8,168.

IV. Counties of Allamakee, Cerro Gordo, Chickasaw, Clayton, Fayette, Floyd, Howard, Mitchell, Winneshiek, and Worth. M. E. Geiser, Dem., 16,296; G. N. Haugen, Rep., 20,020; Thorgvinson, Soc., 218; Smith, Pro., 405. Haugen's plurality, 3,924.

IOWA—*Continued.*

V. Counties of Benton, Cedar, Grundy, Jones, Linn, Marshall, and Tama. Sam'l K. Tracy, Dem., 15,994; James W. Good, Rep., 22,776; Hanson, Soc., 342; Whitmore, Pro., 659. Good's plurality, 6,782.

VI. Counties of Davis, Jasper, Keokuk, Mahaska, Monroe, Poweshiek, and Wapello. D. W. Hamilton, Dem., 18,628; N. E. Kendall, Rep., 18,909; Minnick, Soc., 880. Kendall's plurality, 281.

VII. Counties of Dallas, Madison, Marion, Polk, Story, and Warren. Charles O. Holley, Dem., 17,620; J. A. T. Hull, Rep. 24,931; Wills, Soc., 867; Kellogg, Pro., 1,320. Hull's plurality, 7,311.

VIII. Counties of Adams, Appanoose, Clarke, Decatur, Fremont, Lucas, Page, Ringgold, Taylor, Union, and Wayne. W. D. Jamieson, Dem., 20,436; W. P. Hepburn, Rep., 20,126; Mercer, Soc., 490; Frazier, Pro., 509. Jamieson's plurality, 310.

IX. Counties of Adair, Audubon, Cass, Guthrie, Harrison, Mills, Montgomery, Pottawattamie, and Shelby, R. S. Spencer, Dem., 17,661; Walter I. Smith, Rep., 23,215; Walter Cook, Soc., 364; Kelly, Pro., 392. Smith's plurality, 5,554.

X. Counties of Boone, Calhoun, Carroll, Crawford, Emmet, Greene, Hamilton, Hancock, Humboldt, Kossuth, Palo Alto, Pocahontas, Webster, and Winnebago. Montague Hakes, Dem., 17,256; Frank P. Woods, Rep., 29,608; Bechtel, Soc., 586; Woodman, Pro., 803. Woods' plurality, 12,352.

XI. Counties of Buena Vista, Cherokee, Clay, Dickinson, Ida, Lyon, Monona, O'Brien, Osceola, Plymouth, Sac, Sioux, and Woodbury. W. G. Sears, Dem., 19,033; E. H. Hubbard, Rep., 26,572; Beach, Soc., 435 Hubbard's plurality, 7,439.

PRESENT STATE GOVERNMENT.

Governor, B. F. Carroll; Lieutenant-Governor, George W. Clarke; Secretary of State, W. C. Hayward; Treasurer, W. W. Morrow; Auditor, T. L. Bleakly; Attorney-General, H. W. Byers; Superintendent of Education, J. F. Riggs; Adjutant-General, to be appointed—all Republicans.

JUDICIARY.

Supreme Court: Chief Justice, Wm. D. Evans, Rep.; Judges, Scott M. Ladd, Emil McClain, Rep.; John C. Sherwin, Rep.; Horace E. Deemer, Rep.; S. M. Weaver. Clerk, H. L. Bousquet, Rep.

STATE LEGISLATURE, 1909.

	Senate.	*House.*	*Joint Ballot.*
Republicans	34	79	113
Democrats	16	28	44
Republican majority	18	51	69

VOTE OF THE STATE SINCE 1872.

	Dem.	*Rep.*	*Gr.*	*Pro.*	*Plu.*
1872. Pres.	71,134	131,173	....	....	*60,039 R
1876. Pres.	112,121	171,332	9,400	....	49,721 R
1880. Pres.	105,845	183,904	32,327	....	78,059 R
1884. Pres.	†177,316	197,089	....	1,472	19,773 R
1888. Pres.	179,887	211,598	9,105	3,550	31,711 R
			Pop.		
1892. Pres.	196,367	219,795	20,595	6,402	23,428 R
1895. Gov.	149,433	208,689	32,118	11,052	59,256 R
	D. & Pop.		*N. D.*		
1896. Pres.	223,741	289,293	4,516	3,192	65,552 R
1897. Gov.	194,514	224,501	4,268	8,357	29,987 R
	Dem.		*Pop.*		
1898. Sec. State	173,000	236,524	3,472	7,559	63,524 R
1899. Gov.	183,326	239,543	1,694	7,650	56,217 R
			Soc. D.		
1900. Pres.	209,466	307,785	2,778	9,479	98,606 R
1901. Gov.	143,685	226,839	3,460	15,649	83,154 R
			Soc.		
1903. Gov.	159,708	238,798	6,479	12,378	79,090 R
1904. Pres.	149,141	307,907	14,847	11,601	158,766 R
1906. Gov.	196,143	216,968	9,792	8,901	20,825 R
1908. Pres.	266,358	275,210	8,287	9,837	8,852 R

*Majority. † Democratic and Gr'nb'k Fusion vote.

KANSAS.

Counties. (106.)	President, 1908. Bryan, Dem.	Taft, Rep.	Chafin Pro.	Debs, Soc.	Governor, 1908. Botkin Dem.	Stubbs Rep.
Allen	2,579	3,283	36	204	2,570	3,291
Anderson	1,512	1,722	61	65	1,503	1,722
Atchison	2,592	3,244	18	48	2,946	2,886
Barber	864	1,097	36	45	850	1,107
Barton	2,004	1,729	24	100	2,007	1,746
Bourbon	2,686	2,695	42	211	2,627	2,785
Brown	2,044	2,778	50	61	2,020	2,781
Butler	2,290	3,049	160	149	2,361	3,007
Chase	834	1,021	24	46	816	1,037
Chautauqua	958	1,689	11	148	964	1,666
Cherokee	3,819	3,893	51	1,030	3,807	3,889
Cheyenne	339	486	20	41	325	487
Clark	350	386	12	24	333	407
Clay	1,495	1,858	52	102	1,479	1,866
Cloud	1,663	2,170	76	242	1,620	2,189
Coffey	1,729	2,094	63	35	1,688	2,132
Comanche	245	392	10	10	238	398
Cowley	2,995	3,578	109	396	3,234	3,392
Crawford	4,230	5,152	54	1,631	4,231	5,048
Decatur	1,250	898	41	94	1,244	919
Dickinson	2,782	2,886	94	152	2,321	2,889
Doniphan	1,113	2,307	18	33	1,049	2,344
Douglas	2,010	3,279	70	49	2,032	3,279
Edwards	704	773	35	27	696	783
Elk	1,187	1,454	21	25	1,198	1,459
Ellis	1,421	768	17	20	1,348	821
Ellsworth	1,039	1,213	26	13	1,091	1,173
Finney	551	1,000	18	58	539	1,017
Ford	1,089	1,333	36	44	1,062	1,356
Franklin	2,155	2,658	134	92	2,129	2,716
Geary	1,033	1,257	27	38	1,047	1,257
Gove	456	632	26	33	455	644
Graham	723	911	15	95	722	908
Grant	133	178	2	12	127	183
Gray	338	372	21	64	336	377
Greeley	89	206	3	21	86	208
Greenwood	1,545	2,370	22	69	1,527	2,384
Hamilton	275	415	4	30	271	419
Harper	1,404	1,490	69	112	1,365	1,535
Harvey	1,475	2,305	77	99	1,477	2,304
Haskell	139	172	6	36	136	177
Hodgeman	290	411	12	7	283	421
Jackson	1,494	2,201	39	17	1,480	2,230
Jefferson	1,720	2,270	31	64	1,685	2,301
Jewell	1,932	2,410	110	54	1,920	2,420
Johnson	2,091	2,313	28	88	2,060	2,373
Kearny	304	435	2	26	292	447
Kingman	1,479	1,442	45	84	1,440	1,471
Kiowa	409	699	30	37	399	718
Labette	2,783	3,367	54	643	2,828	3,311
Lane	271	357	16	49	262	365
Leavenworth	3,818	4,846	43	288	4,011	4,630
Lincoln	1,117	1,218	30	58	1,091	1,249
Linn	1,657	1,950	31	126	1,699	1,953
Logan	308	524	18	32	279	558
Lyon	2,562	2,973	147	161	2,544	3,025
Marion	1,747	2,546	80	57	1,712	2,605
Marshall	2,514	3,296	53	32	2,614	3,190
McPherson	1,905	2,708	51	55	1,837	2,781
Meade	386	560	24	26	363	600
Miami	2,256	2,475	26	91	2,301	2,442
Mitchell	1,570	1,765	42	118	1,561	1,797
Montgomery	4,030	5,166	57	661	4,074	5,119
Morris	1,273	1,788	28	19	1,264	1,801
Morton	140	154	5	6	143	154
Nemaha	2,182	2,394	33	32	2,172	2,396
Neosho	2,386	2,929	29	166	2,486	2,840
Ness	461	635	117	109	437	652
Norton	1,337	1,448	66	59	1,367	1,413
Osage	2,288	2,671	86	264	2,188	2,813
Osborne	1,182	1,665	169	45	1,056	1,708
Ottawa	1,265	1,444	65	83	1,245	1,445
Pawnee	961	1,000	36	68	981	986
Phillips	1,490	1,762	55	65	1,503	1,754
Pottawatomie	1,680	2,650	19	11	1,693	2,637
Pratt	1,027	1,193	73	67	1,050	1,189

KANSAS—*Continued.*

Counties.	President, 1908.				Governor, 1908.	
	Bryan, Dem.	Taft, Rep.	Chafin, Pro.	Debs, Soc.	Botkin Dem.	Stubbs Rep.
Rawlins	732	789	7	59	710	734
Reno	3,381	4,092	114	175	3 492	4,032
Republic	1,905	2,156	67	35	1,876	2,200
Rice	1,407	1,832	217	110	1,392	1 877
Riley	1,289	2,276	58	65	1,222	2,379
Rooks	1,003	1,280	51	75	1,003	1,292
Rush	894	764	9	30	878	774
Russell	976	1,360	18	27	974	1,361
Saline	2,134	2,297	38	116	2,218	2,222
Scott	294	324	8	61	272	347
Sedgwick	6,049	6,756	247	390	6,399	6,478
Seward	413	427	15	33	403	446
Shawnee	5,585	7,554	112	170	5,915	7,270
Sheridan	631	639	15	22	632	649
Sherman	508	439	13	46	489	460
Smith	1,593	1 843	78	51	1,612	1 811
Stafford	1,135	1,334	99	48	1,121	1,346
Stanton	107	180	3	6	106	181
Stevens	215	258	23	39	205	272
Sumner	2,772	3,235	95	204	2,860	3,144
Thomas	458	617	20	32	615	578
Trego	630	569	22	44	442	619
Wabaunsee	1,163	1,849	33	24	1,124	1,921
Wallace	206	350	11	23	183	378
Washington	1,904	2,711	53	46	1,893	2,720
Wichita	173	233	1	22	166	238
Wilson	1,777	2,428	40	324	1,770	2,426
Woodson	1,047	1,252	12	41	1,035	1,278
Wyandotte	8,923	8,684	117	528	9,180	8,477
Total	161209	197216	5,033	12,420	162385	196692
Plurality	..	38,007	..	..	..	34,307
Per cent	42.91	52.49	1.08	3.31	45.23	54.77
Scattering	15,696				....	
Whole vote	375,941				359,077	

For President in 1904 Watson, Pop., received 6,156 votes.

The vote for Governor in 1904 was: Dale, Dem., 116,991; Hoch, Rep., 186,731; Louther, Soc., 12,101; Kerr, Pro., 6,584. Hoch's plurality, 69.740.

The vote for President in 1904 was: Parker, Dem., 84,800; Roosevelt, Rep., 210,893.

The scattering vote for Governor in 1908 was: Socialist, 11,721; Prohibition, 3,886; Independent, 68.

VOTE FOR REPRESENTATIVES IN CONGRESS, 1908.

Districts.

I. Counties of Atchison, Brown Doniphan, Jackson, Jefferson, Leavenworth, Nemaha, and Shawnee. F. M. Pearl, Dem., 19,842; D. R. Anthony, Rep., 27,792; J. F. Willets, Soc., 650; Anthony's plurality, 7,950.

II. Counties of Allen, Anderson, Bourbon, Douglas, Franklin, Johnson, Linn, Miami, and Wyandotte B. J. Sheridan, Dem., 26,242; Charles F. Scott, Rep., 28,499: S. M. Stallard, 1,311; D. W. Johnson, 374. Scott's plurality, 2,257.

III. Counties of Chautauqua, Cherokee, Cowley, Crawford, Elk, Labette, Montgomery, Neosho, and Wilson. T. J, Hudson, Dem., 23,377; P. P. Campbell, Rep., 29,207; B. F. Wilson, 5,776; J. B. Cook, 328; F. D. Warren, 2,908; J. H. Roberts, 540. Campbell's plurality, 5,830.

IV. Counties of Chase, Coffey, Greenwood Lyon, Marion, Morris, Osage, Pottawatomie, Wabaunsee, and Woodson. T. H. Grisham, Dem., 16,024; J. M. Miller, Rep., 20,978; W. J. Milliken, 587; E. C. Lindley, 381; Miller's majority, 3,970.

V. Counties of Clay, Cloud, Geary, Dickinson, Marshall, Ottawa, Republic, Riley, Saline, and Washington. R. A. Lovitt, Dem., 18,555; J. D. Calderhead, Rep., 21,093; W. L. Nixon, 824; W. H. Eaton, 439. Calderhead's majority, 1,275.

VI. J. R. Connelly, Dem., 21,922; W. A. Reeder, Rep., 22,200; H. M. Olcott, 961; T. C. Griffith, 617. Reeder's plurality, 277.

KANSAS—*Continued.*

VII. S. T. Hale, Dem., 21,460; E. H. Madison, Rep., 23,615; J. N. Brown, 1,419; H. R. Ross, 893. Madison's plurality, 4,855.

VIII. F. B. Lawrence, Dem., 13,477; Victor Murdock, Rep., 19,029; W. A. Roe, 809; Robert Piatt, 445. Murdock's plurality, 5,582.

PRESENT STATE GOVERNMENT.

Governor, W. R. Stubbs; Lieutenant-Governor, W. J. Fitzgerald; Secretary of State, C. E. Denton; Treasurer, Mark Tullay; Auditor, J. M. Nation; Attorney-General, F. S. Jackson; Adjutant-General, to be named; Superintendent of Education, E. T. Fairchild; Commissioner of Agriculture, F. D. Coburn; Superintendent of Insurance, Chas. Barnes—all Republicans.

JUDICIARY.

Supreme Court: Chief Justice, Wm. A. Johnston; Associate Justices, Chas. B. Graves, Silas Porter, Clark A. Smith, Rousseau A. Burch, Henry F. Mason and Alfred W. Bensen, all Republicans; Clerk, D. A. Valentine.

STATE LEGISLATURE. 1909.

	Senate.	*House.*	*Joint Ballot.*
Republicans	37	94	131
Democrats	3	31	34
Republican majority	34	63	97

VOTE OF THE STATE SINCE 1872.

	Dem.	Rep.	Gr.	Pro.	Plu.
1872. President	32,970	66,805	....	....	*33,835 R
1876. President	37,002	78,322	7,770	....	40,120 R
1880. President	59,789	121,520	19,710	....	61,731 R
1884. President	90,132	154,406	16,341	4,954	64,274 R
1886. Governor	115,697	149,615	....	8,094	33,918 R
			U. L.		
1888. President	102,745	182,904	37,788	6,779	80,159 R
			Pop.		
1892. President	....	157,237	163,111	4,539	5,874 P
1894. Governor	26,709	148,697	118,329	5,496	30,368 R
	Dem.-Pop.		N. D.		
1896. President	171,810	159,541	1,209	1,921	12,269DP
			Soc.L.		
1898. Governor	134,158	149,292	642	1,092	15,134 R
1900. Governor	164,794	181,893	....	2,662	17,099 R
			Soc.D.		
1900. President	162,601	185,955	1,258	3,605	23,354 R
			Soc.		
1902. Governor	117,148	159,242	4,098	6,065	42,094 R
1904. President	84,800	210,893	15,494	7,245	126,093 R
1906. Governor	150,024	152,147	4,463	7,621	2,123 R
1908. President	161,209	197,216	12,420	5 033	38,007 R

* Majority.

KENTUCKY.

Counties. (119.)	President, 1908.				Governor, 1907.	
	Bryan, Dem.	Taft, Rep.	Chafin Pro.	Debs, Soc.	Hager, Dem.	Willson, Rep.
Adair	1,429	1,872	64	..	1,320	1,708
Allen	1,402	1,922	58	4	1,269	1,739
Anderson	1,477	1,040	46	1	1,206	1,039
Ballard	2,117	706	34	63	1,595	592
Barren	3,145	2,308	102	8	2,724	2,034
Bath	1,754	1,471	42	6	1,466	1,349
Bell	925	2,815	30	88	666	1,951
Boone	2,041	631	31	6	1,565	560
Bourbon	2,508	2,312	48	14	2,339	2,229
Boyd	1,950	2,894	63	53	1,548	2,563
Boyle	1,787	1,485	44	10	1,577	1,358
Bracken	1,510	1,100	44	47	1,265	983
Breathitt	1,567	1,620	32	..	1,168	1,395
Breckinridge	2,090	2,603	81	28	1,963	2,262
Bullitt	1,409	726	34	7	1,054	634
Butler	1,012	2,328	55	3	846	2,061
Caldwell	1,541	1,517	42	31	1,306	1,445
Calloway	3,024	808	101	25	2,056	800
Campbell	6,813	7,025	120	810	4,025	6,058
Carlisle	1,625	482	55	22	1,176	365
Carroll	1,514	546	45	2	1,262	590
Carter	1,595	2,620	70	27	1,586	2,349
Casey	1,191	1,878	27	6	1,098	1,616
Christian	3,120	4,618	59	19	2,605	3,925
Clark	2,525	1,859	52	20	2,335	1,806

KENTUCKY—*Continued.*

COUNTIES.	PRESIDENT, 1908.				GOVERNOR, 1907.	
	Bryan, Dem.	Taft, Rep.	Chafin Pro.	Debs, Soc.	Hager, Dem.	Willson, Rep.
Clay	691	1,991	26	9	628	1,691
Clinton	330	1.082	34	18	343	989
Crittenden	1.309	1,714	26	14	1,145	1,494
Cumberland	605	1,172	26	1	525	868
Daviess	5 218	3,922	143	30	3,750	3,138
Edmonson	858	1,291	16	6	722	1,260
Elliott	1 159	618	8	..	1,162	574
Estill	995	1,503	43	..	816	1,264
Fayette	5 247	4,748	108	30	4,912	4,598
Fleming	2,057	1,934	52	3	1,804	1.840
Floyd	1,691	1,557	32	4	1,446	1.151
Franklin	3,233	1,632	32	9	2,856	1,606
Fulton	1,705	636	25	6	1,004	459
Gallatin	958	321	7	2	809	270
Garrard	1,259	1,578	49	5	1,225	1,449
Grant	1,654	1,099	32	5	1.396	1,083
Graves	4 952	1,744	115	108	3,730	1,754
Grayson	1,864	2,360	33	..	1,648	2,140
Green	1,167	1 337	23	10	1,077	1,258
Greenup	1,441	2,142	74	78	1,205	1,480
Hancock	868	1.052	48	11	698	881
Hardin	3,010	1,913	29	30	2,330	1.786
Harlan	252	1,392	17	1	217	1,517
Harrison	2,797	1,571	61	..	2,428	1,556
Hart	1,766	1,950	54	31	1,728	1,824
Henderson	3,735	2,528	85	163	2,479	1.790
Henry	2.253	1,358	51	..	2,027	1,402
Hickman	1,890	658	30	8	1.246	443
Hopkins	3,721	3,315	101	68	2.764	2,756
Jackson	232	1,851	5	2	197	1,686
Jefferson	26.183	27,180	438	653	19,078	28,047
Jessamine	1,574	1,271	95	12	1,256	1,208
Johnson	1,094	2,336	21	40	927	2.076
Kenton	8,683	6,431	135	505	6,370	7,504
Knott	1,110	576	18	..	1,019	504
Knox	867	2,788	28	96	876	2,531
Larue	1,337	1,029	13	4	1,026	960
Laurel	1,165	2 594	42	15	975	2,216
Lawrence	1,878	2,098	47	6	1,829	1,678
Lee	783	1,171	12	2	638	1,018
Leslie	95	1,399	4	3	120	1,246
Letcher	476	1,158	9	2	409	857
Lewis	1,268	2,549	65	23	1.171	2,125
Lincoln	1,994	1,851	94	2	1,619	1,611
Livingston	1,183	997	41	53	1,106	889
Logan	3,114	2,326	67	46	2,433	2,010
Lyon	1 001	759	21	4	746	691
Madison	3,055	3 191	49	16	2,711	2,789
Magoffin	1,005	1,645	29	3	982	1,426
Marion	2 098	3,121	10	2	1,568	1,508
Marshall	1,852	1,217	62	8	1,364	1,040
Martin	240	1,042	11	7	160	749
Mason	2 675	2,126	85	14	2,433	2,151
McCracken	4.127	2 966	64	100	2,944	2,856
McLean	1,430	1,319	75	20	1,164	1,042
Meade	1,295	863	18	15	1,117	721
Menifee	833	451	..	..	680	894
Mercer	1,747	1,567	82	3	1,482	1,494
Metcalfe	968	1,311	25	1	923	1,142
Monroe	770	1,861	20	1	776	1,690
Montgomery	1 549	1,305	32	6	1.257	1,211
Morgan	2,013	1.400	15	..	1,345	1,132
Muhlenberg	2 740	3,063	61	90	2,133	2,612
Nelson	2,452	1,438	26	4	1,813	1,368
Nicholas	1,723	1 085	46	8	1,559	1,049
Ohio	2.785	3,337	91	74	2,348	2,985
Oldham	1,259	625	38	11	744	544
Owen	2,732	735	13	1	2,223	791
Owsley	224	1,240	6	..	245	1.157
Pendleton	1,543	1,177	60	38	1,304	1,201
Perry	524	1,274	13	6	432	1,156
Pike	2,208	3,467	81	5	2,058	2,766
Powell	739	699	24	1	634	566
Pulaski	2,460	4,483	146	25	1,929	3,913
Robertson	688	398	11	3	592	309
Rockcastle	962	1,816	48	2	769	1,533
Rowan	757	1,017	27	5	652	858
Russell	739	1,255	78	18	631	1,027
Scott	2,476	1,794	33	7	2,106	1,801
Shelby	2,742	1,823	87	4	2,192	1,696
Simpson	1,714	913	24	3	1,361	951
Spencer	1 175	563	21	1	882	485
Taylor	1,294	1,218	58	1	1,148	1,107
Todd	1,908	1,555	23	6	1,363	1,436
Trigg	1,680	1,351	20	39	1,347	1,250
Trimble	1,322	344	25	9	1,060	331
Union	2,781	1,312	41	87	2,098	997
Warren	3,742	2,929	100	17	2,734	2,626
Washington	1,615	1,515	16	8	1,416	1,582
Wayne	1,436	1,936	48	2	1,264	1,472
Webster	2,491	1,828	83	11	1,872	1 497
Whitley	1,111	4,023	39	..	823	3,415
Wolfe	1,101	818	21	1	899	653
Woodford	1,690	1,369	36	2	1,419	1,305
Total	244092	235711	5,887	4,060	196428	214481
Plurality	8,381	..		..	..	18.053
Per cent	49.84	48.13	1.20	.83	48.64	51.36
Whole vote	489,750				410,909	

For President in 1904, Parker, Dem., received 217,170 votes; Roosevelt, Rep., 205,277; Debs, Soc., 3,602; Corrigan, Soc. Lab., 596.

The vote for Governor in 1903 was: Beckham, Dem., 229,014; Belknap, Rep., 202,764; Demarc, Pro., 4,830; Nagle, Soc., 2,044; Schmutz, Soc. Lab., 615.

The vote for President in 1900 was: Bryan, Dem., 235,103; McKinley, Rep., 227,128; Woolley, Pro., 3,780; Barker, Pop., 1,861; Debs, Soc., 645; Malloney, Soc. Lab., 390.

For President in 1908, Hisgen, Ind., received 200 votes; Watson, Pop., 353; Gilhaus, Soc. Lab., 404.

VOTE FOR REPRESENTATIVES IN CONGRESS, 1908.

Districts.

I. Counties of Ballard, Caldwell, Calloway, Carlisle, Crittenden, Fulton, Graves, Hickman, Livingston, Lyon, Marshall, McCracken, and Trigg. Ollie M. James, Dem., 37,435; J. M. Porter, Rep., 15,063; Ford, Soc., 210. James's plurality, 12,372.

II. Counties of Christian, Daviess, Hancock, Henderson, Hopkins, McLean, Union, and Webster. A. O. Stanley, Dem., 23,320; John C. Worsham, Rep., 19,302; Farmer, Soc., 299; Stanley's majority, 13,709.

III. Counties of Allen, Barren, Butler, Edmonson, Logan, Metcalfe, Monroe, Muhlenberg, Simpson, Todd, and Warren. R. G. Thomas, Jr., Dem., 20,079; A. D. James, Rep., 19,583; Green, Soc., 377. Thomas's plurality, 496.

IV. Counties of Breckinridge, Bullitt, Grayson, Green, Hardin, Hart, Larue, Marion, Meade, Nelson, Ohio, Taylor, and Washington. Ben Johnson, Dem., 24,344; D. W. Gaddie, Rep., 21,246; Redman, Soc., 165. Johnson's plurality, 3,098.

V. County of Jefferson. Swagar Sherley, Dem., 27,915; R. C. Kinkead, Rep., 25.513; Dobbs, Soc., 658. Sherley's plurality, 2,440.

VI. Counties of Boone, Campbell, Carroll, Gallatin, Grant, Kenton, Pendleton, and Trimble. Joseph L. Rhinock, Dem., 23,945; John R. Inglis, Rep., 18,057; Thobe, Soc., 1,221. Rhinock's plurality, 5,888.

VII. Counties of Bourbon, Fayette, Franklin, Henry, Oldham, Owen, Scott, and Woodford. James C. Cantrill, Dem., 21,157; L. L. Bristow, Rep., 14,706. Cantrill's plurality, 7,441.

VIII. Counties of Anderson, Boyle, Garrard, Jessamine, Lincoln, Madison, Mercer, Rockcastle, Shelby, and Spencer. Harvey Helm, Dem., 17,725; L. W. Bethurum, Rep., 16,049; Johnson, Pro., 442. Helm's plurlity, 1,676.

KENTUCKY—*Continued.*

IX. Counties of Bracken, Bath, Boyd, Carter, Fleming, Greenup, Harrison, Lewis, Lawrence, Mason, Nicholas, Robertson, and Rowan. Jas. N. Kehoe, Dem., 22,107; Joseph B. Bennett, Rep., 22 832; Morris, Pro., 462. Bennett's plurality, 725.

X. Counties of Breathitt, Clark, Elliott, Estill, Floyd, Johnson, Knott, Lee, Martin, Magoffin, Montgomery, Morgan, Menifee, Pike, Powell, and Wolfe. Amos Davis, Dem., 19,567; J. W. Langley, Rep., 22,438; Ward, Soc., 25. Langley's plurality, 2,871.

XI. Counties of Adair, Bell, Casey, Clay, Clinton, Harlan, Knox, Letcher, Leslie, Laurel, Metcalfe, Owsley, Perry, Pulaski, Russell, Wayne, and Whitley A. G. Patterson, Dem., 14,729; D. C. Edwards, Rep. 36,073; Huffaker, Pro., 518. Edwards's plurality, 21,344.

PRESENT STATE GOVERNMENT.

Governor, A. E. Willson; Lieutenant-Governor, W. H. Cox; Secretary of State, Ben H. Bruner; Treasurer, Edwin Farley; Auditor, Frank P. James; Attorney-General, J. B. Breathitt; Superintendent of Education, John G. Crabbe; Commissioner of Agriculture, M. C. Rankin—all Republicans.

JUDICIARY.

Court of Appeals: Chief Justice, Ed. C. O'Rear, Rep.; Justices, W. E. Settle, Dem.; H. S. Barker, Dem.; Thomas J. Nunn, Dem.; John M. Lassing, Dem.; John D. Carroll, Dem.; J. P. Hobson, Dem.; Clerk, Napier Adams, Rep.

STATE LEGISLATURE, 1909.

	Senate.	*House.*	*Joint Ballot*
Democrats	22	51	73
Republicans	16	49	65
Democratic majority	6	2	8

VOTE OF THE STATE SINCE 1876.

	Dem.	*Rep.*	*Gr.*	*N.D.*	*Pro.*	*Plu.*
1876. Pres	159,690	97,156	1,944	....	....	62,634 D
1880. Pres	147,999	104,550	11,498	....	....	43,449 D
1884. Pres	152,961	118,763	1,693	....	3,139	34,198 D
			Lab.			
1888. Pres	183,800	155,134	622	....	5,225	28,666 D
			Pop.			
1892. Pres	175,461	135,441	23,500	....	6,442	40,020 D
1896. Pres	217,890	218,171	....	5,114	4,781	281 R
1899 Gov	191,331	193,714	3,038	....	2,346	2,383 R
1900. Pres	235,103	227,128	1,861	....	3,780	7,975 D
1903. Gov	229,014	202,764	4,830	....	....	27,250 D
1904. Pres	217,170	205,277	2,511	......	6,609	11,873 D
1907. Gov	196,428	214,481	....	....	6,352	18,053 R
1908. Pres	244,092	235,711	....	....	5,887	9,371 D

LOUISIANA.

Parishes. (59.)	President, 1908.			Governor, 1904.	
	Bryan, Dem.	Taft, Rep.	Debs, Soc.	Blanchard, Dem.	Behan Rep.
Acadia	1,017	214	141	877	100
Ascension	551	107	9	775	538
Assumption	511	198	1	785	464
Avoyelles	1,240	50	16	900	10
Baton Rouge, East	1,090	83	20	722	21
Baton Rouge, West	198	9	..	242	15
Bienville	926	65	131	542	34
Bossier	470	8	9	326	1
Caddo	1,733	125	46	1,328	18
Calcasieu	1,975	683	185	1,618	149
Caldwell	314	21	58	245	12
Cameron	660	15	2	222	13
Carroll, East	194	6	1	151	2
Carroll, West	189	11	46	114	3
Catahoula	660	88	114	419	64
Claiborne	874	38	24	589	13
Concordia	288	4	11	209	..
De Soto	881	17	41	506	2
Feliciana, East	589	12	2	285	8
Feliciana, West	350	22	..	247	5
Franklin	456	15	12	300	2
Grant	388	83	52	335	35
Iberia	820	328	52	685	160
Iberville	500	44	..	638	238
Jackson	493	77	51	375	5
Jefferson	1,122	30	..	1,364	53
Lafayette	725	128	121	741	36
Lafourche	1,072	296	5	1,259	267
Lincoln	634	52	26	549	29
Livingston	448	19	30	373	4
Madison	156	6	..	125	..
Morehouse	458	20	19	334	4
Natchitoches	792	143	42	512	83
Orleans	25,678	3,288	253	16,843	1,852
Ouachita	851	60	27	353	15
Plaquemines	416	127	15	663	20
Pointe Coupée	653	23	..	487	1
Rapides	1,302	159	40	839	51
Red River	386	6	72	303	5
Richland	445	9	..	189	3
Sabine	593	47	38	390	7
St. Bernard	356	18	..	529	19
St. Charles	215	22	..	414	30
St. Helena	281	34	1	197	19
St. James	364	123	8	483	301
St. John Baptist	287	33	2	379	28
St. Landry	1,395	238	14	918	71
St. Martin	651	39	18	392	21
St. Mary	767	273	27	949	263
St. Tammany	755	107	73	401	11
Tangipahoa	1,116	240	27	515	49
Tensas	300	7	..	134	5
Terrebonne	634	372	7	979	398
Union	634	53	24	421	4
Vermilion	547	156	50	429	54
Vernon	618	272	241	592	49
Washington	550	49	1	313	15
Webster	853	32	109	346	13
Winn	527	153	206	594	186
Total	63,568	8,958	2,538	48,345	5,877
Majority	..	..	...	42,468	..
Plurality	54,610	..	..	..	..
Per cent	84.59	11.92	.33	89.34	10.66
Whole vote		75,146		54,222	

VOTE FOR REPRESENTATIVES IN CONGRESS, 1908.

Districts.

I. Parishes of Plaquemines and St. Bernard, and part of the City of New Orleans. Adolph Meyer, Dem., 8,667; Henry Seiner, Rep., 681; Alex. Smith, Soc., 284.

II. Parishes of Jefferson, St. Charles, St. John Baptist, and St. James, and part of the City of New Orleans. Robert C. Davey, Dem., 6,349; A. L. Redden, Rep., 409; W. C. Hall, Soc., 154.

III. Parishes of Assumption, Iberia, Lafayette, Lafourche, St. Martin, St. Mary, Terrebonne, and Vermilion. Robt. F. Broussard, Dem., 4,267; S. P. Watts, Rep., 753.

IV. Parishes of Bienville, Bossier, Caddo, De Soto, Natchitoches, Red River, Sabine, Webster, and Winn. John T. Watkins, Dem., 3,210; E. P. Mills, Rep., 88.

V. Parishes of Caldwell, East Carroll, West Carroll, Catahoula, Claiborne, Concordia, Franklin, Jackson, Lincoln, Madison, Morehouse, Ouachita, Richland, Tensas, and Union. Joseph E. Ransdell, Dem., 3,177. No opposition.

LOUISIANA—*Continued.*

VI. Parishes of Baton Rouge, East; Baton Rouge, West; Feliciana, East; Feliciana, West; Livingston, Pointe Coupée, St. Helena, St. Tammany, Tangipahoa, and Washington. George K. Favrott, Dem., 3,370; John Deblieux, Rep., 269.

VII. Parishes of Acadia, Avoyelles, Calcasieu, Cameron, Grant, Rapides, St. Landry, and Vernon. A. P. Pujo, Dem., 3,761; C. C. Duson, Rep., 1,762; James Barnes, Soc., 165.

PRESENT STATE GOVERNMENT.

Governor, J. Y. Sanders; Lieutenant-Governor, P. M. Lambremont; Secretary of State, J. T. Michel; Auditor, Paul Capdeville; Treasurer, O. B. Steele; Attorney-General, Walter Guion; Superintendent of Education, T. H. Harris—all Democrats.

JUDICIARY.

Supreme Court: Chief Justice, J. A. Breaux: Associate Justices, A. D. Land, F. T. Nichols, Frank A. Monroe, O. O. Provosty; Clerk, T. McC. Hyman—all Democrats.

STATE LEGISLATURE, 1909.

Both Houses Democratic; Senate, 41; House, 116.

VOTE OF THE STATE SINCE 1872.

	Dem.	*Rep.*		*Maj.*
1872. President......	66,467	59,975		6,492 D
1872. President......	*57,029	71,634		14,605 R
1876. President......	83,723	77,174		6,549 D
1876. President......	*70,508	75,315		4,807 R
1880. President......	65,067	38,628		26,439 D
1884. President......	62,529	46,347		16,182 D
1888. President......	85,032	30,484		54,548 D
		Fusion.		
1892. President......	87,922	26,563		61,359 D
1896. Governor......	116,216	90,138		26,078 D
		Rep.	*Nat.D.*	*Plu.*
1896. President......	77,175	22,037	1,834	55,138 D
1900. Governor......	60,206	2,449	....	†48,580 D
1900. President......	53,671	14,233	....	†39,438 D
			Soc.	
1904. President......	47,708	5,205	995	42,503 D
1908. President......	63,568	8,958	2,538	54,610 D

* Count of the Rep. Returning Board. † Majority.

MAINE.

COUNTIES. (16.)	PRESIDENT, 1908.				GOVERNOR, 1908.	
	Bryan, Dem.	Taft, Rep.	Chafin Pro.	Debs, Soc.	Gardner, Dem.	Fernald, Rep.
Androscoggin.	3,095	4,381	..	..	5,609	4,907
Aroostook.....	1,157	4,783	..	..	3,102	5,671
Cumberland...	5,735	10,593	..	..	11,656	9,974
Franklin......	930	2,173	..	..	1,492	2,450
Hancock......	1,846	3,169	..	..	3,304	4,033
Kennebec.....	2,842	6,132	..	..	6,135	6,846
Knox........	1,932	2,228	..	..	3,658	2,448
Lincoln........	1,196	1,693	..	..	2,212	2,077
Oxford........	2,093	4,179	..	..	3,030	4,424
Penobscot	3,526	7,336	..	..	8,286	7,217
Piscataquis....	828	2,157	..	..	1,686	2,104
Sagadahoc	838	1,776	..	..	1,513	1,791
Somerset......	1,676	3,688	..	..	3,738	3,800
Waldo	1,335	2,491	..	..	3,022	3,134
Washington ..	2,256	3,507	..	..	3,791	3,861
York	4,076	6,700	..	..	5,523	7,299
Total	35,403	65,987	1,487	1,758	66,075	73,728
Plurality......	..	30,584	..	..	..	7,653
Per cent.......	33.38	62.05	1.39	1.65	..	..
Scattering	1,810				....	
Whole vote..	106,335				142,658	

The vote for Governor in 1904 was: Davis, Dem., 49,791; Cobb, Rep., 75,591; Woodbury, Pro., 2,756; Hopgood, Soc., 1,576.

The vote for President in 1904 was: Parker, Dem., 27,641; Roosevelt, Rep., 64,432.

MAINE—*Continued.*

VOTE FOR REPRESENTATIVES IN CONGRESS, 1908.

Districts.

I. Counties of Cumberland and York. John C. Scates, Dem., 15,615; Amos L. Allen, Rep., 18,887; Joseph Lafontaine, Soc., 373; A. N. Whitam, Pro., 433. Allen's plurality, 3,272.

II. Counties of Androscoggin, Franklin, Knox, Lincoln, Oxford, and Sagadahoc. D. J. McGillicuddy, Dem., 17,115; Jno. P. Swasey, Rep., 18,479; A. J. Dunton, Pro., 376; G. A. England, Soc., 492. Swasey's plurality, 1,264.

III. Counties of Hancock, Kennebec, Somerset, and Waldo. Sam'l W. Gould, Dem., 15,611; Edwin C. Burleigh, Rep., 18,282; W. G. Sterling, Pro., 220; R. G. Henderson, Soc., 350. Burleigh's plurality, 2,661.

IV. Counties of Aroostook, Penobscot, Piscataquis, and Washington. George M. Hanson, Dem., 16 152; Frank E. Guernsey, Rep., 19,659, W. A. Rideout, Pro., 359; D. W. Ross, Soc., 359. Guernsey's plurality, 3,507.

PRESENT STATE GOVERNMENT.

Governor, Bert M. Fernald; Secretary of State, A. I. Brown; Treasurer, P. P. Gilmore; Adjutant-General, A. B. Farnham; Attorney-General, H. E. Hamlin; Superintendent of Education, Payson Smith; Insurance Commissioner, S. W. Carr—all Republicans.

JUDICIARY.

Supreme Judicial Court: Chief Justice, L. A. Emery; Associate Justices, L. C. Cornish, Albert M. Spear, W. P. Whitehouse, G. E. Bird, Albert R. Savage, A. W. King and Henry C. Peabody—all Republicans except Bird: Clerks, E. F. Tompson, C. W. Jones, C. F. Ewert, Reps.

STATE LEGISLATURE, 1909.

	Senate.	*House.*	*Joint Ballot.*
Republicans...........	23	100	123
Democrats	8	51	59
Republican majority	15	49	64

VOTE OF THE STATE SINCE 1872.

	Dem.	*Rep.*	*Gr.*	*Pro.*	*Plu.*
1872. President..	29,087	61,422	....	....	*32,335 R
1876. President..	49,823	66,300	663	....	16,477 R
1880. President..	65,171	74,039	4,408	235	8,868 R
1884. President	51,656	71,715	3,994	2,160	20,060 R
			Lab.		
1888. President..	50,481	73,734	1,344	2,691	23 253 R
1890. Governor..	45,331	64,214	1,298	2,981	18,883 R
			Pop.		
1892. President..	48,044	62,923	2,381	3,062	14,979 R
1894. Governor..	30,621	69,599	5,321	2,730	38,978 R
			N. D.		
1896. President..	34 688	80,465	1,870	1 570	45,777 R
1898. Governor..	29,497	54 266	315	2,335	24,769 R
			Soc. D.		
1900. Governor..	39,823	73,955	632	3,538	34,132 R
1900. President..	36,822	65,435	878	2,585	28,613 R
1902. Governor..	38,349	65,839	1,973	4,376	27,490 R
1904. President..	27,630	64,437	2,103	1,510	36,807 R
1906. Governor..	61,477	69,315	1,553	1,139	7,838 R
1908. President..	35,403	65,987	1,758	1,487	31,584 R

* Majority.

MARYLAND.

COUNTIES. (24.)	PRESIDENT, 1908.		PRESIDENT, 1904.		GOVERNOR, 1907.	
	Bryan, Dem.	Taft, Rep.	Parker Dem.	Roosevelt, Rep.	Crothers, Dem.	Gaither, Rep.
Allegany.	4,791	5,132	3,326	5,232	3,141	4,214
Anne Arund'l	3,435	2,924	3,001	2,849	2,598	2,536
Baltimore C'y	49,139	50,383	47,901	47,444	9,285	6,937
Baltimore Co.	10,297	9,619	9,394	7,570	45,777	41,634
Calvert........	714	1,067	740	1,030	753	952
Caroline......	1,945	1,542	1,809	1,452	1,653	1,397
Carroll	3,641	3,351	3,527	3,357	3,264	3,053
Cecil	2,847	2,317	2,554	2,425	2,292	1,954
Charles.......	1,167	1,538	1,180	1,659	878	1,330
Dorchester...	2,769	2,623	2,087	2,680	2,153	2,270

MARYLAND—*Continued.*

Counties.	President, 1908.		President, 1904.		Governor, 1907.	
	Bryan, Dem.	Taft, Rep.	Parker Dem.	Roosevelt, Rep.	Crothers, Dem.	Gaither, Rep.
Frederick	5,158	5,779	5,004	5,788	4,355	5,443
Garrett	1,121	2,045	947	2,051	836	1,630
Harford	3,143	2,566	3,151	2,561	2,731	2,187
Howard	1,764	1,238	1,914	1,258	1,965	1,026
Kent	1,939	1,731	1,956	1,841	1.616	1,420
Montgomery .	3,351	2,629	3,082	2,711	2,830	2,326
Pr'ce George's	2,680	2,635	2,270	2,845	1,949	1,985
Queen Anne's	2.086	1,130	2,258	1,487	1,682	1,131
Somerset......	1,627	1,907	1,247	1,874	1,659	1,587
St. Mary's....	1,021	1,323	1,580	1,174	922	1,124
Talbot.........	2,025	1,905	1,861	1,999	1 789	1,402
Washington ..	4,518	4,604	4,064	4,581	3,737	3,944
Wicomico	2,751	2,250	2,593	2,179	2,439	1,832
Worcester	1,974	1,515	2,000	1,450	1,747	986
Total	115908	113803	109446	109497	102051	94,300
Plurality	2,105	..	..	51	7,751	..
Per cent	49.51	48.30	48.81	48.81	55.45	44.55
Scattering.....	6,010		5,286		4,215	
Whole vote.	235,821		224,229		208.686	

In 1908, one Taft elector received the highest vote, 116,513. Six Democratic and two Republican electors were chosen. The scattering vote for President was: Chafin, Pro., 3,302; Debs, Soc., 2,323; Hisgen, Ind., 485.

VOTE FOR REPRESENTATIVES IN CONGRESS, 1908.

Districts.

I. Counties of Caroline, Cecil, Dorchester, Kent, Queen Anne's, Somerset, Talbot, Wicomico, and Worcester. James H. Covington, Dem., 19,381; Wm. H. Jackson, Rep., 16,547; Wheatley, Pro., 868. Covington's plurality, 2,734.

II. Baltimore City, counties of Baltimore, Carroll, and Harford. J. F. C. Talbot, Dem., 21,526; R. Garrett, Rep., 19,040; Grill, Pro. 701; Talbot's plurality, 1,468.

III. Baltimore City. Harry B. Wolf, Dem., 14,510; John Kronmiller, Rep., 14,772; Whitehurst, Pro., 267; Jarboe, Soc., 531. Kroumiller's plurality, 262.

IV. Baltimore City. John Gill, Jr., Dem., 18,562; J. P. Hill, Rep., 16,626; Woods, Pro., 449; Gill's plurality, 1,936.

V. Counties of Howard, Anne Arundel, Prince George, St. Mary's, Calvert, and the 21st., 23d and 24th wards of Baltimore City. G. M. Smith, Dem., 14,740; S. E. Mudd, Rep., 15,057; Mahews, Soc., 613. Mudd's plurality, 317.

VI. Counties of Allegany, Frederick, Garrett, Montgomery, and Washington. D. J. Lewis, Dem., 18,073; G. A. Pearre, Rep., 18,619; Cuppett, Pro., 811; Young, Soc., 439. Pearre's plurality, 546.

PRESENT STATE GOVERNMENT.

Governor, Austin L. Crothers; Secretary of State, N. Winslow Williams; Treasurer, Murray Vandiver; Comptroller, Joshua Herring; Adjutant-General, Henry W. Warfield; Attorney-General, Isaac L. Strauss; Superintendent of Education, M. Bates Stevens; Commissioner of Insurance, B. Frank Crouse; Commissioner of Public Lands, Thos. A Smith—all Democrats.

JUDICIARY.

Court of Appeals: Chief Judge, James McSherry; Associate Judges, N. Chas. Burke, A. Hunter Boyd, Henry Page, I. Thomas Jones, John P. Briscoe, S. D. Schmucker, and James A. Pearce; Clerk, Caleb C. Magruder—all Democrats except Schmucker, Republican.

STATE LEGISLATURE, 1909.

	Senate.	*House.*	*Joint Ballot.*
Democrats	17	71	88
Republicans............	9	30	39
Ind. Dem..............	1	..	1
Democratic majority..	7	41	48

MARYLAND—*Continued.*

VOTE OF THE STATE SINCE 1876.

		Dem.	Rep.	Gr.	Pro.	Plu.
1876.	President.	91,780	71,981	....	....	*19,799 D
1880.	President.	93,706	78,515	818	....	15,191 D
1884.	President.	96,866	82,748	578	2,827	11,118 D
1888.	President.	106,168	99,986	....	4,767	6,182 D
				Pop.		
1892.	President.	113,866	92,736	796	5,877	21,130 D
1895.	Governor.	106,169	124,936	989	7,719	18,767 R
				N. D.		
1896.	President.	104,735	136,959	2,507	5,918	32,224 R
1899.	Governor.	125,409	116,286	......	5,275	12,114 D
				S. D.		
1900.	President.	122,271	136,312	908	4,582	13,941 R
1903.	Governor.	108,548	95,923	1,302	2,913	12,625 D
1904.	President.	109,446	109,497	2,247	3,034	51 R
1907.	Governor.	102,051	94,800	....	3,776	7,751 D
1908.	President.	115,908	113,803	....	3,302	2,105 D

* Majority.

MASSACHUSETTS.

Counties. (14.)	President, 1908.				Governor, 1908.	
	Bryan Dem.	Taft, Rep.	Chafin, Pro.	Debs, Soc.	Vahey Dem.	Draper, Rep.
Barnstable....	..	..	..	..	777	5,149
Berkshire.....	..	..	..	..	5.564	8,513
Bristol	..	..	..	..	11,107	17,831
Dukes	..	..	..	..	113	555
Essex	..	..	..	..	20,221	30.724
Franklin......	..	..	..	..	1,624	4,392
Hampden	..	..	..	..	9,515	14,020
Hampshire ..	..	..	..	..	2.555	5.036
Middlesex	..	..	..	..	35,153	50,160
Nantucket ...	..	..	..	..	135	356
Norfolk	..	..	..	..	8,917	15,455
Plymouth	..	..	..	..	6,356	10,956
Suffolk	..	..	..	..	48,011	37,248
Worcester	..	..	..	..	18,114	29,923
Total ......*	155543	265966	4,374	10,779	168162	228318
Plurality......	..	..	..	..	..	...
Per cent	...	..	...	..	..	..
Scattering	......				....	
Whole vote.	....				....	

*Vote by counties on electors not available. Official totals only announced by State canvassers.

For Governor, 1907, Whitney received 13,547 votes on Dem. Citizens, Independent Citizens and no designation tickets; Hisgen, Independence League, 75,489; Prohibition Party, 3,810; Brown, Soc., 7,621; Brennan, Soc. Lab., 2,999.

For President in 1908, Hisgen, Ind., received 19,237 votes; Gilhaus, Soc. Lab., 1,011.

For President in 1904, Corrigan, Soc. L., received 2,359 votes; Watson, Pop., 1.294.

VOTE FOR REPRESENTATIVES IN CONGRESS. 1908.

Districts.

I. Counties of Berkshire, Franklin (part). Hampden (part), Hampshire (part). David T. Clark, Dem., 10,765; George P. Lawrence, Rep., 17,990; Walter Hutchins, Soc. 1,136. Lawrence's plurality, 7,725.

II. Counties of Franklin (part), Hampden (part), Hampshire (part), Worcester (part). John L. Rice, Dem., 7,839; Frederick H. Gillett, Rep., 17,515; Curtis, Ind., 1,623; Orr, Soc., 1,266. Gillett's plurality, 9,676.

III. County of Worcester (part). William I. McLaughlin, Dem., 9,654; Charles G. Washburn, Rep., 18,265; Sturtevant, Ind., 1,456. Washburn's plurality, 8,611.

IV. Counties of Worcester (part) and Middlesex (part). John J. Mitchell, Dem., 15,431; C. Q. Tirrell, Rep., 18,842. Tirrell's plurality, 3,411.

V. Counties of Essex (part) and Middlesex (part). Joseph J. Flynn, Dem., 11,910; Butler Ames, Rep., 16,251; George Conley Ind., 845. Ames's plurality, 4,341.

VI. County of Essex (part). Arthur Withington, Dem., 7,334; Augustus P. Gardner, Rep., 22,093; F. H. Wentworth, Soc., 2,418. Gardner's plurality, 14,759.

MASSACHUSETTS—*Continued.*

VII. Counties of Essex (part), Middlesex (part). George Brickett, Dem., 7,958; Ernest W. Roberts, Rep., 22,179; C. L. McIver, Ind., 2,078. Roberts' plurality, 14,211.

VIII. County of Middlesex (part). Fred'k S. Deetrick, Dem., 9 638; Samuel W. McCall, Rep., 19,147; G. W. Jennings, Ind., 1,320. McCall's majority, 8,439.

IX. County of Suffolk (part). John A Keliher, Dem., 14,060; John A. Campbell, Rep., 6.002; Auerbach, Ind., 2.492. Keliher's plurality, 8,058.

X. Counties of Suffolk (part), Norfolk (part). Joseph F. O'Connell, Dem., 16,553; J. M. Galvin, Rep., 16,549; C. J. Kidney, Ind., 1,187. O'Connell's plurality, 4.

XI. County of Suffolk (part). Andrew J. Peters, Dem., 15,881; Daniel W. Lane, Rep., 15,447; E. M. White, Ind., 1,260. Peters's plurality, 434.

XII. Counties of Bristol (part), Norfolk (part). David W. Murray, Dem., 10,591; John W. Weeks, Rep., 21,097; Jesse C. Joy, Dem., 9,069; A. E. George, Ind., 779. Weeks's plurality, 12,028.

XIII. Counties of Dukes, Nantucket, Bristol (part), and Plymouth (part). John F. McGuiness, Dem., 4,977; Wm. S. Greene, Rep., 16,870; Copeland, Ind., 1,436. Greene's majority, 10,457.

XIV. Counties of Barnstable, Plymouth (part), and Bristol (part). Eliot L. Packard, Dem., 6,709; Wm. C. Lovering, Rep., 20,959; C. B. Drew, Ind., Soc., 1,855. Lovering's plurality, 14,250.

PRESENT STATE GOVERNMENT.

Governor, Eben S. Draper, Rep.; Lieutenant-Governor, Louis A. Frothingham; Secretary of State, Wm. M. Olin; Treasurer, Arthur B. Chapin; Auditor, Henry E. Turner; Adjutant-General, W. H. Brigham; Attorney-General, Dana Malone; Secretary of the Board of Agriculture, J. Lewis Ellsworth; Commissioner of Insurance, Frank C. Hardison—all Republicans.

JUDICIARY.

Supreme Judicial Court for the Commonwealth: Chief Justice, Marcus P. Knowlton; Justices, James M. Morton, Arthur P. Rugg, Henry Newton Sheldon, John W. Hammond, William C. Loring, and Henry K. Braley; Clerk of the Court, Walter F. Frederick—all Republicans.

STATE LEGISLATURE, 1909.

	Senate.	*House.*	*Joint Ballot.*
Republicans	34	172	204
Democrats	6	59	65
Others	...	9	...
Republican majority	28	104	132

VOTE OF THE STATE SINCE 1872.

	Dem.	*Rep.*	*Gr.*	*Pro.*	*Plu.*
1872. President	59,195	138,495	....	....	74,300 R
1876. President	108,777	150,063	....	....	41,286 R
1880. President	111,960	165,205	4,548	682	53,245 R
1884. President	122,352	146,724	24,382	9,923	24,372 R
			Lab.		
1888. President	151,855	183,892	....	8,701	32,037 R
			Pop.		
1892. President	176,813	202,814	3,210	7,539	26,001 R
1894 Governor	123,930	189,307	9,037	9,965	65,377 R
1895. Governor	121,599	186,280	7,786	9,170	64,681 R
	Dem.-Pop.	*Rep.*	*N. D.*	*Pro.*	
1896. Governor	103,662	258,204	14,164	4,472	154,542 R
1896. President	105,711	278,976	11,749	2,998	173,265 R
1897. Governor	79,552	165,095	13,879	4,948	85,543 R
			Soc.		
1899. Governor	103,802	168,902	10,778	7,402	65,100 R
1900. President	156,997	238,866	2,599	6,190	71,869 R
1901. Governor	114,362	185,809	8,898	4,780	71,447 R
1902. Governor	159,156	196,276	39,708	3,538	37,120 R
1903. Governor	163,700	199,684	25,251	5,278	35,984 R
1904. President	165,746	257,822	13,604	4,279	92,076 R
1905. Governor	174,911	197,469	12 874	3,286	22 558 R
1907. Governor	*70,842	188,068	7,621	3,819	103,689 R
1908. President	155,543	265,966	10,779	4,374	110,423 R

*Total Dem. vote, including Independent Citizens', etc., 84,379.

MICHIGAN.

COUNTIES. (85.)	PRESIDENT, 1908.				GOVERNOR, 1908.	
	Bryan, Dem.	Taft, Rep.	Chafin, Pro.	Debs, Soc.	Hemans, Dem.	Warner, Rep.
Alcona	176	826	24	54	205	792
Alger	235	1,006	22	60	271	971
Allegan	2,211	5,479	294	135	3,230	4,451
Alpena	952	2,377	34	116	1,250	2,104
Antrim	576	2,032	101	59	929	1,695
Arenac	717	1,085	60	67	849	971
Baraga	293	770	19	14	305	756
Barry	2,139	3,254	246	21	2,907	2,490
Bay	4,223	6,760	180	403	5,107	5,905
Benzie	555	1,442	210	77	814	1,216
Berrien	4,606	7,269	275	276	5,518	6,520
Branch	2,400	3,721	188	131	3,343	2,836
Calhoun	4,253	6,859	473	530	6,320	4,951
Cass	2,474	3,092	148	128	3,041	2,540
Charlevoix	806	2,538	149	176	1,138	2,243
Cheboygan	1,217	2,081	130	84	1,561	1,788
Chippewa	1,182	2,422	130	37	1,573	2,114
Clare	567	1,350	38	22	788	1,130
Clinton	2,193	3,493	147	23	3,544	2,158
Crawford	248	593	12	28	370	471
Delta	1,101	3,257	84	80	1,192	3,164
Dickinson	549	2,515	176	44	594	2,463
Eaton	3,148	4,883	208	89	4,951	2,639
Emmet	1,016	2,323	204	184	1,281	2,059
Genesee	3,267	7,268	444	303	5,194	5,334
Gladwin	393	1,195	48	31	550	1,029
Gogebic	617	2,265	147	60	726	2,151
Gr'd Traverse	1,301	2,821	134	27	1,937	2,225
Gratiot	2,374	4,164	178	33	3,363	3,209
Hillsdale	2,549	4,517	280	43	4,475	2,463
Houghton	2,421	9,381	627	371	3,102	8,568
Huron	1,481	3,590	164	57	1 775	3,381
Ingham	5,025	6,725	585	157	8,702	3,194
Ionia	3,241	4,598	461	92	4,379	3,544
Iosco	670	1,227	40	9	930	970
Iron	265	2,060	40	22	292	2,037
Isabella	1,666	3.185	133	53	2,450	2,427
Jackson	5,234	6,768	331	161	8,843	3,240
Kalamazoo	4,518	6,571	455	425	6,267	4,931
Kalkaska	359	1,158	105	46	609	951
Kent	11,494	16,668	859	947	18,837	9,979
Keweenaw	64	1,029	16	25	80	1,008
Lake	254	678	14	31	320	620
Lapeer	1,657	3,454	289	34	2,072	3,029
Leelanau	578	1,368	46	23	849	977
Lenawee	4,704	6,607	398	28	6,471	4,553
Livingston	2,418	2,740	219	10	3,238	1,936
Luce	108	357	31	4	132	334
Mackinac	773	1,161	23	10	903	1,028
Macomb	3,158	4,497	226	34	3,709	3,933
Manistee	1,805	2,709	109	139	2.458	2,099
Marquette	1,378	5,635	261	331	1,833	5,104
Mason	1,136	2,590	151	52	1.510	2,237
Mecosta	1,183	2.721	151	80	1,702	2,388
Menominee	1,313	2,862	128	79	1,275	2,903
Midland	889	2,004	53	43	1,222	1,712
Missaukee	446	1,573	51	19	587	1,452
Monroe	3,457	4,208	211	50	4,141	3,534
Montcalm	1,725	4,585	193	116	2,638	3,666
M'ntm'r'ncy	189	588	3	8	240	524
Muskegon	1,863	5,103	149	273	3,774	3,284
Newaygo	962	2,682	148	69	1,391	2,295
Oakland	3,962	6,287	423	107	5,032	5,988
Oceana	808	2,462	259	58	1,197	2,142
Ogemaw	458	1,225	81	25	608	1,083
Ontonagon	429	1,259	18	47	495	1.177
Osceola	769	2,826	146	5	1,409	2,118
Oscoda	114	832	8	3	128	316
Otsego	276	866	34	15	431	725
Ottawa	2,441	5,659	262	165	3,694	4,422
Presque Isle	305	1,722	18	57	412	1,611
Roscommon	149	430	18	18	213	381
Saginaw	7,025	9,464	244	558	10,573	5,884
Sanilac	1,484	4,184	358	43	2,043	3,685
Schoolcraft	295	1,364	42	16	317	1,350
Shiawassee	2,350	4,211	526	171	3,700	2,988
St. Clair	3,754	7,334	332	295	5,110	6,065
St. Joseph	2,773	3,464	173	108	3,870	2,929

MICHIGAN—*Continued*

Counties.	President, 1908.				Governor, 1908.	
	Bryan Dem.	Taft, Rep.	Chafin, Pro.	Debs, Soc.	Hemans, Dem.	Warner, Rep.
Tuscola........	1,575	4,448	331	46	2,338	3,684
Van Buren....	2,335	4,565	195	129	3,265	3,623
Washtenaw ..	4,441	5,845	305	88	7,126	3,168
Wayne........	24,603	50,618	1,446	2,461	35,714	40,456
Wexford	832	2,892	237	89	1,284	2,495
Total........	175771	335580	16,974	11,586	252611	262141
Plurality......	..	160409	..	..	..	109853
Per cent.......	32.34	62.00	313	212	37.13	57.78
Scattering.....		..			..	
Whole vote.		541,230			537,653	

For Governor, 1906, Richtér, Soc. L., received 1,153 votes.

For President in 1904 Swallow, Pro., received 13,308 votes; Debs Soc., 8,941; Watson, Pop., 1,159; Corrigan, Soc. L., 1,012.

The vote for Governor in 1904 was: Ferris, Dem., 223 571; Warner, Rep., 283,799; Shackelton, Pro., 10,375; Lamb, Soc., 6,170; Meyer, Soc. L., 781; Warner's plurality, 60,228.

VOTE FOR REPRESENTATIVES IN CONGRESS, 1908.

Districts.

I. County of Wayne (part). Edwin Denby, Rep., re-elected.

II. Counties of Lenawee, Monroe, Jackson, Washtenaw, and Wayne (part). Chas. E. Townsend, Rep., re-elected.

III. Counties of Branch, Hillsdale, Kalamazoo, Calhoun, and Eaton. Washington Gardner, Rep., re-elected.

IV. Counties of St. Joseph, Cass, Berrien, Van Buren, Allegan, and Barry. Edward L. Hamilton, Rep., re-elected.

V. Counties of Ottawa, Kent, and Ionia. Gerrit J. Diekema, Rep., re-elected.

VI. Counties of Oakland, Genesee, Livingston, Ingham, and Wayne (part). Samuel W. Smith, Rep., re-elected.

VII. Counties of Macomb, Lapeer, St. Clair, Sanilac, Huron, and Wayne (part). Henry McMorran, Rep., re-elected.

VIII. Counties of Clinton, Saginaw, Shiawassee, and Tuscola. Joseph W. Fordney, Rep., re-elected.

IX. Counties of Muskegon, Oceana, Newaygo, Mason, Lake, Manistee, Wexford, Benzie, Leelanaw, and Manitou. James C. McLaughlin, Rep., re-elected.

X. Counties of Bay, Midland, Gladwin, Arenac, Ogemaw, Iasco, Alcona, Oscoda, Crawford, Montmorency, Alpena, Presque Isle, Otsego, Cheboygan, and Emmet. George A. Loud, Rep., re-elected.

XI. Counties of Montcalm, Gratiot, Isabella, Mecosta, Osceola, Clare, Roscommon, Missaukee, Kalkaska, Grand Traverse, Antrim, and Charlevoix. Francis H. Dodds, Rep., elected.

MICHIGAN—*Continued.*

XII. Counties of Delta, Schoolcraft, Chippewa, Mackinac, Ontonagon, Marquette, Menominee, Dickinson, Baraga, Houghton, Keweenaw, Isle Royal, Alger, Luce, Iron, Cass, and Gogebic. H. Olin Young, Rep., re-elected.

PRESENT STATE GOVERNMENT.

Governor, Fred. M. Warner; Lieutenant-Governor, P. H. Kelley; Secretary of State, Fred'k C. Martindale; Treasurer, Al. E. Sleeper; Auditor, Oramell B. Fuller; Attorney-General, John E. Bird; Adjutant-General, William T. McGurrin; Superintendent of Education, Luther L. Wright; Commissioner of Insurance, James V. Barry; Commissioner of State Land Office, Huntley Russell—all Republicans.

JUDICIARY.

Supreme Court: Chief Justice, Claudius B. Grant; Justices, William L. Carpenter, Rep.; Joseph D. Moore, Rep.; Aaron V. McAlvay, Rep.; R. M. Montgomery, Rep.: Frank A. Hooker; Charles A. Blair, Russell C. Ostrander; Clerk, Charles C. Hopkins, Rep.

STATE LEGISLATURE, 1909.

	Senate.	*House.*	*Joint Ballot.*
Republicans	32	98	130
Democrats...............	..	2	2
Republican majority	32	96	128

VOTE OF THE STATE SINCE 1872.

	Dem.	*Rep.*	*Gr.*	*Pro.*	*Plu.*
1872. Pres....	78,350	138,458	....	....	*60,108 R
1876. Pres....	141,595	166,901	9,060	....	*25,306 R
1880. Pres....	131,300	185,190	34,795	....	53,890 R
	Dem.-Gr.†		*Str.-Gr.*		
1884. Gov.....	186,887	190,840	414	22,207	3,953 R
1884. Pres....	189,361	192,669	753	18,403	3,308 R
1886. Gov.....	174,042	181,474	....	25,179	7,432 R
	Dem.		*U. L.*		
1888. Pres....	213,469	236,387	4,555	20,945	22,923 R
			Indus.		
1890. Gov.....	183,725	172,205	13,198	28 651	11,520 D
1891. Sup. Ct.	148,271	153,211	9,121	14,144	4,940 R
			Pop.		
1892. Pres....	202,296	222,708	19,892	14,069	20,412 R
1893. Sup. Ct.	148,712	164,754	14,469	14,526	16,039 R
1894. Gov.....	130,823	237,215	30,012	18,788	106,392 R
1895. Sup. Ct.	108,807	189,294	25,943	18,116	80,487 R
	Dem.-Pop.		*N. D.*		
1896. Gov.....	221,022	304,431	9,738	5,499	83,409 R
1896. Pres....	236,714	293,582	6,879	5,025	56,868 R
			Pop.		
1898. Gov.....	168,142	243,239	1,656	7,006	75,097 R
1899. Sup. Ct..	165,482	216,828	4,856	8,789	51,346 R
			Soc. D.		
1900. Gov.....	226,228	305,612	2,709	11,834	79,384 R
1900. Pres....	211,685	316,269	2,826	11,859	104,584 R
1902. Gov....	174,077	211,261	4,271	11,326	37,184 R
1903. Sup. Ct.	127,582	215,825	6,402	14,611	88,243 R
1904. Gov.....	134,151	361,866	8,941	13,308	227,715 R
1906. Gov.....	129,963	227,557	5,926	9,140	97,594 R
1908. Gov.....	299,394	309,247	....	....	9,853 R
1908. Pres.....	225,057	323,786	....	....	98,729 R

*Majority. † Fusion.

MINNESOTA.

Counties. (85.)	President, 1908. Bryan, Dem.	Taft, Rep.	Chafin Pro.	Debs, Soc.	Governor, 1908. Johnson, Dem.	Jacobson, Rep.
Aitkin	389	1,205	57	143	869	796
Anoka	610	1,577	56	42	1,246	1,049
Becker	728	2,058	186	223	1,535	1,546
Beltrami	648	1,878	45	381	1,387	1,306
Benton	765	1,001	50	230	1,055	805
Big Stone	585	967	89	51	950	670
Blue Earth	2,191	3,297	206	142	3,113	2,708
Brown	1,536	1,518	55	246	2,023	1,371
Clearwater	164	779	46	181	430	628
Carlton	506	1,487	51	833	1,147	930
Carver	1,101	1,739	35	21	1,811	1,234
Cass	461	1,009	16	11	798	774
Chippewa	799	1,409	144	82	1,054	1,309
Chisago	408	2,107	49	71	1,377	1,257
Clay	1,124	1,858	111	65	1,588	1,695
Cook	42	255	1	..	136	172
Cottonwood	526	1,240	93	19	731	1,070
Crow Wing	661	1,681	66	410	1,334	1,219
Dakota	1,778	2,481	131	108	2,622	1,834
Dodge	515	1,454	96	19	846	1,232
Douglas	979	1,844	165	70	1,681	1,341
Faribault	1,039	2,305	357	26	1,363	2,181
Fillmore	1,153	3,259	175	77	1,620	3,003
Freeborn	976	2,465	421	167	1,483	2,310
Goodhue	1,149	4 480	148	198	2,568	3,394
Grant	876	1,099	69	25	668	896
Hennepin	16,169	27,789	145	94	27,456	17,804
Houston	744	1,699	68	11	976	1,485
Hubbard	401	1,288	46	124	742	1,086
Isanti	466	1,198	196	185	1.204	739
Itasca	684	1,883	95	25	1,503	1,195
Jackson	1,013	1,575	58	24	1,289	1,364
Kanabec	242	803	43	65	482	680
Kandiyohi	947	2,312	222	145	1,731	1,802
Kittson	499	968	83	61	928	684
Koochiching	420	826	39	188	722	602
Lac Qui Parle	661	1,894	25	13	791	2,017
Lake	152	584	41	362	571	348
Le Sueur	1,699	1,819	79	199	2,223	1,592
Lincoln	683	891	63	27	888	742
Lyon	1,043	1,618	146	46	1,209	1,530
McLeod	1,506	1,579	131	21	2,045	1,137
Marshall	730	1,644	185	177	1,462	1,165
Martin	1,054	1,922	184	91	1,713	1,422
Meeker	1,111	1,928	44	35	1,894	1,327
Mille Lacs	427	1,119	33	20	849	918
Morrison	1,513	1 936	23	3	2,223	1,361
Mower	1,206	2,629	124	180	1,807	2,161
Murray	762	1,283	55	33	1,068	1,028
Mahnomen	193	265	10	2	308	173
Nicollet	832	1,392	72	50	1,546	858
Nobles	925	1,432	107	58	1,428	982
Norman	661	1,276	195	177	843	1.301
Olmsted	1,621	2,470	21	11	2,163	2,033
Otter Tail	2,320	3,964	321	208	3,669	2,931
Pine	801	1,548	85	303	1,544	968
Pipestone	491	1,057	49	..	731	825
Polk	1,979	3,311	192	556	2.932	2,705
Pope	441	1.794	75	23	760	1,596
Ramsey	11,613	16,556	163	79	18,753	11,132
Red Lake	856	1,428	60	342	1,475	1,121
Redwood	1.076	1,821	88	54	1,474	1,632
Renville	1,364	2,275	110	28	1,943	2,072
Rice	1,614	2,822	111	40	2,607	2,973
Rock	525	1,234	55	17	816	966
Roseau	444	900	61	361	769	747
St. Louis	4,467	12,078	401	1,305	9,082	8,369
Scott	1,548	1,045	52	12	1,995	758
Sherburne	366	1,003	67	42	657	772
Sibley	1,110	1,624	59	12	1,878	1,087
Stearns	3,835	2,614	127	159	4,879	1,881
Steele	1,284	1,899	104	88	1,723	1,631
Stevens	576	877	37	16	798	769
Swift	921	1,343	84	41	1,259	1,140
Todd	1,305	2,334	163	258	1,863	2,027
Traverse	513	685	34	13	734	501
Wabasha	1.416	2,150	77	39	2,135	1,546
Wadena	467	990	29	70	698	800
Waseca	1,085	1,455	59	40	1,458	1,210
Washington	1,120	2,727	68	63	2,180	1,845
Watonwan	537	1,411	45	6	930	1,119
Wilkin	614	779	48	26	792	648
Winona	3,073	3,014	85	69	3,794	2,220
Wright	1,396	2,820	184	37	2,337	2.114
Yellow Med.	786	1,745	130	19	913	1,763
Total	109594	155416	8,658	10,021	173845	153667
Plurality	..	35,822	..	..	20,178	..
Percent	38.73	54.84	2.83	3.60	53.44	46.56
Whole vote.		283,689			327,512	

For President in 1904 Swallow, Pro., received 6,253 votes; Debs, Soc., 11,692; Watson, Pop., 2,004.

The vote for President in 1904 was: Parker, Dem., 55,187; Roosevelt, Rep., 216,651. Roosevelt's plurality, 161,464.

VOTE FOR REPRESENTATIVES IN CONGRESS, 1908.

Districts.

I. Counties of Dodge, Fillmore, Freeborn, Houston, Mower, Olmsted, Steele, Wabasha, Wasecas and Winona. Andrew French, Dem., 17,608; Jas. A. Tawney, Rep., 20,469. Tawney's majority, 2,821.

II. Counties of Blue Earth, Brown, Cottonwood, Faribault, Jackson, Martin, Murray, Nobles, Pipestone, Rock, and Watonwan. W. S. Hammond, Dem., 17,716; Jas. T. McCleary, Rep., 14,091. Hammond's plurality, 3,625.

III. Counties of Carver, Dakota, Goodhue, Le Sueur, McLeod, Nicollet, Rice, Scott, and Sibley. W. H. Leeman, Dem., 13,446. Chas. R. Davis, Rep., 18,896; Davis's plurality, 6,456.

IV. Counties of Chisago, Ramsey, and Washington. David F. Peebles, Dem., 12,395; Fred. C. Stevens, Rep., 21,818. Stevens's plurality, 9,423.

V. County of Hennepin. T. P. Dwyer, Dem., 13,429; Frank M. Nye, Rep., 24,542; Dight, P. O., 1,816. Nye's plurality, 9,297.

VI. Counties of Benton, Cass, Crow Wing, Douglas, Hubbard, Meeker, Morrison, Sherburne, Stearns, Todd, Wadena, and Wright. H. A. Gilkinson, Dem., 13,154; C. A. Lindebergh, Rep., 23,574. Lindebergh's majority, 9,420.

VII. Counties of Big Stone, Chippewa, Grant, Kandiyohi, Lac Qui Parle, Lincoln, Lyon, Pope, Redwood, Stevens, Swift, Traverse, and Yellow Medicine. A. J. Volstad, Rep., 26,597. No opposition.

VIII. Counties of Aitkin, Anoka, Carlton, Cook, Isanti, Itasca, Kanabec, Lake, Mille Lacs, Pine, and St. Louis. C. B. Miller, Rep., 27,873; Alex. Halliday, Pub. O., 6,298. Miller's majority, 21,375.

IX. Counties of Becker, Beltrami, Clay, Kittson, Marshall, Norman, Otter Tail, Polk, Red Lake, Roseau, and Wilkin. Halvor Steenerson, Rep., 17,757; T. T. Braaten, Pub. O., 2,985. Steenerson's plurality, 2,747.

PRESENT STATE GOVERNMENT.

Governor, John A. Johnson, Dem.; Lieutenant-Governor, A. O. Eberhart, Rep.; Secretary of State, Julius A. Schmahl; Auditor, S. G. Iverson; Treasurer, C. C. Dinehart, Rep.; Attorney-General, Geo. T. Simpson, Rep.; Adjutant-General, Fred. B. Wood, Dem.; Superintendent of Education, J. W. Olson, Rep.; Commissioner of Insurance, J. M. Hartigan, Dem.

JUDICIARY.

Supreme Court: Chief Justice, Charles M. Start, Rep.; Associate Justices, Calvin L. Brown, Rep.; Edward A. Jaggard, Rep.; Charles L. Lewis, Rep.; Charles B. Elliott, Rep.; Clerk, C. A. Pidgeon, Rep.

MINNESOTA—*Continued.*

STATE LEGISLATURE, 1909.

	Senate.	*House.*	*Joint Ballot.*
Republicans	43	94	137
Democrats	20	22	42
Prohibition	..	3	..
Republican majority	23	69	92

VOTE OF THE STATE SINCE 1884.

	Dem.	*Rep.*	*Gr.*	*Pro.*	*Plu.*	
1884. Pres	70,065	111,685	3,583	4,684	41,620	R
			U. Lab.			
1888. Pres	104,385	142,492	1,094	15,311	38,106	R
			Pop.			
1892. Pres	100,920	122,823	29,313	14,182	12,367	R
1896. Pres	139,735	193,503	....	4,348	53,768	R
	Fus.					
1898. Gov	131,980	111,796	1,766	5,299	20,184	F
1900. Gov	150,651	152,905	....	...	2,254	R
1900. Pres	112,901	190,461	....	8,555	77,560	R
			Soc.			
1902. Gov	99,375	155,861	3,074	5,735	56,486	R
1904. Pres	55,187	216,651	11,692	6,253	161,464	R
1906. Gov	168,715	92,082	5,006	7,709	76,633	D
1908. Pres	69,594	155,416	10,021	8,658	85,822	R

MISSISSIPPI.

COUNTIES. (78.)	PRESIDENT, 1908.				PRESIDENT, 1904.	
	Bryan Dem.	Taft, Rep.	Watson, Pop.	Debs, Soc.	Parker Dem.	Roosevelt, Rep.
Adams	712	86	8	5	632	30
Alcorn	761	48	6	14	972	66
Amite	1,026	16	30	..	652	15
Attala	1,001	98	17	9	1,074	63
Benton	552	34	1	2	580	49
Bolivar	642	208	10	2	402	185
Calhoun	928	63	19	47	599	25
Carroll	6[illegible]8	31	35	7	617	5
Chickasaw	[illegible]	63	31	3	528	28
Choctaw	559	48	58	13	624	65
Claiborne	436	8	2	1	437	6
Clarke	1,089	40	11	18	824	10
Clay	686	19	16	..	481	7
Coahoma	683	58	..	..	872	44
Copiah	1,346	25	39	4	1,463	23
Covington	774	64	10	11	714	97
De Soto	739	14	2	3	891	20
Forrest	832	59	17	43	..	..
Franklin	311	20	38	15	876	22
Greene	332	43	1	..	282	35
Grenada	523	12	13	4	505	13
Hancock	269	57	2	3	336	85
Harrison	1,399	278	20	84	895	157
Hinds	1,743	68	14	34	1,428	49
Holmes	987	31	9	29	1,103	44
Issaquena	85	11	..	..	96	21
Itawamba	859	67	58	4	838	56
Jackson	648	118	3	24	650	74
Jasper	754	21	30	15	654	20
Jefferson	409	4	1	1	392	4
Jeff. Davis	406	89	6	12	..	..
Jones	1,181	172	71	108	944	143
Kemper	703	46	80	14	633	35
Lafayette	1,028	43	3	5	1,100	48
Lamar	811	68	13	9	233	70
Lauderdale	2,038	72	74	88	1,958	43
Lawrence	397	47	3	5	899	84
Leake	1,005	80	25	47	961	11
Lee	1,336	70	53	8	1,104	15
Leflore	632	21	6	2	490	3
Lincoln	1,068	206	12	5	593	141
Lowndes	877	95	..	..	891	4
Madison	659	60	2	5	719	34
Marion	532	89	7	18	394	141
Marshall	913	29	1	..	1,031	16
Monroe	1,529	50	26	3	617	48
Montgomery	699	8	16	13	789	8
Neshoba	911	61	82	33	932	17
Newton	1,323	16	60	32	1,294	6
Noxubee	626	7	9	2	601	2
Oktibbeha	783	22	19	3	693	12
Panola	903	15	25	8	805	10

MISSISSIPPI—*Continued.*

COUNTIES.	PRESIDENT, 1908.				PRESIDENT, 1904.	
	Bryan, Dem.	Taft, Rep.	Watson, Pop.	Debs, Soc.	Parker Dem.	Roosevelt, Rep.
Pearl River	374	20	2	8	178	6
Perry	144	31	..	12	619	88
Pike	1,284	55	9	15	1,145	76
Pontotoc	879	156	43	5	658	118
Prentiss	716	153	12	9	776	89
Quitman	199	33	..	..	68	24
Rankin	757	13	6	12	883	25
Scott	724	9	5	7	742	8
Sharkey	220	2	1	..	153	7
Simpson	716	61	8	29	649	58
Smith	712	82	12	15	696	21
Sunflower	522	11	1	1	423	9
Tallahatchie	681	2	2	3	639	2
Tate	865	53	7	5	726	22
Tippah	1,021	57	1	5	1,018	69
Tishomingo	588	113	4	5	584	59
Tunica	185	14	1	2	217	11
Union	1,089	103	14	6	939	84
Warren	1,310	169	7	35	1,191	37
Washington	760	72	6	4	792	49
Wayne	430	58	4	14	478	71
Webster	804	191	41	15	557	73
Wilkinson	530	1	..	4	458	5
Winston	729	41	20	4	703	26
Yalobusha	1,085	33	7	10	921	28
Yazoo	979	14	2	11	666	5
Total	60,876	4,505	1,057	1,048	53,376	3,187
Plurality	56,371	..	..	..	50,189	..
Per cent	90.20	6.68	1.56	1.56	91.42	5.46
Whole vote.		67,486			....	

At the State election in 1903 Vardaman, for Governor, received 32,191 votes; Carter, for Lieutenant-Governor, 31,547; Power, for Secretary of State, 32,193; Henry, for Auditor, 31,863; Miller, for Treasurer, 31,768; Williams, for Attorney-General, 31,822—all Democrats, no opposition.

VOTE FOR REPRESENTATIVES IN CONGRESS, 1908.

Districts.

I. Counties of Alcorn, Itawamba, Noxubee, Lee, Lowndes, Monroe, Oktibbeha, Prentiss, and Tishomingo. E. S. Chandler, Jr., Dem., 8,043. No opposition.

II. Counties of Benton, De Soto, Lafayette, Marshall, Panola, Tallahatchie, Tippah, Tate, and Union. Thomas Spight, Dem., 7,511. No opposition.

III. Counties of Bolivar, Holmes, Coahoma, Issaquena, Leflore, Quitman, Sharkey, Sunflower, Tunica, and Washington. B. G. Humphreys, Dem., 4,808. No opposition.

IV. Counties of Attala, Calhoun, Carroll, Chickasaw, Choctaw, Clay, Grenada, Montgomery, Noxubee, Pontotoc, Webster, and Yalobusha. T. U. Sisson, Dem., 7,493. No opposition.

V. Counties of Clarke, Jasper, Kemper, Winston, Lauderdale, Leake, Neshoba, Newton, Scott, Smith, and Wayne. Adam Byrd, Dem., 9,760. No opposition.

VI. Counties of Covington, Greene, Hancock, Harrison, Jackson, Jones, Lawrence, Marion, Perry, Lamar, Pearl River, Forrest, Jefferson Davis, Simpson, and Wayne. E J. Bowers, Dem., 8,702.

VII. Counties of Adams, Amite, Claiborne, Copiah, Franklin, Jefferson, Lincoln, Pike, and Wilkinson. W. A. Dickson, Dem., 6,807; H. C. Turley, Rep., 384.

VIII. Counties of Warren, Yazoo, Madison, Hinds, and Rankin. J. W. Collier, Dem., 5,657. No opposition.

PRESENT STATE GOVERNMENT.

Governor, E. F. Noel; Lieutenant-Governor, Luther Manship; Secretary of State, J. W. Power; Treasurer, Geo. R. Edwards; Auditor, E. J. Smith; Superintendent of Education, P. C. Powers; Attorney-General, R. V. Fletcher; Adjutant-General, Arthur Fridge; Land Commissioner, E. W. Nall—all Democrats.

MISSISSIPPI—Continued.

JUDICIARY.

Supreme Court: Chief Justice, A. H. Whitfield; Associate Justices, Jeff. Truly and S. S. Calhoon; Clerk of the Court, George C. Meyers—all Democrats.

STATE LEGISLATURE, 1909.

The State Legislature is wholly Democratic.

VOTE OF THE STATE SINCE 1884.

	Dem.	Rep.	Gr.	Pop.	Maj.
1884. President...	76,510	43,509	....	....	33,001 D
1885. Governor..	88,783	1,081	....	....	87,702 D
			Pro.		
1892. President...	40,237	1,406	910	10,256	29,981 D
1895. Governor...	46,873	....	....	17,466	*22,407 D
				Nat. D.	Plu.
1896. President...	63,253	4,849	390	1,021	58,404 D
				Pop.	
1904. President...	53,376	3,189	....	1,425	50,187 D
1908. President...	60,876	4,505	....	1,057	56,371 D

*Plurality.

MISSOURI.

Counties. (115.)	President, 1908.				Governor, 1908.	
	Bryan Dem.	Taft, Rep.	Chafin Pro.	Debs, Soc.	Cowherd, Dem.	Hadley, Rep.
Adair	1,992	2,514	75	264	1,959	2,578
Andrew	1,782	2,169	31	15	1,72‸	2,230
Atchison	1,651	1,700	48	18	1,57	1,780
Audrain	3,350	1,732	31	16	3,299	1,772
Barry	2,383	2,526	34	138	2,325	2,588
Barton	1,913	2,154	55	190	1,782	1,767
Bates	3,248	1,673	119	83	3,176	2,846
Benton	1,280	1,924	18	19	1,227	1,962
Bollinger	1,517	1,593	25	27	1,515	1,597
Boone	5,041	2,149	19	28	5,057	2,148
Buchanan	9,836	8,394	96	168	9,224	9,115
Butler	1,893	2,186	27	145	1,890	2,197
Caldwell	1,540	2,161	25	4	1,443	2,261
Callaway	3,878	1,911	39	13	3,824	1,951
Camden	955	1,446	12	33	931	1,480
Cape Gir'rd'u	2,621	3,381	42	28	2,598	3,402
Carroll	2,753	3,015	88	28	2,708	3,049
Carter	591	507	3	57	591	507
Cass	3,143	2,191	48	108	3,064	2,275
Cedar	1,483	1,933	26	61	1,442	1,985
Chariton	3,353	2,249	20	12	3,314	2,296
Christian	956	1,871	60	146	894	1,927
Clark	1,737	1,741	32	5	1,698	1,777
Clay	3,513	1,166	19	25	3,424	1,238
Clinton	2,075	1,578	18	1	2,017	1,632
Cole	2,494	2,402	14	29	2,405	2,489
Cooper	2,555	2,679	12	9	2,502	2,723
Crawford	1,260	1,752	17	51	1,226	1,791
Dade	1,441	1,946	30	41	1,388	2,002
Dallas	955	1,609	3	10	921	1,643
Daviess	2 294	2,388	51	8	2,212	2,468
De Kalb	1,632	1,703	28	2	1,725	1,748
Dent	1,330	1,290	4	31	1,328	1,300
Douglas	699	1,922	16	277	660	1,976
Dunklin	2 734	1,638	22	261	2,711	1,665
Franklin	2,423	4,049	32	121	2,396	4,096
Gasconade	509	2,220	10	13	486	2,267
Gentry	2,236	1,882	52	24	2,181	1,933
Greene	5,830	6,439	143	144	5,672	6,636
Grundy	1,359	2,407	43	12	1,308	2,480
Harrison	1,938	2,842	50	15	1,380	2,898
Henry	3,578	3,854	91	61	3,455	2,960
Hickory	561	1,182	12	32	541	1,204
Holt	1,596	2,246	28	14	1,563	2,272
Howard	2,884	1,141	13	7	2,853	1,163
Howell	1,827	2,164	22	204	1,783	2,220
Iron	931	828	8	5	918	839
Jackson	31,461	26,998	251	903	31,551	27,258
Jasper	8,130	9,143	251	1,024	8,001	9,275
Jefferson	2,698	3,050	19	65	2,645	3,101
Johnson	3,488	2,997	31	69	3,409	3,064
Kansas City	....	....	...	....	....	....
Knox	1,652	1,339	35	25	1,663	1,440
Laclede	1,681	1,902	14	49	1,635	1,954
Lafayette	3,865	3,771	25	98	3,797	3,825
Lawrence	2,532	3,028	54	301	2,471	3,105
Lewis	2,439	1,473	38	20	2,393	1,520
Lincoln	2,555	1,620	17	6	2,521	1,654
Linn	3,000	2,974	40	77	2,897	3,082
Livingston	2,379	2,400	23	42	2,284	2,506
McDonald	1,306	1,333	28	80	1,264	1,377
Macon	3,919	3,542	59	172	3,840	3,635
Madison	1,321	1,248	17	49	1,313	1,322
Maries	1,309	703	10	5	1,287	720
Marion	3,982	2,554	70	149	3,971	2,603
Mercer	852	1,909	26	9	825	1,947
Miller	1 398	2,016	15	61	1,329	2,085
Mississippi	1 589	1,320	19	12	1,580	1,335
Moniteau	1,763	1,691	34	30	1,686	1,764
Monroe	3,772	871	9	14	3,745	910
Montgomery	2,073	2,038	42	11	2,044	2,067
Morgan	1,315	1,663	11	11	1,295	1,682
New Madrid	1,824	1,436	17	73	1,814	1,451
Newton	2,725	2,620	158	281	2,683	2,669
Nodaway	3,595	3,592	45	52	3,475	3,711
Oregon	1,550	729	2	120	1,539	745
Osage	1,439	1,820	29	4	1,420	1,850
Ozark	594	1,233	3	40	559	1,265
Pemiscot	1,725	1,390	6	39	1,720	1,383
Perry	1,569	1,775	28	1	1,548	1,794
Pettis	3,791	3,883	67	195	3,677	4,143
Phelps	1,804	1,520	9	21	1,710	1,594
Pike	3,326	2,403	8	10	3,127	2,504
Platte	2,795	982	16	6	2,781	1,010
Polk	2,139	2,670	35	39	2,101	2,695
Pulaski	1,418	988	11	28	1,382	1,032
Putnam	1,058	2,233	48	52	1,008	2,296
Ralls	1,947	900	9	11	1,993	957
Randolph	4 245	1,953	44	12	4,186	2,027
Ray	3,045	1,919	43	57	2,945	1,975
Reynolds	1,052	544	1	41	1,042	555
Ripley	1,309	946	16	4	1,289	961
St. Charles	1,979	3,480	19	42	1,973	3,505
St. Clair	1,877	1,723	12	72	1,877	1,885
St. François	2,942	3,260	40	439	2,907	3,314
St. Genevieve	1,108	1,064	1	4	1,096	1,066
St. Louis	4,522	10,177	73	512	4,214	10,377
St. Louis City	60,917	74,160	187	4,900	60,109	75,996
Saline	4,189	2,926	22	20	4,108	3,021
Schuyler	1,222	1,007	42	19	1,195	1,031
Scotland	1,564	1,273	25	19	1,526	1,312
Scott	1,853	1,473	17	631	1,823	1,516
Shannon	1,151	849	4	60	1,131	871
Shelby	2,466	1,298	39	17	2,428	1,331
Stoddard	2,736	2,025	35	276	2,709	2,042
Stone	477	1,376	3	123	462	1,399
Sullivan	2,269	2,389	35	20	2,227	2,440
Taney	628	1,080	2	54	600	1,107
Texas	2,328	1,954	18	61	2,346	2,015
Vernon	3,705	2,369	55	172	3,538	2,512
Warren	484	1,714	5	42	467	1,735
Washington	1,330	1,753	20	18	1,317	1,770
Wayne	1,641	1,554	14	84	1,632	1,563
Webster	1,761	1,901	62	75	1,706	1,952
Worth	993	985	45	3	972	1,015
Wright	1,469	2,149	9	57	1,432	2,192
Total	346574	347203	4,198	15,391	340053	355932
Plurality	..	629	..	..	..	15,789
Per cent	48.45	48.55	.57	2.15	48.97	49.78
Whole vote.	715,873				715,618	

For President 1904 Corrigan, Soc. L., received 1,674 votes; Watson, Pop., 4,226.

The vote for Governor in 1904 was: Folk, Dem. 326,652; Walbridge, Rep., 296,552; Hill, Pro., 5,591; Behrens, Soc., 11,031; White, Soc. L., 1,442; Alldredge, Pro., 2,701.

For President in 1908, Watson, Pop., received 1,147 votes; Gilhaus, Soc. Lab., 868; Hisgen, Ind., 399.

Democrats and Republicans claim Lieut-Governorship and Legislature. Will decide in Jan., 1909.

MISSOURI—*Continued.*

VOTE FOR REPRESENTATIVES IN CONGRESS, 1906.

Districts.

I. Counties of Adair, Clark, Knox, Lewis, Macon, Marion, Putnam, Schuyler, Scotland, and Shelby. James T. Lloyd, Dem., 22,133; Chamberlain, Rep., 19,122.

II. Counties of Carroll, Chariton, Grundy, Linn, Livingston, Monroe, Randolph, and Sullivan. William W. Rucker, Dem., 23,263; Haley, Rep., 18,266.

III. Counties of Caldwell, Clay, Clinton, Daviess, De Kalb, Gentry, Harrison, Mercer, Ray, and Worth. Alexander, Dem., 20,387; Eads, Rep., 18,341.

IV. Counties of Andrew, Atchison, Buchanan, Holt, Nodaway, and Platte. Booher, Dem., 21,671; Reed, Rep., 18,908; Wilson, Soc., 216.

V. County of Jackson. William P. Borland, Dem., 31,635; E. C. Ellis, Rep., 27,289.

VI. Counties of Bates, Cass, Cedar, Dade, Henry, Johnson, and St. Clair. David A. De Armond, Dem., 18,532; Atkinson, Rep., 16,372.

VII. Counties of Benton, Greene, Hickory, Howard, Lafayette, Pettis, Polk, and Saline. C. W. Hamlin, Dem., 24,731; John Whittaker, Rep., 23,927; Behrens, Soc., 638.

VIII. Counties of Boone, Camden, Cole, Cooper, Miller, Moniteau, Morgan, and Osage. Dorsey W. Shackleford, Dem., 17,230; Irwin, Rep., 15,691.

IX. Counties of Audrain, Callaway, Franklin, Gasconade, Lincoln, Montgomery, Pike, Ralls, St. Charles, and Warren. Champ Clark, Dem., 23,090; Roy, Rep., 21,702.

X. County of St. Louis, and city (part). Thompson, Dem., 28,634; Richard Bartholdt, Rep., 49,127; Hohen, Soc., 3,557.

XI. St. Louis City. M. J. Gill, Dem., 21,001; F. R. Findlay, Rep., 19,155; Mueller, Soc., 1,072.

XII. St. Louis City. Self, Dem., 15,930; Harry M. Coudrey, Rep., 16,471; Crouch, Soc., 750.

XIII. Counties of Bollinger, Carter, Iron, Jefferson, Madison, Perry, Reynolds, St. François, St. Genevieve, Washington, and Wayne. Smith, Dem., 16,918; Polite E. Elvins, Rep., 17,125.

XIV. Counties of Butler, Cape Girardeau, Christian, Douglas, Dunklin, Howell, Mississippi, New Madrid, Oregon, Ozark, Pemiscot, Ripley, Scott, Stoddard, Stone, and Taney. Joseph J. Russell, Dem., 25,189; Crow, Rep., 25,951; Wilkinson, Soc., 2,363.

XV. Counties of Barry, Barton, Jasper, Lawrence, McDonald, Newton, and Vernon. Hackney, Dem., 22,410; Morgan, Rep., 23,040; Berry, Soc., 2,133.

XVI. Counties of Crawford, Dallas, Dent, Laclede, Maries, Phelps, Pulaski, Shannon, Texas, Webster, and Wright. Robert Lamar, Dem., 16,295; Arthur P. Murphy, Rep., 16,835.

PRESENT STATE GOVERNMENT.

Governor, Herbert S. Hadley; Lieutenant-Governor, in doubt; Secretary of State, Cornelius Roach; Auditor, John P. Gordon; Treasurer, James Cowgill; Attorney-General, H. S. Hadley; Superintendent Public Schools, H. A. Gass; Adjutant-General, James A. De Armond; Commissioner of Insurance, W. D. Vandiver—all Democrats except Hadley.

JUDICIARY.

Supreme Court: Chief Justice, James B. Gantt; Associate Justices: Division 1, Henry Lamm, Walter W. Graves, Leroy B. Valliant; Division 2, A. M. Woodson, Govon D. Burgess, James D. Fox; Clerk, John R. Green—all Democrats except Lamm.

STATE LEGISLATURE, 1909.

	Senate.	*House.*	*Joint Ballot.*
Democrats	23	69	92
Republicans	11	73	84
Democratic majority	12	R 4	8

VOTE OF THE STATE SINCE 1888.

	Dem.	*Rep.*	*Gr.*	*Pro.*	*Plu.*
1888. President	261,974	236,257	....	4,539	25,717 D
			Pop.		
1900. Governor	350,045	317,905	4,356	5,195	32,140 D
1900. President	351,922	314,092	4,244	5,965	37,830 D

MISSOURI—*Continued.*

	Dem.	*Rep.*	*Pro.*	*Soc.*	*Plu.*
1904. President	296,312	321,449	7,191	13,009	25,137 R
1906. Sec. State	292,421	283,417	....	....	9, D
1908. President	346,754	347,203	4,191	15,381	629 R

MONTANA.

COUNTIES. (27.)	PRESIDENT, 1908.				GOVERNOR. 1908.	
	Bryan Dem.	Taft, Rep.	Chafin Pro.	Debs, Soc.	Norris Dem.	Donlin Rep.
Beaverhead	739	878	2	70	980	740
Broadwater	495	326	4	36	486	332
Carbon	814	1,205	17	247	866	1,244
Cascade	1,888	1,935	32	451	2,033	1,789
Choteau	893	1,220	4	109	913	1,180
Custer	531	967	8	84	636	898
Dawson	439	927	10	77	445	899
Deer Lodge	1,611	1,377	33	122	1,789	1,238
Fergus	1,112	1,529	14	257	1,259	1,481
Flathead	1,480	1,838	39	356	1,535	1,859
Gallatin	1,485	1,519	52	160	1,637	1,449
Granite	485	369	2	54	488	392
Jefferson	714	546	20	109	803	501
Lewis & Clarke	2,062	2,033	18	303	2,250	1,910
Madison	1,029	964	13	52	1,128	867
Meagher	314	495	3	17	835	490
Missoula	1,780	1,856	40	341	1,850	1,968
Park	952	1,305	38	264	1,151	1,271
Powell	560	599	7	34	583	573
Ravalli	859	1,045	57	209	1,086	876
Rosebud	235	515	8	19	301	465
Sanders	325	473	4	55	368	485
Silver Bow	6,255	4,618	277	2,126	6,779	4,194
Sweet Grass	264	526	..	35	286	510
Teton	358	622	1	46	394	595
Valley	503	843	12	67	552	868
Yellowstone	1,114	1,803	112	155	1,349	1,718
Total	29,326	32,333	827	5,855	32,282	30,792
Plurality	..	2,997	..	..	1,490	..
Per cent	42.47	46.72	2.14	8.65	47.40	45.07
Whole vote		69,394			68,186	

For President, Pro., 335; Soc. L., 208.

The vote for Governor, 1904, was: J. K. Toole, Dem., 35,377; W. Lindsay, Rep., 26,957; M. G. O'Malley, Soc., 3,431. Toole's plurality, 8,420.

For Governor in 1908, Hazleton, Soc., received 5,112 votes.

VOTE FOR REPRESENTATIVE IN CONGRESS, 1908.

Long, Dem., 29,032; Pray, Rep., 32,819; Duncan, Soc., 5,318. Pray's plurality, 3,787.

STATE LEGISLATURE, 1909.

	Senate.	*House.*	*Joint Ballot.*
Republicans	17	33	50
Democrats	10	38	48
Republican majority	7	D 5	2

PRESENT STATE GOVERNMENT.

Governor, Edwin L. Norris, Dem.; Lieutenant-Governor, Wm. R. Allen, Rep.; Secretary of State, A. N. Yoder, Rep.; Treasurer, Elmer E. Esselstyne, Rep.; Auditor, H. R. Cunningham, Rep.; Attorney-General, A. J. Galen, Rep.; Adjutant-General (to be appointed); Superintendent of Education, W. E. Harmon, Rep.

JUDICIARY.

Supreme Court: Chief Justice, Theo. Brantley, Rep.; Justices, Henry C. Smith, Rep.; Wm. L. Holloway, Rep.; Clerk, John T. Athey, Rep.

VOTE OF THE STATE SINCE ADMISSION.

	Dem.	*Rep.*			*Maj.*
1889. Governor	19,564	18,988			556 D
	Dem.	*Rep.*	*Pop.*	*Pro.*	*Plu.*
1892. President	17,581	11,885	7,334	549	1,270 R
1896. President	42,537	10,494	....	186	32,043 D
	Fus.		*Soc.*		
1900. President	37,146	25,373	708	298	11,773 F
1902. Sup. Jus.	21,204	31,690	2,466	....	10,486 R
1904. President	21,773	34,932	5,676	....	13,159 R
	Dem.	*Rep.*			
1908. President	29,326	32,333	5,855	827	2,997 R

NEBRASKA.

Counties. (90.)	President, 1908. Bryan, Dem.	Taft, Rep.	Chafin Pro.	Debs, Soc.	Governor, 1908. Shallenberger, Dem.	Sheldon, Rep.
Adams	2,337	1,987	119	72	2,452	1,944
Antelope	1,445	1,658	66	28	1,446	1,660
Banner	74	175	2	17	65	182
Blaine	160	220	4	8	146	228
Boone	1,583	1,580	40	12	1,644	1,523
Box Butte	684	600	19	28	680	609
Boyd	891	961	34	27	890	969
Brown	526	588	15	42	534	587
Buffalo	2,520	2,526	75	76	2,590	2,448
Burt	1,215	1,880	49	14	1,194	1,916
Butler	2,129	1,412	41	17	2,192	1,364
Cass	2,387	2,440	85	58	2,291	2,581
Cedar	1,732	1,627	39	5	1,742	1,632
Chase	338	400	34	3	472	280
Cherry	1,031	1,048	41	53	1,071	1,055
Cheyenne	809	886	28	87	785	899
Clay	1,939	1,891	95	31	2,014	1,837
Colfax	1,267	1,159	21	36	1,283	1,157
Cuming	1,722	1,284	29	5	1,812	1,233
Custer	2,898	2,788	98	147	2,826	2,831
Dakota	716	729	22	22	690	756
Dawes	727	836	11	26	740	830
Dawson	1,926	1,737	87	22	2,014	1,646
Deuel	392	526	12	8	382	532
Dixon	1,100	1,257	63	12	1,131	1,234
Dodge	2,694	2,437	108	49	2,725	2,381
Douglas	15,583	14,066	266	798	16,203	13,540
Dundy	394	486	17	26	396	484
Fillmore	1,889	1,756	40	24	2,020	1,721
Franklin	1,298	1,083	51	38	1,341	1,064
Frontier	847	1,098	55	54	881	1,069
Furnas	1,618	1,400	92	15	1,725	1,304
Gage	3,129	3,721	131	69	3,294	3,606
Garfield	363	368	10	23	373	367
Gosper	634	499	32	3	661	481
Grant	101	98	1	1	95	98
Greeley	1 072	691	14	29	1,107	662
Hall	2,329	2,241	102	109	2,410	2,105
Hamilton	1,664	1,633	129	22	1,636	1,652
Harlan	1,158	1,081	31	49	1,324	989
Hayes	277	359	11	42	280	362
Hitchcock	632	683	19	14	637	638
Holt	1,777	1,541	99	63	1,764	1,551
Hooker	91	100	3	3	91	111
Howard	1,435	977	40	31	1,466	945
Jefferson	1.787	1,941	77	39	1,835	1,906
Johnson	1,150	1,357	45	8	1,189	1,322
Kearney	1,174	993	121	28	1,156	1,031
Keith	310	368	6	5	302	372
Keya Paha	354	422	15	49	332	431
Kimball	124	216	7	10	115	225
Knox	2,106	1,871	79	41	2,141	1,858
Lancaster	8,540	7,428	400	85	7,340	8,682
Lincoln	1,382	1,541	80	179	1,462	1,479
Logan	155	140	10	8	147	147
Loup	170	248	10	12	166	244
McPherson	165	234	11	18	149	247
Madison	1,878	2,137	41	14	1,912	2,114
Merrick	1,081	1,133	186	15	1,124	1,128
Nance	926	1,082	45	6	955	1,056
Nemaha	1,674	1,583	49	41	1,688	1,581
Nuckolls	1,523	1,519	35	11	1,528	1,508
Otoe	2,411	2,243	71	18	2,365	2,318
Pawnee	1,115	1,468	80	9	1,171	1,457
Perkins	265	254	1	3	255	254
Phelps	1,238	1,445	116	29	1,224	1,447
Pierce	1,095	1,067	27	9	1,119	1,064
Platte	2,487	1,584	67	8	1,678	1,382
Polk	1,264	1,171	165	43	1,303	1,144
Red Willow	1,317	1,242	53	78	1,335	1,229
Richardson	2,258	2,123	71	17	2,317	2,055
Rock	334	469	14	15	332	469
Saline	2,247	2,048	93	16	2,351	1,994
Sarpy	1,090	912	41	26	1,117	892
Saunders	2,679	2,309	91	31	2,685	2,303
Scott's Bluff	549	789	30	73	512	822
Seward	2,029	1,930	41	2	2,137	1,834
Sheridan	733	809	34	41	733	712
Sherman	925	776	23	50	943	766
Sioux	464	516	24	11	447	526

NEBRASKA—*Continued.*

Counties.	President, 1908. Bryan, Dem.	Taft, Rep.	Chafin Pro.	Debs, Soc.	Governor, 1908. Shallenberger, Dem.	Sheldon, Rep.
Stanton	824	791	9	7	872	752
Thayer	1,703	1,714	53	24	1,783	1,638
Thomas	130	95	2	7	124	101
Thurston	734	895	15	13	734	895
Valley	1,045	1,040	51	10	1,094	1,004
Washington	1,460	1,592	39	40	1,558	1,498
Wayne	1,055	1,297	23	10	1,069	1,258
Webster	1,854	1,408	119	17	1,409	1,350
Wheeler	252	236	10	20	224	236
York	2,042	2,309	124	9	2,049	2,177
Total	131099	126997	5,179	3,524	132960	121076
Plurality	4,102	..	..	..	11,814	..
Per cent	49.01	47.61	1.90	1.31	50.61	46.08
Scattering	....				8 703	
Whole vote	266,799				162,739	

For President in 1904 Watson, Pop., received 20,518; Debs. Soc., 7,412; Swallow, Pro., 6,338; scattering, 7,424.

The vote for Governor in 1904 was: Mickey, Rep., 111,711; Berge, Fus., 102,568; Swander, Pro., 5,488; Vail, Soc., 5,122. Mickey's plurality, 9,143.

For Governor in 1908 Teeter, Pro., received 4,464 votes; Harbough, Soc., 3,069.

VOTE FOR REPRESENTATIVES IN CONGRESS 1908.

Districts.

I. Counties of Cass, Johnson, Lancaster, Nemaha, Otoe, Pawnee, and Richardson. John A. McGuire, Dem., 19,651; Ernest M. Pollard, Rep., 18,716. McGuire's plurality, 935.

II. Counties of Douglas, Sarpy, and Washington. Gilbert M. Hitchcock, Dem., 18,781; A. W. Jefferis, Rep., 16,206; G. C. Porter, Soc., 721. Hitchcock's plurality, 2,575.

III. Counties of Antelope, Boone, Burt, Cedar, Colfax, Cuming, Dakota, Dixon, Dodge, Knox, Madison, Merrick, Nance, Pierce, Platte, Stanton, Thurston, and Wayne: James P. Latta, Dem., 26,832; John F. Boyd, Rep., 24,865; J. M. Woodcock, Soc., 273, Latta's plurality, 1,967.

IV. Counties of Butler, Fillmore, Gage, Hamilton, Jefferson, Polk, Saline, Saunders, Seward, Thayer, and York. C. F. Gilbert, Dem., 21,819; Edmund H. Hinshaw, Rep., 22,674; T. M. Birmingham, Pro., 870. Hinshaw's plurality, 855.

V. Counties of Adams, Chase, Clay, Dundy, Franklin, Frontier, Furnas, Gosper, Hall, Harlan, Hayes, Hitchcock, Kearney, Nuckolls, Perkins, Phelps, Red Willow, and Webster. F. W. Ashton, Dem., 20,627; George W. Norris, Rep., 20,649; G. G. Larkey, Pro., 512; Norris's plurality, 22.

VI. Counties of Boyd, Banner, Blaine, Box Butte, Brown, Buffalo, Cheyenne, Cherry, Custer, Dawes, Dawson, Deuel, Garfield, Grant, Greeley, Holt, Hooker, Howard, Keya Paha, Keith, Kimball, Lincoln, Logan, Loup, McPherson, Rock, Scott's Bluff, Sheridan, Sherman, Sioux, Thomas, Valley, and Wheeler. W. H. Westover, Dem., 23,317; Moses P. Kinkaid, Rep., 25,786; G. W. Hawley, Pro., 790. Kinkaid's plurality, 2,469.

PRESENT STATE GOVERNMENT.

Governor, A. C. Shallenberger, Dem.; Lieutenant-Governor, M. R. Hopewell; Secretary of State, George C. Junkin; Treasurer, L. J. Brian; Auditor, Silas A. Barton; Attorney-General, W. T. Thompson; Superintendent of Education, E. C. Bishop; Commissioner of Public Lands, E. B. Cowlds—all Republicans, except Shallenberger.

JUDICIARY.

Supreme Court: Chief Justice, John B. Barnes; Justices, Chas. B. Letton, Jesse B. Root, Jacob Fawsett, William B. Rose, and M. B. Reese; Clerk, H. C. Lindsay—all Republicans.

NEBRASKA—*Continued.*

STATE LEGISLATURE, 1909.

	Senate.	House.	Joint Ballot.
Republicans	13	31	44
Democrats	20	69	89
Democratic majority	7	38	45

VOTE OF THE STATE SINCE 1876.

	Dem.	Rep.	Gr.	Pro.	Plu.
1876. President.	17,554	31,916	....	....	*14,362 R
1880. President.	28,523	54,979	3,950	....	26,456 R
1884. President.	†54,391	76,903	....	2,899	22,512 R
1888. President.	80,552	108,425	4,226	9,429	27,873 R
			Pop.		
1892. President.	24,943	87.213	83,134	4,902	4,093 R
	Dem.-Pop.	Rep.	N. D.		
1896. President.	115,880	102,304	2,885	1,193	13,576 D
			Soc. D.		
1900. Governor.	113,018	113,879	674	4,315	861 R
1900. President.	114,013	121,835	823	3,655	7,822 R
	Dem.		Soc.		
1902. Governor.	91,116	96,471	3,157	3,397	5,355 R
1903. Sup. J....	87,864	96,991	2,595	4,394	9,127 R
				Pop.	
1904. President.	51,876	138,558	7,412	20,518	86,682 R
				Pro.	
1906. Governor.	84,885	97,858	2,999	5,106	12,973 R
1908. President.	131,099	126 997	3,524	5,179	4,102 D

* Majority. † Democratic and Greenback Fusion.

NEVADA.

COUNTIES. (14.)	PRESIDENT, 1908. Bryan, Dem.	Taft, Rep.	Debs, Soc.	Hisgen, Ind.	PRESIDENT, 1904. Parker Dem.	Roosevelt, Rep.
Churchill	382	389	56	12	165	156
Douglas	173	229	17	..	112	263
Elko	804	737	89	27	510	722
Esmeralda	2,787	2,208	632	157	380	494
Eureka	218	224	26	13	107	236
Humboldt	1,009	823	194	28	356	610
Lander	276	259	34	7	93	227
Lincoln	768	690	139	18	295	409
Lyon	364	458	74	19	165	394
Nye	1,219	1,124	333	97	425	554
Ormsby	343	350	52	6	218	409
Storey	402	447	54	12	337	627
Washoe	1,745	2,053	281	26	721	1,517
White Pine	722	786	222	13	152	279
Total	11,212	10,777	2,208	435	3,982	6,867
Plurality	435	....	....	......		2,885
Per cent.	47.07	40.91	9.32	1.70	32.94	56.66
Scattering	....	...	....	....	1,269	
Whole vote	24,627				11,718	

For Governor in 1906 Sparks, Dem., received 8,686 votes; Mitchell, Rep., 5,338; Cary, Soc., 815.

For President, Debs, Soc., 925; Watson, Pop., 344.

VOTE FOR REPRESENTATIVES IN CONGRESS, 1908.

George A. Bartlett, Dem., 11,333; H. B. Maxon, Rep., 7,552; J. D. Critchfield, Soc., 1,955; A. L. Fitzgerald, Ind. L., 3.037. Bartlett's plurality, 3,801.

PRESENT STATE GOVERNMENT.

Governor, vacancy; Lieutenant-Governor and Acting Governor, D. S. Dickerson; Secretary of State, W. G. Douglas; Treasurer, D. M. Ryan; Comptroller, Jacob Eggers; Superintendent of Public Instruction, Orvis Ring; Attorney-General, R. C. Stoddard—all Dems., except Eggers, Ring, and Douglas, Reps.

JUDICIARY.

Supreme Court: Chief Justice, Frank H. Norcross, Rep.; Justices, George F. Talbot, Dem.; Clerk, W. G. Douglass, Dem.; Clerk ex-officio, Eugene Howell, Dem.

STATE LEGISLATURE, 1909.

	Senate.	House.	Joint Ballot.
Democrats	11	19	30
Republicans	14	16	30

NEVADA—*Continued.*

VOTE OF THE STATE SINCE 1888.

	Dem.	Rep.	Pop.	Silver.	Plu.
1888. President	5,326	7,229	....	....	1,903 R
1892. President	714	2,811	7,264	....	4,453 P
	Dem.	Rep.	Pop.	Soc.	Plu.
1894. Governor	678	3,861	711	5,223	1,362 S
1896. President	....	1,938	....	8,377	6,439 S
1898. Governor	2,060	3,548	883	3,570	22 S
1900. President	6,347	3,849	....	....	2,498 D
1902. Governor	6,529	4,786	....	....	1,743 D
1904. President	3,982	6,867	344	925	2,885 R
			Soc.	Ind.	
1908. President	11,212	10,777	2,203	435	435 D

NEW JERSEY.

COUNTIES. (21.)	PRESIDENT, 1908. Bryan Dem.	Taft, Rep.	Chafin Pro.	Debs, Soc.	GOVERNOR, 1907. K'tzenbach, Dem.	Fort, Rep.
Atlantic	4,577	8,822	342	76	4,615	6,055
Bergen	7,628	14,042	219	575	8,616	10,193
Burlington	6,274	9,020	299	140	5,145	6,576
Camden	10 469	18,999	711	697	8,682	15,237
Cape May	1,553	2,937	111	33	1,322	2,443
Cumberland	4,521	6,770	476	158	3,510	4,945
Essex	30,191	53,687	317	2,205	34,469	34,178
Gloucester	3,707	5,318	322	72	3,034	4,166
Hudson	39,637	41,967	172	2,776	41,018	34,564
Hunterdon	4,737	3.733	140	29	3,760	2,805
Mercer	9,289	14,941	284	687	11,974	11,207
Middlesex	7,940	11,261	134	98	8,605	8,618
Monmouth	9,252	12,519	204	137	9,175	7,797
Morris	5,026	9,089	243	367	4,826	7,007
Ocean	1,634	3,326	89	22	2,033	2,502
Passaic	11.961	17,685	241	1,086	13,000	13.591
Salem	3,173	3,713	88	36	2,752	3,103
Somerset	3,271	5,043	94	24	3,379	3,542
Sussex	3,214	2,653	70	36	2,497	1,888
Union	8,806	15,919	132	912	9,934	10.750
Warren	5 662	3,904	242	83	3,959	3,146
Total	182522	265298	4,930	10,249	186300	194313
Plurality	..	82,776	..	..	..	..
Per cent.	39.08	56.80	1.05	2.19	49.5	50.55
Scattering	4,112					
Whole vote	467,111				380,613	

For Governor, 1907, Mason, Pro., received 5,255 votes; Kraft, Soc., 6,848; Butterworth, Soc. L., 1,568.

The vote for Governor in 1904 was: Black, 179,719; Stokes, Rep., 231,363; Parker, Pro., 6,687; Kearns, Soc., 8,858; Herrschoft, Soc. L., 2.526; Hennecker, Peo., 3,285.

For President in 1908 Hisgen, Ind., received 2,916 votes; Gilhaus, Soc. L., 1,196.

VOTE FOR REPRESENTATIVES IN CONGRESS, 1908.

Districts.

I. Counties of Camden, Gloucester, and Salem. Grosscup, Dem., 17,640; Loudenslager, Rep., 27,443.

II. Counties of Cape May, Cumberland, Atlantic, and Burlington. Grubb, Dem., 20,508; Gardner, Rep., 23,906.

III. Counties of Middlesex, Monmouth, and Ocean. Clark, Dem., 19,776; Howell, Rep., 26,302.

IV. Counties of Hunterdon, Somerset, and Mercer. Steel, Dem., 17,210; Wood, Rep., 23,719.

V. Counties of Union, Warren, and Morris. Barber, Dem., 20,485; Fowler, Rep., 27,948.

VI. Counties of Bergen, Passaic and Sussex. Hughes, Dem., 28,516; Foxhall, Rep., 27.989.

VII. County of Essex (part). Townsend, Dem., 18,104; Parker, Rep., 24,863.

VIII. County of Essex (part). Pratt, Dem., 16,276; Wiley, Rep., 24,536.

IX. County of Hudson (part). Kinkead, Dem., 23,485; Critchfield, Rep., 18,608.

X. County of Hudson (part). Hamill, Dem., 23,820; Dyer, Rep., 16,105.

NEW JERSEY—*Continued.*

PRESENT STATE GOVERNMENT

Governor, John Franklin Fort; Secretary of State, S. D. Dickinson; Treasurer, Dan'l S. Voorhees; Comptroller, Henry T. West; Attorney-General, to be named; Adjutant-General, R. H. Breintnall; Superintendent of Education, C. J. Baxter; Commissioner of Banking and Insurance, David O. Watkins—all Republicans.

JUDICIARY.

Supreme Court: Chief Justice, W. S. Gummere, Rep.; Justices, Charles W. Parker, Rep.; T. W. Trenchard, Rep.; Alfred Reed, Dem.; C. G. Garrison, Dem.; James J. Bergen, Dem.; Willard P. Voorhees, Rep.; James F. Minturn, Dem.; F. J. Swayze, Rep.; Clerk, William Riker, Jr., Rep.

Court of Errors and Appeals: Judges, J. W. Bogert, George R. Gray, Elmer E. Green, W. H. Vreedenburgh, G. D. W. Vroom, Peter V. Voorhees; Chancellor, Wm. J. Magie, and the Supreme Court Justices.

STATE LEGISLATURE, 1909.

	Senate.	*Assembly.*	*Joint Ballot.*
Republicans	13	45	58
Democrats	8	15	23
Republican majority	5	30	35

VOTE OF THE STATE SINCE 1872.

	Dem.	*Rep.*	*Gr.*	*Pro.*	*Plu.*
1880. President	122,565	120,555	2,617	191	2,010 D
1884. President	127,778	123,366	3,456	6,153	4,412 D
1888. President	151,493	144,344	....	7,904	7,149 D
			Soc. Lab.		
1892. President	171,042	156,068	1,337	8,131	14,974 D
			N. D.		
1896. President	133,675	221,367	6,373	5,614	87,692 R
			Soc. D.		
1901. Governor	166,681	183,814	3,489	5,365	17,133 R
1904. President	164,566	265,164	9,587	6,845	80,598 R
1907. Governor	186,300	194,313	....	5,255	8,013 R
1908. President	182,522	265,298	10,249	4,930	82,776 R

*Majority.

NEW HAMPSHIRE.

COUNTIES. (10.)	PRESIDENT, 1908.				GOVERNOR, 1908.	
	Bryan, Dem.	Taft, Rep.	Chafin, Pro.	Debs, Soc.	Carrs, Dem.	Quinby, Rep.
Belknap	1,692	2,916	99	41	1,909	2,628
Carroll	1,591	2,562	37	14	1,739	2,370
Cheshire	1,917	4,160	80	232	2,506	3,476
Coos	2,216	3,294	31	65	2,435	3,015
Grafton	3,582	6,323	95	65	4,492	5,313
Hillsborough	8,701	12,568	151	295	11,379	9,720
Merrimack	4,846	6,932	156	282	6,344	5,503
Rockingham	4,118	6,814	119	161	4,954	5,817
Strafford	3,523	4,822	108	79	3,738	4,491
Sullivan	1,469	2,758	29	65	1,895	2,297
Total	33,655	53,149	905	1,299	41,386	44,630
Plurality	..	19,484	..	..	..	3,244
Per cent	37.84	59.69	1.01	1.44	48.07	51.93
Scattering	585				2,791	
Whole vote	89,008				83,244	

For President in 1908, Hisgen, Ind., received 583 votes.

VOTE FOR REPRESENTATIVES IN CONGRESS, 1908.

Districts.

I. Michael J. White, Dem., 17,400; C. A. Sulloway, Rep., 24,413; Morrill, Pro., 425; Little, Soc., 385.

II. Fred M. Colby, Dem., 16,666; F. D. Currier, Rep., 26,007; Noyes, Pro., 333; McFall, Soc., 684.

PRESENT STATE GOVERNMENT.

Governor, Henry B. Quinby; Secretary of State, Edward N. Pearson; Treasurer, Solon A. Carter; Adjutant-General, Harry B. Cilley; Attorney-General, Edwin G. Eastman; Superintendent of Education, Henry C. Morrison; Secretary Board of Agriculture, Nahum J. Bachelder; Commissioner of Insurance, George H. Adams—all Republicans.

JUDICIARY.

Supreme Court: Chief Justice, Frank N. Parsons, Rep.; Associate Justices, Robert J. Peaslee, Dem.; Reuben E. Walker, Rep.; John E. Young, Rep.; George H. Bingham, Dem.; Clerk A. J. Shurtleff, Rep.

NEW HAMPSHIRE—*Continued.*

STATE LEGISLATURE, 1909.

	Senate.	*House.*	*Joint Ballot.*
Republicans	20	273	293
Democrats	4	116	120
Republican majority	16	157	173

VOTE OF THE STATE SINCE 1884.

	Dem.	*Rep.*	*Gr.*	*Pro.*	*Plu.*
1884. President	39,187	43,250	1,571	552	4,063 R
1888. President	43,382	45,724	....	1,566	2,342 R
				Pop.	
1896. President	21,650	57,444	....	779	35,794 R
			S. Dem.	*Pro.*	
1906. Governor	37,672	40,581	1,011	2,212	2,909 R

NEW MEXICO.

COUNTIES. (25.)	CONGRESS, 1908.		
	Larrazolo, Dem.	Andrews, Rep.	Metcalf, Soc.
Bernalillo	1,730	2,440	128
Chaves	1,421	659	137
Colfax	1,603	1,551	31
Doña Aña	1,021	1,200	4
Eddy	969	285	17
Grant	1,363	871	2
Guadalupe	1,069	977	2
Lincoln	709	763	14
Luna	343	223	20
McKinley	269	395	7
Mora	1,188	1,400	7
Otero	732	627	130
Quay	1,585	1,043	151
Rio Arriba	1,738	1,496	...
Roosevelt	1,707	942	196
Sandoval	214	877	..
San Juan	606	478	60
San Miguel	2,186	2,890	28
Santa Fé	1,333	1,621	4
Sierra	496	384	7
Socorro	1,467	1,610	3
Taos	942	1,183	...
Torrance	1,069	681	106
Union	1,160	1,327	..
Valencia	291	1,482	2
Total	27,217	27,605	1,036
Plurality	..	388	..
Percent	49.39	49.73	1.88
Scattering		2	
Whole vote		55,880	

The vote on joint statehood in 1906 was: Yes, 26,195; No, 14,735.

The vote for Delegate to Congress in 1906 was: Andrews, Rep., 22,915; Larrazola, Dem., 22,649.

PRESENT TERRITORIAL GOVERNMENT.

Governor, George Curry, Rep.; Lieut.-Governor and Secretary of State, Nathan Jaffa, Rep.; Treasurer, J. H. Vaughn, Rep.; Auditor, W. G. Sargent, Rep.; Adjutant-General, A. J. Tarkington, Rep.; Attorney-General, James M. Hervey, Rep.; Supt. Education, J. E. Clark, Rep.; Com. of Insurance, Jacobo Chavez, Rep.; Com. of Agriculture, Robert P. Ervien.

JUDICIARY.

Supreme Court: Chief Justice, William J. Mills; Associate Justices, John R. McFie, Ira A. Abbott, W. H. Pope, E. A. Mann, and F. W. Parker; Clerk, José D. Sena—all Republicans.

TERRITORIAL LEGISLATURE, 1909.

	Senate.	*House.*	*Joint Ballot.*
Republicans	9	20	29
Democrats	3	4	7
Republican majority	6	16	22

VOTE OF THE TERRITORY SINCE 1892.

	Dem.	*Rep.*		*Maj.*
1892	15,799	15,220		579 D
	Dem.	*Rep.*	*Silver.*	*Plu.*
1900	17,857	21,567	....	3,710 R
1902	14,576	24,222	....	7,646 R
1904	17,125	22,305	....	5,180 R
1906	22,649	22,915	....	266 R
1908	27,217	27,605	....	388 R

NEW YORK.

VOTE FOR REPRESENTATIVES IN CONGRESS, 1908.

Districts.

I. Counties of Suffolk, Nassau, and Queens (part). Manson Morris, Dem., 19,419; Wm. W. Cocks, Rep., 29,359; Burgher, Soc., 1,382; Michael, Ind., 1,865.

II. County of Kings (part). Geo. H. Lindsay, Dem., 15,455; Wm. Lieberman, Rep., 9,999; Loske, Soc., 1,305; Walsh, Ind., 1,886.

III. County of Kings (part). James P. Maher, Dem., 15,396; Otto G. Foelker, Rep., 18,614; Hill, Soc., 1,498; Goodman, Ind., 1,485.

IV. County of Kings (part). Edward R. Gilman, Dem., 18,910; Chas. B. Law, Rep., 23,944; Colborn, Ind., 2,542; Wegener, Soc., 2,707.

V. County of Kings (part). J. Harry Snook, Dem., 19,897; Richard Young, Rep., 28,075; Heyer, Soc., 1,309; O'Conner, Ind., 3,327.

VI. County of Kings (part). John E. Eastmond, Dem., 15,917; Wm. M. Calder, Rep., 22,050; Hopkins, Soc., 545; Kinney, Ind., 1,187.

VII. County of Kings (part). John J. Fitzgerald, Dem., 17,773; Wm. A. Koehl, Rep., 10,286; Petrit, Soc., 423; Smith, Ind., 1,841.

VIII. Counties of Richmond and New York (part). Daniel J. Riordan, Dem., 22,329; James E. Winterbottom, Rep., 11,482; Nagel, Soc., 554; Quinby, Ind., 1,200.

IX. County of New York (part). Henry M. Goldfogle, Dem., 6,194; Louis F. Cherey, Rep., 2,312; M. Hilquitt, Soc., 2,483; Salem, Ind., 329.

X. County of New York (part). Wm. Sulzer, Dem., 10,602; Gustav Hartman, Rep., 6,511; Brown, Soc., 1,754; Martin, Ind., 602.

XI. County of New York (part). Chas V. Fornes, Dem., 20,367; L. T. Driggs, Rep., 11,700; Neidig, Pro., 60; Irvine, Soc. 1,161; Porter, Ind., 1,853.

XII. County of New York (part). Michael F. Conroy, Dem., 16,757; Victor H. Duras, Rep., 8,090; Paulitz, Soc., 1,121; Bush, Ind., 1,482.

XIII. County of New York (part). Gerald A. Gray, Dem., 12,380; Herbert Parsons, Rep., 15,108; Newman, Soc., 430; Alson, Ind., 877.

XIV. Counties of New York (part), Queens (part). William Willett, Jr., Dem., 21,643; Emanuel K. Castka, Rep., 14,189; Schmidt, Soc., 3,055; Wade, Ind., 2,485.

XV. County of New York (part). Rhinelander Waldo, Dem., 12,531; Jacob Van Vechten Olcott, Rep., 16,921; Livingston, Soc., 69; Dougherty, Ind., 454.

XVI. County of New York (part). Francis Burton Harrison, Dem., 12,555; Francis A. Adams, Rep., 8,822; Parr, Soc., 1,966; Ackerman, Ind., 1,334.

XVII. County of New York (part). Wm. McAdoo, Dem., 24,736; Wm. S. Bennet, Rep., 32,764; Wilkins, Soc., 1,509; Walter, Ind., 2,105.

XVIII. County of New York (part). Joseph A. Goulden, Dem., 35,569; J. E. Spingham, Rep., 25,590; Staring, Soc., 3,649; McGarry, Ind., 4,144.

NEW YORK—*Continued.*

XIX. County of Westchester. Wm. H. Lynn, Dem., 19,851; John E. Andrus, Rep., 27,966; Walkiel, Soc., 881; Cleary, Ind., 1,237.

XX. Counties of Sullivan, Orange, and Rockland. Richard E. King, Dem., 17,979; Thos. W. Bradley, Rep., 23,997; Pew, Soc., 595; Harrison, Ind., 310.

XXI. Counties of Greene, Columbia, Putnam, and Dutchess. A. C. Zabriskie, Dem., 18,725; Hamilton Fish, Rep., 22,832; Warner, Soc., 141; Lazar, Ind., 525.

XXII. Counties of Rensselaer and Washington. W. A. Huppock, Dem., 19,074; William H. Draper, Rep., 22,980; Nugent, Soc., 294; Lane, Ind., 645.

XXIII. Counties of Albany and Schenectady. Wm. H. Keeler, Dem., 30,008; George W. Southwick, Rep., 30,593; Merrill, Soc., 1,173; Hisgen, Ind., 764.

XXIV. Counties of Delaware, Otsego, Ulster, and Schoharie. E. Hyde Clark, Dem., 23,059; Geo. W. Fairchild, Rep., 28,496; Ostrander, Ind., 1443.

XXV. Counties of Fulton, Hamilton, Montgomery, Warren, and Saratoga. Frank Beebe, Dem., 20,727; Cyrus Durey, Rep., 27,152.

XXVI. Counties of Clinton, Essex, Franklin, and St. Lawrence. Ellis Woodworth, Dem., 14,914; George R. Malby, Rep., 30,635; Thaxer, Soc., 189; Judge, Ind., 394.

XXVII. Counties of Herkimer and Oneida. Curtis F. Williams, Dem., 21,365; Charles S. Millington, Rep., 26,962; A. L. B. Curtiss, Soc., 398; Hoffman, Ind., 380.

XXVIII. Counties of Jefferson, Lewis, and Oswego. A. L. Cornwall, Dem., 15,756; Chas. L. Knapp, Rep., 25,948; Lynch, Soc., 536; Barker, Pro., 2,382; Moore, Ind., 236.

XXIX. Counties of Onondaga and Madison. Alfonso E. Fitch, Dem., 20,527; Michael E. Driscoll, Rep., 33,364; Tower, Soc., 1,569; Smith, Ind., 1,238.

XXX. Counties of Broome, Chenango, Tioga, Tompkins, and Cortland. A. D. Wales, Dem. 19,818; John W. Dwight, Re., 28,622; Beach, Soc., 301; June, Pro., 2,334; Poole, Ind., 254.

XXXI. Counties of Cayuga, Ontario, Wayne, and Yates. John A. Curtis, Dem., 17,891; Sereno E. Payne, Rep., 28,990; Cane, Soc., 956; Ellis, Ind., 937.

XXXII. County of Monroe. Herman S. Searle, Dem., 22,858; James B. Perkins, Rep., 33,025; Swain, Soc., 1,500; Kenfield, Pro., 727; Cox, Ind., 449.

XXXIII. Counties of Chemung, Schuyler, Seneca, and Steuben. James A. Parsons, Dem., 20,319; Jacob S. Fassett, Rep., 24,580; Pettibone, Soc., 376; Mitchell, Pro., 817; Hees, Ind., 410.

XXXIV. Counties of Genesee, Livingston, Niagara, Orleans, and Wyoming. Frank W. Brown, Dem., 23,298; James S. Simmons, Rep., 33,293; Davies, Soc., 1,448; Archer, Ind., 317.

XXXV. County of Erie (part). Daniel A. Driscoll, Dem., 25,886; L. B. Dow, Rep., 20,093; S. Leary, Soc., 626; Dixon, Pro., 108; Reinagel, Ind., 133.

XXXVI. County of Erie (part). W. H. Fallette, Dem., 20,790; De Alvos S. Alexander, Rep., 30,621; Findlate, Soc. 479; Matt, Pro., 511, Price, Ind., 176.

XXXVII. Counties of Allegany, Cattaraugus, and Chautauqua. S. A. Thorne, Dem., 15,718; E. B. Vreeland, Rep., 32,327; Wilson, Soc., 1,210; Rosa, Pro., 2,212; Stone, Ind., 226.

NEW YORK—*Continued.*

Counties. (61.)	Population of New York State.	Governor, 1908. Chanler, Dem.	Hughes, Rep.	Wanhope, Soc.	Shearn Ind.	Lieutenant-Governor. Dix, Dem.	White, Rep.	President, 1908. Bryan Dem.	Taft, Rep.	Debs, Soc.	Hisgen Ind.
Albany	171,497	20,518	23,107	162	416	..	..	18,715	24,763	206	361
Allegany	43,257	3,474	7,508	38	57	..	..	3,390	7,504	46	51
Broome	72,232	7,168	10,361	79	122	..	..	6,672	10,705	99	103
Cattaraugus	66,196	6,320	9,198	248	90	..	..	6,093	9,320	281	79
Cayuga	65,309	6,450	9,288	469	97	..	..	5,790	9,699	595	78
Chautauqua	96'180	7,167	15,049	777	109	..	..	6,157	15,739	988	81
Chemung	51,600	6,205	7,175	71	213	..	..	5,961	7,410	80	197
Chenango	36,783	3,882	5,950	46	52	..	..	3,768	5,949	67	50
Clinton	47,282	4,131	5,241	48	56	..	..	3,868	5,474	54	50
Columbia	42,868	5,305	5,577	12	115	..	..	5,090	5,726	16	121
Cortland	29,503	2,759	5,027	9	34	..	..	2,611	5,090	12	30
Delaware	46,788	4,796	7,190	16	54	..	..	4,640	7,142	21	60
Dutchess	81,633	10,047	10,154	61	217	..	..	8,953	11,132	73	220
Erie	473,700	58'865	46,654	953	368	..	..	45,183	52,182	1,234	249
Essex	32,452	2,237	4,983	54	100	..	..	2,084	5,167	60	94
Franklin	47,012	3,099	5,859	14	67	..	..	2,941	5,999	21	57
Fulton	42,330	4,169	6,104	456	203	..	..	3,507	6,574	565	188
Genesee	35,878	3,350	5,649	12	96	..	..	3,170	5,794	14	93
Greene	31,130	3,848	4,111	55	72	..	..	3,704	4,191	63	74
Hamilton	4,912	644	584	1	2	..	..	587	632	1	2
Herkimer	53,856	6,217	7,872	128	148	..	..	5,917	8,202	156	136
Jefferson	80.459	7,249	11,006	411	190	..	..	6,696	11.477	436	170
Kings	1,358 686	109,832	105,598	7,417	12,889	..	..	96.667	119789	8,422	10,428
Lewis	20,643	3,017	3,972	13	17	..	..	2,810	4,159	13	13
Livingston	36,450	3,938	5,879	11	38	..	..	3,560	5,700	14	29
Madison	39,690	3,786	6,699	116	52	..	..	3,630	6,727	141	46
Monroe	239,434	24,551	31,846	1,298	417	..	..	22,697	33,250	1,521	385
Montgomery	49,928	5,937	6 914	43	202	..	..	5,248	7,571	58	181
Nassau	69,477	5,620	9,123	75	619	..	..	4,879	9,787	86	614
New York	2,384,010	181,325	132,091	14,352	17,919	..	..	160276	154958	15,599	14,121
Niagara	84,744	9,576	10,213	72	62	..	..	8,574	11,145	95	51
Oneida	139,341	15,937	18,493	212	249	..	..	14,968	19,346	250	209
Onondaga	178,441	17,868	26,186	1,006	202	..	..	16,336	27,209	1,116	175
Ontario	52,689	5,616	8,180	69	35	..	..	5,478	8,245	82	30
Orange	108 267	10,962	13,559	159	360	..	..	9,936	14,414	194	361
Orleans	31,323	2,714	4,789	22	81	..	..	2,591	4,885	27	64
Oswego	70,110	6,577	10.144	22	60	..	..	6,170	10,447	76	50
Otsego	48,209	6,202	7.315	17	68	..	..	5,969	7,459	24	58
Putnam	14,169	1,521	2,151	10	48	..	..	1,369	2,275	4	52
Queens	198,240	22,315	17,275	1,685	2,653	..	..	20,252	19,420	1,751	2,288
Rensselaer	122,637	13,978	16,474	183	346	..	..	13,165	17,196	224	337
Richmond	72,845	7,818	6,422	179	562	...	..	7,374	6,831	193	521
Rockland	45,032	4,265	4,591	79	214	..	..	3,937	4,857	88	202
St. Lawrence	90,045	6,208	13,897	49	182	..	..	5,890	14.151	61	170
Saratoga	62,658	7,645	7,721	121	152	..	..	6,519	8,706	155	135
Schenectady	71.334	7.771	9,644	853	271	..	..	7,124	9,944	1,110	249
Schoharie	23,294	3,860	3.433	5	26	..	..	3,839	3,393	5	23
Schuyler	15,122	1,796	2.336	2	8	..	..	1,697	2,417	16	7
Seneca	25,315	3,207	3.732	49	29	..	..	3,138	3,749	54	27
Steuben	81,814	8,875	11,873	205	116	..	..	8,354	12,313	237	111
Suffolk	81,653	6,430	10,273	240	494	..	..	5,871	10,689	283	492
Sullivan	34,795	4,033	4,531	40	47	..	..	3,917	4,593	55	41
Tioga	26,907	2,759	4,228	39	28	..	..	2,700	4,247	45	27
Tompkins	34,151	5,872	5,066	42	31	..	..	3,727	5,090	50	26
Ulster	86,660	8,780	10,407	83	203	..	..	8,545	10,475	107	206
Warren	31,935	3,348	4,532	60	78	..	..	3,020	4,800	60	67
Washington	47,376	4,184	7,450	105	111	..	..	3,586	7,933	110	107
Wayne	48,564	4,463	7.998	45	45	..	..	4,404	8,008	56	46
Westchester	228,950	20,027	27,894	843	1,361	..	..	18,331	29,438	923	1,233
Wyoming	31,355	2,975	5,280	23	36	..	..	2,880	5,308	28	41
Yates	19,408	1,951	3,295	25	23	..	..	1,925	3,275	30	18
Total	8,067,308	735,189	804,651	43,212	33,994	707,701	827,416	667468	870070	38,451	35,817
Plurality			69,462				119,715	..	202602	..	..
Per cent		44.85	49.03	2.21	2.19	42.94	50.32	40.74	53.11	2.34	..
Scattering	..		..			....			..		
Whole vote			1,639,505			1,648,069			1,638,350		

Of the total vote cast for Hearst for Governor. 1906, 17,837 votes were cast under the emblem of the Independence League. Of the total vote for Chanler for Lieutenant-Governor, 17,460 votes were cast under the emblem of the Independence League.

For President in 1908, Gillhaus, Soc. Labor, received 3,877 votes; Hisgen, Ind., 35,817.

For Associate Judge of the Court of Appeals, 1908, Albert Haight, Rep. and Dem., received 1,531,743 votes; Robie Lyon, Ind., 4,232; Block, Soc., 37,874; Hart, Pro., 33,608; Seidel, Soc. Labor, 3,970.

In 1908 the vote of the highest Republican Presidential Elector was 870,070; the highest Democratic, 667,468.

For Governor in 1908, Stockwell, Pro., received 18,802 votes; Armstrong, Soc. Labor, 3,655.

For President in 1904, Corrigan, Soc. L., received 9,127 votes; Watson, Pop., 7,459.

The only State ticket in 1907 was for Judges of the Court of Appeals. E. T. and Willard Bartlett, Dem. and Rep., respectively, received 1,180,275 and 1,165,282, to 114,209 and 121,304 for R. R. Lyon and J. T. McDonough, Independence League candidates, respectively. The highest Socialist vote was 23,798; highest Prohibition, 18,775.

VOTE OF CITY OF NEW YORK FOR GOVERNOR, 1908.

MANHATTAN AND BRONX.

Dist.	Registration.	Chanler, Dem.	Hughes, Rep.	Stockwell, Pro.	Wanhope Soc.	Shearn Ind. L.
1	8,461	5,346	2,096	..	..	290
2	7,685	4,806	1.482	..	..	252
3	9,049	6,284	1,632	..	..	215
4	6,049	3,706	1,221	..	..	219
5	9,796	5,938	2,667	..	..	451
6	9,796	2,742	2.381	..	..	357
7	9,188	5,057	2,878	..	..	434
8	6,458	3,353	1,768	..	..	263
9	8,974	4,932	2,366	..	..	460
10	7,465	3,761	2,259	..	..	401
11	9,615	5,648	2.531	..	..	612
12	9,050	5,865	1,877	..	...	383
13	9,808	4,448	2,684	..	..	410
14	9,393	5,321	2,667	..	..	543
15	12,622	4,680	6,869	..	..	263
16	8.511	4.899	2,198	..	..	492
17	11,750	4.569	5,865	..	..	357
18	9,315	4,714	2,642	..	..	582
19	13.743	5,534	6,450	..	..	543
20	8,521	4,724	2,151	..	..	553
21	14,040	5,332	6,907	..	..	496
22	9,284	4,635	2.623	..	..	583
23	19,627	7,919	9 329	..	..	844
24	6,842	3,667	1,671	...	..	448
25	11,494	4,562	5,526	..	..	408
26	9,522	4,102	3,417	..	..	616
27	10,825	4,135	5,239	..	..	270
28	6,663	3,610	1,920	..	..	415
29	11,668	4,534	5,894	..	..	282
30	15,807	7,765	5,033	..	..	1,058
31	12,512	4,746	6,179	..	..	521
32	20,072	9,958	6,621	..	..	1,439
33	11,754	5,792	3,584	..	..	816
34	15,897	7,472	5,982	..	..	943
35	14,250	6,769	5,884	..	..	698
Total	371,114	181,325	132,091	823	14.352	17,919

BROOKLYN.

Dist.	Registration.	Chanler, Dem.	Hughes, Rep.	Stockwell, Pro.	Wanhope, Soc.	Shearn Ind. L.
1	10,180	4,391	4.607	..	..	283
2	8,729	5.410	2,215	..	..	414
3	8,234	5,124	2,083	..	..	471
4	10,036	4.591	4,213	..	..	470
5	11,927	4,052	6,671	..	..	508
6	9,364	4,005	3,884	..	..	520
7	8,622	4,508	2.978	..	..	467
8	8,695	4,897	2,696	..	..	427
9	13,641	5,771	5,935	..	..	903
10	11,248	4,888	5,405	..	..	330
11	10,985	4,445	5,478	..	..	361
12	12,450	5,163	6,124	..	..	402
13	8,403	4,336	2,800	..	..	509
14	8,185	4,599	2,311	..	..	540
15	9,015	4,437	3,085	..	..	783
16	14,750	6,982	5,775	..	..	679
17	11,273	3,775	6,565	..	..	291
18	14,362	4,937	8,376	..	..	406
19	8,499	3.898	2 853	..	..	681
20	10,741	3,957	5.090	..	..	709
21	6,533	2.883	2,181	..	..	440
22	20,059	7,351	9,026	..	..	1,486
23	13,741	5,408	5,247	..	..	807
Total	249,672	109,832	105,598	319	7,417	12,889

QUEENS.

Dist.	Registration.	Chanler, Dem.	Hughes, Rep.	Stockwell, Pro.	Wanhope, Soc.	Shearn Ind. L.
1	..	..	..	..	..	..
	..	..	..	..	..	..
	..	..	..	..	..	..
	..	..	..	..	..	..
Total	..	22.315	17.275	1.685	92	2.653

RICHMOND.

Dist.	Registration.	Chanler, Dem.	Hughes, Rep.	Stockwell, Pro.	Wanhope, Soc.	Shearn Ind. L.
Total	15.879	7,818	6.422	..	..	..
Gr'd Total	..	..	...	..	..	..

VOTE FOR STATE SENATE, 1908.

RICHMOND—(Forms Twenty-third Senate District with Rockland County.)

District.	Democrat.	Republican.	Socialist.	Prohibition.	Independence League.
2	Bayne...... 12,259	Hurd....... 10,851	Veck.............. 181	Doremus..... 230	Story.......... 524
QUEENS.					
2	Harte....... 21,081	Kupka..... 18,146	Froelich........ 1,780	Farr........... 125	McKeown.. 2,817
BROOKLYN.					
3	Cullen..... 14,170	Boardman. 9,511	Cook.............. 360	Schimpff 44	Duffy......... 1,256
4	Reigelmann 11,646	Gledhill.... 15,851	Lipes.............. 954	Page......... 74	Morrison.... 1,225
5	Cronin...... 14,633	Scheeman.. 12,166	Stifel.............. 666	Brown....... 69	Ross.......... 1,676
6	Harmon... 13,753	Travis..... 17,770	Frazer............ 417	....	O'Loughlin. 981
7	McCarren.. 12,093	Hazlewood 9,380	Stammer......... 781	Irvine........ 42	Holwell..... 1,877
8	Gale........ 14,470	Burling'me 21,933	Hoffstead........ 677	Johnson...... 104	Babcock 1,211
9	Hassenflug. 9,700	Kissell 10,790	Schramm........ 1 865	Reuber....... 40	Schmidt 2,081
10	Tessaro..... 11,301	Alt........ 15,749	Martin........... 2,306	Hirsch....... 62	Geators...... 2,082
MANHATTAN.					
11	Sullivan, C. 11,432	Cebulsky... 4,694	Parker 2,376	Allen.......... 30	Fertig....... 543
12	Sullivan, T. 12.578	Hotz........ 6,650	Guttman........ 1,404	Holden........ 39	McMahon... 640
13	Caffrey..... 15,691	Nowak. ... 8,284	Turk............ 380	Smith......... 50	Rathborne.. 1,114
14	Grady...... 15,493	Hendrick.. 7,311	Willson.......... 940	Lewis......... 26	Domroe...... 1,320
15	McManus.. 13,332	Popper..... 9,012	Wells............ 604	Record........ 25	McCarthy... 1 639
16	Wagner.... 14,026	O'Neill..... 7,646	Rain............. 22,56	Carpenter 21	Griesman... 1,412
17	Liebmann.. 12,507	Agnew..... 17,168	Ghent............ 410	Church........ 73	Govan....... 829
18	Schwab..... 14,144	Brough..... 19,801	Kanely.......... 665	Green......... 58	Rosenthal... 991
19	Markham.. 17,668	Newcomb.. 22,808	Bartholomew... 1,116	Conroy........ 92	Union....... 1.500
20	Frawley... 10,598	Levine 7,759	Coyle............ 1,749	Simmons. 22	Thomas..... 1.314
21	Stillwell ... 16,796	Grimler..... 2,520	Rosch........... 1,671	Huggard...... 39	Kearney.... 2.378
22	Shultz...... 19,923	Tobias...... 15,189	Gall............. 2,178	Lounsberry... 70	V.Rensselaer 2,116

VOTE OF THE STATE OF NEW YORK SINCE 1892

	Dem.	*Rep.*	*Gr.*	*Pro.*	*Plu.*	
1892. Pres....	*654,865	609,350	17,956	38,190	45,518	D
1894. Gov ...	†517,710	673,818	15,868	23,526	156,108	R
1896. Pres....	‡551,369	819,838	17,667	16,052	268,469	R
1897. Ch. Jus.	554,680	493.791	20.854	19,653	60,889	D
1898. Gov	643.921	661.707	23,860	18,383	17,786	R
1900. Gov	693,733	804,859	13,493	22.704	111,126	R
1900. Pres....	§678.386	821,992	12,622	22.043	143,606	R

	Dem.	*Rep.*	*Soc.*	*Pro.*	*Plu.*	
1902. Gov.....	656,347	665,150	15,886	20.490	8,803	R
1904. Pres....	683,981	859,513	36,883	20,787	175,552	R
1904. Gov	733,704	813,964	36,257	20,568	80,560	R
1906. Gov....	691,105	749,002	21,751	15,985	57,897	R
1907. J. Ct. Ap.	1,165,282	1,180,275	23,798	18,775	14,983	R
1908. Gov.....	735,189	864,651	33,994	18,802	69,462	R
1908. Pres.....	667,468	870,070	38,451	22,667	212,602	R

* Populist vote in addition, 16,429. † Populist vote, 11,049. Dem. Reform vote, 27,202. ‡ National Democratic vote, 18,950. § Social Democratic vote, 12,869.

VOTE FOR ASSEMBLYMEN, NEW YORK, 1908.

Assem. Dis.	Democrat.		Republican.		Socialist.		Ind. League.	
1..	Coughlan	5,032	McLain	2,380	Toennies	96	Driscoll	287
2..	Smith	4,703	Robinson	1,572	Mailly	657	Butler	171
3..	Oliver	6,111	Rubin	1,782	Simon	220	Carroll	194
4..	Levy	3,698	Rosenzweig	1,239	Pine	680	Fliashnick	131
5..	Eagleton	5,571	McGann	2,761	Duffie	19	Manning	703
6..	Stern	2,714	Robson	2,396	Hunter	806	Schifter	155
7..	McElligott	4,805	Kelleher	3 112	Techs	138	Langguth	422
8..	Granbard	3,070	Segal	1,699	Stokes	1,250	Perlmann	144
9..	Hackett	4,688	Morton	2,594	Brown	245	Lindsay	457
10..	Speilberg	3,425	McCabe	2,566	Korn	592	Marx	389
11..	Bohan	5,167	Johnston	3,541	Barrett	29	Hillburger	247
12..	Foley	5,799	Lush	1,980	Meyer	337	Ott	333
13..	Hoey	4,027	Fleming	3,136	Plawsky	134	Cahill	356
14..	Herrick	4,836	Conroy	2,865	Herold	285	Hefferman	793
15..	Cohen	4.421	Bennett	7,322	Myers	29	Ackerly	129
16..	McCue	4,655	Marcus	2,320	Pierce	318	Gormley	568
17..	Buckley	4,307	Toombs	6,078	Cassidy	233	Schweitzer	326
18..	Goldberg	4,656	Sussman	2,668	Egerter	558	Holtzman	546
19..	Donihee	5,340	Murray	6,641	Shanahan	305	McInery	485
20..	McGrath	4.738	Kohn	2,195	Kohn	692	Herst	450
21..	Murphy	5,130	Conklin	7,093	Redding	306	Schoeppler	429
22..	Bauman	4,626	Sauer	2,672	Lee	962	Drew	493
23..	Keleher	7,716	Francis	9,520	Crimmins	435	Frellochs	729
24..	Brennau	3,597	Schatzmann	1,776	Stelzer	603	Grahe	370
25..	Wood	4,125	Ward	5,908	Moltman	173	Begg	359
26..	Joseph	3,938	Strauss	3,756	Moore	14	Geariety	788
27..	Riker	3,789	Robinson	5,588	Harris	95	Hanshe	236
28..	Levy	3,284	Kennedy	2,029	Cohn	323	Egan	607
29..	Seligsberg	4,529	Bates	5,890	Halfern	127	Wills	261
30..	Cuvillier	7,222	Caspar	5,641	Jaedicker	670	Donovan	944
31..	Greenberg	4,546	Marks	6,363	Ury	347	Endelman	474
32..	Silberman	9.523	Tonjes	7,012	Holzbauer	964	Niemeyer	1,340
33..	Schmidt	5,696	Horenberger	3,670	Simmons	757	McLoughlin	746
34..	Stein	7,339	Herbst	6.089	Lightbown	860	Levy	791
35..	Sheridan	6,494	Payne	5,708	Eiges	606	Noonan	635

VOTE FOR SURROGATE, NEW YORK COUNTY, 1908.

Cohalan......169,879 | Beckett......144,651 | Mullen...... 15,284 | Palmieri......15,547

VOTE FOR SUPREME COURT JUSTICE, FIRST DISTRICT, 1908.

Lehman..... 173,764 | Bruce..........140,477 | Lichtenstein...15,392 | Mayes.........15,309

VOTE FOR SUPREME COURT JUSTICE, SECOND DISTRICT, 1908.

Stapleton RD300,082 | Whitehouse..138,732 | Stewart........15,696 | Bondin........10.486
Blackmar....162,853 | | Hanson........15,403 | Davidson.....15,043

The Second Judicial District is composed of Kings, Nassau, Queens, Richmond and Suffolk counties.

VOTE FOR JUSTICES OF CITY COURT, NEW YORK COUNTY, 1908.

Lynch........173,145 | Wasservogel.140,961 | Allen..........15,273 | Wolf..........15,441
La Fete......172,492 | Mathewson..141,372 | Block..........15,190 | Kelly..........15,486

GREATER NEW YORK VOTE, 1908, PRESIDENT AND GOVERNOR.

	Manhattan, Bronx.	Kings.	Queens.	Richmond.	Total.
Bryan, Dem.	160,276	96,667	20,252	7,374	284,569
Taft, Rep.	154,958	119,789	19,420	6,831	300,998
Hisgen, Ind.	14,121	10,428	2,288	521	27,358
Debs, Soc.	15,599	8,422	1,751	193	25,965
Chafin, Pro.	506	531	117	103	1,257
Gillhaus, S.L.	1,162	625	93	32	1,812

	Manhattan, Bronx.	Kings.	Queens.	Richmond.	Total.
Chanler, D.	181,325	109,832	22,315	7,818	321,290
Hughes, R.	132,091	105,598	17,275	6,422	261,386
Shearn, Ind.	17,919	12,889	2,653	562	33,803
Wanhope, S.	14,352	7,417	1,685	179	23,633
Stockwell, P.	323	319	92	80	814
Arms'g, S.L	1,114	599	90	33	1,837

VOTE FOR MAYOR OF GREATER NEW YORK.

1897.

	Manhattan and Bronx.	Brooklyn.	Queens.	Richmond.
Van Wyck, Dem.	143,666	76,185	9,275	4,871
Tracy, Rep.	55,834	37,611	5,639	2,779
Low, Cit. Un.	77,210	65,656	5,876	2,798
Sanial, Soc. Lab.	9,786	3,593	921	157
Wardwell, Pro.	650	507	83	119

1901.

	Manhattan and Bronx.	Brooklyn.	Queens.	Richmond.
Shepard, Dem.	156,631	88,858	13,679	6,009
Low, Fus.	162,298	114,625	13,118	6,772
Manierre, Pro.	617	501	74	72
Keinard, Soc. Lab.	4,323	1,638	181	71
Hanford, Soc. Dem.	6,409	2,693	613	120

1903.

	Manhattan and Bronx.	Brooklyn.	Queens.	Richmond.
McClellan, Dem.	188,681	102,569	17,074	6,458
Low, Fus.	132,178	101,251	11,960	6,697
Furman, Soc. Dem.	11,318	4,529	976	133
Hunter, Soc. Lab.	3,540	1,411	178	76
McKee, Pro.	376	394	47	50

1905.

	Manhattan and Bronx.	Brooklyn.	Queens.	Richmond.
McClellan, Dem.	140,264	68,788	13,228	6,127
Ivins, Rep.	64,280	61,192	7,213	4,499
Hearst, M. O. L.	123,292	84,835	13,706	3,096

NORTH CAROLINA.

Counties. (97.)	President, 1908.				Governor, 1908.	
	Bryan Dem.	Taft, Rep.	Chafin Pro.	Debs, Soc.	Kitchin, Dem.	Cox, Rep.
Alamance....	2,113	2,184	..	...	2,220	2,130
Alexander....	793	1,074	...	..	793	1,076
Alleghany...	633	575	...	...	643	541
Anson........	1,490	301	...	..	1,538	263
Ashe..........	1,639	1,674	..	...	1,700	1,701
Beaufort.......	1,828	1,304	...	...	1,914	1,209
Bertie.........	1,258	360	...	...	1,328	274
Bladen........	1,132	660	...	...	1,213	599
Brunswick....	607	841	..	..	671	774
Buncombe....	3,506	3,572	...	...	3,629	3,434
Burke.........	1,310	1,358	..	...	1,353	1,315
Cabarrus......	1,610	1,821	..	...	1,616	1,817
Caldwell.......	1,413	1,745	..	..	1,476	1,665
Camden........	398	164	...	...	405	141
Carteret.......	1,152	1,060	...	...	1,173	998
Caswell........	820	370	...	...	878	323
Catawba.......	1.864	2.010	..	..	1,961	2,012
Chatham.....	1,521	1.497	..	..	1,594	1,428
Cherokee......	782	1,310	...	...	823	1,273
Chowan.......	621	213	...	...	658	176
Clay...........	343	321	..	...	348	318
Cleveland....	2.282	1,459	...	..	2,304	1,452
Columbus.....	1.845	1,381	...	...	2,056	1,192
Craven........	1.399	449	...	...	1,520	340
Cumberland..	1,832	1,453	...	..	2,019	1,250
Currituck.....	701	68	...	...	734	49
Dare..........	416	370	...	...	443	354
Davidson......	2,126	2,340	..	...	2,231	2,481
Davie..........	780	1,185	..	..	802	1,163
Duplin.......	1,508	1,225	...	..	1,642	1,139
Durham......	1,859	1,820	...	...	1,962	1,693
Edgecombe...	1,758	438	..	..	1,839	392
Forsyth......	2,472	2,876	..	..	2,653	2,782
Franklin.....	1.984	561	..	...	2,093	432
Gaston........	2,398	1,970	...	..	2,568	1,820
Gates..........	653	337	...	...	700	278
Graham.......	418	465	...	...	422	461
Granville......	1,561	734	...	..	1,746	592
Greene.........	876	538	...	..	915	504
Guilford......	3.822	2,863	..	..	3,948	2,765
Halifax.......	2,165	880	..	...	2,285	276
Harnett.......	1.501	1,047	..	..	1,550	1,012
Haywood......	1,952	1,304	..	..	1,983	1,253
Henderson....	917	1,602	...	...	998	1,497
Hertford......	839	353	...	..	880	291
Hyde...........	662	223	..	..	701	177
Iredell........	2,465	1,803	...	..	2,533	1,746
Jackson.......	1.022	1,086	..	..	1,028	1,073
Johnston......	2,593	2,827	..	..	2,816	2,596
Jones.........	585	315	...	..	631	272
Lee.............	832	562	..	..	912	501
Lenoir........	1,393	966	..	..	1,490	896
Lincoln........	1,222	1.217	..	..	1,286	1,180
Macon.........	927	1,045	..	..	940	1,017
Madison.......	862	2,027	..	..	878	2,001
Martin........	1,338	421	..	..	1,385	360
McDowell....	950	1,000	..	..	973	984
Mecklenburg.	3,926	1,645	..	..	4,233	1,385
Mitchell......	550	1,808	..	..	575	1,797
Montgomery..	1,008	1,087	..	..	1,047	1,047
Moore.........	1,109	1,077	..	...	1,219	976
Nash..........	1,678	1,334	..	...	1,848	1,222
New Hanover	1,857	511	..	...	2,110	283
Northampton	1,726	186	...	...	1,691	121
Onslow.......	870	710	..	..	988	559
Orange.......	1,017	1,073	..	...	1,077	1,014
Pamlico.......	628	501	..	...	671	478
Pasquotank..	929	405	..	...	1,048	265
Pender.......	930	373	..	...	1,019	294
Perquimans..	568	502	..	..	598	427
Person........	750	969	..	..	890	847
Pitt...........	2,419	890	...	...	2,500	811
Polk..........	511	621	..	..	536	594
Randolph.....	2.472	2,676	...	...	2,546	2,647
Richmond...	1,029	462	..	..	1,106	366
Robeson......	2.698	1,300	..	..	3,005	1,115
Rockingham.	1,887	2,008	..	..	2,039	1,883
Rowan.......	2,392	2,009	..	..	2,719	1,723
Rutherford....	1,978	1,766	..	..	2,011	1,789
Sampson.....	1,835	2,465	..	..	1,409	2,423
Scotland......	714	85	..	...	752	47
Stanly.........	1,491	1,685	...	..	1,587	1,630
Stokes........	1,061	1.711	..	...	1,123	1.671
Surry........	1,709	2,870	...	...	1,820	2,781
Swain........	603	931	...	...	614	902
Transylvania	570	611	...	...	600	579
Tyrrell.......	312	395	...	...	357	345
Union........	2.028	833	...	..	2,086	701
Vance........	1,121	641	...	..	1,187	578
Wake.........	3,718	2,961	..	..	4,149	2,583
Warren......	1,066	296	...	..	1,171	191
Washington..	495	556	...	...	534	526
Watauga.....	962	1.313	...	..	998	1,279
Wayne.......	2,207	1,504	...	..	2,274	1,450
Wilkes......	1,559	3,382	...	...	1,599	3,331
Wilson.......	1,732	1,014	...	...	1,905	831
Yadkin.......	597	1,644	..	..	718	1,649
Yancey.......	978	950	...	..	1,002	912
Total......	136928	114887	..	..	145102	107760
Plurality.....	22,041	..	..	..	37,342	
Percent......	54.37	45.63	..	...	57.34	42.66
Whole vote		251,815			252,862	

For President in 1904 Roosevelt, Rep., received 82,442 votes; Parker, Dem., 124,121 votes.

The vote for Governor in 1904 was: Glenn, Dem., 128,761; Harris, Rep., 79,505; Templeton, Pro., 237; Pegram, Soc., 109. Glenn's plurality, 49,256.

For President in 1900 McKinley, Rep., received 133,081 votes; Bryan, Dem., 157,752 votes.

VOTE FOR REPRESENTATIVES IN CONGRESS, 1908.

Districts.

I. Beaufort, Camden, Chowan, Currituck, Dare, Gates, Hertford, Hyde, Martin, Pasquotank, Perquimans, Pitt, Tyrrell, and Washington. John Small, Dem., 13,119; Isaac M. Meekins, Rep., 5,342. Small's majority, 7,777.

II. Bertie, Edgecombe, Greene, Halifax, Lenoir, Northampton, Warren, and Wilson. Claude Kitchin, Dem., 12,275; McMurray Ferguson, Rep., 3,361. Kitchin's majority, 8,914.

III. Carteret, Craven, Duplin, Jones, Onslow, Pamlico, Pender, Sampson, and Wayne. C. R. Thomas, Dem., 11.544, Eli W. Hill, Rep., 7,896. Thomas's majority 3,648.

IV. Chatham, Franklin, Johnston, Nash, Vance, and Wake. Edw. W. Pou, Dem., 13,463; William G. Briggs, Rep., 8,966. Pou's majority, 4,497.

V. Alamance, Caswell, Durham, Forsyth, Granville, Guilford, Orange, Person, Rockingham, and Stokes. A. L. Brooks, Dem., 18,938; J. M. Morehead, Rep., 19,288; Morehead's majority, 150.

VI. Bladen, Brunswick, Columbus, Cumberland, Harnett, New Hanover, and Robeson. Hannibal L. Godwin, Dem., 12,542; A. H. Slocumb, Rep., 6,385. Godwin's majority, 6,157.

VII. Anson, Davidson, Davie, Montgomery, Moore, Randolph, Richmond, Scotland, Union, and Yadkin. Robt. N. Page, Dem., 15,057; Zeb V. Walser, Rep., 11,732. Page's majority, 3,225.

VIII. Alexander, Alleghany, Ashe, Cabarrus, Caldwell, Iredell, Rowan, Stanly, Surry, Watauga, and Wilkes. Richard N. Hackett, Dem., 15,488; Charles H. Cowles, Rep., 16,863. Cowles's majority, 1,375.

IX. Burke, Catawba, Cleveland, Gaston, Lincoln, Madison, Mecklenburg, Mitchell, and Yancey. Edw. Y. Webb, Dem., 16,530; John A. Smith, Rep., 13,514. Webb's majority, 3,016.

NORTH CAROLINA—*Continued.*

X. Counties of Buncombe, Cherokee, Clay, Graham, Haywood, Henderson, Jackson, McDowell, Macon, Polk, Rutherford, Swain, Transylvania. William T. Crawford, Dem., 14,884; John G. Grant, Rep., 15,245. Grant's majority, 361

PRESENT STATE GOVERNMENT.

Governor, R. B. Glenn; Lieutenant-Governor, F. D. Winston; Secretary of State, J. B. Grimes; Treasurer, B. R. Lacey; Auditor, B. F. Dixon; Attorney-General, R. D. Gilmer; Superintendent of Education, J. Y. Joyner; Commissioner of Agriculture, S. L. Patterson; Commissioner of Insurance, J. R. Young; Adjutant-General, T. R. Robertson—all Democrats.

JUDICIARY.

Supreme Court: Chief Justice, Walter Clark, Rep.; Justices, Geo. H. Brown, Dem; Wm. A. Hoke, Dem.; Henry G. Connor, P. D. Walker; Clerk, Thomas S. Kenan, Dem.

STATE LEGISLATURE, 1809.

	Senate.	*House.*	*Joint Ballot.*
Democrats	46	99	145
Republicans	4	21	25
Democratic majority	42	78	120

VOTE OF THE STATE SINCE 1880.

	Dem.	*Rep.*	*Gr.*	*Pro.*	*Maj.*
1880. President	124,204	115,878	1,136	....	*8,326 D
1884. President	142,952	125,068	....	454	*17,884 D
1888. President	147,902	134,784	....	2,789	13,118 D
			Pop.		
1892. President	132.951	100,342	44.736	2,636	32.609 D
	Dem.	*Rep.-Pop.*			*Maj.*
1894. Ch. Justice	127,593	148,344			20,751 R.-P
	Dem.	*Rep.*	*Pop.*	*Pro.*	*Plu.*
1896. Governor	145,216	154.052	30,932	....	8,936 R
	Fus.	*Rep.*	*N. D.*		
1896. President	174,488	155,222	578	675	19,266 F
	Dem.				
1898. Judge	177,449	159,511	....	....	17,938 D
			Peo.		
1902. Jus. Sup. Ct.	132,239	71,275	....	....	50,964 D
1904. President	124,121	81,442	819	361	41,679 D
1808. Bresident	136,928	114,887	......	....	22,041 D

* Plurality.

NORTH DAKOTA.

Counties. (43.)	President, 1908.				Governor, 1908.	
	Bryan Dem.	Taft, Rep.	Chafin Pro.	Debs, Soc.	Burke, Dem.	Johnson, Rep.
Adams	201	547	19	21	261	575
Barnes	1,002	1,815	60	35	1,541	1,445
Benson	553	1,363	64	30	949	1,126
Billings	236	768	17	21	263	785
Bottineau	1,146	1,951	44	140	1,818	1,490
Bowman	209	452	7	15	334	364
Burleigh	660	1,815	17	37	1,094	1,118
Cass	2,003	3,685	107	94	3,242	2,787
Cavalier	1,191	1,529	24	32	1,520	1,297
Dickey	635	1,062	17	30	830	962
Dunn	160	373	1	8	166	413
Eddy	368	540	16	6	594	394
Emmons	618	951	10	14	733	839
Foster	434	570	7	6	603	444
Grand Forks	1,740	2,740	130	152	2,972	1,820
Griggs	493	605	51	18	680	523
Hettinger	182	568	10	9	211	558
Kidder	251	769	24	26	395	697
La Moure	553	1,104	29	19	824	935
Logan	143	711	3	16	169	708
McHenry	1,296	1,772	33	..	1,836	1,360
McIntosh	140	928	53	55	395	935
McKenzie	212	574	7	4	321	539
McLean	956	2,273	51	46	1,512	916
Mercer	96	430	3	98	138	679
Morton	873	2,021	14	2	1,279	1,746
Nelson	616	1,226	17	60	1,039	961

NORTH DAKOTA—*Continued.*

Counties.	President, 1908.				Governor, 1908.	
	Bryan Dem.	Taft, Rep.	Debs, Soc.	Chafin Pro.	Burke, Dem.	Johnson, Rep.
Oliver	179	325	3	31	279	272
Pembina	1,185	1,389	17	50	1,453	1,217
Pierce	609	884	28	18	978	664
Ramsey	1,072	1,498	72	27	1,556	1,141
Ransom	581	1,308	11	36	911	1,107
Richland	1,502	1,864	14	60	1,901	1,597
Rolette	529	811	99	24	903	550
Sargent	576	1,012	38	20	847	829
Stark	496	922	19	7	599	895
Steele	366	881	17	18	552	787
Stutsman	1,344	1,777	24	45	1,798	1 462
Towner	655	867	60	18	968	664
Traill	490	1,207	33	97	959	943
Walsh	1,641	1,751	117	30	2,075	1,494
Ward	3,165	5,290	563	195	5,272	3,873
Wells	535	1.243	22	19	869	1,025
Williams	1,019	2,039	217	87	1,657	1,673
Total	32,909	57,771	2,411	1,549	49.346	47,093
Plurality	..	24,862	..	..	2,253	..
Per cent	34.77	61.04	2.55	1.64	51.16	48.84
Whole vote		94,640			96.439	

Vote for Governor in 1904 was: M. F. Hegge, Dem., 16,744; E. Y. Searles, Rep., 47,828; H. H. Aaker, Pro., 1,388; A. Basset, Soc., 1,760.

For President in 1904 Roosevelt, Rep., received 52,505; Parker, Dem., 14,273.

VOTE FOR REPRESENTATIVES IN CONGRESS, 1908

At Large.—L. B. Hanna, Fargo, and A. J. Gronna, Lakota, both Republican, elected.

PRESENT STATE GOVERNMENT.

Governor, John Burke; Lieutenant-Governor, R. S. Lewis; Secretary of State, Alfred Blaisdell; Treasurer, G. L. Bickford, Auditor, D K: Brightbell, Attorney-General, Andrew Miller; Superintendent of Education, W. L. Stockwell; Adjutant-General, to be appointed Commissioner of Agriculture, W. C. Gilbrath; Commissioner of Insurance, E. C. Cooper; Commissioner of Public Lands, O. I. Hegge—all Republicans, except Burke, Dem.

JUDICIARY.

Supreme Court: Chief Justioe, David E. Morgan: Justices, Chas J. Fisk, B. F. Spalding, Clerk, R. D. Hoskins—all Republicans.

STATE LEGISLATURE, 1909.

The Legislature is composed of 128 Republicans and 19 Democrats.

VOTE OF THE STATE AND TERRITORY SINCE 1884.

	Dem.	*Rep.*	*F.A.*	*Maj.*
*1884. Congress	3,352	28,906	....	25,554 R
*1886. Congress	15,540	23,567	....	8,027 R
*1888. Congress	15,801	25,290	....	9,489 R
1889. Governor	12,733	25,365	....	12,632 R
1890. Governor	12,604	19,053	4,821	6,449 R
Fusion.	*Pop.*		*Pro.*	
1892. Governor 18,995	....	17,236	.....	1,729 F
1892. President	17,700	17,519	899	181 P
	Dem.		*Pop.*	*Plu.*
1894. Governor	8,188	23,723	9,354	14,369 R
			Pro.	
1896. President	20,686	26,335	358	5,649 R
	Fus.			
1898. Governor	19,496	27,308	....	7,812 R
1900. Governor	22,275	34,052	560	11,777 R
1900. President	20,519	35,891	731	15,372 R
			Soc.	
1902. Governor	17,566	31,621	1,139	4,055 R
1904. President	14,273	52,595	2,005	8,322 R
1906. Governor	34,420	29,359	975	5,115 D
1908. President	32,908	57.771	2,411	24 862 R

*Vote of the north half of Dakota Territory, corresponding to the present State of North Dakota.

OHIO.

Counties. (88.)	President, 1908.				Governor, 1908.	
	Bryan Dem.	Taft, Rep.	Chafin, Pro.	Debs, Soc.	Harmon, Dem.	Harris Rep.
Adams	3,048	3,432	88	17	3,006	3,502
Allen	7,195	5.841	127	373	7,442	5,762
Ashland	3,627	2,804	84	56	3,546	2,934
Ashtabula	3,572	8,213	231	938	3,976	7.974
Athens	3,654	6 449	189	164	3.849	6,342
Auglaize	4 622	3 001	57	102	4,738	2,940
Belmont	7,750	8,193	378	730	7,711	8,472
Brown	4,242	2,638	35	23	4,183	2,686
Butler	9,678	7,320	85	885	10,720	6,490
Carroll	1 590	2,517	83	44	1,603	2 550
Champaign	3 160	4,153	93	46	3,284	4,072
Clark	6 529	8 917	326	1,040	7,324	8,367
Clermont	4,150	4,137	61	107	4,344	3,980
Clinton	2,464	4 107	76	28	2,548	4 079
Columbiana	6,736	9,626	742	948	7,667	9,186
Coshocton	4,106	3,606	83	311	4,310	3,526
Crawford	6,006	3 061	78	166	5,913	3,188
Cuyahoga	39,954	56,344	351	4,818	49,826	48,040
Darke	6,391	4,951	210	70	6,302	5,114
Defiance	3,754	2,531	72	112	3,726	2,604
Delaware	3,330	4,007	186	64	3,398	4,017
Erie	4,983	5,366	41	293	6,198	4,252
Fairfield	5,821	4,023	125	25	5,857	4,035
Fayette	2,451	3,343	49	33	2,568	3,267
Franklin	23.314	28,914	606	1,211	27.149	25,760
Fulton	2 131	3 608	82	69	2,140	3,628
Gallia	2,171	3,914	50	25	2,232	3,906
Geauga	982	2,596	32	32	959	3,633
Greene	2,882	4,902	125	232	3 073	4,843
Guernsey	3,449	5.210	196	798	3,456	5,304
Hamilton	45.429	63,803	317	3,306	64,621	45,685
Hancock	5,420	4,899	93	356	5,249	5,148
Hardin	4,164	4 444	117	99	4,126	4.549
Harrison	1,961	3,069	87	51	1,826	3,265
Henry	3,817	2,425	49	121	3 803	2,461
Highland	3,823	4,149	93	23	3,827	4 221
Hocking	2,864	2 749	47	95	2,891	2,749
Holmes	3,043	1,252	31	29	2,934	1.379
Huron	4,262	4,930	61	90	4,464	4,795
Jackson	3,235	4,489	90	209	3,381	4,402
Jefferson	4,882	7,310	225	355	5,183	7,152
Knox	4,233	4,318	99	139	4,332	4 302
Lake	1,605	3,635	63	121	1,679	3,590
Lawrence	2.654	5,708	65	134	2,896	5,495
Licking	7,685	6,756	119	598	8,100	6,492
Logan	3,186	4 756	116	76	3,219	4,762
Lorain	5,460	8,699	108	944	6,037	8,228
Lucas	16,208	18,715	169	3,394	18,225	16.614
Madison	2,430	3 051	55	17	2,464	3,028
Mahoning	9 312	10,760	298	631	10.523	9,835
Marion	4,657	4 175	116	99	4 682	4 239
Medina	2,378	4,327	52	118	2,428	3,443
Meigs	2,225	4,108	59	222	2 506	3,877
Mercer	4 456	2,148	73	46	4,408	2,233
Miami	5,369	6,558	100	182	5 657	6,348
Monroe	3,961	1,974	57	38	3 909	2,044
Montgomery	20,566	20,069	177	1,780	22,566	18,258
Morgan	1,932	2 445	92	56	1,967	2,425
Morrow	2,239	2,500	121	30	2 137	2.659
Muskingum	6,576	8,080	340	420	6,953	7.885
Noble	2,154	2,707	93	28	2,158	2,728
Ottawa	3,329	2,202	17	75	3,484	2 049
Paulding	2,767	3.049	63	19	2,676	3,170
Perry	3,885	4,304	102	398	4,034	4,261
Pickaway	4,007	3.119	76	22	4,067	3,103
Pike	2,085	1,798	34	24	2,060	1.821
Portage	3,625	4,129	227	183	3,666	4,147
Preble	3,247	3,519	90	42	3,350	3 500
Putnam	4,836	2,483	65	95	1,679	2,687
Richland	6,702	5,301	102	213	6,745	5,403
Ross	5,325	5,432	25	89	5,648	5,158
Sandusky	5,242	4,079	47	172	5,034	4,362
Scioto	4,310	5.790	119	589	4,863	5,367
Seneca	6,138	4 959	88	307	6,180	4 995
Shelby	3,879	2,646	38	38	3,814	2,725
Stark	12,286	14,112	405	1,110	13,957	12,936
Summit	9,930	10,365	328	1.255	10,431	10,205
Trumbull	4,476	6,978	165	397	4,710	6,840

OHIO—*Continued.*

Counties.	President, 1908.				Governor 1908.	
	Bryan, Dem.	Taft, Rep.	Chafin, Pro.	Debs, Soc.	Harmon, Dem.	Harris Rep.
Tuscarawas	6,775	6,717	120	559	7,245	6,426
Union	2,568	3 567	83	31	2,604	3,560
Van Wert	3,783	3,809	55	77	3 703	3,959
Vinton	1,496	1,916	32	25	1 530	1,898
Warren	2.656	4 233	53	50	2,939	4,008
Washington	5.774	5,648	126	58	5,854	5,623
Wayne	5,368	4,388	174	149	5,194	4,711
Williams	3,329	3 625	109	60	3 160	3,824
Wood	5,625	5,904	163	209	5,531	6,112
Wyandot	3,353	2,408	23	32	3,237	2,543
Total	502721	572312	11,402	32,795	552569	533197
Plurality	..	69,591	..	..	19,372	..
Per cent	44.84	51.04	1.01	3.01	50.87	49.13
Scattering		1,322			37,432	
Whole vote		1,121,552			1,123,198	

For Secretary of State, 1,906; Hensler, Soc., received 18,432 votes; Hughes, Pro., 11,970; Eisenberg, Soc. L., 2,211.

For Governor in 1905, Pattison, Dem., received 473,264 votes; Herrick, Rep., 430,617; Cowen, Soc., 17,795: Watkins, Pro., 13,061; Steiger, Soc. Lab., 1,808.

For President in 1904, Corrigan, Soc. Lab., received 2,633 votes; Watson, Pop, 1,392; there were scattering and void ballots not counted, 21,236.

The vote for Governor in 1903 was: Johnson, Dem., 361,748; Herrick, Rep., 475,560; Cowen, Soc., 13,495; Creamer, Pro., 13,502; Gorke, Soc. Lab., 2,071.

VOTE FOR REPRESENTATIVES IN CONGRESS, 1908.

Districts.

I. County of Hamilton (part). Thomas P. Hart, Dem., 23,224; Nicholas Longworth, Rep., 30,444; Robertson, Soc., 1,299; Reid, Pro., 209

II. County of Hamilton (part). C.N. Danenhower, Dem., 27,904; Herman P. Goebel, Rep., 28,008; Monroe, Soc., 1,600; Robertson, Pro., 137.

III Counties of Butler, Montgomery, and Preble. James M. Cox, Dem., 32,524; W. G. Frizzell, Rep., 12,593; Caldwell, Soc., 2,943; Thompson, Pro., 267.

IV. Counties of Allen, Auglaize, Darke, Mercer, and Shelby. Wm. E. Touvelle, Dem., 26,896; Mulligan, Rep., 18,305; Stedke, Soc., 567; Lippincott, Pro., 462.

V. Counties of Defiance, Henry, Paulding, Putnam, Van Wert, and Williams. Timothy T. Ansberry, Dem., 23,712; Wm. W. Campbell, Rep., 16,745; O. Donaldson, Soc., 418; Sleicher, Pro., 234.

VI. Counties of Brown, Clermont, Clinton, Greene, Highland, and Warren. Matt R. Denver, Dem., 23,192; Jesse Taylor, Rep., 21,592; Hypes, Pro., 206.

VII. Counties of Clark, Fayette, Madison, Miami, and Pickaway. O. E. Duff, Dem., 21,503; J. Warren Keifer, Rep., 24,323; Shaffer, Soc., 1,158; Shuman, Pro., 543.

OHIO—*Continued.*

VIII. Counties of Champaign, Delaware, Hancock, Hardin, Logan, and Union. Wm. R. Niven, Dem., 23,271; Ralph D. Cole, Rep., 24,476; Wharton, Soc., 725; McMoran, Pro., 506.

IX. Counties of Fulton, Lucas, Ottawa, and Wood. I. R. Sherwood, Dem., 29,171; Southard, Rep., 27,523; Miller, Soc., 3,285; Braithwaite, Pro., 377.

X. Counties of Adams, Gallia, Jackson, Lawrence, Pike, and Scioto. Thos. H. B. Jones, Dem., 18,918; Adna R. Johnson, Rep., 23.687; Dodge, Soc., 910; Meacham, Pro., 431.

XI. Counties of Athens, Fairfield, Hocking, Meigs, Perry, Ross, and Vinton. L. A. Sears, Dem., 26,650; Albert Douglas, Rep., 27,796; Elswick, Soc., 847; Baker, Pro., 451.

XII. County of Franklin. B. F. Gayman, Dem., 22.813; Edward L. Taylor, Jr., Rep., 29,483; E. O. Jones, Soc., 1,108; Poliny, Pro., 681.

XIII. Counties of Crawford, Erie, Marion, Sandusky, Seneca, and Wyandot. Carl C. Anderson, Dem., 29,736; Grant E. Mouser, Rep., 25,019; Maxwell, Soc., 870; Read, Pro., 298.

XIV. Counties of Ashland, Huron, Knox, Lorain, Morrow, and Richland. Wm. G. Sharp, Dem., 28,525; Frank V. Owen, Rep., 26,799; Storcke, Soc., 1,272; Holton, Pro., 488.

XV. Counties of Guernsey, Morgan, Muskingum, Noble, and Washington. George White, Dem., 22,129, James Joyce, Rep., 22,186; Crawford, Soc., 472; Montgomery, Pro., 686

XVI. Counties of Belmont, Carroll, Harrison, Jefferson, and Monroe. W. A. McCombs, Dem., 19,914 D. A Hollingsworth, Rep., 23,318; Lister Soc 1,103. Johnson, Pro., 656

XVII. Counties of Coshocton, Holmes, Licking Tuscarawas, and Wayne Wm. A. Ashbrook, Dem., 287,512; J F Harrison, Rep., 21.341, Lersch, Pro. 392

XVIII. Counties of Columbiana, Mahoning, and Stark. John J Whitacre, Dem. 29,040; Jas. Kennedy, Rep., 32,287 Wheeler, Soc., 2,551; Jenkins, Pro. 2.998.

XIX. Counties of Ashtabula, Geauga, Portage, Summit, and Trumbull. S. A. Robinson, Dem., 22,529; Wm. Aubrey Thomas, Rep., 32,182; Goodenberger, Soc., 2,641; Crispin, Pro., 864.

XX. Counties of Lake, Medina, and Cuyahoga (part). Charles W. Lapp, Dem., 23,592; Paul Howland, Rep., 32,839; Morgan, Soc., 2,105; Dayton, Pro., 252

XXI County of Cuyahoga (part). Theodore E. Burton, Rep., 31,968; J. E Wertman, Dem., 1[illegible],451; Hayes, Soc., 2,369; McDouough, Pro., 12[illegible].

OHIO—*Continued.*

PRESENT STATE GOVERNMENT.

Governor, Andrew L. Harris; Secretary of State, Corwin A. Thompson; Treasurer, W. S. McKinnon; Auditor, W. D. Guilbert; Commissioner of Education, Edmond A. Jones; Attorney-General, Wade H. Ellis; Adjutant-General, A. B. Critchfield; Commissioner of Insurance, S. J. Vorys—all Republicans.

JUDICIARY.

Supreme Court: Chief Justice, James L. Price; Associate Justices, A. N. Summers, W. B. Crew, John A. Shauck, William Z. Davis, William T. Spear; Clerk, Joseph G. Obermeyre—all Republicans.

STATE LEGISLATURE, 1909.

	Senate.	*House.*	*Joint Ballot.*
Republicans	20	71	91
Democrats	14	45	59
Republican majority.	6	26	32

VOTE OF THE STATE SINCE 1884.

	Dem.	*Rep.*	*Gr.*	*Pro.*	*Plu.*
1884. Pres.	368,286	400.082	5,170	11,269	31,802 R
1888. Pres.	396,455	416,054	....	24,356	19,599 R
			Pop.		
1892. Pres.	404,115	405,187	14,850	26,012	1,072 R
1895. Gov.	334,519	427,141	52,675	21.264	92,622 R
1896. Sec. of S.	473,471	525,020	....	5,469	51,549 R
			N. D.		
1896. Pres.	477,494	525.991	1,857	5.068	48 497 R
1897. Gov.	401,750	429.915	1,661	7,558	28.165 R
1898. Sec. of S.	347,074	408,213	....	7,689	61,139 R
			Ind.		
1899. Gov.	368,176	417,199	106,721	5,825	49,023 R
1900. Pres.	474,882	543,918	....	10,203	69,036 R
			Soc.		
1901. Gov.	368.525	436,092	7,359	9,878	67,567 R
1902. Sec. of S	345,706	436 171	14,270	12,336	90,465 R
1903. Gov.	361,748	475,560	13,495	13,592	113,812 R
1904. Pres.	344,674	600,095	36,260	19,339	255,421 R
1905. Gov.	473,264	430,617	17,795	13,061	42,647 D
1906. Sec. of S.	351,676	408,066	18,432	11,970	56,390 R
1908. Pres	502,721	572,312	33,795	11,402	69,591 R

OKLAHOMA.

COUNTIES. (75.)	PRESIDENT. 1908.			CONSTITUTIONAL CONVENTION. 19[illegible].		
	Bryan, Dem.	Taft, Rep.	Debs. Soc.	Dem.	Rep.	Soc.
Adair	825	782	26	....		.
Alfalfa	1,459	1,732	179	..	..	.
Atoka	784	757	198	:	..	
Beaver	1,212	1,362	197	1,613	1,211	104
Beckham	1,807	866	493	..	..	..
Blaine	1,317	1,598	341	1,291	1,177	139
Bryan	2,215	1,044	462	..	..	..
Caddo	2,964	2,860	423	2,524	2,043	70
Canadian	2,124	1,331	157	1,839	1,233	79
Carter	2 181	1,305	587	..	..	..
Cherokee	913	1,040	47	..	..	..
Choctaw	1,038	878	312	..	..	..
Cimarron	449	871	38	..	..	..
Cleveland	1,437	1,092	414	1,308	141	177
Coal	906	722	524	..	..	..
Craig	1,578	1,296	56	..	..	..
Comanche	3,481	2,437	411	3,054	1,770	63
Creek	1,417	1,761	835	..	..	..
Custer*	1,721	1,579	833	1,311	910	182

OKLAHOMA—*Continued.*

COUNTIES.	PRESIDENT, 1908.			CONSTITUTIONAL CONVENTION, 1906		
	Bryan, Dem.	Taft, Rep.	Debs, Soc.	Dem.	Rep.	Soc.
Delaware	974	625	52	†675	568	..
Dewey	1,075	1,210	486	880	794	30
Ellis	1,260	1,379	224	..	..	..
Garfield	2,618	2,924	254	2,396	1,969	11
Garvin	2,391	1,290	336	..	..	..
Grady	2,826	1,491	258	..	..	..
Grant	1,866	1,796	105	1,868	1,317	56
Greer	2,149	708	472	2,134	433	..
Harper	746	876	201	..	..	..
Haskell	1,401	1,139	363	..	..	..
Hughes	1,649	1,459	380	...	..	..
Jackson	1,905	635	220	..	..	..
Jefferson	1,435	604	288	..	..	..
Johnston	1,274	693	602	..	..	..
Kay	2,511	2,754	138	2,524	2,004	84
Kingfisher	1,541	2,106	226	1,676	1,612	52
Kiowa	2,354	1,591	301	1,665	1,168	34
Latimer	720	616	197	..	..	..
Le Flore	1,872	1,771	230	..	..	..
Lincoln	3,030	3,515	534	2,533	2,354	202
Logan	2,183	3,768	203	1,597	2,427	39
Love	835	413	253	..	..	..
Major	877	1,446	463	...	..	..
Marshall	842	406	406	..	..	..
Mayes	1,186	1,021	44	..	..	..
Murray	1,111	574	280	..	..	..
Muskogee	2,793	3,592	168	..	..	..
McClain	1,234	780	363	..	..	..
McCurtain	565	482	148	..	..	..
McIntosh	1,236	1,606	141	..	..	..
Noble	1,364	1,476	125	1,274	996	46
Nowata	923	1,086	61	..	..	..
Okfuskee	872	1,297	402	..	..	..
Oklahoma	4,876	5,401	493	4,433	3,278	168
Okmulgee	1,103	1,400	295	..	..	..
Osage	1,584	1,528	159	3,061	2,741	74
Ottawa	1,296	1,174	94	..	..	..
Pawnee	1,500	1,556	299	1,572	1,261	256
Payne	1,980	2,244	390	1,710	1,594	200
Pittsburg	2,893	2,735	629	..	..	..
Pontotoc	1,841	860	579	..	..	..
Pottawatomie	3,561	2,609	555	2,919	1,756	189
Pushmataha	625	484	125	..	..	..
Roger Mills	1,168	839	403	962	440	553
Rogers	1,599	1,134	131	..	...	..
Seminole	945	1,168	452	..	..	..
Sequoyah	1,648	2,037	131	..	..	..
Stephens	1,761	725	029	..	..	...
Texas	1,470	1,315	239	..	..	..
Tillman	1,661	732	109	..	..	..
Tulsa	2,292	2,150	226	...	..	..
Wagoner	1,151	2,107	167	..	..	..
Washington	1,409	1,528	124	..	..	..
Washita	1,867	1,118	409	1,121	752	466
Woods	1,421	1,557	288	3,715	2,945	392
Woodward	1,308	1,614	371	2,004	1,866	..
Total	122406	110558	21,729	53,664	40,760	4,040
Plurality	11,848	..	..	12,904	..	..
Per cent	48.02	43.40	8.58	53.58	40.70	5.72
Scattering		......			1,719	
Whole vote		254,693			100,245	

† Day County.

For President in 1908 Hisgen, Ind., received 47 votes; Watson, People's Party, 436.

For Governor in 1907 the vote was: Dem., 137,641; Rep., 110,296; Soc., 9,330.

OKLAHOMA—*Continued.*

VOTE FOR REPRESENTATIVES IN CONGRESS, 1908.

District.

I. Counties of Garfield, Grant, Kay, Kingfisher, Lincoln, Logan, Noble, Osage, Pawnee, and Payne. Dem., 20,501; Bird S. McGuire, Rep., 23,312; Soc., 2,249.

II. Counties of Alfalfa, Beaver, Blaine, Caddo, Canadian, Cimarron, Custer, Dewey, Ellis, *Grady, Harper, Major, Oklahoma, *Roger Mills, Texas, Woods and Woodward. Dem., 25,549; Richard T. Morgan, Rep., 26,273; Soc., 4,443.

III. Counties of Adair, Cherokee, Craig, Creek, Delaware, Hughes, Mayes, *McIntosh, *Muskogee, Nowata, *Okfuskee, Ottawa, Rogers, Seminole, Sequoyah, Tulsa, Wagoner, and Washington. Dem., 23,842; C. E. Creager, Rep., 25,952. Soc., 2,827.

IV. Counties of Latimer, Marshall, Love, Le Flore, *Okfusgee, *Muscogee, McCurtain, Murray, Pontotoc, Atoka, Bryan, Coal, Haskell, Johnston, *Hughes, *McIntosh, Choctaw, Carter, Pittsburg, and Pushmataha, Charles D. Carter, Dem., 23,730; Rep., 15,727; Soc., 5,769.

V. Counties of Kiowa, Washita, *Roger Mills, Beckham, Garvin, Comanche, Jackson, Greer, Cleveland, McClain, Tillman, Pottawatomie, Stephens, *Carter, *Love, *Murray, and Jefferson. Scott Ferris, Dem., 29,355; Soc., 5,478.

*Part of county in district.

PRESENT STATE GOVERNMENT.

Governor, C. N. Haskell; Lieut.-Governor, George Bellamy; Secretary of State, Bill Cross; Treasurer, J. A. Menefee; Auditor, M. E. Trapp; Attorney-General, Chas. West; Adjutant-General, F. M. Canton; Commissioner of Insurance, T. J. McComb; Commissioner of Education, E. D. Cameron—all Democrats.

JUDICIARY.

Supreme Court: Chief Justice, R. L. Williams; Associate Justices, Jesse J. Dunn, M. J. Kane, Jno. B. Turner and Samuel W. Hayes; Clerk of the Court, W. H. L. Campbell—all Democrats.

STATE LEGISLATURE, 1908.

	Senate.	*House.*	*Joint Ballot.*
Republicans	5	18	23
Democrats	39	91	130
Democratic majority.	34	73	107

OREGON.

Counties. (34.)	President, 1908.				President, 1904.	
	Bryan Dem.	Taft, Rep.	Chafin Pro.	Debs, Soc.	Parker Dem.	Roosevelt, Rep.
Baker	1,596	1,689	23	286	938	1,990
Benton	773	1,183	87	68	442	1,107
Clakamas	1,866	2,776	123	364	684	2,783
Clatsop	658	1,482	51	281	336	1,408
Columbia	454	1,242	42	203	221	1,301
Coos	894	1,850	50	427	490	1,712
Crook	548	915	39	106	266	763
Curry	148	268	..	33	87	322
Douglas	1,359	2,092	60	365	908	2,443
Gilliam	242	470	6	40	195	568
Grant	433	748	13	105	316	1,007
Harney	329	450	11	66	190	395
Hood River	359	767	47	58	..	..
Jackson	1,587	2,032	98	380	798	1,992
Josephine	732	967	20	299	327	914
Klamath	427	634	11	79	208	552
Lake	289	465	6	49	115	394
Lane	2,174	3,313	108	424	1,166	3,501
Lincoln	282	595	15	121	179	581
Linn	1,813	2,202	155	334	1,206	2,346
Malheur	543	800	53	70	280	799
Marion	2,239	3,788	275	311	1,034	4,106
Morrow	272	680	24	110	230	875
Multnomah	9,850	17,819	629	1,447	2,324	13,692
Polk	1,113	1,456	75	159	521	1,380
Sherman	252	437	25	36	163	701
Tillamook	253	641	39	129	136	729
Umatilla	1,568	2,328	109	174	840	2,642
Union	1,191	1,510	36	237	775	1,384
Wallowa	506	905	20	108	255	714
Wasco	764	1,309	58	155	536	2,093
Washington	1,153	2,319	124	138	492	2,296
Wheeler	236	418	14	9	161	462
Yamhill	1,246	1,980	236	168	652	2,004
Total	38,049	62,530	2,682	7,339	17,521	60,455
Plurality	..	24,481	..	..	..	42,934
Per cent	34.40	55.78	3.16	6.66	19.42	67.05
Scattering					16,178	
Whole vote					90,154	

For President 1908 Hisgen, Ind., received 289 votes.

For President 1904 Swallow, Pro., 7,806; Debs, Soc., 7,619.

VOTE FOR REPRESENTATIVES IN CONGRESS, 1908.

Willis C. Hawley, Rep., First District, and W. R. Ellis, Rep., Second District, were re-elected by substantial pluralities.

PRESENT STATE GOVERNMENT.

Governor, G. E. Chamberlain, Dem.; Secretary of State and Auditor, F. W. Benson, Rep.; State Treasurer, Geo. A. Steele, Rep.; Superintendent of Public Instruction, J. H. Ackerman, Rep.; Adjutant-General, Wm. E. Finzer, Dem.; Attorney-General, A. M. Crawford, Rep.

JUDICIARY.

Supreme Court: Chief Justice, Robert S. Bean; Justices, Frank A. Moore and Robert Eakin; Clerk, J. C. Moreland —all Republicans.

STATE LEGISLATURE, 1909.

	Senate.	*House.*	*Joint Ballot.*
Republicans	23	51	74
Democrats	6	7	13
Republican majority	17	44	61

VOTE OF THE STATE SINCE 1876.

		Dem.	*Rep.*	*Lab.*	*Pro.*		*Plu.*
1876.	Pres.	14,158	15,208	....	....	....	1,050 R
1880.	Pres.	19,948	20,619	249	....	....	671 R
1884.	Pres.	24,604	26,860	726	492	....	2,256 R
1888.	Pres.	26,522	33,291	363	1,677	....	6,769 R
				Pop.		*Fusion.*	
1892.	Pres.	14,243	35,002	26,965	2,281	35,813	811 F
1896.	Pres.	....	48,779	....	....	46,662	2,117 R
1900.	Pres.	....	46,526	....	2,536	33,385	13,141 R
1902.	Gov.	41,857	41,581	....	3,483	3,771	276 D
				Soc.	*Pro.*		
1904.	Pres.	17,521	60,455	7,619	....	8,806	42,934 R
1906.	Gov.	46,002	43,508	4,468	2,737	....	2,494 D
1908.	Pres.	[illegible]	[illegible]	[illegible]	[illegible]	....	[illegible]

PENNSYLVANIA.

Counties. (67.)	President, 1908.				President, 1904.	
	Bryan Dem.	Taft, Rep.	Chafin Pro.	Debs, Soc.	Parker Dem.	Roosevelt, Rep.
Adams	4,034	3,685	104	19	3,809	4,017
Allegheny	35,655	74,080	4,580	7,311	21,420	90,594
Armstrong	3,212	6,110	738	160	2,260	5,798
Beaver	4,200	7,008	624	662	2,333	7,122
Bedford	3,196	4,784	234	166	3,040	5,364
Berks	17,381	13,642	349	1,858	16,325	15,539
Blair	4,981	10,583	635	535	3,662	12,482
Bradford	3,758	7,997	651	190	2,858	8,303
Bucks	7,233	9,409	191	150	6,706	9,572
Butler	4,698	6,584	721	148	3,183	6,596
Cambria	7,979	12,325	518	434	7,223	13,109
Cameron	533	1,110	28	12	404	1,228
Carbon	3,890	4,486	135	587	2,994	4,505
Centre	3,998	4,927	267	72	4,015	5,291
Chester	6,555	13,118	678	110	4,330	14,200
Clarion	3,291	2,915	447	133	2,463	2,978
Clearfield	5,954	7,726	737	508	4,280	9,541
Clinton	2,547	3,477	136	205	1,941	3,535
Columbia	5,373	3,718	310	78	4,194	3,635
Crawford	5,668	7,679	837	394	3,639	7,450
Cumberland	5,403	6,261	350	160	5,033	7,138
Dauphin	7,546	15,687	663	789	5,026	16,508
Delaware	5,727	15,184	363	168	3,562	15,032
Elk	2,531	2,991	190	77	2,854	3,820
Erie	6,173	10,828	1,519	1,037	5,103	11,951
Fayette	8,220	10,012	873	759	6,779	11,486
Forest	512	1,119	166	37	410	1,328
Franklin	4,682	6,938	247	77	4,110	7,062
Fulton	1,094	974	55	15	1,136	1,100
Greene	3,793	2,438	268	39	3,197	2,442
Huntingdon	1,917	4,503	292	70	1,318	4,587
Indiana	1,965	6,416	889	222	1,544	6,878
Jefferson	2,988	5,652	527	211	2,076	5,860
Juniata	1,414	1,765	55	21	1,201	1,985
Lackawanna	15,451	18,590	420	247	10,066	19,923
Lancaster	8,109	23,523	729	519	7,047	26,083
Lawrence	2,656	5,350	797	1,074	1,888	7,634
Lebanon	2,858	6,874	298	206	2,446	6,938
Lehigh	11,285	11,593	384	415	10,134	11,826
Luzerne	17,379	24,594	572	1,099	13,497	27,809
Lycoming	7,144	8,708	744	536	6,414	8,928
McKean	2,867	5,073	551	229	1,625	5,719
Mercer	5,473	6,497	1,137	607	3,839	8,574
Mifflin	1,799	2,902	124	59	1,374	3,034
Monroe	3,004	1,454	104	17	2,587	1,446
Montgomery	11,899	19,088	881	433	10,401	18,833
Montour	1,490	1,164	81	7	1,352	1,518
Northampton	11,365	10,857	514	346	9,902	11,039
N'thumberl'd	8,590	10,439	392	634	5,921	11,219
Perry	2,184	3,260	72	31	2,094	3,433
Philadelphia	75,317	185263	1,926	5,192	46,875	227709
Pike	1,069	715	17	14	939	592
Potter	1,932	3,603	278	133	1,074	3,976
Schuylkill	15,481	18,758	292	1,106	10,108	1,046
Snyder	1,081	2,401	71	8	971	2,538
Somerset	2,246	6,478	537	215	1,681	6,772
Sullivan	1,076	1,119	140	30	1,185	1,429
Susquehanna	3,230	4,999	439	43	2,562	4,988
Tioga	2,321	6,947	420	51	1,536	7,410
Union	1,154	2,547	98	7	1,031	2,548
Venango	2,815	4,868	1,762	326	1,740	5,892
Warren	2,054	4,672	670	117	1,215	4,737
Washington	7,018	11,430	1,127	696	4,866	11,530
Wayne	2,438	3,650	274	61	2,093	3,386
Westmorel'd	11,101	15,429	1,605	1,468	7,991	17,239
Wyoming	1,629	2,234	120	14	1,575	2,308
York	15,171	14,610	462	499	12,973	14,837
Total	448785	745779	36,694	33,913	335430	840949
Plurality	..	296994	..	..	..	505519
Per cent	35.41	58.86	2.89	2.67	27.12	67.91
Whole vote		1,267,450				

For Governor 1906 Emery received votes: Commonwealth party, 6,094; Lincoln party, 145,657; Referendum party, 784; Union Labor party, 3,675; Stuart received 4,610 votes of the Citizens' party.

For State Treasurer, 1907, only office voted for, Harman, Dem., received 312,737 votes; Sheatz, Rep., 459,965; Stevenson, Pro., 29,830; Clark, Soc., 14,346.

PENNSYLVANIA—*Continued.*

For President, 1908, Hisgen, Ind., received 1,057 votes; Gillhaus, Soc. Lab., 1,222.

VOTE FOR REPRESENTATIVES IN CONGRESS, 1908.

Districts.

I. County of Philadelphia (part). M. J. Geraghty, Dem., 7,773; Henry H. Bingham, Rep., 27,163; I. A. Ramsey, Pro., 212; H. H. McCall, Soc., 607.

II. County of Philadelphia (part). Wm. Schlipf, Jr., Dem., 6,381; Joel Cook, Rep., 24,067; Stitzenberger, Soc., 542.

III. County of Philadelphia (part). Wm. Beerli, Dem., 6,608; J. Hampton Moore, Rep., 23,617; J. Heinz, Soc., 540.

IV. County of Philadelphia (part). H. D. Albright, Dem., 6,594; Reuben O. Moon, Rep., 17,518; Chas. Doerr, Soc., 708.

V. County of Philadelphia (part). Michael Donahue, Dem., 8,488; W. W. Foulkrod, Rep., 21,064; Ed. Moore, Soc., 1,263.

VI. County of Philadelphia (part). Fred T. Bailey, Dem., 10,205; George D. McCreary, Rep., 29,383; C. W. Erwin, Soc., 907.

VII. Counties of Chester and Delaware. D. P. Hibberd, Dem., 10,364; Thos. S. Butler, Rep., 26,684; Walter N. Lodge, Soc., 26.

VIII. Counties of Bucks and Montgomery. Wynne James, Dem., 17,684; Irving P. Wanger, Rep., 26,384.

IX. County of Lancaster. Wm. W. Griest, Rep., 22,022; Geo. B. Wilson, Dem., 7,428.

X. County of Lackawanna. T. D. Nichols, Dem., 16,855; John R. Farr, Rep., 16,138.

XI. County of Luzerne. John H. Bigelow, Dem., 18,569; Henry W. Palmer, Rep., 20,525; Chas. Lavin, Soc., 963.

XII. County of Schuylkill. Robert E. Lee, Dem., 15,339; Alfred B. Garner, Rep., 17,446; C. F. Foley, Soc., 845.

XIII. Counties of Berks and Lehigh. John H. Rothermel, Dem., 27,655; A. N. Ulrich, Rep., 21,416; T. J. Neatherry, Soc., 1,993.

XIV. Counties of Bradford, Susquehanna, Wayne, and Wyoming. George W. Kipp, Dem., 12,980; Chas. C. Pratt, Rep., 15,024; E. H. Meeker, Pro., 1,127; Little, Soc., 1,184.

XV. Counties of Tioga, Potter, Lycoming, and Clinton. Wm. B. Wilson, Dem., 18,592; Elias Deemer, Rep., 16,577; C. H. Lugg, Pro., 1,326; W. J. Brotherton, Soc., 419.

XVI. Counties of Northumberland, Montour, Columbia, and Sullivan. John G. McHenry, Dem., 18,412; E. W. Samuel, Rep., 12,866; J. E. Wolf, Pro., 970.

XVII. Counties of Perry, Juniata, Mifflin, Huntingdon, Fulton, Franklin, Snyder, and Union. Geo. C. Bentz, Dem., 14,044; Benj. K. Focht, Rep., 22,906.

XVIII. Counties of Dauphin, Cumberland, and Lebanon. John L. Whisler, Dem., 13,876; Marlin E. Olmsted, Rep., 27,717; T. H. Hamilton, Pro., 1,488; J. V. Zerby, Soc., 1,023.

XIX. Counties of Blair, Cambria, and Bedford. H. G. Tate, Dem., 15,906; John M. Reynolds, Rep., 26,157.

XX. Counties of Adams and York. Edward D. Zeigler, Dem., 16,928; Daniel F. Lafean, Rep., 19,176; Newcomb, Pro., 434; Pfeiffer, Soc., 339.

XXI. Counties of Cameron, Centre, Clearfield, and McKean. W. H. Walker, Dem., 12,848; Charles F. Barclay, Rep., 15,631; J. D. Blair, Soc., 684; McCoy, Pro., 1,888.

XXII. Counties of Westmoreland and Butler. Silas W. Kline, Dem., 16,234; George F. Huff, Rep., 19,329; R. A. Dornon, Pro., 2,338.

XXIII. Counties of Fayette, Greene, and Somerset. M. R. Traxis, Dem., 12,125; Allen F. Cooper, Rep., 16,769; W. M. Likins, Pro., 3,368; W. Herd, Soc., 820.

PENNSYLVANIA—*Continued.*

XXIV. Counties of Beaver, Lawrence, and Washington. Charles H. Akens, Dem., 10,385; John K. Tener, Rep., 20,538; Frank Fish, Pro., 5,982; C. A. McKeever, Soc., 1,816.

XXV. Counties of Erie and Crawford. John B. Brooks, Dem., 11,995; Arthur L. Bates, Rep., 16,457; McIntyre, Pro., 1,849; Allen, Soc., 970.

XXVI. Counties of Carbon, Monroe, Pike, and Northampton. A. M. Palmer, Dem., 18,865; G. A. Schneebell, Rep., 15,123; Snyder, Pro., 861; Miller, Soc., 910.

XXVII. Counties of Armstrong, Indiana, Clarion, and Jefferson. J. S. Shirley, Dem., 10,088; J. N. Langham, Rep., 19,010; Pender, Pro., 2,739.

XXVIII. Counties of Mercer, Warren, Forest, Venango, and Elk. Till Reiss, Dem., 11,256; Nelson P. Wheeler, Rep., 18,728; J. M. Brown, Pro., 4,018.

XXIX. County of Allegheny (part). J. G. Shirmer, Dem., 5,401; Wm. H. Graham, Rep., 15,616; McConnell, Pro., 1,337; Slayton, Soc., 1,500.

XXX. County of Allegheny (part). E. F. Duffy, Dem., 7,512; John Dalzell, Rep., 15,574; Fidler, Pro., 1,674; Adams, Soc., 2,001.

XXXI. County of Allegheny (part). T. B. Alcorn, Dem., 5,320; James Francis Burke, Rep., 13,380; W. A. Stewart, Pro., 613; J. A. McCarthy, Soc., 779.

XXXII. County of Allegheny (part). John Murphy, Dem., 8,769; A. J. Barchfield, Rep., 16,911; H. S. Gleiss, Pro., 1,648; T. F. Kennedy, Soc., 1,871.

PRESENT STATE GOVERNMENT.

Governor, E. S. Stuart; Lieutenant-Governor, R. S. Murphy; Secretary of the Commonwealth, Robert R. McAfee; Treasurer, J. O. Sheatz; Auditor-General, R. K. Young; Adjutant-General, Thos. J. Stewart; Attorney-General, M. Hampton Todd; Superintendent of Public Instruction, N. C. Schaeffer; Insurance Commissioner, David Martin; Secretary of Agriculture, N. B. Critchfield—all Republicans, except Schaeffer, Dem.

JUDICIARY.

Supreme Court: Chief Justice, James T. Mitchell; Associate Justices, J. Hay Brown, Wm. P. Potter, John Stewart, D. Newlin Fell, S. L. Mestrezat, and John P. Elkin.

STATE LEGISLATURE, 1909.

	Senate.	*House.*	*Joint Ballot.*
Republicans	39	173	212
Democrats	11	34	45
Republican majority	28	139	167

VOTE OF THE STATE SINCE 1872.

	Dem.	*Rep.*	*Gr.*	*Pro.*	*Plu.*	
1872. Pres.	212,041	349,589	....	1,630	137,548	R
1876. Pres.	366,204	384,148	7,204	318	17,944	R
1880. Pres.	407,428	444,704	20,668	1,939	37,276	R
1884. Pres.	392,785	473,804	16,992	15,283	81,019	R
			Lab.			
1888. Pres.	446,633	526,091	3,873	20,947	79,452	R
			Pop.			
1892. Pres.	452,264	516,011	8,714	25,123	63,747	R
			N. D.			
1896. Pres.	433,228	728,300	11,000	19,274	295,072	R
1898. Gov.	358,300	476,306	....	125,746	118,006	R
1899. Treas.	327,512	438,000	....	18,072	110,488	R
			Soc. D.			
1900. Pres.	424,232	712,665	4,831	27,908	288,433	R
			Union.			
1901. Treas.	291,995	423,498	93,213	18,044	131,543	R
			Soc.			
1902. Gov.	436,447	592,867	21,910	23,327	156,410	R
1903. Treas.	235,168	503,775	13,245	24,850	268,607	R
1904. Pres.	335,430	840,949	21,863	33,717	505,519	R
1906. Gov.	301,747	506,392	15,169	24,793	48,485	R
1907. Treas.	312,737	459,965	....	29,830	147,228	R
1908. Pres.	448,785	745,779	33,913	36,694	296,994	R

RHODE ISLAND.

Counties. (5.)	President, 1908. Bryan, Dem.	Taft, Rep.	Chafin, Pro.	Debs, Soc.	Governor, 1908. Arnold, Dem.	Pothier, Rep.
Bristol	..	..	..	..	..	..
Kent	..	..	..	..	..	..
Newport	..	..	..	..	..	..
Providence	..	..	..	..	..	..
Washington	..	..	..	..	..	..
Total	24,706	43,942	..	..	31,406	38,676
Plurality	..	19,236	..	..	..	7,270
Per cent	43.37	56.63	..	..	44.75	55.25
Scattering	...				....	
Whole vote	77,586				....	

For Governor 1907 Remington, Pro., received 831 votes; Johnson, Soc., 681; Leach, Soc. L., 289.

For Governor 1906 Helme, Pro., received 714 votes; Carpenter, Soc., 395; Moran, Soc. L., 320.

The scattering vote for President in 1904 was: Corrigan, Soc. L., 488 votes.

VOTE FOR REPRESENTATIVES IN CONGRESS, 1908.

Districts.

I. Daniel L. D. Granger, Dem., 18,141; Wm. P. Sheffield, Rep., 18,222. Sheffield's plu., 81.

II. Thomas Cooney, Dem., 12 634; Adin P. Capron, Rep., 21,374. Capron's plu., 8,740.

PRESENT STATE GOVERNMENT.

Governor, Aram J. Pothier, Rep.; Lieutenant-Governor, Arthur W. Dennis, Rep.; Secretary of State, Charles P. Bennett; Attorney-General, William B. Greenough; Treasurer, Walter A. Read; Adjutant-General, Frederick M. Sackett; Auditor, Charles C. Gray; Commissioner of Public Schools, Walter E. Ranger; Commissioner of Insurance, Charles C. Gray—all Republicans.

JUDICIARY.

Supreme Court: Chief Justice, vacancy in office; Associate Justices, Clark H. Johnson, C. Frank Parkhurst, John T. Blodgett, Edward C. Dubois. Clerk of the Court, B. S. Blaisdell—all Republicans.

STATE LEGISLATURE, 1909.

	Senate.	House.	Joint Ballot.
Republicans	31	64	95
Democrats	6	6	12
Republican majority	25	58	83

House and Senate each contains 2 Independents.

VOTE OF THE STATE SINCE 1872.

	Dem.	Rep.	Gr.	Pro.	Plu.
1872. President	5,329	13,665	....	....	*8,336 R
1876. President	10,712	15,787	....	....	*5,075 R
1880. President	10,779	18,195	236	....	7,416 R
1884. President	12,391	19,030	422	928	6,639 R
1888. President	17,530	21,968	....	1,250	4,438 R
			Pop.		
1892. President	24,335	26,972	227	1,654	2,637 R
1893. Governor	22,015	21,830	....	3,265	185 D
1894. Governor	22,650	28,957	223	2,241	6,307 R
1895. Governor	14,289	25,098	369	2,624	10,809 R
			N. D.		
1896. President	14,459	37,437	1,166	1,160	22,978 R
1897. Governor	13,675	24,309	....	2,096	10,634 R
1898. Governor	13,224	24,743	....	2,012	11,519 R
			Soc.		
1899. Governor	14,602	24,308	2,941	1,279	9,706 R
1900. Governor	17,184	26,043	2,858	1,848	8,859 R
1900. President	19,812	33,784	1,423	1,529	13,972 R
1902. Governor	32,279	24,541	1,283	1,689	7,738 D
1903. Governor	30,578	29,275	943	936	1,303 D
1904. President	24 839	41,605	....	768	16,766 R
1905. Governor	25,816	31,311	367	882	5,495 R
1906. Governor	33,195	31,877	395	714	1,318 D
1907 Governor	33,300	31,005	....	831	2,295 D
1908 President	24,706	43,942	....	....	19,236 R

SOUTH CAROLINA.

Counties. (42.)	President, 1908. Bryan, Dem.	Taft, Rep.	Governor, 1906. Ansel, Dem.	Chandler, Soc.
Abbeville	1,481	9	684	..
Aiken	1,990	48	930	..
Anderson	2,099	58	878	..
Bamberg	848	33	513	..
Barnwell	1,407	88	767	..
Beaufort	522	272	337	..
Berkeley	609	235	403	..
Calhoun	689	54	..	..
Charleston	1,814	347	1,069	5
Cherokee	1,596	66	482	..
Chester	1,368	37	522	..
Chesterfield	1,458	47	633	..
Clarendon	1,091	62	1,314	..
Colleton	1,899	91	943	..
Darlington	1,279	21	454	..
Dorchester	883	103	309	..
Edgefield	1,097	8	513	..
Fairfield	830	12	320	..
Florence	1,460	28	561	..
Georgetown	544	108	201	..
Greenville	2,774	176	1,303	11
Greenwood	1,765	18	981	..
Hampton	1,328	..	558	..
Horry	1,247	46	507	..
Kershaw	922	5	360	..
Lancaster	1,729	58	831	..
Laurens	2,160	61	1,029	7
Lee	963	58	470	..
Lexington	2,508	80	1,549	..
Marion	2,007	91	834	..
Marlborough	916	16	463	..
Newberry	1,681	44	722	..
Oconee	1,126	172	402	..
Orangeburg	2,686	405	1,888	..
Pickens	1,241	56	403	..
Richland	1,750	236	577	9
Saluda	1,385	8	882	..
Spartanburg	4,162	225	1,710	..
Sumter	1,228	173	413	..
Union	1,389	49	993	..
Williamsburg	1,550	180	913	..
York	1,606	29	569	..
Total	62,288	3,963	30,251	32
Plurality	58,325	..	30,219	..
Per cent	95.99	4.01	..	..
Scattering	152		....	
Whole vote	66,251		30,283	

The vote for Governor in 1908 was: M. F. Ansel, Dem., 61,060. There was only one candidate for Governor voted for.

For President in 1908 Debs, Soc., received 107 votes; Hisgen, Ind., 42.

VOTE FOR REPRESENTATIVES IN CONGRESS, 1908.

Districts.

I. Counties of Berkeley (part), Charleston, Colleton (part), Beaufort, Georgetown, and Williamsburg (part). George S. Legare, Dem., 5,759; Aaron P. Prioleau, Rep., 631. Legare's plurality, 5,128.

II. Counties of Aiken, Barnwell, Saluda, Edgefield, and Hampton. J. O. Patterson, Dem., 8,440; Isaac Myers, Rep., 58. Total, 8,498.

III. Counties of Abbeville, Anderson, Newberry, Oconee, and Pickens. D. Wyatt Aiken, Dem., 10,274. No opposition.

IV. Counties of Fairfield, Greenville, Laurens, Richland, Spartanburg (part), and Union. J. T. Johnson, Dem., 10,806. No opposition.

V. Counties of Chester, Chesterfield, Kershaw, Lancaster, Spartanburg (part), Union (part), and York. D. E. Finley, Dem., 9,468. No op.

VI. Counties of Clarendon, Darlington, Florence, Horry, Marion, Marlborough, and Williamsburg (part). J. E. Ellerbe, Dem., 9,033. No opposition.

VII. Counties of Berkeley (part), Colleton (part), Lexington, Orangeburg, Richland, and Sumter. A. F. Lever, Dem., 9,950; R. H. Richardson, Rep., 998. Lever's plurality, 8,952.

SOUTH CAROLINA—*Continued.*

PRESENT STATE GOVERNMENT.

Governor, M. F. Ansel; Lieutenant-Governor, W. S. McLeod; Secretary of State, R. M. McCown; Attorney-General, J. F. Lyon; Treasurer, R. H. Jennings; Comptroller-General, A. W. Jones; Superintendent of Education, John R. Swearinger; Adjutant-General, J. C. Boyd—all Democrats.

JUDICIARY.

Supreme Court: Chief Justice, Y. J. Pope; Justices, C. A. Woods, Eugene B. Gary, Ira B. Jones; Clerk, U. R. Brooks—all Democrats.

STATE LEGISLATURE, 1907.

	Senate.	*House.*	*Joint Ballot.*
Democrats	42	124	166

VOTE OF THE STATE SINCE 1872.

		Dem.	*Rep.*		*Maj.*
1872.	President	22,683	72,290	....	49,607 R
1876.	President	91,540	92,081	....	641 R
1880.	President	112,312	58,071	....	54,241 D
1884.	President	69,845	21,733	....	48,112 D
1886.	Governor	33,111	.....	....	33,111 D
1888.	President	65,825	13,736	....	52,089 D
				Pop.	*Plu.*
1892.	President	54,692	13,345	2,407	41,347 D
			Ind. Dem.		*Maj.*
1894.	Governor	39,507	17,278	....	22,229 D
			Reorg. Rep.	*Reg. Rep.*	*Plu.*
1896.	Governor	59,424	4,432	2,780	54,999 D
1896.	President	58,798	4,223	5,058	49,517 D
1898.	Governor	28,159	No opposition.		
1900.	Governor	46,457	No opposition.		
1900.	President	47,236	3,579	....	43,657 D
1902.	Governor	31,817	No opposition.		
1904.	President	52,563	2,554	....	50,009 D
1906.	Governor	30,251	32	....	30,219 D
			Rep.		
1908.	President	62,288	3,963	....	58,315 D

SOUTH DAKOTA.

COUNTIES. (53.)	PRESIDENT, 1908.		GOVERNOR, 1908.		PRESIDENT, 1904.	
	Bryan, Dem.	Taft, Rep.	Lee, Dem.	Vessey Rep.	Parker Dem.	Roosevelt, Rep.
Aurora	694	686	732	679	407	632
Beadle	1,048	1,735	1,171	1,654	493	1,818
Bon Homme	1,017	1,324	1,975	1,251	886	1,547
Brookings	588	1,697	692	1,481	353	2,220
Brown	1,772	2,646	1,852	2,450	988	2,737
Brule	826	750	870	713	608	693
Buffalo	69	104	88	89	42	118
Butte	915	1,636	972	1,596	330	793
Campbell	175	627	196	611	120	635
Charles Mix	1,391	1,863	1,527	1,725	823	1,765
Clark	557	1,234	616	1,161	276	1,409
Clay	803	1,291	968	1,159	361	1,723
Coddington	831	1,618	892	1,553	582	1,741
Custer	428	487	432	476	228	536
Davison	1,061	1,276	1,160	1,258	506	1,626
Day	822	1,616	1,111	1,292	383	2,077
Deuel	425	1,022	510	950	279	1,348
Douglas	647	836	725	760	429	859
Edmunds	657	723	693	697	353	786
Fall River	466	726	509	711	248	777
Faulk	421	835	452	805	165	727
Grant	628	1,122	648	1,098	309	1,454
Gregory	1,266	1,550	1,252	1,425	282	675
Hamlin	434	1,095	521	1,019	307	1,197
Hand	655	851	698	815	170	943
Hanson	630	668	645	657	523	745
Hughes	349	795	375	779	335	929
Hutchinson	619	1,507	852	1,297	365	1,752
Hyde	212	455	269	414	91	443
Jerauld	403	582	415	634	130	586
Kingsbury	799	1,537	876	1,472	344	1,896
Lake	636	1,415	757	1,309	260	1,728
Lawrence	1,564	2,735	1,689	2,543	1,347	4,247
Lincoln	699	1,887	781	1,810	378	2,471
Lyman	1,183	1,524	1,317	1,345	306	986
Marshall	453	874	517	830	292	996
McCook	826	1,209	976	1,061	693	1,284
McPherson	157	785	228	714	144	727
Meade	793	953	839	903	268	754

SOUTH DAKOTA—*Continued.*

COUNTIES.	PRESIDENT, 1908.		GOVERNOR, 1908.		PRESIDENT, 1904.	
	Bryan, Dem.	Taft, Rep.	Lee, Dem.	Vessey Rep.	Parker Dem.	Roosevelt, Rep.
Miner	720	906	783	830	475	893
Minnehaha	1,948	4,125	2,613	3,510	1,046	4,[illegible]5
Moody	623	1,275	703	1,212	295	1,471
Pennington	1,166	1,702	1,249	1,586	392	1,126
Potter	400	514	448	563	270	525
Roberts	777	1,562	941	1,402	584	2,282
Sanborn	513	847	558	826	265	1,031
Spink	1,121	1,847	1,177	1,802	492	2,127
Stanley	1,598	2,313	1,656	2,275	396	547
Sully	154	368	148	381	50	364
Turner	793	1,792	896	1,715	521	2,395
Union	1,009	1,392	1,111	1,301	730	1,813
Walworth	351	825	420	764	176	654
Yankton	1,118	1,644	1,225	1,557	788	1,968
Total	40,223	67,352	44,837	62,945	21,969	72,083
Plurality		27,129		18,108	...	50,114
Per cent.	37.39	62.61	41.62	58.38	20.68	71.09
Scattering	..		..		7,343	
Whole vote	107,575		107,182		101,395	

VOTE FOR REPRESENTATIVES IN CONGRESS, 1908.

With several counties missing on Congressional vote of 1908, the candidates received: Republican, C. H. Burke, 67,440; E. W. Martin, 67,652. Democratic, R. E. Dowdell, 38,760; A. H. Olsen, 38,615. No other figures available as ALMANAC goes to press.

PRESENT STATE GOVERNMENT.

Governor, R. S. Vessey; Lieutenant-Governor, H. C. Shober; Secretary of State, R. S. Polley; Treasurer, George Johnson; Auditor, John Herning; Attorney-General, S. W. Clark; Superintendent of Education, H. A. Ustread; Commissioner of Lands, O. C. Dokken—all Republicans.

JUDICIARY.

Supreme Court: Presiding Judge, Dick Haney; Justices, Howard G. Fuller and Dighton Corson; Clerk, Frank Crane—all Republicans.

STATE LEGISLATURE, 1909.

	Senate.	*House.*	*Joint Ballot.*
Republicans	39	95	134
Democrats	6	9	15
Republican majority	33	86	119

VOTE OF THE STATE SINCE 1889.

		Dem.	*Rep.*	*F. A.*	*Maj.*	
1889.	Governor	23,840	53,964	....	30,124	
				Pop.		
1892.	President	9,081	34,888	26,544	18,344	
		Dem.-Pop.	*Rep.*		*Plu.*	
1896.	President	41,225	41,042	683	183	
1898.	Governor	37,319	36,949	....	370	R
		Dem.		*Pro.*		
1900.	President	39,544	54,530	1,542	14,986	R
1902.	Governor	21,396	48,196	2,245	26,800	R
1904.	President	21,969	72,083	2,965	50,114	R
1906.	Governor	28,784	48,709	3,398	19,925	R
1908.	President	40,223	67,352	....	27,129	R

The 1908 vote recorded above is from semi-official figures. The minor parties cast about 6,000 votes in the State.

TENNESSEE.

COUNTIES. (96.)	PRESIDENT, 1908.				GOVERNOR, 1908.	
	Bryan, Dem.	Taft, Rep.	Chafin Pro.	Debs, Soc.	Patterson, Dem.	Tillman, Rep.
Anderson	665	2,030	1	15	696	1,913
Bedford	1,999	7,451	..	4	1,897	1,445
Benton	1,221	860	..	6	1,155	945
Bledsoe	295	435	..	2	274	387
Blount	847	2,568	..	..	841	2,523
Bradley	620	1,063	36	18	657	1,297
Campbell	538	1,806	..	30	539	930
Cannon	904	672	..	..	847	659

TENNESSEE—*Continued.*

Counties.	President, 1908.				Governor, 1908.	
	Bryan, Dem.	Taft, Rep.	Chafin Pro.	Debs, Soc.	Patterson, Dem.	Tillman, Rep.
Carroll	1,802	2,290	..	18	1,697	2,319
Carter	459	3,152	4	..	480	3,126
Cheatham	1,206	526	..	2	1,197	482
Chester	704	580	..	10	621	670
Claiborne	979	1,644	..	..	992	1,401
Clay	764	634	1	4	741	644
Cocke	688	1,752	8	7	676	1,656
Coffee	1,654	656	..	31	1,471	719
Crockett	1,226	1,205	...	..	1,242	1,131
Cumberland	480	1,010	...	..	428	1,036
Davidson	8,309	2,721	..	157	8,021	3,051
Decatur	845	958	..	..	800	976
De Kalb	1,284	1,464	1	2	1,202	1,469
Dickson	1,499	964	2	2	1,489	260
Dyer	1,786	672	..	57	1,732	683
Fayette	1,849	4	..	3	1,863	2
Fentress	332	894	...	15	342	880
Franklin	2,168	716	5	16	1,736	1,997
Gibson	3,173	1,369	..	3	2,898	1,498
Giles	3,042	1,569	..	3	3,010	1,529
Grainger	673	1,311	..	..	621	1,188
Greene	1,886	2,027	5	..	1,736	1,997
Grundy	576	261	...	134	564	268
Hamblen	821	993	..	2	689	910
Hamilton	4,583	4,331	..	208	6,138	2.856
Hancock	370	1,396	...	..	374	1.392
Hardeman	1,570	557	..	16	1,453	549
Hardin	720	1.142	..	9	650	1,097
Hawkins	1,152	1,693	...	..	1,116	1,407
Haywood	1,215	189	..	27	1,172	189
Henderson	912	1,208	...	..	758	1,105
Henry	2,382	1,069	...	18	2,230	1,008
Hickman	1 285	1,065	1	18	1,363	1,004
Houston	665	288	...	25	626	297
Humphreys	1,301	679	..	14	1,249	686
Jackson	1,404	966	...	2	1,392	965
James	217	608	...	1	215	604
Jefferson	677	2,066	...	..	672	1,925
Johnson	232	2,148	1	..	225	2,158
Knox	4,004	5,908	157	159	4,668	5,370
Lake	464	178	..	9	519	186
Lauderdale	1,315	519	..	22	1,259	528
Lawrence	1,591	1,726	2	12	1,653	1,649
Lewis	465	354	9	2	474	343
Lincoln	2,311	692	..	4	2,489	754
Loudon	444	1,006	9	5	13	842
Macon	684	1,594	..	3	653	1,594
McMinn	726	1,326	..	..	719	1,153
McNairy	1,057	1,300	2	..	1,004	1,324
Madison	2,417	1,358	...	29	2,264	1,435
Marion	842	1,074	..	1	822	971
Marshall	1,547	443	..	4	1,446	547
Maury	2,304	627	..	10	2,121	806
Meigs	464	457	..	..	466	448
Monroe	1,406	1,830	..	8	1,327	1,835
Montgomery	2,963	1,903	..	8	2,936	1,735
Moore	678	103	1	...	605	139
Morgan	496	1,236	5	1	471	1,247
Obion	2,258	711	1	1	1,871	825
Overton	1,401	1.008	..	65	1,221	1,102
Perry	756	678	..	12	754	682
Pickett	391	517	..	..	383	516
Polk	747	1,175	..	..	729	1,140
Putnam	1,632	1,419	..	5	1,524	1.476
Rhea	884	1,024	..	..	761	1,080
Roane	644	1,534	..	115	691	1,177
Robertson	2,418	756	1	7	2,199	866
Rutherford	2,764	1,226	..	..	2,455	1,311
Scott	190	1,932	..	25	329	1,770
Sequatchie	394	249	..	..	411	227
Sevier	291	3,130	..	2	346	3,057
Shelby	7.411	3,069	..	239	8,380	1,783
Smith	1,638	1,056	4	..	1,582	1,125
Stewart	1,475	715	..	97	1,322	818
Sullivan	2,393	1,836	19	2	2,280	1,828
Sumner	2,343	693	2	11	2,178	755
Tipton	1,662	1,041	1	3	1,800	533
Trousdale	476	198	..	..	467	213
Unicoi	67	850	..	..	66	851
Union	496	1,685	..	2	334	1,629
Van Buren	329	176	..	4	310	189
Warren	1,587	738	..	20	1,416	890
Washington	1,580	2,267	1	4	1,460	2,195
Wayne	451	1,416	1	..	448	1,374
Weakley	2,976	1,812	12	17	2,718	1,923
White	1,572	835	..	16	1,460	856
Williamson	1,929	605	...	5	1,785	670
Wilson	2,212	902	..	..	1,935	992
Total	135819	118519	268	1,882	133913	113033
Plurality	..	...	...	...	20,880	..
Per cent	44.45	42.05	..	7.25	52.07	47.43
Whole vote	257,946				246,946	

For President in 1908 Watson, Pop., received 1,115; Hisgen, Ind., 343 votes.

The vote for Governor in 1906 was: Patterson, Dem., 101,766; Evans, Rep., 92,804; Ray, Soc., 1,169.

The vote for President in 1904 was: Parker, Dem., 131,653; Roosevelt, Rep., 105,369; Swallow, Pro., 1,889; Debs, Soc., 1,354.

VOTE FOR REPRESENTATIVES IN CONGRESS, 1908.

Districts.

I. Counties of Carter, Claiborne, Cocke, Grainger, Greene, Hamblen, Hancock, Hawkins, Johnson, Sullivan, Unicoi, and Washington. W. P. Brownlow, Rep., re-elected.

II. Counties of Anderson, Blount, Campbell, Jefferson, Knox, Loudon, Morgan, Roane, Scott, Sevier, and Union. R. W. Austen, Rep., elected.

III. Counties of Bledsoe, Bradley, Franklin, Grundy, Hamilton, James, McMinn, Marion, Meigs, Monroe, Polk, Sequatchie, Van Buren, Warren, and White. John A. Moon, Dem., re-elected.

IV. Counties of Clay, Cumberland, Fentress, Jackson, Macon, Overton, Pickett, Putnam, Smith, Sumner, Trousdale, and Wilson. Cordell Hull, Dem., re-elected.

V. Counties of Bedford, Cannon, Coffee, De Kalb, Lincoln, Marshall, Moore, and Rutherford. J. W. Byrnes, Dem., elected.

VI. Counties of Cheatham, Davidson, Houston, Humphreys, Montgomery, Robertson, and Stewart. J. W. Gaines, Dem., re-elected.

VII. Counties of Dickson, Giles, Hickman, Lawrence, Lewis, Maury, Wayne, and Williamson. L. P. Padgett, Dem., re-elected.

VIII. Counties of Benton, Carroll, Chester, Decatur, Hardin, Henderson, Henry, Madison, McNairy, and Perry. T. W. Sims, Dem., re-elected.

IX. Counties of Crockett, Dyer, Gibson, Haywood, Lake, Lauderdale, Obion, and Weakley. Finis J. Garrett, Dem., 11,538, re-elected.

X. Counties of Fayette, Hardeman, Shelby, and Tipton. George W. Gordon, Dem., re-elected.

VOTE FOR GOVERNOR, 1902.

The vote for Governor was: Frazier, [illegible] 98,954; Cambell, Rep., 59,002; Cheeves, Pro., [illegible]. Frazier's plurality, 39,952.

TENNESSEE—Continued.

PRESENT STATE GOVERNMENT.

Governor, Malcolm R. Patterson, Dem.: Secretary of State, John W. Morton; Treasurer, R. E. Folk; Commissioner of Agriculture, John Thompson; Superintendent of Public Instruction, R. E. Jones; Comptroller, Frank Dibrell; Adjutant-General, Tully Brown; Attorney-General, Chas. T. Cates—all Democrats.

JUDICIARY.

Supreme Court: Chief Justice, W. D. Beard; Justices, John S. Wilkes, W K. McAllister, M. M. Neil and John K. Shields; Clerk, Joe J. Roach—all Democrats.

STATE LEGISLATURE, 1909.

	Senate.	*House.*	*Joint Ballot.*
Democrats	27	78	105
Republicans	6	21	27
Democratic majority.	21	57	78

VOTE OF THE STATE SINCE 1886.

	Dem.	*Rep.*	*Gr.*	*Pro.*	*Plu.*
1886. Gov.	126,628	109,835	....	....	16,793 D
1888. Pres.	158,779	138,988	48	5,969	19,791 D
1890. Gov.	113,549	76,081	....	11,082	37,468 D
			I. Dem.		
1892. Gov.	127,247	100,629	31,515	5,427	26,618 D
			Pop.		
1892. Pres.	138,874	100,331	23,447	4,851	38,543 D
1894. Gov.	104,356	105,104	23,092	....	†748 R
	Dem.-Pop.				
1900. Gov.	145,708	119,831	1,269	3,378	25,877 D
1900. Pres.	144,751	121,194	......	......	23,557 D
1902. Gov.	98,954	59,002	...	2,193	39,552 D
1904. Pres.	131,653	105,369	2,401	1,889	26,284 D
1906. Gov.	101,766	92,804	....	....	8,962 D
1908. Pres.	135,819	118,519	......	268	17,300 D

* Majority. † A recount of the vote by the Legislature resulted in the rejection of certain returns for irregularities and elected Turney Governor.

TEXAS.

COUNTIES. (246.)	PRESIDENT, 1908. Bryan Dem.	Taft, Rep.	Chafin Pro.	Debs, Soc.	GOVERNOR, 1908. Campbell, Dem.	Simpson, Rep.
Anderson	1,601	647	..	..	1,592	731
Andrews	...	..	..	..	...	...
Angelina	1,084	197	..	..	938	232
Aransas	193	33	..	..	190	35
Archer	331	63	..	..	327	66
Armstrong	252	32	..	..	252	32
Atascosa	614	142	...	..	614	142
Austin	1,394	572	..	..	1,186	721
Bailey	...	..	..	..	..	..
Bandera	449	283	...	..	442	286
Bastrop	1,232	522	..	...	963	867
Baylor	600	53	..	..	600	53
Bee	333	187	..	..	420	186
Bell	3,067	480	..	..	2,940	560
Bexar	3,886	3,549	...	..	1,896	1,560
Blanco	437	252	..	..	320	456
Borden	135	5	..	..	132	7
Bosque	1,397	268	..	..	1,397	268
Bowie	1,876	705	...	..	1,435	1,120
Brazoria	567	408	..	..	560	415
Brazos	876	138	..	..	890	142
Brewster	583	34	..	..	520	67
Briscoe	117	7	..	..	112	12
Brown	1,557	346	..	..	1,321	367
Burleson	1,501	365	..	..	1,501	364
Burnet	348	265	..	..	326	295
Caldwell	1,546	197	..	..	1,540	204
Calhoun	517	71	..	..	517	71
Callahan	..	..	..	..	..	..
Cameron	1,647	971	..	..	1,620	1,014
Camp	219	324	..	..	219	224
Carson	...	..	..	..	..	..
Cass	1,347	996	..	..	1,239	1,080
Castro	116	8	..	..	116	8
Chambers	293	39	..	..	287	46
Cherokee	1,575	211	..	...	1,438	329
Childress	545	92	..	...	545	92
Clay	1,115	244	..	..	1,115	244
Cochran	356	..	..	..	328	9
Coke	356	56	..	..	356	56
Coleman	1,176	135	..	..	1,030	263
Collin	3,797	792	..	..	3,797	790
Collingsworth	..	..	..	..	..	..
Colorado	1,116	486	..	..	1,108	491
Comal	626	508	..	..	821	708
Comanche	336	292	..	..	306	301
Concho	258	36	..	..	250	39
Cooke	2,439	523	..	..	2,439	523
Coryell	1,658	201	..	..	1,650	203
Cottle	157	18	..	..	153	24
Crane	..	..	..	..	..	..
Crockett	62	13	..	..	62	13
Crosby	148	1	..	...	148	3
Dallam	285	94	..	..	280	99
Dallas	7,324	2,063	..	..	6,890	2,476
Dawson	..	..	..	..	60	32
Deaf Smith	273	48	..	..	271	50
Delta	946	131	..	..	991	123
Denton	2,739	491	..	..	2,736	493
De Witt	966	853	..	..	872	836
Dickens	195	28	..	..	167	49
Dimmit	151	101	..	..	140	112
Donley	..	..	..	..	..	..
Duval	692	605	..	..	542	708
Eastland	1,856	229	..	..	1,856	229
Ector	136	5	..	...	134	9
Edwards	208	232	..	..	207	236
Ellis	4,413	593	..	...	4,411	597
El Paso	2,302	1,019	..	..	2,301	1,020
Erath	2,074	504	..	..	2,074	504
Falls	1,791	503	..	..	1,790	504
Fannin	3,191	614	..	..	3,180	625
Fayette	2,240	1,234	..	..	2,100	1,426
Fisher	776	62	..	..	776	62
Floyd	292	16	...	..	280	28
Foard	..	..	..	..	..	...
Fort Bend	550	858	..	..	542	361
Franklin	650	72	..	...	650	72
Freestone	1,185	302	..	..	1,185	302
Frio	397	112	..	..	380	127
Gaines	93	7	..	..	90	12
Galveston	*2,175	843	..	..	2,060	64
Garza	67	..	..	..	42	30
Gillespie	281	1,332	..	..	176	1,432
Glasscock	75	6	..	..	70	11
Goliad	397	644	..	..	380	665
Gonzales	1,441	609	..	..	1,390	675
Gray	338	82	..	..	338	82
Grayson	4,506	1,388	..	..	4,402	1,467
Gregg	565	273	..	..	565	273
Grimes	973	38	..	...	973	88
Guadalupe	..	..	..	..	..	...
Hale	406	41	..	..	401	43
Hall	508	56	..	..	508	56
Hamilton	1,123	222	...	..	1,121	224
Hansford	98	26	...	..	98	26
Hardeman	664	108	..	..	664	108
Hardin	809	234	..	..	804	239
Harris	5,074	1,722	..	..	4,986	1,960
Harrison	1,143	289	..	..	1,143	289
Hartley	150	30	..	..	150	30
Haskell	1,245	145	..	..	1,165	239
Hays	871	133	..	..	866	147
Hemphill	187	82	...	..	187	82
Henderson	1,143	255	..	..	1,141	257
Hidalgo	554	36	..	..	551	37
Hill	3,330	414	..	..	3,212	516
Hockley	..	..	..	..	...	..
Hood	945	161	..	..	945	161
Hopkins	2,184	271	..	..	2,181	276
Houston	1,310	493	..	..	1,310	739
Howard	504	52	..	..	501	53
Hunt	3,808	518	..	..	3,796	523
Hutchinson	134	30	..	..	134	30
Irion	102	5	..	..	100	7
Jack	780	568	..	..	779	273
Jackson	298	139	..	..	298	139
Jasper	695	187	..	...	690	192

TEXAS—*Continued.*

Counties.	President, 1908.				Governor, 1908.	
	Bryan, Dem.	Taft, Rep.	Chafin Pro.	Debs, Soc.	Campbell, Dem.	Simpson, Rep.
Jeff Davis	121	83	..	..	120	84
Jefferson	1.962	821	..	...	1.920	873
Johnson	2,747	339	..	...	2,740	343
Jones	1,752	206	..	...	1,792	206
Karnes	642	182	..	...	637	186
Kaufman	2,205	387	..	...	2,196	407
Kendall	148	537	..	..	137	543
Kent	194	17	..	..	194	17
Kerr	451	327	..	..	396	348
Kimble	181	60	..	...	189	53
King	69	..	..	...	61	11
Kinney	..	..	..	...	.	..
Knox	798	92	..	..	791	96
Lamar	2,864	482	..	..	2,856	480
Lamb	13	5	..	...	11	7
Lampasas	746	296	..	...	741	297
La Salle	328	224	..	..	311	229
Lavaca	1,666	861	..	..	1,543	910
Lee	820	504	..	..	820	504
Leon	861	351	..	..	861	351
Liberty	534	248	..	..	534	243
Limestone	1,773	247	..	..	1,721	265
Lipscomb	164	66	..	..	163	67
Live Oak	..	...	..	..	..	..
Llano	485	116	..	..	426	159
Loving	3	..	..	..	3	1
Lubbock	224	26	..	..	212	45
Lynn	..	..	...	..	..	..
Madison	540	123	...	..	240	123
Marion	514	414	..	..	514	414
Martin	235	57	...	..	230	61
Mason	424	322	...	..	412	336
Matagorda	590	167	...	..	576	182
Maverick	258	281	..	...	256	290
McCulloch	651	184	..	..	650	185
McLennan	3,778	741	...	..	3,628	812
McMullen	85	35	..	..	80	40
Medina	518	696	..	...	510	701
Menard	152	36	..	..	146	40
Midland	..	..	..	..	..	..
Milam	2,064	460	..	..	2,050	472
Mills	567	401	..	..	560	408
Mitchell	635	73	..	..	635	73
Montague	2,035	322	..	..	2,830	336
Montgomery	752	308	..	..	750	310
Moore	97	12	..	..	97	12
Morris	646	142	.	..	640	148
Motley	...	...	..	..	..	..
Nacogdoches	1,178	186	..	..	1.171	193
Navarro	2,879	618	..	..	2,770	726
Newton	357	94	..	..	350	103
Nolan	433	104	..	..	433	104
Nueces	831	253	..	..	830	254
Ochiltree	...	..	..	..	..	..
Oldham	40	15	..	..	40	15
Orange	534	119	..	..	531	120
Palo Pinto	1,483	269	..	..	1,470	273
Panola	1,242	266	..	..	1,242	266
Parker	..	..	..	..	..	..
Parmer	95	31	..	..	90	37
Pecos	..	..	..	..	..	..
Polk	144	158	..	..	193	159
Potter	233	135	..	..	231	136
Presidio	416	61	..	..	412	66
Rains	233	44	..	..	233	44
Randall	52	3	..	..	56	5
Reagan	1,813	587	...	..	1,812	589
Red River	316	24	..	..	316	20
Reeves	138	178	..	..	136	183
Refugio	125	31	..	..	125	30
Roberts	1,233	394	..	..	1,233	394
Robertson	..	..	..	..	..	..
Rockwall	981	103	..	..	977	108
Runnels	1,595	871	..	..	1,595	870
Rusk	467	54	..	..	467	54
Sabine	423	87	..	...	425	83
San Augustine	..	..	...	...	..	..
San Jacinto	371	299	..	..	370	300
San Patricio	273	115	..	..	265	119
San Saba	744	124	..	..	687	196

TEXAS—*Continued.*

Counties.	President, 1908.				Governor, 1908.	
	Bryan, Dem.	Taft, Rep.	Chafin Pro.	Debs, Soc.	Campbell, Dem.	Simpson, Rep.
Schleicher	126	9	..	..	120	15
Scurry	721	84	..	..	720	85
Shackelford	266	30	..	..	256	40
Shelby	1,727	182	..	..	1,727	187
Sherman	158	37	..	..	156	39
Smith	2,090	863	..	..	2,080	873
Somervell	251	39	..	..	251	39
Starr	901	411	..	..	900	413
Stephens	692	34	..	..	692	34
Sterling	147	5	..	..	146	6
Stonewall	329	14	..	..	329	14
Sutton	79	10	..	..	70	19
Swisher	239	26	..	.	232	31
Tarrant	6,403	1,513	..	..	5,607	2,103
Taylor	1,705	177	..	..	1,705	177
Terrell	110	62	..	..	98	74
Terry	..	..	..	..	..	..
Throckmorton	223	33	..	..	223	33
Titus	960	199	..	..	960	119
Tom Green	920	114	..	..	917	117
Travis	2,440	1,185	..	..	2,440	1,185
Trinity	599	156	..	..	594	154
Tyler	665	122	..	..	652	124
Upshur	898	287	..	..	898	287
Upton	..	..	..	..	..	..
Uvalde	748	320	..	..	742	326
Val Verde	362	182	..	..	360	184
Van Zandt	1,626	179	..	..	1,626	179
Victoria	562	327	..	..	561	328
Walker	613	447	..	..	613	447
Waller	697	349	..	..	697	349
Ward	234	30	..	..	234	30
Washington	1,543	798	..	..	1,542	801
Webb	233	1,109	..	..	233	1,109
Wharton	745	433	..	..	743	435
Wheeler	384	55	..	..	384	55
Wichita	804	255	..	..	804	253
Wilbarger	780	110	..	..	780	110
Williamson	2,430	720	..	..	2,430	720
Wilson	858	252	..	..	858	252
Winkler	12	2	..	..	12	2
Wise	..	..	..	..	..	..
Wood	1,331	375	..	..	1,331	375
Yoakum	36	4	..	..	36	4
Young	813	89	..	..	811	91
Zapata	..	..	..	..	..	498
Zavala	123	29	..	..	123	29
Total	216737	65,602	1,634	4,895	206198	70,850
Plurality	151135	..	..	..	135348	..
Per cent	77.15	22.85	..	..	74.43	25.57
Whole vote	..	..	..	298868	..	277048

Election returns 1906, unofficial vote for Governor: Campbell, Dem., 243,942; Gray, Rep., 42,169; Acheson, Rep., 12,319; Pearson, Pro., 5,910; Edwards, Soc., 7,198; Dowlen, Soc. L., 4 919.

For President in 1904: Parker, Dem., 167,200; Roosevelt, Rep., 51,042.

VOTE FOR REPRESENTATIVES IN CONGRESS, 1908.

Districts.

I. Counties of Bowie, Red River, Lamar, Delta, Hopkins, Franklin, Titus, Camp, Morris, Cass, and Marion. Morris Sheppard, Dem., 9,460.

II. Counties of Jefferson, Orange, Hardin, Tyler, Jasper, Newton, Sabine, San Augustine, Angelina, Cherokee, Nacogdoches, Shelby, Panola, and Harrison. Martin W. Dies, Dem., 9,492.

III. Counties of Wood, Upshur, Gregg, Rush, Smith, Henderson, Van Zandt, and Kaufman. Gordon Russell, Dem., 8,596.

IV. Counties of Grayson, Collin, Fannin, Hunt and Rains. C. B. Randall, Dem., 11,626.

V. Counties of Dallas, Rockwell, Ellis, Hill, and Bosque. J. A. Beall, Dem., 9,125.

VI. Navarro, Freestone, Limestone, Robertson, Brazos, Milam. Rufus Hardy, Dem., 5,429.

TEXAS—*Continued.*

VII. Anderson, Houston, Trinity, Polk, San Jacinto, Liberty, Chambers, Galveston. A. W. Gregg, Dem., 6,426.

VIII. Harris, Fort Bend, Austin, Waller, Montgomery, Grimes, Walker, Madison, Leon. J. M. Moore, Dem., 8,621.

IX. Gonzales, Fayette, Colorado, Wharton, Matagorda, Brazoria, Jackson, Lavaca, De Witt, Victoria, Calhoun, Aransas, Refugio, Bee, Goliad, Karnes. C. F. Burgess, Dem., 11,147.

X. Williamson, Travis, Hays, Caldwell, Bastrop, Bee, Burleson, Washington. A. S. Burleson, Dem., 8,245.

XI. McLennan, Falls, Bell, Coryell, Hamilton. R. L. Henry, Dem., 7,238.

XII. Tarrant, Parker, Johnson, Hood, Somervell, Erath, Comanche. O. W. Gillespie, Dem., 9,820.

XIII. Cook, Denton, Wise, Montague, Clay, Jack, Young, Archer, Wichita, Wilbarger, Baylor, Throckmorton, Knox, Foard, Hardeman, Cottle, Motley, Dickens, Floyd, Hale, Lamb, Bailey, Childress, Hall, Briscoe, Swisher, Castro, Parmer, Deaf Smith, Randall, Armstroug, Donley, Collingsworth, Wheeler, Gray, Carson, Potter, Oldham, Hartley, Moore, Hutchinson, Roberts, Hemphill, Lipscomb, Ochiltree, Hansford, Sherman, Dallam. J. H. Stephens, Dem., 14.652.

XIV. Bexar, Comal, Kendall, Bandera, Kerr, Gillespie, Blanco, Burnet, Llano, Mason, McCulloch, San Saba, Lampasas, Mills, Brown. James L. Slayden, Dem., 12,150.

XV. Cameron, Hidalgo, Starr, Zapata, Webb, Duval, Nueces, San Patricio, Live Oak, Atascosa, Wilson, Guadalupe, McMullen, La Salle, Dimmit, Maverick, Zavala, Frio, Medina, Uvalde, Kinney, Val Verde. J. N. Garner, Dem., 9,421.

XVI. El Paso, Jeff Davis, Presidio, Brewster, Pecos, Crockett, Schleicher, Sutton, Edwards, Kimble, Menard, Concho, Tom Green, Irion, Upton, Crane, Ward, Reeves, Loving, Winkler, Ector, Midland, Glasscock, Sterling, Coke, Runnels, Eastland, Callahan, Taylor, Nolan, Mitchell, Howard, Martin, Andrews, Gaines, Dawson, Borden, Scurry, Fisher, Jones, Shackelford, Stephens, Palo Pinto, Haskell, Stonewall, King, Kent, Garza, Crosby, Lubbock, Lynn, Terry, Yoakum, Cochran, Hockley. W. R. Smith, Dem., 12,766.

PRESENT STATE GOVERNMENT.

Governor, T. M. Campbell; Lieutenant-Governor, A. B. Davidson; Secretary of State, W. R. Davie; Treasurer, Sam Sparks; Comptroller, John W. Stephens; Superintendent of Public Instruction, R. B. Cousins; Land Commissioner, J. T. Robison; Adjutant-General, J. O. Newton; Attorney-General, R. V. Davidson; Commissioner of Insurance, Thos. B. Love—all Democrats.

JUDICIARY.

Supreme Court: Chief Justice, Reuben R. Gaines; Associate Justices, Thomas J. Brown and F. A. Williams; Clerk, F. T. Connerly—all Democrats.

STATE LEGISLATURE, 1909.

	Senate.	*House.*	*Joint Ballot.*
Democrats..........	30	130	160
Republicans.........	1	3	4

VOTE OF THE STATE SINCE 1884.

	Dem.	*Rep.*	*Gr.*	*Pro.*	*Maj.*
1884. Pres...	225,309	93,141	3,321	3,538	*132,168 D
1888. Pres...	234,883	88,422	....	4,749	*146,461 D
			Pop.		
1895. Gov...	241,882	55,405	159,224	‡5,026	*82,658 D
	Dem.-Pop.	*Rep.*	*N. D.*	*Pro.*	*Maj.*
1896. Pres...	370,434	167,520	5,046	1,786	*202,914 D
	Dem.	*Pop.*			
1898. Gov...	285,074	132 348	....	....	152,726 D
		Rep.	*Pop.*	*Pro.*	
1904. Pres...	167,200	51,242	8,062	4,292	*105,958 D
1908. Pres...	216,737	65,602	....	...	151,135 D

* Plurality. ‡ Independent Republican.

UTAH.

COUNTIES. (27.)	PRESIDENT, 1908.				PRESIDENT, 1904.	
	Bryan Dem.	Taft, Rep.	Debs, Soc.	Hisgen, Ind.	Parker Dem.	Roosevelt, Rep.
Beaver........	714	945	27	1	593	869
Box Elder....	1,417	2,401	40	2	1,151	2,400
Caché.........	3,317	3,795	64	3	2,948	4,008
Carbon........	581	1,027	106	..	508	1,244
Davis..........	1,331	1,740	34	5	1,225	1,657
Emery.........	749	1,098	158	..	583	905
Garfield.......	290	728	42	..	252	679
Grand..........	215	233	24	5	165	262
Iron............	488	718	76	..	442	741
Juab	1,421	1,619	300	1	1,206	1,493
Kane..........	102	414	3	..	102	399
Millard	765	1,004	38	..	683	1,001
Morgan.......	306	490	48	..	315	492
Piute..........	157	332	98	1	228	358
Rich....	285	427	5	..	240	439
Salt Lake.....	12,954	20,755	2,059	41	8,389	20,665
San Juan.....	109	131	3	3	36	135
San Pete......	2,307	3,333	129	1	1,741	3,829
Sevier.........	1,272	1,777	187	1	930	1,725
Summit	1,402	1,612	148	9	1,358	2,232
Tooele	808	1,116	59	1	639	1,289
Uintah........	683	782	149	..	630	753
Utah	4,984	6,390	267	2	4,243	6,490
Wasatch......	985	1,265	98	2	656	1,042
Washington..	819	738	5	1	761	718
Wayne.........	184	276	96	..	251	310
Weber........	3,965	5,879	636	8	3,108	6,331
Total........	52,601	61,015	4,895	87	33,413	62,446
Plurality......		18,414	....	...	....	29,033
Per cent......	39.23	56.18	4 51	.08	32.87	61.44
Whole vote..	108,598				101,624	

For President in 1904 Debs, Soc., received 5,767 votes.

The vote for President in 1900 was: Bryan, Dem., 45,006; McKinley, Rep., 47,139; Woolley, Pro., 209; Debs, Soc., 720; Malloney, Soc. L., 106.

The vote for Governor in 1904 was: James H. Moyle, Dem., 38,047; John C. Cutler, Rep., 50,837; Joseph Kauffman, Soc., 4,892; William M. Ferry, American, 7,959.

The vote for Representative in Congress, 1908, was: Lyman R. Martineau, Dem., 35,981; Joseph Howell, Rep., 57,432; Chas. Crane, Soc., 4,372; C. J. Douglas, American, 13,488.

PRESENT STATE GOVERNMENT.

Governor, William Spry; Secretary of State, C. S. Tingey; Treasurer, David Mattson; Auditor, Jesse D. Jewkes; Adjutant-General, E. A. Wedgwood; Attorney-General, A. R. Barnes; Superintendent of Education, A. C. Nelson; Commissioner of Insurance, Secretary of State, ex-officio—all Republicans.

JUDICIARY.

Supreme Court: Chief Justice Daniel N. Straup, Rep.; Justices W. M. McCarty and J. E. Frick; Clerk, H. W. Griffith, Rep.

STATE LEGISLATURE, 1909.

Senate: Republicans 18; total, 18.

House of Representatives: Democrats, 2; Republicans, 43; total, 45.

VERMONT.

COUNTIES. (14.)	PRESIDENT, 1908.				GOVERNOR, 1908.	
	Bryan Dem.	Taft, Rep.	Chafin Pro.	Hisgen, Ind.	Burke, Dem.	Prouty, Rep.
Addison.......	446	2,986	74	84	461	3,534
Bennington ..	749	2,453	56	53	1,009	2,777
Caledonia......	764	2,700	78	76	1,126	3,067
Chittenden.....	1,650	3,807	55	60	3,005	4,181
Essex	327	745	18	5	371	809
Franklin......	1,048	2,360	80	43	1,590	3,535
Grand Isle....	188	364	10	4	319	474
Lamoille......	311	1,456	51	24	369	1,880
Orange.......	668	2,263	69	41	936	2,654
Orleans	384	2,535	34	19	458	3,325

VERMONT—*Continued.*

Counties.	President, 1908.				Governor, 1908.	
	Bryan, Dem.	Taft, Rep.	Chafin Pro.	Hisgen, Ind.	Burke, Dem.	Prouty, Rep.
Rutland	1,542	5,643	103	167	1,916	6,063
Washington	1,610	3,825	71	130	2,160	4,521
Windham	906	3,738	46	68	1,239	4,142
Windsor	907	4,683	62	82	994	4,636
Total	11,496	39,552	799	804	15,953	45,598
Plurality	..	28,056	..	..	..	...
Per cent	21.78	75.12	1.60	1.50	....	..
Whole vote	52,651				64,379	

The vote for Governor in 1906 was: Clement, Dem., 26,912; Proctor, Rep., 42,392; Hanson, Pro., 733; Sullivan, Soc., 512.

The vote for Governor in 1904 was: Porter, Dem., 16,566; Bell, Rep., 48,115; Morse, Soc., 769; Cummings, Pro., 1,175.

VOTE FOR REPRESENTATIVES IN CONGRESS, 1908.

Districts.

I. Counties of Addison, Bennington, Chittenden, Franklin, Grand Isle, Lamoille, and Rutland. Emile Blais, Dem., 8,028; David J. Foster, Rep., 22,190; Edwin R. Towle, Pro., 449.

II. Counties of Caledonia, Essex, Orange, Orleans, Washington, Windham, and Windsor. Andrew J. Sibley, Dem., 6,914; Frank Plumley, Rep., 22,868; W. V. McLaughlih, Pro., 393; Timothy Ivers, Soc., 11.

PRESENT STATE GOVERNMENT.

Governor, George H. Prouty; Lieutenant-Governor, John A. Mead; Secretary of State, Guy W. Bailey; Treasurer, Edward H. Deavitt; Auditor, Horace F. Graham; Attorney-General, J. G. Sargent; Superinteent of Education, Mason S. Stone; Commissioner of Insurance; E. H. Deavitt, and Guy W. Bailey—all Republicans.

JUDICIARY.

Supreme Court: Chief Justice, John W. Rowell; Assistant Justices, Loveland Munson, John H. Watson, Seneca Haselton; Clerk, M. E. Smilie—all Republicans, except Haselton.

STATE LEGISLATURE, 1909.

	Senate.	*House.*	*Joint Ballot.*
Republicans	28	201	229
Democrats	2	39	41
Ind. Democrats	..	3	1
Ind. Republicans	..	1	..
Republican majority	26	158	187

VOTE OF THE STATE SINCE 1872.

		Dem.	*Rep.*	*Gr.*	*Pro.*	*Plu.*
1872.	Pres.	10,927	41,481	....	....	*30,554 R
1876.	Pres.	20,350	44,428	....	....	*24,078 R
1880.	Pres.	18,316	45,567	....	....	*27,251 R
1884.	Pres.	17,331	39,514	785	1,752	22,183 R
1888.	Pres.	16,788	45,192	....	1,460	28,404 R
1890.	Gov.	19,290	33,462	....	1,161	14,163 R
1892.	Pres.	16,325	37,992	....	1,415	21,669 R
				Pop.		
1894.	Gov.	14,142	42,663	740	457	28,521 R
				N. D.		
1896.	Pres.	10,637	51,127	1,331	733	40,490 R
				Soc. D.		
1900.	Gov.	17.129	48,441	567	950	31,312 R
1900.	Pres.	12,849	42,568	....	368	29,719 R
1902.	Gov.	7,364	31,864	....	2,498	24,500 R
1904.	Pres.	9,77	40,459	859	792	30,682 R
1906.	Gov.	26,912	42,332	512	733	15,420 R
1908.	Pres.	11,496	39,552	...	799	28,056 R

* Majority.

VIRGINIA.

Counties and Cities. (118.)	President, 1908.				Governor, 1905.	
	Bryan, Dem.	Taft, Rep.	Chafin Pro.	Debs, Soc.	Swanson, Dem.	Lewis, Rep.
Accomac	1,748	337	...	..	1,263	308
Albemarle	999	380	..	..	1,013	262
Alexandria C.	1,218	247	..	...	270	151
AlexandriaCo	354	165	...	..	272	171
Alleghany	422	488	..	..	688	642
Amelia	247	73	..	..	311	77
Amherst	849	164	..	..	825	99
Appomattox	633	117	..	..	608	94
Augusta	1,435	987	..	...	1,235	863
Bath	310	232	...	..	281	174
Bedford	1,272	463	..	..	1,190	393
Bland	339	397	...	..	401	413
Botetourt	809	793	...	..	833	743
Bristol City	405	187	...	..	380	133
Brunswick	507	123	..	..	594	156
Buchanan	395	635	..	..	462	491
Buckingham	676	333	...	..	654	488
Buena Vista C	137	80	...	..	159	63
Campbell	624	174	..	..	484	149
Caroline	494	326	...	..	578	240
Carroll	859	1,521	..	...	1,130	1,302
Charles City	99	84	..	..	127	33
Charlotte	537	242	..	..	648	217
Charlottesv'le	428	82	..	..	..	134
Chesterfield	608	167	...	..	505	134
Clarke	517	74	..	..	415	68
CliftonForgeC	402	133	..	..	..	..
Craig	364	224	..	..	375	191
Culpeper	962	233	..	..	849	259
Cumberland	374	68	..	...	444	82
Danville	963	206	..	..	790	85
Dickenson	551	671	..	..	671	703
Dinwiddie	445	157	..	..	478	136
Elizabeth C'y	679	253	..	..	519	181
Essex	364	123	..	..	417	147
Fairfax	1,143	404	..	..	784	298
Fauquier	1,354	363	..	..	1,212	424
Floyd	390	1,149	...	..	477	932
Fluvanna	450	135	..	..	458	144
Franklin	1,218	1,101	..	..	1,266	1,025
Frederick	866	354	..	...	532	230
Fredericksb'g	285	252	...	..	438	134
Giles	705	605	..	...	839	557
Gloucester	477	94	..	..	574	109
Goochland	294	246	..	...	344	275
Grayson	844	1,243	..	..	918	1,111
Greene	252	366	..	..	323	338
Greenesville	273	77	..	..	422	117
Halifax	1,268	650	..	..	1,553	452
Hanover	522	204	..	..	580	198
Henrico	626	217	..	..	713	195
Henry	761	716	..	..	979	570
Highland	292	305	...	..	247	254
Isle of Wight	530	199	..	..	656	99
James City	132	62	...	..	131	61
King George	296	199	..	..	332	218
King and Q'n	349	181	..	..	429	153
King William	276	228	..	..	382	221
Lancaster	468	122	..	..	576	110
Lee	805	1,334	..	..	756	1,027
Loudoun	1,570	447	..	..	1,396	413
Louisa	692	290	..	...	691	241
Lunenburg	413	105	..	...	464	68
Lynchburg C.	962	473	...	...	844	270
Madison	466	305	.	..	579	327
Manchester	363	114	..	..	254	39
Mathews	577	86	..	..	514	183
Mecklenburg	1,000	252	..	...	1,232	317
Middlesex	413	164	..	..	379	182
Montgomery	734	795	..	..	787	733
Nansemond	857	271	..	...	778	135
Nelson	742	308	..	..	819	223
New Kent	193	159	..	..	141	91
Norfolk City	2,271	991	..	..	2,393	414
Norfolk Co.	879	739	..	...	1,753	1,030
NewportN'ws	791	498	..	..	1,000	507
Northampton	673	174	..	..	630	168
North'mber'd	410	185	..	..	480	207
Nottoway	481	118	..	..	464	104

VIRGINIA—*Continued.*

Counties and Cities.	President, 1908. Bryan, Dem.	Taft, Rep.	Chafin, Pro.	Debs, Soc.	Governor, 1905. Swanson, Dem.	Lewis, Rep.
Orange	587	198	..	..	742	228
Page	804	802	..	..	1,024	800
Patrick	723	1,092	..	..	841	747
Petersburg	905	205	..	..	880	72
Pittsylvania	1,472	962	..	..	2,101	561
Portsmouth	1.154	407	..	..	963	330
Powhatan	225	146	..	..	234	176
Prince Edward	561	117	..	..	530	137
Prince George	171	88	..	..	198	75
Princess Anne	403	99	..	..	535	143
Prince William	738	200	..	..	726	157
Pulaski	714	780	..	..	793	769
Radford City	204	141	..	..	243	104
Rappahannock	433	158	..	..	467	115
Richmond City	4,143	1,135	..	..	3,038	574
Richmond Co.	338	205	..	..	406	187
Roanoke City	1,408	593	..	..	1,357	455
Roanoke Co.	782	426	..	..	653	411
Rockbridge	1,000	810	..	..	939	779
Rockingham	1,736	1,581	..	..	1,640	1,445
Russell	827	1,173	..	..	1,097	1,326
Scott	1,145	1,781	..	...	1,303	1,656
Shenandoah	1,295	1,449	..	..	1,285	1,325
Smyth	906	1,350	..	..	913	1,191
Southampton	818	206	..	..	975	138
Spottsylvania	346	282	..	..	409	252
Stafford	406	474	..	..	463	486
Staunton	514	347	..	..	507	244
Surry	269	82	..	..	389	106
Sussex	412	115	..	..	389	123
Tazewell	809	1,398	..	..	733	1,256
Warren	562	209	..	..	485	137
Warwick	101	58	..	..	211	78
Washington	1,558	1,741	..	..	1,443	1,512
Westmoreland	353	161	..	..	335	181
Williamsburg	120	48	..	..	151	43
Winchester	449	266	..	..	297	168
Wise	993	1,527	..	..	810	1,441
Wythe	950	1,487	..	..	1,035	1,366
York	214	61	..	..	235	58
Total	82.906	52,573	1,111	256	83,544	45,795
Plurality	30,343	..	..	..	37,749	..
Per cent	60.61	38.35	.81	.27	64.36	35.28
Scattering	....				453	
Whole vote	136,856				129.792	

For Goveruer 1905 Downey, Soc., received 453 votes.

For President in 1904 Watson, Pop., received 359 votes; Corrigan, Soc. L., 56.

The vote for Governor in 1901 was: Montague, Dem., 116,682; Hoge, Rep., 81,366; Rucker, Pro., 1,896; Quantz, Soc., 280; McTier, 285.

For President in 1900 Woolley, Pro., received 2,150 votes.

VOTE FOR REPRESENTATIVES IN CONGRESS, 1908.

Districts.

I. Counties of Accomac, Carolina, Essex, Gloucester, King and Queen, Lancaster, Matthews, Middlesex, Northampton, Northumberland, Richmond, Spottsylvania, Westmoreland, and the City of Fredericksburg. Wm. A. Jones, Dem., 9,733; Wise, Rep., 3,288.

II. Counties of Charles City, Elizabeth City, Isle of Wight, James City, Nansemond, Norfolk, Princess Anne, Southampton, Surry, Warwick, York, and the cities of Norfolk, Portsmouth, Williamsburg, and Newport News. Harry L. Maynard, Dem., 7,358; Groner, Rep., 3,086.

III. Counties of Chesterfield, Goochland, Hanover, Henrico, King William, New Kent, and the cities of Richmond and Manchester. John Lamb, Dem., 8,105; George A. Hanson, Rep., 2,439.

IV. Counties of Amelia, Brunswick, Dinwiddie, Greenesville, Lunenburg, Mecklenburg, Nottoway, Powhatan, Prince Edward, Prince George, Sussex, and the City of Petersburg. Francis R. Lassiter, Dem., 7,200.

V. Counties of Carroll, Floyd, Franklin, Grayson, Henry, Patrick, Pittsylvania, and the City of Danville. E. W. Saunders, Dem., 7,079; Parsons, Rep., 6,988.

VI. Counties of Bedford, Campbell, Charlotte, Halifax, Montgomery, Roanoke, and the cities of Lynchburg, Radford, and Roanoke. Carter Glass, Dem., 8,807; Hartman, Rep., 3,421.

VII. Counties of Albemarle, Clarke, Frederick, Greene, Madison, Page, Rappahannock, Rockingham, Shenandoah, Warren, and the cities of Charlottesville and Winchester. James Hay, Dem., 9,560; Pritchard, Rep., 5,652.

VIII. Counties of Alexandria, Culpeper, Fairfax, Fauquier, King George, Loudoun, Louisa, Orange, Prince William, Stafford, and the City of Alexandria. Carlin, Dem., 10,182; Gregg, Rep., 2,597.

IX. Counties of Bland, Buchanan, Craig, Dickenson, Giles, Lee, Pulaski, Russell, Scott, Smyth, Tazewell, Washington, Wise, Wythe, and the City of Bristol Byars, Dem., 11,592; Campbell Slemp, Rep., 15,693

X. Counties of Alleghany, Amherst, Appomattox, Augusta, Bath, Botetourt, Buckingham, Cumberland, Fluvanna, Highland, Nelson, Rockbridge, and the cities of Staunton and Buena Vista. Hal. D. Flood, Dem., 10,140; Franklin, Rep., 5,281.

STATE LEGISLATURE, 1909.

	Senate.	House.	Joint Ballot.
Democrats	35	86	121
Independents and Republicans	5	14	19
Democratic majority	30	72	102

PRESENT STATE GOVERNMENT.

Governor, Claude A. Swanson, Dem.; Lieutenant-Governor, J. T. Ellyson; Secretary of Commonwealth, D. Q. Eggleston; First Auditor, Morton Marye; Treasurer, A. W. Harman, Jr.; Superintendent of Instructions, J. D. Eggleston; Attorney-General, W. A. Anderson; all Democrats.

JUDICIARY.

Supreme Court of Appeals: President, James Keith; Justices, S. G. Whittle, John A. Buchanan, George M. Harrison, and Richard H. Cardwell; Clerk of the Court, H. Stewart Jones—all Democrats.

VOTE OF THE STATE SINCE 1872.

	Dem.	Rep.	Pop.	Pro.	Maj.
1872. Pres	91,654	93,468	....	....	1,814 R
1876. Pres	101,208	76,093	....	....	25,115 D
1880 Pres	{96,449 / 31,527}	84,020	....	....	*31,527 H
1884. Pres	145.497	139,356	....	138	6,141 D
1885. Gov	152,544	136,510	....	....	16,034 D
1888. Pres	151,977	150,438	....	1,678	†1.539 D
1889. Gov	162,654	120,477	....	897	†42,177 D
			N. D.		
1892. Pres	163,977	113,262	12,275	2,738	†50,715 D
			Pop.		
1893. Gov	127,940	....	81,239	6,962	†39,726 D
1896. Pres	154,709	135,368	2,129	2,350	†19,341 D
1897. Gov	109,655	56,840	....	2,743	†52,815 D
1900. Pres	146,080	115,865	....	2,150	†30,215 D
1901. Gov	116,682	81,366	....	1,896	35,316 D
1904. Pres	80,648	47,880	....	1,383	32,768 D
1905. Gov	83,544	45,795	....	....	37,749 D
1908. Pres	82,916	52,573	256	1,111	30,343 D

* Hancock's actual majority in the State, the Democratic and Readjuster vote both being for him. † Plurality.

WASHINGTON.

Counties. (37.)	President, 1908. Bryan, Dem.	Taft, Rep.	Chafin Pro.	Debs, Soc.	Governor, 1908. .... Dem.	Cosgrove, Rep.
Adams	714	1,033	45	58	750	1,033
Asotin	365	648	38	36	338	993
Benton	465	891	84	151	479	913
Chehalis	1,248	3,128	86	712	1,186	3,422
Chelan	871	1,639	66	160	851	1,776
Clallam	428	938	11	187	459	987
Clarke	1,250	2,416	104	835	1,136	2,525
Columbia	585	887	48	25	632	872
Cowlitz	617	1,573	28	172	623	1,619
Douglas	1,540	1,942	43	191	1,559	2,017
Ferry	393	467	11	115	402	512
Franklin	485	643	27	56	470	638
Garfield	333	556	13	40	354	601
Island	192	450	28	99	157	505
Jefferson	417	859	11	66	392	885
King	14,644	22,297	836	2,173	13,939	23,632
Kitsap	850	1,819	74	494	751	1,987
Kittitas	985	1,752	64	314	1,002	1,772
Klickitat	570	1,245	46	173	549	1,328
Lewis	1,412	3,170	120	528	1,472	3,214
Lincoln	1,443	2 025	73	124	1,453	2,107
Mason	318	553	22	80	322	587
Okanogan	1,074	1,368	22	307	1,028	1,530
Pacific	483	1,492	21	153	537	1,470
Pierce	4,936	10,935	463	1,626	4,701	11,586
San Juan	178	581	10	111	113	621
Skagit	1,449	2,924	113	690	1,367	3,110
Skamania	143	310	7	54	119	350
Snohomish	2,974	5,659	567	958	2,700	5,913
Spokane	6,559	11,719	496	1,184	6,869	11,700
Stevens	1,564	2,546	120	646	1,554	2,613
Thurston	964	1,940	110	367	985	2,001
Wahkiakum	150	485	3	46	132	495
Walla Walla	1,660	2,843	71	102	1,881	2,670
Whatcom	2,398	4,955	296	963	2,273	5,341
Whitman	2,886	3,376	315	337	2,946	3,053
Yakima	1,650	3,998	258	344	1,615	4,032
Total	58,691	106062	4,700	14,177	58,126	110190
Plurality	..	48,371	..	..	...	52,064
Per cent	32.85	57.93	2.30	7.72	33.02	62.26
Whole vote		183,879			171,161	

For Governor 1904: Turner, Dem., 59,119; Mead, Rep., 75,278; Soc., 7,420; Pro., 2,782; Soc. L., 1,070.

For President in 1908, Hisgen, Ind., received 249 votes.

VOTE FOR REPRESENTATIVES IN CONGRESS, 1908.

Districts.

I. Miller, Dem., 26,089; Humphrey, Rep., 39,643; Sherwood, Pro., 26; Burgess, Soc., 1,468.

II. Brown, Dem., 12,006; Cushman, Rep., 29,850; Herman, Soc., 892.

III. Goodyear, Dem., 23,227; Pointdexter, Rep., 38,369; Reinert, Soc., 1,280.

PRESENT STATE GOVERNMENT.

Governor, Samuel G. Cosgrove, Rep.; Lieutenant-Governor, M. E. Hay; Secretary of State, S. H. Nichols, Rep.; Treasurer, John G. Lewis, Rep.; Auditor, C. W. Clausen, Rep.; Adjutant-General, to be named, Rep.; Attorney-General, W. P. Bell, Rep.; Com. Public Lands, E. W. Ross, Rep.

JUDICIARY.

Supreme Court: Chief Justice, Wallace Mount; Associate Justices, R. O. Dunbar, H. D. Crow, M. A. Fullerton, F. A. Rudkin, Stephen J. Chadwick, —all Reps.; Clerk, C. S. Reinhart.

STATE LEGISLATURE, 1909.

	Senate.	House.	Joint Ballot.
Republicans	39	89	128
Democrats	3	6	9
Republican majority	36	83	119

VOTE OF THE STATE SINCE ADMISSION.

	Dem.	Rep.	Pop.	Pro.	Maj.
1892. President	29,802	36,460	19,165	2,542	*6,658 R
			Soc.		
1908. President	58,691	106,062	14,177	4,700	48,371 R

* Plurality.

WEST VIRGINIA.

Counties. (55.)	President, 1908. Bryan, Dem.	Taft, Rep.	Chafin Pro.	Debs, Soc.	Governor, 1908. Bennett, Dem.	Glasscock, Rep.
Barbour	1,634	2,072	78	27	1,685	2,012
Berkeley	2,563	2,675	100	14	2,606	2,641
Boone	1,031	994	7	58	1,032	995
Braxton	2,565	2,365	102	15	2,573	2,365
Brooke	1,074	1,374	58	57	1,147	1,310
Cabell	4,467	4,900	160	111	4,665	4,738
Calhoun	1,212	1,006	44	6	1,243	975
Clay	825	1,320	68	21	832	1,317
Doddridge	990	1,773	46	28	1,045	1,720
Fayette	3,819	5,874	282	464	4,082	5,594
Gilmer	1,512	989	56	1	1,587	918
Grant	336	1,305	25	4	421	1,220
Greenbrier	2,682	2,415	49	46	2 742	2,366
Hampshire	1,773	683	19	1	1,910	561
Hancock	719	1,185	60	20	733	1,179
Hardy	1,219	646	1	4	1,284	593
Harrison	4,004	4,946	397	86	4,404	4,542
Jackson	1,950	2,615	37	19	1,994	2,579
Jefferson	2,490	1,255	76	1	2,519	1,236
Kanawha	7,117	9,663	245	624	7,585	9,018
Lewis	1,832	2,239	149	19	2,081	2,028
Lincoln	1,732	2,202	58	6	1,750	2,183
Logan	1,399	730	11	33	1,409	723
Marion	3,961	4,368	344	222	4,251	4,095
Marshall	2,498	3,680	220	238	2,855	3,415
Mason	1,928	3,116	24	56	2,009	3,063
Mercer	3,006	4,229	24	36	3,468	3,787
Mineral	1,512	1,986	66	17	1,619	1,893
Mingo	1,520	2,058	9	9	1,554	2,028
Monongalia	1,758	3,131	172	187	1,972	2,908
Monroe	1,521	1,523	29	1	1,507	1,480
Morgan	541	1,134	37	4	567	1,115
McDowell	1,916	6,176	45	..	2,491	5,598
Nicholas	1,730	1,795	139	..	1,781	1,763
Ohio	6,497	7,312	153	441	7,550	6,381
Pendleton	1,193	898	3	..	1,204	884
Pleasants	921	987	41	4	936	970
Pocahontas	1,300	1,687	73	8	1,366	1,615
Preston	1,454	3,928	144	81	1,643	3,748
Putnam	1,726	2,098	36	50	1,760	2,073
Raleigh	1,891	2,530	44	122	2,033	2,414
Randolph	2,645	2,363	142	110	2,829	2,220
Ritchie	1,346	2,242	222	38	1,430	2,181
Roane	1,868	2,334	43	9	1,907	2,309
Summers	2,123	1,940	35	3	2,207	1,856
Taylor	1,552	2,106	129	46	1,772	1,901
Tucker	1,265	1,886	122	18	1,380	1,783
Tyler	1,355	2,113	113	69	1,441	2,032
Upshur	846	2,571	174	9	933	2,502
Wayne	2,590	2,410	32	9	2,610	2,392
Webster	1,196	932	32	6	1,216	914
Wetzel	2,874	2,235	96	85	2,953	2,179
Wirt	1,042	1,028	29	7	1,060	1,013
Wood	4,063	4,596	96	127	4,439	4,238
Wyoming	827	1,251	44	2	837	1,244
Total	111418	137869	5,139	3,679	118909	130807
Plurality	..	26,451	..	..	..	11,898
Per cent	42.79	53.43	1.95	1.83	46.08	50.69
Whole vote		258,105			257,991	

For President, 1904, Watson, Pop., had 337 votes.

VOTE FOR STATE OFFICERS, 1904.

For Governor: John Cornwell, Dem., 112,457; W. M. O. Dawson, Rep., 121,540; J. W. Bedford, Pro., 3,999; J. M. Eskey, Soc., 1,279. Dawson's plurality, 9,083.

For President in 1900, Woolley, Pro., received 1,692 votes; Debs, Soc., 268; Barker, Pop., 274.

For President, 1908, Hisgen, Ind., received 46 votes. The scattering vote for Governor was: Soc., 3,308; Pro., 4,967.

VOTE FOR REPRESENTATIVES IN CONGRESS, 1908.

Districts.

I. Counties of Brooke, Hancock, Harrison, Lewis, Marshall, Ohio, and Wetzel. W. R. Hubbard, Rep., re-elected.

WEST VIRGINIA—*Continued.*

II. Counties of Barbour, Berkeley, Grant, Hampshire, Hardy, Jefferson, Marion, Mineral, Monongalia, Morgan, Pendleton, Preston, Randolph, Taylor, Tucker. B. H. Heiner, Dem., 22,771; G. C. Sturgis, Rep., 25,332; Harring, Pro., 1,621; Woodley, Soc., 476.

III. Counties of Clay, Fayette, Greenbrier, Kanawha, Monroe, Nicholas, Pocahontas, Summers, Upshur, Webster. Andrew Price, Dem., 23,355; J. H. Gaines, Rep., 29,268; Hill, Pro., 1,247; Bennett, Soc., 1,153.

IV. Counties of Calhoun, Jackson, Pleasants, Ritchie, Roane, Wirt, Wood, Braxton, Doddridge, Gilmer, and Tyler. W. O. Parsons, Dem., 19,095; H. C. Woodyard, Rep., 16,310; Williamson, Pro, 812; McDougal, Soc., 313.

V. Counties of Cabell, Lincoln, Mason, McDowell, Mercer, Putnam, Raleigh, Wyoming, Wayne, Boone, Mingo, and Logan. L. H. Clarke, Dem., 24,778; J. A. Hughes, Rep., 31,958; Miller, Pro., 414; Crouch, Soc., 381.

PRESENT STATE GOVERNMENT.

Governor, Wm. E. Glasscock; Secretary of State, Stuart F. Reed; Treasurer, E. F. Long; Auditor, John S. Darst; Attorney-General, Wm. G. Conly; Superintendent of Schools, M. P. Shawsley; Adjutant-General, N. S. Burlew—all Republicans.

JUDICIARY.

Supreme Court of Appeals: President, George Poffenbarger, Rep.; Associate Justices, Henry Brannon, Rep.; William N. Miller, Rep.; L. Judson Williams, Rep.; Ira E. Robinson, Rep.; Clerk, W. B. Mathews, Rep.

STATE LEGISLATURE, 1909.

	Senate.	*House.*	*Joint Ballot.*
Republicans	25	60	85
Democrats	5	25	30
Prohibition	..	1	1
Republican majority.	20	34	54

VOTE OF THE STATE SINCE 1872.

	Dem.	*Rep.*	*Gr.*	*Pro.*	*Maj.*
1872. President	2..537	32.283	....	....	2,746 R
1876. President	56,565	42,001	....	....	14,564 D
1880. President	57,391	46,243	9,079	....	*11,148 D
1884. President	67,317	63,096	805	939	*4,221 D
			U. Lab.		
1888. President	78,677	78,171	1,508	1,084	506 D
			Pop.		
1892. President	84,467	80,293	4,166	2,145	4,174 D
			N. D.		*Plu.*
1896. Governor	93,974	105,477	....	1,054	11,503 R
1896. President	92.927	104,414	677	1,203	11,487 R
1900. Governor	100,226	118,807	....	1,373	18,581 R
1900 President	98,807	119,829	....	1,692.	21.022 R
1904. President	100,850	132,608	....	4,413	31,758 R
1908. President	111,418	137,869	3,679	5,139	26,451 R

* Plurality.

WISCONSIN.

Counties. (70.)	President, 1908. Bryan Dem.	Taft, Rep.	Chafin Pro.	Debs, Soc.	Governor. 1908. Aylward, Dem.	Davidson, Rep.
Adams	436	1,167	56	213	402	1,186
Ashland	1,582	2,259	110	32	1,563	2,211
Barron	1,266	3,247	243	128	992	3,434
Bayfield	569	1,957	72	174	500	1,985
Brown	3,353	4,947	129	516	3,249	4,944
Buffalo	1,027	1,937	56	20	982	1,933
Burnett	296	1,181	93	65	201	1,268
Calumet	1,711	1,576	30	85	1,676	1,567
Chippewa	2,203	3,526	148	90	2,160	3,491
Clark	1,576	3,491	152	92	1,503	3,477
Columbia	2,363	4,072	198	140	2,341	4,046
Crawford	1,586	2,041	72	63	1,602	2.014
Dane	7.818	9,441	489	256	7,815	9,341
Dodge	5,883	4,015	162	63	6,033	3,762
Door	778	2,463	53	37	648	2 481
Douglas	1,715	3,509	257	653	1,616	3,612
Dunn	914	3,297	162	119	713	3,369
Eau Claire	1,859	3,980	173	158	1,842	3,903

WISCONSIN—*Continued.*

Counties.	President, 1908. Bryan Dem.	Taf, Rep.	Chafin Pro.	Debs, Soc.	Governor. 1908. Aylward, Dem.	Davidson, Rep.
Florence	102	541	19	5	105	541
Fond du Lac	5,194	5,872	244	230	5,231	5,676
Forest	324	1,023	31	46	283	1,030
Grant	3,696	4,989	288	83	3,666	4,883
Green	1,856	2,617	209	122	1,915	2,439
Green Lake	1,608	2,094	63	32	1,637	2,018
Iowa	2,077	2,986	238	12	2,076	2,933
Iron	314	1,134	43	42	292	1,118
Jackson	631	2 603	65	40	520	2,660
Jefferson	4,492	3,207	161	70	4,580	3,058
Juneau	1,691	2.454	77	37	1,625	2,498
Kenosha	2,006	3,409	239	601	2,029	3.349
Kewanee	1,731	1,590	37	63	1,714	1,603
La Crosse	4,054	4.382	189	112	3,970	4,399
La Fayette	2,100	2,832	105	24	2,079	2,844
Langlade	1,340	1,921	64	33	1,367	1,807
Lincoln	1 813	2,308	63	99	1,849	2,276
Manitowoc	3,952	4,126	61	947	3,993	4.098
Marathon	4.703	5,258	133	276	4,804	5,089
Marinette	1,597	3,454	235	154	1,451	3.477
Marquette	798	1,555	44	17	831	1,521
Milwaukee	26,000	28,625	1,278	17,496	26,917	26,243
Monroe	2,155	3,304	136	91	2,117	3,304
Oconto	1,453	3,020	75	114	1,508	2,944
Oneida	688	1,536	28	354	684	1,453
Outagamie	4,288	5,079	209	118	4,366	4,971
Ozaukee	1,856	1,216	27	60	1,913	1,117
Pepin	447	1,010	36	5	444	995
Pierce	978	2,988	150	56	887	2,984
Polk	816	2.788	146	121	570	3,024
Portage	2,382	3,269	112	50	2,386	3,266
Price	609	1,738	79	236	546	1,707
Racine	3,688	5,490	429	794	4,035	5,029
Richland	1,689	2,464	289	51	1,724	2,343
Rock	3,227	7,839	391	265	3,130	7,781
Rusk	532	1.431	48	96	442	1,439
St. Croix	1,773	3,228	98	83	1,650	3,325
Sauk	2,571	3,854	294	85	2,536	3,788
Sawyer	299	815	18	19	260	849
Shawano	1,750	3.349	102	40	1,709	3,344
Sheboygan	4,405	5,948	245	752	4,486	5,833
Taylor	924	1,627	42	82	896	1,601
Trempealeau	1,085	3,733	117	22	1,122	3,616
Vernon	1,561	4,114	188	39	1,539	4,122
Vilas	278	794	18	33	262	794
Walworth	1,960	4,151	487	73	1,846	4,263
Washburn	396	1,114	35	69	318	1.134
Washington	2,625	2.588	41	77	2,667	2,491
Waukesha	3,206	4,758	346	197	3,282	4,546
Waupaca	1,483	4,785	239	143	1,505	4.728
Waushara	507	2,821	114	82	515	2,749
Winnebago	5.511	6,797	412	288	5,387	6,814
Wood	2,498	3,013	132	274	2,523	3,007
Total	166632	247747	11,564	28,164	165977	242935
Plurality	..	80,915	..	..	..	76.958
Per cent	36.51	54.95	2.54	6.00	36.88	55.20
Scattering		67			8	
Whole vote.		454,488			449,656	

For Governor in 1908: Cox, Pro., received 11,760 votes; Brown, Soc., 28,583; Bottama, Soc. Lab., 293.

For Governor in 1906: Eaton, Pro., received 8,211 votes; Gaylord, Soc. Dem., 24,437: Rosass, Soc. L., 455.

For President in 1904, Watson, Pop., received 530 votes; Corrigan, Soc. L., 223.

The vote for Governor in 1904 was: Peck, Dem., 175,263; La Follette, Rep., 226,995; Arnold, Soc., 24,116; Schofield, N. Rep., 11,920.

VOTE FOR REPRESENTATIVES IN CONGRESS, 1908.

Districts.

I. Counties of Racine, Kenosha, Walworth, Rock, Green, La Fayette. H. A. Moehlenpah, Dem., 14,018; Henry A. Cooper, Rep., 26,728; J. H. Berkey, Pro., 1,576; W. A. Jacobs, Soc., 1,791.

II. Counties of Jefferson, Dane, Columbia, Green, Lake, Marquette, Adams. James E. Jones, Dem., 17,748; John M. Nelson, Rep., 20,926; W. A. Hall, Sr., Soc. Dem., 368.

WISCONSIN—*Continued.*

III. Counties of Grant, Crawford, Richland, Sauk, Juneau, Vernon, and Iowa. James W. Murphy, Dem., 16,004; Arthur W. Kopp, Rep., 21,409; Hardcastle, Pro., 918.

IV. County of Milwaukee (part). W. J. Kershaw, Dem., 14,370; William J. Cary, Rep., 15,509; E. T. Melnes, Soc., 9,788.

V. Counties of Milwaukee (part) and Waukesha. G. H. Daubner, Dem., 12,871; William H. Stafford, Rep., 16,394; Albert F. Welch, Soc., 11,279.

VI. Counties of Sheboygan, Fond du Lac, Dodge, Washington, and Ozaukee. Charles H. Weisse, Dem., 23,317; George Spratt, Rep., 16,184; Edward Damrow, Soc., 866.

VII. Counties of Pepin, Buffalo, Trempealeau, Jackson, Eau Claire, Clark, Monroe, and La Crosse. B. F. Keeler, Dem., 11,466; John J. Esch, Rep., 25,193; Wm. Gray, Soc., 372.

VIII. Counties of Portage, Waupaca, Waushara, Winnebago, Calumet, and Manitowoc. Lyman J. Nash, Dem., 14,984; John H. Davidson, Rep., 23,097; Martin Georgensen, Soc., 1,389; B. E. Van Keuren, Pro., 851.

IX. Counties of Brown, Kewaunee, Door, Outagamie, Wood, Oconto, and Marinette. Luther Lindauer, Dem., 15,249; Gustav Kuesterman, Rep., 18,562; J. E. Harris, Soc., 788.

X. Counties of Iron, Vilas, Oneida, Forest, Florence, Langlade, Lincoln, Shawano, Marathon, Taylor, Price, Ashland, and Wood. W. M. Ruggles, Dem., 16,884; E. A. Morse, Rep., 25,952.

XI. Counties of Barron, Bayfield, Burnett, Chippewa, Douglas, Dunn, Pierce, Polk, Sawyer, St. Croix, Washburn, and Gates. J. S. Konkel, Dem., 10,467; Irvine L. Lenroot, Rep., 30,104; E. B. Harris, Soc., 1,117.

PRESENT STATE GOVERNMENT.

Governor, J. O. Davidson; Lieutenant-Governor, John Strange; Secretary of State, James A. Frear; Treasurer, Andrew H. Dahl; Adjutant-General, C. R. Boardman; Attorney-General, Frank L. Gilbert; Superintendent of Education, C. P. Cary; Commissioner of Insurance, Geo. E. Beedle—all Republicans.

JUDICIARY.

Supreme Court: Chief Justice, John B. Winslow, Dem.; Associate Justices, Wm. H. Tienlin, Rep.; R. G. Siebecker, Rep.; J. E. Dodge, Dem., and Roujet D. Marshall, Rep.; J. C. Kerwin, Rep.; Clerk, Clarence Kellogg, Rep.; John Barnes, Dem.

STATE LEGISLATURE, 1909.

	Senate.	*Assembly.*	*Joint Ballot.*
Republicans	28	80	108
Democrats	4	17	21
Social Dem.	1	3	4
Republican majority	23	60	83

VOTE OF THE STATE SINCE 1872.

	Dem.	*Rep.*	*Gr.*	*Pro.*	*Plu.*
1872. President	86,477	104,988	....	....	18,511 R
1876. President	123,919	130,069	1,506	....	6,150 R
1880. President	114,634	144,397	7,980	....	29,763 R
1884. President	146,459	161,157	4,598	7,656	14,698 R
			U. Lab.		
1888. President	155,232	176,553	8,552	14,277	21,321 R
			Pop.		
1892. President	177,335	170,791	9,909	13,132	6,544 D
1894. Governor	142,250	196,150	25,604	11,240	53,900 R
1896. President	165,523	268,135	....	7,509	102,612 R
1898. Governor	135,353	173,137	8,577	8,078	37,784 R
			S. L.		
1900. Governor	160,764	264,420	6,590	9,707	103,656 R
1900. President	159,285	265,866	524	10,124	106,581 R
1902. Governor	145,818	193,417	15,970	9,647	47,599 R
1904. President	124,107	280,164	28,220	9,770	156,057 R
1906. Governor	103,311	183,558	24,437	8,211	80,247 R
				Soc.	
1908. Governor	165,977	242,935	28,583	11,760	76,958 R
1908. President	166,832	247,747	28,164	11,564	80,915 R

WYOMING.

COUNTIES. (13.)	PRESIDENT, 1908.		GOVERNOR 1906.		
	Bryan Dem.	Taft Rep.	Keister, Dem.	Brooks Rep.	O'N'll, Soc.
Albany	1,152	1,335	767	1,342	204
Big Horn	1,648	2,638	881	1,807	43
Carbon	1,430	1,651	731	1,579	4
Converse	715	1,030	417	1,023	89
Crook	799	1,068	363	747	17
Fremont	1,190	1,838	1,271	722	49
Johnson	604	781	500	666	21
Laramie	2,523	2,965	1,317	2,533	14
Natrona	461	835	399	664	74
Sheridan	1,539	2,158	548	1,010	125
Sweetwater	637	1,299	951	1,411	201
Uinta	1,731	2,525	1,075	2,259	464
Weston	478	723	263	633	5
Total	14,918	20,846	9,483	16,396	1,310
Plurality	...	5,928	..	6,913	..
Per cent	41.70	58.30	34.69	59.99	5.32
Scattering	....			140	
Whole vote	35,764			27,329	

VOTE FOR REPRESENTATIVE IN CONGRESS, 1908.

White, Dem., 13,643; Frank W. Mondell, Rep., 21,531; Morgan, Soc., 2,486.

PRESENT STATE GOVERNMENT.

Governor, B. B. Brooks; Secretary of State, Wm. R. Schnitger; Treasurer, Edward Gillitte; Auditor, Leroy Grant; Adjutant-General, P. A. Gatchell; Attorney-General, W. E. Mullen; Superintendent of Education, A. D. Cook—all Republicans.

JUDICIARY.

Supreme Court: Chief Justice, Chas. N. Potter; Associate Justices, Cyrus L. Beard, Richard A. Scott; Clerk, W. H. Kelly—all Republicans.

STATE LEGISLATURE, 1909.

	Senate.	*House.*	*Joint Ballot.*
Republicans	21	45	66
Democrats	2	5	7
Republican majority	19	40	59

VOTE OF THE STATE SINCE ADMISSION.

	Dem.	*Rep.*	*Pop.*	*Pro.*	*Maj.*
1890. Governor	7,153	8,879	....	....	1,726 R
1892. President	....	8,454	7,722	530	732 R
1892. Governor	8,442	7,446	....	416	1,691 D-P
					Plu.
1896. President	10,655	10,072	....	136	583 D
1900. President	10,164	14,482	....	....	4,318 R
			Soc.		
1902. Governor	10,017	14,483	552	....	4,466 R
1904. President	8,904	20,467	1,077	....	11,563 R
1906. Governor	9,483	16,396	1,316	....	6,913 R
1908. President	14,918	20,846	....	....	5,928 R

HAWAII.

At the Territorial election held 1906 for Delegate to Congress, E. B. McClanahan, Dem., received 3,824 votes; J. K. Kalanianole, Rep., 5,698; C. K. Notley, H. R., 2,889.

Present Territorial Government: Governor, Walter F. Frear; Secretary of Territory, Ernest A. Mottsmith; Treasurer, A. J. Campbell; Delegate in Congress, Jonah Kalanianole; Attorney-General, E. C. Peters. Judiciary: Alfred S. Hartwell, Chief Justice; Associates, Sidney M. Ballou and A. A. Wilder; Clerk, Henry Smith, U. S. District Judge, Sanford B. Dole; U. S. District-Attorney, J. J. Dunne; E. R. Stackable, Collector of Customs.

In the Territorial Legislature the Republicans have 30 on joint ballot Democrats 13, Home Rulers 2.

PORTO RICO.

Governor, Regis H. Post; Secretary, Wm. F. Willoughby; Treasurer, W. J. Groner; Auditor, G. C. Ward; Attorney-General, H. M. Hoyt; Commissioner of Education, E. G. Dexter; Commissioner of the Interior, L. H. Grahame; Resident Commissioner of Territory at Washington, Tulio Larrinaga.

Judiciary—Chief Justice, Jose Quinones. Justices, C. Hernandez, Jose Figueros, J. C. MacLeary, A. Wolfe; U. S. District Judge, B. S. Rodey; U. S. District-Attorney, Jose F. R. Savage.

The Territorial Legislature consists of an upper and lower House. The lower House is the elective branch and has 35 members. All belong to the Unionist party; sits in annual session in January.

LIST OF OFFICIALS AND SALARIES (SUBJECT TO CHANGE).

Mayor.—George B. McClellan ($15,000).
Secretary.—F. M. O'Brien, 6 City Hall ($6,000.)

Bureau of Licenses.—1 City Hall.

Borough Presidents.

Manhattan.—John F. Ahearn, 10 City Hall ($7,500); Bernard Downing, *Secretary* ($4,000).

Bronx.—L. F. Haffen ($7,500), 3d Ave. and 177th St.; H. A. Gumbleton, *Secretary* ($4,000).

Brooklyn.—Bird S. Coler ($7,500), 16 Boro' Hall; Charles F. Adams, *Secretary* ($4,000).

Queens.—Lawrence Gresser ($5,000), L. I. City; John M. Cragen, *Secretary* ($4,000).

Richmond.—George Cromwell ($5,000), New Brighton. Maybury F. Fleming, *Secretary* ($2,500).

Aldermen.

President—Patrick F. McGowan ($5,000). *Vice-Chairman*—T. P. Sullivan. *City Clerk and Clerk of the Board of Aldermen*—P. J. Scully ($7,000). Joseph F. Prendergast, *1st Deputy* ($5,000). *Chief Clerk*—John T. Oakley ($5,000). Aldermen receive $2,000 salary per year.

BOROUGHS AND DISTRICTS.

Manhattan.—1, William Drescher; 2, Michael Stapleton; 3, Timothy P. Sullivan; 4, James J. Smith; 5, Patrick F. Flynn; 6, Adolph Moskowitz; 7, Frank L. Dowling; 8, Max S. Levine; 9, Reginald S. Doull; 10, George J. Schneider; 11, Herman W. Beyer; 12, W. P. Kenneally; 13, J. McCann; 14, J. Loos; 15, L. Barton Case; 16, T. F. Baldwin; 17, J. Schloss; 18, J. J. Nugent; 19, J. Hines; 20, J. J. Reardon; 21, Alexander J. Stormont; 22, J. W. O'Reilly; 23, J. J. McDonald; 24, J. J. F. Mulcahy; 25, C. Delaney; 26, T. B. Johnson; 27, B. Goldsmidt; 28, B. W. B. Brown; 29, John F. Walsh; 30, Joseph D. Kavanagh; 31, Percy L. Davis; 32, P. E. Nagle; 33, Sam'l Marx.

Bronx.—34, James W. Brown; 35, Thomas J. Mulligan; 36, William P. Corbett; 37, John J. Hickey; 38, Arthur H. Murphy; 39, Edward V. Handy; 40, Frederick C. Hochdorffer; 41, M. J. Crowley.

Brooklyn.—42, Robert F. Downing; 43, George A. Colgan; 44, John Mulvaney; 45, J. S. Gaynor; 46, William Wentz; 47, John Diemer; 48, W. J. Heffernan; 49, F. P. Kenney; 50, F. Linde; 51, J. W. Redmond; 52, D. R. Coleman; 53, J. D. Gunther; 54, J. H. Finnigan; 55, T. J. McAleer; 56, T. F. Barton; 57, L. M. Potter; 58, O. Grant Esterbrook; 59, G. A. Morrison; 60, Otto Muhlbauer; 61, F. P. Bent; 62, J. J. Velton; 63, W. P. Sanford; 64, H. F. Grimm; 65, James F. Martyn.

Queens.—66, T. M. Quinn; 67, G. Emener; 68, J. Flanagan; 69, J. J. Hogan; 70, M. J. Carter.

Richmond.—71, J. J. Collins; 72, D. S. Rendt; 73, Charles P. Cole.

Coroners.—Criminal Courts Building.

Manhattan.—Julius Harburger, Peter P. Acritelli, P. Dooly, G. F. Shrady, Jr. ($6,000 each). *Chief Clerk*, J. E. Bausch ($3,000).

Bronx.—Robert F. McDonald, Albert F Schwannecke ($6,000 each).

Brooklyn.—Henry J. Brewer and John F. Kennedy ($6,000 each).

Queens.—Samuel D. Nutt and A. S. Ambler, College Point, L. I. ($4,000 each).

Richmond.—M. J. Cahill, New Brighton, S. I. ($4,000).

Department of Finance.—Stewart Building.

Comptroller.—Herman A. Metz ($15,000).

Deputies.—J. H. McCooey and N. T. Phillips ($7,500 each). *Assistant Deputy.*—Hubert L. Smith ($6,000).

Auditor of Accounts.—P. H. Quinn ($5,000).

Receiver of Taxes.—Manhattan, David E. Austen, ($7,000). *Deputy.*—Bronx—J. B. Underhill ($2,500). Brooklyn—James B. Bouck ($4,000). Queens—George H. Creed ($2,500). Richmond—John De Morgan ($2,500).

Collector of City Revenue and Superintendent of Markets.—Manhattan—John M. Gray ($4,000).

City Paymaster.—John H. Timmerman, 83 Chambers Street ($6,000).

Collector of Assessments and Arrears.—Daniel Moynahan ($4,000).

Bureau of Municipal Investigation and Statistics—Charles S. Hervey ($6,000).

CITY CHAMBERLAIN.—James J. Martin, 63 Stewart Building ($12,000).

Deputy.—Henry J. Walsh ($5,000).

Public Works and Other Departments.

—*Commissioner Public Works.*—Manhattan—John Cloughen ($6,000); Jas. J. Hagan, *Assist.* ($5,000). Bronx—John F. Murray ($5,000). Brooklyn—Desmond Dunne ($6,000). Queens————————, $4,000). Richmond—L. L. Tribus ($8,000).

Bureau of Highways.—Manhattan—G. F. Scannell, *Supt.* ($5,000); Geo. W. Tillson, *Chief Engineer* ($6,000). Bronx.—J. A. Briggs, *Chief Eng.* ($7,500).

Bureau of Sewers.—Manhattan—Frank J. Goodwin ($5,000); Horace Loomis, *Chief Engineer* ($6,000). Bronx—Thomas H. O'Neill, *Supt.* ($4,000). Brooklyn—James Dunne, *Supt.* ($5,000).

Bureau Public Bldgs. and Offices.—Manhattan—John R. Voorhis, *Supt.* ($5,000). Bronx—A. H. Liebenau, *Supt.* ($4,000). Brooklyn—J. Lawrence, *Supt.* ($5,000)

Supt. Baths and Public Comfort.—Manhattan—W. W. Weeks ($2,550). Br'klyn—W. H. Hale ($2,550).

Commissioner of Water Supply, Gas and Electricity.—John H. O'Brien ($7,500). *Deputy.*—M. F. Loughman ($6,000). Bronx—M. Hecht ($4,000). Br'klyn—W. C. Cozier ($5,500). Queens—C. C. Wissel ($3,000). Richmond—John E. Bowe ($2,500).

Commissioner of Bridges—J. W. Stevenson ($7,500). *Deputy*—J. H. Little ($4,500). *Chief Engineer*—Kingsley Martin, ($10,000). *Sec'y*—E. E. Schiff ($4,000).

Commissioner of Street Cleaning.—Foster Crowell ($7,500). *Deputy.*—W. H. Edwards ($5,000).

Chief Clerk—John J. O'Brien ($3,600).

Tenement-House Commissioner.—44 East 23d St.—E. J. Butler ($7,500). *Deputies.*—Manhattan—Wm. H. Abbott, Jr.; Brooklyn—J. McKeown ($4,000 each). Bronx.—*Supt.*, William B. Calvert.

Department of Police.

Central Office, 300 Mulberry Street. House for Detention of Witnesses, 203 Mulberry Street.

Commissioner.—Theodore A. Bingham ($7,500).

Secretary—Daniel G. Slattery ($3,000).

Deputies.—(First) W. F. Baker ($6,000). (Second) F. H. Bugher ($4,000). (Third) Bert Hanson ($4,000). (Fourth) A. Woods ($4,000).

Inspectors.—M. W. Cortright ($5,000), Max F. Schmittberger, R. Walsh, G. F. Titus, J. McCafferty, J. H. Russell, J. E. Dillon, J. F. Thompson, G. R. Holohan, J. J. O'Brien, W. G. Hogan, P. J. Harkins, G. W. McClusky, J. F. Flood, Patrick Corcoran, Miles O'Reilly, Max Steinbruck, Denis Sweeney ($3,500 each).

Chief Clerk.—William H. Kipp ($5,000).

Department of Health.

S. W. cor. 55th St. and 6th Ave.

President and Commissioner.—Thos. Darlington ($7,500). The Commissioner of Police and Health Officer of Port of New York.

Secretary.—Eugene W. Scheffer ($5,000).

Sanitary Supt.—Walter Bensel ($5,000). *Assistants.*—Manhattan—Alonzo Blauvelt ($3,500). Bronx——————— ($3,500). Brooklyn—T. C. Maxfield ($3,500). Queens—John H. Barry ($3,500), Richmond—John T. Sprague ($3,500).

Law Department.—Hall of Records.

Corporation Counsel.—F. K. Pendleton ($15,000).

Secretary.—Edmund Kirby ($3,500).

Assistants.—Theo. Connoly, G. L. Sterling and C. D. Olendorf ($10,000 each).

Assistant.—Brooklyn—James D. Bell ($10,000).

Bureau of Street Openings.—John P. Dunn, 90 West Broadway ($7,500).

Bureau for Collection of Arrears of Personal Taxes.—Geo. O. Reilly, 280 Broadway ($3,500).

Bureau for Recovery of Penalties.—Herman Stiefel, 119 Nassau Street ($6,000).

Tenement-House Bureau.—John P. O'Brien, 44 E. 32d St. ($5,000).

Bureau of Municipal Research.—261 Broadway.

Director.—Henry Bruère.

Secretary.—William H. Allen.

Technical Director.—Frederick A. Cleveland,

Department of Fire.—157 E. 67th St.
Commissioner.—Nicholas J. Hayes ($7,500).
Chief.—Edward F. Croker ($7,000).
Deputy.—Patrick A. Whitney ($5,000).
Brooklyn and Queens.—C. C. Wise ($5,000).
Deputy Chief.—Thomas Lally (Brooklyn and Queens) ($5,000).
Fire Marshals.—Peter Seery ($3,000) (Manhattan, Bronx, and Richmond); William L. Beers ($3,000) (Brooklyn and Queens).
Secretary.—William A. Larney ($4,800).

Department of Parks.—Arsenal, Central Park.
President and Commissioner of Manhattan and Richmond.—Henry Smith ($5,000).
Commissioner of Brooklyn and Queens.—Michael J. Kennedy ($5,000).
Commissioner of Bronx.—Joseph I. Berry ($5,000).
Secretary Park Board.—Wm. J. Fransioli ($4,800).

Bureau of Buildings.
220 Fourth Avenue.
Superintendent.—*Manhattan*—Edward S. Murphy ($5,000). *Assistant.*—Joseph Gordon ($4,000). *Chief Inspector.*—Bernard J. Gorman ($4,000).
Bronx.—P. J. Reville, *Supt.* ($5,000). *Brooklyn.* David F. Moore, *Supt.* ($5,000). *Queens.* — J. P. Powers *Supt.* ($3,000). *Richmond.*—John Seaton, *Supt.* ($2,500).

Department of Taxes and Assessments.
Hall of Records.
President.—Lawson Purdy ($8,000): Commissioners, Frank Raymond, James H. Tully, Chas. A. Putzel, Hugh Hastings, Chas. J. McCormack, John J. Halleran ($7,000 each). *Secretary.*—C. R. Tyng ($4,000).

Department of Charities.—Foot E. 26th St.
Commissioner.—Robt. W. Hebberd ($7,500).
1st Deputy.—Richard C. Baker ($5,000).
Secretary.—J. McKee Borden ($3,500).
2d Deputy (327 Schermerhorn St., Brooklyn).—Thomas W. Hynes ($5,000).

Commissioner of Jurors.—127 Stewart B'ld'g.
Thomas Allison (County of New York) ($6,000).

Commis'rs of Accounts.—115 Stewart B'ld'g.
John Purroy Mitchell and Ernest Y. Gallaher, ($5,000).

Municipal Civil Service Commissioners.
299 Broadway.
Frank L. Polk, *President* ($6,000); R. Ross Appleton, Arthur J. O'Keeffe, Commissioners ($5,000).
Secretary.—Frank A. Spencer ($5,000).

Public Administrator.—119 Nassau Street.
W. M. Hoes ($10,000). F. W. Arnold, *Asst.* ($5,000).
Chief Clerk.—Robert D. Bronson ($2,800).

Department of Correction.—148 E. 20th St.
Commissioner.—John V. Coggey ($7,500).
Deputy.—George W. Meyer ($4,000).
Secretary.—John B. Fitzgerald ($3,000).

Department Docks and Ferries.—Battery Pl.
Commissioner.—Allen N. Spooner ($7,500).
Deputy.—Denis A. Judge ($4,500).
Secretary.—Joseph W. Savage ($4,000).

Department of Education.
Park Ave. and 59th St.
President.—E. L. Winthrop, Jr. *Vice-President.*—John Greene. *Secretary.*—A. E. Palmer ($5,500).
Supt. of School Buildings.—C. B J. Snyder ($10,000).
Supt. of School Supplies.—Patrick Jones ($7,500).
City Supt. of Schools—Wm. H. Maxwell ($10,000).
Associate City Superintendents ($6,500 each).—John Haaren, Edward B. Shallow, Andrew W. Edson, Gustave Straubenmüller, Thomas S. O'Brien, Edward L. Stevens, John H. Walsh, C. E. Meleney.
Examiners ($6,000 each).—James C. Byrnes, Walter L. Hervey, J. A. O'Connell, George J. Smith.

Board of Estimate and Apportionment.
277 Broadway.
Members.—The Mayor, *Chairman;* the Comptroller, the President of the Board of Aldermen, the Presidents of Manhattan, Brooklyn, Bronx, Queens and Richmond (no salary).
Secretary.—Joseph Haag ($7,500).
Bureau of Franchises.—H. P. Nichols, Engineer ($6,000).

Commissioner of Licenses.—277 Broadway.
John N. Bogart ($5,000).

City Improvement Com'n.—21 Park Row.
F. K. Pendleton, Chairman; J. S. Cantor, G. A. Hearn, Whitney Warren, H. P Whitney, F. Bailey, J. W. Alexander, D. C. French, L. F. Haffen, J. A. Wright, J. Cassidy, W. J. La Roche, J. E. Swanstrom, George Cromwell and H. S. Thompson.

Board of Water Supply.—299 Broadway.
John A. Bensel, Chas. A. Shaw, Chas. N. Chadwick ($12,000 each).
Secretary.—Thomas Hassett ($6,000).

City Record.—2 City Hall and 21 Park Row.
Supervisor.—Patrick J. Tracy ($5,000).
Deputy Supervisor.—Henry McMillen ($2,500).

Aqueduct Commissioners.—280 Broadway.
Mayor and Comptroller *ex-officio.*
Commissioners.—John F. Cowan, John J. Ryan, Wm. H. Ten Eyck, John P. Windolph ($5,000 each).
Chief Engineer.—W. H. Sears ($10,000).
Secretary.—H. W. Walker ($4,000).

Board of Assessors.—320 Broadway.
Antonio Zucca, Paul Weimann, James H. Kennedy ($5,000 each).
Secretary.—William H. Jasper ($5,000).

COUNTY OFFICERS.

County Clerk (Court House).—Peter J. Dooling ($15,000). *Deputy.*—John F. Curry ($6,000). *Secretary.*—Joseph J. Glennen ($3,000).
Kings County Clerk (Hall of Records, Brooklyn).—Frank Ehlers ($8,000). *Deputy.*—Robert A. Sharkey ($5,000).
Sheriff New York County (299 Broadway).—Thos. F. Foley ($12,000 and half of fees).
Under Sheriff.—John F. Gilchrist, ($5,000). *Deputies.*—J. J. Murray; F. G. Rinn, F. J. Burnes, T. J. O'Rourke, Joseph Cullen, John McCourt, Max Altman, Max J. Porges, M. J. Cruise, Charles Rader, J. J. O'Neil, F. J. Walgering ($2,500 each).
Warden of County Jail.—Chas. F. Regan ($3,000).
Sheriff Kings County (Court House, B'klyn).—Alfred T. Hobley ($15,000). *Under Sheriff.*—James P. Connell ($6,000).
Deputy Sheriffs.—George A. Owens, John Jaquillard, John Bulck, Jr., Thomas J. Farrell, Chas. D. Kendall, William W. Baird, Edward E. Black, Timothy J. Dady.
Warden.—Richard Wright ($3,000).
Sheriff Queens County (Long Island City).—H. S. Harvey (fees). *Under Sheriff.*—John M. Phillips.
Sheriff Richmond County (Richmond, S. I.).—Joseph J. Barth ($6,000).
Register (Hall of Records).—Frank Gass ($12,000). *Deputy*—Wm. H. Sinnott ($5,000).
Register Kings County (Hall of Records, Brooklyn).—Wm. A. Prendergast ($8,000).
Commissioner of Records (Hall of Rec., B'klyn).—Lewis M. Swasey ($5,000). *Deputy.*—D. H. Ralston ($4,000).

STATE OFFICERS.

EXCISE DEPARTMENT.—1 Madison Avenue.
Special Deputy Commissioners.—Moses M. McKee, Manhattan and Bronx ($5,000); Wm. Watson (Brooklyn) ($3,750); George L. Nichol (Richmond) ($2,000); Edward Dowling (Queens) ($2,500).

STATE BUREAU OF ELECTIONS.—47 W. 42d St.
Superintendent.—William Leary ($5,000).
Chief Deputy.—Collin H. Woodward ($4,500).

QUARANTINE COMMISS'RS.—62 William St.
Commissioners.—F. H. Schroeder, *President;* H. A. Guyon, *Treasurer;* Smith Pine ($2,500 each).
Health Officer.—Alvah H. Doty, M. D. ($12,500).
Secretary.—Geo. Schrader.

Public Service Commission.—154 Nassau St.
For the 1st District.
W. R. Willcox, *Chairman;* W. McCarroll, E. M. Bassett, M. R. Maltbie, John E. Eustis, *Commissioners* ($15,000). Travis H. Whitney, *Secretary* ($5,000).

PILOT COMMISSIONERS.—17 State Street.
Commissioners.—A. F. Higgins, J. H. Winchester, V. H. Brown, Thomas P. Ball, W. I. Comes.
Secretary.—Daniel A. Nash.

PORT WARDENS.—1 Broadway.
Wardens.—John H. Gunner, *President;* Michael Hines, Henry Bradt, Robt. T. Courtney, James F. Pegnam, Charles S. Adler, Harry Jaquillard, Richard O'Brien and Jerome B. Johnson (fees).
Secretary.—A. W. Dodge.

SUPREME COURT.

PART 1, TRIAL TERM (the Criminal Term of the Court for the trial of indictments), held by a Justice of the Supreme Court in the Criminal Courts Building, Centre and Franklin Streets.

GENERAL SESSIONS (Parts 1, 2, 3, 4, and 5).—In the Criminal Courts Building.

Name.	Office.	Term Expires.
Thomas C. T. Crain	Judge of Sessions	Dec. 31, 1920
Edward Swann	" "	" 31, 1921
Joseph F. Mulqueen	" "	" 31, 1921
James T. Malone	" "	" 31, 1921
Thomas C. O'Sullivan	" "	" 31, 1919
Otto A. Rosalsky	" "	" 31, 1920
Warren W. Foster	" "	" 31, 1913

Clerk of Part 1, *Trial Term, Supreme Court, and of the Court of General Sessions* (office in the Criminal Courts Building)—Edward R. Carroll. Judges of General Sessions receive annual salary of $15,000 each.

SPECIAL SESSIONS.

(First Division.)

Criminal Courts Building, Centre Street.

Name. (Salary, $9,000.)	Term Expires.
Judge John B. Mayo	July 1, 1917
" William E. Wyatt	" 1, 1911
" Joseph M. Deuel	" 1, 1913
" Lorenz Zeller	" 1, 1915
" John B. McKean	" 1, 1909
" W. H. Olmsted	May 1, 1912

Court is open daily, except Saturday and legal holidays, from 10 A. M. to 4 P. M.; Clerk's office open Saturdays, 9 A. M. to 12 M. Chas. W. Culkin, *Clerk*. Salary, $5,000.

Children's Part, 66 3d Ave.—Held by one of the Justices of Special Sessions in accordance with assignment of Justices. Court opens at 9.30 daily, except Sunday and legal holidays. Edmund C. Lee, *Clerk*. Salary, $3,000.

CITY MAGISTRATES.

Magistrate. (Salary, $7,000.)	Term Expires.
Frederick B. House	July 1, 1912
Leroy B. Crane	" 1, 1912
Matthew P. Breen	" 1, 1912
Paul Krotel	" 1, 1909
Daniel E. Finn	" 1, 1915
Robert C. Cornell	May 1, 1913
Chas. N. Harris	" 1, 1917
Frederick B. Kernochan	" 1, 1917
Henry Steinert	July 1, 1915
Moses Herrman	" 1, 1909
Joseph F. Moss	" 1, 1915
Peter T. Barlow	May 1, 1913
Arthur C. Butts	" 1, 1917
James J. Walsh	" 1, 1909
Otto H. Droege	July 1, 1917
Joseph E. Corrigan	" 1, 1917

Secretary, Philip Bloch.

MAGISTRATES' COURTS.

First District—Criminal Courts Building, Centre and Franklin Streets; Second District—125 Sixth Avenue (Jefferson Market); Third District—69 Essex Street; Fourth District—151 East 57th Street; Fifth District—170 East 121st Street; Sixth District—East 162d Street, corner Burk and Washington Avenues; Seventh District—314 West 54th Street; Eighth District—Main Street, Westchester; Ninth District (Night Court), 125 Sixth Avenue (Jefferson Market).

DISTRICT ATTORNEY'S OFFICE.

Criminal Courts Building, Centre and Franklin Streets. The salary of the District Attorney is $12,000 per annum; assistants to District Attorney, $7,500; deputy assistants' salaries vary.

Name.	Office.	Name.	Office.	Name.	Office.
Wm. Travers Jerome	Dist. At.	Carl Miner	Deputy.	Frederick B. McNish	Deputy
Charles C. Nott, Jr.	Asst.	Robert S. Johnstone	"	Joseph H. A. Symonds.	"
Charles Albert Perkins	"	Robert E. Manley	"	Alexander Keogh	"
Nathan A. Smyth	"	Robert J. Turnbull	"	Edward L. Tinker	"
James R. Ely	"	Mason Trowbridge	"	Charles A. Dana	"
Isidor J. Kresel	"	W. B. Howe	"	William D. Bosler	"
Robert C. Taylor	"	G. W. Whiteside	"	Alexander Mayper	"
Francis P. Garvan	"	E. C. Kindleberger	"	Joseph Du Vivier	"
John W. Hart	"	Daniel F. Murphy	"	Augustin Derby	"
Harford T. Marshall	"	Theodore H. Ward	"	Wm. Dean Embrie	"
Keyran J. O'Connor	Deputy.	Madison G. Gonterman.	"	John F. O'Neil	"

Secretary, William C. Langdon. Chief Clerk, J. A. Henneberry. Bureau of Special Sessions Information, W. S. McGuire.

Courts of Law in Manhattan.

APPELLATE DIVISION OF THE SUPREME COURT.

FIRST JUDICIAL DEPARTMENT, MADISON AVENUE AND TWENTY-FIFTH STREET.

Justice.	Term Expires.	Justice.	Term Expires.
Edward Patterson, *Pres. Justice*	Dec. 31, 1909	John Proctor Clarke	Dec. 31, 1915
George L. Ingraham	" 31, 1919	James W. Houghton	" 31, 1914
Chester B. McLaughlin	" 31, 1909	Francis M. Scott	" 31, 1911
Frank C. Laughlin	" 31, 1909	John S. Lambert	Temporary

Court opens at 1 P. M. *Clerk*—Alfred Wagstaff. AN APPELLATE TERM to hear appeals from the City and the Municipal Courts will sit in the County Court-House.

SUPREME COURT—APPELLATE, SPECIAL, AND TRIAL TERMS.

Name.	Office.	Term Expires.	Name.	Office.	Term Expires.
Samuel Greenbaum	Justice	Dec. 31, 1915	Philip H. Dugro	Justice	Dec. 31, 1914
Francis M. Scott	"	" 31, 1911	Henry A. Gildersleeve	"	" 31, 1919
James A. Blanchard	"	" 31, 1915	Joseph E. Newburger	"	" 31, 1919
Charles F. MacLean	"	" 31, 1909	Peter A. Hendrick	"	" 31, 1920
Charles H. Truax	"	" 31, 1909	John W. Goff	"	" 31, 1920
Vernon M. Davis	"	" 31, 1916	Samuel Seabury	"	" 31, 1920
Edward E. McCall	"	" 31, 1916	M. Warley Platzek	"	" 31, 1920
Edward B. Amend	"	" 31, 1916	John Ford	"	" 31, 1920
James A. O'Gorman	"	" 31, 1913	Charles W. Dayton	"	" 31, 1920
Henry Bischoff, Jr.	"	" 31, 1917	John J. Brady	"	" 31, 1920
James Fitzgerald	"	31, 1912	Mitchell L. Erlanger	"	" 31, 1920
Leonard A. Giegerich	"	" 31, 1920	Charles L. Guy	"	" 31, 1920
David Leventritt	"	" 31, 1912	James W. Gerard	"	" 31, 1921
Victor J. Dowling	"	" 31, 1918	Irving Lehman	"	" 31, 1922

Clerk—County Clerk Peter J. Dooling, *ex-officio*. Salary of Supreme Court Justices, $17,500.

COURTS OF LAW IN MANHATTAN—*Continued.*

CITY COURT.
CITY HALL.

The Judges are elected for a term of ten years at an annual salary of $12,000.

Name.	Office.	Term Expires.
Edw'd F. O'Dwyer	Chief Judge	Dec. 31, 1917
Edward B. La Fetra	Judge............	" 31, 1920
Lewis J. Conlan ...	"	" 31, 1909
Joseph I. Green	"	" 31, 1915
Richard T. Lynch..	"	" 31, 1920
F. B. Delehanty....	"	" 31, 1910
Thos F. Donnelly...	"	" 31, 1917
Alexander Finelite.	"	" 31, 1917
John V. McAvoy...	"	" 31, 1917
Peter Schmuck.....	"	" 31, 1917

Clerk.—Thos. F. Smith; salary, $6,000.
Deputy.—Edward H. Piepenbring; salary, $3,000.

COUNTY COURT, KINGS COUNTY.
COURT HOUSE.

Judges—Norman S. Dike, Rep., and Lewis L. Fawcett, Rep., $12,500.

SURROGATES' COURT.
COUNTY COURT-HOUSE.

The Surrogates are elected for a term of fourteen years at an annual salary of $15,000.

Name.	Office.	Term Expires.
Abner C. Thomas...	Surrogate.........	Jan. 1, 1914
John P. Cohalan....	"	" 1, 1922

Chief Clerk.—William V. Leary; salary, $10,000.

COURT OF ARBITRATION
OF THE CHAMBER OF COMMERCE OF NEW YORK STATE, 65 LIBERTY ST.

This court was established by act of the Legislature, for the hearing and prompt settlement of controversies among merchants, shipmasters, and others within the Port of New York.

SURROGATE'S COURT, BROOKLYN.
HALL RECORDS.

Surrogate—Herbert T. Ketcham, Dem., $10,000.
Chief Clerk—Edward J. Bergen.

DISTRICT ATTORNEY, KINGS CO.
COURT HOUSE.

District Attorney—John F. Clarke, Dem., $10,000

MUNICIPAL COURTS IN MANHATTAN AND BRONX.

The Justices are elected for a term of ten years at an annual salary of $8,000. The Clerks are appointed by the Justices for six years, and receive annual salaries of $3,000.

Courts.	Location.	Justices.	Clerks.
1st District.....	66 Lafayette St..............	Wauhope Lynn.......... William F. Moore....... John Hoyer.............	Thomas O'Connell. Francis Maugin, Deputy.
2d District......	264 Madison St..............	George F. Roesch........ Benjamin Hoffman..... Leon Sanders.......... Thomas P. Dinnean......	James J. Devlin. Michael H. Looney, Deputy.
3d District	314 W. 54th St...............	Thomas E. Murray....... James W. McLaughlin..	Michael Skelly. Henry Merzbach, Deputy.
4th District.....	151 E. 57th St...............	Michael F. Blake........ William J. Boyhan......	Abram Bernard. James Foley, Deputy.
5th District.....	96th St. and Broadway.......	Alfred P. W. Seaman... William Young.......... Frederick Spiegelberg...	James V. Gilloon. John H. Servis, Deputy.
6th District.....	83d St. and 3d Ave..........	Herman Joseph.......... Jacob Marks.............	Edward F. McQuade. Thos. M. Campbell, Deputy.
7th District.....	70 Manhattan St.............	Phillip J. Sinnott........ David L. Weil........... John R. Davies..........	H. B. Wilson. Robert Andrews.
8th District.....	Sylvan Place and 121st St..	Joseph P. Fallon......... Leopold Prince..........	William J. Kennedy. Patrick J. Ryan.
9th District.....	59th St. and Madison Ave..	Edgar J. Lauer........... Fred De Witt Wells.... Frank D. Sturgis......... William C. Wilson.......	William J. Chamberlain. Charles Healey.
BRONX.			
1st District.....	Town Hall, Westchester......	Peter A. Sheils.............	Stephen Collins.
2d District......	E. 162d St. and Wash'n Ave..	John M. Tierney..........	Thomas A. Maher.

United States Courts in Manhattan.

UNITED STATES CIRCUIT COURT OF APPEALS.—Post-Office Building. *Judges.*—Rufus W. Peckham, Circuit Justice; E. Henry Lacombe, Alfred C. Coxe, Henry G. Ward and Walter C. Noyes, Circuit Judges. *Clerk*—William Parkin; salary, $3,500. *Term.*—Second Monday in October.

UNITED STATES CIRCUIT COURT.—Post-Office Building.

The Judges of the Federal Courts are appointed by the President, and confirmed by the United States Senate, for life.

Associate Justice of the United States Supreme Court and Judge of the Circuit Court.—Rufus W. Peckham; salary, $12,500.

Circuit Judges.—Henry G. Ward, E. Henry Lacombe, Walter C. Noyes and Alfred C. Coxe; salaries, $7,000 each.

Clerk.—John A. Shields; salary, $3,500.

General Terms.—First Monday in April and third Monday in October.

Equity Term.—Last Monday in February.

Terms of Criminal Court.—Second Wednesdays in January, March, May, October, December, and third in June.

UNITED STATES DISTRICT COURT.—Post-Office Building.

Judge of the District Court.—George B. Adams, Chas. M. Hough, Geo. C. Holt; salary, $6,000.

Clerk.—Thomas Alexander.

Stated Term.—First Tuesday in every month. Also first Wednesday of Feb., April, June, Oct. and Dec., for trial of equity suits and actions at law.

Special Term.—Every Tuesday for return of process.

United States District Attorney.—Henry L. Stimson; salary, $10,000.

Assistant District Attorneys.—J. O. Nichols, Goldthwaite H. Dorr, D. Frank Lloyd, Winifred T. Dennison, Lewis O. O'Brien, Thomas D. Thurber, Francis W. Bird, Hugh Govern, Jr., H. A. Wise, F. Frankfurter; salaries range from $2,000 to $5,000.

Marshal.—William Henkel; salary, $5,000.

Chief Deputy.—John Stiebling; salary, $2,750.

Commissioners.—John A. Shields, Samuel R. Betts, Thomas Alexander, Henry P. Butler, Samuel M. Hitchcock, Ed. L. Owen, James Ridgway, Henry W. Goodrich, Herbert Green, Daniel B. Deyo, Alex. Gilchrist, Jr., Avery F. Cushman, Wm. P. Prentice, James L. Williams, D. W. Esmond, Edward J. Collins, Edward T. McEnany.

INFORMATION ABOUT THE CITY OF NEW YORK.

In the following pages information of daily interest to citizens and visitors about the City of New York is given, the subjects, for convenience of reference, being arranged alphabetically. This information is of the date of January 1, 1909, but it must be borne in mind that changes in an active community like that of New York are continuously going on, and that accuracy in details can only be guaranteed for the date of issue of the ALMANAC.

Amusement Places in Manhattan and Bronx.

THEATRES, ETC.	Location.	Proprietors, Lessees or Managers.	Seat. Capacity*
Academy of Music	E. 14th St. and Irving Place	Gilmore & Tompkins	2,510
Alhambra	7th Ave. and 126th St	Percy G. Williams	1,600
American	8th Ave. and 42d St	William Morris Co	2,166
Astor	Broadway and 45th St	Wagenhals & Kemper	1,200
Belasco	42d St. and Broadway	David Belasco	950
Berkeley Lyceum	44th St., near 5th Ave	Walter C. Jordan	458
Bijou	Broadway and 31st St	H. B. Sire	969
Broadway	Broadway and 41st St	Litt & Dingwall	1,700
Carnegie Lyceum	7th Ave. and 57th St	Board of Trustees	639
Carnegie Hall	W. 57th St., near 7th Ave	Board of Trustees	2,800
Casino	Broadway and 39th St	Sam S. & Lee Shubert (Inc.)	1,100
Circle	Broadway and 61st St	Sullivan & Kraus	1,600
Colonial	Broadway and 62d St	Percy G. Williams	1,700
Criterion	Broadway and 44th St	Charles Frohman	912
Daly's	Broadway and 30th St	Sam S. & Lee Shubert (Inc.)	1,150
Dewey	14th St., near 3d Ave	Sullivan & Kraus	1,600
Eden Musee	W. 23d St., near 6th Ave	Eden Musee Co	500
Empire	Broadway and 40th St	Charles Frohman	1,100
Fourteenth Street	W. 14th St., near 6th Ave	J. W. Rosenquest	1,500
Gaiety	Broadway and 46th St	Cohan & Harris	802
Garden	Madison Ave. and 27th St	H. W. Savage	1,110
Garrick	35th St., near 6th Ave	Charles Frohman	850
Gotham	125th St., near 3d Ave	Sullivan & Kraus	1,650
Grand	Grand St., near Bowery	Jacob P. Adler	1,888
Grand Opera House	W. 23d St. and 8th Ave	John H. Springer	2,910
Hackett's	42d St., near Broadway	Henry B. Harris	1,000
Harlem Opera House	W. 125th St., near 7th Ave	Keith & Proctor	1,500
Herald Square	Broadway and 35th St	Sam S. & Lee Shubert (Inc.) & Lew Fields	1,300
Hippodrome	6th Ave. and 44th St	Shubert & Anderson	5,600
Hudson	44th St., near 6th Ave	H. B. Harris	995
Hurtig & Seamon's	W. 125th St. and 7th Ave	Hurtig & Seamon	1,284
Irving Place	E. 15th St. and Irving Pl	Otto Weil	1,096
Kalich	45 Bowery	Leopold Spachner	2,000
Keith & Proctor's Un. Sq	E. 14th St., near Broadway	Keith & Proctor	1,000
Keith & Proctor's	E. 58th St., near 3d Ave	Keith & Proctor	2,200
Keith & Proctor's	W. 23d St., near 6th Ave	Keith & Proctor	1,551
Keith & Proctor's 5th Ave	Broadway and 28th St	Keith & Proctor	1,600
Keith & Proctor's 125th St	125th St. and Lexington Ave	Keith & Proctor	1,800
Knickerbocker	Broadway and 38th St	Al. Hayman & Co	1,352
Liberty	234 W. 42d St	Klaw & Erlanger	1,200
Lincoln Square	Broadway and 65th St	William Morris Co	1,500
London	235 Bowery	Jas. H. Curtin	1,800
Lyceum	45th St., B'way and 6th Ave	Daniel Frohman	937
Lyric	7th Ave. and 42d St	Sam S. & Lee Shubert (Inc)	2,000
Madison Square Garden	Madison Ave., 26th and 27th Sts	Madison Square Garden Co	12,137
Madison Square Garden Concert Hall	26th St. and Madison Ave	Madison Square Garden Co	1,183
Majestic	Broadway and 59th St	The Wilbur-Shubert Co	1,704
Manhattan Opera House	34th St., near 9th Ave	Oscar Hammerstein	3,800
Maxine Elliott	39th St. near Broadway	Sam S. & Lee Shubert (Inc.)	990
Metropolis	142d St. and 3d Ave	Hurtig & Seamon	1,600
Metropolitan Opera House	Broadway, 39th and 40th Sts	Gatti Casazza	3,336
Miner's Bowery	Bowery, near Delancey St	W. H. Isham	1,800
Miner's 8th Avenue	7th Ave., near 25th St	Edwin D. Miner	1,100
Murray Hill	Lexington Ave. and 42d St	Columbia Amusement Co	2,400
New	Central Park West and 62d St	New Theatre Co., W. K. Vanderbilt, Pres	2,318
New Amsterdam	42d St., west of Broadway	Klaw & Erlanger	1,675
New German	Madison Ave. and 59th St	Maurice Baumfeld & Eugen Burg	1,006
New Star	Lexington Ave. and 107th St	Wm. T. Keogh	3,000
New York	Broadway and 45th St	Klaw & Erlanger	1,700
Olympic	E. 14th St., near 3d Ave	David Kraus Amusement Co	1,000
Savoy	34th St. and Broadway	Frank McKee	841
Stuyvesant	44th St., near 7th Ave	David Belasco	1,050
Thalia	Bowery, near Canal St	Sullivan & Woods	1,600
Third Avenue	3d Ave., near 31st St	Charles T Blaney	2,098
Victoria	42d St. and 7th Ave	Oscar Hammerstein	1,000
Wallack's	Broadway and 30th St	Mrs. Theo. Moss	1,200
Weber	Broadway and 30th St	Joseph Weber	1,000
West End	125th St. and 8th Ave	Sam S. & Lee Shubert (Inc.)	2,000
Yorkville	86th St. and Lexington Ave	Hurtig & Seamon	1,450

* Seating capacity is given from information of the best possible authority, but as some theatres are able to add extra seats during important engagements the figures, in a few cases, are likely to vary slightly. There is also, usually, standing room for a limited number of people. Theatre-goers should consult daily papers as to time performances begin.

During the last year the number of moving picture theatres (or nickelodeons) in Manhattan and Bronx has increased to about 200. They are not theatres in the accepted sense of the term, but they furnish harmless entertainment at cheap prices to a great number of people. Their prices of admission are five and ten cents.

Musical entertainments are sometimes given in Cooper Union, Tammany Hall, Atlantic Garden, 50 Bowery; Grand Central Palace, 43d St. and Lexington Ave.; American Institute, 19 West 44th St.; Lexington Opera House, 58th St., near Lexington Ave.; New German Theatre, Madison Ave. and 59th St.

MUSEUMS.—Metropolitan Museum of Art, 5th Ave. and 82d St. (Central Park); open free to the public every week day.

AMUSEMENT PLACES IN MANHATTAN AND BRONX—*Continued.*

(except Mon. and Fri., when admission is 25 cents) from 10 A. M. to half hour before sunset, and on Sundays from 1 P. M. to half hour before sunset, also Saturdays from 10 A. M. to 10 P. M. Museum of Natural History, 8th Ave. and 77th St., open week days from 9 A. M. to 5 P. M., Sunday from 1 to 5 P. M., also on holidays and Tues. and Sat. evenings; admission free. Aquarium, Castle Garden, Battery Park. Zoological Gardens, Central Park, entrance 5th Ave. and 64th St., and at Bronx Park, 182d St. and Southern Boulevard; admission free, except on Mon. and Thurs., when 25c. is charged. Botanical Gardens (Bronx Park) open daily 10 A. M. to 4.30 P. M., free.

The hours for beginning theatrical performances in New York are dictated by the length of the plays. Owing to the increasing lateness of the dinner hour in New York, the beginning of theatrical performances is steadily growing later. Theatre-goers should consult daily newspapers for the time of the rise of curtains, although the doors of all theatres open at 7.30 P. M.

All New York theatres give Saturday matinees, the curtains rising at 2 P. M. Midweek matinees are generally given on Tuesdays, Wednesdays or Thursdays, the day varying in the cases of different attractions. Some of the popular-price theatres and the vaudeville houses give daily matinees.

The standard price for best orchestra seats in New York theatres of the first class is $2. The scale at these houses grades down to 50 cents for seats in the top balcony. Occasionally, when eminent foreign stars visit New York, $3 is charged for best seats, the scale being raised in equal ratio in the balconies. In most theatres of the first class seats may be reserved in any part of the house.

The standard price for best orchestra seats in the so-called popular-price theatres is $1. The scale in these houses grades down to 25 cents for seats in the top balcony. It is not customary to reserve top balcony seats in these theatres.

The standard price for best orchestra seats at the Metropolitan and Manhattan Grand Opera-Houses is $5. The scale at these houses grades down to $1 for seats in the top balcony. At the Metropolitan Opera-House boxes are leased or subscribed for by the season. Some of the privately owned boxes are valued at $100,000.

Seats may be reserved in advance at New York theatres from two to six weeks preceding the date of use. In the case of new productions, managers claim that they fill orders in the order in which they are received. Reservations by mail are filled for out-of-town theatre-goers, but such orders must always be accompanied by a check or money order covering the full amount of the price of such seats.

In the number, beauty and convenience of its theatres New York leads all other cities of the world except, perhaps, London. There are, however, in a few cities of Continental Europe theatres under municipal or State endowment which, as works of architectural art, are more beautiful than the best New York theatres. The New Amsterdam Theatre is the most costly privately owned theatre in the world. The Hippodrome, seating 5,600 people, is the largest theatre of its kind in the world.

The Court of Appeals of the State of New York has decided that the proprietor of a theatre has the right to decide who shall be admitted to witness the plays he sees fit to produce, in the absence of any express statute controlling his action. He derives from the State no authority to carry on his business, and may conduct the same precisely as any other private citizen may transact his own affairs. But the holder of a ticket which entitles him to a seat at a given time and place of amusement, being refused admission, is entitled to recover the amount paid for the ticket and, undoubtedly, such necessary expenses as were incurred in order to attend the performance.

Theatres and Other Places of Amusement in Brooklyn.

Academy of Music, Lafayette Ave., St. Felix St. and Ashland Pl.

Bijou, Smith & Livingston Sts.

Blaney's, Bedford Ave., near S. 9th St.

Broadway, Broadway, near Myrtle Ave.

Brooklyn Inst. Arts and Sciences, East'n Parkway and Flatbush Ave.; office, Lafayette Av.

Clermont Ave. Rink, Clermont Ave., near Myrtle.

Columbia, Washington and Tillary Sts.

Crescent, Flatbush and Fulton Aves.

Fulton, Fulton near Nostrand Ave.

Gayety, B'way & Throop Av.

Grand, Elm Pl., near Fulton St.

Gotham, Fulton St. and Alabama Ave.

Historical Hall, Pierrepont and Clinton Sts.

Hyde & Behman's Olympic, Adams St., near Myrtle Ave.

Keeney's, Fulton St. & Grand Ave.

Majestic, Fulton St. and Ashland Pl.

Memorial Hall, Schermerhorn St. and Flatbush Ave.

New Montauk, Livingston St. and Hanover Pl.

Novelty, 782 Driggs Ave.

Orpheum, Fulton St., near Flatbush Ave.

Payton's, 170 Division Ave.

Star, Jay St., near Fulton.

Young Men's Christian Ass'n 502 Fulton St.

A Shakespearian Table.

PROFESSOR ROLFE, the Shakespearian scholar, has counted the lines which the principal characters in Shakespeare's plays have to speak. His rule was to consider parts of lines, beginnings and endings of speeches as full lines. This is the result:

	Lines to Speak.		Lines to Speak.		Lines to Speak.
Hamlet	1,569	Macbeth	705	Mistress Page	361
Richard III	1,161	Cleopatra	670	Viola	353
Iago	1,117	Prospero	665	Julia ("Two Gentlemen")	323
Othello	888	Romeo	618	Volumnia	315
Coriolanus	886	Petruchio	585	Beatrice	309
Timon	863	Touchstone	516	Lady Macbeth	261
Antony (Cleopatra's)	829	Imogen	541	Katherine (in "The Shrew")	220
Lear	770	Helen ("All's Well")	479	Miranda ("Tempest")	142
Richard II	755	Isabella	426	Perdita	128
Brutus	727	Desdemona	389	Cordelia	115

Henry V. as king and prince (in "Henry IV." and "Henry V.") has 1,987 lines to speak, and Falstaff, in both parts of "Henry IV." and "Henry V." and in the "Merry Wives," has 1,895.

The Stage in New York City During 1908.

A RECORD OF NEW PLAYS AND REVIVALS FROM DECEMBER 1, 1907, TO NOVEMBER 30, 1908, (INC.)

THERE are, in New York City, about sixty-nine theatres devoted to drama, opera, spectacles, concerts, vaudeville, and other forms of stage entertainment (see WORLD ALMANAC, 1909). The total number of events, changes of bill, special performances, trials of plays, etc., in all these theatres during the regular dramatic season of forty weeks approximates 900. Of the above mentioned number of theatres, thirty are producing houses, devoted to productions and runs of their own plays or those of producing managers who are not theatre managers, and also revivals of standard plays. The following summary of dramatic events includes all the productions and revivals in these thirty producing theatres, but excludes the Irving Place and the German (Deutsche) Theatres, where about forty dramas in German are given at each during the regular season. Four producing theatres, now in process of construction, have been added to the list of amusement places in Manhattan and the Bronx, but no plays were acted on their stages prior to January 1, 1909.

SUMMARY OF EVENTS IN PRODUCING THEATRES.

Number of New Plays	63
Number of New Musical Comedies	35
Dramatic Revivals	29
Musical Comedy Revivals	9
Shakespearean Revivals	3
Total events	139

CLASSIFICATION OF NEW PLAYS.

Serious, Sentimental and Problem Plays	22
Melodramas	13
Romantic Comedies	5
Light Comedies	10
Tragedies	3
Farces	10
Total	63

SOURCES OF NEW PLAYS.

Original	42
Adapted from Foreign Plays	10
Dramatized from Novels	11
Total	63

NATIONALITY OF AUTHORS.

By Native Authors	44
By Foreign Authors	19
Total	63

NATIONALITY OF MUSICAL-COMEDY COMPOSERS.

By Native Composers	27
By Foreign Composers	8
Total	35

STARS OF VARYING MAGNITUDES.

Native Stars	44
Foreign Stars	5
Total	49

GENERAL SUMMARY OF SEASON.

Total weeks of New Plays	429
Total weeks of Revived Plays	139
Total weeks of New Musical Comedies	383
Total weeks of Revived Musical Comedies	40
Total weeks of Open Producing Theatres	991

Number of Producing Theatres, 28.

Season reckoned from the general opening of the theatres in the Autumn of 1907 until their closing in the late Spring of 1908, or, in the cases of runs that continued into the Summer, until June 1.

Owing to the great number of theatres in New York and the experimental character of some of the productions, a considerable percentage of which prove either to be failures or of insignificant interest, no attempt has been made in the following lists to include every play offered between November 30, 1907, and December 1, 1908. Care is taken, however, to enumerate the new dramas and the musical comedies, the revivals of classic plays and the reappearances of successful plays of other seasons which, in their success or failure, were conspicuous during the year in the theatrical affairs of New York.

Of the runs of important dramas and musical comedies, produced between August 1 and December 1, 1907, that extended into 1908, "The Thief," a comedy, with Margaret Illington and Kyrle Bellew, lasted 32 weeks at the Lyceum; "The Yankee Tourist," a musical comedy, with Raymond Hitchcock, 13 weeks at the Astor; "When Knights Were Bold," a farce, with Francis Wilson, 16 weeks at the Garrick and Hackett; "The Dairy Maids," an English musical comedy, 12 weeks at the Criterion; "The Round Up," a melodrama, with Macklyn Arbuckle, 19 weeks at the New Amsterdam and Broadway; "Classmates," a comedy, with Robert Edeson, 12 weeks at the Hudson; "My Wife," a comedy, with John Drew and Billie Burke, 16 weeks at the Empire; "Pioneer Days" and "Neptune's Daughter," spectacles, 26 weeks at the Hippodrome; "The Rogers Brothers in Panama," a burlesque, with the Rogers Brothers, 10 weeks at the Broadway and Liberty; "The Master Builder" and other Ibsen plays, with Mme. Alla Nazimova, 14 weeks at the Bijou; "The Girl Behind The Counter," a musical comedy, with Lew Fields and Connie Ediss, 38 weeks at the Herald Square; "The Gay White Way," a musical comedy, 13 weeks at the Casino; "Hip! Hip! Hooray!" a travesty and a burlesque of "The Merry Widow," with Joseph Weber's Stock Company, 25 weeks at Weber's; "The Grand Army Man," a domestic drama, with David Warfield, 19 weeks at the Stuyvesant; "The Hoyden," a musical comedy, with Elsie Janis, 8 weeks at the Knickerbocker and Wallack's; "The Top O' Th' World," a musical comedy, 15 weeks at the Majestic; "The Merry Widow," a Viennese operetta, with a succession of stars, 52 weeks at the New Amsterdam and Aerial; "Artie," a farce, 4 weeks at the Garrick; Arnold Daly's Theatre of Ideas, during which several inconsequential one-act plays were produced, 11 weeks at the Berkeley Lyceum; "Tom Jones," a comic opera, 10 weeks at the Astor; Marie Doro in "The Morals of Marcus," a comedy, 6 weeks at the Criterion; John Mason in the "Witching Hour," a fine drama and one of the year's best plays, 43 weeks at the Hackett; and W. H. Ferguson in "The Toymaker of Nuremberg," a fantastic comedy, 4 weeks at the Garrick.

Dec. 3—Knickerbocker: "The Talk of New York," a musical comedy, 20 weeks.

Dec. 3—Daly's: Lawrence D'Orsay in "The Lanciers," a farce, 3 weeks.

Dec. 3—Belasco: Charlotte Walker and Frank Keenan in "The Warrens of Virginia," a melodrama, 26 weeks.

Dec. 16—Lyric: Josephine Victor in "The Secret Orchard," a melodrama, 3 weeks.

Dec. 16—Wallack's: John Slavin in "A Knight For A Day," a musical comedy, 28 weeks.

Dec. 23—Daly's: James K. Hackett in "John Glayde's Honour," a drama, 2 weeks.

Dec. 23—Liberty: Mabel Taliaferro in "Polly of the Circus," a comedy, 24 weeks.

Dec. 23—Empire: Maude Adams in "Peter Pan," a fantasy, 2 weeks.

Dec. 25—Hudson: Ethel Barrymore in "Her Sister," a comedy, 7½ weeks.

Dec. 25—Garrick: Maxine Elliott in "Under the Greenwood Tree." a romantic comedy, 5 weeks.

Dec. 30—Lyric: Mrs. Minnie Maddern Fiske in "Rosmersholm," a drama, 4 weeks.

Dec. 30—Bijou: Alla Nazimova in "The Comet," a drama, 7 weeks.

Dec. 31—Criterion: Christie MacDonald in "Miss Hook of Holland," a musical comedy, 15 weeks.

Jan. 6—Empire: Maude Adams in "Quality Street," a comedy, 1 week.

Jan. 6—Broadway: Anna Held in "The Parisian Model," a musical comedy, 3 weeks.

Jan. 6—Daly's: E. M. Holland in "The House of a Thousand Candles," a melodrama, 2 weeks.

Jan. 6—Casino: "Funabashi," a musical comedy, 4 weeks.

Jan. 13—Madison Square: Katherine Grey in "Literature" and "The Reckoning," comedies, 3 weeks.

Jan. 15—Empire: Maude Adams in "The Jesters," a poetic comedy, 6½ weeks.

Jan. 18—Daly's: "Society and the Bulldog," a comedy, 3 weeks.

Jan. 20—Astor: Viola Allen in "Irene Wycherly," a comedy, 5 weeks.

Jan. 20—Savoy: Dallas Welford in "Twenty Days in the Shade," a farce, 5 weeks.

Jan. 27—Lyric: Edward H. Sothern in "Lord Dundreary," a comedy, 6 weeks.

Jan. 27—Broadway: "The Waltz Dream," an operetta, 15 weeks.

Jan. 28—New York: Adeline Genee in "The Soul Kiss," a musical comedy, 16 weeks.

Feb. 1—Lyric: Edward H. Sothern in "Hamlet," 1 performance.

Feb. 3—Garrick: Edna Wallace Hopper in "Fifty Miles from Boston," nondescript, 4 weeks.

Feb. 3—Majestic: Williams and Walker in "Bandanna Land," a musical comedy, 11 weeks.

Feb. 10—Daly's: Olga Nethersole in repertoire, beginning with "The Awakening," a drama, 3 weeks.

Feb. 11—Garden: Mrs. Patrick Campbell, in "Electra," a tragedy, 2 weeks.

Feb. 12—Madison Square: Katherine Grey in "The Worth of a Woman," a comedy, 4 weeks.

THE STAGE IN NEW YORK CITY DURING 1908—*Continued.*

Feb. 17—Hudson: Otis Skinner in "The Honor of the Family," a comedy, 15 weeks.
Feb. 17—Bijou: Henry Ludlow in "The Merchant of Venice," 1 week.
Feb. 18—Savoy: Irish players in "A Pot O'Broth," a comedy, 3 weeks.
Feb. 24—Casino: Sam Bernard in "Nearly a Hero," a musical comedy, 14 weeks.
Feb. 25—Astor: "Paid in Full," a comedy (transferred later to Weber's Theatre), 39 weeks.
Feb. 29—Garden: "The Village Lawyer," a comedy, 2 weeks.
March 2—Garrick: Nat C. Goodwin in "The Easterner," a comedy, 2 weeks.
March 2—Empire: William H. Crane in "Father and The Boys," a farce, 16 weeks.
March 2—Daly's. Mme. Komisarzhevsky in repertoire of Russian dramas, beginning with "A Doll's House," a drama, 3 weeks.
March 3—Bijou: Dustin Farnum in "The Rector's Garden," a comedy, ½ week.
March 9—Lyric: Edward H. Sothern in "The Fool Hath Said There Is No God," a comedy, 4 weeks.
March 16—Garrick: John Barrymore in "Toddles," a farce, 3 weeks.
March 19—Bijou: Leo Ditrichstein in "Bluffs," a farce, 3 weeks.
March 23—Daly's: Laura Nelson Hall in "Girls," a farce, 28 weeks.
March 23—Savoy: "The Servant In The House," a symbolical drama, 14 weeks.
March 24—Garden: Bertha Kalish in "Marta of the Lowlands," a melodrama, 2½ weeks.
April 6—Garrick. Cyril Scott in "The Royal Mounted," a comedy, 4 weeks.
April 8—Lyric: Edward H. Sothern in "Don Quixote," a comedy, 3 weeks.
April 18—Bijou: "The Wolf," a melodrama, 14 weeks, (transferred to Lyric).
April 20—Knickerbocker: George Cohan in "The Yankee Prince," a musical comedy, 16 weeks.
April 20—Garden: Edward Vroom in "The Luck of McGregor," a romantic comedy, 1½ weeks.
April 25—Circle: "The Merry Go Round," a musical comedy, 5 weeks.
April 28—Bijou: Henry E. Dixey in "Papa Lebonnard," a comedy, 4 weeks.
May 4—American: Abramson Italian Grand Opera Company, in repertoire, 4 weeks.
May 18—Wallack's: "The Gay Musician," a musical comedy 4 weeks.
May 18—Academy; Edward H. Sothern in a revival of "Lord Dundreary," a comedy, 4 weeks.
May 25—New York: Richard Carle in "Mary's Lamb," a musical comedy, 8 weeks.
June 1—Hammerstein's Roof Garden: season's opening, about 12 weeks.
June 15—New York Roof Garden; "The Follies of 1908" a burlesque, about 12 weeks.
June 20—Madison Square Garden Roof; season's opening, 4 weeks.
Aug. 3—Wallack's; "The Girl Question," a musical comedy 4 weeks.
Aug. 3—New York; Cohan and Harris's Minstrels, 9 weeks.
Aug. 10—Liberty; Frank J. McIntyre in "The Traveling Salesman," a comedy, (later transferred to Gaiety,) 16* weeks.
Aug. 17—Astor; William Hodge in "The Man From Home," a drama, 15* weeks.
Aug. 17—Weber's; transfer of "Paid in Full," to this house (See Astor Theatre, Feb. 25.)
Aug. 18—Criterion; Isadora Duncan in classic dances, 3 weeks.
Aug. 18—Belasco; George Arliss in "The Devil," 15* weeks.
Aug. 18—Garden; Edwin Stevens in "The Devil," 12 weeks.
Aug. 22—Bijou; Douglas Fairbanks in "All for a Girl," a romantic comedy, 4 weeks.
Aug. 24—Hudson; Robert Edeson in "The Call of the North," a melodrama, 5 weeks.
Aug. 27—Lyceum; Billie Burke in "Love Watches," a comedy, 15½* weeks.
Aug. 31—Broadway; "Algeria," a comic opera, 6 weeks.
Aug. 31—Gaiety: dedication, with Frank J. McIntyre in "The Traveling Salesman," (See Liberty Theatre, August 10.)
Sept. 1—Garrick; Joseph Cawthorne and Alexandra Carlisle in "The Mollusc," a satirical comedy, and "The Likes O' Me," a sketch, 12 weeks.
Sept. 1—Wallack's; Arnold Daly in "The Regeneration," a melodrama, 5 weeks.
Sept. 2—Knickerbocker; Gertie Millar in "The Girls of Gottenburg," a musical comedy, 12½ weeks.
Sep. 4—Savoy: Carlotta Nelson in "Diana of Dobson's," a comedy, 2 weeks.
Sept. 5—American; Abramson Grand Opera Company in repertoire, 4 weeks.
Sept. 6—Liberty: Lillian Russell in "Wildfire," a racing comedy, 8 weeks
Sept. 7—Criterion: Hattie Williams in "Fluffy Ruffles," a musical comedy, 6 weeks.
Sept. 10—Hippodrome: "Sporting Days," and "The Battle in the Skies," spectacles, 12½* weeks.
Sept. 14—Empire: John Drew in "Jack Straw," a comedy, 11½* weeks.
Sept. 14—Circle: "School Days," a musical comedy, 3 weeks.
Sept. 21—Hackett: James K. Hackett, in revivals, beginning with "The Prisoner of Zenda," 4 weeks.
Sept. 22—Stuyvesant: Blanche Bates in "The Fighting Hope," a domestic drama, 11* weeks.
Sept. 24—Majestic "Father and Son," a melodrama, 1 week.
Sept. 25—Savoy: "Mater," a satirical comedy, 3 weeks.
Sept. 28—Lyric: Lulu Glaser in "Mlle. Mischief," a musical comedy, 9* weeks.
Sept. 28—Hudson: Robert Edeson in "The Offenders," a melodrama, 2 weeks.
Sept. 29—Bijou: Thomas Wise and Douglas Fairbanks in "A Gentleman from Mississippi," a political comedy, 9* weeks.
Sept. 29—Garrick: May Irwin in "Mrs. Peckham's Carouse," a farce preceding "The Mollusc," 8 weeks.
Oct. 1—Dedication of the New German Theatre at Madison Ave. and 59th St.
Oct. 1—Casino: Louise Gunning in "Marcelle," a musical comedy, 8½ weeks.
Oct. 5—New York: "The American Idea," a combination of musical comedy and vaudeville, 8 weeks.
Oct. 5—Daly's: Maxine Elliott in "Myself—Bettina," a domestic drama, 4 weeks.
Oct. 5—Majestic: Nance O'Neil in "Agnes," a drama, 3 weeks.
Oct. 6—Wallack's: Arnold Daly in "His Wife's Family," an Irish comedy, 2 weeks.
Oct. 12—Broadway: Grace Van Studdiford in "The Golden Butterfly," a comic opera, 6 weeks.
Oct. 12—Hudson: Edgar Selwyn in "Pierre of the Plains," a melodrama, 4 weeks.
Oct. 15—Circle: Louis Mann in "The Man Who Stood Still," 6* weeks.
Oct. 19—Criterion: William Gillette in "Samson," a melodrama, 7* weeks.
Oct. 19—Savoy: Revival of "The Servant in the House," with Henry Miller's associate players in the cast, a satirical and symbolical drama, 7* weeks.
Oct. 20—New Amsterdam: Master Gabriel in "Little Nemo," an extravaganza, 6½* weeks.
Oct. 26—Majestic: Jessie Bonstelle in "The Great Question," a melodrama, 2 weeks.
Nov. 2—Wallack's: Marie Cahill in "The Boys and Bettie," a musical comedy, 4* weeks.
Nov. 2—Daly's: William Faversham's company in "The World and His Wife," a domestic drama, 4* weeks.
Nov. 2—Liberty: "Via Wireless," a scenic melodrama, 4* weeks.
Nov. 9—Hudson: Ethel Barrymore in "Lady Frederick," a comedy, 3* weeks.
Nov. 9—Majestic: "Blue Grass," a racing drama, 3* weeks.
Nov. 17—Hackett: Mrs. Minnie Maddern Fiske in "Salvation Nell," a drama, 2* weeks.
Nov. 23—Weber's: Annie Russell in "The Stronger Sex," a domestic comedy, 1* week.
Nov. 23—Garrick: William Collier in "The Patriot," a farce, 1* week.
Nov. 23—Garden: Henry E. Dixey in "Mary Jane's Pa," a comedy.*
Nov. 30—Savoy: Henry Miller's associate players in "The Winterfest," a symbolical drama.*
Nov. 30—Knickerbocker: Fritzi Scheff in "The Prima Donna," a comic opera.*
Nov. 30—Casino: "The Blue Mouse," a musical comedy.*
Nov. 30—New York: Anna Held in "Miss Innocence," a musical comedy.*

* Still running.

Banks in Manhattan and Bronx.

The Clearing-House is at 77 Cedar Street, Manhattan Borough. Wm. Sherer is manager, Wm. J. Gilpin, assistant manager. Fifty banks are associated for the purpose of exchanging the checks and bills they hold against each other. Other banks, not members of the association, clear through members. The representatives of the members appear at the Clearing-House at 10 o'clock A. M. every business day, with the checks and bills to be exchanged. The resulting balances are ascertained in about an hour, and before half-past one o'clock those indebted pay their balances, and after that hour the other banks receive the amounts due them. The Clearing-House has been in operation since 1853.

Following are extracts from the Manager's annual report for year ending September 30, 1908: The Clearing-House transactions for the year have been as follows: Exchanges, $73,630,971,913; balances, $3,409,632,271; total transactions, $77,040,604,184. The average daily transactions: Exchanges, $241,413,022; balances, $11,179,122; total, $252,592,144. Total transactions since organization of Clearing-House (55 years): Exchanges, $1,930,248,133,349; balances, $89,694,759,171: total, $2,019,942,892,520.

Banks are open from 10 A. M. to 3 P. M., and on Saturdays from 10 A. M. to 12 noon. Commercial paper, except sight or demand bills, falling due on Saturday is payable on the following business day.

NATIONAL BANKS.

Name.	Location.	Capital.	Surplus and Undivided Profits.	President.	Cashier.
Aetna	Greenwich & Warren	$300,000	$325,000	C. E. Finlay	Jas. Dennison.
American Exchange	128 Broadway	5,000,000	4,925,000	Dumont Clarke	Edward Burns.
Bank of Commerce	31 Nassau St	25,000,000	15,667,378	V. P. Snyder	Neilson Olcott.
Bank of New York	48 Wall St	2,000,000	3,369,500	Herbert L. Griggs	Charles Olney.
Battery Park	2 Broadway	200,000	148,000	E. A. de Lima	E. B. Day.
Beaver	In liquidation	......	....	....	....
Bronx	542 Bergen Ave	200,000	....	Geo. N. Reinhardt	Wm. A. Price.
Butchers & Drovers'	683 Broadway	300,000	150,900	D. H. Rowland	William H. Chase.
Chase	83 Cedar St	5,000,000	5,308,511	A. B. Hepburn	S. H. Miller.
Chatham	192 Broadway	450,000	1,000,000	George M. Hard	W. H. Strawn.
Chemical	270 Broadway	3,000,000	5,783,677	William H. Porter	Francis Halpin.
Citizens' Central	320 Broadway	2,550,000	1,381,051	Edwin S. Schenck.	A. K. Chapman.
City	Wall & William Sts.	25,000,000	25,619,293	James Stillman	Arthur Kavanagh.
Coal and Iron	143 Liberty St	500 000	698,000	John T. Sproull	Addison H. Day.
Consolidated	56 Broadway	1,000,000	780,000	William O. Allison.	Thos. J. Lewis.
Copper	115 Broadway	2,000,000	2,445,511	Charles H. Sabin	W. F. Albertsen.
East River	680 Broadway	250,000	110,476	Vincent Loeser	Zenas E. Newell.
European-Am'ican	Dey & Greenwich	100,000	50,000	B. S. Dunn	F. W. Knothoff.
Fifth National	3d Ave. & 23d St.	250,000	450,000	Stephen Kelly	Andrew Thompson
First National	2 Wall St	10,000,000	16,573,000	George F. Baker	C. D. Backus.
Fourth National	14 Nassau St	3,000,000	3,315,590	J. Edwd. Simmons.	C. H. Patterson.
Gallatin	36 Wall St	1,000,000	2,445,776	Sam. Woolverton	G. E. Lewis.
Garfield	71 W. 23d St	1,000,000	1,129,000	R. W. Poor	W. L. Douglass.
Hanover	Nassau St., cor. Pine	3,000,000	9,000,000	Jas. T. Woodward	E. E. Whittaker.
Imp't'rs & Traders'	247 Broadway	1,500,000	7,308,163	Edward Townsend	H. H. Powell.
Irving Nat'l Exc'ge	90 W. Broadway	2,000,000	1,374,951	Lewis E. Pierson	Benj. F. Werner.
Liberty	139 Broadway	1,000,000	2,480,000	F. B. Schenck	Chas. W. Riecks.
Lincoln	32 E. 42d St	1,000,000	1,248,278	Thomas L. James	C. E. Warren.
Market and Fulton	81 Fulton St	1,000,000	1,633,000	Alex. Gilbert	T. J. Stevens.
Mechanics'	33 Wall St	3,000,000	3,723,928	G. W. McGarrah	Frank O. Roe.
Mercantile	195 Broadway	3,000,000	2,490,369	Willis G. Nash	Emil Klein.
Merchants'	42 Wall St	2,000,000	1,621,799	R. M. Gallaway	Joseph Byrne.
Merchants' Exch	257 Broadway	600,000	506,183	P. C. Lounsbury	E. V. Gambier.
National Park	214 Broadway	3,000,000	9,583,404	Richard Delafield	Maurice H. Ewer.
New Amsterdam	B'way, cor. 39th	In liqui	dation.	....	....
New York County	8th Av., cor. 14th St.	500,000	1,145,690	Francis L. Leland	James C. Brower.
Phenix	Nassau & Liberty St.	1,000,000	578,626	F. E. Marshall	Bert L. Haskins.
Seaboard	18 Broadway	1,000,000	1,649,000	Samuel G. Bayne	C. C. Thompson.
Second National	5th Ave., cor. 23d	1,000,000	1,735,000	James Stillman	Joseph S. Case.
Sherman	34th St. & Astor C'rt	200,000	53,343	E. C. Smith	Chas. G. Colyer.

STATE BANKS.

Name.	Location.	Capital.	Surplus and Undivided Profits.	President.	Cashier.
Bank of America	44 Wall St	$1,500,000	$4,804,238	William H. Perkins	W. M. Bennet.
Bank of Metropolis	31 Union Square	1,000,000	2,000,000	C. H. Hackett	E. C. Evans.
Bowery	Bowery, cor. Grand	250,000	775,000	John S. Foster	Charles Essig.
Bronx Bor'gh Bank	440 E. Tremont Ave.	150,000	57,759	C. A. Becker	Jay Lehrbach.
Bryant Park	6th Ave. and 42d St.	200,000	106,000	W. W. Warner	E. F. Giese.
Century §	Fifth Ave. & 20th St.	200,000	149,502	H. L. Crawford	C.S. Mitchell (Ass't)
Chelsea Exchange	34th St. and 8th Av.	200,000	170,343	Irving M. Shaw	A. E. Stilger.
Colonial †	Columbus Av. & 81st.	400,000	225,000	Alexander Walker.	Geo. S. Carr.
Columbia ††	5th Ave., cor. 42d	300,000	438,000	Joseph Fox	W. S. Griffith.
Corn Exchange ‡	13 William St	3,000,000	5,037,169	William A. Nash	Fred'k T. Martin.
Cosmopolitan	803 Prospect Ave	100,000	7,000	C. A. Becker	C. Baunach.
Fidelity	Mad. Ave., c. 75th	200,000	170,000	Edward H. Peaslee.	E. W. Dutton.
5th Av. Bank of N. Y.	530 Fifth Ave.	100,000	2,052,853	A. S. Frissell	B. H. Fancher.

† Branches at 1960, 2199 and 2701 Broadway, Columbus Ave., 92d St., and cor. 105th St.; 116th St., cor. 7th Ave. ‡ Branches, 530, 1178, 2902 B'way, 23 Astor Pl., Columbus Ave. and 72d St., 5th Ave., cor. 19th St.; 42d St., cor. 8th Ave.; 7 E. 42d St., Ave. D, cor. 10th St.; cor. Grand and Norfolk Sts., 34 Union Sq.; 101 W. 125th St., Amsterdam Ave. and 143d St., 522 Willis Ave.; Brooklyn—Court and Montague Sts.; 19 Flatbush Ave.; Queens County Branch, Borden Ave. and Front St.; 75 Fulton Ave., Queens; Franklin St. and Greenpoint Ave.; 116 Main St., Flushing; Jackson Ave. and Fifth St.; also New Brighton, S. I. †† Branch 407 Broadway. § Branch 104th St. and Broadway.

STATE BANKS—MANHATTAN AND BRONX—*Continued.*

Name.	Location.	Capital.	Surplus. (Including Undivided Profits.)	President.	Cashier.
Fourteenth Street ..	1 E. 14th St.(h).......	$1,000,000	$310,000	R. Ross Appleton..	Louis V. Ennis.
German-American .	23 Broad St..........	750,000	627,000	Casimir Tag.........	J. F. Fredericks.
German Exchange..	330 Bowery..........	200,000	850,000	Chas. L. Adrian....	E. F. Swanberg.
Germania...........	190 Bowery..........	200,000	960,000	Edward C. Schaefer	Loftin Love.
Greenwich..........	402 Hudson St.††....	500,000	729,493	Wm. C. Duncan....	Clarence Foote.
Hamilton	Merged with Northern Bank		.....	....	....
Hungarian-Am'c'n	32 Broadway‡........	100,000	100,000	E. S. A. de Lima...	A. Howard Watson
International.......	60 Wall St	500,000	126,000	T. H. Hubbard.....	J. H. Rogers.
Jefferson............	105 Canal St..........	500,000	687,500	Herman Broesel....	Wm. H. Devlin.
Manhattan Compa'y	40 Wall St	2,050,000	3,050,000	Stephen Baker......	D. H. Pierson.
Metropolitan.........	4th Ave. & 23d St.(c)	2,000,000	1,164,800	Henry Ollesheimer.	A. C. Corley.
Mount Morris	85 E. 125th St........	250,000	265,000	L. M. Schwan......	L. H. Hill.
Mutual...............	B'way, c. 33d St.....	200,000	317,000	Charles A. Sackett.	Hugh N. Kirkland.
Nassau...............	9 Beekman St.......	500,000	392,257	Edward Earl........	W. B. Noble, Ass't.
New Netherland....	41 W. 34th St........	200,000	210,000	J. Adams Brown..	Curtis J. Beard.
N. Y. Produce Exch.	Produce Exch. §.....	1,000,000	684,504	Forrest H. Parker..	John R. Wood.
Night and Day......	5th Ave. & 44th St ..	200,000	211,177	S. S. Campbell......	G. L. Wilmerding.
Nineteenth Ward...	3d Ave. & 57th St.(e).	300,000	470,400	W. M. Van Norden	John N. Van Pelt.
Northern............	215 W. 125th St. (j)..	700,000	300,000	F. L. Grant.........	Wm. L. Brower.
Oriental..............	182 Broadway........	In liquidation.		....	....
Pacific...............	470 Broadway	500,000	834,000	H. B. Brundrett....	Sam. C. Merwin.
People's..............	395 Canal St	200,000	457,883	Scott Foster.........	William Milne.
Plaza	5th Ave., c. W. 58th..	100,000	386,404	W. McM. Mills	E. M. Clarke.
Royal.................	95 Nassau St.........	100,000	35,000	Philip Sugerman ...	F. C. Straat.
State..................	378 Grand St.‡‡......	1,000,000	827,726	Oscar L. Richard...	A. I. Voorhis.
Twelfth Ward**.....	125th, c. Lex'n Ave..	200,000	180,000	Frank B. French....	Jas. V. Iverson.
Twenty-third Ward	135th St. & 3d Ave §§.	200,000	88,000	Charles W. Bogart.	Geo. E. Edwards.
Union Exchange....	5th Ave. & 21st St...	750,000	825,000	H. S. Herman.......	David Nevius.
U. S. Exchange.....	In liquidation.......	......	....	....	....
Washington H'ghts.	Amstm. Ave. & 155th	100,000	201,000	John Whalen.......	William Clark.
Wells, Fargo & Co's	51 Broadway........	100,000	40,000	Dudley Evans, V. P.	A. W. Zimmermann
West Side	487 Eighth Ave......	200,000	757,000	C. F. Tietjen	Walter Westervelt.
Yorkville............	85th St., c. 3d Ave....	100,000	400,000	R. Van der Emde..	W. L. Frankenbach.

§ Also Madison Ave., near 60th St., cor. Columbus Ave. and 93d St., cor. 53th St. and 7th Ave., cor. 116th St. and 3d Ave. cor. 103d St. and 1st Ave., and B'way and 86th St., Manhattan St. and Amsterdam Ave., 14th St. and 2d Ave. †† Also at 260 W. B'way, 874, 1531 B'way, 135 William St., 596 Sixth Ave. ‡‡ Also 5th Ave. and W. 115th St. §§ Also 960 Boston Road, and 2803 Third Ave. ** Also 173 East 116th St., and 1925 Third Ave.; (c) also 100 William St., 271 and 565 Broadway; (e) also 242 E. 8oth St., 180 E. 72d St., cor. 34th St. and 3d Ave.; (h) also 356 W. 14th St. and 22 Avenue A.. (j) Also 692 Broadway, 8th Ave and 57th St., 254 Eighth Ave., 2301 Seventh Ave., 1707 Amsterdam Ave., 3d Ave. and 163d St., 505 E. Tremont Ave., 412 E. 138th St.; 194 White Plains Ave.

Banks for Savings in Manhattan and Bronx.

Name.	Location.	President.	No. of Depositors.	Deposits.	Rate Int.‡	Surplus.	Unless otherwise stated, banks close at 12 noon on Saturdays.
American	115 W. 42d St....	Clarence Goadby.....	7,310	$2,242,398	4	$71,630	10 A. M. to 4 P. M. (a)
Bank for Savings...	4th Av., c. 22d St.	Walter Trimble......	160,560	91,459,640	4	6,571,717	10 A. M. to 3 P. M.; Monday 10 A. M. to 6 P. M.
Bowery	130 Bowery......	Henry A. Schenck....	153,882	102,500,499	4	7,969,161	10 A. M. to 3 P. M.
Broadway..........	5 Park Place......	H. F. Hutchinson.....	....	9,615,436	4	574,930	10 A. M. to 3 P. M.
Bronx.	455 Tremont Ave..	Wm. B. Aitken.......	1,800	250,000	4	.....	9 A.M. to 4 P.M.; Mon., 6 to 9 P.M.
Citizens'...........	58 Bowery........	Henry Hasler........	29,138	14,845,843	4	1,438,839	10 A. M. to 3 P. M.
Dollar..............	3d Av. & 148th St.	John Haffen..........	28,700	5,325,000	4	151,000	10 A. M. to 3 P. M.; (a)
Dry Dock..........	341 Bowery.......	Andrew Mills........	67,857	33,981,475	4	2,443,797	10 A. M. to 3 P. M.
East River....... .	280 Broadway....	D. S. Ramsay.........	24,295	22,711,100	4	2,804,604	10 A. M. to 3 P. M.
Emigrant Industrial	51 Chambers St...	Thomas M. Mulry	122,000	96,000,000	4	11,000,000	10 A. M. to 3 P. M.
Empire City.......	231 W. 125th St...	Isaac A. Hopper......	14,500	2,638,218	4	104,043	9 A. M. to 3 P. M.; (a).
Excelsior..........	23d St., c. 6th Av.	William J. Roome....	20,080	7,897,691	4	356,692	10 A. M. to 3 P. M., Mon., 6 to 8 P. M. also. (f)
Franklin............	8th Ave., c. 42d St.	William G. Conklin..	44,205	16,705,426	4	1,040,327	10 A. M. to 3 P. M. (a)
German............	4th Ave., c. 14th St	Casimir Tag..........	131,983	68,171,240	4	5,574,813	10 A. M. to 3 P. M.; Monday, 10 A. M. to 8 P. M. also.
Greenwich.........	248 Sixth Ave....	James Quinlan.......	92,000	59,000,000	4	4,000,000	10 A. M. to 3 P. M.
Harlem	125th St. & Lex. Av	William E. Trotter...	48,190	16,461,460	4	1,048,059	10 A. M. to 8 P. M. (a)
Irving..............	115 Chambers St..	Wm. H. B. Totten....	27,753	19,202,819	4	807,063	10 A. M. to 3 P. M.
Italian..............	64 Spring St.....	Joseph N. Francolini.	12,000	1,750,000	4	45,000	10 A. M. to 3 P. M., Mon. and Sat., 7 to 9 P. M. also.
Maiden Lane.......	170 Broadway....	Louis Windmuller....	3,000	535,000	4	6,107	9 A. M. to 5.30 P. M.
Manhattan.........	644 Broadway....	Joseph Bird..........	21,046	11,851,622	4	726,633	10 A. M. to 3 P. M.
Metropolitan.......	1 Third Ave......	J. B. Currey..........	14,211	9,200,000	4	600,000	10 A. M. to 3 P. M. (a)
New York..........	8th Ave., c. 14th St.	Wm. Felsinger........	....	26,422,489	4	2,054,929	10 A. M. to 3 P. M.; (a)
North River	31 W. 34th St.....	Samuel D. Styles.....	18,028	8,181,592	4	292,290	10 A.M. to 3 P.M. Mon. to 8 P.M.
North Side.........	3196 Third Ave ..	John J. Barry........	1,600	280,000	4	10,000	9 A. M. to 4 P. M.; (a)
Seamen's...........	74 Wall St........	Daniel Barnes........	97,764	67,114,176	4	5,801,928	10 A. M. to 2 P. M.
Union Dime........	B'way, c. 32d St..	Chas. E. Sprague.....	89,652	25,582,808	4	1,929,155	10 A. M. to 3 P. M.; (a)
Union Square......	26 Union Sq. E...	F. M. Hurlbut........	13,836	8,405,925	4	907,536	10 A. M. to 3 P. M. (a)
United States	606 Madison Ave.	Const. A. Andrews ...	9,968	2,715,303	4	73,360	10 A. M. to 4 P. M.; Sat., 10 to 12 noon, and 7 to 9 P.M. (b)
Universal..........	196 E. Broadway.	Wilbur F. Brown.....	....	....	..	....	
Washington	59th St. and Columbus Circle.	Joseph G. Robin......	6,266	1,046,695	4	15,000	9 A. M. to 3 P. M.; Mon. and Sat., 6 to 8 P. M. also. (g)
West Side.	Sixth Av., c. 9th St.	Stephen G. Cook......	9,197	2,160,524	4	72,000	9 A. M. to 3 P. M. (a)

‡Subject to change. (a) Open Monday nights also. (b) Not open Saturday evenings in July, August, September. (f) Except June, July, August and September. (g) Not open Saturday eve. in July and August. (q) Report of December, 1907.

Banks in Brooklyn and Queens.

NATIONAL AND STATE BANKS.

Name.	Location.	Capital.	Surplus and Undivided Profits.	President.	Cashier.
Bank of Long Island	Jamaica §§	$500,000	$725,000	S. R. Smith	W. D. Llewellyn.
Borough	20 Court St.	200,000	124,427	Broc R. Shears	A. K. Moore.
Broadway	12 Graham Ave.	150,000	420,051	H. Batterman	George F. Moger.
Brooklyn	585 Fulton St.†	300,000	185,939	D. O. Underhill	Nelson G. Ayres.
First National	Kent Ave. & B'way.	300,000	347,438	Joseph Huher	William S. Irish.
Homestead	Pen. & Liberty Avs.	200,000	52,229	Solomon Rubin	G. S. Mott.
Manufact'ers' Nat.	84 Broadway	252,000	752,155	A. D. Seymour	J. C. Nightingale.
Mechanics' §	Court & Montague	1,000,000	836,051	Geo. W. Chauncey	Chas. G. Balmanno
Montauk	Fifth Av. & Union St.	100,000	58,506	Henry M. Randall.	Charles J. Lockitt
Nassau National	26 Court St.	750,000	875,000	Thomas T. Barr	Daniel V. Hegeman
National City	350 Fulton St	300,000	580,000	Charles T. Young	Henry M. Wells.
North Side	33, 710 Grand St.‡‡	200,000	84,000	Paul E. Bonner	Henry Billman.
Prospect Park	Flatbush & Ch. Avs.	100,000	51,000	Wm. E. Harmon	Wm. D. Buckner
Terminal	81 Sands Street	100,000	16,000	William P. Reid	George F. Frost.
Union	44 Court St.	1,000,000	800,000	Edward M. Grout	James T. Ashley.
Woodhaven	Woodhaven	25,000	28,111	Wm. F. Wyckoff	H. M. De Ronde.

§Branches at 5th Ave. and 9th St., Schermerhorn St., near Flatbush Ave., Atlantic and Georgia Aves., 4th Ave. and Atlantic. §§ Branches at Jamaica, Flushing, Far Rockaway, Rockaway Beach, Richmond Hill, Elmhurst, College Point, L. I. City. ‡‡ Also Broadway, cor. Lorimer St. † Also at Fulton and Clinton Sts.

Banks for Savings in Brooklyn and Queens.

Name.	Location.	President.	No. of Depositors.	Deposits.	Rate of Int.*	Surplus.	Business Hours. [Unless otherwise stated banks close at 12 noon on Saturdays.]
Brevoort	Nostrand Ave. & Macon St.	Howard M. Smith	10,643	$2,354,090	4	$95,000	9 A. M. to 3 P. M.; also Monday, 7 to 9 P. M.
Brooklyn	Clinton & Pierrepont Sts.	Bryan H. Smith	66,980	44,050,000	4	4,493,000	10 A. M. to 3 P. M.; Monday, 5 to 7 P. M. also.
Bushwick	Grand St., cor. Graham Ave.	Jere. E. Brown	....	3,978,110	4	199,755	10 A. M. to 3 P. M.; Monday, 4 to 7 P. M. also.
City	4th & Flatbush Aves.	R. Rushmore	7,240	1,974,856	4	94,110	9 A. M. to 3 P. M.; Monday, 6 to 8 P. M. also.
College Point.	5th St. & 2d Av.	Fred. W. Grell	2,749	1,106,414	4	87,253	10 A. M. to 3 P. M.; Sat., 10 A. M. to 12 noon; Wed. & Sat., 6 to 8 P. M.
Dime ‼	De Kalb Ave. & Fulton St.	J. L. Marcellus	70,000	3 ,000,000	4	2,250,000	9 A. M. to 3 P. M.; Monday, 5 to 7 P. M. also.
Dime of Williamsburg.	52 Broadway	W. P. Sturgis	12,500	6,803,181	4	347,670	10 A. M. to 3 P. M.; Monday, 5 to 7 P. M. also.
E. Brooklyn	643 Myrtle Ave.	Thos. J. Atkins	14,608	6,083,488	4	418,784	9 A. M. to 3 P. M.; Monday 7 to 9 P. M. also.
East. District	Broadway and Gates Ave.	Lewis E. Meeker	13,729	3,029,945	4	107,272	10 A. M. to 3 P. M.; Mon. & Sat., 6 to 8 P. M. also.
E. New York	Atlantic and Penna. Aves.	Fred. Middendorf	7,000	2,300,000	4	230,000	9 A. M. to 3 P. M.; Monday, 6 to 8 P. M. also.
German	Broadway and Boerum St.	Charles Naeher	31,397	11,980,756	4	689,138	10 A. M. to 3 P. M.; Monday, 5 to 8 P. M. also.
Germania	375 Fulton St. †	Chas. A. Schieren	15,383	7,816,155	4	500,100	9 A. M. to 3 P. M.; Monday, 5 to 7 P. M. also.
Greater New York.	498 Fifth Ave.	C. J. Obermayer	10,242	1,761,137	4	41,716	9 A. M. to 3 P. M.; Monday, 5 to 7 P. M. also.
Greenpoint	845 Manhattan Ave.	Timothy Perry	14,500	5,600,000	4	600,000	9 A. M. to 2 P. M.; Monday 6 to 8 P. M. also.
Hamburg	250 Bleecker St.	James Moffett	2,050	375,000	4	....	9 A. M. to 3 P. M. Mon. 8 P. M.
Jamaica	Jamaica	Wm. A. Warnock.	8,155	3,672,484	4	275,467	9 A. M. to 3 P. M.
Kings County	Broadway and Bedford Ave.	Hubert G. Taylor.	16,000	11,755,600	4	675,141	9 A. M. to 3 P. M.; Monday, 4 to 7 P. M. also.
L. I. City	21 Jackson Ave.	W. J. Burnett	15,500	4,050,000	4	415,000	9 A. M. to 3 P. M.; Monday 5 to 8 P. M. also.
Queens Co.	Flushing	L. M. Franklin	5,944	2,042,001	4	90,880	10 A. M to 3 P. M. ‡
S. Brooklyn.	Atlantic Ave. and Clinton St.	Wm. J. Coombs	....	18,691,567	4	2,084,697	9 A. M. to 3 P. M.; Monday 6 to 8 P. M. also.
Williamsb'rg	B'way & Driggs	Ezra B. Tuttle	99,000	51,500,000	4	7,000,000	10 A. M. to 3 P. M.

* Subject to change. † 354 Adams Street. ‡ Thursday, 7 to 8 P. M.

Safe Deposit Companies in Brooklyn and Queens.

Brooklyn City, Montague and Clinton Streets.
Brooklyn Warehouse and Storage Company, 333 Schermerhorn Street.
Eagle Warehouse and Storage Company, 28 Fulton Street.
Franklin, 166 Montague Street.
Long Island, Fulton and Clinton Streets.
Long Island Storage and Safe Deposit, Nostrand and Gates Aves.
Manufacturers', 84 Broadway.
Pioneer, 41 Flatbush Avenue.

Trust Companies in New York City.

Name.	Location.	Capital.	Surplus & Undiv. Profits.	President.	Secretary.
Astor	Fifth Ave. & 36th St.	$1,250,000	$366,767	E. C. Converse	G. W. Pancoast.
Bankers'	7 Wall St.	1,000,000	1,180,000	E. C. Converse	B. Strong, Jr.
Bowling Green	26 Broadway	1,000,000	2,756,472	Edwin Gould	W. M. Laws.
Broadway	756 Broadway	700,000	336,859	H. M. Belding, Jr.	J. W. H. Bergen.
Carnegie	115 Broadway	1,500,000	750,000	C. C. Dickinson	R. L. Smith.
Central	54 Wall St.	1,000,000	15,338,890	J. N. Wallace	Geo. Bertine.
Columbia	135 Broadway	1,000,000	1,250,000	Willard V. King	L. W. Wiggin.
Commercial	Broadway & 41st St.	500,000	285,335	R. R. Moore	A. Higgins.
Commonwealth	27 Pine St.	250,000	258,434	P. R. Bomeisler	L. A. Rapelyea.
Empire	42 Broadway‡‡	1,000,000	1,000,000	L. W. Baldwin	H. M. Gough.
Equitable	15 Nassau St.	3,000,000	10,432,013	A. W. Krech	F. W. Fulle.
Farmers' Loan & Trust Co.	22 William St., 475 Fifth Ave.	1,000,000	6,276,000	E. S. Marston	A. V. Heely.
Fidelity	Chamb's St. & B'way	750,000	878,511	S. S. Conover	A. H. Mars.
Fifth Avenue	514 Fifth Ave.	1,000,000	1,574,016	Levi P. Morton	James M. Pratt.
Franklin	140 Broadway (*a*)	(See	Brooklyn	table below.)	
Fulton	30 Nassau St. (*q*)	500,000	765,000	H. C. Swords	H. W. Reighley.
Guaranty	28 Nassau St.	2,000,000	7,127,209	....	W. C. Edwards (T)
Guardian	170 Broadway	500,000	512,000	F. W. Woolworth	L. C. Haynes.
Hudson	147 West 42d St.	500,000	640,000	E. R. Chapman	R. A. Purdy.
Italian-American	520 Broadway	500,000	45,000	E. Gerli	A. Baur.
Knickerbocker	358 Fifth Ave.	1,200,000	1,000,125	Charles H. Keep.	Harris R. Dunn.
Lawyers' Title Ins. & Trust Co.	160 Broadway	4,000,000	5,837,000	E. W. Coggeshall.	W. N. Vail.
Lincoln	Madison Square (*a*)	750,000	423,894	Alex. S. Webb, Jr.	Joseph Z. Bray.
Manhattan	Wall & Nassau St.	1,000,000	2,110,436	J. I. Waterbury	G. S. Thomson (T)
Mercantile	120 Broadway	2,000,000	7,012,477	W. C. Poillon, V. P.	H. B. Thorne (T.)
Metropolitan	49 Wall St.	2,000,000	7,430,000	Brayton Ives	G. N. Hartmann.
Morton	38 Nassau St.	2,000,000	7,452,304	Levi P. Morton	H. M. Francis.
Mutual	Portchester	300,000	100,407	Geo. R. Read	Dean Smith.
*Mutual Alliance	66 Beaver St.	700,000	345,117	James H. Parker.	W. F. H. Koelsch.
N. Y. Life Insurance Trust Co.	52 Wall St.	1,000,000	3,859,436	Walter Kerr, V. P.	G. M. Corning.
New York	26 Broad St.	3,000,000	10,461,078	O. T. Bannard	W. E. Drummond (Treas.)
Standard	25 Broad St.	1,000,000	1,200,000	Wm. C. Lane	W. C. Cox.
Title Guarantee & Trust Co.	176 Broadway	4,375,000	8,377,774	C. H. Kelsey	J. W. Cleveland.
Trust Company of America	37 Wall St. §	2,000,000	6,000,000	O. Thorne	....
Union	80 Broadway ††	1,000,000	7,716,574	J. W. Castles	J. V. B. Thayer.
U. S. Mortgage & Trust Co.	55 Cedar St. §§	2,000,000	4,222,238	A. Turnbull (Act.)	C. Brewer.
United States	45 Wall St.	2,000,000	13,121,128	E. W. Sheldon	H. E. Ahern.
† Van Norden	Fifth Ave. & 60th St.	1,000,000	1,622,000	W. M. Van Norden	W. W. Robinson.
Washington	253 Broadway	500,000	1,200,000	D. M. Morrison	M. S. Lott.
Windsor	571 Fifth Ave.**	1,000,000	319,740	J. A. Young	A. G. Norrie.

* Also at 266 Grand Street and Lenox Avenue and 116th Street. † Branch at 320 Grand Street. ‡ Also 184 Montague Street, Brooklyn. § Branch 222 Broadway. †† Also Fifth Avenue and Thirty-eighth Street. ** 65 Cedar Street. ‡‡ Also 242 East Houston Street, 487 Fifth Avenue. §§ Also 125th Street and Eighth Avenue. (*a*) Also Broadway and Lispenard Street and Broadway and Seventy-second Street. (*q*) Report of January 1, 1908. (T) Treasurer.

BROOKLYN TRUST COMPANIES.

Name.	Location.	Capital.	Surplus & Undiv. Profits.	President.	Secretary.
‡ Brooklyn	177 Montague St.	$1,000,000	2,033,519	Theo. F. Miller	S. W. Husted.
* Citizens'	B'way & Sumner Ave.	500,000	165,000	N. S. Jonas	J. H. Conroy.
Flatbush	839 Flatbush Ave.	300,000	217,025	J. Z. Lott	E. D. Fisher.
Franklin	164 Montague St. ††	1,500,000	1,513,455	Arthur K. Wood.	C. W. Ludlum.
Hamilton (*q*)	191 Montague St.	500,000	1,000,000	......	Geo. Hadden.
Home	184 Montague St.	750,000	300,000	F. E. Gunnison	W. K. Swartz.
Lafayette	(In liquidation.)				
Kings County (*q*)	342 Fulton St.	500,000	1,665,211	J. D. Fairchild	Thos. Blake.
L. I. Loan & Trust Co.	44 Court St.	1,000,000	1,800,000	Edw. Merritt	F. T. Aldridge.
** Nassau	B'way & Bedford Ave.	600,000	422,735	A. T. Sullivan	H. F. Burns.
† Peoples'	181 Montague St.	1,000,000	1,425,000	C. A. Boody	C. L. Schenck.
§ Title Guarantee & Trust Co.	196 Montague St.	(See table	above.)		
Williamsburg	B'way & Kent Ave.	700,000	440,000	Brayton Ives	F. H. Hurdman.

* Also 198 Montague Street. † Branches at Bedford Avenue and Halsey Street and Clinton and Myrtle Avenues. ‡ Branches at 1205 Fulton Street; Manhattan Branch, 90 Broadway. ** Branch, 356 Fulton Street. § Branches at 175 Remsen Street, 350 Fulton Street, Jamaica, L. I., and 67 Jackson Avenue, Long Island City. †† Also 140 Broadway, Manhattan. (*q*) Report of January 1, 1908.

Asylums and Homes in Manhattan and Bronx.

Association for Relief of Respectable Aged Indigent Females, 891 Amsterdam Ave.
Babies' Shelter, Church Holy Communion, Reception House, 49 W. 20th St.
Baptist Home for Aged, E. 68th St. and Park Ave.
Bide-a-Wee Home (for animals), 36 Lexington Ave.
Blind Asylum, Blackwell's Island.
Bloomingdale Insane Asylum, White Plains, N. Y. Office, 7 W. 15th St.
Brace Farm School for Boys, 105 E. 22d St.
Brace Memorial Lodging House, 14 New Chambers St.
Brookside Farm Home for Wives and Children of Prisoners, 120 Bible House.
Catholic Protectory, Van Nest Station, office 415 Broome St.
Chapin Home for the Aged and Infirm, 151 E. 66th St.
Charity Organization Society, 105 E. 22d St.
Chebra Hachnosath Orchim. See Hebrew Sheltering House and Home for Aged.
Children's Aid Society, executive office, 105 E. 22d St.
Children's Temporary Home, 442 W. 23d St.
Christian Home for Girls, 217 E. 62d St.
Christian League Women's Industrial Home, 5 E. 12th St.
Christian Workers, 129 E. 10th St.
Christie St. House, 129 Christie St.
Christliches Madchenheim, 217 E. 62d St.
Church of God Missionary Home, 2450 Grand Ave.
Colored Orphan Asylum, W. 261st St., near Riverdale Ave.
Co-operative Home, 444 W. 23d. St.
Crittenton, Florence, Mission, 21 Bleecker St.
Darrach Home for Crippled Children, 118 W. 104th St.
Day School and Home for Crippled Children, 2111 Madison Ave.
Deaconess Home (Baptist), 312 W. 54th St.
Dominican Convent Our Lady of Rosary (Home for Destitute Children), 329 E. 63d St.
Edgewater Creche, C. D. Kellogg, Treas., 105 E. 22d St.
Elizabeth Home for Girls, 307 E. 12th St.
Emergency Shelter for Women with Children, 311 E. 12th St.
Eva Home, 153 E. 62d St.
Five Points House of Industry, 155 Worth St.
Five Points Mission, 63 Park St.
Florence Home for Working Girls, 140 E. 14th St.
Foundling Asylum, 175 E. 68th St., near 3d Ave.
Free Home for Young Girls, 23 E. 11th St.
French Evangelical Home for Young Women, 341 W. 30th St.
German Lutheran Emigrant Home, 4 State St.
German Odd Fellows' Home and Orphan Asylum, Havemeyer Ave., near Watson, Unionport.
Golden Hour Home, 241 E. 19th St.
Grace Church Hospital, 414 E. 14th St.
Heartsease Home for Friendless Girls, 413 E. 51st St
Hebrew Benevolent and Orphan Asylum, Amsterdam Ave., near W. 137th St.
Hebrew Infant Asylum, 907 Eagle Ave.
Hebrew Sheltering Guardian Orphan Asylum, Broadway and W. 150th St., 507 W. 155th St.
Hebrew Sheltering House and Home for Aged, 229 E. Broadway.
Hirsch, Clara de, Home for Working Girls, 225 E. 63d St.
Home for Aged and Infirm, Blackwell's Island.
Home for Aged and Infirm Hebrews, 121 W. 105th St.
Home for Convalescents, 433 E. 118th St.
Home for Crippled and Incurable Children, Broadway, cor. W. 155th St.
Home for Destitute Crippled Children, 141 W. 61st St.
Home for Friendless Children, 936 Woodycrest Ave.
Home for Homeless Boys, Havemeyer Ave., cor. Powell St.
Home for Incurables, 3d Ave., cor. E. 182d St.
Home for Italian Immigrants, 8 Charlton St.
Home for Old Men and Aged Couples, 1060 Amsterdam Ave.
Home for Protestant Immigrant Girls, 9 State St.
Home for Relief of Destitute Blind, 896 Amsterdam Ave.
Home for the Aged, 213 E. 70th St. and 135 W. 106th St.
Home for Unemployed Young Women, 116 E. 106th St.
Home for Young Women, 49 W. 9th St. Branches at 308 2d Ave., 153 E. 62d St.
Home of the Daughters of Jacob, 302 E. Broadway.
Hopper, Isaac T., Home, 110 2d Ave.
House of Calvary (Incurable Cancer, Females), 5 Perry St.
House of Mercy (Protestant Episcopal), W. 214th St., cor. Bolton Rd.
House of Nazareth, W. 236th St., near Spuyten Duyvil.
House of Refuge, Randall's Island.
House of Rest for Consumptives, Inwood-on-the-Hudson, office, 59 E. 59th St.
House of the Good Shepherd, foot of E. 90th St.
House of the Holy Comforter for Incurables, foot W. 139th St.
House of the Holy Family, 136 2d Ave.
Howard Mission and Home for Little Wanderers, 225 E. 11th St.
Huguenot Home of French Church Du St. Esprit, 237 W. 24th St.
Hungarian Relief Society, 3 State St.
Industrial Christian Alliance, 170 Bleecker St.
Industrial Home No. 1, 533 W. 48th St.
Infant Asylum, Amsterdam Ave., cor. 61st St.
Insane Asylum, Ward's Isl'd, office foot E. 116th St.
Institution for the Blind, 9th Ave. and 34th St.
Institution of Mercy, 1075 Madison Ave.
Isabella Heimath, Amsterdam Ave. and W. 190th St
Italian Benevolent Institute, 165 W. Houston St.
Jeanne d'Arc Home for French Girls, 251 W. 24th St.
Jennie Clarkson Home for Children (Valhalla, N. Y.), office 264 Lenox Ave.
Juvenile Asylum, office, 106 W. 27th St.
Leake and Watts' Orphan House, Hawthorne Ave., near City Line.
Leo House for German Catholic Immigrants, 6 State St.
Lincoln Hospital and Home, E. 141st St., cor. Concord Ave.
Loebsolomon & Betty Memorial Home for Convalescents, 356 2d Ave.
Lutheran Pilgrim House, 8 State St.
McAuley's Water St. Mission, 316 Water St.
Margaret Louisa Home of Young Women's Christian Association, 14 E. 16th St.
Messiah Home for Children, Aqueduct Ave. and W. Tremont Ave.
Methodist Episcopal Home, Amsterdam Ave., cor. 92d St.
Midnight Mission and St. Michael's Home, office, 289 4th Ave.
Mission of Our Lady of the Rosary for the Protection of Irish Immigrant Girls, 7 State St.
Mission of the Immaculate Virgin, 375 Lafayette St.
Montefiore Home Broadway and W. 138th St.
National Home for Disabled Volunteer Soldiers, office, 346 Broadway.
National Sunshine Settlement Home, 352 W. 40th St.
Newsboys' Lodging House, 14 New Chambers St.
New York—Asylums and Homes bearing prefix "New York" will be, as a rule, found in this list minus the prefix.
New York Orphan Asylum, Hastings, office 105 E. 22d St.
Orphan Asylum and Home of P. E. Church, cor. Convent Ave. and W. 135th St.
Orphan Home and Asylum of Protestant Episcopal Church, office, 105 E. 22d St.
Our Lady of Grace Hospital and Home for Destitute Mothers, 221 E. 79th St.
Peabody Home for Aged and Indigent Women, 2064 Boston Rd.

ASYLUMS AND HOMES IN MANHATTAN AND BRONX—*Continued.*

Presbyterian Home for Aged Women, 49 E. 73d St.
Protestant Half-Orphan Asylum, 104th St. and Manhattan Ave.
Reformatory for Misdemeanants, Hart's Island.
Rescue Home, 316 E. 15th St.
Robertson, Gilbert A., Home, Scarsdale, N. Y. Secretary, 59 Wall St.
Roman Catholic Orphan Asylum, Sedgwick Ave., cor. Kingsbridge Rd., office, 24 E. 52d St.
Sacred Heart Orphan Asylum, Ft. Washington Ave., cor. W. 190th St.
Sailors' Home, 1 State St.
Sailors' Snug Harbor, S. I., office 31 Nassau St.
St. Agatha's Home for Children, 175 E. 68th St.
St. Ann's Home for Children, 504 E. 90th St.
St. Barnabas's House, 304 Mulberry St.
St. Bartholomew's Girls' Home, 136 E. 47th St.
St. Benedict's Home for Destitute Colored Children, 375 Lafayette St.
St. Elizabeth's Industrial School (female deaf mutes), 237 E. 14th St.
St. Francis's Home for Aged, 609 5th St.
St. Helena's, 311 E. 4th St.
St. John Baptist House, 233 E. 17th St.
St. John's Guild, office 501 5th Ave.
St. Joseph's Home for the Aged, 209 W. 15th St.
St. Joseph's Home for Destitute Children, House of Reception, 12 W. 129th St.
St. Joseph's Home for Poles, 117 Broad St.
St. Joseph's Industrial Home, 65 E. 81st St.
St. Joseph's Night Shelter for Homeless Women, 144 W. 15th St.
St. Joseph's Orphan Asylum, 89th St., cor. Ave. A; Branch, New Road, Throgs Neck.
St. Luke's Home for Aged Women, 2914 Broadway.
St. Mary's Home for Protection and Comfort of Respectable Young Women While Seeking Employment, 143 W. 14th St.
St. Philip's Home for Industrious Catholic Boys, 417 Broome St.
St. Philip's Parish Home, 1119 Boston Rd.
St. Raphael's Home, 10 Charlton St.
St. Rose's Free Home for Incurable Cancer, 426 Cherry St.
St. Saviour's Sanitarium, W. 214th St., cor. Bolton Rd.
St. Vincent de Paul's Orphan Asylum, 215 W. 39th St.
St. Zita's Home for Friendless Women, 125 E. 52d St.
Salvation Army Rescue Home, 316 E. 15th St.; Industrial Home, 229 E. 120th St.
Samaritan Home for the Aged, 414 W. 22d St.
Sanitarium for Hebrew Children, office, 356 2d Ave.
Scandinavian Immigrant Home, 24 Greenwich St.
Scandinavian Mission Home, 252 E. 48th St.
Scandinavian Sailors' Home, 6 Catharine Slip.
Sevilla Home for Children, Lafayette Ave., cor. Barretto.
Shelter for Respeetable Girls, 212 E. 46th St.
Sheltering Arms, 504 W. 129th St.
Sick Children's Mission, 287 E. Broadway, branch of Children's Aid Society.
Society for Prevention of Cruelty to Children, 297 4th Ave.
Strachan, Margaret, Home, 103 W. 27th St.
Swedish Epworth Home, 588 Lexington Ave.
Swedish Lutheran Immigrant Home, 5 Water St.
Swiss Home, 35 W. 67th St.
Temporary Home for Evicted and Homeless Women, 311 E. 12th St.
Thecla Orphanage, Palisades, N. Y. Office, 227 Fulton St.
Training Home for Christian Workers, 127 E. 10th St.
Trinity Chapel Home for Aged Women, 221 W. 24th St.
Trinity Mission House, 211 Fulton St.
Washington Sq. Home for Friendless Girls, 9 W. 8th St.
Webb's Academy and Home for Shipbuilders, Sedgwick Ave., cor. Academy St.
West-Side Boys' Lodging House, 225 W. 35th St.
White Rose Home for Working Girls, 217 E. 86th St.
Woman's Shelter, 243 Bowery.

Commerce of the Port of New York.

IMPORTS AND EXPORTS OF MERCHANDISE AND BULLION.

THE following compilation gives the foreign trade movement of the port for twenty calendar years, ending with 1907. It shows the foreign imports, domestic exports and foreign exports of the Port of New York, as well as the special movement in the form reported from year to year by the Secretary of the Chamber of Commerce:

VALUE OF FOREIGN IMPORTS INTO THE PORT OF NEW YORK FOR THE LAST TWENTY YEARS, ENDED DECEMBER 31.

Years	Dutiable.	Free Goods.	Specie and Bullion.	Total Foreign Imports.
1888..	$301,008,039	$154,865,981	$8,206,303	$464,080,323
1889..	329 210,894	163,920,087	7,948,166	500,979,147
1890..	349,210,717	193,155,771	20,369,499	562,735,987
1891..	254,102,154	268,329,418	35,154,540	557,586,112
1892..	254 360,354	317,939,925	11,407,559	583,707,838
1893..	236,490,931	291,999,022	65,827,758	594,317,711
1894..	198,646,169	239,767,676	20,671,236	459,085,081
1895..	284,036,654	232,250,120	32,856,122	549,142,896
1896..	243,235,760	197,236,035	90,733,968	531,205,763
1897..	248,297,819	218,238,881	28,079,302	494,616,002
1898..	241,921,371	177,770,748	110,580,905	530,273,024
1899..	294,505,183	224,290,748	31,191,223	549,987,154
1900..	304,855,071	221,251,710	29,039,486	555,146,267
1901..	319,912,752	235,107,825	19,367,785	574,388,362
1902..	348,747,880	242,496,808	10,842,054	602,086,742
1903..	339,052,370	259,129,840	29,652,689	627,834,899
1904..	343,684,492	286,168,372	14,101,354	643,954,218
1905..	409,767,035	304,166,382	22,872,970	736,806,380
1906..	456,240,684	333,366,200	99,389,034	888,995,918
1907..	480,413,136	349,331,491	108,913,641	938,658,268

VALUE OF EXPORTS FROM THE PORT OF NEW YORK TO FOREIGN PORTS FOR THE LAST TWENTY YEARS, ENDED DECEMBER 31.

Years	Domestic Exports.	Foreign Exports.	Specie and Bullion.	Total Exports.
1888..	$290,779,161	$9,111,569	$49,565,852	$349,456,582
1889..	336,785,463	9,074,152	71,685,395	417,545,010
1890..	339,458,578	8,184,783	41,646,121	389,289,482
1891..	378,392,937	8,772,099	95,916,277	483,081,313
1892..	368,559,145	9,164,829	93,204,967	470,928,941
1893..	348,097,228	9,900,460	06,397,995	464,395,683
1894..	332,621,123	7,958,095	129,003,594	469,582,812
1895..	323,402,003	8,948,318	139,950,607	472,300,928
1896..	365,570,813	9,450,831	104,036,418	479,058,062
1897..	396,388,942	8,362,182	177,531,109	482,282,233
1898..	460,875,299	9,027,937	58,343,879	528,247,115
1899..	467,554,122	9,059,156	84,729,255	561,342,533
1900..	526 153,270	12,090,402	02,933,991	641,177,663
1901..	498,413,605	12,544,419	100,563,364	611,521,388
1902..	479,634,582	12,096,879	165,411,581	557,143,042
1903..	503,495,265	12,532,984	65,860,849	581,889,098
1904..	490,914,304	13,318,853	44,017,993	648,251,150
1905..	545,708,317	13,980,386	177,922,034	637,610,737
1906..	611,082,425	11,389 037	56,262,355	678,733,817
1907..	670,725,511	12,400,018	87,380,626	770,506,155

Churches in Manhattan and Bronx.

WITH NAMES OF PASTORS.

BAPTIST.

Baptist Ministers' Conference meets every Monday at 11 A. M., at East 31st St., cor. Madison Ave.

Abyssinian, 244 W. 40th St. Chas. S. Morris.
Alexander Ave., cor. E. 141st St. F. W. Blakeslee.
Amity, W. 54th St., bet. 8th and 9th Aves. Leighton Williams.
Ascension, 160th St., bet. Morris and 4th Aves. Isaac W. Goodhue.
Baptist Temple, 11 W. 116th St. D. W. Wisher.
Calvary, W. 57th St., bet. 6th and 7th Aves. R. S. MacArthur; Branch at 67th St., near Amsterdam Ave.
Central, W. 42d St., near 8th Ave. F. M. Goodchild.
Central Park, E. 83d St., bet. 2d and 3d Aves. S. J. Ford.
Collegiate, Amsterdam Ave., cor. W. 92d St.
Creston Ave., E. 189th St., cor. Creston Ave. B. F. Blackwell.
Day Star, 501 W. 157th St.
Eagle Ave., Eagle Ave., near 162d St. L. Rabe.
Ebenezer, 170 E. 105th St. W. A. Lindsay.
Ebenezer (Primitive), 173 8th Ave. John McConnell.
Emanuel, 47 Suffolk St.
Emmanuel, White Plains Rd., Williamsbridge. R. J. Davies.
Fifth Ave., 6 W. 46th St. Chas. F. Aked. Armitage Chapel, 10th Av., cor. W. 50th St. H. W. Hillier.
First, W. 79th St., cor. Broadway. I. M. Haldeman.
First German, 336 E. 14th St. F. A. Licht.
First German, 220 E. 118th St. Frederick Niebuhr.
First Italian, cor. Oliver and Henry Sts. J. Petrelli.
First Swedish, E. 55th St., bet. 3d and Lexington Aves. Emil Froberg.
Galilee, 2475 3d Ave. P. H. Lee.
Grace, 1015 E. 156th St. A. T. Brooks.
Harlem, 215 E. 123d St. Adam Chambers.
Hope, cor. 104th St. and Broadway. R. Hartley.
Immanuel (German), 411 E. 75th St. J. H. Pastoret.
Madison Ave., cor. Madison Ave. and E. 31st St.
Mariner's Temple, 12 Oliver St. G. Dowkontt.
Memorial, Washington Sq. S., cor. Thompson St. Edward Judson.
Mercy Seat, 45 W. 134th St.
Mount Gilead, 307 E. 122d St. L. B. Twisby.
Mount Morris, 5th Ave., near W. 126th St. J. H. Randall.
Mount Olivet, 161 W. 53d St. M. W. Gilbert.
Mount Pleasant, E. 180th St. near Vyse Ave. W. C. Hawes.
North, 234 W. 11th St. E. T. Sanford.
Pilgrim, Boston Road, near Vyse Ave. C. Pittman.
Riverside, 92d St., cor. Amsterdam Ave. A. L. Moore.
Second Ave., 166 2d Ave. R. V. Pierce.
Second German, 407 W. 43d St. E. Umbach.
Sharon, 173 E. 99th St. E. Dromgoole.
Shiloh, 44 Manhattan. E. W. Wainwright.
Sixteenth St., 257 W. 16th St. W. J. Noble.
St. Paul, 352 W. 35th St. H. A. Booker.
Tabernacle, Brook Ave., near E. 165th St. Thos. M. Curry.
Third German, 1127 Fulton Ave. R. Hoefflin
Timothy, 108 W. 30th St. R. R. Wilson.
Tremont, Tremont Ave., cor. Ryer. K. C. MacArthur.
Trinity, E. 224th St., near Barnes Ave. J. W. Brooks.
Union, 204 W. 63d St. G. H. Sims.
Washington Heights, 145th St. and Convent Ave. R. P. Johnson.
West 33d St., 327 W. 33d St. Oscar Haywood.
Zion, 99 6th Av. E. E. Jackson.

CONGREGATIONAL.

Bedford Park, Bainbridge Ave., cor. E. 201st St. A. T. Tamblyn.
Bethany, 10th Ave., near 35th St. W. F. Ottarson.
Broadway Tabernacle, Broadway and 56th St. C. E. Jefferson.
Camp Memorial, 141 Chrystie St. William James.
Christ, E. 175th St., cor. Topping St. H. M. Brown.
Claremont Park, Webster Ave., cor. 167th St., J. C. Whiting.
First of Morrisania, E. 166th St. and Forest Ave. A. Reoch.
Longwood Ave., Leggett Ave., cor. Beck. J. W. Roberts.
Manhattan, W. 76th St. and Broadway. H. A. Stimson.
North New York, E. 143d St., near Willis Ave. W. H. Kephart.
Pilgrim, Madison Ave., cor. 121st St. Fred'k Lynch
Smyrna (Welsh), 206 E. 11th St.
Swedish Evang. Bethesda, 138 E. 50th St. K. F. Ohlson.
Swedish Evang. Immanuel, 308 W. 139th St.
Trinity, Washington Ave., corner E. 176th St. William Milton Hess.

DISCIPLES OF CHRIST.

First, 323 W. 56th St.
Lenox Ave. Union, 119th St., near Lenox Ave. J. P. Lichtenberger.
Second, E. 169th St., near Franklin Ave. S. T. Willis.

EVANGELICAL.

Dingeldein Memorial (German), 429 E. 77th St. D. Schnebel.
Finnish, 29 E. 135th St. G. Blomgren.
First Church of the Evangelical Association, 214 W. 35th St. H. Heine.
German Evangelical Zion, 171 W. 140th St. C. Enders.
Second Church of the Evangelical Association, 424 W. 55th St. J. G. Scharf.
St. Paul's, 159 E. 112th St. H. Rexroth.

FRIENDS.

East 15th St., cor. Rutherford Pl.
Twentieth St., 144 E. 20th St.

GREEK CATHOLIC.

St. George, 332 E. 20th St. N. Pidhorecki.
St. Peter's Chapel (Syrian), Church St., cor. Barclay. A. Bachewate.

JEWISH.

Adereth El, 135 E. 29th St.
Agudath Jeshorim, 115 E. 86th St. D. Davidson.
Ahawath Chesed, 652 Lexington Ave. I. S. Moses.
Ansche Chesed, 7th Ave. and 114th St., Gustav N. Hausmann.
Ansche Sfard, 52 Cannon St.
Ateris Zewi, E. 121st St., near 1st Ave. F. Light.
Atereth Israel, 323 E. 82d St. M. Krauskopf.
Beth-El, 5th Ave., cor. E. 76th St. S. Schulman.
Beth Hamedrash Hagodol, 64 Norfolk St. Simon Jaffe.
Beth Hamedrash Shaarei Torah, 80 Forsyth St.
Beth Israel Bikur Cholim, 72d St. and Lexington Ave. Aaron Eiseman.
Beth Tefila, E. 107th St. and Lexington Ave. S. Distillator.
B'nai Israel, 225 E. 79th St. M. Previn.
B'nai Jeshurun, 65th St. and Madison Ave. Newman Cowen, Pres.
First Galizo Duckler Mogen Abraham, 87 Attorney St.
First Hungarian Cong. Oheb Zedek, 172 Norfolk St. P. Klein.
First Roumanian Am. Congregation, 91 Rivington St.
Kahal Adath Jeshurun, 14 Eldridge St. J. Fried.
Kehilath Jeshurun, 117 E. 85th St. M. S. Margolies.
Kol Israel Ansche Poland, 22 Forsyth St.

CHURCHES IN MANHATTAN AND BRONX—*Continued.*

JEWISH—Continued.

Machzika Torah Anshar Sineer, 34 Montgomery St.
Nachlath Zevl, 59 E. 109th St. H. Kamenetzky.
Rodoph Sholom, 63d St. and Lexington Ave. R. Grossman.
Shaare Berocho, E. 57th St., near 1st Ave. G. Hirsch.
Shaarai Tephilla, W. 82d St., near Amsterdam Ave. F. de Sola Mendes.
Shaari Zedek, 38 Henry St. H. S. Shoher.
Shearith B'nai Israel, 22 E. 113th St. Jacob Mandel.
Shearith Israel, 100 Central Park West, cor. 70th St. H. P. Mendes
Temple Emanu-El, 5th Ave. and 43d St. J. Silverman.
Temple Israel, Lenox Ave., cor. 120th St. M. H. Harris.
Tiffereth Israel, 126 Allen St. Joseph Lotz.
Zichron Ephraim, 67th St., near Lexington Ave. B. Drachman.

LUTHERAN.

Lutheran Synod, George U. Wenner, President, 319 East 19th Street.

Advent, Broadway and 93d St. W. M. Horn.
Ascension, 311 E. Kingsbridge Road.
Atonement, Edgecombe Ave. and 140th St. F. H. Knubel.
Bethany, 14 Teasdale Pl. W. Freas, Jr.
Bethlehem, 239 E. 62d St. A. G. Steup.
Christ, 406 E. 19th St. G. U. Wenner.
Christ, 552 W. 50th St. Carl R. Stolz.
Concordia, 4 Oak Ter., cor. Brook Av. H. Pottberg.
Emanuel, Brown Pl., cor. E. 137th St. A. A. King.
Emigrant House Chapel, 4 State St. G. Doering.
Epiphany, 72 E. 128th St. F. B. Clausen.
Grace, 123 W. 71st St. J. A. Weyl.
Grace, 2924 Valentine Ave. A. Koerber.
Gustavus Adolphus, 151 E. 22d St. M. Stolpe.
Harlem Swedish, 3 E. 118th St. C. E. Hoffsten.
Holy Trinity, Central Park West and W. 65th St. Chas. J. Smith.
Holy Trinity, 1038 Prospect Ave. John Schiller.
Immanuel, 215 E. 83d St. C. J. Renz.
Immanuel, 88th St., cor. Lexington Ave. W. F. Schoenfeld.
Messiah, 314 E. 141st St. G. S. Ohlsund.
Our Saviour, 179th St. and Audubon Ave. W. H. Feldmann.
Our Saviour (Norwegian), 237 E. 123d St. K. Kvamme.
Redeemer, 424 W. 44th St. F. C. G. Schumm.
Reformation, 1335 Bristow St. J. G. M. Ketner.
St. James's, Madison Ave., cor. E. 73d St. J. B. Remensnyder.
St. John's, 81 Christopher St. John J. Young.
St. John's, 217 E. 119th St. H. C. Steup.
St. John's, Fulton Ave. and 170th St. H. Beiderbecke.
St. Luke's, Adams St. and Van Nest. Ave. W. Eickmann.
St. Luke's, 233 W. 42d St. W. F. Koepchen.
St. Mark's, 323 6th St. G. C. F. Haas.
St. Matthew's, 145th St, and Convent Ave. Martin Walker.
St. Matthew's, 354 Broome St. Otto Sieker.
St. Matthew's, E. 156th St., near Courtlandt Ave. W. T. Junge.
St. Paul's, East 178th St., cor. Lafontaine Ave. Karl Kretzmann.
St. Paul's, 313 W. 22d St. Leo Koenig.
St. Paul's, 149 W. 123d St. F. H. Bosch.
St. Paul's, 794 E. 156th St. G. H. Tappert.
St. Peter's, E. 219th St., near White Plains Rd. O. Rappolt.
St. Peter's, Lexington Ave. and 54th St. A. B. Moldenke.
St. Peter's, Alexander Ave. and 141st St. H. A. Steininger.
St. Stephen's, Union-Ave., near 165th St. Paul Roesener.

LUTHERAN—Continued.

St. Thomas (English), 1755 Clay Ave. F. J. Baum.
Trinity, 139 Ave. B. Otto Graesser.
Trinity (Danish) 133 E. 93d St. A. V. Andersen.
Trinity, 164 W. 100th St., near Amsterdam Ave. E. Brennecke.
Washington Heights, W. 153d St., near Broadway. E. A. Tappert.
Zion, 339 E. 84th St. H. Hebler.

METHODIST EPISCOPAL.

Denominational Headquarters, 150 5th Ave.

Battery Swedish, 341 W. 24th St., near 9th Ave. O. W. Johnson.
Bedford St., 28 Morton St. W. P. George.
Beekman Hill, 319 E. 50th St. J. J. Blythe.
Blinn Memorial (German), 103d St. and Lexington Ave. Carl Reuss.
Calvary, 129th St. and 7th Ave. C. L. Goodell.
Centenary, 1074 Washington Ave and E. 166th St. Charles A. Holla.
Chelsea, 331 W. 30th St. A. M. Gay.
Church of the People, 63 Park St. F. J. Belcher.
Church of the Saviour, E. 111th St., cor. Lexington Ave. J. S. Stone.
Cornell Memorial, E. 76th St., near 2d Ave. James H. Lockwood, Jr.
Duane, 294 Hudson St. R. H. Travis.
East Side Parish, 9 2d Ave. J. R. Henry.
Eighteenth St., 307 W. 18th St. G. W. Downs.
Eleventh St. Chapel, 545 E. 11th St. E. L. Fox.
First German, 48 St. Mark's Place. Henry Heck.
Five Points Mission, 63 Park St. F. J. Belcher.
Fordham, Marion Ave., cor. Fordham Road. W. B. Tower.
Forty-fourth St., 461 W. 44th St. W. Ackroyd.
German, Elton Avenue, cor. E. 158th St. John Miller.
German (Second), 346 W. 40th St. J. G. Lutz.
Grace, White Plains Road. John H. Palmer.
Grace, 131 W. 104th St. C. H. Cookman.
Hadley Rescue Hall, 293 Bowery. John Callahan.
Hedding, 337 E. 17th St. A. S. Hagarty.
Jane St., 13 Jane St. Fields Hermance.
John St., 44 John St. J. W. Johnston.
Madison Ave., Madison Ave., cor. 60th St. W. MacMullen.
Metropolitan Temple, 58 7th Ave. J. W. Hill.
Morris Heights, Morris Heights Station. L. B. Longacre.
Mott Ave., Mott Ave., cor. E. 150th St. C. W. McPherson.
Mount Hope, Tremont Ave., cor. E. 177th St. C. W. Inglehart.
Olin, White Plains Ave., Williamsbridge. John Rippere.
Park Ave., Park Ave., cor. 86th St. D. W. B. Thompson.
Perry St., 132 Perry St. John Rowe.
Prospect Ave., Prospect Ave., cor. Macy Pl. W. M. Carr.
Rose Hill, 221 E. 27th St. F. J. Shackleton.
St. Andrew's, 126 W 76th St. G. C. Peck.
St James's, Madison Ave. and 126th St. A. MacRossie.
St. John's (German), Richardson Ave., Wakefield.
St. Mark's, W. 53d St. and 8th Ave. W. H. Brooks.
St. Paul's, 86th St. and West End Ave. G. P. Eckman.
St. Paul's (German), 308 E. 55th St. F. W Boese.
St. Stephen's, Marble Hill Ave., cor. W. 228th St. E. A. Lowther.
Second St., 276 2d St. W. C. Wilson.
Seventh St., 24 7th St. John R. Henry.
Sixty-first St., 229 E. 61st St. F. A. Scofield.
Swedish, Lexington Avenue, cor. E. 52d St. H. Young
Thirty-fifth St., 460 W. 35th St. T. S. Bond.
Thirty-seventh St., 225 E. 37th St. E. C. Hoag.
Tremont, Washington Ave., cor. E. 178th St. A. E. Barnett.

METHODIST EPISCOPAL—Continued.

Tremont (German), Bathgate Ave., near E. 176th St. H. Blesi.
Trinity, 323 E. 118th St. Charles H. Grubb.
Trinity, City Island Ave. Wm. T. Pray.
Twenty-fourth St., 359 W. 24th St. F. H. Carpenter.
Union, W. 48th St., near Broadway. J. Lewis Hartsock.
Washington Heights, Amsterdam Ave., cor. 153d St. J. E. Price.
Washington Sq., 137 W. 4th St. T. H. Baragwanath.
Westchester, West Farms Road. J. J. Snavely.
West Farms, 1004 E. Tremont Ave. J. J. Moffitt.
Willis Ave., cor. E. 141st St. F. B. Stockdale.
Woodlawn, E. 237th St., near Katonah Ave. M. P. Williams.

METHODIST EPISCOPAL (AFRICAN).

Bethel, 239 W. 25th St. R. C. Ransom.
Bishops Chapel, 60 W. 135th St. J. H. Accooe.
Little Zion, 236 E. 117th St. M. A. Bradley.
Metropolitan Union American, 230 E. 85th St. J. Fernandez.
Zion, 127 W. 89th St. J. H. McMullen.

MORAVIAN.

First (English), 154 Lexington Ave. M. W. Leibert.
Second, Wilkins Ave. and Jennings St. C. Hermstaedt.
Third, 224 W. 63d St. V. Flinn.

PRESBYTERIAN.

Denominational Headquarters, 156 5th Avenue.

(Rev. Jesse F. Forbes, Stated Clerk.)

Adams Memorial, 207 E. 30th St. J. F. Forbes.
Alexander Chapel, 7 King St. Hugh Pritchard.
Bedford Park, Bedford Park Boulevard, cor. Bainbridge Ave. B. O. Satterwhite.
Bethany, E. 137th St., near Willis Ave. F. E. Marsten.
Bohemian, 349 E. 74th St. Vincent Pisek.
Brick, 5th Ave., cor. 37th St. W. R. Richards.
Bronx (Bohemian) Washington Ave., near 170th St. V. P. Backoro.
Central, W. 57th St., bet. Broadway and 7th Ave. W. M. Smith.
Christ, 336 W. 36th St. J. M. Farr.
Church of the Puritans, 15 W. 130th St. C. J. Young.
Covenant, 310 E. 42d St. G. S. Webster.
East Harlem, 116th St., bet. 2d and 3d Aves. C. A. Evans.
Emmanuel Chapel, 735 6th St. J. C. Palmer.
Faith, 359 W. 48th St. R. R. White.
Fifth Ave., 5th Ave., cor. 55th St. J. R. Stevenson; Memorial Chapel, E. 62d St., near 1st Ave.
First, 54 5th Ave. Howard Duffield.
First, Ft. Schuyler Road, Throg's Neck. R. B. Mattice.
First, 225th St., Williamsbridge.
First Magyar, 233 E. 116th St. L. Lakasa.
First Union, 147 E. 86th St. J. H. Speer.
Fourth, West End Ave. and 91st St. E. W. Work.
Fourth Ave., 4th Ave. and 22d St. W. D. Buchanan.
Fourteenth St., 14th St., cor. 2d Ave. Geo. E. Merriam.
French Evangelical, 126 W. 16th St. H. L. Grandlienard.
Good Shepherd, 152 W. 66th St. D. E. Lorenz.
Harlem, 17 Mt. Morris Park, West. J. L. Caughey.
Madison Ave., Madison Ave., cor. 73d St. H. S. Coffin.
Madison Square, 24th St. and Madison Ave. C. H. Parkhurst.
Morningside, Morningside Ave. and W. 122d St.
Morrisania, 1203 Washington Ave. M. F. Johnston.
Mount Tabor, 57 W. 134th St. H. G. Miller.
Mount Washington, Broadway, cor. Dyckman St. G. S. Payson.

PRESBYTERIAN—Continued.

New York, 7th Ave. and 128th St. D. J. McMillan.
North, 525 W. 155th St. John R. Mackay.
Northminster, W. 115th St., near St. Nicholas Ave. W. P. Shriver.
Park, 86th St. and Amsterdam Ave. A. P. Atterbury.
Phelps Mission, 314 E. 35th St. E. C. Shaver.
Riverdale, Riverdale. I. S. Dodd.
Rutgers, Broadway and W. 73d St. R. Mackenzie.
St. James's, 357 W. 51st St. C. L. Butler.
St. Nicholas Ave., 141st St. & St Nicholas Ave. T. W. Smith.
Scotch, 96th St. and Central Park W. D. G. Wylie.
Sea and Land, 61 Henry St. O. G. Cocks.
Seventh, cor. Broome and Ridge Sts. J. T. Wilds.
Spring St., Spring St., near Varick St. H. R. Bates.
Thirteenth St., 145 W. 13th St. J. H. Hoadley.
Tremont, Washington Ave., near E. 174th St. J. H. Hartmann.
University Heights, University Heights. Percy B. Wightman.
University Pl., University Pl., cor. 10th St. G. Alexander; Bethlehem Chapel, 196 Bleecker St. J. W. Miller; Emmanuel Chapel, 735 6th St. J. C. Palmer.
West, 42d St., bet. 5th and 6th Aves. A. H. Evans.
West End, 105th St. and Amsterdam Ave. A. E. Keigwin.
West Farms, 980 E. 180th St. M. V. Bartlett.
Westminster, 210-212 W. 23d St. H. G. Mendenhall.
Woodstock, E. 165th St. and Prospect Ave. James Cromie.
Zion (German), 835 E. 165th St. A. F. Hahn.

PROTESTANT EPISCOPAL.

Diocesan House, 416 Lafayette Street.

Rt. Rev. David H. Greer, 7 Gramercy Pk., Bishop; George F. Nelson, Archdeacon, h. 416 Lafayette St.
All Angels, 81st St., cor. West End Ave. S. D. Townsend.
All Saints', 286 Henry St. W. N. Dunnell.
All Souls', 86 St. Nicholas Ave. G. S. Pratt.
Ascension, 36 5th Ave., cor. 10th St. Percy S. Grant.
Ascension Memorial, 243 W. 43d St. J. F. Steen.
Beloved Disciple, 89th St., near Madison Ave. H. M. Barbour.
Calvary, 273 4th Ave. J. L. Parks.
Cathedral of St. John the Divine, W. 113th St., between Amsterdam Ave. and Morningside Ave.
Chapel of Christ the Consoler, foot E. 26th St. (Bellevue Hospital).
Chapel of St. Elizabeth of Hungary, 2 W. 106th St. A. D. Pell.
Chapel of the Good Shepherd, Blackwell's Island. I. W. Beard.
Chapel of the Good Shepherd (General Theological Seminary), Chelsea Square.
Chapel of the Messiah, 206 E. 95th St. F. H. Church.
Christ, Broadway and W. 71st St. G. A. Strong.
Christ, Riverdale. G. A. Carstensen.
Church of the Advocate, Washington Ave., near E. 180th St. G. N. Deyo.
Church of the Resurrection, E. 74th St., near Park Ave. A. D. Pell.
Corpus Christi, 221 W. 69th St. E. C. Rich.
Du St. Esprit, E. 27th St., near 4th Ave. A. V. Wittmeyer.
Epiphany, 259 Lexington Ave. W. T. Crocker.
God's Providence Mission, 330 Broome St.
Grace, 800 Broadway. W. R. Huntington.
Grace, Main St., City Island. Arthur Forbes.
Grace, West Farms, Vyse Ave., near Tremont Ave. A. J. Derbyshire.
Grace Chapel, 414 E. 14th St. Geo. H. Bottome.
Grace Emanuel, 212 E. 116th St. Wm. K. McGown.
Heavenly Rest, 551 5th Ave. Herbert Shipman.
Holy Apostles, 300 9th Ave. A. Grannis.
Holy Comforter, 343 W. Houston St. W. A. A. Gardner.

CHURCHES IN MANHATTAN AND BRONX—*Continued.*

PROTESTANT EPISCOPAL—Continued.

Holy Communion, 324 6th Ave. Henry Mottet.
Holy Cross, 43 Ave. C. M. W. Britton.
Holy Faith, 694 E. 166th St., C. S. Gregg.
Holy Nativity, Bainbridge Ave., cor. Woodlawn Road. H. M. Hopkins.
Holyrood, Broadway, corner W. 181st St. Stuart Crockett.
Holy Trinity (St. James' Parish), 316 E. 88th St. J. V. Chalmers.
Holy Trinity, W. 122d St. and Lenox Ave. H. P. Nichols.
Incarnation, 205 Madison Ave., cor. 35th St. W. M. Grosvenor; Chapel, 242 E. 31st St.
Intercession, 158th St. and Broadway. M. H. Gates.
"Little Church Around the Corner" (Transfiguration), 5 E. 29th St. G. C. Houghton.
Mediator, Kingsbridge Ave. John Campbell.
Our Saviour, foot Market St., East River. A. R. Mansfield.
Redeemer, 136th St., near 7th Ave. W. W. Davis.
St. Agnes's Chapel, 92d St., near Columbus Ave. Wm. C. Rogers.
St. Alban's, Summit Ave., near E. 164th St. H.R. Fell.
St. Andrew's, 127th St., near 5th Ave. G. R. Van De Water.
St. Ann's, St. Ann's Ave., near E. 140th St. C. C. Harriman.
St. Ann's (Deaf Mutes), W. 148th St., near Amsterdam Ave. John Chamberlain.
St. Augustine's Chapel (Trinity Parish), 107 E. Houston St. A. C. Kimber.
St. Barnabas's Chapel, 306 Mulberry St. J. G. Littell.
St. Bartholomew's, 348 Madison Ave. Leighton Parks. Chapel, 209 E. 42d St.; Swedish Chapel, 121 E. 127th St.
St. Christopher's Chapel (Trinity Parish), 213 Fulton St. C. R. Stetson.
St. Chrysostom's Chapel (Trinity Parish), 201 W. 39th St. T. H. Sill.
St. Clement's, 108 W. 3d St. E. H. Van Winkle.
St. Cornelius's, 423 W. 46th St. I. C. Sturges.
St. Cornelius's Chapel, Governor's Island. E. B. Smith.
St. David's, 382 E. 160th St. E. G. Clifton.
St. Edmund's, 177th St., near Morris Ave. J. C. Smiley.
St. Edward the Martyr, 109th St., near 5th Ave.
St. George the Martyr, 222 W. 11th St.
St. George's, E. 219th St., Williamsbridge.
St. George's, 7 Rutherford Pl. Hugh Birckhead.
St. Ignatius's, West End Ave. and W. 87th St. Arthur Ritchie.
St. James's, 71st St., cor. Madison Ave. Frederick Courtney.
St. James's, Fordham, Jerome Ave., cor. E. 190th St. D. L. Pelton.
St. John the Divine Cathedral, W. 113th St., between Amsterdam and Morningside Aves.
St. John the Evangelist, 222 W. 11th St. A. B. Howard.
St. John's (Trinity Parish), 46 Varick St. Chas. L. Gomph.
St. Luke's, Convent Ave., cor. W. 141st St. J. T. Patey.
St. Luke's (Trinity Parish), Hudson St., opp. Grove St. Chas. L. Gomph.
St. Margaret's, E. 156th St., cor. Leggett Ave. C. A. Hamilton.
St. Mark's, 2d Ave. and 10th St. L. W. Batten.
St. Mary's, Alexander Ave., cor. 142d St. B. H. Lee.
St Mary's, Lawrence St., near Amsterdam Ave. H. R. Hulse.
St. Mary the Virgin, W. 46th St. and 6th Ave. G. M. Christian.
St. Matthew's, W. 84th St., near Central Park West. A. H. Judge.
St. Michael's, Amsterdam Ave., near W. 99th St. J. P. Peters.
St. Paul's, Washington Ave., cor. St. Paul's Pl. H. F. Taylor.

PROTESTANT EPISCOPAL—Continued.

St. Paul's (Trinity Parish), Broadway and Vesey St. W. M. Geer.
St. Peter's, 342 W. 20th St. O. S. Roche.
St. Peter's, Westchester Ave. F. M. Clendenin.
St. Philip's, 161 W. 25th St. H. C. Bishop.
St. Priscilla Chapel, 130 Stanton St. Thos. McCandless.
St. Stephen's, 124 W. 69th St. N. A. Seagle.
St. Stephen's, E. 238th St., cor. Vireo Ave. P. McIntire.
St. Thomas's, 5th Ave., cor. 53d St. E. M. Stires.
St. Thomas's Chapel, 230 E. 60th St. R. R. Claiborne.
San Salvatore (Italian), 359 Broome St. E. Knapp.
Transfiguration ("Little Church Around the Corner"), 5 E. 29th St. G. C. Houghton.
Trinity, Broadway and Rector St. Wm. T. Manning.
Trinity, E. 164th St., near Boston Road. A.S. Hull.
Trinity Chapel, 15 W. 25th St. W. H. Vibbert.
Zion and St. Timothy, 332 W. 57th St. Henry Lubeck.

REFORMED CHURCH IN AMERICA.

Denominational Headquarters, Reformed Church Building, 25 E. 22d St.

Anderson Memorial, cor. E. 183d St. and Cambreling Ave.
Bloomingdale, West End Ave. and 106th St. W. C. Stinson.
Church of the Comforter, 279 E. 162d St. Floyd Decker.
Fordham Manor, Kingsbridge Road, cor. Claflin Terrace. J. M. Hodson.
Fourth German, 412 W. 45th St. J. H. Oerter.
German Evangelical Mission, 141 E. Houston St. J. W. Geyer.
German Reformed, 353 E. 68th St. Julius Jaeger.
Grace, 845 7th Ave. J. R. Duryee.
Hamilton Grange, W. 149th St. and Convent Ave. Chalmers P. Dyke.
Harlem Collegiate, 191 E. 121st St. B. E. Dickhaut.
Harbor Mission, Ellis Island. Paul Land.
Lenox Ave., 267 Lenox Ave. E. Tilton, Jr.
Madison Ave., Madison Ave., cor. 57th St. Wm. Carter.
Manhattan, 71 Ave. B. Jacob Schlegel.
Melrose, Elton Ave., cor. E. 156th St. G. H. Miller.
Mott Haven, 3d Ave., cor. 146th St. J. F. Dobbs.
New York Collegiate:
St. Nicholas, 5th Ave., cor. 48th St.
Knox Memorial, 405 W. 41st St. E. G. W. Meury.
Marble, 5th Ave. and 29th St. D. J. Burrell.
Middle, 2d Ave. and 7th St. J. G. Fagg.
North Church Chapel, 113 Fulton St.
Thirty-fourth St., 307 W. 34th St. R. W. Courtney.
Vermilye Chapel, 416 W. 54th St. W. B. Ackert.
West End, 77th St. and West End Ave. H. E. Cobb.
Prospect Hill, 1451 Lexington Ave. H. M. Cox.
South, Madison Ave., cor. 38th St. T. R. Bridges.
Manor Chapel, 348 W. 26th St. James Palmer.
Sunshine Chapel, 550 W. 40th St. H W. Murphy.
Union, Ogden Ave., near 169th St. Simon Blooker.
West Farms, Fairmount Pl., near Prospect Ave. W. R. Hart.

REFORMED CHURCH IN THE U. S.

Bethany, 235 E. 109th St. E. W. C. Brueckner.
Harbor Mission, Ellis Island. Paul H. Land.
Martha Memorial, 419 W. 52d St. Paul H. Schnatz.

REFORMED EPISCOPAL.

First, Madison Ave., cor. 55th St. W. T. Sabine.
St. Paul's, 236th St. and Vireo Ave. W. R. Collins.

REFORMED PRESBYTERIAN.

Fourth, 304 W. 122d St. I. A. Blackwood.
Second, 227 W. 39th St. R. M. Somerville.
Third, 238 W. 23d St. F. M. Foster.

CHURCHES IN MANHATTAN AND BRONX—*Continued.*

ROMAN CATHOLIC.

Most Rev. J. M. Farley, Archbishop, 452 Madison Ave.
All Saints', Madison Av., cor. 129th St. J. W. Power.
Annunciation, B. V. M., Convent Ave., cor. 131st St. W. L. Penny.
Ascension, 107th St., near B'way. E. M. Sweeny.
Assumption, 427 W. 49th St. Henry Nieuwenhuis.
Blessed Sacrament, W. 71st St., near Broadway. M. A. Taylor.
Chapel of the Sacred Heart, Hart's Island.
Corpus Christi, 537 W. 121st St. John H. Dooley.
Epiphany, 373 2d Ave. D. J. McMahon.
Guardian Angel, 513 W. 23d St. J. C. Henry.
Holy Cross, 335 W. 42d St. Chas. McCready.
Holy Family, Castle Hill Ave., cor. Watson Ave. A. N. Stehle.
Holy Innocents, 126 W. 37th St. M. C. O'Farrell.
Holy Name Mission, 157½ Bowery. L. J. Evers.
Holy Name of Jesus, Amsterdam Ave. and 96th St. J. J. Kean.
Holy Rosary, 442 E. 119th St. F. H. Wall.
Holy Spirit, Burnside Ave., cor. Aqueduct Ave. J. D Roach.
Holy Trinity, 229 W. 82d St. M. J. Considine.
Immaculate Conception, 505 E. 14th St. W. G. Murphy.
Immaculate Conception (German), 385 E. 150th St. C. G. Ritter.
Immaculate Conception, Williamsbridge. C. Cassenetti.
Mary, Help of Christians, 431 E. 12th St. J. Ferrazza.
Mary, Star of the Sea, Governor's Island. M. J. Henry.
Most Holy Redeemer, 165 3d St. F. Spiedel.
Most Precious Blood, 115 Baxter St. B. Pollizo.
Nativity, 48 2d Ave. B. J. Reilly.
Our Lady of Good Counsel, 236 E. 90th St. J. N. Connolly.
Our Lady of Guadalupe, 229 W. 14th St. Thos. Darbois.
Our Lady of Loretto, 303 Elizabeth St. W. H. Walsh.
Our Lady of Lourdes, Convent Ave. and W. 142d St. Joseph McMahon.
Our Lady of Mercy, E. 190th St., cor. Webster Ave. P. N. Breslin.
Our Lady of Mount Carmel, 453 E. 115th St. John Do an.
Our Lady of Perpetual Help, 321 E. 61st St. J. G. Kissner.
Our Lady of Pompeii, 214 Bleecker St. A. Demo.
Our Lady of Solace, Van Nest. D. J. Curley.
Our Lady of Sorrows, 105 Pitt St. T. Grossman.
Our Lady of the Rosary, 7 State St. M. J. Henry.
Our Lady of the Scapular of Mount Carmel, 341 E. 28th St. Joseph L. McCabe.
Our Lady Queen of Angels, 228 E. 113th St. Paul Reichertz.
Resurrection, 143d St. and 7th Ave. T. F. Murphy.
Sacred Heart, Shakespeare Ave., near E. 169th St. J. J. Lennon.
Sacred Heart of Jesus, 447 W. 51st St. Joseph F. Mooney.
St. Adalbert's, 424 E. 156th St. Jos. Zaniewicz.
St. Agnes's, 143 E. 43d St. H. A. Brann.
St. Alphonsus's, 312 W. Broadway. Peter Grein.
St. Aloysius's, 215 W. 132d St. John McKenna.
St. Ambrose's, 515 W. 54th St. J. P. Chidwick.
St. Andrew's, Duane St., cor City Hall Pl. Luke Evers.
St. Angela's, Morris Ave. and 163d St. T. W. Wallace.
St. Ann's, 112 E. 12th St. Thos. F. Myhan.
St. Anselm's, 177 Tinton Ave.. B. Kevenhoerster.
St. Anthony's, 1010 E. 166th St. O. F. Strack.
St. Anthony of Padua, 153 Sullivan St. C. Viola.
St. Augustine's, E. 167th St., cor. Fulton Ave. T. F. Gregg.
St. Benedict the Moor, 8 W. 53d St. T. M. O'Keefe.
St. Bernard's, 332 W. 14th St. G. A. Healy.

ROMAN CATHOLIC—Continued.

St. Boniface's, 882 2d Ave. J. S. Braun.
St. Brigid's, 123 Ave. B. P. F. Minogue.
St. Catharine of Genoa, W. 153d St., near Amsterdam Ave. James W. Flood.
St. Catherine of Sienna, 420 E. 69th St. G. I. Conlan.
St. Cecilia's, E. 106th St., near Lexington Ave. M. J. Phelan.
St. Charles Borromeo, W. 141st St., near 7th Ave. H. J. Gordon.
St. Columba's, 339 W. 25th St. Henry Prat.
St. Elizabeth's, W. 187th St., cor. Broadway. T. F. Lynch.
St. Elizabeth of Hungary, 345 E. 4th St. W. Biskorovany.
St. Frances of Rome, Richardson Ave., Wakefield. F. P. Moore.
St. Francis de Sales, 139 E. 96th St. J. L. Hoey.
St. Francis of Assisi, 139 W. 31st St. John B. Stark.
St. Francis Xavier, 36 W. 16th St. T. J. McClusky.
St. Gabriel's, 312 E. 37th St. W. L. Livingston.
St. Ignatius Loyola, Park Ave., cor E. 84th St. W. O'Brien Pardow.
St. James', 32 James St. J. B. Curry.
St. Jean Baptiste's, 159 E. 76th St. A. Letellier.
St. Jerome's, Alexander Ave., cor. 138th St. G. T. Donlin.
St. Joachim's, 24 Roosevelt St. V. Jannuzzi.
St. John Baptist's, 209 W. 30th St. C. Claude.
St. John Chrysostom's, 167th St., near Hoe Ave. B. F. Brady.
St. John Evangelist's, 355 E. 55th St. J. J. Flood.
St. John Nepomuk's, 289 E. 4th St. J. Martincek.
St. John's, 2911 Kingsbridge Ave. D. H. O'Dwyer.
St. John the Martyr, 254 E. 72d St. J. T. Frout.
St. Joseph's, 59 6th Ave. John Edwards.
St. Joseph's, 1943 Bathgate Ave. Peter Farrell.
St. Joseph's (German), 408 E. 87th St. A. Lammel.
St. Joseph's, 125th St., cor. Columbus Ave. G. H. Huntman.
St. Leo's, 11 E. 28th St. Thos. J. Ducey.
St. Lucy's, 340 E. 104th St. E. W. Cronin.
St. Luke's, E. 138th St., near Cypress Ave. J. J. Boyle.
St. Malachy's, 243 W. 49th St. J. F. Delaney.
St. Margaret's, Riverdale. M. J. Murray.
St. Mark, Evangelist, 65 W. 138th St. J. J. Owens.
St. Martin of Tours, E. 182d St., cor. Grote. E. J. O'Gorman.
St. Mary Magdalen's, 527 E. 17th St. E. T. Heinlein.
St. Mary's, 438 Grand St. N. J. Hughes.
St. Mary's, White Plains Road. Jno. J. Carr.
St. Mary's Star of the Sea, City Island. J. B. McGrath.
St. Matthew's, W. 67th St., near Amsterdam Ave. P. F. Maughan.
St. Michael's, W. 34th St. and 9th Ave. J. A. Gleason.
St. Monica's, 409 E. 79th St. J. D. Lennon.
St. Nicholas', 125 2d St. John A. Nageleisen.
St. Patrick's, Mott St., cor. Prince St. J. F. Kearney.
St. Patrick's Cathedral, cor. 5th Ave. and 50th St. M. J. Lavelle.
St. Paul's, 121 E. 117th St. John McQuirk.
St. Paul the Apostle, Columbus Ave. and W. 60th St. G. M. Searle.
St. Peter's, 22 Barclay St. James H. McGean.
SS. Peter and Paul, 159th St. and St. Ann's Ave. W. H. Murphy.
St. Philip Neri's, Grand Boulevard and Concourse., opp. E. 202d St. D. F. X. Burke.
St. Raphael's, W. 40th St., bet. 10th and 11th Aves. M. A. Cunnion.
St. Raymond's, West Farms Road, Westchester. E. McKenna.
St. Rita of Cascia, 442 College Ave. Chas. Ferina.
St. Roch's, 932 E. 150th St. J. Milo.
St. Rose's, Cannon St., near Broome. P. McNamee.
St. Rose of Lima, W. 165th St., near Amsterdam Ave. E. T. McGinley.
St. Stanislaus's, 107 7th St. J. H. Strzelecki.
St. Stephen's, 149 E. 28th St. T. F. Cusack.

CHURCHES IN MANHATTAN AND BRONX—*Continued.*

ROMAN CATHOLIC—Continued.

St. Teresa's, Rutgers, cor. Henry St. J. T. McEntyre.
St. Thomas the Apostle, W. 118th St., near St. Nicholas Ave. J. J. Keogan.
St. Thomas Aquinas's, 1011 Tremont Ave. D. F. Coyle.
St. Valentine's, E. 221st St., Williamsbridge. A. Jaukbowski.
St. Veronica's, Christopher St., near Greenwich. J. F. Flannelly.
St. Vincent de Paul, 127 W. 23d St. T. Wucher.
St. Vincent Ferrer, 871 Lexington Ave. J. R. Meagher.
Transfiguration, 25 Mott St. E. Coppo.

UNITARIAN.

Denominational Headquarters, 104 *E. 20th St.*

All Souls', 4th Av. and 20th St. Thomas R. Slicer.
Lenox Ave., Lenox Ave., cor. 121st St. M. St. C. Wright.
Messiah, E. 34th St., cor. Park Ave. Robert Collyer, Pastor Emeritus.

UNITED PRESBYTERIAN.

Charles St., 41 Charles St. James A. Reed.
First, 16 W. 108th St. T. W. Anderson.
Seventh Ave., 123 W. 12th St. J. H. Tate.
Washington Heights, 172d St. and Audubon Ave. J. L. Hervey.
West 44th St., 434 W. 44th St. H. H. Wallace.

UNIVERSALIST.

Fourth (Divine Paternity), Central Park West and 76th St. F. O. Hall.

MISCELLANEOUS.

Armenian Evangelical, 507 E. 30th St.
Beacon Light Rescue Mission, 2372 3d Ave.
Bethany Gospel Mission, W. 142d St., cor. St. Nicholas Ave.
Broome St. Tabernacle, 395 Broome St.
Catharine Mission, 24 Catharine Slip.
Catholic Apostolic—Central, 417 W. 57th St.; Harlem (German), 202 W. 114th St.
Chinatown Midnight Mission, 17 Doyers St.
Christian Israelites' Sanctuary, 108 1st St.
Christian Reformed, 21 Bank St.
Christ's Mission, 331 W. 57th St.

MISCELLANEOUS—Continued.

Church of Christ (Scientist)—First, Central Park West, cor. W. 96th St.; Second, Central Park West, cor. W. 68th St.; Third, 43 E. 125th St.; Fourth, W. 82d St., near Broadway; Fifth, 228 W. 45th St.; Sixth, 131 E. 34th St.
Church of the Strangers, W. 57th St. and 8th Ave.
Cremorne Mission, 104 W. 32d St.
De Witt Memorial, 280 Rivington St.
Doyers St. Mission, 17 Doyers St.
Eighth Ave. Mission, 291 8th Ave.
Faith Mission, 34 West End Ave.
Free Methodist Mission, 349 E. 10th St.
Gospel Chapel, 305 W. 30th St.
Gospel Tabernacle, 692 8th Ave.
Hungarian Reformed, 121 7th St.
Japanese Mission, 330 E. 57th St.
Mariners', 46 Catharine St.; West Side Branch, 128 Charlton St.
McAuley's Water St. Mission, 316 Water St.
Metropolitan Independent, Carnegie Lyceum.
Mission of the Living Waters, 25 Delancey St.
New Apostolic, 207 E. 120th St.
New Jerusalem (Swedenborgian), 114 E. 35th St.
Olivet Memorial, 63 2d St.
146th St. Gospel Temperance Mission, 146th St., near 3d Ave.
People's Tabernacle, 52 E. 102d St.
Russian St. Nicholas Church, 17 E. 97th St.
Salvation Army, 122 W. 14th St.; 96 Perry St., 2414 Second Ave.; 218 E. 40th St.; 285 E. 142d St.; 434 E. 9th St.; 2256 5th Ave.; 48 W. 10th St.; 967 Washington Ave.; 326 W. 34th St.; 322 W. 4th St.; 206 E. 88th St.; 208 E. 13th St.; 101 W. 99th St.; 915 Eagle Ave.; 158 E. 27th St.; 165 E. 128th St.; 6 Catharine Slip. Slums: 94 Cherry St.; 90 Greenwich St.; 492 10th Ave.; 324 E. 25th St.
Scandinavian Mission, 252 E. 48th St.
Seamen's Christian Association, 399 West St.
Seventh-Day Adventists; (1) 535 W. 110th St., E. H. M. Sell; Berean Chapel, E. 166th St., cor. Trinity Ave., J. J. Kennedy; (4) 1931 Broadway, J. C. Hennessey; (5) 67 E. 125th St. Samuel Gordon.
Strachan, Margaret, Chapel, 105 W. 27th St.
St. Paul's (Evang. Reformed), 608 E. 141st St.
St. Trinity (Greek Orthodox), 153 E. 72d St.
Volunteers of America, 38 Cooper Square W.; 360 Alexander Ave.
West-Side Noonday Prayer, 281 Greenwich St.
Woman's Union Prayer Meeting, Harlem, 101 W. 123d St.
Young People's City Mission, 219 E. 59th St.

Churches in Brooklyn.

WITH NAMES OF PASTORS.

BAPTIST.

Baptist Temple (First in Pierrepont St.), 3d Ave., cor. Schermerhorn St. Cortland Myers.
Bedford Heights, Bergen St., cor. Rogers Ave. F. H. Jacobs.
Berean, Bergen St., near Rochester Ave. L. L. Brown.
Bethany, Clermont and Atlantic Aves. H. Powell.
Borough Park 48th St. and 13th Ave. W. W. Ludwig.
Bushwick Ave., Bushwick Ave., cor. Weirfield St. T. J. Whitaker.
Calvary, 14th St., near 4th Ave. H. A. Tupper, Jr.
Central, Adelphi St., near Myrtle Ave. J. A. Hansen.
Central, Marcy Ave., cor. S. 5th St. J. A. Huntley.
Concord (colored), Duffield St., near Myrtle Ave. W. T. Dixon.
East End, Van Sicklen Ave., near Glenmore Ave. John J. Parsons.
Emmanuel, Lafayette Ave., cor. St. James' Pl. J. Humpstone.

BAPTIST—Continued.

Euclid Ave., Euclid Ave., cor. Hill St. J. V. Osterhout.
First Canarsie, Remsen Ave., Canarsie. W. P. W. Haff.
First, in East New York, Hendrix St., n. Fulton St. J. A. Jones.
First, E. D., Lee Ave., cor. Keap St. Geo. N. Spencer.
First German, E. D., Montrose, near Union Ave. J. C. Grimmell.
First German, Prospect Ave., near 6th Ave. E. Wiesle.
First Swedish, Dean St., near 6th Ave. O. J. Engstrand.
Grace, 47th St., near 3d Ave. Thos. V. Parker.
Greene Ave., Greene Ave., near Lewis Ave. Curtis L. Laws.
Greenwood, 7th Ave. and 6th St. Joel B. Slocum.
Hanson Place, Hanson Pl., cor. S. Portland Ave. W. M. Vines.
Holy Trinity (colored), 595 Classon Ave. S. W. Timms.

CHURCHES IN BROOKLYN—*Continued.*

BAPTIST—Continued.

Lefferts Park, 69th St. and 14th Ave. Herbert Barton.
Lenox Road, Nostrand Ave., cor. Lenox Road. D. A. MacMurray.
Marcy Ave., Marcy Ave., cor. Putnam Ave. W. C. P. Rhodes.
Memorial, 8th Ave. and 16th St. A. S. Barner.
Pilgrim, Patchen Ave., cor. McDonough St.
Prospect Park, Greenwood Ave., cor. E. 7th St. George Stuart.
Redeemer, cor. Cortelyou Road and E. 18th St. A. W. H. Hodder.
Second German, Evergreen Ave., cor. Woodbine. A. P. Mihm.
Sheepshead Bay, E. 15th St., Sheepshead Bay. R. A. Royester.
Sixth Avenue, 6th Ave. and Lincoln Pl. G. O. Griffith.
Strong Pl., Strong Pl., cor. Degraw St. A. H. C. Morse.
Sumner Ave., Sumner Ave., cor. Decatur St. R. M. Greene.
Swedish Ebenezer, Herkimer Ave. and Schenectady Ave. N. E. Johnson.
Tabernacle, Clinton St., cor. 3d Pl. Erwin Dennett.
Trinity, Greene Ave., cor. Patchen. H. Pethic.
Union, Noble, near Manhattan Ave. Wm. E. Monteney.
Washington Ave., Washington Ave., cor. Gates Ave. R. MacDonald.
Williamsburg Jewish Mission, 626 B'way. L. Cohen.

CHRISTIAN SCIENTIST.

First Church of Christ, 404 Lafayette Ave. F. H. Leonard.
Immanuel, 271 Macon St. W. J. Vinall.
Second Church of Christ, Park Pl., near Nostrand Ave.
Third Church of Christ, 199 Lincoln Pl.

CONGREGATIONAL.

Beecher Memorial, Herkimer St., near Rockaway Ave. Charles J. Allen.
Bethesda, Ralph Ave., cor. Chauncey St. G. W. Humphreys.
Borough Park, 41st St., near 13th Ave.
Bushwick Ave., Bushwick Ave., cor. Cornelia St. J. L. Clark.
Central, Hancock St., near Franklin Ave. S. P. Cadman.
Clinton Ave., Clinton Ave., cor. Lafayette Ave. N. Boynton; Atlantic Ave. Chapel, Atlantic and Grand Aves., W. S. Woodworth; Willoughby Ave. Chapel, Willoughby Ave., cor. Grand Ave., S. W. King.
Evangel, Bedford Ave. and Hawthorne. S. H. Cox.
Flatbush, Dorchester Road, cor. E. 18th St. L. T. Reed.
Iglesia (Hispano-American), 756 Quincy St.
Immanuel, Decatur St., near Ralph Ave.
Italian Evan., Henry and Degraw Sts. Emanuel Tealdo.
Lewis Ave., Lewis Ave., cor. Madison St. R. J. Kent.
Nazarene, 1584 Fulton St. H. B. Gantt.
Ocean Avenue, Ocean Ave. and Ave I.
Park, 8th Ave., cor. 2d St. R. W. McLaughlin.
Parkville, 18th Ave., near Ocean Boulevard. H. L. Pyle.
Pilgrim (Swedish), 413 Atlantic Ave. C. G. Ellstrom.
Pilgrim Chapel, Henry St., cor. Degraw St. Chas. M. Calderwood.
Pilgrims, Henry St., cor. Remsen. Marion L. Burton.
Plymouth, Orange St., near Hicks. N. D. Hillis.
Puritan, Lafayette Av., cor. Marcy. J. N. Pierce.
Rockaway Ave., Rockaway Ave., near Blake St.
South, President St., cor. Court St. A. J. Lyman.
St. Paul's Chapel, New York Ave. and Sterling Pl. H. L. Everett.

CONGREGATIONAL—Continued.

Tompkins Ave., Tompkins Ave., cor. McDonough St. N. McG. Waters. Park Ave. Branch, Park Ave., cor. Marcy.
United, Lee Ave., cor. Hooper St. U. G. Warren.

DISCIPLES OF CHRIST.

First, Sterling Pl. and 7th Ave. Herbert Martin.
Second, Humboldt St., near Nassau Ave. J. Keevil.
Third, Dorchester Road and E. 15th St. Walter S. Rounds.

GERMAN EVANGELICAL.

Emanuel, 400 Melrose St. Chas. Philipbar.
Evangelical Salems, 1200 Jefferson Ave. J. Reuber.
Harrison Ave., 125 Harrison Ave. Robt. J. Lau.
St. Paul's, 541 Leonard St. Geo. A. Linder.
Zion's, Liberty Av., near Wyona St. G. F. Schmid.
Zion Evang., Cypress Ave. and Himrod St. Adolph Schmidt.

JEWISH.

Ahawath Scholom Beth Aron, 98 Scholes St. K. Solomon, Cantor.
Ahawath Chesed, cor. Lorimer and Stagg Sts. M. W. Newmark.
Anshe Ernes, 136 Stanhope St.
Asifas Israel, 25 Varet St. L. Shalnfeld.
Beth El, 110 Noble St., Greenpoint. Marcus Rosenstein.
Beth Elohim, State St., near Hoyt. Alex. Lyons.
Beth Israel, Harrison St., near Court St. A. Rosenberg.
Beth Jacob, S., 3d St., near Marcy Ave. S. Rabinowitz.
Bikur Cholim, Wyona, near Fulton St. Israel Sanerstin.
B'nai Sholaum, 327-9 9th St. Cantor J. Schuman.
B'nai Jacob, 167 Prospect Ave. D. Ross.
Chebrah Bnei Sholome, 148 Varet St. S. Newman.
Emanuel Temple, 14th Ave. and 49th St. (now building). I. L. Brill.
Israel, Bedford and Lafayette Avs. Martin Meyer.
Mikro Kodesh Anshe Klodovo, 184 McKibbin St. S. L. Westman.
Ohav Sholom, 135 Thatford St. S. I. Finkelstein.
Ohav Sholom, 19 Varet St.
Shaari Zedek, Quincy St., near Reid Ave. D. H. Wittenberg.
Sons of Israel, Bay 22d St., near Benson Ave. F. Tworger.
Temple Beth Elohim, Keap St., near Division Ave. S. R. Cohen.

LUTHERAN.

Ascension, 55th St. and New Utrecht Ave. F. W. Schaefer.
Bethlehem (German), Marion St., near Reid Ave. E. W. Kandelhart.
Bethlehem, 3d Ave. and Pacific St. F. Jacobson.
Bethlehem (Norwegian), Russell St., near Nassau Ave. C. M. Tolefsen.
Calvary, Rochester Ave., near Herkimer St. E. E. Hoshour.
Christ, 1084 Lafayette Ave. H. S. Knabenschuh.
Emanuel, 7th St., near 6th Ave. Emil Roth.
Emanuel, S. 9th St., near Driggs Ave. John Holthusen.
Finnish Seaman's Mission, 529 Clinton St. T. Hobenthal.
Finnish, 44th St., near 7th Ave. A. A. Rautalahti.
First Scand.-Nor., 184 Kent St. Carl Doving.
German Evangelical, Schermerhorn St., near Court St. J. W. Loch.
Good Shepherd, 3d and Bay Ridge Aves. C. D. Trexler.
Grace, Bushwick Ave. and Weirfield St. C. F. Inteman.
Holy Trinity, Cumberland St., near Lafayette Ave. E. E. Fisher.
Immanuel (Swedish), Leonard St., near Driggs Ave. G. Nelsenius.
Incarnation, 5323 Fourth Ave. Tycho Castberg.

CHURCHES IN BROOKLYN—*Continued.*

LUTHERAN—Continued.

Norwegian Seaman's, 111 Pioneer St. R. Andersen.
Our Saviour (English), 37 Covert St. J. H. C. Fritz.
Our Saviour (Norwegian), Henry St., near 4th Pl. C. S. Everson.
Redeemer, Bedford Ave., cor. Hewes St. S. G. Weiskotten.
Reformation, Barbey St., near Arlington Ave. H. P. Miller.
Resurrection, 236 President St.
Salem's Danish Evangelical, 128 Prospect Ave. T. Beck.
St. Ansgar's (Danish), 47th St. and 3d Ave. K. Samsoe.
St. Jacobi, 46th St., nr. 4th Ave. H. C. A. Meyer.
St. Johannes's, New Jersey Ave., near Liberty St. G. F. Blaesi.
St. Johannes's, 193 Maujer St. A. J. Beyer.
St. John's, 84th St. and 16th Ave. L. Happ.
St. John's, Prospect Ave., near 5th Ave. H. C. Wasmund.
St. John's, E. D., Milton St., near Manhattan Ave. F. W. Oswald.
St. Luke's, Washington Ave., near De Kalb Ave. C. B. Schuchard.
St. Mark's, Bushwick Ave., opp. Jefferson St. J. T. Frey.
St. Matthew's, E. 92d St., near Flatlands Ave. V. Geist.
St. Matthew's (German), N. 5th St., near Driggs Ave. G. Sommer.
St. Matthew's, 6th Ave., cor. 2d St. G. B. Young.
St. Paul's, Knickerbocker Ave., cor. Palmetto St. J. P. Riedel.
St. Paul's, Henry St., near 3d Pl. J. Huppenbauer.
St. Paul's, Ashford St., near Glenmore Ave. J. F. Flath.
St. Paul's, Coney Island, Brighton Chapel. J. F. W. Kitzmeyer.
St. Paul's, E. D., S. 5th St., cor. Rodney St. H. W. Hoffmann.
St. Paul's (Swedish), 392 McDonough St. V. Ljung.
St. Peter's, Bedford Ave., near De Kalb Ave. J. J. Heischmann.
St. Peter's, 94 Hale Ave. A. Brunn.
St. Stephen's, Newkirk Ave., cor. E. 28th St. L. D. Jable.
Tabor (Swedish), Ashford St., near Glenmore Ave. J. C. Westlund.
Trinity, 249 Degraw St. P. Lindemann; Mission, 51st St. and 3d Ave.
Trinity (Norwegian), 27th St., near 5th Ave. P. R. Syrdal.
Wartburg Chapel, Georgia Ave. and Fulton St. R. Herbst.
Zion, Henry St., near Clark St. E. C. J. Kraeling.
Zion, Bedford, near Snyder Ave. P. F. Jubelt.
Zion (Swedish), 59th St. and 11th Ave. J. C. Westlund; Mission, 438 53d St.

METHODIST EPISCOPAL.

Andrew's, Richmond St., near Etna Ave. F. G. Howell.
Bay Ridge, 4th and Ovington Aves. Geo. Adams.
Bethel Ship, 297 Carroll St. A. M. Treistad.
Borough Park, 50th St. and 14th Ave. Howard V. Ross.
Buffalo Ave., Buffalo Ave., cor. Bergen St. H. S. Still.
Bushwick Ave., Bushwick Ave., cor. Madison St. F. W. Hannan.
Cropsey Ave., Cropsey Ave., near Bay 35th. Ralph Keeler.
De Kalb Ave., De Kalb Ave., near Franklin Avè. Dr. W. W. W. Wilson.
Eighteenth St., 18th St., near 5th Ave. L. K. Moore.
Elim (Swedish), 47th St., near 3d Ave. E. N. Hedeen.
Embury, Decatur St., cor. Lewis Ave. W. H. McMaster.

METHODIST EPISCOPAL—Continued.

Epworth, Bushwick Ave., cor. De Kalb Ave. T. L. Price.
Fennimore St., Fennimore St., cor. Rogers Ave. G. W. Osmun.
First, 955 Manhattan Ave. C. H. Grubb.
First Pl., 1st Pl., cor. Henry St. Gordon L. Thompson.
Flatlands, E. 40th St., near Flatlands Ave. Edw. J. Beck.
Fleet St., Fleet St., cor. Lafayette Ave. E. G. Richardson.
Fourth Ave., 4th Ave., cor. 47th St. E. A. Burns.
Goodsell, Sheridan Ave., cor. McKinley Ave. J. Lee Bilby.
Grace, 7th Ave., cor. St. John's Pl. F. F. Shannon.
Gravesend, Neck Road and Van Sicklen St. R. E. Putney.
Greene Ave., Greene Ave., near Central. Henry Schoedel.
Hanson Pl., Hanson Pl., cor. St. Felix St. T. S. Henderson.
Herkimer St., Russell Pl. and Herkimer St. R. S. Povey.
Janes, Reid Av., cor. Monroe St. Robert Bagnell.
Knickerbocker Ave., Knickerbocker Ave., cor. Ralph. F. P. Fisher.
New York Ave., New York Ave., cor. Dean St. F. J. McConnell.
North Fifth St., N. 5th St., near Bedford Ave. L. Richardson.
Nostrand Ave., Nostrand Ave., cor. Quincy St. Chas. W. McCormick.
Prospect Ave., Greenwood and Prospect Aves. W. S. Jackson.
Ridley Memorial, Lawrence Ave., near Ocean Parkway. Gustav Laass.
Salems, E. 38th St. and Ave. D. F. Hagner.
Sands St., Henry St., cor. Clark. F. B. Upham.
Sheepshead Bay, Voorhees Ave., cor. Ocean Ave. H. D. Weston.
Simpson, Clermont Ave., cor. Willoughby Ave. W. J. Thompson.
Sixth Av., 8th St., near 6th Av. W. A. Layton.
South Second St., S. 2d St., near Driggs Ave. I. S. Marsland.
South Third St., South 3d St., near Hewes St. William Hamilton.
St. James's, 84th St., near 20th Av. W. C. Giffin.
St. John's, Bedford Ave., cor. Wilson St. C. H. Priddy.
St. John's, Sumner Pl., near Flushing Ave. J. Shuler.
St. Mark's, Ocean Ave. and Beverly Rd. J. H. Willey.
St. Paul's, Marcy Ave., cor. Penn St. F. H. Rey
St. Paul's, Richards St., near Sullivan St. J. H. Fairchild.
Summerfield, Washington Ave., cor. Greene Ave. J. E. Holmes.
Sumner Ave., Sumner Ave., cor. Van Buren St. G. S. Eldridge.
Swedish Bethany, Troy Ave., cor. Herkimer St. F. E. Broman.
Swedish Immanuel, 422 Dean St. A. J. Lofgren.
Tabernacle, Manhattan Ave. and Noble St. L. H. Caswell.
Union, Leonard, cor. Conselyea. W. P. Estes.
Vanderveer Park, E. 31st St. and Glenwood Rd. W. S. Winans.
Warren St., Warren, near Smith St. A. W. Byrt.
Wesley, Glenmore Av., cor. Atkins. Rowland Hill.
Williams Ave., Williams Ave., near Atlantic Ave. W. W. Gillies.
York St., York St., near Gold St. E. Cunningham.

METHODIST FREE.

Brooklyn, 16th St., near 4th Ave. E. Blews.

METHODIST PRIMITIVE.

First, Park Ave., near N. Elliott Pl. R. Cookson.
Orchard, Oakland St., near Nassau Ave. S. K. Darlington.
Welcome, Classon Ave., near Lafayette Ave. J. J. Lockett.

CHURCHES IN BROOKLYN—*Continued.*

METHODIST PROTESTANT.

Grace, E. 92d St. and Church Lane. H. S. Hull.

AFRICAN METHODIST EPISCOPAL.

Bethel, Schenectady Ave., cor. Dean St. W. H. Lacey.
Bridge St., 315 Bridge St. Albert Cooper.
First Zion, W. 3d St., Coney Island. N. E. Collins.
People's Zion Mission, Atlantic Ave. J. C. Jones.
St. John's, Howard Ave., near Herkimer. I. Wilson.
St. John's, 559 Waverly Ave. Chas. E. McKay.
Zion, Bridge St., near Myrtle Ave. F. M. Jacobs.

PENTECOSTAL.

Bedford Ave., Keap and S. 2d Sts. H. N. Brown.
John Wesley, Saratoga Ave. and Sumpter Ave. Wm. H. Hoople.
Nazarine, Utica Ave., bet. Dean and Bergen Sts. J. A. Ward.
St. Luke's, 18 Erasmus St. A. A. Amos.

PRESBYTERIAN.

Ainslie St., near Manhattan Ave. L. W. Barney.
Arlington Ave., cor. Elton St.
Bay Ridge, 81st St., cor. 2d Ave. M. S. Littlefield.
Fort Hamilton Branch, 94th St. and 4th Ave.
Bedford, Dean St., cor. Nostrand Ave. S. E. Young.
Bensonhurst, 23d Ave. and 83d St. J. MacInnes.
Bethany, McDonough St., near Howard Ave. L. O. Rotenbach.
Borough Park, 46th St. and 15th Ave. H. B. Roberts.
Bushwick Ave., Bushwick Ave. and Ralph St. H. E. Schnatz.
Central, Marcy Ave., cor. Jefferson Ave. J. F. Carson.
City Park Chapel, Concord St., near Hudson Ave. H. K. England.
Classon Ave., Classon Ave., cor. Monroe St. J. D. Burrell.
Cumberland St., Cumberland St., near Myrtle Ave. H. S. Zimmerman.
Cuyler, 358 Pacific St. L. P. Armstrong.
Duryea, Sterling Pl. and Vanderbilt Ave. Wm. Denman.
Ebenezer, Stockholm St., near St. Nicholas Ave. C. C. Jaeger.
Fifth German, Halsey St., near Central Ave. C. H. Schwarzbach.
First, Henry St., near Clark St. L. M. Clarke.
First German, Leonard St., cor. Stagg St. J. G. Hehr.
First Syrian, Henry St. A. T. Baroody.
Flatbush, E. 23d St., near Foster Ave. D. E. Marvin.
Franklin Ave. Church, near Myrtle Ave. S. L. Testa.
Friedens' Kirche, Willoughby Ave., near Broadway. L. Wollerz.
Glenmore Ave., Glenmore Ave., cor. Doscher St. Carl Podin.
Grace, Stuyvesant Ave., cor. Jefferson Ave. R. H. Carson.
Greene Ave., Greene Ave., near Reid Ave. G. H. Eggleston.
Home Crest, cor. Ave. T and E. 15th St. E. L. Tibbals.
Irving Square, Weirfield St. and Hamburg Ave. Ira W. Henderson.
Lafayette Ave., Lafayette Ave., cor. S. Oxford St. C. B. McAfee.
Lefferts Park, 15th Ave. and 72d St. A. J. Brucklacher.
Memorial, 7th Ave., cor. St. John's Pl. T. C. McClelland.
Mount Olivet, Evergreen Ave., cor. Troutman St. F. T. Steele.
Noble St., Noble St., cor. Lorimer St. George C. Edson.

PRESBYTERIAN—Continued.

Olivet, Bergen St., near 6th Ave. J. G. Snyder.
Our Father, 24th St., n. 4th Ave. J. J. MacDonald.
Park Side, Lenox Road, near Flatbush Ave. J. D. Long.
Prospect Heights, 8th Ave., cor. 10th St. H. H. Fisher.
Ross St., Ross St., near Lee Ave. J. E. Adams.
Second, Clinton St., cor. Remsen St. Louis Vanden Berg.
Siloam, Prince St., near Willoughby St. W. A. Alexander.
South Third St., S. 3d St., cor. Driggs Ave. N. W. Wells.
Throop Ave., Throop Ave., cor. Willoughby Ave. A. D. Carlile.
Wells-Memorial, Foster Ave. and E. 13th St. W. B. Gates.
Westminster, Clinton St., cor. 1st Pl. Frederick Campbell.
Wyckoff Heights, Harmon St., near St. Nicholas Ave. J. Oastler.

UNITED PRESBYTERIAN.

Open Church, Eldert's Lane and Etna St. J. I. Frederick.
Bay Ridge, 76th St. and 5th Ave. W. J. Pinkerton.
Central, 80 Covert St. Robert McElroy.
Knox, 6th Ave. and 51st St. R. L. Warnock.
First, S. 1st St., cor. Rodney St. G. H. McClelland.
Second, Atlantic Ave., cor. Bond St. W. M. Nichol.
Westminster, Bainbridge St. and Hopkinson Ave. A. H. Crosbie.

PROTESTANT EPISCOPAL.

Frederick Burgess, Bishop.

Advent, Bay 17th St., near Bath Ave., Bensonhurst H. B. Gorgas.
All Saints', 7th Ave., cor. 7th St. Wm. Morrison.
Ascension, Kent St., near Manhattan Ave. W. E. Bentley.
Atonement, 17th St., near 5th Av. F. J. Keech.
Calvary, 966 Bushwick Ave. J. Williams.
Christ, E. D., Bedford Ave., near Division. W. S. Chase.
Christ, Clinton, cor. Harrison. W. D. Johnson.
Christ Chapel, Wolcott St., near Van Brunt St. C. S. Smith.
Christ, 3d Ave., cor. 68th St. Bishop Falkner.
Epiphany, McCormick Ave. cor. Belmont Ave.
Good Shepherd, McDonough St., near Lewis Ave. Robert Rogers.
Grace, E. D., Conselyea St., near Lorimer St. William G. Ivie.
Grace, Hicks St., cor. Grace St. C. F. J. Wrigley.
Holy Apostles, Greenwood Ave., cor. Prospect. F. A. Wright.
Holy Comforter Chapel, 44 Debevoise St. John Manning.
Holy Cross Mission, 176 St. Nicholas Ave. H. E. Payne.
Holy Spirit, Bay Parkway, cor. 82d St. J. C. Wellwood.
Holy Trinity, Clinton St., cor. Montague St. J. H. Melish.
Incarnation, Gates Ave., near Classon Ave. J. G. Bacchus.
Messiah, Greene Ave., cor. Clermont Ave. St. Clair Hester.
Nativity, Kenilworth Pl., near Ave. F. A. Fleming.
Redeemer, Pacific St., cor. 4th Ave. T. J. Lacey.
St. Alban's, Ave. F, cor. E. 94th St. V. D. Ruggles.
St. Andrew's, 50th St. and 4th Ave. W. N. Ackley.
St. Ann's, Clinton, cor. Livingston St. C. C. Walker.
St. Augustine's, St. Edward's St., near Myrtle Ave. G. F. Miller.
St. Bartholomew's, Pacific St., cor. Bedford Ave. Frank M. Townley.

CHURCHES IN BROOKLYN—*Continued.*

PROTESTANT EPISCOPAL—Continued.

St. Clement's, Pennsylvania Ave., cor. Liberty. F. W. Appleton.
St. George's, Marcy Av., cor. Gates. W. S. Baer.
St. James's, St. James Pl., cor. Lafayette Ave. C. W. Naumann.
St. John's, St. John's Pl., cor. 7th Ave. F. Page.
St. John's, 99th St., cor. Fort Hamilton Ave. W. A. Swan.
St. John's, Parkville. E. A. Osborn.
St. John's Chapel, Atlantic Ave., cor. Albany. E. C. Angell.
St. Jude's, 55th St., near 13th Ave. C. M. Dunham.
St. Luke's, Clinton Ave., near Fulton St. H. C. Swentzel.
St. Mark's, Adelphi St., n. DeKalb Ave. S. S. Roche.
St. Mark's, Brooklyn Ave. and E. Parkway. J. D. Kennedy.
St. Martin's, President St., c. Smith. F. W. Davis.
St. Mary's, Classon, n. Willoughby Av. J. C. Jones.
St. Matthew's, McDonough St. and Tompkins Ave. F. W. Norris.
St. Matthias, E. 23d St., Sheepshead Bay. T. A. Hyde.
St. Michael's, High St., nr. Gold St. W. S. Watson.
St. Michael's, N. 5th St., near Bedford Ave. M. A. Trathen.
St. Paul's, Clinton St., c. Carroll. W. E. L. Ward.
St. Paul's, Church Ave., cor. St. Paul's Pl. T. G. Jackson.
St. Peter's, State St., near Bond St. Henry Blacklock.
St. Philip's, 11th Ave., cor. 80th St. J. H. Sattig.
St. Philip's Chapel, Dean St., near Troy Ave. N. P. Boyd.
St. Stephen's, Patchen Ave., cor. Jefferson Ave. Robert Merriman.
St. Thomas's, Cooper St., cor. Bushwick Ave. D. M. Genns.
St. Timothy's, Howard Ave., near Atlantic Ave. C. A. Brown.
Transfiguration, Ridgewood and Railroad Aves. A. H. Backus.
Trinity, Arlington Ave., near Schenck Ave. N. R. Boss.

REFORMED EPISCOPAL.

Grace, Herkimer St., near Saratoga Ave. G. R. Swartz.
Reconciliation, Jefferson Ave., cor. Nostrand Ave.
Redemption, Leonard St., near Norman Ave. W. V. Edwards.

REFORMED.

Bay Ridge, 2d Ave. and 80th St. F. P. Young.
Bethany Reformed, Clermont Ave., near Willoughby. James Demarest.
Bushwick Avenue, Bushwick Ave., cor. Himrod St. E. Niles.
Church of Jesus, 64 Ralph St. Christian Oswald.
Dutch Evang., Conklin Av., Canarsie. H. J. Herge.
East New York, New Jersey Ave., near Fulton St. F. L. Cornish.
Edgewood, 14th Ave., near 53d St. H. C. Weber.
First, Bedford Ave., cor. Clymer St. A. J. Bailey.
First, 7th Ave., cor. Carroll St. J. M. Farrar.
Flatbush (First), Flatbush Ave., cor. Church Ave. J. E. Lloyd.
Flatbush (Second) (German), Church Ave., cor. Bedford Ave. Louis Goebel.
Flatlands, Kouwenhoven Pl., near E. 40th St. J. S. Gardner.
German Emmanuel, 410 Graham Ave. W. Walenta.
German Evang., 50 Wyona St., near Fulton St. Paul Wienand.
Grace, Lincoln Rd, c. Bedford Av. C. S. Wyckoff.
Gravesend, Neck Road (E. 1st St.). P. V. Van Buskirk.
Greenwood, 41st St., nr. 8th Ave. C. T. Anderson.
Heights, Church on the, Pierrepont St., near Henry. Andrew Magill.
Kent St., Kent St., near Manhattan Ave. R. G. Hutchins.
New Brooklyn, Herkimer St., cor. Dewey Pl. F. C. Erhardt.

REFORMED—Continued.

New Lots, New Lots Road, cor. Schenck Ave. H. C. Hasbrouck.
New Utrecht, 18th Ave., near 83d St. A. H. Brush.
Ocean Hall, Herkimer St., near Hopkinson Ave.
Old Bushwick, Conselyea and Humboldt Sts. J. J. Munro.
People's, Underhill Ave. and Grove St. H. Frech.
South, 4th Ave. and 55th St. W. J. Macdonald.
St. Lucas, 53 Sutton St. Henry Braem.
St. Petri, Union Av., c. Scholes St. G. G. Wacker.
Twelfth St., 12th St., near 5th Ave. J. C. Caton.
Woodlawn Chapel, Av. M. & E. 9th St. J. G. Addy.

ROMAN CATHOLIC.

C. E. McDonnell, Bishop.

All Saints' (German), Throop Ave., cor. Thornton. George Kaupert.
Annunciation of the B. V. M. (German), N. 5th St., cor. Havemeyer St. Peter Henn.
Assumption of the B. V. M., York St., cor. Jay St. W. J. Donaldson.
Blessed Sacrament, Fulton St., cor. Euclid Ave. Joseph E. McCoy.
Chapel of St. John's Home, St. Mark's Ave., cor. Albany Ave. C. F. Vitta.
Chapel of St. Mary's Female Hospital, 155 Dean St.
Chapel of St. Mary's General Hospital, Rochester and St. Mark's Aves. J. Mackiverkin.
Chapel of St. Peter's Hospital, Henry St., cor. Congress St.
Chapel of the Good Shepherd, Hopkinson Ave., cor. Pacific St.
Chapel of the Precious Blood, 212 Putnam Ave.
Chapel of the Visitation Convent, 89th St. & 2d Av.
Epiphany, South 9th St. E. A. Duffy.
Fourteen Holy Martyrs, Central Ave., cor. Covert St. Bernard Kurz.
Guardian Angel, Ocean Parkway, near Neptune Ave. John J. Cullen.
Holy Cross, Church Av., n. Rogers. J. T. Woods.
Holy Family, Rockaway Ave., and 98th St. John Reynolds.
Holy Family (German), 13th St., cor. 4th Ave. F. X. Bettinger.
Holy Name, 9th Ave., cor. Prospect Ave. T. S. O'Reilly.
Holy Rosary, Chauncey St., Reid Av. J. McEnroe.
Immaculate Conception, Leonard St., cor. Maujer. J. F. Crowley.
Immaculate Heart of Mary, Fort Hamilton Ave., cor. E. 4th St. M. T. Tierney.
Most Holy Trinity (German), 132 Montrose Ave. F. M. Schneider.
Nativity, Classon Ave., cor. Madison St. John L. Belford.
Our Lady of Angels, 4th Ave., cor. 74th St. M. J. Flynn.
Our Lady of Charity, Dean St. and Schenectady Ave. B. Puchalski.
Our Lady of Czestohowa (Polish), 25th St., near 4th Ave. Jas. J. Durick.
Our Lady of Good Counsel, Putnam, near Ralph Ave. V. Sorrentino.
Our Lady of Guadalupe, 73d St. and 15th Ave. John J. Durick.
Our Lady of Loretto (Italian), Pacific St., cor. Sackman St. Louis Caporaso.
Our Lady of Lourdes, De Sales Pl., near Broadway. E. H. Porcile.
Our Lady of Mercy, Schermerhorn St., near Bond. J. J. McAteer.
Our Lady of Mount Carmel (Italian), N. 8th St., cor. Union Ave. P. Saponara.
Our Lady of Peace (Italian), 526 Carroll St. Franciscan Fathers.
Our Lady of Perpetual Help, 5th Ave., near 59th St. J. J. Frawley.
Our Lady of Pompeii, Seigel St. O. Silvestri.
Our Lady of the Presentation, Rockaway Ave., cor. St. Mark's Ave. John J. Clarke.
Our Lady of Solace, W. 17th St. and Mermaid Ave., Coney Island. A. Arcese.
Our Lady of Sorrows, Morgan Ave. and Harrison Pl. H. Mertens.

CHURCHES IN BROOKLYN—*Continued.*

ROMAN CATHOLIC—Continued.

Our Lady of Victory, Throop Ave., cor. McDonough St. James J. Woods.

Sacred Heart, Clermont Av., n. Park Av. J. F. Nash.

Sacred Hearts of Jesus and Mary, Degraw and Hicks Sts. John Vogel.

St. Agnes's, Hoyt St., cor. Sackett. J. S. Duffy.

St. Aloysius, Onderdonk Ave. and Stanhope St. J. W. Hauptman.

St. Alphonsus's (German), 177 Kent St. W. Guhl.

St. Ambrose, Tompkins Ave., cor. De Kalb Ave. Thos. F. McGronen.

St. Anne's, Front St., cor. Gold. T. F. Horan.

St. Anthony of Padua, Manhattan Ave., opposite Milton St. P. F. O'Hare.

St. Augustine, 6th Ave. and Sterling Pl. E. W. McCarty.

St. Barbara's, Central Ave., cor. Bleecker St. J. J. Hanselmann.

St. Benedict's (German), Fulton St., near Ralph Ave. Joseph Traenkle.

St. Bernard's (German), Rapelye St., cor. Hicks. John M. Scheffel.

St. Boniface's (German), Duffield St., near Willoughby St. Martin Lang.

St. Brendan's, 1426 E. 10th St. T. A. Hickey.

St. Brigid's, Linden St., cor. St. Nicholas Ave. P. J. Farrelly.

St. Casimir's (Polish), Greene Ave., near Adelphi St. A. Nawrocki.

St. Catherine of Alexandria, 41st St. and Ft. Hamilton Parkway. John J. O'Neill.

St. Cecilia's, N. Henry St., cor. Herbert St. E. J. McGolrick.

St. Charles Borromeo's, Sidney Pl., cor. Livingston St. J. E. Bobier.

St. Edward's St. Edward's St., cor. Leo Pl. J. F. Melia.

St. Elias's, 720 Leonard St. P. Keshelak.

St. Finbar's, Bay 20th St. and Bath Ave. W. A. Gardner.

St. Francis de Chantal, 57th St., near 13th Ave. W. J. McAdam.

St. Francis of Assisi, Lincoln Road and Nostrand Ave. F. X. Ludeke.

St. Francis Xavier's, Carroll St., cor. 6th Ave. D. J. Hickey.

St. Gabriel's, New Lots Road and Linwood St. T. Fitzgerald.

St. Gregory, Brooklyn Ave. and St. John's Pl. M. Fitzgerald.

St. James's Pro-Cathedral, Jay St., cor. Chapel St. Peter Donohoe.

St. Jerome, cor. Newkirk and Nostrand Aves. T. F. Lynch.

St. John's Cantius, Blake and New Jersey Aves. T. Misicki.

St. John the Baptist's, Willoughby Ave., near Lewis Ave. J. W. Moore.

St. John the Evangelist's, 21st St., near 5th Ave. T. S. Duhigg.

St. John's Chapel, Clermont Ave., near Greene Ave. J. J. Coan.

St. Joseph's, Pacific St., near Vanderbilt Ave. P. J. McNamara.

St. Leonard of Port Maurice's (German), Hamburg Ave., cor. Jefferson St. Geo. D. Sander.

St. Louis's (French), Ellery St., near Nostrand Av. Jules Jollon.

St. Lucy's (Italian), 810 Kent Ave. F. Castellano.

St. Malachy's, Van Sicklen Ave., near Atlantic Ave. D. J. Cherry.

St. Mark's, E. 14th St. and Shore Rd. D. J. McCarthy.

St. Martin of Tours, Knickerbocker Ave. and Hancock St. J. J. Donohue.

St. Mary's, 85th St., cor. 23d Ave. C. Wightman.

St. Mary's of the Angels (Lithuanian), S. 4th and Roebling Sts. Vincent Varnagiris.

St. Mary's Star of the Sea, Court St., cor Luquer. J. O'Connell.

St. Matthew's, Utica Ave., cor. Degraw St. J. F. O'Hara.

St. Michael's, 4th Ave., cor. 42d St. W. T. McGuirl.

St. Michael's Archangel (Italian), Lawrence St., cor. Tillary St. G. Garafalo.

St. Michael's (German), Jerome St., near Liberty Ave. P. G. Messmer.

St. Nicholas's (German), Devoe St., cor. Olive St. J. P. Hoffman.

St. Patrick's, Kent Ave., cor. Willoughby Ave. Thomas Taaffe.

St. Patrick's, 95th St., c. 4th Ave. J. P. McGinley.

St. Paul's, Court St., cor. Congress St. M. G. Flannery.

St. Peter's, Hicks St., cor. Warren St. M. A. Fitzgerald.

SS. Peter and Paul's, Wythe Ave., near S. 2d St. J. Doherty.

St. Rose of Lima's, Lawrence Ave., Parkville. J. McAleese.

St. Savior's, 6th St. and 8th Ave. J. J. Flood.

Sts. Simon and Jude, Ave. T. and Van Siclen Ave. J. J. McCarron.

St. Stanislaus' (Scandinavian), 14th St., near 6th Ave. C. H. Dumahut.

St. Stanislaus' (Polish), Driggs Ave., near Humboldt St. Leo Wysiecki.

St. Stephen's, Summit St., cor. Hicks St. J. G. Fitz Gerald.

St. Teresa's, Classon Ave., cor. Sterling Pl. J. McNamee.

St. Thomas Aquinas's, 4th Ave., cor. 9th St. J. Donohue.

St. Thomas Aquinas's, Flatbush Ave., near Av. N. E. W. Dullea.

St. Vincent de Paul's, N. 6th St., near Driggs Ave. Thomas E. Carroll.

Transfiguration, Hooper St., cor. Marcy Ave. W. J. Maguire.

Visitation of the B. V. M., Verona St., cor. Richards St. W. J. White.

SEVENTH-DAY ADVENTISTS.

First German, 1831 Gates Ave. O. E. Reinke.

Scandinavian, 4th Av. & 55th St. M. L. Andreasen.

South Brooklyn, 55th St. & 4th Av. J. L. Johnson.

UNITARIAN.

Church of the Saviour, Pierrepont St., cor. Monroe Pl. J. P. Forbes.

Fourth, E. 19th St., c. Beverly Rd. L. A. Harvey.

Second, Clinton St., cor. Congress St. C. S. S. Dutton.

South Brooklyn, 4th Ave. & 53d St. H. S. Baker.

Unity (Third), Gates Ave., cor. Irving Pl. W. M. Brundage.

Willow Pl. Chapel, Willow Pl. B. J. Newman.

UNIVERSALIST.

All Souls' Church, Ditmas and Ocean Aves. L. W. Brigham.

Church of Our Father, Grand Ave., cor. Lefferts Pl. T. E. Potterton.

Church of Reconciliation, N. Henry St., near Nassau Ave. C. R. Skinner.

Church of the Good Tidings, Madison, cor. Stuyvestant. T. Estler.

MISCELLANEOUS.

Christian Church of the Evangel, Leonard St., near Meserole Ave. S. A. Lloyd.

First Free Baptist, Keap St., cor. Marcy Ave. R. D. Lord.

First German (Swedenborgian), 164 Clymer St.

First German (Swedenborgian—new), Jefferson and Knickerbocker Aves. William Diehl.

Friends, Schermerhorn St., near Boerum Pl.

German People's, Throop Ave., near Myrtle. F. Harlmann.

Grace Gospel, Bainbridge St., near Saratoga Ave.

Latter-Day Saints, Park Pl. and Schenectady Ave. B. R. McGuire.

Moravian, Jay St., near Myrtle Ave. Paul Greider.

Open Door, Halsey St. & Saratoga Av. C. T. Baylis.

People's, 77 Sutton St. W. F. Silleck.

St. Nicholas Greek Orthodox, 301 Pacific St. G. R. Hawaweeny.

Swedenborgian (New Jerusalem), Clark St. and Monroe Pl. W. R. Reece.

Height of Prominent Buildings in Manhattan.

Name and Location.	No. of Stories.	Height.	Dimensions of Buildings.
American Exchange Bank, Broadway and Cedar St.	16	232 ft.	39 ft. 9½ in. x 49 ft. 5 in. x 100 ft.
American Surety Co., Broadway, cor Pine St.	23	306 ft. 1 in.	84 ft. 8 in. x 85 ft. 6 in.
American Tract Society, Nassau, cor. Spruce St.	23	306 ft.	100 ft. 7 in. x 94 ft. 6 in.
Ansonia Hotel, Broadway, 73d and 74th Sts.	16	180 ft.	213 ft. 8½ in. x 239 x 174.
Astoria Hotel, 344-350 Fifth Ave.	16	213 ft.	335 ft. x 98 ft. 9 in.
Atlantic Mutual Insurance, Wall and William Sts., S. W. cor.	18	242 ft.	58 ft. x 89 ft. 6 in. x 143 ft. 5 in.
Bank of Commerce, cor. Nassau and Cedar Sts.	20	270 ft.	106 ft. 2 in. x 109 ft. 6 in.
Battery Park, State and Pearl Sts.	11	145 1-2 ft.	108 ft. 2¾ in. x 127 ft. 101 ft. 9 in. x 93 ft. 9⅛ in.
Bishop Building, William and Liberty Sts., S.E. cor.	12	162 ft.	60 ft. 6 in. x 97 ft. x 121 ft. 7¼ in.
Bowling-Green Building, 5-11 Broadway.	19	272 ft. 6 in.	162 ft. x 201 ft.
Broad Exchange Building, Broad St. and Exchange Pl.	20	276 ft. 8½ in.	106 ft. 8 in. x 102 ft. 4 in. x 236 ft.
Broadway (No. 84)........	12	154 ft.	44 ft. 6 in. x 58 ft. 9 in.
Broadway Chambers, N. W. cor. Broadway and Chambers St.	18	225 ft.	50 ft. 11 in. x 95 ft.
			142 x 96 x 46 ft.
Commercial Cable, 20-22 Broad St.	21	255 ft., exclusive of dome.	45 ft. 1½ in. x 153 ft. 11 in
			86 ft. 8 in. x 110 ft. 7 in.
Downing Building, 106 and 108 Fulton St.	15	To roof top, 179 ft.: pent house, 190 ft	50 ft. x 74 ft. x 103 ft.
Dun (R. G. Dun), 290-294 Broadway.	15	223 ft.	608 ft. x 130 ft. 7⅛ in.
Empire, Broadway and Rector St.	20	293 ft.	78 ft. x 223 ft. 10 in.
Exchange Court (W. W. Astor), Broadway and Exchange Place.	12	160 ft.	129 ft. 9¼ in. x 159 ft. 4½ in.
Fifth Ave. and 45th St.....	13	164 ft.	75 ft. x 150 ft.
Flatiron (Fuller), B'way & 23d St.	20	286 ft.	......
Gillender, cor. Wall and Nassau Sts.	16	To roof top, 219 ft. to tower, 273 ft.	26 ft. x 73 ft. 5½ in.
Home Life Insurance Co., 256 Broadway.	16	To roof top, 219 ft.: to spire top, 280 ft.	55 ft. 6 in. x 109 ft.
Hotel Netherland, cor. 59th St. and Fifth Ave.	17	To roof top, 220 ft.	Mansard roof and bldg., 100 x 125 ft
Hudson Realty Co., 32-34 Broadway.	16	205 ft. 6 in.	53 ft. 9 in. x 203 ft.
International Bank Building, Broadway and Cedar St., N. W. cor.	14	188 ft.	40 ft. 1 in. x 33 ft. 2½ in. x 153 ft.
Johnston Building, 30-36 Broad St.	15	205 ft.	88 ft. ½ in. x 123 ft. 8¾ in.
Maiden Lane (No. 1).......	13	160 ft.	25 ft. 9 in. x 50 ft. 2 in.
Manhattan Life Insurance Co., 64-68 Broadway.	17	To roof top, 246 ft.; to top of tower, 348 ft.	47 x 125 ft.
Metropolitan Life Insurance Co.	46	657 ft. 5 in.	128 ft. 5½ in. x 275 ft. 3 in.
Morton, 110-116 Nassau St.	12	154 ft.	75¾ x 142 x 112 ft.
Mutual Life Insurance Co., Liberty St.	15	To roof top, 210 ft.: to roof garden, 230 ft.	100 x 125 ft.
Mutual Reserve Life Ins. Co., cor. B'way and Duane St.	14	To roof top, 184 ft.	75 x 125 ft.
N. Y. Life Insurance Co., 346-348 Broadway.	12	188 ft. front; to tower, 270 ft.	60 x 196 ft.
New York Realty Co., 9-13 Maiden Lane.	15	203 ft. 6 in.	56 ft. 6 in. x 78 ft. 5 in.
Park Row, 13-21 Park Row.	29	To roof top, 309 ft.; to tower, 382 ft.	104 ft. 2 in. x 153 ft. 11 in
Postal Telegraph Co., cor. Broadway and Murray St.	13	To roof top, 179 ft.; to pent house, 193 ft.	70 x 100 x 155 ft.
Pulitzer Building, Park Row	22	Extreme height, 375½ ft.	115 ft. 4 in. x 136 ft. 8 in.
Queens Insurance Co., cor. William and Cedar Sts.	15	195 ft.	41 ft. 11½ in. x 68 ft.
Singer Mfg. Co., Broadway near Liberty St.	41	612 ft. 1 in.	
St. James, Broadway, cor. 26th St.	16	204 ft.	94 ft. 8½ in. x 149 ft.
St. Paul Building, Ann St. and Broadway.	26	308 ft.	39.4 x 27 x 104.2 x 54.3 x 83.
Standard Oil Building, 24-30 Broadway.	15	263 ft.	114 ft. 1 in. x 207 ft. 11 in.
Times, Broadway and 42d St.	28	419 ft. 9 in. from lowest basement to top of observatory rail.	
Trinity, 111 Broadway.	21	280 ft. 6 in.	
Vincent Building, Broadway and Duane St.	14	205 ft.	50 ft. 11 in. x 110 ft. 7½ in.
Waldorf-Astoria Hotel, 13-19 W. 33d St.	16	214 ft.	85 ft. x 98 ft. 9 in.
Washington Life Ins. Co., Broadway and Liberty St.	19	273 ft.	53 ft. 9 in. x 159 ft. 3 in.

Wanamaker's, B'way, 8th and 9th Streets, 14 stories. 217 ft. 6 in. high; 65 Exchange Place, 16 stories, 211 ft. 6⅛ in. high; Trinity Place, cor. Rector St., 23 stories, 308 ft. high; Fifth Ave., 58th, 59th Sts. (Plaza Hotel), 18 stories, 251 ft. 11 in. high; Cedar and West Sts., 28 stories, 404 ft. high; B'way and Cortlandt St., 26 stories, 360 ft. 6 in. high; B'way and Cedar St., 21 stories, 282 ft. high; 37 Wall St., 25 stories, 318 ft. high; 1 Wall St., 18 stories, 217 ft. high; Cortlandt and Church Sts., 22 stories, 275 ft. 9 in. high; Church and Dey Sts., 22 stories, 275 ft. 9 in. high; Maiden Lane and Liberty St., 20 stories, 250 feet high; 15 Maiden Lane, 264 ft. 5 in. high; 60 Broadway, 22 stories, 306 ft. 3 in. high.

Brooklyn Navy Yard.

UNITED STATES NAVAL STATION ENTRANCE, FOOT SANDS STREET, BROOKLYN.

Commandant—Rear-Admiral C. F. Goodrich.

Captain of the Yard—Capt. T. E. De W. Veeder.
Ordnance Officer—Lt.-Com'd'r W. S. Crosley.
Equipment Officer—Lt. Com'd'r Harry George.
General Storekeeper—Pay Director Reah Frazer.
Pay Office—Pay Inspector F. T. Arms.
Clothing Factory—Pay Inspector T. S. Jewett.
Chief Engineer of the Yard—Capt. Wm. M. Parks.
Civil Engineers—L. E. Gregory in charge, L. F. Bellinger, L. M. Cox, Assistants.
Naval Constructor—W. J. Baxter.

Naval Hospital — Medical Director E. H. Green.
Naval Laboratory—Medical Director Paul Fitzsimons.
Marine Barracks—Col. W. P. Biddle.
Purchasing Paymaster (2 Rector Street, N. Y.)—Pay Director J. A. Mudd.
Labor Board—Commander H. C. Poundstone, retired.

Passes to the Navy Yard will only be recognized on the day stated on the pass. Passes can be secured by writing to the Captain of the Yard, or at Sands Street gate between 9 A. M. and 4 P. M. A stamped and addressed envelope must be inclosed. Visiting hours are between 10 A. M. and 4 P. M. Application to visit the ships in the yard must be made to the executive officers on board.

Pawnbrokers' Regulations in the City of New York.

PAWNBROKERS in New York City are regulated by statute. The rate of interest fixed by law is 3 per cent. a month or any fraction of a month for the first six months, and 2 per cent. per month for each succeeding month upon any loan not exceeding $100, and 2 per cent. a month for the first six months and 1 per cent. a month for each succeeding month on any loan exceeding $100. Pledges cannot be sold until after they have been kept one year, and then at public auction by a licensed auctioneer, after publication of at least six days in two daily newspapers designated by the Mayor. Pawnbrokers pay a yearly license fee of $500 to the city and are under the control of the Mayor. The license is issued through the Bureau of Licenses, and their books must be kept open to the Mayor, Criminal Courts, Magistrates, and Police.

PROVIDENT LOAN SOCIETY (EXECUTIVE OFFICE, 105 EAST 22D ST.) LOANING OFFICES: 279 4TH AVE., 186 ELDRIDGE ST., 119 WEST 42D ST., 105 E. 125TH ST., 409 GRAND ST. BROOKLYN, 24 GRAHAM AVE.

Office hours: 9 A. M. to 5 P. M.; Saturday to 6 P. M. Ticket good for one year only. Loans may be paid by instalments, in sums not less than $1. Rates of interest: One per cent. per month, or any fraction thereof. Only one-half month interest charged on all loans redeemed within two weeks after date of pledge. Condition of loan, agreed to by the holder of the ticket in consideration of interest being charged at less than the rate allowed by law. The Provident Loan Society of New York shall not be liable for loss or damage by fire, breakage, dampness, theft, or moths; nor shall it be liable in any event for more than 25 per cent. in addition to the amount loaned. James Speyer, President; Frank Tucker, Vice-President; Otto T. Bannard, Treasurer; Mortimer L. Schiff, Secretary; M. G. Hopf, Assistant to Treasurer.

When making payment by instalment, the full amount of interest due on the sum loaned must be included, and the ticket must be returned. The interest due on the loan cannot be paid by instalment. The Society has thus far limited the classes of personal property on which it has made loans to clothing and so-called "jewelry," including under that designation all articles of gold or silver, precious stones, opera-glasses, eye-glasses, also men's clothing in good condition, and ladies' and men's furs.

Hospitals in Manhattan and Bronx.

American Vet. See "N. Y. Am. Veterinary."
Babies', 135 E. 55th St.
Bellevue, foot E. 26th St.
Beth Israel, Jefferson and Cherry Sts.
Chinese, 105 Park St.
City, Blackwell's Island, office foot E. 26th St.
Columbus, 226 E. 20th St.
Emergency for Women, 223 E. 26th St.
Flower, Ave. A, cor. E. 63d St.
Fordham, S. Boulevard, cor. Cambreling Ave.
Free Home for Incurable Cancer, 426 Cherry St.
French Benevolent Society, 450 W. 34th St.
General Memorial, 2 W. 106th St.
German, E. 77th St., cor. Park Ave.
Gouverneur, Gouverneur Slip, cor. Front St.
Hahnemann, Park Ave., near E. 67th St.
Harlem Eye, Ear, and Throat Inf., 144 E. 127th St.
Harlem, Lenox Ave., cor. W. 136th St.
Harlem Italian Sanitarium, 281 Pleasant Ave.
Hospital for Consumptive Children, Spuyten Duyvil.
Hospital for Contagious Eye Diseases, 341 Pleasant Ave.
Hospital for Consumptives, Blackwell's Island.
Hospital for deformity and joint diseases, 1917 Madison Ave.
Hospital of the N. Y. Am. Vet. Col., 337 E. 57th St.
House of Relief, 67 Hudson St.
J. Hood Wright Memorial Hospital, W. 131st St., cor. Amsterdam Ave.
King's Park State, office 1 Madison Ave.
Laura Franklin, Free Hospital for Children, 19 E. 111th St.
Lebanon, Westchester Ave., near Cauldwell Ave.
Lincoln, E. 141st St., cor. Concord Ave.
Manhattan Eye, Ear and Throat, 64th St., near 3d Ave.
Manhattan Maternity, 327 E. 60th St.
Manhattan State Hospital, Ward's Island.
Maternity Hospital of the New York Mothers' Home of the Sisters of Misericorde, 5[illegible] E. 86th St.
Merchant Marine, 109 Broad St.
Metropolitan, 248 E. 82d St.
Metropolitan, Blackwell's Island.
Metropolitan Throat, 351 W. 34th St.
Minturn, foot of E. 16th St.
Mt. Sinai, 5th Ave., cor. E. 100th St.
Mount Merijah, 138 2d St.
New Amsterdam Eye and Ear, 230 W. 38th St.
New York, 7 W. 15th St.
New York American Veterinary, 141 W. 54th St.
New York Eye and Ear Infirmary, 218 2d Ave.
New York Homœopathic Medical College and Hospital, Ave. A, near E. 63d St.
New York Infirmary for Women and Children, 321 East 15th St.
New York Medical College and Hospital for Women, 19 W. 101st St.
New York Ophthalmic and Aural Inst., 46 E. 12th St.
New York Ophthalmic, 201 E. 23d St.
New York Orthopœdic, 126 E. 59th St.
New York Polyclinic, 214 E. 34th St.
New York Post-Graduate, 301 E. 20th St.
New York Skin and Cancer, 330 2d Ave.
New York Society for the Relief of the Ruptured and Crippled, 135 E. 42d St.
New York State Institute, 119 W. 81st St.
New York Throat, Nose, and Lung, 229 E. 57th St.
New York Veterinary, 117 W. 25th St.
Nursery and Child's, 571 Lexington Ave.
Our Lady of Grace, 221 E. 79th St.
Pasteur Institute, 313 W. 23d St.
Peoples, 203 2d Ave.
Philanthropin, 2076 Fifth Ave.
Presbyterian, 70th St., near Park Ave.
Riverside, North Brother Island.
Riverside (Reception), foot E. 16th St.
Roosevelt, W. 59th St., near 9th Ave.
St. Andrew's Convalescent Hospital for Women and Children, 213 E. 17th St.
St. Ann's Maternity, 130 E. 69th St.
St. Elizabeth's, 415 W. 51st St.
St. Francis, E. 142d St., cor. Brook Ave.
St. Gregory's Free Hospital, 91 Gold St.
St. John's Guild Floating Hospital for Children, office 501 5th Ave.
St. Joseph's, E. 143d St., cor. Brook Ave.
St. Joseph's Infirmary, E. 82d St., n. Madison Ave.
St. Lawrence, 447 W. 163d St.
St. Luke's, Amsterdam Ave., cor. W. 113th St.
St. Margaret's, 123 E. 27th St.
St. Mark's, 177 2d Ave.
St. Mary's Free Hospital for Children, 407 W. 34th St.
St. Vincent's, 157 W. 11th St.
Sanitarium for Hebrew Children, 356 2d Ave.
Seaside, office 501 5th Ave.
Seton (for Consumptives), Spuyten Duyvil.
Sloane Maternity, W. 59th St., c. Amsterdam Ave.
Society of Lying-in Hospital, E. 17th St., c. 2d Ave.
Sydenham, 339 E. 116th St.
United States Marine (office, Battery).
Vanderbilt Clinic, 60th St. and Amsterdam Ave.
Washington Heights, 554 W. 165th St.
Willard Parker, foot E. 16th St.
Woman's, 110th St., near Amsterdam Ave.
Yorkville, 246 E. 82d St.

Schools in Manhattan.

ELEMENTARY SCHOOLS.

No.	Location.
1	Henry, Catharine and Oliver Sts.
2	116 Henry St.
3	Hudson and Grove Sts.
4	203 Rivington St.
5	141st St. and Edgecombe Ave.
6	Madison Ave. and 85th St.
7	Hester and Chrystie Sts.
8	29 King St.
9	West End Ave. and 82d St.
10	117th St. and St. Nicholas Ave.
11	314 W. 17th St.
12	371 Madison St.
13	239 E. Houston St.
14	225 E. 27th St.
15	728 5th St.
16	208 W. 13th St.
17	335 W. 47th St.
18	121 E. 51st St.
19	344 E. 14th St.
20	Rivington and Forsyth Sts.
21	222 Mott St.
22	Stanton and Sheriff Sts.
23	Mulberry and Bayard Sts.
24	128th St., nr. Madison Ave.
25	330 5th St.
26	124 W. 30th St.
27	206 E. 42d St.
28	257 W. 40th St.
29	Albany, Washington and Carlisle Sts.
30	88th St., bet. 2d and 3d Aves.
31	200 Monroe St.
32	357 W. 35th St.
33	418 W. 28th St.
34	108 Broome St.
35	160 Chrystie St.
36	710 E. 9th St.
37	113 E. 87th St.
38	Clarke, Dominick & Broome Sts.
39	235 E. 125th St.
40	320 E. 20th St.
41	36 Greenwich Ave.
42	Hester, Orchard and Ludlow Sts.
43	Amsterdam Ave. & 129th St.
44	Hubert and Collister Sts.
45	225 W. 24th St.
46	St. Nicholas Ave. & W. 156th St.
47	225 E. 23d St. (School for the Deaf).
48	124 W. 28th St.
49	237 E. 37th St.
50	211 E. 20th St.
51	523 W. 44th St.
52	Broadway and Academy St.
53	207 E. 79th St.
54	Amsterdam Ave. & 104th St.
55	140 W. 20th St.
56	351 W. 18th St.
57	176 E. 115th St.
58	317 W. 52d St.
59	226 E. 57th St.
60	Clinton, Cherry and Water Sts.*
62	Hester, Essex and Norfolk Sts.
63	3d and 4th Sts., e. of 1st Ave.
64	9th and 10th Sts., e. of Ave. B.
65	Eldridge and Forsyth, near Hester St.
66	88th St., near 1st Ave.*
67	114-124 W. 46th St.
68	116 W. 128th St.
69	125 W. 54th St.
70	207 E. 75th St.
71	188-192 7th St.
72	Lexington Ave. and 105th St.
73	209 E. 46th St.
74	220 E. 63d St.
75	25 Norfolk St.
76	Lexington Ave. and 68th St.
77	1st Ave. and 86th St.
78	Pleasant Ave. and 119th St.
79	38 1st St.
80	225 W. 41st St.
81	119th and 120th Sts., near 7th Ave.
82	1st Ave. and 70th St.
83	16 E. 110th St.
84	430 W. 50th St.
85	1st Ave. and 117th St.
86	Lexington Ave. and 96th St.
87	Amsterdam Ave. & W. 77th St.
88	300 Rivington St.
89	Lenox Ave. and 134th St.
90	147th and 148th Sts., w. of 7th Ave.
91	Stanton and Forsyth Sts.*
92	Broome and Ridge Sts.
93	Amsterdam Ave. & 93d St.
94	68th St. and Amsterdam Ave.
95	West Houston and Clarkson Sts.*
96	Ave. A and 81st St.
97	Pitt and Delancey Sts.
98	38 Sheriff St.
100	138th St., w. of 5th Ave.*
101	111th St., west of Lexington Ave.*
102	113th St., east of 2d Ave.*
103	119th St. and Madison Ave.
104	413 E. 16th St.
105	269 E. 4th St.
106	Lafayette St., n'r Spring St.
107	274 W. 10th St.
108	60 Mott St.
109	99th & 100th Sts., e. of 3d Ave.
110	28 Cannon St.
112	83 Roosevelt St.
113	7 Downing St.
114	73 Oliver St.
116	215 E. 32d St.
117	170 E. 77th St.
119	133d & 134th Sts., near 8th Ave.
120	187 Broome St.
121	102d St., bet. 2d and 3d Aves.
122	9th St. and 1st Ave.
124	29 Horatio St.
125	180 Wooster St.
126	536 E. 12th St.
127	515 W. 37th St.
129	433 E. 19th St
130	143 Baxter St.
131	273 E. 2d St.
132	182d St. & Wadsworth Ave.
134	293 Pearl St.
135	51st St. and 1st Ave.
137	Grand and Essex Sts.
140	116 Norfolk St.
141	468 W. 58th St.
144	30 Allen St.
147	Henry and Gouverneur Sts.
150	95th & 96th Sts., e. of 2d Ave.
151	91st St. and 1st Ave.
157	St. Nicholas Ave. & 127th St.
158	Ave. A, 77th and 78th Sts.
159	119th St., bet. 2d and 3d Aves.
160	Rivington and Suffolk Sts.
161	105 Ludlow St.
162	36 City Hall Place.
163	509 E. 120th St.
165	108th and 109th Sts., bet. Amsterdam Ave. and B'way.
166	89th St., bet. Amsterdam and Columbus Aves.
168	104th and 105th Sts., bet. 1st and 2d Aves.
169	Audubon Ave., 168th and 169th Sts.
170	111th St., bet. 5th & Lenox Aves.
171	103d and 104th Sts., bet. 5th and Madison Aves.
172	108th and 109th Sts., bet. 1st and 2d Aves.
174	Attorney, near Rivington St.
177	Market and Monroe Sts.
179	101st and 102d Sts., bet. Columbus & Amsterdam Aves.
180	30 Vandewater St.
183	66th and 67th Sts., east of 1st Ave.
184	116th and 117th Sts., east of Lenox Ave.
186	145th and 146th Sts, near Amsterdam Ave.
188	Manhattan, East Houston, Lewis and E. 3d Sts.
190	82d St., bet. 1st and 2d Aves.
192	136th St. and A'sterd'm Ave.
	Training, 119th St., near 7th Ave.
	Truant, 215 E. 21st St.
	Nautical Schoolship, foot of E. 24th St.

* New buildings in process of construction.

HIGH SCHOOLS.—De Witt Clinton, 10th Ave., 58th and 59th Sts.; Wadleigh, 114th and 115th Sts., w. of 7th Ave.; Washington Irving, 34½ E. 12th St.; Commerce, 65th & 66th Sts., w. of B'way; Stuyvesant, 225 E. 23d St.

THE BRONX.

No.	Location.
1	College Ave. and 145th St.
2	3d Ave., near 170th St.
3	157th St. and Courtlandt Ave.
4	Fulton Av. and 173d St.
5	2436 Webster Ave.
6	Tremont, Bryant and Vyse Aves., West Farms.
7	Kingsbridge Ave. and 232d St.
8	Mosholu P'kwy, Bedford Pk.
9	735 E. 138th St.
10	Eagle Ave. and 163d St.
11	Ogden Ave., Highbridge.
12	Overing St., Densen & Frisby Aves., West Chester. Annex, 5th Ave., East Chester.
13	216th St. and Willett Ave., Williamsbridge.
14	Eastern Boulevard, Throgs Neck.
15	West Chester and St. Lawrence Aves.
16	Matilda St., Wakefield; Annex, 5th Av., East Chester.
17	Fordham Ave., City Island.
18	Courtlandt Ave., n. 148th St.
19	234th & 235th Sts., n. Woodl'n
20	Fox, Simpson, and 167th Sts.
21	225th & 226th Sts., n. White Plains Ave., Williamsb'ge.
22	599 E. 140th St.
23	165th St. and Union Ave.
24	Kappock Rd., Spuyten Duyvil.
25	Union Ave. & 149th St.
26	Andrews and Burnside Aves.
27	St. Ann's Ave., 147th and 148th Sts.

No	Location.	No	Location.	No.	Location.
28	Tremont & Anthony Aves.; Annex, 1787 Weeks Ave., Mt. Hope.	34	Amethyst Ave. and Victor St., Van Nest.	41	Olinville Ave. and Magenta St., Olinville.
29	Cypress Ave. and 136th St.	35	163d St., Grant and Morris Aves.	42	Washington and Wendover Aves.
30	41st St., near Brook Ave.	36	Blackrock Ave., Unionport.	43	Brown Pl., 135th & 136th Sts.
31	Mott and Walton Aves., 144th and 146th Sts.	37	145th and 148th Sts., east of Willis Ave.	44	*Prospect Ave. and 176th St.
				45	*189th and Hoffman Sts. and Lorillard Pl.
32	183d St. and Beaumont Ave. Annex, Boston R'd. Bronxdale.	38	157th St. and 3d Ave.		
		39	Longwood Ave., Kelly and Beck Sts.	46	*196th St., Bainbridge and Briggs Aves.
33	Jerome and Walton Aves., north of 184th St.	40	Prospect Ave., Jennings St. & Ritter Pl.		

HIGH SCHOOL.—Morris, 166th St., Boston Rd., Jackson Ave. *Under construction.

EVENING HIGH SCHOOLS.

20	Rivington and Forsyth Sts. (men).	27	41st St., E. of 3d Av. (women)		Wadleigh, 114th St., near 7th Ave. (women).
	DeWitt Clinton H. S., 59th St. & 10th Ave. (men).	147	Henry and Gouverneur Sts. (women).		Morris, Jackson Ave., Boston Rd. & 166th St.
		184	116th St. n'r Lenox Av. (men).		

EVENING SCHOOLS FOR MALES.

1	8 Henry St.	83	216 E. 110th St.	160	Rivington and Suffolk Sts.
2	116 Henry St.	79	42 1st St.	21	Elizabeth St., near Spring.
8	King St., near Macdougal St.	25	330 5th St.	3	Bronx, 157th St. & Court't Av.
		40	320 E. 20th St.	9	Bronx, 735 E. 138th St.
39	224 E. 126th St.	58	52d St., near 8th Ave.	42	Bronx, Washington & Wendover Aves.
16	208 W. 13th St.	70	207 E. 75th St.		
32	357 W. 35th St.	62	Hester & Norfolk Sts.	109	99th St., near 3d Ave.
49	237 E. 37th St.	77	85th St. and 1st Ave.	65	Eldridge, near Hester St.
22	Stanton and Sheriff Sts.	43	129th St. & Amsterdam Ave.		

FOR MEN AND BOYS, WOMEN AND GIRLS.

29	Albany, Wash'n & Carlisle Sts	67	120 W. 46th St.		

EVENING SCHOOLS FOR FEMALES.

71	190 7th St.	14	225 E. 27th St.	93	Amsterdam Ave. and 93d St.
4	203 Rivington St.	17	335 W. 47th St.	72	Lexington Ave., 105th & 106th Sts.
23	Mulberry and Bayard Sts.	96	Ave. A and 81st St.		
45	24th St., near 8th Ave.	42	Hester, Orchard and Ludlow Sts.	157	St. Nicholas Ave. & 127th St.
19	14th St., near 1st Ave.			177	Market and Monroe Sts.
13	239 E. Houston St.	92	154 Broome St.	10	Eagle Ave. & 163d St., Bronx.
59	E. 57th St., near 3d Ave.	38	Clarke, Domin'k & Br'me Sts.		

NORMAL COLLEGE,
PARK AVE., CORNER EAST SIXTY-EIGHTH ST.

NEW YORK UNIVERSITY,
UNIVERSITY HEIGHTS AND 32 WAVERLEY PLACE.

COLLEGE CITY OF NEW YORK,
AMSTERDAM AVE. AND 138TH STREET.

COLUMBIA UNIVERSITY,
WEST 116TH ST., NEAR AMSTERDAM AVE.

Corporate Schools in Manhattan and Bronx.

Society for the Relief of Half Orphan and Destitute Children, Manhattan Ave. and 104th St.; New York House of Refuge, Randall's Island; Leake and Watts Orphan Asylum, Yonkers, N. Y.; Colored Orphan Asylum and Association for the Benefit of Colored Children, W. 143d St. and Amsterdam Ave.

American Female Guardian Society—Home School, 936 Woodycrest Ave., Bronx. No. 1—303 E. 109th St. No. 2—418 W. 41st St. No. 3—39 Rutgers St. No. 4—4 Willett St. No. 5—4 Charlton St. No. 6—259 E. 4th St. No. 7—225 and 227 E. 80th St. No. 8—523 Morris Ave. No. 9—421 E. 60th St. No. 10—12 Columbia St. No. 11—243 E. 103d St. No. 12—2247 2d Ave.

Five Points Mission, 63 Park St.; Five Points House of Industry, 155 Worth St.; R. C. Orphan Asylum, Female Department, Sedgwick Ave., Bronx; R. C. Orphan Asylum, Male Department, Sedgwick Ave., Bronx.

Children's Aid Society—535 E. 16th St.; 287 E. B'way; 247 E. 44th St.; 552 W. 53d St.; 224 W. 63d St.; 156 Leonard St.; 407 E. 73d St.; 256 Mott St.; 314 E. 35th St.; 28 Pike St.; 350 E. 88th St.; 632 6th St.; 219 Sullivan St.; 295 8th St.; 417 W. 38th St.; 24 Sullivan St.

Hospital for Ruptured and Crippled, 42d St. and Lexington Ave.; House of the Holy Family, 134-136 2d Ave.; New York Institute for the Blind, 34th St. and 9th Ave.

Board of Education in City of New York.

President, Egerton L. Winthrop, Jr.

MANHATTAN MEMBERS.

Until Jan. 1, 1910—Lewis Haase, J. N. Francolini, N. J. Barrett, E. L. Winthrop, Jr.
Until Jan. 1, 1911—T. J. O'Donohue, Clement March, Robert L. Harrison, Frederic R. Coudert.
Until Jan. 1, 1912—Dennis J. McDonald, Cornelius J. Sullivan, Max Katzenberg, Chas. E. Bruce.
Until Jan. 1, 1913—George J. Gillespie, F. P. Cunnion, James E. Sullivan, M. S. Stern, F. W. Crowninshield.
Until Jan. 1, 1914—Hugo Kanzler, L. Haupt, A. Stern, Waller Alexander, R. B. Aldcroftt, Jr.

BROOKLYN MEMBERS.

Until Jan. 1, 1910—James P. Holland, Nathan S. Jonas, John R. Thompson.
Until Jan. 1, 1911—Mitchell May, George Freifield, Joseph E. Cosgrove.
Until Jan. 1, 1912—Thomas M. De Laney, Horace E. Dresser.
Until Jan. 1, 1913—John Greene, Alexander Ferris, Arthur S. Somers.
Until Jan. 1, 1914—Robert E. McCafferty, Frank W. Meyer, George W. Wingate.

BRONX MEMBERS.

Until Jan. 1, 1910—Michael J. Sullivan.
Until Jan. 1, 1911—Thomas J. Higgins.
Until Jan. 1, 1912—Frank D. Wilsey.
Until Jan. 1, 1913—Henry H. Sherman.

QUEENS.

Until Jan. 1, 1910—George A. Vandenhoff.
Until Jan. 1, 1911—A. H. Man.
Until Jan. 1, 1912—Rupert B. Thomas.
Until Jan. 1, 1913—B. Suydam.

RICHMOND.

Until Jan. 1, 1912—A. Hollick.
Until Jan. 1, 1914—R. McKee.

No.	Location.	No.	Location.	No.	Location.
1	Adams and Concord sts.	64	Berriman and Belmont aves.	121	E. 55th st. and Ave. C.
2	47th st., near 3d ave.	65	Richmond, n'r Ridgewood av.	122	Harrison av. & Heyward st.
3	Hancock, near Bedford ave.	66	Osborn, near Sutter ave.	123	Irving ave. and Suydam st.
4	Berkeley pl., near 5th ave.	67	N. Elliott pl., near Park ave.	124	4th ave. and 18th st.
5	Duffield, Johnson and Gold sts.	68	Bushwick ave., corner Kosciusko st.	125	Blake and Thatford aves.
6	Warren, near Smith st.	69	Ryerson st., near Myrtle av.	126	Meserole ave. & Guernsey st.
7	York, near Bridge st.	70	Patchen ave., cor. Macon st.	127	7th ave., 78th and 79th sts.
8	Hicks, Middagh & Poplar Sts	71	Heyward, near Lee ave.	128	21st ave., 83d & 84th sts.
9	Sterling pl. & Vanderbilt av.	72	New Lots rd., cor. Schenck st.	129	Quincy st., near Stuyvesant.
10	7th ave. and 17th st.	73	McDougall, c. Rockaway ave.	130	Fort Hamilton av. & E. 5th st.
11	Washington, near Greene av.	74	Kosciusko st., n'r Broadway	131	Fort Hamilton ave., 43d and 44th sts.
12	Adelphi, near Myrtle ave.	75	Evergreen av., cor. Ralph st.	132	Manhattan and Met. aves.
13	Degraw, near Hicks st.	76	Wyona, near Fulton st.	133	Butler st., bet. 4th & 5th aves.
14	Navy and Concord sts.	77	2d st., near 6th ave.	134	18th ave. & Ocean Parkway.
15	3d ave. and State st.	78	Pacific st., near Court st.	136	4th ave., 40th & 41st sts.
16	Wilson, near Bedford ave.	79	Kosciusko, n'r Sumner ave.	137	Saratoga av. & Bainbridge st.
17	Driggs ave., cor. N. 5th st.	80	W. 17th and W. 19th sts., near Neptune ave.	138	Prospect pl., west of Nostrand ave.
18	Maujer, near Leonard st.	81	Harway, near 25th ave.	139	Ave. C, E. 13th and 14th sts.
19	S. 2d, cor. Keap st.	82	4th ave., cor. 36th st.	140	60th st., west of 4th ave.
20	Union ave. and Keap st.	83	Bergen, cor. Schenectady av.	141	Leonard, McKibbin and Boerum sts.
21	McKibbin, near Manhat. av.	84	Glenmore, cor. Stone ave.	142	Henry and Rapelye sts.
22	Java, near Manhattan ave.	85	Evergreen ave., cor. Cov't st.	143	Havemeyer, N. 6th & 7th sts.
23	Conselyea, n'r Humboldt st.	86	Irving ave., cor. Harman st.	144	Howard ave., Prospect pl. and St. Mark's ave.
24	Arion pl., cor. Beaver st.	87	Herkimer, cor. Radde pl.	145	Central ave. and Noll st.
25	Lafayette, near Sumner ave.	88	Thames st., c. Vanderv'rt pl.	146	18th and 19th sts., bet. 6th and 7th aves.
26	Quincy, near Ralph ave.	89	Newkirk ave., cor. E. 31st st.	147	Bushwick ave., Seigel & McKibbin sts.
27	Nelson, cor. Hicks st.	90	Bedford and Church aves.	148	Ellery and Hopkins sts., near Delmonico pl.
28	Herkimer, near Ralph ave.	91	E. New York & Albany aves.	149	Sutter ave., Vermont and Wyona sts.
29	Columbia, cor. Amity st.	92	Rogers ave. & Robinson st	150	Christopher ave. & Sackman st., near Belmont ave.
30	Conover, Sullivan & Wolcott sts.	93	New York av. & Herkimer st.	151	Knickerbocker ave., Halsey and Weirfield sts.
31	Dupont, n'r Manhattan ave.	94	Prospect ave., opp. Reeve pl.	*	Jamaica ave., opp. Enfield st.
32	Hoyt, cor. President st.	95	Van Sicklen, near Neck rd.	152	Ave. G, E. 23d and 24th sts.
33	Heyward, near Broadway.	96	Ocean ave., near Neck rd.	153†	Ave. T. & E. 12th st., Home'st
34	Norman ave. and Eckford st.	97	Benson, cor. 25th ave.	154†	11th ave., Windsor pl. & Sherman st.
35	Decatur, cor. Lewis ave.	98	Ave. Z, cor. E. 26th st.	155†	Eastern Parkway and Herkimer st.
36	Stagg, near Bushwick ave.	99	Coney Island rd. & Elm ave.	156†	Sutter Ave., Barrett & Grafton sts.
37	S. 4th, near Berry st.	100	W. 3d, between Park pl. and Sheepshead ave.	157†	Kent ave., near Myrtle ave.
38	N. 7th, near Berry st.	101	86th st., near 18th ave.	158†	Belmont ave., Ashford and Warwick sts.
39	6th ave., cor. 8th st.	102	71st st. and 2d ave.	159†	Pitkin ave., Hemlock & Crescent sts.
40	15th st., near 4th ave.	103	14th ave., 53d & 54th sts.	160†	Ft. Hamilton ave., 51st and 52d sts.
41	Dean, cor. New York ave.	104	92d st., cor. 5th ave.	161†	2d ave. and 56th st.
42	St. Mark's and Classon aves.	105	Ft. Hamilton ave., bet. 58th and 59th sts.	162†	St. Nicholas and Willoughby aves. and Suydam st.
43	Boerum, near Manhat. ave.	106	Hamburg and Putnam aves. and Cornelia st.	163†	Benson and 17th aves. and Bay 14th st.
44	Throop, cor. Putnam ave.	107	8th ave. and 13th st.	164†	14th ave., 42d and 43d sts.
45	Lafayette, near Classon ave.	108	Linwood, cor. Arlington ave.	165*	Lott and Hopkinson aves. and Amboy st.
46	Union, near Henry st.	109	Dumont ave., Powell and Sackman sts.		
47	Pacific & Dean sts., n'r 3d av.	110	Monitor st. and Driggs ave.		
48	18th ave. and 67th street.	111	Sterling pl., cor. Vanderbilt ave.		
49	Maujer, near Graham ave.	112	15th ave., 71st and 72d sts.		
50	S. 4th, near Havemeyer st.	113	Evergreen ave. & Moffat st.		
51	Meeker av., cor Humboldt st.	114	Remsen, cor. Ave. F.		
52	Ellery, near Broadway.	115	Canarsie ave., near Ave. M.		
53	Starr, near Central ave.	116	Knickerbocker ave., corner Grove st.		
54	Walworth, near Myrtle ave.	117	Stagg st. and Bushwick ave		
55	Floyd, near Tompkins ave.	118	59th st. and 4th ave.		
56	Bushwick ave., cor. Mad'n st	119	Ave. K and E. 38th st.		
57	Reid ave., cor. Van Buren st.	120	Barren Island.		
58	Degraw, near Smith st.				
59	Leonard, near Nassau ave.				
60	4th ave., cor. 20th st.				
61	Fulton st. and N. Jersey ave.				
62	Bradford, near Liberty ave.				
63	Hinsdale, n'r Glenmore ave.				

* Truant School. † Under Construction.

HIGH SCHOOLS.

Girls'	Nostrand ave., cor. Halsey st.	Erasmus Hall	Flatbush ave., near Church ave.
Boys'	Putnam, cor. Marcy ave.	Eastern District	Marcy av., Rodney and Keap sts.
Annex	Bedford and Jefferson aves.	Commercial	Albany ave., Bergen and Dean sts.
Manual Training	7th ave., 4th and 5th sts.		

Training School for Teachers, Park pl., west of Nostrand ave.

EVENING SCHOOLS.—Night sessions are held for men and boys at Schools Nos. 1, 5, 13, 17, 40, 43, 45, 73, 92, 94, 100, 101, 106, 108, 109, 123, 126, 148. For women and girls: Nos. 2, 15, 18, 22, 26, 54, 92, 100, 101, 108, 120, 123, 142, 150. For men and boys, women and girls, Nos. 5, 92, 100, 101, 108, 123; Eastern Evening High School for men held in P. S. No. 122; Brooklyn Evening High School for men, held in Boys' High School Building; Central Evening High School for women, held in Girls' High School Building; Williamsburg Evening High School for women, held in Eastern District High School; Evening Technical and Trade School, held in Manual Training High School; South Brooklyn Evening High School for Men, held in P. S. 136.

INDUSTRIAL AND ASYLUM SCHOOLS.

Orphan Asylum. 1423-1425 Atlantic ave.
R. C. Orphan Asylum, (Boys), Albany and St. Mark's aves.
R. C. Orphan Asylum (Girls), Willoughby and Sumner aves.
Church Charity Foundation, Albany ave. and Herkimer st.
Howard Colored Orphan Asylum, Dean st. and Troy ave.
Industrial School Association, 141-153 S. 3d st.

Industrial School Ass'n and Home for Destitute Children, Sterling pl., near Flatbush ave.
German Orphan Home, Graham and Montrose aves.
Convent of the Sisters of Mercy, 273 Willoughby ave.
Sheltering Arms Nursery, 157 Dean st.
Hebrew Orphan Asylum, Ralph ave., near Pacific st.

The Public Schools of New York City.

Public education in New York City began with the founding of the Free School Society (after 1826 the Public School Society) in 1805. The society began in a small way, depending upon private subscriptions, but soon received aid from the city. It gradually expanded, and until 1842 had control of the moneys supplied for educational purposes by the city and the common school fund of the State. This condition of affairs was unique. The society, being under the direction of high-minded citizens, enjoyed a large degree of public confidence. So anomalous a system could not last, however, and by an act of the Legislature, passed in 1842, the Board of Education was established. The Public School Society continued to conduct its schools until 1853, when, by mutual consent, they were all taken over by the Board. The society at that time had more than a hundred schools; the value of the property it transferred to the city was estimated at $450,000, and during its existence it educated some 600,000 children. The Board of Education was an elective body from 1842 to 1871, the members being chosen first by wards and from 1863 by school districts; since 1871 they have been appointed by the Mayor. In Brooklyn a Board of Education was created in 1843; the members were chosen by the Common Council until 1862, in which year the appointing power was vested in the Mayor. When consolidation took effect in 1898, separate school boards were provided for the several boroughs (Manhattan and the Bronx being united), with a central Board of Education (a delegated body) having charge of the finances, the erection and repair of buildings, the acquiring of sites, the purchase and distribution of supplies, etc. This system was dropped on the revision of the Charter in 1901, and since 1902 there has been one Board of Education for the city. It consists of forty-six members—twenty-two for Manhattan, fourteen for Brooklyn, four each for the Bronx and Queens, and two for Richmond. Their term of office is five years.

The Board of Superintendents, consisting of the city superintendent of schools and eight associate superintendents, has large powers in the nomination, promotion, and transfer of teachers, the recommendation of text-books and scholastic supplies, the determination of courses of study, the fixing of qualifications for teachers' licenses, etc. Its important acts require the approval of the Board of Education. There are twenty-six district superintendents, whose duties are to visit schools and observe the work of teachers. The Board of Examiners (consisting of the city superintendent and four examiners) conducts all examinations for would-be teachers, and prepares eligible lists. The school superintendents and examiners, as well as the supervisor of free lectures, the superintendent of school buildings, and the superintendent of school supplies (whose duties are indicated by their titles), have terms of six years each. The Board of Education appoints all these officials, and also a secretary and auditor, having no fixed term. Principals and teachers are appointed by the Board of Education on the nomination of the Board of Superintendents. The merit system is in full operation, and teachers are appointed in order of standing. Beginners are on probation for three years, their licenses being renewable from year to year; when permanently licensed, their tenure is assured, and they cannot be removed except on charges. New teachers are appointed only after pursuing a training school course.

The budget appropriation of the Department of Education for 1908 was $26,712,963.59, of which $21,038,075.22 constituted the general school fund (for teachers' salaries). For 1909 the appropriation is $27,470,736.80, the general school fund being $22,044,821.43. A woman teacher now enters the system at $600 a year, and advances, with yearly increments of $40 to $1,240. This applies to the great majority of teachers in elementary schools. In the upper grades the maximum salaries are $1,320 and $1,440. Men teachers in these schools now start at $900 and go up to $2,400. Men principals of elementary schools receive $3,500, and women principals $2,500. In high schools the salaries for women range from $700 to $2,500, and for men from $900 to $3,000. Principals of high schools are paid $5,000, and $5,000 is the salary of district superintendents. Examiners receive $6,000. Associate superintendents receive $6,500. The salary of the city superintendent is $10,000. The number of elementary schools is 498—179 in Manhattan, 157 in Brooklyn, 42 in the Bronx, 86 in Queens, and 34 in Richmond. The number of high schools is fifteen, besides four high school departments in elementary school buildings in Queens. There are also three training schools for teachers and two truant schools. In the elementary schools there are 1,456 men and 13,754 women teachers; in the high schools, 545 men and 592 women. In the evening schools (high and elementary) there are 959 men and 882 women teachers. Eighty-five attendance officers enforce the Compulsory Education law. The latest available figures show the attendance as follows:

	Elementary Schools. (Kindergarten, Primary, Grammar).	High Schools.		Elementary Schools. (Kindergarten, Primary, Grammar).	High Schools.
Manhattan	241,947	8,297	Richmond	11,992	654
Brooklyn	205,064	12,786			
The Bronx......	55,483	2,466	Total	555,525	26,929
Queens	41,039	2,726			

Number on part time (three and three-fourths hours per day), elementary schools:

Manhattan	14,090	Richmond	190
Brooklyn	41,800		
The Bronx	5,849	Total	65,799
Queens	3,870		

Number of sittings:

	Elementary Schools.	High Schools.		Elementary Schools.	High Schools
Manhattan	290,451	11,798	Richmond	17,181	704
Brooklyn	219,953	13,273			
The Bronx.....	63,299	2,326	Total	641,469	31,692
Queens	50,585	3,591			

The number of new sittings supplied since September 1, 1907, has been 76,425, and the reduction in the number of part-time pupils has been 3,234.

Teachers incapacitated after thirty years' service are retired on pensions (half pay); the number of retired teachers is 996.

School buildings and sites are paid for with the proceeds of city bonds (corporate stock); the amount issued since consolidation has been $82,293,849.

Prominent Societies and Associations

(IN MANHATTAN AND BRONX BOROUGHS).

Actors' Society, 133 W. 45th St. Stokes Sullivan, Sec.

Actuarial Society. Arthur Hunter, Sec., 346 Broadway.

Amen Corner, Hoffman House. J. W. McDonald, Sec.

Am. Automobile Association, 437 5th Ave. F. H. Elliott, Sec.

Am. Bankers' Association, 5 Nassau St. Fred E. Farnsworth, Sec.

Am. Bible Society, 6 Bible House. William I. Haven, John Fox and H. O. Dwight, Secs.

Am. Church Missionary Society, 281 4th Ave. Arthur S. Lloyd, Sec.

Am. Fine Arts Society, 215 W. 57th St. C. J. Miller, Sec.

Am. Geographical Society, 15 W. 81st St. A. A. Raven, Sec.

Am. Institute, 19 W. 44th St. R. A. B. Dayton, Sec.

Am. Institute of Banking, 5 Nassau St. George E. Allen, Sec.

Am. Missionary Association, 287 4th Ave. J. W. Cooper and Chas. J. Ryder, Secs.

American Motor League, 132 Nassau St. F. A. Egan, Sec.

Am. Newspaper Pub. Association, 61 Park Row. Herman Ridder, Pres.

Am. Protective Tariff League, 339 Broadway. Charles A. Moore, Pres.

Am. Railway Association, 24 Park Place. W. F. Allen, Sec.

Am. Scenic and Historic Society, 154 Nassau St. E. H. Hall, Sec.

Am. Seamen's Friend Society, 76 Wall St. Geo. McP. Hunter, Sec.

Am. Society for the Prevention of Cruelty to Animals, 50 Madison Ave. R. Welling, Sec.

Am. Society of Civil Engineers, 220 W. 57th St. C. W. Hunt, Sec.

Am. Sunday-School Union, 156 5th Ave. E. P. Bancroft, Sec.

Am. Tract Society, 150 Nassau St. Frederic Judson Swift, Sec.

Am. Water-Color Society, 215 W. 57th St. W. Merritt Post, Sec.

Art Students' League, 215 W. 57th St. Amelia Merritt Ives, Sec.

Association for Befriending Children and Young Girls, 136 2d Ave. Mrs. Wm. E. Fay, Sec.

Association for Improved Instruction of Deaf Mutes, 904 Lexington Ave. Paul M. Herzog, Sec.

Beethoven Maennerchor, 7th Ave., cor. 124th St. Karl Oberbach, Sec.

Board of Foreign Missions, 156 5th Ave. Arthur J. Brown, Sec.

Charity Organization Society, 105 E. 22d St. E. T. Devine, Gen. Sec.

Children's Aid Society, 105 E. 22d St. C. L. Brace, Sec.

Christian and Missionary Alliance, 690 8th Ave. A. E. Funk, Sec.

City Improvement Society. 571 5th Ave.

City Vigilance League, 105 E. 22d St. T. L. McClintock, Sec.

Cooper Union, for Advancement of Science and Art, 8th St. and 4th Ave. R. Fulton Cutting, Sec.

Domestic and Foreign Missionary Society of the Protestant Episcopal Church, 281 4th Ave. A. S. Lloyd and Joshua Kimber, Secs.

Evangelical Alliance, 222 W. 23d St. Leander Chamberlain, Pres.

Friendly Sons of St. Patrick. Alfred J. Tally, Sec., 27 William St.

Gaelic Society, 624 Madison Ave., Jeremiah Lawlor, Sec.

George Junior Republic Assoc. V. E. Macy, Sec.

German Society, 13 Broadway. A. Behrens, Sec.

Hebrew Benevolent and Orphan Asylum Society, Amsterdam Ave., cor. W. 137th St. A. Schiff, Sec.

Hebrew Sheltering Guardian Society, Broadway, cor. W. 150th St. Gustav Eckstein, Sec.

Helping Hand Association, 416 W. 54th St. Mrs. E. H. Herrick, Sec.

Holland Society, 99 Nassau St. H. L. Bogert, Sec.

Home and Foreign Missionary Society of A. M. E. Church, 61 Bible House. H. B. Parks, Sec.

Hospital Saturday and Sunday Association, 105 E. 22d St. Geo. P. Cammann, Sec.

Huguenot Society, 105 E. 22d St. Mrs. J. M. Lawton, Sec.

Industrial Christian Alliance, 170 Bleecker St. Harvey G. Furbay, Sec.

International Order of the King's Daughters and Sons, 156 5th Avenue. Mrs M. L. Dickinson, Sec.

Irish Emigrant Society, 51 Chambers St. Thos. V. Brady, Sec.

Irish Ind. League of America, 20 Vesey St. John Quinn, Sec.

Ladies' Christian Union, 49 W. 9th St.; 308 2d Ave. and 153 E. 62d St. Mrs. Henry Bowers, Sec.

Legal Aid Society, 239 Broadway. A. Leo. Everitt, Sec.

Linnæan Society, Central Park West, cor. W. 77th St. C. G. Abbott, Sec.

Manufacturers' Association, 299 Broadway. P. T. Tunison, Sec.

Merchants' Association, 54 Lafayette St. S. C. Mead, Sec.

Methodist Historical Society, 150 5th Ave. Jas. R. Joy, Sec.

Municipal Art Society, 119 E. 19th St. Charles M. Shean, Sec.

Nat'l Association of Credit Men, 41 Park Row. Chas. E. Meek, Sec.

Nat'l Christian League for Promotion of Purity, 5 E. 12th St. Mrs. E. B. Grannis, Pres.

Nat'l Citizens' Alliance, 41 Park Row. H. Nichols, Sec.

Nat'l Humane Alliance, 105 E. 22d St. H. G. Fiske, Pres.

Nat'l Sculpture Society, 215 W. 57th St. J. S. Hartley, Sec.

Nat'l Society of New England Women, 531 5th Ave. Mrs. E. Thorndike, Sec.

New England Society. G. Wilson, Sec., 65 Liberty St.

N. Y. Academy of Sciences, Central Park West, cor. W. 77th St. E. O. Hovey, Rec. Sec.

N. Y. Association of Working Girls' Societies, 209 E. 23d St. Mrs. Vernon C. Brown, Sec., New Rochelle.

N. Y. Association for Improving the Condition of the Poor, 105 E. 22d St. L. E. Opdycke, Sec.

N. Y. Bible Society, 66 Bible House. Chas. W. Parsons, Sec.

N. Y. City Church Extension and Missionary Soc. of M. E. Church, 150 5th Ave. F. M. North, Sec.

N. Y. City Mission and Tract Society, 105 E. 22d St. W. S. Coffin, Sec.

N. Y. Flower and Fruit Mission, 104 E. 20th St. Miss F. L. Russell, Sec.

N. Y. Genealogical and Biographical Society, 226 W. 58th St. H. R. Drowne, Sec.

N. Y. Historical Society, 170 2d Ave. G. L. Schieffelin, Cor. Sec.

N. Y. Kindergarten Association, 524 W. 42d St. James M. Bruce, Sec.

N. Y. Law Institute, 118 P. O. Building. J. J. Rollins, Sec.

N. Y. Maennerchor Society, 203 E. 56th St. R. Schuler, Sec.

N. Y. Practical Aid Society, 311 W. 45th St. Wm. Crawford, Sec.

N. Y. Society for the Enforcement of the Criminal Law, 106 Fulton St. Edward Insley, Sec.

N. Y. Society for the Prevention of Cruelty to Children, 297 4th Ave. E. F. Jenkins, Sec.

N. Y. Society for the Suppression of Vice, 140 Nassau St. A. Comstock, Sec.

N. Y. Society of Pedagogy, 400 E. 86th St. Edward A. Page, Pres.

N. Y. Sunday-School Association, 105 E. 22d St. J. T. Goodman, Sec.

N. Y. Typographical Society, 32 Union Sq., E,

PROMINENT SOCIETIES AND ASSOCIATIONS—*Continued.*

N. Y. Zoological Soc., 11 Wall St. and E. 183d St., cor. Southern Boulevard. M. Grant, Sec.

Ohio Society, Waldorf-Astoria Hotel. Howard H. Nieman, Sec.

Old Guard, cor. Broadway and 49th St. Charles A. Stadler.

Oratorio Society, 1 W. 34th St. W. B. Tuthill, Sec.

Orphan Asylum Society, office 287 4th Ave. J. C. Bell, Sec.

Philharmonic Society, Carnegie Hall.

Prison Ass'n, 135 E. 15th St. S. M. Jackson, Sec.

Professional Woman's League, 108 W. 45th St. Miss Alice Brown, Sec.

Public Education Ass'n, 105 E. 22d St. Jane E. Robbins, Sec.

Purim Ass'n. J. S. Isaacs, Sec., 7 Pine St.

St. Andrew's Society, 105 E. 22d St. G. A. Morrison, Jr., Sec.

St. David's Soc., 105 E. 22d St. G. M. Lewis, Sec.

St. George's Society, 108 Broad St. Chas. W. Bowring, Sec.

St. Nicholas Soc. C. Isham, Sec., 1286 Broadway.

Society for Instruction in First Aid to the Injured, 105 E. 22d St. J. N. Borland, Sec.

Society for the Prevention of Crime, 105 E. 22d St. T. D. Kenneson, Sec.

Society for the Relief of Half Orphans and Destitute Children, Manhattan Ave., near W. 104th St. Mrs. J. R. Wheeler, Sec.

Society for the Reformation of Juvenile Delinquents, Randall's Island. E. J. Wendell, Sec.

State Charities Aid Association, 105 E. 22d St. Homer Folks, Sec.

Tammany Soc., 143 E. 14th St. Thos. F. Smith, Sec.

Tree Planting Ass'n, 374 Broadway. Charles R. Lamb, Sec.

Unitarian Society, 104 E. 20th St.

United Heb. Charities, 356 2d Ave. F. L. Wachenheim, Sec.

University Settlement Society, 184 Eldridge St. S. L. Cromwell, Sec.

Veteran Firemen's Association, 225 5th Ave. Charles McNamee, Sec.

Women's Prison Association, 110 2d Ave. Mrs. H. M. Guilleudea, Sec.

Young Men's Christian Association, main office, 215 W. 23d St. H. M. Orne, Sec.

Young Men's Hebrew Association, 861 Lexington Ave. F. Younker, Sec.

Young Women's Christian Association, 7 E. 15th St., 460 W. 44th St. Miss J. F. Bangs, Sec.

Parks in Brooklyn and Queens.

SHOWING SIZE, BOUNDARIES, AND VALUE.

Prospect, 516¼ acres, 9th Ave., 15th St., Coney Island, Fort Hamilton, Ocean and Flatbush Aves., value $27,735,000.

Fort Greene, 30 acres, De Kalb Ave., Washington Park, Ashland, Pl., Willoughby St., Canton St. and Myrtle Ave., valne $1,890,000.

Bedford, 4 acres, Brooklyn and Kingston Aves., Park Pl. and Prospect Pl., value $150,000.

Brooklyn Heights, 5 acres, Columbia Heights, fronting on Furman St.

Tompkins, 8 acres, Tompkins, Greene, Marcy and Lafayette Aves., value $400,000.

City, 7⅛ acres, Canton and Navy Sts., Park and Flushing Aves., value $325,000.

City Hall, 1¾ acre, junction of Court and Fulton Sts., value $100,000.

Carroll, 2 acres, President, Court, Carroll and Smith Sts., value $390,000.

Winthrop, 9 acres, Nassau and Driggs Aves., Monitor and Russell Sts., value $325,000.

Highland, terminus of Eastern Parkway Extension, 60 acres, Force Tube Ave., facing Sunnyside Ave., value $250,000.

Sunset, 29½ acres, 41st to 43d St., 5th to 7th Ave., value $200,000.

Red Hook, 25¼ acres, Richards, Dwight, Verona and William Sts., value $150,000.

Bushwick, 7 acres, Knickerbocker and Irving Aves., Starr and Suydam Sts., value $150,000.

Institute Garden, 69 acres, Washington Ave., Eastern Parkway and Flatbush Ave., value $1,250,000.

Parade Ground, 40 acres, Coney Island Ave., Caton Ave., Fort Hamilton Ave. and Parade Pl., value $1,290,000.

Coney Island Concourse, 70 acres, foot of Ocean Parkway, Atlantic Ocean.

Dyker Beach, 140 acres, 7th Ave., New York Bay, Bay 8th St., Cropsey and 14th Aves., value $300,000.

Kings, 11½ acres, Fulton, Alsop and Ray Sts. and Sheldon Ave., Jamaica.

Greenpoint, 43 acres, Perry St., Nassau Ave. and Lorimer St.

McKinley, 11 acres, Fort Hamilton Ave. and 73d St.

Rainey, 4 acres, Vernon Ave., Pierce Ave., Sandford St. and East River.

Bensonhurst Beach, 13 acres, Bay Parkway, Gravesend Bay, 21st and Cropsey Aves., value $38,000.

Lincoln Terrace, 7½ acres, Eastern Parkway, Buffalo Ave., President St. and Rochester Ave., value $120,000.

Canarsie, 30½ acres, Rockaway Parkway and Jamaica Bay, value $105,000.

New Lots Playground, 2¼ acres, Sackman St., Newport, Christopher and Riverdale Aves., value $16,000.

Cooper, 6 acres, Maspeth and Morgan Aves., Sharon and Guilford Sts., value $55,000.

Irving Sq., 3 acres, Hamburg and Knickerbocker Aves., Halsey and Weirfield Sts., value $70,000.

Saratoga Sq., 3¼ acres, Saratoga and Howard Aves., Halsey and Macon Sts., value $121,000.

Linton, 2¼ acres, Bradford St., Blake, Dumont and Miller Aves., value $35,000.

Forest, 536 acres, between Jamaica Ave. and Union Turnpike, Flushing and Myrtle Aves., Richmond Hill, value $1,250,000.

Fort Hamilton, 4½ acres, 4th Ave., De Nyse St., Fort Hamilton Ave., and New York Bay.

PARKWAYS.

Ocean Parkway, 5½ miles, Prospect Park to Coney Island, value $4,000,000.

Eastern Parkway, 2½ miles, Prospect Park to Ralph Ave., value $3,000,000.

Eastern Parkway Extension, 2¼ miles, Ralph Ave. to Highland Park, value $1,300,000.

Fort Hamilton Parkway, 4½ miles, Ocean Parkway to Fort Hamilton, value $1,000,000.

Bay Parkway, 3 miles (formerly 22d Ave.), Ocean Parkway to Bensonhurst Beach, value $1,000,000.

Bay Ridge Parkway (Shore Drive) 3 miles, Fort Hamilton Ave., along shore New York Bay to Fort Hamilton, value $3,500,000.

Rockaway Parkway, 4 miles, Buffalo Ave., to Canarsie Beach.

National Guard, New York.

Headquarters, Stewart Building, 280 Broadway, Manhattan.

Major-General Charles F. Roe, *Commanding.*

Adjutants-General.........Lieut. Frederick Phisterer and Lieut.-Col. George A. Wingate.
Inspectors-General......Lieut.-Col. William H. Chapin and Lieut.-Col. Benjamin B. McAlpin.
Judge-Advocate..............Lieut.-Col. W.W. Ladd.
Ordnance Officers...........Lieut.-Col. Nathaniel B. Thurston and Major William M. Kirby.
Commissary.............Lieut.-Col. Gilford Hurry.
Quartermaster.....Lieut.-Col. John N. Stearns, Jr.
Surgeon............Lieut.-Col. Wm. G. Le Boutillier.
Engineer.......Lieut.-Col. George W. Bunnell, Jr.
Signal Officer.......Lieut.-Col. Frederick T. Leigh.
Aides....Captains Louis M. Greer, Cornelius Vanderbilt and R. K. Prentice.

ATTACHED TO HEADQUARTERS NATIONAL GUARD.

Organization.	Armory.	Numerical Strength.		Commander.	Adjutant.	Headquarter Night.
		Officers.	Men.			
First Co. Signal Corps.	Park Ave. & 34th St., Man..	4	99	Capt. O. Erlandsen....	....	Mon. & Thur.
Second Co. Signal Corps.	801 Dean Street, Brooklyn..	4	70	Capt. E. Bigelow.....	....	Monday.
Twenty-second Eng.....	67th St. & Broadway, Man..	50	704	Col. W. B. Hotchkin .	Capt. R. J. Daly...	Monday.
Squadron A...........	94th St. & Madison Ave., Man.	16	224	Maj. O. B. Bridgman.	Lieut. R. C. Lawrence	Friday.
Squadron C............	Bedford Av. & Union St., B'k	18	177	Maj. C. I. DeBevoise..	Lieut. Chas. Curie..	Monday.
First (Battalion)........	1891 Bathgate Ave., Bronx..	19	301	Maj. D. Wilson......	....	Tuesday.
Thirteenth Ar'y Dist....	Sumner & Jefferson Avs., B'k	56	1111	Col. D. E. Austen....	Capt. T. R. Fleming	Tuesday.
Ninth Ar'y Dist........	125 West 14th St...........	43	759	....	....	....
Eighth Ar'y Dist........	Park Ave. & 94th St.,.......	26	541	....	....	....
Field Hospital.........	56 West 66th St., Manhat'n.	4	50	Maj. W. S. Terriberry	....	Monday.

Total, City of New York, attached to Headquarters, September 30, 1908: Officers and Men, 4,267.

FIRST BRIGADE.

Headquarters, Park Ave. & 34th Street, Manhattan. Brigadier-General George Moore Smith, *Commanding; Assistant Adjutant-General*, Major Thomas J. O'Donohue. Headquarter Night, Monday.

Organization.	Armory.	Numerical Strength.		Commander.	Adjutant.	Headquarter Night.
		Officers.	Men.			
Seventh............	Park Ave. & 67th St.........	47	926	Col. D. Appleton......	Capt. D. W. C. Falls	Friday.
Twelfth............	Columbus Ave. & 62d St.....	41	754	Col. G. R. Dyer.......	Capt. R. A. De Russy	Daily.
Sixty-ninth.........	Lexington Ave. & 26th St. Man	42	656	Col. E. Duffy.........	Capt. J. J. Phelan..	Monday.
Seventy-first........	Park Ave. & 34th St.	42	676	Col. W. G. Bates.....	Capt. C. Greene....	Tuesday.

First Brigade, September 30, 1908: Officers and men, 3,184.

SECOND BRIGADE.

Brooklyn and Queens.

Headquarters, Armory, 23d Regiment, Brooklyn. Brigadier-General John G. Eddy, *Commanding; Adjutant-General*, Major Walter F. Barnes. Headquarter Night, Monday.

Organization.	Armory.	Numerical Strength.		Commander.	Adjutant.	Headquarter Night.
		Officers.	Men.			
Fourteenth.........	8th Ave. and 15th St........	43	779	Col. John H. Foote...	Capt. T. F. Donovan	Monday.
Twenty-third	1322 Bedford Ave..........	50	697	Col. W. A. Stokes.....	Capt. J. H. Ingraham.	Monday.
Forty-seventh......	Marcy Ave. & Heyward St..	35	661	Col. H. C. Barthman..	Capt. H. McCutcheon	Monday.

Second Brigade, September 30, 1908: Officers and men, 2,265.

National Guard, City of New York, September 30, 1908, 9,716; for National Guard, New York State, see Index at "National Guard."

The Naval Militia of New York, headquarters, foot of 97th St., N. R., Manhattan. Total, Naval Militia, New York Officers and men, 735.

Art Galleries in Manhattan.

Name.	Location.	Name.	Location.
American Art Galleries............	E. 23d St. & Madison Sq.	Knoedler & Co.....................	355 Fifth Avenue.
Blakeslee Galleries	358 Fifth Avenue.	Kraushaar, C. W..................	260 Fifth Avenue.
Bonaventure's.....................	5 East 34th Street.	Lenox Library.....................	895 Fifth Avenue.
Clausen, William	7 E. 35th Street.	Macbeth...........................	450 Fifth Avenue.
Cottier............................	3 East 40th Street.	Metropolitan Museum of Art.......	E. 82d Street, Central Park.
Durand-Ruel.......................	5 West 36th Street.	Montrose..........................	372 Fifth Avenue.
Ehrich............................	463 Fifth Avenue.	National Academy of Design.......	Amsterdam Avenue, near 109th Street.
Fifth Av. Art Galleries (Silas)....	546 Fifth Avenue.		
Fine Arts Building................	W. 57th St., nr. Broadway.	National Arts Club................	Gramercy Park, S.
Fishel, Aaron A...................	315 Fifth Avenue.	Noe Art Galleries.................	477 Fifth Avenue.
Gimpel, E. & Wildenstein.........	509 Fifth Avenue.	Oehme, Julius.....................	320 Fifth Avenue.
Keppel, Fr........................	4 East 39th Street.	Schaus, William..................	415 Fifth Avenue.
Klackner Art Gallery..............	7 West 28th Street.	Scott & Fowles...................	295 Fifth Avenue.
Knickerbocker.....................	7 East 28th Street.	Tooth, Arthur & Sons,.............	420 Fifth Avenue.

Postal Letter Carriers in New York City.

TABLE showing number of letter carriers employed in the different boroughs, and the salaries they receive.

(December, 1903.)

BOROUGH.	Number of Carriers.	BOROUGH.	Number of Carriers.
Manhattan and Bronx	2,408	Richmond:	
Brooklyn	1,022	Port Richmond	7
Queens:		West New Brighton	9
Flushing	47	New Brighton	8
Jamaica	42	Rosebank	6
Long Island City	31	Stapleton	10
		Tompkinsville	6

Total number in New York City, 3,596.

The salaries of letter carriers are graded by law as follows: In Manhattan and Bronx, carriers are originally appointed as substitutes and receive pay at rate of 30 cents per hour; when appointed as regular carriers they receive, the first year, $600; second year, $800; third year, $900; fourth year, $1,000; fifth year, $1,100; sixth year, $1,200.

In Brooklyn, carriers receive from $600 to $1,200 per annum each. In Jamaica, carriers receive from $600 to $1,000. In Long Island City, carriers receive $900 each. In Flushing, twenty-four receive $1,000 each, eight $900 each, five $800 each and ten $600 each; also twelve substitute carriers, who receive 30 cents per hour. In Rosebank four carriers receive $1,000, and two $800. In Tompkinsville five carriers receive $1,000 each, and one $600. West New Brighton carriers receive $1,000 per annum each. In New Brighton eight receive $1,000 each, and one $800. In Stapleton nine receive $1,000 each, and three sub-carriers receive 30 cents per hour. In Port Richmond four receive $1,000 each and three $600 each, not including one rural carrier and one R. F. D. carrier.

There is no retirement pay for any of the civil service employés of the United States Government.

Post-Office—Brooklyn, New York.

Postmaster.—Room 2. Office hours, 9 A. M. to 5 P. M. **Assistant Postmaster.**—Room 3. Office hours, 9 A.M. to 5 P.M. **Cashier.**—Room 4. Office hours, 9 A.M. to 5 P.M. **Superintendent City Delivery.**—Room 11. Office hours, 9 A. M. to 5 P. M. **Superintendent of Mails.**—Room 12. Office hours, 9 A. M. to 5 P. M. **Inquiry Dep't.**—Washington Street Corridor. Office hours, 8 A. M. to 6 P. M. **Money-Order Dep't.**—Rooms 6, 7, and 8. Office hours, 9 A. M. to 5 P. M. **Night Window for Money Orders.**—Washington Street Corridor, from 5 P. M. to 10 P. M. **Registry Dep't.**—Room 9. Office hours, 8 A. M. to 6 P. M. **Night Window for Registry Business.**—Washington Street Corridor, from 6 P. M. to 8 A. M. **Poste Restante.**—Window in Johnson Street Corridor. **Postage Stamps, etc., in amounts over $2.**—Wholesale Window, Johnson Street Corridor. **Mail in Quantities.**—Received at Window of Superintendent of Mails in Washington Street Corridor. **Drops.**—In Washington Street Corridor. **Lock Boxes.**—Johnson Street Corridor.

On general holidays the first carrier delivery only is made, and the regular mail is received from 8 A. M. to 10 A. M.

BRANCH POST-OFFICES.

A—14 and 16 Graham Avenue.
B—1266-68 Fulton Street.
C—5121 Third Avenue.
D—1923 Fulton Street.
E—2634 Atlantic Avenue.
F—Flatbush, 830 Flatbush Avenue.
G—860 Manhattan Avenue.
H—Bath Beach, Bath Avenue, near 19th Street.
J—Myrtle Ave., near Wyckoff Ave.
K—Blythebourne, 13th Avenue and 55th Street.
L—L.I.R.R. Depot, Flatbush and Atlantic Aves.
M—Coney Island, Surf Avenue, opp. West 17th Street.
N—Fort Hamilton, Fourth Avenue and 99th St.
O—Sheepshead Bay, 1780 Shore Road.
P—1731 Pitkin Avenue.
R—(Vanderveer) 1574 Flatbush Avenue.
S—1262-1264 Broadway.
T—170 Hamilton Avenue.
V—Fifth Avenue and 9th Street.
W—Broadway and South 8th Street.

[All branch stations are open on week days from 7 A.M. to 9 P.M.; for money-order business from 8 A.M. to 9 P.M.; for the registry of letters from 8 A.M. to 9 P.M. On Sundays stations are open from 10 to 11 A.M., and on holidays from 7 to 11 A.M. No money-order business is transacted on Sundays or holidays. No registry business is transacted on Sundays, but on holidays letters and parcels may be registered from 8 to 10 A.M.]

Public Porters.

EVERY Public Porter must wear, in a conspicuous position, a badge bearing the number of his license, and is not entitled to receive any pay for services unless such a badge is worn, and if he shall demand a greater sum for his services than accords with the rates below, he shall not be entitled to any pay for the service.

Any Public Porter may decline to carry any article, if the distance he shall be required to go shall be more than two miles.

Public Porters shall be entitled to charge and receive for the carrying or conveyance of any article, any distance within half a mile, twenty-five cents if carried by hand, and fifty cents if carried on a wheelbarrow or hand-cart: if the distance exceeds half a mile and is within a mile, one-half of the above rates in addition thereto, and in the same proportion for any greater distance.

Steamships from New York City.

THIS table gives the destination of the steamer, then the street from the foot of which the steamships sail, and the location of the office of the agent in Manhattan. Loading berths are liable to be changed from those here shown.

Antigua, W. 10th St., Quebec S. S. Co., 29 B'way.
Antwerp, foot Fulton St., N. R., Red Star Line, 9 Broadway.
Antwerp, 7th St., Hoboken, Phoenix Line, 22 State St.
Australia, Norton & Son, Produce Exchange, and U. S. & Australasia S. S. Co., 11 Broadway.
Bahamas, Wall St., N. Y. & Cuba Mail S.S. Co., Pier 14, E. R.
Baltimore, Md., foot Old Slip, New York and Baltimore Trans. Co., Pier 11, E. R.
Barbados, Martin Stores, Brooklyn, Booth S. S. Co., 17 Battery Place.
Barbados, W. 10th St., Quebec S. S. Co., 29 B'way.
Barbados, Bethune St., Sanderson & Son, 22 State St.
Barcelona, Pier 8, E. R., Compañia Transatlantica, 8 E. R.
Bermuda, W. 10th St., Quebec S. S. Co., 29 B'way.
Brazil, Lamport & Holt Line, Produce Exchange, Booth S. S. Co., 17 Battery Place.
Bremen, 3d St., Hoboken, North German Lloyd, 5 Broadway.
Bristol, Eng., foot W. 29th St., Bristol City Line, 25 Whitehall St.
Buenos Ayres, Robert's Stores, Brooklyn, Lamport & Holt Line, Produce Exchange.
Buenos Ayres, Norton Line and Prince Line Produce Exchange.
Cadiz, Compañia Transatlantica, 8 E. R.
Calcutta, American & Indian Line, 10 Bridge St.
Callao, Merchants' Line, Hanover Square.
Callao, West Coast Line, 31 Broad St.
Campeche, N. Y. & Cuba Mail SS. Co., 14 E. R.
Cape Town, Norton & Son, Produce Exchange.
Carthagena, W. 25th St., Atlas Line, 45 Broadway
Charleston, S. C., foot of Spring St., Clyde Line, Pier 36, N. R., and 290 Broadway.
China, U. S. & China-Japan Line, 10 Bridge St., Barber & Co., Produce Exchange, American-Asiatic Line, 12 Broadway, Norton & Son, Produce Exchange.
Christiania, 17th St., Hoboken, Scandinavian-American Line, 10 Bridge St., and 1 Broadway.
Colon, foot W. 27th St., Panama R. R. Steamship Line, 24 State St.
Colon, Bethune St., Sanderson & Son, 22 State St.
Colon, W. 25th St., Atlas Line, 45 Broadway.
Copenhagen, 17th St., Hoboken, Scandinavian-American Line, 10 Bridge St. and 1 Broadway.
Costa Rica, W. 25th St., Atlas Line, 45 B'way.
Costa Rica, Bethune St., Sanderson & Son, 22 State St.
Curaçoa, Pier 11, Brooklyn, Red "D" Line, 82 Wall St.
Curaçoa, Royal Dutch Line, 10 Bridge St.
Demerara, Royal Dutch Line, 10 Bridge St.
Demerara, Demerara S. S. Line, 106 Wall St.
Demerara, W. 10th St., Quebec S.S. Co., 29 B'way.
Dominica, W. 10th St., Quebec S. S. Co., 29 B'way.
Galveston, Burling Slip, Mallory Line, 80 South St., and 290 Broadway.
Galveston, N. Moore St., Morgan Line, 349 B'way.
Genoa and Gibraltar, 1st St., Hoboken, Hamburg-American Line, 45 Broadway.
Genoa and Gibraltar, 3d St., Hoboken, North German Lloyd, 5 Broadway.
Genoa and Gibraltar, W. 11th St., White Star Line, 9 Broadway.
Genoa, W. 34th St., Hartfield, Solari & Co., 50 Wall St.
Gibraltar, Jane St., Cunard Line, 21 State St.
Glasgow, W. 24th St., Anchor Line, 17 B'way.
Halifax, Red Cross Line, 17 State St.
Hamburg, 1st St., Hoboken, Hamburg-American Line, 45 Broadway.
Havana, Wall St., New York and Cuba Mail S. S. Co., Pier 14 E. R.
Havana, Pier 8, E. R., Compañia Transatlantica, 8 E. R.
Havre, Barber & Co., Produce Exchange.
Havre, Morton St., French Line, 19 State St.
Hayti, W. 25th St., Atlas Line, 45 Broadway.
Hayti, Royal Dutch Line, 10 Bridge St.
Honolulu, American-Hawaiian S. S. Co., 10 Bridge St.
Hull, foot Bethune St., Wilson Line, 22 State St.
Jacksonville, foot Spring St., Clyde Line, Pier 36, N. R., and 290 Broadway.
Japan, U.S. & China-Japan Line, 10 Bridge St., Norton & Son, Produce Exchange.
Key West, Burling Slip, Mallory Line, 80 South St. and 290 Broadway.
Kingston, Jamaica, W. 25th St., Hamburg-Am. Line (Atlas Line), 45 Broadway.
Kingston, Bethune St., Sanderson & Son, 22 State St.
La Guayra, Pier 11, Brooklyn, Red "D" Line, 82 Wall St.
Leghorn, Union Stores, Brooklyn, Anchor Line, 17 Broadway.
Liverpool, Jane St., Cunard Line, 21 State St.
Liverpool, W. 11th St., White Star Line, 9 B'way.
London, W. Houston St., Atlantic Transport Line, 9 Broadway.
Manchester, Robert's Stores, Brooklyn, Lamport & Holt Line, 301 Produce Exchange.
Manila, American-Asiatic Line, 12 Broadway, and Norton & Son, Produce Exchange.
Marseilles, Fabre Line, 24 State St., and Anchor Line, 17 Broadway.
Martinique, W. 10th St., Quebec S.S. Co., 29 B'way.
Melbourne, American and Australian Line, Produce Exchange.
Melbourne, United States and Australasia Line, 11 Broadway.
Montevideo, lines shown at "Buenos Ayres" call at Montevideo.
Naples, Anchor Line, Fabre Line, North German Lloyd, Hamburg-American, White Star Line, and Cunard Line all call at Naples.
Nassau, Wall St., New York and Cuba Mail S.S. Co., 14 E. R.
New Orleans, North Moore St., Southern Pacific Co., 349 Broadway.
Newport News, Norfolk, and Old Point Comfort. Beach St., Old Dominion S.S. Co., on pier and 81 Beach St.
New Zealand, United Tyser Line, 10 Bridge St., and U. S. and Australasia Line, 11 Broadway.
Para, Martin Stores, Brooklyn, Booth S. S. Co., 17 Battery Place.
Pernambuco, Lloyd Brazileiro, Produce Exchange, and Prince Line, Produce Exchange.
Philadelphia, foot Roosevelt St., Clyde Line, on pier.
Philippine Islands, see "Manila."
Port au Prince, see "Hayti."
Portland, Peck Slip, Maine S. S. Line, 290 Broadway, and on pier.
Port Limon, W. 25th St., Atlas Line, 45 B'way.
Porto Rico, New York and Porto Rico S. S. Line, 12 Broadway.
Porto Rico, Pier 11, Brooklyn, Red "D" Line, 82 Wall St.
Porto Rico, Insular Line, 116 Broad St.
Progreso, Wall St., New York and Cuba Mail S. S. Co., 14 E. R.
Puerto Cabello, Pier 11, Brooklyn, Red "D" Line, 82 Wall St.
Queenstown, Cunard, and White Star Lines call here.

STEAMSHIPS FROM NEW YORK CITY—*Continued.*

Rio de Janeiro, Dock in Brooklyn, Lamport & Holt Line, Prince Line and Lloyd Brazileiro, all in Produce Exchange.

Rotterdam, 7th St., Hoboken, Holland-America Line, 39 Broadway and 10 Bridge St.

San Domingo, Clyde Line, 12 Broadway.

Santiago de Cuba, Prentice Stores, Brooklyn, New York and Cuba Mail Line, Pier 14 E. R.

Savannah, Spring St., Savannah Line; on pier and 317 Broadway.

Savanilla, W. 25th St., Atlas Line, 45 Broadway.

Savanilla, Bethune St., Sanderson & Son, 22 State St.

South Africa, Hansa Line, 10 Bridge St., and Norton & Son, Produce Exchange.

Southampton, Fulton St., N. R., American Line, 9 Broadway, and White Star Line, 9 Broadway.

Southampton, 3d St., Hoboken, North German Lloyd Line, 5 Broadway.

St. John's, N. F., Red Cross Line, 17 State St.

Tampico, Prentice Stores, Brooklyn, New York and Cuba Mail Line, Pier 14 E. R.

Trinidad, Roya Dutch Line, 10 Bridge St.

Trinidad, Trinidad Line, 29 Broadway, Royal Mail Line, 22 State St.

Valparaiso, W. R. Grace & Co., Hanover Square, West Coast Line, 31 Broad St.

Venezuela, Red "D" Line, 82 Wall St.

Vera Cruz, Wall St., New York and Cuba Mail Line, Pier 14 E. R.

Wilmington, N. C., Spring St., Clyde Line, foot Spring St., and 290 Broadway.

Ferries from and to Manhattan.

To Astoria.—From ft. E. 92d St.

" Bedloe's Isl. (Liberty Island).—From Battery.

" Blackwell's Island.—From ft. 26th St., ft. 52d St., ft. 70th St., E. R.

" Brooklyn Borough.—From ft. Catharine St. to Main St., Brooklyn Boro.

" " " From ft. E. 10th and ft. E. 23d St. to Greenpoint Ave., Brooklyn Boro.

" " " From ft. E. 23d St. to B'way, Brooklyn Boro.

" " " From ft. E. 42d St. to B'way, Brooklyn Boro.

" " " From ft. E. Houston St. to Grand St., B'klyn Boro.

" " " From ft. Fulton St. to Fulton St., Brooklyn Boro.

" " " From ft. Grand St. to Grand St. and Broadway, Brooklyn Boro.

" " " From ft. Roosevelt St. to Broadway, B'klyn Boro.

" " " From ft. Wall St. to Montague St., B'klyn Boro.

" " " From ft. Whitehall St. to Atlantic and Hamilton Aves., Brooklyn Boro.

" " " From ft. Whitehall St. to 39th St., Brooklyn Boro.

" College Point (Queens Borough).—From ft. E. 99th St. and E. 134th St.

" Edgewater.—From W. 130th St.

" Ellis Island.—From Barge Office, Whitehall St.

" Hart's Island.—From ft. 26th St., E. R.

" Hoboken.—From ft. Barclay, Christopher and W. 23d Sts. to Newark and Ferry Sts., Hoboken.

To Hoboken.—From ft. W. 23d St. to 14th St., Hoboken.

" Jersey City.—From ft. Chambers and W. 23d Sts. to Pavonia Ave., Jersey City. (Erie, Northern of New Jersey, and N. J. & N. Y. R. R.)

" " " From ft. Cortlandt, Desbrosses, and W. 23d Sts. to Montgomery St., Jersey City. (Pennsylvania R. R., Lehigh Valley R. R., and New York, Susquehanna & Western R. R.)

" " " From ft. Liberty and W. 23d Sts. to Communipaw, Jersey City. (Central R. R. of New Jersey.)

" " " Pennsylvania Annex from ft. Fulton St., Brooklyn Borough, to Jersey City, connecting with Pennsylvania R. R., Lehigh Valley R. R., and New York, Susquehanna & Western R. R.

" North Brother Island.—From ft. E. 132d St.

" Queens Borough (Long Island City).—From ft. E. 34th St. to Borden Ave., Long Island City (L. I. R. R.).

" Randall's Island.—From ft. E. 26th, E. 120th and E. 125th Sts.

" Richmond Borough (Staten Island).—From ft. Whitehall St. to St. George, Staten Island. (Staten Island and Rapid Transit R. R. and Trolley lines.)

" Riker's Island—From ft. E. 26th St.

" Ward's Island.—From ft. E. 116th St.

" Weehawken.—From ft. Desbrosses and ft. W. 42d St. (to W. Shore R. R. Depot.).

" West New York.—From ft. W. 42d St. to Old Slip.

Width of Sidewalks in Manhattan.

In streets 40 feet wide........................10 ft.
" " 50 " " ....13 "
" " 60 " " ....15 "
" " 70 " " ....18 "
" " 80 " " ....19 "
" " above 80, not exceeding 100 feet.20 "
" all streets more than 100 feet...........22 "
" Lenox and 7th Aves., north of W. 110th.35 "
" Grand Boulevard........................24 "
" Manhattan St........................15 "
" Lexington Ave........................18 " 6 in.

In Madison Ave........................19 ft.
" 5th Ave........................30 "
" St. Nicholas Ave........................22 " 6 in.
" Park Ave. from E. 49th to E. 56th St., and from E. 96th St. to Harlem River.15 "
" West End Ave........................30 "
" Central Park West, from W. 59th St. to W. 110th, east side........................27 "
" Central Park West, from W. 59th St. to W. 110th, west side........................25 "

Association of the Bar of New York.

(Bar Association Building, No. 42 West Forty-fourth Street, New York City).

President—Edmund Wetmore. *Vice-Pres.*—John M. Bowers. " Chas. F. Brown. *Vice-Pres.*—Thomas Thacher. " James Byrne. " Edward Shepard. *Rec. Secretary*—S. B. Brownell. *Cor. Secretary*—Henry B. Closson. *Treasurer*—S. Sidney Smith.

At the time of the last report of the Executive Committee there were 1,976 members of the Association. It was instituted in 1869, and its presidents have been as follows: 1870 to 1879, William M. Evarts; 1880 and 1881, Stephen P. Nash; 1882 and 1883, Francis N. Bangs; 1884 and 1885, James C. Carter; 1886 and 1887, William Allen Butler; 1888 and 1889, Joseph H. Choate; 1890 and 1891, Frederic R. Coudert; 1892 to 1894, Wheeler H. Peckham; 1895 and 1896, Joseph Larocque; 1897 to 1899, James C. Carter; 1900 and 1901, John E. Parsons; 1902 and 1903, Wm. G. Choate; 1904 and 1905, Elihu Root; 1906 and 1907, John L. Cadwalader; 1908, Edmund Wetmore. The admission fee is $100, and the annual dues from resident members, $50, and from members having offices in New York City and residing elsewhere, $25; members neither residing nor having offices in New York City shall be exempt from the payment of annual dues.

The Lawyers' Club.—120 Broadway, New York City. *President*—Wm. Allen Butler, Jr. *Secretary and Treasurer*—George T. Wilson. Total membership, 1,900. Membership is not restricted to lawyers. There are no entrance fees, but the annual dues of resident members are $100, and of non-resident members, $50. Non-resident members who are public officials, $25 per annum, and clergymen, whether resident or non-resident, the same. Resident membership limited to 1,350.

Federal Officers in New York City.

CUSTOM-HOUSE.—Bowling Green.

Collector.—Edward S. Fowler ($12,000).

Solicitor to Collector—Harrison Osborne ($5,000).

Chief Clerk of Customs and Special Deputy Collector.—Jos. J. Couch ($6,000). Henry C. Stuart ($5,000).

Deputy Collectors.—John J. C. Barrett, Jesse C. Grant, James H. Johnson, George F. Corts, John C. Williams, Charles A. King, H. L. Swords, and H. E. Esterbrook ($3,000 each).

Cashier.—J. M. Wood ($5,000), Bowling Green.

Acting Disbursing Agt.—Geo. W. Brinck ($3,000).

Auditor.—Josiah S. Knapp ($4,500).

Naval Officer.—Frederick J. H. Kracke ($8,000).

Special Deputy Naval Officers.—H. W. Gourley ($4,000); Thomas J. Skuse ($3,500).

Surveyor.—James S. Clarkson ($8,000).

Special Deputy Surveyor.—F. S. Cooke ($4,000).

Deputy Surveyors.—John M. Bishop, Wm. O. Cloyes, Mathew M. Coneys, J. F. Vail ($2,500 each).

Appraiser.—G. W. Wanmaker ($8,000), Christopher and Greenwich Streets.

Assistant Appraisers.—Chas. W. Bunn, Frank N. Petrie, Harry B. Stowell, Chas. R. Skinner, C. W. MacDonough, S. Krulewitch, A. L. Kline, John D. Smith, Amos M. Knapp ($3,000 each).

Deputy Appraisers.—C. K. Lexow, Michael Nathan, Henry M. Clapp ($3,500 each).

BOARD OF U. S. GENERAL APPRAISERS.—641 Washington Street.

Marion De Vries, H. M. Somerville, E. G. Hay, T. S. Sharretts, R. H. Chamberlain, W. B. Howell, I. F. Fischer, C. P. McClelland, Byron S. Waite ($9,000 each).

SUB-TREASURY.—Wall, corner Nassau Street.

Assistant Treasurer.—George S. Terry ($8,000).

Deputy Assistant Treasurer and Cashier.—George W. Marlor ($4,200).

Assistant Cashier.—Edward W. Hale ($3,600).

POST-OFFICE.—B'way and Park Row. See Index.

NATIONAL BANK EXAMINER.—Custom House.

Examiner.—C. A. Hanna (fees).

U. S. ASSAY OFFICE.—30 Wall Street.

Superintendent.—Kingsbery Foster ($4,500).

Assayer.—Herbert G. Torrey ($3,000).

Melter and Refiner.—Henry B. Kelsey ($3,000).

INTERNAL REVENUE OFFICERS.

(Compensation of Collectors not to exceed $4,500 a year for each district.)

Second District.—1st, 2d, 3d, 4th, 5th, 6th, 8th, 9th, 15th, and parts of the 14th and 16th Wards. Chas. W. Anderson, *Collector*, 150 Nassau Street.

Third District.—7th, 10th, 11th, 12th, 13th, 17th, 18th, 19th, 20th, 21st, 22d, and parts of the 14th and 16th Wards, Blackwell's, Randall's, and Ward's Islands, Ferd. Eidman, *Collector*, 3d Avenue and 16th Street.

Fourteenth District, 7th Division.—From Harlem River north to city line, Borough of Bronx, J. Thomas Stearns, *Deputy Collector*, 534 Willis Avenue, Bronx.

Brooklyn Borough.—First District.—Embracing all of Long Island and Richmond Borough (Staten Island), Edward B. Jordan, *Collector*, Post-Office Building, Brooklyn Borough.

PENSION AGENCY.—65 Bleecker Street.

Pension Agent.—Michael Kerwin.

COM'R OF IMMIGRATION.—Ellis Island.

Commissioner.—Robert Watchorn, ($6,500).

Assistant Commissioner.—Joseph Murray ($4,500).

U.S. SHIPPING COMMISSIONER.—Barge Office.

Commissioner.—Harry A. Hanbury ($5,000).

Deputy.—Albert J. Kenney ($1,860).

LAW COURTS.—See Index.

WEATHER BUREAU.—100 Broadway.

District Forecaster.—Eben H. Emery.

STEAM VESSELS' INSPECTORS.—17 Batt'y Pl.

Supervising Inspector.—Ira Harris ($3,000).

Local Inspectors.—Henry M. Seeley and J. L. Crone ($2,500 each).

U. S. LIFE-SAVING STATIONS.—379 Washington Street.

Customs Collectors at Port of New York.

OFFICIAL LIST OF THE COLLECTORS OF THE PORT OF NEW YORK.

Collector.	Appointed.
John Lamb	March 22, 1784
John Lamb	March 29, 1791
Joshua Sands	April 26, 1797
David Gelston	July 9, 1801
Jonathan Thompson	Nov. 29, 1820
Samuel Swartwout	March 29, 1830
Jesse Hoyt	March 29, 1838
John J. Morgan	March 1, 1841
Edward Curtis	March 18, 1841
C. P. Van Ness	June 29, 1844
Cornelius W. Lawrence	July 1, 1845
Hugh Maxwell	May 16, 1849
D. S. Dickenson	March 30, 1853
Greene C. Bronson	April 8, 1853
Herman J. Redfield	Oct. 23, 1853
Augustus Schell	March 25, 1857
Hiram Barney	March 23, 1861
Simeon Draper	Sept. 7, 1864
Preston King	Aug. 12, 1865
Henry A. Smyth	May 10, 1866
Moses H. Grinnell	March 29, 1869
Thomas Murphy	July 13, 1870
Chester A. Arthur	Nov. 20, 1871
Edwin A. Merritt	July 21, 1878
William H. Robertson	May 18, 1881
Edward L. Hedden	July 1, 1885
Daniel Magone	Aug. 10, 1886
Joel B. Erhardt (Bond)	May 4, 1889
J. S. Fassett (Bond)	Aug. 11, 1890
Francis Hendricks (Bond)	Sept. 22, 1891
James T. Kilbreth (Bond)	Aug. 3, 1893
George R. Bidwell (Bond)	July 12, 1897
Nevada N. Stranahan (Bond)	April 2, 1902
Nevada N. Stranahan (Bond)	April 1, 1906
Edward S. Fowler	Nov. —, 1907

Parks in Manhattan and Bronx.

HEADQUARTERS, THE ARSENAL, CENTRAL PARK.

Battery, foot of Broadway.
Bronx, on Bronx River, lies north of E. 182d St. and White Plains Road, east of Southern Boulevard, 661.60 acres. Zoological Garden.
Bryant, 6th Av. and W. 42d St.
Cedar, Walton Av., 158th St. and Mott Av.
City Hall Park, Broadway, Mail St., Park Row, and Chambers St.
Claremont, Teller Av., Belmont St., Clay Av., and 170th St., in the 24th Ward.
Colonial, 145th to 155th St., Bradhurst Av. to Edgecombe Av.
Corlears Hook Park, Corlears and South Sts.
Crotona, Fulton Av., 3d Av., and Arthur Av.
De Witt Clinton, 52d to 54th St., North River.
East River Park, between Av. B and East River, E. 84th St. to E. 89th St.
Fordham, Fordham Rd., Sedgwick Av. & 188th St.
Fort Washington, Ft. Washington Point, Hudson River.
Hamilton Fish Park, Houston and Willett Sts.
Highbridge Park, 155th St. to Washington Bridge, west of Driveway.
John Jay, 76th to 78th St., East River.
Macomb's Dam, Jerome Av., 162d St., Cromwell's Av., and Harlem River.
Madison Square, Broadway and 23d St.
Morningside Park, between Columbus and Amsterdam Avs. and W. 110th and W. 123d Sts.
Mount Morris Park, between Madison and Mt. Morris Ave. and 120th and 124th Sts.
Park west of Harlem River Driveway and north of Washington Bridge.
Pelham Bay Park, on Long Island Sound and East Chester Bay, northeast end of New York City, 1,756 acres.
Riverside Park, between Riverside Ave. and the N. Y. C. R. R. and W. 72d and W. 129th Sts.
St. Gabriel's Park, 1st Ave. and 35th St.
St. James, Jerome Av., Creston Av., & E. 191st St.
St. Mary's, 149th St., St. Ann's and Robbins Avs.
St. Nicholas, 130th to 141st St., St. Nich'ls to 10th Av.
Seward, Canal and Jefferson Sts.
Stuyvesant, Rutherfurd Pl. and E. 16th St.
Thomas Jefferson, 111th St., 1st Av., 114th St., and Harlem River.
Tompkins Square, Av. A and 7th St.
Union Square, Broadway and 14th St.
Van Cortlandt Park, northern boundary of city. Broadway, Van Cortlandt Av., Jerome Av., and Mt. Vernon Av., 1,132.35 acres.
Washington Bridge, Sedgwick Av., Harlem River, Washington Bridge.
Washington Square, 5th Av. and Waverley Pl.

CENTRAL PARK.

The great park of New York extends from 59th St. to 110th St., being over 2½ miles long, and from 5th Ave. to 8th Ave., being over half a mile wide. It covers 843 acres, of which 185 are in lakes and reservoirs and 400 in forest, wherein over half a million trees and shrubs have been planted. There are 9 miles of roads, 5¼ of bridle paths, and 31 of walks. The landscape architects of the Park were Frederick Law Olmsted and Calvert Vaux. Public park carriages can be found (except in Winter) at the entrances on 5th Ave. and 8th Ave. The fare for an extended ride through the Park is 25 cents. Work was begun on the Park in 1857. The following fanciful names have been officially applied to the several entrances to the Park: 5th Ave. and 59th St., Scholar's Gate; 6th Ave. and 59th St., Artist's Gate; 7th Ave. and 59th St., Artisan's Gate; 8th Ave. and 59th St., Merchant's Gate; 8th Ave. and 72d St., Woman's Gate; 8th Ave. and 81st St., Hunter's Gate; 8th Ave. and 85th St., Mariner's Gate; 8th Ave. and 96th St., Gate of All Saints; 8th Ave. and 100th St., Boy's Gate; 8th Ave. and 110th St., Stranger's Gate; 5th Ave. and 67th St., Student's Gate; 5th Ave. and 72d St., Children's Gate; 5th Ave. and 79th St., Miner's Gate; 5th Ave. and 90th St., Engineer's Gate.; 5th Ave. and 96th St., Woodman's Gate; 5th Ave. and 102d St., Girl's Gate; 5th Ave. and 110th St., Pioneer's Gate; 6th Ave. and 110th St., Farmer's Gate; 7th Ave. and 110th St., Warrior's Gate.

FACTS ABOUT PUBLIC PARKS.

Union Square was purchased by the city in 1833 for $116,051; Madison Square, in 1847, for $65,952; Tompkins Square, in 1834, for $93,358; Washington Square, in 1827, for $77,970, and Manhattan Square, in 1839, for $54,657. The latter is assessed as a part of Central Park. The other four are assessed at over $16,000,000, and are easily worth $20,000,000, while their original cost to the city was only $353,331. Prospect Park, Brooklyn, contains 516 1-6 acres. In woodland, 110 acres; in lakes and watercourses, 77 acres; in meadows, 70 acres; in plantations, 259 1-6 acres; in drives, 9 miles; in bridle roads, 3 1-10 miles; in walks, 12 miles. Ocean Parkway is 5 1-2 miles long and 210 feet wide. Eastern Parkway is 2 1-2 miles long and 210 feet wide. London has 271 public parks, containing 17,876 acres of ground. The largest European city park is in Denmark; it contains 4,200 acres. The great forest of Northern New York covers an area of 3,588,803 acres.

Jury Duty in Manhattan and Bronx.

To be qualified to serve a person must be not less than 21 nor more than 70 years of age, and he must be a male citizen of the United States, and a resident of the county of New York; and he is a resident within the meaning of the jury law if he dwells or lodges here the greater part of the time between the first day of October and the last day of June He must be the owner, in his own right, of real or personal property of the value of $250; or the husband of a woman who is the owner, in her own right, of real or personal property of that value. He must also be in the possession of his natural faculties, and not be infirm or decrepit; intelligent, of good character, and able to read and write the English language understandingly.

THE FOLLOWING PERSONS ARE ENTITLED TO EXEMPTION.

A Clergyman, Minister of any religion officiating as such, and not following any other calling. A practicing Physician, Surgeon, Surgeon-Dentist, or Veterinary Surgeon not following any other calling, and a licensed Pharmaceutist or Pharmacist, or a duly licensed Embalmer, while actually engaged in his profession as a means of livelihood. An Attorney or Counsellor-at-Law regularly engaged in the practice of law as a means of livelihood. A Professor or Teacher in a college, academy, or public school, not following any other calling. Editor, Editorial Writer, or Reporter of a daily newspaper or press association regularly employed as such, and not following any other vocation. The holder of an office under the United States, or the State, or city or county of New York, whose official duties, at the time, prevent his attendance as a juror. A Consul of a foreign nation. A Captain, Engineer, or other officer actually employed upon a vessel making regular trips; a licensed Pilot, actually following that calling. A Superintendent, Conductor, or Engineer employed by a Railroad Company other than a street railroad company, or a Telegraph Operator employed by a Press Association or Telegraph Company who is actually doing duty in an office, or along the railroad or telegraph line of the company or association by which he is employed. Honorably discharged Firemen. Active and honorably discharged Militiamen and active members of the Old Guard. A duly licensed Engineer of steam boilers actually employed as such. Inspectors, Poll Clerks, and Ballot Clerks, or a person who is physically incapable. Grand, Sheriff's, Special, and Municipal Court Jurors.

Bridges in and About the City of New York.

BROOKLYN BRIDGE.

THE bridge connecting Manhattan and Brooklyn over the East River from Park Row, Manhattan, to Sands and Washington Streets, Brooklyn, was begun January 3, 1870, and opened to traffic May 24, 1883. Total cost of the bridge to December 1, 1897, about $21,000,000.

The tolls are: For foot passengers, free; railway fare, 3 cents, or 2 tickets for 5 cents; one horse, 3 cents; one horse and vehicle, 5 cents; two horses and vehicle, 10 cents; each extra horse above two attached to vehicle, 3 cents; bicycles, free. On July 1, 1898, the bridge railway was leased to the elevated railroad companies (now operated by the Brooklyn Rapid Transit), paying therefor $250 per day; trolley cars, 5 cents per round trip. About 120,000 surface cars cross the bridge each month. The carriageways are under control of the Bridge Commissioner, and about $60,000 per annum is derived from this source.

The following are the statistics of the structure: Width of bridge, 85 feet. Length of river span, 1,595 feet 6 inches. Length of each land span, 930 feet. Length of Brooklyn approach, 998 feet. Length of New York approach, 1,562 feet 6 inches. Total length of carriageway, 6,016 feet. Total length of the bridge, with extensions, 7,580 feet.

Size of Manhattan caisson, 172 x 102 feet. Size of Brooklyn caisson, 168 x 102 feet. Timber and iron in caisson, 5,253 cubic yards. Concrete in well holes, chambers, etc., 5,669 cubic feet. Weight of Manhattan caisson, about 7,000 tons. Weight of concrete filling, about 8,000 tons.

Manhattan tower contains 46,945 cubic yards masonry. Brooklyn tower contains 38,214 cubic yards masonry. Depth of tower foundation below high water, Brooklyn, 45 feet. Depth of tower foundation below high water, Manhattan, 78 feet. Size of towers at high water line, 140 x 59 feet. Size of towers at roof course, 136 x 53 feet. Total height of towers above high water, 278 feet.

Clear height of bridge in centre of river span above high water at 90° F., 135 feet. Height of floor at towers above high water, 119 feet 3 inches.

Grade of roadway, 3¼ feet in 100 feet. Height of towers above roadway, 159 feet. Size of anchorage at base, 129 x 119 feet. Size of anchorage at top, 117 x 104 feet. Height of anchorages, 89 feet front, 85 feet rear. Weight of each anchor plate, 23 tons.

Number of cables, 4. Diameter of each cable, 15¾ inches. Length of each single wire in cables, 3,578 feet 6 inches. Ultimate strength of each cable, 12,000 tons. Weight of wire, 12 feet per pound. Each cable contains 5,296 parallel (not twisted) galvanized steel, oil-coated wires, closely wrapped to a solid cylinder, 15¾ inches in diameter. Permanent weight suspended from cables, 14,680 tons.

MANHATTAN BRIDGE.

Manhattan terminal, Bowery and Canal St.; Brooklyn terminal, Nassau, near Bridge St. Estimated cost, $15,833,000; of which $9,552,000 was for structure, $4,000,000 for land in Manhattan, and $2,281,600 for land in Brooklyn.

Width of bridge, 120 ft. Length of river span, 1,470 ft. Length of each land span, 725 ft. Length across each anchorage, 178 ft. 9 in. Length of Manhattan approach 1,293 ft. Length of Brooklyn approach, 1,211 ft. 10 in. Total length between abutments, 5,782 ft. 4 in. Total length of roadway, 6,854 ft. .86 in. Bridge is of double-deck design, 1st deck to have one 35-foot roadway in centre and two trolley tracks on each side, top deck to have four elevated R. R. tracks and one 11-foot footwalk on each side. Approximately 40,000 cu. yds. excavation for each anchor pier; approximately 115,000 cu. yds. masonry and concrete in each anchor pier.

Height of cables at top of tower above mean high water mark, 321 ft. 4 in. Height of roadway at tower above mean high water mark, 138 ft. Grade of roadway 3 ft. in 100 ft. Number of cables four. 37 strands in each cable; 256 wires in each strand; 9,472 wires in each cable; 37,888 wires in four cables. Size of wire 0.192 inches in diameter. Size of cable completed 21¼ inches in diameter. Length of each wire 3,223 ft. 6 in. (anchor to anchor). Ultimate strength of each cable, 27,500 tons.

Weight (in steel only) of cables and suspenders, 8,000 tons. Weight of each tower, 6,300 tons. Weight of main span, 9,000 tons. Weight of each side span, 5,000 tons. Weight of steel in each anchorage, 1,300 tons. Weight of each approach, 8,000 tons.

Work of construction of tower foundation in Brooklyn commenced August 29, 1901. The construction of the cables and the suspended superstructure is now nearing completion.

WILLIAMSBURG BRIDGE.

The tower foundations for the bridge in Manhattan are at the foot of Delancey Slip, and in Brooklyn at a point between South Fifth and South Sixth Streets. The bridge ends at Clinton Street in Manhattan, and at Havemeyer Street in Brooklyn. The dimensions of the bridge are as follows: Main span, 1,600 ft.; entire bridge, between terminals, 7,275 ft.; width of bridge, 118 ft.; minimum height of bridge above mean high water, 135 ft.; height of centre of cables at top of towers above mean high water, 332 ft. 8½ in.; width of carriage ways, each 20 ft.; width of two foot-walks, each 10½ ft.; width of two bicycle paths, each 7 ft.; width of four trolley-car tracks, centre to centre, 9¾ ft.; width of two elevated railroad tracks, centre to centre, 11 ft. New York side—North caisson, 55 ft. below low water mark; south caisson, 66 ft. Brooklyn side—North caisson, 107.5 ft. below low water mark; south caisson, 91.9 ft. The tower foundations are 23 ft. above high water mark and the towers that are placed on top of them are made of steel. The cost is about $12,000,000, exclusive of real estate. The bridge was opened to the public in December, 1903.

QUEENSBORO BRIDGE (UNDER CONSTRUCTION).

Plans approved by the War Department, February 23, 1901. Ordinance providing for the issue of stock to the extent of $550,000 signed by the Mayor, May 21, 1901. Title to land vested in the city December 22, 1901. Work of constructing the piers commenced July 19, 1901. Nearing completion.

NEW YORK AND NEW JERSEY BRIDGE.

Commissioners—F. W. Devoe, R. Somers Hayes, Isidor Straus. *Secretary*—Charles H. Swan. Commissioners' office, 29 Broadway, Manhattan. The Commissioners of the New York and New Jersey Bridge and the Sinking Fund Commissioners of the City of New York selected a location midway between 49th and 51st Streets, Manhattan.. And the State Commissioners have located an elevated freight approach along the marginal wharf, or place, 5 feet west of the westerly line of West Street, with power of the Dock Department saying what docks and turnouts shall be built upon in order that cars can be loaded from ships without extra handling. The maximum length of span is 2,731 feet. Guaranteed cost of the bridge is $20,000,000, and will be a double-deck bridge, as approved by the Secretary of War July 3d, 1900, for trolley and steam traffic. The law provides that the bridge must be completed within ten years. The Union Bridge Company has made a contract with the companies to construct the bridge within six years from the time it commences work, and gave a bond of $1,000,000 for the faithful performance of the contract. It is intended to begin work of construction when the freight approaches to the bridge have been approved by the Sinking Fund Commissioners of New York City.

Army of the United States

STATIONED IN AND NEAR THE CITY OF NEW YORK.

Department of the East—Headquarters, Governor's Island, New York Harbor.

Major-General Leonard Wood, U. S. Army, Commanding.

Aides-de-Camp—Capt. George T. Langhorne, 15th Cavalry; ——————

DEPARTMENT STAFF.

Chief of Staff—Col. George S. Anderson.
Adjutant-General—Col. Henry O. S. Heistand.
Inspector-General—Col. John L. Chamberlain.
Chief Engineer—Col. G. D. Knight.
Department Artillery—Maj. Adelbert Cronkhite.
Judge-Advocate—Lieut.-Col. John A. Hull.
Chief Quartermaster— ——————.
Chief Commissary—Col. James N. Allison.
Chief Surgeon—Col. Charles B. Byrne.
Chief Paymaster—Col. Wm. H. Comegys.
Chief Ordnance Officer—Col. Orin B. Mitcham.
Chief Signal Officer—Lieut.-Col. G. P. Scriven.

Army Building, 39 Whitehall Street, Manhattan, New York City; *Quartermaster's Depot*—Col. Wm. S. Patten, Q. M. D. *Subsistence Depot*—Col. A. L. Smith, D. & P. C. *Medical Depot*—391 Washington Street, Manhattan, New York City; Capt. Edwin P. Wolfe, Medical Corps. *New York Arsenal*—Governor's Island, Col. Orin B. Mitcham, O. D.

Posts in and near New York City, as garrisoned November 15, 1908:

Forts.	*Location.*	*Commanding Officers.*	*Troops.*
Fort Jay	Governor's Island	Col. Wm. H. C. Bowen, 12th Inf.	Headquarters Band and 2d Batt., 12th Infantry.
Fort Hamilton	Narrows, Long Island	Maj. Herman C. Schumm.	4 cos. Coast Artillery.
Fort Hancock	Sandy Hook, N. J.	Col. H. L. Harris, A. C., 5th Band	6 cos. Coast Artillery.
Fort Schuyler	Throgs Neck, N. Y.	Lt.-Col. A. C. Blunt, A. C.	8 cos. Coast Artillery.
Fort Wadsworth	Narrows, Staten Island	Maj. Wm. G. Haan, A. C.	5 cos. Coast Artillery.
Fort Wood	Bedloe's Island	Capt. Daniel J. Carr, S. C.	Co. G, Signal Corps.
Fort Totten	Willet's Point, Whitestone, N. Y.	Col. Albert Todd, A. C., 2th Band	8 cos. Coast Artillery.
Sandy Hook Proving Ground	Sandy Hook, N. J.	Col. Rogers Birnie.	Ordnance Department.

Piers in Manhattan.

NORTH RIVER.

Pier No.	Street.
A, New 1 & Old 1	Battery Pl.
2 & 3	Battery Pl. & Morris.
4	Morris.
5 & 7	Morris & Rector.
8	Rector.
Old 9 & 10	Rector & Carlisle.
New 10	Albany.
Old 11	Carlisle.
New 11	Cedar.
13	Cortlandt & Dey.
14	Fulton.
15	Vesey & Barclay.
Old 16	Liberty & Cortlandt.
New 16	Barclay and Park Place.
17	Park Pl.
18	Murray.
19	Warren.
20	Chambers.
21	Duane.
22	Jay.
23	Harrison.
24	Franklin.
25	North Moore.
26	Beach.
27	Hubert.
28	Laight.
29-30	Vestry.
31	Watts.
32, 33, 34	Canal.
35	Spring.
36	Spring & Charlton.
37	Charlton.
38	King.
39	W. Houston.
40	Clarkson.
41	Leroy.
42	Morton.
43	Barrow.
44	Christopher.
45	W. 10th.
46	Charles.
47	Perry.
48	W. 11th.
49	foot Bank.
50	Bethune & W. 12th
51	Jane.
52	Gansevoort.
53	Bloomfield.
New 54	W. 13th.
Old 54	W. 24th.
Old 55	W. 25th
New 56	W. 14th.
Old 56	W. 26th.
Old 56½	Gansevoort & Bloomfield.
New 57	W. 15th.
Old 57	W. 27th.
New 58	W. 16th.
Old 58	W. 28th.
New 59	W. 18th.
Old 59	W. 29th.
60	W. 19th.
61	W. 21st.
62	W. 22d.
Old 64	W. 34th.
New 64	W. 24th.
New 65	W. 25th.
New 66	W. 26th.
Old 67	W. 37th.
New 67	W. 27th.
New 68	W. 28th.
New 69	W. 29th.
71	W. 31st.
72	W. 32d.
73	W. 33d.
74	W. 34th.
81	W. 42d.
84	W. 44th.
New 89	W. 49th.
Old 89	W. 59th.
91	W. 51st.

EAST RIVER.

Pier No.	Street.
4	Broad.
5, 6, 7, 8,	Coenties Slip
9	Coenties & Old Slip.
10	Old Slip.
11	Gouverneur Lane.
12	Wall.
13	Wall.
14	Maiden Lane.
15	Fletcher & Burling Slip.
16	Burling Slip.
17	Fulton.
18	Beekman.
19	Peck Slip.
20	Peck Slip.
22	Roosevelt.
Old 27	Dover.
New 27	Catharine.
Old 28	Dover & Roosevelt.
New 28	Catharine & Market.
Old 29	Roosevelt.
New 29	Market.
30	Pike & Market.
31	Pike.
Old 32	James Slip.
New 32	Pike.
33	Oliver.
New 33	Pike & Rutgers.
Old 34	Catharine.
New 34	Rutgers.
35	Catharine.
36	Jefferson.
37	Clinton.
38	Clinton & Montgomery.
45	Rutgers & Jefferson.
46	Jefferson.
49	Clinton & Montgomery.
50	Montgomery.
51 & 52	Gouverneur.
53	Jackson.
54	Corlears.
55	Cherry.
60	Rivington.
61	Rivington & Stanton.
62	Stanton.
66	E. 18th.
67	E. 19th.
70	E. 22d.

RECREATION PIERS.

Foot of Market.
Foot of E. 3d.
Foot of E. 24th.
Foot of E. 112th.
Foot of Barrow.
Foot of W. 50th.
Foot of W. 129th.

District Leaders in New York City.

DEMOCRATIC LEADERS AND EXECUTIVE MEMBERS.

Ass'y Dist.
1—D. E. Finn.
2—Thomas F. Foley.
3—Timothy P. Sullivan.
John T. Oakley.
4—John F. Ahearn.
P. J. Scully.
5—C. W. Culkin.
6—Benjamin Hoffman.
7—Frank J. Goodwin.
8—F. J. Sullivan.
9—P. J. Dooling.
William Dalton.
10—Julius Harburger.
11—T. J. McManus.
12—J. J. Murphy.
13—John F. Curry.
14—William J. Boyhan.
15—James J. Hagan.
16—John J. Harrington.
17—Ross Williams.

Ass'y Dist.
18—John V. Coggey.
Bart Dunn.
19—James Ahearn.
20—Maurice Featherson.
21—James J. Walsh.
22—William H. Sinnott.
23—Thomas F. McAvoy.
24—J. J. Dietz.
25—George F. Scannell.
Joseph F. Prendergast.
26—J. J. Frawley.
27—George Donnellan.
28—Nicholas J. Hayes.
29—Thomas E. Rush.
30 S—P. E. Nagle.
30 N—Wallace S. Fraser.
31—William J. Wright.
32—E. J. McGuire.
T. H. O'Neill.
33—Michael J. Garvin.

Ass'y Dist.
34—Arthur H. Murphy.
35—William E. Morris.

Edward Browne.
John J. Delany.
Lewis Nixon.
Charles G. F. Wahle.
Antonio Zucca.
Thomas F. Grady.
John C. Sheehan.
Robert L. Luce.
Daniel F. Cohalan.
William F. Grell.
John R. Voorhis.
George E. Best.
Chairman—Thomas F. McAvoy.
Secretaries—George F. Scannell. Thomas E. Rush. Thomas F. Smith.
Treasurer—Philip F. Donohue.

REPUBLICAN LEADERS AND EXECUTIVE MEMBERS.

Ass'y Dist.
1—William G. Rose.
2—Joseph Levenson.
3—James E. March.
4—Jacob A. Newstead.
5—Joseph T. Hackett.
6—Samuel S. Koenig.
7—William Halpin.
8—Charles S. Adler.
9—Michael H. Blake.
10—Ferdinand Eidman.
11—George W. Wanmaker.
12—William Henkel.
13—Charles B. Page.

Ass'y Dist.
14—John S. Shea.
15—Harry W. Mack.
16—Charles K. Lexow.
17—Abraham Gruber.
18—Joseph E. Nejedly.
19—Wm. S. Bennet.
20—John H. Gunner.
21—Moses M. McKee.
22—Ambrose O. Neal.
23—Collin H. Woodward.
24—Morris Levy.
25—Ezra P. Prentice.
26—Samuel Krulewitch.

Ass'y Dist.
27—B. W. B. Brown.
28—John B. Cartwright.
29—John Henry Hammond.
30—Frank K. Bowers.
31—Harvey T. Andrews.
32 Upper—John J. Knewitz.
32 Lower—William H. Ten Eyck.
33—Edw. H. Healy.
34—Headley M. Greene.
35—Thomas W. Whittle.
President—Herbert Parsons.
Sec'y—Thomas W. Whittle.
Treas.—Otto T. Bannard.

Estimated Population of New York City

AND ITS BOROUGHS, AS NOW CONSTITUTED, 1790 TO 1900.

(UNITED STATES CENSUS REPORT.)

BOROUGHS.	1900.	1890.	1880.	1870.	1860.	1850.	1840.	1830.	1820.	1810.	1800.	1790.
New York City....	3,437,202	2,507,414	1,911,698	1,478,103	1,174,779	696,115	391,114	242,278	152,056	119,734	79,216	49,401
Manhattan..........	1,850,093	1,441,216	1,164,673	942,292	813,669	515,547	312,710	202,589	123,706	96,373	60,515	33,131
Bronx..........	200,507	88,908	51,980	37,393	23,593	8,032	5,346	3,023	2,782	2,267	1,755	1,781
Brooklyn..........	1,166,582	838,547	599,495	419,921	279,122	138,882	47,613	20,535	11,187	8,303	5,740	4,495
Richmond..........	67,021	51,693	38,991	33,029	25,492	15,061	10,965	7,082	6,135	5,347	4,564	3,835
Queens..........	152,999	87,050	56,559	45,468	32,903	18,593	14,480	9,049	8,246	7,444	6,642	6,159

The preceding table shows that the area comprised within the present limits of the City of New York had an estimated population of 49,401 in 1790, which had grown to 696,115 in 1850, representing an increase of 646,714, or 1,309.1 per cent. The population of the present City of New York had grown to 2,507,414 in 1890, or an increase since 1850 of 1,811,299, or 260.2 per cent. Since 1890 there has been an increase of 929,788, or 37.1 per cent., the population in 1900 being 3,437,202.

New York Chamber of Commerce.

ORGANIZED April 5, 1768. Incorporated by George III. March 13, 1770. Reincorporated by the State of New York April 13, 1784. Its object is indicated in the following words of the original charter: "Sensible that numberless inestimable benefits have accrued to mankind from commerce; that they are, in proportion to their greater or lesser application to it, more or less opulent and potent in all countries; and that the enlargement of trade will vastly increase the value of real estates as well as the general opulence of our said colony," and "to carry into execution, encourage, and promote, by just and lawful ways and means, such measures as will tend to promote and extend just and lawful commerce."

During the decade 1760-1770, according to Lord Sheffield's *Observations*, the average yearly value of American Colonial imports from Great Britain was £1,763,409, and of exports to the same country £1,044,591. Up to the evacuation of the city by the British and its occupation by the Americans, on the 25th of November, 1783, the New York Chamber of Commerce had had seven presidents, thirteen vice-presidents, eight treasurers, one secretary, and 135 members. In May, 1763, the Sandy Hook Lighthouse was lighted up for the first time. In 1786 the Chamber of Commerce first suggested the construction of the Erie Canal, and in 1784 petitioned the New York Legislature (which so ordered) that duties should be levied under a specific instead of an *ad valorem* tariff—a system of which the Chamber of Commerce has ever since been the constant advocate.

As a society the Chamber of Commerce consists of fifteen hundred resident and two hundred and fifty non-resident members. Annual dues, $50 per annum. Non-resident members, $25 per annum. The building of the Chamber is at 65 Liberty Street, New York. Officers: *President*, J. Edward Simmons; *Secretary*, vacant; *Treasurer*, William H. Porter.

Clubs in Manhattan.

PRINCIPAL CLUBS AND CLUB-HOUSES. SEE ALSO "SOCIETIES AND ASSOCIATIONS IN NEW YORK CITY."

Name of Club.	Organized.	Club-House.	Membership. Limit. Resident.	Membership. Limit. Non-Resident.	Membership. Present Number. Resident.	Membership. Present Number. Non-Resident.	Initiation Fee. Resident.	Initiation Fee. Non-Resident.	Annual Dues. Resident.	Annual Dues. Non-Resident.	Secretary.
Aldine Association....	1895	Fifth Ave. & 18th St..	500	None.	500	100	$100	$50.00	$75.00	$25.00	Chas. L. Patton.
American Yacht........	1883	Milton Point, Rye, N.Y.	300	....	250	....	50	....	50.00	30.00	W. P. Allen.
Arion............	1854	Park Ave. & 59th St...	....	....	900	20	....	....	60.00	30	C. Wittmann.
Arkwright...........	1893	320 Broadway.........	700	None.	700	200	50	20.00	50.00	20.00	John H. Love, Jr.
Army and Navy	1889	107 W. 43d St.........	None.	None.	289	1,703	25	None.	30.00	5.00	G. W. McElroy.
Authors	1882	7th Ave. c. W. 58th St.	None.	None.	114	67	25	25.00	20.00	10.00	Duffield Osborne.
Automobile..........	1899	54th St., W. of B'way	1,200	None.	1,185	350	100	50.00	50.00	25.00	S. M. Butler.
Barnard...	1894	W. 56th St. & 7th Ave.	700	....	480	39	35	15.00	10.00	5.00	Edward L. Parris.
Calumet	1879	267 Fifth Ave.........	400	None.	375	151	100	50.00	100.00	50.00	E. O. Richards.
Catholic....	1871	120 Central Park South	1,000	None.	835	526	50	None.	50.00	10.00	Charles Murray.
Century Association. ..	1847	7 W. 43d St	1,000	300	1,000	250	150	100.00	60.00	30.00	Wm. M. Sloane.
Chemists............	..	108 W. 55th St........	....	....	....	....	....	....	....	....	Walker Bowman.
City..	1892	55 W. 44th St....... .	None.	None.	966	399	50	15.00	60.00	15.00	Franklin Clarkin.
Columbia Yacht......	1867	Foot W. 86th St.......	None.	None.	515	None.	50	....	30.00	....	George R. Branson.
Coney Island Jockey..	1881	569 Fifth Ave. (d)....	....	....	....	....	50	50.00	25.00	....	Cornelius Fellowes.
Congregational.......	1879	St. Denis Hotel.......	200	None.	170	10	5	None.	10.00	None.	Chas. L. Beckwith.
Cornell University...	1889	58 W. 45th St.........	None.	....	347	144	....	None.	...	....	Frederick Willis.
Downtown Ass'n......	1860	60 Pine St....	1,000	None.	1,000	98	200	75.00	100.00	37.50	Gordon Macdonald.
Drug and Chemical...	1894	100 William St........	500	None.	500	215	50	5.00	50.00	10.00	Ernest Stanffen, Jr.
Engineers...........	1888	32 W. 40th St.........	2,000	....	1,000	1,000	100	100.00	75.00	37.50	M. G. Starrett.
Explorers	1905	29 W. 39th St.........	....	....	65	41	10	5.00	15.00	5.00	H. C. Walsh.
German Liederkranz..	1847	111 E. 58th St........	None.	....	1,140	45	20	...	40.00	20.00	L. L. Breitwieser.
German Press........	1854	21 City Hall Place....	None.	None.	250	....	...	....	....	....	Emil Klaessig.
Green Room..........	1903	139 W. 47th St........	None.	None.	800	....	(c) 25	....	(c) 20	....	C. H. Clarke (Supt.).
Grolier.......	1884	29 E. 32d St..........	250	125	....	....	100	50.00	30.00	15.00	Walter Gilliss.
Hardware...	1892	253 Broadway.........	600	200	600	170	50	50.00	50.00	25.00	Arthur G. Sherman.
Harlem Democratic....	1882	106 W. 126th St.......	None.	None.	600	....	None.	None.	10.00	...	T. E. Dempsey.
Harlem Republican....	1887	23 W. 124th St........	None.	None.	110	None.	1	10.00	30.00	15.00	Wm. H. Rose.
Harmonie............	1852	4 E. 60th St..........	800	None.	800	None.	200	None.	125.00	None.	E. E. Spiegelberg.
Harvard.............	1866	27 W. 44th St..... ...	None.	None.	1,500	1,600	10	10.00	10.40	15.00	L. P. Marvin.
Jockey	1894	Fifth Ave. & 46th St..	50	None.	50	None.	....	....	100.00	....	F. K. Sturgis.
Knickerbocker........	1871	Fifth Ave. & 32d St...	450	None.	450	....	300	....	100.00	....	Jas. W. Appleton.
Knickerbocker Yacht..	1874	College Point, L. I. ..	....	....	147	....	20	....	24.00	...	J. O. Sinkinson.
Lambs..............	1874	130 W. 44th St........	250	300	250	440	200	100.00	75.00	30.00	Maclyn Arbuckle.
Lawyers.........	1887	120 Broadway...... ...	1,350	None.	1,350	500	None.	None.	100.00	50.00	Geo. T. Wilson.
Lincoln.............	1872	12 E. 8th St..........	....	None.	500	....	....	None.	12.00	12.00	J. F. Dornheim.
Lotos...............	1870	558 Fifth Ave.........	600	None.	450	400	100	25.00	75.00	30.00	A. C. Humphreys.
Manhattan..........	1865	26th St. & Madison Ave	....	....	750	450	200	125.00	100.00	25.00	H. D. Macdonald.
Manhattan Chess.....	1877	Carnegie Hall........	None.	None.	220	30	....	....	20.00	10.00	C. H. Hatheway.
Masonic.............	1894	17 E. 22d St..........	1,000	None.	840	....	....	25.00	15.00	5.00	T. C. Lefevre.
Merchants	1871	108 Leonard St........	350	150	350	80	100	75.00	75.00	50.00	Frederic S. Wells.
Metropolitan.........	1891	Fifth Ave. cor. 60th St.	1,000	250	1,000	225	300	300.00	125.00	75.00	Wm. W. Sherman.
National Democrat...	1871	617 Fifth Ave..	3,000	None.	2,420	405	100	25.00	50.00	20.00	John J. Quinlan.
New York...........	1845	20 W. 40th St..	500	None.	450	250	100	50.00	75.00	37.50	Henry Despard.
N. Y. Athletic...... .	1868	W. 59th St.. 6th Ave (g)	3,500	800	3,438	778	200	100.00	60.00	30.00	Chas. L. Burnham.
N. Y. Caledonian	1856	846 Seventh Ave......	None.	None.	375	None.	5	....	6.00	....	Donald Forbes.
N. Y. Press..........	1872	120 Nassau St.........	None.	None.	700	200	10	5.00	24.00	8.00	Walter Scott.
N. Y. Railroad.......	1872	..........(e)...........	None.	None.	1,600	....	3	....	2.00	....	H. D. Vought.
N. Y. Yacht.....	1844	37 W. 44th St. (a).....	None.	None.	2,370	....	200	....	50.00	....	G. A. Cormack.
Players.............	1888	16 Gramercy Park.....	500	550	490	550	100	50.00	50.00	25.00	H. B. Hodges.
Princeton...........	1899	119 E. 21st St........	None.	None.	771	759	10	10.00	30.00	10.00	W. F. McCombs, Jr.
Progress............	1864	1 W. 88th St..........	500	None.	500	40	100	50.00	100.00	50.00	A. M. Guingburg.
Racquet and Tennis ...	1875	27 W. 43d St..........	1,000	300	1,000	300	200	200.00	125.00	62.50	H. C. Mortimer.
Reform..............	1888	42 Broadway..........	None.	2,000	310	620	25	None.	40.00	10.00	Bert Hanson.
Republican	1879	54 W. 40th St.........	1,000	None.	965	982	50	25.00	50.00	28.00	R. L. Maynard.
Saint Nicholas.......	1875	7 W. 44th St..........	500	....	200	100	100	100.00	75.00	37.50	Rutger B. Jewett.
Salmagundi..........	1871	14 W. 12th St.........	500	None.	420	95	50	25.00	35.00	12.50	J. A. Thompson.
Seawanhaka Corinthian Yacht (q)...	1871	Oyster Bay, L. I......	500	None.	500	....	50	....	50.00	....	S. R. Outerbridge.
Strollers	1886	67 Madison Ave.......	400	400	....	....	50	50.00	30.00	15.00	Harold Binney.
Transportation.......	1895	Madison Ave. & 42d St.	500	500	348	392	25	25.00	50.00	25.00	D. W. Pardee.
Turf and Field.......	1895	571 Fifth Ave. (f)....	450	None.	422	....	100	....	50.00	....	E. C. La Montagne.
Underwriters.........	1898	16 Liberty St.........	700	None.	706	54	....	....	25.00	10.00	G. H. Brewer.
Union...............	1836	Fifth Ave. & 51st St...	1,600	None.	1,600	None.	300	....	100.00	....	Franklin Bartlett.
Union League........	1863	1 E. 39th St..........	1,800	....	1,800	....	300	...	100.00	....	Chas. Whitman.
University...........	1865	Fifth Ave. cor. 54th St.	2,000	1,500	2,000	1,500	200	100.00	75.00	35.00	William Manice.
Wool..	1904	W. B'way & Beach St.	450	200	410	99	....	....	50.00	20.00	John N. Stearns, Jr.
Yale................	1897	30 W. 44th St........	None.	None.	1,441	1,296	20	20.00	20.00	10.00	J. McL. Walton.

(a) Rendezvous at Bay Ridge, L. I. (c) Theatrical. (d) and Sheepshead Bay. (e) No club house. Meetings held at 39 W. 29th St. (f) and Belmont Park, Queens.
(g) Country House, Travers Island, Pelham Manor, N.Y. (q) Report of January 1, 1908.

The returns in this table are of January 1, 1909, approximately.

Fire Department in New York City.

(December, 1908.)

TABLE showing number of firemen in active service in New York City, and the salaries they receive:

Manhattan, Bronx and Richmond.	Salary.	Brooklyn and Queens.	Salary.
1 Chief of Department	$7,000	6 Deputy Chiefs	$4,200
8 Deputy Chiefs of Department	4,200	28 Chiefs of Battalion	3,300
31 Chiefs of Battalion	3,300	111 Foremen or Captains	2,160
137 Foremen or Captains	2,160	144 Assistant Foremen	1,800
221 Assistant Foremen or Lieut'ants.	1,800	184 Engineers of Steamers	1,000
247 Engineers of Steamers	1,000	896 Firemen 1st Grade	1,400
1,137 Firemen 1st Grade	1,400	104 " 2d "	1,200
170 " 2d "	1,200	99 " 3d "	1,000
303 " 3d "	1,000	62 " 4th "	800
132 " 4th "	800	5 Medical Officers	.....
50 Men on Probation	800	2 Pilots	1,500
6 Medical Officers	.....	1 Marine Engineer	1,400
8 Pilots	1,500		
5 Marine Engineers	1,400	Making a total of uniformed force, 4,107.	

Pursuant to the provisions of Section 790, Chapter 466, laws of 1903, Greater New York Charter, all uniformed members of the Fire Department are entitled to retire at the expiration of twenty years' continuous service on a pension equal to one-half of the salary they may be receiving at the time of their application. The Fire Commissioner also has the power to retire members of the department who, from any cause, are found to be unable to perform active duty in the department. If the disability occurs from injuries while in the discharge of duty, the pension must equal one-half of the salary; if from natural causes, the Fire Commissioner can decide upon the amount of the pension.

Fire Engine Companies, Manhattan and Bronx.

(Headquarters, 157 and 159 East Sixty-seventh Street.)

1—165 W. 29th St.
2—530 W. 43d St.
3—417 W. 17th St.
4—119 Maiden Lane.
5—340 E. 14th St.
6—113 Liberty St.
7—Duane St. near B'way
8—165 E. 51st St.
9—55 E. Broadway.
10—8 Stone St.
11—437 E. Houston St.
12—261 William St.
13—99 Wooster St.
14—14 E. 18th St.
15—269 Henry St.
16—223 E. 25th St.
17—91 Ludlow St.
18—132 W. 10th St.
19—355 W. 25th St.
20—243 Lafayette St.
21—216 E. 40th St.
22—159 E. 85th St.
23—215 W. 58th St.
24—78 Morton St.
25—342 5th St.
26—220 W. 37th St.
27—173 Franklin St.
28—604 E. 11th St.
29—160 Chambers St.
30—280 Spring St.
31—87 Lafayette St.
32—49 Beekman St.
33—42 Great Jones St.
34—440 W. 33d St
35—223 E. 119th St.
36—1849 Park Ave.
37—83 Lawrence St.
38—1907 Amsterdam Ave.
39—157 E. 67th St.
40—156 W. 68th St.
41—330 E. 150th St.
42—1192 Fulton Ave.
43—Sedgwick Ave., opp. Burnside Ave.
44—221 E. 75th St.
45—925 Tremont Ave.
46—451 E. 176th St.
47—502 W. 113th St.
48—2504 Webster Ave.
49—Blackwell's Island.
50—491 E. 166th St.
51—Ft. E. 99th St. (Boat).
52—Riverdale Ave., near Spuyten Duyvil Parkway.
53—175 E. 104th St.
54—304 W. 47th St.
55—363 Broome St.
56—120 W. 83d St.
57—Battery Park (Boat).
58—81 W. 115th St.
59—180 W. 137th St.
60—352 E. 137th St.
61—1518 W'msbridge Rd.
62—3431 White Plains Rd., Williamsbridge.
63—689 E. 240th St.
64—12th St., Unionport.
65—33 W. 43d St.
66—Ft. Grand St., E. R. (Fire Boat).
67—518 W. 170th St.
68—1080 Ogden Ave.
69—233d St., near Katonah Ave.
70—169 Scofield St., City Island.
71—159th St. & Park Ave.
72—22 E. 12th St.
73—655 Prospect Ave.
74—207 W. 77th St.
75—2085 Jerome Ave.
76—105 W. 102d St.
77—Foot of Main St., Brooklyn.
78—Foot Gansevoort St.
79—Briggs Ave., near 200th St.
80—503 W. 139th St.
81—3045 Albany Road.
82—1215 Intervale Ave.
83—618 East 138th St.
84—513 W. 161st St.
85—Foot of W. 35th St. (Boat).
86—Foot of Gansevoort St. (Boat).
87—Foot of W. 132d St. (Boat).
88—2225 Belmont Ave.

Hook and Ladder Companies, Manhattan and Bronx.

(Headquarters, First Division, 185 Lafayette Street; Eighth Battalion, 160 East Thirty-third Street.)

1—104 Duane St.
2—136 E. 50th St.
3—108 E. 13th St. (Water Tower No. 2).
4—788 8th Ave.
5—96 Charles St.
6—77 Canal St.
7—217 E. 28th St.
8—N. Moore St., c. Varick
9—209 Elizabeth St.
10—191 Fulton St.
11—742 5th St.
12—243 W. 20th St.
13—159 E. 87th St.
14—120 E. 125th St.
15—Old Slip, bet. Water and Front Sts.
16—159 E. 67th St.
17—341 E. 143d St.
18—84 Attorney St.
19—886 Forest Ave.
20—157 Mercer St.
21—432 W. 36th St.
22—766 Amsterdam Ave.
23—504 W. 140th St.
24—113 W. 33d St. (Water Tower No. 3 and Searchlight No. 2).
25—205 W. 77th St.
26—52 E. 114th St. (Water Tower No. 4).
27—453 E. 176th St.
28—250 W. 143d St.
29—620 E. 138th St.
30—104 West 185th St.
31—1213 Intervale Ave.
32—489 East 166th St.
33—2083 Jerome Ave.
34—515 West 161st St.
35—142-144 West 63d St.
36—Sedgwick Ave., opp. Burnside.
37—2930 Briggs Ave.
38—2223 Belmont Ave.

Police Force of New York City.

(December 1, 1908.)

1 *Chief Inspector*, 17 *Inspectors*, 25 *Surgeons*, 1 *Superintendent of Electrical Service*, 1 *Assistant Superintendent of Electrical Service*, 1 *Chief Lineman*, 6 *Linemen*, 2 *Boiler Inspectors*.

Boroughs.	Captains.	Lieutenants.	Sergeants.	Patrolmen.	Doormen.	Police Matrons.	Total.
Manhattan	37	325	276	4,779	80	41	5,538
The Bronx	9	38	45	662	18	4	776
Brooklyn	31	178	171	2,272	65	21	2,738
Queens	10	48	50	528	20	2	658
Richmond	4	18	21	157	6	2	208
Total	91	607	563	8,398	189	70	9,918

On Probation: 41 Patrolmen, 3 Doormen.

SALARIES.

Chief Inspector, Moses W. Cortright, $5,000; 17 other Inspectors, $3,500 each; 25 Surgeons, $3,500 each.

Superintendent of Electrical Service, $4,000; Assistant Superintendent of Electrical Service, $3,000; Chief Lineman, $1,500; Linemen, $1,200 each; 2 Boiler Inspectors, $1,300 each.

Captains, $2,750 each; Lieutenants, $2,000 each; Sergeants, $1,500 each.

Patrolmen, First Grade, five years' service, $1,400 each.

Patrolmen, Second Grade, less than five years and more than four years and six months, $1,350 each.

Patrolmen, Third Grade, less than four years and six months and more than four years, $1,250 each.

Patrolmen, Fourth Grade, less than four years and more than three years, $1,150 each.

Patrolmen, Fifth Grade, less than three years and more than two years, $1,000 each.

Patrolmen, Sixth Grade, less than two years and more than one year, $900 each.

Patrolmen, Seventh Grade, less than one year, $800 each.

Members of the police force may be retired on one-half rate of compensation after service of twenty-five years, having reached the age of fifty-five years, or after twenty years' service upon certificate of police surgeons of permanent disability, or after 20 years' service if a Veteran of Civil War. Members of the police force who have not served twenty years may also be retired upon pension upon certificate of police surgeons of permanent disability or disease contracted without misconduct on the part of the officer, and by reason of the performance of duty, at not to exceed one-half nor less than one-fourth rate of compensation.

Police Station-Houses in Manhattan and Bronx.

PRECINCTS—On January 1, 1909, numbers of Precincts may be changed.

1st. Old Slip. (Temporary, 98 John St.)
2d. Liberty and Church Streets.
5th. 9 Oak Street.
6th. 17 and 19 Elizabeth Street.
7th. 247 Madison Street.
8th. 17 and 19 Leonard Street.
9th. 105 & 107 Eldridge Street.
10th. 24 and 26 Macdougal Street.
12th. 205 Mulberry Street.
13th. Attorney and Delancey Sts.
14th. 135 and 137 Charles Street.
15th. First Ave. and Fifth Street.
16th. 253 Mercer Street.
17th. 130 Sheriff Street.
18th. 230 W. 20th Street.
19th. 127 W. 30th Street.
21st. 327 E. 22d Street.
22d. 434 W. 37th Street.
23d. 134 W. 30th Street.
25th. 160 E. 35th Street.
26th. 345 and 347 W. 47th Street.
28th. 150 W. 68th Street.
29th. 163 E. 51st Street.
31st. 153 E. 67th Street.
32d. 134 W. 100th Street.
33d. The Arsenal, Central Park.
35th. 432 E. 88th Street.
36th. 438 W. 125th Street.
39th. 177 E. 104th Street.
40th. 1854 Amsterdam Avenue.
43d. 148 E. 126th Street.
Traffic A, City Hall.
Traffic B, 36 East 9th Street.
Traffic C, 1 East 27th Street.
Harbor—Station A, Pier A, North River.
" Station B, 122d St. and East River.
61st. Alexander Av. & 138th St.
63d. 160th St. 3d & Washington Avs.
65th. 1925 Bathgate Ave.
66th. Sedgwick Ave. and Wolf St., High Bridge.
68th. Webster Ave. and Mosholu Parkway.
69th. Main St., West Chester.
74th. Boston Ave. and Perot St., Kingsbridge.
77th. City Island.
79th. 229th St. and White Plains Ave., Wakefield.

Police Station-Houses in Brooklyn.

(Headquarters, 269 State Street, Brooklyn.)

PRECINCT AND LOCATION.

104th. 179 Washington St.
143d. 4th Ave. and 43d St.
144th. 5th Ave. and 16th St.
145th. Richards and Rapelye Sts.
146th. 6th Ave. and Bergen St.
147th. 17 Butler St.
148th. Emmett and Amity Sts.
149th. 318 Adams St.
150th. 49 Fulton St.
151st. Grand Ave. and Park Pl.
152d. Atlantic & Schenectady Avs.
153d. Miller and Liberty Aves.
154th. Ralph Ave. and Quincy St.
155th. Gates and Throop Aves.
156th. DeKalb and Classon Aves.
157th. Flushing and Clermont Aves.
158th. Tompkins & Vernon Aves.
159th. Lee Ave. and Clymer St.
160th. Bedford Ave. & N. 1st St.
161st. Manhattan & Greenpoint Aves.
162d. Humboldt & Herbert Sts.
163d. Stagg St. and Bushw'k Av.
164th. Hamburg & De Kalb Aves.
165th. Liberty and E. N. Y. Aves.
166th. E. 95th St. and Ave. G.
167th. 35 Snyder Ave., Flatbush.
168th. Ave. U and E. 15th St.
169th. W. 8th St., near Surf Ave.
170th. Bay 22d St. and Bath Ave.
171st. 86th St. and 5th Ave.
172d. Coney Id. and Foster Avs.
173d. Prospect Park.
182d. Borough Hall.
184th. 191 Broadway.
Branch Bureau Detective Squad, Information and Property Clerk, 269 State St.

Height of Prominent Points in Manhattan and Bronx.

Place	Feet Above Sea Level.
Battery	5
City Hall	36
Fifth Avenue Hotel	38
Central Park Plaza, 59th St. and 5th Ave.	47.5
Mount Morris	100
Central Park Circle	76.5
Reservoir, Central Park (water level)	112
Morningside Park	132
Broadway and 118th Street	135
Kingsbridge Road and 175th Street	200
Washington Bridge Road and 184th St.	250

Hack and Cab Fares in Manhattan Borough.

THE legal rate of fare, of which an official copy shall be furnished by the Bureau of Licenses, and carried by every licensed cabman, shall be as follows:

Mileage rates charged for general driving.

Cabs—

For one mile or any part thereof	$0.50
For each additional half mile or part thereof	0.25
For any stop over five minutes in a trip, for every fifteen minutes or fraction thereof	.25

Coaches—

For one mile or any part thereof	$1.00
For each additional half mile or part thereof	.50
For any stop over five minutes in a trip, for every fifteen minutes or fraction thereof	.40

Hourly Rates.—These hourly rates, except by special agreement, are to apply only to shopping or calling, and shall not include park or road driving, nor driving for more than three miles from the starting point:

Cabs—For one hour or any part thereof, **$1.00**; For each additional half hour or part thereof **50c.**

Coaches—For one hour or any part thereof, **$1.50**; For each additional half hour or any part thereof. **75c.**

No hackman shall demand more than the legal rates of fare or charge for one stop not over five minutes in a single trip.

No hack shall be driven by the time rate at a pace less than five miles an hour.

Line balls, for one or two passengers, **$2** for first mile or part thereof, and **$1** for each additional mile or part thereof. Each additional passenger, 50 cents.

One piece of baggage, not to exceed 50 pounds in weight, shall be carried on a hack without extra charge. Additional baggage carried, 25 cents per piece.

In all cases where the hiring of a hack is not specified in advance to be by time, it shall be deemed to be by distance, and for any detention exceeding fifteen minutes the hackman may demand additional compensation at the rate of **$1** per hour.

REGULATIONS.

Any carriage kept for hire shall be deemed a public hack, and a carriage intended to seat two persons inside shall be deemed a cab, and a carriage intended to seat more than two persons inside shall be deemed a coach, and the term hackman shall be deemed to include owner or driver, or both.

Every license hack, except such as are specially licensed, shall be provided with a suitable lamp on each side, and shall have securely fastened across the middle of the outside of each lamp a metal band not less than two inches in width, out of which the official number of the license shall be cut after the manner of a stencil plate, the component figures of such numbers to be not less than one and one-half inches in height, and the style of the whole to be approved by the Mayor or Chief of the Bureau of Licenses. Every licensed hack shall have the official number of the license legibly engraved or embossed upon a metal plate and affixed inside, as designated and approved by the Mayor or Chief of the Bureau of Licenses, and no licensed hack shall carry or have affixed to it, inside or outside, any number except the official number as aforesaid.

Every licensed hackman, immediately after the termination of any hiring or employment, must carefully search such hack for any property lost or left therein, and any such property, unless sooner claimed or delivered to the owner, must be taken to the nearest police station and deposited with the officer in charge within twenty-four hours after the finding thereof; and in addition a written notice, with brief particulars and description of the property, must be forwarded at once to the Bureau of Licenses.

Every licensed hackman shall have the right to demand payment of the legal fare in advance, and may refuse employment unless so prepaid, but no licensed hackman shall otherwise refuse or neglect to convey any orderly person or persons, upon request, anywhere in the city, unless previously engaged or unable so to do. No licensed hackman shall carry any other person than the passenger first employing a hack without the consent of said passenger.

Distances in Manhattan.—Battery to City Hall, ¾ mile; City Hall to Houston St., **1 mile**; City Hall to Nineteenth St., 2 miles; Avenue Blocks, 20, Street Blocks, 7, are deemed **1 mile**.

Disputes as to rates and distances may be settled by the police, or complaints may be made to the **ELECTRIC TAXAMETER SERVICE.**—Hansom or Coupé may be hailed and engaged on the street when the flag is up. First half mile, 30 cents; each quarter mile thereafter, **10 cents**; each six minutes waiting, 10 cents; for sending cab to address, per mile or fraction, 20 cents.

License Fees in Manhattan and the Bronx.

(BUREAU OF LICENSES, CITY HALL, NEW YORK.)

Hoist, General	$25.00	Driver	$0.50	Junk Boat	$5.00
" " renewal	12.50	" renewal	25	" renewal	2.50
" Special	1.00	Stand, Elevated R. R.	10.00	Junk Cart	5.00
Ticket Speculator	50.00	Common Show	25.00	" renewal	2.50
" " renewal	25.00	" renewal	12.50	Special Hack Stand	25.00
Peddler, Horse & Wagon	8.00	Shooting Gallery	5.00	Special Coach	5.00
" " renew'l	4.00	" renewal	2.50	" renewal	2.50
" Push Cart	4.00	Bowling Alley	5.00	Public Coach	3.00
" " renewal	2.00	" renewal	2.50	" renewal	1.50
" Basket	2.00	Billiard Table	3.00	Special Cab	3.00
" " renewal	1.00	" renewal	1.50	" renewal	1.50
Express	5.00	Gutterbridge	1.00	Public Cab	2.00
" renewal	2.50	Hand Organ	1.00	" renewal	1.00
Public Cart	2.00	Public Porter	1.00	Hack Driver	50
" renewal	1.00	" renewal	25	" renewal	25
Dirt Cart	1.00	Pawnbroker	500.00	Stand, Newspaper	5.00
" renewal	50	Second-hand Dealer	25.00	" Fruit	10.00
Express Driver	50	" renewal	12.50	" Newsp'per & Fruit	15.00
" renewal	25	Junk Shop	20.00	" Bootblack, Chair	5.00
		" renewal	10.00		

Express Offices in the City of New York.

Adams.—Principal office, 71 Broadway. Other offices, 59 Broadway, 154 W. 26th St., Madison Ave. and 48th St., 51 W. 125th St., 2753½ Broadway, 308 W. 124th St., 137 W. Broadway, 309 Canal St., 324 Lafayette St., 11 Wooster St., 29 Seventh Ave., 132 Hamilton Pl., 663 E. 148th St., 25 W. 23d St., 26 E. 42d St., 250 Grand St., 127 Prince St., 13 E. 14th St., 91 Maiden Lane, 1033, 1257 3d Ave., 355 Amsterdam Ave., 1789 Lexington Ave., 2 Reade St., 200 Chambers St., 35 W. 33d St., 242 W. 47th St.: in Brooklyn, 322 Fulton St., 10 Furman St., 787 Flatbush Ave., Jefferson Ave. and Ormond Pl., 89, 2505 Atlantic Ave., 107 Broadway, 71 Jackson Ave., L. I. C.; in Jersey City, 10 Exchange Pl. and Pier D, Pennsylvania R. R. Depot.

American.—Principal office, 65 Broadway. Other offices, 142 W. Broadway, 302 Canal St., 18 Astor Pl., 922, 1434 and 2293 Broadway, 21 Mott St., 22 W. 15th St., 81 Dey St., 1251 3d Ave., 139 Spring St., 251 W. 125th St., 138th St. and Park Ave., Vanderbilt Ave. and 44th St., Madison Ave. and 47th St., 93 Bowery, 2800 Webster Ave., Bronx Park; in Brooklyn, 339, 611, 726, 1392 Fulton St., 26 Dean St., 1055 Flatbush Ave., Lee Ave. and Gwinnett St., 954 Broadway, 2566 Atlantic Ave., 3d Ave. and 25th St., Dock and Water Sts.

American.—European (Foreign) 8 Bridge St.

Borough.—Principal office, 145 W. 125th St. Other offices, 1572 Broadway, 205 W. 74th St., Morris and Greenwich Sts., 296 Canal, foot of Christopher, foot of Liberty, 142 West, 2 Rector St., 127 Franklin St., West Washington Market, 128 Division, 7 E. 14th St., 35 West 3d St., 555 W. 23d St., 24 E. 21st St., 134 W. 38th St., 7 E. 39th St., 128th St., near 3d Ave., West 83d St. near Broadway, 1243 Third Ave., 224, 696 Columbus Ave.

Cuban & Pan-American (Foreign), 52 Broadway, 136 Franklin St.

Davies, Turner & Co. (Foreign).—24 Whitehall St.

Dodd.—Principal office, 1354 Broadway. No. 6 Astor House, 170, 425, 434, 461, 1159, 1354 Broadway, Liberty, Cortlandt, Desbrosses, and W. 23d St. Ferries, Citizens' Line and Metropolitan Line, foot of W. 10th St.; People's Line, foot of Canal St.; Providence Line, foot of Murray St.; Fall River Line, foot of Warren St.; 182, 263 5th Ave., 521 7th Ave., 245 Columbus Ave., Grand Central Depot, 111 W. 125th St., 60 W. 133d St., 2798 3d Ave.; in Brooklyn, 52 Nassau St., 4 Court St., 479 Nostrand Ave., 390 Broadway; in Jersey City, 10 Exchange Pl.

Downing's (Foreign).—120 Broad St.

International (Foreign).—52 B'way, 136 Franklin.

Knickerbocker Express Co.—Main office, 51 Broadway. Orders and parcels will be received at offices of the Wells, Fargo & Co., whose wagons will collect packages for this company.

Long Island.—Principal office, Long Island City. Other offices, foot of James Slip and foot of E. 34th St., 95 Fifth Ave., 304 Canal St., 613 6th Ave., 195 Chambers St., 257 Mercer St., 574 Columbus Ave., 164 E. 77th St., 1047 6th Ave., 133 W. 125th St.; in Brooklyn, 333 Fulton St., 38 Hanson Pl., Atlantic Ave., near Vesta Ave., Bushwick Ave. Depots, 501 Broadway, near Union Ave., Parkville, 5604 3d Ave., near 56th St.

Morris' European Ex.—59 B'way.

National.—Principal office, 141 Broadway. Other offices, 123 Prince St., foot of Desbrosses St., 134 W. 25th St., 9 W. 31st St., 158 Duane St., 114 W. Broadway, 22 Hudson St., 100 Maiden Lane, 105 Bleecker St., 63 Gold St., 96 Worth St., 165 Crosby St., 2293 Broadway, 138th St. and Park Ave., 399 Madison Ave., foot of W. 42d St., Vanderbilt Ave. and 44th St., 1251 3d Ave., 251 W. 125th St., 2800 Webster Ave., Bronx Park; in Brooklyn, same offices American Express; in Jersey City, 109 Hudson St.; in Hoboken and Weehawken, West Shore R. R. depot.

New York and Boston Despatch.—Foot E. 22d St., 304 and 306 Canal St., 100 Maiden Lane, 45 Church St., 63 Gold St., 121 Prince St., 95 5th Ave., 613 6th Ave., 165 Crosby St., 257 Mercer St. Pier 18, N. R.

New York Transfer Company.—See Dodd.

Pitt & Scott (Foreign).—39 Broadway.

Russian Co. (Foreign), 120 Broad St.

Southern.—71 Broadway.—See Adams.

United States.—Principal office, 2 Rector St. Other offices, 134 W. 38th St., 1572 Broadway, 296 Canal St., foot of Christopher St., foot of Liberty St., 12 Fulton St., 100 Maiden Lane; 63 Gold St., 142 West St., 129 Franklin St., West Washington Market, 128 Division St., 205 W. 74th St., 24 E. 21st St., 555 W. 23d St., 7 E. 39th St., 145 W. 125th St., 1243 3d Ave., 224, 696 Columbus Ave., Morris and Greenwich Sts., 7 E. 14th St., 35 W. 3d St., 156 E. 23d St.; in Brooklyn, 339, 611, 1392 Fulton St., Dock, Water and Front Sts., 3d Ave. and 25th St., 1055 Flatbush Ave., 27 Alabama Ave.; in Jersey City, 46 Montgomery St., Depot of Central R. R. of New Jersey at Ferry; in Hoboken, on Ferry St., two blocks from Ferry.

Universal (Foreign).—Metzger & Co., 19 B'way.

Wells, Fargo & Co. (Foreign), 51 Broadway.

Wells, Fargo & Co.—Principal office, 51 Broadway. Other offices, 1159 Broadway, 613, 659, 1047 6th Ave., 310 Canal St., 100 Maiden Lane, 198 W. Broadway, 123 Prince St., 60 E. 8th St., 100 Warren St., 18 Chatham Sq., 174 Mercer St., 1662 Washington Ave., 993 Columbus Ave., 850 E. 169th St., 2621, 2672 Eighth Ave., 3365 Third Ave., 1991 Broadway, 136 W. 22d St., 107 John St., 185 Stanton St., 217 Greene St., 9 Morris St., 128th St. and 3d Ave., 5 Columbus Ave., foot of W. 23d St., 95 5th Ave., 1217 3d Ave., 1734, 2003 Amsterdam Ave., 257 W. 116th St., 133 W. 125th St., 374 Alexander Ave., 3206 3d Ave., 490 Tremont Ave., 156th St. and Union Ave.; in Brooklyn, 331 Fulton St., 524, 780 Broadway, corner Court and Union Sts., 22 Rockwell Pl.; in Jersey City, 299 Pavonia Ave., and at Ferry foot of Pavonia Ave.

Westcott.—Principal office, Madison Ave. and 46th St. Other offices, 84, 149, 399, 415, 429, 922, 1159, 1183, 1216, 1434, 2293 Broadway, foot of Barclay St., foot of Chambers St., foot of Desbrosses St., 18 Astor Pl., foot of W. 23d St., foot of Christopher St., foot of W. 42d St., Grand Central Station, 1251 3d Ave., 121, 251 W. 125th St., 125th Street and Park Ave., 1869 Park Ave., 138th St. and Park Ave., 2800 Webster Ave.; in Brooklyn, 333, 338, 611, 726, 1392 Fulton St., 1055 Flatbush Ave., 2566 Atlantic Ave., 15 Bergen St., 255 Lee Ave., 19 Jackson Ave., L. I. City, 954 Broadway, 3d Ave. and 25th St.

Population of New York City.

GROWTH OF THE CITY SINCE ITS EARLIEST DAYS.

1661	1,743	1800	60,489	1850	515,547	1899 (all Boro's)	3,549,558
1673	2,500	1805	75,587	1855	629,904	1900 " "	3,595,936
1696	4,455	1810	96,373	1860	813,669	1901 " "	3,437,202
1731	8,256	1816	100,619	1865	726,836	1902 " "	3,582,930
1750	10,000	1820	123,706	1870	942,292	1903 " "	3,632,501
1756	10,530	1825	166,136	1875	1,041,886	1904 " "	3,750,000
1771	21,865	1830	202,589	1880	1,206,299	1905 " "	3,850,000
1776	22,861	1835	253,028	1890	1,515,301	1906 " "	4,014,304
1786	23,688	1840	312,710	1893	1,891,306	1907 " "	4,152,860
1790	33,131	1845	358,310	1898 (all Boro's)	3,350,000	1908 " "	4,250,000

U. S. Volunteer Life-Saving Corps.

(Incorporated and Organized in most of the States.)

Officers—James R. Howe, President; Ernest H. Luebbers, Jr., Secretary; K. F. Mehrtens, Assistant Secretary; Wm. P. Jackson, Treasurer. Executive Committee of Consulting Board: Commodore Geo. A. Thormann, chairman; Commodore Aug. G. Miller and Commodore Henry Spitzer.

The United States Volunteer Life Saving Corps has 2,000 patroled stations and 22,000 enrolled members, all expert swimmers, yachtsmen and boatmen, with about 6,000 boats, from dories to expensive sail, steam, naphtha and gasoline launches. (It has saved in the Greater City, approximately, 255 lives; rendered "First Aid" in 302 cases; assisted 277 people on the water, and assisted 88 boats in distress.)

The corps is well organized in New York State, Massachusetts, Connecticut, New Jersey, Maryland, District of Columbia, Pennsylvania, Kentucky and other States as far west as California. It has been giving free instruction in swimming in both male and female departments of all the Public Free Baths of Greater New York—1,700 persons having been taught during the season of 1908, and has built ten life-saving stations, one dock, and placed 36 lifeboats throughout the Greater City.

The corps furnishes its various crews, free of charge, according to the funds available for the various districts and departments, ring life preservers, metallic life preservers, ice balls, medicine chests, flags, signs, charts and boats, and builds life-saving stations at the most dangerous points. It is supported wholly by voluntary contributions, with the exception of the Departments of Greater New York and Rhode Island, which are aided by appropriations from the cities and States, respectively.

The Department of Greater New York is particularly well organized, and is divided into sixteen commodores' and forty-eight vice-commodores' districts, containing 700 patroled stations, with 7,200 members and 1,200 boats devoted to its life-saving work.

LIFE-SAVING STATIONS IN GREATER NEW YORK.

Officers in command of the Greater New York Districts are as follows:

BOROUGH OF THE BRONX.

District No. 1—Fort Morris to Fort Schuyler on the Sound. Commodore, Charles Stahl, 689 East 133d Street, Bronx.

District No. 2—Fort Schuyler to City Line. Commodore, Aug. G. Miller, Tremont Avenue and Theriot Street, Bronx.

District No. 3—All the Harlem River from Port Morris to Spuyten Duyvil, then to Mount St. Vincent or City Line (Bronx shore only). Commodore, E. Harry Seixas, 528 East 149th Street, Bronx.

BOROUGH OF MANHATTAN.

District No. 4—Spuyten Duyvil on Manhattan Island to 100th Street on the Hudson. Commodore, Edw. A. Trede, 773 Eighth Avenue, Manhattan.

District No. 5—100th Street on Hudson, south to Barge Office, including Governor's Island, Ellis Island and Bedloe's Island. Commodore, Henry Spitzer, 249 West 139th Street.

District No. 6—Barge Office to 100th Street, East River. Acting Vice-Commodore, J. Dempsey, 12 Stone Street, Manhattan; Vice-Commodore, Henry Mason, 318 East 9th Street, Manhattan; Vice-Commodore, Henry Smolensky, 106 East 103d Street, Manhattan.

District No. 7—100th Street, East River through the Harlem River to Spuyten Duyvil on the Hudson River. Vice-Commodore, Ernest Hall, 402 East 146th Street, Bronx; Vice-Commodore, George Schmidt, 301 West 154th Street, Manhattan.

BOROUGH OF BROOKLYN.

District No. 8—Broad Channel Station on trestle, Jamaica Bay, following the line of trestle (West side) (Hammels excepted) to Ramblersville, then around the Bay, including all the rest of the Bay, Old Mill, Canarsie, Bergen Beach, Plum Island, Barren Island, Breakwater, etc. Commodore John G. Torborg, 1043 Liberty Avenue, Brooklyn, N. Y.

District No. 9—Coney Island in its entirety. Commodore, Jas. Brennan, foot West 32d Street, Coney Island.

District No. 10—End of Emmons Avenue and Knapp Street, on mainland side of Sheepshead Bay to 39th Street Ferry; Commodore, Charles L. Huson, 16 Bay 23d Street, Brooklyn, N. Y.

District No. 11—39th Street Ferry to Newtown Creek, including both shores of the Creek, Gowanus Canal, Erie Basin, etc. Commodore, Hugh F. Doherty, 152 Douglas Street, Brooklyn.

District No. 12—Newtown Creek, up East River through Hell Gate to City Line, including Little Neck Bay. Commodore, J. M. Finch, 137 Main Street, Astoria, L. I.

BOROUGH OF QUEENS.

District No. 13—Jamaica Bay, east side of trestle to City Line, Rockaway shore excepted. Under temporary command of Commodore John G. Torborg, 1043 Liberty Avenue, Brooklyn, N.Y.

District No. 14—The Rockaways, from Hammels on the trestle, along shore Jamaica Bay side to Rockaway Point, around Point, along Ocean side to point opposite Hammels on trestle. Under temporary command of Commodore Wm. W. Minnis, 36 Kane Avenue, Rockaway, N. Y.

District No. 15—Both shores of Rockaway, east from Hammels to Far Rockaway or City Line, including Arverne, Edgemere, etc. Vice-Commodore W. W. Minnis, 36 Kane Avenue, Hammels, Rockaway.

BOROUGH OF RICHMOND.

District No. 16—Staten Island in its entirety. Vice-Commodore, Arthur Krakehl, 122 First Avenue, New York City.

The Single Tax.

The following statement of the single tax principle was written by Henry George, Sr.:

We assert as our fundamental principle the self-evident truth enunciated in the Declaration of American Independence, that all men are created equal and are endowed by their Creator with certain inalienable rights. We hold that all men are equally entitled to the use and enjoyment of what God has created and of what is gained by the general growth and improvement of the community of which they are a part. Therefore, no one should be permitted to hold natural opportunities without a fair return to all for any special privilege thus accorded to him, and that that value which the growth and improvement of the community attaches to land should be taken for the use of the community; that each is entitled to all that his labor produces; therefore, no tax should be levied on the products of labor.

To carry out these principles, we are in favor of raising all public revenues for national, State, county, and municipal purposes by a single tax upon land values, irrespective of improvements, and all the obligations of all forms of direct and indirect taxation.

Since in all our States we now levy some tax on the value of land, the single tax can be instituted by the simple and easy way of abolishing, one after another, all other taxes now levied and commensurately increasing the tax on land values until we draw upon that one source for all expenses of government, the revenue being divided between local governments, State government, and the general government, as the revenue from direct tax is now divided between the local and State governments, or by a direct assessment being made by the general government upon the States and paid by them from revenues collected in this manner. The single tax we propose is not a tax on land, and therefore would not fall on the use of land and become a tax on labor.

It is a tax not on land, but on the value of land. Then it would not fall on all land, but only on valuable land, and on that not in proportion to the use made of it, but in proportion to its value—the premium which the user of land must pay to the owner, either in purchase money or rent, for permission to use valuable land. It would thus be a tax not on the use and improvement of land, but on the ownership of land, taking what would otherwise go to the owner as owner, and not as user.

In assessments under the single tax all values created by individual use or improvement would be excluded, and the only value taken into consideration would be the value attaching to the bare land by reason of neighborhood, etc., to be determined by impartial periodical assessments. Thus the farmer would have no more taxes to pay than the speculator who held a similar piece of land idle, and the man who, on a city lot, erected a valuable building would be taxed no more than the man who held a similar lot vacant. The single tax, in short, would call upon men to contribute to the public revenues not in proportion to what they produce or accumulate, but in proportion to the value of the natural opportunities they hold. It would compel them to pay just as much for holding land idle as for putting it to its fullest use. The single tax, therefore, would—

1st. Take the weight of taxation off the agricultural districts, where land has little or no value irrespective of improvements, and put it on towns and cities, where bare land rises to a value of millions of dollars per acre.

2d. Dispense with a multiplicity of taxes and a horde of tax-gatherers, simplify government, and greatly reduce its cost.

3d. Do away with the fraud, corruption, and gross inequality inseparable from our present methods of taxation, which allow the rich to escape while they grind the poor. Land cannot be hid or carried off, and its value can be ascertained with greater ease and certainty than any other.

4th. Give us with all the world as perfect freedom of trade as now exists between the States of the Union, thus enabling our people to share through free exchanges in all the advantages which nature has given to other countries, or which the peculiar skill of other peoples has enabled them to attain. It would destroy the trusts, monopolies, and corruptions which are the outgrowths of the tariff. It would do away with the fines and penalties now levied on any one who improves a farm, erects a house, builds a machine, or in any way adds to the general stock of wealth. It would leave every one free to apply labor or expend capital in production or exchange, without fine or restriction, and would leave to each the full product of his exertion.

5th. It would, on the other hand, by taking for public use that value which attaches to land by reason of the growth and improvement of the community, make the holding of land unprofitable to the mere owner and profitable only to the user. It would thus make it impossible for speculators and monopolists to hold natural opportunities unused or only half used, and would throw open to labor the illimitable field of employment which the earth offers to man. It would thus solve the labor problem, do away with involuntary poverty, raise wages in all occupations to the full earnings of labor, make overproduction impossible until all human wants are satisfied, render labor-saving inventions a blessing to all, and cause such an enormous production and such an equitable distribution of wealth as would give to all comfort, leisure, and participation in the advantages of an advancing civilization, in securing to each individual equal right to the use of the earth. It is also a proper function of society to maintain and control all public ways for the transportation of persons and property, and the transmission of intelligence; and also to maintain and control all public ways in cities for furnishing water, gas, and all other things that necessarily require the use of such common ways.

Help in Case of Accidents.

Drowning. 1. Loosen clothing, if any. **2.** Empty lungs of water by laying body on its stomach, and lifting it by the middle so that the head hangs down. Jerk the body a few times. **3.** Pull tongue forward, using handkerchief, or pin with string, if necessary. **4.** Imitate motion of respiration by alternately compressing and expanding the lower ribs, about twenty times a minute. Alternately raising and lowering the arms from the sides up above the head will stimulate the action of the lungs. Let it be done gently but persistently. **5.** Apply warmth and friction to extremities. **6.** By holding tongue forward, closing the nostrils, and pressing the "Adam's apple" back (so as to close entrance to stomach), direct inflation may be tried. Take a deep breath and breathe it forcibly into the mouth of patient, compress the chest to expel the air, and repeat the operation. **7.** DON'T GIVE UP! People have been saved after HOURS of patient, vigorous effort. **8.** When breathing begins, get patient into a warm bed, give WARM drinks, or spirits in teaspoonfuls, fresh air, and quiet.

Burns and Scalds. Cover with cooking soda and lay wet cloths over it. Whites of eggs and olive oil. Olive oil or linseed oil, plain, or mixed with chalk or whiting. Sweet or olive oil and lime-water.

Lightning. Dash cold water over a person struck.

Sunstroke. Loosen clothing. Get patient into shade and apply ice-cold water to head. Keep head in elevated position.

Mad Dog or Snake Bite. Tie cord tight above wound. Suck the wound and cauterize with caustic or white-hot iron at once, or cut out adjoining parts with a sharp knife. Give stimulants, as whiskey, brandy, etc.

Stings of Venomous Insects, etc. Apply weak ammonia, oil, salt water, or iodine.

Fainting. Place flat on back; allow fresh air, and sprinkle with water. Place head lower than rest of body.

Tests of Death. Hold mirror to mouth. If living, moisture will gather. Push pin into flesh. If dead the hole will remain, if alive it will close up. Place fingers in front of a strong light. If alive, they will appear red; if dead, black or dark. If a person is dead decomposition is almost sure to set in after 72 hours have elapsed. If it does not, then there is room for investigation by the physician. Do not permit burial of dead until some certain indication of death is apparent.

Cinders in the Eye. Roll soft paper up like a lamplighter, and wet the tip to remove, or use a medicine dropper to draw it out. Rub the *other* eye.

Fire in One's Clothing. *Don't run*—especially not downstairs or out-of-doors. Roll on carpet, or wrap in woollen rug or blanket. Keep the head down, so as not to inhale flame.

Fire from Kerosene. *Don't use water*, it will spread the flames. Dirt, sand, or flour is the best extinguisher, or smother with woollen rug, table-cloth, or carpet.

Suffocation from Inhaling Illuminating Gas. Get into the fresh air as soon as possible and lie down. Keep warm. Take ammonia—twenty drops to a tumbler of water, at frequent intervals; also, two to four drops tincture of nux vomica every hour or two for five or six hours.

Antidotes for Poisons.

First. Send for a physician.

Second. INDUCE VOMITING, by tickling throat with feather or finger. Drink hot water or strong mustard and water Swallow sweet oil or whites of eggs.

Acids are antidotes for alkalies, and vice versa.

When the Boat Overturns.

DON'T go out in a pleasure boat without being assured that there are life-saving buoys or cushions aboard sufficient to float all on board in case of an upset or collision. All persons should be seated before leaving shore, and no one should attempt to exchange seats in midstream or to put a foot on the edge or gunwale of the boat to exchange seats. Where the waters become rough from a sudden squall or passing steamers, never rise in the boat, but settle down as close to the bottom as possible, and keep cool until the rocking danger is passed. If overturned, a woman's skirts, if held out by her extended arms, while she uses her feet as if climbing stairs, will often hold her up while a boat may pull out from the shore and save her. A non-swimmer, by drawing his arms up to his side and pushing down with widely extended hands, while stair-climbing or treading water with his feet, may hold himself several minutes, often when a single minute means a life; or throwing out the arms, dog fashion, forward, overhand and pulling in, as if reaching for something—that may bring him in reach of help.

Rules in Case of Fire.

CRAWL on the floor. The clearest air is the lowest in the room. Cover head with woollen wrap, wet if possible. Cut holes for the eyes. *Don't get excited.*

Ex-Chief Hugh Bonner, of the New York Fire Department, gives the following rules applying to houses, flats, hotels, etc.:

Familiarize yourself with the location of hall windows and natural escapes. Learn the location of exits to roofs of adjoining buildings. Learn the position of all stairways, particularly the top landing and scuttle to the roof. Should you hear cry of "fire," and columns of smoke fill the rooms, above all KEEP COOL. Keep the doors of rooms shut. Open windows from the top. Wet a towel, stuff it in the mouth, breathe through it instead of nose, so as not to inhale smoke. Stand at window and get benefit of outside air. If room fills with smoke keep close to floor and crawl along by the wall to the window.

Do not jump unless the blaze behind is scorching you. Do not even then if the firemen with scaling ladders are coming up the building or are near. Never go to the roof, unless as a last resort and you know there is escape from it to adjoining buildings. In big buildings fire always goes to the top. Do not jump through flame within a building without first covering the head with a blanket or heavy clothing and gauging the distance. Don't get excited; try to recall the means of exit, and if any firemen are in sight DON'T JUMP.

If the doors of each apartment, especially in the lower part of the house, were closed every night before the occupants retired there would not be such a rapid spread of flames.

Hospitals, Dispensaries, Etc., in Brooklyn.

Bay Ridge Hospital, 60th St. and 2d Ave.
Bedford Dispensary, 343 Ralph Ave.
Bedford Guild Dispensary, 962 Bergen St.
Bethany Deaconesses' Home and Hospital, 237 St. Nicholas Ave.
Bethesda Sanitarium, 952 St. Mark's Ave.
Brooklyn Central Dispensary, 29 3d Ave.
Brooklyn City Dispensary, 11 Tillary St.
Brooklyn Diet Dispensary, 174 Johnson St.; 268 Leonard St.
Brooklyn E. D. Dispensary and Hospital, 106 S. 3d St.
Brooklyn Eye and Ear, 94 Livingston St.
Brooklyn Homœopathic Dispensary (E. D.) 194 S. 3d St.
Brooklyn Hospital, Raymond St., near De Kalb Ave.
Brooklyn Nursery and Infants' Hospital, 396 Herkimer St.
Brooklyn Training School for Nurses, De Kalb Ave., cor. Raymond St.
Bushwick Hospital, 4 Howard Ave.
Bushwick and East Brooklyn Dispensary, Myrtle and Lewis Aves.
Central Homœopathic Dispensary, 15 Columbus Pl.
Coney Island Hospital, Ocean Parkway.
Faith Home for Incurables, Park Pl., corner Classon Ave.
Gates Ave. Homœopathic Dispensary, 13 Gates Ave.
German Hospital, St. Nicholas Ave. and Stanhope St.
Home for Consumptives, Kingston Ave. and St. John's Pl.
Jewish Hospital, Classon and St. Mark's Aves., and 70 Johnson Ave.
Kings County Hospital, Clarkson Ave., near Albany Ave.
Kingston Ave. Hospital, Kingston Ave. and Fenimore St.
Long Island College Dispensary, Pacific St., near Henry St.
Long Island College Hospital, Henry St., near Pacific St.
Long Island Throat Hospital and Eye Infirmary, 55 Willoughby St.
Long Island Veterinary Hospital, 285 Jay St.
Lutheran Hospital, East New York Ave., corner Junius St.
Memorial Dispensary, 811 Bedford Ave.
Memorial Hospital for Women and Children, 827 Sterling Pl.
Methodist Episcopal Hospital (Seney Hospital), 7th Ave., cor. 6th St.
Norwegian Lutheran Deaconesses' Home and Hospital, 46th St., cor. 4th Ave.
Polhemus Memorial Clinic, Amity St., corner Henry St.
Prospect Heights and Brooklyn Maternity, corner Washington Ave. and St. John's Pl.
Reception Hospital, Sea Breeze Ave., near W. 3d St., Coney Island.
Samaritan Hospital and Dispensary, 608 Fourth Ave.
Skene's Sanitarium, 759 President St.
St. Catherine's Hospital, Bushwick Ave., near Ten Eyck St.
St. John's Hospital (Church Charity Foundation), Atlantic Ave., cor. Albany Ave.
St. Mary's General Hospital, Buffalo and St. Mark's Aves. Sisters of Charity.
St. Mary's Maternity and Female Hospital, 155 Dean St. Sisters of Charity.
St. Peter's Hospital, Henry St., cor. Congress St. Sisters of the Poor of St. Francis.
St. Phebe's Mission Guild, 125 De Kalb Ave.
Swedish Hospital, Sterling Pl. and Rogers Ave.
U. S. Naval Hospital, Flushing Ave., opposite Ryerson St.
Williamsburg Hospital, Bedford Ave., cor. S. 3d St.
Willis, 374 Ocean Parkway.

Hotels in Manhattan.

‡Abingdon, 7 Abingdon Square.
*Albany, Broadway and 41st Street.
*Albemarle, Broadway and 24th Street.
*Albert, University Place and 11th Street.
‡America, 102 East 15th Street.
‡Ashland, 4th Avenue and 24th Street.
*Ashton, Madison Avenue and 93d Street.
*Astor House, Broadway, opposite Post-Office.
*Astor, Broadway, 44th and 45th Streets.
*Bancroft House, Broadway and 21st Street.
*Bartholdi, Broadway and 23d Street.
‡Belvedere, 4th Avenue and 18th Street.
*Beresford, 1 West 81st Street.
*Breslin, Broadway and 29th Street.
‡Broadway Central, 673 Broadway.
‡Brunswick, 89th Street and Madison Avenue.
*Buckingham, 5th Avenue and 50th Street.
*Cadillac, Broadway and 43d Street.
†Cecil, 118th Street and St. Nicholas Avenue.
*Colonial, 125th Street and 8th Avenue.
*Continental, Broadway and 20th Street.
*Cosmopolitan, Chambers St. and W. Broadway.
*Empire, Broadway and 63d Street.
‡Endicott, Columbus Avenue and 81st Street.
*Everett House, 4th Avenue and 17th Street.
‡Gilsey House, Broadway and 29th Street.
†Gotham, 5th Avenue and 55th Street.
*Grand, Broadway and 31st Street.
*Grand Union, 4th Avenue and 42d Street.
*Grenoble, 7th Avenue and 56th Street.
*Herald Square, 34th Street, near Broadway.
*Hermitage, 7th Avenue and 42d Street.
*Hoffman House, 1111 Broadway.
*Holland House, 5th Avenue and 30th Street.
*Imperial, Broadway and 32d Street.
*Knickerbocker, Broadway and 42d Street.
*Longacre, 157 West 47th Street.
*Majestic, 4 West 72d Street.
*Manhattan, 42d Street and Madison Avenue.
*Manhattan Square, 56 W. 77th Street.
*Marie Antoinette, Broadway and 66th Street.
*Marlborough, 1355 Broadway.
*Martha Washington, 4th Avenue and 29th Street.
†Martinique, Broadway and 32d Street.
*Metropole, Broadway and 42d Street.
*Mills (No. 1), Bleecker and Thompson Streets.
*Mills (No. 2), Rivington and Chrystie Streets.
*Mills (new), 7th Avenue and 36th Street.
*Murray Hill, Park Avenue and 40th Street.
*Netherland, corner 5th Avenue and 59th Street.
*New Amsterdam, 4th Avenue and 21st Street.
*Park Avenue, Park Avenue and 32d Street.
*Plaza, 5th Avenue and 59th Street.
‡Roland, Madison Avenue and 59th Street.
*St. Denis, Broadway and 11th Street.
‡St. George, Broadway and 12th Street.
†St. Lorenz, 72d Street and Lexington Avenue.
*St. Regis, 5th Avenue and 55th Street.
‡San Remo, 8th Avenue and 75th Street.
‡Savoy, 5th Avenue and 59th Street.
*Seville, corner 29th Street and Madison Avenue.
†Sherman Square, Broadway and W. 71st Street.
*Smith & McNell's, 197 Washington Street.
*Stevens House, 27 Broadway.
‡Sturtevant, 147 W. 35th Street.
*Union Square, 15th Street and Union Square.
*Victoria, 5th Avenue and 27th Street.
*Waldorf-Astoria, 5th Avenue, 33d to 34th Street.
‡Westminster, Irving Place and 16th Street.

*European Plan. †American Plan. ‡American and European Plans.

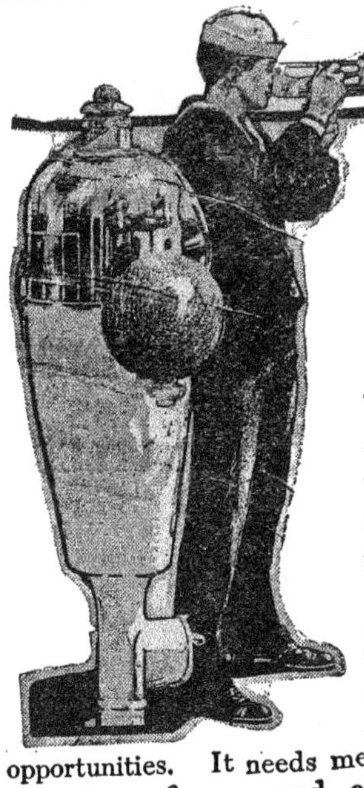

CHANCES IN THE NAVY

EVERY man's ambition is to get into something he enjoys doing. Then his work will be an inspiration to him. Promotion and success follow. He gets to the top.

Few young men have a clear idea of the variety and attractiveness of life in the Navy. This nation is building a powerful and efficient Navy. It needs many young men of more than ordinary ability. It offers them opportunities. It needs mechanics of all kinds---electricians, machinists, carpenters, firemen and coal passers. It needs experienced clerks, musicians, cooks, bakers, stewards, waiters and men for the Hospital Corps, as well as men for the Seamen Branch.

There is an incentive to get to the top in any line of Naval Service. Every encouragement is given a man to improve himself. Good conduct medals, promotion and a raise come to him as the reward for good work. When a man has attained the Navy standard of proficiency in his special line he is assured of continuous employment at good pay.

The Government prefers to enlist young men and train them, at its own expense. Training Stations are located at Newport, R. I., Norfolk, Va., and San Francisco.

The recruit is placed on the pay roll the day he enters.

The work at the schools is practical and intended to prepare a young man in a short time to go on board ship and work at his chosen line.

Send for illustrated booklet, which tells of the chances in the Navy to save money, the duties of bluejackets, their opportunities and how they live. Sent free if you address

Box 70, BUREAU OF NAVIGATION
NAVY DEPARTMENT, WASHINGTON, D. C.

Further information will be found by referring to the Navy classification of the General Index of THE WORLD ALMANAC.

IS BALDNESS DOOMED?

Baltimore hair specialist says it is unnecessary, and proves it. The intense interest in the wonderful work that is being accomplished in Baltimore and other cities by William Chas. Keene, president of the Lorrimer Institute, continues unabated. Many cases of baldness and faded hair of years' standing have been remedied by the remarkable preparation being distributed from Mr. Keene's laboratory, and its fame is spreading far and wide, and thousands of persons are using this remarkable hair food with gratifying results.

What makes this treatment more popular is the fact that free trial outfits are sent by mail prepaid. Those who wish to try it are strongly advised to write to Mr. Keene at the Lorrimer Institute, Branch 127, Baltimore, Md. They will receive the full trial outfit free of charge and much useful information about the hair which will put them on the road to a rapid and certain improvement.

Foreign Consuls in New York City.

Argentine Republic.—José Vicente Fernández, C. G.; Carlos A. Galarce, Asst. C., 80 Wall St.
Austria-Hungary. — Baron Hoenning O'Caroll, C. G.; George de Grivicic, C., 123 E. 17th St.
Belgium.—Pierre Mali, C., 73 Fifth Ave.
Bolivia.—Carlos Sanjines, Act. C. G., 2 Stone St.
Brazil.—José Joaquim Gomes dos Santos, C. G.; F. Garcia Leao, V. C. and Chancellor, 17 State St.
Chile.—Ricardo Sanchez-Cruz. C. G., 43 Exchange Pl.
China.—Wingsshiu S. Ho, C.; L' k Wing, V.C., 18 Broadway.
Colombia.—Carlos M. Sarria, C. G., 78 Broad St.
Costa Rica.—Dr. Juan J. Ulloa, C.G.; A. Monestel, V. C., 66 Beaver St.
Cuba.—Octavio Zayas. y Adan, C. G.; Antonio Altamira, C., 96 Wall St.
Denmark.—J. Clan. C., 130 Pearl St.
Dominican Republic.—Fabio Fiallo, C. G.; J. Esteban Bunols, Chancellor, 31 Broadway.
Ecuador—Felicisimo Lopez, C. G.; R. Zevallos, V. C.; Luis A. Plaza, Chancellor, 11 Broadway.
Egypt.—See "Turkey."
France.—Etienne Lanel, C. G.; L. Bonzom, C., M. Heilmann, V. C., 35 S. William St.
German Em ire.—K. Buenz, C.G.; C. Gneist, C. 11 Broadway.
Great Britain.—Courtenay Walter Bennett, C. G.; Reginald Walsh. C.; E. W. Paget Thurston, V. C.; Norman King, V. C.; Joseph P. Smithers, V. C., 17 State St. Office for shipping seamen, 2 State St.
Greece.—D. N. Botassi, C. G., 35 S. William St.
Guatemala.—Dr. Ramon Bengoechea, C. G.; Luis Padilla, V. C., 4 Stone St.
Hayti.—Geffrard Cesvet, C. G.; E. D. Bassett, V. C., 31-33 Broadway.
Honduras.—Guillermo Moncado. C. G., 66 Beaver St.
Hungary.—See "Austria."
Italy.—A. Raybaudi Massiglia, C. G.; G. di Rosa, V. C.; G. Gentile, V. C., 230 Lafayette St.
Japan.—Kokichi Midzuno, C. G.; Kaichi Yamasaki, V. C., 60 Wall St.
Korea.—See "Japan."
Liberia.—Edward G. Merrill, C., 24 Stone St.
Mexico.—Cayetano Romero, C. G.; A. Leon Grajeda, V. C., 32 Broadway.
Monaco.—M. Heilmann, C., 35 S. William St.
Netherlands.—J. R. Planten, C. G., 116 Broad St. Henry Pluygers, C., 116 Broad St.
Nicaragua.—Pio Bolanos, C.; 66 Beaver St.
Norway.—C. Ravn, C. G; Thj. Klingcuberg, V. C., 17 State St.
Panama—Manuel E. Amador, C. G., 18 Broadway.
Paraguay.—Felix Aucaigne, C. G., Mt. Vernon, N. Y.; W. W. White, C., 309 Broadway.
Persia.—Dikran Khan Kelekian, C., 275 5th Ave.
Peru.—Eduardo Higginson, C. G., 25 Broad St.
Portugal.—Luis Ferreira de Castro, C. G.; A. S. Gouvea, V. C., 17 State St.
Russia.—Baron A. A. Schlippenbach, C. G.; P. d'Adamovitch, V. C.; Paul Tiesenhausen, V. C., 22 N. Washington Sq.
Salvador.—Ernest Schernikow, C.; 42 B'way.
Santo Domingo.—See "Dominican Republic."
Siam.—L. T. Hildreth, C., 48 W. 59th St.
Spain.—Antonio Diaz Miranda, C. G., 18 Broadway.
Sweden—A. E. Johnson, Act. C.; M. Clarholm, Act. V. C., 17 State St.
Switzerland.—J. Bertschmann, C., 18 Exchange Pl.
Trinidad.—J. de la Boissiere, C. G., 102 W. 54th St.
Turkey.—Mundji Bey, C. G., 59 Pearl St.
Uruguay.—Henry H. Jennings, V. C., 17 Battery Pl.
Venezuela.—Gonzalo Picòn-Febres, C.G., 80 Wall St.

Cemeteries in and About the City of New York.

Name.	Location.	Office.	Railroad or Ferry.
Arlington	Arlington, N. J., 4 1-2 miles from J. C.	At Cemetery	Greenwood Lake Div. Erie R. R.
Bay Side and Acacia	Old South Road, Woodhaven, L. I.	At Cemetery	Kings County Elevated or Trolley.
Bay View	Greenville, N. J., 2 1-2 miles from J. C.	At Cemetery	Cent. R.R. of N. J. or trolley from J. C.
Bergen	Bergen, N. J., 1 1-2 miles from J. C.	98 Sip Ave., J. C.	Cortlandt, Desbrosses, W. 23d St. Ferries.
Calvary	Newtown, L. I.	24 E. 52d St., N. Y.	Long Island City or Williamsburg Ferries.
Cedar Grove	Near Corona, L. I., 5 1-2 miles from N. Y.	1 Madison Ave., N. Y.	Long Island R.R. or Bkn. Rapid Transit.
Constable Hook	Bayonne, N. J., 7 miles from J. C.		Cent. R.R. of N. J. or trolley from J. C.
Cypress Hills	Myrtle Ave. and Jamaica Plank Road, Brooklyn Borough.	1 Madison Ave., N. Y.	Grand, Roosevelt, and Fulton Ferries, and also by cars from Brooklyn Bridge.
Evergreens	Bushwick Ave. & Conway St., Brooklyn	At Cemetery	Trolley from Bklyn Ferries, or El. R.R's.
Fair View	Staten Island, near Castleton Corners	W. New Brighton, N. Y.	Trolley from St. George, Staten Island.
Friends'	Prospect Park, Brooklyn Borough	725 E. 31st St., B'k'n	Fulton, Catharine, and Hamilton Ferries.
Greenwood	Brooklyn Boro', N. Y. Main entrances at 5th Ave. and 25th St.	170 Broadway, N.Y.	Cars from Bridge Depot, Fulton, Wall, South, Catharine, and Hamilton Ferries.
Hoboken	New Durham, N.J., 4m. from Hoboken fer.	213 W'sh'gton St., Hob.	Nor. R.R. of N.J.; West Shore; Trolley.
Holy Cross (R. C.)	Flatbush, L. I., Brooklyn Borough	Jay & Chapel Sts., B'k'n	Fulton, Grand, and Roosevelt Ferries.
Holy Name (R. C.)	Westside Ave., Jersey City Heights		Cortlandt, Desbrosses, W. 23d St. Ferries.
Holy Trinity (R. C.)	Central Ave., East New York	At Cemetery	Trolley from Brooklyn Ferries.
Jersey City	Newark Ave., Jersey City, N. J.	At Cemetery	Cortlandt, Desbrosses, W. 23d St. Ferries.
Kensico	Harlem R. R., 25 miles from N. Y.	16 E. 42d St., N. Y.	Harlem R. R.
Linden Hill (M. E.)	East Williamsburg, L. I.	48 St. Mark's Pl., N.Y.	Williamsburg Ferries.
Lutheran	Jamaica Turnpike, near Middle Village	68 William St., N. Y.	Trolley from W'msburg and Fulton Fer.
Machpelah	New Durham, Hudson County, N. J.	At Cemetery	Nor. R.R. of N.J.; N.Y., S. & W.; W.S.R.R.
Machpelah (Heb.)	Adjoining Cypress Hills Cemetery	At Cemetery	Same route as for "Cypress Hills," above.
Maple Grove	Hoffman Boul., 6 miles from L. I. City.	Richmond Hill	East 34th St. Ferry.
Moravian	New Dorp, Staten Island	Located about six miles	from St. George Landing, Staten Island.
Mount Hope	Mount Hope, Westchester County	503 Fifth Ave., N. Y.	Putnam Div., N. Y. Central R. R.
Mount Hope	Jamaica Ave., Brooklyn Borough	155 E. 106th St., N. Y.	Trolley from B'way Ferry, Bkln Borough.
Mount Neboh	Adjoining Cypress Hills Cemetery	2 E. 118th St., N. Y.	Same route as for "Cypress Hills," above.
Mount Olivet	Maspeth, L. I.	82 Wall St., N. Y.	Trolley from foot of Broadway, Brooklyn Borough, or E. 34th St. Ferry Depot.
Mount Zion	Maspeth, L. I.	41 Park Row, N. Y.	Trolley from E. 34th St. Ferry Depot.
New York Bay	Ocean Ave., Greenville, N. J.	At Cemetery	Cent. R. R. of N. J.; or trolley from J. C.
Nyack Rural	Nyack, N. Y.	Nyack, N. Y.	Nor. R. R. of N. J. or West Shore R.R.
Oakland	Yonkers, N. Y.	57 Warburton Ave	Trolley from Yonkers.
Pelham	Lafayette Ave., City Island, N. Y.	Main St., City Island	Horse-car from Bartow, on N. Hav. R.R.
Pine Lawn	Pine Lawn, L. I.	46 W. 34th St., N. Y.	Long Island R.R.
Potter's Field	Flatbush, L. I., Brooklyn Borough	Almshouse, Flatbush	Cars from W'msburg and Fulton Ferries.
Potter's Field	Hart's Island, N. Y.	148 E. 20th St., N. Y.	Boat foot of E. 26th St.
Rockland	Sparkill, Rockland Co., N.Y.	At Cemetery	Northern R.R. of N. J. & West Sh. R.R.
Rosedale and Linden	Linden, N. J., 14 miles from N.Y.	1135 Broadway	Cortland, Desbrosses, W. 23d St. Ferries.
Rosehill and Crematory	Linden, N. J.	1101 Flatiron Bdg., N.Y.	Via Penna. R.R.
St. John's	Yonkers, N. Y.	At Cemetery	N. Y. Central or Putnam Div.
St. Michael's	Flushing Ave., Newtown, L. I.	225 W. 99th St., N. Y.	East 34th and 92d St. Ferries.
St. Peter's (R. C.)	Tonnele Ave., Jersey City Heights		Cortlandt, Desbrosses, W. 23d St. Ferries.
Sleepy Hollow	Tarrytown, N. Y.	130 Main St., Tarryt'n.	N. Y. Central & Hudson R.R.
Staten Island	Richmond Terrace, near W. N. Brighton		Whitehall St. Ferry.
Trinity Church	Amsterdam Ave. and W. 153d St.	187 Fulton St., N. Y.	Sixth or Ninth Ave. Elevated R.R.
Washington	Near Parkville, L. I.	Gravesend	Trolley from Bridge and Ferries.
Weehawken & Palisade	Hoboken, N. J., 2 miles from ferries	At Cemetery	Hoboken and Weehawken Ferries.
Woodlawn	On Jerome Ave. and 233d St.	20 E. 23d St., N. Y.	Harlem Div., N. Y. Central R. R.

New Life --- New Strength

For Run-Down, Worn-Out Men

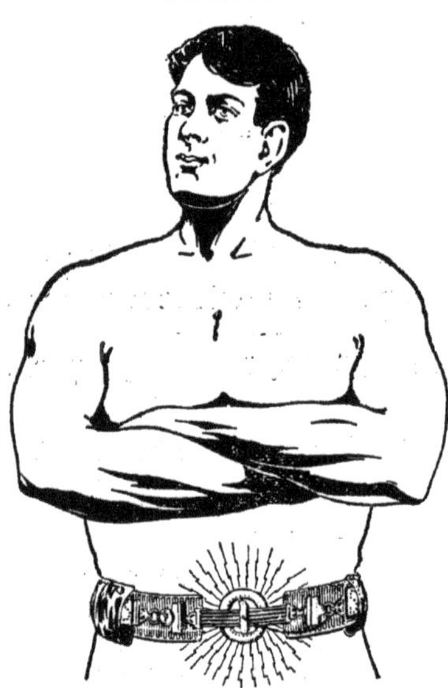

MORE VIM and VIGOR

MORE SNAP and ENERGY

MORE BUSINESS ABILITY

WHAT is strength, vim and energy? What is the force before which obstacles melt and competition fades away? What is that power in man that makes him a leader among men? What is health and strength? In fact, what is life itself but ELECTRICITY? Do not all authorities tell us that they are so closely allied that none can tell where one leaves off and the other begins? Who can say that they are not the same? The strong, healthy man is always full of electricity. The weak man lacks it.

What is more natural then than that electricity should cure when new life and strength is needed, as in Nervous Exhaustion, Weakness, Fatigue, Failing Memory, Poor Circulation, Rheumatic Pains, Backache, Kidney, Liver and Stomach Troubles, etc., caused by overwork or excessive expenditure of nervous force in other directions? There is no question about it. It is a fact that I have demonstrated by curing thousands of such sufferers during my nearly forty years of ceaseless labor in this field. The whole secret is to apply the treatment right, and my experience and success insure that.

ELECTRO-LIFE

Electro-Life is a brand-new invention, containing all that is best in that grand curative triumvirate—Galvanism, Faradism, Magnetism. All three combined in one appliance. It is something new—a step in advance. Nothing like it exists. It is guaranteed for one year, and will cure the most stubborn cases. Price reasonable.

FREE BOOK Let me send you my new "Electro-Life Book." It gives all particulars and contains in a condensed form the knowledge I have amassed during my long experience as a Specialist in Electricity. It is sent post paid, in plain, sealed envelope, upon request. Call at my office, or write for this book to-day.

ALFRED SANDEN, 1151 Broadway, Near 27th Street, New York City
Office hours, 9 to 6; Sundays, 10 to 1.

I Can Cure Cancer

At Home Without Pain, Plaster Or Operation, and I Tell You How, Free.

I Have Proven Cancer Can Be Cured At Home—No Pain, No Plaster, No Knife.—Dr. Wells.

I have discovered a new and seemingly unfailing remedy for the deadly cancer. I have made some most astonishing cures. I believe every person with cancer should know of this marvellous medicine and its wonderful cures, and I will be glad to give full information free to all who write me and tell me about their case.

Peter Keagan, Galesburg, Ill., had cancer of the mouth and throat. Doctors said, "no hope." Mr. Keagan wrote: "It is only a question of a short time—I must die." To-day his cancer is healed up and he is well. My marvellous radiatized fluid did it. It has other just such cures to its credit. It is saving people every day and restoring them to health and strength. If you have cancer or any lump or sore that you believe is cancer, write to-day and learn how others have been cured quickly and safely and at very small expense. No matter what your condition may be, do not hesitate to write and tell me about it. I will answer your letter promptly, giving you, absolutely free, full information and proof of many remarkable cures. Address Dr. Rupert Wells, 325 Radol Bldg., St. Louis, Mo.

Greatest of all Scissors

Eighteen Tools Combined

And Every Tool Practical

6. Ruler
1. Scissors
7. Measure
8. Nail File
9. Screw Driver
2. Buttonhole Scissors
3. Gaspipe Tongs
4. CigarCutter
5. Wire Cutter

Keen Edge

12. Hammer
13. Penknife
14. Glass Cutter
15. Glass Breaker
16. Marking Wheel
11. Cartridge Extractor
10. Cigar Box Opener
17. Ink Eraser
18. Stereoscope

MUCH HANDIER THAN A KNIFE

AN EXCELLENT GIFT

A necessity in every Household, Office, Store, Factory, Afield or Afloat. A Simple—Convenient—Compact—Durable Device. Can be carried in the Pocket or Pocket Book as it is protected by a leather cover. The 18 Tools in one Make a Handsome Gift for Man or Woman.

W. C. HOCKING & CO.

158 Lake Street, Chicago

Used as Souvenirs with Manufacturer's Imprint.

CATARRH CURED. NO CURE, NO PAY

The Paris Medicine Company, 2622-28 Pine Street, St. Louis, Mo., manufacturers of LAXATIVE BROMO QUININE and other standard preparations, have a new discovery—

Grove's New Discovery for Catarrh

And a recently invented device by which this new discovery can be applied to the nose as easily as brushing the teeth. It will cure and prevent CATARRH and bad breath. No matter how clean the mouth may be kept, if the nose is not clean and healthy the breath will be bad. We wish to supply THIS COMPLETE OUTFIT to any sufferer from CATARRH, with the definite understanding that it will cost nothing if you are not satisfied. Price of Grove's New Discovery for Catarrh, 50c; price of Grove's Throat and Mouth Antiseptic, 25c.; price of Grove's Common-Sense Nasal Douche, 25c. If your druggist hasn't it, simply send us 50c. in stamps and mention this book, and we will send the COMPLETE OUTFIT to you by mail. If you are entirely satisfied, after using the treatment, you may send us the balance of 50c., otherwise we will, without question, return the 50c. which you have already sent. Any druggist will tell you we will do exactly what we say.

RUPTURE CURED

That rupture can be cured is admitted. The greatest obstacle has been imperfect appliances that have slipped or are continually moving out of place. It has remained for us to place before sufferers our PERFECT-FITTING, Improved Elastic Truss. IT CAN BE WORN WITH EASE NIGHT AND DAY, and will surely cure where a cure is possible. Of course, there are some cases that have gone too far to be cured by any known process. To those we offer comfort and safety.

Those interested call or send for one of our illustrated books on "Rupture," free.

HENRY NOLL

775 Broadway, New York (opp. Wanamaker's)

☞ Our Trusses are not sold by Agents or Druggists.

Closed Sundays. Lady in attendance for ladies. Examination free.

Established 1882.

THE "NEW CENTURY" GASOLINE FIRE ENGINE

UNEQUALLED FOR FIRE PROTECTION PURPOSES

Built in various sizes.

SUITABLE FOR VILLAGE OR METROPOLITAN FIRE DEPARTMENT SERVICE

HUNDREDS IN SERVICE

PORTABLE POWERFUL DURABLE AND RELIABLE

REASONABLE IN COST

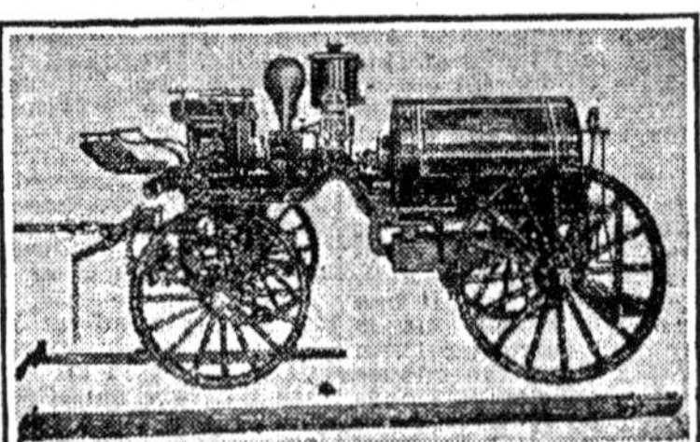

COST OF MAINTENANCE VERY LOW

CAREFULLY PACKED FOR EXPORT, AND PRICE QUOTED F.O.B. FACTORY OR SEABOARD

FOR FULL PARTICULARS ADDRESS THE MANUFACTURERS

WATEROUS ENGINE WORKS CO. :: ST. PAUL, MINN., U. S. A.

Libraries in Manhattan and Bronx.

Academy of Medicine, 17 W. 43d St.—Open 9.30 A. M. to 2 P. M.

American Geographical Society, 15 W. 81st St.

American Institute, 19 W. 44th St.—Open 9 A.M. to 5 P.M.; $5 per annum.

American Law, 60 Wall St.—Open 9 A.M. to 10 P.M.

American Museum of Natural History, Central Park W., cor. W. 77th St.

American Numismatic and Archæological Society, W. 156th St. and Broadway.

Astor.—See "N. Y. Public Library."

Benjamin & Townsend, ft. E. 26th St.—Open daily, 9 A. M. to 5 P. M.; Saturday, 9 A. M. to 12 M.

Booklovers, 5 E. 23d St.—Open 8 A. M. to 6 P. M.

Bryson, W. 120th St., nr. Broadway.—Open, except Sunday, 8.30 A.M. to 5.45 P.M.; Saturday, 8.45 A.M. to 5 P.M.

City, 10 City Hall, free.—Open 10 A.M. to 4 P.M.

Columbia University, W. 116th St. and Amsterdam Ave.

Cooper Union, 7th St. & 4th Ave.—8 A.M. to 10 P.M.

De Witt Memorial, 286 Rivington St.—Open daily, except Sunday, from 3 to 6.30 P. M.

Genealogical and Biographical, 226 W. 58th St.—Open 10 A. M. to 6 P. M.; Mondays, 8 to 10 P. M.

Historical Society, 170 2d Ave.—Open 9 A. M. to 6 P. M., except during August and on Holidays.

Huntington Free Library, Westchester Ave., Westchester.—Open daily, except Sunday, 9 A.M. to 10 P.M.; on Sundays from 2 to 9 P.M.

Law Library of Equitable Life Assurance Society, 120 Broadway.—Open 9 A.M. to 7 P.M.; Summer, 9 A.M. to 5 P.M.

Lenox.—See "N.Y. Public Library."

Loan Libraries for Ships, 76 Wall St.

Masonic, 79 W. 23d St.—Open 7 to 10.30 P. M.

Mechanical Engineers', 29 W. 39th St.—Open daily except Sunday, 9 A.M. to 9 P.M.

Mechanics & Tradesmen, 20 W. 44th St.

Mercantile, 13 Astor Place, 120 Broadway.—Open 8.30 A. M. to 6 P. M. Rates: Clerks, $4 per annum; others, $5.

Mott Memorial Free Medical, 64 Madison Ave.—Open 10 A.M. to 5 P. M.

N. Y. Port Society, 46 Catharine St., 128 Charlton.

New York Public Library.—See Index.

New York Society, 109 University Place.—Open 9 A. M. to 6 P. M.

New York University, Washington Sq., E.

Olivet Memorial, 59 2d St.—Open 8 A. M. to 9 P. M.

Riverdale, Riverdale.—Open Monday, Wednesday, Friday, Saturday, 8 to 10 P. M.

St. Aloysius's, 198 E. 4th St.—Open Sunday afternoons.

Seamen's, 1 State St.; free.—Open 10 A.M. to 10 P.M.

Sociological Reference, 105 E. 22d St.—Open 9 A. M. to 5 P.M.

Squirrel Inn, 131 Bowery.—Open 9 A. M. to 9 P.M.; Sunday, 2 P. M. to 6 P. M.

Tabard Inn, 5 E. 23d St.

Woman's Library, 9 E. 8th St.—Open 9 A. M. to 4 P.M.; $1.50 per annum.

Young Men's Christian Ass'n, 142 2d Ave., 129 Lexington Ave., 5 W. 125th St., 361 Madison Ave., 531 W. 155th St. near Broadway, 317 W. 56th St., 153 E. 86th St., 222 Bowery, foot W. 72d St., 215 W. 23d St., 109 W. 54th St.—Open 9 A. M. to 10 P. M.; Sundays, 2 to 10 P.M.

Young Women's Christian Ass'n, 7 E. 15th St.—Open 9 A.M. to 9.15 P.M., Sundays excepted.

Railroad Passenger Stations in Manhattan.

Baltimore & Ohio, ft. W. 23d and Liberty Sts.

Central of New Jersey, foot of W. 23d and Liberty Streets; New Jersey Southern Division (in Summer), foot of W. 42d and Cedar Streets, also.

Delaware, Lackawanna & Western, foot of Barclay and Christopher Streets.

Erie, foot of Chambers and West 23d Streets.

Lehigh Valley, foot of Cortlandt, Desbrosses and West 23d Streets.

Long Island, foot of East 34th St.

Atlantic Avenue Branch, junction of Flatbush and Atlantic Avenues, Brooklyn.

Manhattan Beach Division, foot of East 34th St.

New Jersey & New York, foot of Chambers and West 23d Streets.

New York & Long Branch, foot Liberty, Cortlandt, Desbrosses and West 23d Streets. In Summer, foot W. 42d and Cedar Sts. also.

New York Central & Hudson River, 42d St. and 4th Ave.; Harlem, 125th St.; Mott Haven, 138th St.; 10th Ave. and 30th St.; Manhattan, 125th St., 152d St.; Harlem Division, 4th Ave. and 42d, 86th, 110th, 125th, 138th and 183d Streets.

New York, New Haven & Hartford, 4th Avenue and 42d Street.

New York, Ontario & Western, foot of Desbrosses and West 42d Streets.

New York, Susquehanna & Western, foot of Cortlandt, Desbrosses and West 23d Streets. Also foot of Fulton Street, Brooklyn, via Annex.

Northern of New Jersey, foot of Chambers and West 23d Streets.

Pennsylvania, foot of Cortlandt, Desbrosses and West 23d Streets. Also foot of Fulton Street, Brooklyn, via Annex.

Philadelphia & Reading, foot of W. 23d and Liberty Streets.

Staten Island, foot of Whitehall Street.

West Shore, foot of Desbrosses and West 42d Streets.

Safe Deposit Companies in Manhattan.

American, 501 Fifth Avenue.
Atlantic, 49 Wall Street.
Bankers 4 Wall Street.
Broadway, 565 Broadway.
Carnegie, 115 Broadway.
Colonial, 220 Broadway.
Empire City, 160 Fifth Avenue.
Federal, 253 Broadway.
Fidelty, 1 Hudson St.
Fifth Avenue, 250 Fifth Avenue.
Garfield, Sixth Avenue and 23d Street.
Hanover, 7 Nassau Street.
Knickerbocker, 358 Fifth Avenue.
Lincoln, 32 East 42d Street, 45 East 41st Street.
Madison, 208 Fifth Avenue, 1128 Broadway, 413 Broadway.
Manhattan Warehouse, 42d Street and Lexington Avenue, Seventh Avenue and 52d Street.
Maiden Lane, 170 Broadway.
Mercantile, 120 Broadway.
Merchants', West Broadway and Beach Street.
Metropolitan, 3 East 14th Street.
Mount Morris, Park Avenue, corner 125th Street.
National Safe Deposit, 32 Liberty Street.
New Amsterdam, 1411 Broadway.
New York County, 79 Eighth Avenue.
Night and Day, 527 5th Avenue.
North America, 45 Exchange Pl.
Produce Exchange, 2 Broadway.
Safe Deposit Co., of New York, 140 Broadway.
Standard, 25 Broad Street.
Stock Exchange, 10 Broad Street.
United States, Broadway and West 73d Street.
Van Norden, 786 Fifth Avenue.
Windsor, 505 Fifth Ave.

Public Buildings in Manhattan.

Army Building, Whitehall and Pearl Streets.
City Hall, City Hall Park.
County Court-House, Chambers St., near B'way.
Criminal Courts Building, Centre & Franklin Sts.
Custom-House Bowling Green.
Hall of Records, Chambers and Centre Sts.
Ludlow Street Jail, near Grand Street.
Post-Office, Broadway and Park Row.
State Arsenal, 7th Avenue and 35th Street.
Sub-Treasury, Wall and Nassau Streets.
Tombs, Centre and Franklin Streets.

NEW YORK POST-GRADUATE MEDICAL SCHOOL AND HOSPITAL

SECOND AVENUE AND TWENTIETH STREET

University of the State of New York : : Winter Session 1908-1909

This College for practitioners offers excellent clinical facilities. There are 225 beds in the Hospital, which is a part of the Institution. The courses are adapted for the general practitioner as well as for those who wish to become proficient in a specialty, such as Eye, Ear, Nose and Throat, Dermatology and Hydrotherapy, Gynaecology and so forth. Special instruction is given in Hydrotherapy, in Phthisiotherapy, and every Department of Medicine and Surgery. The sessions continue throughout the year.

: : FACULTY : :

Surgery—Professors W. B. DeGarmo, M. D.; Willy Meyer, M. D.; Samuel Lloyd, M. D.; Robert T. Morris, M. D.; Carl Beck, M. D.; Theodore Dunham, M. D.; John F. Erdmann, M. D.; Adjunct Professors: Carter S. Cole, M. D.; Franz Torek, M. D.; Edward W. Peterson, M.D.; George E. Doty, M.D.; Aspinwall Judd, M. D.; Charles R. L. Putnam, M. D.

Orthopedic Surgery—Professors W. O. Plimpton, M. D.; Henry L. Taylor, M. D. Adjunct Professor: Charles Ogilvy, M. D.

Diseases of the Rectum and Anus—Professor Samuel G. Gant, M. D. Adjunct Professor—Kenneth K. MacAlpine, M. D.

Medicine—Professors William H. Porter, M.D; Leonard Weber, M. D.; Max Einhorn, M. D.; Edward Quintard, M. D. Adjunct Professors: Robert H. Halsey, M. D.; R. Abrahams, M. D.; Arthur F. Chace, M. D.

Medicine (Diseases of Children)—Professors Henry D. Chapin, M. D.; Augustus Caillé, M. D. Adjunct Professors: Charles O. Maisch, M. D.; Godfrey R. Pisek, M. D.

Pathology, Histology and Bacteriology—Professor Henry T. Brooks, M. D. Adjunct Professor: Benjamin F. Cline, M. D.

Clinical Pathology—Professor Frederic E. Sondern, M. D.

Diseases of Women—Professors Bache McE. Emmet, M. D.; H. St. John Boldt, M. D.; Ralph Waldo, M. D.; James N. West, M. D.; G. G. Ward, Jr., M.D. Adjunct Professors: Abram Brothers, M. D; Grace Peckham-Murray, M. D.; Franklin A. Dorman, M. D.; S. W. Bandler, M. D.; George H. Mallett, M. D.; S. S. Graber, M. D.; E. W. Pinkham, M. D.

Diseases of the Skin—Professor W. Bedford Brown, M. D. Adjunct Professors: Thurston B. Lusk, M. D.; Sigmund Pollitzer, M. D.; William S. Gottheil, M. D.

Diseases of the Eye—Professors Francis Valk, M. D.; A. E. Davis, M. D. Adjunct Professors: Duncan MacPherson, M. D., Ellice M. Alger, M. D.

Diseases of the Ear—Professors Wendell C. Phillips, M. D.; James F. McKernon, M. D.; John B. Rae, M. D.

Diseases of the Nose and Throat—Professors Clarence C. Rice, M. D.; H. Beaman Douglass, M. D. Adjunct Professor: Thomas J. Harris, M. D.

Disease of the Mind and Nervous System—Professors Graeme M. Hammond, M. D.; Wm. J. Morton, M. D.; Joseph Collins, M. D. Adjunct Professors: Abbott C. Combes, M. D.; Edwin G. Zabriskie, M. D.

Obstetrics—Professor George L. Brodhead, M.D. Adjunct Professors: H. P. DeForest, M. D., W. H. W. Knipe, M. D.

Venereal and Genito-Urinary Diseases—Professors Eugene Fuller, M. D.; Ramon Guiteras, M. D.; Follen Cabot, M. D. Adjunct Professors: James Pedersen, M. D.; Winfield Ayres, M. D.

Surgical, Anatomy and Operative Surgery on the Cadaver—Professor John J. McGrath, M. D. Adjunct Professor: Denis A. McAuliffe, M. D.

Phthisiotherapy—Professor S. A. Knopf, M.D.

FOR FURTHER PARTICULARS ADDRESS

GEORGE GRAY WARD, Jr., M.D. Second Ave. and Twentieth St.
Secretary of the Faculty, NEW YORK CITY

GEORGE N. MILLER, M.D., President
ARTHUR F. CHACE, M. D., Secretary of the Corporation
Frederic Louis Brush, M. D., Superintendent

Interborough Rapid Transit Company

13-21 PARK ROW, MANHATTAN BOROUGH.

T. P. SHONTS, Chairman of Executive Committee.	D. W. ROSS, Vice-President.
W. LEON PEPPERMAN, Asst. to Chair'n Ex. Com.	H. M. FISHER, Secretary.
E. P. BRYAN, President.	J. H. CAMPBELL, Treasurer.
FRANK HEDLEY, V.-President & Gen. Manager.	GEO. H. PEGRAM, Chief Engineer.

MANHATTAN RAILWAY DIVISION.

MANHATTAN BOROUGH ELEVATED RAILROADS.

Fare, Five Cents. Children under five years of age, free.

SECOND AVENUE LINE.

Trains will run between South Ferry and 129th Street daily and Sunday at intervals of 2 to 6 minutes from 4.37 A.M. to 12.43 A.M. midnight. Time, 35 minutes. Transfer to and from Third Avenue Line at 129th Street and Chatham Square. Through trains between Canal and Freeman Streets 6.20 and 8.22 A. M. and 4.58 and 6 22 P. M. South Ferry to 129th Street, 8.81 miles.

STATIONS.

South Ferry.	1st St. and 1st Ave.	50th St. and 2d Ave.	111th St. and 2d Ave.
Hanover Square.	8th St. and 1st Ave.	57th St. and 2d Ave.	117th St. and 2d Ave.
Fulton and Pearl Sts.	14th St. and 1st Ave.	65th St. and 2d Ave.	121st St. and 2d Ave.
Franklin Square.	19th St. and 1st Ave.	72d St. and 2d Ave.	127th St. and 2d Ave.
Chatham Square.	23d St. bet. 1st and 2d Aves.	80th St. and 2d Ave.	129th St. (see stations on
Canal and Allen Sts.	34th St. & 2d Ave., branch	86th St. and 2d Ave.	3d Ave. and Subway
Grand and Allen Sts.	to 34th St. Ferry, E. R.	92d St. and 2d Ave.	Division north of 129th
Rivington and Allen Sts.	42d St. and 2d Ave.	99th St. and 2d Ave.	St.).

THIRD AVENUE LINE.

Trains will run daily and Sunday between City Hall and Bronx Park at intervals of $1\frac{1}{2}$ to 4 minutes from 5.30 A.M. to 12.45 A.M., then every 20 minutes to 5.30 A.M. Trains will run daily and Sunday between South Ferry and 129th Street at intervals of 6 minutes from 5.19 A.M. to 12 midnight, then every 20 minutes to 5.14 A.M. Branch to Grand Central Depot every few minutes from 6 A. M. to 12 midnight daily. Branch to 34th Street Ferry every few minutes from 5.30 A.M. to 12 midnight daily. Time between City Hall and Bronx Park, 51 minutes; Chatham Square to 129th Street, $28\frac{1}{2}$ minutes; South Ferry to 129th Street, 34 minutes. Transfer to and from Second Avenue Line at Chatham Square and 129th St.

Trains will run daily and Sunday between 129th Street and Bronx Park at an interval of 2 to 6 minutes from 5 A. M. to 12.45 A.M., then every 10 minutes until 5 A.M. Running time, 21 minutes from 129th Street (Second or Third Avenue) to Bronx Park.

129th Street and Third Avenue to Bronx Park and Third Avenue, 5.15 miles.

Express trains leave Bronx Park for City Hall 6.32 to 8.32 A. M., and from City Hall 4.52 to 6 16 P. M.

South Ferry to 129th St. and Third Ave., 8.53 miles; City Hall to 129th St. and Third Ave, 7.57 miles.

STATIONS.

South Ferry.	23d St. and 3d Ave.	84th St. and 3d Ave.	156th St. and 3d Ave.
Hanover Square.	28th St. and 3d Ave.	89th St. and 3d Ave.	161st St. and 3d Ave.
Fulton and Pearl Sts.	34th St. & 3d Ave., branch	99th St. and 3d Ave.	166th St. and 3d Ave.
Franklin Square.	to 34th St. Ferry, E. R.	106th St. and 3d Ave.	169th St. and 3d Ave.
City Hall.	42d St. and 3d Ave., branch	116th St. and 3d Ave.	Wendover and 3d Aves.
Chatham Square.	to Grand Central Depot.	125th St. and 3d Ave.	174th St. and 3d Ave.
Canal and Bowery.	47th St. and 3d Ave.	129th St. and 3d Ave.	177th St. and 3d Ave.
Grand and Bowery.	53d St. and 3d Ave.	133d St. } between Willis	(Tremont.)
Houston and Bowery.	59th St. and 3d Ave.	138th St. } and Alexander	183d St. and 3d Ave.
9th St. and 3d Ave.	67th St. and 3d Ave.	143d St. } Aves.	Pelham Ave. (Fordham.)
14th St. and 3d Ave.	76th St. and 3d Ave.	149th St. and 3d Ave.	Bronx Park.
18th St. and 3d Ave.			

SIXTH AVENUE LINE.

Trains will run daily and Sunday between South Ferry and 155th Street at intervals of $1\frac{1}{2}$ to 4 minutes from 5.30 A.M. to 12 midnight to 155th Street, and from 12 midnight to 5.30 A. M. every 10 minutes to 155th Street; Rector Street to 58th Street from 8.08 A.M. to 6.20 P.M., 6 minutes interval. The 58th Street station closes at midnight. A shuttle train is run between 58th Street and 50th Street station 5.55 to 7.47 A.M., 10.17 to 3.35 P.M., 6.06 to 12 midnight, all main line trains after 6.20 P.M. from South Ferry going to 155th Street. The through time from Rector Street to 58th Street is $18\frac{1}{2}$ minutes; to 155th Street, $40\frac{1}{2}$ minutes. Passengers transferred at 59th Street to Ninth Avenue Line without extra charge. Crosstown (surface) cars run from Grand Central to 42d Street station.

South Ferry to 155th Street and Eighth Avenue, 10.76 miles; Rector Street to 58th Street and Sixth Avenue, 4.67 miles.

STATIONS.

South Ferry.	14th St. and 6th Ave.	59th St. and 9th Ave.	125th St. and 8th Ave.
Battery Place.	18th St. and 6th Ave.	66th St. & Columbus Ave.	130th St. and 8th Ave.
Rector & N. Church Sts.	23d St. and 6th Ave.	72d St. and Columbus Ave.	(down track only).
Cortlandt & N. Church.	28th St. and 6th Ave.	81st St. & Columbus Ave.	135th St. and 8th Ave.
Park Pl. & Church St.	33d St. and 6th Ave.	93d St. and Columbus Ave.	140th St. and 8th Ave.
Chambers & W. Broadw'y	42d St. and 6th Ave.	104th St. & Columbus Ave.	145th St. and 8th Ave.
Franklin & W. Broadw'y	50th St. and 6th Ave.	110th St., between 8th and	155th St. & 8th Ave., con-
Grand & W. Broadway.	58th St. and 6th Ave.	Columbus Aves.	nects with New York
Bleecker & W. Broadway	53d St. and 8th Ave.	116th St. and 8th Ave.	& Putnam Railway.
8th St. and 6th Ave.			

NINTH AVENUE LINE.

Trains will run daily and Sunday from South Ferry to 135th St. every 2 to 6 minutes, and from 135th St. to South Ferry every 2 to 6 minutes between 5.04 A. M. and 11.55 P.M.; 11.55 P.M. to 5.04 A.M., every 10 minutes. Time, 36 minutes to 135th Street.

Passengers transferred at 59th Street to Sixth Avenue Line without extra charge.

Express trains leave 155th Street for Rector Street 6.53 to 9.09 A. M., and Rector Street for 155th Street 2.21 to 6.30 P. M.

South Ferry to 155th Street and Eighth Avenue, 10.07 miles; South Ferry to 59th Street and Ninth Avenue, 5.08 miles. South Ferry to 135th Street 9 07 miles.

STATIONS.

South Ferry.	Warren & Greenwich Sts.	Christopher & Greenwich.	34th St. and 9th Ave.
Battery Place.	Franklin & Greenwich Sts	14th St. and 9th Ave.	42d St. and 9th Ave.
Rector & Greenwich Sts.	Desbrosses & Gr'nwich Sts	23d St. and 9th Ave.	50th St. and 9th Ave.
Cortlandt & Gr'nwich St	Houston & Greenwich Sts	30th St. and 9th Ave.	59th St. and 9th Ave.
Barclay & Greenwich Sts			

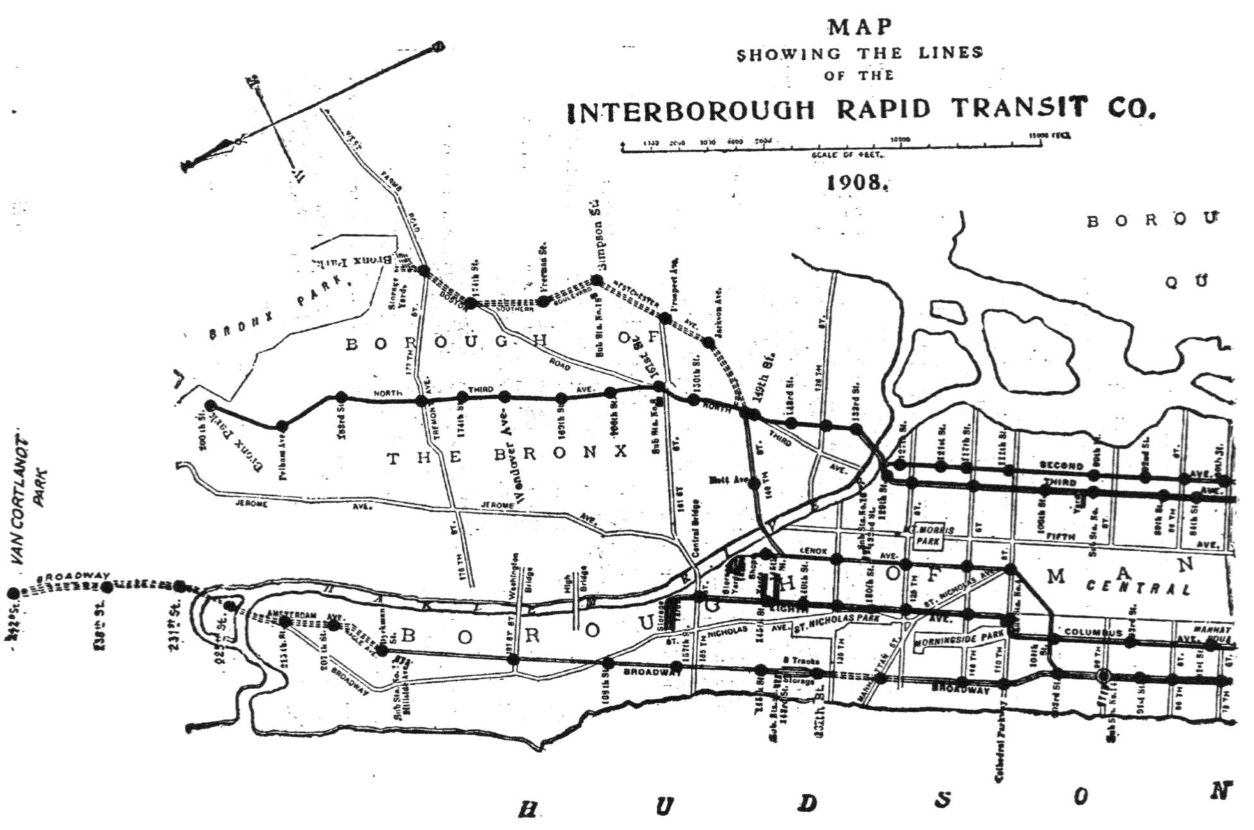
MAP
SHOWING THE LINES
OF THE
INTERBOROUGH RAPID TRANSIT CO.
SCALE OF FEET.
1908.
BOROUGH OF THE BRONX
BOROUGH OF MANHATTAN
CENTRAL
BRONX PARK
VAN CORTLANDT PARK
HUDSON

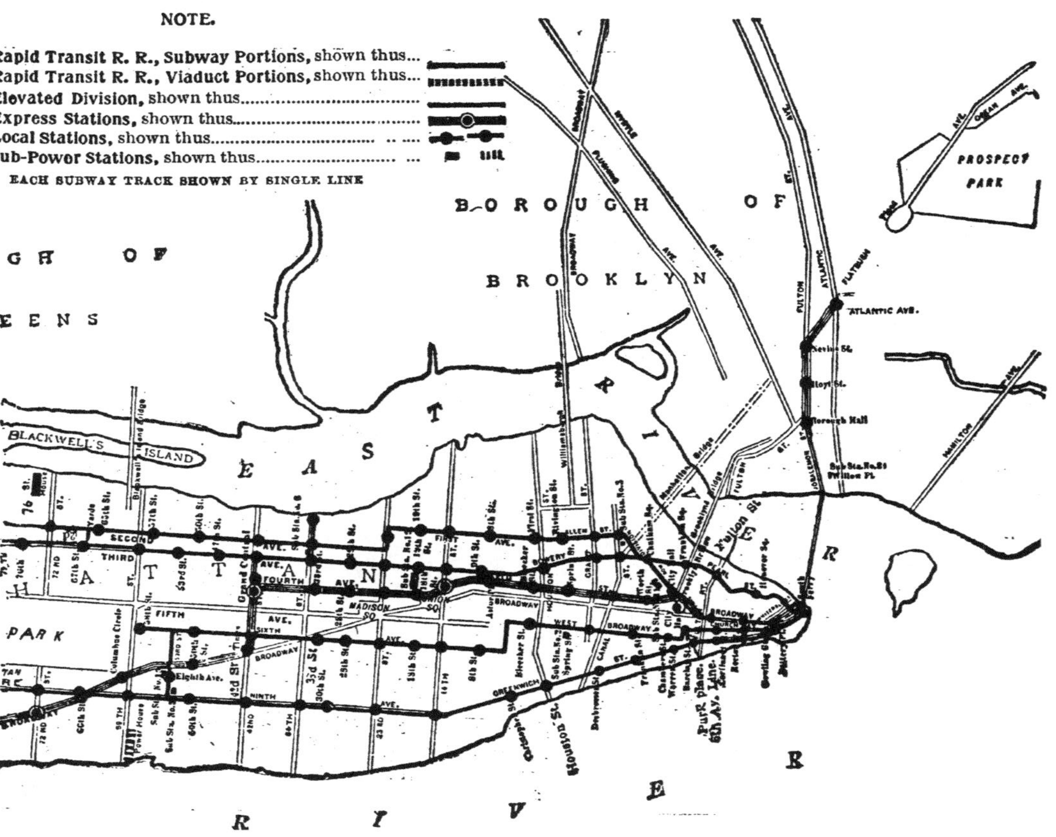
NOTE.
Rapid Transit R. R., Subway Portions, shown thus...
Rapid Transit R. R., Viaduct Portions, shown thus...
Elevated Division, shown thus...
Express Stations, shown thus...
Local Stations, shown thus...
Sub-Powor Stations, shown thus...
EACH SUBWAY TRACK SHOWN BY SINGLE LINE
BOROUGH OF BROOKLYN
EAST RIVER
BLACKWELL'S ISLAND
PROSPECT PARK
ATLANTIC AVE.
Borough Hall
Hoyt St.
FULTON
ATLANTIC
FLATBUSH
HAMILTON
SECOND
THIRD
FOURTH
FIFTH
SIXTH
NINTH
BROADWAY
MADISON SQ.
UNION SQ.
Grand Central
Columbus Circle
PARK
Fulton St.
Park place.
6th Av. Line.
Houston St.
RIVER

INTERBOROUGH RAPID TRANSIT COMPANY

SUBWAY DIVISION—STATIONS.

MAIN LINE.

South Ferry.
Bowling Green.
Wall Street.
Fulton Street.
City Hall Loop.
Brooklyn Bridge.
Worth and Elm Sts.
Canal and Elm Sts.
Spring and Elm Sts.
Bleecker and Elm Sts.
Astor Pl. and 4th Ave.
14th St. and 4th Ave.
18th St. and 4th Ave.
23d St. and 4th Ave.
28th St. and 4th Ave.
33d St. and 4th Ave.
42d St. and Park Ave.
Times Station (42d St. and Broadway).
50th St. & Broadway.
Columbus Circle (60th Street).
66th St. & Broadway.
72d St. & Broadway.
79th St. & Broadway.
86th St. & Broadway.
91st St. & Broadway.
96th St. & Broadway.

WEST BRANCH.

103d St. & Broadway.
110th St. & Broadway.
116th St. & Broadway.
Manhattan St. & B'way.
137th St. & Broadway.
145th St. & Broadway.
157th St. & Broadway.
168th St. & Broadway.
181st St. & Broadway.
Dyckman St. & B' way.
207th St. & Broadway.
215th St. & Broadway.
225th St. & Broadway.
231st St. & Broadway.
238th St. & Broadway.
242d St. & Broadway, Van Cortlandt Park.

EAST BRANCH.

110th St. and Lenox Ave.
116th St. and Lenox Ave.
125th St. and Lenox Ave.
135th St. and Lenox Ave.
145th St. and Lenox Ave.
Mott Av. and 149th St.
149th St. and 3d Ave.
Jackson and Westchester Aves.
Prospect and Westchester Aves.
Simpson St. and South Boulevard.
Freeman St. and South Boulevard.
174th St. and Boston Road.
177th St. and Boston Road.
180th St. and Boston Road.

BROOKLYN BRANCH

Atlantic Avenue.
Nevins Street.
Hoyt Street.
Borough Hall.

Fare, five cents. Children under five years of age, free.

Trains will run daily between City Hall, Atlantic Ave. (Bklyn.), So. Ferry, Bklyn. Bdg., 137th St., Dyckman and 242d Sts. and B'way, and 145th St. and Lenox Ave., and 180th St. and Boston Rd. Trains from the East and West Branches meet at 96th St. Junct., making the interval between that point and Bklyn. Bdg. as follows: Local trains, 12 midnight to 8.30 A. M., 7½ to 2 minutes, and from 8.30 A. M. to 12 midnight, 2 to 3 minutes. Express trains from 6.37 A. M. to 8.25 A. M., 3 to 2 minutes, and from 8.25 A. M. to 12.24 A. M., 2 to 4 minutes. Running time, Local trains: 137th St. and B'way to City Hall, 34 minutes; 180th St. and Boston Rd. to City Hall, 51 minutes. Running time, Express trains: 242d St. to So. Ferry, 48 minutes; Dyckman St. to So. Ferry, 38½ minutes; 180th St. to So. Ferry, 45 minutes; 180th St. to Atlantic Ave., 51 minutes. Bklyn. Bdg. to 242d St. and B'way, 14.12 miles; Bklyn. Bdg. to 145th St. and Lenox Ave., 9.45 miles; Bklyn. Bdg. to 180th St. and Boston Rd., 13.47 miles.

MANY BOOKS IN ONE

WEBSTER'S INTERNATIONAL DICTIONARY

Do you know that the INTERNATIONAL answers with final authority ALL KINDS of questions in The Trades, Arts and Sciences, Geography, Language, Biography, Etc.? Plan of contents as follows:

The International is of constant value and interest to all members of the home, of service to every professional and business man, and indispensable to the student.

Warmly indorsed by President Eliot of Harvard: "The International is a wonderfully compact storehouse of accurate information."

Justice Brewer, United States Supreme Court: "I recommend it to all as the one great standard authority."

Samuel J. Clemens (Mark Twain): "A wonderful book, the most wonderful I know of."

Thousands of similar testimonials are on file with the publishers.

WEBSTER'S COLLEGIATE DICTIONARY

Largest abridgment of the International. The Thin Paper Edition is a real gem of book-making unsurpassed for excellence and convenience. 1,116 pages. 1,400 Illustrations.

Write for specimen pages and "Dictionary Wrinkles." Mention THE WORLD ALMANAC and we will send you a useful set of colored maps, pocket size, of the United States, Cuba, Panama, China, Japan, etc. FREE.

G. & C. MERRIAM CO., Springfield, Mass.

Remember the pleasure and benefit derived in owning an INTERNATIONAL.

"Where the dictionary goes this history should go. The two works come nearer making a complete library than any other two books in the world."

Bishop JOHN H. VINCENT, D.D. & LL.D.

LARNED'S "HISTORY FOR READY REFERENCE AND TOPICAL READING"

A COMPLETE HISTORY of every Nation of the World, of every State in the U. S. A., of all great Social, Religious, Educational and Commercial Movements.

IN THE EXACT WORDS OF THE HIGHEST AUTHORITIES—all sides of controversial subjects being quoted.

SYSTEMATIZED — alphabetically and chronologically—so that any subject can be found at once.

CONTAINS ALSO ....

The full texts of all Constitutions and the great Historical Documents and State Papers of the World's history.

Nearly 150 historical maps. Invaluable Bibliographies, Chronologies, Tables, etc., etc.

INDORSED by leading scholars, librarians, educators, professional and business people everywhere.

This work will answer more questions in history, more authoritatively, with a greater excellence in literary expression and with a greater economy of time than any other ten of the largest and most comprehensive encyclopedic works in the world.

Write for literature, prices and terms.

C. A. NICHOLS CO.
Springfield, Mass.

STUDY LAW AT HOME

The oldest and best school. Instruction by mail adapted to every one. Recognized by courts and educators. Experienced and competent instructors. Takes spare time only. Three courses—Preparatory, Business, College. Law Courses. Prepares for practice. Will better your condition and prospects in business. Students and graduates everywhere. Full particulars and

EASY PAYMENT PLAN SENT FREE

THE SPRAGUE CORRESPONDENCE SCHOOL OF LAW

681 Majestic Bldg., Detroit, Mich.

"Easy Walker" Rubber Heel

WALK EASY Stop that jar on your spine. Prolong your life by wearing EASY WALKER rubber heels. Attached permanently to shoes in five minutes. Re-inforced at the back, which prevents slipping and prolongs the life of the heel. Get the genuine. Name "EASY WALKER" moulded on the face of every heel. Look for the steel holding plate. See how the gum is anchored on the hollow side of the heel. Sold by findings dealers and shoemakers everywhere. If unable to get them from your shoe dealer send us size of shoe you wear and thirty-five cents in coin or postage, and tell us whether you want full or half heels. We will send you a pair postpaid. Mention WORLD ALMANAC.

Manufactured by the

SPRINGFIELD ELASTIC TREAD COMPANY

14-18 N. Lowry Avenue Springfield, Ohio, U. S. A.

ESTABLISHED 1870.

J. C. SCHNOTER'S

SHOULDER BRACE

For Round Shoulders.

Makes the form erect, expands the chest, strengthens the lungs, and is comfortable to wear.

ELASTIC STOCKINGS, KNEE CAPS, AND ANKLETS.

Also **Trusses**, Abdominal Supporters, Crutches, Rubber Tips, Braces, etc.

Competent lady attendants. Separate parlors. See page 730.

"Hernia Trusses"

Scientifically fitted to suit each particular case.

SCHNOTER'S ATHLETIC SUPPORTERS or JOCK-STRAPS are universally used by Professional and Athletic people in general. For Horsemen, Racquet and Tennis players, Golfers, etc. Ask your dealer for the genuine "SCHNOTER'S" and only those bearing our trade-mark—J.C.S.—or we will send direct on receipt of price. Cotton Mesh, 50c.; Linen Mesh, 75c.; Silk, 90c.

J. C. SCHNOTER CO., Makers,
523 Sixth Avenue,
Near 31st St., NEW YORK, N. Y., U.S.A.
Tel. 2699 Mad.

THE ART PRESERVATIVE

IN none of the arts is the advance of the beautiful more pronounced than in that of the art preservative of arts. And it is by a return to the past, idealizing the typography of the Fifteenth Century, that the highest form of the beautiful has been attained. Within ten years the greatest changes for the better have been made. William Morris, of the noted Kelmscott Press, is quoted as saying in 1890 that no good book printing has been done since the middle of the Sixteenth Century, and that the degradation of the art had been largely due to mean types. He urged the use of better types, a tolerance of quaintness, and the revival of mediæval methods.

The adverse criticism of 1890 does not hold good now. A revolution has taken place from the over-ornate to the attractive and restful in typography. America has not been behind in this regard. The Jenson type is, perhaps, the best-known illustration. Between Nicholas Jenson and the American Type Founders' Company stretch nearly 450 years. It was in 1458 that Jenson, an engraver of the Paris mint, was sent to Mainz by Charles VII., King of France, to learn the new art of printing. He studied for three years and returned to Paris. In 1471 Jenson printed four books in Venice. He remained in that romantic city to the end of his life, in 1481. It is said that he was not the first printer to make Roman types, but that he made them better than did his rivals.

In honor of this old typemaker the Jenson type of to-day is named. Like the French pioneer of the craft, the American type founders excel in their time in making the best faced type On reflection, however, it seems strange that this handsome Roman letter, used in Venice in the Fifteenth Century, reached in the highest degree the necessary qualities of legibility and purity of line, and that the Twentieth Century can do no better than borrow its beauties for to-day's readers.

From the inception of printing from movable types, the masters who have handed down the honorable calling have taken pride in their work, like all true artists. Pierre-Simon Fournier, in his Manual Typographique, wrote:

"Type-founding is not like other arts, in which imperfect workmanship may find a use proportionate to its relative value. Printing should tolerate nothing that is bad, nor even that which is mediocre, since it costs as much to found and print bad types as it does to found and print perfect ones."

It is safe to say that the time will never come when the handicraft of the type founder will be a lost art. The demand for the artistic in type, as well as in the other finer fancies of the age, is growing, and is being met by "the founders," by which appellation the printers of the entire country designate the American Type Founders' Company, embracing the best-known and oldest-established concerns of a dozen cities.

This Company is the originator of all the leading type designs, and has unequalled facilities for supplying everything required in printing offices. It has lately issued very attractive specimen books, which cover the widest range in type faces in both plain and original designs. Among the new faces are the Cloister Black, Tabard, and the extensive Cheltenham family.

Additional specimen sheets are constantly being issued from the office, corner of Rose and Duane Streets, New York City, showing the new faces as soon as they are brought out for the public verdict.

OLIVER AIDS ADVERTISERS AND PUBLISHERS

New Oliver Model No. 5 Meets Extraordinary Demands of Voluminous Correspondence and Intricate Accounting Systems

Absolutely unhampered by the limitations of ordinary typewriters and with unrestricted capacity for steady service in all departments of any business, the New Model Oliver No. 5 is a powerful aid to Publishers and Advertisers. When the enormous volume and extreme complexity of present-day business brought about new conditions and requirements, the Oliver rose to meet them.

—Not with a few ***minor*** improvements, but with time-and-labor-saving features of ***major*** importance, which give from 25 to 50 per cent. increase in actual ***working results.*** These innovations of Oliver No. 5, added to the great fundamental advantages already possessed by previous Oliver models, spell

S-U-P-R-E-M-A-C-Y I-N S-E-R-V-I-C-E.

The things that count with Publishers and Advertisers are—getting the work done ***rapidly*** and ***right.***

—And the writing machine that handles the greatest volume of correspondence in shortest time—that expedites the work all along the line—that insures ***accuracy*** as well as ***speed,*** is the New Model No. 5—

The OLIVER Typewriter

The Standard Visible Writer

The basic reasons for Oliver superiority include the great essentials of ***simplicity, durability, speed, accuracy, visible writing, manifolding power*** and ***versatility.*** Upon this groundwork of solid merit we have built up the splendid new Oliver Model No. 5, with its ***Automatic Tabulator, Line-Ruling Device, Disappearing Indicator, Automatic Paper Register, Balance-Shifting Mechanism, Locomotive Base,*** and other epoch-making improvements.

The Oliver is at work to-day in the Editorial Rooms and Business Offices of hundreds of Magazines, Newspapers, Agricultural, Trade and Mail Order Papers throughout the country.

Because it saves time, cuts expense and adds to the efficiency of the working force.

The Oliver Typewriter stands highest in favor of Advertisers for the same vital reasons.

Why not put the Oliver Typewriter to the service test in your office?

A position as Local Agent for the Oliver, in unoccupied territory, awaits the man who can qualify. The salary is commensurate with the high standard of ability required.

The Oliver Typewriter Co., 310 Broadway, New York City, N.Y.

NEW YORK CHICAGO SAN FRANCISCO NEW ORLEANS

Barrow, Wade, Guthrie & Co.

CERTIFIED PUBLIC ACCOUNTANTS
AND
CHARTERED ACCOUNTANTS

BROAD EXCHANGE BUILDING

25-33 Broad Street - - - NEW YORK

18 ST. SWITHIN'S LANE - - - - LONDON, ENGLAND

AGGRAVATED HERNIA—"RUPTURE"

So-called RUPTURE CURES and ill-fitting Trusses cause aggravated Hernia. After your experiments, without any good results, then come and try my method of HONEST TRUSS-FITTING. My long experience in this line enables me to adjust the proper Truss to retain the Hernia in most cases, thereby giving those so afflicted positive relief.

VARICOCELE is the forerunner of RUPTURE. If most men, in time, would wear a well-fitting SUSPENSORY there would be less use for Trusses. I am a SPECIALIST in TRUSSES, SUSPENSORIES, etc. Those that so desire can see their physician before coming to me. The same careful attention given to either ADULT or CHILD. Trusses from $3. Suspensories from 50c. Mail orders executed.

Competent female attendant in Ladies' Department. Hours—9 to 5.

A. PARKS BLACK, G. M.

Dept. T. S. (Expert in Trusses, Suspensories, Etc.)

See pages 718-722 **523 Sixth Avenue, at 31st St., N. Y., U. S. A.**

Do Your Own Printing

AND ADVERTISING

Cards, Circulars : Book : Small Newspaper

Press, $5 • Larger Size, $18

Great Money Savers. Big Profits Printing for Others. Typesetting and All Easy by Printed Instructions Sent. For Old or Young, Business or Pleasure. Write to Factory for Catalogue of Presses, Type, Paper, Cards, Etc.

EXCELSIOR

THE PRESS CO. - - Meriden, Ct.

WHEN YOU PATRONIZE THE ADVERTISERS, KINDLY MENTION THE WORLD ALMANAC.

In writing to advertisers please mention The World Almanac.

THE CLASSIFIED DEPARTMENT

THE WORLD ALMANAC ADDENDA

A list of reliable and enterprising individuals and firms who guarantee to give you the best of anything in each special line

Abdominal Supporters.

J. C. SCHNOTER CO., Abdominal Supporters, Elastic Stockings, etc., Trusses, Suspensories, and effective Shoulder Braces. See pages 715 and 730. Estab. 1870. 523 Sixth Ave., New York.

Addressing.

RAPID ADDRESSING MACHINE CO.
Dun Building,
290 Broadway,
New York.

Artificial Eyes.

Artificial eyes made to order. Large stock on hand. Supply all eye infirmaries of Greater New York and vicinity. Terms reasonable. Write for particulars. Established 1853. MAGER & GOUGELMANN, 104 E. 12th St., New York.

Ash Cans.

ENGINEERS **N. Y. Standard Ash Can M'f'g Co., Inc.**

Angle Ring, Stamped Bottom Engineer, Ash and Garbage Cans, Stable Cans and Ice Cans, Stair Plates, Nosings and Improved Metal Wash Tub Covers. Steamboat Cans made of heavy boiler iron. All kinds of Sheet and Galvanized Iron Receptacles made to order. All cans kept in repair for one year. Send for Illustrated Catalogue.

Dept. 14, 436 E. 10th St., N. Y. Tel., 1137 Orchard

Assayers and Chemists.

RICKETTS & BANKS,
Assayers and Chemists,
104 John St., N. Y. City.
Tests of Ores, Metals, Minerals, Waters and other Materials. Examination of Mines.

Athletic Goods.

The Health Brace; also Physical Culture Goods: Dumbbells, Wrist Machines, Chest Expanders, Punching Bags. In ordering Reborn give chest and waist measures; $1.00, delivered.
New York Physical Culture School.
2 Cooper Square West, opposite Cooper Union, New York City.

Autographic Registers.

Autographic Registers. Manifold Books and Loose Leaf systems. Most modern and practical. Write or call. AUTOGRAPHIC REGISTER CO. New York Salesroom, 44 E. 23d Street. Phone 4481 Gramercy, connecting Factory 10th and Clinton Sts., Hoboken.

Automobile Tires.

TRAUTMAN'S 4 IN 1 ANTI-SKID COVERS prevent skidding, punctures, blowouts and wear and tear on tire. Steam Vulcanizing in all its branches. IRA F. TRAUTMAN, 131 Sixth ave., B'klyn, N. Y. 2 blocks from Flatbush Ave. Tel., 4529 Prospect.

AUTO TIRES
LARGEST STOCK IN THE U. S.
WRITE FOR PRICES STATE SIZE WANTED - WILL QUOTE -
TELEPHONE 2447 CORTLANDT
A. H. KASNER
LARGEST DEALER IN THE U. S.
152 CHURCH ST. NEAR CHAMBERS ST. NEW YORK CITY

Auto Tires Bought.

AUTO TIRES AND TUBES A SPECIALTY.
YES we pay spot cash for scrap rubber, metals and irons.
L. SCHIAVONE & CO.,
Dept. B, 204 W. 18th St.
Telephone 1981 Chelsea.

Bankers and Brokers.

CESARE CONTI.
Letters of Credit. Appointed and authorized correspondent of the Bank of Naples. Est. 1884. 35 Broadway, New York. Importer of Chianti Wines and Olive Oil.

Bowling Alley Supplies.

JOHN G. KLUMPP'S SONS, H. F. Klumpp, John Ebinger. Established 1878. Up-to-date turners in foreign and domestic woods. Cocoa mat makers. Bowling alley builders and alley supply manufacturers. Alley oil. 11-13 Baxter Street, New York. Telephone, 2481 Worth.

Business Opportunities.

PRINTING—5,000 circulars, 6x9, $3.50. 500 letter-heads, envelopes, or business cards, $1. 100 magazines, 20 pages, $2; 1,000, $10. 1,000 post cards from photo or drawing, $4. Write for samples. WALTER & CO., 37 and 39 Dean St., Brooklyn, N. Y.

Cameras and Lenses.

Cameras and Lenses—Kodaks, Premos, Pocos, and a number of other makes always on hand at lowest prices. Send stamp for "Bargain List." NEW YORK CAMERA EXCHANGE, Dept. A, 114 Fulton St., New York City, N. Y.

THE CLASSIFIED DEPARTMENT

THE WORLD ALMANAC ADDENDA

A list of reliable and enterprising individuals and firms who guarantee to give you the best of anything in each special line

Cameras and Lenses.

We are headquarters in buying, selling and exchanging second-hand Cameras and Lenses. Have a full line of the latest Kodaks, Century, Premo and Graflex Cameras, always on hand; also supplies. Write for bargain list. GLOECKNER & NEWBY CO., 171 Broadway, New York.

Car Lighting.

THE SAFETY CAR HEATING & LIGHTING COMPANY, 2 Rector St., New York City. The new mantle lamp increases illumination fourfold with the same consumption of gas—a revolution in car lighting.

Cemeteries.

THE WOODLAWN CEMETERY,
Borough of the Bronx. Lots $150 up.
Write for Descriptive Booklet, or by request a representative will call. Telephone connection.
Office, 20 East 23d St., New York.

Chemicals.

GEO. A. ERKENBRACH CO.,
Mfg. Chemists, 115 Maiden Lane, N. Y.
Chemicals for the Arts, Photographic and Medicinal. Buenos Ayres Hide Poison in Paste.

Chinese and Japanese Goods.

新錦隆

Sun Kim Lung Co., Exporters and Importers of Fine Teas, Chinaware, Fancy Silk and Dry Goods, Silk Shawls, Silk Handkerchiefs; all kinds of Chinaware and Japanese Goods. No 21 Pell Street, New York City, N. Y.

紐約趙晃記

Chu Fong, 93 to 99 Nassau Street, New York, representing the Fong Kee Trading Co., main offices at 37 Queen's Road, Central Hong Kong, China, solicits American manufacturers' lines for China trade. Exporters and Importers.

Cigars.

A. SCHULTE,
Imported Key West and Domestic Cigars, World Bldg., 39 Park Row, 150 Broadway, 1465 Broadway, 49 Cortlandt, 255 Broadway, Nassau and Ann Sts., Maiden Lane and Nassau St., and branches.

Clocks.

A. Cleveland' Magneto AMERICAN WATCHMAN'S CLOCK will Save enough INSURANCE to Pay for Itself in a short time. Costs nothing to maintain. Examined and Approved by National Fire Protection Association. Send for Prices and Catalogue W to PETTES & RANDALL CO., 150 Nassau St., N. Y. Repairs and Supplies for all Watchmen's Clocks.

Coffee.

TRY MY "43" BLEND COFFEE.
None better imported; 35 cents per pound; Callanan's Magazine and price-list mailed on request. L. J. CALLANAN, 41-43 Vesey St., New York City.

Collections.

R. G. DUN & CO.,
Dun Building,
290 Broadway,
New York.

Detective Agencies.

FULLER'S N. Y. DETECTIVE BUREAU.
A service for bankers, lawyers, corporations, firms and individuals. Agents in principal cities of America and Europe. Est. 1870. Tel. 1064 Stuyvesant. J. M. FULLER, Principal, 866 Broadway, New York City.

WESTLOTORN'S Detective Agency—civil and criminal. Thoroughly competent male or female detectives sent to all parts of the world. Suspected persons shadowed, private information, confidential investigations, etc. Correspondence solicited. ALBERT E. WESTLOTORN, Principal, late of Police Department. Offices 229 Broadway, New York. Telephone 6871 Barclay. Established 1890.

Electric Signs.

ELECTRIC SIGN

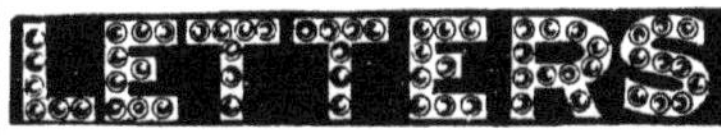

EMPIRE ELECTRIC SIGN CO.
Office and factory: 162 - 164 E. 118th St., New York. Tel. 311 Harlem.

THE CLASSIFIED DEPARTMENT

THE WORLD ALMANAC ADDENDA

A list of reliable and enterprising individuals and firms who guarantee to give you the best of anything in each special line

Felt.

American Felt Co.

Manufacturers of Felt of Every Description.

110 to 116 E. 13TH ST., NEW YORK

Fireworks.

THE PAIN MANUFACTURING CO., Manufacturers of Pain's Manhattan Beach Fireworks. Public and Private Displays. Fireworks at wholesale and retail. No. 12 Park Place, New York.

Gray Hair Restored.

Gray Hair restored any shade, a specialty. Superfluous hair removed from face; $1.00. VELVINE CREAM whitens the skin, removes wrinkles, freckles, $1.00. Invisible face rouge, 50 cents. Combings made up at MME. MALCOM'S Hair Dressing Parlors, 648 Sixth Ave., between 37th and 38th Sts., New York.

"Hernia" Trusses, Obesity Belts, Etc.

For true truss fitting, belts for corpulency and kidney troubles, elastic stockings for varicose veins, crutches, jockey straps, etc., consult A. PARKS BLACK, G. M., Expert Suspensorist, 523 Sixth Ave., New York, U. S. A. See pages 718, 722 and 727.

Invalid Chairs.

WHEEL CHAIRS
WE MAKE OVER 70 STYLES
Catalog "B" Illustrates—Describes—(Free)
SARGENT CO. 279 4th Ave. New York

Lame People.

The Perfection Extension Shoe makes both feet appear exactly alike. Worn with ready made shoes. Shipped on trial. Write for illustrated Booklet. HENRY W. LOTZ. 313 Third Ave., New York.

Old Style. New Style.

Lame People.

Extension Shoes for short limbs made to meet the individual requirements. Orthopedic Appliances. Write for particulars. Distance no barrier.

A. W. SINN, Extension Shoe Manufacturer, 26 Cottage St., Newark, N. J.

Mercantile Agencies.

R. G. DUN & CO.,
Dun Building,
290 Broadway,
New York.

Moving Vans.

Old Gold and Silver.

Worn-Out Gold and Silver Bought by
R. LONGMAN'S SONS,
Gold and Silver Refiners,
8 John Street, New York.

Olive Oil.

Don't forget that my Eclipse Brand of Virgin Olive Oil is absolutely pure; analysis by Agricultural Bureau, Washington, showing absolute purity, in Callanan's Magazine, mailed on request. L. J. CALLANAN, 41-43 Vesey St., N. Y. City.

Packing Boxes.

P. RYAN, Dealer in all kinds of Old and New Packing Cases, Sawdust and Box Straps. Established 1850. Office, 109 Reade St. Yards, Morton and Washington Sts., New York. Telephone, 500 Worth.

Piano Movers.

Koberlein's Transfer operates within a radius of 100 miles of N. Y. Furniture packed and shipped. Office, 221 E. 23d St. Phone 6219 Gramercy. Moving done on short notice.

THE CLASSIFIED DEPARTMENT

THE WORLD ALMANAC ADDENDA

A list of reliable and enterprising individuals and firms who guarantee to give you the best of anything in each special line

Postage Stamps.

UNUSED U. S. BOUGHT at small discount. Old stamp collections wanted. Large Coin Book 10 cents. JOS. NEGREEN, 28 East 23d St., N. Y.

Rheumatism.

RHEUMATISM

Sufferers can send address (no stamp required) and receive FREE a PAMPHLET which tells what Rheumatism really is, the cause of the pain attending it, and how to obtain a lasting and inexpensive cure. S. F. KIMBALL, 3 Union Sq., New York.

Schools and Colleges.

NEW JERSEY MILITARY ACADEMY, FREEHOLD, N. J., prepares for college or business. Special department in separate building for quite young boys.
COL. C. J. WRIGHT, A. M., Principal.

ANNAPOLIS, MARYLAND, St. John's College, established 1696. Classical and scientific courses leading to degrees. Designated by the U. S. Govt. as one of the six leading military colleges. Also Preparatory School for boys. Military department under army officer. Terms $300. THOMAS FELL, LL.D.

CONWAY HALL (COLLEGIATE PREPARATORY SCHOOL), CARLISLE, PA.—Prepares for colleges and technical and professional schools. Terms, $300 per year. Splendid building, located near Dickinson College, and amid healthful surroundings. For catalogue address DR. GEO. EDWARD REED, President.

FLORIDA MILITARY ACADEMY. — A thoroughly equipped military preparatory school in the "Land of Flowers and Sunshine;" excellent climate; tourist town near Jacksonville; best home and social advantages; faculty of university men. Terms, $400. Address THE SUPERINTENDENT, Green Cove Springs, Fla.

HOLY CROSS COLLEGE, Worcester, Mass. —Oldest Catholic College in New England; largest Catholic College in America; location exceedingly healthy and beautiful; classical course only. Terms reasonable. Bulletins on application.

VALLEY FEMALE SEMINARY, Waynesboro, Va., Rev. J. J. Miller, Principal. Climate, scenery and water unsurpassed. Write for Catalogue.

Special Sheet and Metal Workers.

MACHINE PANS AND GUARDS, TANKS, BRASS WASTE CANS.

SPECIAL SHEET METAL WORK of every description, made from blue prints. All kinds of Jobbing done.
Estimates on application.
E. BEHRINGER, 45 Fulton St., New York.

Storage Warehouses.

Columbia Warehouses, Columbus Ave., 66th to 67th St. Office, 149 Columbus Ave. Telephone, 2977 Columbus. The New Columbia, 90th St. and Amsterdam Ave. Unsurpassed facilities. Silver vaults.

Empire Storage Warehouse; furniture removed to city or country. Office 25 First Ave., N. Y. City. 'Phone 2045 Orchard.

Telegraphy.

TELEGRAPHY TAUGHT in the shortest time. The Omnigraph Automatic Transmitter combined with standard key and sounder. Sends you telegraph messages at any speed just as an expert operator would. 5 styles, $2 up; circular free. OMNIGRAPH MFG. CO., 39M, Cortlandt St., New York.

Typewriters.

All makes. Repaired, sold and exchanged. Remington, Hammond, Williams, New Century, Densmore, Yost, Smith Premier, $15 upward. Remington No. 6, Underwood, Oliver, $30 up. Immense stock on hand. Let us quote you. EAGLE TYPEWRITER CO., 79 Duane St., New York. Telephone Worth 1534.

Vault Lights.

VAULT AND SIDEWALK LIGHTS.
JACOB MARK SONS,
Patentees and Manufacturers of Vault Lights, Sidewalk Lights, and Reflecting Prisms of all kinds.
7 Worth St., New York.

Whiskey.

Ask for Callanan's Parrot Brand Rye Whiskey. One of the best distilled in Kentucky. Guaranteed pure. Bottled in Bond for L. J. CALLANAN, 41-43 Vesey St., New York. Price list mailed on request.